Tourist itineraries

Throughout the guide, you will find recommended tourist itineraries. The principal routes are indicated on the regional maps by a numbered box. You will find the description by consulting the pages indicated below.

Agenais, Périgord, Quercy

102 The Bastides of Périgord
108 Dordogne périgourdine
109 Dordogne quercynoise
111 Vézère valley
114 Lot and Célé valleys
122 Aveyron gorges

Alsace

135 The Ridge Road
137 The Hohwald region
141 The Outre-Forêt region
148 The Sundgau region
149 The Wine Road
151 Northern Vosges region

Ardèche, Cévennes

162 Ardèche gorges
165 Cévennes corniche
168 Mont Lozère
174 Tarn and Jonte gorges
177 Vivarais Cévenol corniche

Auvergne

201 Truyère gorges
198 Le Puy Mary
193 Mézenc massif
194 Tour of the Puy de Sancy

Basque country, Béarn, Bigorre

222 Passes of the Pyrénées
211 The Basque country

Berry, Bourbonnais

238 George Sand territory
234 Tour of Upper Berry
235 Bourbonnais mountains

Bordelais, Landes

256 Blayais, Libournais, Entre-Deux-Mers regions
264 Garonne valley, Bazadais and Sauternais regions
269 The Médoc region
267 The Landes girondines coast
266 The Grandes Landes region

Brittany

282 Monts d'Arrée
286 The Blavet river
289 Brière nature park
295 The Rance and Arguenon regions
302 The Léon churchyards
305 Montagnes Noires
311 Forest of Paimpont

Burgundy

337 The Auxerrois region
341 The Brionnais region
351 Morvan lakes
359 Between Tournus and Cluny
360 Along the river Vingeanne

Champagne, Ardennes

369 Champagne Road
375 Meuse valley
379 The Thiérache region

Corsica

390 The Balagne region
396 The Castagniccia heights
398 Bay of Porto

Dauphiné

410 The Chartreuse massif
417 The Queyras valley
422 The Vercors massif

Franche-Comté

436 Esmoulières plateau
436 The Goumois corniche
438 The Loue valley
440 Morez and tour of the gorges

Ile-de-France

459 Chevreuse valley
461 Compiègne forest
475 The Senlis area
479 Tour of the Vexin region

Languedoc-Roussillon

489 The Canigou massif
494 The Espinouse range
495 The Hérault valley
507 The Razès region

Limousin

516 The Dordogne gorges
526 Vassivière lake

Lorraine, Vosges

532 The Argonne region
537 Lakes valley
546 The Donon and the Celles valley
545 From Phalsbourg to the Donon

Lyonnais, Bresse

555 The Beaujolais region
558 The Bresse region
560 The Dombes plateau
571 Tour of Mont Pilat

Maine, Anjou

585 The Angevine Loire and the Layon hills
587 Bercé forest
594 Tour of Upper Maine

Midi toulousain, Pyrénées

607 The Bastides of Armagnac
609 From Couserans to Plantaurel

Normandy

631 The Auge region
638 The Cotentin peninsula
643 The D-Day landing beaches
657 The Perche region
659 Les Quatre Vallées
665 Lower Seine valley

Picardy and the North

675 Round trip of war memorials
678 The Avesnois area
681 Côte d'Opale corniche
684 Canche and Authie valleys
692 Somme valley

Provence, Côte d'Azur

727 The Esterel massif
734 The Lubéron heights
740 Maures massif
765 Grand Canyon of Verdon

Rouergue, Albigeois

778 Lot gorges
783 From Rodez to Conques
785 Sidobre and the Lacaune mountains

Savoy

796 Lake Annecy
799 Lake Bourget
801 The Mont Blanc massif
806 The Grandes Alpes

Touraine, Blésois, Orléanais

829 River Loir near Vendôme
836 The Sologne region

Vendée, Poitou, Charentes

849 Tour of the Champagne Cognac vineyards
858 Marais Poitevin
870 Charente valley
871 Battle sites of the Vendée Wars

Gastronomy

The pleasures of the table are a delightful aspect of a holiday in France. That is why the *Guide* takes particular pains to offer an enticing selection of places to eat. Our list comprises some 5,000 restaurants, so you're sure to find a table to suit your taste — and your budget!

Last year, on the occasion of the election for our fifth GRAND PRIX DES CUISINIERS DE FRANCE, several thoughts on the evolution of cuisine troubled our judges. With the advanced technology that is now available to put meals on our tables, it is necessary to speak boldly of these changes, these revolutionary techniques that threaten the art of cuisine, an art that is officially recognized.

The vacuum-packed preparation of food, which results from many years of research actually assisted by some of the greater chefs, has given us already a perfect marriage between gastronomy and technology. These vacuum-packed dishes (DLC — date limite de conservation — 6-21 days) are unfortunately completely anonymous, and there has been no legislation passed that might require a restaurant to announce that the dish it is serving comes out of an industrial chain. These dishes are now served in some restaurants, enabling them to function with a small number of employees. This — which is a rational evolution — represents a future trap for gastronomic critics, already terribly divided. Who should reap the laurels for a delicious dish? Should it be the employee who heats and serves it or the chef-technician who has put together the ingredients in his kitchen-workshop situated in an industrial area next to any city? This great question has no answer yet.

Obviously, this troubling question is not raised in the establishments of our 121 grand chefs or in Jean-Pierre Vigato's Apicius. He has just been crowned by his peers with the Hachette chefs Grand Prix. He thus brilliantly succeeds our previous laureates:

Bernard LOISEAU — La Côte d'Or Saulieu 1984; Joël ROBUCHON — Jamin, Guy SAVOY both in Paris, first prize divided in 1985; Jacques MAXIMIN — Le Chantecler, Hôtel Negresco Nice 1986; Michel BRAS — Lou Mazuc Laguiole 1987. All of them were younger than 40 when elected.

Jean-Pierre was born in Paris March 20, 1952 and his ambition was formed under the influence of his Italian father and his French mother, with a special mention and thanks to his grandmother from the Pas-de-Calais region, north of France. The old memory of the *ragoût de pommes de terre au lard* cooking slowly on the family stove and pervading all the house with its smell led him to want to create a good cuisine of his own.

After a secondary school education he took his first three years of apprenticeship, by chance and through following a friend, at MOULIN D'ORGEVAL in Villennes-sur-Seine. In 1975, he became a chef's assistant at ALBERT, the famous restaurant of the Ave-

Jean-Pierre VIGATO

nue du Maine, known for its *«carré d'agneau»*. In that venerable institution he was taken in hand by the wonderful Marcel BEAUMONT. He quickly became the "Maître Trancheur" and was able to learn how to deal with clients and, thanks to an exceptional wine cellar, to study wines.

In 1979 he opened, along with his wife Madeleine, a charming little restaurant on avenue Rachel, one of the quietest avenues in Montmartre. His friend Claude MOINS, commercial director of MOET ET CHANDON, helped him to be discovered by Parisian journalists. He achieved success quite rapidly due to the simplicity, high standards and quality of his cuisine, moderate prices and a warm atmosphere. Soon it was apparent that he had to either expend or move. After a year's well-earned rest, he reopened in a more spacious location. The new setting has been supervised with good taste and discretion by Madeleine; in February 1984, APICIUS was born.

Maintaining the same quality and atmosphere, greater success followed. Clients rush to taste and appreciate the excellent cuisine — a light cuisine — with ever-changing flavors: *huîtres spéciales en cressonnette, escalope de foie gras sauté en aigre-doux, saumon rôti avec sa peau craquante, raie vapeur à la civette et au gros sel.* Tripe that clients love and that he loves to make for them contribute a good part to his success, as well as pig's feet without bones and thick slices of veal kidney. For the gourmands, the grand dessert au chocolat is just unforgettable. The wine cellar is at the same high level; among his wines Jean-Pierre particularly likes two wines: Hautes Côtes-de-nuits rouge from Jayer-Gilles and chassagne-montrachet Les Embrazées de Bernard Morey.

Jean-Pierre has also some other passions: family, two young sons, Jérôme, 11 and Maxime, 6, an obligatory name for a chef's son, tennis with his friends and sports cars.

FRANÇOIS ROBOTH

The Hachette Grand Prix Chefs' Panel

The panel members' own restaurants are listed in the guide in red
The gourmet restaurants that panel members particularly recommend are indicated by
a ● Restaurants that offer good food and good value are indicated by a ●

Agde (34) : *La Tamarissière*, Nicolas **Albano**, p. 486
Albertville (73) : Rest. *Million*, Philippe **Million**, p. 795
Angers (49) : Rest. *Le Quéré*, Paul **Le Quéré**, p. 585
Arbois (39) : *Le Paris*, André and Jean-Paul **Jeunet**, p. 430
Auch (32) : *Hôtel de France*, André **Daguin**, p. 605
Auvillers-les-Forges (08 ; → Rocroi) : *Host. Lenoir*, Jean **Lenoir**, p. 377
Les Baux-de-Provence (13) : *l'Oustau de Baumanière*, Raymond **Thuilier** and Jean-André **Charial**, p. 714
Bénouville (14 ; → Caen) : *Le Manoir d'Hastings*, Claude **Scaviner**, p. 636
Biarritz (64) : *Le Café de Paris*, Pierre **Laporte**, p. 215
Bordeaux (33) : Rest. *Jean Ramet*, Jean **Ramet**, p. 260
Bordeaux (33) : *Le Chapon Fin*, Francis **Garcia**, p. 260
Bougival (78 ; → Versailles) : *Le Camélia*, Jean **Delaveyne**, p. 478
Bouliac (33 ; → Bordeaux) : *Saint-James*, Jean-Marie **Amat**, p. 261
N Brive-la-Gaillarde (19) : *La Crémaillère*, Charles **Reynal**, p. 519
Cannes (06) : *Hôtel Gray d'Albion*, Rest. *Royal Gray*, Jacques **Chibois**, p. 720
Chagny (71 ; → Côte de Beaune) : Rest. *Lameloise*, Jacques **Lameloise**, p. 341
Chamalières (63 ; → Clermont-Ferrand) : *Hôtel Radio*, Michel **Mioche**, p. 191
Château-Arnoux (04 ; → Sisteron) : *La Bonne Étape*, Pierre and Jany **Gleize**, p. 759
Châteaufort (78 ; → Chevreuse Valley) : *La Belle Époque*, Michel **Peignaud**, p. 459
Collonges-au-Mont-d'Or (69 ; → Lyon) : Rest. *Paul Bocuse*, Paul **Bocuse**, Roger **Jaloux** and Roger **Fleury**, p. 569
Colmar (68) : *Le Fer Rouge*, Patrick **Fulgraff**, p. 134
Dijon (21) : *Hôtel de la Cloche*, Rest. *Jean-Pierre Billoux*, J.-P. **Billoux**, p. 347
Enghien (95) : *Le Duc d'Enghien*, Michel **Kerever**, p. 463
Eugénie-les-Bains (40) : *Les Prés et les Sources*, Michel **Guérard**, p. 264
Les Eyzies (24) : *Le Centenaire*, Roland **Mazère** and Alain **Scholly**, p. 112
Gennevilliers (92 ; → Paris suburbs) : *Julius*, Julien **Foret**, p. 91
N Grimaud (83 ; → Massif des Maures) : *Les Santons*, Claude **Girard**, p. 741
N Hennebont (56) : *Château de Locguénolé*, Michel **Gaudin**, p. 300
Houdan (78) : *La Poularde*, Pierre and Sylvain **Vandenameele**, p. 466
Illhaeusern (68) : *Auberge de l'Ill*, Paul, Jean-Pierre and Marc **Haeberlin**, p. 137
Joigny (89) : *La Côte Saint-Jacques*, Michel and Jean-Michel **Lorain**, p. 348
Laguiole (12 ; → Monts d'Aubrac) : *Lou Mazuc*, Michel **Bras** (1987 winner), p. 774
Lille (59) : *Le Flambard*, Robert **Bardot**, p. 690
Lille (59) : *Le Paris*, Loïc **Martin**, p. 690
N Loué (72) : *Ricordeau*, Gilbert **Laurent**, p. 591
Lyon (69) : *Léon de Lyon*, Jean-Paul **Lacombe**, p. 567
Maisons-Laffitte (78 ; → Saint-Germain Forest) : *La Vieille Fontaine*, François **Clerc**, p. 474
Marssac-sur-Tarn (81) : Rest. *Francis Cardaillac*, Francis **Cardaillac**, p. 779
Mionnay (01 ; → The Dombes Plateau) : Rest. *Alain Chapel*, Alain **Chapel**, p. 561
N Morlaix (29) : *Hôtel Europe*, Patrick **Jeffroy**, p. 306
Mougins (06 ; → Cannes) : *Le Moulin de Mougins*, Roger **Vergé** and Serge **Chollet**, p. 721
Moulins (03) : *Hôtel de Paris*, François **Laustriat** and Pascal **Bouffety**, p. 241
Nancy (54) : *Le Capucin Gourmand*, Gérard **Veissière**, p. 542
Nantes (44) : Rest. *Delphin*, Joseph **Delphin**, p. 310
Narbonne (11) : *Le Réverbère*, Claude **Giraud**, p. 502
Nice (06) : *Hôtel Negresco*, Rest. *Le Chantecler*, Jacques **Maximin** (1986 winner), p. 748
Orléans (45) : *La Crémaillère*, Paul **Huyart**, p. 831

PARIS (75)
1st arr. : *Le Carré des Feuillants*, Alain **Dutournier**, p. 75
1st arr. : *Chez Pauline*, André **Genin**, p. 76
1st arr. : *Rest. Hubert*, **Hubert**, p. 76
1st arr. : *Chez la Vieille*, Adrienne **Biasin**, p. 76
2nd arr. : *L'Auberge Perraudin*, Claude **Perraudin**, p. 77
5th arr. : *Le Pactole*, Roland **Magne**, p. 78
5th arr. : *La Tour d'Argent*, Claude **Terrail**, p. 78
6th arr. : *Castel, Rest. La Véranda*, Bernard **Chirent**, p. 79
7th arr. : *Rest. Jacques Le Divellec*, Jacques **Le Divellec**, p. 80
7th arr. : *Le Récamier*, Martin **Cantegrit**, p. 80
7th arr. : *La Cantine des Gourmets*, Régis **Mahé**, p. 80
7th arr. : *Le Bistrot de Paris*, Michel **Oliver**, p. 80
N 7th arr. : *Rest. Arpège*, Alain **Passard**, p. 80
8th arr. : *Chiberta*, Louis-Noël **Richard** and Jean-Michel **Bédier**, p. 82
8th arr. : *Le Lord Gourmand*, Daniel **Météry**, p. 82
8th arr. : *Lucas Carton*, Alain **Senderens**, p. 82
8th arr. : *La Marée*, Éric **Trompier** and Gérard **Rouillard**, p. 82
8th arr. : *Taillevent*, Jean-Claude **Vrinat** and Claude **Deligne**, p. 82
14th arr. : *Le Duc*, Jean and Paul **Minchelli**, p. 85
15th arr. : *La Maison Blanche*, José **Lampreia**, p. 86
15th arr. : *Rest. Pierre Vedel*, Pierre **Vedel**, p. 86
15th arr. : *Rest. Morot-Gaudry*, Jean-Pierre **Morot-Gaudry**, p. 86
15th arr. : *Olympe*, Dominique **Nahmias**, p. 86
16th arr. : *Le Pré Catelan*, Gaston **Lenôtre**, p. 88
16th arr. : *Le Petit Bedon*, Christian **Ignace**, p. 88
16th arr. : *Le Toit de Passy*, Yann **Jacquot**, p. 88
16th arr. : *Rest. Henri Faugeron*, Henri **Faugeron**, p. 87
16th arr. : *Rest. Jean-Claude Ferrero*, Jean-Claude **Ferrero**, p. 88
16th arr. : *Rest. Paul Chêne*, Paul **Chêne**, p. 88
16th arr. : *Le Vivarois*, Claude **Peyrot**, p. 88
16th arr. : *Jamin*, Joël **Robuchon** (1985 winner), p. 87
N 17th arr. : *Rest. Sormani*, Pascal **Fayet**, p. 89
17th arr. : *Le Petit Colombier*, Bernard **Fournier**, p. 89
N 17th arr. : *Rest. Paul et France*, Georges **Romano**, p. 89
17th arr. : *Rest. Michel Rostang*, Michel **Rostang**, p. 89
17th arr. : *Rest. Guy Savoy*, Guy **Savoy** (1985 winner), p. 89
N 17th arr. : *Rest. Apicius*, Jean-Pierre **Vigato** (1988 winner), p. 89
18th arr. : *Beauvilliers*, Édouard **Carlier**, p. 90

Pont-de-l'Isère (26 ; → Valence) : *Rest. Michel Chabran*, Michel **Chabran**, p. 420
Puymirol (47 ; → Agen) : *L'Aubergade*, Michel **Trama**, p. 102
N Questembert (56 ; → Rochefort-en-Terre) : *Bretagne*, Georges **Paineau**, p. 319
Reims (51) : *Boyer Les Crayères*, Gérard **Boyer**, p. 377
Roanne (42) : *Rest. Troisgros*, Pierre and Michel **Troisgros**, p. 572
N La Roche-Bernard (56) : *Auberge Bretonne*, Jacques **Thorel**, p. 319
Saint-Étienne (42) : *Rest. Pierre Gagnaire*, Pierre **Gagnaire**, p. 573
Saint-Père-sous-Vézelay (89 ; → Vézelay) : *L'Espérance*, Marc **Meneau**, p. 360
N Saint-Tropez (83) - Courchevel (73) : *Le Chabichou*, Michel **Rochedy**, p. 755, 804
Saulieu (21) : *La Côte d'Or*, Bernard **Loiseau** (1984 winner), p. 357
Strasbourg (67) : *Le Crocodile*, Émile **Jung**, p. 145
Toulouse (31) : *Vanel*, Lucien **Vanel**, p. 620
N Tournus (71) : *Greuze*, Jean **Ducloux**, p. 359
Tours (37) : *Rest. Jean Bardet*, Jean **Bardet**, p. 834
N Tours (37) : *Rest. Charles Barrier*, Charles **Barrier**, p. 835
Valence (26) : *Pic*, Alain and Jacques **Pic**, p. 420
Varetz (19 ; → Brive-la-Gaillarde) : *Castel Novel*, Albert **Parveaux** and Jean-Pierre **Faucher**, p. 519
Versailles (78) : *Les Trois Marches*, Gérard **Vié**, p. 478
Vonnas (01 ; → The Bresse region) : *Rest. Georges Blanc*, Georges **Blanc**, p. 559

N New members of the Hachette Grand Prix Chefs' Panel.

Numbers in parentheses indicate the department in which the restaurant is located (see regional ~ front pages). The → symbol indicates the be consulted.

Gastronomic codes

M.C.F.: maître cuisinier de France
M.O.F.: meilleur ouvrier de France
C.S.H.C.F.: chambre syndicale de la haute cuisine française
J.C.R.C.: jeune chef des relais et châteaux
J.R.: jeune restaurateur

The many faces of France

France is not a country for short-cuts. The culture and atmosphere of the French nation have been developed through centuries of civilization. This is a country that deserves to be savoured. And just as you may linger over a menu before you savour the superb cuisine of France, take time to plan a balanced itinerary that will allow you to sample the rich variety of pleasures France offers.

These introductory chapters have been designed to prepare you for your trip to France. They open up a number of perspectives that may be explored separately or together to give you an overall picture of each region, terrain and site, taking in the climate, ecology, population, history, architecture, culture, technology and daily life. In this way, we hope to turn even the shortest excursion into an adventure, in which the unexpected and the spur-of-the-moment will play an equal role with thoughtful planning and pleasurable anticipation.

It is always a good idea to examine details in their proper context. Looking at the individual regions of France within the context of the French nation helps to explain their place in the entire scheme, as well as to define the distinctive features that set them apart. The regional differences, in turn, help to show how these various elements form a unified whole, with a distinctive identity among the countries of Europe. This unity in diversity springs from a twofold source in nature and in the history of the French people, whereby earth, air and water combine with human settlement and skill to create — and to offer you — a refined manner of living.

France is continuously on the move, and the far-reaching changes of recent years, here as elsewhere, have brought in their wake real risks to the traditional environment together with profound alterations to features once familiar. The latter part of this introduction will draw your attention to certain other developments that, while less immediately apparent, paradoxically seem to blend in with some of the most deep-rooted and characteristic traditions of the French people. These trends include the decentralization of government, the premium placed on culture, and the pursuit of the quality of life.

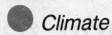

Climate

Averages are only rough guides to the weather. France enjoys a moderate, temperate climate with a relatively limited temperature range. In winter, however, this range widens from west to east, and in summer it narrows from southeast to northwest. The seasons are more marked in eastern than in western France. Atlantic humidity, Siberian air masses in wintertime, summer anticyclones from the Azores, and the Mediterranean influence in the southeast result in **four major climate types.** In Brittany and Normandy to the west, the prevailing climate is oceanic : changeable with frequent rain, often overcast, but with winds that drive away the clouds. The winters are mild and the summers rather cool. The major trends are apparent, although modified by latitude, in the neighbouring regions : hotter summers with more sunshine in Aquitaine, more distinct seasons in the Parisian basin. All of eastern France, has a more continental climate, with more marked contrasts : cold winters, hot summers. The Mediterranean Midi is sunny and dry, with greater extremes : winds, autumn storms. Altitude and exposure play a decisive role in the mountains. Temperatures fall and winters last longer the higher you go.

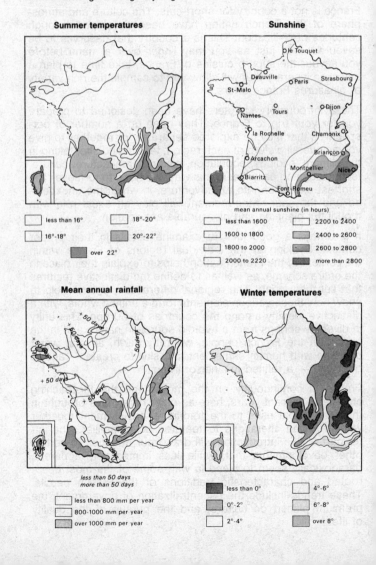

Summer temperatures

	less than 16°		18°-20°
	16°-18°		20°-22°
	over 22°		

Sunshine

mean annual sunshine (in hours)

	less than 1600		2200 to 2400
	1600 to 1800		2400 to 2600
	1800 to 2000		2600 to 2800
	2000 to 2220		more than 2800

le Touquet
Deauville — Paris — Strasbourg
St-Malo
Nantes — Tours — Dijon
la Rochelle — Chamonix
Arcachon — Briançon
Montpellier — Nice
Biarritz
Font-Romeu

Mean annual rainfall

— less than 50 days
more than 50 days

	less than 800 mm per year
	800-1000 mm per year
	over 1000 mm per year

Winter temperatures

	less than 0°		4°-6°
	0°-2°		6°-8°
	2°-4°		over 8°

Beginnings

The territory was populated in the **Palaeolithic Era** by bison- and reindeer-hunters seeking refuge in the Aquitainian basin during the last Ice Age. Notable sites from this era include Les Eyzies, Lascaux and Nas d'Azil. The **Neolithic Era** brought settled populations who cleared forests and established an agricultural economy. Colonization proceeded slowly but steadily from 6 000BC (on the northeastern plains) until 2 000BC (in the mountain massifs). The use of copper and pottery began to spread at the same time. The remarkable megaliths of Brittany still stand as witnesses to these early peoples, and the lesser-known dolmens of the Midi are even more numerous. A population base was established in about 1 000BC with the arrival of the **Celts**, an Indo-European race who came from the East. France owes to them the principal features of the agrarian landscape. Settling down, the Celts established townships that were usually raised and fortified. The original Gallic civilization rose and fell with the Celts. Their early burial mounds *(tumuli)* were succeeded by flat tombs in which urns containing the ashes of the dead were placed, hence the description of the period as "urn-field civilization". Bronze and pottery crafts were perfected at this time. The Celtic civilization was overlaid with the Roman imprint after the conquest by **Julius Caesar.** Celtic tongues were replaced by Latin; the Continental country of Gaul was transformed into a huge Mediterranean province. Over the agricultural foundations rose an urban civilization that is still apparent at Arles, Autun, Fréjus, Lyon, Nîmes, Narbonne, Orange, Vaison and Vienne, among other sites. In the same way, the contributions of **Germanic invaders** were assimilated. Notable among these invaders were the Franks who, after being converted to Christianity, rebuilt Gallic unity during the Merovingian Era. Other important strains were those of the Arabs in southern France, and the Scandinavians who occupied modern-day Normandy in the 10thC.

Prehistoric and Gallo-Roman sites

● Prehistoric sites   ▫ Gaulish sites   ★ Gallo-Roman sites

-600

ca.-300 — Founding of Marseille

-121 — Celtic conquest of S. Gaul

-59-52 — Roman annexation of Provence

-53 — Gallic Wars

12 — Revolt by Vercingetorix

162 — 1st assembly of Gauls

233 — Germanic incursions into Gaul

ca.250 — 1st German invasion

355 — 1st churches founded

373-397 — Invasions by Franks, Germans and Saxons

451 — St. Martin Bishop of Tours

481 — Invasion of Huns

ca.496 — Clovis King of Franks

507 — Clovis converts to Christianity

629 — Clovis defeats Visigoths at Vouillé

ca.630 — Dagobert King of Franks

732 — 1st Benedictine monasteries

751 — Defeat of Moors at Poitiers

800 — Pépin le Bref

814 — Charlemagne Emperor

843 — Louis le Pieux Emperor

885 — Treaty of Verdun

Normans besiege Paris

910 — Cluny Abbey founded

911 — Treaty of St-Clair-sur-Epte sets boundaries of Normandy

975-1000 — Construction of Cluny II

987 — Hugues Capet

1006-1019 — Construction of St-Philibert at Tournus

1066 — England conquered by William the Conqueror

1097 — Foundation of Cîteaux; 1st Crusade

ca.1100 — Moissac Abbey

1115 — Clairvaux Abbey

1222 — Suger Abbot of St-Denis

ca.1132 — Vézelay and Autun

ca.1140 — Cathar heresy develops

1145 — Royal Portal of Chartres

Birth of a nation

Pépin le Bref (Pippin the Short) and his son Charlemagne united the western Germanic peoples of France, Germany and Italy under their sway and established the economic and social institutions of large domains, vassalage and serfdom. In 843, the Treaty of Verdun laid the foundations for the great Western states of the Middle Ages. Western France *(Francia occidentalis)* became a distinct entity. In 987, Hugues Capet was elected King of the Franks, although his power extended no farther than a small area around Paris. Only in the 13thC did the official title of King of France appear, reflecting a growing idea of nationhood that began to emerge during the Hundred Years' War against England.

The Romanesque era

The Norman invasions and powerlessness of the sovereigns brought about a profound crisis in France. Of this crisis and its chief consequence, the weakening of royal power and the disintegration of governmental structures, feudalism was born. Due to its intermediary position between the Mediterranean and barbarian worlds, *Francia,* or land of the Franks, was the cradle of a new art form, from which Romanesque art sprung.

▶ e.g. Germigny-des-Prés; the crypts of Jouarre, Chartres and Auxerre; the choir of Saint-Philbert-de-Grande-Lieu, etc.

For the West, the years from 950 to 1200 were a period of continuous expansion that saw population growth, land clearance, technical advances, the rebirth of trade with fairs and pilgrimages, development of urban centres, and the peak of the Occitanian civilization of Mediterranean France. Villages proliferated, and France became covered in a "white mantle of new churches". The 11thC was the gestation period for Romanesque art, which was derived from the Carolingian heritage enriched and transformed by new influences.

Principal Romanesque monuments

Principal routes of the pilgrimage to Santiago de Compostela

The great innovation was **stone vaulting** : the semicircular barrel vault borne up by stout walls and sturdy pillars and supported on the outside by massive buttresses ; the groined vault formed by barrel vaults intersecting at right angles ; and the domed vault. The central nave, often hemmed in by side aisles, was crowned with a bell tower and extended by an apse. Radiating chapels usually placed in the apse were built over a crypt designed to receive the relics of saints.
▶ e.g. Saint-Benoît-sur-Loire, Vézelay, Autun, Caen, Poitiers, Saintes, Saint-Nectaire, Issoire, Conques.

Sculpture turned the Romanesque churches and basilicas into picture books, where carvings on the capitals, around the arches and on the tympana above the doorways told the story of man from Genesis to Judgment Day. The schools of sculpture were especially outstanding in the **South,** for example around Toulouse, and in Burgundy.

Painting was an important art in the Romanesque period, although few traces remain. Roving schools of painters often depicted the themes of the Apocalypse or the Last Judgment.
▶ e.g. Saint-Savin, Tavant, Berzé-la-Ville.

Romanesque architecture reached its peak early in the **12thC.** Churches of a particular type or "family" were clustered in regions, such as the churches of Auvergne that spread from Notre-Dame-du-Port at Clermont-Ferrand, the hall-churches in Poitou, the domed churches of Aquitaine, the Provençal churches built in imitation of Roman monuments, and the churches of Burgundy. Many churches were built along the pilgrimage routes. Each displays the influence of the monastic order prevalent in the area : either sumptuous **Cluniac** or austere **Cistercian.**
▶ e.g. Cluny, Paray-le-Monial, Fontenay, Sénanque, Le Thoronet.

Music was essentially liturgical. To the basic Gregorian chant, first written down in the 6thC, the 11thC monks at Jumièges added syllabic vocalizations, called tropes, that led eventually to the popular music of the 12thC troubadors.

At the same time, around the formal **literature** written in Latin, there sprang up an oral literary tradition in the vernacular tongue, which marked the beginning of the Old French language. The themes had much in common with myths, as in all such traditions : whereas the lives of the saints were intended to glorify the great figures of Christianity (the Golden Legend), the early epic poems *(chansons de geste),* such as the *Chanson de Roland* and the *Chanson de Guillaume,* praised the deeds of heroes of the feudal world.

The Gothic age

The 12th-13thC was the great age of medieval France. The population burgeoned from 12 million to 20 million, old cities underwent renewal and new towns (such as the walled *bastides* of the Southwest) were built, trade thrived at the great fairs (e.g. Provins), and artistic and intellectual life flourished with the foundation of universities.
Gothic art was first and foremost a **northern** French style, whereas the Romanesque was a southern form. Moreover, Gothic art grew out of the cities, whereas Romanesque art was a rural development. Gothic fashion spread from Île-de-France throughout Europe. Paris was one of the centres of the Western culture that was based on the Christian faith magnificently expressed in the Gothic cathedrals.
The 12thC was an age of experiment, first in Normandy and later in Île-de-France. The **13thC** was an age of achievement, which saw the construction of the four great cathedrals of Chartres, Reims, Amiens, and Beauvais, together with the Sainte-Chapelle in Paris.

Gothic art sprang from a technical innovation, **quadripartite vaulting,** in which pointed arches intersected on the diagonal to form a structural framework. This system, endlessly refined, freed architecture from old restrictions. Churches could be built higher, nearer to heaven, and opened up to light that would stream in like a divine manifestation. While this new art grew out of revolutionary technical progress, it was intended above all to express a new spirituality forged by exultant belief coupled with faith in man, and by fervour and serenity.

1152
Eleanor of Aquitaine marries Henry Plantagenêt

1163
Notre-Dame de Paris

1190
Philippe Auguste and Richard the Lion-Hearted on Crusade

1204
Crusaders take Constantinople

1210
Cathedral of Reims

1214
Bouvines, victory of Philippe Auguste

1218
Crusade against Albigensians

1226-1270
St. Louis (Louis IX)

1245-1248
Sainte-Chapelle

1248
St. Louis on Crusade

1253
University of Paris (Sorbonne) founded

1270
Narbonne and Toulouse Cathedrals

1285-1314
Philippe le Bel

1305
Papacy at Avignon

1314
Condemnation of Templars

1316-1391
Papal Palace built at Avignon

1337
Start of 100 Years' War

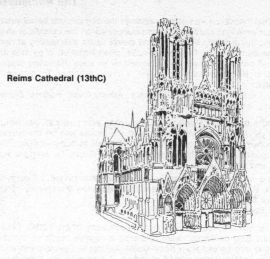

Reims Cathedral (13thC)

The faithful were welcomed at the cathedral doorways by statues that appeared profoundly human and reassuring : Christ triumphing over death, the Virgin-Mother, the saints. Painting declined, replaced by **stained-glass** windows that streamed with light to make translucent pictures outlined by a lacework of stone. ▶ e.g. Amiens, Bourges, Chartres, Laon, Le Mans, Notre-Dame and the Sainte-Chapelle in Paris.

A new music made its appearance along with the early cathedrals. **Polyphony** resounded first at Notre-Dame in Paris, and Adam de la Halle composed the musical Mysteries and Plays that foreshadowed, by several centuries, the light opera.

Principal Gothic monuments

After the 13thC peak, Gothic architecture veered along an exuberantly decorative path. The 14thC Radiant Gothic, such as at Strasbourg and Metz, and the 15thC Flamboyant Gothic were distinguished by a profusion of curves, scrolls, lined vaulting, and brilliantly sculpted ornamentation. The Flamboyant style flourished especially around Normandy, Picardy, eastern France and, especially, Paris (St. Séverin).

Gothic art, symbolizing growing northern French influence, came late to the **Midi**, which had been the homeground of the Romanesque style. The cathedral at Albi is the finest example of the Gothic style adapted to local conditions. In a region rife with heresy and independence movements, high brick walls and a tower-keep symbolized the power of the Church and opened up huge spaces for preaching.

From the Middle Ages to the Renaissance

After the dark period from the mid-14thC to the mid-15thC, which was marked in France by economic stagnation, the Hundred Years' War, famine and plague, the years from 1440 to 1515 were a time of renewal, restoration, and recovery. The country revived, and economy and trade burgeoned along with building, which took on the intensity of a "building fever". Many **city buildings** embellished during the period remain to this day.
▶ e.g. Jacques Cœur Mansion at Bourges, Cluny and Sens mansions and the churches of St. Séverin and St. Merri in Paris, Hospital *(hôtel-dieu)* at Beaune, Town halls *(hôtels de ville)* in Arras and Saint-Quentin, Courthouse *(palais de justice)* at Rouen.

Churches were rebuilt with new, exuberant and often opulent decoration abounding in scrolls and arabesques.
▶ e.g. Cathedrals at Bordeaux, Nantes, Tours, Church of Notre-Dame in Alençon, Abbey of Mont-Saint-Michel, St. Jacques tower in Paris; Cathedrals in Troyes and Rouen.

Castles began to lose their warlike appearance : keeps were turned into lookouts, galleries replaced covered ways, gables and mullioned windows replaced loopholes, and decoration began to slip in everywhere, right up to the mantel piece.
▶ e.g. Châteaux of Chambord, Pierrefonds, Langeais, Ussé, Chaumont.

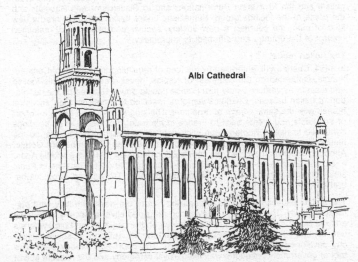

Albi Cathedral

1348 — Black Death

1407 — Civil War : Armagnacs and Burgundians

1415 — Battle of Azincourt

1429-1431 — Joan of Arc

1430-1470 — François Villon

1437 — St-Maclou at Rouen

1451 — Arrest of Jacques Cœur

1453 — End of 100 Year's War

1469 — France's 1st printing house founded

1472 — Château de Plessis-les-Tours; Jeanne Hachette rallies Beauvais

1492 — Columbus discovers America

1494 — 1st Franco-Italian War

1494-1553 — Rabelais

1498

Discovery of routes to Indies; Château de Blois

1515-1547

François I; Leonardo da Vinci at Court

ca.1520

Calvin's writings disseminated

1525

Defeat at Pavia

1531-1570

Fontainebleau decorated

1533-1592

Montaigne

1533

Château de Chambord

1534-1543

Cartier's voyages

1539

Ordinance of Villers-Cotterêts : official French language

1541

Calvin's writings translated

1546-1559

Louvre by Pierre Lescot

1547

Persecution of French Protestants

1547-1559

Henri II

1559

1st Synod of Reformed Church

In the 15thC, **sculpture** achieved independence and sculptors emerged from anonymity. The most renowned sculpture school grew up at the court of the Dukes of Burgundy. Subjects were invariably religious in inspiration : the Virgin and Child, the Virgin embracing the dead Christ, Death.

During the same two centuries, **painting** took an important step forward with the appearance of pictures worked on the easel. The late masterpieces of manuscript illumination are exemplified by the Book of Hours of the Duke of Berry *(Les Très Riches Heures de Jean Duc de Berry)*, and mural painting achieved brilliance with the Dance of Death at Chaise-Dieu. The portrait (ca. 1360) of Jean le Bon (now in the Louvre Museum, Paris) marked the beginning of French portraiture. Painting blossomed under the dual influence of Flanders and Italy. The new flowering of French painting was epitomized in Provence by the Pietà of Avignon (now in the Louvre) and the Coronation of the Virgin by Enguerrand Quarton (at Villeneuve-lès-Avignon), and elsewhere by the portraits of Jean Fouquet and the works of the Moulins Master (at Moulins and Autun). Nevertheless, **tapestry** hangings remained the most important feature of decoration.

The Flemish Guillaume Dufay and Josquin Des Prés dominated the **musical scene.**

By the end of the 15thC, the kingdom was peaceful, and had been enlarged by the entry of Burgundy, Artois, Picardy, Anjou and Brittany into the royal fold. France was ready for the great adventure of the Renaissance. From Plessis-les-Tours to Chambord, the châteaux of the Loire Valley offer a panoply of the development of French art in the 15th and 16thC. The buildings illustrate the blending of late medieval traditions with new forms.

 # The Renaissance

The 16thC was a period of expansion for the economy and the population, stimulated by an influx of precious metals and distinguished by the development of the mercantile system together with the spread of printing.

The great fiefdoms were gradually absorbed by the Crown : Orléans in 1498, Brittany in 1532, the Bourbonnais, Auvergne and Manche in 1527. Territorial unification strengthened royal power. Central administration and royal justice were laid down : one king, one law. Governors and appointed commissioners, forerunners of the royal superintendents, represented the king in the provinces, and the Edict of Villers-Cotterêts, which established the Civil State, made French the official language of the nation.

Humanists and courtiers

The religious civilization that dominated the Middle Ages gave way to humanism that reflected a twofold return to fundamentals : to Christianity, with evangelism and the Protestant Reformation; and to Classicism, with Rabelais and the poets of the Pléiade group. Humanism, under Italian influence, bred a new kind of man, the courtier. A new society, secular and monarchical, assumed control of the country and affirmed its supremacy.

The Italian model

In 1494, Charles VIII, enthralled by the idea of rebuilding the Empire of Constantinople, embarked on the conquest of Naples, never dreaming that his foolish and disastrous venture would turn France upside down. Dazzled by the decoration of Italian palaces, Charles's warlords resolved to embellish their ancestral homes with the same wealth of ornament. The king led the way, luring a cohort of architects and artists back to France in his train. However, just as buildings continued to rise in Romanesque style right up to the High Gothic era, so the blossoming of the Italian style coincided with the **peak of Flamboyant Gothic.** Although decoration evolved, the construction remained that of the Middle Ages.
▶ e.g. St. Etienne-du-Mont, St. Germain-l'Auxerrois, and St. Eustache in Paris, small churches in the Vexin district, churches in Troyes and Brou, cathedral in Auch.

The Italian influence was already apparent before the wars with Italy, and permeated slowly. The Flamboyant style long remained alive, especially in Brittany and the North, but the hub of artistic life was on the banks of the Loire, where a new art and culture were developing around the life at Court. Absolute monarchy developed decisively under François I. The court had already become a tool of government; etiquette was fixed, royal ceremony and the nascent cult of monarchy transformed the nobles into courtiers. The great lords no longer had the means to call up private armies to do battle with the power of the King. They had, therefore, to submit, in exchange for which they were granted the appointments and revenues of the Court and the Church.

The sovereign and his followers launched the fashions. François I played the decisive part. Determined that his court should be no less dazzling than any in Italy, he extended invitations to artists such as Titian and Leonardo da Vinci. Leonardo, who died at Amboise in 1519, spent his last years as "First Painter, Engineer and Architect to the King". In the initial stage, only the **decorative elements** were clearly Italian. The early châteaux of the Loire blended medieval (layout, towers, roofs) and Renaissance (decoration, arcades, gardens) trends. At Amboise, Italian decoration supplanted the original Flamboyant Gothic. Blois, with its large windows and enclosed galleries, sealed the break with the Middle Ages. The style of Blois was soon echoed in the palace of the dukes of Lorraine at Nancy, the *hôtels de ville* in Dreux and Orléans, the Bureau of Finances in Rouen, and the château in Châteaudun. Chambord was the high point of attempts to sever the princely residence from its rough, feudal past.
▶ e.g. Ancy-le-Franc, Azay-le-Rideau, Fontaine-Henry, Le Lude, Beaugency, Montcontour, Assier, Puyguilhem, mansions in Toulouse.

Château de Chambord

The art of building was itself inspired by the lessons of the Italian Renaissance and, hence, by the strict architectural rules inherited from **Antiquity** : symmetry, harmony, balance. Architects adapted these rules to French traditions, bestowing originality on the art of the time, which prefigured Classicism. Anet is the model for such structures.
▶ e.g. Section of the Louvre Palace designed by Pierre Lescot and Jean Goujon (Paris), Anet, church in Gisors, the Gallery Bridge at Chenonceaux, Écouen.

Sculpture

The 16thC was a great age for French sculpture. Examples from the beginning of the century depict subjects typical of the preceding period, interpreted in the Italian manner. Important statuary from the time includes the tomb of the Duke of Brittany at Nantes, the tombs of Louis XII and Anne of Brittany in Saint-Denis, and numerous Virgins whose physical grace has the edge on their spirituality.

The rediscovery of Antiquity dictated the subjects of French sculpture for the next two centuries, when parks and palaces became populated by great mythological figures. Jean Goujon created the first models of this kind, examples of which can be seen in Écouen and in Paris in the Hôtel Carnavalet Museum, the Louvre, and the Innocents fountain. Pierre Bontemps was a more realistic sculptor (see his tomb for François I in Saint-Denis), and Germain Pilon, the Master of the Counter-Reformation, was already working in a near-Baroque idiom (tomb of Henri II and Catherine de Medicis in Saint-Denis). In Lorraine, meanwhile, the works of Ligier Richier (Pietà d'Etain, skeletal monument in the church of St. Etienne in Bar-le-Duc) and the astounding cemetery at Marville, which constitutes an outdoor museum, kept the great Gothic lineage alive, as did the sculpted calvaries of Brittany.

Painting and Music

Italian mannerism triumphed in painting, as can be seen at the châteaux of Fontainebleau and Orion. The portrait painters Jean and François Clouet and Corneille de Lyon took their cue from Fouquet.

The medieval polyphonic tradition was carried on by the great masters Clément Jannequin and Roland de Lassus, among others.

The Age of Louis XIII

1562
Massacre of Wassy; Protestants revolt

1572
St. Bartholomew's Day Massacre

1574-1589
Henri III

1589
Henri of Navarre wars against Catholic League for French crown

1592
Conversion of Henri of Navarre (future Henri IV)

1594
Henri IV crowned

1596-1650
Descartes

1598
Edict of Nantes

1598-1666
François Mansart

1606-1684
Corneille

1610
Henri IV assassinated

1613-1700
André Le Nôtre

1622-1673
Molière

1623-1662
Pascal

1624
Richelieu appointed minister

1629
Edict of Grâce confirmed that of Nantes

1631
French press born with Renaudot's Gazette

The Wars of Religion sounded the knell of the Renaissance. These Wars, begun in 1562 during the Regency of Catherine de Médicis, were marked by atrocities, including the notorious St. Bartholomew's Day Massacre on 24 August 1572. Henri III, assassinated in 1589, was eventually succeeded by Henri de Bourbon, the Protestant King of Navarre, who had to do battle for 5 years to achieve his coronation as **Henri IV** of France. Henri IV re-established religious peace with the Edict of Nantes, which permitted freedom of worship to Protestants, and reaffirmed the authority of the State. In Paris he laid the foundations for the rise of the urban middle class.

▶ e.g. Pont-Neuf, Place Dauphine, Place des Vosges and St. Louis Hospital in Paris, Henrichemont, the town built from the ground up by Sully, Minister to the King, Charleville.

Baroque

The conflicts of the late 16thC revealed a state of deep crisis, stemming from the first rupture between tradition and the modern spirit that revolted against the established rules. The conditions in Europe were translated into the new Baroque art form that was generated by the Counter Reformation. France did not completely escape this influence, and Classicism was reinstated only with the absolutism of Louis XIV, and then only within the court. The first half of the century was witness to the flowering of a much more heterogeneous art, strongly influenced both by the neighbouring countries and by popular traditions.

Château de Balleroy

The more diversified style emerged also in poetry and most of all in the theatre, where a taste for decoration, illusion and metamorphosis reigned in the court ballet, the opera, and the pastoral plays, and held its own until the time of Corneille.

Between 1600 and 1660, many features of French culture became fixed in relation to the Baroque-Classical duality. French Baroque style retained a reserve and severity that were never really at odds with Classicism.

▶ e.g. Sully Mansion and the Luxembourg Palace in Paris, Blérancourt, Rennes Courthouse.

The Counter Reformation

The art of the Counter Reformation was the art of a dominant church, sure of itself and determined to impose a sovereign, organized, hierarchical order. The Jesuits disseminated the model of their Church of Jesus in Rome, a style that

was distinguished by the invariable presence of the three orders of Classicism (Doric, Ionic and Corinthian) and by a large nave designed for preaching. The sumptuousness of the Counter Reformation church, in direct opposition to Protestant rigor, proclaimed it as the anteroom of heaven, as symbolized by the dome.
▶ e.g. Churches of St. Roch, St. Gervais, and St. Paul-St.-Louis in Paris, St. Vincent-de-Paul in Blois.

Louis XIII Style

Under Richelieu, all the powers in the country were forced to submit to the Crown as representative of a State that intended to be paramount in Europe. At this time, the feudal castles, testaments to the old feudal order to which Richelieu had delivered the death blow, assumed a symbolic importance by continuing to proclaim the power of the aristocracy at the very moment when the Crown had challenged it once and for all. New **brick châteaux** with stonework corners went back to the traditional plan of the French castle, symbolizing the aristocrat's desire for independence as he withdrew behind his lofty gateway.
▶ e.g. Vizille, Rosny, Grosbois, Balleroy.

During the reign of Louis XIII, who had little or no interest in city planning, architects working for the Church and for the great Ministers of State gradually consolidated a new mode ; Mansart with Maisons-Laffitte, and Le Vau with Vaux-le-Vicomte, together fathered the Classical style.
▶ e.g. Richelieu, Brouage, Sorbonne chapel, Churches of St. Roch and Val-de-Grace, mansions in the Marais in Paris ; Vaux-le-Vicomte.

French painting entered a period of eclipse before the creative explosion of the 1630s. The Flemish Pourbus the Younger was the official court painter, and minor Flemish masters carried out the decoration of Fontainebleau and the royal châteaux.

The Century of Louis XIV : Classicism

Cardinal Richelieu and Louis XIV, determined to re-establish the supremacy of royal authority, contributed a great deal to the success of Classicism. The order and progression of the straightforward ideas cherished by Cartesian rationalism, which was the philosophical underpinning of French Classicism, were ideally suited to the ceremonial and administrative absolutist government.

Versailles

After the Louvre and Vaux-le-Vicomte, which was designed by Le Vau, the palace of Versailles is the fullest expression of the order that was imposed everywhere in France, and that demonstrated the grandeur of the French monarchy to the rest of Europe. This theatrical assemblage of buildings, which was to fascinate the courts of Europe, was the temple of absolute monarchy. The château and the park, and even the town, were grouped around the Sun-King, representative of God on earth and answerable to Him alone. Strictness of form, majesty of proportions : the Academy ruled by the masterly hand of Le Brun fixed the rules of Classical order.
▶ e.g. Versailles, The Louvre, The Salpêtrière, The Institut, The Invalides, Place Vendôme, Place des Victoires (all in Paris).

Literature and the other arts were also dedicated to the sovereign, although here, Classicism prevailed only after having yielded to several endeavours inspired by Italian Baroque. The Italian influence dominated **painting** until the reign of Louis XIV ; Caravaggio's legacy was much in evidence in the works of the great painters of the beginning of the century, such as Valentin, Simon Vouet, and Georges de la Tour. Philippe de Champaigne and the Le Nain brothers introduced an extremely personal manner of painting, distinguished in the former case by mysticism and in the latter by solemnity. Claude Gelée (known also as Claude Le Lorrain), who lived in Rome for many years, was the first landscape painter, and Poussin, mixing sensitivity with Classical mastery, cast his shadow over the entire century. After 1660, Classical turned to Acade-

1635 — French Academy founded

1637 — Discourse on Method by Descartes ; Convent of Port-Royal

1639-1699 — Racine

1641 — Mazarin appointed minister

1642 — Château Maisons-Laffitte

1643 — Death of Louis XIII ; Mazarin and Anne of Austria co-regents

1646-1708 — Jules Hardouin-Mansart, architect of Versailles, for 30 years

1648-1653 — Frondist revolt

1660 — Pascal's Pensées

1661 — Louis XIV

1664 — Dissolution of Port-Royal

1665 — Colbert Comptroller-General of Finance

1674 — King at Versailles

1683-1764 — Rameau

1684-1721 — Watteau

1685

1694-1778   Revocation of Edict of Nantes

Voltaire

1699   Hardouin-Mansart Superintendent of buildings

1699-1779   Chardin

1702-1704

1707   Camisards' revolt

Steamboat built by Denis Papin

1712-1778   Rousseau

1715   Death of Louis XIV: Louis XV Regent

1721   1st Masonic Lodge founded in France

1743   Louis XV

1748-1825   David

1751   Volume 1 of Diderot's Encyclopaedia published

1762   Rousseau's Social Contract published

1774   Louis XVI

1776-1782   Support for American Revolution

1780-1867   Ingres

1783   Ascent of Montgolfier's balloon

1783-1842   Stendhal

1786   1st ascent of Mont-Blanc

mic; statuary was confined to strict imitation of the Antique mode, and painting witnessed the ascendancy of the ceremonial portrait. Rigaud, however, succeeded in conveying the psychological traits of his models, and Largillière renewed the portrait tradition by applying lessons drawn from Flemish art. Practically all the **sculptors** of the *Grand Siècle* (the Great Century, as this era is called), worked for Versailles under the direction of Girardon. Coysevox was the king's official sculptor, populating the royal palaces with equestrian figures. The two great sculptors of the Baroque age were Pierre Puget and the Italian Gian Lorenzo Bernini.

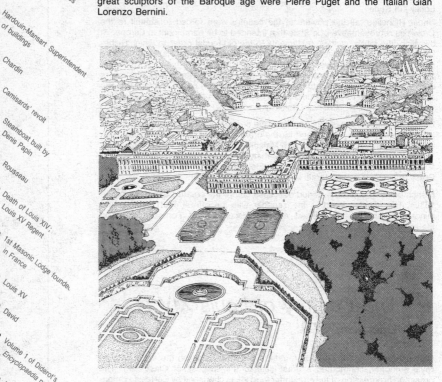

Versailles

Colbert

Jean-Baptiste Colbert (1619-83), who arranged royal patronage for the arts and sciences, also organized the first manufacturing development in France and the first State ventures into capitalism : a proper, planned network of roads radiating like a vast spiderweb from the capital; the tapestry factories of Gobelins, Beauvais, and Saint-Gobain; ropeworks for the royal navy at Rochefort and Rouen; and the first factory towns (Villeneuve).

Vauban

The reign of Louis XIV was also a period of strife, in which one conflict following hard on another exhausted the kingdom. This warfare, however, left a valuable heritage in the form of the remarkable works of Sebastien le Prestre de Vauban (1633-1707). In record time, he redesigned 300 fortresses and built 33 more from the ground up, making outstanding use of local resources not only for defense but also for the comfort of the inhabitants. His models of urban planning combine military logic with the demands of living.
▶ e.g. Bergues, Arras, Neuf-Brisach, Belfort, Fort-St. Vincent, Mont-Dauphin, Seynes-les-Alpes, Colmar, Entrevaux, Briançon, Château-Queyras, Port-Vendres, Montlouis, Socoa, Blaye, Saint-Martin-de-Ré, Belle-Ile.

The Tragic 17thC

It would be a mistake to think of the 17thC as a period of static, sovereign immobility. In fact, Classicism represents only a short spell of balance and harmony in a century that was torn by struggles between opposing forces : tradition versus progress, libertinism versus rigidity. Members of the cultivated upper classes threw themselves violently and passionately into various religious movements and a form of stylized affectation known as "preciousness" *(préciosité)*. Towards the end of Louis XIV's reign, a crisis of conscience, which waxed as the royal prestige waned, was focused on the quarrel that pitted those who continued to profess admiration for the ancient authors, the Latin language and the Classical spirit (typified by Boileau) against others who upheld the superiority of French and the spirit of modernism (Perrault and Fontenelle). The debate soon spread, and criticism of the established institutions (by such as La Bruyère, Fénelon and Vauban), the ideal of progress (Bayle) and claims for freedom of thought heralded the Age of Enlightenment.

The 18thC : Enlightenment

The Regency : salons and gallantry

The strictness of Louis XIV and the austerity that prevailed towards the end of his reign were abruptly succeeded by a joyous frivolity encouraged by an unprecedented economic boom that culminated in the development of major industry by the eve of the Revolution. "Live and enjoy!" was the motto of the day. **Paris** became the capital of pleasure, art and worldliness, the centre of taste and sophistication, as well as the nucleus of art in Europe. This was the age of gallantry, of dazzling receptions and salons where women reigned supreme. The **salons** fostered the spirit — formed by curiosity and the thirst for knowledge — of criticism and daring. Even more than in the days of Preciousness, love and the examination of feelings played the major role.

Construction flourished as never before or since. Châteaux, palaces and mansions changed in appearance, abandoning the rather theatrical grandeur of the previous century in favour of intimacy, gaiety and charm combined with luxurious comfort. The **salon** became the heart of the house, where the emphasis was on decoration; Baroque came back, by way of Italy and Germany, now dressed up in French style, and closely followed by rococo, grotto fantasies *(rocaille)* and the fashion for the exotic. This was the heyday of **gardens** and follies on the outskirts of the large cities, an age of dressing up as shepherdesses and cavorting in romantic ruins. Jean-Jacques Rousseau trumpeted the discovery of Nature as if it were Paradise regained.

The city of light

The growing awareness of the wider world and the passion for knowledge that characterized the Age of Enlightenment were summed up in the *Encyclopaedia* of Denis Diderot, which constituted at one and the same time a summation of politics and philosophy and a mirror of the age.

Concern for public welfare induced many superintendents, governors and prelates to endow their cities with public buildings that rivaled the finest palaces, and with city developments suited to the needs of a population that was growing apace. In Paris and the provincial capitals, the gardens and squares built during this period are still renowned.

▶ e.g. Place de la Concorde, Palais-Royal, Pantheon, Church and Square St. Sulpice, Military School and Champ de Mars, Odéon Theatre in Paris, Place Stanislas in Nancy, city squares at Bordeaux, Rennes, Reims, Peyrou Promenade at Montpellier, Fontaine Gardens in Nîmes.

Religious architecture was no less influenced by fashion. Abbeys and prelates' residences rivaled the palaces of the laity in luxuriousness. **Churches** were decorated like salons, with incrustations of marble and gilt.

In **sculpture,** the Baroque and the Antique remained at odds. The Baroque standard was upheld by Pigalle, Falconet, Pajou, Clodion and Houdon, who were opposed by the Coustou and Adam brothers, Bouchardon and Lemoyne.

Archaeological excavations at Pompeii brought Antiquity before the public eye, and the Louis XVI style managed to blend gracefulness with the Classical style, rediscovering the simplicity of straight lines, geometry and symmetry.

Watteau was the foremost **painter** of the century, imitated more or less successfully by Pater, Lancret, Boucher and Fragonard. Quentin de la Tour, Perronneau and Nattier were brilliant portraitists. While Chardin paid hommage to the Flemish tradition, Hubert Roberts's and Joseph Vernet's impressions of the ruins of Antiquity heralded the neo-Classicism that was later to reach fruition with David.

1789

May : convention of States
General- Jul : storming of
Bastille; Aug : Declaration
of the Rights of Man

1791-1792

Constituent Assembly

1791

Jun : King's flight and
arrest

1792

Proclamation of Republic

1792-1795

Convention

1793

Jan : Louis XVI executed

1793-94

The Terror : royalist
counter-revolt in Vendée

1795-1799

The Directory

1799

Nov : coup d'état of
18 Brumaire

1799-1850

Balzac

1802-1885

Hugo

1803-1869

Berlioz

1804

Napoleon Emperor :
formulates Civil Code

1814

1st Restoration

1815

Napoleon's 100 Days; Waterloo

1815-1816

White Terror : counter-
revolutionary royalist
uprisings following
Waterloo

From the Revolution to the Republic

Three revolutions, two republics, two restorations, two empires : this was the laborious process that gave rise to modern France. Fraught with upheavals, the period nevertheless derived a certain unity from the class newly risen to power : the liberal middle class.

The 1789 Revolution : a decisive turning point

Ideas and criticism propounded by the philosophers, the example shown by the United States of America, the people's misery and a financial crisis culminated inevitably in the Revolution. Louis XIV's successors had attempted to cut back the allowances and privileges that were draining State resources, and to equalize the taxation burden in order to rectify the financial situation, but they encountered opposition from the upper classes, who wrested the Convention of the States General from the King in 1789. Under pressure from the Third Estate, events built up to a revolutionary explosion :
— 5 May : transformation of the States General into a Constituent Assembly
— 14 July : the storming of the Bastille, which symbolized Absolutism
— Night of 4 August : abolition of privilege : middle-class France took the place of the Old French aristocracy
— 26 August : Declaration of the Rights of Man, affirming the principle of equality
— 22 December : provinces replaced by administrative departments
— 22 September 1792 : the Convention elected by universal suffrage proclaimed the Republic.
The King's flight and arrest at Varennes set the seal on the monarchy's death warrant. The mobilization of the European states against Revolutionary France similarly condemned the social revolution set in motion by Robespierre, and the Convention ended in the bloodshed of the Terror. Worn out, France yielded to dictatorship by a victorious general : Bonaparte.

The Napoleonic Era

Under the pretext of seeking to liberate Europe in the name of revolutionary principles, Napoleon Bonaparte, first Consul then Emperor of the French, led France into a series of wars and managed briefly to extend the power of France over almost all the Continent. Napoleon's epic venture will haunt the spirit of the French people and the poetic imagination for a long time to come. Foundering after Waterloo and the 100 Days that followed Napoleon's escape from Elba, the Napoleonic Empire left France impoverished but at the same time enriched by a soundly organized, centralized administration; the system of prefec-

La Madeleine

tures, the schools and civil code still attest to Napoleon's organizational genius. The victorious states restored the Bourbon family to the throne of France. In 1830, however, a new revolution replaced Charles X with the liberal monarchy of Louis-Philippe. The Workers' Revolution of 1848 proclaimed the short-lived Second Republic, which lasted only until Napoleon's nephew became the second Emperor in 1852.

Empire Style

Neo-Classicism began in the reign of Louis XVI and achieved a peak with the First Empire. The taste for Antiquity reigned supreme; architecture boasted triumphal arches, colonnades and the style of the Greek temple, as seen in the Church of the Madeleine, the Chamber of Deputies, and the Bourse (Stock Exchange) in Paris. In painting, **David** introduced the fashion for Roman costume and influenced all the painters of the era, including Isabey, Girodet, Gros, Gérard, and even Ingres.

19th Century France

Neither Louis XVIII nor Charles X managed to reconcile the traditional values of the Old Regime with the demands of the new spirit. After the 1830 revolution, Louis-Philippe's "middle-class monarchy" failed to show itself capable of striking a balance between social order and liberalism, and the revolution of 1848 finally put an end to the Bourbon monarchs.

In the light of the revolutionary and imperial years, the atmosphere of the middle-class France described by the novelist Honoré de Balzac seems stifling and lacking in grandeur. A yearning for adventure intensified by bitterness following the defeats of 1815 fostered the desire for an alternative among the younger generation.

Romanticism

The Romantic movement, filtering down from the Northern countries, marked a turning-point in European culture. It entered France at the beginning of the 19thC along with rupture and revolt : rupture with the Classical tradition and the worship of Antiquity, revolt against withering rationalism; rupture with the society of the time, revolt against convention and mediocrity. Revolt led naturally enough to escapism — escape into nature, back to the legendary Middle Ages, to exotic landscapes, into contemplation.

The watchword everywhere was freedom : in art, in the theatre, where drama ousted tragedy, and in painting, where first Géricault then Delacroix revolted against the Academic style. Painting became suffused with brilliant colour and subjective imagination.

From the Empire to the Republic

The 1848 Revolution ushered in the Second Republic but, after crushing the Workers' Movement during the events of June, the regime took a conservative turn before being abolished in the coup d'état staged by Louis-Napoléon Bonaparte on 2 December 1851. This nephew of the first Emperor restored the Empire on 2 December 1852 and assumed the name of Napoleon III.

The **Second Empire** was as important in terms of the economy as the 1789 Revolution had been in terms of politics : it brought France into the industrial age and provided remarkable economic growth. The ill-thought-out Franco-Prussian War of 1870, however, ended in disaster at Sedan and brought about the regime's downfall.

After 80 years of upheaval and revolution, France enjoyed a period of apparent stability under the **Third Republic,** during which the country amassed a vast colonial empire and passed important legislation that established fundamental freedoms as well as the first social welfare laws.

Starting with the Second Empire, it was no longer possible to refer to "an artistic movement"; rather, a series of successive and superimposed movements gave rise to debate about the very principles upon which modern humanism, art and poetry were founded.

The real winner of the Revolution was the Middle Class; in every regime it has been the Middle Class that has controlled political life and — especially since 1830 — has set the tone for society. A divorce was enacted between artist and public, between "sensitive souls" and "bourgeois society". The Romantic generation suffered through not being understood, but the dividing line was drawn bolder after 1850, and the history of art is punctuated with trials (Balzac, Flaubert,

1819-1877	Courbet
1821-1880	Flaubert
1822-1895	Pasteur
1824	Charles X
1830	Revolution in favour of Louis-Philippe
1830-47	Conquest of Algeria
1840-48	Guizot government
1841-1919	Renoir
1844-1896	Verlaine
1848	Second Republic
1851	Coup d'état by Louis-Napoleon; Second Empire
1854-1891	Rimbaud
1857	Baudelaire's Flowers of Evil published
1870-71	Franco-Prussian War: defeat at Sedan; fall of Empire
1871	Paris Commune
1874	1st Impressionist exhibition
1875	Third Republic
1889	Eiffel Tower
1897	Gide's Fruits of the Earth published
1897-99	Dreyfus Affair
1898-1904	Cézanne's Bathers publicly exhibited
1905	Official separation of church and state

Paris Opéra (1861)

Zola, Manet) and rejections of artists (Courbet and the Realists, Manet and the Impressionists, the Fauvists, the Cubists, and so on).

The former aristocracy henceforth was to look only to the past, clinging to its rejection of the modern world and of the new celebrities of this "industrious century singularly lacking in worthiness", who looked to models of the Old Regime for signals of their success and rise in society. This twofold movement fostered the most traditionalistic Academic art.

Architecture, more dependent than the other arts on financial conditions, erupted in a motley of borrowings; neo-Classicism, neo-Gothic, neo-Renaissance and neo-Romanesque styles sprang up. Nineteenth-century French architecture was primarily an eclectic, archival art, looking for its vocabulary in the history of France and the world. This was an age of archaeological summaries in the fine arts, of expeditions to Greece and Egypt, and of the discovery of historic monuments, notably by Eugène Viollet-le-Duc. Napoleon III's Louvre and Charles Garnier's Paris Opéra are the most remarkable examples of this composite style that mixed Renaissance ceilings with Louis XIII façades and Louis XV decoration.

Industrial architecture partly escaped the pervasive Academic influence by making use of the two great technical innovations of the age : iron and reinforced concrete. These materials were less in evidence in France, however, than in countries such as the United States and Germany. In Paris, an immense urban development programme was carried out in record time under the direction of Baron Haussmann.

▶ e.g. Courthouse, Stock Exchange and Fine Arts Museum in Marseille, Opéra, Gare du Nord and Mayor's Office of the First Arrondissement, National Library (Bibliothèque) in Paris, Meunier chocolate factory in Noisiel.

In the last years of the century, refusing any reference to classical architecture, **Art Nouveau** attempted to blend architecture, decor and furniture in a single style. Developed by Victor Horta and symbolized in France by Hector Guimard, Art Nouveau is characterized by the asymmetry of its forms and the predominance of the curved line.

For a long time, **sculpture** provided an outlet for pretentious effusions, such as can be seen in the endless processions of caryatids supporting the fronts of residential properties and monuments to great men in public squares. The more original sculptors encountered great difficulty in becoming established. Jean-Baptiste Carpeaux was favoured by the patronage of the Imperial family. Auguste Rodin struggled alone against the world but finally dominated the last years of the century with his powerful genius, infused with Romanticism and coupled with incomparable technical mastery. Antoine Bourdelle, a follower of Rodin, produced a considerable body of work that — not entirely successfully — combined exuberant imagination with a return to the archaic Greek style. Aristide Maillol introduced an unadorned, serene simplicity, with sculpture that was close to the earth and embodied goddess-figures brimming with strength and grace.

Painting was undoubtedly the liveliest of the arts. In the course of a half-century, one school succeeded another, each venturing further than the last in the quest for form. Developments were made possible by the enthusiasm of a few rare art-lovers and dealers in paintings, but most of all by the courage of the painters, virtually alone in their questioning of accepted values.

Two main schematic trends evolved. Realism revolted against the conventional Academic view, reaching its peak and exhausting itself with the coming of Impressionism. From then, the painter's subjective imagination asserted itself through the most varied techniques.

From Realism to Surrealism

Courbet was the master of Realism, which is not to say that his was not a highly personal vision of the world. He drew his inspiration from daily life, and the reproach generally addressed to him (that art should not impose ideas) was in fact aimed at **Realism,** this "aesthetic mistake", of which Daumier, Millet and Corot were also accused. Manet, also the subject of violent criticism, created an explosion in painting from 1865. He was the immediate forerunner of the **Impressionists** (Monet, Pissarro, Sisley), who sought to record visual sensation in its pure state. Renoir, Degas and Toulouse-Lautrec followed their own paths. Cézanne, Gauguin and Van Gogh, who overtook Impressionism, laid the foundations of modern painting, in which nature yielded to thought. Rather than breaking up form and volume, Cézanne emphasized them by contrasting colour and geometric shapes. To Gauguin, only the painter's soul mattered; art was an abstraction, a painting was music. Van Gogh was a visionary who expressed himself by means of colour.

Three movements arose directly out of the work of these painters : **Fauvism** (represented by Vlaminck, Derain, Dufy, Matisse), **Cubism** (Braque, Picasso) — which had the deepest influence on our view of the world, going beyond painting to turn the other arts upside down — and **Abstractionism,** which was not restricted to France.

In the 10 years from 1904 to 1914, from one revolution to another, works of art gained a sort of independence within the loose assembly of forms that made them, and active artists shed any specifically national character. Dada (Arp, Picabía, Duchamp), Surrealism (Masson, Tanguy, Chirico, Dali, Max Ernst) and Abstraction (Hartung, De Stael) played an important part in making art international. In addition, artists on the fringe — such as Douanier Rousseau, Bonnard, Rouault, Léger, Chagall, Giacometti and reformers such as Le Corbusier and Brancusi — produced images that ran counter to the art that was being produced in France.

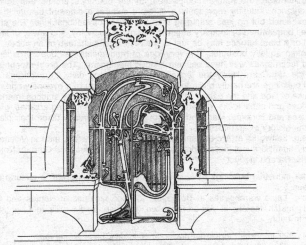

Main gate of the Castel Béranger (Hector Guimard)

Towards a contemporary architecture

Insofar as he was the first to adapt urbanism to the demands of industrial civilization, **Le Corbusier** (1887-1965) is both the pioneer and the symbol of modern architecture. The novelty of his conception of city planning lay in the interpenetration of inner space and outer volume. The house, considered as a "habitable machine", is composed of an ossature of concrete (whose aesthetic qualities were highlighted by Le Corbusier) "dressed" in prefabricated elements.
▶ e.g. Villa Savoye of Poissy; the "Radiant City" of Marseille; the chapel of Ronchamp.

1907 · Picasso's *Demoiselles d'Avignon* publicly exhibited

1913-27 · Proust's *Remembrance of Things Past* published

1914-18 · World War I

1919 · Treaty of Versailles

1925 · 1st Surrealist Exhibition

1930-32 · Great Depression

1936 · Popular Front

1939 · World War II

1940 · Occupation of Paris; De Gaulle calls for resistance; abolition of the Republic; Pétain head of State

1944 · Allied landings in Normandy; Liberation of Paris; De Gaulle transfers provisional government from Algiers to Paris

1945 · Capitulation of German army

1946 · Resignation of De Gaulle; Fourth Republic

1946-1954 · Indochinese War

1954 · Start of Algerian insurrection

1957 · European Common Market

1958 · Riots in Algeria; De Gaulle invested as chief of government

1959 · De Gaulle 1st president of Fifth Republic

1962 · Algerian independence

1965 · De Gaulle re-elected

1968 · Student protests; widespread strikes

1969 · De Gaulle resigns; Pompidou President

1970 · Death of De Gaulle

1974 · Death of Pompidou; Giscard-d'Estaing President

1981 · François Mitterrand President

1986 · Legislative election; beginning of "cohabitation"

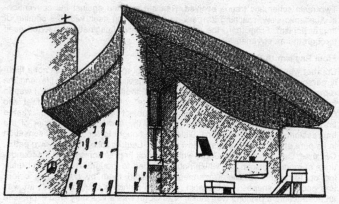

Notre-Dame-du-Haut at Ronchamps

The architecture of the Eighties seems, once again, to be divided between yesterday and tomorrow. Indeed, in reaction to irremediably futuristic constructions, references to Classical art ("post modernism") are re-surfacing, while some architects have chosen to put contemporary art to the service of the renovation of Classical buildings.

 # The industrial heritage

In France, ideas of the past are usually associated with rural life; the French were far behind neighbouring countries in becoming interested in their industrial heritage, the natural complement of the country's artistic and cultural inheritance. Industry represents a different culture, a different beauty that is unexpected but no less engaging than the more conventional kind. The structures bequeathed by industry attest to an era, an economy, and a way of life; a mill or a blast furnace may be just as interesting as a château or an abbey, and is often equally beautiful. The very idea of monuments has been broadened, and factories as well have become historic monuments. The great monuments of the 19thC are really the legacies of industry and daily life, whereas official buildings are hardly more than jumbled leftovers from a bygone world. The house of God and the palace of the King gave way to railway stations, markets, bridges and canal locks, department stores, factories, shopping arcades, glasshouses and libraries. Many industrial buildings have already taken their places in the history of architecture.
► e.g. Saltworks at Arc-et-Sénans, ropeworks in Rochefort, mills in Villeneuve and Sedan, Creusot glassworks, market-place (Les Halles) and Gare du Nord in Paris, Garabit viaduct.

Other industrial buildings have been renovated and converted to cultural purposes.
► e.g. Lainé warehouses at Bordeaux, tobacco factories at Nantes and Colmar, match factory in Aix-en-Provence, Le Blan textile mills in Lille, abattoir in Lyon.

Still other important industrial developments have been preserved.
► e.g. Sawmill at Saint-Sausan-le-Poterie, Meunier chocolate factory at Noisiel, Godin appliance factory at Guise, industrial village at Fontaine-Daniel, Niderviller porcelain factory, Morlaix tobacco factory.

Several obsolete factories have been turned into museums that are to a certain extent responsible for maintaining the industrial landscape. The **working museums** *(écomusées)* are the industrial counterparts of nature parks, or of local and regional museums. The first examples at Le Creusot and Fourmies now have many imitators.
► e.g. Glass museum in a former crystal factory in Sars-Poteries, Woodworking museum in Felleries, Marble museum at Bellignies, Historical mining museum in an old mineshaft at Lewarde near Douai, Regional living museum at L'Isle-d'Abeau.

Practical holiday guide

Information

Every major airline flies to France, either to Paris or to another of the country's **air travel** international airports.

Air France offers the widest range of travel and holiday opportunities, and reservations offices are good information centres for travelers.

The major Parisian airports are **Roissy-Charles de Gaulle** and **Orly**. From Roissy, **Air France shuttle buses** leave every 15 min for Porte Maillot, not far from the Champs-Élysées. **Roissy-Rail** provides trains every 15 min to the Gare du Nord railroad station, then on to the Châtelet metro station.

From Orly, there are **shuttle buses** to Invalides Aérogare terminal in central Paris, with a stop possible at Montparnasse upon request. **Orly-Rail** has trains every 15 min to the Austerlitz, St-Michel and Gare d'Orsay stations.

There is a **helicopter shuttle service** between Roissy and Orly, and also from these airports to a heliport at the Porte de Sèvres (metro : Place Balard) on the S edge of the city. Private air services are available at the **Zone d'Aviation d'Affaires** at Le Bourget Airport, N of Paris, before Roissy.

- **U.K. :** 158 New Bond St., London WIYOA, ☎ (01) 499 8611 ; Heathrow Airport, ☎ (01) 759 2311. **Air France**
- **U.S.A. : New York :** 666 Fifth Ave., 10019, ☎ (212) 247 0100 ; 1350 Ave. of the Americas, **offices** ☎ (212) 841 7300 ; 888 Seventh Ave., ☎ (212) 247 0100 ; Kennedy Airport, ☎ (212) 632 7200. **Chi- abroad cago and the Midwest :** John Hancock Center, 875 N. Michigan Ave., ☎ (800) 237 2747 ; 22 S. Michigan Ave., ☎ (312) 984 0200 ; O'Hare International Airport, ☎ (312) 686 4531. **Los Angeles :** 510 W. 6th St., ☎ (213) 688 9200 ; 8501 Wilshire Bd., Beverly Hills, ☎ (213) 625 7171 ; L.A. Airport, ☎ (213) 646 0028.
- **Canada : Montréal :** 979 Ouest Bd de Maisonneuve, H3A 1M4, ☎ (514) 285 5060 ; Mirabel Airport, ☎ (514) 476 3838. **Ottawa :** 220 av. Laurier, suite 340, ☎ (613) 236 0689. **Québec :** 2, place Québec, suite 742, ☎ (418) 529 0663. **Toronto :** 151 Bloor St. West, suite 600, ☎ (416) 922 3344. **Vancouver :** 1537 W. Eighth Ave., suite 104, ☎ (604) 733 4151.

Roissy-Charles de Gaulle, ☎ (1) 48.62.22.80 ; Orly sud/Orly ouest, ☎ (1) 48.84.32.10 ; Air **information** France, ☎ (1) 46.75.78.00 ; Air Inter, ☎ (1) 46.75.12.12 ; Air France offices : 119, av. des **in France** Champs-Élysées, 75008 Paris, plus numerous offices in other French cities ; Helicopter shuttle : Hélifrance, Héliport de Paris, ☎ (1) 45.54.95.11/45.57.53.67.

France is linked into Europe's extensive rail system and can be reached from such faraway **rail** destinations as Istanbul and even Vladivostock.

There is continuous service between England and France across the Channel. Only in July **ferries** and August are last-minute reservations difficult to obtain. Crossings last approx 35 min by hovercraft, and 90 min by traditional ferry. Overnight crossings with cabins are also available.

Most travel agents can supply information and reservations, or these can be obtained direct- **information** ly from the ferry companies :
- **Brittany Ferries,** Plymouth, ☎ (07) 522 213 31.
- **Hoverspeed,** Dover, ☎ (03) 042 402 02.
- **Sally-The Viking Line,** Ramsgate, ☎ (08) 435 955 66.
- **Sealink,** 179 Piccadilly, London W1V OBA, ☎ (01) 387 12 34.
- **P.O.,** London, 127 Regents St., ☎ (01) 734 44 31 ; Portsmouth, ☎ (07) 057 555 21 ; Dover, ☎ (03) 042 236 05.

Money

The French monetary unit is the **franc,** which subdivides into 100 centimes. The French use both the term "old" franc and "new" franc which can create confusion; however, prices are always quoted in "new" francs.

travelers All major travelers checks are accepted at French banks. Some hotels, restaurants and
checks shops also accept them, but the exchange rate is less favourable than at a bank.

credit cards **Visa,** which is paired with *Carte Bleue* in France, is the most widely accepted. Some, but not all, hotels, restaurants and shops accept American Express, Diners Club or Eurocard.
● In case of loss :
Visa, ☎ (1) 42.77.11.90; American Express, ☎ (1) 47.08.31.21; Diners Club, ☎ (1) 47.62.75.75; Eurocard/Master Charge, ☎ (1) 43.23.46.46.

Emergencies

● Anywhere in France : **Police,** ☎ 17; **Firemen,** ☎ 18.
● In Paris : **ambulances** *(SAMU),* ☎(1) 45.67.00.00; **poisoning,** ☎ (1) 42.05.63.29; **burns,** St-Antoine Hospital, ☎ (1) 43.33.33.33, *poste* (extension) 23.60; **medical assistance** 24 hrs/day (fee charged), *S.O.S. Médecins,* ☎ (1) 43.37.77.77; **dental emergencies** after 8 pm and Sun., hols., *S.O.S. Dentistes,* ☎ (1) 43.37.51.00.

Post and telephone

Postal and telephone services in France are run by a state-controlled organization, *Poste et Télécommunications* (or *P.T.T.*). Most post offices are open 8 am-7 pm weekdays and 8-12 Saturday. The main post office in Paris, open 24 hrs/day, is located at 52, rue du Louvre, 75001. Telephone directories from the world over can be consulted here.

telephone Direct dialing is possible to anywhere in U.K. and U.S. Pavement (sidewalk) phone booths increasingly accept only a special credit card which may be purchased in a post office (where you may also phone). Be warned that hotels and restaurants charge higher rates for calls made by clients.
Reduced rates exist : −30 % for calls in Europe after 6:30 pm and −70 % after 11 pm, and all day Sunday and national hols. Reduced rates to the U.S. : 10 pm-10 am (French time) and all day Sunday.

dialing Telephone numbers in France contain 8 figures. When quoting a number, do it by 10s, e.g. : 42.64.22.22 is "quarante-deux, soixante-quatre, vingt-deux, vingt-deux".
When calling from Paris to the provinces, dial 16 before the 8-figure number.
When calling Paris from the provinces, dial 16.1 before the number.
When calling from province to province, simply dial the 8-figure number.
If in doubt, dial 12 for Information.

Tourist Information

F.G.T.O. The **French Government Tourist Office** is situated in major cities abroad and is, without a doubt, the best source of information for holidays in France. Although the F.G.T.O. does not book travel or accommodation, the staff go out of their way to provide all help necessary for planning holiday arrangements. The F.G.T.O. provides lists of tour operators and travel agents specializing in every holiday field; for example, travel for the disabled, inland waterways, country and farmhouse holidays, châteaux-hôtels, etc.
The **A.N.I.T.** *(Agence Nationale pour l'Information Touristique)* will provide additional help, while the **C.D.T.s** *(Comités Départementaux du Tourisme)* have complementary information for regions and departments of France. **Loisirs-Accueil** lists complete lodgings.

information ● **A.N.I.T.,** 8, av. de l'Opéra, 75001 Paris, ☎ (1) 42.60.37.38.
● **Air France** and **U.T.A.** offices throughout the world.
● **Direction du Tourisme** (for complaints), 2, rue Linois, 75015 Paris, ☎ (1) 45.75.62.16.
French Tourist Offices abroad :
● **Canada** : 1981 av. McGill College, Tour Esso, Street 490, Montreal QCMH3A2 W9, ☎ (514) 288 4264. 1 Dundas St. W., suite 2405, Box 8, Toronto ONTM5G123, ☎ (416) 593 4717.
● **U.K.** : 178 Piccadilly, London W1V OAL, ☎ (01) 629 12 72.
● **U.S.A.** : 610 Fifth Ave., New York, NY 10020-2452, ☎ (212) 757 1125. 645 N. Michigan Ave., suite 630, Chicago, IL 60611-2836, ☎ (312) 757 7800. World Trade Center, N103 2050 Sternmons Freeway, P.O. Box 58610, Dallas, TX 75258, ☎ (214) 742 7011. 9401 Wilshire Blvd., Beverly Hills, CA 90212, ☎ (213) 271 6665. 1 Hallidie Plaza, suite 250, San Francisco, CA 94102-2818, ☎ (415) 986 4161.

Customs, passports and visas

Visitors to France may import limited amounts of perfume, alcohol and tobacco duty-free. **customs**
Details of allowances are available at airports, rail and ferry terminals. Allowances are more
generous for Common Market members. Foreign currency is not subject to restrictions on
entry, but if more than 5 000 French francs are to be re-exported, a "Declaration of Entry"
form must be completed and submitted when leaving France.

● .French Customs Information Centre, 182, rue Saint-Honoré, 75001 Paris, ☎ (1) 42.60.35.90. **information**

Visas are NOT required for EEC member countries. However, a valid passport is required **passports**
to be in your possession when you depart for France. **and visas**
For stays of 3 months or more, a resident's permit *(carte de séjour)* is mandatory. Apply to
nearest French consulate or local *préfecture de police* when in France. EEC members must
have a resident's permit in order to work in France. Citizens of other countries must have a
work permit which is very difficult to obtain at present. Apply to : 93, av. Armen-
tiers, 75011 Paris.
For U.S. and Canadian citizens, a visa IS required. This must be obtained in a French consulate in your country of origin before making airline reservations to France; it cannot be
obtained in France. You don't have to wait and there is a slight fee. You can also do it by
mail. Brochures concerning work permits for American citizens are available at the American
Embassy, 2, rue Saint-Florentin, 75042 Paris Cedex 01, ☎ (1) 42.61.80.75/42.96.14.88. Canadian citizens, contact : Canadian Embassy, 35, av. Montaigne, 75008 Paris,
☎ (1) 47.23.01.01.

 # *Travel in France*

France by plane

With more than 50 routes linking the major cities of France, Air Inter offers travelers the **Air inter**
quickest way to travel at competitive prices. Young people under 25, students under 27,
and senior citizens benefit from reductions of anywhere from 35 % (on flights called "vols
blancs") to 52 % (on flights called "vols bleus"). "Visit France" is another of Air Inter's interesting and economical ways to see France on the weekend or for a brief holiday. Information is available at Air France offices or at your local travel agent. Ask also about their "Carte
Évasion" which pays for itself in less than two round-trips and is advisable for anyone planning to do alot of flying within France.

● **Air France, ☎** (1) 45.35.61.61. **information**
● **Air Inter, ☎** (1) 45.39.25.25.
· For smaller towns private airlines, such as **T.A.T.** (Touraine Air Transport) operate flights. Check
locally at travel agents for regional flight information.
N.B. Remember to compare prices and convenience of air travel with the T.G.V. (high-speed train)
before making travel arrangements.

France by train

The French National railways (*Société Nationale des Chemins de fer Français* or **S.N.C.F.**) **S.N.C.F.**
has an extensive network of trains and very efficient service.
You can either travel by day or by night. For night passengers either couchettes (4-6 beds in
a compartment) or sleeping cars with private accommodation are available.

Food is served in most trains, either at your seat or in the bar or restaurant. Some trains **food &**
offer on-board entertainment by video. Enquire at S.N.C.F. offices in France or at **entertain-**
the F.G.T.O. abroad. **ment**

The high-speed train (*train à grande vitesse,* hence the initials **T.G.V.**) covers long distances **T.G.V.**
in much shorter times than other French trains, e.g., Paris-Marseille by T.G.V. is reached in
4 hours and 40 minutes. A standard 1st- or 2nd-class ticket with **advance booking is required.** Reservations can also be made just before departure at computerized machines provided in T.G.V. railway stations.

Tickets and reservations may be obtained in France at all major railway stations. Outside **tickets**
France, tickets and seat reservations can be purchased from appointed travel agents, cer- **& reser-**
tain railway booking-offices, and from the overseas offices of the French railways. **vations**

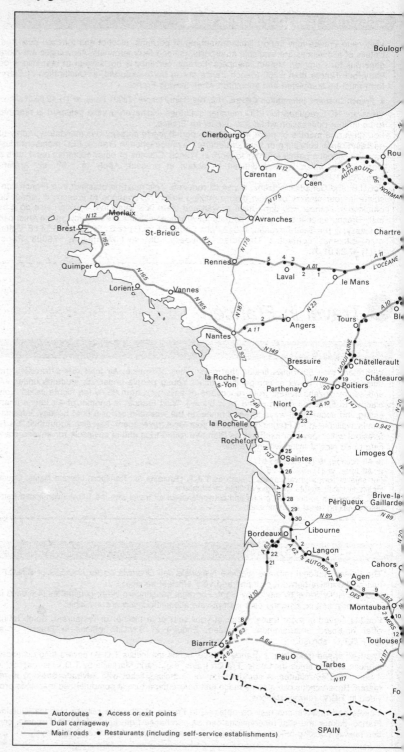

Boulogn

Cherbourg○

N13

Rou

○ *N12*

Carentan ○ *A13* AUTOROUTE DE NORMAN

Caen

N175

Morlaix

Brest○ *N12* ○Avranches

Chartre

St-Brieuc

N175

N165 Rennes○ 5 4 3 *A81* *A11* L'OCÉANE

Quimper○ *N12* 2 1

Laval le Mans

Lorient○ Vannes *N165* *N23* *A10*

N187 2 1○ Tours Bl

Nantes○ *A11* Angers

D937 *N149* L'AQUITAINE

Bressuire ○Châtellerault

la Roche- *N149* 19 Châteauro

s-Yon Parthenay 20○Poitiers

D746 21 *A10* *N147* *N20*

Niort *A10* *D942*

22

la Rochelle○ 23

Rochefort○ *N137* 24

25

N137 ○Saintes Limoges ○

26

27 Brive-la-

28 Périgueux Gaillarde

29 ○ *N89*

A10 30 *N89*

1 Libourne

Bordeaux○ 1 *N20*

A63 2 Langon

22 *A62* 4

21 3 AUTOROUTE Cahors

N10 5

6 Agen

7 *DES* 8 9 *A62*

Montauban *N*

2 *MERS* 10

N10 12

7 8 Toulouse

6 *A63* Tarbes *N117*

Biarritz○ 5 *A64*

6 *A63* Pau ○ *N117*

Fo

═══ Autoroutes ● Access or exit points

─── Dual carriageway

─── Main roads ● Restaurants (including self-service establishments) SPAIN

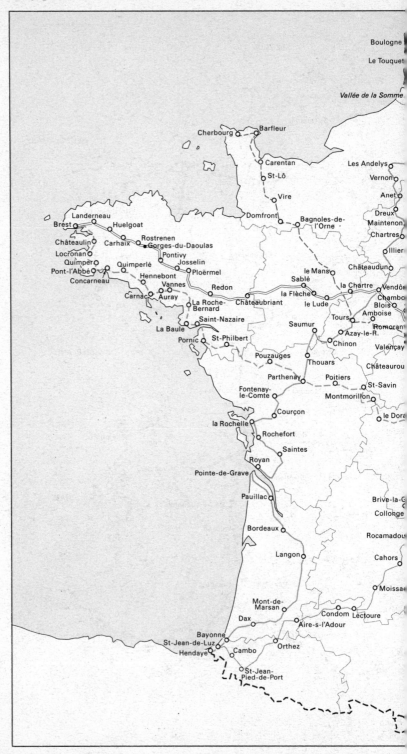

Echelle
0   50   100 km

The itineraries are sketched in different manners in order to distinguish one from another

motorail services Motorcycles, automobiles, and bicycles can be transported by rail within France. Enquire at S.N.C.F. offices.

train reductions Many reductions are offered to train-travelers within France, and herewith are listed the most interesting, but others exist. Enquire at S.N.C.F. stations about all reductions, including those for groups beginning with 6 persons.
Children under 4 go free, children between 4 and 10 pay half price, families traveling together get reductions, as do senior citizens. Other reductions are given for unlimited travel during 1-2 months **(Eurail Pass)**, for young people traveling between June and September, and for traveling during off-peak hours (marked in blue on train schedules.)

"Formule Plus" This is a special round-trip price which includes a theme, e.g. Carnival in Nice or *foie gras* making and tasting in the Périgord.

France-Vacances pass This card entitles any persons residing outside of France and Corsica to travel the whole French rail network for 4, 9 or 16 days within a time limit of 15 days to a month. Other advantages of this pass are : 1-2 days of free transport by bus/métro in Paris, car rentals at reduced prices, reductions at museums, etc. Outside France the pass can be obtained at certain travel agencies and UTA offices; within France it can be bought at S.N.C.F. offices, Orly and Roissy airports, and major rail stations in Paris, Nice, Lyon, and Strasbourg.

information ● **Canada :** *French National Railroads*, 1500 Stanley St., suite 436, Montreal H3A 1R3, ☎ (514) 288 8255/6; 409 Granville St., suite 452, Vancouver V6C 1T2, ☎ (604) 688 6707.
● **U.K. :** *French Railways House Ltd.*, 179 Piccadilly, London W1VOBA, ☎ (441) 493 9731/2/3/4.
● **U.S.A. :** *French National Railroads*, Rockefeller Center, 610 Fifth Ave., New York, NY 10020, ☎ (212) 582 2816/7/8; 360 Post St. on Union Sq., San Francisco, CA 94102, ☎ (415) 982 1993; 9465 Wilshire Blvd., Beverly Hills, CA 90212, ☎ (213) 272 9767; 11 E. Adams St., Chicago, IL 60603, ☎ (312) 427 8691; 2121 Ponce de Leon Blvd., Coral Gables, FL 33134, ☎ (305) 445 8648. Each regional gazetteer section gives telephone numbers of main-line railway stations. In **Paris :** (1) 45.82.50.50.

Motoring

driving in France The French drive on the right and are subject to the same rules practiced elsewhere in Europe. The **right-hand priority** is one significant exception : right-of-way is given to vehicles coming from the right, whether at cross-roads or at T and Y junctions. There is also a **transferred priority to the left** on certain roundabouts (rotaries), marked on street signs. International drivers must be sure that their insurance covers driving in France, green cards no longer being obligatory.

licenses An international driving license is not required for drivers from the U.S., U.K. or Western Europe, but a **valid driver's license** (not a provisional one) from the driver's home country is.

speed limits High-speed autoroutes/highways : 130 km/h; 110 in rain or limited visibility. 4-lane highways/dual carriageways : 110 km/h.
Other roads : 90 km/h; 80 in rain or limited visibility.
Towns : 60 km/h.

car rentals ● **Avis,** ☎ (1) 45.40.32.31.
● **Europcar,** ☎ (1) 30.43.82.82.
● **Hertz,** ☎ (1) 47.88.51.51.
● **Autorent,** ☎ (1) 45.55.53.49.
● **Budget Milleville,** ☎ (1) 43.87.55.55.
● **Citer,** ☎ (1) 43.41.45.45.

assistance ● **U.K. :** *Europ Assistance*, Europ Assistance House, 252 High St., Croydon, Surrey, ☎ (01) 680 1234.
● **U.S.A. :** *World Wide Services*, 21000 Pennsylvania Ave. NW, suite 617, Washington, D.C. 20037, ☎ (202) 429 0655.

France in 7, 15 or 21 days

7 days — **Day 1 : Paris***** : Eiffel Tower, Champs-Élysées, Louvre, Notre-Dame, Ile de la Cité, *bateau mouche* (boat trip) on Seine by night.
— **Day 2 : Paris :** Madeleine Church, Opéra, stroll the Grands Boulevards and shop, Les Halles quarter, historic Marais area, dinner in Montmartre.
— **Day 3 :** Drive to **Chartres***** on A10 and A11 and visit cathedral. On to **Blois**** on N10 and D924, visit château. Drive along **Loire Valley** from **Chambord***** to **Orléans*** and then take autoroute back to Paris.
— **Day 4 : Versailles***** : visit park and château, return to Paris and see Left Bank from Blvd. St-Germain to Montparnasse, hear jazz in left bank club.
— **Day 5 :** Take TGV train to **Mâcon** and hire a car to see abbey at **Cluny****, then visit town

of **Tournus****; take autoroute to **Beaune***** for lunch. Drive to **Dijon***** for dinner. Take night train to Marseille.
— **Day 6 : Marseille**** : visit town and harbour and then on to **Aix-en-Provence***** and Cézanne's *atelier* and lunch. Drive across Les Maures mountains to reach **Saint-Tropez**** for dinner and night.
— **Day 7 :** Visit Saint-Tropez port and museum, drive the Corniche de l'Esterel road** to **Cannes**** and stop at **Nice**** where there are night trains to Paris or night flights.

— **Days 1-7 :** as above.   15 days
— **Day 8 :** Drive Autoroute A13 to **Rouen***** and then on to **Honfleur****. Visit **Deauville*** beaches, **Cabourg** and **Arromanches** (1944 Normandy landings) in afternoon. Then **Bayeux**** (cathedral and tapestry) and evening in **Caen*****.
— **Day 9 :** Visit Caen and **Avranches** and on to **Mont Saint-Michel***** for visit and lunch. Then drive to **Saint-Malo***** and **Dinard** in evening.
— **Day 10 :** Drive to **Rennes**** and **Angers**** for visits. From Angers on to **Le Mans***** on N23. Visit medieval city and automobile museum. Pass by Chartres on way to Paris on A11.
— **Days 11, 12 :** 2 days in Parisian museums, gardens and parks.
— **Day 13 :** Board plane for **Bordeaux*****, rent car, visit vineyards for wine-tasting.
— **Day 14 :** Drive to **Dordogne Valley***** and **Périgord region** through **Bergerac** to **Sarlat***** for lunch. On to **Rocamadour**** and the chasm at **Padirac****. Spend evening at **Figeac***.
— **Day 15 :** From Figeac drive to **Rodez*** for lunch. Then visit **Gorges du Tarn***** on your way to **Nîmes***** for visit to monuments. From Nîmes it's a short distance to **Avignon***** where you visit Palais des Papes and take night train or flight to Paris.

— **Days 1-15 :** as above.   21 days
— **Day 16 :** Leave early by car for visit to **Reims***** cathedral and champagne cellar. On to **Toul**** and **Nancy***** where *art nouveau* originated.
— **Day 17 :** Via **Lunéville**** and **Saverne,** arrive at **Strasbourg*****. Take boat trip on Rhine and visit old city and museums.
— **Day 18 :** Drive Alsace **wine route***** and finish day at **Colmar***** and museum. Spend night at **Mulhouse.**
— **Day 19 :** Visit Mulhouse and then drive down to Burgundy (wine and lunch). On to **Lyon*****; visit Renaissance quarter. Dine gastronomically.
— **Day 20 :** From Lyon drive to **Grenoble**** by autoroute. Drive the **Route Napoléon*** to **Monte-Carlo**,** stopping for lunch in **Gap** or on shores of **Lake Serre-Ponçon*.**
— **Day 21 :** Visit castle (see changing of guard at 11:50) in **Monte-Carlo,** Oceanographic Museum, dine in style, gamble at Casino, then night train to Paris.

— Take advantage of **train** + **auto** and **fly-drive** schemes offered by S.N.C.F. and Air Inter. hints
— See gazetteer sections for regional restaurants, museums to visit and closing days.

Children and young people

Many special services and programs are available to make children's stays more pleasur- hotels &
able in France. The Guide indicates which hotels offer 20 % or more reduction for children restaurants
under 5, the prices of children's menus when available, and babysitting services (consult
also local *Syndicats d'Initiative*).

The following welcome English-speaking children :   camps
● **Vacances-Loisirs,** 33, rue de Beaune, 75007 Paris, ☎ (1) 46.45.04.16 (for 9-12 yr-olds : model
farms where children participate in daily life, including chores).
● **Agriculture et Tourisme,** 9, av. George-V, 75008 Paris, ☎ (1) 47.23.51.50 (farm holidays and wide
range of activities).
● **Loisirs de France,** 30, rue Godot-de-Mauroy, 75009 Paris, ☎ (1) 47.42.51.81 (11 mountain
or seaside centres).
● **Pierre et Vacances,** pl. Ruches, Avoriaz 1800, 74110 Morzine, ☎ 50.74.05.22 (children's mountain holiday village).
● **Centre nautique de Rosbras-Brignau,** B.P. 3, 29116 Moelan-sur-Mer, ☎ 98.39.60.78 (sailing for
8-14 yr-olds ; basic French necessary).

Europe with Children, by Leila Hadley, is an excellent source of information for travelers hint
with children (750 pp., NY 1972, revised ' 84).

The **C.I.D.J.** *(Centre d'Information et de Documentation de la Jeunesse),* 101, quai Branly, young
75015 Paris, ☎ (1) 45.66.40.20, is the most extensive source of information for young travel- people
ers to France.
The **O.T.U.** *(Organisation pour le Tourisme Universitaire),* 137, bd St-Michel, 75005 Paris,
☎ (1) 43.29.12.88, organizes and provides information about travel and holidays in France, including
courses. Consult individual universities about this.

The youth-hostel network *(auberges de jeunesse)* is extensive, but there are many other facil- accommo-
ities for the young as well :   dation

● **A.J.F.** : Gare du Nord railroad station, 75010 Paris, ☎ (1) 42.78.04.82; Beaubourg : 119, rue St-Martin, 75004 Paris, ☎ (1) 42.77.87.80.
● **U.C.R.I.F.** *(Union des Centres de Rencontres Internationales de France)*, 21, rue Béranger, 75003, ☎ (1) 42.27.08.65. (Some have swimming pools, tennis courts, skating rinks as well as language courses and conferences.)
● **U.C.P.A.**, 62, rue de la Glacière, 75013 Paris, ☎ (1) 43.36.05.20.
● **O.C.C.A. J.**, 95, rue d'Amsterdam, 75008 Paris, ☎ (1) 45.26.21.21.
● **O.T.U.** offers single accommodation without reservations at 47 student centres in 32 cities.

general　● **C.I.D.J.** (see above).
information　● **Ligue Française pour les Auberges de Jeunesse**, 38, bd Raspail, 75007 Paris, ☎ (1) 45.48.69.84.
● **Union Française des Centres de Vacances**, 71-77, rue du Théâtre, 75015 Paris, ☎ (1) 45.78.27.45 (provides student holidays and an English-language brochure).

student　For exchanges between France and your home country, consult cultural affairs section of
exchanges　your local French embassy or consulate.
Two well-known organizations specializing in exchanges :
● **Franco-American Cultural Students Exchange**, 108 Westwood Blvd., Los Angeles, CA 90024, ☎ (213) 208 5542.
● **Central Bureau for Educational Visits and Exchange**, Seymour Mews House, Seymour Mews, London W1H 9 PE, ☎ (01) 486 5101.

language　● **Alliance Française**, 101, bd Raspail, 75006 Paris, ☎ (1) 45.44.38.28.
courses　● **Comité d'Accueil**, 166 Piccadilly, London W1V, ☎ (01) 493 2478.
● **Euro-Centre**, 13, passage Dauphine, 75006 Paris, ☎ (1) 43.25.81.40.

Accommodation

Hotels

classifica-　There are approximately 17,500 hotels in France, inspected and supervized on a national
tion　basis. They fall into 5 categories : ★ to ★★★★ (L).
★ = simple but comfortable and ★★★★ (L) = luxury hotel. Expect to pay more the more stars there are.

hints　Most hotels offer special rates for "pension complete" (room plus full meals) or "demi-pension" (room plus breakfast with lunch or dinner). Advanced booking is advised.

reserva-　Some hotels demand an **acompte** (down-payment) or **arrhes** (deposit) withheld in case of
tions　cancellation. Be sure to confirm your reservation on day of your arrival if planning to arrive after 7 pm.

chains　Over the last years different types of hotel chains have developed throughout France. The following have been selected for the quality of their service or originality.
● **Balladins**, 134, rue du Fg-Saint-Honoré, 75008 Paris, ☎ (1) 42.56.30.90 (40 modern, small hotels located on outskirts of cities or on access highways).
● **Campanile**, 40, rue de Villiers, 92300 Levallois, ☎ (1) 47.58.59.50 (135 2-star hotels of human dimensions, called Campanile in cities and Campanile in the countryside).
● **Capitainerie**, 5, av. Marcel-Proust, 28000 Chartres, ☎ 37.35.91.11 (sea ambiance for these hotels near industrial areas).
● **La Castellerie**, Castel Morphée, 2, rue de Lisieux, 61230 Gacé, ☎ 33.35.51.01/05.25.32.80 (52 hotels for castle-style living).
● **Châteaux et Demeures de Tradition**, demeure des Brousses, rue Mas-de-Brousses, 34000 Montpellier, ☎ 67.65.77.66 (70 hotels in the grand style).
● **Châteaux-Hôtels Indépendents et Hostelleries d'Atmosphère**, Château de Pray, 37400 Amboise, ☎ 47.57.23.67 (120 hotels and 13 châteaux to welcome you).
● **Climat de France**, B.P. 93, 91943 Les Ulis Cedex, ☎ 64.46.01.23 (23 medium-size hotels located at city limits).
● **Concorde**, 58, bd Gouvion-Saint-Cyr, 75017 Paris, ☎ (1) 47.58.12.25 (traditional or modern 4-star hotels, at least 100 rooms).
● **Confortel-Louisiane**, 26-30, av. des Frères-Lumière, 78190 Trappes ☎ (1) 30.50.80.03 (20 hotels built of wood for families).
● **Fimotel**, 22, place Vendôme, 75001 Paris, ☎ (1) 05.07.27.27 (22 hotels at city limits).
● **Flatotel**, 52, rue d'Oradour-sur-Glane, 75015 Paris, ☎ (1) 45.54.97.56 (apartments to rent within a hotel).
● **Formule 1**, Hotec, tour Maine-Montparnasse, 33, av. du Maine, 75055 Paris, ☎ (1) 43.20.13.26 (the latest chain of modest 1-star hotels).
● **France-Accueil**, 85, rue du Dessous-des-Berges, 75013 Paris, ☎ (1) 45.83.04.22 (170 hotels from 2 to 4 stars).
● **France-Lodge**, 2, rue de la Bourse, 75002 Paris, ☎ (1) 40.20.92.89 (French families provide lodgings and breakfast for very modest prices).
● **Hexagone**, 2, rue Chaptal, 11000 Narbonne, ☎ 68.32.48.90 (hotels with barbecues and gardens).

● **Hilton-International,** 94544 Orly Aérogare Cedex, ☎ (1) 46.87.33.88 (4-star quality hotels).
● **Holiday Inn,** 61 rue de Malte, 75011 Paris, ☎ (1) 48.06.20.00 (American-style comfortable hotel).
● **Hostellerie du Vignoble français,** Z.A. Pont-de-Joux, B.P. 40, 13360 Roquevaire, ☎ 42.20.04.41.97 (43 hotels in the heart of vineyards).
● **Ibis,** 6-8 rue du Bois-Briard, 91021 Évry Cedex, ☎ (1) 60.77.93.20 (*Ibis* on outskirts and *Urbis* in city centres).
● **Inter-Hôtel,** 31520 Ramonville-Saint Agne, ☎ 61.73.40.63 (more than 200 hotels with good French tradition).
● **International Leading Association (I.L.A.),** 23/6 Schuttersvest, B2800 Mechelen, Belgique, ☎ 32.15.42.07.30. High standards in beautiful private castles.
● **Jet-hôtel,** affiliated with *Meridien* and *Sotair*, by sea and mountains, ☎ 79.09.29.00.
● **Logis et Auberges de France,** 25, rue Jean-Mermoz, 75008 Paris, ☎ (1) 43.59.91.99 (4,600 hotels, often in the countryside; simple but known for local cuisine and quality of welcome).
● **Lucien Barrière,** 9, av. de l'Opera, 75001 Paris, ☎ (1) 42.96.98.59 (a prestigious chain, offering golf passes for weekends in Cannes and Normandy).
● **Mapotel,** 74, av. du Dr-Netter, 75012 Paris, ☎ (1) 43.41.22.44 (150 hotels in cities).
● **Mercure,** autoroute A6, C.E. 1405, 91019 Évry, ☎ (1) 60.77.93.20 (a member of the 2-star *Accor* chain).
● **Méridien,** 81, bd Gouvion-Saint-Cyr, 75017 Paris, ☎ (1) 42.56.01.01 (Hilton-style French chain, for business and pleasure).
● **Moulin Étape,** Moulin de Chameron, 18210 Gannegon, ☎ 48.61.83.80 (fashionable chain of 25 old but modernized mills in the French countryside).
● **Néotel,** 78, rue du Moulin-Vert, 75015 Paris, ☎ (1) 40.44.81.81 (2- and 3-star office/hotels renovated with taste).
● **Novotel,** 2, rue de la Marre-Neuve, 91021 Évry, ☎ (1) 60.77.93.00 (at the city's gates, city centres or tourist areas).
● **Petits Nids de France,** 33, rue Alsace-Lorraine, 53000 Cambrai, ☎ 27.81.30.16 (135 2-star hotels, known for family-style welcome).
● **Pullman International Hotels,** 12, rue Portalis, 75008 Paris, ☎ (1) 05.28.88.00/42.67.27.90 (5 chains with different ratings : *Pullman* (top quality), *Altea* (middle-price range), *PLM-Azur* (hotels with sports and activities), *Arcade* (2 stars, in towns), *Primo* (good quality, modest price).
● **Relais Bleus,** bd Alfred Casil, 13127 Vitrolles, ☎ 42.89.31.88 (best quality at best price).
● **Relais Saint Pierre,** 5, rue Pierre-Vernier, 25290 Ornans, ☎ 81.57.16.44 (70 hotels specializing in fishing).
● **Relais St. Pierre,** 31-33, rue Falguière, 75015 Paris, ☎ (1) 43.21.75.75.
● **Relais du Silence,** Hôtel Les Oiseaux, 38640 Claix, ☎ 76.98.35.79 (250 hotels, from 2 to 4 stars, whose name defines their originality !).
● **Relais et Châteaux,** Hôtel de Crillon, 10, place de la Concorde, 75008 Paris, ☎ (1) 47.42.00.20 (150 prestigious 3- and 4-star hotels).
● **Romantik Hotels,** 3, rue Th.-de-Banville, 75017 Paris, ☎ (1) 42.27.49.18 (European chain that offers stays in 11 historic dwellings).
● **Sofitel,** 2, rue de la Marre-Neuve, 91021 Évry, ☎ (1) 60.77.65.65 (4-star luxury hotels in city centres with gastronomy).
● **Telemark,** 23, rue des Mathurins, 75008 Paris, ☎ (1) 47.42.44.66 (3-star hotels in Alps, a new one due to open in Annecy).
● **Timhotel,** 3, rue de la Banque, 75002 Paris, ☎ (1) 42.61.53.90 (modern 2-star hotels set in old and charming neighbourhoods of Paris).
● **Tradotel,** 1, villa Boissière, 75016 Paris, ☎ (1) 47.27.15.15 (caters to international clientele).
● **Videotel,** 37, av. de l'Opera, 75002 Paris, ☎ (1) 42.97.53.54 (for business people, rooms provide v.c.r's and cable t.v. for American television).

Rural holidays

These are low-cost, self-catering holiday homes in the heart of rural France. Privately-owned, the *gîtes* attract families primarily and are simple accommodations. Minimum stay is two weeks in peak (summer) season.   **Gîtes de France**
● **Fédération Nationale des Gîtes Ruraux de France,** 35, rue Godot-de-Mauroy, 75009 Paris, ☎ (1) 47.42.25.43.

● **Café Couette,** 8, rue d'Isly, 75008 Paris, ☎ (1) 42.94.92.00.   **bed & breakfast**

● **Agriculture et Tourisme,** 9, av. George-V, 75008 Paris, ☎ (1) 47.23.51.50.   **farm stays**

Certain châteaux and manor-houses will provide rooms and dining to paying guests.   **château stays**
● **Château-Accueil,** Mme de Bonneval, Château de Thaumiers, Thaumiers, 18210 Charenton-du-Cher, ☎ 48.61.81.62 (publishes brochure containing 37 châteaux).
● **Châteaux en Vacances,** B.P. 4, 78220 Viroflay, ☎ 30.24.18.16 (for short stays).
● **Châteaux-Hôtels,** Château de Pray, 37400 Amboise, ☎ 47.57.23.67 (13 châteaux).
● **Les Étapes François-Cœur,** 172, Grande-Rue, 92380 Garches, ☎ (1) 47.95.06.47 (quality family dwellings).

Camping

classification · Campsites are either classified into 4 categories (depending on comfort provided) or not at all. For peak-season stays, reservations are strongly recommended.
- **Fédération Française de Camping-Caravaning**, 78, rue de Rivoli, 75004 Paris, ☎ (1) 42.72.84.08.
- **Fédération Nationale de l'Hôtellerie de Plein Air**, 105, rue Lafayette, 75010 Paris, ☎ (1) 48.78.13.77.
- **Campéoles**, 38, bd Edgar-Quinet, 75014 Paris, ☎ (1) 43.22.01.01.
- **Les Huttes de France**, 46, bd. Pasteur, 63001 Clermont-Ferrand, ☎ 73.93.81.10.

farm-camping · **Maison du Tourisme Vert**, 35, rue Godot-de-Mauroy, 75009 Paris, ☎ (1) 47.42.20.20.

château-camping · **Castel-Camping**, Château des Ormes, 35120 Dol-de-Bretagne, ☎ 99.48.10.19

 Calendar, events

Calendar

Despite encouragement to vacation during other months, the French prefer July and August and particularly August is THE holiday month.

hints · If at all possible, avoid traveling on the following dates : 1 Jul., weekend of 14 Jul., 31 Jul., 1 Aug., weekend of 15 Aug.
May, June, September and October are not only less crowded but they are also cheaper.

national holidays · 1 Jan., Easter Mon., 1 May, 8 May, Ascension Day, Pentecost Mon., 14 Jul., 15 Aug., 1 Nov., 11 Nov., 25 Dec.

Cultural events

Few countries offer so much art and culture in such varied surroundings. Local newspapers and tourist offices are excellent sources of information for the cultural festivals of France.

festivals · **Music :** Aix-en-Provence (Jul.), Albi (Jul.-Aug.), Antibes (Jul.), Les Arcs (Jul.-Aug.), Besançon (Sep.), Bordeaux (May), Bourges (May-Jun.), Carpentras (Jul.-Aug.), La Chaise-Dieu (Aug.-Sep.), Chartres (Jul.), Comminges (Jul.-Aug.), Cordes (Jun.-Sep.), Dijon (Jun.-Sep.), Divonne-les-Bains (Jun.-Jul.), Évian (May), Gannat (Jul.), Gourdon (Jul.-Aug.), Ile-de-France (May-Jun.), Lille (Oct.), Lorient (Aug.), Lourdes (Easter), Lyon (May-Jun., Sep.), Menton (Aug.), Metz (Nov.), Mont-Saint-Michel (Jul.-Aug.), Nice (Jul.), Nîmes (Jun.-Jul.) and many, many others.
Dance : Arles (Jul.), Bordeaux (May), Carpentras (Jul.-Aug.), Châteauvallon Toulon (Jul.), Gannat (Jul.), Montpellier (Jun.), Paris (Sep.-Oct.), La Rochelle (Mar.-Apr.).
Theatre : Aigues-Mortes (Aug.), Angers (Jun.), Avignon (Jul.), Bordeaux (May), Nancy (May), Paris (Jun.-Dec.), Quimper (Jul.-Aug.), La Rochelle (May-Jun.), Sarlat (Jul.-Aug.).
Cinema : Avoriaz (Jun.), Cannes (May), Deauville (Sep.), Dinard (Sep.), La Rochelle (Mar.-Apr.).

information · **All F.G.T.O.** offices.
- **La France en Fête :** a brochure published by Direction du Tourisme, 2, rue Linois, 75740 Paris Cedex 15, ☎ (1) 45.75.62.16
- **Saison en Europe :** published by Association Nationale de Diffusion Culturelle, 5 rue Bellart, 75015 Paris, ☎ (1) 47.83.33.58.
- **See gazetteer sections of this guide.**

Festivities in France

food & drink · There are wine festivals, cider celebrations, beer festivities, as well as sauerkraut, *boudin* (blood pudding), cheese and oyster feasts. Consult local tourist offices and the F.G.T.O.

historical festivities · For songs and dances of the past, true Breton folklore and historical pageants, see gazetteer sections of the guide.

traditions · — Mardi Gras and carnival are celebrated from mid-Feb. to end of Mar. Contests of strength can be seen in Basque country in Aug. There are floats, feast-days, bull-running in S France, also bull-fights. See F.G.T.O.

— *Festival de l'Insolite* (weird books, films, etc.) La Garde-Freinet (Var), Mar.
— *Festival de l'Étrange* (science fiction/horror films) Avoriaz (Jan. or Feb.).

unusual to
bizarre

Religious events

The French calendar is still profoundly marked by religious traditions. Christmas, Easter, All Saints and Palm Sunday holy days are celebrated with pilgrimages, processions and church ceremonies. A specific and interesting event, with a religious character, is the Breton "Pardon". See section on Brittany.

 Holiday themes

Nature parks and reserves

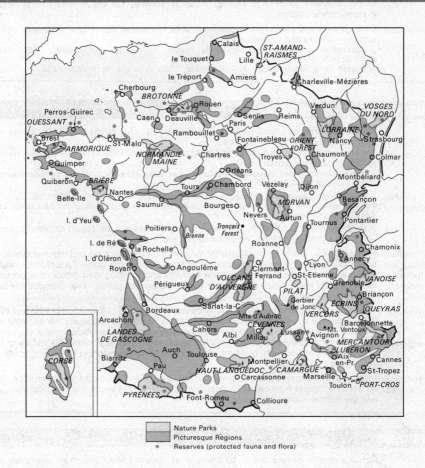

Nature Parks
Picturesque Regions
● Reserves (protected fauna and flora)

● **Société Nationale de Protection de la Nature :** 57, rue Cuvier, 75005 Paris, ☎ (1) 47.07.31.95.
● **Direction de la Protection de la Nature,** Services des Parcs Nationaux, 14, bd du Général-Leclerc, 92524 Neuilly-sur-Seine, ☎ (1) 47.58.12.12.

information

national parks France has six outstanding national parks : Vanoise, Port Cros, Pyrénées Occidentales, Cévennes, Les Écrins, and Mercantour. Visitors are welcome in the "pre-park" where rural life is maintained and developed, but they are frequently prohibited in the "réserve intégrale". Information Centres are situated in and around national parks.
● **Fédération des Parcs Naturels de France,** 4, rue de Stockholm, 75008 Paris, ☎ (1) 42.94.90.84.

nature parks Twenty parks are maintained in France where traditional crafts and skills are pursued : Armorique, Brotonne Forest, Brière, Camargue, Corsica, Orient Forest, Haut-Languedoc, Landes de Gascogne, Lorraine, Luberon, Marais poitevin (marshes), Val de Sèvres et Vendée, Montagne de Reims, Morvan, Normandy-Maine, Mont Pilat, Queyras, Saint-Armand-Raismes, Vercors, Volcans d'Auvergne, Vosges du Nord.

hints — Respect all park regulations : no dogs, follow established paths where indicated, no fires, no camping (except in specific areas).
— Ask for F.G.T.O. booklet "France for sports and leisure" for lists of parks and natural reserves.

Gardens

Visiting gardens in France is a journey through time. From the medieval gardens of Angers to the Japanese gardens at Monet's home in Giverny, the visitor sees natural beauty in museum-like settings.

information Most gardens and parks remain open until dusk in summer. Some offer boat rides, *son et lumière,* concerts and fountain displays.
● **Association des Parcs Botaniques de France,** 15 *bis,* rue de Marignan, 75008 Paris, ☎ (1) 42.56.26.07.
● **Maison de la Nature,** 9, quai du 4-Septembre, 92160 Boulogne, ☎ (1) 46.03.33.56.

Museums and Monuments

France's cultural and artistic heritage is extraordinarily rich. Literally thousands of sites and monuments exist within her borders.
For information concerning all the "châteaux" and classified sites open to the public, as well as cultural voyages, contact :
● **Caisse Nationale des Monuments Historiques et Sites,** Hôtel de Sully, 62, rue Saint-Antoine, 75004 Paris, ☎ (1) 42.74.22.22.

general information ● **Direction des Musées de France,** Palais du Louvre, 75001 Paris, ☎ (1) 42.60.39.26.
For up-to-date information, purchase at newspaper stands *Pariscope, Officiel des Spectacles, Officiel des Galeries,* and *Art Info.*

hints State museums are closed on Tue., and municipal museums are closed on Mon. Opening hours are extremely variable. An entrance fee is charged.

techno-logical and industrial museums Information on sites of technical interest may be obtained from local and regional tourist offices and are described in the regional description section of this guide. Factory visits require a written demand ahead of time and are available only to recognized groups. It is possible to visit a dam, solar station or a nuclear power station with guided visits, provided this permission is granted.

archaeo-logy, eco-museums This most recent form of archaeology concerns the study and conservation of 19th and early 20thC industrial society. This discipline has produced several ecomuseums. For example, the museum at Le Creusot (Burgundy) relates the story of crystal manufacturing and the founding of the Schneider mining empire. In N France, ecomuseums preserve the history of t. e textile industry in Fourmies, glass manufacturing in Sars, woodwork in Felleries, and mining in Lewarde (near Douai).

technical tourism Mulhouse has become the leader in this form of tourism, and among the museums to be visited are : the "Musée National de l'Automobile", the Railway Museum, the Electrical Museum, and the Printed-Fabrics Museum.

Antiques

Genuine antique dealers are to be found in all French towns. The most prestigious are gathered in Paris, Lyon, Strasbourg, Avignon, Grenoble, Toulouse, Nantes and on the Riviera. The better dealers are often recognized experts and are able to provide guarantees or certificates of authenticity.

brocante This term refers to near-antiques, curios, and second-hand goods in general. Real bargains can be found, and prices are always negotiable. There is also alot of pure junk sold.

Most French towns have an auction room *(hôtel de ventes)*, presided over by a certified **auctions** auctioneer *(commissaire-priseur)*. Details of auctions are announced both in the local press and by poster. Goods are exhibited on the preceding day or the morning of the sale. Successful bidders carry their goods away as soon as they are paid for.

— If furniture or objects are preceded by the words "d'époque" or "de style", the goods are **hints** probably recent copies of that period.

— Antique furniture is frequently reconditioned or reassembled, and without a certificate of authenticity, you have no guarantee it is a "real" antique.

— Export of antiques over 100 years old, and whose value exceeds 10 000 F is subject to an export license.

— It is wise to insist upon a detailed invoice for customs purposes, regardless.

— For Paris flea-markets, see gazetteer section. **information**

— For auctions and major sales, consult the following two publications :

● *Gazette de l'Hôtel Drouot* and *Le Moniteur des Ventes*, 99, rue de Richelieu, 75002 Paris, ☎ (1) 42.61.81.78.

— Daily auctions are held at **Hôtel Drouot,** except Sun. and never in Aug. : 9, rue Drouot, 75009 Paris, ☎ (1) 42.46.17.11.

— The **Syndicat National des Antiquaires** publishes the magazine *Art et Curiosités*, 11, rue Jean-Mermoz, 75008 Paris.

— The *Almanach du Chineur* is a goldmine of information published by Hachette.

Many open-air markets, not necessarily listed as flea markets, will have stands by "brocan- **N.B.** teurs" and antique dealers.

Sporting holidays

For a small country, France offers a remarkable variety of sports. The Practical Information section of each region gives local addresses for all sports.

Walking and hiking

France has over 35 000 kilometres of hiking trails. All the *grande randonnée* trails are clearly marked with red and white markers.

— The **F.G.T.O.** booklet *France for sports and leisure* is a useful source for hikers. **information**

— The book *Le Guide du Randonneur* is an invaluable guide, and the **Fédération Française de Randonnée Pédestre** which publishes it organizes walking tours throughout France : 8, av. Marceau, 75008 Paris, ☎ (1) 47.23.62.32.

Riding

Riding and horse-drawn holidays : **information**

● **Association Nationale pour le Tourisme Équestre,** 15, rue de Bruxelles, 75009 Paris, ☎ (1) 42.81.42.82.

Licensed riding schools :

● **Fédération Équestre française,** 164, rue du Fbg Saint-Honoré, 75008 Paris, ☎ (1) 42.25.11.22.

● **Poney-Club de France** (for children), 15, rue du Mesnil, 75116 Paris, ☎ (1) 47.04.65.05.

Tennis and squash

Tennis is a very popular sport in France and there are over 17 000 courts available.

● **Association des Centres de Tennis pour Jeunes,** 69, av. Salvador-Allende, 93290 Trembly-les- **young** Gonesse, ☎ (1) 48.60.72.72. **people**

The U.C.P.A. and O.C.C.A.J. offer tennis for 18-35 yr-olds :

● **U.C.P.A.,** 62, rue de la Glacière, 75013 Paris, ☎ (1) 43.36.05.20.

● **O.C.C.A.J.,** 9, rue de Vienne, 75008 Paris, ☎ (1) 44.94.21.21.

● **Forum Stages,** 46, av. Kléber, 75116 Paris, ☎ (1) 47.04.58.58 (tennis and also music, dance, com- **all ages** puter courses ; welcomes foreigners).

● **Tennis Forest Hills,** 40, av. du Maréchal-de-Lattre-de-Tassigny, 42360 Meudon la Forêt, ☎ (1) 46.30.00.30 (53 covered and 8 outdoor courts in Paris area ; hourly lessons for visitors).

● **Tennis Action,** 145, rue de Vaugirard, 75015 Paris, ☎ (1) 47.34.36.36 (11 centres in Paris and environs).

● **Fédération Française de Squash,** 19, rue Vauthier, 92100 Boulogne, ☎ (1) 46.05.27.32.

Golf

Golf is a developing sport in France, and there are greens springing up everywhere. Among the most famous :
— Golf de Cannes-Mougins, 175, route d'Antibes, 06250 Mougins, ☎ 93.75.79.13.
— New Golf de Deauville, 14800 Saint-Arnoult, ☎ 31.88.20.53.
— Golf de Chantilly, 60500 Vineuil-Saint-Firmin, ☎ 44.57.04.43.
— Golf de Saint-Cloud, 69, rue du 19-Janvier, 92380 Garches, ☎ (1) 47.01.01.85.
— Golf de Saint-Nom-la-Bretèche, Domaine de la Tuilerie, 78860 Saint-Nom-la-Bretèche, ☎ 34.62.54.00.

information ● **Fédération Française de Golf**, 66, av. Victor-Hugo, 75783 Paris Cedex 16, ☎ (1) 45.02.13.55 (has complete list of greens).

N.B. : For additional golf courses and lessons, see :
Golf in France (Éditions Person, 34, rue de Penthièvre, 75008 Paris, ☎ (1) 43.59.46.37).

Mountaineering

● **Fédération Française de la Montagne**, 20, rue La Boétie, 75008 Paris, ☎ (1) 47.42.39.80.
● **Club Alpin Français**, 9, rue La Boétie, 75008 Paris, ☎ (1) 47.42.38.46.
● **Chalets Internationaux de Haute Montagne**, 15, rue Gay-Lussac, 75005 Paris, ☎ (1) 43.25.70.90 (offers courses in mountain climbing for 9-17 yr-olds).

Speleology

The major speleological areas in France are : the Périgord, the Causses, the Haute-Provence, Charentes, and the Pyrénées. The F.F. de Spéléologie will provide lists of clubs with courses in speleology upon demand.
● **Fédération Française de Spéléologie**, 130, rue Saint-Maur, 75011 Paris, ☎ (1) 43.57.56.54.

Motorcycling

permits Mopeds less than 50 cc require no permit and can be driven by persons over 14 yrs. of age. Motorcycles of less than 80 cc require the Al permit for 16 yr. olds. 17 yr. olds can drive 125 cc or 13 horsepower maximum with the same permit. Over 125 cc you need a special permit for up to 100 horsepower.

information ● **Fédération Française de Motocyclisme**, 74, av. Parmentier, 75011 Paris, ☎ (1) 47.00.94.40.

Hunting and shooting

seasons The season for hunting is open from 3-5 mos, from mid-Sep. to late Jan. or Feb. Information is available from local hunting association called **Association Communale de Chasse Agréée.**

types of Three types are practised in France : conventional shoot with beaters, forest-hunting where shooting game is tracked down, and duck and waterfowl shooting in marshes and estuaries.

permits A hunting license is required. Applicants must prove their identity, show a temporary hunting insurance certificate valid in France, and two identity photos. Fee is presently 150 F but can change. Basic fee for hunting is 55 F, plus fees for territory covered and game, also subject to change.

information The National Hunting Office is :
● **Office National de la Chasse**, 85 *bis*, av. de Wagram, 75017 Paris, ☎ (1) 42.27.81.75.
The French Marksmen's Federation is :
● **Fédération Française de Tir**, 16, av. du Président-Wilson, 75016 Paris, ☎ (1) 47.23.72.38.

Aquatic Sports

The visitor may recall that 3/4 of France is coastline and that some 250 000 kilometres of river cross within her borders. Virtually all of France can be visited by water and an enormous choice of water sports is offered.

Sailing

Sailing clubs, regional federations and main marinas are listed in gazetteer sections of this guide. Mayor's offices *(Mairies)* are invaluable sources of information for yachtsmen and surfers.

● **Les Glénans,** C.N.G., quai Louis-Blériot, 75781 Paris Cedex 16, ☎ (1) 45.20.01.40 (rigorous in- **information** struction in sailing, results proven).
● **U.C.P.A.,** 62, rue de la Glacière, 75013 Paris, ☎ (1) 43.36.05.20 (has more than 800 boats in marinas throughout France).

Skin-diving

Underwater fishing requires a license. It is illegal to fish with tanks. Scuba-divers must have **rules** the relevant certificate. Major areas for skin-diving are : Corsica, Gulf of Morbihan, La Seyne-sur-Mer, Hyères, Sanary, Bandol, all of the Riviera.

Scuba instruction and holidays : **information**
● **Océanide,** 4 *bis,* rue Descombes, 75017 Paris, ☎ (1) 46.63.12.72.
● **Jet Tours,** ☎ 45.50.20.75, **Club Med,** ☎ (1) 42.96.10.00.
● **Fédération Française d'Études et de Sports Sous-Marins,** 24, quai de Rive-Neuve, 13007 Marseille, ☎ 91.33.99.31.

Fishing

Regulations vary according to locality and are posted in the local mayor's office *(mairie).* In most cases, local fishing stores are best suppliers of information and can sell necessary permits.

If fishing on private property, you need the owner's permission. If fishing on public property, **permits** you need a permit and payment of annual fishing tax.
Trout water is category 1 and requires payment of supplementary tax. Salmon fishing also requires extra tax as does authorized fishing during closed season. All other fish are category 2. Young people under 16 are exempt of most of these restrictions, excepting the fishing tax. Under-16 yr.-olds are restricted to float fishing.

Category 1 water is closed Sep./Oct.-Feb./Mar. Category 2 water closes on 2nd Tue. in **season** Mar. and opens on last Fri. in Apr. for the S and SE departments. Elsewhere it closes on Tue. following 15 Apr. and re-opens Fri. following 8 Jun.
Amateur sea-fishing is permitted all year round in French maritime waters. Only large nets are subject to regulations. Fishing from boats is regulated : no more than 12 hooks on lines, two lines suspended by floats *(palangres)* may have maximum of 30 hooks each, and two lobster pots. Underwater fishing is strictly regulated. Apply to local port authorities about this.

● **Conseil Supérieur de la Pêche,** 10, rue Peclet, 75015 Paris, ☎ (1) 48.42.10.00 (controls over **information** 250 000 km of French rivers ; enq. about river-fishing only).

Canoes and kayaks

You can bring your own with you, or rent one. We recommend the Ognon (Doubs), Orb (Hérault), Vézère, Dordogne, Ardèche, Ariège and Allier rivers for this sport.

● **Fédération Française de canoë-kayak,** 17, route de Vienne, 69007 Lyon, ☎ 78.61.32.74 (river **information** guides and maps and annual guide to schools and courses called "Vacances en canoë-kayak").

Water skiing

Clubs throughout France, coastal and inland, offer instruction and boat-hire.
● **Fédération Française de Ski Nautique,** 16, rue Clément-Marot, 75008 Paris, ☎ (1) 47.20.05.00 **information** (gives information concerning regulations and clubs ; publishes magazine *Ski Nautique*).
● **Club Med** (water skiing at most clubs), ☎ (1) 42.96.10.00.

Aerial sports

U.S. and U.K. pilot licenses are valid world-wide. Addresses of aeroclubs are given in gazetteer section of this guide.

● **Fédération Nationale Aéronautique**, 52, rue Galilée, 75008 Paris, ☎ (1) 47.20.39.75.

hang-gliding
● **Fédération Française de Vol Libre**, 54 *bis*, rue de la Buffa, 06000 Nice, ☎ 93.88.62.89.

ultralight aviation
● **Fédération Française de Planeurs et Ultra-Légers Motorisés**, chemin de la Sacristie, 84140 Montfavet (near Avignon), ☎ 90.32.56.75.

gliding and ballooning
● **Fédération Française de Vol à Voile**, ● **Fédération Française d'Aérostation**, 29, rue de Sèvres, 75006 Paris, ☎ (1) 45.44.04.78.

parachuting
● **Fédération Française de Parachutisme**, 35, rue Saint-Georges, 75009 Paris, ☎ (1) 48.78.45.00.

Skiing

French ski resorts are considered to be among the finest in the world. In addition to downhill skiing, there is cross-country skiing *(ski de fond)*, rallies *(raids)*, and trekking *(randonnée)*.

hints
— Insurance is essential and can be purchased when booking ski holidays or directly at the ski resort.
— Ski runs are colour-graded according to difficulty : green = easy; blue = intermediate easy; red = intermediate difficult; black = very difficult.
— Useful vocabulary : *téléphérique* = cable car; *télésiège* = chair lift; *teleski* or *tire-fesses* = pomalift; *œuf* = gondola.
— Book out of season where possible as reductions are very advantageous (and you avoid queues (lines) at the lifts!).

Main winter sports stations

● **Fédération Française de Ski,** 81, av. des Ternes, 75017 Paris, ☎ (1) 45.72.64.40.
● **Association des Maires des Stations Françaises de Sports d'hiver,** 61, bd Haussmann, 75008 Paris, ☎ (1) 47.42.23.32 (publishes "Ski-France" in English and can inform about *Stations Villages* where traditional character of life and setting has been maintained to the maximum).
● **France Ski International,** Terminal Air France Maillot, 2, pl. de la Porte-Maillot, 75017 Paris, ☎ (1) 42.99.25.82 (flies to major alpine resorts and publishes informative bilingual ski brochure).
● **Écoles du Ski Français,** Allée des Mitaillères, 38246 Meylan Cedex, ☎ 76.90.67.36 (publishes tri-lingual brochure with special emphasis on instruction facilities).
● **Association Française des "Stations Vertes de Vacances"** et **"Villages de Neige",** Hôtel du Département, 2, rue des Maillets, 72010 Le Mans, ☎ 43.81.72.72 (publishes comprehensive guide to lodgings maintained according to certain standards).

Inland Waterways

No permit is required of foreign visitors who sail or moor along the French coast or inland **permits** waterways for a period of 6 mos. in a single go (or broken up over 12 consecutive mos.). Small yachts and motorboats under 24 m. in length must have a Certificate of Registration, official ship's papers, or the British Small Ships Register. For business and stays exceeding 6 mos., contact French Customs and Information Centre.

Yachts from the U.K. sailing between France (incl. Corsica), Belgium, and Holland require no **health** maritime health declaration. This declaration must be obtained and certified from other ports **control** of departure; yachts arriving from areas of infection should have international vaccination certificate covering all persons aboard.

Main inland waterways

▬ Navigable waterways	▬ Over 5 million metric tons, traffic per year	∿ Rivers ⌒⌒ Canals

speed limits	On rivers : from 10-25 km/h ; on canals and certain canalized rivers : from 6-10 km/h ; within 300 metres of shore : 5 knots. No navigation is permitted in bathing areas.
river-boat rental	● **Syndicat National des Loueurs de Bâteaux,** Port de la Bourdonnais, 75007 Paris, ☎ (1) 45.55.10.47.
cruising holidays	● **Nautic Voyages,** 8, rue de Milan, 75001 Paris, ☎ (1) 45.26.60.80. ● **Quiztour,** 19, rue d'Athènes, 75009 Paris, ☎ (1) 48.74.75.30 (rents houseboats for all of France, offers luxury cruises in *péniche-hôtels* and half- and full-day cruises on the Seine).
maps, charts, guides	● **Établissement Principal du Service Hydrographique et Océanographique de la Marine,** 13, rue du Chatellier, B.P. 426, 29275 Brest. ● **Éditions du Plaisancier,** B.P. 27, 69641 Caluire Cedex (maps in German/Eng). ● **Annuaire du Nautisme,** 30, rue Gramont, 75002 Paris (lists all coastal ports and inland waterways of France). ● **F.G.T.O.** leaflet on navigation.

● *Menu guide*

Agneau lamb.
Aiglefin haddock.
Aiguillette sliver, usually of duck breast.
Aile wing, of poultry or game bird.
Aioli garlic mayonnaise.
Airelle wild cranberry.
Algue edible seaweed.
Aloyau sirloin of beef.
Amande almond.
Andouillette chitterling sausage.
Aneth dill.
Anguille eel.
Anis aniseed.
Araignée de mer spider crab.
Artichaut artichoke.
Asperge asparagus.
Avocat avocado.
Ballotine stuffed, boned, rolled poultry.
Baie berry.
Bar (or Loup) sea bass.
Barbue brill.
Basilic basil.
Basquaise Basque style : Bayonne ham, rice and red or green peppers.
Baudroie anglerfish.
Bavette skirt steak.
Béarnaise tarragon-flavoured sauce with egg yolks, shallots, butter and white wine.
Bécasse woodcock.
Béchamel white sauce.
Beignet fritter.
Bercy sauce based on fish stock, wine and shallots.
Betterave beet.
Beurre blanc butter, shallots, wine and vinegar.
Beurre noir browned butter, vinegar and parsley.
Biche doe.
Bigorneau periwinkle.
Bisque shellfish soup.
Blanc (de volaille) white breast (of poultry).
Blanquette stew with egg and cream sauce.
Blette Swiss chard.
Bœuf à la mode beef braised in red wine with vegetables.

Bœuf à la ficelle beef boiled briefly in stock or water.
Bordelais(e) Bordeaux style with shallots, red wine and beef marrow.
Boudin blood sausage.
Boudin blanc white sausage of veal, chicken or pork.
Bouquet shrimp.
Bourdelot fruit (apple or pear) wrapped in pastry.
Bourguignonne Burgundy style : red wine, onions, bacon.
Bourride white fish and shellfish soup with *aioli.*
Brandade purée of salt cod, mashed potatoes and garlic.
Brocciu Corsican sheep's milk cheese.
Brochet pike.
Brochette skewered meat or fish.
Bulot large sea snail.
Cabillaud cod.
Cabri kid.
Caen (à la mode de) cooked in Calvados, white wine or cider.
Cagouille small land snail.
Caille quail.
Calmar small squid.
Canard duck.
Cane female duck.
Caneton male duckling.
Canette young female duck.
Cannelle cinnamon.
Carbonnade beef braised in beer.
Carré (d'agneau, de veau) rack (of lamb, of veal).
Cassis black currant ; black currant liqueur.
Cassoulet casserole of white beans with pork, goose or duck and sausages.
Céleri celery.
Céleri-rave celery root.
Cèpe boletus mushroom.
Cerfeuil chervil.
Cerise cherry.
Cervelas garlic-flavoured cured pork sausage.
Cervelles brains, of calf or lamb.

Champignon mushroom; **sauvage,** wild; **des bois,** woodland; **de Paris,** cultivated.
Chantilly sweetened whipped cream.
Chapon capon.
Charcuterie cold cuts, smoked, cured or salted meats, terrines, pâtés.
Charlotte moulded dessert with lady fingers and creamy filling, or fruit purée baked in a crust of white bread.
Charolais noted cattle breed; beef.
Chasseur "hunter style" : white wine, mushroom, tomato and shallot sauce.
Châtaigne chestnut.
Chausson pastry turnover.
Chèvre goat or goat cheese.
Chevreuil young roe deer.
Chicorée curly endive or chicory.
Chipiron Basque name for small squid.
Chou cabbage.
Choucroute sauerkraut; **garnie** : with meat.
Chou-fleur cauliflower.
Ciboulette chive.
Citron lemon.
Citron vert lime.
Citronelle lemon grass.
Citrouille pumpkin.
Civelle baby ell, also called **piballe.**
Civet rich stew.
Clémentine small tangerine.
Cochon pig.
Cochonnailles pork products.
Coing quince.
Colin hake.
Colvert wild duck.
Compote stewed fruit or vegetables.
Concombre cucumber.
Confit preserved or candied.
Confiture jam.
Congre conger eel.
Coque cockle.
Coquillage shellfish.
Coquille Saint-Jacques sea scallop.
Coulis purée of raw or cooked vegetables or fruit.
Courgette zucchini.
Crème anglaise custard sauce.
Crépinette small sausage patty wrapped in caul fat.
Cresson watercress.
Crevette shrimp.
Croque-monsieur toasted ham and cheese sandwich.
Crottin firm round goat cheese.
Cru raw.
Crudité raw vegetable.
Crustacé crustacean.
Cuissot haunch, of veal, venison or boar.
Darne slice or steak of fish.
Daube stew.
Daurade sea bream.
Demi-sel lightly salted.
Désossé boned.
Dinde turkey.
Dindonneau young turkey.
Dodine cold, boned, stuffed duck.
Douceurs sweets.
Doux, douce sweet.
Échalote shallot.
Écrevisse crayfish.
Émincé thin slice.
Encornet small squid.
Entrecôte rib steak.
Entremets sweets.
Épaule shoulder.
Épinards spinach.
Escalope thin slice.
Escargot land snail.
Estragon tarragon.
Étrille small crab.

Étuvé(e) braised.
Faisan(e) pheasant.
Farci(e) stuffed.
Farine flour.
Faux-filet sirloin steak.
Fenouil fennel.
Feuille de chêne oak-leaf lettuce.
Feuilletage (en) in puff pastry.
Fève fava bean.
Fine de claire fattened oyster.
Flageolet small, pale green kidney bean.
Flambé(e) flamed.
Flan sweet or savoury custard.
Foie liver.
Foie gras d'oie (canard) fattened goose (duck) liver.
Foie blond chicken liver.
Fond d'artichaut artichoke bottom.
Forestière with mushrooms.
Fourré(e) stuffed or filled.
Frais, fraîche fresh or chilled.
Fraise (des bois) (wild) strawberry.
Framboise raspberry.
Friandise a sweet.
Fricassée stewed or sautéed; braised in wine with cream.
Frisée curly endive.
Frites French fries.
Friture small fried fish.
Froid(e) cold.
Fromage cheese.
Fromage de tête head cheese.
Fruits de mer seafood.
Fumé(e) smoked.
Fumet fish or vegetable stock.
Galantine boned, stuffed rolled poultry, served cold.
Galette pancake or cake, sweet or savoury.
Gamba large prawn.
Gâteau cake or mould.
Gelée aspic.
Genièvre juniper berry.
Gésier gizzard.
Gibelotte rabbit stewed in wine.
Gibier game.
Gigot leg of lamb.
Gigue haunch.
Gingembre ginger.
Girofle clove.
Girolle wild mushroom.
Glacé(e) iced or glazed.
Glace ice cream.
Goujonnette small slice of fish.
Gourmandise a sweet.
Graisse fat.
Grand veneur brown sauce with red currant jelly.
Gras double tripe in wine with onions.
Gratin a dish glazed under the broiler.
Gratin dauphinois potatoes baked with cream and cheese.
Grenadin small veal scallop.
Grenouille (cuisse de) frog's leg.
Grillade grilled meat.
Grillé(e) grilled.
Griotte sour cherry.
Grive thrush.
Gros sel coarse salt.
Groseille red currant.
Hachis minced meat or fish.
Haddock smoked haddock, finnan haddie.
Hareng herring.
Haricot bean.
Homard lobster.
Huile oil.
Huître oyster.
Ile flottante floating island.
Infusion herb tea.
Jambon ham.

Jambon cru salt or smoke-cured raw ham.
Jambonneau pork knuckle.
Jardinière fresh vegetable garnish.
Jarret de veau veal shin.
Julienne slivered vegetables.
Jus juice.
Lait milk.
Laitance roe.
Laitue lettuce.
Lamproie lamprey.
Langouste spiny lobster.
Langoustine Dublin Bay prawns.
Lapereau young rabbit.
Lapin rabbit.
Lard bacon.
Lardon cube of bacon.
Lavaret troutlike lake fish.
Léger(ère) light.
Légume vegetable.
Lieu small salt-water fish.
Lièvre hare.
Limande plaice.
Lisette small mackerel.
Lotte monkfish.
Loup (de mer) Mediterranean fish.
Macédoine diced mixed fruit or vegetables.
Mâche lamb's lettuce.
Madère Madeira.
Magret breast (of duck or goose).
Maïs sweet corn.
Mandarine tangerine.
Mange-tout runner bean.
Mangue mango.
Maquereau mackerel.
Marcassin young wild boar.
Marennes type of oyster.
Mariné(e) marinated.
Marjolaine marjoram.
Marquise mousselike chocolate cake.
Marron large chestnut.
Matelote freshwater fish stew.
Menthe mint.
Merguez spicy sausage.
Merlan whiting.
Merle blackbird.
Mérou grouper.
Mesclun blend of green salad varieties.
Meunière (à la) fish that is rolled in flour, fried in butter and served with lemon, parsley and melted butter.
Meurette in or with a red wine sauce.
Miel honey.
Mijoté(e) simmered.
Millefeuille puff pastry with many thin layers.
Mirabelle yellow plum.
Moelle beef marrow.
Morille morel mushroom.
Mornay cheese sauce.
Morue salt cod.
Mouclade creamy mussel stew.
Moule mussel.
Mousseline airy, creamy mousse or sauce.
Mousseron wild mushroom.
Moutarde mustard.
Mouton mutton.
Mulet mullet.
Mûre blackberry.
Muscade nutmeg.
Museau de bœuf beef muzzle, usually in a vinagrette sauce.
Myrtille bilberry/blueberry.
Nage (à la) served in poaching stock.
Nantua rich truffle and crayfish sauce.
Navarin lamb stew.
Navet turnip.
Noisette hazelnut.
Noix nut, walnut.
Normande (à la) Normandy style : with mushrooms, eggs and cream or with apple cider and/or Calvados.

Nouille noodle.
Œuf à la coque soft-boiled egg.
Œuf brouillé scrambled egg.
Œuf dur hard-boiled egg.
Œuf poché poached egg.
Œuf sur le plat fried egg.
Œufs à la neige floating island.
Oie goose.
Onglet flank of beef.
Ortie nettle.
Os bone.
Oseille sorrel.
Oursin sea urchin.
Paillard thick slice of veal or chicken breast.
Pain bread.
Palmier (cœur de) heart of palm.
Palombe wood or wild pigeon.
Palourde clam.
Pamplemousse grapefruit.
Panaché mixed ; an assortment.
Papillote (en) cooked in parchment or foil.
Parfum flavour.
Parmentier dish with potatoes.
Pastèque watermelon.
Pâte pastry or dough.
Pâtes (fraîches) pasta (fresh).
Pâtisserie pastry.
Paupiette thin slice of meat or fish wrapped around a filling.
Pavé thick slice.
Peau skin.
Pêche peach.
Perdreau young partridge.
Perdrix partridge.
Périgourdine (à la) with truffles and/or *foie gras.*
Périgueux sauce with truffles and Madeira.
Persil parsley.
Petit-gris land snail.
Petits-pois green peas.
Pétoncle small scallop.
Piballe small eel.
Pied de porc pig's trotter.
Pieds et paquets stuffed sheep's tripe and trotters.
Pigeonneau baby pigeon.
Pignon pine nut.
Piment hot pepper.
Pintade guinea fowl.
Pintadeau young guinea fowl.
Pipérade omelette or scrambled eggs with Basque-style filling.
Piquant(e) sharp or spicy.
Pissaladière onion pizza.
Pissenlit dandelion (leaves).
Pistache pistachio.
Pistou purée of basil, garlic and olive oil.
Pithiviers puff pastry filled with almond cream.
Pleurotte oyster mushroom.
Poêlé(e) pan-fried.
Poire pear.
Poireau leek.
Poisson fish.
Poitrine breast of meat or poultry.
Poitrine fumée smoked bacon.
Poivre pepper.
Poivron sweet bell pepper.
Pomme apple.
Pomme de terre potato.
Porc pork.
Porcelet young suckling pig.
Porto port.
Potage soup.
Pot-au-feu boiled beef and vegetables.
Potée boiled pork and vegetables.
Poularde fatted hen.
Poulet chicken.
Poulet fermier free-range chicken.
Poulpe octopus.

Pounti rustic flan of bacon, onions and Swiss chard.
Pousse sprout.
Poussin baby chicken.
Praire clam.
Pralin ground caramelized almonds.
Printanière served with diced vegetables.
Profiterole filled cream puff with chocolate sauce.
Provençale (à la) with garlic, tomatoes and olive oil.
Prune plum.
Pruneau prune.
Quenelle dumpling.
Quetsch Damson plum.
Queue tail.
Râble de lièvre saddle of hare.
Raclette melted cheese dish.
Radis radish.
Ragoût stew.
Raie skate or sting ray.
Raifort horseradish.
Raisin grape.
Raisin sec raisin.
Râpé(e) grated or shredded
Rascasse sculpin.
Ravigote thick vinaigrette sauce.
Reine-claude greengage plum.
Reinette apple.
Rémoulade sauce of mayonnaise, capers, mustard, anchovies and herbs.
Rillettes potted meat.
Ris de veau (d'agneau) veal (lamb) sweetbreads.
Riz rice.
Rognon kidney.
Rognonnade veal loin with kidneys attached.
Romarin rosemary.
Rosette dried sausage from Lyon.
Rouget (rouget barbet) red mullet.
Sablé shortbread.
Safran saffron.
Saint-Pierre John Dory (mild ocean fish).
Sandre river perch.
Sang blood.
Sanglier wild boar.
Saucisse fresh sausage.
Saucisson dried sausage.
Sauge sage.
Saumon (fumé) (smoked) salmon.
Sauté browned in fat.

Sauvage wild.
Scarole escarole.
Seiche cuttlefish.
Sel salt.
Selle saddle (of meat).
Sorbet sherbet.
Sucre sugar.
Suprême boneless breast of poultry or filet of fish.
Tablier de sapeur breaded and grilled honeycomb trip.
Tapenade purée of black olives, anchovies, capers, olive oil.
Tartare (steak) raw minced beef.
Tarte Tatin caramelized upside-down apple tart.
Tendron veal or beef rib.
Terrine baked minced meat or fish.
Thé tea.
Thon tuna.
Thym thyme.
Tian Provençal vegetable casserole.
Tournedos centre-cut beef filet.
Tourteau large crab.
Travers de porc spareribs.
Tripous mutton tripe.
Truffe truffle.
Truite trout.
Turbot(in) (small) turbot.
Vacherin baked meringue with ice cream; strong, creamy cheese.
Vanille vanilla.
Vapeur (à la) steamed.
Veau veal.
Velouté ingredients creamed to make a smooth sauce or soup.
Venaison venison.
Vénus tiny clam.
Verjus juice of unripe grapes.
Verveine lemon verbena herb tea.
Viande meat.
Vinaigre vinegar.
Vinaigre de framboise raspberry vinegar.
Vinaigre de xérès sherry vinegar.
Vinaigrette oil and vinegar dressing.
Vivier fish tank.
Volaille poultry.
Vol-au-vent puff pastry shell.
Yaourt yogurt.
Zeste orange or lemon peel (coloured part only)

French wines

	Exceptional	Very Good	Good
Alsace	71, 76, 85	73, 79, 81, 83	70, 74, 75, 78, 82, 84
Red Bordeaux	75, 82, 85	70, 71, 78, 79, 81, 83	73, 76, 80, 84
White Bordeaux	76, 79, 80, 86	70, 71, 75, 81, 82	74, 78, 83, 84, 85
Red Burgundy	71, 76, 78	85	70, 79, 81, 82, 83, 84
White Burgundy	71, 86	73, 78, 79, 83, 85	70, 72, 74, 76, 82, 84
Rhône Valley	78	76, 79, 83, 85	70, 71, 72, 73, 80, 81,82
Loire Valley	76, 86	71, 73, 78, 85	70, 75, 79, 80, 81, 82
Champagne	75	70, 71, 73, 78, 81, 84	76, 79, 80, 82

Weights and measures : equivalences

Weight		Length	
100 grammes	= 3.527 oz.	1 millimetre (mm)	= .039 inch
1 kilo (kg)	= 2.205 lb.	1 centimetre (cm)	= .033 foot
6.348 kgs	= 1 stone/14 lbs (for body weight only)	1 metre (m)	= 1.094 yard
1 tonne	= 1.102 short ton	1 kilometre (km)	= .621 mile

Surface		Volume	
1 m^2	= 1 197 sq. yard	1 cm^3	= .064 cu. inch
1 km^2	= .386 sq. yard	1 dm^3	= .036 cu. foot
1 hectare (ha)	= 2.47 acres	1 m^3	= 1.309 cu. yard

Liquids

1 litre = 8 454 gills/2.113 pints/1.057 quarts/0.264 gallon

Temperatures

C	F	C	F	C	F
100 =	212	90 =	194	80 =	176
70 =	158	60 =	140	50 =	122
40 =	104	30 =	86	20 =	68
10 =	50	5 =	41	0 =	32
– 5 =	23	– 10 =	14	– 20 =	– 4

Sizes

Men's clothing

Suits :	USA	36	38	40	42	44	46	48
	Eur.	46	48	50	52	54	56	58
Shirts :	USA	14	14$\frac{1}{2}$	15	15$\frac{1}{2}$	16	16$\frac{1}{2}$	17
	Eur.	36	37	38	39	40	41	42
Shoes :	USA	6$\frac{1}{2}$	7	8	9	10	10$\frac{1}{2}$	11
	Eur.	39	40	41	42	43	44	45

Ladies' clothing

Blouses/Cardigans :	USA	32	34	36	38	40	42	44
	Eur.	40	42	44	46	48	50	52
Suits/dresses :	USA	10	12	14	16	18	20	
	Eur.	38	40	42	44	46	48	
Socks/stockings :	USA	8	8$\frac{1}{2}$	9	9$\frac{1}{2}$	10	10$\frac{1}{2}$	11
	Eur.	0	1	2	3	4	5	
Shoes :	USA	5$\frac{1}{2}$	6	7	7$\frac{1}{2}$	8$\frac{1}{2}$	9	
	Eur.	36	37	38	39	40	41	

Paris

When you arrive in Paris, whether it is your first visit or your hundredth, there is always the same thrill of pleasure. The Seine; the lovely grey of Notre-Dame; the long walls of the Louvre; the sweep of the Tuileries, the Concorde and the Champs-Élysées; distant Montmartre; and the dizzying height of the Eiffel Tower. Then, in the evening, the lights and the surging crowds. You probably knew it was like this, even before you saw it: the Paris of the Impressionists — sung, painted and filmed exactly as it is.

But there is a hidden side to this wonderful city. The Parisians have a tendency to keep it to themselves — Paris belongs to them, after all. It's a living city, full of oddities, unexpected pleasures and (sometimes) disappointments; above all, a place with a deep sense of history, which rarely degenerates into nostalgia. This is the Paris we have sought to reveal in this guide.

The sheer amount of sights and experiences offered by this unique city may cause the first-time visitor to feel overwhelmed, and at a loss for a starting point. This is why we have included a number of articles dealing with practical subjects in this chapter, in addition to the regular practical information section at the end. Sites of interest are described in alphabetical order, but are also grouped by district, or *quartier*, in the chapter's opening pages. A full page is devoted to travel, with a list of bus routes that take the visitor through some of Paris' most interesting areas : a novel and authentically Parisian way to see the city. One-, three- and eight-day itineraries are also suggested : naturally these can be modified and adapted to the visitor's own tastes... ☐

● Brief history

53 BC-AD 451
During the Gallic Wars, Caesar's army discovered a small township named **Lutetia** on what is now the Île de la Cité; it was inhabited by a small tribe called the **Parisii.** ● The Romans established themselves there, building a new town on the left bank of the river; with traffic thriving, the Seine boatmen's corporation acquired an importance that lasted for ten centuries. ● **Saint Denis**, bishop of the town, converted the Parisii to Christianity, but was beheaded on the Butte Montmartre in the year 250. Two centuries later, **Saint Geneviève,** a shepherdess from Nanterre, rallied the Parisians in their successful resistance to Attila's invading Huns (451).

5th-10thC
Clovis was the first Christian chieftain of the whole of Gaul; he chose Paris as his capital and died there in 511. His successors extended and beautified the city. **King Dagobert** was buried at Saint-Denis. ● **Charlemagne** preferred Rome and Aix-la-Chapelle to Paris — his descendents signally failed to defend the city against the Norman onslaught. Paris was once more reduced to a small island town during the siege of 885-886.

10th-15thC
With the arrival of the Capetian kings on the throne of France, Paris once more became a centre of political power. Its mercantile prosperity favoured the Seine's right bank, which was low-lying and marshy; **Les Halles** (central markets) were founded in 1137, and remained on the same site for more than eight hundred years. ● The churches and royal palace of the Île de la Cité were joined in the 12thC by the **Cathedral of Notre-Dame,** which was begun in 1163. The City's subsequent development obliged **King Philip Augustus** to build a defensive rampart, culminating in the fortress of the **Louvre** (1190). ● The left bank once more entered the picture with the foundation of the **University.** Meanwhile, the reputation of Paris was

	Advertising Museum	B1, 29
★★	Arc de Triomphe de l'Étoile ...	A1, 23
	Bourse	B2, 10
	Buttes-Chaumont	C1, 30
★★	Carnavalet Museum	B2, 33
	Catacombs	B3, 45
★★	Centre Georges-Pompidou ...	B2, 6
★	Palais de Chaillot	A2, 54
★	Champ-de-Mars	A2, 52
★★★	Champs-Élysées	A1, 21
	Châtelet	B2, 7
★	Ile de la Cité	B2, 1
★★	Cluny Museum	B2, 42
	Cognacq-Jay Museum	B1, 17
★	Museum of Decorative Arts ..	B2, 14
★	La Défense	A1, 60
★★★	Eiffel Tower	A2, 53
	Grands Boulevards	B1, 28
★	Grand Palais, Petit Palais	B2, 22
★	Guimet Museum	A2, 56
★	Les Halles	B2, 8
	Hôtel de Ville	B2, 5
★★	Institut	B2, 48
	Institut du monde arabe	B2, 63
★★★	Les Invalides	B2, 50
★	Jardin des Plantes	B2, 36
	Latin Quarter	B2, 39
★★★	The Louvre	B2, 13
★★	Luxembourg	B2, 43
	Madeleine	B1, 19
★★★	The Marais	B2, 32
★★	Museum of Modern Art	A2, 55
★	Parc Monceau	B1, 24
★★	Montmartre	B1, 27
	Montparnasse	B2, 44
	Parc Montsouris	B3, 46
★	The Mosque	B2, 37
	La Muette	A2, 58
	National Techniques	
★	Museum	B2, 31
★★★	Notre-Dame	B2, 2
	Notre-Dame-de-Lorette	B1, 25
★★	Opéra	B1, 18
★	Orsay Museum	B2, 65
	Palais Omnisport de Paris	
	Bercy	C2, 64
★	Palais Royal	B2, 11
★	Panthéon	B2, 38
	Passy	A2, 57
★★	Père-Lachaise Cemetery	C2, 35
★★	Picasso Museum	B2, 62
	Pigalle	B1, 26

★★	Museum of Popular Arts and	
	Traditions	A1, 59
★★	Rodin Museum	B2, 51
★	Saint-Eustache	B2, 9
	Faubourg Saint-Germain	B2, 49
★★	Saint-Germain-des-Prés	B2, 47
★	Faubourg Saint-Honoré	B1, 20
	Saint-Julien-le-Pauvre	B2, 41
★★	Ile Saint-Louis	B2, 3
★	Saint-Séverin	B2, 40
★★★	Sainte-Chapelle	B2, 4
★★	Tuileries	B2, 15
★★	Place Vendôme	B2, 16
★	Place des Victoires	B2, 12
★	La Villette	C1, 61
★★	Place des Vosges	C2, 34

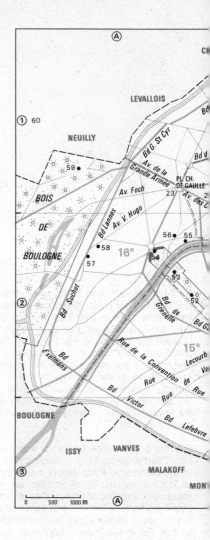

Unusual museums :

Musée du vin

The Wine Museum, situated in a former quarry under the ground, offers an initiation into the art of cultivating vines and the techniques of vinification (Rue des Eaux, 16th arr., 10-6 daily).

spreading. Saint Louis and Philippe le Bel built the **Sainte Chapelle** and extended the royal palace on the Île de la Cité. The population soon surpassed 200 000, and Paris became a focus for political, religious, economic and intellectual power. ● The revolt led by the ambitious merchant-provost Étienne Marcel created a deep and lasting suspicion of the subversive Paris populace in the minds of the French monarchs. Subsequently, the city was brought to the brink of ruin by the **Hundred Years' War.**

16th-18thC
Louis XII established the first grand rules for urban development; François I then tackled the reconstruction of the Louvre Palace, widened streets and forced the municipality to build a **Hôtel de Ville** (town hall) worthy of Paris. His reign marked the beginning of a veritable renaissance, during which the city acquired immense **intellectual prestige.** The Wars of Religion broke out in 1572, and eventually led to the devastation of part of the city. Henri IV quickly rebuilt it after

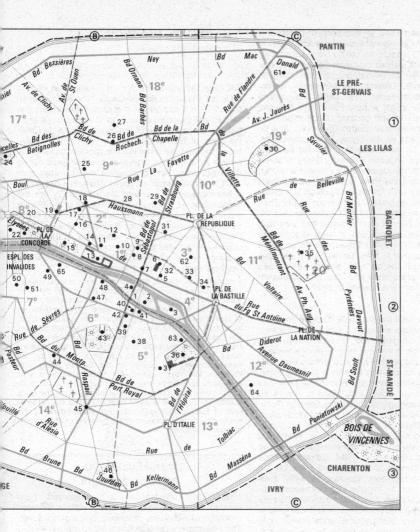

his conversion to Catholicism, leaving, with the able assistance of Sully, a lasting testimonial to his concern for urban planning. Private promoters followed the King's example, and new *quartiers* sprang up all around (Île St. Louis, Faubourg Montmartre, Faubourg St. Germain, Faubourg St. Honoré, with the various mansions built by Mansart) along with religious foundations (Val-de-Grâce) spearheading the reaction against Protestantism. ● Louis XIV cared little for Paris after the **Fronde insurrections**; despite the triumphal arches he erected in the city (Porte St. Denis and Porte St. Martin) and the Paris squares built around his statue (Place des Victoires, Place Vendôme), the Sun King preferred his palace of Versailles. ● The 18thC was a period of unprecedented **economic growth.** For the first time, private houses were built with an eye to real comfort : Louis XV set about a number of major building projects within Paris (Place de la Concorde, Panthéon, Saint-Sulpice, École Militaire). On the eve of the Revolution, the population of Paris had increased to around 650 000.

● The Revolution left no buildings of note. On the contrary, its influence was mainly destructive ; after the Bastille, many convents, churches and aristocratic mansions were pulled down. More seriously in terms of the future, the parks belonging to the nobility and the religious orders were annexed for other purposes — thus Paris was deprived of all its green spaces.

19thC

Napoléon turned Paris into the **capital** of his empire. His **organizational genius** was applied to the city's roads, drains and water supply, as well as to major public building projects like the Arc de Triomphe at the Carrousel, the Arc de Triomphe at the Étoile, the Stock Exchange (Bourse) and the Madeleine. ● Napoléon's ambitious street-widening projects were not realized till the arrival of **Haussmann** during the **Second Empire.** Meanwhile, apartment blocks and buildings swelled the faubourgs of Paris northward and eastward ; these became hotbeds of revolution in 1830 and 1848. ● Napoléon III collected a remarkable team of planners to **reorganize Paris.** In the space of 15 years, he created a modern city. Broad boulevards pierced the tangled alleys of former ages (Saint-Michel, de Sébastopol, de Strasbourg, de Magenta, Voltaire, Diderot, Saint-Germain, Malesherbes and Haussmann). The Baron Haussmann made it possible to get around Paris; and Alphand, with his green parks and gardens, made it possible to breathe (Parc Monceau, Buttes-Chaumont, Bois de Vincennes and Bois de Boulogne). At this period, the city swallowed up its faubourgs and inner suburbs, Auteuil, Passy, La Chapelle, Belleville, Bercy, Grenelle and Vaugirard. ● The **Commune**, a socialist/anarchist insurrection among the Paris populace, was bloodily repressed in May 1871 following Napoléon III's defeat by the Prussians at Sedan. The advent of the Third Republic saw a resumption of the capital's expansion. The Basilica of Sacré-Cœur (Montmartre) was built at this time, with construction in steel enjoying an immense vogue. The **Eiffel Tower,** steel's unrivaled showpiece, appeared in 1889. Development was also underway beneath the surface; drains, water pipes and electricity cables were laid. The first **Metropolitan Railway** (Métro) line opened in 1900.

20thC
The turn of the century, the *Belle Époque* to which a few Métro stations and buildings still bear witness, was quickly submerged in the 1914-1918 War. Paris emerged from this holocaust, only to plunge immediately into profound political and economic crisis. Concrete was used for the first time as a building material (Champs-Élysées Theatre) whilst the first low-rent apartment buildings significantly failed to relieve an acute **housing shortage.** ● During the **German Occupation** (June 1940-August 1944), a time of strict rationing, fear and Gestapo raids was offset by glittering and provocative night-life and real intellectual and artistic creativity. After the resistance uprising of the 19th and 20th August 1944, General Philippe Leclerc's tank division at last entered Paris on the 24th. ● Once it had been liberated by Allied forces, Paris undertook an intense effort of **reconstruction** and **modernization.** The 1950's witnessed a crop of somewhat featureless buildings, and it was only in the 1960s that the "International" architectural style (glass, steel and aluminium) made its first appearance. (U.N.E.S.C.O. building, Maison de la Radio, Maine-Montparnasse complex, Palais des Congrès). ● Traffic and supply problems led to the demolition of the iron-structured Halles de Baltard (Central Market) in 1970, and to the controversial opening of the Seine bank expressways (Voies Express). ● In 1977, for the first time in history, Paris elected a **mayor.**

▶ **ALBERT KAHN Gardens***
9, Quai du 4-Septembre, Boulogne-Billancourt. Métro : Pont-de-Saint-Cloud. Bus : 52, 72.

The Albert Kahn Gardens (Jardins Albert-Kahn) are as filled with contrasts as the life of the turn-of-the-century adventurer for whom they are named. Extraordinary juxtaposition of pinewoods, rock garden, orchard, English park, Japanese garden; astonishingly varied collection of flowers from all over the world. A veritable garden museum *(9:30-12:30 & 2-6; 15 Mar.-15 Nov.).*　☐

▶ **ARC DE TRIOMPHE****
A1 / Place Charles-de-Gaulle. 8th, 16th, 17th arr. Métro and RER : Étoile-Charles-de-Gaulle. Bus : 22, 30, 31, 43, 52, 73, 83, 92. Access to the monument via underground passage at top of Ave. des Champs-Élysées.

For over 150 years, the Arc de Triomphe in what is now the Place Charles-de-Gaulle has been a symbol of French patriotism; it also commemorates the heroes and the fallen of past wars. The colossal arch, built on the raised site of the former "Étoile de Chaillot" (Star of Chaillot) is the hub upon which twelve broad avenues converge like the spokes of a wheel. A project for a national monument was adopted during the Revolution, but construction did not start until 1806 when Napoléon approved Chalgrin's design for a triumphal arch "... except" (in his words), "for the embellishments, which are bad." The fall of the Empire put work on the Arc into abeyance for so long that it became a standing joke for Parisians. Finally, Louis-Philippe inaugurated it, still unfinished, in 1836. The original plans called for the erection of a huge star or quadriga on the top of the building — an idea which has now been abandoned forever.

▶ Nonetheless, the Arc de Triomphe, as it stands, is most impressive. Its massive proportions (50 m high by 40 m wide) combine with the vigour of its decorative reliefs to produce an effect of great power. The best-known of these reliefs is Rude's "La Marseillaise"★ (on the right, from the Champs-Élysées). An idea of the sheer scale of the building is given by the frieze of figures around its top, all of which are larger than life. The Arc may be unfinished, but it amply fulfills its role as a national symbol commemorating the glories of the Empire along with France's "Unknown Soldier", for whom a flame is kept constantly alight within the building by war veterans. Visitors, however, will probably prefer the view from the Arc's summit *(10-5)* to the wreaths, the flags and the ceremonies of Bastille Day (14th of July). **Panorama**★ of the whole city, from the towers of La Défense to Montmartre and the Panthéon.　☐

Unusual museums :
Monocle Museum

Dalaï-lama's eyeglasses are displayed right next to Sarah Bernhardt's, along with a fantastic collection of monocles, pince-nez, opera-glasses, etc. This collection by optician Pierre Marly is worth a look! (Musée des Lunettes et Lorgnettes de jadis, Pierre Marly, 2, Av. Mozart, 16th arr., tel. : 45.27.21.05, 9 :30-12 & 2-6 :30, closed Sun.).

▶ **Musée d'ART MODERNE DE LA VILLE DE PARIS****
(Museum of Modern Art)

A2 / 11, Avenue du Président-Wilson, 16th arr. Métro : Iéna, Alma-Marceau. RER : Pont de l'Alma. Bus : 32, 42, 63, 72, 80, 82, 92.

This museum has been completely refurbished since the National Museum's collections were moved to the Pompidou Centre, better adapted for exhibitions of contemporary art. The Museum of Modern Art now displays important cubist, fauvist and Paris school paintings. Furthermore, the Centre National de la Photographie organizes many shows here.

▶ Matisse's famous triptych, La Danse★ is here, alongside Dufy's gigantic Fée Electricité★, one of the largest murals ever painted. ▶ There is still a whiff of scandal and provocation about the Museum of Modern Art : the ARC section (Animation-Research-Confrontation) organizes demonstrations of contemporary art which are receptive to all the trends of the avant-garde. The plastic arts rub shoulders here with jazz and poetry ; the result is sometimes *"over-contemporary"* — but always exciting *(10-5:30 or 8 Wed. ; closed Mon.).* ☐

▶ Musée des ARTS DÉCORATIFS* and Musée national des ARTS DE LA MODE*

(Museum of Decorative Arts and Museum of the Arts of Fashion)

B2 / 107-109, Rue de Rivoli, 1st arr. Métro : Palais-Royal, Tuileries. Bus : 21, 27, 39, 48, 68, 69, 72, 85.

The Museum of Decorative Arts was opened in 1905 in the Marsan Pavilion, rebuilt after the fire that destroyed the Tuileries Palace in 1871.

▶ Reopened in 1985, the museum exhibits some 80,000 pieces, including furniture, decorative objects, jewelry, *boiseries* (woodwork, especially paneling) and tapestries, from the 15thC to the present day. Other European countries are also represented, along with the art of Islam. A contemporary gallery reuniting for the first time the collections of the 20thC and the Dubuffet gallery. Three documentary rooms : glass, textiles and wallpaper. Art studios open to adults and children *(12:30-6:30 ex Mon. and Tue. ; 11-5 Sun.).*

▶ Opened at the end of 1985, the Museum of Fashion presents the evolution of the arts of dress over an area of 2000 m². Alongside the permanent collections one can trace the contemporary development of fashion day by day *(same hours as above).* ☐

▶ Musée des ARTS ET TRADITIONS POPULAIRES**

(Museum of Popular Arts and Traditions)

A1, 6, route du Mahatma-Gandhi, 16th arr. (Bois de Boulogne). Métro : Porte-Maillot, Sablons. Bus : 73 ; 33 Sat. and Sun.

The aim of this highly individual museum is to breathe new life into the traditions of rural France, to display the wealth and variety of the nation's crafts, and to demonstrate the beauty and value of the tools and skills of an earlier time. The collection touches on every aspect of rural life ; the games, entertainments and dances of provincial France all have their place here, along with traditional tools, utensils, crockery, pottery and a wide range of farm implements *(10-5:15 ex Tue.).* ☐

▶ Place de la BASTILLE

C2 / 4th, 11th, 12th arr. Métro : Bastille. Bus : 29, 65, 69, 76, 86, 87, 91.

The Bastille is a lively, popular *quartier* which used to be a centre for nocturnal revelry among the Paris riffraff. The dance-halls in the Rue de Lappe used to be especially popular with the local *apaches* and *marlous* (hooligans). Today the "Balajo" dance-hall still keeps alive the tradition of the *java* and *bal musette* (accordeon balls).

▶ The **Faubourg St. Antoine** is now almost entirely given over to the sale of reproduction period furniture, but during the last century it seethed with workers and artisans who played an important part in the social upheavals and riots of 1830 and 1848. ▶ The Bastille is the ral-

lying point for workers' unions, which hold their demonstrations around the **Colonne de Juillet** (July Column)★ crowned with its Spirit of Liberty. ▶ The Colonne de Juillet is all that remains of the eight-towered fortress destroyed in the Revolution. ▶ The 1989 opening of the **Opéra de la Bastille** will contribute to the rejuvenation of this popular neighborhood. ☐

Paris-on-the-Seine

On the Canal St-Martin, at the foot of the Bastille column, the dream has become reality : Paris has a port, le port de l'Arsenal. This pleasure-boat marina's amenities include an ultra-modern harbour-master office, a shop selling boating equipment, a restaurant and flowered promenades. A lovely starting-point for river cruisers who wish to explore the Marne, the Seine and even the open sea.

▶ BOIS DE BOULOGNE*

A2 / 16th arr. between Neuilly and Boulogne. Métro : Porte-Maillot, Porte-Dauphine, Porte d'Auteuil, Sablons. Bus : PC, 32, 52, 63 ; 33 Sat. and Sun.

▶ The Bois was ruthlessly cut down during the Revolution and again by the occupying British Army in 1815. Subsequently, it was rearranged according to Second Empire tastes as a park enlivened by **lakes, racecourses** (Auteuil and Longchamp) and a miniature railway track. On fine days, you can go boating on the lakes, which were designed by the engineer Alphand as part of a complicated network of watercourses fed by an artesian well. ▶ The miniature railway still carries children around the **Jardin d'Acclimatation** *(Sablons crossroads ; 9-dusk)*, so called because various exotic creatures are acclimatized here to Paris temperatures : but children seem to prefer the goats, chickens and sheep of the "Farm" to the resident monkeys and parrots. The Jardin also has an extremely well-equipped and varied children's fun fair. ▶ "Papa Meilland", "Princess Ann" and "Sissi" are the stars of the **Bagatelle Park★★** *(Porte-de-Madrid crossroads)*; all three are species of rose. The rose gardens here are the most popular part of this much-loved park, landscaped around a splendid folly. The latter was built by the Count of Artois, who had a bet with the Queen of France that he could finish the job inside two months. The Count requisitioned all the stone and plaster available in Paris and had 900 labourers working round the clock ; the Queen lost her wager. ▶ In the humid **Municipal Greenhouses** (Serres du Fleuriste Municipal, av. de la Porte d'Auteuil, *10-5 or 6*), it's hard to believe that you are only a few metres above the roaring *Boulevard Périphérique* (ring road) and alongside the gigantic **Parc des Princes.** Well-planned and cared for, this garden has a splendid orchid collection and a romantic **jardin des poètes.** ▶ The Bois has sporting facilities (tennis courts at Roland-Garros, clay-pigeon shooting) along with a large number of restaurants. ☐

▶ BUTTES-CHAUMONT

C1 / 19th arr. Métro : Buttes-Chaumont. Bus : 26, 60, 75.

With its sixty acres of rolling parkland, green enough to make a mockery of its name *(monts chauves —* literally, bald hills), the Buttes-Chaumont is perhaps Paris' most picturesque and surprising park, a kind of fantasy garden of the 18th century.

▶ The Buttes-Chaumont Park straddles the twin quartiers of **Belleville** and **Ménilmontant,** which at one time were typically Parisian. After the war, they were taken over by a large North African population which was in turn forced out in recent years by massive construction projects. Édith Piaf and Maurice Chevalier would never recognize their beloved "Ménilmuche" these days, unless they happened upon the hard-to-find entrance to the protected gardens near the Rues des Cascades or Bidassoa. □

▶ CARNAVALET Museum**

B2 / 23, Rue de Sévigné, 3rd arr. Métro : Saint-Paul, Chemin-Vert. Bus : 29, 69, 76, 96.

Four centuries of Paris life (1500-1900) are vividly displayed in this splendid Renaissance mansion, redesigned by Mansart in the 17thC and decorated with large reliefs★ by Jean Goujon, and now a fit setting for the collections of the **Historical Museum of the City of Paris**. As an introduction to the history of Paris, this museum and its new annex in the **Hôtel Le Peletier de Saint-Fargeau** have no equal.

▶ Once the residence of Madame de Sévigné, the Carnavalet Museum has been conceived as a showpiece *(10-5:40; closed Mon.)* : fine furniture (Regency, Louis XV and Louis XVI, boiseries, gilt cabinet★★ painted by Le Brun), also period paintings, street scenes, shop signs, maps, and even an accurately-reconstructed café. □

▶ The CATACOMBS

B3 / Place Denfert-Rochereau, 14th arr. Métro and RER : Denfert-Rochereau. Bus : 38, 68.

A veritable City of Death, the Catacombs can be entered through the E pavilion on the Place Denfert-Rochereau, a vestige of the old Barrière d'Enfer (Hell's Gate) in the city walls erected in 1784. They are really gigantic stone quarries used from 1785 as a dump for corpses from the cemetery of Les Innocents, near Les Halles, which had become so crowded that it was a constant danger to public health.

▶ The mortal remains of some thirty generations of Parisians were deposited in the Catacombs ; some of the bones and skulls were laid out in geometrical patterns by anonymous agents with a taste for the macabre *(2-4, closed Mon. ; 9-11 & 2-4 Sat.).* □

▶ CENTRE GEORGES-POMPIDOU**
(Beaubourg)

B2 / Rue Saint-Martin, 4th arr. Métro : Châtelet, Les Halles, Hôtel-de-Ville, Rambuteau. RER : Châtelet-Les Halles. Bus : 38, 47, 58, 67, 69, 70, 72, 74, 85, 96.

The Centre National d'Art et de Culture Georges-Pompidou, better known as the Beaubourg or Pompidou Centre, was created at the behest of a former French President, Georges Pompidou (1969-1978). The aim of the Centre was to bring together in one place all the various trends in contemporary art forms with a view to acquainting the public at large with modern art and bringing creativity into the museum. This project, spurred on by France's rapid growth and prosperity during the early 1970s, has fulfilled its promise beyond all expectations *(12-10 pm daily ; 10-10, Sat. and Sun. ; closed Tue., call (1) 42.77.11.12 for recorded information).*

▶ On the ground floor **piazza** level, the **forum** is dominated by a portrait of Georges Pompidou by Vasarely. Nearby are the reception and bookshop, next to the **salles d'actualité** (news rooms) of the Centre's library (reviews and recent publications), the CCI (Industrial Creation Centre) and **children's workshops**. On the mezzanine (street level), the CCI organizes original exhibitions which are a must for anyone interested in contemporary topics such as comic-strip art, the media, urban architecture. ▶ On the first, second and third floors, the **Public Information Library** (Bibliothèque Publique d'Information, BPI) displays books and periodicals and operates audio-visual equipment and cassettes in ninety-five foreign languages. The BPI's total surface area, all of which is freely accessible, amounts to something like four acres of floor space.
▶ Part of the third floor, and the whole of the fourth floor is devoted to the works of artists born after 1865. This is the **National Museum of Modern Art★★★**, recently reorganized, which exhibits all the great names of the 20thC : Bonnard, Picasso, Pollock, Mathieu, etc. Works by Kandinsky, along with Matisse's bronzes, and paintings by Max Ernst, the sculptures of Gonzalez and Miró, dominate a slightly uneven collection, which nonetheless demonstrates the fundamentally hesitant, questing nature of contemporary art. ▶ The fifth floor, which is the top, is the home of the **Cinémathèque** (film library and archives), along with certain temporary exhibitions, a bar and a restaurant. The **view★★** from here (40 m above ground level) is superb — the rooftops of all central Paris. ▶ All around the Pompidou Centre, the Piazza (once the **Plateau Beaubourg**) is now a pedestrian precinct. Bookshops, galleries and restaurants have replaced the former sordid haunts of the **Quartier de l'Horloge** (the Clock Quarter). The latter has become a modern building complex, almost a pastiche of the many styles that lurk behind the venerable facades of the **Rue St-Martin**; fittingly, somehow, a clockwork armed man emerges to do battle with a monster, at the stroke of every hour — over the shop of J. Monestier, Rue Bernard-de-Clairvaux. On the other side, toward the Saint-Merri church, see the lively fountain★ designed by Jean Tinguely and Niki de Saint-Phalle (1983), above Pierre Boulez' IRCAM (Contemporary Musical and Acoustical Research Institute). □

Unusual museums :
Musée d'Ennery

The Musée d'Ennery is an "atmospheric" museum, one among many others in Paris. The difference here is that the atmosphere is a very strong one, since the collections are entirely devoted to Far Eastern art, and plenty of it : the rooms are so crammed with statues and objects that their quality is almost submerged. The best items are doubtless the netsukés and kogos, skilfully worked buttons and boxes illustrating everyday scenes in the 17th and 18thC. The sense of detail and decorative precision shown in these objects makes each one a work of art in itself, and gives the Musée d'Ennery its particular distinction as a museum of miniature art (59 Ave. Foch, 16th arr., Thu. and Sun., 2-5 only).

▶ Palais de CHAILLOT*

A2 / 16th arr. Métro : Trocadéro. Bus : 22, 30, 32, 63, 72, 82.

Seen from the Seine, the steep bank of Chaillot has a strangely theatrical air, almost grandiose. The site caught the fancy of Napoléon III, who leveled its summit. The organizers of the Great Exhibition of 1878 were inspired to build a Moorish Palace here ; their successors of 1937 constructed the present enormous building, the Palais de Chaillot, with two wings 200 m long, curving outward toward the Seine.

▶ The **Palais de Chaillot** is a prime example of the sober, somewhat cold architectural outlook of the 1930s. It now houses a huge **theatre**, made famous by Jean Vilar and the Théâtre National de Paris; a **Cinémathèque** (film

library and archives), created by Henri Langlois (entrance Ave. A.-de-Mun); the **Naval Museum★★** (history of navigation : nautical instruments, *10-6; closed Tue. and hols.*); the **Musée de l'Homme★★** (Museum of Anthropology — human evolution and man's origins, *9:45-5:15; closed Tue.*); and the **Museum of French Monuments★★** (anthology of French sculpture, *9:45-12:30 & 2-5; closed Tue.*). All entrances are marked on the **Place du Trocadéro.**
▶ Below the Palais, in a cave built under the sloping gardens, is the **Aquarium★**; freshwater fish in somewhat hallucinatory surroundings *(10-6 daily)*. The terraces of the Place du Trocadéro offer one of the loveliest views of the left Bank : the Eiffel Tower straddling the Champ-de-Mars gardens and École Militaire, the distant Montparnasse skyscraper and, to the right, the modern tower blocks of the Front de Seine. ☐

▶ **CHAMP-DE-MARS***

A2 / 7th arr. Métro : École-Militaire, Bir-Hakeim; RER : Champ-de-Mars. Bus : 28, 42, 49, 69, 80, 82, 87, 92.

The Champ-de-Mars used to be a training ground for military manœuvres, where the soldiers from the **École Militaire★★** (Military Academy; architect : Gabriel; completed 1773) were put through their paces before the king. Here the young Napoléon Bonaparte studied the art of war. The Revolution evicted the army and used the Champ-de-Mars for its own ceremonial purposes, such as the Fête de la Fédération on 14 July 1790, at which the king and no less than 300 000 people from all over France swore fidelity to the nation before General Lafayette. Parades, festivals and horseraces took place here before the great universal exhibitions of 1867 and 1889. The Eiffel Tower, which provoked the furious indignation of the local inhabitants while it was under construction, has since been a magnet for tourists. ☐

Shopping in Paris

Most visitors to Paris see it as the capital of French luxury commerce, fashion and the art of good living. Yet Paris owes a lot to talented foreigners living here, who have become some of its greatest creators : Japanese and Italians for fashion and luxury goods, Greeks for jewelry, even Englishmen for wines! As to fashion, you will always find in Paris the great names of the past, the severe, the outrageous, the avant-garde, haute-couture and ready-to-wear, along with the traditional fashion strongholds like the Faubourg St. Honoré, Place des Victoires, Boulevard des Capucines, St-Germain-des-Prés and Les Halles. One piece of advice : if you want to save time, go straight to see "what people are wearing" in the two leading department stores, Printemps and Galeries Lafayette. See also the list of good shopping addresses in the following pages.

▶ **CHAMPS-ÉLYSÉES***

A1 / 8th arr. Métro : Étoile, George-V, Champs-Élysées-Clemenceau, Concorde. RER : Étoile. Bus : 28, 30, 31, 42, 49, 52, 73, 80, 83, 92.

The Champs-Élysées avenue spans 2 km, from the Imperial and Republican Arc de Triomphe to the Royalist Tuileries gardens. Far off to the west can be seen the modern towers of Porte Maillot and La Défense.

▶ Before Le Nôtre planted his avenue of elms, there was nothing here but scrubland and marshes. Once lengthened and widened, the old Grand Cours became a meeting place for revolutionaries and ruffians, before developing into a site for theatres, puppet shows and gaming houses. In 1800, there were only six buildings on the Avenue; nor did it acquire its present aspect till a hundred years later. Office blocks, stores and cafés stretch from the Rond-Point to the Étoile, whilst among the trees between the Rond-Point and the Tuileries stand a number of theatres and restaurants. ▶ There are few monuments of note in this area, apart perhaps from the gaudy mansion of La Païva★ at No. 25, where the well-known courtesan used to give her famous parties... and the "Lido", a monument of Paris nightlife which has serenely weathered both the vicissitudes of history and the challenge of the daring and modern "Crazy Horse" nearby. The present world-wide fame of the Champs-Élysées is largely due to the superb setting it provides as the centre of Paris-by-night. ☐

▶ **CHÂTELET**

B2 / 1st arr. Métro and RER : Châtelet. Bus : 21, 24, 27, 38, 47, 58, 67, 69, 70, 72, 74, 75, 76, 81, 85, 96.

Around a 19thC fountain ("return from Egypt"), the **Place du Châtelet** marks the convergence of the main north-south and east-west traffic through the capital, both on the surface and underground (two RER lines cross here).

▶ On the Square, the **Théâtre de la Ville** (Municipal Theatre) has been successfully modernized — though it retains the dressing room of the great tragic actress Sarah Bernhardt in its original condition, as a kind of intimate museum. The theatre itself was constructed by Davioud in 1862, like the **Théâtre Musical de Paris** (TMP) opposite. The latter used to be known as the Châtelet Theatre, and was renowned for its operetta productions; now ballet and opera have returned here. ▶ Close by is the **St. Jacques Tower★**, beloved of the Surrealists, which adds a touch of the unusual to this quartier as it submits to the daily nightmarish traffic jams. It was completed in 1522 as the bell tower of the old church of St. Jacques-de-la-Boucherie, headquarters of a once-powerful corporation of butchers. The Revolution would have swept away the entire structure, had it not been for a gunsmith who used it as a shot-tower for making musket balls. ☐

▶ **Île de la CITÉ***

B2 / 1st and 4th arr. Métro : Cité. Bus : 21, 24, 27, 38, 47, 58, 70, 85, 96.

The Île de la Cité, often compared to a boat's hull carried by the Seine, is the original core from which Paris developed. Its inhabitants have to some extent departed; the great mass of the Palais de Justice now overshadows the island's few remaining Louis XIII houses, and its medieval buildings were long ago torn down by Haussmann. Nonetheless, the Île de la Cité remains the living heart of Paris. Here, 20 centuries ago, one of Julius Caesar's lieutenants first set up his headquarters close to a village inhabited by the Parisii...

▶ The **Pont Neuf★** spans the Seine and takes in the western (downstream) end of the Île de la Cité. This bridge is ill-named, because, far from being "Neuf" (new), it is the oldest bridge Paris can boast. It is also the best-loved, most painted, and most praised by poets. ▶ The statue of Henri IV, who inaugurated the Pont Neuf in 1607, dominates what is today the **Square du Vert-Galant,** a delightfully cool little garden on the tip of the island, much frequented on hot summer nights. ▶ The quiet **Place Dauphine★,** between two elegant Louis XIII buildings in brick and stone, was created in honour of the Dauphin. ▶ Enlarged under the Second Empire and at the turn of the century, the **Palais de Justice** (Law Courts)★ retains a considerable proportion of the original Gothic palace inhabited by the first twelve Capetian kings of France. Steer clear of the somewhat forbidding walls of the Quai des Orfèvres : more interesting is the **Quai de l'Horloge★**, to the N of the Palais. On this side, the façade is flanked by three round towers; on the left, the entrance to the **Conciergerie★★**, an imposing edifice which owes much of its medieval haughtiness to 19thC restoration *(10-5 daily)*. Visit here the Prisoner's Gallery (cells occupied by Marie-Antoinette and Robespierre) and a small museum of the Revolution which occupies the chapel. The most remarkable aspect of this gaol-cum-palace, so laden with tragic memories, is the huge **Salle des Gens d'Armes★★**, with its four naves (1315). ▶ At the corner of the Quai de l'Horloge and the Boulevard du Palais stands the massive square tower known as the "Tour de l'Horloge" (Clocktower). This has kept time for the people of Paris since 1334. ▶ From the boulevard, view the monumental Louis XVI façade which glowers over the Cour du Mai — this is the main public entrance to the Law Courts of the Palais de Justice. Constant comings and goings of lawyers, magistrates, and people with nothing better to do; tag along, and you will find yourself in the immense **Salle des Pas-Perdus**, the centre of the City's judicial life. Some of the courtrooms have retained fine elements of their original décor, notably the **Chambre Dorée★** (Gilded Chamber) where Marie-Antoinette was condemned to death. Original *boiseries*. ▶ By now, you will probably be surfeited with gold leaf, stucco and pompous allegories — so take the passage to the left of the Cour du Mai to the breathtakingly lovely **Sainte-Chapelle★★★**. This is a masterpiece of Gothic art, built by Saint-Louis between 1246 and 1248 to house the relic of Christ's Crown of Thorns. Here the two superimposed naves give an impression of airy lightness, almost of fragility. The higher of the two seems to be a reliquary in itself, a jewel-box suffused with filtered light from the 13th and 14thC stained-glass windows *(10-5)*. ▶ At the exit of the Palais de Justice, the Rue de Lutèce leads through to the **Flower Market★**, one of the most picturesque spots in Paris, with its charm heightened by the gloomy surroundings : on one side, the Commercial Tribunal; on the other, the Hôtel Dieu (hospital); behind, the Préfecture de Police. ▶ From here, go back to the Place du Parvis-Notre-Dame and go down into the bizarre **Crypte Archéologique★** *(10-12, 2-6 daily)*; exhibition of steles (inscribed upright stone slabs), reliefs, fragments of statues and inscriptions which bring to life the Paris-that-existed-before-Paris, when the Île de la Cité was merely the site of a small village. ▶ At the upstream end of the island, see the moving **Mémorial de la Déportation★★** (1962), commemorating those who were taken away to labour and concentration camps during World War II *(10-12 & 2-5 daily)*.

▶ CLUNY Museum**

B2 / 6, Place Paul-Painlevé, 5th arr. Métro : Saint-Michel, Odéon, Maubert-Mutualité. RER : Saint-Michel. Bus : 21, 24, 27, 38, 63, 85, 86, 87, 96.

On the ruined thermal baths of Lutetia, built by the Seine boatmen's corporation in the 2nd or 3rdC, the 14thC Abbots of Cluny raised a luxury Paris residence for their own use. On the initiative of A. de Sommerard, a prominent collector and antiquarian, the present building (15thC Flamboyant Gothic) was converted into a museum in 1844.

▶ In the Museum's pleasant and well-lit rooms *(9:45-12:30/2-5:15; closed Tue.)* there is a fine exhibition of medieval ivories, reliquaries, altarpieces, toys and miscellaneous objects in gold. ▶ **Tapestries** are among the Cluny Museum's most important exhibits, especially the famous "Dame à la Licorne"★★ (15thC and rediscovered by George Sand); note also "La Vie Seigneuriale"★★ (16thC) and "L'Offrande du Cœur" (early 15thC). In addi-

tion, numerous 14th and 15thC statues. ▶ The large **Roman Pump Room★** (Salle des Thermes Romains) is the only Roman construction in France which still retains its original arches. Display of archaeological remains, including part of the "Pilier des Nautes", the most ancient sculpture in Paris. □

▶ COGNACQ-JAY Museum

B1 / 25, Blvd. des Capucines, 2nd arr. Métro : Madeleine, Opéra. Bus : 20, 21, 27, 29, 42, 52, 53, 66, 68, 95.

Ernest Cognacq, founder of the La Samaritaine group of stores, created this museum of 18thC France in collaboration with his wife, Louise Jay. It was opened in 1929, foreshadowing the appearance of thorough American-style foundations endowed by private collectors. The Cognacq-Jay Museum contains *boiseries*, precious objects, furniture, porcelain and miniatures, harmonizing perfectly with paintings (Boucher, Chardin, Fragonard) and drawings (Watteau). Nothing is overdone or dull on any of the three floors; the impression is of constant decorative perfection and refinement, the hallmark of the great century of French taste *(10-5:40; closed Mon.)*. □

▶ Place de la CONCORDE***

B2 / 8th arr. Métro : Concorde. Bus : 24, 42, 52, 72, 73, 84, 94.

The Concorde is at the crossroads of two magnificent vistas : the Tuileries to the Champs-Élysées, and the Madeleine to the Palais Bourbon. It is also the largest unencumbered urban space in Paris.

▶ The Place de la Concorde owes its existence to the aldermen of Paris, who commissioned an equestrian statue of Louis XV and began to look for a place to put it; this the king supplied in 1759 by entrusting Gabriel with the reclamation of a marshy area close to the Tuileries. The architect conceived the Place Louis XV to match the surroundings, built the Ambassador's Mansions (now the Hôtel Crillon and the Navy Ministry) and surrounded the square with an octagonal moat which has now been filled in. The square was inaugurated in 1763. During the Revolution, the statue of Louis XV was removed and replaced by the guillotine, and the Place de la Concorde was confirmed in its present name under the July Monarchy. Louis-Philippe, who wished at all costs to avoid any political symbolism, erected the pink granite obelisk★ that stands there today, a gift from the government of Egypt in 1831. ▶ This obelisk was originally taken from the Temple of Rameses II at Thebes; it stands 23 metres high and is covered with hieroglyphs. Two high fountains play around its base. On the perimeter of the square are eight allegorical statues of the great towns of France. Where the Avenue des Champs-Elysées joins the Place de la Concorde you can see the famous rearing horses (Chevaux de Marly★★, 1719) by Coustou, installed here in 1795. At the Tuileries entrance are Coysevox's equestrian statues. □

▶ La DÉFENSE*

Pont de Neuilly, Puteaux. Métro : Pont de Neuilly; RER : La Défense. Bus : 73.

La Défense was originally designed some fifteen years ago as a kind of Paris Manhattan, built in the old quarters of Puteaux, Nanterre and Courbevoie.

▶ La Défense has its commercial centre, exhibition halls (Palais des Expositions★ - Centre National des Industries et des Techniques) and headquarters of giant companies. But of late it has also become a pleasant place to walk about. The areas around the skyscraper towers have been converted to pedestrian precincts, and special efforts have been made to maintain an atmosphere of constant animation. This is supplied by the *CNIT's* exhibitions (computer science, domestic arts, boat show, children's show, etc.), along with jazz and classical music concerts in summer. There are also art exhibitions open to young artists. □

Le Métro

On the 19th of July 1900, after only two years of work, the first line on the Metropolitan railway (designed by the government engineer Fulgence Bienvenüe) was inaugurated. Some Métro entrances still date from the turn of the century; conceived by Hector Guimard, they are characteristic of what was known as the "modern style" — Art Nouveau. By 1945, the network covered 145 km; nowadays it has reached nearly 200 km, with no less than 280 stations, and a number of suburban extensions under construction or at the planning stage. Every day, the Métro's 3500 carriages carry over 4 million travelers with clockwork reliability. The Express Regional Network (RER), operated jointly by the SNCF (National Railway Company) and the RATP (Paris Transport Network) connects the outlying Île-de-France region with the heart of the capital.

▶ EIFFEL TOWER***

A2 / 7th arr. Métro : Bir-Hakeim. RER : Champ-de-Mars. Bus : 42, 69, 82, 87.

Everything has been said, and more, about this "superstar" of Paris tourist attractions, which attracts no less than 3 million visitors each year. The Universal Exhibition of 1889 instigated the building of an iron tower, as a symbol of the triumph of industrial civilization. Gustave Eiffel, an engineer and specialist in metal construction techniques, was chosen from 700 other competitors to make this idea a reality. The work lasted from January 1887 until the spring of 1889; 7000 metric tonnes of iron, two and a half million rivets, 320 metres high... the figures make you dizzy, but perhaps the most astonishing fact of all is that not a single correction was made to the plans during construction, so perfect was Eiffel's final design.

▶ The Eiffel Tower today serves, apart from a favourite subject for painters, as a meteorological station and radio mast; every day its three levels are visited by thousands of people *(9:30 am-11 pm daily for the first and second levels, 9:30-8 daily for the top level)*. Those who go straight to the summit are sometimes disappointed by clouds which obscure the stunning panorama★★★ over Paris; on cloudy days, therefore, the best view is to be had from the second level. Other, taller towers have been built in New York, Moscow and elsewhere. Nevertheless, this old lady of nearly a hundred, who bears her age lightly under forty tons of paint, still retains her power to fascinate. □

▶ FAUBOURG SAINT-GERMAIN*

B2 / 7th arr. Métro : Invalides, Varennes, Chambre-des-Députés, Solférino, Rue-du-Bac. RER : Quai d'Orsay. Bus : 28, 49, 63, 69, 83, 84, 87, 94.

Between the Seine, the Invalides and the Boulevard Saint-Germain lies an elegant quarter which was first inhabited towards the end of the 17thC. As a result, the Faubourg Saint-Germain is a kind of life-size museum of the civil architecture which predominated in that era. On the site of an old game preserve, large numbers of fine houses were constructed in the early 18thC, which later became the homes of important functionaries and rich bourgeois during the Empire, before being turned into an immense complex of embassies and government ministries. Most were built along the same lines : two symmetrical façades enclosing a courtyard, which opens on the street through a decorated gateway. The main part of the building faces in the other direction, onto a park dotted with pavilions, balusters and fountains.

▶ The only two buildings here which are open to the public are the **Hôtel Biron★**, now the Rodin Museum, and the **Hôtel de Salm★** (1782, Museum of the Legion of Honour, 2 Rue de Bellechasse, *2-5; closed Mon.*). However, if you take a walk beginning at the antique shops and art galleries of the Quai Voltaire, taking in Rue du Bac, Rue de Beaune and Rue des Saints-Pères, you can get a sight of the *hôtels* of the **Rue de l'Université** (Nos. 17, 33, 60 and the Hôtel de Soyécourt★, 1707, No. 51), then the *hôtels* of the **Rue St-Dominique** (Hôtel de Brienne, No. 14; Hôtel de Broglie, No. 35; Hôtel de Sagan★, 1715, No. 57). Continue to the Quatre Saisons★ (Four Seasons) Fountain at No. 57, **Rue de Grenelle**, which leads to a group of 18thC houses (Nos. 70, 85, 87, 106-120, 140, 142). On either side of the **Hôtel Matignon** (1720), which is the Prime Minister's residence, the **Rue de Varenne** offers the Hôtel de Boisgelin★ (Italian Embassy), and other *hôtels* at Nos. 45, 47, 50, 56, 60, 73 and 75. At the end of the Rue de Bourgogne stands the **Palais-Bourbon★**, now the Chamber of Deputies. This building dates from 1722, and was enlarged by the addition of the **Hôtel de Lassay★★**, a palace decorated with a number of allegories and statues. Frescoes by Eugène Delacroix in the library. □

▶ FAUBOURG SAINT-HONORÉ*

B1 / 8th arr. Métro : St-Philippe-du-Roule. Bus : 28, 32, 42, 49, 52, 80, 83.

Between the Place Beauvau and the Rue Royale runs the Faubourg Saint-Honoré, which lays serious claim to be the international capital of *haute-couture* and luxury commerce.

▶ Distinguished residences, built in the early 18thC by financiers and businessmen of the period, punctuate the succession of boutiques : in the main, these are now foreign embassies. The British Embassy★ is at No. 39, in Pauline (Bonaparte) Borghese's former town house, amid a cluster of early 18thC mansions in various states of preservation. On the Place Beauvau, the *hôtel* built around 1760 for the Comte de Beauvau is now occupied by the Ministry of the Interior; but the Faubourg's best-known address is unquestionably No. 55-57 — the **Élysée Palace★★**, which originally belonged to the Count of Évreux and later, Madame de Pompadour, became a public dance-hall during the Revolution, and is now (since 1873) the residence of the President of the French Republic. □

▶ GRAND PALAIS, PETIT PALAIS*

B2 / Petit Palais : Avenue Winston-Churchill. Grand Palais : Avenue Winston-Churchill, Avenue de Selves and Avenue Franklin-Roosevelt, 8th arr. Métro : Champs-Élysées-Clemenceau. Bus : 28, 42, 49, 72, 73, 83.

The Grand Palais and Petit Palais stand on the site of the 1900 Universal Exhibition, where marvels from the four corners of the earth were displayed; one of the most talked-about was the moving walkway that circled the pavilions.

▶ The **Grand Palais** was for many years the accustomed venue for Paris's great commercial exhibitions. The huge facilities at the Porte de Versailles and La Défense have now taken over this function, and the Grand Palais is now devoted to art shows *(10-8 daily, 10-10 Wed.; closed Tue.)*. The gigantic glass roof★★ which covers the hall is a masterpiece of Art Nouveau iron architecture. ▶ Behind the Grand Palais, on the Avenue Franklin-Roosevelt, is the **Palais de la Découverte★★** *(10-6, closed Mon. and nat. hols.)*, displaying the various discoveries of modern science; interesting for both children and adults. Popularization of knowledge is the rule here; the major attraction, a **planetarium**, offers a scaled-down version of the night sky, with 9000 stars swimming slowly across it. ▶ The **Petit Palais** has now been transformed into a **Fine Arts Museum★** by the City of Paris. It presents highly diverse collections relative to France in the 19thC : paintings by Delacroix, Géricault, Courbet, Monet, and Cézanne, along with a number of objects from the turn of the century. Also fine antiques and 18thC furniture. Frequent temporary exhibitions *(10-5:40; closed Mon.)*. □

▶ The GRANDS BOULEVARDS

B1 / 1st, 2nd, 3rd, 8th, 9th and 10th arrs. Métro : Madeleine, Opéra, Richelieu-Drouot, Bonne-Nouvelle, Strasbourg-St-Denis. Bus : 20, 21, 22, 24, 27, 29, 38, 39, 42, 47, 48, 52, 67, 85, 95.

▶ The **Boulevard de la Madeleine** and the **Boulevard des Capucines**, between the *Café de la Paix, Fauchon* and the Trois Quartiers department store, still maintain a certain tradition of luxury, even though the beautiful professional *marcheuses* (streetwalkers) of former times no longer walk here to disturb the serenity of Parisian males. ▶ Behind the Opéra, the **Boulevard Haussmann** becomes thoroughly dreary once it has passed the big department stores *(Grands Magasins)* and the vicinity of the St. Lazare railway station. The **Boulevard Malesherbes** peters out in the monotonously genteel 17th arrondissement. ▶ The real Grands Boulevards, which in the 19thC made a fine promenade all the way to the Place de la République, have now been wholly stripped of their original character by the proliferation of fast-food shops, couscous restaurants and other such establishments. ▶ Close by is the business quarter, huddled round the **Bourse★** (Stock Exchange), a somewhat severe Corinthian temple designed by Brongniart in 1825. This district passes into a deep sleep as soon as the offices close down in the evening, in contrast to the adjacent **Strasbourg-St. Denis** neighbourhood which seethes with lovers of Kung-Fu and pornographic movies. There is nothing especially Parisian about the crowds of tourists and seekers of doubtful pleasures around the **Porte St. Denis** and **Porte St. Martin**, but the *quartier* does still have one or two fine 19thC buildings such as the Porte St. Martin Theatre (1829), the Gymnase Theatre (38 Blvd. de Bonne-Nouvelle, 1820), the Variety Theatre (7 Blvd. Montmartre, 1807) and, coming back towards the Opéra, the **Opéra-Comique** (Blvd. des Italiens) or the **Maison Dorée**, on the corner of the Rue Laffitte (1839). □

▶ GUIMET Museum*

A2 / 6, Place d'Iéna, 16th arr. Métro : Iéna. Bus : 32, 63, 82.

The industrialist, musician and traveler Émile Guimet left his collections of Far-Eastern art to the state when he died in 1884. Today they form the core of the newly renovated Guimet Museum, one of the richest exhibitions of Asiatic art on the planet *(9:45-12/ 1:30-5:15; closed Tue. and nat. hols.)*.

▶ Impressive **Cambodian statues★** at the museum's entrance set a religious tone that pervades most of the Cambodian and Southeast Asian works exhibited here, spanning the 6th to the 13thC. The contrast between these idealized and often enigmatic pieces and the **decorative objects** from Pakistan, Afghanistan and India, emphasizes the myriad influences affecting this crossroads between East and West. The 11thC Dancing Shiva★, the Flower Spirit with its Greek overtones, and the 2ndC King of the Snakes are among the greatest masterpieces of the Indian subcontinent. For those who don't care for bronzes, hundred-armed goddesses and painted banners, there is the sumptuous collection of **porcelain and ceramics★★★**, which is unrivaled anywhere in the world for its sheer decorative richness, variety of subject matter, and exquisite craftsmanship. □

▶ Les HALLES*

B2 / 1st arr. Métro : Châtelet-Les Halles, Étienne-Marcel. RER : Châtelet-Les Halles. Bus : 21, 29, 38, 47, 58, 67, 69, 70, 72, 74, 81, 85.

Les Halles are dead; long live Les Halles! The "Ventre de Paris" ("The Belly of Paris") from the 12thC on, the great Halles food and flower market in Baltard's glass-and-metal pavilions at the centre of Paris had been slowly suffocating in an everlasting traffic jam. It continued to do so until the 1970s when the markets were moved to Rungis, well out of town on the main road to Orly Airport. Now the *quartier* is focused on a gigantic crater, where the markets used to stand — the largest urban project attempted in Paris since the Baron Haussmann, and the superb **Fountain of Innocents★★**, a 1549 Renaissance masterpiece by Jean Goujon.

▶ Today's Les Halles is an underground labyrinth, built over a railway station which is itself 25 metres below the surface. It includes some five thousand metres of streets and theatres, the **Grévin Museum** *(10:30-6:45, Sun. and hols. 1-7:15)*, and a **shopping forum★** filled with boutiques, stores and cinemas around a series of lively arcades. The forum is the work of two architects, Vasconi and Penchréac'h, who have taken care that abundant light should penetrate all four underground levels; glass arches, symbolizing the modern Halles, echo the stone arches of the **church of Saint-Eustache** opposite (→), which represent Medieval and Renaissance Paris. Do not miss the **Holographie Museum** on level 1, 15-21 Grand Balcon *(11-7, Sun. and hols. 1-7)*. ▶ On the corner of Rues Pierre-Lescot and Rambuteau, the municipality has created a **cultural centre** housing studios, exhibition halls, poetry workshop (Maison de la Poésie) and, above all, a cultural information service (SVP Culturel) supplying information from a computer bank. ▶ An underground district connecting Saint-Eustache, the Bourse and the Forum, **l'Espace des Halles** offers athletic, educational, social and, above all, cultural activities : **l'Espace photographique de Paris,** photo exhibits and archives open to the public ; the **Maison des Conservatoires,** meeting point for Paris music, dance and theatre conservatories ; an **auditorium** that seats 600 and a **discothèque ;** green spaces such as the **serre panoramique** (greenhouse) displaying 72 plant varieties on 450 square meters, and a 50 m-long **swimming pool** in an elegant setting. ▶ Apartments, a day-nursery and a garden which extends as far as the **Bourse du Commerce** (Commercial Stock Exchange) complete the setting, which is a popular meeting place for the young and the old avant-garde, as well as for artists, marginals and aggressive hooligans. □

▶ HÔTEL DE VILLE

B2 / Place de l'Hôtel-de-Ville, 4th arr. Métro : Hôtel-de-Ville. Bus : 38, 47, 58, 67, 69, 70, 72, 74, 75, 76, 96.

The Hôtel de Ville, headquarters of the mayor's administration, celebrated its centenary in 1982. This occasion was marked by a refurbishment of the former Place de Grève, now the Place de l'Hôtel-de-Ville, which stands in front. This pedestrians-only square was the setting for public executions in the Middle Ages; nowadays it shimmers with flowers and fountains, and below the surface is a huge car park.

▶ The history of the Mairie de Paris (Municipal Authority) goes back to the reign of St. Louis, who in 1260 demanded of the people of Paris that they designate a Provost *(Prévôt)* and Aldermen. The latter deliberated in a salt-merchant's house on the Place de Grève, known as the "Parloir aux Bourgeois". A century later, in 1357, Provost Étienne Marcel bought the "Maison aux Piliers" on behalf of the City of Paris; subsequently greatly enlarged, first under François I, then during the July Monarchy, the building was totally demolished during the revolt of the Commune on the 24th of May 1871, then rebuilt according to a design by Ballu. ▶ The ornate façade of the Hôtel de Ville, with its Renaissance-style statues and decorations, was, for many years, roundly abused by Parisians; nowadays it is recognized for what it is, one of the greatest monuments of the 19thC. The ceremonial rooms inside (sumptuous, but highly impractical) now draw most of the critics' fire. *(Group visits, by request : Accueil de la Ville de Paris, 49, rue de Rivoli.)*   ◻

▶ INSTITUT**

B2 / Quai Conti, 6th arr. Métro : Saint-Germain, Pont-Neuf. Bus : 24, 27, 39, 48, 58, 70, 95.

Under the Institut's august dome, the academicians brood over their interminable dictionary of the French language. Here also the hallowed sages of science and the arts meet in the learned assemblies of the Academy's five branches : Literature, Science, Fine Arts, Moral and Political Science.

▶ These five academies all occupy the serene **Palais de l'Institut de France★★**, designed by Louis Le Vau and completed after his death in 1691 by Lambert and d'Orbay. Before becoming the seat of the French Academy (founded by Richelieu in 1635), this building was occupied by the Collège des Quatre-Nations, as decreed by Cardinal Mazarin — who also bequeathed it his library. The present Bibliothèque Mazarine★ possesses more than 5 000 000 volumes, manuscripts and precious incunabula, stored in its premises in the Tour de Nesle *(10-6; closed Sat. and Sun.).* Students and scholars now work in this tower, from which Queen Margot is said to have had her nightly lovers flung into the Seine. ▶ Close by, on the Quay, stands the **Hôtel de la Monnaie★** (Mint, 1771-77), a fine example of Louis XVI architecture (striking of medals; medal displays; *11-6; closed Mon.*).   ◻

Unusual museums :
Musée de l'Assistance publique

The Public Health Museum, in a fine 17thC aristocratic mansion : a display of ten centuries of medical history, bizarre instruments, anecdotes and curiosities. (47 Quai de la Tournelle, 5th arr. 10-5; closed Mon, Tue. and hols.).

▶ INSTITUT DU MONDE ARABE
(Arab World Institute)

C2 / 5th arr. Métro : Gare d'Austerlitz, Jussieu.

Until recently the centre for Islamic culture was contained in the prestigious **Institut des études musul-**manes across from the Jardin des Plantes (Botanical Gardens). The Institut du Monde Arabe, established by France and nineteen Arab countries, is the new cultural headquarters for an Islamic art and civilization museum, a library with over 40 000 works and an antenna for cultural programming.   ◻

▶ Les INVALIDES***

B2 / 7th arr. Métro : Invalides, Varenne, Latour-Maubourg. RER : Invalides. Bus : 28, 49, 63, 69, 82, 83, 92.

Les Invalides testifies to the military grandeur of France under the Empire and the post-revolutionary Republic. The facade, perhaps the finest in Paris, gives onto a majestic lawn-covered esplanade extending all the way to the banks of the Seine. It was Louis XIV, the Sun King, who announced (in the edicts of 1670 and 1674) the creation of Les Invalides as a home for wounded veterans of his armies.

▶ Les Invalides is the work of two successive architects, Libéral Bruant and Hardouin-Mansart. The latter was responsible for the monumental general design of the building, especially the remarkable **dome★★** on the Place Vauban side, which took 25 years to build (1679-1706). ▶ A more fitting imperial mausoleum could scarcely be conceived for the **tomb of Napoleon I★**, which has lain in the crypt here since 1840 *(10-5 daily, 10-7 Jul.-Aug.)* when the ex-Emperor's body was brought back in triumph from St. Helena. His ashes are contained in six coffins inside an ornate red porphyry monument. Visitors file past in the golden half-light of the crypt, their minds no doubt filled with memories of Austerlitz and Waterloo... ▶ It is almost impossible to visit all of Les Invalides, with its 16 km of corridors. After the obligatory visit to the Dôme church, the royal church, the next stop should be the **church of St. Louis-des-Invalides★**, used by the soldiers. Once again, the former military splendours of France are evoked : tombs of great generals, Napoleonic memorabilia, remains of no less than 1 417 standards captured from assorted enemies. The somewhat less warlike 17thC organ is one of the most beautiful in Paris. ▶ The two buildings of the **Musée de l'Armée★★** (Army Museum; *10-5 or 6 according to season*) enclose the courtyard. ▶ Lost in the garrets of the Invalides are the remarkable and most interesting **Plans-Reliefs★** (relief maps). Here are 1/600 scale models of great cities and fortresses in France and abroad, ranging from Louis XIV to Napoleon III.   ◻

▶ JARDIN DES PLANTES*
(Botanical Gardens)

B-C2 / 5th arr. Entrances : Place Buffon, Place Valhubert. Métro : Jussieu, Place Monge, Gare d'Austerlitz. RER : Gare d'Austerlitz. Bus : 24, 57, 61, 63, 65, 89, 91.

Created by Louis XIII as a "royal medicinal herb garden", and developed by the naturalists Fagon, Jussieu and (especially) Buffon, the Jardin des Plantes is today a haunt of children, students from the vicinity and retired people who wander under the aged trees or around the pits and aviaries of the zoo. In the 18thC this place was a centre for the fashionable aristocratic study of botany.

▶ Galleries devoted to mineralogy, entomology, palaeobotany, palaeontology and comparative anatomy... these names may make you a trifle languid, but the main gallery of the **Museum of Natural History★★** has a magic of its own, with its armies of skeletons and resplendent collections of minerals and butterflies. Some of the greatest names in world biology (Buffon, Daubenton, Cuvier) worked in this museum; nonetheless, it became one of the poorest on earth, though its collections are among the richest. Now it has been renovated and restored, and at last can display its possessions in fit surroundings (57, rue Cuvier, *1:30-5; closed Tue. and nat. hols.*). □

▶ **LATIN QUARTER**

B2 / 5th and 6th arrs. Métro : Odéon, Saint-Michel, Maubert. RER : Luxembourg. Bus : 21, 24, 27, 38, 47, 58, 63, 67, 70, 84, 85, 86, 87, 89, 96.

From the **Odéon Theatre**★ to the "heretical" skyscraper of the Faculty of Sciences (Jussieu), from the Place St-Michel to the Rue Mouffetard, the uniting factor for the Latin Quarter has been the Sorbonne. In the 12thC, Abélard rebelled against the ecclesiastical teachings of the Île de la Cité, and his students followed him across the river to found a new university; subsequently, in 1253, Robert de Sorbon opened a college which offered room and board to poor students. His name was extended to cover an institution grouping no less than four universities on the Left Bank, and the 10 000 students who flocked to the Sorbonne made Paris the intellectual capital of Christendom. Among the most renowned teachers here were St. Bonaventure, Albert le Grand, St. Thomas Aquinas and Malebranche. The Sorbonne was always a turbulent community, opposed to the royal authority; and by 1792 it had declined almost to the point of no return. Napoleon I breathed new life into it, but it was not until the Third Republic that a modern university was established, which the events of May 1968 fragmented into 13 multi-disciplinary universities scattered all over Paris and the suburbs. From the Carrefour de l'Odéon, one continues to the **Place Saint-Sulpice**★★, shaded by chestnut trees. In the centre is the monumental Fountain of the Four Bishops (1844), while to the E is the **Saint-Sulpice church**★, typical of the 17th and 18thC Classical style with a reference to Antiquity *à la* Palladio. Sarvandoni undertook the famous façade whose towers were reworked by Chalgrin. Inside, statues by Bouchardon, Pigalle; paintings by C. Van Loo and especially, the **chapelle des anges**★ (angel's chapel, *1st on right*), decorated by Delacroix and on which he worked until his death in 1863.

▶ The Latin Quarter is today divided up by the Haussmann **boulevards** of **St-Michel** and **St-Germain.** Historically, its main artery was the **Rue St-Jacques**, which follows the lie of an old Gallo-Roman road. ▶ The Boulevard St-Michel, 1.5 km long, begins at Davioud's amazing Second Empire **fountain,** at the centre of the Place St-Michel and for years a great rallying point for Paris marginals. The latter have been drummed off the café terraces of the **St. André-des-Arts** and **îlôt St. Séverin**★ *quartier* by the progressive commercial banality of these ancient streets (fine 18thC houses★ at No. 29, Rue de la Parcheminerie, Rue de la Harpe, odd numbers, Rues des Grands-Augustins, Séguier, Gît-le-Cœur; also Nos. 47 and 52, Rue St-André-des-Arts). ▶ The atmosphere becomes duller in proportion to the growing number of boutiques; around the Sorbonne, however, a few "experimental" cinemas and bookshops maintain a token student presence. The **Sorbonne** itself, a gigantic barrack dating from 1900, deploys its 22 lecture theatres and scores of classrooms around a series of decorated corridors (frescoes and "kitsch" allegories). The main lecture theatre was embellished by Puvis de Chavannes. The only ancient part is the elegant **chapel**★ (by Lemercier, 1635) with its domed façade dominating the Place de la Sorbonne. Inside, paintings by Philippe de Champaigne and Richelieu's tomb, by Girardon. ▶ The **Collège de France** on the Place Marcellin-Berthelot is dedicated to the impartial study of arts and sciences. The first stone of this building was laid by Louis XIII, though it was not completed

until 1780. ▶ On the top of the "Montagne" Sainte-Geneviève, by the **Place du Panthéon** (→), the **church of Saint-Étienne-du-Mont**★★ is dedicated to Geneviève, the saint who saved Paris (late 15thC; choir-screen, tombs of Pascal and Racine). Also the **Sainte-Geneviève Library,** with 1 700 000 volumes. The **Lycée Henri IV** (school) unfortunately bars the access to the remains of the Romanesque abbey of Sainte-Geneviève (kitchens, refectory, tower of Clovis, Library). ▶ The **Place de la Contrescarpe,** behind the Lycée Henri IV, is very lively at night, with a mixture of tramps, students and tourists. Innumerable restaurants and their cosmopolitan clientele are gradually forcing out the traditional inhabitants, who nowadays only manage to get together in the mornings for the provincial market★★ at the bottom of the **Rue Mouffetard.** ▶ The "Mouffe" is now an upscale neighbourhood but has managed to keep the feeling of a protected outpost, especially around the **church of Saint-Médard**★. This curious sanctuary is a blend of Flamboyant Gothic, Renaissance, 17thC and the fashionable Antique style of the 18thC. □

▶ The **LOUVRE***★★★*

B2 / 1st arr. Métro : Louvre, Palais-Royal. Bus : 21, 24, 27, 39, 48, 67, 69, 72, 74, 76, 81, 85, 95.

Seen from the Seine or the Tuileries Gardens, the largest building complex in Paris gives a false impression of unity; this is not far short of miraculous, since the Louvre took no less than eight centuries to reach its present state.

▶ First, the square fortress built by Philippe Auguste (1190), and Étienne Marcel's ramparts; then the "library" of Charles V, the château begun by Pierre Lescot for François I and Henri II, which was carried on by Catherine de Médicis and Henri IV; then the finishing work done by Louis XIV. After this came the museum installed by the Revolution, which was enlarged under Napoléon; the 1871 burning of the Tuileries by the Communards; and finally André Malraux's restoration of the original moats (filled in during the transformation from fortress to palace) in 1965. The Louvre has never ceased to adapt and change. The current challenge is its "Grand Louvre" projet, directed by the Chinese-born American architect I. M. Pei. Its first step is the construction of a transparent pyramid at the entrance to the museum. Then it will renovate the interior of the Ministry of Finance offices. ▶ The Vieux (Old) Louvre (1660-80) with its famous **colonnade**★★ facing the Place du Louvre, surrounds the **Cour Carrée** (Square Courtyard)★ and continues along the Seine as far as the Pont du Carrousel. The W wing of the Cour Carrée is older; this structure is a masterpiece of the French Renaissance, with superb pediments. ▶ The Nouveau (New) Louvre spreads its wings as far as the Pont du Carrousel; its construction dates partly from Napoléon III and partly from the Third Republic, after the burning of the Tuileries (Flore and Marsan Pavilions). Between these two galleries, the gardens are dotted with Maillol's nude statues★, much beloved by photographers.

The Louvre in detail
▶ The **Louvre Museum** is situated in the "Vieux Louvre" around the Cour Carrée (Square Courtyard) and the section of the former palace that follows the Seine *(9:45-5:15 or 6:30, according to the room; museum fully open Mon. and Wed. ; closed Tue., tel. : 42.86.99.00).* It seems futile to attempt any kind of resumé of the Louvre's fabulous collections, of which the small proportion on view to the public is already enough to fill dozens and dozens of immense exhibition rooms. The best way to see the Louvre is the following : spend a half day looking over the principal masterpieces, and then come again in the days following to concentrate exclusively on certain departments. There are six of these, grouping objects broadly according to family. ▶ The **Ancient Greek and Roman pieces** *(ground floor)* which have recently been reorganized, are headed by the famous **Winged Victory of Samothrace,** which was discovered in 1863. This statue

stands at the top of a majestic staircase along with the armless **Venus de Milo**, originally a gift to Louis XVIII. The "Venus" dates from the 2ndC BC. In a special room adjoining are several pieces from the Parthenon, notably the Panathenian Frieze. Roman sculpture achieved an apotheosis with the creation of the Barbarian Princes and the Apollo. ▶ Once known as the "Assyrian Museum", the department of **Oriental Antiquities** *(ground floor, Cour Carrée)* displays treasures from the Near East : the Code of Hammurabi, a basalt stone bearing the laws of Babylon (1750 B.C.) ; Frieze of Archers, representing the King of Persia's bowmen (6thC BC); and statue of the Commissary (intendant) Ebih-Il, from the 3rd millennium BC, with eyes seeming to gaze on eternity. ▶ The **Ancient Egypt section** *(ground floor, basement and first floor, Cour Carrée)* has benefited from the prodigious discoveries made by Champollion and Marielle. Wide variety of figurines and jewelry ; also statues like the colossal Sphinx and the famous Seated Scribe. Fine sarcophagi and steles, along with an entirely reconstructed Mastaba, or funeral chamber. ▶ **The Objets d'Art and Furniture department** *(1st floor, Cour Carrée)* offers an eclectic collection of furniture and objects from the Middle Ages to the 19thC. These include Roman reliquaries, ivories, enamelling, and snuff boxes. It would take hours and hours to give each object here the attention it deserves. Notice especially the lovely Boulle furniture ; Marie Leszczynska's dressing case, given to her in 1729 ; and, in the **Apollo Gallery★★★**, the **Crown Jewels** with the astonishing 137-carat "Regent" Diamond, acquired by Philippe d'Orléans in 1717. ▶ The **Paintings section** is perhaps the best known part of the Louvre. *(1st floor, Grande Galerie, Aile de Flore, etc. 9:45-5, closed Tue.).* It seems to be perpetually undergoing reorganization and contains works covering the development of European painting, from the 14th to the 19thC. **French painting** is represented by such masterpieces as the *Pietà d'Avignon*, Watteau's *Gilles* and Poussin's *Bergers d'Arcadie*. Nonetheless, the public seems to prefer works by the Italian masters, headed by Leonardo's *Mona Lisa* ("La Joconde" in French), a veritable superstar. This mysterious painting tends to overshadow Leonardo's other works in the Louvre, *The Virgin of the Rocks* and *The Virgin, the Child Jesus and Saint Anne*, but it should not distract too much attention from the lovely creations of Fra Angelico, Uccello, Titian and Raphael hanging nearby. The **Flemish and Dutch masters** offer a considerable contrast in style, represented by Van Eyck, Memling, Rubens, Rembrandt and above all, the fascinating Vermeer, to whose *Lacemaker (Dentellière)* has now been added *The Astronomer* from the Rothschild collection. Lastly, the **Cabinet des Dessins** (Drawings department) offers constantly rotating exhibitions from its stock of 80 000 drawings. ▶ **Sculpture** is the last and perhaps the least-visited of the Louvre's sections ; nonetheless, it contains Michelangelo's famous *Slaves* along with important works by Donatello, Jean Goujon, Germain Pilon and Carpeaux. □

▶ **LUXEMBOURG Gardens and Palace****

B2 / 6th arr. RER : Luxembourg. Bus : 21, 27, 38, 58, 82, 84, 85, 89.

The Luxembourg Gardens, once so beloved of Marie de Médicis, is a peaceful spot for the horticulturists to work on the orchids (more than 400 varieties) of the Orangerie, and the gardens' orchards.

▶ After the assassination of Henri IV, his widow, Marie de Médicis, began building a palace (1615) in the gardens she had recently bought from François de Luxembourg and to which she constantly added. ▶ On the Rue de Tournon side, the Palace★★, designed by Salomon de Brosse, retains its original Florentine features. The building now houses the French Senate and was considerably modified in the 19thC. Haussmann was only prevented from destroying the Park by a petition signed by 12 000 people : as it was, the building of the Rue Auguste-

Comte reduced it to its present 60-odd acres. ▶ The Luxembourg is above all a highly civilized park, with its ponds, its terraces, its pretty Fontaine Médicis and its monument to Delacroix. Though it has lost its chair-attendants, the chairs are still there ; alas, the park wardens are implacable about the hour of closing, which is exactly thirty minutes before sunset at all times of year. From the Luxembourg Gardens by the Avenue de l'Observatoire or the Rue Gay-Lussac one reaches the Boulevard Port-Royal and the **Val-de-Grâce** military hospital★★ : the former monastery founded by Anne d'Autriche is one of the most remarkable architectural ensembles of the 17thC. Built to the design of F. Mansart, the dome is one of the finest examples of Roman Baroque in Paris. □

▶ **Church of La MADELEINE**

B1 / Place de la Madeleine, 8th arr. Metro : Madeleine. Bus : 24, 42, 52, 84, 94.

The majestic, slightly ponderous Church of the Madeleine, with its temple facade and its perron 24 steps high, is very much in tune with its smart location at the top of the Rue Royale. This is the core of Paris's luxury commercial area and the crux of the Grands Boulevards.

▶ The church was begun by Napoléon I who wanted a temple dedicated to his Grand Army ; but it was not completed until 1840. □

▶ **Château de MALMAISON*** and de BOIS-PRÉAU***

R.E.R. : Rueil-Malmaison (Line A).

A temporary residence of Napoléon during the Consulate, and later, Empress Josephine's retreat, Malmaison and its "annex", the Bois-Préau, offer a marvelous example of Empire-style decoration : furniture, paintings, memorabilia *(10-12 & 1:30-4:30 or 5)*. In the **park★**, rose garden. ▶ 3 km S. : ponds of Saint-Cucufa. □

▶ **The MARAIS*****

B-C2 / 3rd and 4th arr. Métro : Saint-Paul, Pont-Marie *(S side)*, Bastille, Chemin-Vert, Rambuteau *(N side)*. Bus : 20, 29, 38, 47, 65, 67, 69, 75, 76, 86, 87, 91, 96.

The twisting streets, magnificent private mansions, courtyards and ancient buildings of the Marais quarter cover some 300 acres of protected *(classé)* townscape. This *quartier* is really a huge museum of Paris, a living testimonial to the civil architecture of the 17thC. Not so long ago, it was on the brink of crumbling into ruin, but was saved *in extremis* by the Malraux Law of 1962, which led to a long and ultimately fruitful renovation of the Marais' forgotten treasures. Twenty years later, in the 1980s, accommodation here has become much sought after by wealthy Parisians just as it was in the days of Henri IV when aristocrats and burgers clustered around the Place Royale — now the Place des Vosges — and built themselves houses to match their wealth and ambition. The area is now considerably enlarged, stretching from the Church of St. Gervais to the Bastille and from the Seine to the Temple.

▶ The S end of the Marais between Rue St-Antoine and the Seine is typical of old Paris. The church of **St. Gervais-St. Protais★** (16thC, pure Flamboyant Gothic), is a good starting point for a visit to this side of the quarter; its Classical façade (1620) stands right behind the Hôtel de Ville. It was in this church that a German shell killed 51 people on Good Friday, 1918. ▶ Continuing down the **Rue François-Miron**, lovely houses of the precinct of St. Gervais (1732 : Nos. 2-14). No. 68 on this street is the **Hôtel de Beauvais★** (1655); No. 82, the Hôtel du Président Hénault (1706). ▶ To the right is Rue de Fourcy, then Rue des Nonains-d'Hyeres; on the right, **Hôtel d'Aumont★★** (1648); left, the rear façade of the **Hôtel de Sens★★**, heavily restored but still a fine example of 15thC architecture. This *hôtel* was the home of the eccentric Queen Margot; today, it houses the **Forney Library** *(1:30-8; closed Sun. and Mon.).* ▶ Close by the Quai des Célestins, a part of **Philippe Auguste's city wall** (1180) is still visible (Rue des Jardins-Saint-Paul). ▶ At the end of the quai is the Hôtel Fieubet, built by Mansart in 1678 but loaded with superfluous additions in the 19thC; likewise the mansion at No. 3 Rue de Sully, now occupied by the **Library of the Arsenal.** This building still retains some rooms decorated in the style of Louis XIII, unchanged since the great finance minister Sully lived here *(10-5 daily; closed Sun.)* ▶ Via Rue du Petit-Musc, to the ancient and busily commercial **Rue St-Antoine**, the central artery of the Marais. At No. 17, the circular **Temple of St. Marie★**, built by Mansart in 1634; at No. 21, the Hôtel de Mayenne (1613) and the exceptionally graceful **Hôtel de Sully★★** at No. 62, built by Henri IV's great minister in 1624; today, beautifully restored, this building houses the Historic Monuments Board (C.N.M.H.S. → museums; information centre). Next to the Lycée Charlemagne, further on, is the **church of St. Paul-St. Louis★** (1627-41), in the Jesuit style, rare in Paris. Madame de Sévigné used to come here to listen to the preacher Bourdalone's sermons. ▶ Coming from Rue St-Antoine, the N end of the Marais is entered via the **Rue des Archives** *(to the right, off Rue de Rivoli).* No. 22, next to the Lutheran Church, is the medieval **Cloître des Billettes★** (cloister), built in 1415; the only construction of its kind to be seen in Paris. ▶ At the intersection with the Rue des Francs-Bourgeois stands the **Hôtel Soubise★★** (1705-09), where the National Archives are housed around a fine **courtyard** in the shape of a horseshoe. The superb apartments here (decorated by Boffrand) are open to the public; these are occupied by the **Museum of French History** *(2-5 daily ex Tue.).*

▶ Behind this *hôtel* at No. 60 Rue des Archives, is the **Musée de la Chasse et de la Nature** (Hunting Museum) in the **Hôtel Guénégaud★**, 1650, recently restored *(10-5:30 daily ex Tue. and. hols.)* ▶ **Rue des Francs-Bourgeois** meets **Rue Vieille-du-Temple**; No. 87 of this street is the **Hôtel de Rohan★★**, also a depository for national archives. No. 47, the **Hôtel des Ambassadeurs d'Hollande**, dates from 1655; nearby, No. 31 Rue des Francs-Bourgeois is the **Hôtel d'Albret.** The proximity of these three great houses demonstrates the heavy concentration of aristocratic residences here during the 17thC. ▶ 14-16 Rue des Francs-Bourgeois is the **Hôtel Carnavalet★★** (→) former home of Mme de Sévigné; this architectural masterpiece faces the **Hôtel de Lamoignon★★** (history library) at 24 Rue Pavée... There are many others, too many to enumerate, which mark the apogee of civil architecture in France. A random choice might include the following : the **Hôtel Libéral-Bruant**, Place Thorigny, now the **Bricart de la Serrure** (Lock) **Museum**; the **Hôtel Salé★★**, nearby, 5 Rue de Thorigny, built in 1656 by the seigneur de Fontenay, is now the **Picasso Museum★★** (→) where in superb surroundings the painter's personal collection is on display; the **Hôtel de Marle★**, 11 Rue Payenne.

▶ Rue des Francs-Bourgeois goes back to the **Place des Vosges★★**, the heart and origin of the Marais. This is where it all began : when Henri IV created this fascinating 127 m by 140 m square, he created a whole *quartier,* almost a whole town. The buildings here are uniform in design and the arcaded square is all but totally closed in on itself. The white stone and red brick of the masonry, tempered by dark blue slate roofing, give an impression of purity and harmony. Victor Hugo lived at No. 6, the Hôtel de Rohan-Guéménée, between 1833 and 1848 and wrote some of his most famous works here. The house

is now a **museum** dedicated to the great author *(10-5:30; closed Mon. and Tue.),* containing especially fine examples of his visionary and symbolist drawings.   □

▶ MEUDON

SNCF (Montparnasse station); R.E.R. line C. Bus : 136, 169, 179.

On the edge of its **forest** (wooded parks, play areas), at the foot of the terrace of its former château *(8:30-5:30 or 6;* view★★ of Paris) and its **Observatory**, Meudon is a residential town. **Historical museum** (11 Rue des Pierres) and **Rodin museum**, annex of the one in Paris, with the sculptor's tomb (19 Av. Rodin, *Sat. and Sun., 1:30-5).*   □

▶ Parc MONCEAU*

B1 / 17th arr. Métro : Monceau. Bus : 30, 84, 94.

The Monceau Park is the last remnant of the immense domain belonging to the Orléans family, which at one time covered a large proportion of the land on the western side of Paris. During the Second Empire, when so many of Paris's parks and green spaces were created, the Parc Monceau was landscaped in the English style by the architect Alphand, providing verdant views for the luxurious houses built on its perimeter by notables and favourites of the régime.

▶ Well worth a visit are Nos. 5 and 7, Rue Murillo, and No. 5 **Avenue Van-Dyck.** ▶ Just off the park are two quiet and intimate museums housed in fine specimens of 19thC Paris mansions. At No. 7, **Avenue Vélasquez**, the **Cernuschi Museum★** was donated to the City of Paris by the great collector of Far Eastern art, Henri Cernuschi, in 1896 *(daily 10-5:40; closed Mon. and hols.).* Considerably enlarged since then, notably with the addition of certain archaic pieces which are among the finest examples of their kind in the world. The upper floors contain objects ranging from the 2ndC BC to the 15th and 16thC AD. On the ground floor, courses in calligraphy and temporary exhibition. ▶ At 63, Rue de Monceau, the Camondo family's collection from the French 18thC is now in the possession of the Union des Arts Décoratifs (Decorative Arts Union). The **Nissim de Camondo Museum★** *(10-12 & 2-5; closed Mon., Tue. and hols.)* exhibits bronzes, porcelain objects, Savonnerie carpets, furniture (some from the royal household) and *boiseries.* The former salons are decorated with 23 Aubusson carpets★.   □

Unusual Museums :
Musée Baccarat

Also known as the Crystal Museum, this little establishment has been set up next to the salesrooms of the Baccarat company, Rue de Paradis (No. 30, 10th arr. 9-5; closed Sun.), in the street which is the commercial centre for the glass and porcelain industries. The Musée Baccarat offers a unique demonstration of the French glassworker's art, as practised by a company that has existed since the 18thC and has worked for all the great families of Europe, from the Romanovs to the Hapsburgs. On display are some of Baccarat's most beautiful creations : giant candelabras, flagons, bowls, beakers, and glasses, in every colour and style. This exhibition will make you view the other shop windows in the quartier with a decidedly jaundiced eye...

▶ MONTMARTRE**

B1 / 18th arr. Métro : Blanche, Abbesses, Pigalle, Anvers, Lamarck-Caulaincourt. Bus : 67, 30, 54, 80, 85, 95. A minibus service serves the Butte Montmartre, from the Place Pigalle to the Mairie of the 18th arr., Rue Ordener; funicular railway.

The Butte Montmartre has always been half dream and half reality, a mixture of the best and worst aspects of Paris. On the one hand, it is a mass of clichés and tourists; on the other, if you know how to choose the time and place, it can lead you to delightful discoveries. This ambiguity is the source of its strange fascination.

▶ Nothing in Montmartre's long history ever indicated that it would become a great centre for bohemianism and the arts. The *Mont*, which was once dedicated to the God Mercury, is 130 metres high, one metre taller than the Buttes Chaumont and clearly dominating the Montagne Ste. Geneviève. During the reign of Charlemagne, it was named the "Mont des Martyrs", to commemorate the execution of St. Denis in AD 250. In 1133, a Benedictine abbey was founded here by Queen Adélaïde of Savoy; the fields belonging to the abbey stretched out below, where the Grands Boulevards are now. Henri IV bombarded Paris from Montmartre's strategic heights; later, mills began to appear, as the land grew more heavily cultivated. Montmartre pancakes and wine were consumed in *cabarets* or taverns. The Butte began to acquire a bad reputation; libertine aristocrats built extravagant "follies" here, such as the Château des Brouillards, built by the Marquis de Pompignan in 1772. Then came the tragic events of 1815, when Montmartre put up a bloody resistance to the invading Cossacks. In 1871, hundreds of *Communard* rebels took refuge in the chalk mines of the Butte, where they were immured or blown up by the advancing Versaillais. To expiate their appalling massacre, the Third Republic erected the gigantic Basilica of Sacré-Cœur on the site. Even at this time, after Renoir and Van Gogh, unknown men of genius were beginning to converge on Montmartre from all over Europe : Van Dongen, Juan Gris, Picasso... the legend was born. At the beginning of 1914, Picasso was working on his *Demoiselles d'Avignon*, and Cubism had been founded. Montmartre and the Bateau-Lavoir entered history as the birthplace of modern art. ▶ Like a theatre backdrop, Montmartre has its "street" side and its "garden" side. The street side is mainly the **Boulevard de Clichy**, the **Place Blanche** and the vanes of the **Moulin Rouge** which go round and round all night. Then there is **Pigalle**, with its sex-shops and sordid striptease joints (now being replaced by peep-shows and video-clubs); its vaguely unsavoury fauna, and its overpriced bars and cabarets. ▶ Leaving the bright lights of "Gay Paree" behind, the **Rue Lepic** with its lively market★ leads through to the "garden" side of Montmartre. ▶ At No. 2, Rue Ronsard, in a former covered market is the **Museum d'Art Naïf** (Folk Art Museum), the Max Fourny collection of paintings and sculptures *(daily 10-6).* ▶ The climb to the famous **Moulin de la Galette★** is a steep one; the latter was immortalized by Renoir, and is surrounded by houses from around 1900. Rue d'Orchampt leads down to the side of the Bateau-Lavoir at 5 Rue Ravignan, now demolished. ▶ On the other side of the Rue Lepic, **Avenue Junot** is surrounded by villas and gardens. ▶ In Rue des Saules, the **Lapin Agile Cabaret** still retains its rustic aspect; it stands at the foot of the famous Montmartre vineyards, where the grapes are harvested every year amid all the trappings of country folklore. ▶ At No. 12, Rue Cortot near the **Rue Saint-Vincent** (Aristide Bruant had a song about this street), is the **Vieux-Montmartre Museum** *(2:30-5:30, 11-5 on Sun.; closed Tue.),* possibly the only museum in the world exhibiting a completely reconstructed old-fashioned bistro. ▶ At the top of the long **Rue du Mont-Cenis**, which dips down in a northward direction towards Clignancourt, stands the **Basilica of Sacré-Cœur★** built according to plans by the architect Abadie, between 1876 and 1919. The Basilica makes up for its relative lack of architectural interest by providing

a matchless view of Paris from its terraces — or, even better, from its dome. ▶ It is unfortunate that the Sacré-Cœur sometimes distracts attention from the lovely Romanesque Church of **Saint-Pierre-de-Montmartre★★**, the oldest sanctuary in Paris. There is doubt as to whether this structure embodies the remnant of a Gallo-Roman temple; however, its vaulted Gothic choir dates from 1147. A haven of coolness and peace, only a few steps away from the tourist frenzy of the **Place du Tertre★** with its cluttered café terraces, painters' easels and assembly-line artwork. ▶ The **Place du Calvaire** nearby is a veritable balcony over Paris, which can be both deserted and romantic at some hours. ▶ The steps, or the funicular, take you back down into the turmoil of the **Boulevard Rochechouart.** □

Unusual museums :
the Grevin waxworks

1982 was the centenary year of this museum of historical scenes and waxworks. A new ensemble devoted to 19thC Paris and its spectacles (shows) has now been opened in Les Halles under the same auspices (10, Blvd. Montmartre, 9th arr. 1-7 daily, and Forum des Halles, level 1, 1st arr. 10:30-8 daily).

▶ MONTPARNASSE

B2 / 6th, 14th arrs. Métro : Montparnasse-Bienvenüe, Gaîté, Vavin. Bus : 28, 48, 58, 68, 82, 89, 91, 92, 94, 95, 96.

Montparnasse on the Left Bank, Montmartre on the Right. Their pasts are similar : dance-halls, rendez-vous for artists and exiles who became famous. Here their names are Modigliani, Matisse, Henry Miller, Hemingway, Lenin and Trotsky. Then there is the immense crowd that throngs the many cinemas on the Boulevard du Montparnasse and its periphery, and the terraces of the Dôme and Coupole restaurants (once the headquarters of the avant-garde). The same crowd overflows into the *crêperies* (pancake bars) of the Breton quarter, the Rue Delambre, the Rue de la Gaieté and the Montparnasse station precinct. The **Tour Maine-Montparnasse,** beside the triple-galleried **commercial centre,** in a sense matches the Sacré-Cœur; both are equally decried, but for good or ill their silhouettes are part of the Paris skyline. To the west, the **Bourdelle Museum★** (16 Rue Bourdelle, *10-5:30; closed Mon.)* is housed in a characteristic artist's building, a tangle of *ateliers* (studios) piled with scale models, sketches and plaster casts left by the sculptor. ▶ At No. 100, Rue d'Assas is the **Zadkine Museum★** *(10-5:40 daily ex Mon.),* in the house occupied by the sculptor between 1928 and his death in 1967. Three hundred of his works have been assembled in the building and its small garden, which were first opened to the public in 1982. □

▶ The MOSQUE*

B2 / Place du Puits-de-l'Ermite, 5th arr. Métro : Monge. Bus : 24, 47, 57, 61, 63, 67, 89.

▶ Built between 1922 and 1926 in the Moroccan style, the **Grand Mosque of Paris** *(10-12, 2-5:30; closed Fri. and Muslim holidays)* is decorated with considerable variety. The most diverse motifs in Islamic art have been used here, especially in the remarkable domed prayer hall. Many Parisians come to the *hammam* (baths) here, and greatly appreciate the cakes and mint tea available at the shops of the *souk*. Not far off are the **Arènes de Lutèce** (Rue Monge and Rue des Arènes), the heavily-restored remains of a Gallo-Roman amphitheatre which was destroyed in the 3rdC and rediscovered in the 19thC.   □

▶ La MUETTE and PASSY

A2 / 16th arr. Métro : La Muette, Passy. Bus : 22, 32, 52, 63, PC.

▶ The charming **Ranelagh Gardens** are laid out in the former park of a château lived in by Louis XV and Madame de Pompadour. The present château, hidden discreetly behind a screen of trees, was built at the beginning of the century by Baron de Rothschild. ▶ The resplendent **Marmottan Museum★★** (2 Rue Louis-Boilly, *10-6; closed Mon.*) is devoted to Impressionism; one can see Monet's *Les Nymphéas*, which occupies an entire room. Monet's *Impression, soleil levant* was one of several stolen from the museum's collection. ▶ Discretion is also the hallmark of Balzac's house at No. 47, Rue Raynouard, where the writer used to come to escape his creditors. The resultant **Balzac Museum★** *(10-5:30; closed Tue.)* looks like a country house, with its garden. Balzac was not too happy here, finding it suffocatingly hot in summer and freezing cold in winter. While endeavouring to pursue his somewhat intricate pleasures, and nursing his love for the Polish Mme. Hanska from afar, Balzac nonetheless contrived to finish the last section of his great *Comédie Humaine* in this house. His spartan workroom has been left in its original state, complete with the famous coffee pot. The other rooms are stuffed with the memorabilia of a restless life : portraits, manuscripts, letters and everyday objects. ▶ The **Villa La Roche** (10 Sq. du Dr-Blanche), where the **Le Corbusier foundation** is located, illustrates the theories of the famous architect.   □

▶ NOTRE-DAME***

B2 / 4th arr. Métro : Cité. Bus : 21, 24, 38, 47, 81, 85, 96.

World-famous masterpiece of the Middle Ages, perfect example of Gothic harmony. The Cathedral of Notre-Dame de Paris is more than a monument : it is a "history book", as Michelet has said. It should be visited at different hours of the day, for a full appreciation of the architecture of light embodied in the Gothic nave. Notre-Dame swarms perpetually with visitors, though it takes on a more authentic character during great religious ceremonies or organ recitals. The great organists of Europe come here to play the massive instrument installed in 1730 and rebuilt by Cavaillé-Coll during the 19thC *(free concert, Sun. pm).*

▶ The name of Maurice de Sully is closely associated with the construction of Notre-Dame; after commencing the works, he directed them for thirty-three years until the completion of the choir and transept around 1200. Four more stages of construction had yet to be undertaken before France's largest cathedral was finally completed at the end of the 14thC. From that time onward, Notre-Dame has witnessed many great events : Saint-Louis' lying-in-state (1270); the solemn conversion of Henri IV (1594); the crowning of Napoléon I as Emperor (1804); the singing of the Victory Te Deum (1945); the funeral of General de Gaulle, attended by chiefs of state from all over the world (1970). Notre-Dame's historical importance is matched by its architecture as the symbol of Paris. All Gothic religious art was deeply influenced by it, to the farthest outposts of Europe. The architects Jean de Chelles and Pierre de Montreuil endowed their cathedral with simplicity and harmony, and proportions of 130 m long, 48 m wide and 35 m high from floor to roof. ▶ The **west façade**, enclosed by two massive square towers (69 m high) is divided into three levels : at the base stand the great doorways★★, with on the left a carved Virgin, in the

centre the Last Judgment, and on the right, Saint Anne. This is surmounted by the Gallery of Kings (their heads have been replaced; some of the originals, knocked off by the Revolutionaries in 1793, are now in the Cluny Museum). Above them is the great rose window, 9.6 m in diameter, itself topped by an open gallery joining the two towers *(access to towers 10-4:30).* ▶ The **lateral façades** and **the apse** have three levels backing on to each other; the apse itself is supported by flying buttresses with a span of 15 m. The 90-m spire was replaced by Viollet-le-Duc in 1860. ▶ The **interior** of Notre-Dame *(8-6:30 ex during services)* is composed of five naves, lit by three great rose windows★★ which still have their original 13thC stained glass. The side chapels contain 17th and 18thC paintings. ▶ The wooden choir stalls date from the 18thC; behind them is a magnificent screen decorated with a series of bas-reliefs★★ in polychrome stone. On the right, in the chancel, is the entrance to the Treasury, which displays gold plate, cameos of the various Popes, and a Palatine cross including a fragment of the True Cross. The **archaeological crypt** *(10-5)* displays objects discovered during the construction of the underground parking garage. ▶ Behind Notre-Dame, several parcels of the medieval street network disturbed by the Baron Haussmann are still visible. Rue Massillon, Nos. 4-8, fine 17th and 18thC homes; Rue Chanoinesse, Nos. 22 and 24, odd-looking canon's houses; finally, on the Rue de la Colombe, part of the Gallo-Roman defensive works built around the Île de la Cité.   □

▶ NOTRE-DAME-DE-LORETTE

B1 / 16 Rue Chaptal, 9th arr. Métro : Saint-Georges, Blanche. Bus : 30, 54, 68, 67, 74, 85.

Behind the churches of **Notre-Dame-de-Lorette** (its forbidding exterior, not unlike a Greek temple, hides rich interior decoration) and the **Trinité** was a bustling neighbourhood of artists, painters, writers and musicians, which in the 19thC was referred to as "New Athens".

▶ Restoration and Second Empire buildings surround the Place Saint-Georges (Rues La Bruyère, de la Tour-des-Dames, d'Aumale, Ballu). ▶ The Orléans Square at No. 80, Rue Taitbout was the preferred spot for the love trysts of Chopin and George Sand in the 1840s; and their self-contained housing community was the home of A. Dumas, Delacroix and Heine. The community fall apart when the lovers separated, but the decor hasn't changed : the courtyards, gardens and neighbouring streets (like Rue Chaptal, where G. Sand, Chopin, Liszt and Renan visited the painter Ary Scheffer in his 1820 building) remain the same. The Scheffer home has become the **Renan-Scheffer Museum★**, a record of the intellectual and literary life of the 19thC and the New Athens *quartier (10-5:30, closed Mon.).*   □

▶ OPÉRA**

B1-2 / Place de l'Opéra, 9th arr. Métro : Chaussée d'Antin, Opéra. RER : Auber. Bus : 20, 21, 22, 27, 29, 42, 52, 53, 57, 66, 95.

Built at the behest of Napoleon III, the Paris Opéra boasts that it is the most important example of 19thC theatre architecture. Since the foundation of the Royal Academy of Music by Louis XIV, Paris had had nothing but temporary theatres, which were frequently destroyed by fire. The Second Empire bequeathed to Paris the great opera house it had always dreamed of, in the heart of Haussmann's new quarters.

▶ The original project for the Opéra was devised by Charles Garnier. It was opposed by the Empress Eugénie, who condemned the plans for their lack of style. The architect replied that they were "... in the style of Napoleon III, Madame." The period of construction lasted for 15 years, and incorporated a number of new construction techniques, especially the use of iron; work was interrupted by the Commune's insurrection and a series of financial difficulties. The building was finally inaugurated on 5 January 1875 by Marshal de Mac-Mahon; as of 1881, electric lights replaced the gaslights; and by 1964 Chagall's frescoes covered the ceiling of the opera house. Originally conceived for the social crowds of the Second Empire, the Opéra apportions more space to its public areas and salons than it does to the theatre itself. ▶ The sumptuous marble and onyx staircase★, the grand foyer★ with its mosaic-covered roof and the gigantic six-ton chandelier in the theatre bear witness to an omnipresent concern for display. This is particularly true of the ornate façade, with a replica of Carpeaux's famous sculpture group, *La Danse*. ▶ Lovers of opera and ballet will not overlook the little **Opéra Museum** *(10-5 daily ex Mon.)* in the West Pavilion, where designs, maquettes, decor and costumes recreate the magic of past productions mounted in the "Palais Garnier". ☐

▶ ORSAY Museum*

B2 / Quai Anatole-France, 7th. arr. Métro : Solférino-Gare d'Orsay. RER : Gare d'Orsay. Bus : 24, 68, 69, 73, 84.

Inaugurated in December 1986, the Orsay Museum, built in the former Orsay station, presents works and documents tracing the evolution of the arts and French society from 1848 to 1914. The permanent collection is presented in the new galleries created by the Italian architectural designer Gae Aulenti, and includes paintings, sculptures and *objets d'art* from this period that were formerly displayed in the Louvre, Jeu de Paume Museum and the Palais de Tokyo *(10:30-6, Sun. 9-6, closed Mon.).*

▶ **Painting** : all the Impressionist paintings once housed in the Jeu de Paume are here, representing a wide range from this period. ▶ **Sculpture** : under the high glassed roof, a vivid display from Carpeaux to Maillol. ▶ **Architecture and urbanism** : scale models, drawings, reproductions *(East pavilions).* ▶ **Art deco** : the eclectic tastes of the Second Empire and the tendencies of Art Nouveau are well-represented by furnishings by Hector Guimard, Horta, Majorelle, William Morris. ▶ Photography, graphic arts, publishing, cinema, books and posters are exhibited. ▶ A sumptuous decor and an interesting view can be enjoyed at the **café des hauteurs.** ☐

▶ PALAIS OMNISPORT DE PARIS BERCY

C2 / Quai de Bercy, 12th arr. Métro : Bercy. Bus : 24, 62.

Built over the former wine warehouses of Bercy, the elegant glass and metal construction (and practically vertical lawns!) of P.O.P.B. hide ingenious systems for adapting to athletic or artistic use; from Verdi to the "Six Jours" cycle race.

▶ The P.O.P.B. began the transformation of the Bercy *quartier,* which will continue with building renovation, a Finance Ministry and a 30-acre park. ☐

▶ PALAIS-ROYAL*

B2 / 1st arr. Métro : Palais-Royal. Bus : 21, 27, 29, 39, 48, 67, 69, 72, 74, 81, 95.

The Palais-Royal is a marvelous, timeless enclave, set apart from the surrounding city, which seems to retain something of the 18thC which so loved it. Oddly, Parisians do not know it very well, though foreigners seem to be fully attuned to its charm. Built by Richelieu between 1629 and 1642, it was at first a "Palais-Cardinal", for it was here that Louis XIII's great minister lived and died. It became the Palais-Royal when the young Louis XIV moved in, with Anne of Austria.

▶ The regent Philippe of Orléans turned the Palace and **gardens★★** into a venue for his famous scandalous parties. After the destruction by fire of the Opéra close by, the Palace had to be reconstructed in 1763. The future Philippe-Égalité was so short of money to do this that he built **galleries** all round the gardens, which he rented to tradesmen, along with apartments in the upper stories. A second fire in 1781 destroyed the theatre on the site of today's **Comédie Française.** The Palais-Royal's bad reputation attracted crowds of common people; it was in the gardens that Camille Desmoulins called the populace to arms on 13 July 1789. Subsequently, the Palais Royal's gambling dens and cafés made it a haunt of men-about-town and dandies. Even Napoléon I, who installed the Council of State on the premises, failed to restore its former dignity. But fashion succeeded where authority had failed : the 19thC Paris crowd preferred the Grands Boulevards or the new *quartiers* to the Palais-Royal, and the gardens regained a tranquillity that has remained ever since. ▶ Behind the double portico of the Galerie d'Orléans, which separates the courtyard from the garden, the long galleries house a series of strange little shops selling military decorations, curios and lead soldiers. The main quadrangle is covered with a vast checkerboard by the artist Buren. Their rows correspond to the Palais-Royal colonnades. ☐

▶ The PANTHÉON*

B2 / Place du Panthéon, 5th arr. Métro : Cardinal-Lemoine. RER : Luxembourg. Bus : 21, 24, 27, 38, 84, 85, 89.

The Republic has chosen coldness and austerity to an almost abstract extreme to represent the virtues of its great men *(10-12 & 2-4).*

▶ The history of the Panthéon is hardly one of airy gaiety. Soufflot, the architect of what was then the church of Sainte-Geneviève, died of grief after seeing that his building was fissuring progressively as its dome was raised. The church had hardly been completed when it was turned into a Republican temple, by vote of the Constituent Assembly, in order to "receive the great men of the epoch of French liberty." Mirabeau was the first to enter it, followed by Voltaire, Rousseau and Marat. Some of the great men became less great after their Revolution : Mirabeau and Marat were forced to leave the premises, but the Third Republic installed Victor Hugo, Jean Jaurès and Gambetta. The day after his election, President François Mitterrand paid a visit to the building into which André Malraux had received the ashes of Jean Moulin, the Resistance hero, and where the frescoes of Puvis de Chavannes are in perfect harmony with the solemn, funereal atmosphere. ☐

▶ PASSAGES des GRANDS BOULEVARDS

B2 / 2nd arr. Métro : Bourse, Richelieu-Drouot, Rue Montmartre. Bus : 20, 29, 31, 48, 67, 68, 74, 85.

On the margins of the congested Grands Boulevards (→), are 19thC galleries and covered arcades which offer highly interesting walks; they can be found all over, from the Palais-Royal to the Faubourg St. Denis. With their anachronistic decoration, daring metal-and-glass roofs, old-fashioned shops and tea salons, the "Passages" survive at one remove from the commercial mainstream. Some have been restored and given a new lease on life; others have become a trifle sordid and dilapidated. The oldest, such as the **Pas-**

sage des Panoramas★ (Blvd. Montmartre, opened in 1808), witnessed all the fashionable crowds of the Restoration; figures like Balzac and Chopin used to frequent their shops and restaurants.

▶ The most beautiful gallery in Paris is probably the **Galerie Vivienne★**, which is broad and airy, with monumental decor and elegant paving. Fashion boutiques and tea shops have given this *passage* new life. By contrast, the **Passage Véro-Dodat★** (1826), the **Passage Choiseul** and the **Passage Jouffroy** are devoted to old books, workshops or ... neglect. ▶ Not far from the Grands Boulevards, several galleries have opened in the Rue St-Denis. Most of these do a roaring trade. The **Passage du Caire** is a headquarters for the wholesale cloth trade. The **Passages du Grand Cerf** and **du Bourg-l'Abbé**, on the other hand, have contrived to preserve their original 19thC decor. Between the Rue du Faubourg-Saint-Denis and the Boulevard de Strasbourg, the **Passages Brady, du Désir, de l'Industrie** and **Reilhac** will soon be undergoing restoration of their statues and glassworks. □

▶ **PÈRE-LACHAISE Cemetery★★**

C2 / 20th arr. Métro : Gambetta, Père-Lachaise. Bus : 26, 61, 69, 76.

The 125 acres of the Père-Lachaise Cemetery are half burial ground, half museum of 19thC sculpture. It is also a much-appreciated green area, full of tall trees *(7:30 or 8:30-5 or 6, according to season).*

▶ Opened in 1803 by the Municipality, Père-Lachaise is not unmarked by the publicity surrounding the legendary tomb of Héloïse and Abélard — but it has also had its authentically tragic moments. On 28 May 1871, the last 147 Communard insurgents were lined up and shot here against the **Mur des Fédérés** (Unionist's Wall); every year on the 1st of May, the procession of trade unionists comes to render them symbolic homage. □

▶ **PICASSO Museum★★**

B2 / 5, Rue de Thorigny, 3rd arr. Métro : St-Sébastien-Froissard. Bus : 20, 29, 65, 96.

Inaugurated in September 1985, the Picasso Museum is housed in the Hôtel Salé, built in 1656 by Aubert de Fontenay, the collector of taxes on salt (hence the nickname "Salted Mansion"). The Classical-styled building, superbly restored, is in keeping with the painter's preference for old residences; 6 000 m² were cleared, and Diego Giacometti, the sculptor's brother, created the furniture and light fixtures *(daily 9:45-5:15 ex Tue).*

▶ This exceptional collection, comprised of 203 paintings, 158 sculptures, more than 3 000 drawings and prints, collages and ceramics, was assembled according to a French law which permits payment of inheritance taxes with art works. Furthermore, Jacqueline Picasso contributed the painter's personal collection (paintings and drawings by Renoir, Cézanne, Rousseau, Derain, Braque, Matisse, Miró). The whole, unique in the world, permits a vast overview of the work of one of the century's greatest artists. □

▶ **Musée de la PUBLICITÉ**

(Advertising Museum)

B1 / 18, Rue de Paradis, 10th arr. Métro : Gare de l'Est, Château-d'Eau. Bus : 32, 39, 48.

This unique museum chronicles the precursors of the industry, along with its often neglected masters, whose talents have brightened the walls of city buildings over the years. Collection constantly being

added to *(12-6 ex Tue.).* Posters by Toulouse-Lautrec, Mucha, Erté, Jacno, Colin and Morvan; also fine protest work from 1968 and a mine of cinema and TV publicity footage. Finally, notice the building itself, formerly the store for the Faïenceries de Choisy-le-Roi; in the courtyard and interior, very fine ceramic panels. □

▶ **RODIN Museum★★**

B2 / 77, Rue de Varenne, 7th arr. Métro : Varenne. Bus : 69, 87.

The splendid **Hôtel Biron**, built in 1730 to plans by the architect Gabriel, was originally lent to Rodin in exchange for a donation of his work and collections.

▶ The Rodin Museum is now installed in the surroundings where Rodin lived and worked between 1908 and his death in 1917. It is really a museum-cum-garden, offering a delightful open setting for the sculptor's creations. Here are represented all the phases of Rodin's development, from his youth (around 1875) to his evolution toward modern art in 1895, and his subsequent maturity, covering the years from 1900 onwards. Among the famous works in the museum are : *The Kiss★★*, an astonishing Balzac series, *The Thinker★*, maquettes for the *Bourgeois de Calais★★*, plasters and studies. The collections left by Rodin are of considerable interest : they include Monet *(Paysage de Belle-Isle),* Renoir, and two of Van Gogh's most celebrated canvases, *Le Père Tanguy★★* and *The Harvesters★★.* Temporary exhibits *(10-5:30, 4:30 in winter; closed Tue.).* □

▶ **SAINT-CLOUD**

SNCF (Saint-Lazare station). Bus : 52, 72, 144, 175.

Terraced above Boulogne, Saint-Cloud has lost its château, but the **park★★** remains, where joggers mix with strollers. Steep paths lead down to the spectacular Grande Cascade (view★). □

▶ **Basilica of SAINT-DENIS★★★**

Métro : Saint-Denis-Basilique. SNCF : all lines from Paris-Nord, except Crépy-en-Valois. Bus : 153, 155, 156, 170, 177.

Formerly an abbey church, the Basilica of Saint-Denis is one of the earliest examples of Gothic Art. The 13thC nave and transept are attributed to Pierre de Montreuil. The **narthex** (1130-40) under the towers of the façade marks the first use of the Gothic pointed arch in a large building. Hence the Basilica of St.-Denis is a prelude to the extraordinary flowering of Gothic art in the centuries that followed, though it is visited more for its historical associations than for its architecture.

▶ Legend has it that Saint Denis, after his decapitation in 250, walked all the way up to the north of Paris, head in hands, to be buried there. Here an abbey was founded in 775, and was renowned for its **porches★★**, **choirroom★★** and 12thC **crypt** built by Abbot Suger. Following the example of King Dagobert and Hugues Capet, the Kings of France adopted the habit of having themselves buried in the basilica, which at intervals for over a thousand years resounded with the cry "Le Roi est mort, vive le Roi!" ("The King is dead, long live the King!"). During the Revolution, the royal tombs were desecrated and the statues mutilated; the treasury, which was the richest in all Christendom, was sold or melted down. For better or worse, Louis XVIII restored the basilica, of which he proved to be the last occupant. Among the **tombs★★★** which trace the evolution of funeral art from the Merovingian to the Renaissance eras, can be seen the burial place of Louis d'Orléans★ (16thC), the urn containing the heart of François I and his tomb created by Philibert de l'Orme, the marble tomb of Isabelle d'Aragon, Philippe III le Hardi's 1300 tomb, the monumental tomb of Dagobert in the choir (influenced by Italian art), the tombs of Henri II and Catherine de Médicis, and finally, the recumbent representations of Louis XII and Anne de Bretagne★, quite realistic *(10-4)*. ▶ In the former convent of Saint-Denis, Rue Franciade, is the **Art and History Museum of Saint-Denis**★ which exhibits, alongside Paul Éluard mementos, interesting historical documents on working-class life in the 19thC *(10-5:30; 2-6:30 Sun.; closed Tue.)*. ▶ The famous Christofle factory has been turned into a **museum** tracing the history of the art of goldsmithing (112 Rue A.-Croizat, métro : Porte-de-Paris. *10-5:30, closed Sat. and Sun.*). □

▶ **Church of SAINT-EUSTACHE***

B2 / Rue du Jour, 1st arr. Métro : Les Halles. RER : Châtelet-Les Halles. Bus : 67, 74, 85.

This formidable stone building (1532-1640) has dominated Les Halles' skyline since the demolition of the old market. Its architecture is remarkably unified (considering that the work continued for over a century), the best of Renaissance style combining with the most sophisticated Gothic techniques.

▶ Saint-Eustache is only a church, despite its cathedral proportions. It was altered by Colbert, the parish benefactor (whose imposing tomb★ stands in a chapel behind the choir), then renovated by Baltard in the 19thC (façade); but its main tradition is musical. Rameau is buried here; Berlioz created and performed his Te Deum (1855) at Saint-Eustache, and Liszt gave a recital of his "Messe de Gran". The organ has been heavily restored; today, with its 8000 pipes and broad variety of tones, it is one of the largest instruments of its kind in Paris. ▶ In 1986, a 72-ton sculptured head was installed at the foot of the church by Henri de Miller. □

▶ **SAINT-GERMAIN-DES-PRÉS****

B2 / 6th arr. Métro : Saint-Germain-des-Prés. Bus : 39, 48, 63, 70, 86, 87, 95, 96.

More than just a church, more than just a *quartier,* Saint-Germain-des-Prés is heavily associated with the 1950s, when it was a centre for artists and intellectuals. Boris Vian's trumpet-playing, Juliette Greco's songs, the existentialists and the jazz cellars of Saint-Germain made the area's name, along with its famous cafés (the "Flore" and the "Deux Magots") and the venerable Brasserie Lipp. Places are hard to come by in these establishments, especially ɔp, which is intensely exclusive at lunch and dinne .nes.

▶ Amid the turmoil, the **church of Saint-ᴄ ermain-des-Prés**★★ stands behind its massive bell tower porch (12thC), which has recently been cleaned. This building, though it has frequently been restored and repaired, constitutes the most important vestige of what used to be the oldest and most brilliant abbey in Paris. Saint Germain himself, who was bishop of Paris, inspired King Clovis to build a basilica on the Left Bank of the Seine in the year 545. The abbey that soon grew up around it took the name of Saint-Germain, and the foundations of the present church were laid in about the year 1000. The Romanesque nave is balanced by the early Gothic traits of the choir; the large paintings by H. Flandrin hanging here are somewhat aggressively 19thC. ▶ On the Rue de l'Abbaye side is the tomb of King Casimir of Poland (17thC) and a statue of St. François-Xavier by G. Coustou. ▶ Also nearby, but seeming a hundred miles from the bustle of the **Blvd. Saint-Germain**, is the tiny **Place Fürstenberg**★, with the air of a backward provincial town square. Nothing

here but a lamp post and four catalpas on a small round island in the middle of an 18thC street. A few art galleries : No. 6 was **Delacroix's studio** until his death in 1863 (museum, *9:45-5:15; closed Tue.*). That's all : yet, for many this little square on the former abbey courtyard is one of the most enchanting spots in all Paris. □

Markets and flea markets

Markets play a considerable role in the life of a Paris quarter. Two of the most interesting are the excellently restored Marché Saint-Quentin *(corner of Blvd. Magenta and Rue de Chabrol),* and the Marché du Faubourg Saint-Martin *(Rue Bouchardon).* Both are covered markets, strongly characteristic of turn-of-the-century metal architecture. The open-air markets in Rue Lepic, Place Maubert, Rue Mouffetard, Rue de Buci, Blvd. Raspail *(Métro Rennes)* and Blvd. de la Muette are mostly for food. Place d'Aligre has a food market with a small flea market adjoining. The biggest flea market is on the northern edge of town, at the Porte de Clignancourt (Sat., Sun. and Mon.); alas, few bargains are to be had there nowadays, since "real" antique dealers have moved in, paying high prices for sales locations. More in line with the flea market tradition (and more chancy, perhaps) are the "Puces de Montreuil" *(small furniture, curios and bric-à-brac),* the "Puces de la Porte de Vanves", and the "Puces du Kremlin-Bicêtre", in the inner suburbs (Sat., Sun. am). Note also the secondhand bookstands along the Seine, the flower market on the Ile de la Cité, and the stamp market (Thur., Fri., Sat.) in the gardens off the Champs-Élysées. □

▶ **Church of SAINT-JULIEN-LE-PAUVRE***

B2 / Rue Saint-Julien-le-Pauvre, 5th arr. Métro : Maubert-Mutualité, Saint-Michel, Cité. RER : Saint-Michel. Bus : 21, 24, 27, 38, 47, 63, 85, 86, 87, 96.

The church of Saint-Julien-le-Pauvre has the air of a humble country church that has somehow wandered into one of the noisiest *quartiers* of Paris. The simplicity of this ancient sanctuary, which was once a shrine for pilgrims on their way to Santiago de Compostela, is a powerful contrast to the lavishness of the other great Parisian churches.

▶ Built in the 12thC, the church bears the scars of an eventful history. The style is halfway between Romanesque and Gothic; squat, without flying buttresses, St-Julien nestles in the shadows of its little **square**. Each year, concerts of ancient and modern music are held here, particularly during the Paris summer festival. Saint-Julien-le-Pauvre owes allegiance to the Graeco-Byzantine church (closely akin to Greek Orthodox). ▶ Nearby is another sanctuary of a different kind. On the Rue de la Bûcherie, *Shakespeare and Company* is the temple of Anglo-Saxon literature in Paris, where everyone who was anyone in the small world of letters, from Joyce to Hemingway, came to drink tea under the bookshelves. □

▶ **Île SAINT-LOUIS****

B2 / 4th arr. Métro : Cité, Hôtel-de-Ville, Pont-Marie. Bus : 24, 47, 67, 86, 87.

▶ Originally the Île Saint-Louis was two islands; they were joined together and developed just before the mid-17thC. The most beautiful houses date from this time

(**Hôtel Chenizot★**, 51 Rue St-Louis-en-l'Île : **Hôtel Lauzun★**, 17 Quai d'Anjou : **Hôtel Lambert★**, close by the Pont Sully). Nonetheless, it is the whole ensemble, rather than the individual buildings, which is important. Go down the **Quai d'Anjou**, the **Quai d'Orléans** (Nos. 6, 8, 20 and 22) and the **Quai de Bourbon**. With its glorious views★★ of the Cité, the Seine and the Left Bank, the Île Saint-Louis has managed to preserve its charm, in the face of the restaurants and *brasseries* which would wreck it if they could. Unfortunately, the great houses here are defended with similar ferocity and, with the exception of the sumptuous Hôtel de Lauzun, they are almost impossible to visit. *(Visits to the latter are organized by the Centre d'Accueil de la Ville de Paris, 29 Rue de Rivoli.)*
▶ **Rue Saint-Louis-en-l'Île** is the best introduction to the island's special private atmosphere. No. 21, the **church of Saint-Louis★** (1656-1725) is in the Baroque Jesuit style. The chapels contain a fine selection of Italian paintings. But the street's most popular monument is unquestionably No. 31, which is Berthillon, the ice-cream shop; one of the best in Paris. □

▶ **Church of SAINT-MERRI**

B2 / 78, Rue Saint-Martin. 4th arr. Métro : Châtelet, Hôtel-de-Ville. Bus : 21, 38, 47, 58, 69, 70, 72, 74, 75, 76, 85, 96.

The first period of the Renaissance in France (1515-50) witnessed the building of a number of mansions between the Hôtel de Ville and the Rue Saint-Martin, which espoused the decorative principles of antiquity, as imported from Italy. Religious architecture, notwithstanding, remained faithful to the patterns set out during the golden age of Flamboyant Gothic; and it was as a Gothic church that **Saint-Merri church** was planned. The 18thC to some extent bastardized it, with the copious addition of stucco and pompous motifs. This superimposed decoration has a certain advantage, all the same — looking at it, we may imagine what the vanished choir of Notre-Dame might have looked like. □

▶ **Church of SAINT-SÉVERIN***

B2 / Rue des Prêtres-Saint-Séverin. 5th arr. Metro : Saint-Michel. Bus : 21, 24, 27, 38, 47, 63, 81, 85, 86, 87, 96.

At the centre of this pedestrian precinct, with its medieval street-names (La Huchette, La Bûcherie, Le Chat-qui-Pêche) and pavement artists, the lovely **church of Saint-Séverin**, with its light and elegant nave, broods over the galleries of a 15thC charnel house (labeled a "cloister").

▶ Built between 1414 and 1520, then extended in 1670, Saint-Séverin boasts a singular marvel : the astonishing column in its ambulatory, which is a masterpiece of Flamboyant Gothic, with arches fanning out in the form of palm fronds from its summit. The technical perfection and complexity of this ensemble marks the watershed of several centuries of architectural development. Saint-Séverin's other claim to fame is its magnificent **organ** (used by composers Saint-Saëns and Fauré) with many parts dating from the 18thC. Frequent organ concerts are held here. Also, **stained glass★** (15th and 16thC) and modern windows by Bazaine. □

▶ **SCEAUX**

R.E.R. : line B. Bus : 128, 188, 194, 197, 297.

Colbert's château was destroyed, replaced by a replica which houses the **Ile-de-France Museum** *(9-12 & 4-6, closed Tue.; artistic and historical collections, exhibitions).* The park, very "Grand Siècle", is intact; see the Grand

Canal and the Octogone cascades, the Aurora pavilion (17thC), designed by Perrault, and the Hanover pavilion (18thC) which becomes a concert hall in summer. □

▶ **SÈVRES**

Métro : Pont de Sèvres.

On the edge of the Saint-Cloud park, the **National Ceramics Museum★** retraces the history of this technique — and this art — from its origins to the present *(9:30-12 & 1:30-5, closed Tue.);* Islamic and Chinese pieces, works from Delft, Nevers and, of course, Sèvres. □

▶ **National TECHNIQUES Museum**

B2 / 270, Rue Saint-Martin, 3rd arr. Métro : Arts-et-Métiers, Temple. Bus : 20, 38, 39, 47, 75.

Founded by the 1794 Convention "to explain the construction and use of tools and machines", The **Arts and Trades Conservatory** was created for advanced technical education, but its museum *(1-5:30, 10-5:15 Sun.; closed Mon.)* is meant for the general public, which can discover the long and difficult history of the complex tools and machines now taken for granted. □

▶ **TUILERIES Gardens****

B2 / 1st arr. Métro : Concorde, Palais-Royal, Tuileries. Bus : 21, 24, 27, 39, 48, 68, 69, 72, 81, 95.

The Tuileries Gardens offer one of the most delightful walks in Paris, along the Seine, from the Louvre to the Concorde, a distance of about one kilometre. The terraces beside the river, the garden with its pools and fountains, the merry-go-rounds and children's playgrounds, cover a site where the grim palace of the Kings of France once stood, until it was burned down by the Communard insurgents in 1871.

▶ First, take a stroll round the **Carrousel Gardens**, past Napoléon I's small triumphal arch and the bronzes by Maillol; then walk the whole way along the terraces on the Seine side. ▶ At the top end of the Tuileries (Place de la Concorde) are the **Orangerie★★** *(9:45-5:15, closed Tue.)* and **Jeu de Paume Museums** *(closed for improvements; the collections have been transfered to the Orsay Museum).* Both date from the Second Empire. The Orangerie Museum, which contains *Les Nymphéas* (the Waterlilies) of Monet, has been transformed, and now holds the **Walter-Guillaume collection;** 144 masterpieces mostly of the 20s, by Soutine, Renoir, Cézanne and the Douanier Rousseau. It is a collection without parallel in France. □

▶ **Place VENDÔME****

B2 / 1st arr. Métro : Pyramides, Tuileries. Bus : 24, 42, 52, 84, 94.

Between the arcades of the Rue de Castiglione and the **Rue de la Paix,** the Place Vendôme opens out like a theatre set, starring the Ritz Hotel, Cartier, Van Cleef, Boucheron and others. This is the centre of the world of expensive jewelry and luxury products; the square itself is one of the most balanced and harmonious of the great squares built in honour of the Sun King, Louis XIV, an equestrian statue of whom once stood here — before the Revolution.

▶ Jules Hardouin-Mansart designed the Place Vendôme according to the requirements of Louvois and Louis XIV; the king and his minister were concerned for their future prestige, but they also had an eye for an excellent real-estate operation. The rigorous facades of the Place Vendôme, with their clear-cut horizontal lines, were completed in 1715 : the idea was that rich buyers could lay out their houses behind them just as they liked. Louis XIV's statue was knocked down during the Revolution, and replaced by Napoléon I with a tall column in his own honour. When the Bourbons returned after Waterloo, they appropriated this themselves by crowning it with their emblem, the *fleur-de-lys*. Louis-Philippe put back the statue of Napoléon I; the Commune then pulled the whole thing down, at the instigation of the painter Courbet — and down it remained, for a few months. The unfortunate artist was sentenced to put it up again at his own expense; the business ruined him, but it is to Courbet that we owe the present column and, at its top, the statue of Napoléon in Roman costume. □

Art and antiques

The most prestigious antique dealers are located around the Quai Voltaire *(B2; Métro : Bac)*, the Village Suisse *(A2; Ave. de Suffren; Métro : La Motte-Picquet*, closed Tue. and Wed.*), and the* Faubourg St. Honoré *(No. 54, Antique Market;* closed Sun.*). For* Art Nouveau and Art Deco, Les Halles and the Village St. Paul *(C3, Métro : Sully-Morland,* 11-7*; closed Tue. and Wed.), along with the plush* Louvre des Antiquaires *(11-7; closed Mon.) on the* Place du Palais-Royal.

Among the top art galleries, Artcurial, 9, Ave. Matignon *(B2;* 11-7*; closed Sun. and Mon.) is a kind of contemporary art supermarket, with something to suit every taste and (almost) every pocket. Not so its neighbours :* Bernheim-Jeune, 83, Rue du Faubourg Saint-Honoré; Maeght, 14, Rue de Téhéran; Marcel Bernheim, 35, Rue La Boétie; Wally Findlay, 2, Ave. Matignon. *These galleries deal only in recognized — and expensive — artists. The Left Bank is more open to contemporary art :* Berggruen, 70, Rue de l'Université; Isy Brachot, 35, Rue Guénégaud; Claude Bernard, 9, Rue des Beaux-Arts; Stadler, 51, Rue de Seine. *These establishments deal in modern trends ranging from hyperrealism to the new figurative art. Among the many small galleries in the Beaubourg quartier,* Daniel Templon, 30, Rue Beaubourg, *stands out. For the experienced art lover, the best hunting ground is unquestionably the* Nouveau Drouot *auction rooms (9, Rue Drouot; tel. (1) 42.46.17.11; 11-6 daily).*

▶ Place des VICTOIRES*

B2 / 1st and 2nd arr. Métro : Bourse. Bus : 20, 21, 29, 39, 48, 67, 74, 85.

Designed like the Place Vendôme by Jules Hardouin-Mansart in honour of Louis XIV, the Place des Victoires was abandoned in the 19thC to merchants and tradesmen who installed shop windows in the beautiful 1700 facades.

▶ The Restoration replaced its equestrian statue of Louis XIV, but the whole spirit of the Place des Victoires was considered irretrievably lost when the Rue Étienne-Marcel was driven through in 1883. Fortunately, a concerted renovation project has now restored the Place to its former glory; it has become a centre for high fashion and luxury ready-to-wear clothes. ▶ Nearby is the **church of Notre-Dame-des-Victoires**, founded by Louis XIII and built in the 17th and 18thC. More interesting, perhaps, than the bust of Lully (1702) or the fine *boiseries* in the choir, are the ex-voto tablets that cover the church's walls — there are more than 30 000! □

The canals

Once upon a time, one could float from La Villette to Meaux on a horse-drawn water coach... Those days are gone. All the same, the canals of Paris have mostly retained their curious setting, which made the unforgettable backdrop for Marcel Carné's great movie Hôtel du Nord. The delightful Canal Saint-Martin gives the impression of being lost in Paris, as it wanders close by the roaring traffic of the Place de la République. The anachronistic pace of this waterway is regulated by the lazy barges churning slowly from lock to lock down to the Seine, behind the Ile Saint-Louis, under the Boulevard Richard-Lenoir and the Place de la Bastille and past the new marina in the Bassin de l'Arsenal. Napoléon 1st realized the great dream of Henri IV when he opened his network of canals through the heart of Paris. Nowadays, more than 10 000 barges pass along the various waterways every year, using the Canal Saint-Martin, the Canal de l'Ourcq or the Canal Saint-Denis; all three meet at the immense Bassin de la Villette, with its wharves, warehouses and workshops. Trip round the canals : embarkation La Patache (→ Practical information). Bus : Quai Anatole-France.

▶ LA VILLETTE

C1 / 19th arr. Métro : Porte-de-Pantin, Porte-de-la-Villette. Bus : 75, 150, 151, 152, 251, PC.

The 140 acre park which occupies the site of the former slaughterhouses, constructed in 1866, of which survives the Mérindol★ Grande Halle (250 m long, 81 m wide, 25 m high), is the object of one of the greatest urban projects of our time. The largest attraction is the **Museum of Science, Technology and Industry** which houses permanent and temporary exhibitions, a planetarium *(Tue.-Sun., 2:30-7)*, a discovery centre for children, a media centre and a centre of education; the **"Géode"**★, a highly polished sphere of stainless steel, 36 m in diameter, containing a hemispherical spectacle-hall, equipped with a 1000 m^2 screen *(11-6:30, Tue., Thu., Sun.; 11 am-11:30 pm, Wed., Fri., Sat., closed Mon.);* **Music City** comprises a conservatoire, an Instrument Museum, a centre of education and research and concert halls for both classical and modern music, of which the **"Zenith"** is already in operation. The park of 75 acres, crossed by the Ourcq Canal, will be enlivened by fountains, follies for games, restaurants and a centre for children. □

▶ Forest and Château of VINCENNES

C3 / Avenue de Paris, Vincennes. Métro : Château-de-Vincennes. Bus : 46, 56, 86.

The forest to which Saint Louis used to come to give judgement sitting under an oak-tree was cleared well before the Bois de Boulogne, at the beginning of the 18thC. The present facilities, lakes and rides of the **Bois de Vincennes** were organized during the Second Empire.

▶ The **zoological park**★ *(9-5:30 or 6 in summer)* and **flower gardens** *(parc floral : 9:30-6:30)* attract many visitors from the eastern areas of Paris, as do the many grassy areas and sports grounds of the Bois de Vincennes. ▶ Not far from the flower gardens stand the forbidding walls of the **Château de Vincennes**★, surrounded by moats. □

● *Practical information*

Information : Paris : *Office de Tourisme de Paris,* 127, av. des Champs-Élysées, 75008, ☎ (1) 47.23.61.72. Open daily high season 9 am-10 pm (Sun 9 am-8 pm); low season, 9 am-8 pm (Sun 9 am-6 pm). Gare du Nord office : ☎ (1) 45.26.94.82, at the international train arrival area. Gare de l'Est office : arrival hall, ☎ (1) 46.07.17.73. Gare de Lyon office : "Grandes Lignes" exit area, ☎ (1) 44.43.33.24. Gare d'Austerlitz office : ☎ (1) 45.84.81.70, "Grandes Lignes" arrival area. Offices open daily ex Sun. Queues in summer can be long!

Maison d'information culturelle de la Ville de Paris : 26, rue Beaubourg, 75003. Open daily ex Sun. 10-8.

Bureau d'Accueil de la Ville de Paris, 29, rue de Rivoli, ☎ (1) 42.77.15.40 (ex Sun). **Hauts-de-Seine :** *C.D.T.,* 1, rue Trosy, 92140 Clamart, ☎ (1) 46.42.17.95. **Seine-Saint-Denis :** *C.D.T.,* 2, av. Gabriel-Péri, 93100 Montreuil, ☎ (1) 42.87.38.09. **Val-de-Marne :** *C.D.T.,* 11, av. de Nogent, 94130 Vincennes, ☎ (1) 48.08.13.00.

Entertainment : *Paris Informations Loisirs :* 24-hour service, ☎ (1) 47.20.94.94. In English : ☎ (1) 47.20.88.98. Deutsch : ☎ (1) 47.20.57.58.

Museums : *Paris Info-Musées,* ☎ (1) 42.78.73.81.

Embassies and consulates : *American Embassy,* 2, av. Gabriel, 75008, ☎ (1) 42.96.12.02, the Consulate is at 2, rue St-Florentin, 75008; *British Embassy,* 35, rue du Faubourg-St-Honoré, 75008, ☎ (1) 42.66.91.42, the Consulate is at 105-109; *Canadian Embassy,* 35, av. Montaigne, 75008, ☎ (1) 47.23.01.01 or (1) 47.23.52.20; *Irish Embassy,* 4, rue Rude, 75016, ☎ (1) 45.00.20.87.

S.O.S. : *SAMU* (emergency medical service) **Paris,** ☎ (1) 45.67.50.50. *S.O.S. Médecins,* ☎ (1) 47.07.77.77. *SAMU* **Hauts-de-Seine,** ☎ (1) 47.41.79.11. *SAMU* **Seine-Saint-Denis :** ☎ 17. *SAMU* **Val-de-Marne,** ☎ (1) 42.05.51.41. *Emergency poisoning centre,* ☎ (1) 42.05.63.29. *Police,* ☎ 17. *Lost and found,* 36, rue des Morillons, 75015, ☎ (1) 45.31.14.80.

Going out in Paris : the most detailed sources of information for the visitor are the weeklies *Une semaine de Paris-Pariscope, l'Officiel des Spectacles, 7 à Paris,* which come out on Wed and are sold at all newsstands; these weekly publications provide full information on theatres, shows, cinemas, concerts, exhibitions, festivals, etc., along with practical information and leisure centres. The *Kiosque de la Madeleine* (place de la Madeleine, from noon to 6), sells tickets half-price for same-day events. For restaurant information, ☎ (1) 43.59.12.12 or (1) 43.57.15.00 (Gault and Millau). The monthly English language newspaper *Passion* is also an excellent source of information on Parisian events and topics.

Guided tours : the C.N.M.H.S. (National Monuments Board; Monuments and Museums) organizes daily lectures and visits in Paris. Enq. : 62, rue Saint-Antoine, 75004, ☎ (1) 48.87.24.14, and in numerous daily newspapers. Independent lecturers and associations; see the forementioned weeklies and daily newspapers. *Cassettes Paris auto-guide* (self-guided tours on cassette), Paris T.O., Pompidou Centre, department stores, record stores.

Post Office : *Central Post Office,* 52, rue du Louvre, ☎ (1) 42.33.71.60. Open all night.

Banks : open daily ex Sat, Sun and nat hols. Some foreign exchange offices open on Sat. Banks close at noon on days preceding nat hols, and all day on nat hols.

✗ *Charles-de-Gaulle/Roissy-en-France,* 25 km N, ☎ (1) 48.62.22.80. *Air France :* information, ticket sales and reservations, ☎ (1) 45.35.61.61. *Air Inter :* information, reservations, ☎ (1) 45.39.25.25. Access : R.E.R. line B, direction *Roissy-Rail,* ☎ (1) 48.62.22.17, trains at approx 15 min intervals. R.A.T.P. bus nº 350 Gare de l'Est and Gare du Nord; nº 351 departure pl. de la Nation, ☎ (1) 43.46.14.14. Air France buses ☎ (1) 48.64.30.20 :

terminal at the corner of avenue Carnot, near the Arc de Triomphe. *Orly-Sud* and *Ouest,* 14 km S, ☎ (1) 48.84.32.10. Access : R.E.R. line C, direction *Orly Rail,* ☎ (1) 48.84.38.60; trains at approx 15 min intervals until 9 pm. R.A.T.P. bus nº 215, ☎ (1) 43.46.14.14, departure pl. Denfert-Rochereau; 183A, departure porte de Choisy, and 285, departure porte d'Italie, dir. Savigny-sur-Orge, which passes through the airport. Air France buses, ☎ (1) 43.23.97.10, Invalides terminal; departure every 12 min.

S.N.C.F. (French Railways) Gare du Nord, northern region, ☎ (1) 42.80.03.03. Gare de l'Est, eastern region, ☎ (1) 42.08.49.90. Gare de Lyon, southeast region, ☎ (1) 43.45.92.22. Gare d'Austerlitz, southwest region, ☎ (1) 45.84.16.16. Gare Montparnasse, western region, ☎ (1) 45.38.52.29. Gare Saint-Lazare, western region, ☎ (1) 45.38.52.29. *Central enq. office :* ☎ (1) 45.82.50.50 or on Minitel : 3615 code SNCF. To make reservations at any station, ☎ (1) 45.65.60.60.

Métro : R.A.T.P. Central Enquiries Office : 53, quai des Grands-Augustins, 75006, ☎ (1) 43.46.14.14. Maps of the urban and regional express network are posted and distributed at all stations. The first trains run from 5 or 5:30 am for the regional express network (R.E.R.), and from 5:30 am for the urban metro. The last trains leave the terminus at between 12:30 and 1 am according to the line, all trains being scheduled to arrive at their final destinations by 1:15 am. Apart from the Charenton-Écoles — Créteil sections (line nº 8) and Carrefour Pleyel — St-Denis (line nº 13), cost of the Métro ticket (1st or 2nd class) is fixed, independent of the length of the journey or the number of changes of line.

R.E.R. : the Regional Express Network comprises three lines : Line A : Saint-Germain-en-Laye-Boissy-Saint-Léger or Marne-la-Vallée. Line B : Saint-Rémy-lès-Chevreuse or Robinson-Châtelet-Roissy or Mitry-Claye. Line C : Saint-Quentin-en-Yvelines-Dourdan, Massy or Étampes.

City bus service : the map of the city bus network is posted on Métro station quays, bus shelters and main bus stations. Except for the "PC" line (Petite Ceinture — inner ring-road), the lines are numbered. Tariff : 1 2nd-class Métro ticket for 1 or 2 section trips, 2 Métro tickets for any trips exceeding 2 sections. Special tariffs for the PC line.

Tourist passes : these allow an unlimited number of trips for 2, 4 or 7 day periods on all R.A.T.P. lines (Métro, R.E.R., buses), and are sold in 50 Métro stations, in Paris ralway stations and at the Paris Tourism Office. If you are staying a while in Paris, it might be worth buying a *carte orange,* allowing unlimited travel for a 1 week calendar month on the R.A.T.P. networks, within the allocated zones; or a *coupon jaune* valid (Mon-Sun). The R.A.T.P. proposes *Formule 1* coupons, valid for one day.

Taxis : a few of the many taxi service numbers : ☎ (1) 47.39.33.33, (1) 42.03.99.99, (1) 42.05.77.77, (1) 42.70.41.41.

Driving in Paris : do not use your car in Paris unless it's absolutely necessary; traffic is extremely dense, with numerous traffic jams. Parking places, if there are any, must be paid for. It is thus preferable to use public transport and to leave your vehicle at one of the many carparks at the "portes de Paris" (the main entrances to the city on the ring-road, the Boulevard Périphérique).

Car-hire : *Avis,* 5, rue Bixio, 75007, ☎ (1) 45.50.32.31; 60, rue de Ponthieu, 75008, ☎ (1) 43.59.03.83; Gare St. Lazare, Quai No. 27, 75008, ☎ (1) 42.93.35.67; Gal. Élysées Rond-Point, 47, av. Franklin-Roosevelt, 75008, ☎ (1) 45.62.18.68; 184, rue du Fg-St-Martin, ☎ (1) 42.00.72.03; Gare de l'Est, 75010, ☎ (1) 42.00.72.03; Gare du Nord, Track No. 19, 75010, ☎ (1) 42.85.55.08/42.85.76.69; Gare de Lyon, 75012, ☎ (1) 43.42.10.41/43.43.14.52; 24, av. d'Ivry, 75013, ☎ (1) 45.83.21.93; Gare d'Austerlitz, Porte No. 25, 75013, ☎ (1) 45.84.22.10; 105, rue Lourmel, 75015, ☎ (1) 45.54.33.65; Gare de Montparnasse, Quai No.

19, 75015, ☎ (1) 43.21.62.12 ; 105, rue de Lourmel (with driver), ☎ 45.54.33.65 ; 59, rue Pierre Demours, 75017, ☎ (1) 43.80.21.01 ; 8, bd Davout, ☎ 40.24.10.20 ; 78, av. Pierre Grenier, 92100 Boulogne-sur-Seine, 46.09.04.30 ; 99, av. Charles-de-Gaulle, 92200 Neuilly-sur-Seine, ☎ (1) 47.47.10.70. **At the airports :** Le Bourget, 1, av. du 8 mai 1945, ☎ (1) 48.38.51.00 ; Orly Ouest, ☎ (1) 48.84.44.91 ; aérogare de Roissy I, ☎ (1) 48.62.34.34 ; aérogare de Roissy II, ☎ (1) 48.62.59.59.

Aerial views of Paris : *Paris-Hélicoptère,* héliport de Paris, ☎ (1) 45.54.12.55 ; Métro Balard.

Paris by bus : *France Tourisme Paris Vision,* 214, rue de Rivoli, 75001, ☎ (1) 42.60.30.01 and 42.60.31.25. *Cityrama Rapid-Pullman,* 4, pl. des Pyramides, 75001, ☎ (1) 42.60.30.14.

Excursions on the Seine : *bateaux-mouches* (Seine pleasure boats) : pont de l'Alma, 75007, ☎ (1) 42.25.96.10. *Bateaux parisiens/Tour Eiffel,* pont d'léna, 75007, ☎ (1) 45.51.33.08. *Vedettes* (launches) du Pont-Neuf, pont Neuf, 75001, ☎ (1) 46.33.98.39. *Nautic Croisières,* quai du Point-du-Jour, pont de Boulogne, 92100 Boulogne, ☎ (1) 46.21.48.15. *Vedettes de Paris et de l'Ile-de-France,* pont de Suffren, 75007, ☎ (1) 47.05.71.29.

Bicycle rental : in many R.E.R. stations. *Le Bicy-club de France* organizes rambles and rents bicycles, info : 8, place de la Porte-de-Champerret, 75017 Paris, ☎ (1) 47.66.55.92. Bike paths, info : *Direction régionale de l'équipement,* 21, rue Miollis, 75032 Paris Cedex 15, ☎ (1) 45.67.55.03.

On the Paris canals : *Patache Eautobus,* a 3-hour morning excursion, leaving from the quai Anatole-France (Métro : Solférino) to the Villette basin, up the Seine and the Canal St-Martin ; vice versa in the afternoon, daily ex nat hols from May to Nov. Reservation essential : ☎ (1) 48.74.75.30. *Canauxrama :* from the Villette basin (Métro : Jean-Jaurès) to the Arsenal port (Métro : Bastille) ; the Canal de l'Ourcq, from Paris to Meaux. Reservations : 9 am-1 pm, ☎ (1) 46.24.86.16.

Markets : *Clignancourt flea-market,* avenue de la porte de Clignancourt, Sat, Sun and Mon, 7-7. *Flower-market :* Place des Ternes, 17th arr., daily ex Mon, 8-7 and at place de la Madeleine, 8th arr., same days and hours. *Bird market :* place Louis-Lépine, 4th arr., Sun. 9-7.

Auction rooms : *Nouveau Drouot,* 9, rue Drouot, 75009, ☎ (1) 42.46.17.11. Daily ex Sun, 11-6.

Cultural events : Apr-May : *Paris poetry festival,* place Saint-Sulpice ; *traditional arts festival.* **Jun :** *Mozart festival.* **Jul-Aug :** *festival du Marais ; festival estival de Paris ; festival de l'Orangerie de Sceaux.* **Sep-Dec :** *Paris chamber music festival.* **Oct :** *jazz festival.*

Other events : these are many and varied, including such events as the *Foire de Paris,* the *Salon du Prêt-à-Porter* and the *Paris Marathon.* Lists of these events can be found in the brochures published by the Paris Tourist Office and the Ville de Paris, and in the weeklies *Pariscope, L'Officiel des Spectacles,* etc.

Lodging for young people : *U.C.R.I.F.,* 20, rue J.-J.-Rousseau, 75001, ☎ (1) 42.36.88.18. *A.J.F.,* 12, rue des Barres, 75004, ☎ (1) 42.72.72.09.

Baby-sitting : *C.R.O.U.S.,* ☎ (1) 43.29.97.10 ; *Kid Service,* ☎ (1) 42.96.04.16.

Camping : ★★★*Paris-Ouest-Bois de Boulogne,* rte du Bord-de-l'Eau (500 pl.), ☎ (1) 45.06.14.98. *Paris-Issy-les-Moulineaux* (48 pl.), ☎ (1) 46.38.07.66. ★★★*Le Tremblay-Champigny-sur-Marne* (330 pl. ; access N4, A4), ☎ (1) 42.83.38.24.

In preparing for your trip, consult the pages pertaining to the regions. You will find there the description of the region you wish to visit, as well as a list of sites that must be seen, a brief history and practical information.

● *Hotels-restaurants*

✉ 75001

Hotels :

★★★★(L) *Intercontinental,* 3, rue de Castiglione, ☎ (1) 42.60.37.80, AE DC Euro Visa, 472 rm 27 apt ▦ ⌕ & 1650. Rest. ● ♦♦ *La Rôtisserie Rivoli* In summer, the terrace blooms with flowers ; very nice food by J.-J. Barbier and his kitchen brigade, 270-320♦ *Le Café Tuileries* Discothèque *Estrela.* 150-210.

★★★★(L) *Jolly Hôtel Lotti,* 7, rue de Castiglione, ☎ (1) 42.60.37.34, Tx 240066, AE DC Euro Visa, 130 rm ⋙ 1520. Rest. ♦♦ Grill as well, 210-320.

★★★★(L) *Meurice Inter-Continental,* 228, rue de Rivoli, ☎ (1) 42.60.38.60, Tx 230673, AE DC Euro Visa, 187 rm ≪ ⌕ & 1950. Rest. ♦♦♦♦ ⌕ & ⅋ 200-380.

★★★★(L) *Ritz,* 15, pl. Vendôme, ☎ (1) 42.60.38.30, Tx 220262, AE DC Euro Visa, 164 rm Ⓟ ≪ ▦ ⌕ ⌖ Favoured by Coco Chanel and Hemingway, 2460. Rest. ● ♦♦♦♦ *L'Espadon* ≪ ⌖ ⅋ Even as we speak, work continues on a huge underground site where a pool, sports room and squash court, hair salon and late-night bar are under construction. Rooms and suites, of course, and the famous dining room where Guy Legay and his staff pamper their faithful patrons : *brandade de morue truffée, homard à la broche, steack "Coco Chanel", délice glace Vendôme.* Prestigious cellar, 265-500 ; child : 230.

● ★★★★ *Saint-James et Albany,* 202, rue de Rivoli, ☎ (1) 42.60.31.60, Tx 213031, AE DC Euro Visa, 207 rm 3 apt ▦ ⌖ 600. Rest. ♦♦ *Saint-James,* 140-300.

★★★★ *Cambon,* 3, rue Cambon, ☎ (1) 42.60.38.09, Tx 240814, AE DC Euro Visa, 44 rm Ⓟ ⌕ ⌖ 820.

★★★★ *Castille,* 37, rue Cambon, ☎ (1) 42.61.55.20, Tx 213505, AE DC Euro Visa, 76 rm, 1080. Rest. ♦♦ *Le Relais Castille* & closed Sat and Sun , hols, 60-150.

★★★★ *Royal Saint-Honoré,* 13, rue d'Alger, ☎ 42.60.32.79, Tx 680429, AE DC Euro Visa, 80 rm ≪ 700. Rest. ♦ ⌖ ⅋ closed Sat and Sun hols, 130-180.

★★★ *Les Halles,* (Novotel), pl. Marguerite-de-Navarre, ☎ (1) 42.21.31.31, Tx 216389, AE DC Euro Visa, 285 rm ≪ ⌕ ⌖ ⋙ & 625. Rest. ♦♦ *La Rôtisserie* ≪ ⌖ & 130 ; child : 45.

★★★ *Molière,* 21, rue Molière, ☎ (1) 42.96.22.01, AE DC Euro Visa, 32 rm 3 apt ⌕ 380.

● ★★ *Le Louvre,* 4, rue Croix-des-Petits-Champs, ☎ (1) 42.60.34.86, Tx 216405, AE DC Euro Visa, 56 rm ⋙ & A quiet street just a few steps from the Louvre, 370.

★★ *Agora,* 7, rue de la Cossonnerie, ☎ (1) 42.33.46.02, Tx 260717, AE, 28 rm Ⓟ ≪ ⅋ 310.

★★ *Ducs de Bourgogne,* 19, rue du Pont-Neuf, ☎ (1) 42.33.95.64, Tx 216367, Euro Visa, 49 rm ⌖ ⅋ 290.

Restaurants :

● ♦♦♦♦ *Le Grand Véfour,* 17, rue de Beaujolais, ☎ (1) 42.96.56.27, AE DC Euro Visa, closed Sat noon and Sun , Aug. Jean-Claude Lhonneur, formerly of *Le Céladon,* succeeds André Signoret who has left the *Véfour* to replace Jean-Paul Bonin at the *Crillon.* And so it goes, the waltz of the chefs in the Taittinger-owned restaurants. Here, the great tradition of Raymond Oliver is scrupulously respected : *oeufs Louis Oliver, sole Grand Véfour, pot-au-feu de pigeon Gauthier, soufflé au chocolat,* 250-550.

● ♦♦♦ *Carré des Feuillants,* 14, rue de Castiglione, ☎ (1) 42.86.82.82, Visa Ⓟ & closed Sat and Sun. In a pretty setting decorated by Slavik, Alain Dutournier and his staff are really cooking. The *carte* is quite different from the old *Trou Gascon* (now ably managed by Mme Dutournier), but allusions to the chef's native Southwest abound : *raviolis de foie gras à la truffe, croustade légère d'anguille à l'oseille et aux pruneaux, agneau de Pauillac rôti à la broche, pièce de bœuf de Bazas grillée au charbon de bois*. The cellar, Dutournier's pet passion, holds over 500 different great and modest vintages, 400-500.

● ◆◆◆ *Gérard Besson*, (I.L.A.), 5, rue du Coq-Héron, ☎ (1) 42.33.14.74, Visa ⌕ க ✍ closed Sat noon and Sun, 3 wk in Jul, 2 at Xmas. Gérard Besson, a prize-winning pupil of the late, great Georges Garin, has just freshened up his quarters. The delicious food hasn't changed, we're glad to report : *ragoût d'huîtres, chipolatas et champignons à la crème de crevette*, game in season, 220-350.

● ◆◆◆ *Hubert*, 25, rue de Richelieu, ☎ (1) 42.96.08.47, AE DC Visa ♪ closed Mon noon and Sun. Hubert and his sweet spouse Joëlle have finally made their dream come true. In a handsome setting, he devotes all his energy to making his food-loving patrons happy : *galette de pommes Maxim's au saumon, sauce cressonnette, sole aux oranges, baron de lapin rôti aux fines de claires d'Isigny*, 250-350.

● ◆◆◆ *Le Mercure Galant*, 15, rue des Petits-Champs, ☎ (1) 42.97.53.85, closed Sat noon and Sun , hols. A spacious 19thC restaurant serving savoury cuisine : *champignons farcis aux escargots et basilic, fricassée de volaille*. Special fixed-price meal in the evening, 300.

● ◆◆◆ *Le Poquelin*, 17, rue Molière, ☎ (1) 42.96.22.19, AE DC Visa ♪ க closed Sat noon and Sun, 1-21 Sep. Loiseau, Perraudin and other great young chefs who got their start here with Claude Verger, would surely approve the new decor and Michel Guillaumins'cuisine : *rognons de veau à l'ail confit, daurade rôtie à la peau de canard*, 150-280.

● ◆◆◆ *Pierre Traiteur*, 10, rue de Richelieu, ☎ (1) 42.96.09.17, AE DC Euro Visa, closed Sat and Sun, Aug. Guy Nouyrigat is taking a well-deserved rest. His trusty staff is now directed by M. and Mme Dez, a couple of pros. Nothing has changed : *terrines*, roast rabbit, generous and delicious *bœuf ficelle*. Excellent wines from the Loire, 250-300.

● ◆◆◆◆ *Vert Galant*, 42, quai des Orfèvres, ☎ (1) 43.26.26.76, AE DC Euro Visa ℙ ≮ closed Sat. With a view of the Seine, a few steps away from the Courthouse. Arguing cases and courtroom emotions make a person hungry! Spec : *sole grillée, caneton rôti, andouillette de Saint-Pierre*. Prices are reasonable - if you've just won your suit, 200-290.

◆◆◆ *Prunier-Madeleine*, 9, rue Duphot, ☎ (1) 42.60.36.04, AE DC Euro Visa ≮ ♪ க Wonderful seafood : *filet de turbot, filet boston*, 200-400.

● ◆◆ *Chez la Vieille*, 37, rue de l'Arbre-Sec, ☎ (1) 42.60.15.78, closed eves. Adrienne Biasin, the eponymous 'vieille' is now a media darling, but none of it has gone to her head - her restaurant has always enjoyed capacity crowds. The prices at her tiny bistro are just the same - don't forget to reserve if you want to sample the generous hors d'oeuvre and dessert buffets. *Rognons, foie de veau, pot-au-feu, plat de côte*, etc... A good place for a final blow-out before you start that diet, 250-300.

● ◆◆ *Chez Pauline*, 5, rue Villedo, ☎ (1) 42.96.20.70, Visa, closed Sat eve and Sun, 27 Jun-28 Jul, 24-31 Dec. André Génin brilliantly maintains the bistro quality of his father's hearty cuisine : Game in season, stuffed cabbage, *lapereau en gelée*. But in this new decor, he is inspired to add a few creations of his own : *queues de langoustines en bouillabaisse, salade de homard breton, pigeonneau rôti en croûte de sel*. All the Beaujolais *crus* are on hand, to quench your thirst, 300.

● ◆◆ *Le Globe d'Or*, 158, rue St-Honoré, ☎ (1) 42.60.23.37, AE Euro Visa ♪ closed Sat and Sun, Aug. Gérard Constiaux and his wife Christiane are able to have food-lovers rushing to try their tasty, hearty Southwestern cookery : *jambon de pays grillé à l'échalote*, all kinds of duck dishes and good Madiran wine, 230.

● ◆◆ *A la Grille Saint-Honoré*, 15, pl. du Marché-St-Honoré, ☎ (1) 42.61.00.93, AE DC Visa ℙ ₩ ♪ closed Sat and Sun. D. Cassagnes' savoury cuisine : *raviolis de crabe beurre blanc et herbes, filet de dorade grillé aux légumes frits, pot-au-feu "la Grille"*, 145-240.

● ◆◆ *Goumard*, 17, rue Duphot, ☎ (1) 42.60.36.07, AE DC Euro Visa, closed Sun. Lovely fish well prepared and tariffed at what the market will bear, 350.

● ◆◆ *Les Bouchôleurs*, 34, rue de Richelieu, ☎ (1) 42.96.06.86 க closed Sat noon and Sun, 15 Apr-15 May. Mussels direct from Aiguilllon-sur-mer make fresh and delicious *mouclades*, 130.

● ◆◆ *Pharamond*, 24, rue de la Grande-Truanderie, ☎ (1) 42.33.06.72, AE DC Visa ₩ closed Mon noon and Sun , Jul. Here's where to come for wonderful tripe and an authentic Belle-Epoque decor. Cider, *Poiré*, choice vintages, 150.

● ◆◆ *Véro-Dodat*, 19, galerie Véro-Dodat, ☎ 45.08.92.06, AE DC Visa ⌕ ♪ closed Mon noon and Sun, Sep. An adorable little restaurant in a famous pedestrian gallery (the gates close at 10pm). As in bygone days, one must ring at the entrance, 75-180.

◆◆ *Caveau François Villon*, 64, rue de l'Arbre-Sec, ☎ (1) 42.36.10.92, Euro Visa ₩ ♪ க closed Mon, Sat noon, Sun, 15-31 Aug. Simple, savoury fare served in a handsome 15thC cellar : *coquilles Saint-Jacques fraîches à la vanille en gousse* (in season), *rognons de veau à l'effilochée d'endives*, 170-200.

◆◆ *L'Escargot Montorgueil*, 38, rue Montorgueil, ☎ (1) 42:36.83.51, AE DC Euro Visa க closed 8 days around Aug 15. Lovely interior. Six featured snail dishes, *turbot Montorgueil*, 250.

◆◆ *Righi Palais Royal*, 2, pl. du Palais-Royal, ☎ (1) 42.61.16.00, AE DC Euro Visa ⌕ ♪ Luxurious decor ; pretty girls and fashionable regulars come for the enjoyable, quality Italian food. Piano-bar, 180.

● ◆ *Porte du Bonheur*, 8, rue du Mont-Thabor, ☎ (1) 42.60.55.99, AE DC Visa, closed Sat noon and Sun eve. Charmaine's exquisite welcome and Félix Chong's delicate cuisine make for a memorable meal, or astounding banquet (order in advance) : *crevettes aux gousses d'ail et sel parfumé, agneau sauté à la sauce d'huîtres*, 55-150.

● ◆ *Saudade*, 34, rue des Bourdonnais, ☎ (1) 42.36.30.71, AE DC Visa ⌕ ♪ closed Sun, 1 Aug-6 Sep, 23-27 Dec. Portugal in Paris : plaintive fado music and *bacalhau*, the traditional salt-cod specialty, 160.

◆ *Au Pied de Cochon*, 6, rue Coquillière, ☎ (1) 42.36.11.75, AE DC Visa ℙ ♪ A Venetian look prevails in this veritable institution that never closes, 200.

◆ *Carr's*, 18, rue Thérèse, ☎ (1) 42.96.04.29, AE DC Euro Visa ⌕ ♪ க closed Sun eve. Conall Carr has followed his heart's desire and opened a restaurant. Galway Bay oysters, Irish stew. You'll never feel lonely here. Rare Irish whiskeys, 95-130 ; child : 60.

◆ *La Main à la Pâte*, 35, rue St-Honoré, ☎ (1) 45.08.85.73, AE DC Visa ♪ closed Sun. Pleasant Italian food, served till late at night. Spec : *carpaccio, jardinet des Quatre-Pâtes*, 80-180.

◆ *La Vigne*, 30, rue de l'Arbre-Sec, ☎ (1) 42.60.13.55, Visa ℙ ♪ A young woman cooks traditional favourites in this old market-district bistro : *œufs en meurette, andouillette et tête de veau*, 150-180.

PARIS II

✉ 75002

Hotels :

★★★★(L) *Westminster*, 13, rue de la Paix, ☎ (1) 42.61.57.46, Tx 680035, AE DC Euro Visa, 102 rm ℙ ♪ ⌂ 1350. Rest. ● ◆◆◆ *Le Céladon*, closed Sat and Sun, 2 Aug-2 Sep. The decor is still pale green, to harmonize with the 17thC porcelain, but the chef is new : Joël Boilleaut who is 30 years old and loaded with talent, trained by Robuchon and Kéréver. Wonderful food : *ravioles de tourteaux au basilic, millefeuille de saumon et d'épinards à la moëlle, filet d'agneau de Pauillac rôti à la coriandre et pâtes fraîches, gratin de fruits rouges et son sorbet*, 190-240.

Send us your comments and suggestions; we will use them in the next edition.

● ★★★★ *Edouard VII*, 39, av. de l'Opéra, ☎ (1) 42.61.56.90, Tx 680217, AE DC Visa ♪ 760. Rest. ♦ ♪ ఉ closed Sat and Sun, 220-350.
★★★ *Ascot Opéra*, 2, rue Monsigny, ☎ (1) 42.96.87.66, AE DC Euro Visa, 36 rm, 450.
★★★ *Favart*, 5, rue Marivaux, ☎ (1) 42.97.59.83, Tx 213126, 38 rm ⟊ ⬩♪ ఉ 376. Rest. ♦ *New-Yorker* ♪ closed Mon eve, Sat noon, Sun, 100.
★★★ *François*, 3, bd Montmartre, ☎ (1) 42.33.51.53, Tx 211097, AE DC Euro Visa, 64 rm 11 apt ⍩ 600.
● ★★ *Timhotel La Bourse*, 3, rue de la Banque, ☎ (1) 42.61.53.90, Tx 214488, AE DC Visa, 46 rm ⍩ The latest link in the chain, near the Grands Boulevards, 370.
★★ *Nouveau Monde*, 98, rue de Cléry, ☎ (1) 42.33.22.37, 48 rm, 200.

Restaurants :
● ♦♦♦ *Auberge Perraudin*, 164, rue Montmartre, ☎ (1) 42.36.71.09, AE DC Visa ♪ closed Sun. Claude Perraudin is proud to announce that he soon will have a new decor. His generous, straightforward cooking will doubtless gain a brand-new crowd of patrons, but the regulars will remain for the fabulous *foie gras* (on sale to take out), kidneys, lobsters, etc...At the usual reasonable prices, 150-300 ; child : 50.
● ♦♦ *La Corbeille*, 154, rue Montmartre, ☎ (1) 42.61.30.87, AE Euro Visa ♪ ఉ closed Sat noon (l.s.), Sun, New Year's Day, 15-22 Aug. Good food by gifted chef J.-P. Cario : *duo de poissons crus à l'aneth, raviolis de foie gras de canard aux morilles, noisettes de marcassin Saint-Hubert*, 150-280.
♦♦ *Coup de cœur*, 19, rue St-Augustin, ☎ (1) 47.03.45.70, AE DC Euro Visa ♪ ఉ closed Sat noon and Sun. A sweetheart of a restaurant; excellent value, but a bit more effort is needed in the kitchen, 115-170.
♦♦ *Drouant*, 18, rue Gaillon, ☎ (1) 47.42.56.61 This restaurant famed as site of the "Goncourts», has opened again, completely restored, with the artistry of James Baron (formerly of Cholet), 400-600.
♦♦ *Le Vaudeville*, 29, rue Vivienne, ☎ (1) 42.33.39.31, AE DC Visa Charming, old-fashioned brasserie serving a chic clientele, 105-140.
♦ *Dona Flor*, 10, rue Dussoubs, ☎ (1) 42.36.46.55, AE Visa, closed Mon. A favourite with the capital's Brazilian community, from 8pm to 2am, 150-200.
♦ *Hollywood Savoy*, 44, rue N.-D.-des-Victoires, ☎ (1) 42.36.16.73, closed Sat noon. Where the stockbrokers meet and greet over lunch; at dinner, jazz and American cuisine, 80-120.
♦ *L'Amanguier*, 110, rue de Richelieu, ☎ (1) 42.96.37.79, AE DC Visa ♪ closed 1st May. Winter garden, patio. Good food, quick service, 130.
♦ *Pile ou Face*, 52 bis, rue N.-D.-des-Victoires, ☎ (1) 42.33.64.33 ♪ closed Sat and Sun , Aug. Snappy waiters, fashionable food, 250.

PARIS III

✉ 75003

Hotels :
● ★★★★ *Pavillon de la Reine*, 28, pl. des Vosges, ☎ (1) 42.77.96.40, Tx 216160, AE DC Euro Visa, 49 rm Ⓟ ⍩ ⬩ ♪·ఉ An enchanting hotel, 850.
★★★ *Little Palace Hotel*, 4, rue Salomon-de-Caus, ☎ (1) 42.72.08.15, 59 rm ⍩ 250. Rest. ♦ 70-100.
★★ *Roubaix*, 6, rue Greneta, ☎ (1) 42.72.89.91, 53 rm, 210.
★ *Grand Hôtel des Arts et Métiers*, 4, rue Borda, ☎ (1) 48.87.73.89, 34 rm ⟊ ⬩ ఉ 125.

Restaurants :
● ♦♦ *Ambassade d'Auvergne*, 22, rue du Grenier-St-Lazare, ☎ (1) 42.72.31.22, Visa, closed Sun. Outstanding, hearty cuisine that takes you right to the heart of Auvergne : *charcuteries, saucisse fraîche, aligot, soupe aux choux*... and good Auvergnat wines. Service until 1am, 170.

♦♦ *La Guirlande de Julie*, 25, pl. des Vosges, ☎ (1) 48.87.94.07, AE Visa, closed Mon and Tue, Feb, 160-240.
● ♦ *L'Ami Louis*, 32, rue du Vertbois, ☎ (1) 48.87.77.48, closed Mon and Tue , Jul, Aug. The bill is as big as the servings, 120-260.

PARIS IV

✉ 75004

Hotels :
★★★ *Deux Iles*, 59, rue St-Louis-en-l'Ile, ☎ (1) 43.26.13.35, 17 rm, 485.
★★★ *Lutèce*, 65, rue St-Louis-en-l'Ile, ☎ (1) 43.26.23.52, 23 rm ⍩ 485.
★★★ *Saint-Merry*, 78, rue de la Verrerie, ☎ (1) 42.78.14.15, 12 rm Ⓟ ⟊ ⬩ A 17thC presbytery, 420.
★★ *Célestins*, 1, rue Charles-V, ☎ (1) 48.87.87.04, 15 rm, closed Aug, 300.
★★ *Place des Vosges*, 12, rue de Birague, ☎ (1) 42.72.60.46, AE DC Euro Visa, 16 rm ⬩ ⍩ 230.

Restaurants :
● ♦♦♦ *L'Ambroisie*, 9, pl. des Vosges, ☎ (1) 42.78.51.45, closed Mon noon and Sun, 2 wks in Aug. Bernard Pacaud has fallen in love with the discreet, provincial charm of this handsome square. Patrons agree that his fine cooking is all the better for the change of scene : *mousse de poivron, effeuillé de raie aux choux, millefeuille de framboises*, 220-400.
● ♦♦ *Au Quai des Ormes*, 72, quai de l'Hôtel-de-Ville, ☎ (1) 42.74.72.22, Visa ⟊ closed Sat and Sun, 1-26 Aug. A skip and a jump from the mayor's office, the Masraffs keep their many customers very happy : *dos de Saint-Pierre grillé, poêlée de langoustines aux artichauts, rognons de veau rôti*. Low-calorie dishes, 140-280.
● ♦♦ *Le Dômarais*, 53 bis, rue des Francs-Bourgeois, ☎ (1) 42.74.54.17, AE Euro Visa ⬩ ♪ closed Mon noon, Sat noon, Sun, 2-28 Aug. The unusual decor is a 15thC chapel, with an 18thC dome. Young Patrice Bougerol has people talking about his enjoyable cuisine : *estouffade d'escargots à l'ail doux, saumon à la moelle de bœuf, symphonie de chocolats*, 120-180.
♦♦ *Au Franc Pinot*, 1, quai de Bourbon, ☎ (1) 43.29.46.98, DC Euro Visa ♪ closed Mon and Sun. No fewer than 24 wines can be tasted at the bar of this handsome 17thC edifice, accompanied by tempting gourmet snacks. Light and original cuisine can be had in the splendid vaulted cellar : *filet d'agneau rôti aux langoustines*, 130-250.
♦♦ *Bofinger*, 5, rue de la Bastille, ☎ (1) 42.72.87.82, AE DC Euro Visa ⍩ The oldest brasserie in Paris : seafood year round, *choucroutes*. Varied *à la carte* offerings and a fine selection of Alsatian wines, 140-150.
♦♦ *Chez Julien*, 1, rue du Pont-Louis-Philippe, ☎ (1) 42.78.31.64, AE Visa, closed Mon, Sat noon, Sun, 10 Aug-3 Sep, 250.
♦♦ *Coconnas*, 2 bis, pl. des Vosges, ☎ (1) 42.78.58.16, AE DC Euro Visa Ⓟ ⟊ ⍩ closed Mon and Tue, 15 Dec-15 Jan. Claude (*La Tour d'Argent*) Terrail's pet restaurant, 160-250.
♦♦ *Wally Saharien*, 16-18, rue Le Regrattier, ☎ (1) 43.25.01.39, DC Visa, closed lunch and Sun. The culinary subtleties of the desert are to be found here. All the wine you can drink, 230.
● ♦ *Le Monde des Chimères*, 69, rue St-Louis-en-l'Ile, ☎ (1) 43.54.45.27, Visa, closed Sun , Sep. The tradition continues; a feminine touch in the kitchen and the dining-room, 100-150.

In preparing for your trip, consult the pages pertaining to the regions. You will find there the description of the region you wish to visit, as well as a list of sites that must be seen, a brief history and practical information.

♦ *Chez Benoît*, 20, rue St-Martin, ☎ (1) 42.72.25.76 Ⓟ closed Sat and Sun , Aug. Hearty food : *rosette du Beaujolais, compotier de bœuf en salade, boudin maison*, 350.
♦ *Jo Goldenberg*, 7, rue des Rosiers, ☎ (1) 48.87.20.16, DC Euro Visa ♪ The gathering spot of Paris's Jewish community : *zakouski*, pastrami, smoked salmon, 120.

PARIS V

⊠ 75005

Hotels :

★★★ *Nations*, 54, rue Monge, ☎ (1) 43.26.45.24, Tx 205139, AE DC Euro Visa, 38 rm 🐾 Beflowered little patio, 400.
★★★ *Sélect Hôtel*, 1, pl. de la Sorbonne, ☎ (1) 46.34.14.80, Tx 201207, AE DC Visa, 69 rm Ⓟ ⏴ ♪ 420.
● ★★ *Collège de France*, 7, rue Thénard, ☎ (1) 43.26.78.36, 29 rm, 320.
● ★★ *Grandes Ecoles*, 75, rue du Cardinal-Lemoine, ☎ (1) 43.26.79.23, 35 rm ⏴ ⅏ ⚶ Flower garden; charming hotel near the Place de la Contrescarpe, 220.
★★ *Carmes*, 5, rue des Carmes, ☎ (1) 43.29.78.40, 38 rm ⅏ 250.
★★ *Esmeralda*, 4, rue St-Julien-le-Pauvre, ☎ (1) 43.54.19.20, Tx 270105, 19 rm ⏴ ⚶ 270.
★★ *Trois Collèges*, 16, rue Cujas, ☎ (1) 43.54.67.30, Tx 206034, AE DC Euro Visa, 44 rm Ⓟ ⏴ ⅏ 316.

Restaurants :

● ♦♦♦♦ *La Tour d'Argent*, 15-17, quai de la Tournelle, ☎ (1) 43.54.23.31, AE DC Visa Ⓟ ⏴ ⅋ closed Mon. For centuries, the *Tour d'Argent* has lived in close harmony with the Seine and Notre-Dame. Time cannot slow energetic Claude Terrail, the master of the tower, who trains his staff to honour the principles of perfect hospitality that his patrons have come to expect. Presiding over the pots (silver, naturally) in the kitchen is Dominique Bouchet, an exceptionally gifted young chef, who spent five years with Joël Robuchon : *persillé de homard en gelée aux aromates, petit homard froid Lagardère, marinière de rougets.* Nor are the classics forgotten : *foie gras des trois empereurs* and *le festival des canetons "Tour d'Argent", "Marco Polo", orange*, etc. Do visit the cellar and its memorable wine museum. Across the street, *Tour d'Argent* goodies are sold at the "Comptoir de la Tour", (tel. 46.33.45.58), 250-750.
● ♦♦♦ *Abélard*,. 1, rue des Grands-Degrés, ☎ (1) 43.25.16.46, AE DC Euro Visa Ⓟ ⏴ ⅏ ⚶ ♪ closed Feb. Little by little, *Abélard* has made a place for itself, thanks to Patrick Pontoiseau's youthful style of cookery. The menu changes regularly, 100-200.
● ♦♦♦ *Dodin-Bouffant*, 25, rue Frédéric-Sauton, ☎ (1) 43.25.25.14, DC Visa, closed Sun , Aug. Dany and Maurice Cartier continue in Jacques Manière's tradition. Seawater tank for shellfish. Exemplary prices, 180-300.
● ♦♦♦ *Le Pactole*, 44, bd St-Germain, ☎ (1) 43.26.92.28, AE Euro Visa, closed Sat noon and Sun. The place is getting too small for all the diners who bid for a table. Roland Magne and his wife (who offers the smiling welcome, arranges flowers, pictures..) yearn for a new setting and new horizons. In the meantime, life goes on as does the fine cuisine that could benefit, we think, from a bit more diversity, 160-300.
● ♦♦ *Auberge de la Bûcherie*, 41, rue de la Bûcherie, ☎ (1) 43.54.78.06, AE DC Visa Ⓟ ⏴ ♪ � closed Mon noon. Cosy atmosphere with a fireplace and Lurçat tapestries, an appetizing menu and B. Bosque's refined cuisine : *langoustines au chou*, 280.
● ♦♦ *Clavel*, 65, quai de la Tournelle, ☎ (1) 46.33.18.65, Visa, closed Mon noon and Sun. All new, both management and decor. Outstanding food : *ravioles de homard, carré d'agneau rôti, pigeon farçi*, 160-300.

Be advised that hotels and restaurants in this Guide have perhaps changed addresses; prices indicated are also subject to modifications.

● ♦♦ *La Truffière*, 4, rue Blainville, ☎ (1) 46.33.29.82, AE DC Euro Visa ⚶ ♪ ⅏ closed Mon, 20 Jul-24 Aug. The Sainsard brothers perpetuate a solid culinary tradition : *foie gras, cassoulet, carré d'agneau farçi aux champignons.* Splendid Bordeaux vintages, 120-250.
● ♦♦ *Les Fêtes Gourmandes*, 17, rue de l'École-Polytechnique, ☎ (1) 43.26.10.40, Visa, closed Tue, 1-15 Jan. Let the feasting begin! Everyone's talking about young Vincent Gérard's affordably priced cuisine, 130.
● ♦♦ *Sud Ouest "L'Escarmouche"*, 40, rue de la Montagne-Ste-Geneviève, ☎ (1) 46.33.30.46, AE DC Euro Visa ♪ closed Sun, Aug. G. Bourgain's rich and generous cooking, served in a 13thC crypt : *magret, foie gras, cassoulets* (meat or fish), 200.
♦♦ *Auberge des Deux Signes*, 46, rue Galande, ☎ (1) 43.25.46.56, AE DC Euro Visa ⏴ ⚶ ♪ closed Sun. Historic decor, contemporary food : seafood, fish, 180-300.
♦♦ *Chez René*, 14, bd St-Germain, ☎ (1) 43.54.30.23, closed Sat and Sun, 26 Jul-3 Sep. Beaujolais wines and regional fare, 180-200.
● ♦ *Chez Toutoune*, 5, rue de Pontoise, ☎ (1) 43.26.56.81, Visa, closed Mon and Sun, 10 Aug-7 Sep, 24 Dec-2 Jan. An unbeatable fixed-price meal for 85F and a gourmet take-out shop (for pocket money?) next door, 85-110.
● ♦ *Restaurant "A"*, 5, rue de Poissy, ☎ (1) 46.33.85.54, AE Don't miss it : 18thC chinese cooking. Noble and traditional dishes, artistically carved vegetables that deserve to be displayed in a gourmet museum, 65-150.
● ♦ *Salut l'Artiste*, 22, rue Cujas, ☎ (1) 43.54.01.10, AE DC Euro Visa ♪ ⅏ closed Sun, Aug. Paul Chêne is understandably proud of his children and their nice little restaurant. Fair prices, 60-200.
● ♦ *Vivario*, 6, rue Cochin, ☎ (1) 43.25.08.19, closed Mon and Sun, 25 Dec-1 Jan. Good wines from the Corsican cooperative and specialties of similar origin make a great combination, 140-160.
♦ *Balzar*, 49, rue des Écoles, ☎ (1) 43.54.13.67, closed Tue, 1 Aug-2 Sep. A superb decor, great daily specials attract the scholars of the Collège de France and many Hachette employees : *foie de veau niçoise, bœuf gros sel, pieds de porc* and good beer, 140-185.
♦ *Bouquet du Port*, 4, bd de Port-Royal, ☎ (1) 47.07.08.99, AE DC Euro Visa ⏴ ♪ ⅏ closed Mon, Tue noon, Sun eve, 8 Aug-8 Sep. Fish, oysters, seafood, 180-220.
♦ *L'Estrapade*, 15, rue de l'Estrapade, ☎ (1) 43.25.72.58, AE DC Euro Visa ⏴ ♪ ⅏ closed Sat and Sun. Excellent seasonal fare at incredible prices. Limited space, 150.

PARIS VI

⊠ 75006

Hotels :

● ★★★★(L) *Guy-Louis Duboucheron*, 13, rue des Beaux-Arts, ☎ (1) 43.25.27.22, Tx 270870, AE DC Euro Visa, 27 rm A most beautiful hotel, where O. Wilde stayed, 1700. Rest. ♦♦♦ closed Aug. Handsome bar. Well-conceived menu and fine cuisine, 220-310.
● ★★★★ *Relais Christine*, 3, rue Christine, ☎ (1) 43.26.71.80, Tx 202606, AE DC Euro Visa, 51 rm Ⓟ ⅏ ⚶ ♪ A superb hostelry in the heart of Saint-Germain-des-Prés, 1090.
★★★★ *Littré*, 9, rue Littré, ☎ (1) 45.44.38.68, Tx 203852, AE Euro Visa, 120 rm Ⓟ ♪ ⅏ 600. Rest. ♦♦ 125.
★★★★ *Lutétia-Concorde*, 43, bd Raspail, ☎ (1) 45.44.38.10, Tx 270424, AE DC Visa, 300 rm 17 apt Ⓟ ⏴ 🐾 800. Rest. ● ♦♦♦ *Le Paris* ♪ closed Mon and Sun , Aug. Jacky Fréon (Joël Robuchon's lieutenant at *les Célébrités*) and his staff wish you an excellent appetite in the stunningly decorated (Sonia Rykiel and Slavik) dining room : *piccatas de lotte, filet de canette nantaise, nougat glacé au coulis de framboise*, 220-340 ; child : 30.
★★★★ *Victoria Palace*, 6, rue Blaise-Desgoffe, ☎ (1) 45.44.38.16, Tx 270557, AE Euro Visa, 110 rm Ⓟ ⅏ 545. Rest. ♦♦ ⅏ ⅏ 120-160.

● ★★★ *Latitudes Saint-Germain*, 9, rue Saint-Benoît, ☎ 42.61.53.53, AE DC Euro Visa, 117 rm ♪ A handsome job of renovation, providing every modern amenity, 720.

● ★★★ *Sainte-Beuve*, 9, rue Sainte-Beuve, ☎ 45.48.20.07, Tx 270182, 23 rm A small but comfortable and charming establishment, 650.

● ★★★ *Saints-Pères*, 65, rue des Saints-Pères, ☎ (1) 45.44.50.00, Tx 205424, Euro Visa, 40 rm ⬛ ◑ 🐎 ⬛ ⬷ 500.

★★★ *Abbaye Saint-Germain*, 10, rue Cassette, ☎ (1) 45.44.38.11, 45 rm ⬛ ◑ ⬷ 600.

★★★ *Madison Hôtel*, 143, bd Saint-Germain, ☎ (1) 43.29.72.50, Tx 201628, AE Visa 55 rm ◑ 🐎 ◔ ⬷ 700.

★★ *Balcons*, 3, rue Casimir-Delavigne, ☎ (1) 46.34.78.50, Euro Visa, 55 rm ♪ 255.

★★ *Molière*, 14, rue de Vaugirard, ☎ (1) 46.34.18.80, AE Euro Visa, 15 rm, 250.

Restaurants :

● ◆◆◆ *Jacques Cagna*, (I.L.A.), 14, rue des Grands-Augustins, ☎ (1) 43.26.49.39, AE DC Euro Visa, closed Sat and Sun , Aug, 23 Dec-3 Jan. The most discreet of today's great young chefs will pamper you in his delightful and refined modern decor. Some of the dazzling possibilities : *pétoncles en coquille crémées au caviar, côte de bœuf "Angus", gâteau au chocolat et noix crème anglaise*. Great and simple wines, 195-500.

● ◆◆◆ *La Véranda*, 15, rue Princesse, ☎ (1) 43.26.90.22, AE DC Visa ⅙ closed Mon, Sat noon, Sun, 1-8 Feb, Jul. Way up atop the Club Princesse, Bernard Chirent, vice-president of the Troisgros alumni, cooks at the peak of his form (nothing less would do) for his demanding boss, Jean Castel, his friends and clients. Simple, very good food, 250.

● ◆◆◆ *Relais Louis XIII*, 8, rue des Grands-Augustins, ☎ (1) 43.26.75.96, AE DC Euro Visa ♪ closed Mon noon and Sun, 1-11 Jan, 3-31 Aug. Period atmosphere in this splendid old classified dwelling. Chef Martinez enlivens tradition with a youthful zest. The emphasis is on seafood : *assiette dégustation, rougets aux olives, millefeuilles de rognons*. Splendid cellar supervised by prize-winning sommelier, J. Chauché, 165-300.

● ◆◆ *Chez Dumonet*, 117, rue du Cherche-Midi, ☎ (1) 45.48.52.40, Visa, closed Sat and Sun, 30 Jun-1 Aug, 19-27 Dec. J. Dumonet, a seasonal sailor, cooks hearty straightforward dishes here in his handsome bistro, when he isn't out taming the seas. Exceptional cellar. Next door, charcoal-grilled specialties, 270.

● ◆◆ *Chez Gramond*, 5, rue de Fleurus, ☎ 42.22.28.89, closed Sun, 31 Jul-2 Sep. Where the Senate takes a lunch- or dinner-break : *escalopes de saumon sauce ciboulette*, 250.

● ◆◆ *Guy*, 6, rue Mabillon, ☎ (1) 43.54.87.61, Visa ♪ closed Mon noon and Sun, 10-20 Aug. There's a sweet samba in the air here : *feijoada, frigideira de langouste, rabada* and such pretty girls, especially at lunch on Saturday, 100-195.

● ◆◆ *Xavier Grégoire*, 80, rue du Cherche-Midi, ☎ (1) 45.44.72.72, AE Visa, closed Sat noon and Sun, 7-24 Aug. Xavier Grégoire's savoury cuisine is served in tiny, flower-filled dining rooms. Incredible fixed meal for 108 F. Spec : *filet de rouget au foie gras, escalope de saumon fumé*, 110-230.

● ◆◆ *Brasserie Lipp*, 151, bd St-Germain, ☎ (1) 45.48.53.91, closed Mon , Easter, Jul, 1 Nov, 22 Dec-5 Jan. Simply everyone comes here. You can't smoke a pipe but, illogically, cigars are acceptable, 160-220.

● ◆◆ *L'Apollinaire*, 168, bd St-Germain, ☎ (1) 43.26.50.30, AE DC Euro Visa ◑ ♪ ⬷ closed 18 Dec-5 Jan. From the outside, it looks like a *brasserie*, but it is first-rate. Fine wines, 150-200.

Be advised that hotels and restaurants in this Guide have perhaps changed addresses; prices indicated are also subject to modifications.

● ◆◆ *La Foux*, 2, rue Clément, ☎ (1) 43.54.09.53, AE DC ◑ ♪ ◔ closed Sun, 1 Jan, 25 Dec. A publishers' hangout. Big-hearted A. Guini, with an assist from his spouse, maintains the Lyonnais traditions : *tablier de sapeur, foie de veau des terreaux*. Real Lyonnais lunches on winter Saturdays. The Brouilly flows freely. In summer, Niçoisstyle snacks, 125-250.

● ◆◆ *La Petite Cour*, 8, rue Mabillon, ☎ (1) 43.26.52.26, Euro Visa ⅙ ◑ ◑ closed Mon and Sun , open Mon eve in summer, 20 Dec-5 Jan. Stéphane Oliver extends a smiling welcome : *morue fraîche aux artichauts et pommes pailles, chartreuse de pigeon de Bresse*, 150-300.

● ◆◆ *Le Caméléon*, 6, rue de Chevreuse, ☎ (1) 43.20.63.43, closed Mon and Sun , Aug. Lots of good humour and bonhomie here. Great food and delicious pastries. Nice wine list, 130.

● ◆◆ *Le Muniche and le Petit Zinc*, 25-27, rue de Buci, ☎ (1) 46.33.62.09, AE DC Euro Visa Quantity and quality. Spacious dining room, booths, basement bar with a jazz trio. *Choucroutes, foie gras, confits*, oyster bar. Take-out shop open until 3am just a few steps away, 110-150.

◆◆ *Allard*, 41, rue St-André-des-Arts, ☎ (1) 43.26.48.23, AE DC Euro Visa, closed Sat and Sun, 1 Jan, Aug, 25 Dec. Mme Allard is gone, but the Burgundian tradition persists in this well-known bistro, 280.

◆◆ *L'Echaudé St-Germain*, 21, rue de l'Echaudé, ☎ (1) 43.54.79.02, AE DC Euro Visa, 110-150.

◆◆ *La Closerie des Lilas*, 171, bd du Montparnasse, ☎ (1) 43.54.21.68, AE DC Euro Visa. Montparnasse atmosphere, for a price, 200-500.

◆◆ *La Grosse Horloge*, 22, rue St-Benoît, ☎ (1) 42.22.22.63, AE DC Euro Visa. Time for fresh fish and oysters all year round, 140.

◆◆ *Lapérouse*, 51, quai des Grands-Augustins, ☎ (1) 43.26.68.04, AE Euro Visa ⅙ 'We feed your passion', say the ads. True enough, what with the delightful, romantic decor renovated by Pierre Pothier. But they aren't nearly so good at feeding the patrons, 200-300.

◆◆ *La Vigneraie*, 16, rue du Dragon, ☎ 45.48.57.04, AE DC Euro Visa ♪ closed Sun. Bruno Fava's outstanding cuisine raises this wine bar above the ordinary : *foie gras, pot au feu, saumon à l'unilatéral*, 60-150.

◆◆ *Les Arêtes*, 165, bd du Montparnasse, ☎ (1) 43.26.23.98, closed Mon and Sat noon. Fresh from the ocean, fish as you like it, 120-250.

● ◆ *Chez Tante Madée*, 11, rue Dupin, ☎ (1) 42.22.64.56, AE DC ♪ ◔ closed Sat noon and Sun. Unusually affordable prices for truly enjoyable fare. Spec : *ris de veau au coulis de langoustines et aux asperges, canette fermière aux navets sautés et à la menthe*, 150-250.

● ◆ *Le Gourmet Gourmand*, 72, rue du Cherche-Midi, ☎ (1) 42.22.20.17, closed Mon and Sun, 19-26 Apr, Aug. Excellent cuisine and the dynamism of J.-C. Adib, 200.

◆ *Drugstore Publicis Saint-Germain*, 149, bd St-Germain, ☎ (1) 42.22.92.50, AE DC Euro Visa, 50-70.

◆ *L'Epicerie Landaise*, 10, rue Princesse, ☎ (1) 43.26.02.96, Euro Visa, closed Sun , hols and Aug. The owner provides warm and generous Southwestern dishes until 7am, 180-220.

PARIS VII

✉ 75007

Hotels :

★★★(L) *Pont-Royal*, (Mapotel), 7, rue de Montalembert, ☎ (1) 45.44.38.27, Tx 270113, AE DC Euro Visa, 75 rm 5 apt Ⓟ ⅙ ♪ ◔ Library bar in the basement, 1100. Rest. ◆◆ *Les Antiquaires* ♪ ◑ closed Sun , Aug. Spec : *magret de canard au confit d'oignon*, 150-200.

★★★★(L) *Sofitel-Paris-Invalides*, 32, rue St-Dominique, ☎ (1) 45.55.91.80, Tx 250019, AE DC Euro Visa, 112 rm Ⓟ ◑ ♪ 🐎 ◔ 1250. Rest. ● ◆◆ *Le Dauphin* ♪ ◔ Competently managed by Michel André Potier, this fine restaurant boasts light and inspired cuisine by Jacques Hébert (a gifted Robuchon protégé), 200-350.

★★★★ *Montalembert*, 3, rue Montalembert, ☎ (1) 45.48.68.11, Tx 200132, Euro Visa, 61 rm ◔ 600.

● ★★★ **Saint-Simon**, 14, rue de Saint-Simon, ☎ (1) 45.48.35.66, 34 rm ⋙ ⌕ ⌘ 600.

★★★ **Cayré**, 4, bd Raspail, ☎ (1) 45.44.38.88, Tx 270577, AE DC Euro Visa, 130 rm Ⓟ ⌕ 716.

★★★ **L'Académie**, 32, rue des Saints-Pères, ☎ (1) 45.48.36.22, Tx 205650, AE DC Euro Visa, 34 rm ♪ 440.

★★★ **Quai Voltaire**, 19, quai Voltaire, ☎ (1) 42.61.50.91, 33 rm ≼ ⌘ Exceptional view. Wilde and Wagner slept here, 350.

★★★ **Résidence Elysées-Maubourg** (I.L.A., Mapotel), 35, bd de Latour-Maubourg, ☎ (1) 45.56.10.78, Tx 206227, AE DC Euro Visa, 30 rm Ⓟ ⋙ ⌕ ♪ Antique reproductions. Individual safes in the rooms, 500.

★★★ **Thoumieux**, 79, rue St-Dominique, ☎ (1) 47.05:49.75, Tx 205635, 10 rm ⌕ 375. Rest. ◆◆◆ ⌖ closed Mon. A neighbourhood institution, recently freshened up, 41-120.

★★★ **Université**, 22, rue de l'Université, ☎ (1) 4Ƶ.61.09.39, 28 rm ⌕ ⌘ 450.

★★★ **Varenne**, 44, rue de Bourgogne, ☎ (1) 45.51.45.55, AE, 24 rm ⌕ Two steps away from parliament, 350.

★★★ **Verneuil Saint-Germain**, 8, rue de Verneuil, ☎ (1) 42.60.24.16, Tx 205650, AE Euro Visa, 26 rm ⌕ ♪ 420.

● ★★ **Solférino**, 91, rue de Lille, ☎ (1) 47.05.85.54, Euro Visa, 33 rm ⌕ ⌘ closed 22 Dec-3 Jan, 340.

★★ **Lindbergh**, 5, rue Chomel, ☎ (1) 45.48.35.53, AE DC Euro Visa, 26 rm ⌕ ⌖ 320.

★★ **Résidence Latour-Maubourg**, 150, rue de Grenelle, ☎ (1) 45.51.75.28, 12 rm ≼ ⌕ ⌘ A former private mansion, 300. Rest. ◆ ⌘ 68.

★★ **Vaneau**, 85, rue Vaneau, ☎ (1) 45.48.25.09, DC Euro Visa, 52 rm ⌖ 300.

Restaurants :

● ◆◆◆◆ **Jacques Le Divellec**, 107, rue de l'Université, ☎ (1) 45.51.91.96, AE DC Euro Visa ⌖ ⌘ closed Mon and Sun, 26 Jul-26 Aug, 23 Dec-3 Jan. Sporting fresh yachtclub colours, Jacques Le Divellec's restaurant near Les Invalides manages to bring the best of the sea to the city. Fresh fish, simply (beautifully) prepared : *rougets poêlés en laitue, dorade braisée au gamay, bar rôti à l'écaillé crème d'échalote*, 195-400.

● ◆◆◆◆ **Le Jules Verne**, Tower Eiffel, 2nd floor (elevator, south pillar), ☎ (1) 45.55.61.44, Tx 205789, AE Euro Visa Ⓟ ≼ ♪ ⌘ The world's most fabulous view, with an equally breathtaking decor by Slavik and wonderful food by Louis Grondard. Reservation necessary, 220-400.

● ◆◆◆ **Ravi**, 50, rue de Verneuil, ☎ (1) 42.61.17.28, AE DC Euro Visa Ⓟ ♪ ⌘ Decor, service, table settings worthy of the greatest establishments. Ravi Gupta's entrancing Indian cuisine is absolutely first-rate. Fabulous tandoori curry, 105-300.

● ◆◆◆ **Arpège**, 84, rue de Varenne, ☎ (1) 45.51.20.02, AE DC Euro Visa ⌕ ♪ closed Sat noon and Sun, 1-17 Aug. On the site of Alain Senderens's former *Archestrate*, a talented young chef, Alain Passard, late of the *Duc d'Enghien*, has struck out on his own. Our nostalgia for bygone days quickly dissipates when we taste his light, personal style of cooking. Reasonable prices, 130-225.

● ◆◆◆ **Bistrot de Paris**, 33, rue de Lille, ☎ (1) 42.61.16.83, Euro Visa, closed Sat noon and Sun. A successful author and technical consultant to many important firms, Michel Oliver still finds time to manage his Bistrot, which for 20 years has played to capacity crowds. Excellent value here, witness the perfectly aged rib of beef and one of the least expensive wine lists in town, 200-300.

● ◆◆◆ **Duquesnoy la Bourgogne**, 6, av. Bosquet, ☎ (1) 47.05.96.78, AE DC Euro Visa Ⓟ ⌕ closed Sat noon and Sun. A new start for the Duquesnoy couple, who leave the 5th arrondissement behind. Everything here is brand-new, from dining room to kitchen. Best of luck to them! *Terrine tiède de poireaux et langoustines, raviolis de homard et tourteaux, chartreuse de pigeon, feuillantine au citron*. Fine wines, 280-450.

● ◆◆◆ **La Cantine des Gourmets** (I.L.A.), 113, av. de La Bourdonnais, ☎ (1) 47.05.47.96, AE DC Visa Ⓟ ♪ closed Mon and Sun. With surprising speed and maestria Régis Mahé, a close friend of super-chef Jacques Maximin, has conquered Paris with his refined, delicious cuisine. Attentive and smiling hostess Micheline Coat provides the perfect welcome and warm decor. *Soufflé d'artichaut au foie gras, pot-au-feu de pigeon, langue et rognon d'agneau, terrine aux trois chocolats*, 200-400.

● ◆◆◆ **La Ferme Saint-Simon**, 6, rue de Saint-Simon, ☎ (1) 45.48.35.74, Euro Visa, closed Sat noon and Sun, 3-24 Aug. Thanks to his well-trained staffs, F. Vandehende successfully runs two Parisian eateries (*Le Manoir de Paris*). Inspired, varied *carte*, fabulous pastries. Smiling Denise Fabre, a television personality (and Mme Vandehende) can often be seen supervising the dining room service, 150-270.

● ◆◆◆ **Le Récamier**, 4, rue Récamier, ☎ (1) 42.22.51.75, DC Euro Visa ⋙ ⌕ closed Sun, 24-31 Dec. For politicians, publishers and plain old gourmets. You'd almost think you're in the country here in summer, at a table on the quiet terrace banked with flowers. Food is good, hearty and generously served. Owner Martin Cantegrit picks the best ingredients that the Rungis market has to offer : *œufs en meurette, fritures d'équilles, foie de veau*. The cellar holds some nicely-priced treasures, 300.

● ◆◆◆ **Tan Dinh**, 60, rue de Verneuil, ☎ (1) 45.44.04.84, closed Sun, 1-15 Aug. In a brand-new and striking Asian setting, the Vifians serve their exciting Oriental specialties. The cellar is a veritable treasure trove. Take their advice when ordering wine : they are knowledgeable indeed, 300.

◆◆◆ **Chez les Anges**, 54, bd de Latour-Maubourg, ☎ (1) 47.05.89.86, AE DC Euro Visa Ⓟ ⌕ ♪ ⌖ closed Mon and Sun eve. These angels are gourmets, 275-320.

● ◆◆ **Chez Françoise**, aérogare des Invalides, ☎ (1) 47.05.49.03, AE DC Visa ⌖ closed Mon and Sun eve , Aug. When the Assemblée takes a break, many of the members come here to refuel. Don't worry, regular folks are welcome too. Consistent quality : *foie gras frais maison, barbue grillée sauce vierge*, 100-170.

● ◆◆ **La Boule d'Or**, 13, bd de Latour-Maubourg, ☎ (1) 47.05.50.18, closed Mon , Aug. Young Serge Barbey has got the ball rolling here with outstanding cuisine. His mentor, Bernard Loiseau, would surely approve. *Feuilleté de sole, symphonie de poissons marinés, pigeonneau rôti compote d'oignons, tarte fine Verger*, 170-300.

● ◆◆ **Labrousse**, 4, rue Pierre-Leroux, ☎ (1) 43.06.99.39, AE Visa ⌕ ⌖ closed Sat noon and Sun, 1-21 Aug. After the luxury of the *Grand Véfour* where he presided in the kitchen, Yves Labrousse has opted for the almost provincial peace of a little side street to practice his culinary art : *œufs en meurette, feuilleté de rouget, pigeonneau en aumonière*, 125-270.

● ◆◆ **La Flamberge**, 12, av. Rapp, ☎ (1) 47.05.91.37, AE DC Euro Visa, closed Sat noon and Sun. A great but modest chef at work here : *brochettes de Saint-Jacques au poivron doux*, game in season, *tarte chaude aux fruits*, 300-350.

● ◆◆ **La Sologne**, 8, rue de Bellechasse, ☎ (1) 47.05.98.66, AE DC Visa Ⓟ ⌕ ⌖ The best selection of fresh game in season. Excellent Loire Valley wines. Next door at *Le Crik*, take-out foods and snacks, 100-210.

● ◆◆ **Chez Gildo**, 153, rue de Grenelle, ☎ (1) 45.51.54.12, closed Mon and Sun Jul-Aug. Italian cuisine, 160-280.

● ◆◆ **La Famiglia**, 34, rue de Bourgogne, ☎ (1) 45.55.80.75, AE DC Euro Visa. Pasta and more pasta... yes, but made by La Famiglia. They know what they're doing, Zoo.

● ◆◆ **Le Perron**, 6, rue Perronet, ☎ (1) 45.44.71.51 ⌕ closed Sun, 1-30 Aug. A little side street well known to lovers of pasta and good Sicilian cooking, 120-150.

● ◆◆ **Vin sur Vin**, 20, rue de Montessuy, ☎ (1) 47.05.14.20, closed Sun. This friendly wine bar has become a full-fledged restaurant. Good food at affordable prices. Good wines, 150.

Send us your comments and suggestions; we will use them in the next edition.

♦♦ *Le Galant Verre*, 12, rue de Verneuil, ☎ (1) 42.60.84.56, AE DC Euro Visa ⌂Ġ closed Sat noon and Sun, 225-260.

♦♦ *Relais Saint-Germain*, 190, bd St-Germain, ☎ (1) 42.22.21.35, Euro Visa. As ever, an excellent fixed-price meal, 80-170.

● ♦ *Au Pied de Fouet*, 45, rue de Babylone, ☎ (1) 47.05.12.27, closed Sat eve and Sun, 5-20 Apr, 2 Aug-6 Sep, 22 Dec-2 Jan. Hard to secure a table here, and hostess Andrée, by her own admission has something of a temper. Simple fare, but the homemade pastries are remarkable. Martial mans the bar, serving coffee and selected wines, 100-120.

● ♦ *Le Bellecour*, 22, rue Surcouf, ☎ 45.51.46.93, AE DC Euro Visa, closed Sat eve and Sun , Sat lunch, Oct-Jun, 10 Aug-1 Sep. Good Lyonnais fare, 200-250.

♦ *Aux Fins Gourmets*, 213, bd St-Germain, ☎ (1) 42.22.06.57, closed Sun, Aug. A good, inexpensive little place, 80-130.

♦ *Chez Germaine*, 30, rue Pierre-Leroux, ☎ (1) 42.73.28.34 ⅋ closed Sat eve and Sun, 28 Jul-1 Sep. Oil-cloth napery and simple, home-style fare, 40-70.

♦ *L'Oeillade*, 10, rue de Saint-Simon, ☎ (1) 42.22.01.60, AE DC Euro Visa, closed Sun. Good, inexpensive food with a feminine touch : *noix de coquilles Saint-Jacques, raie aux capres, magret d'oie au poivre*, 130.

♦ *La Belle France*, Eiffel Tower, 1st floor, ☎ (1) 45.55.20.04, Tx 205789, Euro Visa ℗ ≼ ⅋ 80-180; child : 40.

PARIS VIII

✉ 75008

Hotels :

● ★★★★(L) *California*, 16, rue de Berri, ☎ (1) 43.59.93.00, Tx 660634, AE DC Euro Visa, 188 rm ℗ ⬭ ⬭ 🐎 995. Rest. ♦♦ closed Sun, 120-210.

● ★★★★(L) *Claridge Bellman*, 37, rue François-Ier, ☎ (1) 47.23.54.42, Tx 641150, AE DC Visa, 42 rm, 875. Rest. ♦♦ *Relais Bellman* ♪ Ġ ⅋ closed Sat and Sun, Aug, 24 Dec-2 Jan. Handsome antique furniture, and a warm ambience rarely found in luxury hotels. Interesting food. Spec : *salade de crabe pamplemousse, suprême de barbue à l'orange, cœur de filet à l'estragon*, 230.

★★★★(L) *Crillon*, (Concorde), 10, pl. de la Concorde, ☎ (1) 42.65.24.24, Tx 290204, AE DC Euro Visa, 189 rm ℗ ≼ ⬭ ⬭ ♪ Ġ 1750. Rest. ● ♦♦♦ ♦ ♪ Ġ ⅋ The bright and lively decor devised by Sonia Rykiel contrasts picturesquely with the marble stateliness of Gabriel's 18thC palace. André Signoret, late of the *Grand Véfour*, returns to the *Crillon's* kitchens : *Saint-Pierre aux poires et basilic, coeur de pigeonneau glacé de céleri, feuilles de chocolat aux épices*, 360-450. ♦♦ *L'Obélisque* Light fare from the grill, 120-210.

● ★★★★(L) *Le Bristol*, 112, rue du Fbg-Saint-Honoré, ☎ (1) 42.66.91.45, Tx 280961, AE DC Euro Visa, 200 rm ℗ ⬭ ⬭ ⅋ 🖂 Discreet luxury in a former 18thC cloister, 1800. Rest. ♦♦♦♦ ≼ ⅋ Outstanding table, worthy of the hotel, 320-430.

● ★★★★(L) *Le Warwick*, 5, rue de Berri, ☎ (1) 45.63.14.11, Tx 642295, AE DC Euro Visa, 148 rm ℗ ⬭ ⬭ ♪ 1650. Rest. ● ♦♦♦ *La Couronne* ♪ closed Sun eve , hols and Aug. Chef Bodiguel staunchly defends tradition : *ravioles d'écrevisses à la feuille d'estragon, fin ragoût de ris et rognons de veau*, 195.

★★★★(L) *Balzac*, 6, rue Balzac, ☎ (1) 45.61.97.22, Tx 290298, AE DC Euro Visa, 70 rm ⬭ 1400. Rest. ● *Le Sallambier* ♪ closed Sat and Sun. Pleasant decor, cuisine of Southwestern inspiration, prepared by a disciple of André Daguin. Nice selection of modest wines, 250-300.

★★★★(L) *George V*, 31, av. George-V, ☎ (1) 47.23.54.00, Tx 650082, AE DC Euro Visa, 288 rm ⬭ ⬭ 2100. Rest. ♦♦♦ *Les Princes* ♪ closed hols. The surprising, flavourful cuisine, of chef Pierre Larapidie is now featured here, in a luxurious setting, 220-400.

★★★★(L) *Lancaster*, 7, rue de Berri, ☎ (1) 43.59.90.43,

AE DC Euro Visa, 66 rm 10 apt Ġ 1600. Rest. ♦♦♦ closed Sat and Sun. Outstanding food, 160-300.

★★★★(L) *Plaza-Athénée*, 25, av. Montaigne, ☎ (1) 47.23.78.33, Tx 650092, AE DC Euro Visa, 218 rm ≼ ⬭ ⬭ ♪ Ġ 2000. Rest. ♦♦♦♦ *Le Régence* ♪ Ġ ⅋ 600.

★★★★(L) *Prince de Galles*, (Marriott), 33, av. George-V, ☎ (1) 47.23.55.11, Tx 280627, AE DC Euro Visa, 171 rm 🐎 Ġ 1650. Rest. ● ♦♦♦ ≼ ♪ ⅋ Pierre-Dominique Cecillon, sidekick of Joël Robuchon at the *Concorde* and the *Nikko*, is shooting off sparks in his new kitchen : *petits gris et grenouilles au pourpier, ravioles de loup au jus de truffes, pied d'agneau farci, mousse vanille aux griottes*, 165-320; child : 100.

★★★★(L) *Pullman Windsor* (I.L.A.), 14, rue Beaujon, ☎ (1) 45.63.04.04, 135 rm, 950. Rest. ● ♦♦♦ *Le Clovis*, closed Sat and Sun , Aug and hols. Chef Roue, a former player on the Robuchon team, heads the side here in a new decor : *tartare de dorade rose et saumon mariné, grenouilles et écrevisses au sauternes, pigeonneau à la feuille de vigne*, 125-300.

★★★★(L) *Royal Monceau*, 37, av. Hoche, ☎ (1) 45.61.98.00, Tx 650361, AE DC Euro Visa, 220 rm ⬭ ⬭ 🖂 2140. Rest. ● ♦♦♦♦ *Le Jardin* ● Light, innovative cooking. Spec : *gourmandises de veau aux aromates, suprême de volaille aux coquilles Saint-Jacques*, 240-400♦♦♦ *Le Carpaccio* ⅋ closed Aug. Italian cuisine, 230-360.

● ★★★★ *Atala*, 10, rue Chateaubriand, ☎ (1) 45.62.01.62, Tx 640576, AE DC, 49 rm ⬭ ⬭ ⬭ Ġ 650. Rest. ♦♦ Ġ closed Sat and Sun , Aug, 180.

● ★★★★ *Résidence du Roy*, 8, rue François-1er, ☎ (1) 42.89.59.59, Tx 648452, AE DC Euro Visa, 36 rm ℗ ⬭ ⬭ ♪ Ġ 1300.

● ★★★★ *Résidence Maxim's*, 42, av. Gabriel, ☎ (1) 45.61.96.33, Tx 642794, AE DC Euro Visa, 4 rm 39 apt. Luxury and refinement : just don't ask the price. Rest. ♦♦♦ *Caviarteria* The first link of an international chain of prestigious hotels bearing the stamp of Pierre Cardin : suites from 50 to 250 m^2, 2 bars, caviarteria, health club and relaxation centre. So luxurious that price simply isn't a consideration. Breakfast and tea served under an arbour in a decor that resembles a painting by Fragonard or Boucher. Maximum's bar open from noon to 1am, 200-400.

★★★★ *Astor l'Horset*, 11, rue d'Astorg, ☎ (1) 42.66.56.56, Tx 642737, AE DC Euro Visa, 128 rm ⬭ ♪ 710. Rest. ♦♦ *La Table de l'Astor*, closed Sat and Sun, 170-230.

★★★★ *Napoléon*, 40, av. de Friedland, ☎ (1) 47.66.02.02, Tx 640609, AE DC Euro Visa, 140 rm, 1150. Rest. ♦♦ *Baumann Napoléon* ♪ Business specials, *saumon au vert, saucisson froid de poissons à l'estragon, rognons de coq en raviolis*, 215-300.

★★★★ *Royal Hôtel*, 33, av. Friedland, ☎ (1) 43.59.08.14, Tx 280965, AE DC Euro Visa, 57 rm ≼ 723.

★★★★ *San Régis*, 12, rue Jean-Goujon, ☎ (1) 43.59.41.90, Tx 643637, AE DC Visa, 44 rm ≼ ♪ Entirely renovated in 1986. Antique furniture, 1400. Rest. ♦♦ ♪ ⅋ 190.

● ★★★ *Résidence Saint-Honoré*, 214, rue du Fbg-St-Honoré, ☎ (1) 42.25.26.27, Tx 640524, AE DC Euro Visa, 91 rm ♪ 🐎 630.

★★★ *Franklin*, 19, rue Buffault, ☎ (1) 42.80.27.27, AE DC Euro Visa, 64 rm ⬭ Ġ 540. Rest. ♦ closed Sat and Sun , hols, 85-220.

★★ *Buckingham*, 45, rue des Mathurins, ☎ (1) 42.65.81.62, AE DC Euro Visa, 35 rm ⅋ 360. Rest. ♦ 70-200.

★★ *Ceramic Hôtel*, 34, av. de Wagram, ☎ (1) 42.27.20.30, AE DC Euro Visa, 53 rm Astonishing façade covered with ceramics, an Art-Deco hotel, 350.

★ *Bellevue*, 46, rue Pasquier, ☎ (1) 43.87.50.68, 48 rm ⅋ 140.

Restaurants :

● ♦♦♦♦ *Lamazère*, 23, rue de Ponthieu, ☎ (1) 43.59.66.66, AE DC Euro Visa ℗ ⬭ ♪ ⅋ closed Sun , Jul, Aug. 31 Jul-1 Sep. The temple of truffles, *foie gras*, and *confits* presided over by high priest and magician Roger Lamazère, 500-600.

● ◆◆◆◆ *Lasserre*, 17, av. Franklin-Roosevelt, ☎ (1) 43.59.53.43 ⌘ closed Mon noon and Sun, 2-31 Aug. Valiant René Lasserre deserves a special salute as a champion of classic French cuisine : *queues de langoustines rôties sauce sabayon, cassolette de ris de veau et crêtes de volailles au thym sauvage, nougat glacé aux fruits*, 400-600.

● ◆◆◆◆ *Le Bacchus Gourmand*, 21, rue François-1er, ☎ (1) 47.20.15.83, closed Sat and Sun. The new restaurant of the *Maison de la vigne et du vin*, is now a star in the gastronomic firmament thanks to the talents of Thierry Coué (a former colleague of Senderens at the latter's *Archestrate*), who gives full measure of his gifts in this plush setting. Flawless service. *Raviolis de pied d'agneau au safran, sole meunière aux oursins et oignons frits* (prepared tableside), *glace au miel*, pastries. Soon, a wine list representing the great French vintages, 250-450.

● ◆◆◆◆ *Le Pavillon Elysée*, 10, av. des Champs-Élysées, ☎ (1) 42.65.85.10, AE DC Visa ℙ ⌘ ⌘ closed Sat noon and Sun , Aug. A little shuffling of staff has taken place. Gaston Lenôtre remais in command, while young Didier Lanfray will henceforth preside in the kitchen preparing : *langoustines rôties sur jonchée de saumon, rougets à la fricassée de fenouil, canard rouennais , les mignardises* and chocolats, memorable pastries. *Les Jardins :* open every day all year round, with a 2-wk respite around Xmas, 300-450.

● ◆◆◆◆ *Lucas Carton (Alain Senderens)*, 9, pl. de la Madeleine, ☎ (1) 42.65.22.90, Tx 281088, Visa ℙ ⌘ ⌘ closed Sat and Sun, 1-23 Aug, 23 Dec-4 Jan. Hard by the Madeleine, a unique decor of blond paneling attributed to Majorelle (1859-1926). Eventhia oversees the flowers, the smiles, the welcome. Your tastebuds are catered to by Alain Senderens, explorer in the realm of French cuisine, who devotes an entire page of his menu to listing some 60 recipes he has created since 1968. Two other pages offer 6 *prix-fixe* meals (550-1000F, not incl. service); subtle harmonies of food and wines ; another page pairs wines and cheeses (18 varieties). To give you an idea : *raviolis de pétoncles, foie gras de canard aux choux à la vapeur, canard Apicius*. Old vintages. Private club upstairs, 550-1 000.

● ◆◆◆◆ *Taillevent*, 15, rue Lamennais, ☎ (1) 45.61.12.90 ♪ ⌘ closed Sat and Sun, 14-22 Feb, 25 Jul-24 Aug. The Duc de Morny would surely have enjoyed hosting the gourmet patrons who reserve far in advance to lunch or dine in his handsome town house. But J.-C. Vrinat does an impeccable job of it, assisted by chef Claude Deligne : *filet de sole artichauts et curry, noisettes d'agneau en chevreuil*. One of the world's best cellars, 530.

● ◆◆◆◆ *Maxim's*, 3, rue Royale, ☎ (1) 42.65.27.94, AE DC Euro Visa ⌘ closed Sun. Pierre Cardin sets the tone, chef Menant and his brigade do their best to follow : it's starting to jell. Upstairs, dinners and late suppers. Close by, *Minim's* and its (far) lower prices, 600-700.

◆◆◆◆ *Laurent*, 41, av. Gabriel, ☎ (1) 42.25.00.39, AE DC ℙ ⌘ ♪ ⌘ closed Sat noon and Sun. The pearl of the Golden Triangle of restaurants on the Champs-Élysées. Lobster salad, *langouste tiède en salade, canard nantais aux deux cuissons, soufflés Laurent*, 320-610.

◆◆◆◆ *Ledoyen*, (I.L.A.), Carré des Champs-Élysées, ☎ (1) 42.66.54.77 ℙ ⌘ ⌘ ♪ ⌘ closed Sun , Aug. Under new management. Wait and see, 300-500.

● ◆◆◆ *Alain Rayé*, 49, rue du Colisée, ☎ (1) 42.25.66.76, DC Euro Visa ⌘ ⌘ closed Sat noon and Sun. Alain Rayé, late of Albertville, serves outstanding cuisine at very Parisian prices, 165-290.

● ◆◆◆ *Chiberta*, 3, rue A.-Houssaye, ☎ (1) 45.63.77.90, closed Sat and Sun , hols and Aug. Louis-Noël Richard has many faithful clients whom he welcomes with flawless hospitality in his handsome establishment (the sober decor is by Jean Dives). The cuisine of impish, discreet Jean-Michel Bedier keeps all these customers satisfied, 350-420.

● ◆◆◆ *La Fermette Marbeuf 1900*, 5, rue Marbeuf, ☎ (1) 47.23.31.31, AE DC Visa ♪ Pleasant interior with a turn-of-the-century decor. Capable, sly Jean Laurent, his chef Gilbert Isaac and their dependable staff never cease to amaze us with their attention to detail. New menu : cheese tray, vintage wine list, cigars, smiles etc..., 125-190.

● ◆◆◆ *La Marée*, 1, rue Daru, ☎ (1) 47.63.52.42, AE DC ℙ closed Aug. The quality here is as regular as the tides that the restaurant is named for. Eric Trompier, the young owner-director has infused an agreeably youthful feel here, much to the patrons' approval (Mama quietly keeps an eye on things too). In the kitchen, Gérard Rouillard and his expert brigade send forth splendidly simple fish and seafood dishes : *belons au champagne, loup Marie-Do, turbotin, rougets grillés, farandole gourmande du chef pâtissier*. For the regulars, a few meat dishes. More than 600 wines on hand in the cellar, with the spotlight on Bordeaux in all price ranges, 250-400.

● ◆◆◆ *Le Bonaventure*, 35, rue Jean-Goujon, ☎ (1) 42.25.02.58, AE Visa ♪ closed Sat noon and Sun. An unobtrusive eatery in a quiet spot near the Alma. The little inner courtyard holds tables in fine weather. Noël Gutrin prepares some interesting dishes : *saumon à la tahitienne, poêlée de langoustines et Saint-Jacques aux cèpes, fricassée de ris et de rognons de veau au vinaigre de framboise*, 250.

● ◆◆◆ *Le Lord Gourmand*, 9, rue Lord-Byron, ☎ (1) 43.59.07.27, AE Euro Visa, closed Sat and Sun , Aug, 24-31 Dec. Model student Daniel Météry has caught up with his teachers (Bocuse, Troisgros). He pays them homage every day with his dazzling cuisine : *roulade de Saint-Jacques* (in season), *magret fumé, souris d'agneau aux pâtes fraîches, tarte tiède aux pommes et abricots*. Ask Brigitte for a cocktail, 160-300.

● ◆◆◆ *Fouquet's*, 99, av. des Champs-Élysées, ☎ (1) 47.23.70.60, AE DC Euro Visa ⌘ ⌘ closed Sat and Sun , for *Fouquet's Elysées*, 18 Jul-23 Aug. The denizens of the theatre and film world come for the warm welcome of Maurice Casanova, for his daughter, Jenny Paule's charming smile and for P. Ducroux's good cooking. On the terrace, Paris and the Champs-Élysées are at your feet, 200-240.

◆◆◆ *Francis*, 7, pl. de l'Alma, ☎ (1) 47.20.86.83 Fish are the favoured food in this handsome, classy *brasserie*, 250.

● ◆◆ *Al Amir*, 66, rue François-1er, ☎ (1) 47.23.79.05, AE DC Visa ♪ ⌘ The charm of the East and the Arabian nights, just off the Champs-Élysées. Wonderful hot and cold *mezzes*, charcoal-grilled dishes and Le banese wines, 165-250.

● ◆◆ *Au Petit Montmorency*, 5, rue Rabelais, ☎ (1) 42.25.11.19, Euro Visa ⌘ closed Sun , Aug. In a quiet, propitiously named street, D. Bouché cooks up a stunning array of delicate flavours : *foie gras de canard au caramel poivré, canard Lucifer à la semoule, soufflé au chocolat*, 280.

● ◆◆ *Chez Edgard*, 4, rue Marbeuf, ☎ (1) 47.20.51.15, AE DC Euro Visa, closed Sun. A favourite with politicians, stars and radio personalities. Reserve, 230.

● ◆◆ *Jean-Charles et Ses Amis*, 7,rue de la Trémoille, ☎ (1) 47.23.88.18, closed Sat noon. Jean-Charles Diehl has lots of friends who appreciate his warm welcome and the cooking of chef J.-C. Billebault, 150-250.

● ◆◆ *Le Grenadin*, 46, rue de Naples, ☎ (1) 45.63.28.92, AE Euro Visa ♪ closed Sat and Sun , 3 wks in Aug, 23 Dec-2 Jan. Young Patrick Cirotte is a chef with a future : *émincé de rable de lapin à la crème d'ail, marinade de blanc de volaille*. His restaurant now holds more lucky diners since its recent facelift, 135-350.

● ◆◆ *Le Marcande*, 52, rue de Miromesnil, ☎ (1) 42.65.19.14, AE DC Visa ⌘ ⌘ closed Sat and Sun, 1-26 Aug. The cuisine of this handsome restaurant is supervised by superchef Michel Lorain of Joigny's *Côte Saint-Jacques*, 180-320.

● ◆◆ *Les Thermes du Royal Monceau*, 39, av. Hoche, ☎ (1) 42.25.06.66, AE DC Visa ⌘ ⌘ ♪ ☐ In the luxuriously sophisticated and over-equipped Roman baths, unlike any a real Roman might have seen, you can purchase a membership for a year or a day. The restaurant features pleasant, light fare by Thierry Couchot. Spec :

filet de turbot au sauternes et foie gras, éventail de magret de canard, soufflé léger au citron vert, 120-185.

● ◆◆ **Tong Yen**, 1 bis, rue Jean-Mermoz, ☎ (1) 42.25.04.23, AE DC Euro Visa, closed 1-25 Aug. A crowded Chinese spot, favoured by local celebrities whom Thérèse Luong greets warmly. Peking duck, 250.

● ◆◆ **Chez Vong**, 27, rue du Colisée, ☎ (1) 43.59.77.12, AE DC Visa Ⓟ ♩ closed Sun. A chic Chinese eatery with a Hollywood decor. Refined cuisine and the service can be very good indeed. Spec : Peking duck, Vietnamese dumplings *(banh cuon)*, sautéed crab Cantonese, 200.

● ◆◆ **Flora Danica**, 142, av. des Champs-Élysées, ☎ 43.59.20.41, AE DC Euro Visa ⚕ closed 24 Dec and 1 May. Danish salmon in all possible guises (smoked, marinated, grilled, etc), herring, 300.

● ◆◆ **Hédiard**, 21, pl. de la Madeleine, ☎ (1) 42.66.09.00, AE DC Euro Visa ♩ closed Sun. So you won't die of hunger or thirst. Take-out, gourmet shop, wines, 260.

● ◆◆ **L'Espace**, 1, av. Gabriel, ☎ (1) 42.66.11.70, AE DC Euro Visa, closed Sat noon. A high-class crush guaranteed daily, overseen by Jacques Collart : buffet, daily specials, pastries, inexpensive wines. Pierre Cardin lunches here on his home turf —how reassuring! Pianobar, 130-240.

● ◆◆ **La Ligne**, 30, rue Jean-Mermoz, ☎ (1) 42.25.52.65, DC Euro Visa ♩ closed Sat and Sun , Aug, 25-31 Dec. Cross the line *(la ligne)* to find excellent food by Jean Speyer, 185.

● ◆◆ **Le Drugstorien**, 1, av. Matignon, ☎ (1) 43.59.38.70, AE DC Visa The Publicis chain's very good restaurant : *foie gras frais maison, sole à la ciboulette*, 120-210.

◆◆ **Androuet**, 41, rue d'Amsterdam, ☎ (1) 48.74.26.90 A comeback for the restaurant of this shrine to French cheese. *Tourte au roquefort, croquettes Marie Harel* (she invented camembert), *raviolis de chèvre, fondues* (order in advance), 250-300.

◆◆ **Baumann-Marbeuf**, 15, rue Marbeuf, ☎ (1) 47.20.11.11, AE DC Euro Visa ♩ The place to come for good meat and *choucroute*, 170-200.

◆◆ **Copenhague**, 142, av. des Champs-Élysées, ☎ 43.59.20.41, AE DC Euro Visa ⚘ closed Sun and hols, 1 wk Jan, 2-30 Aug. Spec : salmon marinated with dill, reindeer steaks with blackberries in sweet-and-sour sauce, 340.

◆◆ **Le Vanillier**, 90, rue la Boétie, ☎ (1) 42.89.28.28, closed Sat and Sun. Excellent Malgasy cuisine, closer than Madagascar, 200.

● ◆ **Chez Tante Louise**, 41, rue Boissy-d'Anglas, ☎ (1) 42.65.06.85, AE DC Euro Visa, closed Sat and Sun, Aug. In this cosy setting, Bernard Lhiabastres serves enjoyable food that is bound to attract crowds to his handsome establishment. As always, pains are taken with the quality, choice and pricing of wines, 170-250.

● ◆ **Le Boeuf sur le Toit**, 34, rue du Colisée, ☎ (1) 43.59.83.80, AE DC Visa. If you don't mind waiting in line...oyster bar and irreproachably fresh seafood, 140-160.

● ◆ **Savy**, 23, rue Bayard, ☎ (1) 47.23.46.98, Visa, closed Sat and Sun, 1-30 Aug. Where radio personalities gather. It's good, simple and not too expensive. Cuisine of Auvergne : *choux aveyronnais, farçou, jambonneau aux lentilles*, 120-210.

◆ **Grand Pub Lady-Hamilton**, 82, av. Marceau, ☎ (1) 47.20.20.40, Visa ⚘ ♩ A fine English pub, known as the site of many a 'third half' for football players and fans, 70-110.

◆ **Le Bar des Théâtres**, 6, av. Montaigne, ☎ (1) 47.23.34.63, closed Aug. A hangout for television journalists. After-theatre suppers. More-than-decent *brasserie fare*, 150-200.

◆ **Le Bistrot de la Gare**, 73, av. des Champs-Élysées, ☎ (1) 43.59.67.83, Visa, 50-100.

◆ **Théâtre du Rond-Point**, • av. F.-Roosevelt, ☎ (1) 42.56.22.01, Visa. Where the Renaud-Barrault theatre troupe meets after the show, 50-150.

The arrow (→) is a reference to another entry.

PARIS IX

✉ 75009

Hotels :

● ★★★★(L) **Scribe** (I.L.A., Sofitel), 1, rue Scribe, ☎ (1) 47.42.03.40, Tx 214653, AE DC Euro Visa, 217 rm 🏍 ♿ 1490. Rest. ● ◆◆◆ **Les Muses** ♩ ♿ closed Sat and Sun , Aug and hols. A fresh, new decor and a young, new chef, Christian Massault, for this eminently agreeable hotel restaurant. Light, flavourful cuisine : *tagliatelle aux escargots et à la sauge, sole au vermouth, navarin de canette de Challans, délice de chocolat au coulis d'orange*, 160-220◆◆ **Le Jardin des Muses** ♩ ♿ A coffee shop serving low-calorie specialties for the fitness-minded, 100.

★★★★(L) **Grand Hôtel**, 2, rue Scribe, ☎ (1) 42.68.12.13, 583 rm 12 apt ♿ 1250. Rest. ◆◆◆ **Le Patio**, closed eves and Aug, 185-230◆◆ **Café de la Paix** A traditional spot for after the theatre or ballet, 250-330.

● ★★★ **Léman**, 20, rue de Trevise, ☎ (1) 42.46.50.66, Tx 281086, AE DC Euro Visa, 24 rm ♩ 🏍 An enchanting decor, peace and quiet, 650.

★★★ **Aston**, 12, cité Bergère, ☎ (1) 47.70.52.46, AE DC Euro Visa, 34 rm ⚕ ♿ 450.

★★★ **Casino**, 41, rue de Clichy, ☎ (1) 48.74.74.99, AE Euro Visa, 40 rm, 225. Rest. ● ◆◆ ♩ closed Sat and Sun , hols. Chef J.-C. Jarrault presides in the kitchen, and is resposible for the delectable cuisine : *salade Christine, dos de sandre à la vapeur d'algues et aux queues de langoustines, tournedos 'Yella'*, 120-260.

★★★ **Franklin**, 19, rue Buffault, ☎ (1) 42.80.27.27, Tx 640988, AE DC Euro Visa, 64 rm ⚕ 🏍 490. Rest. ◆ ♩ closed Sat and Sun, 15 Jul-15 Aug, 150-200.

★★ **Résidence Sémard**, 15, rue Pierre-Semard, ☎ (1) 48.78.26.72, 41 rm ⚕ 210.

Moulin Rouge, 39, rue Fontaine, ☎ (1) 42.82.08.56, Tx 660055, AE DC Euro Visa, 50 rm ⚕ 🏍 480.

Restaurants :

● ◆◆◆◆ **Café de la Paix Opéra**, 3, pl. de l'Opéra, ☎ (1) 47.42.97.02, Tx 670738, AE DC Euro Visa ⚘ ♿ closed Aug. Gil Jouanins' authentic "grande cuisine" is perfectly suited to Garnier's decor and frescoes : *petite nage froide de crustacés aux concombres et menthe poivrée, filet de canette poêlé aux petits légumes nouveaux, assiette aux trois cacaos*. Fine cellar, 350.

● ◆◆◆ **Charlot**, 12, place Clichy, ☎ 48.74.49.64 Seafood, shellfish, super-fresh fish in this, the jewel in the Blanc family's crown, superbly decorated by Pierre Pothier. Open until 2 am, 200.

● ◆◆ **La Table d'Anvers**, 2, pl. d'Anvers, ☎ (1) 48.78.35.21, Visa Ⓟ Excellent quality here! They're young and talented, working in a modern decor, charging agreeably affordable prices. Who are they? Christian and Philippe Conticini. Father Roger oversees the dining room and the cellar (a little paradise for good bottles). *Salade tiède de moules, céleri et fenouil croquant au safran, rouget poêlé sur une fondue de pied de porc et céleri frais*. Dreamy desserts, original dishes, lots of spices, sweet-and-sour combinations, earthy fare..., 100-180.

● ◆◆ **Café de la Paix Relais Capucines**, 12, bd des Capucines, ☎ (1) 42.68.12.13, Tx 670738, AE DC Euro Visa ♩ ♿ Classified frescoes by Charles Garnier adorn this pleasant winter garden. The traditional Burgundy cuisine overseen by Gil Jouanin is delicious. The terrace, the Foyer Bar Opéra open till 10pm, 150.

● ◆◆ **Cartouche-Edouard VII**, 18, rue Caumartin, ☎ (1) 47.42.08.82, AE Visa, closed Sun, 25 Jul-23 Aug. Hurry for the Southwest and its generous cuisine, served in this annex of the *Repaire de Cartouche. Confits, foie gras*, etc..., (served until 2am), 210.

● ◆◆ **Le Grand Café Capucines**, 4, bd des Capucines, ☎ (1) 47.42.75.77, AE DC Euro Visa Ⓟ ⚘ ♩ ♿ Open day and night, just like in the Belle Époque. Seafood and other delicious fare, 180.

◆◆ **Au Petit Riche**, 25, rue Le Peletier, ☎ (1) 47.70.68.68, AE Visa ♩ closed Sun, 1-27 Aug. This authentic turn-of-the-century bistro offers a wealth of good Loire Valley vintages, but the food needs some bucking up, 110-180.

♦♦ *Le Square*, 6, sq. de l'Opéra, ☎ (1) 47.42.78.50, AE Visa, closed Sat noon and Sun. An actors rendezvous. Lots of men - and a few pretty girls. Period woodwork and contemporary cuisine, 140-200.

♦♦ *Savoie-Bretagne*, 21, rue Saint-Lazare, ☎ (1) 48.78.91.94, Euro Visa, closed Sat and Sun , eves, 15-30 Aug. Spec : *cœur d'artichaut frais aux crevettes, filets de sole aux pâtes fraîches et au basilic, blanc de turbot au gratin*, 105-200.

♦♦ *Taverne Kronenbourg*, 24, bd des Italiens, ☎ (1) 47.70.16.64, Euro Visa 🅿 ♪ ♿ An authentic Alsatian enclave on the busy Grands Boulevards. Spec : *haddock sur choucroute, pied de cochon grillé sauce béarnaise, brochette de lotte*. Music, 90-140.

● ♦ *Ty Coz*, 35, rue St-Georges, ☎ (1) 48.78.42.95, AE DC Visa, closed Mon and Sun. Sparkling seafood for genuine Breton cuisine, 220.

● ♦ *Bar Romain*, 6, rue Caumartin, ☎ (1) 47.42.98.04, AE DC Euro Visa ♪ ♿ closed Sun, 3-29 Aug. Where showbiz personalities gather to tuck into Paris's best steak tartare. Open until 2 am, 160.

♦ *Le Bœuf Bourguignon*, 21, rue de Douai, ☎ (1) 42.82.08.79 ♪ closed Sun, 3-17 Aug. Good, simple bistro featuring *bœuf bourguignon*. Ex-actors Nathalie Nattier and Robert Willar welcome you, 50-100.

♦ *Pagoda*, 50, rue de Provence, ☎ (1) 48.74.81.48, Visa, closed Sun in Aug. Spec : crab claws, sauteed shrimp, Peking duck, 55-150.

PARIS X

✉ 75010

Hotels :

★★★★ *Chamonix*, 8, rue d'Hauteville, ☎ (1) 47.70.19.49, Tx 641177, AE DC Euro Visa, 35 rm, 600.

★★★ *Gare du Nord*, 33, rue St-Quentin, ☎ (1) 48.78.02.92, AE Euro Visa, 49 rm ॐ 370.

★★★ *National Hôtel*, 224, rue du Fbg-St-Denis, ☎ (1) 42.06.99.56, AE DC Euro Visa, 58 rm ♿ 340.

★★ *Baccarat*, 19, rue des Messageries, ☎ (1) 47.70.96.92, AE DC Euro Visa, 31 rm ♨ ♧ 320.

★★ *Frantour-Château-Landon*, 3, rue de Château-Landon, ☎ (1) 42.41.44.88, AE DC Euro Visa, 161 rm ♿ 340.

Restaurants :

● ♦♦ *Au Chateaubriant*, 23, rue de Chabrol, ☎ (1) 48.24.58.94, AE Visa ॐ closed Mon and Sun , Aug, 1 wk in winter. For more than a decade, Guy Bürkli, that excellent chef, formerly with J. Forno, has been preparing pasta. Spec : *scampi fritti, paglia e fieno alla contadina, zabaglione al marsala*, Italian wines, 250.

● ♦♦ *Chez Michel*, 10, rue de Belzunce, ☎ (1) 48.78.44.14, AE DC Visa 🅿 closed Fri and Sat , 15 days in Feb, 1-24 Aug. A master of classic cuisine, M. Tounissoux upholds the great traditions and prices... Spec : *salade de foie gras à l'effilochée d'endives, filet de bar sur fondue de tomates au basilic, fondant au chocolat*, 300-400.

● ♦♦ *Le Louis XIV*, 8, bd St-Denis, ☎ (1) 42.08.56.56, AE DC Visa 🅿 ♿ closed Mon and Tue, 31 May-1 Sep. A fine establishment serving cuisine in the grand tradition. The spit-roasted meats and charcoal grills are textbook examples of what such fare should be, 220-310.

● ♦♦ *Le New-Port*, 79, rue du Fbg-St-Denis, ☎ (1) 48.24.19.38, AE Visa 🅿 ♧ closed Mon and Sun, 2-24 Aug, 20 Dec-5 Jan. Fish and seafood get top billing : *charlotte de rougets, sole farcie à l'ail et tomate légèrement anisée*, 200.

♦♦ *Brasserie Terminus-Nord*, 23, rue de Dunkerque, ☎ (1) 42.85.05.15, AE DC Visa. A Bucher *brasserie*, complete with turn-of-the-century decor : oysters all year round, *choucroute paysanne, gâteau glacé au caramel*, 100-140.

♦♦ *Casimir*, 6, rue de Belzunce, ☎ (1) 48.78.32.53, AE DC Euro Visa 🅿 closed Sat noon and Sun. Classic dishes, as rich as the bill..., 140-240.

♦♦ *Julien*, 16, rue du Fbg-St-Denis, ☎ (1) 47.70.12.06, AE DC Visa. A long wait, but the welcome and service are quite capably handled. But careful! One meal brought us overcooked sole and mussels, nearly raw french fries. Keep an eye on things, Monsieur Bucher! Thank you, 105-140.

● ♦ *Brasserie Flo*, 7, cour des Petites-Ecuries, ☎ (1) 47.70.13.59, AE DC Visa, closed Aug. Chic, fashionable, up-to-the-minute and everyone waits in line. Uneven cuisine. Oyster and piano bars, 150-250.

● ♦ *La P'tite Tonkinoise*, 56, rue du Fbg-Poissonnière, ☎ (1) 42.46.85.98, Visa ♪ closed Mon and Sun, 1 Aug-15 Sep, 22 Dec-5 Jan. For the cognoscenti, one of the capital's best examples of Vietnamese cuisine, prepared by the Costa family : *nems*, stuffed crab, filet of goose or duck roasted with five flavours, 160.

♦ *Aux Deux Canards*, 8, rue du Faubourg-Poissonière, ☎ 47.70.03.23 The first restaurant for non-smokers in Paris. More will surely follow. Classic cooking : Barbary ducks *à l'orange* or *au poivre vert*, 90-180.

PARIS XI

✉ 75011

Hotels :

★★★★ *Holiday Inn*, 10, pl. ' de la République, ☎ (1) 43.55.44.34, Tx 210651, AE DC Euro Visa, 333 rm 🅿 ♪ ♠ ॐ 1280. Rest. ♦♦ *La Belle Epoque* ♪ ♿ ॐ 150-195 ; child : 45.

★★★ *Le Méridional*, 36, bd Richard-Lenoir, ☎ (1) 48.05.75.00, AE DC Euro Visa, 36 rm, 450.

★★ *Nord et de l'Est*, 49, rue de Malte, ☎ (1) 47.00.71.70, Visa, 44 rm ॐ closed 25 Jul-1 Sep, 24 Dec-3 Jan, 210.

★★ *Royal Voltaire*, 53, rue Richard-Lenoir, ☎ (1) 43.79.75.67, AE DC Euro Visa, 55 rm, 230.

Restaurants :

● ♦♦ *A Sousceyrac*, 35, rue Faidherbe, ☎ (1) 43.71.65.30, AE Visa ॐ closed Sat and Sun , Aug. Since 1923, good food has been a family affair with the Asfaux. It's delicious, not too expensive and generously served : *terrine de foie gras frais, ris de veau entier aux champignons*, cassoulet on Wed and Fri, 120-220.

● ♦♦ *Chez Philippe*, 106, rue de la Folie-Méricourt, ☎ (1) 43.57.33.78 🅿 closed Sat and Sun , Aug. Warm, friendly Philippe Serbource directs family members and charming colleagues. Rich, splendid Southwestern fare. The cellar is the boss's pride, 220.

● ♦♦ *Chez Fernand*, 17, rue de la Fontaine-au-Roi, ☎ (1) 43.57.46.25, closed Sat noon and Sun , Aug. Fernand is inspired by good things from Normandy : *raie au camembert, émincé de canard au cidre et pommes*, camemberts aged on the premises, *tarte aux pommes, crêpes*. The prices are modest, and the little fixed meal is nearly a giveaway, 85-150.

● ♦♦ *Le Pêché Mignon*, 5, rue Guillaume-Bertrand, ☎ (1) 43.57.02.51, Visa ♪ ♿ closed Mon and Sun , Aug, 1 wk at Easter. Cuisine in tune with the seasons and the tides : *mosaïque de trois poissons, panaché de poissons fins à la julienne de légumes, rouelles de ris de veau braisé*, 195.

● ♦ *Le Repaire de Cartouche*, 8, bd des Filles-du-Calvaire, ☎ (1) 47.00.25.86, AE Visa ♿ closed Sun, 25 Jul-23 Aug. A fine place for Southwestern fare, 90-210.

● ♦ *Astier*, 44, rue J.-P.-Timbaud, ☎ (1) 43.57.16.35, Visa, closed Sat and Sun , Aug. Michel Picquart continues to watch over his kitchen and cellar, and to keep prices down, 95.

● ♦ *La Maison des Antilles (Restaumagre)*, pl. des Antilles, ☎ (1) 43.48.77.17, Tx 213810, AE DC ♨ ♪ ♿ A market just like in the islands, an exotic *brasserie* dubbed *Les Quatre Vents*, and a restaurant, Le *Beauharnais*. Refresh your vacation memories, or just get to know Martinique, Guadeloupe, Guyana and the Réunion islands, 50-170.

♦ *Chez Paul*, 13, rue de Charonne, ☎ (1) 47.00.34.57, closed Sat and Sun , hols, Aug, 2 wks in Sep. M. and Mme Paul's generous cuisine, 70-120.

PARIS XII

⊠ 75012

Hotels :
★★★ *Azur*, 5, rue de Lyon, ☎ (1) 43.43.88.35, AE Visa, 62 rm, 360.
★★★ *Modern'Hôtel Lyon*, 3, rue Parrot, ☎ (1) 43.43.41.52, AE Visa, 53 rm 🏊 385.
★★★ *Paris-Lyon Palace*, (Inter-Hôtel), 11, rue de Lyon, ☎ (1) 43.07.29.49, AE DC Euro Visa, 128 rm ♿ 420.
★★★ *Terminus Lyon*, 19, bd Diderot, ☎ (1) 43.43.24.03, Tx 230702, AE Euro Visa, 61 rm, 370.
★★ *Frantour-Gare de Lyon*, 2, Pl. Louis-Armand, ☎ (1) 43.44.84.84, Tx 217094, AE DC Euro Visa, 315 rm ♿ 450.

Restaurants :
● ◆◆◆ *Au Pressoir*, 257, av. Daumesnil, ☎ (1) 43.44.38.21, Euro Visa Ⓟ closed Sat and Sun, Aug and Feb school hols. A brand-new decor, and delicious cuisine by Henri Seguin : *terrine de deux foies, bar en peau, ris de veau aux noix et au lard*, 280-300.
◆◆◆ *Le Train Bleu*, 20, bd Diderot, ☎ (1) 43.43.09.06, DC Euro Visa Ⓟ The landmark turn-of-the-century dining room is alone worth the trip ; the food is not, 195-230.
● ◆◆ *Trou Gascon*, 40, rue Taine, ☎ (1) 43.44.34.26, Visa Ⓟ ♿ closed Sat and Sun, 15 Jul-15 Aug, 25 Dec-1 Jan. Now the annex of Alain Dutournier, installed rue Castiglione at the *Carré des Feuillants*, the Trou Gascon is in the capable hands of Mme Dutournier. Southwestern specialties : *raviolis de crabe au basilic, saumon rôti au chou tendre, cassoulet "Trou Gascon"*. Wonderful collection of Armagnacs, 250.
● ◆◆ *Epicure 108*, 22, rue Fourcroy, ☎ 47.63.34.00, Visa - closed Sat noon and Sun. Just 30 places here, their occupants carefully pampered by M. and Mme Pequignot : *spirale de poissons crus, lotte rôtie à la gentiane, rognonnade d'agneau, gâteau opéra chocolat à l'orange*. An elegant fixed-price offering available in the evening, 175.
● ◆◆ *La Gourmandise*, 271, av. Daumesnil, ☎ (1) 43.43.94.41, AE DC Visa Ⓟ ♪ ♿ closed Sat noon and Sun, 12-19 Apr, 9-23 Aug. Alain Denoual is a worthy chef who deserves your encouragement : *salade d'épinards et de magret fumé, fricassée de langoustines en feuille de choux, agneau au miel*, 135-220.
◆◆ *La Tour d'Argent*, 6, pl. de la Bastille, ☎ (1) 43.49.90.32 The "other one". A pretty *brasserie* decorated by Slavik. Seafood, *choucroute*, moderate prices, 150.

PARIS XIII

⊠ 75013

Hotels :
★★ *Gobelins*, 57, bd St-Marcel, ☎ (1) 43.31.79.89, 45 rm, 280.
★★ *Résidence des Gobelins*, 9, rue des Gobelins, ☎ (1) 47.07.26.90, Tx 206566, AE DC Euro Visa, 32 rm ♪ 280.
★★ *Véronèse*, 5, rue Véronèse, ☎ (1) 47.07.20.90, 66 rm 🏊 170.

Restaurants :
● ◆◆◆ *Les Vieux Métiers de France*, 13, bd Auguste-Blanqui, ☎ (1) 45.88.90.03, AE DC Euro Visa ♪ A talented and inventive chef, Michel Moisan. More than 1000 bottles in the cellar to go with his specialties : *cocotte d'oursins, turbotin belle Gabrielle, langoustines maraîchères*, 185-350.
● ◆◆ *Le Petit Marguery*, 9, bd de Port-Royal, ☎ (1) 43.31.58.59, AE DC Euro Visa, closed Mon and Sun, Aug, 24 Dec-2 Jan. The Cousin brothers shop, cook and run their restaurant with exemplary good humour : *wild mushrooms, game in season, coquilles Saint-Jacques*, 120-230.
● ◆◆ *Le Ti Koc*, 13, pl. de Vénitie, ☎ (1) 45.84.21.00, Visa. The Asian community's cabaret for the whole family. Music and singers, just like back home. Chinese food, *dim sum*, 200.

● ◆◆ *Les Algues*, 66, av. des Gobelins, ☎ (1) 43.31.58.22, AE Visa Ⓟ ♿ closed Mon and Sun, 2-24 Aug, 20 Dec-5 Jan. Sparkling fresh fish : *nage de rougets, plie soufflée au crabe sauce basilic*, 90-200.
◆◆ *Chinatown Olympiades*, 44, av. d'Ivry, ☎ (1) 45.84.72.21, Euro Visa. Chic Chinese cooking at brasserie prices, 120-210.
◆◆ *Le Traiteur*, 28, rue de la Glacière, ☎ (1) 43.31.64.17, AE DC Euro Visa Ⓟ ♪ ♿ 🏊 closed Sat and Sun, 1-20 May, 20 Dec-10 Jan. Classic cuisine with a terrace in fine weather, 90-175.
● ◆ *Hawaï*, 87, av. d'Ivry, ☎ (1) 45.86.91.90, Visa ♪ 🏊 closed Thu. The Asiatic version of Lipp : a-see-and-be-seen brasserie. Spec : *soupe Tonkinoise*, beef *tau bay*, skewered shrimp, rice with spare ribs, 80.
◆ *Berges (Chez Jacky)*, 109, rue du Dessous-des-Berges, ☎ (1) 45.83.71.55 🍷 ♪ closed Sat and Sun, 31 Jul-1 Sep. A friendly spot worth seeking out. The owner shops at the Rungis market, 250.

PARIS XIV

⊠ 75014

Hotels :
★★★★(L) *Le Méridien Montparnasse*, 19, rue du Cdt-Mouchotte, ☎ (1) 43.20.15.51, Tx 200135, AE DC Euro Visa, 952 rm Ⓟ 🍷 🏨 ♪ ♿ 🏊 1250. Rest. ● 🍷 *Le Montparnasse "25"* ♪ ♿ 🏊 closed Sun, 3-31 Aug. Overseen by chef Raoul Gaïga, a real pro. In a 1920s setting, comfortable, contemporary food : *bourride à la provençale, dos de turbot rôti*, 195-400 ◆ *La Ruche* 🍷 ♪ ♿ Open all day. Buffet until 10pm, 140-200 ; child : 70. ◆ *Le Park* 🍷 ♪ ♿ (l.s.). In fine weather, dine in the pretty garden. Buffet, grills, barbecue. *Le Corail* - Piano-bar, 120-150.
★★★★(L) *Pullman Saint-Jacques* (ex P.L.M.), 17, bd St-Jacques, ☎ (1) 45.89.89.80, Tx 270740, AE DC Euro Visa, 797 rm Ⓟ 🍷 ♪ ♿ 900. Rest. ◆ *Le Café Français* ♪ 160-215 ◆ *Le Patio* ♪ 100.
★★ *Le Châtillon*, 11, sq. de Châtillon, ☎ (1) 45.42.31.17, 31 rm 🍷 ♿ closed Aug, 190.
★★ *Midi*, 4, av. René-Coty, ☎ (1) 43.27.23.25, 50 rm, 260.
★★ *Moulin Vert*, 74, rue du Moulin-Vert, ☎ (1) 45.43.65.38, Tx 260818, AE DC Euro Visa, 28 rm 🍷 ♪ 290.

Restaurants :
● ◆◆◆ *Chez Albert*, 123, av. du Maine, ☎ 43.20.05.19, closed Fri eve and Sat. This is obviously a lucky restaurant (André Daguin, J.-P Vigato practiced here). Stéphane Pruvot knows his way around a kitchen, and his future looks bright. *Tête de veau ravigote, ris de veau poêlé*. Excellent meat, 250-300.
● ◆◆◆ *Le Duc*, 243, bd Raspail, ☎ (1) 43.22.59.59, Tx 204896, closed Mon, Sat, Sun. Depending on what's best and freshest at the Rungis market (the world's biggest port), Paul and Jean Minchelli serve a dazzling array of fresh fish and seafood. They 'invented' raw fish (sea bass, scallops, salmon) and lots of other good things : *rougets en vessie, sole au vinaigre. soupe tiède de langoustines*. Branches in Geneva and the Seychelles, 300-500.
● ◆◆◆ *Les Armes de Bretagne*, 108, av. du Maine, ☎ (1) 43.20.29.50, AE DC Euro Visa Ⓟ 🍷 ♿ closed Mon and Sun eve ex hols, 4-31 Aug. Fine seafood in a Napoléon-III setting, 200-300.
● ◆◆ *Aux Iles Marquises*, 15, rue de la Gaîté, ☎ (1) 43.20.93.58, AE Visa ♪ ♿ closed Sat noon and Sun. Mathias Thery, a Troisgros alumnus, presides in the kitchen. Hurry now to try his fish and seafood dishes before the neighbourhood is overrun (the *Bobino* just reopened!), 105-230.
● ◆◆ *Gérard et Nicole*, 6, av. Jean-Moulin, ☎ (1) 45.42.39.56, Visa Ⓟ closed Sat and Sun , wk of Aug 15. In a decor that they and their patrons admire, Gérard and Nicole are as friendly as ever, and their cooking just as delicious : *raviolis de langoustines, filets de rouget à l'huile d'olive*. Loire Valley wines, 250-280.
● ◆◆ *La Cagouille*, 10-12, place Brancusi, ☎ (1) 43.22.09.01, closed Mon and Sun, Jul. Everything

here is spanking new, including (especially) the luminously fresh fish purchased nightly at the Rungis wholesale food market. Owner Gérard Allemandou selects the engaging wines and prepares the simple, simply marvelous food. A Charentes native, he collects fine Cognacs - some date back to 1805! 250-300.

● ◆◆ *L'Assiette*, 181, rue du Château, ☎ (1) 43.22.64.86, AE DC Euro Visa, closed Mon and Tue. 'Lulu' has redecorated. Prices haven't risen in consequence, quality is high as ever, and portions of her excellent Béarnais cuisine are just as generous. Wear your *béret basque*, 180-230.

● ◆◆ *Lous Landès-Hervé Rumen* , 157, av. du Maine, ☎ (1) 45.43.08.04, Euro Visa ♪ ♿ closed Mon noon and Sun. Georgette has taken her well-deserved rest; now Hervé Rumen oversees the harmony of the kitchen and dining room. Hearty cuisine, 180-300.

● ◆◆ *La Chaumière des Gourmets*, 22, pl. Denfert-Rochereau, ☎ (1) 43.21.22.59, DC Euro Visa Ⓟ ⪦ ⼌ closed Sat and Sun , 8-15 Mar, Aug. Freshened decor for Jean Becquet's delicious cuisine : *salade de ris de veau aux navets, marmite dieppoise*, game in season, 150-205.

● ◆◆ *Le Dôme*, 108, bd du Montparnasse, ☎ (1) 43.35.25.81, closed Mon. On the walls, 75 years' worth of photos record the history of this Montparnasse hot spot. Owner Claude Bras bought a nearby fish market to make sure his seafood is super-fresh. For a decade now, chef Paul Canal has cooked it expertly. Good wines, 200-300.

◆◆ *André Provost*, 1, rue de Coulmiers, ☎ (1) 45.39.86.99, AE Euro Visa Ⓟ closed Sat and Sun. Spec : *salade de pied de cochon, andouillette tirée à la ficelle, foie de veau au citron vert*, 260.

◆◆ *La Chaumière Paysanne*, 7, rue Léopold-Robert, ☎ (1) 43.20.76.55, AE DC Euro Visa ⪦ ♪ ♿ closed Mon noon and Sun, 8-25 Aug. Didier Bondu's nicely executed cuisine changes often. Spec : *tartare de langouste, paupiette de lotte, pied de veau braisé au foie gras*, 150-220.

◆◆ *La Coupole*, 102, bd du Montparnasse, ☎ (1) 43.20.14.20, Euro Visa, closed Aug. A 1925 decor, picturesque patrons, and the food is quite good, 120-180.

◆◆ *La Guérite du Saint-Amour*, 209, bd Raspail, ☎ (1) 43.20.64.51 A *guérite* is a shelter, and this one is newly decorated. Fish is the specialty, and the Saint-Amour (a Beaujolais *cru*) flows, 120-230.

◆◆ *Le Moniage Guillaume*, 88, rue de la Tombe-Issoire, ☎ (1) 43.27.09.88, AE DC Euro Visa Ⓟ ⼌ ⪦ ♪ 5 rm, closed Sun. Spec : fish, seafood, shellfish (kept live in a tank), seafood *cassoulet*, 185-280.

◆◆ *Sarava*, 160, av. du Maine, ☎ (1) 43.22.23.64, AE DC Euro Visa ♪ closed Mon, 24 Dec-15 Jan. Brazilian atmosphere. Cuisine and service need improvement, 160-200.

● ◆ *Au Feu Follet*, 5, rue Raymond-Losserand, ☎ (1) 43.22.65.72 ♪ ♿ closed Sun and lunch, 18 Jul-18 Aug. A friendly little place where the hostess does the cooking. *Bœuf mode, brandade de morue* served until late at night, 140.

◆ *Le Bar à Huîtres*, 112, bd du Montparnasse, ☎ (1) 43.20.71.01, AE Visa ♪ Spec : seafood platter, *filet de turbot au caviar d'aubergines, choux à la crème chantilly*, 200.

◆ *Le Flamboyant*, 11, rue Boyer-Barret, ☎ (1) 45.41.00.22, closed Mon, Tue noon, Sun eve , Easter and Aug. The sun of the Antilles at your table, 150-250.

◆ *Léni Restaurant*, 7, rue Francis de Pressensé, ☎ (1) 45.41.06.17, closed Mon noon and Tue noon , Xmas school hols. Quite decent family-style food near a popular art film house, 110-130.

◆ *Les Petites Sorcières*, 12, rue Liancourt, ☎ (1) 43.21.95.68, Euro Visa, closed Mon, Sat noon, Sun , Aug, 1 wk at Xmas. Simple, pleasant cooking. Delightful reception, 70-150.

> For the translation of a name of a meat, a fish or a vegetable, for the composition of a dish or a sauce, see the Menu Guide in the Practical Holiday Guide; it lists the most common culinary terms.

PARIS XV

✉ 75015

Hotels :

★★★★(L) *Hilton International Paris*, 18, av. de Suffren, ☎ (1) 42.73.92.00, AE DC Euro Visa, 480 rm 29 apt Ⓟ ⪦ ⪦ ♿ ⵰ 1100. Rest. ◆◆◆ *Le Toit de Paris* ⪦ ⵰ closed Sun and at lunch, 27 Jul-28 Aug. A view of the Eiffel Tower comes free with the good cooking in this panoramic dining room, 235-325◆ *La Terrasse* Upgraded coffee-shop, 100-140◆ *Le Western* American meat cooked U.S.-style, 155-200.

★★★★(L) *Nikko*, 61, quai de Grenelle, ☎ (1) 45.75.62.62, 777 rm 9 apt Ⓟ ⪦ ⵰ ⊠ 900. Rest. ● ◆◆◆ *Les Célébrités* ♿ M. Poncet in the dining room and J. Sénéchal in the kitchen make an admirable team. The food is in the tradition of Joël Robuchon, who once headed up the kitchen here. Pastries by J.-P. Hévin, who took first prize in the French chocolate Olympics, 245-475◆◆ *Le Benkay* Traditional Japanese food and *teppenyaki* (food cooked on a hot steel burner), 120-210.

★★★★(L) *Sofitel Paris*, 8-12, rue Louis-Armand, ☎ (1) 45.54.95.00, Tx 200432, AE DC Euro Visa, 635 rm Ⓟ ⪦ ♪ ⊠ A modern luxury hotel near the 'périphérique' highway, 850. Rest. ● ◆◆◆ *Le Relais de Sèvres* R. Durand is a modest but highly competent chef, as his cooking plainly shows. Spec : *saumon en carpaccio et petite friture d'encornets, saumon gratiné à la crème de noix, pruneaux glacés au mascara*, 240-350◆ *La Tonnelle* Simple, carefully cooked food, 110-250.

★★★ *Suffren La Tour*, 20, rue Jean-Rey, ☎ (1) 45.78.61.08, AE DC Euro Visa, 407 rm Ⓟ ⪦ ⼌ ♿ 440. Rest. ◆◆ 150-210.

★★ *Lecourbe*, 28, rue Lecourbe, ☎ (1) 47.34.49.06, Tx 205440, AE DC Euro Visa, 47 rm ⼌ ♪ ♠ 330.

★★ *Pacific Hôtel*, 11, rue Fondary, ☎ (1) 45.75.20.49, Euro, 66 rm, 240.

Restaurants :

● ◆◆◆ *La Maison Blanche*, 82, bd Lefèbvre, ☎ (1) 48.28.38.83, AE ♪ ♿ closed Mon, Sat noon, Sun, 1-15 Sep. In a chic and sober off-white decor a bit larger than before, José Lampreia finally has room to move. Amid a riot of greenery and white blossoms he serves forth delicious specialties that delight his ever more numerous patrons. Surprisingly reasonable prices : *farcis d'oursin au pied de porc, tendron de veau aux épices, cabillaud au chou et lard, gâteau au chocolat*, 150-250.

● ◆◆◆ *Ravi*, 214, rue de la Croix-Nivert, ☎ (1) 45.31.58.09. The sumptuous, appetizing annex of Ravi Gupta. Just like the old days of the Raj. Spec : grills, 300.

● ◆◆◆ *Morot-Gaudry*, 6, rue de la Cavalerie, ☎ (1) 45.67.06.85, Visa ⪦ ⪦ closed Sat and Sun. With a picture-postcard view of the Eiffel Tower and the rooftops of Paris, Jean-Pierre Morot-Gaudry's is a captivating spot, where he will entice you with subtle cuisine and choice wines : over 600 different vintages, some available by the glass. *Mousseline d'huître au coulis de homard, crépinette de pieds aux pommes, roast grouse* (in season), 200-250.

● ◆◆◆ *Olympe*, 8, rue Nicolas-Charlet, ☎ (1) 47.34.86.08, AE DC Visa, closed Mon, Sat noon, Sun noon, 1-22 Aug, 22 Dec-4 Jan. Charming Dominique Nahmias now cooks lunches too. Evenings draw her fashionable fans who rave about creations like : *daurade aux artichauts et pommes de terre sautées à la sauge, terrine de pied de veau vinaigrette de poivrons tièdes.* Husband Albert oversees the list of pleasant little wines : white Burgundies, Côtes du Rhône, 180-420.

● ◆◆◆ *Pierre Vedel*, 19, rue Duranton, ☎ (1) 45.58.43.17 ⵰ closed Sat and Sun, 5 Jul-2 Aug, 24 Dec-3 Jan. In a bistro full of friends and acquaintances, chef Pierre Vedel (a weight-lifting buff) prepares fine classic dishes at moderate prices : *tête de veau, côte de bœuf aux champignons, blanquette d'huîtres de bouzigues* (in winter), *bourride.* Remarkable list of inexpensive wines, 180-250.

● ◆◆ *Aux Senteurs de Provence*, 295, rue Lecourbe, ☎ (1) 45.57.11.98, AE DC Euro Visa ♿ closed Mon and

Sun. A new little spot for fresh fish, reasonably tariffed. Genuine *bouillabaisse, bourride, aïoli,* 135-210.

● ◆◆ **Aux Trois Horloges**, 73, rue Brancion, ☎ (1) 48.28.24.08, AE DC Euro Visa ♪ Genuine Franco-Algerian food just like his late mother used to make, prepared by Bernard Pons : *couscous, paëlla, méchoui, sepia, brochettes.* Home delivery, 150.

● ◆◆ **L'Aquitaine**, 54, rue de Dantzig, ☎ (1) 48.28.67.38, AE DC Euro Visa ♪ closed Mon and Sun. Seven young women, all capable cooks, serve forth fine Southwestern fare under the direction of Christiane Massia. *Petits gris d'Aquitaine, marmite du pêcheur aux fines herbes, faux-filet de Chalosse aux cèpes.* Regional wines, 300.

● ◆ **La Petite Bretonnière**, 2, rue de Cadix, ☎ (1) 48.28.34.39, AE Visa ♪ closed Sat noon and Sun, 3-24 Aug. Little by little, Alain Lamaison is building his nest, a very pretty one that sets off his cuisine to perfection, 230.

● ◆◆ **Restaurant du Marché**, 59, rue Dantzig, ☎ (1) 48.28.31.55, AE DC Euro Visa. The Massia family's first restaurant. Excellent, generous cuisine of the Landes region. Wines of Chalosse, Tursan, Madiran. Wine and food items to take out, 250.

● ◆◆ **Yvan Castex**, 15, rue Desnouettes, at the corner of 2, rue de Langeac, ☎ (1) 48.42.55.26, AE DC Euro Visa ♪ ৬ closed Sun, 20-28 Feb, 10-31 Aug. Outstanding fare at utterly reasonable prices, 120-200.

● ◆◆ **Au Petit Mirabeau**, 3, rue de la Convention, ☎ (1) 45.77.95.79 ♪ closed Sat and Sun hols, 1 Jan, Aug, 25 Dec. Good, traditional fare by chef Bessière (*le Mouton Blanc)*, 70-200.

● ◆◆ **La Gauloise**, 59, av. de la Motte-Picquet, ☎(1) 47.34.11.64, AE DC Visa, closed Sat and Sun. Friendly spot, pleasant food, 250.

● ◆◆ **Le Clos de la Tour**, 22, rue Falguière, ☎ (1) 43.22.34.73, AE DC Euro Visa ও ♪ closed Sat noon and Sun, 3-26 Aug. A profusion of paintings and flowers, a short, well-designed menu, 240.

◆◆ **Bermuda Onion**, 16, rue Linois, ☎ (1) 45.75.11.11, AE DC Visa ঌ ⬜ ♪ closed 1 May. P. Derderian's latest brainchild. American decor, with white sand on the terrace in summer. Beautiful girls, good food, 220.

◆◆ **Bistrot "121"**, 121, rue de la Convention, ☎ (1) 45.57.52.90, AE DC Euro Visa ৬ closed Mon and Sun eve, 12 Jul-18 Aug, 20 Dec-1 Jan. A Parisian institution, in the Moussié family tradition, 190-350.

◆◆ **Chez Maître Albert**, 8-10, rue de l'Abbé-Groult, ☎ (1) 48.28.36.98, AE DC Euro Visa ও ♪ closed Mon. Pictures by Beaux-Arts students adorn the walls. Spec : *filets de sardines marinés au citron, bouillabaisse en filets*, 150-200.

◆◆ **Le Clos Morillons**, 50, rue des Morillons, ☎ (1) 48.28.04.37, Visa, closed Sat noon and Sun, 1-21 Jan. Pierre Vedel's old place is now home to a couple of worthy young restaurateurs : *terrine de lentilles vertes au foie gras, escalope de sandre*, 145-180.

◆◆ **L'Etape**, 89, rue de la Convention, ☎ (1) 45.54.73.49, Euro Visa ♪ ৯ closed Sat noon and Sun. Reasonably inexpensives, 110-220.

◆◆ **Marcel Prout**, 19, av. Félix-Faure, ☎ (1) 45.57.29.89, Visa, closed Sun. For lovers of Southwestern specialties, a restaurant with show-biz connections : *foie gras, salades au magret, confit.* Nicely chosen little Bordeaux wines, 120-150.

● ◆ **La Gitane**, 53 bis, av. de la Motte-Picquet, ☎ (1) 47.34.62.92, closed Sat and Sun. A real neighbourhood bistro, annex of *La Gauloise*. Patronized by journalists and politicians, 120-150.

● ◆ **Le Carouzier**, 8, av. du Maine, ☎ (1) 45.48.14.38, Visa, closed Mon and Sun, 15 Jul-2 Sep. All kinds of *couscous*. Good *merguez* sausages and *pastillas*, 120.

● ◆ **Le Volant**, 13, rue Béatrix-Dussane, ☎ (1) 45.75.27.67, Visa, closed Sat noon and Sun,

1-15 Aug. This friendly restaurant is the H.Q. of racing drivers. Warm, smiling young G. Houel dispenses tasty, robust cuisine : *foie de veau au vinaigre de xérès, pruneaux à l'orange*, 75-130.

● ◆ **Napoléon et Chaix**, 46, rue Balard, ☎ (1) 45.54.09.00, Visa ও ♪ ৬ closed Sat noon and Sun , Aug. 'Dédé' Pousse takes time out between a film shoot and a cycling competition to help out his wife, Jocelyne, in their little restaurant. G. Magnan is in the kitchen : homemade pasta, catch of the day, 140-280.

◆ **L'Amanguier**, 51, rue du Théâtre, ☎ (1) 45.77.04.01, AE DC Visa ♪ closed 1 May. Quick service, tasty, inexpensive food. Other branches at Ternes, tel. 43.80.19.28; Neuilly, tel. 47.45.79.73 ; Richelieu, tel. 42.96.37.79, 130.

◆ **La Datcha Lydie**, 7, rue Dupleix, ☎ (1) 45.66.67.77, Visa ও ♪ ৬ closed Wed, 15 Jul-31 Aug. A friendly Russian restaurant-cum-grocery : borscht, *chashlik*, smoked salmon, 90-150.

◆ **La Pastilla**, 7, rue d'Alençon, ☎ (1) 45.48.40.96 Moroccan specialties : excellent *couscous* and *pastilla*, 85-140.

◆ **Le Pacifico**, 50, bd du Montparnasse, ☎ (1) 45.48.63.87, closed Mon noon. Mexican food : *tacos, enchiladas, guacamole*, 80-120.

PARIS XVI

⊠ 75016

Hotels :

★★★★(L) **Raphaël**, 17, av. Kléber, ☎ (1) 45.02.16.00, Tx 610356, AE DC Euro Visa, 87 rm ঌ ♪ ক ৬ 990. Rest. ◆◆ ♪ ৬ 180-250.

● ★★★★ (L) **St-James Club**, 5 pl. Chancelier-Adenauer, ☎ (1) 47.04.29.29, Tx 643850, AE DC Euro Visa, 38 rm ⬜ ঌ ⬜ How times change! Admission requirements to the St-James Club also Henceforth they are open with rooms and suites discreetly decorated by Renée Putman who has greated one of the Capital's loveliest residences. Billiards, sauna, gym, 2 000. Rest. ● ◆◆◆◆ Quality cuisine restricted to hotel guests and club members, 220-400.

★★★★ **Alexander**, 102, av. Victor-Hugo, ☎ (1) 45.53.64.65, Tx 610373, 62 rm ৯ 710.

★★★★ **Baltimore**, 88 bis, av. Kléber, ☎ (1) 45.53.83.33, Tx 611591, AE DC Euro Visa, 119 rm, 1080. Rest. ● ◆◆◆ **L'Estournel**, closed Sat and Sun , Aug. For your pleasure, a disciple of J. Robuchon is at work in the kitchen : *raviolis de crabe à l'orange, Saint-Pierre en habit vert au velouté de pistaches*, 185-350.

★★★★ **Résidence du Bois** (R.C.), 16, rue Chalgrin, ☎ (1) 45.00.50.59, 19 rm ⬜ ঌ 1000.

★★★ **la Muette**, 32, rue de Boulainvilliers, ☎ (1) 45.25.13.08, AE DC Euro Visa, 13 rm ⬜ ঌ ♪ 380.

★★ **Villa d'Auteuil**, 28, rue Poussin, ☎ (1) 42.88.30.37, 17 rm, 195.

Restaurants :

● ◆◆◆◆ **Faugeron**, 52, rue de Longchamp, ☎ (1) 47.04.24.53, closed Sat and Sun , Aug, 24 Dec-2 Jan. Three cheers! And our sincere congratulations. For the second consecutive time, a French sommelier is named 'world champion' : J.-C. Jambon. For more than a decade, he has capably administered *Faugeron*'s exceptional cellar, where affordable bottles are also to be found. Guests are welcomed by the charming Gerlinde, and chef Henri Faugeron combines flavours and scents in an ideal symphony of which the Corrèze region provides the earthy notes. What a team! *Œufs coque à la purée de truffes, cervelas de ris de veau, filet de bœuf rané à la vinaigrette de champignons, sablés à l'anis et aux framboises.* Business lunches, 350-400.

● ◆◆◆◆ **Jamin**, 32, rue de Longchamp, ☎ (1) 47.27.12.27, AE DC Visa ♪ closed Sat and Sun, Jul. What else can we say about gifted Joël Robuchon, the vice-president of our chefs'panel, about his capable and charming wife Janine, his peerless young brigade, the dining-room staff directed by J.-J. Kement, a tight team if ever there was one. We can only urge you to reserve (far in advance), and rejoice at the treat in store : *gelée*

Be advised that hotels and restaurants in this Guide have perhaps changed addresses; prices indicated are also subject to modifications.

de caviar à la crème de chou-fleur, galette de truffes aux oignons et lard fumé, agneau pastoral aux herbes en salade. Great wines of course, but you'll find inexpensive bottles too, 420.

● ♦♦♦♦ *Jean-Claude Ferrero*, 38, rue Vital, ☎ (1) 45.04.42.42, AE DC Visa ⬜ 🔺 🏵 closed Sat and Sun, 15 Aug-8 Sep, 24 Dec-5 Jan. It's like a breath of the country in Paris : a cosy little town house entirely redone by J.-C. Ferrero who, when he's not supervising the remaining workmen, performs his instinctive culinary magic in the kitchen. A knowledgeable mycologist, Ferrero serves a staggering array of truffles and mushrooms all year round. Andrée extends a smiling welcome. Garden dining room, private rooms, 350-400.

● ♦♦♦♦ *La Grande Cascade*, Bois de Boulogne, ☎ (1) 45.27.33.51, AE DC Euro Visa ℗ 🔺 ⬜ ♪ ⅙ closed eves (15 Oct-15 Apr), 20 Dec-20 Jan. Napoléon III has abandoned his hunting lodge, but André Menut and his brigade have attracted a very posh crowd of clients to fill the gap. Jean Sabine presides over the kitchen. Splendid cellar and lovely terrace for summer days, 195-400.

● ♦♦♦♦ *Le Pré Catelan*, rte de Suresnes, Bois de Boulogne, ☎ (1) 45.24.55.58, DC Euro Visa ℗ ⬜ 🔺 ⅙ closed Mon and Sun eve, 5 Feb-3 Mar. A tireless globetrotter, Gaston Lenôtre's thoughts are never far from his cherished Pré Catelan, capably managed by his wife, Colette. When the sun shines, it's paradise, 480-500.

● ♦♦♦♦ *Le Vivarois*, 192, av. Victor-Hugo, ☎ (1) 45.04.04.31, AE DC Visa ♪ ⬜ ⅙ closed Sat and Sun , Aug. Attention, please! We are here in a shrine to gustatory pleasures. A high priest of seasonal cooking, Claude Peyrot firmly believes in buying fresh foodstuffs at the Rungis market, his appetizing menu attests : *coquilles Saint-Jacques saisonnières en crème de Noilly, poissons au gré de la marée, queue de bœuf au vin rouge.* Luscious pastries, and a wealth of wines, 255-450.

● ♦♦♦ *Le Petit Bedon*, 38, rue Pergolèse, ☎ (1) 45.00.23.66, Visa ♪ closed Sat and Sun , Aug. His many satisfied customers have not swelled Christian Ignace's head. He remains a capable, modest chef, who avoids fads and trends. Be sure to reserve a table : *tourteau frais tante Louise, pigeon au vinaigre de miel, filet de sole au coulis de moules et morilles,* 300.

● ♦♦♦ *Le Toit de Passy*, 94, av. Paul-Doumer, ☎ (1) 45.25.91.21, Visa ℗ 🔺 ⬜ ⅙ closed Sat noon and Sun, 20 Dec-13 Jan. A superb restaurant in the sky, with a lovely outdoor terrace that affords an unbeatable view of the Eiffel Tower. The site inspires chef Yann Jacquot who is very nearly one of the city's best chefs : *soupe d'huîtres au jus de truffes et à l'aneth, langoustines rôties au beurre d'agrume, pigeonneau en croûte de sel.* Exceptional cellar, cigars, 170-300.

● ♦♦♦ *Michel Pasquet*, 59, rue La Fontaine, ☎ (1) 42.88.50.01, AE DC Euro Visa 🔺 ♪ ⅙ closed Sat noon and Sun, 14 Jul-15 Aug. Still the same excellent cuisine and service by members of the family. The elegant new decor is a plus, 160-300.

● ♦♦♦ *Patrick Lenôtre*, 28, rue Duret, ☎ (1) 45.00.17.67, Euro Visa 🏵 closed Sat and Sun, 15 Jul-5 Aug. At last he has his own restaurant, carrying on his family's tradition, 400-450.

● ♦♦♦ *Paul Chêne*, 123, rue Lauriston, ☎ (1) 47.27.63.17, AE DC Visa ℗ closed Sat and Sun, 30 Jul-2 Sep. This restaurant is as solid as an oak, and its wonderful cuisine never goes out of style. In fact, it appears to be coming back into fashion. What a treat to sit down in this pleasant room to a generously served meal. *Maquereaux frais au muscadet, terrine, rognon de veau aux trois moutardes, beignets de pomme, gelée de groseilles.* Appealing wines, 300-350.

● ♦♦♦ *Prunier-Traktir*, 16, av. Victor-Hugo, ☎ (1) 45.00.89.12, AE DC Euro Visa, closed Mon and Tue. Fresh fish served in the 1925 decor, at the bar or to take out. Quality and tradition, 220-360.

● ♦♦♦ *Ramponneau*, 21, av. Marceau, ☎ (1) 47.20.85.40, AE DC Euro Visa ⅙ closed Aug. Stylish and solid. *Terrine, œuf cocotte, côte de bœuf, gigot, charlotte au chocolat.* Fine wines, 350.

● ♦♦♦ *Shogun*, the *Nomadic*, port Debilly,

☎ (1) 47.20.05.04, AE DC Euro Visa ♪ ⅙ 🏵 Europe's biggest Japanese restaurant floats aboard the *Nomadic*. At night, an unforgettable view of the illuminated Eiffel Tower. A guaranteed change of pace : *sashimi, sushi, tempura, teppanyaki, saké* and kimonos. Prices according to the value of the yen, 130-550.

♦♦♦ *Ile de Kashmir*, quai Debilly, accross from 32, av. de New-York, ☎ (1) 47.23.50.97, AE DC Euro Visa ℗ 🔺 ♪ 🏵 Two floating restaurants : *Le Lotus* and *Le Jardin de Shalimar.* Arabian nights setting, Kashmiri cuisine, 125-230.

♦♦♦ *Le Chandelier*, 4, rue Paul-Valéry, ☎ (1) 47.04.55.22, AE DC Visa 🔺 ♪ closed Fri and Sat noon , Sat eve Apr-Sep. Luxurious kosher restaurant in an 18thC town house, supervised by the Paris Beth-Din. Light dishes, 230-350.

● ♦♦ *Le Conti*, 72, rue Lauriston, ☎ (1) 47.27.74.67, AE Visa, closed Sat and Sun. Michel Ranvier, a Troisgros alumnus, fixes fabulous pasta, 250.

● ♦♦ *Le Mouton Blanc*, 40, rue d'Auteuil, ☎ (1) 42.88.02.21, Euro Visa ♪ ⅙ closed 20 Jul-20 Aug. A literary shrine, formerly frequented by Molière and Boileau, where chef Bessières serves a food-lover's feast of quality fare at low prices : *panaché de saucisson, salade de moules, rognons d'agneau.* Fixed-price starter and main course option, 110-170.

● ♦♦ *Le Relais d'Auteuil*, 31, bd Murat, ☎ (1) 46.51.09.54, AE DC Euro Visa ♪ ⅙ closed Sat noon and Sun. Patrick Pignol serves light, youthful, inspired cuisine. Sampling menu, fine wines, 150-250.

● ♦♦ *Pantagruel*, 11, rue de la Tour, ☎ 45.20.09.31, closed Sun. A new home for Christiane and Freddy Israel. Classic, copious dishes : *escargots en cassolette, foie de canard chaud aux myrtilles, turbot au Bouey,* game in season, 250-300.

● ♦♦ *Sous l'Olivier*, 15, rue Goethe, ☎ (1) 47.20.84.81, Visa 🏵 ⬜ 🔺 closed Sat and Sun , hols. The young chef's efforts make this an agreeable place to pause for a meal : *émincé de paleron braisé à la roquette, rable de lapereau au gratin de champignons,* 130-220.

● ♦♦ *Chalet des Iles*, Lac Inférieur, Bois de Boulogne, ☎ (1) 45.88.04.69, DC Visa ℗ 🔺 ♪ ⅙ closed 30 Nov-1 Mar. For canoe buffs ; a real change of scene deep in the Bois de Boulogne. Very pleasant, 130-200.

● ♦ *Aux Trois Obus*, 120, rue Michel-Ange, ☎ (1) 46.51.22.58, Visa A friendly neighbourhood *brasserie* where sports fans gather. Wines chosen by the owner, oyster bar in winter, 150-250.

● ♦ *Brasserie le Stella*, 133, av. Victor-Hugo, ☎ (1) 47.27.60.54, closed 1 wk in Feb and Aug. Chic *brasserie* for power brokers, likable yet furiously fashionable. The owner buys his wines direct from the growers, 160-210.

PARIS XVII

✉ 75017

Hotels :

★★★★(L) *Concorde La Fayette*, 3, pl. du Gal-Koenig, ☎ (1) 47.58.12.84, Tx 650892, AE DC Euro Visa, 1000 rm ℗ ♪ 🔺 ⌄ 1200. Rest. ♦♦♦ *L'Etoile d'Or* ♪ ⅙ Spec : *tartare de poissons fins au caviar,* 210-320. ♦♦ *L'Arc-en-Ciel* in fine weather, the terrace *le Barbecue,* 150-200.

★★★★(L) *Méridien Paris*, 81, bd Gouvion-St-Cyr, ☎ (1) 47.58.12.30, AE DC Euro Visa, 1027 rm 16 apt ℗ Chef Brazier can be proud of his team, 1000. Rest. ● ♦♦♦ *Le Clos Longchamp*, closed Sat and Sun. Featuring J.-M. Huard's light specialties : *filet de lotte et son foie avec algues et pistou, mignon de veau glacé "Orloff",* 180-360. ● ♦♦ *Le Yamato* For regulars and numerous Japanese tourists, 100-160. ♦ *La Maison Beaujolaise* Wash down hearty *charcuterie* with cool Beaujolais, 140-220. ♦ *Le Café Arlequin* An excellent *brasserie,* 100-160. ♦ *Salle Lionel Hampton* ♪ The loss of our friend, the late, lamented Moustache is irreplaceable, but the good jazz keeps rolling along, just as he would have wanted. Every Sun from noon to 3 pm, 'Jazz sur Brunch', big band and an abundant buffet, 230; child : 115.

★★★★ *Splendid Etoile*, 1, av. Carnot, ☎ (1) 47.66.41.41, Tx 280773, 57 rm 🅿 ≪ ♤ ఉ ⚘ 690. Rest. ♦♦ ≪ ఉ closed Sat and Sun , Aug, 250.

● ★★★ *Regent's Garden*, (Mapotel), 6, rue Pierre-Demours, ☎ (1) 45.74.07.30, Tx 640127, AE DC Euro Visa, 40 rm 🅿 ▨ ♤ ♨ Pleasure of a blooming garden in a Napoléon-III residence, 600.

★★★ *Belfast*, 10, av. Carnot, ☎ (1) 43.80.12.10, AE DC Euro Visa, 54 rm 🅿 ≪ ఉ At the foot of the Arch of Triumph, 450.

★★★ *Etoile Pereire* (R.S.), 146, bd Pereire, ☎ (1) 42.67.60.00, Tx 305551, AE DC Euro Visa, 26 rm 🅿 ♤ ⚘ 520.

★★ *Prima Hôtel*, 167, rue de Rome, ☎ (1) 46.22.21.09, AE Visa, 30 rm, 240. Rest. ♦ 80-100.

★★ *Résidence Villiers*, 68, av. de Villiers, ☎ (1) 42.27.18.77, Tx 642613, 28 rm, 255.

Restaurants :

● ♦♦♦ *Michel Rostang*, 20, rue Rennequin, ☎ (1) 47.63.40.77, Tx 649629, Visa 🅿 closed Sat noon and Sun, 1-18 Aug. Michel Rostang thrives in Paris, as does his pretty wife. Their new decor is a most attractive setting for his perfectly executed, inventive cuisine : *canette de Bresse au sang, œufs de caille en coque d'oursin* (Oct-Mar), *filet de sole vapeur au persil*, 200-550. ● ♦♦ *Bistrot d'à Côté*, 10, rue Gustave-Flaubert, ☎ 42.67.05.81. In a turn-of-the-century grocery store, Michel and Marie-Claude Rostang have opened a bistro featuring Lyonnais specialties, 180.

● ♦♦♦ *Alain Morel*, 143, av. de Wagram, ☎ (1) 42.27.61.50, closed Sat noon and Sun. A calm, sober setting in a prestigious neighbourhood worthy of chef Morel's talent. In fine weather, enjoy his light, inspired cuisine on the magnificent terrace. *Salade de pommes de terre au foie gras, pudding à la moelle, côte de boeuf, millefeuille*. Appealing wines, 250-400.

● ♦♦♦ *Apicius*, 122, av. de Villiers, ☎ (1) 43.80.19.66, AE Visa 🅿 closed Sat and Sun, 30 Jul-30 Aug. The new darling of Parisian gourmets, J.-P. Vigato is without doubt a chef on the rise. We welcome him to our chefs'panel. Lucky man : he has a lovely wife and a very pretty restaurant. Fish and *abats* are the house specialties, *Tête de veau remoulade, pied de porc rôti aux cèpes*. Interesting wines, 250-300.

● ♦♦♦ *Guy Savoy*, 18, rue Troyon, ☎ (1) 43.80.40.61, Euro Visa, closed Sat and Sun, 15-31 Jul. In the former Bernardin restaurant Guy Savoy (C.S. H.C.F.) continues to offer his excellent cuisine in a new decor. M. Savoy proposes some excellent choices : *poêlée de moules aux champignons du moment, pommes de terre et lotte rôties à l'échalote confite*, 400-450.

● ♦♦♦ *La Barrière de Clichy*, 1, rue de Paris, ☎ (1) 47.37.05.18, DC Euro Visa, closed Sat noon and Sun, 7-21 Aug. Gifted chef Yves Le Gallès is on his own now, in a fresh, bright decor : *émincé de champignons aux choux, ris de veau aux escargots*, 250-350.

● ♦♦♦ *Le Manoir de Paris*, 6, rue Pierre-Demours, ☎ (1) 45.72.25.25, AE DC Euro Visa 🅿 ♤ closed Sat and Sun, 6 Jul-3 Mar. The new decor signed Pierre Pothier is a much-needed improvement. Francis Vandenhende and his wife, Denise Fabre, now own a fresh, inviting restaurant, a perfect setting for Philippe Groult's fine cooking : *rissoles de lotte aux épices, soupe de homard aux herbes fraîches, pied de porc rieuse à la sauvage*. Appealing wines. Coming soon : a Niçois eatery on the upper floor, 250-300.

● ♦♦♦ *Ma Cuisine*, 18, rue Bayen, ☎ (1) 45.72.02.19, AE Euro Visa 🅿 ♤ ♪ closed Sat noon and Sun. René Sourdeix succeeds Alain Donnard, 205-300.

● ♦♦♦ *Paul et France*, 27, av. Niel, ☎ (1) 47.63.04.24, AE DC Visa, closed Sat and Sun, 14 Jul-15 Aug. Honorary Chef to the Paris soccer team, jovial Georges Romano accompanies the players to all official 'away' matches. A former footballer himself, Romano knows all about competition. He is a fierce defender of fine cuisine, and we are

happy to welcome him as a new member of our chefs' panel. Light, spontaneous creations in tune with the seasons : *raviolis de tourteaux, filet de Saint-Pierre aux coques, pigeon de ferme rôti*. Good wines and Armagnacs. A true southerner, the chef always has a good story to tell, 300.

● ♦♦♦ *Sormani*, 4, rue du Gal-Lanrezac, ☎ (1) 43.80.13.91, Visa, closed Sat and Sun, 18-25 Apr, 2-22 Aug, 23 Dec-4 Jan. In a setting of blue velvet, under the watchful eyes of a plaster Caesar, Pascal Fayet prepares first-rate Italian cuisine, including a gourmet array of pasta : *raviolis, lasagne, spaghettis*... and of course *carpaccio, jambon, rouget*, served with a carefully chosen list of Italian wines, 300.

● ♦♦ *Auberge de Recoules*, 150, bd Pereire, ☎ (1) 43.80.63.22, AE DC Euro Visa ఉ closed Sat and Sun , Aug. When you go in, you see it's really a bistro chic. Simple but high-quality cuisine prepared by Bernard Maire : seafood, remarkable *foie gras*, delicious *andouillette* and very good meats at affordable prices. To satisfy his patrons, owner Pierre Le Hors plans to redecorate, 200-250.

● ♦♦ *Chez la Mère Michel*, 5, rue Rennequin, ☎ (1) 47.63.59.80, Visa, closed Sat and Sun , Aug. The true believer's temple of *beurre blanc*, whipped up by M. Gaillard in his genuine little bistro, 240.

● ♦♦ *Chez Laudrin*, 154, bd Pereire, ☎ (1) 43.80.87.40, AE Euro Visa, closed Sat and Sun. Jacques Billaud, aided and abetted in his new decor by young Jean Jouhanneau serves hearty fare along with tasty wines and Champagne - you are billed only for what you drink : fish, kidneys, tripe, rabbit, 250-300.

● ♦♦ *La Braisière*, 54, rue Cardinet, ☎ (1) 47.63.40.37, Visa, closed Sat and Sun , Aug. Very nice food by talented B. Vaxelaire : *farci de barbue au crabe, délice à la rhubarbe*, 175-230.

● ♦♦ *La Côte de Bœuf*, 4, rue Saussier-Leroy, ☎ (1) 42.27.73.50, AE DC Visa, closed Sat and Sun, 2 Aug-1 Sep. Beef of course, but try the daily specials too, or the seasonal game and the *confits*, all beautifully prepared by S. Delmond, 150.

● ♦♦ *Lajarrige*, 16, av. de Villiers, ☎ (1) 47.63.25.61 ♪ closed Sat noon and Sun, 4 Aug-1 Sep. J.-C. Lajarrige welcomes you into his 17thC decor like the musketeer he is. Southwestern specialties executed by E. Marrottaf, a disciple of André Daguin : *magret de mulard, brandade de morue, grand cassoulet Lajarrige*, 115-185.

● ♦♦ *La Petite Auberge*, 38, rue Laugier, ☎ (1) 47.63.85.51, DC Euro Visa 🅿 closed Mon and Sun, 3 Aug-1 Sep. No words can suffice to describe Léo Harbonnier's delightful cooking. Go see for yourself. Fabulous *millefeuille*, 180-250.

● ♦♦ *La Toque*, 16, rue de Tocqueville, ☎ (1) 42.27.97.75, Visa ♪ closed Sat and Sun, 10 Jul-10 Aug, 23 Dec-5 Jan. Young, talented Jacky Joubert keeps a lid on the prices here. Spec : *escalope de saumon poêlée, cuisse et râble de lapereau au chou*, 170.

● ♦♦ *Le Gouberville*, 1, pl. Charles-Fillion, ☎ (1) 46.27.33.27, Visa ≪ ♤ ♪ closed Mon and Sun, 1-18 Aug. Discreet, provincial charm in the capital. A church, a square and a terrace surrounded by summer greenery. In the pretty dining room, a homey air prevails. *Foie gras frais maison, marmite dieppoise*, 90-200.

● ♦♦ *Le Petit Colombier*, 42, rue des Acacias, ☎ (1) 43.80.28.54, Visa 🅿 closed Sat and Sun noon, 1-17 Aug. A businessman as well as a chef (he heads up the restaurateurs' union), Bernard Fournier practices his craft with brio in a rustic, family-style inn where he keeps a close eye on everything, especially the generous leg of lamb carved tableside, calf's liver, honestly priced, 180-250.

● ♦♦ *Le Relais d'Anjou*, 15, rue de l'Arc-de-Triomphe, ☎ (1) 43.80.43.82, DC Visa ♤ ♪ closed Sat noon and Sun, 20 Jun-17 Jul. Outstanding example of Anjou's regional cuisine. The owner, a real perfectionist, makes his own *rillettes*. Wonderful wines, 200.

● ♦♦ *Le Santenay*, 75, av. Niel, ☎ (1) 42.27.88.44, AE DC Euro Visa ≪ ♤ ♪ closed Mon and Sun eve, 1-20 Aug.

In a pleasant Napoléon-III decor, Francis Vallot serves traditional cooking; his wife provides smiles and lovely bouquets. Spec : *brochet maraîchère*, great red Bordeaux and Burgundies, 250.

● ♦♦ *Michel Comby*, 116, bd Péreire, ☎ (1) 43.80.88.68, AE DC Visa Ⓟ ঙ closed Sat and Sun (open Sat eve Jun-Oct), 23 Feb-16 Mar, 20 Jul-2 Aug. Candlelight and flowers for Michel Comby, happy to be in his own place at last, after years of service at *Lucas Carton*, Here, he expresses his talent freely, to loud applause : *feuilleté de grenouilles au confit de poireaux, cassolette d'escargots chablisienne, rognons de veau*, 135-300.

● ♦♦ *Andrée Baumann*, 64, av. des Ternes, ☎ (1) 45.74.16.66, AE DC Euro Visa ♪ ঙ Delicious *choucroute* in myriad guises : Alsatian, fish, Oriental, with boiled beef, etc...Oyster bar in winter, 100-200.

● ♦♦ *Chez Georges*, 273, bd Pereire, ☎ (1) 45.74.31.00, Visa, closed Aug. Georges Mazarguil maintains his tradition of excellent daily specials; meats carved at your table : *gigot rôti aux flageolets, petit salé aux choux*, 160-220.

● ♦♦ *Chez Guyvonne*, 14, rue de Thann, ☎ (1) 42.27.25.43, Visa ♪ closed Sat and Sun, 10 Jul-3 Aug, 24 Dec-5 Jan. In a peaceful spot near the parc Monceau, refined cuisine. Spec : *émincé de rognons de veau au vin de cornas*, 240.

● ♦♦ *Épicure 108*, 22 rue Foureroy, ☎ (1) 47.63.34.00, Visa closed Sat. noon and Sun. Just 30 places here, their occupants carefully pampered by M. and Mme Pequignot. *Spirale de poissons crus, lotte rôtie à la gentiane, rognonnade d'agneau, gâteau opéra*, chocolat à l'orange. An elegant fixed-price offering avalaible in the evening, 250.

● ♦♦ *La Coquille*, 6, rue du Débarcadère, ☎ (1) 45.72.10.73, AE Visa, closed Mon and Sun , 1 Jan, Aug, Xmas. C. Lansecker continues in the fine tradition of Paul Blache. Fresh shellfish in season, 300.

● ♦♦ *La Soupière*, 154, av. de Wagram, ☎ (1) 42.27.00.73, AE Euro Visa, closed Sat and Sun, 7-23 Aug. Outstanding soups by C. Thuillart, 130-180.

● ♦♦ *Michel Clave*, 10, rue Villebois-Mareuil, ☎ (1) 45.73.29.30 After the *Crillon*, the *Bristol* and the *Café de la Paix*, experienced chef Michel Clave has settled down here to serve you delightful dishes like *crêpes d'oeufs brouillés, blanquette de turbot, glace au chocolat amer*, 250.

● ♦♦ *Pétrus*, 12, pl. du Mal-Juin, ☎ (1) 43.80.15.95, AE DC Euro Visa Ⓟ closed Mon and Sun , Aug. Oyster bar, excellent fish prepared by G. Dugast. *Navarin de homard, petite marmite du pêcheur à la nage*. Impressive cellar supervised by Jean Frambourt, president of the Sommeliers de France, 300.

● ♦ *Le Beudant*, 97, rue des Dames, ☎ (1) 43.87.11.20, AE DC Visa Ⓟ ♪ closed Sat noon and Sun. Tiny, but the regionally inspired cuisine is tasty and well prepared : *foie gras frais maison*, fish, 200-280.

● ♦ *Pommeraie Jouffroy*, 36, rue Jouffroy, ☎ (1) 42.27.39.41, AE DC Visa Ⓟ ♪ closed Sun , Aug. Norman cuisine in all its glory : cider, Calvados, *gratin de pomme*, 120-220.

♦ *Dessirier*, 9, pl. du Mal-Juin, ☎ (1) 43.80.50.72, DC Euro Visa Ⓟ Superb oyster bar all year round, fish prepared the old-fashioned way, 250-350.

♦ *L'Amanguier*, 43, av. des Ternes, ☎ (1) 43.80.19.28, AE DC Visa ♪ closed 1 May, 130.

PARIS XVIII

✉ 75018

Hotels :
● ★★★★ *Terrass* (Mapotel), 12, rue Joseph-de-Maistre, ☎ (1) 46.06.72.85, Tx 280830, AE DC Euro Visa, 108 rm 〆 ๓ 620. Rest. ♦♦ *La Guerlande* ♪ ঙ At the foot of Montmartre, reliable cooking, 180. ♦ *L'Albaron* Fast service until 1am, 75-130.

★★★ *Résidence Montmartre*, 10, rue Burcq, ☎ (1) 46.06.45.28, Visa, 46 rm In a typical street of Old Montmartre, 250.

● ★★ *Tim Hôtel Montmartre*, 11, pl. Émile-Goudeau,

☎ (1) 42.55.74.79, Tx 650508, AE DC Euro Visa, 63 rm 〆 ঙ ♪ ๓. On a charming tree-shaded square, 295.

★★ *Capucines Montmartre*, 5, rue Aristide-Bruant, ☎ (1) 42.52.89.80, Tx 205139, AE DC, 30 rm ঙ ♪ 250.

★★ *Prima-Lepic*, 29, rue Lepic, ☎ (1) 46.06.44.64, Tx 281162, Visa, 38 rm ♪ ❀ 200.

★★ *Royal Montmartre*, 68, bd de Clichy, ☎ (1) 46.06.22.91, 48 rm, 165. Rest. ♦ *Le Chat Noir* Brasserie, 70-80.

Restaurants :
● ♦♦♦♦ *Beauvilliers*, 52, rue Lamarck, ☎ (1) 42.54.54.42, Euro Visa Ⓟ ♪ ❀ closed Mon noon and Sun, 30 Aug-15 Sep. The most blooming decor in Paris (terraces for fine days). Édouard Carlier, a most capable restaurateur (like the figure for whom his house is named) invites you to celebrate the joys of contemporary cuisine : *filets de rougets en fine escabèche, saumon sauvage au curry et julienne d'endives, cassolette de petits gris aux mousserons*. Édouard loves good sherries, so will you. His cellar holds great Châteaux and the best Burgundies, 300.

● ♦♦ *Clodenis*, 57, rue Caulaincourt, ☎ (1) 46.06.20.26, AE DC Euro Visa, closed Mon and Sun. Up on the 'butte' of Montmartre, a young, competent team serves light, inventive dishes in a rosy dining-room. Game in season, 210-300.

● ♦♦ *Les Chants du Piano (Michel Derbanne)*, 10, rue Lambert, ☎ 42.62.02.14. Michel Derbane is back on his feet, playing the 'piano' (a.k.a. the stove) in his usual inspired style : *sorbet de foie gras, médaillon de lapin, cocotte de poulet de Bresse truffé, croustillant de chocolat*, 130-210.

● ♦♦ *Les Fusains*, 44, rue Joseph-de-Maistre, ☎ (1) 42.28.03.69, Visa ঙ ঙ closed Mon and Sun , lunch and Sep. In a warm, friendly atmosphere, dine at the foot of Montmartre, on the terrace in summer. Bernard Mathys serves a fixed-price menu with delights like : *cuisses de grenouilles au vin d'Alsace, pigeonneau aux trois choux*, 230-350.

● ♦♦ *Les Semailles*, 3, rue Steinlen, ☎ (1) 46.06.37.05, AE DC Visa ♪ ঙ closed Mon and Sun, 1-15 Feb, 1-31 Jul. The talented Jean-Jacques Jouteux has moved again. Telephone in advance to be sure that he is here; his presence guarantees an excellent meal, 350-400.

● ♦♦ *Poulbot Gourmet*, 39, rue Lamarck, Visa ♪ his many regulars are enthusiastic about J.-P. Langevin's tasty specialties : *étuvée d'escargots, marmite de poissons*, 180-200.

● ♦♦ *Moucharabieh*, 4, rue Aimé-Lavy, ☎ (1) 42.64.48.70, AE Visa ঙ ♪ closed Mon and Sat noon. The annex of *Wally le Saharien*, serving the famous desert *couscous* and new *tajines* : fish, gambas, lobster, spiny lobster, 150-220.

● ♦♦ *Grandgousier*, 17, av. Rachel, ☎ (1) 43.87.66.12 Ⓟ ঙ closed Sat and Sun , 1 wk in Aug. Excellent food in a delightful little setting : *salade d'écrevisses et foie gras, magret de canard au miel de lavande*, 110-220.

♦ *Le Bateau Lavoir*, 8, rue Garreau, ☎ (1) 46.06.02.00 ঙ ঙ closed Jun. Decent food at decent prices, 65-100.

PARIS XIX

✉ 75019

Hotel :
★★ *Parc*, 1, pl. Armand-Carrel, ☎ (1) 42.08.08.37, 51 rm ๓ 250.

Restaurants :
● ♦♦♦ *Le Pavillon Puebla*, Parc des Buttes-Chaumont, ☎ (1) 42.08.92.62, Visa Ⓟ ๓ ঙ ♪ closed Sat noon and Sun. The Vergès family has changed address. Quiet, greenery, luxury and a new decor for this Belle-Époque house. Original culinary creations : *bouillabaisse glacée, matelote de filets de sardines à la moelle, sole et langoustines aux champignons sylvestres*. Tasty wines, 200-250.

● ♦♦ *La Pièce de Boeuf*, 7, rue Corentin Cariou, ☎ 40.05.95.95, closed Sat and Sun. Guy Cardon's cooking is an excellent reason to head up to La Villette. Fine meat specialties washed down with appealing little house wines, 200.

♦♦ *Au Cochon d'Or*, 192, av. Jean-Jaurès, ☎ (1) 46.07.23.13, AE DC Euro Visa. A new setting for grilled beef *spéciale Cochon d'Or, salade de tête de veau*, 200-360.

♦♦ *La Chaumière*, 46, av. Secrétan, ☎ (1) 46.07.98.62, AE DC Euro Visa ℙ closed Sun , Aug. Spec : *tartare de langue de veau, lotte au coulis de langoustines*, game in season, 70-160.

PARIS XX

✉ 75020

Hotels :
★★ *Pyrénées-Gambetta*, 12, av. du Père-Lachaise, ☎ (1) 47.97.76.57, 30 rm ⌂ 265.
★★ *Unic Hôtel*, 6, rue du Pont-de-l'Eure, ☎ (1) 43.61.93.10, 35 rm ℙ ⌂ closed Aug, 200.

Restaurants :
♦♦ *Relais des Pyrénées*, 1, rue du Jourdain, ☎ (1) 46.36.65.81, AE DC Euro Visa, closed Sat and Aug. Spec : *confit d'oie comme en Béarn, saumon frais au champagne*, 220-310.
● ♦ *Aux Becs Fins*, 44, bd de Menilmontant, ☎ (1) 47.97.51.52, Visa ♪ The local crowd and those in the know adore Laurence Lefebvre's generous bistro cooking : *foie gras frais, cassoulet du Périgord, Saint-Jacques Laurençais*, 120-240.

NEARBY

BOULOGNE-BILLANCOURT, ✉ 92100.

Restaurants :
● ♦♦ *Au Comte de Gascogne*, 89, av. J.-B.-Clément, ☎ (1) 46.03.47.27, AE DC Visa ⌂ closed Sat and Sun , Aug and hols. Beneath the palm trees, delight in the lightened cuisine of the French Southwest : *foie frais de canard, gigotin de lapereau*, 350.
● ♦♦ *L'Auberge* (ex Petite Auberge Franc-Comtoise), 86, av. J.-B.-Clément, ☎ (1) 46.05.67.19, AE DC Euro Visa ⌂ ♪ ⌂ closed Sun and Aug. The peace of Franche-Comté on the banks of the Seine near the Bois de Boulogne. Spec : *blanc de turbot poché au beurre de homard, culotte de lapereau aux pruneaux*, 150-230.
● ♦♦ *La Bretonnière*, 120, av. J.-B.-Clément, ☎ (1) 46.05.73.56, AE DC Euro Visa ℙ ♪ closed Sat and Sun. Marc Laurens plans a facelift for his Breton decor. We can only approve. Classic fare, 240-310.
♦♦ *L'Avant-Seine*, 1, rd-pt Rhin-et-Danube, ☎ (1) 48.25.58.00, Visa, closed Mon and Sun. Just outside Paris, a little spot owned by Gérard Vié, 170-250.

CHENNEVIÉRES-SUR-MARNE, ✉ 94430.

Restaurant :
♦♦ *L'Ecu de France*, 31, rue de Champigny, ☎ (1) 45.76.00.03 ℙ ≼ ⌂ ♪ ✿ closed Mon and Sun eve, 1-7 Sep. A blooming terrace by the riverside, 250.

CLICHY, ✉ 92110.
Car rental : *Avis*, 18, bd Jean-Jaurès, ☎ (1) 47.37.46.53.

Restaurant :
● ♦♦ *La Bonne Table*, 119, bd Jean-Jaurès, ☎ (1) 47.37.38.79, closed Mon and Sun, 20 Aug-20 Sep. Gisèle Berger cooks only sparkling fresh fish, 250.

COURBEVOIE, ✉ 92400.
Car rental : *Avis*, 82, bd de la Mission Marchand, ☎ (1) 43.34.05.00.

Restaurant :
● ♦♦ *Helodidi*, 46, bd de Verdun, ☎ (1) 43.33.53.09, AE DC Visa ℙ ⌂ ♪ closed Sun, 20 Aug-6 Sep. Top-drawer

seafood specialties by J.-P. Crème : *marmite du pêcheur, cassoulet de poisson, turbot fruit de la passion*, 120-200.

GENNEVILLIERS, ✉ 92230.

Hotel :
● ★★ *Résidence Julius*, 14, rue Eugène-Varlin, ☎ (1) 47.92.05.62, Visa, 30 rm ⌂ ⌂ ♪ ⌂ ✿ 400.

Restaurant :
● ♦♦♦ *Julius*, 6, bd Camelinat, ☎ (1) 47.98.77.32, closed Sat and Sun. Top-quality establishment with the accent on comfort. Julien (Julius) Forêt was determined to make his renowned hostelry an equally reputed restaurant. After some extensive construction work, he now supervises an outstanding kitchen : *roulé de saumon au citron vert, suprême de barbue au beurre de tomate, nougat glacé au chocolat amer chaud*, 210-310.

ISSY-LES-MOULINEAUX, ✉ 92130.

Restaurant :
● ♦♦ *Auberge d'Armaillé*, 42, rue Guynemer, ☎ (1) 45.54.70.69, AE DC Euro Visa ℙ ⌂ ⌂ ⌂ closed Sat noon and Sun, 3-27 Aug. Russia on the Seine : caviar, vodka, *koulibiak de saumon frais, poulet à la kievski*, 300.

LEVALLOIS-PERRET, ✉ 92300.

Restaurants :
● ♦♦ *Le Basilic*, 20, rue Ernest-Cognacq, ☎ (1) 47.58.62.06, Visa, closed Sat noon and Sun. Good food in a fresh, green setting, and nice cool wine to accompany it all, 85-200.
♦♦ *Pointaire*, 46, rue de Villiers, ☎ (1) 47.57.44.77, AE DC Visa ♪ closed Sat noon and Sun , Aug. New management. Spec : *savarin de brochet au coulis d'étrilles, sandre au beurre blanc*, 150-230.
● ♦ *La Forge*, 51, rue Louis-Rouquier, ☎ (1) 47.57.87.24, closed Sat noon and Sun. Food grilled over vine-cuttings, 150-200.

LIVRY-GARGAN, ✉ 93190.

Restaurant :
● ♦♦ *Auberge Saint-Quentinoise*, 23, bd de la République, ☎ (1) 43.81.13.08, AE Visa ♪ closed Mon and Sun eve. Michel Nicoleau is an outstanding chef ; now in his own place, he gives his all : *fricassée de homard à l'ail doux, suprême de volailles gratiné aux morilles, truffé au chocolat amer*, 125-220.

MEUDON, ✉ 92190.

Restaurant :
● ♦♦ *Relais des Gardes*, 42, av. du Gal-Gallieni, ☎ (1) 45.34.11.79, AE DC Visa ℙ ♪ closed Sat and Sun eve , Aug. The house is a venerable one, but the cooking is decidedly modern, based on the catch of the day : *chausson à la bénodétoise, pot-au-feu de canard à la Saintongeaise*, 160-250 ; child : 70.

NEUILLY-SUR-SEINE, ✉ 92200.
Car rental : *Avis*, 99, av. Charles-de-Gaulle, ☎ (1) 47.47.10.70.

Hotels :
★★★★ *Hôtel International*, 58, bd V.-Hugo, ☎ (1) 47.58.11.00, Tx 610971, AE DC Euro Visa, 330 rm ℙ ⌂ ⌂ ♪ ⌂ ⌂ 875. Rest. ● ♦♦ *Le Club* ♪ ⌂ vacation going with the famous Club buffet. Occasional theme or ethnic evenings, 140-210.
★★ *Parc*, 4, bd du Parc, ☎ (1) 46.24.32.62, 71 rm, 270.

Restaurants :
● ♦♦♦ *La Truffe Noire*, 2, pl. Parmentier, ☎ (1) 46.24.94.14 ♪ ⌂ ♪ ⌂ closed Sat noon and Sun. A new address for Chantal and Jenny Jacquet. Regional specialties from the Loire Valley accompanied by local wines : *beuchelle tourangelle, mousseline de brochet beurre blanc*, 200.
● ♦♦ *Jacqueline Fénix*, 42, av. Charles-de-Gaulle, ☎ (1) 46.24.42.61, Visa ♪ closed Sat and Sun, 31 Jul-1 Sep, 23 Dec-2 Jan. Jacqueline Fénix extends a charming welcome, and serves very nice cuisine as well, 290-350.

● ♦♦ *La Rascasse*, 10, av. de Madrid, ☎ (1) 46.24.05.30, AE DC Visa, closed Sat and Sun , hols. M. Franza haunts Rungis market nightly, seeking out the freshest fish : *timbale de maquereaux en gelée, lotte à la chartreuse*, 250.

● ♦♦ *La Tonnelle Saintongeaise*, 32, bd Vital-Bouhot, ☎ (1) 46.24.43.15 ≼ ₥ ⌕ ♪ ⅃ closed Sat and Sun , one wk at Easter, 8-30 Aug, 24 Dec-8 Jan. A delightful spot by the water. Summer terrace. Regional cooking : *chaudrée saintongeaise, lapereau sauté au pineau des Charentes*, 150-220.

● ♦♦ *Le Manoir*, 4, rue de l'Église, ☎ (1) 46.24.04.61, AE Visa A. Albert and his wife take good care of you in their handsome establishment. Next door, *L'En-Cas*, the Manoir's wine bar annex, with a fine selection of wines and tasty little snacks, 200-250.

♦♦ *Café de la Jatte*, 67, bd de Levallois, ☎ (1) 47.45.04.20, AE Visa ℗ ≼ closed Sat noon. Terribly fashionable, by the water's edge, and for 150F it's not bad. Reserve, 75-180.

♦ *L'Amanguier*, 12, av. de Madrid, ☎ (1) 47.45.79.73, AE DC Visa ♪ closed 1 May, 130.

♦ *La Chevauchée*, 209 ter, av. du Gal-de-Gaulle, ☎ (1) 46.24.07.87, AE DC Visa ♪ closed Sat noon and Sun, 11 Jul-9 Aug, 100-145.

NOGENT-SUR-MARNE, ⊠ 94130.

Hotel :
★★★ *Nogentel*, 8, rue du Port, ☎ (1) 48.72.70.00, Tx 210116, AE DC Euro Visa, 61 rm ℗ ≼ ♪ 🐎 360. Rest. ♦♦ ♪ closed Aug, 150.

ORLY-AÉROGARE, ⊠ 94390.

Restaurants :
● ♦♦♦ *Maxim's*, Orly aérogare ouest, BP 404, ☎ 46.87.16.16, AE DC Euro Visa Chef Jean Jorda and dining room manager Roger Godeau goes like clockwork, in the great tradition : *sole Albert, terrine Maxim's, colinot rôti aux lardons*, 350-400.

♦♦ *Grill Maxim's*, Aérogare Orly ouest, BP 404, ☎ 46.87.16.16, AE DC Euro Visa, 250.

PUTEAUX, ⊠ 92800.

Restaurant :
● ♦♦ *Gasnier*, 7, bd R.-Wallace, ☎ (1) 45.06.33.63, AE DC Visa ♪ closed Sat and Sun , hols, 1 wk Feb school hols, 26 Jun-3 Aug. Hubert Gasnier, an award-winning chef, cooks good, hearty fare : *foie gras, petits gris, cassoulet*, and a little extravagance, truffle ragoût, 300.

RUEIL-MALMAISON, ⊠ 92500.
Car rental : *Avis*, 31, av. Paul-Doumer, ☎ (1) 47.49.39.29.

Restaurant :
♦♦♦ *El Chiquito*, 126, av. Paul-Doumer, ☎ (1) 47.51.00.53, Euro Visa ₥ ⅃ closed Sat and Sun , Aug. Spec : *gigot de mer aux pâtes fraîches, saumon frais beurre de homard*, 250-280.

SAINT-CLOUD, ⊠ 92210.

Hotel :
★★★ *Villa Henri IV*, 43, bd de la République, ☎ (1) 46.02.59.30, Visa, 36 rm ℗ ⅃ 400. Rest. ♦ ⸙ closed Sat and Sun eve , Aug, 70-200.

Restaurant :
● ♦♦ *Le Florian*, 14, rue de l'Eglise, ☎ (1) 47.71.29.90, AE Visa ℗ ♪ closed Sat noon and Sun eve. The young Outhiers have left their niche on the Ile St-Louis for Saint-Cloud, trading one saint for another. Maybe this one will answer their prayers. Avant-garde dishes : raw salmon, bass with *foie gras* (why not?), 300-350.

SAINT-OUEN, ⊠ 93400.

Restaurant :
● ♦♦ *Le Coq de la Maison Blanche*, 37, bd Jean-Jaurès, ☎ (1) 42.54.01.23, Visa ♪ ⅃ closed Sun. A spacious suburban dining room serving daily specials, 250.

SCEAUX, ⊠ 92330.

Restaurant :
● ♦♦ *L'Orangerie*, 13, rue Michel-Charaire,

☎ (1) 43.50.83.00, Visa ⌕ ⅃ closed Mon and Sun eve, 10 Aug-2 Sep. Young J.-P. Beaudouin is a chef to cultivate for his light, savoury cuisine : *cassolette de ris et rognons de veau aux morilles, foie gras frais maison*, 220.

La VARENNE-SAINT-HILAIRE, ⊠ 94210.

Restaurant :
● ♦♦ *La Bretèche*, 171, quai de Bonneuil, ☎ (1) 48.83.38.73, Euro Visa ⅃ closed Aug. For a nostalgic hour on the banks of the Marne. No more deep-fried minnows, but Max Lamoureux serves many another tasty dish : *œufs pochés à la lie de morgon, andouillettes de saumon*. Great Burgundies, 250-350.

VILLE D'AVRAY, ⊠ 92410.

Restaurant :
● ♦♦ *Le Jardin de Gauvain*, 147, rue de Versailles, ☎ (1) 47.09.63.24, DC Euro ℗ ≼ ₥ ⌕ closed Mon and Sun eve. A likable young team serves a 'menu of the week', 160-190.

 Recommended

Open at night :
Au Pied de Cochon, 6, rue Coquillère, 75001, ☎ (1) 42.36.11.75. Never closes.
Bar Romain, 6, rue Caumartin, 75009, ☎ (1) 47.42.98.04. Where show-biz folk gather until 2am.
Drug Night, 55, bd des Batignolles, 75008, ☎ (1) 42.93.47.49. 6pm-3am, Sat 5am. All-night grocery.
Grand Pub Lady-Hamilton, 82, av. Marceau, 75008, ☎ (1) 47.20.20.40. Where sports fans meet.
L'Epicerie Landaise, 10, rue Princesse, 75006, ☎ (1) 43.26.02.96. Until 7am (closed Sun and Aug).
Le Grand Café Capucines, 4, bd des Capucines, 75009, ☎ (1) 47.42.75.77. Seafood and good daily specials, night and day.
Le Hangar, 12, imp. Berthaud, 75002, ☎ (1) 42.74.55.44. Business dinners until 2am.
Le Muniche et le Petit Zinc, 25-27, rue de Buci, 75006, ☎ (1) 46.33.62.09. Wine and food to go until 3am.
Méridien Paris "Nouveau St-Hilaire", 81, bd Gouvion-Saint-Cyr, 75017, ☎ (1) 47.58.12.30. Night-club, spaghetti fest around 3am.
Théâtre du Rond-Point, av. F.-Roosevelt, 75008, ☎ (1) 42.56.22.01. Where the Renaud-Barrault theatre troupe pauses to dine.

Wine bars :
♦ *Au Duc de Richelieu*, 110, rue de Richelieu, 75002, ☎ (1) 42.96.38.38, closed Sun, 28 Jul-1 Sep. Sandwiches made with regional *charcuterie* washed down with an admirable selection of tasty wines.
♦ *Au Père Tranquille (Jean Nouyrigat)*, 30, av. du Maine, 75015, ☎ (1) 42.22.88.12, closed Mon and Sun. No menu, just terrines and daily specials. Two choice cheeses. Loire Valley wines : Champigny, Gamay, Bourgueil. Food served in the evening. Check out the reception! Terrace and sunflowers in summer.
♦ *Au Soleil d'Austerlitz*, 18, bd de l'Hôpital, 75005, ☎ (1) 43.31.39.36, closed Sat and Aug. Excellent country wines, snacks.
♦ *Aux Négociants*, 27, rue Lambert, 75018, ☎ (1) 46.06.15.11, closed Sat and Sun , mid-Jul-mid-Aug, 25 Dec-1 Jan. Good wines from Beaujolais, Bourgueil, varied daily specials at friendly prices.
♦ *Chez Serge (Serge Cancé)*, 7, bd Jean-Jaurès, 93003 Saint-Ouen, ☎ (1) 42.54.06.42, closed Sat and Sun. A bistro : yes or no ? Go see for yourselves, taste the owner's wines and delicious cooking (at lunch). Snacks and wine, until 9pm. Beaujolais, Burgundies, Champagnes.
♦ *Club Amical du Vin*, 292, rue Saint-Jacques, 75005, ☎ (1) 46.34.69.78. Two or three wines for tasting and comparing each Saturday. Wines to go.
♦ *Gaîté Bar*, 7, rue Papin, 75003, ☎ (1) 42.72.79.45. A future wine-tasting maven. Priceless decor. Beaujolais, Bordeaux.

◆ **Jacques Melac**, 42, rue Léon-Frot, 75011, ☎ (1) 43.70.59.27, closed Sun and Jul. By acquiring the shop next door, J. Melac doubled his floor space. The grape vine that grows here is lovelier every year. Fine wines, wisely chosen. Wine and *charcuterie* to take out.

◆ **J.-P. Chastang**, 8, av. A.-Briand, 92160 Antony, ☎ (1) 46.66.01.14, closed Wed and Sun , Aug. Mama's cooking, her son's choice of excellent wines : Beaujolais, Bordeaux, *charcuterie* from the Rouergue and Lot regions.

◆ **L'Echalote**, 14, rue Chabanais, 75002, ☎ (1) 42.97.47.10. Bistro food and Georges Dubœuf's Beaujolais wines. Smoked wild salmon, to try on the spot or take home. *Foie gras*. 100.

◆ **L'Entre-Deux-Verres**, 48, rue Sainte-Anne, 75002, ☎ (1) 42.96.42.26. In a vaulted 17thC cellar, outstanding Bordeaux wines accompany regional dishes and grilled meats. On Tuesdays, Loïc de Roquefeuil gives tasting courses.

◆ **L'Oenothèque**, 20, rue Saint-Lazare, 75009, ☎ (1) 48.78.08.76, closed Sat and Sun , hols. Intelligent way to eat lightly and drink a glass or two. Wines to go.

◆ **La Bergerie**, 21, rue Galilée, ☎ (1) 47.20.48.63, Visa & closed Sat and Sun. An impressive list of tasty little wines (Beaujolais, Touraine, Vouvray) bottled by capable young Christian Baudy. A friendly neighbourhood bistro frequented by local football (soccer) players. Two specials daily, as well as : *confit maison, carré d'agneau*. Lovely red and white Bordeaux, *vin jaune*, 80-120.

◆ **La Boutique des Vins**, 31-33, rue de l'Arcade, 75008, ☎ (1) 42.65.27.27, closed Sat and Sun. Daily specials, wines by the glass and by the bottle, all in a well-bred ambience. Service by the owner.

◆ **La Cave Drouot**, 8, rue Drouot, 75009, ☎ (1) 47.70.83.38, closed Sun. With his impish Basque smile, J.-P. Cachau cultivates a public of appraisers from the nearby auction centre, and rugby fans. Beaujolais, Bordeaux, Côtes du Rhône, Sancerre, Madiran.

◆ **La Cloche des Halles (Serge Lesage)**, 28, rue Coquillère, 75001, ☎ (1) 42.36.93.89, closed Sun. Ever in a good humour, Serge Lesage is still waiting to win the wine-bar award. Hams, quiches, *charcuterie* accompanied by Beaujolais, Brouilly, and top-notch Burgundies.

◆ **La Devinière**, 70, rue Alexandre-Dumas, 75011, ☎ (1) 43.73.22.97, closed Mon and Sun, 5 Aug-5 Sep. A selection of Loire Valley wines and snacks. Rabelais (for whose birthplace the bar is named) would surely approve.

◆ **La Nuit des Rois**, 3, rue Pasteur-Wagner, ☎ (1) 48.07.15.22, Visa ᠁ ♪ closed lunch. A princely selection of 50 Champagnes by the glass or the bottle. A piano is on hand daily, from 2pm - 2am. 130-150.

◆ **La Royale (Roger Aygalenq)**, 80, rue de l'Amiral-Mouchez, 75015, ☎ (1) 45.88.38.09, closed Sun and Aug. Tastings of Touraine and Beaujolais vintages, with sage comments from the owner.

◆ **La Tartine (Jean Bouscarel)**, 24, rue de Rivoli, 75004, ☎ (1) 42.72.76.85, closed Tue and Aug. Lots of regulars appreciate the wide selection of good wines served around a cold buffet featuring delicious cheeses.

◆ **La Tassée d'Argent (Pierre Bourdut)**, 24, av. Gabriel-Péri, 94100 Saint-Maur, ☎ (1) 48.83.00.14 Food prepared by the owner (lunch only). All the crus of Beaujolais.

◆ **Le Beverly**, 9, rue de l'Ancienne-Comédie, 75006, ☎ (1) 43.26.78.48, closed Sun. J.-C. Fragnier and H.-P. Marboutin were the proud winners of the 'best glass of wine' award for 1986. Wines selected by the two owners include : Menetou-Salon, Reuilly, Quincy, Pecharmants ; to keep the wine company, try the house *charcuteries, boudin, terrine de couenne*, pig trotters and daily specials.

◆ **Le Bistrot à Vin**, 2, espl. de la Défense, 92400 Courbevoie, ☎ (1) 47.76.11.94. Amid the skyscrapers of La Défense, good wines from Auvergne's Pierre Pecoul. 100-150.

◆ **Le Bistrot du Sommelier**, 97, bd Haussmann, 75008, ☎ (1) 42.65.24.85, closed Sat eve and Sun, 25 Dec-1 Jan. A genuine, enjoyable little eatery where wines are given top billing. Pay these young oenophiles a visit.

◆ **Le Blue Fox**, Cité Berryer, 25, rue Royale, 75008, ☎ (1) 42.65.10.72. Lots of tourists. Chic and expensive.

◆ **Le Café Parisien**, 15, rue d'Assas, 75006, ☎ (1) 45.44.41.44, closed Mon and Sun , 1 wk in winter, 2 in Aug. Growers'wines and daily specials. View of traffic and the prettiest girls in Paris.

◆ **Le Maconnais**, 10, rue du Bac, 75007, ☎ (1) 42.61.21.89, closed Sat noon and Sun. Hearty Lyonnais snacks, Beaujolais, Côtes du Rhône and Mâcon wines to quench your thirst.

◆ **Le Millésime**, 7, rue Lobineau, 75006, ☎ (1) 46.34.22.15, closed Sun. Top-flight French wines, and wines from elsewhere which are sometimes uneven. Music in the evening, thanks to a gypsy guitarist.

◆ **Le Pain et le Vin**, 1, rue d'Armaillé, 75017, ☎ (1) 47.63.88.29, closed Sat and Sun and Aug. A. Dutournier, H. Faugeron, B. Fournier et J.-P. Morot-Gaudry are on hand from time to time, to raise a glass. Wines by the glass and by the bottle from noon to 2am. *Charcuterie* snacks, cheeses, daily specials.

◆ **Le Petit Bacchus**, 13, rue du Cherche-Midi, 75006, ☎ (1) 45.44.01.07, closed Mon and Sun. Talented English wine pro Steven Spurrier hoists the Union Jack over an outstanding selection of French wines. Snacks, and the Poilâne bakery is right across the street.

◆ **Le Rallye (Antoine Deconquand)**, 267, rue du Fbg-Saint-Martin, 75010, ☎ (1) 46.07.22.83, closed Sun and Aug. Hurray for Auvergne and its tasty *charcuteries*. Daily specials cooked up by the owner's wife, Beaujolais crus. Choice wines on sale. The owner is looking for singers to join his chorale.

◆ **Le Rallye (Bernard Perret)**, 6, rue Daguerre, 75014, ☎ (1) 43.22.57.05, closed Mon , Sun and 14 Jul. Bernard Peret is an undisputed prince of good Beaujolais crus. Wines to go.

◆ **Le Rubis (Albert Prat)**, 10, rue du Marché-Saint-Honoré, 75001, ☎ (1) 42.61.03.34, closed Sat and Sun and Aug. Never empty. Good Beaujolais, friendly prices.

◆ **Le Sauvignon (Henri Vergne)**, 80, rue des Saints-Pères, 75007, ☎ (1) 45.48.49.02, closed Sun and Aug. A few square metres is all, but the place is an institution, drawing all the neighbourhood's fashion retailers. The most refined sandwiches in town. Beaujolais, Bordeaux, Sancerre.

◆ **Le Val d'Or (Gérard Rongier)**, 28, av. Franklin-Roosevelt, 75008, ☎ (1) 43.59.95.81, closed Sun. Everything here is first rate. Brasserie and restaurant at lunchtime : *terrines*, ham, homemade pastry. Beaujolais and Aloxe-Corton for connoisseurs.

◆ **Le Verre et l'Assiette**, 1, rue du Val-de-Grâce, 75005, ☎ (1) 46.33.45.96. Bookstore specializing in gastronomy and oenology.

◆ **Les Bacchantes**, 21, rue Caumartin, 75009, ☎ (1) 42.65.25.35, closed Sun. From 11am to midnight. Wines by the glass or the bottle. Daily specials, *charcuterie*, omelettes, cheese, snacks.

◆ **Les Caves Angevines**, 2, pl. Léon-Deubel, 75016, ☎ (1) 42.88.88.93. Friendly wines at friendly prices. A judicious selection of wines by the glass or to take out, bottled by the owner. Six tables for the daily special, prepared by the owner's wife. What is the 'best glass of wine' jury waiting for?

◆ **Les Domaines**, 56, rue François-1er, 75008, ☎ (1) 42.56.15.87, closed Sun. From 8am to 1am : Madiran, Savennières and many other wines by the glass or the bottle, from 8 to 60 F. Restaurant and light snacks.

◆ **Ma Bourgogne (Louis Prin)**, 133, bd Haussmann, 75008, ☎ (1) 45.63.50.61, closed Sat and Sun and Aug. Remarkably cordial welcome from Louis Prin and his staff in their handsome, brand-new setting. Brasserie and restaurant at lunch. Selected Beaujolais and Burgundies for your pleasure.

◆ **Nicolas**, 8, av. de Wagram, 75008, ☎ (1) 42.27.22.07. Good and great bottles from 9am to midnight.

◆ **Relais Beaujolais (Alain Mazeau)**, 3, rue Milton, 75009, ☎ (1) 48.78.77.91, closed Sun and Aug. With Alain Mazeau, formerly of *Ma Bourgogne*, consistent quality is a given. Selected wines and elegant snacks. Beaujolais, Loire Valley wines.

♦ *Taverne Henri IV (Robert Cointepas)*, 13, pl. du Pont-Neuf, 75001, ☎ (1) 43.54.27.90, closed Sat and Sun , hols, Easter, Aug. Where members of the Bar gather for lunch or a drink with their detective buddies. Beaujolais, Touraine, Muscadet, and the rare wine of Suresnes, regional products served as snacks or in assortments.

Good things :
A l'An 2000, 82, bd des Batignolles, 75017, ☎ (1) 43.87.24.67. Caterer, food to go.
Androuet, 41, rue d'Amsterdam, 75009, ☎ (1) 48.74.26.90. The master is gone, but the good cheeses remain.
Battendier, 8, rue Coquillière, 75001, ☎ (1) 42.36.95.50. Caterer-charcutier. Mme de Gaulle's favourite.
Bon Marché, 38, rue de Sèvres, 75007, ☎ (1) 45.48.47.94. The best department store supermarket in town.
Cantin, 12, rue du Champ-de-Mars, 75007, ☎ (1) 45.50.43.94. For traditional cheeses.
Caraïbos, 21, rue de la Roquette, 75011, ☎ (1) 47.00.51.47. Exotic foods. Fruits, vegetables, rum, pork products.
Charcuterie Vignon, 14, rue Marbeuf, 75008, ☎ (1) 47.20.24.26.
Coesnon, 30, rue Dauphine, 75005, ☎ (1) 43.54.35.80. Said to be the best charcutier in Paris.
Duval, 55, rue Marcelin-Berthelot, 93700 Drancy, ☎ (1) 48.32.03.17. The best andouillette in France.
Fauchon, 26, pl. de la Madeleine, 75008, ☎ (1) 47.42.60.11. Incredible turnover, prices as high as their overhead.
Hédiard, 21, pl. de la Madeleine, 75008, ☎ (1) 42.66.44.36. Tropical fruits a specialty, jams.
La Maison des Antilles, Guyane, Réunion, pl. des Antilles, 75011, ☎ (1) 43.48.77.20. West Indian foodstuffs.
Le Coq Saint-Honoré, 3, rue Gomboust, 75001, ☎ (1) 42.61.52.04. Poultry, game in season.
Legrand, 1, rue de la Banque, 75002, ☎ (1) 42.60.07.12. Gourmet grocery. Excellent little wines. Splendid cellar.
Le Manguier, 5-7, pl. de Vénitie, 75013, ☎ (1) 45.83.58.88. Tropical produce of the Antilles and Réunion Island.
Paul Corcellet, 46, rue des Petits-Champs, 75002, ☎ (1) 42.96.51.82. Exotic foodstuffs : from bear pâté to ostrich steak.
Poilâne, 8, rue du Cherche-Midi, 75006, ☎ (1) 45.48.42.59. Celebrated rustic loaves.
Pétrossian, 18, bd de Latour-Maubourg, 75007, ☎ (1) 45.51.59.73. A temple of caviar and smoked salmon.
Verlet, 256, rue Saint-Honoré, 75001, ☎ (1) 42.60.67.39. The oldest coffee and tea merchant in Paris.

Tea-rooms :
Cador, 2, rue de l'Amiral-Coligny, 75001, ☎ (1) 45.08.19.18. View of the Louvre colonnade.
Dalloyau, 2, pl. Ed.-Rostand, 75006, ☎ (1) 43.29.31.10. View of the Luxembourg Gardens.
Feyeux, 56, rue de Clichy, 75009, ☎ (1) 48.74.37.64.
La Gerbe d'Or, 8, rue de Ponthieu, 75008, ☎ (1) 43.59.27.91.
Ladurée, 16, rue Royale, 75008, ☎ (1) 42.60.21.79. Elegant decor and wonderful macaroons.
Le Flore-en-l'Ile, 42, quai d'Orléans, 75004, ☎ (1) 43.29.88.27.
Le Jardin de Thé, 10, rue Brise-Miche, 75004, ☎ (1) 42.74.35.26. Near the IRCAM and Beaubourg. Outstanding tarts.
Pandora, 24, passage Choiseul, 75002, ☎ (1) 42.97.56.01.

Ice cream :
Baggi, 38, rue d'Amsterdam, 75009, ☎ (1) 48.74.01.39.

Berthillon, 31, rue St-Louis-en-l'Ile, 75004, ☎ (1) 43.54.31.61.
Glacier de France, 48 bis, av. d'Italie, 75013, ☎ (1) 45.80.23.75.
La Sorbetière, 12, rue Gustave-Courbet, 75016, ☎ (1) 45.53.59.59.
Le Bac à Glaces, 109, rue du Bac, 75007, ☎ (1) 45.48.87.65.
Raimo, 61, bd de Reuilly, 75012, ☎ (1) 43.43.70.17.

Music-halls and cabarets :
Alcazar, 62, rue Mazarine, 75006, ☎ (1) 43.29.02.20. A traditional night out on the town.
Crazy Horse Saloon, 12, av. George-V, 75008, ☎ (1) 47.23.32.32. Racy and slightly crazy.
Don Camillo, 10, rue des Saints-Pères, 75007, ☎ (1) 42.60.82.84. Dinner-show, stars of today and tomorrow.
Folies-Bergères, 32, rue Richer, 75009, ☎ (1) 42.46.77.11. The birth of the nude.
Lido, 116 bis, av. des Champs-Élysées, 75008, ☎ (1) 45.63.11.61. Ooo là là!. Two shows nightly.
Michou, 80, rue des Martyrs, 75018, ☎ (1) 46.06.16.04. Best drag show in town.
Moulin-Rouge, pl. Blanche, 75009, ☎ (1) 46.06.00.19. Super-cabaret. Wear a tie.
Paradis Latin, 28, rue du Cardinal-Lemoine, 75005, ☎ (1) 43.25.28.28, closed Tue. The audience is a show in itself.

Clubs, discothèques :
Adison Square Gardel, 23, rue du Cdt-Mouchotte, 75014, ☎ (1) 43.21.54.58. From 5 o'clock tea dances to Fri night frenzy.
Bains-Douches, 7, rue du Bourg-l'Abbé, 75003, ☎ (1) 48.87.01.80. Wade through the crowd. Restaurant for hip night-owls.
Bus Palladium, 6, rue Fontaine, 75009, ☎ (1) 48.74.54.99. Rockers only.
Caveau de la Huchette, 5, rue de la Huchette, 75005, ☎ (1) 43.26.65.05. A jazz institution.
Chez Castel, 15, rue Princesse, 75006, ☎ (1) 43.26.90.22. Very famous, very private.
Elysées-Matignon, 2, av. Matignon, 75008, ☎ (1) 42.25.73.13. Everyone is there.
Keur Samba, 79, rue La Boétie, 75008, ☎ (1) 43.59.03.10. Black is beautiful.
La Main Jaune, pl. de la Porte-de-Champerret, 75017, ☎ (1) 47.63.26.47. Roller disco.
La Table d'Harmonie, 8, rue Thénard, 75005, ☎ (1) 43.54.59.47. Piano bar, videos until 2am.
Le Palace et le Privilège, 8, rue du Fg-Montmartre, 75009, ☎ (1) 42.46.10.87. Punks and princesses.
Régine's Club, 49, rue de Ponthieu, 75008, ☎ (1) 43.59.21.60. The high priestess of the night.
Washington Square, 47, rue de Washington, 75008, ☎ (1) 45.63.45.10, Euro Visa, closed Sun, Aug, 24 Dec-2 Jan. From 6pm to 2am. Piano-bar and singalongs.

cheap chic : bargain outlets :
Cacharel Stock, 114, rue d'Alésia, 75014.
Emmanuelle Khanh, 6, rue Pierre-Lescot, 75001.
Givenchy, 3, rue George-V, 75008.
Mic-Mac, 13, rue Laugier, 75017.
Nina Ricci, 39, av. Montaigne, 75008.
Paris-Nord Diffusion (D.Hechter outlet), 62, rue de Pelleport, 75020.
Pierre d'Alby, 60, rue de Richelieu, 75002.

Agenais, Périgord, Quercy

▶ Art and man have their roots here in the Cro-Magnon past. In Périgord and Quercy there are traces of history dating back for tens of thousands of years : the history of the earth, where slow drops of water patiently carved out the famous rock shelters, and the history of man himself. In the world-famous limestone caves and grottos, the paintings left by prehistoric man float eerily among stalactites and stalagmites. Some of these paintings show the landscape we can see today : fertile valleys basking in the shadow of great limestone plateaus known as *"causses"* are alive with spiny, sweet-smelling shrubs.

This landscape, with its many quick-flowing rivers and streams is astonishingly diverse : there are hundreds of castles and churches, stone sentinels bearing witness to heroic and crueller times marked by religious wars and harshly-repressed peasant revolts. This very beautiful region is also fragile and poor, and has suffered more than any other from the rural exodus. The rural architecture of Périgord and Quercy is justly famous, and throughout the ages the inhabitants have made excellent use of the region's good stone.

Périgord is a paradise for gourmets, renowned for its fattened poultry, *foie gras*, truffles, boletus mushrooms and nuts, not to mention the excellent wine of Cahors, popular both in France and abroad for hundreds of years. A hint : perhaps the best and most memorable meals are to be had in Périgord's many picturesque villages. □

Don't miss

★★★ The Dordogne périgourdine B2-3, the Dordogne quercynoise C2, Les Eyzies-de-Tayac-Sireuil C2, the Lot and Célé valleys C-D3, Moissac B4, Monpazier B3, Sarlat C2.

★★ Auvillar B4, the Bastides of Périgord B3, Beynac-et-Cazenac C2, Bonaguil B3, Brantôme B1, Domme C3, Figeac D3, Hautefort C2, Jumilhac B1, Lascaux C2, Montauban C4, Rocamadour C3, Saint-Amand-de-Coly C2, Saint-Cirq-Lapopie C3, Souillac C2, Trémolat B2.

★ Agen B4, Assier D3, Beaulieu-en-Rouergue D4, Cahors C3, Caylus C4, Céou Valley C3, Chancelade B2, Double Forest A2, Gourdon C3, Lanquais B3, Lauzerte C4, Montpezat-de-Quercy C4, Nérac A4, Gouffre de Padirac C2, Périgueux B2, Saint-Antonin-Noble-Val C4, Saint-Céré D2, Villefranche-du-Périgord B3.

Weekend tips

Spend a Friday evening at Sarlat and the rest of the weekend in the valleys of the Dordogne, the Lot and the Célé, with a stopover in Cahors. The caves at Pech Merle and Font de Gaume are truly worth a detour.

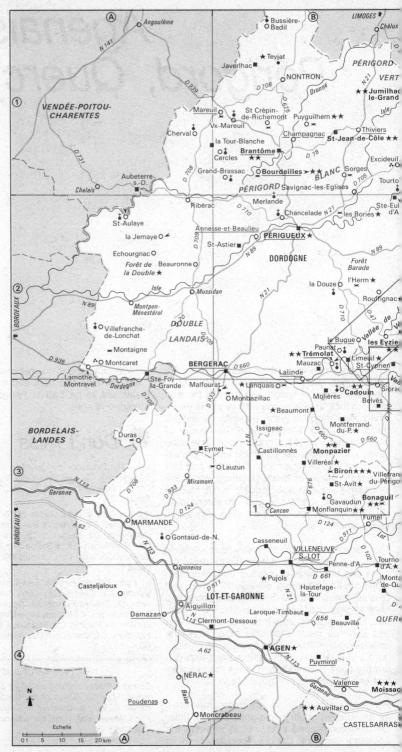

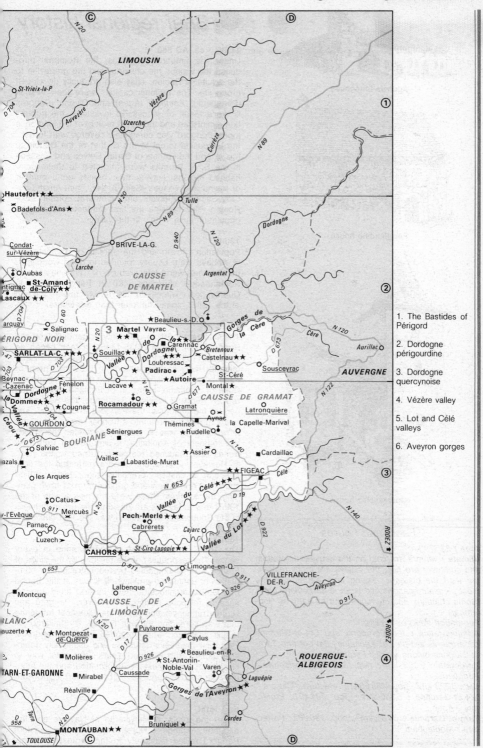

1. The Bastides of Périgord
2. Dordogne périgourdine
3. Dordogne quercynoise
4. Vézère valley
5. Lot and Célé valleys
6. Aveyron gorges

Agenais farmhouse

Périgourdine house

Quercynoise house

Facts and figures

Area : 23 379 km²
Climate : *winters are cold on the causses (plateaus) and summers are hot; the valleys are more temperate than the plateaus; spring and autumn are the most pleasant seasons, the latter is particularly calm. (Some châteaux and churches shut as early as September).*
Population : *approx 1 million.*
Administration : *the Dordogne and Lot-et-Garonne departments are part of Aquitaine; the Lot and Tarn-et-Garonne belong to Midi-Pyrénées.*
Dordogne : *9 060 km²; pop. 385 772; Prefecture : Périgueux.*
Lot : *5 228 km²; pop. 159 663; Prefecture : Cahors.*
Lot-et-Garonne : *5 360 km²; pop. 304 491; Prefecture : Agen.*
Tarn-et-Garonne : *3 731 km²; pop. 196 232; Prefecture : Montauban.*

Brief regional history

27 BC - ca. AD 350
Under the Emperor Augustus, the **Romans** introduced the walnut, the chestnut and the grapevine to the Aquitaine Region. They also gradually developed urban life. The regional capitals were then *Vesona* (Périgueux), *Aginnum* (Agen) and *Divona* (Cahors).
● As a result of successive invasions, the population diminished and the forest took over the land once more. Périgord was completely covered with forest : the Limousine forest to the N, that of the Double to the W, and the Forests of Sarlat, Belvès and Bessède in the S. ● **Hermits** were attracted to these uninhabited regions, leaving their names on a number of towns and villages (Saint-Astier, Saint-Amand-de-Cloy, Saint-Avit-Sénieur, among others). Former Gallo-Roman villas became the first **monasteries** and the population lived largely in the valleys.

12thC
Population growth and the spread of monasticism. ● Abbeys were usually founded in deep woodland; the earliest were later rebuilt. ● The number of **Romanesque churches** (400 in Périgord; 200 in Quercy) bears witness to this renewal toward the end of the 12thC, somewhat later than elsewhere.

13thC
The constant political instability engendered by the Hundred Years' War (1335-1445), in fact, began as early as 1154 with the marriage of Eleanor of Aquitaine to Henry II of England. ● In 1259 the **Treaty of Paris** between Louis IX of France (St. Louis) and the Duke of Aquitaine, Henry III of England, divided the region. Henry III received Saintonge, the Agenais, a part of the Limousin, the Périgord and Quercy. The treaty turned the area into a frontier region, constantly **ravaged by war**. ● Instability affected the artistic development of Aquitaine; it was cut off from new trends and remained resolutely turned to the past. ● However, intermittent warfare permitted the construction of castles, fortifications (including fortified churches) and a new and original form of town planning, the *bastide*. These were the new towns of the 13thC that today still are basic to the urban network in the Southwest. Montauban was the first *bastide*.

16thC
The 16thC was a period of **renaissance** in every sense. The reconquest of the territory by the kings of France was accompanied by reconstruction or completion of unfinished projects. ● It was at this period that Gothic architecture made its first timid appearance in religious buildings; however, Périgord and Quercy remained aloof from the **Classical influence** that was spreading through France. ● Similarly, the rebuilt châteaux, which reached into the hundreds, kept their mediaeval structure and essentially defensive aspect; the Hundred Years' War gave way to clashes of the Protestant Reformation and the innumerable popular uprisings that tore apart 17thC Périgord.

End 16thC
Under the aegis of Marguerite of Navarre and her daughter, Jeanne d'Albret, Aquitaine and western Périgord rallied massively to the Protestant cause.

● From 1570 to 1590, war was continuous. Bergerac, Sainte-Foy-la-Grande and Montauban became bastions of the **Reformation,** while Périgueux and Cahors were strongholds of the Holy Catholic League *(Sainte-Ligue).* ● In opposition to the mood of fanaticism that gripped both sides, the great writer Montaigne retired to his estate near Monbazillac to work on his *Essays.*

17thC
In the Périgord, land of great estates, the dominant agricultural system was that of sharecropping, as reflected by the castles positioned in the centre of landholdings. ● Between 1635 and 1685, **peasant rebellions** succeeded one another from year to year. Peasants of Protestant and Catholic factions rose against heavy taxation, landowners and army levies, attacking châteaux and attempting to organise general uprisings, only to be crushed by the armed retainers of the landowners.

18thC
The end of the Monarchy *(Ancien Régime)* was marked by a brief industrial expansion : metalworking in Périgord (the Nontronnais Region), and textile industries in Montauban and Agen. ● The central administration, or its representatives, helped to develop the towns of Périgueux and Montauban. ● In the countryside, the principle of **speculative mixed crops** took root and today is typical of the Southwest : grapevines, fruit (prunes, walnuts), tobacco, fattened geese and so on. ● **The French Revolution** created the Department of the Dordogne, an area that corresponded almost exactly to the boundaries of the ancient Province of Périgord. Through the purchase of church lands, the urban *bourgeoisie* became integrated with the ancient landowning aristocracy, who preserved the greater part of their possessions. The basic system of great estates and tenant farmers remained the same, and, with the acquisition of political power, the gentry also acquired control. The lord of the manor simply became the elected representative.

19thC
The beginning of the Second Empire in 1852 coincided with the apogee of rural civilisation. Population density reached its maximum. ● Grape-growing was highly labour-intensive, and was extended mainly through forest clearance at the instigation of the great landowners. The **phylloxera crisis** that ruined the grapevines was a shattering disaster, precipitating a massive rural exodus. ● Between 1886 and 1921, three-quarters of the population left the land, but the towns did not benefit in any real sense. ● Peasants and rural craftsmen, deprived of their markets, left for manufacturing centres ; the gentry departed for well-placed administrative posts in Paris.

20thC
After the loss of its work force (depopulation was further aggravated by massive losses in WWI), Périgord vegetated and has only recently begun a successful agricultural revolution. Certain regions have not yet been touched and the contrast between carefully cultivated valleys and the plateaus covered in light woodland and scrub is very marked. ● The Lot and Dordogne are still regions from which people tend to emigrate : today there are hardly more inhabitants in these areas than there were in Roman times.

● **Practical information**

Information : **Dordogne** : *Comité Départemental de Tourisme (C.D.T.),* 16, rue du Pdt-Wilson, 24000 Périgueux, ☎ 53.53.44.35. **Lot** : *C.D.T.,* Chambre de Commerce, 46000 Cahors, ☎ 65.35.07.09. **Lot-et-Garonne** : *C.D.T.,* B.P. 158, 47005 Agen, ☎ 53.66.14.14. **Tarn-et-Garonne** : O.D.T., Hôtel des Intendants, pl. Foch, 82000 Montauban, ☎ 63.63.31.40. In **Paris** : *Maison du Périgord,* 30, rue Louis-le-Grand, 75002, ☎ (1) 47.42.09.15 ; *Maison du Lot-et-Garonne,* 15-17, passage Choiseul, 75002, ☎ (1) 42.97.51.43. *Dir. régionale de la Jeunesse et des Sports :* **Aquitaine** : Cité administrative, Tour A, 65, rue Jules-Ferry, 33090 Bordeaux Cedex, ☎ 56.44.84.64. **Midi-Pyrénées** : 44, rue des Couteliers, 31072 Toulouse Cedex, ☎ 61.25.60.13. *Dir. rég. des Affaires culturelles :* **Aquitaine** : 26-28, pl. Gambetta, 33074 Bordeaux Cedex, ☎ 56.52.01.68. **Midi-Pyrénées** : 56, rue du Taur, 31000 Toulouse, ☎ 61.23.20.39.

Reservations : *Loisirs-Accueil (L.A.) :* **Dordogne** : 16, rue du Pdt-Wilson, 24000 Périgueux, ☎ 53.53.44.35 ; **Lot** : 430, av. Jean-Jaurès, 46000 Cahors, ☎ 65.22.55.30 ; **Tarn-et-Garonne** : Hôtel des Intendants, pl. Foch, 82000 Montauban, ☎ 63.63.31.40, 63.93.59.15.

S.O.S. : **Dordogne** : *SAMU* (Emergency Medical Service), ☎ 53.08.81.11. **Lot** : *SAMU,* ☎ 65.30.01.01. **Lot-et-Garonne** : *SAMU,* ☎ 53.96.39.39. **Tarn-et-Garonne** : *SAMU,* ☎ 63.04.03.80. *Poisoning Emergency Centre :* Toulouse, ☎ 61.49.33.33 ; Bordeaux, ☎ 56.96.40.80.

Weather forecast : **Dordogne,** ☎ 53.53.99.91 ; **Lot,** ☎ 65.41.14.34 ; **Lot-et-Garonne,** ☎ 53.95.18.28 ; **Tarn-et-Garonne,** ☎ 63.03.03.66.

Holiday villages : enq. : *C.D.T.*

Farmhouse holidays : numerous accommodation possibilities, including rural lodging, camping, farmhouse-inns. List of addresses at the *T.O., Loisirs-Accueil* and *Relais Dép. des Gîtes Ruraux :* **Dordogne,** 16, rue du Pdt-Wilson, 24000 Périgueux, ☎ 53.53.44.35 ; **Lot,** Chambre d'Agriculture, 46000 Cahors, ☎ 65.22.55.30 ; **Lot-et-Garonne,** Chambre d'Agriculture, 1, rue du Pechabout, 47000 Agen, ☎ 53.96.44.99 ; **Tarn-et-Garonne,** enq. : *O.D.T.*

Festivals : May : *concerts* in Chancelade-Périgueux. **May-Jun :** *dance festival* in Brantôme ; *spring music festival* in Marmandais. **Jun :** *horse week* in Agen. **Jul :** *French song festival* in Moirac ; *music festivals* in Monflanquin, Moissac ; *gastronomy festival* in Villefranche-de-Gueyzan ; *organ festival* in Castelsarrasin ; *blues festival* in Cahors ; *dance festival* in Brantôme ; *jazz festival* in Cahors. **Mid-Jul :** *music* at La Rougerie in Sarlat. **End Jul :** *Périgord Noir music festival* in Saint-Léon-sur-Vézère. **Jul-Aug :** *music festivals* in Duras, Clairac, Saint-Amand-de-Coly (chamber), Beaulieu Abbey (contemporary) ; *theatre games* in Sarlat ; *music and theatre* in Lanquais ; *jazz festival* in Souillac ; *dance* in Biron ; *summer encounters* in Gourdon-en-Quercy ; *festival* in Bonaguil. **Aug :** *music festivals* in Montricoux, Saint-Céré ; *mime festival* in Périgueux ; *summer encounters* in Sarlat ; *festival* in Gramont ; *dance festival* in Montauban ; *international folklore festival* in Casseneuil.

Events : May : *Périgord potters' get-together* in Bussière-Badil ; *wooden clog fair* in Brantôme ; *horse fair* in Montclar-de-Quercy. **End Jun :** *textile fair* at Varaignes. **Jul :** *meat-pie fairs* in Penne d'Agenais, Tournon ; *bric-à-brac fairs* in La Mothe-Montravel, Belvès, Montflanquin ; *international horse-show* in Le Bugue. **Jul-Aug :** *liars' festival* and *world grimace championships* in Moncrabeau. **Aug :** *regional products fair* in Marcillac-sur-Célé ; *bric-à-brac fair* and *market of old illustrated magazines* in Thiviers ; *old-time market* in Nontron. **1st Sun. in Oct :** *departmental agricultural show* at Montauban. **Nov :** *European endurance horse trials* in Moutenq.

Markets : principal markets for *foie gras* and truffles (Nov-end-Feb) : Beaumont-de-Lomagne (Sat), Bergerac (Wed, Sat), Cahors (Sat), Excideuil (Thu), Lalbenque (Tue),

Limogne (Tue, Fri), Lisle (Tue), Montauban (Wed, Fri), Mussidan (Sat), Périgueux (Wed, Sat), Ribérac (Fri), Sarlat (Sat), Sauzet (Thu), Terrasson (Thu), Thenon (Tue), Thiviers (Sat), Tocane-Saint-Apre (Mon), Valence-d'Agen (Tue), Vergt (Fri).

Truffles

The truffle is a black mushroom, strongly yet delicately flavoured, growing in chalky soil and generally beneath oak trees. Truffle hunting (cavage) is seasonal from November to March and since the 'black diamond of haute cuisine' grows underground, truffle hunters use trained dogs or (more rarely) sows to help them in their efforts. One oak may yield up to 2 kilos of truffles; the best are found late in the season. Périgord markets around 4 tons of truffles a year out of a national total of 15 tons; the markets in the Lot, especially at Lalbenque (Tue. during Jan. and Feb.) are much the best source both for quantity and quality. Research has not yet discovered the secret of growing this marvellous and extremely valuable mushroom, but a 25-acre experimental truffle farm has been established near Coly. Visit the Truffle Museum at Sorges on N21 between Périgueux and Thiviers (pm only; closed Tue.).

Perigord gastronomy

*Plump poultry, Boletus mushrooms (cêpes), truffles : Périgord is justly famous as a gastronomic paradise. A few marvellous dishes have made its reputation : foie gras, omelette with truffles or with cêpes, confit (goose or duck cooked and preserved in its own fat) served with sorrel or pommes sarladaises (potatoes cooked in goose fat), salade aux noix (salad garnished with walnuts) and cabécou (goat cheese); these make up the traditional menu in all the area's restaurants. Sometimes there may be tourin (garlic soup), tourtières (meat pies), coq au vin or au verjus (juice of white grapes), les farcies (stuffed poultry, goose neck, hare). Unfortunately, lazy cooks tend to rely on the can-opener and the Périgord reputation rather than following the traditional recipes. Apart from a few great restaurants, you will find your best meals in unpretentious village inns or farms.
There are good local wines to go with the meal : Coteaux de Bergerac, Monbazillac with the foie gras, Côtes de Duras and Côtes de Buzet (1979 and 1982 were very good years) and the neighbouring Cahors.*

Rambling and hiking : the region is traversed by numerous G.R. tracks (n°s 4, 636, 646, 64, 46, 65, 651, 652), which may also be used as bridlepaths, particularly on the Quercy causses (plateaus). Enq. : *Comité départemental des Sentiers de Grande Randonnée,* résidence Vésuna, 7, imp. Vésone, 24000 Périgueux. **Lot** : enq. : *C.D.T.* **Tarn-et-Garonne** : Touring the Aveyron Gorges, enq. : *O.D.T.* **Lot-et-Garonne** : enq. : *C.D.T.*

Riding holidays : lists of riding centres and gîtes are available at *O.T., S.I.* and *C.D.T.*

Horse-drawn holidays : *Loisirs-Accueil,* **Dordogne** and **Lot** : *Les Attelages d'Armagnac,* Domaine de Cézaou, 47170 Mezin, ☎ 53.65.70.61. *Les Roulottes de l'Agenais,* 47370 Cazideroque, ☎ 53.71.72.65. *Les Attelages de la*

vallée du Lot, Duravel, 46700 Puy-l'Évêque. *Hobby Voyages,* 8, rue de Milan, 75009 Paris, ☎ (1) 45.26.60.80, 42.80.04.96, 42.80.42.82.

Cycling holidays : **Lot** : *C.D.T.* and *Comité départemental de Cyclotourisme,* av. de la Dordogne, 46600 Martel, ☎ 65.37.30.82. **Tarn-et-Garonne** : 12 clubs, enq. *O.D.T.* **Dordogne, Lot-et-Garonne** : *C.D.T.*

Crafts courses : **Dordogne** : lithography, sculpture, dance, pottery, weaving, music, instrument-making; enq. : *C.D.T.* and *L.A.* **Lot-et-Garonne** : spinning, tapestry, bookbinding, pottery, photography; enq. : *C.D.T.* and *L.A.* **Tarn-et-Garonne** : sculpture, metal working, painting, painted furniture, woollen crafts : enq. : *C.D.T.* and *L.A.* **Lot** : pottery, weaving, basket-weaving, folklore, geology, introduction to prehistory : enq. : *C.D.T.*

Cooking and Wine courses : **Dordogne** : numerous beginners' courses in the specialities of Périgord : enq. : *C.D.T.* and *L.A.* **Tarn-et-Garonne** : beginners' courses in the preparation of *foie gras* and *confits* : M. André Pochat, les-Vignes-de-Brassac, 82190 Bourg-de-Visa, ☎ 63.94.24.30. Other courses : enq. *O.D.T.* **Lot** : enq. *C.D.T.* and *L.A.*

Children : riding courses, farm holidays, sports holidays : enq. : *C.D.T., L.A.* and *Relais des Gîtes Ruraux.*

Aquatic sports : wind-surfing, sailing, canoeing in Tarn-et-Garonne.

Canoeing : on the Lot, the Célé, the Dordogne and the Dronne. Enq. : *C.D.T.* **Lot** : SAFARAID, ☎ 55.28.80.70. **Tarn-et-Garonne** : CAPSA, ☎ 63.30.64.47.

Rowing : enq. at the *Maison du Lot-et-Garonne.*

Golf : Barbaste (9 holes), Bon-Encontre-Capitouls (9 holes), Castelnaud (27 holes), La Chapelle-Auzac (6 holes), Espalius (5 holes), Périgueux-Marsac (9 holes).

Flying : **Dordogne** : at Condat, enq. : *L.A.;* Cahors-Lalbenque aero club, ☎ 65.21.05.96, Périgueux-Bassillac aerodrome; enq. : *C.D.T.* Rodez-Marcillac, ☎ 65.42.21.95. Aerial tour of the bastides, ☎ 53.36.85.99. **Lot-et-Garonne** : U.L.M. flying school, ☎ 53.95.08.81. **Tarn-et-Garonne** : Montauban aero club, ☎ 63.03.27.44; beginners courses in delta-plane at St-Antonin-Noble-Val.

Caves

There are innumerable caves in this country of limestone cliffs. Many contain calcite deposits (stalactites and stalagmites) formed by the continuous interaction of the limestone with water. These caves were too damp for prehistoric man to live in, but some of them probably served as sanctuaries. Apart from the famous Lascaux Cave, now closed, the most beautiful are at Font de Gaume, Rouffignac, and Pech Merle in Quercy.

Potholing and spelunking : *Comité Dép.,* **Dordogne** : c/o M. Vidal, 7, rue de la Cité, 24000 Périgueux. **Lot** : local committee : M. Lafaurie, 46150 Catus, ☎ 65.22.70.49. **Tarn-et-Garonne** : 1468, av. de Foueneve, 82000 Montauban. CAPSA : introduction and sports holidays, ☎ 63.30.64.47.

Hunting and shooting : *Féd. Dép. des Chasseurs :* **Dordogne**, 4, rue Arago, 24000 Périgueux, ☎ 53.08.75.38; **Lot** : 22, rue Brives, 46000 Cahors, ☎ 63.35.13.22. **Lot-et-Garonne** : 111, bd de la Liberté, 47000 Agen, ☎ 53.47.05.44. **Tarn-et-Garonne** : 4, rue Denfert-Rochereau, 83000 Montauban, ☎ 63.03.46.51.

Fishing : *Féd. Dép. des Associations de Pêche et de Pisciculture :* **Dordogne** : 31, rue Wilson, 24000 Périgueux, ☎ 53.53.44.21; **Lot** : 40, bd Gambetta, 46000 Cahors, ☎ 65.35.50.22; **Lot-et-Garonne** : 4 bis, rue Floirac, 47000 Agen, ☎ 53.66.16.68; **Tarn-et-Garonne** : 160, fg Toulousain, 82000 Montauban, ☎ 63.63.01.77.

● *Towns and places* ═══════════

Toulouse 114, Bordeaux 139, Paris 735 km
pop 32893 ⊠ 47000   B4

Agen is famous for its prunes; also for its rugby team, perennially among the best in France. Agen retains much of the charm of a past provincial era.

▶ The **cathedral of St. Caprais** (B1) is something of a mixture — Romanesque choir, Gothic nave, the whole completed in the 16thC — but the Romanesque *chevet* is beautiful and the choir is finely decorated with carved capitals.
▶ The **Quartier des Cornières**, between the cathedral and the market, is classified of historic importance; the restored houses are half-timbered with brickwork in between; the prettiest is the Seneschal's House (13thC), which serves as a show window for Agen's museum. ▶ The **museum★** itself is remarkable. It occupies a group of 16thC town houses, and has some good 18thC paintings and a number of Impressionist works — but above all, five Goyas and the famous *Venus du Mas*, a Hellenistic marble discovered in the region *(10-12 & 2-6 ex Tue.)*. ▶ Promenade along the banks of the river Garonne among the plane trees, and admire the 19thC **canal-bridge★** (A1), which carries the canal across the river. Downstream, the Garonne and its canal are bordered by a forest of poplars, which supplies wood for crates for the fruit and vegetables grown in the area.

Nearby

▶ **Manor of Prades** *(8 km on Valence road)* : 16th-17thC *(visit on request)*. ▶ **Port-Sainte-Marie** *(20 km NW)* : timber-faced houses (15th-18thC) and two Gothic churches. Make a detour through **Clermont-Dessous**, charming stronghold of the 13thC : view. ▶ **Beauville★** *(26 km E)* : fortified bastide admirably suited to the site; 16thC church; 13th-16thC château; nearby, church of **Marcoux**. ▶ **Saint-Maurin** : built around an ancient abbey, a dependency of Moissac.

Excursion south of Agen *(40 km)*

▶ **Château d'Estillac★** : largely reconstructed by Montluc (1502-1577), who headed the royal armies against the Protestants and was a forerunner of the great military architect Vauban. Still a family home *(visit on request)*. ▶ **Aubiac** : 12thC church of somewhat severe aspect. ▶ **Moirax**, old fortified village, possesses the most beautiful Romanesque church★ in the Agenais region : pure, clean lines, faithfully restored; remarkable capitals; 17thC panelling with fine patina. ▶ **Layrac★** overlooking the junction of the rivers Gers and Garonne; arcaded town square; Romanesque church with painted dome (18thC).   □

Practical Information ─────────────

AGEN
ℹ 107, bd Carnot (B-C2), ☎ 53.47.36.09.
✈ *La Garenne*, 3 km SW, ☎ 53.96.21.77.
SNCF (B1), ☎ 53.66.50.50/53.66.01.63.
Car rental : *Avis*, 29, av. du Gal-de-Gaulle (A1), ☎ 53.47.17.51 ; Train station.

Hotels :

● ★★★ **Résidence des Jacobins** (L.F.), 1 ter, pl. des Jacobins (A2), ☎ 53.47.03.31, Tx 560800, 15 rm ℗ 🏧 🌊 300.
★★ *Atlantic*, 133, av. J.-Jaurès (C2), ☎ 53.96.16.56, Tx 560800, AE DC Euro Visa, 30 rm ℗ ♪ closed Aug, 170.
★★ *Le Quercy* (L.F.), 10, rue de la Grande-Horloge (B1), ☎ 53.66.35.49, 12 rm ℗ 🌊 ❀ closed Sun, 6-28 Aug, 130. Rest. ◆ Good, simple cooking : *truite rosée au beurre de vinaigre, mousseline de Saint-Jacques au coulis de poisson, confit de canard aux cerises de vin*, 55-90 ; child : 35.

Prunes and plum trees

Prunes have been part of the French diet for almost 1000 years. Introduced from Persia by returning Crusaders, and planted in the valley of the Lot by the tireless monks of Clairac, the plum tree was one of the earliest and most successful of agricultural "speculations", since the fruit could easily be preserved by drying. The name of Agen has become synonymous with prunes, not simply because they are grown nearby but also because it has been the principal point of dispatch for other regions. Faced with competition from California, the growers between Agen and Villeneuve-sur-Lot have modernised their operations and modern hillside orchards are one of the dominant features of the landscape.

Restaurants :

◆◆ *L'Aéroport*, La Garenne airport, ☎ 53.96.38.95, Tx 550225, AE DC Euro Visa ℗ ≰ closed Sat , Sun eve. and Aug. Regional cooking, 95-200.
◆ *L'Absinthe*, 29 bis, rue Voltaire (A-B2), ☎ 53.66.16.94, Visa ♪ closed Sat noon and Sun, 1-15 Sep. A good little eatery, 160.
◆ *Le Voltaire*, 36, rue Voltaire (A-B2), ☎ 53.47.27.01, AE DC Euro Visa ♪ ও A country-style setting in a farmer convent.*Foie gras à la croque au sel, saumon à l'oseille, filets de sole aux morilles*, 50-200 ; child : 25.

Recommended
Baby-sitting : Info at the Syndicat d'Initiative.
Events : *Pine Fair*, in Sep ; *Foire du gravier*, in Jun.
Guided tours : (Jul-Aug), info at the Syndicat d'Initiative.
Riding gîte : Info at the Syndicat d'Initiative.
Youth hostel : 17, rue Léo-Lagrange, ☎ 53.66.18.98.
♥ antiques : *Au Bon Vieux Temps*, 12, rue des Corniches (B1), ☎ 53.66.92.61 ; candy : *Boisson*, 20, rue Grande-Horloge (B1), ☎ 53.66.20.61, closed Sun ; pastry, chocolates : *Maison Maufferon*, bd Carnot, ☎ 53.66.37.65 ; regional specialities : *J.P. Caban*, 175, bd Carnot (B-C2), ☎ 53.66.47.20.

Nearby

AIGUILLON, ⊠ 47190, 30 km from **Agen**.
ℹ rue Bazin, ☎ 53.79.62.58.
SNCF ☎ 53.79.64.60.

⚠ ★★★*Municipal* (75 pl), ☎ 53.79.61.43.

Recommended
Events : *fair featuring regional specialities*, in Aug.

BON-ENCONTRE, ⊠ 47240, 5 km E.

Hotel :
★★ *Le Parc* (L.F.), 41, rue de la République, ☎ 53.96.17.75, Euro Visa, 10 rm ℗ 🏧 🌊 closed 25 Feb-2 Mar, 25 Oct-2 Nov, 23 Dec-3 Jan, 170.

COLAYRAC, ⊠ 47450, 5 km W.

Hotel :
★★★ *La Corne d'Or* (L.F.), RN 113, ☎ 53.47.02.76, Tx 560800, AE DC Euro Visa, 14 rm ℗ ≰ ♪ closed Sat and Sun eve, 12 Jul-12 Aug, 210. Rest. ◆◆ ♪ ও Spec : fish and shellfish, 90-180 ; child : 55.

GALIMAS, ⊠ 47340 Laroque-Timbaut, 11 km N on the RN 21.

Hotel :
★★★ *La Sauvagère*, ☎ 53.95.60.39, 12 rm ℗ 🏧 🌊 closed Sun eve (l.s.), 270. Rest. ◆ ♪ 55-145.

PUYMIROL, ⊠ 47270, 16 km E.

Restaurant :
● ◆◆◆ *L'Aubergade*, (R.C.), 52, rue Royale,
☎ 53.95.31.46 ▩ ♪ closed Mon ex Jul-Aug and hols. With
no undue hoopla, Michel Trama continues his exemplary
progress among the ranks of this country's top chefs. The
restaurant is housed in a fine old 12th-C "bastide", decorated by his capable wife, Maryse. The little garden is delightful. Food is unfussy, with a southwestern accent : *langoustines aux oignons et petits lardons, brandade de
canard.* Smokers take note of the exceptional cigar selection, 100-250 ; child : 80.

Recommended
♥ at Lafox, PC 47270, antiques : *M. Martini,*
☎ 53.68.50.97.

ASSIER*

Figeac 16, Cahors 57, Paris 598 km
pop 863 ⊠ 46320   D3
This little village on the edge of the Gramat Causse
(plateau) was endowed with a sumptuous **château★**
(of which one wing remains) and **church★** by Galiot
Genouillac (Henri IV's artillery master, 1465-1546), a
grand seigneur of the Renaissance *(Jun.-Sep., 10-12
& 2:30-6:30, closed Tue. ; rest of the year on request ;
tel : 65.40.57.31).*   □

AUVILLAR**

Moissac 20, Agen 46, Paris 675 km
pop 863 ⊠ 82340   B4
A sleepy, magical village overlooking the river
Garonne. The **market building**, with bulbous columns
and rounded arches, is strongly reminiscent of Tuscany. Auvillar was formerly a great producer of
faience.   □

BARADE Forest

                                                            B2
Between Rouffignac and Montignac in the country of
the 17thC rebel, Jacqou le Croquant. Classic Périgord countryside : groves of trees following hill contours, grassy valleys and stony plateaus perfumed by
heather, broom and gorse.
▶ D31 runs along the Barade Forest between Rouffignac
(→) and Thenon ; for walkers, GR36 serves this purpose.
The TO has signposted a path along the route taken by
Jacqou, but it is enough to see Fanlac, where he spent
his childhood, and the château de l'Herm, which he
burned down. ▶ **Fanlac** is deserted but remains an
archetypal Périgord village, with ochre houses, a square,
bordered by the church (12th-17thC) and the squire's
house. ▶ Deep in the woods, abandoned, gloomy and
austere, stands the **château de l'Herm** (15thC), home
of the wicked Lord of l'Herm *(Jun.-Sep.).*   □

The BASTIDES of PÉRIGORD**

                                                            B3
Round-trip *(approx 130 km, full day ; see map 1)*

The *bastides*, sited apparently at random all over this
gentle countryside, are charming, old-world surprises
for travellers in Périgord. They were built during the
Franco-English wars of the 13thC and have prospered ever since ; today they form an important
network of market towns throughout SW Aquitaine.
Bastides were fortified walled towns inhabited by
freemen. All were built according to the same plan : a

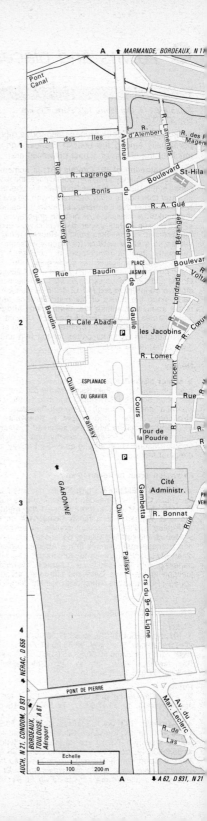

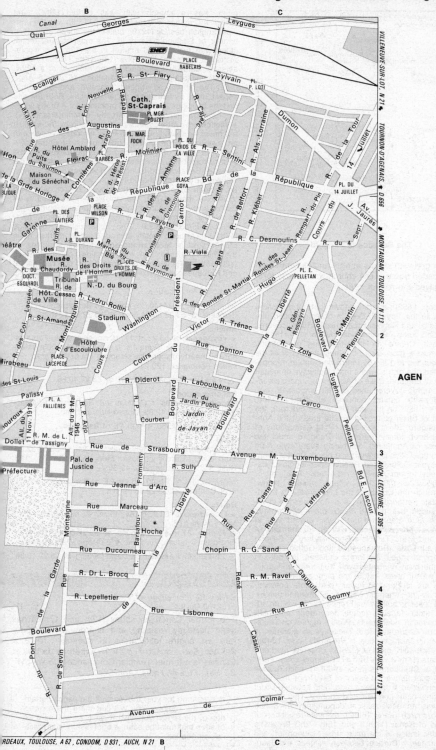

1. The Bastides of Périgord

rectangular grid with streets at right angles centred on a large, arcaded square. The church was usually fortified and played the role of keep.

▶ **Belvès** (pop. 1 652) : a fortified town (but not a *bastide*) at the entry to the Pays au Bois, a broad, wooded plateau. Mediaeval and Renaissance houses; 15thC covered market; 12thC keep; Benedictine church (13th-15thC); belfry (15thC). Centre for the marketing of walnuts. ▶ **Monpazier★★★** (pop. 533) : the most perfect of all the *bastides*. Founded in 1284 by Pierre de Gontaut, Monpazier controlled one of the area's main highways on behalf of Edward I of England, Duke of Aquitaine. Superb arcaded square. 16thC covered market with embossed roof, and church with carved doorway of same period. ▶ **Biron★★★** : high on its *pech* (limestone outcrop), the huge **castle** of Biron controlled a wide area of the Agenais and Périgord. Biron was built by 14 generations of the Gontaut-Biron family (barons of Périgord under the English dukes of Aquitaine), combining every style from the 12thC to the 18thC in a charming blend. Double chapel★ (Flamboyant Gothic) and Renaissance loggia★; vistas of pretty green valleys *(daily ex Tue., tel. : 53.53.44.35/53.22.62.01).* The village nestles below. ▶ Down through the woods of the Lède Valley to **Saint-Avit★** : classic Périgord houses and Romanesque chapel. ▶ **Gavaudun** : a rugged keep above the gorges of the Lède *(Jun.-Sep. and nat. hols., guided visit at 2:30; Jul.-Aug., unaccompanied visit at 10)*, remains of almshouse and 14thC Templars Commandery. ▶ Beyond **Montagnac-sur-Lède** (Romanesque and Gothic church), the landscape changes, the forest vanishes, the horizon broadens, the plain undulates with fruit trees and grain fields. The walnut gives way to the plum and the grape, the houses are longer and lower; tiled roofs predominate : this is the Agenais Region. ▶ **Monflanquin★★** (pop. 2 356) : *bastide* built by the French (1279), with arcaded square, stone façades (some decorated), and half-timbered houses in side streets. Poultry market on Thursdays and, on Saturdays and Tuesdays in summer, a small market for farm produce. ▶ **Villeréal★** (pop. 1 340) : another French-built *bastide* (1269). Covered market : wooden pillars (14thC) with 16th-17thC upper story. Fortified church. ▶ **Castillonnès** (pop. 1 400) : French *bastide* (1259) on a spur above the valley of the Dropt, like Villeréal and Monpazier. ▶ **Issigeac** (pop. 686) between Dropt and Dordogne, plum and vineyard country. This mediaeval town was an ecclesiastical dependency of Sarlat. Late Gothic church (early 16thC), summer residence of the Bishops of Sarlat (17thC) and 16th-17thC Provost's house. Gothic house in the main street; pigeon loft and outside staircase. ▶ **Bardou**, between Issigeac and Beau-

mont, has a church with wall belfry (12thC) and 15th-17thC manor. ▶ **Beaumont** (pop. 1 300) was the principal English *bastide* (1272), built in the shape of an H in honour of England's Henry III. The main square, rebuilt along with the covered market in the 18thC, is incomplete, but the fortified church★ (13th-14thC) is full of character. ▶ **Saint-Avit-Sénieur★** is the offshoot of a 12thC Benedictine abbey (mineral collection; *15 Jul.-15 Aug., 3-6).* The church is rugged, massive and military in aspect; it is, nevertheless, rather beautiful. Both the site and the buildings are classified monuments. A pretty winding road by the river runs directly to Montferrand (→). ▶ **Molières** : a little country *bastide* begun by the English but never finished. ▶ **Cadouin★★** is a modest village with an oversized church, surrounded by chestnut-tree-covered hills. Ruins of a Cistercian abbey here exemplify the best of regional architecture. The first monks cleared the forest of Bessède and founded the villages in the vicinity. A piece of the Holy Shroud brought from Antioch attracted crowds of pilgrims, and a lovely church was built to receive them (1154). The cloister mingles Flamboyant Gothic and Renaissance styles and contains some highly realistic sculptures *(daily ex Tue. off season; tel. : 53.53.44.35/53.22.06.53).* The other abbey buildings (17thC) have been greatly altered. Covered market, as in Montferrand. ▶ **Montferrand-du-Périgord★** straggles up the hill, crowned by the remains of a fortress (12th-15thC); Renaissance houses, 16thC covered market and Romanesque church in the cemetery. □

Practical Information

BEAUMONT, ✉ 24440, 29 km SE of **Bergerac**.
ⓘ mairie, ☎ 53.22.30.24 (l.s.); ☎ 53.22.39.12 (h.s.).

Hotel :
★ *Voyageurs*, ☎ 53.22.30.11, 10 rm, closed Jan-Feb, Oct-Nov, 180. Rest. ♦ "Popaul's" is a little-known little eatery serving hearty dishes like steaming soups,*foie gras, filet sauce Périgueux*, 120-210.
▲ ★★★*Les Remparts*, (70 pl), ☎ 53.22.40.86.

Recommended
Chambres d'hôtes : *Château de Régagnac (Château-Accueil),* ☎ 53.22.42.98, closed Nov and Feb.

ISSIGEAC, ✉ 24560, 12 km SE of **Bergerac**.

Hotel :
★ *Voyageurs* (L.F.), Bouniagues, RN 21, ☎ 53.58.32.26, Euro Visa, 13 rm Ⓟ 盤 closed Mon, 15 Oct-15 Nov, 113. Rest. ♦ ♪ Shaded terrace, 45-80.

MONPAZIER, ✉ 24540, 45 km SE of **Bergerac**.
ⓘ pl. Centrale, ☎ 53.22.68.59 (h.s.). ♥

Hotels :
★★ *Londres*, ☎ 53.22.60.64, 10 rm ⌗ closed Mon (l.s.), Nov-Easter, 105.
★ *France*, 21, rue St-Jacques, ☎ 53.22.60.06, 14 rm ⌕ Fine 13th-C house, 70. Rest. ♦ ♪ closed Wed, 45-160.
▲ at Gaujac, ★★*Moulin de David* (100 pl), ☎ 53.22.40.86.

BEAULIEU-EN-ROUERGUE*

Caylus 10, Montauban 44, Paris 655 km
✉ 82160 Caylus   D4

The former Cistercian abbey (12th and 17thC) has been perfectly restored and is now a contemporary art centre (exhibitions in summer; *10-12 & 2-6 Apr.-Sep.; closed Tue.)* ▶ The **château de Cas** at Espinas is a former Templar Commandery *(5 km SW; 2-7 Sat., Sun. and hols., Apr.-Oct.).* □

In preparing for your trip, consult the pages pertaining to the regions. You will find there the description of the region you wish to visit, as well as a list of sites that must be seen, a brief history and practical information.

BEAUMONT-DE-LOMAGNE

Montauban 36, Toulouse 57, Paris 692 km
pop 3949 ⊠ 82500   B4

Capital of white garlic, Beaumont-de-Lomagne is equally known for its equestrian events. Streets, squares, half-timbered houses and, especially ▶ the medieval market (14thC) and the church in meridional Gothic style are worthy of a stop.

Nearby

▶ In the church of **Bouillac** *(14 km SE)* the treasury of the former Cistercian abbey of Grand-Selve (13thC).   □

Practical Information ————————————

Hotel :
★ *Le Commerce* (L.F.), 58, rue Mal-Foch, ☎ 63.02.31.02, Euro Visa, 14 rm Ⓟ ⅏ closed Sun eve and Mon, 20 Dec-15 Jan, 130. Rest. ♦ ♪ & ఞ Regional fare, 40-100; child : 30.

⚠ ★★★*du Lac* (100 pl), ☎ 63.65.26.43.

BERGERAC

Périgueux 47, Bordeaux 92, Paris 555 km
pop 28617 ⊠ 24100   B2-3

On the banks of the Dordogne where it enters the plain, Bergerac has always been a port, a ford and a cross-roads. It is also the capital of southern Périgord. Today little remains of Bergerac's commercial importance or its intellectual activity as the capital of Protestantism. There are a few timbered houses, here and there a Renaissance dormer window, but the winding, narrow streets of the old port and the wide, straight avenues in the centre of town retain a certain charm.

▶ The **Récollets Cloister** (Renaissance and 18thC galleries) houses the offices of the Bergerac Regional Wine Council *(daily in summer).* ▶ In a bend of the Rue du Château there is a pretty balustraded balcony; **Rue de l'Ancien-Pont** boasts a 14thC house, Louis XIII (17thC) building and the Maison Peyrarède, known as the Château Henri IV (16thC), which houses the **Tobacco Museum**★ *(Musée du Tabac)* : bright and lively, this display provides a wealth of information on the major SW product *(10-12 & 2-5 or 6, closed Sun. am and Mon.).* ▶ Also see **town hall**, former Convent of the Dames de la Foi; **museum of sacred art** and **museum of wine and boat-making**; 17thC Cordeliers mill (exhibitions, *10-30-11:30 & 1:30-4:30, tel. : 53.57.12.57).*   □

Practical Information ————————————

BERGERAC
ⓘ 97, rue Neuve-d'Argenson, ☎ 53.57.03.11.
✈ *Roumanières*, 5 km SE, ☎ 53.57.00.09.
🆂🅽🅲🅵 ☎ 53.57.26.71/53.57.72.79.
Car rental : *Avis*, 1, av. du 108e-R.-I., ☎ 53.57.69.83; train station.

Hotels :
● ★★ *Le Cyrano*, 2, bd Montaigne, ☎ 53.57.02.76, AE DC Visa, 11 rm Ⓟ ♪ closed Mon eve and Sun eve, 26 Jun-11 Jul, 3-27 Dec, 140. Rest. ♦ ♦ ♪ Old-fashioned recipes given a new slant. Spec : *salade de lapin confit aux pointes d'asperges, mignon de veau et son ris aux morilles, suprême de pigeonneau aux pignons*, 70-200.
★★ *Bordeaux*, 38, pl. Gambetta, ☎ 53.57.12.83, Tx 550412, AE DC Euro Visa, 42 rm Ⓟ ⅏ ⊟ closed 20 Dec-30 Jan, 200. Rest. ♦ ♪ & ⊟ 70-180; child : 50.
★★ *Europ-Hôtel*, 20-22, rue Petit Sol, ☎ 53.57.06.54, Euro Visa, 22 rm Ⓟ ⅏ 150.
★★ *La Flambée* (L.F.), 3 km rte de Périgueux, ☎ 53.57.52.33, 21 rm Ⓟ ⅏ ⚄ ఞ ♪° closed Sun eve,

2-22 Jan, 9-23 Jun, 190. Rest. ♦ ♦ ఞ closed Mon and Sun eve, 60-160.
⚠ ★★*La Pelouse* (70 pl), ☎ 53.57.06.67.

Recommended
Auction house : *auctions*, pl. Gambetta, ☎ 53.57.38.16.
Events : Easter fair, fair of St Martin (Nov.).
Guide to wines : Château de Monbazillac, 6 km S., ☎ 53.57.06.38, tasting and sale of Monbazillac, Bergerac wines.
Market : *flea market*, in old Bergerac, 1st Sun of month.
Sports : *Gaule Bergeracoise*, ☎ 53.57.13.71, fishing; *Centre école de parachutisme sportif*, aérodrome de Bergerac-Roumanières; *Compagnie d'Arc du Périgord*, ☎ 53.57.16.33, archery.

Nearby

SAINT-JULIEN-DE-CREMPSE, ⊠ 24140 Villamblard, 12 km N.

Hotel :
★★★ *Manoir du Grand Vignoble*, (C.H., R.S.), ☎ 53.24.23.18, Tx 541629, AE DC Visa, 30 rm Ⓟ ⅏ ⚄ ⊠ ♪° closed 22 Dec-14 Feb, 450. Rest. ♦ ♦ ♪ & ఞ 140-250.

BONAGUIL**

Fumel 10, Villeneuve-sur-Lot 34, Paris 580 km
⊠ 47500 Fumel   B3

The **castle** of Bonaguil, the "mad castle" (its defensive sophistication borders on paranoia), is fascinating as the quintessence of late feudal architecture.

▶ The castle stands alone, perched on a forbidding outcrop between two wooded valleys, representing a last futile challenge to the centralised power of French monarchs. It was built when the châteaux of a more easygoing world were already appearing along the banks of the Loire *(guided tours hourly from 10 am and 3 pm; out of season : Sun. only, 3 pm; closed Jan.-Feb.).*

Nearby

▶ **Sauveterre-la-Lémance**★ feudal castle of the Kings of England and Dukes of Aquitaine, built on the lines of Welsh fortresses (13th-14thC; *visits).*   □

BRANTÔME

Périgueux 27, Angoulême 58, Paris 483 km
pop 2100 ⊠ 24310   B1

The river Dronne runs merrily around the town; on the opposite bank stands an abbey, home to the writer Brantôme (1540-1614), courtier, soldier and one-time escort of Mary, Queen of Scots. ▶ Like Périgueux cathedral, the church was restored by the architect Abadie; fine 11thC bell-tower, 17th and 18thC convent buildings. The crudely-carved (16thC) caves are the setting for the Brantôme Dance Festival. An angled bridge leads to the **monks' garden** ★ with benches dating from the Renaissance. Charm and culinary renown. ▶ Don't miss the **Château de Richemont** (16thC ; *7 km NW ; 15 Jul.-31 Aug., 10-12 & 3-6; closed Fri., Sun. a.m.).*

Trip around Brantôme★★ *(approx 50 km, half-day)*

▶ **Brantôme.** ▶ **Champagnac-de-Belair :** a well-known restaurant in an old oil-pressing mill beside the river. ▶ The Cistercian **abbey of Boschaud**★ (1163) has been restored by the MH (historical monuments) board and the younger members of the Club du Vieux Manoir voluntary organisation *(guided visits, 14 Jul.-15 Aug.; off season, unaccompanied visits).* ▶ The **château de Puyguilhem**★★ is on a par with many châteaux of the Loire. The sculpture and decoration of its monumental chimneys were probably done by local craftsmen *(daily ex Tue.; off season,* *tel. : 53.53.44.35/53.54.82.18).* ▶ **Villars** : the Grotte de Cluzeau contains cave paintings contemporary with those of Lascaux (→) *(15 Jun.-15 Sep., 9-12 & 2-7; out of season Sun. and nat. hols.)* ▶ **Saint-Jean-de-Côle★★**, another village masterpiece on the banks of the river; Gothic bridge, mill, faded gold and brown tiles and potbellied houses straight out of the Middle Ages. Around the enormous square : interesting church with figured capitals (12thC), Renaissance cloister, covered market and the château de Marthonie (15th-16thC; *Jul.-Aug. 10-12 & 2-7).* Museum : Musée du Vieux St.-Jean. ▶ Pretty road along the river Col which flows around the ruins of the **castle of Bruzac** (15thC). ▶ **Saint-Pierre-de-Côle** huddles around a poorly-restored Romanesque church. ▶ The château at **La Chapelle-Faucher**, perched atop a cliff over the river, was devastated by fire. Crude Romanesque church in the village. ▶ Between Brantôme and Bourdeilles flows the **Dronne★**, bordered by poplar and walnut trees. The river passes beneath impressive cliffs pocked with shelters hollowed out by prehistoric man. ▶ **Bourdeilles★★** (pop. 728) : ravishing site. The river flows under a Gothic bridge. The seigneurial mill projects over the river like the prow of a boat, and the château itself stands hard by, anchored to an enormous rock shelf; this was a 13th-15thC fortress, later a Renaissance palace designed by a sister-in-law of Brantôme; antique furnishings★ *(daily ex Tue.; off season, tel : 53.53.44.35).*

Practical Information ─────────────────

BRANTÔME
ⅰ pavillon des Gardes de l'abbaye, ☎ 53.08.80.52 (h.s.).

Hotels :
● ★★★★ **Le Moulin de l'Abbaye** (R.C.), 1, rte de Bourdeilles, ☎ 53.05.80.22, Tx 560570, AE Euro Visa, 12 rm Ⓟ ∉ ⚏ ⚑ ♪ closed 15 Nov-5 May, 500. Rest. ● ◆◆◆◆ ∉ ♪ closed Mon. This mill on the banks of the Dronne is a pure delight! The personalized rooms (each bears the name of a famous château of Bordeaux) guarantee idyllic peace, with the murmur of water in the background. Dynamic mill-owner Régis Bulot, an award-winning chef isn't one to doze on his flour sacks. Chef Christian Ravinel (formerly of Troisgros) serves up flawless food : *foie gras en terrine, filet de bœuf aux échalotes au vin de Cahors.* Great desserts featuring a cake named for race-driver "Alain Prost". Great wines, too. In winter, the entire staff moves up to Courchevel's Hôtel des Neiges, 160-320.
★★★ **Chabrol**, 57, rue Gambetta, ☎ 53.05.70.15, AE DC Euro Visa, 20 rm Ⓟ ∉ ⚘ closed Sun eve and Mon (l.s.), Feb school hols, 15 Nov-12 Dec, 220. Rest. ● ◆◆ ∮ ⚘ River view. There's some fine cooking done here in the Charbonnel brothers' handsome restaurant. Alas , the menu is over-long and the list of notices forbidding things like dogs, shorts, bermudas, etc.. (in high season!) is ridiculously old-fashioned, 100-250.
Auberge du Soir, rue Georges-Saumande, ☎ 53.05.82.93, AE DC Euro Visa, 9 rm Ⓟ ⚏ ⚑ pens (h.s.), closed 15 Jan-26 Feb, 370. Rest. ◆ 65-100.

▲ ★★*Municipal* (56 pl), ☎ 53.05.75.24.

Recommended
Chambres d'hôtes : Le Chatenet, à 1 km, ☎ 53.05.81.08, pleasant rooms in a manor house with a pool.
♥ at Montplaisir, goose confit factory : ☎ 53.54.83.13.

Nearby
BOURDEILLES, ⊠ 24310 Brantôme, 10 km SW.

Hotel :
● ★★★ **Les Griffons** (C.H.), Le Pont, ☎ 53.05.75.61, Euro Visa, 10 rm Ⓟ ∉ ⚑ ♪ closed Tue lunch (15 Apr-30 Jun), 1 Oct-14 Apr. 16th-C residence, 250. Rest. ◆◆ ∉ ♪ 95-150; child : 60.

▲ *Municipal Fonseigner* (35 pl), ☎ 53.05.74.17.

CHAMPAGNAC-DE-BELAIR, ⊠ 24530, 6 km NE.

Hotel :
● ★★★★ **Moulin du Roc** (R.C.), ☎ 53.54.80.36,

Tx 571555, AE DC Euro Visa, 12 rm Ⓟ ∉ ⚏ ⚑ ♂ closed 15 Jan-15 Feb, 15 Nov-15 Dec, 400. Rest. ● ◆◆◆ ∉ ♪ ♂ closed Tue and Wed noon. Spec : *foie gras au vinaigre de framboise, truite aux cèpes,* 190-240.

CAHORS**

Montauban 61, Agen 92, Paris 595 km
pop 20774 ⊠ 46000   C3
A remarkable site on a loop of the river Lot, surrounded by wild, bare hills. Twenty centuries of history are represented in this little capital of one of the most rural departments in France. The town is cosy and affable, a little sleepy, but its people are fond of life. Cahors is especially proud of Léon Gambetta (1838-82), the founder of Occitanian Radicalism. Visit on market days *(Wed. or Sat.)* when town meets country on the square in front of the cathedral.

▶ **Pont Valentré★★** (bridge; A2) is the principal monument in Cahors. Built at the time of the Franco-English wars, a prime example of a fortified mediaeval bridge (14thC). ▶ The **cathedral★** bell-tower keep (C2; 11th-12thC) dominates the pink-tiled roofs of the old town. Its massive façade was added in the 14thC and the **Romanesque tympanum★**, similar to Moissac's and already showing hints of Gothic design, was moved to the N side near the Prefecture (the 18thC Episcopal Palace). On the S side, the 16thC **cloister** has satirical sculptures in the style of Cadouin (→) and paintings in 16thC Italian style. ▶ NE of the cloister, pretty Renaissance decor in the former **Archdeaconry of St. Jean.** ▶ The **Badernes sector★** to the S (C3) is now being restored. During the great days of the 13thC this was the commercial centre of Cahors and today it is still a lively and picturesque area. ▶ The **Hôtel de Roaldès** on the Place Henri IV (C2) was probably decorated by the cathedral sculptors (ca. 1500). ▶ The upper quarter of the town, **Soubirous**, where Catholics and Protestants once clashed, was the site of the university, founded by Pope John XXII (ca. 1244-1334; last Pope at Avignon and native of Cahors), and closed in the 18thC. One of the towers of the **Collège Pellegri** (15thC) is still standing, masked by modern buildings. ▶ If you go up towards the **church of St. Barthélemy** (B1; 14thC), you will see many architectural details from the 13th, 14th and 15thC; next to the church the stocky **Tower of Pope John XXII** is a remnant of the former Duèze Palace, built by the Pope's brother and never finished (14thC). ▶ The **Diane Gate** on the Place Thiers bears vestiges of the old Roman Baths. ▶ N of the town, standing watch over the Lot, are the 15thC Barbican and the **Tour** (tower) St. Jean, outside the walls (B1). The museum in the old Episcopal Palace honours the famous men of Cahors, Pope John XXII, the poets Clément Marot (1493-1544) and de Magny (ca. 1530-1561), Gambetta himself *(high season 10-7 ex Mon.).* ▶ The walk to **Mont Saint-Cyr★** rewards the visitor with a view over the whole town.

Also... ▶ **Château de Roussillon** *(3 km N)* : a mediaeval fortress containing a small museum of rural life in Quercy *(summer, groups only; 2-7 ex Tue.).*

Round-trip of the Cahors vineyards *(107 km from Cahors to Bonaguil via the lower valley of the Lot; sign-posted on each bank, but the right bank carries much more motor traffic).*

No more cliffs but plenty of bends in the river, with villages perched on hills or by the water's edge, their Romanesque churches and châteaux surveying the vineyards from above. ▶ **Cahors.** ▶ From **Mercuès** onward (château of the Bishops of Cahors, now a hotel), the vine is predominant. ▶ **Parnac** : headquarters of the Winegrowers' Cooperative. ▶ **Luzech** is a small industrial centre, superbly sited; the mediaeval village is clustered at the keep; behind is the hill of Impernal, one of the numerous possible sites of the Roman town of *Uxellodunum.* ▶ **Puy-l'Évêque,** another production centre for Cahors wine, is a fortified town in a natural amphitheatre by the Lot; Gothic

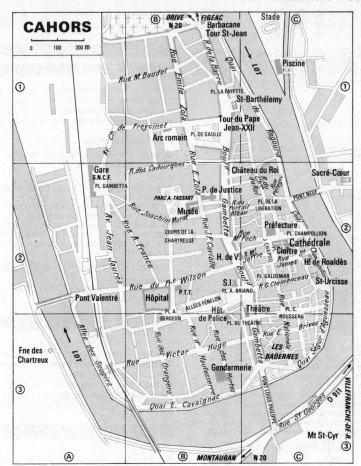

CAHORS

0   100   200 m

BRIVE   FIGEAC   Stade
N 20   Barbacane
Tour St-Jean

Piscine

Rue M. Baudel

PL. LA FAYETTE
St-Barthélemy

Tour du Pape
Jean-XXII
Arc romain   PL. DE GAULLE

Gare   R.des Cadourgues   Château du Roi   Sacré-Cœur
S.N.C.F.
PL. GAMBETTA   P. de Justice
PARC A.-TASSART   PONT NEUF
Musée   PL. DE LA
LIBÉRATION
COURS DE LA   Préfecture
CHARTREUSE   PL. CHAMPOLLION
Cathédrale
Cloître
H. de V.   Rue   Hl de Roaldès
James
S.I.   St-Urcisse
Pont Valentré   Hôpital   PL. GALDEMAR
P.T.T.   R.G.Clemenceau
PL. A.-BRIAND
PL. A.   ALLÉES FÉNELON   Théâtre
-BERGEON   Hôt.   PL. C.
de Police   ROUSSEAU
PL. DU THÉÂTRE
Fne des   LES
Chartreux   BADERNES
Gendarmerie

Quai E. Cavaignac   Rue St-Georges   D 911
Mt St-Cyr

MONTAUBAN   N 20

church (sculptures) which was part of the town's defence system, opposite a 13thC keep (view). ▶ 15thC frescos in the church at **Martignac** *(4 km N)*. ▶ The country here is more level and roofs are lower : this is the Agenais Region. ▶ Return to **Bonaguil**★★ (→) along a lovely road through **Duravel** (11thC church with figured capitals and archaic crypt) and **Montcabrier,** 13thC *bastide* with an attractive church. ☐

Practical Information _____

CAHORS
ⓘ pl. A.-Briand (B2), ☎ 65.35.09.56.
✈ Cahors-Lalbenque, ☎ 65.21.00.48.
🚆 (A2), ☎ 65.22.50.50.
Car rental : Avis, 512, av. J.-Jaurès Pl. de la Gare, ☎ 65.30.13.10; train station.

Hotels :
● ★★★ **Moulin de la Source Bleue**, La Source Bleue, Touzac, ☎ 65.36.52.01, Visa, 9 rm 🅿 ♨ 🍴 closed 15 Nov-7 Apr, 210. Rest. ♦ closed Tue, 95-150.
★★★ **France**, (Inter-Hôtel), 252, av. J.-Jaurès (A2), ☎ 65.35.16.76, Tx 520394, 80 rm 🅿 🍴 ⎕ ⌦ closed 23 Dec-2 Jan, 200.
★★★ **La Chartreuse** (L.F.), fg St-Georges (C3), ☎ 65.35.17.37, 34 rm 🅿 ♨ closed 24 Dec-1 Jan, 180. Rest. ♦♦ closed Mon, 120-210.

★★★ **Terminus**, 5, av. Ch.-de-Freycinet (B1), ☎ 65.35.24.50, AE Euro Visa, 30 rm 🅿 🍴 200. Rest. ● ♦♦♦ **Le Balandre** ⌦ closed Mon and Sun eve , Sat lunch (h.s.), 10 Feb-5 Mar, 1-8 Jun. Young Gilles has hit his stride cooking in this pleasant 1900-style eatery. Fine selection of vintage Cahors wines, 75-200.
★ **Paix**, 30, pl. St.-Maurice (C2), ☎ 65.35.03.40, 22 rm, closed Sun, 15 Dec-15 Jan, 100. Rest. ♦ 50-150.

Restaurants :
♦♦ **La Taverne**, 1, rue J.-B. Delpech (B-C2), ☎ 65.35.28.66, AE DC Visa ♪ ⌦ closed Sun eve. A fresh new look worthy of the noble truffles served here under many guises by P. Lannes, 95-250.
♦♦ **Sénéchal du Quercy**, St.-Henri, RN 20, ☎ 65.35.52.97, Euro Visa 🅿 ♨ ♫ ⎕ ♪ closed Wed , Jan, 75-200.
♦ **Marie-Colline**, 173, rue Clemenceau (C2), ☎ 65.35.59.96, closed eve, 1-15 Sep. Vegetarian, 50.

⋀ ★★**St. Georges** (50 pl), ☎ 65.35.04.64.

Recommended
Bicycle-rental : Ets Combes, 117, bd Gambetta, ☎ 65.35.06.73.
Guide to wines : M.J.C., imp. de la Charité, B.P. 42, ☎ 65.35.06.43, typical Quercy cuisine, tasting of Cahors wines.
Guided tours : Office de tourisme, C.N.M.H.S., in Jul-Aug.

Night-clubs : *Le Look*, rte de Paris.
Sports : *M.J.C.*, imp. de la Charité, ☎ 65.35.06.43, canoë-kayak excursions on the Lot, Célé, Dordogne rivers; hiking; lectures.
♥ gastronomy, crafts : *La Tour du pape Jean XXII*, 3, bd Gambetta, ☎ 65.35.39.52; local products : *Sudreau*, 91, bd Gambetta, ☎ 65.35.26.06; pastry : *Larguille*, 21, bd Gambetta; truffles : *Pebeyre*, rue F. Suisse, ☎ 65.35.24.80.

Nearby

DOUELLE, ⊠ 46140 Luzeek, 12 km W.

Restaurant :
♦♦ **Marine**, Luzech, ☎ 65.20.02.06, Visa Ⓟ ♿ closed Mon eve and Tue, 2 Jan-1 Apr. Fish and seafood, 65-120.

LABÉRAUDIE, ⊠ 46090 Cahors, 3 km NW.

Hotel :
★ **Le Clos Grand** (L.F.), "Pradines", ☎ 65.35.04.39, Euro Visa, 21 rm Ⓟ ∰ ⌕ 130. Rest. ♦ ♪ closed Fri eve, Sat noon, Sun eve, 29 Jun-7 Jul, 21 Aug-13 Sep, 24 Dec-5 Jan, 50-110.

LAMAGDELAINE, ⊠ 46090 Cahors, 7 km E.

Restaurant :
● ♦♦♦ **Marco**, ☎ 65.35.30.64, AE DC Euro Visa Ⓟ ∰ ⌕ ♪ ♿ closed Mon and Sun eve (h.s.), 12 Jan-3 Mar, 21-29 Oct. Three cheers for the cuisine of Cahors in Claude Marco's light, tasty interpretations : *salade de queue de bœuf, émincé de bar aux huîtres*, 100-230; child : 50.

MERCUÈS, ⊠ 46090, 7 km NW of **Cahors**.

Hotel :
● ★★★★(L) **Château de Mercuès** (R.C.), ☎ 65.20.00.01, AE DC Euro Visa, 23 rm Ⓟ ∰ ⌕ ♿ 🖃 ♪ closed 3 Nov-1 Apr, 600. Rest.● ♦♦♦♦ **L'Aigle d'Or** ⌕ ♪ ♿ G. Vigouroux had to blow up some vineyards in the course of restoring (quite tastefully) this handsome aerie. The château boasts magnificent cellars and is endowed with a fine chef in Hervé Guérin, whose fine cooking harmonizes nicely with the surroundings : *petites salades châtelaines, escalope de foie gras au château de haute serre, magret de canard au cassis*. Cahors wines featured, 155-230.

Le MONTAT, ⊠ 46090 Cahors, 9 km NW on the D 47.

Restaurant :
♦♦ **Templiers**, ☎ 65.21.01.23, Visa Ⓟ ♪ closed Mon , Sun eve ex Jul-Aug, 15 Jan-15 Feb, 1-12 Jul. 12th-C commander's residence : *foie gras, filet de barbue*, 75-145.

PUY-L'ÉVÊQUE, ⊠ 46700 Cahors, 31 km W.
Ⓘ Mairie, ☎ 65.30.81.45.

Hotels :
● ★★★ **Le Relais de la Dolce** (R.S.), rte de Villefranche-du-Périgord, Montcabrier, ☎ 65.36.53.42, AE DC Euro Visa, 12 rm Ⓟ ∰ ⌕ ♿ 🖃 300. Rest. ● ♦ ⌕ ♪ ♿ ♻ closed Wed. Peace and relaxation await you in this attractive establishment. Low season : 24-hour advance reservation required, 130.
● ★★ **Bellevue**, pl. de la Truffière, ☎ 65.21.30.70, Visa, 15 rm Ⓟ ∰ ⌕ ♪ closed Sun eve and Mon (l.s.), 15 Nov-15 Mar, 160. Rest. ♦♦ ♪ 50-120.
● ★★ **Hostellerie Le Vert** (L.F.), Mauroux, ☎ 65.36.51.36, Visa, 7 rm Ⓟ ∰ ⌕ closed 15 Nov-15 Mar, 210. Rest. ♦ ⌕ ♪ closed Wed, 75-120; child : 35.

⚐ ★★**de la Plage** (100 pl), ☎ 65.30.81.45.

Recommended
Guide to wines : *M. Delgoulet*, château Chambert, Flousors, Cahors wines.
Sports : *Safaraid*, pl. du Rampeau, ☎ 65.36.30.39.

SAINT-MÉDARD-CATUS, ⊠ 46150, 18 km NW.

Restaurant :
♦♦ **Le Gindreau**, ☎ 65.36.22.27, Visa ⌕ ♪ ♿ closed Tue

eve and Wed (l.s.), Mon in Jul-Aug, 2-28 Feb, 2 Nov-2 Dec. Spec : *sweetbreads, foie gras, fish*, 100-200.

CAUSSADE

Montauban 22, Cahors 39, Paris 634 km
pop 6132 ⊠ 82300   C4
Former Protestant stronghold, latterly a hat-making centre. Hôtel de Maleville (17thC mansion). ▶ Three bastides nearby : **Réalville** *(7.5 km S)*, **Mirabel** *(6.5 km W of Réalville)* and **Puylaroque**★ *(13 km NE)*.   □

Practical Information _____

Ⓘ rue de la République, ☎ 63.93.10.45 (h.s.).
SNCF ☎ 63.93.10.21/63.63.50.50.

Hotels :
● ★★ **Larroque** (L.F.), av. du 8-Mai, ☎ 63.93.10.14, AE DC Euro Visa, 27 rm Ⓟ ⌕ ♿ closed Sun eve (l.s.), 23 Dec-15 Jan, 145. Rest. ♦♦ ♪ ♿ closed Sat noon and Sun eve (l.s.). Regional cooking, 60-110; child : 45.
★★ **Dupont**, 25, rue des Récollets, ☎ 63.65.05.00, Euro Visa, 31 rm Ⓟ ⌕ ♻ closed Fri eve , Sat, 1-7 May, 1-30 Nov, 150. Rest. ♦ ♿ closed Sat noon, Fri eve (l.s.), 60-150.

⚐ ★★★**La Piboulette** (100 pl), ☎ 63.93.09.07.

Recommended
♥ truffles : *Gaillard*, 5, pl. du Gal-de-Gaulle, ☎ 63.93.09.61.

CÉOU Valley*

                                                    C3
Between Quercy and Périgord, from the **Causse de Gramat** (→) to the **château de Castelnau** (→) in the Dordogne, this valley provides one of the most agreeable walks imaginable. The Céou is, in fact, a stream winding beneath poplars through a plain chequered with crops and studded with villages.   □

CÈRE Gorges

                                                    D2
The Cère is a minor tributary of the Dordogne, rising in the Plomb du Cantal; between **Laroquebrou** and the **château de Castelnau** (→), the Cère plunges through wild and wooded rocks. Its course is followed by the railway and by GR652, a trail through oak and beech along the hilltops.   □

DORDOGNE PÉRIGOURDINE***

                                                    B2-3
From Souillac to Badefols-sur-Dordogne *(90 km, full day; see map 2)*

In the Périgord sector of the Dordogne Valley, the river curves slowly around high limestone cliffs; villages and châteaux face one another across the river, and rich crops spread away over the plain.
▶ The Dordogne, largest river in France, rises in the Puy de Sancy (alt. 1 886 m), and enters Périgord-Dordogne at Cazoulès, downstream from **Souillac** (→). ▶ Just after the charming church in **Carsac** (Romanesque, ogive vaulting from the 16thC) on the right bank, the road runs above the river bend known as the **Cingle de Montfort**★. The 15thC castle (heavily restored) is perched on a bluff high above the river; village with stone-tiled roofs at cliff-foot.
▶ **Cénac** crouches below the *bastide* of Domme. The church is not typical of Périgord but its 12thC *chevet* is very fine; carved corbels and capitals. ▶ **Domme**★★ : here everything is exceptional — the site, the view from the Barre, terrace, the quality of the architecture, the

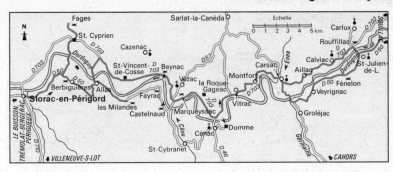

2. Dordogne périgourdine

colour of the stone. This is a French *bastide* (1383) built on an irregular plan to accommodate the terrain. 13thC ramparts, 17thC covered market, 16thC governor's house on the square, stalactite caves *(Apr.-Sep.)*. ▶ Starting from Domme, visit the town of **La Roque-Gageac**, a former inland port, built right against the cliffs. ▶ **Marquayssac** is a 17thC château-belvédère opposite those of **Lacoste** (19thC) and **Castelnaud** (12th and 15thC). ▶ **Beynac-et-Cazenac**★★ is a gem : the village is built over a lovely bend in the river, and the **castle** — one of the Four Baronies of Périgord — sits atop the cliff; this was once (13th-16thC) a formidable fortress, despite its idyllic setting; 13th-18thC decoration; 14thC frescos *(1 Mar.-15 Nov., 10-12 & 2:30-6:30, 4:30 low season).* ▶ Beyond Beynac, the valley reveals more beautiful scenery; the left bank is recommended. ▶ The river flows past the **château de Fayrac** (14th-17thC) and through an experimental walnut plantation. ▶ **Les Milandes** : the country château (end 15thC, much restored) of the Caumont family made famous when purchased by the late American singer-dancer Josephine Baker *(Jul.-Aug., 9-11:30 & 2-6:30; rest of year 9:30-11:30 & 2-6; closed Nov.-Feb.).* ▶ At **Berbiguières**, the 17thC château is hidden behind high walls. ▶ **Saint-Cyprien** spreads along a hillside. Pretty houses surround the church (12thC bell-tower keep) former abbey (16thC) occupied by the State Tobacco Board *(Régie des Tabacs).* N of the village on a wooded hill is the lovely restored **château de Fages**; superb site; view. ▶ Another château (15th-17thC) above **Mouzens** *(10-12 & 3-6, 15 Jul.-30 Aug.).* ▶ At **Limeuil** the road rejoins the valley of the **Vézère**. ▶ Superb route towards **Trémolat** (→) and **Badefols-sur-Dordogne**★, a protected site. ☐

Practical Information ────────────

BADEFOLS-SUR-DORDOGNE, ✉ 24150 Lalinde, 5 km E of **Lalinde**.

Hotel :
★★ **Lou Cantou** (L.F.), ☎ 53.22.50.36, 12 rm 🅿 ⬙ 𝕃 closed Oct-Mar, 120. Rest. ◆ 80-130.

DOMME, ✉ 24250, 29 km SW of **Souillac**.
ℹ 50, pl. de la Halle, ☎ 53.28.37.09 (h.s.).

Hotel :
★★ **L'Esplanade** (L.F.), ☎ 53.28.31.41, AE, 20 rm ⬚ ♨ pens (h.s.), closed Mon, Feb and Nov, 580. Rest. ◆ ⬚ ♪ 80-200.

⚐ ★★**La Croix des Prés** (33 pl), ☎ 53.28.30.18 ; ★★**Le Perpetuum** (85 pl), ☎ 53.28.35.18.

La **ROQUE-GAGEAC,** ✉ 24250 Domme, 13 km S of **Sarlat**.

Hotel :
★★ **La Belle Etoile**, ☎ 53.29.51.44, 15 rm ⬚ ⬙ closed 15 Oct-Palm Sun, 150. Rest. ◆ ⬚ 70-130.

⚐ ★★★*Beau Rivage* (190 pl), ☎ 53.28.32.05 ; ★★*Verte Rive* (60 pl), ☎ 53.28.30.04.

SAINT-CYPRIEN, ✉ 24220, 21 km W of **Sarlat**.
ℹ ☎ 53.30.36.09.

Hotels :
● ★★★ **L'Abbaye,** ☎ 53.29.20.48, AE DC Euro Visa, 24 rm 🅿 ⬙ ▭ closed Wed lunch (1st 2 wks of Apr), 15 Oct-30 Mar, 400. Rest. ◆◆ ♪ 110-160.
● ★★ **Bonnet,** Beynac et Cazenac, ☎ 53.29.50.01, Visa, 22 rm 🅿 ⬚ half pens (h.s.), closed 15 Oct-15 Apr, 460. Rest. ◆ ⬚ ⬙ Pleasant cooking on the banks of the Dordogne river, 80-130.

⚐ ★★*Les Deux Vallées* (80 pl), ☎ 53.29.53.55 ; ★*La Cabane* (33 pl), ☎ 53.29.52.28.

VÉZAC, ✉ 24220, 2 km S of **Beynac**.

Hotels :
● ★★★ **Manoir de Rochecourbe,** D 57, ☎ 53.29.50.79, Euro Visa, 7 rm 🅿 ⬚ 𝕃 closed 1 Nov-18 Apr, 250.
● ★★★ **Oustal de Vézac,** ☎ 53.29.54.21, AE Euro Visa, 20 rm 🅿 ⬙ 𝕃 ♨ ⬚ closed 1 Nov-Easter, 220.

DORDOGNE QUERCYNOISE★★★

C2-3
From Souillac to Saint-Céré *(60 km, half-day; see map 3)*

As in Périgord, narrow passes give way to luxuriant meadows, dominated by villages and hilltop châteaux. The country is well-watered and peaceful, planted with alders, poplars and tobacco.

▶ **Souillac** (→). ▶ At the end of the Pinsac bridge is the **château de La Treyne** (17thC), built on a rock above the river; at the junction of the Dordogne and the greenbanked Ouysse is **Belcastel château** (14th, 19thC), with an incomparable view *(visit the terrace in summer only).* ▶ Stalactite caves at **Lacave** *(Palm Sun.-end Sep.).* ▶ Good view over **Meyronne** (former residence of the Bishops of Tulle), and **Saint-Sozy.** ▶ **Creysse**★ is superb ; interesting Romanesque church with twin apses from different periods. ▶ View over the **Cirque de Montvallon** (natural amphitheatre) from the wayside cross at **Copeyre ;** visible on another loop of the river are the château de Mirandol (16thC), the bell-tower of Floirac (18thC) and, in the distance, the Puy d'Issolud, another possible site of *Uxellodunum.* ▶ **Martel**★★, on the *causse* (plateau) to the N is charming. The entire town centre is classified, with numerous 14th, 15th and 16thC houses ; the Town Hall and Raymondie Palace, (14thC; *Jul.-Aug., p.m.*) ; 13thC mint ; covered markets (18thC) ; fortified Gothic church with Romanesque tympanum. ▶ **Carennac**★★, a delightful, brown-tiled town, grew up around the priory where the author François Fénelon (1651-1715) was abbot. The 15th-17thC château stands above the island-studded river. The doorway★ of the church (12th, 15thC)

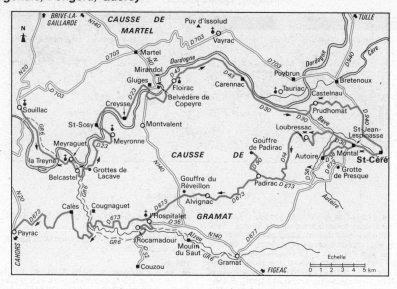

3. Dordogne quercynoise

echoes the motifs of Moissac (→); satirical carvings on the capitals, 16thC statues and 15thC murals. Gothic cloister with Romanesque gallery. The village contains numerous Renaissance vestiges. ▶ The formidable red bulk of the **château de Castelnau-Bretenoux★** on a wooded hillock dominates all the surrounding valleys *(30 Jun.-14 Sep., 10-1 & 2-7)*. ▶ At its foot is the village of **Prudhomat**, scattered among the greenery. ▶ **Bretenoux** is a former *bastide* founded by the Lord of Castelnau. ▶ **Saint-Céré** (→).

Practical Information ―――――――――――

CARENNAC, ⊠ 46110 Vayrac, 33 km SE of **Souillac**.

Hotel :
★ **Fenelon** (L.F.), ☎ 65.38.67.67, Visa, 21 rm ℗ ≼ half pens (h.s.), closed Fri and Sat lunch, 1 Feb-10 Mar, 170. Rest. ♦ ≼ 55-130.

LACAVE, ⊠ 46200 Souillac, 15 km SE of **Souillac**.

Hotel :
★★★ **Pont de l'Ouysse**, ☎ 65.37.87.04, Visa, 11 rm ≼ ⏷⏷⏷ ⚶ closed Mon (l.s.), 11 Nov-1 Mar, 170. Rest. ♦♦ 100-200.

MARTEL, ⊠ 46600, 15 km NE of **Souillac**.

Hotel :
● ★★ **Les Falaises** (L.F.), Gluges, ☎ 65.37.33.59, Visa, 15 rm ℗ ≼ ⏷⏷⏷ ⚶ ⏿ half pens (h.s.), closed 1 Dec-1 Mar, 360. Rest. ♦ ≼ 60-120.

DOUBLE Forest*

A2
This is true forest country★, in contrast to the nearby Landes region, where trees are farm cultivated; many of the streams that wind beneath oak and pine have been dammed to make ponds. This ancient forest long had a reputation as the haunt of wolves and fantasy or maleficent creatures; the ponds spread malaria and even animals had rheumatism. Drained, improved and planted with pines, the region now resembles the Sologne, south of Orléans. There

are few villages, but a sprinkling of half-timbered farmhouses and hamlets on the dryer slopes. For walkers, this is a poetic landscape, and for bird-watchers a treasure trove.

▶ **Échourgnac** is the capital of the Double; important fairs, almost unchanged since the last century, are held here four times a year. ▶ The **La Jemaye Lake★** has now become a leisure centre. ▶ Don't miss **Saint-Astier★** on the edge of the forest. Here, at the end of autumn, farmers and merchants spread coloured umbrellas over the squares, and crowds come to buy poultry, *foie gras* and truffles for the Christmas and New Year festivities. A massive church and bell-tower (15thC) dominate the town and overlook the valley of the river Isle. Several houses have kept Renaissance elements — turrets, half-timbering. ▶ The area is richly supplied with fire clay; tilers working in the traditional manner have replaced the 19thC potters.

DURAS

Bergerac 44, Marmande 23, Paris 596 km
pop 1245 ⊠ 47120   A3
Situated above the valley of the Dropt, Duras is the centre of a wine-growing district that is beginning to acquire a solid reputation.

▶ 17thC château *(9-12 & 2-6); popular arts and traditions museum and arcaded square.*

Practical Information ―――――――――――

Hotel :
★ **Auberge du Château** (L.F.), pl. Jean-Bousquet, ☎ 53.83.70.58, AE DC Euro Visa, 10 rm ≼ ⚶ ⏿ pens, closed Wed, 15 Nov-15 Dec, 180. Rest. ♦ ≼ 45-135; child : 40.

For the translation of a name of a meat, a fish or a vegetable, for the composition of a dish or a sauce, see the Menu Guide in the Practical Holiday Guide; it lists the most common culinary terms.

EYMET

Bergerac 25, Périgueux 72, Paris 579 km
pop 2943 ⊠ 24500   A3

Visit this ancient French *bastide* on Thursday, market day, when the local country folk meet in the Place des Arcades around the tall 17thC fountain. This is no longer truly Périgord, but the humps and hillocks of Guyenne, kingdom of tobacco, the grapevine and fruit. Eymet is famed for conserves.   ☐

Practical Information ——————————

ℹ au château, ☎ 53.23.81.60.

Hotel :
★ *Château*, rue du Couvent, ☎ 53.23.81.35, 10 rm ℗ ⌕ closed 12-30 Nov, 80. Rest. ♦ closed Sun eve in Jan and Feb ex school hols, 45-85; child : 30.

⚠ ★★*Municipal* (33 pl), ☎ 53.23.80.28.

Les EYZIES-DE-TAYAC-SIREUIL★★★

Sarlat 21, Périgueux 45, Paris 532 km
pop 858 ⊠ 24620   B2

The science of prehistory originated in this village, between holm oak-covered cliffs at the confluence of the Vézère and the Beune. The first drawing of a mammoth was discovered here along with the first skeleton of Cro-Magnon Man, 30 000 years old.

▶ The **National Prehistory Museum**★★★ *(9:30-12 & 2-6, 5 off season; closed Tue.)*, an essential introduction to the prehistoric sites of Périgord. ▶ The **fortress church**★ of **Tayac** (12thC; Limousin doorway) was built by the monks of Paunat. ▶ The Roc de Tayac (troglodyte dwellings) houses a **speleological museum** *(May-Sep.)*. ▶ The **Font de Gaume Cave**★★★ *(9-11 & 2-5, Apr.-Sep.; 10-11 & 2-3 rest of year; closed Tue. and nat. hols.)* : this is the most beautiful collection of polychrome cave paintings open to the public in France. ▶ The **Combarelles Cave**★★★ *(same hours and conditions as above)* contains France's most important collection of rock engravings. ▶ The **Abri du Cap Blanc** has a lifesize bas-relief of horses★ *(permission to view at the hamlet of La Grèze)*. ▶ The **Grand Roc Cave**★ above the river Vézère in the **Laugeries Cliffs** (prehistoric remains) is famous for its coral-like mineral deposits.

Prehistoric Périgord : the Vézère Valley★★★ *(see map 4)*

During the past 100 years, 25 caves, 150 sites and thousands of vestiges have been found in the Vézère Valley, demonstrating man's persistent presence in these white cliffs; the place is a sort of Cro-Magnon version of Egypt's Valley of the Kings.

S of Les Eyzies *(16 km)*

▶ The road follows the left bank of the Vézère. ▶ **Campagne** : the 15thC castle is over-restored, but the site, with the stream, wash-house and wall-belfryed church (12th-15thC), is very pretty. ▶ **Le Bugue** : between hills and river (spoiled by heavy traffic). ▶ The engravings in the **Bara-Bahau Cave** are hard for non-experts to decipher *(23 Mar.-Sep., 10-12 & 2-6; Jul.-Aug., 9-6:30)*. ▶ The **Gouffre de Proumeyssac** *(same hours; open Sun. in Oct., tel. : 53.06.28.82)* offers impressive cave scenery. ▶ The hilltop road to Limeuil has broad views over the valley and the hills. ▶ **Limeuil**★, on the hilltop where the Vézère joins the Dordogne, is a former fortified town turned inland port. It is now one of the Périgord's most charming villages. ▶ The country chapel of **Saint-Martin-de-Limeuil** (in the cemetery) is an endangered masterpiece.

N of Les Eyzies *(approx 30 km)*

On the right bank, the site of **La Madeleine** has given its name to the Higher Paleolithic culture of the Lascaux

4. Vézère valley

artists. ▶ **Tursac** : church with a row of cupolas and bell-tower keep. Fortified house at **Reignac**. ▶ **La Roque-Saint-Christophe**, a long, natural *corniche* (ledge) that once served as a rampart. In the cliff is a **troglodyte village** with a 15thC chapel and a feudal castle. At **Pas du Miroir**, there are five levels of habitation occupied since the Gallo-Romans *(Palm Sun.-15 Sep., 10-12 & 2-6)*. ▶ On the other bank, the **Moustier** site has given its name to a stone-working period. ▶ **Peyzac** : 14thC chapel in the cemetery. ▶ **Saint-Léon-sur-Vézère**★ : delightful village by the river; stone-roofed church and two châteaux (14th and 16thC). ▶ On the other bank, **Sergeac** has stone-roofed houses around a 13thC manor, the remains of a Templar Commandery and an astonishing 13th-14thC fortress church. Viewpoint at **Castel-Merle**. ▶ **Thonac** : Le **Thot Prehistoric Centre** on the wooded hillside *(4 km)* : introduction to Prehistory *(Jul.-Aug., 9:30-7:30; rest of year 10-12 & 2-5:30; closed Jan. and Mon.)*. ▶ W of Thonac, superb village of **Plazac**★ and **Côte de Jor**★ (viewpoint). ▶ To see the **château de Losse**★ (16thC; *1 Jul.-15 Sep.*) on a rock above the green river, follow the left bank. ▶ **Montignac**, astride the river, was just another inland port (galleried houses on the quays) before it became famous with the discovery of **Lascaux** (→). ▶ The tour of prehistoric Périgord would not be complete without a visit to **Rouffignac** (→). □

Practical Information

Les **EYZIES-DE-TAYAC-SIREUIL**
① ☎ 53.06.97.05.

Hotels :
● ★★★ *Cro-Magnon*, (Mapotel), ☎ 53.06.97.06, Tx 570637, AE DC Euro Visa, 27 rm 𝕻 ≪ ⌂ half pens (h.s.), closed 15 Oct-15 Apr, 630. Rest. ● ♦♦♦ ⅋ A delightful halt : good, top-quality food with a Périgord accent : *gâteau de légumes (du jardin), sole au foie gras.* Good cellar, 100-280.
● ★★★ *Le Centenaire* (R.C.), ☎ 53.06.97.18, Tx 541921, AE DC Euro Visa, 30 rm 𝕻 ≪ ⌂ closed 5 Nov-1 Apr, 300. Rest. ● ♦♦♦ ⅋ closed Tue noon. An enchanting spot in prehistoric Périgord. The Mazère and Scholly families make their house more comfortable each year. No stone-age cooking here, just delicate regional specialities like : *variation sur les foies gras, tourtière de volaille, raviolis d'escargots à l'oie fumée, pot-au-feu et sa mique,* 135-350.
★★★ *Les Glycines*, ☎ 53.06.97.07, AE Visa, 25 rm 𝕻 ≪ ⌂ ⌀ closed 6 Nov-11 Apr. Lovely house furnished with antiques, 250. Rest. ♦♦ ⅋ & ⅋ Inventive cuisine that follows the chef's mood and the market's offerings : *bouquet d'asperges, papillote de sole,* 90-190.
★★ *Centre* (L.F.), pl. de la Mairie, ☎ 53.06.97.13, Visa, 18 rm 𝕻 ≪ ⌂ ⌀ ⅋ half pens (h.s.), 190. Rest. ♦♦ ⅋ ⅋ closed 15 Nov-15 Mar. Spec : *assiette périgourdine, tournedos nouveau, pot-au-feu de lotte aux légumes,* 65-200 ; child : 40.
★★ *Moulin de la Beune*, ☎ 53.06.94.33, 20 rm 𝕻 ≪ ⌂ ⌀ closed 4 Nov-21 Mar, 200.
★★ *Roches* (L.F.), ☎ 53.06.96.59, 19 rm 𝕻 ⌂ ⅋ closed 1 Nov-Palm Sun, 145.

△ ★★*l'Etang Joli* (33 pl), ☎ 53.06.96.62 ; ★★*la Rivière* (65 pl), ☎ 53.06.97.14 ; at Sireuil (10 km), ★★*Le Mas de Sireuil* (100 pl), ☎ 53.29.68.06.

Recommended
Sports : Canoe-Kayak, ☎ 53.29.66.95.
♥ at Lavesque, bakery : ☎ 53.29.24.08, some of the best bread in France,.

Nearby

Le **BUGUE**, ⊠ 24260, 9 km SW.
① Hôtel-de-ville, ☎ 53.07.20.48 (h.s.).
SNCF ☎ 53.07.20.05.

Hotels :
● ★★★ *L'Auberge du Noyer*, Le Récaud de Bouny Bas, ☎ 53.07.11.73, Euro Visa, 8 rm 𝕻 ⌂ ⌀ ⅋ ⌂ closed 1 Jan-30 Mar, 2 Nov-31 Dec, 240. Rest. ● ♦♦ ⅋ ⅋ closed Mon noon and Tue noon. English innkeepers welcome you to this old 18th-C farmhouse... just like in a novel : *écrevisses du Vergt, truite aux pleurotes, magret aux airelles.* "Nice cup of tea", 60-150.
● ★★★ *Royal Vézère*, (Mapotel), pl. de l'Hôtel-de-Ville, ☎ 53.07.20.01, Tx 540710, AE DC Euro Visa, 53 rm 𝕻 ≪ ⌂ ⌀ closed 1 Oct-29 Apr, 325. Rest. ● ♦♦ *l'Albuca* ⅋ ⅋ closed Wed noon and Thu noon. Christian Rouffignac's flower-bedecked terrace overlooks the Vézère. Good food, discothèque, 95-250.
★★ *Château*, Campagne, 4 km S., ☎ 53.07.23.50, 18 rm 𝕻 ≪ ⌂ ⌀ closed 15 Oct.-15 Mar, 175. Rest. ♦ 55-110.

△ ★★*Le Part* (135 pl), ☎ 53.07.24.60.

Recommended
Sports : horse club, Parc Royal Vézère, ☎ 53.07.21.67.

CONDAT-SUR-VÉZÈRE, ⊠ 24750 Condat-le-Lardin, 11 km NE of **Montignac**.

Restaurant :
● ♦ *L'Aérodrome*, ☎ 53.51.27.80, AE Euro Visa 𝕻 ≪ ⌂

⅋ & ⊡ closed Tue eve and Sun eve (l.s.) , Mon. Cheers for the likable cuisine served on lovely Haviland china with an airplane motif, 60-200.

Le **LARDIN SAINT-LAZARE**, ⊠ 24570 Condat, 11 km NE of **Montignac**.

Hotel :
★★ *Sautet* (L.F.), rte de Montignac, ☎ 53.51.27.22, AE Visa, 35 rm 𝕻 ⌂ ⊡ ⅋ closed Sat and Sun (l.s.), 20 Dec-15 Jan, 180. Rest. ♦♦ ⅋ ⅋ ⅋ 75-180.

MONTIGNAC, ⊠ 24290, 31 km NE.
① pl. B.-de-Born, ☎ 53.51.82.60.

Hotels :
★★★ *Château de Puy-Robert*, rte de Valojoux, à 1,5 km, ☎ 53.51.92.13, AE DC Euro Visa, 40 rm 𝕻 ≪ ⌂ ⌀ ⊡ 620. Rest. ♦♦♦ ⅋ The most recent of Albert Parveaux's Relais : a delightful little château for fans of Napoléon III. Light, modern, regional cuisine, 200-300.
★★★ *Le Relais du Soleil d'Or*, 16, rue du 4-Septembre, ☎ 53.51.80.22, Visa, 38 rm 𝕻 ≪ ⌀ ⅋ ⅋ & ⊡ closed 1 Nov-Palm Sun, 210. Rest. ● ♦♦ ⅋ ⅋ & You'll acquire a taste for earthy foods from the markets of Périgord, 75-250 ; child : 60.

△ ★★*Le Bleufond* (80 pl), ☎ 53.51.83.95.

Recommended
Guide to wines : Claude Dallis, Rare white plum brandy.

SERGEAC, ⊠ 24290 Montignac.

Restaurant :
♦ *Auberge de Castel-Merle*, ☎ 53.50.70.08, AE Visa 𝕻 ⅋ ⌀ ⌀ closed Mon ex Jul-Aug, 31 Oct-1 Apr. Classic cooking of Périgord, 55-110 ; child : 35.

TAMNIES, ⊠ 24620 Les Eyzies-de-Tayac-Sireuil, 12 km W.

Hotel :
★★ *Laborderie* (L.F.), ☎ 53.29.68.59, Euro, 30 rm 𝕻 ⅋ ⌀ ⌀ & ⌂ closed 15 Nov-15 Mar, 200. Rest. ♦♦ ⅋ & Spec : *foie gras aux reinettes, terrine de foie gras frais, saumon à l'oseille,* 60-100.

FIGEAC**

Cahors 71, Brive 92, Paris 584 km
pop 10500 ⊠ 46100   D3

Once a Protestant refuge, Figeac still has the air of a lively town of the Middle Ages, when it was a trading centre and staging post for pilgrims to Compostela. The town is now undergoing intensive restoration.

▶ There are few monuments here other than the **Mint** (dedicated to Champollion, decipherer of the Rosetta Stone, born at Figeac in 1790) constructed in local 13thC style : arcades forming a covered market, columned windows and open gallery beneath a flat roof. ▶ The **church of St. Sauveur**, a Benedictine abbey church (12th-14thC) was completely remodelled in the 17th and 19thC ; 13thC chapter-house with 17thC polychromed wood. ▶ Something interesting in every street : the great arcades in front of ancient shops, half-timbering and corbelled upper stories, soft-hued brickwork. ▶ Place Carnot is a former market-place ; the Rue Gambetta full of ogives, the Rue Colomb, which was the town's aristocratic street in the 17thC, and the Rue Boutaric are full of antique shops. ▶ Fine restoration of the **Enclos des Carmes** to the N. ▶ **Champollion Museum** *(15 Jun.-15 Sept., 10-12 & 2:30-6:30).* ▶ The **Aiguilles de Figeac** are 13thC obelisks planted S and W of the town. ▶ **Cardaillac** *(11 km NW)* was a fortified village, home of one of the most powerful feudal families in Quercy, and a Protestant refuge. □

Practical Information

FIGEAC
① pl. Vival, ☎ 65.34.06.25.
SNCF ☎ 65.34.10.37.

Car rental : *Avis*, 10, quai Bessières, ☎ 65.34.10.28; train station.

Hotels :
● ★★★ *Carmes*, enclos des Carmes, ☎ 65.34.20.78, Tx 520794, AE DC Euro Visa, 32 rm ℗ ⬚ ▭ ⌇ closed Sun eve and Sat (Oct-Apr), 15 Dec-15 Jan, 240. Rest. ◆◆◆ ⅃ ᶑ 85-200; child : 45.
★★ *Bains* (L.F.), 1, rue du Griffoul, ☎ 65.34.10.89, Euro Visa, 20 rm ℗ ≼ ⬚ ᵓ ᶑ closed 15 Dec-15 Mar, 127.

⚠ ★★★*Le Lido* (85 pl), ☎ 65.34.12.58; ★★★*Les Carmes* (60 pl), ☎ 65.34.08.56.

Nearby

CRANSAC, ⊠ 12110 Aubin, 33 km S.
⚐ (1 Apr-31 Oct), ☎ 65.63.09.83.
ⓘ mairie, ☎ 65.63.03.55.
SNCF ☎ 65.63.00.70.

Hotel :
★★ *Parc* (L.F.), 11, rue Gal-Louis-Artous, ☎ 65.63.01.78, 25 rm ℗ ⬚ ᵓ ᶑ closed 15 Oct-15 Apr, 130. Rest. ◆ ≼ ⍟ 50-100; child : 35.

⚠ ★★*Municipal* (35 pl), ☎ 65.63.03.55.

LACAPELLE-MARIVAL, ⊠ 46120, 21 km.
ⓘ château, ☎ 65.40.81.11 (h.s.).

Hotel :
★★ *La Terrasse*, rte d'Aurillac, ☎ 65.40.80.07, AE DC Euro, 23 rm ℗ ≼ ⬚ ᵓ closed 20 Dec-1 Apr, 200. Rest. ◆◆ ≼ 80-160.

⚠ ★★*Bois de Sophie* (65 pl), ☎ 65.40.82.59.

Recommended
Sports : *horse riding lessons*, Château d'Aynac, ☎ 65.38.93.16.

LATRONQUIÈRE, ⊠ 46210, 28 km S.
ⓘ mairie, ☎ 75.40.26.62 (h.s.).

Hotel :
● ★★★ *Tourisme*, ☎ 65.40.33.60, 30 rm ≼ ᵓ ⅃ closed Jan-Feb, 150. Rest. ◆◆ ⅃ ⍟ Spec : *cassolette d'escargots au beurre d'orties, pièce de bœuf au jus de truffe*, 60-100.

GOURDON*

Cahors 46, Brive 66, Paris 558 km
pop 5096 ⊠ 46300   C3
Gourdon's high hill can be seen from 20 km around. It is the principal town of a green, wooded district, the **Bouriane**. The old town has been spring-cleaned; its stonework now rivals that of Sarlat (→).

▶ The prettiest square is framed by the 17thC town hall, overlooking covered arcades; there is also a powerful Languedoc Gothic church. ▶ 360° view from the site of the château (destroyed).

Also... ▶ **Cougnac Caves★** *(3 km N)* : decorated with Magdalenian paintings, very similar to those of Pech Merle (→) *(Palm Sun.-1 Nov., 9-11 & 2-5:30; Jul.-Aug., 9-6:30).*

S. of Gourdon : the Bouriane region. Round trip *(approx 80 km; half-day)*

This is a hidden land, all hills, hollows, meadows, streams and woods. Ruined feudal buildings litter the limestone peaks, and many villages have pretty Romanesque churches bearing witness to the vigour of rural life at the end of the 11thC. ▶ **Gourdon.** ▶ In the **Céou Valley** are the ruins of the Cistercian **Abbaye Nouvelle** (new abbey). ▶ **Salviac** : a village reminiscent of the Midi ; 14thC stained glass★ in the church; **Lacoste Manor** (13th-16thC). ▶ **Cazals★**: above the valley of the Masse. ▶ The **château de Montcléra** was remodelled in the 16thC. ▶ The churches in **Arques** and **Saint-André-des-Arques** owe much to the Franco-Russian sculptor Zadkine, who dis-

covered the frescos in the latter and had the former restored. ▶ **L'Herm** is a delightful village; the priory at **Goujounac★** is overrun by vegetation. ▶ **Catus** in the Vert Valley was once a fortified town and has an 11thC priory. ▶ The beautifully aged church at **Rampoux** is marred by clumsily restored frescos.   □

Practical Information _____

ⓘ allée de la République, ☎ 65.41.06.40.
SNCF ☎ 65.41.02.19.

Hotels :
● ★★ *Bouriane*, pl. du Foirail, ☎ 65.41.16.37, 22 rm ℗ ⬚ ᵓ ⍟ closed 2 Jan-15 Mar, 200. Rest. ● ◆ ᵓ ⍟ closed Mon and Sun eve, 60-200.
★★ *Bissonnier* (L.F.), 51, bd des Martyrs, ☎ 65.41.02.48, Euro Visa, 24 rm ℗ ≼ ᵓ ⍟ closed Fri eve, 27 Nov-3 Jan, 160. Rest. ◆ ᵓ 50-160.
★★ *Promenade*, bd Galiot-de-Genouilhac, ☎ 65.41.05.41, 15 rm ℗ ≼ ⬚ ᵓ closed 1-15 May, 105.

⚠ ★★★ *"Ecoute s'il Pleut"* (110 pl), ☎ 65.41.06.19.

Recommended
Sports : *Cyclo-Club*, pl. de l'Ancienne-Gendarmerie, ☎ 65.41.00.36.

GRAMAT

Figeac 35, Cahors 56, Paris 549 km
pop 3828 ⊠ 46500   C3
The principal town of the Gramat *causse* (plateau), on the banks of the Alzou. Important sheep fairs are held here. ▶ A wildlife park★ shows the animals of the region at liberty *(pm only, low season).*

▶ On the Figeac road : **Beaulieu Hospice,** almshouse for pilgrims to Compostela; **Thémines** (covered market★); **Rudelle** and its fortress church★; **Le Bourg** early 12thC Romanesque church. ▶ At the other end of the *causse*, **La bastide-Murat** was the home of Joachim Murat (1767-1815; marshal under Napoléon; small museum, *1 Jul.-15 Sep., 10-12 & 2-6, closed Tue.)*; important fairs are held here. ▶ Beautiful villages nearby : **Vaillac, Soulomès, Montfaucon, Séniergues.**   □

Practical Information _____

GRAMAT
ⓘ pl. de la République, ☎ 65.38.73.60.
SNCF ☎ 65.38.71.27.

Hotels :
● ★★★ *Lion d'Or*, pl. de la République, ☎ 65.38.73.18, Euro Visa, 15 rm ℗ ≼ ⬚ closed Mon am, 15 Dec-15 Jan, 200. Rest. ● ◆◆ ≼ ⅃ ᵓ closed Mon noon. Keeping alive the flame of Quercy cuisine and the wines of Cahors : *mignon de boeuf au foie gras et jus de truffes*, 70-250.
★★ *Centre* (L.F.), pl. de la République, ☎ 65.38.73.37, Euro Visa, 14 rm ℗ ≼ closed Sat (l.s.), Feb school hols, 150. Rest. ◆ ⅃ 60-125; child : 30.

Recommended
♥ cheese : *Mme V. Pégourié*, pl. de la Halle, ☎ 65.38.71.09.

Nearby

RIGNAC, ⊠ 46600 Martel, 5 km NW.

Hotel :
★★★ *Château de Roumégouse* (R.C.), ☎ 65.33.63.81, AE DC Euro Visa, 14 rm ℗ ≼ ⬚ ⅃ ᵓ half pens (h.s.), closed 2 Nov-1 Apr, 430. Rest. ● ◆◆ ≼ ⅃ ᵓ ⍟ closed Tue noon. The rich fare of Quercy served in a château : *sauté de truffes au foie gras*, 110-200.

┌───┐
For the translation of a name of a meat, a fish or a vegetable, for the composition of a dish or a sauce, see the Menu Guide in the Practical Holiday Guide; it lists the most common culinary terms.
└───┘

Causse de GRAMAT

C-D3

The Causse de Gramat is the largest and wildest of the *causses* in the Lot area. It is scarred by the canyons of the Alzou and the Ouysse where a number of mills still can be seen. This is a mountain landscape, swept by a remorseless wind, with here and there a drystone hut or sheepfold. In the clearings, a few grey houses with brown-tiled roofs huddle around fortified churches. To the E, a remarkable site : the Desert of La Baunhie★. □

HAUTEFORT**

Périgueux 35, Limoges 65, Paris 459 km
pop 1035 ⊠ 24390   C1-2

The grand **château de Hautefort** *(Palm Sun.-1 Nov., 9-12 & 2-7; rest of the year, 2-6; closed 15 Dec.-15 Jan.)* is surrounded by an enormous park. Recently restored after a fire in 1968.
▶ The château is built on a spur overlooking broad woodlands and heath country. Two famous people lived in this château : the warrior-troubadour Bertrand de Born in the 12thC, and much later, Marie de Hautefort, a mistress of Louis XIII and hostess of a famous 17thC literary *salon*.
▶ The architecture of the village church recalls that of the château.

Nearby

▶ **Badefols-d'Ans★** *(6 km S)* : on the edge of the Périgord, this feudal castle was enlarged in the 15th and 18thC. Church with cupolas (12thC). □

JUMILHAC-LE-GRAND**

Limoges 53, Périgueux 56, Paris 447 km
pop 1450 ⊠ 24630   B1

This village is in fact part of the Limousin region and centres around a vast market-place (famous at the turn of the century for pig fairs).
▶ The **château,** hanging over the **Gorges de L'Isle,** is straight out of a fairy-tale, bristling with towers, belfries and pepperpot turrets (note the herringbone ridge tiles). Various portions of the building date from the 14th-18thC *(Easter-Nov., Sun. 2-6; 15 Jun.-15 Sep., 10-12 & 2-6:30).*
▶ The **church** was once the castle chapel. □

LALINDE

Bergerac 22, Périgueux 59, Paris 576 km
pop 2954 ⊠ 24150   B2

ⓘ ☎ 53.61.08.55.
SNCF ☎ 53.61.04.39.

Hotels :
● ★★★ *La Métairie* (R.C.), Mauzac, 6 km E., ☎ 53.22.50.47, Euro Visa, 11 rm Ⓟ ⟨⟨ ⚌ ⚘ ⊠ half pens, closed Tue eve, 2 Jan-11 Apr. From 15 Oct. Closed Wed lunch, 760. Rest. ◆◆ ⟨⟨ ♪ ⚘ 95-200.
★★ *Château* (L.F.), 1, rue de Verdun, ☎ 53.61.01.82, AE DC Visa, 9 rm ⟨⟨⚘ half pens (h.s.), closed 15 Nov-1 Mar, 140. Rest. ◆◆ ⟨ closed Fri ex Jul-Aug, 55-160.
★★ *La Résidence,* rue du Pr-Testut, ☎ 53.61.01.81, 11 rm Ⓟ ⚌ ⚘ closed 16 Sep-14 May, 125.

Restaurant :
● ◆◆ *Le Relais St-Jacques,* pl. de l'Eglise, St-Capraise-de-Lalinde, 4 km W., ☎ 53.23.22.14, Visa ♪ closed Mon eve and Tue eve, 1-16 Apr, 1-15 Dec. A gourmet feast with the flavour of Périgord. Incredibly affordable prices : *salade de gésiers confits, escalope de foie de canard chaud au monbazillac,* 55-180 ; child : 40.

▲ ★★*Le Moulin de la Guillou* (100 pl), ☎ 53.61.02.91.

LANQUAIS*

Bergerac 25, Brive-la-Gaillarde 106, Paris 596 km
pop 526 ⊠ 24150 Lalinde   B3

A tiny village (market, interesting grainstore) with a superb unfinished **château,** now very dilapidated. Feudal keep and Renaissance structure by the same masons responsible for the Louvre in Paris *(9-11:30 & 2-5 or 6, Apr.-Oct. ; closed Thu.).*
▶ On the other bank of the Dordogne, feudal castle of **Baneuil** *(1 Jul.-20 Sep., 10-12 & 3-6 ; closed Sun.).* □

LASCAUX**

C2

The famous cave discovered in 1940 has been closed to the public for the past 20 years. The 1 500 drawings and paintings could only be saved by such measures. Recently an astonishing facsimile, Lascaux II★★, was opened ; it was created over 10 years by artists using the same methods as the painters of the Palaeolithic era. *(Jul.-Aug., 9:30-7:30 ; rest of year, 10-12 & 2-5:30 ; closed Jan. and Mon.)* □

LAUZERTE*

Montauban 37, Agen 52, Paris 635 km
pop 1700 ⊠ 82110   C4

A *bastide* on a hill. Square houses with flat roofs currently undergoing restoration.
▶ NE, **Barguelonne Vale,** pretty villages. ▶ **Montcuq★** : old fortified village, capital of the **Quercy Blanc Region,** white as the limestone of the plateaus ; in the little valleys, a wide variety of crops. On the hillside, the *chasselas* grape predominates. □

Causse de LIMOGNE

C3-4

Fields of lavender and a *maquis* (heath) of holm-oak and aromatic plants in hot sun on stone give the *causse* a Mediterranean atmosphere. Dolmens, little stone huts, local architecture, and here and there a mill, a well, or a washhouse are reminders of an active community in this region.
▶ The capital, **Limogne,** is right in the middle of the *causse,* the crossroads and centre of the truffle industry.
▶ **Lalbenque :** site of the biggest market in the district. □

Practical Information _____

LALBENQUE, ⊠ 46230, 23 km S of **Cahors.**
SNCF ☎ 65.37.62.07.

Hotel :
★★★ *L'Aquitaine,* on the RN 20, ☎ 65.21.00.51, AE DC Euro Visa, 44 rm Ⓟ ⟨⟨ ⚘ ⊠ closed 24 Dec-8 Jan, 242. Rest. ◆ ⚗ closed Tue lunch and Sun eve, 80-120.

Recommended
Market : *truffle market,* Tue.

LOT and CÉLÉ Valleys***

C-D3

Round-trip from Cahors *(160 km, full-day ; see map 5).*

These narrow slots between golden cliffs separate the *causses* of Gramat and Limogne. The road follows them with difficulty and at each bend you may

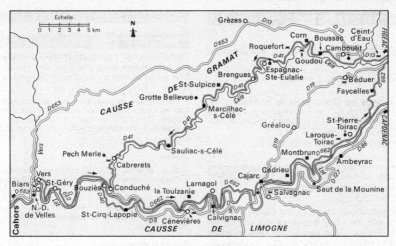

5. Lot and Célé valleys

discover a château, fortress church or village perched on high like an eagle's eyrie.

▶ **Cahors.** ▶ At Vers, **Notre-Dame de Velles** : pretty apse with rustic corbels. ▶ The Célé and Lot rivers meet at **Conduché.** ▶ The writer André Breton (1896-1966 ; founder of Surrealism) spent his summers in **Saint-Cirq-Lapopie★★** (pop. 179), and compared its charms to the poetry of Rimbaud. Renaissance church and charming museum in the château de la Gardette. ▶ **Château de Cénevières★** *(Apr.-Sep., 10-12 & 2-6 ex Tue. ; Oct.-Mar., closed at 5) :* overlooking the Lot, this feudal fortress was transformed during the Renaissance. Opposite, troglodyte village of **La Toulzanie.** ▶ **Calvignac** : on the edge of the cliff overlooking **Larnagol.** ▶ **Cajarc** was once an inland port : seamen's chapel ; charming holiday spot. ▶ 8 km from Cajarc, there is a remarkable but little-known site called **Le Saut-de-la-Mounine.** ▶ **Montbrun★** clusters high around its fortress. ▶ **Laroque-Toirac** : 15thC château *(19 Jul.-19 Sep.).* ▶ The warlike church of **Saint-Pierre-Toirac** (11th-12thC, fortified 14th-15thC) looks like a feudal keep. ▶ Return to **Figeac** (→) across the *causse.* ▶ The châteaux of **Ceint d'Eau** (15thC) and **Béduer** (13thC) have been much restored. ▶ After **Boussac,** the Célé disappears into a canyon and narrow gorges alternate with cropland. ▶ **Espagnac-Sainte-Eulalie★,** on the edge of the *causse,* its pointed roofs grouped around a priory, (17th-18thC). The principal sight here is the church (12th-14th-15thC) ; 14thC tombs and remarkable gilded woodwork (17thC). ▶ **Marcilhac-sur-Célé★** was a rich Benedictine abbey ; magnificent ruins. The Romanesque portion has not been rebuilt but the Gothic part is in use as a church (frescos). In a nearby valley, Bellevue cave (view of the village). ▶ **Fontaine-de-la-Pescalerie** is one of the most delightful sites in the region. ▶ **Cabrerets** : through the valley of the Sagne★ (a little ecological paradise), to the **Pech-Merle Caves★★★,** a beautiful Paleolithic sanctuary open to the public ; remarkable site, very instructive museum *(Palm Sun.-Oct. and by appt. off-season).* □

Practical Information ────────────

CABRERETS, ⊠ 46330, 33 km NE of **Cahors.**

Hotel :
● ★★ *Grottes* (L.F.), ☎ 65.31.27.02, Visa, 18 rm Ⓟ ⛌ 🅡 🍽 ▣ closed 15 Oct-4 Apr, 155. Rest. ♦ ♪ ⅋ closed Sat noon, 1 Oct-4 Apr, 55-100.

Recommended
Canoe-kayak rental : *les Amis du Célé,* ☎ 65.31.26.73, daily May-Sep.

CAJARC, ⊠ 46160, 51 km W of **Cahors.**

Restaurant :
♦♦ *La Ferme de Montbrun,* 9 km via D 662, ☎ 65.40.07.71, Euro Visa ⅋ ♪ closed Wed ex Jul-Aug, 1 Oct-1 May. "Nouvelle" country cuisine, 150-220.

FONTAINE-DE-LA-PESCALERIE, ⊠ 46330 Cabrerets, 2 km NE of **Cabrerets.**

Hotel :
● ★★★ *La Pescalerie* (R.C.), ☎ 65.31.22.55, AE DC Euro Visa, 10 rm Ⓟ ⛌ 🏠 🅡 closed 1 Nov-1 Apr. 17th-C manor, 480. Rest. ● ♦♦ 🅑 Hélène Combette welcomes you to her pretty little paradise. Happiness awaits you in her very lovely home. Family-style cuisine, featuring the best of the Quercy markets, 185-250.

SAINT-CIRQ-LAPOPIE, ⊠ 46330, 33 km W of **Cahors.**

Hotels :
★ *Auberge du Sombral,* ☎ 65.31.26.08, 10 rm 🅡 closed Tue eve and Wed, 15 Nov-15 Mar, 200. Rest. ♦♦ 🅑 closed 15 Nov-15 Feb, 60-200.
● *Pélissaria,* ☎ 65.31.25.14 Ⓟ ⛌ 🏠 🅡 half pens, closed 3 Nov-1 Apr, 500. Rest. ♦ ⅋ 80-120.

MAREUIL

Brantôme 20, Limoges 86, Paris 494 km
pop 1215 ⊠ 24340   B1

One of the outposts of the province and one of the four Baronies of the ancient Province of Périgord. Unusually, the **castle** is built in the plain, completely surrounded by moats ; Flamboyant Gothic chapel *(2-6, Easter-1 Nov. ; low season and nat. hols., Sun. 2-5:30 only).* □

Nearby

▶ A number of châteaux provide excellent destinations for walks, though most are not open to the public : ▶ **Beaulieu** *(3 km, very near the Riberac road).* ▶ **Beauregard** *(3 km along a path on the left of the Riberac road).* ▶ **Repaire** *(2 km on the first road left from the Ribérac road).* Several pretty churches nearby : ▶ **Vieux Mareuil** *(5 km E ; D939) :* 13thC Romanesque church fortified in the 14thC. ▶ **Cherval** *(10 km SW ; D708) :* fortress church with four cupolas★. ▶ **Cercles** *(10 km S D99) :* part of an old priory ; figured capitals (12thC) on W door. ▶ On a neighbouring bluff, fine houses reminiscent of the Renaissance in **La Tour Blanche★** : 10thC keep ; 17thC manor.

Also... ▶ **Château des Bernardières** (14th, 15th and 17thC; *Jul.-Sep., 10-11 & 3-6)*, near Champaux *(10 km E)*.

□

Practical Information

Nearby

VIEUX-MAREUIL, ⊠ 24340, 5 km SE.

Hotel :
● ★★★ *Auberge de l'Etang Bleu*, ☎ 53.60.92.63, AE DC Euro Visa, 11 rm Ⓟ ⊀ ⩍ ⚲ half pens (h.s.), closed Sun eve and Mon (All Saints Day–Easter), 15-31 Jan, 400. Rest. ◆◆ ⊰ ⅋ 75-200 ; child : 40.

⚠ ★★★*L'Etang Bleu* (165 pl), ☎ 53.56.62.63.

MARMANDE

Agen 58, Bordeaux 89, Paris 684 km
pop 17758 ⊠ 47200   A3
The main agricultural centre of the Garonne Valley, which vies with the Loire Region for the title of "the garden of France". The landscape here is often compared to that of Tuscany in Italy. A.-Marzelles Museum (local history, *tel. : 53.64.42.04*).

▶ On the Agen road : ▶ **Le Mas-d'Agenais** : covered market and Rembrandt painting in the Benedictine church. ▶ **Clairac**, along the Lot where, in the 16thC, the Benedictines pioneered tobacco and prunes, now the principal crops of the region (museum, *summer, Tue. and Sat. p.m.*). ▶ **Gontaud-de-Nogaret** : Gibra mill.   □

Practical Information

MARMANDE
ⓘ 21, rue de la République, ☎ 53.64.32.50.
✈ *Virazeil*, 3 km E, ☎ 53.64.26.36.
SNCF ☎ 53.66.50.50.

Hotels :
★★ *Capricorne* (L.F.), rte d'Agen, ☎ 53.64.16.14, AE DC Euro Visa, 33 rm Ⓟ ⩍ ⚲ ⊠ closed Sun eve and Fri lunch, 15 Dec-10 Jan, 170. Rest. ◆ ⅃ 100-200.
★ *Auberge de Guyenne*, 9, rue Martignac, ☎ 53.64.01.77, Euro Visa, 16 rm Ⓟ ⚲ closed Mon (l.s.), 26 Oct-13 Nov, 120. Rest. ◆ ⅃ ⅋ 45-80 ; child : 30.

⚠ ★★*Municipal* (75 pl), ☎ 53.64.63.05.

Recommended
Guide to wines : at Meilhan-sur-Garonne, *Labeau*, ☎ 53.94.31.29, clear plum and pear brandies.
♥ at St-Sernain-de-Duras CP 47120, artisanal canning and courses : *Béatrice Donon*, Ferme "Les Savoys", 26 km N. D 708, ☎ 53.94.76.34.

Nearby

CASTELJALOUX, ⊠ 47700, 23 km S.
SNCF ☎ 53.93.00.45.

Hotels :
★★ *Cordeliers* (L.F.), 1, rue des Cordeliers, ☎ 53.93.02.19, Euro Visa, 24 rm Ⓟ ⚲ ⅋ 200.
Vieille Auberge, 11, Posterne, ☎ 53.93.01.36, AE Visa, 4 rm Ⓟ ⚲ closed Sun eve and Mon, 130. Rest. ◆ B. Daniel's good cooking : *terrine de foie gras de canard, salade gourmande*, 50-160.

⚠ ★★*Municipal* (66 pl), ☎ 53.93.00.24.

DAMAZAN, ⊠ 47160, 30 km S.

Hotel :
● ★★ *Canal* (L.F.), ☎ 53.79.42.84, 20 rm Ⓟ ⊀ ⩍ ⚲ 130. Rest. ◆◆ ⅃ 65-200:

⚠ ★★*Du Lac* (66 pl), ☎ 53.79.42.98.

Recommended
Guide to wines : at Buzet-sur-Baïze CP 47160, *wine cooperative*, ☎ 53.84.74.30, côtes de Buzet.

MOISSAC★★★

Montauban 29, Agen 43, Paris 657 km
pop 11410 ⊠ 82200   B4
The distribution centre for *chasselas* grapes and all the fruit grown along the Tarn and Garonne rivers. The **abbey church** here is one of the greatest achievements of European religious art.

▶ Its **majestic doorway**★★★ is a perfect expression of Cluniac ideals and had considerable influence in southern France. The church itself is ordinary, but the **cloister**★★ is superb. ▶ Moissac Museum in the former abbot's residence.

Nearby

▶ From **Boudou** *(7 km W)* view over both river valleys. ▶ **Castelsarrasin** *(8 km S)* : important agricultural market; former *bastide*, priory attached to Moissac. ▶ **Abbaye de Belleperche** (12th-13th-17thC ; *6 km S from Castelsarrasin)*. ▶ **Castelsagrat** *(13 km NW)* : well-preserved little *bastide*, and **château de Brassac** (13th-15thC ; *Easter-1 Nov., 2-7/30)*.   □

Practical Information

ⓘ pl. Durand-de-Bredon, ☎ 63.04.01.85 (h.s.).
SNCF ☎ 63.04.01.61.

Hotel :
★★★ *Relais du Moulin*, 1, pl. du Moulin, ☎ 63.04.03.55, Visa, 45 rm Ⓟ ⩍ ⚲ ⋌ 350. Rest. ◆◆ ⊰ ⅋ 85-175.

⚠ ★★★*L'Ile de Bidounet* (140 pl), ☎ 63.32.29.96.

MONBAZILLAC

Périgueux 54, Bordeaux 99, Paris 562 km
pop 837 ⊠ 24240 Sigoulès   B3
Monbazillac produces wine as famous as Sauternes and both have suffered from the current preference for dry wines. ▶ The Renaissance **château** belonging to the wine-making cooperative is now a museum *(9-12 & 2-5)*. One room is consecrated to wine, another devoted to Protestantism, equally important to local people. ▶ The **vineyards** cover the surrounding hills (30 km²). Planted by monks at the end of the 11thC, they blossomed under the influence of Bergerac merchants and exiled Protestants. This fertile agricultural region marks the transition from the Dordogne to the opulent Bordelais Region. Even the more ordinary houses have handsome, dignified façades, and the Roman-tiled roofs projecting over their verandahs echo this feeling. Farms and small holdings are sprinkled throughout the area, and the market towns, with their population of independent growers, are focal points of the region.

Nearby

▶ **Sainte-Foy-la-Grande** *(25 km W)*, astride the Dordogne, was a French *bastide* (arcaded square) and Protestant stronghold. ▶ **Montcaret**★ *(13 km W)* : Gallo-Roman mosaics and Romanesque church (the capitals are re-used Gallo-Roman sculptures). ▶ **Saint-Michel-de-Montaigne** *(4 km NW)* : in the centre of the Montravel vineyards, (velvety *demi-sec* wines). The château where Montaigne lived was destroyed by fire and rebuilt during the 19thC, but the **library tower** where he wrote his *Essays* (1580-1585) is the original *(9-12 & 2-7; closed Mon., Tue. and 6 Jan.-19 Feb.)*. ▶ In the N of the Dordogne, vineyards give way to small fields, orchards and tobacco plantations. ▶ **Montpeyroux** *(6 km N)* : the U-shaped château of Montecoulon (17th-18thC) makes a pretty picture with the neighbouring church and its beautiful apse in Saintonge Romanesque. ▶ **Carsac-de-Gurson** *(6 km N)* : a pretty church in similar style. Ruins of feudal castle at Gurson. ▶ **Saint-Martin-de-Gurson** *(2 km)* : another church in Saintonge Romanesque, its flat façade enlivened by stylised arches; the *chevet* was fortified in the 15thC, but damaged during restoration. □

Practical Information _____

Hotel :
★★ *Relais de la Diligence*, rte d'Eymet, ☎ 53.58.30.48, Euro Visa, 8 rm ≪ closed Tue eve and Mon (l.s.), 15-28 Feb, 24 Jun-10 Jul, 140. Rest. ♦ ♪ 80-180.

MONTAUBAN**

Toulouse 53, Auch 86, Paris 656 km
pop 53147 ⊠ 82000   C4

Montauban is the rose of the Midi, its pink brick gleaming in the sunlight. It was also a *bastide;* the central square, Place Nationale★★ (B2), was rebuilt in the 17th and 18thC in Italian style (under restoration).

▶ Fine view over the Tarn from the **Pont Vieux** (14thC bridge; B2). ▶ **Ingres Museum**★★ in the former Episcopal Palace (17thC) : exceptional collection bequeathed by the painter; works by Bourdelle and Desnoyer. *(Palm Sun. - Jun., Sep.-15 Oct., closed Mon.; 16 Oct.-Palm Sun., closed Sun.; 10-12 & 2-6; Jul.-Aug. 10-12 & 1:30-6, closed hols.)* ▶ Numerous streets are lined with town houses★ from the French Classical period. ▶ A rare classical **cathedral**, gleaming white in this town of pink brick, symbolises the Counter-Reformation against the Protestant heresy; Montauban was the capital of the "Protestant Republic" of the Midi. Inside, a painting by Ingres, "Le vœu de Louis XIII". ▶ One private town residence, the **Hôtel Lefranc-de-Pompignan** (17th-18thC) is a fine example of Montalbanais architecture *(visits; enq. : SI).* ▶ W of the town is a fertile plain watered by the Tarn and the Garonne; good land shimmering with heat in the summers at the foot of landscape is changing, and industry is starting to oust agriculture as the area's economic mainstay. ▶ **Natural History and Prehistoric Museum** *(10-12 & 2-6, closed Mon., Sun. am and hols.)* across from the Ingres

Museum; also **regional museum** *(Tue., Fri., 10-12 & 2-6).* Rose garden in Chambord park, near the municipal pool. □

Practical Information _____

MONTAUBAN
ⓘ Ancien Collège, 2, rue du Collège (B-C2), ☎ 63.63.60.60.
✈ 2 km NE, ☎ 63.03.27.44.
SNCF (A2), ☎ 63.63.50.50.
Car rental : *Avis*, Train station (C1); 5, rue de la Briqueterie, ☎ 63.66.23.06.

Hotels :
★★★ *Ingres*, (Mapotel), 10, av. Mayenne (A2), ☎ 63.63.36.01, 34 rm P 🅿 280.
★★ *Le Prince Noir* (L.F.), pl. Prax-Paris (C2), ☎ 63.63.10.10, Tx 520362, Euro Visa, 34 rm P ♪ Flowery terrace, 160.
★★ *Midi*, (Inter-Hôtel, L.F.), 12, rue Notre-Dame (B2), ☎ 63.63.17.23, Tx 531705, AE DC Euro Visa, 48 rm P ≪ 🕮 & 180. Rest. ♦♦ ♪ & closed Sun (Oct-May), 15 Dec-15 Jan. Spec : *demoiselles de canard assaisonnées, parfait glacé aux pêches caramélisées et au miel,* 65-170; child : 35.
★★ *Orsay*, across from the station (A2), ☎ 63.63.00.57, Tx 520362, AE DC Euro Visa, 20 rm P ♪ closed Sun and Mon lunch, 24 Dec-1 Jan, 200. Rest. ● ♦♦ ♪ & closed 24 Dec-1 Jan, 1-15 Jul. Spec : *foie gras aux pommes, turbot à la verveine, magret au cassis,* 80-180.

Restaurants :
♦♦ *Le Ventadour*, 23, quai Villebourbon (A2), ☎ 63.63.34.58, AE DC Euro Visa ≪ closed Sat noon and Sun Feb, Aug. In a 17thC vaulted room. Spec : *aiguillettes de canard au vinaigre de framboises, ris de veau sautés aux cèpes,* 80-130.
♦ *Le Pitzou*, 24, rue de la Comédie (B1), ☎ 63.63.02.83, AE DC Euro Visa ♪ closed Wed eve and Sun. Spec : *fromage chaud aux cèpes, ragoût de St-Jacques et de grenouilles, foie gras aux pointes d'asperges,* 60-120.

Recommended
Baby-sitting : *fédération des Oeuvres Laïques,* ☎ 63.63.04.20.
Market : esplanade Prax-Paris, Sat am.
♥ candy : *Les Délices*, 10, rue de la République,

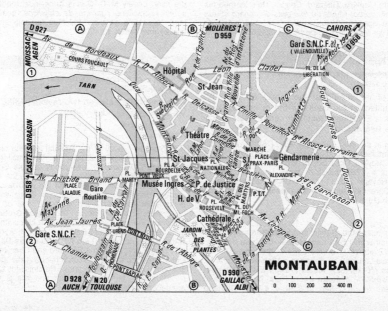

☎ 63.63.06.38 ; chocolates, tea : *Laplace*, 52, rue de la Résistance, ☎ 63.63.06.08 ; pastry : *Robert Marty*, 70, rue Léon-Cladel, ☎ 63.03.46.52 ; *Péries*, 7, rue des Carmes, ☎ 63.63.06.85.

Nearby

GRISOLLES, ⊠ 82170, 24 km.

Hotel :
★★ *Relais des Garrigues*, N 20, ☎ 63.67.31.59, Visa, 27 rm Ⓟ ⁂ ⌕ closed 4 Jan-10 Feb, 190. Rest. ♦ closed Wed noon, 120-150.

⚠ ★★★*Aquitaine* (35 pl), ☎ 63.30.33.22.

MONTBETON, ⊠ 82290 La Ville-Dieu-du-Temple, 5 km W.

Hotel :
★★★ *Les Coulandrieres*, rte de Castel-Sarrasin, ☎ 63.67.47.47, Tx 520200, AE DC Euro Visa, 21 rm Ⓟ ⁂ ⅘ ⌧ half pens (h.s.), closed Sun eve, 604. Rest. ♦♦ ♪ Spec : *escalope de bar aux poireaux et aux truffes, carré d'agneau aux pleurotes*, 90-250.

MONTPEZAT-DE-QUERCY*

Cahors 29, Montauban 34, Paris 625 km
pop 1412 ⊠ 82270   C4
Montpezat is built on a ridge along the edge of the Limogne Causse and owes its treasures to a dynasty of outstanding prelates, the des Prés.
▶ Arcaded square ; Languedoc Gothic church : 16thC Flemish tapestries and beautiful statue of the Virgin.
Also... ▶ Church at **Saux** *(4 km NW)* deep in the woods and decorated with murals (15thC). **Castelnau-Montratier★** *(12 km NW)* former fortified town on a hill.   □

Practical Information ⎯⎯⎯⎯⎯⎯⎯⎯⎯⎯⎯

ⓘ pavillon d'accueil de l'Union touristique du Bas-Quercy RN20, ☎ 63.02.05.65 (h.s.).
SNCF ☎ 63.02.07.16.

Hotel :
● ★ *Depeyre*, rue de la République, ☎ 63.02.08.41, AE DC Euro Visa, 7 rm Ⓟ ⁂ ⌕ closed Sun eve (l.s.) and Mon, 6-30 Jan, 9-19 Jun, 120. Rest. ● ♦ ♪ closed Mon (Jul-Aug) and Sun eve. Jacques Depeyre hasn't wasted his time with Manière, Guérard, Chapel. He's learned his lessons well : *turbot fourré au foie gras de canard et aux poireaux de vigne nouveaux, poulet fermier au coulis de truffes, délicat à la pulpe de pruneaux*, 80-250.

NÉRAC*

Agen 30, Bordeaux 124, Paris 719 km
pop 7270 ⊠ 47600   A4
Domaine of the d'Albrets, the family of Henri IV, Nérac, situated on the banks of the delightful Baïse River, was a European Humanist centre, later a hotbed of the Reformation.

▶ **Museum** in the only remaining wing (15thC) of the old château : interesting documentation on life in Nérac *(9-12 & 2-6, 9-6 May-15 Oct. ; closed Mon. ; off season, tel. : 53.65.21.11)*. ▶ 1780 **church** by Victor Louis, architect of the Palais Royal in Paris. ▶ Gothic bridge ; attractive walk along the Garenne ; mediaeval area (petit Nérac) ; château de Bournac (16thC).

Nearby

▶ Fortified mill★ and Gothic bridge at **Barbaste** *(6 km NW)*. ▶ Another mill S of **Lavardac**. ▶ **Château de Xaintrailles★** *(12 km NW)* : on the edge of the Landes forest (→ Bordelais-Landes). ▶ *Bastides :* **Vianne★** *(9 km N)*, **Mézin** *(13 km SW)*. ▶ **Poudenas★** *(17 km SW)* : château where Henri IV used to hunt *(guided visits 14 Jul.-1 Sep. at 3:30, 4, 4:30)* ▶ **Château**

de **Buzet-sur-Baïse** *(15 km N)*, surrounded by the *Côtes de Buzet* vineyards. ▶ 12 km S, **Moncrabeau** is celebrated locally for its liars and storytellers.   □

Practical Information ⎯⎯⎯⎯⎯⎯⎯⎯⎯⎯⎯

NÉRAC
ⓘ sq. des Bains, ☎ 53.65.21.22 (h.s.) ; hôtel de ville, ☎ 53.65.00.54.
SNCF ☎ 53.65.00.34.

Hotels :
★★ *Albret* (L.F.), 40-42, allées d'Albret, ☎ 53.65.01.47, Tx 560800, 20 rm Ⓟ ⌕ closed Mon (l.s.), Sep, 2-9 Mar, 180. Rest. ♦ 45-160.
★★ *Château* (L.F.), 7, av. Mondenard, ☎ 53.65.09.05, 20 rm, closed Oct, 150. Rest. ♦ ⅌ closed Mon noon and Sun eve (Nov-Jun), 60-150.

Recommended
Guide to wines : *Pallas*, Domaine de Casseneuil, ☎ 53.65.01.51, vintage Armagnacs ; at Mezin, PC 41170, Domaine de Cazeaux Lannes.

Nearby

FRANCESCAS, ⊠ 47600 Nérac, 11 km SE.

Restaurant :
♦ *Le Pot aux Roses*, 3-5, Grande-Rue, ☎ 53.65.41.59, AE Euro Visa ♪ ⅊ closed Wed and Sun eve (ex Jul-Sep), 23 Jun-10 Jul. R. Assimon, a gifted pupil of A. Senderens, is now own boss. Good luck ! : *gâteau de roquefort au floc de Gascogne, salade de queues d'écrevisses aux pêches blanches* (in season), 90-125.

MONCRABEAU, ⊠ 47600 Nérac, 12 km SE.

Hotel :
● ★★ *Le Phare* (L.F.), ☎ 53.65.42.08, AE DC Visa, 7 rm ⅌ ⁂ ⌕ closed Tue, 15 Feb-8 Mar, 12-30 Oct, 180. Rest. ● ♦ ⅌ Generous, inexpensive regional dishes : *gâteau de cèpes aux noix, écrevisses flambées à l'armagnac, feuilleté de fruits de saison*, 60-160.

⚠ ★★★*Municipal* (150 pl), ☎ 53.65.42.11.

POUDENAS, ⊠ 47170 Mézin, 17 km SW.

Restaurant :
● ♦♦ *A La Belle Gasconne*, ☎ 53.65.71.58, AE DC Visa ⅌ ⁂ ♪ closed Mon and Sun eve, 1-15 Dec. Boat rides on the river. Lovely M.-C. Gracia turns local foodstuffs into subtle specialities : *terrine de chipirons*, geese, homemade jams and pastries. Produce for sale on the spot and by mail order, 100-200.

NONTRON

Périgueux 49, Limoges 69, Paris 477 km
pop 4000 ⊠ 24300   B1
A beautiful site between two ravines. 18thC château. View over the Bandiat Valley.

Nearby

▶ Explore the valley of the Bandiat and the old smithies that give a special character to this small district ; at **Javerlhac** *(10.5 km W)*, everybody speaks Occitan, the ancient dialect of the S. The 13thC church, the 15thC castle with its dovecote, the mill and the willows combine to create a beautiful rustic landscape. ▶ Romanesque chapel at **Saint-Robert** *(16 km NW)* has one of the finest bell-towers in the region. ▶ The **Teyjat Grotto** is decorated with remarkable Magdalenian rock carvings. ▶ Leisure centre on the **Saint-Estèphe Lake**, in woods strewn with rocky outcrops *(10 km N)*. ▶ **Bussière-Badil** *(15 km W)* : on the borders of the Périgord and Charente regions, with a fine Romanesque church mingling the architectural characteristics of both regions. Reminiscent of Cadouin (→ Bastides), but the W porch and the S tympanum are decorated with carvings.   □

Practical Information _____

NONTRON
ⓘ pl. du Champ-de-Foire, ☎ 53.56.00.53 (h.s.).   ♥

Hotel :
★★ *Grand Hôtel* (L.F.), 3, pl. Alfred-Agard, ☎ 53.56.11.22,
Euro Visa, 26 rm Ⓟ ⬤ ⬤ ⬤ ⬤ half pens (h.s.), closed
15-31 Jan, 360. Rest. ♦ ⬤ 45-160.

Nearby

JAVERLHAC, ✉ 24300 Nontron, 11 km NW.

Hotel :
★ *Auberge des Tilleuls* (L.F.), ☎ 53.56.30.12, Euro Visa,
8 rm ⬤ ⬤ ⬤ half pens (h.s.), 220. Rest. ♦ 40-60;
child : 30.

SAINT-ESTÈPHE, ✉ 24300 Nontron, 9 km NW.

Restaurant :
♦ *Gérard Dutin*, ☎ 53.56.83.24, Euro Visa ♪ closed Tue,
15 Oct-10 Nov. Fixed-price meals centred around Périgord specialities, 45-90.

The NONTRONNAIS Region

B1

This is Périgord Vert — called green, for its ubiquitous grass and chestnut trees. A centre for the manufacture of barrels, baskets and other functional items.
The westerly wind carries a tang of Brittany, blowing across the heather and over the massive granite
rocks (Roc Branlant, Roc Poperdu). This is an outpost of the Limousin, with a more boisterous climate
than elsewhere in Périgord and more lakes and rivers.
Don't miss Chalard Waterfall *(Saut du Chalard)*.   ☐

Gouffre de PADIRAC*

(Padirac Chasm)
C2

The most famous chasm in France, plunging onto the
heart of the Causse de Gramat.

▶ The river running through the Gouffre joins the Dordogne at Montvalent, but its source is still unknown. Visit
the Gouffre by boat; the water's surface is smooth and
unruffled *(spring hols.-Oct., 9-12 & 2-6; 8-12 & 2-7 in Jul.;
8-7 Aug.)*.   ☐

The PÉRIGORD BLANC Region

A-B1

Aquitaine and the western part of the Midi begin
around Ribérac and Périgueux. Here are riverside
limestone plateaus similar to those of the Sarladais
region — the **Isle**, the **Auvézère**, the **Loue** and the
Dronne — but the valleys are wider, the slopes
gentler, the farms more opulent. The middle reaches of
the Isle extend into a different region S of Périgueux,
where the little hamlets are so isolated in the woods
that the country seems overrun by oak and chestnut.
☐

The PÉRIGORD NOIR Region

C2
Round trip *(68 km; approx half-day)*

Sarlat in the ideal departure for exploring the **Périgord
Noir** region, a country of round hills covered in oak
woods, chestnut groves and pine forests, and where
the finest stone-roofed houses are to be found.

▶ Sarlat. ▶ **Temniac** : the chapel of Notre-Dame, in the
simple Périgord style of the 12thC, on a superb site. **Châ-**

teau ruins *(10-12 & 2-6 or 7)*. ▶ **Saint-Geniès** : Romanesque church with broad stone-tiled roof; 16thC fortified
bell-tower; in the cemetery, Gothic chapel decorated with
frescos. ▶ **Saint-Crépin** : classic Périgord village beside a
stream, with Romanesque church and small 17thC manor-
house. **Caducet** also has a Romanesque church, and an
interesting 17thC cemetery. ▶ **Salignac-Eyvignes** clings
close to the **château de Fénélon**, an imposing 12th-17thC
fortress with a commanding view of Périgord Noir.
(Jul.-Aug. ex Tue.). ▶ **Château du Claud** : a wild site in
the woods; stone roofs and great character. ▶ **Eyvignes** :
16thC manor house, 12th and 16thC church. ▶ **Eybènes** :
12thC church, two manors (16th and 18thC). ▶ **Orla-
guet** : small Romanesque church in typical countryside.
▶ **Carlux** : little squares planted with lime trees, a fortress
in ruins since the end of the Hundred Years' War and a
Gothic fireplace. S, the **château de Rouffilhac** has been
over-restored, but the site is wonderful, a hillside of evergreen oaks above the Dordogne. ▶ **Calviac** : 12th and
15thC church belonging to the abbey where Sacerdos,
patron saint of Sarlat, was a monk. ▶ **Sainte-Mondane** :
on the other bank of the Dordogne in the centre of a large
agricultural estate with classified historic 17thC farm buildings, you will find the 15thC **château★** where the writer
Fénélon (1651-1715) was born; it has retained a marked-
ly military character (collection of old cars; *daily 10-12
& 2-6 or 7*). View over the vales of the Sarladais. ▶ **Veyrignac** : on the left bank of the Dordogne, with a little
church and a large château over the river *(1 Jul.-15 Sep.
10-12 & 2-7)*. ▶ **Groléjac** : a wide bridge over the Dordogne, a manor house, old buildings and a Romanesque
church with a big, square bell-tower (17thC woodwork and
repoussé leatherwork). ▶ **Carsac★** : a ravishing stone-
tiled village, with its château surrounded by greenery
and a beautifully-proportioned Romanesque church (but
modern stained glass; ogive vaulting from 16thC). ▶ Pleasant walk or bicycle ride up the **vale of the Enea★** lined
with country houses, to **Sainte-Nathalène** with its 16thC
manor and Romanesque church.
Also... ▶ **Saint-André-d'Allas** *(4,5 km W of Sarlat)* : on a
rock above the Allas is a large 18thC (Louis XV) château.
The rustic church at **Allas** with its wall-belfry and stone
roof was remodelled in the 15thC, whereas the church
at **Saint-André**, also stone-tiled, was rebuilt in the 16thC.
In the hamlet of **Bussiéral**, the **huttes gauloises** of **Le
Vreuil★** are an intriguing collection of drystone huts.   ☐

Nearby

CARLUX, ✉ 24370, 18 km E of **Sarlat**.

Hotel :
★★ *Aux Poissons Frais* (L.F.), ☎ 53.29.70.24, 20 rm Ⓟ ⬤
⬤ ⬤ ⬤ ⬤ closed Oct, 170. Rest. ♦ ⬤ ⬤ 50-180.

⬤ at Rouffilhac, ★★*Ombrages de Dordogne* (80 pl),
☎ 65.29.70.24.

GROLÉJAC, ✉ 24250 Domme, 11 km SE of **Sarlat**.

Hotel :
★★ *Le Grillardin*, ☎ 53.28.11.02, AE Euro, 14 rm Ⓟ ⬤ ♪
⬤ closed Feb school hols and Nov, 160. Rest. ♦ closed
Wed, 85-110.

⬤ ★★★★*Les Granges* (135 pl), ☎ 53.28.11.15.

SALIGNAC-EYVIGNES, ✉ 24590, 19 km NE of **Sarlat**.

Hotel :
★ *La Terrasse*, pl. de la Poste, ☎ 53.28.80.38, Euro,
13 rm Ⓟ closed 10 Nov-1 Apr, 125. Rest. ♦ 50-100.

PÉRIGUEUX*

Brive 73, Angoulême 85, Paris 530 km
pop 35400 ✉ 24000   B2

A vigorous regional capital that has made great
efforts to restore its old buildings (now comparable
with those at Sarlat). Périgueux always had everything
necessary for status as the kingpin of the Périgord,

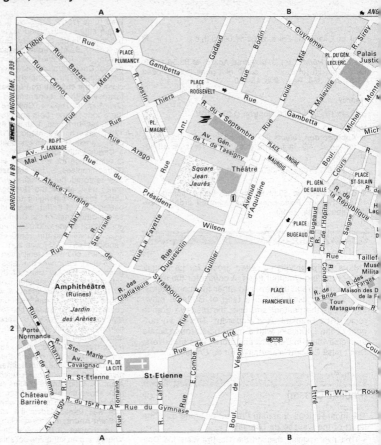

PÉRIGUEUX

in particular a central position, where all roads meet. The huge Place Francheville (B2; car park) is the link between the old town around the cathedral (C2) and the lower town (A2), with vestiges of the Gallo-Roman town *Vesona.* Visitors keen on archaeology should begin here and climb up the streets of Saint-Front. Otherwise, head for the cathedral and the classified historical area, especially on Wednesday or Saturday (market days) when all the little squares have a holiday air.

Vesona, Gallo-Roman capital of the Pétrocores (inhabitants of Roman Périgord) was, to judge by the excavations, a rich city with luxurious villas. An amphitheatre for 30 000 people was dismantled to build ramparts in the 3rdC, together with a huge temple of which only the **Vesone Tower** (A2), formerly the *Cella* or Holy of Holies, remains. The Gallo-Roman city was succeeded by two rival cities, each behind ramparts : the city of the count and the bishop (built on the ancient ruins of Vesona) and the town of the merchants and artisans. The Quartier Saint-Front is still the dynamic heart of Périgueux, and the old buildings along the winding streets are gradually being restored. The cathedral is spectacular and somehow anachronistic, seeming to belong more to the 19thC than to the 12thC. In Renaissance times, merchants built their houses along the banks of the Isle. The modern town has grown out from the wide 18thC boulevards and rather dreary developments around the station.

▶ The **church of St. Etienne** (A2) was long a cathedral and the model for numerous diocesan churches with cupolas; it is a good example of Périgord Romanesque, spare and stern, even if the nave is a 17thC reconstruction. ▶ At the back of the **Place Francheville** (B2), which was once a sort of no-man's-land between the two rivals, the **Mataguerre Tower** (end 15thC), the last of the 28 towers that fortified the bourgeois town of Saint-Front. ▶ The preserved area has been admirably restored (pedestrian precinct). ▶ On the **Place de la Clautre,** in front of the cathedral façade formed by the original 10th-11thC church, is a bustling open-air market *(Wed., Sat.).* ▶ The **Cathedral of St. Front** (C2) is the greatest of cupola churches, its grandiose dimensions inspired by Venice with five oriental-style cupolas and bell-towers dreamed up in the late 19thC by Abadie, architect of Sacré Coeur in Paris. ▶ Many 15th and 16thC mansions in the **old town★** (preservation area) : — Rue Aubergerie : No. 8, Hôtel de Sallegourde (15th-16thC); No. 11, Hôtel d'Abzac de Ladouze (15thC); No. 20 (17thC); No. 23 (15thC); — No. 7 Rue de la Constitution, Hôtel Gamensan★ (end 15thC); — Nos. 1-3-5 Rue Limogeanne : Renaissance; — No. 1 Rue de la Sagesse : Renaissance staircase★. — No. 17 Rue Éguillerie : maison Tenant (14th-15thC). — Rue de la Miséricorde : Renaissance staircase★ (No. 2), Nos. 4 and 7, interesting doors (15th and 17thC); — Rue du Plantier : 17th and 18thC *hôtels.* ▶ **Les Allées Tourny** (1743) separate the old town from the new town that developed along the Bordeaux road before the arrival of the railway (1856). ▶ The **Péri-**

939

Musée du Périgord (Bibliothèque)

C *BERGERAC, AGEN, N 21 ↘ BRIVE, CAHORS, N 89*

2-7, Jul.-Aug.). Château d'Escoire (18thC). ▶ **Le Change** *(15 km E)* : at a bend in the Auvézère, Romanesque church, two châteaux, interesting bridge with cutwaters and mill. ▶ **Agonac** *(15.5 km N)* : fortified Romanesque church with cupolas (11th-13thC); 15thC manor. ▶ **Château de Jaillac** *(17 km N)* : feudal fortress, frequently remodelled *(Easter-29 Sep., 3-6:30).* ☐

Practical Information ─────────────

PÉRIGUEUX
ℹ av. d'Aquitaine (A2), ☎ 53.53.10.63; O.T., 16, rue Wilson (A-B1), ☎ 53.53.44.35.
✈ *Bassillac*, ☎ 53.54.41.08.
SNCF (off map A1), ☎ 53.09.50.50.
🚌 pl. Francheville (B2), ☎ 53.08.76.00.
Car rental : *Avis*, 18, rue du Pdt-Wilson, ☎ 53.53.39.02; train station.

Hotels :
● ★★★ ***Bristol***, 37, rue Antoine-Gadaud (B1), ☎ 53.08.75.90, Tx 540131, Visa, 29 rm Ⓟ ⌕ ♪ 205.
★★★ *Domino*, (Inter-Hôtel, C.H.), 21, pl. Francheville (B2), ☎ 53.08.25.80, Tx 570230, AE DC Euro Visa, 37 rm ♪ Ġ 200. Rest. ● ♦ ♪ Ġ ⌘ Spec : *mignonnette de foie de canard aux pommes, ragoût d'écrevisses aux pâtes fraîches, tournedos périgueux*, prepared by a gifted young chef, 75-200.

Restaurants :
● ♦♦♦ *L'Oison*, 31, rue Saint-Front (C1), ☎ 53.09.84.02, AE DC Visa ♪ Ġ closed Mon and Sun eve, 10 Feb-15 Mar. The fixed meal offers outstanding value. You're sure to find something appealing among the "à la carte" dishes : *foie gras de canard mi-cuit, panaché de poissons au beurre d'herbes, le grand dessert de l'Oison*. Affordable Duras and Buzet wines, 100-280.
♦♦ *La Flambée*, 2, rue Montaigne (B-C1), ☎ 53.53.23.06, Euro Visa ♪ closed Sun. A restaurant to reckon with : *foie frais, tournedos périgueux*, grilled turbot, 90-250.

▲ at Périgueux-Boulazac, ★★*Barnabé* (80 pl), ☎ 53.53.41.45; at Périgueux-Lesparat, ★*l'Isle* (100 pl), ☎ 53.53.57.75.

Recommended
♥ antiques : *Salle des ventes*, 32, rue Gadaud, ☎ 53.53.11.15, many antique dealers in the preserved section of town; foies gras : *Pierre Champion*, 21, rue Taillefer, ☎ 53.53.43.34.

Nearby

ANNESSE-ET-BEAULIEU, ✉ 24430 Razac-sur-l'Isle, 14 km SW.

Hotel :
● ★★ *Château de Lalande* (L.F.), ☎ 53.54.52.30, AE DC Euro Visa, 22 rm Ⓟ ⌂ ⌕ half pens (h.s.), closed 15 Nov-15 Mar, 210. Rest. ♦♦ ⌕ ♪ Ġ closed Wed noon (l.s.), 65-140.

ANTONNE-ET-TRIGONANT, ✉ 24420 Savignac-les-Eglises, 10 km NE.

Hotel :
★★ *Hostellerie la Charmille*, Laurière, ☎ 53.06.00.45, Visa, 18 rm Ⓟ ⌂ ⌘ closed Mon, 150. Rest. ♦ ♪ 80-130.

BASSILLAC, ✉ 24330 Saint-Pierre-de-Chignac, 6 km W.

Hotel :
★★ *Château de Rognac* (L.F.), ☎ 53.54.40.78, 12 rm Ⓟ ⌕ ⌂ ⌂ closed Sun eve and Mon (l.s.), 1-15 Feb, 1-31 Nov, 190. Rest. ♦♦ ⌕ Ġ 75-170.

CHANCELADE, ✉ 24650, 5 km NW.

Hotel :
★★ *Pont de la Beauronne*, ☎ 53.08.42.91, AE, 24 rm Ⓟ ⌘ closed Sun eve and Mon lunch, 20 Sep-20 Oct, 130. Rest. ♦ 45-100.

gord Museum (C1) is excellent for regional archaeology★. Important section on prehistory, complementing the Eyzies Museum (→); Gallo-Roman finds, popular arts and traditions *(10-12 & 2-5; closed Tue.)*. ▶ On the **quays** (C2) with the best view of the cathedral and the old town : Hôtel de Lur (mid-16thC), Maison des Consuls (15thC), Maison Lambert (early 16thC) and, on the other side, the old Moulin du Chapitre (chapter house mill).

Nearby

▶ **Chancelade**★ *(6 km W)* : admirably restored Romanesque abbey in deep woodland. Cupola church partly rebuilt in the 17thC (14thC frescos and painting by Georges de la Tour). Abbey buildings around a pretty garden *(Feb.-15 Dec., daily ex Tue.; Jun.-7 Sep., 9-12 & 2-7)*; 15thC fermenting room where exhibitions and concerts are held in summer; stables and workshops (17thC), fortified mill (15thC); Bourdeilles apartments (15th-17thC); abbot's apartments (18thC). On the other side of the square, tiny Romanesque chapel★. A late Magdalenian tomb was found at Chancelade. ▶ The priory of **Merlande**★ *(6 km N)* was founded by the monks of Chancelade in a clearing of Feytaud Forest. The Romanesque church was fortified in the 16thC. Remarkable carved capitals. To one side, the prior's house. ▶ **Bassillac** *(9 km E)* : in a loop of the Isle, mill and château of Rognac; Romanesque church. ▶ **Antonne-et-Trigonant** *(12 km, Limoges road)* : **château des Bories**★ on a terrace above the Isle, a typical 15thC Périgord manor *(10-12 &*

RIBÉRAC

Périgueux 37, Angoulême 58, Paris 503 km
pop 4290 ⊠ 24600   A2

No grand monuments, simply a charming site, a good fishing river, green valleys, woods full of birds and the soft sky of Aquitaine. The Charentes Region lies in the far distance.

Nearby

▶ **Saint-Privat-des-Prés** *(12 km W)* : fortified church★ with the same façade, copied from the nearby Saintonge Region, as Saint-Martin-de-Gurson (→ Monbazillac). ▶ **Saint-Aulaye** *(10 km from Saint-Privat)*, another *bastide* on a hill rising out of the Dronne, a little to one side, another Saintonge-style church★ with figured capitals. ▶ On the Brantôme (→) road is the fortified church of **Grand-Brassac** *(20 km)* with characteristic line of cupolas ; 16thC sculptures reused on the N doorway. □

Practical Information _____

ⓘ pl. du Gal-de-Gaulle, ☎ 53.90.03.10 (h.s.).

Hotel :
★★ **France** (L.F.), 3, rue M.-Dufraisse, ☎ 53.90.00.61, AE Euro Visa, 20 rm ▨ ⌕ 130. Rest. ♦ ♪ ය 50-125 ; child : 30.

⚠ ★*La Dronne* (100 pl), ☎ 53.90.50.08.

Recommended
♥ foie gras : *Charcuterie Raynaud*, 35, rue du 26-Mars, ☎ 53.90.00.47.

ROCAMADOUR**

Brive 55, Cahors 59, Paris 545 km
pop 795 ⊠ 46500 Gramat   C3

Inseparable from Padirac (→) and much like it. This village, built into the cliff beneath a comic-opera château, boasts its charms on billboards and road signs. After so much publicity, *"le deuxième site de France"* (the second most-visited site in France) might easily be disappointing. However, the site★★ itself is remarkable (see it from the Hospitalet Road), while the seven sanctuaries of Rocamadour have a number of treasures, in particular two 12thC frescos. These sanctuaries were frequented by pilgrims on their way to Compostela, although their origins go back to pagan times *(guided tour Jun.-Sep. and spring school hols.)*. ▶ View★ over the town, the canyon and the *causse* from the château terrace.

Nearby

▶ **Hospitalet** : Grotte des Merveilles (Cave of Marvels) is decorated with figures like those in Pech Merle (→ Valley of the Lot) but much deteriorated *(Jul.-Oct., 9-8)*. ▶ The road★ to **Calès** on the edge of the *causse* follows the meandering Alzou and leads to the **moulin de Cougnaguet★** (14thC mill) on the river. ▶ Lovely walks to the sources of the Ouysse★ *(3 hr round-trip)*, the biggest underground river in the region, and to the **Alzou Gorges★**, marked by old mills *(3 hr round-trip on GR 6)*. □

Practical Information _____

ROCAMADOUR
ⓘ Grande-Rue, ☎ 65.33.62.59 (h.s.).
SNCF ☎ 65.33.63.05.

Hotels :
★★★ **Beau Site**, (Mapotel), ☎ 65.33.63.08, Tx 520421, AE DC Euro Visa, 55 rm ▨ ⌕ 𝄞 closed Nov-Mar, 270. Rest. ♦♦ **Jehan de Valon** ⌕ ♪ ය Praiseworthy efforts in the kitchen, instigated by young D. Menot : *civet de canard au vin de coteaux, feuilleté de ris d'agneau aux*

champignons des bois. Interesting wines, 80-180 ; child : 45.
● ★★ **Les Vieilles Tours** (L.F.), Lafage, ☎ 65.33.68.01, Euro Visa, 8 rm ▨ ⌕ ⫙ ⌕ half pens, closed 20 Nov-31 Mar, 350. Rest. ♦ ♪ ය 𝄞 closed lunch ex Sat and Sun. Spec : *caille farcie au foie gras et truffée, charlotte de brochet*, 70-120 ; child : 35.
★★ **Sainte-Marie**, pl. des Senhals, ☎ 65.33.63.07, Visa, 22 rm ▨ ⌕ ⌕ closed Oct-Mar, 165. Rest. ♦ ♪ ය 45-110.

Nearby

CALÈS, ⊠ 46200, 14 km.

Hotels :
★★ **Le Pagès**, rte de Payrac, ☎ 65.37.95.87, 15 rm ▨ ⌕ ⫙ ⌕ half pens, closed Tue (l.s.), 3 Jan-3 Feb, 1-29 Oct, 320. Rest. ♦ ⌕ 𝄞 *Brochet farci aux herbes*, 50-200.
★ **Le Petit Relais** (L.F.), ☎ 65.37.96.09, DC Euro Visa, 9 rm ▨ ⌕ closed Sat lunch , Feb school hols, 110. Rest. ♦ ⌕ ය 40-80 ; child : 30.

Grotte de ROUFFIGNAC**
(Rouffignac caves)   B2

A pantheon of prehistory with 11 km of galleries and more than 200 rock carvings, half depicting mammoths *(Palm Sun.-1 Nov., 10-11:30 & 2-5, 6, 1 Jul.-15 Sep. ; Sun. only low season)*.

▶ In the village of Rouffignac only the Renaissance church★ escaped destruction by the Nazis.

Nearby

▶ **Plazac★** *(6 km E)* : a touching cemetery surrounds the Romanesque church with its beautiful square bell-tower (16thC frescos) ; the presbytery is the former 14thC episcopal palace. ▶ View from the **Côte de Jor★** (steep bank) over the Vézère Valley (→).

SAINT-AMAND-DE-COLY**

Brive-la-Gaillarde 36, Périgueux 55, Paris 526 km
pop 300 ⊠ 24290 Montignac   C2

The former abbey church of the Augustinian canons, perhaps the most beautiful church in the Périgord, rises out of the woods of Sarlat.

▶ This building was originally intended as a fortress with gate-house, keep, fortification and ramparts. ▶ The village it protected is now empty but remains beautiful with its ochre walls and stone-tiled roofs. The buildings are now being restored and exhibitions and concerts are staged here in summer. □

Practical Information _____

Hotel :
● **Manoir d'Hautegente**, Terrasson, à 3 km N., ☎ 53.51.68.03, AE Visa, 6 rm ▨ ⌕ ⫙ ⌕ 𝄞 ය half pens (h.s.), closed 12 Nov-1 Apr, 850. Rest. ♦ ⌕ ය Deep in the heart of Périgord, Edith Hamelin's flower-bedecked manor welcomes you with specialities like : *paupiettes de poulet aux pleurotes, fonds d'artichauts aux foie gras et morilles*, 160-220 ; child : 40.

SAINT-ANTONIN-NOBLE-VAL*

Villefranche-de-Rouergue 41, Montauban 42, Paris 659 km
pop 1870 ⊠ 82140   C4

Located on the banks of the Aveyron between the Quercy and Rouergue regions, the sun-bleached roofs of this small village recall those of the Midi. Between the quay and the Town Hall★ (12thC ; small prehistory museum) you will find a mediaeval town★ of merchants' houses from the 13th, 14th and 15thC.

Nearby

▶ **Varen★** : fortified château (14th-15thC) and church (12thC); ▶ **Verfeil★** : old village and covered market; ▶ **Beaulieu Abbey★** (→). ▶ **Bosc Cave** *(Grotte du Bosc; Easter-Oct.)*. ▶ A pretty road running N up the **valley of the Bonnette★** will bring you to two beautiful villages : **Caylus★**, a mediaeval township with fortified church, 14thC market and feudal keep, and **Lacapelle-Livron★**, a former Templar Commandery between the Causse de Limogne (→) and the army training ground of Les Espagots.

Aveyron Gorges★★ *(34 km; approx 3 hr; C-D4)*

Downstream from **Saint-Antonin** the river abruptly penetrates the **causse**; a *corniche* (cliff road) follows it closely and hillside villages appear. ▶ **Penne★** balanced on the cliff with a notable fortress. ▶ **Bruniquel★** : Gothic houses and château. ▶ S of Bruniquel in the **Vère Vale** are other fine fortified villages, while to the E stretch the tall oaks of the **La Grésigne Forest★**, which for years supplied the French navy with timber. Beyond Bruniquel, the valley opens out into a plain. ▶ **Montricoux** is the last of the hill villages, with corbelled and half-timbered houses along the right bank, guarded by a 13thC Templars' keep.   □

Practical Information _____

Nearby

CAYLUS, ⊠ 82160, 44 km NE of **Montauban**.
Ⓘ av. Père-Huc (h.s.).

Hotel :
★ *Bellevue*, ☎ 63.67.06.57, Visa, 11 rm Ⓟ ≪ ⌂ closed Wed, 1-15 Jan, 105. Rest. ♦ ≪ ♪ ₺ 50-150; child : 30.

SAINT-CÉRÉ*

Brive 54, Cahors 76, Paris 546 km
pop 4210 ⊠ 46500   D2
Picturesque old houses with wooden facings (15th, 16th, 17thC) and, in the background, the towers of St. Laurent (12th, 15thC) where Jean Lurçat (1892-1966; tapestry artist influenced by Cézanne) had his workshop; tapestry exhibition in the casino.

Nearby

▶ **Ségala** is a mountainous region stretching W to join the Auvergne. ▶ The **château de Montal★** *(1.5 km W)* is a great Renaissance work. *(Jun., Jul., Sep., 9-11:30 & 2:30-5:30; Aug., 9:30-11:30-3-6).*

Tour of the Merveilles area *(20 km)*

▶ **Saint-Céré**. ▶ **Grotte de Presque** : "the cave of columns" *(la grotte des colonnes; Apr.-Oct.)*. ▶ **Autoire★★**, a fairy-tale village at the mouth of the **Autoire Gorges★**, is as discreet and perfect as Rocamadour is flashy. ▶ **Loubressac★**, fortified village at the uppermost junction of three valleys. The **château** (15th-17thC) is, in fact, an overgrown manor-house.   □

Practical Information _____

Ⓘ pl. de la République, ☎ 65.38.11.85.

Hotels :
★★★ *Coq-Arlequin* (L.F.), 1, bd du Dr-Roux, ☎ 65.38.02.13, Visa, 30 rm Ⓟ ≪ ⌷ ♪° half pens (h.s.), closed Jan-Feb, 500. Rest. ♦♦ ⅋ 65-200.
★★ *Parc*, av. J.-Mouliérat, ☎ 65.38.17.29, 24 rm Ⓟ ≪ ⌂ closed Fri eve and Sat, Dec, 200. Rest. ♦ ⅋ 70-100.

Restaurant :
♦ *Jean-Pierre Ric*, rte de Leyme, Saint-Vincent-du-Pendit, ☎ 65.38.04.08 ≪ ≪≪≪ ♪ closed Mon ex Jul-Aug and hols, 1 Mar-1 Apr, 70-170.

⚠ ★★★*de Soulhol* (200 pl), ☎ 65.38.12.37.

SARLAT***

Brive 51, Périgueux 66, Paris 539 km
pop 10627 ⊠ 24200   C2
The Renaissance and the Middle Ages still live in this town, one of the rare sites in France to remain intact since the 17thC; and on this account entirely restored by the Historical Monuments Board *(CNMHS)*. At one time girded with ramparts, it has kept its heart-shaped ground plan and is divided in two by *la traverse*, the busy commercial Rue de la République. Sarlat is the capital of France for walnuts and *foie gras*, as any shop window in the old town will confirm. On Saturdays, there is a market in the Place de la Grande Rigaudie and, once a month, a fair that attracts people from miles around. On other days, this square serves as a car park. The entire eastern part has already been restored and is brought to life by the TO *(guided visits, evenings, Easter-15 Sep.)*.

▶ **Place du Peyrou** (B2) : surrounded by the Renaissance façade of the former episcopal buildings now used as a theatre, by old shops with bow-fronted windows and by the cathedral of St. Sacerdos, a blend of 16th-17thC architecture. The **Hôtel La Boétie**, where the writer Étienne La Boétie (1530-63) was born, is also located on the square. ▶ **The Chapelle des Pénitents Blancs** (White Penitents' Chapel; B2) is purest Romanesque architecture. ▶ The Penitents' garden is a former cemetery with an enigmatic **light-tower** *(lanterne des morts; C2)*. ▶ The charm of Sarlat lies in its coherent style, the elegance of even its humblest houses, its ochre tones and its stone roofs, rather than in its monuments. Note the **Renaissance houses** on Rue de la Salamandre and Rue Landry. ▶ At the back of a garden is the former **Présidial** (Tribunal of Justice) crowned with a curious turreted lantern tower. ▶ The **Place de la Liberté**, now given over to luxury shops, is an extension of the Place du Marché and the Place du Marché Aux Oies, which overflow into it on Saturdays with cages of ducks and geese, fresh goose liver or mushrooms, according to season. In summer a theatre festival takes over this square. **Maleville House★** *(Hôtel de Maleville)* has two very different façades; it is, in fact, three houses run together and remodelled in the 16thC by a finance official of Henri IV, hence the portraits of the king and his mistress Gabrielle d'Estrées (1573-99). Town Hall (17thC); church of Sainte-Marie (14th-16thC); Gisson House *(Hôtel de Gisson;* 16thC). ▶ All the **mansions** in the **Rue des Consuls★** are worthy of mention; the street of a perfect example of urban architecture of the 16th-17thC. ▶ The W sector (B2) has not yet been restored, and is therefore ignored by tourists and business alike; it has the flavour of old towns, full of bustling, chaotic and unreconstructed streets. Here are Récollets Convent (Rue Rousseau) and Ste Claire Convent★ (Rue de la Boétie, *Jul.-Aug., 9-12 & 2-6)*, built in the 17thC.   □

Practical Information _____

SARLAT
Ⓘ pl. de la Liberté (B1-2), ☎ 53.59.27.67.
🚃 (off map B3), ☎ 53.59.00.21.

Hotels :
● ★★★ *Hostellerie de Meysset* (C.H.), lieu-dit Argentauleau, rte des Eyzies, ☎ 53.59.08.29, AE DC Visa, 26 rm Ⓟ ≪ ⌂ ₺ half pens (h.s.), closed 4 Oct-17 Apr, 630. Rest. ♦♦ ₺ 105-220.
● ★★★ *La Salamandre*, rue Abbé-Surguier (off map B3), ☎ 53.59.35.98, AE DC Euro Visa, 23 rm ⅋ closed 1 Nov-15 Apr, 260.
★★★ *La Hoirie* (R.S.), La Giragne, rte de Souillac, ☎ 53.59.05.62, AE DC Euro Visa, 15 rm Ⓟ ≪ ⌂ ⌷ closed 15 Nov-15 Mar, 280. Rest. ♦ ♪ Spec : *émincé de magret à la fleur de pêche*, 130-180.
★★★ *La Madeleine*, 1, pl. de la Petite-Rigaudie (off map A1), ☎ 53.59.12.40, Tx 550689, Euro Visa, 22 rm

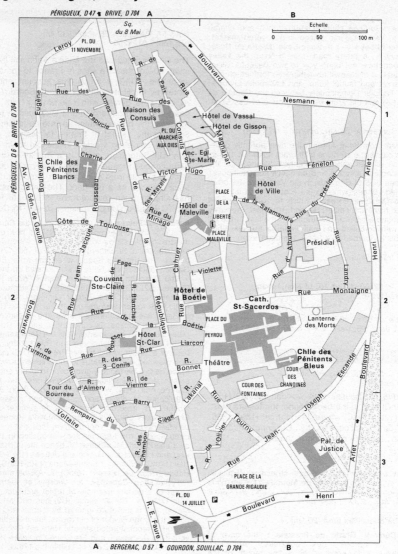

SARLAT

Map of Sarlat with labels: PÉRIGUEUX, D 47; BRIVE, D 704; Sq. du 8 Mai; Echelle 0 50 100 m; Leroy; PL. DU 11 NOVEMBRE; Rue de la paix; Boulevard; Rue; Nesmann; Rue des Armes; Rue Papucie; Maison des Consuls; Hôtel de Vassal; Hôtel de Gisson; PL. DU MARCHÉ AUX OIES; Chlle des Pénitents Blancs; R. de la Charité; Anc. Egl. Ste-Marie; R. Victor Hugo; Fénelon; Arlet; Rousseau; Côte de Toulouse; R. des Mazeis; Rue du Minage; Hôtel de Maleville; PLACE DE LA LIBERTÉ; Hôtel de Ville; R. de la Salamandre; Rue du Présidial; Présidial; Henri; PLACE MALEVILLE; Fage; I. Violette; Canuet; Couvent Ste-Claire; R. Blanchet; Hôtel de la Boétie; Cath. St-Sacerdos; Rue Montaigne; Landry; R. d'Albusse; Rue; Boétie; PLACE DU PEYROU; Lanterne des Morts; Hôtel St-Clar; Liarçon; Théâtre; Chlle des Pénitents Bleus; Escande; Boulevard; R. de Turenne; R. des 3 Conils; R. Bonnet; COUR DES CHANOINES; R. d'Almery; R. de Vienne; R. Lakanal; COUR DES FONTAINES; Joseph; Tour du Bourreau; Rue Barry; Siège; Tourny; Jean-; Pal. de Justice; Arlet; Remparts du; Voltaire; R. des Chambon; R. E. Faure; l'Ollivier; Rue; PLACE DE LA GRANDE-RIGAUDIE; PL. DU 14 JUILLET; Henri; Boulevard; BERGERAC, D 57; GOURDON, SOUILLAC, D 704; Av. du Gén. de Gaulle; Boulevard Eugène; PÉRIGUEUX, D 6; BRIVE, D 704; Magnanat; Consuls; Jacques; Jean; Rue des; Rue; PLACE DE LA; Boulevard

P 🏛 half pens (h.s.), closed 1 Jan-15 Mar, 540. Rest. ♦♦ ⴟ closed 3 Nov-15 Mar, 75-250.

● ★★ **Hostellerie La Verperie**, allée des Acacias (off map A1), ☎ 53.59.00.20, AE, 15 rm P 📶 🏛 🌲 🐾 half pens (h.s.), closed 1 Dec-1 Jan, 320. Rest. ♦ 📶 🐾 closed Sun, 65-110.

★★ **Mairie**, 13, pl. de la Liberté (B1-2), ☎ 53.59.05.71, Visa, 11 rm 📶 closed 15 Nov-1 Apr, 140.

★★ **St-Albert** (L.F.), 10, pl. Pasteur (off map B3), ☎ 53.59.01.09, AE DC Euro Visa, 52 rm 🐾 closed Sun eve , Mon., 4 Nov-15 Apr, 180. Rest. ♦♦ Regional dishes. Spec : escalope de foie de canard aux échalotes, foie gras frais maison non truffé, ris de veau sauce Périgueux, 80-220.

La Couleuvrine, (L.F., C.H.), 1, pl. de la Bouquerie

(off map B1), ☎ 53.59.27.80, AE DC Euro Visa, 18 rm P closed 15-31 Jan, 185. Rest. ♦ 60-120.

Restaurant :
● ♦ **La Ferme**, Caudon-de-Vitrac, 8 km S, ☎ 53.28.33.35 📶 🏛 ⴟ closed Mon , Oct. At this genuine Périgord farm, robust, rustic dishes : bean soup, omelette with truffles, 55-150.

▲ ★★★★Les Grottes de Roffy (125 pl), ☎ 53.59.15.61 ; ★★★★Les Périères (90 pl), ☎ 53.59.05.84 ; at Saint-André-d'Allas, 10 km W., ★★★★Moulin du Roch (160 pl), ☎ 53.59.20.27.

Recommended
Bicycle-rental : M. Faure, 8, rue de la République, ☎ 53.59.21.78.

Guided tours : info at the S.I.
Sports : *Fournier equestrian centre*, Sarlovèze, Bonnefond, rte de Vezac, ☎ 53.59.15.83.
♥ foie gras : *Boutique Rougier*, rue des Consuls, ☎ 53.59.24.68; truffles : *Aux Armes du Périgord*, 1, rue de la Liberté, ☎ 53.59.10.22.

Nearby

MARQUAY, ⊠ 24620, 11 km N.

Hotel :
● ★★ *Bories*, Le Bourg, ☎ 53.29.67.02, Euro Visa, 19 rm P ≼ ₪ ◌ ▱ closed 15 Nov-15 Mar, 160.

SOUILLAC

Brive 37, Cahors 66, Paris 529 km
pop 4062 ⊠ 46200   C2

The town itself has little character, but the **doorway**★★ of the **abbey church**, mutilated and then rebuilt inside the church, is a major work of Southern Romanesque art, very close in style to Moissac (→). Tobacco warehouse in the former 18thC abbey.   ☐

Practical Information _____

⓵ 9, bd Malvy, ☎ 65.37.81.56.
SNCF ☎ 65.32.78.21.

Hotels :
● ★★★ *Les Granges Vieilles*, rte de Sarlat, ☎ 65.37.80.92, 11 rm P ≼ ₪ ◌ ⨯ closed Nov. Peace and quiet guaranteed in a large park with tall trees, 200. Rest. ♦♦ ♪ ♪ 70-180.
★★★ *Puy d'Alon*, av. J.-Jaurès, ☎ 65.37.89.79, 11 rm P ≼ ₪ ◌ ⅟ 185.
★★ *Ambassadeurs* (L.F.), 7-12-14, av. du Gal-de-Gaulle, ☎ 65.32.78.36, Euro Visa, 28 rm P ₪ closed Fri eve and Sat ex Jul-Sep, 21 Feb-1 Mar, 28 Sep-28 Oct, 160. Rest. ♦♦ ♪ ⅟ 45-95.

Château de la Treyne, (C.H., I.L.A.), ☎ 65.32.66.66, AE DC Euro Visa, 12 rm ≼ ₪ ◌ ♪ ♪ᵖ half pens (h.s.), closed 2 Jan-1 Apr, 1000. Rest. ♦ ≼ ♪ By reservation, 180-220.

⚊ ★★★★*La Paille Basse* (220 pl), ☎ 65.32.73.51.

Recommended
♥ *charcuterie Maury*, 13, rue de la Halle, ☎ 65.37.00.22.

THIVIERS

Périgueux 37, Limoges 64, Paris 457 km
pop 4215 ⊠ 24800   B1

⓵ pl. Mal-Foch, ☎ 53.55.12.50 (h.s.).
SNCF ☎ 53.55.00.21.

Nearby

EXCIDEUIL, ⊠ 24160, 19 km E.

Hotel :
★★ *Host. du Fin Chapon* (L.F.), pl. du Château, ☎ 53.62.42.38, 10 rm P ₪ ⨯ closed Sun eve and Mon (l.s.), 20 Dec-25 Jan, 115. Rest. ♦ 50-140.

⚊ ★*Le Pont Rouge* (33 pl), ☎ 53.55.40.02.

MAVALEIX, ⊠ 24800 Thiviers, 11 km N.

Hotel :
● ★★★ *Château de Mavaleix* (C.H.), RN 21, ☎ 53.52.82.01, Tx 540131, Euro Visa, 22 rm P ≼ ₪ ◌ closed 2 Jan-7 Feb. 23-ha park beside a river (hunting, fishing), 320. Rest. ● ♦♦♦ ≼ Courses in the preparation of *foie gras*, 80-200; child : 50.

┌─────────────────────────────────────┐
│ Send us your comments and suggestions; we will │
│ use them in the next edition.   │
└─────────────────────────────────────┘

TONNEINS

Agen 41, Bordeaux 106, Paris 701 km
pop 10146 ⊠ 47400   A4

SNCF ☎ 53.79.00.60.

Hotel :
★★★ *Castel Ferron* (L.F.), RN 113, ☎ 53.84.59.99, AE DC Euro Visa, 17 rm P ≼ ₪ ◌ ♪ ⨯ In an 18th-C dwelling, 350. Rest. ♦ ♪ closed Sat noon (l.s.), 90-200.

⚊ ★★*Robinson* (53 pl), ☎ 53.79.02.28.

Recommended
Sports : *UST Kayak*, 22, quai Barre, ☎ 53.84.52.22.

TOURTOIRAC

Périgueux 37, Brive 55, Paris 472 km
pop 756 ⊠ 24390 Hautefort   B1

In the greenery along the banks of the Auvézère are the imposing remains of a **Benedictine abbey**★ (11thC), girdled with 14thC ramparts.

▶ The church has been partly rebuilt; of the original structure there remain the transept, a square bell-tower, a cupola on pendentives and some ancient capitals. In the garden★ is a small Romanesque chapel with acoustic chambers, part of the enclosure wall, the abbey building (17thC) and, under the presbytery, the chapter, with amusing capitals. ▶ Tourtoirac was the home of Antoine Tounens, an obscure lawyer turned adventurer who made himself King of Patagonia in 1860.   ☐

TRÉMOLAT★★

Bergerac 34, Périgueux 54, Paris 639 km
pop 543 ⊠ 24510 Saint-Alvère   B2

The horseshoe bend known as the **"Cingle de Trémolat"**★★, one of the most famous sites on the Dordogne River, is now a yacht basin. The village★ with the stream tumbling along between the houses, and manor-houses with their pointed roofs, has a thoroughly French air.

▶ The **fortress church** (12thC) has much character, its bare façades interspersed with buttresses, and bell-tower keep, decorated in the 18thC. Beautiful Romanesque chapel in the cemetery.

Also... ▶ **Belvédère de Sors**★★ *(4 km E, downstream from Limeuil)*, above another bend in the Dordogne; an extraordinarily peaceful landscape. ▶ **Paunat**★ *(2.5 km N)* : Romanesque **church** fortified in the 15thC; similar to that of Trémolat.

Practical Information _____

Hotel :
● ★★★ *Le Vieux Logis* (R.C.), ☎ 53.22.80.06, Tx 541025, AE DC Euro Visa, 22 rm P ₪ ◌ ♪ half pens. A 16th-C dwelling hidden in the greenery, 1090. Rest. ● ♦♦♦ ♪ ♪ Happiness has inhabited this spot for over 35 years, thanks to Mme Giraudel-Destord, who with taste and talent turned this small farm into a delightful stopover. Her son, Bernard, a knowledgeable promoter of Périgord's charm, continues her efforts. Chef Pierre-Jean Duribreux performs culinary magic, assisted in the dining-room by his wife. Splendid cellar, 85-300; child : 40.

VALENCE

Montauban 46, Cahors 66, Paris 760 km
pop 4734 ⊠ 82400 Valence-d'Agen   B4

Restaurant :
● ♦♦ *La Campagnette*, rte de Cahors, ☎ 63.39.65.97, Visa P ◌ ♪ ♪ Don't miss out on Gérard Lerchundi's tasty

cooking, so light and creative : *salade de goujonnettes de rouget, rognon de veau entier aux échalotes*, 75-250.

VILLEFRANCHE-DU-PÉRIGORD*

Cahors 40, Périgueux 85, Paris 584 km
pop 800 ⊠ 24550   B3

Villefranche is an isolated *bastide* village with an arcaded square and a covered market (early 19thC) on heavy pillars, overlooking a minor tributary of the Lémance and surrounded by wooded hills in the heart of the 100-km² forest of pine, oak and chestnut stretching between the Périgord and the Quercy regions.

Nearby

► **Besse** *(8 km N)* : delightful grouping of 16th-17thC château and stone-tiled fortified church; the porch is a rare example of Romanesque sculpture in the Périgord.   □

VILLENEUVE-SUR-LOT

Agen 29, Cahors 75, Paris 614 km
pop 23730 ⊠ 47300   B3-4

A *bastide* (→) that expanded over the fertile plain, where fruit of all kinds, especially plums, grow in abundance.

► The classic checkerboard pattern is clearly apparent around the arcaded square where the market is still held. Good view over the town and houses on the quay from the Pont-Vieux (Old Bridge; 13thC). Small local museum (**musée Rapin**; *summer, 3-7; winter, 2-6*).

Nearby

► **Pujols★** with Renaissance houses; ► **Casseneuil★** : former inland port on the Lède; ► **Penne d'Agenais** *(8 km E)* : restored mediaeval village perched high above the Lot; ► **Hautefage-la-Tour★** *(10 km S of Penne)* : as fine as any Tuscan village; ► **Laroque-Timbaut** : old houses huddled around the covered market. **Frespech★** *(5 km)* : miniature fortified village. ► Caves at **Lestournelles** and **Fontirou** *(Apr.-Sep., 9-12:30 & 1:30-7:30; off season, Sun. and nat. hols.)*.   □

Practical Information _____

VILLENEUVE-SUR-LOT
ⓘ behind the theatre, ☎ 53.70.31.35.
𝗦𝗡𝗖𝗙 ☎ 53.70.00.35.

Hotels :

★★★ *Parc*, (Mapotel), 13, bd de la Marine, ☎ 53.70.01.68, Tx 550379, AE DC Euro Visa, 40 rm Ⓟ ▥ ⌕ ♪ ♨ ໄ. 220. Rest. ♦♦ ♪ ໄ closed Mon. Spec : *brochette de queues de langoustines beurre blanc, filet de bœuf au St Amour*, 70-220; child : 50.

★★ *Résidence*, 17, av. L.-Carnot, ☎ 53.40.17.03, 18 rm Ⓟ ▥ ⌕ closed 10 Dec-15 Jan, 105.

★ *L'Espoir*, 5, pl. de la Marine, ☎ 53.70.71.63, 9 rm Ⓟ ⌕ closed 15 Dec-15 Jan, 120.

Recommended

♥ *La Maison du Pruneau d'Agen (prunes)*, 5, porte de Paris, ☎ 53.70.30.86.

Nearby

CANCON, ⊠ 47290, 19 km N.

Hotel :

★★★★   *Château   de   Monviel*   (R.C.),   Monviel, ☎ 53.01.71.64, AE DC Visa, 9 rm Ⓟ ⌕ ▥ ⌕ ♨ ▤ closed Wed, 3 Jan-30 Mar, 15 Nov-15 Dec. A 17th-C dwelling, 400. Rest. ♦♦ ♪ 100-180.

PUJOLS, ⊠ 47300, 4 km SW.

Hotel :

● ★★★ *Chênes*, Bel-Air, ☎ 53.49.04.55, AE DC Euro Visa, 21 rm Ⓟ ⌕ ▥ ⌕ ♪ ໄ closed Sun eve (l.s.), 2-15 Jan, 23-30 Jun, 24-30 Nov, 270.

Restaurant :

● ♦♦ *Auberge La Toque Blanche*, ☎ 53.49.00.30, AE DC Euro Visa ▥ ♪ ໄ ⍨ closed Mon (l.s.) , Sun, Feb school hols, 22 Jun-6 Jul, 23-30 Nov. The fine regional foostuffs come from the nearby market : *escalope de foie de canard à l'échalote, paupiette de sole farcie aux langoustines*, 95-230.

Le TEYSSET, ⊠ 47380 Monclar, 20 km W on the D667/D13.

Restaurant :

♦♦ *Le Teysset*, ☎ 53.84.95.56, Visa Ⓟ ⌕ ▥ ⌕ ♪ closed Thu and Fri noon, 15 Jan-1 Mar, 80-190.

TONNEINS, ⊠ 47400, 3 km NW of **Agen.**

Hotel :

★★★ *Castel Ferron*, RN 113, ☎ 53.84.59.99, AE DC Euro Visa, 17 rm Ⓟ ⌕ ▥ ⌕ ▤ ⌀ ♪ 300. Rest. ♦ ▥♪ 90-200.

⚓ ★★*Robinson* (54 pl), ☎ 53.79.02.28.

Alsace

▶ Between the Vosges forest and Germany lies Alsace, perhaps the most unusual of all the French provinces. Even the French tourist sometimes feels as if he has entered a foreign country : landscape, architecture, lifestyle and even language (a Germanic dialect mixed in some parts with French to create a picturesque blend known as *frangermal*) are different from those he has left behind. But the hospitality of the inhabitants quickly dispels any feeling of strangeness. The Alsatian has always been conscious of his region's position as a hub of European civilization and despite his fight to retain his individuality and annexations by the region's powerful neighbour, he has remained open to the outside.

The picturesque streets of Colmar, studded with museums, churches and charming old buildings, combine cosmopolitan bustle with quiet provincial charm. Strasbourg has the jovial atmosphere of its wine bars or *winstubs*, the famous cathedral of Notre-Dame, Gothic splendour in delicately-worked pink sandstone, and the prestige associated with the presence of the European Parliament. The half-timbered houses of the region contribute a great deal to the charm of its villages. The countryside is densely populated and most of the inhabitants live in villages, where each house is separated from its neighbours by a narrow passageway.

Alsace is famous too for its cuisine : sausages, black puddings, *foie gras*, vegetable and fruit tarts, the famous *choucroute* (sauerkraut), based on chopped cabbage marinated in brine, but differing subtly from one town to another, and the region's excellent white wines. □

● Don't miss

★★★ Colmar A3, Kaysersberg A3, Riquewihr A3, Strasbourg B2, Route du Vin B2.

★★ Murbach A3, Obernai A-B2, Outre-Forêt B1, La Petite-Pierre A1, Sundgau A-B4, Turckheim A3, Northern Vosges A-B1, Wissembourg B1.

★ Ballon d'Alsace A4, Barr A2, Route des Crêtes A3-4, Haut-Kœnisbourg A3, the Hohwald Region A2, Marmoutier A2, Mont-Sainte-Odile A2, Munster Valley A3, Neuf-Brisach B3, Ribeauvillé A3, Ridge Road A3-4, Rosheim A-B2, Rouffach A3, Sélestat B3, Wangenbourg A2.

Weekend tips

Two suggestions : Strasbourg offers the flea-market in Rue du Vieil-Hôpital ; cathedral and surroundings ; the Rohan palace or the Musée de l'Oeuvre Notre-Dame (museum of medieval art) ; lunch at a brewery or restaurant, followed by a historical or regional museum, Petite France, the lively canal area, and the obligatory visit to a winstub (wine tavern). On Sunday, excursion to Obernai, Mont Sainte-Odile, Rosheim and Molsheim.
Alternatively : Colmar, where the town and the Unterlinden Museum will take up all of Saturday, then a Sunday trip along the Wine Road to Kaysersberg, Riquewihr and Ribeauvillé with, if time allows, a climb to Haut-Koenigsbourg (note the timetable).

● Brief regional history

Up to the 9thC
Alsace has distinct geographical characteristics, but little historical identity before the Roman era. The Celtic inhabitants established important market-towns and sanctuary cities. ● Fortified border towns built during the **Pax Romana,** following the conquest by Julius Caesar (58BC), emphasised the territory's position as a border state. The agricultural and trading system that grew in response to the demands of the garrisons laid the foundations for the **economy** that remains the basis of prosperity to this day. ● Christianity began to take root during the Roman era. A troubled period marked by successive invasions of **Germans** (Alemanni) and Huns (453) was finally ended in 596 with the conquest of **Clovis,** king of the Franks. The name Alsace appeared for the first time in the 7thC : its origin is uncertain but at that time it was used to indicate the independent Duchy of Alsace.

9th-11thC
Under Frankish protection, the church prospered and the **Carolingian Renaissance** gave rise to magnificent buildings, including the bishop's palace at Strasbourg and Murbach Abbey. As Charlemagne's empire crumbled, the two counties of Nordgau and Sundgau replaced the Duchy of Alsace. ● Two sons of Louis the Debonair, Charles and Louis, allied themselves against their brother Lothar in the **Oath of Strasbourg** (842), the earliest historical text known to have been written in Romance and Germanic languages. ● In 870, Charles conceded Alsace to Louis, and the territory would remain under the sway of the **Holy Roman Empire** until 1648.

12th-14thC
The feudal era in Alsace culminated in the "**Hohenstaufen Century**", which ended with the death of the Emperor Frederick II in 1250. During this period, trade thrived, towns expanded and **Romanesque art** and architecture flourished. ● Many fortified towns united to form boroughs. In 1354, Haguenau, Wissembourg, Obernai, Rosheim, Sélestat, Colmar, Turckheim, Kaysersberg, Munster and Mulhouse (later to unite with the Swiss cities) formed a cooperative alliance known as the **Decapol** ("ten cities"); trade with the Rhineland enabled Strasbourg to remain independent. ● During the Hundred Years' War only minor incidents disturbed the peace, by virtue of the region's relative remoteness from the English territories in France.

14th-16thC
The later Middle Ages were marked by religious intensity and municipal pride. The magnificent spire was erected on Strasbourg cathedral, and the Issenheim altarpiece was created. In 1434, the German Gutenberg (1400-68) moved to Strasbourg, where he worked until 1448 on his "secret process" that, as the printing press, was soon to revolutionize the world. As the **Renaissance** dawned, Alsace was pledged to the Dukes of Burgundy; the tyranny of their bailiff, Pierre de Hagenbach, brought about revolt. ● The bloodily-suppressed peasants' revolt was followed by the **"peasants' war"** (1525) in which 40 000 died. ● During these upheavals, humanist thought and the **Protestant Reformation** took root; Strasbourg was an intellectual centre. Many buildings from this era are still standing.

Outre-Forêt

Sundgau

Vineyard areas

Facts and figures

Location : *At the eastern end of France on the Swiss and German borders, Alsace covers the eastern slopes of the Vosges mountains and the plain on the left bank of the Rhine. Three distinct regions : the Vosges mountains, the Vosges foothills (vineyards); the plain. North and South, the Outre-Forêt and the Sundgau (on the edge of the Jura mountains); NW, Alsace Bossue (hillocky Alsace) similar to Lorraine (→).*
Area : *8 280 km².*
Climate : *Continental with wide temperature variations; the Vosges act as a barrier to Atlantic influence; little difference between North and South. Dry, hot summer (20°-30°C); misty but often beautiful autumn; dry, cold winter (av. 0°); mild, bright spring.*
Population : *1 566 000; more than 400 000 in Strasbourg.*
Administration :
*Department of the **Haut-Rhin** (Upper Rhine), Prefecture Colmar; Department of the **Bas-Rhin** (Lower Rhine), Prefecture Strasbourg.*

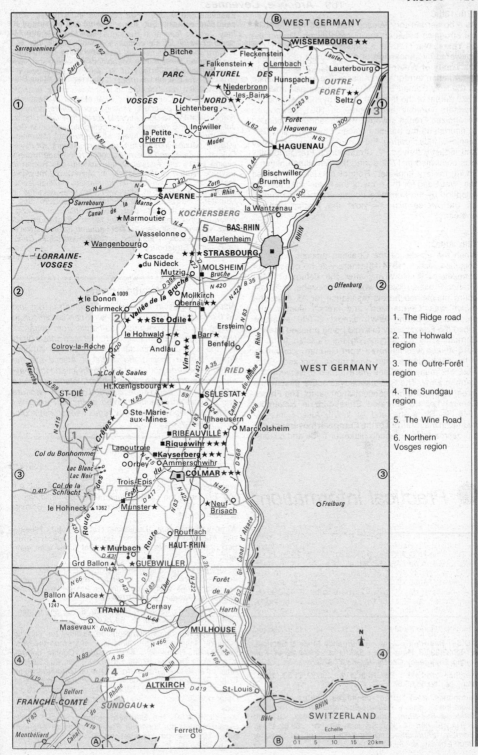

1. The Ridge road

2. The Hohwald region

3. The Outre-Forêt region

4. The Sundgau region

5. The Wine Road

6. Northern Vosges region

17th-18thC

As a border territory, Alsace was a pawn in the political struggles between the Great Powers. During the **30 Years' War** (17thC), a request for French aid was answered by annexation of a substantial region. With the **Treaty of Westphalia,** France took possession of the Austrian territories in Alsace. The feeble influence of the Holy Roman Empire was extinguished after the 1679 defeat of the Imperial forces by the French commanders Turenne and Condé; in 1681, Strasbourg recognized French sovereignty. Strasbourg continued to flourish as the meeting place of the Latin and Germanic worlds; during the Enlightenment, art, trade and industry thrived. ● Strasbourg's French identity was confirmed in 1792 during the Revolution, when a young military engineer, Rouget de l'Isle, composed the "War Song for the Army of the Rhine" that, after its adoption by the Marseille Volunteers, became known as the *Marseillaise* — now the French national anthem.

19th-20thC

When the armies of the Coalition against Napoleon occupied Alsace (1814-18), there was no question of annexation. ● However, after the defeat of 1870 (Franco-Prussian War), when the citizens of Strasbourg maintained heroic resistance for 45 days, the region was "Germanized" and French identity suppressed. ● During **WWI,** almost 20000 Alsatians joined the French army to avoid being pressed into the German army for service on the Russian front. In 1918 Alsace was liberated from German occupation. ● In **1940** Alsace was once more annexed. From 1942 on, many Alsatians were forced to serve in the German army. The Resistance was active despite the threat of the Struthof concentration camp. The French General Leclerc liberated Strasbourg in November 1944. ● Since the end of WWII, Alsace has remained in the forefront of the **European movement,** still a crossroads and meeting place for trade and culture.

Festivals and events : Feb : *carnival* in Mulhouse; *Passion play* in Masevaux. Apr : *snail festival* in Osenbach. May : *street festival* in Huningue; *antiques fair, international chamber music competition, international fair* and *folklore show* in Colmar; *pig festival* in Ungersheim. Jun : *rose festival* in Saverne; *kougelhopf* (local dessert) *festival* in Ribeauvillé; *"fires of St. John"* in numerous villages; *Paris-Colmar on foot; Fête-Dieu procession* in Geispolsheim; *Bach festival* in Mulhouse; *music festivals* in Strasbourg, Colmar. Jul : *rural festival* in Seebach; *"Sans-Culottes" parade* in Mutzig; *woodcutters' competition* in Saint-Pierre-Bois; *morello cherry festival* in Uffoltz. Jul-Aug : *music festivals* at the collegiate church in Colmar, the Dominican convent in Guebwiller, Masevaux (organ); *nautical jousting* in Strasbourg; *sauerkraut day* in Colmar; *popular and folk music concerts* in Niederbronn's casino park; *folk festival* at the château des Rohan in Saverne. Aug : *crafts festival* in Masevaux; *mountain festival* in Grandelbruch; *frying festival* in Illhaeusern; *almond-tree festival* in Mittlewihr; *folklore evenings* in Munster; *"marriage of l'Ami Fritz"* in Marlenheim. Sep : *hops festival* in Haguenau; *beer fountain* in Mutzig; *onion fair* in Brumath; *European fair* in Strasbsuorg; *fiddlers' festival* in Ribeauvillé. Oct : *autumn textile festival* in Sainte-Marie-aux-Mines. Dec : *christkindelsmärik; Christmas fair* in Strasbourg.

Alsatian crafts

Alsace abounds in folklore, and tradition is not lost on the souvenir industry. At times it can be difficult to distinguish true from false, authentic from imitation. Nevertheless, you can trust craftsmen and shops bearing the sign Souvenir de France - Alsace Authentique. Notable among the crafts of Alsace are the brightly-coloured pottery of Soufflenheim and the grey-and-blue earthenware of Betschdorf, intended for use and not mere decoration; painted wooden furniture and household objects; printed cloth; folk art glass paintings; wood and stone (Vosges sandstone) sculpture; inlaid wood.

 Practical information

Information : Bas-Rhin : *Office Départemental du Tourisme (O.D.T.),* 9, rue du Dôme, 67061 Strasbourg Cedex, ☎ 88.22.01.02. Haut-Rhin : *Association Départementale du Tourisme (A.D.T.),* 68020 Colmar, ☎ 89.23.21.11. In **Paris** : *Maison de l'Alsace,* 39, av. des Champs-Élysées, 75008, ☎ (1) 42.56.15.94. *Regional products* : 10, rue du Colisée, 75008 Paris, ☎ (1) 45.62.54.85. *Dir. Rég. de la Jeunesse et des Sports,* 17, rue Goethe, 67083 Strasbourg Cedex, ☎ 88.61.62.01. *Dir. Rég. des Affaires culturelles,* palais du Rhin, 3, pl. de la République, 67082 Strasbourg Cedex, ☎ 88.32.28.37. Attention : Good Friday and Dec 26 are nat hols in Alsace.

S.O.S. : Bas-Rhin : *SAMU* (Emergency Medical Service), ☎ 88.33.33.33. Haut-Rhin : *SAMU,* ☎ 89.44.22.44. *Poisoning Emergency Centre,* ☎ 88.37.37.37.

Weather forecast : Bas-Rhin : ☎ 88.71.11.33. Haut-Rhin : ☎ 89.56.68.68.

Farmhouse, rural "gîtes" chambres d'hôtes and farmhouse-inns : enq. : *Relais Départemental du Tourisme Rural du Bas-Rhin,* Maison de l'Agriculture, 103, rte de Hausbergen, 67300 Schiltigheim, ☎ 88.62.45.09. *Chambre d'Agriculture du Haut-Rhin,* 3, pl. de la Gare, 68000 Colmar, ☎ 89.41.35.33.

Wine guide : list of producers and cellars at the *S.I.* and *T.O.* or at the *Centre d'Information du Vin d'Alsace (C.I.V.A.),* 12, av. de la Foire-aux-Vins, 68003 Colmar, ☎ 89.41.06.21.

Wine festivals : Jun : Dorlisheim (1st Sun). Jul : Ribeauvillé. Aug : Turckheim, Colmar, Eguisheim, Gueberschwir. Sep : *harvest festivals* everywhere. Oct : *new wine festivals.*

Nature parks : many activities are offerred Apr.-Oct. in the Vosges Nature Park. Enq. : *Syndicat mixte du parc naturel régional des Vosges du Nord,* La Petite-Pierre, 67290 Wingen-sur-Moder, ☎ 88.70.44.30.

Leisure centre : *Nautiland Haguenau,* 8, rue des Dominicains, 67500 Haguenau, ☎ 88.73.49.59.

Hiking and Rambling : numerous possibilities for "walking holidays," thanks to the chalets and refuges on the Vosges Massif. Enquiries : *Club vosgien,* Comité central, 4, rue de la Douane, 67000 Strasbourg, ☎ 88.32.57.96. *Amis de la Nature-Strasbourg,* 10, rue du Gard-Hoenheim, 67000 Strasbourg, ☎ 88.33.45.03. — *Vosges-Trotter Colmar,* 16, av. de l'Europe, 68000 Colmar, ☎ 89.79.10.33. Other possibilities : crossing of the Vosges mountains on foot : *T.O.* and *S.I.* in Sainte-Marie-aux-Mines, ☎ 89.58.80.50. The Northern Range on foot : *Relais Départemental du Tourisme Rural,* Maison de l'Agriculture, 103, rte de Hausbergen, 67300 Schiltigheim, ☎ 88.62.45.09.

Alsace cuisine

"... one of the regions of Europe where my mouth watered the most", wrote the 18thC gastronomist *Jean-Antheime Brillat-Savarin (1755-1826) about Alsace. The food is very rich, and pork products (charcuterie) abound : saveloy (served as a salad with Gruyère cheese), liver sausages, Strasbourg sausages, black pudding, and Alsatian foie gras (livers of specially-fed geese) served in a pastry crust or with veal or bacon added, as a pâté. The farm-inns of the Munster Valley serve a typical local meal : onion tart (tourte), sauerkraut, Munster cheese and rhubarb or apple pie. The traditional baeckaoffe is a particularly fortifying dish of potatoes baked slowly (formerly in the baker's oven) with pork, beef and mutton marinated in wine. Around Strasbourg, a tart called flammenkueche is usually made with onion, less often with fresh fruit. Sauced dishes (stews, chicken braised in Riesling) are often accompanied by egg noodles. Also served with Riesling is a freshwater fish stew called the matelote, made with fish from the Ill or the Rhine; fried carp is traditional in the Sundgau. Springtime asparagus is the speciality of Hoerdt, N of Strasbourg. To finish the meal, a favourite dessert : the kugelhopf, a yeasty raisin cake followed by another Alsatian speciality, eau-de-vie (brandy) flavoured with fruit or berries.*

The wines of Alsace

The vineyards of Alsace cover a total of 110 km^2 fragmented into about 12000 holdings. The wines are classified not by grades within district of origin, as in the rest of France, but rather according to the seven permitted grape varieties, plus an eighth wine blended from a selection of the seven. Varieties are : Sylvaner, fruity, light and fresh; Riesling, fruity, delicately perfumed; Gewürztraminer, flowery, spicy and elegant; Muscat d'Alsace, dry, the ideal aperitif; Tokay (Pinot Gris), opulent and full; Pinot Blanc, rounded and balanced; Pinot Noir, dry, fruity red or rosé. The eighth, Edelzwicker, combining several varieties, is the white wine for everyday consumption. All the wines of Alsace, in distinctive slender bottles, are consumed young and cool.

Technical tourism : homemade fruit brandy distillery at Lapoutroie (visits from May to Sep, ☎ 89.47.50.16). Breweries : *Heineken* at Mutzig, *Kronenbourg* at Obernai and Strasbourg, ☎ 88.29.90.00. Rose stone quarries at Petersbach, ☎ 88.70.45.66.

Scenic railways : *Rhine tourist railway (C.F.T.R.)*, Neuf-Brisach-Marckolsheim. From Jul-Sep, Sun and nat hols; — *Vallée de la Doller.* Departure from Cernay or Sentheim. Sun and nat hols, and daily ex Mon and Tue in Jul-Aug. Duration : 1 hr; — *Rosheim-Ottrott :* Sun and nat hols in Jul-Aug. Duration : 1 hr; round trip, ☎ 88.95.81.14, ext. 16. — *Minitrain from Saverne to the Château du Haut-Bau :* Jul-15 Sep, Sat, Sun and nat hols. Duration : 2 hr 30, ☎ 88.91.13.08.

Cycling holidays : *O.D.T.* **Bas-Rhin;** *A.D.T.* du **Haut-Rhin.** Fédération Française de Cyclotourisme, ligue d'Alsace de Cyclotourisme, M.-P. Wanner, 1, rue F.-Kuhllmann, 68000 Colmar.

Riding holidays : Enq. *O.D.T.* **Bas-Rhin,** the *A.D.T.* du **Haut-Rhin** and *Association Alsacienne de Tourisme Equestre,* 2, rue Landwasser, 68000 Colmar, ☎ 89.41.52.82.

River and canal cruises : discover Alsace by traveling up the Marne canal to the Rhine. Enquiries and bookings : *O.D.T.* **Bas-Rhin** and *A.D.T.* du **Haut-Rhin.**

Handicraft courses : sculpture, model-making, weaving, pottery, polychrome painting, spinning and natural dyes, wickerwork, copper enamelling, silk painting. Enq. : *O.D.T.* **Bas-Rhin** and *A.D.T.* du **Haut-Rhin.**

Peasant cookery courses : Bas-Rhin : Lembach, Marlesheim, Mutzig, Niederbronn-les-Bains, Obersteigen, Strasbourg. Enrollments : *Relais Dép. du Tourisme Rural,* Maison de l'Agriculture, 103, rte de Hausbergen, 67300 Schiltigheim, ☎ 88.62.45.09.

Other courses : nature and environmental discovery courses, *Centre Permanent d'Initiation à l'Environnement Régional d'Alsace (C.P.I.E.),* 36, rue de Sélestat-Muttersholtz, 67600 Sélestat, ☎ 88.85.11.30.

Children : for all information about children's holidays (music, sports, farm holidays, etc.) and children's activities throughout the year, consult the *Centre d'Information Jeunesse Alsace (C.I.J.A.),* 7, rue des Écrivains, 67000 Strasbourg, ☎ 88.37.33.33.

Aquatic sports : list of centres at *O.T., S.I.* and *C.D.T. Ligue d'Alsace de Canoë-Kayak,* 15, rue de Genève, 67000 Strasbourg, ☎ 88.35.27.20.

Winter sports : resorts : col des Bagenelles, ballon d'Alsace, le Bonhomme, Champ du Feu, Cote 1000, Dolleren, Donon, le Frenz, Gaschney, Grand-Ballon, Grendelbruch, le Hohwald, Markstein, Saales, la Schlucht, Schnepfenried, Tanet, Trois-Fours, Wangenbourg-Engenthal. **Cross-country skiing.** In Champ du Feu, Donon, Grendelbruch, La Petite-Pierre, Plaine, Saales, Wangenbourg-Engenthal. Enq. *A.D.T.* du **Haut-Rhin.** Ski trek across the Vosges mountains : *S.I.* Sainte-Marie-aux-Mines. "Forfait Hautes-Vosges" : *S.I.* in Munster. Cross-country ski schools : *S.U.A.* Tourisme et Propagande, Chambre d'Agriculture du Haut-Rhin, 3, pl. de la Gare, 68000 Colmar, ☎ 89.41.35.33.

Golf : Strasbourg, Illkirch-Graffenstaden, Chalampé, golf de l'Ile-du-Rhin (18 holes).

Flying, gliding, etc. : enq. : *O.D.T.* and *A.D.T.*

Storks

The Alsatians are attached to these birds, the emblem of their province, and were extremely concerned when only three pairs of storks returned to Alsace for the summer of 1981. The main reasons for this disappearance seem to be the draining of marshes and winter-time hunting in Africa. The Alsatians are attempting to rebuild the population by mating wild birds with storks reared in captivity; the baby storks migrate as do their wild forebears. There are several "stork parks" in Alsace, the main one at Kintzheim (→ Route du Vin).

Hunting and shooting : local legislation on hunting is fairly restrictive. Enq. at the *Féd. dép.* **Bas-Rhin :** Résidence Lafayette, 5, rue Staedel, 67000 Strasbourg, ☎ 88.79.12.77. **Haut-Rhin :** 2, av. A.-Wicky, 68100 Mulhouse, ☎ 89.45.60.28.

Fishing : *Féd. Dép. des Associations de Pêche et de Pisciculture :* **Bas-Rhin,** 2, rue de Nomeny, 67000 Strasbourg, ☎ 88.34.51.86. **Haut-Rhin,** 29, rue de Colmar, 68200 Mulhouse, ☎ 89.59.06.88.

Towns and places

AMMERSCHWIHR

Colmar 7, Saint-Dié 49, Paris 508 km
pop 1639 ⊠ 68770   A3

Hotels :
★★ **Aux Armes de France**, 1, Grand'Rue, ☎ 89.47.10.12,
Tx 880666, AE DC Euro Visa, 10 rm ℗ closed Wed and
Thu lunch, 5-30 Jan, 270. Rest. ● ◆◆ The Gaetners are
really cooking! Alsatian wine by the litre. Interesting fixed-
price meals, 325-350; child : 120.
★★ **L'Arbre Vert** (L.F.), 7, rue des Cigognes,
☎ 89.47.12.23, Euro Visa, 13 rm ⌇ half pens (h.s.),
closed Tue, 10 Feb-25 Mar, 20 Nov-10 Dec, 190. Rest. ◆
Good food in an Alsatian setting. Regional specialities,
60-110.

Recommended
Guide to wines : *Caves Schaetzel*, 3, rue de la 5e-D.-B.

BALLON D'ALSACE*

                                                   A4
A peak at the S end of the Vosges mountains, seeming to guard the Belfort Gap, the Ballon d'Alsace is
easily accessible via three winding roads from Lorraine, Franche-Comté and Alsace.
▶ From the Pass where these roads converge (restaurant; monument to WWII bomb disposal experts), 20 min
walk to the summit (orientation table, view★); walks.   ☐

BARR*

Strasbourg 35, Colmar 39, Paris 493 km
pop 4600 ⊠ 67140   B2
On the Wine Road, the houses of Barr are arranged
around the 17thC **town hall★**; the square is the scene
of many local festivities.
▶ In the town, **Folie Marco Museum** : furniture, pottery,
pewter, local souvenirs, in an 18thC mansion so luxurious
that it was nicknamed *Folie* (madness); wine-tasting in the
cellar *(daily ex Tue., 10-12 & 2:30-6, Jul.-Sep.; Jun., Oct.,
Sat., Sun., rest of year by appt.).* ▶ W on D854, then
a forest road to **châteaux of Spesbourg** and **Andlau**
(12thC; 14th-16thC; *30 min and 1hr round trip walk,
respectively).* ▶ **Château de Landsberg★** : 12thC *(D854,
D109 then GR5; 1hr walk round trip).*

Practical Information ───────────

BARR
ⓘ pl. de l'Hôtel de Ville, ☎ 88.08.94.24.
SNCF ☎ 88.08.90.15.

Hotel :
★★ **Maison-Rouge** (L.F.), 1, av. de la Gare,
☎ 88.08.90.40, Visa, 13 rm ℗ half pens, closed Mon and
Feb, 170. Rest. ◆◆ Terrace dining, 35-120.

⚠ ★★*Wepfermatt* (70 pl), ☎ 88.08.02.38.

Recommended
Chambres d'hôtes : at Heiligenstein, *Maison Ruff*, 1.5 km
N, ☎ 88.08.10.81.

Nearby
ITTERSWILLER, ⊠ 67140 Barr, 6 km S.

Hotel :
★★★ **Arnold**, rte du Vin, ☎ 88.85.50.58, Tx 870550, AE
Visa, 28 rm ℗ ⌇ ⏠ ⌀ ⌇ 300. Rest. ● ◆◆ ⌇ ⌇ closed
Mon and Sun eve. In the heart of the wine country, tradi-
tional *choucroute* (sauerkraut) is the specialty, along with

*noisette de marcassin aux airelles, filet de sandre au
riesling* 95-160.

MITTELBERGHEIM, ⊠ 67140, 2 km S.

Hotel :
★ **Gilg**, 1, rue Rotland, ☎ 88.08.91.37, AE DC, 10 rm ℗
⌇ closed Tue eve , Wed, 6 Jan-5 Feb, 25 Jun-4 Jul, 135.
Rest. ◆ ⌇ 115-190.

Recommended
Guide to wines : *Caves Wantz*, 3, rue des Vosges.

BRUCHE Valley

                                                   A2
From Molsheim (→ Route du Vin) to the **Saales Pass**
(alt. 556 m), the valley follows the course of the river
Bruche, between the sandstone of the northern Vosges and the crystalline rocks of southern Vosges.
▶ **Mutzig** : breweries. Follow the valley by N420 *(left
bank)* rather than the motorway. **Niederhaslach** *(3 km
N)* : at the edge of a forest, a 13th-14thC **abbey church★**
showing influence of Strasbourg cathedral; stained glass ;
tomb ; 18thC stalls. ▶ **Guirbaden** *(7 km S)* : ruined castle on a rock; important fortress until the 17thC; view★.
▶ **Schirmeck** : summer and winter resort; capital of the
valley ; the textile industry replaced by engineering ; **historical museum** *(1-6, Sun., hols. in season); walks.* Excursion to Donon (alt. 1 009 m ; *12-km drive and 15-min walk*)
view★★★, via **Grandfontaine** : old **iron mine** open to the
public *(2-6, Sat., Sun.).* ▶ **Struthof** : the only WWII **concentration camp** in France held 40 000 prisoners, of whom
10 000 were killed ; huts, barbed-wire enclosure, watchtowers, gas-chamber ; museum *(May-Sep., 8-11:30 &
2-4:30; rest of year, 9-11:30 & 2-4:30);* National Deportation Cemetery.   ☐

Practical Information ───────────

COLROY-LA-ROCHE, ⊠ 67420 Saales, 11 km NE.

Hotel :
● ★★★ **Cheneaudière** (R.C.), ☎ 88.97.61.64, Tx 870438,
AE DC Euro Visa, 28 rm ℗ ⌇ ⌇ ⌀ ⌇ ⌀ ⌀ closed
1 Jan-1 Mar, 590. Rest. ● ◆◆◆ ⌇ ⌀ Chef Jean-Paul
Bossée is building up solid experience in the kitchen
and will soon be a force to reckon with : *tartare de saumon frais d'Ecosse, millefeuilles de foie gras et de truffes*, 190-300.

Col du DONON, ⊠ 67130 Schirmeck, 10 km NW of **Schirmeck.**

Hotel :
★★ **Donon** (L.F.), Grandfontaine, ☎ 88.97.20.69, Visa,
21 rm ℗ ⌇ ⌀ ⌇ ⌁ ⌀ closed Thu (l.s.), 10 Nov-10 Dec,
155. Rest. ◆ ⌇ ⌀ 60-100.

MOLLKIRCH, ⊠ 67190 Mutzig, 9 km SW.

Hotel :
★★ **Fischhütte** (L.F.), 30, rte de la Fischhütte,
☎ 88.97.42.03, Visa, 18 rm ℗ ⌀ ⌇ closed Mon eve and
Tue, 26 Jan-7 Mar, 200. Rest. ◆ ⌇ 50-170.

⚠ ★★*Fischhütte* (50 pl), ☎ 88.97.42.03.

Recommended
Youth hostel : ☎ 88.93.42.23.

MUTZIG, ⊠ 67190, 3 km W of **Molsheim.**
SNCF ☎ 88.38.13.06.

Hotel :
★★ **Hostellerie de la Poste** (L.F.), 4, pl. de la Fontaine,
☎ 88.38.38.38, 19 rm ⌇ 170. Rest. ◆ 50-100.

Restaurant :
● ◆◆ **Au Nid de Cigognes**, 25, rue du 18-Novembre,

☎ 88.38.11.97, Visa, closed Tue eve and Wed. For traditional Alsatian fare, 45-130.

NATZWILLER, ⊠ 67130 Schirmeck, 10 km SE of **Mutzig.**

Hotel :
★★ *Auberge Metzger*, 70, rue Principale, ☎ 88.97.02.42, Visa, 10 rm Ⓟ ≼ ⑳ ⚲ ♩ half pens (h.s.), closed Mon, 5-30 Jan, 130. Rest. ♦ ♩ 40-120.

NIEDERHASLACH, ⊠ 67190 Mutzig, 15 km W of **Molsheim.**

Hotel :
★★ *La Pomme d'Or* (L.F.), 36, rue Principale, ☎ 88.50.90.21, AE DC Euro Visa, 20 rm Ⓟ ⚲ ⑳ half pens (h.s.), closed Mon eve and Tue (l.s.), 1 Feb-1 Mar, 310. Rest. ♦ ♩ ⑳ 45-120.

OBERHASLACH, ⊠ 67190 Mutzig, 16 km W of **Molsheim.**
ℹ mairie, ☎ 88.50.90.15.

Hotel :
★★ *Aux Ruines du Nideck* (L.F.), 2, rue de Molsheim, ☎ 88.50.90.14, DC Euro Visa, 13 rm Ⓟ ≼ ⑳ closed Tue eve and Wed, 1-15 Mar, 11 Nov-7 Dec, 180. Rest. ♦ ≼ ♩ 60-150.

SCHIRMECK, ⊠ 67130, 25 km SW of **Molsheim.**
ℹ ☎ 88.97.00.02.
🚆 ☎ 88.97.00.68.

Hotels :
★★ *La Charbonnière* (L.F.), Col de la Charbonnière, Bellefosse, ☎ 88.08.31.17, DC Euro Visa, 20 rm Ⓟ ≼ ⑳ ⚲ ⑳ sauna, 178. Rest. ♦ ≼ ♩ 65-120.
★★ *La Rubanerie* (L.F.), La Claquette-Rothau, ☎ 88.97.01.95, AE DC Euro Visa, 16 rm Ⓟ ≼ ⑳ ⚲ ó 205. Rest. ♦ ≼ ♩ ⑳ 85-135.
★★ *Neuhauser* (L.F.), Les Quelles, ☎ 88.97.06.81, AE DC Visa, 10 rm Ⓟ ≼ ⑳ ⚲ 🖃 closed Wed, 15-30 Jan, 15-30 Nov, 180. Rest. ♦ ≼ ♩ 80-125.

△ ★★*Municipal* (50 pl), ☎ 88.95.01.61.

BRUMATH

Haguenau 11, Saverne 30, Paris 468 km
pop 7702 ⊠ 67170   B1

🚆 ☎ 88.51.10.11.

Hotel :
★★ *A l'Ecrevisse* (L.F.), 4, av. de Strasbourg, ☎ 88.51.11.08, AE Euro Visa, 21 rm Ⓟ ⑳ closed Mon eve and Tue, 14 Jul-7 Aug. Sauna, 150. Rest. ● ♦♦ ♩ ó
This superb establishment has been the home of the Orth family since 1780. Excellent crayfish, and saddle of roe deer in season, 120-185.

Nearby

MOMMENHEIM, ⊠ 67670, 6 km NW.

Restaurant :
♦♦ *Manoir de la Tour-St-Georges*, 165, rte de Brumath, ☎ 88.51.61.78, AE DC Euro Visa ⑳ ♩ ó closed Mon and Tue eve, 40-150.

COLMAR***

Strasbourg 71, Nancy 148, Paris 531 km
pop 63700 ⊠ 68000   A3

A popular French illustrator known as Hansi (a leader of French Resistance during WWI) was born in Colmar. The charm of this typical Alsatian town inspired his art. Capital of the Haut-Rhin department, Colmar is a busy city with a constant flow of business and tourism, a city of art and good living whose earlier prosperity bequeathed churches fine mansions and works of art.

▶ Leave your car near the Champ-de-Mars (A-B2) under the protection of General Rapp, sculpted (like New York's Statue of Liberty) by Frédéric Bartholdi, and enter the **old town** by the Rue des Augustins. ▶ **Place du Marché-aux-Fruits** : pink sandstone façade of the **Conseil Souverain d'Alsace★** (Supreme Council of Alsace, 1765 now a law court) and Kern house with scrolled gable. ▶ **Krutenau district** (B3) : follow Rue St-Jean (house of the Knights of St. John, showing Italian influence); from the bridges over the River Lauch, views of flowered balconies and weeping willows; this area, known as **"Little Venice"★★**, is illuminated at night. Quai de la Poissonnerie, **natural history museum** (*Apr.-Oct., 9-12 & 2-6; rest of year, closed Tue.*). ▶ Between the Lauch and the Old Customs House is the **tanners' district** (B-C2) : the restored elegance of this flower-laden old quarter makes a pleasant backdrop to modern life. ▶ **Ancienne Douane★★** (Old Customs House, 15th-16thC) : the municipal magistrates and town council used to meet on the first floor ; a passage through the building leads to the **Grand'Rue★** (B2) with interesting houses (No. 15, Maison des Arcades 1606) and the Protestant **church of St. Mathieu** : choir-screen★, 14th-15thC stained glass ; behind the church, Louis XV façade of the former hospital. ▶ Rue des Marchands (B2) **half-timbered houses★★** and mansions : **Pfister House★★** at the corner of Rue Mercière (1537 ; frescos, oriel window, galleries); Nos. 32, 34, 38, 44, 48; at No. 30, **Bartholdi Museum** (sculptor's work ; local history; *10-12 & 2-6, Apr.-Oct.; Sat., Sun. rest of year);* Rue Schongauer, the **Maison du Cygne★.** ▶ Former Guardhouse (1575 ; B2) and other old houses line the cathedral square ; the cathedral is the former **collegiate church of St. Martin★★** (13th-14thC ; sculptures on the E and S doorways ; 19thC choir stalls★). ▶ **Dominican church★★** (B2) : nave, typical Rhineland Gothic ; 14thC stained-glass windows★ ; Schongauer's **Virgin with Rose Bush★★★** (*1473*). **Maison des Têtes★★** (17thC), in the street of the same name. ▶ **Unterlinden Museum★★★** (B1 ; *Apr.-Oct., 9-12 & 2-6, 5 rest of year; closed Tue. and hols*). Unterlinden ("under the lime trees"), a Dominican convent from the 13thC to 1790, now a superb museum ; **cloister★** ; archaeology, medieval and Renaissance sculpture, stained glass windows, medieval paintings (Martin Schongauer altarpiece★★, Nativity★ ; **Issenheim altarpiece★★★ →**), modern art, Alsatian folk art (furniture, ironwork, toys, winepresses). □

The Issenheim altarpiece

The Colmar museum is the most popular French museum outside of Paris, largely because of the altarpiece painted by Mathias Grünewald (1460-1528), for the Issenheim hospital chapel. The sick were shown scenes from the altarpiece appropriate to the phases of the liturgical calendar, or the sections carved by the contemporary Nicolas de Haguenau. According to chroniclers of the time, the impact of the work was therapeutic.
The subjects portrayed are medieval in character, but the use of form and colour shows Renaissance influence.

Practical Information _____

COLMAR
ℹ 4, rue des Unterlinden (B1), ☎ 89.41.02.29.
✈ Houssen, 3 km N, ☎ 89.23.99.33.
🚆 (A3), ☎ 89.24.50.50/89.23.23.22.
🚌 train station.
Car Rental : Avis, 49, rue de la 1ʳᵉ armée française (A2), ☎ 89.23.21.82.

Hotels :
★★★★ *Terminus Bristol*, (Mapotel), 7, pl. de la Gare (A3), ☎ 89.23.59.59, Tx 880248, AE DC Euro Visa, 70 rm Ⓟ

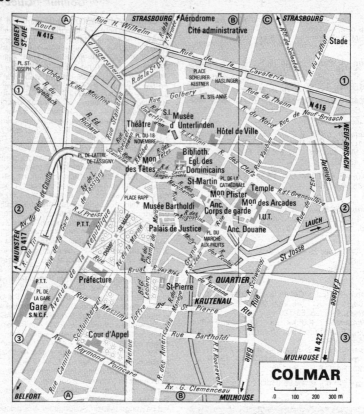

COLMAR

.0   100   200   300 m

---

380. Rest. ● ◆◆ *Le Rendez-vous de Chasse* ♪ ♣ Fish, seafood, game in season, 190-300.

★★★ *Champ-de-Mars*, (P.L.M.), 2, av. de la Marne (A2), ☎ 89.41.54.54, Tx 880928, AE DC Euro Visa, 75 rm P ▦ ♣ ♪ ♨ 300.

★★★ *Maréchal*, 4-6, pl. des Six-Montagnes-Noires (B3), ☎ 89.41.60.32, Tx 880949, AE Euro Visa, 40 rm P ⟨ ▦ ♣ ♪ closed Jan, Feb, 250. Rest. ◆◆ ♪ ♣ 75-120.

★★★ *Romains*, 13, rte de Neuf-Brisach, Horbourg-Wihr, ☎ 89.23.46.46, Tx 880294, Euro Visa, 63 rm P ⟨ ▦ ♣ ♪ closed 22-31 Dec, 205. Rest. ◆ ♪ closed Sat eve, 50-80.

★★★ *Saint-Martin*, 38, Grand'Rue (B2), ☎ 89.24.11.51, Euro Visa, 12 rm P ⟨ ♣ closed Jan, 200.

★★ *Cerf* (L.F.), 9, Grand'Rue, Horbourg-Wihr, ☎ 89.41.20.35, Visa, 27 rm P ▦ ♪ ※ closed Mon, 15 Jan-1 Mar, 185. Rest. ◆◆ ⟨ ♪ ※ closed Mon and Sun eve, 70-120.

★★ *Fecht* (L.F.), 1, rue de la Fecht (off map B1), ☎ 89.41.34.08, 39 rm P 200. Rest. ◆ ♪ closed Mon and Sun eve, 70-110.

★★ *Majestic* (L.F.), 1, rue de la Gare (A2), ☎ 89.41.45.19, 40 rm P closed Mon eve and Sun, 15 Dec-10 Jan, 230. Rest. ◆ ♪ 120-160.

★ *Rapp*, 16, rue Berthe-Molly (B2), ☎ 89.41.62.10, AE DC Euro Visa, 14 rm, closed 21 Jun-5 Jul, 1 Dec-8 Jan, 110. Rest. ◆ closed Wed, 55-100; child : 30.

Restaurants :

● ◆◆◆ *Au Fer Rouge*, 52, Grande Rue (B2), ☎ 89.41.37.24 ♣ ♪ closed Mon and Sun eve, 6-27 Jan, 28 Jul-4 Aug. We would have liked to reveal Patrick Ful- graff's impressions as a new member of our chefs'pa- nel : -but discretion is a virtue, especially in a chef. His is an intelligent, high-quality cuisine served in a splendid

setting. Spec : *nouilles tièdes et salpicon de langoustes, chausson à la truffe "André Pic", morue fraîche poêlée au Noilly*. Luscious desserts and great Alsatian wines, 170-250.

● ◆◆◆ *Schillinger*, 16, rue Stanislas (A2), ☎ 89.41.43.17, AE DC Euro Visa ♪ ♣ closed Mon and Sun eve, 4 Jul-1 Aug. Excellent updated regional cuisine, 170-250.

◆◆ *Maison des Têtes*, 19, rue des Têtes (B2), ☎ 89.24.43.43, AE DC Euro Visa ▦ ♪ ♣ closed Mon and Sun eve, 15 Jan-15 Feb, 80-160.

● ◆ *S'parisser Stewwele*, 4, pl. Jeanne-d'Arc (C2), ☎ 89.41.42.33 P ♪ closed Tue eve, 9 Feb-4 Mar, 22 Jun-1 Jul, 23 Nov-2 Dec. A Winstub in a classified 16th- C dwelling ; regional dishes, 100-140.

◆ *Caveau Saint-Pierre*, 24, rue de la Herse (B3), ☎ 89.41.99.33, Euro Visa ♪ ♣ closed Sun eve, 20 Feb-9 Mar, 1-15 Jul, 20 Dec-3 Jan, 70-80.

⚠ ★★★*III* (100 pl), ☎ 89.41.15.94.

Recommended
Youth hostel : 7, rue Sint-Niklaos, ☎ 89.41.33.08.
Guide to wines : *Caves Martin-Jund*, 12, rue de l'Ange ; at Soultzmatt, 15 km N., *Léon Boesch et fils*, ☎ 89.47.01.83.
Guided tours : *Old Colmar*, in a mini-train from June to Oct, info and reservations at t, he tourist office.
♥ bakery : *Léonard Helmstetter*, 11-13, rue des Serruriers (B2), ☎ 89.41.27.78 ; fine pork products : *Glasser*, 18, rue des Boulangers (B2), ☎ 89.41.23.69 ; pastry : 3, rue des Têtes (B2), ☎ 89.23.34.72 ; pastry-tea room : *Clergue*, 21, pl. de la Cathédrale (B2), ☎ 89.41.82.60 ; take-out foods : *Kempf*, 21, rue des Clers (B-C2), ☎ 89.41.32.07.

Nearby

WETTOLSHEIM, ⊠ 68000 Colmar, 5 km SW.

Hotel :
★★★ *Auberge du Père Floranc* (R.S.), 9, rue Herzog, ☎ 89.41.39.14, AE DC Euro Visa, 32 rm ℗ ⇘ ⋙ ⚲ ❦ half pens (h.s.), closed Sun eve (l.s.) and Mon (l.s), 1-16 Jul, 12 Nov-18 Dec, 510. Rest. ● ♦♦ ⇘ Peace in a lovely park nestled in the wine country. The whole Floranc family cooks for you : *foie gras de l'auberge, la tourte de caille Père Floranc,* 85-180.

Route des CRÊTES

(The Ridge Road) A3

From Cernay to the Bonhomme Pass *(77 km ; see map 1)*

Partly built during WWI to serve the Front, the Ridge Road is now the main tourist route in the Upper Vosges, with views of the hillside fields (Hautes Chaumes), and pine and beech woods. Roads and footpaths connect, and farm-inns are dotted along the way.

1. The Ridge road

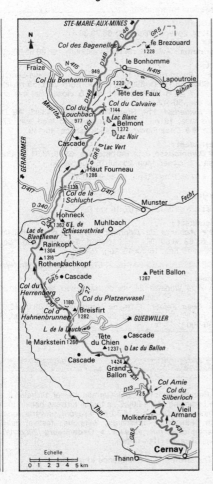

▶ **Cernay** (pop. 10300), badly damaged during the two World Wars, now an industrial and wine-making centre at an important crossroads ; 13thC town gate ; stork park ; Doller Valley tourist steam-train *(at the level crossing on D66, Sun. and nat. hols., May-Oct., daily ex Mon. and Tue. in Jul.-Aug. ; 1hr round trip to Sentheim ; info. tel. 89.82.88.48).* ▶ Leaving **Mount Molkenrain** (alt. 1 125 m) on the left, the road winds up to **Vieil-Armand**★★, site of an 8-month battle in 1914-15 : National Monument ; cemetery ; from the summit, view★ over the battlefield. **Ballon de Guebwiller**★★ (alt. 1 424 m) : highest point of the Vosges *(15-min hike to the top, view★★)* ; Diables Bleus (Blue Devils) monument to Hunters' Battalions ; signposted paths (e.g., Ballon lake). ▶ **Le Markstein** : a renowned summer and winter resort ; starting point for hikes (road★★ to the valley of the Lauch and Guebwiller). ▶ **Col de Hahnenbrunnen** (pass, alt. 1 180 m) : from the farm, view★ over the Fecht Valley. **Col de Herrenberg** (alt. 1 186 m) : to the right, **Mont Rainkopf** (alt. 1 304 m). ▶ **Mont Honeck** (alt. 1 362 m) : 1.5 km access road ; orientation table at one of the best **panoramas★★★** in the Vosges. ▶ **Col de la Schlucht** : winter sports and excursion centre ; highest pass in the mountains (alt. 1 139 m). **Haut-Chitelet** *(2 km SE)* : alpine garden *(Jun.-Oct.).* ▶ To the right, paths, views over the **lakes (Vert, Noir, Blanc)** ; **Col du Calvaire** (alt. 1 134 m). ▶ The road descends to the **Bonhomme** (alt. 949 m), Franco-German border in 1871. To the right, road down to **Le Bonhomme** (can also be reached via **Col des Bagenelles,** *11 km de tour*). □

Practical Information _____

Le **BONHOMME,** ⊠ 68650 Lapoutroie, 24 km NW of **Colmar.**

Hotels :
★★ *Poste* (L.F.), rue du 3e-Spahi, ☎ 89.47.51.10, Euro Visa, 21 rm ℗ ⋙ closed 12 Nov-20 Dec, 180. Rest. ♦ ♪
★ *Lion d'Or,* 64, rue Principale, ☎ 89.47.51.18, Euro Visa, 12 rm ℗ ⇘ ⚲ closed Wed, 12 Nov-1 Dec, 105. Rest. ♦ ⇘ 60-100.

CERNAY, ⊠ 68700, 19 km NW of **Mulhouse.**
ⓘ 1, rue Latouche, ☎ 89.75.50.35 (h.s.).
SNCF ☎ 89.75.40.02.

Hotels :
★ *Belle-Vue,* 10, rue Mal-Foch, ☎ 89.75.40.15, Euro Visa, 12 rm ℗ ⋙ ⚲ half pens (h.s.), closed Sun, 20 Dec-20 Jan, 145. Rest. ♦ 40-100.
★ *Hostellerie d'Alsace,* 61, rue Poincarré, ☎ 89.75.59.81, AE DC Euro Visa, 10 rm ℗ ⋙ closed Sun eve and Mon, 14-31 Jul, 100. Rest. ♦ ♪ 60-145.

⚎ ★★★★*Les Acacias* (145 pl), ☎ 89.75.56.97.

GOLDBACH, ⊠ 68760, 8 km from **Thann.**

Hotel :
★ *Goldenmatt,* ☎ 89.82.32.86, 12 rm ℗ ⇘ ⋙ ⚲ closed 15 Nov-Easter, 250. Rest. ♦ ⇘ Isolated manor-house in a splendid natural setting, 80-110.

Le **GRAND BALLON,** ⊠ 68760 Willer-sur-Thur, 42 km NW of **Mulhouse.**

Hotel :
★ *Grand Ballon,* ☎ 89.76.83.35, 20 rm ℗ ⇘ ⚲ half pens, closed 15 Nov-15 Dec, 310. Rest. ♦ ⇘ 60-100.

MARKSTEIN, ⊠ 68610, 49 km NW of **Mulhouse.**

Hotel :
★★ *Wolf,* ☎ 89.82.64.36, DC Visa, 22 rm ℗ ⇘ half pens (h.s.), closed 10 Nov-10 Dec, 530. Rest. ♦ ⇘ ♪ 70-110.

GUEBWILLER

Colmar 26, Belfort 53, Paris 548 km
pop 11080 ⊠ 68500 A3

Three churches, three styles : three ages in the history of Guebwiller, an industrial town (textiles, engineering) at the entrance to the Lauch Valley, once controlled by the abbey of Murbach.

▶ **Church of Notre-Dame**★★ : 18thC French neo-Classical structure, now a Protestant church; Baroque choir★ (stalls★) showing Austrian influence. ▶ **Dominican church**★ : Gothic, medieval frescos; concerts. **Florival Museum** : art and local history displays in the church *(May-Oct., weekdays ex Tue., 2:30-5, weekends and hols. 10-12 & 2-5:30; Nov.-Apr., weekends, hols. only, same hours).* ▶ Church of **St. Léger**★ : oldest in town (12th-13thC), Romanesque façade★, doorway★ and nave; Gothic choir. ▶ 16thC town hall (Hôtel de Ville).

Nearby

▶ **Lauch Valley**★, called "Florival" (Vale of Flowers) for its floral charm. The ridge road leads to **Buhl** : 15thC altarpiece★ in neo-Romanesque church; then to **Lautenbach** : restored Romanesque church, portico★, Baroque pulpit★★, Gothic cloister. ▶ **Ungersheim** *(8 km SE)* : the Upper Alsace Ecomuseum displays about twenty peasant houses which recreate an Alsatian village. *(Jun.-21 Sep., daily 10-8; 22 Sep.-21 Dec., 10-7; 22 Dec-May, 11-5 on request.)* □

Practical Information _____

GUEBWILLER
ⓘ 5, pl. St-Léger, ☎ 89.76.10.63.
SNCF ☎ 89.46.50.50.

Hotels :
★★ *Alsace* (L.F.), 140, rue de la République, ☎ 89.76.83.02, 29 rm, 160. Rest. ◆◆ ♪ closed Fri eve and Sat noon ex summer, Dec. Nice cooking, 80-130.
★★ *Lac* (L.F.), rue de la République, ☎ 89.76.63.10, Euro Visa, 43 rm Ⓟ ⪜ ∰ ♪ ⌕ ⫽ 150. Rest. ◆ ♪ closed Mon. *Choucroute, civet de chevreuil,* 35-70.

Restaurant :
◆ *Taverne de l'Eco-Musée de Haute Alsace,* Musée des maisons paysannes d'Alsace, ☎ 89.48.22.28, AE DC Euro Visa Ⓟ ⪜ closed Mon between 1 Nov-1 May, 55-120.

Recommended
♥ Painted wood furniture : *Mme Halterbach*, 8, rue Verdun.

Nearby

BUHL, ⊠ 68530, 3 km NE.

Hotel :
★★ *A la Vigne* (L.F.), 141, rue Florival, ☎ 89.76.92.99, 12 rm Ⓟ ⪜ ∰ closed Mon (l.s.), Jan, 100. Rest. ◆ ♪ ⫽ 60-120.

JUNGHOLTZ, ⊠ 68500, 7 km S.

Hotels :
● ★★★ *Résidence les Violettes,* (L.F., R.S.), Thierenbach, ☎ 89.76.91.19, DC Euro Visa, 12 rm Ⓟ ⪜ ⫽ closed 6-31 Jan, 300. Rest. ◆◆◆ closed Mon eve and Tue (l.s.). Renowned food, 150-280.
★ *Biebler* (L.F.), 2, rue de Rimbach, ☎ 89.76.85.75, AE DC Euro Visa, 12 rm Ⓟ ⪜ ∰ ⫽ ⫽ closed Thu eve and Fri, 130. Rest. ◆ 55-130; child : 35.

LAUTENBACH, ⊠ 68610, 8 km NW.

Hotel :
★ *Mark* (L.F.), 68, rue Principale, ☎ 89.76.32.03, 12 rm Ⓟ ∰ closed Mon (l.s), 1-15 Mar, 1-30 Nov, 70. Rest. ◆ ♪ 60-100.

⚎ ★*Saint-Gangolf* (100 pl), ☎ 89.76.32.02.

HAGUENAU

Strasbourg 32, Sarreguemines 75, Paris 477 km
pop 38000 ⊠ 67500 **B1**

This medieval town on the river Moder is the gateway to Northern Alsace.

▶ Activity is centred on the pedestrian precinct around the **Grand'Rue** : 18thC houses on the Place d'Armes.
▶ **Church of St. Georges**★, built over 5 centuries; Romanesque nave, Flamboyant Gothic vaulting and tabernacle★ in the choir; 15thC altarpiece in the right transept.
▶ **Alsatian Museum**★ : furniture, shop signs, tools, costumes, folk art *(8-12 & 2-6; Sat., Sun. 2-5; closed Tue.).*
▶ **Library** (early 20thC) : historical museum of archaeology, coins *(9-12 & 3-6; weekends 3-5:30; closed Tue.).*
▶ **Church of St. Nicolas** : 14th-15thC; statues, furnishings.

Nearby

▶ N of town : **Haguenau Forest,** the largest in Alsace (137 km²). At the edge of the forest, church of **Walbourg**★ (15thC). ▶ **Soufflenheim** *(14 km E)* : pottery industry, as at Betschdorf (→ Outre-Forêt). ▶ **Sessenheim** *(4 km farther)* : place of pilgrimage for admirers of the German poet Johann Wolfgang von Goethe (1749-1832), who stayed here long enough to have an affair with the daughter of the pastor in 1770-71 ; Protestant church; Goethe memorial *(9-12 & 2-6).* ▶ **Marienthal** *(5.5 km SE)* : site of pilgrimage to the Virgin since the 12thC. ▶ **Pfaffenhofen** *(14 km W),* centre of peasant revolts in 1525; **museum of folk art**★★ *(2-5, Wed., Sat., Sun. and by appt, tel :* 88.07.70.33); Bertrand Uberech distillery. ▶ 11 km N, **Morsbronn-les-Bains** : spa and leisure park (Fantasialand). □

Practical Information _____

HAGUENAU
ⓘ 1, pl. Joseph-Thierry, ☎ 88.73.30.41.
SNCF ☎ 88.93.77.05.
Car rental : Avis, 46, rte de Strasbourg,, ☎ 88.93.30.30.

Hotels :
★★ *Europ-Hôtel*, 15, av. du Pr-René-Leriche, ☎ 88.93.58.11, Tx 880566, AE DC Euro Visa, 55 rm Ⓟ ⪜ ∰ ⪡ ♪ ⪡ ⅋ ⌕ 215. Rest. ◆ ♪ ⅋ closed Sat eve and Sun eve, 60-105.
★★ *Kaiserhof,* 119, Grand'Rue, ☎ 88.73.43.43, AE DC Euro Visa, 10 rm, closed Tue eve and Wed eve, 170. Rest. ◆◆ *Chez Pierre* ♪ ⅋ Quick service, 40-140.

Restaurant :
◆◆ *Barberousse*, 8, pl. Barberousse, ☎ 88.73.31.09, Euro Visa ♪ ⅋ closed Mon, 25 Jul-15 Aug, 40-95.

⚎ ★★*Les Pins* (70 pl), ☎ 88.93.90.57.

Nearby

DRUSENHEIM, ⊠ 67410, 16 km E.

Restaurant :
◆◆◆ *Auberge du Gourmet,* 707, rte de Herrlisheim, ☎ 88.63.30.60 Ⓟ ∰ ♪ closed Tue eve and Wed, 30 Jan-10 Feb, 15 Jul-15 Aug, 75-200.

MORSBRONN-LES-BAINS, ⊠ 67360 Wœrth, 11 km NW.

Hotels :
★★ *A la Vignette*, 24, rte de Haguenau, ☎ 88.09.30.50, 30 rm Ⓟ ∰ closed Jan, 125.
★★ *Beau Séjour,* 3, rte de Haguenau, ☎ 88.09.42.55, 40 rm Ⓟ ∰ ⌕ closed 20 Dec-1 Jan, 160. Rest. ◆ ♪ 50-100.

HAUT-KOENIGSBOURG★★

A3

▶ Remodeled to suit the German Kaiser Wilhelm II at the beginning of the 20thC ; a feudal fortress behind triple ramparts *(9-12 & 1-6, 4:30 off season);* several rooms with 15th-16thC furnishings; weapons; festival hall★; chapel, forge, mill; **view**★★. ▶ **Oedenbourg** *(200m W)* : ruins of **castle** (12th-13thC). □

_____
The arrow (→) is a reference to another entry.

2. The Hohwald region

Le HOHWALD*

A2

Round trip *(59 km, half-day, see map 2)*

The land of the cherry-flavoured liqueur kirsch (Val de Villé; *visit to the distilleries in Bassemberg, Steige and on the "kirsch route", D 39),* and the heart of central Vosges; a tour through the range of Vosges landscapes.

▶ **Villé** : tourist centre at the junction of several valleys *(signposted hikes).* **Albé,** 1 km N : traditional houses; **museum of Val de Villé** *(2:30-6 Sun. and Wed., Sat. in summer).* ▶ The road climbs to Kreuzweg Pass (alt. 768 m; view★), then drops to **Le Hohwald★★,** attractive summer and winter resort with scattered villas and chalets between alt. 600 m and 1 100 m; walks (Hohwald waterfall★★, *45 min;* Ungersberg summit, *2hr).* ▶ The road climbs the side of **Neuntelstein** (alt. 971 m; view★★). Leave right D310 to Struthof (→ Bruche Valley). ▶ **Champ du Feu** plateau★ : downhill and cross-country skiing; view★★ from the lookout tower. ▶ Other lookouts on the way down to **Col de Steige** (pass, alt. 534 m). ▶ **Urbeis** : country town at the foot of Bilstein castle ruins. □

Practical Information

Le HOHWALD, ⊠ 67140 Barr, 26 km NW of **Sélestat.** ⓘ ☎ 88.08.30.90.

Hotels :
● ★★★ **Grand-Hôtel,** (Inter-Hôtel), rue principale, ☎ 88.08.31.03, Tx 890555, AE DC Euro Visa, 73 rm ℙ ⊰ ⏁⏁⏁ ⫶ 🌲 ఉ ⁊ closed 5 Jan-3 Feb, 10 Nov-20 Dec, 255. Rest. ♦♦ 65-155; child : 40.
★★ **Marchal,** ☎ 88.08.31.04, Euro Visa, 17 rm ℙ ⊰ ⫶⫶⫶ ⁊ pens (h.s.), closed Tue am, 5-15 Mar, 5 Nov-20 Dec, 400. Rest. ♦♦ ⊰ ♨ ⚘ 80-115.

△ ★★★★Municipal (100 pl), ☎ 88.08.30.90.

Col de STEIGE, ⊠ 67420 Ranrupt, 24 km NW of **Sélestat.**
Hotel :
★ **Col de Steige,** ☎ 88.97.60.65, 15 rm ℙ ⊰ ⫶⫶⫶ ⚘ ఉ closed Mon, Tue (l.s.), Oct-Jan, 130. Rest. ♦ ⊰ ఉ 55-120.

VILLÉ, ⊠ 67220, 12 km NW of **Sélestat.**
ⓘ mairie, ☎ 88.57.11.57.

Hotel :
★★ **A la Bonne Franquette** (L.F.), 6, pl. du Marché, ☎ 88.57.14.25, 10 rm ఉ half pens (h.s.), closed Wed eve, Thu, 10 Feb-20 Mar, 24 Dec-3 Jan, 350. Rest. ♦ ⚘ 50-150.

△ ★★Municipal (100 pl), ☎ 88.57.13.44.

ILLHAEUSERN

Saint-Dié 51, Strasbourg 60, Paris 521 km
pop 557 ⊠ 68150 Ribeauvillé   B3
ILLHAEUSERN

Restaurant :
● ♦♦♦♦ **Auberge de l'Ill,** rue de Collonges, ☎ 89.71.83.23, AE DC ℙ ⊰ ⫶⫶⫶ ⚘ ఉ closed Mon and Tue open Mon lunch in summer, Feb, 1-8 Jul. "Hard work, family..." and loads of talent are the secrets of success at this idyllic spot on the banks of the Ill. Father Paul and son Marc man the kitchen with creative fervour : *salade de joues de porc aux lentilles vertes, saumon soufflé, feuilleté de pigeonneau aux choux et truffes, strudel aux pommes.* Jean-Pierre and the rest of the clan manage the dining room and the business end. Rare vintages (19-45-49-53-61), 350-500.

Recommended
Chambres d'hôtes : *Maison d'hôtes Jehl,* 33, rue du 25-Janvier, ☎ 89.71.83.76, 6 rm.

Nearby
GUÉMAR, ⊠ 68970.
Hotel :
● ★★★ **La Clairière,** 46, rte d'Illhaeusern, ☎ 89.71.80.80, 25 rm ℙ ⊰ ⚘ ⁊ closed Jan-Feb, 320.

The KOCHERSBERG Region

A-B2

Kochersberg, once the granary of Strasbourg, is a rich agricultural region NW of the city; cereals, tobacco and hops trained on high trellises create a distinctive checkered landscape.

▶ **Truchtersheim** : local **museum** *(Sun. 2:30-6).* ▶ **Wasselonne** : on the edge of the Kochersberg; medieval remains and old houses. ▶ **Hohatzenheim,** *(16 km NE)* : Romanesque church★. □

Practical Information

WASSELONNE, ⊠ 67310, 14 km SE of **Saverne.**
ⓘ pl. du Gal-Leclerc, ☎ 88.87.17.22.
Hotel :
★ **Au Saumon,** 69, rue du Gal-de-Gaulle, ☎ 88.87.01.83, 18 rm ℙ ⊰ closed Sun eve (l.s.) and Mon, 15-30 Jun, 100. Rest. ♦ 60-120.

△ ★★Municipal (100 pl), ☎ 88.87.00.08.

MARMOUTIER*

Saverne 6, Strasbourg 33, Paris 452 km
pop 2000 ⊠ 67440   A2

Benedictine monastery founded in the 6thC; Rhineland Romanesque abbey-church **façade★★** (1150); Gothic nave with 18thC choir; Louis XV stalls★; 18thC organ (concerts). Small **country museum** in the village *(May-Sep., Sun., 10-12 & 2-6).* □

Practical Information

Hotel :
★ **Aux Deux Clefs,** 30, rue du Gal-Leclerc, ☎ 88.70.61.08, Euro Visa, 15 rm ℙ   half pens (h.s.), closed Mon, Jan-Feb, 270. Rest. ♦ ⊰ 45-150.

MULHOUSE

Colmar 41, Strasbourg 118, Paris 537 km
pop 113700 ⊠ 68100   A4

The town and district of Mulhouse can be seen from the top of the *Tour de l'Europe* (C2). Traditional industries include textiles and potash mining *(NW of town)*. Dynamic cultural life includes music, theatre, dance, museums.

▶ **Hôtel de Ville**★ (1552 ; B2); historical museum *(10-12 & 2-5 or 6, closed Tue.; Thu. 8:30 pm-10:30 pm)*; ▶ Protestant **church of St. Etienne** : 14thC stained glass★. ▶ **Fine Arts Museum** and Lapidary Museum in the chapel of St. Jean (murals). ▶ **Fabric Printing Museum**★★, (C3; *10-12 & 2-6 Tue. and hols; demonstrations Mon., Wed. in Jul., Aug.)* : no fewer than ten million samples from which manufacturers still derive inspiration; techniques and motifs since the 18thC; demonstration of machinery *(Mon. & Wed. am)*. ▶ **Musée du Chemin de Fer** (Railway Museum)★★★, *(Apr.-Sep., 9-6; Oct.-Mar., 10-5; closed hols)* signposted from the Belfort road; the largest railway museum in Europe; small-scale models, miniature network; exceptional items on 860 m of rails in the great hall : first European steam locomotive; Napoleon III's private car★★ decorated by the 19thC architect Eugène Viollet-le-Duc (1814-79); carriages from the great European express trains; locomotive "Pacific 231"; posters; platform equipment, accessories. ▶ Annex with **Musée du Sapeur-Pompier** (Firemen's Museum) : equipment, uniforms and vehicles from 18thC to present day. ▶ **National Automobile Museum**★★★ (192 Avenue de Colmar; *11-6*

ex Tue.) The Schlumpf brothers' collection of 440 European cars of all periods, in working order.

Nearby

▶ **Rixheim** *(2 km E)* : **wallpaper museum** in a former commandery (18thC; *10-12 & 2-6 Apr.-11 Nov., daily ex Tue. and nat. hols.; 12 Nov.-Mar., weekends only)*. ▶ **Kingersheim** : tropical aquarium *(2-6)*. ▶ To the E, the dense **Hardt Forest** (hornbeam, oak). ▶ **Ottmarsheim** *(11 km)* : octagonal Romanesque **church**★★ inspired by the 11thC Imperial chapel at Aix-la-Chapelle (Aachen). ▶ **Ensisheim** *(14 km N)* : town **hall**★ and Renaissance houses.   □

Practical Information _____

MULHOUSE
ℹ 9, av. Foch (C2-3), ☎ 89.45.68.31.
✈ *Bâle-Mulhouse*, 27 km SE, ☎ 89.69.00.00. *Air France office*, 7, av. Foch (C2), ☎ 89.46.10.18.
SNCF (C3), ☎ 89.46.50.50/89.45.62.83.
🚌 av. du Gal-Leclerc (C3), ☎ 89.45.36.56.
Car rental : *Avis*, 116, rue de Bâle, ☎ 89.44.18.18 ; Airport, ☎ 89.69.00.00.

Hotels :
★★★ *Altéa de la Tour* (ex Frantel), 4, pl. du Gal-de-Gaulle (C3), ☎ 89.46.01.23, Tx 881807, AE DC Euro Visa, 96 rm 🅿 ♢ 🖰 ♨ 400. Rest. ♦♦ *L'Alsace* ♨ ♪ ♿ closed Sat noon and Sun, 24 Dec-2 Jan, 70-120.
★★★ *Europe*, 11, av. du Mal-Foch (C2-3), ☎ 89.45.19.18, 50 rm, 250.
★★★ *La Bourse*, 14, rue de la Bourse (C3), ☎ 89.56.18.44, Tx 881720, Euro Visa, 50 rm, closed 21 Dec-4 Jan, 285.

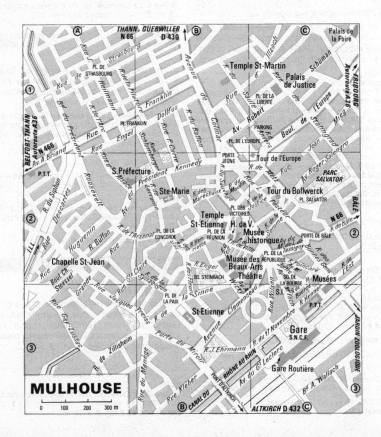

MULHOUSE

★★ *Musée*, 3, rue de l'Est (C2), ☎ 89.45.47.41, Tx 881188, DC Euro Visa, 43 rm Ⓟ ⦰ ⬚ closed 20 Dec-5 Jan, 200.

Restaurants :
◆◆ *Auberge Alsacienne du Parc Zoologique*, 31, av. de la 9e-D.I.C. (C3), ☎ 89.44.26.91, AE DC Euro Visa ⦰ ♪ closed Mon eve and Sun eve, Mon lunch (l.s.), 1 Feb-1 Mar, 20 Dec-1 Jan, 45-200.
◆◆ *Le Belvédère*, 80, av. de la 1re-D.-B. (C3), ☎ 89.44.18.79, AE DC Euro Visa ⦰ closed Mon eve and Tue , Feb school hols, 1-15 Aug, 135-190.
◆◆ *Rest. du Musée National de l'Automobile*, 192, av. de Colmar (B1), ☎ 89.43.44.20 ⦗ For vintage-car fans, 95-140.
◆ *Restaurant du Musée du Chemin de Fer*, 2, rue A.-de-Glehn, ☎ 89.43.44.20, DC Euro Visa Ⓟ ⬚ closed Mon, Tue eve, Wed eve, Thu eve, Fri eve dinner only (h.s.), 30-100.

Nearby

DIEFMATTEN, ⊠ 68780, 13 km SW.

Restaurant :
◆ *Cheval Blanc*, ☎ 89.26.94.40, AE DC Euro Visa ⦗ ⦰ closed Mon and Tue, 7-28 Jan, 15-31 Jul, 90-220; child : 75.

ILLZACH-MODENHEIM, ⊠ 68110, 3 km N.

Restaurant :
● ◆◆ *Le Parc*, 8, rue V.-Hugo, ☎ 89.56.61.67, Euro Visa ⦗ ⦰ ♪ closed Mon, Sat noon, Sun eve. A view of the park and J.-P. Huffschmitt's enjoyable cuisine : *mignonnette d'agneau poêlée menthe fraîche ou ail, feuilleté de fruits de saison chaud*, 110-220.

RIEDISHEIM, ⊠ 68400, 1 km S.

Restaurant :
◆◆ *Auberge de la Tonnelle*, 61, rue du Mal-Joffre, ☎ 89.54.25.77, AE DC Euro Visa ♪ closed Sat noon and Sun. A young couple on the rise. Seasonal fare : *terrine chaude de turbot et écrevisses, canette rôtie aux griottes*, 130-210.

STEINBRUNN-LE-BAS, ⊠ 68440 Habsheim, 9 km S.

Restaurant :
● ◆◆◆ *Moulin du Kaegy*, ☎ 89.81.30.34, AE DC Euro Visa ⦗ ⦰ も closed Mon and Sun eve, Jan. A 16thC mill. Poetic menus : feast, Tradition. Today. Spec : *foie d'oie confit à l'ombre, salade tiède de pois gourmands et rognons, ris de veau aux carottes primeurs et au jus*, 220-300.

MUNSTER Valley*

A3

A valley watered by the Fecht and dotted with farm-inns where you can sample *tourte* (meat pie) and the celebrated Alsace cheeses.

▶ **Soultzbach-les-Bains** : spa, table waters; flowers; church and 15thC chapel inside the ramparts. ▶ **Gunsbach**, on the left bank of the Fecht : house of Albert Schweitzer (1875-1965), doctor, musician, winner of the Nobel Peace Prize (museum, *9-12 & 2-6*; African art museum, *weekdays 2-5, 15 Jul.-15 Sep.)*; ecumenical church, used by both Catholics and Protestants. ▶ **Munster** (pop. 5 000) : grew around a 7thC abbey; ideal stopover; signposted walks; covered market and town hall; weaving factory; spa. ▶ **Muhlbach** : Log Transport (Schlitte) Museum *(7 Jul.-1 Sep., 3-6)*. Farther on, after Metzeral : walk to the lakes of Fischboedle and Schiessrothried *(1 hr & 2 hr walk, respectively, round trip)*. □

Practical Information ⎯⎯⎯⎯⎯⎯⎯⎯⎯

LUTTENBACH, ⊠ 68140 Munster, 3 km SW of Munster.

Hotels :
● ★★ *Au Chêne Voltaire*, rue Voltaire, ☎ 89.77.31.74,

19 rm Ⓟ ⦗ ⦰ ⬚ ⥁ closed 10-21 Mar, 15 Nov-10 Jan, 280. Rest. ◆ ⦗ ♪ Guests only, 50-80.
★ *Le Chalet* (L.F.), 85, rue de la Mairie, ☎ 89.77.38.33, 18 rm Ⓟ ⦗ ⦰ ⬚ ⥁ closed 2-25 Jan, 160. Rest. ◆ closed Tue eve and Wed (l.s.), 40-85 ; child : 30.

MUHLBACH, ⊠ 68380 Metzeral, 24 km SW of **Colmar**.

Hotel :
★★ *Perle des Vosges* (L.F.), 22, rue du Gaschney, ☎ 89.77.61.34, 25 rm Ⓟ ⦰ ⥁ closed 3 Jan-2 Feb, 160. Rest. ◆ closed Wed (l.s.), 60-100.

Recommended
Farmhouse-inn : *Braunkopf*, ☎ 89.77.60.53.

MUNSTER, ⊠ 68140, 19 km SW of **Colmar**.
ⓘ pl. de la Salle-des-Fêtes, ☎ 89.77.31.80.
🚆 ☎ 89.77.34.17.

Hotels :
★★ *La Cigogne*, 4, pl. du Marché, ☎ 89.77.32.27, Visa, 10 rm Ⓟ ⦰ ⥁ half pens, closed Sun eve and Mon, 15-22 Jun, 16 Nov-6 Dec, 280. Rest. ◆◆ ⥁ 60-120.
★★ *Le Val St-Grégoire* (L.F.), 5, rue St-Grégoire, ☎ 89.77.36.22, Visa, 30 rm Ⓟ ⦰ ⦰ ♪ 🏍 closed Fri and Sat lunch, 4-25 Jan, 1-21 Dec, 175. Rest. ◆ ♪ 55-80.
⚹ ★★★*Muncipal* (205 pl), ☎ 89.77.31.08.

SOULTZBACH-LES-BAINS, ⊠ 68230 Turckheim, 13 km SW of **Colmar**.

Hotel :
★ *Saint-Christophe*, 1, rue de l'Église, ☎ 89.71.13.09, AE DC, 10 rm Ⓟ ⦗ ⦰ ⬚ closed Wed. Rest. ◆ ⦗ ♪ 35-65.

MURBACH**

Colmar 32, Belfort 59, Paris 554 km
pop 666 ⊠ 68530 Buhl   A3
Abbey church of pink sandstone amid the valley greenery, although damaged (nave destroyed in the 18thC), the most beautiful Romanesque church in Alsace.

▶ Hermits lived at the site before the abbey was founded in 727. A century later its influence extended to the Palatinate (West Germany) and Switzerland. The abbots of Murbach, always from the higher nobility, were Princes of the Holy Roman Empire. The abbey was sacked during the French Revolution (1789). ▶ Choir and transept, flanked by two towers framing the square apse, are decorated with blind arcades and pierced with semicircular bays. □

Practical Information ⎯⎯⎯⎯⎯⎯⎯⎯⎯

Hotels :
● ★★★ *Domaine Langmatt* (L.F.), ☎ 89.76.21.12, Euro, 18 rm Ⓟ ⦗ ⦰ ⬚ ▱ 370. Rest. ◆◆ ⦗ も ⥁ closed Wed noon, 75-160.
★★★ *Hostellerie St-Barnabé* (L.F.), 25, Grande-Rue, ☎ 89.76.92.15, AE DC Euro Visa, 29 rm Ⓟ ⦗ ⦰ 240. Rest. ◆◆ 100-200.

NEUF-BRISACH*

Colmar 16, Strasbourg 72, Paris 467 km
pop 2200 ⊠ 68600   B3
A fortress built in the late 17thC by Louis XIV's military engineering genius Sébastien de Vauban (1633-1707). Neuf (new) Brisach faces Vieux (old) Brisach on the opposite river bank, once Austrian, now German.

▶ Octagonal **fortifications**★★ with canals, bastions and forts surrounds the symmetrical town centred on the Place d'Armes (church of St. Louis, altarpiece★). Two of the four gates still remain; in the Belfort Gate, the **Vauban museum** *(Mar.-Nov., 9-11 & 2-5 ex Tue.;* model★ of the town). □

Practical Information

NEUF-BRISACH
ℹ 6, pl. d'Armes, ☎ 89.72.56.66 (h.s.); mairie, ☎ 89.72.51.68 (l.s.).

Hotels :
★★ ***Cerf***, 11, rte de Strasbourg, ☎ 89.72.56.03, Euro Visa, 30 rm closed 22 Dec-15 Jan, 210. Rest. ♦ ♪ 70-150.
★★ ***Soleil*** (L.F.), 6, rue de Bâle, ☎ 89.72.51.28, AE DC Euro Visa, 25 rm, closed Sun eve and Mon, 130. Rest. ♦♦ ♪ 80-150.

⛺ ★★*Vauban* (135 pl), ☎ 89.72.54.25; at Biesheim, ★★★★*Ile du Rhin* (265 pl), ☎ 89.72.57.95.

Nearby

ARTZENHEIM, ✉ 68320 Muntzenheim, 11 km N.

Hotel :
★★ ***Auberge d'Artzenheim***, 30, rue du Sponeck, ☎ 89.71.60.51, Euro Visa, 11 rm Ⓟ closed Mon eve and Tue, 15 Feb-15 Mar, 135. Rest. ● ♦♦ ♪ ♿ The Hüsser's table is known for its quality and moderate prices : *panaché de poissons à la crème de ciboulette, sorbet de tomates fraîches.* Alsatian wines, 70-110.

NIEDERBRONN-LES-BAINS

Haguenau 21, Strasbourg 53, Paris 449 km
pop 4440 ✉ 67110 B1

Two springs gave rise to the town; both Celts and Romans bathed in the waters (municipal museum : *on request, tel. 88.09.08.40).* Alsace's only casino.

▶ Walks; parks and gardens in the town; **Wasenbourg castle** (15thC; *1 hr walk;* view); **Ziegenberg :** Celtic campsite *(NW, 1 hr).*

Nearby

▶ **Vieux-Windstein castle** *(7 km N) :* 1212, partly hollowed out of the rock; 500 m away, **Nouveau-Windstein castle** (1340); 10 km away *(still on D53)* ruins of **Wineck** and **Schoeneck castles.** □

Practical Information

⚕ ☎ 88.09.60.55 (year round).
ℹ hôtel de ville, ☎ 88.09.17.00.
SNCF ☎ 88.09.01.08.

Hotels :
★★★ ***Grand Hôtel***, (Inter-Hôtel), 16, av. Foch, ☎ 88.09.02.60, AE DC Euro Visa, 60 rm Ⓟ 300. Rest. ♦♦ ♪ closed Thu, 100-200.
★★ ***Bristol***, 4, pl. de l'Hôtel-de-Ville, ☎ 88.09.61.44, AE DC Euro Visa, 28 rm Ⓟ 200. Rest. ● ♦♦ ♪ ♿ closed Wed, Jan. Light, enjoyable fare : *terrine de poularde au foie gras, saumon au vinaigre de Xérès, râble de lapereau*, 60-180.

Restaurant :
♦♦♦ ***Parc***, pl. des Thermes, ☎ 88.09.68.88, Tx 890151, AE DC Euro Visa, closed Thu, 27 Jan-20 Feb, 140-250.

⛺ *Heidenkopf* (70 pl), ☎ 88.09.08.46.

OBERNAI★★

Strasbourg 30, Colmar 45, Paris 485 km
pop 9440 ✉ 67210 A-B2

At the foot of Mont Sainte-Odile, on the Wine Road. **Place du Marché★ :** the heart of town; old houses behind ruined ramparts; **corn market★** (Halle aux Blés); 16thC town hall; Renaissance well★ . The town was the 7thC birthplace of St. Odile (patron saint of Alsace), and a member of the 14thC Decapol (→ Brief regional history). Active industries are located outside the town walls.

Nearby

▶ **Erstein** *(15 km W) :* handsome peasant houses, tobacco barns. 4 km further S, **Osthouse :** 16thC château *(no visits).* □

Practical Information

OBERNAI
ℹ Chapelle du Beffroi, ☎ 88.95.64.13.
SNCF ☎ 88.95.52.34.

Hotels :
● ★★★ ***Le Parc***, (R.S.), 169, rue Gal-Gouraud, ☎ 88.95.50.08, Tx 870615, Euro Visa, 50 rm Ⓟ ♪ pens (h.s.), closed 22 Jun-6 Jul, 1 Dec-1 Jan, 590. Rest. ● ♦♦♦ ♪ ♿ closed Mon and Sun eve. For 30 years Marc Wucher and his chef R. Schaeffer have served rich cuisine respecting both tradition and market-fresh ingredients, 200-240.
★★★ ***Le Grand Hôtel***, rue Dietrich, ☎ 88.95.51.28, AE DC Euro Visa, 24 rm Ⓟ closed Feb, 190. Rest. ♦ closed Mon and Sun eve, 83-160.
★★ ***Hostellerie la Diligence*** (L.F.), 23, pl. de la Mairie, ☎ 88.95.55.69, AE Euro Visa, 50 rm 2 apt, closed 22 Nov-15 Dec, 200. Rest. ♦♦ closed Wed and Tue (l.s), 100-170.
★★ ***Vosges***, 5, pl. de la Gare, ☎ 88.95.53.78, Euro Visa, 15 rm Ⓟ 153. Rest. ♦ closed Mon and Sun eve (l.s.), 12-31 Jan, 15-29 Jun, 55-130.

Restaurants :
♦♦ ***Au Boeuf***, 183, rue du Mal-Foch, Blaesheim, ☎ 88.68.81.31, AE DC Euro Visa Ⓟ ♿ closed Mon and Sun eve, 1-21 Feb, 1-15 Aug, 100-170.
♦ ***La Halle aux Blés***, pl. du Marché, ☎ 88.95.56.09, Visa ♪ Authentic Alsatian decor, 80-120.

⛺ ★★*Municipal* (150 pl), ☎ 88.95.38.48.

Nearby

ERSTEIN, ✉ 67150, 15 km W.
SNCF ☎ 88.98.00.06.

Hotel :
A l'Agneau, 50, rue du 28-Novembre, ☎ 88.98.02.12, 8 rm closed 1-21 Jul, 80. Rest. ♦ closed Wed, 36-70.

⛺ ★★*Wagelrott* (100 pl), ☎ 88.98.13.51.

RHINAU, ✉ 67230 Benfeld, 14 km SE.

Hotel :
★★ ***Bords du Rhin***, 10, rte du Rhin, ☎ 88.74.60.36, AE DC Visa, 15 rm Ⓟ closed Mon eve and Tue, 15 Jan-15 Feb, 160. Rest. ♦ 80-130.

Restaurant :
♦♦ ***Au Vieux Couvent***, 6, rue des Chanoines, ☎ 88.74.61.15, AE DC Euro Visa Ⓟ closed Tue eve and Wed, 1-15 Jan, 6-17 Jul, 28-31 Dec, 100-210.

⛺ ★★*Ziegelhof* (100 pl), ☎ 88.74.60.45.

SAND, ✉ 67230 Benfeld, 6 km S.

Hotel :
★★ ***Hostellerie La Charrue*** (L.F.), 4, rue du 1er-Décembre, ☎ 88.74.42.66, Visa, 26 rm Ⓟ closed Sun eve and Mon lunch, 16 Feb-9 Mar, 14-24 Dec, 140. Rest. ♦ ♪ ♿ 65-150.

ORBEY

Colmar 20, Saint-Dié 42, Paris 500 km
pop 3140 ✉ 68370 A3

Orbey, like the neighbouring commune of **Lapoutroie**, is an ideal stopover for peace and quiet and country walks (Grand Faudé *45 min;* Pierre-du-Loup *20 min;* Noirmont *3 km + 15 min;* Tête-du-Faux *2 hr).*

▶ The **Orbey Valley (Orbey, Fréland, Lapoutroie, Hachimette, Le Bonhomme** and **Labaroche**), has been a French-speaking enclave since the 16thC; Munster cheese production centre. ▶ **Lakes Noir** and **Blanc** *(8 km and*

10 km) : pleasant, among firs and rocks ; the lakes, linked by a force-feed duct, produce 60 000 kW/hr ; water from the first lake is pumped back into the second during off-peak periods. ☐

Practical Information ───────────

ORBEY
ℹ Mairie, ☎ 89.71.30.11.

Hotels :
★★★ *Motel Au Bois-le-Sire* (L.F.), 20, rue Ch.-de-Gaulle, ☎ 89.71.25.25, Euro Visa, 36 rm ℗ ≼ ₳ ♪ ₲ ☒ closed Sun eve and Mon, 3 Jan-2 Feb, 29 Nov-26 Dec, 185. Rest. ♦ 80-165.
★★ *Les Bruyères* (L.F.), 35, rue Ch.-de-Gaulle, ☎ 89.71.20.36, DC Visa, 28 rm ℗ ♨ half pens (h.s.), closed 31 Oct-31 Mar. ex Feb school hols, 264. Rest. ♦ ♪ 55-95.

⚠ ★★*Municipal* (65 pl), ☎ 89.71.20.07.

Nearby

LABAROCHE, ☒ 68910, 7 km E.

Hotel :
★★ *Les Evaux*, ☎ 89.49.80.06, 13 rm ℗ ≼ ₩ ₲ closed 15 Nov-15 Dec, 190.

LAPOUTROIE, ☒ 68650, 5 km N.

Hotels :
● ★★ *Les Alisiers* (L.F.), 5, Faudé, ☎ 89.47.52.82, Visa, 15 rm ℗ ≼ ₩ ₲ closed Mon eve , Tue, 15 Nov-24 Dec, 190. Rest. ♦ ≼ ♪ 80-110 ; child : 40.
★★ *Faudé* (L.F.), 28, rue du Gal-Dufieux, ☎ 89.47.50.35, Euro Visa, 27 rm ℗ ≼ ₩ ₲ ☒ closed 1-15 Mar, 12 Nov-5 Dec, 158. Rest. ♦ ≼ 59-120 ; child : 40.

⚠ ★★*Le Clos des Biches* (70 pl), ☎ 89.47.50.86.

Recommended
♥ cheese (Munster) : *Harcaine*, 18, rue Gal-Dufieux.

The OUTRE-FORÊT Region**

B1
Round trip *(approx 75 km, full day ; see map 3)*

In the extreme NE of France, between Wissembourg and the forest of Haguenau, this borderland of cultivated hillsides has often been a battleground ; here and there can be seen the structures of the **Maginot Line**. Today, the villages are peaceful and flowery, with half-timbered houses (18th-19thC) in tidy streets. In this devoutly Protestant area with long-standing traditions, regional costumes are still occasionally worn.

3. The Outre-Forêt region

▶ **Seebach**★ (formerly Oberseebach and Niederseebach), one of the first villages on the itinerary, with traditional houses among less distinctive buildings. ▶ **Hunspach**★★★, the most uniform village, with sloping streets leading to public buildings grouped in the square. ▶ **Schoenenbourg**★★ *(2 km E)*, on the Maginot Line *(open weekends)*. ▶ **Hoffen**★★★ : town hall with wooden columns. ▶ **Soultz-sous-Forêts** belonged to the powerful Rohan-Soubise family in the 18thC. **Merkwiller-Pechelbronn** *(4 km W)* : thermal spa once exploited for oil (museum : *3-5, Sun., 15 Apr.-15 Nov.)*. ▶ **Surbourg** : Rhenish Romanesque church★, remainder of the abbey that once stood here. ▶ **Betschdorf**★ : pottery (blue decoration on a grey ground) in shops and workshops on the main street (museum, Rue Kuhlendorf : *May-Jun., Sep. 2-5 ex Mon. ; Jul.-Aug., Sun., hols., 10-12 & 2-5)* ; 15thC frescos in the church ; half-timbered houses. ▶ **Kuhlendorf** *(2 km N)* : church. ▶ **Hatten**, entirely destroyed in 1945. ▶ **Seltz**, Roman in origin ; tourist centre with shore, sailing, ferry across the Rhine. On the right of the road to **Munchhausen** and **Mothern** : marshy forest area, with unusual flora and fauna now fast disappearing. ▶ **Lauterbourg** (pop. 2 460), once fortified by Vauban. ▶ **Schleital**, one-street village with houses lined up for 4 km. ☐

Practical Information ───────────

LAUTERBOURG, ☒ 67630, 41 km of **Haguenau**.
▰▰▰▰ ☎ 88.54.60.00.

Hotel :
★ *A la Poêle d'Or*, 39, rue Gal-Mitiklhauser, ☎ 88.94.80.59, AE DC Euro Visa, 7 rm ℗ closed Thu, 15-31 Jul, 150. Rest. ♦♦♦ ♪ ₲ 115 ; child : 30.

RIBEAUVILLÉ*

Colmar 15, Strasbourg 62, Paris 524 km
pop 4600 ☒ 68150   A3

Modest but attractive town on the Upper Rhine, once headquarters of the itinerant musicians' guild. The **Grand'Rue** is straddled by the **Tour des Bouchers**★ (Butchers' tower, 13th-16thC) ; flower-decked fountains and carefully restored houses ; Gothic church (organ casing★) ; small **museum** in the town hall (silver and silver-gilt goblets), unfortunately rarely open.

Nearby
▶ Three castles : 45-min walk to **castle of St. Ulrich**★ (12th-14thC, once the residence of the powerful Ribeaupierre family) ; opposite, ruins of **Girsberg castle**, or "Petit Ribeaupierre" ; another 15-min walk to the **castle of Haut-Ribeaupierre** (Altenkastel ; 13thC ; 15thC keep★) ; view★. ▶ From Ribeauvillé, good roads to Sainte-Marie-aux-Mines and, via Aubure, to **Fréland Pass**, in the heart of the Vosges. ☐

Practical Information ───────────

ℹ Grand'Rue, ☎ 89.73.62.22 ; mairie, ☎ 89.73.60.26.
▰▰▰▰ ☎ 89.73.60.20.

Hotels :
● ★★★★(L) *Clos St-Vincent* (R.C.), rte de Bergheim, ☎ 89.73.67.65, Euro Visa, 11 rm ℗ ≼ ₩ ₲ closed Nov-Mar, 640. Rest. ♦♦♦ ♪ closed Tue and Wed. Great cellar, gourmet cuisine : *émincé de lapin aux choux, foie chaud de canard aux noix*, 120-220.
● ★★★ *La Pépinière*, rte de Sainte-Marie-aux-Mines, ☎ 89.73.64.14, AE Euro Visa, 19 rm ℗ ≼ ₩ ₲ ♪ closed 4 Jan-4 Apr. A warm and rustic decor in an old country house, 250. Rest. ♦ ≼ ♪ closed Tue noon and Wed noon, Tue eve in (l.s.). Spec : *truite du strengbach en pot-au-feu, rosace d'agneau au fumet de coriandre*, 85-180 ; child : 50.
★★★ *Les Vosges* (L.F.), 2, Grand'Rue, ☎ 89.73.61.39, AE DC Euro Visa, 16 rm 2 apt ℗ ♨ closed Mon and Tue lunch, 1-21 Feb, 24 Nov-7 Dec, 270. Rest. ● ♦♦ Joseph Matter serves delicate, refined fare : *escalope de foie*

d'oie poêlée à la rhubarbe, filet d'agneau en croûte de sel, fruits rouges à la glace au miel, 150-250.
★★★ **Seigneurs de Ribeaupierre**, 11, rue du Château, ☎ 89.73.70.31, 10 rm, closed 1 Dec-15 Mar. A 17thC house, 300.
★★ **Cheval Blanc** (L.F.), 122, Grand'Rue, ☎ 89.73.61.38, Euro Visa, 25 rm ℗ ⇖ ⚲ pens, half pens (h.s.), closed 1 Dec-1 Feb, 280. Rest. ♦ ⸝ ♿ closed Mon, 40-80.
★★ **Tour** (L.F.), 1, rue de la Mairie, ☎ 89.73.72.73, DC Euro Visa, 32 rm ℗ ⇖ ♨ ⚘ ⸝° closed 10 Jan-15 Mar, 190.

Restaurant :
♦ **Zum Pfifferhuss**, 14, Grand'Rue, ☎ 89.73.62.28 ⸝ ⚘ closed 15 Feb-15 Mar, 80-120.

⚠ ★★★★*Pierre de Coubertin* (300 pl), ☎ 89.73.66.71 ; ★*Trois Châteaux* (100 pl), ☎ 89.73.60.26.

RIQUEWIHR★★★

Colmar 13, Saint-Dié 46, Paris 529 km
pop 1040 ⊠ 68340   A3

This town is described as a "pearl" among the vineyards that surround it. For several centuries it was the property of the eccentric dukes of Wurtemberg. Houses built by wine-growers in the 16th and 17thC, like the rest of the town, are exceptionally well-preserved. Riquewihr produces excellent Riesling.

▶ The houses are built against the rectangular **fortifications**. The town offers many treasures for the eye : **oriel windows**, sculpted galleries, doorways, **fountains** and wells, yards and passages, shop signs, and flowers everywhere from May to Oct. The **main street** (Rue du Général-de-Gaulle) leads from the town hall to the **Dolder★** (13thC gate; small museum, as also in the Tour des Voleurs (Thieves' Tower); *9-12 & 1:30-6 Sat., Sun., Easter-1 Nov. ; daily Jul.-Aug.)*, and the Obertor, gate of the second enclosure. ▶ Château of the Wurtemberg-Montbéliard : (16thC) now an attractive historical **Museum of the French Post, Telegraph and Telecommunications** (PTT) : documents, costumes, models from early times to the present day *(10-12 & 2-6, 3-7 Sun. and nat. hols. ; closed Tue. ex Jul.-Aug. and nat. hols.)*.   ☐

Practical Information ────────────

ℹ rue du Gal-de-Gaulle, ☎ 89.47.80.80 (h.s.).

Hotels :
★★ **Au Riesling** (L.F.), 93, rte du Vin, Zellenberg, 1 km E, ☎ 89.47.85.85, Euro Visa, 36 rm ℗ ⇖ ⚲ ♿ ⚘ half pens (h.s.), closed 5 Jan-28 Feb, 390. Rest. ♦ ⇖ ⸝ ♿ ⚘ closed Mon and Sun eve, 70-130 ; child : 35.
★★ **Le Riquewihr**, rte de Ribeauvillé, ☎ 89.47.83.13, Tx 881720, AE DC Euro Visa, 49 rm ℗ ⇖ ⚲ ⚲ ⸝ Sauna, 190.

Restaurants :
● ♦♦ **Auberge du Schoenenbourg**, 2, rue de la Piscine, ☎ 89.47.92.28, Euro Visa ⇖ ⚲ closed Wed eve and Thu, Feb. A shady garden, a view of the wine country : a recipe for happiness : *rouelles de sole aux poivrons doux, suprême de faisan aux foie gras et aux navets confits*. Good wines, 200-260.
♦♦ **L'Ecurie**, cour des Cigognes, ☎ 89.47.92.48, AE DC Euro Visa ⚲ closed Mon , Dec. Spec : *marbré aux foies de volailles, grenadin de sandre farci aux morilles fraîches*, 125-150 ; child : 25.
♦ **Au Tire-Bouchon**, 33, rue du Gal-de-Gaulle, ☎ 89.47.92.58, AE DC Euro Visa ⸝ closed Tue eve and Wed (l.s.), 12 Nov-15 Dec. Pleasant country-inn decor, 40-65.

⚠ ★★★★*Intercommunal* (100 pl), ☎ 89.47.90.08.

Recommended
Guide to wines : *Caves Mittnach-Klack*, 8, rue des Tuileries.

SAINTE-MARIE-AUX-MINES

Saint-Dié 23, Colmar 34, Paris 411 km
pop 6530 ⊠ 68160   A3

Although mines supplying silver, lead, copper, cobalt and arsenic gave the town its name, the weaving of fine woolen cloth has been the source of its prosperity since the 18thC. Small factories and workshops do not detract from the beauty of the site, which is a widening of the Liepvrette Valley. Passage to Lorraine has become easier with the opening of the road tunnel to Saint-Dié *(toll)*.

▶ **Museum of Mining and Local Traditions** (70 Rue Wilson; *10-12 & 2-6 Jul.-Aug.*). Mineral Exhibition and Exchange *(1st weekend in Jul.)*. Disused **St. Barthélemy silver mine★★**, worked in the 16thC *(Jul.-5 Sep. ; 9-12 & 2-6, Sun., Mon. Whitsun, 2 last Sun of Jun.).* ▶ Sainte-Marie is a good base for excursions in the Vosges.   ☐

Practical Information ────────────

ℹ 1, pl. de la Gare, ☎ 89.58.80.50.

Hotel :
★★ **Cromer** (L.F.), pl. Foch, ☎ 89.58.70.19, AE DC Euro Visa, 38 rm ℗ ⚲ ♨ closed Sun eve and Mon, Mar, 15 Nov-15 Dec, 170. Rest. ♦ ⸝ ⚘ 60-100.

Recommended
Youth hostel : 21, rue Reber, ☎ 89.58.75.74.

Mont SAINTE-ODILE★★

Strasbourg 42, Colmar 52, Paris 501 km
⊠ 67530 Ottrott   A2

Mount Sainte-Odile, the patronal shrine of Alsace, was probably a sacred place before Christianity entered the region. Its history and location make it not just a pilgrimage site for the pious but a must on any itinerary.

▶ **Convent of Ste. Odile :** a Roman site (alt. 761 m) founded in the 8thC, restored in the 12thC ; devastated many times, reoccupied from the mid-19thC on. The buildings have no special distinction, apart from the chapels of the Holy Cross (11th-12thC) and Ste. Odile (12thC ; 8thC tomb of the saint) ; almshouse. From the terraces, **view★★★** over the plain. ▶ **Mur Païen★** (pagan wall) : originally Bronze Age, remodeled by the Romans, a 10-km long wall completely enclosing the mount ; the most apparent remains are near D426, from where you can also reach the ruined **castles of Birkenfels, Dreysteim** and **Hagelschloss.** ▶ Via the road to Saint-Nabor : St. Odile's spring *(600 m away);* farther on, remains of the abbey of Niedermunster, founded in 707 by St. Odile. ▶ **Ottrott** *(8 km) :* produces one of the few red Alsatian wines ; **tourist train** from Ottrott to Rosheim *(16 km ; 1 hr round trip Sun., Jul.-Sep.).*

Practical Information ────────────

Mont SAINTE-ODILE

Hotel :
★ **Mont-Sainte-Odile**, at the summit, ☎ 88.95.80.53, Euro Visa, 132 rm ℗ ⇖ ⚲ ⚲ ⚘ closed 7-20 Jan, 16-30 Nov, 110. Rest. ♦ ⇖ ⚘ 45-85.

Nearby

OTTROTT, ⊠ 67530, 8 km N.

Hotels :
★★★ **Beau Site**, 1, rue du Gal-de-Gaulle, ☎ 88.95.80.61, Tx 870445, AE Euro Visa, 14 rm ℗ ⚘ closed Sun eve, 200. Rest. ♦♦♦ ⸝ Traditional opulence : game in season, fish, 180-280.
● ★★ **Hostellerie des Châteaux**, (L.F., R.S.), 11, rue des Châteaux, ☎ 88.95.81.54, AE Euro Visa, 36 rm ℗ ⚲ ♿

St. Odile

Odile was born in the 7thC, the blind daughter of a cruel duke of Alsace who had hoped for a son and wanted the infant killed. Spirited away from the court by a nurse, Odile recovered her sight when she was baptized in a convent in the Jura mountains. She came back to Alsace and miraculously escaped the marriage planned for her by her father, now reconciled to having a daughter and hoping to profit from the fact. The father eventually became resigned to the Divine Will as interpreted by Odile, and had a convent built for her. The flood of aspirants drawn by Odile's faith necessitated a second convent, which was built below the first (Niedermunster). Odile was canonized in the 11thC by the Alsatian Pope Leo IX; in 1946 she was proclaimed patron saint of Alsace.

closed 15 Jan-15 Feb, 200. Rest. ♦♦ ♪ closed Tue (l.s.). Spec : *salade d'épinards, raviole de foie gras sur lit d'oignon, sole au coulis d'écrevisses*, 80-165.

SAVERNE

Strasbourg 39, Lunéville 80, Paris 446 km
pop 10480 ⊠ 67700   A1
When in 1770, Goethe (→ Sessenheim) was invited to the palace of Cardinal de Rohan, he was astonished by the luxury of the stables. Goethe's surprise suggests the splendour of the "Alsatian Versailles", surrounded today by a town that was for 5 centuries the property of the Rohan family.

▶ On the banks of the Marne-Rhine canal (pleasure craft), flowered paths lead to the most beautiful façade of the **palace★★**, built in red sandstone in the late 18thC in neo-Classical style. Place du Général-de-Gaulle : more austere, but still elegant *(being restored : no visits).* ▶ Old houses near the town hall in the **Grand'Rue.** ▶ **Rose garden** (1 300 varieties) on the bank of the river Zorn *(9-12 & 2-7, Jun.-Sep.;* **Rose Festival***, Jun.);* **botanical garden** *(3.5 km NW via N4; 9-5 Jul.-Aug.).*

Nearby

▶ W of Saverne : ruined **château du Haut-Barr★** (12th-16thC, "the Eye of Alsace"), and Géroldseck, attractive sites facing the plain. Not far from Haut-Barr : restored optical telegraph installed by the engineer Claude Chappe (1763-1803) in 1794 (museum). From the ruins, GR53 takes hikers S towards the summit of Mont Brotschberg *(30 min; 531 m),* then to the ruins of **Ochsenstein castle** *(3 hr 30).* ▶ Church of **St. Jean-Saverne** *(5 km;* worth a visit) : Romanesque building (only remains of Benedictine abbey) with 18thC gatetower; inside, 16thC tapestries. ▶ Artzwiller inclined plane (→ Sarrebourg, Lorraine).   ☐

Practical Information _____

SAVERNE
ⓘ château des Rohan, ☎ 88.91.80.47 (h.s.); mairie, ☎ 88.91.18.52.
SNCF ☎ 88.91.16.72.

Hotels :
★★ **Bœuf Noir**, 22, Grand'Rue, ☎ 88.91.10.53, Euro Visa, 20 rm 🅿 🔍 closed Sun eve and Tue, 1-25 Oct, 80. Rest. ♦ 40-135.
★★ **Fischer** (L.F.), 15, rue de la Gare, ☎ 88.91.19.53, Visa, 19 rm 🅿 ❁ 🕏 closed Fri eve and Sat, 26 Apr-4 May, 21 Dec-12 Jan, 155. Rest. ♦ ♪ 40-80.
★ **Le National**, 2, Grand'Rue, ☎ 88.91.14.54, 30 rm 🅿 ❁ 🕏 half pens (h.s.), closed Fri, Nov-Dec, 330. Rest. ♦ ❁ ♪ closed Sat noon, 59-135.

🔺 ★★★*Municipal* (100 pl), ☎ 88.91.35.65.

Nearby

LANDERSHEIM, ⊠ 67700 Saverne, 12 km on the D 41.

Restaurant :
● ♦♦ **Auberge du Kochersberg**, rte de Saessolsheim, ☎ 88.69.91.58, Tx 870974, AE DC Euro Visa ❁ 🎖 ♪ 🔍 closed Tue, Wed, Sun eve, 17 Feb-11 Mar, 21 Jul-12 Aug. A. Roth and P. Klipfel make a winning team in the kitchen : *foies gras maison, ravioles aux queues d'écrevisses*, 140-270.

SÉLESTAT*

Colmar 22, Strasbourg 47, Paris 508 km
pop 15400 ⊠ 67600   A-B3
An old city supposed to have been founded by a giant. It was a residence of Charlemagne, later part of the Holy Roman Empire and a member of the Decapol (→ Brief regional history). From the Middle Ages, Sélestat was renowned for its university and school of Humanism in the 15th-16thC.

▶ **Humanist Library★★** : books from the 7thC on : manuscripts, incunabula and works of art. *(9-12 & 2-5; closed Sat. pm and Sun.).* ▶ **Church of St. Georges** : Gothic (13th-15thC); ancient and modern stained glass, Renaissance pulpit★. Nearby, **abbey church of Ste. Foy★★**, one of the finest Romanesque churches in Alsace despite 19thC restoration. ▶ Walk through the winding streets in the heart of the town to admire towers, old houses and sculpted doorways, with boulevards following the line of the ancient fortifications.

Nearby

▶ **Ebermunster** *(8 km NE)* : domed **abbey church★★** in the middle of the Alsatian plain; this Austrian Baroque sanctuary (1719) replaced a church destroyed during the Thirty Years' War; gold, stucco, frescos, curves and countercurves form a theatrical monument. ▶ **Benfeld** *(11 km farther on),* main centre for Alsatian tobacco (festival end Aug.); town hall with 16thC Jack-o'-the-Clock. ▶ Not far from the Rhine in **Marckolsheim** *(15 km SE)* : **Maginot Line** pill-box, now a memorial museum with Sherman tank, Soviet cannon *(9-12 & 2-6, Sun. and nat. hols.; daily 15 Jun.-15 Sep.; closed 15 Nov.-15 Mar.);* **Rhine tourist train** (→ Neuf-Brisach).   ☐

Practical Information _____

SÉLESTAT
ⓘ La Commanderie Saint-Jean, bd Leclerc, ☎ 88.92.02.66.
SNCF ☎ 88.82.50.50.

Hotels :
★★ **Vaillant**, pl. de la République, ☎ 88.92.09.46, AE Visa, 47 rm 🅿 🕮 🔍 210. Rest. ♦ ♪ 🕏 ❁ 60-120.
★ **Auberge des Alliés**, 39, rue des Chevaliers, ☎ 88.92.09.34, 7 rm 🅿 closed Mon, 18 Feb-5 Mar, 17 Jun-2 Jul, 135. Rest. ♦ 90-190.

Restaurants :
● ♦♦ **Jean-Frédéric Edel**, 7, rue des Serruriers, ☎ 88.92.86.55, AE DC Euro Visa 🅿 🔍 ♪ closed Tue eve and Wed , Sun eve (l.s.), 26 Jul-12 Aug, 23 Dec-6 Jan. A house with character, where J.-F. Edel, a pupil of Jean Delaveyne, upholds the family tradition. Spec : *fondant tiède de saumon au beurre clarifié, croustillant de foie de canard à l'alsacienne*, 140-260.
♦ **Vieille Tour**, 8, rue de la Jauge, ☎ 88.92.15.02, Euro Visa ♪ 🕏 closed Mon and Sun eve, 23 Feb-8 Mar, 29 Jun-12 Jul, 60-160; child : 50.

🔺 ★★*Les Cigognes* (50 pl), ☎ 88.92.03.98.

┌───┐
│ Looking for a locality? Consult the index at the back │
│ of the book.   │
└───┘

Nearby

BERGHEIM, ⊠ 68750, 11 km S.

Restaurant :

♦ **Winstub du Sommelier**, 51, Grand'Rue, ☎ 89.73.69.99
⌀ closed Sun, 15 Feb-15 Mar, 1-10 Jul, 80-130.

KINTZHEIM, ⊠ 67600 Selestat, 6 km W.

Restaurant :

● ♦ **Auberge Saint-Martin**, 80, rue de la Liberté,
☎ 88.82.04.78 ℙ closed Wed noon and Thu noon (l.s.),
Feb. The Haeberlin family's favourite *winstub*, 80-100.

MARCKOLSHEIM, ⊠ 67390, 15 km SE.
ⓘ 27, rue du Mal-Foch, ☎ 88.92.56.98.

Hotel :

★★ **L'Aigle**, 28, rue du Mal-Foch, ☎ 88.92.50.02, Euro
Visa, 17 rm ℙ closed Mon, 1-15 Feb, 180. Rest. ♦
100-170.

STRASBOURG★★★

Nancy 145, Metz 162, Paris 486 km
pop 252200 ⊠ 67000   B2

Strasbourg is irrigated by the two arms of the Ill River
and the canals that flow into it. It is a city with two
identities, one European and international, the other
Alsatian and full of provincial charm. Under the lofty
vaults of the cathedral, on the flowery quays of Petite
France where picturesque 16thC houses line the
canals, or in the warm atmosphere of a wine tavern
where the tantalizing smell of ham baked in a crust
mingles with the bouquet of a glass of Edelzwicker,
past and present blend in harmonious well-being.

▶ **Place Kléber** (C3) : a popular meeting place disfigured
by unattractive shopfronts; even the **Aubette★**, an 18thC
guardhouse, has been defaced. A better starting point for
a walking tour is **place Gutenberg** (C3; carpark; TO in the
Renaissance **Chamber of Commerce★★★**). ▶ **Rue Mercière**, half-timbered houses, leads to the cathedral : in
front, the **Pharmacie du Cerf** (1268)★★ and **Kammerzell
House★★** (1589). ▶ **Cathedral of Notre-Dame★★★** (C3),
now free of all scaffolding after 32 years (1,500,000 hours)
of work : 142-m spire; red sandstone façade of Gothic
lacework; statuary (right doorway : Tempter and Foolish
Virgins★★★); beautiful side doors; at 12:30 enter by the S
door (tympanum of the Virgin★★) and see the **astronomical clock★★** (16thC) in operation in the transept. Inside,
Romanesque foundations have been re-used (choir over
the 11thC crypt), but the architecture and decoration are
pure Gothic; 14thC stained glass★; Pillar of the Last
Judgement★★; 15thC pulpit★, baptismal fonts and altarpiece; 17thC tapestries of the Life of the Virgin exhibited
in the nave in May and June *(Apr.-Sep., daily 10-12 & 2-6;
Oct.-Mar., 2-6, Sun also 10-12; son et lumière at 9 pm in
French, 8 pm in German 15 Apr.-30 Sep.; 330 steps to
the top of the tower; view★★).* ▶ **Place du Château** (C3;
tourist mini-train) : 18thC Jesuit college, now a secondary
school. **Palais Rohan★**, palace of the Prince-Archbishops,
built by Armand Cardinal de Rohan-Soubise in 1732
(façade★★★ on the Ill River); medieval and Renaissance
houses of the Oeuvre-Notre-Dame. ▶ **Museums of the
Palais Rohan : State Apartments★★ ; Fine Arts★★** (Italian paintings; El Greco, Goya, Flemish masters, 18thC
French school); **Decorative Arts** (ceramics by the celebrated 18thC Hannong family of potters); **Archaeology★**
*(10-12 & 2-6, Apr.-Sep.; Sun., weekdays pm, rest of year;
closed Tue.).* ▶ **Museum of the Oeuvre-Notre-Dame★★★**
(same hours) : art and documents from the 11th to the
17thC relating to the cathedral; stained glass, paintings,
furniture, religious art. ▶ Nearby, three more museums
(same hours) : the **Historical Museum★★**, in the old
Grande Boucherie (C3; religious collections; relief map
of the city); **Museum of Modern Art★**, in the Ancienne
Douane★ (Old Customs House; C3); across the Ill, the
Alsatian Museum★★★ (C4) in three old houses, interior

decoration, popular arts and traditions. Quai des Bateliers
(D3) : **Cour du Corbeau★★**, 14th-16thC hostelry. ▶ Past
the **church of St. Thomas★** (C3; the Protestant cathedral,
Gothic); tomb of Maréchal de Saxe by the 18thC sculptor Pigalle★★), **Petite France** district★★★ (B3) : half-timbered houses with galleries overhanging the Ill; **covered
bridges★** with towers; dam. ▶ **St. Pierre-le-Vieux** (B3) :
two churches in one, Catholic (15thC paintings★★) and
Protestant (choir-screen★). **Grand'Rue** (16th and 18thC
houses) or Rue du 22-Novembre (B-C3) leads back to the
city centre; **church of St. Pierre-le-Jeune** (C2). Rest of
the visit by car. ▶ **Place Broglie** (C2) : **town hall★** and
surrounding area (civic offices, officers' club, Rue Brûlée) reveal the prosperity of Strasbourg in the 18thC. ▶ A
century later, the Administration moved to the other side
of the Ill, around the **Place de la République** (D2), built
by the Germans : Palais du Rhin, library, music conservatory, theatre, post office. ▶ The 20thC appears farther
on : synagogue at the **Contades Park★** (D1; 1961), **Music
and Convention Palace** (N of Radio
House; 1975). ▶ Opposite the **Orangery Park★★** (F1;
zoo, farm, well-known restaurant, Josephine Pavillon),
the **Palais de l'Europe★★** (1977) : the Council of Europe,
sessions of the European Parliament, and offices *(9-12 &
2:30-5; tel. in advance 88. 61.49.61 ext. 30 33).* ▶ Near
the University : **zoological museum★** (E3; *2-6, Wed. and
Sun. 10-12 & 2-6; closed Tue.).* ▶ **Boat trips** (landing stages by the Rohan Palace and Dauphine Promenade →;
Apr.-Oct.) : 3-hr cruise on the Rhine, visit to **Free Port of
Strasbourg**, the most important river port in France after
Paris. ▶ Two local industries may be visited : Brasserie
Kronenbourg (brewery, 68, route d'Oberhausbergen) and
Seita (cigarette factory, 7, rue de Krutenau).

Nearby

▶ **La Wantzenau** *(12 km NE)*, on the bank of the Ill; popular with gourmets. ▶ Two notable agricultural regions :
N, **Hoerdt** is the asparagus centre (served everywhere
in Apr. & May); S, cabbage used for sauerkraut is cultivated as far as **Eschau** (11thC Romanesque **abbey
church★★**).   ⯀

The wine tavern

*The wine tavern is an institution - associated espe-
cially with Strasbourg - that is indispensable for getting to know Alsace. The proprietor often serves wine
from his own vineyard. A popular meeting place at
the end of the afternoon and in the evening, with the
warm atmosphere of a wood-lined room, where a
ham baked in a pastry crust, a knuckle of pork with
horseradish or an onion tart will bring out the best in
a young wine. Each tavern has a loyal group of regulars who meet at the stammtisch (regulars' table); this
is the place of honour where the proprietor may invite
you to join in.*

Practical Information _____

Maison du Bœuf ♪ & ℀ Dominique Michou pleases the most demanding of his patrons : *filet de bœuf au pinot noir à la moëlle, saumon et lotte fumés*, 145-200 ♦♦ **Le Jardin** ♪ & Grill. Take-out foods, 80-120.

★★★★(L) **Terminus Gruber**, (Mapotel), 10, pl. de la Gare (A2), ☎ 88.32.87.00, Tx 870998, AE DC Euro Visa, 78 rm 𝒫 ⩜ & 460. Rest. ♦♦ ♪ & closed 21 Dec-3 Jan. With a brasserie, 125-230.

● ★★★ **France**, 20, rue du Jeu-des-Enfants (B3), ☎ 88.32.37.12, Tx 890084, AE DC Euro Visa, 70 rm 𝒫 ⩜ 310.

● ★★★ **Orangerie**, 58, allée de La Robertsau (F1), ☎ 88.35.10.69, 25 rm 𝒫 280.

● ★★★ **Rohan**, 17-19, rue Maroquin (C3), ☎ 88.32.85.11, Tx 870047, 36 rm ⩜ ⩘ ℀ 315.

★★★ **Hannong**, 15, rue du 22-Novembre (B3), ☎ 88.32.16.22, Tx 890551, AE DC Euro Visa, 70 rm 𝒫 ⩜ ♪ 𝄞 & closed 23-30 Dec, 350. Rest. ● ♦♦ **Wyn' Bar** ♪ & closed Sat and Sun, Aug. Pleasant food, quick service : superb selection of wines by the glass, 100-160.

★★★ **La Villa d'Est**, (I.L.A.), 12, rue Jacques-Kablé (D1), ☎ 88.36.69.02, Tx 870669, AE DC Euro Visa, 32 rm 𝒫 ♪ & closed 23 Dec-2 Jan, 325.

★★★ **Monopole-Métropole**, (I.L.A.), 16, rue Kuhn (B2), ☎ 88.32.11.94, Tx 890366, AE DC Euro Visa, 94 rm 𝒫 𝄞 closed 24 Dec-1 Jan, 320.

★★★ **Princes**, 33, rue Geiler (F1), ☎ 88.61.55.19, Euro Visa, 43 rm 𝒫 ⩜ ♪ 250.

● ★★ **Europe**, 38, rue du Fossé-des-Tanneurs (B3), ☎ 88.32.17.88, Tx 890220, AE DC Euro Visa, 60 rm ⩜ 250.

● ★★ **Gutenberg**, 31, rue des Serruriers (C3), ☎ 88.32.17.15, 50 rm ℀ closed 1-10 Jan, 195.

★★ **Louis-XIII**, 133, rte de Colmar (A5), ☎ 88.34.34.28, AE DC Euro Visa, 16 rm, closed 27 Dec-4 Jan, 130. Rest. ♦♦ ♪ closed Sat noon and Sun. It's very good and not too expensive, 130-150.

★★ **Suisse**, 2-4, rue de la Râpe (C3), ☎ 88.35.22.11, 25 rm 𝒫 ♪ 210. Rest. ♦ **Horloge Astronomique** ⩜ ♪ & closed Mon and Tue noon, 15 Dec-15 Jan, 75-130.

★ **Au Cycliste**, 8, rue des Bateliers (D3), ☎ 88.36.20.01, 18 rm ⩜ ℀ closed 23 Dec-2 Jan, 115. .

★ **Michelet**, 48, rue du Vieux-Marché-aux-Poissons (C3), ☎ 88.32.47.38, 16 rm 𝒫 ⩜ 125.

★ **Patricia**, 1 a, rue du Puits (C3), ☎ 88.32.14.60, 20 rm ⩜ 100.

★ **Victoria**, 7-9, rue du Maire-Kuss (A-B3), ☎ 88.32.13.06, 37 rm, 110.

Restaurants :

● ♦♦♦ *Crocodile*, 10, rue de l'Outre (C3), ☎ 88.32.13.02, AE DC Euro Visa ♪ ℀ closed Mon and Sun, 5 Jul-3 Aug, 24 Dec-1 Jan. A gifted native son, Émile Jung serves a harmonious blend of classic and Alsatian cuisine : *caille confite Brillat-Savarin, gratins de langouste, oie rôtie à la choucroute, râble de lièvre au raifort, sorbet Adelaïde*. The great wines of Alsace hold pride of place. Courteous welcome from Monique, 210-350.

● ♦♦♦ **Buerehiesel**, 4, parc de l'Orangerie (F1), ☎ 88.61.62.24, AE DC Euro Visa ⩜ closed Tue eve and Wed , Tue lunch (Nov-Mar), 25 Dec-1 Jan. Celebrated table. "Nouvelle cuisine", 195-400.

♦♦♦ **Valentin Sorg**, 6, pl. de l'Homme-de-Fer (B3), ☎ 88.32.12.16, AE DC Euro Visa ⩜ ♪ closed Tue and Sun eve, 15 Feb-1 Mar, 15-31 Aug. Remarkable view. Classic cooking, 150-290.

● ♦♦ **Aux Mille Pâtes**, 8, pl. St-Etienne (D3), ☎ 88.35.55.23, AE DC Euro Visa, closed Mon noon and Sun, 9-22 Feb, 10-24 Jan. Just pasta? Oh, but what pasta! 110-140.

● ♦♦ **Julien**, 22, quai des Bateliers (D3), ☎ 88.36.01.24, AE DC Euro Visa ⩜ closed Sat and Sun , Feb school hols, 1-21 Aug, 150-220.

● ♦♦ **Kammerzell**, 16 pl. de la Cathédrale (C3), ☎ 88.32.42.14 Guy-Pierre Baumann has returned to his roots, determined to make a success of this temple of traditional Alsatian cuisine. *Winstub* on the ground floor. All sorts of *choucroute*, 200-300.

♦♦ **Au Dauphin**, 13, pl. de la Cathédrale (C3), ☎ 88.32.86.95, AE DC Euro Visa, closed Mon and Sun

eve , Feb. The tranquillity of a flowery courtyard and intimate dining rooms : *petit ragoût de sandre en meurette, rognonnade d'agneau aux aubergines*. Appealing wine list, 150-200.

♦♦ **L'Orangerie**, parc de l'Orangerie (F1), ☎ 88.61.36.24, AE Euro Visa ⩜ ⊞ ♪ & closed Mon. An excellent value, 100-120.

♦♦ **Le Renard Prêchant**, 34, rue de Zurich (D3), ☎ 88.35.62.87, Euro Visa 𝒫 ⩜ ⩘ & closed Sun, Aug. In a former church, a cult for good cooking, 50-135.

♦♦ **Zimmer-Sengel**, 8, rue du Temple-Neuf (C3), ☎ 88.32.35.01, AE DC Euro Visa, closed Sat and Sun, Aug, 140-225.

● ♦ **A l'Arsenal**, 11, rue de l'Abreuvoir (D3), ☎ 88.35.03.69, AE DC Euro Visa ♪ closed Sat and Sun. Outstanding value for traditional Alsatian cuisine, lightened for contemporary tastes : *salade de choucroute au cervelas rôti, veau au raifort*, 120-210.

♦ **Jean dit Carolis**, 16, rue de Zurich, ☎ 88.35.44.93, Visa, closed Sat and Sun, 15 Jul-15 Aug. By the water's edge, outstanding fish, 40-100.

Bierstub :

● ♦ **Gurtlerhoft**, 13, pl. de la Cathédrale, ☎ 88.75.00.75 A 14thC cellar, 45-90.

Brasseries :

● ♦ **A l'Ancienne Douane**, 6, rue de la Douane (C3-4), ☎ 88.32.42.19, AE DC Euro Visa ⩜ ♪ One of Strasbourg's last big brasseries in a house dating from 1358, on the banks of the Ill. The menu is varied, prices are low! Spec : *sandre à la strasbourgeoise, foie gras, choucroute*, 55-95.

● ♦ **Au Romain**, 6-8, rue du Vieux-Marché-aux-Grains (C3), ☎ 88.32.08.54, AE DC Euro Visa, closed Mon and Sun eve, 22 Dec-5 Jan. Spec : *choucroute garnie, bäckeoffe strasbourgeoise, matelote aux quatre poissons*, 40-80.

● ♦ **Bague d'Or**, 7, rue de l'Eglise (C2), ☎ 88.32.47.42, closed Sat eve and Sun, 1 week before Easter, 60-95.

Winstubs :

● ♦ **Au Coin des Pucelles**, rue des Pucelles (D3), ☎ 88.35.30.85, closed Sun and lunch, 120-210.

● ♦ **Le Clou**, 3, rue du Chaudron, ☎ 88.32.11.67 ♪ & closed Sun noon, hols, 14-23 Aug, 70-100.

● ♦ **Le Saint-Sépulcre**, 15, rue des Orfèvres ☎ 88.32.39.97, Euro Visa, closed Mon and Sun, 1-21 Jul, 60-90.

● ♦ **Pfifferbriader**, 9, pl. de la Grande-Boucherie, ☎ 88.32.15.43, closed Sun, 31 Jul-31 Aug, 35-80.

● ♦ **S'Burjerstuewel, Chez Yvonne**, 10, rue du Sanglier, ☎ 88.32.84.15, closed Mon noon and Sun, 14 Jul-10 Aug, 25 Dec-1 Jan, 80-130.

● ♦ **Zum Strissel**, 5, pl. de la Grande-Boucherie, ☎ 88.32.14.73, closed Sun and Sun , Feb school hols, 7-31 Jul, 40-80.

⚲ ★★★★*Montagne Verte* (200 pl), ☎ 88.30.25.46 ; ★★★*Baggersee* (250 pl), ☎ 88.39.03.40.

Recommended
Youth hostel : F.U.A.J., 9, rue de l'Auberge-de-Jeunesse, ☎ 88.30.26.46.
Farmhouse-gîte : at Breuschweckersheim PC 67112, *Diemer*, 11 km W, ☎ 88.96.02.89.
Leisure activities : boat rides on the illuminated Ill (Apr-Oct). Château des Rohan, promenade Dauphine.
♥*La Boutique du Foie Gras*, 6, rue Friesé, ☎ 88.32.28.42 ; 125 different beers : *Les 12 Apôtres*, rue Mercière ; Alsatian costumes, embroidery : 11 bis, quai Turckheim ; bakery : *Au Vieux Strasbourg*, 10, rue de la Division-Leclerc, ☎ 88.32.00.88 ; *A. Walter*, 32, Grand'Rue ; pastry, ice cream, tea-room : *Christian*, 10, rue Mercière and 12, rue de l'Outre, ☎ 88.22.12.70 ; Swiss herbalist shop : 22, quai des Orfèvres ; take-out foods : *Kirn*, 19, rue du 22-Novembre, ☎ 88.32.16.10 ; tea-room : *Beyler*, 5, pl. de la Cathédrale, ☎ 88.32.73.66.

Nearby

PFULGRIESHEIM ⊠ 67370 Truchtersheim, 10 km NW.

Restaurant :
● ♦♦ **Bürestubel**, 8, rue de Lampertheim, ☎ 88.20.01.92

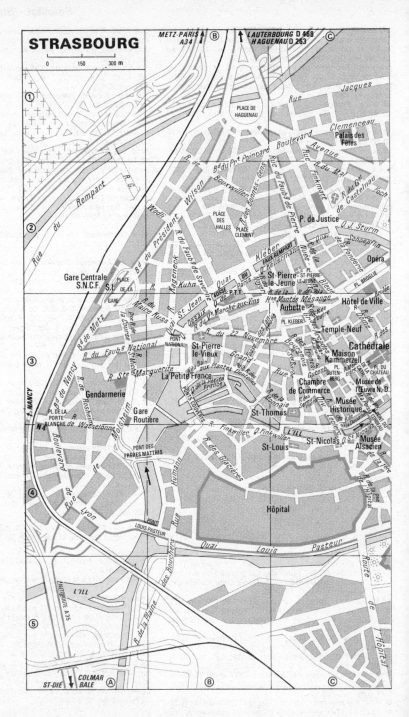

STRASBOURG

0   150   300 m

⨳ ⚒ closed Mon and lunch, 18 Aug-1 Sep. A typically Alsatian gourmet feast beneath a beamed polychrome ceiling : *tarte flambée au feu de bois, boudin, palets de pommes de terre*. Regional wines and clear brandies. Catering, 55-100.

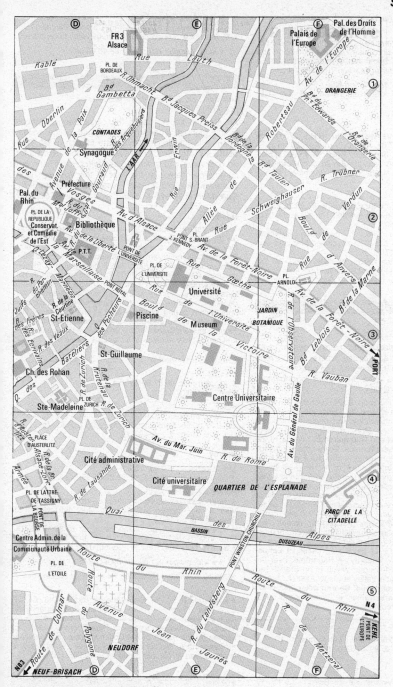

REICHSTETT, ⊠ 67460 Souffelweyersheim, 9 km N.

Hotels :
★★★ **A l'Aigle d'Or**, 5, rue de la Wantzenau,
☎ 88.20.07.87, 18 rm 🅿 320.

★★ **Paris** (L.F.), 2 c, rue du Gal-de-Gaulle, ☎ 88.20.00.23,
16 rm 🅿 closed 5-31 Aug, 150. Rest. ♦ ♪ 80-120.

The arrow (→) is a reference to another entry.

SCHILTIGHEIM, ⊠ 67300, 6 km N.

Restaurant :
● ♦♦ **La Table Gourmande**, 43, rte du Gal-de-Gaulle, ☎ 88.83.61.67, AE DC Euro Visa ♪ closed Mon noon and Sun, 27 Jul-18 Aug, 24 Dec-6 Jan. A pupil of Jacques Le Divellec prepares wonderful seafood, 160-250.

La WANTZENAU, ⊠ 67610, 12 km NE.
ⓘ pont international de Gambsheim, 8 km NE, ☎ 88.96.44.08.
SNCF ☎ 88.96.20.16.

Hotel :
● ★★ **Le Moulin de la Wantzenau** (R.S.), 27, rte de Strasbourg, ☎ 88.96.27.83, AE DC Euro Visa, 20 rm 🅿 〰 🖫 ♪ closed 24 Dec-2 Jan, 260. Rest. ● ♦♦ craft closed Thu and Sun eve, 6-16 Jan, 25 Jun-20 Jul. Worthwhile restaurant : *poussin "Mère Clauss"*, *matelote au vin blanc*, 115-230.

Restaurants :
♦♦ **A la Barrière**, 3, rte de Strasbourg, ☎ 88.96.20.23, AE DC Euro Visa ♪ closed Wed eve and Thu, 15 Aug-6 Sep. Worth a detour, 185-250.
♦♦ **J. Schaeffer et Fils**, 1, quai des Bateliers, ☎ 88.96.20.29, AE DC Visa 〰 〰 ⌘ closed Mon and Sun eve, 15 Jul-1 Aug, 95-170.
♦♦ **Zimmer**, 23, rue des Héros, ☎ 88.96.62.08, AE DC Euro Visa 〰 craft closed Mon and Sun eve, 1-16 Aug. Spec : *foie d'oie aux reinettes*, *matelote au riesling*, 120-200.

The SUNDGAU Region**

A-B4
Round trip *(110 km ; full day)*
Southern country of ponds and rivers abounding with carp, with half-timbered houses where bread-ovens protrude from the walls ; peaceful and not much visited, it attracts those who like quiet countryside, fishing and reflective walks.

▶ **Altkirch**, a modest town (pop. 6 120) over the Sundgau ; an old house on the Place de l'Hôtel-de-Ville is the **Sundgau Museum** (archaeology and popular traditions ; *(3:30-5:30 Sun. ; daily ex Mon., Jul.-Sep.)*; remains of ramparts. ▶ **Ballersdorf** and **Gommersdorf** : typical of the region with 18thC peasant houses. Follow the Grumbach Valley. ▶ **Feldbach** : Romanesque church★★ of a former priory (12thC). ▶ **Ferrette** : site★ on a steep hill below two ruined castles *(10-min walk)* on the edge of the Swiss Jura, near the few remains of the Cistercian **abbey of La Lucelle** *(11 km S, on the border)*. ▶ Beyond the chapel of Hippoltskirch, **Oltingue** is characteristic of Sundgau : peasant museum★ *(3-6 Tue., Thu., Sat. ; 11-12 and 2:30-6 Sun., 15 Jun.-1 Oct. ; 2-5 Sun. rest of year, closed Jan., Feb.).* ▶ **Bouxwiller** : church furnishings. **Werentzhouse** : cross the upper Ill Valley (beautiful houses at **Grentzingen**) to reach the site★ of the ruined castle of **Landskron**; macaque monkeys nearby. ▶ **Hagenthal**, near the Basel (Switzerland) golf-course, which is on French territory ; crafts. ▶ Thalbach Valley leads to Altkirch ; typical Sundgau houses at **Knoeringue**, **Berentzwiller**, and *(4 km N of the road)* **Obermorschwiller**. ▶ Saint-Morand : hospital chapel : 12thC sarcophagus. □

Practical Information ────────

ALTKIRCH, ⊠ 68130, 20 km SW of **Mulhouse**.
ⓘ pl. Xavier-Jourdain, ☎ 89.40.02.90 (h.s.).
SNCF ☎ 89.40.96.44.

Hotel :
★★ **Auberge Sundgovienne**, rte de Belfort, 3,5 km W, ☎ 89.40.97.18, AE DC Euro Visa, 31 rm 🅿 〰 〰 ♪ craft closed Mon eve, 160. Rest. ♦ ♪ craft closed Mon and Tue eve. A stopover worth a detour, 55-155.

HIRTZBARCH, ⊠ 68118, 4 km S of **Altkirch**.

Hotel :
★ **Ottié-Baur**, 9, rue de-Lattre-de-Tassigny,

☎ 89.40.93.22, Visa, 13 rm 🅿 〰 〰 ♪ half pens (h.s.), closed Mon eve and Tue, 1 wk for Carnival, 23 Jun-17 Jul, 170. Rest. ♦♦ ♪ Fried carp is the specialty here, 50-100.

A ★★**Les Acacias** (80 pl), ☎ 89.40.00.04.

THANN

Mulhouse 22, Colmar 44, Paris 537 km
pop 7780 ⊠ 68800   A4
An Alsatian saying has it that "Strasbourg's steeple is the highest, Fribourg-en-Brisgau's is the widest, Thann's is the finest." **Collegiate church of St. Thiébaut★★** (14th-15thC) : a beautiful steeple plus sculpted doorways and stained glass windows. Thann is a commercial centre at the foot of the Vosges : signposted walks ; old houses ; **historical museum** in the Corn Market *(10-12 & 2:30-6:30, 15 May-30 Sep.).*

Nearby
▶ **Thur Valley**, industrial, but with a few worthwhile stops on the way to the Col de Bussang (pass, alt. 731 m). Downstream, the church at **Vieux-Thann** has a 16thC Entombment ; upstream, **Saint-Amarin**, known for its "fires of St. John" festival *(Jun.);* small historical and folklore museum *(2-6, May-Oct.).* Further, to the right, **Kruth-Wildenstein Lake** *(D13b, 18 km from Thann) :* leisure centre (beach, sailing, fishing) at the foot of the château de Wildenstein. ▶ **Joffre Road**, from Bitschwiller to Masevaux, constructed during WWI ; views★ of the Trouée de Belfort, the Sundgau and Jura. ▶ **Masevaux** *(18 km SW of Thann)*, at the entrance of the Doller Valley : a small industrial centre ; few remains of its famous abbey. □

Practical Information ────────

THANN
ⓘ pl. Joffre, ☎ 89.37.00.43 (h.s.).
SNCF ☎ 89.37.11.13.

Hotel :
★ **Moschenross** (L.F.), 42, rue du Gal-de-Gaulle, ☎ 89.37.00.86, Euro Visa, 25 rm 🅿 ♪ craft closed Mon, Feb , Oct, 120. Rest. ♦ ♪ craft 40-120.

Nearby

MASEVAUX, ⊠ 68290, 18 km SW.
ⓘ 36, Fossé-Flagellants, ☎ 89.82.41.99 (h.s.).

Hotels :
★ **Host. Alsacienne**, 16, rue du Mal-Foch, ☎ 89.82.45.25, Visa, 9 rm 🅿 closed Sun eve and Mon, Jul-1 Nov, 120. Rest. ♦ ♪ craft 60-160.
★ **L'Aigle d'Or**, 9, pl. Clemenceau, ☎ 89.82.40.66, DC Euro Visa, 9 rm 🅿 ♪ closed Mon eve and Tue, 1-30 Jan, 8 Sep-15 Oct, 105. Rest. ♦ ♪ craft 50-150.

A ★★★**Municipal** (60 pl), ☎ 89.82.42.29.

SEWEN, ⊠ 68290 Masevaux, 8 km SW of **Masevaux**.

Hotel :
★★ **Vosges** (L.F.), 38, Grand'rue, ☎ 89.82.00.43, AE DC Euro Visa, 22 rm 🅿 〰 〰 ⌘ craft closed Sun eve and Thu (l.s.), 15 Jan-7 Feb, 15 Oct-30 Nov, 100. Rest. ♦ ♪ craft Young J.-M. Kieffer, a pupil of Paul Bocuse, heads this kitchen on the banks of the Doller : *soupe de grenouilles au concombre*, *filet de truite à la crème d'aneth*, *dodine de pintadeau farcie aux petits légumes*, 65-150.

Les TROIS-ÉPIS

Colmar 12, Saint-Dié 54, Paris 519 km
pop 564 ⊠ 68410   A3
At only 15 km from Colmar, this is a notable excursion centre for the Vosges and the Colmar region ; the health resort was entirely rebuilt after 1945. □

Practical Information

ℹ ☎ 89.49.80.56.

Hotels :

★★★★(L) ***Le Grand Hôtel***, (I.L.A., Mapotel), ☎ 89.49.80.65, AE DC Euro Visa, 50 rm 🅿 500. Rest. ● ♦♦♦ ***Le Hollandsbourg*** ♪ A bouquet of delectable, light flavours arranged by chef François Stephan : *bouchon de foie gras, soufflé d'écrevisses, filet de bœuf ficelle*, 200-300.

★★★ ***Marchal*** (L.F.), ☎ 89.49.81.61, Euro Visa, 40 rm 🅿 half pens (h.s.), closed 5 Dec-15 Jan, 530. Rest. ♦♦ ♪ ♿ 80-165 ; child : 40.

● ★★ ***La Chêneraie*** (L.F.), 4, chemin du Galz, ☎ 89.49.82.34, Visa, 25 rm 🅿 closed Wed, 20 Dec-1 Feb, 190.

★★ ***La Croix d'Or*** (L.F.), ☎ 89.49.83.55, 12 rm 🅿 closed Wed, 2 Jan-4 Feb, 210. Rest. ♦ 70-120.

Route du VIN★★★

(The Wine Road) B2

From Thann to Marlenheim *(120 km ; 2 days)*

The prettiest villages in Alsace appear in this itinerary, on flowering, vine-covered hillsides at the foot of the Vosges. The route runs from S to N ; the most attractive part lying between Turckheim and Châtenois. Wine-tasting in the cellars.

▶ **Thann** (→) and **Cernay** (→ Route des Crêtes). ▶ After **Wattwiller,** view on the right of the Mulhouse potash basin. ▶ **Hartmannswiller :** fortified church, old castle. ▶ **Soultz★ :** pretty square town hall, houses, remains of ramparts ; W, chapel of Notre-Dame de Thierenbach (site★). ▶ **Guebwiller** (→); castle in **Orschwihr;** houses and old fountains in **Wethalten.** ▶ **Soultzmatt,** just after the **château de Wagenbourg :** prestigious vineyard ; mineral spring ; Romanesque steeple. ▶ **Rouffach★** (pop. 4900) : "Witches' Tower" crowned by a stork's nest ; 12th-14thC **church of Notre-Dame★★ ;** medieval and Renaissance **Place de la République★★ ;** museum in the wheat market ; on the way out of town, 19thC Issenbourg castle. ▶ **Hattstatt :** church, town hall. **Gueberschwihr :** old houses, Romanesque bell tower. ▶ **Husseren-les-Châteaux :** start of the Road of the Five Castles — the three **towers** of **Eguisheim, Hohlandsbourg** (view★), and **Pflixbourg** (supposedly haunted by a White Lady) ; all date from the 13thC. ▶ **Eguisheim★** : walk around the ramparts ; old houses ; remains of castle and church doorway. ▶ **Colmar** (→). ▶ **Turckheim★★** : three gates, a square ; and the last town-crier in Alsace still calls the hours *(10 pm, from May to the grape harvest).* **Niedermorschwihr★** : houses with oriel windows, Romanesque bell tower. ▶ **Kaysersberg★★★,** charming village (pop. 2710), banners flying from the castle opposite the **fortified bridge★★** over the river Weiss ; 16th and 17thC houses, Renaissance town hall★, **church★** (12th, 15thC) ; gilded wood **altarpiece★★ ; birthplace of Albert Schweitzer;** small **museum** *(10-12 & 2-6 daily, Easter, 2 May-31 Oct.).* **Kientzheim** : castle with **vineyard museum** *(10-12 & 2-6, Jul.-Oct.) ;* 16thC tombstones in the church. ▶ **Sigolsheim :** church★ (1200) escaped destruction in 1944 ; National War Cemetery. **Bennwihr :** modern church. **Mittelwihr** : wines. ▶ **Riquewihr** (→). ▶ **Hunawihr :** fortified church surrounded by 14thC fortifications ; **Centre de Réintroduction de la Cigogne★** (stork preserve ; *10-12 & 2-6, Apr.-Oct. ; closed Sun. am ; Wed., Sat. and Sun. in good weather in autumn),* deer park *(Apr.-Oct.).* ▶ **Ribeauvillé** (→). ▶ Road from **Bergheim** (medieval towers, gates and fortifications) to **Thannenkirch** *(7 km)* : summer resort. ▶ **Saint-Hippolyte** : houses, fountain, red wine. ▶ **Kintzheim :** the Sélestat road leisure park *(Wed., Sat., Sun., 16 Sep.-end Oct. ; daily, Jun.-15 Sep.).* At the château on the Haut-Koenigsbourg road : **Volerie des aigles** (falconry displays, *2-5, Apr.-Sep. ; Wed., Sat., Sun. in autumn ; demonstrations daily 3, 4 and Sun., Jun., Jul., 5 ; Aug., 2:30, 3:30, 4:30, 5:30*). Farther on, **Montagne des Singes** (Monkey Mountain nature park, *10-12 & 2-6, Apr.-Oct.).* ▶ **Châtenois :** towers, gates and old buildings. ▶ **Scherwiller :** excursion to **Ramstein** and **Ortenbourg★★ castles** *(1 hr 15 walk).* ▶ **Dambach-la-Ville★ :** vine-growing, knitwear ; circular ramparts (gates, wooden houses). NE, **Epfig :** Romanesque chapel of Ste. Marguerite★★. ▶ **Andlau★ : church★★** of an abbey founded by St. Richarde (11thC crypt, Romanesque frieze★★, doorway★★). ▶ After **Barr** (→) and **Obernai** (→), the vines are less dense. **Boersch :** gates and square★. ▶ **Rosheim★ :** typical Alsatian Romanesque **church★★★** (outside sculpture, apse, Rhenish-style capitals) ; town gates ; 12thC Maison du Païen, oldest house in Alsace ; **tourist train** to Ottrott *(Sun. and nat. hols., Jul.-Aug., 1 hr).* ▶ **Molsheim** (pop. 6990) : once site of the *Bugatti* motor factory, now **Bugatti Museum** (Cour du Chartreux, *8-10 & 2-6, summer*) ; ramparts ; stork park. **Metzig★ :** Renaissance museum *(2-6, Sat. and Sun. ; Apr.-Sep.).* **Altorf** *(E) :* Romanesque and Baroque church. ▶ **Avolsheim :** 11th-12thC chapel of St. Ulrich, among the oldest in the province, and, a bit further, the church of **Dompeter,** in the middle of the cemetery. ▶ **Traenheim. Westhoffen :** Rosenbourg castle ; cherry festival in June. **Wangen★ :** fountain festival (wine flows free) in July. **Marlenheim :** rosé wines ; Friend Fritz's Wedding Festival *(Aug.).* These are the last villages on the Wine Road, which continues to the small vineyard S of Wissembourg (→) : wine tasting at Cleebourg. □

Practical Information

ANDLAU, ✉ 67140 Barr, 16 km N of **Sélestat.**
ℹ pl. de la Mairie, ☎ 88.08.22.57.

Hotels :

★★★ ***Kastelberg*** (L.F.), rue du Gal-Kœnig, ☎ 88.08.97.83, Euro Visa, 28 rm 🅿 200. Rest. ♦ closed lunch, Nov-Easter, 80-180.

★ ***Au Canon*** (L.F.), 2, rue des Remparts, ☎ 88.08.95.08, AE Euro Visa, 10 rm 🅿 closed Tue, Feb, 150. Rest. ♦♦ ♪ 90-150.

Restaurant :

♦♦ ***Au Bœuf Rouge***, 6, rue du Dr-Stoltz, ☎ 88.08.96.26, AE DC Euro Visa 🅿 ♪ ♿ closed Wed eve and Thu, Jan, 20-30 Jun. Spec : *jambonneau au raifort sur choucroute, pochade de sandre.* Annex : *Winstub du Bœuf*, 75-180 ; child : 30.

Recommended

Guide to wines : *Catherine Lacoste*, 12, rue Deharbe, ☎ 88.08.95.83, wine shop.

EGUISHEIM, ✉ 68420 Herrlisheim, 6 km S of **Colmar.**
ℹ 22, Grand'Rue, ☎ 89.23.40.33.

Hotel :

★★ ***Auberge Alsacienne***, 12, Grand'Rue, ☎ 89.41.50.20, Euro Visa, 20 rm 🅿 closed 15 Dec-1 Feb, 220. Rest. ♦♦ closed Mon eve and Tue dinner only, 70-130.

Restaurant :

● ♦♦ ***Caveau d'Eguisheim***, 3, pl. du Château, ☎ 89.41.08.89 🅿 ♿ closed Wed eve and Thu, 15 Jan-1 Mar, 1-9 Jul. Traditional Alsatian dishes (*tarte à l'oignon, choucroute, cuisses de grenouilles au riesling*), and the fine cuisine of a Bocuse alumnus. Great Alsatian wines, 110-130.

⛺ ★★*Municipal* (100 pl), ☎ 89.23.19.39.

Recommended

Guide to wines : *Caves Hertz*, 1, porte des Chevaliers ; *Caves Sorg*, 8, rue Stumpf.

KAYSERSBERG, ✉ 68240, 11 km NW of **Colmar.**
ℹ 44, rue du Gal-de-Gaulle, ☎ 89.47.10.16.

Hotels :

★★★ ***Remparts*** (L.F.), 4, rue de la Flieh, ☎ 89.47.12.12, 31 rm 🅿 230.

★★★ ***Résidence Chambard***, 9-13, rue du Gal-de-Gaulle, ☎ 89.47.10.17, Tx 880272, AE DC Euro Visa, 20 rm 🅿 ♪ closed 1-20 Mar, 1-15 Dec, 400. Rest. ● ♦♦ ♿ closed Mon and Sun eve. Two dining rooms for P. Irmanns' tasty cooking : *foie gras frais en boudin, turbot* grillé au gingembre, mousse Chambard. Riesling, Tokay, 180-300.

★★ **Arbre Vert** (L.F.), 1, rue Haute-du-Rempart, ☎ 89.47.11.51, 24 rm ⌖ closed Mon (l.s.), 5 Jan-5 Mar, 160. Rest. ◆◆ 75-130.

★ **Château** (L.F.), 38, rue du Gal-de-Gaulle, ☎ 89.78.24.33, Euro Visa, 10 rm ⌖ closed Wed eve (l.s.) and Thu, 26 Feb-7 Mar, 25 Jun-4 Jul, 3-19 Dec, 150. Rest. ◆ ♪ ⅃ ♿ 50-100.

Restaurant :

◆◆ **Au Lion d'Or**, 66, rue du Gal-de-Gaulle, ☎ 89.47.11.16, DC Euro Visa, closed Tue eve and Wed, 15 Jan-21 Feb. Spec : foie gras maison, mousseline de brochet aux cuisses de grenouilles, 75-140.

⅄ ★★★★Municipal (100 pl), ☎ 89.47.14.47.

KIENTZHEIM, ⊠ 68240 Kaysersberg, 9 km NW of **Colmar**.

Hotels :

★★ **Hostellerie de l'Abbaye d'Alspach** (L.F.), 2-4, rue Foch, ☎ 89.47.16.00, Euro Visa, 20 rm ℗ ⌖ ⚲ ⌖ closed 6 Jan-9 Feb, 170. Rest. ◆◆ 80-160.

★★ **Hostellerie Schwendi** (L.F.), 2, pl. Schwendi, ☎ 89.47.30.50, Euro Visa, 7 rm ℗ ⚲ closed Wed, Nov-Easter, 165. Rest. ◆ ♪ Regional fare, 90.

MARLENHEIM, ⊠ 67520, 20 km W of **Strasbourg**.
ℹ pl. Kaufhaus, ☎ 88.87.51.09.

Hotels :

★★ **Hostellerie du Cerf**, 30, rue du Gal-de-Gaulle, ☎ 88.87.73.73, AE Visa, 17 rm ℗ ⚲ closed Mon and Tue, 9 Feb-3 Mar, 220. Rest. ● ◆◆ ♿ Very fine food. Spec : suprême de sandre lardé braisé au riesling, rognonnade de quasi de veau à l'Ache de montagne et crème d'échalotes, 220-350.

★★ **Hostellerie Reeb** (L.F.), 2, rue du Dr-Schweitzer, ☎ 88.87.52.70, AE DC Euro Visa, 35 rm ℗ ⌗ ⌖ closed Thu, 7-31 Jan, 200. Rest. ◆◆ 90-200.

Restaurant :

◆◆ **Auberge du Kronthal**, 2, rue du Kronthal, ☎ 88.87.50.25, Visa ℗ ⌗ ♿ closed Mon and Sun eve, 15 Jul-15 Aug, 20-28 Dec. Spec : canard à l'orange, 50-120.

MITTELWIHR, ⊠ 68630, 10 km N of **Colmar**.

Restaurant :

◆◆ **La Couronne d'Or**, 19, rte du Vin, ☎ 89.47.90.47, AE DC Euro Visa ♪ closed Mon and Sun eve , Jan. Fish is a specialty, 70-120.

Recommended
Guide to wines : Caves Goeker, 24, rue de Riquewihr.

MOLSHEIM, ⊠ 67120, 27 km SW of **Strasbourg**.
ℹ hôtel de ville, ☎ 88.38.52.00 ; Caveau de la Metzig (h.s.).
SNCF ☎ 88.38.14.31.

Hotels :

★★★ **Diana**, pont de la Bruche, ☎ 88.38.51.59, AE DC Euro Visa, 45 rm ℗ ⌖ ⌗ ⚲ ♪ ♿ 200. Rest. ◆◆ ♪ ⌖ Spec : raviolis d'escargots crème de riesling et ail, délice de sandre au pinot noir et pâtes fraîches, 85-150 ; child : 35.

★★ **Centre** (L.F.), 1, rue St-Martin, ☎ 88.38.54.50, Euro Visa, 29 rm ℗ ⚲ 160.

★ **Le Cheval Blanc**, 5, pl. de l'Hôtel-de-Ville, ☎ 88.38.16.87, AE DC Euro Visa, 13 rm ℗ half pens (h.s.), closed Feb, 260. Rest. ◆◆ ♪ closed Tue eve and Wed. Spec : canard au muscat, kougelhopf de légumes à la crème d'avocat, 70-100.

⅄ ★★Municipal (100 pl), ☎ 88.38.11.67.

NIEDERMORSCHWIHR, ⊠ 68230 Turckheim, 7 km W of **Colmar**.

Hotel :

★★ **L'Ange**, 125, rue des Trois-Épis, ☎ 89.27.05.73, Euro, 15 rm ℗ ⌗ half pens (h.s.), closed 5 Jan-28 Mar, 330. Rest. ◆ closed Tue eve and Wed, 50-80.

Restaurant :

◆ **Caveau du Morakopf**, 7, rue des Trois-Épis, ☎ 89.27.05.10 ♪ closed Sun, 15-30 Jun, 1-7 Jul, 70-110.

ROSHEIM, ⊠ 67560, 29 km SW of **Strasbourg**.
ℹ hôtel de ville, ☎ 88.50.40.10.
SNCF ☎ 88.50.40.18.

Hotels :

Auberge du Cerf, 120, rue du Gal-de-Gaulle, ☎ 88.50.40.14, Euro Visa, 3 rm ♿ closed Fri, Sat, 1-25 Aug, 15 Dec-2 Jan, 155. Rest. ◆ ♪ 60-150.

Le Relais de Rosheim, 34, rue des Vosges, ☎ 88.50.23.07, 9 rm, 5 apt ℗ ⌖ ⌗ ⚲ ⚘ ♿ 160.

Restaurant :

◆ **La Petite Auberge**, 41, rue du Gal-de-Gaulle, ☎ 88.50.40.60, Euro Visa ♪ closed Wed, 8 Jan-8 Feb, 50-130.

⅄ ★★Fackenthal (35 pl), ☎ 88.97.45.20.

ROUFFACH, ⊠ 68250, 15 km S of **Colmar**.
SNCF ☎ 89.49.60.09.

Hotels :

● ★★★★ **Château d'Isenbourg** (R.C.), ☎ 89.49.63.53, Tx 880819, Euro Visa, 40 rm ℗ ⌖ ♿ ⌴ ☞ closed Jan-Feb, 600. Rest. ● ◆◆◆ **Les Tommeries** ⌖ ♪ Classic fare. Panoramic dining room. Flawless service. Spec : foie gras, canard rôti à l'orange, 200-280.

★★ **Bollenberg**, ☎ 89.49.62.47, Tx 880896, AE DC Euro Visa, 50 rm ℗ ⌗ ⚲ ♿ 210. Rest. ◆ ♿ closed 21-31 Dec, 125-160 ; child : 45.

Recommended
Guide to wines : at Soultzmatt, PC 68570, 3 km W, caves Boesch, 4, rue du Bois.

SAINT-HIPPOLYTE, ⊠ 68590, 20 km N of **Colmar**.

Hotels :

★★★ **Munsch Aux Ducs de Lorraine**, (L.F., R.S.), 16, rte du Vin, ☎ 89.73.00.09, AE DC Euro Visa, 41 rm ℗ ⌖ ⌗ ⚲ ♪ ♿ half pens (h.s.), closed 10 Jan-15 Mar, 15-31 Dec, 330. Rest. ◆◆ ⌖ ♪ closed Mon. Spec : poêlée de coquilles Saint-Jacques à la tomate fraîche, noisette de chevreuil St-Hubert, 90-250 ; child : 65.

★★ **La Vignette** (L.F.), 66, rte du Vin, ☎ 89.73.00.17, 16 rm ℗ half pens (h.s.), closed Thu, Dec-15 Feb, 310. Rest. ◆ 75-120.

★★ **Parc** (L.F.), 6, rue du Parc, ☎ 89.73.00.06, DC Euro Visa, 22 rm ℗ ⌗ ⚲ ♿ half pens (h.s.), closed 15 Jun-1 Jul, 21 Dec-1 Jan, 210. Rest. ◆ ⌖ ♪ ♿ closed Wed eve (l.s.) and Mon, 50-100.

Recommended
Guide to wines : at Orshwiller, PC 67600, 2 km N, Engel, 1, rte du Vin.

SOULTZ, ⊠ 68360, 17 km NW of **Mulhouse**.

Hotel :

★ **Belle-Vue** (L.F.), 28, rte de Wuenheim, ☎ 89.76.95.82, DC Euro Visa, 7 rm ℗ ⌖ half pens (h.s.), closed Mon, 300. Rest. ◆ ⌖ ♪ 60-110 ; child : 30.

Recommended
Farmhouse-gîte : Schmitt, ☎ 88.38.21.09.

THANNENKIRCH, ⊠ 68590 Saint-Hippolyte, 21 km N of **Colmar**.

Hotel :

★★ **La Meunière**, 30, rue Ste-Anne, ☎ 89.73.10.47, Visa, 12 rm ℗ ⌖ ⌗ ⚲ ♿ closed Wed, 15 Nov-15 Mar, 160. Rest. ◆ ♪ 60-80.

TURCKHEIM, ⊠ 68230, 7 km W of **Colmar**.
SNCF ☎ 89.27.06.37.

Hotel :

★★ **Vosges**, pl. de la République, ☎ 89.27.02.37, Euro Visa, 32 rm ℗ ⌖ ⌗ ⚲ ♪ closed 15 Nov-Easter, 200. Rest. ◆ ♪ 50-80.

⅄ ★★★★Municipal (130 pl), ☎ 89.27.02.00.

Northern VOSGES Region**

A-B1

Round trip *(approx 172 km; 1 or 2 days)*

Across the Vosges massif and the **Northern Vosges Nature Park** with a detour through the Moselle department. Romantic landscapes and ruins in forests where folklore is part of daily life.

▶ **Niederbronn-les-Bains** (→); on the right, forest road to **Wintersberg★**. ▶ **Château du Falkenstein★★** *(15-min walk)* : ruins; **Lake Hanau★** (shore, woods) near the **Waldeck** ruins (site★). ▶ **Zinsel Valley** : lakes and woods. ▶ **Offwiller** : **museum** of popular art in half-timbered house *(Sun. 2-6, Jul.-Sep.)*. ▶ **Lichtenberg** : hilltop castle once owned by the Counts of Hanau, renovated by Vauban in the 17thC *(9-12 & 1:30-6, Mar.-Nov.)*; the village is a summer resort. ▶ **Bouxwiller**, capital of Hanau-Lichtenberg county, but the Revolution destroyed most traces of the past; Renaissance town hall★ (museum : *8-11 & 2-5)*; old houses. ▶ **Neuwiller-lès-Saverne** : square in front of the medieval **abbey church** (18thC façade and steeple); inside, 15thC **tapestries★★★** (story of St. Adelphe) in an **upper chapel★★** (11thC; *Sun. pm, ask at the presbytery)*. Protestant 13thC collegiate church of Ste. Adelphe behind the abbey. **Weiterswiller** *(3.5 km N)* : 15thC frescos in church; fossil and mineral museum *(9-12 & 2-6)*. ▶ A winding forest road (animal park) leads to **La Petite-Pierre★★**, picturesque village : 13th and 17thC château; regional nature park centre; **Museum of the Seal of Alsace** *(10-12 & 2-5, 6 in season; closed Mon., Jul.-Sep.)*. ▶ **Wingen-sur-Moder** : Lalique crystal-works. **Meisenthal : Glass and Crystal Museum** *(2-6 in summer, Sun. Apr.-May and Sep.-Oct.)*. **Saint-Louis-lès-Bitche** : displays at former royal glassworks (founded 1767) and at **Lemberg**. ▶ **Bitche** (pop. 7 860; Moselle Department) : medieval fortress turned into a citadel★ by Vauban (museum : *9-12 & 2-6, Feb.-Oct.; closed Mon.)*. Along the mountain road, several medieval ruins in the woods to the left : **Lutzelhardt, Wasigenstein★, Petit-Arnsberg, Froensbourg★** (paths). ▶ A road leads to semi-underground **Fleckenstein★★** : museum *(8-7, Apr.-Oct.)*; beyond, path to **Hohenbourg castle**. ▶ 1 km S of **Lembach** : **limekiln★★** of the **Maginot Line** recently opened to the public; visit to the underground installations *(8-6, May-Oct.)*. ▶ **Woerth** : château of the Counts of Hanau; museum of 1870-71 Franco-Prussian war *(2-5, Apr.-Oct.)*; battlefields nearby (Reichshoffen). ☐

Practical Information

BITCHE, ⊠ 57230, 3 km E of **Sarreguemines**.
⊡ porte de Strasbourg, ☎ 87.96.00.13 (h.s.).
🚃 SNCF ☎ 87.96.00.18.

Hotel :
★★ **Strasbourg** (L.F.), 24, rue Teyssier, ☎ 87.96.00.44, Euro Visa, 11 rm 🅿 ⌘ closed 4-26 Jan, 9-23 Sep, 180. Rest. ♦ closed Mon and Sun eve. Good little eatery, 45-120.

GRAUFTHAL, ⊠ 67320 Drulingen, 10 km S.

Hotels :
★ **Au Vieux Moulin**, ☎ 88.70.17.28, Euro Visa, 18 rm 🅿 ⌘ ⌘ closed 11 Nov-26 Dec, 105. Rest. ♦♦ ⌘ ⌘ closed Mon eve and Tue, 60-120; child : 25.
★ **Aux Maisons des Rochers** (L.F.), 26, rue Principale, ☎ 88.70.17.09, 12 rm 🅿 ⌘ ⌘ ⌘ closed Mon, Jan, 120. Rest. ♦ 80-120.

LEMBACH, ⊠ 67510, 24 km N of **Haguenau**.
⊡ 45, rte de Bitche, ☎ 88.94.43.81.

Hotels :
★★ **Vosges du Nord**, 59, rte de Bitche, ☎ 88.94.43.41, 8 rm 🅿 ⌘ closed Mon and Tue, 20 Aug-15 Sep, 110.
★ **Auberge du Cheval Blanc**, 4, rue de Wissembourg, ☎ 88.94.41.86, Euro Visa, 7 rm 🅿 closed Mon and Tue, 2-21 Feb, 17 Aug-5 Sep, 100. Rest. ● ♦♦ The Mischlers' opulent cuisine does justice to the 1740 decor. Spec :

escalope de foie gras au fumet de truffes, blanc de turbot aux huîtres, médaillons de chevreuil, 120-250.

⋏ ★★★*Fleckenstein* (250 pl), ☎ 88.94.40.38.

NIEDERSTEINBACH, ⊠ 67510 Lembach, 8 km W.

Hotel :
● ★★ **Cheval Blanc** (L.F.), 11, rue Principale, ☎ 88.09.25.31, Euro Visa, 31 rm 🅿 ⌘ ⌘ ⌘ 🖃 closed 20 Jan-1 Mar, 1-15 Dec, 150. Rest. ♦ ⌘ ⌘ closed Thu, 65-160.

OBERSTEINBACH, ⊠ 67510 Lembach, 10 km W of **Lembach**.

Hotel :
★ **Anthon**, 45, rue Principale, ☎ 88.09.25.01, Euro Visa, 7 rm 🅿 ⌘ ⌘ closed Mon and Tue, 2 Jan-1 Feb, 180. Rest. ♦ ⌘ ⌘ Very good food. Spec : foie gras frais, filets de soles aux nouilles fraîches, selle de chevreuil grand veneur, 70-150.

La PETITE-PIERRE, ⊠ 67290 Wingen-sur-Moder, 16 km N of **Saverne**.
⊡ ☎ 88.70.44.30.

Hotels :
● ★★ **Auberge d'Imsthal**, (R.S., L.F.), rte forestière d'Imsthal, ☎ 88.70.45.21, AE DC Euro Visa, 23 rm 🅿 ⌘ ⌘ ⌘ ⌘ ⌘ 200. Rest. ♦ ⌘ ⌘ ⌘ 50-180; child : 15.
★★ **La Clairière** (L.F.), 63, rte d'Ingwiller, on D 7, ☎ 88.70.47.76, AE DC Euro Visa, 18 rm 🅿 ⌘ ⌘ ⌘ ⌘ closed 15 Jan-28 Feb, 170. Rest. ♦ ⌘ ⌘ ⌘ 70-100.
★★ **Lion d'Or** (L.F.), 15, rue Principale, ☎ 88.70.45.06, DC Euro Visa, 35 rm 🅿 ⌘ ⌘ ⌘ 🖃 ⌘ closed Wed eve and Thu, 5 Jan-15 Feb, 210. Rest. ♦ ⌘ ⌘ ⌘ 55-150; child : 40.
★★ **Vosges** (L.F.), 30, rue Principale, ☎ 88.70.45.05, Euro Visa, 30 rm 🅿 ⌘ ⌘ ⌘ closed Tue eve and Wed, 15 Nov-15 Dec, 240. Rest. ♦ ⌘ 60-150.

WOERTH, ⊠ 67360, 15 km N of **Haguenau**.
⊡ 2, rue du Moulin, ☎ 88.09.30.21.

Hotel :
★ **La Chaumière**, rte de Lembach, ☎ 88.09.30.06, AE DC Euro Visa, 20 rm 🅿 ⌘ closed 20 Dec-10 Jan, 100. Rest. ♦ closed Mon and Tue eve, 60-110.

WANGENBOURG*

Saverne 20, Strasbourg 41, Paris 464 km
pop 230 ⊠ 67710   A2

Evergreen forests, game-filled woods, meadows, waterfalls and medieval fortresses.

▶ **Wangenbourg castle**, a stone's throw from the town centre, 13thC fortifications, keep destroyed by Swedish troops in 1663. Walks : SW, **Schneeberg** peak (alt. 960 m; panorama★); N, **Obersteigen** : 13thC **priory**; S along D218, **Nideck : castle** and **waterfall★**; **Hohenstein, Birkenwald** and **Freudeneck castles**. ☐

Practical Information

⊡ 47, rue du Gal-de-Gaulle, ☎ 88.87.32.44 (h.s.); mairie, ☎ 88.87.31.46 (l.s.).

Hotel :
● ★★ **Parc Hôtel** (L.F.), 39, rue du Gal-de-Gaulle, ☎ 88.87.31.72, DC, 24 rm 🅿 ⌘ ⌘ ⌘ ⌘ ⌘ 🖃 ⌘ closed 3 Nov-22 Dec, 205. Rest. ♦♦ ⌘ ⌘ 65-85; child : 50.

WISSEMBOURG**

Strasbourg 64, Sarreguemines 80, Paris 509 km
pop 7340 ⊠ 67160   B1

Flowery quays, gardens on the ramparts, and brown-tiled roofs lend colour to Wissembourg, originally the site of an abbey.

▶ Stroll along the Lauter through the **Bruch district★★** to **Anselmann Quay★** (Renaissance houses), or past the **Maison du Sel★** (salt house, 1450). ▶ 18thC town hall;

Hôpital Stanislas, residence of ex-king Stanislas Leszczynski of Poland, whose daughter Maria was married to Louis XV in 1725. ▶ **Church of St. Pierre-et-St. Paul★,** Gothic with Romanesque tower; frescos; stained glass; furnishings. ▶ **Westercamp Museum★** in a 16thC mansion to the N of town : historical collections, furniture, old kitchen, wine-press *(10-12 & 2-5; closed Sun., Wed., hols. and Jan.).*

Nearby

▶ **Altenstadt★,** *(1 km E)* : 11th-12thC Romanesque church. ▶ S, **Cleebourg vineyard** : Tokay, Pinot blanc. □

Practical Information ───────────────────

WISSEMBOURG
ⓘ hôtel de ville, ☎ 88.94.15.55.
SNCF ☎ 88.94.00.52.

Hotels :
★★ *L'Ange,* 2, rue de la République, ☎ 88.94.12.11, Visa, 8 rm, closed Sun eve and Mon, 19 Jan-17 Feb, 160. Rest. ◆ 95-120.

★★ *Le Cygne* (L.F.), 3, rue du Sel, ☎ 88.94.00.16, Euro Visa, 16 rm Ⓟ ⌕ ⚘ closed Wed, Thu lunch, Feb, 10-31 Jul, 160. Rest. ◆◆ ♪ ⚘ 85-150.
★ *La Rose,* 4, rue Nationale, ☎ 88.94.03.52, 7 rm, closed Sun eve and Wed, 1-25 Sep, 25 Dec-5 Jan, 100. Rest. ◆ ら 40-70.

Nearby

DRACHENBRONN, ⊠ 67160 Wissembourg, 11 km SW on the D 77.

Recommended
Farmhouse-inn : *Moulin des 7 Fontaines,* ☎ 88.94.50.90, 5 rm, closed 18 Feb-4 Mar, 26 Aug-9 Sep. Mon and Thu eve. Spec : *tarte flambée,* regional dishes.

ROTT, ⊠ 67160 Wissembourg, 7 km W.

Hotel :
★★ *La Cave de Cleebourg,* ☎ 88.94.52.18, Euro Visa, 20 rm Ⓟ ⌕ ⚒ ⌕ closed Sun eve and Mon, 15 Dec-15 Jan, 120. Rest. ◆ ♪ ら 100-180.

Ardèche, Cévennes

▶ The region is built on three kinds of rock and stone — granite, limestone and schist — which have formed three different cultures and civilizations; two peoples who were enemies for many years, but who now share the same destiny.

Schist underlies mountain torrents, rugged peaks and chestnut trees and has given birth to a freedom-loving society characterized by religious dissent. The pink and grey granite of the high crests provides a backdrop to the breeding of hardy animals able to withstand storms and snow. The great limestone plateaus, or *causses,* swept by wind and clouds, are the home of sheep and wool, crosses and religious rebels. Hardworking and rebellious Cévennes, poor and pious Lozère, and unlike either of them, the wine-growing country with its individualist and anti-clerical tradition.

Despite their differences, these regions complement each other. Highlanders have always been drawn to the plain, towards the distant horizon of the sea. The Cévennes mountains surge up from the *garrigue* over the ochre villages of the vineyards, like waves emerging from purple mist. With its sharp peaks and steep, narrow valleys, it is an austere, almost haughty country, both fierce and fragile, intimidating and fascinating.

At the edge of the purple plains, bordering the saltmarshes, is Aigues-Mortes, a walled city at the edge of the Rhône delta. Saint Louis wanted to make it the major port of the Levant, but nature defeated his efforts and Aigues-Mortes became instead a prison for Protestants in the 17th and 18th centuries. The visitor can still read their names and sentences — some exceeding fifty years' imprisonment — in the register of the Constance tower.

Nîmes is a postcard dream of the South — sun and aniseed aperitifs, markets under the plane trees, pines and cypresses, fountains and squares still impregnated with the memory of its Roman past.

The region's gorges and plateaus are perfect for hiking and canoeing, and its hundreds of underground caverns and rivers attract many speleologists. The great peaks and cliffs have been carved over the centuries into fantastic and eery shapes. The Cévennes *corniche,* or winding roadway, passes through one of the most rugged landscapes in France; in spring its sharp peaks and weathered rocks are softened by cherry blossom and narcissus. ☐

Don't miss

★★★ Mont Aigoual A3, Ardèche Gorges C2, Cévennes Corniche B3, Gard Aqueduct C3, Mont Lozère B2, Nîmes C4, Tarn and Jonte Gorges A2-3, Uzès C3.

★★ Aigues-Mortes B4, La Garde-Guérin B2, Mont Gerbier de Jonc B1, Causse Méjean A3, Rhône Corniche C1, Causse de Sauveterre A2, Vivarais Corniche B2.

★ Anduze B3, Antraigues C1-2, upper valley of the Ardèche B2, Beaucaire C4, Eyrieux Corniche and Gorges C1, Florac A2, Largentière C2, Lussan C3, the Margeride Region A2, Marvejols A2, Mende A2, Pont-Saint-Esprit C3, Saint-Gilles-du-Gard C4, Saint-Jean-du-Gard B3, Sommières B4, Tournon C1, Valleraugue A-B3, Les Vans B2, Villeneuve-de-Berg C2.

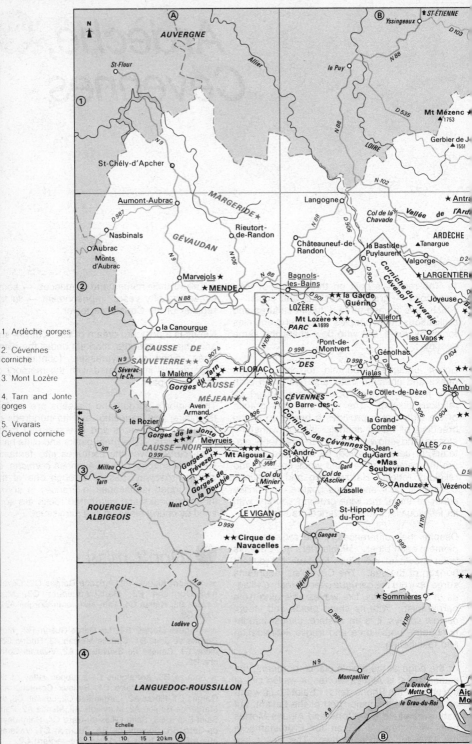

1. Ardèche gorges

2. Cévennes corniche

3. Mont Lozère

4. Tarn and Jonte gorges

5. Vivarais Cévenol corniche

On the Sauveterre Causse

Cévennes region

Facts and figures

Location : *South of the Massif Central Mountains*
Area : *16 545 km²*
Climate : *Varied, depending on relief, latitude and prox-imity to the sea.*
Sunny Mediterranean climate on the coastal plain; Mont Aigoual, only 70 km from the sea, is one of the wettest places in France, and often foggy; the Lozère region suffers long snowy winters; the causses (pla-teaus) have mountain winters and Mediterranean summers; the Cévennes mountains benefit from a coastal climate with occasional heavy rain and storms.
Population : *894 140*
Administration : *Department of the* **Ardèche,** *Pre-fecture : Privas; Department of the* **Gard,** *Prefec-ture : Nîmes; Department of the* **Lozère,** *Prefecture : Mende.*

● Brief regional history

The Romans

The Romans conquered the region in 121BC. Under Emperor **Augustus** (27-14BC), **Nîmes** became one of the showpieces of the Roman Empire, for the benefit of the colonists and retired veterans of his Egyptian campaigns against Anthony and Cleopatra. Beaucaire, Uzès, Anduze and Le Vigan were also founded by the Romans. ● Roman cultural influence made a profound and lasting impression on the country's language, customs and infrastructure. Roman first names are still common in Nîmes and in the Cévennes.

11th-13thC

● Convents and abbeys (principally **Benedictine**) were the major instruments of development in the area. The Knights Hospitallers of Lozère extended their influence throughout the Gévaudan area. Vineyards regained the importance they had under the Gallo-Romans, and **chestnut trees** started to spread throughout the Cévennes. Trade expanded: the fair of St. Gilles became a major annual trading event. ● Unlike the Midi-Toulousain (→), the Languedoc area remained firmly Catholic; it was made part of the **Royal Domain** and, with the stewardships of Beaucaire (created 1229) and Aigues-Mortes (1246), formed a defensive zone to counteract the effects of the heretical tendencies of the South. ● Guillaume de Grimoard, born at Bougès, became Pope Urban V in 1362.

The Reformation

Together with the Roman influence, the **Protestant Reformation** constitutes the major cultural event in the region. Directly or indirectly, the Reformation affected every sector of society and every part of the region, even including neighbouring areas such as Gévaudan and Rouergue, which remained Catholic. Protestantism spread along trade-routes down the Rhône Valley and into the mountains; the combination of Protestantism and a strongly **latinized rural population** is typical of Languedoc, and was to influence its development. Protestants, also known as Huguenots or Camisards, hastened the spread of Northern French culture, since they were completely divorced from their Catholic neighbours, having different feast days, first names, meals and cultural orientation, taking the Bible as their cultural basis, while the Catholics emphasized processions, rituals and crosses. ● There was soon a vigorous **Catholic reaction**, leading to the foundation of numerous missions. ● The Revocation of the Edict of Nantes signalled the start of religious persecution, and popular Protestant resistance remains firmly rooted in local memory; finally, in July 1702, the **Camisards** revolted against State-imposed religion. ● During the **Revolution**, the Protestants were on the side of the Republic, while the counter-revolutionary Catholics supported the Church and Crown. ● Under the 3rd Republic (1870-1940), this division acquired a new look: the Protestant areas always voted to the left, while the Catholics remained firmly legitimist. This cultural difference is still visible today.

18th-19thC

The **local economy was at its height** in the 18thC, when the valleys of the Cévennes produced a large proportion of French silk. ● During the **first industrial revolution,** the Péchiney factories were built at Salindres, near Alès, developing an important steel industry around the coal-mines and stimulating the building of one of the first railway lines (La Grand-Combe to Beaucaire). ● The wine trade also benefitted from new means of transport, and more acres of **vineyards** were planted; this was the period of great **trade-fairs** at Beaucaire, Barre-des-Cévennes and Alès. ● In the middle of the 19thC, the traditional economy of the area was hit by silk-worm disease, which was not overcome until Pasteur's discoveries later in the century. Around the same period, Phylloxera destroyed the vines, and a fungus attacked the chestnut trees. Redevelopment of the **vineyards** at the end of the century was paralleled by the appearance of great estates and an emphasis on monoculture. Languedoc became a wine factory.

Today

At the beginning of the 20thC, disquieting signs began to appear : competition from artificial textiles, poor wine sales, the coal crisis and the fall in agricultural prices, followed by the blood-bath of WWI. In the back country, disaster was not far off; silk producers and factories closed, and the coal mines too were threatened. The **rural exodus** accelerated, and by 1970 there were only 500 inhabitants in the Cévennes Nature Park. ● But while the back country was dying slowly, the coast was undergoing development : major engineering projects on the Rhône, irrigation helping the expansion of fruit production, and the growth of the tourist industry. ● Today, there are encouraging signs of growing **interest in preserving the cultural and agricultural identity** of the region. Steps have been taken to encourage traditional activities including silk production and goat-breeding, together with country holidays that spread the benefits of the tourist industry inland.

The Garrigues

The Garrigues form the last plateau between the causses and the coastal plain. These low limestone plateaus stretch around the SE of the Massif Central mountains, limited by the plain of the Vistre (S), the Cévennes (N) and the Ventoux (E). Clumps of holm-oak alternate with stony areas of aromatic herbs : thyme, savory, laurel, rosemary and lavender, and of course, kermes oak (garric which gives the area its name). The Protestants used to worship in the valleys, when their religion was outlawed; the textile workers built their mazets in the shade of the cyprus and almond trees. The perfume and dyeing industries find their raw materials here; the sheep graze on buckthorn and honeysuckle, and provide fertilizer for the vineyards. Near the towns the land is cultivated, but the surroundings are left wild (woods).
There are more dolmens in the Garrigues than anywhere else in France, as well as the dry-stone huts known as capitelles *in Languedoc. The beautiful Uzès-Nîmes road crosses this unusual sun-drenched landscape, where it is always summer.*

● *Practical information*

Information : **Languedoc-Roussillon :** *Comité Régional de tourisme (C.R.T.),* 12, rue Foch, 34000 Montpellier, ☎ 67.60.55.42. **Rhône-Loire :** *C.R.T.,* 5, pl. de la Baleine, 69005 Lyon, ☎ 78.42.50.04. **Ardèche :** *Comité Départemental de tourisme (C.D.T.),* 8, cours du Palais, 07002 Privas Cedex, ☎ 75.64.04.66. **Gard :** *C.D.T.,* 3, pl. des Arènes, B.P. 122, 30011 Nîmes Cedex, ☎ 66.21.02.51. *Office de tourisme d'Alès et des Cévennes,* hôtel consulaire, B.P. 49, 30101 Alès Cedex, ☎ 66.52.21.15. **Lozère :** *Office Départemental de Tourisme (O.D.T.),* pl. Urbain-V, B.P. 4, 48002 Mende Cedex, ☎ 66.65.34.55. In **Paris,** *Maison de la Lozère,* 4, rue Hautefeuille, 75006, ☎ 43.54.26.64. In **Lyon :** *Maison de la Lozère,* 9, rue du Plat, 69002 Lyon, ☎ 78.38.28.23.

Reservations : *Loisirs-Accueil Lozère,* B.P. 4, 48002 Mende Cedex, ☎ 66.65.34.55. *Maison de la Lozère* in Paris.

S.O.S. : Ardèche : ☎ 17. **Gard :** *S.A.M.U.* (Emergency Medical Service), ☎ 66.67.00.00. **Lozère :** ☎ 17. *Poisoning Emergency Centres :* Montpellier, ☎ 67.63.24.01, and Grenoble, ☎ 76.42.42.42. *Ocean Rescue :* ☎ 66.51.43.09 (headquarters at Port-Camargue).

Weather forecast : Ardèche, ☎ 75.01.83.50. **Gard,** ☎ 66.26.08.88. **Lozère,** ☎ 66.49.13.69.

Rural gîtes, chambres d'hôtes, farmhouse accomodation : Ardèche : *Relais dép. des Gîtes de l'Ardèche, C.D.T.,* 8, cours du Palais, B.P. 221, 07002 Privas Cedex, ☎ 75.64.04.66. **Gard :** *Gîtes ruraux du Gard,* S.D.T.R. at *C.D.T.,* ☎ 66.21.02.51. **Lozère :** *Relais dép. des gîtes de l'Ardèche* at *C.D.T.*

The Cévennes-Ardèche cuisine

The Cévennes, a poor region of Protestant traditions, is not really a gastronomic area, and simply makes use of local produce (trout, game and charcuterie). Chestnuts were long the staple food of the region, and marrons glacés (crystallized chestnuts) are still a speciality of the Ardèche. A local cheese of interest is the Pélardon, a round goat cheese; try the sharp-tasting Clinton wine. In the Lozère, tripoux (tripe), game and mushrooms are traditional, together with cheese and charcuterie (as in the Rouergue and Auvergne). On the Languedoc plain, cooking has a Mediterranean character, based on olives, fish and seafood. It is also, like the Ardèche, a fruit, salad and vegetable area (Remoulins cherries, Eyrieux peaches). At Aigues-Mortes, the sandy soil grows good asparagus. The most popular dishes are brandade (salt cod creamed with mashed potatos and garlic) and boeuf à la gardiane (the recipe for this stew is a closely-kept secret among families of the area). Brasucades (grilled mussels) and sardinade (sardines grilled on vine-cuttings) are popular tourist dishes.

Wine

Languedoc wines have undergone improvement because of selection of the grape varieties and more control over the processing of vine and wine. Try Côteaux du Languedoc, Costières du Gard, Muscat de Lunel, Côteaux de l'Ardèche. Many cooperatives sell direct. Biggest regional producer : Les Salins du Midi (Listel rosé).

Holiday villages : Centers for handicapped persons in Mejannes, Villeneuve-lès-Avignon, Le Vigan. Enq. : *C.D.T.* Gard.

Festivals and other events : Apr : Lussas *cinema festival.* **Jun :** *féria de Pentecôte* in Nîmes. **Jul :** Uzès *festival nights;* Alès *young theatre festival; jazz festival* in Nîmes; *summer festival* in Saint-Thomé. **Mid-Jul :** *festival of violets* at Sainte-Eulalie. **End of Jul :** *festival of olives* at Les Vans. **Mid-Jul-end of Aug :** *festival of jousters* at Serrière. **Jul-Aug :** *international summer festival* at the charterhouse in Villeneuve-lès-Avignon; *theatre festival* in Aigues-Mortes; *classical music festival* in Le Vigan; *musical evenings* at the château de Villevieille; Nîmes *folk festival.* **Aug :** *theatre and poetry festival* in Valvignères; *concerts* in Annonay. **Early Sep :** *Protestant gathering* in Mialet, at musée du Désert; *féria des vendanges* in Nîmes; *wine festival* at Saint-Péray. **Mid-Nov :** *festival of chestnuts* at Privas; **end of Nov :** *wine festival* at Cornas.

Rambling and hiking : the region is traversed by GR trails 4, 6, 7, 42, 44, 427, 420, 60, 65, 66, 68, 67, 72 and 73 (topoguides). *Assn. de Tourisme de Randonnée Languedoc-Roussilon (A.T.R.),* 8-10, rue du Pont-Juvenal, 34000 Montpellier, ☎ 67.65.38.51. *Comité de Coordination des Randonnées non motorisées,* 8, cours du Palais, 07002 Privas Cedex, ☎ 75.64.04.66 (hiking, horseback, riding, biking, canoeing, cross-country, skiing : see the *Guide to Walking and Rambling*). The *Gard C.D.T.* publishes a brochure which describes approx 28 short and medium-distance hikes. The *Association des Randonnées en Cévennes et Vivarais Largentiérois (R.C.V.L.)* has published a descriptive guide which presents all the different aspects of the region, and can be purchased at the *Largentière S.I.,* ⌧ 07110. The *Mende S.I.* provides a list of associations which propose hiking and rambling ideas and the *Cévennes National Park* publishes particularly informative documentation.

Leisure centre : numerous activities : rowing, patholing-spelunking, climbing. Centres : La Canourgue, 48500, ☎ 66.32.87.46, Sainte-Énimie, 48210, ☎ 66.48.53.55, Malzieu-Ville, 48140, ☎ 66.32.87.94 and 66.31.70.16. In summer *Centre d'Animation Vacances* (C.A.V.), enq. *Dir. de la jeunesse et des sports, Lozère :* 12, bd L. Arnault, 48000 Mende ☎ 66.49.04.20 which publishes a pamphlet on youth hostels and the C.A.V.

National and nature parks : *Cévennes National Park :* information service in Florac, ☎ 66.45.01.75 and 66.45.10.60 (summer). In Jul-Aug an office is open at the château de Florac along with six other information centres : Pont-de-Montvert, Meyrueis, Saint-Jean-du-Gard, Le Vigan, Génolhac and Villefort. The Cévennes National Park publishes leaflets called *Sentiers de découverte des paysages* (Discovering Country Trails), which provide interesting maps and descriptions. *Gévaudan Nature Park,* Sainte-Lucie, NE of Marvejols, ☎ 66.32.09.22.

Scenic railways : *Vivarais Railway,* Tournon-Lamastre line : Sun and nat hols, Apr-Oct, several days weekly during high season. Enq. and bookings : *Société C.F.T.M.,* 8, rue d'Algérie, 69001 Lyon, ☎ 78.28.83.34. *Le Transcevenol,* the Cévennes steam-powered locomotive, from Anduze to Saint-Jean-du-Gard, runs May-Oct. Enq. and bookings : ☎ 66.85.13.17, or T.V.C. station, 30270 Saint-Jean-du-Gard.

Technical tourism : Gard : Viticultural estates, *Cie des Salins du Midi et des Salines de l'Est,* 30220 Aigues-Mortes. **Lozère :** local information in the S.I. Source Perrier, 30310 Vergèze, ☎ 66.84.60.27. *Oil-mill* at Martignargues, 30360 Vézenobres, ☎ 66.83.54.52. *Spinning* at Monoblet, 30170 Saint-Hippolyte-du-Font, ☎ 66.85.22.33. **Ardèche :** *Bès Calixte,* 07240 Vernoux : sausage factory, from 15 Jun-15 Sep ; sales.

Riding holidays : *Comité gardois de Tourisme équestre et de Loisirs,* 3, pl. des Arènes, B.P. 122, 30011 Nîmes Cedex. *Le Beaucent,* 30190 Vic-Saint-Anastasie, ☎ 66.81.00.98. Enq. concerning riding *gîtes,* horse hire and trails at the Cévennes National Park information service, château de Florac. *Assn. régional pour le Tourisme* équestre et l'équitation de loisirs en Cévennes, Roussillon et Languedoc, M. Ségui, 14, rue des Logis, Loupian, 34140 Mèze, ☎ 67.43.82.50. and C.D.T.

Cycling holidays : the *Gard Conseil Général* has published a brochure listing approx 20 circuits (available at each C.D.T.).

Motoring and motorcycling : Ledenon circuit, 20 km from Nîmes, ☎ 66.37.15.31 and 66.37.18.38.

River and canal cruises : houseboat hire on the Rhône Canal in Sète : *Nautic Voyages*, marina, 30220 Aigues-Mortes, ☎ 66.51.04.34; *le Cygne*, a yacht : Enq. and reserv., 15, rue Circulaire, 30300 Beaucaire, ☎ 66.59.35.62 in season, 66.59.45.08 rest of the year.

Handicraft and Cookery Courses : Enq. C.D.T.

Children : *Assn. lozérienne mutuelle d'Animation et de Formation agricole*, 10, cité des Carmes, 48000 Mende, ☎ 66.65.18.30, and *Assn. d'Accueil en milieu rural de la Basse-Ardèche*, M. Dutruit, hameau des Salelles, 07170 Saint-Maurice-d'Ibie, ☎ 75.37.84.10, propose holidays for children in rural family homes. The *Mas du Pont*, 30360 Vézénobres, ☎ 66.83.61.19, caters to 5 to 15 year old children with various activities : workshops for painting, modeling, audiovisual; sports.

Aquatic sports : centres : Camboux Lake, at Sainte-Cécile-d'Andorge; at the Sénechas Dam, near Bessèges; Ponaut Lake and Villefort Lake. Cruises, boat races at the *Ecole de Mer*, Port-Camargue, 30240 Le Grau-du-Roi, ☎ 66.51.43.09 and at Naussac and Moulinet Lakes.

Canoeing : Ardèche, Lozère and **Gard :** canoe trips down the Ardèche, the Lot, the Allier, the Truyère, the Jonte and the Tarn : see the *C.D.T.* and *C.R.T.*

Rowing : at Saint-Gilles, on the Rhone canal at Sète; enq. at *Rowing-club* 3 bis, rue du Soleil, 30800 Saint-Gilles, ☎ 66.87.27.31.

Potholing and spelunking : *Comité dép. de spéléo en Ardèche :* enq. at the *C.D.T.;* underground safari in the Trabuc Cave, enq. : *S.C.M.S.*, B.P. 121, 34003 Montpellier, ☎ 67.89.79.12. *Spéléo club Lozère*, mairie de Chirac, 48100 Marvejols, ☎ 75.39.61.56.

Climbing : *Club Alpin Français*, 14, rue F.-Pelloutier, 30000 Nîmes. *Ardèche escalade* at Pradons (Mr. Termine), ☎ 75.39.61.56.

Winter sports : *Assn. ardéchoise des Centres-écoles et Foyers de ski de fond*, M. Duvert, 07510 Saint-Cirgues-en-Montagne. *Ski Club mendois*, ☎ 66.65.02.69. The **Ardèche** and **Lozère** C.D.T. publish brochures which provide

Weekend tips

The round trip of the Tarn and Jonte Gorges can easily be combined with the ascent of the Aigoual. Return to Millau via the Dourbie Gorges (→ *Rouergue*), or to Nîmes along the Cévennes Corniche; but Nîmes - Pont-du-Gard - Uzès is an itinerary worth a weekend in itself.

Cévennes nature park

Created in 1970, in an area seriously depopulated by rural exodus, this is the largest of the nature parks, and the only inhabited one : 840 km^2 at the centre of the park cover the Cévennes and Lozère uplands (Mount Lozère, Bougès, Aigoual, Lingas and the Méjean causse). There are 120 landholdings, 52 administrative communes and 117 hamlets in the Gard and Lozère regions; these are sustained by a total population of barely 500 people. The periphery of the park consists mainly of the Cévennes causses, which are more thickly populated : 2 280 km^2, with 41 000 inhabitants.

The park management provides agricultural and sheepfarming advice and guidance, and ensures that the inhabitants participate in the protection of the environment, through the maintenance of footpaths and hiking trails, farm holidays, sale of local produce etc.

There is an ecological museum at Mount Lozère with exhibitions, events, monument restoration etc. The park has the same rules as the other French nature parks, with special status for the inhabitants. Fauna and flora are protected and several species have been re-introduced (red and roe deer, grouse, griffon vulture, golden eagle, beaver). Seven different information centres welcome visitors : Florac, Villefort, Pont-de-Montvert, Meyrueis, Saint-Jean-du-Gard, Le Vigan, Génolhac. 750 km of GR paths, 500 km of horse-riding paths, 200 km of ski-trails (all with stopover cabins) run through the park. Half-day hikes are indicated on the information sheets.

lists of resorts and propose various ski holiday possibilities. Gard : Espérou/Prat-Peyrot resorts, ☎ 67.82.22.78, and Mas de la Barque, ☎ 66.48.80.26.

Parachuting : *Centre régional de Parachutisme Provence-Méditerranée*, aérodrome, 30150 Pujaut, ☎ 90.25.19.20.

Ballooning : *Vol découverte*, 16, pl. des Cordeliers, 07100 Annonay.

Golf : Nîmes, rte de St-Gilles (18 holes), ☎ 66.70.10.01.

Hunting and shooting : enq at *Féd. dép. des chasseurs*. **Ardèche :** 5, av. C.-Faugier, 07000 Privas, ☎ 75.64.30.53; **Gard :** 21, rue Dhuoda, 30000 Nîmes, ☎ 66.84.01.65; **Lozère :** 16, bd Soubeyran, 48000 Mende, ☎ 66.65.04.44.

Fishing : the *Féd. de Pêche et de Pisciculture de l'Ardèche*, 12, bd de la République, 07100 Annonay, ☎ 75.33.26.20, publishes a fishing and tourism map. **Gard :** *Féd. dép. des Assn. de Pêche et de Pisciculture*, 8, rue Sully, 30000 Nîmes, ☎ 66.67.56.29. **Lozère :** *Féd. dép. de la Pêche*, av. Paulin-Daudé, 48000 Mende, ☎ 66.65.36.11. *C.D.T.*, ☎ 66.65.34.55.

 Towns and places ═══════

Mont AIGOUAL***

A3

Round trip *(32 km from Mayrueis to the meteorological station at Aigoual; approx 1 hr.)*

▶ Mont Aigoual is the highest point in the Cévennes; to the S, the Hérault Valley appears 1 000 m below. It is the source of rivers running to both the Atlantic and the Mediterranean. The Parc National Cévenol (Cévennes Nature

Park) has recently re-introduced a number of vanishing species in its forests (red and roe deer, *mouflons*). The winter pasturage trails make this a paradise for hikers.

▶ **Valleraugue**, on the Hérault River : the **Sentier "des 4 000 marches"** (path of 4 000 steps) leads directly to the summit of the Aigoual, shortest and most direct route *(full day; difficult walk)*, first through chestnut trees, then through a forest of beech and firs (more mountainous).

The standard excursion can be combined with one to the Tarn or the Jonte Gorges (→).

▶ **Meyrueis** (→ Tarn Gorges). ▶ Hairpin roads up the Causse Noir (→). Nestled in the greenery, by the Bétuzon River★, is the **château de Roquedols** (15th-17thC), one of the largest in the Cévennes : the Cévennes Nature Park information centre *(mountain paths; Jul.-Sep., 10-12 & 3-7).* ▶ **Monjardin Pass** (alt. 1 090 m) : transition from the limestone of the Causse Noir to the granite and schist of the Aigoual; view★ over the Trévezel Valley.▶ **Abîme de Bramabiau** : resurgence of the Bonheur River, which disappears in the Camprieu Causse to reappear as water-falls *(visit).* On the *causse :* remains of the **abbaye du Bonheur,** former overnight stop for travelers *(access on foot from the GR62).* ▶ The Mount Souquet road joins the Dourbie Gorges★★ (→ Rouergue) under the fir trees. ▶ **Serreyrède Pass★★** (alt. 1 300 m) on the ridge-line : E, an enormous natural amphitheatre, source of the Hérault (narrow path to the waterfall) overlooked by the Céven-nes mountains; W, valley of Bonheur, which disappears into the peat bogs. The pass is on the great Languedoc winter pasture trail.▶ Superb excursion to the summit of the Aigoual, but mist and snow are frequent.▶ **Aigoual Meteorological Station,** a century old : orientation table; **panorama★★** from the Alps to the Pyrénées. All the paths pass the Observatory. ▶ Descent to **Le Vigan** *(32 km)* via **L'Espérou** : spectacular views of the Mediterranean. ▶ This ski-resort is the communications centre for the Massif. ▶ Pleasant walk to the Maison Forestière de Montals *(forestry centre; 5 km)* and the Orgon waterfall *(25 min).*

▶ From the top of the Aigoual, the picturesque but difficult **Cabrillac** road joins the Meyrueis-Florac road at the **Per-juret Pass** *(13 km NW).* ▶ The **Valleraugue** road★ plunges down 20 km of hairpin bends to the Hérault amphitheatre : fir, beech and chestnut woods. □

Practical Information ⎯⎯⎯⎯⎯⎯⎯⎯⎯⎯⎯⎯

L' ESPEROU, ⊠ 30570 Valleraugue, 10 km S.

Hotel :
Touring, ☎ 67.82.60.04, 20 rm ℗ ⌘ ☖ ⌕ pens, closed Fri (l.s.), 10 Nov-25 Dec, 155. Rest. ♦ 50-70.

VALLERAUGUE, ⊠ 30570, 30 km SE.

Hotel :
★ **Les Bruyères,** rue André-Chanson, ☎ 67.82.20.06, Visa, 28 rm ℗ ⌘ ☖ ⌕ closed 30 Oct-1 Apr, 160. Rest. ♦ ⌕ ☖ 45-80.

AIGUES-MORTES★★

Montpellier 29, Nîmes 41, Paris 749 km
pop 4475 ⊠ 30220   B4

Aigues-Mortes is surrounded by ramparts, at the extreme point of the Rhône delta, in a strange land-scape of lagoons, saltmarshes and vineyards.

▶ The town is a well-preserved example of medieval mili-tary architecture, symbolizing the religious and political conquests of the Capetian dynasty in Languedoc. In the 13thC, St. Louis (Louis IX) wanted to make this town France's principal port to the Holy Land and the Eastern Mediterranean; it would have been a rival to Marseille in a still-independent Provence. However, in spite of the efforts of numerous kings, the harbour silted up; by the 17th and 18thC it had become no more than the king-dom's principal prison for Protestants.

▶ **Ramparts★★,** built by Philippe the Bold at the end of the 13thC; the rest of the town had been built around the religious buildings. Access to the ramparts via the **Cons-tance Tower** *(9-12 & 2-6, Apr.-Sep.; 10-12 & 2-5 Oct.-Mar) :* excellent view of the town (festival shows at the foot of the tower).▶ Gothic parish **church** rebuilt in the 17th-18thC. ▶ Two other 17thC churches. ▶ Place St-Louis (statue of the king) : former 17thC Capuchin convent, now exhibition hall. ▶ Visit the **saltmarshes★**

(marais salants), where salt has been made since the Middle Ages *(Tue.-Fri.; Jul.-Aug., from the TO at Aigues-Mortes or Grau-du-Roi).* Listel rosé vineyards between the salt-pans. □

Practical Information ⎯⎯⎯⎯⎯⎯⎯⎯⎯⎯⎯⎯

ℹ pl. St-Louis, ☎ 66.53.73.00.
SNCF ☎ 66.51.99.78.

Hotels :
● ★★★ **Les Remparts,** 6, pl d'Armes, ☎ 66.53.82.77, AE DC Euro Visa, 19 rm ℗ ⌘ ⌕ ☖ closed 1 Nov-15 Mar. Beautiful house from the 18thC, 335. Rest. ♦♦♦ ⌘ ⌕ ☖ closed Mon ex Jul-Aug, 105-165; child : 55.
★★★ **Saint-Louis,** 10, rue de l'Amiral-Courbet, ☎ 66.53.72.68 ℗ ⌘ ☖ closed Jan-Feb, 210. Rest. ♦♦ ⌕ ☖ closed Wed (l.s.), 80-230.

Restaurants :
♦♦ **Les Arcades,** 23, bd Gambetta, ☎ 66.53.81.13, AE Euro Visa ℗ ⌘ ⌕ ☖ closed Mon ex Jul-Aug, 15 Nov-15 Dec. "Authentic" is the word for this old stone structure, and for P. Merquiol's fine cooking : *filet de sole au château-chalon, fricassée de homard aux mousserons.* Local wines, 90-170.
● ♦ **La Camargue,** 19, rue de la République, ☎ 66.53.86.88, AE DC Euro Visa ⌘ ⌕ ☖ closed Mon , lunch ex Sun, 2 Jan-4 Feb. Gypsy guitarists play in this superb old house, typical of the Camargues. Regional specialities : *crudités, terrines à la provençale, bœuf guar-diane aux olives noires.* Costières du Gard, 80-120.
♦ **Le Minos,** 7, pl. St-Louis, ☎ 66.53.83.24, Euro Visa ⌕ ⌘ ☖ closed 20 Oct-30 Mar. Fish have pride of place : catch of the day, live lobsters and spiny lobsters, 60-150.

⚠ ★★★★*Petite Camargue* (350 pl), ☎ 66.53.84.77.

ALÈS

Nîmes 44, Montpellier 70, Paris 709 km
pop 44345 ⊠ 30100   B3

Alès, the most important town in the Cévennes, has a long industrial tradition : these days, cloth and silk have given way to coal and iron. Little remains of the old town except a few prestigious buildings recalling Protestant resistance to state-imposed religion.

▶ 18thC Meridional Gothic **cathedral;** 18thC town hall, once the Languedoc Parliament; 18thC bishop's palace, now the chamber of commerce; prison-fortress built by Vauban. **Château-museum** : archaeology, mineralogy, 17th-18thC French painters, triptych attributed to Jean Bellegambe (late 15thC) and two paintings by Brueghel. **Mining Museum** *(Apr.-Sep. 10-12:30/2-7:30) :* 600-m gal-leries telling the story of coal extraction.

Nearby

▶ **Château de Rousson★** *(10 km on Aubenas road) :* typi-cal Languedoc manor (17thC). ▶ Densely-wooded coun-tryside all around; the road from Alès to Saint-Jean-du-Gard via the **Uglas Pass★** is like a tunnel through oaks and chestnuts *(30 km).* ▶ **Vézénobres★** *(11 km S),* beautiful village; remains of ramparts; Romanesque hous-es; feudal ruins; Louis XV château hidden in the trees. ▶ **Grotte de la Cocalière** *(25 km N; Palm Sund.-end Oct. 9-12 & 2-6) :* cave pearls and hanging discs (rock formations). □

Practical Information ⎯⎯⎯⎯⎯⎯⎯⎯⎯⎯⎯⎯

ALÈS
ℹ 2, rue Michelet, ☎ 66.52.21.15; pl. G.-Péri, ☎ 66.52.32.15 (h.s.).
SNCF ☎ 66.23.50.50/66.30.12.43.
Car rental : Avis, 31, av. Carnot, ☎ 66.86.35.19; train sta-tion.

Hotels :
★★★ **Grand Hôtel,** 17 bis, pl. G.-Péri, ☎ 66.52.19.01,

43 rm Ⓟ 190. Rest. ♦♦ closed Sat eve and Sun (l.s.), 60-130.
★★★ *Orly*, 10, rue d'Avéjan, ☎ 66.52.43.27, DC Euro Visa, 43 rm Ⓟ ⌕ ⚡ 170.
★★ *L'Ecusson* (L.F.), rte de Nîmes, Saint-Hilaire de Brethmas, ☎ 66.30.10.52, 26 rm Ⓟ ▥ ⌕ ♿ 135.
Parc, 174, rte de Nîmes, ☎ 66.30.62.33, Euro Visa, 5 rm Ⓟ ≼ ⌕ In a park, 155. Rest. ♦♦ ♪ 70-200.

Restaurant :
♦ *Le Clou de Girofle*, 58, rte de Saint-Martin, ☎ 66.86.22.46, closed Sun, Jan, 20 Aug-5 Sept. Spec : feuilleté de Saint-Jacques aux deux purées, filet mignon de porcelet à la confiture d'oignons, 120-210.

△ ★★Châtaigniers (76 pl), ☎ 66.52.53.57 ; at Allègre, PC 30500 St-Ambroix, ★★★Château de Boisson (90 pl), ☎ 66.85.65.61 ; ★★★Domaine des Fumades (100 pl), ☎ 66.85.70.78.

Nearby
La FAVÈDE, ⊠ 30110 La Grand-Combe, 15 km N.

Hotel :
● ★★★ *L'Auberge Cévenole*, (L.F., R.S.), ☎ 66.34.12.13, Euro, 16 rm 2 apt Ⓟ ≼ ⌕ ♿ ⚡ closed 16 Nov-14 Mar, 250. Rest. ♦♦ ≼ Spec : escargots à la cévenole, feuilleté au roquefort, 130-150.

LASALLE, ⊠ 30460, 30 km SW.

Hotel :
★★ *Les Camisards*, 51, rue de la Croix, ☎ 66.85.20.50, Euro Visa, 20 rm Ⓟ ▥ ♿ closed 15 Nov-30 Mar, 145. Rest. ♦ ♿ 45-80 ; child : 30.

△ ★★Val de la Salendrinque (75 pl), ☎ 66.85.24.57.

Recommended
▼ local products : la S.I.C.A., (oyster mushrooms) on road leading out of village.

SAINT-AMBROIX, ⊠ 30500, 19 km NE.

Hotel :
● *Croquembouche* (L.F.), Courry, ☎ 66.24.13.30, Euro Visa, 5 rm Ⓟ ▥ ⌕ ⚡ ⊡ closed Tue, 1-15 Oct. Beautifully restored 18thC farmhouse with pool, 200. Rest. ♦ ⚡ 60-120.

ANDUZE*

Alès 13, Nîmes 47, Paris 722 km
pop 2790 ⊠ 30140   B3
Anduze has an old tradition of Protestant independence.

▶ **Protestant church,** one of the largest in France, on the central square opposite the **clock tower** (1320) and a 17thC château. ▶ The **old quarter★** was the craftsmen's district until the 19thC ; many 17thC houses ; 15thC covered market ; **fountain-pagoda** (1648) in green and yellow tile — the same colour as Anduze pottery.

Nearby

▶ **From Anduze to Saint-Jean-du-Gard via Mas-Soubeyran** *(25 km)*

▶ **Bambouseraie de Prafrance★** (bamboo plantation) : botanical garden like a Far Eastern jungle *(Mar.-Nov., 9-12 & 2-7; Jul.-Aug., 9-7).* ▶ **Générargues :** fork to the Gardon de Mialet in a narrow **canyon★.** ▶ The **Mas-Soubeyran★★** was one of the centres of French Protestantism : **Désert Museum** dedicated to the Cévennes resistance to State-imposed religion *(Mar.-Nov., 9:30-12 & 2:30-6).* ▶ Picturesque cul-de-sac leads to the **Trabuc grotto★** : lake and interesting formations *(Jun.-Sep. : 9:30-6; 15 Mar.-15 Oct. 10:30-12:30/2:30-5:30; closed 15 Oct.-15 Mar).* ▶ Return to Luziers crossroads. ▶ **Pont des Abarines★** (bridge over the Gardon de Mialet). ▶ **Saint-Jean-du-Gard★,** the other gateway to the Cévennes ; built along the Gardon in a valley of vines and olive trees : 17thC bridge. Some 20 spinning factories here

were still working at the end of the 19thC ; today, it is a major tourist centre. Market on Tuesdays ; concerts at the church ; exhibitions at the town hall ; **Musée des Vallées Cévenoles** (regional history museum, *May-Sep., 10:30-12:30 & 2-7, closed Mon. and Sun. ; Oct.-Apr. Mon. 2-6 Tue. and Thu. on request).* ▶ The clock tower is all that remains of the Benedictine priory.   ☐

Practical Information _____

ANDUZE
ⓘ plan de Brie, ☎ 66.61.98.17 (h.s.).

Hotel :
★★ *La Porte des Cévennes*, 3 km N, rte de Saint-Jean-du-Gard, ☎ 66.61.99.44, AE Euro Visa, 18 rm Ⓟ ≼ ▥ ⌕ ⚡ closed 30 Oct-30 Mar, 150. Rest. ♦ ≼ closed Sat noon and Sun noon, 45-90.

△ ★★★Les Fauvettes (60 pl), ☎ 66.61.72.23 ; ★★★Malhiver (102 pl), ☎ 66.61.76.04 ; ★★3 terrains (500 pl).

Recommended
Events : concerts at the Temple, in summer.
Leisure activities : Cevennes steam train, from Anduze to Saint-Jean-du-Gard, ☎ 66.85.13.17.
▼ *La vitrine Cévenole*, on the St-Jean-du-Gard road ; pork products : *Dhombre*, on the square of the Château ; pottery : *d'Anduze*, on the St-Jean-du-Gard road, ☎ 66.61.80.86.

Nearby

GÉNÉRARGUES, ⊠ 30140, 4 km N on the D 129.

Hotel :
★★★ *Les Trois Barbus*, ☎ 66.61.72.12, AE DC Euro Visa, 32 rm Ⓟ ≼ ▥ ⌕ ⊡ half pens (h.s.), closed Mon eve and Sun eve, 3 Nov-3 Apr. Tranquil setting, 600. Rest. ♦♦ ≼ ♪ ⚡ 125-180.

Recommended
Leisure activities : Bambouseraie de Prafrance, floral park, ☎ 66.61.70.47. The Far East in the Cévennes : daily 30 Mar-31 Oct (9-12 & 2-7) and Jul-Aug (9-7).

MIALET, ⊠ 30140 Anduze, 10 km NW on the D 129.

Hotel :
★ *Les Grottes de Trabuc*, ☎ 66.85.02.81, 8 rm Ⓟ ≼ ▥ half pens (h.s.), closed Tue eve and Wed lunch, 7 Oct-1 Apr, 240. Rest. ♦ ≼ closed Tue, 55-90.
△ ★★La Rouquette (133 pl), ☎ 66.85.32.97 ; ★★les Plans (230 pl), ☎ 66.85.32.46.

SAINT-JEAN-DU-GARD, ⊠ 30270, 14 km N.
ⓘ av. R.-Boudon, ☎ 66.85.32.11 (h.s.).

Hotels :
★★ *Auberge du Péras* (L.F.), La Bastide, rte de Nîmes, ☎ 66.85.35.94, 10 rm Ⓟ closed 2 Jan-10 Feb, 165. Rest. ♦ ♪ 40-90.
★★ *L'Oronge* (L.F.), 103, Grand'Rue, ☎ 66.85.30.34, AE DC Euro Visa, 40 rm Ⓟ ▥ ⚡ closed Sun eve and Mon (l.s.), 2 Jan-1 Apr. Former 18thC coach house, 200. Rest. ♦ 45-120.

△ ★★★La Forêt (60 pl), ☎ 66.85.37.00 ; ★★la C.A.M. (200 pl), ☎ 66.85.32.06 ; ★★les Sources (100 pl), ☎ 66.85.38.03.

Recommended
▼ The Grand'Rue boasts an antiques shop, lambskin clothing, a wrought iron shop, and silk weavers.

TORNAC-ANDUZE, ⊠ 30140 Anduze, 5 km SE.

Restaurant :
♦♦ *Le Ranquet*, rte de St-Hippolyte, ☎ 66.77.51.63, AE DC Visa ▥ ♪ ⚡ closed Tue eve and Wed ex Jul-Aug, 10 Jan-24 Mar. A good place to eat, with Anne Majourel's straight-from-the-heart cuisine : salade d'aiguillettes de caille, turbotin braisé à l'oseille, magret à la confiture d'oignons. Piano-bar, French billiards, art gallery, 85-150.

ANNONAY

Saint-Etienne 43, Valence 53, Paris 532 km
pop 20085 ⊠ 07100   C1

In the 15thC, the leather and wool industries made use of the Deûme and Canse rivers at Annonay. In the 17thC, they were joined by the paper industry (Montgolfier, Canson).

▶ Annonay was built in the narrow Deûme gorge (old bridge) : 19thC factories currently being modernized.
▶ Château; monument to the Montgolfier brothers who made the first balloon ascent here in 1783. ▶ **César Filhol Museum** behind the town hall (15 Rue Béchetoille; *Fri., Sat., Sun., 2-6; daily in summer*) : art, folklore, Montgolfier brothers memorabilia); Christ★ in the church of Veyrine (17thC).

Nearby

▶ *(6 km NE)* **Peaugres** : **safari park** *(summer 9:30-6; winter 11).* ▶ **Terney Dam** : lake surrounded by cedars.
▶ *(5 km N)* **Boulieu** : fortified town. ▶ **Serrières**, riverharbour on the Rhône *(15 km NE)* : museum *(weekends, Easter-Oct., 3-6, hols. 3-7).* ▶ **Romanesque church**★ at **Champagne** : cupola vaulting★; carved tympanum and lintels; 15thC stalls. ▶ **Quintenas** : 12th-14thC fortified church; 10 km S, chapel of Notre-Dame d'Ay above the Ay Gorge *(7 km, then 4km).*

Round trip through the upper Vivarais *(approx 120 km; full day)*

Annonay. ▶ *Corniche* (cliff road) above the Canse Gorge.
▶ **Péréandre rock** (40 m) above the stream. ▶ S of **Saint-Vallier**, the **Rhône Pass** is particularly spectacular : ruins of **Arras** and **Serves**. ▶ **Vion** : striated capitals in the church. ▶ **Hermitage vineyards** on the opposite bank.
▶ **Tournon★**, opposite Tain-Hermitage : beautiful town; the oldest **lycée** (school) in France (1536; rebuilt in the 18thC); 17thC Jesuit chapel★ where symbolist poet Mallarmé taught; 15th-16thC **château** where the son of François I died in childhood; small museum *(Apr.-May 2-6; Sep.-Oct. 2-5; summer 10-12 & 2-6);* terraces★★ overlooking the Rhône. Flamboyant Gothic church : 16thC frescos and triptych; 17thC organ. ▶ Bridge over the Doux (14th-18thC). ▶ *Corniche* to Lamastre along the **Doux Gorges★**. ▶ **Small steam train★** between Tournon and Lamastre along the bottom of the valley *(C.F.T.M. tel. : 78.28.83.34).* ▶ **Boucieu-le-Roi** : 13th-16thC church.
▶ **Lamastre** : small industrial town and renowned gastronomic site; rebuilt Romanesque church above the old quarter of Macheville. ▶ Louvesc *corniche* : views over the watershed between the Doux and Eyrieux valleys.
▶ **Château de Rochebloine** : panorama over the upper Doux Valley★, with the Alps on the horizon. ▶ **Buisson Pass** (reconstructed miniature Ardèche village; view) : winding road to the right to **Pailharès** and Romanesque church at **Saint-Félicien** *(detour 25 km if returning via Faux Pass).* ▶ **Lalouvesc**, mountain resort in pine woods above the **Ay gorges**; 19thC basilica of St. François-Régis (museum : relics of the saint; *open year round but on request Dec.-Mar., tel. : 75.67.82.00).* ▶ Modest Romanesque church at **Veyrines** *(6 km from Satillieu).*
▶ Return to **Annonay**.   ☐

Practical Information ⎯⎯⎯⎯⎯⎯⎯⎯

ANNONAY
ℹ 5, bd de la République, ☎ 75.33.24.51.
SNCF ☎ 75.33.31.24.

Hotel :
★★ **Midi** (L.F.), 17, pl. des Cordeliers, ☎ 75.33.23.77, AE DC Euro Visa, 40 rm Ⓟ closed Sun in winter, 20 Dec-20 Jan, 130.

Restaurant :
◆ **Marc et Christine Julliat**, 29, av. Marc-Seguin, ☎ 75.33.46.97, Visa ⪽ ♪ closed Mon and Sun eve, 2-23 Feb, 27 Jul-10 Aug, 85-155.

Recommended
Farmhouse-inn : at Saint-Jacques-d'Atticieux, *Le Miron*, ☎ 75.33.35.78. Pool, camping. Farm produce for sale. Open weekdays by appointment.
Market : *flea market*, 2nd Sun of the month.

Nearby

DESAIGNES, ⊠ 07570, 7 km W of **Lamastre** on D 533.

Hotel :
★ **Voyageurs** (L.F.), ☎ 75.06.61.48, 20 rm Ⓟ ⪽ ⫘ 〰 ♘ ⊗ ♪ half pens (h.s.), closed 1 Oct-15 Mar, 280. Rest. ◆ ⪽ ⊗ 45-120.

LALOUVESC, ⊠ 07520, 25 km SW.
ℹ ☎ 75.67.84.20.

Hotels :
★★ **Beau Site** (L.F.), ☎ 75.67.82.14, AE DC, 33 rm Ⓟ ⪽ 〰 ⫘ ♞ half pens (h.s.), closed 1 Oct-10 Apr, 165. Rest. ◆ ⪽ 55-100; child : 35.
★★ **Le Relais du Monarque** (L.F.), ☎ 75.67.80.44, AE DC, 20 rm Ⓟ ⪽ 〰 ⫘ ♞ half pens (h.s.), closed 15 Oct-1 May, 460. Rest. ◆ ⪽ ♪ 55-85; child : 35.

LAMASTRE, ⊠ 07270, 45 km S.
ℹ rue Ferdinand-Herold, ☎ 75.06.43.99.

Hotels :
● ★★★ **Château d'Urbilhac**, rte de Vernoux, 2 km, ☎ 75.06.42.11, AE DC Euro Visa, 14 rm 2 apt Ⓟ ⪽ 〰 ⫘ ♪ closed 1 Oct-1 May. Antique furnishings, 350. Rest. ◆◆ ⪽ 125-190.
★★★ **Midi**, pl. Seiguobos, ☎ 75.06.41.50, AE Euro Visa, 20 rm Ⓟ 〰 ⫘ half pens (h.s.), closed Sun eve Sun and Mon, 15 Dec-1 Mar, 530. Rest. ● ◆◆ **Barattero** The Perrier brothers have ably taken over the reins here : *pain d'écrevisses sauce cardinal, soufflé glacé aux marrons.* Wines of the Ardèche, 135-210; child : 90.
★★ **Grand Hôtel du Commerce** (L.F.), pl. Rampon, ☎ 75.06.41.53, 23 rm Ⓟ 〰 closed 30 Oct-25 Feb, 205. Rest. ◆ ⪽ ⊗ 50-140.
⚘ ★★**Municipal** (130 pl), ☎ 75.06.44.33.

PEAUGRES, ⊠ 07340 Serrières, 7 km SW of **Serrières** on the N 82.

Hotel :
★ **Le Bon Gîte** (L.F.), ☎ 75.34.80.44, 11 rm Ⓟ 〰 ⫘ closed Sat, 15 Jan-1 Mar, 100. Rest. ◆ 45-75.

SAINT-MARCEL-LES-ANNONAY, ⊠ 07100 Annonay, 7 km W on the D 82.

Hotel :
★ **Auberge du Ternay**, barrage du Ternay, ☎ 75.67.12.03, AE DC Visa, 7 rm Ⓟ ⪽ ⫘ closed Mon ex Jul and Aug, 3 Nov-3 Dec, 85. Rest. ◆ ⪽ ♪ Meals served on a terrace at the lake's edge, 40-130; child : 20.

SATILLIEU, ⊠ 07290, 11 km NE of **Lalouvesc** on D 578.

Hotel :
● ★★ **La Gentilhommière**, (France-Accueil), rte de Lalouvesc, ☎ 75.34.94.31, Tx 345548, AE Euro Visa, 49 rm Ⓟ 〰 ⪽ ♞ ⊡ ♪ ♫ 250. Rest. ◆◆ closed Fri eve and Sun eve, 1 Nov-1 Apr, 70-90; child : 35.
⚘ ★★**Granjeon** (100 pl), ☎ 75.34.96.64.

SERRIÈRES, ⊠ 07340, 15 km NE.
ℹ quai jules-Roche, ☎ 75.34.06.01.

Hotel :
★ **Schaeffer**, ☎ 75.34.00.07, AE DC, 12 rm Ⓟ closed Mon eve and Tue eve ex Jul, Aug, Jan, 115. Rest. ◆ 90-190.

Recommended
Guide to wines : at Saint-Désirat-Champagne, *Wine co-operative*, ☎ 75.34.22.05, syrah for sale.
▼ **M. Gautier**, ☎ 75.34.23.11, artisanal distillery, apples and pears.

TOURNON, ⊠ 07300, 39 km SE.
ℹ imm. la Tourette, ☎ 75.08.10.23.
SNCF ☎ 75.08.31.77.

Hotels :
★★★ *Paris* (L.F.), 12, quai Marc-Seguin, ☎ 75.08.01.11,
Tx 345156, AE DC Euro Visa, 36 rm ⫽ closed Sun (l.s.),
230. Rest. ♦♦ ⫽ ♪ closed Sat and Sun (l.s.), 1-15 Feb,
1-15 Nov, 80-180; child : 55.
★★ *Manoir*, 226, rte de Lamastre, ☎ 75.08.20.31, 10 rm
℗ ⚏ ☒ closed 15 Sep-15 Mar, 160.

Å ★★★*Manoir* (80 pl), ☎ 75.08.02.50; ★★★*Municipal*
(100 pl), ☎ 75.08.05.28; ★★*Foulons* (70 pl),
☎ 75.08.22.72; ★★*Sables* (100 pl), ☎ 75.08.20.05.

Recommended
Guide to wines : at Mauves, *Domaine J.-L. Chave*, wines.

ARDÈCHE Gorges***

C2
From Vallon to Saint-Martin *(48 km; 2 hr; see map 1)*

Rock, water, sun, wind, light and silence : unsullied
nature. Perched on top of the cliff and overlooking
the tourist road, the Ardèche Gorges follow the river
200 m below for a distance of 32 km. Discover the
grandiose spectacle of nature untouched and untamed — a paradise for climbing, canoeing and camping in caves. Numerous viewpoints have been constructed allowing one to admire the silken curves of
the river from the edge of the Gras plateau, above
the towering cliffs sculpted in a myriad of forms, and
innumerable grottoes sparkling in the sun. The Ardèche is an excellent region for speleologists and pothol-
ers (spelunkers).

► **Vallon-Pont-d'Arc :** busy tourist centre. ► Two keeps
overlook the entrance to the canyon between the Gras
Plateau and the Orgnac Aven Plateau; easy parking *(lock
car doors)* : viewpoints at Serre de Tours, Gaud, La Madeleine, Les Templiers. ► **Pont-d'Arc**★, huge natural stone
arch across the river *(beach, canoe rental)*. ► After Pont-
d'Arc, the canyon is really spectacular. ► **La Madeleine
grotto :** classic karst cave with wide variety of stalactites and stalagmites *(daily Apr.-Oct., 9:30-12 & 2-6:30)*.
► **Saint-Martin-d'Ardèche**, in the Côtes du Rhône
vineyards, is the other tourist centre for the region.
► **Saint-Marcel-d'Ardèche :** Romanesque church; cardinal de Bernis' castle.   □

Practical Information ————————————

SAINT-MARCEL-D'ARDÈCHE, ☒ 07700 Bourg-Saint-
Andéol.

Hotel :
Auberge de la Source, RN 86, ☎ 75.04.65.66, 4 rm ℗ ⫽

⚏ ⬡ ⅃ half pens (h.s.), closed Jan-Feb, 260. Rest. ♦ ⫽
♪ ⅃ 40-130.

SAINT-MARTIN-D'ARDÈCHE, ☒ 07700 Bourg-Saint-
Andéol, 12 km S of **Bourg-Saint-Andéol**.
ⓘ pl. du Champ-de-Mars, ☎ 75.54.54.20.

Restaurant :
♦ *L'Echiquier*, rue du Candelas, ☎ 75.98.70.81, Visa ⫽
closed Tue, 2-30 Nov, 50-100; child : 40.

Å ★★★*Le Moulin* (200 pl), ☎ 75.04.66.20; ★★*Municipal*
(70 pl), ☎ 75.04.65.25.

Recommended
Canoes-kayaks rental : *Lafet*, Gorges road,
☎ 75.04.62.17; *Raoux*, in the village, ☎ 75.04.67.00.
Market : Sun (h.s.) : local produce and crafts.

VALLON-PONT-D'ARC, ☒ 07150, 9 km S of **Ruoms**.
ⓘ ☎ 75.88.04.01.

Hotels :
★★ *Tourisme* (L.F.), bd Peschaire-Alizon, ☎ 75.88.02.12,
DC Visa, 26 rm ℗ half pens (h.s.), closed Mon,
15 Dec-15 Jan, 170. Rest. ♦ 50-90; child : 35.
Manoir de Raveyron, rue Henri-Barbusse, ☎ 75.88.03.59,
Visa, 11 rm ⚏ ⬡ ⌖ pens (h.s.), closed 1 Oct-1 Mar, 330.
Rest. ♦ 50-105; child : 20.

Å ★★★*Arc-en-Ciel* (100 pl), ☎ 75.88.04.65; ★★★*Beau
Rivage* (100 pl), ☎ 75.88.03.54; ★★★*Mondial* (250 pl),
☎ 75.88.00.44; ★★★*Plage-Fleurie* (150 pl),
☎ 75.88.01.15; ★★★*Provençal* (315 pl), ☎ 75.88.00.48;
★★★*Roubiné* (135 pl), ☎ 75.88.04.56; ★★*8 terrains*
(690 pl).

Recommended
Canoes-kayaks rental : adresses available at the *S.I.*
Market : Sat am.

Upper ARDÈCHE Valley*

B2
From La Chavade Pass to Aubenas *(43 km; approx. 3 hr)*

The Ardèche river drops 1 000 m in the space of a few
miles; small stone bridges and, after Thueyts, black
basalt rock.

► **La Chavade Pass**★ (alt. 1 271 m) on the watershed
between the Atlantic and the Mediterranean slopes. The
river rises in the nearby **Mazan forest :** numerous mountain paths; ruins of 12thC abbey. ► The Aubenas road
runs along the mountain side : views★ over the gorge.
Mediterranean influence in the villages : vines are trained
up the walls.► Ruins of the Montlaur château.► **Malbos :**
pretty medieval **bridge** at the foot of the former mining
village of **Mayres.** ► **Thueyts**, fruit-growing village on a
lava outflow from the **Gravenne de Montpezat** volcano★

1. Ardèche gorges

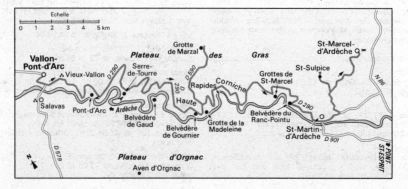

(2 hr 30 excursion to the N); view over the lava field and the Devil's Bridge *(Pont du Diable; marked path; approx. 1 hr 30).* ▶ **Neyrac-les-Bains,** small spa, volcanic waters. ▶ **Château de Ventadour** at the entrance to **Pont-de-Labeaume.** ▶ The road runs through chestnut woods and past abandoned spinning factories. ▶ **Vals-les-Bains** (→). ▶ **Aubenas** (→). ☐

Practical Information ───────────────

JAUJAC, ⊠ 07380 Lalevade, 10 km SE of **Thueyts** on the N 108.

Hotel :
★ **Le Caveau** (L.F.), ☎ 75.93.22.29, AE, 20 rm Ⓟ ☖ ▨ closed Dec-Feb, 120. Rest. ♦ ♪ ✵ 50-90.

THUEYTS, ⊠ 07330, 50 km of **Privas**.

Hotels :
★★ **Les Platanes** (L.F.), ☎ 75.93.78.66, Visa, 26 rm Ⓟ ≶ ∭ ☖ ⌘ ♿ closed 10 Nov-10 Feb, 165. Rest. ♦ ≶ 50-90; child : 40.
★★ **Marronniers** (L.F.), pl. du Champ-de-Mars, ☎ 75.36.40.16, Visa, 19 rm Ⓟ ∭ ✵ closed Mon, 15 Dec-5 Mar, 180. Rest. ♦ ♿ ✵ 55-125.
★★ **Nord** (L.F.), ☎ 75.36.40.38, 25 rm Ⓟ ≶ ∭ ☖ closed Tue (l.s.), Oct-1 Apr, 170. Rest. ♦ 60-100.

⚠ ★★*De Belos* (67 pl), ☎ 75.36.44.35.

AUBENAS

Privas 30, Le Puy 91, Paris 633 km
pop 13700 ⊠ 07200   C2

Aubenas has the charm of a large Provençal village : Saturday market held on the château square, old-fashioned shops in faded colours and a splendid view over the river.

▶ Good view of the town from the south : old ramparts round the town centre, the many-coloured château roofs and the St. Benoît Dome. Take a short walk through the arcaded streets and see the gargoyles and mullioned windows of the old houses. ▶ The strategic position of the 12thC **castle** gave it control over the region : rebuilt in the 17thC, now the town hall; 15thC spiral staircase; 16thC gallery in a courtyard★; 1750 Grand Staircase; 18thC decor; terrace overlooking the valley *(Jul.-Aug., 10-12 & 3:30-6:30 closed on Sun. pm; Easter-1 Nov., Sat. 3-6 and Sun.10-12).* ▶ The **St. Benoît Dome**★ is an elegant Italianate 17thC building; the mausoleum of the Maréchal d'Ornano, Lord of Aubenas, who was involved in all the plots against Cardinal Richelieu; he died in the Vincennes prison in Paris (exhibitions of religious art; *same hours*).

Nearby

▶ **Vals-les-Bains** *(5 km N),* delightful old-fashioned spa. ▶ The **Volane Valley** runs between the lava fields of the Aizac volcanos. ▶ **Antraigues**★ *(10 km N from Vals),* at the junction of three rivers. ▶ **Castle of Boulogne**★ (14thC, *18 km N) :* abandoned. ▶ **Jastres** viewpoint *(7.5 km W).* ▶ **Largentière**★ *(20 km SW),* a medieval silver mining town, that now extracts lead and zinc; astonishing site : pink-tiled roofs at the bottom of the Ligne gorge, overlooked by 12thC castle ruins and the impressive Law Courts (Palais de Justice) which look like a Greek temple; the bishop's **castle** is now an almshouse. **Récollets Gate,** remains of the ramparts, leads into the old town★ : narrow streets and stone steps. Gothic church with Flamboyant chapels and 19thC spire; Hôtel de Ville (town hall) and arcaded square. ▶ All the villages in the area were fortified to defend the mines : **Chassiers**★ has a fortified church (14thC) and a 14th-16thC château. ▶ **Montréal** : 13th-16thC keep. ▶ **Sanilhac** *(W) :* 15thC château. ▶ Farther up, the **Brizon Tower** (orientation table and panorama★) used to communicate by signals with the Loubaresse Tower in the Baume Valley.

Through the Ardèche Valley★ *(from Aubenas to Vallon-Pont d'Arc, 40 km, 2-3 hr)*

▶ Soft fertile hills of vineyards, orchards, and southern-looking villages. In central Ardèche, there are villages in green pastures between the cliffs, or nestled on the edge of the plateau. ▶ **Sauveplantade**★ : delightful 12thC Romanesque church. ▶ **Rochecolombe**★, **Lagorce**★. ▶ **Voguë**★★ : feudal castle, rebuilt in the 17thC *(Jul.-Aug., 10-12 & 2-6, Sun. 3-6; Mar.-Jun., Sep.-Nov., Sun. only; closed Nov.-Mar.).* ▶ **Balazuc**★, old fortified village in grey stone. ▶ **Ruoms**★, fortified town at the mouth of three gorges; the old centre★ is worth restoring : ramparts; Romanesque church (mosaic in volcanic stone), Gothic houses. ▶ N, the **Ruoms Pass**★ is one of the best natural curiosities in the region. ▶ Another pass through the **Beaume Gorges**★★, where the river drops 1 500 m in 40 km; past the beautiful village of **Labeaume**★, you must go on foot. ▶ The lower **Chassezac Valley**★ is typically Mediterranean with vineyards stretching out of sight; cypress and olive trees. ▶ Don't miss the **Mas de la Vignasse**★, where writer Alphonse Daudet lived; his parents were wealthy silk merchants (Daudet museum and agronomy museum in former silk-worm rearing building; *1 May-1 Oct., daily 9-12 & 2-6:30).* ▶ **Vallon-Pont-d'Arc** (→ Ardèche Gorges). ☐

Practical Information ───────────────

AUBENAS
ℹ 4, bd Gambetta, ☎ 75.35.24.87.
SNCF ☎ 75.35.01.67.

Hotels :
★★ **La Pinède** (L.F.), rte du Camping-des-Pins (D 235), ☎ 75.35.25.88, Visa, 30 rm Ⓟ ≶ ∭ ☖ ✵ ♪ᵒ 200. Rest. ♦ ≶ ♿ ✵ closed Mon, 15 Dec-21 Jan, 55-135; child : 40.
★★ **Le Cévenol** (L.F.), 77, bd Gambetta, ☎ 75.35.00.10, 45 rm Ⓟ ♿ ✵ 190.
★★ **Le Panoramic Escrinet** (L.F.), col de l'Escrinet, 14 km NE on N 104, ☎ 75.87.10.11, AE, 20 rm Ⓟ ≶ ∭ ☖ ▨ half pens (h.s.), closed 16 Nov-15 Mar, 220. Rest. ♦ *Le Col de l'Escrinet* ≶ ♪ ✵ 85-220.

Restaurant :
♦ **Le Fournil,** 34, rue du 4-Septembre, ☎ 75.93.58.68, Visa ✵ closed Mon and Sun eve, 1 Jan-3 Feb, Jun, 80-130.

⚠ ★★*Pins* (200 pl), ☎ 75.35.18.15.

Recommended
Market : Sat am around the square of the Château : regional specialities for sale (cheese, fruit, honey, jam).
♥ local produce : Les Halles, rue Radal, ☎ 75.35.07.07, fruit, vegetables, wines, pork products; Château de Bourgneuf, ☎ 75.35.13.39, glazed chestnuts, chestnut purée.

Nearby

ANTRAIGUES, ⊠ 07530, 14 km N.
ℹ mairie, ☎ 75.38.72.46/75.38.70.10.

Hotel :
L'Oeil-de-Boeuf, pont de l'Huile, ☎ 75.38.71.12, AE DC Visa, 9 rm Ⓟ ∭ ☖ half pens (h.s.), closed Tue eve , Mon ex Jul-Aug and Feb, 315. Rest. ♦ ≶ ♪ 65-135.

Restaurants :
♦♦ *Lo Podello,* ☎ 75.38.71.48 ∭ ☖ closed Thu, Oct-Mar. This former château offers a rustic decor and a permanent exhibition of the owner's paintings. Local savoury specialties, 100-125; child : 45.
● ♦ *La Brasucade,* on the Place, ☎ 75.38.72.92 ≶ ♪ closed Wed. Eye-popping fixed-price meal and eye-pleasing paintings, 90.

LAVIOLLE, ⊠ 07530, 7 km N of **Antraigues** on the D 578.

Hotel :
★ *Les Plantades,* ☎ 75.38.71.58, 10 rm Ⓟ ∭ ☖ half pens (h.s.), closed 5 Nov-15 Dec, 120. Rest. ♦ 45-55.

RUOMS, ⊠ 07120, 24 km S.
ℹ pl. de la mairie, ☎ 75.93.91.90.

Hotels :

● ★★★★ *Le Caléou*, domaine du Rouret, Grospierres, on D 111, ☎ 75.93.60.00, Tx 345478, AE DC Euro Visa, 117 rm Ⓟ ⌁ ⚌ ⌕ ♪ ♨ ᕃ ⌷ ⌁ closed 20 Dec-2 Feb. Sports centre covering 210 acres, 420. Rest. ♦ ⌁ ♪ ᕃ 110-185.

★ *Le Savel*, rte des Brasseries, ☎ 75.39.60.02, 15 rm Ⓟ ⚌ ⌕ pens (h.s.), closed Mon, 1 Feb-3 Mar, 440. Rest. ♦ ♪ 55-130.

⚠ ★★★Chapoulière (100 pl), ☎ 75.39.64.98 ; ★★★La Plaine (62 pl), ☎ 75.39.65.83 ; ★★★Mas du Barry (80 pl), ☎ 75.39.67.61 ; ★★Grand-Terre (200 pl), ☎ 75.39.64.94 ; ★★Municipal (100 pl), ☎ 75.39.62.38.

Recommended
Market : Fri.

VALGORGE, ⊠ 07110 Largentière, 19 km NW of Largentière.

Hotels :

● ★★ *Le Tanargue* (L.F.), ☎ 75.93.68.88, AE Euro, 25 rm Ⓟ ⌁ ⚌ ᕃ half pens (h.s.), closed 4 Jan-6 Mar, 220. Rest. ♦ ⌁ ♪ 80-200 ; child : 40.

★ *Chez Michel* (L.F.), ☎ 75.88.98.90, Euro, 20 rm Ⓟ ⚌ ⌕ ⌁ half pens (h.s.), closed Dec, 100. Rest. ♦ 40-65 ; child : 20.

VALS-LES-BAINS, ⊠ 07600, 6 km NW.
⌖ ⌁ ☎ 75.37.46.68.
ⓘ 12, av. Farincourt, ☎ 75.37.42.34.
⚎⚎ ☎ 75.37.40.06.
⚎⚎ ☎ 75.37.44.62.

Hotels :

★★★ *Grand Hôtel des Bains*, 3, montée du Grand-Hôtel-des-Bains, ☎ 75.94.65.55, AE DC Visa, 54 rm Ⓟ ⌁ ⚌ ⌕ ♨ ᕃ closed 5 Oct-20 May, 340. Rest. ♦♦ ⌁ ♪ ᕃ 125-200 ; child : 70.

★★★ *Le Vivarais*, (Mapotel), rue Claude-Expilly, centre des Parcs, ☎ 75.94.65.85, AE DC Euro Visa, 41 rm Ⓟ ⌁ ⚌ ⌕ ♪ 280. Rest. ♦ ⌁ ♪ closed Sun eve, 15 Nov-31 Dec, 85-120.

● ★★ *L'Europe*, (France-Accueil), 86, rue Jean-Jaurès, ☎ 75.37.43.96, Tx 346256, AE DC Euro Visa, 35 rm Ⓟ ♨ closed 10 Oct-10 Apr, 180. Rest. ♦ ᕃ ⚘ Spec : mousseline de truite, comtasso, 75-200 ; child : 30.

★★ *Grand Hôtel de Lyon*, (Inter-Hôtel), 11, av. Farincourt, ☎ 75.37.43.94, Tx 346256, AE DC Euro Visa, 35 rm Ⓟ closed Nov-Mar, 185. Rest. ♦ *Les Arcades* ᕃ 80-175 ; child : 35.

★★ *Saint-Jacques* (L.F.), 8, rue Auguste-Clément, ☎ 75.37.46.02, AE Visa, 28 rm Ⓟ ⌁ ⚌ ⌕ 210. Rest. ♦ closed 15 Oct-Easter, 70-90 ; child : 40.

★★ *Saint-Jean* (L.F.), 112 bis, rue Jean-Jaurès, ☎ 75.37.42.50, AE DC Euro Visa, 32 rm Ⓟ ⌕ ᕃ closed 15 Oct-Easter, 150. Rest. ♦ ᕃ 70-120.

Recommended
Casino : ☎ 75.37.42.12.
Farmhouse-inn : at St-Andéol-de-Vals, *Mas de la Pierre*, 7,5 km N on D 257, ☎ 75.37.56.12, weekdays in winter. Local specialties.

Mende 42, Le Puy 91, Paris 535 km
pop 1049 ⊠ 48130   A2

⚎⚎ ☎ 66.31.80.30.

Hotels :

★★★ *Chez Camillou*, 10, rte du Languedoc, ☎ 66.42.80.22, AE Euro Visa, 41 rm Ⓟ ⌁ ⚌ ᕃ closed 10 Nov-20 Dec, 170. Rest. ♦ ⌁ ᕃ 55-120.

★★★ *Grand Hôtel Prouhèze*, 2, rte du Languedoc, ☎ 66.42.80.07, AE Visa, 30 rm Ⓟ ⌁ ♪ closed Sun eve ,Mon ex school hols, Nov-Feb, 250. Rest. ● ♦♦ ♪ ᕃ A lovely stopping-place in the Gévaudan. The owner does the cooking : *sac d'os à la tuée du cochon, fricassée d'écrevisses*. Over 500 entries on the wine list, 80-250.

⚠ ★★Municipal (100 pl), ☎ 66.42.80.02.

Nearby

SAINT-CHÉLY-D'APCHER, ⊠ 48200, 10 km N.
ⓘ bd Guérin-d'Apcher, ☎ 66.31.03.67 (h.s.).
⚎⚎ ☎ 66.31.00.16.

Hotels :

★★ *Rocher Blanc*, La Garde, ☎ 66.31.90.09, 21 rm Ⓟ ⌁ half pens (h.s.), closed Sun eve (l.s.), 1 Dec-10 Feb, 140. Rest. ♦ ♪ ᕃ ⚘ 50-100.

★ *Lion d'Or*, 132, rue T.-Roussel, ☎ 66.31.00.14, 30 rm Ⓟ ♪ closed 20 Dec-15 Jan, 100. Rest. ♦ Good food, 45-80.

⚠ ★★Municipal (80 pl), ☎ 66.31.03.24.

Recommended
Events : *rock and fossil exchange*, in Aug.

Avignon 33, Alès 50, Paris 659 km
pop 17780 ⊠ 30200   C3

Life in the old town known and loved by the painter Renoir was drastically altered by the development of the modern Marcoule district, but the ancient *bastide* is still there, and the Place des Arcades★ is being restored.

▶ Small **museum** created by painter Albert André, friend of the Impressionists, with an important collection of modern art *(10-12 & 2-5:30; closed Tue.)* : good collection of Renoirs, 19thC Lyonnais school, Besson collection of figurative painters : Pignon, de Koninck, Cueco.▶ Rue Crémieux and neighbouring streets : dilapidated town **mansions** still worth seeing.

Nearby

▶ **Marcoule**, most important plutonium production centre in France (viewpoint and exhibition).▶ Lovely villages on a hilltop among the Côtes du Rhône vineyards : **Laudun** *(9 km SE)* : Gothic church transformed in the 17thC. ▶ **Château de Lascours**, E (16thC). ▶ On the edge of the Gard forest★ : **Saint-Laurent-des-Arbres** : fortified Romanesque church and much-restored château ; **Saint-Victor-la-Coste**★.

Down the Cèze Valley★★ *(from Bagnols to Les Vans 66 km, half day)*

▶ **La Roque-sur-Cèze**★ : Romanesque church ; château ; ▶ Downstream, the spectacular **Sautadet waterfall**★. ▶ **Cornillon**★ : Romanesque church among the remains of the castle and fortification wall (view★).▶ **Goudargues**★, former site of a Benedictine abbey : canal, washhouse, fountains, remains of three churches including the former **abbey church**★, one of the most remarkable Romanesque buildings in the Gard Department (nave restored in the 17thC, vaulting and doorway in the 19thC). ▶ Dry heath country on the plateau. ▶ The road runs above the **Cèze Gorges**★ *(access on foot)*. ▶ **Barjac** is a tourist centre for the Ardèches gorges : 17thC church ; château ; old houses. ▶ **Saint-Paul-le-Jeune**, old mining village N of the Cévennes Valley. ▶ Through the **Païolive woods** before reaching **Les Vans** (→). □

Practical Information ──────────────

BAGNOLS-SUR-CÈZE
ⓘ esplanade Mont-Cotton, ☎ 66.89.54.61.
⚎⚎ ☎ 66.23.50.50.

Hotels :

● ★★★★ *Château de Coulorgues*, rte d'Avignon, ☎ 66.89.52.78, AE Euro Visa, 23 rm Ⓟ ⌁ ⚌ ⌕ ⌷ ⌁ closed Sun eve and Mon (l.s.), Jan-Feb. Very pleasant setting, 390. Rest. ♦♦ ♪ ⚘ 90-150.

★★ *Valaurie*, St-Nazaire, ☎ 66.89.66.22, DC Euro Visa, 22 rm Ⓟ ⌁ ⚌ ᕃ closed 20 Dec-20 Jan, 185.

Restaurant :

♦ *Le Florence*, 16, pl. Bertin-Boissin, ☎ 66.89.58.24, Visa

♪ closed Mon and Sun eve, 27 Apr-4 May, Oct. Italian specialities, 60-100; child : 45.

⛺ ★★★*Genêts d'or* (95 pl), ☎ 66.89.58.67.

Recommended
Farmhouse-inn : *Venejean*, 5 km on N86 and D148, ☎ 66.89.65.16, charcoal-grilled specialities.

Nearby

CONNAUX, ✉ 30330, 9 km S on the N 86.

Restaurant :
● ♦♦ ***Maître Itier***, N 86, ☎ 66.82.00.24, AE Ⓟ ♪ closed Mon and Sun eve, 1-15 Feb, 15-31 Jul. Flawless cooking by a master chef : *saumon frais mariné aux herbes et à la vodka, gratin de langoustes*. Dinner by reservation only, 90-210.

GOUDARGUES, ✉ 30630, 15 km NW on the D 980.

Hotel :
★★ ***Le Commerce***, quai du Canal, ☎ 66.82.20.68, DC Euro Visa, 55 rm Ⓟ ♪ half pens, 180. Rest. ♦ ♪ Terrace service, 75-120.

BEAUCAIRE*

Nîmes 24, Avignon 25, Paris 710 km
pop 13000 ✉ 30300 C4

On the banks of the Rhône, at the foot of an impressive keep, opposite the castle of Tarascon (→ Provence). In the 18thC, this was an important textile town.

Sign-posted tour of the town starting from the castle. ▶ The triangular keep built into the rock and the Romanesque chapel (dismantled in the 17thC) are the only remains of the fortifications; viewpoint★. ▶ **Vignasse Museum :** archaeological and historical collections in the château buildings *(10:15-12 & 2-6)*. ▶ **Rue de la République :** 17th and 18thC mansions. ▶ Place de la République : arcades and French Classical mansions; the ground floors were used as warehouses. ▶ Franciscan church of St. Paul (15thC). ▶ Sunday market in front of the late 17thC **Hôtel de Ville**★ (town hall), copied from the Lunaret mansion in Montpellier (→). ▶ Church of **Notre-Dame des Pommiers**★ (1744) by Franque, the architect of Avignon; the re-utilized Romanesque frieze★ was inspired by St. Gilles (→); inside : 18thC furnishing; pictures by Parrocel.

Nearby

▶ Abbey of **Saint-Roman-l'Aiguille**★ *(5 km NW)* on the cliff above the Rhône; fortified in the 17thC *(1 Jul.-15 Oct., 10-7, closed Thu.; 16 Oct.-Jun., weekends, nat. hols, school hols, 3-6)*. ▶ **Villeneuve-lès-Avignon** (→ Provence). ▶ The Nîmes road runs through the **Costières-du-Gard** vineyards : circuit, follow arrows starting at the Costières house on the Générac road. □

Practical Information

ℹ 6, rue de l'Hôtel-de-Ville, ☎ 66.59.26.57.
SNCF ☎ 66.59.10.27.

Hotels :
★★★ ***Les Vignes Blanches***, (Inter-Hôtel), rte de Nîmes, ☎ 66.59.13.12, Tx 480690, Visa, 62 rm Ⓟ ♿ closed 15 Oct-1 Apr, 250. Rest. ♦♦ ♪ ♿ 80-115.
● ★★ ***Les Doctrinaires*** (C.H.), quai du Gal-de-Gaulle, ☎ 66.59.41.32, Tx 480706, Euro Visa, 34 rm Ⓟ half pens (h.s.), closed Mon eve and Sun eve (l.s.), 15 Jan-4 Feb. 17thC hotel, 540. Rest. ♦♦ ♪ ♿ closed Sun eve. Handsome vaulting overhead, 90-200; child : 45.

⛺ ★★*Le Rhodanien*, (80 pl), ☎ 66.59.25.50.

CÉVENNES Corniche***

B3

From Saint-Jean-du-Gard to Florac *(50 km; see map 2)*

▶ **Saint-Jean-du-Gard** (→ Anduze). ▶ Winding road up through the pine forest, running along the crest of the mountains. ▶ **Saint-Roman-de-Tousque** is the only village between Saint-Jean and Le Pompidou, a stopover on the winter pasture route from Languedoc, and a former post-relay on the Gévaudan road. Two roads lead out of it, one to the pretty village of **Saumane**, in the Borgne Valley, and the other to **Sainte-Croix-Vallée-Française.** ▶ **Le Pompidou,** at the foot of the **Can de l'Hospitalet** mountain (superb view from the top over the Saint-Jean river, the Borgne Valley, and the Gardon de Sainte-Croix river - Vallée Française) : Romanesque chapel of **Saint-Flour-du-Pompidou**★ in the old cemetery; 16thC side chapels; concerts in summer. ▶ The Gardon de Sainte-Croix river starts at the **Faïsses Pass** (alt. 1 018 m); to the N, the Can Noire. ▶ Romanesque church in **Barre-des-Cévennes,** to the E. ▶ The road follows the Tarnon to Florac; schist and limestone houses; hump-backed bridge at the entrance to Florac (→).

▶ The **Vallée Française,** along the Gardon de Sainte-Croix river, is typical of the Cévennes. Silk-worm breeding was once a major industry in the region. Today, young farmers are trying to revive the abandoned hamlets. ▶ **Sainte-Croix-Vallée-Française :** school in the 12th-17thC château; Romanesque church; stone bridge. ▶ **Moissac :** ruins of the château and of the church destroyed during the Camisards war (Protestant resistance to State-imposed religion); Protestant church of **La Boissonnade**★ in an old Romanesque church; pélardon cheese-making. ▶ **Pont-Ravagers :** small local museum. ▶ The 14thC tower of **Saint-Étienne-Vallée-Française** once communicated with the one at Lancize. □

2. Cévennes corniche

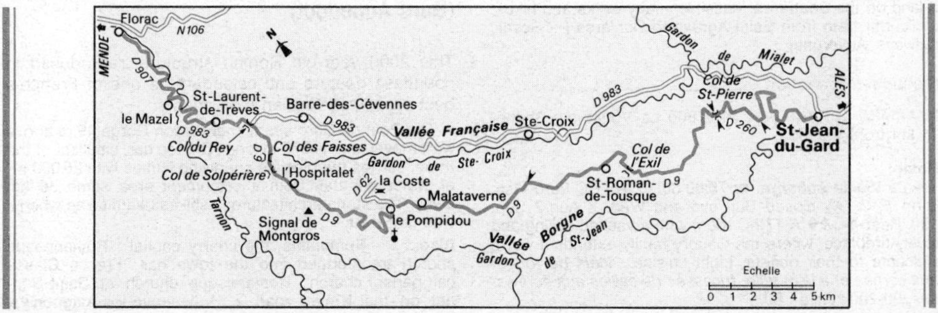

COIRON Plateau

Created by lava from the Massif Central mountains, a volcanic plateau between Privas (→) and Aubenas (→) : black cliffs, low houses of dark stone, stretches of grassland and many streams.

▶ **Balmes de Montbrun★** *(13 km N from Saint-Jean-le-Centenier) :* cliffs riddled with volcanic caves. ▶ The dykes of **Rochemaure★**, by the Rhône, and the giant rocks of **Chenavari★** are the extreme limits of the lava field. ▶ The villages★ are built both of black basalt and white stone : **Saint-Jean-le-Sentenier, Mirabel, Saint-Laurent-sous-Coiron** (panoramas across the Cévennes). □

Le COLLET-DE-DÈZE

Alès 32, Mende 80, Paris 706 km
pop 562 ⊠ 48160   B3

Hotel :
★ **Le Vieux Moulin,** ☎ 66.45.52.62, Visa, 14 rm P closed Wed (l.s.), 15 Dec-15 Jan, 120. Rest. ♦ 90-150.

Recommended
Farmhouse-inn : *Pennens Bas,* St-Frezale-de-Ventalon, CP 48240, 8 km, ☎ 66.45.52.45, reserve, 80-130.

EYRIEUX Corniche and Gorges*

Round trip from La Voulte to Saint-Agrève *(74 km ; half day)*

A scenic road on the high Ardèche plateaus among the chestnut trees and the spruce. At its foot, the vineyard-covered Eyrieux Valley, best seen in spring when the peach and cherry trees are in bloom.

▶ **La Voulte-sur-Rhône,** small industrial town on the Rhône by the reservoir of the Loriol dam : enormous Renaissance château (damaged in 1944) ; in the chapel, pretty ornamentation *(ask at the SI, Jun.-Oct., closed Sun. and nat. hols).* Remains of ramparts around the old town (15th-16thC houses). ▶ **Saint-Symphorien-sous-Chomerac,** wickerwork museum *(1 May-15 Oct., 10-7 ; low season and weekends on request, tel. 75.65.02.07).* ▶ **Saint-Laurent-du-Pape,** surrounded by orchards. ▶ **Fortress of Pierre-Gourde★** : impressive views over the Rhône, the Ventoux, the Vivarais ridges and Mount Mézenc *(11 km N from Saint-Laurent on a winding road).* ▶ The **Eyrieux Corniche★** is breathtaking : many viewpoints over the valley and the mountain ridges. The road climbs towards Le Cheylard, above the gorges. ▶ **Pont-de-Chervil :** Gothic bridge over the river. ▶ **Le Cheylard,** between Gerbier de Jonc and Mount Mézenc. ▶ Beautiful road going up to Saint-Agrève : views down to the Saint-Julien Valley, and up to the Gerbier de Jonc, Mount Mézenc and the Suc de Sara ; hike *(1/2 hr)* up to the feudal ruins of **Rochebronne castle★** (site), among pine trees, juniper and heather. ▶ **Saint-Agrève,** small mountain resort in the high pastureland on the **Boutières** Massif★ ; many walks and hikes. ▶ Tourist **train** from Saint-Agrève to Dunières (→ Scenic railways, Auvergne). □

Practical Information

CHARMES-SUR-RHÔNE, ⊠ 07800 La Voulte-sur-Rhône, 11 km from **Valence.**

Hotel :
★★ **La Vieille Auberge,** ☎ 75.60.80.10, AE DC Euro Visa, 7 rm P ♦ closed Sun eve and Wed, 2 Aug-2 Sep, 130. Rest. ● ♦♦ A 17thC room with a vaulted ceiling and lovely fireplace, where the Gaudry family extends a warm welcome to their guests. Light cuisine : *filets de rouget aux cornes et à la moëlle, fricassée de cailles à écrevisses,* 90-200 ; child : 60.

Le CHEYLARD, ⊠ 07160, 21 km SW of **Lamastre.**

Hotel :
★ **Voyageurs,** 2, rue du Temple, ☎ 75.29.05.88, AE DC Euro Visa, 17 rm, closed Sun eve (l.s.) , Feb school hols, 15 Sep-15 Oct, 55. Rest. ♦ ♦ ♦ 40-75.

⋏ *La Chèze* (120 pl), ☎ 75.29.09.53.

SAINT-AGRÈVE, ⊠ 07320, 25 km N of **Cheylard.**

Hotel :
★ **Le Clair Logis** (L.F.), ☎ 75.30.13.24, Visa, 12 rm P ♦ ♦ closed Wed, Apr, 10 Oct-15 Dec, 85. Rest. ♦ ♦ ♪ 40-70.

La **VOULTE-SUR-RHÔNE**, ⊠ 07800, 19 km S of **Valence.**

Hotel :
★★ **Le Musée** (L.F.), pl. du 4-Septembre, ☎ 75.62.40.19, Euro Visa, 15 rm P ♦ ∰ ♪ closed Feb, 200. Rest. ♦ ♦ ♪ ♦ 70-90 ; child : 35.

FLORAC*

Mende 39, Alès 71, Paris 611 km
pop 2104 ⊠ 48400   A2

A small frontier town between the Huguenot (Protestant) areas and the fortresses of the Papal States ; also a crossroads between the Cévennes mountains and the limestone region of the Tarn Gorges. With a combination of mountain and Mediterranean climates, Florac is ideally situated to be the HQ of the Cévennes Nature Park.

▶ Built at the foot of the **Méjean** (→), by the bed of the Tarnon River. ▶ Protestant church and market-place *(Sat.)* mark the town centre. ▶ Good view from the bridge of the source of the Pêcher river. ▶ **Château,** at the top of the town (keep rebuilt in 17thC) : HQ of the Cévennes Nature Park (introduction to the park ; annual exhibitions ; *8-12:30 & 2-8).* Also see 1583 convent with carved façade.

▶ From Florac, direct ascent of the Aigoual possible via the Tarpoul Gorges★ *(difficult road),* or descent to Saint-Jean-du-Gard (→ Anduze) via the Borgne Valley, Saumane and the narrow Estrêchure defile. □

Practical Information

ℹ av. J.-Monestier, ☎ 66.45.01.14.

Hotel :
★★ **Grand Hôtel du Parc,** 47, av. Jean-Monestier, ☎ 66.45.03.05, 58 rm P ♦ ∰ ♦ ♦ half pens (h.s.), closed Mon, 1 Dec-15 Mar, 165. Rest. ♦ ♦ ♪ Regional cooking, 55-120.

⋏ ★★*La Tière* (35 pl), ☎ 66.45.01.14 ; ★★*Municipal* (130 pl), ☎ 66.45.00.53.

Recommended
Farmhouse-inn : *Blajoux,* Quézac, 12 km NW on N 107 and 107 bis, ☎ 66.48.51.95. Reserve.

Le pont du GARD***
(Gard Aqueduct)

This 2000 year-old Roman structure, reproduced in countless posters and calendars, is one of France's best-preserved Roman monuments.

▶ The Pont du Gard spans the Gardon Gorge 49 m above water-level, and is 275 m long. The top tier, smallest of the three, carries the pipeline supplying Nîmes with $20\,000 \text{ m}^3$ of water per day from a catchment area some 50 km away. The stone architecture is still as beautiful as when it was first built.
Also... ▶ **Remoulins,** the cherry capital : Romanesque church transformed into the town hall ; French Classical parish church ; Romanesque church at Saint-Bonnet on the Nîmes road. ▶ **Villeneuve-lès-Avignon★★**

(→ Provence). ▶ *16 km NE*, the famous **Tavel** vineyards (rosé). □

Practical Information

CASTILLON-DU-GARD ⊠ 30210 Remoulins, 4 km NE of **Remoulins** on the D19, D222.

Hotel :
● ★★★★(L) *Le Vieux Castillon* (R.C.), ☎ 66.37.00.77, Tx 490946, Visa, 35 rm ℙ ⫽ 🏊 🏞 ♫ closed 2 Jan-15 Mar. In the heart of a genuine medieval village, 600. Rest. ♦♦♦ ⫽ ♪ 210-300.

PONT-DU-GARD ⊠ 30210 Remoulins, 3 km W of **Remoulins** on the N 100.
🛈 ☎ 66.37.00.02.

Hotel :
★★★ *Le Vieux Moulin*, left bank, ☎ 66.37.14.35, 17 rm ℙ ⫽ 🏊 🏞 closed 11 Nov-15 Mar. Private beach on the banks of the Gardon, 270. Rest. ♦♦ closed Mon noon and Tue noon, 70-115.

REMOULINS ⊠ 30210, 20 km NE of **Nîmes**.
🚂 ☎ 66.37.13.42.

Hotels :
★★ *Le Colombier* (L.F.), rte du Pont du Gard, ☎ 66.37.05.28, 12 rm ℙ 🏊 🏞 170. Rest. ♦♦ 65-120.
★★ *Moderne*, pl. des Grands-Jours, ☎ 66.37.20.13, AE DC Euro Visa, 25 rm ℙ half pens (h.s.), closed Sat (l.s.), Feb school hols, 17 Oct-15 Nov, 130. Rest. ● ♦ ♪ A treat for you and your budget. Three attractive fixed meals or à la carte, with service included. Inexpensive wines, 45-100.

Restaurant :
♦ *Ourika-Scholmès*, rte d'Avignon, ☎ 90.31.73.43, AE Visa 🖃 closed Mon, Nov-Feb. The setting is from the Arabian nights : a tent fit for a king (in fine weather) and authentic Moroccan food, 120-210.

⚠ ★★★★*La Soubeyranne* (200 pl), ☎ 66.37.03.21 ; ★★*Camp-Plage du Pont-du-Gard* (80 pl), ☎ 66.37.03.00 ; ★★*La Valive*, ☎ 66.22.81.52.

Recommended
Canoes-kayaks rental : *Collias*, ☎ 66.22.84.83.

TAVEL ⊠ 30124, 14 km NW of **Avignon**.
🛈 mairie, ☎ 66.50.04.10.

Hotels :
★★★ *Auberge de Tavel*, voie Romaine, ☎ 66.50.03.41, AE DC Euro Visa, 11 rm ℙ 🖃 closed 1 Feb-15 Mar, 285. Rest. ♦♦ ♪ closed Mon ex Jul-Aug. Agreeable terrace, 120-250 ; child : 50.
★ *Hostellerie du Seigneur*, pl. du Seigneur, ☎ 66.50.04.26, Euro Visa, 7 rm ℙ half pens (h.s.), closed Thu, 15 Dec-15 Jan, 150. Rest. ♦ 60-120.

La GARDE-GUÉRIN***

Alès 60, Mende 65, Paris 606 km
pop 781 ⊠ 48800 Villefort   B2

The village, right on the edge of the Chassezac gap★, is a classified site. It was formerly a fortress guarding the Régordane, the ancient road linking Nîmes to the Auvergne. In the 10thC this was a dangerous route, because the local robber barons habitually captured travelers and held them for ransom. Eventually, the Bishop of Mende took control of the situation by giving these brigands official duties, including the protection of travelers, for which they received a toll. La Garde-Guérin was made their official headquarters.

▶ These robber barons were known as *Seigneurs pariers*, i.e. equals in power and privilege ; there were 27 of them. Today, their tall houses (14thC), the sheepfolds, and the square keep of the castle (11th-13thC) can be seen inside the ramparts. Fine capitals in the Romanesque chapel.

Also... ▶ Attractive Romanesque churches at **Prévenchè-**

res (12th-15thC ; *9 km N*) and **Puylaurent** *(10 km W of Prévenchères)*. □

Mont GERBIER DE JONC**

B1

Volcanic Mont Gerbier de Jonc — similar views to Mont Mézenc (→) — stands like a dome on the Cévennes ridge : one of the sources of the Loire River... But the mountain where France's longest river starts looks bone dry. It is anybody's guess which of the streamlets running out of the surrounding heath is the true source....

▶ From **Estables**, the road follows the ridge-line between the Loire and Rhône, running through forests with views on both sides. It winds round the upper **Bonnefoy Valley** (remains of the Bonnefoy Charter-House), among spruce forests (raspberry and blueberry bushes). Easy climb of the Gerbier de Jonc *(10-20 min)*. ▶ **Isarlès Lake** *(25 km W)* : craterlake surrounded by peaks and forests ; swimming, wind-surfing. ▶ To the S *(15 km, then 1 hr round trip)* : **Ray Pic** waterfalls. ▶ Beautiful route (view★★) from Gerbier de Jonc to Aubenas by **Usclades-et-Rieutord** and through the **Pal Pass**, around the **Suc de Bauzon**★ (lava outcrop). ▶ Small Romanesque church at **Saint-Cirgues-en-Montagne**. *Corniche* above the **Fontolière Gorges**★. ▶ Back in the **Ardèche Valley** (→) at **Pont-de-Labeaume** *(50 km)*. □

Practical Information

USCLADES-ET-RIEUTORD ⊠ 07510 Saint-Cirgues, 15 km S.

Hotel :
Ferme de la Besse, ☎ 75.38.80.64, 18 rm ℙ ⫽ 🏞 ♫ closed 1 Oct-20 Dec, 10 Apr-1 Jun. Typical Ardèche house. Cross-country skiing, 120. Rest. ♦ 70.

Recommended
Farmhouse-inn : *Sablouze*, ☎ 75.38.80.93, lodging and cross-country skiing. Regional fare. By reservation during high season.

GRANGES-LÈS-VALENCE

Privas 39, Saint-Etienne 90, Paris 562 km
pop 9556 ⊠ 07500   C1

Hotel :
★★ *Alpes Cévennes*, 641, av. de la République, ☎ 75.44.61.34, AE DC Visa, 28 rm ℙ ♿ closed 4-21 Aug, 28 Dec-3 Jan, 165.

Restaurant :
♦ *Auberge des Trois Canards*, 565, av. de la République, ☎ 75.44.43.24, AE DC Euro Visa ℙ ♫ ♿ closed Mon and Sun eve, 4-25 Aug, 90-180 ; child : 45.

Nearby
SAINT-PÉRAY, ⊠ 07130, 4 km W on the N 532.

Hotels :
★★★★(L) *Château du Besset* (R.C.), Saint-Romain-de-Lerps, ☎ 75.58.52.22, Tx 345261, Visa, 12 rm ℙ ⫽ 🏊 🏞 ♪ ♿ 🖃 ♫ closed 1 Jan-26 Mar, 1700. Rest. ♦ ⫽ ♿ Spec : *saumon frais aux truffes du Tricastin, canon d'agneau à la crème d'ail douce*, 300.
★★ *Bains* (L.F.), 14, av. du 11-Novembre, ☎ 75.40.30.13, AE DC Euro Visa, 35 rm ℙ 🏞 ♫ closed 20 Dec-30 Jan, 150. Rest. ♦ closed Mon noon, 65-90.

For the translation of a name of a meat, a fish or a vegetable, for the composition of a dish or a sauce, see the Menu Guide in the Practical Holiday Guide; it lists the most common culinary terms.

LANGOGNE

Le Puy 42, Mende 50, Paris 581 km
pop 4025 ⊠ 48300   B2

An austere, mountainous, sheep breeding region.
▶ The town centre is clearly marked by the five round
towers of the ramparts, and the square clock-tower.
▶ Romanesque **church**★ with Gothic façade; Cistercian ground-plan; interesting capitals. ▶ Close
by : late Gothic houses (17thC) and superb covered market★.

Nearby

▶ Beautiful walk in the Mercoire Forest *(S)* to the
Mercoire abbey (13th-17thC). ▶ **Châteauneuf-de-Randon**
(21 km SW), overlooking the valley of Boutaresse, is the
main cattle market in the area; on the Place du Champ de
Foire : statue of Constable Du Guesclin (→ Brittany) who
died during the siege of Châteauneuf in 1380. Remains of
ramparts. ▶ The road to La Bastide-Puylaurent *(20 km S)*
follows the meandering upper **Allier River**★.   □

Practical Information _____

ℹ 15, bd des Capucins, ☎ 66.69.01.38 (h.s.).
SNCF ☎ 66.69.10.80.

Hotels :
★★ **Voyageurs**, 9, av. Joffre, ☎ 66.69.00.56, Visa, 14 rm
ℙ closed Sun (l.s.), 20 Dec-26 Jan, 100. Rest. ♦ ♪ 40-70.
★ **Gaillard**, quartier du pont d'Allier, ☎ 66.69.10.55,
20 rm ℙ closed Sat eve and Sun eve (l.s.) ex hols,
15 Dec-20 Jan, 80. Rest. ♦ ♣ 45-135.

⚑ ★*Municipal* (300 pl), ☎ 66.69.10.33.

Mont LOZÈRE***

                                                   B2

This a bare granite peak projecting above the Cévennes Mountains, overlooking extensive peat-bogs and
closely-cropped turf strewn with granite rocks.

▶ The Saint-John's Hospitallers (or Knights of Malta)
owned thousands of acres on the Lozère; their **commandery** (at the hamlet of **l'Hôpital,** near Pont-de-Montvert)
is on the territory of the **Ecomusée de Lozère**★, an outdoor museum which illustrates the agro-pastoral past of
the mountain. Two old farms are examples of traditional
architecture : Mas Camargues and Mas Troubat. ▶ One
of the highest points (alt. 1 680 m) is **Cassini Peak**, near
the source of the Tarn river★ : in fine weather, the
view stretches from the volcanic mountains of southern
Auvergne (Chaîne des Puys) to the Alps and Mount Ventoux, and from the Languedoc plain to Canigou.

Trip around Mont Lozère *(160 km ; full day ; see map 3)*

▶ **Pont-de-Montvert**, on the upper reaches of the Tarn
River, was an important Calvinist centre; 17thC bridge;
clock tower and old houses; **Ecomusée information centre.** ▶ From Pont-de-Montvert to **Le Bleymard**, via the
Finiels Pass★ (alt. 1 541 m) : wind-swept rocky pasture
land and woods. ▶ **Croix de Berthel Pass.** ▶ Beautiful
views over the Cévennes along the ridge road★ (route
des Crêtes) leading to Alès via **Portes**★ (14th-17thC château). ▶ **Vialas** is almost Mediterranean; one of the few
remaining Protestant churches (17thC); former lead mine.
▶ **Génolhac**, on the Régordane road (→ La Garde-Guérin) : 17thC houses; church with 11thC tower; Cévennes
Nature Park information centre. ▶ From Génolhac to Villefort the road climbs 1 000 m through chestnut, oak and
beech woods, to emerge among upland pastures and pine
trees. ▶ **Villefort** was a fortified town : 14th and 16thC
houses; Nature Park centre. ▶ **Reservoir** on the Altier
River outside town; **château de Castanet** (1578; *exhibitions).* The road from Villefort to Mende along the valleys
of the Altier and Lot Rivers replaces the mule-track along
the passes (GR68). ▶ **Altier :** 17thC church, Romanesque
nave; castle ruins; views★. ▶ On the opposite bank, **château du Champ**, rebuilt during the Romantic period. ▶ **La
Prade** fortified farm. ▶ **Les Tribes Pass** (alt. 1 131 m), highest point on the Altier; separating the Altier and the Lot
rivers running respectively to the Mediterranean and the
Atlantic. ▶ **Le Bleymard** has an Auvergne look. ▶ **Saint-
Jean-du-Bleymard** : former Benedictine priory; Romanesque church and fortified 13thC farm. ▶ **Château du
Tournel** (12thC). ▶ **Saint-Julien-du-Tournel**★ : Romanesque church★. ▶ **Bagnols-les-Bains** : miniature spa;

3. Mont Lozère

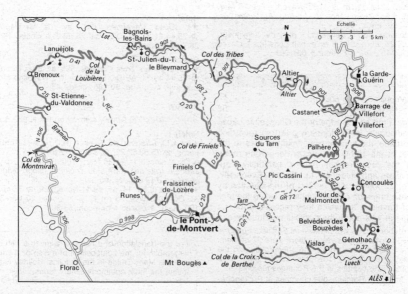

18th-19thC façade on the spa buildings. ▶ Return to Mende (→) along the river, or detour to **Lanuéjols** : Gallo-Roman mines; 3rdC funeral monument★; Auvergnat Romanesque church★; 16thC fountain. ▶ **Balsièges,** at the foot of the Lion rock, typical Lot village with fish-scale tiling. ▶ **Montmirat Pass,** between the Lot and Tarn valleys : view over the Cévennes and the Aigoual. ▶ Serpentine road; excellent view over **Florac** (→). Beautiful route along the Tarn, to Pont-de-Montvert.   □

Practical Information _____

BAGNOLS-LES-BAINS, ⊠ 48190, 21 km E of **Mende.**
⌇ (1 May-31 Oct), ☎ 66.47.60.02.
ⓘ ☎ 66.47.64.79.

Hotel :
● ★★ *Commerce*, 2, av. de la Gare, ☎ 66.47.60.07, Euro Visa, 28 rm ℗ ▥ ⌖ ♨ ⌀ closed Sun eve , Mon (l.s.), Nov-Mar, 150. Rest. ♦ ⌇ ♪ ⌀ Home-cured pork, 50-200.

⚠ ★★*Municipal* (100 pl), ☎ 66.47.64.79.

GÉNOLHAC, ⊠ 30450, 30 km N of **Alès.**
ⓘ Mairie, ☎ 66.61.10.55.
SNCF ☎ 66.61.10.35.

Hotel :
★ *Mont Lozère*, 13, av. de la Libération, ☎ 66.61.10.72, AE Visa, 15 rm ℗ ⌇ ⌀ half pens (h.s.), closed Tue eve, 1 Nov-1 Dec, 280. Rest. ♦ ⌇ ⌀ 55-130♦ ⌇ ⌀ 55-130.

VIALAS, ⊠ 48220 Le Pont-de-Montvert, 8 km W of **Génolhac.**
ⓘ mairie, ☎ 66.41.00.05.

Hotel :
★★ *Chantoiseau*, rte du Haut, ☎ 66.41.00.02, AE DC Euro Visa, 15 rm ⌇ ▥ ⌖ ⌀ half pens (h.s.), closed Tue eve and Wed, 4 Jan-1 Feb, 20 Nov-20 Dec, 340. Rest. ● ♦♦♦ ⌇ ♪ ⌀ In a lovely 17thC Cévennes residence works a chef-cum-sommelier-cum-poet! Only local produce used. Gourmet specialities. Cooking lessons during high season. Coal and home-canned foods sold, 80-180; child : 55.

VILLEFORT, ⊠ 48800, 59 km E of **Mende.**
ⓘ rue de l'Eglise, ☎ 66.46.80.26.   ♥
SNCF ☎ 66.46.80.03.

Hotels :
★★ *Balme* (L.F.), pl. du Portalet, ☎ 66.46.80.14, AE DC Euro Visa, 23 rm ℗ half pens (h.s.), closed Sun eve and Mon (l.s.), 1-5 Oct, 5 Nov-31 Jan, 330. Rest. ● ♦♦ Very good, bountiful, inexpensive food. Michel and Micheline go all out to please. *Terrine d'aubergines au coulis de basilic, pied de veau farci aux girolles*, 60-125; child : 35.
★ *Régordane*, La Garde-Guérin, ☎ 66.46.82.88, Visa, 16 rm ℗ ▥ ⌖ closed Oct-Apr ex Easter school hols, 110. Rest. ♦ ♪ A 16thC manor in the heart of an historical village, 70-100.

⚠ ★★*Le Petit Paradis* (35 pl), ☎ 66.46.80.26.

The MARGERIDE Region*

A2

This abandoned and unpopulated region of dark pine forests, granite and porphyry, heather and pasture-land, is made for lovers of open spaces and unspoilt nature.

▶ The mountain was once divided into vast land-holdings but the forests and pasture-land were too heavily taxed for farmers to exploit satisfactorily : this explains the low population and the scarcity of villages. Ironically, the southern plateau was known as the **Plateau du Palais du Roi★** (plateau of the King's Palace).   □

On the maps, a town's name underlined <u>Saulieu</u> means that the locality possesses at least one recommended establishment (blue or red point).

Practical Information _____
Le MALZIEU-VILLE, ⊠ 48140.

Recommended
Farmhouse-inn : *Le bon accueil*, Paulhac-en-Margeride, ☎ 66.31.73.46.

MARVEJOLS*

Mende 29, Rodez 85, Paris 558 km
pop 6000 ⊠ 48100   A2
Three fortified gates still guard this town, rebuilt by Henri IV after the destruction of the Wars of Religion (16thC; statue). 17thC houses recall the prosperous merchants who sold the wool and cloth produced by the shepherd families of the Margeride and the Gévaudan.

Nearby

▶ Two Romanesque churches : **Chirac** *(5.5 km S)* and former Benedictine abbey of **Monastier** in the Colagne Valley★ *(6 km S)*. ▶ **Gévaudan Park** *(10 km N)* at Sainte-Lucie : European animals, especially wolves *(Easter-Oct., 10-6).* ▶ Near **Moulinet Lake★** *(17 km NW)*, **château de La Baume★** has surprisingly luxurious ornamentation by Montpellier artists (early 18thC; *10-12 & 2-6, 15 Jun.-15 Sep.; 2-5 rest of year, closed Tue.*).   □

Practical Information _____

ⓘ av. de Brazza, ☎ 66.32.02.14 (h.s.).

Hotel :
★★ *Gare et Rochers*, pl. de la Gare, ☎ 66.32.10.58, AE DC Euro Visa, 30 rm ℗ ⌇ ▥ ⌖ ♿ closed 15 Jan-15 Feb, 140. Rest. ♦ ⌇ ♿ closed Sat noon, 45-120; child : 25.

Restaurant :
● ♦♦ *Viz Club*, rte du Nord, ☎ 66.32.17.69, AE DC Visa ⌇ ▥ ♿ closed 16 Nov-1 Feb. Louis-XIII dining room. Spec : *filets de truite en chemise verte, suprême de pintade farcie au fromage de chèvre cuite en papillote*, 50-120.

Causse MÉJEAN**

A3

The highest of the Grands Causses (plateaus); only 13 % is cultivated, 10 % is forest land, and the remainder is bare : sheep grazing to the E, and wood to the W : follow the grazing trails using the brochure provided by the Méjean Association (in local *mairies*) to discover the beauty of the *causse*, and understand the shepherds' life and the local stone architecture. Here and there, dolmens and carved stone crosses; birds of prey wheel in the sky. Good view over the Park from the **Can de l'Hospitalet★** mountain.

▶ The **Armand aven★★** is the most spectacular site, an enormous underground cavern : rock formations include a "forest" of 400 stalagmites *(Easter-Palm Sunday).* ▶ Villages on the *causse :* **Hyelzas** (rural museum), **La Parade** (13 thC church, old mill), **Drigas, Hures** (Romanesque churches★). Views over the gorges from **Hourtous Rock** (by the Tarn) and **Saint-Pierre-des-Tripiers** (on the Jonte).   □

MENDE*

Le Puy 92, Rodez 108, Paris 573 km
pop 12100 ⊠ 48000   A2
Mende is very much a country town : pasture-land is close by, and at this stage the Lot River is just a little trout stream with cows grazing on its banks. You can smell the mountain air and the pine forest.

▶ Capital of the Lozère Department, a tiny cathedral town : narrow streets with old corbelled houses, stone doorways with wooden doors, elaborate staircases, 15th and 16thC oriel windows on the façades ; pretty fountains. ▶ **Cathedral of St. Pierre**★★, a Catholic watchtower over the nearby Protestant areas : begun in the 15thC by Pope Urban V (native of the region), it took nearly five centuries to build : the two great Flamboyant doorways were installed at the beginning of the 20thC. View over the old town★ from the two 16thC towers ; inside : 17thC stalls, woodwork and altars, organ, tapestries and parts of choir-screen. ▶ Ignon-Fabre museum : regional folk art and archaeology *(10-12 & 2-5, closed Sun.)*. ▶ In the former Carmelite convent (Rue de l'Ange), exhibition and sale of Lozère craftwork. ▶ Rue Notre-Dame : 13thC former synagogue ; see courtyard. ▶ **Tour des Pénitents** (tower) : remains of 12thC rampart, 17thC chapel. ▶ 16thC **bridge**★ over the Lot.   □

Practical Information _____

ℹ 16, bd du Soubeyran, ☎ 66.65.02.69.
✈ *Brenoux*, 4 km SE, ☎ 66.65.14.61.
SNCF ☎ 66.65.00.39/66.65.15.37.

Hotels :
● ★★★ *Le Lion d'Or*, (Mapotel), 12-14, bd Britexte, ☎ 66.49.16.46, Tx 480302, AE DC Euro Visa, 40 rm 🅿 ₠ 🏠 🗐 ♬ ♿ 🖼 half pens (h.s.), closed 15 Nov-15 Mar, 535. Rest. ♦ ₠ ♿ 🕸 80-160.
● ★★ *Urbain V*, 9, bd Th.-Roussel, ☎ 66.49.14.49, 59 rm 🅿 closed 15 Dec-7 Jan, 220. Rest. ♦ ♪ 🕸 closed Sun. Self-service, 40-65.
★★ *France* (L.F.), 9, bd L.-Arnault, ☎ 66.65.00.04, Visa, 27 rm 🅿 ♿ closed 15 Dec-31 Jan, 160. Rest. ● ♦♦ closed Mon and Sun eve (l.s.). Quality food, 50-120.

⚠ ★★*Sirvens* (300 pl), ☎ 66.65.16.93 ; *Tivoli* (100 pl), ☎ 66.65.00.38.

Recommended
Farmhouse-inn : at Saint-Étienne-du-Valdonnez, *La Fage*, ☎ 66.47.05.36.

NÎMES***

Avignon 43, Montpellier 51, Paris 712 km
pop 140000 ⊠ 30000   C4

For the northerner, Nîmes is the archetypal Southern town : sun, *pastis* (anis-flavoured liquor), markets under the plane trees, pines and cypresses, fountains and squares where venerable Romans nod to you graciously. The monuments are beautiful and photogenic ; in the evening you might imagine yourself in Italy or Spain.

▶ *Guided tours with the CNMHS (National Monuments Board ; in summer ; comprehensive ticket for the Roman monuments : 9-12 & 2-5 or 7 according to season.*

Nîmes was a major city under the Romans, at the cross-roads of the Domitian Way between Arles and Narbonne and the Régordane Way to the mountains. The Emper-or Augustus made Nîmes a showplace of the Roman Empire. Later, the city was to be the scene of bitter struggles between the Protestant and Republican mer-chants and the Royalist Catholic working classes during the Revolution. Since the Protestants were forbidden to hold public office, they channeled their energies into trade, and quickly dominated the wool and silk industry in the Cévennes. Nîmes is one of the three or four towns which claim to have supplied Levi Strauss with the cloth to make his first blue jeans (denim : *de Nîmes*).

▶ **Esplanade** (C2), the main thoroughfare of the town. Two steps away is the **Roman arena**★★ (corridas), slight-ly smaller than the arena at Arles : four entrances, two superimposed arcaded stories of 60 arches, and 24 000 seats arranged in thirty-four tiers ; from the Middle Ages to the 18thC it was developed into housing for some 2 000 people. ▶ 500 m away is the **Maison Carrée**★★ (Square

House, B2), a Roman temple to the grandsons of the Emperor Augustus which may have formed part of the forum. Carved entablature supported by columns spaced at varying intervals. Inside : **antiquities museum**★ of dis-coveries from the same period as the temple : mosaics, marble statue of Apollo★, bronze head of Apollo★, eagle frieze in Augustan Empire style, a Venus reassembled from 103 fragments. ▶ Go down the residential **Quai de la Fontaine**★ along the canal to the delightful **Fountain Gardens**★★ (Jardins de la Fontaine ; A1-2) : a masterpiece of 18thC garden planning, around the ruins of the first Roman buildings, including the **Temple of Diana**★ (2ndC) and the Nemausus spring. ▶ Through the alleys of cedar and pine walk up to the **Magne Tower**★, remains of the Roman ramparts (A1 ; panorama★ over the town, the Cévennes, and Ventoux as far as the Pyrénées). ▶ Flea-market *(Sun.)* and Monday market under the nettle trees of Bd. Gambetta (B1). ▶ Bd Amiral-Courbet (C2), the main avenue in Nîmes with shops, cafés and inexpensive res-taurants ; on the right hand side : **Porte Auguste**, city gate built in 16BC as part of the Roman ramparts ; Protestant church (former Dominican church ; 17thC) ; **archaeologi-cal museum**★ in the former church of the Jesuit college (17thC chapel) : ancient civilizations from the early Iron Age to the end of the Roman occupation ; the neces-sary background for understanding the Nîmes of Clas-sical times ; Grésan warrior★, frieze from Nagès★, mosaic of Bellepheron killing the Chimaera ; Natural History Museum in same building *(10-12 & 2-5, Oct.-Palm Sun. ; 3-7 in summer, closed Sun. am).* ▶ **Place aux Herbes** (C2) : Romanesque house ; cathedral and former bishop's palace. The **cathedral of St. Castor**★ (C2) was rebuilt in the 19thC in Romano-Byzantine style. 11thC façade : upper frieze★ of the Creation (Romanesque and 17thC). The former bishop's palace★ (17thC) houses the Music Conservatory and the **Museum of Old Nîmes** *(same hours as above)* : folk art including local forms of bull-fighting ; beautiful silk shawls★ ; traditional furniture★ ; cera-mics. ▶ Wander through the narrow streets of **medie-val Nîmes**, around the cathedral : upper class houses (16th-18thC), fashionable shops (pedestrian zone).

Also... ▶ **Fine Arts Museum**★ Rue Cité-Foulc (C3 ; *9-12 & 2-6 ; closed Tue. Oct.-May and Sun. am)* : temporary exhi-bitions of various painters. ▶ Extraordinary **aqueduct**★★ built by the Romans ca. 19BC to bring water to the city, snaking through 50 km of rugged countryside from the Eure springs near Uzès (→) : a masterpiece of Roman civil engineering like the Pont du Gard *(guided tours, enq. at SI).*

Nearby

▶ **Gardon Gorges**★, between **Dions** and the **Gard aque-duct** (→). The river Gard runs through a narrow canyon, high cliffs overlooked by the GR6 ; many caves. ▶ View★ over the gorges from the Uzès road by **Saint-Nicolas bridge**★ (13thC) and the priory of **Saint-Nicolas-de-Cam-pagnac**★ (half-farm, half-fortress ; 12th-13thC).   □

Practical Information _____

NÎMES
ℹ 6, rue Auguste (B1-2), ☎ 66.67.29.11.
✈ *Nîmes-Garons*, 6 km S, ☎ 66.70.06.88. Air France office, Nîmes-Garons airport, ☎ 66.70.02.52.
SNCF (C3), ☎ 66.23.50.50.
Car Rental : *Avis*, train station ; 1 bis, rue de la Républi-que (B3-4), ☎ 66.21.00.29 ; Airport ; 1800, av. Mal-Juin, ☎ 66.29.05.33.

Hotels :
★★★ *Cheval Blanc*, 1, pl. des Arènes (C3), ☎ 66.67.20.03, AE DC Euro Visa, 47 rm ♪ 350. Rest. ♦♦ 120-210.
★★★ *Imperator* (Concorde), quai de la Fontaine (A1-2), ☎ 66.21.90.30, Tx 490635, AE DC Euro Visa, 62 rm 🅿 ₠ 🖼 ♪ 🐎 closed Feb, 310. Rest. ♦♦ *L'Enclos de la Fon-taine* ♪ ♿ 🕸 closed Sat noon. The town's finest hotel is in need of a facelift. Lovely shaded terrace. Three fixed-price meals available : 'English', businessman's special and gourmet sampler, 130-200.

NÎMES

0   100   200 m

★★★ *Tuileries*, 22, rue Roussy (C2), ☎ 66.21.31.15, AE DC Euro Visa, 11 rm [P] ▦ ⚲ ♪ ♨ ♿ 290.

★★ *Le Louvre*, 2, sq. de la Couronne (C2), ☎ 66.67.22.75, Tx 480218, AE DC Euro Visa, 33 rm [P] ≼ ▦ ⚲ ♨ ♿ A renovated town house, 150. Rest. ♦ ≼ ♿ 85-180.

Restaurants :

● ♦♦ *Le Magister*, 5, rue Nationale (B-C1), ☎ 66.76.11.00, AE DC Visa ♪ closed Sun, 16 Feb-1 Mar, 2-16 Aug. Martial Hocquart loves light and tasty recipes : *brandade, gardianne sous la cendre*, 115-200 ; child : 60.

♦♦ *Au Cocotier*, 15, rue P.-Semard (C1), ☎ 66.67.83.29, Euro Visa ♪ closed Sun Aug. Exotic specialties from Madagascar, the Reunion and Seychelles islands. A free glass of punch for Hachette guide readers, 95-110.

♦ *Le Jardin d'Hadrien*, 11, rue Enclos Rey, ☎ 66.21.86.65, AE DC Euro Visa ▦ ⚲ closed Sat noon and Sun, 130-175.

♦ *Le Lisita*, 2, bd des Arènes (B2), ☎ 66.67.29.15, Visa ≼ closed Sat, Sun eve and Aug, 80-160.

♦ *Les Jardins du Couvent*, 21, rue du Grand-Couvent (B2), ☎ 66.67.54.08, AE DC Euro Visa ▦ ♪ ♿ closed Mon and Sun eve. Spec : *filet de daurade en gratin, ris de veau bonne femme, pellardon grillé*, 80-100 ; child : 45.

♦ *Lou Mas*, 5, rue de Sauve (A2), ☎ 66.23.24.71 ♪ ♿ ❀ closed Sun, 1-15 Aug. Enjoyable food served near a splashing fountain, 80-150.

The arrow (→) is a reference to another entry.

△ ★★★*Domaine de la Bastide* (230 pl), ☎ 66.38.09.21.

Recommended

Market : *flowers and bric à brac*, bd J.-Jaurès, Mon ; *flea market*, around the church of St-Baudille, Sun am.

Nightclubs : *Le Liberty*, bd Amiral-Courbet, ☎ 66.21.02.15 ; *Le Marinella*, 150, rte de Sauve, ☎ 66.64.78.67, closed Mon ; *La Tosca*, 3, rue Corneille, ☎ 66.21.80.59.

♥ *bodega : Emilio Munoz*, 6, rue Thoumayne. 'The poet is never mistaken'. The Vidals respect the wisdom of that adage and welcome the cream of Nîmes ; Sevillan music and dance ; *La pena to Mas Campuzano*, 38, rue de la Porte France, ☎ 66.26.16.95. Meeting place of the "Viva el Toro" club. Aficionados, sangria and tapas. Crowded and jolly, olé ! 50F ; at Caladon, pastry, ice cream, chocolates : *G. Courtois*, 8, pl. du Marché, ☎ 66.67.20.00.

Nearby

GARONS, ✉ 30128, 12 km SE on the N113-D442.

Hotel :

★★★★ *Alexandre*, 1, rue de l'Aéroport, ☎ 66.70.08.99, Visa, 4 rm [P] ≼ ▦ ⚲ ♪ ❀ closed Sun eve and Mon, 2-17 Jan, 17-31 Aug, 250. Rest. ● ♦♦ ♪ ❀ The well-known Alexandre has left, but the tradition continues, 185-210 ; child : 60.

SAINT-COME, ⊠ 30870, 12 km W.

Restaurant :
● ◆◆ *La Vaunage*, ☎ 66.81.33.29 ⨂ closed Mon and Tue, 1-18 Mar, 1-18 Sep. An interesting little spot not yet known to the masses : *loup aux senteurs des garrigues, gratin de framboises*, 130-170.

Causse NOIR

A3

Surrounded by the rivers Tarn, Jonte and Dourbie, this is the smallest of the Grands Causses (plateaus).

▶ W : dark forests (hence the name; *noir* = black), hills, sinkholes and choked *avens* (caves); NW : landscapes like ruined towns around Montpellier-le-Vieux; E : sheepfolds and flocks.   ▫

PRIVAS

Montélimar 33, Le Puy 118, Paris 603 km
pop 10638 ⊠ 07000   C1-2

The capital of the Ardèche was an important Protestant centre, destroyed by royal troops in 1629. Only three years later it was rebuilt.

▶ Close to Mont Toulon, above the Ouvèze River (17thC stone bridge), and facing the Coiron plateau. ▶ **Agricultural Museum of the Verdus★** *(5 km S)* in a country inn *(Mr. Clair, tel. : 75.64.27.40, daily in summer)*. ▶ Pretty village at **Coux** *(3 km E)*; **Jaubernie Caves** : shelter for Protestants in the 16th-17thC *(3.5 km E, then 30 min on foot)*.

Also... ▶ **Pranles** *(15 km N)* : Museum of Protestant Vivarais in the house of Pierre and Marie Durand, 17thC martyrs *(10-12 & 2:30-6:30, 15 Jun.-15 Sep.; Palm Sun. - 1 Nov., weekends only 10-12 & 2-6)*; interesting example of a Cévennes farm.

From Privas to Vernoux-en-Vivarais via the Dunière Gorges *(40 km; approx. 3 hr)*

Spectacular winding mountain road and *corniche* above the valleys; nice views of terraced hillsides and isolated hamlets. ▶ **Privas.** ▶ Between **Moulin-à-Vent** and **Olllières-sur-Eyrieux** : road through chestnut trees. ▶ Turn right on the La Voulte road, to **Dunière** at the entrance to the **gorges**; up to the ruins of the **château de Tourette★**, impressive keep in untouched setting. ▶ **Vernoux-en-Vivarais.**

▶ From Privas to Aubenas via the **Escrinet Pass★** (alt. 788 m) : beautiful road; mountain panoramas.

▶ From Privas to Gerbier-de-Jonc on the **Quatre Vios** (Four Winds) **Pass** road★★ : one of the most spectacular in Upper Vivarais.   ▫

Practical Information ───────────────

PRIVAS
ℹ️ 1, av. Chomérac, ☎ 75.64.33.35.
SNCF ☎ 75.64.11.87 (am only).

Hotel :
★★★ *Chaumette*, av. Vanel, ☎ 75.64.30.66, AE DC Euro Visa, 36 rm ℗ ⅏ ᨏ 260. Rest. ◆ 60-100.

⚠️ ★★*d'Ouvèze* (170 pl), ☎ 75.64.05.80.

Nearby

OLLIÈRES-SUR-EYRIEUX, ⊠ 07360, 19 km N.

Hotel :
★★ *Auberge de la Vallée* (L.F.), Bas Pranles, ☎ 75.66.20.32, Euro Visa, 8 rm ℗ ⅏ ⨂ closed Sun eve and Mon (l.s.), 1 Feb-15 Mar, 15-21 Sep, 150. Rest. ◆ ♪ 70-120.

The RHÔNE Corniche★★

C1

From Tournon to Saint-Péray *(26 km)*

Between Tournon (→) and Valence (→ Dauphiné), there is a series of beautiful landscapes as the valley narrows; the Rhône *corniche* (cliff road) gives excellent views over the river, the orchards in the plain, and the Vercors mountains on the horizon.

▶ **Tournon.** ▶ Steep climb along the cliff edge : Doux Gorges to the W. ▶ **Saint-Romain-de-Lerps** : two orientation tables pin-point 13 departments. Above **Saint-Péray** is the eagle's nest castle of **Crussol★**, 200 m above the plain *(one hour round trip : narrow road, then path)* : impressive 12thC ruins. Below, on the riverbank, 17thC **château de Châteaubourg.**   ▫

Practical Information ───────────────

SAINT-ROMAIN-DE-LERPS, ⊠ 07130, 28 km SW of **Tournon.**

Hotel :
★★★★(L) *Le Château de Bessef* (R.C.), ☎ 75.58.52.22, 10 rm ℗ ⅏ ᨏ ⊡ ♪ closed 26 Oct-28 Mar. A 15thC château, 1800. Rest. ◆◆◆ ♪ Two handsome dining rooms and cooking that does them proud. Spec : *salade ardéchoise aux langoustines, tartare de daurade rose au caviar*, 250-330.

The RHÔNE Valley★★

C2

From La Voulte to Pont-Saint-Esprit *(65 km; half day)*

This was one of the great North-South highways of European civilization. Every stopover became a town, and in the wake of the merchants came ideas, art, new customs... and wars. The hill-top villages with their towers and crenellations recall old rivalries. Each rock carries a fortress, as in the Rhine Valley. Over the ages, the river boatmen were the mainspring of valley life — until the arrival of the railway and the construction of the great dams which tamed the river. Today, the Rhône Valley is an industrial and commercial centre with factories, warehouses, refineries and nuclear power stations. Fortunately, the orchards and vineyards are only a few miles away.

▶ **La-Voulte-sur-Rhône** (→ Eyrieux). ▶ **Baix**, downstream from the Loriol dam. ▶ **Cruas★** : on the banks of the river canal : remarkable Romanesque **abbey church★** (Lombard influence; 11thC mosaic; one pre-Romanesque crypt with fine capitals★, one Gothic crypt); 12th-16thC fortified chapel and fortress built by the monks; access through medieval streets. ▶ **Meysse** : medieval town centre. ▶ **Mélas** : Romanesque chapel. ▶ **Rochemaure** : feudal castle★ (13th-16thC); **Pic de Chenavari** : volcanic dyke on a basalt base★ (views★ from the top, *45 min round trip*). ▶ **Viviers★** (pop. 3290), former episcopal city on a rock above the river : traditionally, the *Midi* (the South of France) begins here. The rounded roof-tiles, steeply sloping streets and balconies of wrought iron give the place a Provençal look. At the entrance to the lower town, the Bishop's palace, the Hôtel de Roqueplane and the Dominican chapel of Notre-Dame du Rhône form a charming 18thC group; the **old town★★** takes you straight back to the Middle Ages. The Place de l'Ormeau★ is overlooked by the superb cathedral apse★★ (12thC, rebuilt 17th-18thC); the tower in front seems to be a fortified gateway from an earlier period; remarkable **Renaissance house** (Maison des Chevaliers) on the Place de la République; wrought-iron balconies in the Grand'Rue; view of the Rhône and the Alps from the esplanade. ▶ Beyond Viviers, the Rhône runs through the **Donzère defile★**. Viewpoint above the **Donzère-Mondragon** complex (canal, electricity generating station, Pierrelatte nuclear power station). ▶ **Saint-Baume Gorges★** to the W : villages of **Saint-Montant★** and **Larnas**, each with a typical Vivarais Romanesque church. ▶ **Bourg-Saint-Andéol** (pop. 7 665), by the banks of the Rhône : view from the quays, plane trees, church towers and ramparts of the episcopal palace. **Church of St. Andéol** (12thC chevet★) partially rebuilt in 18thC; 2ndC Gallo-Roman sarcophagus, said to be that of St. Andéol; Adoration of the Magi (primitive, Portuguese); French Classical mansions; convents; Renaissance loggia of the **Hôtel Nicolaï**. 10 min SW, **Tournes fountain**, with Gallo-Roman bas-relief dedicated to Mithras. ▶ **Pont-Saint-Esprit★** (pop. 8 135) grew around a **bridge★** (*pont :* bridge) dedicated to the Holy Spirit, one of four such on the Rhône. On the terrace★ above the river are three churches : St. Saturnin (15thC), the Baroque chapel of the Penitents★ (17thC) and the former church of St. Pierre, in French Classical style (17thC); monumental staircase leading to the quay. Renaissance house at the foot of the bridge. Remains of Vauban's citadel and the former collegiate church (15thC). P. Raymond Museum (archaeology and local traditions; *10-12 & 2-6; closed Tue.*)

Also... ▶ The **Charterhouse of Valbonne★** *(10 km W)* : set in a forest of oak and beech, roofed with varnished tiles★, a perfect example of French Classical monastic architecture; built on a medieval ground-plan; superb Baroque church. And of course, the gorges of the Ardèche (→) and the Cèze (→). □

Practical Information ───────────────

BAIX, ⊠ 07210 Chomérac, 11 km E of **Chomérac**.

Hotel :
● ★★★★(L) *La Cardinale* (R.C.), ☎ 75.85.80.40, Tx 346143, AE DC Visa, 15 rm Ⓟ ≮ ▩ ⌀ ▣ closed Wed, Thu lunch (Nov-Mar), 3 Jan-20 Feb. Former manor-house on the Rhône, 750. Rest. ◆◆ ⊗ 130-205.

BOURG-SAINT-ANDÉOL, ⊠ 07700, 14 km S of **Viviers**.
ⓘ pl. Champs-de-Mars, ☎ 75.54.54.20.
SNCF ☎ 75.04.50.70.

Hotels :
★★ *Moderne*, pl. Champs-de-Mars, ☎ 75.54.50.12, AE Euro, 21 rm ▩ closed 30 Nov-1 Mar, 170. Rest. ◆ ⊗ closed Sat noon and Sun eve (l.s.), 55-110.
★★ *Prieuré*, quai Madier-de-Montjau, ☎ 75.54.50.97, 10 rm Ⓟ Former priory, 145.

⚐ ★★★*Camp du Lion* (140 pl), ☎ 75.54.53.20.

PONT-SAINT-ESPRIT, ⊠ 30130, 15 km S of **Bourg-Saint-Andéol**.
ⓘ la Citadelle, ☎ 66.39.13.25.
SNCF ☎ 66.39.09.87.

Hotel :
★★ *Le Vieux Moulin* (L.F.), RN 86, Saint-Alexandre, ☎ 66.39.18.44, Euro Visa, 9 rm Ⓟ ▩ 130. Rest. ◆ 50-100.

Recommended
Chambres d'hôtes : at Saint-Paulet-de-Caisson, 5 km, *La Cantarelle*, ☎ 66.39.17.67.

VIVIERS, ⊠ 07220, 11 km S of **Montélimar**.
ⓘ ☎ 75.52.77.00.

Hotels :
★★ *Le Provence*, pl. de la Mairie, ☎ 75.52.60.45, AE Visa, 10 rm Ⓟ ≮ ♪ closed Sun eve and Mon, 3 Jan-4 Feb. Rest. ◆ ≮ ♪ ⊗ 85-170.
★ *Relais du Vivarais*, ☎ 75.52.60.41, 10 rm Ⓟ ≮ ▩ ⌀ closed 20 Dec-20 Jan, 90. Rest. ◆ ≮ & 70-110.

⚐ ★★★★*Rochecondrie* (80 pl), ☎ 75.52.74.66; ★★*Roqueplane* (70 pl), ☎ 75.52.64.43.

┌─────────────────────────────────────┐
│ Be advised that hotels and restaurants in this Guide │
│ have perhaps changed addresses; prices indicated │
│ are also subject to modifications. │
└─────────────────────────────────────┘

SAINT-GILLES-DU-GARD*

Nîmes 19, Montpellier 57, Paris 732 km
pop 10850 ⊠ 30800   C4

The modern town is a crossroads, but the old Saint-Gilles on the hillside has kept its character.

▶ The 12thC abbey church of St. Gilles was damaged during the Wars of Religion (16thC); after the Revolution, only the triple **doorway★★** and magnificent W façade were left. The general restoration carried out in the 17thC was clumsy, but the façade is a marvel, inspired by Classical architecture and, in turn, frequently copied in Languedoc and Provence. The theme illustrated is the Passion of Christ. ▶ The triple-vaulted **crypt** houses the tomb of St. Gilles. ▶ The **spiral staircase** of the N bell tower was an obligatory part of the curriculum for apprentice stonemasons. ▶ Covered market like the old Baltard markets of 19thC Paris. ▶ Small museum in much-restored Romanesque house *(Mon., Wed., Fri., 9-12 & 2-7).* □

Practical Information ───────────────

ⓘ Maison Romane, ☎ 66.87.33.75 (h.s.).
SNCF ☎ 66.87.32.83.

Hotels :
★★ *Le Cours*, 10, av. F.-Griffeuille, ☎ 66.87.31.93, AE DC Euro Visa, 26 rm Ⓟ ▩ ⌀ half pens (h.s.), closed 20 Dec-1 Feb, 240. Rest. ◆ Spec : *rouille d'encornets provençale, filet de dorade à la crème, gardiane de bœuf*, 40-80.
★ *Le Globe*, pl. Gambetta, ☎ 66.87.30.41, Visa, 23 rm, closed 15 Nov-14 Dec, 100. Rest. ◆ 60-100.

Restaurant :
◆◆ *La Rascasse*, 16, av. F.-Griffeuille, ☎ 66.87.42.96 ♪ & 5 rm, closed Wed, 55-170.

⚐ ★★★*La Chicanette* (100 pl), ☎ 66.87.28.32.

Causse de SAUVETERRE**

A2

The most northerly of the great *causses,* and also the most wooded : the west of the plateau is a natural forest of oak, beech and fir ; a further 12 000 acres have been planted.

▶ **Sauveterre** is one of the main villages of the *causse;* farms are usually scattered. Typical Sauveterre dormerwindows. ▶ Fortified farm of **Choisal** (17thC). ▶ **La Canourgue** has lost some of its character but the narrow streets around the church have been restored : modest cob-walled houses, vaulted street-passages, fountains. It was once a weaving village, producing coarse woollen cloth. Benedictine church★ (11th-14thC; pink and white sandstone mosaic; 18thC statues). Small Gallo-Roman museum : ceramics from Banassac, like Millau an important pottery centre in the 1st, 2nd and 3rdC. ▶ Beautiful road★★ from **Chanac** (château of the Bishops of Mende; 13thC church, Gothic bridge) and Boyne, on the Tarn; particularly spectacular from **Le Massegros**, by the Point Sublime★★★ on the Tarn Gorges. □

Practical Information ───────────────

La CANOURGUE, ⊠ 48500, 49 km SW of **Mende**.
ⓘ ☎ 66.32.83.67 (h.s.); mairie, ☎ 66.32.81.47.
SNCF ☎ 66.32.81.68.

Hotels :
● ★★ *Commerce* (L.F.), ☎ 66.32.80.18, Visa, 32 rm Ⓟ ▩ & closed Sun eve and Mon, 15 Nov-1 Mar, 140. Rest. ◆ & 45-90.
★ *Citadelle*, av. des Gorges-du-Tarn, ☎ 66.32.80.11, 10 rm ▩ closed 1 Oct-6 Nov, 140. Rest. ◆ ♪ & 45-80.

Recommended
Farmhouse-inn : *Le Mazelet*, ☎ 66.32.83.16; *Les Hermaux*, ☎ 66.32.60.78.

CHANAC, ⊠ 48230, 15 km S of **Marvejols**.
i pl. Triadou, ☎ 66.48.20.08.
SNCF ☎ 66.48.20.19.

Hotel :
★ **Voyageurs** (L.F.), ☎ 66.48.20.16, 18 rm P ⋙ ♨
half pens (h.s.), 230. Rest. ♦ 45-70.

SOMMIÈRES*

Montpellier 28, Nîmes 28, Paris 740 km
pop 3000 ⊠ 30250   B4
Beautiful and somewhat neglected, near the stony
hills where Lawrence Durrell found the same light and
olive trees as in Greece.

▶ On the banks of the Vidourle, Sommières is a former
stronghold : elegant French Classical mansions★ round
an arcaded square★ behind the dismantled ramparts. On
the hill, castle ruins ; remains of the Roman bridge under
the one in use. **Also...** ▶ **Château de Villevieille★★**
(2 km), a harmonious blend of several periods (12th, 16th,
18thC) ; Louis XIII furniture ; small Gallo-Roman museum ;
summer concerts *(Jul.-15 Sep., 2-7:30 ; Sun. off-season)*.
▶ Charming cypress-flanked Romanesque chapel at **Saint-
Julien-de-Salinelles★** *(5 km N ; concerts in summer)*.

The Silk route★ *(approx. 65 km ; half day)*
N of Sommières are the southern Cévennes : vines,
olive trees, pine woods, holm-oak and mastic in the
fields ; charming towns showing the influence of the
Midi. These were weaving towns but the handsome
silk factories are now deserted.

▶ **Sommières.** ▶ On the edge of the cliff, **Sauve★** : from
the old bridge, nice view of the village ; since the Middle
Ages, speciality of pitchforks made from hackberry wood.
▶ Surrounded by vineyards, **Saint-Hippolyte-du-Fort★** :
Mediterranean atmosphere, but typical Cévennes houses
(17th-18thC), large Protestant church, Louis XIV fort, silk
factories. The Margaride winter pasture trail starts from
Saint-Hippolyte : today it is a hiking trail through the
Asclier Pass *(panorama★★)*, Aire de Côte, Can de l'Hos-
pitalet and Florac. ▶ The road through **Monoblet** and
Saint-Félix-de-Pallières (two pretty villages) is more difficult than the direct route, but the landscapes are typical of
the Cévennes although the vegetation is Mediterranean.
Silkworm breeding is being revived in Monoblet. ▶ **Ganges** (→ Languedoc). ▶ **Le Vigan★**, at the foot of the
Aigoual (→) : Place du Quai and Place d'Assas (lime trees
and fountains) are the town's social centres ; walk in the
Promenade des Chataigniers (park) by the former ramparts. The **Cévenol Museum** recalls the prosperous
period of silk production *(10-11:30 & 2-6:30, Apr.-Oct.,
closed Tue. and Sat., ex Jul.-Aug. ; off-season, Wed. only)*.
                                                                    □

Practical Information ————————————
SOMMIÈRES
i 1, pl. de la République, ☎ 66.80.99.30.
SNCF ☎ 66.80.96.63.

Hotel :
● ★★★ **Auberge du Pont Romain** (C.H.), 2, rue Emile-
Jamais, ☎ 66.80.00.58, AE DC Euro Visa, 14 rm P ⁞
⌧ half pens (h.s.), closed 15 Jan-15 Mar, 240. Rest. ♦♦
⁞ closed Wed. Savoury dishes, 135-180.

Restaurant :
● ♦♦♦ **L'Enclos Montgranier**, rte de Gallargues-le-Mon-
tueux, ☎ 66.80.92.00, AE Euro ⁞ ⋙ & closed Mon and
Sun eve ex Jul-Aug, 15 Nov-15 Mar. The entire Deste-
nay family works together to welcome their guests with
warmth and generosity ; rooms and a pool may be in the
offing. Their sincere, earthy cookery has the genuine tang
of Languedoc ; prices are moderate. Spec : fresh Junas
truffles (in season) and lots of good light dishes, lamb
from Nîmes and ratatouille, 95-295 ; child : 75.

⚔ ★★★*International Club*, Mus (50 pl), ☎ 66.35.07.06 ;
★★*Municipal* (60 pl), ☎ 66.80.33.49.
Recommended
♥ olive oil : *oil cooperative.*

Nearby

PONT-D'HÉRAULT, ⊠ 30570 Valleraugue, 6 km E
of **Vigan** on the D 999.

Hotel :
★★ **Maurice**, ☎ 67.82.40.02, Visa, 18 rm P ⁞ ⋙ ⌧ ⁂ ♨
closed 23 Dec-1 Feb, 160. Rest. ♦ ⁞ & ⁂ 85-120.

Le REY, ⊠ 30570, 5 km E of **Vigan** on the D 999.

Hotel :
★★ **Château du Rey**, ☎ 67.82.40.06, Euro Visa, 12 rm
P ⋙ ⁂ closed 15 Nov-1 Apr. A 13thC château, 250.
Rest. ♦♦ **L'Abeuradou**, closed Mon (l.s.). An array of
light, regional dishes prepared by Yves Thenin in a 16thC
sheepfold. Spec. : *feuilleté de brandade, sauté d'agneau
aux fougères*, 120-210.

Le VIGAN, ⊠ 30120, 68 km NW.
i ☎ 67.81.01.72.
SNCF ☎ 67.81.03.01.

Hotel :
★★ **Auberge Le Mas Quayrol** (C.H.), Aulas, 6 km,
☎ 67.81.12.38, DC Euro Visa, 16 rm P ⁞ ⋙ ⌧ & ⌧
closed 31 Oct-Easter, 230. Rest. ● ♦♦ ⁞ ♪ Out in the
country with a splendid view of the Cévennes foothills
: *morilles au vin jaune flambées à la fine champagne*,
90-170.

⚔ ★★★*Val de l'Arre* (120 pl), ☎ 67.81.02.77.

TARN and JONTE Gorges***

                                                                    A2-3
From Florac to Millau *(84 km ; half day)*
The Tarn Gorges have long been a major tourist
attraction, but the few villages and the dramatic landscape have remained unspoilt. The many caves in the
area served as refuges for Protestants, Catholics and
aristocrats at different times in history.

The road follows the bottom of the gorge between the
coloured cliffs of the Sauveterre and Méjean *causses*
(plateaus). Flourishing vegetation *(boat-trips Easter-Sep.,
from La Malène to Les Baumes amphitheatre).*

▶ **Florac** (→).▶ **Ispagnac★**, fortified in the 15thC : bridge ;
Romanesque church and Benedictine priory ; Gothic houses ; 17th-18thC château. ▶ Gothic **bridge★** near **Qué-
zac★** ; large 14th-16thC church. The canyon begins at
Molines. ▶ **Rocheblave** manor (16thC). ▶ Another 16thC
château below **Montbrun bridge.** ▶ Viewpoint above
Castelbouc★★. ▶ **Prades** : village and 16thC château.
▶ **Sainte-Énimie**, in a pretty setting at the mouth of the
ravine : narrow cobbled streets, terraced slopes, 14thC
Romanesque church, small regional museum ; above,
13thC Benedictine priory, Romanesque chapel. ▶ **Mas-
Saint-Chély**, beside a waterfall : 12thC Romanesque
church (Gothic doorway) ; houses with Renaissance decoration. ▶ **Pougnadoires** Amphitheatre★. ▶ **La Caze** château (15th-17th-19thC) : now a hotel. ▶ **Hauterive★**, on
the opposite bank. ▶ **La Malène**, where two ravines
meet : a stone bridge links it to the left bank, overlooked by the hair-pin bends of the Méjean road★★ (spectacular) ; 15thC château-hotel ; Romanesque church ; marvelous excursions to the **Hourtous rock★★** and **Point
Sublime★★★.** *(Departure for the boat-trip★★★).* ▶ The
Tarn runs over rapids and through **Les Détroits★** (series
of narrows), and into **Les Baumes amphitheatre★★.**
▶ **Pas du Souci**, overlooked by the **Aiguille rock.** ▶ **Les
Vignes**, where the valley broadens. ▶ The Sévérac road
(→ Rouergue) leads to the **Point Sublime★★★**, fabulous
view over the canyon and the *causse* (plateau) *(13 km,
including 5 km tight bends).* ▶ **La Sourde rock** : view
over Pas du Souci. ▶ From Les Vignes to Le Rozier, the

canyon straightens out : marvelous rock formations such as the **Bastion de Cinglegros** on the left bank.▶ The Sauveterre cliffs widen to form the **Saint-Marcellin amphitheatre.** ▶ **La Muse bridge** (500 m upstream from the junction with the Jonte River) leads to Le Rozier where the Promenade de la Jonte begins (*see below*). ▶ Towards Millau, the road is less spectacular ; the Tarn leaves the gorges after it joins the Jonte.▶ Pretty medieval villages of **Liaucous** and **Mostuéjouls** (12-17thC château). ▶ Two views over the valley : the ruins of **Caylus** castle and **Compeyre**, once a rival to Millau. ▶ **Aguessac,** junction with N9. ▶ **Millau** (→).

Jonte Gorges★★★ (*56km; approx. 2 hr;* A3)

▶ **Le Rozier,** at the junction of the Tarn and the Jonte : like **Peyreleau,** one of the main tourist centres of the gorges ; pretty Romanesque church near La Muse bridge ; view-point from **Capluc rock★★** on the Méjean *causse* (*45 min*). ▶ The Jonte canyon, separating the Méjean *causse* (N) from the Noir *causse* (S), is just as beautiful as the Tarn Gorges, with two levels of vertical red cliff, divided by a green glacis. *Corniche* (cliff road), many viewpoints : ▶ **Vase de Sèvres** ▶ **Fabié and Curvelier rocks** ▶ **Belvédère des Terrasses.** ▶ **Les Douzes,** overlooked by the Saint-Gervais rock, like a ruined tower : Romanesque chapel. Fontaine des Douzes, resurgence of the Jonte River. ▶ The river disappears in summer at the Sourguettes mill. ▶ **Meyrueis,** important tourist centre : excursion to the Aigoual (→), the Dargilan cave (→) and the Armand aven (cave ; →).▶ Further on, the Florac road runs up the Jonte Valley between the Méjean *causse* and Mont Aigoual ; cultivated areas. ▶ After **Gatuzières,** the road climbs along the side of the Aigoual. **Perjuret Pass** (alt. 1 028 m), on a narrow ridge between the *causse* and the Cévennes. Panorama over the Cévennes and the Lozère. Aigoual road to the S ; **Nîmes-le-Vieux★** road to the N ; spectacular rocks around Veygalier. ▶ The road runs down into the Lozère : open horizons, grass-covered slopes and woods. ▶ **Fraissinet-de-Fourques** (bridge). ▶ Limestone cliffs. ▶ **Les Vanels :** down the Tarnon to Florac (→).

Practical Information

La CAZE, ⊠ 48500 La Canourgue, 6 km NE of **La Malène.**

Hotel :
● ★★★★ *Château de la Caze* (I.L.A.), ☎ 66.48.51.01, AE DC Visa, 20 rm P ≮ ▒ ⌂ ♪ ♨ closed 15 Oct-1 May. A 15thC château, in a 124 acres park, 620. Rest. ♦♦♦ ♨ ▒ closed Tue. A table of high repute. Spec : crayfish, trout, 180-250.

La MALÈNE, ⊠ 48210 Sainte-Enimie, 35 km S of **Mende.**
ⓘ ☎ 66.48.53.44.

Hotel :
★★★ *Manoir de Montesquiou,* ☎ 66.48.51.12, DC, 12 rm P ≮ ▒ ⌂ ♨ closed 16 Oct-15 Apr, 270. Rest. ● ♦♦♦ ≮ ♪ ▒ closed Mon noon. A family-run manor deep in the Tarn Gorges. Regional specialities star : *truite au jambon de pays, ris de veau à la crème de laitue, pêche du manoir,* 90-200 ; child : 50.

⅄ ★*Le Clos* (70 pl), ☎ 66.48.51.24.

MEYRUEIS, ⊠ 48150, 42 km NE of **Millau.**
ⓘ rue de l'Horloge, ☎ 66.45.60.33 (h.s.) ; mairie, ☎ 66.45.62.64.

Hotels :
● ★★★ *Château d'Ayre* (C.H.), ☎ 66.45.60.10, AE DC Visa, 24 rm P ≮ ▒ ⌂ ♪♂ closed 1 Jan-29 Mar. A Benedictine monastery from the 12thC. Comfortable rooms, 335. Rest. ♦♦ ♨ 100-180 ; child : 50.
● ★★★ *Renaissance* (Inter-Hôtel, C.H.), ☎ 66.45.60.19, AE DC Euro Visa, 20 rm ▒ ⌂ closed 2 Jan-15 Mar. Period reproduction furniture, old engravings, 240. Rest. ♦♦ Good regional food. Spec : *godiveau de truite aux écrevisses, musquette au miel,* 80-180 ; child : 40.
★★ *Europe et du Mont-Aigoual,* quai d'Oréans,

☎ 66.45.60.05, 50 rm P ▒ ⌂ ⊠ half pens (h.s.), closed 1 Nov-1 Apr, 260. Rest. ♦ ♪ 60-80.
★★ *France,* ☎ 66.45.60.07, Euro Visa, 46 rm P ▒ ⌂ ♪♂ closed Oct-Mar, 120. Rest. ♦ ♨ 50-105.
★★ *Saint-Sauveur,* pl. d'Orléans, ☎ 66.45.62.12, Euro Visa, 14 rm ▒ ⌂ ♨ closed 10 Nov-15 Mar, 110. Rest. ♦ closed 30 Sep-15 May. A shady terrace to enjoy in fine weather, 55-70 ; child : 40.

⅄ ★★★*Capelan* (80 pl), ☎ 66.45.60.50 ; ★★*Champ d'Ayres* (70 pl), ☎ 66.45.60.51 ; ★★*Le Pré de Charlet* (70 pl), ☎ 66.45.63.65.

Recommended
Farmhouse-inn : at Hures-la-Parade, *Les Hérans,* ☎ 66.45.64.42 ; at Saint-Pierre-des-Tripiers, *La Viale,* ☎ 66.48.82.39.

PEYRELEAU, ⊠ 12720, 21 km NE of **Millau.**

Hotel :
★★★ *Muse et Rozier* (I.L.A.), La Muse, ☎ 65.62.60.01, Tx 531917, AE DC Euro Visa, 38 rm P ≮ ▒ ⌂ half pens (h.s.), closed 6 Oct-Easter, 580. Rest. ● ♦♦♦ ▒ Extremely modern decor in this renovated feudal manor on the banks of the Tarn : *escalope de foie gras chaud aux amandes, selle d'agneau en croûte de sel,* 110-180 ; child : 40.

⅄ ★★*Les Peupliers* (35 pl), ☎ 65.62.61.33.

Le ROZIER, ⊠ 48150 Meyrueis, 1 km from **Peyrelau.**

Hotel :
★★ *Les Voyageurs,* ☎ 65.62.60.09, 24 rm ▒ closed Oct, 110. Rest. ♦ 65-75.

SAINTE-ENIMIE, ⊠ 48210, 21 km S of **Mende.**
ⓘ mairie, ☎ 66.48.50.09 (h.s.).

Hotels :
★★ *Burlatis,* ☎ 66.48.52.30, Visa, 18 rm ▒ closed Oct-Apr, 160.
★★ *Commerce,* ☎ 66.48.50.01, AE Euro Visa, 20 rm P ≮ closed Oct-Easter school hols. Private beach on the banks of the Tarn, 160. Rest. ♦ 55-100.
★★ *Paris* (L.F.), ☎ 66.48.50.02, 15 rm P ≮ ▒ ♨ closed 15 Sep-15 Jun, 150. Rest. ♦ ♪ 40-80 ; child : 30.

Restaurant :
♦ *Auberge du Moulin,* ☎ 66.48.53.08 ≮ ▒ closed Nov-Apr, 40-100.

Les VIGNES, ⊠ 48210 Sainte-Enimie, 31 km S of **Mende.**

Hotel :
★★ *Gévaudan,* ☎ 66.48.81.55, 18 rm P ≮ closed 31 Oct-15 Mar, 180. Rest. ♦ 50-120.

⅄ ★★*Beldoire* (100 pl), ☎ 66.48.82.79.

UZÈS★★★

Nîmes 25, Avignon 38, Paris 707 km
pop 7826 ⊠ 30700   C3

Uzès is one of France's prettiest towns, thanks to government grants for the restoration of its architectural heritage : narrow streets and Renaissance or French Classical mansions, arcaded square and pleasant fountains. Concerts and CNMHS (National Monuments Board) guided tours in summer. In the Middle Ages, this was a textile town and a Protestant citadel : its overlord, Antoine de Crussol, was the leader of the Protestant armies in Languedoc, and to bring him back to the Catholic fold, Uzès was elevated to the rank of Duchy in 1565. The playwright Racine stayed here in his youth, as did the writer André Gide.

▶ **Place aux Herbes★** (Pl. de la République) : arcades and 16th, 17th and 18thC mansions. ▶ The **Fenestrelle Tower★★** is the only remnant of the old Romanesque cathedral, rebuilt in the 17thC after the Wars of Religion (paintings attributed to Simon de Châlons, Avignon, 16thC). The 17th-18thC bishop's residence is very dilapi-

UZÈS

0   50   100m

dated. ▶ Fine view of the town and countryside from the **Promenade Racine,** built on the ancient fortifications above the Alzon ravine (17thC Racine Pavilion). 19thC Hôtel de Castille (mansion). ▶ **The Duché**★★, residence of the Dukes of Uzès *(9-12 & 2-6 in season; 10-12, 2:30-5 in winter).* It is overlooked by the enormous **Bermonde Tower** square keep, (11thC); in the courtyard, Renaissance façade. Inside : Louis XV and Louis XVI furniture. ▶ 18thC Hôtel de Ville (town hall). ▶ 3rdC crypt on the Place du Duché. ▶ The tour de l'Horloge (Clock tower, 11thC), representing the power of the church; opposite, the Tour du Roi. ▶ Renaissance Hôtel Dampmartin (mansion). ▶ French Classical church of **St. Étienne**★ : trefoil ground-plan and curved façade (18thC).
Also... ▶ Stud-farm (Alès road), and Agricultural and Locomotion Museum at Arpaillargues *(4.5 km W, 9-12 & 2-7, closed Mon.).*

Nearby

▶ The woods and orchards in the countryside around Uzès alternate with the former vine-growing villages, now active holiday resorts. Nearly all of them have a château or pretty church. ▶ **Saint-Siffret**★, hilltop village around a Templar castle and attractive church *(4 km W).* ▶ **La Capelle** and **Masmolène** *(15 km NE)* each have a château. ▶ **La Bastide-d'Engras** *(12 km NE)* : feudal castle. ▶ **Argilliers** : typical Languedoc château remodeled in the 18thC by the Baron de Castille in neo-Classical style. ▶ Picturesque hermitage at **Collias** on the Gardon River *(5 km S).* Superb hilltop village of **Lussan**★ overlooking the Garrigue *(17 km NW)* and **Guidon du Bouquet rock** (alt. 629 m) between Uzès and Alès (wide view★). □

Practical Information _____

UZÈS
ⓘ av. de la Libération (A2), ☎ 66.22.68.88.
🚃 ☎ 66.22.12.52.

Hotel :
● ★★★ **Entraigues,** 8, rue de la Calade (B-C2), ☎ 66.22.32.68, DC Visa, 18 rm ℗ ⬒ ⬚ ⬚ closed 2 Jan-2 Feb. A 15thC mansion, 300. Rest. ♦♦ closed Tue and Wed noon. Spec : *feuilleté d'escargots aux morilles, médaillon de lotte à la provençale,* 65-130.

Restaurant :
♦ **L'Alibi,** 1, pl. Dampmartin (B2), ☎ 66.22.01.32 🚾 closed Wed. The count of Dampmartin's 15thC town house. Jazz concerts, 80-130.

⚠ ★★★**Mas Fran Val** (50 pl), ☎ 66.22.27.62; ★★**Municipal** (70 pl), ☎ 66.22.11.79.

Nearby

ARPAILLARGUES, ☒ 30700 Uzès, 5 km W.

Hotel :
● ★★★ **Marie d'Agoult,** (C.H., R.S.), château d'Arpaillargues, ☎ 66.22.14.48, AE DC Euro Visa, 25 rm 2 apt ℗ 🚾 ⬚ ⬚ ╱○ closed 1 Nov-15 Mar, 440. Rest. ♦♦♦ closed Wed (l.s.). Remarkable interior decor in this 17th-18thC house where Marie d'Agoult once dwelt. Spec : *médaillon de lotte au safran, parfait de banane aux violettes, filets de morue fraîche "à la d'Uzès",* 170-280.

LUSSAN, ☒ 30580, 18 km N.

Hotel :
● ★★ **Auberge de la Treille,** rte de Bagnols-sur-Cèze, Andabiac, ☎ 66.72.90.26, Visa, 8 rm ℗ ⬚ ⬚ 140. Rest. ♦ ⬚ 60-100.

Le ROUX, ☒ 30700 Uzès.

Restaurant :
♦ **Auberge de la Valcroze,** 6 km N of Lussan on D 787, ☎ 66.72.90.73 ℗ ⬚ ⬚ closed Mon and Tue , Nov-Mar. In a charming village, 90-250.

Les VANS*

Alès 43, Privas 66, Paris 670 km
pop 2580 ☒ 07140   B2

Between Upper and Lower Ardèche, Les Vans is a tourist centre : bright stone houses, square, fountains, 17thC church.

Nearby

▶ The Vans region is attractively situated at the foot of the Cévennes; the **Chassezac Valley** changes character as it runs from the schist of the Cévennes to the limestone of the Vivarais. ▶ **Païolive woods**★ is a natural curiosity :

immense labyrinth with amazing formations in a tumble of rocks and trees; numerous marked paths. ▶ Nearly all the surrounding villages have a pretty church and interesting architecture. ▶ Don't miss **Naves★** *(2.5 km SW)*, nor ▶ **Brahic** in the little Gagnière Valley *(7 km SW)*. ▶ **Joyeuse★** *(15 km NE)*, former stronghold and trading place between the valley and the mountain : château of the Duc de Joyeuse; 17thC church; old town centre. ☐

Practical Information

Les VANS
ⓘ ☎ 75.37.24.48.

Hotels :
★★ *Château Le Scipionet* (C.H., R.S., L.F.), on D 104, ☎ 75.37.23.84, Tx 345790, Euro Visa, 23 rm 3 apt Ⓟ ⪕ ⪦ ♪ ⪕ ☐ ♨ half pens (h.s.), closed 1 Oct-15 Mar. A solitary, romantic château set in a 30 acres park, 650. Rest. ♦ ⪕ ♪ ⪕ ❄ 130-180; child : 55.
★ *Château*, pl. Ollier, ☎ 75.37.23.16, Euro Visa, 19 rm Ⓟ closed Fri (l.s.) and Nov, 120. Rest. ♦ 80-130.

Recommended
Farmhouse-inn : at Les Armas-le-Haut, *La Pomponnette*, ☎ 75.37.22.83. Riding centre. An old Sarrasin dwelling where Honoré regales his guests,.

Nearby

CHANDOLAS-MAISONNEUVE, ⊠ 07230, 13 km S of **Joyeuse** on the N104/D 208.

Hotel :
★★ *Relais de la Vignasse* (L.F.), ☎ 75.39.31.91, Euro Visa, 17 rm Ⓟ ⪕ ♨ ⪦ ⪕ pens, half pens (h.s.), 460. Rest. ♦ ⪕ ♪ ⪕ 60-120; child : 35.

JOYEUSE, ⊠ 07260, 14 km NE.

Hotel :
★★ *Les Cèdres* (L.F.), ☎ 75.39.40.60, AE DC Euro, 40 rm Ⓟ ♨ ⪦ ♪ closed 10 Oct-10 Apr, 250. Rest. ♦ ⪕ ♪ ⪕ 50-100.

LABLACHÈRE, ⊠ 07230, 3 km SW of **Joyeuse** on N 104.

Hotel :
★ *Commerce*, ☎ 75.36.61.80, 20 rm Ⓟ ♨ ❄ closed Sat, Sun (l.s.), 20 Dec-6 Jan, 110. Rest. ♦ 55-130.

ROSIÈRES, ⊠ 07260 Joyeuse, 2 km NE on the N 104.

Hotel :
★ *Cévennes* (L.F.), ☎ 75.39.52.07, Euro Visa, 14 rm Ⓟ ⪕ ♨ ⪦ closed Sun eve and Mon, 15 Feb-15 Mar, 10-20 Oct, 100. Rest. ♦ ♪ ⪕ 50-80.
⛺ ★★★★*Le Sous-Perret* (75 pl), ☎ 75.39.50.54.

VILLENEUVE-DE-BERG*

Aubenas 16, Privas 46, Paris 632 km
pop 2083 ⊠ 07170   C2

This former *bastide* (13thC) is situated between the basalt plateau of Coiron and the limestone of the Gras — two very different landscapes.
▶ It was once the juridical capital of the Vivarais and still has beautiful 17thC mansions from this period. Cistercian church rebuilt in the 17thC; panorama over the Vivarais. ▶ Small museum in the farm-school at **Le Pradel** *(5 km N)*. ▶ **La Villedieu** *(6 km)* : small museum of the bizarre, Bayssac quarter *(year-round, daily)*.

Nearby

▶ S from Villeneuve : **Gras Plateau★**. ▶ **Saint-Maurice-d'Ibie**, ▶ **Saint-Andéol-de-Berg**, ▶ **Les Salelles**. ▶ **Alba** *(13 km E)*, was a Roman town; 11th-16thC keep. Opposite, medieval village of **La Roche★**. Farther S, another hill-village : **Saint-Thomé★** (ramparts, remains of two châteaux and 15thC cloister). ☐

VIVARAIS CÉVENOL Corniche**

B2

La Bastide to Les Vans *(45 km; see map 5)*

Less traffic than on the Cévennes *corniche* (cliff road), with beautiful views in a changing landscape, running from the mountains to the lower plateau.

▶ **La Bastide-Puylaurent** : brought into existence by the railway. ▶ **Trappe-de-Notre-Dame-des-Neiges** : R. L. Stevenson stayed here on his "Travels with a Donkey". ▶ **Saint-Laurent-les-Bains** : small spa. ▶ The route crosses the **Borne Ravine**, then runs through the **Chap del Bosc forest**. ▶ **Montselgues** was a dependency of the Benedictine Abbey of Monastier, which played an important role in developing the mountain area; Romanesque church★. ▶ **Thines** *(see below)*, appears on its rocky outcrop. ▶ After **Peyre**, the Mediterranean climate leaves its mark : chestnut trees replace firs, and vineyards are more common. ▶ Turn towards **Chambonas** and its château, down a very winding road running through marvelous villages clustered around their churches : **Saint-Jean-de-Pourcharesse★**, **Faugères**, **Payzac**, **Brès**, surrounded by miles of terraced hillsides. ▶ On the twisting road from Les Vans to La Bastide, take the detour to **Thines★★** :

5. Vivarais Cévenol Corniche

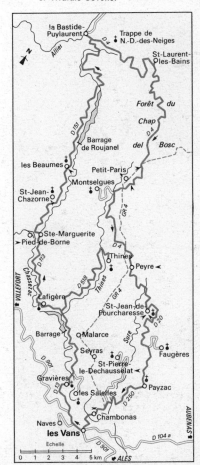

isolated village with an outstanding church; a stopover for pilgrims between Le Puy and Provence; stone-tiled roofs, multicoloured stonework, and carved ornamentation inspired by St. Gilles (→). The most beautiful part is the chevet, built of red-sandstone and white limestone.▶ **Pied-de-Borne** : lovely site at the junction of three gorges. The generating station is the key element in the Chassezac complex.▶ Delightful Romanesque chapel at **Sainte-Marguerite-Lafigère.** ▶ This narrow sloping valley is covered in chestnut trees and irrigated by a very sophisticated system installed in the 19thC. The best illustration of the extraordinary work of the Cévennes farmers.▶ Romanesque church at **Saint-Jean-Chazome.**

▶ **Beaumes** : Romanesque chapel and small bridge. ▶ The **Roujanel dam** has transformed the mountain stream into a peaceful lake.▶ **Alzons,** in the heart of the chestnut woods.▶ **La Bastide.** □

Auvergne

▶ The awe-inspiring volcanic relief of Auvergne, with its giant massifs and mountain chains, has long given it a reputation for isolation and self-sufficiency. This citadel in the very heart of France has often been described as the museum of a past and a tradition long stripped of their original dynamism. But modern communications have triumphed over geographical and climatic barriers, and commerce and tourism have further opened up a region which possesses attractions rivaling the better-known beauty spots of France. Many of Auvergne's sons and daughters have "emigrated" to the large cities, particularly Paris, where they opened up little corner cafés and bars, selling wood and domestic coal as profitable sidelines.

Auvergne has five of the ten leading thermal resorts in France and excels in country holidays : trekking in the Cantal mountains, pony-trekking, country inns and camping on farms, amidst lakes, splendid scenery and mountains. Auvergne also boasts excellent ski resorts, attracting skiers from all over France and Europe. Cross-country skiing at Mont-Dore, Super-Besse and Super-Lioran is perhaps the greatest drawcard, although downhill skiing is also popular.

Auvergne is the site of one of the most original and important schools of Romanesque art in France — here 12th-century architecture and sculpture show perhaps their most personal expression. Castles and country houses, popular traditions and crafts and the gastronomic specialties of Auvergne further explain its popularity with tourists. The region is noted for its cheeses : Cantal, Auvergne blue, creamy Saint-Nectaire, and a number of goat cheeses, the best-known being the *cabecou* of Salers and Aurillac. Sausages, salami and the famous Auvergne ham find willing buyers

all over France, and the local wines provide an earthy and very palatable accompaniment.

The capital, Clermont-Ferrand, is an important automobile manufacturing center, specializing in tyres. It has always been a meeting place for inhabitants and tourists alike, a busy, lively city with more than a drop of southern blood in its veins, and blessed with many fine buildings including a number of well-preserved Gothic and Renaissance dwellings.   □

Don't miss

★★★ La Chaise-Dieu B-C2, Le Puy C3.

★★Brioude B2-3, Orcival A2, Puy-de-Dôme B2, Salers A3, Truyère Gorges A-B3.

★ Arlempes C3, Blesle B2, Billom B2, Clermont-Ferrand B1, Issoire B2, Mont-Dore A2, Riom B1, Saint-Flour B3, Saint-Nectaire B2, Thiers B1.

Weekend tips

Visiting Clermont-Ferrand will take all morning, and can be followed by an afternoon spent driving up the Puy-de-Dôme peak and touring the Dôme Mountains; return to Clermont via Royat or the plateau of Gergovie. On the second day, drive out to the Dore Mountains, climb the Sancy peak and visit the spa and ski villages of Mont-Dore and La Bourboule; see the old village of Besse-en-Chandesse and drive back to Clermont via Saint-Nectaire or, if you have the time, through Issoire. Another excellent idea for a summer weekend is to drive from Puy-en-Velay to Clermont-Ferrand, taking in Brioude, the Allier Gorges, Saint-Flour (lunch), the Garabit Viaduct, the upper Truyère Valley and the Cantal Mountains (stay the night at Vic-sur-Cère or Aurillac). On the second day tour via Anjony, Salers, Mauriac, Bort-les-Orgues and the romantic Château de Val; end the day with a drive around the Dore Mountains and up the Puy-de-Dôme peak.

Near Brioude

In the Haut-Loire region

In South Cantal

"Jasserie" in the Puy-de-Dôme region

Near Murat

● *Brief regional history*

Up to 1stC BC.

There was human life in the Auvergne Region even before the Cantal volcano became extinct, apparently going back some two million years. The Chilhac deposits (near Brioude, Haute-Loire), appear contemporary with the middle Villafranchian epoch; the largest palaeolithic deposits in the Auvergne date, however,

from the **Magdalenian era** (15 000-8 000 BC). ● The **Neolithic era** (megaliths) was succeeded by the various **metal-working periods,** during which the **Celtic invasions** occurred. ● Towards 800 BC the **Arvernes** - pastoral nomads - settled the plains of the Allier River and neighbouring mountains. Their dominance rapidly extended from the Rhine to the Atlantic, and in 124 BC they annexed the territory of the *Vellaves* (Velay). But this was the Arvernian Empire's last effort. For in 121 BC King Bituit was defeated by the Roman armies, and the resistance of Vercingetorix, culminating in the victory of the Gallic cavalry at Gergovie before Bituit's final defeat at Alesia, was not sufficient to save the Gauls from Roman domination.

1st-5thC
Rome attached Auvergne to the **Province of Aquitaine,** and immediately began to build roads and baths ; agricultural development was encouraged, and Lezoux became an important producer of ceramics.

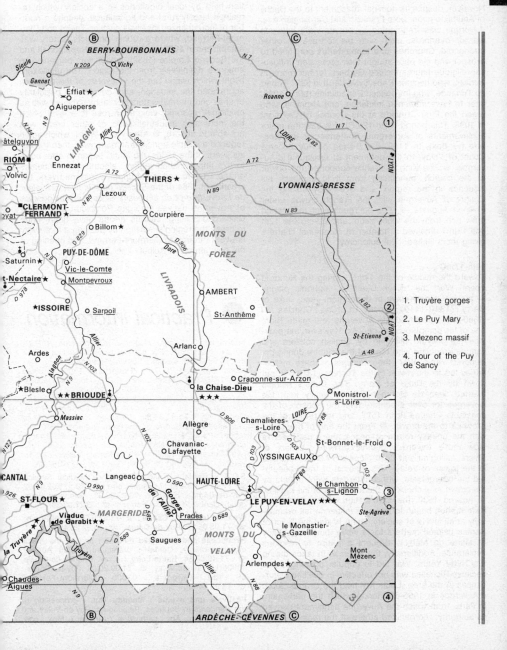

1. Truyère gorges

2. Le Puy Mary

3. Mezenc massif

4. Tour of the Puy de Sancy

● Toward the middle of the 3rdC, Christian colonies came to be established in urban centres, notably Austremoine, Nectaire, Mary, Genès, Florus and Julien. Although the invasion of the Visigoths widely spread the Arian heresy, Christianity and the long-standing influence of Roman civilization retained its hold, largely due to personalities such as Sidonius Apollinaris, man-of-letters and Bishop of Clermont (where he died in 487).

6th-13thC
However, despite its nominal attachment to the Duchy of Aquitaine under both Frankish and Carolingian rule, Auvergne was fragmented by private wars between warrior overlords, each with his fortress or other stronghold. **Churches and monasteries** continued to prosper and the poor sought their protection. Influential religious figures include Gerbert, former monk at Aurillac, who became Pope Sylvester II in 999; Robert de Turlande, who introduced Benedictine rule in 1043, later to have immense influence, and Urban II, who urged the First Crusade at the Council of Clermont in 1095. This period (11th-12thC) also saw the major achievements of **Auvergnat Romanesque architecture** (→ box). In 1169, the Bishop of Puy became Count of Velay, to the detriment of Guillaume d'Auvergne. ● The King of France supported the power of the church, benefitting from it to establish his influence in the region, and eventually uniting the County of Auvergne with the French crown, under Philippe Auguste. ● The bourgeoisie at this period grew rich from the wool trade, and during the 12th and 13thC obtained a number of communal charters giving them limited local autonomy.

14th-17thC
Toward the middle of the 14thC, during the Hundred Years' War, the "Black Death" — bubonic plague — brought a **new wave of desolation.** Jean, Duke of Berry (1340-1416), uncle of King Charles VI (1380-1422), received the Auvergne and made Riom one of his sumptuous residences. However, the province fell prey to pillaging by English soldiers and various irregulars who roamed the country during the Hundred Years' War; the exactions of these mercenaries led to the revolt of the Tuchins (1378-85), put down by the Duke of Berry. The Duke's heiress married Jean de Bourbon, whose family kept the Auvergne for over a century until the treason of the constable Charles III in 1527, and the return of the province to the crown. ● From the end of the 15thC with the uneasy return of peace, there had been a slow move toward economic growth : cutlery at Thiers, fulling mills at Saint-Flour and Aurillac and lace in the towns of Velay. This renewal of trade benefitted the bourgeoisie, whose interests were upheld by the crown as a check on the ambitions of the nobility. ● Around 1530, the introduction of the **Protestant Reformation** began to make its influence felt dramatically at all levels of society. Henri IV and the Edict of Nantes calmed matters for a while, but the regency of Marie de Médicis brought a return to religious intolerance. Additionally, the increase in taxes during the Thirty Years' War led to popular uprisings; and because Richelieu was not effective in quelling disturbances in the area, Louis XIV held the *Grands Jours d'Auvergne* in 1665-66, during which the parliament in Paris, from which the Auvergne parliament derived its authority, reorganized affairs of the region.

18th-20thC
Despite good management by royal administrators, Auvergne underwent a period of general shortages at the beginning of the 18thC; overpopulation in the mountain regions led to temporary emigration to other parts of France. Politically, the **French Revolution and the Empire** found little enthusiasm in the Auvergne Region, where the mountains became the natural refuge of non-conformists. ● At the time of the restoration of the monarchy in 1814, daily life in the Auvergne was characterized by the privileged position held by local dignitaries in a society which remained largely rural and agricultural, despite a number of industrialized localities such as Thiers and Clermont-Ferrand, where a rubber products factory was established in 1832. ● By the time of Napoleon III and the **Second Empire** (1852), labour was beginning to emigrate definitively from the region. The phylloxera blight which wiped out the vineyards of the province aggravated the situation, and, despite the popularity of spas and thermal waters (for fashionable as well as medicinal reasons), emigration rose to a level which the increasing industrialization of other areas was not able to absorb. ● After World War I, which again reduced available agricultural manpower, then the crisis years of the 1930s, the 20thC began to offer hope to this impoverished region : electrification schemes on the Truyère and in the upper Dordogne rivers, the creation in 1964 of the *Société pour la mise en valeur de l'Auvergne et du Limousin.* Since the presidencies of Auvergne natives Georges Pompidou and Valéry Giscard d'Estaing, serious efforts have been made to break the region's isolation by pushing a motorway network through to Clermont-Ferrand, and opening of the new airport at Aulnat.

● *Practical information*

Information : *Comité Régional du Tourisme (C.R.T.),* 45, av. Julien, B.P. 395, 63011 Clermont-Ferrand Cedex, ☎ 73.93.04.03. Cantal : *Comité Départemental du Tourisme Cantalien (C.D.T.),* Préfecture, 15000 Aurillac, ☎ 71.48.53.54. Haute-Loire : *C.D.T.,* Hôtel du Département, av. Ch.-de-Gaulle, 43000 Le Puy, ☎ 71.09.26.05. **Puy-de-Dôme** : *Comité départemental du Tourisme et du Thermalisme,* 69, bd Gergovia, 63038 Clermont-Ferrand Cedex, ☎ 73.93.84.80. *Direction Régionale de la Jeunesse et des Sports,* 34, rue de A.-Thomas, 63000 Clermont-Ferrand, ☎ 73.35.09.56. *Dir. régionale des Affaires culturelles,* hôtel de Chazerat, 4, rue Pascal, 63000 Clermont-Ferrand, ☎ 73.92.40.41. In Paris : *Maison de l'Auvergne,* 194 *bis,* rue de Rivoli, 75001, ☎ 42.61.82.38.

S.O.S. : **Cantal** : *SAMU,* Emergency Medical Service, ☎ 71.48.45.45 and 17. **Haute-Loire** : *SAMU :* 71.02.02.02. **Puy-de-Dôme** : *S.M.U.R.,* 73.27.33.33. Poisoning Emergency Centre : Clermont-Ferrand, ☎ 73.27.33.33.

Weather forecast : Cantal : ☎ 71.63.67.48. Haute-Loire, ☎ 71.08.66.96. Puy-de-Dôme : ☎ 73.92.28.49.

Farmhouse and chambres d'hôtes : enq. at the *Relais départementaux.* Cantal : préfecture, 15006 Aurillac, ☎ 71.48.53.54. Haute-Loire : 4, av. Charles-de-Gaulle, 43000 Le Puy-en-Velay, ☎ 71.09.26.05. **Puy-de-Dôme** : 69, bd Gergovia, 63000 Clermont-Ferrand, ☎ 73.93.84.80.

Festivals and events : **Maundy Thu.** : *procession of the Penitents* in Saugues, Paulhaguet, Puy-en-Velay and Puy-Valcivières. **Apr** : *carnival* in Yssingeaux. **May** : *con-*

certs and musical attractions daily in Aurillac; *daffodil festival* in Chambon-sur-Lignon; Clermont *festival* (odd-numbered years). **Jun** : 1st Sun, *cherry festival* in Vieillerie; *children's folkore festival* in Clermont (even-numbered years); *fortune-telling festival* in Aigueperse; *gentiane festival* in La Tour d'Auvergne; *spring festival* in Cournon; *curiosity and collectors' festival* in Billom; *French bowls championships* in Clermont-Ferrand. **Jun-Aug** : *International Folk Festival of Spas* at La Bourboule, Châtelguyon, Le Mont-Dore, etc. **Jul** : *concerts* at Vollore. **14 Jul** : *tourist festival* in Olliergues. **End Jul** : *Le Velay International Folk Festival* in Gannat; *Auvergnat vigil* in Saint-Pierre-la-Bourlhonne; *Les Médiévannes* in La Tour-d'Auvergne-Saint-Pardoux. **Jul-Aug** : *festival of French music* in La Chaise-Dieu. **Aug** : *Auvergnat Days* in Issoire; *country festival* in Thiers; *national moto-cross* in Ambert; *French hill-climb motor-racing championships* at Mont-Dore; *International hill-climb motor-racing championships* in Châtelguyon. **15 Aug** : *procession* in Notre-Dame du Puy. **End of Aug** : *hang-gliding festival* at Puy-de-Dôme. **Early Sep** : *National Fair* at Clermont-Ferrand; *bachelors' fair* in Marat; last Thu, *shepherds' pilgrimage* in La Font-Sainte; *artistic and cultural festival* in Saint-Germain-l'Herm.

Fairs and markets : **Jun** : *strawberry and regional products fair* in Teilhede. **Jul** : *Saint-Nectaire festival* in La Tour-d'Auvergne. Aigueperse : *market* Sat; Picherande : *cheese market* every other Fri.

The cheeses of Auvergne

"Auvergne is one huge cheese-board!" exclaims a promotional poster, disputing this title with France itself! For good reason : Cantal *(fresh or aged), especially from* Salers, *the blue-veined* bleu d'Auvergne *and* fourme d'Ambert *(taking its name from the moulds used to shape the cheese) and the smooth and creamy* Saint-Nectaire *are known to all gourmets. Other names should be added to these well-known cows-milk cheeses :* fourme de Montbrison, fourme de Saint-Anthème, Saingorlon, Murol, *and* Gaperon à l'ail *(with garlic), as well as a number of goats-milk cheeses such as* Cabecou, *from the Salers and Aurillac areas.*

Nature parks : *Park naturel régional des volcans d'Auvergne,* administrative centre : Montlosier près Randanne, Aydat, 63210 Rochefort-Montagne, ☎ 73.21.27.19. Information centres : *«Maisons du Parc»* (open daily ex Sun, Mon) at Égliseneuve d'Entraigues, Laveinire; in Aurillac : 10, rue du Pdt-Delzons, ☎ 71.48.68.68; in Salers *(Jun-15 Sep)* : pl. Principale, ☎ 71.40.70.68; at the peak of Puy-de-Dôme *(15 Jun-15 Sep).* Parc Livradois-Forez, Saint-Gervais-sous Meymont, 63880 Olliergues, ☎ 73.95.54.31.

Rambling and hiking : Auvergne is one of France's best regions for rambling and hiking, being traversed by G.R.'s numbers 3, 30, 33, 330, 4, 40, 400, 412, 441, 65 (topoguides). Le *Chamina*, 5, rue Pierre-le-Vénérable, 63000 Clermont-Ferrand, ☎ 73.92.82.60, publishes numerous pedestrian guides and itineraries, together with the yearly updated list of gîtes and relais. *Chamina* also organizes a number of hikes with guides. Further enq : *Bureau des accompagnateurs de la Haute-Auvergne,* 43 bis av. de la Tronquière, 15000 Aurillac, ☎ 71.63.40.84. *Comité départemental de la Randonnée,* préfecture de la **Haute-Loire,** 43000 Le Puy, ☎ 71.09.24.12, ext 319. *Assn. pour la pratique des Sports de Plein air (A.P.S.-P.A.),* 17, pl. Lafayette, 43100 Brioude, ☎ 71.50.00.70.

Scenic railways : *la Galoche, small tourist train* in Velay-Vivarais, Dunières-Saint-Agrève (37 km). From May to Oct, Sun and nat hols; from 15 Jul to end Aug, Sun and Wed; Round the Cantal, ☎ 71.48.08.56. Tour of Cantal, enq. ☎ 71.48.08.56.

Auvergne cuisine

Auvergne culinary specialities are simple and hearty, shunning pretention. Traditional produce, regionally grown for centuries, predominates, almost as if foods imported into Europe from faraway places had not yet penetrated the Massif Central. Similarly, the culinary traditions, although differing from area to area, mostly remain solidly based on long and very gentle simmering. Thus, traditional soups (cabbage-based) and stews blend local produce, to which are added different preparations of lentils, chestnuts or mushrooms. Among the meats, charcuterie excels : rissoles, fricandeaux, saucissons, and, of course, the famous Auvergne ham. *Charolais beef is a speciality, and the celebrated cheese of Salers is another bovine product not to be missed. The delicately flavoured mutton of the region appears in dishes such as* gigot brayaude *(larded, cooked with white wine and herbs), and in* tripou d'Auvergne *made from tripes and paunch. Then, there is poultry, game in season (hare, venison, boar, pheasant, partridge, quail...) and lake fish (trout, char, even salmon — which fortunately have been protected and flourish around Langeac). However lavish your meal, it is inconceivable to skip the cheese course (→ box), nor that it should end without locally-grown fruit, possibly in a* tarte *or a* clafoutis *(flan). To eat as they do in Auvergne, remember to have some tasty rye bread with your meal, and a local wine - even if the wine list is not the equal of other regions in scope and prestige; certainly, you should try* Boudes, Châteaugay, Corent, Dallet, Madargue, *or* Saint-Pourçain, *from the* Allier; *and finally, let us not omit the* Gentiane, *as apéritif, and the Marc d'Auvergne or Prunelle du Velay as a digestif to complete the meal.*

Cycling holidays : *Chamina,* 5, rue Pierre-le-Vénérable, 63000 Clermont-Ferrand, ☎ 73.92.82.60, proposes 15 itineraries departing from the «le Cévenol» S.N.C.F. line, and currently being published; circuits with guides : tour of the Auvergne lakes (7 days). The *Tour cycliste du Puy-de-Dôme* (Jul) is an event open to all. Enq. : M.B. Gounel, 62 *bis,* rue de l'Oradou, 63000 Clermont-Ferrand, ☎ 73.91.63.99. There are numerous organized touristic cycling circuits. Enq : *Ligue Auvergne-Velay de Cyclotourisme,* 27, rue des Chandiots, 63100 Clermont-Ferrand, ☎ 73.25.29.03. M. Charles Rolland, president of the groupe cyclotouriste, Les Bouleaux, bât E, b3, av. Foch, 43000 Le Puy, ☎ 71.09.49.65.

Riding holidays : **Cantal** : enq. : *Assn. Départementale du Tourisme Équestre (A.D.T.E.),* B.P. 423, 15000 Aurillac, ☎ 71.63.54.41. **Haute-Loire** : enq. : *A.D.T.E. Velay-Auvergne,* 5, rue de la Gazelle, 43000 Le Puy, ☎ 71.09.17.48; *Chamina,* see above. List of riding centres at the *C.D.T.*

Technical tourism : *Société thermal de La Bourboule,* bd G.-Clemenceau, 63150 La Bourboule, ☎ 73.81.02.92. *Toys : Manufacture européenne de jouets,* Z.I., 15100 Saint-Flour, ☎ 71.60.11.61. *Société des Eaux de Volvic,* ☎ 73.38.12.66 (for appt.). Farm tours (manufacture of Saint-Nectaire cheese) enq. and listings at C.D.T. Puy-de-Dôme.

Handicraft courses : lace-making, basket-making, the making of straw chair-bottoms, copper-work, etc : *Maison de l'Artisanat,* Bilhac-Polignac, 43000 Le Puy, ☎ 71.09.50.94. Calligraphy, artistic binding, beginners' courses in traditional building techniques : *Assn. «Château-Rocher»,* Saint-Rémy-de-Blot, 63440 Saint-Pardoux, ☎ 73.85.53.00. Pottery, painting on china and glass :

K. Phalippon, *atelier d'expression artistique manuelle*, 63160 Égliseneuve-près-Billom, ☎ 73.68.48.30. Weaving, pottery, porcelain-making : *Les Compagnons du Buffadou*, Faverolles, 15390, Loubaresse, ☎ 71.23.40.84. Beginners' courses in weaving, macramé, lace-making with a spindle, in an old farm in the Livradois mountains : M. Sauvage, «la Fontaine des Thiolles», 63630 Saint-Germain-l'Herm, ☎ 73.72.02.16.

Other courses : cinema-communication (theory and practical, super-8) photography, make-up, masks, introduction to astronomy and astronomical photography; canoe-kayak, sailing : enq. at the *Dir. dép. de la Jeunesse et des Sports.* Wind-surfing : *Club des Sports de Clermont-Ferrand*, 19, av. de la Libération, ☎ 73.93.93.59. Tennis : *Tennis-Club de Pradelles*, 63200 Marsat, ☎ 73.38.58.68. Hang-gliding : *Aéro-club de Brioude Chamina* (see "Rambling"). Archaeology, rural architecture, spinning, etc. : *Groupe de recherches historiques et archéologiques de la vallée de la Sumène*, Antignac, 15240 Saignes, ☎ 71.40.23.76. Squash : *Club Squash-Tonic*, Le Puy, ☎ 71.02.22.97. Geology : *La maison des volcans*, Château Saint-Étienne, 15000 Aurillac, ☎ 71.48.49.09.

Children : "riding holidays" : Montcelet riding farm, Saint-Gervazy, 63340 Saint-Germain-Lembron, ☎ 73.96.44.51; Zanières riding centre, 63420 Ardes-sur-Couze, ☎ 73.71.84.30. Sailing instruction for beginners in Gournon, from 2 until 6 pm. Enq. : *Direction Départementale de la Jeunesse et des Sports*, cité administrative, rue Pélissier, 63034 Clermont-Ferrand Cedex, ☎ 73.92.42.68.

Aquatic sports : numerous stretches of water. Enq : *C.D.T., S.I., O.T.* and *Club des Sports de Clermont-Ferrand*, 19, av. de la Libération, ☎ 73.93.93.59.

Diving : *Club de Plongée Aurillacois*, Centre nautique, ☎ 71.48.26.80. *Club Arverne de Plongée* (ex Aug.), M. Dondainas, 23, rue A.-Fallières, 63000 Clermont-Ferrand, ☎ 73.37.37.44. *Club de Plongée Sous-Marine Clermontois*, B.P. 406, 63011 Clermont-Ferrand Cedex. *Club Vellave de Plongée*, Coopérative d'habitat rural, bd Bertrand, 43000 Le Puy-en-Velay ☎ 71.09.28.01.

Canoeing : Auvergne offers numerous and varied possibilities for canoeing. *Ligue Auvergne de Canoë-Kayak*, M. Jeanmougin, pl. Jos.-Gardet, 63800 Cournon, ☎ 73.84.81.33. *Association sportive de la vallée d'Olt*, 15120 Vieillerie, ☎ 71.49.95.81.

Motoring and motorcycling : *Ligue motocycliste régionale d'Auvergne*, 1, rue J.-Prugnard, 63100 Cébazat, ☎ 73.24.00.83. *Moto-club d'Auvergne*, 40, bd Charles-de-Gaulle, 63000 Clermont-Ferrand, ☎ 73.93.19.84.

Golf : Royat (9 holes) and Le Mont-Dore (9 holes), Chambon-sur-Lignon (4 holes), Orcines (14 holes).

Facts and figures

Location : in the centre of France covering most of the Massif Central. A number of rivers rise in its mountains and flow down to the Atlantic and the Mediterranean.

Area : 18700 km²

Climate : Auvergne has a reputation for harsh weather especially in winter, when the temperatures drop sharply and the mountains are covered in snow. Spring temperatures vary from one extreme to the other; summer tends to be heavy and hot, although higher up the mountains the air is refreshing; autumn is usually the best season of the year.

Population : 967000, mainly in Puy-de-Dôme and Clermont-Ferrand.

Administration : Department of the **Cantal**, Prefecture : Aurillac; Department of the **Haute-Loire**, Prefecture : Le Puy; Department of the **Puy-de-Dôme**, Prefecture : Clermont-Ferrand.

Skiing in Auvergne

Thanks to prolonged and ample snow during the winter months, the Auvergne region and the Massif Central mountains are remarkably well-suited to winter sports, and excellent facilities have been installed since the early 1950s. There are a number of alpine skiing centres, but the emphasis is on cross-country skiing, at cosy family resorts. Mont-Dore, Super-Besse and Super-Lioran are the main centres in Auvergne, popular with the French as well as with visitors. But Chastreix-Sancy, Chambon-les-Neiges and Saint-Anthème (22 km from Ambert) are also well frequented. At Alberoche-Collandres and La Bourboule-Charlannes a start has been made with ski-trekking.

Hot baths and volcanos

The Auvergne is a truly spectacular region, shaped in the fierce volcanic activity of the tertiary era after the shock of the geological upheaval which created the Alps. Several volcanic massifs piled on top of each other over some 30 million years; the gigantic mass of the Cantal, which is, in fact, an enormous, eroded volcanic cone, probably reached 75 km in circumference and some 3000m high. The next act was the appearance of the Dore, Cézallier and Aubrac peaks and those of Mégal and Mézenc of Velay, some 12 million years ago. The second phase of the phenomenon, which, comparatively speaking, occurred only yesterday, was relatively minor in size; the Devès chain, and the Puys (or Dômes) developed during the quarternary era some 50000 years ago, in a burst of volcanic activity which continued until about 5000 BC, resulting in a chain 30-km long from north to south and 3 to 4 km wide. But the Puy is no ordinary volcano; the giant of the chain, is a massive pyramid dominating some 60 extinct craters. Volcanos like this, Stromboli-type or ejection cones, sometimes give the effect of nested craters — one inside the other — when there have been several eruptions; other times breached craters have split to allow the formation of rugged lava fields spreading over several miles. A third type, solid-walled explosion craters, today form lakes, or marshes. As for the Puy-de-Dôme itself, it is a crater-less Pelean volcano which produced "domite", a clear lava that solidified rapidly and here accumulated to form the dome, while elsewhere characteristic volcanic dykes, necks or spines were produced.

Potholing and spelunking : *Société Aurillacoise de Spéléologie*, 1, rue Jean Moulin, 15000 Aurillac, ☎ 71.64.24.40. *Groupe Spéléologique Auvergnat*, 62, rue Alexis-Piron, 63170 Aubière.

Winter sports : cross-country skiing : the entire Massif central can be safely crossed on skis, thanks to excursions organized by *Chamina*, 5, rue P.-le-Vénérable, 63000 Clermont-Ferrand, ☎ 73.92.82.00. Enq. concerning winter sports resorts at the *T.O.*

Climbing-mountaineering : *Club Alpin Français*, 3, rue Mal-Joffre, salle n° 7, 63000 Clermont-Ferrand, ☎ 73.92.16.37. *Groupe des alpinistes gaulois*, 40, av. A.-Elisabeth, 63000 Clermont-Ferrand, ☎ 73.26.50.75.

Hang-gliding : *Féd. Française de Vol à Voile Libre,* Ligue du Centre, M. Lacombe, 10, bd de Lafayette, 63000 Clermont-Ferrand. *Assn. de Vol Libre d'Auvergne,* M. A. Molia, 20, av. J.-Jaurès, 63400 Chamalières, ☎ 73.35.32.84. *Les Ailes de Plomb du Cantal,* M. Dourel, allée de la Promenade, 15800 Le Puech-Vic-sur-Cère, ☎ 71.47.56.56.

Aerial sports : flight school at flying club in Le Puy, ☎ 71.05.76.42 and Brioude, ☎ 71.50.13.53.

Parachuting : *Para-Club,* Mlle Malbec, Aéro-Club de Tronquière, 15000 Aurillac, ☎ 71.64.22.00. *Aérodrome Le Puy/Loudes,* M. Dursapt, 2, rue de Sébastopol, 43300 Langeac, ☎ 71.77.11.41.

 Towns and places

AIGUEPERSE

Clermont-Ferrand 31, Montluçon 74, Paris 359 km
pop 2740 ⊠ 63260   B1

Former capital of the Duchy of Montpensier, a modest linear town in the centre of the rich agricultural region of Limagne.

▶ **Sainte Chapelle★,** built in 1475 by Louis I of Bourbon-Montpensier («Louis le Bon», 1402-86); excellent 14thC statues. ▶ Hôtel de Ville (17thC) : belfry with jack o' the clock (animated clock). ▶ 13th-14thC church (rebuilt nave) with 15thC **"Mourning of the Dead Christ"** (wood polychrome group) and remnants of frescos.

Nearby

▶ Above **Chaptuzat** *(3 km NW),* château de la Roche★ on the edge of the plateau (view★), 11th-12thC fortress rebuilt in the 15th-16thC *(9-12 & 2-7).* ▶ **Montpensier** *(3 km NE),* a tiny village despite the historical splendour of the family that bore its name, hidden away among vineyards at the foot of a butte (view★). **Effiat,** 3 km farther, has a pretty Louis XII château★; don't miss the Grand Salon *(9-12 & 2-7, daily Jun.-Sep. ; Sat., Sun. and nat. hols. Mar.-May and Oct.-Nov.);* 1 km farther on : **château de Denone,** 16thC *(2-7 Easter school hols. and Jul.-Aug.);* in the 12thC church at **Biozat,** figured capitals★ and 15thC frescos. From here, return to Aigueperse via **Saint-Genès-du-Retz** (Romanesque church). ▶ **Artonne** *(5.5 km SW)* with a Romanesque church in part, dating to the 10thC. At **Saint-Myon,** church★ with a superb apse.   ☐

Practical Information _____

SNCF ☎ 73.63.60.35.

Hotel :
★ **Marché,** pl. du Marché, ☎ 73.63.61.96, Euro Visa, 20 rm ℗ closed 1-15 Oct, 115. Rest. ♦ ♪ ♿ closed Wed eve, 30 Sep-15 Oct, 50-75 ; child : 30.

ALLIER Gorges

                                                                            B3
From Vieille-Brioude to Monistrol-d'Allier *(63 km, approx 2 h 30)*

The fish-filled River Allier runs over rocks and gravel, snaking its way between mountains speckled with ancient villages perched on hillsides.

▶ **Vieille-Brioude.** ▶ **Saint-Ilpize,** a typical valley village, ranged along an escarpment, with a modest church and a ruined castle. ▶ **Blassac :** 11th-12thC church with 14thC frescos. ▶ **Lavoûte-Chilhac,** on a peninsula linked to the left bank by a 15thC bridge; important 18thC buildings from a former Benedictine monastery; 15thC church (see treasure room, *8 or 9-12 & 2-6 or 7).* ▶ **Saint-Cirgues :** 15thC frescos★ in the church choir; 10 km W, on the **Ally Plateau** are a number of windmills, including one still in working order. ▶ Frescos, sculptures or architec-

ture make almost every church in the valley worth stopping for : **Aubazat, Arlet** *(off the road),* **Peyrusse, Langeac** (pop. 4733 ; small capital of this region ; ancient houses). **Chanteuges** is a pretty village clustering around an old priory (see the cloister). On the other bank, **Sainte-Marie-des-Chazes** Romanesque chapel. ▶ Leave the valley at **Prades** (basalt colonnades) to **Monistrol-d'Allier** by the ruins of the Rochequde Château, in a superb setting★ ; nearby, more basalt colonnades at Escluezis ; 9 km N, **Mercoeur Château :** Renaissance, with 12th-14thC keep (prison ; *visit possible).*   ☐

Practical Information _____

LANGEAC, ⊠ 43300, 41 km W of **Le Puy.**
ⓘ pl. Aristide-Briand, ☎ 71.77.05.41.
SNCF ☎ 71.77.05.63.

▲ ★★*Le Prado* (133 pl), ☎ 71.77.05.01.

Recommended
Chambres d'hôtes : *Chez M. Simon,* Lestival, ☎ 71.77.04.99, table d'hôtes.
Events : *Feast of Saint Gal,* 1st Sun in Jul ; *Midsummer's Eve bonfire,* in June.

PRADES, ⊠ 43300, 13 km SE of **Langeac.**

Hotel :
● ★★ **Chalet de la Source,** rte de St-Julien, ☎ 71.74.02.39, Visa, 17 rm ℗ ♿ ▩ ♨ pens (h.s.), closed 1 Oct-16 Apr. Trout fishing. Friendly place to stay, 360. Rest. ♦ ♿ Good food : *escalope de saumon au cerfeuil, étuvée de pintade au xérès,* 65-110 ; child : 35.

AMBERT

Le Puy 74, Clermont-Ferrand 78, Paris 436 km
pop 8026 ⊠ 63600   C2

A variety of small industries has taken over from the paper mills which were once the focus of wealth for this modest regional capital of the Livradois : more than 300 watermills fed by the streams and rivers of the area to make paper at the end of the 16thC.

The only tangible remains of the fortunes accumulated by the papermakers is the imposing Gothic **church** (one of the few in this style in the Auvergne), built of granite at a period and in a region where the norm was *pise* (a clay, stone and mud mix). ▶ Numerous **15th-16thC houses** in the narrow, twisting streets of the old town. ▶ Circular town hall. Museum of Agricultural machinery and steam engines *(15 Jun.-15 Sep., 9-12 & 2-6 ; low season on request).*

Nearby

▶ **Richard de Bas Mill★** *(4 km E)* : a perfect example of the paper-mills of yesteryear, with manufacturing processes dating to the 14thC and a whole floor of stretched lines open to the wind to dry the sheets *(9-12 & 2-6 ; Jul.-Aug. 9-8 ;* museum, history of paper). From the mill you can take a pleasant trip through the **Forez Mountains**

Gliding : *Centre de vol à voile du Velay,* ☎ 71.09.64.33. *Aéroclub de Brioude,* M. J.-C. Brun, ☎ 71.50.04.67. *Centre de vol à voile,* aéro-club P. Herbaud, 63500 Issoire, ☎ 73.89.16.62.

Hunting and shooting : enq. at the *Féd. dép. des Chasseurs.* **Cantal :** 14, allée du Vialenc, ☎ 71.48.62.66. **Haute-Loire :** 17, bd A.-Clair, ☎ 71.09.10.91. **Puy-de-Dôme :** 42, rue Morel-Ladeuil, ☎ 73.93.76.27.

Fishing : enq at the *Féd. dép. des Assn. de Pêche et de Pisciculture.* **Cantal :** 14, allée du Vialenc, ☎ 71.48.19.25. **Haute-Loire :** 32, rue Henri-Chas, 43000 Le Puy, ☎ 71.09.09.44. **Puy-de-Dôme :** 65, rue Oradou, 63000 Clermont-Ferrand, ☎ 73.91.42.33.

(55 km; approx. 2 hr), taking D996 to the left; a good run over Pradeaux Pass to **Saint-Anthême**, a little summer resort and winter-sports centre. Go N up the valley of the Ance River by D139 to reach the **Grand Genèvrier**, where the mountain farm of Coq Noir has been transformed into a museum★ celebrating *Fourme*, a local country cheese (tastings; *1 Jul.-15 Sep.*). Past Supeyres Pass (alt. 1 366 m), view★ on the way down of the **Cirque de Valci-vières** (steep hollow). □

Practical Information ─────────────

AMBERT

ⓘ 4, pl. de l'Hôtel-de-Ville, ☎ 73.82.01.55; pl. G.-Courtial, ☎ 73.82.14.15 (h.s.).

🚋 ☎ 73.92.50.50/73.82.09.60.

Hotels :

★★ *Le Livradois*, 1, pl. du Livradois, ☎ 73.82.10.01, AE DC Euro Visa, 14 rm Ⓟ closed Mon eve and Sun eve (Oct-Easter), 190. Rest. ♦ ♪ Lots of good traditional fare : *œufs brouillés aux mousserons, fricassée de volaille aux écrevisses.* Local wines, 70-200; child : 50.

★ *La Chaumière* (L.F.), 41, av. du Mal-Foch, ☎ 73.82.14.94, AE DC Euro Visa, 15 rm Ⓟ ♨ closed Sat eve and Sun eve, 6 Mar-5 Apr, 31 Aug-6 Sep, 150. Rest. ♦ ♪ 55-140.

★ *La Gare*, 17, av. de la Gare, ☎ 73.82.00.27, 21 rm Ⓟ ≼ pens (h.s.), closed Sat, 15 Oct-15 Nov, 300. Rest. ♦ 45-95.

▲ ★★*Trois Chênes*, on the banks of the Dore, rte de Puy (120 pl), ☎ 73.82.34.68.

Nearby

La CHAULME, ⊠ 63660 Saint-Anthême, 22 km E on the N 496.

Hotel :

Creux de l'Oulette (L.F.), ☎ 73.95.41.16, Euro Visa, 11 rm Ⓟ 🐾 80. Rest. ● ♦ ♪ closed Tue eve and Wed 20 Nov-20 Mar ex Xmas wk. Simple and appealing, this pretty little Auvergnat eatery is known for its home-cured pork, 35-90.

ARLANC

Ambert 16, Saint-Etienne 80, Paris 452 km
pop 2300 ⊠ 63220   B-C2

A little city with two hearts; in the north it clusters around a Romanesque church (remodeled 15th-16thC); in the south, the town has its commercial activity; on the Place de l'Hôtel de Ville is a lacemaking museum *(Jul.-Sep. 10-12 & 3-6; rest of the year : 3-6)*.

Nearby

▶ 13thC ironwork on the door of the church★ at **Dore-l'Église** *(4 km SE)*. ▶ The 15thC church of **Marsac-en-Livradois** *(7 km N)* has an evident southern character; S, chapel housing the Musée des Pénitents Blancs du Livradois (Museum of the White Penitents; *Jun.-Sep., 9:30-11:30 & 2-6; Sat., Sun., Mon. low season).* 9 km SW, walks around **Saint-Sauveur** in the Dore gorges; houses and ruins of a 15thC castle; protected site★. □

ARLEMPDES*

Le Puy 28, Aubenas 76, Paris 544 km
pop 182 ⊠ 43490 Costaros   C3

A curious and spectacular fortified village, above which perch the ruins of a 12th-14thC castle *(apply at Hôtel du Manoir)* on a volcanic rock over the rugged gorges of the Loire : site★. Small Romanesque church.

Nearby

▶ **Goudet** *(10 km)*, another pleasant site above the gorges at the foot of the ruins of Beaufort Castle. □

AURILLAC

Brive 98, Clermont-Ferrand 160, Paris 546 km
pop 33197 ⊠ 15000   A3

The name itself tells you that you are now in southern or Occitanian, France; the flat tiled roofs, a jumble of houses with wooden balustrades and the inhabitants' different approach to life : all emphasize the fact that this is the Midi.

▶ The old town is clearly marked, clustering around the **church of St. Géraud** (mainly 17thC). ▶ 400 m N, the **St. Etienne Château**, rebuilt in 1880, houses the **Maison des Volcans★** : exhibitions on volcanos in the Auvergne region and other parts of the world. *(Jul.-Aug., 10-12 & 2-7; closed Sun. am; Sep.-Jun. 9-12 & 2-6; closed Sun.).* ▶ The 16thC Maison des Consuls★ is today given over to the **Musée du Vieil Aurillac**, the old city *(Apr.-Sep., 2-6 Wed.-Sat.)*. ▶ On Place Gerbert (Gerbert was a former monk of St. Géraud and first French Pope as Sylvester II in 999), is the wax museum (Historial; *daily 2-7)*. View★ upstream from the neighbouring bridge of old houses bordering the Jordanne. ▶ 17thC Flemish tapestries★ in the **Palais de Justice** (law courts; *9-12 & 2-6; closed Sat. pm and Sun.)*. ▶ In the church of Notre-Dame-des-Neiges (14th-16thC) : 17thC Black Virgin. ▶ **Rames Museum★** *(2nd floor, 10-12 & 2-6; closed Sun. am, Tue. and nat. hols.)* : exhibition on life in the Cantal Region; **Parieu Museum** *(3rd floor, same hours)* : Fine Arts.

Nearby

▶ **Château de Conros**, 4 km SW of **Arpajon-sur-Cère** *(4 km S)*, old feudal manor, housing a museum of arts and traditions of Cère Valley *(14 Jul.-Aug., 2-7).* ▶ **Route des Crêtes★** (ridge road), NE, above the right bank of the Jordanne River : views★; continue down into the **Mandailles Valley★** before climbing to Puy Mary peak. ▶ **Laroque-brou** *(25 km W)*, on the right bank of the Cère below feudal ruins; 14thC church; small archaeological collection at the *mairie* ; 16thC Messac Château *(visit on request).* 5 km upstream, the **Saint-Étienne-Cantalès** dam turns the Cère into a 12 km long lake (view★). □

Practical Information ─────────────

ⓘ pl. du Square, ☎ 71.48.46.58.
✈ *Aurillac-Tronquières*, ☎ 71.63.56.98.
🚋 71.48.50.50/71.48.10.12.
Car rental : *Avis*, 35, av. Pupil.-de-la-Nation, ☎ 71.48.08.84; train station.

Hotels :

★★★ *Grand Hôtel de Bordeaux* (L.F., Mapotel), 2, av. de la République, ☎ 71.48.01.84, Tx 990316, AE DC Euro Visa, 37 rm Ⓟ ♪ closed 20 Dec-20 Jan. Warm welcome, 240.

★★★ *La Thomasse*, 48, rue du Dr-Mallet, ☎ 71.48.26.47, AE DC Euro Visa, 22 rm Ⓟ ♨ & 250.

★★ *L'Univers*, 2, pl. P.-Sémard, ☎ 71.48.24.57, AE Euro Visa, 42 rm Ⓟ ♨ ✷ 160. Rest. ♦ *L'Etoile d'Or* ✷ 80-130.

★★ *La Ferraudie*, 15, rue Bel-Air, ☎ 71.48.72.42, DC Euro Visa, 22 rm Ⓟ ≼ & 180.

Restaurant :

♦♦ *La Reine Margot*, 19, rue G.-de-Veyre, ☎ 71.48.26.46, Euro Visa ♪ & closed Mon ex Aug. Regional decor and delicious food. Don't miss it : *ris de veau aux cèpes, filet de bœuf au poivre, filet de turbot.* Friendly service, 55-120.

▲ ★★★*L'Ombrade* (200 pl), ☎ 71.48.28.87.

Recommended

♦ pastry-candies : *Favre*, 11, rue des Carmes, tourte auvergnate; sweetmeats : *chez Vernande*, 16, rue des Frères.

─────────────

Looking for a locality? Consult the index at the back of the book.

BILLOM*

Clermont-Ferrand 27, Ambert 55, Paris 412 km
pop 4164 ⊠ 63160   B2

A few small industries and an important position in
the garlic and spice markets haven't yet restored its
medieval importance : at that time it had 5 000 inhabitants, and was, in the 13thC, an important university
town with more than 2 000 students.
▶ A number of beautiful **old houses** still survive from the
period of glory and prosperity : see the **Corporation of
Butchers** (trade guild), and the Dean's House (16thC ; Rue
des Boucheries), the **Chapter House** (façade of the old
university, 1447), the 16thC houses of the Échevin (magistrate) and the Bailli (bailiff). ▶ The **church** has a remodeled Romanesque choir, surrounded by 12thC **grillwork★** ;
in a chapel, 14thC frescos★ ; 11thC crypt★ ; in the left
aisle : frescos and sculptured group of the Burial of
Christ (15thC).

Nearby

▶ **Chauriat** *(7 km NW)* has an interesting Auvergnat
Romanesque church★ ; note the remarkable mosaic work
on the S transept gable ; figured capitals. ▶ The capitals
of the church in **Espirat** *(4 km)* are no less interesting.
▶ **Ravel** *(12 km NE)* has a fine château rebuilt during
17th-18thC on the remains of a medieval fortress :
18thC apartments★, paintings *(Easter-1 Nov., 10-12 &
2-7);* 2.5 km W, the church of **Moissat-Bas** has a wooden
shrine★ sheathed in copper (13thC); 5 km S, **Glaine-Montaigut** : Romanesque church with notable capitals.▶ 5 km
SE of Billom : remains of **Montmorin Castle** (12thC) on a
hilltop ; the main building has been turned into an Auvergnat museum *(2-7 daily Jul.-Oct., Sat.-Sun. rest of year);*
return to Billom making the round trip through **Saint-Dier-
d'Auvergne** (Romanesque church); 5 km S, **château des
Martinanches**, 15th-16thC *(2-7 daily 15 Jun.-15 Sep.)* and
ruins of the **château de Mauzun★** (12th-16thC ; *10 min
climb;* panorama).   □

BLESLE*

Saint-Flour 39, Le Puy 83, Paris 456 km
pop 851 ⊠ 43450   B2

A country town with many stone monuments, indicating a prosperous past due mainly to an abbey which,
in the 16thC, became a chapter of canonesses.
▶ Ruins of fortifications and massive 13thC square
keep★, 14thC bell tower★, remains of a church. ▶ The
Romanesque **abbey church★** dates back to Carolingian
times ; stalls, treasure room★. ▶ The town hall now occupies the 15thC main building of the abbey. ▶ Several
15th-16thC houses.

Nearby

▶ **Massiac** *(9 km S)*, country holiday centre ; 15thC church
with beautiful 15thC reliquary Virgin. ▶ **Léotoing** *(16 km
NE)* : 11thC chapel decorated with 15thC murals ; ruins of
13thC château, large cylindrical keep overlooking the gor-
ges★ of the Alagnon River ; a little to the N, at the opening of the gorge, **Lempdes** has an original semicircular
market hall on Doric pillars ; 6 km farther on, the church
of **Saint-Gervazy** has a Romanesque statue of The Virgin
Enthroned★★, without doubt the most beautiful in the Puy-
de-Dôme.   □

Practical Information _____

Nearby

MASSIAC, ⊠ 15500, 9 km S.
⬧ rue de la Paix, ☎ 71.23.03.93.   ⬦
SNCF ☎ 71.23.02.69.

Hotel :
★★ **Mairie** (L.F.), rue Albert-Chalvet, ☎ 71.23.02.51, Euro

Visa, 22 rm ℗ ⬜ ⬠ closed Mon, 15 Nov-15 Mar, 170.
Rest. ♦ ⫶ ⬠ 50-85.

⚓ ★★*L'Allagnon* (85 pl), ☎ 71.23.03.93.

La BOURBOULE

Clermont-Ferrand 53, Mauriac 70, Paris 439 km
pop 2403 ⊠ 63150   A2

A well-known spa resort (specializing in the relief of
asthma, skin disorders and allergies), with all attendant leisure facilities.
▶ **Grands Thermes** : a sort of pseudo-Byzantine palace.
▶ On the opposite bank of the Dordogne River, **Fenestre
Park★**, departure point for a cable-car up to **Charlannes
Plateau** *(closed Oct.-15 Dec.; also accessible by road :
7 km),* a pleasant wooded park overlooking the valley of
the Dordogne. ▶ N of the resort, excursion *(7 km by car
and 1/2 hr on foot)* to **Banne d'Ordanche** (alt. 1 515 m ;
panorama★).   □

Practical Information _____

⚴ (2 May-30 Sep), ☎ 73.81.02.90.
⛰ 850-1500m.
⬧ pl. de l'Hôtel-de-Ville, ☎ 73.81.07.99.
SNCF ☎ 73.81.03.64.

Hotels :
★★ **Aviation** (L.F.), rue de Metz, ☎ 73.81.09.77, Visa,
48 rm ℗ ⬠ closed 15 Apr-1 May, 1 Oct-20 Dec, 190.
Rest. ♦ ⫶ ⬥ ⬠ 60-90.
★★ **International**, av. d'Angleterre, ☎ 73.81.05.82, 16 rm
⬟ ⬠ closed 20-30 Apr, 3 Nov-18 Dec. In 42-acre
Fenestre Park, 400. Rest. ♦ ⫶ ⬠ 75-100.
★★ **Parc**, quai Mal-Fayolle, ☎ 73.81.01.77, AE DC Euro
Visa, 54 rm ℗ ⬠ ⬜ ⫶ pens (h.s.), closed
25 Sep-15 May, 450. Rest. ♦ ⫶ ⬠ 70-95.
★ **Le Pavillon** (L.F.), av. d'Angleterre, ☎ 73.81.01.42,
26 rm ⬥ ⬠ ⬥ ⬠ closed 20 Sep-20 May, 120.
★ **Poste**, bd G.-Clemenceau, ☎ 73.81.09.66, 50 rm ⬠ ⫶
pens (h.s.), closed 29 Sep-9 May. Across from the hot
springs, 325. Rest. ♦ ⫶ ⬠ 50-70; child : 35.
Auberge Tournebride, rte de Murat-le-Quaire,
☎ 73.81.01.91, 8 rm ℗ ⬠ ⬟ ⬜ ⬠ half pens, closed Mon
ex school hols (l.s.), 14-21 Apr. Family atmosphere, 450.
Rest. ♦♦ ⬠ ⬠ 75-160; child : 50.

⚓ ★★★*Les Clarines* (920 m) (100 pl), ☎ 73.81.02.30;
★★*Le Piquetou*, rte de la Tour (80 pl), ☎ 73.95.03.02;
★★*Les Cascades* (850 m) (165 pl), ☎ 73.81.10.20; at
Murat-le-Quaire, *Natural camping area*, ☎ 73.81.01.59; at
Saint-Sauves, ☎ 73.81.17.08.

Recommended
Baby-sitting : info *S.I.*
Rural-gîte : villa *l'Eau-Vive*, bd Mal-Leclerc,
☎ 73.81.05.28; at Grand-Tertre, villa *les Tamaris*, at
Buguette (1 km), ☎ 73.81.02.52.

BRIOUDE**

Le Puy 60, Clermont-Ferrand 70, Paris 456 km
pop 7854 ⊠ 43100   B2-3

A terraced market town above the valley of the Allier
River ; once an ecclesiastical seigniory (feudal estate)
of considerable financial importance. It is today an
important veal and agricultural market and a popular
salmon-fishing centre.
▶ The **Basilica of St. Julien★** (11th-12thC) is the biggest Romanesque church in Auvergne, its majesty reinforced by impressive polychrome stone work ; the S
porch★ retains its original metalwork ; the nave, heightened in the 13thC, is preceded by a narthex★ with Romanesque frescos in the gallery ; other frescos in the nave,
where the capitals★ are not to be missed ; 16thC stone
floor ; 15th-16thC statues. ▶ Old houses ; from the terrace
of the town hall, view★ over the valley.

Nearby

▶ **Lavaudieu** *(10 km SE)* : Romanesque abbey church; the nave still has an important group of frescos★ from the 14thC; sober cloister *(10-12 & 2-5 or 6)*, with wooden upper floor, leads directly into the refectory (12thC fresco). Small museum of popular arts and traditions. ▶ 5 km farther on, **Domeyrat** : Romanesque church; dominated by the ruins of a 15thC castle. ▶ **Auzon**, 12 km N, was once a fortified town; Romanesque church : see S porch★ and works of art inside.　□

Practical Information —————————————

ⓘ pl. de Champanne, ☎ 71.50.05.35.
SNCF ☎ 71.50.11.51.

Hotels :
★★ *Hôtel Moderne* (France-Accueil), 12, av. V.-Hugo, ☎ 71.50.07.30, AE DC Euro Visa, 17 rm Ⓟ half pens (h.s.), closed Sun eve , Mon ex in season and hols, 1 Jan-15 Feb, 370. Rest. ● ♦ *Marius* Foies and confits to take out, but also *saumon à l'ail confit, canard à la moutarde douce*, to enjoy on the spot, 115-250.
★★ *Le Brivas* (Inter-Hôtel), rte du Puy, ☎ 71.50.10.49, Tx 392817, AE DC Euro Visa, 30 rm Ⓟ ⌕ ⌂ ⌐ closed Fri eve, Sat lunch (15 Oct-15 Mar), 20 Nov-28 Dec. Surrounded by flowers with a view of the Livradois mountains, 205. Rest. ♦ ⌂ 60-150; child : 45.
★ *Poste et Champanne*, 1, bd Dr-Devins, ☎ 71.50.14.62, 22 rm Ⓟ ⌐ ⌘ closed Sun eve (l.s.), 140. Rest. ♦ ⌂ Spec : *potée auvergnate*, delicious *petit salé aux lentilles*, 50-80.

La CHAISE-DIEU★★★

Le Puy 41, Saint-Etienne 79, Paris 469 km
pop 953 ⊠ 43160　　　　　　　　　　　　　　　B-C2

At the heart of an immense forested area, a few scantily populated hamlets; as its name — literally, the throne of God — indicates, this was once the seat of an influential abbey : one of its former monks became Pope.

▶ **Church of St. Robert★★**, superb 15thC Gothic edifice, built at the order of Pope Clement VI, boasts a majestic interior with a Flamboyant Gothic choir screen★ (15thC); 17thC organ case; important works of art in the choir *(9 or 10-12 & 2-5 or 7; closed Tue. Nov.-May)* : tomb of Clement VI★ (d. 1353); 156 Gothic stalls★; early 16thC tapestries★★; 15thC mural of the *Danse Macabre*★ in N side aisle. ▶ S, only two galleries of the **cloister** remain. Over the apse, **Clémentine Tower** looks like a fortified keep. ▶ Next to the cloister, the convent buildings (17th-18thC) house the **Historial** (wax museum, *Jun.-Sep. 9-12 & 2-7*) and the **"Echo Room"** (two people in opposite corners with their backs turned can talk quietly together). ▶ Old houses.

Nearby

▶ **Signal de Saint-Claude** (peak, *1 km E*; alt. 1 112 m; view★). ▶ **Malaguet Lake** *(10 km S)* in the heart of a pine forest. ▶ **Craponne-sur-Arzon** *(19 km E)*, summer resort and mechanized lacemaking centre; 16thC church, with Romanesque tower for belfry; old houses and remains of fortifications.　□

Practical Information —————————————

La CHAISE-DIEU
✠ 1080m.
ⓘ pl. de la Mairie, ☎ 71.00.01.16.

Hotels :
● ★★ *L'Echo et Abbaye* (L.F.), pl. de l'Echo, ☎ 71.00.00.45, AE Euro Visa, 12 rm Ⓟ ⌕ ⌂ ⌐ ⌂ ⌘ closed 5 Nov-10 Apr, 190. Rest. ♦ ⌂ ⌂ ⌘ In the former abbey's refectory. Terrace service, 65-175; child : 55.
★★ *Au Tremblant* (L.F.), ☎ 71.00.01.85, Visa, 28 rm Ⓟ ⌕ ⌂ ⌐ closed 16 Nov-31 Mar, 150. Rest. ♦ ⌂ ⌂ Spec : *coquelet au vin*, 55-95.

Nearby

CRAPONNE-SUR-ARZON, ⊠ 43500, 19 km E.
ⓘ pl. du Fort, ☎ 71.03.23.14.
SNCF ☎ 71.02.50.50.

Hotels :
★★ *Mistou* (L.F.), Pontempeyrat, ☎ 77.50.62.46, 22 rm Ⓟ ⌕ ⌂ ⌂ closed Tue eve and Wed, 11 Nov, Mar, 180. Rest. ● ♦♦ ⌘ The forest, the trout-filled river and a peaceful inn that serves good food by Bernard Roux (and let's not forget the fine cellar!)... Who could ask for more? 85-180; child : 60.
★ *Au Grandgousier* (L.F.), 3, pl. de la Grenette, ☎ 71.03.21.90, 9 rm Ⓟ closed Mon eve (l.s.), 1-8 Sep, 21 Oct-15 Nov, 90. Rest. ♦ ⌂ ⌂ 45-70.

△ ★★★★*Parc des Sports* (14 pl), ☎ 71.00.23.09.

Recommended
Gîte à la ferme : 8 km, le Maisonny-Saint-Georges-Lagricol, ☎ 71.03.25.87.

CHÂTEAUNEUF-LES-BAINS

Clermont-Ferrand 49, Montluçon 55, Paris 375 km
pop 374 ⊠ 63390 St-Gervais d'Auvergne　　　　A1

Tiny mineral water spa on both banks of the Sioule River; a trout fisherman's paradise.

▶ Shady park of Sequoias; porphyry (crystalline) rocks on the right bank, granite on the left.

Nearby

▶ **Sioule Gorges★**, towards Ébreuil (→ Berry); to one side, **Menat** : Romanesque church, very much restored in the 19thC but still preserving carved capitals★ with leaves, interlacings and animals, and a 15thC cloister gallery. ▶ **Saint-Gervase-d'Auvergne** *(8 km W)* : 15thC church with Romanesque apse; from there, visit the **Viaduc des Fades★** (viaduct; *10 km S*), built in 1908, the highest in France (132.5 m above the River Sioule).　□

Practical Information —————————————

⌂ (2 May-30 Sep), ☎ 73.86.67.49.
ⓘ ☎ 73.86.67.86.
SNCF　St-Gervais-Châteauneuf, 8 km, ☎ 73.85.71.85.

Hotel :
★ *Château* (L.F.), ☎ 73.86.67.01, Visa, 38 rm Ⓟ ⌂ ⌂ ⌘ closed Oct-May, 150. Rest. ♦ 55-110; child : 30.

△ ★★*Le Got* (55 pl), ☎ 73.86.67.85.

Recommended
Farmhouse-gîte : at Saint-Gervais d'Auvergne, 7 km, Le Fél, ☎ 73.85.72.35, camping, fishing.
Farmhouse-inn : at Saint-Pardoux CP 63440, *Les Labbis*, 11 km NE on D 122 and D 5, Pouzols, ☎ 73.97.45.56, tasty regional fare.

CHÂTELGUYON

Clermont-Ferrand 20, Montluçon 75, Paris 378 km
pop 4588 ⊠ 63140　　　　　　　　　　　　　　B1

About 100 m above the plain of Limagne on a spur of the Puys chain, this is a health resort for those with digestive problems.

▶ The old town is centred around the church (modern frescos) to the N; **spa★** in the park on either side of the Sardon River, with pine-covered **Chalusset Hill** to the S; from the top, view over the Puys, Limagne and Forez mountains.

Nearby

▶ **Château de Chazeron★** *(3 km W)*, overlooking the W bank of the Sardon : 16th-17thC building with 14thC keep *(May-Sep. 3-6)*. From there, tour the foothills of the Puys Mountains *(50 km, approx. 2 hr)* via **Manzat** (Renaissance woodwork in church), Gour de Tazenat (a perfectly circular crater lake), Charbonnières-les-Vieilles, **Combronde** (18thC town hall), **Davayat** (Louis XIII-style château; *May-15 Oct.10-12 & 2-7; Sat. and Sun. pm rest of year*) and **Saint-Bonnet** (12th-14thC church). ▶ **Enval** *(3.5 km S)*, at the exit from the gorges *(15 min on foot)*, where the Ambène River comes down in a chain of miniature cascades; farther on, **Volvic** and **Tournoël château** (→ Volvic). □

Practical Information _____

♨ (3 May-15 Oct), ☎ 73.86.00.08.
ℹ parc Etienne-Clementel, ☎ 73.86.01.17.
SNCF ☎ 73.86.00.29.

Hotels :
● ★★★★ *Pullman Splendid*, (ex Mapotel), 5-7, rue d'Angleterre, ☎ 73.86.04.80, Tx 990585, AE DC Euro Visa, 88 rm ℙ ≼ ⓜ ⌕ ♪ ⅋ ⌧ closed 16 Oct-24 Apr Near the hot springs, a renovated residence in a park. Rest. ◆◆ ⅋ Delicious omelettes, 125-180.
★★★ *International*, rue A.-Punett, ☎ 73.86.06.72, 68 rm ≼ ⓜ ⌕ ♪ closed Jan-Apr, Oct-Dec, 250. Rest. ◆ ⅋ 90-125; child : 45.
★★★ *Mont-Chalusset*, ☎ 73.86.00.17, Tx 392679, AE DC Euro, 70 rm ℙ ≼ ⓜ ⌕ ♪ closed 30 Sep-2 May, 225. Rest. ◆ ≼ ♪ ⅋ 95-165.
★★★ *Paris*, 1, rue du Dr-Levadoux, ☎ 73.86.00.12, 62 rm ⓜ closed Sun eve, Jan-Feb, 230. Rest. ● ◆ ⅋ Savoury fare, 90-150.
● ★★ *Manoir Fleuri*, rte de Chazeron, ☎ 73.86.01.27, 15 rm ℙ ≼ ⓜ ⌕ closed 5 Oct-25 Apr, 145. Rest. ◆ ≼ ⅋ closed 5 Jan-7 Mar, 85-160.
★ *Bellevue*, 4, rue Punett, ☎ 73.86.07.62, 40 rm ≼ ⓜ ⌕ pens (h.s.), closed 31 Oct-1 Mar, 360. Rest. ◆ ≼ ⅋ 55-120.

Restaurant :
◆ *La Grilloute*, 33, av. Baraduc, ☎ 73.86.04.17, Visa ♪ closed Tue, 1 Oct-5 May. Succulent Auvergnat pork products, excellent terrines and trout in Champagne sauce, 70-140.

⚠ ★★★*Clos de la Balanède* (250 pl), ☎ 73.86.02.47.

Rodez 87, Aurillac 94, Paris 552 km
pop 1267 ⊠ 15110   B3-4
A fortified city in times past, now cautiously developing into a health resort; very much a leader in matters of energy saving, thanks to its hot springs (70-82°C). The majority of buildings have long enjoyed hot water and central heating at very low cost.

▶ 15thC church. ▶ Each of the eight districts of the town has a niche sheltering a statue of its patron saint. ▶ Château de Couffour (14thC, restored) to the S. ▶ 4 km NW, château de Montvallat, of solid granite with corner towers (16th-17thC). □

Practical Information _____

♨ (1 May-17 Oct), ☎ 71.23.51.06.
ℹ 1, av. G.-Pompidou, ☎ 71.23.52.75.

Hotels :
★★ *Aux Bouillons d'Or*, 10, quai du Remontalou, ☎ 71.23.51.42, Euro Visa, 12 rm ≼ ⓜ ⅋ closed Mon eve, Tue (l.s.), Dec-Easter, 190. Rest. ● ◆◆ ⅊ ⅋ Simple and tasty, J.-M. Cornut's cooking is nicely priced : *palette d'agneau sur la mousse de navets, jarret de porc demi-sel à la potée*, 55-220.
★★ *Beauséjour*, 9, av. G.-Pompidou, ☎ 71.23.52.37, 47 rm ℙ ⓜ closed Fri eve and Sat (l.s.), 1 Dec-15 Mar, 170. Rest. ◆ ♪ 45-130.
★★ *Valette*, 29, pl. du Gravier, ☎ 71.23.52.43, 45 rm, closed 15 Oct-1 May, 220. Rest. ◆ ⅋ 70-130.

⚠ ★★*Le Couffour* (170 pl), ☎ 71.23.57.08.

Moulins 96, Saint-Etienne 150, Paris 390 km
pop 151092 ⊠ 63000   B1
Clermont has a very staid appearance (the town of Volvic and its quarries are not far away), but it is by no means dreary. It came late to industrialization (the principal industry is tyre manufacture, developing after the automobile at the end of the last century). But it is now, and has always been, the hub of the region, where the Auvergnat people living in the mountains meet those from the plain, and where health-resort visitors come on excursions. For this is a town full of bustle with a definite flavour of the Midi Region.

▶ **Place de Jaude** (B2) is the link between old and new Clermont, with cafés, theatre and shopping centre and, as is fitting, a statue of the Gallic hero Vercingetorix (Bartholdi, 1902). ▶ The Classical church of **St. Pierre des Minimes** has elegant 18thC woodwork in the choir. ▶ **Rue des Chaussetiers** has been renovated and is now a pedestrian street leading past ancient houses (No. 3, Hôtel Savaron, 1513) to the **cathedral★** (C1; 13th-14thC; facade and spires 19thC). This is an elegant Gothic building, with a light and graceful interior due to extremely slender pillars made possible by using solid basalt stone. 13th-14thC stained glass, frescos of the same period in radiating chapels. From the transept, paid access to Bayette Tower; panorama★ . ▶ Other beautiful old houses in **Rue Pascal** (No. 4, Hôtel de Chazerat) and **Rue du Port★**. ▶ **Notre-Dame-du-Port★★**, excellent example of Auvergnat Romanesque (11th-12thC) with superb choir and figured capitals★★ which are among the most beautiful in the region. ▶ Place de la Poterne, the **Ambroise Fountain★** (1515) in Volvic stone. ▶ **Rue des Gras** (B1-2), interesting houses and a 16thC mansion housing the **Ranquet Museum** (history of the town, *objets d'art*, including medieval sculpture; *10-12 & 2-5 or 6; closed Mon. and nat. hols.*). ▶ Nearby, the St. Pierre Market and the narrow streets make an agreeable stroll (Rue de la Boucherie).

Also... ▶ **Bargoin Museum** (C3; *10-12 & 2-5 or 6; closed Mon. and nat. hols.*) : prehistoric and Gallo-Roman archaeology, paintings and sculpture. ▶ **Lecoq Museum** *(same hours)* : natural history, interesting regional collections. Opposite, **Lecoq Garden★** (7 acres) where a fortified 15th-16thC gate has been re-erected. ▶ **Church of St. Genès** (C2; 14th-15thC) with Flamboyant Gothic side chapels. ▶ **Fontaines Petrifiantes** (petrifying springs) at Saint-Alyre (off map, B1) where in the Peru grotto highly mineralized water leaves carbonate deposits on small objects, which appear like ivories or cameos after two or three months *(9-12 & 2-6; 8-7 Jul.-Aug.)*.

Montferrand *(3 km NE)*

▶ A city of grape growers and merchants and, until the beginning of the 17thC, seat of a court of law. Incomparable collection of **Gothic and Renaissance houses★**. ▶ Among many others, see : **Maison de l'Annonciation** (16thC), **Maison du Notaire** (end of 15thC), **Maison du Sire de Beaujeu** (with pretty Henri II courtyard), **Maison de l'Apothicaire** (15thC). ▶ In the church of Notre-Dame (13th-14thC), fine sculptures from the 17thC.

Chamalières *(1.5 km W)*

▶ Industrialized (iron and steel, paper) long before Clermont, and now its residential annex, halfway between the Auvergnat capital and the hot-spring spa at Royat (→). ▶ The narthex and nave of the church go back to Carolingian times; lovely choir with ambulatory, 12th-13thC.

Nearby

▶ Royat (→) and the Puy-de-Dôme peak. ▶ N of the village, the **Côtes de Clermont** (view★ of the town), where some theories site the Gallic stronghold of Gergovie.

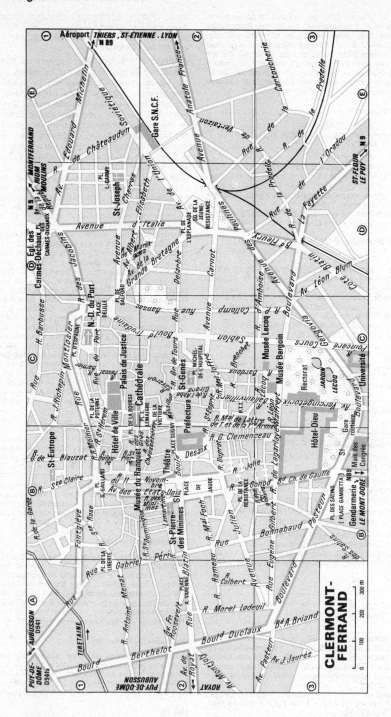

▶ **Gergovie** *(14 km S)* : a monument vigorously recalls the Gauls' dubious victory over Caesar ; overlooking the black basaltic village of the same name (called Merdogne until the last century), this basalt plateau has not yielded any convincing proof of the events reputed to have occurred there ; view★.

Tour of Serre Mt. *(approx 60 km ; 2hr30)*

Leave Clermont by the N89 and D3 to the south ; **Opme,** a truly archaic hamlet, dominated by its château★, a fortress in volcanic rock, 11th-13thC, with 17thC main building. Near **Chanonat,** the château de la Bâtisse (15th-18thC) ; gardens, apartments★ *(May-Sep. 10-12 & 2-7 ; Sat. and Sun. 2-6 rest of year).* From **Crest** (13th-15thC church, remains of fortifications and tower ; view★), descend to the valley of the Veyre River and cross the Gothic bridge at **Saint-Amand-Tallende.** The church★★ of **Saint-Saturnin★** expresses the spirit of monastic poverty ; its bell tower served as a model for many others in the Auvergne. 15thC *Pietà* in the crypt. Imposing 14th-15thC château *(Easter-1 Nov., 9-7)* ; remains of ramparts. 2 km SW, the **abbey of Notre-Dame-de-Randol** (1971) : geometric architecture★, startling in this calm nook of the gorges of the Monne. **Aydat Lake★,** retained by a wall of lava, is surrounded with pleasant forest. Return to Clermont by D145 across the Serre Mountain (views), then by the N89. 9 km NW of the lake is the **château de Montlosier** (near Randanne), administrative centre of the Volcans d'Auvergne nature park (→) : exhibition and models of volcanic activity, audiovisuals *(15 Jun.-30 Sep., 10-12:30 & 2-7).* ☐

Practical Information ⎯⎯⎯⎯⎯⎯⎯⎯

CLERMONT-FERRAND
ℹ 69, bd Gergovia (B3), ☎ 73.93.30.20.
✈ *Clermont-Ferrand-Aulnat*, 6 km, ☎ 73.91.71.00. Air-France office, at the airport, ☎ 73.91.84.84.
SNCF (E2), ☎ 73.91.87.89.
🚌 bd Gergovia (C3), ☎ 73.93.13.61.
Car rental : *Avis*, train station (E2) ; Aulnat airport, ☎ 73.91.18.08 ; Pl. Gallieni, ☎ 73.93.39.90.

Hotels :
★★★ **Altea Gergovia** (ex Frantel), 82, bd Gergovia (B3), ☎ 73.93.05.75, Tx 392658, AE DC Euro Visa, 124 rm [P] ⅃ ⅋ closed Sat lunch and Sun, 400. Rest. ♦♦ **La Rétirade** ⅃ Distinguished cuisine in a comfortable setting. Chef Truchetet is a real pro : *terrine de légumes au foie gras, poulet de Bresse aux écrevisses,* 125-220 ; child : 50.
★★ **Minimes,** 10, rue des Minimes (B2), ☎ 73.93.31.49, 28 rm [P] ⅃ 115.
★★ **St-André,** 27, av. de l'Union-Soviétique (D2), ☎ 73.91.40.40, 25 rm, 180. Rest. ♦ *l'Auvergnat* ⅃ closed Sun. Fine regional fare : *potée, coq au vin, pâté de pommes de terre,* 100-190.
★ **Foch,** 22, rue du Mal-Foch (B2), ☎ 73.93.48.40, Euro Visa, 19 rm ⅋ 80.

Restaurants :
● ♦♦ **Boutron,** 48, rue des Chandiots (off map C3), ☎ 73.24.76.18, Visa ⅋ ⅃ closed Sun, 14 Jul-1 Aug. Reserve one of the 25 seats in this intimate eatery, for a delicate, enjoyable meal : *aiguillette de canard au miel d'acacia, gâteau de lapereau au noisettes et sa confiture d'oignons,* 125-250.
● ♦♦ **Buffet de la Gare Routière,** 69, bd Gergovia (C3), ☎ 73.93.13.32, AE DC Euro Visa [P] ⅃ closed Sat in Jul-Aug. Functions both as a *brasserie* and a restaurant. Spec : seafood, fish, *émincé de filet de bœuf au bleu d'auvergne,* 115-250.
♦♦ **La Table d'Hôte,** 42, rue Fontgiève (B1), ☎ 73.30.95.23, AE DC Euro Visa ⅃ closed Sat noon and Sun eve. Good, fashionable and relatively cheap : *chausson de tomates au coulis de courgettes, confit de lapereau,* 130-220.
● ♦ **Le Brezou,** 51, rue St-Dominique (B2), ☎ 73.93.56.71, Visa [P] ⅋ ⅃ closed Sat and Sun, 20 Dec-5 Jan. Marie-Anne Duchet cooks up superior specialties. Two fine fixed-price menus feature *filet de loup au beurre blanc, ris de veau aux mousserons,* game in season, 60-130.
● ♦ **Clavé,** 10-12, rue St-Adjutor (B1-2), ☎ 73.36.46.30, Euro Visa ⅃ ⅋ Friendly atmosphere, likable food. Spec : *salade de caille aux deux foies gras, pied de veau farci sauce périgourdine,* 110-250.
♦ **Le Bougnat,** 29, rue des Chaussetiers (B2),

☎ 73.36.36.98, Visa ⅃ closed Mon noon and Sun, 6-13 Jul. Folksy regional fare, 70-100.
▲ at Ceyrat, 6 km on N 89, ★★★*Chanset* (210 pl), ☎ 73.61.30.73.

Recommended
Bicycle rental : *Mazeyrat,* 3, bd Gergovia, ☎ 73.91.44.74.
Events : *feast of Notre-Dame du Port,* in May.
Guided tours : daily 15 Jun-15 Sep. info. S.I..
Night clubs : *Le Monos,* 12, rue Ramond, ☎ 73.93.34.35 ; *L'Aquarius,* Pont-du-Château, ☎ 73.23.57.64 ; at Ocet, *New Country,* ☎ 73.84.57.71 ; at Villars-Orcines, *L'Artishow,* ☎ 73.62.17.80.
Youth hostel : 55, av. de l'Union-Soviétique, ☎ 73.92.26.39.
♥ cheese : *Quinty,* Halles St-Pierre ; Mme *Madœuf,* Marché St-Pierre ; chocolates : *Vieillard,* 13, rue Pascal ; pork products : *Marchandon,* 3, rue Blatin ; *Rullière,* 31 bis, rue Gras.

Nearby

Col de CEYSSAT, ✉ 63870 Orcines, 14 km E on D 68.

Restaurant :
● ♦♦ **Auberge des Muletiers,** ☎ 73.87.11.18 [P] ⅋ closed Mon and Sun eve, 23 Aug-8 Sep, 24 Dec-5 Jan. Friendly little mountain inn. Hearty, rustic dishes : *aiguillettes aux pleurotes, cassoulet,* 65-125.

CHAMALIÈRES, ✉ 63400, 5 km W.

Hotels :
★★★ **Radio,** 43, av. Pierre-Curie, ☎ 73.30.87.83, AE DC Euro Visa, 27 rm [P] ⅋ ᨢ ⅋ ⅃ closed 11 Nov-1 Mar, 370. Rest. ● ♦♦♦ ⅋ ⅃ ⅋ closed Mon and Sun eve. Michel Mioche and his wife have settled here for good, after extensive improvements were made on their inn. Show them you approve of the newly decorated "art deco" rooms and the excellent cuisine by stopping in. Regional cooking : *saumon aux lentilles vertes du Puy, civet de caneton orcival, tourte de viande,* local cheeses, 220-340.
★★ **Chalet Fleuri,** 37, av. Massenet, ☎ 73.35.09.60, 40 rm [P] ⅋ 180. Rest. ♦ ⅋ 75-130.

DURTOL, ✉ 63830, 5 km NW on the D 941 A.

Restaurants :
● ♦♦ **L'Aubergade,** rte de la Baraque, ☎ 73.37.84.64, Euro Visa ⅃ closed Mon and Sun eve, 1-21 Mar, 1-21 Sep. Louis-XIII decor, family-style service : *turbot à la crème d'estragon, rognon de veau entier à l'étouffée,* 90-150.
● ♦ **Auberge des Touristes,** rte de la Baraque, ☎ 73.37.00.26, AE Euro Visa ⅃ ⅋ closed Mon and Sun, 27 Apr-5 May, 10-30 Aug. Fresh ocean fish in the hills of Auvergne, ham and *foie gras* as well. Interesting wine list, 130-360.

PÉRIGNAT-LÈS-SARLIÈVE, ✉ 63170 Aubière, 5 km S.

Hotel :
★ **Le Petit Bonneval,** ☎ 73.79.11.11, 4 rm [P] ⅋ ⅋ closed Sun eve , Fri, Easter, 20 Jul-10 Aug, 25 Dec-2 Jan, 120. Rest. ● ♦ ⅃ The pleasure of old-fashioned cooking : *truites aux lardons,* 75-100.

CONDAT

Saint-Flour 59, Clermont-Ferrand 84, Paris 502 km
pop 1568 ✉ 15190   A2

In a delightful basin of meadows surrounded by wooded hills, Condat's first summer villas were built by successful traveling salesmen from the linen trade, a traditional regional activity.

⎯⎯⎯⎯⎯⎯⎯⎯⎯⎯⎯⎯⎯⎯⎯

In preparing for your trip, consult the pages pertaining to the regions. You will find there the description of the region you wish to visit, as well as a list of sites that must be seen, a brief history and practical information.

Nearby

Few vestiges remain of the 12thC Cistercian abbey of **Féniers** *(3 km S)* which was rebuilt in 1686. ▶ **Montboudif** *(6 km NW)* is the village birthplace of Cantal schoolteacher's son Georges Pompidou (1911-74; President of France 1969-74). ▶ **Égliseneuve-d'Entraigues** *(12 km NW)*, up the pretty valley of the Rhue : small Romanesque church, rustic and full of character with interesting capitals; Maison des Fromages d'Auvergne★ (regional cheeses exhibition : audiovisuals; tools; tastings; *15 Jun.-30 Sep. 10-11 & 2-6 daily; hourly visits, tel : 71.78.51.22).* **Rhue Valley★**, downstream *(32 km to Bort-les-Orgues, →* Limousin), by a *corniche* (cliff road) through the Maubert Forest. □

ISSOIRE*

Clermont-Ferrand 37, Le Puy 97, Paris 423 km
pop 15383 ⊠ 63500   B2

A small island of urban life inhabited mainly by technicians in a predominantly rural region; this ancient city is an important industrial centre, producing 50 % of France's aluminum; it is also the site of a Soviet-made hydraulic press, capable of forging parts under 65 000 tons of pressure.

▶ The old town remains a captive of its ancient fortifications, long since disappeared; narrow streets and old buildings, one of which, the *Maison des Échevins*, houses the **Historial** (wax museum) retracing the city's past *(10-7 or 2:30-7)*. ▶ In the town centre, the **church of St. Austremoine★★** (12thC) is a worthy example of the Romanesque art and architecture in the Auvergne region; clumsy restorations effected during the last century; look instead at the scope and imagination of the design and the quality of the architectural detail. Apse★★ remarkable for its architecture and ornamentation; crypt★★, fresco★ of the Last Judgement (15thC) in the narthex.

Nearby

▶ **Parentignat** *(4 km SE)* has a classic 17thC château richly furnished with pieces from the French Regency and Louis XV periods; paintings★; *(2-6; May-Jun., Sun. and nat. hols.; 15 Jun.-20 Sep., daily ex Wed.).* ▶ At **Nonette** *(7 km S of Parentignat)*, ruins★ of a 14thC château on a conical spur; admirable view★ over the valley; in the village, remains of ramparts, ancient houses and 11th-16thC church housing 14thC Christ figure★ of great quality (only the bust remains). 6 km E of Nonette, graceful Romanesque church at **Mailhat** (12thC) is decorated in a vigorous, even earthy style. ▶ **Usson** *(12 km E)*, the flank of a basalt peak bearing a statue (1892) of the Virgin, offers a fine view; old houses, 12th-14thC church, remains of the château where Queen Margot, wife of Henri IV, was exiled from 1585-1605 for "conduct unbecoming of a Queen", a surprising reason when we consider the license permitted at the court (Henri is known to the French as *Vert Galant,* kindly translated as a man who doesn't know his years with women).

Around the Couzes *(approx 110 km; 1/2 day)*

▶ From Issoire, go up the valley of the Couze de Pavin. ▶ At the entrance to **Perrier**, a vertical flow of basalt has been pierced to produce artificial grottos. ▶ In **Saint-Floret**, remains of 13thC château (Gothic hall; 14thC frescos); on a rock, the church of Chastel with 15thC frescos. ▶ **Saurier** : site★, a medieval bridge and fortified gates. Farther on, the **Courgoul Gorges**, through which runs the Couze de Valbeleix; follow the road to Besse-en-Chandesse for a few miles for **Moulin Neuf**, where there is small Auvergnat museum of 19thC rural tools and traditions *(Jun.-Sep. 9-12 & 2-7)*, and, a little farther on, the **Jonas★**, 60 artificial grottos dug out at some unknown, possibly prehistoric, period, much used and fortified during the Middle Ages *(15 May-Sep. 9-12 & 2-7; Sun. pm rest of year)*. ▶ **Compains** : Romanesque church with elegant Gothic choir. ▶ **Saint-Alyre-ès-Montagne**, where

you rejoin the valley of the Couze d'Ardes (or Vallée des Rentières★) with spectacular basalt rock structures; rare 13thC graveyard lantern. ▶ **Ardes-sur-Couze** is the former capital of this modest duchy; in the church the main altar (17thC) includes eight 15thC painted bas-reliefs on wood; stone *Pietà*, paintings, all 15thC. ▶ **Saint-Germain-Lembron**, amid vineyards; 6 km NW, fine Renaissance château★ at **Villeneuve**, with 16th-17thC frescos illustrating tales and fables *(Apr.-Sep. 10-12 & 2-6, closed Tue.; Oct.-Mar., 10-12 & 3-5; closed Tue. and Wed.).* □

Practical Information _____

ISSOIRE
ⓘ pl. Gal-de-Gaulle, ☎ 73.89.15.90.
SNCF ☎ 73.89.20.06.

Hotels :
★★ **Le Pariou**, 18, av. Kennedy, ☎ 73.89.22.11, Euro Visa, 30 rm Ⓟ ⌂ ⌰ closed 20 Sep-10 Oct, 120. Rest. ♦ Flowery terrace. Spec : *poulet au St-Pourçain*, 50-70.
★ **Les Vigneaux**, Le Broc, 5 km S on N 9, ☎ 73.89.10.90, 8 rm Ⓟ ≼ ⌂ ⌰ 150. Rest. ♦ ♪ 120-210.

Nearby

MONTPEYROUX, ⊠ 63730, 13 km N.

Hotel :
● **Auberge de Tralume** (C.H.), ☎ 73.96.60.09, AE DC Euro Visa, 4 rm Ⓟ ≼ ⌂ ⌰ 150. Rest. ● ♦♦ ♪ Charm, character and delectable seasonal cuisine : *ris de veau aux écrevisses, turbot à la moutarde*, 130-220.

PARENTIGNAT, ⊠ 63500 Issoire, 4 km SE.

Hotel :
★★ **Tourette** (L.F.), ☎ 73.55.01.78, 31 rm Ⓟ ⌂ ⌰ ⌰ closed Fri eve and Sat ex Jul-Aug, Feb, 5 Nov-1 Dec, 150. Rest. ♦ 50-150.

SARPOIL, ⊠ 63490 Sauxillanges, 11 km SE.

Restaurant :
● ♦ **La Bergerie**, ☎ 73.71.02.54 Ⓟ ⌂ closed Wed and Sun eve, 2 Jan-1 Mar, 8-15 Jun. Good country cooking goes on here : *chou farci, turbot au four, filet de bœuf au parfum de morilles*, 200-280.

Le LIORAN

Saint-Flour 37, Aurillac 39, Paris 507 km
pop 623 ⊠ 15300 Murat   A3

At the end of one of the oldest road tunnels in France (1839), this simple hamlet has grown into the winter sports resort of **Super-Lioran**, created in 1963 to take advantage of one the Auvergne's best alpine skiing locations.

Nearby

▶ **Cère Pass** (alt. 1 285 m; *45 min on superb road;* views), from here an easy ascent to the Puy de Lioran (1 368-m peak; *15 min)*. ▶ **Plomb du Cantal★** (alt. 1 858 m; *2-3 h ascent, 1hr15-1hr30 descent; or 50 min there and back by cable car from Super-Lioran)*, second highest peak in the Massif Central after Sancy; remarkable panorama★★. ▶ **Alagnon Valley★**, towards Murat; 1.5 km from Lioran on the right, buron de Belles-Aigues (shepherd's hut for making cheese) : cheese-making *(15 Jun.-30 Sep., 10-12:30 & 2:30-7)*. □

Practical Information _____

Le LIORAN
⌘ 1250-1850m (Super-Lioran).
ⓘ ☎ 71.49.50.08.
SNCF ☎ 71.49.50.05.

Hotel :
★ **Auberge du Tunnel** (L.F.), ☎ 71.49.50.02, DC Euro Visa, 18 rm Ⓟ ⌂ closed 1 May-1 Jul, 1 Oct-22 Dec, 160.

Rest. ♦ ⅃ ᕇ Good regional fare : *potée auvergnate, tripous cantaliens*, 50-100.

Nearby

SUPER-LIORAN, ⊠ 15300 Murat, 2 km SW on the D 67.

Hotels :
★★★ *Anglard et du Cerf*, ☎ 71.49.50.26, AE Euro Visa, 38 rm Ⓟ ⅏ ⅃ closed 20 Apr-30 Jun, 30 Sep-19 Dec, 180. Rest. ♦♦ ⅏ View of the Cantal hills. Spec : *foie gras du chef*, pastries, 70-180.
★★ *Remberter Saporta*, ☎ 71.49.50.28, Euro Visa, 32 rm Ⓟ ⅏ ₪ closed 20 Apr-28 Jun, 15 Sep-20 Dec, 170. Rest. ♦ ⅏ ᕇ Set amidst pines at the foot of the slopes, 45-70.
★ *Rocher du Cerf*, ☎ 71.49.50.14, 11 rm Ⓟ ⅏ ₪ ⌕ half pens (h.s.), closed 15 Apr-15 Jun, 15 Sep-18 Dec, 155. Rest. ♦ ⅏ Set in a pine grove at the foot of the Cantal slopes. Regional dishes, 45-95.

MAURIAC

Aurillac 56, Tulle 70, Paris 486 km
pop 4776 ⊠ 15200   A3

The enormous cattle markets held twice a month hardly seem to dent the calm of this pleasant country town, its black basalt houses contrasting sharply with the surrounding greenery.

Despite archaeological restoration, **Notre-Dame-des-Miracles Basilica★** (12thC) has kept its charm : carved Ascension (mutilated) on the tympanum ; in the apse, very freely-inspired corbel work ; inside, walnut statue of the Virgin★ (12thC) to which the church owes its name. ▶ **Puy Saint-Mary** *(NW, 15 min)*, grassy knoll with broad view over the plains of Cantal and Corrèze.

Nearby

▶ On the road to Bort-les-Orgues (→ Limousin), stop at the site★ of the **Charlus ruins** *(18 km)* and at **Ydes-Bourg** *(22 km)*, where the Romanesque church★ has some interesting 12thC bas-reliefs under the porch, with delightfully-carved corbelling of ribald faces ; 2.5 km E, **Saignes :** pretty summer resort.   □

Practical Information ─────────────

ⓘ pl. G.-Pompidou, ☎ 71.67.30.26.   🕊
𝗦𝗡𝗖𝗙 ☎ 71.68.01.21.

Hotels :
★★ *L'Ecu de France* (L.F.), 6, av. Ch.-Périé, ☎ 71.68.00.75, Visa, 26 rm 🍴 ⅋ half pens (h.s.), closed 15 Dec-15 Mar, 380. Rest. ♦ 70-150 ; child : 45.
● ★ *Au Rendez-Vous des Pêcheurs* (L.F.), Pont du Chambon, St-Merd-de-Lapleau, ☎ 55.27.88.39, Euro Visa, 9 rm Ⓟ ⅏ ₪ ⌕ closed Fri eve and Sat lunch, 12 Nov-20 Dec, 130. Rest. ♦♦ ⅏ ᕇ A perfect spot for a tranquil vacation, 55-120.

△ ★★★ *Coste Mauve* (70 pl), ☎ 71.68.08.73 ; ★★ *La Roussille* (100 pl), ☎ 71.68.06.99.

Recommended
Chambres d'hôtes : *château de Bassignac*, 16 km N, ☎ 71.40.82.82.
Events : *pilgrimage of Our Lady of Miracles*, 1st 2 wks in May.

MEZENC Massif★★

                                    C3-4

Between the Velay and Vivarais regions, the Mézenc volcano, the Meygal (NW) and Coiron (→) Massifs form a long volcanic chain from the Loire to the Rhône. To the east, by the Rhône, erosion has eaten deeply into the chain, forming the Boutières Amphitheatre and numerous valleys ; to the west, by

the Loire, the peaks are more gently rounded and covered with rich pasture.

Round trip from Monastier-sur-Gazeille to Le Puy *(103-120 km ; half day)*
▶ **Le-Monastier-sur-Gazeille** (pop. 2 093) traces its ancestry to an abbey founded in the 7thC ; remains include a remodeled 12thC church (polychrome, treasure room★) and, behind it, the former castle of the abbey (14th-17thC), a massive construction in black basalt. ▶ A detour to **Moudeyres★** is a must : thatched roofs, and the Perrel brothers' farm, restored to create the atmosphere of 18thC rural life *(Jul.-15 Sep. 9-2 & 3-7, ex Wed.)*. ▶ **Les Estables :** excellent for cross-country skiing ; starting point for the **Mont Mézenc** (alt. 1 753 m ; *by Croix de Peccata, 3 km, then 20 min on foot ; by Croix des Boutières, 2.5 km, then 15 min*) : from the top of the Mézenc (→ Ardèche, Cévennes), broad horizons★★ — as far as the Alps in good weather. ▶ Only the priory remains of the former **Bonnefoy charterhouse ;** superb wooded site★ ; 7 km farther, is **Mont Gerbier de Jonc** (→ Cévennes ; *20-min climb ;* view) : at its foot, a monument to the sources of the Loire River. ▶ Snaking down the E flank of the Mézenc, the road gives views of the **Boutières region**, with sharper peaks and deeper valleys running down to the Rhône. ▶ After **Fay-sur-Lignon**, take a short turn around St. Front Lake, through **Saint-Front** to **Maziaux★**, a hamlet where stone tiling still strongly rivals thatched roofs. ▶ Romanesque churches at **Saint-Julien-Chapteuil** (musée Jules Romains ; *Jul.-Aug.* on request, tel. 71.08.70.14) and **Saint-Pierre-Eynac**.   □

Practical Information ─────────────

MOUDEYRES, ⊠ 43150 Laussonne, 13 km NE of **Monastier-sur-Gazeille.**

Hotel :
★★ *Le Pré Bossu* (R.S., L.F., C.H.), ☎ 71.05.10.70, AE Visa, 10 rm Ⓟ ⅏ ₪ ⌕ closed 15 Nov-Easter ex school hols, 175. Rest. ● ♦ ⅃ ⅋ A pleasant cottage in a natural setting ; fishing and mushrooming. Spec : *truite sauvage aux algues, écrevisses au pistou*, 95-200 ; child : 55.

MONISTROL-SUR-LOIRE

Saint-Etienne 30, Le Puy 48, Paris 549 km
pop 5438 ⊠ 43120   C2-3

This former secondary residence of the bishops of Puy, 2 km from the Loire River, is now a little industrial township in the development area of Saint-Étienne. Romanesque church enlarged in the 17thC ; former 17thC episcopal château *(hospice) ;* its former gardens form a terrace above the gorges of the Bilhard (waterfalls ; views over the Loire Valley).

Nearby

▶ **Saint-Didier-en-Velay** *(10 km E)* : Museum of Arts and Crafts of the Massif Central (collection of wheels and plows ; *Jul.-Aug., 3-6 ; closed Mon.* ; annex at La Séauvesur-Semène, *3 km*). ▶ From **Bas-en-Basset**, climb to the ruined château of Rochebaron (14th-15thC ; *entrance free ;* view) ; 8 km W, the **château de Valprivas** (15th-16thC ; court of honour with Italian-influenced decoration ; *10-12 & 3-6).* ▶ Via **Beauzac** *(11 km SW ;* Romanesque-Gothic church★) and **Retournac**, overlooking the Loire, go up the river valley to **Chamalières-sur-Loire** (Romanesque church★), and from there by **Roche-en-Régnier** to the foot of a volcanic peak surmounted by a feudal keep (view) ; continue N to **Chalençon★**, an ancient village on a splendid site★ with medieval keep, 12thC chapel, old houses, bridge from the Middle Ages ; cultural activities in summer.   □

Looking for a locality? Consult the index at the back of the book.

Practical Information ───────────────

Nearby

SAINT-DIDIER-EN-VELAY, ⊠ 43140, 10 km E.

Hotel :
★ *Auberge du Velay*, ☎ 71.61.01.54, AE DC Euro Visa, 8 rm, closed Mon eve and Sun eve, 15-28 Feb, 20 Jul-12 Aug, 85. Rest. ♦ ♪ In this rustic 17thC inn, you can sample *crème de lentilles au saumon, magret de canard*, 80-200.

MONT-DORE*

Clermont-Ferrand 47, Mauriac 73, Paris 437 km
pop 2394 ⊠ 63240   A2

The thermal springs of Mont-Dore, forgotten like so many others since Roman days, began their return to fashion at the beginning of the 18thC. But this resort of repentant smokers and victims of respiratory ailments is also an important winter sports centre. The lavishly-equipped slopes at Sancy offer a wide choice of trails for skiers at all levels.

▶ The spa★ was considerably enlarged at the end of the last century and totally renovated some years ago; it has now reached monumental proportions. Gallo-Roman ruins on view *(guided tours in season; closed Sun. and nat. hols.)*. ▶ Many walks; reception room at Pic du Capucin (peak, *8 min by cable-car and 35 min on foot;* alt. 1 463 m; panorama★); big waterfall SE, *45 min-1 h;* waterfalls at Queureilh (site★) and Saut du Loup *(3 hr round trip).* ▶ Puy de Sancy★★ *(S; 4 km by road, 5 min in cable-car and 20 min on foot);* the summit (alt. 1 886 m) is the highest in the Massif Central; fantastic view★★.

Around the Puy de Sancy *(approx 80 km; 1/2 -1 day; see map 4)*

▶ Go to La Bourboule and take the D88 to the left. ▶ Overlooking the hamlet of Vendeix-Haut is **Roche Vendeix**, a solid block of basalt with ruins of a fortress *(access in a few minutes);* fine panoramic view. ▶ A pleasant drive down the D88; here make a rapid detour *(12 km round trip)* to the Roc Courlande (alt. 1 577 m; view) and the resort of **Chastreix-Sancy**. ▶ At **Chastreix**, Gothic church (13th-14thC). ▶ **Super-Besse** is a resort built in 1961, departure point for a cable-car over the valley of Chaudefour★ to reach the Puy de la Perdrix (alt. 1 824 m; view). ▶ From the D978/D149 crossroads there are excursions to **Lake Pavin★**, one of the most typical circular crater lakes in the Auvergne, surrounded by steep basalt walls below the Puy de Montchal (alt. 1 411 m; *30 min;* wide view); at **Notre-Dame-de-Vassivière** *(10 km round trip),* a chapel of 1515 with a Black Virgin, still an

4. Around the Puy de Sancy

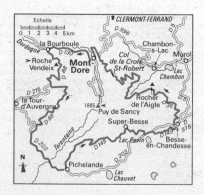

important centre of pilgrimage *(2 Jul. and Sun. after 21 Sep.).* ▶ **Besse-en-Chandesse** (pop. 1 860), a dairy-farming centre (Saint-Nectaire cheese is made here) and a winter and summer resort; church★ with Romanesque nave and figured capitals ; market building ; old château ; Rue de la Boucherie with old houses and market stalls from 15th-16thC; belfry ; 3 km S, the Anglard Waterfall. ▶ **Courbanges**, attractive lintels over the doors; shortly after, view★ from the Rocher de l'Aigle. ▶ The road descends to the **Chaudefour Valley★**, surrounded by wooded slopes with high, strangely-shaped peaks. ▶ Back to Mont-Dore over the Croix St. Robert Pass (alt. 1 425 m; panorama★).   ☐

Practical Information ───────────────

MONT-DORE
⚓ (15 May-30 Sep), ☎ 73.65.05.10.
☒ 1050-1846m.
ℹ av. du Gal-Leclerc, ☎ 73.65.20.21.
SNCF ☎ 73.65.00.02.

Hotels :
★★★ *Panorama*, 27, av. de la Libération, ☎ 73.65.11.12, Visa, 40 rm Ⓟ ⚒ ⚑ ♪ ☜ pens, half pens (h.s.), closed 10 Apr-15 May, 30 Sep-20 Dec, 460. Rest. ♦ ♦ ♪ ♿ ☜ 85-150; child : 60.
● ★★ *Puy Ferrand* (R.S., L.F.), at the foot of Sancy, 4 km on D 983, ☎ 73.65.18.99, Tx 990332, AE Euro Visa, 40 rm Ⓟ ♦ ⚑ ♪ closed 15 Apr-15 May, 20 Sep-15 Dec. Close to the ski lifts, in a natural setting. Sauna, 185. Rest. ♦ ♦ ♪ ♿ Spec : *pot-au-feu de la mer aux petits légumes*, 90-140.
★★ *Cascades*, 26, av. G.-Clemenceau, ☎ 73.65.01.36, 23 rm Ⓟ ♦ ♪ closed 2 Apr-15 May, 1 Oct-20 Dec, 130. Rest. ♦ ♪ ☜ 45-100.

▲ ★★*Domaine de la Grande Cascade*, 9 km N on D 983 (60 pl), ☎ 73.65.06.23; ★★*les Crouzets* (250 pl), ☎ 73.65.21.60.

Recommended
Baby-sitting : *halte-garderie des neiges*, in winter for children 3-8 years; *municipal activities centre,* in summer for children 4-12 years. Info at *S.I.*
Casino : 12, rue Meynadier, ☎ 73.65.00.58, closed Oct-Nov and Apr-May.
Farmhouse-gîte : at Le Genestoux, 3.5 km, *M. Lacombe,* ☎ 73.65.00.67; at Le Rigolet-Haut, 3 km, *M. Sauze,* ☎ 73.65.03.38.
Farmhouse inn : *ferme de l'Angle,* Le Pitsounet, ☎ 73.65.02.11.
Youth hostel : rte de Sancy, ☎ 73.65.03.53.

Nearby

BESSE-ET-SAINT-ANASTAISE, ⊠ 63610, 19 km SE.
ℹ pl. Gd-Mèze, ☎ 73.79.52.84.

Hotels :
★★★ *Les Mouflons*, rte de Super-Besse, Besse-en-Chandesse, ☎ 73.79.51.31, AE Visa, 50 rm Ⓟ ⚒ half pens (h.s.), closed 25 Sep-31 May. Well-situated, comfortable establishment, 460. Rest. ● ♦♦ ♦ ☜ Nearly at the foot of the ski trails, Antoine Sachapt gives pride of place to regional recipes : *feuilleté de grenouilles aux escargots, saumon de fontaine aux champignons sylvestres.* Cheese and wines of Auvergne 85-200.
★★ *Gazelle* (L.F.), rte Compains, ☎ 73.79.50.26, 30 rm Ⓟ ⚒ ⚑ ♿ closed 30 Oct-20 Dec, 140. Rest. ♦ 45-90.
★★ *Petite Ferme* (L.F.), Le Fau, ☎ 73.79.51.39, AE DC Euro Visa, 32 rm Ⓟ ⚒ closed 20 Apr-20 May, 20 Sep-1 Nov, 190. Rest. ♦ 60-85.

Restaurant :
● ♦♦ *La Bergerie*, ☎ 73.79.61.06 ⚒ ♪ closed 15 Apr-30 Jun, 15 Sep-15 Dec. At the foot of the slopes, for hurried skiers at lunch, gourmets at dinner : *saumon au fenouil, ris de veau à la crème, poulet à l'estragon,* 60-200.

SUPER-BESSE, ⊠ 63610 Besse-et-Saint-Anastaise, 7 km W of **Besse.**

⚡ 1350-1850m.

Hotel :
★★★ *Gergovia*, 1, rue M.-Gauthier, ☎ 73.79.60.15, 53 rm ⋄ ◊ closed 11 Apr-12 Jun, 4 Oct-20 Dec, 250. Rest. ♦ Spec : *truite à l'auvergnate*, 90-150.

MONTSALVY

Figeac 57, Rodez 60, Paris 581 km
pop 1035 ⊠ 15120   A4

ⓘ rue du Tour-de-Ville, ☎ 71.49.21.43.

Hotels :
★★ *Nord*, (L.F., Inter-Hôtel), pl. du Barry, ☎ 71.49.20.03, AE DC Euro Visa, 30 rm Ⓟ closed Jan-Mar. Cordial comfort, 140. Rest. ♦ ⵏ ⭘ Spec : *canard de Barbarie au cidre, nougat glacé au cointreau et au miel*, 55-140; child : 35.
★ *Auberge Fleurie*, (L.F.), pl. du Barry, ☎ 71.49.20.02, AE DC Euro Visa, 18 rm Pleasant rustic house, annex 1 km away with 5-acre park, 130. Rest. ♦ closed 1 Nov-1 Mar. Good regional fare : *tripous, truite meunière, omelette aux cèpes*, 40-100.

Å ★★*La Grangeotte* (165 pl), ☎ 71.49.20.10.

Recommended
Farmhouse-inn : *Sunezergues*, ☎ 71.49.92.01; at Junhac, *Aubesfeyre*, ☎ 71.49.22.70; at Lacapelle-del-Fraysse, *Lacaze*, ☎ 71.62.55.07.

Nearby
CALVINET, ⊠ 15340, 15 km W.

Hotel :
★ *Le Beauséjour*, rte de Maurs, ☎ 71.49.91.68, 19 rm Ⓟ ⑊ ◊ pens, half pens (h.s.), closed Sun eve and Mon ex hols (Apr-May), 10 Oct-25 Mar, 220. Rest. ● ♦♦ ⭘ ⭙ A wide array of earthy dishes generously apportioned by M. Puech : *assiette de charcuterie maison, étuvé de blanc de volaille à l'ail doux et au vinaigre*. Local products for sale, 60-150; child : 35.

MURAT

Saint-Flour 25, Aurillac 51, Paris 495 km
pop 2813 ⊠ 15300   A3

A good summer base below the Rocher de Bonnevie on the left bank of the Alagnon River for exploring the Cantal Region.

▶ **Maison Rodier** (16thC) and **Maison Tallandier** (15thC) in the heart of the old town; in the neighbouring church (15thC, remodeled) is a Black Virgin, said to have been brought back from Palestine by Louis IX. ▶ NW, the **Rocher de Bonnevie** *(30-min climb)* is the pedestal for a colossal cast-iron Virgin; view★ over the town and valley. ▶ From the opposite side of the valley, **Bredons** *(1 hr round trip; 2.5 km road)* has a lovely site★ for its church★ on a turf-covered terrace; Romanesque edifice, Renaissance stalls, Baroque altarpiece and a small treasure room.

Nearby
▶ **Château de Massebeau,** with two principal buildings flanked by machicolated towers (with openings for dropping molten lead, stones, etc.) and roofed in stone *(20 Jul.-end Aug., 10-12 & 2-4)*. ▶ Château d'**Anterroches,** 15thC keep overlooking the Lioran road. ▶ **Dienne** *(10 km N)* is a robust mountain village on one of the roads to the Pas de Peyrol (→ Mauriac, Puy Mary circuit); remarkable capitals with *naïf* carvings bear witness to a vigorous popular art; the church also houses a strikingly realistic 13thC wooden Christ figure. ▶ Magnificent view★ over Murat from Laveissenet *(6 km S).*   ☐

ⓘ av. Dr-Mallet, ☎ 71.20.09.47; Hôtel-de-Ville, ☎ 71.20.03.80.
SNCF ☎ 71.20.07.20.

Å (85 pl), ☎ 71.20.01.83.

Recommended
Farmhouse gîte : M. **Lacueille**, 4, route d'Allanche, ☎ 71.20.00.33.

MUROL

Clermont-Ferrand 37, Mauriac 96, Paris 433 km
pop 624 ⊠ 63790   A2

The château★ (14th-15thC), an irregular dodecahedron, is mounted on a basalt formation; muted, red-hued lava blocks used in its construction add to the romantic ambience of this ruin *(Jun.-Sep. 10-12 & 2-7; Sun. only low season).*

Nearby
▶ **Lake Chambon** *(2 km SW),* a marvelous 140-acre lake with beach bordered by meadows and pine woods. Above to N, the Dent du Marais, a sheer cliff face, also called the Saut de la Pucelle (Virgin's Leap). ▶ **Chambon-sur-Lac**, little Romanesque church partly buried by silt from the Couze River.   ☐

Practical Information

MUROL
ⓘ mairie; pl. Coudert, ☎ 73.88.62.62.

Hotels :
★★ *Dômes*, Groire, 0,5 km E. on D 146, ☎ 73.88.60.13, 30 rm Ⓟ ⑊ ◊ ⭘ ⭙ ▤ ⌀ closed Sep-May ex Feb hols, Easter, 150. Rest. ♦ Fixed-price menu, 70-130.
★★ *Parc* (L.F.), ☎ 73.88.60.08, Visa, 40 rm Ⓟ ⑊ ▤ ⌀ pens (h.s.), closed 30 Sep-1 May, 420. Rest. ♦ 75-110.
★ *Relais des Montagnes*, Beaune-le-Froid, 4 km NW, alt. 1000 m, ☎ 73.88.61.48, Visa, 12 rm Ⓟ ⑊ ◊ ⵏ ⭘ closed 30 Sep-1 Feb, 100. Rest. ♦ ⑊ ⵏ ⭘ ⭙ Bountiful cuisine, 45-80.

Å ★★★*La Ribeyre* (200 pl), ☎ 73.88.64.29; ★★*André Auserve* (350 pl), ☎ 73.88.60.46; ★★*La Plage*, Lake Chambon (450 pl), ☎ 73.88.60.27; ★★*La Rivière*, rte de St-Nectaire (40 pl), ☎ 73.88.60.95.

Recommended
Bicycle rental : ☎ 73.88.63.08.
Rural-gîte : M. **Espy**, ☎ 73.83.54.90; at Beaune-le-Froid, M. **Roux**, ☎ 73.79.12.57.

Nearby
CHAMBON-SUR-LAC, ⊠ 63790, 3 km W.
⚡ 1250-1800m, at Chambon-des-Neiges.

Hotels :
★★ *Bellevue*, on Lake Chambon, D 996, ☎ 73.88.61.06, 25 rm Ⓟ ⑊ ⭘ half pens (h.s.), closed Mar, Oct-Jan, 160. Rest. ♦ ⭘ 50-85.
★★ *Le Grillon* (L.F.), ☎ 73.88.60.66, Euro Visa, 20 rm Ⓟ ⑊ ▦ pens, half pens (h.s.), 190. Rest. ♦ ⑊ closed Nov-Apr ex wkends and Feb hols, 50-100; child : 25.

ORCIVAL★★

Clermont-Ferrand 27, Mauriac 84, Paris 416 km
pop 381 ⊠ 63210 Rochefort-Montagne   A2

In the upper valley of the Sioulet, stock-rearing country; a key site for medieval sacred art.

▶ The Romanesque (12thC) **church★★**, restored in the 15thC and 19thC, is remarkably homogeneous; inside, light, slender and very elegant, a seated silver-gilt covered 12thC wooden statue of the Virgin★★; beautiful capitals (one figured); enormous crypt; note the 13thC iron work on the doors. ► Gothic houses in the village.

Nearby

► **Château de Cordès★** *(2.5 km N)*, 15thC, remodeled in the 17thC with 18thC interiors. Bowers and arbours designed by Le Nôtre *(10-12 & 2-6; closed Feb.)*. ► 11 km S, **Lake Servière** surrounded by pines and spruce. Farther S on the road to Mont-Dore, the **Guéry Pass** (alt. 1 264 m) above Guéry Lake; 500 m away : viewpoint overlooking the **Tuilière and Sanadoire rocks★**, gigantic phonolitic dykes. □

Practical Information _____

Hotel :
★ *Au Vieux Logis*, ☎ 73.65.82.03, Euro Visa, 9 rm ♙ ᵶ closed Tue eve and Wed, 25 Oct-10 Dec, 85. Rest. ♦ 40-90.

⚑ ★★*Etang de Fléchat* (65 pl), ☎ 73.65.82.96; ★*Ferme des Planchettes* (65 pl), ☎ 73.21.22.75.

Recommended
Rural-gîte : M. Coehndy, ☎ 73.65.81.46; at Douharene, 5 km, M. Ceyssat, ☎ 73.65.85.70.

PONTAUMUR

Clermont-Ferrand 44, Le Mont-Dore 63, Paris 409 km
pop 992 ⊠ 63380   A1

Hotel :
★ *Poste* (L.F.), av. du Marronnier, ☎ 73.79.90.15, Euro Visa, 17 rm ❧ closed Sun eve and Mon, 24-30 Jun, 15 Dec-1 Feb, 140. Rest. ● ♦ Tasty, straightforward, down-home cooking : *salade d'andouille à l'huile de noix, pigeon à l'ail et son gâteau de courgettes*, 65-140.

Nearby

PONTGIBAUD, ⊠ 63230, 23 km E.

Hotel :
★ *Poste* (L.F.), pl. de la République, ☎ 73.88.70.02, AE Euro Visa, 11 rm 🅿 closed Sun eve and Mon (l.s.), 1 Jan-2 Feb, 1-15 Oct, 140. Rest. ● ♦♦ ᵶ Cheers for J.-Y. Andant's savoury, hearty Auvergnat dishes : *truites des volcans, lapin farci*, 50-120; child : 25.

Le PUY***

Saint-Etienne 78, Mende 92, Paris 516 km
pop 29024 ⊠ 43000   C3

In the centre of a natural amphitheatre ringed by volcanic mountains, dotted with unusual rock formations, each serving as the pedestal for a statue or monument, Le Puy, capital of the Velay area, is foremost a religious centre, owing its origins to an important Marian Order pilgrimage.

► The **Place du Breuil** (A-B3) is the heart of the modern town, with cafés, a market and municipal offices; S is Vinay. ► At the rear of the garden is the **Crozatier Museum** (A3) : archaeology, fine arts, regional arts and traditions; above all, see the lace room★ *(10-12 & 2-4 or 6; closed Tue. and Feb.)*. ► The old town still has many **medieval, Gothic and Renaissance houses** : don't miss (B2) Rues Porte-Aiguière, Chaussade, du Collège, Pannessac. ► The **cathedral★★** (11th-12thC) is an exceptional building, with cupolas over the nave and bold construction : the steep street (actually a stairway) passes right under the church, between doorways with 12thC leaves. Note 13thC frescos; 11thC frescos in the left transept and the gallery; in a relics chapel *(visit with Cloister daily ex Tue., 8-12 & 2-6)* is a large 15thC fresco; the room next door is the treasure room. Romanesque **cloister★★** *(same hours)*. The Porche du For★ overlooks the square of the same name from the right transept (view over the

town), beside the 16thC bishop's palace. From the left transept, the Porche St. Jean leads to an 11thC baptistry adjoining the prior's house. ► N of the cathedral, the chapel of the Penitents (coffered painted ceiling, 1630; important pictures by local painters, 18thC). ► **Corneille Rock** (B1), 130 m above the Place du Breuil, offers a good view of the town and its environs *(9 or 10-5,6,7 or 8; closed Tue. low season and Dec.-Jan., ex school hols. and Sun. pm)*; the view from the crown of an enormous statue of Notre-Dame de France (1860) is equal. ► A little way out of the centre, the 14th-15thC **Gothic church of St. Laurent** (A1); nearby the **Centre d'Initiation à la Dentelle du Puy** (lacemakers at work, exhibition; *weekdays only).* ► Perched on an 85-m volcanic dyke is the 10th-12thC **church of St. Michel d'Aiguilhe★** (B1) with a polychrome façade★ of Eastern inspiration *(9 or 10-12 & 2-6 or 7, ex Christmas and 1 Jan., 15 Mar.-Oct.; winter school hols., pm only)*; important fragments of paintings, probably 10thC.

Nearby

► **Espaly Saint-Marcel** *(1.5 km W)* is dominated by two volcanic rock formations one of which bears the remains of a château and the other a number of pious but unattractive constructions, and a gigantic statue of St. Joseph *(entry fee; diorama)*; from the terrace, view of Le Puy and the basalt colonnades known as the **Orgues d'Espaly.** ► SW of Puy, basalt **Mons Plateau**, with steep flanks partially enclosed by a loop of the Loire River. Near **Coubon**, the château de **Volhac** *(15 Jun.-15 Sep., 2-8; closed Tue.)* and the **Daniel Tower**, a 14thC square keep to which has been added a Renaissance logis *(Jul.-Sep., Tue.-Thu. 2-6)*; 3.5 km S, the château de Poinsac (16th-18thC); return to Le Puy via **Bouzols** (another château, 12th-13thC, partially in ruins). ► **Saint-Germain-Laprade** *(11 km)*, little Romanesque church with fortified bell tower.

Around the châteaux of Velay *(50 km; approx half day)*

► At **Polignac**, on an enormous flat-topped basalt formation, reinforced by a 13thC wall, rest the remains of a 14thC château★ *(May-Sep., 9:30 or 10-12 & 2-5:30 or 7)*, powerful keep 32-m high (view★); church partially Romanesque, 12th and 14thC frescos; 3 km E : 16thC fortified house at **Cheyrac** with curious painted decoration *(high season, by appt.).* ► Another imposing fortress, the 14th-16thC **château de Saint-Vidal** *(Jul.-Aug., 2-6:30)*. ► **Saint-Paulien**, early centre of the Velay area, has a 12thC church, remodeled and fortified and small museum in a former chapel. ► The **château de Rochelambert** (16thC), sober volcanic rock structure, is, in fact, a romantic 16thC residence on a pretty site over the right bank of the Borne River *(Mar.-Sep., 10-12 & 2-6)*; 14 km NW, from the castle ruins of **Allègre** *"Gallows of Allègre"* view of the Velay Mts. and the Mézenc Massif to the S. ► On a steep rock outcropping over the Loire is the **château de Lavoûte-Polignac** (rebuilt 19thC), with superb furnishings and picture gallery *(Easter-1 Nov.; 9:30-12:30 & 2-6:30)*; 1 km farther, the church of **Lavoûte-sur-Loire** has a 13thC Christ figure★. Return to Le Puy along the Loire, which flows for 9 km through the **Peyredeyre Gorge★**. □

Practical Information _____

Le PUY
🛈 pl. du Breuil (B3), ☎ 71.09.38.41.
✈ Le Puy-Loudes, ☎ 71.08.62.28.
SNCF (C3), ☎ 71.02.50.50/71.02.75.05.
🚌 courtyard of train station (C3), ☎ 71.09.25.60.
Car rental : Avis, 18, bd de la République (C2), ☎ 71.02.71.46; train station.

Hotels :
★★★ *Chris'tel*, 15, bd Alexandre-Clair (A3), ☎ 71.02.24.44, AE Euro Visa, 30 rm 🅿 ᶜ 240. Rest. ♦♦ *Le Chavaniac* ♪ ᵶ closed Fri noon and Sat noon, 15 Dec-15 Jan, 55-90.
★★ *Le Val-Vert* (L.F.), 6, av. Baptiste-Marcet (off map B3), ☎ 71.09.09.30, 26 rm 🅿 ❉ ᵶ half pens (h.s.), closed Sun, 15 Dec-15 Jan, 145. Rest. ♦ ❉ ♪ Eves, residents only, 55-70.

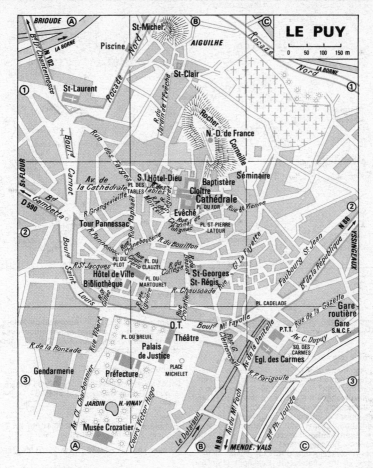

LE PUY

0 50 100 150 m

Lacemaking

The delicate craft made its appearance in Puy and Velay during the 16thC. Women began very young, working with a needle or on a frame with bobbins. The craft became widespread in country districts. The manufacturer, a businessman in town, organized the distribution of work, provided the thread (linen, wool, silk, gold or silver) and patterns, which were renewed as fashion changed. Although underpaid, lacemaking played an important economic role as additional income; it could even be essential in times of scarcity. No doubt for this reason, the trade prospered in the region during the 17thC, aided by the Jesuit François Régis, a stubborn defender of social causes; as a result, an important part of the production went for religious ornamentation.

Restaurants :

♦♦ *Le Bateau Ivre*, 5, rue Portail-d'Avignon (C2), ☎ 71.09.67.20, DC Euro Visa ♪ closed Mon and Sun, 1-15 Jul. Elegant ambience and quality cuisine : *foie gras de canard, rouget à la moelle, marmite au Velay*, 70-120.

♦♦ *Sarda*, 12, rue Chênebouterie (A-B2), ☎ 71.09.58.94,

Visa ✍ closed Mon and Sun eve, 28 Sep-5 Nov. This 13thC building boasts two 17thC frescoes, 60-130.

▲ ★★★*Bouthezard*, RN 102 (83 pl), ☎ 71.09.55.09.

Recommended
Auction house : 10, bd de la République, ☎ 71.09.03.85.
Events : *procession through town*, 15 Aug at 3pm ; *pilgrimage to Our Lady of Puy*, 14-15 Aug.
Leisure activities : 2, rue Duguesclin, ☎ 71.02.01.68, lacemaking centre (lessons).
♥ pastry-candy : *Le Bergerac*, 43, pl. du Breuil and 8, pl. Crozatier, ☎ 71.09.05.72 ; Velay liqueurs and apéritifs : *La Verveine du Velay*, fg St-Jean, ☎ 71.05.68.11 ; Velay raspberry and sloe liqueurs : *Tour Pannessac*, ☎ 71.09.06.57.

Nearby

BLAVOZY, ✉ 43700 Brives-Charensac, 6 km E on N 88.

Hotel :
★★ *Le Moulin de Barette*, Pont de Sumène, ☎ 71.03.00.88, Visa, 43 rm Ⓟ 🏠 ⚲ ↗ closed Jan-Feb, 180. Rest. ♦ ♪ closed Mon (Nov-Mar), 50-130.

For the translation of a name of a meat, a fish or a vegetable, for the composition of a dish or a sauce, see the Menu Guide in the Practical Holiday Guide; it lists the most common culinary terms.

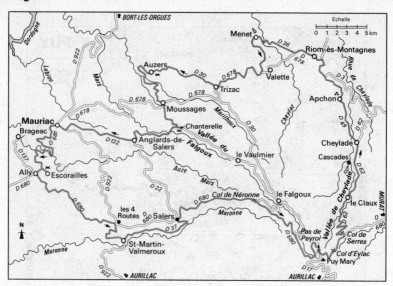

2. Le Puy-Mary

Le PUY-MARY

A3

(150 km; approx 1 day; See map 2)

▶ From Mauriac, follow D681 S. ▶ Before **Ally**, Château de la Vigne★, roofed with stone; built in 1450 with added *logis* from the 18thC *(Jul.-Aug. 2:30-7)*; 6 km N, in a remarkable setting★ above the gorges of the Auze River is **Brageac★**; the church, although restored, is well worth a look (capitals, bases of columns, small treasure room); nearby, former abbey chapel with fine stone roof and large tower. ▶ **Saint Martin-Valmeroux** : old town with attractive market buildings and turreted houses (15th-16thC). ▶ A pleasant ride down the valley of the Maronne : site★ of the château de Palemont (15thC); 2 km S, **Fontanges** (15thC church). ▶ **Salers** (→). ▶ The road★ to Neronne Pass runs along a corniche (cliff road) over basalt escarpments above pastures and shepherds' huts before reaching the upper valley and the steep hollow, **Cirque du Falgoux★**. ▶ From the **Pas de Peyrol** (alt. 1 589 m), easy climb up the **Puy Mary★★** (alt. 1 787 m; 25 mins) : spectacular view of the nearer valleys, separated by narrow ridges. After the **Col d'Eylac** (pass; alt. 1 500 m) view of the Impradine Valley, which runs down towards Dienne and Murat (→). ▶ From the **Col de Serres** (pass; alt. 1 364 m) there is an oblique view of the valley of Cheylade before the road goes hairpinning down. Church at **Cheylade** : wooden paneling★ consisting of 1 428 small, painted panels (18thC); waterfalls★ nearby. Site★ of the chapel of font-Saint (alt. 1 250 m), a very important place of Marian pilgrimage. ▶ The stone-roofed houses of **Apchon** are typical of the region; castle ruins *(10-min climb)*, oblique view★ over the valley. ▶ **Riom-ès-Montagne**, important dairy centre; figured capitals★ in the 11thC choir of the church; Maison de la Gentiane et de la flore★ (gentian and flora; *15 jun.-15 Sep., 10-12:30 & 2:30-7; tel. : 71.78.10.45)*. ▶ Several ruined châteaux around **Trizac**, and the *Cases de Cotteughe*, remains of what are said to be Gallic houses. ▶ Remarkable *Pietà* in the church at **Auzers**; castle★ with stone roofing (14th-15thC; *1 Jul.-15 Sep., 2-6:30)*. ▶ **Moussages** : church housing the most beautiful Romanesque statue in Upper Auvergne, Notre-Dame de Claviers★★. From here, reach the end of **Falgoux Valley★** via the château de

Chanterelle (17thC). ▶ **Anglards-de-Salers** : Romanesque church of Limousin region influences; château de la Trémolière (15thC; *Jul.-Aug. 2:30-7)* : good collection of Aubusson tapestries★ (16thC). ☐

Practical Information

RIOM-ES-MONTAGNES, ☒ 15400, 36 km NE of **Mauriac**.
ℹ pl. du Gal-de-Gaulle, ☎ 71.78.07.37.
SNCF ☎ 71.78.00.66.

Hotel :
★ **Panoramic** (L.F.), ☎ 71.78.06.41, 11 rm ℙ closed Sun eve (l.s), 110. Rest. ♦ 50-100.

⚠ ★★★*Le Sedour* (176 pl), ☎ 71.78.05.71.

RIOM*

Clermont-Ferrand 15, Moulins 81, Paris 375 km
pop 18901 ☒ 63200   B1

Riom holds itself aloof on its butte like a magistrate in court; lofty facades and monumental fountains recall the past of this city of lawyers, sculpted in the sombre stone of Volvic, black as the rich soil of the Limagne plains.

▶ **The church of St. Amable,** heavily restored, has a nave and transept in the purest Auvergne Romanesque style, and a Gothic choir; in the sacristy are wooden paneling from 1687 and a collection of chasubles. ▶ In the **Rue de l'Horloge** there are a number of old *hôtels particuliers* (private mansions; nos. 3,7,15,19,21,28,22,20,4); note No.12, the **Hôtel Guimoneau★** *(closed Sun. and Aug.)* the staircase of which is decorated with an Annunciation; opposite is a Gothic and Renaissance belfry. ▶ In the Rue de l'Hôtel-de-Ville are other mansions (**Maison des Consuls★**, 1527) and the Hôtel de Ville (town hall; 18thC restored). ▶ The **Mandet Museum**, in a 17thC mansion *(daily ex Tue., 10-12 & 2-5:30)*, is principally devoted to painting (Flemish and Dutch schools; 17thC Italian and Spanish; 18thC French). ▶ The **Auvergne Museum** *(same hours)* provides a remarkable exhibition of popular arts and traditions. ▶ The *Palais de Justice* (Law Courts) occupies the site of the ducal palace, of which the **Sainte Cha-**

pelle★ remains (14thC; *10-11:30 & 2-5:30, ex Sun. and nat. hols.*; 15thC stained glass). ▶ **Notre Dame du Marthuret** (14th-15thC) : Flamboyant Gothic façade houses a Virgin with Bird★★, a masterpiece of 14thC sculpture.

Nearby

▶ **Mozac** (pop : 3 080, *1.5 km W*) has an interesting abbey church★ (Romanesque nave, Gothic choir and transept), particularly good figured capitals★★ and a treasure room★ (12thC shrine of St. Cadmin); 2 km farther, the church at **Marsat** has a Black Virgin★ of the 12thC.
▶ 9 km E : 11th-12thC church★ at **Ennezat** stands as a prototype of Romanesque art in the Auvergne (see capitals and 15thC frescos). From here you can go for a walk in the **Limagne Plain**, an area carpeted with alluvial silt, and so flat that water flows very slowly among willows and populars; a sharp contrast with the nearby ragged mountains. **Maringues**, partially Romanesque church, lovely wooden tanneries★ on the banks of the Morge; view over the Limagne from the Butte de Montgaçon. Push on to **Randan** on the edge of a fine forest, returning via **Villeneuve-les-Cerfs** (dovecote) and **Thuret**; 11th-12thC church★ with figured capitals. □

Practical Information

ⓘ 16, rue du Commerce, ☎ 73.38.59.45.
🚃 ☎ 73.38.20.14.

Restaurants :

● ♦♦ **Les Petits Ventres**, 6, rue A.-Dubourg, ☎ 73.38.21.65, AE Euro Visa ♪ closed Mon, Sat noon, Sun eve, 1-28 Sep. Original, light cuisine in an elegant, nostalgic setting, 80-235.
♦ **Le Moulin de Villeroze**, 144, rte de Marsat, ☎ 73.38.58.23 ⓦ ♪ ⌖ closed Mon and Sun eve, 4-13 Jan, 80-165.

ROYAT

Clermont-Ferrand 4, Montluçon 95, Paris 393 km
pop 4094 ⊠ 63130   B1-2

Like many spas, Royat was developed by the Romans, forgotten by the Barbarians and resurrected by Napoléon III during the mid-19thC. Specializes in cardio-vascular treatments.

▶ Pleasant walks in the **Parc Thermal** (spa), typical architecture. Nearby, the **Grotte du Chien** (Dog's Grotto) *(15 Apr.-Sep., 9-12 & 2-6)*... but don't take your dog — there's a layer of carbon dioxide close to the ground and it won't get enough air. ▶ Uphill, the old town stands around the **church★** (12thC, fortified 13thC) built onto a priory (much remodeled); 10thC crypt. ▶ 150 m along on the banks of the Tiretaine River, a **stonecutter's workshop** *(mid-Jun.-Sep., 9:30-12 & 2-6; closed Sun. and nat. hols.)*.

Nearby

▶ Walks through three gorges opening W on the Royat Valley. ▶ The best excursion is to **Puy de Dôme★★** *(6-km toll road)*, on whose flanks the ruins of a Gallo-Roman Temple of Mercury have been unearthed. The summit (alt. 1 465 m), highest peak in the chain of the Puys, towers nearly 1 000 m over Clermont; vast and unrivaled panorama★★★. Close by, information office of Volcans d'Auvergne regional nature park *(15 Jun.-15 Sep., daily 10-12:30 & 2:30-7; exhibitions).* □

Practical Information

ROYAT
♨ ☎ 73.35.80.16/73.35.80.28 (Apr.-Oct.).
ⓘ pl. Allard, ☎ 73.35.81.87.
🚃 ☎ 73.30.11.93.

Hotels :

★★★ **Métropole**, 2, bd Vaquez, ☎ 73.35.80.18, Euro Visa,

---

77 rm ⌖ ら half pens (h.s.), closed Oct-May, 660. Rest. ♦♦ ♪ ら ⌖ 105-200.
★★ **La Belle Meunière**, 25, av. de la Vallée, ☎ 75.35.80.17, AE DC Euro Visa, 10 rm Ⓟ ♪ closed Sun eve, Wed, Feb school hols, Nov, 180. Rest. ● ♦♦♦ ♪ ら A Belle-Epoque setting where the ghost of Général Boulanger still wanders; he would surely approve Jean-Claude Bon's light, regional cooking, 130-250; child : 80.
★ **Royat-Restaurant** (L.F.), bd J.-B.-Romeuf, ☎ 73.35.82.72, Visa, 14 rm ⌖ closed Sun eve (l.s.), Mon, 15 Jan-15 Feb, 100. Rest. ♦ Spec : *foie gras*, 100-140.

Restaurants :

♦♦♦ **Le Paradis**, ☎ 73.35.85.46, AE Euro Visa ⌖ ⌖⌖ closed Mon and Sun eve, 2 Jan-10 Feb. Spec : *truite farcie à l'auvergnate, médaillon de veau au basilic*, 75-150; child : 40.
♦♦ **L'Hostalet**, 47, bd Barrieu, ☎ 73.35.82.67, Visa, closed Mon, Tue noon, Sun eve, 2 Jan-10 Apr, 80-130.
ᚼ ★★★★**L'Oclède**, rte de Gravenoire (90 pl), ☎ 73.35.97.05.

Recommended

Casino : ☎ 73.35.80.81, Rest. *La Martingale*. Dancing. Cinema.

Nearby

ORCINES, ⊠ 63870, 17 km W.

Hotel :

● ★★ **Le Dôme** (L.F.), summit of Puy-de-Dôme, ☎ 73.91.49.00, 10 rm Ⓟ ⌖⌖ closed 1 Oct-15 May, 165. Rest. ♦♦ ⌖ 70-150.

SAINT-CERNIN

Aurillac 22, Mauriac 36, Paris 522 km
pop 1271 ⊠ 15310   A3

On the slopes above the Doire River, a large village very typical of the Cantal area; Romanesque church with massive wall-belfry; in the choir, 15thC wood paneling and stalls.

Nearby

▶ **Château d'Anjony★** *(7.5 km E)*, 15thC with high keep comprised of four towers close together; at the foot, graceful 17thC addition. *(Palm Sun.-1 Nov., 2-6:30)*; frescos in **Tournemire** church. ▶ **Saint-Chamant** *(10.5 km NE)* has beautiful painted 15thC stalls★ in its church; 17th-18thC château with 15thC keep *(15 Jun.-15 Sep., 9-7).* ▶ Salers (→). □

SAINT-FLOUR*

Aurillac 76, Le Puy 92, Paris 490 km
pop 9148 ⊠ 15100   B3

Once the capital of Haute (upper) Auvergne. The look of this old town with its fortress-like presence, perched on a basalt terrace 100 m above the valley of the Lander, confirms the pride felt by inhabitants who willingly proclaim themselves "the most Auvergnat of the Auvergne".

▶ Picturesque streets lined with 16thC town houses (Rue des Lacs, Rue Marchande) run from the Allées Pompidou to the Place d'Armes. ▶ 15thC **cathedral** has the dour lines of a real fortress; 17th-18thC paintings; fragments of murals; large 13thC wooden Christ figure★, the black *Bon Dieu Noir.* ▶ In the former episcopal palace (17thC), is the Hôtel de Ville (town hall) and the **Haute Auvergne Museum** (archaeology, medieval art, folklore; *9-12 & 2-6; closed Sat. and Sun. Oct.-May).* ▶ Left of the cathedral, the former Maison Consulaire (16thC; *Jul.-Aug., 9-12 & 2-7)* now housing the Douet Decorative Arts Museum.

Nearby

▶ Walks through the **Lander Gorges** *(SE)*. ▶ **Sailhant Waterfall** *(8 km, plus 10 min on foot),* at the foot of a château (restored), return via **Roffiac** : little Romanesque church★, former chapel of a château, now in ruins. ▶ **Vil-ledieu** *(5.5 km S)* : church (1363) with handsome doorway (ironwork and knocker) and carved stalls. ▶ **Les Ternes** *(12 km SW)* : 15thC church, château★ (15th-16thC, re-stored, *Jul.-Aug. 2-7; closed Sun.).* ▶ Many dolmens and *menhirs* on the **Planèze**, a wind-swept plateau 1 000 m above sea level. ☐

Practical Information ──────────────

🛈 2, pl. d'Armes, ☎ 71.60.22.50.
SNCF ☎ 71.60.03.37.

Hotels :
★★ *Europe*, 12-13, cours Spy-des-Ternes, upper town, ☎ 71.60.03.64, Euro Visa, 45 rm ℙ ≼ 🝙 � closed Dec-Feb. Nicely situated, 180. Rest. ♦ ≼ ♪ 𝅘 Cordial welcome. Spec : *choux farcis et pounti, ris de veau aux moril-les,* 50-140.
★★ *Grand Hôtel des Voyageurs*, 25, rue du Collège, upper town, ☎ 71.60.34.44, 38 rm ℙ 🝙 ⚿ half pens (h.s.), closed 15 Oct-30 Mar, 355. Rest. ♦♦ ♪ Good Auver-gnat cooking, 55-130 ; child : 35.
★★ *Le Panoramic*, Garabit, on RN 9, 10 km, ☎ 71.23.40.24, Euro Visa, 30 rm ℙ ≼ 🝙 ⚿ 𝅘 ☐ 🏊 half pens (h.s.), closed 2 Nov-23 Mar, 360. Rest. ♦ ≼ ♪ 𝅘 45-65 ; child : 25.
★ *Au Rendez-Vous des Pêcheurs*, Bout du Monde, com-mune de St-Georges, ☎ 71.60.15.84, 16 rm ℙ ≼ 🝙 🝙 half pens (h.s.), 210. Rest. ♦ 𝅘 Friendly Auvergnat inn ; local specialties *(tarinette, aligot, potée)* for every bud-get, 35-60.

⚑ ★★★*International*, RN 9 (130 pl), ☎ 71.60.43.63 ; ★★★*Les Orgues*, upper town (105 pl), ☎ 71.60.22.50 ; ★★*Le Lander*, lower town (50 pl), ☎ 71.60.22.50.

Recommended
Farmhouse-gîte : at 3 km, *La Chaumette,* ☎ 71.60.41.02.

SAINT-NECTAIRE*

Clermont-Ferrand 93, Mauriac 102, Paris 428 km
pop 650 ⊠ 63710   B2

Despite the still-existing famous *fromage* called *Saint-Nectaire,* this is no longer a cheese market, but a spa (kidney treatments) linked by a string of villas and hotels to a small mountain town.

▶ **Saint-Nectaire-le-Haut** : 12thC church★★ of modest but perfectly harmonious proportions, the epitome of Auvergnat Romanesque, with 103 capitals, including 6 with figures in the choir ; remarkable treasures on view in the left transept. ▶ **Saint-Nectaire-le-Bas** looks like other spas ; visit the **Fontaine pétrifiante** (fossilizing spring ; *8:30-12 & 2-7* in summer ; *9:30-12 & 2-6, ex Mon. low season*).

Nearby

▶ **Puy de Mazeyres** *(3 km E ;* 919 m ; view, especially). ▶ **Châteauneuf Caves** *(NW ; 1 hr round trip) ;* on the flank of the Puy also called Châteauneuf, nine artificial caves served as a fortress during the Norman invasions. ▶ **Couze de Chambon Valley** : downstream by **Sail-lant** (waterfall) to **Montaigut-le-Blanc**, fortified town with medieval appearance at the foot of 13th-15thC château ruins, and **Champeix★**, surrounded by vineyards, village with a profusion of old houses (see the upper town or Marchidial). ▶ **Murol** (→) and Lake Chambon. ☐

Practical Information ──────────────

SAINT-NECTAIRE
♨ (25 May-30 Sep), ☎ 73.88.50.01.
🛈 parc des Grands-Thermes, ☎ 73.88.50.86.

Hotel :
★★ *Paix* (L.F.), ☎ 73.88.50.20, 27 rm ℙ ≼ 🝙 closed 30 Sep-25 May ex for groups, 150. Rest. ♦ 40-75.

⚑ ★★★*Oasis* (80 pl), ☎ 73.88.52.68 ; at Saillant, ★★*Hutte des Dômes* (60 pl), ☎ 73.88.50.22.

Recommended
Farmhouse-inn : at Freydefond, 5 km NW, *Chez Mme et M. Rassion,* ☎ 73.88.52.76. Pleasant setting and delicious Saint-Nectaire cheese.

Nearby

MONTAIGUT-LE-BLANC, ⊠ 63320, 7 km E.

Hotel :
★★ *Le Rivalet* (L.F.), rte de Besse-Saint-Nectaire, ☎ 73.96.73.92, AE DC Visa, 7 rm ℙ 🝙 ⚿ closed Mon eve and Tue, 5 Jan-3 Feb, 180. Rest. ● ♦ ♪ 𝅘 Outstanding classic, regional cuisine served at a country inn. *Choux et saumon frais à la gentiane, rouget barbet aux spaghet-tis de courgettes, filet de canette au châteaugay,* 75-180 ; child : 50.

SALERS**

Mauriac 19, Aurillac 49, Paris 505 km
pop 470 ⊠ 15410   A3

On a superb site overlooking the valley of the Maronne, Salers was from the 15thC the seat of the *bailliage* (administrative region) of Haute-Auvergne. This official role made the town's fortune, and the remains of ramparts, the sober walls of volcanic rock, stone roofs and sombre doorways still give an impression of aristocratic luxury behind the facade of a country town. Whether a city the size of a village, or a village with the pretensions of a city, Salers is one of the most attractive places in the Auvergne.

▶ The **church★** (15th-16thC) in the lower town houses a polychrome Holy Sepulchre★ of 1495, two paintings attrib-uted to the Spaniard José Ribera and five 17thC Aubus-son tapestries. ▶ Among the beautiful buildings in the upper town on the **Grande-Place★** (Place Tyssandier d'Escous) and nearby, see the **Maison du Bailliage** (15thC ; *open May-Oct.,* tel. : 71.40.70.59), the **Hôtel de Bargues** (16th-17thC ; *Apr.-Sep. 10-12 & 2-7),* the **Maison de la Ronade** (end 14th-early 15thC) and the **Maison des Templiers★** *(Jul.-Aug., 10-12 & 2-6 ;* exhibition of cheese-making and folklore). ▶ From the **Promenade de la Barouze**, 250 m above the valley of the Maronne, view★ E over the Puy Violent Peak.

Nearby

▶ Around the Puy Mary peak (→ Mauriac). ▶ Down the **valley of the Maronne** : Palemont and Saint-Martin-Val-meroux (→ tour of the Puy Mary) ; **Saint-Eulalie** (church) ; fine ruins of château de Branzac ; **Saint-Christophe-les-Gorges** (site★ of Romanesque chapel of Notre-Dame-du-Château) ; **Saint-Martin-Cantalès** (hexagonal 12thC bell tower) ; Bertrande Gorges ; **Saint-Illide** (16thC woodwork in church) ; return via Saint-Cernin (→). ☐

Practical Information ──────────────

SALERS
🛈 pl. Tissandier-d'Escous, ☎ 71.40.70.68 ; mairie, ☎ 71.40.72.33.

Hotels :
★★ *Bailliage* (L.F.), ☎ 71.40.71.95, Euro Visa, 35 rm ℙ 🝙 🝙 closed 12 Nov-20 Dec, 190. Rest. ♦ ♪ Tripe and boiled pork nicely prepared, generously served, 90-130.
★ *Remparts* (L.F.), espl. de Barrouze, ☎ 71.40.70.33, AE Euro Visa, 26 rm ℙ ≼ 🝙 ᬠhalf pens (h.s.), closed 12 Oct-15 Dec, 360. Rest. ♦ ≼ 𝅘 Good location. Warm welcome and enjoyable food. Spec : *pounti aux pruneaux, truffade, clafoutis,* 45-80.

Recommended
Events : at Trinité, *pilgrimage to Notre-Dame-de-Lorette*, 3rd wk in Jul, tourist festival.
Farmhouse-inn : at Récusset, *Mme Geneix*, 11 km E, in the high valley of the Maronne, ☎ 71.40.73.55.

Nearby

Le **THEIL**, ⊠ 15140 Saint-Martin-Valmeroux, 6 km SW on the D 35.
Hotel :
★★ *Maronne* (R.S.), ☎ 71.69.20.33, Euro Visa, 20 rm 🅿 ⋘ ░ ⌕ 🕹 ⌂ ⏚ half pens, closed 25 Apr-4 Nov, 360. Rest. ♦ ⋇ ⋏ 🕹 90-140.

SAUGUES

Le Puy 44, Mende 74, Paris 506 km
pop 2497 ⊠ 43170   B3
One of the strongholds of the Gévaudan region. Today this is a market town for the northern part of the Margeride Mountains (→ Cévennes) and a summer resort.

▶ **Church** with Romanesque gatetower, 12thC Virgin Enthroned, 15thC *Pietà*; treasure room. ▶ Huge 12th-13thC keep, the **Tour des Anglais**, with forestry museum. Holy Thursday, Easter Week penitents' procession.

Nearby

▶ **Esplantas** *(7 km S)*, pretty hill village with granite houses and ruins of a 14thC château. ▶ 28 km W, **Mont Mouchet** was a bulwark of the WWII Resistance; monument to the *Maquis* (partisans); Mont Mouchet Museum in neighbouring forester's lodge *(15 May-Oct., 9-12:30 & 1:30-8)*.   □

THIERS*

Clermont-Ferrand 45, Lyon 137, Paris 387 km
pop 16820 ⊠ 63300   B1
Congesting the gorges of the Durolle are factories and workshops, some old and blackened, others freshly painted, defining this town of steps and zigzagging streets. Thiers has for centuries provided France's eating implements (70% of the national production, one-quarter for export).

▶ A few old houses in the Rue Conchette, leading to the **Terrasse du Rempart** (panorama★). ▶ More old houses in the Rue du Bourg and the **Place du Pirou**; see Maison (also called Château) du Pirou (15thC, restored; SI) : temporary exhibitions on local history and folklore; No.11 on the street of the same name, the **Maison des Sept Péchés Capitaux** (House of the Seven Deadly Sins). ▶ In the Rue de la Coutellerie★ see Nos. 12 and 14; at No. 21, known as La Maison de l'Homme de Bois (The Wooden Man's House, 15thC), knife-grinding and polishing workshops have been reconstituted as an annex to the **Maison des Couteliers** (Cutlery House, No. 58, *Jun.-Sep. daily, 10-12 & 2-6; Oct.-May, daily ex Mon., 2-6)*. Workshops and large collections of cutlery and associated tableware. ▶ Church of St. Genès (11thC, much restored) has 12thC frescos in the choir and cupola. ▶ From the church of St. Roch to the church at Le Moûtier (12thC; disfigured 19thC; capitals★), go down the **Durolle Valley★**, with a number of series of factories exploiting the many falls in the river.

Nearby

▶ **Saint-Rémy-sur-Durolle** *(8.5 km NE)* near a pool in a lovely location★. ▶ **Château d'Aulteribe** *(14 km SW)*, an old medieval house "enriched" in the 19thC with troubadour decorations; good collections *(9 or 10-12 & 2-5 or 6, daily ex Tue.)*. ▶ **Courpière** *(15 km S)* : Romanesque Vir-

gin★ and Holy Sepulchre in the 15thC church; 2.5 km N, **château de la Barge** (16th-18thC ; *early Jul.-end Sep., 2-5)*; 7 km NE, **Vollore-Ville**, an old town on a fine site★ : 17thC château in the shadow of a 12thC keep, housing souvenirs of Lafayette and the American War of Independence *(Jul.-5 Sep., 2-7)*. ▶ **Lezoux** *(16 km W)*, an important ceramics centre during the Gallo-Roman period; traces of more than 200 kilns; municipal ceramics museum *(Jul.-Aug. 2:30-6 ex Mon.; open Sun. and Mon. Easter-Whitsun; Sun. only Jun. and 1-15 Sep.)*; very rich collection, including the Mithras Vase★.   □

Practical Information _____

THIERS
ℹ pl. du Pirou, ☎ 73.80.10.74 ; pl. de la Mutualité (h.s.). **SNCF** ☎ 73.80.19.62.
Car rental : *Avis*, Garage Alfa-Roméo RN 89, Pont de Doré, ☎ 73.80.10.07.

Hotel :
★★ **Chez la Mère Dépalle**, RN 89, ☎ 73.80.10.05, AE Euro Visa, 10 rm 🅿 ⋇ ⋘ ░ ⌂ closed Sun eve (l.s.), 1 Oct-31 Mar, 200. Rest. ♦ ⋇ Spec : *poulet crémé aux morilles, grenouilles à la provençale, écrevisses à la nage*, 70-120.

Nearby

COURPIÈRE, ⊠ 63120, 15 km S.
Hotel :
★ **Au Bon Coin** (L.F.), Aubusson d'Auvergne, 8 km, ☎ 73.53.55.78, Euro Visa, 7 rm, half pens (h.s.), closed Mon, 15 Jan-1 Feb, 250. Rest. ● ♦♦ A good spot to sample Auvergnes'specialties, 50-180.
LEZOUX, ⊠ 63190, 16 km W.
Hotels :
★★★★ **Château de Codignat** (R.C.), Bort-l'Étang, 8 km SE on D 223 and D 115, ☎ 73.68.43.03, Tx 990606, AE DC Euro Visa, 14 rm 🅿 ⋇ ⋘ ░ ⌂ half pens (h.s.), closed 4 Nov-15 Mar, 1500. Rest. ♦♦ ⋏ 🕹 closed Tue noon and Thu noon ex hols. Remarkable 15th-C château. Cordial welcome. Spec : *terrine de raie sauce grelette, panard de lancelot, magret de canard fumé (canardise)*, 220-350 ; child : 130.
★★ **Les Voyageurs**, pl. de la Mairie, ☎ 73.73.10.49, 10 rm ⋇⋘ closed Sun eve and Mon, Feb, 15 Sep-20 Oct, 160. Rest. ♦ Spec : *terrine de foie gras frais, omelette du curé Brillat Savarin, paupiettes de sole aux écrevisses*, 75-140.

Recommended
Sports : *Les Cavaliers Arvennes*, Les Bradoux, Sermentizon, 63120 Courpière, ☎ 73.53.11.38.

TRUYÈRE Gorges**

                                                               A3
Two circuits are possible, depending on whether you start from Chaudes-Aigues or Entraygues.

From Chaudes-Aigues *(122 km ; half day)*

▶ Leave Chaudes-Aigues by the Garabit road (D13). ▶ From the **Belvédère du Cheylé**, view★ over the cirque de Mallet (steep hollow) and the lake created on the Truyère River by the Grandval Dam ; views all the way to **Auriac**. Descend via **Faverolles** (craft exhibition at the Compagnons du Buffadou ; château du Chassan 14th-18thC, *Jul.-Sept., 2:30-7)* to the **Garabit Viaduct★★** with a superb 564 m arch, by Gustave Eiffel (1884) ; carrying the Paris-Béziers road 90 m above the water. At **Loubaresse** *(7 km S)* is the Eco-musée de la Margeride on an old farm ; nearby, château de Pompignac (14thC ; *daily in season 10-12 & 2-7 ex Sun. am ; off season, tel. : 71.73.70.15)* overlooking the Arcomie Valley. ▶ Return as far as Fridefont to see the **Grandval Dam★**, an impressive structure with vaults 85 m high which backs up the waters of the Truyère for 27 km. ▶ Ruins of the **château d'Alleuze★** (13thC) on the edge of a cliff. ▶ Through

Lavastrie and Neuvéglise to the **château de Roche-brune★** (15thC; 13thC keep; *14 Jul-1 Sep. 2:30-6 ex Tue.; tel. : 71.23.82.72).* ▶ Superb drive along D56. ▶ Hamlet of **Sainte-Marie** : modest church with stained-glass windows by Jean Cocteau. ▶ At **Pont-de-Tréboul** Bridge, continue along the lower part of the gorge (in Rouergue) : wonderful scenery; you may wish to go on to the **Belvédère du Vézou** (view★), or even the **château de Bohal★** (13thC; *12.5 km N of Pierrefort; visit on request in Aug. and Sep., tel. : 71.73.40.82).* ▶ Return to Chaudes-Aigues with a detour to **Espinasse** *(3.5 km round trip),* built on a spur (view★). ☐

From Entraygues to Thérondels *(50 km, twisting road, half-day)*

The Truyère River winds between two lava plateaus from the Cantal volcano (Tertiary Era); hydroelectric dams have not spoilt its beauty.

▶ **Couesque Dam** : 15 km² Reservoir fed by the Goul and Truyère rivers. ▶ **Pons** : Gothic church. ▶ **Rouens** : panorama over the Couesque reservoir and **Vallon★**, crowned by the ruins of a 13thC castle. ▶ **Mur-de-Barrez★** : a boundary marker between Carladès Plateau and the Bromme Valley (view★). In the 17thC Mur belonged to the Grimaldi family, Princes of Monaco; note the ogival door on the clock tower; old houses flanked by towers on the square and along the Grand'Rue; church with Romanesque capitals, Gothic doorway, 17thC furnishings. ▶ **Brommat** : church with 13thC arcaded bell tower, 17th-18thC statues; 15thC priory. Hydroelectric complex (three dams and two generating stations). ▶ **Albinhac** : 15thC manor; attractive houses; 1478 Gothic church (Annunciation on the doorway, key-stone vaulting, carved coats of arms, bas-relief of Death★, 16thC polychrome wood statue of St. Martin, maternal figure of St. Anne). ▶ **Laussac** : site★; 11thC Romanesque chapel. ▶ **Sarrans Dam**, built in the 1930s, one of the biggest in France; 35 km² reservoir. ▶ **Thérondels**, northernmost village in the Rouergue; the church blends Romanesque and Flamboyant Gothic (compare the capitals). ▶ If time permits, return via **Orlhaguet** : Romanesque church★ converted in the 15thC into a fortress; collection of 16thC wayside crosses★. **Mels★** : painted walnut altarpiece, a sort of 15thC strip cartoon. **Bès-Bédène★★**, abandoned village in a superb setting; Gothic church and bridge, communal oven, old houses.

Practical Information

GARABIT, ⊠ 15390 Loubaresse, 30 km NE of **Chaudes-Aigues**.
SNCF Loubaresse, ☎ 71.73.70.55.

Hotels :
★★ **Beau Site** (L.F.), RN 9, ☎ 71.23.41.46, Euro Visa, 20 rm 🅿 ₩ 🄺 closed 1 Nov-1 Apr, 120. Rest. ♦ ₹ ᚼ 60-90.
★★ **Garabit** (L.F.), ☎ 71.23.42.75, Euro Visa, 48 rm 🅿 ₩ ⊟ closed 1 Nov-1 Apr, 190. Rest. ♦ ♪ 80-100.
★★ **Viaduc** (L.F.), ☎ 71.23.43.20, 20 rm 🅿 ₩ closed 2 Nov-1 Apr, 140. Rest. ♦ ₹ ♪ 40-90.

VIC-LE-COMTE

Clermont-Ferrand 24, Le Puy 105, Paris 414 km
pop 3787 ⊠ 63270   B2

In a region of hillocks where the Allier River winds through the Limagne Plain; Middle Ages stronghold and capital of the County of Auvergne.

▶ **Sainte Chapelle★**, built in 1510, serves as the choir of a 19thC church; Italian altarpiece of 1520, 17thC stalls and a painting on wood from the 15thC.

Nearby

▶ Imposing dimensions of ruined **château de Buron** *(5 km S).* ▶ **Château de Montfleury** *(2 km N),* large 13th-18thC country mansion (furniture; collection of horse-drawn car-

riages; *15 Jun.-15 Sep. 10-12 & 2-7);* 4 km farther on, 12thC **château de Bosséol** *(15 Jun.-15 Sep. 10-12 & 2-7);* view★ over the area. ☐

Practical Information

SNCF ☎ 73.39.92.18.

Restaurant :
● ♦♦ **Le Comté**, 186, bd de Longues, Longues, 4 km NW, ☎ 73.39.90.31, Euro Visa ₩ closed Mon and Sun eve, 1-15 Feb. Regional fare in tune with the seasons : *potillon d'escargots et grenouilles, pied de porc farci aux foies gras et morilles,* 80-160.

Recommended
Bicycle rental : Angelvy, ☎ 71.47.51.84.
Chambres d'hôtes : at La Croix, Saint-Clément, M. Amilhaud, 1,5 km E., ☎ 71.47.52.05; at Olmet, 63880, Olliergues, 4 km, Mme Benech, ☎ 71.47.50.54.

VIC-SUR-CÈRE

Aurillac 21, Saint-Flour 55, Paris 525 km
pop 2113 ⊠ 15800   A3

A rising summer resort; long ago, capital of the little region of Carladès.

▶ The old town contains a number of **old houses** including that of the Princes of Monaco★ (15thC).

Nearby

▶ 3 km N by N122 is the **Cère Pass**, where the river hurtles abruptly from a narrow gorge; farther on is a path leading *(30 min)* to Roucole Waterfall. ▶ **Thiézac** *(6 km N)* is a small summer holiday resort; in the Gothic church is a curious seated Christ figure★ in painted wood (16thC); on a butte, the chapel of Notre-Dame-de-Consolation (16thC; 17thC painted vaulting).

Around Carladès *(65 km; approx 3 h)*

▶ From Vic, follow the road to Mur-de-Barrez (D 54). ▶ From Curebourse Pass, up to the **Rocher des Pendus** (alt. 1 068 m; view★). ▶ **Lou-sous-Monjou**, Romanesque church with wall-belfry. ▶ **Château de Cropières**, dilapidated, at the bottom of the valley. ▶ But the **château de Messilhac** (14thC-16thC) is in perfect condition, with interesting furnishings *(Jul.-early Sep., 2-6:30; tel. : 71.49.55.55).* ▶ Turn around to reach **Carlat** at the foot of a basalt formation★ once crowned by a fortress that was later razed by Henri IV *(20-min round trip);* view★. ▶ Return to Vic along the left bank of the Cère, crossing the river at **Polminhac** : 12thC church with wall-belfry; château de Pesteils with square 14thC keep★ (14thC-15thC frescos; *15 Jun., 2:30-5:30, 16-30 Jun., 10-12 & 2:30-5:30; Jul.-Aug. 10-12 & 2:30-6; May, Sep., 2:30-5:30; tel. : 71.47.44.36).* ☐

Practical Information

ℹ av. Mercier, ☎ 71.47.50.68.
SNCF ☎ 71.47.51.74.

Hotels :
● ★★ **Bains** (L.F.), av. de la Promenade, ☎ 71.47.50.16, Tx 393160, Euro, 38 rm 🅿 ₩ 🄺 ⊟ half pens (h.s.), closed Nov-Apr ex Xmas school hols, 400. Rest. ♦ ♪ Spec : *terrine de truite saumonée sauce ciboulette, potée de lotte et de saumon en feuilletine,* 55-120.
★★ **Auberge des Monts**, Col de Curebourse, 6 km SE, ☎ 71.47.51.71, 31 rm 🅿 ₩ ᚼ closed Sun eve and Mon, 1 Nov-15 Dec, 200. Rest. ♦ ᚼ ᚼ ⅋ 65-140.
★★ **Bel Horizon**, rue Paul-Doumer, ☎ 71.47.50.06, 30 rm 🅿 ₩ ᚼ pens (h.s.), closed 1 Nov-10 Dec, 180. Rest. ♦ ᚼ ᚼ ⅋ 50-75.
★★ **Family** (L.F.), av. Émile-Duclaux, ☎ 71.47.50.49, Tx 393160, AE DC Euro Visa, 39 rm 🅿 ᚼ ₩ ⅋ half pens (h.s.), closed Oct-Apr ex Xmas hols and wkends. Rest. ♦ ᚼ ᚼ Family cooking with a regional accent : *chou farci, potée, tripous,* 50-90.

VOLVIC

Clermont-Ferrand 20, Montluçon 83, Paris 382 km
pop 3936 ⊠ 63530   B1

The black stone of Volvic is hard and solid, yet light; it first appeared during the 13thC in the construction of the cathedral at Clermont, and from then on began to replace other construction materials. Volvic became the major source of building stone, hence the rather severe appearance of towns in the vicinity.

▶ The **Maison de la Pierre** (Stone House), at the entrance to underground quarries, displays the volcanic origins of Volvic rock (andesite) and the often wretched lives of the quarry workers of former times, together with uses of the quarried stone *(guided tours every 45 min; 10-11:30 & 2:15-6 ex Tue., 15 Mar.-15 Nov.; take warm clothing).* ▶ Nearby, bottling plant for Volvic mineral water *(May-Sep.; weekdays 9-12 & 2-6; Sat. and Sun. am only; tel. : 73.38.12.66).* ▶ Romanesque choir with ambulatory in the church; capitals★. ▶ From the town hall, 20-min ascent to Notre-Dame-de-la-Garde (panorama★). From here, a good path *(20 min, or 2 km by road from the town)* leads to the **château de Tournoël★★** (13thC), dismantled by Cardinal Richelieu; pretty 15thC turreted staircase, chapel, keep, superb cylindrical tower 32 m high (marvelous view; *Easter-Oct., 9-12 & 2-7 ex Tue.).* ▶ Near Les Goulots *(1.2 km after the station, which is 6 km from Volvic)* : the **Maison du Miel★** (Honey House) shows the life of a bee-keeper *(May-Sep. 2-6:30 daily; rest of year, Sun. only 2-5:30).* ▶ 7 km SE, **Châteaugay**, dominated by a powerful square keep★ of the château (14th-16thC; *10-12 & 2-7);* tasting of Côtes d'Auvergne wines).   □

Practical Information ――――――――――――――

SNCF ☎ 73.33.51.71.

Hotels :
★ *Rose des Vents*, Luzet, 3 km, ☎ 73.33.50.77, AE DC Euro Visa, 28 rm ℗ ⨳ ▥ ⬚ ⌂ ✧ 180. Rest. ♦ ♪ closed Mon (l.s.) , Mon lunch only (Jul-Aug), 65-120.
La Chaumière (L.F.), Tournoël, 1 km N, ☎ 73.33.50.37, 6 rm ℗ ⨳ ▥ closed (l.s.) and Wed, 70. Rest. ♦ 40-90.

⚠ ★*Municipal* (50 pl), ☎ 73.33.50.38.

Recommended
Events : *pilgrimage to N.-D.-de-la-Garde,* late May.

YSSINGEAUX

Le Puy 27, Saint-Etienne 51, Paris 570 km
pop 6718 ⊠ 43200   C3

A modest town that lives from meat-curing and sub-contracting for industries in the Saint-Étienne area.

▶ The town hall occupies the former Gothic (14thC) living quarters of an old château. ▶ W, a 922-m butte provides a view over the area *(15-min walk).*

Nearby

▶ **Puy de Glavenas** *(6 km, plus 15 min on foot)* : a flat-topped-mountain; 2 km NE, the château de Mortessagne (15thC). ▶ **Versilhac** *(9 km NE)* : museum of local and art traditions *(Jul.-Aug.; 2:30-6 ex Tue.);* nearby, two dams on the Lignon (view★ from Lavalette), source of Saint-Étienne's water supply. ▶ E, pleasant summer resorts in

unspoiled countryside : **Montfaucon-en-Velay, Saint-Bonnet-le-Froid, Tence** and **Le Chambon-sur-Lignon.** ▶ S, the **Massif du Meygal,** bristling with volcanic cones and dykes. Their clear-cut silhouettes overlook lava-shingled roofs of the little villages; leaving the forest, there is a view from the peak of Grand Testavoyre, (alt. 1 436 m); more spectacular the view from **Queyrières★★.**   □

Practical Information ――――――――――――――

YSSINGEAUX

Hotels :
● ★★ *Clair Matin* (L.F.), Les Barandons, 3.5 km on D 157 and D 185, ☎ 71.59.73.03, AE DC Euro Visa, 30 rm ℗ ⨳ ▥ ⚘ ♪ ⬚ ✧ pens (h.s.), closed 5-20 Jan, 1-15 Mar, 20 Nov-20 Dec, 230. Rest. ♦ ⨳ ♪ ✧ A pleasant hotel in a beautiful location, 70.
★★ *Le Cygne*, 8, rue Alsace-Lorraine, ☎ 71.59.01.87, Visa, 18 rm ℗ ▥ ⚘ ♪ ✧ closed Sun eve and Mon, 27 Aug-5 Oct, 20 Dec-7 Jan, 125. Rest. ♦♦ ✧ 55-95.

Nearby

Le CHAMBON-SUR-LIGNON, ⊠ 43400, 28 km SE.
ℹ la Place, ☎ 71.59.71.56.

Hotels :
★★★ *Bel-Horizon* (L.F.), chem. de Malle, ☎ 71.59.74.39, 19 rm ℗ ⨳ ▥ ⚘ ⬚ ✧ half pens (h.s.), closed 1 Jan-22 May, 16 Nov-31 Dec, 500. Rest. ♦ ⨳ ♪ ⚅ ✧ 75.
★★ *Central*, ☎ 71.59.70.67, 25 rm ℗ ⚘ half pens (h.s.), closed Mon eve and Tue (l.s.), 29 Sep-29 Oct, 300. Rest. ♦ Generous family-style cooking : *saucisson chaud, crêpes aux morilles, gratin dauphinois,* 45-90.

⚠ ★★★★*Les Hirondelles* (50 pl), ☎ 71.59.73.84; ★★*Le Lignon* (130 pl), ☎ 71.59.72.86.

Recommended
Events : *Jonquil festival,* 1st Sun in May; *local fair,* 2nd Sun in Sep.

SAINT-BONNET-LE-FROID, ⊠ 43290 Montfaucon, 34 km E.

Hotel :
★★ *Auberge des Cimes* (L.F.), ☎ 71.59.93.72, AE DC Euro Visa, 11 rm ℗ ⨳ ▥ ⚅ ✧ ⬚ closed Sun eve and Mon, 1 Nov-14 Apr, 105. Rest. ● ♦♦ ⨳ ♪ ✧ The new place that all the guides and food writers claim to have discovered. We told you about it in our first edition! Régis Marcon is responsible for the outstanding, inventive cuisine : *gâteau de pigeon en gelée, navets farcis aux escargots à l'ail doux, filets de rougets au beurre d'artichauts,* 70-200; child : 25.

Recommended
Events : *mushroom festival,* in Nov.

TENCE, ⊠ 43190, 9 km of **Chambon** on the D 103.

Hotel :
★★ *Grand Hôtel* (R.S.), rue d'Annonay, ☎ 71.59.82.76, Visa, 20 rm ℗ ▥ ⚘ closed Sun eve and Mon, 1 Dec-1 Mar, 230. Rest. ♦ ⨳ ✧ Traditional cooking by P.-M. Placide, a former pupil of R. Vergé : *foie gras chaud au coulis de cèpes, amandine de loup au safran, crépinette de lapin au jus de truffe,* 110-300.

――――――――――――――――――――――――――――

Send us your comments and suggestions; we will use them in the next edition.

Basque Country, Béarn, Bigorre

▶ Perhaps the most striking thing about the Pyrénées is their aura of coolness and greenery. The word mountain usually conjures up images of gravel and scree, silence and vast stretches of empty land — but these mountains are as green and lush as any idyllic painter's landscape. The far-off bluish haze of the high peaks melts into the watercolor tints of the Labourd region, and the countryside is full of bubbling streams and rivers running through valleys large and small. Other mountains have rivers — this country has a whole glossary of special terms for its waterways to translate all possible variations in size, speed and color.

On the road from Mont-de-Marsan to Pau, the traveler can stop to watch the peaks of the Pyrénées rearing up like a crenellated fortress over the low plains of Aquitaine. Everywhere, sea, mountains and sky converse before the Pyrénées come to a head in one last masterful surge near the Spanish border.

The clear sky of Bayonne floats over the sharp spires of the cathedral. Biarritz, once a simple fishing village enriched by whale-hunting, is now a center of tourist attraction whose perfect climate also draws an increasing number of retired people.

Despite the differences between the Basque country and the Béarn region, these two regions, with their strong centuries-old traditions, live in perfect harmony in the shadow of the Atlantic Pyrénées. Bigorre, too, has its own special personality, its own history and

traditions as befits the native land of Henri IV, born in Pau in 1553. Bigorre's prestige is increased by the four million visitors and tourists who each year come to Lourdes, the town where the Virgin Mary appeared to a young village girl named Bernadette and left behind the miraculous springs. Here, the infirm and the healthy bathe together; piety and rosary beads, plastic statuettes and tourist buses coexist peacefully in the shadow of the Pyrénées. □

Don't miss

★★★ Basque Country A1, Biarritz A1, Laruns and the Ossau Valley C2, Passes of the Pyrénées C2, Saint-Jean-de-Luz A1.

★★ Arreau and the upper valley of the Aure D2, Bayonne A1, Oloron-Sainte-Marie B1, Pau C1, Saint-Jean-Pied-de-Port A-B1, Western Pyrénées National Park C2.

★ Aïnhoa A1, Arette-la-Pierre-Saint-Martin B2, Bagnères-de-Bigorre D2, Espelette A1, Hendaye A1, Lescar C1, Lourdes C2, Mauléon-Licharre B1, Saint-Étienne-de-Baïgorry A1, Salies-de-Béarn B1, Sauveterre-de-Béarn B1.

Weekend tips

Leave Bayonne or Biarritz, explore Bidache, Salies and Sauveterre-de-Béarn, château de Laàs, Barcus (lunch), Saint-Engrâce and Mauléon-Licharre. Stopover at Saint-Jean-Pied-de-Port. Next day, visit the Aldudes, Cambo, Saint-Pée and Sare (lunch), then Rhune and Saint-Jean-de-Luz. A visit to Lourdes (full day) could be rounded off by an excursion to Cauterets and the Gavarnie natural amphitheatre.

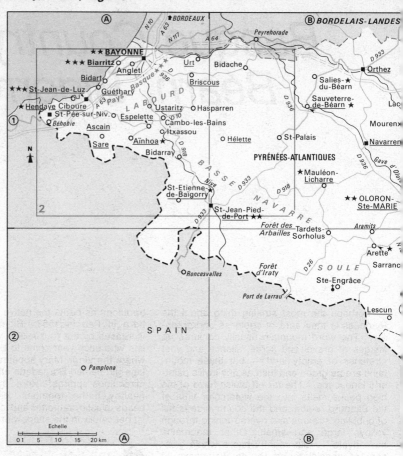

Basque house

Béarn house

Bigorre mountain house

● *Brief regional history*

Prehistory - Roman occupation

The Pyrénées have been inhabited since the earliest prehistoric times. By the Neolithic Era, a linguistic and ethnic identity had been established. The principal resources were agricultural and pastoral, based mainly on stock rearing.

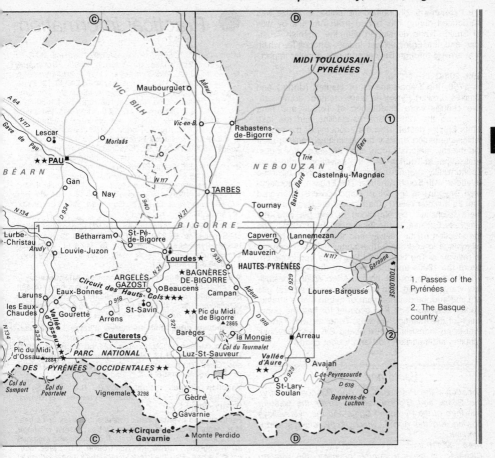

1. Passes of the Pyrénées

2. The Basque country

1st-9thC

The arrival of **Roman troops** drove the local population into the western mountains; Roman influence weighed most heavily around *Beneharnum* (Lescar), which, together with *Iluro* (Oloron), became the seat of a bishopric soon after the establishment of Christianity (6th-7thC). ● The Visigoths, who assumed the region in the 5th-7thC, were replaced in the 9thC by the Frankish Emperor Charlemagne.

9th-15thC

The Carolingian Dynasty was in turn overthrown by the 9thC Norman invaders, but control of the free-spirited mountain population was at best nominal, and the inhabitants of the former Roman Province of *Novempopulanie* paid little more than lip-service to historical developments. ● The Viscounty (Vicomté) of Béarn, created in 820, moved the regional capital from Lescar *(Beneharnum)* to Morlaàs. The states of Soule, Bigorre and Labourd were established between the 9th and the 11thC. ● Political control of the region was complicated by the 1154 marriage of Eleanor of Aquitaine (divorced wife of the French Louis VII) to Henri II Plantagenêt of England, which gave the English a hold on Eleanor's dowry ter-

ritories in SW France. The regions of Labourd, Soule and Bigorre came under English rule, and Bayonne developed into an important port. ● In 1290, the Counts of Foix were granted Béarn and began a **policy of neutrality** — especially under Gaston Fébus in the 14thC — that resulted in the formation of an independent Béarn state. The English were driven out of western France at the conclusion of the Hundred Years' War (early 15thC). At the end of the 15thC, the Albret family assumed the crown of Navarre, a kingdom straddling both sides of the Pyrénées. The Protestant Albrets, who established a new capital at Pau, tended to the French side, and the Catholic rulers of Spain (Ferdinand and Isabella) confiscated Upper Navarre at the beginning of the 16thC.

16th-18thC

Henri of Navarre, heir to Jeanne d'Albret, Queen of Navarre, succeeded to the throne of France as Henri IV in 1589, uniting his old and new kingdoms (1607) along with the three northern Basque provinces of Soule, Labourd and Bigorre. In 1620 Henri's son, Louis XIII, created the **Parliament of Navarre,** which conferred a degree of autonomy on the region. In 1659, during the reign of Louis XIV, the **Treaty of** the **Pyrénées** finally ratified the union. ● Maize was introduced during this period from America by way of Spain. Trade developed with the Spanish Americas and the French West Indies. Chocolate, which first arrived through Bayonne, was a popular import.

19th-20thC
In 1790, the Départements of Hautes (Upper) and Basses (Lower) Pyrénées were created; administrative centres were established at Tarbes and Pau. ● During the 19thC, Spain's decline and the loss of its Empire destabilized the economy of the region, which depended entirely on agriculture, lacking as it did the raw materials (iron, coal) necessary for industrialization. ● Tourism was the salvation of the area, economically stagnant despite the revival of trade relations with South America. The English, who occupied Bayonne at the fall of Napoléon (1814) favored Pau as a winter resort; Biarritz and the Basque coast were "launched" by Napoléon III and his wife, the Empress Eugénie, in the latter half of the 19thC. The introduction of the railway and the institution of the pilgrimage to Lourdes further stimulated this economic revival. ● The two World Wars, the economic crisis of the 1930s and the effects of the Spanish Civil War halted the tourist boom. After WWII, possibilities were enlarged with the discovery of natural gas at Lacq and the development of hybrid maize strains. Today, Bayonne and Pau account for half the population of the Atlantic Pyrénées. Together with Tarbes, Pau is an industrial centre of the SW, and Bayonne remains an important port and tourist centre.

Facts and figures

Location : *the Pays Basque (the Basque Country), the Béarn and Bigorre regions cover the western one-third of the Pyrenean Chain and the river valleys flowing into the Adour, which is the chain's northern limit.*
Area : *12 110 km².*
Climate : *in general, sunny; however, the western Pyrénées are affected by their proximity to the ocean. The Pays Basque is known for mild autumns, but also for summer showers. Frequent heavy rain keeps summer temperatures low, even in Bigorre.*
Population : *approx. 766 000.*
Administration : *The Pyrénées-Atlantiques Department (prefecture : Pau) is part of the economic region of Aquitaine, whereas the Hautes-Pyrénées Department (prefecture : Tarbes) is part of the Midi-Pyrénées economic region.*

The wine of kings

The king of wines, or at least the wine of kings since it was served at the baptism of Henri IV, is **Jurançon** : *white, dry or sweet, firm, clean-tasting, with little perfume. Another dry regional wine,* **Pacherenc** *from the Vic-Bilh region, has a higher alcohol content than most table wines. Béarn wines, red, rosé or dry white, are pleasant and have a full bouquet;* **Irouléguy** *rosé, red and the occasional white should be savoured young. People who enjoy an uplifting, simple red wine should try* **Madiran**. *Good years : 1975, 1981, 1982, 1983.*

 Practical information

Information : *Comité Régional de Tourisme (C.R.T.) Aquitaine,* 24, allées de Tourny, 33000 Bordeaux, ☎ 56.44.48.02. **Midi-Pyrénées** : *C.R.T. Midi-Pyrénées,* 12, rue Salambô, 31200 Toulouse, ☎ 61.47.11.12. **Pyrénées-Atlantiques** : *Comité Départemental de Tourisme (C.D.T.),* Parlement de Navarre, rue Henri-IV, 64000 Pau, ☎ 59.83.92.37. **Béarn** : *C.D.T.,* building des Pyrénées, 64000 Pau, ☎ 59.32.84.32. ext. 45-10. **Pays basque** : *C.C.T.P.B.,* 17, rue V.-Hugo, 64108 Bayonne Cedex, ☎ 59.59.28.77. **Hautes-Pyrénées** : *C.D.T.,* 6, rue Eugène-Ténot, 65000 Tarbes, ☎ 62.93.03.30. In **Paris** : *Maison des Pyrénées,* 15, rue St-Augustin, 75002, ☎ (1) 42.61.58.18 and **Bordeaux** : 8, rue Ausone, 33000, ☎ 56.44.05.65. *Dir. régionale de la Jeunesse et des Sports,* cité administrative, tour «A», rue Jules-Ferry, B.P. 65, 33090 Bordeaux Cedex, ☎ 56.44.84.64. *Dir. des Affaires culturelles,* 26-28, pl. Gambetta, 33074 Bordeaux, ☎ 56.52.01.68.

S.O.S. : **Pyrénées-Atlantiques** : *SAMU* (Emergency Medical Service), ☎ 59.27.15.15 (Pau); 59.63.33.33 (Bayonne). **Hautes-Pyrénées** : *SAMU* ☎ 62.34.44.44. *Poisoning Emergency Centre* : ☎ 62.32.97.77 (Bordeaux); 61.49.33.33 (Toulouse).

Weather forecast : **Pyrénées-Atlantiques** : ☎ 59.27.50.50 (Pau); ☎ 59.22.03.30 (Bayonne); *Ocean Search and Rescue* : ☎ 59.59.82.00. *Road and snow conditions* : ☎ 59.66.21.68 and 56.96.33.33. **Hautes-Pyrénées** : ☎ 62.34.77.77 and 62.34.44.18.

Farmhouse gîtes and chambres d'hôtes : **Pyrénées-Atlantiques** : *Association Départementale des Gîtes Ruraux,* Maison de l'Agriculture, 124, bd Tourasse, 64000 Pau, ☎ 59.80.19.13. **Hautes-Pyrénées** : *Relais Dép. des Gîtes Ruraux,* 22, pl. du Foirail, 65000 Tarbes, ☎ 62.34.52.82 and *C.D.T.*

Vacation villages : Enq. : *V.V.F.,* B.P. 236, 64108 Bayonne, ☎ 59.55.84.06. **Hautes-Pyrénées** : at Genos, Sanary. Enq. : *C.D.T.*

Festivals and events : **Jan** : *café-theatre week* in Tarbes. **Mar** : *week of Occitan culture* in Tarbes; *festival of image and sound* in Pau. **Easter** : *festival of music and religious art* in Lourdes, Tarbes and Saint-Savin. **Jun** : *jazz festival* in Tarbes; *Pau theatre festival; international industrial film festival* in Biarritz. **Jul** : *Pyrénées folk festival* in Oloron-Sainte-Marie (even-numbered years). **Aug** : *international festival of Basque folklore* in Bayonne; *Basque festival* in Saint-Palais; *cheese fair* in Loures-Barousse; *cartoon festival* in Anglet; *flower festival* in Bagnères-de-Bigorre. **Sep** : *international bridge festival and Iberian and Latin-American film festival* in Biarritz; *session of the Maurice Ravel international academy of music* in Saint-Jean-de-Luz; *music festival on the Basque Coast* (concerts in numerous towns); *parachuting festival* in Tarbes.

National and nature parks : *parc national des Pyrénées-Occidentales,* 56, rte de Pau, 65013 Tarbes-Ibos, ☎ 62.93.30.60. *Assn. des Amis du parc national des Pyrénées,* 20, rue Samonzet, 64000 Pau, ☎ 59.27.15.30. The National Park Centres in Etsaut, Gabas, Arrens, Cauterets and Saint-Lary propose a different exhibition in each valley, together with all documents published by the park.

Rambling and hiking : maps *I.G.N.* parc national des Pyrénées 1/25000. Pays basque-Soule, Pays basque Ouest (topoguide) and Béarn parc national au 1/50000. The G.R.10 crosses the region, linking the Atlantic and the Mediterranean (topoguide). For all rambles, hikes and courses, practical information at the : *C.I.M.E.S.* Pyrénées *(Centre d'Information Montagnes et Sentiers),* 3, sq. Balagué, 09200 Saint-Girons, ☎ 61.66.40.10; every morning ex Wed. *Assn. des Amis du parc national des Pyrénées,* hiking rambling club, 32, rue Samonzet, 64000 Pau, ☎ 59.27.15.30. *Assn. Départementale des Sentiers d'Excursion,* 83, av. des Lauriers, 64000 Pau. *Cie des gui-*

Pyrenean flora and fauna

The Western Pyrénées National Park (parc national des Pyrénées occidentales) protects countless specimens of native fauna, of which the Pyrenean bear is probably the most intriguing. There is little likelihood of finding yourself face-to-face with one, as only about 30 are in existence. There are, however, about 1500 isard (Pyrenean mountain goat, the park's symbol) as well as lynx, civet, marten, ermine, marmot and other species. The park shelters many varieties of birds : Egyptian vulture, griffon vulture, golden eagle, bearded vulture and sparrow hawk. Smaller birds include ptarmigan (similar to the Scottish grouse), capercaillie, water ouzel, and others. The rivers abound with char and several species of trout. Flora include blue iris, rhododendron, jonquil, asphodel, turk's cap lily, anemone, and scented daphne, as well as alpine varieties such as gentian, edelweiss, ramondia, Pyrenean buttercup, and dwarf plants such as catch-fly and Pyrenean willow.

---

des des Pyrénées, Maison du Tourisme, 6, rue Eugène-Ténot, 65000 Tarbes, ☎ 62.93.03.30 and *C.D.T.*

Cycling holidays : a guide, "Cycling holidays in Béarn" is available at the *Comité touristique Béarn,* ☎ 59.32.84.32, ext. 54-10. **Hautes-Pyrénées :** ☎ 62.95.03.97.

Riding holidays : *Association Départementale de Randonnées Équestres,* Escos, 64270 Salies-de-Béarn, ☎ 59.38.40.16. Introduction, trekking : *Société hippique rurale du Val d'Adour,* 65140 Bazillac, ☎ 62.96.82.97. Also *C.D.T.*

Scenic railways : the *Artouste scenic railway,* daily mid-Jun-end Sep, ☎ 59.05.36.99. *Rhune rack railway :* from the Saint-Ignace Pass to the Rhune summit, Jul-Sep daily ; Easter hols, May-Jun, 1 Oct-15 Nov : Sat, Sun and nat hols with departures at 10 am and 3 pm. *Avré Funicular railway* in Barèges. Enq. : ☎ 62.92.68.19 and 62.92.68.26.

Technical tourism : *Fromagerie des Chaumes* (local cheese producer) in Jurançon, 155, av. Rauski, ☎ 59.06.17.20. *Distillerie Izarra,* 9, quai Bergeret, 64108 Bayonne, ☎ 59.55.09.45. *Stendhal Cosmetics* in Mourenx, ☎ 59.60.01.55. Basque béret : *Entreprise Laclau,* Z.I., Oloron-Sainte-Marie, ☎ 59.39.04.41. *Pyrénéenne de textiles,* in Bagnères-de-Bigorre, ☎ 62.95.01.79.

Handicraft courses : enq. : *C.R.T. Aquitaine* and *C.D.T. Pyrénées-Atlantiques.* Pottery, weaving in Pau, fabric painting in Bayonne, weaving in Louhossoa. Enq. : *C.D.T. Pyrénées-Atlantiques.* Reupholstery, poster design at Tarbes *(youth hostel).*

Other courses : cooking, photography, yoga, mountain discovery... enq. : *L.A. Hautes-Pyrénées.*

Jai alai (pelota) : *Féd. française de Pelote Basque,* Trinquet moderne, 64100 Bayonne, ☎ 59.22.22.34.

Skittles : game with 6 or 9 large wooden pins, popular in Béarn, *Assn. de quilles de 9,* M. Bert-Lariga, Lalonguette, 64450 par Thèze, ☎ 59.04.83.04.

Aquatic sports : *Assn. Nautique de Biarritz,* port des Pêcheurs, ☎ 59.24.11.41. Surfing and wind-surfing : *Bidassoa Surfing-Club,* 8, rue de la Forêt, 64700 Hendaye, ☎ 59.20.14.35. *Biarritz Surfing-Club,* 78, av. Kennedy, ☎ 59.23.10.05. *Féd. française surf et skate,* plage nord, 40150 Hossegor, ☎ 58.43.55.88.

Scuba diving : *Centre de Plongée de la Côte Basque,* rue des Usines, Ciboure, 64500 Saint-Jean-de-Luz.

Canoeing : *Comité Départemental de canoë-kayak des Hautes-Pyrénées,* ☎ 62.95.16.29. Haut-Louron, ☎ 62.99.68.02. Saint-Pé-de-Bigorre, ☎ 62.41.81.48.

U.S.S. Canoë-Kayak, Sauveterre-de-Béarn, ☎ 59.38.57.58.

Rafting : *Béarn rafting Eaux-Vives,* ☎ 59.39.29.40 or 59.06.31.10, Hautes-Pyrénées, ☎ 62.94.48.28.

Golf : 18-hole courses in Anglet, Artiguelouve, Biarritz, Ciboure, Lannemezan, Pau-Billère, Saint-Jean-de-Luz ; 9-hole at Laloubère.

Potholing-spelunking : *Centre International de spéléologie des Pyrénées-Atlantiques,* B.P. 5, Arette-la-Pierre-Saint-Martin, ☎ 59.66.20.09.

Climbing-mountaineering : *Club alpin français,* 5, rue R.-Fournets, 64000 Pau, ☎ 59.27.71.81. *Club Pyrénéiste Jurançonnais,* 12, rue J.-P.-Toulet, ☎ 59.06.22.86. **Hautes-Pyrénées :** *Cie des Guides* (see Rambling).

Auto sports : *Automobile-Club basco-béarnaise,* sq. Aragon, 64000 Pau ☎ 59.27.01.94. *Assn. sportive automobile des montagnes de Soule,* 18, rue V.-Hugo, 64130 Mauléon-Licharre, ☎ 59.28.01.56. Bigorre, *Promo Course,* 33, rue Branhauban, 65000 Tarbes, ☎ 62.93.04.06.

Winter sports : Cross-country skiing : *Assn. Dép. de Ski de Fond des Pyrénées-Atlantiques,* Parlement de Navarre, rue Henri-IV, 64000 Pau, ☎ 59.83.12.37. Also *C.D.T.* and *T.O.*

Gliding and hang-gliding : *Delta-Club du Centre de vol à voile,* Hiribarne aérodrome, Itxassou, 64250 Cambo-les-Bains, ☎ 59.29.75.36. *Labourd,* 109, bd de la Mer, 64700 Hendaye. *École Pyrénéenne de vol libre* (Pyrénées gliding school), 65240 Vieille-Louron, ☎ 62.99.68.55 ; enq. and enrollments : Central Reservation, 65590 Borderes-Louron, ☎ 62.98.64.12. *Delta-Club bigourdan,* 22, rue St-Blaise, enq. : ☎ 62.95.04.83. *École de vol libre du Cavedan,* ☎ 62.95.04.83 (evenings). *Club deltaplane Gourette,* M. Bouille, 9, rue Corisandre, 64290 Gan, ☎ 59.21.54.24.

Hunting and shooting : enq at the *Féd. Dép. des Chasseurs.* **Pyrénées-Atlantiques :** rue Jean-Zay, 64000 Pau,

---

Basque cuisine

Jambon de Bayonne is prized far and wide. Traditionally, this ham is cured simply by being rubbed with salt. Fried with eggs or used in cooking Basque style, it is delicious. Chocolate was introduced into France and Europe by way of Bayonne in 1670. The mouth-watering fattened goose or duck livers (foie gras) are equally good au naturel or as confits (preserved in their own fat). Garbure is a delectable thick green vegetable soup. Fish dishes make free use of tunny, sea bream, turbot and whiting ; specialities are fried sardines with egg yolk, fish stew (matelote) and chipirones (baby squid) served in various ways. Salmon from the mountain streams (saumon des gaves), particularly the Adour, is exquisite. Ewe's milk cheese is excellent as, for the sweet tooth, is touron (rich marzipan, with nuts).

☎ 59.84.31.55. **Hautes-Pyrénées :** 6, rue G.-Clemenceau, 65000 Tarbes, ☎ 62.34.53.01.

Fishing : *Féd. des Assn. de Pêche des Pyrénées-Atlantiques,* 29, rue A.-Briand, 64000 Pau, ☎ 59.02.38.27. The *Féd. Dép. des A.P.P., Féd. Dép. de Pêche,* résidence Bigerrions, bd Martinet, 65000 Tarbes, ☎ 62.36.62.09, publishes a brochure which lists the federal fishing reserves and associations, and dates for the season. Sea fishing : *Yacht-Club Adour Atlantique,* Section Pêche, av. de l'Adour, 64600 Anglet, ☎ 59.63.16.22. World salmon-fishing championships in Navarrenx. Enq : *S.I.* Navarrenx, ☎ 59.66.10.22.

Towns and places

ARETTE-LA-PIERRE-ST-MARTIN*

Oloron 20, Pau 53, Paris 838 km
pop 1120 ⊠ 64570   **B2**

Arette (alt. 1 650 m), westernmost winter resort in the Pyrénées (open also in summer, hikes and rambles) forms a kind of balcony on Anie Peak (alt. 2 504 m).

▶ At the **Pierre-Saint-Martin Pass** *(3 km SW; alt.* 1 760 m; *open mid-May-mid-Oct.)*, a ceremony has taken place every 13th of July since 1375 : the shepherds of Barétous pay a tribute of three heifers to their Spanish neighbours from Roncal in exchange for grazing rights. Nearby, the **gouffre de la Pierre-Saint-Martin** (world's deepest pothole, more than 1 760 m ; *inaccessible to the public*). □

Practical Information ————————————

⚐ 1650-2000m, (la Pierre-Saint-Martin).
ℹ ☎ 59.66.20.09.

Hotel :
★ *Salies*, 8, pl. de l'Eglise, ☎ 59.34.61.03, 21 rm Ⓟ ⬱
closed 15 Nov-10 Dec, 120. Rest. ♦ ⬱ 40-90.

ARGELÈS-GAZOST

Tarbes 33, Pau 53, Paris 838 km
pop 3460 ⊠ 65400   **C2**

Argelès (alt. 465 m), a spa specializing in the relief of skin diseases and rheumatism, is set in a lush valley where the rivers Cauterets and Gavarnie combine to form the Haut Gave de Pau (upper reaches of the river). Mild, sunny climate ; mineral springs on extensive grounds.

Argelès Valley

▶ **Saint-Savin** : 12thC monastery on the site of a Gallo-Roman camp ; fortified **Romanesque church**★ (organ casing 1557, museum of religious art in the Chapterhouse) ; view over the houses. The 12thC **château d'Arcizans-Avant**, above the town, has commanded the Auzun and Saint Savin valleys since the 12thC *(daily pm Jul.-21 Sep. ; Sun. and school hols. pm Apr.-Oct.)*.▶ **Pierrefitte-Nestalas** : at the exit of the Luz and Cauterets gorges ; 16th-18thC houses.▶ **Beaucens** : imposing ruins of 13th-14thC château now house **Donjon des Aigles**★ (Falconry Museum, *daily pm Apr.-Oct.*). Other keeps near **Agos-Vidalos** *(4 km N ;* 12thC) and at **Sère-Argelès** *(4 km NW ;* 13thC).▶ 20 km drive E on the Hautacam mountain road.   □

Practical Information ————————————

ARGELÈS-GAZOST
⚐ (1 Jun-30 Sep).
ℹ pl. de la Mairie, ☎ 62.97.00.25.
⟁⟁ ☎ 62.97.00.28.

Hotels :
● ★★ *Le Miramont*, bd des Pyrénées, ☎ 62.97.01.26, 29 rm Ⓟ ⬱ ⟋ ⬰ half pens (h.s.), closed 25 Oct-22 Dec, 300. Rest. ♦ ⟋ ⬰ Good value, 60-135.
★★ *Bon Repos* (L.F.), 13, rue du Stade, ☎ 62.97.01.49, 20 rm 3 apt Ⓟ ⬱ ⬰ half pens (h.s.), closed 15 Oct-15 May. ex Xmas, Feb school hols and Easter, 260. Rest. ♦ ⬱ 45-60 ; child : 35.
★★ *Les Cimes* (L.F.), 1, pl. Ourout, ☎ 62.97.00.10, Euro Visa, 27 rm Ⓟ ⬱ ⬰ & half pens, closed 10 Oct-18 Dec, 230. Rest. ♦ ⬱ 100 ; child : 25.
★ *Nord*, 22, av. Gal-Leclerc, ☎ 62.97.08.84, 18 rm Ⓟ ⬱ ⬰ closed Mon, 26 Sep-1 Nov, 100. Rest. ♦ 45-100.

⟁ ★★★*Les Trois vallées* (250 pl), ☎ 62.90.35.47.

Nearby

AGOS-VIDALOS , ⊠ 65400 Argelès-Gazost, 5 km NE.

Hotel :
★★ *Chez Pierre d'Agos*, ☎ 62.97.05.07, 53 rm Ⓟ ⬱ ⟋ & half pens, 270. Rest. ♦ ⬱ ⟋ 40-70.
⟁ ★★★*La Tour* (120 pl), ☎ 62.97.08.59 ; ★★*La Châtaigneraie* (65 pl), ☎ 62.97.07.40.

ARCIZANS-AVANT , ⊠ 65400 Argelès-Gazost, 5 km S.

Hotel :
★ *Le Cabaliros* (L.F.), ☎ 62.97.04.31, 9 rm Ⓟ ⬱ ⬰ ⬰ half pens, closed 6-31 Jan, Oct, 215. Rest. ♦ ⬱ ⬰ 50-120 ; child : 40.
⟁ ★★*Le Lac* (66 pl), ☎ 62.97.01.88.

BEAUCENS , ⊠ 65400 Argelès-Gazost, 8 km SE.
⚲ (1 May-31 Oct), ☎ 62.97.04.01.

Hotel :
★★ *Thermal* (L.F.), parc thermal, ☎ 62.97.04.21, 32 rm Ⓟ ⬱ ⬰ ⊡ half pens (h.s.), closed 1 Oct-1 Jun. 20 acres of wilderness, 170. Rest. ♦♦ *Thermes* ⬱ ⟋ ⬰ 55-85 ; child : 35.

⟁ ★★*Le Viscos* (100 pl), ☎ 62.97.05.45.

SAINT-SAVIN , ⊠ 65400 Argelès-Gazost, 3 km S.

Hotels :
★★ *Le Viscos* (L.F.), ☎ 62.97.02.28, AE Euro Visa, 16 rm Ⓟ ⬱ ⟋ ⬰ closed Mon, 1-26 Dec, 190. Rest. ♦♦ ⬱ Fresh air and good food : *filets de canard au foie gras frais et cèpes*, 100-170.
★★ *Panoramic*, ☎ 62.97.08.22, AE Visa, 22 rm Ⓟ ⬱ ⬰ ⟲ pens, half pens (h.s.), closed 10 Oct-1 Apr, 310. Rest. ♦ ⬱ & 55-100 ; child : 30.

The Upper AURE Valley**

D2

Arreau was once the principal town for four valleys, at the junction of the rivers Aure and Louron. Walks.

▶ Church of **St. Exupère** ; 16thC houses (especially noteworthy, Maison du Lys (Lily) near the covered market).

Nearby

▶ 7 km along the **Neste de Louron Valley**, overshadowed by the 3 130-m high snow-covered Gourgs Blancs Peak to **Loudervielle** (Romanesque church) and **Peyresourde Pass**, then down to Bagnères-de-Luchon (→ Midi-Toulousain-Pyrénées).▶ **Aure Valley** *(approx. 70 km round trip)*. **Cadéac** : 16thC Gothic church, Romanesque doorway, ruined 12th-13thC tower.▶ **Ancizan** : church with 1554 Entombment of Christ.▶ **Bazus-Aure** : Gothic church with noteworthy keystone vaulting. **Bourisp** : church (late 16thC paintings).▶ **Vieille-Aure** : church with Romanesque E end, 16thC nave, 15th-16thC murals.▶ **Saint-Lary-Soulan** : in the heart of the valley, a winter sports resort ; **Maison du Parc National** (Park Office) offers an audiovisual program on the fauna of the Pyrénées *(daily during school terms, or by request to the Field Director, tel 62.39.40.91)*.▶ Take the cable car to **Pla d'Adet** (alt. 1 700 m) : from that plateau a gondola runs to **Soum de Matte** (alt. 2 377 m). Excursions on foot or by car, especially in the vicinity of **Orédon**★ (alt. 1 850 m) and **Cap-de-Long**★★ **Lakes** (alt. 2 160 m), the latter held by the largest dam in the Pyrénées. From the lodge (Châlet-Refuge), interesting walks through the **Néouvielle Nature Reserve**★ (23 km²), next to the National Park ; or climb up Long Peak (alt. 3 194 m ; guide essential), the highest peak in the French Pyrénées.▶ Upstream of Saint-Lary the road runs through the **resort** and **plateau of Aragnouet** : Romanesque former chapel of the Hospitallers (warrior-monks who guarded the pilgrimage routes) on one of the roads to the Spanish shrine of Santiago de Compostela. From here, reach the winter sports centre of **Piau-Engaly** (alt. 1 880-2 380 m) and the **Bielsa tunnel** into Spain. □

Practical Information _____

ARREAU, ⊠ 65240, 32 km NW of **Bagnères-de-Luchon**.
ⓘ pl. du Monument, ☎ 62.98.63.15.
SNCF ☎ 62.98.64.23.

Hotel :
★★ **Angleterre** (L.F.), rte de Luchon, ☎ 62.98.63.30, Euro Visa, 20 rm Ⓟ ⌇ ⅏ closed 15 Apr-1 Jun, 10 Oct-26 Dec, 170. Rest. ♦ ⌇ ♪ ⩌ 50-100 ; child : 35.

HÈCHES, ⊠ 65250 La Barthe-de-Neste, 13 km N of **Arreau**.

Hotel :
★ **Hostellerie de la Neste**, rue de la Gare, ☎ 62.98.83.04, 15 rm Ⓟ ⌇ ⅏ ⌔ closed Mon, Tue, Oct-May, 100. Rest. ♦ ⌇ ♪ ᴧ 50-105.

SAINT-LARY-SOULAN, ⊠ 65170, 12 km S of **Arreau**.
⌇ 830-2380m.
ⓘ ☎ 62.39.40.29/62.39.50.81.

Hotels :
★★ **Christiana**, le Pla d'Adet, 13 km on D 123, ☎ 62.98.44.42, AE DC Visa, 24 rm Ⓟ ⌇ ⌔ closed 20 Apr-1 Dec, 195.
★★ **Terrasse Fleurie**, ☎ 62.39.40.26, Tx 520360, AE, 28 rm Ⓟ ⌇ ♪ closed 10 May-1 Jul, 20 Sep-15 Dec, 150. Rest. ♦ ♪ 60-120 ; child : 30.

⚠ ★★★★*Municipal* (100 pl), ☎ 62.39.41.58 ; ★★★*Le Luston*, ☎ 62.39.40.64.

BAGNÈRES-DE-BIGORRE*

Tarbes 21, Saint-Gaudens 57, Paris 826 km
pop 9850 ⊠ 65200   D2

Bagnères (alt. 550 m) offers a range of interests : thermal springs (sulphur, calcium, iron and other mineral waters), a summer resort, industrial weaving, slate and marble quarries. Other activities include the manufacturing of equipment for the aviation, railway and electrical industries ; flower festival in summer.

▶ Casino, **spa facilities** and the **Salies Museum** (*daily ex Tue. and Sun. in season ; Thu. and Fri. out of season*; fine arts, natural history) at the edge of the Thermal Park★ ; the houses in town are faced with marble ; 15th-16thC church of St. Vincent ; ruined 12thC cloister ; the Jacobins Tower, now a bell-tower, formerly part of a 15thC convent. ▶ 2 km S, Bagnères Gateway and the **Médous Caverns★** : 760 m of galleries ; 160 m accessible by boat (*daily Jun.-Sep.*), discovered in 1948. ▶ Above the town to the W, the **Bédat lookout★** (alt. 880 m), a one-hr walk on woodland paths. □

Practical Information _____

⚕ (7 May-20 Oct), ☎ 62.95.00.23.
ⓘ pl. La Fayette, ☎ 62.95.01.62.
SNCF ☎ 62.95.01.19.

Hotels :
★★★ **La Résidence** (R.S.), Parc Thermal de Salut, ☎ 62.95.03.97, Euro Visa, 40 rm Ⓟ ⌇ ⅏ ⌔ ♨ ⊗ ▱ 〳 pens (h.s.), closed 15 Oct-1 Apr, 315. Rest. ♦ ♪ 70-100.
★ **Bellevue**, **Thermes de la Reine**, Lacets des Thermes, ☎ 62.95.24.58, 20 rm Ⓟ ⅏ ⌔ ⊗ closed 20 Oct-5 May, 170.
★ **France**, 7, bd Carnot, ☎ 62.95.08.16, 21 rm Ⓟ closed 20 Oct-1 Jun, 115.
★ **Petites Vosges**, (Pierre Lestage), 17, bd Carnot, ☎ 62.95.28.31, 8 rm Ⓟ ⌇ ♨ pens, closed 1 Oct-1 Dec, 130. Rest. ♦ ⌇ ♪ ᴧ 45-75.

⚠ ★★★*Les Fruitiers* (100 pl), ☎ 62.95.25.97 ; ★★★*Les Tilleuls* (100 pl), ☎ 62.95.26.04 ; ★★*Les Palomières* (40 pl), ☎ 62.95.59.79.

Recommended
Bicycle-rental : M. Couture, rue du Mal.-Foch, ☎ 62.95.03.93.
Casino : pl. des Thermes, ☎ 62.95.20.42.
Events : *flower festival*, in Aug.
Farmhouse-gîte : at Orignac (5 km on RN 117), J. Pujo, ☎ 62.95.48.18.
▼ antiques : M. Sayous, pl. Ramond ; ceramics : Cazalas, ☎ 62.95.28.37 ; pastry : Pâtisserie Bordelaise, allée des Coustous, ☎ 62.95.00.36.

Pays BASQUE***

(The Basque Country)   A1

From Bayonne to Biarritz (*approx 205 km, 2-3 days ; see map 2*)

The Basque Country encompasses the Atlantic seaboard (75 % of French Basques live between Biarritz and Hendaye), as well as the mountainous inland area stretching southwest of the Gave d'Oloron to the Spanish border. The distinctive character of the Basque country and people is most apparent in the backcountry villages and deep valleys. The landscape is superb. The valleys of the Nive, the Aludes and the Saison (Soule) are described in itineraries from Saint-Étienne-de-Baïgorry (→) and Mauléon-Licharre (→).

▶ From **Bayonne** (→) leave the Adour Valley and climb to the **Mouguerre Cross** (panorama★★ of the town, the mouth of the Adour, the coast and the Pyrénées). The **Route Impériale des Cimes** (Imperial Peak Road) offers splendid views. ▶ **Cambo-les-Bains** : a spa and winter resort best viewed from the terrace in front of the church, which is in traditional Basque style (17thC altarpiece). The Emperor Napoléon III, his wife, the Empress Eugénie, and the actress Sarah Bernhardt were among the habitual clients. **Villa Arnaga★** : 1.5 km W on the Bayonne Road, where the poet Edmond Rostand (1619-55, author of the verse drama *Cyrano de Bergerac*) lived ; garden, museum. ▶ The **Isturitz** and **Oxocelhaya★ Caves** are just off the road between Isturitz and Saint-Martin-d'Arberoue (*visits ; traces of prehistoric habitation*). ▶ **Garris** : charming church in village of Basque houses. ▶ **Saint-Palais** : annual Basque Festival in summer at this crossroads of former pilgrimage routes to Compostela. ▶ **Osquich Pass** (alt. 392 m) separates the provinces of Soules and Basse (lower) Navarre : view over Béarn. ▶ **Saint-Jean-le-Vieux** and **Saint-Jean-Pied-de-Port** (→). ▶ **Saint-Étienne-de-Baïgorry** (→). ▶ Before reaching **Bidarray** you reach Pont d'Enfer (Hell's Bridge) ; Nive Gorges (trout fishing). ▶ From **Itxassou** (pretty church) to the opening of Pas de Roland (mountain pass), from where you can reach **Mont Urzumu**★ and **Artzamendi** (*difficult road ;* alt. 926 m ; panorama★). ▶ **Espelette** : a typical Basque village★ with 17thC wooden galleries in the church and discus-shaped tombstones dating from the 13thC. Winter, *pottoks* fair (Basque ponies). ▶ **Aïnhoa★** : one of the most typical Basque villages in Labourdes ; Romanesque church, 17thC houses. ▶ **Sare★** : at the foot of Saint-Ignace Pass, attractive village, church with 17th-18thC galleries ; from here, you can reach the Sare Forest (11 km², pigeon shooting in autumn) ; prehistoric caves. A cog railway goes from the Saint-Ignace Pass to the top of the **Rhune** (alt. 900 m), best vantage point★★ in the Basque country. ▶ **Ascain★** : traditional Basque church, 17thC houses. ▶ **Urrugne** : fortified town whose church (entirely remodeled in the 16thC) borrows the Guipuzcoan style from the neighbouring province in Spain. ▶ Nearby, **château d'Urtubie** : 16th-18thC, with 14thC keep (*daily ex Tue., 3-7, mid-Jul.-early Sep.*); panorama★ from the pilgrim chapel of Notre-Dame-de-Socorri. ▶ **Hendaye★** rises steeply above the River Bidassoa, which forms the border with Spain. On the **Île des Faisans** in the middle of the river, the Treaty of the Pyrénées was drawn up in 1659

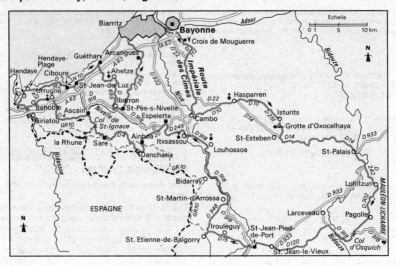

2. The Basque country

(linking Roussillon and the Cerdagne with France) as was the marriage contract of Louis XIV and Maria-Teresa of the Hapsburg Dynasty. Since that time, the control of the island has alternated between France and Spain every six months. In the town, the St. Vincent church (16th-17thC) has a beautiful 12thC crucifix. ► To the N, the seaside resort of **Hendaye-Plage** and the coast road of the **Corniche des Basques★**. ► **Socoa** : one of the great Atlantic surfing beaches. ► **Ciboure** and **Saint-Jean-de-Luz (→)**. ► **Guéthary** : view★ NE as far as Biarritz; remodeled 17thC church. ► **Saint-Pée-sur-Nivelle★** : on the edge of an 18 km² forest; old houses, galleried Basque church, remains of 16thC château with keep dating from 1403. □

Practical Information

AINHOA, ⊠ 64250 Cambo-les-Bains, 26 km S of **Bayonne**.

Hotels :
● ★★★ *Argi-Eder*, (Mapotel), ☎ 59.29.91.04, Tx 570067, AE DC Euro Visa, 36 rm 🄿 ≶ ₩ ⌂ ♪ 🖃 closed Wed, 15 Nov-15 Mar, 450. Rest. ♦♦ ♪ ኔ Spec : *truite "Ainhoarra", tournedos "Argi-Eder", tarte chaude aux fruits.* Renowned restaurant, 125-190.
★★★ *Ithuria* (C.H.), ☎ 59.29.92.11, AE DC Visa, 28 rm 🄿 ≶ ₩ ⌂ closed Tue eve and Wed, 15 Nov-15 Mar, 290. Rest. ♦♦♦ ♪ ኔ On the road to Compostela, pilgrims are still searching out good restaurants. Here's one, in a historic monument : *louvine grillée, foie gras, saumon sauvage, confits* and some good (or great) Bordeaux wines to quench your thirst, 120-180.
★★ *Oppoca*, rue Principale, ☎ 59.29.90.72, Visa, 12 rm 🄿 ≶ ₩ half pens (h.s.), closed Tue, 17 Nov-9 Apr, 400. Rest. ♦♦ Spec : *saumon frais tartare, cailles confites sur canapés aux pruneaux*, 85-150; child : 50.

⚠ ★★★*Xokoan* (33 pl), ☎ 59.29.90.26.

ASCAIN, ⊠ 64310, 27 km S of **Bayonne**.
ⓘ mairie, ☎ 59.54.00.84.

Hotels :
★★★ *L'Hacienda*, RN 618, ☎ 59.54.02.47, AE Visa, 26 rm 🄿 ≶ ₩ ⌂ 🖃 closed 15 Nov-15 Mar, 280. Rest. ♦♦ *Le Ranchero Grill* ≶ ኔ closed Wed and Sun eve, 5 Jan-1 Mar, 100.

● ★★ *La Rhune*, ☎ 59.54.00.04, 42 rm 🄿 ≶ ₩ ⌂ 🖃 closed 5 Jan-15 Mar. Squash, 230. Rest. ♦ ≶ ኔ 70-120.
★ *Achafla-Baïta*, rte d'Urrugne, 2 km, ☎ 59.54.00.30, 14 rm 🄿 ≶ ₩ ⌂ closed 15-30 Nov, 110. Rest. ♦ ኔ closed Mon (l.s.), 60-150.

⚠ ★★★*Zelaia* (170 pl), ☎ 59.54.02.36.

BIDARRAY, ⊠ 64780, 36 km SE of **Bayonne**.

Hotels :
★★ *Pont d'Enfer*, ☎ 59.37.70.88, 16 rm 🄿 ≶ ₩ half pens, closed 1 Nov-20 Mar, 350. Rest. ♦ Nice little eatery, 75-120.
★ *Erramundeya*, ☎ 59.37.71.21, 10 rm 🄿 ≶ ⌂ closed Tue (l.s.), 1 Dec-1 Mar, 110.

BIRIATOU, ⊠ 64700 Hendaye, 4 km SE of **Hendaye**.

Hotel :
● ★★ *Bakea*, ☎ 59.20.76.36, AE DC Euro Visa, 15 rm 🄿 ≶ ♪ ኔ ⌘ half pens (h.s.), closed 30 Sep-1 May, 465. Rest. ● ♦♦ ♪ ኔ closed Oct-Apr. No lowering of quality or standards in this spacious chalet, but prices are rising. Spec : *terrine de foie gras frais, homard grillé à l'estragon, turbot poché au beurre blanc*, 100-160.

CAMBO-LES-BAINS, ⊠ 64250, 19 km SE of **Bayonne**.
♨ (1 Feb-22 Dec), ☎ 59.29.78.54. ⚑
ⓘ parc Saint-Joseph, ☎ 59.29.70.25.
SNCF ☎ 59.25.71.24.

Hotel :
★★★ *Errobia*, av. Chantecler, ☎ 59.29.71.26, Visa, 15 rm 🄿 ≶ ₩ ⌂ closed 30 Oct-1 May, 230.

⚠ ★★★*Bichta Eder*, ☎ 59.29.94.23; ★★★*Ur-Hégia* (120 pl), ☎ 59.29.72.03.

ESPELETTE, ⊠ 64250 Cambo-les-Bains, 20 km S of **Bayonne**.

Hotel :
● ★★ *Euzkadi* (L.F.), ☎ 59.29.91.88, Euro Visa, 28 rm ₩ closed Mon, 15 Nov-15 Dec, 20-28 Feb, 140. Rest. ♦ The "academy" of Basque cuisine : *ttoro, axoa, pipérade, tripoxa...* André Darraïdou does both the cooking and the translating, 55-120.

Restaurants :
♦ *Le Relais du Labourd*, rte de Saint-Jean-de-Luz, ☎ 59.29.90.70, AE DC Euro Visa 🄿 ≶ ₩ ⌂ ♪ ኔ closed

Wed and Sun eve, 15 Jan-15 Feb. Excellent farm-style food in a 17thC setting : *pâtés, terrines, saucisses confites, magrets*, 50-150.

♦ *Pottoka*, ☎ 59.29.90.92 Ⓟ ▦ & closed Mon , 10 days in Feb and in Oct, 50-90.

Recommended
Events : *chili festival*, in Oct ; *pottok festival*, late Jan.

GUÉTHARY, ⊠ 64210 Bidart, 15 km SW of **Bayonne**.
ⓘ pl. de la Mairie, ☎ 59.26.56.60.
𝗦𝗡𝗖𝗙 ☎ 59.26.50.41.

Hotel :
★★★ *Briketenia*, rue de l'Empereur, ☎ 59.26.51.34, AE Visa, 21 rm Ⓟ ≼ ▦ pens (h.s.), closed Tue, 1 Nov-15 Dec, 520. Rest. ● ♦♦ The Ibarboure brothers' gastronomic festival : an excellent fixed-price meal featuring fish, steamed bass, 90-230.

HASPARREN, ⊠ 64240, 24 km SE of **Bayonne**.
ⓘ pl. Saint-Jean, ☎ 59.29.62.02 (h.s.). ♥

Hotel :
★★ *Les Tilleuls*, pl. Verdun, ☎ 59.29.62.20, Euro Visa, 12 rm Ⓟ pens (h.s.), closed Fri eve , Sat lunch, Sun eve, 6-28 Oct, 400. Rest. ♦ ♪ ☜ 60-130.

⚠ ★★★*Chapital* (100 pl), ☎ 59.29.62.94.

Recommended
Events : *cattle races*, in the streets, Jul.

HÉLETTE, ⊠ 64640 Iholdy, 15 km SE of **Cambo-les-Bains**.

Hotel :
● ★★ *Auberge Aguerria*, ☎ 59.37.62.90, AE DC Euro Visa, 12 rm Ⓟ ▦ ◟ pens (h.s.), closed 5 Sep-5 Oct, 290. Rest. ♦♦ ♪ A pleasant, peaceful place to stop, 50-100.

HENDAYE, ⊠ 64700, 32 km of **Bayonne**.
ⓘ 12, rue des Aubépines, ☎ 59.20.00.34.
𝗦𝗡𝗖𝗙 ☎ 59.20.70.11.
Car-rental : Avis, train station ; 107, bd Général-de-Gaulle, ☎ 59.20.79.04.

Hotels :
★★★ *Liliac*, rd-pt de la Plage, ☎ 59.20.02.45, AE DC Euro Visa, 24 rm Ⓟ ≼ closed 1 Oct-1 Mar, 235.
● ★★ *Gitanilla* (L.F.), 52, bd Gal-Leclerc, ☎ 59.20.04.65, AE DC Euro Visa, 7 rm ▦ ⚘ half pens (h.s.), closed Mon eve and Sun eve, 15 Oct-30 Nov, 280. Rest. ♦♦ ♪ Simple and good : *pantxeta d'agneau, brochette de lotte grillée*, 80-130.
● ★★ *Pohoténia*, rte de la Corniche, ☎ 59.20.04.76, Visa, 52 rm Ⓟ ⚘ ⊡ pens (h.s.), closed Jan, 480. Rest. ♦ ⚘ 80-125.
★ *Chez Antoinette* (L.F.), pl. Pellot, ☎ 59.20.08.47, 24 rm Ⓟ ▦ ◟ ⚘ half pens (h.s.), closed 20 Sep-1 Jun, 280. Rest. ● ♦ ≼ ♪ ⚘ Regional fare : *pantxeta d'agneau, magret de canard*, 70-80.

Restaurant :
♦ *Sotua*, 5, bd du Gal-de-Gaulle, ☎ 59.20.63.68, AE DC Euro Visa ♪ closed Mon eve and Tue eve (l.s.). Fresh fish, spiny lobster, terrific fixed-price meals, 50-150.

⚠ ★★★*Acacias* (120 pl), ☎ 59.20.78.76.

ITXASSOU, ⊠ 64250 Cambo-les-Bains, 24 km SE of **Bayonne**.

Hotels :
★★ *Le Fronton* (L.F.), ☎ 59.29.75.10, DC Visa, 15 rm Ⓟ ≼ ▦ ⚘ half pens, closed Wed, 1 Jan-15 Feb, 320. Rest. ♦♦ ≼ ⚘ 50-135.
★ *Le Txistulari*, ☎ 59.29.75.09, 17 rm Ⓟ ≼ ▦ ◟ & 85. Rest. ♦ Terrace dining, 50-110.

Recommended
Farmhouse-gîte : *Arosteya*, ☎ 59.29.98.28, pool.

LARCEVEAU, ⊠ 64620, 15 km SW of **Saint-Palais**.

Hotel :
★ *Espellet*, ☎ 59.37.81.91, Visa, 19 rm Ⓟ ≼ ▦ ⚘ closed Tue ex Jul-Aug, 1-15 Mar, 140. Rest. ♦ ≼ & ▦ 40-110.

SAINT-PALAIS, ⊠ 64120, 54 km SE of **Bayonne**.
ⓘ pl. de l'Hôtel-de-Ville, ☎ 59.65.71.78. ♥

⚠ ★★★★*Ur-Alde* (80 pl), ☎ 59.65.72.01.

Recommended
Events : *Basque festival*, in Aug.

SAINT-PÉE-SUR-NIVELLE, ⊠ 64310 Ascain, 19 km S of **Bayonne**.

Hotel :
★ *Le Fronton* (L.F.), Ibarron, ☎ 59.54.19.82, AE DC, 15 rm Ⓟ ≼ ▦ ◟ ⚘ & pens (h.s.), closed Wed (l.s), 15 Jan-15 Feb, 330. Rest. ♦♦ ≼ & Terrace and winter garden. Spec : *langoustines aux asperges, aiguillettes de canard aux écrevisses*, fresh salmon, 100-200 ; child : 40.

⚠ ★★★*Goyetchea* (100 pl), ☎ 59.54.11.68.

SARE, ⊠ 64310 Ascain, 35 km S of **Bayonne**.

Hotels :
★★★ *Arraya*, ☎ 59.54.20.46, AE Euro Visa, 20 rm Ⓟ ≼ ▦ ♪ ⚘ half pens (h.s.), closed 4 Nov-24 May, 660. Rest. ● ♦♦ ≼ ♪ & A good restaurant with a few local specialties. Spanish and local wines, 75-230.
★★ *Picassaria* (L.F.), Lehembiscay, ☎ 59.54.21.51, 36 rm Ⓟ ≼ ▦ ◟ pens (h.s.), closed Wed, 30 Nov-1 Mar, 340. Rest. ♦ closed Wed, 30 Dec-1 Mar, 65-110.

⚠ ★★*Petite Rhune* (36 pl), ☎ 59.42.21.51.

BAYONNE★★

Pau 107, Bordeaux 184, Paris 773 km
pop 42970 ⊠ 64100   A1

Seen from Bayonne's point of view, Pau is merely the capital of the Béarn, whereas Bayonne is the capital of the Basque country. An ancient town of quays, picturesque streets and ramparts, a port (sulphur from Lacq, maize, cement, phosphates) at the mouth of the Adour. The town is also a centre for the chemical and aeronautical industries as well as a tourist resort. Local specialities include smoked ham, chocolate, nougat with pine nuts *(touron)* and (less recently) the namesake bayonet ; cultural festival in August.

▶ The Adour and its tributary the Nive cut the town into three : **Grand Bayonne, Petit Bayonne** and the **Faubourg-Saint-Esprit**; the first two are surrounded by formidable ramparts★. ▶ Place Général-de-Gaulle and Place de la Liberté separate the Adour from the old town ; walk down **Rue du Port-Neuf** (A2 ; pedestrian precinct ; restaurants) and up towards the cathedral. ▶ **Ste Marie Cathedral★** (A2), in Northern French Gothic style (13th-14thC) ; 16thC stained glass, 13thC **cloister**; spires added in the 19thC. ▶ **Château-Vieux** (A2), rebuilt by the military engineer Sébastien de Vauban (1633-1707) in 1680, occupies the NW corner of the fortifications, incorporating medieval defensive walls. ▶ In Petit Bayonne, **Bonnat Museum★** of collections donated by the painter Léon Bonnat (1833-1922) (B2 ; 15th-19thC paintings, drawings, antiquities ; *in season, daily ex Tue. 10-12 & 4-8; low season, daily ex Tue., Sat. and Sun., 10-12 & 3-7)*; **Basque Museum★★** in a 16thC house (B2 ; regional art, Basque folklore ; *in season, daily ex Sun. and nat. hols. 9:30-12:30 & 2:30-6:30; low season, 10-12 & 2:30-5:30)*. Near the 17thC Mousserolles Gateway, **Château-Neuf** (B2) ; 15th-17thC. ▶ On the right bank of the Adour, at 9, quai de l'Amiral-Bergeret, **Izarra Distillery** for the local liqueur *(visits tel. 59.55.09.45)*. ▶ Visits to the **port** : *enquire at Chamber of Commerce, tel. 59.25.75.75*. In summer, cruises on the river Adour (Société Nautique, Mousserolles Quay, *tel. 59.59.21.93)*.

Nearby

Ustaritz *(13 km S)*, capital of Labourde until 1790, on the left bank of the Nive ; the Seminary of St. François-

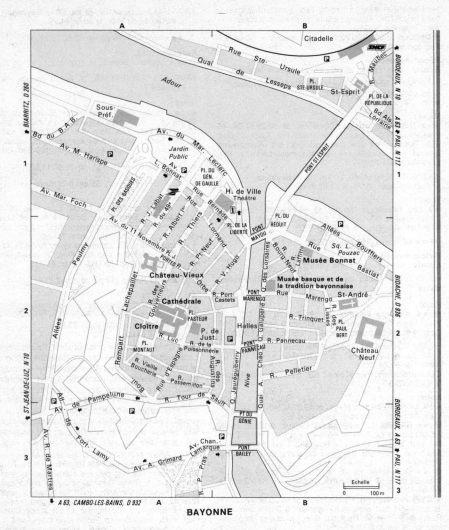

BAYONNE

Xavier has played an important role in preserving the Basque language. □

Practical Information

BAYONNE
ⓘ pl. de la Liberté (B2), ☎ 59.59.31.31.
✈ Biarritz-Bayonne-Anglet, ☎ 59.23.90.67.
SNCF (B1), ☎ 59.55.50.50/59.55.11.88.
Car-rental : *Avis*, 1, rue Sainte-Ursule (C1),
☎ 59.55.06.56 ; train station.

Hotels :
★★★ *Agora*, av. J.-Rostand, ☎ 59.63.30.90, Tx 550621,
AE DC Euro Visa, 105 rm P ♨ ☼ ⌕ ↕ ☝ ఈ 280. Rest. ♦ ♪
70-80 ; child : 45.
● ★ *Le Cheval Blanc*, 68, rue Bourg-Neuf (B2),
☎ 59.59.01.33, AE DC Euro Visa, 24 rm P ♪ ఈ 80.
Rest. ● ♦♦ ♪ ఈ closed Mon (l.s.), 5-27 Jan. Good, cheap
food by I. Teilechea : *ravioles de langoustes au beurre de
tomate*, 110-175.

Restaurants :
♦♦ *Euskalduna*, 61, rue Pannecau (B2), ☎ 59.59.28.02,
closed Mon and eves ex Sat. Spec : fish soup, 80-130.
♦ *La Chistera*, 42, rue Port-Neuf (B2), ☎ 59.59.25.93 ⌕
♪ ఈ closed Tue, 20 Oct-10 Nov. Terrace dining, 65-120.

⚐ ★★★★*La Chêneraie* (170 pl), ☎ 59.55.01.31.

Recommended
Events : *ham festival*, Easter ; *bullfights*, in Aug.
Guided tours : *C.N.M.H.S.*, (1 Jul-31 Aug, ex Sun), check
with S.I.
♥ *Hôtel des ventes*, 22, av. Dubrocq, ☎ 59.59.88.73 ; choc-
olates and tourons (almond meringues) : *Cazenave*, rue
Port-Neuf, ☎ 59.59.03.16.

Nearby

BRISCOUS, ⊠ 64240, 14 km E.

Restaurant :
● ♦♦ *Auberge Ama-Lur*, ☎ 59.31.52.38 ♪ ⌖ closed
Mon and Tue (l.s.), Nov-Dec. In fine weather only, authentic local cuisine : *civet de canard, poularde bressane au
porto*, local wines, 80-200.

MOUGUERRE, ⊠ 64990 Saint-Pierre d'Irube, 8 km on the D 936.

Hotel :
★★ *Kuluska* (L.F.), ☎ 59.31.83.60, 10 rm Ⓟ ⅊ ∭ ⟨
half pens, closed Fri eve, 1-15 Nov, 320. Rest. ♦ ⅊ ⅊
⅋ 60-120.

URT, ⊠ 64670, 10 km SE.

Restaurant :
● ♦♦ *La Galupe*, quartier du Port, ☎ 59.56.21.84, Visa Ⓟ
⟨ ⅊ ⅋ closed Mon and Sun eve , 2 wks in Nov and Feb.
On the banks of the Adour. Good regional fare, 120-180.

USTARITZ, ⊠ 64480, 12 km S.
ℹ mairie, ☎ 59.93.00.32.
ⓢⓝⓒⓕ ☎ 59.31.00.35.

Hotel :
★★★ *La Patoula* (C.H.), ☎ 59.93.00.56, AE Visa, 9 rm Ⓟ
⅊ ∭ ⟨ ⅋ closed 5 Jan-1 Mar, 300. Rest. ● ♦♦ ⅊ ⅋ ⅊
closed Mon and Sun eve, 5 Jan-15 Feb. On the banks of
the Nive, a pleasant park and an excellent gourmet restaurant featuring fish prepared by P. Guilhem : *salade
Patoula, escalope de saumon sauvage*, 115-180.

⚠ ★★*Kapito-Harri* (50 pl), ☎ 59.31.00.32.

VILLEFRANQUE, ⊠ 64990, 4 km.

Hotel :
★★★★ *Château de Larraldia*, rte d'Hasparren,
☎ 59.44.00.10, Tx 540831, AE DC Euro Visa, 23 rm Ⓟ ⅊
∭ ⟨ ⅌ ⅊ ⅃ closed Nov-11 Apr, 800. Rest. ♦♦ ⅊ ⅊
⅋ 180-220.

BIARRITZ★★★

Pau 115, Bordeaux 184, Paris 780 km
pop 26650 ⊠ 64200   A1

Biarritz, Anglet and Bayonne form a vast urban agglomeration separated by green spaces ; it is difficult to
say where one town ends and another begins. Biarritz was long a simple fishing village to which the whal-
ing industry brought a degree of prosperity, but starting with the second Empire (*ca.* 1850) wealthy Europeans flocked to spend their leisure time near the
Villa Eugénie, built for the wife of Napoléon III. Soon
they commissioned architects to build residences in
the surrounding areas. Later, the gentle winter climate attracted the retired, who now represent about
20 % of the population. The two casinos, three beaches (Côtes des Basques, Port Vieux and Grande
Plage) and outdoor activities (underwater fishing, surfing, wind surfing) make Biarritz equally popular with
tourists.

▶ Start exploring the town from **Place Georges-Clemenceau**, a busy square near the **Place Bellevue** and the
Summer Casino (Casino d'Été). N of the **Municipal Casino**
and the **Grande Plage** (main beach) is the former Villa
Eugénie, now the **Palais Hôtel**; farther on, the almost
equally old **Hôtel Miramar**, now a salt-water treatment
centre. ▶ On the **Atalaye Plateau** separating the fishing
port from Port Vieux beach is the **Musée de la Mer**★
(Marine Museum) : ancient and modern seafaring (*daily
9-7 Jul.-Aug.*). **Aquarium**★ : principal species found in the
Bay of Biscay. Spectacular promontory, the **Rocher de la
Vierge**★ (Virgin's Rock). ▶ View★ the length of the Basque coast from the perspective on the seafront.

Nearby

▶ **Anglet** : industrial Bayonne meets residential Biarritz ;
16thC church, 17th-18thC furnishings ; distinctive Basque
wooden galleries. Since the late 19thC, many imposing
weekend houses have been built. The principal attractions are 4 km of sandy beach and the Chiberta Forest
(170 acres ; footpaths, bridle paths, lake, golf course).
▶ The other side of the Négresse Quarter (Biarritz railway

station), between Mouriscot Lake and the ocean, is **Ilbaritz.** ▶ 5 km SW, from the **Bidart** cliffs (chapel of the
Madeleine), view of the Pyrénées and the Bay of Biscay. ☐

Practical Information _____

BIARRITZ
ℹ sq. d'Ixelles (C2), ☎ 59.24.20.24.
✈ *Biarritz-Bayonne-Anglet*, 4 km SE, ☎ 59.23.90.67. *Air
France office*, Parme airport, ☎ 59.23.93.82.
ⓢⓝⓒⓕ ☎ 59.23.58.95/59.23.58.97.
Car-rental : *Avis*, Anglet airport, ☎ 59.23.67.92 ; 25, av.
Edouard-VII, ☎ 59.24.33.44 ; train station.

Hotels :
● ★★★★(L) *Palais*, 1, av. de l'Impératrice,
☎ 59.24.09.40, Tx 570000, AE DC Euro Visa, 138 rm Ⓟ ⅊
∭ ⟨ ✿ ☐ closed 10 Nov-1 Apr, 1300. Rest. ● ♦♦♦♦
⅊ ⅊ One of the last grand hotels of the Napoléon III era.
The cooking is in much the same register : *filets de rougets aux haricots verts, homard à la compote de poivrons*.
Poolside service, 220-320.
★★★★(L) *Miramar*, av. de l'Impératrice, ☎ 59.24.85.20,
Tx 540831, AE DC Euro Visa, 122 rm Ⓟ ⅊ ⅊ ⅊ ☐ 1300.
Rest. ● ♦♦♦ ⅊ ⅊ ⅋ Enjoyable food : *salade de homard,
magret aux fruits*, low-calorie dishes for those taking the
cure, 220-350 ; child : 80.
● ★★★★ *Eurotel*, 19, av. de la Perspective,
☎ 59.24.32.33, Tx 570014, AE DC Euro Visa, 60 rm Ⓟ ⅊
closed 1 Nov-15 Mar, 520. Rest. ● ♦♦♦ ⅊ ⅊ closed Mon
noon and Sun. Efficient M. Dubroscq and his staff serve
quality fare on an upper floor that opens onto a stupendous view, 170-250.
● ★★★ *Windsor*, (Inter-Hôtel), Grande-Plage,
☎ 59.24.08.52, AE DC Euro Visa, 37 rm ⅊ closed
1 Oct-20 Mar, 300. Rest. ♦ 85-150.
★★★ *Clair de Lune* (C.H.), 48, av. Alan-Seeger, rte
d'Arbonne, ☎ 59.23.45.96, AE Visa, 9 rm Ⓟ ⅊ ⅊ 380.
★★★ *Plaza*, av. Edouard-VII, ☎ 59.24.74.00, AE DC Euro,
60 rm Ⓟ ⅊ ⅊ 480. Rest. ♦ ⅊ Rest. bar-pub. 120-180.
● ★★ *Atalaye*, plateau de l'Atalaye, ☎ 59.24.06.76, Euro
Visa, 25 rm Ⓟ ⅊ closed 18 Oct-10 Apr, 210.
★★ *Auberge du Relais*, 44, av. de la Marne,
☎ 59.24.85.90, AE DC Visa, 14 rm, pens (h.s.), closed
1 Feb-1 Mar, 390. Rest. ● ♦♦ ⅊ Excellent seasonal fare
at low prices, 55-150.

Restaurants :
● ♦♦♦♦ *Café de Paris*, (Pierre Laporte) 5, pl. Bellevue, ☎ 59.24.19.53, AE DC Visa ⅊ ⅊ closed Mon (l.s.),
20 Nov-1 Apr. To silence detractors, Pierre Laporte has
put extra energy into his cooking, to show his faithful
clients that his is a truly great table. *Petit homard à la
coque, canard aux citron vert*. Splendid desserts. Great
Bordeaux wines await you, 250-350.
● ♦ *Alambic*, 5, pl. Bellevue, ☎ 59.24.53.41 ⅊ ⅊ closed
Mon (l.s.), 11 Nov-15 Mar. Prepared by Pierre Laporte's
staff, an hors-d'œuvre buffet, grills, daily specials. Young
crowd, low prices, 120-150.
● ♦ *Auberge de la Négresse*, 10, bd de l'Aérodrome,
☎ 59.23.15.83, Euro Visa ⅊ ⅊ closed Mon, 6 Oct-11 Nov.
A fashionable bistro serving simple, tasty, copious meals :
boudin aux pommes, fresh salmon in parchment, 45-100.
● ♦ *Relais de Parme*, airport, ☎ 59.23.93.84, AE DC
Euro Visa, closed Sat. A branch of the *Café de Paris*. In
an agreeable setting, the fine cuisine of Pierre Laporte.
For folks in a hurry, there is the "Silver Flight", 200-400.
● ♦ *Chez Albert*, Vieux Port des Pêcheurs,
☎ 59.24.43.84, Euro Visa ⅊ closed Wed (l.s.),
15 Dec-6 Mar. With the colourful Albert, the atmosphere is
warm and the show is non-stop. Fresh fish, 160-180.

⚠ ★★★*Biarritz* (267 pl), ☎ 59.23.00.12 ; ★★★*Splendid*
(135 pl), ☎ 59.23.01.29 ; ★★*Aldabenia* (80 pl),
☎ 59.23.72.25.

Recommended
Auction house : 6, rue du Centre, ☎ 59.24.21.88.
Casino : pl. Bellevue, ☎ 59.24.11.22.
Night-clubs : *Baobab et Plantation*, at the Casino,
☎ 59.24.11.22.
Thalassotherapie : *Institut Louison Bobet*, av. de l'Impé-

ratrice, ☎ 59.24.20.80, rhumatology, post-surgical therapy, fitness training.
Thermal baths : rue de Madrid, ☎ 59.24.13.80.
♥ chocolates : *Mirmont*, 3, rue Mazagran ; *Henriet*, av. Edouard-VII ; gourmet groceries : *Arosteguy*, 5, rue V.-Hugo, ☎ 59.24.00.52 ; pastry and bread : *Dodin-Garrigue*, 7, rue Gambetta (B2), ☎ 59.24.16.37 ; tourons (almond meringues) : *Daranatz*, 12, rue du Mal-Foch, ☎ 59.24.21.91.

Nearby

ANGLET, ⊠ 64600, 4 km E.
ℹ 1, av. de la Chambre-d'Amour, ☎ 59.03.77.01.
✈ *Biarritz-Parme*, 3 km SW, ☎ 59.23.90.67.

Hotels :
★★★★(L) **Château de Brindos** (R.C.), rte de l'Aviation, ☎ 59.23.17.68, Tx 541428, AE DC Visa, 15 rm ℙ ⫽ ⫻ ⫻ ⫽° half pens (h.s.), 1500. Rest. ♦♦♦ ⫻ ⌁ Great food : blancs de turbot aux raviolis, assiette de la mer, poussin en surprise, 250-300.
● ★★★ **Chiberta et Golf**, 104, bd des Plages, ☎ 59.63.88.30, Tx 550637, AE DC Euro Visa, 80 rm ℙ ⫻ ⫻ ⫽ ⫽ ⫻ ⫻ ⫻ half pens (h.s.), 725. Rest. ♦♦ ⌁ ⫻ ⫻ 100-155.

Restaurant :
♦♦ **La Concha**, 299, av. Adour, ☎ 59.63.49.52 ⫻ A new approach to fast food in a Spanish cider-factory decor. *Dorade à l'espagnole, côte de bœuf grillée au charbon de bois*, 110.

⅄ ★★★*Parme* (200 pl), ☎ 59.23.03.00.

BIDART, ⊠ 64210, 6 km SW.
ℹ Grande Plage, ☎ 59.54.93.85 (h.s.).
SNCF ☎ 59.54.92.91.

Hotels :
● ★★★ **Bidartea**, (Mapotel), N 10, ☎ 59.54.94.68, AE DC Euro Visa, 36 rm ℙ ⫻ ⫻ ⫻ ⫻ ⫻ ⫻ closed Nov-Dec, 290. Rest. ♦ ⫻ ⌁ ⫻ ⫻ closed Mon and Sun eve, 80-120.
★ **Pénélope**, av. du Château, ☎ 59.23.00.37, 20 rm ℙ ⫻ ⫻ ⫻ ⌁ ⫻ half pens (h.s.), 135. Rest. ♦ ⫻ ⌁ ⫻ closed 30 Oct-1 May, 55-90.

⅄ ★★★★*Le Pavillon royal* (250 pl), ☎ 59.23.00.54 ; ★★★★*Le Ruisseau* (300 pl), ☎ 59.23.54.56 ; ★★★*Itsasoa la Mer* (200 pl), ☎ 59.26.52.21.

Recommended
♥ spices from the world over, teas : *Marcel Prévot Charlemagne*, RN 10, ☎ 59.54.94.21, open daily. Spice museum, a curiosity.

Bayonne 32, Mont-de-Marsan 93, Paris 778 km
pop 1015 ⊠ 64520   B1
This village overlooking the valley of the Bidouze between Béarn and Navarre was once the independent fiefdom of the Gramont family, one of the most illustrious in France.

▶ 16thC **church**. Ruined **château de Gramont★**, parts of which date from the 16thC *(daily ex Tue., Mar.-Sep.).*

Nearby

▶ **Château de Guiche** *(7 km NW)*, rebuilt in the 18thC, was also the property of the Dukes of Gramont *(same hours)*; ruined 13thC keep. ▶ View★ over the Adour Valley and the Pyrénées from **Miremont Ridge** *(6 km W).*
▶ **Labastide-Clairence** *(15 km SW)* : a walled town founded in 1312, with typical roofs of the region ; also a Gothic church fitted in the 17th-18thC with Basque-style wooden galleries.   □

For the translation of a name of a meat, a fish or a vegetable, for the composition of a dish or a sauce, see the Menu Guide in the Practical Holiday Guide; it lists the most common culinary terms.

Tarbes 50, Pau 70, Paris 855 km
pop 1110 ⊠ 65110   C2
Cauterets and the neighbouring valleys are among the leading Pyrenean winter sports and excursion areas. Cauterets is also a spa, with 11 sulphur-rich springs. The 16thC author Rabelais, the 18th-19thC statesman Talleyrand, the 19thC authors Chateaubriand, George Sand and Flaubert, and the turn-of-the-century actress Sarah Bernhardt were among the famous visitors.

▶ In the town centre, Place Clemenceau is built over the River Cauterets ; at the heart of the left bank is the **Casino Esplanade**. The **Cauterets Museum** is also the HQ of **the Western Pyrénées National Park** (exhibitions of flora, fauna, insects, geology, ecology ; *daily 9-12 & 3-7).* On the right bank, a path above the park leads to the **Bains** (Baths) **de la Raillère** and the **Cascades de Lutour★** (waterfalls).

Nearby

▶ The surrounding mountain woods are ideal for cross-country hikes and rambles. ▶ SW (paths ; *road to the Pont d'Espagne)* **Jeret valley★★** : waterfalls★ at **Cérisey**, the Pas de l'Ours and Boussès. From the Pont d'Espagne continue along the **Marcadeau valley** or towards **Lake Gaube★★**, with the snowy peaks of Vignemale (alt. 3 298 m) and the adjacent mountains in the background. □

Practical Information _____

⌁ ☎ 62.92.51.60.
⌁ 1500-2000m, closed May-Oct.
ℹ pl. de la Mairie, ☎ 62.92.50.27.

Hotels :
● ★★★ **Bordeaux**, (Mapotel), 23, rue de Richelieu, ☎ 62.92.52.50, Tx 521425, AE Visa, 26 rm ℙ ⫻ ⌁ half pens (h.s.), closed 1 Oct-10 Dec, 480. Rest. ♦ ⌁ 90-180.
● ★★★ **Trois Pics**, av. Leclerc, ☎ 62.92.53.64, AE, 30 rm ℙ ⫻ closed May, 1 Nov-18 Dec, 200. Rest. ♦ ⌁ 55-110.
● ★★ **Etche Ona** (L.F.), 20, rue Richelieu, ☎ 62.92.51.43, AE Visa, 35 rm ⫻ half pens (h.s.), closed 30 Sep-20 Dec, 180. Rest. ♦ ⌁ 65-150.
★ **Centre Poste**, 11, rue de Belfort, ☎ 62.92.52.69, 39 rm ⫻ closed 20 Apr-10 May, 22 Sep-19 Dec, 100. Rest. ♦ ⫻ 55.

⅄ ★★★*Mamelon Vert* (100 pl), ☎ 62.92.51.56 ; ★★*Les Bergeronnettes* (50 pl), ☎ 62.92.50.69 ; ★★*Les Glères* (100 pl), ☎ 62.92.55.34.

Recommended
Casino : espl. des Oeufs, ☎ 62.92.52.14.
♥ candy : *l'Avalanche*, La Raillère, ☎ 62.92.52.97 ; le Royalty, espl. du Casino, ☎ 62.92.52.24.

Orthez 16, Pau 25, Paris 784 km
pop 710 ⊠ 64170 Artix   B1
A thicket of metal towers and pipelines, flames flickering in the sulphur-laden air. Treated by the *SNEA* and *Elf-Aquitaine* (visits : tel. : 59.60.07.78), the sulphur is either exported or used in the aluminium plant at Noguères and in other chemical plants. But how much longer will this complex exist ? The gas reserves will probably have run out by the year 2000.
                                                                    □

Be advised that hotels and restaurants in this Guide have perhaps changed addresses ; prices indicated are also subject to modifications.

LANNEMEZAN

Tarbes 35, Auch 66, Paris 840 km
pop 7400 ⊠ 65300   D2

Industrial centre, without doubt the busiest of the Pyrénées (chemicals, reinforced concrete; institute of atmospheric studies nearby), Lannemezan has no tourist pretentions. The city is built on this plateau of the same name, source of the rivers which flow into the Garonne.

▶ View of the city and mountains from the psychiatric hospital above. ▶ The upper valley of the Gers forms the Magnoac region : former pilgrimage chapel of **Notre-Dame-de-Garaison**★ (16th-17thC; *17 km NE*) has interesting furnishings. ▶ **Monléon-Magnoac** *(22 km NE) :* the church of Saint-Jean-Baptiste was fortified during the Gothic period. ▶ The collegiate church of **Castelnau-Magnoac** *(25 km NE)* is dominated by a monumental bell tower (old statues and 16thC stalls).

Nearby

▶ After **Mourenx** *(2 km SW)*, a new town created in 1957-61 (lookout and orientation table), the countryside soon sheds the industrial air of Lacq; the Gave de Pau and surrounding villages have a traditional appearance. ▶ **Monein** *(13 km S) :* vineyards, orchards on a road to Compostela; largest Gothic church in Béarn (15th-16thC, 12thC tympanum). ▶ **Château de Morlanne**★ *(21 km NE);* 18thC furnishings, paintings *(pm daily Mar.-Oct.);* was used in the 14thC to defend Béarn's northern border. The village church (14thC bell tower; 17th-18thC furnishings) was also part of the defenses.   ☐

Practical Information ――――――――――――――

LANNEMEZAN
ℹ pl. de la République, ☎ 62.98.08.31.
SNCF ☎ 62.98.00.49.

Hotel :
★★ **Pyrénées** (L.F.), rue Diderot, ☎ 62.98.01.53, AE DC Euro Visa, 30 rm ℙ ≼ �️ ◌ 170. Rest. ♦ ⸴ & 55-75.

Nearby

AVENTIGNAN ⊠ 65660, 16 km SE.

Hotel :
★ **Grottes de Gargas**, ☎ 62.99.02.38, 10 rm ℙ �️ ◌ ⸙
closed (l.s.), 120. Rest. ♦ ⸙ 40-100.

LARUNS and the Ossau Valley

Pau 37, Tarbes 71, Paris 822 km
pop 1465 ⊠ 64440   C2

Laruns, in the Valentin Valley (→ Pyrenean Passes), is the best place to begin a visit to the upper valley of the Gave d'Ossau, where many mountain village traditions are still maintained.

▶ Annual folklore festival *(15 Aug.)* in the main square; the inhabitants don traditional Béarnais costume. Walks. ▶ **Béost** *(1.5 km NE) :* a charming mountain village; Romanesque church★, enlarged in the 15thC.

Ossau Valley★★★ *(approx 60 km round trip)*

▶ **Eaux-Chaudes**, a spa in a narrow, wooded gorge; excellent base for excursions. ▶ **Gorges de Bitet**★ : pleasant walks, **Miégebat** hydroelectric station. ▶ **Gabas :** the Bious and the Brousset meet here to form the Gave d'Ossau; **Maison du Parc National** (Park Office) provides information on mountain ecology; life at high altitudes *(daily pm 15 Jun.-15 Sep.)* or by request to the Field Director, tel. *59.05.32.13).* Climbs and excursions in the mountains (guide essential); lakes★ Bious, Ayous; **Midi d'Ossau Peak** (alt. 2 885 m; panorama★★). ▶ The cable car at **Sagette** (winter sports), between Gabas and Lake Fabrèges, takes you to the **Artouste tourist train**★

(15 Jun.-15 Sep.), the highest in Europe. After about 10 km, **Lake Artouste**★ (alt. approx. 2 000 m). From here, climb **Balaïtous** (guide; alt. 3 146 m). ▶ Splendid view of the surrounding peaks from the **Col du Pourtalet**★★ (pass) on the Spanish border (alt. 1 792 m).   ☐

Practical Information ――――――――――――――

Hotel :
★★ **Ossau**, pl. de la Mairie, ☎ 59.05.30.14, Visa, 12 rm ≼ closed Wed, 130. Rest. ♦ ⸴ closed Tue (l.s.), 55-130.

Recommended
Events : *local festival*, 15 Aug; *cheese fair*, in Oct.

LOURDES*

Bayonne 143, Toulouse 169, Paris 824 km
pop 17620 ⊠ 65100   C2

A sleepy hamlet and former stronghold of the County of Bigorre, Lourdes, in 1858, saw its destiny change in the Massabielle Cave where Bernadette Soubirous, then a 14-year-old peasant girl claimed to have had several visions of the Virgin Mary. Four million visitors and pilgrims now make their way to Lourdes each year; the pious and the ailing from all over the world contribute to the town's incongruous admixture of bustle, contemplation and commerce.

▶ The **Processions Esplanade** (A1) passes close to the **underground Basilica of St. Pius X**★ (capacity 20 000) built in 1958 for the Centenary of the Visions. ▶ **Basilica of the Rosary :** the lower church, in neo-Byzantine style (1885), is set beneath a neo-Gothic basilica (1876); remarkable pipe organ. Pilgrims crowd around the lower church to collect water from taps next to the **Massabielle Cave**. Farther on are baths for immersing the sick. In the Prairie de la Grotte (Cave forecourt), a slide-show, *"Un jour, Bernadette..."* is shown in megavision on six screens *(daily until 7 pm in season).* ▶ Above the basilica, the **chemin du Calvaire** (road to Calvary) leads past a spur; view★. ▶ **Museum of Petit Lourdes :** (68 Avenue Peyramale) model of the town in 1858 *(daily in season).* ▶ Rue de la Grotte (B2) leads to the **Gemmail Museum of Sacred Art** (N° 72, *daily, Palm Sun.-15 Oct.*) and the **Wax Museum** (N° 87 *daily, Mar.-Oct.; until 9:30 pm in season).* ▶ The **Boly Mill** on Rue Bernadette-Soubirous (B1) is the birthplace of St. Bernadette *(daily ex Sat, Easter-15 Oct.).* ▶ The **Municipal Hospice** (C1) displays mementoes of Bernadette, who spent some time there in retreat before entering a convent at Nevers, where she died in 1879. Rue des Petits Fossés, the *cachot* (lock-up; B1, *daily; closed am in winter)* was the humble home of the Soubirous at the time of the visions. At 38 Rue de la Grotte and 14 Rue du Fort, films are shown on the life of St. Bernadette *(daily in season).* ▶ **Château of the Counts of Bigorre :** (B1) 11thC, 14thC keep, over-restored in the 19thC, with the **Pyrenean Museum** *(daily; closed Jan.;* history of Lourdes; Basque, Béarn and Bigorre folklore; natural history). ▶ 1.5 km S, cable-car to **Béout** (alt. 700 m); farther on, cable railway to **Jers Peak** (alt. 900 m); views★. ▶ 2 km NW : **Lake Lourdes** in a charming setting. ▶ **Bartrès** *(4 km N) :* the sheep farm (Maison de Lagüe) where Bernadette spent her childhood.   ☐

Practical Information ――――――――――――――

ℹ pl. du Champ-Commun (B-C2), ☎ 65.94.15.64.
✈ *Tarbes-Ossun*, 10 km NE, ☎ 62.34.42.22.
SNCF (C1), ☎ 62.94.10.47/62.34.35.36.
🚌 av. du Mar.-Juin (C1).
Car-rental : *Avis*, Train station (C1).

Hotels :
● ★★★★ **Grand Hôtel de la Grotte**, (Mapotel), 66-68, rue de la Grotte (B2), ☎ 62.94.58.87, Tx 531937, AE DC Euro Visa, 85 rm ℙ ≼ ⸴ ⸙ & closed 25 Oct-Palm Sun, 420. Rest. ♦♦ ≼ & 90-130.

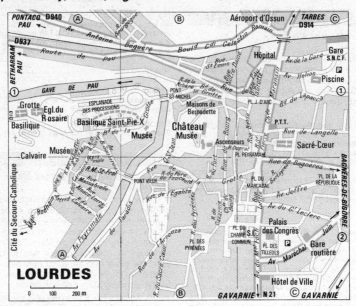

LOURDES

0   100   200 m

★★★★ *Impérial*, 3, av. du Paradis (A2), ☎ 62.94.06.30, AE DC Euro Visa, 100 rm 🅿 ⌇ ⛪ ⚃ ⚄ closed 20 Oct-15 Apr, 400. Rest. ♦♦ ⌇ ⚃ ⚌ 100-150; child : 50.

● ★★★ *Auberge Provençale*, (Inter-Hôtel), 4, rue Baron-Duprat (B-C1), ☎ 62.94.31.34, 62 rm, 300. Rest. ♦♦ 70-80.

● ★★★ *Espagne*, (Mapotel), 9, av. du Paradis (A2), ☎ 62.94.50.02, AE DC Euro Visa, 92 rm 🅿 ⌇ ⚌ closed 15 Oct-15 Apr, 300. Rest. ♦♦ ♪ 70-250.

● ★★★ *Excelsior*, (Mapotel), 83, bd de la Grotte (B2), ☎ 62.94.02.05, AE DC Euro Visa, 80 rm 🅿 ⌇ closed Nov-Easter, 290. Rest. ♦♦ ♪ 80-200.

★★ *Albret*, 21, pl. du Champ-Commun (C2), ☎ 62.94.75.00, Euro Visa, 27 rm 🅿 ⌇ closed 10 Dec-7 Feb, 165. Rest. ● ♦♦ *La Taverne de Bigorre* ♪ Claude Moreau's good classic and regional dishes : *garbure bigourdane, sole aux cèpes*, 40-130.

⚕ ★★★★*Plein Soleil* (50 pl), ☎ 62.94.40.93 ; ★★★*De Sarsan* (65 pl), ☎ 62.94.43.09 ; ★★*Anclades* (100 pl), ☎ 62.94.10.37 ; ★★*L'Arrouach* (65 pl), ☎ 62.94.25.75 ; ★★*La Scierie* (75 pl), ☎ 62.94.29.24 ; ★★*Moulin du Monge* (66 pl), ☎ 62.94.28.15.

Recommended
Leisure activities : *lac de Lourdes*, 3 km NW on rte de Pau, ☎ 62.94.26.50, surf, yachting, pedal boats.

LUZ-SAINT-SAUVEUR

Lourdes 31, Bagnères-de-Bigorre 47, Paris 850 km
pop 1160 ⊠ 65120   C2

Luz is a mountain spa above the Saint-Sauveur Gorge. Access from here to beautiful sites around Gavarnie (→ below), Barèges or Tourmalet (→ Passes of the Pyrénées).

▶ **Romanesque church★** : late 12thC, with 14thC surrounding wall, formerly part of a Hospitallers' Commandery; **museum** of religious art, archaeology, ethnography *(open on request daily pm ex Sat. and Sun., tel. 62.92.81.75)*. ▶ **Maison de la Vallée** (cultural centre) : various exhibitions and events. ▶ **Spa** (alkaline sulphur springs) in the upper area of Saint-Sauveur. ▶ **Winter**

sports centre at **Luz-Ardiden** (alt. 1 700-2 200 m ; *12 km NW).*

Gavarnie Valley *(approx 40 km round trip)*

▶ **Pont Napoléon** (bridge) crosses 65 m above the river in the **Saint-Sauveur Gorge★.** ▶ The hydroelectric station at **Pragnères** is the largest in the Pyrénées *(visits in summer).* ▶ From **Gèdre** at the junction of the Gavarnie and the Héas, you can go up the Héas Valley to the **Cirque de Troumouse** (natural amphitheatre)★★, less well known but just as impressive as that at Gavarnie. ▶ **Gavarnie** (alt. 1 360 m) : beyond the **Chaos de Coumely** (rockfall), the best base for excursions on foot, horse or donkey to the **Cirque★★★** *(approx. 2hr).* This magnificent amphitheatre, 10 km in circumference, is formed by concentric circles of rock rising to 1 200-1 500 m. It is crowned with glaciers and numerous waterfalls ; the **Grande Cascade★** falls 240 m. The **Botanical Gardens** contain more than 400 species of Pyrenean plants, almost half of which come from the locality. Among the mountain walks and climbs *(guide often essential)*, the **Tantes Peak** (alt. 2 322 m), the **Bouchara Pass** (alt. 2 270 m ; *on the Spanish border road),* the **Brèche de Roland** (alt. 2 807 m), the **Cirque d'Estaubé** and the **Cirque de Troumouse** (also called the **Pimené**, alt. 2 801 m) provide the best views★★.   ☐

Practical Information ─────────────────

LUZ-SAINT-SAUVEUR
ⵜ (15 May-30 Sep), ☎ 62.92.81.58.
ⵜ 1, pl. du 8-Mai, ☎ 62.92.81.60.

Hotels :
★★ *Londres*, Esquieze-Sère, 2 km N, ☎ 62.92.80.09, Euro Visa, 30 rm 🅿 ⌇ ♪ ⚄ closed May, Nov, 130. Rest. ♦ ⌇ ♪ 50-100.

★ *Terminus*, Esquieze-Sère, 2 km N, ☎ 62.92.80.17, 18 rm 🅿 ⚌ closed 20 Sep-30 May ex school hols, 100. Rest. ♦ 75-65.

⚕ ★★★*International* (135 pl), ☎ 62.92.82.02.

Recommended
Farmhouse-gîte : *J. Castagne-Cloze*, rue de Lart, ☎ 62.92.81.19, pool, fishing, farm produce for sale.

Leisure activities : *Maison de la Montagne*, ☎ 62.92.87.28, guides offer program of mountain excursions.

Nearby

GAVARNIE, ⊠ 65120 Luz-Saint-Sauveur, 20 km S.
⚡ 1400-2500m.
ℹ mairie, ☎ 62.92.49.10.

Hotels :
★★ *Cîmes*, ☎ 62.92.48.13, 13 rm ⌘ closed Nov, 170. Rest. ♦ ♪ 45-200.
★ *Astazou*, ☎ 62.92.48.07, 13 rm ⌐ closed 15 Oct-1 Feb, 90. Rest. ♦ 50-80.
★ *Taillon*, ☎ 62.92.48.20, AE DC Euro Visa, 19 rm Ⓟ ⌘ ⌘ closed 1 Nov-20 Dec, 100. Rest. ♦ ⌘ 45-80.
★ *Voyageurs*, ☎ 62.92.48.01, 20 rm Ⓟ ⌘ half pens (h.s.), closed 15 Apr-1 Jun, 4 Nov-22 Dec, 125. Rest. ♦ ♪ ⌘ ⌘ 60-140.

GÈDRE, ⊠ 65120 Luz-Saint-Sauveur, 12 km S.

Hotel :
★ *Brèche de Roland*, ☎ 62.92.54.48, 24 rm Ⓟ ⌘ ⌐ closed May, 1 Oct-20 Dec, 130. Rest. ♦ ⌘ ♪ ⌘ 50-60.

△ ★★*Le Relais d'Espagne* (40 pl), ☎ 62.92.47.70.

MAULÉON-LICHARRE*

Bayonne 77, Pau 63, Paris 817 km
pop 4310 ⊠ 64130   B1

Mauléon, in a wide valley, is the capital of Soule (one of the three French Basque provinces) and a town with thriving traditions, including the manufacture of the rope-soled canvas shoes called espadrilles.

▶ The little town, dominated by the ruins of a fortified château (view), has several beautiful buildings; arcades around the Place du Marché. At Nᵒ 9 Rue du Jeu-de-Paume, the **Anduran Manor**★ (17th-18thC furniture; *Jul.-15 Sep. ex Thu., Sun. and nat. hols., tours at 11, 3, 4, 5*). ▶ Ruins of the **château de Mongaston** *(10 km N)* : 16thC; *(daily ex Tue., 3-6:30, Jul.-Sep.)*. ▶ **Aussurucq** *(10 km SW)* : a good base for walks in the Arbailles or Soule woods (numerous paths).

Saison Valley★★ *(approx 80 km round trip)*

▶ **Gotein** : the church has a Virgin and Child of Spanish origin. ▶ **Trois-Villes** : château d'Élicabia (17thC; park). ▶ **Tardets-Sorholus** : a *bastide* (fortified town) of 1280; several of the surrounding villages have Romanesque churches. ▶ **Licq-Athérey** : recreational facilities, including trout-fishing, jeep racing in the mountains, hang gliding, walks and pigeon shoots. ▶ Higher up, the junction where the valleys of Larrau and Uhaïtxa meet to form the Saison; continuing up the Uhaïtxa you come to the narrow **Kakouetta Gorges**★, the **Ehujarre Ravine**★ (trails), and the village of **Sainte-Engrâce**, its 11th-12thC Romanesque church★ one of the most interesting in the region (carved decoration; 18thC Spanish altarpiece), on a pilgrim road to Compostela. Beyond, GR 10 leads to the **Holcarté Crevasses** *(access difficult)*. ▶ Paths to the winter pastures throught **Larrau** (14thC church); walks in the **Iraty** and **St. Joseph woods** (pigeon shooting in autumn). ☐

Practical Information _____

MAULÉON-LICHARRE
ℹ 10, rue J.-B.-Heugas, ☎ 59.28.02.37.
SNCF ☎ 59.28.07.80.

Hotels :
● ★★ *Château*, 25, rue de la Navarre, ☎ 59.28.19.06, AE Euro Visa, 36 rm Ⓟ ⌘ ⌘ ⌐ closed 15 Jan-1 Mar, 115. Rest. ♦ ⌘ ⌘ 50-65.
★★ *Bidegain*, 13, rue de la Navarre, Mauléon-Soule, ☎ 59.28.16.05, AE DC Euro Visa, 30 rm Ⓟ ⌘ ⌘ ⌐ closed

Sun eve, 25-30 Nov, 15 Dec-15 Jan, 140. Rest. ♦ closed Fri eve and Sun (l.s.), 50-130.

△ ★★*Du Saison* (30 pl), ☎ 59.28.18.79.

Nearby

BARCUS, ⊠ 64130 Mauléon-Soule, 14 km SE.

Hotels :
★★ *Fronton*, ☎ 59.28.91.88, 21 rm Ⓟ ⌘ ⌘ closed 16-28 Feb, 2-21 Nov, 100. Rest. ♦ ⌘ ♪ closed Mon eve and Tue. Remarkable Basque cuisine, 40-120.
★ *Chilo*, ☎ 59.28.90.79, AE DC Euro Visa, 11 rm Ⓟ ⌘ ⌘ closed Mon, 4-29 Jan, 30 Sep-15 Oct, 70. Rest. ♦ ⌘ ♪ 40-170.

TARDETS-SORHOLUS, ⊠ 64470, 13 km S.
ℹ cité administrative, ☎ 59.28.50.26.

Hotel :
★★ *Gave*, ☎ 59.28.53.67, Euro Visa, 14 rm Ⓟ ⌘ ⌐ ⌘ closed 15 Nov-28 Feb, 180.

OLORON-SAINTE-MARIE**

Pau 33, Bayonne 99, Paris 818 km
pop 12237 ⊠ 64400   B1

The ancient Basque town called *Iluro*, at the junction of the Aspe and the Ossau, is now known as Oloron and linked with the episcopal city of Sainte-Marie. High points of the year are the May and September agricultural fairs. Town industries also include household linen, Basque bérets and chocolate. Biennial international folklore festival in Aug.

▶ From Place Mendiondou at the centre of town between the bridges over the rivers Aspe and Ossau, climb through the old **quarter of Sainte-Croix** (15th and 18thC houses) to the **Romanesque church**, with its sturdy bell tower and keep; view. ▶ On the left bank of the Aspe, the **Cathedral** (rebuilt 13th-14thC) : romanesque doorway; sculpture; treasury in the sacristy.

Nearby

▶ The church at **Lucq-de-Béarn** *(12th-16thC; 13 km N)* is part of a Benedictine monastery founded in the 10thC; inside, handsome Paleo-Christian sarcophagus (5th-6thC). ▶ The ruins of the **château de Moumour** *(5 km NW)* rise above a spur overlooking the Oloron. ▶ The **château d'Aren** *(13 km NW; pm ex Sun., Jun.-15 Sep.)* belonged to the Lords of Aren. ▶ 17 km NW, church (12th-13thC) at **L'Hôpital-Saint-Blaise** reveals a Mozarabic influence. ▶ **Aramits** *(15 km SW)* : international speleology centre of the Pyrénées-Atlantiques. 3 km further, **Lanne** offers paths for woodland walks.

Aspe Valley★★ *(approx 110 km round trip)*

▶ A link between French Béarn and Spanish Aragon via the Somport Pass (alt. 1 630 m), and one of the last holdouts of mountain sheep-farming; much of the Pyrenean cheese is made here; towards the upper end of the valley, the flora and fauna are protected by the national park. ▶ **Lurbe-Saint-Christau** : spa used for the treatment of skin disorders *(Apr.-Oct.)*. ▶ 18thC altarpiece in church at **Escot**. ▶ **Sarrance** : the church is a 14thC Premonstratensian foundation, rebuilt after the late- 16thC Wars of Religion (17thC two-story cloister). Just off the Somport road, the village of **Lescun** : huddled around the church and enclosed by jagged peaks (**Anie Peak**, alt. 2 504 m; panorama★). The **Maison du Parc National d'Estaut** (Park Office) : exhibition on the Pyrenean bear *(11-7 daily, Jul.-Aug. or by request to the Field Director at Bedous, tel. 59.34.70.87)*. Beyond the Pont d'Enfer and the Fort de Portalet, where Léon Blum (1872-1950; socialist statesman) and Marshall Pétain (1856-1951; WWI hero who led the pro-Nazi Vichy government during WWII) were imprisoned, is **Urdos**, the last village before the **Col du Somport** (pass; Customs post). Somport was known to the

Romans as *Summus Portus* (High Gate); it was used by the Arabs as a gateway to Europe in the medieval epic poem, the *Chanson de Roland*. □

Practical Information _____

OLORON-SAINTE-MARIE
ℹ pl. de la Résistance, ☎ 59.39.98.00.
𝗦𝗡𝗖𝗙 ☎ 59.39.00.61.

Hotel :
● ★★ *Béarn*, 4, pl. G.-Clemenceau, ☎ 59.39.00.99, AE DC Euro Visa, 26 rm P ⧓ 𝄞 closed Sun, Mon (l.s.), Sat lunch (h.s.), 15 Nov-15 Dec, 195. Rest. ♦♦ ♪ In a 30s-style winter garden, a star performance by the Darrozes : *saumon au coulis de crabe, rognons de veau aux morilles.* Armagnac from the family collection, 65-105.

Ⓐ ★★*Municipal* (100 pl), ☎ 59.39.11.26.

Recommended
Events : *International folk festival*, in Aug (biannual).

Nearby
FÉAS, ⊠ 64570 Aramits, 8 km SW.

Hotel :
★ *Forgerie du Beau Site*, ☎ 59.39.24.87, DC Euro Visa, 10 rm P ⧓ 𝄞 closed Tue eve and Wed lunch (l.s.), 15 Nov-20 Dec, 80. Rest. ♦ ♪ 40-90.

Ⓐ ★★*Vieux Moulin* (50 pl), ☎ 59.39.81.18.

LANNE, ⊠ 64580 Aramits, 5 km NW.

Hotel :
★ *Lacassie* (L.F.), ☎ 59.34.62.05, AE DC Euro Visa, 11 rm P ⧓ closed Mon, 120. Rest. ♦ ♪ 80-130.

LESCUN, ⊠ 64490 Bedous, 36 km S.
⚓ ☎ 59.34.40.04, closed Apr-Oct.

Hotel :
● ★★ *Pic d'Anie*, ☎ 59.34.71.54, 21 rm ⧓ 𝄞 ⚞ closed 20 Sep-1 Apr, 190. Rest. ♦ 60-120.

LURBE-SAINT-CHRISTAU, ⊠ 64660 Asasp-Issor, 9 km S.

Hotels :
★★★ *Résidence du Parc*, ☎ 59.34.40.04, 43 rm P ⧓ ⚞ ⊟ ♫ closed 31 Oct-1 Apr, 310. Rest. ♦♦ ♪ 70-120.
★★ *Vallées*, ☎ 59.34.40.01, 20 rm P ⧓ ⧓ ⊟ closed 11 Jan-25 Mar, 180. Rest. ♦ 40-70.

ORTHEZ

Dax 36, Bayonne 51, Paris 787 km
pop 11540 ⊠ 64270   B1

Vines, maize and livestock are raised in the surrounding area. Orthez is an important market town *(every Tue.)* where poultry, *foie gras (Nov.-Feb.)* and *jambon de Bayonne* (smoked, air-cured ham) are the specialities. Furniture is also manufactured in the town.

▶ The Counts of Foix-Béarn favoured this fortified town in a strategic position. A hump-backed **bridge★** (13th-14thC) with a central tower crosses the Gave de Pau ; the remains of the concentric fortifications around the **Moncade keep** lie to the N of the town. **Church of St. Pierre** (13th-14thC) was also part of the defense system. In Rue du Bourg-Vieux, old houses and mansions, including one said to have belonged to Jeanne d'Albret, Protestant Queen of Navarre from 1555 to 1572 and mother of Henri IV.

Nearby

▶ **Sault de Navailles** *(10 km NE)* : ruins of the château overlook tracks that were once pilgrimage and trading routes as well as trails to the winter pastures. **Bellocq** *(15 km NW)* : 13thC fortified town ; remains of the château of the Viscounts of Béarn. ▶ **Salies-de-Béarn★** *(17 km W)* in the **Saleys Valley** : a spa, 15thC church, old bridge and houses.   □

Practical Information _____

ORTHEZ
ℹ rue des Jacobins, ☎ 59.69.02.75.
𝗦𝗡𝗖𝗙 ☎ 59.69.93.24.

Restaurant :
♦♦ *Auberge Saint-Loup*, 20, rue du Pont-Vieux, ☎ 59.69.15.40, AE DC Visa ⧓ ♪ ⚞ closed Mon and Sun lunch (Jun-Sep), 15-30 Jun, 15-30 Oct. In the restored former hospice Saint-Loup. Spec : *feuilletés d'asperges, pleurotes and foie gras poêlé "en chemise"*, 98-145.

Ⓐ ★★*Source* (65 pl), ☎ 59.69.02.75.

Recommended
Market : Tue (*foies gras* and ham).

Nearby
BÉRENX, ⊠ 64300, 8 km.

Hotel :
★★ *Auberge du Relais*, ☎ 59.38.13.09, Euro Visa, 20 rm P ⧓ ⊟ closed Sat eve Oct, 110. Rest. ♦ 38-120.

PUYOO, ⊠ 64270 Salies-de-Béarn, 9 km N of **Salies-de-Béarn**.

Hotel :
★★ *Voyageurs*, RN 117, ☎ 59.38.10.98, 15 rm P ⧓ closed Sun eve and Mon, 3-20 Feb, 23 Dec-2 Jan, 135. Rest. ♦ ♪ Good little restaurant, 50-120.

SALIES-DE-BÉARN, ⊠ 64270, 17 km W.
⚓ ☎ 59.38.10.11, (t.a.).
ℹ 4, bd Saint-Guily, ☎ 59.38.00.33.
𝗦𝗡𝗖𝗙 ☎ 59.38.08.02.

Hotels :
● ★★ *Golf*, Helios, rte d'Orthez, ☎ 59.65.02.10, AE Visa, 33 rm P ⧓ ⧓ ⚞ ⚐ ⊟ ♫ ♪ half pens (h.s.), 480. Rest. ● ♦♦♦ ⚞ In a lovely green setting, discover Francis Barrat's varied cuisines : regional, traditional, low-calorie. *Râble de lapin aux 12 épices, ravioles d'huîtres au curry, soufflé glacé au café*, 75-200.
★★ *Blason*, 6, pl. J.-d'Albret, ☎ 59.38.00.53, 27 rm P ⧓ closed Jan, 110. Rest. ♦ 50-80.

Restaurant :
♦♦ *La Terrasse*, 2, rue Loumé, ☎ 59.38.09.83, AE DC Visa, closed Mon (l.s.), 100-150.

Ⓐ ★★★*Mosqueros* (60 pl), ☎ 59.38.12.94 ; ★*Al Cartero* (20 pl), ☎ 59.38.29.66.

Recommended
Youth hostel : stade Al Cartero, ☎ 59.38.29.66.

PAU★★

Bordeaux 190, Toulouse 194, Paris 785 km
pop 90020 ⊠ 64000   C1

Having visited the château where the "good king Henri" was born, you may be disappointed at not being able to see, from the Balcon des Pyrénées, the splendid view of the mountains — it is highly likely that the summer light, heavy with humidity, has drawn a veil over this famous vista. It was the English, as far back as the beginning of the last century, who found that the late autumn and almost non-existent winter is the best period to discover Pau. At the centre of an agglomeration counting more than 100 000 inhabitants, it is the largest town close to the mountains. Pau is the regional capital of the Pyrénées-Atlantiques, a university town, an important army base and an agricultural market centre. During recent decades, this former capital of the Béarn has received an economic boost from the exploitation of natural gas deposits at Lacq (→).

▶ **Château★** (A2 ; *daily 9:30-11:45 & 2-5:45 or 6:45*), built on a spur in the 12thC, enlarged in the 13th-14thC, com-

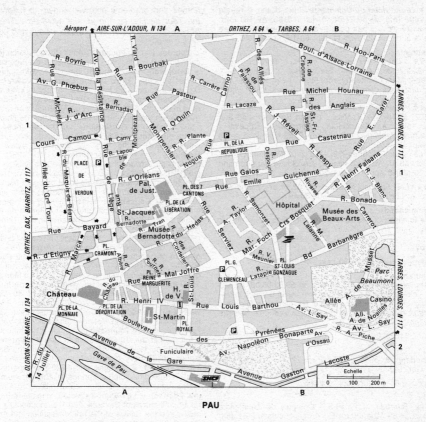

Aéroport ↖ *AIRE-SUR-L'ADOUR, N 134* **A**   *ORTHEZ, A 64* ↖ *TARBES, A 64* **B**

PAU

pletely remodeled in the 19thC; **National Museum** (tapestries, furniture, memorabilia of Henri IV (→ box); **Béarnais Museum** (prehistory, archaeology, natural sciences, ethnography). Opposite is the General Council, formerly the **Parliament of Navarre.** ▶ The **Boulevard des Pyrénées**★★ (late 19thC) overlooks the 200 Chamerop (dwarf) palms of the Joantho gardens and offers an exceptional view in clear weather over 150 km of the mountain chain. ▶ The boulevard runs past the Place Royale (statue of Henri IV) to end at **Beaumont Park**★, a 30-acre English garden around the casino *(open all year).* **Fine Arts Museum**★ (B1-2, Rue Mathieu-Lalanne; *daily ex Tue., 10-12 & 2-6)* : 17th-20thC European paintings. ▶ **Place Clemenceau** (Palais des Pyrénées conference centre) and the surrounding streets form the busy town centre, with banks, hotels, restaurants and shops. ▶ **Bernadotte Museum** : in the 18thC Maison Balagué (A2; *10-12 & 2-6; closed Mon. and 1 Jan.),* birthplace in 1763 of Napoléon's General Bernadotte, who became (1818) King Charles XIV of Sweden. ▶ From here, walk through the old streets of the restored **Hédas Quarter,** full of attractive restaurants and shops, to reach the château and the **Tour de la Monnaie,** formerly the government mint.

Nearby

▶ **Jurançon** : on the left bank of the Gave de Pau, the name given to the wine of the region; visit the wine cooperative at **Gan** *(tel. 59.21.57.03),* 8 km away. ▶ **Lescar**★ *(8 km NW)* was a bishopric from the 6thC until the French Revolution. The kings of Navarre were buried in the **cathedral**★★; Romanesque E end (sculpted corbels); inside, capitals (partly reworked in the 17th and 19thC), 12thC mosaic in the choir. In the former Bishop's Resi-

dence, the **Musée Béarnais** *(9:30-12:30 & 2:30-5:30; 6:30 in season);* opposite the cathedral, 14thC **Fort Esquirette;** view★ of the Pyrénées from the neighbouring terrace. In the lower town, **church of St. Julien,** rebuilt in the 17thC. Lescar is a major maize-growing centre; the Agricultural Cooperative *(Coopérative Agricole)* is open to visitors *(tel. 59.32.84.46).* ▶ **Nay** *(18 km SE)* : local products are cow- and sheep-bells *(sonnailles)* and Basque berets. Arcades around the square, where a Renaissance house is said to have belonged to Jeanne d'Albret; the bell tower of the 15thC southern Gothic church is built into the town walls. 3 km away on the other bank, the medieval **keep** of **Coarraze** where Henri IV spent a carefree childhood; other parts of the château were rebuilt in the 18thC *(Jul.-15 Aug.).* □

Practical Information

PAU
ℹ️ pl. Royale (A2), ☎ 59.27.27.08.
✈ *Pau-Uzein,* 10 km N, ☎ 59.27.97.44. *Air France office,* 6, rue Adoue, ☎ 59.27.27.28.
SNCF (A-B2), ☎ 59.30.50.50.
Car-Hire : *Avis,* Airport; Train station (B3); 80, rue d'Étigny (A3), ☎ 59.32.97.97.

Hotels :
● ★★★ *Continental,* (Mapotel), 2, rue du Mal-Foch (B2), ☎ 59.27.69.31, Tx 570906, AE DC Euro Visa, 100 rm ℗ 250. Rest. ♦ 95-150.
★★★ *Agora,* bd Cami-Salié (off map A1), ☎ 59.84.29.70, Tx 541852, AE DC Euro Visa, 92 rm ℗ 〰 ⌣ ♪ 🚴 ♿ 280. Rest. ♦ ♪ ♿ 80-90; child : 45.
★★★ *Paris,* 80, rue Émile-Garet (B1), ☎ 59.27.34.39, Tx 541595, AE DC Euro Visa, 41 rm ℗ ⌣ ♪ 🚴 ♿ 350.

● ★★ **Grand Hôtel du Commerce**, (Inter-Hôtel), 9, rue du Mal-Joffre (A2), ☎ 59.27.24.40, Tx 540193, AE DC Euro Visa, 51 rm ℗ ⌕ ♪ half pens (h.s.), 365. Rest. ♦ ♪ closed Sat eve and Sun, 20 Dec-11 Jan, 60-130 ; child : 40.

Restaurants :
● ♦♦♦ **Chez Pierre**, 16, rue L.-Barthou (B2), ☎ 59.27.76.86, AE DC Euro Visa ♪ closed Sun, 14 Feb-3 Mar. For hearty appetites : fresh salmon, *garbure, cassoulet, canard aux truffes fraîches*. Local wines, Bordeaux, 180-220.
● ♦♦♦ **Patrick Jourdan**, 14, rue Latapie (B2), ☎ 59.27.68.70, AE DC Visa ♪ closed Sat noon and Sun (h.s.), 15-31 Jul. Outstanding gastronomic stopover : *salade tiède landaise, sole fourrée Patrick, émincé de ris de veau*, 135-180.
♦♦ **Le Saint-Jacques**, 9, rue du Parlement (A2), ☎ 59.27.58.97, AE Euro Visa ⸤⸥ ♪ ⅋ closed Sat noon and Sun, 23 Mar-5 Apr, 1-15 Jul, 50-140.

Å ★★★**Les Sapins** (30 pl), ☎ 59.02.34.21 ; *Plaine des Sports et Loisirs* (70 pl), ☎ 59.02.30.49.

Recommended
Guide to wines : *Cave Coopérative des vins de Jurançon*, 53, av. Henri-IV, ☎ 59.21.57.03.

Nearby

ARTIGUELOUVE, ⊠ 64230 Lescar, 10 km W.

Restaurant :
♦♦ **Mariette**, quartier du Château, ☎ 59.83.05.08, AE DC Visa ⟨ closed Wed (l.s.) and Sun eve. Alain Bayle, a prize-winning chef, is making a name for himself : *foie gras frais aux raisins, turbot au miel et aux oranges, noisette de magret forestière*, 85-200.

GAN, ⊠ 64290, 8 km S.

Hotel :
★ **L'Horizon**, ☎ 59.21.58.93, 12 rm ℗ ⸤⸥ ⌕ closed Mon (l.s.), Oct, 140. .

GELOS, ⊠ 64110 Jurançon, 1 km S.

Hotel :
★★ **Le Bourbail**, (L.F., R.S.), Coteaux de Guindalos, ☎ 59.21.54.60, Visa, 20 rm ℗ ⟨ ⌕ ♪ ⅋ closed 2-31 Jan, 160. Rest. ♦ ⟨ ♪ ⅋ ⅋ closed Sat, 75-110.

JURANÇON, ⊠ 64110, 2 km S.

Restaurant :
● ♦♦ **Ruffet**, 3, av. Ch.-Touzet, ☎ 59.06.25.13, AE DC, closed Mon, Sun eve and Aug. Handsome and cozy, this traditional inn features food by Milou Larrouy : *terrine chaude de cèpes au fumet de Porto, confit d'oie à l'ancienne, crêpes à la béarnaise*, local wines, 75-170.

NAY, ⊠ 64800, 18 km SE.

Hotels :
★★ **Chez Lazare** (L.F.), Arros, ☎ 59.61.05.26, Euro, 7 rm ℗ ⸤⸥ ⌕ closed Sun, 15-31 Oct, 150. Rest. ♦ 55-100.
★★ **Voyageurs** (L.F.), 12, pl. Marcadieu, ☎ 59.61.04.69, 22 rm ℗ ⟨ ⅋ ⅋ 155. Rest. ♦ ⅋ 45-80.

SOUMOULOU, ⊠ 64420, 17 km E.

Hotel :
★★ **Béarn**, 18, rue Las-Bordes, ☎ 59.04.60.09, AE DC Euro Visa, 13 rm ℗ ⸤⸥ closed Sun eve and Mon (l.s.), 15 Jan-15 Feb, 200. Rest. ♦♦ ♪ 50-90.

Passes of the PYRÉNÉES★★★

C2
Round trip from Lourdes *(approx 280 km, 2-3 days ; see map 1)*

Several valleys north from the **Western Pyrénées National Park :** Gave d'Ossau, Arrens, Cauterets and Gavarnie, which make up the Gave de Pau, the Adour and the Neste d'Aure. They are linked by high passes as Aspin, Tourmalet, Soulor and Aubisque, whose

names and gradients are well known to followers of the *Tour de France*, the annual cycle race. The town of Lourdes is a gateway to these valleys and passes.

▶ **Lourdes** (→). ▶ **Pouzac :** 16thC Gothic church (Classical woodwork inside). ▶ **Bagnères-de-Bigorre** (→). ▶ **Beaudéan :** 16thC church, bell tower with noteworthy timber structure. Drive up the **Lesponne Valley★** along D29 to Chiroulet, and from there on foot to **Lake Bleu★**. ▶ **Campan :** 16thC church ; 18thC woodwork ; 16thC covered market. ▶ **Asté :** 16thC church ; remains of 13thC fortress ; keen walkers can climb the Casque de Lhéris (alt. 1 595 m ; view). ▶ **Escaladieu★ :** Cistercian abbey (1142) where the Counts of Bigorre were buried ; chapterhouse ; church rebuilt in the 17thC. ▶ **Mauvezin :** view of the Pyrénées from the former **fortress** (10th-14thC), where the English Edward the Black Prince and Gaston Fébus (1331-91, gentle poet and violent Count of Foix) stayed. The 36 m-high keep houses a local museum *(daily May-Sep. ; Sun. and nat. hols. out of season ; group visits by request)*. ▶ **Capvern-les-Bains :** mineral springs rich in magnesium and calcium sulphate. ▶ **La Barthe-de-Neste :** remains of 12thC keep. ▶ **Sarrancolin★ :** 12th-13thC Romanesque church (Renaissance choir stalls ; 13thC reliquary of St. Ebons ; 12th-15thC monastic buildings ; remains of fortifications, houses. ▶ **Arreau** (→). ▶ **Col d'Aspin** (pass ; alt. 1 490 m) : views★★ of the Pyrénées and the Aure Valley (→ Arreau). ▶ **Espiadet :** quarry of green marble veined with red and white. ▶ **La Mongie** (alt. 1 800 m) : major winter resort, with Barèges on the other side of the Tourmalet, offering a total of 40 ski lifts. Cable-cars *(Dec.-end Apr.)* from **Taoulet** (alt. 2 340 m ; views★★) ; walks to the Garet waterfall, Lake Gréziolles and the Néouvielle Reserve, and the Aure Valley (→ Arreau). ▶ **Col du Tourmalet** (pass ; alt. 2 115 m) : site★★ ; a toll road *(1 Jul.-10 Oct.)* leads to **Midi du Bigorre Peak** (alt. 2 865 m ; view★★★ of the Pyrénées and the Gascony plain) ; observatory, Geophysical Institute *(visits)* established in 1880. ▶ **Barèges** (alt. 1 220 m) : sports resort and spa (alkaline sulphur springs). Cable-car from Lienz Plateau (alt. 1 600 m ; skiing) ; cable railway to Airé Peak (alt. 2 418 m). ▶ **Luz-Saint-Sauveur** (→) leads to the natural amphitheatres of Gavarnie and Troumouse. **Luz Gorge** opens into the valleys of Pierrefitte-Nestalas and Argelès-Gazost (→ Argelès). ▶ **Arras-en-Lavedan :** château de Castelnau d'Azun with wall and ruined keep (13th-15thC). ▶ **Aucun :** Romanesque church extended with the addition of a Gothic sanctuary. ▶ **Arrens-Marsous :** church surrounded by a 15thC crenellated wall. Arrens is a gateway to the national park, along the Gave d'Arrens Valley ; it is a base for many walks and climbs to high mountain lakes. The isards (Pyrenean mountain goats) are unfortunately still prey to unscrupulous hunters. ▶ **Col du Soulor★** (pass ; alt. 1 450 m), **Pyrénées corniches** (cliff roads) and **Litor Amphitheatre** (sites★★) lead up to the **Col d'Aubisque** (pass ; alt. 1 710 ; panorama★★). ▶ **Gourette** (alt. 1 400 m) : oldest winter resort in the Pyrénées, with 25 ski runs and numerous lifts, one of which goes to Pène Blanque (alt. 2 550 m), from where you can continue to the **Ger Peak** (alt. 2 613 m ; view★★). ▶ **Valentin Valley** with woods and waterfalls★, links Gourette to **Eaux-Bonnes** (alt. 750 m) : mineral springs with chloride, sulphur and trace metals ; 12thC Romanesque church with rather ribald decoration on the corbels. Mountain walks from spring to autumn (marked forest paths). ▶ **Laruns** (→), mouth of the Ossau Valley. ▶ Horses graze at the foot of the Benon Plateau near **Bielle**, once the main town of the valley ; the valley archives used to be kept in the *sagrari* (chamber) over the sacristy in the 15th-16thC church ; 16thC houses. ▶ **Arudy :** near marble quarries ; 15th-16thC church ; Maison d'Ossau (local museum), natural history of the National Park. ▶ **Sainte-Colome :** typical Béarnais village, 16thC Gothic church. ▶ **Louvie-Juzon :** 15thC church with 17th-18thC woodwork decoration. ▶ **Mifaget :** on the road through Ossau to Santiago de Compostela, a 12thC almshouse chapel. ▶ **Bruges :** departure point for steep and arduous mountain hikes ; lodgings can be reserved ahead at farmhouses *(information from National Park Offices)*. **Asson :** another stop-

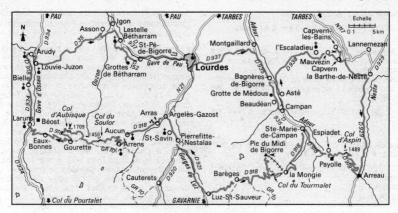

1. Passes of the Pyrénées

over on the road to Compostela; château; church with five-sided E end. ▶ Near **Lestelle-Bétharram** : church of Notre-Dame, a 17thC place of pilgrimage; a bridge dating from 1687 crosses the Gave de Pau; site. ▶ The **Bétharram Caverns★★** : vaulted caverns on five levels; underground river (boat on the lake), cable-car and tourist train in summer *(daily, Easter-mid-Oct.)*. ▶ **Saint-Pé-de-Bigorre** : a halt on the pilgrimage road to Compostela. The abbey (founded in the 11thC) was burnt during the late-16thC Wars of Religion; vestiges of the original church next to another built in the 17thC; view over the area from the Gave de Pau. □

Practical Information

ARRAS-EN-LAVEDAN, ⊠ 65400 Argelès-Gazost, 3 km SW of **Argelès**.

Hotel :
★ *Auberge de l'Arragnat* (L.F.), ☎ 62.97.14.23, 18 rm ℗ ⬤ ⬤ closed 20 Dec-6 Jan, 110. Rest. ♦ ♪ 30-120.

⚲ ★★*L'Idéal* (40 pl), ☎ 62.97.03.13; ★★*Le Pircoulet* (40 pl), ☎ 62.97.02.11.

BARÈGES, ⊠ 65120 Luz-Saint-Sauveur, 38 km SE of **Lourdes**.
⚓ (1 Jun-30 Sep), ☎ 62.92.68.19.
⚑ 1250-2350m.
🛈 mairie, ☎ 62.92.68.64.

Hotels :
★★ *Europe* (L.F.), ☎ 62.92.68.04, 53 rm ⬤ closed 6 Apr-7 Jun, 23 Sep-21 Dec, 180. Rest. ♦ ⬤ 60-120.
★ *Grand Bivouac*, ☎ 62.92.68.20, 20 rm, half pens, closed 15 Apr-15 May, 140.

CAMPAN, ⊠ 65200 Bagnères-de-Bigorre, 28 km S of **Tarbes**.
🛈 ☎ 62.95.35.01.

Hotels :
★★ *Chalet-Hôtel*, Sainte-Marie-de-Campan, 6 km SE, ☎ 62.91.85.64, 25 rm ℗ ⬤ ⬤ ⬤ half pens (h.s.), 310. Rest. ♦ ⬤ ⬤ 50-115.
★ *Deux Cols*, Sainte-Marie-de-Campan, 6 km SE, ☎ 62.91.85.60, 20 rm ℗ ⬤ ⬤ closed 30 Apr-30 May, 15 Nov-15 Dec, 120. Rest. ♦ ♪ ⬤ 50-120; child : 30.

⚲ ★★★*Orée des Monts* (90 pl), ☎ 62.91.83.98; ★★*Le Layris* (50 pl), ☎ 62.95.35.34; ★★*Les Bulanettes* (50 pl), ☎ 62.95.85.90.

CAPVERN-LES-BAINS, ⊠ 65130, 27 km SW of **Tarbes**.
🛈 ☎ 62.39.00.46.
SNCF ☎ 62.39.03.82.

Hotels :
⬤ ★★★ *Le Laca*, rte de Mauvezin, ☎ 62.39.02.06, Tx 521929, AE Visa, 60 rm ℗ ⬤ ⬤ ♪ ⬤ ⬤ closed 30 Oct-1 Apr, 305. Rest. ♦ ⬤ ♪ ⬤ 80-220.
★★ *Lac Saint-Martin*, RN 117, ☎ 62.39.04.13, Euro Visa, 20 rm ℗ ⬤ ⬤ ⬤ closed 1 Dec-1 Apr, 185. Rest. ♦ ⬤ ♪ ⬤ 60-110.
★ *Bellevue* (L.F.), Le Laca, ☎ 62.39.00.29, AE, 34 rm ℗ ⬤ ⬤ ⬤ ⬤ closed 6 Oct-2 May, 100. Rest. ♦ ⬤ ⬤ ⬤ 50-120.

EAUX-BONNES, ⊠ 64400 Laruns, 43 km S of **Pau**.
⚓ (15 May-30 Sep), ☎ 59.05.34.02.
🛈 ☎ 59.05.33.08.

Hotels :
★★ *La Poste*, ☎ 59.05.33.06, AE DC Euro Visa, 20 rm ℗ ⬤ ⬤ closed 10 Apr-15 May, 30 Sep-20 Dec, 140. Rest. ♦ ⬤ ♪ ⬤ 55-115.
★ *Richelieu et Thermes*, rue du Dr-Creignoux, ☎ 59.05.34.10, 24 rm ℗ ⬤ closed 30 Apr-15 May, 30 Sep-15 Dec, 130. Rest. ♦ 35-80.

⚲ ★★★*Ecy* (50 pl), ☎ 59.05.11.47.

GAILLAGOS, ⊠ 65400 Argelès-Gazost, 30 km SW of **Lourdes**.

Hotel :
★ *Au Relais des Cols* (L.F.), ☎ 62.97.05.53, 17 rm ℗ ⬤ ⬤ ⬤ closed Oct-Apr ex Feb school hols and Easter weekend, 110. Rest. ♦ ⬤ ⬤ ⬤ 55-130; child : 30.

GOURETTE, ⊠ 64440 Laruns, 51 km S of **Pau**.
⚑ 1400-2400m.
🛈 ☎ 59.05.12.17 (h.s.).

Hotels :
★★ *Boule de Neige*, ☎ 59.05.10.05, 18 rm ⬤ ⬤ ⬤ closed Easter-10 Jul, 1 Sep-20 Dec, 250. Rest. ♦ ♪ closed in summer, 60-150.
★★ *Pène-Blanque*, (Inter-Hôtel), ☎ 59.05.11.29, Euro Visa, 20 rm ℗ ⬤ ⬤ ⬤ closed Easter-early Jul, 1 Sep-20 Dec, 220. Rest. ♦ ⬤ 60-150.
★ *Le Glacier*, ☎ 59.05.10.18, Euro Visa, 10 rm ⬤ pens, closed 20 Apr-20 Jun, 20 Sep-15 Dec, 260. Rest. ♦ ⬤ 40-100.

LESTELLE-BÉTHARRAM, ⊠ 64800, 16 km NW of **Lourdes**.

Hotel :
★ *Le Vieux Logis*, rte des Grottes, ☎ 59.71.94.87, Euro Visa, 15 rm ℗ ⬤ ⬤ ⬤ ⬤ closed Nov-Mar, 120. Rest. ♦ ⬤ ♪ closed Mon eve and Tue (l.s.), 15 Jan-1 Mar, 60-140.

△ *★Du Saillet* (50 pl), ☎ 59.61.29.07.

LOUVIE-JUZON, ✉ 64260 Arudy, 3 km S of **Arudy**.

Hotels :
★★★ La Forestière, rte de Pau-Laruns, ☎ 59.05.62.28, AE DC Euro Visa, 15 rm ℗ ⊰ ∰ ⎯ 190. Rest. ♦ ⊰ ♪ 75-150; child : 50.
★★ Dhérété, 9, rue Gambetta, ☎ 59.05.61.01, 18 rm ℗ ⊰ ∰ ⎯ ➫ half pens (h.s.), closed Mon, 15 Oct-1 Dec, 350. Rest. ♦ ⊰ ➫ 60-125.

MAUVEZIN, ✉ 65130 Capvern-les-Bains, 5 km SW of **Capvern**.

Hotel :
★ **Auberge de l'Arros**, ☎ 62.39.05.05, Visa, 16 rm ℗ ∰ ⎯ 150. Rest. ♦ ⚸ Local fare, 40-110.

La MONGIE, ✉ 65200 Bagnères-de-Bigorre, 25 km S of **Bagnères**.
𝔖 1800-2400m.
ⓘ ☎ 62.91.94.15.

Hotels :
● ★★★ **Mandia**, ☎ 62.91.93.49, 50 rm ℗ ⊰ ∰ ⎯ pens, closed Easter-15 Dec, 500. Rest. ♦♦ 70-150.
● ★★★ **Sol Y Neou** (L.F.), ☎ 62.91.93.22, 36 rm ⊰ closed 30 Apr-15 Dec, 370. Rest. ♦ ♪ 60-150.
● ★★ **Crête Blanche**, ☎ 62.91.92.49, AE Visa, 25 rm ℗ ⊰ closed 30 Apr-15 Dec, 280. Rest. ♦ ♪ 70-100.

SAINT-PÉ-DE-BIGORRE, ✉ 65270, 10 km W of **Lourdes**.
ⓘ mairie, ☎ 62.41.80.07.

Hotel :
★★ **Pyrénées**, 11, av. Gal-de-Gaulle, ☎ 62.41.80.08, AE Visa, 43 rm ℗ ∰ ⎯ closed 15 Nov-15 Dec, 135. Rest. ♦♦ ⊰ 45-150.

△ ★★**La Grotte aux Fées** (65 pl), ☎ 62.41.81.63; ★★**Les Rives du Gave** (35 pl), ☎ 62.41.80.29.

SAINT-ÉTIENNE-DE-BAIGORRY*

Bayonne 51, Pau 114, Paris 822 km
pop 1690 ✉ 64430   A1
From Saint-Étienne, with its hump-backed bridge, galleried Basque church and 17thC château, the **Nive Valley** or **vallée des Aldudes★**, a fisherman's paradise, narrows to a wooded gorge. The local activities are tourism and agriculture. ► **Banca**, a hamlet, formerly a copper-smelting centre. **Aldudes**, an autumn rendez-vous for hunters, out for the migrating pigeons that fly up through the valley and over Spain.   □

Practical Information
ⓘ pl. de la Mairie (closed Feb), ☎ 59.37.43.11.

Hotel :
● ★★★ **Arcé**, ☎ 59.37.40.14, Euro Visa, 26 rm ℗ ∰ ⎯ ⌂ ⌷ closed 11 Nov-15 Mar, 290. Rest. ● ♦♦ A great restaurant on the banks of the Nive. Regional cuisine : *saumon de l'Adour poché au beurre blanc, ris d'agneau sautés provençales, tournedos navarrais*, 120-200; child : 60.

△ ★★**Irouléguy** (70 pl), ☎ 59.37.43.96.

Recommended
Guide to wines : *cave coopérative, Irouléguy wines*, ☎ 59.37.41.33.

SAINT-JEAN-DE-LUZ***

Bayonne 21, Pau 128, Paris 793 km
pop 12920 ✉ 64500   A1
Saint-Jean-de-Luz is a relatively new town, whose finest hours came in the 17thC with a Treaty of the Pyrénées and the marriage of Louis XIV. A whaling-station since the 11thC, Saint-Jean is today a tuna-

fishing port. In winter, the anchovy fleet takes over (the cannery is the leading French producer). Seaside resort with casino.
► The **Place Louis-XIV**, with its bandstand and café terraces, overlooks the quay where the tuna fleet is moored. Next to the town hall (1657), the **château Lohobiaque** (1635) was Louis XIV's residence during his marriage solemnities (memorabilia; furniture; *daily ex Sun. pm, 8-15 Jun. and Jul.-21 Sep.*). ► Maria Teresa, future Queen of France, stayed in a 17thC mansion along the quay. ► The **Barre Quarter**, between the Place, the quay and the raised dyke along the edge of the beach, was once the shipowners' district; it is now partly a pedestrian precinct with restaurants, galleries and fashionable shops. ► **Church of St. Jean-Baptiste★**, where the royal marriage took place, was built in the 14th-15thC (traditional Basque wooden galleries, altarpiece★). ► At the mouth of the Nivelle, on the other side of the port, is **Ciboure★**, whose fortified 16thC church and old houses give it a typically Basque appearance. The composer of *Bolero*, Maurice Ravel (1875-1937), was born at No. 12 on the quay.   □

Practical Information

SAINT-JEAN-DE-LUZ
ⓘ pl. du Mal-Foch, ☎ 59.26.03.16.
✈ *Biarritz-Parme*, 16 km NE, ☎ 59.23.90.67.
SNCF ☎ 59.26.02.08.
Car-Hire : Avis, 31, bd Thiers, ☎ 59.26.17.43; train station.

Hotels :
● ★★★★(L) **Le Grand Hôtel**, (Mapotel), 43, bd Thiers, ☎ 59.26.12.32, Tx 571487, AE DC Euro Visa, 48 rm ℗ ⊰ ♪ ⚸ ⌷ closed 8 Jan-28 Feb, 900. Rest. ● ♦♦♦♦ ⊰ ♪ ⚸ ➫ The coast's newest luxury hotel is a force to be reckoned with. Bruno Cirino, advised by top chef Alain Ducasse (of the Hachette panel), produces remarkable dishes : *piments et petits rougets de pays sautés au basilic, agneau des Pyrénées rôti en cocotte à l'infusion de thym*. Extensive wine list, 170-380.
★★★★(L) **Chantaco**, golf de Chantaco, ☎ 59.26.14.76, Tx 540016, AE DC Euro Visa, 24 rm ℗ ⊰ ∰ ♪ ⁄ ➤ ⌿ closed 16 Oct-31 Mar. A handsome Spanish-style residence in a tranquil setting, 370. Rest. ♦♦ ⊰ ♪ ⚸ Spec : *piperade basquaise, caneton aux pêches fraîches*, 120-200.
★★★ **Madison**, 25, bd Thiers, ☎ 59.26.35.02, Tx 540140, AE DC Euro Visa, 25 rm ♪ 225.
★★★ **Plage**, 33, rue Garat, ☎ 59.51.03.44, 35 rm ℗ ⊰ ⎯ closed 15 Oct-1 Apr, 240. Rest. ♦ 50-60.
★★ **Commerce**, 3, bd V.-Hugo, ☎ 59.26.31.99, 36 rm ⊰ closed 1 Dec-1 Mar, 240.
★★ **La Fayette** (L.F.), 18-20, rue de la République, ☎ 59.26.17.74, AE DC Euro Visa, 19 rm, 170. Rest. ♦
Kayola ♪ ⚸ 80-120; child : 40.

Restaurants :
● ♦♦ **Kaïku**, 17, rue de la République, ☎ 59.26.13.20, AE Visa ♪ closed Mon eve (h.s.), Wed in winter, 12 Nov-25 Dec. In the town's oldest edifice (1580), sample fresh fish nicely prepared by M. Ourdanabia : *louvine braisée au madiran, Saint-Pierre aux raisins et aux cèpes, magret aux fruits frais*, 160-250.
♦ **Au Chipiron**, 4, rue Etchegaray, ☎ 59.26.03.41, AE ♪ closed Mon, Jan, 55-115.
♦ **Chez Pablo**, 5, rue Mlle-Etcheto, ☎ 59.26.37.81, closed Wed , Oct. Large, oilcloth-covered tables set with tasty *angulas, chipirons à l'encre, pibales* (in season), local wines, 50-130.
♦ **La Vieille Auberge**, 22, rue Tourasse, ☎ 59.26.19.61, Visa, closed Wed, 3 Jan-1 Apr. Top-notch food, and generous too! Seafood platter, grilled fish, local wines, 60-120.
♦ **Le Pavillon de l'Infante**, rue de l'Infante, ☎ 59.26.09.49. Fresh, lively cuisine near the port, 120-250.
♦ **Léonie**, 6, rue Garat, ☎ 59.26.37.10, AE DC Visa ♪ closed Mon, 1-27 Feb. Pleasant bar-restaurant, 130-180.

△ ★★★**Chibaou-Berria** (220 pl), ☎ 59.26.21.90; ★★★**Inter-Plages** (100 pl), ☎ 59.26.56.94; ★★★**Itsas-**

Mendi (300 pl), ☎ 59.26.56.50; ★★*Maya* (115 pl), ☎ 59.26.54.91; ★★*Plage Soubelet* (115 pl), ☎ 59.26.51.60.

Recommended
Casino : pl. de la Pergola, ☎ 59.26.09.09.
Events : *tuna festival*, in Jul; *Basque Xmas*; *ttoro festival*, early Sep.
Leisure activities : *boat rides*, ☎ 59.26.25.87.
Night-clubs : *le Look and le Beach*, at the casino.
♥ Basque linens : *Iparralde*, rue Gambetta; chocolates : *Paries*, 15, rue Gambetta; espadrilles : *Bayona*, 60, rue Gambetta, ☎ 59.26.05.40; macaroons : *Adam*, 6, pl. Louis-XIV, 49, rue Gambetta, ☎ 59.26.21.98.

Nearby

CIBOURE, ⊠ 64500 Saint-Jean-de-Luz, 2 km W.

Hotel :
★★ *La Caravelle*, bd P.-Benoît, ☎ 59.47.18.05, Euro Visa, 16 rm P ⦿ half pens (h.s.), 320. Rest. ♦ ⦿ ⌖ closed 15 Jan-30 Mar, 15 Apr-15 Jun, 15 Oct-15 Dec, 60-90.

Restaurants :
♦♦ *Chez Mattin*, 63, rue E.-Baignol, ☎ 59.47.19.52, Euro Visa, closed Mon , Jan-Feb, 100-150.
● ♦ *Dominique*, quai M.-Ravel, ☎ 59.47.29.16, closed Mon and Sun eve , Oct, 3 wks after Easter. At the port, fish from the sea to your table, 120-210.

SAINT-JEAN-PIED-DE-PORT★★

Bayonne 54, Pau 103, Paris 825 km
pop 1770 ⊠ 64220   A-B1
Formerly a stronghold and a staging post on the pilgrim road, at the foot of the *port* (pass) of Roncevaux; today, a pleasant winter resort, and a busy tourist and fishing centre.

▶ Ramparts surround the 17thC area around the **Rue d'Espagne,** which runs N to the **old bridge** on the Nive (view★). The Rue de la Citadelle, lined with 16th and 17thC red sandstone houses, runs N through the upper town★ surrounded by 15thC walls. Near the bridge, the church of the Assumption, rebuilt in the 18thC with a 16thC doorway. Almost opposite, in Rue de l'Église, the former almshouse is now a **Museum of Basque Pelota.** Beyond the 15thC house known as the bishops' prison *(Prison des Évêques)* you reach the St. Jacques gateway on the way up to the 17thC **citadel;** valley view.▶ On the edge of the old town, the France gateway opens on to an avenue lined with bustling sidewalk cafés.

Nearby

▶ Upstream from Saint-Jean, the valley of the Petite Nive becomes the **Défilé de Valcarlos★** marking the border with Spain. ▶ Along the valley of the Nive itself you can go up to the excursion centre of **Béhérobie** *(13 km).* ▶ Down the Laurhibar Valley SE, you come to the 12thC Romanesque church of **Saint-Sauveur** and *(approx. 30 km)* the **Iraty Forest** (23 km²) : flora and fauna; footpaths, bridle-paths and cross-country skiing. ▶ Finally, from **Saint-Jean-le-Vieux** (red sandstone church; Romanesque doorway, 17th-18thC galleries), you can follow route GR65, one of the most trodden of the former pilgrim routes to Compostela, which runs parallel to D933. It passes through **Osterbat** and **Harambels** (Chapel of St. Nicolas★), which were also pilgrim halts. □

Practical Information _____
ⓘ pl. du Marché, ☎ 59.37.03.57.
SNCF ☎ 59.37.02.00.

Hotels :
● ★★★ *Les Pyrénées*, 19, pl. Ch.-de-Gaulle, ☎ 59.37.01.01, AE Visa, 25 rm 2 apt ⦿ ⌕ ⌖ closed Mon eve (Nov-Mar), Tue (Sep-Jun), 5-25 Jan, 25 Nov-22 Dec, 280. Rest. ● ♦♦♦ ♪ ⌖ ⌗ Authentic Basque gastronomy by F. Arrambide : *foie gras frais de*

canard poché et servi au naturel, pigeon rôti à l'ail doux et raviolis aux cèpes, 110-280.
★★★ **Continental**, 3, av. Renaud, ☎ 59.37.00.25, 22 rm P ⦿ closed 15 Mar-11 Nov, 230.
★★ **Central Hôtel,** (France-accueil), 1, pl. Ch.-de-Gaulle, ☎ 59.37.00.22, AE DC, 14 rm P ⦿ ⌗ closed 28 Dec-10 Feb, 160. Rest. ♦ ⦿ 65-160.
★★ **Etche Ona**, 15, pl. Floquet, ☎ 59.37.01.14, 13 rm P ⦿ ⌗ half pens (h.s.), closed Fri (l.s. ex school hols), 6 Nov-15 Dec, 350. Rest. ● ♦♦ ⌕ Savoury, original cuisine by J.-C. Ibargaray : *blanc de barbue aux endives confites et safran, saumon frais de l'Adour, pigeonneau à plat dans son jus,* 70-160.
★ **Ramuntcho** (L.F.), 1, rue de France, ☎ 59.37.03.91, DC Euro Visa, 17 rm P ⦿ ⌕ ♪ ⌗ closed 1-22 Dec, 110. Rest. ♦ ⦿ ♪ closed Wed, 55-125.

Recommended
♥ at Ispoure, pork products : *Ferme Abotia*, ☎ 59.37.03.99, ham, pâtés, *boudins* by mail.

SAUVETERRE-DE-BÉARN★

Dax 45, Bayonne 62, Paris 795 km
pop 1668 ⊠ 64390   B1
An 11thC viscount of Béarn granted a charter of independence to this delightful city on the road to Compostela. The name is pronounced locally as *Sauveté.*

▶ Beautifully situated on an escarpment overlooking the Gave d'Oloron, Sauveterre has retained parts of its medieval walls and the ruins of the 12th-13thC **château de Montréal,** as well as an arch of a fortified bridge. From the terrace of the church, with its 12th-13thC bell tower keep, view★ over the Pyrénées; 16thC **château de Nays.**

Nearby

▶ **Château de Laàs** *(8 km E;* 1775) : furniture and works of art from the Middle Ages to the early 19thC; gardens *(Jul.-Sep.; Sat. and Sun. Mar-Jun.).* ▶ **Navarrenx** *(18 km SE)* : 16thC **ramparts** (St. Antoine Gateway; 15thC church); the world salmon-fishing championship is held in the Gave d'Oloron every year between Mar. and Jun.-Jul.; a good departure point for cross-country treks with pack ponies. The town is a regional centre for furniture production. □

Practical Information _____
SAUVETERRE-DE-BÉARN
SNCF ☎ 59.38.52.63.

Hotel :
● ★ *A Boste* (L.F.), rue L.-Bérard, ☎ 59.38.50.62, AE Visa, 10 rm P ⌗ half pens (h.s.), closed Sun eve and Mon, 1 Oct-15 Nov, 300. Rest. ♦ ⌗ Savoury cuisine, 50-170.
▲ ★★*Gave* (100 pl), ☎ 59.38.53.30.

Nearby

NAVARRENX, ⊠ 64190, 18 km SE.
ⓘ porte St-Antoine (h.s.); mairie, ☎ 59.66.10.22. ♥

Hotel :
● ★★ *Commerce*, ☎ 59.66.50.16, 30 rm, closed Mon eve, Jan, 110. Rest. ♦ 50-120.

Recommended
Events : *world salmon fishing competition*, info S.I., in Mar, Apr, Jul.

TARBES

Auch 73, Toulouse 154, Paris 805 km
pop 54055 ⊠ 65000   D1
The rich soil here is drained by the upper valley of the Adour; wheat and maize are cultivated, and lush grass provides pasture for the National Stud. Tarbes

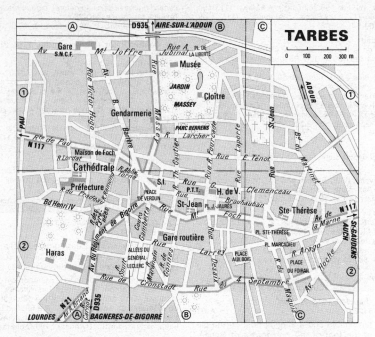

TARBES

0 100 200 300 m

is the major agricultural market of the region, as well as an industrial centre (electricity from generating stations in the mountains; engineering and chemical industries). High-level technical schools have been established in the area.

▶ The main thoroughfares of the town meet at the **Place de Verdun** (B2), where townspeople gather in the evenings. Rues Brahauban and Maréchal-Foch are shopping centres. ▶ Main attraction is the **Massey Garden★** (B1), one of the most beautiful parks in SW France, with medieval architectural vestiges (capitals from Trie-sur-Baïse, Gothic cloister from Saint-Séver-de-Rustan →), as well as an 1850 villa in Italian style, with art collections and a **Museum of Cavalry and Horses** (*daily ex Mon., Tue. and nat. hols, 10-12 & 2-6*). Birthplace of **Maréchal Foch** (1851-1929 WWI hero) at N° 2 Rue de la Victoire, a Louis XV mansion (*daily ex Tue. and Wed.; memorabilia*). ▶ **Cathedral of Notre-Dame-de-la-Sède** : (A2) 12thC structure with Gothic ogive vaulting added in the 14thC; 18thC furnishings. ▶ The *Haras National* (National Stud Farm; A2)★ : some of the finest stallions in France (*visit park and stables daily pm ex Tue., Jun.-Feb., 2:30-5:30*).

Nearby

▶ **Ibos** *(6 km N)* was one of the main strongholds of Bigorre; Gothic collegiate church dominated by bell tower-keep (14th-15th-C; 17th-18thC furnishings). ▶ **Château de Montaner★** *(15 km NW in the Atlantic Pyrénées)* : on a site fortified as early as the 11thC; transformed by Gaston Phébus (→ *Passes of the Pyrénées*), 40-m high keep, polygonal brick surrounding wall (*Sat. and Sun. pm Apr.-Sep., or by appt. with the organization* Pierres et Vestiges, *64110 Jurançon, tel. 59.32.37.39*). In the village church, 15th-16thC frescoes. ▶ **Saint-Séver-de-Rustan** *(25 km NE)* : remains of a Benedictine abbey; the cloister has been reassembled at Massey Gardens at Tarbes, together with capitals from the 15thC collegiate church of **Trie-sur-Baïse** *(30 km NE)*, much of which is now in the Cloisters division of the Metropolitan Museum of Art in New York; remains of the 13thC fortified town.□

Practical Information _____

TARBES
ℹ️ pl. de Verdun (B2), ☎ 62.93.36.62.
✈ Tarbes-Ossun-Lourdes, 9 km SW, ☎ 62.32.92.22.
SNCF (A1), ☎ 62.37.50.50.
🚌 pl. au Bois (B2), ☎ 62.34.71.21.
Car-Hire : Avis, Train station (A1); av. de Lourdes, ☎ 62.34.26.76; Airport.

Hotels :
● ★★★ **Le Président**, (Mapotel), 1, rue G.-Fauré (A2), ☎ 62.93.98.40, Tx 530522, AE DC Euro Visa, 57 rm Ⓟ ≶ ⬛ ♪ 🏊 ♿ 🖵 280. Rest. ♦♦ **Le Toit de Bigorre** ≶ ♪ ♿ ☜ 50-100; child : 30.
★★★ **Henri IV**, 7, av. B.-Barère (A1), ☎ 62.34.01.68, AE DC Euro Visa, 24 rm Ⓟ ≶ ♿ 190.
★★ **Le Martinet**, 13, bd du Martinet (off map C2), ☎ 62.37.96.30, AE Euro Visa, 24 rm Ⓟ ⬛ ♪ 150.
★★ **Normandie**, 33, rue Massey (B1), ☎ 62.93.08.47, 21 rm Ⓟ ≶ 130.
★★ **Terminus**, 42, av. Joffre (A1), ☎ 62.93.00.33, Visa, 32 rm ☜ ⚘ 190. Rest. ♦ ♪ closed Sat, Sep, 60-120.

Restaurants :
● ♦♦ **L'Amphitryon**, 38, rue Larrey (B2), ☎ 62.34.08.99, AE DC Visa ♪ ♿ closed Sat noon and Sun, 3-23 Aug. Light, modern food for Tarbes' demanding diners : cannellonis de homard et Saint-Jacques, grande assiette de pigeon, saumon aux truffes en sabayon de poireaux, 130-220.
● ♦♦ **La Caravelle**, at the Airport, Juillan, 5 km SW, ☎ 62.32.99.96, AE DC Visa ≮ ⬛ ♪ ♿ closed Mon and Sun eve, 4-27 Jan, 13-29 Jul. Regional dishes by L. Rouzaud : œufs Caravelle, filets de sole au pamplemousse. Fine stock of Bordeaux wines. Cocktails at the "Guépard" bar, 130-165.
♦♦ **Toup'ty**, 86, av. B.-Barère (A1), ☎ 62.93.32.08 ♪ closed Mon and Sun eve , Jul, 75-160.
● ♦ **Buffet de la Gare**, 21, av. du Mal-Joffre (A1), ☎ 62.93.16.22, closed Sat. In the best French "buffet de gare" tradition, 40-100.

Nearby

CHIS, ⊠ 65800 Aureilhan, 9 km NE.

Hotel :
★★ *Ferme de Saint-Ferréol* (L.F.), ☎ 62.36.22.15, AE DC
Euro Visa, 22 rm ℗ ⫞ ▥ ◠ ⋌⁰ closed Fri eve and Sun eve
(l.s.), 150.

IBOS, ⊠ 65420, 6 km W.

Hotel :
★★ *La Chaumière du Bois*, rte de Pau, ☎ 62.31.02.42,
AE Euro Visa, 11 rm ℗ ⫞ ▥ ◠ & ▤ closed 30 Mar-6 Apr,
21 Dec-6 Jan, 260. Rest. ◆◆ ⫞ ♪ & closed Mon and Sun
eve. Regional dishes : *saumon en papillote, ris de veau
aux pâtes fraîches*, 65-100 ; child : 40.

ODOS, ⊠ 65310 Laloubère, 4 km S.

Hotel :
★★★ *Concorde*, (Inter-Hôtel), RN 21, ☎ 62.93.51.18, AE
DC Euro Visa, 42 rm ℗ 250. Rest. ◆ 60-120.

TRIE-SUR-BAISE, ⊠ 65220, 30 km NE.
i mairie, ☎ 62.35.52.39.   ♥

Hotel :
★★ *Tour*, ☎ 62.35.52.12, AE DC Euro Visa, 11 rm ℗ ▥ ◠
closed 2 Jun-14 May, 1-15 Oct, 160. Rest. ◆ closed Mon
noon, 50-100.

⅄ ★*Municipal* (33 pl), ☎ 62.35.52.39.

Recommended
Events : *horse races*, in Aug ; *foie gras competition*, mid-
Dec.

The VIC-BILH Region

C1

An agricultural region best known for the Madiran
vineyards, first planted during the Gallo-Roman
period. The area includes numerous valleys that run
more or less parallel between the Gave de Pau and
the Adour.

▶ **Morlaàs** : on the edge of the Vic-Bilh *(12 km NE from
Pau on D943)*, one of the leading towns in medieval
Béarn. The church was part of a Cluniac priory founded in
the 11thC and rebuilt between the 14th and 16thC. ▶ The
Romanesque church at **Sévignacq-Thèze** *(7 km NW on
D943, between Morlaàs and Lembeye)* was also rebuilt
in the 15thC ; wall belfry ; Romanesque sculptures in the
doorway, much medieval detail. ▶ **Lembeye** *(32 km NE
of Pau)* : 16thC church (Flamboyant Gothic doorway) ;
Madiran wine-making cooperative, *tel. 59.68.10.93.*   ☐

VIC-EN-BIGORRE

Tarbes 17, Auch 62, Paris 788 km
pop 5065 ⊠ 65500   C-D1
Vic is a typical medieval walled town *(bastide)*, and
provides an excellent centre for exploring the Adour
valley.

Nearby

▶ **Rabastens-de-Bigorre** *(8 km E)* : a walled town founded
in the 14thC near the Alaric Canal, the name of which is

derived from the Visigothic occupation of the area in the
5thC ; large Gothic church. ▶ **Maubourguet** *(9 km N)* : the
church, near the extensive marketplace, was formerly part
of an 11thC Benedictine priory. ▶ **Madiran** *(21 km N)* :
12thC Romanesque apse and crypt in the church ; Benedictines were also established here, where they contributed significantly to the development of the vineyards.
▶ Nearby is **Castelnau-Rivière-Basse** *(23 km N)* :
former stronghold overlooking the Adour valley (ruined
13thC keep ; Gothic church with massive gate tower).
▶ **Mazères** *(2 km E in the plain)* : a Romanesque church
fortified in the 15thC.   ☐

Practical Information

VIC-EN-BIGORRE
i rue Mal-Foch, ☎ 62.96.81.33.
SNCF ☎ 62.96.71.64.

Hotels :
★★ *Baloc*, rte de Bordeaux, ☎ 62.96.73.95, Euro Visa,
21 rm ℗ ▥ 180. Rest. ◆ closed 9 Oct-1 Nov. Spec : *foie
gras frais aux pêches*, 50-100.
★★ *Tivoli*, ☎ 62.96.70.39, Visa, 24 rm ▥ 150. Rest. ◆ ♪
closed Mon, 7-20 Jan, 5-20 Sep, 60-140.

Nearby

MAUBOURGUET, ⊠ 65700, 9 km N.
i mairie, ☎ 62.96.30.09.
SNCF ☎ 62.96.31.56.

Hotel :
★ *France*, allées Larbanès, ☎ 62.96.30.10, 19 rm, 90.
Rest. ◆ ♪ 40-100.

Recommended
Events : *cattle show*, 1st Tue in May.
Farmhouse-inn : at Labatut-Rivière, 5 km NE, *R. Larrieu*,
canoe-kayak, river-skiing, tennis, pony rides.

RABASTENS-DE-BIGORRE, ⊠ 65140, 8 km E.
i mairie, ☎ 62.96.60.22.

Hotels :
● ★ *Platanes*, ☎ 62.96.61.77, 6 rm, closed Sat, 120.
Rest. ◆ ♪ 50-90.
★ *Chez Yvonne* (L.F.), ☎ 62.96.60.20, Visa, 10 rm ℗
closed Sun eve and Fri, 1 May, 15 Oct-3 Nov, 80.
Rest. ◆ 40-100.

Recommended
Riding center : ☎ 62.96.59.44, camping.

WESTERN PYRÉNÉES NAT. PARK**

The park, created in 1967, covers 457 km² at an altitude of 1 070-3 300 m. It includes the high valleys of
Aspe, Ossau, Azan, Cauterets, Barèges and Aure.
At the southern boundary it crosses the border to
become the Spanish national park of Ordesa. A great
variety of plant and animal species are protected
here. Guided walks slanted towards ecology, fauna
and flora, and history, start from the valleys ; information available from the various park offices *(Maisons du Parc)* or the Regional HQ at Tarbes.   ☐

Berry, Bourbonnais

▶ This largely unknown region, set in the middle of France, is a harmonious combination of many of the country's features : immense wheatfields, alternating forests and pastureland, grassy mountain slopes irrigated by hundreds of little streams, ponds and forests, narrow, snaking valleys and pebble-strewn hills. Berry-Bourbonnais has borrowed aspects from all its neighbours and it is often hard to say exactly where the region begins or ends. But there is a spiritual unity nonetheless, composed of calm and moderation, a natural tendency towards balance in art and in all the details of daily life. Here are churches and châteaux, half-timbered houses, gorges, country paths, scenic panoramas — but all in moderation : a few masterpieces and hundreds of minor treasures to discover at every turn of the path.

The magnificent cathedral of Bourges rises up above the tiled roofs of its parish huddled on a slight rise in the plain of Champagne. Despite the industrial and urban bustle of the newer part of the city, the narrow, winding streets of the old town have retained much of their charm. The writer George Sand, who spent 41 years of her life in Nohant, and was revered by the local people both for her charity and her genius, described Bourges cathedral as "a blend of the delicate and the colossal, both gracious and untamed, simultaneously heavy and airborne." Many consider it the most beautiful cathedral in France.

The Benedictine abbey of Fontgombault, founded in the 11th century, still resounds to the purity of Gregorian chant, and the countryside is dotted with Romanesque and Gothic churches. Near the border with Auvergne is Vichy, with its Belle Époque architecture, where jaded colonials used to come to recover their dissipated health and restore their dwindling fortunes at the casino.

Bourbonnais and Berry may not figure among the most famous wine-producing regions of France, but there are excellent local vintages, mainly white : Sancerre, a fruity dry white sauvignon, with a palatable red counterpart; Quincy, Reuilly, Pouilly — especially Pouilly Fumé — and a host of others. The region is famous for its goat cheeses, the best-known being the round *crottin* of Chavignol and the ash-covered *pyramides* of Valençay and Levroux. Regional cooking is hearty, but far from plain, featuring delicious stews of game and chicken, meat pies and *pâtés* — recipes simmered and perfected over the centuries in the low-roofed farmhouses of this harmonious region. □

 ## Don't miss

★★★ Bourges B1, Nohant-Vicq B2.

★★ Fontgombault A2, Sancerre B1, Valençay A1, Vichy C3.

★ Argy A2, Creuse Gorges A2, Lapalisse C3, Moulins C2, Nançay B1, Souvigny C2, Tronçais Forest B2.

Weekend tips

Starting from Moulins, where you can find an excellent lunch, a Saturday afternoon itinerary will take you to beautiful churches at Souvigny and Saint-Menoux; continue through Bourbon-l'Archambault to Ygrande (stopover in the forest of Tronçais). On Sunday, to Ainay-le-Vieil and the country around Saint-Amand-Montrond : Drevant, Noirlac, the château de Meillant.

In Sologne berrichonne

In Indre

In Champagne berrichonne

Facts and figures

Location : *geographical centre of France.*
Area : *21 400 km².*
Climate : *mixture of continental and coastal influences; quite cold in winter, with late springs, pleasant summers and autumns that are usually long and sunny.*
Population : *943 000.*
Administration : *departments : Allier, Prefecture Moulins; Cher, Prefecture Bourges; Indre, Prefecture Châteauroux.*

● *Brief regional history*

Before 52BC
Two Celtic tribes (the Biturigi) inhabited the Berry and Bourbonnais regions after immigrations of the 8thC BC. The territory of the northern Biturigi extended as far as Bourges *(Avaric)*, reputedly the most beautiful city in Gaul, while the southern kingdom of Arverne was based in Gergovia, and included part of the Allier Plain.

52BC-10thC
When Gaul was partitioned in 27BC, the region was included in the province of Aquitaine, with Avaric as its capital. The Romans developed the countryside and built roads. Thermal springs (Vichy, Néris) prospered from rich clients. When Christianity began to spread during the 3rdC, **Bourges** became the Metropolitan See for the dioceses of Aquitaine. ● In 270, Germanic tribes began to invade, but neither the Franks nor the Visigoths reached Berry-Bourbonnais in sufficient numbers to impose their authority. ● The

Duchy of Aquitaine, constituted in 614, remained independent of the Frankish Merovingian kings until the reign of Pepin the Short (761). The region was finally broken up by the development of the feudal system in the 10thC.

10th-13thC

The former **county of Bourges** was divided into two principal seigneuries : the **viscounty of Bourges,** which was sold to the king of France in 1101 and elevated to the status of duchy; and the **viscounty of Déols,** which remained under Aquitaine until conquered by Philippe Auguste at the end of the same century. ● The seigneury of **Bourbonnais,** based around Bourbon-l'Archambault, was formed at the same period, and prospered through marriages, legacies and the king's favour.

14th-15thC

The most famous Duke of Berry was **Jean** (1340-1416), uncle of Charles VIII, and brother of King Charles V. He surrounded himself with an elegant court and patronized the arts. Some of the most

exquisite manuscript miniatures of the Middle Ages were created on his order, including the famous book of hours, the **"Très Riches Heures du Duc de Berry"** (now in the Condé Museum, Château de Chantilly). ● Bourges was an important mediaeval centre of artistic achievement. King Charles VII of France resided there, and Bourges remained his capital, thanks to the financial aid of Jacques Coeur (→ box), until Joan of Arc in 1428 rallied the French to drive out the occupying English. ● The Bourbon dukes who made **Moulins** the capital at the end of the 15thC lived in luxury.

16thC to the present day

King François I, humiliated by the splendid court of Charles III, **Duke of Bourbon,** sequestrated some of the duke's possessions. In retaliation, Charles joined forces with Holy Roman Emperor Charles Quint, and played a decisive role in defeating the French at Pavia. This provoked François I to attach all Bourbon estates to the crown on the death of Charles in 1527. Berry followed in 1601; since that time the Berry and Bourbonnais regions have formed an integral part of France.

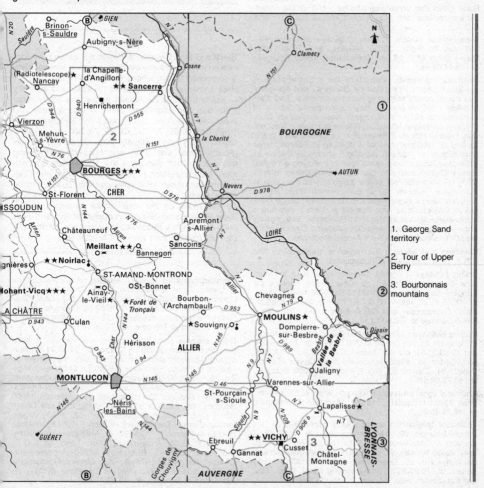

1. George Sand territory

2. Tour of Upper Berry

3. Bourbonnais mountains

Practical information

Information : *Comité Régional de Tourisme* **Auvergne** *(C.R.T.),* 43, av. Julien, 63011 Clermont-Ferrand, ☎ 73.93.04.03. *C.R.T.* **Val de Loire,** 9, rue Pierre-Lentin, 45041 Orléans Cedex 1, ☎ 38.62.68.48. **Allier :** *Office Bourbonnais du Tourisme et du Thermalisme,* 35, rue Belle-Croix, 03400 Yzeure, ☎ 70.44.41.57. **Cher :** *Comité Départemental de Tourisme (C.D.T.),* 10, rue de la Chappe, 18000 Bourges, ☎ 48.70.71.72. **Indre :** *C.D.T.,* bus station, rue Bourdillon, 36000 Châteauroux, ☎ 54.22.91.20. *Dir. régionale de la Jeunesse et des Sports :* **Centre :** 1, bd de la Motte-Sanguin, B.P. 14, 45015 Orléans Cedex, ☎ 38.62.70.80. **Auvergne :** 8, pl. de Regensburg, 63000 Clermont Ferrand, ☎ 73.35.10.10. *Dir. rég. des Affaires culturelles :* **Centre :** 6, rue Dupanloup, 45043 Orléans Cedex, ☎ 38.68.11.86. **Auvergne :** hôtel de Chazerat, 4, rue Pascal, 63000 Clermont Ferrand, ☎ 73.92.40.41.

S.O.S. : Allier : ☎ 70.46.46.46. **Cher :** *SAMU* (emergency medical service), ☎ 48.65.15.15. **Indre :** *S.M.U.R.,* ☎ 54.27.01.64. *Poisoning Emergency Centre :* Tours, ☎ 47.66.15.15. Clermont-Ferrand, ☎ 73.27.33.33.

Weather forecast : Allier : ☎ 70.03.00.00. **Cher :** ☎ 48.50.15.91. **Indre :** ☎ 54.34.05.13.

Rural gîtes and chambres d'hôtes : enq at the *Relais départementaux des gîtes ruraux* and at the *O.T.* and *C.D.T.*

Camping-car rentals : Allier : garage St-Christophe, 119, rue de Paris, 03000 Moulins, ☎ 70.44.13.60. **Cher :** Sobal ELS, 29, av. Jean-Jaurès, 18000 Bourges, ☎ 48.24.02.94.

Festivals and events : Feb : wine fair at Saint-Pourçain-sur-Sioule. **Apr :** *Printemps de Bourges;* **mid-Apr-early Jun :** *rural poetry festival* in Aubigny-sur-Nère. **End Apr-mid-Sep :** *Été de Noirlac.* **May :** *international festival of experimental music* in Bourges; *snail festival* in Cluis (1 May); *céréalia* in Issoudun; *fête de la Louée* in Vesdun. **Jun. :** *Grand Prix de Formule III* in La Châtre. **Jul :** *grape festival* in Verdigny; *festival of folklore* in Gannat; *fêtes romantiques* in Nohant. **Jul-Aug :** *theatrical festival* in Valençay; *Bourbonnais music festival* in Souvigny; *music festival* Châteaumeillant; *fête des ânes (donkey fete)* in Garigny; *ancestral fete of the bargemen of the Loire* in Saint-Satur; *wizards' fair* in Bué; *French Wines Fair* in Sancerre. **Aug :** *music festival* in Gargilesse; *dance festival* in Châteauroux; *lyric festival* in Vichy; **mid-Aug :** *marionnette festival* in Mayet-de-Montagne. **Sep :** *Slide-show Festival* in Vichy. **Sep-Oct :** *Autumn Days* in Moulins. **Oct :** *Orval fairs* in Saint-Amand-Montrond.

Rambling and hiking : the region is traversed by the G.R.3, 31, 41, 46 and 412 (topoguides).

Riding holidays : *Comité Départemental pour le Tourisme Équestre (C.D.T.E.) du* **Cher** (riding centre), La Rongère, Saint-Éloy-de-Gy, 18110 Saint-Martin-d'Auxigny, ☎ 48.25.43.97. **Indre :** *C.D.T.E.,* 43, rue de Mousseaux, 36000 Châteauroux and *C.D.T.* **Allier :** enq. : Dr Millen, 03800 Gannat, ☎ 70.90.13.18.

Cycling holidays : Allier : *Comité Dép. de Cyclotourisme,* M. Sarrazin, 21, rue Darcin, 03300 Cusset, ☎ 70.98.64.44 and 70.98.01.51, ext 397. **Indre :** *C.D. de Cyclo :* M. Blenert, Cedex 35, 36500 Neuillé-les-Bois. **Cher :** *C.D. de Cyclo :* M. Cherer, 67, rue E.-Vaillant, 18000 Bourges, ☎ 48.70.03.97.

River and canal cruises : cruise on canals of the region : *Blue Line,* L'Équerre, 18320 Marseille-lès-Aubigny, ☎ 48.76.48.01.

Technical tourism : *Cérame* (Berry porcelain), 16, av. Raoul-Aladenize, 18500 Mehun-sur-Yèvre, ☎ 48.57.48.05 *(by appt.). Observatoire de Paris* (radio-astronomy station), 18330 Nançay, ☎ 48.51.82.41. *Compagnie fermière de Vichy,* 1-3, av. Eisenhower, B.P. 312, 03201 Vichy Cedex, ☎ 70.98.95.37 (Vichy mineral water, Wed., Thu. and Sat. ex nat. hols, 3-5 and 15 May-15 Sep.).

Berry and Bourbonnais cuisine

Simple country cooking which makes the most of local produce. Apparent simplicity, however, masks skills developed throughout generations in farmhouse kitchens. Not everyone can make a successful oyonnade (chicken in a sauce combining eau-de-vie, wine); braised chicken Berry-style (with the blood and liver of the bird) or a poulet en barbouille (barbouille means daub and tells you that this is the sort of chicken you want to eat with your fingers). Chicken is also prepared with verjuice (unsweetened grapejuice) and in pies. Pâtés and meat pies with crackling are also popular. Both Berry and Bourbonnais claim to have invented the sanciau, a cross between a pancake and an omelette, which may be sweet or savoury. Other regional specialities are paupiettes au bouillon (meat "olives" braised in wine), tête de veau berrichonne (braised head of veal), excellent local beef, and game of many kinds from the woods of Berry. The Indre and Cher valleys provide goat's milk cheese, among which the charcoal-dusted pyramides of Valençay and Levroux are famous, as are the crottins of Chavignol.

Wines

Berry and Bourbonnais, although not among the top-ranked wine-producing districts, produce several highly-esteemed wines, whites for the most part.
Best known is white Sancerre — fruity and very dry — made from the Sauvignon grape; the finest come from Bué and Chavignol. There is also a fresh and lively red Sancerre. Good years for Sancerre red : 1962, 64, 66, 69, 70, 71, 73, 76, 78, 83.
Quincy (very dry), Reuilly (like Sancerre), Pouilly (Pouilly-Fumé, still fresh and light, despite having more body than Sancerre) are also widely appreciated. Menetou-Salon (a golden white wine) and Châteaumeillant (both "gris" rosé and red) deserve to be better known.
To the south, on the edge of the Auvergne region, Saint-Pourçain-sur-Sioule produces whites and reds (akin to the spicy Beaujolais) in vineyards traditionally claimed to date from the pre-Christian era.

Handicraft courses : pottery, weaving : *Assn. Rencontres et Loisirs,* O. et A. Delouche, 9 rue Chassagne, 18160 Lignières, ☎ 48.60.20.08 and enq. at *C.D.T.* **Cher.** *Château de Lys,* Bressolles, ☎ 70.46.69.86. Discover nature : *Centre Permanent d'Initiation à l'Environnement (C.P.I.E.),* 03360 St-Bonnet Tronçais, ☎ 70.06.14.69.

Other courses : sport car racing and formula 3, hotel du Lion d'Argent, 36400 La Châtre, ☎ 54.48.11.69. Hurdygurdy, diatonic accordion at Ennordres, the *Ateliers du Gué de la Pierre,* Ennordres, 18380 La Chapelle-d'Angillon, ☎ 48.58.00.60. Musical and theatrical expression, Ballads, South American music : Theatre at St-Florent-sur-Cher : *Fed. des Œuvres laïques,* 5 rue Samson, 18000 Bourges, ☎ 48.24.34.93. Water skiing on Lake Chambon : *Club nautique d'Eguzon,* B.P. 52, 36200 Argenton-sur-Creuse. Environment initiaton : *C.P.I.E.,* château d'Azay-le-Ferron, 36290 Mézières-en-Brenne, ☎ 54.39.23.43. Archaeology **Cher :** enq. at *C.D.T.; A.S.S.A.A.,* B.P. 3, St-Marcel, 36200 Argenton-sur-Creuse; Hang-gliding : *flying club Moulins-Montbeugny,* ☎ 70.20.04.56. Parachuting at *Lapalisse flying club,* 03120 and at Bourges, ☎ 48.50.41.83.

Children : riding course : Enq. *C.D.T. Cher.* Pony-club : château de la Roche, rte de Graçay (children's leisure centre), Anjouin, 36210 Châbris. *Le lieu-Cheval,* Agonges, 03210 Souvigny, ☎ 70.43.97.49.

Lakes : Enq. *C.D.T.*

Aquatic sports : on the lakes of St-Bonnet, ☎ 70.67.50.01 ; Sault, ☎ 70.51.50.03 ; Goule, ☎ 70.66.60.77 ; Vichy, ☎ 70.98.71.94. Vieure, ☎ 70.07.20.82 ; Chambon, ☎ *S.I. ;* Ejuzon, ☎ city hall.

Canoeing : Enq. : *C.D.T.* Indre and *C.R.T. Auvergne.*

Golf : Nassigny (9 and 18 holes), Vichy (18 holes), Hérisson (9 holes).

Hang-gliding : *Aéroclub de Moulins-Montbeugny,* ☎ 70.20.04.56. *Union Aéronautique du Centre,* 18000 Bourges, ☎ 48.50.41.83. *Aéroclub d'Issoudun,* ☎ 54.21.21.27. *Aéroclub* at Le Blanc, ☎ 54.37.06.97.

Parachuting : *Centre Aéroparachutiste,* M. Eskenazi, aérodrome de Lapalisse, 03120 Lapalisse, ☎ 70.99.18.03. *École de parachutisme* at Le Blanc, ☎ 54.37.06.97.

Winter sports : Enq. : *S.I.* of the Montagne Bourbonnaise, *Maison de la Montagne Bourbonnaise,* 03250 Le Mayet-de-Montagne, ☎ 70.41.75.24. Cross-country skiing in Saint-Nicolas-des-Biefs, Lavoine, La Loge-des-Gardes.

Hunting and shooting : enq. at the *Féd. Dép. des Chasseurs.* **Allier** : 6, av. V.-Hugo, 03000 Moulins, ☎ 70.44.07.71. **Cher** : 9, pl. de la Nation, 18000 Bourges, ☎ 48.24.28.46. **Indre** : 46, bd du Moulin-Neuf, 36000 Châteauroux, ☎ 54.22.15.98.

Fishing : **Allier** : *Féd. Dép. de Pêche et Pisciculture,* 25, bd du Gal-de-Gaulle, 03300 Cusset, ☎ 70.97.90.42. **Cher** : *Féd. de Pêche,* 59, rue Barbès, 18000 Bourges, ☎ 48.50.53.07. **Indre** : *Féd. Dép. de la Pêche,* 19, rue des États-Unis, 36000 Châteauroux, ☎ 54.34.59.69.

● *Towns and places*

AIGURANDE

Guéret 35, Châteauroux 48, Paris 316 km
pop 2182 ⊠ 36140   A2

SNCF ☎ 54.30.30.36.

Hotel :
★ *Relais de la Marche* (L.F.), Pl. du Champ-de-Foire, ☎ 54.30.31.58, 7 rm Ⓟ ⚏ ⚲, closed Mon (off-season), Nov, 100. Rest. ♦ Spéc. : *cuisses de grenouilles et écrevisses,* 80-130.

Recommended
Events : crayfish festival, last Sun in Aug ; pilgrimage to *Notre-Dame de la Bouzanne,* on Tue after Pentecost.

ARGENTON-SUR-CREUSE

Châteauroux 31, Limoges 94, Paris 302 km
pop 6141 ⊠ 36200   A2

Charming houses with wooden porches on the banks of the river Creuse.

▶ SI in a lovely old house not far from the **Vieux Pont** (Old Bridge)★ ; view★ over the river and the town. ▶ On the far side of the bridge, a 15thC house and the **chapel of St. Benoît** (Virgin and Child, 1485).

Nearby
▶ **Prunget**★ *(8 km NE) :* the **donjon** (keep), a large square 14thC tower, near those at **Mazières★** and **La Chaise-Saint-Éloi.** ▶ **Saint-Marcel** *(2 km N),* on the site of a Gallo-Roman town called *Argentomagus ;* artifacts in the museum *(15 Jun.-15 Sep., 10-12 & 2-6:30 ; Sun. pm or daily on request rest of year) ;* remains of frescos in 12th-15thC church ; crypt (pre-Romanesque chancel) and treasury★. ▶ **Chazelet** *(12 km SW) :* a 15thC château. 10 km farther lies **Saint-Benoît-du-Sault** : mediaeval houses★ on a granite spur ; fortified gateway (14thC) ; Romanesque church. **Roussines** *(3 km N) :* vaulting in the church is decorated with 15thC paintings. ▶ 20 km W, **Château-Guillaume★,** 11th-14thC fortress heavily restored in the 19thC. □

Practical Information

ARGENTON-SUR-CREUSE
ⓘ hôtel de Scévolle, ☎ 54.24.05.30.
SNCF ☎ 54.24.15.72.

Hotels :
★★ **Cheval Noir,** 27, rue Auclert-Descottes,

☎ 54.24.00.06, Tx 251183, Visa, 32 rm Ⓟ & closed Sun eve , Mon lunch, Dec-Feb, 210. Rest. ♦ ♪ & 75-150.
★★ **Manoir de Boisvillers,** 11, rue Moulin-de-Bord, ☎ 54.24.13.88, Euro Visa, 15 rm Ⓟ ⚏ ⚟ ⚲ closed 25 Dec-15 Jan, 155.
★★ **Moulin du Vivier,** Le Pêchereau, on D 48, ☎ 54.24.03.23, 14 rm Ⓟ ⚏ ⚟ ⚲ closed Mon, 20 Jan-28 Feb, 145.
★ **France** (L.F.), 8, rue J.-J.-Rousseau, ☎ 54.24.03.31, AE DC Euro Visa, 24 rm Ⓟ closed Sat (l.s.), 15 Nov-15 Dec, 120. Rest. ♦ ♪ closed Sun and Sat (l.s.), 50-80.
★ **Le Petit Roy,** 6, rue Le Bourgoin, Le Menoux, 5 km SE. on D 48, ☎ 54.47.87.09, Visa, 8 rm Ⓟ ⚏ ⚲ ⚘ pens (h.s.), 260. Rest. ♦ ♪ closed Wed (l.s.), 50-150.

Restaurant :
♦ *Chez Maître Jean,* 67, av. Rollinat, ☎ 54.24.02.09, Visa, closed Wed, 15-30 Jan, 13-28 Oct, 50-100.

⚠ ★★★*Les Chambons* (35 pl), ☎ 54.24.15.26.

Recommended
Events : pilgrimage of the Bonne-Dame, 1st Sun of July.
▼ cabinetry : G. Dorangeaon, ☎ 54.47.85.26 ; pottery : F. Baudat, ☎ 54.47.86.28 ; wood sculpture : A. Bonithon, La Damielle, ☎ 54.47.80.97 ; at Gargilesse, wrought iron : S. Bachelier, ☎ 54.47.83.28.

Nearby

TENDU, ⊠ 36200 Argenton-sur-Creuse, 9 km NE on the N 20.

Restaurant :
● ♦♦ **Moulin des Eaux Vives,** ☎ 54.24.12.25, AE DC Euro Visa ⚟ ♪ closed Mon ex Jul-Aug, 26 Jan-14 Feb, 14-24 Sep. A bit of paradise, this terrace at the water's edge. Spec : calf liver with acacia honey, salmon, 90-115 ; child : 50.

ARGY*

Châteauroux 31, Blois 83, Paris 275 km
pop 687 ⊠ 36500   A2

A square keep bracketed by four 14thC turrets and a gallery with Renaissance decoration make the **château★** worth a visit *(exterior only, 9-12 & 2-6) ;* exhibition of 19thC agricultural implements in outbuildings.

▶ **Pellevoisin** *(5 km N)* is the site of an important Marian pilgrimage ; church with 12thC choir ; 3 km SW, feudal castle at Le Mée. □

AUBIGNY-SUR-NÈRE

Bourges 46, Orléans 75, Paris 181 km
pop 5693 ⊠ 18700   B1

14thC ramparts, **wooden houses** (15th-16thC); Maison du Bailli (magistrate's house)★ near the 12th-15thC church (16thC choir stalls).

Nearby

▶ **Argent-sur-Sauldre** *(10 km N)* : 15thC church; 18thC château with 15thC towers. ▶ **Blancafort** *(9 km NE)* : 15thC church with an interesting timbered gate-tower; 15th-17thC château★ with a formal French garden and a large park *(15 Mar.-2 Nov., 10-12 & 2-6)*. ▶ **Château de la Verrerie★** in *Oizon (10 km SE)* : by a lake on the river Nère; the Scottish family of Stuart (not the royal Stuarts) rebuilt it in the 15th-16thC; graceful Italian courtyard, furniture, tapestries; chapel *(daily, 10-12 & 2-7, 15 Feb.-15 Nov.)*.   □

Practical Information

AUBIGNY-SUR-NÈRE
ℹ️ mairie, ☎ 48.58.00.09.
SNCF ☎ 48.58.04.89.

Hotel :
★★ *La Chaumière* (L.F.), 1, pl. Paul-Losnier, ☎ 45.58.04.01, AE DC Euro Visa, 16 rm ℗ ⬚ ⬚ ♪ half pens, 350. Rest. ♦ ♪ Spec : *tourte à l'oeuf, poulet en barbouille*, 65-150.

Restaurant :
♦ *Auberge de la Fontaine*, 27, av. Ch.-de-Gaulle, ☎ 48.58.02.59, AE DC Euro Visa ℗ closed Mon and Sun eve. In a setting typical of the Sologne region, Paulette Massé cooks up specialities like : *cake aux fruits de mer, ris de veau du chef*, 50-140.

⚐ ★★*Parc des Sports* (100 pl), ☎ 48.58.02.37.

Recommended
Bicycle-rental : *M. Barré*, rue Charbon, ☎ 48.58.00.29.

Nearby

OIZON, ⊠ 18700 Aubigny-sur-Nère, 10 km SE.

Hotel :
Château de la Verrerie, (I.L.A., C.H.), ☎ 48.58.06.91, AE DC, 7 rm ℗ ⬚ ⬚ ♪ closed Dec-Feb, 600. Rest. ♦♦ *La Maison d'Hélène* ⬚ closed Tue, 1 Oct-15 Jun. In the park surrounding the château. Spec : *terrine de foies de volailles aux truffes, truite saumonée hollandaise*, 75-150; child : 25.

BANNEGON

Bourges 42, Nevers 57, Paris 269 km
pop 297 ⊠ 18210   B2

Hotel :
● ★★★ *Moulin de Chameron*, (R.S., L.F.), ☎ 48.61.83.80, Visa, 10 rm ℗ ⬚ ⬚ ⬚ ⬚ closed Thu (l.s.), 1 Jan-14 Mar, 3 Nov-31 Dec. A museum devoted to the milling trade in this 18th-C mill, 230. Rest. ♦♦ ♪ ⬚ 85-187.

Upper BERRY

                                    B1

From La Chapelle-d'Angillon to Saint-Martin-d'Auxigny *(approx. 50 km; 2 hr 30; see map 2)*

From the Paris-Bourges road, which runs straight through the Sologne, the gentle hills of Boischaut can be seen to the E as you approach the Pays-Fort and the district of Sancerre. Hedges, copses and thickets between stands of forest are steadily being cleared for open-field cultivation.

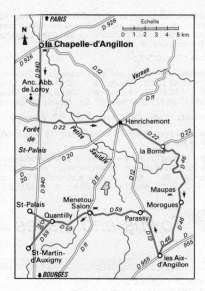

2. Upper Berry

▶ **La Chapelle-d'Angillon** : 15thC church, old houses; château de Béthune, 17thC mansion, 11thC keep *(9-12 & 2-6, closed Sun. am and Tue.)*. ▶ **Henrichemont**, a town started by the Duke of Sully (Prime Minister to Henri IV) but never completed; there are no important buildings. ▶ **La Borne** : a clay subsoil provides building material for half-timbered houses, as well as raw material for the local potters★, who for the past 20 years have been reviving a craft that brought renown to La Borne for more than three centuries. ▶ **Morogues** : the church (14thC) has a 15thC wooden canopy★; old houses. **Château de Maupas** (15thC, much restored) : important collection of ceramic plates★, mainly from Nevers and Moustiers *(1 Jul.-15 Sep., 10-12 & 1-7; rest of the year : 2-7, am Sun. and nat. hols.)*. ▶ **Aix-d'Angillon** church has a 12thC Burgundian choir. ▶ **Château de Menetou-Salon** (remodeled in 19thC; *Apr.-Oct., 10-11:45 & 2-6*); 15thC tapestries and, in the outbuildings, a collection of old cars. The local white wine is excellent. ▶ Get back on the road to Bourges at **Saint-Martin-d'Auxigny**. ▶ **Saint-Palais** *(3 km N)* : 12th-13thC church and grape-press (15thC).   □

Valley of the BESBRE

                                    C2-3

From Lapalisse to Dompierre *(36 km; 90 km with detours; half-day)*

The valley contains a surprising number of châteaux.

▶ **Lapalisse** (→). ▶ **Château de Gléné** : 4 km away, remodelled in 18thC (14thC towers). ▶ **Cindré** : 18thC château; 3 km S, château de Puyfol (15th-16thC). ▶ Pass château du Verger (left) and château de la Pouge (right) and continue to **Chavroches★** : ruins of a 13thC fortress surround a 15thC building. ▶ **Château du Vieux-Chambord★** : a square keep with turrets (13thC) towers over the 14th-16thC château. ▶ **Jaligny-sur-Besbre** : large Renaissance château; poultry market on Wed. ▶ Near **Chapeau**, 10 km WNW from Vaumas : château de la Cour (15th-16thC), a typical Bourbonnais structure with tapered black and red brick *(ext. visits all year)*. ▶ After **Vaumas** (15thC church with wooden porch), the 15thC **château de Beauvoir★** : gardens *(daily)* and a 17thC façade. ▶ **Château de Toury★**, a miniature fortress in pink granite

(15thC); hunting museum *(Apr.-Oct., Sat., Sun. and nat. hols., 10-12 & 2-6)*. ▶ **Dompierre-sur-Besbre**, the largest town in the valley; 5 km SW : **Le Pal** amusement park *(May-Sep., 10-7)* and game farm *(same hours and, off season, 11-dusk)*. Trappist **Abbey of Sept Fons** *(4 km N)*, audio-visual show only. **Beaulon** *(7 km N from Sept-Fons)* : regional museum *(Sun. and nat. hols. Jun.-Sep., 3-7)*. ◻

Practical Information

DOMPIERRE-SUR-BESBRE, ⊠ 03290, 19 km N of **Jaligny-sur-Besbre**.

Hotel :
★ **Paix** (L.F.), pl. du Commerce, ☎ 70.34.50.09, 10 rm ✒ closed Sun eve and Mon, 15 Oct-15 Nov, 100. Rest. ◆ 50-150.

BOURBON-L'ARCHAMBAULT

Moulins 48, Nevers 51, Paris 291 km
pop 2550 ⊠ 03160   C2
A spa whose origins lie in Celtic times; subsequently the seat of the Bourbons, who eventually became the largest royal family in Europe.

▶ Opposite the spa, the **Logis du Roi** (King's Lodgings) : built in 1645, now housing the SI and the Augustin-Bernard Museum (regional history, folk arts and customs; *15 Apr.-15 Oct., 3-6)*. ▶ Three of the 14thC **castle's** 24 towers★ remain; steps by the lake down to a rather disfigured 14thC fortified mill; view of the massive **Quiquengrogne Watchtower** (1317), remains of the external fortifications.

Nearby

▶ **Saint-Menoux** *(9 km E)* : a beautiful Romanesque church★ (12thC), carved decoration, capitals and frieze; choir★; stonework in the 11thC narthex; sarcophagus of St. Menoux in the choir. ▶ **Ygrande** *(10 km WSW)* : another 12thC church★ (octagonal 14thC bell-tower). ◻

Practical Information

ⓘ 1, pl. des Thermes, ☎ 70.67.09.79 (h.s.).   ♥

Hotel :
★★ **Thermes**, av. Ch.-Louis-Philippe, ☎ 70.67.00.15, 22 rm ⬭ closed 1 Nov-21 Mar, 205. Rest. ◆◆ ⬭ ♨ ✒ Traditional fare : *foie gras maison, noix de lotte florentine*, 65-148.

Restaurant :
◆ **L'Oustalet**, av. E.-Guillaumin, ☎ 70.67.01.48, Euro Visa ⬭ ♪ closed Fri eve and Sun eve , hol eves, 1-18 Mar, 12-30 Oct, 75-165.

⚠ ★★**Parc de Bignon** (157 pl), ☎ 70.67.08.83.

BOURBONNAIS Mountains

                                                          C3

Round trip from Châtel-Montagne *(approx. 90 km; half-day)*

▶ **Châtel-Montagne** : unusually well-preserved 12thC Romanesque church★★; 15thC houses. ▶ Drive to **Le Mayet-de-Montagne** and up the Sichon Valley. ▶ **Glozel** : a hamlet famous for prehistoric discoveries whose authenticity has been the subject of controversy (museum : *daily ex Sun. and nat. hols. out of season)*. ▶ Near **Ferrières** : Grotte des Fées (fairy cavern; *2 km downstream)*; chapel squeezed into a crack in the rock known as Pierre Encize *(2 km upstream)*. ▶ **Rocher Saint-Vincent** is 40 min. on foot from **Lavoine** (clog-making). ▶ **Puy de Montoncel** (alt. 1 287 m; view★), a 2-hr ride. ▶ The valley of the Boen leads to a ford at La Chaux, 2 km from the **Rocher de Rochefort** (view★). ▶ Hill road along the Monts de la Madeleine to La Trapière at the foot

of the **Pierre du Charbonnier** (alt. 1 031 m, panorama★). ▶ A little way off the route *(1.5 km to Biefs, then 30 min. on foot)* is the **Pisserotte waterfall**.   ◻

BOURGES★★★

Châteauroux 67, Orléans 106, Paris 227 km
pop 80379 ⊠ 18000   B1
The first landmark from any direction is the cathedral, standing watch over the tiled roofs on a low hill rising from the plain. Once past the plain suburbs of this industrial and administrative centre, beyond the junction of the Yèvre and Auron rivers, discover the picturesque streets of the old section; in this beautiful and historic city the religious reformer John Calvin studied law.

▶ **Cathedral★★★** (B-C3; *8-12 & 2-6:30, Jul.-Aug., 8-7)*, famous for its five doorways, is exceptionally beautiful; built between 1192 and 1324, with double side-aisles instead of a transept; carvings★ around the doorways (scenes from the Old and New Testaments, lives of the saints, a Last Judgment★★ on the central doorway) are from the apogee of Gothic art; a Romanesque doorway★ on either side. Stained glass★★ (13thC) in ambulatory and choir (prophets and apostles); 14thC window in the façade; 16thC window in the side chapels. The large crypt *(daily ex Sun. am and nat. hols. 9-10:2-6;* diaporama : "Trésors d'art du Cher") : 1543 Entombment of Christ; recumbent effigy of Jean Duke of Berry (15thC). Access to the N tower (view★; *same hours as the crypt)*. On the corner of Rue Molière is the 13thC **Grange aux Dîmes★** (tithe barn). ▶ **Rue Bourbonnoux** : 15th and 16thC houses, among the most attractive streets in Bourges. ▶ **Hôtel Lallement** (early 16thC) museum of decorative arts *(1 Apr.-15 Oct., 10-11:15 & 2-5:15; 16 Oct.-31 Mar., 10-11:15 & 2-4:15; closed Mon.)*. ▶ **Place Gordaine** : half-timbered houses (15thC). ▶ **Rue Mirabeau** (B2; pedestrian) : gabled dwellings. ▶ Passage to Rue Branly which leads to the **Hôtel des Échevins** (Council House; B2)★ : Renaissance building, octagonal staircase tower with bracketed arches. ▶ Next to the church of Notre-Dame (rebuilt in 1520), the **Maison de Pellevoysin**, a 15thC Gothic mansion in stone, surrounded by half-timbered houses; courtya'd at N° 3 Rue Cambournac. ▶ **Hôtel Cujas★**, built in 1515; it has an interior courtyard and corbelled turrets, and now houses the **Berry Museum★★** (prehistory, antiques, folk art and traditions : *10-11:30 & 2-5:30; ex Tue. and nat. hols.)*. ▶ **Palais de Justice** (courthouse; A3) : 17thC convent built by Jules Hardouin-Mansart (the architect who worked for 30 years on the Palace of Versailles; → Ile-de-France). ▶ **Palais Jacques Cœur★★** (B3) : situated on Gallo-Roman fortifications, which are partly visible. Jacques Cœur (→ box) built the palace in 1443-51; it is a superb example of Gothic civil architecture *(May-Oct., 9-11:15 & 2:15-5:15; Nov.-Apr., 10-11 & 2-4:15; closed nat. hols.)*. ▶ On Rue des Armuriers (16thC house at the corner of Rue d'Auron), the **Prefecture** (B4; 18thC), which incorporates part of the 15thC ducal palace where Louis XI was born. ▶ Follow the Rue du 95°-de-Ligne (11thC doorway★ at the corner of the Rampe Marceau), past the **Cultural Centre** (Maison de la Culture,1964) to the **Archepiscopal Gardens★** (Jardins de l'Archevêché; B-C4; view★ of the cathedral), in front of the town hall (hôtel de ville, 17thC).

▶ **Also...** ▶ The **church of St. Bonnet** (C2) : 16thC choir; 15th-16thC stained glass. ▶ The **Marais de la Voiselle** (the Voiselle Marshes) : the "water rats" (market gardeners) use flat-bottomed boats to get about. ▶ **Prés-Fichaux rose garden** (B1-2). ▶ The **Infirmary** (Hôtel-Dieu; A2) : Renaissance entrance; Maison de La Reine Blanche with carved wooden exterior (16thC). ▶ **Natural History Museum** *(Oct.-Mar., 2-5:30; Apr.-Sep. 2-6; closed Sat.)*, ornithological collection.

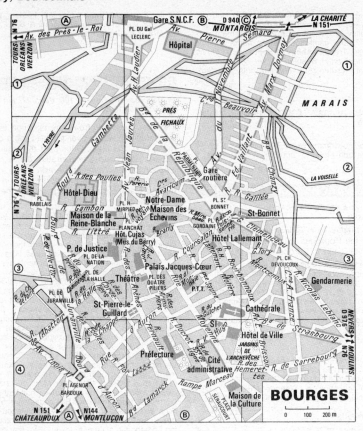

BOURGES

0   100   200 m

Nearby

▶ **Maubranches** *(12 km E on N151)* : 15th-17thC château★ *(ext. visits only)*. **Sainte-Solange** *(4.5 km NE)* : site of annual pilgrimage on Whit Monday ; Aubusson tapestries (1704) in the 12th-13thC church. ▶ **Savigny-en-Septaine** *(14 km SE on D976)* : 12thC church. **Avord** *(7.5 km farther)* : Romanesque doorway★ on church. ▶ **Jussy-Champagne** *(5.5 km S of Avord)* : 11th-12thC Romanesque church★ ; château★ *(1590-1650)* in Louis XIII style *(25 Mar.-15 Nov., 9-11:45 & 2-6:30)*. ▶ **Plaimpied** *(11 km SE on D106)* : 15thC buildings and Romanesque church★ with fine capitals, remainder of an abbey.   □

Practical Information

ⓘ pl. E.-Dolet (B4), ☎ 48.24.75.33, closed Sun (l.s.).
SNCF (B1), ☎ 48.65.50.50/48.70.10.52.
▒▒▒ *Le Prado* (A3), ☎ 48.24.36.42.
Car rental : *Avis*, train station (B1) ; 23,av. H.-Laudier (B1), ☎ 48.24.38.84.

Hotels :

★★★ *Angleterre*, 1, pl. des Quatre-Piliers, ☎ 48.24.68.51, AE DC Euro Visa, 31 rm ℙ ♪ closed 20 Dec-20 Jan, 280. Rest. ♦ ♪ ⦸ 60-130.
★★ *Grand Argentier*, 9, rue Parerie (Avaricum) (B2), ☎ 48.70.84.31, AE DC Visa, 14 rm ℙ ◔ ◈ closed 22 Dec-31 Jan. 15th-C house, 205. Rest. ♦ ♪ ⅋ closed Mon noon and Sun eve. Generous portions of family-style food served on the flowery terrace, 75-120.
★★ *Les Tilleuls*, 7, pl. de la Pyrotechnie (C4),

Jacques Cœur

Jacques Cœur *(cœur : heart)* was without doubt the greatest financier of his age. Born in modest circumstances at Bourges in 1395, he demonstrated a gift for commerce and built an immense fortune, becoming expert in trade with the East. His wealth was such that he was able to support the State of France out of his own pocket after the Treaty of Troyes ceded most of northern France to the English in 1420. Charles VII appointed Cœur minister of finance in 1436, and in 1441 ennobled him. He carried out important commissions for the king and won fame and honours, but his success and magnificent mode of living aroused jealousy at the court, leading to downfall and imprisonment in 1451. Inspired by his motto, "To the valiant Heart, nothing is impossible", he escaped from France and entered the service of the Pope, who put him in command of a fleet against the Turks. He died at Chios in Greece in 1456.

☎ 48.20.49.04, Tx 782026, DC Euro Visa, 29 rm ℙ ▦ ♪ 180.
★★ *Monitel*, (Inter-Hôtel) 73, rue Barbès (A4), ☎ 48.50.23.62, Tx 783397, AE DC Euro Visa, 48 rm ℙ closed 24 Dec-2 Jan, 200. Rest. ♦ *La Braisière* ᕷ closed Sat noon, 65-100.

★★ *Saint-Jean*, 23, av. M.-Dormoy (C1), ☎ 48.24.13.48, Euro Visa, 24 rm P closed 1 Feb-1 Mar, 110.

Restaurants :
● ♦♦♦ *Jacques Cœur*, 3, pl. J.-Cœur (B3), ☎ 48.70.12.72, AE DC Visa ⟨ ♪ closed Sat and Sun eve, 14 Jul-13 Aug, 24 Dec-2 Jan. Classic cuisine signed F.Bernard : *coquilles Saint-Jacques sautées, rognons de veau, saumon frais,* Cher wines, 170-210.
♦♦ *L'Ile d'Or*, 39, bd Juranville (A3), ☎ 48.24.29.15, AE DC Euro Visa ♪ & closed Mon noon and Sun, 1-16 Mar, 1-16 Sep, 80-200.

⚠ ★★*Municipal* (75 pl), ☎ 48.20.16.85.

Recommended
Youth hostel : 22, rue Henri-Sellier, ☎ 48.24.58.09.
♥ candy : *la Maison des Forestines*, 3, pl. Cujas (A-B3), ☎ 48.24.00.24, delicious praline-filled bonbons ; ceramics : *M. Levêque*, 9, av. E.-Renan, ☎ 48.20.07.92 ; enamels, jewelry : *Boutique des Artisans*, 89, rue d'Auron, ☎ 48.24.59.66 ; pastry, tea room : *Aux Trois Flûtes*, 13, rue Bourbonnoux, ☎ 48.24.24.28.

La BRENNE

(The Brenne Marshes)
A2

Malaria was endemic here until the 19thC, despite attempts — as far back as the 13thC — to drain the marshes. Waterholes left from these unsuccessful efforts have been turned to good purpose as bird sanctuaries and recreation areas.

▶ **Mézières-en-Brenne** : 14thC church★, 15thC choir stalls ; 14th and 16thC stained glass. ▶ **Paulnay** *(6 km NW of Mézières)* : Romanesque church★. **Azay-le-Ferron**★ *(12 km)* : **château** blending architectural styles of the 15th to the 19thC *(Apr.-Sep. : daily ex Tue., 10-12 & 2-6 ; rest of the year, Wed., Sat. and Sun., 10-12 & 2-6 ; closed 11 Nov.-25 Dec.)*; Empire (Napoléon I, ca. 1800) furnishings★. ☐

Round trip *(35 km)*
From **Subtray** *(3 km E from Mézières)*, take route D 14ᴮ (on your right, château de Beauregard). ▶ Further on, **château du Bouchet**★ (13th, 15th, 16thC ; *Jul.-15 Sep.* on request, ☎ 54.37.80.14) ; to the S, the great **étang de la Mer Rouge** (190 ha lake). ☐

BRINON-SUR-SAULDRE

Orléans 57, Bourges 64, Paris 188 km
pop 1249 ⊠ 18410
B1

Hotel :
★★ *Solognote*, (L.F., R.S.), Grande-Rue, ☎ 48.58.50.29, Euro Visa, 10 rm P ⸱⸱⸱ closed Tue eve in season and Wed, 1-28 Feb, 11-21 May, 15-30 Sep, 220. Rest. ● ♦♦ closed Tue eve and Wed. Good cooking by G. Dominique in a pleasant country inn : *petit salé de canard en potée, salade tiède de Saint-Jacques*, 130-220.

Recommended
Bicycle-rental : at Argent-sur-Sauldre, *M. D. Trémeau*, pl. du Marché, ☎ 48.73.60.04.
Events : at Argent-sur-Sauldre, *rose festival*, last Sun in May.

CHÂTEAUNEUF-SUR-CHER

Bourges 26, Montluçon 71, Paris 263 km
pop 1663 ⊠ 18190
B2

Château★ (16th-17thC), Renaissance carving in the courtyard ; French Regency, Louis XIV and Louis XVI furniture *(ca. 1650-1790)* ; antique copper kitchenware★ ; zoo park *(Apr.-Oct., daily 10-12 & 2-7 ; rest of the year, Sat., Sun. and nat. hols 2-5)*.

Nearby
▶ *Lignières (16 km SW)* : remodelled Romanesque church (15thC stalls) ; château★ rebuilt in 1660. **Château du Plaix** : museum of folk art and traditions (costumes ; *Sun. 3-8, 24 Jun.-29 Sep.*). ☐

CHÂTEAUROUX

Bourges 67, Guéret 89, Paris 269 km
pop 53967 ⊠ 36000
A2

Manufactory of the "Gitane", the French cigarette made from black tobacco, with an aroma more like that of a cigar. SEITA (the French tobacco monopoly ; *vis. on request, tel.* 54.34.33.86) produces more than 30 million/day, not far from château Raoul (15thC) which gave the town its name. View★ of the Indre River from the Pont-Neuf.

▶ **Museum** *(daily ex Mon. 9:30-12 & 2-6 Jun.-Sep. ; 2-6 rest of year ;* archaeology, Napoleonic memorabilia, fine arts, local folklore). ▶ **Déols** : once the site of a powerful abbey ; 12thC bell-tower★★ ; 3rdC marble sarcophagus in the church crypt. ☐

Practical Information _____

ℹ pl. de la Gare, ☎ 54.34.10.74.
🚆 **SNCF** ☎ 54.27.50.50/54.34.44.17/54.22.13.22.
🚌 ☎ 54.22.13.22.
Car rental : *Avis*, 72, av. de Paris, ☎ 54.27.45.46 ; Train station.

Hotel :
★★★ *Elysée Hôtel*, 2, rue de la République, ☎ 54.22.33.66, AE DC Euro Visa, 18 rm P ⸱⸱⸱ closed Sun, 15 Aug, Christmas, hols, 280.

Restaurants :
● ♦♦♦ *Jean-Louis Dumonet (ex Jean Bardet)*, 1, rue Jean Jacques Rousseau, ☎ 54.34.82.69. Like father, like son : Jean-Louis Dumonet, offspring of Sailor Jean of the Parisian restaurant Joséphine, has taken over the kitchen lately occupied by Jean Bardet, now in Tours. The tradition of good food goes on. Rooms available at neighboring hotel Elysée, 120-300.
● ♦ *Ciboulette*, 42, rue Grande, ☎ 54.27.66.28, Euro Visa ♪ closed Mon and Sun, 55-115.

⚠ ★★★★*du Rochat* (100 pl), ☎ 54.34.26.56.

Recommended
Events : *annual fair*, exhibits, parade of flowered floats, mid-sep ; *spring fair*, Art and gastronomy show (early May) ; *Cheese festival*, Aug ; *Saint-Christophe's pilgrimage*, Sun after 14 Jul ; *pilgrimage to the Bonne-Dame-du-Chêne*, (forêt de Châteauroux), Mon after Pentecost.
♥ jewelry : *D. Prudhomme*, 11, rue Cazala, ☎ 54.34.03.11 ; wood sculpture : *J. Loyrette*, ☎ 54.27.11.44, (by appt.).

CHÂTILLON-SUR-INDRE

Châteauroux 67, Blois 76, Paris 256 km
pop 3560 ⊠ 36700
A1

A market town on one of the rare hills in this generally flat landscape.

▶ 12thC Romanesque **church** with graphically carved capitals★ (doorway, pillars in nave, columns in windows and arcades). ▶ The mantled **keep** is all that remains of the 11th-12thC castle *(9 or 10-12 & 2-4 or 7)*.

Nearby
▶ Near Clion *(6.5 km SE)* : château de l'**Isle-Savary**★ (15thC). ▶ **Palluau-sur-Indre** *(12 km SE)* : 12th-15thC château★ (restored ; *vis. on request*) ; 12th-16thC church with stained glass, stalls, statuary★ from 16thC. ▶ Continuing up the Indre Valley, **Saint-Genou** : the choir and transept,

in the purest Berrichon Romanesque style (12thC) are all that remains of the church (interesting capitals). ☐

Practical Information _____

ⓘ 81, rue Grande, ☎ 54.38.70.96.
SNCF ☎ 54.38.71.63.

Hotel :
★ *Auberge de la Promenade*, 88, rue Grande, ☎ 54.38.71.95, Euro Visa, 7 rm Ⓟ ◌ closed Sun eve , Wed ex summer, 1-15 Jun, 1-15 Oct, 105. Rest. ◆ ♪ ♿ 50-125.

La CHÂTRE

Châteauroux 36, Montluçon 62, Paris 301 km
pop 5142 ⊠ 36400   B2

Little changed since the novelist George Sand (→ box) wrote about it more than a century ago : square tower, remains of the seigneurial castle, and a gate-tower serving as belfry and porch for the church.

▶ Tower : now the **Museum of George Sand and the Vallée Noire** *(daily ex Thu. am; 9:30-11:30 & 2-5:30, Apr.-15 Oct.; Wed., Sun. and nat. hols. 3-6 rest of year)* : life and work of the writer; ornithological collection; view★ from the tower.

The Vallée Noire (Black Valley) : George Sand country *(round trip, sign-posted; approx. 85 km; half-day; see map 1)*

▶ **Nohant★★★** : a centre of the Romantic movement, and a memorial to George Sand. The large 18thC mansion surrounded by greenery was home to the writer for more than 40 years *(9 or 10-11:45 & 2-4 or 6; closed Tue., nat. hols. and Wed. ex Apr.-Sep.).* ▶ **Vic** : Romanesque church★ (11th-12thC) has exceptional 12thC frescos★★ that were saved by the efforts of George Sand. ▶ A little off the route, **Saint-Chartier** : 15thC château, where every July an international gathering of lutenists and bellringers is held. ▶ **Verneuil-sur-Igneraie** : a village of potters. ▶ **Berthenoux** : large Romanesque church with sculpted capitals★ ; 18thC *trompe-l'œil* paintings. ▶ **Thévet-Saint-Julien** : church of St. Martin (12thC); frescos★★ more beautiful than those at Vic. ▶ Château du Magnet (15th-16thC). ▶ **Lys-Saint-Georges** : 15thC castle★ surrounded by moats ; ruined 12thC keep *(ext. visit).* ▶ **Neuvy-Saint-Sépulchre**, named for the circular church★ (late 11th-12thC) modelled on that of the Holy Sepulchre in Jerusalem. ▶ **Château de Sarzay★** : massive 14thC keep *(daily ex Tue., 10-12 & 2-7 Apr.-Sep.).* ▶ **Château de Montgivray**, once the property of Solange, daughter of George Sand ; campsite in the park.

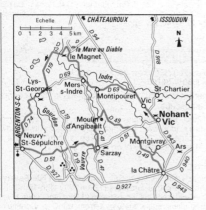

1. George Sand territory

South of La Châtre *(round trip approx. 60 km; 2 hr 30)*

▶ **Chassignoles :** bell-tower on the church. ▶ **Saint-Denis-du-Jouhet :** 12th-13thC stained glass in the choir. ▶ **Crevant :** above the church doorway, 15thC bas-relief (Adoration of the Magi). ▶ **Sainte-Sévère-sur-Indre :** ruined keep ; charming market square (1696 covered market★ ; 1543 stone cross). ▶ **La Motte-Feuilly :** church (15th-16thC), remarkable recumbent effigy (1521) of Charlotte d'Albret whose château★ (14th-15thC) stands by the lake.   ☐

_____

George Sand

George Sand was born Aurore Dupin, the great-granddaughter of the Maréchal de Saxe (brilliant military commander in the service of Louis XV). In 1808, at the age of five, after the sudden death of her father, Aurore was taken to live at Nohant with her grandmother. She married the Baron Dudevant, a man of gloomy disposition, but often found a chance to slip away to dances with the villagers at La Châtre, sometimes even accompanying poachers on their rounds. Throughout 40 years of upheavals, Nohant remained her safe harbour, and she drew extensively on her childhood haunts to add colour and depth to her writings. At Nohant she entertained the cultural elite of her day, including Liszt and Marie d'Agoult, Delacroix, Balzac, Chopin, Flaubert, Turgenev and many others. George Sand (the pen-name she adopted with her first novel) remained close to the peasant friends of her childhood, providing both financial and medical help (she studied anatomy and herbal medicine). At her death in 1876, she was mourned throughout the countryside.

_____

Practical Information _____

La CHÂTRE
ⓘ sq. G.-Sand, ☎ 54.48.22.64 (h.s.).
SNCF ☎ 54.48.00.06.

Hotels :
★★ *Les Tanneries*, Pont du Lion-d'Argent, ☎ 54.48.21.00, Tx 130960, AE DC Visa, 10 rm Ⓟ ◌ ◌ 200. Rest. ◆ ◌ ♪ closed Mon and Sun eve, 80-130.
★★ *Lion d'Argent* (L.F.), 2, av. du Lion-d'Argent, ☎ 54.48.11.69, Tx 130960, AE Euro Visa, 26 rm Ⓟ 135. Rest. ◆ ♪ 50-70 ; child : 30.
★★ *Notre-Dame* (L.F.), pl. Notre-Dame, ☎ 54.48.01.14, AE DC Euro Visa, 17 rm Ⓟ ◌ ◌ ♪ ◌ closed 25 Dec-1 Jan, 185.

Restaurant :
◆ *Poste*, 10, rue Basse-du-Mouhet, ☎ 54.48.05.62, AE DC Euro Visa ◌ ◌ ♪ ♿ closed Mon and Sun eve, 15-22 Jun, 10-30 Sep, 25-31 Dec, 75-120.

▲ at Montgivray, 4 km N., ★★*Solange Sand* (100 pl), ☎ 54.48.11.09.

Recommended
Events : *Lute-makers and bell-ringers*, 14 Jul; *Dog show*, Aug; at Cluis, *fête du Luma*, in May.

Nearby

NOHANT-VIC, ⊠ 36400, 8 km N.

Hotel :
★ *Petite Fadette*, ☎ 54.31.01.48, 15 rm Ⓟ ◌ ◌ 150. Rest. ◆ ♪ 70-120.

Recommended
Events : *festival des fêtes romantiques de Nohant*, in Jun (concert).
Son et lumière : entertainment at the château (in summer).

SAINT-CHARTIER, ⊠ 36400 La Châtre, 9 km N.

Hotel :
● ★★ *La Vallée Bleue*, (C.H., L.F.), rte de Verneuil, ☎ 54.31.01.91, Euro Visa, 13 rm P ⧉ ∰ ⊕ closed Sun eve and Mon (l.s.) ex hols, 15 Jan-28 Feb, 200. Rest. ◆ ⧉ ⊗ The charm of an old dwelling and family-style fare, 90-130 ; child : 50.

CHEVAGNES

Nevers 74, Vichy 74, Paris 314 km
pop 719 ⊠ 03230   C2

Hotel :
★ *Cheval-Blanc*, rte Nationale, ☎ 70.43.40.15, Euro Visa, 18 rm P ∰ ⊕ closed 20 Dec-15 Jan. Beside the river, 115. Rest. ◆ 50-100.

CREUSE Gorges*

                          A2
From Argenton to Fresselines *(62 km ; half-day)*
There is no single, continuous road running the length of the Creuse Valley. Numerous dams that have halted the flow of rushing streams by no means detract from the natural beauty of the area.
▶ **Argenton-sur-Creuse** (→). Drive up the right river bank past **Menoux** : old church, the interior covered with brightly-coloured paintings★ of Hell and Paradise by the Columbian painter Carasco (1976). ▶ View★ over the valley from **Chocats.** ▶ **Gargilesse★** : old gateway with two towers ; ancient château ; church★ (12thC) with some of the finest capitals★★ in Berry ; in the crypt, 13th, 15th, 16thC frescos ; Villa Algira : once George Sand's, now a museum *(Easter-30 Sep, 9:30 or 10-12 or 12:30 & 2 or 2:30-6 or 7)*. ▶ Near Pommiers *(7 km from Gargilesse)* : **château du Châtelier★** (15th-16thC ; *exit. visits 9-12 & 2-5, closed Sat., Sun. and nat. hols., Sep.-Mar.)*. ▶ View of the valley from the ruined **château de Châteaubrun** (13thC). ▶ **Éguzon** forms a lake★ 15 km long on the Creuse ; panorama★ from the viewing-area *(access by D45A)*. 11 km E of the dam, **château de Breuil-Yvain** (15th-18thC ; *exit. visits Aug.-15-Sep., 9-12 & 2-6)*. ▶ **Éguzon** : castle ruins. ▶ **Crozant** : near the S end of the lake, ruins of an 11th-15thC fortress *(entrance fee ; Easter-Oct.)*. ▶ From **Fresselines**, between the Grande and the Petite Creuses, it is a 15-min walk to the junction of the two streams : site★.   ▯

Practical Information _____
CROZANT, ⊠ 23160 Saint-Sébastien, 10 km S of **Eguzon**.

Hotel :
★*Lac*, pont du Crozant, ☎ 55.89.81.96, 10 rm P ⧉ ⊕ ⊗ ♪, closed Oct-Mar, 130. Rest. ◆ ⧉ ♪ 45-100.
⚑★★ *Font bonne* (33 pl), ☎ 55. 89.80.34.

CULAN

Guéret 68, Châteauroux 69, Paris 302 km
pop 1055 ⊠ 18270   B2

▶ 13th-15thC **castle★** with rare wooden galleries on the towers ; well-appointed interior, tapestry collection★ (15th-17thC ; *9-11:30 & 2-5, 6:30 in season ; closed Wed. ex in season)*.

Nearby
▶ **Vesdun** *(6.5 km E)* : claimed by some as the exact centre of France, a lively village with many exhibitions and events. **Saint-Désiré** *(5 km S of Vesdun)* : Romanesque church (11th-12thC) enhanced by the use of pink and ochre sandstone ; eastern end, crypt. ▶ **Châteaumeillant** *(12 km W)*, a small market town surrounded by vineyards (sign-posted route), producing V.D.Q.S (government clas-

sification as *"Vins Délimités de Qualité Supérieure"*, i.e. not top-grade, but pleasant to drink and often good value) white, red and rosé wines ; the 12thC church★ of St.-Genès is noteworthy for six apsidal chapels on each side of the choir, graphically carved capitals. Émile Chenon Museum : archaeological museum in 14th-16thC house *(10-12 & 2-6, 15 Jun.-15 Sep.)*. ▶ **Saint-Jeanvrin** *(5 km NE)* : Romanesque church by a lake. ▶ **Châtelet** *(12 km from Châteaumeillant)* : another beautiful Romanesque church.   ▯

Practical Information _____
SNCF ☎ 48.56.60.59.

Hotel :
★ *La Poste*, Grande-Rue, ☎ 48.56.66.57, 14 rm P ⧉ closed Mon, 3 Jan-15 Feb, 120. Rest. ◆ ⧉ ⊗ 40-85.
⚑ ★*La Guinguette* (35 pl), ☎ 48.56.64.57.

Recommended
♥ crafts : M. Prudhomme, rue du Château, ☎ 48.56.63.91, art objects ; at Saint-Maur, painting on silk : M. Cl. Baramin, "lavret", ☎ 48.56.74.24, lessons.

ÉBREUIL

Montluçon 58, Moulins 66, Paris 360 km
pop 1224 ⊠ 03450   C3

▶ This town grew up around an abbey whose 18thC buildings are now a hospital (collection of pharmacist's jars★). ▶ The church is Auvergne Romanesque ; 12thC statues★ in the narthex, frescos★ in the gallery.

Nearby
▶ **Saint-Quintin-sur-Sioule** *(4 km SW)* : 12th-13thC castle incorporating a 10thC Romanesque chapel *(Jul.-Sep., 10-12 & 2-7)*. ▶ **Gannat** *(10 km E)* : 12th-14thC castle, now a museum *(Jun.-Sep., 3-7 ; closed Mon.)* : gospel★ with 10th-12thC bindings ; crafts, etc. ; the Gothic church incorporates a Romanesque building (capitals★). ▶ From **Vicq** *(4 km N ; Romanesque church)*, go to see the church★ at **Veauce** (11thC, eastern end★), also the 14th-15thC château, poorly restored *(10:30-12 & 2:30-6 ; closed 5 Dec.-5 Jan.)*. ▶ NE on D350 **château de Rochefort★** (13th-15thC ; *4 km)*.

Sioule Gorges *(18 km to Pont de Menat)*
▶ D915 climbs to a cliff road above the left river bank before droppping to the foot of a 13thC château and village of **Chouvigny★**, also the name of the most beautiful part of the Gorges.★ ▶ Continue to **Pont de Menat**, a mediaeval hump-backed bridge close to the ruined **Château-Rocher** (11thC, refortified in 13thC ; *Jun.-Sep., 9-12 & 2-7 ; Nov.-Apr., 2-5)*. ▶ The excursion into Auvergne can be extended to Châteauneuf-les-Bains (→ Auvergne).   ▯

Practical Information _____
ÉBREUIL
ℹ Hôtel-de-ville, ☎ 70.90.71.33.   ♥

Hotel :
★★ *Commerce*, rue des Fossés, ☎ 70.90.72.66, 20 rm P ∰ ⊕ ⊗ closed Mon, Oct, 120. Rest. ◆ 60-100.
⚑ ★★★★*La Filature* (50 pl), ☎ 70.90.72.01 ; ★★*Les Nières* (33 pl), ☎ 70.90.71.33.

Nearby
GANNAT, ⊠ 03800, 10 km E.
ℹ pl. Rantian, ☎ 70.90.17.78.
SNCF ☎ 70.90.01.41.

Hotels :
★ *Château*, 9, pl. Rantian, ☎ 70.90.00.88, 10 rm P ♪ closed Jan. Rest. ◆ 80-130.
★ *L'Agriculture*, 3, pl. Rantian, ☎ 70.90.00.17, 28 rm P closed Mon, Oct-May. Rest. ◆ 70-130.
⚑ ★★*Municipal* (66 pl), ☎ 70.90.12.16.

FONTGOMBAULT**

Châteauroux 68, Poitiers 68, Paris 296 km
pop 267 ⊠ 36220   A2

▶ The abbey **church★** (11th-12thC, 19thC nave) is an important centre of Gregorian chant *(mass at 10:15, vespers at 6 daily, 5 Sun. and hols.)*; splendid Romanesque choir★★ with double side aisles and ambulatory with three radiating chapels; capitals★ with carved foliage; 15thC convent buildings. ▶ **Le Blanc** *(8 km SE)* : view★ from the upper town; Romanesque bell-tower of St-Génitour; ornithological museum *(1st and 3rd Sat., Jun.-Sep., 3-6).*   ☐

Practical Information

Nearby
Le **BLANC**, ⊠ 36300, 8 km SE.
⎀ pl. de la Libération, ☎ 54.37.05.13 (h.s.); hôtel de ville, ☎ 54.37.23.40.
SNCF ☎ 54.37.07.01.

Hotel :
● ★★ **Domaine de l'Etape** (C.H.), rte de Belâbre, ☎ 54.37.18.02, AE DC Euro Visa, 21 rm ℙ ≮ ⚱ ◿ Private 44-acre pond, 180. Rest. ◆ evening only, 50-75.

Recommended
Events : summer concerts. Early Sep : Bons Saints pilgrimage. Nov : St Martin's fair.
Sports : *Villa Varsovie*, 73, rue de la République, ☎ 54.37.29.03, Sports and leisure. Fishing; *La Virevolte*, *domaine du Fresne-Douadic*, ☎ 54.37.10.28, horse riding and pony club.
♥ Enamel jewelry : *A. Jubard*, Les Chezeaux, rte d'Avant, ☎ 54.37.32.17; sculpture and pottery : *F. Taillandier*, 16, quai Aubépin, rte de Belâbre, ☎ 54.37.17.94.

ISSOUDUN

Châteauroux 29, Bourges 38, Paris 243 km
pop 15166 ⊠ 36100   B2

An ancient stronghold at the confluence of two rivers on the edge of the plateau.

▶ The **belfry★** (12th-14thC) was formerly part of the city gate, and is flanked by two towers of unequal size. ▶ **Tour Blanche★** (White Tower) : cylindrical keep 27 m high, built by Richard the Lion-Heart (King of England, 1189-99; his territory included all of western France); panorama★ as far as Bourges *(38 km).* ▶ **Church of St-Cyr** : 16thC stained-glass★ in the choir. ▶ **Museum★** in the former Hospice St-Roch (almshouse; *10-12 & 2-7 daily ex Tue.)* : fine buildings, dispensary★ (379 pharmacist's jars in Nevers earthenware); chapel with two (originally four) 16thC carved Trees of Jesse★ (genealogies of Christ).

Nearby
▶ **Charost** *(12 km NE)* : 19thC château (remains of 13thC keep), Romanesque church, 14 km NE, **château de Castelnau★** (16thC). **Chezal-Benoît** *(17 km SE)* : only the nave remains of the 12thC abbey church (carved foliage on capitals★); the 18thC abbey buildings now house a psychiatric hospital; walks in the **Chœurs-Bommiers forest★; Bommiers** : 12thC church (stalls★ from 1515, capitals).

Practical Information

⎀ pl. du Dr-Guilpain, ☎ 54.21.13.23.
SNCF ☎ 54.21.01.54.

Hotels :
★★★ **Auberge La Cognette** (R.S.), 26, rue des Minimes, ☎ 54.21.21.83, AE DC Euro Visa, 14 rm ℙ ◿ ⎖ ふ closed 4-26 Jan, 31 Aug-17 Sep, 300. Rest. ● ◆◆◆ ⎖ closed Mon and Sun eve ex hols, 4-26 Jan, 31 Aug-17 Sep, 110-320.

★★★ **France Commerce**, 3, rue P.-Brossolette, ☎ 54.21.00.65, Tx 751422, AE DC Euro Visa, 24 rm ℙ ≮ ⚱ ◿ ふ closed 21 Jan-1 Mar, 255. Rest. ◆ **les Trois Rois** ≮ ⎖ 50-190; child : 50.
★ **Berry**, 88, rue P.-Brossolette, ☎ 54.21.20.51, 16 rm ℙ ⚱ closed Sun eve (l.s.) and Xmas hols (l.s.), 140.

Recommended
Events : wine fair, Apr.

LAPALISSE*

Moulins 50, Clermont-Ferrand 79, Paris 344 km
pop 3673 ⊠ 03120   C3

Lapalisse offers the discreet charm of its river and the historic celebrity of its castle : the main building of this Italianate Renaissance château (15th-16thC) is built against the original 11th-13thC castle and a Gothic chapel; inside, paintings, furnishings★ from Renaissance to Empire, 15thC Flemish tapestries★★ *(Palm Sunday-1 Nov., 9-12 & 2-6; closed Tue. ex Jun.-Aug.).*

Nearby
▶ **Saint-Gérand-le-Puy** *(9 km W)* : 12thC church with 13thC frescos; 5 km N from here are the spectacular ruins of the château de **Montaigu-le-Blin** (14thC; restoration in progress; *visits during school hols.).* In the town hall, small historical museum *(open Sun. pm in summer).* ▶ **Montaiguët-en-Forez** *(15 km E)* : 15thC city gate and castle *(ext. visits daily).*   ☐

Practical Information

⎀ pl. Ch.-Bécaud, ☎ 70.99.08.39 (h.s.); ☎ 70.99.00.86.
SNCF ☎ 70.99.00.42.

Hotel :
★★ **Galland**, 20, pl. de la République, ☎ 70.99.07.21, Euro Visa, 8 rm ℙ closed Wed, Jan, 180. Rest. ◆ 50-200.

Recommended
Events : *La mémoire du Temps*, at the château, ☎ 70.99.22.65, entertainment every Fri and Sat night in Jul-Aug.

LEVROUX

Blois 76, Châteauroux 96, Paris 257 km
pop 3126 ⊠ 36110   A2

▶ 13thC **church★** built on the ruins of the Roman governor's palace; 15thC statues and organ casing★. ▶ Near the church, wooden houses and tiled gateway (Porte de Champagne; 1435-1506).

Nearby
▶ **Château de Bouges** *(9 km NE)* : 18thC building, furniture★; park; in the outbuildings, collection of saddles, harnesses★ and horse-drawn carriages *(daily 9 or 10-12 & 2-6, Apr.-Oct.; closed Tue. ex Jul. and Aug.; Wed. pm, Sat. and Sun. rest of year).* ▶ **Villegongis★** *(9 km S)* : 16thC château, architecture and decoration similar to Chambord (→), although on a lesser scale *(ext. visits free).*   ☐

Practical Information

Hotel :
★★ **La Cloche** (L.F.), 3, rue Nationale, ☎ 54.35.70.43, Euro Visa, 28 rm ℙ ふ closed Mon eve and Tue, 15 Feb-15 Mar, 200. Rest. ◆ ⎖ ふ 50-105.

In preparing for your trip, consult the pages pertaining to the regions. You will find there the description of the region you wish to visit, as well as a list of sites that must be seen, a brief history and practical information.

MEHUN-SUR-YÈVRE

Bourges 17, Châteauroux 61, Paris 226 km
pop 7178 ⊠ 18500 B1

Once the favourite of Jean, Duke of Berry (→ Brief regional history), Mehun today is a small industrial center for porcelain and ceramics.

▶ A tower★ of the 14thC château houses a **museum** *(10-12 & 2-7:30 ex Tue. Jul.-Aug.; Sun. Jun. and Oct.; Apr., Mon. and weekends only, 10-12 & 2:30-5:30).* ▶ 16thC Porte de l'Horloge (Clock Gate). ▶ 11thC-12thC church. ▶ Visits to porcelain factory. □

Practical Information

ℹ pl. du 14-Juillet, ☎ 48.57.35.51 (h.s.).
SNCF ☎ 48.57.30.22.

Hotel :
★ ***La Croix Blanche*** (L.F.), 164, rue Jeanne-d'Arc, ☎ 48.57.30.01, Visa, 20 rm Ⓟ half pens (h.s.), closed Sun eve and Mon, 20 Dec-20 Jan, 260. Rest. ♦ ♿ 50-95; child : 30.

MONTLUÇON

Clermont-Ferrand 91, Bourges 93, Paris 320 km
pop 51765 ⊠ 03100 B2-3

Until the 19thC this was a very small town perched on a hill. The opening of the Berry Canal and the development of local coal-mines rapidly industrialized and greatly enlarged the town.

▶ Grand'Rue (numerous 15th-16thC houses) leads to the 15thC **church of Notre-Dame** (15thC statues★). ▶ Château of the dukes of Bourbon (15th-16thC, much restored) houses the **Musée de la Vielle** (hurdy-gurdy museum; *15 Mar.-15 Oct., 10-12 & 2-6 ex Tue.; 16 Oct.-14 Mar., 2-6 ex Mon. and Tue.)* : hurdy-gurdies★ and ceramics; archaeology; history; folklore. From the terrace, view★ over the city. ▶ **Church of St. Pierre :** Romanesque and 15thC; 16thC statues and 15thC wooden crucifix. ▶ Every Saturday, flower market in the streets of Old Montluçon.

Nearby

▶ **Domérat** *(6 km NW) :* Romanesque church with 11thC crypt. ▶ **Huriel (***6 km further) :* 12thC church. Two 15thC towers and a magnificent square keep (105 steps; view★; *8:30-6 ex Sat. and Sun.*) are all that remains of the castle. ▶ **Magnette** *(5 km N) :* a warehouse and a barge are the main attractions at the museum of water transport on the Berry canal *(end Jul.-early Sep., Sat., Sun. and 15 Aug., 2-8).* □

Practical Information

MONTLUÇON
ℹ 1ter, av. Max-Dormoy, ☎ 70.05.05.92.
SNCF ☎ 70.05.05.50/70.28.19.02.
🚌 quai Rouget-de-Lisle, ☎ 70.05.39.97.
Car rental : *Avis*, 30, rue A.-Allier, ☎ 70.05.59.02; train station.

Hotels :
★★★ ***Château Saint-Jean*** (C.H.), parc Saint-Jean, rte de Clermont-Ferrand, ☎ 70.05.04.65, 8 rm Ⓟ Historic dwelling, 350. Rest. ♦♦♦ ♪ 125-230.
● ★★ ***Saint-Victor***, 6 km rte de Bourges, N 144, ☎ 70.28.80.64, AE Euro Visa, 28 rm Ⓟ ♿ 155. Rest. ♦ ♪ ♿ Spec : *coq au vin d'Auvergne, pâté de pommes de terre à la crème fraîche*, 50-90.
★ ***Hostellerie du Théâtre***, 1, rue de la Croix-Verte, ☎ 70.05.07.27, AE Euro Visa, 8 rm pens, closed Sun, 5-25 Jul, 310. Rest. ♦ ♪ ♿ 45-90; child : 30.

Restaurants :
♦♦ ***Ducs de Bourbon***, 47, av. Max-Dormoy, ☎ 70.05.22.79 ♪ closed Mon and Sun eve. Louis-XVI dining room and an English-style pub, 75-150.
♦♦ ***Le Grenier à Sel***, 10, rue Notre-Dame, ☎ 70.05.53.79, AE DC Visa, closed Mon and Sun eve, 1-15 Aug. 17th-C decor. Refined regonal dishes. Spec : *ris de veau aux morilles, cassolette de grenouilles à la crème d'ail et cresson*, 100-240.

Nearby

DOMÉRAT, ⊠ 03410, 6 km NW.

Hotel :
★★ ***Novelta*** (L.F.), rte de Guéret, ☎ 70.03.34.88, Euro Visa, 40 rm Ⓟ 225. Rest. ♦ ♪ ♿ closed Sun eve, 1-20 Aug. Family-style cooking, good value, 60-110.

MOULINS*

Clermont-Ferrand 96, Bourges 98, Paris 294 km
pop 25548 ⊠ 03000 C2

At the end of the 15thC, Moulins became the capital of the Duchy of Bourbon and was for a while a centre of cultural activity.

▶ Rue d'Allier (B2) : the busiest street, lined with 15th and 16thC mansions. ▶ Rue de l'Horloge : **bell-tower** (1455) topped with a gallery and a 16thC belfry; mechanical figures (the Jacquemart family) strike the hours and quarters. ▶ Left of the tower, **rue des Orfèvres★ :** half-timbered houses. Rue and Place de l'Ancien Palais : a 15thC mansion is now the **Museum of Folklore and Old Moulins** (Musée du Folklore et du Vieux Moulins; history; *daily ex Thu.; 9-12 & 3-6:30*). ▶ **Cathedral** (B1) : in the 19thC, a pseudo-Gothic nave was grafted onto the late 15thC Flamboyant Gothic choir; stained glass★ in the apse; treasury-room *(daily 9-12 & 2-6 ex Tue. out of season)* with triptych★★★ (1498-1501) by the Moulins Master (→ box), portraying Anne of France (daughter of Louis XI) and her husband Pierre, Duke of Bourbon, donors of the painting; also a beautiful triptych by the Flemish painter Joos van Cleve (16thC). ▶ Only the 15thC Mal Coiffée tower and a Renaissance pavilion remain of the Château (**Museum of Art and Archaeology :** *10-12 & 2-5 or 6 daily ex Tue.*). ▶ Rue F.-Péron and Rue de Paris : handsome old mansions. Continue to the school chapel (*lycée*, A-B1) to see the **mausoleum of Henri II de Montmorency★★** (1652). ▶ Cours Anatole-France and Jean-Jaurès (B-C1) : avenues lined with typical Bourbonnais mansions decorated with diapered black and red brick.

Nearby

▶ **Yzeure** *(1 km E) :* Romanesque church with 11thC crypt; small historical museum of the Bourbonnais *(closed Sat., Sun. and nat. hols.; am Nov.-Mar.).* ▶ **Allier Valley** upstream to **Châtel-de-Neuvre :** Romanesque churches at **Chemilly, Besson, Châtel-de-Neuvre** (site★, view over the valley and the Monts de la Madeleine), **Bessay-sur-Allier** and **Toulon-sur-Allier;** 13thC and 15thC castles at **Bressolles** (châteaux du Lys; *no visits*); near **Besson,** castles of Ris (14th-15thC), Rochefort (ruins), Vieux Bostz (15th-16thC) and Fourchaud★ (14thC; one of the best preserved fortresses in Bourbonnais). ▶ **Allier Valley,** downstream : château d'Avrilly (16thC, much restored); **château du Riau** (15th-17thC), near 1584 barn with exquisite keel-form timberwork★ *(3-6 ex Tue., Apr.-Sep.; 2-7 ex Sun. rest of year);* N from Villeneuve-sur-Allier, the **Arboretum de Balaine★** (botanical park specialising in trees; est. 1804; *2-7 May-Oct; closed Tue. and Fri.).* □

Practical Information

MOULINS
ℹ pl. de l'Hôtel-de-Ville (B2), ☎ 70.44.14.14.
SNCF (C3), ☎ 70.44.23.73/70.46.50.50.
🚌 av. Mal-de-Lattre-de-Tassigny (B3), ☎ 70.44.06.31.
Car rental : *Avis*, train station (C3); 21, rue M.-de-Dombasle, ☎ 70.48.58.24.

Hotels :
★★★ ***Paris*** (R.C.), 21, rue de Paris (B1), ☎ 70.44.00.58, Tx 394853, AE DC Euro Visa, 27 rm Ⓟ half pens (h.s.),

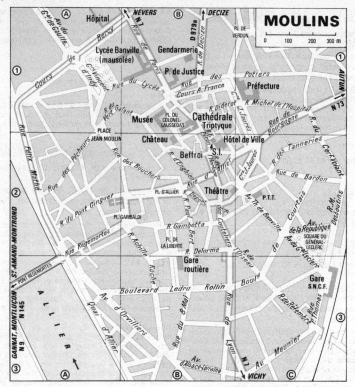

The Moulins Master

The most important late-15thC French painter long remained anonymous, although his work was often favourably compared to that of his Italian contemporaries Leonardo da Vinci, Bellini and Perugino.
After much research, art experts and historians have recently agreed that he was almost certainly Jean Hey, a painter of Flemish origin. Born around 1450 and active from 1480 to 1501 (date of his master-piece, the Moulins triptych), he was employed at the court of the dukes of Bourbon in 1490; his portraits of several members of the ducal family are now in the Louvre Museum in Paris. The museum at Autun in nearby Burgundy cherishes a superb Nativity by this master painter.

550. Rest. ● ◆◆◆ ♪ ᴔ closed Mon and Sun eve. A revivifying stopover. Flawlessly managed by François Laustriat, excellent cooking from Pascal Bouffety. A happy blend of regional specialities and modern dishes : *foie gras aux gousses d'ail rôties, noisette d'agneau aux rouelles de pieds de cochon, boeuf charolais cru en salade.* Excellent cellar, 70-250.
● ★★ **Le Chalet**, (L.F., R.S.), Coulandon, 6 km W on D 945, ☎ 70.44.50.08, AE DC Euro Visa, 21 rm ℗ ♦ ▨ ⬗ closed Sun (l.s.), 16 Nov-31 Jan. A pleasant chalet in an immense park with a pond ; fishing, 210. Rest. ◆ ⬗ closed lunch and Sun, 60-110.
● ★★ **Le Parc** (L.F.), 31, av. Gal-Leclerc (C2), ☎ 70.44.12.25, Visa, 28 rm ℗ closed 1-15 Oct,

22 Dec-5 Jan, 210. Rest. ◆ ♪ ᴔ A great spot, excellent value, 70-150.
★ **Agriculture**, 15, cours Vincent-d'Indy (A1), ☎ 70.44.08.58, 24 rm ℗ 100.

Restaurant :
● ◆◆ **Jacquemart**, 10, pl. de l'Hôtel-de-Ville (B2), ☎ 70.44.32.58, AE DC Euro Visa ᭜ ▨ ♪ closed Mon and Sun eve, 21-27 Apr, 3-17 Aug, 21 Dec-4 Jan. Louis de Roberty is a proud alumnus of Senderens's kitchen, and an excellent cook : *coquilles Saint-Jacques* (season) *en infusion de consommé de boeuf à la moelle, "sole courgettes et truffes ne font qu'un", noisette et foie d'agneau au laurier et persil frit,* 120-300.

⅄ ★*Plage* (66 pl), ☎ 70.44.19.29.

Recommended
♥ *crafts gallery,* hôtel de Moret, rue d'Allier, ☎ 70.46.78.34 ; chocolates, candy : *Au Palet d'Or, M. Ceardy* ; pastries : *le Moulin de la Galette,* pl. de la Liberté ; pork products : *Giraud,* pl. d'Allier.

Nearby

BRESSOLLE, ⊠ 03000 Moulins, 5 km S.

Restaurant :
◆◆ **Le Bateau Ivre**, ☎ 70.44.48.00 ♪ ᴔ 75-200 ; child : 55.

VILLENEUVE-SUR-ALLIER, ⊠ 03000 Moulins, 13 km N on the N7.

Hotel :
Château du Riau, (I.L.A., C.A.), ☎ 70.43.30.74, 3 rm ℗ ▨ ⅄ A 15th-C château of the Popillon family faithful to Bourbons, 280.

NANÇAY*

Bourges 36, Châteauroux 68, Paris 201 km
pop 790 ⊠ 18330 Neuvy-sur-Barangeon   B1

Charming village in the Sologne region with a castle (15th-16thC, much restored), woods, lakes and a population of craftsmen. It is also a radio-astronomy station, with a giant mirror★ *(200 x 40 m; 4 km N; visit on written request; 2nd Sat. of the month; parking).*   □

Practical Information _____

Hotels :
● ★★★ *Auberge Les Meaulnes* (C.H.), ☎ 48.51.81.15, AE DC Euro Visa, 10 rm ░░ ↻ ⌣ closed Tue (l.s.), 15 Jan-15 Mar, 300. Rest. ♦♦♦ ♪ ⌣ Quality cooking in a lovely setting, 150-225; child : 80.
● ★★★ *Relais de Vouzeron* (C.H.), pl. de l'Eglise, Vouzeron 6 km SE., ☎ 48.51.61.38, AE DC Visa, 9 rm ℙ ↻ closed Sun eve and Mon, 1 Aug-1 Sep, 310. Rest. ♦♦ ♪ ⌣ Spec : *rillettes de saumon, harengs des mers du Nord,* 180-220.

NÉRIS-LES-BAINS

Montluçon 8, Clermont-Ferrand 83, Paris 327 km
pop 2996 ⊠ 03310   B3

A spa since pre-Roman days, when the Gauls made use of the healing properties of the hot springs.
▶ Roman remains at the **Rieckotter Museum.** *(5-7 daily ex Sun. and nat. hols., May-Sep.)* in the spa buildings.
▶ Romanesque **church** (11th-12thC) and octagonal bell-tower roofed with chestnut shingles, built on top of Gallo-Roman remains; nearby, Merovingian burial ground.   □

Practical Information _____

♨ (2 May-23 Oct), ☎ 70.03.10.39.   ♥
ⓘ carrefour des Arènes, ☎ 70.03.11.39.

Hotels :
★★★ *Parc*, 40, rue Boisrot-Desserviers, ☎ 70.03.22.22, Tx 990029, Euro Visa, 59 rm ⌣ ░░ ↻ ♨ ⌣ 250. Rest. ♦ ⌣ ♪ ⌣ closed Sun eve , Nov-Apr, 70-120; child : 35.
● ★★ *Parc des Rivalles* (L.F.), 7, rue Parmentier, ☎ 70.03.10.50, 32 rm ℙ ⌣ ░░ ↻ half pens (h.s.), closed 30 Sep-1 May, 400. Rest. ♦ ⌣ ⌣ ⌣ 50-110.
★★ *Le Garden* (L.F.), 12, av. Marx-Dormoy, ☎ 70.03.21.16, Euro Visa, 19 rm ℙ ⌣ ⌣ closed Fri eve and Sun eve (10 Nov-1 May), 5-20 Jan, 20 Oct-10 Nov, 150. Rest. ♦ ♪ 55-120; child : 35.
★ *Centre* (L.F.), 10, rue Capitaine-Migat, ☎ 70.03.10.74, 24 rm ░░ ↻ closed 5 Oct-2 May, 105. Rest. ♦ 50-100.

Recommended
Casino : 2, bd des Arènes, ☎ 70.03.10.32.

SAINT-AMAND-MONTROND

Bourges 44, Montluçon 49, Paris 271 km
pop 12770 ⊠ 18200   B2

On Wednesdays and Saturdays, lively market in the heart of the old town.

▶ In a 15th-16thC building, **St.-Vic Museum** *(10-12 & 2-6 ex Mon. and Tue. am);* history, folk art of lower Berry.
▶ Close by is the church of St. Amand (11th-13thC).

Nearby

▶ **Noirlac Abbey★★** *(5 km N) :* founded in 1136, one of the most beautiful and best-preserved Cistercian abbeys; 12thC church of perfect simplicity and balance, Gothic cloister★ (13th-14thC), chapterhouse (12thC), store-room, refectory, dormitory *(daily 10-12 & 2-5 or 6; closed Tue. Oct.-Dec.).* ▶ **Bruère-Alléchamp,** and its houses with round towers screening outside staircase. In the middle of

the village, the centre of France is indicated by a Roman stone. ▶ **La Celle :** Romanesque church with Carolingian carvings set in the façade. ▶ **Meillant :** castle★★ (rebuilt 15th-16thC), mediaeval W façade contrasts with the exuberant Renaissance E side and the Tour du Lion, a tower famed for its decoration of interlaced "C"s and the lead lion that stands at its head; furnishings *(daily 9-11:45 & 2-6:45).* Dun-sur-Auron *(13 km N of Meillant) :* Tour de l'Horloge (clock-tower) and old houses; 12th-15thC church. ▶ **Thaumiers** *(10 km SE of Dun) :* the château, an elegant 18thC building, is now a "chambre d'hôte" *(tel. : 48.60.87.62).* ▶ **Ainay-le-Vieil** *(10 km S of Saint-Amand) :* château★★ is worth a special trip; Renaissance building surrounded by walls and towers, encircled by moats *(10-12 & 2-7, daily ex Tue. am., 7 Feb.-31 Mar. and Nov.-Jan).* ▶ **Drevant,** a flowery village between Saint-Amand and Ainay : excavations of Roman amphitheatre and baths.   □

Practical Information _____

ⓘ pl. de la République, ☎ 48.96.16.86.   ♥
SNCF ☎ 48.96.04.50.

Hotels :
★★ *La Poste* (L.F.), 9, rue du Dr-Vallet, ☎ 48.96.27.14, 24 rm ℙ ↻ closed Mon ex hols, 20 Nov-1 Jan, 200. Rest. ♦ ♪ ⌣ 55-180.
★ *Pont du Cher*, 2, av. de la Gare, Orval, 5 km N, ☎ 48.96.00.51, Visa, 13 rm ℙ ⌣ ░░ half pens (h.s.), closed Mon (l.s.), 220. Rest. ♦♦ ⌣ Spec : *saumon à l'oseille, truite Pont du Cher, sandre au sancerre, coq du Berry,* 50-110.

Restaurant :
♦ *Le Bœuf Couronné*, 86, rue de Juranville, ☎ 48.96.42.72, AE Euro Visa ⌣ closed Wed, 2 Jan-16 Feb, 50-125.

SAINT-POURÇAIN-SUR-SIOULE

Moulins 31, Clermont-Ferrand 65, Paris 325 km
pop 5433 ⊠ 03500   C3

The town grew around the 11thC Romanesque abbey church (15thC carved choir stalls), which was rebuilt several times between the 14th and the 19thC. A 15thC bell-tower and several half-timbered houses remain of the abbey buildings. Viticulture Museum *(15 Jun.-10 Sep.).*

Nearby

▶ **Saulcet** *(3 km NW) :* fine 12th-13th and 15thC murals in the Romanesque church (14thC); handsome bell-tower★. ▶ **Verneuil-en-Bourbonnais** *(2.5 km farther) :* one of the most picturesque villages in the region; Romanesque church, castle ruins, fortifications and gateways; at the former 10thC church of Notre-Dame-sur-l'Eau, exhibitions in summer. 16thC château de Boucherolles *(9 km NW of Verneuil near* **Tréban***) :* park *(daily 15 Jun.-15 Aug.).*

Practical Information _____

SAINT-POURÇAIN-SUR-SIOULE
ⓘ bd Ledru-Rollin, ☎ 70.45.32.73 (h.s.).   ♥
SNCF ☎ 70.45.31.20.

Hotels :
★★ *Deux Ponts* (L.F.), (France-Accueil), llot de Tivoli, fbg Paluet, ☎ 70.45.41.14, AE DC Euro Visa, 28 rm ℙ ⌣ ░░ half pens (h.s.), closed Sun eve (l.s.), 1-16 Mar, 15 Nov-20 Dec. By the riverside, 345. Rest. ♦ ⌣ closed Mon and Sun eve, 55-120; child : 40.
★★ *Le Chêne Vert*, (L.F., France-Accueil), 35, bd Ledru-Rollin, ☎ 70.45.40.65, AE DC Euro Visa, 35 rm ℙ ♪ closed Tue and Wed lunch (l.s.), 5 Jan-7 Feb, 30 Sep-10 Oct, 170. Rest. ♦ ♪ Classic cuisine in tune with the seasons, 70-200; child : 35.

▲ ★★★*lle de la Ronde* (50 pl), ☎ 70.45.45.43; *La Moutte* (33 pl), ☎ 70.45.91.94.

Recommended
Bicycle-rental : at Bayet, *M. Marchand*, ☎ 70.45.31.62.
Guide to wines : *wine festival*, late Aug.

Nearby

VARENNES-SUR-ALLIER, ✉ 03150, 11 km E.

Hotel :
★★★ ***Auberge de l'Orisse*** (L.F.), ☎ 70.45.05.60, AE Euro Visa, 23 rm closed Sun eve, Mon lunch (Nov-Mar), 225. Rest. ♦ 85-250; child : 35.

SANCERRE**

Bourges 46, Nevers 50, Paris 204 km
pop 2286 ✉ 18300 B1

A wine-growing district, between the Loire Valley and the Berry and Nivernais regions.

▶ A network of twisting streets (several 15th-16thC houses) runs to the **Tour des Fiefs,** a striking cylindrical 15thC keep. Close by is a 19thC pseudo-Renaissance château. From the Caesar Gate, magnificent view★.

Nearby

▶ At the foot of Sancerre hill is **Saint-Satur;** only the Gothic choir★ of the church was completed. ▶ **Sens-Beaujeu** *(11 km W) :* 16th-17thC château (with additions from 1810); 4 km from there, **château du Boucard** rebuilt in the 16thC; severe exterior conceals an elegant Renaissance courtyard *(daily 10-12 & 2-6, 7).* ▶ **Jars** *(5 km farther) :* Renaissance church and fortified mediaeval manor-house. ▶ **Tour de Vèvre** *(12 km SW) :* a massive 12thC keep rebuilt in the 15thC. ▶ 12 km S, **château de la Grange** (late 16thC). □

Practical Information

SANCERRE
ℹ mairie, ☎ 48.54.00.26.

Hotels :
★★ ***Le Panoramic***, rempart des Augustins, ☎ 48.54.22.44, Tx 783433, AE, 57 rm 190.
★★ ***Rempart*** (L.F.), rempart des Dames, ☎ 48.54.10.18, AE DC Euro Visa, 12 rm 150. Rest. ♦ 55-130.

Restaurants :
♦ ***La Tour***, 31, pl. de la Halle, ☎ 48.54.00.81, AE Visa closed Mon and Sun eve (h.s.), 5-16 Jan, 100-155.
♦ ***La Treille***, Chavignol (3 km SW), ☎ 48.54.12.17, closed Tue eve and Wed (l.s.), Jan-Feb. A simple, savoury village restaurant in goat-cheese country, 85-130.

Recommended
Events : *fête de la "Sabotée sancerroise"*, Sury-en-Vaux, 15 Aug; *Grape festival*, Verdigny, last Sun in Jul; *crottin festival*, weekend of 1 May; *wizards' festival*, Bué, 1st Sun in Aug.
Guide to wines : *wines G. de Cholot*, Château de Thauvenay; *French wines days*, last weekend in Aug; *A.-Mellot*, restaurant, tasting, sale : 3, rue Porte-César; *wine fair*, 1st weekend in Jun, presentation of the Sancerre vintage.
♥ crafts : *la Poterie de Sancerre*, 3, pl. de la Halle, ☎ 48.54.10.34; honey wax : *J.-P. Senée*, farmer, av. de Verdun.

Nearby

SAINT-SATUR, ✉ 18300 Sancerre, 4 km NE.

Hotels :
★★ ***Le Laurier*** (L.F.), 29, rue du Commerce, ☎ 48.54.17.20, Euro Visa, 9 rm closed Mon, 2-28 Feb, 130. Rest. ● ♦ Rustic inn. Regional cuisine accents local wines : *lapereau en gelée, sandre au beurre blanc*, 50-130.
Etoile, 2, quai de Loire, ☎ 48.54.12.15, 11 rm closed 15 Nov-10 Mar, 140. Rest. ♦♦ Local cuisine of Sancerre, best regional wines (Sancerre, Pouilly), 75-180.

Restaurant :
♦ ***Saint-Roch***, quai de Loire, ☎ 48.54.01.79 closed Tue (l.s.), 20 Dec-20 Mar. Boat on the Loire, 85-130.

SAINT-THIBAULT, ✉ 18300 Sancerre, 5 km NE on the D 955, D 4.

Hotel :
L'Auberge, ☎ 48.54.13.79, AE DC Euro Visa, 5 rm closed Tue eve (l.s.), 140. Rest. ♦♦ Very tasty red Sancerre from Verdigny; *coq en barbouille, aiguillette de jambon en gelée*, 55-100; child : 30.

SANCOINS

Nevers 39, Bourges 51, Paris 265 km
pop 3667 ✉ 18600 B2

One of the largest cattle markets in Europe; 500 000 head annually pass through the Parc des Grivelles (salesyards). In town, the Jean Baffier art centre *(daily ex Sat. pm and Sun.).*

Nearby

▶ Along D76 to **Apremont-sur-Allier :** mediaeval village; in the château outbuildings (15th-17thC), display of horse-drawn carriages *(7 Apr.-15 Sep., 2-6 ex Tue.);* flower garden *(10-12, 2-6).* ▶ **Château de Saint-Augustin** *(8.5 km SE) :* 18thC; 87-acre zoo-park *(2-6, school hols., Wed., Sat. and Sun.).* □

SOUVIGNY*

Moulins 12, Montluçon 55, Paris 306 km
pop 1929 ✉ 03210 C2

Priory chosen by the dukes of Bourbon as their burial place : magnificent church★★ with Gothic exterior and Romanesque interior.

▶ Noteworthy architecture (double side-aisles, elevation with fine carved decoration) : **capitals★,** ornamental arches on the supposed tomb of St. Mayeul (12thC), **tombs of Louis II and Charles I of Bourbon** (15thC). ▶ 16th-18thC priory buildings. ▶ **Stonework Museum** *(10-12 & 3-6, daily ex Tue., Jul.-Aug.; Sat., Sun. only in May, Jun., Sep., Oct.)* in the former church of St-Marc (12th-17thC).

Nearby

▶ **Autry-Issards** *(5 km W) :* a small Burgundian-Romanesque church (inside, Flemish painting, late 15thC); château des Issards (15th-19thC; *15 Jun.-15 Sep., daily from 4 pm).* ▶ **Le Montet** *(18 km SW) :* remains of fortified church; **Buxières-les-Mines** *(12 km N of Montet) :* Romanesque church with steepled bell-tower; doorway. Elegant Manoir de la Condemine (manor-house, *May-Sep., Sat. and Sun. 2-7).* □

Practical Information

SNCF ☎ 70.43.61.47.

Hotel :
Auberge des Tilleuls, pl. St-Eloi, ☎ 70.43.60.70, AE DC closed Mon eve and Tue, 9-25 Feb, 12-28 Oct. Rest. ♦ 75-110.

TRONÇAIS Forest*

B2

Beautiful, dense forest 105 km^2 in area; avenues through stands of oak (70 %) and beech. Replanted by Jean-Baptiste Colbert (1619-83; Louis XIV's prime minister).

▶ Picnic areas, camping grounds, lakes with leisure facilities. Numerous walks; take the routes past the **300 year-old oaks** (some over 35m high and 3.5m in circumference). ▶ S, **Hérisson** : a charming village in the shadow of a ruined 13th-14thC castle (panorama). ☐

Practical Information ⸻

HÉRISSON, ⊠ 03190, 16 km SW of **Cérigny**.

Hotel :
Château de la Roche-Othon, (C.A.), ☎ 70.06.80.31 Ⓟ ⋙
⟍ 3 ch. d'hôtes, 400. Rest. ◆ Guests only, 90-300.

SAINT-BONNET-TRONÇAIS, ⊠ 03360, 43 km N of **Montluçon**.

Hotel :
★★ *Le Tronçais* (L.F.), lieu-dit Tronçais, ☎ 70.06.11.95, 12 rm Ⓟ ≼ ⋙ ⟍ ↗ closed Sun eve and Mon (l.s.), 1 Dec-1 Mar, 170. Rest. ◆ ≼ ও ⅗ 80-115.

⚖ ★★★*Champ Fossé* (120 pl), ☎ 70.06.11.30.

Recommended
Bicycle-rental : *association du pays de Tronçais*, ☎ 70.67.56.89; *foyer rural*, ☎ 70.06.11.15.

VALENÇAY**

Châteauroux 43, Blois 55, Paris 235 km
pop 3139 ⊠ 36600   A1

The **château**★★ presents a uniform architectural style, even though construction spanned more than 200 years.

▶ French Regency, Louis XVI and Empire furnishings in the apartments *(15 Mar.-15 Nov., daily 9-12 & 2-6; rest of the year weekends only).* ▶ Animals roam the park *(open all year 9-12 & 2-7).* ▶ In the outbuildings, **Automobile Museum :** 50 models★ from 1898-1945 *(same hours as the park).* ☐

Practical Information ⸻

ⓘ rte de Blois, ☎ 54.00.04.42 (h.s.).
𝘚𝘕𝘊𝘍 ☎ 54.00.12.34.

Hotel :
● ★★★★ *Espagne* (R.C.), 9, rue du Château, ☎ 54.00.00.02, Tx 751675, AE Euro Visa, 18 rm Ⓟ ⋙ ⟍ ও closed 15 Nov-15 Mar, 450. Rest. ● ◆◆◆ ও A perfect welcome and delicious food. Don't miss : *terrine aux cinq légumes, coquelet à la crème de ciboulette, noisettes d'agneau à l'estragon,* 170-280.

Restaurant :
◆ *Le Chêne Vert*, 55, rte Nationale, ☎ 54.00.06.54, Euro ⋙ ও closed Sat and Sun eve (l.s.), 10-29 Jun, 7 Dec-17 Jan. Friendly service. Good game in season, 50-120.

Recommended
Son et lumière : at the château, Jul-Aug.
♥ at Parpeçay, 7 km from Chabris, virgin olive oil : *Maison Givert-Marchal.*

VICHY**

Moulins 57, Clermont-Ferrand 59, Paris 351 km
pop 30554 ⊠ 03200   C3

This health resort preserves the charm that drew fashionable clients long before the turn of the century; it is equipped with up-to-date leisure and sports facilities; casino; attractive gardens; antique shops; luxurious hotels.

▶ **Maison du Bailliage,** or Chastel Franc (magistrate's court; B4) (1531) displays art and archaeology collections; near the church Saint-Blaise, the Centre for Archaeological Research has exhibits on the history of Vichy (2 Rue Porte de France; *in season,* Sat. 2-6). ▶ The **spa buildings** (A2) can be visited on certain afternoons in season; Missionary Museum, 18 Avenue Thermale *(May-Sep., daily ex Mon. 3-6).*

Nearby

▶ **Cusset** *(3 km E)* : an industrial suburb; houses of Charles VII and Louis XI (both 15thC) and other old houses; historical museum in the Tour Prisonnière (prison tower final remains of 15thC fortifications; *May-Sep., Wed., Sat., Sun. 3-7).* ▶ 8.5 km S, **Saint-Yorre :** château★ de Busset (15th-19thC; 15th-16thC murals★ in the SE tower; *groups only, on request).* ▶ **Billy** *(15 km N)* : at the foot of a rock crowned with the ruins of a 13th-14thC fortress *(pm Jun.-15 Sep.).* ☐

Practical Information ⸻

VICHY
⚘ Mar-Dec., ☎ 70.98.95.37, springs open all year. ♥

ⓘ 19, rue du Parc (A3), ☎ 70.98.71.94.
✈ Vichy-Charmeil, 6 km N, ☎ 70.32.34.09.
𝘚𝘕𝘊𝘍 (C2), ☎ 70.98.41.06.
🚌 pl. Ch.-de-Gaulle (B3), ☎ 70.98.41.33.
Car rental : Avis, 53, av. P.-Doumer (C2), ☎ 70.98.92.81; train station.

Hotels :
★★★★ *Aletti Thermal Palace*, 3, pl. Joseph-Aletti (A3), ☎ 70.31.78.77, DC Euro, 57 rm ♪ 1 Oct-14 May. Vichy's single old-fashioned luxury hotel. Bridge club, 415.
★★★★ *Pavillon Sévigné* (Mapotel), 10-12 pl. Sévigné (A4), ☎ 70.32.16.22, Tx 990393, AE DC Euro Visa, 40 rm Ⓟ ⋙ ও closed Feb-Mar. Former residence of Mme de Sévigné 600. Rest. ● ◆◆◆ ♪ ও closed Mon and Sun eve. Young G. Raimbault's cooking style, learned at the side of Jean Delaveyne, Bougival's resident wizard, is downright bewitching : *pomme de ris de veau aux écrevisses, terrine de foie gras frais de canard, suprême de fumaison de saumon frais,* 180.
★★★ *Amérique*, 122 bis, bd des Etats-Unis (A2-3), ☎ 70.31.88.88, Visa, 48 rm ♪ pens (h.s.), closed 5 Oct-17 Apr, 500. Rest. ◆ ♪ ⅗ 80-95.
★★★ *Grignan*, 7, pl. Sévigné (A4), ☎ 70.32.08.11, Visa, 121 rm Ⓟ ⟍ ও ⅗ half pens (h.s.), 385. Rest. ◆ ♪ ও ⅗ 55-150.
★★★ *La Paix*, 13, rue du Parc (A3), ☎ 70.98.20.56 ≼ ⋙ ⟍ closed 30 Sep-20 Apr, 240. Rest. ◆◆ ⅗ 110.
★★ *Gallia*, 12 av. P.-Doumer (B3), ☎ 70.31.86.66, 72 rm ⋙ pens (h.s.), closed Nov-Feb, 31 Oct-1 Mar, 435. Rest. ◆ 75-120.
★★ *Magenta*, 21, rue Stucki (A2), ☎ 70.31.80.99, 62 rm ⋙ closed 1 Oct-1 May, 250. Rest. ◆◆ ♪ ⅗ 85-210.
★★ *Tiffany*, 59, av. P.-Doumer (C2), ☎ 70.31.82.99, AE DC Euro Visa, 10 rm Ⓟ ⟍ closed Fri (l.s.), 15-30 Nov, 180. Rest. ◆ closed Fri eve and Sat. lunch (l.s.).

Restaurants :
● ◆◆◆ *Violon d'Ingres*, 5, rue du Casino (A-B3), ☎ 70.98.97.70, AE DC Euro Visa ⋙ ⟍ ♪ closed Tue. Now in roomier quarters, J. Mulher cooks in the grand tradition of Belle-Epoque Vichy, to the delight of spa-goers. Spec. : *salade de pigeon au fois gras, noisette d'agneau à la crème d'ail,* 100-200.
◆◆ *La Grillade-Strauss*, 5, pl Joseph-Aletti (A3), ☎ 70.98.56.74, AE DC Euro Visa ⋙ ♪ closed Mon and Sun eve. The fashionable place to be seen : a lovely villa alive with memories of Napoléon III and G. Hilmer, the former chef. Spec. : *pot-au-feu de poissons, ris de veau aux champignons sauvages,* 120-200.
◆◆ *Rotonde du Lac,* bd Mal-de-Lattre-de-Tassigny, at the Yacht-Club (A1), ☎ 70.98.72.46 Ⓟ ≼ ⋙ ও closed Tue, 150-300.

Recommended
Youth hostel : 19, rue du Stade, ☎ 70.32.25.14.
Bicycle rental : *M. Marchand*, 13-15, allée Mesdames, ☎ 70.31.87.10; *M. Gayet*, 8, rue Source-de-l'Hôpital, ☎ 70.32.12.37; *Ets Brière*, 48, bd Gambetta, ☎ 70.31.52.86.
Nearby
ABREST, ⊠ 03200 Vichy, 4 km S on D 906.

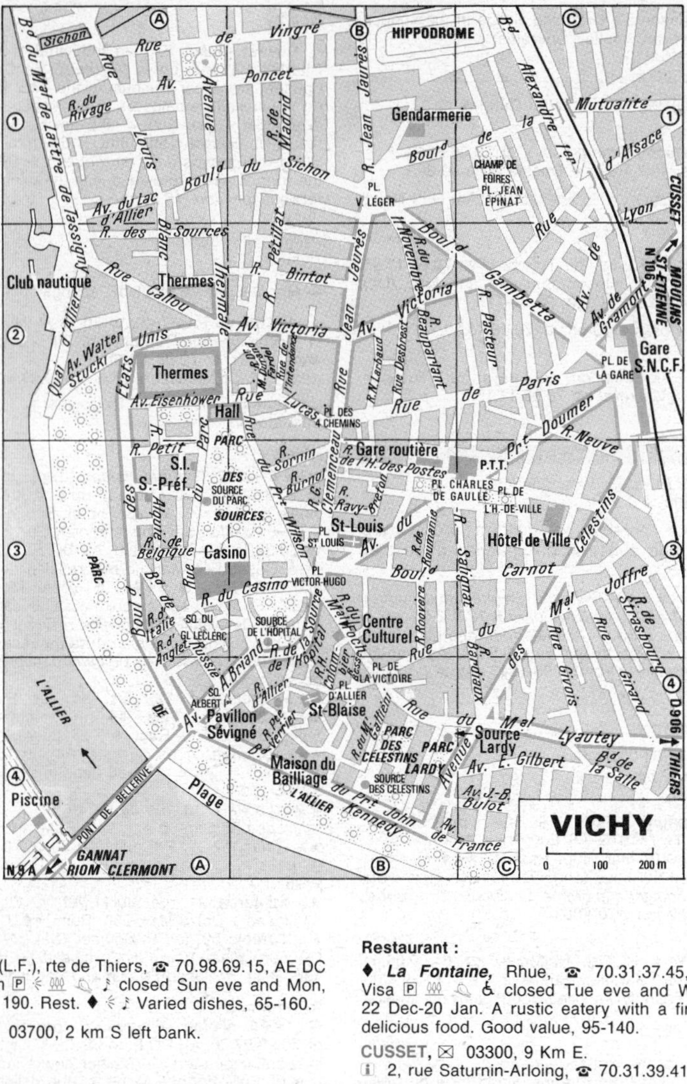

Hotel :

La Colombière (L.F.), rte de Thiers, ☎ 70.98.69.15, AE DC Euro Visa, 4 rm P closed Sun eve and Mon, 10 Jan-15 Feb, 190. Rest. ♦ Varied dishes, 65-160.

BELLERIVE, ✉ 03700, 2 km S left bank.

Hotels :

★★★ ***Marcotel,*** rue de la Grange-aux-Grains, ☎ 70.32.34.00, AE DC Euro Visa, 38 rm P closed Sun eve (l.s.), 15-29 Dec, 305. Rest. ♦ closed Sun eve (l.s.), and Mon lunch, 120-210.

★★ ***Chez Mémère,*** chemin de Halage, ☎ 70.32.35.22, 10 rm P closed 10 Sep-10 May. By the water's edge, 165. Rest. ♦♦ closed lunch ex Sun. Carefully prepared food, 120-150.

★★ ***Résidence,*** rue de la Grange-aux-Grains, ☎ 70.32.37.11, Visa, 114 rm P 180.

CHARMEIL, ✉ 03110, 8 km N.

Restaurant :

♦ ***La Musarde,*** ☎ 70.32.09.76 P closed Mon, 24 Jun-2 Jul, 25 Oct-3 Nov. Mosey on in and sit down to a good meal prepared by the Piastras : *andouillette, saucisson chaud de grenouilles.* Wines of Auvergne, 100-170.

CREUZIER-LE-VIEUX, ✉ 03300 Cusset, 5 km N on N 209.

Restaurant :

♦ ***La Fontaine,*** Rhue, ☎ 70.31.37.45, AE DC Euro Visa P ♿ closed Tue eve and Wed, 15-28 Oct, 22 Dec-20 Jan. A rustic eatery with a fireplace. Simple, delicious food. Good value, 95-140.

CUSSET, ✉ 03300, 9 Km E.

ℹ 2, rue Saturnin-Arloing, ☎ 70.31.39.41.

Hotel :

★★ ***Le Globe,*** 1, rue Pasteur, ☎ 70.97.82.31, AE DC Euro Visa P half pens (h.s.), closed 1-15 Nov, 365. Rest. ♦ ♿ 55-110.

Restaurant :

♦♦ ***Taverne Louis XI,*** près de l'église, ☎ 70.31.37.45, closed Mon and Sun eve, Feb school hols, 3-27 Oct, 80-150.

VIERZON

Châteauroux 58, Orléans 79, Paris 210 km
pop 34886 ✉ 18100 B1

Industrial centre for agricultural implements and ceramics.

▸ Several old houses near the town hall (17th-18thC) and church (17thC); museum of Old Vierzon.

Nearby

▶ **Massay** *(10 km SW, N 20)* : a fine 12 th-14thC church and extensive remains of a Benedictine abbey (chapter, storehouse, dormitory, 12th-13thC ; exhibits and concerts in summer). ☐

Practical Information ————————————

ⓘ pl. M.-Thorez, ☎ 48.75.20.03.
SNCF ☎ 48.75.08.61.
Car rental : *Avis*, train station ; station Total, rte de Neuvy.

Hotels :

● ★★★ **Sologne,** rte de Châteauroux, 2 km SW, ☎ 48.75.15.20, Euro Visa, 24 rm Ⓟ ♨ ≾ 240. Rest. ◆ **La Grillade** ⨪ ♿ closed Sun, 60-120.

★★ **Château de la Beuvrière** (I.L.A., C.H.), Sainte-Hilaire-de-Court, 7 km SW on RN 20, ☎ 48.75.08.14, AE DC Euro Visa, 15 rm Ⓟ ⨪ ♨ ≾ ⨯ closed 5 Jan-27 Feb. A private home that takes in joying guests, 280. Rest. ◆◆ ⨪ closed Sun. Spec. : *effiloché de lottine à la tomate et au thym, pigeonneau rôti à la fondue de choux verts,* 60-120.

★★ **Terminus et Bordeaux,** pl. de la Gare, ☎ 48.75.00.46, Euro Visa, 42 rm Ⓟ 130.

Bordelais, Landes

A triangular-shaped region with a wide stretch of coast as its hypotenuse, infinite beaches of fine sand and a hinterland containing the largest forest in France, dotted with large, tranquil lakes fringed with pine-trees. Along the valleys of the Gironde, the Garonne and the Dordogne lie great stretches of vineyards, where almost half of France's best wines are produced. We could divide the region in two : to the east is Entre-Deux-Mers — "between two seas" — named for the great ocean tides which swell the Garonne and the Dordogne; the fertile cornfields and pastureland of Bazadais, the forests of Albret, and the farmlands of Marsan and Chalosse with their hot springs. To the west, the ocean and wine-growing Médoc, with its industry and summer tourism; the Arcachon basin, famous for its oysters; Buch and Born — army, petrochemicals and tourism, and the resorts along the southernmost part of the coast, which live on fresh air and holiday-makers.

The city of Bordeaux is both an ocean and river port, with installations stretching along one hundred kilometres — oil tankers, cargo ships, shipyards and barges all have their appointed places. The city also boasts magnificent 18th-century administrative and private buildings, beautiful churches and cathedrals and many fine museums, including the Centre Jean Moulin, a Resistance museum and centre of documentation on the Second World War.

Bordeaux wines grow in an area of 1 000 square kilometres, producing 500 million bottles a year, and including the most famous vintages in the world : Château-Lafite-Rothschild, Château-Latour, Château Margaux, Château-Mouton-Rothschild, Château-Haut-Brion and Château Yquem. Médoc is a country of châteaux, ranging from simple farm buildings to genuine castles and grandiose mansions built by the *chartrons*, merchants of English descent who still dominate the Bordeaux wine-trade. And to accompany the wine there is the excellent cooking of the region : eels and oysters, lamb from the salty meadows of Pauillac, goose — and duck — liver *pâtés* and rich *confit* from the Landes region and the excellent, yellow, corn-fed poultry for which the region is famous. □

 ## Don't miss

★★★ Bordeaux B2, Saint-Émilion B2.

★★ The Bazadais Region B2, Entre-Deux-Mers Region B2, Garonne Valley B2, the Grandes Landes Region A-B3, the Marensin Region A3, the Médoc Region A1, Saint-Macaire B2, the Sauternais Region B2.

★ Arcachon Basin A2, the Blayais Region B1, Cap-Ferret A2, the Chalosse Region A-B4, Dax A3-4, Hossegor A4, the Libournais Region B2, Maubuisson A1, Mimizan A3, Mont-de-Marsan B3, Peyrehorade A4, Soulac-sur-Mer A1, Soustons A3.

Weekend tips

Spend the first night at Bordeaux (city monuments magnificently illuminated); then be on the quay in the morning in time for a boat trip round the harbour. Afterwards cross the Garonne and the Dordogne, then on to Saint-André-de-Cubzac and Blaye via the Gironde corniche (hill road). At Blaye, cross the Gironde and enter the Médoc district, where you will see some of the famous châteaux and perhaps taste the wines. From the Médoc, continue towards the Arcachon Basin via the lake road, and spend the night there. The second day, explore the immense Landaise forest, going from N to S, crossing the regional park of the Landes de Gascogne to Sabres, departure point for a tour of the remarkable Marquèze Eco-museum. On the return route, make a detour if you have time towards Bazas and the château de Roquetaillade; then, from Langon, return to Bordeaux along the Garonne Valley, preferably by the right bank.

Gironde peasant's house

Châteaux in the Bordeaux region

Châteaux are obviously not unique to the Bordeaux region, but here the name takes on a special meaning linked to the production of wine rather than the style of the building. There are around 3 000 châteaux in the Gironde, of which some 300 are particularly well known. In the Bordeaux region, to have the right to the title of château, a wine must meet the following conditions : The wine must come from an appellation d'origine contrôlée (AOC) area; it must come from a producing vineyard with the name of a château earned through past and continual use; and, in theory, it must have been made at the château. However, private vineyards are allowed to have their grapes made into wine at a cooperative while retaining their own appellation, but in this case the product cannot be labeled mise en bouteille au château (château-bottled).

Landes house

Facts and figures

Area : the Gironde (10 626 km²) and the Landes (9 364 km²) are the two largest French departments, together forming a region of 20 090 km².
Population : 1 425 000; 1 127 000 in the Gironde, 297 500 in the Landes.
Climate : mild with a warm, early spring. In this season, the Côte d'Argent (Silver Coast) fully deserves its name when a barely perceptible haze softens contours and colours the seascape. Beautiful days are frequent in autumn, the time of the grape-harvest. Winter, mild on the coast, is hardly more severe inland.
Administration : the Gironde and the Landes belong to the Aquitaine region. Gironde Department, prefecture : Bordeaux; Landes Department, prefecture : Mont-de-Marsan.

● Brief regional history

10th-1stC BC

In the first millennium BC, **Iberians** from Spain established themselves between the Garonne and the Pyrénées. ● Invading **Celts** subsequently pushed them back to the mountains in the 6th and 5thC. ● In 56BC **Publius Crassus,** Julius Caesar's lieutenant, fought a victorious campaign against the Celts in the Aquitaine basin.

1st-4thC AD

In the 1stC AD, **Roman colonization** was in full swing in the area. Prosperous Gallo-Roman **villas** were built throughout Aquitaine at this time. ● The 4thC saw the flowering of a brilliant cultural **elite** that included the poet and grammarian Ausonius (309-394) and **St. Paulinus of Nole,** bishop and poet, born in 353.

5th-8thC

The great barbarian **invasions** began in the 5thC, reaching a climax when the **Visigoths** forced the Emperor **Honorius** to cede them an empire in the SW with Toulouse as its capital. In the early 6thC, however, the Frankish king **Clovis** defeated the Visigoth **Alaric;** this led to the absorption of Aquitaine into the Frankish kingdom. ● At the end of the century, the **Vascons** (Iberians who had not been colonized by Rome) came down from their Pyrenean fortresses and systematically ravaged the region. ● However, in the mid-7thC an alliance between the Vascons and the Aquitaines led to the restoration of the Kingdom of Toulouse now ruled by the **Dukes of Aquitaine.** ● The Saracens invaded Aquitaine in 729; Duke **Eudes** sought help from **Charles Martel** (viceroy of the king of the Franks) who crushed the Arab invading force at Poitiers (732). ● Charles Martel occupied the entire Bordeaux region when, in 735, Duke **Hunald,** son of Eudes, refused to recognize his suzerainty. Martel's son, **Pépin le Bref,** the first king of the Carolingian Dynasty, completed the conquest of Aquitaine in 759. ● In 780 Charlemagne made Aquitaine a kingdom for his son Louis the Pious and entrusted **Guilhem,** Count of Toulouse, with the defense against Muslim invaders.

9th-12thC

In 817 **Louis the Pious** made his son Pépin Viceroy of Aquitaine. ● But in the 10thC anarchy spread and the country broke up for a time into numerous **independent baronies.** ● A period of relative security in the 11thC favoured the expansion of **monastic foundations,** which cleared the land and increased agricultural development. **Pilgrims** flocked to the shrine of Santiago da Compostela in Spain, and various religious orders established numerous hostelries along the roads they traveled. ● In 1036 the Duchy of Gascony was amalgamated with the **Duchy of Aquitaine,** now ruled by the **Counts of Poitiers.** ● In 1137, **Eleanor of Aquitaine,** sole heiress and daughter of Duke Guillaume X, married the King of France, **Louis VII,** who repudiated her in 1152. She then married **Henry Plantagenêt,** heir to the English throne (who already possessed Anjou, Touraine, and Normandy), bringing him a priceless dowry. ● In 1169, Henry ceded Aquitaine to his son, **Richard the Lionheart.**

12th-15thC

The death of Richard the Lionheart in 1199, followed by Eleanor's death in 1204, began a period of instability; **King John,** Richard's younger brother, was unable to maintain power in his distant duchy. ● But in the mid-13thC the Gascon **stewards** appointed by **King Henry III** achieved a return to order with the help of the Church. The King of England granted the Gascon towns important **freedoms** to consolidate his control. ● The period of peace that followed brought about **changes in the patterns of rural population;** from 1250 to 1350 numerous walled towns (*bastides*) were built. ● At the beginning of the Hundred Years' War, the **Black Prince,** Duke of Aquitaine and son of

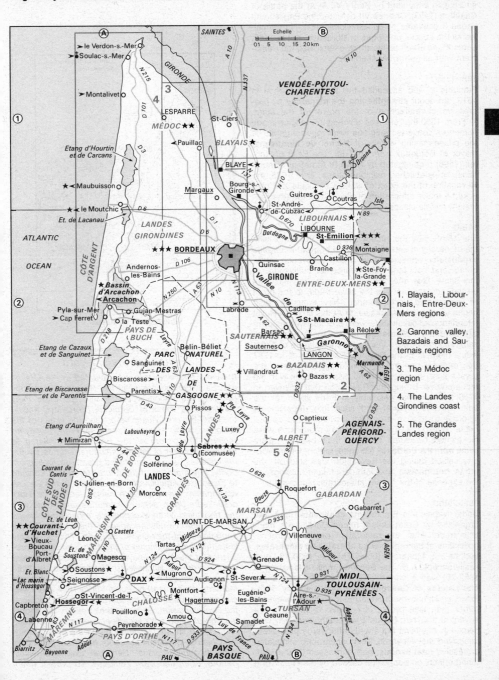

1. Blayais, Libournais, Entre-Deux-Mers regions

2. Garonne valley, Bazadais and Sauternais regions

3. The Médoc region

4. The Landes Girondines coast

5. The Grandes Landes region

Edward III of England, defeated the French at Poitiers in 1356. ● His death in 1376 led to the emergence of the **Guyenne parliament** and the **city government of Bordeaux** as the real centres of power in the region. ● In 1451 Bordeaux recognized the suzerainty of the French king, but the following year rallied to an English army sent by **Henry VI**. ● At the battle of **Castillon** (1453), **Charles VII** defeated the English and ended 3 centuries of English domination. He cancelled all the special privileges of Bordeaux, but in 1462, **Louis XI**, an adroit politician, re-established the Parliament with all its former liberties.

16th-17thC

François I, who ascended the throne of France in 1515, set about **strengthening the monarchy** by progressive **centralization** of the power of the state. ● From 1550 the reformed (Protestant) religion made numerous converts; **religious wars** raged, in spite of the peace-making efforts of **Michel de Montaigne,** mayor of Bordeaux from 1581-85. The Edict of Nantes (1598) promulgated by **Henri IV** (a native of Aquitaine), re-established religious peace. ● In 1685, the Revocation of the Edict of Nantes by **Louis XIV** provoked a major **emigration** of the Huguenots (the Protestant middle class).

18thC

The 18thC saw the **reconciliation** of Bordeaux with the monarchy. It was also a period of great **economic expansion;** vineyards and maize cultivation prospered, and new land was cleared for cultivation. At the same time the wine trade with England was on the increase, as was the slave trade, to the profit of Europe and North America. New industries also began to appear in Aquitaine. ● At this time the Royal Intendants (administrators) were profoundly transforming Bordeaux; **Montesquieu,** whose ideas on the separation of powers inspired the legislators of 1791, was a member of the Guyenne Parliament. ● In 1787 this regional parliament, in refusing to register the royal edicts, signalled general dissatisfaction with the monarchy. ● During the Revolution that followed in 1789, the National Assembly at Paris voted for the administrative division of France into **departments** in order to abolish provincial privileges and special rights. ● In 1792, the Revolutionary moderates were nicknamed *Girondins* because their best speakers came from the Bordeaux (Gironde) region. When property seized during the Revolution was sold off, the **urban bourgeoisie** acquired large land-holdings, at the expense of the former aristocratic landowners.

19th-20thC

Under Napoleon's Empire, the **continental blockade** organized by Great Britain ruined Bordeaux's maritime trade. After the restoration of the Bourbons, politicians of the region were **liberals** and **moderates,** and the July Monarchy (Louis-Philippe, 1830-48) was easily accepted. ● The Second Empire (Napoleon II, 1852-70) was a period of great **economic change.** The **Landes of Gascony** were systematically developed, and landowners preferred to cultivate vineyards rather than less profitable cereals. ● In 1870, the advent of the Third Republic was enthusiastically welcomed in Aquitaine but shortly afterwards **phylloxera** destroyed the vineyards. This catastrophe stimulated a massive **rural exodus,** only surpassed by the shattering effects on population caused by the First World War. ● Since WWI, successive French governments have sought to encourage **industrial development** in the area. At the same time, **agriculture** has undergone a **revolution :** the grape no longer monopolizes the land. Other crops, especially maize, vegetables and fruit, have developed well.

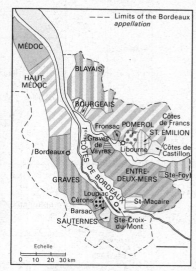

Vineyards of Bordeaux

History of the vineyard

It seems that vineyards were planted in the Graves and Saint-Émilion areas by the Romans when they occupied the region around 50BC. The Elder Pliny mentions the wines of Burdigala (Bordeaux) and in the 4thC the poet Ausonius praised the wines of the Garonne Valley. As with all the great French vineyard regions, the history of the Bordelais is related to the development of large agricultural estates by the monasteries, which contributed greatly to their prosperity. The marriage of the future Henry II of England to Eleanor of Aquitaine (1152) resulted in the English ascendancy over Aquitaine, which led to the Hundred Years' War, some 2 centuries later. This was the beginning of an exceptionally prosperous period for Bordeaux wines because of the strong English appreciation of their clairet, or claret. This prosperity lasted until the beginning of the 13thC, when the production of the Aunis vineyards farther north was sent directly from La Rochelle to Flanders and England, but the conquest of Aunis (now part of the Charente Maritime department) by Louis VIII in 1224 eventually closed this route, and the Bordeaux wines regained the English market. To insure their delivery in London, the English fitted out a wine fleet numbering 300 ships in 1370. To satisfy the demands on the other side of the Channel, Bordeaux asked for help from producers in neighbouring regions : Bergerac, Gaillac, Moissac, Cahors, Agen and even Toulouse. To protect them-

selves from possible competition, they obtained important privileges and tax deductions from the King of
England. These were abolished by Charles VII after
France reconquered Guyenne, but later re-established
by the shrewd Louis XI.
Although Bordeaux appears to have been the wine-
making capital of the civilized world during the Middle Ages, the region had yet to become pre-eminent
in terms of quality. At that time a wine's geographical origins were not considered important and the
idea of classification by growth was unknown. In the
same way that Châteauneuf-du-Pape was used to
improve Burgundy wines, the red wines of Gaillac and
the black wine of Cahors were frequently used to give
body to the lighter clarets of Bordeaux. The Bordeaux wineries showed their gratitude to the Gaillac
producers by allowing them privileges that prohibited
Cahors and Bergerac winemakers from competing.
In the 17thC, land ownership progressively passed
to parliamentary aristocrats, recently ennobled and
financially more sound than the old landowning families. The land they accumulated was made into large
vineyards, notably in the Médoc. However, even at
that time, the Bordeaux vineyards produced only
young wine that aged poorly. In 1647, when prices for
red wines were fixed by the authorities in Bordeaux,
the palus wines (from the marshland on the edge of
the Gironde) were given the highest value, followed
by Graves and Médoc. Today, these evaluations
seem completely topsy-turvy, given that nowadays
the palus wines do not even have a special appellation. In the 18thC, thanks to the industrial production of glass and corks, it became possible to age
wine under suitable conditions. The Duc de Richelieu,
governor of Guyenne, introduced Bordeaux wines to
Louis XV's court, and the writer Montesquieu used
connections gained through his philosophical works
to spread the taste for wines produced on his property among Europe's most refined palates. Based
upon the quality of their conservation and their capacity to improve with age, a hierarchy was established
among competing wines according to their district of
origin. Thus began the idea of crus, or growths. In the
19thC the identification of a growth with a particular
piece of land became so precise that it became possible to distinguish the wine of one estate or château
from another. (The use of the word château in a wine-
producing area may denote either a castle or mansion, or simply a vineyard and out-buildings.) In 1885,
at the request of Napoleon III, the Médoc wines were
classified at last. They included one Graves, the Haut-
Brion, but excluded those that at the time were considered to be "from the wrong side of the river" -
Saint-Émilion and Pomerol. It was only in 1911, after
endless quarreling and litigation, that the limits of the
Bordeaux wine region became those of the Gironde
department. In contrast with the 19thC, the practice of
bottling wine at its vineyard of origin became general-
ized after 1925, encouraged by merchants who were
thus able to be sure of the quality of the wine
they bought. Today, however, only 10% of the producers within the Appellation Contrôlée of the Bordeaux region, created in 1936, bottle their own wine.
The production of Bordeaux wines currently varies
between 90 and 100 million gallons per annum. One-
third of this is white, and the total represents about
half the entire French production of Appellation Contrôlée wines.

 # Practical information

Information : Aquitaine : Comité Régional du Tourisme
(C.R.T.), 24, allées de Tourny, 33000 Bordeaux,
☎ 56.44.48.02; **Gironde :** Comité Départemental du Tourisme (C.D.T.), 21, cours de l'Intendance, 33080 Bordeaux
Cedex, ☎ 56.52.61.40; **Landes :** C.D.T., 22, rue V.-Hugo,
40011 Mont-de-Marsan, ☎ 58.75.38.67. Dir. régionale de
la Jeunesse et des Sports, Cité administrative, tour
«A», B.P. 65, rue Jules-Ferry, 33090 Bordeaux Cedex,
☎ 56.24.33.33. Dir. rég. des Affaires culturelles, 26-28,
pl. Gambetta, 33074 Bordeaux Cedex, ☎ 56.52.01.68.

Youth information : C.I.J.A., 5, rue Duffour-Dubergier,
33000 Bordeaux, ☎ 56.48.55.50.

S.O.S. : Gironde : SAMU (Emergency Medical Service),
☎ 56.96.70.70. **Landes :** SAMU, ☎ 58.75.44.44 (Mont-
de-Marsan) and 58.74.22.22 (Dax). Poisoning Emergency
Centre : ☎ 56.96.40.80. Ocean rescue centre :
☎ 56.52.26.23.

Weather forecast : Gironde : ☎ 56.34.26.74.; **Landes,**
☎ 58.75.28.44. Marine Forecast : ☎ 56.83.17.00.

Rural gîtes and chambres d'hôtes : Gironde : Relais
départementale des gîtes ruraux, 38, rue Ferrère, 33000
Bordeaux, ☎ 56.81.54.23.

Camping-car rentals : Gironde : Centour Aquitaine, 32,
bd de la Plage, 33120 Arcachon, ☎ 56.83.06.37; Caravan Park, 853, cours Gal-de-Gaulle, 33000 Draguignan,
☎ 59.89.12.69.

Festivals : Apr : music festival week in Saint-André-de-
Cubzac; Albret Musical (Apr-Aug), ☎ 58.46.40.40, ext
2202. **May :** music in Bazadais; May music festival in Bordeaux, ☎ 56.90.91.60, ext 1259. **Jun-Sep :** music season in the Guîtres Abbey, ☎ 57.49.12.74; abbey festival,
☎ 58.74.74.33. **Jul-Aug :** music weeks. **Aug :** Chalosse
musical monuments, ☎ 58.97.71.93. **Oct :** music in Eysi-
nes, ☎ 56.28.03.33. **Nov :** SIGMA in Bordeaux (contemporary art works).

Sporting events : mid-Mar : coastal regatta in Cagnotte.
Apr : cow-running in most Landes communities, enq. :
C.D.T., S.I. and O.T. **14 Jul :** Haute-Lande marathon (race
on stilts). **Aug :** Cesta Punta international tournament in
Hossegor. **Dec :** international show jumping in Bordeaux.

Exhibitions and trade fairs : Feb : salon des antiquaires
in Bordeaux. **Apr :** exhibition fair in Biscarosse. **May :** Bordeaux international fair. **Jun :** wine fete in Carcans-Mau-
buisson. **Aug :** pony and draught horse fair in Saubusse;
honey fair in Pissos; wine fair in Sainte-Croix-du-Mont;
oyster fair in Gujan-Mestras and Claoney. **Sep :** Ousse-
Suzan grand fair (St-Michel). **Oct :** radio, television, elec-
troacoustic and audiovisual show in Bordeaux.

Rural and traditional festivals and fairs : Feb : carnival in
Saubusse. **Mar :** fatted oxen parade in Bazas. **Jun :** fête
de la Jurade in Saint-Émilion. **Jul :** Landes coast festival
in the beach resorts; oyster festival around the Arcachon
Basin. **Aug :** jeux floraux (flower show) in Contis; traditional festival in Hagetmau, Dax, Roquefort, Pomarez, Soustons, Saint-Sever and Arcachon. **Sep :** festival of the new
wine in Cadillac, Barsac-Sauternes. **Oct :** grape harvest
festivals. **24 Dec :** feu de la Torelle in Capbreton.

Nature park : Parc régional des Landes de Gascogne,
park office : 13, pl. Jean-Jaurès, 40011 Mont-de-Marsan,
☎ 58.06.24.25.

Rambling and hiking : topoguides (G.R.6) 662/65. The
C.D.T. Landes and Gironde provide useful information on
marked trails in the Landes Nature Park as well as numerous short hikes. Assn. de tourisme pédestre, S.I. du
Pyla, ☎ 56.22.53.83 and Dir. Dép. Jeunesse et Sports
Gironde, ☎ 56.52.13.52; Landes, ☎ 58.75.52.22. Orientation courses : enq. : C.D.T.

Scenic railways : Guîtres-Marcenais line, ☎ 56.39.10.78,
or 56.49.00.89; Sabres-Marqueze line runs on Sat, Sun
and nat hols, Apr-Oct and daily 15 Jun to 20 Sep.

Labouheyre-Marqueze-Sabres line : Sun and nat hols, Jun-15 Sep; *A.B.A.C.*, 40630 Sabres, ☎ 58.07.52.70.

Cycling holidays : the *Comité Dép. de Cyclotourisme des Landes* proposes twenty-five 50-100 km itineraries and a number of permanent circuits; enq : 12, rue Gabriel-Fauré, 40990 Saint-Paul-lès-Dax, ☎ 58.74.27.52, and *C.D.T.* in Mont-de-Marsan. In the **Gironde** region : bookings : *C.D.T.*

Riding holidays : **Gironde** : *Association Régionale de Tourisme Équestre (A.R.T.E.)*, domaine de Volcelest, 33830 Joué-Belin, ☎ 56.88.02.68, and *Ligue Régionale de la Féd. Franç. d'Équitation*, 51, quai de Queyries, 33100 Bordeaux-Bastide, ☎ 56.56.01.38. **Landes** : *A.D.T.E., Chambre d'Agriculture*, 40000 Mont-de-Marsan, ☎ 58.75.15.62 and *C.D.T. Landes* : these organizations give information on the excursion possibilities, itineraries and lodgings.

Technical tourism : manufacture of playing cards : *Boechat Frères S.A.*, Z.I. du Phare, 33700 Mérignac, ☎ 56.34.36.30 by appt.

River and canal cruises : Bordeaux wine cruises on the Garonne and Dordogne rivers and the Midi canal : bookings : *C.D.T.* ☎ 56.52.61.40. Cruises on the Adour River at Dax, ☎ 58.74.87.07.

Instruction courses : In the Landes Nature Park : canoeing, riding and cycling tours, crafts : *Bureau des activités de pleine nature du parc*, ☎ 58.06.24.25. *Centre d'initiation à l'environnement*, B.P. 11, Le Teich, 33470 Gujan-Mestras, ☎ 56.22.80.93. *Centre d'initiation au milieu naturel*, 32, rue de Doumerc, 33000 Bordeaux, ☎ 56.89.45.79. Also, enq. : *C.D.T. Gironde*.

Wine guide : *Conseil interprofessionnel du vin de Bordeaux*, 1, cours du 30-Juillet, 33000 Bordeaux, ☎ 56.52.82.82.

Aquatic sports : sailing, wind-surfing, surfing : for information concerning sailing schools and regattas, contact the *C.D.T.*

Speed-sailing : *Féd. Franç.* : 96, rue Etchenique, 33200 Bordeaux, ☎ 56.02.09.81.

Canoeing : In **Gironde** on the Lège, the Ciron, the Dropt, the Eyre, the Jalle, the Larrit. **Landes** : streams of Contis, Ste-Eulalie and Muchet on the Douze, the Gorbas, the Leyre and the Luy. *C.D.T. Landes* and *Gironde* will give you information about schools and activities.

Golf : *18 holes* : Arcachon, Bordeaux-Caudéran, Bordeaux-Cameyrac, Hossegor, Lacanau; *9 holes* : Bordeaux-Lac, Moliets, Mont-de-Marsan.

Flying, gliding and parachuting : flying : *Union Régionale*, 79, av. du Mal-Leclerc, 33200 Sainte-Foy-la-Grande, ☎ 56.46.15.82; gliding : *Ligue Régionale*, 10, cours Alsace-Lorraine, 33000 Bordeaux, ☎ 56.44.22.81, and

Association Aéronautique Aquitaine, ☎ 56.21.75.57; parachuting : *Ligue Régionale de Parachutisme Sportif d'Aquitaine*, stade Vangermez, 33140 Villenave-d'Ornon. **Gironde** : La Teste, ☎ 56.66.09.72; Soulac, ☎ 56.59.84.50. **Landes** : *C.D.T.*

Potholing and spelunking : *Comité Spéléo de Gironde*, hôtel des Sociétés Savantes, 71, rue du Loup, 33000 Bordeaux.

Cow running : *Féd. Franç. de Course Landaise*, 2, rue des Archers, 40100 Dax, ☎ 58.74.70.10, and *C.D.T. Landes*.

Hunting and shooting : *Fédération Dép. des Chasseurs de Gironde*, 82, quai des Chartrons, 33000 Bordeaux, ☎ 56.81.24.45. *Féd. Dép. des Chasseurs des Landes*, 151, av. G.-Clemenceau, B.P. 172, 40130 Dax Cedex, ☎ 58.90.18.69.

Fishing : enq at the *Féd. Dép. des Assoc. de Pêche et Pisciculture (F.D.A.P.P.)*. **Gironde** : 299, cours de la Somme, 33800 Bordeaux, ☎ 56.92.59.48. **Landes** : pl. A.-Briand, 40400 Tartas, ☎ 58.73.43.79. Sea fishing : *Direction des Affaires Maritimes du Littoral Sud-Ouest*, 3, rue Fondaudège, 33000 Bordeaux, ☎ 56.52.10.71, and *Affaires Maritimes*, at the port, 33120 Arcachon, ☎ 56.83.06.47.

Bordeaux cuisine

Bordeaux and its region, well known as the world capital of wine, also enjoy superb food; the two are inseparable. First, there are the sea and its products : plentiful fish, oysters from the Arcachon Basin (gravettes are the youngsters) served at any hour with bread, butter and small sausages. The Gironde and its tributaries provide lamprey, shad, and eel, sometimes even caviar-bearing sturgeon, though this is rare. For gourmets, there is salt-meadow lamb from Pauillac and, in season, mushrooms à la bordelaise (cooked in oil with parsley and garlic); shallots and wine, are used for other dishes à la bordelaise, including the famous entrecôte steak, grilled by preference over vine prunings. Other marvelous products of the Bordeaux area are foie gras (goose and duck livers), confit (any meat preserved in its own fat) and magret (the fresh breast meat of a goose or duck), and excellent 'yellow' chicken (poulet jaune) raised on high quality maize only. You can sometimes find ortolan (a small bird fattened on millet), although it is a protected species. Salmon can still be caught in the Adour and Gaves Réunis. Excellent beef from Saint-Vincent-de-Tyrosse.

Towns and places

A2

From Arcachon to Cap Ferret *(approx 70 km, half day)*

The Arcachon Basin is the only wrinkle in an otherwise straight coastline. It is connected to the ocean by a narrow channel partially obstructed by sand but never entirely blocked, unlike other adjacent basins that have become inland lakes. It is best to explore this area by boat as the scenery changes with the shore : dunes around the pass, stands of pines and modern construction at Arcachon, unusual oyster-farms and vast stretches of sand revealed by low tide.

▶ **Arcachon★** : marine and forest resort, villas; Thiers jetty at the centre of the town's seafront offers views of the Ile aux Oiseaux (an island bird sanctuary) and the entire sea-basin to the N; **Aquarium Museum** *(daily, Easter-1 Nov.)* ▶ 9 km S beyond **Pyla-sur-Mer** is the **Pilat Dune**, rising to a height of about 115 m; shining white sand constantly transformed by the wind. The Dune has been growing for over 100 years. ▶ **La Teste** : oyster farming and fish reservoirs by the landing stage. **La Hume★** *(3 km NE)*, another small oyster harbour, zoological park and village craftwork. ▶ **Gujan-Mestras** : the principal oyster-breeding centre in the basin, a port of tile-roofed cabins; a picturesque place, with channels full of *pinnaces*

(the local type of small fishing vessel) and oyster boats.
▶ **Le Teich,** small town near the Eyre delta; **ornithology reserve,** local and migrating species *(guided visits daily in season).* ▶ **Facture :** large pinewood conversion factory. The route continues through **Audenge, Taussat-les-Bains, Andernos-les-Bains,** the Arcachon Basin's number two resort, and finally **Arès.** At **Lège,** a small road goes through the pines to the wild **Grand-Crohot beach** (bathing sometimes dangerous). Between Lège and Cap-Ferret, several oyster ports; then, at **Cap Ferret★,** luxurious villas scattered among the pines; a tall lighthouse (52 m high, 258 steps) marks the entrance of the basin (from the top, magnificent view). Farther on from Lège, itinerary continues along the **Landes coast** (→) to Grave Point. □

Practical Information ───────────

ANDERNOS-LES-BAINS, ⊠ 33510, 35 km NE of **Arcachon.**
ℹ 33, av. du Gal-de-Gaulle, ☎ 56.82.02.95.

Hotels :
★★ **Central** (L.F.), 20, av. Thiers, ☎ 56.82.02.10, Visa, 12 rm Ⓟ ᐳ ᐸ half pens (h.s.), closed Sun eve and Mon lunch, 15-31 Jan, 15-28 Feb, 320. Rest. ♦ *Le Rétro* ♪ 65-150 ; child : 35.
★★ **Le Coulin,** 3, av. d'Arès, ☎ 56.82.04.35, Visa, 11 rm Ⓟ ᐳ ᐸ half pens (h.s.), closed lun., janv., 370. Rest. ♦ ♪ ᐸ 45-125.
★ **Étoile,** 13, pl. de l'Étoile, ☎ 56.82.00.29, 8 rm, closed Wed (l.s.), 100. Rest. ♦ ♪ 45-90.

⚠ ★★★*Pleine Forêt* (210 pl), ☎ 56.82.17.18.

ARCACHON, ⊠ 33120.
ℹ quinconces de la gare, ☎ 56.83.01.69.
SNCF ☎ 56.83.88.88.
Car rental : *Avis,* 35, av. du Général de Gaulle, ☎ 56.83.89.49.

Hotels :
★★★★ **Arc-Hôtel,** 89, bd de la Plage, ☎ 56.83.06.85, AE DC Euro Visa, 30 rm Ⓟ ᐳ ♪ ❄ □ 420.
★★★ **Grand Hôtel Richelieu,** 185, bd de la Plage, ☎ 56.83.16.50, Tx 540043, AE DC Euro Visa, 45 rm Ⓟ ᐸ ᐳ ᐸ closed 1 Nov-15 Mar, 240. Rest. ♦ ᐸ ♪ ᐸ 50-90.
★★★ **Les Ormes,** 77, bd de la Plage, ☎ 56.83.09.27, Tx 570503, Visa, 24 rm Ⓟ ᐸ ᐳ ᐸ half pens (h.s.), 730. Rest. ♦♦ ᐸ ♪ ᐸ 75-130.
★★★ **Les Vagues,** 9, bd de l'Océan, ☎ 56.83.03.75, AE DC Visa, 21 rm Ⓟ ᐸ ᐳ ♪ half pens (h.s.), closed 15 Nov-1 Apr, 665. Rest. ♦♦ ᐸ ♪ ❄ closed Oct-Easter, 125.
★★★ **Roc Hôtel et Hôtel Moderne,** 200-202, bd de la Plage, ☎ 56.83.05.01, Tx 570503, 55 rm ᐳ ᐸ 200. Rest. ♦ ♪ ᐸ 50-100.
★★ **Gascogne,** 79, cours Héricart-de-Thury, ☎ 56.83.42.52, AE DC Visa, 38 rm ᐳ ᐸ pens (h.s.), 460. Rest. ᐸ 65-130.
★★ **Lamartine,** 28, av. de Lamartine, ☎ 56.83.95.77, AE Euro Visa, 31 rm Ⓟ ᐸ ᐳ ᐸ closed 1 Oct-2 Mar, 210.
★★ **Les Buissonnets,** 12, av. L.-Garros, Le Moulleau, ☎ 56.22.00.83, 8 rm ᐳ ᐸ ❄ pens (h.s.), closed Oct, 240. Rest. ♦ ♪ Spec : seafood, breast of duck, 70-140.

Restaurants :
♦♦ *Chez Boron,* 15, rue Pr-Jolyet, ☎ 56.83.29.96, AE DC Euro Visa ♪ ᐸ closed Wed , last 2 weeks in Feb. Spec : seafood platter, *bouillabaisse royale, filet Saint-Pierre aux morilles,* 140-180.
♦♦ *Le Boucanier,* 222, bd de la Plage, ☎ 56.83.41.82, Euro Visa ♪ ❄ closed Mon (l.s.), 20 Nov-20 Dec. Spec : seafood, *la sole en soufflé de langoustines au blanc de poireaux et la tarte fine aux pommes,* 200.
● ♦ *L'Ecailler,* 1, bd Veyvrien, Montagnère, ☎ 56.83.84.46, Visa Ⓟ ♪ ᐸ closed 6 Oct-1 May. For the exceptionally fresh oysters and seafood, 80-130.
♦ *Chez Yvette,* 59, bd Gal-Leclerc, ☎ 56.83.05.11 ♪ closed 2 Jan-9 Feb. Spec : seafood, 140-180.

⚠ ★★*Les Abatilles* (240 pl), ☎ 56.83.24.15.

Recommended
Casino : 210, bd de la plage, ☎ 56.83.41.44.
Events : *basin festival,* 15 Aug.
Leisure activities : sports, info. *A.P.A.C.S.,* ☎ 56.83.44.02 ; flat-bottomed boat rides in the Arcachon Basin.
♥ *La maison des produits régionaux,* rest stop Cestas, autoroute d'Arcachon, Bernard Lafon's home-canned foods.

CAP-FERRET, ⊠ 33970, 62 km E of **Arcachon.**
ℹ pl. du Marché, ☎ 56.60.63.26.

Hotel :
★★ **Dunes,** 119, av. de Bordeaux, ☎ 56.60.61.81, 13 rm Ⓟ ᐸ ᐸ closed 25 Sep-25 Apr, 155.

⚠ ★★★*Les Sables d'Or* (230 pl), ☎ 56.60.62.73.

GUJAN-MESTRAS, ⊠ 33470, 10 km E of **Arcachon.**
ℹ 41, av. de-Lattre-de-Tassigny, ☎ 56.66.12.65.
SNCF ☎ 56.66.00.68.

Hotels :
★★ **La Guérinière,** 18, cours de Verdun, ☎ 56.66.08.78, Tx 541270, AE DC Euro Visa, 57 rm Ⓟ ♪ ᐳ □ 260. Rest. ♦♦ ᐸ ♪ Seasonal specialities served around the pool, 75-250 ; child : 55.
★ **Il Bacio,** 8, av. de-Lattre-de-Tassigny, La Hume, ☎ 56.66.12.12, 17 rm Ⓟ ᐳ ᐸ half pens (h.s.), closed Wed, Feb and Oct-Nov, 300. Rest. ♦ ♪ 45-105.

Restaurant :
♦ *Les Viviers,* Port-de-Larros, ☎ 56.66.01.04, Tx 560912, AE DC Euro Visa Ⓟ ᐸ ᐳ ♪ closed 1-15 Oct. Seafood, 100-150.

Recommended
Events : *oyster festival,* Aug.
Leisure activities : flat-bottomed boat rides in the harbour ; *Aqua-City,* ☎ 56.66.39.39, closed Oct-May.
♥ oysters : *Orvart,* port de Lauros, ☎ 56.66.01.04 ; *Beynel-Daney,* av. de la Gare, port du Canal, ☎ 56.66.00.37.

PYLA-SUR-MER, ⊠ 33115, 4 km SW of **Arcachon.**
ℹ mairie, rd-pt du Figuier, ☎ 56.22.53.83/56.22.53.83 ; ☎ 56.22.02.22.
SNCF ☎ 56.92.50.50.

Hotels :
★★★ **La Guitoune,** 95, bd de l'Océan, ☎ 56.22.70.10, AE DC Euro Visa, 21 rm Ⓟ ᐸ ᐳ pens, 840. Rest. ♦♦ ᐸ ᐸ Spec : grilled fish, *bouillabaisse,* 120-250.
★★ **Beau Rivage,** 16, bd de l'Océan, ☎ 56.22.01.82, AE DC Visa, 21 rm Ⓟ ᐸ closed 25 Sep-1 Apr, 260. Rest. ♦ closed (l.s.), 60-120.
★★ **La Corniche,** 46, av. L.-Gaume, ☎ 56.22.72.11, 15 rm ᐸ ᐳ pens (h.s.), closed Wed (l.s.), 23 Oct-27 Mar, 660. Rest. ♦♦ ᐸ 80-120.
★★ **Oyana,** 52, av. L.-Gaume, ☎ 56.22.72.59, 17 rm ᐸ ♪ half pens (h.s.), closed 30 Sep-1 Apr, 220. Rest. ♦ 70-90.

Restaurant :
♦♦ *Les Embruns,* 65, bd de l'Océan, ☎ 56.22.50.67 ♪ Spec : fish and shellfish, 120-210.

⚠ ★★★*La Dune* (335 pl), ☎ 56.22.72.17.

La TESTE, ⊠ 33260, 4 km S of **Arcachon.**
ℹ pl. J.-Hameau, ☎ 56.66.55.49 (h.s.).
SNCF ☎ 56.66.29.70.

Hotel :
★★ **Basque** (L.F.), 36, rue du Mal-Foch, ☎ 56.66.26.04, 8 rm ᐳ closed Sun eve and Mon (l.s.), 1 Oct-15 Nov, 180. Rest. ♦ ♪ 80-130.

Restaurant :
♦ *Chez Tintin,* rte de Biscarrosse, ☎ 56.22.74.82 ᐸ ᐳ closed Mon in Sept, 15 Oct-15 Mar, 120-190.

Recommended
♥ oysters : *Cameleyre,* port de La Teste, ☎ 56.66.27.94.

The BAZADAIS Region**

B2
Round trip from La Réole to Roaillan *(approx 60 km, half day; see map 2, Garonne Valley)*

Rolling countryside, in which maize production is gradually encroaching on vineyards. Agricultural enclave bordered to the S and W by the Landes Forest. ▶ From **La Réole** (Garonne Valley →) to **Auros** *(15 km SW)*, gateway to the Bazadais. 4 km NW, remains of 14thC Cistercian **Abbey of Le Rivet.** ▶ The capital of the Bazadais, **Bazas** : on high ground overlooking the small and narrow valley of the Beuve. Above the russet rooftops soars the elegant nave of the **cathedral of St. Jean★,** facing a broad arcaded square. This cathedral is one of the most beautiful Gothic edifices of Aquitaine; built in 1233, partially remodeled in the 16th and 17thC; beautiful **façade★,** three doorways (13thC) with medieval statuary. Christ in the central doorway, flanked by the Virgin Mary (right doorway) and St. Peter (left doorway); fine figured arches. Although rebuilt after the Huguenot damage, the **nave** retains its original Gothic character; in the choir, Louis XV altar in polychrome marble. To the right of the cathedral, pleasant terraced **garden** overlooking the Beuve Valley. Nearby, **Porte Gisquet** (gateway), with two 15thC towers; ancient ramparts. ▶ **Beaulac** : take the road out towards Préchac. To the right, small road to fortified mill (15thC) at **Cossarieu,** at the entry to the **Ciron gorges,** full of greenery, difficult access. ▶ **Préchac** has an original Romanesque church, remodeled 15thC (apse★, capitals). ▶ **Uzeste** *(6 km N)* : former Gothic **collegiate church;** apse, shrine of Pope Clement V (who was born in this region); in the apse chapel, beautiful Virgin of the same period. ▶ **Villandraut★,** birthplace of Pope Clement, who built the town's imposing château, typical of 14thC lowland fortifications *(open daily).* **Roaillan** : Romanesque church. Nearby, **Roquetaillade château★** built in early 14thC by Cardinal de la Mothe (nephew of Clement V); interior restored and decorated by Viollet-le-Duc in the 19thC *(Jul.-Sep., daily 9:30-12 & 2-7; out of season, Sun. pm, 2-6; closed 15 Dec.-15 Jan.)* : very beautiful square keep, 35 m tall; nearby 14thC chapel and ruins of 12th-13thC castle. From Roaillan, take D125 NW to Sauternes and the Sauternais region (→). □

Practical Information _____

BAZAS, ⊠ 33430, 59 km SE of **Bordeaux.**
ℹ️ pl. de la Cathédrale, ☎ 56.25.00.02.

Hotels :
★★★ **Relais de Fompeyre,** rte de Mont-de-Marsan, ☎ 56.25.04.60, AE DC Visa, 32 rm ⌂ ▤ ℘ 275. Rest. ♦ closed Sun eve (l.s.), 60-160.
★★ **Hostellerie Saint-Sauveur** (L.F.), 14, cours du Gal-de-Gaulle, ☎ 56.25.12.18, AE Euro Visa, 10 rm Ⓟ closed Sun, 1-10 Oct, 130.

Recommended
Chambres d'hôtes : *château d'Arbieu,* ☎ 56.25.11.18, 5 rm, 100-180.
Events : *parade of fatted steers,* in Mar.
Farmhouse-inn : at Gajac, 6 km E, *Piquetuge,* ☎ 56.25.10.62.
♥ *Château de Cazeneuve,* 33730 Villandraut, weekend at the château for hog-butchering and lessons in how to make *charcuterie.* Fri to Mon (2 pers.) : 3500-5000F.

The BLAYAIS Region*

B1
From Bordeaux to Saint-Savin *(approx 70 km, half-day; see map 1)*

The Blayais is a transitional region between the Charentes and Entre-Deux-Mers along the right bank of the Gironde, with sharp chalk outcrops that contrast with the smooth, rolling Médoc opposite. The coast is well endowed with natural harbours. This zone along the Gironde produces excellent wines (Côtes de Bourg and Côtes de Blaye), and various crops are produced in the rest of the Blayais.

▶ From **Bordeaux** (→) along the right bank to the Dordogne via the Cubzac viaduct, built by Eiffel in 1882. ▶ **Saint-André-de-Cubzac** : church with Romanesque apse, raised and fortified in the 15thC. **Château de Bouilh,** 2 km N in the heart of the wine country, built in 1787 but not finished, by Victor Louis, architect of the Grand Theatre of Bordeaux *(Thu., Sat., Sun. pm May-Sep.);* wine-tasting room and cellar *(Mon.-Fri.).* ▶ **Saint-Gervais** : fortified Romanesque church. ▶ **Prignac** : to the right, road to the **Pair-non-Pair grotto** in a limestone slope of the Moron Valley, which later joins the Dordogne; inside, paintings from the Aurignacian period. ▶ **Bourg★,** suspended on the edge of a limestone cliff, possesses remains of its 13thC fortifications and several old houses. In the upper city, the *District* terrace offers a superb view of the Gironde. To the W, the **Citadelle château** (17thC), former residence of the Archbishops of Bordeaux, built over a maze of galleries now used as cellars. On the approach to the hill, the **Gironde corniche** (hill road) provides splendid views of the river; beyond Bayon, the route goes past cliffs riddled with galleries and cave dwellings. **Blaye★★,** because of its strategic position on the Gironde, long an active harbour. Impressive fortifications : **citadel** with streets, squares and gardens that have remained unchanged for centuries; convent and cloister (1610); remains of old fortified castle, birthplace of the troubadour Jaufré Rudel; ancient ruins of the St. Romain basilica; according to tradition, the crypt contains the body of the Chevalier Roland, killed fighting the Moors at the legendary battle of Ronceval. The ancient house of the Master-at-Arms, now the Blayais Museum of Art and History *(daily).* ▶ **Saint-Christoly-de-Blaye,** Romanesque church. ▶ **Saint-Savin** : remains of Saujan château. ▶ From Saint-Savin, D18 turns SW towards the **Libournais** region. □

Practical Information _____

BLAYE, ⊠ 33390, 51 km N of **Bordeaux.**
ℹ️ allées Marines, ☎ 57.42.02.45 (h.s.); mairie, ☎ 57.42.10.70. ✈
SNCF ☎ 57.92.50.50.

Hotel :
● ★★ **La Citadelle** (C.H.), pl. d'Armes, ☎ 57.42.17.10, AE DC Visa, 21 rm Ⓟ ⌂ ⌂ ♪ ▤ half pens (h.s.), 440. Rest. ♦♦ ♪ 70-150; child : 55.

⚑ ★★*La Citadelle* (30 pl), ☎ 57.42.00.20.

BORDEAUX***

Agen 139, Bayonne 184, Paris 583 km
pop 208200 ⊠ 33000   B2

Bordeaux is the great tidal port of the Gironde River. Thanks to innovative town planning imposed by the *Intendants Royaux* (administrators), the city's 18thC architecture remains an impressive whole. The quays fronting the river form a broad crescent, hence the nickname *port de la lune* ("moon port") and the coat of arms of Bordeaux, a silver crescent and blue waves.

▶ The town's unique 18thC character is exemplified by the Place de la Comédie at its centre and the **Grand Theatre★** (C2), built between 1773 and 1780 by Victor Louis. To the S, the Rue Ste.-Catherine, commercial centre of Bordeaux, links the Place de la Comédie with the **Porte d'Aquitaine** (1755); to the NW stretch the Allées de Tourny, 200 ft. wide. ▶ The **Quinconces Esplanade** (C1) built 1818-28 on the site of the château Trompette, forms a semicircle as far as the 130-ft high **Girondins monument** (1895), topped by its statue of Liberty. Also, immense statues of Montaigne and Montesquieu and, on the quayside, columns (1829) with allegorical figures representing Commerce and Navigation. Nearby, the **public gardens** (B1), 25 acres laid out by Tourny in

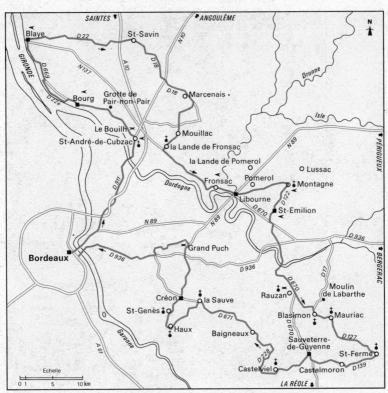

SAINTES • ANGOULÊME • N

Blaye   D 22   St-Savin

GIRONDE   D 669   N 137   A 10   D 18   Dronne

Bourg   Grotte de   Pair-non-Pair   D 18   Marcenais •   Isle

Le Bouilh   Mouillac   PÉRIGUEUX

St-André-de-Cubzac   la Lande de Fronsac   N 89

la Lande de Pomerol

Lussac

Fronsac   Pomerol   Montagne

Dordogne   Libourne   D 122   St-Emilion

N 89   N 89   D 670

Bordeaux   Grand Puch   D 936   BERGERAC

D 936   D 936   D 17

Créon   la Sauve   Rauzan   D 670   Moulin   de Labarthe

St-Genès   Blasimon   Mauriac

Garonne   Haux   Baigneaux   D 671   D 670   D 127

A 61   Sauveterre-   de-Guyenne   D 139

Echelle   Castelviel   Castelmoron   St-Ferme

0 1   5   10 km   LA RÉOLE

Blayais, Libournais, Entre-Mer Regions

1746-56, a favourite promenade for the people of Bordeaux. **Museum of Natural History** *(pm daily ex Tue.).*
► Rue Ferrère (C1), the former Lainé warehouses now contain the CAPC **Contemporary Art Museum** *(11-7, closed Mon.)* which is enhanced by remarkable 19thC architecture. ► The **Gallien Palace** (B2) : 3rdC Roman amphitheatre, the only remains of ancient Burdigala, as the Romans called the city; farther on, **St. Seurin church★**, original edifice of the 12th-15thC, one of the city's oldest sanctuaries. A modern façade hides the 12thC porch; crypt from the 11thC, sarcophagi and Merovingian remains. ► **Place Gambetta** (B2), the city's loveliest square, has a pleasant garden surrounded by Louis XV houses. ► Elegant stores stretch along the **Cours de l'Intendance,** smart shopping precinct. (The closest equivalent to *Cours* in English is "mall".) To the left of Rue Martignac is the **church of Notre-Dame** (B2), 17thC; former Dominican chapel, fine example of the "Jesuit" style (French Baroque). ► On Place Pey-Berland (C3) is the **Jean Moulin Centre** : Museum of the Resistance coupled with a documentation centre on WWII *(pm; closed Sat., Sun. and nat. hols.).* **Cathedral of St. André★★** : two spires 250ft tall; single nave (mid-12thC); Gothic transept and choir (14thC). On the N side, the royal door (13thC) : the statuary here is among the most beautiful examples of Gothic art. Next to the apse, in a square, is the bell tower of the cathedral, the **Tour Pey-Berland,** built 1440-46. ► On the Place de Rohan, the **Hôtel de Ville** (town hall; B3) occupies what used to be the Archbishop's residence. At 39 Rue Bouffard, the **Museum of Decorative Arts** depicts life in Bordeaux from the Middle Ages to the 18thC *(pm daily ex Sun. and Tue.).* In the gallery to the N, the **Fine Arts Museum★★** contains a rich collec-

tion of painting and sculpture from the 15thC to the present; numerous contemporary works *(10-12 & 2-6 daily ex Tue.).* ► The **Place de la République** is bordered by the Law Courts (Palais de Justice, 1846) and the St. André hospital. To the right, Rue Jean-Burguet leads to the **church of Ste. Eulalie,** 12th-16thC Gothic. From here, Rue Paul-Louis-Lande continues to the Cours Pasteur, opposite the building that used to house the Bordeaux Faculty of Letters (1886); vestibule with tomb of Michel de Montaigne. ► **Cours Victor-Hugo** (C-D3) : to the right, the **Lycée Montaigne,** a former Jesuit college (17th and 19thC façade); to the left at the top of Rue St-James stands the **Grosse Cloche Gate★;** nearby, the **church of St. Eloi,** 13th-15thC. ► **Church of St. Michel** (D4), a broad, triple-naved edifice dating from the 14th-16thC : aisle chapels closed off with 18thC iron grilles; inside, fine works of art. Nearby, the **Tour St. Michel** : hexagonal bell tower (1472-92) with 330-ft spire. ► **Church of Ste. Croix** (D4; 12th-13thC), famed for its Romanesque façade (restored). The Fine Arts Academy now occupies the former abbey (18thC). Along the Garonne quays to the left, the **Pont de Pierre** (501 m long); this was the first bridge built here (1882), connecting the city to the *bastide* area on the other side of the river. The Burgundy Gate (1775) stands on the Bordeaux end of the bridge at the centre of a graceful crescent formed by Louis XV buildings. Buildings in the same style stand along the quays. Downstream from the bridge, the **Cailhau Gate** (D3; 1495) recalls the stone ballast unloaded on the neighbouring quay (*cailhau* is Gascon dialect for "pebble" or "stone"). It is now the **Museum of Old Bordeaux.** ► **Place de la Bourse★★★** (D3) opens on to the Garonne quayside. This is an interesting ensemble of 18thC architecture. To the left is the

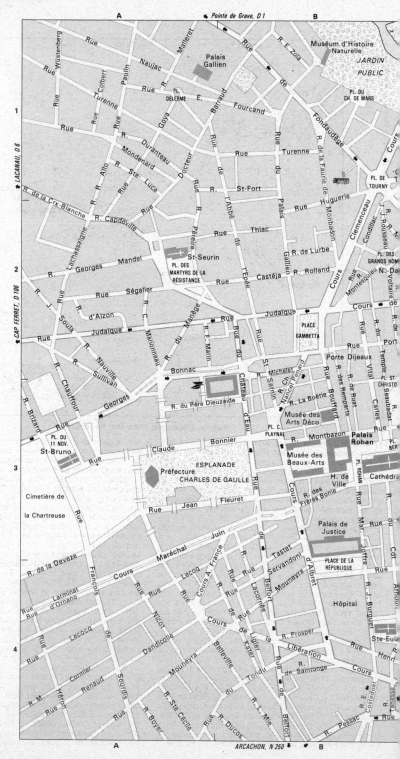

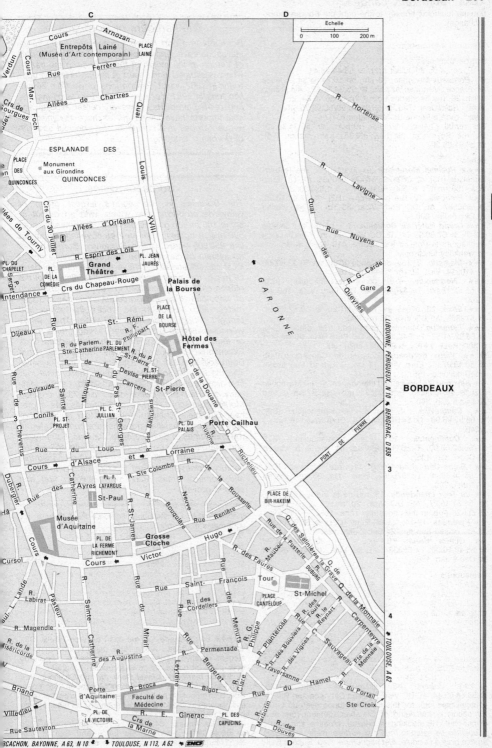

Douane (customs house), to the right the **Bourse** (stock-exchange). □

Practical Information _____

BORDEAUX

ⓘ 12, cours du 30-Juillet (C2), ☎ 56.44.28.41.
✈ *Bordeaux-Mérignac*, 10 km, ☎ 56.34.84.84. Agence Air France, Mérignac Airport, ☎ 56.34.32.32; *Air France* office, 29, rue Esprit-des-Lois (C2), ☎ 56.44.64.35.
SNCF Saint-Jean (D4), ☎ 56.92.50.50/56.92.76.56.
🚌 rue La Raurie-Monbadon (B1).
Car rental : *Avis*, Mérignac Airport, ☎ 56.34.38.22; 59, rue Peyronnet, ☎ 56.92.69.38; train station (F5), ☎ 56.91.65.50.

Hotels :
★★★★ *Pullman Meriadeck* (ex Frantel), 5, rue Robert-Lateulade (B3), ☎ 56.90.92.37, Tx 540565, AE DC Euro Visa, 196 rm P ♪ ⚴ 560. Rest. ♦♦ ♪ 135-220.
★★★ *Français*, 12, rue du Temple (B2), ☎ 56.48.10.35, Tx 550587, AE DC Euro Visa, 36 rm ⚲ ♨ closed 20 Dec-6 Jan, 200.
★★★ *Grand Hôtel de Bordeaux*, 3-5, pl. de la Comédie (C2-3), ☎ 56.90.93.44, AE DC Visa, 98 rm P ⚴ Classical architecture in front of the theatre, 410. Rest. ♦ Brasserie weekday lunch only.
★★★ *Majestic*, 2, rue de Condé (C3), ☎ 56.52.60.44, Tx 410214, Visa, 50 rm P ♪ ⚲ ⚴ 245.
★★★ *Normandie*, 7-9, cours du 30-Juillet (C2), ☎ 56.52.16.80, Tx 570481, AE DC Euro Visa, 100 rm ⚲ 200.
★★★ *Sèze*, 23, allées de Tourny (C2), ☎ 56.52.65.54, Tx 572808, AE DC Visa, 25 rm, 290.
★★★ *Terminus* (Mapotel), Saint-Jean train station (D4), ☎ 56.92.71.58, Tx 540264, AE DC Euro Visa, 80 rm P ♪ ⚴ 360. Rest. ♦♦♦ ♪ ⚴ 90-100; child : 45.
● ★★ *Vieux Bordeaux*, 22, rue du Cancéra (C2-3), ☎ 56.48.07.27, Euro Visa, 11 rm ⚲ closed Sun lunch. 18thC building, 165.
★★ *Bayonne*, 15, cours de l'Intendance, 4, rue Martignac (C2), ☎ 56.48.00.88, Tx 570362, Euro Visa, 37 rm, closed 20 Dec-5 Jan, 160.
★★ *Campaville*, 4, cours G.-Clemenceau (B3), ☎ 56.52.98.98, Tx 541079, AE DC Euro Visa, 45 rm ⚲ ♪ 240.
★★ *Continental*, 10, rue Montesquieu (B2), ☎ 56.52.66.00, Tx 571288, Visa, 51 rm P ⚴ closed 20 Dec-7 Jan, 185.
★★ *Etche-Ona* (Inter-Hôtel) 11, rue Mautrec (C2), ☎ 56.44.36.49, Tx 570362, Euro Visa, 33 rm, closed 1-11 Jan, 200.
★★ *La Tour Intendance*, 16, rue de la Vieille-Tour (B2), ☎ 56.81.46.27, AE DC Visa, 20 rm P ⚲ ⚴ closed 25 Jul-25 Aug. In the pedestrian zone, 195.
★★ *Pyrénées*, 12-14, rue St-Rémi (C2), ☎ 56.81.66.58, 19 rm, closed Sun pm, 24 Dec-2 Jan, 185.
★★ *Quatre Sœurs*, 6, cours du 30-Juillet (C2), ☎ 56.48.16.00, Tx 560334, AE DC Visa, 35 rm ⚲ closed 20 Dec-6 Jan, 190.

Restaurants :
● ♦♦♦ *Le Chapon fin*, 5, rue Montesquieu (D4), ☎ 56.79.10.10, AE DC Visa ♪ ⚴ closed Mon and Sun, 15-23 Feb, 19-27 Apr, 15-30 Jul. Francis Garcia should hang his name over the door, since such is the fashion...It would be that much easier to discover and enjoy his ingenious, inventive cuisine, enjoyably light, yet with a regional accent : *homard tiède sur une petite salade aux parfums des champs, filets de sole aux carottes fondantes, lapereau à la Royale*. The decor is charming, hostess Géraldine Garcia even more so. Some 500 great wines to quench your thirst, 250.
● ♦♦♦ *Dubern*, 42, allées de Tourny (C2), ☎ 56.48.03.44, AE DC Visa ♪ closed Sat noon and Sun. A youthful new look for this local institution (historic Louis XV decor) is the doing of Christian Clément, the new owner-chef. His cooking is original, creative and light : *paupiettes de saumon frais aux huîtres, filets de rougets au foie gras à l'acidulé, filet mignon de veau*. Superb well-

---

The harbours of Bordeaux

Bordeaux is a port for both ocean and river; its installations cover approximately 100 km from the port of Verdon at the mouth of the Gironde to the barge-wharves situated in the heart of the city. Total harbour traffic in 1982 was 17 million tons, down from 20 million tons in 1981, because of the drop in oil imports and related products; however, cereal exports and coal imports have increased, as have the miscellaneous cargoes that constitute the principal strength of Bordeaux shipping.

Bordeaux wines

The Bordelais is the world's largest group of vineyards producing fine wines, with an output of some 100 million gallons per year. That means about 500 million bottles, from an area covering something like 250 000 acres. Unlike Burgundy, Bordeaux has no system of classification by quality, only a set of local classifications that have no common standard. Of these, the most famous is the classification of the Médoc châteaux, organized in 1855 during the reign of Napoleon III by the Bordeaux Chamber of Commerce, and based on the prices the wines had brought during the previous 100 years. Thus, wines were classified as First (premier), second, third, fourth or fifth growths (crus). To these were added Crus Exceptionnels, Crus Bourgeois Supérieurs, Crus Bourgeois and later Crus Artisans and Crus Paysans. The old list still holds good today. The original four first-growth châteaux (Lafite-Rothschild, Latour, Margaux and Haut-Brion) were joined in 1973 by château Mouton-Rothschild. Only one Sauternes has a premier cru title : Château Yquem. Most of the other crus classés (classified growths) are concentrated in the communes of Saint-Estèphe, Pauillac, Saint-Julien and Margaux, all on the deep gravelly soil of the Gironde's south bank. To these should be added this century's classifications of the Graves, Saint-Émilion and Pomerol areas, each with its own first and second growths.

---

stocked cellar. On the upper floor, **Le Petit Dubern**, for light meals at low prices, 100-120.
● ♦♦♦ *Jean Ramet*, 7-8, pl. Jean-Jaurès (C2), ☎ 56.44.12.51, Visa P ♪ closed Sat and Sun. Pure delight in this attractive modern decor !... With his young kitchen staff, Jean Ramet serves extraordinary food in tune with his mood and the market. Contemporary dishes like poached wild cèpe and girolle mushrooms (in season), *salade de moules et coques, côte de bœuf de Bazas à la moelle, tarte chaude aux pommes "Tel Quel"*, as well as more classic preparations. The dining room and cellar (great Bordeaux wines) are overseen by Mme Ramet, 155-400.
● ♦♦♦ *La Chamade*, 20, rue des Piliers-de-Tutelle (D3), ☎ 56.48.13.74, Visa ♪ A fine 18thC cellar is the setting for elegant, creative cuisine : *salade de poissons à l'huile de noix, pavé de turbot, ris de veau poché*, 135-250.
● ♦♦ *Le bistrot du Clavel Gare*, 44, rue Ch.-Doumercq (D4), ☎ 56.92.91.52 ♪ ⚺ closed Mon noon, Sat noon, Sun. Bistro cooking by Francis Garcia for a crowd of regulars, as well as the local soccer team and its fans. Atmosphere, 100-150.
● ♦♦ *Le Rouzic*, 34, cours du Chapeau-rouge (C2), ☎ 56.44.39.11 ♪ closed Sat lunch and Sun in winter. Tranquil elegance and excellent cuisine prepared by

Michel Gautier : *feuilleté léger de queues de langoustines aux morilles et ris de veau*, lamprey. Attractive cellar. On the first floor, the *Bolchoï*, for Russian folklore, food and 25 different vodkas, 195-250.

● ♦♦ *Philippe*, 1, pl. du Parlement (C2), ☎ 56.81.83.15, AE DC Euro Visa ⏧ ♪ closed Mon and Sun , Aug. Fresh from the ocean, fish and seafood : *bar aux raisins frais*, 200-300.

● ♦♦ *Le Cailhau*, 3, pl. du Palais (C3), ☎ 56.81.79.91, AE DC Visa ♪ closed Sat noon and Sun, Aug. An "in" bistro, 135-250.

● ♦♦ *Le Pavillon des Boulevards*, 120, rue de la Croix-de-Seguey (off map A1), ☎ 56.81.51.02, AE DC Euro Visa ⏧ ♿ closed Sat noon and Sun. In a lovely Bordelais residence : *rouget, bar au vinaigre de vin, filets de canette*, 280-320.

♦♦ *Le Vieux Bordeaux*, 27, rue Buhan (D4), ☎ 56.52.94.36, Euro Visa ♪ closed Sat noon and Sun , Feb and Aug, 95-200.

● ♦ *La Tupina*, 6, rue Porte-de-la-Monnaie (D4), ☎ 56.91.56.37, Visa ♿ closed Sun. J.P. Xiradakis, président of the "Association for the Preservation of Southwestern Culinary Traditions", practices what he preaches : *foie gras frais*, duck, baby eels, lamprey and fabulous Bazas beef. And he may soon be serving woodcock and buntings, if ever the law allows. Interesting cellar, 170-210.

● ♦ *Bistrot Du Clavel Centre*, 7, rue Montesquieu (B2), ☎ 56.51.28.81, Visa ⌘ closed Sat and Sun (h.s.) Sat, Sun, Mon lunch (l.s.). Francis Garcia's second bistrot, 100-150.

♦ *La Forge*, 8, rue du Chai-des-Farines (D3), ☎ 56.81.40.96, closed Mon and Sun, 15 Aug-15 Sep, 65-100.

♦ *Le Mably*, 12, rue Mably, ☎ 56.44.30.10, Visa, closed Sun. Friendly and trendy in the centre of town, 55-110.

Recommended
Events : *Grand Théâtre de Bordeaux*, pl. de la Comédie (C2-3); *May music festival*, info at Grand Théâtre, ☎ 56.90.91.60, reserve.
Guide to wines : *Le Cellier Bordelais*, quai de la Monnaie, ☎ 56.31.30.30 ; *Caves de Mujniac*, 180, cours de la Marne, ☎ 56.94.02.03, great and modest Bordeaux wines, F. Darroze's armagnacs ; *Bar des Grands-Hommes*, 10, pl. des Grands-Hommes ; *Hôtel des Vins*, 106, rue Abbé-de-l'Epée, ☎ 56.48.01.29, tastings, sale of Bordeaux wines, wine paraphernalia and museum ; *Cellier des Chartrons*, 41, rue Borie, ☎ 56.81.52.99 ; *Magnum*, 3, rue Gobineau, ☎ 56.48.00.06, tastings, shipping of Bordeaux wines ; *Badie*, 62, allée du Tourny, ☎ 56.52.23.72, wines, brandies.
Guided tours : *le Vieux Bordeaux*, C.N.M.H.S., S.I. (17 Jun-30 Sep). The history of Bordeaux told through the river's history on a boat ride. Departures : embarcadère des Quinconces, quai Louis-XVIII.
Leisure activities : *Grands Bateaux d'Aquitaine*, restaurant boat *Aliénor*, across from 27 quai de Queyries, ☎ 56.86.50.00 ; *Bordeaux leisure activities*, ☎ 56.48.04.68, 24 hours a day.
Youth hostel : 22, cours Barbey (E5).
♥ candies : *Cadiot-Badie*, 26, allées de Tourny, ☎ 56.44.24.22 ; cheese shop : *Jean d'Alos*, 4, rue Montesquieu ; chocolates : *Saunion*, 56, cours G.-Clemenceau, ☎ 56.48.05.75 ; engravery : *M. Mauzauque*, 10, rue des Bahutiers, ☎ 56.52.94.14, Bordeaux glasses custom-engraved ; gourmet groceries : *Le Coin Gourmand*, pl. des Grands-Hommes, ☎ 56.44.00.73 ; *Cerutti*, pl. des Grands-Hommes ; at Le Mouréou, at Cabanac, home-cooked *foie gras* : *F. Chabrette*, 33650 Labrède, 30 km S, ☎ 56.20.24.87.

Nearby

BÈGLES, ⊠ 33130 Bègles-Dorat.

Restaurant :
♦♦ *Erbia*, 1, rte de Courréjean, ☎ 56.85.88.87, Visa Ⓟ ⌕ ♪ ♿ closed Sat noon and Sun. A regional repertory prepared by a lady chef : lamprey, baby squid, scallops in season, 80-200.

BOULIAC, ⊠ 33270 Floirac, 9 km SE.

Restaurants :
● ♦♦♦ *Saint-James*, pl. Camille-Hostein, ☎ 56.20.52.19, AE DC Visa ⏧ ⌕ ♿ ⌘ Jean-Marie Amat serves whatever strikes his fancy at the market, prepared with talent in an avant-garde style. The clients who dine in his lovely, austere restaurant with its superb view of Bordeaux are always enraptured. *Tartare de homard ciboulette, civet de canard à la cuillère, crème au miel au safran*, Pauillac lamb. Good Bordeaux wines, 120-350.
● ♦♦ *Auberge du Marais*, 22, rte de Latresne, ☎ 56.20.52.17, Euro Visa ⏧ ♿ closed Wed, Feb school hols, Aug. Good breeding will out. Honest family cooking at easy-going prices by the family of J.-M. Amat : *saumon au gros sel, lotte rôtie au jambon de canard*. Good Bordeaux wines, 100-170.

CAMBES, ⊠ 33880, 24 km S.

Hotel :
★★ *Hostellerie A la Varenne*, Esconac, ☎ 56.21.31.15, Visa, 12 rm Ⓟ ⏧ ⌕ ♿ closed Wed, 2 Feb-2 Mar, 175. Rest. ♦ ⌕ ♪ ♿ 80-180 ; child : 50.

MACAU, ⊠ 33460, 14 km NW on the D2.

Restaurant :
♦♦ *Château Desplats*, ☎ 56.30.47.77 ⌕ ⏧ ⌕ ♿ closed Mon, 2-16 Jan, 100-200.

PESSAC, ⊠ 33600, 5 km SW.

Hotels :
★★★★ *La Réserve* (R.C.), 74, av. du Bourgailh, ☎ 56.07.13.28, Tx 560585, AE Euro Visa, 20 rm Ⓟ ⏧ ⌕ ⌘ ♫ closed 15 Nov-15 Mar, 400. Rest. ● ♦♦ ⌕ ♪ ♿ The gourmet institution of Flourens (*Dubern* restaurant) in a 17-acre park with a pond and swans, 190-245.
★★★ *Royal Brion*, 10, rue du Pin-Vert, ☎ 56.45.07.72, AE DC Euro Visa, 26 rm Ⓟ ⏧ ⌕ ♿ closed 20 Dec-15 Jan, 220.

SALAUNES, ⊠ 33160, 19 km NW.

Hotel :
★★★ *Les Ardillières*, rte de Lacanau, ☎ 56.05.20.70, AE, 40 rm Ⓟ ⏧ ⌕ ♣ ♿ ⌖ ♫ half pens (h.s.). 15-acre park, 235. Rest. ♦♦ 85-150.

The CHALOSSE Region*

A-B4
From Dax to Mont-de-Marsan *(approx 130 km, full day ; see map 5, Grandes Landes)*

The Chalosse Region covers the green and undulating southern Landes, a totally different landscape from that of the heavily-wooded north. This is the home of *foie gras* (goose and duck liver), free-range chickens and milk-fed veal. This opulent region offers warmth and hospitality and its towns are frequently gastronomic stops.

▶ **Dax** (→). ▶ **At Pontonx** D10 crosses the river Adour into the Chalosse. This road passes first through the *barthes*, low meadows along the left bank of the Adour. ▶ **Poyanne** : beautiful Louis XV château, with a façade composed of five separate pavilions. ▶ **Laurède**, once a stopover for pilgrims to Santiago de Compostela, Spain ; church with striking rococo furnishings (marble pulpit, lectern and altar). ▶ **Near Mugron**, a pretty village overlooking the Adour Valley. **Nerbis** : interesting church, partly 11thC. ▶ **At Montaut**, remains of medieval fortifications, with a church backed up against them ; two naves, one 14thC, the other 15th. ▶ **Saint-Sever★**, which straddles the Adour Valley, was built around an important Benedictine abbey (10thC) ; the abbey church★ (11thC) was damaged by Protestants during the 16thC, but retains the original capitals ; the presbytery and the *hôtel de ville* (town hall) now occupy parts of the former monastic building. The church of the Jacobins is another former abbey church, with an especially beautiful cloister, now under restoration after a long period of use as a grain market. To the S of Saint-Sever, take the narrow road to **Audignon** : church★, bell tower-porch, Romanesque apse. ▶ Country holiday resort of **Hagetmau** : this town is known for chair manufacturing. On the outskirts, the **crypt** of St. Girons is the only vestige of the 12thC abbey which was built around the sepulchre of this saint who evangelized SW France. Inside : beautifully sculpted capitals. ▶ From Hagetmau, go E along D2 to **Samadet**, famous for the pottery made here between 1732 and 1840. See the house of the Abbé de Roquépine, founder of the industry ; small museum *(daily)*. ▶ Beyond Samadet lies the pleasant enclave of **Tursan**, which produces a fine wine classified "VDQS" (*Vin Délimité de Qualité Supérieure ;* → Wine) ; its capital, **Geaune**, was a *bastide* built by a Genoese seneschal for Edward II of England ; the town's church (Languedoc Gothic, 15thC) has a large bell tower-porch. ▶ **Aire-sur-l'Adour★**, founded during the Roman conquest ; 11thC cathedral, later remodeled (beautiful furnishings from the 18thC). In the **Mas d'Aire** suburb, S of this small market town, is the original Romanesque church of Ste. Quitterie, elegantly remodeled : crypt with magnificent 6thC marble sarcophagus★, carved with biblical scenes. ▶ From Aire, continue up the Adour Valley taking N124 towards Mont-de-Marsan. **Grenade-sur-Adour**, a former *bastide* built in the 14thC : church completely redone in the 18thC, except for the apse. On the other bank of the Adour, above the village of **Larrivière**, is the old chapel of St. Savin, built in the 11thC with large stones taken from the Adour ; now dedicated to Notre-Dame of Rugby! ▶ Between Grenade and Mont-de-Marsan, detour towards **Bascons** *(3 km N of Grenade)* : fortified church. At **Bostens**, N of the village : chapel (15thC) Notre-Dame-de-la-Course-Landaise, where participants in the local sport of bull-running can solicit the protection and assistance of the Virgin Mary. The *Courses Landaises* are akin to the annual Pamplona bull-running ; young heifers race the *écarteurs* (dodgers) who try to avoid being butted or trampled. **Mont-de-Marsan** (→) ☐.

Practical Information ─────────────

AIRE-SUR-L'ADOUR, ☒ 40800, 31 km SE of **Mont-de-Marsan**.
ℹ️ pl. Ch.-de-Gaulle, ☎ 58.71.64.70 (h.s.).
SNCF ☎ 58.76.64.65.

⚠️ ★★*Les Ombrages de l'Adour* (100 pl), ☎ 58.76.64.70.

Recommended
Canoes-kayaks rental : *M. Bourrec*, bd Lamothe, ☎ 58.76.67.88.
Leisure activities : excursions on the Adour in canoe-kayaks, info *S.I.*

AMOU, ☒ 40330, 18 km of **Hagetmau**.
ℹ️ mairie, ☎ 58.89.00.22.

Hotel :
★★ *Commerce*, pl. de la poste, ☎ 58.89.02.28, 18 rm ℗ closed Mon eve (l.s.), Nov, 170. Rest. ♦♦ Spec : seafood, 150-200.

Recommended
Bicycle rental : *Larrey*, ☎ 58.57.02.26 ; *Capdeville*, ☎ 58.57.02.99.
Farmhouse-gîte : at Castel-Sarrazin, 4 km N, *Les Pins*, ☎ 58.89.30.31.

GRENADE-SUR-L'ADOUR, ☒ 40270, 30 km from **Mont-de-Marsan**.

Restaurant :
● ♦♦ *Pain Adour et Fantaisie*, 7, pl. des Tilleuls, ☎ 58.45.18.80, closed Mon, 1 Jan-15 Feb. Didier Oudil, a protégé of Michel Guérard since the old days in Asnières at the *Pot-au-Feu*, and kitchen manager at the celebrated establishment in Eugénie-les-Bains, has opened a large, handsome place of his own on the banks of the Adour (terrace in good weather). Three unusual fixed-price menus : one based on crusty bread, another on fish from the river, and the third on the best that the seaso-

nal market has to offer. Wide selection of Bordeaux and other Southwestern wines. Bravo Didier! 115-185.

HAGETMAU, ☒ 40700, 29 km SW of **Mont-de-Marsan**.
ℹ️ ☎ 58.79.38.26.
SNCF ☎ 58.79.33.30.

Hotels :
● ★★ *Auberge Lacs d'Halco*, ☎ 58.79.56.56, 23 rm ℗ ⚠️ 🕸 ⚲ 100. Rest. ♦ ♪ 80-130.
★ *Jambon*, 27, rue Carnot, ☎ 58.79.32.02, Visa, 9 rm ℗ ⚠️ ♪ closed Mon, Jan, 125. Rest. ♦ ♪ ♨ 55-170.
★ *Relais Basque*, 1, rue Pascal-Duprat, ☎ 58.79.30.64, Euro Visa, 6 rm ℗ ♨ closed Fri eve, 85. Rest. ♦ ♪ ♨ 45-60.

⚠️ ★★★★*Les Loussets* (25 pl), ☎ 58.79.33.14.

Recommended
Farmhouse-inn : at Geaune PC 40320, *Colette and Pierre Labrouche*, "Pigon", Vielle Tursan, ☎ 58.79.17.37 ; at Maylis PC 40250, *Armand and Colette Laborde*, "Caoubet", ☎ 58.97.72.91 ; at Morganx PC 40700, *Charlotte and René Lalanne*, "Bontemps", ☎ 58.79.20.04 ; at Mugron PC 40250, *Rosette and René Cabannes*, "Marquine", rte d'Hagetmau, ☎ 58.97.74.23.
Farmhouse-inn : at 2 km on N 133, *César*, ☎ 58.79.41.45.

SAINT-SEVER, ☒ 40500, 17 km SW of **Mont-de-Marsan**.
ℹ️ pl. Tour-du-Sol, ☎ 58.76.00.10 (h.s.).
SNCF ☎ 58.76.00.45.

Hotels :
● ★★ *Relais du Pavillon* (Inter-Hôtel), quartier de Péré, ☎ 58.76.20.22, AE DC Euro Visa, 14 rm ℗ ⚠️ ♪ half pens (h.s.), closed Sun eve , Nov-Mar, 380. Rest. ♦ ♪ ♨ Spec : foie gras, brochette gourmande, wine from the property, 80-170.
★ *France et Ambassadeurs*, pl. Cap.-du-Pouy, ☎ 58.76.00.01, AE DC Euro Visa, 22 rm ℗ ♨ closed Sun eve and Mon, Oct, 100. Rest. ● ♦ Goose and duck star here, 40-150.

⚠️ ★★*Rives de l'Adour* (100 pl), ☎ 58.76.04.60.

Recommended
Events : *historic entertainments*, rue Lamarque, ☎ 58.76.01.38, at the Jacobin abbey. Info *S.I.* in Jul-Aug.

DAX*

Bayonne 50, Bordeaux 142, Paris 736 km
pop 18650 ☒ 40100　　　　　　　　　　　A3-4

Dax (the name derives from the Latin *aquae* - "waters") is today the second-most important thermal spa in France after Aix-les-Bains. Ever since the visit of the Roman Emperor Augustus in the 1stC, Dax has attracted visitors to its hot springs ; combined with mud from the Adour (the celebrated *dacquoise* or *peloïde*), they work wonders for the health.

▶ From the old **bridge** (B1) over the Adour, there is a beautiful view of the town, framed by the green islands of the **Parc Théodore-Denis** (B1 ; Roman arenas) upstream, and the **Parc des Baignots** downstream. At the end of the Latter are the mud basins. ▶ On **Place Thiers** (B2) is a statue of the navigator and mathematician Charles de Borda. Below, mists rise above the **Fontaine Chaude** (B2 ; hot springs daily produce 400 cm³ metres of water at a constant 64°C). ▶ Above the Théodore-Denis park are the remains of **Gallo-Roman fortifications** (B1) from the 4thC, almost entirely destroyed in the last century and converted into a promenade under the plane trees. ▶ The **cathedral★** (B2) was rebuilt in the 17thC in the French Classical style and afterwards restored ; however, the Apostles doorway (13thC) of the former Gothic sanctuary still remains, while inside the church there are 16th-17thC stalls, 18thC furniture and paintings from the 17th and 18thC ▶ In the St-Martin-d'Ages mansion (17thC, Rue Cazade) is the **Borda museum** (archaeology, arts and traditions of the Landes ; *Apr.-Oct. 2-7, Mon.-Fri. ; Nov.-Mar. 2-7, Tue., Wed., Thu. ; closed nat. hols.)*. ▶ The **church**

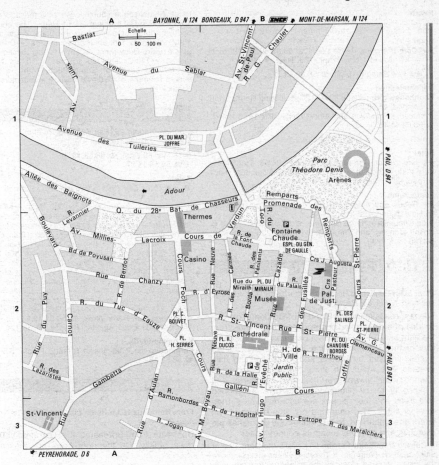

DAX

of **St. Vincent-de-Xaintes** (A3 ; 19thC) has a Gallo-Roman mosaic in the choir.

Nearby

▶ On the right bank of the Adour is **Saint-Paul-lès-Dax**. The **church** has a decorated Romanesque apse★ (frieze★ in marble ; bestiary and religious scenes) running above arcatures, with figured capitals. ▶ **Berceau-de-Saint-Vincent-de-Paul** (Cradle of St. Vincent), 7 km NW : on the church square, by the large oak where Vincent kept his father's flock, is the house in which he was born *(Sat., Sun.).* ▶ **Oeyreluy** *(5 km S) :* the doorway of the village church here is decorated with interesting pre-Romanesque sculpture. ☐

Practical Information _____

DAX
⚓ (year round).
ⓘ pl. Thiers (B1), ☎ 58.74.82.33.
🚉 (B1), ☎ 58.74.50.50/58.74.38.75.
Car rental : *Avis*, av. de la Gare, ☎ 58.74.48.51 ; train station.

Hotels :
● ★★★ *Parc* (Mapotel) 1, pl. Thiers (B2), ☎ 58.74.86.17, AE DC Euro Visa, 40 rm ℗ ♪ & 230. Rest. ♦♦♦ ⌀ closed Sun, 75-200.
★★★ *Grand Hôtel*, rue de la Source (B2), ☎ 58.74.91.75, Tx 540516, AE DC Euro Visa, 138 rm ℗ ⌀ ♪ & ⌧ ⌀ 210. Rest. ♦ ♪ & ⌀ 70-90.
★★★ *Regina*, bd des Sports (B2), ☎ 58.74.84.58, AE DC Euro Visa, 131 rm ℗ ⌀ ♪ closed 4 Dec-3 Mar, 140. Rest. ♦♦ ♪ ⌀ 85-120.
★★ *Miradour*, av. E.-Millies-Lacroix (A2), ☎ 58.74.98.86, AE DC Euro Visa, 120 rm ℗ ♪ ⌀ 210. Rest. ♦ 80-130.
★★ *Richelieu* (L.F.), 13, av. V.-Hugo (B3), ☎ 58.74.81.81, AE Visa, 20 rm ℗ 280. Rest. ♦ Good value. Spec : *homard à la Marensine*, 80-160.
★ *Nord* (L.F.), 68, av. St-Vincent-de-Paul (B1), ☎ 58.74.19.87, 19 rm ℗ ⌀ closed 20 Dec-12 Jan, 100.

Restaurant :
● ♦♦ *Bois de Boulogne*, allée du Bois de Boulogne, ☎ 58.74.23.32, Visa ⌀ ♪ closed Mon, 1 Oct-16 Nov. Excellent grills served in a delightful wooded setting : foie de canard, terrine de queues de langoustes, fresh fish, 50-130.

Recommended
Casino : cours de Verdun, ☎ 58.74.21.35, 58.74.34.40.
♥ woolens : Mme Marès, ☎ 58.74.60.29.

Nearby

CASTETS, ⊠ 40260.

Hotel :
★★ *Côte d'Argent*, rte de Léon, ☎ 58.89.40.33, 12 rm ℙ ⅏ ⚓ ⚄ closed 1 Nov-1 Apr, 100. Rest. ◆ 60-80.

⚠ ★★★*Le Galan* (210 pl), ☎ 58.89.43.52.

Recommended
Farmhouse-gîte : ☎ 58.89.42.17 ; at Jouand'Herm, 5 km S, *Lelanne*, ☎ 58.89.41.89.
♥ stucco : *Françoise and Albert Lesca*, RN 10, 5 km N, ☎ 58.89.41.45.

SAINT-PAUL-LÈS-DAX, ⊠ 40990, 2 km N.

Hotel :
★★ *Lac*, rue du Centre Aéré, ☎ 58.91.84.84, Tx 560690, Euro Visa, 250 rm ℙ ⅏ ⅏ ⚓ ♪ ⚄ ⊡ closed Dec-Jan. Heated pool, 205. Rest. ◆ ⅏ ♪ ⚄ ⚄ 70-90.

Restaurants :
◆◆ *Relais des Plages*, ☎ 58.74.08.86 ⊡ closed Mon, 15 Nov-15 Dec, 120-210.
◆ *La Chaumière*, rte de Bayonne, ☎ 58.91.79.81 ⅏ ⅏ ♪ ⚄ closed Mon eve and Tue (l.s.), 1-15 Nov, 23 Feb-15 Mar, 80-160.

ENTRE-DEUX-MERS Region**

B2
From Saint-Émilion to Bordeaux *(approx 130 km, full day ; see map 1, Blayais Region)*

The fast roads leading NE and E of Bordeaux give little idea of the charming countryside that extends from the right bank of the Garonne. Between the broad valleys of the Garonne and the Dordogne the country is criss-crossed by brooks and small, winding millstreams. The roads run along the crest, each bend offering fresh views over meadows, orchards and tobacco or maize plantations. The hills are topped with trees and their slopes are covered with serried rows of vines. This charming but little-known region offers the unhurried tourist numerous Romanesque churches and *bastides* along its country roads.

▶ Coming from **Saint-Émilion** (→), cross the Dordogne at **Saint-Jean-de-Blaignac**. ▶ The road climbs steeply above the valley, passing close by the village of **Rauzan**, with imposing ruins (13th-14thC) of a feudal castle long held by the Duras family ; fine cylindrical keep. ▶ **Blasimon :** below the town, on the other bank of the River Gamage is the former abbey church of St. Maurice (12th-13thC) : Romanesque façade and wall-belfry ; doorway with elegant carvings ; ruins of the cloister and the chapter house (12thC). 2 km NE on the Gamage is the fortified **mill** of **Labarthe**, built in the 14thC by the Benedictine monks of Blasimon. ▶ 4 km E, **Mauriac**. This town has an interesting Romanesque church fortified in the 14thC. ▶ From there, rejoin D127 to **Saint-Ferme :** church, ancient Benedictine abbey with Romanesque apse (inside : sculpted capitals). ▶ Continue past **Castelmoron-d'Albret**, a picturesque fortified town on rocky hillside coming out at **Sauveterre-de-Guyenne**, a *bastide* built in 1281 by Edward I of England : broad arcaded square and four town gateways. ▶ 8 km SW, **Castelvieil**, on its hill, boasts a 12thC church with a S doorway in perfect Saintonge Romanesque style. ▶ **Saint-Brice.** ▶ Today, the site of the great forest *(silva major)* that gave its name to the little village of **La Sauve**★★ is cloaked with vineyards ; it was cleared by Benedictine monks from the **abbey** founded here by St. Gérard in 1079. The imposing ruins★ of the church and monastic buildings clearly show the importance of this religious establishment on the route of the pilgrims to Compostela. On a neighbouring hilltop is the parish **church of St. Pierre :** Gothic style (early 13thC) ; square apse adorned on the outside with four very fine statues ; inside, interesting 16thC frescos. ▶ From La Sauve, slight detour towards **Haux** *(8 km S ;* another Sain-

tonge Romanesque church, with sculpted doorway) and **Saint-Genès-de-Lombaud**, N of Haux. The church has been a shrine for pilgrims to the Black Virgin since the 13thC ; doorway with amusing sculptures. ▶ **Créon**, heart of the Entre-Deux-Mers region : former *bastide* built in the early 14thC ; arcaded square. ▶ 10 km N stands the fortified **castle of Grand Puch**, 14thC, a well-preserved example of medieval military architecture. ▶ Bordeaux (→).　　　　□

EUGÉNIE-LÈS-BAINS

Mont-de-Marsan 26, Pau 53, Paris 743 km
pop 408 ⊠ 40320 Geaune　　　　B4
⚕ (1 Mar-30 Nov), ☎ 58.58.19.01.
ℹ ☎ 58.58.15.37.

Hotels :
● ★★★★(L) *Les Prés d'Eugénie* (R.C.), ☎ 58.51.19.01, Tx 540470, AE DC, 35 rm ℙ ⅏ ⚓ ♪ ⚘ ⚄ ⊠ ♪ closed 1 Jan-8 Mar, 16 Nov-31 Dec, 1000 Rest. ◆◆◆ *Michel Guérard* ⅏ ♪ ⚄ ⚄ Second Empire charm appreciated by the Empress Eugénie herself and contemporary comfort. Fairy tales still do come true : once upon a time, in the rich land of Chalosse, there was a marvelous mansion, flowery fields, springs and a couple named Michel and Christine Guérard ; you know the rest. If not, a visit is worth any number of words. Discover his surprising slimming cuisine or the richer creations of cuisine *douceur* (or both) executed by Guérard and his lieutenant, Edgar Duhr : *raie en conque marine, suprême de caneton, corne d'abondance aux fruits glacés.* Cooking lessons, 380-430.
★ *Lalanne*, rue René-Vielle, ☎ 58.51.19.17, 10 rm ℙ ⅏ ⚄ closed 31 Oct-1 Apr, 90. Rest. ◆ ⚄ 55-120.

Recommended
Farmhouse-inn : at Vieille-Tursan, *Pigon*, 8.5 km W, ☎ 58.58.16.51.

The GARONNE Valley**

B2
From Bordeaux to La Réole *(approx 70 km, half-day ; see map 2)*

Upstream from Bordeaux, the Garonne Valley narrows rapidly. On the right bank are the limestone

2. Garonne valley, Bazadais and Sauternais regions

hills of **Entre-Deux-Mers** (→). The vineyards here produce both red and white wines and have the appellation "Premières Côtes de Bordeaux". As for the sweet white wines of Loupiac and Sainte-Croix-du-Mont, although belonging to the Premières Côtes, they are sold under their own names. Lastly, the wines produced around Saint-Macaire have the specific appellation "Côtes de Bordeaux Saint-Macaire".

▶ **Bordeaux** (→). ▶ From **Floirac**, where there is an observatory open to the public, the D10 offers excellent views over the river, notably at **Bouliac** (from the terrace of the small Romanesque church, fortified in the 15thC) and at **Quinsac**. ▶ To the N of **Langoiran** is La Peyruche Botanical Park, which includes a small zoo (birds and snakes). On the way out of the village the ruins of a fortified castle (13thC) loom over the Garonne. ▶ **Rions**, village sited on the ruins of a rich Gallo-Roman villa; it was fortified in the 14thC. ▶ **Cadillac★**, another *bastide* made easier to defend by virtue of its position on a hillside above the river, still preserves a segment of the walls that formerly girdled the town. Beautiful gateway (Porte de Mer) and arcaded square.The church (15thC) is flanked by a chapel (1606) containing the tombs of the Dukes of Épernon. Immediately opposite is the imposing **château** (early 17thC) built by the first Duke of Épernon, a friend of Henri III, who became governor of Guyenne under Louis XIII *(daily ex Tue.)*. ▶ **Loupiac** : Roman villa, possibly that of the poet Ausonius, who was full of praise for the wines of the Garonne. ▶ **Sainte-Croix-du-Mont** is built on a knoll surrounded by vineyards. From the church terrace, view of the valley of the Garonne and the Sauternais ; cliff formed by massive piles of fossilized oyster shells from the late Tertiary Age ; cave dwellings. ▶ **Verdelais**, a famous place of pilgrimage to the Virgin since the 14thC. The walls of the church of Notre-Dame, rebuilt after the Religious Wars, are covered with ex-voto plaques. In the cemetery is the gravestone of the painter Henri de Toulouse-Lautrec, who died aged 37 in a nearby château. From the Calvary hill, the view is similar to that of neighbouring Malagar, described by the writer François Mauriac (1883-1970), who lived 1 km from the village. ▶ Opposite **Langon**, an important wine centre on the right bank of the Garonne, is **Saint-Macaire★★**, named after a 6thC bishop. This town is built on limestone rock overlooking the right bank of the river ; its three fine fortified gateways lead into a charming and intact medieval city. A labyrinth of cool, narrow streets centres on the long **Place du Mercadieu** (partly 15thC), which is surrounded by beautiful houses resting on arcades (*couverts*). One of these houses, a post-house in the time of Henri IV, has been made into the **Postal Museum of Aquitaine** : history of the postal service from the Renaissance to the 20thC *(Apr.-15 Oct., 2-6:30 daily ; out of season, Sat., Sun., nat. hols. only)*. St. Sauveur church : panoramic terrace, former Benedictine church (12th-14thC) : in the dome of the apse, **paintings** (14thC) include the Apocalypse of St. John. ▶ **Saint-André-du-Bois** *(5 km from Saint-Macaire)* : the **château de Malromé★**, birthplace of the Counts of Béarn and final home of Toulouse-Lautrec, now houses the Institut Toulouse-Lautrec in one wing (collection of rare drawings, *15 Jun.-15 Sep., 2:30-7)*. ▶ **La Réole★**, a strategic position during the Roman era. Church of St. Pierre : Benedictine monastery built in the 10thC, abbey church rebuilt in the late 18thC. The monastic buildings open on to a terrace (view). To W, the château includes the remains of an English fortress. Perhaps the most intriguing monument, at the highest part of the city, is the ancient *Maison Communale* (12thC), one of the rare Romanesque edifices still remaining in Aquitaine, composed of a hall on the ground floor and the *Salle des Échevins* (aldermen's hall) on the first floor. S of La Réole, beyond the Garonne Valley, is the **Bazadais** region (→). ☐

Practical Information ─────────

LANGON, ⊠ 33210, 46 km SE of **Bordeaux**.
ⓘ allée Jean-Jaurès, ☎ 56.62.34.00. ✦

SNCF ☎ 56.63.32.83.

Hotel :
● ★★★ *Claude Darroze*, 95, cours du Gal-Leclerc, ☎ 56.63.00.48, AE DC Euro Visa, 16 rm Ⓟ ▥ ❦ closed 10 Oct-5 Nov, 285. Rest. ● ♦♦♦ & ❦ In the family birthplace, the Oliviers maintain their fine traditions : lamprey, game in season. Graves wines and Armagnac, 160-250.

Restaurants :
● ♦♦ *Grandgousier*, rte d'Auros, ☎ 56.63.30.59, AE DC Euro Visa Ⓟ ▥ ♪ Local specialties fixed by an alumnus of Darroze ᵇ hure de baudroie, salades aux triquandilles *(tripes)*. Remarkable list of Bordeaux wines, 60-140.
♦♦ *Les Erables*, RN 13, Preignac, ☎ 56.62.20.94, Visa Ⓟ ♪ closed Wed, 55-120 ; child : 40.
▲ ★★*des Allées Marines* (100 pl), ☎ 56.63.50.82.

Recommended
Chambres d'hôtes : at Villandraut, 15 km SW, *les Berdicots*, ☎ 56.25.30.79, tables d'hôtes.

QUINSAC, ⊠ 33360 Latresne, 15 km SE of **Bordeaux**.

Restaurant :
♦♦ *Hostellerie Robinson*, ☎ 56.21.31.09 Ⓟ ∢ ▥ ⌀ & closed Tue, 160-200.

Recommended
Guide to wines : *cave coopérative vinicole*, ☎ 56.20.86.09, closed Sun and Mon.

La RÉOLE, ⊠ 33190, 66 km SE of **Bordeaux**.
ⓘ pl. de la Libération, ☎ 56.61.13.55 (h.s.). ✦
SNCF ☎ 56.61.00.56.

Hotel :
★★ *Centre*, 42, rue A.-Caduc, ☎ 56.61.02.64, AE Euro Visa, 12 rm Ⓟ ⌀ closed Jan, 115. Rest. ♦ ♪ closed Tue, 50-110 ; child : 30.

Restaurant :
● ♦♦ *La Fontine*, rte de l'Église, Fontet, ☎ 56.61.11.81 Ⓟ ∢ ▥ ⌀ ♪ closed Tue eve and Wed. This friendly spot features savoury regional fare, good value : civet de lotte au romarin et genièvre, daube de manchons de canard aux pâtes fraîches maison, 60-140.
▲ ★★*Le Rouergue* (60 pl), ☎ 56.61.10.11.

SAINT-MACAIRE, ⊠ 33490, 49 km SE of **Bordeaux**.
ⓘ Le Prieuré, ☎ 56.63.34.52.

Hotel :
★ *Arts* (L.F.), allée des Tilleuls, ☎ 56.63.07.40, DC Visa, 9 rm Ⓟ ⌀ half pens (h.s.), 270. Rest. ♦♦ *Le Gerbaude* ♪ closed Wed and Sun eve. Duck is the star here, 55-135.

Recommended
Farmhouse-inn : at Verdelais, *Le Roy*, ☎ 56.63.25.26.

The GRANDES LANDES Region★★

A-B3
From Mont-de-Marsan to Lit-et-Mixe *(approx 100 km, full day ; see map 5)*

The Grandes Landes is an immense expanse of forest, entirely artificial : most of it was planted in the last century. The forester remains indispensable : there is no natural equilibrium in the area and if it were left to nature, scrub would gain the upper hand, the sand dunes would start to move, ponds would silt up, and marshes would return due to lack of drainage. This fragile environment is threatened not only by fire and numbering, but also by the encroaching corn plantations and increasing tourist resorts.

▶ **Mont-de-Marsan** (→) : take the road straight through the forest to **Garein** : factory where pine by-products are processed. ▶ 28 km NE, **Luxey** : a former processing plant for resin products open to the public *(same hours as the Ecomusée de Marquèze)*. ▶ **Sabres** : beautiful Renaissance doorway to the church and tall arcaded bell tower. Leave your car at the station if you want to go to Mar-

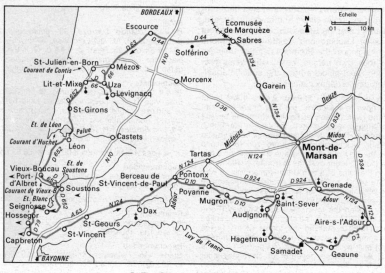

5. The Grandes Landes region

quèze - the train is the only way to get there. ▶ The **Eco-musée de Marquèze★★**, one of the principal attractions of the **Landes de Gascogne regional park★★**; situated 5 km NE of Sabres, Marquèze is a clearing in the heart of the forest, a new museum of faithfully reconstructed 19thC village life in the once-numerous small agricultural communities of the Grandes Landes (horses, watermill, barn, chicken houses; *Jun.-mid-Sep. daily; end Mar.-May and mid-Sep.-end Oct., Sat. pm, Sun. and nat. hols.; closed early Nov.-Mar.*) ▶ **Solférino**, on the road to Mimizan, the former model village founded by Napoleon III in 1857 during his intensive afforestation of the Grandes Landes. Small museum *(daily)* : souvenirs and memorabilia. ▶ On the road from Solférino to **Escource**, the forest gives way in places to intensively cultivated maize fields. ▶ The forest continues from Escource to **Mézos** : church, fortified bell tower (14thC). ▶ From Mézos, leaving **Saint-Julien-en-Born** to the right, the road continues to **Uza**, a village buried in the greenery next to a small lake formed by the Vignac River; remarkable old statues (painted wood) in the church. ▶ 5 km SE, **Levignac★** : another valley formed by the Vignac : traditional Landais half-timbered houses; remarkable 14thC fortified church : wooden vaulting with naif 18thC fresco by local artists; Renaissance doorway installed in the 18thC. ▶ From **Lit-et-Mixe**, D652 runs N towards Mimizan (→), or S towards the *étangs* (ponds) of the **Marensin** (→). □

Practical Information _____

LUXEY, ⊠ 40430 Sore, 43 km N of **Mont-de-Marsan**.
ⓘ mairie, ☎ 58.08.02.28.

Hotel :
Relais de la Haute Lande, ☎ 58.08.02.30, Euro Visa ℗ closed Sun eve and Mon, 15 Jan-20 Feb, 120. Rest. ♦♦ Enjoyable food. Spec : *sole au foie gras, sauce de cèpes*, 65-150.

MÉZOS, ⊠ 40170 Saint-Julien-en-Born, 6 km from **Saint-Julien**.

Restaurant :
♦♦ **Boucau**, ☎ 58.42.61.38, AE DC ℗ ⇆ 🍴 & ⅋ closed Mon and Sun eve , Nov-Feb, 50-150.

SABRES, ⊠ 40630, 35 km NW of **Mont-de-Marsan**.

Hotel :
★★ **Auberge des Pins** (L.F.), rte de la Piscine, ☎ 58.07.50.47, Visa, 14 rm ℗ ⅏ ⤳ ⅋ closed Mon, 15 Jan-15 Feb, 190. Rest. ♦ ⇆ 🍴 & ⅋ 55-120.

⚂ ★★**Les Cigales** (30 pl), ☎ 58.07.52.51.

SAINT-JULIEN-EN-BORN, ⊠ 40170, 18 km S of **Mimizan**.
ⓘ ☎ 58.42.89.80.

Hotel :
★★ **Le Neptune**, Contis-Plage, ☎ 58.42.85.28, 16 rm ℗ closed 15 Sep-1 Jun, 195.

LABENNE

Bayonne 13, Mont-de-Marsan 83, Paris 756 km
pop 2172 ⊠ 40530   A4

ⓘ ☎ 59.45.40.99.
SNCF ☎ 59.31.40.15.

Hotel :
★★ **Européen**, ☎ 59.45.41.49, AE DC Euro Visa, 24 rm ℗ ⅏ closed 15 Jan-1 Mar, 200. Rest. ♦ 🍴 55-100.

⚂ ★★★**La Mer** (300 pl), ☎ 59.45.42.09.

The LANDES GIRONDINES Coast*

A1-2
From Lège to the Pointe de Grave *(approx 130 km, full day; see map 4)*

From the Arcachon Basin to the Pointe de Grave stretches an endless beach of fine sand, backed by dunes. Behind it, other dunes have disappeared under the immense pine forests. The white sand beaches, inland lakes and pines stretch S as far as the mouth of the Adour. Along the coast, the growth of beach resorts is controlled by a master plan formulated by the committee charged with overseeing the development of the Aquitaine coast. This has also initiated construction of new communities around some of the lakes such as Lacanau and Hourtin-Carcans.

The beaches are reached by access roads as there is no coastal road except near Montalivet.

► From **Lège**, at the top of the **Arcachon Basin** (→), head N towards **Le Porge**, a village receded several times because of the advancing dunes. ► From **Lacanau**, a small market-town set in the heart of the pine forest with a beautiful 18thC church, the route leads you to the charming resort of **Moutchic** which extends to the shore of the vast **Lacanau Lake**, a windsurfers' paradise. Waterskiers have their own stretch of water at **Pitrot Lake** very close-by. ► Beyond Moutchic, the road runs alongside the very handsome golf-course at Ardilouse, an exceptional links, before reaching the ocean. On entering **Lacanau-Océan**, the large bathing resort of the "Médoc Atlantique", the route bears to the N by the forest road to arrive at Maubuisson. ► To the left, road to the beach of **Carcans-Plage**. ► **Maubuisson★** : villas and new residences on the edge of **Lake Hourtin-Carcans**, the largest of the Landes lakes (15 000 acres, 19 km long and 3-4 km wide), bordered with marshes to the N and SE; the W bank consists of high, pine-covered dunes. Pleasant open-air centre at **Bombannes**. ► **Hourtin** : sailing, canoes, kayaks. The road then crosses a marsh in the direction of **Hourtin-Plage** (beach), for which development is planned. ► **Pin-Sec**, deserted beaches popular with naturists. ► **Montalivet-les-Bains** : excellent swimming; France's first naturist beach was opened here in 1950. ► **Soulac-sur-Mer★** : exceptional and safe family beach on the ocean; formerly an important harbour on the Gironde, which has gradually silted up since the 16thC; **Notre-Dame-de-la-Fin-des-Terres basilica★** was engulfed by the dunes in 1757. A century later it was unearthed : a fine example of Romanesque architecture, with Saintonge-style apse, and Poitou-style nave; in the interior, beautiful figured capitals depicting the burial of St. Véronique at Soulac; polychrome wood statue of Notre-Dame de la Fin des Terres. ► **Le Verdon-sur-Mer**, to the N of Soulac, a deepwater **port** for tankers and container ships. ► Still farther N, a pine-covered dune marks the **Pointe de Grave** at the entrance to the Gironde Estuary. On the sea wall at the site of the American landings in 1917, is a plaque commemorating the departure of La Fayette to the United States. Pointe de Grave may be reached all the year round from **Royan** (→). In season, a ferry carries visitors to the **Cordouan lighthouse** *(approx 8 km from Pointe de Grave;* the building dates from the Renaissance; superb view). ☐

Practical Information _____

CARCANS-PLAGE, ✉ 33121, 13 km W of **Carcans**.

Hotel :
★★ *Océan* (L.F.), rue de la Plage, ☎ 56.03.31.13, 14 rm, closed Oct-Mar, 180. Rest. ♦ ♪ 120-210.

▲ ★★★*Le Pin Franc* (45 pl), ☎ 56.03.33.57.

HOURTIN, ✉ 33990, 20 km NE of **Maubuisson**.
ⓘ pl. de l'Église, ☎ 56.41.65.57.

Hotel :
★★ *Le Dauphin*, 1, pl. de l'Église, ☎ 56.09.11.15, Visa, 20 rm Ⓟ ♨ ▤ closed Mon, Nov, 190. Rest. ♦ ➾ 55-65; child : 40.

▲ at Hourtin-Plage, ★★★*La Côte d'Argent* (750 pl), ☎ 56.41.60.25.

LACANAU-OCÉAN, ✉ 33680, 12 km SW of **Maubuisson**.
ⓘ pl. de l'Europe, ☎ 56.03.21.01.

Hotel :
★★ *Étoile d'Argent* (L.F.), pl. de l'Europe, ☎ 56.03.21.07, 14 rm Ⓟ ♨ pens (h.s.), closed 1 Dec-15 Jan, 200. Rest. ♦ 65-100; child : 30.

MAUBUISSON, ✉ 33121 Carcans, 9 km W of **Carcans**.
ⓘ rte de l'Océan, ☎ 56.03.31.16.

Hotel :
★★ *Lac*, ☎ 56.03.30.03, Visa, 39 rm Ⓟ ⟜ closed 15 Nov-15 Mar, 205. Rest. ♦ ♪ ᵭ 70-110.

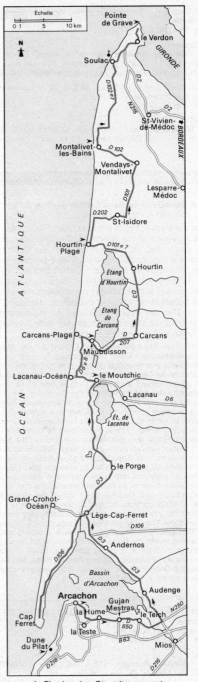

4. The Landes Girondines coast

If you enjoy sports, consult the pages pertaining to the regions; there you will find addresses for practicing your favorite sport.

MONTALIVET-LES-BAINS, ⊠ 33930 Vendays, 35 km NW of **Hourtin.**
ⓘ ☎ 56.41.30.12.

Restaurant :
♦♦ *Clef des Champs*, rte de Vendays, 5 km SE, ☎ 56.41.71.11, Visa 〰 ᴹᴹ ♪ ゟ closed Tue eve (l.s.) and lunch (l.s.), Feb. Reserve. Regional specialties, 150-200.

SOULAC-SUR-MER, ⊠ 33780, 30 km NW of **Lespierre.**
ⓘ pl. du Marché, ☎ 56.59.86.61.
SNCF ☎ 56.59.85.56.

Hotel :
★★ *Molière*, 22, rue F.- Laffargue, ☎ 56.09.82.69, Euro, 17 rm 〰 ᴹᴹ ᕲ ⅋ 🖼 half pens (h.s.), closed 1 Oct-10 Apr, 390. .

The LIBOURNAIS Region*

B2
From Saint-Savin to Saint-Emilion *(approx 60 km half day; see map 1, Blayais Region)*

After the Medoc, this is the next most important wine-growing region of the Bordelais. On both sides of the Isle Valley, and on the right bank of the Dordogne, there is a succession of famous wine-producing districts. From the W to the E : Canon Fronsac, Fronsac, Pomerol and Lalande-de-Pomerol, coupled with Saint-Émilion and its satellite *appellations*. These districts constitute a vast area, exclusively producing red wines. They are nearly as famous as the competing wines from the Médoc, although not distinguished by the same illustrious classification.

▶ D18 from **Saint-Savin** to the E edge of the **Blayais** (→) to **Marcenais** : 13thC Romanesque Templar church. ▶ **Mouillac** : Romanesque church enlarged in the 16thC. ▶ **Lalande-de-Fronsac** : Romanesque church decorated with superb carved tympanum (Apocalypse of St. John). ▶ Beautiful views of the valley of the Dordogne, especially from the hillfort of **Fronsac**; below, in the village, there is a Romanesque church. ▶ **Libourne** is a former English *bastide*, of which the old ramparts have been replaced by a shady promenade. The town borrows its name from the seneschal Roger de Leyburn who founded it in the 13thC. The harbour here for wine boats from Saint-Émilion and Pomerol dates from when lighters came down on the current to meet larger ships entering with the tide. Libourne still has an important role in the wine trade. From the long stone bridge there is an excellent view of the city. Where the Dordogne and the Isle rivers meet, the **Grand-Port tower** (14thC) controls access to the old harbour. The heart of the city is a large arcaded square, very lively on market days. The *Hôtel de Ville* was rebuilt in 1910 : inside is a **museum** of archaeology along with a picture gallery containing works by René Princeteau, one of Toulouse-Lautrec's masters. ▶ Beyond Libourne, a list of prestigious names : **Pomerol, Château Pétrus, Néac,** and finally **Montagne-Saint-Émilion,** with its Romanesque church, much restored. ▶ **Saint-Émilion** (→). ▢

Practical Information

CASTILLON-LA-BATAILLE, ⊠ 33350, 18 km SE of **Libourne.**
ⓘ mairie, ☎ 57.40.00.06.
SNCF ☎ 57.40.00.28.

Hotel :
★★ *Bonne Auberge*, 12, rue du 8-Mai-1945, ☎ 57.40.11.56, AE DC Visa, 10 rm, closed Sat lunch and Mon, 1-21 Nov, 130. Rest. ♦ ♪ Regional foods, 60-155.

🄰 ★★*La Pelouse* (45 pl), ☎ 57.40.04.22.

Recommended
Events : *historic show*, reenactment of the Battle of Castillon, in Aug, info S.I.
Farmhouse-gîte : at Blanzas, ☎ 57.40.25.57.

COUTRAS, ⊠ 33230, 18 km N of **Libourne.**
ⓘ mairie, ☎ 57.49.04.60.
SNCF ☎ 57.49.08.01.

Hotel :
★★★ *Auberge de la Rollandière*, Rolland, 6 km NE, ☎ 57.49.11.63, 9 rm ℗ 〰 ᴹᴹ ᕲ closed Mon, 31 Mar-1 May, 195. Rest. ♦ ♪ ゟ 35-95.

🄰 at Rolland, 6 km NE, ★★*Municipal Frais Rivage* (57 pl), ☎ 57.49.12.00.

LIBOURNE, ⊠ 33500, 31 km E of **Bordeaux.**
ⓘ 1, pl. A.-Surchamp, ☎ 57.51.15.04.
SNCF ☎ 57.51.11.80/57.51.41.50.
Car rental : *Avis*, train station, ☎ 56.91.65.50.

Hotels :
★★★ *Loubat*, 32, rue Chanzy, ☎ 57.51.17.58, Tx 540436, AE Euro Visa, 25 rm ℗ 〰 ᕲ ♪ 235. Rest. ♦♦ Spec : *lamproie à la libournaise, cèpes, entrecôte maître de chai,* 85-170.
★★ *Gare*, 43, rue Chanzy, ☎ 57.51.06.86, 11 rm ℗ 〰 closed Nov, 200. Rest. ♦ closed Sun, 80-120.

Restaurant :
● ♦ *Le Landais*, 15, rue des Treilles, ☎ 57.74.07.40 〰 ゟ Down-home cooking, good and cheap, 35-60.

🄰 ★★*Le Ruste* (100 pl), ☎ 57.51.01.54.

Recommended
Guide to wines : *hospitaliers de Pomerol* wine-tasting and societies : Château de Tailhas, ☎ 57.51.26.02; at Fronsac, 2 km SW, Château Canon de Breur, ☎ 57.51.30.60; at Saint-Michel-de-Fronsac, 6 km, Château la Rivière.

MAGESCQ

Dax 16, Bayonne 45, Paris 728 km
pop 1149 ⊠ 40140 Soustons   A3

ⓘ ☎ 58.47.70.19.

Hotel :
● ★★★ *Relais de la Poste*, ☎ 58.47.70.25, AE DC Visa, 10 rm 2 apt ℗ 〰 ᴹᴹ ᕲ ♪ ⅋ 🖼 ℘ closed Mon eve and Tue, 12 Nov-25 Dec, 350. Rest. ● ♦♦ ゟ The Coussau family performs in the kitchen : *foie gras de canard aux raisins,* fresh grilled salmon, great Bordeaux wines, 200-300.

Restaurant :
● ♦ *Le Cabanon*, RN 10, ☎ 58.47.71.51, Tx 540660, AE Euro Visa 〰 ♪ ゟ closed Mon, 15-30 Oct. Good eating guaranteed. Spec : *pâté chaud de gibier en croûte,* 60-300.

The MARENSIN Region**

A3
From Lit-et-Mixe to Dax *(approx 100 km, full day; see map 5, Grandes Landes)*

This region covers the S section of the Landes coast. Afforested in the 19thC, sparsely populated except in the seaside resorts, the Marensin is dotted with ponds which drain off to the ocean through the dunes.

▶ **Lit-et-Mixe,** where the **Grandes Landes** (→) meet the coastal strip. ▶ **Saint-Girons,** 5 km W : Romanesque fortified church; immense beach of very fine sand. ▶ **Léon** : picturesque Landais half-timbered houses around the church. ▶ **Lake Léon** *(2 km W)* : a paradise for fishermen and windsurfers, and the departure point for boat trips down the capricious **Courant d'Huchet**★★★, through beautiful greenery with rare hibiscus amid the alders, tamarisk and willows *(enq. : Bureau des Bateliers, the boatmen's office, tel. 58.48.75.38).* ▶ **Moliets** : rustic houses among cork-oaks. 3 km W, limitless sandy beach. W and S of the village, **Moliets** and **Prade ponds,** both easily accessible. ▶ **Vieux-Boucau,** once the busy **Port d'Albret,** at the mouth of the Adour; today an active tourist resort on the banks of a 180-acre lake. ▶ The route follows the **Courant de Vieux-Boucau**. ▶ **Soustons★**, founded in the 14thC by the English (its name comes from the English "south town"), small bustling centre (corks, plastic, wood) of an agricultural region (asparagus, maize, chicken); alley of plane-trees to **Soustons Lake**, fringed with rushes. ▶ **Tosse : Romanesque church**, square tower and 12thC apse. ▶ Several kilometres of pinewoods separate the old town of **Seignosse** from **Penon**, a brand-new seaside resort. ▶ **Hossegor★** grew around a lake in the forest before expanding to the ocean. Fine villas in the Basque-Landais style, set in the middle of the pine woods contrast oddly with the modern buildings of Hossegor. ▶ **Capbreton**, situated at the mouth of the Adour; as early as the 10thC it was an important maritime city, its sailors going as far as the North American coast in search of whales. The church tower served as a landmark to navigators, who have venerated the Pietà in the porch since the 15thC; today a large marina has been built where the Bourret and Boudigau rivers meet. The beach here is safe and well protected from ocean swells. ▶ **Saint-Vincent-de-Tyrosse** : cattle-breeding centre. ▶ **Dax** (→). ☐

Practical Information

CAPBRETON, ⊠ 40130, 18 km N of **Bayonne**.
ⓘ av. G.-Pompidou, ☎ 58.72.12.11.

Hotels :
★★ *L'Atlantic*, 75, av. de-Lattre-de-Tassigny, ☎ 58.72.11.14, 53 rm Ⓟ ⟨⟨ 🔲 half pens (h.s.), closed 30 Sep-15 May, 440. Rest. ♦ closed 10 Sep-31 May, 85-100.
★★ *L'Océan* (L.F.), 85, av. G.-Pompidou, ☎ 58.72.10.22, DC Euro Visa, 48 rm Ⓟ ⟨⟨ ⅄ half pens (h.s.), closed Oct-Mar, 420. Rest. ♦♦ ⟨⟨ ⅄ ⅄ ⅋ closed Tue (l.s.), 50-150; child : 30.
★★ *Miramar*, bd Front-de-Mer, ☎ 58.72.12.82, AE Euro, 44 rm Ⓟ ⟨⟨ ⅋ half pens (h.s.), closed 25 Sep-15 May, 380. Rest. ♦ ⟨⟨ ⅄ ⅋ 70-160.

Restaurant :
♦♦ *La Sardinière*, 87-89, av. G.-Pompidou, ☎ 58.72.10.49, AE DC Euro Visa ⟨⟨ ⅄ ⅄ closed 16 Nov-22 Dec, 135-150.

⅄ ★★★*La Civelle* (600 pl), ☎ 58.72.15.11.

HOSSEGOR, ⊠ 40150, 20 km N of **Bayonne**.
ⓘ pl. Pasteur, ☎ 58.43.72.35.

Hotels :
★★★ *Beauséjour*, av. du Tour-du-Lac, ☎ 58.43.51.07, 45 rm Ⓟ ⟨⟨ ⅄ ⅄ ⅋ half pens (h.s.), closed 18 Sep-4 Jun, 280. Rest. ♦ ⅄ ⅋ closed lunch, 125-165.
● ★★ *Les Huîtrières du Lac*, 1187, av. du Touring-Club, ☎ 58.43.51.48, 9 rm Ⓟ ⟨⟨ ⅄ half pens (h.s.), closed Wed (l.s.), Dec-Feb, 400. Rest. ♦ ⅄ ⅄ ⅋ Private oyster park, fish and seafood, 90-150.
★★ *Ermitage*, allée des Pins-Tranquilles, ☎ 58.43.52.22, 12 rm Ⓟ ⟨⟨ ⅄ ⅄ ⅄ half pens (h.s.), closed 20 Sep-30 Mar, 190. Rest. ♦ ⅄ ⅋ closed lunch, 80-150.

Recommended
Baby-sitting : info *S.I.*

LÉON, ⊠ 40550, 28 km NW of **Dax**.
ⓘ rue de la Poste, ☎ 58.48.76.03.

Hotel :
★ *Lac*, ☎ 58.48.73.11, 16 rm Ⓟ ⟨⟨ ⅄ ⅋ half pens (h.s.), closed Oct-Mar, 170. Rest. ♦ ⟨⟨ ⅋ 50-110.

⅄ ★★★★*Lou Puntaou* (720 pl), ☎ 58.48.74.05.

SAINT-VINCENT-DE-TYROSSE, ⊠ 40230, 24 km SW of **Dax**.
ⓘ mairie, ☎ 58.77.00.21.
SNCF ☎ 58.77.03.53.

Hotels :
★★ *Côte d'Argent*, rte d'Hossegor, ☎ 58.77.02.16, 22 rm Ⓟ ⟨⟨ 180. Rest. ♦ 80-130.
★ *Touristes*, av. Nationale, ☎ 58.77.03.28, 10 rm Ⓟ ⟨⟨ 130. Rest. ♦ ⅄ closed Mon, 15 Dec-5 Jan, 60-150.

Restaurant :
● ♦♦ *Le Hittau*, RN 10, ☎ 58.77.11.85, AE DC Euro Visa ⟨⟨ ⅄ ⅄ closed Mon and Sun eve, 15 Feb-10 Mar, 15-30 Oct. In a converted sheepfold, renowned local cuisine, 100-275.

Recommended
♥ at Saint-Geours-de-Marenne, foie gras, magrets : Ets Labeyrie, 7 km NE, ☎ 58.57.30.11.

SEIGNOSSE, ⊠ 40510, 27 km N of **Bayonne**.
ⓘ av. des Lacs, ☎ 58.43.32.15.

Hotel :
● ★★ *Golf*, av. de la Braserade, ☎ 58.43.12.72, Tx 560203, DC Euro Visa, 29 rm Ⓟ ⟨⟨ ⅄ ⅄ 🔲 235. Rest. ♦♦ *L'Assiette landaise* ⅄ For the savoury, flavourful cuisine prepared by Bernard Lacarrau : *pigeon de ferme aux fèves et jambon, turbot en vert et blanc de blettes*, 80-120.

⅄ ★★★★*Les Oyats* (380 pl) ☎ 58.43.37.94 ; ★★★*Penon* (350 pl), ☎ 58.43.30.30.

SOUSTONS, ⊠ 40140, 28 km W of **Dax**.
ⓘ mairie, ☎ 58.41.52.62.

Hotels :
★★★ *Pavillon Landais*, 26, av. du Lac, ☎ 58.41.14.49, AE DC Visa, 8 rm Ⓟ ⟨⟨ ⅄ half pens (h.s.), closed Sun eve , Mon (Oct-Jun) ex school hols, 22 Dec-1 Mar, 440. Rest. ● ♦♦ ⟨⟨ ⅄ On a lakeside, across from Latché and its illustrious owner (François Mitterrand), a delightful stopover for rest and regional repasts : duck, foie gras, salmon from the Adour river, 110-190.
● ★★ *La Bergerie*, av. du Lac, ☎ 58.41.11.43, Visa, 12 rm Ⓟ ⟨⟨ ⅄ ⅋ half pens (h.s.), 440. Rest. ♦ Reserved for guests, 110-220.
★★ *Château Bergeron*, rue du Vicomte, ☎ 58.41.58.14, Visa, 17 rm Ⓟ ⟨⟨ ⅄ ⅋ half pens (h.s.), closed 15 Sep-15 Jun, 400. Rest. ♦ Reserved for guests, 100-220.
★ *Hostellerie du Marensin*, pl. Sterling, ☎ 58.48.05.16, 14 rm ⅋ 95. Rest. ♦ 40-105.

⅄ ★★★★*L'Airial* (400 pl), ☎ 58.48.02.48.

Recommended
Bicycle rental : M. Nicolas, ☎ 58.48.01.10.

VIEUX-BOUCAU-LES-BAINS, ⊠ 40480, 36 km NW of **Dax**.
ⓘ port d'Albret, ☎ 58.48.13.47.

Hotels :
★ *Côte d'Argent*, rue Principale, ☎ 58.48.13.17, 45 rm Ⓟ ⅋ 100. Rest. ♦ closed Mon (l.s.). Spec : *salmis de palombes*, 60-130.
★ *La Marenne*, av. de la Plage, ☎ 58.48.12.70, DC Euro Visa, 38 rm Ⓟ ⟨⟨ ⅋ closed Nov-Mar, 110. Rest. ♦ 90-150.

The MÉDOC Region★★

A1
Circuit Bordeaux to Bordeaux (approx 150 km full day; see map 3)

Bathed·in a special light, the vine-growing Médoc is geographically different from the rest of the Bordeaux region. Its narrow, enclosed valleys provide a wide variety of growing conditions. There is a local saying that the wine is best when the grape "sees" the water (i.e. the Gironde), but this is by no means the case with the great *Premiers Crus*. The stony Médoc soil retains the warmth of the sun well into the night; the vine-growers capitalize on this phenomenon by cutting the vines short to avoid damage from spring frosts. The Médoc is a country of châteaux, which may range from simple farm buildings to the splendid residences of great landowners.

▶ **Blanquefort** on the N edge of Greater Bordeaux : ruins of **château Duras** (14thC) S of the village; a tower-flanked polygonal enclosure razed by order of Louis XIII. ▶ **Mar-**

3. The Médoc region

gaux is celebrated the world over for its red wines, especially **Château-Margaux**, first of the *premiers crus classés*; vineyard of 150 acres; visit cellars *(daily ex Sat., Sun., and nat. hols.)* and winery; exterior of the **château** only (1802) : façade with projecting Ionic porch.▶ **Lamarque** (ferry to Blaye) has a bell tower like a lighthouse; the Château-Lamarque vineyards surround their 13th and 17thC château. ▶ 3 km E by the Gironde is **Fort-Médoc** *(daily 10-7, Jun.-Sep.)*, built by Vauban ca. 1689. Together with the fortress of Blaye on the other bank of the Gironde and Fort-Paté on an island in the estuary, Fort-Médoc formed part of a very effective line of defense for the port of Bordeaux. A beautiful carved gate leads into the bastions; view of the Gironde. ▶ On the right stands **château de Beychevelle★** (1757), its pediment carved with garlands and palm leaves; visit the wine cellars *(daily ex during grape-picking)*. ▶ Beyond **Saint-Julien**, the route runs through famous vineyards. ▶ **Pauillac**, gateway to Bordeaux and centre of the wine trade (visit the Maison du Vin); this district has seen a renewal of activity since the construction of an oil refinery. ▶ In the hamlet of **Pouyalet, château Mouton-Rothschild★★** produces one of the most famous *crus* of the Médoc, and has been a premier cru classé since 1973; visit wine cellar *(closed Sat., Sun. and nat. hols.)*. Wine museum in spectacular ancient cellars *(write or tel. 56.59.22.22)*. From Pouyalet the road goes downhill again toward **château Lafite-Rothschild**, to the left; the wine produced here has graced the finest tables since the 18thC; visit the cellar *(daily, ex during grape harvest in Sep., Oct.)*▶ The **manoir de Cos d'Estournel** *(right)*, bizarre oriental folly dating from the last century. ▶ **Saint-Estèphe**, a large market town surrounded by vineyards ; behind it flows the

Gironde, bordered by fishermen's huts on pilings.▶ **Saint-Seurin-de-Cadourne**, N from Saint-Estèphe, marks the N limit of the *Haut-Médoc* appellation, which covers nearly all the most prestigious châteaux of the region. ▶ **Cadourne** : good view of the Gironde.▶ At **Port-de-By** the road leaves the riverbank and climbs toward the village of **By**. ▶ **Begadan** : of the original Romanesque church only the apse remains. ▶ At **Civrac** : 12thC church. ▶ **Lesparre-Médoc** : handsome square keep, the remains of a 14thC château known as *L'Honneur de Lesparre* ("the pride of Lesparre").▶ **Vertheuil** : former abbey building, 18thC ; Romanesque church★ with remarkable Saintonge Romanesque doorway ; facing the church, alley to fortified gate of the former château (15thC ; square keep and ruins on small wooded hill). ▶ **Saint-Laurent** : church, composite style, Romanesque apse, 14thC façade and 16thC spire. ▶ **Listrac**, known for its Haut-Médoc wine. ▶ At **Moulis**, Romanesque church★ : sculpted corbels, apse, figured capitals inside, fortified chamber above the transept crossing.▶ **Avensan** : in the church, Romanesque apse, interesting 15thC *bas-reliefs* in the altarpiece. ▶ At **Castelnau-de-Médoc** : 15thC church ; stained glass of the same period and several carved wood panels of the 17thC.▶ Bordeaux (→). □

Practical Information ─────────────────

LESPARRE-MEDOC, ⊠ 33340, 38 km S of **Royan**.
ℹ pl. de la Mairie, ☎ 56.41.05.02 (h.s.).
SNCF ☎ 56.41.06.67.

Hotel :
★ *Paris*, 16, cours du Gal-de-Gaulle, ☎ 56.41.00.22, Visa, 10 rm Ⓟ ♨ ⚲ ⅟ closed Feb school hols, 85.

Restaurant :
♦♦ *La Mare aux Grenouilles*, rte de Soulac, ☎ 56.41.03.46, AE DC Visa ⚄ ♨ ♪ ⅟ closed Mon, 1 Oct-10 Mar, 60-85 ; child : 35.

Recommended
Guide to wines : at Bégadan, 7 km N, *cave St-Jean*, ☎ 56.41.50.13 ; *Château la Tour de By*, ☎ 56.41.51.53 ; *Château Patache d'Aux*, ☎ 56.41.50.18.

MARGAUX, ⊠ 33460, 22 km NW of **Bordeaux**.
ℹ mairie, ☎ 56.88.71.36.

Restaurants :
● ♦♦ *Le Lion d'Or*, Arcins, ☎ 56.58.96.79, AE ⚲ closed Mon and Sun eve. The warm and jovial J.-P. Barbier is full of talent. Hurry and discover his honest and generous cooking : *pibailles, lièvre à la royale, palombe à la goutte de sang, col vert à la sauvagine, omelettes aux cèpes ou aux truffes*. You can bring your own wine which, in the heart of wine country, is a fine idea, 45-140 ; child : 20.
● ♦♦ *Le Savoie*, ☎ 56.88.31.76 ♨ ☀ closed Sun and hols, 20 Dec-20 Jan. In the midst of the vineyards, a restaurant people are talking about. Spec : *blanc de bar au soupe de ravioles aux huîtres, rable de lièvre aux betteraves rouges*. Great Bordeaux wines, 50-150.

Recommended
Guide to wines : 20 km S, *Château Lanescan*, ☎ 56.58.91.01, wine and horse museum ; *Château Margaux*, ☎ 56.88.70.28 ; at Cantenac, *Château-Pouget*, ☎ 56.88.30.58.

PAUILLAC, ⊠ 33250, 42 km N of **Bordeaux**.
ℹ ☎ 56.59.03.08.
SNCF ☎ 56.92.50.50.

Hotel :
★★ *France et Angleterre*, 4 quai Albert-de-Pichon, ☎ 56.59.01.20, AE DC Visa, 15 rm Ⓟ ♨ ⚲ 280. Rest. ♦ closed in winter, 120-210.

Recommended
Guide to wines : *Château Lafite-Rothschild*, ☎ 56.59.01.74 ; *Château Mouton-Rothschild*, ☎ 56.59.26.00, wine museum. Visits on written request ; *Château Pichon-Longueville*, ☎ 56.59.19.40 ; at Moulis, 23 km S, *Château Moulin à Vent*, ☎ 56.58.15.79 ; at Saint-

Estèphe, 11 km N, *Château Cos d'Estournel*,
☎ 56.59.25.50.

MIMIZAN*

Mont-de-Marsan 75, Bordeaux 114, Paris 702 km
pop 7410 ⊠ 40200   A3
Two roads from either side of the river link this small
town to the seaside resort of Mimizan-Plage. Until the
17thC there was an active harbour here, the *Segosa*
of the Roman era, which finally disappeared under the
moving sand dunes.

▶ The stabilization of the dunes at the end of the 18thC
enabled the **bell tower★** of a former Benedictine abbey
church to be saved; magnificent Romanesque doorway
(12thC); tympanum (Adoration of the Magi). Around the
abbey were four stone pyramids *(garluch)*, only one of
which remains. They marked the limits of the old sanctuary, where fugitives or the oppressed could find inviol-
able safety. To the W of the old bell tower, the Papeteries
de Gascogne paper mill : documentation room *(pm, season only)*.

Nearby

A pleasant road links Mimizan to **Parentis-en-Born** *(18 km
NE)* : fine views of **Aureilhan lake**, and its larger neighbour at **Parentis** and **Biscarrosse**; derricks of the last of
the Parentis oil wells. The Esso-Rep group, which holds
the well concession, has a permanent exhibition in the
village of Parentis *(Jun.-Aug., 9-8)*. ▶ **Biscarrosse** *(10 km
NW of Parentis)* : renewed activity since the creation of
the Landes testing centre for the aerospace industry.   □

Practical Information _____

MIMIZAN
ⓘ av. M.-Martin, Mimizan-Plage, ☎ 58.09.11.20.

Hotels :
● ★★★ *La Côte d'Argent*, 4-6, av. M.-Martin, Mimizan-
Plage, ☎ 58.09.15.22, AE DC Euro Visa, 40 rm ℗ ⊁ ♪
half pens (h.s.), closed 1 Oct-15 May, 590. Rest. ♦♦ ⊱ ♪
⅋ 110-200.
★★ *Au Bon Coin du Lac*, Le Bourg, ☎ 58.09.01.55, AE
Visa, 9 rm ℗ ⊱ ⑭ ⚭ ⊱ ♪ ⅋ half pens (h.s.), closed Sun
eve and Mon, 840. Rest. ● ♦ ⊱ ♪ ⚭ ⅋ Delicious cuisine
served lakeside : *paupiettes de magret de canard, gâteau
de chou au foie de canard*, 100-280 ; child : 40.
★★ *Mermoz* (L.F.), 16, av. du Courant, Mimizan-Plage,
☎ 58.09.09.30, AE DC Euro Visa, 18 rm ℗ ♪ ⑭ ⊱ ♪
half pens (h.s.), closed 30 Sep-15 May, 435. Rest. ♦ ⊱ ♪
ᵴ ⅋ 80-140.
★★ *Parc* (L.F.), 6, rue des Papeteries, Mimizan-Plage,
☎ 58.09.13.88, Visa, 16 rm ℗ ⑭ ⚭ pens (h.s.), closed
Fri eve and Sat (l.s.), 15 Dec-1 Feb, 460. Rest. ♦ ᵴ
⅋ 70-140.
★★ *Taris*, 19, rue de l'Abbaye, Mimizan-Bourg,
☎ 58.09.02.18, Euro Visa, 23 rm ℗ ⑭ ♪ half pens (h.s.),
175. Rest. ♦ ♪ closed Oct-May, 65-150.

⚓ at south beach ★★★★*Club Marina*, a lot of activities
and services (630 pl), ☎ 58.09.12.66.

Recommended
Casino : ☎ 58.09.05.02.

Nearby

BISCARROSSE-PLAGE, ⊠ 40520, 9 km NW.
ⓘ 19 ter, av. de la Plage, ☎ 58.78.20.96.

Hotels :
★★ *La Forestière* (L.F.), rte d'Arcachon, ☎ 58.78.24.14,
Visa, 34 rm ℗ ⊱ ⑭ ⚭ ᵴ half pens (h.s.), 535. Rest. ♦ ⊱
♪ ᵴ closed Fri and Sat noon , Nov, 70-150 ; child : 70.
★ *Auberge Regina*, 2, av. de la Libération, ☎ 58.78.23.34,
11 rm ℗ ⊱ ⑭ ⚭ pens (h.s.), closed 25 Sep-22 Mar, 520.
Rest. ♦ ⊱ ♪ ᵴ 55-100.

⚓ ★★★*de la Rive* (345 pl), ☎ 58.78.12.33.

GASTES, ⊠ 40160 Parentis-en-Born, 7 km SW.

Hotel :
★ *L'Estanquet* (L.F.), ☎ 58.09.74.00, AE DC Euro Visa,
8 rm ℗ ⑭ ⚭ half pens (h.s.), closed Tue ex summer,
30 Sep-15 May, 170. Rest. ● ♦♦ ♪ Like mother, like
daughter : Pépette Descat cooks as heartily and as well
as mother Georgette, 50-200.

ISPE, ⊠ 40600 Biscarrosse, 6 km N.

Hotel :
★★ *La Caravelle* (L.F.), ☎ 58.78.02.67, 11 rm ℗ ⊱ ⑭ ⚭
⅋ closed 1 Dec-1 Mar, 210. Rest. ♦ ⊱ ♪ ᵴ 80-190.

MONT-DE-MARSAN*

Pau 80, Bordeaux 126, Paris 721 km
pop 27330 ⊠ 40000   B3
Situated at the junction of the Douze and Midou
rivers, which together form the Midouze. This is the
administrative centre of the Landes, with a busy military aircraft testing centre on the outskirts. Particularly lively in mid-July, during the *Fête de la Madeleine*, with *Courses Landaises* and *Corridas*.

▶ Behind the square of the *Hôtel de Ville* (town hall), you
can see picturesque 18thC houses straddling the Ruelle
des Arceaux. ▶ The **Lacataye keep**, only vestige of a
14thC castle built by Gaston Phébus, Count of Béarn,
now transformed into a **Fine Arts museum★** dedicated to
two local sculptors, Charles Despiau and Robert Wiérick
(9:30-12 & 2-6 daily ex Tue.). Nearby is a former **Romanesque chapel** overlooking the Midou, well restored. It
houses the **Dubalen Museum** of prehistory and natural
science *(9:30-12 & 2-6 ex Tue.)*.   □

Practical Information _____

MONT-DE-MARSAN
ⓘ 22, rue V.-Hugo, ☎ 58.75.38.67.
SNCF ☎ 58.75.11.28/58.75.37.69.
Car rental : *Avis*, 5, rue du Mal-Bosquet, ☎ 58.46.10.50;
train station.

Hotel :
★★ *Richelieu*, ☎ 58.06.10.20, Tx 550238, AE DC Euro
Visa, 70 rm ℗ ⚭ ᵴ 150. Rest. ♦ ᵴ closed 15-25 Jan,
65-135.

Restaurant :
♦ *Auberge des Clefs d'Argent*, 333, av. des Martyrs-de-
la-Résistance, ☎ 58.06.16.45, AE Visa ⊱ ♪ ⅋ closed
Mon, 2-9 Jan, 15-30 Oct, 65-150.

Nearby

VILLENEUVE-DE-MARSAN, ⊠ 40190, 17 km E.
ⓘ mairie, ☎ 58.45.22.68.

Hotels :
● ★★★ *Europe* (L.F.), pl. de la Boiterie, ☎ 58.45.20.08,
AE Visa, 15 rm ℗ 180. Rest. ● ♦♦ ♪ Robert Garrapit is
a renowned local personality. His cooking is too : here
chickens and ducks don't die in vain : *salade de cèpes
aux aiguillettes d'oie*, feather-light *tourtière*, a cellar
stocked with fine Armagnacs and Bordeaux, 80-220.
● ★★ *Darroze*, Grande-Rue, ☎ 58.45.20.07, AE Visa,
35 rm ℗ closed Sun eve and Mon (ex Jul-Aug), 1-15 Feb,
200. Rest. ● ♦♦♦ The Darrozes are to Armagnac and
good food what singer/song writer Pierre Perret (a regular
patron here) is to French song : they are stars! 115-250.

MORCENX

Mont-de-Marsan 39, Bordeaux 110, Paris 700 km
pop 5814 ⊠ 40140   A3

ⓘ ☎ 58.07.80.29.
SNCF ☎ 58.07.84.18.

Hotel :
★★ *Bellevue* (L.F.), 2, rue Carnot, ☎ 58.07.85.07, 24 rm ℗ 🏨 🗔 🍽 closed 20 Dec-15 Apr, 160. Rest. ♦ 🍽 closed Sat (l.s.). Old-fashioned cooking, 50-120 ; child : 40.

Å ★★★*Le Clavé* (50 pl), ☎ 58.07.83.11.

PEYREHORADE*

Dax 23, Bayonne 36, Paris 770 km
pop 3090 ✉ 40300   A4
Peyrehorade, capital of the **Orthe region**, faces Bayonne rather than the wooded Landes or Chalosse areas. Its name means "pierced stone" and it stands on the banks of the *Gaves Réunis*, a tributary of the Adour formed by the mountain streams *(gaves)* of Pau and Oloron.

▶ At the foot of a hill crowned by the keep of the ruined **château d'Apremont**★ is a small village around the **château Montréal**★ (late 16thC), built by the viscounts of Orthe. This is a large building flanked by four round towers, with remarkable entrance gates. Behind it, a pleasant shady walk along the banks of an artificial lake fed by the Gaves ; small **port** for pleasure-craft.

Nearby

▶ **Arthous abbey**★, 3 km SW, built by Premonstratensian monks in 1160, a stopover on one of the pilgrim roads to Santiago de Compostela : Romanesque church ; apse with remarkable exterior decoration ; **archaeology museum** in former monastic building *(15 Jun.-15 Sep., daily 9-12 & 2-6)*. ▶ **Sorde-l'Abbaye**★★ *(3 km SE)*, on the pilgrim road between the Landes and the Pyrénées, which was successively traveled by Neolithic man, the Roman legions, Charlemagne's troops and the pilgrims of St. James. The village developed around an abbey built on the foundations of a large 4thC Gallo-Roman villa ; it later became a fortified *bastide* (13thC) ; remains of ramparts. **Church** with Romanesque apse and doorway ; Gothic transept and nave ; in the choir, fragments of a mosaic (11thC hunting scenes). Nearby, the 16thC **abbot's house** with polygonal turret, built on the site of a Gallo-Roman spa ; foundations and fragments of mosaic. Other abbey remains : part of a cloister ; a long subterranean gallery (1710) by the stream (once used as a cellar and fishpond). ▶ **Cagnotte** *(8 km NE)* : Romanesque **church**, formerly the mausoleum of the viscounts of Orthe ; interesting funerary monuments.   □

Practical Information _____

PEYREHORADE
ℹ️ pl. du Sablot, ☎ 58.73.00.52.
🚄 ☎ 58.73.03.38.

Hotel :
★ *Central*, pl. A.-Briand, ☎ 58.73.03.22, AE Visa, 10 rm ℗ ◁ 🗔 closed Sun eve and Mon, Nov-Mar, 320. Rest. ♦♦ ⅍ A food lover's paradise. An array of enjoyable fixed-price menus, 45-250.

Recommended
Farmhouse-gîte : at Cauneille, 3 km E, *l'Oustaou*, ☎ 58.73.07.43.
♥ 12 km W, charcuterie : *Christian Barucq*, ☎ 58.98.00.10, cooked ham.

Nearby

CAGNOTTE, ✉ 40300 Peyrehorade, 8 km NE.

Hotel :
★★ *Boni*, ☎ 58.73.03.78, 10 rm ℗ 🏨 🗔 🗔 closed Sun eve and Mon (l.s.), 1 Dec-5 Mar, 140. Rest. ● ♦♦ ⌁ Annie Demen cooks way out in the country, in a pretty dining room that was once a bread oven, 95-130.

ESCOS, ✉ 64270, 10 km S.

Hotel :
● ★ *Relais des Voyageurs*, ☎ 59.38.42.39, DC Euro

Visa, 9 rm ℗ 🏨 🗔 🐾 closed Sun eve and Mon (16 Sep-14 Jun), 10 Dec-20 Jan, 170. Rest. ♦ ⅍ In a peaceful village, a charming, inexpensive country stopover, 50-110.

LABATUT, ✉ 40300 Peyrehorade, 10 km E.

Restaurant :
● ♦♦ *Auberge du Bousquet*, carrefour du Maou, on RN 117, ☎ 58.98.18.24, AE DC Visa 🏨 ⅍ ⅍ closed Mon eve , Tue and Jan. One of Alain Dutournier's gifted colleagues while in Paris, Ḃ. Lacarrau has now struck out on his own : *gésiers de canard confits, filet d'anguilles, magret grillé au coulis de cèpes*. Local wines, 45-150 ; child : 30.

Recommended
♥ pork products : *Jean-Pierre Lamaison*, ☎ 58.98.19.00. Dried Landes ham.

PORT-DE-LANNE, ✉ 40300 Peyrehorade, 7 km NW.

Hotel :
★★ *La Vieille Auberge* (L.F.), pl. de l'Église, ☎ 58.89.16.29, 7 rm ℗ 🏨 ◁ ⅍ 🗔 half pens (h.s.), closed 26 Sep-26 Jun, 400. Rest. ● ♦♦ ⅍ closed lunch. This early-18thC inn has kept its period furniture. For foodlovers : *confits de porc et de canard, foies gras*, fresh salmon, 110-190.

SAINT-ÉMILION***

Bordeaux 39, Bergerac 56, Paris 611 km
pop 3010 ✉ 33330   B2
In the hills above the Dordogne basin, this vineyard village is one of the most beautiful sites of France and one of the strangest, for its golden limestone buildings are rooted in a network of subterranean galleries. The Gallo-Roman poet Ausonius praised the site. In the 8thC, the Breton monk Émilion made his hermitage in one of the numerous grottoes, and later a community of Benedictine monks founded a monastery. The village and its ramparts grew up around this foundation. During the Revolution, Saint-Émilion was the last refuge of the unfortunate Girondins (→ *Brief regional history*).

▶ N, the **Dominican wall**, ruins of a convent outside the walls ; two of the town gates ; considerable remains of the ramparts ; remains of Romanesque and Gothic houses. ▶ Enter the town by Rue Guadet ; a road leads off to the **convent of the Cordeliers ;** square, 14thC cloister *(daily)*. The **Porte de la Cadène** leads to the centre of the town : picturesque **Place du Marché** (market square), closed by a rocky wall with pierced windows lighting a **church** quarried out of **solid rock** *(guided tours : ask at SI)*. A beautiful doorway (14thC) leads to this large and unique subterranean church built by the monks (9th-12thC) out of several caves. On the cliff, the **bell tower** (12thC and 16thC) seems isolated from the rest of the church. ▶ From the Place du Marché, visit the **catacombs** *(ask at SI)* : former charnel house with cemetery on the cliff. ▶ At the end of the square : angular apse (13thC) of the **Trinité chapel** *(visits, ask at SI)*, above the **hermitage of Saint-Émilion** (see the "furniture" cut in the rock) ; a spring rises in the oratory. ▶ Behind the Trinité chapel, an alley leads to the **château du Roi** : massive 13thC keep. Another steep alley links the Place du Marché with the **Place des Créneaux,** which is surrounded by the monastery buildings : bell tower of the underground church. Also see the collegiate church's beautiful 14thC **cloister** with its Gothic arcades. W of the former **deanery** (office of the SI) is the **Chapter chapel** (13thC). Go round the chapel to the former **Maison de l'Abbé ;** small **museum** *(daily)*. ▶ The **collegiate church,** which was built in the 12thC, replaced the underground church : Romanesque nave, Gothic gate-tower, choir and transept.   □

Practical Information _____

ℹ️ pl. des Créneaux, ☎ 57.24.72.03.
🚄 ☎ 57.24.72.12.

Hotels :

● ★★★★ *Hostellerie de Plaisance*, pl. du Clocher, ☎ 57.24.72.32, AE DC Euro Visa, 12 rm ℗ ⬚ 475. Rest. ◆◆◆ Regional fare : *magret de canard aux orties, feuilleté aux pommes tièdes.* Incomparable Saint-Émilion wines, 140-180.

★★ *Auberge de la Commanderie*, rue des Cordeliers, ☎ 57.24.70.19, 15 rm ⦗ ♪ ⨝ closed 15 Dec-31 Jan, 145. Rest. ◆ ♪ ᵬ ⨝ closed Tue, 70-250.

Restaurants :

● ◆◆ *Logis de la Cadène*, pl. du Marché-aux-Bois, ☎ 57.24.71.40 ⬚ closed eves. Tidy, rustic family-run restaurant. Spec : *lamproie à la bordelaise, poulet crapaudine, millas girondins,* 90-210.

◆ *Chez Germaine*, pl. du Clocher, ☎ 57.24.70.88, AE DC Euro ⦗ ⬚ closed Mon and Sun eve, 10-24 Jan, 70-180.

⅄ ★★★*La Barbanne* (70 pl), ☎ 57.24.75.80.

Recommended

Guide to wines : *Wine confraternity*, Château Figeac, ☎ 57.24.72.26, wine tasting; at Lussac, 10 km N, Château Ausone, Maison Vauthier, ☎ 57.24.70.94.
♥ pottery : *Galerie Jean Guyot*, rue Guadet.

The SAUTERNAIS Region**

B2

From Roallan to Bordeaux *(approx 70 km, half-day; see map 2, Garonne Valley)*

Region of sweet white wines (Sauternes and Barsac). Pretty winding roads between vine-covered hillsides dotted with châteaux. The Sauternes wines of five communes are obtained by a special (natural) process : the grapes are picked in an advanced state of ripeness when they have been attacked by the tiny fungus that causes *pourriture noble,* noble rot. This causes the grapes to diminish in size while their sugar content increases, giving the resultant wine a unique flavor.

▶ W from **Roaillan**, D125 crosses the wooded region up to the **Bazadais** (→), then suddenly enters the Sauternais vineyards, where even the smallest plot of land is reserved for the precious grapes. ▶ Not far from **Sauternes** (partly Romanesque church) is the winery of **château**

Filhot (19thC), neo-Classical style; taste the wines of the vineyard. ▶ On the other bank of the Ciron, on the W limit of Sauternes, is **Budos :** ruins of the 14thC fortified château. ▶ **Château Yquem** occupies a site at the top of the slope *(admission free to the estate and interior courtyard of the château);* built in the early Renaissance and remodeled in the 17thC, it stands in the centre of a vineyard that produces the most prestigious and the most expensive of the great *crus* of Sauternes : each vine produces only one glass of wine annually. ▶ On the road to the Garonne Valley, see the ravishing **château de Malle★★,** Classical style (early 17thC), with French gardens; inside, rare furniture, good paintings *(late Mar.-mid-Oct. daily ex Wed, 3-7).* The Malle vineyards produce wines of two different *appellations*, being located at the limits of Graves (reds) and Sauternes (whites). ▶ **Barsac,** one of the five wine-making communes with the Sauternes appellation; the church with three naves dates from the early 17thC (inside, 18thC furniture). ▶ Around **Cérons,** a very ancient port on the Garonne, an *A.C.* wine is produced that is close to Sauternes : Romanesque church with interesting carvings on the doorway. ▶ Across the **Graves region,** the vineyards extend all along the left bank of the Garonne up to Bordeaux. ▶ **Labrède :** beautiful Romanesque church façade : Montesquieu was born in 1689 at the **château de Labrède★** *(mid-Mar.-mid-Nov. 9:30-11:30 & 2:30-5:30 daily ex Tue.; out of season 2:30-5 Sat., Sun. only; closed mid-Dec.-end Jan.).* Montesquieu also designed the park of the fortified manor, 13th and 15thC. Visit the salons and the writer's bedroom and library. ▶ **Bordeaux** (→). ☐

Practical Information ──────────

BARSAC, ⊠ 33720 Podensac, 8 km NW of **Langon.**

Hotel :

★★★ *Hostellerie du Château de Rolland* (C.H.), RN 113, ☎ 56.27.15.75, AE DC Euro Visa, 8 rm ℗ ⦗ ⬚ ◷ ♪ half pens (h.s.), closed 15 Nov-30 Dec, 600. Rest. ◆◆ ⦗ ♪ closed Wed noon, 160-250; child : 60.

SAUTERNES, ⊠ 33210, 10 km SW of **Langon.**

◆ *Auberge les Vignes*, pl. de l'Église, ☎ 56.63.60.06 ℗ ◷ ᵬ closed Mon eve, 15 Jan-15 Feb. Southwestern dishes : steaks and duck breast grilled over vine-cuttings, *lamproie bordelaise,* seasonal fruit tarts. Sauternes holds pride of place, 45-120.

Brittany

Brittany is a region with a personality both strong and mysterious. For Brittany is several regions in one, and diversity is the rule, in language and landscape alike. The natural parks of Brière and the salt marshlands of Guérande cover 70 square kilometres of low-lying land drained by canals and a multitude of channels. The inhabitants — who occupy the higher-lying islands — live from fishing, hunting, peat — and reed-gathering and animal-breeding. The ancient fortified city of Concarneau now lives from trawler fishing and tourism. Along the Emerald Coast, the infinite variations of sea-green reflections and a succession of capes, bays, rocks, cliffs and estuaries lead to Saint-Malo, with its ramparts and narrow streets, and Cap Fréhel. Dinand preserves its character as a favourite holiday spot for post-Victorian English aristocrats — boasting luxurious villas with Mediterranean gardens of fig trees, palms and camellias. Brest is a naval base and the most important nuclear submarine base in France. Nantes is a busy port and the largest city in Western France, but it is also worth a visit for its shady avenues, its cathedral, its massive buildings. The imposing city of Rennes is the administrative capital of the region and possesses many fine museums and dwellings.

Popular traditions, such as *Fest Noz*, the nocturnal festival marking the successful completion of collective activities, the mediaeval *pardons* which only Brittany has kept alive, the saints still remembered for their miraculous powers of healing, the strange musical instruments played only here and the unusual language of *brezhoug* spoken by 800 000 people in the South — all contribute to Brittany's very special, individual character. The region's healthy, outdoor attractions and its great seafaring traditions make it one of France's most popular holiday spots. □

Don't miss

★★★ Carnac B3, Cap Fréhel C1, Gulf of Morbihan C3, Nantes D4, Saint-Malo D1.

★★ Belle-Ile B3-4, Brière Nature Park C3-4, Concarneau B2, Côte d'Émeraude C-D1, Dinan C-D2, Le Faouët B2, Le Folgoët A1, Kernascléden B2, Locmariaquer C3, Locronan A2, Menez-Bré B1, Pleyben B2, Quimper A2, Raz Point A2, Rennes D2, Saint-Pol-de-Léon A-B1, Tréguier B1, Vannes C3.

★ Côte des Abers A1, Aber Wrac'h A1, Armorique Nature Park B2, Monts d'Arrée A-B2, La Baule C4, Ile de Bréhat C1, Brest A2, Clisson D4, Le Croisic C4, Dol-de-Bretagne D2, Fougères D2, Ile de Groix B3, Guérande C3-4, Huelgoat B2, Josselin C2, Lannion B1, Menez-Hom A2, Montagnes Noires B2, Ile d'Ouessant A1, Forest of Paimpont C2, Perros-Guirec B1, Plougastel-Daoulas A2, Pont-Aven B2, Port-Louis B3, Quintin C2-3, Rochefort-en-Terre C3, Saint-Castle-Guildo C1, Saint-Philbert-de-Grand-Lieu D4, Trégastel B1, Vitré D2.

Weekend tips

On Friday evening, take a plane to Quimper; on Saturday, visit the town, then tour the Bigouden region and/or go to the Pointe du Raz; stop over in Locronan. On Sunday, drive through the Monts d'Arrée (→ round trip from Le Faou to Roc'h Trévezel), and return towards Brest via a number of traditional churchyards (→ round trip from Roc'h Trévezel to Landerneau). Fly back from Brest.

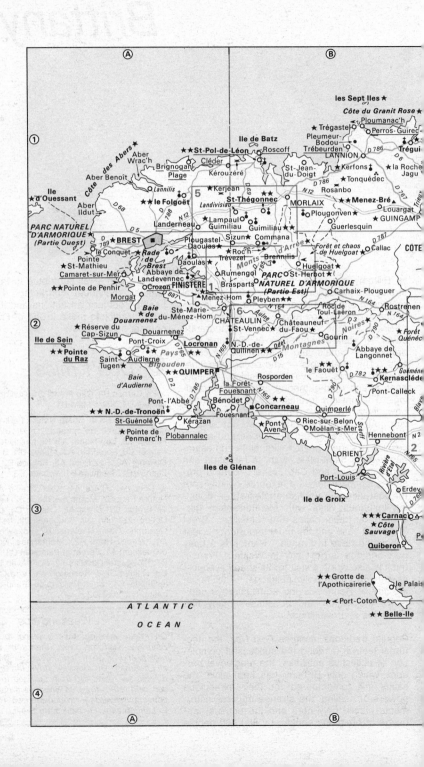

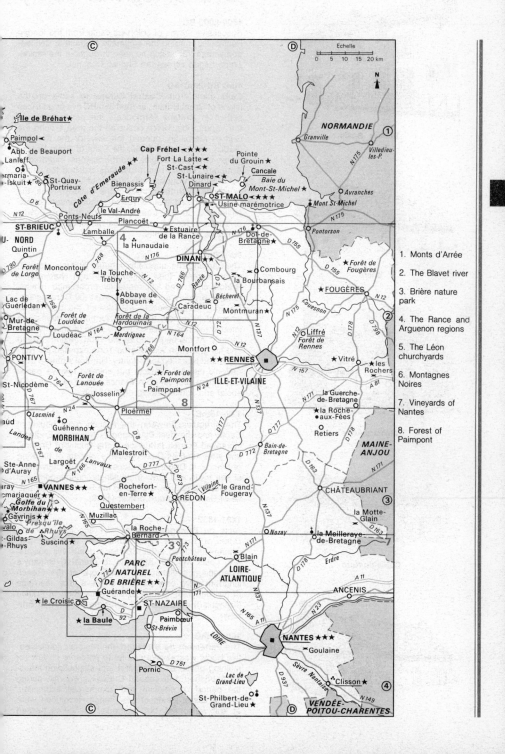

Echelle

0 5 10 15 20 km

N

Île de Bréhat★

Paimpol◄

Abb. de Beauport
Lanleff
ermaria-
-Iskuit   St-Quay-
         Portrieux
D 6   Bienassis
                         Erquy
N 12
Ponts-Neufs   le Val-André
ST-BRIEUC   Plancoët
U- NORD   Lamballe
Quintin   la Hunaudaie
D 790   Forêt
de Lorge   Moncontour   la Touche-
                          Trébry
Lac de   Abbaye de
Guerlédan   Boquen ★
Mur-de-   Forêt de   Forêt de la
Bretagne   Loudéac   Hardouinais
           Loudéac N 164   Merdrignac
PONTIVY
D 767   Forêt de
St-Nicodème   Lanouée
                      Josselin
Locminé
aud   Guéhenno ★
Landes   **MORBIHAN**
de
Ste-Anne   Largoët   Lanvaux
d'Auray
ray N 165 **VANNES ★★**
cmariaquer ★★
Gâvrinis ★★
valo Presqu'île
Gildas- de Rhuys
-Rhuys   Suscinio ★

Côte d'Emeraude ★★

Cap Fréhel ◄ ★★★
Fort La Latte
St-Cast ◄★
St-Lunaire ★★
Dinard
◯ST-MALO ★★★
Usine marémotrice

Pointe
du Grouin ★
Cancale
Baie du
Mont-St-Michel ★

★ Estuaire
de la Rance
Dol-de-
Bretagne ★

DINAN ★★

Combourg
la Bourbansais
Bécherel
Caradeuc   Montmuran ★

Montfort ◯

★★ **RENNES**
ILLE-ET-VILAINE

★ Forêt de
Paimpont
Paimpont

Ploërmel

Malestroit

Rochefort-
en-Terre ★
Questembert
Muzillac   ◯REDON
la Roche-
Bernard
Pontchâteau
**PARC
NATUREL
DE BRIÈRE ★★**
Guérande ★
ST-NAZAIRE
★ la Baule
Paimbœuf
St-Brévin
le Croisic ★

Pornic

NORMANDIE
Granville   Villedieu-
             les-P.
N 175

Avranches ★
Mont St-Michel ★

N 175
Pontorson

D 155
★ Forêt de
Fougères
N 155
★ **FOUGÈRES**
N 12

Liffré ◯
Forêt de
Rennes
★ Vitré
★ les
Rochers
A 81
la Guerche-
de-Bretagne ★
★ la Roche-
● aux-Fées
Retiers
**MAINE-
ANJOU**
CHÂTEAUBRIANT
la Motte-
Glain
★ la Meilleraye-
de-Bretagne
**LOIRE-
ATLANTIQUE**
Nazay
Blain
Erdre
ANCENIS
A 11
N 23
NANTES ★★★
Goulaine
Clisson ★
St-Philbert-de-
Grand-Lieu ★
**VENDÉE-
POITOU-CHARENTES**

Lac de
Grand-Lieu

1. Monts d'Arrée

2. The Blavet river

3. Brière nature
park

4. The Rance and
Arguenon regions

5. The Léon
churchyards

6. Montagnes
Noires

7. Vineyards of
Nantes

8. Forest of
Paimpont

Rennes Basin

Brière

Monts d'Arrée

Côtes-du-Nord

Morbihan

 # Brief regional history

4500-2000 BC
Successive waves of colonists came from the Iberian Peninsula, bringing the enigmatic **Megalithic Civilisation** whose traces can be seen throughout the region. Trade began across the English Channel.

4thC BC-9thC AD
Celts came from **Central Europe** to settle on the island of Great Britain; around 350 BC five great tribes settled in Brittany (Armorica); the naval defeat of the Veneti tribe, which occupied the area around the Gulf of Morbihan, opened the way for the **Romans** (56BC). ● In about AD460, the Celts of Great Britain, driven out by the Angles and the Saxons, migrated to **Armorica**; legend has it that they crossed the Channel in "stone troughs" with their chiefs, usually priests or monks. With the retreat of the Gallo-Romans, the Celts organised themselves into independent principalities. ● In the East of Brittany the key towns of Vannes, Rennes and Nantes remained part of the Kingdom of the Franks.

9th-12thC
The Carolingians, unable to conquer Brittany, attempted to increase their influence through **Nominoë**, a Breton chief who subsequently proclaimed himself **King of Brittany** and turned against the Carolingians. He and his successors established the boundaries where they remain today. ● Norman invasions and internal rivalries left Brittany in a state of anarchy for a century. At the beginning of the 10thC Alain le Grand and his grandson Alain Barbe-Torte expelled the Normans and reunified the country. Brittany suffered from periodic internal conflicts but enjoyed relative peace and independence from France, developing its own social and administrative organisation.

12th-15thC
The struggles between the French royal house of Capet and the rival Plantagenêts (Kings of England) increased **French influence** in the Duchy of Brittany, and after 1250 its Dukes became vassals of the King of France. ● Brittany developed a thriving international sea trade and grew increasingly independent until Charles VIII of France crushed the Bretons at the battle of Saint-Aubin-du-Cormier (1488).

1491-1532
Anne de Bretagne, heiress of François II, the last Duke of Brittany, was compelled to marry first Charles VIII then, after Charles's death, his successor, Louis XII. Her attempts to preserve Brittany's independence within the framework of the French kingdom were only partially effective. The marriage of her daughter Claude to the future King of France (François I) put an **end to self-determination in Brittany.**

16th-19thC
The **Parlement de Bretagne**, the regional administrative body, was always careful to preserve its few remaining privileges. The ports and shipbuilding industry flourished and coastal Brittany grew rich during the period of colonial and commercial expansion. ● The liberal ideals of the French Revolution were at first welcomed, but unpopular measures passed

by the Revolutionary Government of the Convention (military conscription, religious intolerance) gave rise to the **Chouannerie,** the revolt of the Bretons.

19th-20thC
Arrival of the railway brought competition from industrialised areas and hastened the region's economic decline, simultaneously encouraging emigration. ● To the problems of a neglected region were added the ravages of WWII, and Brittany had to wait until 1968 before modernising its agriculture and emerging from a state of virtual isolation. Since then, the development of maritime and tourist activities together with increasing industrialisation, has given impetus to economic growth.

Facts and figures

Location : *At the westernmost point of France, a 250-km long peninsula whose breadth varies from 75 to 150 km, separating the English Channel from the Atlantic Ocean.*
Area : *34 077 km².*
Climate : *Maritime, thus variable. Generally clement, due to the influence of the Gulf Stream. Bracing on the coast, with little frost, even inland; few really hot spells (mean summer temperatures between 18 and 25°C), but high rate of sunshine (2 000 hours per year : as much as the Mediterranean Coast).*
Population : *3 349 183.*
Administration : *Côtes-du-Nord Department, Prefecture Saint-Brieuc. Finistère Department, Prefecture Quimper. Ille-et-Vilaine Department, Prefecture Rennes. Loire-Atlantique Department, Prefecture Nantes. Morbihan Department, Prefecture Vannes.*

Megaliths

Megaliths date from the Neolithic Era and the Bronze Age (4500-2000 BC). They are not restricted to Brittany, but are so numerous here that most of the names used to describe them are Breton words. A dolmen (stone table), apparently a group burial chamber, consists of a corridor with a circular vault, sometimes covered with earth (tumulus) or rocks (cairn); some have no terminal chamber. Menhirs (standing stones) vary in size; the largest known (now broken) was found at Locmariaquer; it stood 20.3-m tall and weighed 350 tons. Menhirs occur both alone and grouped in cromlech (stone rings) or in rows (→ Carnac).

Visitable Breton lighthouses

A whole row of lighthouses has for a long time marked off shipping-routes and indicated passes and ports with great precision along the rock-strewn Breton coastline. Some of them are open to the public.
Roscoff, ☎ 98.69.70.06; Batz, ☎ 98.61.77.87; Stiff, ☎ 98.48.90.93; Trézien, ☎ 98.89.60.16; Ile Vierge, ☎ 98.04.78.01; Kermorvan, ☎ 98.04.01.68; Saint-Mathieu, ☎ 98.89.00.17; Sein, ☎ 98.70.90.10; Eckmühl, ☎ 98.58.61.17; Belle-Ile, ☎ 97.31.82.08; Cap Fréhel, ☎ 96.41.40.03; Ouessant, ☎ 98.44.24.96.

● Practical information

Information : *Délégation régionale au tourisme,* 3, rue d'Espagne, B.P. 2275, 35022 Rennes Cedex, ☎ 99.50.11.15. **Côtes-du-Nord** : *Comité Départemental du Tourisme (C.D.T),* 1, rue Chateaubriand, 22000 Saint-Brieuc, ☎ 96.61.66.70. **Finistère** : *C.D.T.,* 34, rue de Douarnenez, 29000 Quimper, ☎ 98.53.72.72. **Ille-et-Vilaine** : *C.D.T.,* 1, rue Martenot, 35032 Rennes Cedex, ☎ 99.02.97.43. **Loire-Atlantique** : *C.D.T.,* 34, rue de Strasbourg, 44035 Nantes Cedex, ☎ 40.89.50.77. **Morbihan** : *C.D.T.,* Hôtel du Département, B.P. 400, 56009 Vannes Cedex, ☎ 97.54.06.56. In **Paris** : *Maison de la Bretagne,* Maine-Montparnasse shopping centre, 75737, ☎ 45.38.73.15. Well-stocked bookshop. *Dir. régionale de la Jeunesse et des Sports,* B.P. 79, 35000 Rennes Cedex, ☎ 99.79.30.23, and Château de l'Étaudière, B.P. 936, 44075 Nantes Cedex, ☎ 40.49.41.24. *Dir. rég. des Affaires culturelles,* hôtel de Blossac, 6, rue du Chapitre, 35000 Rennes, ☎ 99.79.21.32.

Reservations : *Service Loisirs-Accueil (S.L.A.)* **Ille-et-Vilaine,** 1, rue Martenot, 35000 Rennes, ☎ 99.02.97.41. *S.L.A.* **Loire-Atlantique,** 34, rue de Strasbourg, 44000 Nantes, ☎ 40.89.50.77. *S.L.A.* **Morbihan** : *C.D.T.,* ☎ 97.42.61.80.

S.O.S. : **Côtes-du-Nord,** *SAMU* (Emergency Medical Service), ☎ 96.94.40.15. **Finistère,** *SAMU,* ☎ 98.46.11.33. **Ille-et-Vilaine,** *SAMU,* ☎ 99.59.16.16. **Loire-Atlantique,** *SAMU,* ☎ 40.48.35.35. **Morbihan,** *SAMU,* ☎ 97.54.22.11. *Poisoning Emergency Centre* : Rennes, ☎ 99.59.22.22. Nantes, ☎ 40.48.38.88.

Weather forecast : **Finistère** : ☎ 98.84.63.00. *Marine forecast* : ☎ 98.84.82.83. **Ille-et-Vilaine** : ☎ 99.31.90.00. **Morbihan** : ☎ 97.84.83.44.

Rural gîtes, chambres d'hôtes and farmhouse camping : enq and reservations at the *Relais départementaux* : **Côtes-du-Nord,** 5, rue Baratoux, 22000 Saint-Brieuc, ☎ 96.61.82.79. **Finistère,** 5, allée Sully, 29332 Quimper Cedex, ☎ 98.95.75.30. **Ille-et-Vilaine** : *C.D.T.* Ille-et-Vilaine. **Loire-Atlantique,** 46bis, rue des Hauts-Pavés, 44024 Nantes Cedex, ☎ 40.76.39.90. **Morbihan,** 11, pl. Mal-Joffre, B.P. 78, 56400 Auray, ☎ 97.56.48.12, and *C.D.T.,* Vannes.

Holiday villages : enq. : *C.D.T.;* the *C.R.T. Bretagne* publishes a complete list.

Camping-car rentals : **Côtes-du-Nord** : André See, Z.A. Pommeret, 22120 Yffiniac, ☎ 96.34.32.98; **Finistère** : *Brittany loisirs,* 3, av. de Coran, 29000 Quimper, ☎ 98.57.32.32; **Ile-et-Vilaine** : *Sun loisirs,* route de Saint-Malo, 35630, Hédé, ☎ 99.45.49.74; **Loire-Atlantique** : *Camping de la Gavelle,* route de la Côte-Sauvage, 44740 Batz-sur-Mer, ☎ 40.23.91.63.

Festivals and events : **Mar** : *golf tournament* in Dinard. **Apr** : *festival of traditional arts* in Rennes; *Toulfoelen folk festival* in Quimperlé. **May** : *le mai breton* in Saint-Brieuc. **Jun** : *Gallic musical competition* in Monterfil; *Brocéliande festival* in Paimpont; *cultural activities* in Vitré. **Jul** : *festival of Breton creation* in Rennes; *embroidery festival* in Pont-l'Abbé; *Clos Poulet festival* in Saint-Malo; *tour de France sailing regatta; tennis tournament* in Dinard; *gorse festival* in Lamballe; *folklore festival* in Plozévet; *apple-tree festival* in Fouesnant; *fêtes de Cornouaille* in Quimper. **Jul-Aug** : *abbey festival* in Redon; *classical music festival* in Locronan; *Ille-et-Vilaine festival; horse races* in Saint-Malo (week-ends and nat. hols.). **Aug** : *Celtic festival* in Lorient; *mediaeval festival* in Pontivy; *sea festival* in Plougasnou; *international jumping competition* in Dinard; *Saint-Loup festival* in Guingamp; *seagull festival* in Saint-Briac-sur-Mer; *living book spectacle* in Fougère; *musical weeks* in Quimper. **15 Aug** : *Grandes Fêtes d'Arvor* in Vannes; *festival* in Menez-Hom. **3rd Sun in Aug** : *fête des filets bleus* in Concarneau. **End Aug-early Sep** : *youth and the sea festival* in Dinard. **3rd Sun in Aug** : *grande fête des menhirs* in Carnac. **Dec** : *Rock music* in Rennes.

The vineyards of Nantes

126 km² of vineyards, in the S and SE parts of the Department of the Loire-Atlantique and spilling over slightly into the Vendée and the Maine-et-Loire, produce Muscadet (white, AOC.; 12°) Gros Plant (white, VDQS; 11°) Grolleau, rosé or gris, extends over the Retz countryside (VDQS under examination) and Coteaux d'Ancenis-Gamay (VDQS; 12°). The last can be produced in red, white or rosé according to choice. Muscadet is subdivided by regions : Muscadet Sèvre-et-Maine, Muscadet Coteaux de la Loire, and Muscadet AOC. Muscadet sur lie has spent only one winter in the barrel and is bottled early while still on the lees, to preserve the freshness, delicacy and bouquet of the wine. Muscadet and Gros Plant go extremely well with seafood and fish ; they should be taken at 8.5°C ; the Gamay can be drunk chilled or at room temperature.

Brittany cuisine

Food in Brittany depends more on quality and freshness than on a tradition of haute-cuisine ; all the vegetables are locally grown, and fish or seafood will have been caught the same day. In earlier times, the inland Bretons ate mainly cereals and vegetables ; meat (in stews or charcuterie), was for feast days ; fish was eaten only by the coastal population.

More recently, a number of traditional preparations have made their way outside Brittany, among them the Kauteriad (or Côtriade), a fish soup quite unlike bouillabaisse, and the Kouign, of which the best known variety is the Kouign Amân (with butter), a sweet fried cake of wheat flour, eggs and honey. Crêpes (pancakes made with wheat flour) and galettes (a thick variety made with buckwheat) were usually eaten plain or with butter or, in Upper Brittany, with eggs or grilled sausages. Other ways of serving them are recent inventions, but nonetheless delicious.

Pardons (traditional religious feast-days) : 2nd Sun in May : in Quintin, Pardon Notre-Dame de Délivrance. End May : Tréguier, Pardon Saint-Yves. Trinity Sun : Rumengol, Pardon Notre-Dame de Rumengol; La Trinité-Porhoet, Pardon de la Trinité. End Jun : Le Faouët, Pardon Sainte-Barbe. 1st Sun in Jul : Guingamp, Pardon Notre-Dame de Bon Secours. 2nd Sun in Jul : Locronan, la Troménie. 25 and 26 Jul : Sainte-Anne-d'Auray, Pardon de Sainte-Anne. End Jul : Guérin, Notre-Dame du Méné Guen; Saint-Quay-Portrieux, Pardon de Sainte-Anne; Vieux-Marché, at the chapelle des Sept-Saints, Islamic Christian pilgrimage. 15 Aug : Rochefort-en-Terre, Pardon Notre-Dame de la Tronchaye; Perros-Guirec, Pardon Notre-Dame de la Clarté. Last Sun in Aug : Plonevez-Porzay, Pardon de Sainte-Anne-la-Palud. 1st Sun in Sep : Le Folgoët, Pardon Notre-Dame. 8 Sep : Josselin, Pardon Notre-Dame du Roncier. 15 Sep : Carnac, Saint-Cornély, Pontivy, Notre-Dame de la Joie. 20 Sep : Saint-Jean-Trolimon, Pardon Notre-Dame-Tronoën; Plouha, Pardon de Kermaria-en-Isquit.

Nature parks : Parc naturel régional d'Armorique, Balaneg-Huella Saint-Éloi, 29224 Daoulas, ☎ 98.21.90.69. Parc naturel régional de Brière, Administrative Centre, 180, île de Fédrun, 44720 Saint-Joachim, ☎ 40.88.42.72.

Rambling and hiking : the GR34, 37, 38 and 39 cross Brittany, along with two alternative routes on the GR341 and 347 (topoguides). The Association Bretonne des Relais et Itinéraires (A.B.R.I.), 3, rue des Portes-Mordelaises, 35000 Rennes, ☎ 99.31.59.44, 10, rue Lafayette, 44000 Nantes, ☎ 40.73.91.69, and 69, rue de Kerbriand, 29200 Brest, ☎ 98.41.90.41, provide appropriate gîtes for hikers.

Cycling holidays : S.L.A. Ille-et-Vilaine; other enq : A.B.R.I. Rennes, ☎ 99.79.36.26. See also Nantes, 3, pl. Saint-Pierre, ☎ 40.48.24.20. The S.L.A. organises cycling tours in the Loire-Atlantique area, ☎ 40.89.50.77. Morbihan : Comité Départemental du Cyclotourisme.

Riding holidays : Association Régionale pour le Tourisme Équestre en Bretagne (A.R.T.E.B.), 1, rue Gambetta (afternoon), 56300 Pontivy, ☎ 97.25.31.36. Also enq at C.D.T., O.T., S.I. and S.L.A. Visits at the national stud in Lamballe.

River and canal cruises : Brittany is doted with 600 km of navigable waterways. Excursions on the Odet : Vedettes de l'Odet, B.P. 8, 29118 Bénodet, ☎ 98.57.00.58. For boat hire, enq at the Comité de Promotion Touristique des Canaux Bretons et Voies Navigables de l'Ouest, 3, rue des Portes-Mordelaises, 35000 Rennes, ☎ 99.79.36.26. S.L.A. Loire-Atlantique and S.L.A. Morbihan for the Erdre Valley and the Breton canals, ☎ 40.89.50.77, and S.L.A. Côte-du-Nord.

Technical tourism : lighthouse visits (see box); Centre d'Étude de Valorisation des Algues, presqu'île de Pen-Lan, 22610 Pleubian, ☎ 96.22.93.50; Centre culturel des métiers de Bretagne, 22210 Plemet.

Handicraft courses : among others : cabinet-making, sculpture in wood, weaving, cooking (château-hôtel de Coatguelen); enq. : C.D.T. Côtes-du-Nord. Introduction to ship building ; intro. to stone sculpture and granite-carving in Sant-Goazec, Monhault (S.L.A. Ille-et-Vilaine); making of stringed instruments : Chambre de Commerce et de l'Industrie du Morbihan, Z.I., quai des Indes, 56100 Lorient, ☎ 97.21.00.46; audio-visual in Sizun; crêpe-making at the Institut de la Crêpe bretonne in Rochefort-en-Terre.

Traditional Breton churchyards

Until the end of the 15thC, the churchyard was only an enclosure around the church, a transitional zone between the sacred and the secular. Here, processions began and ended at the foot of a Calvary, which sometimes served as a pulpit. On pardon days, stalls of various kinds were erected against the outside wall. The dead were buried in the church, and later transferred to a building outside, known as the reliquary. During the 16thC, this was replaced by a larger ossuary that also served as a mortuary chapel. Later still, epidemics and population growth caused the tombs to be moved into the churchyard. Parishioners themselves took care of the churchyard, which had become a symbol of community life. In the 17thC, economic expansion enabled them to indulge in extravagant expenditure, often with one eye on their neighbours' activities : churchyards were elaborated with continual rebuilding and the addition of ornate decoration. Craftsmen and artists of great talent were frequently engaged.

Golf : Côtes-du-Nord : 18 holes : Pleumeur-Bodou, Saint-Quay-Portrieux; 9 holes : Plehedel, Sables-d'Or-Frehel, Saint-Cast-le-Guildo. **Finistère** : 18 holes : Landernau; 9 holes : Clochars-Fouesnant-Bénodet, La Forêt-Fouesnant. **Ille-et-Vilaine** : 18 holes : Saint-Briac, 9 holes : Rennes. **Morbihan** : 18 holes : Ploërmel. **Loire-Atlantique** : 18 holes : La Baule, La Bretesche.

Sailing : list of sailing clubs and schools at the *Ligue Haute-Bretagne* (for the **Ille-et-Vilaine** and **Côtes-du-Nord**), 1, rue des Fours-à-Chaux, 35260 Cancale. *Société anonyme de gestion du Morbihan*, Hôtel de Département, 56000 Vannes, 97.42.63.44. Sailing schools at Quiberon and La Trinité; enq. : *C.D.T.*; *École J.-Riguidel*, 40, rue du Port-Maria, 56170 Quiberon, ☎ 97.50.19.64. The *U.D.N.E.F.* in Quimper, ☎ 98.95.71.18, publishes a list of all schools and centres including *Les Glénans*, ☎ 98.97.14.84. In **Paris** : 1, quai Louis-Blériot, 75781 Paris Cedex 16, ☎ (1) 45.20.01.40. *C.D.T.* Nantes (for the **Loire-Atlantique**).

Wind-surfing : Instructional courses at La Baule; reservations, *S.L.A.* in Nantes.

Water skiing : *Ligue de Bretagne de Ski Nautique*, B.P. 99, 49303 Cholet.

Healers and protecting saints

Guardian saints and healers, making up for the almost total lack of doctors, occupied an important place in popular religion, and pardons (→ box) drew great crowds to the saints' sanctuaries. A random selection of the saints and their special talents : Alar and Noyale protect horses; Cornély and Herbot, horned beasts; Briac cures nervous ailments; Cado helps the deaf; Guirec helps girls to find a husband; Egarec cures ear infections; Gurloës, gout; Hervé is visited for scalp infections and protects against fear; Ivy guards new-born children, especially their eyes; Livertin and Tujanne cure headaches; Mamert relieves stomachaches; Méen takes care of the insane; Tugen looks after rabies cases; Vennec helps rheumatism; and the Virgin is good for any complaint.

Scuba diving : enq. at *C.D.T.*, *C.R.T.*, *O.T.* and S.I.

Canoeing : enq. : *Comité de Promotion Touristique des Canaux Bretons et des Voies Navigables de l'Ouest*, 3, rue des Portes-Mordelaises, 35000 Rennes Cedex, ☎ 99.79.36.26; in **Morbihan** : *Comité Départemental de Canoë-Kayak*, 14, rue du Blavet, 56650 Lochrist, ☎ 97.36.09.05. Also courses in Bréhat, Quimper, Carantec.

Speed-sailing : *Ligue régionale de char à voile*, 26 bis, rue Belle-Fontaine, 56100 Lorient et *C.D.T. Finistère*, ☎ 98.83.50.16, essentially at Ploudalmezeau.

Hunting and shooting : enq. at the *Fédérations Départementales de Chasse*, **Côtes-du-Nord** : 19, rue de Brest, 22000 Saint-Brieuc, ☎ 96.33.15.92; **Finistère** : rue Turgot, 29000 Quimper, ☎ 98.95.85.35; **Ille-et-Vilaine** : 178, rue Antrain, 35000 Rennes, ☎ 99.63.20.21; **Loire-Atlantique** : 13, bd François-Blancho, 44005 Nantes, ☎ 40.89.59.25; **Morbihan** : rue Cap.-Jude, 56000 Vannes, ☎ 97.47.10.32.

River fishing : 10 000 km of rivers and canals open to the public. *Fédérations Départementales des Associations de Pêche :* **Côtes-du-Nord** : 6, rue des Buttes, 22000 Saint-Brieuc, ☎ 96.33.23.26; **Finistère** : 1, rue Poher, 29000 Quimper, ☎ 98.53.16.61; **Ille-et-Vilaine** : 149, rue d'Antrain, 35000 Rennes, ☎ 99.63.03.95; **Loire-Atlantique** : 80, rue Hector-Berlioz, 44005 Nantes, ☎ 40.59.38.01; **Morbihan** : mairie de Ploërmel, ☎ 97.63.10.92. And *Fédération des Associations de Pêche et de Pisciculture du Morbihan* : Pisciculture de Gouarnais, 56000 Saint-Avétel, ☎ 97.60.70.18. Regional information centre : *la Maison de la Rivière, de l'Eau et de la Pêche*, Moulin de Vergraon, 29237 Sizun, ☎ 98.68.86.33.

Sea fishing : enq. at harbour-masters and *S.L.A.*, *O.T.* and *S.I.*

Towns and places

Côte des ABERS*
(Abers Coast)
A1

From Le Conquet to Brignogan *(approx 120 km, full day)*
The banks of the estuaries, with rounded cliffs covered in pale heather, are less steep than in the N; the creeks and beaches are popular with shell and seaweed collectors.

▶ Via **Ploumoguer** (Cohars Manor, E) as far as the sandbanks at Porsmoguer; **Corsen Point** (view★, *1 km on foot*) is the westernmost outcrop of continental France. ▶ **Plouarzel** *(4 km E;* polychrome Pietà in church) has the tallest menhir in France (12 m high). ▶ **Brélès** overlooks the Aber Ildut; 16th-18thC church with St. Isidore in Breton costume accompanied by angels playing bagpipes. ▶ 11 km from Brélès, the museum of local history at **Saint-Renan** *(daily, Jul.-Aug.)*. ▶ Beyond **Aber-Ildut**, at the mouth of the estuary, the village of **Melon** lives by seaweed harvesting. ▶ Menhirs, chapels and manor-houses ring the resort of **Porspoder**. ▶ Near **Kersaint** and **Portsal**, a cliff road *(corniche)* runs past **château de Trémazan** (12th-15thC). ▶ 3 km from **Ploudalmézeau** : church at **Lampaul-Ploudalmézeau** with a Renaissance bell-tower★ and porch. ▶ Cross the Aber Benoît to **Sainte Marguerite Peninsula** to visit **Aber Wrac'h★**, a lobster and deep-sea fishing port in a ring of reefs and islets. ▶ Near **Lannilis**, château de Keroüartz (Breton Renaissance; *no visits*). ▶ **Plouguerneau** : in a region notorious in the 16th-17thC for ship plunderers and wreckers. ▶ **Kerlouan** an important chicory-growing centre; drive through to reach the sea at **Brignogan-Plage** : sandy beaches and rock out-

crops; 5.5 km S behind a sandbank : the church★ of **Goulven**. ☐

Practical Information _____

BRIGNOGAN-PLAGE, ⊠ 29238, 37 km NE of **Brest**.
🛈 rue du Gal-de-Gaulle, ☎ 98.83.41.08.

Hotel :
● ★★ *Castel Régis*, pl. du Garo, ☎ 98.83.40.22, 17 rm
ℙ ⨉ ⏲ ⅏ ⎘ ⌂ closed Oct-Easter, 230. Rest. ♦♦ ⅏ ⌘
closed Wed noon. Light, classic cuisine starring local fish and shellfish, 110-270.

⚕ ★★*Keravezan* (250 pl), ☎ 98.83.41.65.

LANNILIS, ⊠ 29214, 5 km SE of **l'Aberwrac'h** on the D128.

Hotel :
★ *Voyageurs*, 3, rue J.-Tromelin, ☎ 98.04.00.28, AE DC Euro Visa, 13 rm ℙ 90. Rest. ♦ closed Mon, 60-100.

PLOUIDER, ⊠ 29260 Lesneven, 6 km S of **Brignogan-Plage** on the D770.

Hotel :
★ *Butte*, 10, rue de la Mer, ☎ 98.83.10.54, 15 rm ℙ ⏲
⎘ closed Sun eve and Mon, 1-20 Jan. Charm; two-star comfort, 150. Rest. ♦ ⨉ ♪ ⅏ 60-220.

Be advised that hotels and restaurants in this Guide have perhaps changed addresses; prices indicated are also subject to modifications.

ANCENIS

Nantes 42, Rennes 102, Paris 342 km
pop 7263 ⊠ 44150   D3-4

Small city on the right bank of the Loire; light industry. Fine remains of the château (15th-17thC; *visits during school summer hols.*) where François II of Brittany and Louis XI of France signed their 1468 treaty that paved the way for the union of the two countries.

▶ 3 km across the Loire is the village of **Liré**, birthplace of the poet Joachim du Bellay (1522-60); small museum devoted to him in an old house (*9-12 & 2-6 ex Mon.;* memorabilia, regional arts and traditions).   ▢

Practical Information _____

〔SNCF〕 ☎ 40.96.21.30.

Hotel :
★★ **Val de Loire** (L.F.), on the Angers road, 1 km from RN 23, ☎ 40.96.00.03, Tx 711592, Euro Visa, 40 rm ℗ ᨨ ᨩ ₺ 185. Rest. ♦ ♪ closed Sat, 50-100.

ARMORIQUE Nature Park*

                                                            A1-2
This nature park was created in 1967, not only to protect natural sites and their flora and fauna, but also to provide information and research facilities for agricultural development and to broaden the potential of rural resources.

▶ The park, 650 km² in area, includes more than 30 towns and villages in four sectors: The Monts d'Arrée (→), the estuary of the Aulne and the Menez-Hom (→), the Roscanvel Peninsula (→ Camaret) and Ouessant Island (→).

Nearby

▶ **Menez-Hom★** the last rise of the Montagnes Noires (Black Mountains). ▶ **Sainte-Marie-du-Menez-Hom :** churchyard with 16thC chapel (3 altarpieces★ with twisted columns decorated with leaves). ▶ Near **Saint-Nic** (16thC church), chapel of Saints Côme and Damien (sculpted floral trusses★, rustic floral and animal motifs). Nearby, **Pentrez-Plage** (beach). ▶ At the foot of the N slopes of Menez-Hom, **Trégarven** on the banks of the Aulne; on the outskirts, rural school museum created by the Park (*Jul.-Aug., daily ex Tue., 2-6*). ▶ Downstream, the Aulne provides **Landevennec** with a protected verdant site★; remains of 5thC abbey; small historical museum.   ▢

Monts d' ARRÉE

                                                            A-B2
Round trip (*110-130 km, one day; see map 1*)
These are substantial hills rather than mountains, the highest being only 384 m. Sandstone, schist and granite lie close to the surface of the soil, where sparse grazing and stunted vegetation do little to soften the rugged countryside. This underdeveloped region has preserved many aspects of traditional, rural Brittany.

▶ **Le Faou,** far inland on the Aulne estuary, was once a prosperous little trading port (merchants' houses in the main street); 16thC church with 1628 bell-tower. ▶ **Rumengol** (church 1536; Renaissance doorway; remarkable statues in S porch; 17thC altarpieces★). The church is too small to cope with the influx of pilgrims to its popular *pardons* (→ box) (*Trinity Sunday, 15 Aug., 8 Sep.*). ▶ **Pen Ar Hoat** (alt. 210 m), after the **forest of Cranou**, overlooks the estuary of the Aulne, towards Brest and the bay of **Douarnenez**. ▶ The **Domaine de Menez-Meur**, at the heart of the Park (→), provides information for visitors (exhibitions, zoo, *crêperie; daily ex Mon. 15 Jun.-15 Sep., 10:30-7; Sat., Sun. and nat. hols. rest of year; closed Dec., Jan.*); walks. ▶ **Saint-Rivoal :** exhibi-

tion of rural techniques and traditions on an 18thC farm (*Jun.-15 Sep. 1:30-6:30, ex Tue.*), typical houses from various regions in Brittany; museum of tools and architecture. ▶ **Menez Mikel (Mont Saint-Michel-de-Brasparts,** alt. 380 m; view★ for 60 km around in fine weather); at its foot, the **Ferme (farm) St. Michel** houses the Brittany Craftsmen's Center (*daily ex Tue., 10-12 & 2-6:30*). ▶ From **Roc'h Trévezel★**, skirt the bowl of **Yeun Ellez** ("the mouth of Hell"), with its sinister winter fogs. The marshes formerly here have been inundated by a lake created to cool the nuclear reactor of Brennelis, a modern substitute for the will o'the wisps and peat bogs of earlier days. At **Kerbérou :** former Templar Commandery. ▶ **Huelgoat★ :** one of the most beautiful sites in inland Brittany, between a 1.5 km² lake and a forest★★ with granite rocks, streams and luxuriant undergrowth; 16thC church and chapel of Notre-Dame-des-Cieux; endless possibilities for walks in the Chaos du Moulin (rockfall)★ or to the Pierre Tremblante (Shivering Stone), the Ménage de la Vierge Cavern, the Artus Cavern, La Mare aux Sangliers (Wild Boar Pond), the Gouffre★ (sinkhole), etc. ▶ Outside the **chapel of Saint Herbot★★** (15th-16thC), an elaborate figured cross★ (1571). Statues of the Apostles in the porch (1498), square 15thC tower and small ossuary. Fine furnishings (carved wood chancel★ (16thC), stalls, altarpieces, stained glass (1556). ▶ Interesting furnishings in the churches of **Loqueffret** (16thC), **Brennilis** (end of 15thC) and **Lannédern** (porch, 1662; cross and 17thC ossuary in the cemetery). ▶ **Brasparts** churchyard (→) is typical : church (1551) with Renaissance porch★ (1589), Calvary★ with Pietà, and ossuary with two figures of Ankou (Death) at the corners.   ▢

Practical Information _____

Le FAOU, ⊠ 29142, 30 km SE of **Brest**.
ⓘ 10, rue du Gal-de-Gaulle, ☎ 98.81.90.44.

Hotels :
★★ **La Vieille Renommée**, 11, pl. de la Mairie, ☎ 98.81.90.31, Euro Visa, 38 rm ℗ ₺ closed Sun eve and Mon, 16 Feb-3 Mar, 10 Nov-1 Dec, 155. Rest. ♦ ♪ ₺ 65-120.
★★ **Relais de la Place**, 7, pl. de la Mairie, ☎ 98.81.91.19, Euro Visa, 38 rm ℗ ⁂ closed Sat, 15 Sep-15 Oct, 140. Rest. ♦ Spec : seafood, 65-120.

HUELGOAT, ⊠ 29218, 29 km S of **Morlaix**.
ⓘ 14, pl. Aristide-Briand, ☎ 98.99.72.32.

Hotel :
★ **An Triskell**, rue des Cieux, ☎ 98.99.71.85, 11 rm ℗ ᨪ ᨨ ᨩ ₺ closed 15 Nov-15 Dec, 125.

ᚼ ★★**Fao** (100 pl), ☎ 98.99.71.55.

Recommended
♥ *Le Temps des Cerises*, folk cabaret at 2,5 km; at Brasparts, crafts : la Ferme Saint-Michel, ☎ 98.81.41.13; at La Feuillée, *Auberge de la Crêpe*, ☎ 98.99.61.70, attractive Breton setting.

LOCMARIA-BERRIEN, ⊠ 29218 Huelgoat, 4 km N of **Huelgoat**.

Restaurant :
● ♦ *Auberge de la Truite*, ☎ 98.99.73.05 ᨨ closed Sun eve and Mon ex Jul-Aug, 2 Jan-1 Mar. At the age of 86, Mlle Lucie Le Guillou watches over the quality of her folksy eatery. Try the trout terrine and her famous quails, 110-290.

Recommended
Leisure activities : *excursions in horse-drawn carriages,* from the station.

AUDIERNE

Quimper 35, Brest 75, Paris 591 km
pop 3094 ⊠ 29113   A2

This pretty lobster port has a fine beach and provides access to the **Île de Sein** (→).

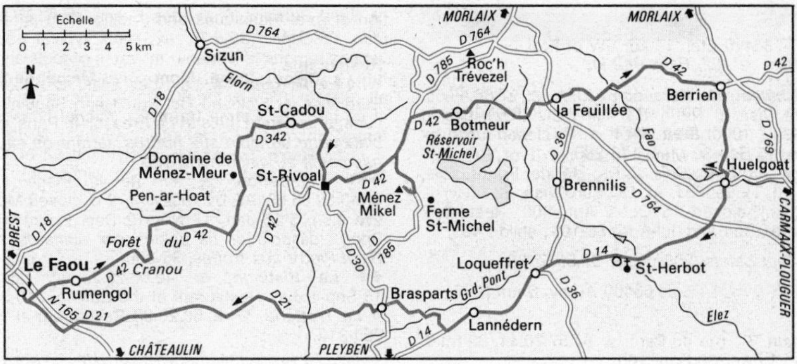

1. Monts d'Arrée

▶ You will see lobster traps piled at the watergate. Rue du Môle, **La Chaumière Bretonne** *(Jun.-Sep., 9 or 10-7 or 8).*

Nearby

▶ 4.5 km W : the **chapel of Saint Tugen★** (1535), 17th-18thC furnishings. ▶ **Pont-Croix :** a little town with ancient paved alleys. Church of Notre-Dame de Roscudon, rebuilt 15thC; 13thC nave; S porch★ and bell-tower with 67-m stone steeple. ▶ **Plozévet** (15th-16thC) : Romanesque arcades; chapel of La Trinité★ (16thC, *1 km N*), fine statuary. □

Practical Information

AUDIERNE

ⓘ pl. de la Liberté, ☎ 98.70.12.20.

⛴ ☎ 98.70.02.38, in 1 : 10 hr, The crossing takes 70 min . Connection with île de Sein.

Hotels :

★★★ ***Le Goyen***, pl. Jean-Simon, ☎ 98.70.08.88, Tx 941300, Visa, 34 rm Ⓟ ☀ half pens (h.s.), closed 15 Nov-15 Dec, 15-31 Jan, 270. Rest. ● ♦♦ ☀ ♿ closed Mon ex hols and Jul-Aug. Pleasant, very well-kept hotel. The restaurant has a panoramic view of the port, and the boats that bring their bounty to chef Basser for his fine, classic dishes : *coquilles et bar marinés aux baies roses* (why not?), *bar sauce tomate* and lots of other good things. Nice cellar; the young staff is eager to please but inexperienced, especially in season, 120-265.

★★ ***Le Cornouaille***, across from the port, ☎ 98.70.09.13, 10 rm 4 apt ☀ closed 30 Sep-30 Jun, 200.

★★ ***Roi Gradlon*** (L.F.), 3, bd Manu-Brusq, sur la plage, ☎ 98.70.04.51, AE Euro Visa, 20 rm Ⓟ ☀ ♪ half pens (h.s.), closed Mon (l.s.), 2 Jan-15 Mar, 260. Rest. ♦ ☀ ♪ 60-150; child : 35.

⛺ ★★*Kerhuon* (50 pl), ☎ 98.70.10.91; ★★*Kerivoas* (20 pl), ☎ 98.70.26.86.

Recommended

♥ gourmet groceries : *De Vigne en Vin*, ☎ 98.70.22.05.

Nearby

PLOZEVET, ⊠ 29143 Plogastel-Saint-Germain, 10 km SE.

ⓘ ☎ 98.58.30.73.

Hotel :

★★ ***Moulin de Brénizenec***, 4 km S. on the Pont-l'Abbé road, ☎ 98.58.30.33, 10 rm Ⓟ ♨ closed Oct, 270.

⛺ ★★*Cornouaille* (110 pl), ☎ 98.58.30.81.

Recommended

Guide to wines : *de Vigne en Vin*, ☎ 98.70.22.05, fine wines and chocolates.

♥ at Lesneut, *Ateliers d'Art de Bretagne*; crêperie : *L'Arc-en-Ciel*, ☎ 98.54.34.33.

POULDREUZIC, ⊠ 29134, 7 km SE.

Hotels :

★★★ ***Ker Ansquer*** (L.F.), Lababan, 2 km NW on D 40, ☎ 98.54.41.83, 11 rm Ⓟ ☀ ♨ ♿ half pens (h.s.), closed 1 Oct-14 May, 215. Rest. ♦ ☀ 60-120.

★★ ***Breiz-Armor***, plage de Penhors, ☎ 98.54.40.41, Euro Visa, 23 rm Ⓟ ☀ half pens (h.s.), closed Mon (l.s.), 15 Oct-1 Apr, 245. Rest. ♦ ☀ ♪ closed 2 Jan-1 Apr, 55-120.

AURAY

Vannes 18, Quimper 98, Paris 474 km
pop 10185 ⊠ 56400 C3

An unpretentious town on the banks of the Loch, where the tide comes 12 km inland.

▶ The church of St. Gildas (1641) mixes styles, with a preference for the Renaissance (side porch). ▶ Through the Place de la République (Hôtel de Ville, late 18thC), and down the Rue du Père-Éternel (stalls★ in the chapel) to the Promenade du Loch★ overlooking the river and the estuary. ▶ From here, visit **St. Goustan quarter★** across a 17thC stone bridge : 15thC half-timbered houses★ by the old port.

Nearby

▶ **Sainte-Avoye** *(4.5 km SE) :* 16thC chapel with choir screen★ (1554) in carved wood. ▶ The bridge at **Bono** *(6 km)* gives a fine view of the port, where the principal occupation is raising oysters. ▶ **Sainte-Anne-d'Auray** *(6 km NE; pilgrim influx, 15-16 Jul.);* neo-Renaissance basilica; behind, former Carmelite convent with 17thC cloister; treasury and ex-votos★ *(daily 10-12 & 2-6, Jul.-Sep.; Sun. and Wed. only in May-Jun.).* Gallery of Breton religious art (statues; *same hours*). Near the Breton War Memorial (1932), the La Fontaine Museum (dolls in Breton costumes); wax museum *(Apr.-Oct., 8-8);* Nicolazic House (mobilier). Nicolazic Gallery, display case of processional banners. □

Practical Information

AURAY

ⓘ pl. de la République, ☎ 97.24.09.75.

SNCF ☎ 97.24.02.02.

⛴ Excursions on Morbihan bay (stops at Locmariaquer, Port-Navalo, l'ile aux Moines), daily in season, depending on tides.

Hotel :

★★ ***Loch***, La Petite-Forêt, Lorient road, ☎ 97.56.48.33, Tx 951025, Euro Visa, 30 rm Ⓟ ☀ ♨ ♪ ♿ 225. Rest. ♦ ***La Sterne*** ☀ ♪ closed Mon noon, 60-190.

Nearby

ERDEVEN, ⊠ 56410 Etel, 14 km SW of **Etel**.

Hotels :
● ★★★★ *Château de Kéravéon* (C.H.), ☎ 97.55.68.55, AE DC Euro Visa ℗ ⑾ 🔍 ☒ half pens (h.s.), closed 15 Sep-15 May, 1000. Rest. ♦♦♦ 👍 ⊗ closed lunch ex Sat and Sun, 15 Sep-30 May, 170-280.
★★ *Auberge du Sous-Bois* (L.F.), rte de Pont-Lorois, ☎ 97.55.66.10, Tx 950581, AE DC Euro Visa, 22 rm ℗ ⑾ half pens (h.s.), closed 15 Oct-1 Apr, 400. Rest. ♦ ♪ closed lunch ex Sun and Jul-Aug, 55-100; child : 45.

⚠ ★★*Les Sept Saints* (200 pl), ☎ 97.55.52.65.

SAINTE-ANNE-D'AURAY, ⊠ 56400 Auray, 6 km NE.

Hotel :
★★ *Le Myriam*, 37, rue du Parc, ☎ 97.57.70.44, 30 rm ℗ ⑾ 🔍 closed 15 Apr-30 Sep, 160.

La BAULE*

Nantes 74, Rennes 136, Paris 445 km
pop 14688 ⊠ 44500   C4

The most popular seaside resort in Brittany, on a par with Royan and Biarritz, the other major resorts on the Atlantic Coast. La Baule claims to have the most beautiful beach in Europe.

▶ A broad promenade with flower gardens flourishing in the mild climate starts at **Pornichet**, created 20 years ago on the edge of an 8-km crescent of fine sand (the **Côte d'Amour**, Guérandaise peninsula). The luxury hotels and imposing mansions vary in style from quaintly old-fashioned (La Baule became a resort in 1880) to up-market modern. Behind them, rows of pines protect comfortable villas from the ocean winds. Hotels, leisure facilities and entertainment are calculated to please a sophisticated clientele ; families tend to stay in the little white houses at **Le Pouliguen**, an old fishing port separated from La Baule by a canal that feeds the salt marshes. ☐

Practical Information —————————

La BAULE
ⓘ 9, pl. de la Victoire, ☎ 40.24.34.44.
✈ Saint-Nazaire-Montoir, 22 km E, ☎ 40.22.35.06.
SNCF ☎ 40.60.13.20/40.60.01.97.
🚌 pl. de la Victoire, ☎ 40.60.25.58.
Car rental : Avis, Train station ; 17, av. Clémenceau, ☎ 40.60.36.28 (open from 15th Jun to 15th Sep).

Hotels :
★★★★(L) *Castel Marie-Louise* (R.C.), 1, av. Andrieu, ☎ 40.60.20.60, Tx 700408, AE DC Euro Visa, 31 rm ℗ ⑾ ⑾ 🔍 👍 1160. Rest. ● ♦♦ 🍴 ♪ ⊗ The taste of the ocean at your table : *marinade de coquilles Saint-Jacques au citron vert sur mousse d'avocat, fricassée de turbot et de ris de veau aux pleurotes, sauce gingembre*, 120-250 ; child : 85.
★★★★(L) *Hermitage*, esp. F.-André, ☎ 40.60.37.00, Tx 710510, AE DC Euro Visa, 237 rm ℗ 🍴 ⑾ 🔍 ♪ ☒ 🏊 closed 15 Oct-15 Apr, 1400. Rest. ♦♦♦ 🍴 ♪ ⊗ Attractive all-inclusive 'relaxation' package. Fitness centre. Golf and tennis lessons. Sessions with sports pros (tennis, windsurfing, golf). As in other hotels of the Barrière chain, this one managed by energetic Yves Le Naour, there is good food, here prepared by François Sierra, 230-280.
★★★★ *Royal*, espl. F.-André, ☎ 40.60.33.06, Tx 701135, AE DC Euro Visa, 100 rm ℗ 🍴 ⑾ 🔍 half pens (h.s.), closed Nov-Mar, 850. Rest. ♦♦ 180-200.
★★★ *Alizés* (L.F.), 10, av. de Rhuys, ☎ 40.60.34.86, AE DC Euro Visa, 30 rm ℗ 🍴 ⑾ ♪ 🐾 half pens (h.s.), 680. Rest. ♦ 🍴 ♪ ⊗ 110-190.
● ★★ *La Palmeraie* (L.F.), 7, allée des Cormorans, ☎ 40.60.24.41, 23 rm ⑾ 🔍 pens (h.s.), closed Oct-Mar, 470. Rest. ♦ ⊗ 90-110.
★★ *Concorde*, 1, av. de la Concorde, ☎ 40.60.23.09, Euro Visa, 47 rm ℗ 🍴 ⑾ 🔍 ⊗ closed 1 Oct-1 Apr, 280.

★ *Saint-Bernard*, 6, av. des Evens, ☎ 40.60.32.02, 7 rm ℗ ⑾ ⊗ 190.

Restaurants :
● ♦♦♦ *Pergola*, 147, av. des Lilas, ☎ 40.24.57.61, AE Euro Visa ℗ ♪ closed Oct-Apr. Henri Seguin's attractive summer quarters (he's at Le Pressoir in Paris, otherwise) : *blanquette de lapin aux huîtres, tartare de saumon, ananas confit au gingembre*, 180.
♦♦♦ *L'Espadon*, 2, av. de la Plage (5th floor), ☎ 40.60.05.63, AE DC Visa 🍴 ♪ 👍 closed Mon and Sun eve (l.s.), 5-16 Jan, 17 Nov-12 Dec. Room with a view. Spec : *cassolettes de belons aux épinards, éventail de Saint-Pierre aux truffes*, 95-300.
♦♦ *Le Bistingo*, ☎ 40.60.20.23 ℗ closed lunch, 15 Sep-1 Jun. Restaurant at the Casino, 210-320.
♦ *La Trattoria*, ☎ 40.60.20.23 Restaurant at the Casino, 220-310.

⚠ ★★★★*Pré du château Careil* (43 pl), ☎ 40.60.22.99 ; ★★★*Ajoncs d'Or* (200 pl), ☎ 40.60.33.29 ; ★★★*Caravaning l'Eden* (105 pl), ☎ 40.60.03.23.

Recommended
Casino : ☎ 40.60.20.23, closed 15 Sep-1 Jun. With two restaurants, Le Bistingo and la Trattoria.
Events : folk ballet festival, Jul-Aug ; Breton week ; 'pardon' at la Baule, late Aug ; international horse trials, Jul ; automobile parade, 14 Aug.
Night-clubs : Le Sako, at the Casino, ☎ 40.60.20.23, closed (l.s.) ; Le Tropicana, at the Casino, ☎ 40.60.20.23, closed (l.s.) ; at Saint-André-des-Eaux, Club Saint-Denac, 8 km NE, ☎ 40.60.46.18, Jun-Sep, 11pm till dawn.
Thalassotherapie : 28, bd de l'Océan, ☎ 40.24.30.97.

Nearby

PORNICHET, ⊠ 44380.
ⓘ pl. Aristide-Briand, ☎ 40.61.08.92.
SNCF ☎ 40.61.08.28.

Hotel :
★★★ *Sud Bretagne* (L.F.), 42, bd de la République, ☎ 40.61.02.68, AE DC Euro Visa, 33 rm ℗ ⑾ ♪ ☒ 🏊 half pens (h.s.), closed 31 Oct-31 Mar, 700. Rest. ♦♦ *La Piscine* 🍴 ♪ 100-200.

⚠ ★★★*Bel Air* (230 pl), ☎ 40.61.10.78 ; ★★★*Bugeau* (170 pl), ☎ 40.61.02.02 ; ★★★*Forges* (170 pl), ☎ 40.61.18.84.

Recommended
Casino : bd des Océanides, ☎ 40.61.05.48.
Marina : ☎ 40.61.03.20.

Le POULIGUEN, ⊠ 44510.
ⓘ port Sterwitz, ☎ 40.42.31.05.
SNCF ☎ 40.60.51.35.

Hotels :
● ★★★ *Domaine de Cramphore*, bd de l'Atlantique, ☎ 40.42.23.61, DC Visa, 22 rm ℗ 🍴 ⑾ 🔍 ☒ 🏊 closed 15 Oct-30 Nov, 350. Rest. ♦♦ *Les Farnientes* 🍴 closed Mon eve and Tue. Tranquil and charming. Spec : *salade farnientes, escalope de bar, ris de veau à l'orange*, 60-170.
★★ *Grand Hôtel Neptune*, 14, quai Jules-Sandeau, ☎ 40.60.50.05, Visa, 27 rm 🍴 closed Wed (l.s.), 15 Nov-1 Apr, 200. Rest. ♦ 🍴 ♪ ⊗ 60-140.

Restaurant :
♦♦ *Voile d'Or*, av. de la Plage, ☎ 40.42.31.68 ℗ 🍴 ♪ closed Tue eve and Wed, 5 Jan-2 Feb, 70-200.

⚠ ★★*Mouettes* (230 pl), ☎ 40.42.10.29 ; ★*Clein*, rue de Kerlis (100 pl), ☎ 40.42.43.99.

BELLE-ÎLE-EN-MER**

pop 4191 ⊠ 56360 Le palais   B3-4

This largest island of Brittany is little more than a bare plateau stubbornly cultivated by its inhabitants. Its many valleys protect crops from waves that thunder against the cliffs. Some of the beaches are dangerous, but the remoteness of Belle-Île attracts many visitors.

▶ **Le Palais** : a port fortified 1st half 19thC. Citadel (museum) dating from 1572 *(free entrance ; 9-6)*.

Tour of the island *(57 km ; an easy day ; take care when walking near the edge of the cliffs)*

▶ Start from **Sauzon**, a little fishing port; go to **Poulains Point★** at the northernmost tip of the island; the **Apothecairerie Cave★★**, a natural marvel; after a quick visit to **Port Donnant** (cliffs★) and a brief stop at the **Grand Phare** (lighthouse; panorama★ ; *1 Jul.-15 Sep. 9:30-12:30 & 2-6;* 256 steps; 85 m above sea level), see the rock needles★ at **Port-Coton**. Via **Bangor** and **Locmaria** (superb ex-voto model in the church) you can reach Lilliputian **Port-Maria** on the E tip of the island. Return to Le Palais along the beach (Les Grands Sables). ☐

Practical Information ——————————

ℹ️ quai Bonnelle, ☎ 97.31.81.93.
🚢 ☎ 97.31.80.01, from Quiberon, in 45 mn, 4 to 10 daily connections depending on season, passagers and cars.

Hotels :
★★★ *Manoir de Goulphar*, Bangor, ☎ 97.31.80.10, Tx 730750, 52 rm P ⏳ ░ half pens (h.s.), closed 5 Nov-15 Mar, 520. Rest. ♦ ⏳ 🕏 90-200.
★★★ *Le Cardinal*, Port de Sauzon, pointe du Cardinal, ☎ 97.31.61.60, Tx 730750, 85 rm P ⏳ ♪ half pens (h.s.), closed 1 Oct-15 Apr, 580. Rest. ♦ ⏳ 🕏 90-180.
● ★★★ *Castel Clara* (R.C.), Goulphar, Bangor, ☎ 97.31.84.21, Tx 730750, AE Visa, 43 rm P ⏳ 🕳 ♪ 🐾 ⏳ 🖃 ⏳ closed 15 Oct-15 Mar, 625. Rest. ● ♦♦ ⏳ ♪ ⏳ 120-260 ; child : 65.

Restaurant :
● ♦ *La Forge*, rte de Goulphar, ☎ 97.31.81.33, AE Euro Visa 🕳 ♪ closed 11 Nov-1 Apr. Spec : *feuilleté d'huîtres au beurre de cassis, embeurrée de fettucine aux crustacés,* 85-160 ; child : 50.

Recommended
♥ crêperie : *Chez Renée*, at Bangor, ☎ 97.31.52.87 ; *du Moulin*, ☎ 97.31.83.96 ; pleasure port : Le Palais, ☎ 97.31.42.90, 300 slips ; youth hostel : *Hauts de Boulogne*, Le Palais, ☎ 97.31.81.33 ; at Sauzon, crêperie : *Les Embruns*, rue du Lt Riou, ☎ 97.31.64.78.

BÉNODET

Quimper 16, Lorient 71, Paris 556 km
pop 2286 ✉ 29118   A-B2
The population increases to around 30 000 in summer ; the site★★ (picture-postcard marina on the Odet Estuary) and lush vegetation are very attractive. Marvellous views from the lighthouse, the banks of the Odet and the **Cornouaille Bridge.** ☐

Practical Information ——————————

BÉNODET
ℹ️ 51, av. de la Plage, ☎ 98.57.00.14.
🚢 to the îles des Glénans daily in Jul-Aug.

Hotels :
● ★★★ *Gwell-Kaër*, 3, av. de la Plage, ☎ 98.57.04.38, Visa, 24 rm P ⏳ ♪ 🕏 pens (h.s.), closed Mon, 15 Dec-31 Jan, 700. .
★★★ *Ker Moor*, av. de la Plage, ☎ 98.57.04.48, Tx 941182, Euro Visa, 65 rm P ⏳ 🕳 ░ 🖃 🐾 pens (h.s.), 380. Rest. ♦ ⏳ 🕏 90-200.
★★ *Le Cornouaille* (L.F.), 62, av. de la Plage, ☎ 98.57.03.78, 30 rm 🐾 closed Oct-Apr, 190. Rest. ♦ 70-110.
★★ *Le Minaret* (L.F.), corniche de l'Estuaire, ☎ 98.57.03.13, Euro Visa, 21 rm P ⏳ 🕳 half pens (h.s.),

closed Oct-Mar, 255. Rest. ♦ ⏳ ♪ 🕏 Moroccan architecture and Breton cuisine, 60-210.

Restaurant :
● ♦ *La Ferme du Letty*, Le Letty-Izella, ☎ 98.57.01.27, AE Euro Visa ♪ 🕏 closed Wed and Thu noon , Feb school hols, 4-31 Oct. In keeping with the farmhouse theme, the menu is a little overloaded, but J.-P. Guilbault serves enjoyable food : *feuilleté de tourteau, saumon soufflé.* Cellar now being stocked, 175-200.

🏕 ★★★★*Letty* (500 pl), ☎ 98.57.04.69 ; ★★★*Pointe Saint-Gilles* (476 pl), ☎ 98.57.05.37 ; ★★*Plage* (300 pl), ☎ 98.57.00.55.

Recommended
♥ crêperie : *La Boulange*, 11, rue de l'Eglise, ☎ 98.57.17.71 ; at Combrit, antiques : *Nédélec*, ☎ 98.56.36.03 ; *Le Courtil*, ☎ 98.56.46.64.

Nearby
SAINTE-MARINE, ✉ 29120 Combrit, 10 km E of **Pont-l'Abbé.**

Hotel :
★ *Le Jeanne-d'Arc*, 52, rue de la Plage, ☎ 98.56.32.70, 9 rm P ⏳ half pens (h.s.), closed Mon eve (l.s.) and Tue, Oct-Mar, 320. Rest. ● ♦♦ Seafood carefully cooked by Burgundian René Fargette : *foies blonds au coulis de homard, jardinière de homard bressane,* 130-230.

The BIGOUDEN Region

                                                                A2
Typical Breton countryside around Pont-l'Abbé, mixing tradition (the tall white caps of the women) and modernity (tractors and market gardening, tourism and rows of identical little white houses).

▶ **Pont-l'Abbé** (pop. 7 729) is 6 km upriver. The **Bigouden Museum★** in a round 15thC tower by a lake *(Jun.-Sep., daily 9-12 & 2-6:30 ex Sun. and nat. hols.)* : costumes and headdresses. ▶ Church (1383, two rose windows★) near shady walk on right bank. ▶ On left bank, ruins★ of the churchs of Lambour (13th-16thC). ▶ **Kerlever** *(5 km NE)*, Cornouaille botanical garden *(in season, 10-12 & 2-6).*

Round trip along the coast *(43 km, 2 1/2 hr)*

▶ Follow D2. The pretty Bigouden farm at **Kervagégan** has been transformed into an ecomuseum. ▶ **Kérazan Manor** (16th-18thC) in a park ; 18th-19thC furniture, 16th-20thC paintings and drawings *(Jun.-15 Sep. ; 10-12 & 2-6 ; ex Tue.).* ▶ **Loctudy** (pop. 3 560) : an ideal seaside resort for children. The church★ is one of the most beautiful Romanesque buildings in Brittany ; the port (fishing, pleasure craft) faces **L'Ile-Tudy,** a fishing port on the end of a narrow peninsula. ▶ Busy little ports along the coast : **Lesconil** (sardines and langoustines), **Lechiagat** and **Le Guilvinec** (third most active fishing port). ▶ The church★ at **Penmarc'h** is a fine example of Breton Flamboyant Gothic architecture (1508) ; the one at the port of **Kérity** is more modest. ▶ The **Eckmühl lighthouse** (64 m, 1897) on the tip of Penmarc'h is one of the most powerful in France ; superb view *(May-15 Sep., 10-12 & 2-7 ; pm only rest of year).* ▶ **Saint-Guénolé** : a coastal and deep sea fishing port ; to the N, the sea boils around the rocks ; **museum of prehistory** *(10-12 & 2-6, Jun.-Sep.),* surrounded by megaliths ; reconstructed burial chambers inside. ▶ Dolmens, menhirs, and cromlechs (→ box) line the road to **Plomeur** (18thC church). ▶ **Château de Kernuz** (now a hotel) stands in a park, and possesses a 15thC guardroom. 🌾

Round trip inland *(approx. 50 km ; 3 hr)*

▶ Tour of the churches and chapels : **Tréminou★** (15thC ; Calvary in the form of a pulpit) ; **Saint-Jean-Trolimon** (16thC, rebuilt) ; **Notre-Dame de Tronoën★★** (15thC ; Calvary★★ on the heath, prototype of the Breton Calvaries). ▶ **Plonéour-Lanvern** : surrounded by churches and chapels; chapels of Languivoa (14th-16thC) and Lanvern (16thC); churches at Tréguennec (15th-16thC; stained glass, altarpieces, beams), Trégoat (15thC) and Peumerit (13thC); ruined 13thC chapel at Languidou★. The manorhouses are hardly less numerous : manor-farm at Minven (16thC door), fortified manor at Penquelenec; Trévilit Manor★ (15thC; *exterior visit only*). ☐

Practical Information ─────────────

Le GUILVINEC, ⊠ 29115, 8 km E of La Pointe de Penmarc'h.
ⓘ ☎ 98.52.10.79.

Hotel :
★★ *Port*, (France-Accueil), Léchiagat, ☎ 98.58.10.10, Tx 941200, AE DC Euro Visa, 40 rm ℗ ⸖ ⸜ ♫ ᵫ half pens (h.s.), closed 24 Dec-5 Jan. Boat rides and deep-sea fishing organized by the hotel, 230. Rest. ♦ ⸖ ♪ ᵫ ⚘ 70-150; child : 35.

Recommended
Events : *sea festival*, 15 Aug.

L' ILE-TUDY, ⊠ 29157, 11 km SE of Pont-l'Abbé.
ⓘ ☎ 98.56.43.11.

Hotel :
★ *Dunes*, 9, av. de Bretagne, ☎ 98.56.43.55, 12 rm ℗ ᵯ ᵫ ♪ pens, closed 15 Sep-1 Jun, 420. Rest. ♦ ♪ ⚘ Guests only.

⚠ ★★*Bois d'Amour* (74 pl); ★★*Pen ar Palud* (70 pl), ☎ 98.56.39.27; ★★*Sillon* (170 pl), ☎ 98.56.42.57.

LESCONIL, ⊠ 29138, 8 km S of Pont-l'Abbé.
ⓘ rue Pasteur, ☎ 98.87.86.99.

Hotel :
★★ *La Plage*, (France-Accueil), 10, rue Joliot-Curie, ☎ 98.87.80.05, Tx 941200, AE DC Euro Visa, 29 rm ℗ ᵯ ᵯ ᵫ ♪ ᵫ closed Mon (l.s.), 15 Oct-1 Apr. Excursions and deep-sea fishing, 140. Rest. ♦ ⸖ ♪ ᵫ ⚘ 70-150; child : 35.

LOCTUDY, ⊠ 29125, 6 km SE of Pont-l'Abbé.
ⓘ pl. de la Mairie, ☎ 98.87.53.78.

Hotel :
★★ *Rafiot*, at the port, ☎ 98.87.42.57, 9 rm 3 apt ᵯ closed Sun, Oct, 180.

⚠ ★★*Kergall* (100 pl), ☎ 98.87.45.93; ★★*Mouettes* (60 pl), ☎ 98.87.43.51.

PLOBANNALEC, ⊠ 29138 Lesconil, 6 km S of Pontl'Abbé.

Restaurant :
● ♦♦ *Petit Kéroulé*, rte de Pont-l'Abbé, ☎ 98.82.22.55, Visa ᵯ ♪ ᵫ closed Mon eve and Tue ex Jul-Aug, Oct. Lots of fresh, house-smoked and marinated fish, 100-200.

PLOMEUR, ⊠ 29120 Pont-l'Abbé, 6 km SW of Saint-Guénolé.

Hotel :
★★ *La Ferme du Relais Bigouden* (L.F.), rte du Guilvinec, Pendreff, ☎ 98.82.04.79, Euro Visa, 16 rm ℗ ᵯ ᵯ ♪ ᵫ closed 10 Dec-20 Jan, 165.

Restaurant :
♦♦ *Le Relais de Ty Boutic*, Ty Boutic, ☎ 98.87.03.90, Visa ᵫ closed Wed , Feb, 50-180.

⚠ ★★*Moulin* (80 pl), ☎ 98.58.18.93; ★★*Pointe de la Torche* (155 pl), ☎ 98.58.62.82.

PONT-L'ABBÉ, ⊠ 29120, 20 km SW of Quimper.
ⓘ Château, ☎ 98.87.24.44.

Hotel :
★★ *Château de Kernuz* (C.H.), 10, rte de Penmarc'h, ☎ 98.87.01.59, Euro Visa, 12 rm ℗ ᵯ ᵯ ♬ 🖼 half pens (h.s.), closed 1 Nov-1 Apr. 16th-C château, 460. Rest. ♦♦ ♪ 80-120.

Restaurant :
● ♦♦ *L'Enclos de Rosveign*, Ménez-Kerlaouarn, ☎ 98.87.02.90, Euro Visa ᵯ ♪ ᵫ closed Wed. Excellent

food with a local accent, expertly prepared by J.-P. Stephan : *homard braisé, bavaroise d'araignées de mer, palette de poissons aux coquillages*, 85-250; child : 65.

⚠ ★★*Ecureuils* (130 pl), ☎ 98.87.03.39; at Kerseoch, ★★*Châtaigniers* (100 pl), ☎ 98.87.11.90.

Recommended
♥ at Plonéour-Lanvern, crêperie : *Tachen-ar-Groag*, 2, rte St-Jean, ☎ 98.87.70.58.

SAINT-GUÉNOLÉ, ⊠ 29132 Penmarc'h.
ⓘ pl. A.-Dupany, ☎ 98.58.81.44.

Hotels :
● ★★ *La Mer*, 184, rue François-Péron, ☎ 98.58.62.22, Visa, 17 rm ℗ ᵯ ᵫ closed Mon eve and Sun eve, 11 Jan-27 Feb, 190. Rest. ♦ ᵯ Set before the ocean, at what looks like the end of the earth, here is savoury, hearty fare : *homard à la bigoudène cuit aux algues*, 105-200.

★★ *Sterenn*, rte du Phare-d'Eckmühl, plage de la Joie, ☎ 98.58.60.36, Euro Visa, 16 rm ℗ ᵯ ᵬ ⚘ half pens (h.s.), closed Wed ex 10 Jun-17 Sep, 5 Oct-11 Apr, 520. Rest. ♦ ᵯ ⚘ 65-165.

The BLAVET River

B-C2
From Mur-de-Bretagne to Pluvigner (*148 km, full day*)

A dark, peaceful river running through quiet countryside, with here and there a grove of trees or a clump of golden furze among the potato fields that stretch to Pontivy.

▶ An interesting route from N to S through the centre of Brittany. ▶ **Mur-de-Bretagne** (pop. 2 165) on a hilltop, 17thC chapel surrounded by old oaks; 2 km W, **Lake Guerlédan★** (4 km², boat trips); wooded banks; producing electricity since 1929 in the Blavet Gorges. ▶ Through the rock-strewn **Poulancre Gorges** to **Saint-Gilles-Vieux-Marché** (lakes, menhirs) and **Saint-Mayeux** (Calvary surrounded by old yews in the cemetery). D76 runs from here along the ridge line; views. ▶ In **Laniscat**, furnishings and wheel of bells in the church (1691); continue to the **Daoulas Gorges★**, with almost vertical schist formations (*in summer*, mineralogical exhibition). ▶ Ruins of the Cistercian **abbey of Bon Repos** near an old, ivy-covered bridge (doorway, 18thC buildings, remains of 13thC chapel). ▶ Delightful walks in the woodlands around **Forges-des-Salles**. ▶ GR34 runs through the **forest of Quénécan★**, a beautiful itinerary along the S bank of the lake, with a steep rock wall on the opposite side; by car to the bay at **Sordan**; view from the dam. ▶ The Tree of Jesse (genealogy of Christ) is often represented in Breton churches : at **Saint-Aignan** (12thC), carved; St. Mériadec Chapel (16thC), **Stival**, in stained glass. ▶ After **Pontivy** (→) and environs, leave the Blavet : **Quelven**, depopulated by a rural exodus, an old village that is still crowded every 15 August at the *pardon* (→ box), on one of the rare days when the sides of an opening Virgin in the Notre-Dame chapel (15th-16thC) are unfolded to reveal 12 bas-reliefs of Christ's Passion. ▶ The road zig-zags back to the Blavet at **Rimaison** (remains of château). ▶ The chapel of **Saint-Nicodème★** is of remarkable proportions (46 m bell-tower); built in 1537 in Flamboyant Gothic style; furnishings. Nearby, a consecrated fountain (1608). ▶ **Saint-Nicolas-des-Eaux** : on the banks of the Blavet Canal, old granite houses, some with thatched roofs. ▶ The road follows the river in a tight bend around **La Couarde "peninsula"** : view★ of both sides of the valley; La Trinité chapel (15th-16thC) at **Castennec**; old hermitage of St. Gildas at the foot of the hamlet. ▶ **Bieuzy** : church retaining 16thC beams and stained glass; Renaissance houses with wells; 16thC fountain. ▶ **Melrand** : typical old inland Brittany village with granite houses (several from the Renaissance); 200 m from the church, unusual Calvary★ (18th-19thC). ▶ The road criss-crosses the Blavet through neatly-tended countryside where thatched roofs are still common; menhirs

(3.5 m and 5 m high) at **Saint-Barthélemy**; the water from the fountains at the **chapel of Saint-Adrien** (15thC) is reputed to cure stomach pains. Visit the **château de Villeneuve-Jacquelot** and the exhibition of regional arts and traditions in the Poul Fétan Museum at **Quistinic**; catch your breath in refreshing **Pont Augan**. ▶ Before you reach **Baud** (pop. 4 962; 16thC church), visit the statue known as the **Vénus de Quinipily**, which gave the local clergy sleepless nights for centuries in their struggle to overcome popular superstition and the cult that surrounds the goddess. ▶ Choice of walks in the **forest of Camors** (beech, megaliths). ▶ The château de Kéronic (16thC; *private*) is worth a detour on the way to **Pluvigner** (many chapels). ☐

Practical Information _____

MUR-DE-BRETAGNE, ⊠ 22530, 21 km W of **Loudéac**.

Hotel :
★★ *Auberge Grand'Maison*, 1, rue Léon-le-Cerf, ☎ 96.28.51.10, AE, 15 rm, closed Sun eve and Mon, 23-30 Jun, 30 Sep-25 Oct, 120. Rest. ● ◆◆◆ ♪ ᕍ
A comfortable inn where Brigitte Guillo oversees the efficient service while husband Jacques prepares tasty, original dishes : *blanc de turbot mariné, huîtres tièdes aux bigorneaux, pigeon au choux de foie gras.* A curiosity : *le coulommiers rôti au caramel poivré,* 110-250.

Recommended
Farmhouse-inn : at Glomel, 33 km W by N 164, *Manoir de Saint-Penan*, ☎ 96.29.60.04, chambres d'hôtes.

Île de BRÉHAT*
(Bréhat Island)

pop 511 ⊠ 22870 Paimpol   C1

An island 1.5 by 3.5 km, 10 min from Arcouest Point among scattered reefs and islets; jagged coastline, no cars allowed (a few tractors only). Camellias and hydrangeas, mimosa and rose laurel brighten the gardens; roads wind through heather to bays and creeks inhabited by guillemots and cormorants, curlews and seagulls, where fishermen bring in lobster, king prawns and crab. The village is clustered around church (remodelled 17th, 18thC; small wallbelfry★; porch opening on to flowered cemetery). ☐

Practical Information _____

⛴ ☎ 96.20.00.66, from Saint-Quay-Portrieux, Jun-Sep., 1h30 crossing; ☎ 96.20.82.30, from la pointe de l'Arcouest (h.s.), frequent daily service (about every 1/2 hr in summer), 10 mn crossing.

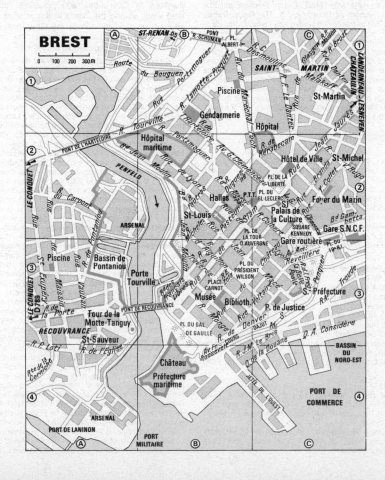

Hotels :
● ★★ *Bellevue*, Le Port-Clos, ☎ 96.20.00.05, Euro Visa, 18 rm ≪ ⌂ ⅃ & half pens (h.s.), closed 15 Nov-30 Mar, 560. Rest. ♦♦ ≪ ♪ & 65-130.
● ★★ *La Vieille Auberge* (L.F.), ☎ 96.20.00.24, 15 rm ⌂ ⌂ & ⚄ half pens (h.s.), closed Nov, Easter school hols, 430. Rest. ● ♦♦ & 60-120.

BREST*

Quimper 71, Rennes 244, Paris 597 km
pop 160355 ⊠ 29200   A2
(see map on previous page)
Brest successfully disguised its post-war development as well as its military-industrial activities; it is not a tourist town in the traditional sense, but its superb roadstead, the romantic names of streets and bistros and the mild climate attract numerous visitors, in addition to admirers of the French Navy.

▶ Brest, originally a Roman military outpost, became an important port under Cardinal Richelieu (1631). During WWII it was France's principal naval dockyard; it became a German submarine base, as a result of which the port was heavily bombed. After the D-Day landings in 1944 (→ Normandy), a devastating siege of 43 days obliterated the town centre.
▶ **Museum** (B3; *10-11:45 & 2-6:45 ex Tue.*) : paintings from the 17th, 18th and 19thC; Dutch, Flemish and Italian schools; school of Pont-Aven. ▶ The **Recouvrance Bridge★** (A-B3) has an 87-m centre span which rises 29 m in 2 min 28 sec. View★ of the Penfeld and the **arsenal buildings** *(visits for French citizens only).* ▶ In La Motte-Tanguy Tower (16thC; A3) is the **Old Brest Museum** *(daily Jul.-Aug., 10-12 & 2-7; Jun. and Sep., 2-7; Thu., Sat. and Sun. pm rest of the year)* military history; dioramas. The **Naval Museum** is in the 15th-16thC **château** (B4; *daily ex Tue. and nat. hols, 9-11:30 & 2-5:30*). ▶ From the Cours Dajot (B4-C3) on the S side of the ramparts (built in 1683 by Louis XIV's military engineer Sebastien de Vauban), view★★ of the harbour.   □

Practical Information _____

ⓘ 6, rue Augustin-Morvan (C2), ☎ 98.44.24.96.
✈ *Guipavas*, 9 km NE, ☎ 98.84.61.49. *Air France office*, 12, rue Boussingault, ☎ 98.44.15.55; *Brest-Ouessant*, ☎ 98.84.64.87.
SNCF (C2), ☎ 98.80.50.50.
▨▨ pl. Franklin-Roosevelt (C2-3), ☎ 98.44.46.73.
▭▭ ☎ 98.80.24.68, Excursions : Ouessant, Camaret, les Tas de Pois, l'île de Sein, le Conquet, l'île Molène (all year).
Car rental : *Avis*, Guipavas airport; 3, bd des Français-Libres, ☎ 98.43.37.73; Train station (C2).

Hotels :
★★★ *Continental*, (France-Accueil), 22, rue de Lyon (B-C2), ☎ 98.80.50.40, Tx 940575, AE DC Euro Visa, 75 rm ♪ closed Sat lunch and Sun, 280. Rest. ♦ closed Sat noon and Sun, 55-100.
★★★ *Voyageurs*, 15, av. G.-Clemenceau (B2), ☎ 98.80.25.73, Tx 940660, AE DC Euro Visa, 40 rm, closed 1-15 Jan, 22 Jul-13 Aug, 300. Rest. ● ♦♦ closed 1-15 Jan, 22 Jul-13 Aug. A gourmet centre with the 'Grand Large' brasserie on the ground floor and the 'Panoramique' upstairs. Meat and fish dishes, 150-200.
★★ *Bellevue*, 53, rue V.-Hugo (C2), ☎ 98.80.51.78, Euro Visa, 26 rm ≪ 130.

Restaurants :
● ♦♦♦ *Le Frère Jacques*, 15 bis, rue de Lyon (B2), ☎ 98.44.38.65, Euro Visa ♪ closed Sat noon and Sun, 27 Jul-9 Aug. Jacques Peron's innovative cuisine : *demoiselles de Loctudy, sole au foie gras*, 130-250.
♦♦ *Le Poulbot*, 26, rue d'Aiguillon (B3), ☎ 98.44.19.08, AE DC Euro Visa ♪ closed Sat noon and Sun, 18 Aug-6 Sep, 70-210.

♦♦ *Les Antilles*, 12, rue de Siam (B2), ☎ 98.46.05.52, Euro Visa ≪ ♪ child : 30.
♦ *Le Panoramique*, (station buffet) pl. du 19e-R.I. (C2), ☎ 98.46.03.97, AE DC Euro Visa ≪ closed Fri eve and Sat, 15-30 Jun, 45-120.

Recommended
Marina : *Moulin-Blanc*, ☎ 98.02.20.02.
Youth hostel : *Au Moulin-Blanc*, ☎ 98.41.90.41.

BRIÈRE Nature Park**

                                                                  C3-4
From Montoir-de-Bretagne to Guérande *(96-138 km, full day; see map 3)*
The Grande Brière is a 200 km² peat bog drained by numerous ditches. The inhabitants of the 21 communes in the area own the marshes collectively, as they have since the letter of patent of the Duke of Brittany, François II, signed in 1461. The people live by netting fish, wildfowling, stock-rearing and the sale of peat and reeds, supplemented by boat trips and other tourist activities. Today, however, these are only secondary livelihoods; many are employed in the shipyards at Saint-Nazaire or the workshops at Trignac. Not far from the summer excitement of the Côte d'Amour *(5 km from La Baule)*, which shows signs at present of an increased activity (the school of marsh-dwellers at Guérande), 300 *paludiers* (marshdwellers) work among the reeds in the shallow marshes, keeping up the tradition of the Guérande salt pans. Because of industrial competition, the area being worked has been reduced to only 8 km².

▶ 70-acre bird sanctuary at **Saint-Malo-de-Guersac**; Maison de l'Éclusier at **Rosé** *(Jun.-Sep. 10-12:30 & 3-7)* : life in the marshes and on the waterways of the Brière region. ▶ Typical Brière village at **Île de Fédrun** : squat houses with thick walls of stone or cob, whitewashed every year. No. 308, *La Chaumière Briéronne (same hours as the Maison de l'Éclusier)* is a perfect example. Landing stages project from the ring road into the parallel canal; facilities for boat trips. Visitor's information from No. 180 (La Maison du Parc). ▶ Past **Crossac** (old château) and **La Madeleine** (Calvary and menhir), to **Missillac** (16thC stained glass in church); visit the park of **château de la Bretesche★** *(closed Mon. in winter).* ▶ La **Chapelle-des-Marais** : S.I.; Maison du Sabotier (wooden shoe-maker; *Jun.-Sep. ; off season, Wed. pm*). ▶ The ruins of the **château de Ranrouët** (12th-13thC), which was dismantled by Cardinal Richelieu, are being restored. ▶ Boat trips at **Fossés Blancs**, and at **La Pierre-fondue**; ▶ More boats at **Saint-Lyphard**; splendid view★ from the bell-tower *(Jul.-Aug., ex Sun. am and nat. hols.).* ▶ Close to the **Kerhinet★★** road is the dolmen of **Kerbour**. Kerhinet itself is a village-museum (inn; museum : *same hours as the Maison de l'Éclusier*); traditional Brière houses. **Bréca** and **La Chaussée Neuve** : boat trips, views★ over the Brière. Through **Guérande** (→) to **château de Careil★** : Renaissance façades in the courtyard *(20 Mar.-Sep., 10:30-12 & 2:30-7:30; candlelight visits Wed. and Sat. at 9:30 pm, 15 Jun.-Aug.).* ▶ **Kervalet** is a marvellous little marshdwellers' village. ▶ **Saillé** : Maison des Paludiers offers an introduction to the world of the salt marshes; costumes, furnishings, tools, explanatory models *(Jul.-15 Sep., 10-12 & 2-7; pm only in Jun.).* ▶ **Batz-sur-Mer** (pronounced "Ba") : 15th-16thC church with unusual carved keystones; view★ over saltings from the tower (1677; 60 m; *15 Jun.-Aug.*); the **Musée des Marais Salants** (Marshdwellers' Museum; *Jun.-Sep., school hols., 10-12 & 3-7; Oct.-May, Sat., Sun., 3-7)* is one of the oldest museums of folk arts and traditions in the region; nearby, ruins of a Gothic chapel. ▶ Pretty road around the point at **Croisic** (→); squat salt barns in wood or stone, their walls supported by buttresses, line the road. Drive or walk carefully along this low dyke between tidal reservoirs and mud flats to explore the marshes. ▶ La **Tur-**

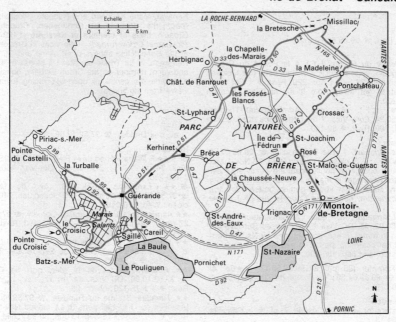

3. Brière nature park

---

balle : a sardine port linked by a lovely road to **Piriac-sur-Mer** (13thC crypt under the church; attractive old houses); extensive view★ of the coast from **Castelli Point.** □

Practical Information

BATZ-SUR-MER, ⊠ 44740, 3 km SE of **Missillac**.

Hotel :
★ **Marais Salants** (L.F.), 24, pl. de la Gare, ☎ 40.23.92.15, 10 rm ⬚ ⬚ closed Tue, 1 Oct-1 Apr, 160.

MISSILLAC, ⊠ 44160 Pontchâteau, 8 km NW of **Pontchâteau**.

Hotel :
★★★ **Golf de la Bretesche** (C.H.), Domaine de la Bretesche, ☎ 40.88.30.05, Visa, 27 rm ⬚ ⬚ ⬚ ⬚ ⬚ ⬚ ⬚ half pens (h.s.), closed Feb. A superb setting at the edge of a 13-ha pond, 570. Rest. ♦ ⬚ ⬚ ⬚ ⬚ 90-160.

Practical Information

ⓘ pl. Kléber, ☎ 98.27.93.60 (h.s.).
⚓ ☎ 98.27.22.50, excursion to Tas de Pois bird sanctuary.

Hotels :
● ★★ **France** (L.F.), overlooking the port, ☎ 98.27.93.06, 22 rm ⬚ ⬚ ⬚ closed Fri (l.s.) and school hols, 11 Nov-1 Apr, 170. Rest. ● ♦♦ ⬚ ⬚ 60-180.
★★ **Jacques Moreau** (L.F.), 19, quai G.-Toudouze, ☎ 98.27.93.06, DC Euro Visa, 22 rm ⬚ ⬚ ⬚ ⬚ half pens (h.s.), closed Fri, 11 Nov-1 Apr, 270. Rest. ♦ ⬚ ⬚ ⬚ ⬚ 60-120; child : 40.
★★ **Styvel**, quai du Styvel, ☎ 98.27.92.74, 14 rm ⬚ closed Thu, Oct-Apr, 200. Rest. ♦ 75-100.

⚑ ★★★**De Lambézen** (83 pl), ☎ 98.27.91.41.

Recommended
Leisure activities : *boat excursions with commentary*, ☎ 98.27.22.50, excursions to Tas des Pois sanctuary. "Sirènes" boats.

CAMARET-SUR-MER

Quimper 64, Brest 66, Paris 594 km
pop 3064 ⊠ 29129   A2

France's leading source of langoustes; a pleasant town protected by a 600-m natural dyke on which stand the chapel of Notre-Dame de Rocamadour (16th-17thC) and the Château Vauban (1689; naval and historical museum; *daily Jun.-Sep.*).

▶ 1 km W, **rows of menhirs** (143 altogether) at **Lagat Jar;** 2 km W, Toulinguet Point (lighthouse, fort, caves); 3 km SW, **Pen Hir Point**★★, a 70 m sheer cliff with the enormous rocks of the Tas de Pois extending out to sea; a magnificent and popular site. ▶ View★★ over Brest Channel and roadstead from the Pointe des Espagnols on **Roscanvel Peninsula,** covered with gorse, small forts and army training grounds. □

CANCALE

Dinan 34, Avranches 59, Paris 396 km
pop 4693 ⊠ 35260   D1

Oysters are the main product of Cancale : *creuses* (concave shell) are the most numerous; *plates* (flat) are less common; *pieds de cheval* (shaped like horse hooves) are rare. The seafront★ is a long line of restaurants looking across to Mont-Saint-Michel Bay *(25 km).*

▶ **Views**★ from three headlands linked by GR34. Another view from the church tower *(15 Jun.-15 Sep.; ticket from S.I.);* next door, carved-wood museum *(Jul.-Aug., daily ex Sun. pm, 10-12:30 & 3:30-6:30; rest of the year, enq. : S.I.);* museum of folk arts and traditions *(Jul.-Aug., daily ex Mon. am, 10:30-12:30 & 3:30-7:30; off season, 3:30-7:30 ex Sun.).* □

Practical Information _____

CANCALE
ℹ️ rue du Port, ☎ 99.89.63.72 (h.s.).

Hotels :
● ★★ *Pointe du Grouin* (L.F.), à la Pointe du Grouin, ☎ 99.89.60.55, Visa, 17 rm 🅿 ⬗ 🛆 half pens (h.s.), closed Tue ex Jul-Aug, 28 Sep-1 Apr, 220. Rest. ◆ ⬗ For those who want to get away from it all, an ideal vacation spot, 80-200.
★ *Phare* (L.F.), 6, quai Administrateur-Thomas, ☎ 99.89.60.24, Euro Visa, 7 rm ⬗ half pens (h.s.), closed Wed, Jan, 300. Rest. ◆ 60-140.

Restaurants :
● ◆◆ *De Bricourt*, 1, rue Duguesclin, ☎ 99.89.64.76, Euro Visa 🔲 🛆 ♪ 🛆 closed Tue and Wed, 30 Nov-1 Mar. An attractive bourgeois house featuring family-style service. Olivier Roellinger is the young chef bound for glory. His quality cuisine just keeps getting better : *tourteau frais au coriandre, huîtres de Cancale, turbot à l'arète*, 100-300.
● ◆◆ *L'Armada*, 8, quai Administrateur-Thomas, ☎ 99.89.60.02, AE DC Visa ⬗ 🔲 ♪ closed Sun eve and Mon, eves in winter. Fresh, crisp cuisine by Nadine Perrigault and her charming staff. The sea is just outside the door : oysters and fish, 150-200.

⚚ ★★★*Port-Mer* (83 pl), ☎ 99.89.63.17 ; ★★*Bel Air* (280 pl), ☎ 99.89.64.36 ; ★★*Pointe du Grouin* (165 pl), ☎ 99.89.63.79.

Recommended
♥ bay oysters for sale : *M. Désirée*, 7, pl. de la Chapelle, ☎ 99.89.64.13.

Nearby
SAINT-MÉLOIR-DES-ONDES, ✉ 35350, 6 km SW.

Hotel :
★★ *La Gare* (L.F.), ☎ 99.89.10.46, Tx 740896, AE DC Euro Visa, 63 rm 🅿 🛆 🛆 half pens (h.s.), closed 15 Dec-15 Jan, 400. Rest. ◆ ◆◆ 🛆 closed Sun eve (1 Oct-31 Mar). The peaceful countryside is often roused by the rumble of passing trains. In season, diners and lodgers cause a bit of crowding. But it's all in good fun, as is the family atmosphere and the fine cooking : *faux-filet vigneronne aux poires vin de cassis, suprême de barbue à l'acidulé*, 90-250.

CARNAC★★★

Vannes 31, Lorient 37, Paris 487 km
pop 3964 ✉ 56340   **B3**
Across the scrub-covered heath, 2935 menhirs are lined up apparently to correspond to specific dates of sunrise and sunset ; the oldest stones may date from the Middle Neolithic Period, whereas the most recent may be from the Early Bronze Age (*ca.* 2500-2000 BC) ; little more is known. These mysterious and spectacular standing stones have made Carnac, with its sheltered beaches, one of the most important seaside resorts on the S coast of Brittany.

▶ In town, 17thC **church** with a stone canopy over the porch ; the covered beams in the three naves are decorated with paintings★. **Miln-le-Rouzic Museum**, a new museum opened in 1985 (prehistory collection, *daily ex Tue., 10-12 & 2-5*). Nearby, the **St. Michel Tumulus★**, a large burial chamber from 3000 BC (*daily Apr.-Sep.*), surmounted by a chapel (view★). ▶ From the Plouharnel road, a turning which runs alongside the lines of standing stones ; **Menec Alignments★★** (1099 menhirs in 11 lines 1167 m long, starting from a cromlech of 70 menhirs) ; **Kermario Alignments★** (1029 menhirs in 10 rows 1120 m long) ; **Kercado Tumulus** (*Easter hols. and Jun.-Sep.*) ; **Kerlescan Alignments★** (594 menhirs in 13 rows of 880 m) ; return to Carnac via the **Moustoir Tumulus**. The region is dense with megaliths (*signposted*) : dolmens at Kériaval, Mané Kérioned and Runesto (*Plouharnel-Auray road*), the dolmens at **Rondossec, Crucuno,** Mané Groac'h, **lines of menhirs at Kerzhero** (1129 menhirs ; *Plouharnel-Erdeven road*). ▶ Services in Gregorian chant at the Benedictine abbeys of St. Anne and St. Michel in **Kergonan. ▶ La Trinité-sur-Mer :** a pleasant fishing port and yacht harbour on the Crash Estuary, considered for a decade the centre of open-sea racing (oyster beds ; view★ from the bridge).   □

Practical Information _____

CARNAC
ℹ️ av. des Druides, ☎ 97.52.13.52.

Hotels :
● ★★★★ *Diana*, 21, bd de la Plage, ☎ 97.52.05.38, Euro Visa, 34 rm 🅿 ⬗ 🛆 ♪ 〰 closed Oct-Mar, 400. Rest. ◆ ♪ 100-250.
● ★★ *Lann-Roz* (L.F.), 36, av. de la Poste, ☎ 97.52.10.48, 13 rm 🅿 ⬗ 🔲 〰 closed Jan, 240. Rest. ◆ closed Wed, 100-210.
★★ *Alignements* (L.F.), 45, rue St-Cornely, ☎ 97.52.06.30, 27 rm 〰 closed 25 Sep-25 May, 193. Rest. ◆ ♪ closed lunch, 45-100.
★★ *Genêts*, 45, av. de Kermario, ☎ 97.52.11.01, 35 rm 🅿 🔲 ♪ pens (h.s.), closed 30 Sep-10 Apr, 3-27 May, 570. Rest. ◆ ♪ 〰 85-145.
★★ *Rochers*, 6, bd de la Mer, port de Plaisance, ☎ 97.52.10.09, DC Visa, 14 rm 🅿 ⬗ 🛆 ♪ 〰 190. Rest. ◆ ⬗ ♪ 75-120 ; child : 25.
★★ *Tumulus*, 31, rue du Tumulus, ☎ 97.52.08.21, Euro Visa 🅿 ⬗ 🔲 ♪ half pens (h.s.), closed Nov-Mar, 406. Rest. ◆ ⬗ ♪ closed 15 Sep-15 Jun, 50-90 ; child : 20.

Restaurant :
◆ *La Calypso*, Le Pô, ☎ 97.52.06.14, Euro Visa 🅿 ⬗ 🛆 ♪ 〰 closed Wed noon, Wed eve Jul-Aug, 3 Nov-15 Mar. Seafood abounds in this oyster-farming area, 85-140.

⚚ ★★★★*Grande Métairie* (352 pl), ☎ 97.55.71.47 ; ★★★★*Menhirs*, rte D 119 (400 pl), ☎ 97.52.94.67 ; ★★*Beaumer* (100 pl), ☎ 97.52.93.52.

Recommended
Night-clubs : *Les Chandelles*, av. de l'Atlantique, ☎ 97.52.13.80.
♥ antiques : *M. Le Paih*, 2, bis av. Salins, ☎ 97.52.95.43 ; oyster-farmer : *M. Jenot*, ☎ 97.52.08.15.

Nearby
PLOUHARNEL, ✉ 56720, 3 km.

Hotels :
★★ *Chez Michel* (L.F.), av. de l'Océan, ☎ 97.52.31.05, Visa, 24 rm 🅿 〰 closed Wed, Jan-Mar, 3 Nov-31 Dec, 150. Rest. ◆ ♪ 50-90 ; child : 35.

⚚ ★★*Goëlands* (80 pl), ☎ 97.52.31.92 ; ★★*Sables Blancs* (565 pl), ☎ 97.52.31.92 ; ★*Bois d'Amour* (200 pl), ☎ 97.52.35.39.

La TRINITÉ-SUR-MER, ✉ 56470, 5 km E.
ℹ️ cours des Quais, ☎ 97.55.72.21 (h.s.).

Hotel :
★★ *Le Rouzic* (L.F.), 17, cours des Quais, ☎ 97.55.72.06, AE DC Euro Visa, 32 rm ⬗ half pens (h.s.), closed 15 Nov-15 Dec, 405. Rest. ◆ ⬗ 🛆 closed Mon and Sun eve Oct-May, 75-110.

Restaurants :
● ◆◆ *Les Hortensias*, 4, pl. Yvonne-Sarcey, ☎ 97.55.75.11, AE Euro Visa ⬗ 🔲 🛆 closed Wed and Thu (l.s.) ; Nov-Feb. One of food critic Henri Gault's 50 favourite restaurants. Hydrangeas are much in evidence at this charming establishment with a view of the port. Very good but too-classic cuisine by Patrick Le Guen : he should take a lesson from his young colleagues and innovate a bit. *Cervelas de poissons, bar fumé minute*, cheese is too expensive (40 Frs), airy, sublime desserts. Pricey wines, 100-240 ; child : 60.
◆◆ *L'Azimut*, 1, rue du Men-Dû, ☎ 97.55.71.88, Euro

Visa P ⪍ ♪ closed Mon and Sun eve (l.s.), hols, Dec-Jan, 100-210.

⚠ ★★★★*Baie* (185 pl), ☎ 97.55.73.42 ; ★★★*Plijadur* (100 pl), ☎ 97.52.72.05.

Recommended
♥ antiques : *La Carène*, 4, rue Marie-Rohr, ☎ 97.55.76.04.

CHÂTEAUBRIANT

Rennes 55, Nantes 70, Paris 355 km
pop 14415 ⊠ 44110   D3

Capital of the Mee Region, guarded by an imposing fortress, Châteaubriant remains tied to its rural past : famous livestock market dating from the Middle Ages ; slaughter-house ; manufacture of farm machinery.

▶ The **château★** is in two parts : Vieux Château (11th, 13th and 15thC), with 13thC entrance, 12th-13thC chapel and 15thC main building attached to a large square keep ; and Château Neuf (Renaissance, 1533-39, restored) ; the parts are linked by a gallery to a lodge with projecting bays that shelters a staircase *(15 Jun.-15 Sep., daily 9-12 & 2-7 ex Mon.).* ▶ 15th-16thC houses. ▶ In the suburb of Béré (take the Rennes road) : 11thC **church★** with wooden 15thC porch, three 17thC altarpieces and a 14thC Virgin.

Nearby

▶ 17 km SE, through Saint-Julien-de-Vouvantes : **château de La Motte-Glain★** (end 15thC), a blend of limestone and sandstone on the lake shore housing a unique collection of African and European hunting trophies, temporary exhibitions of painting *(2:30-6:30, Sat., Sun. and nat. hols. Easter-14 Jun. ; daily ex Tue. 15 Jun.-15 Sep.).* ☐

Practical Information _____

ⓘ 40, rue du Château, ☎ 40.81.04.53.
𝗦𝗡𝗖𝗙 ☎ 40.81.10.52.

Hotel :
★★★ *Ferrière*, rte de Nantes, ☎ 40.28.00.28, AE DC Euro Visa, 25 rm P ⸿ ⚊ ♪ ⅔ closed 25-31 Dec, 210. Rest. ♦♦ ⪍ ♪ ⅔ 80-130 ; child : 40.

CHÂTEAULIN

Quimper 29, Brest 47, Paris 551 km
pop 6102 ⊠ 29150   A-B2

Châteaulin on the river Aulne is renowned for salmon fishing ; the salmon forms part of the town's coat of arms. Pleasant walks along the riverbanks.

▶ On the left bank on a rocky peak is the **church of Notre-Dame** (15th-16thC) ; Renaissance tower ; 1722 porch ; 16thC ossuary, 15thC Calvary. Excellent view.

Nearby

▶ 6.5 km N : overlooking the Aulne, the **chapel of Saint-Sébastien★** with octagonal sacristy (1772), in a churchyard with Calvary★ (mid-16thC) ; inside, 18thC altarpieces and decorated rood beam. ▶ Next to the 16thC church in Cast *(7 km SW on D7)* , a sculptural group★ showing St. Hubert being converted while out hunting. ▶ 12 km S on D770 : a Calvary★ of 1556 in front of the Gothic **chapel of Saint-Vennec★**, where a polychrome group depicts St. Gwen (St. Blanche) with three breasts to feed her sons, Gwenolé, Jacut and Vennec. ☐

Practical Information _____

CHÂTEAULIN
ⓘ quai Cosmao, ☎ 98.86.02.11 (h.s.).
𝗦𝗡𝗖𝗙 ☎ 98.86.00.52.

Hotels :
★★ *Bon Accueil* (L.F.), Port-Launay, 2 km NE, ☎ 98.86.15.77, Tx 940501, Euro Visa, 59 rm P ⸿ ⪍ ⸿ ⚞

⅔ closed Sun eve and Mon (l.s.), Jan, 180. Rest. ♦ ⪍ ♪ ⅔ 50-135.

Auberge des Ducs de Lin, anc. rte de Quimper (1,5 km), ☎ 98.86.04.20, DC Euro Visa, 5 rm P ⪍ ⸿ ⚊ half pens, closed Sun eve and Mon (l.s.), 2-20 Mar, 21 Sep-5 Oct, 400. Rest. ♦ ⪍ ♪ Spec : salmon, 130-190.

Nearby

LOPÉREC, ⊠ 29117 Pont-de-Buis, 13 km N.

Restaurant :
♦ *Auberge bretonne*, 5, pl. de l'Eglise, ☎ 98.73.05.03 ⸿ ♪ ⅔ closed lunch ex Sat. Reserve. In a neo-Breton setting, Marie Avan cooks simple dishes : very fresh fish, garden-fresh fruit *sorbets*. Jean Avan offers great wines at moderate prices, 65-160.

PLOMODIERN, ⊠ 29127, 12 km W on the D887, D47.

Hotel :
★★ *Motel-Relais Porz-Morvan*, 3 km, ☎ 98.81.53.23, Visa, 12 rm P ⸿ ⚊ ⚞ ♪ closed late Sep-Easter. Crêperie, 235.

CLISSON*

Nantes 28, Cholet 33, Paris 377 km
pop 5032 ⊠ 44190   D4

Two rivers meet at the foot of an old château. Local economy depends on uranium and livestock.

▶ The town was levelled during the French Revolution of 1794 and rebuilt in an oddly Italianate style. ▶ Opposite the **Pont de la Vallée** (Valley Bridge, 14thC) across the Sèvre is a staircase leading through the pedestrian precinct (wood-framed **covered market★**) to the **château★** *(9-12 & 2-6 or 7 ; closed Tue.) ;* a bridge across the moat leads to the 15thC entrance ; the W part (to the right as you enter) was built in the 15thC by François II, last Duke of Brittany. The E half dates from the 13th and 14thC ; 16thC additions reinforce it to the S.

Nearby

▶ 7.5 km NW, near the Sèvre, stained glass in the church at **Monnières** depicts the surrounding vineyards. ▶ The Pierre Abélard Museum, at **Pallet** on the opposite bank : arts and traditions of the vineyard and tasting of Muscadet and gros-plant *(May-Nov., Sat., Sun. and nat. hols., 2:30-6:30).* ▶ 9 km N : **Vallet** specialises in Muscadet wine. 3 km further : the **château La Noë de Bel-Air** : a Palladian villa of 1836 in an English-style park *(exterior visit on request).* ☐

Practical Information _____

ⓘ 1, pl. du Minage, ☎ 40.78.02.95.
𝗦𝗡𝗖𝗙 ☎ 40.36.11.70.

Hotel :
★★ *Gare*, pl. de la Gare, ☎ 40.36.16.55, Euro Visa, 34 rm P ⸿ 165. Rest. ♦ 50.

Restaurant :
♦♦ *La Bonne Auberge*, 1, rue Olivier-de-Clisson, ☎ 40.78.01.90, closed Mon and Sun eve , hols, 15 Feb-3 Mar, 9 Aug-1 Sep. Refined cuisine, 70-250.

⚠ ★★*Municipal* (65 pl), ☎ 40.78.35.14.

COMBOURG

Dinan 24, Rennes 37, Paris 369 km
pop 4763 ⊠ 35270   D2

The **château★** is a 14th-15thC fortress, remodelled in Romantic style between 1876-1900 ; the machicolated towers can be seen through the trees.

▶ The writer Chateaubriand (1768-1848) passed his childhood here ; memorabilia *(2-5:30, Mar.-Nov. ; park also 9-12 ; closed Tue.).* ▶ 5 km E : **château de Lanrigan** (15th-16thC), Flamboyant Gothic with flanking turrets in grey granite (park only, Jun.-Sep., 8-12 & 2-7). 6.5 km SE, **château de La Chapelle-aux-Filzméens** (15th-17thC) : dovecote; collection of antique lace (daily May-Oct.). ▶ At **Dingé**, 7 km S of Lanrigan, **Ville-André Manor** (exterior only, 8-12 & 2-8; closed Sun.), a rectangular granite building with square turrets. 13 km E, **château de la Ballue** (17thC), remarkable Baroque gardens★★ and, inside the château, collections concerning gardens (10-12 & 2:30-5:30 Jul.-Aug., closed Tue.). ☐

Practical Information —————————

COMBOURG
ⓘ Maison de la Lanterne, pl. Albert-Parent, ☎ 98.73.13.93; ☎ 98.73.00.18. ₵
SNCF ☎ 98.73.00.43.

Hotels :
★★ **Château** (L.F.), 1, pl. Chateaubriand, ☎ 99.73.00.38, AE DC Euro Visa, 32 rm ℗ ⅋ ▒ half pens (h.s.), closed 15 Dec-25 Jan, 225. Rest. ♦♦ ⅋ closed Mon (l.s.), 55-250; child : 37.
★★ **Lac** (L.F.), 2, pl. Chateaubriand, ☎ 99.73.05.65, Tx 740802, AE DC Euro Visa, 30 rm ℗ ⅋ ▒ ♪ half pens (h.s.), closed Sun eve (l.s.), 26 Oct-2 Dec, 130. Rest. ♦ ⅋ ♪ 75-150.

Recommended
Guide to wines : at La Favrais, Bonnemain, Les Tastevins, Claude Berthe, ☎ 99.73.86.76, advice on wine.

Nearby
HÉDÉ, ⊠ 35630, 7 km S.

Hotel :
★★ **Vieux Moulin** (L.F.), ☎ 99.45.45.70, DC Euro Visa, 14 rm ℗ ⅋ ▒ ♪ half pens (h.s.), closed Sun eve and Mon, 22 Dec-22 Jan. In the valley of windmills, a historic site, 360. Rest. ♦ ⅋ ♪ Ġ 65-120.

Restaurant :
♦♦ **Vieille Auberge**, RN 137, ☎ 99.45.46.25, Visa ⅋ ▒ ♪ Ġ closed Mon and Sun eve , Feb, 115-140.

CONCARNEAU★★

Quimper 24, Lorient 52, Paris 543 km
pop 18225 ⊠ 29110   B2

This ancient city combines tourism with trawler fishing. The boats return every 10 to 15 days from the waters off Scotland, Ireland or the African coast; Concarneau boasts the third-largest fresh-fish landings and the biggest tuna catch in France.

▶ The **Ville Close** (Walled Town)★★; fortified in the 13th-14thC, 300 m long; illuminated on summer evenings. This little island was given new granite ramparts★ in the 16thC and was further fortified in the 17thC by Vauban (sentry-walk open Easter-Sep., 9-7). ▶ Narrow alleys open off Rue Vauban, which is lined with souvenir shops. **Musée de la Pêche** (Fishing Museum : daily 9:30-8:30 Jul.-Aug.; 10-12:30 & 2:30-6 out of season) : 47 aquariums, models and displays of the history and commercial activity of the town. ▶ Another sea-oriented exhibition at the **Marinarium** (15 Jun.-15 Sep., 10-12 & 2-6:30) in front of the yacht harbour, at Port de la Croix. On the N side of the inner harbour, the **fish auction** (criée) where tons of fish are unloaded, starting at 10 pm; the criée gets into full swing around 7 am, although nowadays the procedure is automated and much less noisy than it used to be. ▶ 1.5 km N of the town centre on the La Forêt Bay is the seaside resort of **Les Sables Blancs.** ▶ 5 km S : good views from **Cabellou Point**; elegant villas in the woods. ▶ At the exit from the town : **château de Kériolet**, built in 1870 in late-15thC style.

Nearby

▶ 70 min away by boat (tel. 98.97.01.44; in summer, service also from Beg Meil and Bénodet, tel. 98.57.00.14), the **Glénan Islands** form an archipelago of 9 small islands,

one of which boasts an impressive fort (18thC), while the others offer a bird sanctuary, a lighthouse and, especially, a well-known nautical centre.   ☐

Practical Information —————————

CONCARNEAU
ⓘ pl. J.-Jaurès, ☎ 98.97.01.44.
SNCF ☎ 98.97.00.66.

Hotels :
★★★★ **Belle Etoile**, (I.L.A., C.H.), Le Cabellou-Plage, ☎ 98.97.05.73, AE DC Euro Visa, 30 rm ℗ ⅋ ▒ ◿ ⅋ Ġ ♪ half pens (h.s.), closed Feb, 1140. Rest. ♦♦♦ ⅋ ▒ closed Tue (l.s.), 5 Jan-15 Mar. Fish is the specialty, 170-200.
★★★ **Promotel du Cabellou**, 7, av. du Cabellou, ☎ 98.97.32.18, 39 rm ℗ ⅋ ◿ closed 30 Sep-1 Apr, 215. Rest. ♦ ⅋ ♪ closed Tue (l.s.), 60-160.
★★★ **Ty Chupen Gwenn**, plage des Sables-Blancs, ☎ 98.97.01.43, DC Visa, 15 rm ℗ ⅋ ▒ ◿ ♪ closed Sat eve and Sun (Nov-Mar), 1 Dec-4 Jan, 11-17 May, 300.
★★ **Sables Blancs**, plage des Sables-Blancs, ☎ 98.97.01.39, AE DC Euro Visa, 48 rm ▒ ◿ ♪ ♨ Ġ half pens (h.s.), closed 4 Nov-25 Mar, 470. Rest. ♦♦ ⅋ ♪ Ġ 60-95; child : 40.

Restaurants :
● ♦♦♦ **Galion**, (I.L.A.), 15, rue St-Guénolé, ☎ 98.97.30.16, Tx 940336, AE DC Euro Visa ♪ Ġ closed Mon , Sun (late Sep-early Jun), 18 Jan-15 Mar, 30 Nov-16 Dec. A very fine table in the heart of the walled city, with delicate cuisine starring fish by Henri Gaonac'h . Bar-grill, 125-230.
● ♦♦ **Douane**, 71, av. Alain-Le-Lay, ☎ 98.97.30.27, Euro Visa ♪ Ġ closed Sun, 20 Feb-1 Mar, 1-15 Nov. New decor, friendly, casual atmosphere. The bar attracts many friends and patrons. J.-M. Peron is a disciple of noted chef Jean Delaveyne, the 'wizard' of Bougival. Fresh local fish, big prawns with sauce diable, turbot grillé sauce échalote. Generous desserts, 80-200.
● ♦♦ **La Coquille**, 1, rue du Moros, ☎ 98.97.08.52, AE Euro Visa ℗ ⅋ ◿ ♪ closed Mon and Sun eve (l.s.), 11-24 May, 22 Dec-13 Jan. Across from the port, try the fresh fish prepared by M. Le Maître. Seafood salad, mussels and cod tongues, 110.

△ ★★★Cabellou (100 pl), ☎ 98.97.10.40; ★★★Les Prés Verts (150 pl), ☎ 98.97.09.74; ★★Lanadan (100 pl), ☎ 98.97.17.78; ★Loc'h Ven (200 pl), ☎ 98.97.68.00; at Trégunc, ★★★Pendruc (170 pl), ☎ 98.97.66.28.

Recommended
Events : fish festival, next-to-last Sun in Aug.
Youth hostel : pl. de la Croix, ☎ 98.97.03.47.
♥ Antiques : Galerie Henry Depoid, 11, rue Vauban en Ville-Close, ☎ 98.97.31.36; pork products : Le Brigant, 91, av. de la Gare, ☎ 98.97.02.31, Pâté de campagne.

Nearby
TRÉGUNC, ⊠ 29128, 5 km E.

Hotel :
★★ **Le Menhir** (L.F.), 17, rue de Concarneau, ☎ 98.97.62.35, Euro Visa, 28 rm ℗ ▒ ♨ closed Sun eve and Mon, 16 Oct-14 Mar, 410. Rest. ♦ ♪ 65-175.

Le CONQUET

Brest 24, Morlaix 84, Paris 536 km
pop 2011 ⊠ 29217   A2

This fishing port, weekend resort for the people of Brest and point of embarkation for boats to Ouessant (→), maintains a radio station that broadcasts weather reports and messages to the fishing fleet.

▶ View★ of the coast and the islands from **Kermorvan Point.** From **Renards Point,** you can see the beams from 13 lighthouses. ▶ 4 km away, **Saint-Mathieu Point★** view; ruins of a large 13thC abbey.   ☐

Practical Information

Le CONQUET

Hotel :
★★ *Pointe Sainte-Barbe*, ☎ 98.89.00.26, DC Euro Visa, 33 rm P ⊰ ⚲ closed 2 Jan-5 Feb. Rooms with sea view, 235. Rest. ◆ ⊰ ♪ ⚹ ⚶ closed Mon ex Jul-Aug, 65-250.

Restaurant :
◆ *Pointe Saint-Mathieu*, Plougonvelin, ☎ 98.89.00.19, Visa ♪ ⚹ closed Tue and Sun eve, 20 Jan-4 Mar, 50-150.

⚐ ★★*Le Theven* (300 pl), ☎ 98.89.06.90; ★★*Presqu'île de Kermorvan* (65 pl), ☎ 98.89.01.64.

Nearby

LAMPAUL-PLOUARZEL, ✉ 29229, 12 km.

Restaurant :
◆◆◆ *Auberge du Kruguel*, 7, rue de la Mairie, ☎ 98.84.01.66, Visa P ⚿ ⚲ ♪ ⚶ closed Wed, Thu noon, Sun eve Sep-Feb. Rustic inn serving classic fare. Spec : *huîtres chaudes, bar aux artichauts, selle d'agneau en croute.* A la carte choices are weak, 120-160.

Le CROISIC*

Vannes 75, Nantes 84, Paris 455 km
pop 4365 ✉ 44490   C4

Next to La Baule and the Côte d'Amour, the port of Le Croisic is more involved with fishing (sardines, prawns, oysters and mussels) than with tourism.

▶ The picturesque **port★** is separated by little islands, called *jonchères*, into a number of basins. It was reshaped in the 18thC and is surrounded by **houses** of the period, stretching between two moles created with ballast left by boats loading salt from the nearby marshes. The **Aquarium of the Côte d'Amour★** *(10-8, Jul.-Sep. ; 10-12 & 2-7 rest of the year; closed Mon. and 15-31 Jan.)* : more than 3000 shells, in addition to live specimens from all over the world. Nearby, the Town Hall (end 16thC) has a small naval museum *(Jun.-Sep., 10-12 & 3-7; closed am Mon. and Thu.).* Flamboyant Gothic church (1494-1507) with 56-m tower.

Nearby

▶ Besides the trip to Guérande (→) and salt marshes (→ Brière), take a trip around **Croisic Point**; a *corniche* runs along the cliffs of the **Grande Côte.**   □

Practical Information

ⓘ pl. de la Gare, ☎ 40.23.00.70.
SNCF ☎ 40.23.00.68.

Hotels :
● ★★ *Grand Hôtel de l'Océan*, Port Lin, ☎ 40.42.90.03, DC, 15 rm ⊰ ⚲ ⚶ 250. Rest. ● ◆◆ ⊰ ⚶ The ocean at your table ; a splendid view of the Atlantic. One of the coast's best seafood spots, 170-220.
★ *Perthuy du Roy*, pl. Croix-de-Ville, ☎ 40.23.00.95, Visa, 12 rm ⊰ closed Thu, 15 Nov-15 Dec, 85.

⚐ ★★*Océan* (260 pl), ☎ 40.23.07.09 ; ★★*Paradis*, plage Castouillet (100 pl), ☎ 40.23.07.89 ; ★★*Stella Maris*, plage Castouillet (185 pl), ☎ 40.23.03.71 ; at Batz-sur-Mer, ★★★*La Govelle* (50 pl), ☎ 40.23.91.63 ; ★★*Municipal* (400 pl), ☎ 40.23.91.71.

CROZON Peninsula

                              A2

This sparse extension of Brittany projects into the Atlantic at the mercy of the heavy seas. Corn is grown wherever shelter can be found. At the base of the peninsula, the bald mountain of Ménez-Hom (→) is similar to many others found further inland. On the tip is Camaret (→), with lobster boats sheltered

behind one of the innumerable headlands. The peninsula is a microcosm of Brittany.

▶ **Crozon-Morgat★** (Morgat is the port) lives more from tourism than from sardine fishing ; a superb beach★, admirably sheltered and surrounded by cliffs, together with attractive sites in the vicinity, makes it a popular resort. Near the beach are the **Grottes Marines★** (seacaves), some accessible only by boat. **Dinan Point** *(6 km WSW)* : a mass of rocks (known as the Château de Dinan) resembling a ruined castle, linked to land by two natural bridges. Close by, Les Korrigans★ caves can be reached only during the season of spring tides *(guide essential);* **Cap de la Chèvre★★** : no less impressive with 100-m sandstone-and-quartz cliffs. ▶ In **Crozon** itself, the church has an altarpiece★ dating from 1602, with 400 carved and painted wooden figures, full of vigour and expression.   □

Practical Information

CROZON-MORGAT, ✉ 29160, 55 km NW of **Quimper.**
ⓘ bd de la Plage, à Morgat, ☎ 98.27.07.92/98.27.21.65.

Hotels :
★★ *Hostellerie de la mer* (L.F.), Le Frêt, sur le Port, ☎ 98.27.61.90, Euro Visa, 28 rm P ⊰ ⚿ ⚲ ⚛ ⚶ closed 5 Nov-10 Apr, 215. Rest. ◆ ⊰ ♪ ⚲ ⚶ 85-250.
★★ *Moderne* (L.F.), 61, rue Alsace-Lorraine, ☎ 98.27.00.10, Euro Visa, 34 rm P half pens (h.s.), 505. Rest. ◆ 55-135.
★ *Kador*, 42, bd de la plage, Morgat, ☎ 98.27.05.68, Euro Visa, 18 rm P ⊰ ⚿ ⚲ half pens (h.s.), closed 15-30 Jan, 15 Nov-15 Dec, 195. Rest. ◆ ⊰ closed Mon (l.s.), 65-145.

Restaurants :
◆◆ *Le Roof*, bd de la France-Libre, ☎ 98.27.08.40, Euro Visa ⊰ ⚿ ♪ ⚲ closed Mon (l.s.), Oct. Terrace service. The decor sports a nautical theme in tune with the excellent fish served here, 80-220.
◆ *Auberge du Gerdann*, rte de Crozon, D 887, ☎ 97.27.78.67, Euro Visa P ⚿ closed Tue , Mon eve (l.s.), 1-15 Feb, 15-30 Oct, 65-140.
◆ *Les Echoppes*, quai du Kador, ☎ 98.27.00.93 ⊰ closed (l.s.), open w.e. May-Jun. Nany Gleize cares for her cuisine and her clients ; excellent seafood, 70-150 ; child : 40.

⚐ ★★★*Plage de Goulien* (90 pl), ☎ 98.27.17.10 ; ★★*Pen Ar Menez* (200 pl), ☎ 98.27.12.36.

DINAN**

Rennes 51, Avranches 67, Paris 393 km
pop 14157 ✉ 22100   C-D2

Dinan is fortified and crenellated, girded with ramparts, paved with cobblestones and full of old houses. It is built almost entirely of light grey granite, yet the houses do not seem austere. Window-boxes and gardens, the deep green valley of the Rance with its little yacht marina, together with a busy country market make this an extremely attractive town.

▶ In the heart of town, the Place des Cordeliers (B1), the Rue de l'Apport and the **Place des Merciers★** have retained **timber houses★**. Close by, the church of St. Malo (choir and transept from 1490, remainder rebuilt in the 19thC), and the former convent of the Cordeliers (private school ; restored 15thC cloister ; *visit during school hols.*). Opposite is the lively market. ▶ The steep **Rue du Jerzual★★** (C1), lined with 16thC houses occupied by craftsmen, runs down to the 14th-15thC port of the same name and continues into Rue du Petit-Fort, equally steep and quaint, with craft workshops and crêperies. Continue on to the **port** (Gothic bridge) where the sails woven nearby used be shipped to Saint-Malo. ▶ **Basilica of St. Sauveur** (C2) : an interesting mixture of styles ; Romanesque (façade and right half of the nave ; 12thC), Flamboyant Gothic, and Renaissance. The heart of Du Guesclin (14thC Constable of France and probably its ablest leader during the Hundred Years' War) is buried here. Around the E end is the Jardin Anglais★ (English gar-

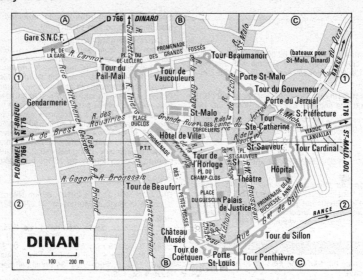

den; view★); tour of the ramparts. ▶ Almost opposite the SI (C1), in the Kératry Mansion★ (1559), are the **Tour de l'Horloge** (clock-tower; end 15thC; *Jul.-Aug. 10-12 & 2-6 ex Sun.)* and a former stone mason's workshop. ▶ **Castle★★** : a handsome oval keep (1382) standing 34 m high astride the ramparts; inside is a museum of life in Dinan through the ages *(daily 9-12 & 2-7 in summer; shorter hours, closed Nov. and Tue. out of season)* : bonnets and regional costumes; view★ from the platform; at the foot of the ramparts, Petits-Fossés Promenade★.

Nearby

▶ **Léhon★** *(2 km S)* : fine church★, formerly a priory chapel (tombs, tablets and funerary statues from 13th, 14th and 15thC); 15thC refectory and remains of 17thC cloister. Walks along the Rance. ▶ **Valley of the Argentel** *(40 min on foot along Rue St.-Malo, C1)*, shady site with fountain. ▶ 2 km N : ruins of 16thC **château de la Garaye.** ▶ **Aublette** *(3 km W)* : automobile museum *(daily Jun.-Sep. 3-6).*

Round trip through the Rance and Arguenon regions *(approx 160 km; one long day; see map 4)*

▶ Dinan. ▶ On the road from **Pleslin,** with one of the rare lines of menhirs in Upper Brittany, watch for charming manor-house of Bois de La Motte (16th-17thC). 500 m from the Dinan road, near a farm : ruins of a Roman **temple of Mars;** more interesting Roman remains can be found at **Corseul** (Jardin des Antiques, museum in the town hall). ▶ **Pléven** : a pretty village near **Vaumadeuc Manor★** (15thC, now a hotel) and ruins of the 14thC **château de la Hunaudaie★,** a surprising fortress in this quiet countryside. ▶ **Saint-Esprit-des-Bois** : a farm-museum displaying various aspects of Breton life. ▶ **Plancoët** is surrounded by charming, secret châteaux, hidden manors and farms which sometimes look like mansions. ▶ **Jugon-les-Lacs** : an ideal country holiday spot between a lake (upstream) and a reservoir (downstream). ▶ **Mégrit** : churchyard. ▶ Massive Romanesque church in **Yvignac.** ▶ After **Caulnes,** you can see *(but not visit)* the **château de Couëlan★** and, beside a lake that supplies drinking water to Rennes, the 15thC **château de Beaumont.** ▶ The **manor du Hac** (14thC; *2:30-6:30; closed Feb., 1 Nov. and Mon. out of season)* is worth the detour unless you prefer an alignment of 30 dolmens. ▶ Beyond **Saint-Pern** (18thC château), **Caradeuc★** : an extensive French Classical country house; French gardens★ *(8-8).*

▶ **Bécherel** : fortifications and old houses; close by, the **château de Montmuran,** where Du Guesclin was knighted (12th-14thC; *hourly from 2 until 7 and every 1/2 hour on Sun.; Sat. and Sun. 2-6, 1 Nov.-Easter);* 500 m away : the Flamboyant Gothic church★ (15th-16thC) of **Les Iffs,** with nine 16thC stained-glass windows. ▶ **Hédé** (remains of a large château; heavily restored Romanesque church) : walks in the Vallée des Moulins (valley of the mills) and along the Ille-et-Rance canal. ▶ **Château de la Bourbansais★** : aristocratic 14th and 17thC residence with 18thC interiors; French park; zoo *(3-6, 15 Jun.-15 Sep.; Sun. and nat. hols. rest of year).* ▶ If you have time left, take a short detour in the **Coëtquen Forest★** to see the ruins of a château and **La Chesnaie Manor.** ☐

Practical Information _____

DINAN
ℹ 6, rue de l'Horloge (B2), ☎ 96.39.75.40.
✈ Dinard-Pleurtuit, 16 km N, ☎ 99.46.16.82.
SNCF (A1), ☎ 96.39.00.78/96.39.22.39.
🚌 pl. Duclos (B1).
🚢 ☎ 99.46.10.45, from Dinan to Dinard, via la Rance (daily in season).

Hotels :
● ★★★ *Avaugour*, 1, pl. du Champ-Clos (B2), ☎ 96.39.07.49, AE DC Euro Visa, 27 rm P ⬚ ⟨⟨⟨ ⟩⟩⟩ 🔒 ♿ 280. Rest. ● ♦♦ ⟨⟨ A lovely, flowery garden on the ramparts, and an up-dated traditional menu prepared by G. Quinton : turbot, sole, John-Dory, brill, salmon, 60-250♦ *La Poudrière* ♪ 80-130.
★★ *Marguerite* (L.F.), 29, pl. Du Guesclin (B2), ☎ 96.39.47.65, AE DC Euro Visa, 19 rm P ♪ half pens (h.s.), closed Sun eve and Mon (l.s.), Jan, 420. Rest. ♦♦ ♪ 50-150.
★ *La Caravelle*, 14, pl. Duclos (B1), ☎ 96.39.00.11, AE DC, 11 rm P ♪ closed Wed (1 Oct-1 Jul), 15 Oct-8 Nov, 110. Rest. ♦♦ ♪ Believe it or not, behind this café's modest façade is an excellent restaurant : clams, oysters, spiny lobster, etc. at rather stiff prices, 100-250.

Restaurant :
♦♦ *Chez la Mère Pourcel,* 3, pl. des Merciers (B1), ☎ 96.39.03.80, AE DC Euro Visa ⟨⟨ ⟨⟨⟨ ⟩⟩⟩ ♪ 🔒 closed Mon, 23 Dec-20 Feb, 90-200; child : 60.

Recommended
Farmhouse-inn : at Trévon 10 km S. on D 78,

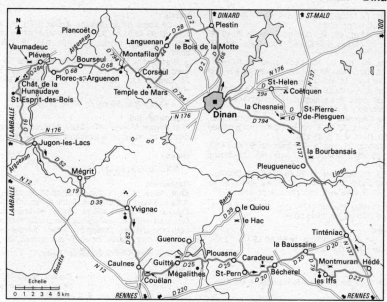

4. The Rance and Arguenon regions

☎ 96.83.56.89, spec : *canard aux navets et potée campa-gnarde.*
Handicrafts : rue du Jerzual, many workshops.
Youth hostel : *moulin de Méen,* vallée de la Fontaine-des-Eaux, ☎ 96.39.10.83.
♥ crêperie : *Artisans,* 6, rue du Petit-Fort, ☎ 96.39.44.10.

Nearby

PLANCOËT, ✉ 22130, 17 km NW.
ⓘ ☎ 96.84.10.48.
SNCF ☎ 96.31.64.64.

Hotel :
★★ *Gare* (L.F.), les Quais, ☎ 96.84.10.24, AE DC Euro Visa, 12 rm ℗ ⚡ ∰ ◑ ♪ ❄ closed Sun eve and Mon, 130. Rest. ● ◆◆ *Chez Crouzil* ❄ ♪ A banal road-side eatery-cum-banquet room has become a quality res-taurant thanks to J.-P. Crouzil's skill with the remarkable farm-fresh produce he procures from neighbouring grow-ers, 70-200 ; child : 50.

PLEUGUENEUC, ✉ 35720, 15 km E.

Hotels :
★★★★ *Château de la Bourbansais,* ☎ 99.45.20.42, 1 apt ℗ ⚡ ∰ ⚒ ❄ ⌂ closed Nov-Feb. Horse riding. Renowned stopping-place in Brittany, 650.
● ★ *Château de la Motte-Beaumanoir,* (I.L.A.), ☎ 99.45.26.37, 4 rm 2 apt ℗ ⚡ closed Oct-Easter, 500.

PLÉVEN, ✉ 22130 Plancoët, 12 km SW of **Plancoët.**

Hotel :
★★★ *Manoir du Vaumadeuc* (C.H.), ☎ 96.84.46.17, 9 rm ℗ ⚡ ∰ ⚒ ♿ closed 5 Jan-20 Mar. Elegant decor in a medieval setting, 460. Rest. ◆◆◆ ♿ ❄ Spec : *pigeon laqué au miel, escalope de truite saumonée,* 185-220.

QUÉDILLAC, ✉ 35290, 25 km S.

Hotel :
★★ *Relais de la Rance,* 6, rue de Rennes, ☎ 99.07.21.25, AE DC Euro Visa, 18 rm ℗ ⚡ ❄ closed Sun eve (l.s.) and Feb, 170. Rest. ◆ ♪ ❄ Spec : *barbue à l'oseille, poêlée de langoustine à l'estragon,* 50-150.

Rennes 72, Saint-Brieuc 68, Paris 413 km
pop 10016 ✉ 35800   D1

The English aristocracy made Dinard fashionable at the end of the Victorian Era. In the turn-of-the-century atmosphere, the luxury hotels have an old-fashioned charm and the villas are set in Mediterranean-style gardens with fig-trees, palms, camellias, tamarisks and other exotic trees.

▶ Stroll around the **Écluse Beach★** and the Casino. It is almost obligatory to take a walk along the **Clair de Lune Promenade★,** which runs past the **Sea Museum and Aquarium** *(Pentecost Sun.-Sep., 10-12 & 2-6 ; 7 pm Sun. and nat. hols).* ▶ View★ from the Vicomté over the Rance, Saint-Servan, and the *tidal generating station (8:30-8 ; entry on the left bank downstream from the lock).*

Boat trips

▶ **Cézembre Island** *(approx 4-hr round trip, including 2hr30 stopover ; in season only) :* take your swimsuit but beware of strong currents. ▶ **Cap Fréhel** (→) *(3-hr round trip, in season only).* ▶ **Trip up the Rance★** *(2hr30 to Dinan ; the return journey depends on the tide and is not always possible the same day).* Excursion through a valley winding among green banks dotted with little ports ; the fishermen have yielded to boating enthusiasts since the construction of the dam.   □

Practical Information

DINARD
ⓘ 2, bd Féart, ☎ 99.46.94.12.
✈ *Dinard-Pleurtuit,* 7 km S, ☎ 99.46.18.46.
SNCF ☎ 99.46.10.04.
⚓ *Vedettes vertes,* ☎ 99.46.10.45, to Saint-Malo and Islands, (Chausey, Anglo-Norman) and cap Fréhel.
Car rental : *Avis,* Airport, ☎ 99.46.25.20.

Hotels :
● ★★★★ *Reine Hortense* (C.H.), 19, rue de la Malouine,

☎ 99.46.54.31, Tx 740802, AE DC Visa, 10 rm Ⓟ ⋞ ⫶ ⚘
♪ closed 10 Nov-1 Apr, 800.
★★★★ **Grand Hôtel**, 46, av. George-V, ☎ 99.46.10.28,
100 rm Ⓟ ⋞ ⫶ closed Nov-Easter, 700. Rest. ♦♦ ⊗
140-240.
★★ **Balmoral**, 26, rue du Mal-Leclerc, ☎ 99.46.16.97,
Tx 730800, AE Euro Visa, 30 rm ⚘ & closed Sun eve and
Mon (2 Nov-19 Apr), 15 Nov-1 Mar, 210.
★★ **La Plage** (L.F.), 3, bd Féart, ☎ 99.46.14.87, Visa,
18 rm ⋞ ♪ half pens (h.s.), closed 15 Jan-31 Mar, 440.
Rest. ♦ **Le Trezen** ♪ & 55-200.
★★   **Roche-Corneille**,   4,   rue   G.-Clemenceau,
☎ 99.46.14.47, Visa, 27 rm ⋞ ♪ & half pens (h.s.), closed
Nov-Mar, 460. Rest. ♦ ♪ & 85-200.
★★ **Vieux Manoir**, 21, rue A.-Gardiner, ☎ 99.46.14.69,
Euro Visa, 26 rm Ⓟ ⋞ ⫶ ⚘ ♪ & ⊗ ▭ closed
15 Oct-15 Mar, 310.
★ **Altaïr** (L.F.), 18, bd Féart, ☎ 99.46.13.58, AE DC Visa,
22 rm ⫶ half pens (h.s.), closed Sun eve and Wed ex
school hols, 15 Dec-15 Jan, 160. Rest. ♦ 55-230.
△ ★★★★**La Ville Mauny** (174 pl), ☎ 99.46.94.73;
★★★★**Prieuré** (100 pl), ☎ 99.46.20.04.

Recommended
Night-clubs : Jet 7, 4, bd Wilson, ☎ 99.46.15.71.
Son et lumière : info. S.I., Jun-Sep.

Nearby

La GOUGEONNAIS, ⊠ 35780 La Richardais, 4 km SE.

Restaurant :
♦♦ **Le Petit Robinson**, ☎ 99.46.14.82, AE DC Euro Visa
♪ closed Tue eve and Wed, 5-20 Feb, 15 Nov-20 Dec,
55-120 ; child : 40.

DOL-DE-BRETAGNE*

Saint-Malo 24, Rennes 54, Paris 373 km
pop 4974 ⊠ 35120   D2
A long street that broadens as it descends the hill,
lined with **houses**★ dating back to the 11th and 12thC
(Nᵒˢ 17 and 18) and 13thC (Nᵒ 27, antique shop★).
▶ The **cathedral**★ attests to the religious importance of
the city during the High Middle Ages ; the kings of Brittany
made it the religious capital of the country despite Papal
objections. It is a majestic 13thC Gothic edifice, more Norman than Breton in style, with an elegant S porch and a
noteworthy 13thC window★ in the choir. ▶ Opposite, the
historical **museum**★ *(Easter-Sep., 9:30-5:30).* ▶ To the E :
the **Douves Promenade** follows the ramparts (view★ over
the marshes and Mont Dol).

Nearby

▶ **Mont Dol** *(4 km N)* : site of a mythical combat between
St. Michael and the Devil ; magnificent view over the
marsh where the legendary forest of Scissy was engulfed
by the sea in the 8th and 9thC. The land was progressively reclaimed through the efforts of monks from the
12thC on ; it was dried out for good after the 18thC, and
is now extremely fertile. ▶ Continue to the coast *(5 km
farther)* where villages such as **Le Vivier-sur-Mer** shelter with mills behind a dyke : panoramic views★ over the
bay of Mont-Saint-Michel. ▶ Through **Épiniac** (16thC bas-
reliefs in the church) to see the outside of **château de
Landal** (15th-19thC) in a romantic setting of woods and
lakes ; return via Ormes (similar attractions) or detour via
the 15thC church of **Broualan** in typical lower-Brittany
style. ▶ 10 km SW on the edge of a lake : remains of the
Benedictine **Le Tronchet Abbey** with a monumental 17thC
cloister ; the nearby **Mesnil Forest** is ideal for walks : châteaux, dolmens, and other diversions.   ▢

Practical Information _____

DOL-DE-BRETAGNE
𝗂 hôtel de ville, ☎ 99.48.15.37 (h.s.).
🚆 ☎ 99.48.00.86.

Hotels :
★★ **Le Logis de la Bresche Arthur** (L.F.), 36, bd Demi-
niac, ☎ 99.48.01.44, AE DC Euro Visa, 24 rm Ⓟ ⫶ ♪ ☞
half pens (h.s.), closed Feb, 380. Rest. ♦ ♪ & 65-110 ;
child : 45.
★ **Bretagne** (L.F.), 17, pl. Chateaubriand, ☎ 99.48.02.03,
Euro Visa, 29 rm Ⓟ ⚘ & half pens (h.s.), closed
26 Sep-18 Oct, 130. Rest. ♦ & closed Sat, 50-70 ;
child : 30.
△ ★★**Municipal** (90 pl), ☎ 99.48.14.68.

Recommended
♥ at Baguer-Morvan, PC 35120, *Museum of peasantry,* a
century of evolution in peasants' lives and customs.

Nearby

CHERRUEIX, ⊠ 35120, 13 km E.

Restaurant :
● ♦ **Parcs**, pl. de l'Eglise, ☎ 99.48.82.26, AE DC Visa ⫶
& closed Wed and Sun eve, 5 Jan-5 Feb, 30 Nov-15 Dec.
Popular with speed sailors. Robert Abraham is off to a
fast start with his fresh, enjoyable cuisine that celebrates
both land and sea. Tasting bar. Spec : *rillettes de poisson,
feuilletés aux moules, omelette aux coques,* 80-170.

Le VIVIER-SUR-MER, ⊠ 35960, 8 km N.

Hotel :
★★ **Bretagne** (L.F.), rd-pt du Centre, ☎ 99.48.91.74, AE
DC Euro Visa, 30 rm Ⓟ ⋞ closed Sun eve and Mon,
1 Nov-1 Apr, 165. Rest. ♦ ⋞ ♪ 60-200.

Recommended
Leisure activities : discovery of the bay of Mt-St-Michel,
aboard the 'Sirène de la Baie', ☎ 99.73.00.14, Shellfish can be sampled during the cruise (Easter to late Sep),
reserve at the Gare Maritime, ☎ 99.48.82.30.

DOUARNENEZ

Quimper 22, Brest 74, Paris 578 km
pop 17813 ⊠ 29100   A2
Deep in a bay★ where the legendary city of Ys
is said to lie beneath the waves, the fishing port of
Douarnenez rivals Guilvinec as the third French tuna-
fishing port. Expansion around **Tréboul** has given the
town an interest in tourism.
▶ Between the new port and Rosmeur Harbour, visit the
fish auction *(criée)*, opposite. **Boat Museum,** on the banks
of the river of Port-Rhu. ▶ In town : chapels of Ste. Hélène
(Flamboyant Gothic) and St. Michel (17thC). ▶ The
16th-17thC church in the Plouaré District has a 45-m bell
tower (16thC). ▶ View★ from the viaduct to **Tréboul,** set
above the harbour, and stretching towards rocky Leydé
Point *(3 km ; view★)* along Les Sables Blancs beach.

Nearby

▶ In **Kerlaz** *(5 km E)*, 16th-17thC church with ossuary and
lacy spire. Return to **Pouldavid** (14th-16thC church ; 16thC
painted panelling inside) through **Le Juch** (in the church,
Annunciation in recesses with painted shutters, old
stained glass). ▶ 11 km W : inside the Flamboyant Gothic
church★ at **Confort,** a wheel of bells said to restore
speech to the dumb. 2 km from here : the open-air pulpit
and consecrated fountain in front of the chapel of **Notre-
Dame de Kérinec** (13th-14thC).   ▢

Practical Information _____

𝗂 rue du Dr-Mével, ☎ 98.92.13.35, closed Sun.
✈ Quimper-Pluguffan, 21 km SE, ☎ 98.94.01.28.
🚆 ☎ 98.92.00.88.

Hotels :
★★   **Auberge   de   Kerveoc'h**,   Kerveoc'h road,
☎ 98.92.07.58, Euro Visa, 14 rm Ⓟ ⫶ ⚘ half pens (h.s.),
closed Oct-Easter, 405. Rest. ♦ ♪ & ⊗ 60-150.
★★ **Grand Hôtel de la Plage**, Tréboul, ☎ 98.74.00.21,

102 rm P ⌠ ▨ half pens (h.s.). Private beach, 180. Rest. ♦
♨ 80-130.

Restaurants :
♦♦ *Le Petit Marquis*, 83, rue du Véret, ☎ 98.74.18.49,
Euro Visa ⌠ ▨ ♪ closed Mon noon, Tue eve, Wed noon
(l.s.) Mon and Wed lunch (h.s.). Spec : *fricassée de Saint-
Jacques, goujonnettes de sole*, 80-140 ; child : 35.
● ♦ *L'Armorial*, 3, rue Jakez-Riou, ☎ 98.74.31.77, DC
Euro Visa ▨ ♪ ⌂ closed Mon, 1-24 Feb. Simple, very
good food. Steamed fish, baked lobster, 80-200.

⚠ ★★*Ferme de Kerleyou* (70 pl), ☎ 98.74.03.52.

Recommended
♥ at the Ris beach, on D 7, antiques : *Le Berrre*, toward
Locronan, ☎ 98.92.86.26.

Côte d' ÉMERAUDE**

(Emerald Coast) C-D1

This part of the North Brittany coast is named for the
infinite variety of green shades ("emerald") reflected
by the sea. From Grouin Point to Val-André, a succession of capes and bays with rocks, inlets, cliffs,
estuaries, beaches and islets, not to mention Saint-
Malo and Cape Fréhel.

Eastern sector, Saint-Malo to Cancale *(23 km ; approx
1hr30).*

► Leave **Saint-Malo** (→) via Paramé and the beach at
Minihic (18thC fort reused by the Germans). ► **Rothéneuf :** 300 carved rocks★, a masterpiece of naïf art by a
local priest, the Abbé Fouré (early 20thC) ; marine aquarium ; 500 m S from the church, **Limoëlou Manor★**, once
the property of Jacques Cartier (1491-1557 ; discovered Canada in 1534), restored and refurnished (exhibition *daily ; pm ex Tue. in season ; pm Sat. and Sun. rest
of year).* ► The harbour of Rothéneuf is an enclosed
bay that almost entirely empties at low tide ; above it
stands the **Malouinière de Lupin★** (1692, private mansion). ► Beyond the **anse Du Guesclin** (inlet ; site★,
beach, 1758 island fort) and Verger Beach, is **Grouin
Point★**, a 49-m high rocky crest with a superb view, from
Mont-Saint-Michel and the Cotentin Peninsula to Cape
Fréhel ; pretty coast road back to Cancale (→).

Western sector from Dinard to Val-André *(87 km ; full
day)* (Côtes-du-Nord)

► Leave **Dinard** (→) on the road to **Saint-Lunaire★**, where
Claude Debussy composed *La Mer* ; Décollé Point : one of
the best views★ on the coast ; charming old church in the
town. ► After **La Garde-Guérin Point** (view★), to **Saint-
Briac** at the entrance to the Frémur, which drains at low
tide (view★ of the estuary from the bridge). ► At **Lancieux**
(family beach★) the road leaves the coast briefly. ► Water-
tower at **Ploubalay** (1970 ; 54 m ; lift ; *9-midnight
Apr.-Sep. ; Sat. pm, Sun. and nat. hols. Oct.-Nov.)* ; terrace
with the most beautiful view★★ in the region. ► Between
two deep bays that dry out at low tide is the long **Saint-
Jacut** Peninsula. ► **Le Guildo** : ruins of 15thC château.
► Cross the estuary of the Arguenon (view downstream of
mussel beds) and, at the foot of **Notre-Dame du Guildo**,
throw pebbles to hear the "ringing stones" ring. ► **Saint-
Cast-le-Guildo★**, a gracious resort with one of the most
attractive beaches in North Brittany ; pleasant walks to
Saint-Cast and La Garde Points. ► **Matignon :** home town
of the family that built the Matignon Palace in Paris, now
the Prime Minister's residence. The big event here is the
market *(Wed.) ; galettes* (buckwheat cakes) and sausage
are sold on street corners (the *Café-Charcuterie Samson*
is particularly good). ► Salt-meadow sheep graze around
the deep bay at Le Frênaye, which you must skirt to see
Fort La Latte and Cap Fréhel (→). ► The beaches of **Plé-
herel-Plage** and **Sables-d'Or-les-Pins★** are widely known
for silky sand and pine woods. ► Reach Val-André (→) by
Erquy, a little port specialising in scallops. □

Practical Information ――――――――――

ERQUY, ✉ 22430, 35 km NE of **Saint-Brieuc**.
ℹ bd de la Mer, ☎ 96.72.30.12.

Hotel :
★★ *Plage*, ☎ 96.72.30.09, 24 rm P ⌠ closed Oct-Easter, 190.

Restaurant :
● ♦♦ *L'Escurial*, bd de la mer, ☎ 96.72.31.56, AE DC
Euro Visa P ⌠ ♪ ♨ closed Mon and Sun eve, 1-24 Oct.
Madame Bernard cooks very nice food : *tresse de sole et
saumon au beurre de ciboulette, paupiette barbue, magret
de canard au caramel et à l'armagnac*, 70-180.

⚠ ★★★*Les Pins* (400 pl), ☎ 96.72.31.12 ; ★★★*Saint Pabu*
(280 pl), ☎ 96.72.24.65 ; at les Hôpitaux, ★★★*Le Vieux
Moulin* (170 pl), ☎ 96.72.34.23.

Recommended
♥ *Poissonnerie Le Gall*, 8, rue Foch, ☎ 96.72.32.25.

Les SABLES-D'OR-LES-PINS, ✉ 22240 Fréhel, 8 km SW
of **Cap Fréhel**.
ℹ pl. des Fêtes, ☎ 96.41.51.97.

Hotels :
★★ *Ajoncs d'Or*, ☎ 96.41.42.12, 75 rm P ⌠ ▨ 🏊
half pens (h.s.), closed 25 Sep-27 May, 450. Rest. ♦ ⌂
60-165 ; child : 45.
★★ *Au Bon Accueil* (L.F.), ☎ 96.41.42.19, Visa, 39 rm P
⌠ ▨ ♪ ♨ pens, half pens (h.s.), closed 30 Sep-12 Apr,
225. Rest. ♦ ♪ ⌂ 60-85 ; child : 45.
★★ *Diane* (L.F.), ☎ 96.41.42.07, 42 rm P ⌠ ▨ ♨ 🏊 ⌂
closed 30 Sep — Palm Sun, 265.
★ *Les Pins*, ☎ 96.41.42.20, Euro Visa, 22 rm P ⌠ ▨ ♪
pens (h.s.), closed 10 Nov-20 Mar, 170. Rest. ♦ ⌠ ⌂
closed 10 Nov-20 Mar, 60-100 ; child : 35.

SAINT-CAST-LE GUILDO, ✉ 22380, 50 km NE of **Saint-
Brieuc**.
ℹ ☎ 96.41.81.52.
🚂 *Lamballe*, 30 km SW, ☎ 96.31.00.56.

Hotels :
★★★ *Ar Vro*, 10, bd de la Plage, ☎ 96.41.85.01, AE DC
Euro Visa, 47 rm P ⌠ ▨ 🏊 half pens (h.s.), closed
1 Sep-1 Jun, 320. Rest. ♦ ⌠ ♨ 150-200.
★★ *Dunes*, rue Primauguet, ☎ 96.41.80.31, Euro Visa,
27 rm 2 apt P ▨ ♨ ♪ half pens (h.s.), closed Sun eve ,
Mon (Oct), Nov-Mar, 500. Rest. ♦ ♨ 80-210.
★ *Angleterre et Panorama* (L.F.), 33, rue de la Fosserole,
☎ 96.41.91.44, 38 rm P ⌠ ▨ 🏊 🏊 ♪ half pens (h.s.),
136. Rest. ♦ ⌠ ♨ 76-62.

⚠ ★★★*Mielles* (100 pl), ☎ 96.41.03.60 ; ★★*Ferme de Pen
Guen* (300 pl), ☎ 96.41.92.18 ; ★★*La Clôture Goudeoir*
(100 pl), ☎ 96.41.80.18.

Recommended
Chambres d'hôtes : *Château du Val d'Arguenon*,
☎ 96.41.07.03, a park on the seashore.
♥ at Saint-Jaquel, cider : *Francis Renouard*, fairy grotto,
☎ 96.47.00.19.

SAINT-JACUT-DE-LA-MER, ✉ 22750, 15 km N of **Plancoët**.
ℹ rue du Châtelet, ☎ 96.27.71.91.

Hotel :
★★ *Vieux Moulin*, ☎ 96.27.71.02, 30 rm P ▨ ⌂ ♨
closed Nov-Mar, 190. Rest. ♦ 80-130.

⚠ ★★*Grands Hotieux* (100 pl), ☎ 96.27.73.20 ; ★★*Man-
chette* (370 pl), ☎ 96.27.70.33.

ÉTEL Estuary

B3

A miniature Gulf of Morbihan ; the S coast is strewn
with many islets that offer challenging obstacles to
windsurfers.

▶ The estuary is barred at its mouth by a sandbank, the Barre d'Étel, which causes dangerous currents; visible in high seas. ▶ **Étel** (pop. 2 699) is a busy sardine- and tuna-fishing port as well as a small bathing resort. ▶ **Saint-Cado** *(5 km N)*, on a peninsula linked to an islet with a partly Romanesque chapel (site★). ▶ Highway crosses the **Lorois Bridge**; view★ over the coastline. ▶ 8.5 km N of Étel, **Plouhinec** : surrounded by megaliths; Roman-esque church★ at **Merlevenez**, 4 km farther on. ☐

Le FAOUËT**

Lorient 40, Quimper 51, Paris 508 km
pop 3185 ✉ 56320   B2

The town is built around a large square with a cov-ered market★★ (end 16thC; timber construction on granite pillars).

Nearby

▶ Several superb chapels (15th-16thC) in nearby hamlets are worth a visit, not only for their artistic qualities but also for the sites★ on which they stand : **Sainte-Barbe** *(3 km NE by road; more pleasant on foot)* in Baroque setting (oratory, main building, bell and staircase); **Saint-Fiacre** *(3 km S)* with a wall belfry and lacy choirscreen★★ (1480); the choirscreen at **Saint-Nicolas** *(8.5 km E)*, dating from the Renaissance, is a masterpiece of naïf art; the chapel of **Saint-Sébastien** is also worth a visit *(5.5 km N)* : carved beams show a saraband danced by demons in court cos-tume. **Saint-Jean** *(3.5 km W of Saint-Nicolas)* rustic, with a touching Pietà. ▶ 11 km N : the **Langonnet Abbey** (rebuilt 18thC) has a 13thC chapterhouse. ▶ 13 km S : site★ of the **Rochers du Diable** (Devil's Rocks), a tumble of huge boulders among greenery overlooking the Ellé River. ☐

Practical Information ⎯⎯⎯⎯⎯⎯⎯⎯⎯

ⓘ ☎ 97.23.08.37.   ⅏

Hotel :
★ **La Croix d'Or**, 9, pl. Bellanger, ☎ 97.23.07.33, 16 rm P pens (h.s.), closed Sat, 20 Dec-20 Jan, 360. Rest. ♦ ♪ ♿ Nice little eatery, 45-160.

Le FOLGOËT**

pop 2826 ✉ 29260 Lesneven   A1

One of Brittany's most important pilgrimages, dating from the 14thC, brings the main square (Grand'Place) to life every 7-8 September.

▶ The Flamboyant Gothic **church of Notre-Dame★★**, built 1422-60, began the fashion for scalloped windows and doorways. Inside : fine statues; 15thC altars; beautiful rose window (choir); kersantite (regional stone) choir-screen, once polychrome. Close to the presbytery, in a tur-reted 16thC manor house, the pilgrim hostel (1929 neo-Gothic) is the setting for the **Folgoët Museum** (religious art). ▶ 2 km NE : **Lesneven** (pop. 7 087) : an important cattle and pig market; old houses and pretty 1678 cloister. The **Léon Museum** has just opened. ▶ 4.5 km SE : close to Ploudaniel, **Trébodennic Manor** (16thC, restored 1880; 8-12 Apr.-Sep.). ☐

FOUESNANT

Quimper 15, Lorient 59, Paris 549 km
pop 5430 ✉ 29170   B2

Famous for its cider and the girls' headdresses at the Fête des Pommiers (apple festival, *3rd Sun. in Jul.*), the town is close to the coastline of rocks and beach-es. Romanesque church★ (nave, transept).

Nearby

▶ **La Forêt-Fouesnant** *(3.5 km E)* : country holidays; golf; site★★. ▶ **Beg Meil** *(4 km S)*, surrounded by greenery,

with inlets and a broad beach; view★ over the bay, Con-carneau *(regular 30-min crossings in season)* and the Glénans Islands. ▶ To either side of **Mousterlin Point** stretch long, uncluttered beaches. ☐

Practical Information ⎯⎯⎯⎯⎯⎯⎯⎯⎯

FOUESNANT
ⓘ rue Kérourgué, ☎ 98.56.00.93 (h.s.).

Hotels :
★★ **Celtique**, plage du Cap-Coz, ☎ 98.56.01.79, 53 rm P ⪦ ⌘ ⍾ pens (h.s.), closed 4 Oct-31 May, 380. Rest. ♦ ♪ ♿ 60-130.
★★ **La Pointe de Mousterlin** (L.F.), ☎ 98.56.04.12, Visa, 47 rm P ⪦ ⌘ ⍾ ♿ ⌀ half pens (h.s.), closed 20 Sep-27 May, 190. .
★ **Auberge de la Croix**, ☎ 98.56.00.95, 25 rm P ⌘ ⍾ half pens (h.s.), closed 30 Sep-15 May, 160. Rest. ♦ ♿ 45-75.

Restaurant :
♦♦ **L'Huîtrière**, 2,5 km on the Saint-Evarzec route, ☎ 98.56.01.10 ⌘ ♪ ♿ closed Sep-Jun. Spec : lobsters, seafood, 115-300.

△ ★★★**Grand Large**, Mousterlin (300 pl), ☎ 98.56.04.06.

Recommended
♥ crêperie : *L'Epi d'Or*, rte de Quimper, ☎ 98.91.62.71.

Nearby

BEG-MEIL, ✉ 29170, 6 km S.

Hotel :
★★ **Thalamot** (L.F.), 4-6, le Chemin-Creux, ☎ 98.94.97.38, AE Euro Visa, 35 rm ⪦ ⌘ ⍾ ♿ half pens, closed 10 Oct-15 Apr, 500. Rest. ♦ ♿ 65-180.

La FORÊT-FOUESNANT, ✉ 29133, 7 km NE of **Concar-neau**.

ⓘ 2, rue du Port, ☎ 98.56.94.09 (h.s.); ☎ 98.56.96.57 (l.s.).

Hotels :
● ★★★★ **Manoir du Stang** (C.H.), 1.5 km on the D 783, ☎ 98.56.97.37, 26 rm P ⪦ ⌘ ⍾ ♿ ♿ half pens (h.s.), closed 26 Sep-9 May, 880. Rest. ♦♦♦ ⪦ ♿ 190.
★★ **L'Espérance** (L.F.), pl. de l'Eglise, ☎ 98.56.96.58, 30 rm P ⪦ ⌘ half pens (h.s.), closed 30 Sep-1 Apr, 305. Rest. ♦ ♿ 50-150.

△ ★★★★**St-Laurent**, Kerléven (300 pl), ☎ 98.56.97.65; ★★★**Pen-ar-Steir** (103 pl), ☎ 98.56.97.75; ★★**Kerantérec** (210 pl), ☎ 98.56.98.11; ★★**Saules** (110 pl), ☎ 98.56.98.57.

FOUGÈRES*

Rennes 48, Laval 48, Paris 322 km
pop 25131 ✉ 35300   D2

A centre of the French shoe industry and an impor-tant cattle market, one of the most modern in Europe *(every Fri. in the Parc de l'Aumaillerie)*. For the tourist, the walled town and castle are perhaps the most inter-esting features.

▶ From the **Place aux Arbres★**, with shady, flowered terraces, a good view★ of the 14th-16thC Hôtel de Ville (town hall), the Gothic church of St-Léonard (15th-16thC) and the castle, set against the Nançon Valley. ▶ At 51 Rue Nationale is **La Villéon Museum** (Impressionist paint-er; *Apr.-Jun., Sep., weekends and hols.; Jul.-Aug., daily 2-7*). ▶ **Castle★★** (12th-15thC) : on a rocky outcrop at the bottom of the valley, an apparently impregnable fortress, with 13 towers. It was nevertheless captured and recap-tured a number of times. The interior has been turned into an open-air theatre; guided tour of the sentry-walk and some of the towers *(9, 10, 11, 2, 3, 4, 5 or 6, Mar.-Oct.; closed Tue. off season; Sat. and Sun. only in Nov.; Sun. only in Feb.)*. **Shoe Museum** *(same hours as the cas-tle)*. Near the entrance is the **Maison des Artisans** (local crafts). ▶ **Church of St. Sulpice** (15th-18thC) : at the foot of the fortress, has two big altarpieces carved in the granite wall itself; Louis XV (18thC) furnishings; a village priest was burnt at the stake because of suspicions aroused by the twisted spire. Many **old houses** in the neighbouring Marchix quarter. To the N, the Urbanist Convent (17thC) has been converted into a cultural centre.

Nearby

▶ Beyond the N gates of the city, the **Fougères Forest★** offers 4 marked paths and interesting remains : see the curious Landéan cellar★ (12thC). ▶ To the W stretches the **Coglès region,** with streams, old mills and pleasant valleys. At **Saint-Brice-en-Coglès** : two marked châteaux (Le Rocher Portail, 17thC and La Motte ; *no visits*). Farther S is the **château La Haye** (15th-17thC ; *ext. visit only*) at **Saint-Hilaire-des-Landes**; the **château de Belinaye** (18thC ; *on request, 8-12 & 2-6 ; closed Sat. and Sun. Mar.-Oct., Sun. rest of year*) can be seen at **Saint-Christophe-de-Valains.** ▶ 20 km SW : **Saint-Aubin-du-Cormier,** a strategic promontory between the Ille and Couesnon rivers, site of the dramatic defeat of the Breton army by the French that marked the end of independent Brittany. The ruins of the 12th-15thC castle are still struggling, but against ivy now.   □

Practical Information _____

FOUGÈRES
ⓘ pl. A.-Briand, ☎ 99.94.12.20.
SNCF ☎ 99.99.01.40.

Hotels :
★★ **Voyageurs**, 10, pl. Gambetta, ☎ 99.99.08.20, AE DC Euro Visa, 36 rm Ⓟ closed 20 Dec-6 Jan, 150. Rest. ♦ closed Sat and Sun eve (l.s.), 5 Aug-6 Sep, 15-25 Feb, 80-140.
★ **Commerce** (L.F.), pl. du Grand-Marché, ☎ 99.94.40.40, 23 rm Ⓟ ⌂ ⌘ closed Xmas and Sun (l.s.), 160. Rest. ♦ ♪ 60-120.

🅐 ★★★*Municipal* (90 pl), ☎ 99.99.40.81.

Recommended
♥ *Maison des Artisans d'Art (crafts),* rue de la Fourchette, 7 Jun-15 Sep, 9am-12noon and 2-7 pm.

Nearby

LOUVIGNÉ-DU-DÉSERT, ✉ 35420, 28 km N.

Hotel :
● ★★ **Le manoir**, (L.F.,France-Accueil), 1, pl. Ch.-de-Gaulle, ☎ 99.98.53.40, Tx 741235, Euro Visa, 20 rm Ⓟ ⌂ ⌂ ♿ closed Sun eve , Mon, 10 Jan-20 Feb, 160. Rest. ♦ ♪ ♿ 65-170.

Cap FRÉHEL★★★

C1

A windswept plateau 70 m above the waves, with walls of red granite. The view is most impressive from the sea *(boats from Saint-Malo and Dinard);* on a clear day you can see as far as the island of Jersey in the English Channel.

▶ The **Grande Fauconnière★** is sugar-loaf hill on the right, where thousands of herring gulls, guillemots, kittiwakes and cormorants nest. Like the treeless, gorse-grown plateau itself (the **Lande de Fréhel**), it is a classified nature reserve. ▶ 3 km E : **Fort La Latte★** (14th-19thC) stands on an isolated rocky knoll *(Jun.-Sep., school hols. ; 10-12:30 & 2:30-6:30).*   □

GRAND-FOUGERAY

pop 2032 ✉ 35390   D3

A frontier town between Brittany and Anjou; partly Romanesque church. The park surrounds the only tower left of a fortress captured from the English by

Du Guesclin and his soldiers, who disguised themselves as woodcutters to perform this notable feat.

Nearby

▶ Châteaux and manors are plentiful throughout the region, especially to the W, along the banks of the Vilaine. Near **Guipry,** N, you can visit the 17th-18thC château des Champs★ *(9-12 & 2-6, 10 Jul.-20 Aug.).* ▶ Farther S, the Vilaine runs past **Langon,** whose partly-Romanesque church has a 12thC fresco ; the chapel appears originally to have been a Gallo-Roman sanctuary dedicated to Venus ; a damaged fresco shows the goddess rising from the waves. St. Agathe, patron saint of nursing mothers, has taken her place. Close to the town are 28 menhirs, said to be girls who were turned to stone for missing the evening service. ▶ 14 km N, **Bain-de-Bretagne** : 14th, 15thC houses.   □

Île de GROIX★
(Groix Island)

pop 2605 ✉ 56590   B3

The Sorcière (Witch's) Island is 45 min by ferry from Lorient, Enez or Groarc'h. It is a flat undulating plateau, girded with cliffs rising out of the sea. A tunafish on the church steeple replaces the traditional rooster as a weather vane (to draw attention to the importance of tuna-fishing at the beginning of the century). To the S, a beautiful section of coast looks out to sea ; walks along the headland and to the local landmark known as the Trou d'Enfer ; return to Port Saint-Nicolas.

▶ **Port Tudy,** Groix ecomuseum *(in season, daily 9:30-12:30 & 3-7 ; out of season, 10-12:30 & 2-5 ex Mon.).*
□

Practical Information _____

ⓘ 4, rue Gal-de-Gaulle, ☎ 97.05.81.75.
⛴ ☎ 97.21.03.97, from Lorient, in 45 mn, between Lorient and Port-Tudy, several crossings daily. In summer, reserv. nec. for auto.

Hotel :
★★ **Ty-Mad**, à Port-Tudy, ☎ 97.05.80.19, Euro Visa, 12 rm Ⓟ ⌂ pens (h.s.), closed Apr-Sep, 200. Rest. ♦ 65-150.

🅐 ★★★*Les Sables Rouges* (120 pl), ☎ 97.05.81.32 ; ★*Fort du Méné* (45 pl), ☎ 97.05.80.15.

Recommended
Youth hostel : batterie du Méné, ☎ 97.21.41.87.

GUÉRANDE★

Vannes 65, Nantes 77, Paris 450 km
pop 9475 ✉ 44350   C3-4

The old city huddles behind almost intact ramparts that serve as wind-breaks ; the cobbled streets come to life for the Saturday market.

▶ Tour of the granite **ramparts★** (14th-15thC) to see the six towers and four gateways, one of which, the Porte St. Michel (E, with massive machicolated towers), now houses the **Musée du Vieux Guérande★** (local historical museum ; *Easter-Sep., 9-12 & 2-7*) : furniture, costumes★, Le Croisic ceramics (1602-1734), model of the salt-marshes. ▶ The **church★** *(Friday organ concerts in summer)* has been frequently remodelled but retains its Flamboyant Gothic structure; amusing rustic capitals and interesting furnishings (tombs, altarpieces, statues); 17th-18thC houses.   □

Practical Information _____

Hotel :
★ **Roc Maria**, 1, rue des Halles, ☎ 40.24.90.51, Euro Visa, 9 rm ✵ closed Sep-Apr. A 15th-C dwelling, 180.

Restaurant :
♦♦ **La Collégiale**, 63, fg Bizienne, ☎ 40.24.97.29, AE DC ⚏ ⌕ ♪ ఉ closed Tue and Wed noon , Xmas wk, Feb, 150-240.

La GUERCHE-DE-BRETAGNE

Laval 40, Rennes 41, Paris 326 km
pop 4075 ⊠ 35130   D3
The square on the W side is almost as large as the town itself; 12th-15thC church with amusing carvings in the stalls; old pillared houses in and around the Place de la Mairie.

Nearby

▶ 3 km NW of **Rétiers** : the **Roche aux Fées (Fairies' Rock)**, 22 m long, is one of the largest megalithic monuments in France. ▶ 16 km NW : the **château de Monbouan** (18thC), with its balustrades reflected in a little lake *(15 Jul.-Aug., 9-12 & 2-6)*; 3 km farther : the church at **Louvigné-de-Baix** has stained-glass windows★ (1542) that are among the oldest of their kind in Brittany.   ☐

Practical Information _____

ℹ pl. du Gal-de-Gaulle, ☎ 99.96.30.78.   ♥
SNCF ☎ 99.96.21.51.

Hotel :
★ **La Calèche** (L.F.), 16, av. Gal-Leclerc, ☎ 99.96.20.36, DC Euro Visa, 13 rm ℗ ⚏ ⌕ pens (h.s.), closed Sun eve (l.s.) and Fri, Xmas, 30 Sep-11 Oct, 170. Rest. ♦ ♪ 50-150.

GUINGAMP

Saint-Brieuc 31, Morlaix 53, Paris 484 km
pop 9519 ⊠ 22200   B1
Once a thriving cloth market, the city has recaptured some of its former prosperity through successful cattle and pig farming in the district.

▶ Old houses around the Renaissance fountain in the central square; close by, an imposing half-Gothic, half-Renaissance **basilica**★ with a Black Virgin whose *pardon*, celebrated with fireworks on the first Saturday night in July, draws enormous crowds.

Nearby

▶ 7 km SE from Bourbriac is **Plésidy** : the 15th-16thC Toul Al Gollet Manor★ *(vis. on written request : Mme Anne de Boxtel, 11, rue Chabanais, 75002 Paris)*. ▶ Towards Saint-Brieuc, **Châtelaudren** is known for apples and the brown trout from the Leff River; in the cemetery chapel, more than 120 15thC wooden panel paintings, early "cartoon strips" illustrating the Old and New Testaments and the legends of St. Marguerite and St. Fiacre. ▶ Renaissance church at **Bulat-Pestivien** *(pardon Sun. after 8 Sep.)* : notable 66-m tower, porch and sacristy (sculpted "Dance of Death" frieze); 16thC Calvary★ in Pestivien cemetery.   ☐

Practical Information _____

GUINGAMP
ℹ pl. du Vally, ☎ 96.43.73.89.
SNCF ☎ 96.43.70.53.
Car rental : Avis, 8, rue de la Pompe, ☎ 96.44.36.32; train station.

Hotels :
★★★ **Le Relais du Roy**, 42, pl. du Centre, ☎ 96.43.76.62, AE DC Visa, 7 rm ℗ ⚏ ♪ half pens (h.s.), closed Xmas

school hols, 750. Rest. ♦♦ ♪ ఉ ✵ closed Sun , Nov-Mar, 80-250; child : 65.
★★ **Le Goéland**, La Chesnaye, ☎ 96.21.09.41, Visa, 30 rm ℗ ⚏ ⚏ ⚏ ఉ 160. Rest. ♦ ⚏ ♪ ఉ 60-80; child : 35.

Recommended
Events : *Saint-Loup festival*, Breton folk dancing. Week before last in Aug.
♥ at Plouisy, 4 km NW, celtic harps.

Nearby

LOUARGAT, ⊠ 22450, 14 km W on the anc. RN12.

Hotel :
★★ **Manoir du Cleuziou**, ☎ 96.43.14.90, 29 rm ℗ ⚏ ⚏ ⚏ ☐ ⌖ closed 15 Nov-10 Mar, 245. Rest. ● ♦♦ ⚏ ఉ The 17th-C manor house is a setting worthy of A. Le Rest's expertly prepared cuisine : *salade de homard au basilic, soupière de Saint-Jacques et langoustines*, 135-205; child : 95.

HENNEBONT

Lorient 10, Vannes 46, Paris 487 km
pop 13103 ⊠ 56700   B3
One third of this old town, nestled in the Blavet estuary, was destroyed in WWII.

▶ The **church** is a Flamboyant Gothic building dating from 1513, with a 72-m spire. ▶ Remnants of the ramparts around the **walled town**★ (Bro Erec'h gate, 15thC, flanked by massive towers); pretty gardens at the foot of the walls. Botanical gardens at Kerbihan. ▶ Large **stud-farm** on the grounds of the former abbey of la Joie *(visits in summer, 10, 11, 2 and 4)*.   ☐

Practical Information _____

ℹ pl. du Mal-Foch, ☎ 97.36.24.52.
SNCF ☎ 97.36.20.08.

Hotel :
● ★★★★ **Château du Locguénolé** (R.C.), rte de Port-Louis, ☎ 97.76.29.04, Tx 950636, AE DC Euro Visa, 35 rm ℗ ⚏ ⚏ ⚏ ☐ ⌖ closed 15 Nov-1 Mar, 640. Rest. ● ♦♦♦♦ ⚏ ♪ ఉ closed Mon noon. An elegant, tastefully furnished house that overlooks the Blavet estuary. For hunters, a 100-ha park. Alyette de la Sablière and her family welcome you like a guest into their happy home. As a proof of our esteem, we welcome her and her talented chef Michel Gaudin, to our chefs' panel. We hope shy Michel will be pleased, not embarrassed, by our gesture. Like him, his cooking is dicreet, most agreeable and of a high order : *salade de queue de bœuf et d'ailerons de volaille, poissons de petit bateau, selle d'agneau fourrée en rognonnade*, fabulous desserts. Great and modest wines. Stylish service, 120-250; child : 95.

Recommended
♥ crêpes : *créperie des Remparts*, 27, rue Trottier, ☎ 97.36.28.18; *créperie Hent Er Mor*, 30, av. des Plages, Kervignac, 6 km S., ☎ 97.65.77.17.

JOSSELIN*

Loudéac 34, Vannes 42, Paris 422 km
pop 2740 ⊠ 56120   C2
The best-known picture postcard of inland Brittany shows pleasure craft at the foot of this formidable castle with tall, pointed towers and soaring walls.

▶ The **castle**★★, on a sheer rock over the river Oust, is the very image of a mediaeval fortress *(30 Mar.-May : Wed., Sun. and nat. hols. 2-6; June and 1-22 Sep. : daily 2-6; Jul.-Aug. : daily 10-12 & 2-6; closed in winter)*. Within the walls is a long, low building★★ (1490-1505) facing a courtyard, richly decorated in the style of the period. The 19thC interior★★ owes its warmth and charm to the fact that the Rohan family still lives here. In the stables *(separate entrance)*, the Old Doll Museum presents the Rohan private collection *(May-Sep. 10-12 & 2-6, closed Mon.; 1 Oct.-15 Nov. and Mar., Apr., Wed., Sat., Sun. and hols. 2-6).* ▶ The rest of the town lives up to the castle : charming 16th and 17thC **houses**, many half-timbered, with caryatids or carved woodwork. ▶ The Flamboyant Gothic **church★** has pinnacled buttresses, gargoyles and a series of gables pierced with large windows.

Nearby

▶ The 9 836-acre **Lanouée Forest** *(7 km N)* is one of the most beautiful in Brittany. ▶ **Guéhenno** *(12 km SW) :* Calvary★ (1550, restored 1853) unique in the Morbihan. ▶ **Ploërmel** *(12 km E) :* a crossroads town that was much fought over in the 14th and 16thC. The ramparts have been converted into houses. The 16thC Renaissance and Flamboyant Gothic church★ has a carved N doorway★ and 16thC stained glass.★ At La Mennais college, a 19thC astronomical clock. ▶ 8 km S, **La Chapelle-Caro** : château de Crévy (costume museum, 1720-1930; *Easter-1 Nov., Wed., Sat., Sun. 2-6 ex Jul.-15 Sep.; Jun. 10-12 & 2-6 daily).* □

Practical Information

JOSSELIN
🛈 pl. Congrégation, ☎ 97.22.36.43.

Hotel :
★★ **Château**, 1, rue du Gal-de-Gaulle, ☎ 97.22.20.11, Euro Visa, 36 rm ℗ ≪ closed Sun eve and Mon, Feb, 205. Rest. ♦ ≪ ♪ 55-150.

Nearby

PLOËRMEL, ✉ 56800, 46 km NE of **Vannes**.
🛈 pl. Lamennais, ☎ 97.74.02.70.
SNCF ☎ 97.74.05.35.

Hotel :
● ★★ **Commerce** (L.F.), 70, rue de la Gare, ☎ 97.74.05.32, Euro Visa, 30 rm ℗ ≪ ♪ half pens (h.s.), closed Mon (Oct-Jun), 2-25 Jan, 310. Rest. ● ♦ *Le Reberminard* ♪ ᕁ After Rennes, the Cruaud brothers have open their second restaurant here : *bavarois d'avocat au crabe, suprême de colin aux trois crèmes*, 55-140 ; child : 40.

⚓ ★★★*Belles Rives*, on the edge of the pond, boating centre (135 pl), ☎ 97.74.01.22.

KERNASCLEDEN★★

Lorient 32, Rennes 139, Paris 487 km
pop 434 ✉ 56540 Le Croisty   B2

The murals★★ in the Gothic chapel (1420-64) are among the most beautiful collections of French 15thC painting : scenes from the Life of the Virgin and the Childhood of Christ, *Dance of Death*, depiction of Hell. Their evocative character, composition and range of colours show great artistic skill.

▶ S, **Pont-Calleck** : forest and 16th-17thC château reflected in a pretty pond.   □

LAMBALLE

Saint-Brieuc 21, Rennes 81, Paris 431 km
pop 10078 ✉ 22400   C2

Capital of Penthièvre before Guingamp, now a market town and the summer gateway to the beaches at Val-André, Erquy and Les Sables-d'Or.

▶ **Old houses** line the Place du Martrai, including the Maison du Bourreau (executioner's house), now used by the SI and housing the **Mathurin Meheut museum** and the **Old Lamballe museum** *(Jun.-15 Sep. ex Sun. and nat. hols.), 10-12 & 2:30-6:30).* ▶ A steep street runs up to the collegiate church (13th-15thC) and the surrounding shady walk. ▶ Large **stud-farms** *(10 Jul.-15 Sep., week-days 2-4:30, Sun. 10-12 & 2-5; off season by appt., tel. :*

96.31.00.40).* In the distance the attractive **church of St. Martin★** (11thC arcades ; carved 1519 wooden porch). ▶ 23 km S : in Cistercian solitude, the **Boquen Abbey★** (12thC church, restored).   □

Practical Information

🛈 1, pl. du Martray, ☎ 96.31.05.38 (h.s.).   ♥
SNCF ☎ 96.31.00.56.

Hotels :
★★★ *Angleterre* (L.F.), 29, bd Jobert, ☎ 96.31.00.16, Tx 740994, AE DC Euro Visa, 22 rm ℗ ≪ ᄤ ♪ ≋ half pens, 250. Rest. ♦ ♪ ᕁ ≋ closed Mon noon and Sun eve, 1 Nov-1 Apr, 60-115 ; child : 30.

● ★★ *Manoir des Portes* (R.S.), La Poterie, ☎ 96.31.13.62, Tx 950750, AE DC Euro Visa, 16 rm ℗ ≪ ᄤ ᕁ ♪ closed 15 Jan-28 Feb, 260. Rest. ♦♦ ♪ ᕁ closed Mon ex Jul-Aug, 15 Jan-28 Feb, 80-150 ; child : 40.

Restaurant :
● ♦♦♦ *Lorand-Barre*, Les Ponts-Neufs, 11 km NW, ☎ 96.32.78.71, AE DC ≪ ᕁ closed Mon and Sun eve, 1 Dec-3 Mar. The region's best-known table, 285-400.

LANDERNEAU

Brest 20, Quimper 62, Paris 580 km
pop 15531 ✉ 29220   A1

An inland town linked to the sea by the river Élorn, prospering from cloth and leather in the 16th-17thC (old houses) ; today trade centres around meat, milk and cauliflowers.

▶ **De Rohan Mansion★** (9 pl du Général-de-Gaulle, *now a tea shop*), in golden granite with slate shingles, one of the loveliest buildings in the town ; see also the de Léon Quay. The **Pont de Rohan★** (bridge ; best view from upstream) and Rue St.-Thomas (left bank). ▶ Church of St. Thomas (16thC). ▶ 6.5 km N : **Trémaouézan★** has a 15thC church with porch★ that was its gallery. ▶ E : round trip of the Léon churchyards (→).   □

Practical Information

🛈 Pont de Rohan, ☎ 98.85.13.09.
✈ *Guipavas*, 12 km W.
SNCF ☎ 98.85.00.30.

Hotels :
★★ *Clos du Pontic* (L.F.), rue du Pontic, ☎ 98.21.50.91, Euro Visa, 32 rm ℗ ᄤ ≪ ᕁ 190. Rest. ♦ ♪ closed Mon, Sat noon, Sun eve, 70-190.

★★ *L'Amandier*, 55, rue de Brest, ☎ 98.85.10.89, AE DC Euro Visa, 8 rm ℗ ≪ ≋ half pens (h.s.), 415. Rest. ♦♦ ♪ ᕁ ≋ Spec : *gratin d'huîtres au champagne, feuilletés de ris de veau au beurre de truffes, noix de St-Jacques en habit vert*, 95-140.

Restaurant :
♦ *La Mairie*, 9, rue de la Tour d'Auvergne, ☎ 98.85.01.83, Euro Visa ≪ ♪ closed Tue, 1-15 Jul, 15 Nov-1 Dec. At the very tip of Europe : *blanquette de fruits de mer, Kig au Farz*, (a complete Breton meal), 50-150 ; child : 25.

LANNION★

Morlaix 38, Saint-Brieuc 63, Paris 515 km
pop 17228 ✉ 22300   B1

Where the valley of the river Léguer turns into an estuary, close to the resorts of the Côte de Granit Rose (Pink Granite Coast ; → Perros-Guirec), this old country town does its best to profit from the presence of the National Telecommunications Research Centre.

▶ **Old houses** on the Place du Général-Leclerc, corbelled, slate-roofed or decorated with caryatids ; near the church of St. Jean (16th-17thC) visit the Romanesque **church of Brélévenez★** (12th-13thC, remodelled).

Nearby

▶ 2.5 km W : **Loguivy** has a charming churchyard. ▶ **Le Yaudet** *(7.5 km W)* : a little port at the mouth of the Léguer; pretty site★; unusual Nativity in the church. ▶ 10 km N : the **Pleumeur-Bodou** space communications station *(guided tours : tel. : 96.48.41.49)*; the key attraction is the 50-m tall Dacron dome (Radome) housing one of the antennae.

Round trip to Tonquédec and Rosanbo *(approx 60 km, 1/2 day)*

▶ On the road to Pouaret *(D11)* and a number of small roads to the left, you can see : the ruins of château de Coat-Frec (16thC); the **chapel at Kerfons★** (1559, polychrome wood choirscreen★), in a charming valley; the imposing ruins of the feudal **château de Tonquédec★** (14th-16thC); the gardens of the **château de Kergrist★** *(9-12 & 2-6)* and the **chapelle des Sept Saints** (Seven Saints' Chapel), built on a dolmen, and a pilgrims' shrine for both Catholics and Muslims on the 4th Sun. in July. ▶ After **Plouaret** (old houses, 16thC church), the **château de Rosanbo★**, a severely aristocratic 15thC residence, enlarged in the 17thC. Interesting furnishings *(10-12 & 2-6, Jul.-Aug.; off season, tel. : 96.35.18.77)*. ▶ Return via Saint-Michel-en-Grève (→ below).

Armorique Corniche (cliff road ; *24 km to Locquirec*)

▶ The Morlaix road is especially attractive past **Saint-Michel-en-Grève** along the 5-km beach of the Lieue de Grève; it continues along the **Corniche de l'Armorique★★** that skirts **Plestin-les-Grèves** (Lesmaës manor, early 16thC, *early Aug.-mid-Sep. 2-6)* to provide an infinite variety of views over the sea, the cliffs, the shoreline and the rocks, finally reaching **Locquirec** (panel paintings in the church, 1712). □

Practical Information ─────────────

LANNION
ℹ 1, quai d'Aiguillon, ☎ 96.37.07.35, closed Mon and Sat (l.s.).
✈ *Lannion-Servel*, 3 km N, ☎ 96.37.42.92.
SNCF ☎ 96.37.03.01.
Car rental : *Avis*, Rte de Perros-Guirec (AP), ☎ 96.48.52.71; train station.

⚠ ★★★*Beg-Léguer* (200 pl), ☎ 96.48.75.20.

Nearby

LOCQUIREC, ⊠ 29241, 23 km W.
ℹ at the harbour, ☎ 98.67.40.83.

Hotel :
★ *Port* (L.F.), ☎ 98.67.42.10, 10 rm ⚞ ⚘ closed 3 Sep-25 Mar, 150. Rest. ♦ ♪ 70-100.

⚠ *Toul ar Goué* (250 pl), ☎ 98.67.40.85.

PLOULEC'H, ⊠ 22300 Lannion, 4 km W.

Hotel :
★ *Genêts d'Or* (L.F.), Le Yaudet, ☎ 96.35.24.17, Euro Visa, 15 rm ℙ ▦ ⚞ ♪ ⚘ ♿ ⚘ half pens, closed Mon eve, Jan, Feb, 300. Rest. ♦ ♪ ⚘ 55.

SAINT-MICHEL-EN-GRÈVE, ⊠ 22300, 11 km SW.

Hotel :
★★ *Plage* (L.F.), ☎ 96.35.74.43, AE Euro Visa, 38 rm ℙ ⚞ ⚞ ♪ closed Jan, 160. Rest. ♦ ⚞ ♪ ♿ 60-100.

The LÉON Churchyards

A-B1
Round trip from Morlaix *(approx 107-121 km, full day; see map 5)*

Traditional Breton churchyards (→ box), although not exclusive to the Léon region, can be seen here at their most elaborate, showing both the skill of the artisans and the wealth of the parishes.

▶ **Saint-Thégonnec,** one of the most complete : 17thC ossuary★★ in Breton Renaissance style; Calvary of 1610; doorway of 1587; church (16th-17thC) with noteworthy panelling★. ▶ **Guimiliau :** unusual size and richness for so small a village; Calvary★★ with more than 200 statuettes; 17thC church with a wealth of carved furnishings. ▶ **Lampaul-Guimiliau :** without doubt the most richly-decorated church★ in Brittany; polychrome altarpieces★★ attributed to joiners from the French Royal Navy. ▶ If you have time after visiting **Landivisiau** (cattle market; naval air base), detour to see the 16th-17thC church★ at **Bodilis** and the churchyard at **Saint-Servais**; return via Brézal, with a mill opposite a ruined church (site★). ▶ **La Roche-Maurice :** beneath the ruins of a château (view★), a rustic churchyard. ▶ Above Landerneau (→) : little-known **Pencran**, with expressive sculptures. ▶ **La Martyre :** once famous for horse fairs, has a Renaissance ossuary with a well-known and oddly menacing caryatid on the corner. ▶ **Ploudiry :** a fine collection of wooden statues; more at **Sizun★**, also a monumental archway. ▶ **Ker Hoad :** the **mills,** now an ecomuseum, demonstrate the many uses of water in traditional rural economies *(Apr.-Jun., daily 2-6; Jul.-15 Sep., 11-7; 16 Sep.-end Oct., Sun. 2-6)*. ▶ **Commana :** an interesting churchyard; the ornate altarpieces★ in the church illustrate "rustic Baroque". ▶ Continue along the foot of Roc'h Trévezel (→ Monts d'Arrée) and through **Plounéour-Ménez** (churchyard) to reach the former Cistercian abbey church at **Le Relecq** (Romanesque and Gothic, partially rebuilt), returning to Morlaix via **Pleyber-Christ** (churchyard ; carved beams and stalls).

Also...

▶ **Plougonven** *(12 km SE from Morlaix)* : fine and complete churchyard; vibrant carved figures on the Calvary★. Others at **Plében** (→) and Sainte-Marie-du-Ménez-Hom (→ Ménez-Hom), to name only the largest. □

Practical Information ─────────────

LAMPAUL-GUIMILIAU, ⊠ 29230 Landivisiau, 4 km S of **Landivisiau.**

Hotel :
★★ *L'Enclos* (L.F.), ☎ 98.68.77.08, AE DC Euro Visa, 36 rm ℙ ▦ ⚞ ♿ 180. Rest. ♦ ♪ 60-150.

Recommended
♥ sculpture : *Guy et Jeanne Jeffroy,* ☎ 98.68.72.09.

LANDIVISIAU, ⊠ 29230, 38 km NE of **Brest.**
ℹ rue G.-Clemenceau, ☎ 98.68.03.50.
SNCF ☎ 98.68.00.04.

Hotel :
★★ *L'Etendard,* 8, rue du Gal-de-Gaulle, ☎ 98.68.06.60, DC Euro Visa, 30 rm ℙ ♿ ⚘ closed Sun eve, 15 Dec-15 Jan, 180.

SAINT-THÉGONNEC, ⊠ 29223, 12 km E on the anc. RN 12.

Hotel :
★ *Auberge Saint-Thégonnec* (L.F.), 6, pl. de la Mairie, ☎ 98.79.61.18, Euro Visa, 6 rm ▦ half pens, closed Mon eve and Tue, 15 Dec-5 Feb, 250. Rest. ● ♦♦ ♪ ♿ ⚘ Quick, visit Alain Le Coz for his very good cooking and the genial service overseen by his spouse. Fixed menus at very nice prices. Home-smoked fish, fisherman's *potau-feu*, 60-150.

SIZUN, ⊠ 29237, 37 km E of **Brest.**
ℹ ☎ 98.68.81.70. ♥

Hotel :
★ *Voyageurs,* 2, rue de l'Argoat, ☎ 98.68.80.35, 16 rm ℙ closed Sat eve (l.s.), 6-29 Sep, 100. Rest. ♦ 45-65.

Recommended
♥ at Hanvec, Parc Naturel Régional d'Armorique : *Maison de la Rivière, de l'Eau, de la Pêche,* Moulin de Vergraon, ☎ 98.68.86.33.

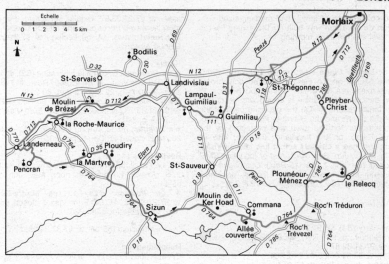

5. The Léon churchyards

LOCMARIAQUER**

Quiberon 31, Vannes 32, Paris 487 km
pop 1279 ⊠ 56740   C3

Like Carnac (→), this holiday resort is close to numerous megaliths.

▶ Dolmens at Kercadoret and Kervérès, Mane-Réthual★ and Mane-Lud; decorated chambers at the **Table des Marchands★★** (one of the most famous) and the covered alley at Pierres Plates★; broken menhir at **Men-er-Hroëc'h**, formerly one of the largest in the world (20.3 m, 347 tons); tumulus at Mane-er-Hroëc'h; dolmen at Kerlut. ▶ View★ over the Gulf of Morbihan and the sight from **Kerpenhir Point.** □

Practical Information _____

ℹ pl. de la Mairie, ☎ 97.57.33.05.

Hotel :
★★ *Relais de Kerpenhir*, Kerpenhir, ☎ 97.57.31.20, Euro Visa, 17 rm ℗ ≼ ⊞ ◔ ♪ ✵ half pens, 250. Rest. ♦ ≼ ♪ ⴺ ✵ 40-65.

⚠ ★★*Kerpenhir* (115 pl), ☎ 97.57.31.92; ★★*Locker* (65 pl), ☎ 97.57.32.74.

LOCRONAN**

Quimper 17, Brest 63, Paris 567 km
pop 704 ⊠ 29136 Plogennec   A2

It is rare to find such architectural quality and unity so well preserved. Locronan, formerly a city of weavers and textile merchants, is now thriving due to tourism.

▶ The granite Renaissance houses (16th-17thC) around the well in the **town square★★** have elegant pediments above dormer windows. ▶ Stained glass★ (end 15thC) in the apse of the **church★** (same period; *closed 12:30-1:30*). On the right, in the **Pénity Chapel,** a Burial of Christ (16thC naïf masterpiece), and the 15thC tomb of St. Ronan. ▶ On the second Sunday in July participants in the *pardon* make their way in a great procession to the top of the Montagne de Locronan (alt. 289 m; view★) : this is the *Petite Troménie* (*tro minihy*, procession around the monastery); every 6th year (1989), a longer route is used and the procession is called the *Grande Troménie*.

Nearby

▶ 4 km NW : **Moëllien Manor** (17thC, *now a hotel*). ▶ 8 km W, **Sainte-Anne-la-Palud,** where the *pardon* is one of the most famous (*last Sun. in Aug.*). □

Practical Information _____

LOCRONAN
ℹ pl. de la Mairie, ☎ 98.91.70.14 (h.s.).

Hotels :
★★ *Fer à Cheval*, rte du Bois-de-Nevet, 1 km SW on D 63, ☎ 98.91.70.67, AE DC Euro Visa, 35 rm ℗ ≼ ⊞ ◔ ♿ 200. Rest. ♦ ≼ ♪ ⴺ ✵ 60-135; child : 30.

★ *Prieuré* (L.F.), rue du Prieuré, ☎ 29.91.70.89, Euro Visa, 15 rm ℗ ≼ ⊞ ◔ ✵ half pens, closed Mon (l.s.), 1 Oct-2 Nov, 180. Rest. ♦ ♿ 50-120.

⚠ ★*Municipal* (155 pl), ☎ 98.91.87.76.

Nearby

SAINTE-ANNE-LA-PALUD,   ⊠   29136   Plogonnec, 4 km NW.

Hotel :
★★★★ *La Plage* (R.C.), ☎ 98.92.50.12, Tx 941366, AE DC Euro Visa, 30 rm ℗ ≼ ⊞ ◔ ♿ ☐ ⴺ half pens (h.s.), closed 15 Oct-10 Apr, 1100. Rest. ● ♦♦♦ ≼ ✵ A variety of Breton foods generously served and simply prepared : *bar fumé, langouste grillée aux herbes des dunes,* 150-250.

LORIENT

Quimper 64, Rennes 147, Paris 496 km
pop 64675 ⊠ 56100   B3

Three centuries ago, the newly-created French East India Company, needing more warehouses and dockyards, founded the Port de l'Orient (Port of the East). Since then, Lorient has always lived by and from the sea, and now, rather than one harbour, there are four.

▶ Between the town hall (B2-3) and the church of Notre-Dame de la Victoire (C2), a broad pedestrian precinct is centred around the lively **Place Aristide-Briand.** ▶ Only French citizens may visit the **arsenal,** which specialises in repair and construction of small- and medium-sized vessels. ▶ **Port de Keroman** was built for the fishing fleet in 1919-27; best seen in early morning.

Nearby

▶ 6 km S, **Larmor Plage** : two lovely beaches; 16thC church; the figures on the Flemish-inspired polychrome wooden altarpiece are full of life; 15th-16thC frescos. W of Larmor, the tranquil coastline is dotted with ports that double as family resorts. ▶ On the opposite bank of the estuary of the Scorff and the Blavet is **Port-Louis★** (pop. 3700). This former fortified town was protected by the château de Kerso, on the headland; the city, with its 17thC ramparts, has a **citadel★★** that juts into the roadstead (16th-17thC; *Jun.-Sep. 10-7; rest of the year, 10-12 & 2-7; closed Tue. and 1 Nov.-15 Dec.*). Compagnie des Indes Museum and Marine Museum (boats, paintings, weapons; *in season, 10-7; off season, 10-12 & 2-5*). ☐

Practical Information

LORIENT
🛈 pl. Jules-Ferry (B3), ☎ 97.21.07.84.
✈ *Lann-Bihoué*, 6 km NW, ☎ 97.82.32.93. *Lorient-Belle-île*, ☎ 97.31.82.87.
▰▰▰ (B1), ☎ 97.31.08.23/97.21.21.04.
▰▰▰ bd Mar.-Joffre (B2), ☎ 97.21.02.48.

▰▰ ☎ 97.21.03.97, regular service for Pen-Mané, Larmor, Kernével, Port-Louis and l'île de Groix.
Car rental : *Avis*, 14, bd Leclerc, ☎ 97.21.00.12; Lann-Bihoué Airport.

Hotels :
★★★ *Bretagne*, 6, pl. de la Libération (B2), ☎ 97.64.34.65, AE DC Euro Visa, 34 rm ℙ 260. Rest. ♦ ♪ ♿ ⌘ closed Sun, 24-30 Aug, 22 Dec-18 Jan, 80-215.
★★★ *Mercure Lorient*, 31, pl. Jules-Ferry (B3), ☎ 97.21.35.73, Tx 950810, AE DC Euro Visa, 58 rm ≋ ◍ ◌ ♪ ▦ ♿ 340.
★★ *Atlantic*, 30-33, rue du Couédic (B2), ☎ 97.64.13.27, 26 rm ℙ closed 20 Dec-5 Jan, 235.

Restaurants :
♦♦ *Le Pic*, 2, bd Franchet-d'Esperey (B2), ☎ 97.21.18.29 ♪ ♿ closed Thu and Sat noon Mar, Jun, 15-31 Dec, 55-140.
♦ *Le Poisson d'Or*, 1, rue Maître-Esvelin (B3), ☎ 97.21.57.06, AE DC Euro Visa ♪ closed Sat noon and Sun. Enjoyable food, 80-220.

▲ ★★*Municipal* (65 pl), ☎ 97.37.34.98.

Recommended
Events : *theatre festival*, in Jul-Aug; *interceltic festival*, 1st 2 wks in Aug.

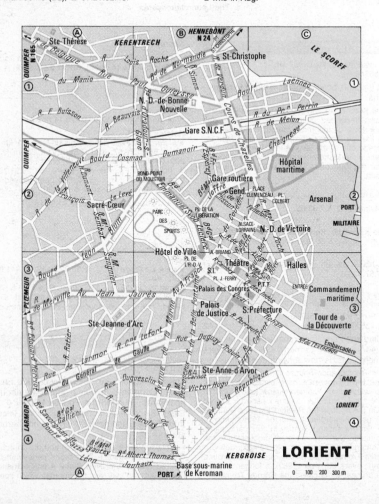

LORIENT

0   100   200   300 m

Guided tours : guided cruises on the Blavet and the port of Lorient.
♥ crêperie : *St-Georges*, 14, rue Paul-Bert, ☎ 97.64.28.11.

Nearby

GUIDEL, ✉ 56520, 12 km NW.
Hotel :
★★★ *La Châtaigneraie*, rte de Moëlan-sur-Mer, ☎ 97.65.99.93, Euro Visa, 10 rm P ♨ ♒ ♪ ⚱ 280.

⚊ ★★*Bas Pouldu* (265 pl), ☎ 97.65.98.05.
LARMOR-PLAGE, ✉ 56260, 6 km S.
Hotel :
★★ *Beau Rivage* (L.F.), plage de Toulhars, ☎ 97.65.50.11, AE DC Euro Visa, 18 rm P ⚱ ♒ ♿ pens (h.s.), 500. Rest. ♦ ⚱ ♪ closed Mon and Sun eve, 27 Oct-2 Dec, 65-220.

⚊ ★★*Phare* (75 pl), ☎ 97.65.53.22.
PORT-LOUIS, ✉ 56290, 19 km SE.
🚢 Boats for Lorient, Groix and Gâvres.
Hotel :
★★★ *Avel Vor*, (L.F., France-Accueil), 25, rue de Loc-malo, ☎ 97.82.47.59, Tx 950826, AE DC Euro Visa, 19 rm P ⚱ half pens (h.s.), closed Mon and Sun eve (l.s.), 460. Rest. ● ♦♦ ⚱ ♪ 50-180 ; child : 40.

⚊ ★★*Remparts* (135 pl), ☎ 97.82.47.16.

Recommended
♥ *musée de la Compagnie des Indes*, Citadelle de Port-Louis.

LOUDÉAC

Saint-Brieuc 41, Rennes 85, Paris 436 km
pop 10756 ✉ 22600   C2

ℹ️ ☎ 96.28.25.17.
🚆 ☎ 96.28.00.29.

Hotel :
★★ *Les Voyageurs*, 10, rue de Cadelac, ☎ 96.28.00.47, AE DC Euro Visa, 30 rm P ⚱ ♪ closed Sat, 20 Dec-14 Jan, 160. Rest. ♦ ⚱ ♪ ♿ 45-155 ; child : 35.

Restaurant :
♦ *Auberge du Cheval Blanc*, 6, pl. de l'Eglise, ☎ 96.28.00.31 ♪ closed Mon eve and Sun eve, 15 Sep-15 Oct, 45-110.

⚊ ★*Municipal* (75 pl), ☎ 97.28.14.92.

MENEZ BRÉ**

                                                            B1
This peak (alt. 302 m) is high enough to give a view★ of the sea.

► 8 km W : **Belle-Isle-en-Terre** is surrounded by woods, hills and ravines. In this beautiful setting, the Breton wrestling championships are held *(3rd Sun. in Jul.)*. 15 km N : the **chapel of Locmaria** has an early-16thC choirscreen★, as has the church of the same period in **Loc Envel**. □

Practical Information _____

BELLE-ISLE-EN-TERRE, ✉ 22810, 8 km E.
ℹ️ ☎ 96.43.30.38.

Hotel :
★★ *Relais de l'Argoat* (L.F.), rue du Guic, ☎ 96.43.00.34, Euro Visa, 10 rm P ⚱ half pens (h.s.), closed Mon, Feb, 170. Rest. ♦ ♿ Spec : *huîtres tièdes aux blancs de poireaux, rouget en fenouillette*, 50-90.

Recommended
Events : *Breton wrestling tournament*, in Jul.

MONCONTOUR-DE-BRETAGNE

Lamballe 16, Saint-Brieuc 23, Paris 435 km
pop 1015 ✉ 22510   C2

On a promontory girdled with ramparts and greenery, flower-decked shops and fine old houses, some in granite, others in wood.

► **St. Mathurin Church** : six magnificent stained-glass windows★ (1520-49, Flemish influence). ► On the hill opposite : château des Granges (18thC, 13thC tower). ► 2 km S : the **chapel of Notre-Dame-du-Haut** with statues of seven healing saints (pardon, *15 Aug.*) ; 5 km further, highest point of **Le Méné Landes** (alt. 339 m) : vast panorama (as far as Saint-Malo in good weather). ► 5.5 km E : **château** and lake of **La Touche-Trébry★**, 16thC *(daily ex Sun. and nat. hols. 2-6)*. ► Near **Hénon** *(6 km NW)*, Le Colombier Manor (15th-17thC) in a romantic setting *(visit by request)*. ► Numerous other manors and **châteaux** in the area, including **La Houssaye** *(12 km NW)*, in a large park *(20 Jul.-31 Aug., ex 15 Aug., 10-12 & 3-7)*. □

Les MONTAGNES NOIRES*
(The Black Mountains)   B2

Round trip *(127 km, full day)*

Not so high as the Monts d'Arrée (→), the Black Mountains offer wooded valleys and winding roads ; trout and salmon in the rivers.

► **Carhaix-Plouger** (→). Leaving the Gourin road at **Port-de-Carhaix** and passing the unusual Calvary★ at **Kerbreuden** (15thC), you arrive at **Saint-Hernin** : churchyard (16th-17thC, ossuary 1697, Calvary). ► Almost on the ridge of the Montagnes Noires is the chapel of Saint-Hervé★, protector of horses. ► **Gourin** hosts the annual *bagadou* championship *(1 May)*, an affirmation of Celtic customs, with lively music and wrestling. In the church (17thC), 15thC Pietà. Several slate quarries in the vicinity. ► The **Toul Laëron Rock**, 326 m high, gives a wide view over the region. ► The **chapel of Notre-Dame-du-Crann★** (1535 ; *1 km from Spézet*) has a charming exterior ; inside, the original stained glass★ (1548), evidently inspired by German engravings, shows the extent of Brittany's cultural awareness at this period. ► Short detour : view from Notre-Dame-du-Cudel ; churchyard and yew-tree at **Roudouallec** ; covered alley at Castel-Ruffel. ► In the heart of the **forest of Laz★**, the **Domaine de Trévarez★** *(Apr.-Jun., Sep., 1-7 ex Tue. ; Jul.-Aug., 11-7 ; Sat., Sun. and nat. hols. 2-6 rest of year)* provides wonderful walks through its 185 acres of camellias, azaleas and rhododendrons. ► As you leave the forest, there is a fine view over the bell-tower-studded landscape of the Aulne Valley and the Monts d'Arrée. Calvary★ in the cemetery. ► Pretty winding road to **Tréguron** (chapel), **Gouézec** (16thC stained-glass Passion★ in the church), and **La Roche du Feu** (alt. 281 m ; panorama). ► One 16thC fountain is left at the **Trois Fontaines Chapel** ; Calvary, fine woodwork, gallery, carved beams, statues). ► After **Pleyben** (→), which is worth a prolonged visit, the return trip is shorter. ► Stop at **Châteauneuf-du-Faou**, on top of a hill over the Aulne ; immense panorama★ over the Montagnes Noires. ► **Cléden-Poher** ; 15thC church ; woodwork, ossuary, elegant Calvary. □

Practical Information _____

CHÂTEAUNEUF-DU-FAOU, ✉ 29119, 36 km NE of **Quimper**.
ℹ️ 7, rue de la Mairie, ☎ 98.81.83.90 (h.s.).   ⚘

Hotel :
★ *Gai Logis* (L.F.), rte de Quimper, ☎ 98.81.73.87, 12 rm P closed Mon (winter only), 20 Dec-15 Jan, 100. Rest. ♦ closed Mon (l.s.), 45-70.

Don't forget to consult the Practical Holiday Guide: it can help in solving many problems.

MONTFORT

Rennes 22, Dinan 39, Paris 370 km
pop 4378 ⊠ 35160   D2

This is a country-holiday resort with remains of ramparts and a 14thC keep from the mediaeval town.

▶ The **Ecomuseum** *(closed Sat. and Sun. in summer)* has a fascinating collection★ of country costumes (originals, and scale reproductions on dolls).

Nearby

▶ **Château de Montauban**★ *(15 km NW, closed Tue.)* : at the edge of the forest; 5 km onwards : the **Manoir de la Louverie** (17thC; *Jul.-Aug. ex Sun. and nat. hols.*). From here, continue to **Saint-Méen-le-Grand** and see the 13th-14thC **church**. ▶ 6.5 km W : **Iffendic** (15thC church with 16thC stained glass), not far from the Étang de Trémelin (lake; leisure centre). ▶ 10 km S : in **Monterfil**, the annual Upper-Brittany music competition *(end Jun.)* is accompanied by enthusiastic festivities.   □

Gulf of MORBIHAN★★★

                                                      C3

Mor Bihan (the "little sea") is sprinkled with isles and islets at water level which are sometimes accessible on foot at low tide. The bay is almost closed by the Rhuys (→) and Locmariaquer (→) peninsulas. Wind surfers, sailing boats, tourist excursions and the ferries to the larger islands can be glimpsed between the white houses and the little gardens with their clumps of trees.

▶ The **Ile d'Arz**★ is an island only 3 km long; partially Romanesque church. ▶ **Ile aux Moines**★★, somewhat longer, is covered with pinewoods; many charming sites; see the château de Guéric, the road along the ridge (views★ over the bay), Pen Hap Point, etc. ▶ **Ile de Gavrinis** *(access from **Larmor Baden** in 15 min; daily 15 Jun.-15 Sep.)* has a tumulus★★ (8 m high, 100 m circumference); an astonishing size, with esoteric signs engraved on the walls; further S, the **Islet of Er Lanic** has two cromlechs, one of which is visible only at low tide. The bay was formed when the ground subsided after the prehistoric era.   □

Practical Information _____

LARMOR-BADEN, ⊠ 56790, 24 km W of **Vannes**.

Hotel :
★★ *Auberge Parc Fetan* (L.F.), 17, rue de Berder, ☎ 97.57.04.38, AE DC Euro Visa, 23 rm 8 apt 🅿 ≼ ⌂ ⌕ ♪ closed 5 Nov-15 Mar, 175. Rest. ♦ ≼ ♪ 🔆 55-150.

⚠ ★★*Ker-Eden* (100 pl), ☎ 97.57.05.23.

MORLAIX

Brest 60, Quimper 82, Paris 536 km
pop 19541 ⊠ 29210   B1

Morlaix is situated at the back of a deep narrow estuary, and crowned with a viaduct. Pleasure craft have taken the place of the *feluccas*, *caracks* and *nefs* and other craft that made this town the rival of Nantes and Saint-Malo, and the most important port in lower Brittany during the 18thC heyday of the French East India Company. The old town is still lively, especially on market days.

▶ Wooden houses decorated with statuettes or slate shingles line the old streets. The **Grande-Rue**★ with its old-fashioned boutiques is the best example. ▶ Allow a good hour for exploring; see the Maison de la Duchesse Anne (Duchess Anne's house; end 15thC); carved wooden staircase inside. **Museum** *(10-12 & 2-6 in summer, 5*

in winter; *closed Tue.*), paintings of the French, Italian and Dutch schools; some modern works but particularly good on rural life in times past. Church of St. Melaine (1489).

Nearby

▶ **Carantec** *(15 km N)* : very much a family resort, reached by a lovely *corniche* (cliff road)★. ▶ Enjoyable excursion along the right bank *(48 km round trip)* beginning at the **château de Keranroux** (18thC; *visit on request*), following the coastline to the **Cairn de Barnenez**★, a large stone tumulus with eleven funerary chambers *(9-12 & 2-6; Jun.-Sep.)* and continuing to the magnificent red rocks at Primel Point★, near **Primel-Trégastel**; return via **Plougasnou** (16thC church), **Saint-Jean-du-Doigt**, site of an important *pardon* on 23/24 June (15th-16thC church; see the treasure room; 1691 fountain; 1577 chapel), and **Lanmeur** (pre-Romanesque crypt beneath the church; chapel of Kernitron with Romanesque doorway, nave and transept). ▶ SW : tour of traditional churchyards (→).   □

Practical Information _____

MORLAIX
🛈 pl. des Otages, ☎ 98.62.14.94.
✈ Morlaix-Ploujean, 6 km SE, ☎ 98.62.16.09.
🚆 ☎ 98.88.08.88.

Hotels :
★★ *Europe*, 1, rue d'Aiguillon, ☎ 98.62.11.99, Tx 940696, AE DC Euro Visa, 68 rm, closed 15 Dec-15 Jan, 230. Rest. ● ♦♦♦ ♪ 🔆 ⌕ Talented young Patrick Jeffroy, a member of our chef's panel, has three passions : his family, books, and cooking. A stint with Jacques Maximin, the 'Napoléon of the kitchen' has renewed Jeffroy's enthusiasm. Back at home in his dreary restaurant, he needed it! Fortunately, owner M.Feunteuna is a realist, and hired local architect Thierry Mostini to give the place a needed facelift. The better to honour the light, tasty, inventive food served here : thin scallops of salmon that you cook yourself on a hot stone, *bar poché au cidre aux artichauts et chips pommes fruits, sardines marinées aux peches blanches, salade tiède à l'andouille de Guéméné*. Savoury tiny vegetables grown locally by François Le Lagadec, farm-raised chicken rubbed with curry. Lovely cellar, moderately priced. Fabulous *figues rôties au vin de framboise et cassis, miroton de fruits frais*, 80-190.
★★ *Menez*, Plouezoc'h, 8 km, rte de Plougasnou, ☎ 98.67.28.85, 10 rm 🅿 ≼ ⌂ ⌕ ⌕ closed Mon lunch, Sat eve and Sun, 1-31 May, 15 Sep-27 Oct, 150.

Restaurants :
● ♦ *Au Passé Simple*, 21, rue Ch.-de-Gaulle, ☎ 98.88.71.02, AE Euro Visa ♪ closed Mon, 15-30 Oct. Savoury, fresh, modern cuisine, 50-120.
♦ *Bistrot Boeuf*, 7, pl. de Viarmes, ☎ 98.88.61.18, Euro Visa ≼ ⌂ closed Mon noon and Sun. For not much money, enjoy one of the fine meat dishes served in this nostalgic decor, supervised by P. Jeffroy. Spec : *beignets de boeuf J. Cocteau, miroton sous feuilletage*, 70-110.

Recommended
Guide to wines : *La Maison du Vin*, pl. des Viarmes, ☎ 98.88.72.43, Wines, liqueurs, brandies.
Handicrafts : at Brasparts, 7 km, *Breton creative crafts centre*, La Ferme Saint-Michel, ☎ 98.81.41.13, quality handicrafts.
Youth hostel : 3, rte de Paris, ☎ 98.88.13.63.
♥ crêperie : *Grall*, 6, rue au Fil, ☎ 98.88.50.51 ; at Sainte-Melaine, Breton cakes : *Au Four Sainte-Melaine*.

Nearby

CARANTEC, ⊠ 29226, 10 km SE of **Saint-Pol-de-Léon**.
🛈 pl. Ch.-de-Gaulle, ☎ 98.67.00.43.

Hotel :
★ *Falaise*, plage du Kelenn, ☎ 98.67.00.53, 26 rm 🅿 ≼ ⌂ ⌂ ⌕ half pens (h.s.), closed 25 Apr-25 May, 20 Sep-12 Apr, 265. Rest. ♦ ≼ ⌕ 60-115.

⚠ ★★★*Mouettes* (140 pl), ☎ 98.67.02.46 ; ★★*Méneyer* (58 pl), ☎ 98.67.00.13.

PLOUNÉRIN, ⊠ 22780, 23 km E on the anc. RN12.

Hotel :
★★ *Relais de Bon Voyage*, ☎ 96.38.61.04, AE DC, 3 rm P
◳ closed Tue eve and Wed, 5-28 Jan, 220. Rest. ● ♦♦
♪ Patrick Fer, formerly of la Pyramide in Vienne, cooks up some pretty fair specialties using fine Breton products. Spec : *turbot braisé au champagne, salade de choux aux filets de canard*, 85-220.

TAULÉ, ⊠ 29231, 11 km W.

Hotel :
★ *Le Relais des Primeurs*, 17, rue de la Gare, ☎ 98.67.11.03, 16 rm P ⬓ ◳ half pens (h.s.), closed Fri eve and Sat lunch, 30 Aug-27 Sep, 290. Rest. ♦ ♪ ◌ 50-115.

Recommended
♥ at Land'C'Hoat, syrups : *du Merle Fruitier*. Exceptional fruit syrups.

NANTES***

Angers 89, Rennes 107, Paris 377 km
pop 247227 ⊠ 44000   D4

Nantes is the principal city in western France, the link between the Atlantic and the rest of the country; during the days of Brittany's autonomy, Nantes was its capital city. Today it is a town of shady courtyards, alleyways and boulevards; it has a cathedral, a château, massive towers and balconied mansions. The busy port takes ships of up to 20 000 tons.

▶ Pedestrian precinct of **old streets** around the **church of Sainte-Croix** (D3; 17thC); 15th-16thC timbered houses (SI in the former Apothecaries' Hall; 16thC); others, more recent, in stone with carved human and animal heads. Second-hand shops, *croissanteries*, fashion boutiques in this most lively quarter. ▶ The **fortress**★★ (E2) dates from 1466; buildings of various periods around the inner courtyard, including the Grand Logis★ (*SW; Gothic*); note the Flamboyant pinnacled gables over the dormer windows, in contrast with the severe mass of the building. 12thC keep, with three museums *(daily, 10-12 & 2-6; closed Tue. ex Jul.-Aug.)* : the **Musée d'Art Populaire Régional**★ (Regional Folk Art Museum : the five Breton départments, plus the Vendée), the **Musée d'Art Décoratif** (Decorative Art Museum : furniture, lace, 16thC Rhodes ceramics), and the **Naval Museum** ("Musée des Salorges"). ▶ The **cathedral**★ (E2) is still undergoing renovation after a fire in 1971. This superb, soaring Gothic building (begun in 1434) has 15thC carvings on the inner façade; tomb of François II★★ by Michel Colombe, Brittany's greatest sculptor. ▶ On the S side of the cathedral, see the **Psalette**, former 16thC chapter-house; on the N side, the 15thC Gate of St. Pierre. Remains of the Gallo-Roman surrounding wall have been uncovered nearby. ▶ **Musée des Beaux-Arts**★★★ (Fine Arts Museum; E1 ; *daily ex Tue. and nat. hols., 9:15-12 & 2-6, 5 out of season*); excellent French, Flemish and Italian paintings (three major works by Georges de La Tour, two paintings by Monet; Rubens, Tintoretto, Guardi, and an anonymous Florentine triptych); a number of contemporary works. ▶ **Jardin des Plantes**★ (botanical gardens; F1-2) has marvellous magnolias and camellias; glass-houses of rare plants recall French colonial days. ▶ W of the Cours des Cinquante Otages (D1-2-3) is the **18thC part of town**, built with the wealth gained through colonial enterprise and triangular trading : trade goods exchanged for African slaves, slaves sold in Louisiana and the Antilles, and a return to Nantes with sugar cane. ▶ **The Place Royale**★ (C3) is one of the centres of this quarter, but don't miss **Passage Pommeraye**★★ (at the beginning of the Rue Santeuil), a delightful late 19thC shopping arcade with staircases, mirrors, statues and plaster work. ▶ The **Cours Cambronne**★ (B3; *to the W*) is surrounded by magnificent 18th-19thC houses with pilasters and balustrades. ▶ The **museum** *(daily 2-6 and Wed. 10-12; closed Mon. and Fri.)*; collections from Nantes' merchants and

travellers. ▶ The **Dobrée Museum**★★ occupies three buildings, one of which is the former Bishops' country house (15thC; *daily ex Tue., 10-12 & 2-6)* : antiquities, Romanesque and Gothic treasures, religious paintings and 15th-16thC sculptures. ▶ The former **Feydeau Island** (D3), now surrounded by asphalt, consists almost entirely of **mid-18thC mansions** built by merchants; fine façades looking on the Cours Franklin-Roosevelt, the Allée Turenne and the Rue Kervégan. ▶ Other fine buildings and mansions from the time of the French East India Company along the **Quai de la Fosse** (A-B-C4). ▶ Further to the W : view over the port, Beaulieu Island and the S banks of the Loire from **Sainte-Anne Butte**; nearby, a 19thC town house is now the **Jules Verne Museum** *(daily ex Tue., 10-12:30 & 2-5)* : life and work of this famous Nantes writer, who would no doubt have liked to visit the neighbouring **Planetarium** *(daily ex Mon., Tue. and Sun. am).*

Also... ▶ The **prefecture** (E-D1 ; 17thC) and surrounding area is strictly Classical, softened by the shady planetrees and terraces on the Erdre; 18thC private mansions in the Place du Maréchal-Foch. ▶ The **Town Hall** (hôtel de ville) and annexes : largely 17thC; on other side of the Bd de Strasbourg, Saint-Aignan mansion (15th-16thC).

Nearby

▶ The **Erdre Valley**★ *(to the N)*, best seen by boat (promenade and luncheon cruises : *24 Quai de Versailles, D1; daily Apr.-Aug.; rest of year* : tel. 40.20.24.50*; duration approx 3hr30)*. Numerous country houses can be seen on the trip, including the château de la Gâcherie (right bank, 15thC, much restored). ▶ The banks of the Loire★, upstream : a narrow road running along a dyke (good restaurants), parallels the S bank as far as **Champtoceaux** (in Anjou; *3 km from Nantes*; see the Promenade de Champalud★). Off the road, château de **Goulaine**★ (15th-16thC), last château on the Loire, the furthest downstream *(Jun.-Sep.)*, conservatory★★ of exotic butterflies, unique in continental Europe *(daily ex Tue., 16 Jun.-15 Sep.; rest of the year, Sat., Sun. and nat. hols., 2:30-6:30)* and church at **Loroux-Bottereau** (13thC frescos).   □

Practical Information ─────────────

NANTES
ⓘ pl. du Change (D2), ☎ 40.47.04.51.
✈ *Château-Bougon*, 10 km SW, ☎ 40.84.80.00. *Air France* office, pl. Neptune, ☎ 40.47.12.33; Château-Bougon airport, ☎ 40.84.02.17.
🚈 (F2), ☎ 40.50.50.50/40.74.63.65.
🚌 Champ-de-Mars (D3).
Car rental : *Avis*, Train station (F2), ☎ 40.74.39.74; Airport, ☎ 40.84.81.01.

Hotels :
★★★★(L) *Sofitel*, bd Alexandre-Millerand (B5), ☎ 40.47.61.03, Tx 710990, AE DC Euro Visa, 100 rm P ◄ ⬓ ◳ ❏ ♞ 430. Rest. ♦♦ ♪ 105-180.
● ★★★ *France*, 24, rue Crébillon (C3), ☎ 40.73.57.91, Tx 700633, AE DC Euro Visa, 76 rm P A hotel with character across from the Opera, 350. Rest. ♦♦ ◌ 70-135.
★★★ *Astoria*, 11, rue de Richebourg (C2), ☎ 40.74.39.90, 45 rm P ⬓ ◌ closed Aug, 230.
★★★ *Le Jules Verne*, (Mapotel), 3, rue du Couëdic, pl. Royale (C3), ☎ 40.35.74.50, Tx 701166, AE DC Euro Visa, 65 rm P ⬓ ◌ ♞ 240.
★★★ *Mapotel Central*, 4, rue du Couëdic (C3), ☎ 40.20.09.35, Tx 700666, AE DC Euro Visa, 125 rm, 290. Rest. ♦ 60-150.
★★ *Paris*, 2, rue Boileau (C3), ☎ 40.48.78.79, Tx 700615, Euro Visa, 50 rm P ♪ closed 24 Dec-2 Jan, 235.

Restaurants :
● ♦♦♦ *Le Manoir de la Comète*, 21, av. de la Libération, Saint-Sébastien-sur-Loire (off map F5), ☎ 40.34.15.93, DC Visa ⬓ closed Sat noon and Sun, 14 Feb-30 Mar, 3-18 Aug. Perfect peace and comfort in a large park, and the refined cuisine of Christian Thomas : *filets de sole crème d'oursin, pigeon en becasse*. Wines of the month, 100-280.

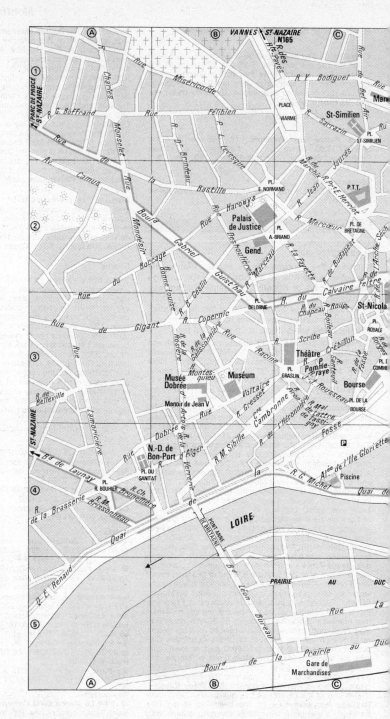

● ◆◆◆ *Maraîchers*, 21, rue Fouré (E-F3), ☎ 40.47.06.51, AE DC Visa ♪ closed Mon, Sat noon, Sun. Contemporary cuisine served until midnight, 145-240.

◆◆◆ *L'Esquinade*, 7, rue St-Denis (D2), ☎ 40.48.17.22,

AE DC Visa ♪ & closed Mon and Sun eve, 105-180.

● ◆◆ *Le Colvert*, 14, rue Armand-Brossard (D2), ☎ 40.48.20.02, AE DC Euro Visa, closed Sat noon and Sun, 31 Aug-23 Sep. Young Didier Macouin has a

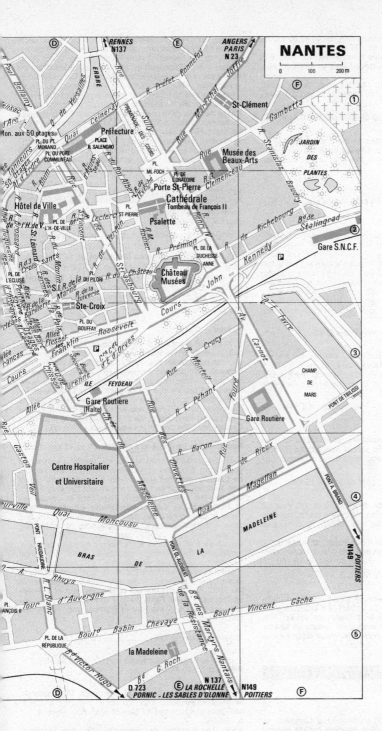

weakness for the cuisine of bygone eras. Why not ? It's pleasant enough, 100-250.
- ● ◆◆ **Mon Rêve**, Basse-Goulaine, on the route following the Loire (D 751), ☎ 40.03.55.50, AE DC Visa ⇐ 000 ♪ ♿

closed Wed and Sun eve , Feb school hols. Gérard Ryngel is faithful to his region : *brochet beurre blanc, cuisses de grenouilles au vin de pays*, 100-200 ; child : 70.

◆◆ **La Sirène**, 4, rue Kervégan (D3), ☎ 40.47.00.17, AE DC Euro Visa ♪ 50-100; child : 35.
◆◆ **Le Nantais**, 161, rue des Hauts-Pavés (off map B1), ☎ 40.76.59.54, Visa ▨ ♪ & closed eves ex Sat, 1-25 Aug, 80-160.
◆ **Brasserie de Talensac**, 14 bis, rue de Talensac, ☎ 40.89.55.59, Euro Visa ♪ & closed Mon and Sun eve , Aug, 65-110.

△ ★★★★*Val de Cens*, on D 69 (200 pl), ☎ 40.74.47.94.

Recommended
Leisure activities : *excursions on the Erdre*, info S.I..
♥ chocolates : *Gautier*, 9, rue Fosse et 18 bis, av. Emile-Boissier; at Pont-de-Bellevue, *foie gras* and smoked salmon : at the Rest. Delphin.

Nearby

Le pont de BELLEVUE, ⊠ 44470 Sainte-Luce-sur-Loire, 9 km E.

Restaurant :
● ◆◆◆ *J.-J. Delphin*, (Joseph Delphin), ☎ 40.25.60.39, AE DC Euro Visa ≼ closed Mon , Sun eve, Xmas hols, 10-31 Aug. Joseph Delphin is proud of his M.O.F. prize and his membership in this 'Académie culinaire'. His delicious cuisine is inspired by the local ingredients available in this fortunate region. Many original creations (indicated on the menu by the initials JD) : *royale de homard crème de noisette, estouffade de turbot au muscadet, ragoût de saumon frais au bonnezeaux*. Great Muscadets and other Loire Valley wines, 145-300.

ORVAULT, ⊠ 44700, 7 km NW on the D 42.

Hotel :
★★★★ *Le Domaine d'Orvault* (R.C.), chemin des Marais-du-Cens, ☎ 40.76.84.02, AE DC Visa, 30 rm ℗ ▨ ⌂ & ⤴ closed Mon lunch and Feb, 425. Rest. ● ◆◆◆ ♪ & A green and peaceful stopover. Spec : *blanc de turbot*. Fine list of Loire wines, 145-300.

SAINT-JEAN-DE-BOISSEAU, ⊠ 44640 Le Pellerin, 15 km W on the D 723-D 58.

Restaurant :
● ◆◆ *L'Enclos de la Cruaudière*, ☎ 40.65.66.10, Visa ▨ & closed Mon , Sun, Feb school hols, 20 Jul-20 Aug. G. Durand serves varied and imaginative seasonal cuisine, 220-250.

SAINT-JULIEN-DE-CONCELLES, ⊠ 44450, 15 km.

Restaurants :
◆◆ *Clémence*, La Chebuette, ☎ 40.54.10.18, DC Visa ≼ ♪ closed Sun eve , Feb. The cult of *beurre blanc*, invented by Clémence Praud in the late 19thC, is celebrated here, 125-200.
◆ *Auberge Nantaise*, Le Bout-des-Ponts, ☎ 40.54.10.73, AE Euro Visa ≼ ♪ closed Mon and Sun eve, 4-15 Jan. Nostalgic decor, attractive fixed meals, 80-180; child : 50.

Les SORINIÈRES, ⊠ 44400, 12 km S.

Hotel :
● ★★★★ *Abbaye de Villeneuve* (R.C.), rte des Sables-d'Olonnes, ☎ 40.04.40.25, Tx 710451, AE DC Euro Visa, 16 rm 1 apt ℗ ▨ ⌂ ▭ In a Cistercian abbey, 750. Rest. ◆◆ Spec : *jambon de magret de canette en salade, émincé de Saint-Jacques cressonnière aux légumes croquants*, 150-250.

pop 1255 ⊠ 29242   A1

▶ The centre of this island community is **Lampaul**. Its granite houses with their blue shutters huddle around the church; in the neighbouring cemetery, a mausoleum (1668) houses little wax crosses, each made when a man was lost at sea. The cross, known as "Croix de Broëlla" (*Bro:* country; *Ela:* return) replaced the man during funer-

al rites and was deposited in a reliquary in the church, before being solemnly transferred to this collective memorial. ▶ In the hamlet of **Niou Huella** *(barely 1 km W)*, is France's first **Ecomuseum**, two houses devoted to the island's way of life and traditions *(daily ex Tue.; Christmas school hols., Feb., Apr.-Jun. : 2-6; Easter hols., Jul.-Sep. : 11-6:30)* : see the furniture, made entirely of shipwreck wood (there are no trees on the island). ▶ To the W, the **Phare de Créac'h** is one of the most powerful lighthouses in the world (theoretical range 200 km; the foghorn can be heard 18 km away). This black and white-striped tower symbolises the island's identity. ▶ Walk across the heath : little black or white sheep, attached in pairs to low windbreaks shaped like three-armed stars, graze the salt grass (hence their delicious meat).   □

Saint-Brieuc 45, Morlaix 72, Paris 496 km
pop 8367 ⊠ 22500   C1

Paimpol is an unpretentious port and seaside town, the centre of the cod-fishing industry in the second half of the 19thC : **Musée Municipal de la Mer** (Maritime Museum : *daily Apr.-15 Sep., 10-12 & 3-7*). ▶ At the gates of the town is the **Abbey of Beauport★** *(guided tours at Easter, Whitsun and Jul.-20 Sep., 9-12:30 & 2-7);* important 13thC remains (chapter and the *salle au Duc*).

Nearby

▶ **Arcouest Point★★** *(6 km N);* boats for Bréhat Island (→) leave from the foot : marvellous view of the island and the reef-strewn sea. From both sides of the highway between Paimpol and Arcouest, little roads run towards the shore, where tiny ports are hidden among the hollyhocks, the broom and the pinewoods. ▶ **Loguivy-de-la-Mer** *(5 km N)* is one of them, a king prawn fishing port by the mouth of the Trieux (view★ from the heath). ▶ Fine walks along the coast to the S. ▶ Good view of the Trieux Estuary from the bridge at **Lézardrieux** *(5 km W)*.

Round trip to Lanleff and Kermaria *(28 to 40 km, 2 hr)*

Take the Lanvollon road for 9.5 km, reaching **Lanleff** on your right : a curious circular ruin known as the **Temple de Lanleff**, attributed successively to the Romans, Gauls and Templars, is in fact a church, almost certainly 11thC, built on the plan of the Holy Sepulchre in Jerusalem. ▶ The **chapel of Kermaria-an-Iskuit★** (House of Mary, restorer of health) dates principally from the 14th and 15thC; attractive porch and collection of interesting murals (end of 15thC); see the terrifying Danse Macabre★★ (47 pictures accompanied by naive captions, expressing the haunting presence of Death, the Great Leveller) : numerous sculptures★. ▶ **Lanloup** (16thC church) is only 2 km from the shore where, according to legend, the first Celtic immigrants from Britain landed in the 5thC. The site is marked by the tiny port of **Bréhec-en-Plouha**. ▶ **Bilfot Point**, 4 km from **Plouézec** : fine view over the islands in the Bay of Paimpol and, in the distance, Bréhat.   □

⓵ pl. de la République (closed pm), ☎ 96.20.83.16 (l.s.).
SNCF ☎ 96.20.81.22.

Hotels :
● ★★★ *Le Barbu*, pointe de l'Arcouest, Ploubazlanec, ☎ 96.55.86.98, Euro Visa, 20 rm ℗ ≼ ▨ ⌂ & ▭ ⤴ half pens (h.s.), closed 11 Nov-31 Mar, 650. Rest. ◆ ≼ ♪ & 100-260.
★★★ *Le Repaire de Kerroc'h*, 29, quai Morand, ☎ 96.20.50.13, AE Euro Visa, 7 rm ≼ ◈ ♪ 300. Rest. ◆◆ ♪ A new start for this typical 18th-C St-Malo dwelling. Wonderful fish, 120-200.
★★★ *Relais Brenner*, (I.L.A.), Pont de Lézardrieux,

☎ 96.20.11.05, Tx 740676, AE DC Euro Visa, 28 rm Ⓟ ⬩
♨ ⚲ ♪ ♿ half pens, closed Mon (l.s.), 410. Rest. ♦ ⬩ ♪
♿ In a pleasant setting, enjoy lobster, warm oysters with
seaweed, 140-220.

Restaurants :
♦♦ *Cotriade*, quai Dayot, ☎ 96.20.81.08, Euro Visa ⬩
closed Wed ex Jul-Aug, 15 Nov-15 Mar, 60-220.
♦♦ *La Vieille Tour*, 13, rue de l'Eglise, ☎ 96.20.83.18,
Visa ♪ ♿ closed Tue eve and Wed, 15 Nov-7 Dec, 70-150.

⚠ ★★*Cruckin* (100 pl), ☎ 96.20.78.47 ; at Lézardieux CP
22740, 5 km W, *Municipal* (70 pl), ☎ 96.20.17.22.

Recommended
Marina : at Lézardieux, ☎ 96.20.14.22.
Youth hostel : *Château de Keraoul*, ☎ 96.20.83.60.

Nearby

PLÉHÉDEL, ✉ 22290 Lanvollon, 7 km S on the D 7.

Hotel :
● ★★★ *Château de Coatguelen* (R.C.), D 7,
☎ 96.22.31.24, Tx 741300, AE DC Euro Visa, 16 rm Ⓟ ⬩
♨ ⚲ ▣ ♪ ♫ half pens (h.s.), closed 5 Jan-3 Apr, 1200.
Rest. ● ♦♦♦ ⬩ ♪ ℀ closed Tue noon and Wed noon.
In a handsome castle dating from 1850, Louis Le Roy
steams away with his usual force and talent, doing wonders with seaweed and sea salt. Spec : *huîtres chaudes
au cidre et aux poireaux, éventail de ris de veau et de
homard*, 130-300 ; child : 70.

Forest of PAIMPONT

C2
Round trip to Plélan-le-Grand *(signposted; 66 km; 1/2
day; see map 8)*

The largest of Brittany's forests (70 km^2) is only a
remnant of the great forest of **Brocéliande**, mentioned in the legends of King Arthur and his knights. The
forest covered the whole of central Armorica (Brittany), and was reputedly the scene of some of
the adventures of the knights of King Arthur's Round
Table. This magnificent forest site today includes no
fewer than 14 lakes.

▶ The **château de Brocéliande,** in Norman style, and the
château at Le Pas du Houx, are set on either side of a
lake. Both date from early this century. ▶ Rather than
stopping for the too few remnants of Telhouët priory
along the D71, turn left coming out of the forest : "Merlin's
tomb" and a "fountain of youth" (two slabs of schist and,
150 m away, a spring). ▶ The 15th-19thC **château de
Comper** *(ext. visit Easter-Oct., ex Wed. and Thu.; rest of
year, ex Sat. and Sun.)* stands silhouetted between three

lakes. ▶ The ivy-covered **château du Rox** backs onto the
forest. ▶ **Tréhorenteuc** has a church unusually "restored"
some years ago by a parish priest, an amateur of legends
and symbols. The **Val sans Retour** (Valley of No Return)
is a rocky ravine reached from the foot of a little 16thC
manor ; here, according to the Arthurian legend, the
wizard Merlin was held captive in a prison of air...
▶ Looking down from the road you can see the **château
de Trécesson★**, an austere and unusual castle in brown
rock. ▶ **Paimpont**, in a large clearing by a lake★, owes its
origin to an abbey ; 17thC building (temporary exhibitions
in season) and large 13thC church. ▶ The **Paimpont Forges** used to produce steel of the highest quality from
local iron ore and charcoal. All that is left today among
the ancient trees by the two lakes are two small châteaux
(modern), two chapels, and the remains of the workshops
and furnace. □

Practical Information

PAIMPONT, ✉ 35380.
ⓘ Office touristique de Brocéliande at the mairie of Plélan,
☎ 99.06.86.07. ♥

Hotel :
Manoir du Tertre, 4 km on the D 71, ☎ 99.07.81.02, Visa,
8 rm Ⓟ ⬩ ♨ ⚲ ℀ half pens (h.s.), closed Tue, Feb. A
16th-C manor house, 160. Rest. ♦ ⬩ ♪ ℀ 60-170.

Recommended
Bicycle-rental : ☎ 99.06.83.03.

PERROS-GUIREC*

Morlaix 50, Saint-Brieuc 74, Paris 526 km
pop 7497 ✉ 22700   B1
Despite the crowds that fill its forty hotels and flock
to the beaches and casino, this, the second-largest
resort on the North Brittany Coast, has not succumbed
to expansionism. Excellent harbour, strange rock
formations and elegant 1900s-era houses.

▶ Sheltered by the Pointe du Château, **Trestrignel
beach★** is lined with villas, some of extravagant size ;
near the beach at **Trestraou★** is the Palais des Congrès
(Convention Hall), Seawater Institut de Cure Marine and
the yachting centre. Superb views of Tomé Island, reefs
and islets from the Sentier des Douaniers, which links the
two beaches and continues west towards Ploumanac'h
(1 hr from Trestraou).

Nearby

▶ **Les Sept Iles** (the Seven Islands) are some 4.5 km
off the coast. The main island is the **Ile aux Moines ;** lighthouse and 1720 fort. The remainder, in particular the
Ile Rouzic (to seaward) and the **Ile Malban,** are now
bird sanctuaries *(no visits)* where gulls, cormorants, guillemots and especially puffins, gannets, oyster catchers and
petrels can be seen in the distance.

**The Côte de Granit Rose★★ (Pink Granite Coast), from
Perros Guirec to Trébeurden** *(18 km)*

After Perros, the road runs past the chapel of Notre-Dame
de Clarté (1445, *Pardon* 15 Aug. ; panorama★ from neighbouring orientation table) and cuts across the **Ploumanac'h** peninsula : see the strangely shaped coppery-pink
rocks on Squewel Point★, a protected area ; 500 m W,
lighthouse *(Jul.-Aug., 2-5).* ▶ Similar rocks around **Tré-
gastel★ ;** near Coz-Porz beach are caves with a small
archaeological museum and an aquarium *(Easter holidays
and May : week-ends and nat. hols. ; Jun., Sep. daily :
2-6:30; Jul.-Aug., 9-9).* ▶ 3 km S : **Trégastel-Bourg** has a
16thC church and 17thC ossuary, surrounded by a cemetery. In front of it stands a menhir, known locally as the
"Menhir of Virility". ▶ The Pleumeur-Bodou road (→ Lannion) will take you to see a number of menhirs ; almost
opposite this road is another leading to **Ile Grande,** linked
to the mainland by a bridge ; nearby on the little **island
of Aval** is a megalith supposed to be the tomb of King

8. Forest of Paimpont

Arthur. ▶ More rocks, white sand and a *corniche* (cliff road) overlooking islands and peninsulas at **Trébeurden,** a large family resort. □

Practical Information

PERROS-GUIREC
ⓘ 21, pl. de l'Hôtel de Ville, ☎ 96.23.21.15.
✈ *The pink granite coast,* Lannion, 9 km S, ☎ 96.48.42.92.
⛴ ☎ 96.23.22.47, To les Sept Iles daily, Easter-late Sep; for same period, Guernesay twice a week.

Hotels :
● ★★★ ***Le Sphinx***, 67, chem. de la Messe, ☎ 96.23.25.42, AE DC Euro Visa, 11 rm ⚘ ♨ ♘ ♪ ♿ closed 3 Jan-15 Mar, 15 Nov-20 Dec, 250. Rest. ♦♦ ⚘ ♪ ♿ Private fish-pond, 110-200.
★★★ ***France***, 14, rue Rouzig, ☎ 96.23.20.27, 30 rm Ⓟ ⚘ ♨ ♘ ♪ half pens (h.s.), closed Sun eve and Mon lunch, 3 Jan-1 Feb, 1 Nov-15 Dec, 400. Rest. ♦ ♪ closed 1 Nov-15 Mar, 65-170; child : 55.
★★★ ***Grand Hôtel de Trestraou***, bd Joseph-Le-Bihan, ☎ 96.23.24.05, AE DC Euro Visa, 71 rm Ⓟ ⚘ 300. Rest. ♦ 80-130.
★★★ ***Morgane***, (Inter-Hôtel), pl. de Trestraou, ☎ 96.23.22.80, AE DC Euro Visa, 30 rm Ⓟ ⚘ ♨ ♘ ▣ half pens (h.s.), closed 30 Oct-1 Apr, 240. Rest. ♦ ⚘ ✗ 75-150; child : 35.
★★★ ***Printania***, 12, rue des Bons-Enfants, ☎ 96.23.21.00, DC Euro Visa, 38 rm Ⓟ ♨ ♘ ⚲ closed 20 Dec-5 Jan, 280. Rest. ♦ ♪ ✗ closed Mon noon and Sun eve, 100-200.
★★ ***Les Feux des Iles*** (L.F.), 53, bd Clemenceau, ☎ 96.23.22.94, DC Euro Visa, 15 rm Ⓟ ⚘ ♨ ♘ ♪ ⚲ half pens (h.s.), closed Sun eve , Mon (l.s.), Feb, 15 Oct-20 Nov, 440. Rest. ♦ ⚘ ♪ ✗ 75-250.
★ ***Ker Ys*** (L.F.), 12, rue du Mal-Foch, ☎ 96.23.22.16, DC Euro Visa, 30 rm Ⓟ ♨ ✗ half pens (h.s.), closed Tue, 10 Oct-15 Feb, 180. Rest. ♦ 80-130.

Restaurants :
♦♦♦ ***Le Homard Bleu***, plage de Trestraou, ☎ 96.23.24.55, Euro Visa ⚘ ♨ ♪ ♿ closed Jan, 75-160.
♦ ***Crémaillère***, 13, pl. de l'Eglise, ☎ 96.23.22.08, AE DC Euro Visa ♪ closed Mon, 1-15 Feb. Spec : *ragoût de homard au champagne*, 70-200.

⛺ ★★★★*Le Ranolien*, ☎ 96.23.21.13; ★★★*Claire Fontaine*, rue du Pont-Hélé (180 pl), ☎ 96.23.03.55; ★★★*Trestraou*, av. du Casino (180 pl), ☎ 96.23.08.11.

Nearby

PLOUMANAC'H, ⊠ 22700 Perros-Guirec, 5 km W.
ⓘ pl. du Centre (in summer), ☎ 96.23.06.63.

Hotel :
● ★★ ***Rochers*** (L.F.), chem. de la Pointe, ☎ 96.23.23.02, Euro Visa, 15 rm ⚘ ♘ ♪ ✗ half pens (h.s.), closed Sep-Easter, 600. Rest. ♦♦ ⚘ ♪ ✗ closed Wed (l.s.), 100-250; child : 55.

TRÉBEURDEN, ⊠ 22560, 11 km S of **Trégastel**.
ⓘ pl. Crech-Hery, ☎ 96.23.51.64, closed Sun.
✈ *Lannion-Servel*, 8 km SE.
⛴ ☎ 96.23.51.64, sea excursions.

Hotels :
● ★★★ ***Manoir de Lan Kerellec*** (R.C.), allée centrale de Lan Kerellec, ☎ 96.23.50.09, AE Euro Visa, 14 rm Ⓟ ⚘ ♨ ♘ ♪ ⚲ closed Mon, Tue lunch, 15 Nov-15 Mar, 450. Rest. ● ♦♦ ⚘ ♪ Your happiness will be complete with J.-L. Danjou's good cooking and the warm welcome that G. Daubé extends to visitors at his adorable manor house, 120-220.
● ★★★ ***Ti Al-Lannec*** (R.S.), allée de Mézo-Guen, ☎ 96.23.57.26, Tx 740656, AE Visa, 22 rm Ⓟ ⚘ ♨ ♘ half pens (h.s.), closed 15 Nov-15 Mar, 690. Rest. ♦ ⚘ ♪ ✗ closed Mon noon, 95-250; child : 60.

⛺ ★★★*Hostiou Kerdual* (35 pl), ☎ 96.23.54.86; at Penvern, ★★★*Espérance* (50 pl), ☎ 96.23.95.35; at Pors Mabo, ★★★*Armor-Loisirs* (120 pl), ☎ 96.23.52.31.

Recommended
Youth hostel : *Pors Toëno*, corniche de Goas-Treiz, ☎ 96.23.52.22.

TRÉGASTEL, ⊠ 22730, 7 km E.
ⓘ pl. Sainte-Anne, ☎ 96.23.88.67.
✈ *Lannion-Servel*, 8 km S.

Hotels :
★★★ ***Belle Vue***, (France-Accueil), 20, rue des Calculots, ☎ 96.23.88.18, Euro Visa, 33 rm Ⓟ ⚘ ♨ ♘ 🏇 half pens (h.s.), closed 5 Nov-16 Apr, 600. Rest. ♦♦ ***Le Souper du Pêcheur Gourmand*** ♪ closed 15 Nov-15 May, 95-180.
★★ ***Beau Séjour***, (Inter-Hôtel), plage du Coz-Pors, ☎ 96.23.88.02, AE DC Euro Visa, 20 rm Ⓟ ⚘ half pens (h.s.), closed 30 Sep-1 Apr, 480. Rest. ♦ ⚘ 80-180.
★ ***La Corniche***, 38, rue Ch.-Le Goffic, ☎ 96.23.88.15, 20 rm Ⓟ ⚘ half pens (h.s.), closed (l.s.), 295. Rest. ♦ closed lunch, 55-80.

⛺ ★★★*Golven*, baie de Kervalos (160 pl), ☎ 96.23.87.77; ★★*Tourony* (100 pl), ☎ 96.23.86.61.

PLEYBEN**

Châteaulin 10, Brest 57, Paris 541 km
pop 3897 ⊠ 29190 B2

The parish churchyard here has the same structure and richness as those of the Léon region, testifying to the creativity of Breton art and the wealth of the farmers who made up the parish councils in the 16th and 17thC.

▶ Even before you reach the entrance (1725) you will be struck by the **Calvary**★★ (mid-16thC with later additions), one of the most impressive of its kind. ▶ The Flamboyant Gothic **ossuary** houses pieces of stonework and statues; exhibitions in summer. ▶ The Flamboyant Gothic **church**★ (1564) contrasts with the solidity of the Renaissance bell-tower. Timberwork★ from late 16thC; beams carved with rustic, macabre or burlesque scenes; interesting furniture and numerous old statues. ▶ Within a 3-km radius are seven other chapels; see those at **Gard-Maria** (*SE;* 17thC) with a small Calvary, and, to the N, **Lannéleg.** □

PLONÉVEZ-PORZAY

Quimper 21, Brest 62, Paris 565 km
pop 1645 ⊠ 29127 Plomodiern A2

ⓘ ☎ 98.92.53.57.

Hotel :
● ★★ ***Manoir de Moëllien*** (R.S.), ☎ 98.92.50.40, DC Euro Visa, 10 rm Ⓟ ⚘ ♨ ♘ ♿ half pens (h.s.), closed Wed (l.s.), 12 Nov-20 Mar, 530. Rest. ● ♦♦ ♪ ♿ In a manor house dating from 1642 set in the Porzay countryside, are tastefully furnished rooms and enjoyable food : an excellent value, 60-180; child : 35.

⛺ ★★★*Kervel* (250 pl), ☎ 98.92.51.54; ★★*Le Porzay* (80 pl), ☎ 98.92.50.51; ★★*Sainte-Anne* (100 pl), ☎ 98.92.51.17; ★★*Treguer-Plage* (333 pl), ☎ 98.92.51.91.

PLOUGASTEL-DAOULAS*

Brest 11, Quimper 62, Paris 593 km
pop 9611 ⊠ 29213 A2

Renowned for its strawberries and its gentle climate, in the centre of a wide peninsula jutting into the Brest roadsteads; panoramic views. The town has one of the most beautiful **Calvaries**★★ (1602) in the region, with more than 150 figures.

▶ 3 km E, **Kergoff Manor,** a former hunting lodge of the Rohan family; chapel of St. Christine (*4 km W;* 16thC) with a churchyard; **pointe de l'Armorique** (view★); chapel of St. Guénolé (15thC) on road to **Keraménez.** ▶ 10 km E from Plougastel : Daoulas★ has a Romanesque church next to monastic buildings of great elegance (12thC cloister); a rare and beautiful example of Romanesque architecture in Finistère. ▶ 7 km SE of Daoulas : don't miss the little-known **chapel** of **Notre-Dame de Lorette;** curious Calvary★, like a stylised anchor. □

Practical Information ───────────

Restaurant :
♦♦ *Le Chevalier de l'Auberlac'h,* 5, rue Mathurin-Thomas, ☎ 98.40.54.56 ♪ closed Sun eve. Serge Bonnamour's cooking is a real treat : *Assiette de l'Océan, fricassée de langoustines,* 115-200.

⚘ ★★*Clé des Champs* (57 pl), ☎ 98.40.36.14 ; ★★*Saint-Jean* (100 pl), ☎ 98.40.32.90.

PONT-AVEN*

Quimper 32, Lorient 38, Paris 527 km
pop 3295 ⊠ 29123   B2-3
Best known for its associations with the painter Paul Gauguin. He first stayed here in 1886 and soon attracted a group of young painters, subsequently known as the School of Pont-Aven, who followed him some three years later to Le Pouldu.

▶ **Municipal Museum** *(Apr.-Sep.)* : temporary exhibitions of regional painters. ▶ ▶ Former **Mill** (15thC), Breton furniture and decor. ▶ **Tremals** : 16thC chapel (inside, 18thC wood Christ, model for Gauguin's "Christ jaune"). ▶ **Nizon** : Romanesque Calvary also inspired Gauguin. ▶ Pleasant walks along the **banks of the Aven** to the S; château de Hénan *(4 km;* 15th-16thC), fine site above the estuary. ▶ **Port-Manec'h** *(10 km S),* site★ at the mouth of the Aven. ▶ 4.5 km E : **Riec-sur-Bélon** owes its fame to exquisite oysters and a famous restaurant. □

Practical Information ───────────
PONT-AVEN
ℹ ☎ 98.05.04.70.
Hotel :
★ *Les Ajoncs d'Or,* pl. de l'Hôtel-de-Ville, ☎ 98.06.02.06, Euro Visa, 14 rm, closed Sun eve and Mon (l.s.), 160. Rest. ♦ 70-160 ; child : 25.
Restaurants :
● ♦♦♦ *Moulin de Rosmadec,* on the edge of the river Aven, ☎ 98.06.00.22 ꝲ ♪ ☜ closed Wed , Feb, 15 Oct-11 Nov. In a handsome Breton setting, a classic menu with the accent on seafood, 90-220.
● ♦♦ *La Taupinière,* rte de Concarneau, ☎ 98.06.03.12, AE DC Euro Visa ♪ ☜ closed Mon eve and Tue, 3-31 Jan, 3 Sep-15 Oct. Lots of charm and good cooking in a lovely cottage. Spec : *langoustines grillées sauce à l'estragon, le millefeuille aux tourteaux, filet de Saint-Pierre à la crème de poireaux,* 180-260.

⚘ ★★*Roz-Pin,* rte de Névez (600 pl), ☎ 98.06.03.13.

Nearby
MOËLAN-SUR-MER, ⊠ 29116, 13 km SE.
ℹ rte des Moulins, ☎ 98.96.67.28.
Hotels :
● ★★★★ *Les Moulins du Duc* (R.C.), at 2 km NW on the banks of Belon, ☎ 98.39.60.73, Tx 940080, AE DC Euro Visa, 27 rm ℗ ꝲ ♤ ☐ closed 15 Jan-28 Feb, 460. Rest. ● ♦♦ ꝲ ♪ Xavier Gabarit, a young pupil of Charles Barrier, mans the kitchen. Sophisticated fish specialties, 150-220.
Manoir de Kertalg, (I.L.A., C.H.), ☎ 98.39.77.77, Euro Visa, 9 apt ℗ ꝲ ꝲꝲ ♤ ♪ ⁄⁰ closed 5 Jan-1 Apr, 500.

⚘ ★★*Ile Percée* (65 pl), ☎ 98.56.98.92 ; at Kerfany-les-Pins, ★★*Tal ar Moor* (66 pl), ☎ 98.71.01.43.

┌──┐
│ Be advised that hotels and restaurants in this Guide │
│ have perhaps changed addresses; prices indicated │
│ are also subject to modifications. │
└──┘

PORT-MANECH, ⊠ 29139 Névez, 13 km S.

Hotel :
★★ *Ar-Moor,* ☎ 98.06.82.48, Visa, 36 rm ℗ ꝲ ꝲꝲ closed Oct-Mar, 230. Rest. ♦ 75-200.

RAGUENES-PLAGE, ⊠ 29139 Névez, 12 km SW.

Hotel :
★★ *Le Men-Du,* rue des Iles, ☎ 98.06.84.22, 14 rm ℗ ꝲ ꝲꝲ ♤ ☜ closed 25 Sep-1 Apr, 200.

RIEC-SUR-BELON, ⊠ 29124, 5 km E.
ℹ ☎ 98.06.97.65.

Hotels :
★★★ *Kerland* (C.H.), D 24, rte de Moëlan, ☎ 98.06.42.98, Euro Visa, 20 rm ℗ ꝲ ꝲꝲ ♤ closed Sun eve , Mon lunch, Feb school hols, 350. Rest. ♦♦ ꝲ ♪ ♿ closed Mon noon and Sun eve (l.s.), 85-150 ; child : 55.
★ *Chez Mélanie,* pl. de l'Eglise, ☎ 98.06.91.05, 7 rm ℗ ꝲꝲ closed Jan, 15 Nov-15 Dec, 180. Rest. ● ♦♦ closed Tue. Mélanie is no longer in the kitchen, but life goes on, and so do the lobster specialties in this handsome Breton inn, 90-130.

⚘ ★★*Belon* (150 pl), ☎ 98.06.90.58.

PONTIVY

Vannes 52, Saint-Brieuc 64, Paris 460 km
pop 14224 ⊠ 56300   C2
The old town and its 15thC château have a distinctly Breton character; the new town dates from 1805 and was built on almost military lines at the orders of Napoleon.

▶ In the heart of old Pontivy are the **Place du Martray★,** the Rues du Pont and du Fil, lined with old 15th-16thC houses. 16thC Flamboyant Gothic church. ▶ The **château de Rohan★** (15thC fortress ; *15 Apr.-15 Oct., 10-12 & 2-6 ; 2-4 out of season ex Mon. and Tue. ; closed Nov.-Dec.);* set on a hillside, with outer fortifications intact. ▶ 17th-18thC bourgeois houses in the Rue de Lourmel.

Nearby
▶ Naïf statues in the porch of the 15th-16thC church at Noyal-Pontivy *(7 km E).* ▶ 2 km further on, **Sainte-Noyale** is the scene of a *Pardon* for horses *(last Sun. in Jun.).* Fine religious buildings★ : oratory, fountain, ornate cross, Flamboyant Gothic chapel (painted 17thC panelling★). □

Practical Information ───────────
PONTIVY
ℹ rue du Gal-de-Gaulle, ☎ 97.25.04.10 (h.s.).
SNCF ☎ 97.25.00.20.
Hotels :
★★ *Martin* (L.F.), 1, rue Leperdit, ☎ 97.25.02.04, Euro Visa, 30 rm ℗ ♪ closed Sun in winter, 15 Dec-15 Jan, 130. Rest. ♦ ♪ ♿ 50-120 ; child : 35.
★ *Robic,* 2-4, rue J.-Jaurès, ☎ 97.25.11.80, Euro Visa, 26 rm ℗ ꝲꝲ 120. Rest. ♦ 40-110.

Nearby
BUBRY, ⊠ 56310, 22 km SW.
Hotel :
★★ *Auberge de Coët-Diquel* (L.F.), ☎ 97.51.70.70, Euro Visa, 20 rm ℗ ꝲꝲ ♤ ♪ ♿ ☐ ⁄⁰ half pens (h.s.), closed 1 Dec-15 Mar, 485. Rest. ♦ ꝲ ♪ ♿ 60-120 ; child : 50.

PORNIC

Nantes 51, La Roche-sur-Yon 79, Paris 428 km
pop 8709 ⊠ 44210   C4
This small natural port at the end of a deep inlet is a cosy seaside resort and capital of the Jade coast. The port★ is the most attractive area with sailing boats at the foot of the 13th-14thC castle and its surrounding

greenery; its tiled roofs give it a slightly Mediterranean air.

Nearby

▶ **Bourgneuf-en-Retz** *(15 km SE)* : at the back of a wide sandy bay; museum of the Retz area *(9-12 & 2-5, Jun.-Sep.; closed Tue.; Wed., Sat., Sun. only out of season).* ▶ **Saint-Gildas Point** *(NW; panorama*★*)* marks the end of the rocky coast; from here to the mouth of the Loire, the **Jade Coast** (Côte de Jade) becomes a 16-km long, gently sloping beach, lined with pine-covered dunes. Principal resorts : **Tharon-Plage, Saint-Brévin-les-Pins**, which offers a sudden air of Provence with its dunes, 8 km of beach and lovely stretch of pine after the bridge at Saint-Nazaire. **Mindin** is part of Saint-Brévin; a part of 1861 is now a small Naval Museum (models, temporary exhibitions; *3-6:30 daily, Easter hols. and 15 May-15 Sep.; Sat. and Sun. Easter-15 May).* ☐

Practical Information ───────────────

PORNIC
ⓘ pl. du Môle, ☎ 40.82.04.40.
SNCF ☎ 40.82.00.06.

Hotel :
★★ **Sablons**, Sainte-Marie-sur-Mer, 3 km W, ☎ 40.82.09.14, Euro Visa, 30 rm Ⓟ ◫ ◌ 170. Rest. ♦ ♪ ❀ 85-160.

△ ★★★*Patisseau* (150 pl), ☎ 40.82.10.39; ★★*Bleuets* (170 pl), ☎ 40.82.11.07; ★★*Boutinardière* (323 pl), ☎ 40.82.05.68; ★★*Madrag ue* (400 pl), ☎ 40.82.06.73; ★★*Source* (100 pl), ☎ 40.82.04.37.

Recommended
Casino : quai Leray, ☎ 40.82.26.87.

Nearby

SAINT-BRÉVIN-LES-PINS, ⊠ 44250, 17 km N.
ⓘ 10, rue de l'Eglise, ☎ 40.27.24.32.

Hotels :
★★ **Le Débarcadère** (L.F.), pl. de la Marine, ☎ 40.27.20.53, AE DC Euro Visa, 17 rm Ⓟ ◄ ◫ ◌ pens (h.s.), closed Sun eve, 15 Nov-15 Jan, 360. Rest. ♦ ◄ ♪ 40-150.
★ **Le Kayac** (L.F.), 119, av. Mal-Foch, ☎ 40.27.22.37, 11 rm Ⓟ ◌ ♭ half pens (h.s.), closed 15 Oct-15 Mar, 340. Rest. ♦ ♪ 45-100.

△ ★★*Farandole* (200 pl), ☎ 40.27.92.95; ★★*Pierre Attelée* (600 pl), ☎ 40.27.80.32; ★★*Pierres Couchées* (250 pl), ☎ 40.27.85.64; ★★*Rochelets* (300 pl), ☎ 40.27.40.25.

QUIBERON

Vannes 46, Lorient 49, Paris 502 km
pop 4812 ⊠ 56170   B3

Quiberon is a tourist town on a peninsula (normal population 7 000) which receives more than 100 000 visitors each year. This is the Côte Sauvage (Wild Coast) : Quiberon and its beach, sheltered by Belle-Île; Port Haliguen, Saint-Pierre and Kerhostin face inland across the bay.

▶ At the entrance to the peninsula, the **Galion Ship Museum**, dedicated to the art of shell design *(15 Apr.-Sep., 9:30-12:30 & 2-7:30).* ▶ **Trip around the peninsula :** 16.5 km to Port-Blanc. ▶ The *corniche* starts at **Port-Haliguen** : at the SE end of the peninsula, Conguel Point provides a lovely view of the bay, Houat and Belle-Île. Return past Quiberon via **Goulvars Point** (Thalassotherapy Institute founded in 1964) and follow the **Côte Sauvage★**, a long succession of rugged cliffs, pierced by caves, arches and tunnels filled with the din of wind and sea. ☐

Practical Information ───────────────

ⓘ 7, rue de Verdun, ☎ 97.50.07.84.
SNCF ☎ 97.50.07.07.
⬤➤ ☎ 97.50.06.90, to Belle-Ile, in 45 mn, (in season, reserve for cars). For Houat and Hoédic (1h and 1h30).

Hotels :
★★★★(L) **Sofitel Thalassa**, pointe de Goulvars, ☎ 97.50.20.00, Tx 730712, AE DC Euro Visa, 113 rm Ⓟ ◄ ◫ ◌ ♪ ◫ ❀ closed 2 Jan-1 Feb, 930. Rest. ♦♦♪ ◌ ❀ 175-250; child : 80.
★★★★ **Sofitel Diététique**, ☎ 97.50.20.00, AE DC Euro Visa, 76 rm Ⓟ ◄ ◫ ◌ ◫ ♪◌ closed 4 Jan-8 Feb, 1000. Rest. ♦ ❀ 200-300.
★★★ **Ker Noyal**, chemin des Dunes, ☎ 97.50.08.41, AE DC Euro Visa, 100 rm Ⓟ ◌ ❀ closed 31 Oct-15 Mar, 370. Rest. ♦ ♪ ❀ 120-140.
★★ **La Petite Sirène**, 15, bd René-Cassin, ☎ 97.50.17.34, Tx 950538, AE DC, 14 rm 5 apt ◄ ◌ ♪ ❀ closed 5 Nov-20 Mar. 15 independent studio apartments equipped with kitchenette, 200. Rest. ♦ ◄ ♪ ◌ ❀ closed Wed (l.s.), 80-190; child : 60.
★★ **Plage** (L.F.), 25, quai d'Orange, ☎ 97.30.92.10, 44 rm Ⓟ ◄ half pens, closed 6 Oct-1 Apr, 250. Rest. ♦ ♪ ❀ 75-150.
★ **Deux Mers**, rue Surcouf, Penthièvre-Plage, ☎ 97.52.33.75, Visa, 27 rm Ⓟ ◄ ◫ ◌ pens (h.s.), closed Oct-Mar, 360. Rest. ♦ 55-100.
★ **L'Océan** (L.F.), 7, quai de l'Océan, ☎ 97.50.07.58, 38 rm Ⓟ ◄ pens (h.s.), closed 15 Nov-1 Apr, 325. Rest. ♦ ◄ 60-90.

Restaurants :
♦♦ **Le Relax**, 27, bd de Castéro, ☎ 97.50.12.84, AE DC Euro Visa ◄ ◌ ♪ closed Tue and Sun eve, 15 Nov-31 Mar, 50-130.
● ♦ **La Goursen**, 10, quai de l'Océan, ☎ 97.50.07.94, AE Visa ♪ closed Tue, 15 Nov-20 Mar. Fish and more fish, fresh-caught nearby, prepared in a dozen appealing ways and affordably priced, 190-250.
♦ **La Taverne**, Portivy, by St-Pierre, ☎ 97.30.91.61 ◄ ◫ ♪ ◌ closed Wed, 4 Nov-1 Mar. Spec : broiled lobster, 65-170.

△ ★★★*Do-mi-si-la-mi* (170 pl), ☎ 97.50.22.52; ★★★*Joncs du Roch*, rue de l'Aérodrome (110 pl), ☎ 97.50.24.37; ★★*Bois d'Amour* (335 pl), ☎ 97.50.13.52; ★★*Conguel* (200 pl), ☎ 97.50.19.11; ★★*Goviro* (200 pl), ☎ 97.50.13.54; at Saint-Pierre, ★★★*Park er Lann* (135 pl), ☎ 97.50.24.93; ★★*De Kerhostin* (150 pl), ☎ 97.30.95.25; ★★*Le Petit Rohu* (165 pl), ☎ 97.50.27.85; ★★*Penthièvre* (665 pl), ☎ 97.52.33.86.

Recommended
Thalassotherapie : Centre Louison Bobet, ☎ 97.50.20.00, all year.
Youth hostel : 45, rue du Roch-Priol, ☎ 97.50.15.34.
♥ Viviers du Portivien, Saint-Pierre, ☎ 97.30.93.81, spiny lobsters, lobsters, crabs; candy : Le Roux, 18, rue du Port-Maria, for their famous caramels; Niniches, bd Chanard, caramels.

QUIMPER★★

Brest 72, Vannes 115, Paris 556 km
pop 60162 ⊠ 29000   A2

This former capital of Cornouaille has prospered in the 20thC, while preserving its Breton character and atmosphere.

▶ The **cathedral of St. Corentin★** (B1, *8-11:45 & 1:45-6:30*) is dedicated to the city's patron saint. The 13th-15thC building shows the different phases of Breton Gothic architecture; between the two spires (19thC), the legendary King Gradlon watches over the town he founded after the destruction of his city of Ys (→ box). Inside, numerous tombs and effigies; don't miss the splendid stained glass★ (end 15thC). ▶ In the former bishop's palace (Gothic and Renaissance) is the **Musée Départemental Breton** (Brittany Museum; *10-7 ex Tue.*) : wood-

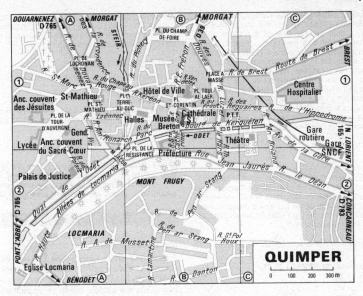

carvings, tombstones, traditional interior and costumes★ from Cornwall. ▶ The **Musée des Beaux-Arts** (Fine Arts Museum) in the Hôtel de Ville *(9:30-12 & 2-6:30, May-15 Sep.; 9:30-12 & 2-6, 16 Sep.-Apr.; closed Tue. and nat. hols.)* is one of the richest provincial museums : 17thC Flemish and Dutch paintings and superb canvasses by the School of Pont-Aven. ▶ NW from the square, walk through the Rue Élie-Fréron and the neighbouring streets with their appetizing names : Rue du Sallé, Place au Beurre (butter), Rue des Boucheries (butchers), Venelles du Poivre (pepper) and du Pain-Cuit (baked bread); the old houses along these streets become more numerous in the **Rue Kéréon**★ opposite the cathedral façade. ▶ Fine view over the old town from the wooded hill of Mont Frugy (B2), on the left bank of the Odet; pleasant walks. ▶ 500 m downstream from the town centre is the **Loc-maria** Quarter (A2), where Quimper began; Roman-esque church★ (11th-12thC). Since the 17thC Locmaria has been a centre of ceramics production with an internation-al reputation : **Faïenceries HB-Henriot** *(Mon.-Fri. 9-11:30 & 2-5:30);* **Faïencerie Keraluc** *(Mon.-Fri., 9:30-12 & 1:30-4:30).* 16thC church in the Ker-feunteun District *(1 km N);* 1550 stained glass★.

Nearby

▶ Downstream, the **Odet** widens into an attractive estuary★★ lined with numerous châteaux among rhodo-dendron, camellias, and Virginia tulip trees; this is a trip to make by boat *(daily service May-Sep.; 1 hr 15 from Quimper to Bénodet).* ▶ 6.5 km E, **Ergué-Gabéric** : in the church, 16thC stained-glass window of the Passion; 3.5 km further on : chapel of Notre-Dame de Kerdévot, excellent example of 15thC Cornish architecture, with late 15thC Flemish altarpiece★. ▶ 7 km NE, the **Stangala**★ : the Odet flows through a wooded ravine *(5-6 min on foot from car-park at the Pointe du Griffonez; walks).* ▶ 12.5 km N : there is a remarkable pyramidal Calvary of 1550 in front of the chapel of **Notre-Dame de Quilinen**★★ (16thC; 1520 Descent from the Cross). □

Practical Information

ℹ rue du Roi-Gradlon (B1), ☎ 98.95.04.69.
✈ Pluguffan, 6 km SW, ☎ 98.94.01.28.
SNCF (C2), ☎ 98.90.50.50.
🚌 2, bd de Kerguelen (B1), ☎ 98.95.02.36.

🚢 ☎ 98.57.00.58, to Bénodet, Loctudy, les îles de Glénan.
Car rental : *Avis*, Airport; 8, av. de la Gare (C1-2), ☎ 98.90.31.34; train station (C1-2).

Hotels :
★★★ **Le Griffon**, 131, rte de Bénodet, 2 km S (A2), ☎ 98.90.33.33, Tx 940063, AE DC Euro Visa, 50 rm Ⓟ ▥ 🏊 ≵ 🖵 closed 20 Dec-6 Jan, 260. Rest. ◆◆◆ **Le Creach Gwenn** ≵ ঔ closed Sat eve and Sun (l.s.), 20 Dec-12 Jan, 65-160.
★★ **Gradlon**, 30, rue de Brest (B-C1), ☎ 98.95.04.39, AE Euro Visa, 25 rm ▥ 🏊 ⌘ closed 19 Dec-19 Jan, 220.
★★ **Sapinière**, 286, rte de Bénodet (A2), ☎ 98.90.39.63, Tx 940034, AE DC Euro Visa, 40 rm Ⓟ ≶ ▥ 🏊 ঔ ⌘ 🖵 🞍 closed Mon lunch in winter, 20 Sep-18 Oct, 160.

Restaurants :
◆◆◆ **Capucin Gourmand**, 29, rue des Réguaires (B-C1), ☎ 98.95.43.12 ≵ closed Sat noon and Sun , Feb school hols, 15 Aug-1 Sep, 135-230.
◆◆ **Tritons**, allées de Locmaria (A2), ☎ 98.90.61.78 ≶ ≵ ঔ closed Mon. Enjoyable food. Spec : *potée de boeuf à la bretonne, confit de canard*, good value, 70-100.

△ ★★★★ *Orangerie de Lanniron* (100 pl), ☎ 98.90.62.02.

Recommended
Events : *Musical weeks*, 1st 3 wk in Jul; *Cornwall festi-val*, 4th Sun in Jul.
♥ *Au Costume Breton*, 11, rue Madec, dolls, hats, coifs; antiques : *Brocantic*, 56, quai de l'Odet, ☎ 98.55.43.34, antique faïence; crêperie : *Vieux Quimper*, 20, rue Verde-let, ☎ 98.95.31.34; *St-Marc*, 2bis, rue St-Marc, ☎ 98.55.53.28; Quimper faïence : *La Civette*, 16 bis, rue du Parc, ☎ 98.95.34.13.

QUIMPERLÉ

Lorient 21, Quimper 46, Paris 511 km
pop 11697 ⊠ 29130   B2-3

Here, the Ellé and Isole rivers meet to form the Laïta, which meanders down to the sea *(14 km S);* won-derful walks along its banks. At Pentecost, Quimperlé celebrates the *Pardon de Toulfoën* (a feast day for birds).

▶ From the cloister buildings of the former 17thC abbey on the **Place Nationale**, good view of the church of Saint-Croix (rotunda, rebuilt 19thC). One of the three apses dates from 11thC; crypt with interesting capitals; finely-carved stone Renaissance altarpiece★ (1541) behind the entrance door. ▶ To the N, the aristocratic **Rue de Brémond-d'Ars** runs through the old town, bordered by ancient houses; in the Rue Dom-Morice, opposite the ruins of the church of St. Colomban, see the 15thC **Maison des Archers** (small museum of history and local traditions : *Jul.-Aug. ex Sun. and nat. hols.)*. ▶ Across the Isole, climb the steep old-fashioned Rue Savary to the **Place St.-Michel** in the heart of the upper town; square-towered church (13thC nave, square 15thC choir) with Flamboyant Gothic N porch.

Nearby

▶ To the S, 1852-acre **Carnoët Forest** hides a few châteaux *(no visits)*; also ruins of **château de Carnoët** and former **abbey** of St. **Maurice** (founded 12thC; *no visits).* ▶ **Le Pouldu**, at the mouth of the Laïta, is a pleasant town which still remembers the period (1889-94) when Gauguin and his friends used to stay here.   □

Practical Information ────────────

QUIMPERLÉ
🛈 pont de Bourgneuf, ☎ 98.96.04.32 (h.s.).
SNCF ☎ 98.39.24.24.

Hotels :
★★★ **Hermitage**, 2 km on the D 49, ☎ 98.96.04.66, 32 rm
ℙ 🎴 ▭ 220. Rest. ◆◆ **Le Relais du Roch**, closed Feb school hols, 20 Dec-1 Jan, 65-180.
★ **Auberge de Toulfoën**, rte du Pouldu, 3 km, ☎ 98.96.00.29, AE DC Euro Visa, 9 rm ℙ 🎴 🔣 Ó ⅋ closed Mon, 25 Sep-Oct, 165. Rest. ◆ 🕏 🕭 Ó closed Nov-Easter ex Sun, hols, 80-140.

Restaurant :
● ◆ **Ty-Gwechall**, 4, rue Mellac, ☎ 98.96.30.63, Euro Visa 🕭 closed Wed ex summer, Dec-Jan. A classic example of a Breton crêperie, 25-45.

Nearby

Le POULDU, ⊠ 29121, 15 km S.
🛈 bd de l'Océan, ☎ 98.39.93.42 (h.s.).

Hotels :
★★ **Armen** (L.F.), (anc. Quatre Chemins), rte du Port, ☎ 98.39.90.44, DC Euro Visa, 38 rm ℙ 🎴 🕭 half pens (h.s.), closed 21 Sep-May, 470. Rest. ◆ 🕭 ⅋ 55-140; child : 40.
★★ **Bains**, plage des Grands Sables, ☎ 98.39.90.11, Euro Visa, 49 rm 🕏 245. Rest. ◆ 🕭 ⅋ 70-200.
⚠ ★★*Les Embruns* (200 pl), ☎ 98.39.91.07.

RAZ Point★★

A2

A long rocky spur beaten by the waves and swept by the wind, a marvel to be visited outside the holiday season, or when poor weather has discouraged visitors...

▶ Go past the enormous car-park *(paying)*, the shopping centre and the semaphore, for a view★★ of the Point and its reefs, the light-house (le Phare de la Vieille) and, 12 km out, the Île de Sein. ▶ A path runs around the Point *(non-slip soles recommended, guide advised);* see the sinkhole **(Enfer de Plogoff)** and other chasms. ▶ The **Baie des Trépassés★** (beach) : when Druids died, they were taken by boat from here to the Île de Sein for burial; according to some, the drowned city of Ys is here (→ box). From the opposite end, you can reach the **Pointe du Van★★**, no less impressive but with fewer facilities, and the Pointe de Brézellec. ▶ **Cléden-Cap-Sizun** : church with 1550 bell-tower★ and Renaissance porch. ▶ As you go towards Douarnenez (→), make a detour to see the **Réserve**

Ornithologique du Cap Sizun★ (bird sanctuary; *10-12 & 2-6, 15 Mar.-Aug.*) on the Catel-ar-Roch promontory; with luck and binoculars, you can see interesting species such as razor-billed auks, puffins and shags.   □

Practical Information ────────────

CLÉDEN-CAP-SIZUN, ⊠ 29113 Audierne, 10 km W on the D 784.

Restaurant :
● ◆ **L'Etrave**, 1, pl. de l'Eglise, ☎ 98.70.66.87 ⅋ closed Wed, 29 Sep-1 Apr. Lobsters and fish at attractive prices, 50-150.

PLOGOFF, ⊠ 29113 Audierne.

Hotel :
● ★★ *Baie des Trépassés* (L.F.), ☎ 98.70.61.34, Euro Visa, 27 rm ℙ 🎴 🔣 closed 15 Nov-1 Mar, 240. Rest. ◆ 🕏 🕭 A good place for seafood by the shore : seafood assortment, grilled lobsters with cream, 60-100.

REDON

Vannes 57, Rennes 65, Paris 401 km
pop 10252 ⊠ 35600   C3

Redon is a small town at the junction of the Vilaine River and the canal from Nantes to Brest. Only pleasure craft pass through here, and the town's light industries are closely linked to agricultural activity of the surrounding countryside.

▶ The 14thC Gothic bell-tower★ (67 m high) of **St. Sauveur** overlooks the town centre. The church lost 25 m of nave in a fire; what remains is a fine 12thC Romanesque building with a second (central) bell-tower : it is a squat building despite its three arcaded stories and rounded angles. To see it at its best, go to the cloister, rebuilt in 17thC; the 13thC choir is darkened by the enormous altarpiece given by Cardinal Richelieu; remains of Romanesque frescos. ▶ Numerous **old houses** in the Grande-Rue, the streets nearby, and the lively Rue du Port.   □

Practical Information ────────────

🛈 rue des Etats, ☎ 99.71.06.04.
SNCF ☎ 99.71.10.70.

Hotels :
★★ **Bretagne** (L.F.), pl. de la Gare, ☎ 99.71.00.42, DC Euro Visa, 17 rm ℙ 🎴 🔣 closed Mon, 175.
★ **Gare**, 10, av. de la Gare, ☎ 99.71.02.04, AE DC Euro Visa, 7 rm 🕏 closed Sun eve , Sat lunch (15 Sep-15 Jun), 100. Rest. ◆ **Le Relais du Gastronome** 🕭 95-250; child : 55.

RENNES★★

Nantes 107, Brest 244, Paris 348 km
pop 200390 ⊠ 35000   D2

This ancient city was partially rebuilt after a catastrophic fire in 1720. The French Classic architecture of the period contrasts stongly with the appearance of other Breton towns : nothing Celtic or regional about it, but very suitable for a Breton Parlement that wanted to affirm its independence in the face of an absolute monarch. Nonetheless, the area around the cathedral and the Rue Saint-Georges maintain a mediaeval look.

▶ **Place de la République** (B2), overlooking the river Vilaine, is the heart of the town. The Palais du Commerce, an imposing building in the style of Louis XIV, was built between 1886 and 1932. ▶ The **Hôtel de Ville★** (1732-62) is in the purest Louis XV style, with two pavilions linked by a central block to form a horseshoe, and topped by a bell-tower. See the monumental staircase and the 18thC tapestries in the S pavilion; opposite is the **theatre** (1856). ▶ The **Place du Parlement★** is surrounded by classi-

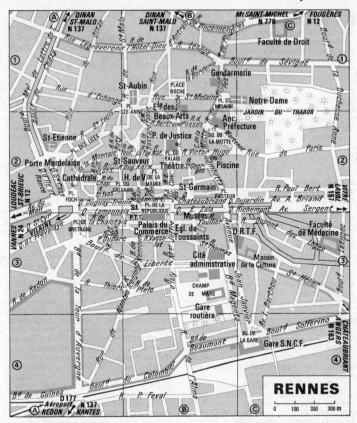

DINAN
ST-MALO
N 137

DINAN
SAINT-MALO
N 137

Mt SAINT-MICHEL
N 776

FOUGÈRES
N 12

Faculté de Droit

Gendarmerie

St-Aubin

PLACE
HOCHE

Notre-Dame

Eᴸᵉ des
Beaux-Arts

Anc.
Préfecture

St-Étienne

P. de Justice

Porte Mordelaise

St-Sauveur

Théâtre

Piscine

Cathédrale

H. de V

St-Germain

St-Georges

Musées

Palais du
Commerce

Egl. de
Toussaints

O.R.T.F.

Faculté
de Médecine

Cité
administrative

Maison
de la Culture

CHAMP
DE MARS

Gare
routière

Gare S.N.C.F.

Aéroport
REDON NANTES

N 137

RENNES

0   100   200   300 m

cal façades. The fourth side is occupied by the **Palais de Justice** (courthouse)★, built 1618-54 for the Parlement de Bretagne. The façade is typical of Rennes : grey granite, with white stone for the upper stories. Inside, the decoration★★ (by painters who also worked in Versailles) dates from the reign of Louis XIV. Ask the Concierge de la Cour (the official court attendant) to show the Salle des Assises (panelling), the Première Chambre Civile (paintings) and the Grand'-Chambre du Parlement de Bretagne★ (panelling, decorated ceiling and Gobelin tapestries). ▶ The old houses in the **Rue St-Georges★** are noteworthy. ▶ The church of St. Germain (15th-16thC Flamboyant Gothic) has 16thC stained glass in the S transept. ▶ Art Nouveau ceramics in the 1926 **swimming pool** by Emmanuel Le Ray, who also designed the Halle de la Poissonnerie (fish market ; 1912 ; rue de Nemours, B3). ▶ The **church of Notre-Dame** (B-C1), also known as the church of St. Mélaine, is a former abbey church ; partly Romanesque with charming cloister gallery of 1683. Behind the church is the colourful Thabor Garden. ▶ Enjoy the lively bustle of the pedestrian streets (Rues Le Bastard, La Fayette and Nationale, B2), then walk towards the old town near the **cathedral** (A2 ; 1787-1844 ; altarpiece★, Antwerp 1520), where a number of **old mansions** and **wood houses** escaped the fire of 1720 ; see Rue St-Sauveur (Nº 3, 1557 ; Nº 5, 18thC) to the left of the 18thC basilica of the same name. Rue St-Guillaume, the so-called Maison du Guesclin★, is occupied by a restaurant. See also the Rues de la Psalette and du Chapitre, one of the most handsome (Nᵒˢ 22, 20, 18, 11, 8, and especially 6). ▶ The **Porte Mordelaise** (A2) was the city's State Entrance for the Dukes of Brittany. Astride an ancient street, this gateway, entire-

ly restored, was once part of the city ramparts (15thC). ▶ Du Guesclin is reputed to have entered his first tournament in the **Place des Lices** ; lined with tall houses (mostly 17thC), it is now a thriving marketplace. ▶ In the Rues St-Michel and du Champ-Jacquet, there are pretty half-timbered houses. ▶ On the left bank, see the Palais des Musées (B3 ; two museums ; *daily ex Tue., 10-12 & 2-6*) : the **Musée de Bretagne** (pre-history, history, art, ethnology, costumes★, furniture ; lively setting) is the best introduction to a trip around Brittany ; the **Musée des Beaux-Arts** (Fine Arts) is one of 15 great regional museums created in Year IX of the French Revolution (1801) ; don't miss the Newborn Child★★ by Georges de La Tour, canvasses by the painters of the School of Pont-Aven, the regional artists' room, and the Rennes ceramics (17th-19thC). ▶ In the **Maison des Métiers** (B3, Champ de Mars), exhibitions and sale of regional crafts. **Also...** Urban expansion in the 70's has provided several interesting modern constructions : at Bourg l'Évêque (W ; 100-m elliptical towers of **Les Horizons**) ; Villejean (NW ; **church of St. Marc**) ; the **Barre Saint-Just Quarter** (*rue de Fougères, NE*).

Nearby

▶ **Rennes Forest** (9-15 km NE) : 30 km² of oaks, a pleasant picnic place for those who do not care to try the famous restaurant in **Liffré** ; half-way between Rennes and the forest is the Musée Automobile de Bretagne : 80 vehicles in running order from 1895 to 1925 (*daily ex Tue. 9-12 & 4-6*). ▶ In the valley of the Vilaine, downstream from Rennes, is the site★ of the **Moulin du Boël** (mill ;

17 km S, right bank). On the other bank, pleasant walks along the GR 39. ▶ **Châteaugiron** *(16 km SE)* : imposing remains of a castle★ with moats, walls and ivy-covered keep (12th-13thC); main buildings date from the 17th-18thC (restored). Pretty houses in the town. ☐

Practical Information ─────────────

RENNES
ⓘ pont de Nemours (B2), ☎ 99.79.01.98.
✈ *Saint-Jacques-de-la-Lande*, 7 km SW, ☎ 99.31.91.77.
Air France office, 7, rue de Bertrand, ☎ 99.63.09.09.
SNCF (C4), ☎ 99.65.50.50.
🚌 bd Magenta (B3-4), ☎ 99.30.87.80.
Car rental : *Avis*, 24, av Janvier (B-C3), ☎ 99.30.01.19 ; Train station (C4) ; Airport.

Hotels :
★★★ *Altea Parc du Colombier*, (ex Frantel), 1, rue Cap-Maignan (B4), ☎ 99.31.54.54, 140 rm, 360. Rest. ♦♦ *La Table Ronde*, closed Sat noon and Sun, 22 Dec-1 Jan, 155-200.
★★★ *Central*, 6, rue Lanjuinais, angle quai Lamennais (A3), ☎ 99.79.12.36, Tx 741259, AE DC Euro Visa, 43 rm 1 apt 🅿 🔍 ♨ 235.
★★★ *Le Président*, 27, av. Janvier (C3), ☎ 99.65.42.22, Tx 730004, AE DC Euro Visa, 34 rm 🅿 🔍 ♪ ♿ 240.
★★ *Astrid*, 32, av. Louis-Barthou (C3-4), ☎ 99.30.82.38, Euro Visa, 30 rm 🔍 180.
★★ *Garden*, 3, rue Duhamel (C3), ☎ 99.65.45.06, Tx 730772, AE Visa, 22 rm 🅿 🔍 180.

Restaurants :
● ♦♦ *Le Palais*, 6-7, pl. du Parlement-de-Bretagne (B2), ☎ 99.79.45.01, AE DC Euro Visa ♪ closed Mon and Sun eve , Feb school hols, 8-31 Aug. The best restaurant in Rennes. Light, original fare by two former colleagues of Michel Kéréver : *foie gras de canard poêlé aux poireaux, aiguillettes de caneton mi-sauvage, soufflé au citron vert coulis de fraises parfumées*, 75-220.
● ♦♦ *Le Piré*, 18, rue du Mal-Joffre (B3), ☎ 99.79.31.41, AE DC Euro Visa 🏛 ♪ ♿ closed Sat noon and Sun , hols. M. Angelle, formerly of Beauvilliers in Paris, serves forth simple yet refined dishes : *brick de foie gras chaud, tarte de ris de veau au corail d'oursins, chaud froid de poire et pamplemousse jus de genièvre*, 80-200.
● ♦♦ *Chouin*, 12, rue d'Isly (B3), ☎ 99.30.87.86, Visa ♪ closed Mon and Sun , Feb school hols, 3-25 Aug, 25 Dec-5 Jan, 90-140.
● ♦♦ *Le Reberminard*, 67ter, bd de la Tour-d'Auvergne (A3-4), ☎ 99.30.19.71, Euro Visa ♪ ♿ closed Mon. Varied, interesting fixed meals : *chateaubriand au beurre vert, noisette d'agneau sur lit d'oignons rouges*, 55-150 ; child : 40.
♦♦ *L'Ouvrée*, 18, pl. des Lices (A2), ☎ 99.30.16.38, AE DC Euro Visa ♪ 🏛 closed Mon and Sat noon, 18-28 Apr, 2-26 Aug. A varied selection of dishes featuring fish, served in a pretty 16th-C house : *filet de boeuf en pot-au-feu cuit dans le consommé et sa lamelle de foie gras, aiguillettes de turbot aux huîtres et à la crème de poireaux*, 90-160 ; child : 40.

Recommended
♥ pastry : *Duchesse de Bretagne*, 3-5, rue de Toulouse, ☎ 99.79.35.78 ; pork products : *Hesteau*, 28, rue de Nemours, ☎ 99.79.49.23 ; take-out food : *Cerbet*, 11, rue des Dames, ☎ 99.30.26.56.

Nearby

CHÂTEAUBOURG, ✉ 35220, 21 km E.

Hotels :
★★★ *Ar Milin'*, 30, rue de Paris, ☎ 99.00.30.91, Tx 740083, AE DC Euro Visa, 33 rm 🅿 ≼ ♿ ♪ closed 15 Dec-7 Jan. Relaxation room, sauna, whirlpool, 220. Rest. ♦♦ ≼ closed Sun eve ex Apr-Sep, 90-175 ; child : 50.
★★ *Pen'Roc* (L.F.), La Peinière, Saint-Didier, ☎ 99.00.33.02, AE DC Euro Visa, 15 rm 🅿 ≼ 🏛 🔍 ♪ closed Sun eve, 21 Feb-8 Mar, 25 Oct-5 Nov, 175. Rest. ♦ ♪ ♿ 🏛 65-210 ; child : 50.

LIFFRÉ, ✉ 35340, 17 km NE.

Hotel :
● ★★ *La Reposée*, La Quinte, 2 km SW on the N 12, ☎ 99.68.31.51, AE Euro Visa, 25 rm 🅿 ≼ 🏛 🔍 ♪ 🌙 ♪ closed 22-28 Dec. Peace and quiet in a spacious park near Rennes, 250. Rest. ♦ ≼ ♿ 60-110.

Restaurant :
● ♦♦♦ *Lion d'Or*, 8, rue de Fougères, ☎ 99.68.31.09, AE Euro Visa 🏛 closed Mon and Sun eve, 29 Jul-13 Aug. No rooms in this hostelry, but good cooking by Jean-Claude Demonceau, successor to Michel Kéréver now at the Duc d'Enghien : *cassolette de langoustines à la menthe, suprême de pigeon en paupiettes de chou au foie gras, gratin de fruits*, 120-225.

RHUYS Peninsula

C3

This low peninsula which shelters the Gulf of Morbihan from the wind, has recently developed a number of yacht harbours, created the resort of Le Crouesty, and built a highway : this is perhaps a way of protecting the remainder.

▶ At the base of the peninsula, the **château de Kerlévenan** (end 18thC) is surprisingly Italianate. ▶ **Sarzeau** (pop. 4 443) is surrounded by campsites ; near the church (1626) are a number of 17th-18thC granite houses★ with decorated dormer windows. ▶ The **château de Suscinio**★ has been restored and made into a museum *(out of season 9:30-12 & 1:30-7 ex Tue., Sat. and Sun. ; Apr.-Sep. daily ; closed Feb.)*. However, to preserve its well-known silhouette, the roofs were not altered. This superb fortified building (13th-15thC) was once the residence of the Dukes of Brittany. ▶ Partially Romanesque church at **Saint-Gildas-de-Rhuys** (12thC capitals, 11th-18thC tombstones) housing one of the largest treasure rooms★ in Brittany *(5-7, Sun. 4-6)*. ▶ The 20-m high **tumulus of Tumiac** or **Butte de César**, beside the road, gives a splendid view over the bay and the ocean. ▶ Another view from the Pointe du Petit Mont above the developing town of **Kerjouanno** and the port of **Le Crouesty**. ▶ The shady little harbour of **Port-Navalo** overlooks the neck of the bay. ☐

Practical Information ─────────────

PORT-NAVALO, ✉ 56640 Arzon.
ⓘ old train station, ☎ 97.41.31.63.

Hotel :
● ★ *Ruys*, 2, rue de la Douane, ☎ 97.41.20.01, Visa, 14 rm 🅿 ≼ closed 30 Sep-1 Apr, 220.

Recommended
Marina : *Le Crouesty*, ☎ 97.41.23.33, 1.200 pl.

SARZEAU, ✉ 56370, 22 km SE of **Vannes**.
ⓘ ☎ 97.41.82.37.

Hotel :
★ *La Chaumière de la Mer*, Pointe de Penvins, ☎ 97.67.35.75, 17 rm 🅿 ≼ 🏛 🔍 pens, half pens (h.s.), closed Oct-Mar, 200. Rest. ♦ ≼ ♪ 40-100.

Restaurant :
♦ *L'Espadon*, La Grée, Penvins, ☎ 97.67.34.26, AE DC Euro Visa ♪ ♿ closed Tue eve and Wed (h.s.), 60-150 ; child : 50.

⛺ ★★★★*Madone* (380 pl), ☎ 97.67.33.30 ; ★★★★*Ty an diaoul* (36 pl), ☎ 97.67.33.57 ; ★★★*Kersial*, rte de Saint-Jacques (100 pl), ☎ 97.41.75.59.

La ROCHE-BERNARD

Vannes 40, Nantes 70, Paris 441 km
pop 838 ✉ 56130
C3

La Roche-Bernard, situated on a headland★, was, in the 17thC, a moderately important naval dockyard. Today, it is a yacht harbour, linked to the sea by

the lock at the Arzal Dam (1970; *7 km downstream*).
Attractive 15th and 16thC wooden houses.

Nearby

▶ 16 km W, **Pénestin** : an unpretentious seaside resort
where the coastline alternates between beaches and
cliffs. ▶ 12 km NE, **Cadouzan Manor** preceded by two
15thC towers. ▶ 14 km NW is the **château de Branféré**,
surrounded by a park; zoo★ with 1 000 animals in semi-
liberty *(9-12 & 2-6:30, Apr.-Sep., or 5:30, 26 Sep.-14 Nov.).*
▶ Boat trips on the Vilaine River.   ☐

Practical Information

La ROCHE-BERNARD
ⓘ ☎ 99.90.67.98.   ♥

Hotels :
★★ **Auberge des Deux Magots**, 1-2, pl. du Bouffay,
☎ 99.90.60.75, Visa, 15 rm Ⓟ closed Sun eve (l.s.) and
Mon, 15 Dec-15 Jan, 210. Rest. ♦♦ ♪ 50-85.
● ★ *Auberge Bretonne*, 2, pl. Duguesclin,
☎ 99.90.60.28, AE DC Euro Visa, 6 rm Ⓟ ♧ ♪ closed
Thu and Fri lunch, 15 Nov-15 Dec, 170. Rest. ● ♦♦♦ ♪ ♧
Joël Robuchon, an excellent judge of his peers, declares
that Jacques Thorel will go far. A rosy future is surely in
store for this young chef whom we are happy to welcome to our chefs' panel. Solange assists her husband in
their fresh, pretty inn with her smiling, discreet efficiency.
A wide selection of fixed-price meals allows you to
sample an array of modern, clean-lined dishes : *St-Jacques en croustille, spirale de sole aux pissenlits, rouelle
de homard légèrement fumée, court-bouillon de lotte avec
tomates farcies aux coquillages, fine crêpe de langouste,
cannellonis de dorade, jambon de marcassin aux cêpes,
agneau au serpolet, soupe de cerises, gratin de pommes.*
The cellar attests to a passion for wine; theme menus
centred around a great bottle. 75-180.

Nearby

PEAULE, ✉ 56130 La Roche-Bernard, 9 km N.

Hotel :
★★ **Auberge Armor-Vilaine** (L.F.), ☎ 97.42.91.03, Euro
Visa, 21 rm Ⓟ ∰ ♧ ✻ closed Sun eve and Mon lunch
(l.s.), 15 Dec-15 Jan, 160. Rest. ♦ ♪ ♧ ✻ 50-190.

ROCHEFORT-EN-TERRE*

Vannes 34, Rennes 78, Paris 414 km
pop 613 ✉ 56220 Malansac   C3
In a beautiful setting of rocks and woodland, this old
fortified town is filled with cheerful people, *crêperies,*
and antique shops; there are geraniums at the windows, and more flowers in the old wells and horse
troughs.

▶ The old covered market now houses the town hall.
▶ Close by, the main street has a number of **17thC granite houses,** one of which is flanked by a pentagonal corbelled turret. Others, even more delightful, stand around
an old well in a tiny square. ▶ The **church** dates from
the 12thC but was rebuilt during 16th-17thC; interesting
furnishings (stalls, 1592, and altarpiece of painted stone,
1610). ▶ The **castle** is only a heap of ruins (view★) with
the exception of the out-buildings, rebuilt stone by stone
with material from other ruined castles and now refurbished to make a museum *(11-12 & 2-6, Jun.-15 Sep.;
Sun. and nat. hols. only rest of year).*

Nearby

▶ **Questembert** *(10 km SW; pop. 4 900)* : several 16th
and 17thC houses with carved façades, fine timber-built
market★ of 1675.   ☐

┌───┐
If you enjoy sports, consult the pages pertaining to
the regions; there you will find addresses for practicing your favorite sport.
└───┘

Practical Information

ROCHEFORT-EN-TERRE

Restaurant :
♦♦ *Au Vieux Logis*, ☎ 97.43.31.71, Euro Visa ≼ ♪ ♧
closed Mon, 85-140.

Nearby

QUESTEMBERT, ✉ 56230, 10 km SW.

Hotel :
● ★★★ *Le Bretagne* (R.C.), 13, rue Saint-Michel,
☎ 97.26.11.12, AE Visa, 8 rm Ⓟ ∰ ♧ ♪ ♧ closed Sun eve.
and Mon, 3 Jan-15 Mar, 350. Rest. ● ♦♦♦ ♪ ♧ Undisputed leader of Brittany's culinary clan, mischievous, mustachioed Georges Paineau is an honoured member of our
chefs' panel. Paineau is a wise man. His cuisine is creative and light, with a focus on fish and other carefully
chosen ingredients : *huîtres paquets à la vapeur, ravioles de coquillages, turbot rôti au jus de veau, ragoût
de sole, canette de Challans.* Low-calorie meals for spa-
goers from nearby Quiberon. The comfortable old house
was tastefully renovated and decorated by M. Paineau,
who oversees his antiques and gourmet food shop (jams,
oils), yet still finds time to paint very pretty tablecloths,
140-330.

ROSCOFF

Morlaix 28, Brest 62, Paris 565 km
pop 3787 ✉ 29211   B1
This old port became a health-spa centre in 1899 and
later, a seaside resort. It is surrounded by market gardens and has regained its youth since local growers
established the Brittany Ferries line to export their
onions and import tourists!

▶ The Gothic **church** has an over-decorated bell-tower;
the wooden ceiling and monumental carved wood altarpiece are more interesting. ▶ **Aquarium★** *(22 Mar.-
31 Oct., tel. : 98.69.72.30).*

Batz Island
(15-min crossing hourly; extra sailings in summer)

▶ Flat, ringed with beaches and reefs that appear at
low tide; an exceptionally gentle climate. Specialises in
market gardening and sea-weed gathering.   ☐

Practical Information

ⓘ chapelle Saint-Anne, rue Gambetta, ☎ 98.69.70.70.
🚃 ☎ 98.69.70.20.
⛴ ☎ 98.61.79.66, to l'île de Batz, in 15 mn, connections with Plymouth, 8 h crossing, daily year round, and
with Cork (10h), once a week, 98.69.07.20.

Hotels :
★★★ **Le Gulf Stream**, ☎ 98.69.73.19, Euro Visa, 32 rm
Ⓟ ≼ ∰ ♧ ♪ ♧ half pens (h.s.), closed 15 Oct-Mar, 500.
Rest. ● ♦ ≼ ♪ ♧ ✻ Jacques Creach's fine cooking
keeps getting better. A little more simplicity and it will be
perfect. The sea stretches out before you, 95-250.
★★ *Bellevue* (L.F.), rue Jeanne-d'Arc, ☎ 98.61.23.38,
Visa, 20 rm Ⓟ ≼ ∰ ♧ closed 15 Oct-15 Apr, 180. Rest. ♦
♪ ✻ 60-200.
★★ *Le Triton*, rue du Dr-Bagot, ☎ 98.62.24.44, Euro Visa,
45 rm Ⓟ ∰ ♧ ✻ closed 15 Nov-Jan, 200.
★★ *Talabardon*, pl. de l'Eglise, ☎ 98.61.24.95, Euro Visa,
41 rm Ⓟ ≼ ♧ closed 15 Oct-15 Mar, 195. Rest. ♦ ≼ ♪
♧ closed Sun eve, 80-150.
★ *Bains*, ☎ 98.61.20.65, Euro Visa, 50 rm ≼ ∰ 🐟 ♧
closed 15 Oct-15 Mar, 190. Rest. ♦ ♪ ♧ ✻ 65-90; child : 50.

△ ★★*Manoir de Kerestat* (100 pl) ☎ 98.69.71.92;
★★*Per'haridy* (200 pl), ☎ 98.69.70.86.

┌───┐
On the maps, a town's name underlined <u>Saulieu</u>
means that the locality possesses at least one
recommended establishment (blue or red point).
└───┘

ROSPORDEN

Quimper 22, Lorient 47, Paris 538 km
pop 6752 ⊠ 29140   B2
On the edge of a 110-acre lake formed by the Aven;
the church, largely rebuilt in the 17thC, has a 14thC
bell-tower with very pure lines.

Nearby

▶ 9 km W : **Saint-Yvi** has a beautiful parish churchyard★
planted with old yew-trees; church and Calvary (16thC),
ossuary (15thC) and fountain. ▶ 14 km NW : **Scaër** is
famous for its Breton wrestling *(last Sun. in Aug.)*; 15thC
figured cross in front of the church.   ☐

Practical Information _____

⚙ ☎ 98.59.27.26.
SNCF ☎ 98.59.20.15.

Hotel :
● ★★ *Bourhis* (L.F.), 3, pl. de la Gare, ☎ 98.59.23.89,
AE DC Euro Visa, 27 rm ℗ ♪ Ġ closed Sun eve and Mon
(l.s.), 15 Feb-8 Mar, 15 Nov-1 Dec, 250. Rest. ♦ ♪ Ġ Seafood carefully cooked by M. Bourhis, 120-250.

ROSTRENEN

Pontivy 37, Loudéac 38, Paris 480 km
pop 4391 ⊠ 22110   B2
A quiet little country town on a hill, with a lake to the
S, in the heart of Brittany. Walks along the GR37
and by the Nantes-Brest canal; the canal cutting crosses the watershed between the Aulne and the Blavet
rivers at Glomel, not far from here.

Nearby

▶ 6 km SW : the **Manor of Coatcouraval** (15thC), in a
woodland setting *(Jul.-Aug.)*. ▶ 9 km N : **Kergrist-Moëlou** is worth a detour for its 16thC Flamboyant Gothic
church, surrounded by aged yew-trees, with a 1578 Calvary (damaged). ▶ 11 km E, **Gouarec** : schist houses by
the junction of the river Blavet and the Nantes-Brest
canal; 4 km S : the chapel of Notre-Dame de la Croix at
Plélauff has a rood-screen★ whose paintings are masterpieces of naïf art. ▶ 14 km NE, **Saint-Nicolas-du-Pélem** :
beside the church (1470 stained glass) is the St. Nicholas
Fountain, one of the most charming you could find; in the
vicinity of the town, you will see pretty chapels, megaliths and rocky outcrops; at **Toul-Goulic**, the Blavet goes
briefly underground. En route, **Lanrivain** : 15thC ossuary,
16thC Calvary★   ☐

Practical Information _____

Nearby

GOUAREC, ⊠ 22570, 12 km E.

Hotel :
★★ *Blavet* (L.F.), RN 164bis, ☎ 96.24.90.03, Euro Visa,
15 rm ℗ ∰ closed Sun eve and Mon ex Jul-Aug,
3 Feb-3 Mar, 22-29 Dec. Rustic furnishings, 160. Rest. ♦♦
♪ 70-130.

▲ ★★★*Municipal* (100 pl), ☎ 96.24.90.22.

SAINT-BRIEUC

Rennes 99, Quimper 139, Paris 452 km
pop 51399 ⊠ 22000   C2
On a headland between the Goët and Gouédic rivers,
formerly a quiet market town, the seat of a bishopric, a
stopover in the Tro Breiz, a small fishing port. Under
the pressures of immigration from the countryside
and recent industrialisation, Saint-Brieuc is changing
fast.

▶ The town centre with its narrow streets is very lively.
▶ The 14th-15thC **cathedral** (rebuilt in 18th and 19thC;
A3) has an unusually austere appearance for so important
a sanctuary, due to the two tower-like mediaeval keeps.
▶ The neighbouring streets have a number of fine **old
timber-fronted houses**, often carved, as in the Rue Fardel (A2). ▶ Fine **views** from many points around the headland : the **Rond-Point Huguin** (C2) overlooking the Gouédic Ravine (pleasant walks). The Tertre Aubé★ (B-C1),
surveys the Gouët Valley, the port and the bay.

Nearby

▶ 3.5 km NE is the **Cesson Tower**, a ruined 14thC keep
dominating the mouth of the Gouët. ▶ **Roselier Point**
(8.5 km NE; view★ over the bay) is reached through **Le
Légué** (port of Saint-Brieuc) and Saint-Laurent-de-la-Mer;
a pleasant road continues to **Les Rosaires beach**, surrounded by cliffs. ▶ 19 km SW : **Quintin**★ is a charming
ancient town above a lake; 15thC gate, 16th-18thC houses and the 17th-18thC wings of an uncompleted château. 2 km S : visit the park of the **château de Robien**
(18thC).   ☐

Practical Information _____

SAINT-BRIEUC
ⓘ Pavillon du Tourisme, 7, rue Saint-Gouéno,
☎ 96.33.32.50/96.33.42.29.
✈ *Saint-Brieuc-Trémuson*, 3 km W, ☎ 96.94.95.00.
SNCF (A4), ☎ 96.94.50.50/96.94.04.79.
🚌 rue Waldeck-Rousseau (B3), ☎ 96.33.36.60.
Car rental : *Avis*, 2, bd Clémenceau (B4), ☎ 96.33.44.14.

Hotels :
● ★★ *Le Pignon Pointu*, 16, rue J.-J.-Rousseau (B4),
☎ 96.33.02.39, Euro Visa, 17 rm ℗ 🔍 ♺ closed
19 Dec-4 Jan, 170.
★★ *Mon Hôtel*, 19, rue Jean-Métairie (A3), ☎ 96.33.01.21,
Euro Visa, 46 rm ℗ 🔍 ♺ closed 20 Dec-5 Jan, 200.

Restaurant :
● ♦♦ *Le Quatre Saisons*, 61, chem. des Courses
(off map C3), ☎ 96.33.20.38, Visa ∰ ♪ closed Mon and
Sun eve, 16-28 Feb, 16 Aug-2 Sep. In a former race-
course restaurant, M. P. Faucon and chef D. Quay are
surefire winners. Seafood and seasonal cuisine. Scrumptious pastries, 60-230.

▲ ★★*de Brezillet* (150 pl), ☎ 96.61.29.33.

Recommended
Youth hostel : *Ty Coat*, rue A.-Daudet, ☎ 96.61.91.87,
Bicycle touring.

Nearby

PLÉRIN, ⊠ 22190, 3 km N.

Hotel :
★★ *Le Chêne Vert*, (L.F., France-Accueil), rte de St-Lau-
rent-de-la-Mer, ☎ 96.74.63.20, AE DC Euro Visa, 52 rm ℗
≪ ∰ 🔍 ♪ Ġ ♺ closed 20 Dec-3 Jan. Squash, 200. Rest. ♦
≪ ♪ closed Sat noon and Sun noon, 55-110.

Restaurants :
● ♦♦ *La Vieille Tour*, 75, rue de la Tour, ☎ 96.33.10.30,
AE DC Euro Visa ≪ ♺ closed Sat noon and Sun,
15 Jun-1 Jul, 23 Dec-4 Jan. The view of the bay and the
little fishing boats never let one forget that this is seafood
country, 125-250; child : 50.
● ♦ *Le Relais des Rosaires*, rte des Rosaires,
☎ 96.74.54.55, DC Euro Visa ∰ ♪ ♺ closed Mon and Sat
noon. Serge Arboli is inspired by Le Divellec's way with
seafood. Oysters, roast lobster or spiny lobsters, *pavé de
bœuf au chèvre chaud*, 160-300.

QUINTIN, ⊠ 22800, 19 km SW.
ⓘ mairie, ☎ 96.74.84.01.
SNCF ☎ 96.74.87.85.

Hotel :
★★ *Commerce*, 2, rue Rochonen, ☎ 96.74.94.67, Visa,
14 rm 🔍 ♪ ♺ closed Sun eve , Mon lunch (ex Jul-Aug),
15 Dec-15 Jan, 160. Rest. ♦ ♪ 50-145.

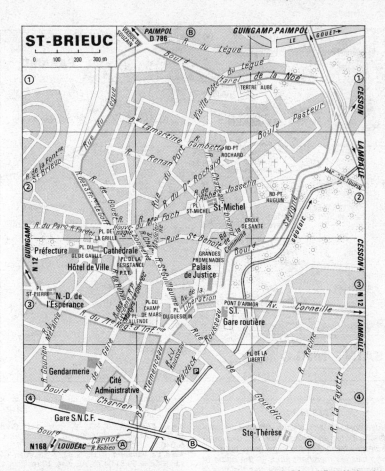

ST-BRIEUC

0   100   200   300 m

PAIMPOL
D 786 ⒝

GUINGAMP,PAIMPOL
LE ◀GOUËT▶

R. du Légué

Bould

du tégué

① Vieille Côte... Farel de la Noë ①

TERTRE AUBÉ

Bould Pasteur

CESSON

LAMBALLE

R. de la Fontne St-Brieuc

R. du ... Lamartine

R. Renan

R. du Pont Gambetta

RD-PT ROCHARD

② R. dessinerie-Goff R. de Goüet R. du Dr Rochard R. de l'Abbé Josselin ② VIAC DE TOUPIN

RD-PT HUGUIN

② R. du Parc R. Fardel PL DE ... magie R. Mal Foch PL ST-MICHEL St-Michel

Séveigné CESSON

GUINGAMP N 12

Préfecture GL DE GAULLE PL DU Cathédrale PL DE LA RESISTANCE

CROIX DE SANTÉ

Hôtel de Ville P.T.T. GRANDES PROMENADES

③ PL ST-PIERRE N.-D. de l'Espérance PL DU CHAMP DE MARS PL DU GUESCLIN Palais de Justice

Bould Commune

Av. de la Libération

PONT D'ARMOR Av. Corneille

③ N 12 LAMBALLE

S.I. Gare routière

R. Rousseau

Gendarmerie Cité Administrative

PL DE LA LIBERTÉ

R. Waldeck P

④ Bould Charner ④

Gare S.N.C.F.

R. la Fayette

Bould Carnot

N168 ◀ LOUDÉAC R. Robien ⒜ ⒝ Ste-Thérèse ⒞

SAINT-MALO***

Avranches 66, Rennes 69, Paris 411 km
pop 47324 ⊠ 35400   D1

It is almost impossible to believe that Saint-Malo was totally rebuilt in its present form after WWII. The ramparts and narrow streets of the Ville Close (walled city) are lined by houses in the severe style of the 17th and 18thC, and it is very easy to imagine the place as it was in the days of the great sailing ships.

▶ The best place for an overall view of Saint-Malo is the **Esplanade Saint-Vincent** (E1). To the W is the ancient walled city, proud of its history; to the N and NW lies the seaside resort with beach, hotels, casino and Palais des Congrès. To the E and SE you can see the port with its busy trade in cod and coal; S, behind the yacht harbour, are the wooded heights of Saint-Servan and the estuary of the Rance, gateway to the high seas... ▶ The **castle★** is a mighty pentagonal fortress flanked by round towers, now housing the town hall and the **City Museum** *(10-12 & 2-6, Jun.-Sep.)*: history of the town and its great men. Also in the castle is the **Galerie Quiquengrogne** *(Easter-15 Sep., 9:30-12 & 2-6:30)*: wax museum of the town's famous men including Cartier (1491-1557), discoverer of Canada, and Chateaubriand. ▶ **Tour of the ramparts★★** for a series of splendid views over the sea and its islets: at high tide the waves beat on the ramparts; at low tide you can reach the **islands of Grand Bé** (A1; Chateau-

briand's tomb), **Petit Bé** and **Fort National** *(guided tour, view★* of the Ville Close). ▶ Wander around the pedestrian precinct inside the ancient **walled city★**; souvenirs, antiques, curiosities, cafés, *crêperies*... ▶ The **cathedral★** (D-E2) is a contrast in styles where every century is represented, from the 12th to 18th; modern stained-glass windows in blazing colours. ▶ **Aquarium** in the ramparts (Place Vauban; E1; *daily*); opposite, **Exotarium** *(combined tickets)*. ▶ The **Pointe de la Cité** (A3) is crowned by a fort (1759), rebuilt during the German occupation *(ext. visit only;* orientation table). The **Corniche d'Aleth★** *(path;* pedestrians only; view★) runs around the point. ▶ The **Solidor Tower★** (1382; there are in fact three towers) houses the **Musée International des Long-Cours Cap-Horniers,** illustrating the lives of the seamen who sailed three-masted ships around Cape Horn *(guided tours at 2, 3:15 and 4:30, Jan.-Mar. and Oct.-Dec; at 10:30, 2, 3:30 and 5, Apr.-14 Jun. and 15-30 Sep.; at 10:30, 11, 2, 2:30, 3:30, 4, 5, 15 Jun.-14 Sep.).* ▶ Excellent **view** over the estuary from the path round Corbières Park (B3; *8-8).* ▶ **Paramé** (C1) is the seaside resort of Saint-Malo; walk along the wave-battered sea-wall (view★).

Nearby

▶ As from Dinard (→), boat trips to Cézembre Island, Cap Fréhel and Dinan. ▶ The Côte d'Émeraude (→) E of Saint-Malo is a short but indispensable walk. ▶ Around Saint-Malo, many 18thC *Malouinières* (mansions built by the sea-traders of the period), all on the same pattern;

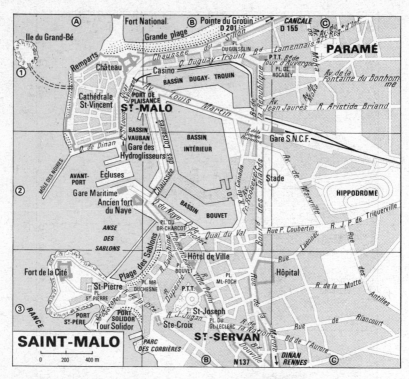

SAINT-MALO

0   200   400 m

Corsairs

Never confuse corsairs with pirates, those unscrupulous rogues who looted and pillaged for their own profit; the corsair may behave in the same way, but he is a patriot who pillages merchant ships in the name of his King... **Duguay-Trouin** *(1673-1736) was the first of the famous French corsairs, who captured more than 300 English ships between 1689 and 1709, with the support of the ship owners of Saint-Malo. During one period of ten years, the Malouin corsairs captured 3 800 commercial vessels. Other famous corsairs were* **Jean Bart** *(1650-1732, born and died in Dunkerque) and* **Robert Surcouf** *(1773-1827).*

only one is open to visitors : the **château du Bosq**★ *(7 km S on the N137 and a narrow road on the right).* □

Practical Information

ℹ️ au port de plaisance (E2), ☎ 99.56.64.48.
✈ *Dinard-Pleurtuit*, 17 km SW, ☎ 99.46.16.82.
SNCF (C1), ☎ 99.56.08.18/99.56.15.53.
🚌 esplanade Saint-Vincent (E1).
⚓ to Excursions to the Channel Islands Portsmouth, Chausey Islands, Channel Islands; excursions : Dinan via la Rance, île de Cézembre, cap Fréhel; info S.I.
Car rental : *Avis*, Train station (C1); Gare Maritime de Naye (A2), ☎ 99.81.73.24.

Hotels :

★★★ *Central*, (Mapotel), 6, Grande-Rue (E2), ☎ 99.40.87.70, Tx 740802, AE DC Euro Visa, 46 rm ♪ half pens (h.s.), 600. Rest. ♦ ♪ ♿ closed Mon eve and Sun eve, 6 Jan-15 Feb, 80-120.

★★★ *Digue*, 49, chaussée du Sillon (B1), ☎ 99.56.09.26, Tx 730736, AE DC Euro Visa, 53 rm Ⓟ ≼ closed 30 Oct-30 Mar, 285.
★★★ *Elizabeth* (C.H.), 2, rue des Cordiers (E2), ☎ 99.56.24.98, Tx 730800, AE DC Euro Visa, 17 rm ♨ ♿ 340.
★★★ *Le Valmarin*, (C.H., R.S.), 7 rue Jean-XXIII, St-Servan (B3), ☎ 99.81.94.76, AE Visa, 10 rm Ⓟ ♨ ♨ ♪ closed Jan-Feb, 360.
★★★ *Thermes*, 100, bd Hébert, Grande Plage (E1), ☎ 99.56.02.56, AE DC Euro Visa, 98 rm Ⓟ ≼ ♨ ♪ ♿ ☒ pens, closed 4 Jan-1 Feb, 695. Rest. ♦ ≼ ♿ ♨ Three restaurants : home-style, low-calorie, gourmet, 80-150.
● ★★ *France et Chateaubriand*, pl. Chateaubriand (E1), ☎ 99.56.66.52, Tx 740802, AE DC Euro Visa, 84 rm Ⓟ ≼ ♪ ♿ half pens (h.s.), 440. Rest. ♦ ♪ ♿ closed 11 Nov-10 Mar, 75-120.
★★ *Bristol-Union*, 4, pl. de la Poissonnerie (E2), ☎ 99.40.83.36, Euro Visa, 27 rm ♪ ♿ closed 15 Nov-31 Jan, 225.
★★ *Le Rochebonne*, 15, bd Chateaubriand (E1), ☎ 99.56.01.72, Tx 740802, Euro Visa, 39 rm ⎧⎭ closed Mon (l.s.), Feb, 160. Rest. ♦ ♪ Spec : *feuilleté d'escargot, blanquette de poissons nobles, foie de canard au muscat*, 65-150.
★ *Annick*, 13, rue du Boyer (D2), ☎ 99.40.88.57, Visa, 11 rm ≼ ♨ half pens, closed Wed, 1 Dec-15 Jan, 230. Rest. ♦ ♪ 40-100.
★ *Porte Saint-Pierre* (L.F.), 2, pl. du Guet (D2), ☎ 99.40.91.27, Euro Visa, 29 rm ≼ ♨ half pens (h.s.), closed Tue eve, 15 Nov-1 Feb, 360. Rest. ♦ ≼ ♪ closed Tue, 50-125.

Restaurants :

● ♦♦♦ *La Métairie de Beauregard*, Bourg de St-Etienne, on the rte de Rennes (C3), ☎ 99.81.37.06, AE DC Visa ⎧⎭ ♪ closed 1 Sep-12 Jun. Spec : *foie gras frais de canard, broiled lobster, blanquette de homard*, 130-200.

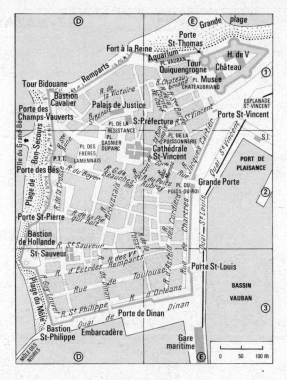

SAINT-MALO (intra-muros)

● ◆◆ *A la Duchesse Anne*, pl. Guy-la-Chambre (E1),
☎ 99.40.85.33 ⊞ ❀ closed Wed , Dec-Jan. Spec : lobster, *foie gras de canard*, 160-220.
◆ *Gilles*, 2, rue de la Pie-qui-Boit (D2), ☎ 99.40.97.25,
Euro Visa, closed Thu and Sun eve (l.s.), 1-15 Mar,
11 Nov-15 Dec, 80-130.

⚠ ★★*Cité d'Aleth*, Saint-Servan (400 pl), ☎ 99.81.60.91 ;
★★*Nielles*, bd de Rothéneuf (95 pl), ☎ 99.40.26.35 ; at
Rothéneuf, ★★*Illots* (130 pl), ☎ 99.56.41.36.

Recommended
Boat rental : *Locaguen*, ☎ 99.82.30.06.
Marina : Bas Sablons, ☎ 99.81.71.34.
Thalassotherapie : ☎ 88.56.02.56.
Youth hostel : av. du R.-P.-Humbricht, ☎ 99.40.29.80.
♥ crêperie : *Chez Gaby*, 2, rue de Dinan ; *Corps de Garde*,
3, montée N.-D.

SAINT-NAZAIRE

Nantes 62, Rennes 124, Paris 433 km
pop 68947 ⊠ 44600
C4

This harbour was built a century ago for ships too
large to enter Nantes. It was destroyed during WWII,
when it served as a German submarine base. The
town is now the leading French naval dockyard (70 %
of national production) and a major commercial port.

▶ Everything here converges on the port★★ where a **viewing terrace** has been built above the old submarine pens
(C3 ; *9:30-7:30, Jul.-Aug. ; 9:30-12 & 2-6 ex Mon. in Jun.
and 1-15 Sep.*). View over the outer port, protected by
two 500-m jetties and the Saint-Nazaire Basin (550 m x
160 m) ; the submarine base is still intact and this 10-acre
concrete rectangle is now used by industry ; you can also

see the Penhoët Basin (1100 x 230 m) and surrounding
shipyards. The skilled workforce and high performance
equipment can build tankers of up to 500 000 metric
tons. A sizeable proportion of their output today consists of motors, compressors, boilers and equipment for
nuclear power-plants and aerospace. ▶ The town has
been rebuilt on a generous scale ; the most interesting
architectural achievement is the **Salle Omnisport★** (1975 ;
sports stadium) where an enormous concrete shell,
roofed with plastic-coated steel cable stands in the middle
of the sports ground.

Nearby

▶ **Donges**, 16.5 km E, is the third-largest oil port in
France ; see the refineries with flares at night. The modern
church has a monumental Calvary★ on the façade, inspired by Breton traditions. ▶ **Montoir de Bretagne**, 8 km
away, the foremost methane port of Europe, completes this industrial complex. ▶ From the **Saint-Nazaire
Bridge★** (1965 ; 3356 m ; 60 m above the Loire ; *toll*) you
have a wide view★ over the town and the estuary.   □

Practical Information _____

⃞ pl. de l'Hôtel-de-Ville (A3), ☎ 40.22.40.65.
✈ *Montoir*, 7 km NE, ☎ 40.90.15.89.
SNCF (A1), ☎ 40.66.50.50.
▭ 17, rue Henri-Gautier (B2), ☎ 40.22.21.07.
Car rental : *Avis*, 126, av. de la République (A1-2),
☎ 40.66.65.44.

Hotels :
★★★ *Berry*, 1, pl. de la Gare (B1), ☎ 40.22.42.61,
Tx 700952, AE DC Euro Visa, 27 rm ℗ ⓑ 230. Rest. ◆◆ ♪
ⓑ 100-130.
★★★ *Bon Accueil* (L.F.), 39, rue Marceau (B3),

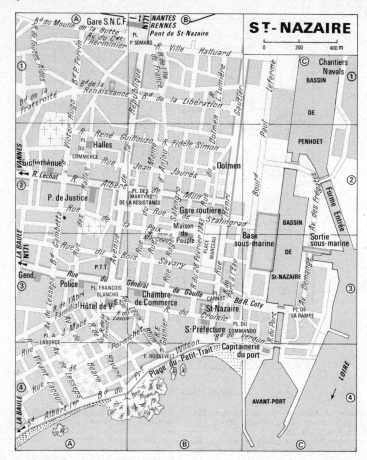

ST-NAZAIRE

☎ 40.22.07.05, AE DC Euro Visa, 12 rm Ⓟ closed Jul, 290. Rest. ♦ ♪ closed Sat, 60-140.
★★ **Dauphin**, 33, rue J.-Jaurès (A-B2), ☎ 40.66.59.61, AE DC Euro Visa, 21 rm Ⓟ ⬙ 125.

⚠ ★★★L'Eve (404 pl), ☎ 40.91.90.65; ★★Les Jaunais (70 pl), ☎ 40.91.90.60.

ST-PHILBERT-DE-GRAND-LIEU*

Nantes 23, Rennes 130, Paris 400 km
pop 4182 ⊠ 44310   D4

Red tiles instead of slates, white tufa instead of granite... Muscadet or Gros Plant white wines instead of cider. Nevertheless, the Retz region has been part of Brittany since the year 851.

▶ In 815 the monks of Noirmoutier, fleeing the Normans, founded an abbey a few kilometres from a marsh-bordered lake in this remote spot. The **church**★ is still there, a rare example of Carolingian architecture, with pillars based alternately on stone and brick, and a crypt containing the 7thC sarcophagus of St. Philbert; 16th-17thC priory and monastic buildings.

Nearby

▶ **Machecoul** *(15 km SW)* : old houses and ruins of the 14thC castle of Gilles de Retz, the valiant companion at arms of Joan of Arc; he later became one of history's worst criminals, the inspiration for Perrault's "Bluebeard". ▶ 19 km S, in Legé : **château de Bois-Chevalier**★ (1655; Apr.-Oct., 9-12 & 2-7).   □

SAINT-POL-DE-LÉON**

Morlaix 20, Brest 58, Paris 557 km
pop 7998 ⊠ 29250   A-B1

Lacy stonework and a pointed bell-tower set among cultivated fields... This is a region famous for its artichokes and other vegetables, and also for the flowers, shrubs, and conifers grown for replanting in private gardens.

▶ The chapel of **Notre-Dame du Kreisker**★★ (14thC; *summer, 10-11:30 & 1:30-5:30*) is of astonishing size; the 15thC bell-tower★★ is 77 m high, with an openwork spire flanked by pinnacles which has been much copied in the region. ▶ **Old houses** in the street leading to the **cathedral**★★ (13th-16thC; *8:30-11:45 & 1:30-7*), a sober Gothic edifice showing signs of Norman influence. Inside, see the 15th and 16thC stained glass, the Renaissance organs, the carved stalls (1512) and the unusual *Etagères de la Nuit* behind the left-hand stalls : these are small chapel-shaped reliquaries containing skulls. ▶ The Hôtel de Ville is in the former bishop's palace (18thC). ▶ The **Promenade du Champ de la Rive** (riverside walk) ends at a

Calvary where there is an excellent view over the estuary of the Penzé and its islets. The port of Pempoul and the Sainte-Anne beach are at the head of a shallow bay.

Round trip of the châteaux in Léon *(65 km approx)*

▶ Take the road from **Saint-Pol** to Plouescat; after crossing the Landivisiau road, you drive alongside a crenellated wall *(right)* surrounding the Manor of Pontplancoët; further on is the Manor of Kerautret, on the left. ▶ The **château de Kérouzéré★** *(ext. visit only, 1 Jul.-15 Sep.)* is one of the region's best examples of 15thC military architecture. ▶ 1 500 m from Cléder, the **château de Tronjoly** is an elegant Renaissance mansion. ▶ Leaving **Plouescat**, a town specialising in garlic and shallots (see the *cohue* - 16thC covered market), take the D30 which passes the château de Maillé (1570) towards Kerjean. A short detour to the left takes you to see *(from the road only)* the spectacular ruins of the château de Kergornadeac'h, near a lake in the middle of the woods. ▶ **Kerjean★★** is one of the finest 16thC Breton châteaux *(10-12 & 2-6 Ap-Sep; 5 rest of year; closed Tue. and nat. hols.).* This luxurious mansion is surrounded by fortifications, reflecting both the uncertainty of the times and the independent spirit of wealthier Bretons. In the chapel, see the beautiful chestnut-panel vaulting and the carved beams; in the rooms that have been restored, 16th and 17thC Breton furniture of interest. ▶ Through **Berven** (15th-16thC church★ in a churchyard with Renaissance gateway), to **Tréflaouénan** (in the church, decorated nave panelling showing fourteen scenes from the Life of Christ); ruins of the **Manor of Créac'h Ingar** (15thC, under restoration, *free admission*). ☐

Practical Information ─────────────

SAINT-POL-DE-LÉON
ⓘ pl. de l'Evêché, ☎ 98.69.05.69.
SNCF ☎ 98.69.14.55.

Nearby

CLÉDER, ✉ 29233, 5 km W of **Plouescat** on the D 10.

Restaurant :
● ◆◆ *Le Temps de Vivre*, 9, rue de l'Armorique, ☎ 98.69.42.48, AE Euro Visa ♪ closed Mon and Wed eve. Good times in store with J.-Y. Crenn's wonderful cooking *choux farcis de lotte, millefeuille de pigeon à l'artichaut*, 95-220.

PLOUESCAT, ✉ 29221, 6 km NE of **Folgoët**.
ⓘ ☎ 98.69.62.18.

Hotels :
★★ *La Caravelle* (L.F.), 20, rue du Calvaire, ☎ 98.69.61.75, Euro Visa, 16 rm Ⓟ ♪ closed Mon eve (l.s.), 180. Rest. ◆ ♪ 50-150.
★ *L'Azou*, 8 bis, rue du Gal-Leclerc, ☎ 98.69.60.16, AE DC Euro Visa, 5 rm ♨ ♪ ♿ closed Tue and Wed lunch, 13-23 Jan, 25 Sep-15 Oct. Rest. ◆ ♪ ♿ Spec : seafood assortment, *salade de Saint-Jacques léonarde, goujonnette de sole au noilly*, 50-200.

▲ ★★*Pors-Meur* (88 pl), ☎ 98.69.63.16; ★*Poulfoën* (88 pl), ☎ 98.69.81.80.

SAINT-QUAY-PORTRIEUX

Saint-Brieuc 21, Guingamp 28, Paris 472 km
pop 3399 ✉ 22410   C1

A family seaside resort with beaches, facilities and a good location.

▶ Beaches and cliffs, sand and rocks, paths among the gorse and pines, stretching along the coast which seems to be a continuous holiday area from **Binic** (local history museum, *daily pm, Jun.-Sep.*) through **Étables-sur-Mer** and Saint-Quay, to **Portrieux**.

Nearby

▶ 9 km SW : chapel of **Notre-Dame de la Cour★** (15thC) with stained glass★ in the apse, illustrating the Life of the Virgin in eighteen scenes *(guided tour, 8-8, Jul.-Sep.)*. ☐

Practical Information ─────────────

SAINT-QUAY-PORTRIEUX
ⓘ 17 bis, rue Jeanne-d'Arc, ☎ 96.70.40.64.
⛴ ☎ 96.70.40.64, l'île de Bréhat.

Hotels :
★★★ *Ker Moor*, 13, rue du Pdt-Le-Sénécal, ☎ 96.70.52.22, AE DC Euro Visa, 28 rm Ⓟ ♨ ♨ ⚄ ♪ ♿ ♭ closed Sun eve and Mon, 15 Dec-15 Mar, 300. Rest. ◆ ♪ ♿ 95-190.
★★ *Gerbot d'Avoine* (L.F.), 2, bd du Littoral, ☎ 96.70.40.09, 26 rm Ⓟ ♨ ♨ closed Sun eve and Mon, 6-24 Jan, 23 Nov-24 Dec, 185. Rest. ◆ ♪ 50-90.

▲ ★★★*Bellevue* (220 pl), ☎ 96.70.41.84.

Nearby

ÉTABLES-SUR-MER, ✉ 22680, 3 km S.

Hotel :
● *La Colombière*, bd du Littoral, ☎ 96.70.61.64, Euro Visa, 5 rm Ⓟ ♨ ♨ ⚄ ♫ closed Mon eve and Tue, 15-30 Nov, 300. Rest. ◆ ♪ ♫ 80-250; child : 65.

▲ ★★*Abri Côtier* (140 pl), ☎ 96.70.61.57.

Île de SEIN
(Sein Island)

pop 504 ✉ 29162   A2

This flat (highest point : 8 m) 140-acre rock has no trees, no springs (the inhabitants rely on rainwater), a few cows, and some potatoes or other vegetables grown in the shelter of low stone walls. The houses huddle along narrow streets barely 2 m wide. A fierce current rushes between the mainland and this windswept island. The only resources are scallops, lobsters, and other sea-food.

▶ The **Sénans libres** monument recalls the departure for England of the entire male population in response to the appeal of 18 June 1940; 36 never returned. ▶ The **lighthouse** *(visits)*, seen up to 50 km, offers a panorama★ of the island and mainland. ☐

Practical Information ─────────────

⛴ ☎ 98.70.02.37, from Audierne, in 1hr10, 1 connection daily (3 in Jul-Aug) ex Wed.

Hotel :
Rozen-Fouquet, 32, rue F.-Croûton, ☎ 98.70.90.77 ♨ ⚄ closed 1 Nov-1 Jun, 80.

Restaurant :
● ◆◆ *Auberge des Senans*, 6, quai Français-Libres, ☎ 98.70.90.01 ♨ closed 1 Oct-15 Apr. The famous *ragoût de pommes de terre et de homards* that inspired so many great chefs, 50-155.

TRÉGUIER★★

Guingamp 36, Saint-Brieuc 60, Paris 511 km
pop 3400 ✉ 22220   B1

A former bishopric and stop of the Tro Breiz this is a quiet city, its streets sloping down to a superb estuary uniting the Jaudy and Gumdy.

▶ **Cathedral of St. Tugdual★★** : one of the most beautiful 14th-15thC Gothic buildings in Brittany *(Easter-end Sep., 9-12 & 2-7)*; inside, see the carved choir-stalls and the neo-Gothic tomb of St.Yves, a very popular saint, whose *pardon (19 May)* attracts thousands. In the N transept is the entry to the treasure room and the 15thC cloister★ *(admission charged)*. ▶ **Ernest Renan's birthplace** *(10-12 & 2-7, Apr.-Sep.; closed Tue., Wed.)*, a handsome 17thC half-timbered house. ▶ Other fine **old houses** towards the Quai du Jaudy.

Nearby

▶ 2 km S : **Minihy-Tréguier** is the birthplace of St. Yves (1253-1303); 15thC church. ▶ **Pleubian** *(9 km NE)* in the centre of a peninsula; seaweed gathering. ▶ 7 km N : **Plougescrant;** fantastically-shaped rocks; chapel of St. Gonéry, with an astonishing bent spire covered with lead; panelling with naïf paintings★. ▶ All along the Tégor coast★ are little resorts surrounded by rocks, reefs, islets and inlets : **Port Blanc, Trestel** and **Trévou-Tréguignec.** ▶ 11 km SE, **château de la Roche-Jagu★** : a 14th-15thC fortified mansion surrounded by greenery above the left bank of the Trieux *(daily 1 Jul.-15 Sep., 9-12:30 & 2-7)*. □

Practical Information _____

TRÉGUIER
ℹ mairie, ☎ 96.92.30.19.

Hotels :
★★★ *Kastell Dinec'h*, (L.F.), rte de Lannion, ☎ 96.92.49.39, Euro Visa, 15 rm Ⓟ 𝄞 🍽 🔇 ♪ ♿ closed Tue eve and Wed, 12-27 Oct, 31 Dec-15 Mar, 210.
★ *Estuaire*, 5, quai du Gal-de-Gaulle, ☎ 96.92.30.25, Euro Visa, 15 rm 𝄞 ✿ closed Sun eve and Mon (l.s.), 130. Rest. ♦ 50-100.

Nearby

PORT-BLANC, ✉ 22710 Penvénan, 11 km NW.

Hotel :
★ *Grand Hôtel* (L.F.), bd de la Mer, ☎ 96.92.66.52, AE DC Euro Visa, 30 rm Ⓟ 𝄞 🍽 🔇 🚲 ♪° half pens (h.s.), closed Oct-Easter, 140. Rest. ♦ 𝄞 ♪ 50-75.

TRÉVOU-TRÉGUIGNEC, ✉ 22660 Trélévern, 13 km NW.

Hotel :
★ *Trestel-Bellevue*, rte de Trestel, ☎ 96.23.71.44, 14 rm Ⓟ 𝄞 🍽 🔇 half pens (h.s.), closed 30 Sep-Easter, 190. Rest. ♦ 𝄞 ♪ Shellfish, 65-100; child : 35.

⚠ ★★★*Anciennes Dunes* (120 pl), ☎ 96.23.76.09; ★★★*Mât* (70 pl), ☎ 96.23.71.52.

Le VAL-ANDRÉ

Saint-Brieuc 29, Dinan 43, Paris 436 km
pop 3801 ✉ 22370 Pléneuf　　　　　　　　　C1
2 km from the town of **Pléneuf**, a century-old resort by a marvellous beach. Yacht harbour at Dahouët (site★).

▶ 6 km NE, **château de Bienassis★** (1620) : a fine mansion in pink sandstone with double moats (15th-17thC) and French formal gardens *(8 Jun.-15 Sep., ex Sun. and nat. hols. 10:30-12:30 & 2-6:30)*. □

Practical Information _____

ℹ arcades du Casino, ☎ 96.72.20.55.

Hotel :
★★ *Grand Hôtel du Val-André*, 80, rue A.-Charner, Pléneuf, ☎ 96.72.20.56, Euro Visa, 39 rm Ⓟ 𝄞 🔇 half pens (h.s.), closed Wed and Thu lunch (l.s.), 12 Nov-1 Mar, 270. Rest. ♦ 𝄞 ♿ ✿ 75-200.

Restaurant :
● ♦♦ *Cotriade*, in the port of Piégu, Pléneuf, ☎ 96.72.20.26 𝄞 closed Mon eve and Tue, 15 Dec-15 Jan. Panoramic view of the pleasure port and excellent food by J.-J. Le Saout, 110-300.

⚠ ★★*Monts Colleux* (300 pl), ☎ 96.72.95.10; ★★*Salines de Mercœur* (133 pl), ☎ 96.72.95.09.

VANNES**

Rennes 106, Quimper 116, Paris 456 km
pop 45397 ✉ 56000　　　　　　　　　　　C3
A quiet country town at the back of the Gulf of Morbihan. Charming old buildings and narrow twisting streets, flower-beds at the base of the ramparts.

▶ Starting from the **port** (B3), Rue Le Pontois is probably the best way to approach the old city : **ramparts★** studded with towers and gate-ways, formal French garden, old wash houses on the Ruisseau de Rohan (Rohan Brook), all of which are illuminated on summer evenings. The view★ is even more beautiful from the Garenne Promenade. ▶ You reach the *chevet* of the cathedral through the **Porte Prison** (B2; 15thC, machicolated tower). Around the cathedral, old buildings★ house many antique shops and boutiques : Rue Saint-Guenhaël is the most typical. ▶ The **cathedral★** (B2), principally 15th and 16thC, has a Flamboyant Gothic N doorway with Renaissance recesses; inside is the tomb of St. Vincent Ferrier (tapestries of his miracles); chapels with altarpieces, statues and paintings; don't miss the treasury★ in the former chapterhouse. ▶ Opposite the cathedral is the **cohue** (12th-14thC covered market) looking on old houses; on the first floor, a Fine Arts Museum. ▶ Place Henri-IV, Rue Salomon and Rue des Halles in the pedestrian precinct are also lined by fine **old houses.** ▶ In the château Gaillard (1400, former seat of the Parliament of Brittany), is the **Archaeology Museum** *(daily ex Sun., 9:30-12 & 2-6)*, especially rich in pre-historic finds★ from the Gulf of Morbihan. ▶ Close by, in the Place Valancia, is the Maison de Vannes, decorated with two carved wood grotesques. ▶ In the Louis XIV-style Hôtel de Limur (Rue Thiers, B2) is the TO. At N° 1 of the same street, near the port, is the Gulf and Sea Museum. ▶ Interesting and important **Aquarium** (the second-largest in Europe) at the end of the bridge : species from the Gulf, the tropical coral reefs and the great lakes of Africa *(daily 10-6:30; Jul., Aug. 9-9)*. ▶ 5 km S, **Conleau island** : lovely shady spot with pine trees, where people go to eat oysters. Regular boat service to the Ile d'Arz.

Nearby

▶ 9 km SW the **Pointe d'Arradon★** gives a good view of the many islands and inlets in the Gulf of Morbihan (→). ▶ In **Saint-Avé** *(4 km NE),* chapel of Notre-Dame du Loc★ : figured cross with carved alabaster panels (15thC). ▶ 15 km E, **château du Plessis-Josso★** (14th-16thC) : vast manor-house with ramparts, towers, mill and pond *(10 Jul.-30 Aug., pm)*. 4 km further on : the 18thC **château de Trémohar-en-Berric** has kept its 14th-15thC fortified out-buildings *(visit on request 1 Jul.-15 Sep., 9-12 & 2:30-6)*. □

Practical Information _____

VANNES
ℹ 1, rue Thiers (B2), ☎ 97.47.24.34.
✈ *Meucon*, 10 km NE, ☎ 97.60.78.79.
SNCF (C1), ☎ 97.42.50.50/97.54.11.48.
⚓ *Navispace*, ☎ 97.63.79.99, gastronomic cruise, candlelight dinner-cruises; *Vedettes vertes (boats)*, ☎ 97.63.79.99, from pont Vert to golfe du Morbihan, Houat, Hoëdic.
Car rental : *Avis*, 4, rue J.-le-Brix (B2), ☎ 97.47.47.43; train station.

Hotels :
★★★ *La Marebaudière*, 4, rue A.-Briand (C2), ☎ 97.47.34.29, AE DC Euro Visa, 40 rm Ⓟ 🍽 🔇 half pens (h.s.), closed Sun eve (l.s.), 18 Dec-8 Jan, 205. Rest. ♦ *La Marée Bleue* ♪ ♿ 60-170.
★★★ *Manche-Océan*, 31, rue du Lt-Colonel-Maury (B2), ☎ 97.47.26.46, AE DC Visa, 42 rm Ⓟ 🔇 🚲 ♿ 170.

Restaurants :
● ♦♦ *Le Lys*, 51, rue Mal-Leclerc (C2), ☎ 97.47.29.30, AE DC Euro Visa Ⓟ closed Mon and Sun eve (l.s.), 15 Nov-13 Dec. Good cooking in a subdued atmosphere.

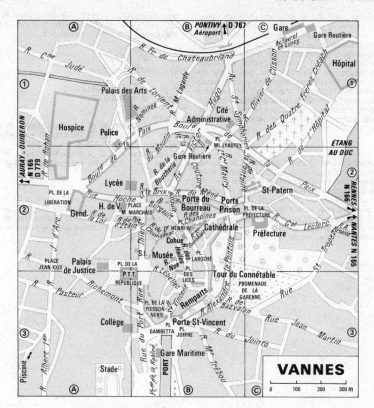

Ⓐ PONTIVY Ⓑ D 767 Aéroport Ⓒ Gare Gare Routière
R. Cne R. Fr. de Chateaubriand Hôpital
Judé
Ⓐ① Av. Favrel et Liney ①
Palais des Arts
Hospice Police Cité Administrative ÉTANG AU DUC
PL. MAL LYAUTEY
AURAY - QUIBERON N 165 D 779 Gare Routière
Lycée St-Patern ②
PL. DE LA LIBÉRATION Porte du Porte RENNES N 166 NANTES N 165
Gend. H. de V. Bourreau Prison
PL. DE LA PRÉFECTURE
Cathédrale Préfecture
Cohue
Palais Musée Tour du Connétable
PLACE JEAN-XXIII de Justice PL. DE LA
P.T.T. RÉPUBLIQUE Remparts PROMENADE DE LA GARENNE Rue
Collège Porte St-Vincent
GAMBETTA PL. JOFFRE Rue du Jointo
Piscine Gare Maritime
Stade PORT
Ⓐ Ⓑ Ⓒ

VANNES
0   100   200   300 m

Spec : *fricassée de sole et palourdes, picata de lotte enrubanné au lard fumé sur lit d'oseille, ris de veau braisés au cidre*, 90-250 ; child : 45.
♦♦ *L'Epée*, 2, rue Joseph-le-Brix (B2), ☎ 97.47.10.11, AE Euro Visa ♪ ঙ closed Sat noon and Sun, 45-120.

⚐ ★★★*Conleau* (290 pl), ☎ 97.63.13.88.

Nearby
ARRADON, ⊠ 56610, 9 km SW.
Hotels :
★★ *Hesperie*, La Lande du Bourg, ☎ 97.44.72.25, 25 rm ℙ ≼ ⚟ ♪ ঙ 180.
★★ *Vénètes*, à la Pointe d'Arradon, ☎ 97.44.03.11, 12 rm ≼ ⚐ ⚒ closed Nov-Feb, 310. Rest. ♦ ♪ ⚒ closed Mon and Sun eve, 100-190.

L'Île d' ARZ, ⊠ 56840.
Hotel :
★ *L'Escale*, on the wharf, ☎ 97.44.32.15, Visa, 11 rm ≼⚐ pens (h.s.), closed 30 Sep-1 Apr, 196. Rest. ♦ ≼ ♪ 50-110.

La presqu'Île de CONLEAU, ⊠ 56000 Vannes, 5 km SW.
Hotel :
★★ *Roof*, ☎ 97.63.47.47, AE DC Euro Visa, 12 rm ℙ ≼⚐ ⚒ closed 5 Jan-15 Feb, 170. Rest. ♦ ♪ closed Mon (l.s.), 70-140.

LOCMINÉ, ⊠ 56500, 28 km.
ⓘ pl. Anne-de-Bretagne, ☎ 97.60.00.37.
Hotel :
★★ *L'Argoat* (L.F.), 34, rue de Clisson, ☎ 97.60.01.02, Visa, 22 rm ℙ ⚟ ⚐ ♪ ⚘ closed Fri eve and Sat lunch, 25 Dec-20 Jan, 180. Rest. ♦ ♪ 45-90 ; child : 40.

⚐ ★★*Beaulieu* (45 pl), ☎ 97.60.02.16.
MUZILLAC, ⊠ 56190, 25 km SE.
Hotels :
★★★★ *Domaine de Rochevilaine* (R.C.), pointe de Pen-Lan, 4 km S on D 5, ☎ 97.41.69.27, Tx 950570, AE DC Euro Visa, 28 rm ℙ ≼ ⚟ ⚐ ☐ closed 1 Jan-7 Mar, 600. Rest. ● ♦♦ ≼ ♪ ⚒ P. Caillaut cooks in the finest Breton tradition, 220-300.
★★ *Auberge de Pen Mur*, 20, rte de Vannes, ☎ 97.41.67.58, AE DC Euro, 24 rm ℙ ⚟ ♪ ⚙ half pens (h.s.), closed 15-30 Nov, 210. Rest. ♦♦ ♪ Seafood, fish, 60-170.

⚐ at Billiers, ★★*Guérandière*, 3 km S. (150 pl), ☎ 97.41.64.83.

VITRÉ*

Rennes 36, Nantes 118, Paris 311 km
pop 13491 ⊠ 35500   D2

One of the gateways to Brittany, Vitré is part of a line of defensive sites between Clisson and Fougères. Because of its defensive role, Vitré acquired an impressive castle and a ring of ramparts ; with quaint narrow streets and old houses the town looks much like a mediaeval woodcut.

▶ Enter the **old city** by the **Rue d'Em-Bas** lined, like the **Rue Baudrairie★**, with ancient houses. ▶ The pride of the city is the **castle★★**, a perfect example of mediaeval military architecture. Built on a triangular plan with three broad round towers, it opens onto the square through a gatehouse, itself flanked by several towers and today housing the town hall and a museum *(daily Jul.-Sep., 10-12 & 1:30-6; rest of year, 10-12 & 2-5:30; Oct.-Mar., closed Mon. am, Tue., Sat., Sun.; Apr.-Jun., closed Tue.)*. ▶ The **church of Notre-Dame** (15th-16thC) is very characteristic of Flamboyant Gothic in Upper Brittany : façade is studded with gables and pinnacles, while an outside 15thC pulpit recalls the important role played by the Church in the public life of those days; ask in the sacristy to see the series of 32 Limousin enamels★ (1544). ▶ Walk down the Rue Notre-Dame (old houses) and the neighbouring streets to the Place de la République where the **Promenade du Val** starts, and continues along the N and E **ramparts★**.

Nearby

▶ From the **Rachapt** District (15thC chapel of St. Nicolas with 16thC frescos) you can walk up to the **Tertres Noirs** *(15 min) :* view★ over town and castle. ▶ 6 km SE : the **château des Rochers-Sévigné★** (16th-17thC) would still look familiar to the Marquise de Sévigné (1626-96), who wrote some of her famous letters here *(daily ex Sun. am, 9-12 & 2-6)*. ▶ **Champeaux** *(9 km NW);* square, old granite houses★ grouped around a 1601 well, and a collegiate 15th-16thC church★; inside, Renaissance works of art : canopied stalls (1530-35), mausoleum of Guy d'Espinay (1553), stained glass; 1.5 km S of the village, **château d'Espinay** (14th-16thC; *no visitors).*   ☐

Practical Information _____

ⓘ pl. St-Yves, ☎ 99.75.04.46.
SNCF ☎ 99.75.00.47.

Hotels :
★★ *Petit Billot*, 5, pl. du Gal-Leclerc, ☎ 99.75.02.10, Euro Visa, 23 rm ⌘ closed Fri eve and Sat lunch, 15 Dec-15 Jan, 175. Rest. ♦ ♪ ⌘ 55.
★ *Le Chêne Vert*, 2, pl. du Gal-de-Gaulle, ☎ 99.75.00.58, 22 rm Ⓟ ⌘ closed Fri eve and Sat, 22 Sep-22 Oct, 120. Rest. ♦ 50-130.

Restaurants :
♦ *Le Pichet*, 17, bd de Laval, ☎ 99.75.24.09, Visa ⏧ ⌘ closed Mon and Sun eve, 10-24 Aug, 75-180.
♦ *Taverne de l'Ecu*, 12, rue Beaudrairie, ☎ 99.75.11.09, Euro Visa Ⓟ ⌘ ♪ closed Mon and Sun eve, 1-15 Feb, 1-15 Sep, 60-150.

Burgundy

▶ It is sometimes difficult to ascertain where Burgundy begins and where it ends : its borders are vague and it encloses a multitude of different regions. There is Celtic, rugged Morvan, the Romanesque and mystical tradition of its mediaeval abbeys, the sensuality of the Côte-d'Or and the magnificent city of Dijon. For tourists, its major attractions are just as diverse. For many, Burgundy is first and foremost the prestigious domain of the great wines from the 210 square kilometres of vineyards along the purple and gold banks of the river. More than 150 of these produce wine bearing the coveted *A.O.C.* label. It is divided up into some 5 000 separate vineyards producing wine of the most varied nature, depending on the particular microclimate, soil and exposure. The most famous Burgundies come from the Côte-d'Or with its two great vineyards, the Côte de Nuits and the Côte de Beaune.

For others, Burgundy represents a soil fertilized by mediaeval faith, the site of Romanesque architecture's finest masterpieces : Vézelay, Autun, and Cluny, and the modest country churches of the Brionnais and Mâconnais regions. In 910 Bernon founded a Benedictine abbey on the banks of the Grosne, and Cluny very quickly became the center of mediaeval Catholicism. Its abbots enjoyed an influence greater than that of popes and kings. Two centuries after it was founded, Cluny had 1 200 brother and sister houses throughout Europe.

For still others, Burgundy is a mosaic of landscapes, generous and severe by turns, studded with forests, waterways and canals. Dotted too with the imposing châteaux of feudal lords and the cultivated noblemen of the Age of Enlightenment. Burgundy has traditionally been a place of exchanges and encounters, of summer holidays and weekend escapades; hunting, fishing, sporting activities and cultural marvels, excellent cooking and specialities which flavor the whole of French cuisine : snails, Dijon mustard, gingerbread, cassis (black currant) liqueur and the famous *kir* — an aperitif of white wine and cassis.

The capital city, Dijon, houses the splendid palaces of Burgundian aristocracy, a Fine Arts Museum testifying to the genius of the Flemish artists who lived and painted here under the patronage of the Great Dukes, and a bevy of churches and private mansions. ☐

 Don't miss

★★★ Ancy-le-Franc B1, Autun B3, Beaune C3, Dijon C2, Fontenay B2, Vézelay A2.
★★ Auxerre A1-2, Avallon B2, Côte de Beaune C3, Châteauneuf B4, Châtillon-sur-Seine B1, Cluny B-C4, Cure Valley A-B2, Morvan Lakes and Nature Park B2-3, Nevers A3, Côte de Nuits C2-3, Semur-en-Auxois B2, Solutré C4, Tournus C4, between Tournus and Cluny C4.
★ Alise-Sainte-Reine B2, the Chalonnaise Region C3, La Charité-sur-Loire A3, Joigny A1, Paray-le-Monial B4, the Puisaye Region A2, Saulieu B2, Sens A1, Serein Valley B2, Tonnerre B1, Villeneuve-sur-Yonne A1, along the river Vingeanne C2.

Weekend tips

Full Saturday morning at Dijon, then follow the Vineyard Road to Beaune, and stop for the night at Tournus or Cluny. Early morning drive to Autun, then Saulieu (where you should have lunch). Continue to Avallon and Vézelay, and end the day at Auxerre. If you are taking the train, go to Laroche-Migennes (direct lines).

In the Auxerrois region

In the Nivernais region

Wine grower's house

In the Mâconnais region

Facts and figures

Location : *East of the centre of France, a crossroads and passage way on the North-South axis.*
Area : *31 582 km²*
Population : *1 596 000*
Climate : *temperate; colder in Morvan; wet in the mountains; very sunny west of Dijon. Winter often cold but clear; variable spring; summer often wet; mild, clear autumn (grape harvest), the most beautiful season in Burgundy.*
Administration :
— *Department of Côte-d'Or, Prefecture Dijon;*
— *Department of Nièvre, Prefecture Nevers;*
— *Department of Saône-et-Loire, Prefecture Mâcon;*
— *Department of Yonne, Prefecture Auxerre.*

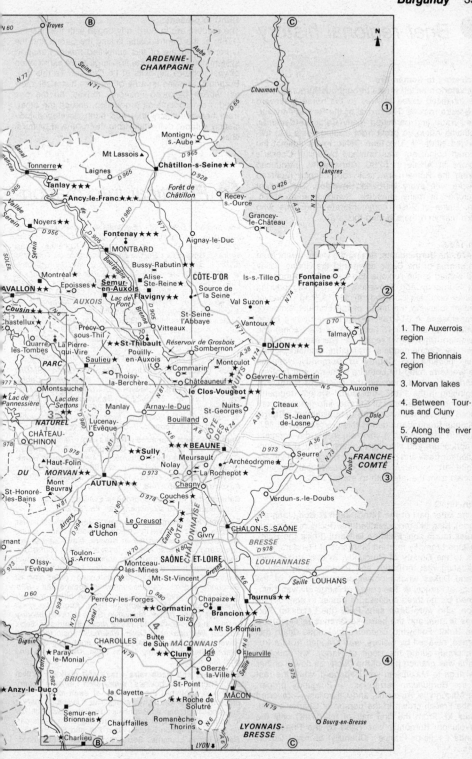

1. The Auxerrois region

2. The Brionnais region

3. Morvan lakes

4. Between Tournus and Cluny

5. Along the river Vingeanne

Brief regional history

Prehistory to Roman Era

Prehistoric man left traces throughout Burgundy, from the inhabited caves at Arcy to the horse graveyard at Solutré rock. ● The arrival of the Romans encouraged trade and permitted many **Celtic settlements**, including Autun, to grow from trading posts into full-fledged cities. ● The **final Gallic revolt** against the Roman colonisers was crushed by Julius Caesar's legions at **Alésia** in 52BC. **Christianity**, introduced during the Roman era, took root despite repeated checks with every Barbarian **invasion**. The ancient churches at many sites (St. Symphorien at Autun, Ste. Reine at Alise) commemorate Christians who were martyred there during this era.

5th-14thC

In **470**, the **Burgundians**, fleeing the Huns, swept from the shores of the Baltic down into the Rhône Valley and settled in the regions corresponding to modern-day Burgundy and Provence. ● The neighbouring **Franks** occupied Burgundy in 534. A long period of conflict following the death of the Frankish Emperor Charlemagne in 814 resulted in the territory's **being divided** into an eastern (left bank of the Saône) and a western (right bank) region. ● The eastern region, ruled by Charlemagne's grandson, Lothaire, eventually became the **County of Burgundy**, whereas the western, ruled by Lothaire's enemy and brother, Charles the Bald, became the **Duchy of Burgundy**. Beginning in the 11thC, the feudal system fragmented Burgundy, like most of Europe, into fiefdoms controlled by local warlords. The **establishment of large religious foundations** during this era (Vézelay in 867, Cluny in 910) played a vital role in the development of agriculture and viticulture, which laid a solid foundation for trade and prosperity. ● Burgundian Romanesque Art flourished in the ecclesiastical buildings erected from the late 10th to early 13thC.

14th-18thC

In the latter part of the 14thC, **Jean le Bon** (John the Good), King of France, settled the Duchy of Burgundy on his fourth son, **Philippe le Hardi** (Philip the Bold). Philippe promptly married Margaret of Flanders, heiress to the County of Burgundy, in one stroke consolidating vast territories and founding a dynasty of Grand Dukes whose power surpassed that of the Kings of France. ● The power of Burgundy was maintained by the three successors (father to son) of Philippe, who were **Jean sans Peur** (the Fearless), **Philippe le Bon**, and the bellicose **Charles le Téméraire** (the Bold). Following Charles's inglorious death (his corpse, ravaged by wolves, was dragged from a frozen pond) during his siege of Nancy, his daughter Marie was granted part of the Duchy as dowry on her marriage to Maximilian von Hapsburg, while the rest of the Burgundian territories — Burgundy proper, the Mâconnais, Auxerrois and Charollais — reverted to the French crown in the person of Charles's rival, **Louis XI**. From the first half of the 17thC until the Revolution, Burgundy was ruled by the Princes de Condé (→ Ile-de-France : Chantilly) as royal Governors.

19thC to present

The modern era in Burgundy began with the opening (1794) of the Centre Canal linking the Saône and the Loire. The advent of this simplified freight transport system coincided with the first large-scale exploitation of vast iron-ore deposits at Le Creusot. To this day, Burgundy remains an area of limitless historical interest whose balanced economy thrives, on the one hand, from agricultural production, and on the other, from heavy industry that has been developed judiciously without detracting from the rural and pastoral charm of the region.

Practical information

Information : *Délégation Régionale au Tourisme (D.R.T.),* 53, rue de la Préfecture, 21041 Dijon Cedex, ☎ 80.55.24.10. *Comité régional de Tourisme,* same address. **Côte-d'Or :** *Comité Départementale de Tourisme (C.D.T.),* 53, rue de la Préfecture, 21041 Dijon Cedex, ☎ 80.73.81.81. **Nièvre :** *C.D.T.,* 64, rue de la Préfecture, 58019 Nevers, ☎ 86.57.80.25. **Saône-et-Loire :** *C.D.T.,* 389, av. de Lattre-de-Tassigny, 71025 Mâcon, ☎ 85.39.47.47. **Yonne :** *Association départementale de Tourisme,* Maison départementale du Tourisme, 1 et 2, quai de la République, 89000 Auxerre, ☎ 86.52.26.27. *Dir. régionale de la Jeunesse et des Sports,* 22, rue Audro, B.P. 1530, 21033 Dijon Cedex, ☎ 80.30.47.73. *Dir. rég. des Affaires culturelles,* Hôtel Chartraire de Montigny, 41, rue Vannerie, 21000 Dijon, ☎ 80.67.22.33.

S.O.S. : Côte-d'Or : *Medical Emergency Centre (SMUR)* Dijon, ☎ 80.41.12.12; *Poisoning Emergency Centre* Dijon, ☎ 80.41.12.12. **Nièvre :** *SAMU (Emergency Medical Service),* ☎ 86.59.22.00. **Saône-et-Loire :** *SMUR Chalon-sur-Saône,* ☎ 85.48.85.00, and Mâcon, ☎ 85.96.03.03; *Poisoning Emergency Centre* Lyons, ☎ 78.54.14.14. **Yonne :** *SMUR* Auxerre, ☎ 86.46.45.67.

Rural Gîtes and chambres d'hôtes : enq. : *Relais départementaux des Gîtes ruraux :* **Côte-d'Or :** *C.D.T.;* **Nièvre :** *C.D.T.;* **Saône-et-Loire :** *Chambre d'Agriculture,* bd Henri-Dunant, 71010 Mâcon Cedex, ☎ 85.38.99.78; **Yonne :** *Service Promotion rurale,* 14 bis, rue Guynemer, 89000 Auxerre, ☎ 86.46.47.48, and *C.D.T.*

Camping-car rentals : *Bourgogne Evasion,* 156, av. de la République, 71210 Montcharin, ☎ 85.78.52.11.

Festivals and events (→ also wine) : **Jan :** *musical winter* in Dijon. **Feb :** *carnival* in Chalon-sur-Saône. **Mar :** *spring fair* in Dijon; *exhibition fair* in Nevers. **May :** *sale of antiques and bric-à-brac* and *ring festival* in Dijon; *course des chausses* in Semur-en-Auxois; *antiques show* in Tournus. **Jun :** *music festival* in Dijon; *boating festival* and *great pardon of sailors* in Saint-Jean-de-Losne; *great days of Burgundy* and *musical encounters* in Beaune. **Jul :** *Burgundy nights festival* in Autun; *Morvan music festival; international music academy* in Dijon. **Aug :** *the great hours of Cluny flower festival* in Saint-Honoré; *bilberry festival* in Glux-en-Glenne; *horse racing* in Vitteaux. **Sep :** *48-hour flea market* in Dijon. *Nivernais music festival* in Nevers. **Oct :** *chestnut fair* in Saint-Léger-sous-Beuvray, Nevers. **Dec :** *crafts and gifts fair* in Dijon.

Exhibitions and trade fairs : fairs and markets of livestock, horses and bovines ; **every Mon :** *Bresse poultry market* in Louhans; **the 2nd Tue. of each month :** *livestock market* in Corbigny; **every Thu :** *livestock market* in Saint-Christophe-en-Brionnais; **10 Feb :** *livestock fair* in Fours; **Sat and Sun following 15 Aug :** *Charollais cattle show and fair* in Saulieu; **last Sat and Sun in Aug :** *Balme fair* in Louhans; **Sep :** *regional fair* in Montbard; **Dec :** *agricultural competition* in Nevers.

Burgundy wines

The Romans found vines already flourishing when they conquered Burgundy, but Burgundian wines came into their own during the Middle Ages. The Cluniac and Cistercian monks systematically cultivated and improved vines while, at the same time, improving techniques of fermentation and aging. Many vineyards today yielding excellent wines originated as dependencies of abbeys.

Burgundian vineyards cover a total of 52 500 acres, of which 38 000 are entitled to the superior status of A.O.C. (controlled place-name of origin). Nearby 5 000 growers cultivate plots that are called "climats". There may be as many as 50 climats in a single "place of origin" but it is essential to bear in mind that in Burgundy, more than anywhere else, quality counts above quantity. Plots as small as a single row of vines may change hands for fabulous sums.

Like all the vineyards in France, those of Burgundy were completely laid waste during the 19thC by the American vine louse, Phylloxera vastatrix, which destroyed the vines at the root. Phylloxera was finally overcome by grafting French vines onto the root stocks of resistant American varieties, but only after an appalling toll had been exacted of French vine-growers and workers in related industries.

The finest Burgundian wines are described as appellations communales (of community origin). Wines of lesser quality are appellations régionales (of regional origin), i.e. less specific, including wines that are defined not by locality but by some other peculiarity, such as Bourgogne aligoté (a white Burgundy wine made from aligoté grapes) or Bourgogne passe-tout-grains (a red made from a mixture of grape varieties). Others may be described as Bourgogne ordinaire, grand ordinaire or simply Bourgogne (Burgundy).

The two widely used grape varieties are the pinot noir (black) and the pinot chardonnay (white). To a much lesser extent, the aligoté and (mainly in Beaujolais) the gamay are also used.

The most illustrious Burgundian wines come from the Côte-d'Or ("golden coast"), which is divided into two main areas. The Côte de Nuits produces superb reds (Chambertin, Clos-de-Bèze, Bonnes-mares, Musigny, Clos-de-Vougeot, Grands-Échézeaux, Romanée-Conti, Romanée-Saint-Vivant, Richebourg). The Côte de Beaune produces both reds and whites, including the whites generally acknowledged as the very greatest by wine lovers; the reds include Corton-Charlemagne and Les Bressandes; the whites are Montrachet, Chevalier-Montrachet, Bâtard-Montrachet, Bienvenues-Bâtard-Montrachet and Criots-Bâtard-Montrachet.

There are also two vine-growing regions in Saône-et-Loire. The Côte Chalonnaise produces the whites of Rully, Montagny and the reds of Givry and Mercurey; the Mâconnais is home mostly to whites, including the widely acclaimed Pouilly-Fuissé. The reds and rosés from the Mâconnais are also light, fruity and very pleasant.

In Basse Bourgogne (lower Burgundy), the official name of the vine-growing regions around the Yonne, the term appellations communales is reserved for Chablis (always white). Other wines from the region (Irancy, Saint-Bris, Vincelottes) are only appellations régionales. The best recent Burgundy years are 61, 69, 71, 76, 78, and 83.

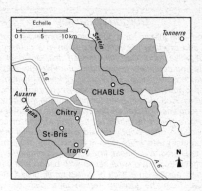

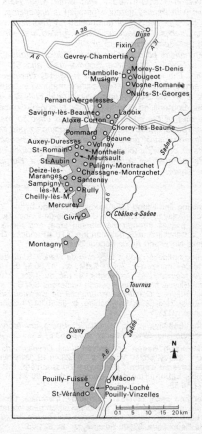

Son et lumière : Côte-d'Or : circuit de la Côte de Nuits, circuit de la Côte de Beaune; enq. : O.T. Beaune, ☎ 80.22.24.51. **Yonne :** grand historical spectacle in Saint-Fargeau; enq. : Maison de la Puisaye, ☎ 86.74.15.72. Autun's 100 faces, 15 May-30 Sep, enq. : O.T./S.I.

National and nature parks : nature park of the Morvan region; enq. : Maison du Parc, Saint-Brisson, 58230 Montsauche, ☎ 86.78.70.16. One-day excursions in the Morvan; enq. : Ecotour, résidence le France, 2, av. Colbert, 58000 Nevers, ☎ 86.61.56.78. Inclusive holidays : Chaîne hôtelière du Morvan, le Relais des Lacs, Planchez-en-Morvan, 58230 Montsauche, ☎ 86.78.41.68.

Burgundy cuisine

Good wine makes for a good table. Burgundian cooking and produce are renowned even in a country of superlative food. Carefully tended soil, an ideal climate and countless generations of know-how add up to matchless dining. Escargots, almost a symbol of the province, are particulary good when prepared with Chablis. Red wine is used for braising the internationally renowned Charollais beef (en daube). Chambertin is the red wine favoured for the preparation of coq-au-vin, too often poorly served elsewhere. Fish stew (pôchouse) with white wine is a speciality of Verdun-sur-le-Doubs. A delicious first course is poached eggs en meurette, in red wine sauce with bacon and small onions, served on a slice of grilled garlic bread. Saupiquet from the Morvan region is a dish of ham served in a cream sauce with white wine. Ham in aspic with parsley (jambon persillé) is appetizing, as are the tripe sausages (andouillettes) from Arnay-le-Duc, Chablis, Clamecy or Mâcon, grilled and served with the aromatic mustard of Dijon.
The cheeses produced on the border of Champagne are excellent : Chaource, Soumaintrain and St. Florentin. The undisputed king of Burgundy cheeses is the strong Époisses, which is often matured in brandy (marc). In the South, firm, sharp goat cheeses are called boutons de culotte (trouser buttons). Gougère is a ring of the same kind of dough used to make cream puffs, baked into a golden ring and topped with a glazed crust of grated Gruyère or Comté cheese.
Tarts or puddings (clafoutis) prepared with black currants or cherries make a fine end to a Burgundian dinner.

Rambling and hiking : Burgundy is traversed by the G.R. 7 from Nolay to Beaujeu, the G.R. 13 Ile-de-France-Bourgogne passes through the Morvan area, and the G.R. 137, a transverse axis between the G.R. 13 and the G.R. 7, links Nolay and Autun (topoguides).

Cycling holidays : enq. : *Bicy-club de France*, 8, pl. de la Porte-de-Champerret, 75017 Paris, ☎ 47.66.55.92, and *Ligue régionale de Bourgogne*, 8, rue du Tillor, 21000 Dijon. Bicycle hire : train + bike in numerous S.N.C.F. stations. **Nièvre :** *Comité départemental de Cyclotourisme*, rue Émile-Zola, 58260 La Machine, ☎ 86.50.84.73. **Saône-et-Loire :** *C.D.T.*

Riding holidays : enq. : *A.R.T.E. Bourgogne-Morvan*, 9, Grande-Rue, 89120 Charny, ☎ 86.63.67.25.

Horse-drawn wagon or caravan : *les Cavaliers de la nature*, Marcy, 58210 Varzy, ☎ 86.29.40.19. **Wild West style covered wagon :** *Bourgogne Buissonnière*, B.P. 1, 21820 Labergerment-lès-Seurre, ☎ 80.21.00.16/ 80.21.10.58.

River and canal cruises : Burgundy, Nivernais, Centre, Yonne, and Saône canals, and canal which runs lateral to the Loire. Enq. : *Voies navigables de Bourgogne*, 1-2, quai de la République, 89000 Auxerre, ☎ 86.52.26.27.

Courses : Nièvre : pottery in Saint-Amand-de-Puisaye, spinning in Chevannes, weaving in Montigny-aux-Amognes; enq. : *C.D.T.* **Yonne :** ceramics in Poilly-sur-Serein, weaving in Avallon, yoga in Villeneuve-sur-Yonne; enq. : *C.D.T.* Restoration of monuments : *Sites et monuments de Bourgogne du Sud*, 38, rue des Forges, 21000 Dijon, ☎ 80.30.72.01. Œnology : see "wine guide".

Wine guide : Apr : *Almshouse wine auction* in Nuits-Saint-Georges. **May :** *French wines fair* in Mâcon. **Aug :** *wine fair* in Pouilly-sur-Loire. **Sep :** *"trinquée"* in Meursault. **Nov :** *Sauvignon festival* in Saint-Bris-le-Vineux; the *"Trois glorieuses"*, a major 3-day festival : *le Chapitre*

at Clos-de-Vougeot (1st day), *Vente des hospices* at the Beaune Almshouse (2nd day), and the *Paulée* at Meursault (3rd day); enq. : *Comité interprofessionnel de la Côte-d'Or et de l'Yonne pour les vins d'appellation contrôlée de Bourgogne*, rue Henri-Dunant, 21200 Beaune, ☎ 80.22.21.35. *Comité interprofessionnel des Vins de Bourgogne et du Mâconnais* : Maison du Tourisme, av. du Mal-de-Lattre-de-Tassigny, 71000 Mâcon, ☎ 85.38.20.15. Mâconnais wine route *"Follow the grape"*, enq. : Mairie de Solutré-Pouilly, 71960 Pierreclos, ☎ 85.35.81.00. *Maison des vins de Chablis*, 26, rue Auxenoise, 89800 Chablis. Course (1 session fall, spring), enq. : *Maison des Vins*, promenade Sainte-Marie, 71100 Chalon-sur-Saône, ☎ 85.41.64.00.

Young people : enq. *C.R.I.*, 1, bd Champollion, 21000 Dijon, ☎ 80.71.32.12.

Golf : 18 holes : Chalon-sur-Saône, Norges-la-Ville; 15 holes : Mâcon; 9 holes : Magny-Cours, Savigny-sous-Clairis.

Canoeing : in the Morvan, La Cure and Le Chalaux areas, with the Chameçon lake station. Enq. : *C.D.T.* **Nièvre**.

Potholing and spelunking : Yonne, enq. : mairie, Chablis, and *Centre Social Balzac*, rue Balzac, 21000 Dijon, ☎ 80.32.58.46.

Climbing : *Club Alpin Français*, 5, rue de Strasbourg, 71100 Chalon-sur-Saône, and 7, rue des Cordiers, 71000 Mâcon. **Yonne :** Saussois rock, 25 km S of Auxerre; **Nièvre :** Surgy rock, N of Clamecy; **Côte-d'Or :** Saffres cliffs near Vitteaux; and **Saône-et-Loire :** famous Solutré rock.

Cross-country skiing : 5 marked circuits in the Haut-Folin mountains (Morvan).

Flying, gliding and ballooning : ballooning, enq. : *The Bombard Society*, hôtel de la Poste, 3, bd Clemenceau, 21100 Beaune, ☎ 80.22.08.11. Balloon ascents, enq. : Apr, *Centre aérostatique de Bourgogne*, 8, rue Jules-Merey, 21200 Beaune, ☎ 80.22.21.03, and from May-Jan, M. Pierre Bonnet, résidence du Lac, Les Hêtres, 21200 Beaune, ☎ 80.22.62.25. Other flying activities : **Nièvre**, Cosnes-sur-Loire, Nevers, aérodrome de la Sangsue, ☎ 86.57.03.92. **Saône-et-Loire :** Chalon, *aéroclub de Bourgogne*.

Hunting and shooting : *Fédérations départementales des chasseurs*. **Côte-d'Or :** 47, rue Verrerie, 21000 Dijon, ☎ 80.73.24.11. **Nièvre :** rte du Terrain de karting, 58000 Nevers, ☎ 86.61.27.91. **Saône-et-Loire :** *Maison de l'Agriculture*, bd Henri-Dunant, 71000 Mâcon, ☎ 85.38.32.37. **Yonne :** 19, rue Moreaux, 89000 Auxerre, ☎ 86.51.06.44.

Fishing : *Fédérations départementales des Associations de Pêche et de Pisciculture.* **Côte-d'Or :** 6, rue Ch.-Durmont, 21000 Dijon, ☎ 80.67.46.61 ; **Nièvre :** 7, quai de Mantoue, 58000 Nevers, ☎ 86.61.18.98. **Saône-et-Loire :** 334, résidence du Parc, rue Claude-Debussy, 71000 Mâcon, ☎ 85.38.38.52. **Yonne :** 3, rue du 24-août, 89000 Auxerre, ☎ 86.51.03.44.

Monks

The landscape of Burgundy, a treasury of Romanesque architecture, was in large part fashioned by monks. Between the 10th and 13thC, offshoots of the Burgundian mother-houses of Cluny and Cîteaux diffused the monastic principles defined by St. Benedict in the 6thC throughout the Western world. The Cluniac foundations sought to proclaim the glory of God through splendid churches and influential abbots. The Cistercians on the other hand, formed by St. Bernard in the 12thC, assumed the simplicity and rigor of the original monastic Rule. The foundation of Cîteaux in 1092 marked the beginning of Cluny's decline.

● *Towns and places*

ALISE-SAINTE-REINE*

Montbard 16, Dijon 57, Paris 253 km
pop 718 ⊠ 21150 Venarey-les-Laumes   B2

Vercingetorix, leader of the Gauls, was defeated by Julius Caesar in 52BC after a siege of 6 weeks at **Alésia**, a site now generally acknowledged to be the Gallo-Roman ruins on **Mont Auxois**. The village was named in the 4thC AD in honour of a Christian martyr of the region.

▶ Above the village, which is also the site of a large regional hospital established by St. Vincent-de-Paul (founder of the Sisters of Charity) in 1660, Roman theatre, forum, temples; Merovingian basilica *(10-6, Apr.-Oct.; 9-7 summer)*; statue of Vercingetorix; orientation table **(view★★)**. ▶ In the village : archaeological museum *(same hours)*; Ste. Reine's spring; church of St. Léger (7th-11thC) ▶ Early Sep. : Ste. Reine pilgrimage.

Nearby

▶ **Château de Bussy-Rabutin★★** *(5 km N; 9-12 & 2-6, Apr.-Nov.; 10-11 & 2-3 Dec.-Mar.; closed Tue. and Wed.)*: 15th-16thC mansion to which the 17thC proprietor, Roger de Rabutin, was banished for having lampooned the love-life of Louis XIV; painted decoration★. ▶ **Bussy-le-Grand** : Romanesque church. ▶ **Flavigny-sur-Ozerain★★** *(7 km S)* : Renaissance and mediaeval houses, partly restored; abbey founded in the 7thC, where Saint Reine was buried (Carolingian crypt★; *8-11:15 & 1:30-5:30*); parish church of St. Genest (13th-15thC; statues; 15thC choir stalls). ▶ Numerous châteaux near **Venarey-les-Laumes** : **Grignon★** (11th-16thC; *summer ex Tue., 3-6:30*); **Lantilly** (18thC), "château of 100 windows" *(10-12 & 2:30-6, 25 Mar.-15 Oct. ex Tue.)*. **Marigny-le-Cahouët** : 12th-16thC fortified farmstead *(ext. only, Jun.-Oct., Wed., Sat., Sun., 9-12 & 2-6)*.   □

ANCY-LE-FRANC***

Tonnerre 19, Auxerre 54, Paris 218 km
pop 1065 ⊠ 89160   B2

The **château** on the outskirts of town is a charming example of Italian Renaissance architecture.

▶ It was built in 1546 for the Clermont-Tonnerre family by an Italian artist working at the court of François I : quadrilateral building around **courtyard★★**; pilasters, alcoves, dormer-windows *(9:30-6:30 Apr.-Nov.)*. ▶ Magnificent decoration in the apartments, salons, chapel, library, kitchens, and **murals★★** in the "Pharsale" and "Sacrifices" galleries. ▶ 125-acre park. ▶ **Nuits-sur-Amançon** *(SE)* : 16thC château *(9-12 & 2-6:30, May-Nov.)*. **Ravières** : church, old houses.   □

ARNAY-LE-DUC

Autun 28, Dijon 57, Paris 290 km
pop 2335 ⊠ 21230   B3

In 1570 during the Wars of Religion, Henri of Navarre (later Henri IV) fought his first battle near this small town above the river Arroux. Church of St. Laurent (15th-16thC; restored).

▶ Almshouse (17thC) now a gallery for exhibition and sale of **regional crafts and specialities** *(Apr.-Nov. 10-12 & 2-6, closed Mon. ex summer)*. ▶ Place Bonaventure-des-Perriers : town hall, turreted house.   □

Practical Information

ℹ 15, rue Saint-Jacques, ☎ 80.90.11.59.
🚃🚌 ☎ 80.90.19.99.   📌

Hotels :

★★★ **Chez Camille**, (I.L.A., C.H.), 1, pl. E.-Herriot, ☎ 80.90.01.38, AE DC Euro Visa, 12 rm 🅿 🍴 closed 5-25 Jan, 265. Rest. ● ◆◆ 🍴 The Poinsot family welcomes you into their old Burgundian home : *tartare de saumon frais à l'aigrelette, croûte de filet de bœuf aux truffes*, 110-230; child : 60.
★ **Relais Saint-Jacques**, 27, rue St-Jacques, ☎ 80.90.07.33, 10 rm 🅿 closed Sat, 70. Rest. ◆ ◆ 45-100.
★ **Terminus** (L.F.), 2, rue de l'Arquebuse, ☎ 80.90.00.33, Euro Visa, 12 rm 🅿 closed Wed, 6 Jan-6 Feb, 150. Rest. ◆ ₺ 60-120.

AUTUN***

Chalon-sur-Saône 53, Dijon 85, Paris 293 km
pop 22156 ⊠ 71400   B3

Napoleon and his brothers briefly studied at the Jesuit college; mediaeval ramparts protect the town (A2-B3).

▶ The **Arroux★** (A1) and **St. André** (C1) **Gates**, two of the original four Roman gates to the city; remains of a large Roman **theatre** (15000 spectators) overlooking a stadium and artificial lake (C2). Nearby, **Bonaparte** (formerly Jesuit) **College** (17thC); Marbres promenade. ▶ Leave the modern city at the Champ de Mars (B2) and walk past mansion façades to reach the **cathedral of St. Lazare★★★** (B3) : early 12thC, remodelled in Gothic times; doorway with **tympanum of the Last Judgement★★★** signed on the lintel by the renowned 12thC sculptor Gislebertus, carved medallions showing signs of the zodiac and the labours of the months; Romanesque **capitals★★★** in the nave (some, replaced by copies, are displayed in the chapterhouse); third chapel on left, martyrdom of St. Symphorien by Ingres; view★ from the bell tower. ▶ **Rolin Museum★★** on the other side of Place St-Louis : Recumbent Eve★★★ by Gislebertus; 15thC Virgin of Autun★ (polychrome stone); Nativity★★★ by the Master of Moulins *(9:30-12 & 2-6:30, 15 Mar.-Sep.; 10-12 & 2-4, Oct.-14 Mar.; closed Sun. am, Tue. and hols.)*. ▶ Chapel of St. Nicolas (B1) : garden, **lapidary museum** *(enq. : tel. : 85.52.35.71)*. ▶ Rue St-Antoine (B2-3) : **natural history museum** *(tel. : 85.52.09.15)*.

Nearby

▶ **Temple of Janus** at the city gates *(between D978 and D980 N)*; **Couhard Rock** *(D120 S)*; **Cross of Liberation** lookout *(D120 and D287)*. ▶ **Briscou waterfall** and **Planoise Forest** *(D120 and D287)*. ▶ **Château de Montjeu** *(5 km S)* : splendid park. ▶ **Château de Sully★★** (B3) : superb 16th-18thC edifice with skewed corner towers *(exterior visits 8-6 Palm Sunday-Oct.)*. ▶ S of Sully, **Val-Saint-Benoît** priory recently reoccupied by nuns.

Round trip to Mont Beuvray★ *(approx 80 km in the S of the Morvan Nature Park)*

▶ W from Autun via N81, take D3 to right. **Château Monthelon** : 15thC. ▶ La grande Verrière : **Morvan Mineral Museum** *(2-6 Sat., Sun., nat. and school hols. Mar.-Oct.)*. ▶ **Saint-Léger-sous-Beuvray**, at the foot of Mont Beuvray (alt. 821 m; *one-way road*) : chestnut cultivation. **Bibracte** : Gallic hill-fort and capital of the Edueni (→ Alesia; view★★). ▶ Beyond the source of the Yonne river, through Saint-Prix Forest *(D18, D500)*, **Haut-Folin peak** (alt. 901 m), the highest point in Morvan. ▶ Return to Autun via **Canche Gorge** and D78.   □

Practical Information _____

ℹ 3, av. Charles-de-Gaulle (B2), ☎ 85.52.20.34.
🚆 *SNCF* (A1), ☎ 85.52.28.01.

Hotels :

★★★ **Vieux Moulin**, porte d'Arroux (B1), ☎ 85.52.10.90,

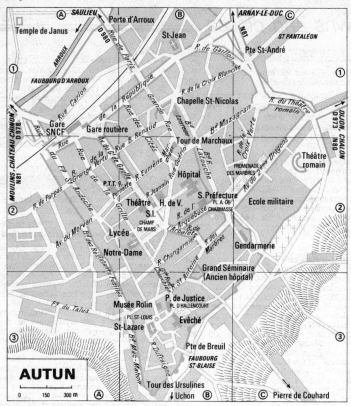

AUTUN

0   150   300 m   (A)

AE Euro Visa, 16 rm P ▩ ♨ closed Sun eve (l.s.), Mon, Jan-Feb, 200. Rest. ♦♦ ≶ ♪ ♿ 110-120.
★★ *Les Arcades* (L.F.), 22, av. de la République (A1), ☎ 85.52.30.03, AE DC Euro Visa, 40 rm P closed 1 Jan-15 Mar, 160.
★★ *Tête Noire* (L.F.), 1-3, rue de l'Arquebuse (B2), ☎ 85.52.25.39, Euro Visa, 20 rm P half pens (h.s.), closed Sat (l.s.), Mar, 270. Rest. ♦ 55-130.
★ *France* (L.F.), pl. de la Gare (A1), ☎ 85.52.14.00, 23 rm P closed Sun eve, 100.
La Clef des Champs, Bellevue, rte de Château-Chinon, ☎ 85.52.12.30, Euro Visa, 8 rm P ▩ closed Sun eve and Mon, 16 Feb-1 Mar, 100. Rest. ♦♦ ♪ 95-200.

Restaurant :
♦ *Le Chalet bleu*, 3, rue Jeannin (C1), ☎ 85.52.25.16, Visa, closed Mon eve and Tue, 80-130 ; child : 45.

⚠ ★★★*du Pont-d'Arroux* (104 pl), ☎ 85.52.10.82.

Recommended
Events : *Morvan music festival*, Jul.
Guided tours : Roman ruins and the historic district ; visit and commentary.
Leisure activities : *Aéroclub du Morvan*, Aérodrome de Bellevue, ☎ 85.52.14.40.
Son et lumière : *the 100 faces of Autun*, 15 May-30 Sep.
♥ antiques : *Raoul Metra*, ☎ 85.52.37.22.

AUXERRE★★

Sens 57, Dijon 148, Paris 168 km
pop 41164 ✉ 89000   A1

Auxerre, famous in the Middle Ages for its St. Germain abbey, in a beautiful site★ on the left bank of the Yonne, has been a thriving commercial centre since the Gallo-Roman era.

▶Walk from the quays through the old quarter towards the **cathedral of St. Étienne**★★ (B2) : flamboyant Gothic façade (damaged 13th-14thC sculptures★ on doorways), **stained glass**★★ (16thC rose windows in the transept, 13thC windows in the ambulatory). 11thC **crypt**★★, with 11th-13thC **frescos**★★ (Christ on a white horse) ; Treasury of illuminated manuscripts, enamels, ivories *(9-12 & 2-6)*. ▶**St. Germain abbey church**★, founded in the 6thC : Gothic structure (13th-15thC) ; remains of 6thC abbey ; elements of the 12thC Romanesque cloister were found in the 18thC buildings now used as a cultural centre (exhibitions). Two levels of **Carolingian crypts**★★★ : ancient (AD850) **frescos**★★ depicting the life and martyrdom of St. Stephen *(9-11:30 & 2-5:30 ex Tue. and nat. hols.)* ; numerous tombs including that of St. Germain, 5thC bishop of the city. ▶ Rue de Paris leads to the central **Surugue** (A2) and **Hôtel-de-Ville** (B2) squares connected by **Rue de l'Horloge**★ : fine buildings ; 15thC clock-tower. ▶ **Leblanc-Duvernoy Museum** (A2) : tapestries, pottery, historical items in a mansion *(10:30-12 & 2-6 or 5 in winter ; closed Tue., nat. hols. and 1-15 Nov.)*.

Also... ▶ **St. Eusèbe church** (A2) : 15thC ; Renaissance choir, fine late-Romanesque bell-tower. ▶ **St. Pierre**

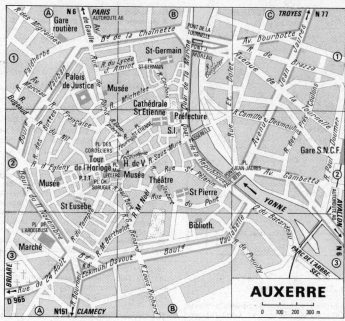

AUXERRE

0   100   200   300 m

church (B2) : 16th-17thC. ▶ Paul Bert nature conservatory (Bd Vauban, A1 ; *daily*). ▶ **Museum of Art and History** at the Coche d'Eau Mansion on Quai de la Marine (B1 ; temporary exhibitions).   □

Practical Information _____

AUXERRE
ℹ 1-2, quai de la République (B2), ☎ 86.52.06.19.
✈ *Auxerre-Branches*, 5 km N, ☎ 86.53.24.79/ 86.53.02.65.
SNCF (C2), ☎ 86.46.50.50.
🚌 rue des Migraines (A1), ☎ 86.46.90.66.
Car rental : *Avis*, 1, rue E.-Dolet (B1-2), ☎ 86.46.83.47/ 86.46.48.74 ; train station (C2).

Hotels :
★★★ *Le Maxime*, 2, quai de la Marine (B1), ☎ 86.52.14.19, AE DC Euro Visa, 25 rm 🅿 250.
★★ *De Seignelay*, 2, rue du Pont (B2), ☎ 86.52.03.48, Euro Visa, 23 rm 🍴 🛏 closed Mon (l.s.), 10 Jan-10 Feb, 190. Rest. ♦ ♪ 55-115.
★★ *Normandie*, 41, bd Vauban (A1), ☎ 86.52.57.80, AE DC Euro Visa, 48 rm 🅿 🍴 🛏 🕷 170.

Restaurants :
♦♦♦ *Le Jardin Gourmand*, 56, bd Vauban (A1), ☎ 86.51.53.52, AE DC Euro Visa, ♪ 🛏 closed Mon and Sun eve , Nov. Spec : *Langoustines rôties, carrelet au beurre*, 95-260.
♦♦ *Le Saint-Hubert*, 3, rue de la Poterne (B2), ☎ 86.52.10.57, Tx 800997, Euro Visa 🕷 closed Fri eve (l.s.) and Sat. Quality and simplicity : *puits d'escargots au chablis, estouffade de bœuf*, 35-90.

⚠ ★★★*Municipal* (220 pl), ☎ 86.52.11.15.

Recommended
Auction house : 21, av. Pierre-Larousse, ☎ 86.52.17.98, Fri am.
Guide to wines : at Coulanges-la-Vineuse PC 89580, *Raymond Dupuy*, ☎ 86.42.24.20.

Nearby

CHEVANNES, ✉ 89240 Pourrain, 8 km SW.
Restaurant :
● ♦♦ *La Chamaille*, La Barbotière, ☎ 86.41.24.80, AE DC Visa 🍴 🍷 🛏 closed Tue eve, Wed, Sun eve, 3 Feb-5 Mar, 31 Aug-9 Sep, 22-26 Dec. An old farmhouse in the heart of the country, at the water's edge. Seasonal cuisine, 110-220 ; child : 60.

VAUX, ✉ 89290, 6 km S.
Restaurant :
● ♦♦ *La Petite Auberge*, 2, pl. du Passeur, ☎ 86.53.80.08, Visa 🍴 🍷 🕷 closed Mon and Sun eve, 1-15 Jul, 23 Dec-15 Jan. On the riverbank. Elegance, comfort, and food with the true flavour of Burgundy, 100-200.

The AUXERROIS Region

A1-2
Round trip from Auxerre *(105 km, full day ; see map 1)*
On both sides of the Yonne Valley, villages nestled into the hillsides ; vineyards gradually recapturing lost prestige : this is the Auxerrois region which is also known for its beautiful churches.

▶ **Auxerre** (→). ▶ Beyond the A6 motorway interchange, **Appoigny** : 13th-16thC church★, Renaissance choirscreen. ▶ **Seignelay** : timber-built covered **market★**; church of St. Martial (15th-16thC). ▶ **Pontigny★★** : Romanesque **church** (108 m long) with Gothic arches, second "daughter" (founded 1114) of the abbey of Cîteaux (→ Côte de Nuits) ; 17thC choir stalls★ ; an important mediaeval abbey that provided refuge for three exiled Archbishops of Canterbury : Thomas Becket from 1164 to 1166, Stephen Langton (1208-13) and Edmund Rich (venerated here where he died in 1240, as St. Edme). ▶ **Ligny-le-Châtel** : church with Romanesque nave, Renaissance choir. ▶ **Chablis★**, where a renowned white wine is produced ; **wine cellar** in the former chapel of the 13thC infirmary (Hôtel-Dieu) ; S of town, **churches of St. Martin** (13thC) and the partly Romanesque **St. Pierre.**

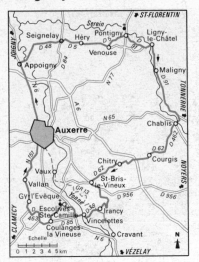

1. The Auxerrois region

▶ Via **Chitry** (fortified church), **Saint-Bris-le-Vineux** (church 13th-16thC; 16thC fresco and furniture), and **Irancy** (old houses), through the Yonne vineyards (lower Bourgogne); before the phylloxera crisis (→ box, "Wines of Burgundy") this was a more important wine-producing region than the Côte d'Or. Wines were sent to Paris from **Vincelotte** (13thC storehouse). ▶ **Escolives-Sainte-Camille** : Romanesque church with porch and brick bell-tower; Gallo-Roman archaeological excavations, Merovingian cemetery. ▶ **Coulanges-la-Vineuse,** where both wine and cherries are produced. ▶ **Gy-l'Évêque** : ruined church, 12thC bell-tower still standing. ▶ **Vaux** : a favourite of anglers; an excellent restaurant draws gourmets from Auxerre; attractive porch on the church.   □

Practical Information ⎯⎯⎯⎯⎯⎯⎯⎯⎯⎯⎯

APPOIGNY, ⊠ 89380, 10 km N of **Auxerre**.

Restaurant :
● ◆◆ *Relais Saint-Fiacre*, 4, rte de Paris, ☎ 86.53.21.80, AE DC Visa ⪡ ♪ ▣ closed Mon and Sun eve, 5-27 Jan. The best of Burgundy on your plate and in your glass, thanks to award winning chef M.Moret, 95-250 ; child : 40.

CHABLIS, ⊠ 89800, 19 km E of **Auxerre**.
SNCF ☎ 86.46.50.50.

Hotels :
★★ *Hostellerie des Clos* (L.F.), rue Jules-Rathier, ☎ 86.42.10.63, AE DC Euro Visa, 26 rm ▣ ░░░ ⌕ ♪ � closed Wed eve (l.s.), 5 Jan-7 Feb, 260. Rest. ◆◆ *Michel Vignaud* ♪ closed Wed and Thu noon (l.s.). M. Vignaud's traditionally tasty fare : *terrine de sandre à l'irancy, rognons de veau aux raisins et ratafia de chablis,* 130-280 ; child : 50.
★ *Etoile*, 4, rue des Moulins, ☎ 86.42.10.50, Euro Visa, 15 rm ▣ closed Mon and Tue lunch, 15 Dec-15 Feb, 140. Rest. ◆ 60-120.

Recommended
Events : wine festival, 4th Sun of Nov.
Guide to wines : Cave coopérative, ☎ 86.42.11.24.

LIGNY-LE-CHÂTEL, ⊠ 89144, 22 km NE of **Auxerre**.

Hotel :
★★ *Relais Saint-Vincent* (L.F.), 14, Grande-Rue, ☎ 86.47.53.38, DC Euro Visa, 10 rm ▣ ░░░ ⌕ ㋫ 200. Rest. ◆ closed lunch, 60-100.

Restaurant :
◆ *Auberge du Bief*, 2, av. de Chablis, ☎ 86.47.43.42, AE DC Euro Visa ░░░ ♪ closed Mon eve and Tue, 2-15 Jan, 2-15 Oct. Simple fare from good, fresh produce, 90-200.

AVALLON**

Auxerre 51, Dijon 105, Paris 225 km
pop 8904 ⊠ 89200   B2

Reach Avallon via the Cousin Valley (→ below) to discover this ancient town at its most picturesque. Sensible planning has placed the modern development of Avallon far enough from the old town to preserve the charm promised by the sight of its ivy-covered ramparts and weathered watchtowers.

▶ Behind the **ramparts★** : Petite-Porte promenade ; Fort-Mahon and Fontaine-Neuve streets ; numerous 15th-17thC houses line the main street (Rue Aristide-Briand). ▶ Near the 15thC **Sires de Domecy mansion,** the **church of St. Lazare★** : the two 12thC **doorways★★,** although damaged, are beautifully carved ; inside, figured capitals, statuary in the nave. ▶ Left, past the 15thC **tour de l'Horloge** (clock-tower), **Avallon museum** : geology and local archaeology, paintings, engravings, goldsmith's work *(Easter school hols., 2:30-6:30 ex Tue. ; 15 Jun.-15 Sep. 10-12 & 3-7, ex Tue. ; closed Mon. in Jun.).* ▶ Near Place Vauban : former post house, now a prestigious restaurant ; beginning of the commercial part of town (market Thu. & Sat. am).

The Cousin Valley★★ *(38 km round trip ; approx half-day)*

▶ 6 km down the Saulieu road, turn right towards Magny and **Moulin-Cadoux** *(D75),* to cross the Cousin River. ▶ **Marrault** : a rural setting by a pond ; ivy-covered chapel, 18thC château, small inn. ▶ D10 runs down to the valley *(D427),* below the walls of Avallon. **Cousin-le-Pont** : glass-works. Beautiful riverside road amid trees, numerous water mills turned into restaurants. ▶ **Pontaubert** : the mediaeval Hospitallers of St. John of Jerusalem controlled this "bridge-town" on the Vézelay (→) pilgrimage road : **church★** in perfect 12thC Burgundian Romanesque style (14th and 16thC statues). ▶ **Vault-de-Lugny** : moated castle★ (partly 15thC) ; church with 70m-long 16thC **fresco★** of Christ's Passion. ▶ Return via **Annéot** (12th-15thC church), D128 and D166.   □

Practical Information ⎯⎯⎯⎯⎯⎯⎯⎯⎯⎯⎯

AVALLON
ℹ 4, rue Bocquillot, ☎ 86.34.14.19.   ♥
SNCF ☎ 86.34.01.01/86.34.09.22.

Hotels :
★★★★(L) *Poste* (R.C.), pl. Vauban, ☎ 86.34.01.12, Tx 351806, AE DC Euro Visa, 23 rm ▣ ░░░ ⌕ closed 20 Nov-10 Mar, 520. Rest. ◆◆◆ In summer, enjoy lunch in the pretty courtyard of this former coach house : *petite marée au fumet de caviar, magret de canard aux poireaux et aux amandes,* 180-330.
★★★ *Le Relais Fleuri* (L.F.), RN 6, exit autoroute A6, ☎ 86.34.02.85, Tx 800084, AE DC Euro Visa, 48 rm ▣ ░░░ ⌕ ㋫ ▣ 250. Rest. ◆◆ ⌕ L. Schiever serves his good moderately-priced cooking out in the country : *turbotin beurre blanc, jambon à l'os au vin rouge,* 90-150.
★★★ *Moulin des Ruats* (C.H.), vallée du Cousin (4.5 km S), ☎ 86.34.07.14, AE DC Euro Visa, 20 rm ▣ ⌕ ♪ half pens (h.s.), closed Mon, Tue lunch, 30 Oct-1 Mar, 690. Rest. ◆◆ ⪡ ㋫ Spec : *truite au bleu, salade du Moulin,* 180-190.
● ★★ *Vauban*, 53, rue de Paris, ☎ 86.34.36.99, 26 rm ▣ ░░░ ㋫ closed 16 Nov-8 Dec, 240.
● *Château de Vault-de-Lugny,* Vault-de-Lugny, ☎ 86.34.07.86, Euro Visa, 8 rm ▣ ⪡ ░░░ ⌕ ♬ ♣ A 38-acre estate, with 800 m of river front, 800.
Les Capucins (L.F.), 6, av. Paul-Doumer, ☎ 86.34.06.52, Euro Visa, 8 rm ▣ ░░░ ⌕ closed Tue eve and Wed ex hols, 15 Dec-20 Jan, 240. Rest. ● ◆◆ Generous, fresh and

tasty. The starters are practically meals in themselves; ham in Chablis, 80-160.

Restaurant :
● ◆◆ *Le Morvan*, 7, rte de Paris, ☎ 86.34.18.20, AE DC Euro Visa ⬚ ♪ ♿ closed Mon and Sun eve, 6 Jan-1 Mar, 17-27 Nov. Updated regional fare : *escargots aux noisettes et chablis, escalope de ris de veau à l'oseille*, 110-150.

⚁ ★★★*Sous-Roche* (100 pl), ☎ 86.34.10.39.

Nearby

PONTAUBERT, ⊠ 89200 Avallon, 4 km W.

Hotel :
● ★★ *Moulin des Templiers*, vallée du Cousin, ☎ 86.34.10.80, 14 rm ℗ ⬚ ♿ closed Oct-15 Mar, 200.

Recommended
▼ antiques : *M. Lafosse*, ☎ 86.34.02.13.

SAINTE-MAGNANCE, ⊠ 89200 Avallon, 14 km SE.

Restaurant :
● ◆◆ *La Chênevotte*, RN 6, ☎ 86.33.14.79 ⬚ ♪ ♿ closed Tue eve and Wed. The Bregeot family receives very simply in their home. Spec : charcoal-grilled meat and poultry, 60-140.

BEAUNE★★★

Chalon-sur-Saône 30, Dijon 45, Paris 316 km
pop 20207 ⊠ 21200   C3

Beaune is the wine-trading centre of Burgundy and also one of France's most charming towns, with a wealth of historical and artistic treasures.

▶ **Hôtel-Dieu★★★** (B2) : mediaeval infirmary, in continuous use as a hospital from its founding in 1443 until 1971; part of it still serves as a home for the aged. The splendid **courtyard★★** is often photographed as a symbol of Burgundy (glazed-tile roof, turrets and dormer-windows, galleries, wrought-iron well). The mediaeval decoration and furniture are preserved in the infirmary proper (52 m long; polychrome timber vaulting). A polyptych of the **Last Judgement★★★** (Roger Van der Weyden, 1443), formerly in the infirmary and now displayed in the museum, is a masterpiece of primitive Flemish painting. **Pharmacy★** (pewter and ceramics); habits worn by the nursing nuns until 1961 (window in courtyard); tapestries and furniture *(9-6:45, 5:30 in winter).* ▶ **Mansion of the**

Dukes of Burgundy★ (B2) : among other old houses and mansions, built in the 14th, 15th and 16thC, has two wooden galleries, now the **Burgundy Wine Museum★★** *(10-12:30 & 2-6:15)* : vine-growing techniques, history of the vineyard, tools, bottles, paintings and sculptures, contemporary tapestries; fermentation room *(son et lumière, Thu., Fri., Sat., ; enq. at SI).* ▶ **Collegiate church of Notre-Dame★** (B2) : 14thC porch, Romanesque nave reminiscent of Autun (→); choir remodelled in the 13thC, side-chapels added later (frescos; sculpture; 15th-16thC paintings); 15thC silk and wool **tapestries** depicting the **Life of the Virgin★★** exhibited behind the altar; admire the exterior of the E end of the church. ▶ Around Place Monge : interesting mansions, such as the 16thC La Rochepot Mansion (B2). ▶ Not far from there is a former orphanage founded in the 17thC **(Hospice de la Charité**, B1; *temporarily closed)*. ▶ In the Town Hall (former Ursulines Convent, 17thC) : **Museum of Fine Arts** : archaeology, history, painting and **Étienne-Jules Marey** (1830-1904; inventor of chronophotography) **collection** *(May-Nov. 10-12:15 & 3-6:30 ex Tue.).* ▶ Stroll the streets to discover the many old houses of Beaune, before visiting the Saint-Nicolas district, N of town. ▶ **Church of St. Nicolas** : in the vineyard area, 12thC doorway and tower, 15thC wooden porch; the rest of the church is mostly 13thC.

Nearby

▶ Easily accessible from Beaune *(D18 and D23 ; or highway A6)*, the **Archéodrome★** (archaeological information centre) : models, documents, outdoor reconstructions of prehistoric and Gallic dwellings, tombs, Roman fortifications for the siege of Alésia, Roman villa *(10-8 or 6, Sep.-Oct.).*   ☐

Practical Information _____

BEAUNE
ℹ rue de l'Hôtel-Dieu (B2), ☎ 80.22.24.51 ; autoroute A6, rest stop of Beaune-Merceuil, 21190 Meursault, ☎ 80.21.46.43/80.21.46.78.
🚆 (C2), ☎ 80.41.50.50.
Car rental : *Avis*, 4 bis, rue J. Ferry, ☎ 80.22.87.88 ; train station.

Hotels :
● ★★★★ *Le Cep*, 27, rue Maufoux (A2), ☎ 80.22.35.48, Tx 351256, AE DC Euro Visa, 50 rm, closed 30 Nov-15 Mar, 550.
★★★★ *La Poste*, bd Clemenceau (A2), ☎ 80.22.08.11, Tx 350982, AE DC Euro Visa, 25 rm ℗ ⬚ ♿ half pens

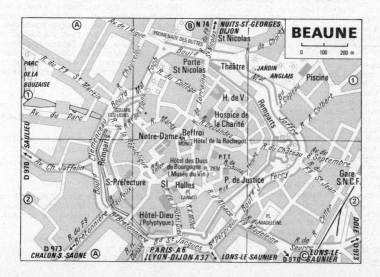

(h.s.), closed 17 Nov-1 Apr, 1483. Rest. ● ◆◆◆ ≶ A grand institution for a fine Burgundian cuisine : *tartare de saumon, filet de bœuf à la vigneronne, poire bourguignonne.* Great Burgundies, 200-330.

★★★ *Central*, 2, rue Victor-Millot (B2), ☎ 80.24.77.24, Euro Visa, 22 rm, closed Wed (l.s.), 20 Nov-20 Mar, 260. Rest. ◆◆ ♪ 107-250.

★★★ *Closerie* (L.F.), 61, rte de Pommard (A2), ☎ 80.22.15.07, Tx 351213, AE DC Euro Visa, 30 rm P ▥ ⌂ ♪ ⊡ closed 24 Dec-31 Jan, 300.

● ★★ *Grillon* (L.F.), 21, rte de Seurre (C2), ☎ 80.22.44.25, AE DC Visa, 18 rm P ▥ half pens (h.s.), closed 15 Jan-15 Feb, 360. Rest. ◆ closed Wed and lunch, 65-95.

★★ *Au Raisin de Bourgogne* (L.F.), 164, rte de Dijon (B1), ☎ 80.24.69.48, AE DC Euro Visa, 11 rm P ♪ closed Sun. Piano-bar, 195.

★★ *Auberge Bourguignonne*, 4, pl. Madeleine (C2), ☎ 80.22.23.53, Visa, 8 rm P closed Mon, 20 Dec-21 Jan, 10-17 Jun, 175. Rest. ◆ ♪ Traditional cuisine, 76-130.

★★ *Bourgogne*, 27, av. Charles-de-Gaulle (off map B2), ☎ 80.22.22.00, Tx 350666, AE DC Euro Visa, 120 rm P ▥ ♪ ⌂ ⊡ closed Sun eve and Mon in winter, Jan, 223. Rest. ◆ ♪ ⌂ 82-132.

★★ *Bretonnière*, 43, fg Bretonnière (A2), ☎ 80.22.15.77, 22 rm P ▥ ⌂ 200.

Restaurants :

◆◆◆ *Les Gourmets*, 17, rue Monge (B1), ☎ 80.22.15.99 ♪ 120-210.

◆◆◆ *Relais de Saulx*, 6, rue Louis-Véry (B2), ☎ 80.22.01.35 ⌂ ⌂ ⋇ closed Mon and Sun eve, 15 Feb-15 Mar. In wine country, *escalope de saumon tiède à l'embeurrée de choux vert*, 71-180.

● ◆◆ *Alain Billard*, 3, rue Nicolas-Rolin (B2), ☎ 80.22.64.20, Euro Visa ≶ ⌂ closed Mon and Sun eve. Pleasant food, wines, 70-250.

● ◆◆ *Hostellerie de l'Ecusson*, pl. Malmédy (C2), ☎ 80.22.83.08, AE DC Visa ⌂ ♪ closed Wed. Updated regional fare : *filets de sole au beurre d'olives, gelée de lapereau à la badiane*. Terrace dining, 75-200.

● ◆◆ *Jacques Lainé*, 10-12, bd Foch (A-B1), ☎ 80.24.76.10, AE DC Euro Visa P ≶ ⌂ In his sumptuous turn-of-the-century dwelling, J. Lainé is bound for success with his tasty seasoned specialties. Burgundies, 85-250.

◆◆ *Auberge St-Vincent*, pl. de la Halle (B2), ☎ 80.22.42.34, AE DC Euro Visa ♪ closed Sun eve (l.s.), Dec. Traditional cuisine in a venerable building, 100-150.

● ◆ *Rôtisserie de la Paix*, 47, fg-Madeleine (C2), ☎ 80.22.33.33, AE DC Euro Visa ▥ ♪ ⌂ closed Mon and Sun eve, 1-15 Jan. A friendly young couple who deserve encouragement. Tasty fish specialties, 85-170.

◆ *Au petit Pressoir*, 15, pl. Fleury (B2), ☎ 80.22.07.31, Visa ♪ closed Tue eve and Wed, 18 Jun-10 Jul. Most interesting regional fare, 67-110.

⚓ ★★★★*Les Cent Vignes* (120 pl) ☎ 80.22.03.91.

Recommended

Events : at hospices de Beaune, *baroque and classical music festival*, ☎ 80.22.24.51, from the last wk of Jun until the 14 Jul. Reservation at the tourist office of Beaune, Dijon, Châlon, Lyon, Paris,.

Guide to wines : *Cave du Bourgogne*, 28, rue Sylvestre-Chauvelot, ☎ 80.22.18.34 ; *Reine Pédauque*, 2, fg St-Nicolas, ☎ 80.22.23.11, cellar tours ; *Cave des Baptistines*, pl. de la Madeleine, ☎ 80.22.09.05, cellar tours ; *Bistrot Bourguignon*, 8, rue Monge, ☎ 80.22.23.24, excellent wines chosen by specialists ; *Maison Calvet*, ☎ 80.22.06.32, cellar tours ; *wine market*, rue Nicolas-Rolin, ☎ 80.22.27.69, unlimited tastings.

Guided tours : *C.N.M.H.S.*, 10am and 4pm ex Sun.

Leisure activities : at Meursanger, *Balloon trips*, Château Laborde, ☎ 80.26.63.30, Apr-Oct.

Son et lumière : Hôtel des Ducs de Bourgogne (B2).

♥ *Le Galion*, 5, pl. Ziem, ☎ 80.22.65.21, the fashionable watering-hole ; *Maison Denis Perret*, 40, rue Carnot, ☎ 80.22.35.47, all local specialties ; Antiques : *M. Javouhey*, ☎ 80.22.76.77 ; Candies : *A. Bouché*, 1, pl. Monge, for local sweet specialties.

Nearby

CHOREY-LES-BEAUNE, ⊠ 21200 Beaune, 8 km NE.

Hotel :

● ★★★★(L) *Ermitage Corton*, (I.L.A., C.H.), rte de Dijon, ☎ 80.22.05.28, AE DC Euro Visa, 7 rm 5 apt P ≶ ▥ ⌂ ♪ ♨ closed Sun eve and Mon, 15 Jan-20 Feb, 1900. Rest. ● ◆◆◆ ≶ ♪ ⌂ The Parra family restaurant has a new look, with Champagne-coloured walls and great wines from neighbouring vineyards in the guests' glasses. While the fixed-price meals are still available : "Evasions Gourmandes" (7 courses), "Autour d'un plat", "La Cuisine du Marché", "La route des grands crus", you can also try the *effeuillée de raie au chou, la cuisse de volaille à la lie de Corton* and the unforgettable "Grand Dessert", 200-350 ; child : 35.

LEVERNOIS, ⊠ 21200 Beaune, 6 km SE.

Hotel :

● ★★ *Parc*, ☎ 80.22.22.51, 20 rm P ≶ ▥ ⌂ ⌂ closed 1-17 Mar, 17 Nov-4 Dec, 150.

VIGNOLES, ⊠ 21200 Beaune, 4 km.

Restaurant :

● ◆◆ *Au Petit Truc*, pl. de l'Eglise, ☎ 80.22.01.76, Euro ▥ ⌂ closed Mon and Tue , 2 wks in Feb and in Aug. Reserve. Appealing good, simple food, just like home, though a bit more expensive.*Terrine de veau au chablis, poulet au vinaigre, gigot rôti*, and wonderful jams on sale to take away, 140-250.

The côte de BEAUNE Region**

C3

From Serrigny N to Santenay S, the Côte de Beaune is one of the most densely cultivated and — square metre for square metre — most valuable tracts of land in the world.

▶ **Serrigny** : 18thC château, beautiful farms. ▶ **Aloxe-Corton** and **Pernand-Vergelesses** : great red wines. **Savigny-lès-Beaune★** : 12thC Romanesque bell-tower ; 15th-18thC church ; 17th-18thC **château★** with cellars, stables, motorcycle museum of 250 models *(9-12 & 2-6:30; closed 15-31 Dec.);* Louis XIV pavilion, French gardens. ▶ **Pommard** : old houses, château (14thC cellars) and Volnay : château — both great red wine names. ▶ **Auxey-Duresses** both red and white wines. **Meursault** : site of the annual *Paulée* (→ Trois Glorieuses); 15th-18th-19thC château, glazed-tile roof. ▶ **Saint-Romain** *(6 km W of Meursault)* : summertime exhibition of local history in the town hall. ▶ **Puligny-Montrachet** and **Chassagne-Montrachet** : revered as the sources of the finest white wines in the world. ▶ **Santenay** : château at the foot of cliffs (15thC keep) ; 13th-15thC church ; salt and lithium hot spring. ▶ **Chagny** *(15 km S of Beaune)* : commercial town and gastronomic stopover ; Romanesque elements in the church. □

Practical Information ――――――

ALOXE-CORTON, ⊠ 21420, 10 km N of **Beaune**.

Hotel :

★★★ *Hôtel Clarion*, ☎ 80.26.46.70, Tx 351229, AE DC Visa, 10 rm P ▥ Rustic charm, 475.

AUXEY-DURESSES, ⊠ 21190 Meursault, 2 km W of **Meursault**.

Restaurant :

◆◆ *La Crémaillère*, ☎ 80.21.22.60 P ⋇ closed Mon eve and Tue, 1 Feb-15 Mar. Spec : *cassolette d'escargots bourguignonne, dodines de caneton aux cinq poivres*, 75-150.

CHAGNY, ⊠ 71150, 15 km S of **Beaune**.
ⓘ rue des Halles, ☎ 85.87.25.95.
▦ **SNCF** ☎ 85.87.16.95.

Hotels :

★★★ **Château de Bellecroix** (L.F.), (R.S.), RN 6, ☎ 85.87.13.86, AE DC Visa, 19 rm P ▥ ◿ closed Wed, Jan, 21-31 Dec, 435. Rest. ♦ ≼ ♪ ㆆ 85-190.

★★★ *Lameloise*, 36, pl. d'Armes, ☎ 85.87.08.85, Tx 801086, Euro Visa, 21 rm P ㆆ closed Wed and Thu lunch, 22 Dec-22 Jan, 450. Rest. ● ♦♦♦♦ ℘ "One for all and all for one" could well be the Lameloise family motto. With young chef Jacques, they all do their utmost to welcome you into their very pleasant home. They offer you great but simple dishes, sagely concocted with an eye to the season's and the market's bounty. The dessert menu and wine list are required reading for gourmets, 230-450.

★★ *La Ferté*, 11, bd de la Liberté, ☎ 85.87.07.47, Euro Visa, 14 rm P ▥ ♪ 180.

⚠ ★★★*Pâquier-Fané* (85 pl), ☎ 85.87.21.42.

Recommended

♥ Montgolfière : *Air Escargot*, ☎ 85.87.12.30, balloon rides over Burgundy.

MEURSAULT, ⊠ 21190, 8 km S of **Beaune**.
SNCF ☎ 80.21.23.75.

Hotels :

★★ *Au Soleil Levant*, (Motel), 5, rte de Volnay, ☎ 80.21.23.47, 35 rm P ㆆ 150. Rest. ♦ ≼ ♪ ㆆ closed 20 Nov-20 Dec, 50-90.

★★ *Centre* (L.F.), 4, rue du Mal-de-Lattre-de-Tassigny, ☎ 80.21.20.75, Euro Visa, 7 rm P ◿ 92. Rest. ♦ closed Sun eve (l.s.), 70-95.

★★ *Le Chevreuil - Mère Daugier*, facing Hotel de Ville, ☎ 80.21.23.25, AE DC Visa, 20 rm P ⚗ half pens (h.s.), closed 15 Dec-1 Mar, 555. Rest. ♦ *Le Pâté Chaud* ㆆ In a typical wine country setting, the Thévenots uphold the gastronomic traditions of la Mère Daugier : the famous hot *pâté chaud persillé*, *escargots* and Meursault, of course. No cover for children, 140-170.

⚠ ★★★*Grappe d'Or* (115 pl), ☎ 80.21.22.48.

Recommended

♥ pork products : *Bourgogne, jambon persillé* ; at Puligny-Montrachet, fine wines : *Ramonet-Proudhon*.

PULIGNY-MONTRACHET, ⊠ 21190, 12 km from **Beaune**.

Hotel :

Le Montrachet, pl. des Marronniers, ☎ 80.21.30.06, 22 rm, closed Wed, 1 Dec-10 Jan, 245. Rest. ♦♦ Pleasant and well-conceived regional repertory : *oeufs en meurette, sandre, poulet de Bresse au vinaigre de vin*. Fine wines, 100-225 ; child : 40.

Recommended

♥ fine wines : *Ramonet-Proudhon*.

BOURBON-LANCY

Moulins 36, Autun 62, Paris 312 km
pop 6507 ⊠ *71140*   A4

With a view to the Loire Valley, town with five hot springs for treating rheumatism and circulatory problems ; substantial industry ; casino ; park.

▶ Near the springs, **Hospice d'Aligre** : chapel has 17thC pulpit donated by Louis XIV. ▶ Near the square, picturesque 16thC half-timbered house, fountain, clock-tower. ▶ N, Romanesque former church of St. Nazaire, now **museum of local antiquités** *(3-7 ex Mon. and Wed., Jul.-Sep.)*

Nearby

▶ **Saint-Aubin-sur-Loire**★★ *(6.5 km S, past Germigny forest)* : **château** in 18thC French Classical style, with elegant outbuildings *(2.5 ex Tue., Jul.-Sep.).* ▶ **Signal du Mont** (alt. 469 m ; *7 km W of Bourbon-l'Archambault)* : **view** to the Auvergne peaks in clear weather. ▶ **Ternant** *(18 km N)* : church with two Flemish sculpted wood **triptychs**★★ *(1432-1435 ; 9-6 or 4 in winter).*   □

Practical Information _____

☿ (10 May-30 Sep).
i pl. d'Aligre, ☎ 85.89.18.27.
SNCF ☎ 85.38.50.50.

Hotel :

★★ *Raymond* (L.F.), 8, rue d'Autun, ☎ 85.89.17.39, DC Euro Visa, 20 rm P ◿ half pens (h.s.), closed Fri eve , Sat lunch, Sun eve (l.s.), 25 Apr-2 May, 14 Nov-4 Dec, 200. Rest. ♦ ♪ ℘ Seasonal offerings, 85-250.

⚠ ★★★*Saint Prix* (128 pl), ☎ 85.89.14.85.

Recommended
Casino : *des thermes*, ☎ 85.89.09.04.

The BRIONNAIS Region

B4
Round trip *(approx 127 km, full day ; see map 2)*

Between the Loire and the wooded Mâconnais hills, a little-visited pastoral area dotted with churches dating from the era of Cluniac expansion (11th-12thC).

▶ **Paray-le-Monial** (→). ▶ **Saint-Yan** : Romanesque choir and bell-tower. ▶ **Montceaux-l'Étoile** : church with noteworthy Ascension on the tympanum★★ and lintel. ▶ **Anzy-le-Duc**★ : jewel of the Brionnais ; bell-tower★★ ; church★★★, supposedly the model for Vézelay (→) ; **carvings**★★★ (tympanum, capitals) among the earliest in Burgundy ; frescoed apse ; walk around the farm *(no entry)* occupying the former priory outbuildings to see more primitive tympanum (11thC). ▶ **Marcigny** : commercial town, 15thC houses ; partly Romanesque church (bell-tower) ; Tour du Moulin (Mill Tower) museum with fine woodwork (statues, ceramics : *2-6, closed Dec.-Jan.).* ▶ **Semur-en-Brionnais**★ : château where St. Hugues, a 12thC abbot of Cluny (→) was born ; remains of late-12thC church★★ : octagonal 13thC bell-tower ; carved doorway★★. ▶ **Saint-Christophe-en-Brionnais** *(8 km NE)* : cattle market (Thu. am). ▶ **Saint-Julien-de-Jonzy** : tympanum★★ (Last Supper and Christ Washing the Disciples' Feet, on the lintel) ; mid-12thC bell-tower★ and doorway★★ (partly damaged during the Revolution) ; view★ from behind the church. ▶ **Iguerande**, on the banks of the Loire : figured capitals★ in the church. ▶ **Fleury-la-**

2. The Brionnais region

Montagne : tympanum★ depicting Christ, the Virgin and St. John. ▶ **Charlieu★** (→ Lyonnais-Bresse). ▶ **Château-neuf** : hillside site★ ; Romanesque church★ overlooking old bridge ; château du Banchet (partly 16thC). **Saint-Maurice-lès-Châteauneuf** *(D8)* : cemetery chapel with bell-tower and Romanesque E end. ▶ **La Clayette** (pron. "clette") : small market town ; moated castle★★ (14th-19thC) ; **Automobile Museum★** in the 15thC outbuildings *(9-12 & 2-7 ex Sun., Easter-1 Nov. ; 2-6 ex Sat., Sun. rest of year)*, an annex of the larger museum at **Chaufailles** *(7 km E ; same hours)*. ▶ **Bois-Sainte-Marie** : one of the oldest (11thC) churches★ in the Brionnais ; side tympanum ; capitals ; unusual ambulatory. ▶ **Château de Drée★★** (17thC) among trees at the end of a beautiful walk. ▶ **Vareilles** : Romanesque bell-tower. ▶ **Saint-Germain-en-Brionnais** : solid country church. ▶ **Varenne-l'Arconce** : bell-tower ; decoration carved from hard local sandstone. ▶ Beyond château de Montessus, **Charolles** : cattle market and centre of the Charollais ; remains of the château of the counts of Charollais ; museum of the works of local sculptor René Davoine (1888-1962 ; *closed Tue.*). ▶ Paray-le-Monial (→). □

Practical Information

CÉRON, ⊠ 71110 Marcigny, 7 km from **Marcigny**.

Hotel :
E. Charlier, (I.L.A., Château-Accueil), La Fredière, ☎ 85.25.19.67 ℗ 〰 〰 closed Xmas, 200.

CHAROLLES, ⊠ 71120, 55 km NW of **Mâcon**.
ℹ couvent des Clarisses, ☎ 85.24.05.95.
SNCF ☎ 85.24.38.50/85.24.12.41.

Hotel :
★★ *Le Moderne* (L.F.), Av. de la Gare, ☎ 85.24.07.02, AE DC Visa, 18 rm ℗ 〰 〰 ⅋ ⊡ half pens (h.s.), closed Sun eve and Mon lunch, 24 Dec-1 Feb, 250. Rest. ◆◆ 〰 ⅋ Spec : *terrine de foies de volailles*, 80-200 ; child : 35.

⚑ ★★*Municipal* (60 pl), ☎ 85.24.04.90.

Recommended
Events : folklore evenings, Jul-Sep, info S.I.
♥ regional foods and crafts : *la Maison du Charolais*, RN 79, ☎ 85.24.00.46, Charolais afternoon tea daily.

CHAUFFAILLES, ⊠ 71170, 13 km S of **La Clayette**.
ℹ the Château, ☎ 85.26.07.06. ♥
SNCF ☎ 85.26.04.05.

Hotel :
★★ *Paix* (L.F.), pl. de la République, ☎ 85.26.02.60, 19 rm ℗ closed 1 Nov-25 Mar, 180. Rest. ◆◆ Excellent food : *cuisses de canard marinées en cocotte*, 80-130.

Recommended
♥ at Iguérande, 30 km W., oils : *Leblanc*, ☎ 85.84.07.83, walnut and hazelnut oils.

La CLAYETTE, ⊠ 71800, 57 km W of **Mâcon**.

Hotel :
★★ *Poste et Dauphin*, 17, rue Centrale, ☎ 85.28.02.45, AE DC Euro Visa, 15 rm ⌖ closed Fri eve , Sat and Sun eve (l.s.), 22 Dec-15 Jan, 120. Rest. ◆ 60-120.

⚑ ★★*Les Bruyères* (100 pl), ☎ 85.28.09.15.

Recommended
Chambres d'hôtes : at Céron par Marcigny, 30 km W., *Le Fredière (C.A.)*, 30 km W, ☎ 85.25.19.67.

MARCIGNY, ⊠ 71110.

Hotel :
Badin, (I.L.A., Château-Accueil), Les Récollets, ☎ 85.25.05.16, 8 rm ℗ 〰 〰 〰

CHALON-SUR-SAÔNE

Dijon 69, Lyon 126, Paris 340 km
pop 57967 ⊠ 71100   C3

An important market since the Middle Ages, where each year before the carnival (Mardi Gras), the "cold"

fair attracts trappers from all over France, and fur-buyers from all over the world, to trade in pelts.

▶ On the island in the Saône, the **Hospital** (C2) : 16thC refectory★ ; 15thC Doyenné Tower, formerly near the Cathedral, rebuilt here in 1907 *(Wed., Sat. and Sun., Apr.-Oct.)*. ▶ On the right bank of the river, 18thC Messageries Mansion housing the **Nicéphore Niepce Museum★★** : scientist and inventor of photography (1765-1833), born and died at Chalon ; equipment, helio-graphy, daguerreotypes, contemporary photographs (B2 ; *9:30-11:30 & 2:30-5:30 ex Tue. and nat. hols.*). ▶ Cathedral of St. Vincent (C1) : Romanesque transept, Gothic apse, Renaissance chapels, 19thC façade ; among half-timbered houses. ▶ **Denon museum★** (B2) : archaeology (Gallo-Roman bas-relief★) ethnology (lighterage, craftwork), paintings (16thC altarpiece, pre-Impressionists) *(9:30-12 & 2-5:30 ex Tue. and nat. hols.)*. ▶ **The House of Wines** of the Chalonnaise Region *(N, N6)* and an important **rose garden** (Plaine Saint-Nicolas) round off Chalon's attractions. ▶ On the left bank of the Saône, **Saint-Marcel** : Cluniac Romanesque priory church commemorating a regional martyr ; the philosopher Peter Abé-lard (b. 1079) died here in 1148. □

Practical Information

CHALON-SUR-SAÔNE
ℹ square Chabas, bd de la République (A1), ☎ 85.48.37.97.
SNCF (A2), ☎ 85.48.28.37/85.48.09.12/85.93.50.50.
Car rental : Avis, 34, av. Victor Hugo, ☎ 85.48.30.52 ; train station.

Hotels :
★★★ *Royal Hôtel*, (Mapotel), 8, rue du Port-Villiers (B2), ☎ 85.48.15.86, Tx 801610, AE DC Euro Visa, 51 rm ℗ 〰 〰 〰 250. Rest. ◆◆ *Les Trois Faisans* ♪ closed Mon noon and Sun (l.s.), 75-120.
★★★ *Saint-Georges*, 32, av. Jean-Jaurès (A2), ☎ 85.48.27.05, Tx 800330, AE DC Euro Visa, 48 rm ℗ 〰 ♪ 240. Rest. ● ◆◆ ♪ A stopover known for it high quality : *feuilleté d'escargots de Bourgogne, loup au vin rouge*, 85-240.
★★★ *Saint-Régis*, (Mapotel), 22, bd de la République (A1), ☎ 85.48.07.28, Tx 801624, AE DC Euro Visa, 38 rm ℗ 〰 〰 half pens (h.s.), 520. Rest. ◆◆ ♪ closed Sat noon and Sun, 21 Dec-21 Jan, 70-185.
★★ *Nouvel Hôtel* (L.F.), 7, av. Boucicaut (A1), ☎ 85.48.07.31, Euro Visa, 27 rm ℗ 130.
★★ *Saint-Hubert*, 35, pl. de Beaune (B1), ☎ 85.46.22.81, Tx 801177, AE DC Euro Visa, 51 rm ℗ 〰 closed 24 Dec-2 Jan, 200.
★★ *Saint-Jean*, 24, quai Gambetta (B2), ☎ 85.48.45.65, 25 rm 〰 ⅋ 175.
★ *Gloriette*, 27, rue Gloriette (B2), ☎ 85.48.23.35, 16 rm ℗ 〰 closed Sun, 80.

Restaurants :
● ◆◆ *Luc Pasquier*, pl. de la Gare (A2), ☎ 85.48.29.33, Visa ♪ closed Mon and Sun eve. Luc Pasquier's culinary gift grows with the years : *bisque d'écrevisses, pigeonneau de Bresse au jus de truffes*, 70-200.
◆◆ *Marché*, 7, pl. St-Vincent (C2), ☎ 85.48.62.00, DC Euro Visa ⅋ closed Mon and Sun eve, 15 Aug-15 Sep. In the old city, 65-150.

⚑ at Saint-Marcel, ★★★*La Butte* (92 pl), ☎ 85.48.26.86.

Recommended
Events : carnival, info. *Comité des fêtes*, ☎ 85.43.07.75, late Feb-early Mar.
Guided tours : old city, quartier St-Vincent, ☎ 85.48.37.97.
Leisure activities : balloon rides, aéroclub de Bourgogne, ☎ 85.41.82.64.
Youth hostel : rue d'Amsterdam, ☎ 85.46.62.77.
♥ Chocolates : *Alex*, pl. Saint-Pierre ; pork products : *Chambade*, 13, rue Grange Vadot, ☎ 85.48.20.85.

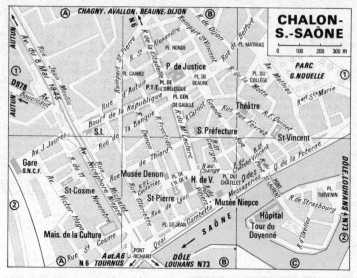

Nearby

SAINT-RÉMY, ⊠ 71100 Chalon-sur-Saône, 3 km SW of **Chalon-sur-Saône**.

Restaurant :
● ♦♦ *Le Moulin de Martoray*, ☎ 85.48.12.98, DC Euro Visa Ⓟ ⟨⟨⟨ closed Mon and Sun eve , Feb school hols, late Aug. The reputation of the talented J.-P. Gillot will soon spread beyond the food lovers of Burgundy due to his fine cuisine : *saumon fumé maison, sandre à la canelle, poires rôties sauce café*, 80-200.

The CHALONNAISE Region*

C3

W of Chalon-sur-Saône, the Côte Chalonnaise extends N and S of Mercurey between the districts of Beaune and Mâconnais. The vineyards produce red and white wines of great quality.

▶ **Chassey-le-Camp** *(SW of Chagny)* : "camp" refers to a Neolithic hillfort. ▶ **Rully** *(W of D981)* : 13th and 15thC fortress★ with large towers and square keep *(Sat., Sun., Apr.-Oct.)*; white wines. ▶ **Mercurey** : red wine tastings. ▶ **Château de Germolles★** : 13th-14thC *(10-12 & 2-6:30 ex Tue.; Jul-Aug.)*. ▶ **Givry** *(D981)* : commercial town and red wine centre ; 18thC layout ; monumental gates, fountains, covered markets, church★. ▶ **Buxy★** : mediaeval fortifications, old houses, Romanesque church ; white wine tastings. ▶ S of **La Ferté** Forest, a Louis XIII abbey building and farm remain from the first "daughter" foundation of Cîteaux (→ Côtes de Nuits). ▶ **Saint-Martin-de-Laives★** *(7 km farther, above the A6 motorway)* : 11thC church. In same direction, **Sennecey-le-Grand** : Romanesque church. ▶ **Saint-Julien** *(1 km S : church 11th-12thC)*. □

Practical Information _____

MERCUREY, ⊠ 71640 Givry, 12 km NW on the Givry.

Hotel :
★★★ *Hostellerie du Val d'Or* (L.F.), Grande-Rue, ☎ 85.47.13.70, Visa, 11 rm Ⓟ ⟨⟨⟨ ⟩⟩ closed Mon eve and Sun eve , Tue lunch (l.s.), 23 Aug-4 Sep, 13 Dec-8 Jan, 220. Rest. ♦ 130-280 ; child : 60.

Recommended
Guide to wines : *Jeannin-Naltet*, owner-grower. Red and (rare) white Mercurey.

La CHARITÉ-SUR-LOIRE

Nevers 24, Auxerre 95, Paris 216 km
pop 6416 ⊠ 58400   A3

Pilgrims on the road from Vézelay to the Spanish shrine of Santiago de Compostela were entitled to stop for a night's board and lodging at the Cluniac abbey, which thereby earned the name of "Charity on the Loire".

▶ On the banks of the Loire (view★ from the bridge), La Charité surrounds the remains of the abbey. The **church★★**, despite the destruction of the first bays of the nave, remains a splendid example of Cluniac architecture. Ste. Croix tower was part of the 12thC façade (tympanum) ; nave rebuilt in the 18thC ; choir and transept★ 11th-12thC ; capitals ; outside, E end★★. ▶ Museum of local mediaeval archaeology *(3-6 ; Jul.-Aug. 10-12 & 3-7 ; closed Tue.)*.

Nearby

▶ 7 km E, beautiful Bertranges Forest (oak). ▶ **Pouilly-sur-Loire** *(13 km N)* : centre of a sign-posted route around a white wine region. □

Practical Information _____

La CHARITÉ-SUR-LOIRE
ⓘ 49, Grande-Rue, ☎ 86.70.16.12.
SNCF ☎ 86.70.03.02.

Hotel :
★★ *Grand Monarque*, 33, quai Clemenceau, ☎ 86.70.21.73, AE DC Euro Visa, 9 rm Ⓟ ⟨⟨⟨ ♪ half pens (h.s.), closed Wed (Nov-Mar), 15 Feb-1 Mar, 410. Rest. ♦♦ ⟨ ♪ 90-190.

⚠ ★★*La Saulaie* (50 pl), ☎ 86.70.00.83.

Recommended
♥ sweets : *Confiserie du Prieuré*, 11, pl. des Pêcheurs.

Nearby

POUILLY-SUR-LOIRE, ⊠ 58150, 13 km N.
⓵ rue Waldeck-Rousseau, ☎ 86.39.12.55.
SNCF ☎ 86.39.13.33.

Hotels :
★★★ *L'Espérance*, 17, rue René-Couard, ☎ 86.39.10.68,
AE DC Euro Visa, 4 rm ℗ ≼ ₩ ও closed Sun eve and
Mon, 5-31 Jan, 1-20 Dec, 180. Rest. ♦♦ ≼ ♪ ও closed Sun
eve ex Jul-Aug and Mon. Terrace overlooking the Loire.
Spec : *écrevisses au pouilly, émincé de bar au vinaigre
xérès, aiguillettes de canard au sancerre rouge*, 130-250.
★★ *Relais Fleuri* (L.F.), 42, av. de la Tuilerie,
☎ 86.39.12.99, Euro Visa, 9 rm ℗ ≼ ₩ ও closed Wed
eve (l.s.) , and Thu, 15 Jan-15 Feb, 140. Rest. ♦♦ *Le Coq
Hardi* ≼ ♪ ও 50-120.

Restaurant :
♦ *La Vieille Auberge*, hamlet of Charenton, RN 7,
☎ 86.39.17.98, Euro Visa ℗ ₩ ও ✍ closed Tue eve and
Wed eve, 15 Feb-1 Mar. Refined cuisine in a venerable
residence, 60-160 ; child : 40.

⩗ ★★*Malaga*, on the banks of the Loire (100 pl),
☎ 86.39.14.54.

Recommended
♥ Cave coopérative.

CHÂTEAU-CHINON

Autun 36, Nevers 66, Paris 287 km
pop 2463 ⊠ 58120   B3
The town motto says "Small town, great renown";
on a hillside once inhabited by Gauls, good base for
excursions to the Morvan Nature Park (→).

▶ From the château promenade, view★ over the Morvan and the Yonne Gorges; climb **Calvaire ridge** (butte;
view★★). ▶ Rue St-Christophe, **Morvan Costume and
Folklore museum★**, with memorabilia of Napoleon III.
▶ In the former Saint-Claire convent, **Septennat museum**
opened in 1986 : gifts offered to the French President.

Nearby

▶ To the N, Morvan lakes (→). ▶ **Château de Besne**
(12 km W) : 12th-15thC *(ext. only)*. 25 km further, **Châtillon-en-Bazois** : mediaeval château *(am ex. Tue.)*. ▶ Along
D978 E, then at **Arleuf** by D177 to the **Anost Forest★** :
signposted trails not far *(20 km)* from **Anost** : wild-boar
reserve and lookout at **Notre-Dame-de-l'Aillant**
(alt. 625 m). **Cussy-en-Morvan** *(7.5 km farther)* : site★. □

CHÂTILLON-SUR-SEINE★★

Auxerre 83, Dijon 84, Paris 248 km
pop 7963 ⊠ 21400   B1
The Seine flows under the Perthuis-au-Loup bridge in
a city that retains a great deal of charm despite extensive damage inflicted in 1940.

▶ Town life is centred around Rue Maréchal-de-Lattre-de-
Tassigny and the Place de la Résistance. Tourists flock to
the **museum★★** (7 Rue du Bourg; *9-12 & 2-6; Nov.-Feb.,
weekends only, 10-12 & 2-5, 7 in summer; closed Mon.)*.
In the Renaissance Philandrier★ mansion : archaeological
collection (Gallo-Roman domestic objects, tools) including
the **Vix Treasure**, unearthed in 1953 in the burial mound
of a Gallic noblewoman, the prize exhibit a **bronze urn**
dating from the 6thC BC, 1.64 m high, 208 kg, with
a magnificent frieze; also gold and silver jewellery (dia-
dem★★). ▶ Left on Rue du Bourg, overlooking the town
near the château ruins, **church of St. Vorles★★** : 10thC
Romanesque, built of small stones and stone tiles, 13thC
bell-tower; 16thC Holy Sepulchre in spare interior.
▶ Nearby, pleasant walk to the **source of the Douix★** at
the foot of a rocky slope.

Nearby

▶ **Vix** *(7 km NW)* : small village at the foot of **Mont Las-
sois**, remembered for the treasure (→ above) unearthed
near the hill-fort; church of St. Marcel, partly Romanesque. ▶ SE, the 85 km² **Châtillon Forest** (oak, beech,
conifers); 18 km of forest road; via D928, another
forest route to **Marots lakes** and **Val des Choues abbey**
ruins. ▶ Down the **Seine** and **Coquille valleys** *(N71)* past
remains of 14thC castle at Brémur then D32 and D954 to
Aignay-le-Duc *(33 km from Châtillon)* : Gothic church with
16thC altarpiece. **Étalante** *(5 km farther)* : **source of the
river Coquille★**. **Duesme** *(4 km from Aignay)* : remains
of 14thC château; waterfall. **Quemigny-sur-Seine** : 18thC
château. Farther W to **Jours-les-Baigneux** : Renaissance
château *(Easter and school hols. ex Tue.)*. ▶ **Montigny-
sur-Aube** extreme N of Côte-d'Or *(22 km NE)* : 16thC
château. ▶ In a small valley between two forests, ruined
abbey of **Molesmes** *(24 km NW; 2-6, Apr.-Nov. ex Mon.)* :
the first abbey of the Cistercian order (1098), which exert-
ed profound effects on both architecture and religious
thought.   □

Practical Information _____

⓵ pl. Marmont, ☎ 80.91.13.19.
SNCF ☎ 80.91.08.29.

Hotels :
★★★ *Côte d'Or*, rue Ch.-Ronot, ☎ 80.91.13.29, AE DC
Euro Visa, 11 rm ℗ ₩ ও half pens, closed Sun eve and
Mon (l.s.), 18 Dec-19 Jan, 490. Rest. ♦♦ 65-130.
★★ *Sylvia Hôtel*, 9, av. de la Gare, ☎ 80.91.02.44, Euro
Visa, 21 rm ℗ ₩ ও 145.

⩗ ★★★*Essi* (66 pl), ☎ 80.91.03.05.

CLUNY★★

Mâcon 25, Chalon-sur-Saône 52, Paris 391 km
pop 4734 ⊠ 71250   B-C4
William the Pious, Duke of Aquitaine, founded the
Benedictine monastery here on the banks of the
Grosne in 910. Cluny quickly became the most
famous and powerful abbey in Christendom; its
abbots — Odon, Mayeul, St. Hugues and Peter the
Venerable — at times surpassed popes and kings
in influence. Numerous country churches, in a rustic but accomplished Romanesque style, remain from
this period. Two centuries after its foundation, Cluny
had spawned 1 200 daughter-abbeys throughout
Europe. The abbey church, still a magnificent building,
was systematically demolished in 1798 after the
Revolution.

▶ The city grew up around the abbey *(reached by D15 to
E)*; remains of the **ramparts** can still be seen. ▶ Place
du 11-Août : **stables of St. Hugues** (summer exhibitions);
opposite, the Gothic façade of the **abbey** (over-restored
in the 19thC; *10-12 & 2-5, 9-12 & 2-6 in summer)*; most
of the existing buildings were reconstructed in the 18thC;
they frame the cloister facing the gardens (School of Arts
and Crafts, national thoroughbred stud-farm; *9-11 & 2-5;
enq. : tel. 85.59.07.85)*, shadowed by the 62m-high octagonal **Clocher de l'Eau Bénite★★** (Holy-Water bell-tower)
and the clock-tower. With the Gothic **Bourbon chapel**,
these are the only remains of the **abbey church of
St. Pierre-St. Paul**. The scope of the original can be ima-
gined from the fact that these great structures once
formed a single crosspiece of one of the two transepts.
This church, built between 1088 and 1130, was 177 m
long, with five naves, five bell-towers and 301 windows;
for several centuries it was the largest church in Christendom. ▶ At the rear of the gardens in the 13thC **Farinier**
(flour store) are the figured **capitals★★★** from the choir :
Adam & Eve, Abraham's sacrifice, beekeepers, seasons,
musical modes, and many others, all carved in 1095.
▶ Right, on leaving the abbey, Rue A.-K.-Conant follows the line of the former nave : the two square Baraban

towers mark the former façade. ▶ Farther along on the right, in a 15thC abbey building, the **Ochier Museum★** : sculpture and souvenirs of the abbey; local history; work by the painter Pierre Prud'hon (1758-1823) who was born at Cluny *(10-12 & 2-4 or 6:30 in summer; closed 20 Dec.-15 Jan.).* ▶ Nearby, the former 15thC **abbey palace,** now the town hall. ▶ 12th and 13thC **houses;** Hôtel de la Monnaie : exhibitions; 13thC **church of Notre-Dame** (pretty parvis with fountain); late Romanesque **church of St. Marcel★** (1159; bell-tower★★). Then to the land of the poet Alphonse de Lamartine (1790-1869) (→ Mâcon), or the Cluny area towards Tournus (→).

Nearby

▶ **Azé caves** *(12 km E)* : underground river; prehistory museum *(10-12 & 2-7, Palm Sunday-1 Oct.; Oct. : Sun. only).* ▶ **Grosne Valley** (→ between Tournus and Cluny). **Suin Ridge** *(21 km W)* : 592 m high; view★★. **Pézanin Arboretum** *(13 km S)* : 45 acres of exotic trees. **Chaumont** *(8 km NW)* : Renaissance and 19thC **château,** neo-Gothic; 17thC **stables★.** ☐

Practical Information _____

ℹ 5, rue Mercière, ☎ 85.59.05.35.
SNCF ☎ 85.38.50.50/85.59.07.72.

Hotels :

● ★★★ *Bourgogne,* pl. de l'Abbaye, ☎ 85.59.00.58, AE DC Euro Visa, 18 rm ℙ ◁ ⌇ ♪ half pens (h.s.), closed Tue, Wed lunch, 15 Nov-15 Mar, 665. Rest. ♦♦ ♪ ⅋ Quality fare. Spec : *coquilles St-Jacques fraîches au beurre fondu fines herbes,* 100-200.
★★ *Moderne,* pont de l'Etang, ☎ 85.59.05.65, AE DC Euro Visa, 16 rm ℙ ⅋ half pens (h.s.), closed Sun eve, 3-15 Mar, 15-30 Nov, 400. Rest. ♦♦ ⅋ ♪ ⅋ closed Mon noon and Sun eve. Top-drawer cooking, 75-200.
★ *Abbaye* (L.F.), av. de la Gare, ☎ 85.59.11.14, Euro Visa, 18 rm ℙ ⅋ ⦿ half pens (h.s.), closed Dec-Feb, 350. Rest. ♦ ♪ closed Mon noon and Sun eve, 70-100.

▲ ★★★*Saint-Vital,* rue des Griottons (90 pl), ☎ 85.59.08.34.

Recommended
Events : *art exhibits,* St-Hugues stables and Hôtel de la Monnaie, all summer; *"Les Grandes Heures",* five concerts held in the abbey cloister, Aug.

COSNE-SUR-LOIRE

Nevers 52, Auxerre 84, Paris 196 km
pop 12463 ✉ 58200   A2

Small town on the Loire, shopping centre on N7; **museum** of river boats *(15 Jun.-15 Sep. 10-12 & 3-7 ex Mon. and Tue.).* **Church of St. Agnan :** former Cluniac priory (Romanesque apse and doorway).
▶ **Saint-Père :** *(2 km E)* : 12th-16thC Commandery of Villemoison (Knights-Templars' residence; *Jun., Jul., Sep., Sat. 2-7, Sun. 10-12; Aug. daily 2-7).*

Nearby

▶ **Cadoux farm** *(11 km N on N7)* : exhibition of country traditions in summer. Farther on, view *(left)* of the **Belleville-sur-Loire Nuclear Centre.** ▶ At the gates of **Donzy** *(17 km E)* is **Donzy-le-Pré** : 12thC tympanum of the Cluniac priory is considered a masterpiece of Burgundian Romanesque sculpture. **Château de La Motte-Josserand** *(4 km N),* a mediaeval fortress remodelled in the 17thC *(10-12 & 2-6, Jul.-Aug.; interior visit by appt.).* SE, the forests of Donzy and Bellary.   ☐

Practical Information _____

COSNE-SUR-LOIRE
ℹ ☎ 86.28.11.85.
SNCF ☎ 86.28.05.12.

Hotels :
★★ *Grand Cerf,* 43, rue St-Jacques, ☎ 86.28.04.46, Euro Visa, 21 rm ℙ half pens, closed Sun eve and Mon lunch, 15 Dec-1 Jan, 140. Rest. ♦ 90-140.
★ *Saint-Christophe,* pl. de la Gare, ☎ 86.28.02.01, Euro Visa, 15 rm ℙ closed Fri, 80. Rest. ♦ ⅋ 50-100.

Restaurants :
♦♦ *La Panetière,* 18, pl. de la Pêcherie, ☎ 86.28.11.70 ♪ closed Mon, Feb school hols, 1-15 Aug, 90-120.
♦♦ *Le Sévigné,* 16, rue du 14-Juillet, ☎ 86.28.27.50, AE DC Euro Visa ⦿ ♪ ⅋ ⨝ closed 1-21 Oct. A noted woman chef mans the kitchen : *paté de thon, canard aux pêches,* 70-110; child : 40.

▲ ★★★*Ile de Cosne* (200 pl), ☎ 86.28.27.92.

Nearby

DONZY, ✉ 58220, 17 km SE.
ℹ mairie, ☎ 86.39.30.28.

Hotel :
★★ *Ermitage Hôtel,* rue Gal-Leclerc, ☎ 86.39.30.62, 20 rm ℙ ⦿ 100. Rest. ♦ *Talvanne,* closed Fri (l.s.), 80-130.

▲ ★★*Municipal* (33 pl), ☎ 86.39.32.93.

Le CREUSOT

Autun 29, Mâcon 90, Paris 378 km
pop 32309 ✉ 71200   B3

Le Creusot, Montchanin and Montceau-les-Mines : an industrial conglomeration (urban pop. 120 000) that has much of interest tourists. The substantial remains of 17th and 18thC industry have contributed greatly to understanding the developments that paved the way for the industrial revolution.

▶ Iron was exploited S of the Morvan from the Middle Ages; the 17thC discovery of extensive coal seams permitted large-scale development in the form of steel mills and other industries dependent on readily available fuel, such as ceramics and glass-making. ▶ **Château de la Verrerie** : the name commemorates the former glassworks transferred to Le Creusot in 1787 and continuing throughout the 19thC under the aegis of the renowned St. Louis and Baccarat crystal manufacturers (→ Vosges). From 1834 to 1970, the château was the home of the Schneider family, whose steel mills enlarged the town and its factories several times over during the 19th and first half of the 20thC. It is now a cultural center composed of three institutes : the **Centre for creativity in the plastic arts,** the **J.-B. Dumay Institute,** and the **Écomusée of the Creusot-Montceau-les-Mines urban community,** the latter housing permanent exhibits as well as temporary exhibitions *(10-12 & 2-6 ex Mon.).* In the courtyard, 2 conical ovens were transformed into a chapel and a theatre, the latter restored. Behind the château, a magnificent park★.

Nearby

▶ In summer *(Jun.-Sep.),* the Museum offers displays at various locations, including a mine entrance at **Blanzy** *(16 km S),* lock-keeper's house at **Ecuisses** *(9 km SE),* school-house at **Montceau-les-Mines** (→ ; *info. from Château de la Verrerie).* ▶ **Saint-Sernin-du-Bois** *(7 km N)* : keep and partly Romanesque priory near a reservoir. ▶ **Couches** *(16 km NE; D1)* : **château** belonged to Marguerite of Burgundy, widow of Charles d'Anjou, King of Naples and Sicily, and brother of St. Louis (13thC); 11thC keep, 13thC wall. In the village : 15th and 16thC church; old houses *(Jul.-Aug., 3-6 daily).* ▶ **Signal d'Uchon** *(18 km W)* : alt. 681 m, orientation table, one of the best vantage points on the massif.   ☐

_____

On the maps, a town's name underlined <u>Saulieu</u> means that the locality possesses at least one recommended establishment (blue or red point).

Practical Information _____

Nearby

Le BREUIL, ⊠ 21670, 1 km S.

Hotel :
★★ *Moulin Rouge* (L.F.), rte de Montcoy, ☎ 85.55.14.11, AE DC Euro Visa, 37 rm P ∢ ⅏ ⊡ closed Sun eve , Fri, 20 Dec-10 Jan, 250. Rest. ♦♦ ♪ 65-150.

COUCHES, ⊠ 71490, 15 km NE.

Hotel :
★ *Trois Maures* (L.F.), pl. de la République, ☎ 85.49.63.93, 10 rm P ⅏ ⊾ half pens, closed Mon, 15 Feb-15 Mar, 135. Rest. ♦ 50-85.

TORCY, ⊠ 71120, 8 km SE.

Restaurant :
● ♦♦ *Le Vieux Saule*, ☎ 85.55.09.53, AE DC Euro Visa ♪ ᕃ closed Mon and Sun eve, 15 Jul-5 Aug. Inventive, varied cuisine : *salade d'asperges au confit de canard huile de truffe, panaché de poissons en papillote aux aromates du jardin*. Good cellar, 85-200.

CURE Valley**

A-B2
From Cravant to Chastellux *(85 km, full day)*

Ideal for weekends away from Paris (2 hr away) : river, meadows and woods, caves, Vézelay.

► The Cure and Yonne rivers meet at **Cravant** and join the Seine, near Paris. A stopover for loggers with timber from the forests ; Renaissance church ; old houses. ► **Accolay** *(left bank)* 12thC church. ► **Vermenton :** large market-village ; church, 12thC towers. ► **Arcy-sur-Cure :** caves★ (large Grotto with mineral formation, lake ; *9-12 & 2-6, Mar.-Nov.*) ; stroll on the riverbank. Left bank : **Chastenay manor** (14thC and Renaissance ; *school hols., Easter, 15 Jun.-Sep., 10:30-11:30 & 2:30-5:30*). ► **Saint-Moré :** caves, Gallo-Roman ruins of Nora ; wall, tower. ► After **Sermizelles,** leave N6 for D951 on the left. ► **Asquins,** at the foot of the Vézelay hill (→). ► **Saint-Père-sous-Vézelay** (→ Vézelay). ► **Pierre-Perthuis :** ruined mediaeval castle ; modern bridge over the **Cure Gorges (site★)** ; old hump-backed bridge. ► Leave the Cure for a detour to **Bazoches** ; the military engineer Sébastien de Vauban (1633-1707) is buried in the church (his heart is in the Invalides Museum in Paris) ; 12th-15thC **castle★.** ► Via D127, **Cure** (site★) and D20, reach **Chastellux** (→ the Morvan Lakes). ☐

Practical Information _____

VERMENTON, ⊠ 89270, 24 km SE of **Auxerre.**
🚈 ☎ 86.53.50.90.

Restaurant :
♦ *L'Espérance*, 3, rue du Gal-de-Gaulle, ☎ 86.53.50.42, AE DC Euro Visa ♪ closed Mon and Sun eve. Spec : *escargots en meurette*, 60-180 ; child : 40.

⚐ ★*Municipal les Coulemières* (35 pl), ☎ 86.53.50.01.

Recommended
Boat rental : at Accolay, 89460 Cravant, *Burgundy Cruisers,* ☎ 86.53.54.55.

DECIZE

Nevers 34, Autun 78, Paris 274 km
pop 7437 ⊠ 58300   A3

Decize is a charming town on an island at the junction of the Aron and the Loire, where the Nivernais canal ends.

► **Church of St. Aré :** 11thC, over a 7thC Merovingian crypt dedicated to St. Aré, Bishop of Nevers. ☐

Practical Information _____

ℹ mairie, ☎ 86.25.03.23.   ♥
🚈 ☎ 86.25.08.53.
⚐ ★★★★*Les Halles* (208 pl), ☎ 86.25.14.05.

Recommended
Boat rental : *Champvert-Plaisance,* ☎ 86.25.38.43 ; at Breuil, *Camping fluvial,* 4, rue Morambeau, ☎ 85.55.21.10.

DIJON***

Auxerre 148, Lyon 192, Paris 313 km
pop 145549 ⊠ 21000   C2

Dijon is an elegant, busy city, former capital of the Grand Dukes of Burgundy who brought the finest artists of Flanders to adorn it. It is a cross-roads, where all the Burgundian regions converge.

Between the train station (A2 ; near Arquebuse gardens and Natural History Museum) and the town centre, **Place Darcy** (A2) : heart of Dijon ; 18thC Guillaume gate and Darcy garden with fountains. ► Left of the lively **Rue de la Liberté :** market district ; **Rue des Forges** lined with exquisite houses (nos. 52, 56, 40 : Aubriot Mansion★★, 38, 34) leading to **Place de la Libération★★** (B2) 1690, designed by Jules Hardouin-Mansart (1647-1708), who succeeded his grandfather as Royal Architect at Versailles. ► Courtyard of Honour of the **Grand Duke's Palace★★** (now the Town Hall) opens onto the square ; staircase★★, 18thC State Room. Right of the courtyard, passageway to Bar courtyard : Bar tower (14thC) flanked by Renaissance Bellegarde stairway. ► The **Fine Arts Museum★★★** (B2) : one of the richest in France *(10-6 ex Tue.)*; partly in the 15thC ducal kitchens★, near the sculpture collection of works of the sculptors François Rude (1784-1855) and François Pompon (1855-1933), born at Dijon. In the Guards' Hall★, the remarkable 15thC **tombs★★★** of Philippe le Hardi and Jean sans Peur ; carved and painted **altarpieces** illustrate the golden age of Flemish art. Important painting collections include : Flemish Primitives, Dutch Masters (Teniers, Hals, Rubens) ; Italian (Lotto, Veronese, Tintoretto, Tiepolo) ; 17th-18thC French (Champaigne, Rigaud, Mignard) ; 19thC (Géricault, Delacroix, Corot, Monet, Vuillard) ; 20thC (Delaunay, de Staël, Messagier, Vieira da Silva) and many others. ► Behind the Ducal Palace, **Place des Ducs** (B2), with old houses : **Rues Verrerie** and **Chouette** are lined with 15th-17thC houses and mansions (Voguë **Mansion★** with glazed-tile roof ; B2). ► **Church of Notre-Dame★★** : façade with fine Gothic arches ; the nave is a beautiful example of Burgundian Gothic (1210-40) ; in the right transept, 13thC Black Virgin. Outside, bell-tower : Jack-o'-the-clock with his wife and children (the Jacquemart family) strikes the hours. ► **Lantenay Mansion★★** (1759 ; B1) : now administrative offices ; in the street, 18thC mansions. ► **Church of St. Michel★** (B2) : behind a Renaissance façade, a Flamboyant Gothic building. ► **Lantin Mansion** (17thC), now **Magnin Museum,** retains most of its furniture ; paintings (Hieronymus Bosch : Christ Crowned with Thorns★ ; Vouet ; Gros ; *9-12 & 2-6 ex Tue.*). ► Many houses and mansions dating from the 16th-18thC in Rue Vauban (No. 21 : Liégard Mansion★★), Rues de l'Amiral-Roussin, du Petit-Potet, Berbissey, Place Bossuet. ► **Palais de Justice** (Courthouse) in the former Parliament of Burgundy (B2) : Renaissance doorway ; ceiling★ in the 17thC court of assizes. ► Past the churches of St. Jean (15thC) and St. Philibert★ (12th ; 16thC spire), the **cathedral★** of **St. Bénigne** (A2) : a glazed-tile roof on the Gothic former abbey church (1280-1314) ; the circular **crypt★★★** is in fact the Romanesque basilica built by Abbot Guillaume of Volpiano (10thC) ; pre-Romanesque capitals★★★. ► **Archaeological Museum★★** in the 12thC dormitory of the former abbey ; on the ground floor, Gallo-Roman votive statues★★ found at the source of the Seine ; on the first floor, Romanesque and Gothic sculpture *(9-12 & 2-6 ; 9:30-6 in summer ; closed Tue.)*. ► At the W exit from town, former **Champmol Charterhouse,** now a psychiatric hospital, built by Philippe le Hardi ; burial site of the

DIJON

0 100 200 300 m

TROYES N 71
Av. V. F. Spuller
R. J. Cellerier
R. des Roses
R. Montchapet
R. Gagnereaux
PL. DUPUIS
Devosge
Bd de la Trémouille
PL. ST-BERNARD
PL. DE LA RÉPUBLIQUE
R. de Mulhouse

↑ LANGRES
N 74
R. Marceau
R. Garibaldi
Bd. G. Clemenceau
Champagne
Bd de
PL. DES CONGRÈS
Palais des Congrès
D 70
BESANÇON

PL. A.-DUBOIS
R. V. Hugo
Rue
Bd de brosses
R. Bannelier
Préfecture
Gare Porte-Neuve
S.N.C.F.

Gare routière
M. Foch
PL. DARCY
B. Sévigné
P.T.T.
Pte Guillaume
PL. GRANGIER
R. Musette
Notre-Dame
R. Chaudronnerie
Gare routière
PL. DU 30-OCTOBRE

Gare de Dijon-Ville
N 5
S.N.C.F.
Musée Archéologique
R. des forges
PL. DES DUCS DE BOURGOGNE
Théâtre
R. Rameau
St Michel

PARIS
AUTOROUTE A6
Av. Albert 1er
Ancienne Chartreuse
CHAMPMOL
PROMENADE DE L'ARQUEBUSE
St Bénigne
St Philibert
St Jean
H. de V.
PL. DE LA LIBÉRATION
Musée Magnin
PL. BOSSUET
Palais des Ducs de Bourgogne
(Musée des Beaux-Arts)

OUCHE
R. de l'Arquebuse
Hôtel Bouchu
PL. ÉMILE-ZOLA
P. de Justice
PL. DES CORDELIERS
Biblioth.
Cité administrative

Hôpital
Musée Bourguignon
Rue de Tivoli
PL. PRÉSIDENT-WILSON

Voltaire
Carnot

PL. DU 1er MAI
R. du Pont
Tanneries
Hôtel de Police
Rue du Transvaal
Bd de Brosses
Cr. gal de Gaulle
Rue d'Auxonne
N 5
AUXONNE DOLE

A 37 BEAUNE
N 74

Dukes of Burgundy, destroyed during the Revolution. The only remains are : chapel **doorway★** (1390) and **Puits de Moïse★★** (Moses Well), base of a Calvary by the 14thC master-sculptor Claus Sluter (the original polychrome stressed the realism of the masterpiece). ► Out of town, Lake Kir (beach, leisure centre, sailing, restaurant) named after a canon and mayor of Dijon who favoured the drink of white wine enlivened by black-currant liqueur *(cassis)* named Kir in his honour.
Also... ► **Perrin-de-Puycousin Museum of Burgundian life** (17 Rue St-Anne, B3 ; *9-12 & 2-6 ex Tue.*). ► **Museum of Religious Art** (15 Rue St-Anne ; B3) : goldsmiths' work, textiles *(9-12 & 2-6, ex Tue. and nat. hols.)*. ► **Hospital Museum**, in 17thC hospital (15thC chapel) : works of art, illuminated manuscripts *(by appt., tel. : 80.41.81.41)*. ► Natural history museum *(2-6, 5 in winter ex Tue.)*.

Nearby

► **Mont Afrique** *(10 km SW; alt. 600 m)* : park; view★. ► **Rouvres-en-Plaine** *(14 km SE)* : Cistercian Gothic church (13th-14thC) with sculptures by Sluter; treasury. ► Narrow road along the **Souzon Valley★** *(NW; D996 and D7; or GR7 and GR2)* : 1790 **château de Vantoux★**.

Ouche Valley★ from Dijon to Bligny *(47 km ; half-day)*

► The highway and the Bourgogne canal run through this valley in the Dijon countryside. ► Beyond **Velars-sur-Ouche** (small Côte-d'Or tourist train which follows the canal to Plombières, *tel. : 80.23.83.75*) turn right at **Fleury-sur-Ouche**, towards the **château de Lantenay** (18thC; *Thu., 1st and 3rd Sun. in month, Apr.-Oct.)*. ► **Pont-de-Pany :** left, road to 18thC **château de Montculot★.** ► Before **Saint-Victor-sur-Ouche**, ruins of Marigny castle on the right. ► **La Bussière-sur-Ouche :** remains of 13thC Cistercian abbey *(by appt., tel. 80.33.02.29)*. ► Beyond the motorway viaduct at **Pont-d'Ouche**, the valley ends just

past **Bligny-sur-Ouche** (Gothic church with Romanesque doorway; tourist train). □

Practical Information _____

DIJON
ℹ pl. Darcy (A2), ☎ 80.43.42.12.
✈ Longvic-Dijon, 7 km SE. *Air France office*, 7, pl. Darcy (A2), ☎ 80.41.15.30.
SNCF ☎ 80.41.81.35/80.41.50.50/80.43.52.56.
(C2), ☎ 80.43.58.97.
Car rental : *Avis*, 5, av. Mal-Foch, ☎ 80.43.60.76; train station.

Hotels :
● ★★★ *Chapeau Rouge*, (Mapotel), 5, rue Michelet (A-B2), ☎ 80.30.28.10, Tx 350535, AE DC Euro Visa, 33 rm ♨ Fine furnishings, 375. Rest. ♦♦♦ ♪ ⅊ ⅋ Spec : *fricassée d'escargots à l'ail doux, filet de jeune canard au citron vert*, 160-300.
★★★ *Cloche*, 14, pl. Darcy (A2), ☎ 80.30.12.32, Tx 350498, AE DC Euro Visa, 80 rm Ⓟ ⅓ ⅊ closed 30 Jan-2 Mar, 490. Rest. ● ♦♦♦♦ *Jean-Pierre Billoux* Already renowned as a great hotel (the building is a classified historic monument), thanks to J.-P. Billoux, *La Cloche* is becoming a gastronomic landmark in Burgundy. These new premises (a magnificent bar and three dining rooms, including a winter garden) are a perfect setting for the discreet chef (a pupil of the famed Dumaine) and his wife, who, to their surprise, have discovered they are bound for glory. Their success is richly deserved. Do pay them a visit for their lovely house, their distinguished reception and the remarkable food, 300-450.
★★★ *Jura*, (Inter-Hôtel), 14, av. Mal-Foch (A2), ☎ 80.41.61.12, Tx 350485, AE DC Euro Visa, 75 rm Ⓟ ⅋ ⅊ ⅓ closed 20 Dec-15 Jan. Video in the rooms, 260.
● ★★ *Le Jacquemart*, 32, rue Verrerie (B2), ☎ 80.73.39.74, Euro Visa, 32 rm ⅓ 160.

★★ **Allées**, 27, cours Gal-de-Gaulle (B3), ☎ 80.66.57.50, Visa, 37 rm 🅿 ⬜ 🔾 closed 2-16 Aug, 140.
★★ **Le Chambellan**, 92, rue Vannerie (B2), ☎ 80.67.12.67, AE DC Euro Visa, 21 rm 🅿 closed 20 Dec-4 Jan. Video in the rooms, 150.
★★ **Nord**, pl. Darcy (B2), ☎ 80.30.58.58, Tx 351554, AE DC Euro Visa, 26 rm, closed 23 Dec-14 Jan, 140. Rest. ♦♦ ♪ Tastings at the wine bar, 90-145.
★★ **Poste**, 5, rue du Château (B2), ☎ 80.30.51.64, 59 rm 🅿 160. Rest. ♦ **Grand Café** ♪ 60-120.
★★ **St-Bernard**, 7 bis, rue Courtépée (B1), ☎ 80.30.74.67, Visa, 19 rm 🅿 ⬜ 🔾 155.

Restaurants :
♦♦♦ **Le Pré-Aux-Clercs et Trois Faisans**, 13, pl. de la Libération (B2), ☎ 80.67.11.33, Tx 350394, AE DC Euro Visa ⬚ ♪ closed Tue and Sun eve, 120.
● ♦♦ **Le Rallye**, 39, rue Chabot-Charny (B2), ☎ 80.67.11.55, AE DC Visa, closed Mon noon and Sun , nat. hols, 14 Feb-1 Mar, 13 Jul-1 Aug. Fine cooking supervised by François Minot, 70-160.
♦♦ **Breuil**, 1, rue de la Chouette (B2), ☎ 80.30.18.10, AE DC Euro Visa ♪ closed Mon eve and Tue Jan. Elegant fare served in a venerable house in the heart of town, 140-230.
♦♦ **Le Vinarium**, 23, pl. Bossuet (B2), ☎ 80.30.36.23, AE DC Visa ♪ closed Mon noon and Sun , Feb. Boasts a very fine 13th-C crypt, 80-150.
♦♦ **Les Oenophiles, La Toison d'or**, 18, rue Ste-Anne (B3), ☎ 80.30.73.52 ⬜ ♪ closed Sat noon and Sun and Feb school hols, Aug. Wine cellar-museum in a historic dwelling, 80-120.
● ♦ **Chez Thibert**, 10, pl. Wilson (B3), ☎ 80.67.74.64, AE Euro Visa ⬚ closed Mon noon and Sun , Feb, Aug. A talented young chef offers escargots au bouillon, filets de poisson en paupiettes au caramel, 85-250.
● ♦ **Le Chabrot**, 36, rue Monge (A2), ☎ 80.30.69.61, Euro Visa ♪ closed Mon noon and Sun. Friendly mustachioed C. Bouy invites you to pour a bit of one of his splendid Burgundies into your soup as the locals do ("faire chabrot"). Hearty regional cooking : saumon grillé à l'unilatérale, foies de volailles au vin rouge, 70-180.
♦ **Le Duché**, 52, rue Verrerie, ☎ 80.72.30.50, Euro Visa, closed Tue, 65-120.
♦ **Lou Pescadou**, 30, rue Berbisey (A3), ☎ 80.30.34.71, AE DC Euro Visa ♪ & closed Mon noon. Guaranteed freshness all year round for oysters and other seafood, 110-180.

▲ ★★**Municipal du lac** (249 pl), ☎ 80.43.54.72.

Recommended
Bicycle-rental : Cycles Pouilly, 3, rue de Tivoli and 3, rue Sysley, ☎ 80.66.61.75; Rousseau, 3, pl. Notre-Dame, ☎ 80.30.91.52.
Events : Folk festival, in Sep; Summer dance, theatre and music festivals, 1 Jul-13 Aug.
Guide to wines : La Cour aux vins, ☎ 80.67.85.14, tastings at the cellar.
Guided tours : S.I. pl. Darcy, 1-30 Sep, daily at 4pm. A single card grants access to Dijon's museums : 10 F, valid 1 year.
River and canal cruises : Duc de Bourgogne, port de plaisance, ☎ 80.41.51.99, hotel barge.

Nearby

PLOMBIÈRES-LÈS-DIJON, ✉ 21370, 6 km NW.

Restaurants :
♦♦ **Auberge Gourmande**, Velars-sur-Ouche, ☎ 80.33.62.51 ⬚ ⬜ ♪ & closed Mon and Sun eve. A flower-filled house, seasonal cuisine : coq au vin, grilled turbot, 80-140.
♦♦ **Le Cygne**, Lake Kir, ☎ 80.41.02.40, Visa ⬚ ♪ & closed Mon and Sun eve , Feb, 75-150.

PONT-DE-PANY, ✉ 21410, 21 km W.

Hotel :
★ **Pont de Pany**, RN 905, ☎ 80.33.62.51, 16 rm 🅿 ⬜ ♪ closed Wed, Jan-Feb, 100. Rest. ● ♦♦ Robert André is proud of his tasty Burgundian cooking accompanied by

extraordinary local wines (one of the finest selections of Burgundies in all France), 60-200.

VAL-SUZON, ✉ 21121 Fontaine-les-Dijon, 17 km NW.

Hotel :
★★★ **Hostellerie du Val Suzon**, RN 71, ☎ 80.35.60.15, 18 rm 🅿 ⬜ 🔾 closed 2 Jan-2 Feb, 210. Rest. ♦♦ ♪ closed Wed and Thu noon (Oct-Easter), 125-250.

FONTENAY Abbey***

B2

The 12thC monastic reformer St. Bernard of Clairvaux laid down stringent rules for his builder-monks. The abbey he founded here illustrates the virtuosity of Romanesque architecture within the Cistercian strictures on austerity and sobriety, where nothing should distract from prayer; the beauty of the buildings springs entirely from the fundamental design and materials.

▶ The abbey was begun in about 1120. Behind the entrance building (15thC upper floor) left, not far from the dovecote, the **church★** (1140-1147) : simple doorway; the pillars and arches of the nave draw the eye to the choir and square apse (12thC floor tiling); the Virgin★ of Fontenay (13thC) stands in the left transept. Opposite, staircase to the dormitory (chestnut beams★) and the entrance to the chapterhouse. ▶ This leads to the **cloister★★** with massive yet elegant arcades. Up to 300 monks and laybrothers at a time lived in the abbey. ▶ Through the prison (the monks had rights of justice on abbey lands) to the forges, restored like the rest of the buildings, at the beginning of this century. The abbey was used as a paper mill after the Revolution (1789) until 1906 (guided tours every hour — half-hour, Jul.-Aug. — 9-12 & 2 or 2:30-6:30). □

JOIGNY*

Auxerre 27, Sens 30, Paris 148 km
pop 9644 ✉ 89300   A1

Gateway to Burgundy on the river Yonne, Joigny, with its bell-towers rising above old roofs, is a stopover for shopping and excellent dining.

▶ Park on the quay, then walk to the churches of **St. Thibault★** (15thC Flamboyant Gothic; Flemish paintings; 14thC Smiling Virgin★) or of **St. Jean** (Renaissance; 13thC tomb of a countess of Joigny) among half-timbered houses. ▶ N of town, remains of ramparts; from D20, view over the town.

Nearby

▶ **Saint-Cydroine** church (11th-12thC Romanesque; 4 km E) : octagonal bell-tower, near **Laroche-Migennes** (train-station). ▶ **La Ferté Loupière** (18 km SW) : church with late-15thC mural **dance of death★★**. **Bontin** (6 km S) : 17thC **château**, residence of Sully, minister to Henri IV (10-12 & 2-6, Jul.-Aug.). □

Practical Information

JOIGNY
ⓘ bus station, quai Ragobert, ☎ 86.62.11.05.
SNCF ☎ 86.62.07.66.

Hotels :
★★★★ **A la Côte Saint-Jacques** (R.C.), 14, fg de Paris, ☎ 86.62.09.70, AE DC Visa, 33 rm 🅿 ⬚ ⬜ & ✉ closed 5-28 Jan, 475. Rest. ● ♦♦♦♦ ♪ Both the older establishment and the residence (with its very luxurious rooms) on the banks of the Yonne, connected by a tunnel carved out beneath the highway (that's right!) are charming, pleasurable stopovers. The Lorain family, Michel and son Jean-Michel, are on hand to welcome you with light, wonderful food. Spéc. : gaspacho de langoustines à la crème de courgettes, bar au beurre de truffe, millefeuil-

les tièdes aux framboises. Jacqueline oversees the cellar and service, aided by her daughter and daughter-in-law. Wine and food shop, 430-450.
★★★ **Modern'Hôtel**, (Mapotel), av. Robert-Petit, ☎ 86.62.16.28, AE DC Euro Visa, 21 rm 🅿 🎜 ♪ 🖳 ⍋ half pens (h.s.), 720. Rest. ● ♦♦ **Les Frères Godard** ⪕ ♪ ය A brilliant group of appealing gourmet menus : *canard à la Gaston Godard, tournedos maillet d'or*, 175-220 ; child : 100.

Nearby

La CELLE-SAINT-CYR, ⊠ 89970, 10 km N.

Hotel :
★★ **Auberge de la Fontaine aux Muses** (L.F.), ☎ 86.73.40.22, 14 rm 🅿 ⪕ 🎜 ⍒ ⫸ 🖳 ⍋ closed Mon eve, 250. Rest. ● ♦♦ ⪕ ♪ closed Mon and Tue noon. Enjoyable setting and quality fare, 100-200.

⚘ ★★*Municipal* (60 pl), ☎ 86.62.07.55.

Recommended
Boat rental : *Locaboat Plaisance*, quai du Port-au-Bois, ☎ 86.62.06.14.

LOUHANS

Châlon-sur-Saône 40, Dijon 83, Paris 380 km
pop 6923 ⊠ 71500   C3-4
On the left bank of the Saône, a charming town with arcaded main street, old houses and handsome 18thC infirmary (pharmacy★ ; *guided vis. daily ex Tue., Sun., 10:30, 2:30 & 4*). Renowned markets for cattle, pigs and poultry.   □

Practical Information

🅸 av. du 8-Mai-1945, ☎ 84.75.05.02.
SNCF ☎ 85.75.12.35.

Hotels :
★★ **Moulin de Bourgchâteau**, rte de Châlon, ☎ 85.75.37.12, AE Euro Visa 🅿 ⪕ 🎜 ⍒ ය 185. Rest. ♦ ♪ closed Mon and Sun eve, 70-200.
★ **Cheval Rouge** (L.F.), 5, rue d'Alsace, ☎ 85.75.21.42, AE Euro Visa, 13 rm 🅿 closed 20 Dec-4 Jan, 90. Rest. ♦ closed Mon and Sun eve, 70-90.

Recommended
Events : *F.Point gastronomic exhibit*, last Sun in Nov.
Market : *Bresse poultry market*, every Mon.

MÂCON

Châlon-sur-Saône 58, Lyon 68, Paris 396 km
pop 39866 ⊠ 71000   C4
The curved tile roofs of Mâcon (birthplace of Lamartine) suggest that the Midi is not far away. A busy commercial town on the right bank of the Saône, and an important wine centre *(wine sales in May)*.

▶ Near the prefecture, **Old St. Vincent★** (C2), narthex (porch) of a Romanesque church destroyed in 1795. ▶ **Ursulines Museum** (B2) : archaeology (Solutré →; excavations), ethnography, art (Dutch, Flemish and French paintings, contemporary art ; *10-12 & 2-6 ex Tue. and Sun. am*). ▶ On the other side of Rues de La Barre and Sigorgne (main thoroughfares), **Lamartine Museum** (B2) : 19thC furniture and art ; mementos of Lamartine *(2-5 ex Tue., May-Oct.)*. ▶ Place aux Herbes : wooden house (D-C1).

Nearby

▶ **Saint-André-de-Bâgé★** *(9 km W)* : 11thC church with octagonal bell-tower in a small cemetery, interesting capitals. ▶ On the S edge of the Department, **Romanèche-Thorins** *(14 km S)* in the renowned Moulin-à-Vent wine-producing region of Beaujolais ; Guillon Museum of Crafts *(Easter-1 Nov. Sun. and nat. hols.)* ; zoo *(10-6:30)*.

Lamartine territory
Round trip from Mâcon *(approx 64 km, half-day)*

▶ Distinctive silhouette of **Solutré Rock★★** *(9 km W :* alt. 495 m), where prehistoric men chased wild horses over the cliff ; the site abounds in prehistoric remains and has lent its name to the Solutrean Era (18 000-15 000BC). ▶ **Pouilly** and **Fuissé** are joined in the name of a great white wine ; **Chasselas** has given its name to a variety of table grapes. ▶ Via Grand Vent Pass and D22 (leisure centre on Lake Saint-Point) to **Saint-Point★** : chateau, Romanesque church and funerary chapel of Lamartine and his family *(Mar.-15 Nov., 10-12 & 2-6, ex. Sun. am and Wed.).* ▶ **Berzé-le-Châtel★** : triple-walled mediaeval castle *(D22, N79)*. 2 km farther, **Berzé-la-Ville** : monk's chapel★, Cluniac 12thC former priory church ; **murals★★** *(9:30-12 & 2-6, Palm Sunday-1 Nov.).* ▶ On the other side of the valley, **Milly-Lamartine★** (Romanesque church) : village where the poet stayed in his childhood ; **château de Pierreclos★** (rebuilt 17thC), mentioned in Lamartine's work. ▶ Cross the valley again to **château de Montceau** : summer residence of the Lamartine family in the middle of their vineyards.   □

Practical Information

MÂCON
🅸 187, rue Carnot (B2), ☎ 85.39.71.00.
✈ *Charnay*, 3 km SW, ☎ 85.34.15.15.
SNCF *Gare T.G.V. Mâcon-Loché* (A3), ☎ 85.38.50.50.
Car rental : *Avis*, 23, av. E.-Herriot (A-B3), ☎ 85.38.68.75 ; train station (A3).

Hotels :
★★★ **Mapotel Bellevue**, 416-420, quai Lamartine (B2), ☎ 85.38.05.07, Tx 800837, AE DC Euro Visa, 28 rm 🅿 ♪ 390. Rest. ♦♦ ♪ ය 90-120.
★★ **Host. du Château de la Barge**, Crèches-sur-Saône, 12 km S, ☎ 85.37.12.04, AE DC Euro Visa, 24 rm 🅿 ⪕ 🎜 ⍒ ⫸ ය closed Sun, 25 Oct-10 Nov, 20 Dec-10 Jan, 205. Rest. ♦ ⪕ 65-115 ; child : 35.
★★ **La Promenade** (L.F.), 266, quai Lamartine (B2), ☎ 85.38.10.98, AE DC Euro Visa, 21 rm 🅿 ⪕ 🎜 closed Wed and Thu, Jan, 165. Rest. ♦ ⪕ ♪ 65-95.

Restaurants :
♦♦♦ **Auberge Bressane**, 114, rue du 28-Juin (C1), ☎ 85.38.07.42, AE DC Visa ♪ closed Wed. Spec : *feuilleté d'escargots à la crème d'ail*, 110-200.
● ♦♦ **Au Rocher de Cancale**, 393, quai Jean-Jaurès (C1-2), ☎ 85.38.07.50, AE DC Euro Visa ⪕ closed Mon, Sat noon, Sun eve, 2-16 Jan, 6-26 Jul. On the banks of the Saône, J.-F. Mabon's enjoyable cooking : *sandre à la cancalaise, gâteau de foie blond au sabayon de langoustines*, 65-160.
● ♦ **Le Saint-Laurent**, 1, quai Bouchacourt, Saint-Laurent-sur-Saône, ☎ 85.38.32.03, AE Euro Visa ⪕ ♪ closed Mon and Sun eve, 1-18 Aug, 20 Nov-15 Dec. Simple and good : fish, poultry, 110-175.

⚘ ★★★*Municipal Les Varennes* (200 pl), ☎ 85.38.16.22.

Recommended
Events : *national wine fair*, 1st Sun in Sep.
Guide to wines : *La Maison mâconnaise des Vins*, av. de Lattre-de-Tassigny, ☎ 85.38.36.70, tastings, sales, regional meals.
Market : *régional*, prom. Lamartine, Sat am.
Sports : at Mâcon-Charnay, *aéroclub du Mâconnais*, ☎ 85.34.18.54.

Nearby

FLEURVILLE, ⊠ 71260 Lugny, 13 km S of **Tournus**.

Hotel :
● ★★★ **Château de Fleurville** (C.H.), ☎ 85.33.12.17, AE DC Euro Visa, 15 rm 🅿 🎜 ⍒ ය closed Feb ex weekends, 15 Nov-25 Dec, 280. Rest. ♦♦ ♪ ය ⫸ closed Mon noon, 100-200 ; child : 45.

MÂCON

0   100   200 m

IGE, ⊠ 71960 Pierreclos, 14 km W.

Hotel :
● ★★★★ *Château d'Igé* (R.C.), ☎ 85.33.33.99,
Tx 351915, AE DC Visa, 14 rm ℗ ⬚ ⬚ ♪ closed
5 Nov-5 Feb. 13th-C Château, 550. Rest. ◆◆◆ ♪ 120-250.

ROMANÈCHE-THORINS, ⊠ 71150 la Chapelle-de-Guin-
chay, 14 km S.
SNCF ☎ 85.35.50.18.

Hotel :
★★★ *Les Maritonnes*, ☎ 85.35.51.70, AE DC Euro Visa,
20 rm ℗ ⬚ ⬚ closed Sun eve , Mon (l.s.), Tue (h.s.),
15 Dec-25 Jan, 1-30 Jun, 280. Rest. ◆◆ Flower garden,
refined cooking. Spec : *turban de sole au zeste de citron
confit, ragoût de lotte au pistil de safran,* 140-250.

Recommended
Guide to wines : *les Vins Georges Dubœuf,*
☎ 85.35.51.13.

SOLUTRÉ, ⊠ 71960 Pierreclos, 9 km W.

Hotel :
★★ *Relais de Solutré,* ☎ 85.35.80.81, Tx 351996, Euro
Visa, 32 rm ℗ ⬚ 220. Rest. ● ◆◆ Fernand Bucchianeri,
a former journalist, has been around. He knows what
he's talking about. Spec : *sandre à l'oseille, cassolette de
queues d'écrevisses à l'estragon, andouillette de veau au
Pouilly fuissé,* 65-100.

Restaurant :
◆ *Auberge de la Grange du Bois,* la Grange-du-Bois,
Euro Visa ⬚ ⬚ ♪ & closed Tue eve and Wed , Feb, 70-100.

> For the translation of a name of a meat, a fish or a
> vegetable, for the composition of a dish or a sauce,
> see the Menu Guide in the Practical Holiday Guide;
> it lists the most common culinary terms.

MONTBARD

Auxerre 73, Dijon 81, Paris 237 km
pop 7707 ⊠ 21500   B2

Between the Brenne River and the Burgundy canal,
the town was once home to Dukes of Burgundy (Jean
sans Peur spent his youth here). It was the birthplace of the celebrated 18thC naturalist Georges-
Louis Leclerc de Buffon (1707-88).

▶ **Place Buffon :** the mansion of the naturalist had
direct access to the **chateau park★,** which he remodelled ; archaeology and history **museum** (mediaeval and
19th-20thC sculpture ; local painters); Buffon's study ;
13thC St. Louis and Aubépin towers *(8:30-12 & 2-5
Apr.-Oct. ex Tue.).* ▶ In town, **fine arts museum** (Rue
Piron ; *2:30-5, Apr.-Dec.).*

Nearby

▶ **Buffon Forges★★** *(6 km NW via D905 then left) :*
18thC industrial centre ; exhibits on steel-making in Burgundy *(2:30-6, Jun.-Sep. ex Tue.).* ▶ **Vausse** *(20 km W),*
between the forests of St. Jean and Châtel-Gérard :
12thC former Cistercian priory ; cloister *(daily ex Tue.,
15 Jun.-15 Sep., 2-7)*   □

Practical Information _____

ℹ Pavillon, rue Carnot, ☎ 80.92.03.75 ; mairie,
☎ 80.92.01.34 (l.s.).   ♥
SNCF ☎ 80.92.06.77/80.92.09.21.

Hotel :
★★ *L'Ecu* (L.F.), 7, rue Auguste-Carré, ☎ 80.92.11.66, AE
DC Euro Visa, 25 rm ℗ ⬚ closed Sat (15 Nov-1st Feb),
480. Rest. ◆ 85-195 ; child : 40.

Restaurant :

◆◆◆ **Le St-Rémy**, ☎ 80.92.13.44, AE DC Euro Visa ⊰ 쌀
♪ closed Mon and eves ex Sat, 2 Jan-10 Feb. Spec : *sau-piquet Montbardois à la façon de M. Belin*, 50-150.

⚠ ★★★★*Municipal* (53 pl), ☎ 80.92.21.60.

MONTCEAU-LES-MINES

Autun 42, Mâcon 68, Paris 384 km
pop 26949 ⊠ 71300   B3-4

A 19thC industrial town bred from the coal mines of Blanzy, part of the Le Creusot complex.

▶ Two branches of the Le Creusot Museum (→; *school hols.*) recall an earlier life : the school house (37 Rue Jean-Jaurès, *last Sun. of month, 3-7*); and, at **Blanzy** *(3 km NE)*, St. Claude mine-shaft (Rue du Bois-Clair, *Sun. 3-7*).

Nearby

▶ **Gourdon** *(7 km SE, D980)* : hilltop village with Romanesque church★, frescos and carved capitals. **Mont-Saint-Vincent** butte *(8 km farther;* alt. 603 m) : view★★ sometimes as far as the Alps ; 11th-12thC Romanesque church in the village with transverse barrel-vaulted nave and small archaeological museum. ▶ **Bissy-sur-Fley** *(28 km E, D90 and D28)* : 15thC castle where the poet Pontus de Thiard was born in 1521. ▶ **Perrecy-les-Forges** *(17 km SW)* : 12thC church ; in the upper narthex★★, Le Creusot Museum exhibit *(Sat. and Sun. 3-7, Jun.-15 Sep.)*.
▶ **Toulon-sur-Arroux** *(20 km W)* : Romanesque church and old bridge ; not far from there, a Buddhist community and pagoda at the **château de Plège.** ▶ **Issy-l'Évêque** *(16 km W)* : 11th-12thC church, frescos, capitals. ☐

Practical Information

ℹ 1, pl. de l'Hôtel-de-Ville, ☎ 85.57.38.51.
SNCF ☎ 85.57.14.15.

Hotel :

★ *Lac*, 58, rue de la Loge, ☎ 85.57.18.22, 22 rm Ⓟ ⊰ 쌀
♨ ☒ 110.

Recommended

Sports : *aéroclub du Bassin minier*, aérodrome Pouilloux, CP 71320 Saint-Vallier, ☎ 85.79.10.83.

MORVAN Lakes**

                                                      B2-3
Round trip from Quarré-les-Tombes *(approx 134 km, full day; see map 3)*

In the heart of the Morvan massif and nature park (→), these lakes are an added attraction in this wooded landscape.

Quarré-les-Tombes : named after the numerous sarcophagi found near the church, which posed a mystery until it was discovered that 6th-9thC stonemasons working at local quarries had kept up a thriving trade in funerary monuments. S, **Duc Forest** : forest roads, hiking trails ; deer reserve ; Roche des Fées (Fairies' rock) ; Pérouse rocks★. ▶ **Chastellux★** : the **château★**, in a superb site★ overlooking the Cure, has belonged to the same family for 1 000 years ; restored in the 19thC, but retains a 15thC appearance. ▶ **Crescent Dam** (1930, 14 million m³, 407 acres : hydroelectric station ; beach ; sailing) and the **Chaumecon Reservoir** (333 acres) indirectly regulate the level of the Seine. ▶ **Saint-Martin-du-Puy** : 14th-18thC **château de Vésigneux.** Lormes : panoramas near the church and at Mont Justice *(1.5 km N)*; view★ ; walks. Narvau Gorge, Goulot pond. ▶ Across the Yonne channel, 15th-17thC **château de Chassy** *(4-7, Jul.-Aug.)*. ▶ **Pannesière-Chaumard Reservoir★** : the biggest in Morvan (1950, 85 million m³), 1 284 acres ; hydroelectric station ; aquatic sports. **Ouroux-en-Morvan** *(8 km NW).* ▶ Despite numerous man-made tourist attractions, **Lake Settons★★** remains beautiful ; the reservoir (1861, 21 million m³, 887 acres ; aquatic sports) regulates the level of the

3. Morvan lakes

Yonne. ▶ **Montsauche**, a mountain village (alt. 650 m). **Savault** *(5 km W)* : crafts in summer. Just off the road, **Saut de Gouloux** : waterfall running into the Cure ; site★★. ▶ **Saint-Brisson** : park office (→ Nature Park); resort for hiking and angling. ▶ **Dun-les-Places**, on the other side of the Breuil-Chenue forest : nature trail and angling. ▶ **Saint-Agnan** : the 350-acre **lake** is little frequented despite an attractive shore. ▶ **La Pierre-qui-Vire** (Balancing Rock) : at the Benedictine **abbey** founded in 1850, the monks publish informative books on Romanesque art (catalaque series); exhibits *(weekday mass at 9:30; Sun. at 10)*. ▶ **Saint-Léger-Vauban** : birthplace of the military architect Sébastien de Vauban, who is buried in Bazoches (→ Cure Valley); exhibits *(10-12 & 2-7, 15 Jun.-15 Sep.)*. ☐

Practical Information

QUARRÉ-LES-TOMBES, ⊠ 89630, 19 km SE of **Avallon**.

Hotels :

★★ **Nord et Poste** (L.F.), 25, pl. de l'Eglise, ☎ 86.32.24.55, 35 rm, half pens. 340. Rest. ◆ ⏚ Spec : *parfait de foie blond tiède de canard aux champignons noirs, soufflé de brochet sauce cardinal*, 70-125.
★ **Brizards** (L.F.), 7 km S. ☎ 86.32.20.12, DC Visa, 26 rm Ⓟ 쌀 ♪° closed 2 Jan-2 Feb, 195. Rest. ◆ 110-165.

Restaurant :

◆◆ **Auberge de l'Atre**, Lavaults, ☎ 86.32.20.79, AE DC Euro Visa ⊰ 쌀 ♪ ⏚ closed Tue eve and Wed , 2 Jan-Feb, 85-200.

MORVAN Nature Park**

                                                      B2-3

A region once renowned in Paris for two essential resources : timber floated down the Cure and Yonne rivers, and wet nurses. A wet, hilly, thickly wooded region (beech, hornbeam, oak, and conifers on the hilltops) that today is France's main source of Christmas trees.

▶ The nature park created in 1970 comprises 1 730 km² overlapping four Burgundy departments. The park has fostered redevelopment of the human and natural resources of the region; ample signposting and equipment encourage environmental exploration and nature-related activities. ► The **Maison du Parc** (office) at Saint-Brisson (→ Morvan lakes) is in a 19thC lakeside mansion, with information, exhibits, activities; essential stop. □

Practical Information ───────────

ⓘ Maison du Parc, Saint-Brisson, 58230 Montsanche, ☎ 86.78.70.16.

Recommended
Holiday villages : Saint-Agnan, 58230 Montsanche, ☎ 86.78.72.00. Holidays for all. Info and reservations : ☎ 42.77.11.40.
Youth lodgings : *chalet refuge du Brenil, Parc naturel régional du Morvan*, ☎ 86.78.72.34, 34 beds year round.

NEVERS**

Moulins 54, Dijon 188, Paris 240 km
pop 44700 ⊠ 58000   A3
Nevers is situated in a bend on the right bank of the river Loire. Famous for its faience, it had belonged to the Dukes of Burgundy until François I made it and the entire Nivernais region an independent duchy.

► The town is centred on **Place Carnot** (B2, Rue St-Martin, **Chapel of Ste Marie** with Louis XIII façade★) and **Rue du Commerce** (C2; partly pedestrian; 15thC belfry). ► Near the Prefecture, **church of St. Pierre★** (C1; 1612) and 18thC **Paris Gate.** ► **Church of St. Étienne★★** (C1) : Cluniac Romanesque, late 11thC; noteworthy E end. ► **Ducal Palace★** (B2) : now the Courthouse; 15th-16thC, combining mediaeval strength with Renaissance delicacy (stairway, dormer-windows, chimneys). ► **Cathedral of St-**

Cyr-et-St Julitte (B3) : an apse at either end of the nave; W end, Romanesque over an 11thC crypt (excavated 6thC baptistery); E end, 13thC Gothic nave; 15thC chapels. ► Rue St-Genest, **Municipal Museum** (A3) : **faïence collection★★** from Nevers and elsewhere; ivories, enamels, glass, modern painting *(10-12 & 3-7 ex Tue. and Jan.)*. ► On the 12thC ramparts, **Croux Gate★★** (A3; 14thC) : lapidary museum, Roman era, Romanesque *(daily 10-12 & 3-7 in season; in winter, by appt.)*. From there, one can walk as far as the Loire along the particulary well preserved collection of ramparts.
Also... ► **St. Gildard Convent** (A1) where Bernadette Soubirous (→ Lourdes) lived as a nun from 1860 to 1879; her embalmed body lies in a glass casket in the chapel. ► **Church of St. Bernadette** (*N of map*; Bd de Lattre-de-Tassigny) : contemporary architecture (1966).

Nearby

► **Pougues** *(11 km NW)* : at one time a thermal spa on the banks of the Loire. ► **Guérigny** *(14 km N; on the way, two châteaux near Urzy)* : 18thC château and state forges. ► **Marzy** *(4.5 km W)* : 12thC Romanesque church (bell-tower★); local ethnographic museum in town hall. ► **La Machine :** Mine museum *(Jun.-Sep., 10-12 & 3-7 ex Tue.; Oct.-May, Sat. and Sun., 2-6).*

Between the Loire and Allier rivers *(75 km round trip, half-day)*

► Near the **Bec d'Allier** *(D976, SW)*, where the Allier meets the Loire, **château du Marais** (14th-16thC) and **Guétin canal-bridge** (the Loire canal flows over the Allier after a series of three locks). ► Farther S, 13thC fortress at **Meauce**, and *(via D134)* ruined Cluniac priory at **Mars-sur-Allier** (12thC church). ► **Saint-Pierre-le-Moutier** *(A3,*

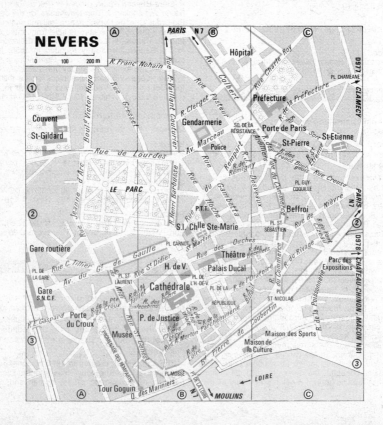

via D108) : old houses (Renaissance); 12th-15thC church.
► Via N7 N, then right by the **château de Villars**
(14th-15thC), **Saint-Parize-le-Châtel** : church over a
Romanesque crypt (capitals★); 2 km away, golf course
and motor-racing track at **Magny-Cours** (racing school).
► From **Rozemont** (*D133;* remains of 13thC fortress), D13
leads back to Nevers via **Chevenon** (14thC castle) along
the Loire canal; on the opposite bank, **Imphy** forges. ☐

Practical Information _____

NEVERS
ⓘ 31, rue du Rempart, ☎ 86.59.07.03.
SNCF ☎ 86.61.50.50.
Car rental : *Avis,* 5, rue de la Passière, ☎ 86.57.51.03;
train station (A3).

Hotels :
★★★ *Diane,* (Mapotel), 38, rue du Midi (A3),
☎ 86.57.28.10, Tx 801021, AE DC Euro Visa, 30 rm Ⓟ ▨
⬧ ♨ closed 20 Dec-20 Jan, 270. Rest. ♦ ⅃ & closed
Mon and Sun noon, 90-130.
● ★★ *Château de la Rocherie,* RN 7, Varennes-Vauzel-
les, ☎ 86.38.07.21, AE DC Euro Visa, 15 rm Ⓟ closed Sun
eve (Nov-late Mar), 1-15 Jan, 1-15 Nov, 180. Rest. ♦♦
80-230.
★★ *La Folie* (L.F.), rte des Saulaies (off map A3),
☎ 86.57.05.31, Euro Visa, 27 rm Ⓟ ⅃ ☐ closed
15 Dec-6 Jan, 175. Rest. ♦ ⅃ & closed Fri and Sun
eve, 55-95.
★★ *P.L.M. Loire,* quai de Médine (C3), ☎ 86.61.50.92,
60 rm Ⓟ ⬧ ♨ closed Oct-Easter, 295. Rest. ♦♦♦ closed
Sat, 15 Dec-15 Jan, 100-165.
★ *Morvan* (L.F.), 28, rue de Mouësse (C2), ☎ 86.61.14.16,
Visa, 11 rm Ⓟ closed Tue eve and Wed, 2-15 Jan,
1-21 Jul, 110. Rest. ♦ 80-160.
Auberge de la Porte du Croux, 17, rue de la Porte-du-
Croux (A3), ☎ 86.57.12.71, AE DC Euro Visa, 3 rm Ⓟ ⬧
▨ ♨ closed Fri eve and Sun ex hols, 10-31 Aug, 120.
Rest. ♦♦ ⬧ Nicely-prepared food, fresh fish direct from
La Rochelle, 95-170.

Restaurant :
♦ *Le Gambrinus,* 37, av. du Gal-de-Gaulle, ☎ 86.57.19.48,
Visa ⅃ closed Sat noon and Sun , Sep, 55-80.

⚠ ★★*Municipal* (70 pl), ☎ 86.57.56.95.

Nearby

BONA, ✉ 58330 Saint-Saulze, 23 km NE.

Hotel :
★ *La Réunion,* ☎ 86.58.63.71, 7 rm ▨ ♨ closed Feb,
100. Rest. ♦ closed Mon in winter. Seasonal cuisine
that Claude Perraudin prepares wonderfully well, like his
famous, elder, Pierre, 120-310.

MAGNY-COURS, ✉ 58470, 12 km S.

Hotel :
★★★ *La Renaissance,* Le Bourg, ☎ 86.58.10.40, AE DC
Euro, 10 rm Ⓟ & closed Sun eve and Mon, 30 Jan-1 Mar,
1-7 Jul, 350. Rest. ● ⬧ ♦♦ Succulent eating : *jambon
d'Arleuf en saupiquet mode nivernaise, filet de Charolais
à la crème et morilles.* Bar : Le François 1er, 180-420;
child : 100.

SAINT-PIERRE-LE-MOUTIER, ✉ 58240, 23 km S.
SNCF ☎ 86.68.40.35.

Restaurant :
♦♦ *La Vigne-Le Relais Gastronomique,* rte de Decize,
☎ 86.37.41.66, Euro Visa ⬧ ⅃ & closed Tue eve and Wed,
Feb school hols. In the great culinary tradition : *terrine
au foie gras de canard, cassolette de lotte à la russe,*
110-160; child : 60.

⚠ ★★*Municipal* (40 pl), ☎ 86.37.42.09.

If you enjoy sports, consult the pages pertaining to
the regions; there you will find addresses for practicing your favorite sport.

NOLAY

Beaune 20, Mâcon 90, Paris 315 km
pop 1582 ✉ 21340   B3

Below walls, among meadows and vineyards : 14thC
covered **market★** roofed with stone tiles; in the
church, bell-tower with 16thC Jack-o'-the-clock.

Nearby

► **Cirque du Bout du Monde★** (World's End natural
amphitheatre; *5 km N, D111) :* **Cormot** limestone **escarpments** overlooking the Tournée River (rock-climbing).
► **La Rochepot★★** : above trees and vineyards, beautiful
château, birthplace of Philippe Pot (1428; his tomb is in
the Louvre Museum in Paris), ambassador of the Grand
Dukes of Burgundy; château was restored during the
19thC on the 12th and 15thC remains ; Renaissance wing;
furniture and works of art in several rooms *(9:30-11:30 &
2:30-5:30 ex Tue.).* In the village, Romanesque church
(12thC capitals ; Renaissance bell-tower).   ☐

Practical Information _____

ⓘ 98, rue St-Pierre, ☎ 80.21.70.86.

Hotels :
★★ *Chevreuil* (L.F.), pl. de l'Hôtel-de-Ville, ☎ 80.21.71.89,
AE DC Euro Visa, 14 rm Ⓟ ⬧ ▨ ♨ half pens (h.s.), closed
Wed, Dec, 420. Rest. ♦ ⬧ ⅃ & 45-80 ; child : 30.
★ *Sainte-Marie* (L.F.), 36, rue de la République,
☎ 80.21.73.19, AE DC Euro Visa, 12 rm Ⓟ closed Mon ex
summer, 6 Jan-6 Feb, 160. Rest. ♦ ⅃ & 65-100 ; child : 45.

⚠ ★★*Municipal,* rte de Couches (70 pl), ☎ 80.21.73.00.

The côte de NUITS Vineyards★★

C2-3

Great wine names appear at every turn on the Côte
de Nuits road through a region that rivals the Côte de
Beaune for prestige and quality.

► From **Chenôve,** at the S exit of Dijon (→), the hillsides are covered with vine rows, often in walled enclosures (the *clos* of many vineyard names). The Dukes of
Burgundy maintained an estate here; the **Cuverie des
Ducs★** (fermenting room) still has two huge wine presses
(13thC originals or 15thC copies; *daily*). ► **Marsannay** :
rosé wines. ► **Fixey :** Romanesque church with glazed-tile
bell-tower. ► **Fixin,** known both for wine and for a statue,
the "Awakening of Napoleon" commissioned in 1846 by a
former captain of the Imperial guard ; Napoleonic museum
(9-12 & 2-5, 7 in summer ; closed Tue. and Fri. am).
► **Chambertin** and **Clos-de-Bèze** : great wines. **Gevrey :**
10thC castle★ rebuilt in the 13thC *(10-12 & 2-6, 11 Sun.);*
church with Romanesque doorway. **Collonges-lès-Bévy :**
17th-18thC château *(2-6 Sat., Jul.-Sep.).* W, D31
follows the **Lavaux Valley.** ► **Morey-Saint-Denis,** Cham-
bolle-Musigny, Vougeot : famous vineyards and great
red wines. **Château du Clos-Vougeot★★,** built by Cistercian monks in 1551, stands in their vineyards *(9-11:30
& 2:30-5:30; closed 20 Dec.-5 Jan.);* nearby, 12thC wine
store and 13thC fermenting room (wine presses); today
the château is the headquarters of the promotional
brotherhood of the Chevaliers du Tastevin (→ box).
► **Gilly** *(1 km E) :* 15th-17thC **château,** former residence
of Cistercian abbots *(daily).* ► The **Vosne-Romanée** holdings include Romanée-Conti, the rarest and most expensive of red wines (less than 5 acres of vineyard). ► **Nuits-
Saint-Georges,** once a Gallo-Roman township, now a
prosperous Burgundian village; archaeological museum
in the 17thC clock-tower (Gallo-Roman and Merovingian
exhibits ; *9-12 & 2-6 daily May-Sep.);* Romanesque church
in the cemetery. ► **Cussigny** *(6 km S) :* 17th-18thC châ-
teau *(10-12 & 2:30-7, Jul.-15 Sep.).*

Nearby

▶ **Cîteaux Abbey** *(12 km E)* : founded in 1098, visited by St. Bernard (→ Fontenay) in 1112; nucleus of the dynamic expansion of the Cistercian order (more than 1 000 abbeys throughout Christendom by the 13thC) advocating rigorous application of the Benedictine rule, in reaction to the laxity of Cluny (→); reformed again in the 18thC, the Order has since been known as the Trappists; 15th-18thC buildings, audiovisual presentation *(9:30-12 & 2:30-6)*.

The Côte Hinterland

▶ **St. Vivant Abbey** (at **Curtil-Vergy**, *8 km via D25 and D35)* : 10thC ruins; signposted trails. **Reulle-Vergy** *(1 km farther)* : church of St. Saturnin; **museum of folk arts and crafts of the Upper Côtes**★ *(Sun. 2-6 and daily 15 Jul.-15 Sep.;* nature trail). Beyond, between **Ternant** and **Rolle** : two dolmens *(D104b)*. ▶ Via D25 (Serrée Valley), cultivation of black currants and raspberries near **Arcenant**, then Pertuis Valley. ▶ **Bouilland** *(22 km from Nuits via D25 then left on D2, or 16 km from Beaune)* : charming site★, many walks; ruins of Ste. Marguerite abbey; Percée (pierced) rock; La Vieille Valley. □

Practical Information _____

BOUILLAND, ⊠ 21420 Savigny-lès-Beaune, 16 km N of **Beaune**.

Hotel :
★★★ **Hostellerie du Vieux Moulin**, ☎ 80.21.51.16, AE DC Euro Visa, 13 rm ℙ ⫯ ⑩ ⫫, 14 Dec-22 Jan, 375. Rest. ● ♦♦ ⫯ ⅃ ⅍ closed Wed and Thu noon ex hols. First-class rustic luxury, reasonably priced : *lasagne de truite de mer, pigeonneau aux fèves fraîches*, 130-220.

CHAMBOLLE MUSIGNY, ⊠ 21220, 25 km N of **Beaune**.

Hotel :
★★★★(L) **Relais de Chambolle**, ☎ 80.62.80.94, Tx 351603, AE DC Euro Visa, 36 rm ℙ ⫯ ⑩ ⫫ ⅃ ⅍ 750. Rest. ♦♦♦ ⫯ ⅃ ⅍ A prestigious new stopover in the heart of the wine country. 160-300.

GEVREY-CHAMBERTIN, ⊠ 21220, 27 km NE of **Beaune**.
ⅈ pl. de la Mairie, ☎ 80.34.38.40.
SNCF ☎ 80.34.30.59.

Hotel :
★★★ **Les Grands Crus**, rte des Grands-Crus, ☎ 80.34.34.15, 24 rm ℙ ⫯ ⑩ ⫫ closed 1 Dec-15 Feb, 235.

Restaurants :
● ♦♦♦ **La Rôtisserie du Chambertin**, rue du Chambertin, ☎ 80.34.33.20 ⅃ closed Mon and Sun eve , Feb, 3-10 Aug. There's everything to like at Pierre Menneveau's lovely place. Great Burgundy vintages and good cooking by J.-P. Nicolas, a former assistant to Louis Outhier : *escargots, coq au vin, côte de bœuf vigneronne*, 230-300.
● ♦♦ **Les Millésimes**, 25, rue de l'Eglise, ☎ 80.51.84.24, AE DC Euro Visa ⅃ ⅍ closed Tue and Wed noon, 1 Jan-11 Feb. Set in the wine country, the Sangoy family's restaurant serves delicious food : *galette de truffes, bar à la vapeur* and good wines (over 27 000 bottles in the cellar); all the great Burgundies are on hand, 175-280.

MARSANNAY-LA-CÔTE, ⊠ 21160, 6 km S of **Dijon**.

Restaurant :
● ♦♦ **Gourmets**, 8, rue du Puits-de-Têt, ☎ 80.52.16.32, AE DC Euro Visa ⑩ ⅃ closed Mon eve and Tue , Jan, 15-22 Jul, 145-220.

MOREY-SAINT-DENIS, ⊠ 21220 Gevrey-Chambertin, 4 km S of **Gevrey**.

Hotel :
★★ **Castel de Très Girard** (L.F.), rue Très-Girard, ☎ 80.34.33.09, AE DC Euro Visa, 14 rm ℙ ⫯ ⑩ ⫯ ⅃ ⅍ ⊠ Rest. ♦♦ ⫯ ⅃ 130-260; child : 75.

NUITS-SAINT-GEORGES, ⊠ 21700, 17 km NE of **Beaune**.
ⅈ Maison du Tourisme, ☎ 80.61.22.47.
SNCF ☎ 80.61.05.84/80.61.10.80.

Hotels :
★★★ **Côte-d'Or** (L.F.), 37, rue Thurot, ☎ 80.61.06.10, Euro Visa, 7 rm ☼ closed Sun eve and Wed, 1-21 Feb, 1-21 Jul, 360. Rest. ♦♦♦ Remarkable food, light and elegant, by Jean Crotet. Interesting cellar, 220-380.
★★★ **La Gentilhommière**, 13, rte de la Serrée, CD 25, ☎ 80.61.12.06, Tx 350401, AE, 20 rm ℙ ⫯ ⑩ ⫫ ⅃ ⫳ ⅍ half pens (h.s.), closed 1-20 Jan, 460. Rest. ♦♦ ⫯ ⅃ 95-200; child : 55.

Recommended
Guide to wines : *wine auction at the hospices*, info. mairie, ☎ 80.61.12.54, Sun before Palm Sun; at Magny-les-Villiers, M. Jayer.

OTHE Forest

A1

Forested massif between Sens and Troyes (→ Champagne, Ardennes), dotted here and there by apple and cherry orchards; vestiges of prehistoric habitation.

▶ The region offers numerous resorts and excursion centres such as **Dixmont** (13th-16thC church), **Cerisiers** (partly 12thC church), **Arces**, **Vaudeurs**, and the many villages in the Vanne, Yonne and Armançon valleys.

Practical Information _____

VAUDEURS, ⊠ 89320, 14 km S of **Villeneuve-l'Archevêque**.

Hotel :
● ★★ **Vaudeurinoise** (L.F.), rte de Grange-Sèche, ☎ 86.96.28.00, AE Visa, 7 rm ℙ ⫯ ⑩ ⫫ closed Tue eve and Wed, Feb, Oct, 160. Rest. ♦ ⫯ ⅃ ⅍ Young C. Ballu is a talented, capable chef : *crêpe soufflée au saumon, timbale de nouilles fraîches aux Saint-Jacques et œufs de lump*, 115-220.

PARAY-LE-MONIAL*

Mâcon 68, Autun 79, Paris 372 km
pop 11312 ⊠ 71600

B4

Paray-le-Monial is a religious centre and an important market town; the Romanesque basilica of Sacré-Cœur has been a focus of Roman Catholic devotion since the 17thC.

▶ On the banks of the Bourbince, **abbey church of Notre-Dame**★★ (now the basilica) built between 1090 and 1110 in golden stone; two towers flank the doorway; beautiful **eastern end**★★★ with octagonal tower at the transept crossing : inside, slender columns, capitals, 15thC fresco; the plan resembles that of the now-demolished church of Cluny. ▶ Annual pilgrimage to **relics** of 17thC St. Marguerite-Marie Alacoque *(9-12 & 2-7, Mar.-Oct.;* park, diorama). ▶ Place Guignaud : Renaissance **Town Hall**★, 16thC St. Nicolas Tower. ▶ Rue de la Paix, **Hiéron Museum**★ of religious art : 12thC tympanum★ from Anzy-le-Duc; paintings (Italian, French, Flemish) on the theme of the Eucharist *(15 May-8 Sep., 9-7)*.

Nearby

▶ 18thC **château de Digoine**★★ *(16 km NE)* can be seen from D128 or, on the other side of the Centre Canal, D974. ▶ **Digoin** *(12 km NW)* : a paradise for anglers at the junction of the Arroux, Loire, Arconce and Bourbince rivers, and the intersection of several canals. Ceramics Centre : techniques, exhibits of Digoin ceramics and others *(Jun.-Sep., 2:30-7)*. □

Practical Information ⎯⎯⎯⎯⎯⎯⎯⎯⎯⎯

PARAY-LE-MONIAL
ⓘ pl. de la Poste, ☎ 85.81.10.92.
SNCF ☎ 85.81.07.97/85.81.13.25.

Hotel :
★★ *Trois Pigeons*, 2, rue Dargaud, ☎ 85.81.03.77, Euro Visa, 33 rm Ⓟ ⑭ closed 1 Dec-1 Mar, 150. Rest. ◆◆ 75-100.

⚐ ★★★*Le Pré Barret* (57 pl), ☎ 85.81.05.05.

Recommended
Events : *Sacred-Heart pilgrimage*, late Jun-early Jul; *procession, feast of St Marguerite-Marie*, ☎ 85.81.11.72, in Oct, Sun after 16th.
Leisure activities : *aéroclub du Charollais*, ☎ 85.81.08.19, aerial sports.

Nearby
DIGOIN, ✉ 71160, 12 km NW.
ⓘ 8, rue Guilleminot, ☎ 85.53.00.81.
SNCF ☎ 85.53.12.61/85.53.17.39.

Hotel :
★★ *Commerce et Diligences* (L.F.), 14, rue Nationale, ☎ 85.53.06.31, AE DC Visa, 10 rm Ⓟ ≼ closed Mon eve and Tue, 4-13 May, 3 Nov-4 Dec, 125. Rest. ◆ Spec : *parfait aux foies de volailles*, 80-200.

⚐ ★★★*La Chevrette* (100 pl), ☎ 85.53.11.49.

GUEUGNON, ✉ 71130, 16 km NE.

Hotel :
★★ *Le Relais Bourguignon* (L.F.), 47, rue de la Convention, ☎ 85.85.25.23, AE DC Euro Visa, 8 rm Ⓟ ♪ closed Sun eve and Mon, 21 Feb-2 Mar, 3-25 Aug, 130. Rest. ◆◆◆ ♪ Spec : *salade bressane aux foies de volailles sautés*, 70-160.

VITRY-EN-CHAROLLAIS, ✉ 71600 Paray-le-Monial, 2 km W.

Hotel :
★★★ *Le Charollais*, RN 79, ☎ 85.81.03.35, Tx 801801, AE Visa, 20 rm Ⓟ ⑭ ≼ ♪ ⅄ 200. Rest. ◆◆ ♪ ⅄ Grill, 50-110.

POUILLY-EN-AUXOIS

Dijon 42, Autun 45, Paris 273 km
pop 1396 ✉ 21320   B2
A road transport intersection in S Auxois near the Burgundy canal, which passes through a tunnel. Church of **Notre-Dame-Trouvée** (14th-15thC) with miraculous statue.

Nearby
▶ **Chailly-sur-Armançon** *(6.5 km W)* : 12thC remains; 16thC château★. ▶ **Grosbois Reservoir** *(11 km N)* : fishing. ▶ **Thoisy-le-Désert** *(3.5 km S)* : 14thC spire on the church. ▶ **Châteauneuf★★** *(10 km SE)* : above the canal and motorway A6 (site★), a picturesque village★ sheltered by a castle (12th-15thC; *10-12 & 2-4 or 6, ex Tue. and Wed. in winter*); ramparts, 14th-16thC houses. ▶ **Commarin** *(5 km N of Châteauneuf)* : on the edge of the village, 17th-18thC château★ flanked by 15thC towers (tapestries, 18thC furniture; *10-12 & 2-6 ex. Tue., Palm Sun.-1 Nov.*).   □

Practical Information ⎯⎯⎯⎯⎯⎯⎯⎯⎯⎯

POUILLY-EN-AUXOIS
SNCF ☎ 80.41.50.50.

Hotels :
★★★ *Motel du Val Vert*, rte d'Arnay-le-Duc, ☎ 80.90.82.34, Euro Visa, 30 rm Ⓟ ≼ ⑭ ⚐ 220.
★ *Bassin* (L.F.), Le Bassin, ☎ 80.90.83.98, 7 rm Ⓟ ⍟ closed Sun eve , Mon, Oct, 130. Rest. ◆ ⍟ 60-90.

⚐ ★★*Municipal* (70 pl), ☎ 80.90.85.44.

Nearby
CHÂTEAUNEUF, ✉ 21320 Pouilly-en-Auxois, 10 km SE.

Hotel :
● ★★ *Host. du Château*, (L.F., R.S.), ☎ 80.33.00.23, AE Euro Visa, 15 rm ⑭ ≼ half pens, closed Mon eve and Tue (l.s.), 15 Nov-15 Mar, 170. Rest. ◆◆ ♪ ⍟ An attractive stopover in a charming village, 105-215 ; child : 50.

PRÉMERY

Nevers 29, Château-Chinon 56, Paris 236 km
pop 2603 ✉ 58700   A3
On the banks of the Nièvre, in the heart of a wooded massif, the 14th-17thC **château** once belonged to the counts of Nevers : Gothic collegiate church.

Nearby
▶ **Giry** *(4.5 km N)* : 12th, 15th, 18thC château *(10-12 & 2-5, Jul.-Oct. ex Tue.)*. ▶ **Montenoison Butte** *(8.5 km NE)* : feudal ruins and panorama. **Saint-Révérien** *(13 km NE)* : **church★** with Romanesque apse (capitals★). ▶ **Champallement** *(N)* : 15thC castle and Gallo-Roman site of Compierre. 8 km further, **Brinon-sur-Beuvron** : 13th-17thC moated castle. ▶ **Saint-Saulge** *(17 km SE)* : Gothic church over a Romanesque crypt. Jailly *(4 km W)* : Romanesque church.   □

The PUISAYE Region*
                                         A2
A region of woods, meadows, ponds and hedges often mentioned by the writer Colette (1873-1954) who was born in Saint-Sauveur. The clay soil gave rise to a pottery-making tradition dating from the Middle Ages.

▶ **Saint-Sauveur-en-Puisaye** (pop. 1 149) : capital of the region ; old streets, birthplace of Colette (Rue des Vignes), 12th-16thC church ; 11 km NE, site of the **Battle of Fontenoy**, where Charles the Bald was defeated by his brother Lothaire in 841. ▶ **Treigny** : the church is referred to as the "cathedral of Puisaye" ; pottery exhibit in the Maison du Chanoine. ▶ **Ratilly★** : 13thC feudal castle ; pottery workshop, courses ; contemporary art exhibits in summer. ▶ **Saint-Armand-en-Puisaye** (pop. 1 314) : pottery workshops ; Renaissance château. ▶ **Saint-Fargeau** : old houses ; Gothic and Renaissance church (stalls, triptych, 15thC Pietà) ; 15th-17thC clock-tower ; and 15th-17thC **château★★**, a pink brick, slate-roofed pentagon flanked by fat towers ; here, Mme de Montpensier (the "Grande Mademoiselle"), first cousin to Louis XIV, was exiled for her persistent involvement in anti-government plots ; the 17thC composer Jean-Baptiste Lully worked here as a kitchen helper before becoming court composer to Louis XIV *(10-12 & 2-7, Easter-11 Nov. ; son et lumière show some summer evenings)*. Beyond the park *(4 km SE)*, **Bourdon Reservoir★** (beach, sailing). Farther *(10 km, D185)* at Boutissaint, 988-acre **St. Hubert Animal Park★** : red and roe deer, bison ; camera safari courses ; riding excursions *(daily 7 am-8 pm)*. ▶ 20 km NE from Saint-Fargeau *(D90)*, **Rogny-les-Sept-Écluses** : gigantic 17thC steplocks on the dried-out Briard canal ; at **Dicy**, the Fabuloserie, unusual art museum *(May-2 Nov., 2-6)*.

Round trip from Ouanne to Charny *(38 km, approx 2hr)*

Favoured by Parisians as a weekend retreat, this valley irrigated by the Ouanne River (D950) still has an unspoilt rustic charm.

▶ **Ouanne** *(26 km SW of Auxerre)* : 16thC church. ▶ **Toucy** (pop. 2 665) : home town of the lexicographer Pierre Larousse (1817-75) ; commercial centre ; church rebuilt 16thC ; two 12thC defensive towers. ▶ **Villiers-Saint-Benoît** : regional museum of folk art★★ displaying interior of an 18thC Puisaye home ; 12th-16thC Burgundian sculpture; Auxerrois and Puisaye ceramics *(10-12 & 2-6 ex Tue.; closed 15 Dec.-15 Jan.).* ▶ **Château de Grandchamp** (16thC). ▶ **Charny** : agricultural and market town.　☐

Practical Information ―――――――――

TOUCY, ⊠ 89130, 24 km SW of **Auxerre**.
ᴤᴺᴄꜰ　☎ 86.46.50.50/86.44.15.48.

Hotel :
Lion d'Or, 37, rue Lucile-Cormier, ☎ 86.44.00.76, Visa, 8 rm Ⓟ closed Mon eve and Tue, 5-20 Jan, 5-15 Dec, 65. Rest. ♦ ♪ 65-150.

⚠ ★★*Le Patis* (50 pl), ☎ 86.44.13.84.

SAINT-FLORENTIN

Auxerre 31, Sens 44, Paris 174 km
pop 6757 ⊠ 89600　　　　　　　　　　　　　A1

Close to the Champagne region (→ Ardennes-Champagne), Saint-Florentin is a pleasant stopover above the Armançon River and the Burgundy canal. Saint-Florentin and Soumaintrain cheeses are produced in this area.

▶ **Church**★★ : 15th-17thC **stained glass**★ (The Creation); nave and chapel with Renaissance decoration; choirscreen and statues by sculptors of the Champagne school.

Nearby

▶ Same influence in the churches at **Sormery, Vénizy, Soumaintrain** and **Neuvy-Sautour**★. ▶ **Brienon-sur-Armançon** *(8 km W)* : collegiate church (16thC choir★); round 17thC wash-house★.　☐

Practical Information ―――――――――

SAINT-FLORENTIN
ᴤᴺᴄꜰ　☎ 86.35.02.74.

Hotels :
★★★ *La Grande Chaumière* (L.F.), 3, rue des Capucins, ☎ 86.35.15.12, AE DC Visa, 10 rm Ⓟ closed 1-8 Sep, 20 Dec-20 Jan, 230. Rest. ♦ ♪ closed Wed, 85-250.
★★ *Les Tilleuls* (L.F.), 3, rue Descourtives, ☎ 86.35.09.09, Visa, 10 rm Ⓟ ♨ closed Sun eve, Mon, 2 Nov-2 Dec, 175. Rest. ♦ ♿ ⚘ 60-200.

⚠ ★★*Plage* (150 pl), ☎ 86.35.08.13.

Nearby

VENIZY, ⊠ 89210, 6 km N.

Hotel :
● ★★ *Moulin des Pommerats* (L.F.), ☎ 86.35.08.04, DC Euro Visa, 20 rm Ⓟ ♨ ♿ ♨ closed Sun eve and Mon (l.s.), 250. Rest. ● ♦♦ ♪ ♿ The mill is on a trout stream. Good value : *cailles aux airelles, rognons sautés à la moutarde de Dijon, gambas flambés au marc,* 80-170.

SAINT-HONORÉ-LES-BAINS

Moulins 66, Nevers 67, Paris 307 km
pop 831 ⊠ 58360　　　　　　　　　　　　　B3

This thermal spa for the treatment of asthma and respiratory problems, on the edge of the Morvan Nature Park, is a pleasant place to stay; walks, excursions.

Nearby

▶ **Château de Vandenesse**★ *(6 km W)* : 15thC towers. ▶ 9 km SE, **La Bussière** : 15thC castle. ▶ **Moulin-Engilbert** *(11 km N)* : cattle-market; old houses around the Gothic church. ▶ **Commagny** *(2 km SW)* : priory with 12thC church, 15thC buildings. ▶ **Limaton** and **Brinay** *(6 km and 11 km W)* : 14th-17thC and 13thC castles.

▶ Above the Roche Valley, **Larochemillay**★ *(18 km E)* : 18thC château at the foot of Mont Beuvray (→ Autun).　☐

Practical Information ―――――――――

♨ (27 Mar-30 Sep), ☎ 86.30.73.27.
ᴤᴺᴄꜰ　☎ 86.30.84.57.

Hotel :
★★ *Henry-Robert* (L.F.), 47, av. du Gal d'Espeuilles, ☎ 86.30.72.33, AE Visa, 15 rm Ⓟ ♨ ♨ ♿ ♿ closed 1 Jan-18 Apr, 160. Rest. ♦ ♪ ♿ 70-110; child : 45.

⚠ ★★★*Des Bains* (100 pl), ☎ 80.30.73.44 ; ★★*Bonneau* (33 pl), ☎ 80.30.76.00.

Recommended
Casino : ☎ 86.30.70.99.

SAINT-SEINE-L'ABBAYE

Dijon 27, Avallon 79, Paris 304 km
pop 309 ⊠ 21440　　　　　　　　　　　　　C2

Early 13thC church, Romanesque in appearance, constitutes the remains of the abbey that once was the source of the village's prosperity; choirscreen; paintings, 18thC stalls. Attractive fountains, including "La Samaritaine" (1715).

Nearby

▶ **Source of the Ignon** (rebuilt 16thC manor-house at **Poncey-sur-l'Ignon;** *Sat., Sun. pm*). **Source of the Seine**★ *(10.5 km NW),* maintained by the City of Paris; close by, Gallo-Roman excavations of a temple to the goddess Sequana (divinity of the Seine).　☐

The SAÔNE Valley

　　　　　　　　　　　　　　　　　　　　C3-4

From Franche-Comté (→), the Saône runs through a pleasant valley, past small towns (fishing; shores; sailing); from N to S, D20, D976.

▶ **Pontailler-sur-Saône** (→ along the Vingeanne). ▶ **Auxonne** (pop. 7 121) : a town of character, on the Dijon-Dole road; 16thC **Comté Gate; 15thC Town Hall; Gothic church of Notre-Dame** (Romanesque tower; 15th-16thC statues); 15thC château with **Bonaparte museum** (Napoleon served here as a lieutenant of artillery; *2:30-4:30 ex Thu.; daily Jul.-Aug.; closed 15 Oct.-1 May*) and arsenal built by Vauban. ▶ **Saint-Jean-de-Losne** (pop. 1 476) : small craft port at the mouth of the Burgundy canal and close to the Rhône-Rhine canal junction; 15th-16thC church. ▶ **Seurre** (pop. 2 694) : 16thC family home of the preacher and writer Jacques-Bénigne Bossuet (1624-1704), now an **environmental museum of the Saône**★ (geology, history, ethnology; *10-12 & 3-7, Jul.-Oct.*); 17thC hospital. ▶ **Verdun-sur-le-Doubs** (pop. 1 139) : at this junction of two rivers the specialty is *pôchouse* (→ Burgundy cuisine); **Grain and Bread Museum** (Musée du Blé et du Pain, Rue du Pont-St.-Jean; *3-7, Sat., Sun.*); old houses. ▶ **Terrans**★ *(21.5 km W of Verdun)* : 18thC château. ▶ **Pierre-de-Bresse** *(3 km farther)* : 17thC château; **Bresse environmental museum** (the N of this region is part of Burgundy; *2-6 ex Tue.*); lakes.　☐

Practical Information ―――――――――

AUXONNE, ⊠ 21130, 16 km NW of **Dôle**.
ⓘ bd Pasteur, ☎ 80.36.34.46.　　　　　♥
ᴤᴺᴄꜰ　☎ 80.37.30.31.

Hotel :
★★ *Corbeau* (L.F.), 1, rue de Berbis, ☎ 80.31.11.88, AE DC Euro Visa, 10 rm Ⓟ closed Sun eve (l.s.), 21 Dec-26 Jan, 125. Rest. ♦ 55-100.

△ ★★★*Arquebuse* (100 pl), ☎ 80.37.34.36.

SAINT-JEAN-DE-LOSNE, ⊠ 21170, 22 km W of **Dôle**.
🗓 ☎ 80.29.05.44.
SNCF ☎ 80.29.05.64.

△ ★★*les Herlequins* (67 pl), ☎ 80.29.05.44.

Recommended
Boat rental : *Saône Line*, ☎ 80.29.12.86; *Plaisance et Tourisme fluvial*, Saint-Usage, ☎ 80.29.11.06.
Events : *river boat festival*, Jun.

SEURRE, ⊠ 21250, 26 km E of **Beaune**.
SNCF ☎ 80.21.14.13.

Hotel :
★★ **Castel** (L.F.), 20, av. de la Gare, ☎ 80.20.45.07, 20 rm 🅿 closed Mon (l.s.), 2 Jan-15 Feb, 185. Rest. ◆◆ ᵹ 70-145.

△ ★★*La Piscine* (190 pl), ☎ 80.21.15.92; ★★*Raie Mignot* (33 pl), ☎ 80.21.14.61.

Recommended
Boat rental : *Bourgogne Buissonnière*, B.P. 1, 21820 Labergement-lès-Seurre, ☎ 80.21.10.58.

VERDUN-SUR-LE-DOUBS, ⊠ 71350, 22 km SE of **Beaune**.
🗓 mairie, ☎ 85.91.52.52. ◗
SNCF ☎ 85.93.50.50/85.91.51.05.

Hotels :
● ★★★ *Moulin d'Hauterive*, (C.H., R.S.), Saint-Gervais-en-Vallière, Chaublanc, ☎ 85.91.55.56, Tx 801391, AE DC Euro Visa, 21 rm 🅿 ﹘ ⚲ ▱ ♪° half pens (h.s.), closed Sun eve and Mon, 1 Jan-6 Feb, 800. Rest. ◆◆ ♪ 120-350.
★★★ *Hostellerie Bourguignonne*, av. du Pdt-Borgeot, ☎ 85.91.51.45, AE DC Euro Visa, 14 rm 🅿 ﹘ ⚲ closed Tue eve and Wed (l.s.), 15 Jan-15 Feb, 220. Rest. ◆ ♪ ᵹ Reservations advised, 110-220.

△ ★★*Municipal* (170 pl), ☎ 85.42.55.50.

SAULIEU*

Autun 41, Dijon 73, Paris 252 km
pop 3084 ⊠ 21210   B2
Countless pilgrims and travellers over the ages have halted at Saulieu, gateway to the Morvan (→). Writers François Rabelais (ca. 1490-1553) and the Marquise de Sévigné (1626-96) stopped at Saulieu and praised the quality of the food and wine. Mme de Sévigné confessed to having been tipsy for the first time in her life and made an expiatory offering to the local church. Saulieu is still today a gastronomic attraction.

▶ **Basilica of St. Andoche**★★ (12thC) on a charming square; noteworthy figured **capitals** (Flight into Egypt★, Christ and Mary Magdalene, Hanging of Judas) in the Romanesque nave (rebuilt 1704); 14thC stalls. ▶ Next door, **museum** of archaeology, local history, rural crafts and traditions, religious art, sculpture by Pompon (→ Dijon; *10-12 & 2-6 ex Tue.*). ▶ SE of town, 15thC church of St. Saturnin.

Nearby
▶ **La Roche-en-Brénil** *(12 km N)* : 16th-18thC **château**★.
▶ **Thoisy-la-Berchère** *(10 km E)* : 15thC château built over a feudal manor (Renaissance façade). **Mont-Saint-Jean**★ *(6.5 km further NE)* : **site**★ and old village (ramparts, Romanesque church over crypt, mediaeval houses, château). ▶ **Menessaire** *(11 km S)* : 12th-17thC **château** with glazed-tile roof *(9-6, Jul.-Aug.)*.   □

Practical Information
🗓 rue d'Argentine, ☎ 80.64.00.21 ; mairie, ☎ 80.64.09.22.
✈ *Saulieu-Liernais*.
SNCF ☎ 80.64.05.32.

Hotels :
● ★★★★ *La Côte d'Or* (R.C.), 2, rue d'Argentine, ☎ 80.64.07.66, Tx 350778, AE DC Euro Visa, 13 rm 9 apt 🅿 ﹘ ❄ 560. Rest. ● ◆◆◆ Bernard Loiseau, our first Hachette grand prix des Cuisiniers winner, isn't just resting on his laurels in his handsome, newly -renovated establishment. He assures us that a pool and tennis court will soon be completed. In the kitchen, this inspired pupil of the Troisgros brothers is preparing further creative gastronomic surprises : *escargots aux orties, merlan au jus de veau, lapin braisé aux navets émincés, tarte aux pommes chaude et légère.* Burgundies star in the fine cellar, 230-450.
● ★★ **Poste**, (Inter-Hôtel), 1 rue Grillot, ☎ 80.64.05.67, Tx 350540, AE DC Euro Visa, 48 rm 🅿 ♪ ᵹ 190. Rest. ◆ ♪ ᵹ 95-200; child : 45.
★ **Borne Impériale** (L.F.), 14-16, rue d'Argentine, ☎ 80.64.19.76, AE Euro Visa, 7 rm 🅿 closed Mon eve and Tue, 15 Nov-15 Dec, 180. Rest. ● ◆ A temple of Burgundian cuisine : *jambon à la crème, escargots*, 80-210.
★ **Tour d'Auxois**, 10, rue Sallier, ☎ 80.64.13.30, 30 rm 🅿 closed Sun eve and Mon, 1 Dec-1 Jan, 100. Rest. ● ◆ ♪ Fixed-price meals much appreciated by neighbour Bernard Loiseau: *œufs en meurette, poulet de ferme*, 55-210.

Recommended
♥ bakery : *Deschaumes*, ☎ 80.64.18.72.

SEMUR-EN-AUXOIS**

Avallon 42, Dijon 81, Paris 250 km
pop 4619 ⊠ 21140   B2
Approached from the W, the spire and mediaeval towers of the town suddenly appear on a spur on the river Armançon. Once inside the gates, this proves to be one of the most attractive towns in Burgundy.

▶ The 14thC Sauvigny Gate leads along the Rue de la Liberté (elegant buildings) to the heart of the old town.
▶ **Church of Notre-Dame**★★ : Burgundian Gothic, 13thC transept and choir; 14th-15thC chapels, tympanum on N doorway; 14thC stained glass; 15thC entombment of Christ; furnishings. ▶ View from the ramparts. ▶ **Municipal Museum** in former Dominican convent (Rue J.-J.-Collenot) : sculpture, paintings, archaeology, natural sciences *(3-7, Wed. and Fri.; 10-12 & 2-6 Jul.-Aug.)*. ▶ Orle d'Or Tower : remains of 14thC keep.

Nearby
▶ **Lake Pont** *(4 km S)* : shore, sailing. ▶ **Thil** : 9th-12thC castle, 14thC collegiate church, both damaged in the late-16thC Wars of Religion; site★★ *(15 km S)* is a landmark on A6 motorway. ▶ In the Serein Valley, **Bourbilly** *(9 km SW)* : 14thC castle★ restored in the 19thC (Venetian chandeliers) *(10-12 & 3-6, ex Mon., Apr.-1 Sep.)*; here Mme de Sévigné (→ Saulieu) stayed here, and at the **château d'Époisses**★ *(11.5 km E)* : 11th, 16th and 18thC; double fortifications with moats, dovecote, interior decoration and furniture *(10-12 & 3-6; ext. visits 10-6)*. Époisses produces a cheese praised by the 18thC gastronomist Jean-Anthelme Brillat-Savarin (1755-1826) as the "king of cheeses".   □

Practical Information
🗓 2, pl. Gaveau, ☎ 80.97.05.96.   ◗
SNCF ☎ 80.97.11.04.

Hotels :
★★ **Cymaises**, 7, rue du Renaudot, ☎ 80.97.21.44, Euro Visa, 11 rm 🅿 ﹘ ⚲ closed Feb school hols, 90.
★★ **La Côte d'Or** (L.F.), 3, pl. Gaveau, ☎ 80.97.03.13, AE DC Euro Visa, 15 rm 🅿 ﹝ half pens, closed Wed, 3 Jan-25 Mar, 330. Rest. ◆ 60-130.
★ **Les Gourmets**, ☎ 80.97.09.41, Euro Visa, 15 rm 🅿 ﹘ ⚲ closed Mon eve , Tue and Nov, 140. Rest. ◆ ♪ 60-110.

Restaurants :
◆◆ **La Cambuse**, 8, rue Févret, ☎ 80.97.06.78, AE DC

Euro Visa ♪ ઙ closed Wed eve and Thu, 16 Nov-15 Mar. Friendly atmosphere, regional dishes, 80-150.
● ♦ **Le Carillon**, 13, rue Buffon, ☎ 80.97.07.87, Euro Visa ⟨ ⚲ ♪ closed Mon eve and Tue, 5-27 Oct. Trained by Bernard Loiseau, 100-150.

Recommended
♥ antiques : *M. Pere*, ☎ 80.97.02.51.

SENS*

Auxerre 57, Troyes 65, Paris 119 km
pop 27900 ⊠ 89100   A1
Sens, 1 hr 15 from Paris on the banks of the Yonne, is the point where Ile-de-France, Gâtinais, Champagne and Burgundy meet. The history of the town reaches back to the Romans.

▶ **Cathedral of St. Étienne★★** : earliest of the great Gothic cathedrals (1130-1164), site of the wedding of St. Louis (Louis IX) and Marguerite de Provence. The **nave** looks Romanesque, but the **transepts** (15th-16thC) are Flamboyant Gothic ; the outer doorways lost their carvings during the Revolution ; Renaissance belfry on the S tower. Inside : rose windows in the transepts ; **stained glass★★** from 12thC (ambulatory) to 16thC ; 18thC choir enclosure gate ; **mausoleum★** of the Dauphin Louis de Bourbon (1729-65), only son of Louis XV and father of Louis XVI ; **treasury★★** is one of the richest in France : textiles, ivories, ornaments, liturgical objects. ▶ Right of the cathedral, 13thC **Synod Palace★** : restored by architect Eugène Viollet-le-Duc (1814-79), roofed with glazed tiles, now museum of stonework, tapestries and furniture. Renaissance and 18thC buildings nearby. ▶ Opposite, covered market in 19thC ironwork ; close by, neo-Renaissance Town Hall of 19thC. ▶ Among old mansions, **Municipal Museum**, Place de la République : Gallo-Roman inscriptions ; archaeology, mediaeval sculpture, 17th-19thC paintings *(9-12 & 2-6 or 5, ex Tue.)*.
Also... ▶ **Strolls** near the former **ramparts** (remains *S of town centre ;* base built with re-used Roman stones). ▶ **Old houses** in Rue Jean-Cousin. ▶ **Church of St. Jean** at former hospital : Champenois Gothic style. Farther on, **church of St. Savinien** : partly 11thC.

Nearby

▶ On the Gâtinais Plateau W, **Chéroy** *(22 km) :* 13thC tithe-barn ; 6 km farther, château de Vallery. ▶ **Pont-sur-Yonne** *(12 km NW) :* 13th and 15thC church ; old bridge. ▶ **Fleurigny** *(15 km NE) :* mediaeval **château★** with Renaissance additions ; chapel with coffered ceiling *(Apr.-15 Sep., 2:30-5:30 daily ex Wed. in Aug. ; off season, Sat., Sun. and nat. hols.).*   ☐

Practical Information ─────────────

SENS
ⓘ pl. Jean-Jaurès, ☎ 86.65.19.49.
SNCF ☎ 86.65.06.44.
Car rental : *Avis*, 7, rue du Gal-Leclerc, ☎ 86.95.27.29 ; train station.

Hotels :
★★★ **Paris et Poste**, (Mapotel), 97, rue de la République, ☎ 86.65.17.43, Tx 801831, AE DC Euro Visa, 31 rm ℗ ▒ 240. Rest. ♦♦ ઙ 100-250.
★★ **Relais de Villeroy** (L.F.), rte de Nemours, Villeroy, 6 km W, ☎ 86.88.81.77, AE DC Visa, 8 rm ℗ ▒ closed Sun eve and Mon lunch, 27 Jul-12 Aug, 22 Dec-6 Jan, 150. Rest. ♦ ઙ closed Mon and Sun eve, 100-200.
★ **Regina** (L.F.), rte de Nogent-sur-Seine , Soucy, ☎ 86.86.64.62, Euro Visa, 7 rm ℗ ▒ closed 20 Aug-25 Sep, 90. Rest. ♦ ♪ closed Mon and Sun eve, 80-110.

Restaurants :
♦♦ **Auberge de la Vanne**, 176, rte de Lyon, ☎ 86.65.13.63, AE Euro Visa ⟨ ▒ ♪ closed Fri eve and Sat, 20 Dec-10 Jan. At the water's edge. Spec : *demi-caneton au poivre vert*, 65-175.

♦♦ **Palais**, 18, pl. de la République, ☎ 86.65.13.69, Euro Visa ⟨ ♪ closed Mon and Sun eve, 5-26 Jan, 60-150.
⚿ ★★*Entre-deux-Vannes*, rte de Lyon (85 pl), ☎ 86.65.64.71.

Nearby

CHÉROY, ⊠ 89690, 22 km W.

Restaurant :
♦♦ **La Tour d'Argent**, 3, pl. de la Concorde, ☎ 86.97.53.43, Visa ℗ ♪ closed Mon and Tue open in season, 15 Jan-15 Feb, 15 Mar-22 Jun, 60-120.

PONT-SUR-YONNE, ⊠ 89140, 12 km NW.
SNCF ☎ 86.67.15.87.

Hotel :
★★ **L'Ecu** (L.F.), 3, rue Carnot, ☎ 86.67.01.00, AE DC Euro Visa, 8 rm ℗ ▒ closed Mon eve and Tue (l.s.), 15 Jan-5 Mar, 110. Rest. ♦ ♪ ઙ Likable food, casual atmosphere, 60-130 ; child : 45.

⚿ ★★*de l'Ile d'Amour* (100 pl), ☎ 86.67.03.62.

SAINT-VALÉRIEN, ⊠ 89150, 8 km E of **Chéroy**.

Restaurant :
● ♦ **Le Gâtinais**, 22, rue de la République, ☎ 86.88.62.78, Visa ♪ closed Tue and Wed, 1-20 Feb, 1-20 Sep. The heart-warming food of Southwestern France in a Burgundian eatery : *foie gras, bavarois aux asperges et son coulis de tomates*, 135-200.

SEREIN Valley*

A1
From Auxerre to Avallon *(approx 90 km ; full day)*
An excursion through green landscape dotted with pretty villages between two of Burgundy's loveliest towns.

▶ From **Auxerre** (→), reach the Serein River at Pontigny, and follow it to Chablis *(D91).* ▶ From **Chablis** (→ Auxerrois Region), D45 follows the Serein. ▶ **Pailly-sur-Serein :** Flamboyant Gothic church. ▶ Just after **Annay-sur-Serein :** 16thC château de Moutot. ▶ **Noyers-sur-Serein★★** (pop. 837) : fortified mediaeval town, 15th-16thC half-timbered houses ; place de l'Hôtel-de-Ville★ ; 15thC church ; 13thC ramparts E of town. ▶ **L'Isle-sur-Serein** *(D96) :* island in the river ; remains of 15thC castle, old houses. ▶ **Montréal★** *(D11) :* early 12thC Gothic **church★★** on hilltop ; carved choir stalls★★ (1526), 14th-16thC statues and furnishings ; view★. Nearby *(NE),* **Talcy** : Romanesque church. **Thizy** : 13thC castle. **Pizy** : 15thC fortified farmstead. ▶ SW, **Avallon** (→).   ☐

TILLE Valley

C2
In the N of Burgundy the river Tille runs through thickly wooded countryside S towards the Saône.

▶ **Grancey-le-Château**, on the edge of the Côte-d'Or : old city gate, 17th-18thC château★. ▶ **Villey-sur-Tille** and **Crecey-sur-Tille** : castle ruins. ▶ **Is-sur-Tille** : two Renaissance houses ; 14thC church. ▶ **Courtivron** *(13 km W) :* 14th-18thC **château** *(ext. visits 14 Jul.-1 Sep.) ;* village between the forest of Mouloy and Is-sur-Tille. ▶ **Til-Châtel** : old houses, 12thC **church★** (doorway and tympanum ; capitals★). ▶ **Lux** : 16thC château *(Sun. am, Jun. and Sep. ; daily Jul.-Aug.).*

TONNERRE*

Auxerre 35, Troyes 57, Paris 200 km
pop 6181 ⊠ 89700   B1
A well-placed trading town on the banks of the Armançon and the Bourgogne canal.

▶ In the lower town, a spring, the **Fosse Dionne★★**, runs into a pool used as a public laundry, before joining the Armançon. ▶ Former **hospital**, founded in 1293 by Marguerite of Burgundy (→ Couches) : infirmary★ 80 m long; timber vault★; tombs of Marguerite and Louvois★, Count of Tonnerre (minister to Louis XIV); Entombment of Christ★, a masterpiece of 15thC Burgundian sculpture *(10-11:30 & 2-5:30 ex Tue., Jun.-15 Sep.)*. ▶ In town, **Uzès Mansion★** (1533), now a savings bank; birthplace in 1728 of the notorious Chevalier d'Eon, brilliant soldier and diplomat. Municipal Museum of local history *(Wed., Sat. 2-5)*. Collegiate church of St. Pierre : 14th and 16thC (furnishings).

Nearby

▶ **Tanlay** *(9.5 km E)* : **château★★★** (1643-48) down a lime-tree walk, through a 1630 pavilion to a formal courtyard, then the buildings; left, protected by the moat, another pavilion (Portail Neuf); beyond, the Court of Honour and the main building. Inside : Grand Gallery decorated with illusionist paintings; furniture; 16thC fresco from the school of Fontainebleau (→ Ile-de-France; *9:15-11:30 & 2:15-5:15 ex Tue., Palm Sun.-1 Nov.)*. □

Practical Information ────────────

ⓘ pl. Marguerite-de-Bourgogne, ☎ 86.55.14.48 (h.s.), closed Tue.
〓 ☎ 86.55.16.99.

Hotel :
● ★★★★ **L'Abbaye Saint-Michel** (R.C.), Montée de St-Michel, ☎ 86.55.05.99, Tx 801356, AE DC Euro Visa, 16 rm Ⓟ ≪ ⃰ ♪⁰ half pens, closed Sun eve and Mon (Oct-Apr), 2 Jan-15 Feb. A 12th-C Benedictine abbey, 1060. Rest. ● ♦♦♦ ♪ In the name of the father...and of the son, Christophe Cassac, a gifted, observant pupil of Joël Robuchon, whose masterly cuisine is more polished every year : *tête de veau, sandre mariné au chou vert, blanc de poulet en vessie*. Superb desserts, 210-350.

⅄ ★★*la Cascade*, av. A.-Briand (135 pl), ☎ 86.55.14.44.

Recommended
Guide to wines : *Lucien Beau*, ☎ 86.55.11.15; at Epineuil, PC 89700, *J.-C. Michaut*, ☎ 86.55.24.99, a terrific red wine and a fragrant rosé.

TOURNUS**

Chalon-sur-Saône 27, Lyon 102, Paris 365 km
pop 7338 ⊠ 71700   C4

A stopover on the main road S to the Mediterranean, rich in Romanesque architecture.

▶ Fleeing the Normans, monks from Noirmoutier (→ Poitou, Vendée, Charentes) settled here with relics of St. Philibert (9thC) and rebuilt the 300-year-old abbey. The **church★★★** : 9thC façade; 10thC crypt and ground floor of the narthex; 11th and 12thC nave and choir; three 12thC towers. Past the **narthex** (1st floor; 11thC chapel of St. Michel★) the **nave** has sturdy pillars and unusual transverse barrel vaulting. The **choir★** and chapels are in accomplished Romanesque style. ▶ To the side of the church : abbey buildings around the cloister (summer exhibitions). ▶ Place de l'Abbaye (old houses); **Perrin de Puycousin museum** : domestic interiors, furniture, costumes *(Apr.-1 Nov., 9-12 & 2-6 ex Tue.)*. ▶ Farther S, a street and **museum** named for the painter **Jean-Baptiste Greuze** (1725-1805), who was born here (paintings, archaeology; *9:30-12 & 2-6:30 ex Tue. and Sun. am)*. ▶ S of town, church of Ste. Madeleine★ : 12th, 15thC nave and Renaissance chapel.   □

Practical Information ────────────

TOURNUS
ⓘ pl. Carnot, ☎ 85.51.13.10.
〓 ☎ 85.38.50.50.

Hotels :

★★★★ **Le Rempart**, 2-4, av. Gambetta, ☎ 85.51.10.56, Tx 351019, AE DC Euro Visa, 30 rm Ⓟ ≪ ⃰ ♪ ⓑ half pens (h.s.), 600. Rest. ♦♦ ⃰ ⓑ A new address run by young folks who deserve your encouragement : snails, frogs. Excellent Burgundies, 125-270; child : 30.

★★★ **Greuze**, 1, rue Thibaudet, ☎ 85.51.13.52, AE Euro Visa, 21 rm ≪ closed 15 Nov-15 Dec. Rest. ● ♦♦♦ closed Thu eve. Jean Ducloux is one of the greatest cooks in France. And he knows it : with his inimitable sense of humour, he grants top marks to his authentic, opulent, generous cuisine, ⃰ washed down with great Burgundies and refreshing Dubœuf Beaujolais. At age 60, he is a genuine monument to good food and amply deserves his seat on our chefs' panel. His menu is mouthwatering, a masterpiece of gastronomic prose : *pâté en croûte Alexandre Dumaine, véritables quenelles de brochet sauce écrevisse, grenouilles fraîches, escargots, entrecôte charolaise "non parée", poulet au vinaigre*. Meals in a pleasant setting. The hôtel Greuze (21 rooms) is just a few steps away, 290-380.

★★★ **Le Sauvage**, (Mapotel), pl. du Champ-de-Mars, ☎ 85.51.14.45, Tx 800726, AE DC Euro Visa, 31 rm Ⓟ ≪ ♪ 🐎 ⓑ half pens (h.s.), closed 15 Nov-15 Dec, 460. Rest. ♦♦ ⃰ ⓑ 75-165; child : 45.

★★ **Aux Terrasses** (L.F.), 18, av. du 23-Janvier, ☎ 85.51.01.74, Visa, 12 rm Ⓟ closed 5 Jan-5 Feb, 1-30 Jun, 130. Rest. ♦ closed Mon and Sun eve (l.s.), 80-200.

★★ **Paix** (L.F.), 9, rue J.-Jaurès, ☎ 85.51.01.85, AE DC Euro Visa, 23 rm Ⓟ ⓑ closed Tue eve (Sep-Jun), 10 Jan-3 Feb, 4-12 May, 19-27 Oct, 200. Rest. ♦ ⃰ ⓑ closed Tue and Wed noon (Sep-Jun), 60-95.

★ **Nouvel Hôtel**, 1 bis, av. des Alpes, ☎ 85.51.04.25, Euro Visa, 6 rm Ⓟ closed Sun eve and Wed, 2-9 Jan, 26 Nov-29 Dec, 85. Rest. ♦ ⃰ 60-120.

Recommended
Events : *antiques show*, late May-early Jun; *Religious works performed*, in the abbey's nave and cloister, in Aug. ♥ *la Manufacture*, slightly imperfect cookware for sale.

Nearby

BRANCION, ⊠ 71700, 13 km W on D 14.

Hotel :
★★ **La Montagne de Brancion**, ☎ 85.51.12.40, Euro Visa, 20 rm Ⓟ ≪ 〰 ◌ ⃰ closed 11 Nov-1 Mar, 205.

Between TOURNUS and CLUNY

                                    C4
Round trip from Tournus *(95 km; full day)*

Throughout the rolling region between the Saône and the Grosne, the Romanesque period built a large member of charming rural churches. In addition, there are châteaux and lovely scenery.

▶ **Tournus** (→). ▶ **Ozenay** and **Martailly-lès-Brancion** : 10th-14thC castle. Detour recommended to **Cruzille** *(6 km S)* : museum of Burgundian rural craft tools *(9-11:30 & 1:30-6:30, Easter-Oct.)*. Then road right towards **Brancion★★** : mediaeval village beneath a 10th-14thC castle; houses, market; on the spur (view★★), attractive 12thC Romanesque **church★★** (stone tiles; Gothic murals). Below and opposite, **La Chapelle-sous-Brancion** : partly Romanesque church. ▶ **Chapaize★** : 11thC church with 12thC chapels; bell-tower★★ appears at the end of a straight run through the forest. NE, **Lancharre** : ruin of Romanesque abbey. ▶ **Chissey-lès-Mâcon** : capitals★ in 13thC church. ▶ View★★ from **Mont Saint-Romain** (alt. 579 m); **Blanot Caves** below *(Mar.-Nov. 9-12 & 1:30-7)*. ▶ **Blanot** : very narrow roads; 12thC Romanesque church, 14thC priory buildings. ▶ **Azé Caves** (→ Cluny). ▶ **Donzy-le-Pertuis** : 11thC church. ▶ **Cluny** (→). D981 runs by the Grosne River. ▶ **Taizé** : œcumenical religious community made up of men of many Christian denominations from all over the world; Romanesque church★ in the village. ▶ **Ameugny** : Romanesque church. ▶ **Cormatin** :

Renaissance **château★★** (1600) with exceptional interior decoration, paintings, furniture *(10-12 & 2:30-6:30).* ▶ Beyond **Malay** (Romanesque church), possible detour to **Sercy** (15thC château) and **Saint-Gengoux-le-National** (Romanesque church, château, old houses), to the N. ▶ Return via D215 and Chèvres Pass. □

VARZY

Nevers 53, Dijon 161, Paris 213 km
pop 1475 ☒ 58210 A2

Former residence of the bishops of Auxerre. **Museum** of archaeology, sculpture, religious art, furniture, ceramics *(10-12 & 2-6, Mar.-Oct.).* Church of St. Pierre (13th-14thC), statues and Renaissance triptychs.

Nearby

▶ **La Chapelle-Saint-André** *(6 km NW)* : 13thC and Renaissance **Corbelin Manor. Menou** *(10 km W)* : 17thC **château★ ;** 18thC entrance gates. ▶ **Entrains-sur-Nohain** *(18 km NW)* : Gallo-Roman dig, museum *(3-7, Jul.-Aug.).* ▶ In **Champlémy** *(10 km S)* : 14th-16thC château, near the source of the Nièvre. □

VÉZELAY★★★

Avallon 15, Auxerre 51, Paris 225 km
pop 582 ☒ 89450 A2

Vézelay is a Romanesque masterpiece that has been designated by UNESCO as an international treasure. Founded in 878, the abbey of Vézelay (harboring relics of Christ's disciple St. Mary Magdalene) became a major place of pilgrimage in its own right, but was also an important stopover on the pilgrim road to the Spanish shrine of Santiago de Compostela.

▶ Stroll from Place du Champ-de-Foire (fairground, now the carpark) up winding streets to the **basilica of Ste. Madeleine★★★** on the hilltop. **Tympanum★★★** in the narthex (Christ in Glory; Apostles); luminous nave (1120-40), the arches in two contrasting light shades of stone; pillars, graphic **capitals★★★** (nearly 100, including the Mystic Mill, Moses and St. Paul, St. Eustache, the Golden Calf, Adam and Eve); early Gothic choir (1185). The abbey declined after the 16thC and the church had been abandoned when the 19thC restorer Viollet-le-Duc (→ Sens) undertook to rebuild it. Concerts and illuminations in summer. ▶ Right of the basilica, chapterhouse and cloister (restored); remains of abbey buildings. ▶ In the former dormitory, **lapidary museum★** (sculpture unearthed during restoration; exhibits, *Jul.-15 Sep., 10-12:30 & 3-7 ex Mon.).* ▶ Rampart walk. At the E end of the basilica, terraced garden (view★). Numerous old houses, often over huge vaulted halls where pilgrims stayed.

Nearby

▶ **Saint-Père-sous-Vézelay :** at the foot of the hill, efforts are being made to reintroduce vines; 13th-15thC Gothic **church★★** with tall spire and elaborate porch; elegant interior architecture, combining Champenois and Burgundian influences. Close by, **Archaeological Museum of Fontaines Salées :** finds from the Gallo-Roman site *(3 km SE)* in the Cure Valley (→; *9:30-12:30 & 2:30-6:30, Mar.-Dec. ex Wed.).* ▶ 7 km away, **Cordeland de Chamoux** shows the development of life over 600 million years *(Jul.-Oct., 9:30-12:30 & 2-8; tel. 86.33.28.33).* □

Practical Information

VÉZELAY
ℹ mairie, ☎ 86.33.24.62/86.33.23.69.
SNCF ☎ 86.46.50.50.

Hotels :
● ★★★ ***Résidence Hôtel le Pontot***, ☎ 86.33.24.40, closed 15 Nov-15 Mar, 450-600.

● ★★★ ***Poste et Lion d'Or***, ☎ 86.33.21.23, 49 rm Ⓟ half pens (h.s.), closed in winter, 400. Rest. ♦♦ 200-250.
★ ***Relais du Morvan***, pl. du Champ-de-Foire, ☎ 86.33.25.33, Visa, 9 rm closed Tue eve and Wed, Jan. Rest. ♦ ♿ 70-100.

Nearby

SAINT-PÈRE-SOUS-VÉZELAY, ☒ 89450, 2 km E.

Hotel :
● ★★★ ***Espérance*** (R.C.), ☎ 86.33.20.45, AE DC Visa, 19 rm Ⓟ closed Jan, 600. Rest. ● ♦♦♦♦ closed Tue and Wed noon. *L'espérance* means hope, and all of yours will be met and more in Françoise and Marc Meneau's warm and handsome house at the foot of the hill, an ideal spot for a restful and rewarding gourmet retreat. The self-taught chef offers a festive variety of dishes : *cromesquis, moules farcies, truffade de soles, vol au vent*, rich desserts (*glace au Zan*) and glorious Burgundies, 200-300.

⛺ ★★*Municipal* (60 pl), ☎ 86.33.26.62.

VILLENEUVE-L'ARCHEVÊQUE

Sens 24, Auxerre 57, Paris 139 km
pop 1234 ☒ 89190 A1

In the Vanne Valley (which sends drinking water via an aqueduct to Paris), Villeneuve (New Town) was founded in 1163 by an archbishop (archevêque) of Sens. Saint Louis came here to receive Christ's supposed Crown of Thorns, brought from the East, which he later housed in the Sainte-Chapelle in Paris.

▶ 13th-14thC **church :** Gothic doorway★; 16thC Entombment of Christ showing Champenois influence. ▶ Walks in the Othe forest (→). □

VILLENEUVE-SUR-YONNE★

Sens 13, Auxerre 44, Paris 135 km
pop 4980 ☒ 89500 A1

Created from scratch in 1163 as a royal residence by King Louis VIII, the town was originally called Villefranche-le-Roy. A pleasant centre for excursions to the Othe Forest (→), and a week-end resort.

▶ At either end of Rue Carnot, a handsome gate (13th and 16thC). Opposite an 18thC post-house, **church of Notre-Dame :** Renaissance **façade★★,** Gothic nave, 13th-16thC stained glass, 16thC Entombment of Christ. ▶ **Saint-Julien-du-Sault** *(7 km S)* : church with 13thC and Renaissance stained glass; old houses : steep walk to the hilltop chapel of Vauguillan with a view over the Yonne Valley. □

Practical Information

ℹ 4 bis, rue Carnot, ☎ 86.87.36.28.
SNCF ☎ 86.87.15.44.

Hotel :
★★ ***L'Hostellerie du Dauphin***, 12-14, rue Carnot, ☎ 86.87.18.55, 11 rm Ⓟ closed Feb school hols, 1 Nov, 210. Rest. ♦♦ Spec : *turbot à l'oseille mousse de céleri, pintade pochée aux morilles, pruneaux aux aromates et au vin*, 70-220.

⛺ ★★*Le Saucil* (100 pl), ☎ 86.87.00.69.

Along the river VINGEANNE★

C2

Round trip from Pontailler-sur-Saône *(approx 66 km, full day)*

Parallel with the Marne-Saône canal, the Vingeanne flows through a little-frequented valley to the extreme NE of Burgundy, on the edge of Franche-Comté (→).

▶ **Pontailler-sur-Saône** : at the foot of Mount Ardoux, a hill rising gently from the plain. ▶ **Talmay** : 18thC **château** with 13thC keep; Louis XV style embellished in the "Chinese" fashion of the mid-18thC; furnishings *(3-4:30 Jul., Aug.; closed Mon.).* ▶ The road crosses and re-crosses the canal before reaching **Beaumont-sur-Vingeanne** : 1724 folly★ visible from the street *(no visits).* ▶ On the other bank, château de **Rosières★**, fortified, 15th-17thC; painted ceiling★. ▶ **Saint-Seine-sur-Vingeanne** : Romanesque church, 16th-18thC château. Farther on, **Mornay** : 16thC château. ▶ The road passes a beautiful washhouse on the left before reaching **Fontaine-Française** : Henri IV defeated the Spaniards and the Catholic League here in 1595; 18thC lakeside **château★★** where the 18thC luminaries Voltaire, Rousseau, Mme de Staël and Mme Récamier all stayed *(2-6, Jul.-Sep. ex Tue. and Thu.).* ▶ **Bèze** : fortified town with towers, church, 13thC houses; source of the river Bèze in caverns *(Apr. and Oct., 10-7; Sat., Sun.; May-Sep., 10-8 daily ex Mon. and Tue. am).* ▶ **Mirebeau** : stopover town; 13th and 16thC church. □

VITTEAUX

Montbard 33, Dijon 45, Paris 270 km
pop 1097 ⊠ 21350   B2

At a point where the river Brenne is joined by several streams, Vitteaux is a pretty town with old houses, Gothic market and church (15thC organ loft, stalls).

Nearby

▶ **Posanges★★** *(3 km N)* : feudal castle, recently restored; four 15thC towers. ▶ **Church of Saint-Thibault★★** : a "stone reliquary"; 13thC doorway on tympanum, late-15thC carved doors (Life of St. Thibault); choir★ with 14thC vaulting; carved and painted altarpiece★★ (Virgin and Child, same period). □

The YONNE Valley

                                                                A2

The Yonne rises near Château-Chinon in the Morvan region, and flows into the Pannesière-Chaumard reservoir (→ Morvan Lakes). It runs through a valley parallel to the Nivernais canal before widening near Auxerre to join and augment the Seine.

▶ **Montreuillon Aqueduct** (152 m long) carries water from the Yonne channel across the river to the canal. ▶ **Mar-**

cilly : 15thC castle. **Lantilly** *(S of Corbigny)* : 15th and 17thC castle with moats, keep and furnished rooms *(tours at 3,5 ex Tue., Jul.-Aug.).* ▶ **Corbigny** (pop. 1 997) : Flamboyant Gothic church; market town. ▶ Nearby, **château de Chitry** : 16th-18thC; Italian gallery *(2-6, 15 Jun.-1 Oct.);* **château de Villemolin** *(6 km NE)* : 16thC *(11-6, Apr.-Oct.).* ▶ W of the valley, 17thC **château Pignol; Tannay**, a white wine village : St. Léger church (13th-16thC). ▶ Farther, on the right bank, **Metz-le-Comte★** : Romanesque church. ▶ **Clamecy** (pop. 5 590) : busy town between the Yonne and Mont Beuvron; old houses; 12th-14thC church of St. Martin; **museum** in the Bellegarde Mansion (Rue Bourgeoise; regional ethnography, archaeology, painting; *10-12 & 3-7, May-15 Oct.; closed Tue.).* ▶ **Coulanges-sur-Yonne** : stopover; 4 km E, along the right bank, 15thC **château de Faulin.** ▶ 12 km W, partly destroyed château of **Druyes-les-Belles-Fontaines** (12thC; *3-6, Jul.-15 Sep.).* ▶ **Châtel-Censoir** : site★; road to Vézelay (→); **church★** with Romanesque choir, crypt; 16thC nave. ▶ **Saussois Rocks★** : rock-climbing school above the canal; **Mailly-le-Château** : site; old bridge. ▶ **Cravant** : junction of the Yonne and the Cure rivers (→ Cure Valley). □

Practical Information _____

CLAMECY, ⊠ 58500, 69 km NE of **Nevers**.
ⓘ rue du Grand-Marché, ☎ 86.27.02.51 (h.s.); ☎ 86.27.16.70 (l.s.).
🚆 *SNCF* ☎ 86.46.50.50.

Hotel :
★ *Hostellerie de la Poste*, 9, pl. E.-Zola, ☎ 86.27.01.55, Visa, 17 rm P ⸱ ⸱ ⸱ closed Mon, 20 Jun-4 Jul, 15 Dec-15 Jan, 135. Rest. ♦ ♪ 55-100.

⋏ *Pont Picot* (70 pl), ☎ 86.27.05.97.

Recommended
Events : *andouillette fair*, in Aug.
Farmhouse-inn : *La Poussaudière*, ☎ 86.27.15.68.

MAILLY-LE-CHÂTEAU, ⊠ 89660 Châtel-Censoir, 22 km NE of **Clamecy**.

Hotel :
★★ *Le Castel*, (L.F., R.S.), pl. de l'Eglise, ☎ 86.40.43.06, Euro Visa, 12 rm P ⸱ ⸱ ⸱ closed Tue eve and Wed, 15 Nov-15 Mar, 200. Rest. ● ♦ ⸱ A quiet spot to savour fine cuisine : *escargots aux noisettes, pavé de charolais à la moutarde ancienne, gratin de framboises et sa liqueur*, 70-150.

⋏ ★★ *Pré du Roi* (50 pl), ☎ 86.40.44.85.

Champagne, Ardennes

▶ A region whose reputation is dominated by its most famous product — champagne — fruit of a second fermentation in the bottle and a skillful blend of different varieties of grape. But Champagne produces red wines, rosés and whites as well, no less palatable for being less well-known.

Champagne is a region of forests — the Ardenne, Saint-Gobain, Villers-Cotterêts; lakes — Der Chantecoq is the largest in France — and fertile valleys, dotted with beautiful towns and cities. Langres, with its ramparts and towers dominating the surrounding countryside, was the birthplace of the writer Diderot. The centre of Laon, built on a hill overlooking the great plain of Champagne, has retained its medieval streets and character, and boasts a cathedral built in the early Gothic period. The citizens of Troyes have started to painstakingly rebuild a city full of historical treasures dating from the Middle Ages to the Renaissance, the "golden age" of Troyes. The city of Reims has twice played a central role in the history of France : first in 496 when Clovis was baptized there and founded the Frankish monarchy, and again in 1429 when the valiant Joan of Arc had the Dauphin crowned in Reims cathedral.

In ages past, Champagne was famous for its great fairs which attracted visitors from all over Europe and even from as far afield as Constantinople. The benches or *bancs* that the moneychangers sat on to ply their trade gave their name to our modern banks. □

Don't miss

★★★ Reims B2, Troyes B4.

★★ Champagne Road B2-3, Langres C4, Laon A2, Orient Lake and Forest B4.

★ Châlons-sur-Marne B3, Chaource B4, Château-Thierry A2-3, Fère-en-Tardenois A2, Meuse Valley B1, Rocroi B1, Saint-Quentin A1, Soissons A2, Thiérache Region A-B1, Villers-Cotterêts A2.

Weekend tips

The mansions, museums and churches of the old town of Troyes are well worth a day. Detour through the Othe countryside to the S, then turn back NE along the lakes of the Orient and Der-Chantecoq forests. Stopover at Châlons-sur-Marne or Épernay. Next day, visit the Champagne country, with a lunch break at Reims. Another weekend, visit the Ardennes.

Facts and figures

Location : *The region stretches between the outcrops of the Ile-de-France in the west and Lorraine in the east, the mountains of the Ardennes in the north and Burgundy in the south.*
Area : *32 978 km².*
Climate : *More temperate in the west (2º-18º C and 550-700 mm annual rainfall) than in the Ardennes and the Haute-Marne, which are colder and wetter (1 000-1 200 mm rainfall).*
Population : *1 870 695.*
Administration : *Department of the* **Marne**, *Prefecture Châlons-sur-Marne ; Department of the* **Haute-Marne**, *Prefecture Chaumont ; Department of the* **Ardennes**, *Prefecture Troyes ; Department of the* **Aisne** *(officially part of the administrative region of Picardy), Prefecture Laon.*

Southern ("wet") Champagne

Wooden stud construction, Aube region

● *Brief regional history*

BC
More than 1 000 sites dating from between 3000 and 4000 BC have been excavated in the region, and 80 megaliths have been uncovered, 69 of them in the Aube sector. ● Even then, Champagne was a crossroads and scene of territorial dispute between Danubians and Celts.

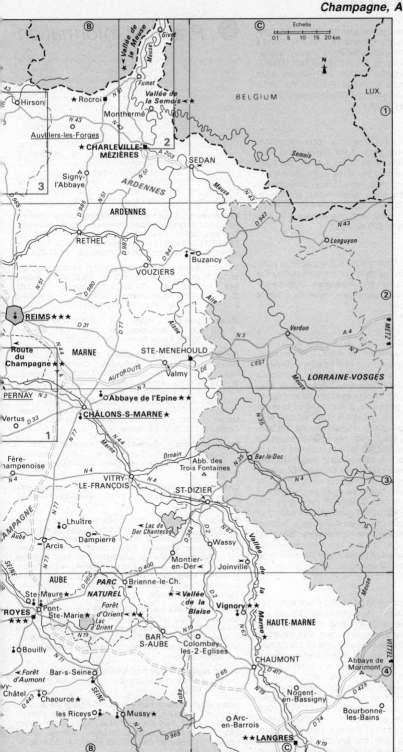

Echelle
01 5 10 15 20 km

1. Champagne Road

2. Meuse valley

3. The Thiérache region

Roman Era

The arrival of Julius Caesar and the Roman occupation brought peace and prosperity. Invading **Franks** and **Teutons** remained to settle in an uneasy coexistence. When, however, in 451 **Attila the Hun** threatened the region, Visigoths, Franks and Romans were obliged to join forces to defeat Attila at the battle known as the "Champs (fields) Catalauniques" 20 km north of present-day Troyes.

3rd-10thC

The encroachment of Christianity received official sanction when **Clovis**, King of the Franks, was baptized at Reims in 496. ● At Clovis's death, the kingdom was divided among his three sons, then partitioned further among their heirs. The empire disintegrated after Charlemagne's death in 814, and Champagne became a buffer region, suffering invasions from both east and west, with the **Normans** in 883, and the **Hungarians** in 926 and 954.

10th-13thC

The advantages of Champagne's geographical position came to the fore as trading increased during the Middle Ages. The success of the regular Champagne Fairs consolidated the value of the region as a hub of European commerce.

13th-17thC

The Gothic cathedrals built at Troyes, Laon and Reims were an inspiration to 13thC Christendom. In the 14thC Jean Sans Peur (the Fearless), Duke of Burgundy, decided to annex Champagne to forge a link between his territories in Flanders and Burgundy. To enhance his military strength, he formed an alliance with the English who, in turn, wished to press their claim to the throne of France. The resulting conflict put a stop to prosperity. Rallied around the banner of Joan of Arc, the French managed to expel the English in 1429, and Charles VII was crowned King of France at Reims. ● The region again flourished until the 16thC, when the Holy Roman Emperor Charles V invaded eastern France. Throughout the latter half of the 16thC, the country was torn apart by the Wars of Religion, which pitted Catholic against Protestant. The Edict of Nantes (1598), which guaranteed freedom of religion to Protestants, resolved the internal conflict, but France was at war with Spain from 1635 until 1643, and Champagne did not see true peace until 1652. ● The coronation of Louis XIV at Reims in 1654 marked the return of Champagne to French rule.

20thC

From the very beginning of WWI, the Front was fixed in Champagne, between the Chemin des Dames and Saint-Mihiel. Despite a determined attack, Germany failed to capture Verdun in 1916, and was forced to retreat. In 1918, Germany once more took the Chemin des Dames and thrust toward Reims and the Marne, where the advance was repulsed in a horrific battle. In September 1918, when the Allied army freed the Ardennes, the Ardennes-Champagne region emerged devastated by conflict. ● During WWII, the French Front was pushed back to Sedan on 13 May 1940, and Champagne was occupied for 4 years. The invasion caused heavy damage (Rethel, Vitry-le-François, Châlons, Vouziers), and the bombings during and after the Allied landing in 1944 devastated the region.

● *Practical information*

Information : Champagne-Ardennes : *Comité Régional du Tourisme (C.R.T.),* 5, rue de Géricault, 51100 Châlons-sur-Marne, ☎ 26.64.35.92. *Office régional culturel de Champagne-Ardennes,* 33, av. de Champagne, 51000 Épernay, ☎ 26.54.32.19. **Aisne :** *Comité Départemental de Tourisme C.D.T. :* 1, rue Saint-Martin, 02000 Laon, ☎ 23.20.45.54. **Ardennes** *C.D.T. :* Résidence Arduinna, 8, av. Georges-Corneau, 08000 Charleville-Mézières, ☎ 24.56.06.08. **Aube** *C.D.T. :* Hôtel du Département, 10026 Troyes, ☎ 25.73.48.01. **Marne** *C.D.T. :* 2 bis, bd Vaubécourt, 51100 Châlons-sur-Marne, ☎ 26.68.37.52. **Haute-Marne** *C.D.T. :* Hôtel de la Préfecture, 52000 Chaumont, ☎ 25.32.65.00. *Direction rég. de la Jeunesse et des Sports,* 20, rue Simon, 51100 Reims, ☎ 26.05.10.83. *Dir. Rég. des Affaires culturelles,* 5, rue Jéricho, 51022 Châlons-sur-Marne Cedex, ☎ 26.65.00.06.

Reservations : *Loisirs-Accueil* **Ardennes** (enrollments for instruction courses, leisure centres) : 18, av. Georges-Corneau, 08000 Charleville-Mézières, ☎ 24.56.00.63. Tx 840016 Chamco (Tourism). **Marne :** *Office du Tourisme de Reims,* 1, rue Jadart, 51100 Reims, ☎ 26.47.25.65.

S.O.S. : Aisne : *SAMU* (emergency medical service), ☎ 23.20.20.20. **Aube :** *SAMU,* ☎ 25.82.33.33. **Ardennes :** *SAMU,* ☎ 24.57.21.21. **Marne :** *SAMU,* ☎ 26.06.07.08. **Haute-Marne :** *SAMU,* ☎ 17. Poisoning Emergency Centre : Paris, ☎ (1) 42.05.63.29.

Weather forecast : Aisne : ☎ 23.68.84.33. **Aube :** ☎ 25.74.65.00. **Ardennes :** ☎ 24.88.74.91. **Marne :** ☎ 26.88.63.63. **Haute-Marne :** ☎ 25.05.21.12.

Farmhouse gîtes and chambres d'hôtes : enq. at the Relais Départementaux. **Ardennes :** Chambre d'Agriculture, 1, av. du Petit-Bois, 08000 Charleville-Mézières, ☎ 24.33.38.66. **Aube :** Chambre d'Agriculture, 2 bis, rue Jeanne-d'Arc, 10000 Troyes, ☎ 26.73.25.36. **Marne :** Complexe Agricole du Mt-Bernard, rte de Suippes, B.P. 1505, 51002 Châlons-sur-Marne, ☎ 26.64.08.13. **Haute-Marne :** Hôtel du Conseil Général, 52011 Chaumont Cedex, ☎ 25.32.65.00. **Aisne :** *C.D.T.*

Farmhouse-inns : Haute-Marne : *Association pour le Développement Rural,* 26, av. 109e-R.I., 52011 Chaumont, ☎ 25.03.13.35. **Marne :** see Relais Départemental gîtes ruraux.

Camping-car rentals : Aube : *Pref' Aub Equipements,* route de Brienne, 10150 Pont-Sainte-Marie, ☎ 25.81.18.90.

Festivals and events : May : *pilgrimage* to Notre-Dame de l'Épine (near Châlons-sur-Marne); *Joan of Arc Festival* in Reims; *folklore festival* in Sainte-Marie-du-Lac. **Jun :** *popular festival* in Troyes. *International folk festival* in Châlons-sur-Marne; *jazz festival* in Reims. **End Sep** (every 3 years) : *world marionette festival* in Charleville-Mézières. **Early Oct :** *detective novel and film festival* in Reims. **Dec :** *Shepherds' Christmas festival* in Braux-Sainte-Cohière (Marne).

Markets and rural events : *andouillette market* (chitterling sausage) in Signy-l'Abbaye (Ardennes). **Jun :** *cheese market* in Rocroi. **3rd week-end in Sep :** *Sauerkraut days* in Brienne-le-Château (Aube); *mushroom festival* in Sainte-Ménehould (Marne). **Oct** (every 2 years) : *cheese market* in Chaource (Aube).

Scenic railway : *«petit train touristique du Vermandois»;* departure from Saint-Quentin : *S.I.,* hôtel de ville, ☎ 23.67.05.00.

National and nature parks : *Parc Régional de la Montagne de Reims :* Maison du Parc, 51160 Pourcy, ☎ 26.59.44.44. *Parc Régional de la Forêt d'Orient (Orient Forest;* including a 5 500-acre lake : fishing, sailing, bathing) : Maison du Parc, 10220 Piney, ☎ 25.41.35.57 and 25.41.34.90.

Leisure centre : *Parc nautique des vallées de l'Ailette et de la Bièvre*, Chamouille, 02000 Laon, ☎ 23.24.83.03.

Rambling and hiking : several GRs cross Champagne-Ardennes : G.R. 2 (148 km traversing the Othe region and the length of the Seine Valley); G.R. 24 (141-km circuit, starting from Bar-sur-Seine, and crossing the Orient Forest Regional Park); G.R. 12, part of the European Walkway n° 3 from the Atlantic to Bohemia; G.R. 14 (vineyards and forests of Reims Mountain). The G.R. 78 forms a large circuit around Langres, on the plateau. Addresses of associations : *C.D.T.* Topoguides for sale at the *Maison des Sociétés Sportives*, 2, bd Carnot, 10000 Troyes, ☎ 25.78.23.27.

Technical tourism : Cutlery : *Chambre Syndicale de la Coutellerie*, pl. du Collège, 52800 Noyent-en-Bussigny, ☎ 25.31.85.20. Basket weaving and wickerwork school, 52500 Fayl-la-Forêt, ☎ 25.88.63.02 (summer). Glassmaking : *Compagnie française du Cristal*, 10310 Bayel, ☎ 25.27.05.02. *Centrale nucléaire de Choar*, ☎ 24.55.05.26.

Champagne

The champagne process, which puts the bubbles in the wine, is a second fermentation that takes place in the bottle. The best champagnes are careful blends of one or more of three authorized varieties of grape (Pinot Noir and Meunier, red; Chardonnay, white). Blanc de Blancs (white from whites), the exception to the rule, is a very pale champagne made from Chardonnay grapes. Dom Pérignon (1638-1715), the cellar master-monk at Hautvillers, is credited with the development of the champagne process. The details of his experiments are hard to sort out, but it seems that he was the first to blend wines in a systematic fashion, and among the first to use the classic mushroom-shaped cork that keeps the seal despite tremendous pressure in the bottle. The region also produces excellent still wines.

Riding holidays : Extensive selection of bridle-paths (weekend, 4-5 days), rallies, instruction courses, stays at riding centres. Enq at the *Association Champagne-Ardenne de Tourisme Équestre*, info : *C.D.T.* **Horse-drawn wagons :** *C.D.T.* **Aisne.**

Cycling holidays : circuits with specific themes of interest over Reims Mountain (see Nature Parks). Cycling tours and stays around the Der-Chantecoq Lake : *Maison du Lac*, Giffaumont-Champaubert, 51920 Saint-Rémy-en-Bouzemont, ☎ 26.41.62.80 and 87. Weekends in the Langres region : *Office du Tourisme*, pl. Bel'Air, 52200 Langres, ☎ 25.85.03.32). For further information : *Fédération Française de Cyclotourisme*, 8, rue Jean-Marie-Jego, 75013 Paris, ☎ (1) 45.80.30.21. Bicycle hire : see *C.D.T.*

River and canal cruises : from Berry-au-Bac (20 km N of Reims) to Château-Thierry and beyond, by house-boat : *Champagne-Navigation*, rte Nationale, 02190 Berry-au-Bac, ☎ 23.79.95.01. By canal, traversing the **Haute-Marne**, leaving from Saint-Dizier : *Double Écluse*, port de plaisance (pleasure-boat port), rue Alfred-de-Musset, 52100 Saint-Dizier, ☎ 25.06.10.56. On the Meuse : enq. : *C.D.T.;* reserv. : *L.A.*

Handicraft courses : the courses at the natonal institute of puppetry, in Charleville-Mézières are famous (reservations *L.A. Ardennas*). Weaving in Ay, wood sculpture in Sainte-Méhéhould, carpentry and linen painting in Aix-en-Othe, beekeeping in Saint-Rémy-en-Bouzemont; basketweaving courses, especially in Haute-Marne and in the Ardennes. Enq. : *C.D.T.*

Wine guide : *Comité interprofessionnel du vin de Champagne*, 51200 Épernay, ☎ 26.54.47.20.

Golf : three 18-hole courses : château de la Cordelière, 10210 Chaource, ☎ 25.46.11.05; Reims en Champagne, château des Dames de France, Gueux, 51140 Joncherysur-Vesle, ☎ 26.48.60.40; Parc de l'Ailette (Aisne), ☎ 23.24.83.03.

Aquatic sports : Aisne : sports centres at Tréou-sur-Marne and Monampteuil; motorboating at Villeneuve-Saint-Germain; **Ardennes :** Bairon and Vieilles-Forges lakes; **Aube :** Orient Forest Lake, enq. : *Maison du Parc;* **Haute-Marne :** motorboating on 4 lakes around Langres and **Marne :** Lake Der-Chantecoq.

Canoeing : *Ligue Champagne-Ardennes de la Féd. Française de Canoë-kayak*, 81, rue du Gal-Leclerc, Fagnières, 51000 Châlons-sur-Marne. **Aisne :** *Comité Départemental de Canoë-kayak*, Erloy, 02260 La Capelle, ☎ 23.97.42.90.

Climbing : principal sites in the **Ardennes** Mountains, at the spot known as Roc-la-Tour, near Monthermé. In the **Marne** region : Vertus and Grauves cliffs, not far from Épernay. Enq. : *C.D.T.*

Flying, gliding and ballooning : light aircraft, U.L.M., enq. at the Charleville-Mézières aerodrome, 08540 Tournes, ☎ 24.33.14.89, and *Troyes Gliding Centre*, B.P. 4074, 10013 Troyes Cedex, ☎ 25.43.39.13. Ballooning : *Club Aérostatique de Champagne*, 5, rue du Pistolet, 51100 Reims, ☎ 26.87.59.87. Hang-gliding : three established sites : near Revin, Joigny-sur-Meuse **(Ardennes)** and Bar-sur-Aube **(Aube).** Information : *Féd. Française de Vol Libre*, 73220 Aiguebelle, and *Directions Dép. de la Jeunesse et des Sports :* **Ardennes :** 16, rue Porte-de-Bourgogne, 08000 Charleville-Mézières, ☎ 24.57.22.11. Parachuting : *Centre de Parachutisme de la* **Marne**, B.P. 410, 51004 Reims Cedex, ☎ 26.88.32.11; and **Aisne :** in Laon, ☎ 23.23.00.87.

Cuisine in and with champagne

Champagne is used in the preparation of regional delicacies, such as poached pike (brochet) or braised chicken. Other regional specialities are andouillettes (tripe sausages) from Troyes, served sizzling hot with potatoes, fried onions or red beans, and pig's foot à la Sainte-Menehould (first braised then coated with breadcrumbs). Popular dishes include pork and cabbage stew (la potée champenoise), breaded ham hock (jambonneau) from Reims, white pudding (boudin blanc), and sauerkraut (choucroute) from Brienne. The cheeses of Chaource and Thiérache are well known, and local confectionery includes chocolate pebbles (rocaillons) from Sedan, pink ratafia biscuits from Reims, and almond meringues made in Bar-sur-Aube and Wassy.

Hunting and shooting : reserve at *Loisirs-Accueil* in Ardennes, *Féd. Dép. des Chasseurs :* **Aisne :** 133, rue Crécy, 02000 Laon, ☎ 23.23.30.89. **Ardennes :** 15, rue Kennedy, 08000 Charleville-Mézières, ☎ 24.56.07.35. **Aube :** 17, bd Victor-Hugo, 10000 Troyes, ☎ 25.73.71.22. **Marne :** 24, bd Justin-Granthille, 51000 Châlons-sur-Marne, ☎ 26.65.17.85. **Haute-Marne :** 22, rue Ampère, 52000 Chaumont, ☎ 25.03.60.60.

Fishing : enq. at the *Féd. Dép. des Associations de Pêche et de Pisciculture.* **Aisne :** 4, rue Porte-d'Ardon, 02000 Laon, ☎ 23.20.23.33. **Ardennes :** 52, av. d'Arches, 08000 Charleville-Mézières, ☎ 24.57.34.14. **Aube :** 10-12, rue F.-Gentil, 10000 Troyes, ☎ 25.73.36.96. **Marne :** 32, rue des Lambards 51250 Sermaize-les-Bains, ☎ 26.41.21.26. **Haute-Marne :** 8, rue de la Convention, 52000 Chaumont, ☎ 25.03.10.78.

Towns and places

ARCIS-SUR-AUBE

Troyes 27, Châlons-sur-Marne 50, Paris 163 km
pop 3258 ⊠ 10700   B3
The centre of Arcis is the 15th-16thC **church**; the
heart of the town is a shady walk along the banks
of the Aube. The 17thC **château** (now the town hall)
stands in a riverside park.

▶ **Lhuître** *(9 km NE)* : the church★ (12th, 16thC) is among
the most beautiful in the region; 16thC stained glass.   ☐

BAR-SUR-AUBE

Chaumont 42, Troyes 52, Paris 217 km
pop 7146 ⊠ 10200   B4
Two churches in a hilly region of streams and rivers.
One, **St. Pierre**, surrounded by a pretty wooden gallery; inside, 14thC polychrome statue, Virgin with a
Bouquet. ▶ The other, **St. Maclou**, is closed; stroll
along the Aube (mill).

Nearby

▶ **Bayel** *(7.5 km SE on D396)* : in the church, polychrome
15thC Virgin and Child★, a regional masterpiece attributed to the "Master of St. Martha". At the Cristalleries de
Champagne showroom, overhead view★ of crystal manufacture (founded in 1661; *visits by appt., tel. :
25.92.05.02*), last bastion of a regional craft. ▶ **Clairvaux**
(14 km SE) : the Cistercian abbey founded by St. Bernard in 1125, rebuilt in the 18thC, is now a prison *(abbey
buildings may be visited 1st Sat. of month, 3:15; tel. :
25.27.06.19).* ▶ **Trémilly** *(19 km N)* : 18thC château with a
Renaissance well *(Easter hols. and 15 Jun.-15 Sep., 10-12
& 2-5 ex Mon.).*   ☐

Practical Information _____

BAR-SUR-AUBE
Ⓘ hôtel de ville, ☎ 25.27.04.21.
SNCF ☎ 25.27.09.92.

Hotel :
★★★ **Commerce**, 38, rue Nationale, ☎ 25.27.08.76, AE
DC Euro Visa, 15 rm Ⓟ closed 2 Jan-10 Feb, 170.
Rest. ◆◆ ♪ 65-200.

⚠ ★★*La Gravière* (43 pl), ☎ 25.27.12.94.

Nearby

ARSONVAL, ⊠ 10200 Bar-sur-Aube, 6 km NW.

Restaurant :
◆ *Hostellerie de la Chaumière*, RN 19, ☎ 25.26.11.02,
AE Euro Visa Ⓟ ⚘ ⚱ ♪ ⚙ closed Mon and Sun eve,
7 Dec-14 Jan, 75-150.

BOURBONNE-LES-BAINS

Langres 43, Dijon 111, Paris 312 km
pop 3146 ⊠ 52400   C4
The springs were known to the Gauls and Romans,
and the waters are still sought after for the treatment
of rheumatism, respiratory infections and the after-
math of broken bones; Romanesque church; Gallo-
Roman remains, thermal spa.

Nearby

▶ **Coiffy-le-Haut** *(7.5 km SW)*, a wine-producing village
with a view★ as far as the Jura mountains. ▶ **Côte des
Noues :** *(5 km N,* alt. 425 m, panorama★). ▶ **Morimond**
(NNW) : vestiges of one of the first four daughter abbeys

of Cîteaux *(Cistertium,* the Latin form of the name, gives
rise to "Cistercian") founded in 1115 and razed after
the Revolution (1789); its influence throughout Christian
Europe was considerable. Return to Bourbonne via the
château de Parnot *(by appt., tel. : 25.90.80.25).*   ☐

Practical Information _____

♨ ☎ 25.90.07.20 (Mar-Nov).   ♥
Ⓘ pl. des Bains, ☎ 25.90.01.71.
SNCF ☎ 25.03.50.50.

Hotels :
★★ **Hérard** (L.F.), 29, Grande-Rue, ☎ 25.90.13.33, AE
DC Euro Visa, 45 rm Ⓟ ⚘ ⚱ ㅎ pens, 150. Rest. ◆ ♪ ㅎ
50-120; child : 45.
★★ **Lauriers-Roses**, pl. des Bains, ☎ 25.90.00.97, 80 rm
Ⓟ ⚘ ⚱ ㅎ closed 2 Oct-29 Mar, 140. Rest. ◆ ㅎ 45-90.

⚠ ★★★*Le Montmorency* (60 pl), ☎ 25.90.08.64.

BRIENNE-LE-CHÂTEAU

Troyes 40, Bar-le-Duc 70, Paris 198 km
pop 4112 ⊠ 10500   B4
Napoleon studied at the military academy here from
the age of 9 (1779) until at 16 he was commissioned
as an artillery lieutenant.

▶ The former academy buildings and the 18thC château
are still standing; the town centre, demolished in WWII,
has been rebuilt in stone; covered market in wood, with
tiled roof. ▶ Brienne celebrates its main local product,
sauerkraut, with a festival the third weekend in September. ▶ **Napoleon Museum** : war room, miscellaneous
documents and memorabilia *(daily ex Mon., 9-11:30 &
2-5).* ▶ Church of St. Pierre-St. Paul (15th-16thC) : grisaille
(monotone grey) stained glass in the 16thC apse.

Nearby

▶ **Brienne-la-Vieille** *(2 km S)* : church★ (12th, 16thC);
Romanesque doorway from a nearby abbey. ▶ **Rosnay-
l'Hôpital** *(9 km N)* : 12th, 15thC church, crypt; 16thC
stained glass, 16th-18thC statuary.   ☐

Practical Information _____

SNCF ☎ 25.77.80.34.

Hotel :
★ **Voyageurs**, 30, av. Pasteur, ☎ 25.92.83.61, AE Euro
Visa, 14 rm Ⓟ ⚱ half pens (h.s.), 220. Rest. ◆ ㅎ ⚙
closed Sun (Oct-May), 45-70.

CHÂLONS-SUR-MARNE*

Reims 45, Troyes 77, Paris 187 km
pop 54359 ⊠ 51000   B3
An interesting mixture of ancient and modern architecture in the "dry" (less rainy) region of Champagne.
The very fine religious monuments make a stop
worthwhile.

▶ **Notre-Dame-en-Vaux**★★ (B1) : elegant specimen of
early-12thC Gothic; stained glass★ from Troyes (although
Châlons had its own glass-makers); ring of 56 bells.
▶ The **cloister** behind the church, destroyed in the 18thC,
was partly rebuilt from 1963 to 1978; rare carved capi-
tals★★; 50 lifelike column-statues★★ *(10-12 & 2-5 or 6;
closed Tue.).* ▶ **Cathedral**★ (A2) : a neo-Classical façade
on the 12thC triple nave and Romanesque tower; 13th,
14th and 16thC stained glass★; 12thC baptismal font;
numerous tombstones. ▶ **Church of St. Alpin** (B2, pedestrian precinct) : grisaille windows right of the entrance.
Also... ▶ Pleasant shady Promenade du **Jard** (B2).
▶ **Municipal Museum** (B1, Place Godart) : archaeology,

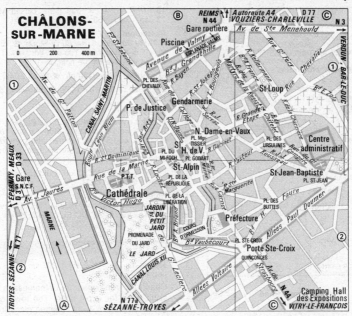

12th-15thC sculpture, a traditional Champenois interior, paintings, ornithology, Hindu religious statuary★. ▶ **Garinet Museum** (19thC town-dweller's interior); and **Goethe-Schiller Museum** (personal effects of the German poets Johann Wolfgang von Goethe [1749-1832] and Friedrich von Schiller [1759-1805]) in rue Pasteur (B2). ▶ **Church of St. Jean** (C2) : 11thC Romanesque nave. ▶ To the S, near the civic offices, 13thC mansion of the former Intendants de Champagne (Regional Governors); **St. Croix gateway** (C2) built in 6 weeks (unfinished) to greet Marie-Antoinette of Austria on her arrival in France to marry the future Louis XVI.

Nearby

▶ **Notre-Dame-de-l'Épine**★★ *(7 km E on N3)*, a jewel of Flamboyant Gothic (1410-1524) and a site of pilgrimage since the 100 Years' War; elegant choir screen with 14thC Virgin; decorated crossbeam; entombment of Christ, *ca.* 1500; the choir is Renaissance on the left and Gothic on the right; outside, interesting gargoyles. ☐

Practical Information ‾‾‾‾‾‾‾‾‾‾

CHÂLONS-SUR-MARNE
🅸 3, quai des Arts (B1), ☎ 26.65.17.89.
SNCF (A2), ☎ 26.88.50.50/26.65.18.35.
Car rental : Avis, 9, av. de la Gare, ☎ 26.68.56.39.

Hotels :
★★★ *Angleterre*, 19, pl. Mgr-Tissier (B1), ☎ 26.68.21.51, AE DC Euro Visa, 18 rm ⓟ ⌖ half pens (h.s.), closed Sun eve, 29 Jun-20 Jul, 20 Dec-7 Jan, 590. Rest. ♦♦ *Jacky Michel*, closed Sun ex hols, 140-280.
★★ *Pot d'Etain*, 18, pl. de la République (B2), ☎ 26.68.09.09, Visa, 26 rm ⓟ ♪ closed 20 Dec-18 Jan, 120.

⚠ ★★★★*Municipal* (96 pl), ☎ 26.68.38.00.

Recommended
Youth hostel : rue Kellermann, ☎ 26.68.13.56 (season).

Nearby

CHERVILLE, ⊠ 51150 Tours-sur-Marne, 8 km W on N 3.
Restaurant :
♦♦ *Le Relais de Cherville*, ☎ 29.69.52.76 ▩ 💺 closed Sat and Sun, 150-250.

L' ÉPINE, ⊠ 51000, 7 km NE.

Hotel :
★★★ *Aux Armes de Champagne*, ☎ 26.68.10.43, Tx 830998, AE Euro Visa, 40 rm ⓟ ⌖ ▩ 💺 ⌖ closed 5 Jan-11 Feb, 290. Rest. ♦♦ ⌖ ♪ 💺 ⌖ The roses that brighten the nearby church are a delight to the eye. The palate, however, does not share in the pleasure, 80-300.

La route du CHAMPAGNE**

(Champagne Road)
B2-3

From Reims to Vertus *(125 km; full day; see map 1)*

A major attraction around Reims and Épernay, covering the three regions that represent 80% of the Champagne vineyards : the Montagne de Reims, the Côte des Blancs and the Marne Valley. The fourth region — in the Aube S of Bar-sur-Aube and including Bar-sur-Seine together with 3200 acres in the departments of Aisne and Seine-et-Marne — makes up a total champagne-producing area of 340 km², of which only 250 km² are currently planted. This represents 2% of the total vine-growing area of France. The vineyards of Champagne are very fragmented : 120 champagne firms (only 10 are really important) own about 13% of the vineyards. Nevertheless, they account for two-thirds of total production by purchasing grapes from other growers. The remaining one-third comes from about 14300 smallholdings averaging just under 4 acres in area. Almost one-third of the smallholders make their own wine. After the bad years of 1978, '80 and '81, excellent harvests in '82 and '83 enabled producers to reconstitute their stocks

1. Champagne Road

and stabilize prices. Stocks normally represent 3 years' sales (450-500 million bottles stored in 200 km of cellars dug into the chalk). Champagne brings in more foreign currency than any other French wine. Even so, 60 % of production is sold in France. More than 10 000 salaried workers are directly or indirectly employed in production and distribution.

▶ **Montagne de Reims :** leaving Reims, take the road for Épernay; the champagne road is signposted from Mont Chenot. After **Rilly**, on a hill road (corniche) above Reims at the foot of Mount Joli (alt. 274 m), the great names appear one after the other : **Mailly-Champagne** : 13thC church. **Verzenay :** mill, view★. **Verzy :** church with 11thC statue of the Virgin; nearby, twisted beech trees known as "faux de Verzy"; Sinaï Observatory at 288 m, view. **Ambonnay. Bouzy** produces a light red wine. **Louvois :** park of former château built by a minister to Louis XIV, later owned by a daughter of Louis XV.

▶ **Marne Valley** (N of Épernay) : from E to W, two great vineyards at **Mareuil-sur-Ay** (12thC church), and **Ay** (house known as Henri IV's wine press). **Hautvillers :** prettiest site in the vineyards; with a rebuilt abbey church and a restored building where illuminated medieval manuscripts are on display, as well as a reconstruction of Dom Pérignon's laboratory (private property, visits by request). Continuing westwards, **Damery :** 13thC church★. **Châtillon-sur-Marne :** statue of Urban II, the Pope of the Crusades, born here in 1042. **Dormans :** swimming in the Marne; Chapelle de la Reconnaissance (burial site of 1 500 unknown soldiers).

▶ **Côtes des Blancs★ :** marked route S of Épernay, the most respected vineyards (planted almost exclusively with Chardonnay grapes) : **Cramant, Avize, Oger, Le Mesnil-sur-Oger. Vertus :** a spring wells up at the E end of the 12thC church of St. Martin. □

Practical Information _____

DORMANS, ⊠ 51700, 38 km SW of **Reims**.
⃞ rue du Pont, ☎ 26.58.21.45.
SNCF ☎ 26.58.21.95.

Hotel :
★ **Demoncy** (L.F.), 10, rue de Châlons, ☎ 26.58.20.86,

10 rm Ⓟ ⌨ ⌕ ⌘ half pens, closed Mon eve , Tue, 23 Jan-1 Mar, 150. Rest. ◆ ⌕ & 90-120.

Restaurant :
◆ **Table Sourdet**, 6, rue du Dr-Moret, ☎ 26.58.20.57, Euro Visa Ⓟ & closed Mon, Tue eve, Wed eve, Thu eve, Fri eve, ex Sat and eve before hols, 55-160.

Å ★★*Essi Plage* (120 pl), ☎ 26.58.21.45.

Le MESNIL-SUR-OGER, ⊠ 51190 Avize, 5 km N of **Vertus**.

Restaurant :
● ◆◆ **Le Mesnil Jaillant**, 2, rue Pasteur, ☎ 26.57.95.57, AE DC Euro Visa & closed Mon eve and Wed , Feb school hols, 15 Aug-5 Sep. Refined and generous cooking by C. Jaillant : homemade terrine, game in season, 90-250; child : 50.

VERTUS, ⊠ 51130, 20 km S of **Epernay**.
SNCF ☎ 26.52.12.31.

Hotel :
★★★ **Reine Blanche**, (Inter-Hôtel), 18, av. Louis-Lenoir, ☎ 26.52.20.76, AE DC Euro Visa, 23 rm Ⓟ ⌕ ⌇ closed Feb, 220. Rest. ◆ ⌇ 120-250.

CHAOURCE*

Troyes 33, Dijon 120, Paris 200 km
pop 1106 ⊠ 10110   B4

Chaource, renowned for a namesake cheese, is a good base for exploration. The town boasts several fine examples of 16thC stained glass from Troyes.

▶ Church★★ : in the crypt a sculpted **Entombment of Christ★★** (1515 eight-figure group) is a superb example of the Troyes style of the period; funerary frescos, statuary, wooden crèche.

Nearby

▶ **Ervy-le-Châtel** (21 km W on the Saint-Florentin road) : covered market, old houses, stained glass★ in the church. **Neuvy-Sautour** (10 km farther on) : church★ with Renaissance choir and large, ornate cross. ▶ **Bar-sur-Seine** (21 km E) : church with bas-reliefs, woodwork, 16thC stained glass★; nearby (100 m) Renaissance house of brick and carved wood. ▶ **Les Riceys** (22 km SE) : a group of three villages and an important vineyard. **Ricey-Bas** : 16thC church★, Troyes Renaissance style, stained glass, 16th-17thC sculpture. **Ricey-Haute-Rive** : 16thC church with stained glass, 15thC pulpit. **Mussy-sur-Seine** (13 km E, on D17) : 13thC church★, 14th-15thC statuary, 16thC Pietà; château (15th, 18thC) now the town hall; several 15th and 16thC houses; Museum of the Resistance (Rue Boursault; Sat. and Sun. pm, May-Oct.).   □

Practical Information _____

CHAOURCE

Hotel :
★★ **Aux Maisons** (L.F.), Maisons les Chaource, ☎ 25.40.11.77, Euro Visa, 14 rm Ⓟ ⌨ ⌕ 120. Rest. ◆ ⌕ & closed Sun eve, 70-120; child : 35.

Nearby

BAR-SUR-SEINE, ⊠ 10110, 21 km E.
⃞ mairie, ☎ 25.29.80.35.

Hotel :
★ **Barsequanais**, 6, av. Gal-Leclerc, ☎ 25.29.82.75, 24 rm Ⓟ ⌨ ⌕ closed Sun eve and Mon lunch (l.s), 25 Dec-25 Jan, 150. Rest. ◆ 70-120.

Å ★★*La Motte Noire* (65 pl), ☎ 25.38.86.38.

On the maps, a town's name underlined Saulieu means that the locality possesses at least one recommended establishment (blue or red point).

CHARLEVILLE-MÉZIÈRES

Reims 83, Saint-Quentin 119, Paris 225 km
pop 61558 ⊠ 08000   B1

Two cities in one on the banks of the Meuse. Mézières has conserved most of its ramparts (14th, 16thC; *signposted tour*), while Charleville was created from scratch at the beginning of the 17thC. The poet Arthur Rimbaud (1854-1891) was born and raised here; his grave is in the cemetery. Place Ducale★, urban architecture (Louis XIII-Henri IV) similar to that of the renowned Place des Vosges in Paris. Nearby, the **Vieux Moulin** (old mill, Louis XIII); Ardenne Museum, regional folklore *(9-12 & 2-6 ex Mon.)*; Rimbaud Museum (quai Arthur-Rimbaud).

▶ **Mézières** was almost entirely rebuilt in red brick after WWII. Church of **Notre-Dame-de-l'Espérance★** (15th-16thC Flamboyant Gothic) : the black image of the Virgin is the object of an annual pilgrimage; modern stained glass.   ☐

Practical Information _____

⑴ 2, rue Mantoue, ☎ 24.33.00.17.
SNCF ☎ 24.33.50.50/24.33.01.08.
Car rental : *Avis*, train station; 6, av. G.-Corneau, ☎ 24.56.14.18.

Hotel :
★★★ **Relais du Square** (L.F.), 3, pl. de la Gare, ☎ 24.33.38.76, Tx 841196, AE DC Euro Visa, 49 rm ℗ 🏧 ⌡ 🍴 ὦ 200.

Restaurant :
◆◆ **La Cigogne**, 40, rue Dubois-Crancé, ☎ 24.33.25.39, Euro Visa 🏧 ὦ closed Mon and Sun eve, 1-15 Aug. Spec : *pâté de truite en brioche*, 60-150; child : 50.

⚠ ★★★*Mont Olympe* (180 pl), ☎ 24.33.23.60.

Recommended
Youth hostel : 3, rue des Tambours, ☎ 24.57.44.36.
♥ shops on the rue de la République (pedestrian zone) and pl. Ducale (game, *andouillettes, boudin blanc*, blood sausage.

CHÂTEAU-THIERRY*

Reims 58, Troyes 110, Paris 96 km
pop 14920 ⊠ 02400   A2-3

The French Aesop, Jean de la Fontaine (1621-1695) was born here; small museum at 12 Rue La Fontaine *(10-12, 2 or 2:30-5, 6 or 6:30; closed Tue.)*; church of St. Crépin (15th-16thC). Through the streets (or up 104 steps) to the 14thC **Porte St. Jean** leading to the promenade of the château overlooking the valley.

Nearby

▶ **Bois Belleau** *(10 km NW along N3 and D9)* : WWI military cemeteries. ▶ **Essômes** *(3 km S)* : 13th-14thC church★. ▶ SE : drive through the **Surmelin Valley.** ▶ **Condé-en-Brie** *(15 km)* : château, with apartments of the Prince de Condé, remodeled in the 18thC *(Jul.-Aug. daily 10-12 & 2:30-6:30; Easter-Jun. and Sep.-Oct. : Sun. and nat. hols. only, 2:30-6:30).* ▶ **Orbais** *(26 km)* : 12th-13thC church (choir★ with triforium and seven rose windows) built by Jean d'Orbais who was one of the builders of Reims cathedral. ▶ Return to Château-Thierry through Dormans and the valley of the Marne.   ☐

Practical Information _____

⑴ pl. de l'Hôtel de Ville, ☎ 23.52.10.79.
SNCF ☎ 23.83.11.27/23.83.14.08.
Car rental : *Avis*, 2, rue Chierry, BP 123, ☎ 23.70.92.51.

Restaurant :
● ◆◆◆ **Auberge Jean de La Fontaine**, 10, rue des

Filoirs, ☎ 23.83.63.89, Visa ⌡ ὦ closed Mon and Sun eve. With great dazzle and fanfare, chef Guy Girard is back, assisted by two promising young cooks. In an agreeable rustic decor, where the fabulist Jean de La Fontaine is much in evidence, inventive cuisine is served with a flourish : *canard au sel en pot-au-feu, foie gras, choucroute au poisson, cassoulet* and every weekend, the cheapest fixed meal in France; take-out shop, 140-200.

Recommended
Guide to wines : *Caves Pannier*, tour and tasting daily, 9-12, 2:30-6:30 ex Sun.

CHAUMONT

Troyes 94, Dijon 103, Paris 259 km
pop 29552 ⊠ 52000   C4

Houses with distinctive staircase towers and corbelled turrets cluster around the keep and basilica. The newer areas are pleasant and well laid out.

▶ **Basilica of St. Jean** : a mixture of Gothic and Renaissance, with interesting triforium and openwork tower staircase; statuary including polychrome Entombment of Christ★ (15thC), Tree of Jesse★ (genealogy of Christ, Troyes 16thC) in St. Nicolas chapel. ▶ **Old houses**, courthouse; only the 12thC **dungeon** remains from the château of the Counts of Champagne. ▶ **Municipal museum** *(Apr.-Oct. : Thu., Sat., Sun. 10-12 & 2-6).* ▶ Extensive view★ from the Square Philippe-le-Bon. ▶ **Viaduct★** : 19thC railway engineering at its best, 654 m long, three stories towering 52 m above the Suize and the road to Châtillon-sur-Seine.

Nearby

▶ **Nogent-en-Bassigny** *(22 km SE through the valley of the Marne and down D107)*, centre for the manufacture of scissors and cutlery.   ☐

Practical Information _____

⑴ bd Thiers, ☎ 25.03.04.74.
SNCF ☎ 25.03.50.50/25.03.33.91.
Car rental : *Avis*, Pl. A.-Briand, ☎ 25.32.00.79; train station.

Hotels :
★★★ **Terminus Reine**, (Mapotel), pl. du Gal-de-Gaulle, ☎ 25.03.66.66, Tx 840920, AE DC Euro Visa, 63 rm ℗ ὦ 270. Rest. ♦ ⌡ ὦ closed Sun eve , 1 Nov, Easter, 35-200.
★★ **L'Etoile d'Or** (L.F.), rte de Langres, ☎ 25.03.02.23, Euro Visa, 15 rm ℗ ὦ closed Sun eve and Mon lunch, 150. Rest. ♦ ⌡ ὦ 50-95; child : 40.

Restaurant :
◆◆ **La Clé des Champs**, 33, fg de Bruxereilles, ☎ 25.03.48.72 ℗ closed Mon and Sun eve, 80-150.

⚠ ★★*Municipal* (100 pl), ☎ 25.32.11.98.

Recommended
Youth hostel : rue Decres, ☎ 25.03.73.18, Jul-Aug.

COLOMBEY-LES-DEUX-ÉGLISES

Chaumont 27, Troyes 68, Paris 232 km
pop 688 ⊠ 52330   C4

Since 1979 visitors have been allowed into the four main ground-floor rooms of **La Boisserie**, the personal residence of the former President of France, General Charles de Gaulle (1890-1970), who lived here from 1946 to 1958, retiring here in 1969. The books and furniture are in place in the library and in the General's corner study. Visitors are often surprised by the simplicity of the house. De Gaulle is buried in the cemetery around the village church. A **memorial cross** of Lorraine, 44 m high, overlooks the hills.   ☐

Practical Information ⎯⎯⎯⎯⎯⎯⎯⎯⎯⎯

Hotels :
★★★ *Les Dhuits*, (Mapotel), ☎ 25.01.50.10, AE DC Euro
Visa, 30 rm ℙ ⊰ ᕟᕟ ᕟ ᕟ closed 20 Dec-10 Jan, 195.
Rest. ♦ ⊰ᕟ 50-120; child : 35.
★ *Auberge de la Montagne*, rue d' Argentolles,
☎ 25.01.52.69, 11 rm ℙ ᕟᕟ closed 26 Jan-3 Mar, 80.
Rest. ♦ closed Mon eve and Tue (l.s), 50-200.

Lake DER-CHANTECOQ

B3

The region was once an immense oak forest of which
only a fragment remains. The name of Der comes
from the Celtic world for oak. In 1974, the largest
artificial lake in France (48 km²) was created here to
regulate the flow of the Marne and the Seine. Three
villages were inundated in the process, but the most
interesting buildings were reconstructed along the
north shore.
▶ **Sainte-Marie-du-Lac :** Museum-village with traditional
wood-faced buildings; church★ at Nuisement, smithy,
barns, activities Apr.-Oct. (enq. : C.D.T. Marne).
▶ Round trip *(45 km S and SW)* of the churches of the
Der. **Montier-en-Der :** former abbey church★ with timber structure reminiscent of early Saxon churches; choir
based on that of St. Rémi at Reims. **Ceffonds** :
early-16thC church. **Puellemontier** *(6.5 km NW)* : numerous farmhouses with wood facings; 16thC stained glass
in church. **Lentilles★** *(W, beyond Lake Horre)* : pretty
wood-faced church with timbered porch and high, steep
roof. **Chavanges** *(4 km NW)* : 12th and 16thC church.
Outines *(9 km NE)* : church with shingles and studding. □

ÉPERNAY

Reims 27, Troyes 111, Paris 143 km
pop 28876 ⊠ 51200 B2-3
Épernay, the heart of the vineyard country around the
Montagne de Reims, is where many champagne merchants maintain cellars. The regional **museum** has
an extensive display related to viticulture and wine
making.
▶Church of Notre-Dame (early 20thC neo-Gothic) : 16thC
stained glass; interesting regional sculptures. ▶**Champagne cellars :** Moët et Chandon, Mercier. ▶Nearby, the
Champagne road (→). □

Practical Information ⎯⎯⎯⎯⎯⎯⎯⎯⎯⎯

ÉPERNAY
ⓘ7, av. de Champagne, ☎ 26.55.33.00.
SNCF ☎ 26.51.39.07/26.88.50.50.
Car rental : *Avis*, 70, rue Champrot, ☎ 26.54.11.92.

Hotel :
★★★ *Les Berceaux*, 13, rue des Berceaux,
☎ 26.55.28.84, AE DC Euro Visa, 29 rm, 215. Rest. ● ♦♦
♪ closed Sun eve. Good classic cuisine : *terrine de ris de
veau, tournedos en croûte*; great champagnes, 115-190;
child : 45.

Restaurants :
● ♦♦ *La Terrasse*, 5-7, quai de la Marne, ☎ 26.55.26.05,
AE Euro Visa ♪ closed Mon and Sun eve, 1-23 Feb,
1-15 Jul. Good food, enjoyable view, 50-130.
● ♦ *Jean Burin*, 8, pl. Mendès-France, ☎ 26.51.66.69,
AE DC Euro Visa. Jean Burin has got back to basics,
75-110.

⚕ ★★★*Municipal* (100 pl), ☎ 26.55.32.14.

Nearby
CHAMPILLON-BELLEVUE, ⊠ 51160, 6 km N on N 51.

Hotel :
★★★ *Royal Champagne* (R.C.), Bellevue, ☎ 26.51.11.51,
Tx 830111, AE DC Euro Visa, 23 rm ℙ ⊰ ᕟᕟ ᕟ ᕟ closed
4-27 Jan. Pleasant bungalows, 500. Rest. ● ♦♦♦ ⊰ Moët
et Chandon's gastronomic stopover, with an unimpeded
view over the Champagne region. Spec : *trois saumons
panachés en sauce tiède, grenadine de sandre au champagne*, 200-300; child : 85.

MONTMORT, ⊠ 51270, 18 km SW on the D 51.

Hotel :
★ *Cheval Blanc*, ☎ 26.59.10.03, Euro Visa, 12 rm,
closed Fri, 15 Feb-15 Mar, 100. Rest. ● ♦ P. Cousinat's
enjoyable cooking in a small village. Spec : *coq au
vin*, 75-150.

FÈRE-CHAMPENOISE

Epernay 37, Troyes 66, Paris 139 km
pop 2518 ⊠ 51230 B3
Totally destroyed by fire in 1756, much damaged in
1914, and burned out again in 1940, the town has
only one church left (13thC tower, 15thC choir).
▶ National Cemetery and War Memorial commemorating
the first battle of the Marne (WWI). ▶ **Corroy** *(7 km SSW
on D9)* : church dating from 1070; porch. ▶ **St. Gond
marsh** *(10 km NNW)* : a 30 km² wasteland that saw heavy
fighting in 1914 (memorial at **Mondemont**); now partly cultivated. □

FÈRE-EN-TARDENOIS*

Château-Thierry 26, Reims 45, Paris 110 km
pop 3295 ⊠ 02130 A2
A large covered market and an oddly-shaped church
built in several stages (15th-16thC); 3 km off, the
seven round towers of the château de la Fère.
▶ **The Forteresse de la Fère★** *(no entrance fee)*, on a
sandstone mound in the forest; the five-arched viaduct
topped with a two-storey gallery dates from the 16thC;
entrance attributed to the sculptor Jean Goujon
(1510-1569).

Nearby
▶Remains of fortresses incorporated into several farmsteads : **Nesles** *(4 km E on D2);* **Armentières** *(13 km W
on D310 and D80);* via **Coincy** (beautiful church) and
3 km from **Oulchy-le-Château** : church★ with Romanesque nave, 11thC bell tower, noteworthy capitals). □

Practical Information ⎯⎯⎯⎯⎯⎯⎯⎯⎯⎯

SNCF ☎ 23.82.24.50.

Hotel :
★★★★*Hostellerie du Château* (R.C.). ☎ 23.82.21.13. Tx
145526. AE Euro Visa, 23 rm ℙ ⊰ ᕟᕟ ᕟ ᕟ ♪ half pens.
closed 1 Jan-1 Mar. 1470. Rest. ● ♦♦♦♦⊰ ♪ ᕟ After a
fruitful tour of the most renowned restaurants in France,
the young chief Christophe Blot rejoined the historic chateau (1260) of his family, 240, 500.

Restaurant :
♦♦ *Auberge du Connétable*, rte du Château,
☎ 23.82.24.25, AE ᕟᕟ ♪ ☐ closed Mon, 2 Jan-15 Feb.
70-160.

⎯⎯⎯⎯⎯⎯⎯⎯⎯⎯⎯⎯⎯⎯⎯⎯⎯⎯⎯⎯
For a complete picture on the gastronomy featured
in the Guide, see p. 8.
⎯⎯⎯⎯⎯⎯⎯⎯⎯⎯⎯⎯⎯⎯⎯⎯⎯⎯⎯⎯

⎯⎯⎯⎯⎯⎯⎯⎯⎯⎯⎯⎯⎯⎯⎯⎯⎯⎯⎯⎯
Don't forget to consult the Practical Holiday Guide: it
can help in solving many problems.
⎯⎯⎯⎯⎯⎯⎯⎯⎯⎯⎯⎯⎯⎯⎯⎯⎯⎯⎯⎯

JOINVILLE

Chaumont 43, Troyes 93, Paris 243 km
pop 5091 ⊠ 52300   C3
A compact and lively country town with narrow streets and fine Renaissance or neo-Classical houses on a wooded hill overlooking the flowering banks of the river Marne.

▶ **Château du Grand Jardin★** : 16thC; rare trees.

Nearby

▶ Near Rupt *(via D117 right)*. **Blécourt★** : 12th-13thC church in serene Cluniac style; Virgin and Child (copy of 13thC statue stolen in 1965). **Vignory** *(23 km)* : Romanesque church★★ is one of the major 11thC buildings in eastern France; timbered nave, figured capitals, 15th-16thC sculpture (Virgin and Child, Nativity, Vision of St. Hubert, altarpiece of Christ's Passion). ▶ **Poissons** *(6 km SE on D47)* in the valley of the Rongeant; 16thC church, sculpture.   □

Practical Information

ℹ️ mairie, ☎ 25.96.13.01.
SNCF ☎ 25.96.14.77.

Hotel :
★★ **Poste**, pl. de la Grève, ☎ 25.96.12.63, AE DC Euro Visa, 11 rm Ⓟ ⛧ closed 10 Jan-10 Feb, 130. Rest. ♦ ċ. Attractive prices. Spec : *mousseline de sole Virginie*, 80-130.

Ⓐ ★*Petit Bois* (100 pl), ☎ 25.96.06.64.

Recommended
♥ at Biencourt-sur-Orge, 25 km NE, Brie de Meaux : *Renard-Gillard*, ☎ 29.75.91.82.

LANGRES★★

Chaumont 35, Dijon 68, Paris 294 km
pop 11359 ⊠ 52200   C4
A town that invites exploration on foot : seven gates, six towers, ramparts crowned with a sentry walk, view over the countryside where the Marne, the Aube and the Meuse arise.

▶ Place Diderot (named for the philosopher Denis Diderot born here 1713). ▶ **Cathedral★** : 12thC Burgundian Romanesque with 18thC façade; 14thC Virgin in a Renaissance chapel; pulpit and organ casing from Morimond abbey. Close by : the chapterhouse, formerly the walled "Ville Capitulaire"; former Canons' houses. 20 Rue Cardinal-Morlot : Renaissance house★ *(guided visits)*. ▶ **St. Didier Museum** : Gallo-Roman life in the region (13 Roman roads fan out from Langres). ▶ **Museum of the Breuil de St. Germain Mansion** : furniture, ceramics, Diderot memorabilia *(10-12 & 2-5 or 6; closed Tue.)*. ▶ Gallo-Roman gateway.

Nearby

▶ Four 19thC reservoirs, feeding the Marne-Saône canal : sailing, especially on Lake Liez. ▶ **Pailly** *(12 km S)* : Renaissance château★. ▶ **Faylé-Billot** *(26 km SE on the Vesoul road)* : basket-weaving, craft shops, exhibitions in the École de Vannerie *(daily in summer ex Sun)*.   □

Practical Information

LANGRES
ℹ️ pl. Bel-Air, ☎ 25.85.03.32.
SNCF ☎ 25.85.05.21/25.03.50.50.
Car rental : Avis, pl. des Etats-Unis, ☎ 25.32.00.79.

Hotels :
● ★★ **Europe** (L.F.), 23-25, rue Diderot, ☎ 25.87.10.88, AE DC Euro Visa, 28 rm Ⓟ half pens (h.s.), closed Sun eve, 4-17 May, 1-27 Oct, 300. Rest. ♦ ċ. closed Mon noon

and Sun eve. Fine 17thC house. Spec : *truite soufflée au bourgogne blanc*, 50-120.
● ★★ **Le Cheval Blanc**, 4, rue de l'Estres, ☎ 25.87.07.00, AE Euro Visa, 23 rm Ⓟ ⛤ ⛧ ♪ closed Tue eve, Wed lunch, 5 Jan-6 Feb, 140. Rest. ♦♦ ♪ Former abbey. Spec : *tournedos aux morilles*, 55-150; child : 40.
★ **La Poste**, 8-10, pl. Ziegler, ☎ 25.85.10.51, 35 rm Ⓟ ⛧ closed Sun eve and Mon lunch, 21 Feb-2 Mar, 19-28 Sep, 8-29 Nov, 150.

Restaurant :
♦ **Rôtisserie Lingonne**, 2, rue du Gal-Leclerc, ☎ 25.87.63.82 ♪ ċ. closed Wed, 100-200.

Ⓐ ★★*Navarre* (65 pl), ☎ 25.85.37.80.

Nearby

AUBERIVE, ⊠ 52160, 20 km SW.

Hotel :
● ★★ **Le Relais du Lys**, Château de Vivey, ☎ 25.86.20.22, Visa, 7 rm Ⓟ ⛧ closed Wed, 15 Jan-1 Mar, 350. Rest. ♦ 95-260.

LAON★★

Reims 47, Cambrai 95, Paris 138 km
pop 29074 ⊠ 02000   A2
On an isolated hill overlooking the Champagne plain, Laon has some of the finest monuments in northern France. The upper town, a network of narrow medieval streets and beautiful houses, is linked to the lower town by a revolutionary French transport system, POMA 2000.

▶ **Cathedral★★★** (B-C2) built in a single stage starting in 1155, except for the 13thC choir. As one of the first Gothic buildings, it introduced many new ideas. The arcaded gallery inspired that of Notre-Dame-de-Paris; the triangular gables over the porches prefigured those at Chartres; the towers were models for Reims and others. The carved oxen pay tribute to the beasts that hauled thousands of blocks of stone from quarries in the plain. The four-storey nave (118 m from east end to doorway, 24 m high) is lit east-west by two symmetrical rose windows and by the openings in the clerestory above the galleries. The cathedral, chapterhouse, cloister *(under repair)* and former episcopal palace★ still look much as they did in the Middle ages. ▶ **Citadel** : (C2) view. ▶ **Porte d'Ardon** : (S, B-C2) 13thC gateway and rampart walk. **Museum** (42 Rue G.-Ermant; C2) Greek and Roman antiquities★; 12thC chapel of the Templars★. ▶ W through the medieval town centre lies the **church of St. Martin★** (A2), a former abbey church built on Cistercian lines (12th-13thC); farther on, the Soissons gateway★.

Nearby

▶ **Notre-Dame de Liesse★** *(15 km NE on N377)* : pilgrimage site. ▶ W, round trip through the **Saint-Gobain Forest★**. Ruined abbeys of Tortoir and St. Nicolas-aux-Bois. At **Saint-Gobain** (13th-14thC church), a sheet-glass and mirror industry was founded at the instigation of Jean-Baptiste Colbert (1619-1683) minister to Louis XIV. **Coucy-le-Château** : surrounded by ramparts, was guarded by one of the largest medieval châteaux, (damaged in WWI; *Jun.-Sep. 9-12 & 2-6; Oct.-May 10-12 & 1:30-4; closed Tue.*). Return to Laon via the **Abbey of Prémontré★**, birthplace of the Premonstratensian Order of White Canons (18thC buildings; magnificent spiral staircase★); **Merlieux** : freshwater nature information centre created in 1982 (aquaria, botany trail along the lakes, *Sat. and Sun. pm)*. **Mons-en-Laonnois** : country town with 13th-14thC church. ▶ S, a 25-km tour of the churches of the Laonnois through attractive countryside : **Bruyères** and **Vorges**, both fortified; **Presles** : 11th, 12thC porch; **Nouvion-le-Vineux** : Romanesque bell tower. ▶ 16 km S of Laon on D967 : the **Chemin des Dames**. This narrow crest is followed by D18 from its western crossroads with N2; scene of heavy fighting in WWI; memorial chapel and mili-

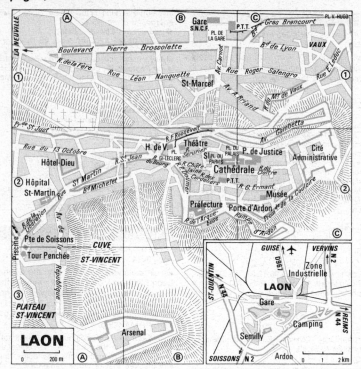

tary cemetery at **Cerny**; the Caverne du Dragon *(signposted)*, subterranean fortress and museum; 1 km N of the cavern are the remains of the Cistercian abbey of **Vauclair** (12th-13thC); interesting garden of medicinal plants; small museum of local ceramics *(Apr.-Oct., 8-8)*. ▶ **La Fère** *(21 km NW)* : Jeanne d'Aboville museum (paintings★). ▶ **Bois-lès-Pargny** *(20 km N)* : 17thC château *(ext. visits free; interior by request).* ▶ **Tergnier** : Resistance and deportation museum *(Sat., Sun.).*   □

Practical Information

LAON
ℹ️ pl. du Parvis (B2), ☎ 23.23.45.87.
🚆 (B1), ☎ 23.79.10.79/23.23.23.35.
🚌 pl. de la Gare (B1), ☎ 23.23.04.13.

Hotels :
★★★ *Angleterre*, 10, bd de Lyon (lower city; C1), ☎ 23.23.04.62, Tx 145580, AE DC Euro Visa, 30 rm 🅿️ closed Sun (l.s), Sat lunch all year, 190. Rest. ♦ closed Sat noon Dec, 60-170.
★★ *La Bannière de France*, 11, rue Franklin-Roosevelt (B2), ☎ 23.23.21.44, AE DC Euro Visa, 19 rm 🅿️ 🍴 ⌗ half pens (h.s.), closed 1 May, 20 Dec-20 Jan, 360. Rest. ♦ ⌗ A coach house dating from 1685. Spec : *rognons de veau au Bouzy*, 70-170.

Restaurant :
♦♦ *La Petite Auberge*, 45, bd Brossolette (lower city; A-B1), ☎ 23.23.02.38, AE DC Euro Visa ♪ ⌗ closed Sat. After a journeyman's tour of France, young Willy-Marc Zorn has returned to aid his father in the kitchen. House-smoked salmon, *roulade de saumon et sole à la gentiane*, 90-250.

▲ ★★★*Municipal* (71 pl), ☎ 23.23.29.07.

Recommended
Leisure activities : at Chamonille, *Parc Nautique des*

vallées de l'Ailette, ☎ 23.24.83.03, a 395-acre man-made lake in a 1111-acre park, daily 10-8, May-Oct with horseback riding, golf, fishing, lodging available.
♥ candy, take-out foods : *Rojer*, 7, rue Châtelaine, spec in town : *pâté de perdreaux en croûte.*

Nearby

BERRY-AU-BAC, ✉️ 02190 Guignicourt, 27 km SE.

Restaurant :
● ♦♦ *La Cote 108*, ☎ 23.79.95.04, AE DC Euro Visa 🍷 ♪ closed Mon and Sun eve, 23 Dec-30 Jan. The Champagne countryside and S. Courville's excellent cooking : *émincé de Bresse aux pleurotes*, 115-250.

La FÈRE, ✉️ 02800, 21 km NW.
🚆 ☎ 23.23.23.35.

Hotel :
★★ *Relais de Champagne*, ☎ 23.56.21.39, AE DC Euro Visa, 24 rm 🅿️ ♪ ⌗ closed Jan-feb, 280. Rest. ● ♦♦ ⌗ closed Nov-Mar. According to his mood, André Peudecoeur may cook up seafood, meats, *foie gras*, and all sorts of home-made terrines. Great Bordeaux vintages, 200-400.

URCEL, ✉️ 02000 Laon, 13 km.

Restaurant :
♦ *Host. de France*, RN 2, ☎ 23.21.60.08, Visa 🍷 ♪ closed Wed , Feb school hols, 17 Aug-4 Sep, 55-150.

VENDEUIL, ✉️ 02800 La Fère, 7 km N of **La Fère** on N 44.

Hotel :
★★ *Auberge de Vendeuil*, (L.F., R.S.), ☎ 23.66.85.22, 22 rm 🅿️ 🍴 🍷 ⌗ 240. Rest. ♦ Family-style welcome. Spec : *papillote de saumon rose à l'ail confit, médaillon de turbot en cassolette*, 80-200.

MEUSE Valley*

B1
Round trip from Charleville *(approx 130 km, full day)*

The appearance of factories, cement works and silos in the industrialized Meuse Valley has not spoilt the Ardennes Forest, which teems with game and has a rich folklore.

▶ 15 km N of Charleville, the crests known as the **Quatre Fils-Aymon** (the four sons of Aymon), brothers reputed to have escaped together from Charlemagne on the legendary steed Bayard. ▶ **Monthermé** : summer resort; church of St. Léger, Laval-Dieu : former abbey of White Canons, 12thC church, 18thC wood paneling. **Rock of the tower** *(3.5 km N and 20 min walk round trip)* : view★★ over the Ardennes. **Rock of the Seven Villages** *(3 km S)* : panorama★★ over the river valley. You can drive 18 km down D31 along the river **Semoy★** to the Belgian frontier : reedy banks and old mills in an area much appreciated by fishermen and nature lovers. ▶ The valley runs between the **Roches de Laifour** (waterfall) and the ravine of the **Dames de Meuse★** *(1 hr 30 to the top round trip)*. ▶ **Revin** : village built across two loops of the Meuse. Nearby, Mont Malgré Tout★ (Mont In Spite of Everything; *30min walk round trip)* overlooking the town. ▶ After **Fumay** (slate works), the valley widens. ▶ **Haybes.** ▶ **Hierges** : ruins of medieval château in a grand setting. ▶ **Chooz** : Franco-Belgian nuclear power station. ▶ **Givet** : fortified town at the foot of the stronghold of Charlemont *(15 Jun.-15 Sep., 10-12 & 2-6)*; the narrow streets are busy during the season; church of St. Hilaire, built by the 17thC military engineer Sébastien de Vauban (1633-1707). ▶ Return to Charleville through the Ardennes forest★ between Vireux and Monthermé. ☐

Practical Information

MONTHERME, ⊠ 08800, 17 km N of **Charleville.**
SNCF ☎ 24.32.11.67.

Hotel :
★★ *Franco-Belge* (L.F.), 2, rue Pasteur, ☎ 24.53.01.20, Visa, 14 rm �◊ ⌂ ≋ closed Fri eve and Sun eve, 10-25 Jan, 270. Rest. ♦ ♪ 45-140.

⚠ ★★*Au Port à Diseur* (100 pl), ☎ 23.53.01.21 ; ★★*Rapides de Phades* (100 pl), ☎ 23.53.06.73 ; *Echina "Chez Marius"* (50 pl), ☎ 23.53.05.56.

REVIN, ⊠ 08500, 23 km NW of **Charleville.**

Hotel :
★★ *François 1er*, quai Camille-Desmoulins, ☎ 23.40.15.88, Euro Visa, 20 rm ℗ ⋖ closed Sun eve, 155. Rest. ♦ ⋖ ♪ 50-110 ; child : 35.

MONTMIRAIL

Château-Thierry 18, Epernay 37, Paris 114 km
pop 3696 ⊠ 51210   A3

The site of battles in 1814 and during WWI, Montmirail is perched above the valley of the Petit Morin (walks). Louis XIII-style château *(private)*. ☐

NOGENT-SUR-SEINE

Sens 42, Troyes 56, Paris 109 km
pop 5103 ⊠ 10400   A3

Meadows, willows, poplars, a mill and, near the quay, a sturdy half-timbered dwelling known as Henri IV's house. Upstream, a nuclear power plant *(visit by appt., tel. : 25.39.00.78).*

▶ **Church of St. Laurent★** : 15th-16thC, Renaissance tower; 16thC organ casing; 16th-17thC sculpture and painting. ▶ Behind the apse, Rue de la Halle : old houses. ▶ Rue Gustave-Flaubert leads to the **museum** : works by

local sculptors P. Dubois and A. Boucher; Gallo-Roman pottery.

Nearby

▶ **Le Paraclet** *(6 km SE on the Troyes road)* : site of the convent founded in 1129 by the theologian Pierre Abélard, whose beloved Héloïse was the first abbess. Parts of the wall still stand, together with the crypts, dovecote and storehouse. The kitchens are incorporated in a wing of the 17thC château *(ext. visit Jul.-Sep., 2-6 ex Sun.)*. ▶ **Ferreux** *(3.5 km farther)* : 17thC château *(visit by appt.)*. ▶ **Pont-sur-Seine** *(8 km E)* : 17th-18thC château. ▶ 18thC **château de la Motte-Tilly★** : superb furnishings★ *(Apr.-Sep. daily ex Tue. 10-11:30 & 2-6:15 ; off season, Sat., Sun., nat. hols ; son et lumière, tel. : 25.39.84.54).* ☐

Practical Information

SNCF ☎ 25.25.81.61.

Hotel :
★ *Beau Rivage* (L.F.), 20, rue Villiers-aux-Choux, ☎ 25.39.84.22, Visa, 7 rm ⋖ ⌂ ⌂ closed Mon eve, Fri eve, Sun eve (in winter), 105. Rest. ♦ ⋖ ♪ 55-140.

Restaurant :
♦♦ *La Chapelle Godefroy*, 3 km E via N 19, ☎ 25.39.88.32, AE Visa ⌂ closed eve ex Sat, 1-21 Aug. A mill. Good food, 75-220.

ORIENT Lake and Forest**

B4

The artificial Lake Orient (23 km²) was created in 1966 to regulate the flow of the Seine. It is bordered by an oak forest (13 km²); recreational facilities attract tourists. 30 km scenic route.

▶ The reservoir protects the town of Troyes from flooding and regulates the water level in Paris when the Seine is in spate; small hydroelectric station. ▶ Near **Géraudot** : bird sanctuary. ▶ **Mesnil-Saint-Père** : game reserve 5 km N (boar, red and roe deer; *open Sat. and Sun. 4-dusk Apr.-Sep. ; 1st and 3rd Sun. 3-dusk Oct.-Mar.).* Information from the Maison du Parc (office) at main forest crossroads; info. on fishing (pike), accommodation, sporting and leisure facilities *(daily ; tel. : 25.41.35.57).* ☐

REIMS***

Châlons-sur-Marne 45, Charleville 83, Paris 141 km
pop 181985 ⊠ 51100   B2

Two key events in French history took place at Reims (Rheims in English). The first was the baptism of Clovis, king of the Franks, in AD496, which legitimized the monarchy and laid the foundation for a national identity. The second was the coronation of Charles VII in the cathedral on 17 July 1429. This confirmed the success of Joan of Arc in rallying the French to shake off 9 years of English rule, during which France had virtually ceased to exist as a separate entity. Reims was rebuilt twice during the first half of this century to repair war damage. The growth of Champagne exports since 1970 has enabled the town to expand at a dizzy rate.

▶ **Place Drouet-d'Erlon** (A1-2), a pedestrian precinct lined with cafés, restaurants, cinemas and shopping arcades, is the hub of social activity. Church of St. Jacques : 13th-16thC, with modern abstract stained glass★ by Vieira da Silva and Joseph Sima. ▶ **Cathedral★★★** (B2) : 6650 m² in area, 81.5 m high, 149 m in overall length; the nave is 138.7 m long and 38 m high. Planned by Jean d'Orbais (→ Orbais), building began in 1211 and was mostly completed a century later. The immediate impression is of extreme lightness and elegance : the three arched doorways, the gallery of kings and the delicate openwork

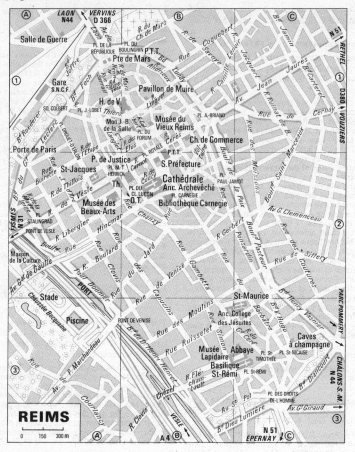

REIMS

0   150   300 m

towers and flying buttresses are so perfectly proportioned that they appear weightless. Lessons learned from Chartres, begun 20 years earlier, resulted in a brilliant fusion of space and light. The perspective leads the eye towards the choir, and the windows appear as integral parts of the ogives, creating a curtain of light around the sanctuary. On the inside W wall★★, superb sculpture (the knight's communion★); outside on the W face, sculptural groups of the Visitation★, the Presentation in the Temple, the Last Judgement, and the famous smiling angel★★ (left doorway), a masterpiece of Champenoise style; ▶ The **Tau Museum** (B2, right of the cathedral; *10-12 & 2-5 or 6*) : formerly the King's coronation residence; treasures and statues★ from the cathedral (Crowning of the Virgin, Goliath). ▶ **Museum of St. Denis** (A2, 8 Rue Chanzy) : exceptional collection of 15thC paintings★, drawings★ by the German artist Lucas Cranach the Elder, 19thC paintings, including 20 by Camille Corot★ (→ Ile-de-France) and 9 by Eugène Boudin (1824-98). ▶ **Basilica of St. Rémi★★** (B-C3), important pilgrimage site (St. Rémi was the bishop who baptized King Clovis); the choir★★ (1162-90) is the earliest example of ogival architecture in Champagne; fine E end. ▶ Next door, the former abbey (rebuilt 17th-18thC) now the **archaeological museum** (prehistory to end of Middle Ages; entrance 53 Rue St-Simon, B-C3) : 16th-19thC weapons, Romanesque archaeology, tapestries★ illustrating the life of St. Rémi.

Also... ▶ **Porte Mars★** (A1) : superb Roman triumphal arch. ▶ **Salle de Guerre** (War Room), where the German

surrender was signed on 7 May 1945 (Collège Technique, 10 Rue Franklin-Roosevelt, A1; *15 Mar.-11 Nov., 10-12 & 2-6; closed Tue.).* ▶ **Museum of Old Reims★** (Vergeur Mansion, 16th-18thC; B1) : history of the town, documents, illustrations of coronations, furnished rooms, engravings by the German artist Albrecht Dürer of Christ's Passion and the Apocalypse★ *(2-6; closed Mon.).* Opposite, underground **Roman galleries** (3rdC, Place du Forum). Figures by the 18thC sculptor Jean-Baptiste Pigalle surrounding a statue of Louis XV in Place Royale. ▶ **Foujita Chapel** (35, Rue du Champ-de-Mars; B1) frescos by the Japanese artist Tsugouharu Foujita (1886-1968) who was baptized at Reims. **Church of St. Nicaise** *(entry via C2),* decorated with Lalique glass, in a housing estate built in the 1920s. ▶ Former Jesuit college (B-C3), vast 17thC ensemble (refectory, kitchens, salons, library). ▶ **Maison de la Culture** (cultural centre, A2; Rue de Vesle, over the bridge). Round **church of St. Vincent-de-Paul** in the new Quartier de l'Europe. The University is on the edge of town. ▶ The **Centre historique de l'automobile française**, transferred from Saint-Dizier, has been installed at 84, Rue G.-Clemenceau (B2; *daily 10-7*).

Nearby

▶ **Fort de la Pompelle** *(9 km E on the Châlons road)* : museum, German helmets and uniforms from WWI. ▶ **Montagne de Reims** (regional nature park; *10 km S on* *the Épernay road*) : woods, Saint-Imoges Lake, Ardre Valley. ▶ Champagne Road (→). ☐

Practical Information

REIMS
ⓘ 1, rue Jadart (B1), ☎ 26.47.25.69/26.47.04.60.
✈ *Reims-Champagne*, ☎ 26.07.18.35. Air France office, 11, rue Henri-Jadart, ☎ 26.47.17.84.
SNCF (A1), ☎ 26.88.50.50/26.47.84.30.
▦ pl. du Forum (B1), ☎ 26.65.17.07.
Car rental : *Avis*, 14, bd du Mal-Joffre (A1), ☎ 26.47.10.08.

Hotels :
● ★★★★(L) *Boyer Les Crayères* (R.C.), 64, bd Henry-Vasnier (C3), ☎ 26.82.80.80, Tx 830959, AE DC Euro Visa, 16 rm ⊀ ▦ ◿ ≀ ⅃ ℘ closed 21 Dec-13 Jan, 1000. Rest. ● ◆◆◆◆ ⅃ ⅄ closed Mon noon and Tue noon. Champagne is an occasion all by itself, but a visit to Gérard Boyer, in his enchanting establishment, tastefully decorated by his wife, Elyane, is a real celebration! First-rate food : *feuilleté de foie gras chaud, poissons grillés au beurre de caviar, canard aux poires et gingembre, les délices de Marjorie.* The cellar is stocked with a wealth of regional riches, 320-450.
★★★ *L'Assiette Champenoise*, 40, av. P.-V. Coutu, Tinqueux, ☎ 26.03.14.94, AE DC Euro Visa Rest. ● ◆◆◆ Colette and J.-P. Lallement invite you to enjoy their new decor and their light, inventive cuisine, 100-250.
★★★ *La Paix*, (Inter-Hôtel), 9, rue Buirette (A2), ☎ 26.40.04.08, Tx 830974, AE DC Euro Visa, 105 rm ℗ ▦ ⌧ 260. Rest. ◆ *Taverne de Maître Kanter* ≀ ⅄ 50-130.

Restaurants :
● ◆◆◆ *Le Florence*, 43, bd Foch (A1), ☎ 26.47.12.70, AE DC Euro Visa ≀ closed Sun eve, 20 Jul-11 Aug. Elegance and quality. Spec : *mêlée de sole et rouget au beurre de vinaigre, fricassée de volaille de Bresse aux langoustines, gratin de fruits rouges au sabayon de champagne,* 180-300.
● ◆◆ *Le Chardonnay*, 184, av. d'Epernay (off map A3), ☎ 26.06.08.60, AE DC Euro Visa ⅄ closed Sat noon and Sun , Aug, 20 Dec-13 Jan. There's good food still here at the Boyer family's birthplace : *côte de boeuf, confit de canard,* 180-210.
◆◆ *Le Continental*, 95, pl. Drouet-d'Erlon (A1), ☎ 26.47.01.47 A fine place to stop in the centre of town, featuring G. Lantenois's good cooking : *foie gras au ratafia, lobster, spiny lobster (in tanks) au champagne, filet de boeuf au bouzy,* 70-140.
◆◆ *Le Vigneron*, pl. P.-Jamot (B2), ☎ 26.47.00.71, closed Sat noon and Sun. Regional decor. The restaurant-museum represents a typical winegrower's house. Old-fashioned fare, 120-250.

△ ★★★*Airotel de Champagne* (115 pl), ☎ 26.85.41.22.

Recommended
Events : *"Cathédrale de Lumière et de Son",* info. S.I., spectacle in the cathedral.
Guide to wines : *Taittinger,* 9, pl. Saint-Nicolas, ☎ 26.85.45.35 ; *Veuve Clicquot-Ponsardin,* 1, pl. des Droits-de-l'Homme, ☎ 26.85.24.08 ; *Pommery,* 5, pl. du Gal-Gouraud, ☎ 26.05.05.01 ; *Piper-Heidsieck,* 51, bd Henry-Vasnier, ☎ 26.85.01.94, cellar tours.
Market : *Flea market,* pl. du Boulingrin, 1st Sun of month. ♥ candy : *Petite Friande,* 15, cours J.-B.-Langlet, chocolates shaped like Champagne corks ; *A Dom Pérignon,* 13, rue du Cadran-St-Pierre ; gourmet grocery : *Fossier,* 25, cours J.-B.-Langlet, cookies ; pork products : *Au Cochon sans rancune,* maison Coeuriot, 47, rue de Vesle.

Nearby
MONTCHENOT, ⊠ 51500 Rilly-la-Montagne, 11 km S.

Restaurant :
● ◆◆ *Le Grand Cerf*, RN 51, ☎ 26.97.60.07, AE Euro Visa ▦ ≀ closed Tue eve and Wed, 2-22 Aug, 20 Dec-6 Jan. For country charm and fine cuisine : *escalope de bar au beurre d'étrilles, ris de veau à la fondue d'oignons,* 130-250.

SEPT-SAULX, ⊠ 51400, 18 km SE.

Hotel :
★★★ *Le Cheval Blanc* (R.S.), 2, rue du Moulin, ☎ 26.61.60.27, Tx 830885, AE DC Euro Visa, 21 rm ℗ ⊀ ▦ ◿ ⅄ ℘ ⅃ half pens, closed 15 Jan-15 Feb, 800. Rest. ◆ ⊀ A lady's in the kitchen preparing excellent dishes like : *écrevisses au vin de champagne, brochet beurre champenois ;* fine cellar, 150-250.

SILLERY, ⊠ 51500 Rilly-la-Montagne, 8 km SE.

Restaurant :
◆◆ *Le Relais de Sillery*, 3, rue de la Gare, ☎ 26.49.10.11, Euro Visa ⊀ ▦ ⅄ closed Mon and Sun eve , Feb. Jeannine Adin is a lion-trainer (animal park open in summer) as well as a chef : *régal d'escargots forestière, mousse de lotte coulis de crevettes, noix de veau aux morilles,* 120-160.

ROCROI*

Charleville 29, Laon 83, Paris 234 km
pop 2789 ⊠ 08230 B1

Guided tours of the fortifications (begun 1555, finished 17thC). The eight perfectly linear streets radiating from the wide central square are lined with slate-roofed houses.

▶ **Lake Vieilles-Forges** *(12 km SE)* : sailing, swimming. **Renwez** *(3 km S of Lake)* : 15thC church. **Montcornet** *(1.5 km farther)* : ruined 12th-14thC château *(museum, 2-6 Sat., Sun., Easter-Oct. ; daily ex Mon., Jul.-15 Sep.).* ☐

Practical Information

ROCROI
ⓘ pl. A.-Hardy, ☎ 24.54.10.22/24.54.24.46 (h.s.).

Hotel :
★★ *Commerce*, pl. A.-Briand, ☎ 24.54.11.15, AE DC Euro Visa, 12 rm, half pens (h.s.), closed Mon (Oct-Mar), 5 Jan-10 Feb, 260. Rest. ◆ ≀ ⅄ 60-100.

△ ★★*Les Remparts* (50 pl), ☎ 24.54.10.22.

Nearby

AUVILLERS-LES-FORGES, ⊠ 08260 Maubert-Fontaine, 13 km SW on D 877.

Hotel :
★★★ *Hostellerie Lenoir* (R.S.), 21 rm ℗ ▦ ◿ ⅄ closed Fri, 1 Jan-1 Mar, 260. Rest. ● ◆◆ ≀ ⅄ The discreet charm of the bourgeoisie nestled in a great house. Four-handed duets in the kitchen, where Jean Lenoir (M.C.F.) cooks with his sister, Ginette : *feuilleté de grenouilles cressonnière, champignons des Ardennes.* Champagnes featured on the wine list. Cooking lessons, 210-350.

SAINT-DIZIER

Bar-le-Duc 24, Chaumont 74, Paris 212 km
pop 37445 ⊠ 52100 C3

An important crossroad town and typical of French town planning since the 1950s.

▶ "Au Petit Paris" : house in the main street, decorated with shards of ceramics.

Nearby

▶ **Trois-Fontaines**★ *(11 km on D16)* : ruins of 13thC Cistercian abbey, outbuildings rebuilt in the 18thC *(15 Jun.-15 Sep. 2:30-7 ; park open all year).* ☐

Practical Information

ⓘ pavillon du Jard, ☎ 25.05.31.84.
SNCF ☎ 25.05.67.68.
Car rental : *Avis*, 61, av. d'Alsace-Lorraine, ☎ 25.58.31.22.

Hotel :
★ *Picardy*, 15, av. de Verdun, ☎ 25.05.09.12, 12 rm P ⋙
⌕ closed 14-24 Aug, 125.

Recommended
Youth hostel : rue des Capucines, open all year.

SAINT-QUENTIN*

Laon 46, Valenciennes 70, Paris 155 km
pop 65067 ⊠ 02100   A1
The town had to be almost entirely rebuilt after WWI,
but several interesting buildings were saved, together
with an important collection of pastels by Quentin
de La Tour (1704-88), who was born and died here.
A 30-acre public park in the centre of town, sailing on
Lake Isle, barges on the Somme canal.

▶ **Basilica** (12th-15thC) in the town centre looks stolid
from outside but is surprisingly airy and elegant inside ;
13thC choir★ with five radiating chapels ; magnificent
18thC organ. ▶ Nearby : façade of the 1509 Hôtel de Ville
with three gables and a fine bell tower (ring of 37 bells).
▶ **Museum of Entomology★** in the library : unique European collection of 600 000 butterflies *(daily ex Mon.,
Apr.-Aug.).* ▶ **Antoine-Lécuyer Museum** (28, Rue Antoine-
Lécuyer ; *daily ex Tue.)* : 87 pastel portraits★ by Quentin
de La Tour ; paintings, tapestries, porcelain.   ▢

Practical Information _____

SAINT-QUENTIN
ⓘ hôtel de ville, ☎ 23.67.05.00.
▰▰▰ ☎ 23.62.34.03/23.62.51.45.
Car rental : *Avis*, Train station ; 36, rue des États-Géné-
raux, ☎ 23.62.62.80.

Hotels :
★★★ *Grand Hôtel*, 6, rue Dachery, ☎ 23.62.69.77,
Tx 140225, AE DC Visa, 41 rm P 245. Rest. ● ♦♦♦ *Le
Président* ♪ closed Mon and Sun eve, 2-15 Feb, 3-23 Aug.
Ever more stylish cuisine from Raymond Brochard : *nava-
rin de homard breton, bar aux courgettes, canard aux her-
bes fraîches*, 145-300.
★★ *France-Angleterre*, (Inter-Hôtel), 28, rue E.-Zola,
☎ 23.62.13.10, Tx 140986, AE DC Euro Visa, 30 rm P ⌕
& closed 25 Dec-1 Jan, 225.

Restaurants :
● ♦♦ *Le Château*, Neuville-Saint-Amand, 3 km SE,
☎ 23.68.41.82, AE DC Euro Visa ⋞ ⋙ ♪ closed Mon, Wed
eve, Sun eve 1 wk in Feb, 3-24 Aug, 24-31 Dec. Good
cooking by the Meiresonne brothers : seasonal menus
and carte, 130-250.
♦♦ *Au Petit Chef*, 31, rue E.-Zola, ☎ 23.62.28.51, AE Visa
♪ & Spec : *truite farcie au champagne*, 55-130.
♦ *Café Riche*, 10, rue des Toiles, ☎ 23.64.12.12, Euro
Visa ♪ closed Tue and Sun eve, 5-20 Jan, 20 Jul-10 Aug.
Spec : seafood, *turbot sauce hollandaise, steack au
poivre flambé*, 60-150.

Nearby

BLÉRANCOURT, ⊠ 02300 Chauny, 23 km NW on D 6.

Hotel :
★★★ *Le Griffon* (C.H.), 25, pl. Gal-Leclerc, ☎ 23.39.60.11,
AE DC Euro Visa, 21 rm P ⋞ ⋙ ⌕ & ⅋ closed Sun eve
and Mon, 23-30 Dec, 230. Rest. ♦ ⋞ ♪ ⅋ 90-165 ;
child : 55.

GUISE, ⊠ 02120, 27 km.

Hotel :
★★ *Champagne-Picardie*, 41, rue André-Godin,
☎ 23.60.43.44, Visa, 14 rm P ⋙ ⌕ ⅋ 175.

For the translation of a name of a meat, a fish or a
vegetable, for the composition of a dish or a sauce,
see the Menu Guide in the Practical Holiday Guide ;
it lists the most common culinary terms.

SAINTE-MENEHOULD

Châlons-sur-Marne 46, Verdun 47, Paris 220 km
pop 5807 ⊠ 51800   B-C2
The town is known for more than breaded pig's foot.
The lower town of Sainte-Menehould (pron. *Sainte-
Menou*) retains an 18thC urban appearance (town
hall, Place du Général-Leclerc) in contrast to the vil-
lage-like upper town clustered around the 12th-14thC
church (15thC sculpture, the Dormition of the Virgin).
On 21 June 1791, Louis XVI was recognized in the
post house (now the Gendarmerie) during his flight
from Paris. He was arrested a little farther on at
Varennes-en-Argonne. Sainte-Menehould was also
the birthplace of Dom Pérignon (→ box).

▶ **Municipal museum :** geological collection *(daily Palm
Sun.-11 Nov. ; Sat. pm and Sun. rest of year).*

Nearby

▶ **East :** **Argonne forest** (→ Lorraine). ▶ **Givry-en-
Argonne** *(16 km S)* : lakes in the Belval Forest. ▶ **Braux-
Sainte-Cohière★** *(5.5 km W)* : 16th-17thC château, Regional Museum of the Argonne (exhibitions and events,
20 Jun.-4 Sep., 9-12 & 2-7 ; closed Tue.). ▶ **Valmy**
(11 km NW), site of 1792 victory by French Revolutionary
army over invading Prussians ; reconstructed historic mill.
▶ **La Neuville-au-Pont** *(6 km NW on Vouziers road)* :
14th-16thC church.   ▢

Practical Information _____

SAINTE-MENEHOULD
ⓘ Pl. du Général Leclerc, ☎ 26.60.85.83.

Nearby

GIVRY-EN-ARGONNE, ⊠ 51330, 16 km S.

Hotel :
★ *L'Espérance*, pl. de la Halle, ☎ 26.60.00.08, 7 rm P ⌕
closed Sun eve, 90. Rest. ♦ ♪ 45-105 ; child : 35.

SEDAN

Charleville 22, Verdun 80, Paris 237 km
pop 24535 ⊠ 08200   B-C1
Massed ramparts and bastions, built in stages beginning in the 15thC, on a rock overlooking the Meuse
valley. Extremely interesting for students of military
architecture ; inside, noteworthy vaulting and timber
framework, models from various periods (Sedan
Museum and temporary exhibitions *Apr.-Oct. 10-5:30 ;
15 Sep.-25 Oct. 1:30-5:30).* ▶ **Church of Saint
Charles,** Place d'Armes, former Protestant church
(16thC.). ▶ **Old houses** around the Rues du Ménil and
de l'Horloge, Place de La Halle.

Nearby

▶ 30-acre lake to the S : sailing, swimming. ▶ **Bazeilles**
(3.5 km SE) : rebuilt after 1870 ; small museum ; 1730 château de Dorival★ *(10-12 & 2-6 closed Mon.).* ▶ **Chéhéry**
(10 km W) : 16thC château du Rocan *(visits).* ▶ **Mouzon**
(17 km SE) : old country town ; Burgundy gateway, remnants of fortifications *(Jun.-Sep., Sat. and Sun. 2-6)*
13thC Benedictine abbey church (tympanum, galleries and
clerestorey, choir★ with ambulatory and five radiating chapels).   ▢

Practical Information _____

ⓘ pl. Crussy, ☎ 24.29.31.14.
▰▰▰ ☎ 24.27.14.84.
Car rental : *Avis*, train station.

Restaurant :
♦♦ *Au Bon Vieux Temps*, 1-3, pl. de la Halle,

☎ 24.29.03.70, AE DC Euro Visa ♪ ➾ closed Mon and Sun eve, 2 Feb-2 Mar. Hearty regional dishes. Spec : *tournedos Curnonsky*, 110-270.

⚠ ★★*Prairie de Torcy* (150 pl), ☎ 24.27.13.05.

SOISSONS*

Laon 36, Reims 56, Paris 100 km
pop 32236 ⊠ 02200   A2

Soissons was largely rebuilt to repair the destruction of the Franco-Prussian War of 1870-71 and the two world wars. Several admirable buildings have somehow survived.

▶ **Cathedral★★**, built over 3 centuries, most of it dates from the 13thC; the S transept★ (1177) is the most beautiful part; Adoration of the Shepherds★ by the Flemish painter Peter Paul Rubens; 13thC stained glass in the choir. ▶ Place du Cloître (cloister) with 13thC houses; behind the church, Romanesque remains of St. Pierre-au-Parvis, now a memorial to the Deportation of WWII. ▶ N on the Grand' Place : no. 16 is the 17th-18thC **Barral Mansion** *(visits by request).* ▶ Nearby, the 18thC **Town Hall**, formerly the governor's residence; former abbey church of St. Léger (11thC crypt, 13thC chapterhouse and cloister); in the abbey buildings, **Museum** of regional art and archaeology, 19thC painting★, statuary *(10-12 & 2-5; closed Tue.).* ▶ Across the Aisne *(500 m E of Place Alsace-Lorraine)* : ruined **abbey of St. Médard** within a school; 13thC chapterhouse, 11thC crypt, where the tombs of St. Médard and of Clovis's successors, Clothaire and Sigisbert, were found. ▶ S *(400 m NW of the Paris crossroads)* : 13th-14thC façade★ of the former **abbey of St. Jean-des-Vignes**; cloister, refectory, storehouse (13thC), 16th-18thC abbot's residence *(Mar.-Oct. daily ex Tue., 10-12 & 2-5 or 6; Nov.-Feb., Wed., Sat., Sun. only).*

Nearby

▶ **Septmonts** *(7 km S on D1 then D95 left)* : ruins of medieval château. ▶ Near **Condé-sur-Aisne** *(13 km E)* : fort of Condé-Chivres-Val *(1877; 8:30-7 pm).* ▶ **Braine** : 13thC abbey church★ of St. Yved, fine example of early Gothic. ☐

Practical Information ――――――――――

ℹ av. du Gal-Leclerc, ☎ 23.53.08.27.
SNCF ☎ 23.53.07.45/23.53.34.05.

Hotels :
★★★ **Le Picardie**, 6-8, rue Neuve-St-Martin, ☎ 23.53.21.93, AE DC Euro Visa, 33 rm Ⓟ ⚑ ♿ 225. Rest. ♦♦ ♪ ♿ closed Sun eve, 60-200.
★★ **Lion Rouge**, 1, rue G.-Alliaume, ☎ 23.53.31.52, Visa, 33 rm Ⓟ ♨ 200. Rest. ♦ closed Sun (l.s), 70-100.

Restaurant :
♦♦ **Le Grenadin**, 19, rte de Fère-en-Tardenois, ☎ 23.73.20.57, Visa ♨ ♪ closed Mon and Sun eve , Aug, 45-105.

⚠ ★★*Municipal* (100 pl), ☎ 23.59.12.00.

The THIÉRACHE Region*

A-B1
Round trip from Vervins *(75 km, half-day)*

The peaceful countryside is divided by hedges and dotted with black and white cows, whose milk is used to make Maroilles cheese. Along the banks of the Brune or the Heureau, however, fortified churches with turrets and keeps often rise in the midst of the villages. Until the 17thC, the Thiérache was a frontier that suffered from frequent invasion and pillage. The churches served as refuges for both man and beast, equipped with wells and bread ovens in the buildings themselves. About 50 such buildings still exist from

the 12th-15thC. Nine are included in this itinerary; others can be seen near Hirson (near Wimy) and NW of Vervins between Étréaupont and Guise (→ Vervins).

▶ Take the road to Hirson. ▶ **La Bouteille** : rectangular church★ built in sandstone by the Cistercians (ruined abbey of Foigny). ▶ **Plomion** : pink church (16thC) has a square keep with round towers; a chimney leads from the hall of the keep to the roof space, converted into a strongroom. ▶ Nearby, at **Jeantes** : the church of St. Martin (façade framed by solid square towers), modern paintings and stained glass by Charles Eyck (1962). ▶ **Dagny** : farm buildings in cob, latticework barns. ▶ **Brunehamel** : ruined 16thC château. ▶ **Parfondeval** : old houses around a brick church. ▶ **Montcornet** : 12th-13thC church with 16thC turrets on the transept and E end. ▶ **Vigneux** : church with keep and fortified apse. ▶ **Burelles** : keep replaces the bell tower; the upper story of the fortified transept could shelter the entire village. ▶ **Prisces** : four-storey square keep. ▶ **Gronard** : 16thC church with keep and two round towers; attractive square shaded by lime trees. ▶ **Aubenton** : Jean-Mermoz museum *(Sat., Sun.).*☐

TROYES***

Reims 130, Dijon 152, Paris 165 km
pop 64769 ⊠ 10000   B4

Troyes has a rich architectural heritage from the Middle Ages to the Renaissance; mansions, cathedral, churches, and residential quarter are all in good condition. Until the 1970s, much of the half-timbering that gives the town its charm was hidden under plaster; a change in fashion fortunately has brought to light much of the original material.

▶ The **Saint-Jean quarter** : this pedestrian precinct is the centre of life in Troyes. Note : *For security reasons all the churches in Troyes and the environs are closed except for the hours of service and the summer season; keys available from the SI, from 16, Boulevard Carnot (A2), or from the caretakers. Guided tours available.* ▶ The maze of restored streets and alleys (Rues Champeaux, Paillot-de-Montabert, Charbonnet, des Chats) converge on Place Maréchal-Foch (B2) and the **Town Hall** (17thC; B1-2). ▶ **Church of St. Urbain★** (B1, Rue Clemenceau), a 13thC architectural feat whose walls seem no thicker than the stained glass★ (also 13thC), especially in the choir; numerous statues including 16thC Virgin with Grapes★. ▶ **Ste. Madeleine★** (A1-2) : 12thC nave and transept, Renaissance choir and tower, Flamboyant Gothic choir screen★★ (early 16thC, 10 years in the making) with arches as delicate as lace. Statue of St. Marthe★★, a 15thC masterpiece by a master sculptor; in the apse, stained glass★ typical of Renaissance Troyes. ▶ On the other side of Dampierre quay, beyond the infirmary (B1), **Pharmacy museum★** *(daily, 10-12 & 2-6, ex Tue. and nat. hols.),* the **cathedral★★** (C1) : 4 centuries (1208-1638) of brilliant architectural achievement; 13th-14thC stained glass★ in the choir, 15th-16thC in the nave (including the "Mystical Pressing" 1625 by Linard Gontier, symbolically representing Christ as a grapevine); treasury. ▶ To the right of the cathedral, Museum of Modern Art★★, inaugurated in 1982 in the former episcopal palace : the Lévy Collection of Fauvist paintings, including works by Marinot, La Fresnay, Soutine; sculpture by Degas, Maillol, Picasso, Rodin; African and Oceanic art.
Also... ▶ **St. Jean** (B2) : stained glass★ (Martyrdom of Ste Agathe). ▶ **St. Pantaléon** (A2) : 16thC Troyes statuary. ▶ Opposite, **Vauluisan Museum★** : mansion with interesting collection including statuary and costumes. **Maison de l'Outil** (B2, Maurois mansion★) : unique collection of woodworking tools maintained by the Compagnons du Devoir, a craft guild with origins in the Middle Ages *(daily ex nat. hols., 10-12 & 2-6).* ▶ **Library** (Bibliothèque)★ : stained glass by Linard Gontier (Life of Henri IV); **Fine Arts Museum** (same building, different entrance; B1) : archaeology, painting, natural history.

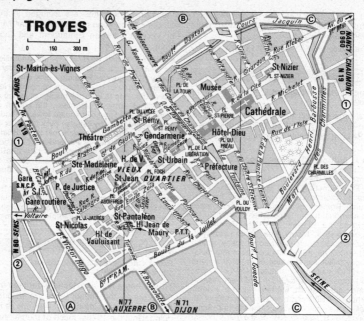

Nearby

▶ To the N and W *(via A1)* : churches of **St. Martin-ès-Vignes** *(1 km N)* : 16th-17thC stained glass★★; **Sainte-Savine** *(1.5 km W)* : paintings on wood panels; **St. André-les-Vergers** *(3 km SSW)* : doorway, 16thC altarpiece. ▶ Church★ of **Pont Sainte-Marie** *(3 km NE)* : stained glass★. ▶ **Barberey-Saint-Sulpice** *(7 km NW)* : Louis XIII château *(exterior visits Aug.-15 Sep., 10-12 & 2-6)*. ▶ **Feuges** *(12 km N)* : Christ★ attributed to the Master of Ste-Marthe. ▶ **Villemaur-sur-Vanne** *(27 km W)* : bell tower; carved wood choirscreen★, stalls. ▶ **Bouilly** *(15 km S on N77)* : altarpiece★ (16thC Troyes), Piétà, statue of Ste. Marguerite. ▶ Church of **Isle-Aumont** : Carolingian choir, Romanesque apse ("nailheads" of oriental origin around the outside window) and Gothic choir *(visits Sun. at 3)*. ▶ **Rumilly-lès-Vaudes** : church★ (painted altarpiece and stained glass); 16thC Tourelles manor house★ with wooden galleries, now the town hall *(groups only)*. □

Practical Information _____

TROYES
ℹ 16, bd Carnot (A2), ☎ 25.73.00.36/25.73.17.24.
✈ *Barberey-Saint-Sulpice*, 5 km N, ☎ 25.72.08.50.
SNCF pl. Mal.-Joffre (A2), ☎ 25.72.50.50/25.72.50.08.
Car rental : *Avis*, 4, av. P.-Brossolette, ☎ 25.73.02.40; train station (A2).

Hotels :
★★★ *Le Grand Hôtel*, (Inter-Hôtel), 4, av. Mal-Joffre (A2), ☎ 25.79.90.90, Tx 840582, Euro Visa, 100 rm ♨ 270. Rest. ♦ *Brasero*, 60-110 ♦*Brasserie le Croco*, 50-100 ♦*Le Champagne* ♪ 90-200 ♦*Louisiane*, closed Mon, 100-150.
★★★ *Poste*, 35, rue E.-Zola (B2), ☎ 25.73.05.05, Tx 840995, AE Euro Visa, 34 rm ♪ 230. Rest. ♦ ♪ ♿ closed Mon and Sun eve. Nicely prepared seasonal dishes, 160-220.
★★★ *Royal*, 22, bd Carnot (A2), ☎ 25.73.19.99, Tx 841015, AE DC Euro Visa, 37 rm ℙ closed 19 Dec-12 Jan, 200. Rest. ♦ ♪ closed Mon noon and Sun eve, 65-120.
★★ *Le Champenois*, 15, rue Pierre-Gauthier (A1),

☎ 25.76.16.05, Visa, 26 rm ℙ ♦ ♨ ♿ ♨ closed Sun eve, 1-23 Aug, 19 Dec-3 Jan, 150.

Restaurant :
♦♦ *Le Bourgogne*, 40, rue Gal-de-Gaulle (A1), ☎ 25.73.02.67 ♨ closed Mon eve and Sun, 2-31 Aug. Predictable, but good. Spec : *biscuit aux fruits de mer et aux pistaches, escalope de foie de canard au vinaigre de framboises*, 100-160.

Recommended
Auction house : 1, rue de la Paix.
♥ crafts : *Les Métiers d'Art*, 1, pl. J.-Jaurès; sweets : *Confiserie de Champagne*, 28, rue Auger, Sainte-Savine.

Nearby

AIX-EN-OTHE, ✉ 10160, 31 km SE.

Hotel :
● ★★★ *Auberge de la Scierie* (L.F.), La Vove, ☎ 25.46.71.26, AE DC Euro Visa, 14 rm ℙ ♦ ♨ ♨ ♪ ♿ ☐ closed Mon eve and Tue (Oct-Mar), 15 Feb-1 Mar, 260. Rest. ● ♦♦ ♦ ♪ ♿ Gastronomy took over this little 17thC mill (see the old works) in 1966 : *andouillette à la fondue de chaource, aiguillettes de canard au vinaigre de cerises*, 105-220; child : 50.

VERVINS

Laon 36, Charleville 72, Paris 172 km
pop 2989 ✉ 02140   A1

The former "capital" of the Thiérache region offers attractive paved streets, slate roofs and the remains of medieval fortifications.

▶ **Church of Notre-Dame** (13th-14thC) : stone and brick gatetower; inside, painting by Jouvenet, Christ in the House of Simon (1699). ▶ **Town Hall** (17thC). ▶ **Coigny Mansion** (16thC) : where Philip II of Spain and Henri IV signed a treaty to end hostilities in 1598; now the sub-prefecture.

Nearby

▶ **Hirson** *(18 km NE)*, an important railway junction; 4 km E, **Benedictine abbey of St. Michel** *(visits by request)* founded 944, rebuilt in 1715 in brick and stone (early Gothic choir, transept with Renaissance triple nave). The valley of the Gland is 30 km² of forest stretching to the Belgian frontier. **Wimy** *(8 km W of Hirson)* : fortified church★ with well, chimney and bread oven. ▶ Between Vervins and Guise to the W, follow the Maubeuge road 8 km to Étréaupont. On the left, the Oise Valley : fortified churches at **Autreppes, Saint-Algis, Englancourt, Marly-Gomont** (turrets, façade with loopholes), **Malzy, Beaurain.** ▶ **Guise** : former fief of the powerful Guise family (château★ incorporating the medieval citadel, under restoration; *9-12 & 2-5:30, 6 or 7 ex Christmas hols.)*; **municipal museum** *(Tue., Fri. 1:30-8, Wed., Thu. 1:30-6:30, Sat. 1:30-6).* **Vadencourt** *(7 km NW)* : collection of 2 500 traditional tools and implements at the Atelier du Bois (woodworking shop; *Sat. and Sun. 9-12 & 2-6).* □

Practical Information ⎯⎯⎯⎯⎯⎯⎯⎯⎯

ⓘ pl. du Gal-de-Gaulle, ☎ 23.98.09.92 (h.s.).
SNCF ☎ 23.98.03.54.

Hotel :
★★★ **La Tour du Roy**, 45, rue du Gal-Leclerc, ☎ 23.98.00.11, AE DC Euro Visa, 15 rm Ⓟ ∰ ⚑ ఈ closed Sun eve, 15 Jan-15 Feb. Henri IV is said to have stayed here, 200. Rest. ● ♦♦ ఈ closed Mon noon and Sun eve (l.s.). The cordial welcome is worthy of the outstanding regional cuisine : *lapin au cidre de Thiérache, ris de veau aux morilles, crêpes soufflées,* 120-250.

VILLERS-COTTERÊTS*

Soissons 23, Meaux 42, Paris 77 km
pop 8402 ⊠ 02600   A2

Museum, rue Desmoutiers *(pm ex Tue.; 1st 3 Sun. of month, 9-12 & 2-5).* **Château** *(open daily)* completed in 1535 for François I by Philibert Delorme, 17thC park designed by Le Nôtre; galleried façade, staircase. At 46 Rue Alexandre-Dumas, birthplace of the writer Alexandre Dumas the elder (1803-1870).

Nearby

▶ **Longpont** *(11 km NE)* : ruins of an abbey consecrated in 1227 in the presence of St. Louis (Louis IX); the 13thC storehouse was turned into a château, rebuilt in the 18thC and restored after 1918 *(10-12 & 2:30-7 ex Thu., Mar.-Oct.; Sat., Sun. and hols., Nov.-Feb.);* 15thC painted panels in parish church, remains of cloister; **Vierzy** *(8 km farther)* : ferme (farm) du Vieux Château (15thC keep, *Jul.-Sep., Sun. pm)* ▶ **Retz Forest** (13 km²) : mostly beech with oak and hornbeam, red and roe deer, boar, pheasants; the northern part is the most attractive. Marked trails to **Montgobert** (woodworking museum in the château; *Apr.-Oct. 10-12 & 2-6 ex Tue., Sun. 2-6).* ▶ **Soucy** : fortified church. ▶ **Saint-Pierre-Aigle.** ▶ **Cœuvres** : château, salt barns, 12th-15thC church. ▶ **La Ferté-Milon** *(10 km S),* birthplace of the author Jean Racine (1629-1699), ruins of 14thC fortress; church of St. Nicolas with fine Renaissance choir. □

Practical Information ⎯⎯⎯⎯⎯⎯⎯⎯⎯

VILLERS-COTTERÊTS
SNCF ☎ 23.96.01.85.

Hotels :
★★★ **Le Régent**, 26, rue du Gal-Mangin, ☎ 23.96.01.46, Tx 150747, AE DC Visa, 17 rm Ⓟ ∰ ⚑ 🏇 ఈ A former coach house with an 18thC façade, 245.
★ **Commerce**, 17, rue du Gal-Mangin, ☎ 23.96.19.97, Visa, 7 rm ⚑ closed Sun eve and Mon, 15 Jan-15 Feb, 130. Rest. ♦ Spec : *fricassée d'escargots forestière, gratin de fruits,* 70-170.

Nearby

La FERTÉ-MILON, ⊠ 02460, 10 km S.

Hotel :
★★ **Racine**, pl. du Port-au-Blé, ☎ 23.96.72.02, 8 rm Ⓟ ∰ ∰ ⚑ A 16thC mansion, 220. Rest. ♦ ∰ ♪ A fixed menu served only for conferences or training sessions. Introductory and advanced painting courses.

LONGPONT, ⊠ 02600, 12 km NE.

Hotel :
★★ **L'Abbaye** (L.F.), rue des Tourelles, ☎ 23.96.02.44, 11 rm Ⓟ ∰ ⚑ View of the abbey and the forest, 200. Rest. ♦ ♪ 70-170.

VITRY-LE-FRANÇOIS

Châlons-sur-Marne 32, Troyes 74, Paris 183 km
pop 18290 ⊠ 51300   B3

An important crossroads town, junction of the Marne-Rhine and Marne-Saône canals, rebuilt after WWII on the ground plan used for its creation under François I.
▶ 17th-18thC cathedral with neo-Classical interior.

Nearby

▶ 10 km N on the Châlons road and right : **Saint-Amand-sur-Fion** : 12th-13thC church with porch, choir★. Numerous timber-framed farmhouses in the village and on the roads *(D60 and D14)* to Vitry.

Practical Information ⎯⎯⎯⎯⎯⎯⎯⎯⎯

ⓘ pl. Giraud, ☎ 26.74.45.30.
SNCF ☎ 26.74.71.86/26.05.50.50.

Hotels :
★★ **Cloche**, 34, rue A.-Briand, ☎ 26.74.03.34, 24 rm Ⓟ ∰ ⚑ 210. Rest. ♦ 90-190.
★★ **Poste**, pl. Royer-Collart, ☎ 26.74.02.65, AE DC Euro Visa, 30 rm, 210. Rest. ♦ closed Sun, 1-21 Aug, 20 Dec-2 Jan, 80-130.

▲ ★★**La Peupleraie** (70 pl), ☎ 26.74.11.00.

VOUZIERS

Charleville 51, Reims 56, Paris 197 km
pop 5214 ⊠ 08400   B2

Birthplace of the historian Hippolyte Taine (1828-1893), an important trade centre in the 16thC, heavily damaged in the two world wars.
▶ **Church of St. Maurille** : 16thC, with Renaissance triple doorway★. ▶ ▶ In the cemetery, monument to Roland Garros, first man to fly the Mediterranean.

Nearby

▶ **Grandpré** *(17 km SE)* : 17thC entrance gates of former château; 15th-16thC church. **Saint-Juvin** *(5 km farther)* : 17thC fortified church. ▶ **Buzancy** *(22 km E on D947)* : 13th-15thC church in Champenois style; château de la Cour, former residence of the dukes of Lorraine. ▶ **Vision de Belval park** *(30 km NE on D947 then 16 km on D6)* : 2 500 acres of forest; animals living wild *(Apr.-15 Nov. 9 or 10-8 or 9 pm).* □

Practical Information ⎯⎯⎯⎯⎯⎯⎯⎯⎯

ⓘ pl. Diderot, ☎ 24.71.76.63 (h.s.); ☎ 24.71.84.59 (l.s.).
SNCF ☎ 24.30.80.13.

Hotel :
★★ **La Ville de Rennes**, 18, rue Chanzy, ☎ 24.71.84.03, Euro Visa, 20 rm Ⓟ ∰ 150. Rest. ♦ ♪ 60-125.

⎯⎯⎯⎯⎯⎯⎯⎯⎯⎯⎯⎯⎯⎯⎯⎯⎯⎯⎯
If you enjoy sports, consult the pages pertaining to the regions; there you will find addresses for practicing your favorite sport.
⎯⎯⎯⎯⎯⎯⎯⎯⎯⎯⎯⎯⎯⎯⎯⎯⎯⎯⎯

WASSY

Saint-Dizier 18, Troyes 75, Paris 228 km
pop 3596 ⊠ 52130   C3

On Sunday 1 March 1562 in a barn near the church, the troops of François de Guise massacred 250 Pro-testants. This "Wassy massacre" began 35 years of internecine religious warfare throughout France.

▶ 17thC **Town Hall** with astronomical clock.

Nearby

▶ Drive through the valley of the Blaise *(38 km)* to **Juzennecourt**. Château de **Cirey-sur-Blaise** *(private)* with medieval keep.   □

Corsica

▶ Corsica, an island with the astonishing diversity of a continent : the snowy peaks of Cinto, the palm trees of the capital Ajaccio, the luminous gulf of Porto, the cool forests of Vizzavona and the burning desert of Les Agriates. It is almost as if the gods had decided to give it a little of everything : mountain torrents, rivers and alpine lakes, alpine pastures and deep chestnut groves, scented *maquis* and immense laricio pinetrees, white limestone cliffs and red rocks. The eye travels in an instant from icy slopes to orange groves, from vineyards to the ever-present sea.

Corsica is a mountain in the Mediterranean, bearing traces of human presence and human labor since Antiquity : terraced hillsides, olive groves and sheep-pens abandoned in the *maquis*, which covers two-thirds of the island in a dense, perfumed mantle. It has always served as a hiding place for bandits, outlaws and those bent on the vendettas that characterized Corsican society.

From the 11th to the 13th century, Corsica was placed under the authority of the Republic of Pisa, and Tuscan architects and masons erected Romanesque churches and chapels, small and perfectly proportioned. Corsica's most famous son is Napoléon Bonaparte, of Italian descent. The island has its own Romance language, which has been undergoing a revival since the early 1970s as a symbol of the region's cultural identity.

Corsican wines are solid and colorful like the island itself. The food is excellent : sausages, smoked hams and salamis with an Italian influence. Wild boar, goat and lamb are popular, and fish and shellfish are found in abundance. Cheese and dishes prepared with sweet chestnuts round off a cuisine that should not be thought inferior to that of the mainland. Corsican craftsmen, supported by craft associations, produce high-quality pottery, wickerwork, wood sculpture, jewelry, knives and woven garments. □

Don't miss

★★★ Bavella Pass B3, The Castagniccia Heights B2, Girolata Bay A2, Porto Bay A2.

★★ Asco Valley B2, Balagne A2, Bonifacio B4, Calvi A2, Cape Corse B1, Casinca B2, Corsican Regional Nature Park A-B2-3, Filitosa A3-4, Niolo A2, Porto-Vecchio Bay B4.

★ Ajaccio A3, Bay of Ajaccio A3, Aléria A3, Bastelica A-B3, Bastia B1, Cargèse A3, Evisa A2, Mariana B2, Ospedale Forest B4, Propriano A4, Saint-Florent B1, Sartène A4, Vizzavona B3.

Weekend tips

First visit : Ajaccio by night, the port, Place Maréchal-Foch, the old town. Next day, drive to Porto : Piana inlet, bay of Porto (lunch) and La Croix pass. Take the inland road back to Ajaccio : Spelunca Gorges, Evisa (stopover), Vico, then via Sagone (quicker) or the Écoliers road : Arbori and Sari d'Orcino.

Brief regional history

6500-ca. 565BC
The first traces of **prehistoric man** in Corsica are relatively recent, dating from the Early Neolithic era. An immigrant, he was principally a hunter-gatherer before progressing to the use of primitive agricultural techniques. ● The **Megalithic period,** ca. 3000-1000BC, saw the arrival of various civilizations, which left traces of their culture in the form of **dolmens** and **menhirs** (stone monuments), forts, and burial vaults. The most interesting are the **menhirs** dating from around 1500BC. Their stylized human forms resemble the stone figures found in the Cyclade Islands.

Facade embellished by staircase

565BC-AD455
Recorded history in Corsica began with the **Phoceans** (Greeks from Asia Minor) who also founded Marseille on the mainland. They founded the city of Alalia (modern Aléria), introduced the cultivation of wheat, olives and vines, and established mining and international trade as well as written communication. ● The subsequent **Roman occupation** of Corsica lasted 6 centuries from 260BC, but remains from this period are meagre, apart from the discoveries at **Aléria** and less significant finds at Mariana, Rome's second colony on the island. ● Even fewer traces were left by the conquered inhabitants. This is not surprising, since they were largely shepherd tribes, who supplemented their staple diet by gathering honey and hunting boar.

Near Porto-Vecchio

455-1077
Successive **invasions** (Vandals, Ostrogoths, Byzantines and Lombards) brought anarchy and poverty after the relative security of Roman rule. This turbulent period saw the rise of an aristocracy of native Corsicans. As they fought for land and power, these aristocrats did not hesitate to form alliances with one or other of the foreign powers — namely, **Pisa** or **Genoa** — that were contending for possession of Corsica.

1077-1755
Long after the **Pax Romana**, the **Pax Pisana** — rule by the Italian city-state of Pisa — was established (1077-1284). ● Trade increased greatly during this period, and many churches were built (→ box). **Genoa** took over the island after finally defeating Pisa in the naval battle of Méloria (1284). ● The Genoese held sway for 484 years, and founded or fortified the towns of Calvi, Ajaccio, Porto-Vecchio, Bastia and Saint-Florent. Watchtowers erected by the Genoese for defense are still in existence on many parts of the coast. ● Faced with both anarchy and Genoese exploitation, the native Corsicans made various attempts to seize control of their destiny. The **Terre du Commun** revolt of 1384, the struggles led by **Sampiero Corso** in 1564 and the War of Independence between 1729 and 1769 (the 40 Years' War) ultimately led to annexation by France, which had already intervened several times, either on her own account (1553) or at the request of Genoa (1737, 1747).

1755 to the present day
In 1755 the Corsicans declared **Pascal Paoli** "General of the Nation"; a new constitution was proclaimed, the economy was reorganized, the Univer-

Cape Corse

Facts and figures
Location : *82 km from Italy, 180 km from mainland France.*
Area : *8721 km² (vs. Sardinia, 24089 km²); max. length 183 km; max. width 83 km.*
Climate : *Mediterranean. Av. temp. > 12 °C : Ajaccio 14.7°, Bastia 15.2°; sea temp. : May 16 °C, Jun. 19°, Jul. 22°, Aug. 23°, Sep. 22°, Oct. 20°.*
Population : *240178; working : 81310; towns 125000 (Ajaccio and Bastia 100000).*
Administration : *Department of* **Southern Corsica,** *Prefecture Ajaccio; Department of* **Upper Corsica,** *Prefecture Bastia.*

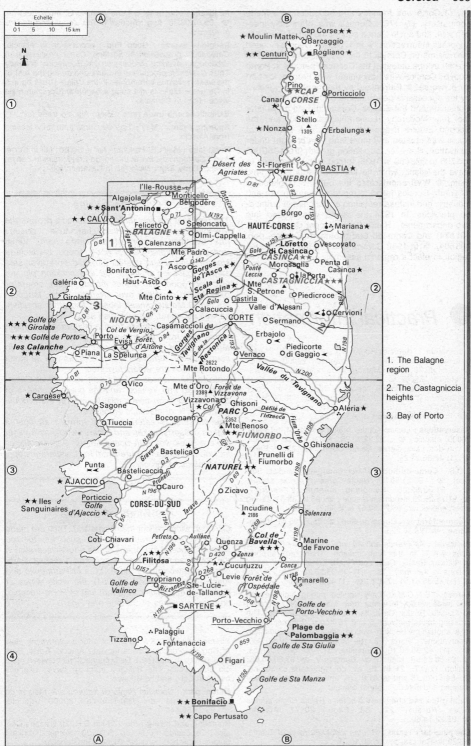

Echelle
01 5 10 15 km

N

★ Moulin Mattei — Cap Corse ★★
○ Barcaggio
★★ Centuri ○ ■ Rogliano ★

Pino ○
★★ CAP ○ Porticciolo
Canari ○ CORSE
★★
Stello
★ Nonza ○ ▲ ○ Erbalunga ★
1305

Désert des St-Florent ★ ___
Agriates ○ ★ BASTIA ★
NEBBIO

l'Ile-Rousse
Algajola ○ Monticello ○ Borgo ○
★★ Sant'Antonino ■ ○ Belgodère
★★★ CALVI ○ Feliceto ○ HAUTE-CORSE ○ ·★· Mariana ★
BALAGNE ★★ ○ Spelontato
○ Olmi-Cappella ★★ Loretto
Calenzana ○ Golo *di Casinca* ○ ○ Vescovato
Mte Padro ○ *CASINCA* ★★
Bonifato ○ Asco ○ *Gorges* Ponte Morosaglia ○ Penta di
Haut-Asco ○ *de l'Asco* Leccia ○ ○ ○ la Porta Casinca ★
Galéria ○ *Scala di* Mte ○ *CASTAGNICCIA* ★★★
Girolata ○ Mte Cinto ★★ *Sta Regina* S. Petrone ○ Piedicroce
★★★ *Golfe de* Golo ○ Castirla ○
Girolata *NIOLO* ★★ ○ Calacuccia Valle d'Alesani
★★★ *Golfe de Porto* ○ Col de Vergio ○ Casamaccioli *du* CORTE ○ Sermano ○ Cervioni ★
les Calanche Porto ○ Forêt ○ *Gorges* Erbajolo ○
★★★ Evisa ○ *d'Aitone* *du* ○ Piedicorte
○ Piana ○ La Spelunca *Restonica* ○ *Tavignano* ○ di Gaggio
2622 Venaco ○
Mte Rotondo ▲ *Vallée du Tavignano*

○ Vico Mte d'Oro *Forêt de* *N 200*
★ Cargèse ○ 2389 ▲ *Vizzavona*
○ Sagone Vizzavona
Bocognano ○ Ghisoni ○ *Défilé de*
○ Tiuccia ★ Col *PARC* *l'Inzecca* Aléria ★
2352 ▲ Mte Renoso
FIUMORBO
★ Bastelica ○ Ghisonaccia ○
Punta Prunelli di
Bastelicaccia ○ *NATUREL* ★★ Fiumorbo
★ AJACCIO ○ ○ Cauro ○ Zicavo
★★ Iles Porticcio *Golfe*
Sanguinaires ○ *d'Ajaccio* ★ Incudine
2186 ▲ ○ Solenzara
Coti-Chiavari ○ Petreto ○ Aullène *Col de*
Quenza ○ *Bavella* Marine
★★★ Filitosa ○ Zonza ○ ★★★ de Favone
Golfe de Propriano ○ Cucuruzzu ○ ○ Levie *Forêt de* Pinarello ○
Valinco Ste-Lucie- *l'Ospédale*
de-Talland ★ *Golfe de*
★ SARTENE ★ *Porto-Vecchio* ★★
Porto-Vecchio ○
○ Palaggiu *Plage de*
○ Fontanaccia *Palombaggia* ★★
Tizzano ○ *Golfe de Sta Giulia*
○ Figari
Golfe de Sta Manza

★★ Bonifacio ■
★★ Capo Pertusato

CORSE-DU-SUD

1. The Balagne region
2. The Castagniccia heights
3. Bay of Porto

sity of Corte was founded and education was made compulsory. By 1762, Corsica was practically independent, and again Genoa sought the aid of France to suppress insurrection. ● In 1768, the Genoese ceded their claims on Corsica to the French. On **8 May 1769** French troops defeated the Corsican patriots at **Ponte Nuovo**; Corsica was now united with France, for better or worse. ● Patronized by the monarchy, ignored by the successive governments of the Revolution, the Consulate and the Empire, Corsica thrived only under the July Monarchy (Louis-Philippe, 1830) and the Second Empire (Napoléon III, 1852). A network of roads was created and more land was brought under cultivation. However, population growth (from 150 000 in 1796 to 322 000 in 1936) forced many Corsicans to leave the island, which lacked the resources to feed them. ● **WWI accelerated the outflow.** Depleted of its youth, Corsica failed to modernize agriculture and industry, and instead remained entrenched in outmoded practices. In 1974 the island was divided into two departments : **Haute Corse** (Upper Corsica, pop. 131 574) and **Corse du Sud** (Southern Corsica, pop. 108 604). ● In 1982 Corsica became the first French region to elect a regional assembly.

 Practical information

Information : *Agence Régionale du Tourisme et des Loisirs (A.R.T.L.),* 22, cours Grandval, 20000 Ajaccio, ☎ 95.51.00.22 ; **Paris** : *Maison de la Corse,* 12, rue Godot-de-Mauroy, 75009, ☎ (1) 47.42.04.34. *Dir. régionale de la Jeunesse et des Sports,* résidence Triana, 15, av. Colonel-Colonna-d'Ornano, 20000 Ajaccio, ☎ 95.23.38.52. *Dir. rég. des Affaires culturelles,* 19, cours Napoléon, B.P. 301, 20179 Ajaccio Cedex, ☎ 95.21.70.27.

Reservations : *Loisirs-Accueil région Corse,* 24, bd Paoli, 20000 Ajaccio, ☎ 92.22.70.79. *Paris Corse Accueil,* 3, rue des Lavandières, Sainte-Opportune, 75001 Paris, ☎ (1) 42.36.23.29.

S.O.S. : **Corse-du-Sud** : *SAMU* (Emergency Medical Service), ☎ 95.21.50.50. **Haute-Corse** : *police station,* ☎ 91.33.52.06. *Poisoning emergency centre :* ☎ 91.75.25.25. *Mountain rescue :* ☎ 95.23.30.31. *Diving emergencies,* ☎ 95.21.52.67 and 95.21.37.02.

Weather forecast : Corse-du-Sud : ☎ 95.21.05.81. **Haute-Corse :** ☎ 95.36.22.97.

Air travel : *Air France* and *Air Inter* offer daily flights, as does *T.A.T.* in the high season. There are airports at Ajaccio, Bastia, Calvi and Figari. Enquiries and reservations : *Air Inter,* ☎ (1) 45.39.25.25 ; *Air France,* ☎ (1) 45.35.61.61 ; *T.A.T.,* ☎ (1) 42.61.85.85.

Ferries : *S.N.C.M. :* Daily service during high season and twice weekly in winter from Marseille, Nice, Toulon to Ajaccio, Bastia, Calvi, Ile-Rousse and Propriano. The crossing takes between 5 and 10 hours. Summer crossings should be booked well in advance. Enquiries and reservations : Paris, 12, rue Godot-de-Mauroy, 75009, ☎ (1) 42.66.60.19 ; Marseille, 61, bd des Dames, ☎ 91.56.34.96 ; Nice, 3, av. Gustave-V, ☎ 93.88.60.63 ; Toulon, *C.M.T.,* 21 et 49, av. de l'Infanterie-de-Marine, ☎ 94.41.25.76 and 94.41.01.76, and in all major railway stations and *S.N.C.F.* tourist offices.

Rural gîtes and chambres d'hôtes : *Relais Régional des Gîtes Ruraux,* 22, bd Paoli, 20177 Ajaccio, ☎ 95.22.14.60.

Camping-cars rental : *Routes insolites,* road of Bastia, 20220 Ile-Rousse, ☎ 95.60.16.01.

Festivals : end of jul : *Aléria in Allegria,* music festival, ☎ 95.57.03.73. **Aug :** *festival of folk songs and dances in Ajaccio.*

Religious events : Good Frid : *procession* in Ajaccio, *Catenacciu procession* in Sartène, *Cerca procession* in Erbalunga, *evening procession* in Bonifacio ; **Maundy Thu :** *Canistrelli procession* in Calvi, and during the rest of the week, religious ceremonies in the Uniate Greek church in Cargèse. Mass is still sung *a paghiella* (Corsican male voice choir) in Sermano.

Exhibitions and trade fairs : May : Ajaccio *trade fair.*

Sporting events : May : *Tour de Corse* auto rally, leaving from Ajaccio.

Rural fairs : May : *St-Pancrace fair* in Sorbo ; *fair in Corte.* **Aug :** *Castagniccia fair* at the col de Prato ; *fairs* in Zonza, Renno. **Early Sep :** *Niolo fair* in Casamaccioli.

Corsican cuisine

The pigs that run wild through the maquis provide the raw material for an excellent charcuterie : prisuttu (the Corsican version of prosciutto ham), lonzu *(rolled and smoked fillet of pork),* coppa, salciccie *(a kind of salami) and* figatelli *(smoked pork liver sausage). Roast leg of lamb, kid and suckling pig are also very good. Fish dishes include mullet, bream or bass baked or grilled over aromatic herbs, langoustes (small Mediterranean lobster) and other shellfish, as well as* azimu, *the local fish soup.*
Brocciu, *a cheese made from a mixture of whey and whole milk from either ewes or goats, is an important ingredient in Corsican cooking. It adds flavour to soups, cakes, turnovers and fritters, as well as pasta dishes, which are widely favoured.*
Noteworthy cheeses are the soft varieties of Calenzana, Niolo and Venaco, and the pressed cheese of Sartène. Corsican ewe's milk is used in the production of 10 % of mainland Roquefort.
The chestnut is eaten in many forms : as flour it makes desserts, cakes and fritters ; whole as a vegetable it goes well with boiled fennel. Popular dishes include omelettes flavoured with mint, asparagus tips, mushrooms, or brocciu.

The wines of Corsica

Corsican wines reflect their homeland. They are made from recognized grape varieties, such as, for red wine, "nielluccio" in Upper Corsica and "sciacarello" in the south, and for white, muscat and malmsey. Particularly noteworthy are the A.O.C.s of Patrimonio and Ajaccio (first classified in 1984), the white wines of Cape Corse (Rogliano, Centuri) and of Porto-Vecchio, and the red wines of Sartène and Figari.

Scenic railways : *S.N.C.F.* lines offer a captivating view of Corsica. Principal towns served : Ajaccio, Corte, Bastia, Ile-Rousse and Calvi. Daily connections between Ajaccio and Bastia. The *Balagne tramway* serves beaches between Calvi and Ile-Rousse.

Nature park : *Corsican Regional Nature Park,* Maison du Parc, 4, rue du Gal-Fiorella, 20000 Ajaccio, ☎ 95.21.56.54.

Rambling and hiking : the 173-km G.R. 20 crosses Corsica. Topoguide *I.G.N.* du G.R. 20, Michel Fabrikant guides published by Didier Richard in Grenoble.

Riding holidays : 1 000 km trails with gîtes, *Association Régionale du Tourisme Équestre Corse*, M. Giorgi, 9, bd Pugliesi-Conti, 20000 Ajaccio, ☎ 95.21.48.79.

Instructional courses : mountain ecology and photography, climbing : *Muntagne corse in liberta*, parc Billelo, imm. Girolata, av. Napoléon-III, 20000 Ajaccio, ☎ 95.23.17.42 after 7:30 pm. **Paris** : ☎ (1) 47.26.03.84.

Beautiful beaches

In July and August empty beaches exist only in the imagination. However, certain parts of the Corsican coast are so difficult to reach by land that they remain the preserve of boating enthusiasts : Saleccia (→ Agriates Desert), Girolata (→ Porto). On Cape Corse, Barcaggio and Nonza beaches are usually quiet even at the height of the season. The most beautiful beaches of fine sand are in the bay of Valinco (→ Propriano) and around Porto-Vecchio (→), but first prize goes to Palombaggia, with its red rocks and umbrella pines. Another superb seascape is the cove at Ficajola, near Piana (→ Porto). On the east coast, the beaches are huge stretches of sand, bordered by hotels and holiday villages; they are particularly suitable for children, since the sea is warm and shallow. Calvi beach (→) has 7 km of sand surrounded by pine forest.

Wine guide : *Groupement interprofessionnel des vins de l'Ile de Corse*, 6, rue Gabriel-Péri, 20200 Bastia, ☎ 95.31.37.36.

Children : rambling and hiking for families with young children organized by *Montagne corse in liberta* (address above). Day care provided for infants.

Aquatic sports : Sailing : *Ligue corse de voile*, President, M. J. Frigara, fossés de la Citadelle, 20000 Ajaccio, ☎ 95.21.07.79. Marinas : *Fédération corse des ports de plaisance*, 24, rue Napoléon, 20200 Bastia, ☎ 95.31.01.15.

Scuba diving : *Fédération Française d'Études et de Sports sous-marins*, M. J. Bellan, 25, bd Dominique-Paoli, 20000 Ajaccio, ☎ 95.22.23.78.

Canoeing : especially in Mar, Apr and May. M. Santonacci, rte des Sanguinaires (Barbicaja), 20000 Ajaccio, ☎ 95.52.01.46.

Potholing and spelunking : *Association Spéléologique Corse*, 2, rue Martinetti, 20000 Ajaccio, ☎ 95.21.68.21.

Climbing-mountaineering : *Associu di i Muntagnoli Corsi*, quartier Santa-Maria, 20122 Quenza, ☎ 95.78.61.25 and in Sollacaro, ☎ 95.74.62.28.

Winter sports : Dec-Apr. : info. at resorts at the Col du Vergio, Haut-Asco and Ghisoni-Capannelle. Cross-country skiing in Bastelica, Quenza, Evisa and Zivaco; enq. : *S.I.* Ajaccio, Bastia.

Hunting and shooting : *Féd. Dép. des Chasseurs de la Corse-du-Sud,* 19, av. Beverini, 20000 Ajaccio, ☎ 95.23.16.91. *Féd. Dép. de la Haute-Corse,* M. D. Mezzadri, résidence Nouvelle-Corniche, Saint-Joseph, 20200 Bastia, ☎ 95.32.25.99.

Fishing : *Féd. Dép. de Pêche et de Pisciculture*, President M. Martini, 7, bd Paoli, Bastia, ☎ 95.31.47.31. *Féd. inter-dép. de Pêche et de Pisciculture*, 13, rue du Dr-Del-Pellegrino, 20000 Ajaccio, ☎ 95.23.13.32.

 Towns and places

AGRIATES Desert

B1

D81 runs through 30 km of parched landscape that was once the granary of Corsica. Apart from a few houses at **Casta** *(12 km W of Saint-Florent)*, a few shepherds' stone huts are the only habitations in the 160 km².

▶ From Casta, a difficult road *(12 km, negotiable at low speed)* leads to **Saleccia Beach★★** (restaurant). ☐

AJACCIO*

Corte 83, Bastia 153, Calvi 159 km
pop 55000 ⊠ 20000   A3

The colours in the magnificent bay change with the hours and the weather. New white buildings rise above red-tiled roofs and terra-cotta façades that have scarcely changed since the young Napoléon played in a cave on the site of the Place d'Austerlitz.

▶ **Place Maréchal-Foch★** (C2) : palm trees, fountain and restaurant terraces a few steps from the car-ferry dock. This is the social centre of Ajaccio where local residents traditionally stop for a *pàstis* (anise-flavoured alcoholic drink) before lunch. ▶ In the Town Hall, the **Napoleonic Museum** *(9-12 & 2:30-5:30; 2-5 in winter)* commemorates the Emperor (Napoléon's baptismal certificate and other memorabilia). ▶ Each morning the neighbourhood market bustles with noise and colour as choice Corsican produce (cheese, *charcuterie, beignets,* fritters) is laid out for the day. ▶ **Fesch Palace** (C2), built in 1827 by Cardinal Fesch

(Napoléon's uncle); Imperial Chapel, burial vault of the Bonaparte family. The Fesch Museum★★ *(closed for restoration)* boasts 1200 paintings covering 5 centuries of Italian art. ▶ The **Bonaparte House★** (C2; *9-12 & 2-6, summer; 10-12 & 2-5, winter; closed Sun. pm and Mon. am)* : Napoléon I was born here on 15 Aug. 1769. The whitewashed walls of his room contrast with the luxurious decoration of the adjacent rooms. ▶ **Cathedral** (C3), built in 1593 in the Venetian style; the first chapel on the left displays the Virgin of the Sacred Heart★ by Eugène Delacroix.

Nearby

▶ **Les Milelli** *(4 km NW)* : the Bonaparte family property, in an olive grove above the bay of Ajaccio (festival in summer). ▶ **Punta Castle** *(13 km NW; closed due to fire damage)* : 19thC copy of a pavilion in the Tuileries in Paris. View★★ of the bay of Ajaccio. ☐

Practical Information _____

AJACCIO
ⓘ hôtel de ville, pl. Mal-Foch (C2),
☎ 95.21.53.39/95.21.40.87.
✈ *Campo dell'Oro*, 7 km E, ☎ 95.21.07.07. Air France desk, at airport, ☎ 95.20.36.60; Air France office, 3, bd du Roi-Jérôme (C2), ☎ 95.21.16.36.
SNCF (C1), ☎ 95.23.11.03.
⛴ *S.N.C.M.*, quai Lherminier (C2), ☎ 95.21.90.70.
Car rental : Avis, Campo dell Oro airport, ☎ 95.23.25.14; Diamant-III building, av. de Paris (B2), ☎ 95.21.01.86.

Hotels :
★★★★ *Campo dell'Oro,* (Mapotel), Ricanto beach, ☎ 95.22.32.41, Tx 460087, AE DC Euro Visa, 140 rm Ⓟ ⦃

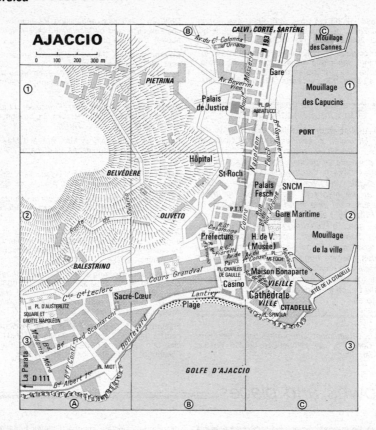

〰 ♪ ⅙ 🖃 650. Rest. ♦♦♦ ♪ ⚘ closed Jan-Feb. A good restaurant that gets better all the time : another plus for this fine hotel, 180-250 ; child : 90.
● ★★★ *Albion*, 15, av. Gal-Leclerc (A3), ☎ 95.21.66.70, Tx 460846, AE DC Euro Visa, 63 rm ℗ ♪ 270.
● ★★★ *Costa*, 2, bd Colomba (B3), ☎ 95.21.43.02, AE DC Euro Visa, 53 rm ⅙ 〰 ⚘ 245.
★★★ *Fesch*, 7, rue Cardinal-Fesch (C2), ☎ 95.21.50.52, Tx 460084, AE DC Euro Visa, 77 rm, 265.
★★★ *Napoléon*, 4, rue Lorenzo-Véro (B2), ☎ 95.21.30.01, Tx 460625, AE DC Euro Visa, 62 rm, 290.
● ★★ *San-Carlu*, (I.L.A.,L.F.), 8, bd Danielle-Casanova (C3), ☎ 95.21.13.84, AE DC Euro Visa, 44 rm ⅙ ⚘ 250.
★★ *Spunta di Mare*, Saint-Joseph (C2), ☎ 95.22.41.42, AE DC, 64 rm ℗ ⅙ 〰 ♪ half pens (h.s.), closed 20 Dec-20 Jan, 380. Rest. ♦ ♪ closed 15 Dec-15 Jan, 60-110.

Restaurants :
● ♦♦ *L'Amore Piattu*, 8, pl. du Gal-de-Gaulle (B2), ☎ 95.51.00.53, closed Sun and lunch, 1-20 Aug. You simply must dine at Marie-Louise Maestracci's delightful little restaurant for the straight-forward family-style fare offered on the single set-price menu, 140.
♦♦ *Les Palmiers*, 3, pl. Foch (C2), ☎ 95.21.02.45, AE DC Euro Visa ⅙ closed 1 Nov-1 Apr. A fashionable eatery near the port, 70-110.
♦♦ *Point U*, 59 *bis*, rue Fesch (C2), ☎ 95.21.59.92 ♪ closed Wed, 15 Mar-15 Apr. Regional cooking and fresh fish, 80-170.
● ♦ *Côte d'Azur*, 12, cours Napoléon (C3), ☎ 95.21.50.24, AE DC Visa ♪ closed Sun, 20 Jun-20 Jul. Marc Lamic cooks for mainland folk stuck in their ways as well as for finicky, food-loving Corsicans : *terrine de*

poulet aux foies de volailles, cuisse de canard rôtie. Corsican dessert wines, muscat and malvoisie, 95-170.
♦ *A Tinella*, 86, rue Fesch (C2), ☎ 95.21.13.68, AE DC Euro Visa ♪ ⚘ closed Mon, 25 Oct-18 Nov. Nestled in an old house, the kitchen produces fresh, ever-more-polished cuisine : *marmite du pêcheur, ris de veau aux pâtes vertes,* 75-200.
♦ *France*, 59, rue Fesch (C2), ☎ 95.21.11.00 ♪ closed Sun, Nov. The unexpected but pleasant marriage of Corsican and Périgourdine cuisines, 50-150.
♦ *U Scalone*, 2, rue du Roi-de-Rome (C2-3), ☎ 95.21.50.05, Euro Visa, closed Sun, 1-21 Dec. In the heart of the city, good Lyonnais cooking. Splendid meat, 130-150.

Recommended
Bicycle rental : airport, ☎ 95.23.22.19 ; Ets Solvet, 5, rue Maglioli, ☎ 95.23.20.31 ; *Centre commercial Castellani*, ☎ 95.22.27.68.
Camping-car rental : *Campo dell'Oro* airport.
Casino : bd Lantivy (B3), ☎ 95.21.41.44.
Diving rental : *Aux Pêcheurs*, Commercial port, ☎ 95.21.68.07. Air pump and spare parts.
Events : crafts fair, in Jul ; folk festival, in Aug.
Guide to wines : Alzeto, *Sari d'Urcinu*, Cinarca road, ☎ 95.28.20.67 ; *Comte Peraldi*, ☎ 95.22.37.30 ; at Pisciatella, *Bianchetti*, clos Capitoro, Sartene road.
Leisure activities : *Au Son des Guitares*, 7, rue du Roi-de-Rome (C3). Traditionnal Corsican songs and cooking served up by Antoine Bonelli, formerly a guitarist with the late Tino Rossi.
Marina : *La Citadelle*, ☎ 95.21.23.01, (250 pl.) ; *l'Amirauté*, ☎ 95.22.31.98, (440 pl.).
Nightclubs : *Dolce Vita*, ☎ 95.21.35.20 ; *Le Roi Jérôme*,

☎ 95.21.39.66; *L'Octogone*, ☎ 95.21.41.14; *Le Week-End*, ☎ 95.52.01.39; *Palm Beach*, ☎ 95.52.01.03.
♥ *Loviconi Valérie*, 6, rue Fesch; Corsican crafts : *Casa di l'Artigiani*, 9, rue Notre-Dame (C2); Corsican specialities : *Y. Leca*, 3, rue Fesch.

Nearby

BALEONE, ⊠ 20167, 8 km NE on the N 193.

Restaurant :
♦♦ *Chez Maïsetti*, ☎ 95.22.37.19 ⧉ closed Sun. Pierrette runs a veritable showcase for Corsican family cooking. In season : *artichaut au brocciu, cabri à la corse grillé, truite de torrent, beignets à la farine de châtaigne*. Local wines, 80-150.

FAVONE, ⊠ 20144, 9 km SE.

Hotel :
★★ *U Dragulinu*, ☎ 95.57.20.30, Visa, 26 rm ℗ ⟨ ⚇ ⌇ half pens (h.s.), 475. Rest. ♦ ⟨ ⌇ ⧉ ⚘ 85-160; child : 35.

⚠ ★★*Bon Annon* (100 pl), ☎ 95.57.24.35.

Bay of AJACCIO*

A3

The bay of Ajaccio, angular in the N, more tortuous in the S, is comparable in beauty to the bay of Naples. Encircling mountains present a majestic backdrop to the sea. Inlets, beaches and natural anchorage make this one of the most popular vacation spots on the island.

Sanguinaires Road *(12 km W)*

▶ Along the cliff road *(corniche)*, hewn from the granite around the bay, villas and luxury hotels stand incongruously next to the grandiose funerary chapels that face the roads and highways, according to Corsican custom. The beaches at Scudo and Vignola offer superb aquatic sports. The road ends at a tower built by the Genoese at **Parata Point**. The view★ takes in the entire bay and the **Sanguinaires Islands** beyond. ▶ **Sanguinaires Islands**★★ *(motorboats leave from Ajaccio, opposite Place Maréchal-Foch; 9 and 2, Apr.-Oct.; 3hr round trip)* : the French author Alphonse Daudet (1840-97) lived for a year at the lighthouse on the largest of these islets. He left a vivid record of his impressions in his humorous sketches of Provençal life, *Lettres de mon moulin*. □

Porticcio and the mountain road★ *(83 km round trip, half-day)*

▶ Beyond the airport at **Campo dell'Oro** the S coast of the Bay of Ajaccio has been extensively developed for tourism. ▶ **Porticcio**, across from Ajaccio : the focal point of seafront development. ▶ Port of **Chiavari** and **Verghia** beach backed by pine forest. 6 km of narrow road leads to **Castagna Point** (view★). ▶ Leaving the bay, the road plunges into thick *maquis* (→ box) with glimpses of the sea★ along the way. ▶ **Coti-Chiavari** : a village on the hillside above the bay. ▶ Drive to the TV relay station, where the view★ takes in the bays of Ajaccio and **Valinco**. ▶ To take the road across the mountains go back 1.3 km on the Ajaccio road then follow D55 *(right)* through a terrain covered with heather, arbutus, filaria and cistus, the combination known to local people as *le maquis dense*. ▶ The passes at Cortone (625 m), Chenova (629 m) and Belle-valle (522 m) offer impressive views. □

Practical Information _____

BASTELICACCIA, ⊠ 20166 Porticcio, 8 km NE.

Restaurant :
♦♦ *Auberge Seta*, ☎ 95.20.00.16 ℗ ⟨ closed Wed , Jan. Food to delight Corsicans and mainlanders alike : *charcuterie, terrine de merle*, charcoal-grilled lamb, boar in season, 120-180.

Recommended
Holiday cottages : *Les Amandiers de Fontanaccia*, ☎ 95.20.02.58.

PORTICCIO, ⊠ 20166, 17 km SE.
⑴ ☎ 95.25.05.74.
Car rental : *Avis*, Hôtel Résidence Marina Viva, ☎ 95.25.03.15. (Open from 1st Jan. to 1st Oct.)

Hotels :
● ★★★★(L) *Sofitel Thalassa*, ☎ 95.25.00.34, Tx 460708, AE DC Euro Visa, 100 rm ℗ ⟨ ⚇ ⌇ ⌂ ⚘ half pens (h.s.). Private beach, water skiing, diving, ocean spa, 1680. Rest. ● ♦♦♦ *Le Caroubier* ⟨ ⌇ ⚘ Chef Dulucq carries on the Sofitel's culinary tradition with a happy blend of Corsican and continental specialities : *cassolette d'escargots à la corse, omelette de bruccio à la menthe, andouillette de mérou au jus de persil*. Corsican and other French wines, 195-350.
★★★★ *Maquis*, (I.L.A.), ☎ 95.25.05.55, 20 rm 2 apt ℗ ⟨ ⚇ ⌂ ⚘ half pens. A group of attractive old houses and a private beach, 360. Rest. ♦♦ The overloaded menu could use a little pruning, and the young staff lacks experience, but the home-made tagliatelle are a treat. Corsican wines, 170-260.
★★ *Isolella*, ☎ 95.25.41.36, Visa, 32 rm ℗ ⟨ ⌇ ⚘ half pens (h.s.), 440. Rest. ♦ ⟨ ⌇ ⧉ closed Nov-Mar, 65-240.

Restaurant :
♦ *Le Club*, on the beach, ☎ 95.25.00.42 ⚇ ⌇ Fresh fish buffet, 100-180.

⚠ ★★★★*Benista* (200 pl), ☎ 95.20.04.41; at U Prunelli, ★★★*Pisciatello* (300 pl), ☎ 95.20.00.51.

Recommended
Nightclubs : *Liberty*, ☎ 95.25.07.00; *Blue Moon*, ☎ 95.25.07.70.

Route des SANGUINAIRES.

Hotels :
● ★★★★ *Eden Roc* (R.C.), ☎ 95.52.01.47, Tx 460486, AE DC Visa, 34 rm ℗ ⟨ ⚇ ⌂ ⚘ pens (h.s.), closed 30 Sep-4 May, 1200. Rest. ♦♦♦ ⟨ ⌇ ⚘ Excellent varied fare for pampered lodgers, 230.
★★★ *Dolce Vita*, ☎ 95.52.00.93, AE DC Euro Visa, 33 rm ℗ ⟨ ⚇ ⌂ pens, half pens (h.s.), closed 20 Sep-30 Mar, 915. Rest. ♦♦ Spec : assorted marinated fish, *timbale de pâtes fraîches, civet de langouste*, 70-150.
★★★ *Sun Beach*, ☎ 95.21.55.81, Tx 460088, AE DC Euro Visa, 87 rm ℗ ⟨ ⚇ ⌇ ⚘ ⌂ ⚘ half pens (h.s.), closed 1 Nov-21 Mar, 250. Rest. ♦ ⟨ ⌇ ⧉ 80-150; child : 40.

Restaurants :
♦ *Auberge de la Terre Sacrée*, ☎ 95.52.00.92 ⟨ ⚇ ⚘ closed Oct. It's authentically Corsican, tasty and cheap, 120-150.
♦ *I Sanguinari*, at Parata Point, ☎ 95.52.01.70 ⟨ closed eve (l.s.). In 1863, Alphonse Daudet, showing excellent taste, stayed on the largest of these islets. Today, the Corsican fare is simple and good, the sun is always shining and smiles would be appreciated. Sea urchins in season, 100-150.

⚠ ★★★*Château de Barbicaggia* (100 pl), ☎ 95.52.01.17.

ALÉRIA*

Corte 50, Bastia 72, Ajaccio 112 km
pop 2410 ⊠ 20270   B3

In ancient times, Aléria was the capital of Corsica by virtue of its strategic position straddling sea-routes to the eastern Mediterranean. Alalia, as the port was known to the Greeks who founded it in about 565BC, prospered through trade with Greece, Italy, Sicily, Gaul, Spain and Carthage. In 259BC the Romans took Alalia and used it as their base of operations for the colonization of Corsica.

▶ **Museum★** *(8-12 & 2-7, 5 in winter)* : permanent display of archaeological finds from ancient Alalia; funerary relics, weapons and ceramics★ illustrate the importance of the E coast of Corsica to economic and military expansion in the ancient world. The entrance ticket also covers the Roman excavations (forum, temple, baths, law courts). □

Practical Information ⎯⎯⎯⎯⎯⎯⎯⎯⎯⎯⎯

ℹ mairie, ☎ 95.57.00.73.

Hotel :
★ *Les Orangers*, Cateraggio, ☎ 95.57.00.31, Visa, 13 rm
Ⓟ ⌂ ✿ closed Sun eve (l.s.), 130. Rest. ♦ 50-120.

▲ ★★★*Marina d'Aléria* (100 pl), ☎ 95.57.01.42.

ASCO Valley**

B2
Road through the Asco Valley *(30 km from Ponte Leccia)*

The river Asco winds through the austere but magnificent landscape of the highest mountains in Corsica. Rugged snow-covered peaks exceeding 2000 m in altitude, pine forest, granite walls channeling the torrent, a low scrub-covered valley, holm oak and alders rising out of a barren plain : such drastic changes within only a few kilometres are typical of Corsica. The Asco Valley subsists on a mountain economy based on forestry and livestock ; the rich countryside of Balagne provides pasturage during the winter. Formerly, the women of the valley wove goat hair and wool, while the men made wooden buckets, milkpails, spoons, ladles and moulds for the *brocciu* cheese. Asco is the habitat of the bearded vulture, an endangered species with a wingspan exceeding 2.5 m. Wild sheep *(mouflons)* are protected in a nature reserve in the upper valley.

▶ 2 km along the Calvi road, then straight down D47.
▶ **Asco**, at the mouth of the river gorges, the only village in the valley : the area attracts hunters, anglers, botanists and climbers ; honey from the region is especially prized.
▶ **Haut-Asco** : skiing from Dec. to Apr. ; in summer Haut-Asco becomes a base camp for mountaineers' assaults on **Monte Cinto** (2710 m), the highest peak in Corsica ; an easy but time-consuming climb *(6hr up, 4hr down)*; panorama★★. □

Practical Information ⎯⎯⎯⎯⎯⎯⎯⎯⎯⎯⎯

ASCO ET HAUT-ASCO, ⊠ 20276.
☳ 1450-1820m.
ℹ mairie d'Asco, ☎ 95.47.82.07.

Hotel :
★ *Le Chalet*, Haut-Asco, ☎ 95.47.81.08, 22 rm Ⓟ ⌂ ⓓ half pens (h.s.), closed 31 Sep-1 Jan. View over the Cinto Massif, 320. Rest. ♦ ⌂ 60-70.

The BALAGNE Region**

A2
Round trip *(99 km, full day ; see map 1)*

This oil and wheat-growing region was once the garden of Corsica. Olives, figs and oranges from Balagne were exported via Calvi and Ile-Rousse. Low hills and fertile plains lie between the sea and the mountains. The golden-grey villages cluster around slender bell towers, and each hillside echoes the next in a landscape enlivened by the distant sea. Here and there you may pick out traces of abandoned agricultural terraces. Although attempts have been made to resume olive-growing on a commercial basis, livestock and grapevines are the principal resources today. Endowed with a climate in which palms, agave and Barbary figs flourish, Balagne has also succeeded in developing its coastline for tourism. Popular resorts include Calvi, Algajola, Île-Rousse, the marinas at Davia and Sant'Ambroggio and an extensive holiday village at Lozari, stretching over 50 acres along a beautiful sandy beach. Handicrafts, too, have been developed in Balagne in recent years through the efforts of promotional associations such as *La Corsicada*. At villages such as Pigna and Lumio, peasant crafts have been revived, and attractive items (pottery, weaving, wood and wickerwork) are available.

▶ **Calvi** (→). ▶ **Calenzana**, long a base for independence movements, claims to be Corsican at heart, in contrast to neighbouring Calvi, which was the seat of the occupying Genoese. Start of GR20 hiking trail. ▶ **Church of Sta. Restituta** rises above groves of sturdy olives. The frescos★ in the 15thC cenotaph are reminiscent of miniatures. ▶ **Zilia** : view★ over the valley and Montemaggiore. ▶ **Cassano** : in the church, a triptych★ of the Virgin and Child by a local painter, Simonis de Calvi (1505). ▶ **Montemaggiore★** : imposing Baroque church overlooking Calenzana and Calvi Bay. 1 km N, Romanesque church (12thC) of San Rainiero with walls of black and white granite. ▶ **Sant'Antonino★★** *(2 km right)*, perched high in the hills of Balagne ; a maze of narrow streets and steps among façades of dark granite (craftshops, small restaurants) is worth exploring. ▶ **Aregno**, surrounded by orange and lemon trees, with 13thC church of the Trinity★ in Pisan Romanesque style (frescos★). ▶ **Pigna★**, among olive groves overlooking the bay of Algajola ; craftshop run by *La Corsicada* (pottery). ▶ **Convent of Corbora** : starting point for a 1hr climb to **Monte Sant'Angelo** (alt. 562 m ; view★). ▶ **Corbora**, a Moorish-looking village below a ruined castle. ▶ **L'Ile-Rousse**, named for its islets of red granite linked to the shore by a jetty, this seaside resort is much appreciated for pleasant weather and a beach of fine sand. ▶ **Belgodère** : the ruins of an old fort overlook the valley. ▶ **Speloncato**, named for the numerous caves *(spilunca)* in the surrounding hillsides. Superb view★ of Balagne. ▶ Road continues through the villages of Nessa, Feliceto, Muro, Cateri (crafts *on right*) and Lavatoggio.

The Pisan churches

From the 11th to the 13thC Corsica was governed by the city-republic of Pisa, which brought architects, sculptors and stone masons from Tuscany. These builders were responsible for most of the Romanesque churches of Castagnicia, Nebbio and Balagne. Pisan sanctuaries in Corsica are recognisable by their small size and perfect proportions. The buildings are roofed with flat stones (teghje); the alternation of dry-jointed blocks of limestone, schist or granite gives a beeautiful polychrome effect to the walls. Today many churches and chapels are lost in the maquis. Of those still accessible the most interesting are : La Trinité at Aregno, La Canonica at Mariana, St. Jean at Carbini, San Michele at Murato and the old cathedral of Nebbio at Saint Florent.

Practical Information ⎯⎯⎯⎯⎯⎯⎯⎯⎯⎯⎯

CALENZANA, ⊠ 20214, 12 km SE of **Calvi**.

Hotel :
★ *Bel Horizon*, 4, pl. Prince-Pierre, ☎ 95.62.71.72, 17 rm Ⓟ ⌂ ⌂ closed 30 Sep-1 Apr, 160.

Restaurant :
♦ *U'Spuntini*, rte de Bonifato, ☎ 95.65.07.06 ⌂ closed 15 Oct-1 Jan. Hearty snacks at a pig farm, 60-170.

▲ ★★*Morsetta* (90 pl), ☎ 95.62.70.08 ; ★★*Paradella* (150 pl), ☎ 95.65.00.97.

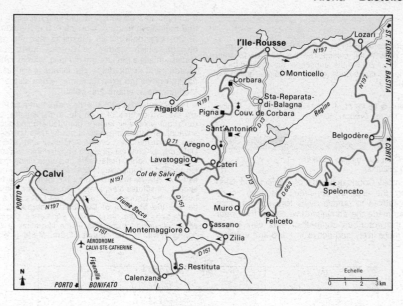

1. The Balagne region

Recommended
♥ *Casa di l'Artigiani*, Coop. de Calanzana-Balagne, ☎ 95.65.09.08, flavoured wines, natural products made from almonds.

CATTERI, ⊠ 20225 Muro, 11 km SW of **L'Ile Rousse**.

Restaurant :
♦ *Chez Léon*, ☎ 95.61.73.95 P ◿ 90-120 ; child : 50.

FELICETO, ⊠ 20225 Muro, 12 km SW.

Hotel :
● ★★ *Mare e Monti* (L.F.), ☎ 95.61.73.06, 18 rm P ⚶ ◿ closed 1 Oct-1 May, 150. Rest. ♦ 65-100.

L' ÎLE-ROUSSE, ⊠ 20220, 24 km NE of **Calvi**.
ⅱ av. J.-Calizzi, ☎ 95.60.04.35.
SNCF ☎ 95.60.00.50, L'Ile-Rousse-Calvi : frequent daily service in summer.
🚢 *S.N.C.M. at the Agence Tramar.*

Hotels :
★★★ *La Pietra*, rte du Port, ☎ 95.60.01.45, AE DC Euro Visa, 40 rm P ≼ ♪ closed 1 Nov-31 Mar. A hotel nestled in the seaside cliffs, 360.
● ★★ *A Pasturella*, Monticello, ☎ 95.60.05.65, 15 rm P ≼ ◿ closed Sun eve , Mon, 1 Nov-15 Dec, 170. Rest. ♦ ≼ 85-140 ; child : 75.
★★ *Grillon*, av. Paul-Doumer, ☎ 95.60.00.49, 16 rm P ◿ 180. Rest. ♦ 70-160.
★★ *L'Isola Rossa*, rte du Port, by the sea, ☎ 95.60.01.32, 20 rm P ≼ ⚶ closed 1 Feb-15 Mar, 170.
★ *La Bergerie*, rte de Monticello, ☎ 95.60.01.28, 13 rm P ⚶ closed 15 Dec-1 Mar, 200. Rest. ● ♦ ♪ Maroccan cuisine : *tagine de mérou à la juive, mouton, brochettes*, broiled fish, 120-160.

Restaurant :
♦♦ *Le California*, rte du Port, ☎ 95.60.01.13 P ≼ ◿ ♪ ⅾ ⊗ closed Wed, 1 Oct-1 May. Terrace dining. Sea view. Spec : lobsters and grilled fish, 80-180.

PIOGGIOLA, ⊠ 20259, 7 km S of **Speloncato**.

Hotel :
Auberge Aghjola, ☎ 95.61.90.22, AE Visa, 10 rm P ≼ ◿ ♪ 🏇 ⅾ half pens (h.s.), closed Tue, 15 Oct-15 Nov, 355.

Rest. ♦ ♪ ⅾ ⊗ Deep in the peaceful heart of Corsica, cheap, hearty fare featuring : pork products, game, wild trout, baby lamb, 50-130 ; child : 30.

SANT'ANTONINO, ⊠ 20220, 14 km SW of **L'Ile-Rousse**.

Restaurant :
♦ *La Taverne Corse*, ☎ 95.61.70.15, Visa ≼ ♪ ⅾ closed 15 Oct-15 Apr, 70-150.

Recommended
Cabaret : *La Lanterne*, folk music.
Camping-car rental : rte de Bastia, ☎ 95.60.16.01.
♥ wines and malmsey : *Clos Petra Rossa*, rue du Gal-Graziani.

SPELONCATO, ⊠ 20281, 32 km E of **Calvi**.

Hotel :
● ★ *Spelunca*, ☎ 95.61.31.21, 15 rm ≼ ◿ closed Oct-May, 160. Rest. ♦ Spec : Corsican cuisine, 70-100.

BASTELICA*

Ajaccio 41, Corte 62, Sartène 84 km
pop 796 ⊠ 20119   A-B3

An hour's drive from Ajaccio amid rivers, dense forests and mountains, the six hamlets of Bastelica are spread over a valley covered with chestnut trees. Bastelica is revered as the birthplace of the Corsican hero Sampiero (1498-1567). This "most Corsican of Corsicans" led a long struggle against the Genoese.

Nearby

▶ **Prunelli Gorges★** *(14 km by D27 and D3)* : the road runs through Tolla, where the houses overlook a reservoir. Farther on, **Bocca di Mercuio** commands a view of a natural amphitheatre in the mountains. Climb left *(300 m)* : view★ of the dam and the gorges. ▶ **Monte Renoso** (alt. 2 352 m), one of the most commanding lookout points in Corsica *(7 hr 30 up, 4-5hr down)*.   □

Practical Information _____

Hotel :
★★ *U Castagnetu*, ☎ 95.28.70.71, AE DC Visa, 15 rm ℗
⫷ ◿ half pens (h.s.), closed Tue (l.s.), 3 Nov-15 Dec,
250. Rest. ♦ ⫷ ♪ & Like the landscape, the cooking has a
mountain tang : *charcuterie*, grilled blackbirds, grilled leg
of lamb, 50-120.

Restaurant :
♦ *Chez Paul*, ☎ 95.28.71.59 ⫷ ◿ ♪ & Simple, tasty, family-
style fare. Try the *brocciu*, 40-65.

BASTIA*

Corte 70, Calvi 93, Ajaccio 153 km
pop 45000 ⊠ 20200   B1

The two great Corsican towns of Ajaccio and Bastia, facing the sea in opposite directions, once
seemed destined to remain rivals forever. But since
Bastia was made the administrative centre for Upper
Corsica, the notorious competition has diminished.
Bastia is more lively and active in trade and industry
than Ajaccio. The people would also have you believe
that their town is more "Corsican". It is the barometer
of Corsican political life. Bastia is also the gateway
through which visitors to Corsica hurry to other
places; this is a pity, for the old port, with its crumbling
façades and its citadel — the Genoese fortress *(bastia)* that gives the town its name — has all the classic
Mediterranean charm and colour.

▶ **Place St-Nicolas** (B2) and the **Vieux Port** (Old Port; B3)
are the two centres of town life. In the square, children
run about while their fathers, grandfathers and uncles are
solemnly engaged in games of bowls. Café terraces buzz
with talk of the latest events in football and politics. The
Old Port, by contrast, is more popular with tourists, who
frequent the cafés, restaurants and night clubs that flourish around the imposing 17thC church of St. Jean Bap-
tiste. ▶ Above the Old Port, the **citadel quarter** (B4)
almost constitutes a separate town, sheltered within walls
built by the Genoese in 1521. ▶ The Governor's Palace
houses the **Museum of Corsican Ethnography.** Among
the exhibits is the turret of the submarine *Casabianca*,
which played a crucial role in the liberation of Corsica
during WWII. ▶ The **church of Ste. Marie** (1495-1604)

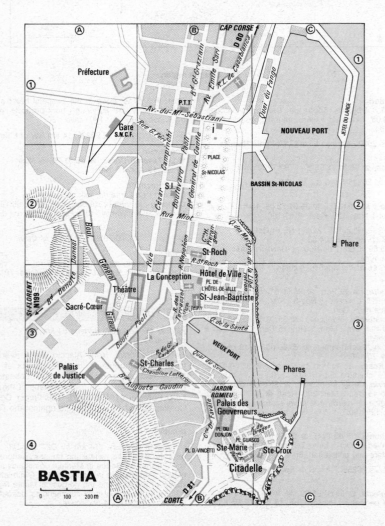

displays a sculpted-silver Assumption★ (1856). ▶ The nearby **chapel of Ste. Croix** is richly decorated with gilded stucco; the water-blackened image of Christ★ was found floating in the sea in 1428. ▶ Works of art in the **chapel of the Conception** (B3). ☐

Practical Information

ⓘ 35, bd Paoli (B2-3), ☎ 95.31.02.04; pl. St-Nicolas (B2), ☎ 95.31.00.89.
✈ *Bastia-Poretta*, 20 km S, ☎ 95.36.03.52. *Air France office*, at the airport (B1), ☎ 95.36.03.21; 6, av. E.-Sari (B1), ☎ 95.32.10.29.
SNCF (A1), ☎ 95.31.20.09.
⛴ S.N.C.M., Nouveau Port (C1), ☎ 95.31.36.63.
Car rental : *Avis*, Poretta Airport, ☎ 95.36.03.56; 2, rue N.-D. de Lourdes, ☎ 95.32.57.30.

Hotels :
★★★ *Ostella*, RN 193, exit S, Montecro, ☎ 95.33.51.05, 30 rm P ⇔ ⚜ ᯲ 270. Rest. ♦ ♪ 60-120.
★★ *Bonaparte*, 45, bd Gal-Graziani (B1), ☎ 95.34.07.10, AE DC Euro Visa, 24 rm P ᯲ 240.
★★ *Cyrnéa*, Pietranera, ☎ 95.31.41.71, 20 rm P ⇔ ⚜ ᯲ ㄟ ❀ closed 23 Dec-1 Feb. Sea view, beach 50m away with direct access, 215.
★★ *Posta Vecchia*, quai des Martyrs (B2), ☎ 95.32.32.38, AE DC Euro Visa, 44 rm P ⇔ ᯲ 300.

Restaurants :
● ♦♦ *Chez Assunta*, 4, pl. Fontaine-Neuve (B2), ☎ 95.31.67.06 P ᯲ ♪ closed Sun noon, 1 Jan-15 Feb. In a cool and discreetly-decorated former 17thC chapel, Assunta Cianelli embodies the perfect Corsican cook. She keeps an eye on everything, yet manages to turn out fresh pasta, breads and ice cream. Fresh fish and fritters are her husband's department. Everything is a treat : seafood, baked rabbit, home-made desserts. Local wines.
● ♦♦ *Le Bistrot du Port*, rue Posta-Vecchia (B2), ☎ 95.32.19.83 ᯲ ♪ closed Sat noon and Sun, 8-15 Feb, 1-30 Oct. An intimate atmosphere, friendly service in a nostalgic setting, plus J. Rovinalti's excellent food. Vast selection of fish and meats. Local and other French wines, 150-200.
♦♦ *La Taverne*, 9, rue du Gal-Carbuccia (B3), ☎ 95.31.17.87, AE DC Visa ᯲ ♪ ❀ closed Mon. Corsican cuisine, 85-130.
♦♦ *Lavezzi*, 8, rue St-Jean (B3), ☎ 95.31.05.73, closed Sun noon, 10 Feb-10 Mar. Very good Corsican food served in a handsome village house. Stuffed capon, *macaroni à la langouste, sardines au brocciu*, 75-200.
♦♦ *Le Romantique*, 4 bis, rue du Pontetto (B3), ☎ 95.32.30.85, AE DC Euro Visa ⇔ ᯲ ♪ closed Sat noon and Sun noon, 1-28 Feb. A pleasant little restaurant. Lovely terrace. Fish, 80-180; child : 40.

Recommended
Bicycle rental : *Locanautic*, 1, rue Cdt-L'Herminier, ☎ 95.31.37.38.
Marina : *Le Vieux Port*, ☎ 95.31.62.24.
♥ Corsican crafts : *Casa di l'Artigiani*, 5, rue des Terrasses, ☎ 95.32.65.21.

BAVELLA Pass***

B3

The Col de Bavella (alt. 1 243 m) cuts through the dorsal mountain chain to provide one of the most spectacular landscapes on the island. The granite needles of Bavella rear above a plateau covered with grass and sparsely strewn with windswept pines. To the N stretches the Incudine Massif, whereas to the E, the sea is framed between walls of red rock.

▶ The Bavella Pass is reached by D268 linking Solenzara to Zonza *(39 km)*. The road crosses **Larone Pass** (view★★) and winds through the coniferous **Bavella Forest★**. With luck you may glimpse a flock of mouflons on the rocky slopes above 1 000 m. ▶ The inn on the pass will supply full information about hiking around Bavella;

GR20, the main hiking trail, crosses the pass *(red/white markers)*. ▶ **Zonza**, surrounded by forests, a favourite with trout fishermen. ☐

Practical Information

ZONZA, ⊠ 20124, 37 km from **Sartène**.

Hotels :
★★ *Incudine* (L.F.), ☎ 95.78.67.71, Visa, 10 rm P half pens (h.s.), closed 30 Sep-1 Apr, 350. Rest. ♦ 85-130.
● ★ *Les Touristes*, ☎ 95.78.42.31, 10 rm, closed 1 Nov-15 Mar, 110. Rest. ♦ Corsican cuisine at interesting prices. Orchard fruit, 60-120.

Recommended
♥ Crafts : *Casa di l'Artigiani*, ☎ 95.78.44.50, open Apr-Sep and Xmas.

BOCOGNANO

Ajaccio 40, Corte 43, Bastia 113 km
pop 315 ⊠ 20136
B3

Hotel :
★ *Monte d'Oro*, col de Vizzavona, ☎ 95.47.21.06, 45 rm P ⚜ ᯲ ㄟ 🐾 closed 15 Sep-31 Dec. Rest. ♦ ⇔ ㄟ ❀ 90-185; child : 60.

Restaurant :
♦ *L'Ustaria*, ☎ 95.27.41.10 ⇔ ⚜ ♪ ❀ A good place to eat inland, 75-200.

BONIFACIO**

Sartène 54, Ajaccio 140, Bastia 170 km
pop 2736 ⊠ 20169
B4

Did Ulysses make landfall at Bonifacio, as *The Odyssey* suggests? No matter whether the legendary voyager took shelter there, today the Marina is a popular harbour for pleasure craft. The upper town, set firmly on white limestone, is an irresistible site. Bonifacio, isolated on the southernmost point of Corsica, has always been a world apart. Even the dialect differs from other Corsican speech and is derived from the Italian of old Liguria.

▶ The **Marina★**, tucked away in an extraordinary cleft between the limestone cliffs; shops, cafés, and seafood restaurants draw tourists, fishermen and the boating fraternity. ▶ **Ville Haute★★** : in the upper town, a network of narrow streets within ancient walls offers striking views★★ seaward, even taking in neighbouring Sardinia. ▶ **Place Manichella** : old houses★ are perched on the extreme edge of the cliff.
Also... ▶ The **church of Ste. Marie Majeure** (12th-13thC); marble tabernacle (1465). ▶ The Citadel, now a base for the French Foreign Legion, is closed to visitors, but the Gothic **church of St. Dominique★** and the cemetery may be seen by arrangement *(apply to the SI)*.

Nearby

▶ **Marine caves★★** *(grottes marines; 45 min by motorboat from the Quai de la Marine)* : best way to see the cliffs of Bonifacio. ▶ **Cape Pertusato★★** *(5.5 km SE)* : spectacular view of Bonifacio, the islands of Cavallo and Lavezzi and the Sardinian coast. ▶ **Santa Manza Bay** *(6 km NE)* : rocky inlets and isolated beaches, sea views and restaurant. ☐

Practical Information

ⓘ pl. d'Arme, ☎ 95.73.03.48.
⛴ quai J.-Comparetti, ☎ 95.73.01.28, to Sardinia.
Car rental : *Avis*, quai Comparetti, ☎ 95.73.01.28.

Hotels :
● ★★★ *Solemare*, ☎ 95.73.01.06, 57 rm ⊰ closed 30 Sep-1 Apr, 340.
★★★ *La Caravelle*, 11, quai Comparetti, ☎ 95.73.00.03, AE DC Euro Visa, 25 rm ⊰ & ⤴ closed 20 Oct-1 Apr, 280.
★★ *Résidence du Club Nautique*, ☎ 95.73.02.11, 10 rm ℙ closed 1 Nov-27 Mar, 230.

Restaurants :
● ♦♦ *Stella d'Oro (Chez Jules)*, 7, rue Doria, ☎ 95.73.03.63 ♪ closed 30 Sep-15 Apr. A gold star for the cooking at this enjoyable gourmet eatery. Don't miss it, 80-300.
♦♦ *La Calanque*, Tonnara-Plage, ☎ 95.73.02.24, AE Visa ⊰ ♪ closed Nov-Feb. Spec : fish, spiny lobsters, *bouillabaisse*, 180.
♦ *U Ceppu*, Santa-Manza, ☎ 95.73.05.83 ⊰ ▥ ♪ closed 15 Oct-30 Apr. An uncomfortable mix of meat and fish cooking; maybe they should choose one or the other, 75-150.

Å ★★★*Campo di Liccia* (120 pl), ☎ 95.73.03.09.

Recommended
Baby-sitting : *Mme Rezé*, ☎ 95.73.07.66, 9 am - 8 pm.
Marina : ☎ 95.73.03.13, (250 empl.).

BORGO

Corte 58, Calvi 110, Ajaccio 140 km
pop 3413 ⊠ 20290
B2

Hotel :
★★★ *Isola*, rte du Bord-de-Mer, ☎ 95.33.19.60, Tx 460695, AE DC Euro Visa, 70 rm ℙ ⊰▥ ◡ ▩ ⚘ ▱ ⤴ closed Nov-Mar, 370. Rest. ♦ ⊰ ♪ & ⚘ 80-120.

Nearby
CASAMOZZA , ⊠ 20290 Borgo, 8 km S.

Hotel :
★★★ *Chez Walter*, ☎ 95.36.00.09, Tx 488141, AE DC Euro Visa, 32 rm ℙ▥ ◡ ▱ ⤴ 300. Rest. ♦ ♪ closed Mon noon and Sun eve, 85-100.

CALVI**

Bastia 93, Corte 96, Ajaccio 160 km
pop 3636 ⊠ 20260
A2
Calvi dramatically combines past and present : the semi-deserted citadel crumbles with age, while the Marina spills over with summer life. The setting of sea, palm-trees and broad beach bordered with umbrella pines against the **Cinto Massif** (snow-covered until early summer), make Calvi one of the most popular seaside resorts.
▶ The **Marina** and Rue Georges-Clemenceau (running parallel), are the traditional promenades. Restaurants and cafés, vantage points for watching the comings and goings of yachts and fishing boats, keep up a brisk trade until late at night.▶ The **Citadel**, between the bays of Calvi and Revellata, symbolises almost 5 centuries of Genoese occupation. Walk on the remparts★, sea views.
▶ **Church of St. Jean-Baptiste** (18thC) : triptych★ (15thC) by Barbagelata; **Treasury of Religious Art of Balagne** in oratory of St. Antoine.▶ It is highly questionable that Christopher Columbus was born in Calvi, despite the assertive inscription in Rue Colombo.

Nearby
▶ **Chapel** of the **Madona di a Serra★** *(6 km SW)* : on a hilltop overlooking Calvi Bay and the mountains.▶ **Marinas of Saint'Ambroggio** and **Algajola** *(12.5 km and 15 km NE)* : beaches, swimming pools, scuba diving, sailing, tennis, hotels, Club Mediterranée holiday village.▶ **Cave of the seals★** *(Grotte des Veaux Marins ; motorboat from the Marina, 1hr45 round trip)* : on the other side of the Revel-

lata Peninsula, a 200 m-deep cave named for the seals that once frequented it. ▶ **Calvi to Girolata by sea★★** *(daily from the Marina, 9 am, Easter-Oct. full day, lunch at Girolata :* view from Revellata to the Bay of Porto and Piana inlet, via the Bay of Girolata. ▶ **Bonifato amphitheatre★** *(cirque : 20.5 km SE) :* beyond the Calvi Ste-Catherine airport the road enters the **Calenzana Forest** (recently ravaged by fire), ending at the **Auberge de la Forêt**, where the porphyry walls of the naturel amphitheatre of Bonifato rise above the treeline. The road turns into a path rejoining GR20. ▢

Practical Information _____

CALVI
ℹ chemin de la Plage, ☎ 95.65.05.87.
✈ *Calvi-Sainte-Catherine*, 7 km S.E, ☎ 95.65.08.09.
🚆 ☎ 95.65.00.61, Calvi-Bastia and Calvi-Ajaccio lines. In summer : serv for l'Ile-Rousse.
🚢 *Corsica Ferries*, ☎ 95.65.10.84 ; *S.N.C.M.*, quai Landri, ☎ 95.65.02.81.
Car rental : *Avis*, Sainte-Catherine Airport; 6, av. de la république, ☎ 95.05.06.74.

Hotels :
● ★★★ *Balanea*, 6, rue Clemenceau, ☎ 95.65.00.45, Tx 460540, AE DC Visa, 40 rm ⊰ ♪ 420.
● ★★★ *Résidence des Aloès*, quartier Donatéo, ☎ 95.65.01.46, AE CD Euro Visa, 26 rm ℙ ⊰▥ ◡ & closed 1 Oct-1 May, 210.
★★★ *Kallisté*, 1, av. du Cdt-Marche, ☎ 95.65.09.81, AE DC Visa, 27 rm ⊰▥ ♪ closed 30 Sept-1 Jun, 220. Rest. ♦ & 70-150.
★★★ *Le Magnolia*, pl. du Marché, ☎ 95.65.19.16, AE-DC, 12 rm ▥ ⚘ 420.
★★★ *Le Saint-Erasme*, rte de Porto, ☎ 95.65.04.50, AE, 32 rm ℙ ⊰▥ ♪ closed 10 Oct-1 Apr, 253.
★★ *Corsica*, rte de Pietra-Maggiore, ☎ 95.65.07.36, 48 ch. ℙ ⊰▥ ◡ ⚘ half pens (h.s.), closed Nov-Apr, 360. Rest. ♦ ⚘ For guests only.
★★ *Cyrnea*, 200 m beach, ☎ 95.65.03.35, 36 rm ℙ▥ ⚘ closed 20 Oct-1 Mar, 200.

Restaurants :
● ♦♦ *Ile de Beauté*, quai Landry, ☎ 95.65.00.46, AE DC ⊰ ♪ closed Wed lunch, 23 Sep-1 May. One Corsicas' finest tables, starring seafood specialties by a brilliant chef, supervised by M. Caumeil : *millefeuille de soie, escalope de saumon, fricassée de homard*. On the upper floor, *le Bœuf en Terrasse :* fine meats, 85-280.
♦♦ *Le Comme Chez Soi*, quai Landry, ☎ 95.65.00.59, AE DC Euro Visa ⊰ ♪ & closed 20 Jan-10 Mar, 230.
♦ *U Spuntinu*, rte de Bonifato, ☎ 95.65.07.06 ℙ▥ ◡ & closed 1 Oct-30 May, 180.

Å ★★★*Bella Vista* (160 pl), ☎ 95.65.11.76 ; ★★★*Clos du Mouflon* (80 pl), ☎ 95.65.03.53 ; ★★★*La Dolce Vita* (200 pl), ☎ 95.65.05.99 ; ★★★*La Pinède* (240 pl), ☎ 95.65.02.42 ; ★★★*Paduella*, (74 pl), ☎ 95.65.06.16 ; ★★*Campo-di-Flori* (24 pl), ☎ 95.65.02.43.

Recommended
Bicycle rental : *Balagne Cycles*, Laniella 2, ☎ 95.65.12.44.
Marina : ☎ 95.65.10.60 (350 empl.).

Nearby
ALGAJOLA , ⊠ 20290, 9 km SW.

Hotel :
★ *Plage*, ☎ 95.60.72.12, 36 rm, ℙ ⊰▥ ◡ ♪ ⚘ pens (h.s.), closed 1 Oct-1 May, 420. Rest. ♦ ⊰ ♪ ⚘ 65.

Å ★★*Cala di Sole* (120 pl), ☎ 95.31.68.26 ; ★★*Plage* (70 pl), ☎ 95.60.71.76.

BONIFATO, ⊠ 20214, 21 km SE.

Hotel :
★ *Auberge de la forêt*, Calenzana, ☎ 95.65.09.98, 7 rm ♦ ▥ ⚘ closed Nov-Mar, 135. Rest. ♦ 60-100.

GALERIA, ⊠ 20245, 33 km SE.

Hôtels :
★★ *Filosorma,* ☎ 95.62.00.02, 14 rm, P ⊀ ⌘ closed 5 Nov-15 Apr, 190. Rest. ♦ ⌘ 70-110.
★★ *Spinosi,* in front of bay, at 30 m from the beach ☎ 95.62.00.02, 14 rm P ⊀ ⚲ ⚰ half pens (h.s.), closed 15 Oct-15 Apr, 380. Rest. ♦ ⸽ 75-110.

⚠ ★★*Idéal Camping* (67 pl), ☎ 95.62.01.46.

Le CAP CORSE**

B1

Round trip from Bastia to Saint-Florent *(113 km, full day)*

Cape Corse is the northern extremity of the 40-km chain of mountains forming the spine of the island. In this harsh setting, *maquis* has reclaimed the hillsides where once fruit trees, vines and olives grew; abandoned villages and feudal ruins look like outcrops of the mountains. The sea views are astounding, especially on the W coast where the cliff road runs high above the saw-tooth coastline. Cape Corse natives, unlike other Corsicans, have always been drawn to the sea and distant lands, such as South America and the West Indies. Imposing houses *(palazzi)* attest to the profitability of these sojourns abroad. Characteristic of the peninsula are the *marines,* or marinas, once village extensions for fishing and trading, now given over to tourism.

▶ **Bastia** (→). ▶ **Lavasina,** renowned for pilgrimages to the Virgin Mary. From here you can reach **Monte Stello★★** *(4 km by road to Pozzo then a 5hr walk round trip)* : highest point on the cape (1 307 m).▶ **Sisco** *(7 km left)* : 17 hamlets surrounded by myrtle, heather, arbutus, chestnut and holm oak; church of St. Martin (reliquary of St. John Chrysostom★★, 13th or 14thC); 15-min walk to the **church of St. Michele★** (Romanesque, 11thC); view★. ▶ Romanesque **church of Santa Catarina** : oriental-style ceramic decorations.▶ **Macinaggio,** long a port, now an important marina; **Tomino** *(3.5 km SW)* : panorama★. ▶ **Rogliano★** : three castles, three churches, eight hamlets, fortified towers clinging to the rock; once a powerful stronghold that controlled all the north of Cape Corse. ▶ **Ersa** : 16 km round trip to **Tollare★** and **Barcaggio★**, a few stone houses isolated on the point facing a small island of green serpentine marble. ▶ **Moulin Mattei** : panorama★ over cape and sea.▶ **Centuri-Port★★** *(5 km right)* : prettiest marina on the peninsula.▶ **Pino,** a village perched above the sea; narrow road to **Bocca di Santa Lucia★** *(5 km)* and Seneca's Tower *(30-min walk)* : panorama★★. ▶ **Canari★** on the mountainside; churches of Santa Maria★ (12thC) and St. François. ▶ Pass the disused asbestos mine at Albo to reach **Nonza★**, an ancient stronghold built on sheer black rock. ☐

Practical Information ─────────────────

BARCAGGIO, ⊠ 20275 Ersa, 47 km N of **Bastia**.

Hotel :
★★ *La Garaglia,* ☎ 95.35.60.54, 24 rm P ⊀ ⚱ ⚲ closed 25 Sep-3 Apr, 170. Rest. ♦ 80-105.

CENTURI-PORT, ⊠ 20238, 12 km SW of **Barcaggio**.

Hotel :
● ★ *Vieux Moulin,* by the harbour, ☎ 95.35.60.15, AE DC Visa, 14 rm P ⊀ ⚱ ⸽ ⍟ half pens (h.s.), closed Oct-Feb, 500. Rest. ♦ ⊀ Spec : *langoustes grillées à l'armoricaine, mérous,* 90-170.

Restaurant :
♦ *U Fanale,* across from the island of Giraglia, ☎ 95.35.62.72 ⸽ closed Wed, 20 Sep-31 May. Spec : fish soup, Corsican wines, 80-160.

PINO, ⊠ 20228 Luri, 43 km N of **Bastia**.

Restaurant :
♦ *Allard,* ☎ 95.35.01.76, closed Sep-Apr. Family-style cuisine, 60-95.

PORTICCIOLO, ⊠ 20228 Luri, 18 km SE of **Pino**.

Hotel :
● ★★★ *Caribou,* ☎ 95.35.00.33, AE DC Euro Visa, 40 rm P ⊀ ⚱ ⚲ ⸽ ⊟ ⍟ half pens, closed 15 Sep-15 Jun, 920. Rest. ♦ ⊀ ⸽ ⚰ 200-250.

CARGÈSE*

Ajaccio 51, Corte 106, Calvi 108 km
pop 898 ⊠ 20130   A3

Cargèse, on a granite promontory between the bays of Sagone and Pero, is reminiscent of Greece where, indeed,, many of the inhabitants have their origins. The people maintain the cultural and religious traditions of their forebears who fled from Ottoman oppression in the 17thC. Opposite the Catholic church stands an Orthodox church decorated with icons in the Byzantine style.

▶ **Sagone** *(13 km SE)* and **Tiuccia** *(21 km SE)* in the curve of the **bay of Sagone★** : pleasant resorts on a fine sandy beach. ☐

Practical Information ─────────────────

CARGÈSE
ℹ rue du Dr-Dragacci, ☎ 95.26.41.31.

Hotels :
● ★★★ *Lentisques,* rte du Pero, ☎ 95.26.42.34, 20 rm P ⊀ ⚱ ⌘ half pens (h.s.), closed 30 Sep-30 Apr, 200. Rest. ♦ ⸽ 100-190.
★★ *La Spelunca,* ☎ 95.26.40.12, 20 rm P ⊀ ⚲ ⸽ closed Nov-Easter, 250.
★ *Thalassa,* Pero beach, ☎ 95.26.40.08, 22 rm P ⊀ ⚱ ⚲ half pens (h.s.), closed 30 Sep-15 May. Family atmosphere,, 350.

⚠ ★★*Torrace* (70 pl), ☎ 95.26.42.39.

Recommended
♥ carved gourds : *Casa di l'Artigiani,* chemin de Paomia, Apr-Sep and Christmas.

Nearby
SAGONE, ⊠ 20118, 13 km SE.

Hotel :
★★ *Marine,* on the beach, ☎ 95.28.00.03, AE, 17 rm P ⊀ ⚱ half pens (h.s.), closed Dec-Feb, 400. Rest. ♦ ⊀ ⸽ ⚰ 50-220.

TIUCCIA, ⊠ 20111 Calcatoggio, 21 km SE.

Hotel :
● ★★★ *Cinarca,* ☎ 95.52.21.39, AE DC Euro Visa, 46 rm P ⊀ ⚲ ⸽ ⚰ ⊟ half pens (h.s.), closed Nov-Mar, 460. Rest. ♦♦ ⸽ closed lunch and hols, 80-130.

The CASINCA Region**

B2

This is one of the most fertile regions of Corsica and one of the most densely populated. Between the sea and the mountains — Monte Sant'Angelo — lie fields of corn, vegetables, citrus, vines and tobacco.

Tour of the Casinca *(35 km, narrow roads)*

▶ **Vescovato★** (pop. 2 129), the principal town of this little region, is reached by D237, which branches off 2.5 km SE of **Casamozza**.▶ Continue through **Venzolasca** to **Loreto-di-Casinca★★** *(detour 16 km round trip on D6)* and **Penta-**

di-Casinca and **Castellare-di-Casinca★** : exceptionally well-situated villages with typical Corsican architecture. □

Practical Information

FOLELLI, ✉ 20213, 30 km S of **Bastia**.

Hotel :
★★ ***San Pellegrino*** (L.F.), ☎ 95.36.90.61, Tx 460398, AE DC Euro Visa, 105 rm 🅿 ♨ ✂ ⚲ half pens (h.s.), closed Oct-Apr, 480. Rest. ♦♦ ⚘ ♪ ✗ 80-140.

Restaurants :
♦ ***Castelli***, ☎ 95.36.90.09 🅿 ♨ ♿ A genuine little Corsican inn; family-style food by Mme Castelli : *tarte aux herbes, beignets au fromage*, 50-120.
♦ ***Chez Mathieu***, rte d'Orrezza, ☎ 95.36.93.16, Euro Visa 🅿 ⚘ ♪ ♿ closed Sat , Feb, 45-65.

The CASTAGNICCIA Heights***

B2

From Ponte Leccia to the east coast *(76 km, full day; see map 2)*

A garden fortress in a maze of mountains, Castagniccia is difficult to reach but worth the effort. This was a stronghold of island resistance, where the signal was given for revolt against the Genoese. Pascal Paoli (18thC leader of Corsican independence) was born here. Narrow roads twisting through the rocky landscape offer glimpses of hidden valleys. The chestnut trees that gave Castagniccia its name (bot. *Castanea :* chestnut) and former prosperity (flour, timber) are still plentiful, but this "bread tree", as it is known locally, is no longer economically important. The villages scattered along the mountain crests today are almost deserted; the villagers have left to work in the plain or on the Continent.

▶ **Ponte Leccia.** ▶ Follow D71 : at the Col de Serna, turn left for **Santa-Maria-de-Valle-di-Rostino** *(5 km by road then a 15-min walk) :* pre-Romanesque church (10thC) in ruins and **St Tomoso de Pastoreccia** *(6 km by road, then a 10-min walk)* and a pre-Romanesque chapel with 15th-16thC frescos★. ▶ **Morosaglia** (pop. 854), birthplace of Pascal Paoli (museum : documents, personal effects); his remains are buried in the chapel. ▶ **Porta** *(8 km left) :* Baroque church (1720), bell tower★; concerts in summer on the Italian-style organ (1780). ▶ **Campana** (pop. 20) : church (Adoration of the Shepherds★★, 17thC school of Seville). ▶ **Campodonico** *(3.5 km right) :* path up Monte San Petrone (alt. 1767 m; *5-hr round trip),* panorama★★. ▶ **Convent of Orezza** (ruins), formerly a centre of Corsican resistance (Paoli met Napoléon here in 1790). ▶ **Piedicroce** (pop. 164) : oldest pipe-organ★ (17thC) in Corsica; *verde di Corsica* (Corsican green), a type of marble found only in this region, was used to decorate the Medici chapel in Florence, Italy. ▶ **Carcheto** (pop. 39) : Baroque bell tower★. ▶ **Valle d'Alesani** (pop. 192), another stronghold of resistance against the Genoese. A German adventurer had himself proclaimed King Theodore I of Corsica here in the 18thC; church (15thC Sienese painting : the Virgin of the Cherries★★). ▶ **Cervioni** (pop. 1 254) : vineyards, view★ of the eastern plain. ▶ **Chapel of Sta. Cristina** *(1 km to Valle di Campoloro then 45-min walk round trip, rocky path) :* twin Romanesque apses decorated with frescos★ (1473). ▶ Route along the cliff road of Castagniccia★. **San Nicolao** (pop. 867), terraced village surrounded by orchards, chestnut and olive trees. □

Practical Information

PIEDICROCE, ✉ 20229.

Hotel :
★ ***Le Refuge*** (L.F.), ☎ 95.35.81.08, AE DC Visa, 23 rm ⚘ ✂ closed Oct, 190. Rest. ♦ ⚘ ♪ ♿ Spec : *charcuteries maison, beignets de fromage, gâteau de farine de châtaigne*, 70.

VALLE D'ALESANI, ✉ 20234, 17 km W on the Cervioni.

Restaurant :
♦ ***Auberge des Deux Vallées***, col d'Arcarotta, 9 km NW, ☎ 95.35.91.20 🅿 ⚘ ♨ ✂ ♪ ♿ closed Tue. Mountain specialities, goat-cheese fritters (*buglidicce*), 50-70.

CAURO

Sartène 64, Corte 88, Bastia 158 km
pop 595 ✉ 20117 A3

Restaurant :
♦♦ ***U Barracone***, Eccica Suarella, RN 196, ☎ 95.28.40.55, AE DC Visa 🅿 ♨ ✂ ♪ ♿ closed Mon (l.s.), 15 Jan-28 Feb. A pleasant inn serving savoury fireside fare : soup, *tripette*, 85-180.

CORSICAN REGIONAL PARK**

AB2-3

200 km² (a quarter of the island) stretching from the Bay of Porto to the Ospedale Forest, this sampler of Corsica's natural assets offers deep creeks, beaches, lakes and rivers, rocks, woods, and mountain heaths. The objective is to protect flora and fauna, but the park is also designed to encourage agricultural development and the prevention of forest fires. Native species include *moufflon,* bearded vulture, osprey, golden

2. The Castagniccia heights

eagle and kite. More easily spotted : wild boar, the Corsican nuthatch (which climbs pine trees), pigeon, woodcock and trout.

GR20 *(see marked route on sightseeing map)*

▶ Hiking on GR20 is the best and most energetic way to explore the reserve : 200 km from Calenzana (near Calvi) to Conca (above Porto-Vecchio). Eleven equipped lodges and chalets; hotels and private huts near the route. GR20 is passable from mid-Jun. (snow still possible) to the beginning of Nov. Time for the journey : about 15 days. Take proper equipment, including warm clothing and good mountain- or rock-climbing boots. Certain stretches are very difficult and sometimes dangerous. □

CORTE

Bastia 70, Ajaccio 83, Calvi 96 km
pop 5446 ⊠ *20250* B2

Corte is a symbol of independence in the heart of the island. From 1755 to 1769 it was Paoli's capital. As the seat of the Corsican university, it embodies the island's cultural identity.

▶ On the Cours Paoli, the main artery of Corte, students debate the latest news in the Rex-Bar. ▶ From Place Paoli walk through the **Old Town** *(Vieille Ville)* to the Place Gaffori (bullet marks on façades are reminders of violent fighting during the 18thC war of independence). ▶ The **National Palace** (seat of the independent government of Corsica), the **Citadel** and the **Belvédère★** overlook the Tavignano and Restonica gorges.

Nearby

▶ **Restonica Gorges★★** *(15 km SW first towards Ajaccio then turn right).* ▶ The gorges are the starting point for several hikes : **Lake Melo** and **Lake Capitello★** *(pleasant; 1hr15 for the former, 2hr for the latter)*; **Monte Rotondo★** (alt. 2262 m; *recommended but rather difficult towards the top; 5hr up, 4hr down).* ▶ **Tavignano Gorges★** *(no road; 6hr30 to the pass)* : wild and splendid country. ▶ **Popolasca** *(20 km NNW; Bastia road and left on D18)* : a pleasant drive in the countryside around Corte; the village is overshadowed by red rock needles★ similar to those at Bavella. ▶ **Sermano★** *(23 km E; Bastia road and right on D41)*, one of the rare villages where Mass is still sung in the old Corsican settings for male voices *(a paghiella)* : chapel of San Nicolao *(15-min walk from the village;* frescos★). Roads from **Sermano** invite exploration : **Casardo Pass★; Zuani** (old houses★); **San Cervone Pass★**. □

Practical Information ─────────

CORTE
🚋 🕿 95.46.00.97.

Hotel :
● *Auberge de la Restonica*, at the entrance of the gorges, 🕿 95.46.09.58, 6 rm ℗ ⚏ ⌕ closed Thu, 170. Rest. ♦♦ ♪ closed 1 Nov-1 Feb. Spec : *tarte aux herbes, cabri rôti aux herbes,* 80-150.

⚠ **★★★**Tuani (35 pl), 🕿 95.46.11.65.

Recommended
♥ Corsican crafts : *Casa di l'Artigiani,* 13, rue du Colonel-Ferracci.

Nearby

Le pont de CASTIRLA, ⊠ 20218, 12 km N.

Restaurant :
● ♦ *Costa Santucci*, 🕿 95.47.42.04, closed Jan-1 Apr. Take the mountain road for carefully-prepared Corsican family cooking with a flair. Single menu with choice of 3 main courses. Homemade canneloni, daily specials, cheese and dessert for 60 F.Yes, 60F.

VENACO, ⊠ 20231, 13 km S.

Hotel :
● **★★★** *Paesotel E Caselle*, 5 km via D 43, 🕿 95.47.02.01, Tx 460145, AE DC Visa, 47 rm ℗ ⚏ ♪ ⌕ ⊟ ⸌° half pens (h.s.), closed 1 Oct-30 Apr. Cottages in the *maquis*, 675. Rest. ♦ ⚏ ⌕ ⚘ A mountain shepherd's shelter, 150-200.

ÉVISA*

Corte 63, Ajaccio 72, Calvi 99 km
pop 248 ⊠ *20126* A2

Between Corte and Porto, a stopover 830 m high among chestnut trees and swift streams.

Nearby

▶ **Spelunca Gorges★★** *(3hr walk to Ota)* : leave by the Porto road and turn right past the cemetery wall to arrive at the Genoese bridge at **Zaglia★** (base of the **Spelunca amphitheatre★★**). ▶ **Aïtone Forest** *(4.5 km on the Corte road to the forester's lodge)* : pine, beech, fir and holm oak (4200 acres); the lodge is the starting point for walks to **Bocca di Salto** *(1hr)* and **Bocca di Cocavera** *(3hr);* panorama★★. ▶ Follow the D70 over Sevi Pass to **Vico** *(21 km SE),* then take D23 left to the spa at **Guagno-les-Bains** and **Guagno** *(42 km SE),* in the heart of the forest; up to **Orto★** and on to **Soccia★**. □

Practical Information ─────────

ÉVISA

Hotels :
★★★ *U'Castellu*, 🕿 95.26.20.71, 8 rm ℗ ⚏ closed l.s., 230.
★★ *Scopa Rossa*, 🕿 95.26.20.22, 20 rm ℗ ⚏ ⌕ ⚏ ⸌° closed 1 Nov-10 Feb, 200. Rest. ♦ 70-140.
★ *L'Aïtone*, rte Principale, 🕿 95.26.20.04, AE Visa, 17 rm ℗ ⚏ ⚏ ⚘ ⌕ closed 10 Nov-31 Dec, 190. Rest. ● ♦♦ ⚏ ♪ The chestnut trees of the Spelunca Valley are at your feet. Two lovely dining rooms separated by a huge fireplace are where you'll enjoy Toussaint Ceccaldi's good family-style cooking : *terrines maison* (boar, black bird), trout, chestnut *crêpes,* 60-120.

Recommended
♥ *Casa di l'Artigiani*, 🕿 95.26.22.24, Apr-Sep and Christmas.

Nearby

SOCCIA, ⊠ 20125, 18 km NE.

Hotel :
● **★★** *U Paese* (L.F.), 🕿 95.28.31.92, 22 rm ℗ ⚏ ⌕ ⚏ ⚘ closed 1-27 Dec, 200. Rest. ♦ 80-140.

Col de VERGIO, ⊠ 20224 Calacuccia, 12 km NE.

Hotel :
● **★** *Castel de Vergio*, Albertaccio, 🕿 95.48.00.01, 40 rm ℗ ⌕ closed Oct-Nov. Deep in the state forest, 140. Rest. ♦ 60-120.

VICO, ⊠ 20160 Evisa, 21 km.

Hotel :
★★ *U Paradisu*, rte du Couvent, 🕿 95.26.61.62, AE Visa, 20 rm ℗ ⚏ ⚏ ⌕ ⚘ half pens (h.s.), 370. Rest. ♦ ⚏ 60-70.

FILITOSA**

A3-4

The face of prehistoric Corsica can be seen in the stone warriors of Filitosa. The men who appeared in the Taravo Valley as early as 6000BC were shepherd warriors. Towards 2000BC the inhabitants of Filitosa had created a structured society and had built strongholds such as Torre and Cucuruzzu. Their crowning achievement was the creation of statues of armed men on which the fame of the region rests. It has been suggested that the indigenous people might have been conquered by the Shardanes (*Torréens* in Corsican), skilled navigators who plied the Mediterranean *(8-sunset; better light am).*

▶ The **Museum** near the entrance displays excavated artifacts. ▶ 70 m ahead to the right is **Filitosa V★**, most representative of this type. ▶ The **oppidum** (town) : a group of fortifications and religious monuments fashioned from large boulders. Above and to the right of the entrance is **Filitosa IX★**, the megalithic masterpiece. ▶ The remains of a **Torréen village** and five menhirs in a quarry are still visible. ☐

The FIUMORBO Region

B3

An isolated stretch that takes its name from the Fiumorbo River. The local people were renowned for their independence and unceasing resistance to foreign occupation. Hemmed in by mountains and chestnut forests, the villages look across to **Aléria.**

▶ Walk through **Fiumorbo** from **Ghisonaccia** to **Prunelli-di-Fiumorbo** *(19 km; pop. 2 050).* ☐

GHISONI

Corte 42, Ajaccio 83, Sartène 99 km
pop 385 ⊠ 20227   B3
In a deep valley, unlike most Corsican villages, Ghisoni lies below the Verde and Sorba Passes.

▶ 27 km of beautiful road, running between the green serpentine walls of the **Inzecca Defile★**, then through the **Strette★**, links Ghisoni to **Ghisonaccia.** Ghisonaccia has thrived since modern cultivation was introduced to the eastern plain. ☐

LEVIE

Sartène 28, Ajaccio 103, Corte 137 km
pop 752 ⊠ 20170   B4
The archaeological museum *(9-12 & 2-6, Jun.-Sep.; 10-12 & 2-5 winter)* shows that man lived on the Levie plateau from Neolithic times until the Bronze and Iron Ages ; 15thC ivory Christ★ in the presbytery.

Nearby

▶ **Cucuruzzu★** *(3.5 km on D268, then 3.5 km right and 700 m on foot; guided tours in season)* : fortified Torréen stronghold (→ Filitosa) from the Bronze Age. View★ to the Bavella needles. ▶ **Sainte-Lucie-de-Tallano** *(8.5 km SW;* pop. 362) : one of the best Corsican wines is produced here. A rare variety of greenstone★ (orbicular diorite) is quarried nearby. Church (**holy water stoup★** and **marble bas-relief**, 15thC). **Crucifixion★★** and the **Virgin and Child altarpiece★** are currently in restoration. ▶ **Carbini** *(8 km SE;* pop. 125) : in the Middle Ages a sect called the Giovannali preached and practised communal living here ; they were massacred. **Church of San Giovanni★** (12thC). ☐

MARIANA*

B2
Named for Marius who founded it in 92BC during the Roman colonisation of Corsica.

▶ Only a few sections of brick wall remain from Roman times. In the 12thC the Pisans built **La Canonica★★**, the Romanesque cathedral *(key in nearby café).* ▶ 50m S, remains of an earlier cathedral (4th-10thC) and baptistery decorated with **mosaics★.** ▶ **Church of San Parteo** *(300m SW)* has a noteworthy apse (11thC). ☐

The NIOLO Region**

A2
Niolo is a region of superlatives. Bounded on the W by the Vergio Pass and the upper Golo basin and on the E by the Scala di Santa Regina, here are the grandest mountains (the Cinto Massif), the biggest river (the Golo), the most extensive pine forests, the highest villages, and the oldest traditions. Sheep and goats, always the mainstay of the region, are still more economically important than forestry.

▶ **Calacuccia** (pop. 418), the main town in the region alongside the reservoir; a base for excursions to the Cinto massif. ▶ **Casamaccioli** *(3 km SW;* pop. 500) : view of the Cinto from the other side of the lake. ▶ **Scala di Santa Regina★** *(10 km NE)* : the Corte road runs through a pass hewn from granite. ▶ **Valdo-Niello Forest★** *(24 km SW to the Vergio pass on the Porto road)* : 46 km² of stone pine, alder and beech; Corsica's largest forest. ▶ **Lake Nino★** *(2hr30 drive)* : 14 km along D84 towards Porto, then left on a track joining GR20. ▶ **Monte Cinto★★** *(4hr30 to the glacier edge round trip; 7hr to the top)* : D218 via Lozzi, drive for 10 km, then hike. ☐

OSPÉDALE Forest*

B4
Spread above the bay of Porto-Vecchio, this 45 km² pine forest looks on to granite needles.

▶ **Porto-Vecchio** (→) to **Zonza** *(40 km)* : D368 runs through wooded peaks and the Barocaggio-Marghese forest, crossing the Ospedale dam; 800 m past the dam, an unmarked path on the right leads to the **Piscia di Gallo waterfall** (often dry in summer; *2hr round trip).* ☐

Bay of PORTO***

A2
(see map 3)
The most beautiful spot is in the Bay of Girolata; farther on, the granite needles and columns of the Calanche rise 300 m above the water.

3. Bay of Porto

▶ **Porto** : restaurants and hotels deep in the bay and at the end of the valley; climb *(5 min)* the Genoese tower on the promontory to watch the sunset★★; eucalyptus wood along the pebble beach. ▶ **Sea excursions**★★ leave Porto for the Calanche *(2hr)* or Girolata *(3hr)*.

From Porto to the Calanche and Capo Rosso *(approx 22 km)*

▶ Drive to the chalet at Roches Bleues *(8 km from Porto)*, where you can obtain all the directions you need for walks around the Calanche; **castle** *(60-75 min return, blue markers)*; former **mule track** *(chemin des Muletiers★; 60-90 min return, blue markers)*. ▶ **Piana** : D624 (right) runs down to **Ficajola cove**★★ *(4 km)*, and D824 runs towards **Capo Rosso** *(9 km;* splendid view★★) and the beach at Arone. ▶ **Lava pass**★★ *(1 km S from Piana by D81)* : view over the Calanche and the **bays of Porto and Girolata.**

From Porto to Girolata *(23 km then 4hr walk round trip)*

▶ D81 leaves the red rocks of Bussaglia beach on the left. Beyond Partinello, pebble beach at Caspio. ▶ **La Croix Pass** *(272 m)* : view★★★ of the bays of Porto and Girolata. ▶ From the pass, a mule track leads to a fishing hamlet deep in the Bay★★★ of **Girolata**; rendez-vous for pleasure craft (inns). □

Practical Information ――――――――――――

PIANA, ⊠ 20115, 11 km SW of **Porto.**

Hotel :
★★★ **Capo Rosso**, ☎ 95.26.82.40, AE DC Visa, 57 rm 🅿 🕮 ⚲ 🕸 closed l.s. View of the sea and the bay, 300. Rest. ♦♦ ⦉ 80-170.

PORTO, ⊠ 20150 Ota, 76 km SW of **Calvi.**
ⓘ rte de la Marina, ☎ 95.26.10.55.

Hotels :
★★★ **Flots Bleus**, at the Marina, ☎ 95.26.11.26, 20 rm 🅿 ⚲ half pens (h.s.), closed 15 Oct-1 Apr, 550. Rest. ♦♦ ♪ 85-180.
★★ **Capo d'Orto**, rte de Calvi, ☎ 95.26.11.14, 30 rm 🅿 ⦉ 🕸 🔳 closed Nov-Mar, 220. Rest. ♦ ♪ 70-140.
★★ **Cyrnée**, at the Marina, ☎ 95.26.12.40, 10 rm ⦉ ⚲ closed Nov-Mar, 200. Rest. ♦ 80-160.
★★ **Le Porto**, rte de Calvi, ☎ 95.26.11.20, AE DC Euro Visa, 30 rm 🅿 ⦉ 🕸 closed 30 Sep-1 May, 240.
⚶ ★★★**Les Oliviers** (140 pl), ☎ 95.26.14.48.

SERRIERA, ⊠ 20147, 6 km N.

Hotels :
● ★★ **L'Aiglon**, Bussaglia beach, ☎ 95.26.10.65, 18 rm 🅿 ⦉ 🕮 ⚲ half pens (h.s.), closed Oct-Apr, 420. Rest. ♦ ⦉ 65-100.
★ **Maquis**, rte de Calvi, ☎ 95.26.12.19, 6 rm ⦉ closed 1 Nov-15 Dec, 170. Rest. ♦ ♪ 80-140.

Bay of PORTO-VECCHIO**

B4
White sand, emerald sea, umbrella pine and cork-oak forests are the setting for the inlets and sun-filled creeks of this bay. Before WWII **Porto-Vecchio** was a malaria-ridden village. Today, free of malaria, it is a town (pop. 8 103, inflated to 40 000 in summer) whose old streets and Genoese fortifications are steadily being turned into a seaside resort. It is the third largest port on the island and exports locally harvested cork as well as wine. There is an attractive olive grove by the marina *(1 km).*

▶ **Piccovagia peninsula**★★ *(28 km round trip)* closes the S end of the bay. Take the Bonifacio road *(N198 S)*, and proceed left on V7. **Palombaggia beach**★★, looking over to the Cerbicale Islands. ▶ **Santa Giulia Bay**★ *(8 km S)* : Club Méditerranée, and a white sand beach. ▶ **Sogno**

Bay, Saint Cyprien and **Pinarello**★★ beaches *(approx 15 km)*. D468 (narrow) leads to creeks and inlets on the N coast of the bay : holiday villages, campsites and small hotels. ▶ **Torre** and **Arraggio**★ *(8 km and 10 km N)* : stone fortresses built during the Bronze Age (2000BC). □

Practical Information ――――――――――――

PINARELLO, ⊠ 20144, 14 km NE.

Hotel :
★★ **La Tour Génoise**, ☎ 95.71.44.39, 28 rm 🅿 ⦉ ⚲ closed Oct-May, 220. Rest. ♦ 75-140.

PLAGE DE PALOMBAGGIA, ⊠ 20137, 14 km SE.

Hotel :
● ★★ **Le Hameau de Palombaggia**, ☎ 95.70.03.65, 20 rm 🅿 🕮 ⚲ closed Nov-Mar, 220.

PORTO-VECCHIO, ⊠ 20137, 63 km E of **Sartène.**
ⓘ pl. de l'Hôtel de Ville, ☎ 95.70.09.58.
Car rental : Avis, 7, bd J.-Jaurès, (Open 10.04/01.10) ☎ 95.70.14.77.

Hotels :
★★★ **Cala Rossa**, Lecci, 8 km, ☎ 95.71.61.51, Tx 460394, AE DC Visa, 50 rm 🅿 ⦉ 🕮 ♪ ⚲ half pens (h.s.), closed 1 Nov-10 May, 1900. Rest. ● ♦♦ ⦉ 🕸 Excellent cuisine : *chapon braisé, cabri rôti aux herbes, omelette au brocciu et menthe fraîche*, 180-230.
★★★ **Ziglione** (R.S.), rte de Palombaggia, ☎ 95.70.09.83, 32 rm 🅿 ⦉ 🕮 ⚲ half pens (h.s.), closed 15 Sep-15 May, 500. Rest. ♦ ⦉ ♪ 160-200.
★★ **Le Goéland**, at the Marina, ☎ 95.70.14.15, 21 rm 🅿 ⦉ 🕮 ⚲ 🕸 Private port, 180.
★★ **Les Roches Blanches**, rte du port de Commerce, ☎ 95.70.06.96, 15 rm 🅿 ⦉ ⚲ 🕸 half pens (h.s.), closed Oct-Apr, 180. Rest. ♦ 🕸 90-150.
★★ **San Giovanni**, rte d'Arca, ☎ 95.70.22.25, AE Visa, 26 rm 🅿 🕮 ⚲ ♿ 🔳 ♫ half pens (h.s.), closed 16 Oct-31 Mar, 270. Rest. ● ♦♦ ⦉ ♪ 80-130.
● **U Stagnolu**, rte de Cala-Rossa, la Trinité de Porto-Vecchio, ☎ 95.70.02.07, AE DC Visa, 30 rm 🅿 ⦉ 🕮 ⚲ half pens (h.s.), closed 15 Oct-Easter, 485. Rest. ♦ ⦉ ♪ 100-150.

Restaurants :
● ♦♦ **Le Baladin**, 13, rue du Gal-Leclerc, ☎ 95.70.08.62, AE DC Euro Visa ♪ closed Sat noon and Sun, 15 Dec-1 Feb. Colette and Toussaint Matteï are fond of good things, much to the pleasure of their patrons : *marinade de saumon au coulis d'huîtres, filet de daurade au beurre rouge, mignon de veau à l'orange*, 140-180.
♦♦ **Le Troubadour**, 13, rue du Gal-Leclerc, ☎ 95.70.08.04, AE DC Euro Visa 🕮 ♪ closed Sat noon and Sun, 15 Dec-1 Feb. Tanks of live lobsters, 130-160.
♦ **Le Lucullus**, 17, rue du Gal-de-Gaulle, ☎ 95.70.10.17, AE DC Euro Visa ♪ closed Mon noon and Sun (Oct-May), 15 Jan-28 Feb. Good regional cooking, 70-180.

⚶ ★★★★**Golfo di Sogno** (500 pl), ☎ 95.70.08.98; ★★★**Arutoli** (50 pl), ☎ 95.70.12.73; ★★★**La Baie des Voiles** (100 pl), ☎ 95.70.01.23; ★★★**Les Ilots d'Or** (100 pl), ☎ 95.70.01.30.

Recommended
Marina : ☎ 95.70.01.83, (450 empl.).

PROPRIANO*

Sartène 13, Ajaccio 73, Corte 138 km
pop 3098 ⊠ 20110   A4
On Valinco Bay, kilometres of fine sand border a placid sea, ideal for underwater fishing and aquatic sports.

Nearby

▶ **Valinco Bay**★, north coast : Porto-Pollo and Filitosa★★ *(28 km)*. Cliff road above the bay; after 14 km, road to the right for Filitosa (→) : prehistoric statues. **Porto-Pollo** : a family resort where sailing boats used to load charcoal.

▶ **Valinco Bay★, south coast :** Belvédère and **Campo-moro** *(16 km; light best in the evening).* Portigliolo : 1.5 km of sand. **Belvédère** overlooking the bay. **Campomoro★ :** a Genoese watchtower at the end of the cape. ▶ **Olmeto** *(9.5 km N) :* Prosper Mérimée (1803-70; author of *Carmen*) featured the town in *Colomba*, a novel that traced the course of a *vendetta*. Nearby, **Fozzano, Santa Maria-Figaniella, Arbellara** and **Viggianello** overlook the Bay of Valinco. □

Practical Information ―――――――――――――

PROPRIANO
ⓘ 17, av. du Gal-de-Gaulle, ☎ 95.76.01.49.
Car rental : *Avis*, rue du Gal-de-Gaulle, ☎ 95.76.00.76.

Hotel :
★★ **Lido**, ☎ 95.76.06.37, 17 rm Ⓟ ✦ ⬟ closed in winter, 220. Rest. ♦♦ ♪ Beside the sea. Spiny lobsters in tanks prepared to order by Antoine Pettilloni, 80-140.

Restaurant :
♦♦ **Le Cabanon**, av. Napoléon, ☎ 95.76.07.76, AE DC Visa ✦ ♪ closed 30 Oct-15 Mar, 70-210.

△ ★★★*Colomba* (100 pl), ☎ 95.76.06.42; ★★★*Le Corsica* (120 pl), ☎ 95.76.00.57; ★★★*Tikiti-Campeoles* (200 pl), ☎ 95.76.08.32.

Recommended
Marina : ☎ 95.76.10.40, (360 empl.).

Nearby

PORTO-POLLO, ⊠ 20140 Petreto-Bicchisano, 20 km NW.

Hotel :
★ **Les Eucalyptus**, ☎ 95.74.01.52, AE DC Euro Visa, 24 rm Ⓟ ✦ ⬟ ◿ ✿ ◢ half pens (h.s.), closed 1 Oct-15 May. On Valinco bay, 360. Rest. ♦ ✦ ♪ Spec : fish and seafood, 65-150; child : 40.

△ ★★*Alfonsi* (116 pl), ☎ 95.74.01.80; ★★*Valinco* (70 pl), ☎ 95.74.02.12.

QUENZA

Sartène 44, Ajaccio 84, Bastia 150 km
pop 229 ⊠ 20122 B3

The Bavella needles *(aiguilles)* rear like fangs above the horizon; to the N lies the Cuscione plateau, among southern Corsica's finest high pastures, and a centre for cross-country skiing, horseback riding and hiking; church (carved pulpit and panels, 16thC).

▶ **Aullène** *(15 km W) :* church with pulpit whose carving recalls the pirate raids that ravaged the coast until the 18thC. □

Practical Information ―――――――――――――

QUENZA
ⓘ mairie, ☎ 95.78.62.11.

Hotel :
★★ **Sole a Monti**, ☎ 95.78.62.53, 20 rm ✦ closed 15 Sep-1 May, 200.

Nearby

AULLÈNE, ⊠ 20116, 14 km W.

Hotel :
★ **Poste**, ☎ 95.78.61.21, 20 rm Ⓟ ✦ ◿ closed Oct-Apr, 100. Rest. ♦ ✦ ⓖ ✿ A place to keep in mind, offering a single fixed-price menu of specialties, 75.

SAINT-FLORENT*

Bastia 23, Calvi 70, Ajaccio 176 km
pop 1217 ⊠ 20217 B1

Base for pleasure craft and scuba diving; the regional capital of Nebbio along the shoreline deep in a pic-

ture-postcard bay★ : Place des Portes, marina, and old town around the Genoese citadel.

▶ **Nebbio Cathedral★** *(1 km; key from the SI on the Bastia road) :* this handsome Romanesque building (early 12thC Pisan) is the only vestige of the city of Nebbio; carved stylized animals on some capitals.

Around Nebbio★★ *(60 km round trip, approx. 4hr)*

▶ The region fans out from the Bay of Saint-Florent to a semicircle of mountains on the horizon; vineyards (including those of Patrimonio), orchards and olive groves alternate with pastureland and sheepfolds. ▶ Take D81 towards Calvi; after 5 km, take D62 left. ▶ **Santo-Pietro-di-Tenda :** a red stone church (17thC); 800 m farther on, the ruins of the Romanesque St. Pietro (13thC). ▶ **Sorio.** ▶ **Rapale.** ▶ Romanesque church of **San Michele★★ :** unusual gate-tower; white and green (serpentine) walls. ▶ **San Stefano Pass★★** *(road right towards Bastia via Lancone Pass★) :* the sea on either side. ▶ **Oletta,** known for a Roquefort-like cheese. ▶ **Teghime Pass★★ :** view of both flanks of Cap Corse is even better if you go up to the **Serra di Pigno★★** *(4 km of narrow road; left just after the pass towards Bastia).* ▶ **Patrimonio,** renowned for wine. □

Practical Information ―――――――――――――

SAINT-FLORENT
ⓘ at the Centre administratif, ☎ 95.37.06.04.

Hotels :
★★★ **Bellevue**, ☎ 95.37.00.06, Tx 460290, AE DC Euro Visa, 27 rm Ⓟ ⬟ ☐ ◢ closed Oct-Mar, 450.
● ★★ **Dolce Notte**, rte de Bastia, ☎ 95.37.06.65, 25 rm Ⓟ ✦ ⬟ ◿ ✿ closed Nov-Mar, 250.
★★ **Europe**, pl. des Portes, ☎ 95.37.00.03, 22 rm, closed Nov-Easter, 230. Rest. ♦ ♪ 80-140.

Restaurants :
● ♦ **La Rascasse**, prom. des Quais, ☎ 95.37.06.99, AE Euro Visa ✦ ♪ ⓖ closed Mon (Mar-May), Nov-Feb. Only a few tables available for top-quality fish and seafood in this up-and-coming restaurant, 120-180.
♦ **La Gaffe**, at the port, ☎ 95.37.00.12, AE DC Euro Visa ✦ ⬟ ♪ ⓖ closed Mon, Nov-Feb, 75-150; child : 40.

△ ★★★*Camp d'Olzo* (60 pl), ☎ 95.37.03.34; ★★★*Kalliste* (160 pl), ☎ 95.37.03.08; ★★★*U Pezzo*, rte de la Plage (145 pl), ☎ 95.37.01.65; ★★*Acqua Dolce* (70 pl), ☎ 95.37.08.63.

Recommended
Guide to wines : *Dominique Gentille*, ☎ 95.37.01.54. Muscat wines.
Marina : ☎ 95.37.00.79, (550 slips).
▼ *Casa di l'Atrigiani*, pl. de la Poste.

Nearby

PATRIMONIO, ⊠ 20253, 5 km NW.

Restaurant :
♦ **L'Osteria di San-Martino**, ☎ 95.30.11.93, Visa ⬟ ♪ closed 25 Sep-Jun, 80-100; child : 30.

Recommended
Bicycle rental : *Locacycles*, ☎ 95.37.07.87, motor scooters, motorized bicycles, bicycles (Mar-Nov).
Boat rental : *Locanautic*, ☎ 95.37.07.87, motor boats, water scooters, wind surfers, pedal boats (May-Sep).
Guide to wines : *cave Marsifi*, outside the village.

SARTÈNE*

Ajaccio 86, Corte 140, Bastia 178 km
pop 3184 ⊠ 20100 A4

The austere medieval buildings are typically Corsican; flowered window-boxes and garlands of washing brighten the sombre granite walls in the old town★.

▶ **Church :** cross and chains carried by the Grand Penitent during the penitential procession *(Procession du*

Catenacciu) on Good Friday evening; this ritual is often compared to that of Holy Week in Seville. ▶ **Museum of Prehistoric Corsica★** *(10-12 & 2-5 or 6; winter, closed Sat. and Sun.)* : artifacts dating from the early Mediterranean Neolithic (6000BC) to the early Iron Age. ▶ **Panorama★** from the rocky outcrop overlooking the village from the E.

Nearby

▶ **Belvédère de Foce★** *(5 km E)* : view of the Rizzanèse basin and Valinco Bay. ▶ The **Palaggiu megaliths** *(16 km SW)* : 258 menhirs, the largest single group in the Mediterranean. The road continues to the marina at **Tizzano** *(5 km)* : beach, creeks, scuba diving. ▶ The **Fontanaccia dolmen** *(17 km SSW)* : six vertical stones supporting a horizontal slab 3.40 m long. Nearby : **Rinaiu** (45 menhirs) and **Stantari** (25 menhirs). □

Practical Information —————————————

ⓘ cours Saraneli, ☎ 95.77.05.37.

Hotels :
● ★★ *Roches*, ☎ 95.77.07.61, Visa, 66 rm Ⓟ ≼ ⋘ ⚘ 200. Rest. ✦ ♪ 70-130.
★★ *Villa Piana*, rte de Propriano, ☎ 95.77.07.04, DC Visa, 32 rm Ⓟ ≼ ⋘ ⚘ ♪ ⚘ ⚘ closed 30 Sep-8 May, 210.

Restaurant :
◆◆ *La Chaumière*, 39, rue Louis-Cap.-Bededetti, ☎ 95.77.07.13, AE DC Visa ≼ ♿ closed Mon (Oct-May), 2 Jan-2 Mar. Spec : *tripe, cabri en sauce, porcelet à la corse*, 70-180.

⚠ ★★★*L'Avena*, domaine de Zivia, Tizzano (280 pl), ☎ 95.77.02.18.

Recommended
Guide to wines : *cave coopérative Santa Barba*, ☎ 95.77.01.05; *Cave des grands vins sartenais*, on the Propriano road.
♥ *Casa di l'Artigiani*, rue Bonaparte, ☎ 95.77.02.26, open Apr-Sep and Christmas.

SOLENZARA

Sartène 77, Bastia 103, Ajaccio 131 km
⊠ 20145 Sari-di-Porto-Vecchio   B3
SOLENZARA
ⓘ mairie annexe, ☎ 95.57.43.75.

Hotels :
★★★ *Maquis et Mer*, ☎ 95.57.42.40, 7 rm Ⓟ ⋘ closed Nov, 290.
★★ *La Solenzara*, ☎ 95.57.42.18, AE DC Euro Visa, 33 rm Ⓟ ≼ ⋘ ⚘ 150.

Recommended
Marina : ☎ 95.57.46.42, 350 slips.

Nearby

FAVONE, ⊠ 20144, 9 km SE.

Hotel :
★★*U Dragulinu*, ☎ 95.57.20.30. Visa, 26 rm. ⋘ ≼ Ⓟ ⚘ half pens (h.s.), 475. Rest. ✦ ♿ 85-160; child : 35.

⚠ ★★*Bon Annon* (100 pl), ☎ 95.57.24.35.

TARCO, ⊠ 20137, 14 km S.

Hotel :
★★ *Au Rêve*, ☎ 95.57.20.93, 21 rm Ⓟ ≼ ♿ ⚘ closed 30 Sep-1 May, 210. Rest. ✦ ⚘ A pleasant place to stop. Exceptional *bouillabaisse* prepared by Mme Mancha, from her fisherman husband's catch, 100-160.

Restaurant :
◆◆ *Fonderie*, ☎ 95.57.40.21 ♿ closed Tue and Wed (l.s.). Spec : fish and Corsican dishes, 100-190.

⚠ ★★★*Côte des Nacres* (100 pl), ☎ 95.57.40.65.

TAVIGNANO Valley

B2-3
The Tavignano River winds through rocky gorges between Corte and Aléria before running into the eastern plain. Ancient villages clinging to the northern slopes are linked by cliff roads.

Along the Tavignano *(84 km, leave Corte by D14)*

▶ **Erbajolo** : panorama★★. ▶ **Altiani.** ▶ **Piedicorte-di-Gaggio** : view★. ▶ **Pancheraccia.** ▶ Return to Corte by N200 beside the river. □

VIZZAVONA*

B3
Just off the Bastia-Ajaccio road, this hideaway in the heart of the forest consists of a minuscule railway station and a few hotels. As a stopover on GR20, Vizzavona is popular with hikers. ▶ The **forest★**, 3 700 acres of pine and beech, is crisscrossed with walking trails. **Col de Vizzavona** (pass, alt. 1 168 m; *3 km towards Ajaccio*) links the schist region of NE Corsica to the crystalline rocks of the SW.

Nearby

▶ Excursions on foot ranging from easy strolls to cross-country treks : ▶ Chemin des Ponts *(45 min)*. ▶ Madonuccia *(1hr)*. ▶ Cascade des Anglais *(45 min)*. ▶ Punta di u Ceppa *(1hr30)*. Monte d'Oro★ *(8hr30 round trip)*. □

Practical Information —————————————

Col de VIZZAVONA, ⊠ 20219 Vivario, 9 km NE.

Hotel :
★ *Monte d'Oro*, ☎ 95.47.21.06, 47 rm Ⓟ ≼ ⋘ ⚘ ⚘ closed Oct-Jun, 100. Rest. ✦ ⚘ 60-120.

ZICAVO

Sartène 60, Ajaccio 63, Corte 81 km
pop 269 ⊠ 20132   B3
Among mountains covered in beech and chestnut, this large village is a base for hiking and cross-country skiing excursions towards the Coscione and the incudine ranges.

▶**Incudine★★** (2 128 m) : vantage point of southern Corsica, accessible by a forest road and GR20 *(4hr30 round trip)*. □

Dauphiné

▶ In Dauphiné — between mountains and Midi, between Alps and Mediterranean — the green fields and dark forests of the Vercors meet up with the dry mountains and lavender fields of the Diois region. At Chamrousse, L'Alpe-d'Huez and Les Deux Alpes, the winter skier can enjoy mountain scenery and southern sun, or can ski through the snow-covered pasturelands of Vercors and the forests of Chartreuse. In summer, the tourist can hike through villages, hamlets and sheep-folds nestled in high mountain passes, past torrents of clear mountain water where marmots come to drink and play.

The Drôme Valley, bathed in a light reminiscent of Tuscany, unfolds its centuries-old villages with their southern beechtrees and oleanders. The Chartreuse Massif climbs towards immense banks of dark pinetrees studded with strange limestone formations. In 1085 Saint Bruno founded the monastery which became the mother house of his order. The monks still make the famous Chartreuse liqueur — yellow and green — which was originally intended for pharmaceutical use, from 130 plants carefully combined according to a secret recipe.

Grenoble, the capital of Dauphiné, is a dynamic city with a high-tech reputation in industry and scientific research, and it played a leading role in the great hydroelectric power adventure of the last century. It is characterized by the intellectual ferment of its university campuses and research centres.

The area around Valence produces wines belonging to the great Côtes-du-Rhône family.

Châtillons-en-Diois produces light, fruity, elegant wines which are mostly drunk in the region. Dauphiné's most famous recipe is the *gratin dauphinois*, a delicious dish of potatoes baked with eggs and cheese. But there are all kinds of *gratins*, using macaroni, eggplant, and many other specialities of the region. □

 Don't miss

★★★ The Oisans Massif B2, the Queyras Valley C2, the Vercors Massif A-B2.

★★ The Briançonnais Region C2, the Chartreuse Massif B1, Grenoble B2, Saint-Véran C2.

★ L'Alpe-d'Huez B2, Briançon C2, Chamrousse B2, the Devoluy Massif B3, Valley of the Drôme A3, Serre-Ponçon C3, the Valbonnais Valley B2, Vallouise Valley C2, Vienne A1, Villard-de-Lans A-B2.

Weekend tips

Visit Grenoble first of all, an hour from Lyon by motorway. See the Musée des Beaux-Arts (Fine Arts Museum) and the old quarters of the town; lunch in the Rue St-Laurent. After a few hairpin bends and over the Porte pass, you're in La Chartreuse, with splendid landscapes and a famous monastery, not open to visitors, but at La Correrie you will learn everything about the monks and their liqueur. On returning to Grenoble, dine at La Bastille overlooking the lights of the town.

The next day see the Vercors Massif : a real mountain trip. From Villard-de-Lans return either by Pont-en-Royans and the Isère Valley or go back the same way through Sassenage.

Brief regional history

BC
Starting around 650 BC the **Celts,** the ancestors of the Gauls, began to settle in Dauphiné; the best-known tribe was the **Allobroges,** famous for their resistance to the Romans.

121BC-AD5
The **Roman occupation** of the Dauphiné lasted 575 years, and Vienne, the capital of the conquered Allobroges, became a rich and brilliant Roman city (commerce, industry).

6th-13thC
As the feudal system took hold during the **Middle Ages,** certain seigneurs dominated the others, by force or through suitable alliances. Thus **Guigues le Vieux,** Comte d'Albon, would seem to be the founder of the Dauphiné. His descendants continued his policy of expansion; Guigues IV was the first to bear the title of Dauphin.

14thC
But two centuries later, **Humbert II,** last of the third line of Dauphins, ruined and childless, negotiated the sale of his domains (200 000 florins and a life's income) to the King of France. This was the famous *Transport du Dauphiné.* The agreement stipulated that the Dauphiné should be the province of the eldest son of the King of France, which is why the Crown Prince was known as the Dauphin until the fall of the French monarchy.

15th-17thC
The Crown's **newly-acquired province** was a **well-administered territory,** with a diversified economy : cattle, arable farming (at altitudes up to 2 000 m), wine, fruit, hemp, wood and wool were the Dauphiné's principle products. ● During the wars of religion (16thC), the Dauphiné was on the whole favourable to the Protestant Reformation. At this point there appeared the formidable and destructive Baron des Adrets and the great Protestant war-chief, **Lesdiguières** (1543-1626).

18thC
Politically, the old **Delphinal Council** instituted by Humbert II (14thC) was **transformed into a Parliament** (1453) by the future Louis XI, the only royal Dauphin to have visited his province in order to govern it. The Parliament of Grenoble, as it was known, was to play a major role in the early stages of the French Revolution. ● In 1791 the Dauphiné was divided into three departments : the Isère, the Drôme and the Hautes-Alpes.

19thC
This century was marked principally by **economic change,** and by the building of roads and railways (greatly benefitting Valence, on the Paris-Marseille line). 1869 saw Aristide Bergès' first use of water power, which he called "white coal", to operate a paper mill in Graisivaudan. Grenoble was also to profit from this new energy source, and the developing electrochemical and metallurgical industries, large consumers of electricity, sprang up near generating stations built in the valleys of the Graisivaudan, the Romanche, Maurienne and the Tarentaise.

20thC
This spirit of imaginative research and capacity for invention characterizes the Dauphiné today. The local character is one of tenacity and resistance; during the last war the **Maquis** (partisans) of Oisans, Chartreuse and Vercors demonstrated this to the full.

Drôme region farmhouse

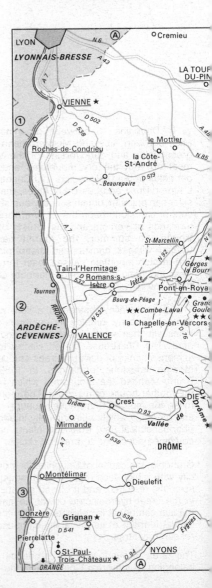

Briançon area

Dauphiné region

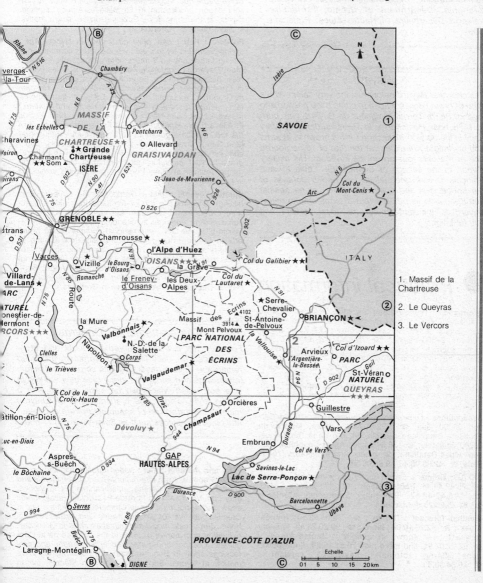

1. Massif de la Chartreuse

2. Le Queyras

3. Le Vercors

Facts and figures

Location : *The Dauphiné region is the hinge linking the northern and southern Alps, joining Savoie and Italy in the northeast to the Alps of Haute-Provence in the south. In the west, the Dauphiné is bounded by the Rhône.*
Area : *19219 km².*
Climate : *Except in the extreme south and the lowest valleys, the mountains dictate the weather. The Dauphiné's position between northern and southern Alps is evident in the region's marked temperature changes.*
Population : *1319583; Isère : 860378; Drôme : 361847; Hautes-Alpes : 97358.*
Administration : *Department of Isère, Prefecture : Grenoble. Department of Drôme, Prefecture : Valence. Department of Hautes-Alpes, Prefecture : Gap.*

Bayard

The chevalier Bayard belongs in the very select Who's Who of great heroes whose exploits have passed into legend. Pierre Terrail, Seigneur de Bayard, was born in 1476 near Pontcharra, in Graisivaudan (→). Very early in life he won distinction for his prowess at arms and his knightly exploits; at the age of 16 he floored one of the best jousters in the kingdom. His military career, in the service of Charles VIII, Louis XII and François I, was unequalled. His heroic defense of the bridge over the Garigliano River, alone against 200 Spaniards, is but one feat of arms among many. Bayard is the epitome of the loyal servant and faithful knight.

 # Practical information

Information : Hautes-Alpes : *Comité Départemental du Tourisme (C.D.T.)*, 5 ter, rue Capitaine-de-Bresson, 05002 Gap Cedex, ☎ 92.53.62.00. **Drôme :** *C.D.T.*, 1, av. de Romans, 26000 Valence, ☎ 75.43.27.12. **Isère :** *C.D.T.*, same address as the *C.R.T. Dir. Rég. Jeunesse et Sports*, 15, rue de la République, B.P. 1145, 38022 Grenoble Cedex, ☎ 76.42.75.90. In *Paris :* Maison **Alpes-Dauphiné,** 2, pl. André-Malraux, 75001, ☎ 42.96.08.56. *Maison de la* **Drôme,** 14, bd Haussmann, 75009, ☎ 42.46.66.67. *Maison des* **Hautes-Alpes,** 4, av. de l'Opéra, 75002, ☎ 42.96.05.08.

Reservations : *Loisirs-Accueil* **Hautes-Alpes,** 16, rue Carnot, 05000 Gap, ☎ 92.61.73.73; **Isère,** Maison du Tourisme Dauphiné-Grenoble, 14, rue de la République, 38000 Grenoble, ☎ 76.54.34.36; **Alpes-Dauphiné,** Maison Alpes-Dauphiné, 2, place André-Malraux, 75001 Paris, ☎ 42.96.08.43/49.96.08.56.

S.O.S. : Drôme : *SAMU (emergency medical service),* ☎ 75.42.44.44. **Hautes-Alpes :** ☎ 17; **Isère :** *SAMU,* ☎ 76.42.42.42. Poisoning Emergency Centre : ☎ 91.75.25.25 in Marseille.

Weather forecast : Drôme : ☎ 75.01.83.50; **Hautes-Alpes :** ☎ 92.20.10.00; **Isère :** ☎ 92.20.20.40. *Weather forecast — snow conditions,* **Hautes-Alpes :** ☎ 92.21.07.91, and **Isère :** ☎ 76.51.19.29. *Snow conditions* (24-hr automatic answering service) : ☎ 76.54.30.80.

Rural gîtes and chambres d'hôtes : enq. : *Relais Départementaux;* **Hautes-Alpes :** 5 ter, rue Capitaine-de-Bresson, B.P. 55, 05002 Gap Cedex, ☎ 92.51.31.45; **Drôme :** av. Georges-Brassens, 26500 Bourg-lès-Valence, ☎ 75.43.01.70, ext 18; **Isère :** *Maison du Tourisme,* 14, rue de la République, 38000 Grenoble, ☎ 76.44.42.28.

Camping-car rentals : Isère : *Carloc,* rue de la Mairie, Bresson, 38320 Eybend, ☎ 76.25.71.63; *Vienne camping-car,* route de Leveau, 38200 Vienne, ☎ 74.85.74.51; *Ducros,* Centre Dauphiné-Survoie, quartier de l'Egala, Z.I. de Voreppe, 38430 Moirans, ☎ 76.53.70.89.

Cultural events : Apr-May : *chamber music festival* at the château de Grignan. **Mar :** *music festival* in Saint-Antoine-l'Abbaye; *humourous film festival* in Chamrousse; *pilgrimage* at Notre-Dame-de-Lans; *festival* at the château de Vizille. **Jul :** *jazz festival* in Vienne, *festival of film shorts* in Grenoble; *Mont-St-Guillaume pilgrimage* in Embrun; *Notre-Dame-des-Neiges festival* in L'Alpe-d'Huez; *torchlight canoe procession* in La Salle-les-Alpes; *"summer nights"* at the château de Suze-la-Rousse. **Aug :** *festival* in Saint-Pierre-de-Chartreuse.

Folklore : Feb : *new olive oil festival* in Nyons. **Apr :** *spring festival* in Nyons. **Jul :** *wood-cutter's competition* in Allevard and Lans-en-Vercors; *international folk festival* in Mont Severoux; *linden flower festival* in Buis-les-Baronnies; *picodon festival* in Saou. **Aug :** *wood-cutters' festival* in Chamrousse; *world assembly of Dauphinois kinsmen* in Grenoble; *mountain festival* in L'Alpe-d'Huez; *mountain pasture festival* in Gresse-en-Vercors and Arvieux; *festival of the Saint-Hilaire funicular railway; beer festival* in Allevard; *threshing festival* in Fressinières; *festival of the mountain and guides* in La Chapelle-en-Valgaudemar (2nd Sun.); *lavender festival* in Lesches-en-Diois. **Sep :** *colt fair* and *horse festival* in Saint-Sorlin-en-Valloire; *grape-harvest festival* in Tain-l'Hermitage. **Oct :** *démontagnage festival* in Saint-Bonnet; *gastronomic exhibition* in Laragne.

Sporting events : Mar : *Grand Prix de L'Alpe-d'Huez* (skiing), *Chamrousse 6-hour* (cross-country ski competition); *"white tread"* in Autran. **Apr :** *auto race* in Crémieu. **Jun :** *cycling criterium* in Grenoble; *foot race* in Saint-Martin-d'Uriage. **Jul :** *international summer skiing grand prix* in L'Alpe-d'Huez; *pedestrian rally* from Oisans to Bourg-d'Oisans. **Aug :** *Trophée des Écrins* in Venosc; *auto-cross* in Bourg-d'Oisans; *speleology* (spelunking) *film festival* in La Chapelle-en-Vercors (28 Aug-2 Sep). **Sep :** *international hang-gliding film festival* in Saint-Hilaire. **Oct-Nov :** *6 cyclists' days* in Grenoble.

The craftsmen of Queyras

Formerly the peasants carved the tools and utensils needed for daily life, while craftsmen produced remarkable chests decorated with scrollwork, foliage, interlacings and suns. The stone pine they worked in is a soft wood which can be easily carved with a simple knife. Today, the craftsmanship of Queyras maintains the tradition of beautiful furniture and beautiful objects in places such as Saint-Véran and Abriès.

Fairs and markets : Mar : *paper industry fair* and *spring fair* in Grenoble. **Apr :** *international market of minerals and crystals* in Bourg-d'Oisans; *used-car market* in Vienne. **May :** *postcard salon* in Pont-de-Beauvoisin; *scale model show* and *agricultural fair* in Chapareillan; *antique fair* in Crémieu; *festival of artistic trades and professions* in Rives. **Jun :** *scale model and miniature show* in Grenoble; *exhibition and market of arms* in the château de la Condamine, Corenc; *bric-à-brac and artistic trades and professions show* in Beaucroissant. **Jul :** *international olive market* in Nyons. **Sep :** *bric-à-brac* in Vienne; *fair* in

Lans-le-Vercors; *antique fair* in Chapareillan; Beaucroissant *fair.* Oct : *honey fair* in Vienne. **Nov** : *Alpexpo and autumn fair* in Grenoble. **Dec** : *motor show* in Grenoble.

National and nature parks : *Parc Naturel National des Écrins,* 7, rue du Colonel-Roux, B.P. 142, 05004 Gap Cedex, ☎ 92.51.40.71, and *Maison du Parc,* 05290 Vallouise, ☎ 92.23.32.31. *Parc Naturel Régional du Vercors,* 38250 Lans-en-Vercors, ☎ 76.95.40.33, and *Maisons du Parc,* 38650 Gresse-en-Vercors, ☎ 76.34.08.40; in La Chapelle-en-Vercors and Chamaloc, ☎ 75.22.11.82. *Parc régional du Queyras,* rte de la Gare, 05600 Guillestre, ☎ 92.45.06.23. *Le Jardin des oiseaux,* Lepie, ☎ 75.84.45.90.

Chartreuse

The secret has been well kept. We know only that 130 plants go into the composition of the famous elixir given to the Charterhouse monks in 1607 and known as Chartreuse. Pinks, absinthe, fir buds and balm are among the ingredients, but the proportions are a secret. Today the Carthusian monks are still active (in Voiron → Chartreuse) around their great stills. Green Chartreuse (55°) and yellow Chartreuse (43°) are made directly from this mysterious mixture, which was originally for medicinal use only.

Rambling and hiking : topoguides G.R. 5-54/541, 549-58/541, G.R. 9/91/93/95, 9/429, G.R. 91, G.R. 94/946. The *Briançon Guide Office* organizes accompanied excursions : tours of the Cerces, of Champsaur, of the Rochebrune peak, in Queyras, of Viso and South Oisans; enq and enrollments, ☎ 92.20.15.73. *Centre d'Information Montagne et Sentiers (C.I.M.E.S.),* ☎ 76.54.34.36. Tour of the Alps, enq. *Maison du Tourisme,* B.P. 227, 14, rue de la République, 38019 Grenoble, ☎ 76.42.08.31/76.51.76.00. Hike with packhorse, enq. : *Bureau des accompagnateurs d'Embrun,* ☎ 92.43.02.75; *Maison de la nature,* 05460 Abriès, ☎ 92.45.73.54, and *Terre-Rouge,* 05100 Cervières, ☎ 92.21.01.37.

Scenic railways : Saint-Georges-La Mure line : runs every Sun. from end May to end Sep., enq. : *Chemin de Fer de La Mure,* ☎ 76.46.12.51. Saint-Hilaire-du-Touvet funicular railway : daily ex Tue. 15 May-15 Oct., enq. : ☎ 67.08.00.02. Bréda-Pontcharra-La Rochette line : runs on the first Sun. of each month from May to Oct., 1 hr 30 trip (allow approx 6 hours return for day-trip). Enq. : M. Vargel, ☎ 76.21.02.10, and M. Portenart, ☎ 76.27.21.56.

Riding holidays : *Assn. Régionale Rhône-Alpes de Tourisme Équestre,* 47, av. A.-Briand, 38600 Fontaine, ☎ 76.27.10.61. *Association la Drôme à cheval,* 21, rue de Royans, 26100 Romans, ☎ 75.05.15.50.

Cycling holidays : *Ligue Régionale Dauphiné-Savoie,* hameau d'Allières, 38640 Claix. *Comité Dép. des Hautes-Alpes,* ☎ 92.51.57.45. *Tour de la Drôme,* enq : M. Mazan, Beauséjour, av. Lupin, 26300 Bourg-de-Péage, ☎ 75.70.36.01.

River and canal unises : at Valence, port de l'Epervière, excursions on the Rhône, ☎ 75.42.38.93.

Technical tourism : *Station météorologique de St-Martin d'Hères,* ☎ 76.54.29.63. Tour of ancient nougat factory, *Escobar,* pl. Léopold Blanc, 26200 Montélimar, ☎ 75.01.25.53; Traditional oil-mill, enq. : Mme Autran, la Digue, 26110 Nyons, ☎ 75.26.02.52 or S.C.A. du Nyonsais, B.P. 9, 26110 Nyons, ☎ 75.26.03.44. Liqueur : *Cave de la Grande Chartreuse,* bd E.-Kofler, 38500 Voiron, visits every day from Easter to Toussaint (8-11:30; 2-6:30) and from Toussaint to Easter, every day except Sat, Sun and hols. Skis : *Rossignol,* Le Menon, 38500

Voiron, ☎ 76.05.40.22 : visits every working day, enq. at public relations office.

Handicraft courses : silk and wood painting, drawing, mosaic work, pottery, porcelain, weaving, wood sculpture, carpentry, book-binding, wicker-work and photography : see *Maisons du Tourisme* in Grenoble and Paris to obtain the list, and the *Ateliers du Canet,* 38590 Saint-Martin-le-Vinoux, ☎ 76.87.61.17, which organize most of these courses.

Dauphinois cuisine

This is the country of the gratin, the most famous of the breed being potato-based gratin dauphinois. There is no room here to list all the possible variations and explain the different points of view of Dauphiné cooks; but here is the recipe considered (by many, if not all!) as the basic starting point : thickly butter a gratin dish and cover it in fine slices of good quality potato. Salt and pepper. Beat a whole egg, and add whole milk. Moisten the potatoes with the mixture and sprinkle with dabs of butter. Cook in a slow oven. Grated Gruyère cheese is optional. The list of possible gratins is unlimited — macaroni, eggplant, crayfish, etc. As for other delicacies, olive trees grow in profusion around Dignes and Nyons. Truffles can be found, during the season, in the Drôme. The local pastry is known as la pogne, half-way between a brioche and a tart, and garnished with fruit or squash according to season. Numerous liqueurs including the famous Chartreuse, and génépi, are made from the aromatic plant of that name.

The wines of the Dauphiné

North of Valence, the wines of L'Ermitage and Crozes-Ermitage belong to the great family of Côtes-du-Rhône. These wines taste strongly of their origins, a flavour of blackberries and hawthorns. Among the reds : Bessards, Croze and Larnage; among the whites, Chante Alouette and Le Clos des Hirondelles (great years : 1945, 49, 54, 57, 61, 67, 71, 76, 78, 83). Also worthy of attention are the reds of Haut-Comtat around Nyons, solidly structured and generous, and those of the Coteaux du Tricastin, light and fruity. Clairette de Die is a sparkling wine, admired for its freshness and finesse.

Other courses : botany and apiculture at the *Maison de la Flore,* near Die, ☎ 75.22.11.82; the *Hutte aux Pies Association* organizes circuits to discover minerals, plant-life and habitat, ☎ 92.66.25.40. Instructional courses in mountain bird-watching, observation of mountain wildlife and flora : enq at the *A.N.C.E.E.S.F.,* Maison de la Nature, 05460 Abriès, ☎ 92.45.73.54. The *Maison du Parc des Écrins* proposes summer courses in ornithology, plant-life, botanical fauna, geology and ethnology. Courses in expression, dance, theatre, music : list from *Maisons du tourisme en Dauphiné* in Grenoble and Paris. Dance : *Conservatoire de la danse de Grenoble,* ☎ 76.87.82.82, and info : *C.D.T. Drôme.* Theatre : *Compagnie de la Tour Brune* in Embruns, ☎ 92.43.02.61.

Sports courses : spelunking : *Maison du parc et de la spéléo,* 26420 La Chapelle-en-Vercors, ☎ 75.48.22.38, and *Centre national de la spéléologie,* 26420 Saint-Martin-en-Vercors, ☎ 75.45.50.05. Climbing : *Maison du parc et du Royans,* ☎ 75.48.70.59, and *Maison des Gui-*

des, Embrun, ☎ 92.43.02.75. Cross-country skiing and hiking : *Maison de la transhumance*, ☎ 76.34.10.13 (Tue., Fri. pm). Horse-trekking : Barcillonnette, ☎ 92.54.24.62. Also list from *les Maisons de tourisme du Dauphiné* and the *Club Alpin Français*, section Dauphiné, 32, av. Félix-Viallet, 38000 Grenoble, ☎ 76.87.03.73, and section Hautes-Alpes, B.P. 61, 64, Grand-Rue, 05102 Briançon Cedex, ☎ 92.21.18.77.

Wine guide : *Université du vin*, 26130 Suze-la-Rousse, ☎ 75.04.86.09.

Children : courses in competitive downhill skiing and tennis in Les Orres, enq. : *comité de la station*, ☎ 92.44.01.61; courses in hiking, mountain discovery, botany, etc. : *Parc des Écrins*, O.T. Embrun, ☎ 92.43.02.75, and S.I. Savines, ☎ 92.44.20.44. Also enq : *Dir. régionale de la Jeunesse et des Sports*.

Sailing and wind-surfing : *Féd. Régionale Dauphiné-Savoie* **(Isère + Drôme)**, M. Duclot, clos des Gentons, 38570 Theys, ☎ 76.54.41.27. *Féd. Alpes-Provence* **(Hautes-Alpes)**, M. Bouveyron, C.N.M., Pavillon Flottant, quai Rive-Neuve, 13007 Marseille, ☎ 91.33.73.55. *Base de l'Épervière* in Valence.

Water skiing : *Ligue Régionale Dauphiné*, M. Cortez, 14, rue Charrel, 38000 Grenoble, ☎ 76.23.35.36, and for the **Hautes-Alpes :** *Ligue Régionale Méditerranée*, Mme F. Lion, 8, rte de Cannes, 06650 Opio, ☎ 93.77.31.71.

Canoeing : *Ligue Régionale Dauphiné*, M. Thiel, 1, rue du Vercors, 38800 Le Pont-de-Claix, and centre at the Briançon *Parc des sports et des loisirs*, ☎ 92.20.17.56.

Potholing and spelunking : *Comité Régional C* **(Isère + Drôme)**, 28, quai St-Vincent, 69000 Lyon, ☎ 78.39.71.78, and *Comité Régional D* **(Hautes-Alpes)**, Acquaviva, 29, bd Rodocanachi, 13008 Marseille. Also see *Spéléo Club Alpin*, 9, rue Bayard, 05000 Gap, ☎ 92.51.55.14.

Climbing : *Comité Régional de la Féd. de la Montagne pour le Dauphiné*, M. Féasson, 15, av. de la Boisse, 73000 Chambéry. The *Centre-école d'Embrun* organizes courses for groups, instructional courses in climbing on ice, a snow school, climbing school; enq. : ☎ 92.43.02.75.

Skiing : *Comité Régional F.F.S. Dauphiné* **(Drôme + Isère)**, B.P. 193, 38005 Grenoble Cedex, ☎ 76.46.32.46; *A.D.E.P.S.* avenue Piétri, 38250 Villard de Lans, ☎ 76.95.15.89; *Maison Alpes-Dauphiné*, 2, place André Malraux 75001 Paris, ☎ 49.96.08.43/49.96.08.56; *Comité Régional Alpes-Provence* **(Hautes-Alpes)**, 30, rue Sénac, 13001 Marseille, ☎ 91.48.21.28. Excursions in the Écrins massif, in Oisans, standard races, snow-ski races and summer-skiing down the long slopes of the Écrins massif. Information at *O.T. Montgenèvre*, ☎ 92.21.90.22, and *Cie des guides de l'Oisans*, Serre-Chevalier, ☎ 92.24.74.54. For the Vercors ski crossing, enq. at *C.D.T. de la Drôme* which publishes a brochure.

Ice sports : *Féd. Régionale Dauphiné*, M. Moyencourt, ☎ 93.81.12.05.

Golf : La Chapelle-en-Vercors (9 "compact" holes, practice), Montgenèvre-Clavière (18 holes), Saint-Didier-de-Charpey (9 holes), Valence (9 holes).

Hang-gliding : *Centre-école* at Mevouillon in the Baronnies, enq. : ☎ 75.28.50.80.

Hunting and shooting : enq. at the *Féd. Dép.* **Hautes-Alpes :** quartier Lareton, 05000 Gap, ☎ 92.51.16.25, and imm. Montjoie, chemin Bonne, 05000 Gap, ☎ 92.51.33.62; **Drôme :** 60, av. Sadi-Carnot, 26000 Valence, ☎ 75.43.05.36; **Isère :** 6, rue St-François, 38000 Grenoble, ☎ 76.43.11.01, and 12, rue Montorge, 38000 Grenoble, ☎ 76.46.20.23.

Fishing : enq at the *Féd. Dép. de Pêche et Pisciculture*, **Hautes-Alpes :** 18, rue Arène, 05000 Gap, ☎ 92.51.11.40; **Drôme :** 3, pl. Dragonne, 26000 Valence, ☎ 75.43.17.98; **Isère :** 1, rue Cujas, 38000 Grenoble, ☎ 76.44.28.39.

Towns and places

AUTRANS

Grenoble 36, Valence 76, Paris 590 km
pop 1595 ⊠ 38880   B2

⚹ 1050-1610m.
ⓘ ☎ 76.95.30.70.

Hotels :
★★ *Buffe* (L.F.), La Côte, ☎ 76.95.33.26, AE DC Euro Visa, 18 rm ℗ ≼ ⚌ closed Wed (l.s.), 20 Apr-20 May, 1-30 Sep. Sauna, solarium, 230. Rest. ♦ ✤ 55-150.
★★ *Poste* (L.F.), ☎ 76.95.31.03, Euro Visa, 30 rm ⚌ ⚘ ☒ closed 15 Oct-15 Dec, 140. Rest. ♦ ♪ 60-120.

⚐ ★★★*Joyeux Réveil* (100 pl), ☎ 76.95.33.44; ★★★*Vercors* (63 pl), ☎ 76.95.31.88.

BOCHAINE

                                                      B3
At Bochaine you are moving into the south, though the vegetation still remains in some parts Alpine, with forests and meadows. The village, in the high valley of the Buëch River, lies at this turning point between the north and the south of the Alps.

▶ The **pass of the Croix Haute** (1 179 m), on the N75, carries you over to such new regions. ▶ Easy excursions can be made from **Lus-la-Croix-Haute** (pop. 548) to the valley of the Jarjatte where splendid views of the ridge of the

Aiguilles may be had. ▶ The road goes on through **Saint-Julies-en-Beauchêne, Aspres-sur-Buëch** and **Serres,** an old Protestant stronghold with houses overhanging the river.   □

Practical Information _____

LUS-LA-CROIX-HAUTE, ⊠ 26620, 51 km NW of **Gap.**
ⓘ ☎ 92.58.51.85 (h.s.).

Hotel :
★ *Le Chamousset*, ☎ 92.58.51.12, Euro Visa, 20 rm ℗ ≼ ⚌ ⚘ closed 15 Nov-25 Dec, 135. Rest. ♦ ≼ ♪ 55-120.

⚐ ★★*Champ de la Chèvre* (100 pl), ☎ 92.58.50.14; ★★*La Condamine* (60 pl), ☎ 92.58.50.86.

SERRES, ⊠ 05700, 42 km SW of **Gap.**
ⓘ mairie, ☎ 92.67.03.50.
SNCF ☎ 92.67.00.39.

Hotel :
● ★★ *Fifi Moulin*, rte de Nyons, ☎ 92.67.00.01, AE DC Euro Visa, 25 rm ℗ ≼ ⚌ ⚘ ☒ half pens, closed Wed, 11 Nov-6 Feb, 314. Rest. ● ♦ ≼ ♭ Simple, generous fare, 70-110.

⚐ ★★★★*Deux Soleils* (75 pl), ☎ 92.67.01.33; ★★★*les Barillons* (66 pl), ☎ 92.67.01.16.

Be advised that hotels and restaurants in this Guide have perhaps changed addresses; prices indicated are also subject to modifications.

BRIANÇON*

Gap 87, Grenoble 116, Paris 681 km
pop 11831 ⊠ 05100   C2

Briançon, formerly the guardian of the valleys, has always been something of a fortress.

▶ Overlooking the modern part of the town (Sainte-Catherine), the **Ville Haute★★** (upper town) has hardly changed since Vauban, Louis XIV's great military architect, surrounded it with ramparts. ▶ The main shopping area, on the other side of the Porte de Pignerol gate, is the **Grand-Rue★**, where the waters of the Grand Gargouille hurtle through the town. ▶ Behind the church of **Notre-Dame**, also built by Vauban (1718), the highest peaks of the Briançonnais are visible. ▶ Visits to the citadel are organized by the TO. Panorama★. ▶ Note the **Pont d'Asfeld★** (1734), bridge with a fifty-six-metre span above the river Durance.   □

Practical Information ―――――――――――

ℹ Vieux-Colombier, ☎ 92.21.08.50/92.21.08.21.
▆▆▆▆ ☎ 92.21.03.84/92.21.00.50.
Car rental : Avis, 2, rte de Gap, Garage Peugeot Talbot, ☎ 92.21.10.02 ; train station.

Hotels :
★★★ **Vauban**, 13, av. Gal-de-Gaulle, ☎ 92.21.12.11, Visa, 44 rm 🄿 ⪌ 🕮 ⅋ half pens (h.s.), closed 10 Nov-19 Dec, 230. Rest. ♦♦ 80-140.
★★ **Le Mont Prorel**, 5, rue R.-Froger, ☎ 92.20.22.88, AE DC Euro Visa, 19 rm 🄿 ⪌ 🕮 ⅋ half pens (h.s.), 230. Rest. ♦ ♪ 60-120.
★★ **Mont-Brison**, 3, av. Gal-de-Gaulle, ☎ 92.21.14.55, 44 rm 🄿 ⪌ ⅋ closed 3 Nov-20 Dec, 170.

▲ ★★★*Cinq Vallées* (116 pl), ☎ 92.21.06.27 ; ★★*Municipal* (80 pl), ☎ 92.21.04.32.

Recommended
Baby-sitting : at Villeneuve-la-Salle, 6 km, ☎ 92.24.71.88.

The BRIANÇONNAIS Region**

                                                      C2
▶ Briançon, at the heart of a cluster of valleys, is the chief town in the basin of the upper Durance. The sky is almost always clear and sunny for skiing in this area. ▶ **Puy-Saint-Pierre** (4 km SW) and **La Croix de Toulouse** (6.5 km N) have good views★★ over Briançon and the valley of the Durance. ▶ The **Valley of the Clarée★** (Névache road, 20.5 km N) : this is the first of these luminous and uninhabited valleys which are more and more frequent on the way S. Take a look in passing at the beautiful houses of the Briançonnais ; also the churches, which are often decorated with murals★. Beyond **Névache**, the route continues (9.5 km) to the chalets of Laval (flowers★). ▶ **Route de Montgenèvre** (2 km NE to the pass) : since the turn of the century the sunny slopes of **Montgenèvre** have been popular for skiing. In the past almost all the conquerors of Italy and Gaul, including Caesar, took this historic passage. ▶ **Route de l'Izoard★★** (21 km SE from the pass). The last of the Dauphinois passes on the road to the Grandes Alpes (→ Savoie). The Izoard road leads through to Queyras (→). From the pass the view★★ is superb and the **Casse Desert** looks like a lunar landscape. ▶ **Valley of the Guisane★** (28 km NW to the Lautaret Pass). **Serre-Chevalier** is the name given to the associated hamlets of the valley, which have banded together to take advantage of the white gold on the mountain slopes. From **Chantemerle**, a road leads 12 km to the Granon Pass (alt. 2 413 m ; view★★) and the cable-car to Serre-Chevalier (alt. 2 483 m) ; view over the massif du Pelvoux and the Briançonnais. **Le Monêtier-les-Bains** (pop. 970) is a rendez-vous for walkers and mountaineers.   □

Practical Information ―――――――――――

Le MONÊTIER-LES-BAINS, ⊠ 05220, 8 km S of **Serre-Chevalier**.

Hotel :
★★ **Auberge du Choucas** (L.F.), ☎ 92.24.42.73, DC, 13 rm 🕮 ⪍ half pens (h.s.), 610. Rest. ♦ ♪ ⅋ closed 15 Apr-20 Jun, 1 Oct-20 Dec, 85-270.

La SALLE-LES-ALPES, ⊠ 05240, 3 km NW on the N 91.

Hotel :
★★ **Le Lièvre Blanc**, Villeneuve, ☎ 92.24.74.05, AE DC Visa, 26 rm 🄿 ⪌ 🏊 ⊡ half pens (h.s.), closed May, Sep, 240. Rest. ♦ ⪍ 65-110 ; child : 30.

Recommended
Youth hostel : Le Bez, ☎ 92.24.74.54.

SERRE-CHEVALIER, ⊠ 05330 Saint-Chaffrey, 8 km W of **Briançon**.
⚐ 1350-2660m.
ℹ Chantemerle-Saint-Chaffrey, ☎ 92.24.00.34.

Hotels :
★★ **La Balme**, Chantemerle, Saint-Chaffrey, ☎ 92.24.01.89, AE DC Visa, 25 rm 🄿 ⪌ 🕮 ⪍ closed May, Oct-Nov, 350.
★ **Boule de Neige**, 15, rue du Centre, ☎ 92.24.00.16, Visa, 10 rm 🏊 half pens, closed Easter-Xmas, 480. Rest. ♦ ♪ Hearty family-style food, 80-120.

The CHAMPSAUR Region

                                                      C3
The Champsaur road, Saint-Bonnet to Orsières-Merlette (24 km E, D945, D944)

The lower Champsaur around Saint-Bonnet is another active agricultural district, mostly dairy farming, while the upper Champsaur, deforested and rugged, has a distinctly mountainous aspect.

▶ **Saint-Bonnet-en-Champsaur** makes a charming picture, its brown roofs clustering round the slate steeple of the bell tower. This is a good starting point for exploring the upper Champsaur, the Valgaudemar (→), Trièves (→) and Dévoluy (→). From Saint-Bonnet, the D23 and a forest road run through the wild valley of **Séveraissette★** up to **Molines-en-Champsaur** (12.5 km), the starting point for walks in the Suzerre and Londonière forests. ▶ **Pont du Fossé**, 2 km W, ruins of the château de Montorsier (12thC) and ancient aquaduct. ▶ **Pont des Corbières**; then road left to Champoléon going up the harsh **Drac Blanc** ravine★. ▶ **Orcières-Merlette** is built on the sunny slopes of the Drouvet (alt. 2 655 m ; cable car ; spring skiing).   □

Practical Information ―――――――――――

CHAILLOL, ⊠ 05260 Chabottes, 10 km E on the D 43.

Hotel :
★ **Etable**, Saint-Michel-de-Chaillol, ☎ 92.50.48.35, 9 rm 🄿 ⪌ 🕮 ⪍ closed 15 Apr-29 Jun, 15 Sep-20 Dec, 100. Rest. ♦ ⅋ 50-70.

ORCIÈRES-MERLETTE, ⊠ 05170, 33 km NE of **Gap**.

Hotel :
★ **Poste**, ☎ 92.55.70.04, 31 rm 🄿 ⪌ 100. Rest. ♦ 80-130.

Recommended
Youth hostel : la Fruitière, les Tourengs, ☎ 92.55.44.30.

SAINT-BONNET-EN-CHAMPSAUR, ⊠ 05500, 15 km N of **Gap**.
ℹ ☎ 92.50.02.57.   ♥

Hotels :
★★ **Chenets** (L.F.), Saint-Julien-en-Champsaur, ☎ 92.50.03.15, Euro Visa, 20 rm 🄿 ⪌ 🕮 half pens (h.s.), closed 30 Sep-1 Dec, 160. Rest. ♦ ⪍ 55-70.
★★ **Le Mauberret-Combassive** (L.F.), pl. du Champ-de-Foire, ☎ 92.50.00.19, 27 rm ⪌ 🕮 ⪍ ♪ closed 20 Apr-20 May, 10 Oct-20 Dec, 115. Rest. ♦ ♪ 50-100.

The CHARTREUSE Massif**

B1

From Grenoble to Chambéry *(80 km, half-day; see map 1)*

The Chartreuse appears like a citadel between the peaks of Chambéry and Grenoble, surrounded by huge carpets of dark pines from which emerge twisted outcrops of rock. In this solitary wilderness St. Bruno founded the monastery of the Grande Chartreuse in 1085, later to become the mother house of the order of Carthusian monks. A few minutes from Grenoble, the Chartreuse Massif is ideal for cross-country skiing and medium altitude mountain hikes.
▶ **Grenoble** *(→)*. ▶ **Fort du Saint-Eynard** *(4 km)* view★★. From **Sappey-en-Chartreuse** *(alt. 1 000 m)* to the Col de Porte stretches the immense limestone table of **Chamechaude** *(alt. 2 082 m)*, the highest point of the Massif. From the pass a road leads *(4.5 km, then 30 min on foot)* to the top of **Charmant Som★★** *(1 867 m)* with

1. The Chartreuse massif

a remarkable view. ▶ **Saint-Pierre-de-Chartreuse** *(right, 1 km)*, among firs and alpine meadows, a pleasant retreat in the heart of the Massif. Nearby you will find : the **chapel of St. Hugues** *(2.5 km S)* decorated with paintings (1953) by J. M. Pirot; **Perquelin** *(3 km E)* : for lovers of forest walks (GR9); **Scia** *(cable-car, then 15 min on foot)* : view★; **Sangles★★** *(2 km W, then 1 hr on foot)* : view of the Grande Chartreuse and the Guiers Mort Gorges.
▶ The road continues down the **Guiers Mort Gorges★★**.
▶ **La Correrie** *(1 km right)*, a dependency of the Grande Chartreuse, is the intermediary for all contacts with the outside world, since visits to the monastery are forbidden. La Correrie has a museum devoted to the life and history of the Chartreuse monks *(Easter-1 Nov., 9-12 & 2-6:30, sale of liqueurs and souvenirs of La Chartreuse)*. ▶ **Saint-Laurent-du-Pont** *(pop. 4 125)*, a tiny tourist resort at the gates of the Chartreuse. Saint-Laurent is linked to Grenoble by the little road over the **La Charmette Pass★★** *(30 km)*, through the woods and along the hilltop road *(view★)*; **Voiron** *(15 km SW of Saint-Laurent; pop. 19 700)* makes skis (Rossignol) and also distills the famous Chartreuse liqueur (Caves de la Chartreuse, *8-11:30 & 2-6:30, 5:30 off season*; *closed Sat. and Sun., Nov.-Easter)*.
▶ Beyond Saint-Laurent, take the road through the **Guiers Vif Gorges★** (see the Pas du Frou★★ promontory). ▶ **Saint-Pierre-d'Entremont** *(pop. 459; 3 km W)* : view★ and especially, the **Cirque de Saint-Même** *(4.5 km SE)* : two superb waterfalls★ which give birth to the Guiers Vif. ▶ **Granier Pass** *(alt. 1 164 m, view★★, chalet-hôtel)*. □

Practical Information

SAINT-LAURENT-DU-PONT, ⊠ 38380, 33 km N of **Grenoble**.

Hotel :
★ **Voyageurs** (L.F.), rue Pasteur, ☎ 76.55.21.05, Euro Visa, 20 rm ♪ half pens, closed Fri eve, Oct, 95. Rest. ♦ ♪ 50-115.

SAINT-PIERRE-D'ENTREMONT, ⊠ 73670, 50 km N of **Grenoble**.
ⅰ ☎ 79.65.82.85.

Hotel :
★★ **Château de Montbel** (L.F.), ☎ 79.65.81.65, Euro, 16 rm ℗ ♿ ≋ ⚶ 🐕 closed Sun eve, Mon (l.s.) and school hols, 1 Nov-15 Dec, 170. Rest. ♦ ♪ ⚶ 80-150; child : 40.

⚑ ★★**Cozon** (33 pl), ☎ 79.65.82.85.

SAINT-PIERRE-DE-CHARTREUSE, ⊠ 38380 Saint-Laurent-du-Pont, 29 km N of **Grenoble**.
⚡ 900-1700m.
ⅰ ☎ 76.88.62.08.

Hotels :
★★★ **Beau Site**, ☎ 76.88.61.34, AE Euro Visa, 33 rm ℗ ⚶ ♿ ❏ closed Wed, 30 Sep-15 Dec, 220. Rest. ♦ ⚶ ♪ ⚑ ⚶ 65-80; child : 40.
★ **Nord**, ☎ 76.88.61.10, 18 rm ℗ ⚶ ♨ ⚶ ♪ pens (h.s.), closed May, Oct, 180. Rest. ♦ ♪ 50-120.

⚑ ★★★**Martinière** (100 pl), ☎ 76.88.60.36.

Recommended
Youth hostel : St-Hugues, ☎ 76.88.62.37.

Le SAPPEY-EN-CHARTREUSE, ⊠ 38128, 13 km S of **Saint-Pierre-de-Chartreuse** on the D 512.
⚡ 1000-1350m.

Hotel :
★★ **Skieurs**, ☎ 76.88.80.15, Tx 320245, 18 rm ℗ ⚶ ⚶ ⚶ closed Mon ex school hols, 1 Oct-1 Dec, 200. Rest. ♦ ⚶ ♪ 85-140.

VOIRON, ⊠ 38500, 29 km NW of **Grenoble**.
ⅰ Voiron Chartreuse, pl. de la République, ☎ 76.05.00.38.
SNCF ☎ 76.05.50.50/76.05.06.14.
Car rental : Avis, 5, av. de D.-Valois, ☎ 76.05.06.22; train station.

Hotels :
★★★ **Castel Anne**, 73, av. Dr-Valois, ☎ 76.05.86.00, AE

Euro Visa, 18 rm ℗ ⬠ closed 8-28 Feb, 280. Rest. ◆◆
♪ 90-160.
★ *La Chaumière* (L.F.), rue de la Chaumière,
☎ 76.05.16.24, 25 rm ℗ ⪉⪍ ⅋ half pens, 280. Rest. ◆ ♪
⅁ 60-80.

⚠ ★★★*Porte de Chartreuse* (70 pl), ☎ 76.05.14.20.

The DÉVOLUY Massif*

B3

Amid the harsh scenery of this area, the little oases
of Saint-Disdier, Saint-Étienne and the forest of Bois-
Rond are the only relief. The Dévoluy is riddled with
underground cavities known as *chourums*.

▶ The **Souloise defile★** to the N, to the **Noyer pass★★**
and the **Potrachon defile** to the S are the entrances to the
natural fortress which surrounds **Saint-Étienne-en-Dévoluy** (pop. 527) and the winter sports station of **Superdévoluy**. To the NW, the **Étroits defile★★** and *(6.5 km)*
Saint-Disdier, noteworthy for its 12thC church★. ☐

Practical Information _____

SAINT-ÉTIENNE-EN-DÉVOLUY, ⊠ 05250, 35 km N
of Gap.
⚓ 1500-2500m.
ⓘ ☎ 92.58.80.48 ; Superdévoluy, ☎ 92.58.82.82.

Hotel :
★ *La Souloise*, ☎ 92.58.82.05, 8 rm ℗ ⪉⪍ ⅋ pens, 245.
Rest. ◆ ⪉ 50-80.

DIEULEFIT

Orange 58, Valence 78, Paris 635 km
pop 2990 ⊠ 26220   A3

ⓘ pl. de l'Église, ☎ 75.46.42.49.

Hotels :
★ *L'Escargot d'Or* (L.F.), rte de Nyons, ☎ 75.46.40.52,
Euro Visa, 15 rm ℗ ⪉⪍ ⪍ ▭ pens (h.s.), closed Wed,
15 Nov-15 Dec, 400. Rest. ◆ ⪉⪍ ♪ 70-100.
★ *Les Brises*, rte des Raymonds, ☎ 75.46.41.49, 9 rm ℗ ⪉
⬠ ⪍ pens (h.s.), closed Tue eve and Wed, 1 Jan-2 Feb,
300. Rest. ◆ 55-120.

Nearby

Le POËT-LAVAL, ⊠ 26160, 5 km W.

Hotel :
★★★ *Hospitaliers* (L.F.), ☎ 75.46.22.32, AE DC Euro Visa,
20 rm ℗ ⪉⪍ ⪍ ▭ closed 15 Nov-1 Mar. Medieval commander's residence, overlooking the valley, 400. Rest. ◆
The reception runs hot and cold. Seasonal cooking,
150-300.

Valley of the DRÔME*

From Crest to Cabre Pass *(82 km, approx. 4 hr)*

The valley of the Drôme should be better known.
Bathed in a light like that of Tuscany, it is a lovely
mixture of Dauphiné and Provence. D93 takes you
from Crest to ancient villages with plane trees and
rose laurel, reminiscent of the Midi.

▶ **Crest** (pop. 7 844) is crowned by a superb 12thC keep★
(summer, 9-12 & 2-7; winter, 1:30-5). ▶ **Pontaix** (site★).
▶ **Die** (pop. 4 047), overlooked by the escarpment of
the Glandasse, famous for its *Clairette*, a sparkling wine
which you will be invited to taste all along the road ;
cathedral (12th-17thC), museum (Gallo-Roman remains).
▶ 6 km beyond Die, road left to **Châtillon-en-Diois** where
you can see *(10 km N)* the **Cirque d'Archiane★**, a magnificent limestone amphitheatre *(GR93)*. 7 km E of Châtillon :
the **Gorges des Gas★** near Lus-la-Croix-Haute. ▶ After
Luc-en-Diois, the road crosses the site of Claps★ (land-

slide), leaves the Drôme and climbs towards the Col de
Cabre (alt. 1 180 m).   ☐

Practical Information _____

CHÂTILLON-EN-DIOIS, ⊠ 26410, 79 km SE of **Valence**.

ⓘ rue Reclus, ☎ 75.21.10.07.
Hotel :
★ *France* (L.F.), ☎ 75.21.12.02, 19 rm, closed Fri eve and
Sun eve, 15 Nov-26 Dec, 100. Rest. ◆ closed Sat
eve, 60-90.

⚠ ★★*Municipal* (133 pl), ☎ 75.21.10.21.

CREST, ⊠ 26400, 28 km SE of **Valence**.
ⓘ 1 bd de Belgique, ☎ 75.25.11.38.
〽 ☎ 75.25.05.81.

Hotels :
★★ *Grand Hôtel* (L.F.), 60, rue de l'Hôtel-de-Ville,
☎ 75.25.08.17, Euro Visa, 20 rm ⪍ closed Mon eve and
Sun eve (Nov-Feb), 2-31 Jan, Dec, 125. Rest. ◆ ♪ closed
Mon noon and Sun eve, 50-80 ; child : 40.
★ *Kléber*, 6, rue Aristide-Dumont, ☎ 75.25.11.69, 9 rm ⪍
closed Mon eve and Sun eve, 18 Jan-1 Feb, 120.
Rest. ◆ 65-220.

Restaurant :
◆ *Porte Montségur*, av. des Trois-Becs, E exit,
☎ 75.25.41.48 ⬠ ♪ closed Mon eve and Wed (l.s.),
15-28 Feb, 60-400.

⚠ ★★*Clorinthe* (200 pl), ☎ 75.25.05.28.

DIE, ⊠ 26150, 65 km SE of **Valence**.

ⓘ pl. St-Pierre, ☎ 75.22.03.03 (h.s.) ; ☎ 75.22.26.57 (l.s.).
〽 ☎ 75.22.05.42.

Hotels :
★★ *Relais de Chamargues* (L.F.), av. de la Clairette,
☎ 75.22.00.95, 9 rm ℗ ⬠ closed Mon eve and Sun eve,
25 Jan-1 Mar, 140. Rest. ◆ 70-90.
★★ *Saint-Dominique* (L.F.), 44, rue C.-Buffardel,
☎ 75.22.03.08, 26 rm ℗ ⪉ ⬠ ⪍ ♪ ▭ 140. Rest. ◆ ♪ ⅁
closed 5 Nov-5 Dec, 45-80 ; child : 30.
★ *Alpes*, 87, rue C.-Buffardel, ☎ 75.22.15.83, Euro Visa,
22 rm ⪉ ⪍ ♪ 100.

⚠ ★★★*Glandasse* (100 pl), ☎ 75.22.02.50 ; ★★*Chamar-
ges* (100 pl), ☎ 75.22.14.13 ; ★★*du S.I.* (133 pl),
☎ 75.22.03.03 ; ★★*Piscine* (160 pl), ☎ 75.22.06.19.

Recommended
guide to wines : *Coopérative de Clairette-de-Die*, av.
Clairette, ☎ 75.22.02.22, tasting.

GRANE, ⊠ 26400, 8 km W on the D104.

Hotel :
★★ *Giffon*, pl. de l'Église, ☎ 75.62.60.64, AE DC Euro
Visa, 9 rm ⬠ ⪍ ♪ closed Mon eve and Sun eve (Oct-Apr),
15 Nov-8 Dec, 200. Rest. ◆ ♪ 90-210 ; child : 45.

LUC-EN-DIOIS, ⊠ 26310, 12 km S of **Châtillon-en-Diois**.

Hotel :
★★ *Levant* (L.F.), ☎ 75.21.33.30, 16 rm ℗ ⪉ ⬠ ♪⁰
half pens (h.s.), 320. Rest. ◆ ♪ ⅁ 65-80 ; child : 40.

⚠ ★★*Municipal* (133 pl), ☎ 75.21.10.21.

TRESCHENU-CREYERS, ⊠ 26410 Châtillon-en-Diois,
11 km NE of **Châtillon** on the D120.

Hotel :
★★ *Le Mont Barral* (L.F.), Hameau des Nonnières,
☎ 75.21.21.24, 24 rm ℗ ⬠ ⪍ ▭ ♪⁰ closed Tue eve,
15 Nov-20 Dec. Sauna, solarium, 110. Rest. ◆ ♪ 50-90.

In preparing for your trip, consult the pages pertaining to the regions. You will find there the description of the region you wish to visit, as well as a list
of sites that must be seen, a brief history and practical information.

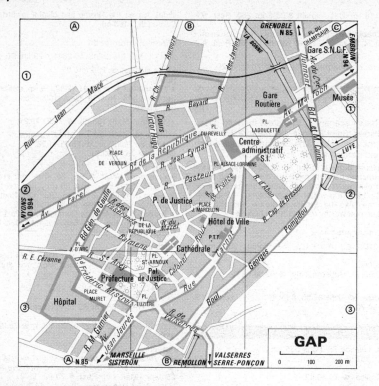

GAP

GAP

Digne 87, Grenoble 103, Paris 668 km
pop 32000 ⊠ 05000   B3

Dauphiné with a touch of the South — a busy, animated crossroads on the holiday trail. Pleasant walks in pedestrian precincts in the shadow of the cathedral (interesting polychrome stonework). The museum contains the mausoleum★ of de Lesdiguières, last Constable of France (16th-17thC, by Jean and Jacob Richier). ▶ 15 km S : **Tallard** is overlooked by a 14th-16thC château★.   □

Practical Information

ℹ 5, rue Carnot (B2), ☎ 92.51.57.03.
✈ *Gap-Tallard*, ☎ 92.54.10.38.
SNCF (C1), ☎ 92.51.50.50/92.51.00.93/92.51.24.84.
Car rental : *Avis*, train station (C1) ; 9, av. du Cdt-Dumont (C1), ☎ 92.51.26.09.

Hotels :
● ★★ *La Ferme Blanche*, Villarobert, ☎ 92.51.03.41, AE Euro Visa, 30 rm ℙ ⚍ ▥ ⚏ 150.
★★ *Clos*, 20 *ter*, av. du Cdt-Dumont (C1), ☎ 92.51.37.04, 42 rm ℙ ▥ ⚏ closed Sun eve, 25 Oct-25 Nov, 150. Rest. ♦ ♪ 60-110.
★★ *Fons Regina* (L.F.), 13, av. de Fontreyne, ☎ 92.53.98.99, AE DC Euro Visa, 21 rm ℙ ▥ ⚏ half pens (h.s.), 185. Rest. ♦ ⚄ ♪ 65-115 ; child : 45.

Restaurants :
● ♦♦♦ *Roseraie*, rte de Romette, Villarobert, 2 km on D 92, ☎ 92.51.43.08, AE DC Euro Visa ℙ ⚄ ▥ ♪ closed Thu and Sun eve, 90-220.
♦♦ *Le Carré Long*, 32, rue Pasteur (B2), ☎ 92.51.13.10, AE DC Euro Visa ℙ ♪ closed Mon and Sun, 1-15 May, 10-31 Oct. Spec : *feuillantine de saumon aux blancs de*

poireaux, filet de loup à la vapeur de citron, 65-110 ; child : 45.

⌂ ★★★*Alpes Dauphiné* (66 pl), ☎ 92.51.29.95 ; ★★★*Essi Provence* (83 pl), ☎ 92.51.57.03 ; ★★*Napoléon* (70 pl), ☎ 92.52.12.41.

The GRAISIVAUDAN Valley

B-C1

The Graisivaudan, through which the Isère runs today, is a large valley hollowed out by glaciers, and formerly occupied by a lake, which was linked with the Lac du Bourget. This is one of the most fertile regions in the Alps.

▶ To see the majestic mountains of the Chartreuse and Belledonne to best advantage, follow the little roads between Grenoble and Pontcharra at the foot of the two massifs. ▶ **Chartreuse** *(D30) :* look for the **Bec du Margain★** *(15 min on foot)* with a remarkable panorama from Vercors to Mont Blanc and **Saint-Hilaire-du-Touvet**, famous for its funicular railway (1924), with a slope of 83°. ▶ **Belledonne** *(D280) :* in **Lancey** *(13 km NE of Grenoble)* the Museum of Aristide Bergès and hydroelectric power. For an overall view of Graisivaudan and the Chartreuse Massif go up to the **Croix de Revollat★★** peak. From Laval to **Allevard** (thermal spa ; museum of the olden days, *daily ex Tue., 10-12 & 3-6:30*), the communes on the slope of Belledonne have grouped together to create the station of **Sept Laux★** (alt. 1350-2200 m) : the charm of little mountain villages with the facilities of a major summer and winter resort. ▶ 1 km S of Pontcharra : **château Bayard** was the birthplace of the knight of the same name (museum, view★).   □

Practical Information _____

ALLEVARD, ⊠ 38580, 35 km SW of **Chambéry**.
⌘ (17 May-24 Sep), ☎ 76.97.56.22.
ⓘ pl. de la Résistance, ☎ 76.45.10.11.

Hotels :
★★ *Parc*, parc des thermes, ☎ 76.97.54.22, 49 rm P ≪ ⋙ ≫ ⌡ closed 26 Sep-14 May, 190.
★★ *Les Pervenches*, (L.F., R.S.), av. Davallet,, ☎ 76.97.53.62, Tx 305551, Euro Visa, 34 rm P ≪ ⋙ ⌂ ⌘ & ⌀ ⌡ closed Wed eve and Sun eve, 25 Sep-1 Feb, 10 Apr-10 May, 205. Rest. ♦ ≪ ⌂ ⊗ closed Wed and Thu noon, 26 Sep-1 Feb, 65-130♦ ⊗ 70-105 ; child : 45.
★★ *Pic de la Belle Etoile*, Pinsot, 7 km S on D525, ☎ 76.97.53.62, Tx 305551, Euro Visa, 34 rm P ≪ ⋙ ⌂ ⌘ & ⌀ ⌡ closed Wed eve and Sun eve, 18 Oct-1 Dec, 205. Rest. ♦ ⊗ 70-105 ; child : 45.

▲ ★★★*Le Collet d'Allevard* (90 pl), ☎ 76.45.10.32 ; ★★*Clair Matin* (150 pl), ☎ 76.97.55.19 ; ★★*Idéal Camping* (60 pl), ☎ 76.97.50.23.

> In preparing for your trip, consult the pages pertaining to the regions. You will find there the description of the region you wish to visit, as well as a list of sites that must be seen, a brief history and practical information.

Chambéry 55, Lyon 104, Paris 567 km
pop 160000 ⊠ 38000   B2

Grenoble is the capital of the Dauphiné, straddling the junction of the Drac and the Isère rivers. The birthplace of Stendhal, Grenoble is a centre of Dauphiné industry, with an international reputation for metallurgy, electronics, scientific research, and advanced energy research. It was one of the earliest towns to develop hydroelectric power, and it is at the forefront in the fields of tourism and sport (Olympic city 1968).

▶ If you want to see how Grenoble lives, stroll around the **Place Grenette** (B3) and the neighbouring pedestrian precincts to the **Place Victor-Hugo** (B3). ▶ The **Stendhal Museum** (B2 ; life of the writer) is in the former town hall (10-12 & 2-6 ex Mon.), with the church of St. André nearby (13thC, tomb of Bayard) and the **Palais de Justice★** (law courts), former Parliament of the Dauphiné, a beautiful Gothic and Renaissance building (woodwork★). ▶ **Grenoble Museum★★** (12:30-7 ex Tue.) : active, unexpected, always full of ideas, this is a permanent centre of research. See the famous gallery of contemporary art★, and also the Francisco de Zurbarans★★ (17thC), Philippe de Champaigne and the painters of the 19th and 20thC★ :

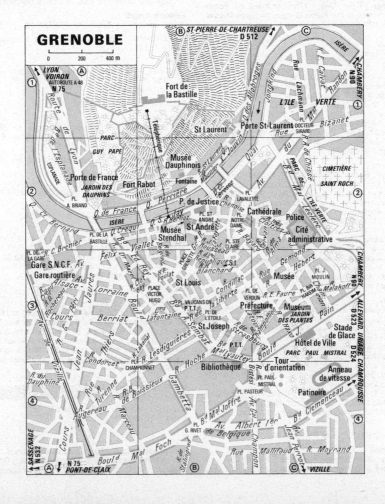

Corot, Boudin, Renoir, Monet, Bonnard, Picasso. And don't forget the Egyptian room★. ▶ **Fort de la Bastille**★★ (B1, *Apr.-Oct., 9 or 10-midnight; Nov.-Mar., 10-7:30; closed Jan.*) : from this magnificent spot there is a fine view across Grenoble and the Belledonne (Restaurant; old car museum); descent possible on foot through Guy-Pape Park★ and the Garden of the Dauphins★ *(consult timetables).* ▶ **Dauphinois Museum**★ (B2; *10-12 & 2-6 ex Tue.*) installed in an ancient 17thC convent, is the best introduction to the life, art and popular traditions of the province. In the same quarter, the **Merovingian crypt**★ (6thC) of the church of St. Laurent (B1) is one of the oldest Christian monuments in France *(Jun.-Sep., 10-12 & 2:30-6:30; Oct.-Jun., by appt.; closed Tue).*
Also... ▶ The **hôtel de ville**★ (town hall;C3) by architects Novarina and Welti (1967), the Paul-Mistral Park with its Olympic facilities (sports stadium, speed-skating rink), the Perret tower (87 m) and modern sculptures. ▶ The **Maison de la Culture**★ (Cultural Centre; 1968 arch. Wogensky). ▶ Ernest Hébert Museum : works of this Dauphinois painter. ▶ **Natural history museum** *(daily ex Tue.).* ▶ **Centre national d'art contemporain,** Cours Berriat (A3), in a turn-of-the-century factory *(tel. : 76.21.95.84).*

Nearby

▶ **Chamrousse**★ *(30 km SE)* : favourite haunt of skiers from Grenoble. A cable-car takes you to the Croix de Chamrousse★★ peak (2 225 m) with a fabulous view. ▶ **Sassenage** *(6 km NW)* : 17thC château de Bérenger *(visits);* walks in the Furon Gorges. ▶ **Saint-Marcel-lès-Valence** *(RN 532 towards Valence)* : old car museum *(9-12 & 2-7).* ☐

Practical Information ─────────────────

GRENOBLE
ⓘ 14, rue de la République (B3), ☎ 76.54.34.36.
✈ *Grenoble-St-Geoirs*, 29 km NW, ☎ 76.65.48.48. *Air France office*, 4, pl. V.-Hugo (B3), ☎ 76.87.63.41.
SNCF (A3), ☎ 76.57.50.50/76.47.09.45.
☞ pl. de la Gare (A3), ☎ 76.87.90.31.
Car rental : *Avis*, train station; 35, bd Langevin-à-Fontaine, ☎ 76.27.06.54; 55, av. de Vigny, ☎ 76.09.71.18; 22, cours J.-Jaurès (A3-4), ☎ 76.47.52.72; St Étienne-de-St-Geoirs, ☎ 76.65.41.96.

Hotels :
★★★★ *Park Hotel* (R.S.), 10, pl. Paul-Mistral (C4), ☎ 76.87.29.11, Tx 320767, AE DC Euro Visa, 59 rm 🄿 ✦ 𝄪 🕭 ⅋ closed 24 Dec-3 Jan, 710. Rest. ✦✦ *Taverne de Ripaille* ⅃ ⅊ closed Sat eve and Sun noon, 180.
● ★★★ *Angleterre*, 5, pl. Victor-Hugo (B3), ☎ 76.87.37.21, Tx 320297, AE DC Euro Visa, 70 rm ✦ 𝄪 𝄪 335.
● ★★★ *Lesdiguières*, 122, cours de la Libération (off map A4), ☎ 76.96.55.36, Tx 320306, AE DC Euro Visa, 36 rm 🄿 𝄪 closed 30 Jul-2 Sep, 18 Dec-3 Jan, 300. Rest. ✦ ✧ Hotel school, 100-135.
● ★★ *Alpes*, 45, av. Félix-Viallet (A2), ☎ 76.87.00.71, AE Euro Visa, 42 rm 🄿 165.

Restaurants :
● ✦✦ *La Poularde Bressane*, 12, pl. Paul-Mistral (C4), ☎ 76.87.08.90, AE DC Euro Visa 🄿 ⅃ ⅊ closed Sat noon and Sun, 26 Jul-27 Aug. Two young cooks put their training with Delaveyne and Troisgros to excellent use : *mosaïque de légumes, soyeux d'agneau*, 100-220.
✦✦ *Le Pommerois*, 1, pl. aux Herbes (B2), ☎ 76.44.30.02, closed lunch in Aug and Mon. Excellent food, 210-320.
✦✦ *Thibaud*, 25, bd Agutte-Sembat (B3), ☎ 76.43.01.62, AE DC Euro Visa ⅃ 80-140.
✦ *L'Escale*, 4, pl. de Gordes, ☎ 76.44.64.14, Euro Visa 𝄪 ⅃ closed Mon, 1-15 Aug. Fast, family-style service, quality food. In summer, an hors d'oeuvre buffet, 50-150; child : 30.

⚐ ★★*Municipal* (133 pl) ☎ 76.96.19.87.

Recommended
Baby-sitting : *Baby Sitting Contact*, ☎ 76.49.45.65.
Guided tours : *"Grenoble Historique"*, C.N.M.H.S. daily

Jun, Aug, Sep ex Wed, meet at tourist office at 10am, 2:30pm, 4:30pm. St-Laurent Church, crypt and excavations, ☎ 76.87.72.87.
Youth hostel : *La Quinzaine*, av. du Grésivaudan, ☎ 76.09.33.52.
♥ walnut candies : *Miland*, 17, pl. Grenette.

Nearby

BRESSON, ⊠ 38320 Eybens, 8 km S on the D 5.
Hotel :
★★★★ *Chavant*, ☎ 76.25.15.14, Tx 980882, AE Euro Visa, 7 rm 🄿 𝄪 closed 26-31 Dec, 500. Rest. ● ✦✦✦ ✧ closed Wed and Sat noon. J.-P. Chavant has succeeded his father, but upholds the same fine culinary traditions. Spec : *escalope de foie de canard tiède aux noix, filet de boeuf au foie gras frais et jus de truffes, mille-feuille d'agneau aux champignons des bois*, 155-220.

CHAMROUSSE, ⊠ 38410 Uriage, 29 km SE.
⚑ 1450-2250m.
ⓘ Le Recoin, ☎ 76.97.02.65; Roche Béranger, ☎ 76.97.20.88.
☞ ☎ 76.97.02.06.
Hotels :
★★★ *Hermitage*, ☎ 76.89.93.21, Visa, 50 rm 🄿 closed 20 Apr-15 Dec, 270. Rest. ✦✦✦ 110-160.
★★ *Le Virage*, Le Recoin, ☎ 76.89.90.63, Visa, 18 rm 🄿 ⅊ 𝄪 closed 15 Apr-15 Jun, 15 Oct-15 Dec, 180.
Recommended
Youth hostel : *Le Recoin*, ☎ 76.97.01.14.

CORENC-MONTFLEURY, ⊠ 38700 La Tronche, 3 km N on the D 512.
Hotel :
★★★ *Les Trois Roses*, (Mapotel) 32, av. du Grésivaudan, ☎ 76.90.35.09, AE DC Euro Visa, 50 rm 🄿 ✦ 𝄪 𝄪 𝄪 closed 24-31 Dec, 280.

EYBENS, ⊠ 38520, 3 km SE.
Hotel :
★ *L'Aubergade*, rte Napoléon, Herbeys, ☎ 76.73.67.52, 6 rm, closed Sun eve and Mon, 200. Rest. ✦ ⅃ Family atmosphere and tasty food, 50-100.

SAINT-MARTIN-LE-VINOUX, ⊠ 38950, 2 km N on the A 48 N 75.
Restaurant :
✦✦ *Pique-Pierre*, 1, rue Konrad-Killian, ☎ 76.46.12.88 🄿 𝄪 closed Aug., 120-210.

URIAGE-LES-BAINS, ⊠ 38410, 10 km SE.
Hotels :
★★★ *Grand Hôtel*, ☎ 76.89.10.17, 51 rm 🄿 𝄪 𝄪 ✧ 🖂 ⅊ closed 25 Sep-1 May, 210. Rest. ✦ 80-130.
★★ *Le Manoir*, rte de Premol, ☎ 76.89.10.88, 18 rm 🄿 𝄪 𝄪 pens (h.s.), closed Sun eve and Mon, 5-31 Jan, 20 Nov-12 Dec, 420. Rest. ✦ ⅃ 𝄪 50-150.

VARCES, ⊠ 38760, 13 km S on the N75.
Hotel :
★★★★ *Escale* (R.C.), pl. de la République, ☎ 76.72.80.19, AE Euro Visa, 12 rm 🄿 𝄪 𝄪 closed Sun eve, Mon (l.s.), Tue (h.s.), Jan, 320. Rest. ● ✦✦ ⅃ René Brunet decided to take life a little easier; he now advises his young successor, chef Frédéric Buntinx : *filet de dorade à la crème de concombre, émincé de boeuf aux noix sauce morille*, 135-450.

GRIGNAN*

Nyons 23, Montélimar 28, Paris 632 km
pop 1147 ⊠ 26230   A3

This pretty Tricastin Town was made famous by the letters of Marquise de Sévigné to her daughter, Countess of Grignan; 14thC gate with 17thC belfry; impressive château, mostly Renaissance (visits) : furniture, tapestries; view; collegiale church of St. Sauveur (concerts in summer); municipal museum.

Nearby

▶ **Donzère-Mondragon canal**★ *(18 km S.)* ▶ Romanesque churches★ of **Saint-Paul-Trois-Châteaux** *(7.5 km SE)*, **St. Restitut** *(10.5 km SE)* and **La Baume-de-Transit** *(15.5 km E)*.

Hotel :
★★ *Sévigné*, ☎ 75.46.50.97, Visa, 20 rm ℗ closed Mon (l.s.), 1 Dec-15 Jan, 180.

Restaurant :
● ♦ *L'Eau à la Bouche*, rue St-Louis, ☎ 75.46.57.37 ♪ closed Mon and Sun eve, 15 Jan-15 Feb, 85-140.

Recommended
Events : *Carmentran*, carnival and Provençal songs in Feb.
♥ pumpkin bread : *boulangerie de la Mère Peyrol*; at Montjoyer, trappist distillery, Château d'Aiguebelle, 12 km NW.; at Roussas, wines of Tricastin : *Domaine de Grangeneuve*, rte de Grignan, ☎ 75.98.50.22.

Nearby

DONZÈRE, ⊠ 26290, 16 km S of **Montélimar**.
🛈 ☎ 75.51.71.50.
SNCF ☎ 75.51.60.42.

Hotel :
★★★ *Roustan*, 26, Basse-Bourgade, ☎ 75.51.61.27, Visa, 11 rm ℗ ⚏ 🍴 closed Sun eve and Mon, 31 Jan-1 Mar, 155. Rest. ♦ ♪ 75-120.

La GARDE-ADHÉMAR, ⊠ 26100 Pierrelatte, 8 km W of **Pierrelatte**.

Hotel :
L'Escalin, ☎ 75.04.41.32, Euro Visa, 6 rm ℗ ≼ ⚏ 🍴 half pens (h.s.), closed Mon and Sun, Aug-May. Rest. ♦♦ ♪ & 90-250.

SAINT-PAUL-TROIS-CHÂTEAUX, ⊠ 26130, 8 km SE of **Pierrelatte**.

Restaurant :
● ♦♦ *La Chapelle*, imp. Ludovic-de-Bimard, ☎ 75.96.60.88, Visa ⚏ ♪ closed Mon and Sun eve, 90-260; child : 40.

Recommended
♥ *SICA France Truffes*, rte de Valréas, fresh and canned truffles.

SAINT-RESTITUT, ⊠ 26130 Saint-Paul-Trois-Châteaux, 12 km SE of **Pierrelatte**.

Hotel :
★★★ *Auberge des Quatre Saisons* (L.F.), pl. de l'Église, ☎ 75.04.71.88, AE DC Euro Visa, 10 rm ⚏ 🍴 ♪ ℘ closed Mon eve and Tue am, 12 Nov-10 Dec, 300. Rest. ♦ ♪ closed Mon eve and Tue noon (l.s.). Medieval vaulted ceiling and fine regional fare, 70-200.

SOLERIEUX, ⊠ 26130 Saint-Paul-Trois-Châteaux, 14 km E of **Pierrelatte** on the D59, D71.

Hotel :
★ *Ferme Saint-Michel*, rte de la Baume, ☎ 75.98.10.66, Visa, 10 rm ℗ ⚏ 🍴 �️ ▭ closed 15 Dec-15 Jan, 170. Rest. ♦♦ closed Mon noon and Sun eve. Enjoyable family-style food, 65-110.

SUZE-LA-ROUSSE, ⊠ 26790, 18 km SE of **Pierrelatte**.

Hotel :
★★ *Relais du Château*, ☎ 75.04.87.07, AE Euro Visa, 38 rm ℗ ⚏ 🍴 & 🌝 ▭ ℘ closed 20 Dec-10 Jan, 200. Rest. ♦ 60-100.

Recommended
♥ oenology, wine tasting : *Université du vin*, ☎ 75.04.86.09.

MONTÉLIMAR

Valence 45, Avignon 82, Paris 606 km
pop 30200 ⊠ 26230   A3
Hard or soft, nougat has made the name of this quiet little town world famous. The château des Adhémar (12th-14th-16thC; *10-12 & 2-7 ex Tue., Wed. am*) from which it takes its name is situated on a bluff to the east.

Nearby

▶ **Puygiron** *(8 km E)*, **La Bégude-de-Mazenc** *(15 km E)* and **Le Poët-Laval** *(23 km E)* should be seen for their location and medieval character. ▶ **Notre-Dame d'Aiguebelle** *(17 km SE)* is an ancient Cistercian abbey (12thC).   □

Nougats

Black nougat is an old Provençal delicacy; almonds bound together by lightly caramelized honey and eaten between two wafers. The better-known white Montélimar nougat is a refined cousin : egg white for smoothness, a few pistachios and various flavours are added to make this delicious candy that Montélimar exports all over the world.

Practical Information

MONTÉLIMAR
🛈 Champ-de-Mars, ☎ 75.01.00.20.
SNCF ☎ 75.01.50.50/75.01.09.88.
Car rental : *Avis*, 84, bd Saint-James, ☎ 75.51.86.20; train station.

Hotels :
● ★★★★ *Parc Chabaud*, 16, av. d'Aygu, ☎ 75.01.65.66, AE DC Visa, 22 rm ℗ ⚏ closed 24 Dec-1 Feb, 450. Rest. ♦♦♦ closed Sat and Sun, 210-250.
★★★ *Relais de l'Empereur*, (Mapotel), pl. Marx-Dormoy, ☎ 75.01.29.00, Tx 345537, AE DC Euro Visa, 40 rm ℗ ⚏ closed 10 Nov-20 Dec, 450. Rest. ♦♦ & Traditional and a bit stiff, 165-200.
★★ *Printemps*, (L.F., R.S.), 8, chemin de la Manche, ☎ 75.01.32.63, 16 rm ℗ ⚏ 🍴 & half pens (h.s.), closed Sun, Nov-Jan, 450. Rest. ♦ ≼ & closed lunch, 75-100.
★ *Pierre* (L.F.), 7, pl. des Clercs, ☎ 75.01.33.16, 11 rm, 125.

Restaurants :
♦♦ *Le Grillon*, 40, rue Cuiraterie, ☎ 75.01.79.02, AE Euro Visa ♪ 🌝 closed Wed and Sun noon, 15 Dec-15 Jan. Spec : *émincé de truite à la crème d'oseille, jambonneau de canard confit maison au vinaigre d'estragon*, 80-160.
● ♦ *Papillote*, 2, pl. du Temple, ☎ 75.01.99.28 ⚏ ♪ & closed Mon and Sun, 1-15 Jan, 1-21 Oct, 55-80.
▵ ★★★*International* (100 pl) ☎ 75.01.88.99.

Recommended
♥ nougat : *Chabert et Guillot*, 1, rue Ducatez; at Espeluche, ⊠ 26740, 9 km SE, decorated bread : *Bernard Augier*.

Nearby

CHÂTEAUNEUF-DU-RHÔNE, ⊠ 26840 Malataverne, 9 km S.

Restaurant :
● ♦♦ *La Savinière*, ☎ 75.90.72.52 & closed Mon and Sun, 1-30 Jun. A good, reasonably-priced restaurant in a pretty house, 75-130.

MALATAVERNE, ⊠ 26780, 9 km S on the N7.

Hotels :
★★★ *Domaine du Colombier*, rte de Donzère, ☎ 75.51.65.86, AE DC Visa, 12 rm ℗ ≼ ⚏ ⚘ ▭ closed

Mon lunch, Feb, 360. Rest. ♦♦ ♪ Spec : *paupiettes de lotte*, 110-180.
Mas des Sources, D144, ☎ 75.51.74.18, Visa, 6 rm ⸙ ⣿ ◿ ⌂ ↗ half pens, closed Sun eve , Feb, Nov, 450. Rest. ● ♦♦ closed Wed and Sun eve. A new beginning for Jean-Marie and Nicole Picard (*le petit Bacchus* in Paris) here amid 100 acres of wine country in a sports complex (tennis, squash, pool, volley-ball, sauna). Excellent Provençal cooking by a gifted young chef. Weekend packages, wine-tasting courses, 140-200 ; child : 70.

MIRMANDE, ⊠ 26270 Loriol, 20 km N.

Hotel :
● ★★ *Capitelle* (R.S.), ☎ 75.63.02.72, AE DC Visa, 15 rm ℙ ⣿ ◿ ❀ closed Tue, 15 Jan-1 Mar, 185. Rest. ♦ ♪ Handsome Renaissance house, 70-100.

Restaurant :
● ♦ *Resto du Port*, rue du Boulanger, ☎ 75.63.00.70, Visa, closed Tue, lunch ex Sat, Sun, Jan. Spec : *brochette de porc au thé et au miel, filet de poisson à la laitue de mer*, 75-130.

MONTBOUCHER-SUR-JABRON, ⊠ 26740, 5 km E on the D 169.

Hotel :
● ★★★ *Le Castel*, Château de Montboucher, ☎ 75.46.08.16, AE DC Visa, 10 rm ℙ ⣿ ⌂ closed Tue, 12 Nov-21 Dec. 13thC house, 280. Rest. ♦♦ ⸙ ♪ 110-180.

NYONS

Orange 42, Gap 106, Paris 657 km
pop 6293 ⊠ 26110   A3

Olives, truffles and jam are the specialities of Nyons, also known for the mildness of its climate. See the Forts★, an area of narrow streets and staircases, and the bridge (14thC) over the Aygues.

Nearby

▶ SE : the little **Baronnies Massif★** with its principal town **Buis**, pokes its limestone crest through a decor of vines, olive trees and fields of lavender. ▶ Discover old fortified villages★ such as : **Sainte-Jalle** *(17 km E)*, **Saint-Auban-sur-l'Ouvèze** *(40 km SE)* and **Verclause** *(35 km NE)*.   ◻

Practical Information ———————————————
NYONS
ⓘ pl. de la Libération, ☎ 75.26.10.35.

Hotels :
● ★★ *Auberge du Vieux Village*, (I.L.A.), Aubres, 4 km E, ☎ 75.26.12.89, AE DC Euro Visa, 15 rm ℙ ⸙ ⣿ ◿ ⌂ 300. Rest. ♦ closed Wed noon, 90-160.
● ★★ *Picholine* (L.F.), prom. de la Perrière, ☎ 75.26.06.21, AE DC Euro Visa, 16 rm ℙ ⸙ ⣿ ◿ ⌂ closed Mon, 250. Rest. ♦ ⸙ ♿ 100-120 ; child : 25.
★★ *Colombet*, 53, pl. de la Libération, ☎ 75.26.03.66, 30 rm ℙ ⸙ ⣿ closed 5 Nov-10 Jan, 220. Rest. ♦ Reserve, 70-160.

Restaurant :
♦ *Le Petit Caveau*, 9, rue V.-Hugo, ☎ 75.26.20.21, DC Visa ♿ closed Mon, 75-200.

⚠ ★★★*Municipal* (97 pl), ☎ 75.26.22.39 ; ★★*Saint-Rim-bert* (80 pl), ☎ 75.26.03.81.

Nearby

BUIS-LES-BARONNIES, ⊠ 26170, 30 km SE.
ⓘ pl. du Champ-de-Mars, ☎ 75.28.04.59.

⚠ ★★*Municipal* (55 pl), ☎ 75.28.04.96.

Recommended
Events : lime tree festival, mid-Jul.
♥ cheese, honey, olive oil : *La Savoilane*, 2.5 km, ☎ 75.28.03.39 ; Picodons (goat cheese) : Wed at the market.

CONDORCET, ⊠ 26110, 6 km NE.

Restaurant :
♦♦ *La Charrette Bleue*, rte de Gap, ☎ 75.27.72.33, AE Visa ⣿ ♪ closed Wed. A former coaching inn. Flowery terrace. Spec : *sauté d'escargots aux girolles, carré d'agneau à la crème de thym*, 55-120 ; child : 35.

The OISANS Massif★★★

B2

The Oisans is to the Dauphiné what the Mont Blanc Massif is to the Savoie, a sanctuary for climbers. Apart from the road from Grenoble to the Lautaret pass up the Romanche Valley, only vertiginous paths lead into this fortress of peaks and frozen land.

Valley of the Romanche★★ : from Le Bourg-d'Oisans to the Lautaret pass *(39 km, 2 hr)*

▶ **Le Bourg-d'Oisans★** (pop. 3 071) is well known to amateur geologists, who find a wealth of mineral samples in the area. ▶ Anyone who likes crazy little mountain roads should go up to **Villard-Reculas★**, **Auris★**, **Villard-Reymond★** (ascent of Prégentil promontory★★ *40 min*) and **Villard-Notre-Dame★★** for the view and charming character of these villages. ▶ The road which continues to **L'Alpe d'Huez★** (peak *13 km*) is easier. Facing full S, one thousand metres above the Romanche River, the ancient hamlet of **Huez** faces the sparkling Meije glaciers. An international winter sports resort, and also an excursion centre : to the Pic du Lac Blanc★★★ *(access by cable-car)* the Dôme des Petits Rousses★★ peaks, and to Lake Besson★. ▶ Hydroelectric reservoir of **Chambon★.** ▶ Right : the D213 goes up *(10 km)* to **Les Deux-Alpes** ski-resort among the high reaches where you can ski even in summer on the glacier of Mont de Lans (3 160 m). ▶ **La Grave★** (pop. 453) seems to live only for the Meije★★ peak, shining from all its glaciers above this important mountaineering centre. The cable-car from the Ruillans Pass★★★ (alt. 3 200 m) enables you to see this marvel of ice.

Vénéon Valley★★★ and La Bérarde *(26 km, leave from 5 km SE of Le Bourg-d'Oisans, 2 hr)*

▶ This is an area reserved for high mountain guides and mountaineers. ▶ From the hamlet of **La Bérarde** on foot *(1 hr 15, easy)* to the **Plan du Carrelet** *(chalet-hôtel;* wood and stone construction) one of the most beautiful sights in the Écrins Nature Reserve. From La Bérarde, 2:30 hr to climb *(hiking shoes recommended)* to the **Tête de la Maye** (alt. 2 519 m ; panorama★★★).   ◻

Practical Information ———————————————
ALLEMOND, ⊠ 38114, 11 km N on the on N 91.

Hotel :
★ *Giniès*, ☎ 76.80.70.03, 18 rm ℙ ⸙ ⣿ ◿ 100. Rest. ♦ ⸙ closed 2 May-15 Sep, 75-145♦ closed 2-15 Sep, 75-145.

L' ALPE-D'HUEZ, ⊠ 38750, 62 km SE of **Grenoble**.
⚡ 1860-3350m.
ⓘ pl. Paganon, ☎ 76.80.35.41.
Car rental : Avis, garage Bel Alpe (closed Jun-Nov), ☎ 76.80.45.06.

Hotels :
★★★★ *L'Ours blanc*, ☎ 76.80.31.11, Tx 520807, Euro Visa, 37 rm, half pens (h.s.), closed 1 May-20 Dec, 940. .
★★★ *Chamois d'Or*, ☎ 76.80.31.22, 41 rm, closed 25 Apr-15 Dec, 400. Rest. ● ♦♦ ⸙ ♿ The cooking remains light for skiers : *huîtres chaudes aux épinards frais, émincé de blanc de Bresse en papillotte* ; terrace service, 98-250.
★★★ *Vallée Blanche*, ☎ 76.80.30.51, 41 ch. ℙ ⸙ ◿ closed 24 Apr-15 Déc, 500. Rest. ♦ Piano-bar, discothèque, 130-190.

Restaurant :
♦♦ *La Cordée*, rue de la Meije, ☎ 76.80.35.39 ♪ closed 1 May-1 Jul, 1 Sep-11 Nov, 90-180.

Recommended
Leisure activities : *summer skiing*, ☎ 66.29.00.99 ; at Alti Bar, *summer skiing*, ☎ 76.80.41.15.
Youth hostel : *Marc Sangnier*, ☎ 76.80.37.37.

Le BOURG-D'OISANS, ⊠ 38120, 49 km from **Grenoble**. ⚡ 720m. ↩
ℹ quai Girard, ☎ 76.80.03.25.
🚒 ☎ 76.80.00.90.

Hotel :
★★ *L'Oberland* (L.F.), av. de la Gare, ☎ 76.80.24.24, AE DC Euro Visa, 30 rm P ⊱ ≋ ♨ ♨ half pens (h.s.), closed 15 Apr-15 May, 30 Sep-15 Dec, 360. Rest. ♦ ⚶ 60-140 ; child : 40.

⚠ ★★★★*Belledonne* (130 pl), ☎ 76.80.07.18 ; ★★★★*Rencontre du Soleil* (73 pl), ☎ 76.80.00.33.

Recommended
Events : *international market of minerals and crystals*, Easter weekend.
Holiday villages : ☎ 76.80.02.03.

Les DEUX-ALPES, ⊠ 38860, 65 km NW of **Briançon**. ⚡ 1650-3423m.
ℹ maison des Deux-Alpes, ☎ 76.79.22.00.
🚒 ☎ 76.80.51.22.

Hotels :
★★★★ *La Farandole*, ☎ 76.80.50.45, Tx 320029, AE DC Euro Visa, 60 rm P ⊱ ≋ ♨ ♪ ⊡ ♫ half pens (h.s.), closed 4 May-20 Jun, 14 Sep-28 Nov, 1200. Rest. ♦♦ ⊱ ♪ ♨ 160-200.
● ★★★ *La Mariande* (L.F.), ☎ 76.80.50.60, Tx 320883, 25 rm P ⊱ ≋ ♨ ♪ ⊡ ♫ pens, closed 25 Apr-20 Jun, 1 Sep-20 Dec, 940. Rest. ♦♦ ⊱ ♪ ♨ ⚶ Seasonal cuisine, 130.
★★★ *La Bérangère* (R.C.), ☎ 76.79.24.11, Tx 320878, AE Euro Visa P ⊱ ♨ ♪ ♨ ⊡ half pens (h.s.), closed 4 May-28 Jun, 31 Aug-12 Dec, 860. Rest. ♦♦ ⊱ ♪ ♨ ⚶ 150-220.

⚠ ★★*Deux Alpes* (80 pl), ☎ 76.79.20.47.

Le FRENEY-D'OISANS, ⊠ 38142, 14 km E of **Bourg-d'Oisans** on the N 91.

Hotel :
● ★★ *Panoramique*, Mizoen, ☎ 76.80.06.25, 9 rm P ⊱ ≋ ♨ closed Sep-May, 180. Rest. ♦ ⚶ 70.

La GARDE-EN-OISANS, ⊠ 38520, 2 km N of **Bourg-d'Oisans**.

Hotel :
★ *Forêt de Maronne* (L.F.), Le Chatelard, ☎ 76.80.00.06, 13 rm P ⊱ ≋ ♨ half pens (h.s.), closed 30 Apr-15 Jun, 20 Sep-20 Dec, 316. Rest. ♦ ♪ 45-140 ; child : 35.

La GRAVE, ⊠ 05320, 39 km NW of **Briançon**.
ℹ ☎ 76.79.90.05.

Hotel :
★★ *Castillan*, ☎ 76.79.90.04, Visa, 43 rm P ⊱ ≋ ♨ ⚶ ⊡ closed 4-27 May, 27 Sep-20 Dec, 140. Rest. ♦ ⊱ ♪ ♨ 60-125.

⚠ ★★*Ermitage* (66 pl), ☎ 76.79.90.33.

The QUEYRAS Valley***

C2
(see map 2)

Clear rushing water, rolling pebbles of green and mauve marble, woods of larch and stone pine filtering the southern light ; and the slopes are dotted with thousands of flowers. Flora and fauna are all protected within the Regional Park. The Queyras is a country of high villages (all are over 1 300 m alt.) with a long tradition of woodworking, where craftsmen still produce toys, furniture and decorated wooden chests.

From Guillestre to Abriès *(31 km, 2 hr)*

▶ A stopover on the Grandes Alpes route, **Guillestres** (pop. 2 009) is also the principal town in the Queyras region. 4 km NW : **Mont-Dauphin★**, a fortified city in pink marble, designed by Vauban. 10 km S, **Vars :** winter sports resort based on several villages strung out along the road to the Vars Pass. ▶ **Château-Queyras★**, medieval fortress (13thC) framed between the two slopes of the valley ; 11 km to the Bucher Summit (view★★). 5.5 km NW, **Arvieux** (pop. 351) : on the road to the Izoard Pass★★, a centre for master-toymakers. ▶ **Aiguilles** (pop. 310) and **Abriès** (pop. 322) : surrounded by forests, for winter skiing and summer walks to high meadows covered with

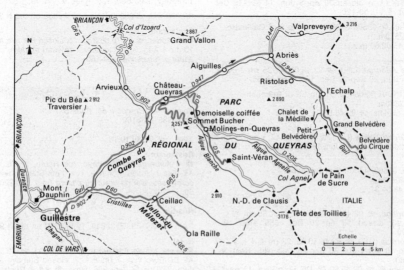

2. The Queyras valley

flowers. The road continues *(16 km)* dawdling along with the Guil River to the **Mount Viso** belvedere★★.

From Guillestre to Ceillac★ *(road 14 km)*

▶ Pines and larches accompany you from the enclosed valley of Cristillan to **Ceillac** (beautiful isolated chapel). Excursion into the Mélezet Valley★ (GR5).

From Château-Queyras to Saint-Véran★★ *(14 km)*

▶ The houses typical of the region first appear at **Molines-en-Queyras** (pop. 375) in the valley of the Aigue Blanche. ▶ **Saint-Véran★★** (pop. 275) : famous for its European altitude record (1 990-2 040 m) and its houses★ crowned with huge lofts.   □

Practical Information ────────────

ARVIEUX, ⊠ 05350 Château-Ville-Vieille, 32 km SE of **Briançon**.
ⓘ La Chalp, ☎ 92.45.75.76.

Hotel :
★★ *La Borne Ensoleillée*, ☎ 92.45.72.89, Euro, 18 rm
ⓟ ⫕ ∭ ⚲ half pens (h.s.), closed 2 May-15 Jun, 15 Sep-20 Dec, 310. Rest. ♦ ⫕ 60-90.

GUILLESTRE, ⊠ 05600, 35 km S of **Briançon**.
ⓘ pl. Salva, ☎ 92.45.04.37.

Hotels :
● ★★ *Barnières 1* (L.F.), ☎ 92.45.05.07, 35 rm ⓟ ⫕
▭ ♪ 180. Rest. ♦ 120-210.
★★ *Barnières 2* (L.F.), ☎ 92.45.04.87, 39 rm ⓟ ⫕ ⚲ ⫘
▭ ♪ 200. Rest. ♦ 120-210.

⚠ ★★★★*Le Villard* (83 pl), ☎ 92.45.06.54 ; ★★★*La Rochette* (233 pl), ☎ 92.45.02.15 ; ★★★*Saint-James les Pins* (100 pl), ☎ 92.45.08.24 ; ★★*Serre Altitude 1000* (100 pl), ☎ 92.45.00.40.

Recommended
Youth hostel : *Les Quatre Vents*, rte de la Gare, ☎ 92.45.04.32.

MOLINES-EN-QUEYRAS, ⊠ 05390, 46 km SE of **Briançon**.
ⓘ ☎ 92.45.83.22.

Hotel :
★★ *L'Equipe* (L.F.), ☎ 92.45.83.20, AE DC Euro Visa, 21 rm ⓟ ⫕ ∭ ⚲ closed 30 Apr-5 Jun, 14 Sep-19 Dec, 200. Rest. ♦ ⫕ ♪ 50-120.

Le RISOUL, ⊠ 05600 Guillestre, 3 km S of **Guillestre**.
⚡ 1850-2570m.
ⓘ ☎ 92.45.02.60 (h.s.).

Hotel :
★ *Bonne Auberge* (L.F.), ☎ 92.45.02.40, 35 rm ⫕ closed 15 Mar-1 Jun, 20 Sep-20 Dec, 160. Rest. ♦ 65.

SAINT-VÉRAN, ⊠ 05490, 51 km SE of **Briançon**.
⚡ 2040-2560m.
ⓘ at the ski lifts, ☎ 92.45.82.21.

Hotel :
★★ *Le Grand Tétras* (L.F.), ☎ 92.45.82.42, Visa, 21 rm ⓟ ⫕ ∭ ⚲ closed 3 May-14 Jun, 15 Sep-20 Dec, 175. Rest. ♦ ⫕ 50-110.

VARS, ⊠ 05560, 47 km S of **Briançon**.
⚡ 1650-2250m.
ⓘ ☎ 92.45.51.31.

Hotels :
★★★ *Caribou*, ☎ 92.45.50.43, Euro Visa, 35 rm ⓟ ⫕ ⚲ pens (h.s.), closed 10 Apr-20 Dec, 855. Rest. ♦ ⫕ ♪ 155-200.
★★ *Escondus* (L.F.), ☎ 92.45.50.35, 23 rm ⓟ ⫕ ∭ ⚲ ⫘ ♪ closed 10 Apr-1 Jul, 30 Sep-15 Dec, 185. Rest. ♦ ♪ ⫘ 60-150.
★★ *L'Ecureuil*, ☎ 92.45.50.72, DC Euro Visa, 17 rm ⓟ ⫕ ♪ ＆ closed 15 Apr-1 Jul, 31 Aug-20 Dec, 250.

ROMANS-SUR-ISÈRE

Valence 18, Grenoble 81, Paris 562 km
pop 34000 ⊠ 26100   A2

Feet have always been the major preoccupation here, and by the 15thC the guild of *sabotiers* and *grolleurs* (clog- and shoemakers) was prospering. Today the town remains the French capital of quality footwear.

▶ From Egypt to the present day, the march of history is retraced in the **Musée de la Chaussure★** (Shoe Museum) which also includes a section on regional ethnography *(closed Tue. and nat. hols.).* ▶ Don't miss the **collegiate church of St. Barnard★** (12th-13th-14thC) and its Flemish hangings★★ of 1555 ; old streets★ behind the church.   □

Practical Information ────────────

ROMANS-SUR-ISÈRE
ⓘ pl. Jules-Nadi, ☎ 75.02.28.72.
SNCF ☎ 75.02.31.75.
Car rental : Avis, 8 av. du maquis, ☎ 75.05.18.10.

Hotel :
★★ *Magdeleine*, 31, av. P.-Sémard, ☎ 75.02.33.53, Euro Visa, 16 rm, 160.

Restaurant :
♦♦ *Ponton*, 40, pl. Jacquemart, ☎ 75.02.29.91, Visa ♪ closed Mon and Sun eve, 12-31 Jul. Regional fare : *ravioles de Romans*, 100-180.

⚠ ★★*des Chasses* (40 pl), ☎ 75.72.35.27 ; .

Recommended
Baby-sitting : *le Dauphiné Libéré*, ☎ 75.02.09.66.

Nearby

BOURG-DE-PÉAGE, ⊠ 26300, 3 km S.

Hotel :
★★ *Yan's* (L.F.), ☎ 75.72.44.11, AE Visa, 25 rm ⓟ ∭ ▭ 280.

GRANGES-LES-BEAUMONT, ⊠ 26600 Tain-l'Hermitage, 5 km W on the D 532.

Hotel :
★★ *Lanaz*, ☎ 75.71.50.56, 8 rm ⓟ ⫕ ∭ ⚲ ＆ closed Sat, 1-12 May, 1-23 Sep, 135. Rest. ♦ ⫕ ＆ 40.

PIZANCON, ⊠ 26300 Bourg-de-Péage on the N 351.

Restaurant :
● ♦ *Astier*, ☎ 75.70.06.27 ∭ ＆ closed Sat eve and Sun, 10 Jul-4 Aug. Spec : *rognons de veau madère, chevreau sauté à l'ancienne*, 100-160.

SAINT-MARCELLIN

Valence 44, Grenoble 55, Paris 571 km
pop 6935 ⊠ 38160   A2

SNCF ☎ 76.38.10.10.

Restaurant :
● ♦ *Auberge de l'Abbaye*, rue Haute, ☎ 76.36.42.83, AE Visa ♪ closed Mon eve, Tue, Feb. Spec : *ravioles aux écrevisses, filet de bœuf au chèvre frais*, 100-220 ; child : 50.

Nearby

SAINT-LATTIER, ⊠ 38840, 12 km SW on the N 92.

Hotel :
● ★★★ *Lièvre Amoureux*, (I.L.A., R.C.), ☎ 76.36.50.67, AE DC Euro Visa, 7 rm ⓟ ⫕ closed Sun eve and mon (l.s.), 25 Dec-17 Jan, 280. Rest. ● ♦♦ ⫕ Rustic setting. Spit-roasted hare, *ravioles*, 130-300.

SERRE-PONÇON Lake*

C3

Today hundreds of little coloured sails brighten this enormous sheet of water *(30 km²)*. The lake's prime function since 1960 has been to regulate the flow of the Durance, irrigating the Alps of Haute-Provence and producing electricity.

▶ Near the enormous dam (viewpoint★★) of packed earth (14 million m³) is the **underground generating plant**★ *(visits at 2 and 4, Jun.-Sep.)*. ▶ **Savines-le-Lac** (pop. 859) has replaced the old village, now submerged under the lake. ▶ **Embrun** (pop. 5813) has a remarkable church of Notre-Dame★ (Romanesque, end 12thC; treasure room★); market *(Wed., Sat.)* 10 km S : ancient abbey★ (12thC) and **forest of Boscodon**★★, pines, spruce and larch. □

Practical Information _____

EMBRUN, ⊠ 05200, 38 km E of **Gap**.
🛈 pl. Dosse, ☎ 92.43.01.80.
SNCF ☎ 92.43.00.61.

Hotels :
★★★ **Bartavelles**, Crots, 3 km SW on N 94, ☎ 92.43.20.69, AE Visa, 43 rm 7 apt Ⓟ ≶ ♨ ⌂ closed 30 Sep-7 Nov, 270. Rest. ♦♦ ♪ closed 11 Nov-10 Dec, 70-160.
★ **Notre-Dame** (L.F.), av. Gal-Nicolas, ☎ 92.43.08.36, 15 rm ♨ closed 15 Nov-15 Dec, 120. Rest. ♦ 120-210.

⚠ ★★★★*La Clapière* (446 pl), ☎ 92.43.01.83; ★★★*La Tour* (113 pl), ☎ 92.43.17.66; ★★★*Les Tourelles* (100 pl), ☎ 92.43.15.31; .

SAVINES-LE-LAC, ⊠ 05160, 28 km E of **Gap**.
🛈 ☎ 92.44.20.44.
SNCF ☎ 92.44.20.34.

Restaurant :
♦ **Relais Fleuri**, ☎ 92.44.20.32 Ⓟ ≶ ♨ closed Mon ex Jul-Aug, 30 Sep-15 May, 60-130.

⚠ ★★★*Chaumettes* (50 pl), ☎ 92.44.20.16; ★★★*Les Sources* (46 pl), ☎ 92.44.20.52; ★★*Eygoires* (333 pl), ☎ 92.44.20.48; ★★*Grand Morgon* (80 pl), ☎ 92.44.22.15.

La TOUR-DU-PIN

Lyon 55, Grenoble 67, Paris 518 km
pop 7037 ⊠ 38110   A1

The triptych★ in the church is by a pupil of Dürer (1541). 15thC Renaissance house, known locally as the Maison des Dauphins★.

Nearby

▶ *Bourgoin-Jallieu (15 km W)* : museum with 19th-20thC paintings and drawings. One room devoted to tapestries and printing on cloth, specialities of Bourgoin *(Wed., 2-5; Thu., 2-6; Sat. 4:30-7:30)*. ▶ **L'Isle-d'Abeau** *(27 km W)*, a new city features some interesting modern architecture. At Villefontaine, next to a lake, **Ecomuseum of Northern Dauphiné** (numerous exhibitions ; *2-6 ex Sat.)*. ▶ **La Côte-Saint-André** *(36 km NW)* : Hector Berlioz Museum★ in the house where the composer was born *(9-12 & 3-6; Feb. 2-5; closed Mon. and Jan.)*. ▶ **Château de Virieu**★ *(12 km SE)* an 11thC fortress *(summer, 2-6; closed Mon.)*. ▶ **Paladru Lake**★ *(20 km SE)*. Neolithic man lived around the shores of this emerald lake, now the hunting-ground of wind-surfers from Lyon and the Dauphiné. □

Practical Information _____

La TOUR-DU-PIN
SNCF ☎ 76.97.04.34.

Hotel :
★ **Dauphiné-Savoie** (L.F.), 2-4, rue A.-Briand,

☎ 74.97.03.87, Euro Visa, 12 rm Ⓟ closed 16-24 Mar, 15-31 Oct, 100. Rest. ♦ ♪ closed Mon noon, 55-110.

⚠ ★★*Coin Tranquille*, Les Abrets (117 pl), ☎ 76.32.13.48.

Nearby

Les AVENIÈRES, ⊠ 38630, 17 km.

Hotel :
★★ **Relais des Vieilles Postes** (R.S.), ☎ 74.33.62.99, AE DC Euro Visa, 17 rm ≶ ♨ ⌂ ♿ closed Sun eve and Mon lunch ex Jul-Aug, 21 Apr-4 May, 24 Nov-14 Dec, 195. Rest. ● ♦♦ ♪ ✾ Top chef Guy Savoy declares that his friend Laurent Thomas will soon have people talking. In a lovely rustic inn with loads of character he serves a felicitous selection of dishes : *salade de langoustines aux pâtes fraîches et agrumes, paupiette de saumon aux écrevisses, ragoût de ris et rognons de veau aux ravioles et foie gras*. We wish him much success, 100-250.

CESSIEU, ⊠ 38110, 6 km W on the N 6.

Hotel :
★★ **La Gentilhommière** (L.F.), ☎ 74.88.30.09, AE DC Euro Visa, 6 rm Ⓟ ♨ closed Sun eve and Mon, 15-30 Nov, 120. Rest. ♦ A friendly stopover between Lyon and Chambéry, 100-150; child : 40.

CHARAVINES, ⊠ 38850, 22 km S.
🛈 rte Nationale, ☎ 76.06.60.31.   ♥

Hotels :
★★ **Host. du Lac Bleu** (L.F.), Lake Paladru, ☎ 76.06.60.48, 15 rm Ⓟ ≶ ♨ closed Tue (l.s.), Oct-Easter, 175. Rest. ♦ ≶ ♪ (l.s.) 60-105.
★★ **Poste** (L.F.), ☎ 76.06.60.41, Visa, 20 rm Ⓟ ♨ ♿ closed Sun eve and Mon, 28 Oct-15 Dec, 210. Rest. ♦ ♪ ♿ 70-150; child : 40.

⚠ ★★*Bord du Lac* (85 pl), ☎ 76.06.64.70.

CRÉMIEU, ⊠ 38460, 34 km NW.
🛈 mairie, ☎ 74.90.70.92.

Hotels :
★★ **Petite Auberge**, 7, rue de la Juiverie, ☎ 74.90.75.45, Visa, 14 rm Ⓟ ♨ 180. Rest. ♦ 75-210.
★ **Auberge de la Chaite**, cours Baron-Raverat, ☎ 74.90.76.63, AE DC Euro Visa, 11 rm Ⓟ ≶ ♨ closed Mon, Dec, 115. Rest. ♦ ♪ ♿ 50-110; child : 35.

Restaurant :
● ♦ **Chez Roby**, Villemoirieu, 2 km W, ☎ 74.90.73.90, Visa ♨ ♪ closed Mon eve, Tue, Sun eve, 1-30 Dec. Copious, savoury country cooking, prepared with fresh farm produce. Spec : *foie de la ferme au cidre et aux pommes*, 125-185.

FAVERGES-DE-LA-TOUR, ⊠ 38110, 10 km E on N 516.

Hotel :
● ★★★★(L) **Le Château** (R.C.), ☎ 74.97.42.52, AE DC Visa, 43 rm Ⓟ ≶ ♨ ⌂ ♪ ⌂ ♐ closed 19 Oct-16 May, 1100. Rest. ♦♦ ♪ ✾ closed Mon, 175-210.

Le MOTTIER, ⊠ 38260 La Côte-Saint-André, 10 km N of **La Côte-Saint-André** on the D 71.

Restaurant :
● ♦ **Les Dommières**, ☎ 74.54.42.06, AE ♪ ♿ closed Wed, Thu, Sun eve , Jan, 15 Jul-15 Aug. Competition is tough for the limited number of seats in this old renovated barn; J.-L. Boland's dishes are crowd-pleasers : *gâteau de foie de volaille, noisettes de chevreau, biscuit glacé à l'orange*, 90-120.

The TRIÈVES Region

B2

▶ **Monestier-de-Clermont** (pop. 774) is the best starting point for exploring the Trièves, a green land deeply scored by the waters of the Drac and the Ebron. ▶ A pleasant trip by car to **Mens** *(21 km SE)* via the **Pont de Brion**★ (bridge), and from there to **La Mure** *(19 km N)* via the **Accarias Pass**★ or the **Sautet Dam**★ and Corps

(25 km E) via the Saint-Sébastien Pass. ▶ From Monestier, you can also reach the upper valley of the Gresse via the **Allimas Pass**★ *(17 km SW);* view★★ of Mont Aiguille (alt. 2 086 m). ◻

Practical Information ───────────────

GRESSE-EN-VERCORS, ⊠ 38650 Monestier-de-Clermont, 36 km S of **Grenoble.**

Hotel :
● ★★ *Le Chalet* (L.F.), ☎ 76.34.32.08, AE Euro, 31 rm ℙ ⫷ ⚇ ⌕ ⯰ ▣ ⌁ half pens (h.s.), closed 3-28 May, 15 Oct-20 Dec, 465. Rest. ◆ ⯰ Regional fare, 60-150; child : 40.

MONESTIER-DE-CLERMONT, ⊠ 38650, 33 km S of **Grenoble.**
ⓘ parc municipal, ☎ 76.34.06.20.
SNCF ☎ 76.34.08.13.

Hotel :
★ *Modern*, ☎ 76.34.07.35, Visa, 21 rm ℙ ⚇ ⌕ ⯰ closed 5 Nov-1 Feb, 200. Rest. ◆ 60-100.

SAINT-PAUL-LES-MONESTIER, ⊠ 38650 Monestier-de-Clermont, 2 km NW on the D 8.

Hotel :
★★ *Au Sans-Souci* (L.F.), ☎ 76.34.03.60, AE Euro Visa, 16 rm ℙ ⫷ ⚇ ⌕ ♪ ▣ closed Sun eve and Mon, Jan, 180. Rest. ◆ ⫷ 60-160; child : 40.

The VALBONNAIS Valley*

B2

From La Mure, the road crosses these two little regions which are in fact the lower and upper reaches of the River Bonne. Dark larch and bright birch clothe the slopes around **La Chapelle-en-Valjouffrey**★ *(24 km);* from here you can reach Le Désert *(8.5 km),* in an amphitheatre★ of snowy peaks. Trips to the **Valsenestre**★ (gorges and forests★). ◻

VALENCE

Lyon 100, Grenoble 100, Paris 668 km
pop 68000 ⊠ 26000 A2

Valence is the main market (fruit and vegetables) for the Drôme and the Ardèche regions ; it is easy to appreciate the charms of Valence in the narrow streets and alleys of the old town around the cathedral.

▶ The **cathedral**★ (A-B2) is a handsome 12thC Romanesque building well reconstructed in the 17thC. ▶ Nearby, the **museum** *(2-5:45)* has a remarkable series of 96 sanguines★★ (red ochre crayon sketches) and drawings of Italy (1755-75) by Hubert Robert. ▶ N of the cathedral, the Pendentif is a graceful Renaissance structure (1548). Also... ▶ The **Maison Dupré-Latour**★, early 16thC (7 Rue Pérollerie, B1-2) and the **Maison des Têtes**★, Renaissance (57 Grande-Rue, B1-2). ◻

Practical Information ───────────────

VALENCE
ⓘ pl. du Gal-Leclerc (B2), ☎ 75.43.04.88.
✈ *Valence-Chabeuil*, 5 km SE, ☎ 75.44.48.80/ 75.41.50.50.
SNCF (B2), ☎ 75.56.33.33.
Car rental : *Avis*, 164, av. de Romans (C1), ☎ 75.42.58.91; train station (B2); 51, rue D.-Papin (B3), ☎ 75.44.54.69.

Hotels :
★★★ *2000*, av. de Romans (C1), ☎ 75.43.73.01, Tx 345873, AE DC Euro Visa, 31 rm ℙ ⚇ ⌕ 250. Rest. ◆ *Lys* ⫷ ♪ ⅄ ⯰ 90-130.
★★★ *Pic* (R.C.), 285, av. V.-Hugo (A3), ☎ 75.44.15.32, AE DC, 4 rm ℙ ⚇ closed Sun eve , Wed, 10 days in Feb, Aug, 350. Rest. ● ◆◆◆◆ ⫷ At the "Pic" of their form, Jacques

and Alain are happy men. Their house is lovely, the family hospitality exceptionally warm. The food is in peak form too, simple yet outstanding : *salade de pêcheurs au xérès, foie de canard au marc de l'hermitage, pigeon de Bresse aux aubergines.* To quench your thirst, all the great Rhône Valley wines, 200-450.
★★ *L'Europe*, 15, av. F.-Faure (B2), ☎ 75.43.02.16, Euro Visa, 26 rm ℙ Provençal furnishings, 250.

Restaurants :
● ◆◆ *L'Epicerie-Restaurant*, 18, pl. St-Jean (B1), ☎ 75.42.74.46, Visa ℙ ⫷ ⚇ ♪ closed Sun and 25 Dec. In his venerable 15thC home with its 1920s decor, Pierre-Camille Vernet improves your mind (with exhibits and jazz) while he feeds you. Interesting fixed meals : *pastel de la mer à la vapeur sur deux beurres, filet mignon caramélisé aux raisins et petits légumes,* Côtes-du-Rhône wine, 55-150.
◆ *La Taverne*, 4, pl. des Clercs, ☎ 75.43.10.59, AE DC Euro Visa ℙ ⚇ ♪ closed Sun, 90-120; child : 35.

Recommended
Guided tours : *C.N.M.H.S.*, info tourist office, by appt.
♥ chocolates, pastry : *Giraud*, 5, pl. de la République, ☎ 75.43.05.28; fish, poultry, game, *foie gras : Fullana*, 5, av. V.-Hugo, B2, ☎ 75.44.24.32; local brioche cake and other pastries : *Dragon*, 12, av. de Chabreuil, ☎ 75.43.11.71.

Nearby

BOURG-LES-VALENCE, ⊠ 26500, 3 km NE on the N 7.

Hotel :
★★ *Seyvet*, 24, av. Marc-Urtin, ☎ 75.43.26.51, AE DC Euro Visa, 34 rm ℙ ⚇ ⌕ closed 7-27 Jan, 240. Rest. ◆◆ closed Sun eve (l.s.), 60-190.

CHABEUIL, ⊠ 26120, 11 km E on the D 68/N 538.

Hotel :
★ *Commerce*, pl. Genissieu, ☎ 75.59.00.23, 21 rm ℙ closed Sat, Nov, 145. Rest. ◆ 60-100.
🅐 ★★ *L'Espervière* (170 pl), ☎ 75.43.63.01.

ÉTOILE-SUR-RHÔNE, ⊠ 26800 Portes-lès-Valence, 8 km S.

Hotel :
★★★ *Château de Clavel* (I.L.A.), ☎ 75.60.61.93, AE Euro Visa, 24 rm ℙ ⫷ ⚇ ⌕ ▣ ⯰ closed Sun eve, 350. Rest. ◆ ⫷ ♪ ⅄ closed Sun (l.s.), 95-125; child : 60.

MONTMEYRAN, ⊠ 26120, 14 km SE on the N 538 A.

Restaurant :
◆◆ *La Vieille Ferme*, Quartier Dorelons, D 125, ☎ 75.59.31.64, AE DC Visa ℙ ⫷ ⚇ ⌕ ♪ closed Mon eve, Tue, Sun eve, 31 Jul-30 Aug. A real working farm that serves rustic cuisine to those who reserve in advance, 130-150.

PONT-DE-L'ISÈRE, ⊠ 26600 Tain-l'Hermitage, 9 km N.

Hotel :
★★ *Chabran* (R.C.), ☎ 75.84.60.09, Tx 346333, Visa, 12 rm ℙ ⚇ closed Sun eve and Mon (Sep-Easter), 350. Rest. ◆ ◆◆◆ ⫷ The extensive improvements point up the delectable cooking of tireless, dynamic Michel Chabran. Once a modest inn, it is now a trim modern restaurant bursting with patrons : *ravioles de Royans pochées au bouillon de poule, flan de moules aux jeunes légumes, râble de lapereau rôti aux échalotes.* The cellar holds treasures from the Rhône Valley. To work off the meal, sports facilities steps away (pool, tennnis, golf, karting), 200-400.

SAINT-VALLIER, ⊠ 26240, 32 km N.

Hotels :
● ★★ *Voyageurs*, 2, av. Jean-Jaurès, ☎ 75.23.04.42, AE DC Euro Visa, 9 rm ℙ ⫷ ♪ closed Sun eve and Mon, 5-15 Jan, 1-24 Jun, 135. Rest. ◆◆ ♪ Classic dining. Wide choice of wines, 60-165.
● ★ *Terminus*, 116, av. Jean-Jaurès, ☎ 75.23.01.12, AE DC Euro Visa, 20 rm ℙ closed Tue eve , Wed, Feb school hols,, 4-28 Aug, 90. Rest. ◆ ♪ In a simple setting, fine

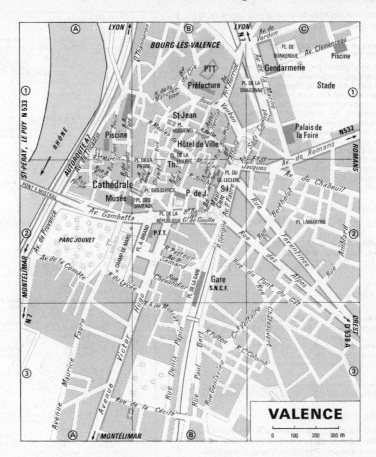

VALENCE

0   100   200   300 m

food by A. Lecomte : *feuilleté d'asperges aux coquilles Saint-Jacques et rouget, émincé de volailles aux écrevisses*, 100-240 ; child : 50.

⚐ ★★*Les Lucs* (150 pl), ☎ 75.08.32.82.

Recommended
♥ wine : *cave coopérative*, ☎ 75.08.20.87.

TAIN-L'HERMITAGE, ⊠ 26600, 26 km N.
ⓘ rue Jean-Jaurès, ☎ 75.08.30.43.

Hotel :
★★ *L'Abricotine*, rte de Romans, 3 km, ☎ 75.07.44.60, Euro Visa, 9 rm ℗ ᠁ ♨ closed Sun (Nov-Mar), 10 Nov-10 Dec, 170. Rest. ♦ ⫶ ᕓ 55-70.

Restaurant :
♦ *Reynaud*, 82, av. Président-Roosevelt, ☎ 75.07.22.10, AE DC Visa ⫶ ᠁ ⚘ closed Mon and Sun eve, Jan, 16-23 Aug, 120-280.

The VALGAUDEMAR Valley*

B2

Valgaudemar is hidden deep in the Massif des Écrins, on the fast-running Séveraisse. Downstream there are fresh meadows where curtains of poplars scintillate in the sunshine. The scenery changes completely with the houses of Villar-Loubière, clinging to the rock : the valley is suddenly surrounded by bright

walls and dark shaded woods as the mountains close in.

▶ From **La Chapelle-en-Valgaudemar** *(18 km on N85)* climb to the hamlet of Portes : view★★ over the Olan Peak. ▶ Continue 9 km to the chalet-hotel of Gioberney, shortly after the Cascade du Voile de la Mariée (Bride's Veil Falls) site★ ; numerous excursions from the chalet. □

Practical Information ───────────

La **CHAPELLE-EN-VALGAUDEMAR**, ⊠ 05800 Saint-Firmin, 48 km N of **Gap**.
ⓘ ☎ 92.55.23.21.

Hotel :
★ *Mont Olan*, ☎ 92.55.23.03, Euro Visa, 36 rm ℗ ⫶ ᠁ ♨ pens, half pens (h.s.), closed 25 Mar-15 Sep, 155. Rest. ♦ 55-85.

⚐ ★★*Les Mélèzes* (80 pl), ☎ 92.55.23.17.

The VALLOUISE Valley*

C2

The Vallouise leads up to the foot of the highest peaks in the Dauphiné. The villages of the region are typically Dauphinois : around the Romanesque bell tower, the large stone houses, sometimes adorned with arcades and crowned with wooden storage lofts, are backed against the hillside so that you can walk in on the upper level.

Vallouise Route★ : from Argentière to Le Pré de Madame Carle *(24 km)*

▶ The village churches of the Vallouise strike a charmingly rustic note among the houses. Inside they are frequently decorated with frescos (**Les Vigneaux,** Vallouise), while the doors are equipped with locks★ and ironwork peculiar to this valley. Above the beautiful houses with their large wooden galleries in the village of **Vallouise** (pop. 512) stands the winter sports resort of **Puy-Saint-Vincent.** Going up the valley via **Saint-Antoine** as far as **Ailefroide,** in the middle of the meadows, one passes by numerous hamlets of the commune of **Pelvoux** which are all mountaineering centres. ▶ From the village of **Le Pré de Madame Carle★** you can climb in 2 hr 30 *(beware of icy surfaces)* to the mountain refuge on the Glacier Blanc (view★★). □

Practical Information _____

AILEFROIDE, ✉ 05340, 38 km W of **Briançon.**

Hotel :
★ *Chalet Rolland* (L.F.), ☎ 92.23.32.01 P ≼ ໝ 泉 closed 10 Sep-20 Jun, 150. Rest. ♦ 60-130.

PUY-SAINT-VINCENT, ✉ 05290 Vallouise, 28 km SW of **Briançon.**
彡 1400-2700m.
ⓘ ☎ 92.23.38.97.

Hotels :
★★ *La Pendine,* Les Prés, ☎ 92.23.32.62, 32 rm P ≼ ໝ 泉 ❀ half pens, closed 15 Apr-15 Jun, 15 Sep-10 Dec, 390. Rest. ♦ ≼ ♪ ❀ 60-110; child : 45.
★★ *Saint-Roch,* ☎ 92.23.32.79, 12 rm P ≼ 泉 ❀ ▭ pens, half pens, closed 15 Apr-25 Jun, 1 Sep-20 Dec, 210. Rest. ♦ ≼ ♪ ❀ 70-100; child : 45.

The VERCORS Massif***

A-B2
Circuit *(142 km, 1 day; see map 3)*
There are two Vercors : the visible and the invisible. The first, accessible to all, is the country of wide pastures and silent forests. The other Vercors, the invisible one, is the subterranean world carved out by the waters, a hidden world reserved for the speleologist : sink-holes, grottos and chasms (such as the Gouffre Berger) abound. Between the Isère and the Drôme rivers, Vercors is a natural citadel. Near Grenoble, the Montagne de Lans is cattle country, open to tourism (Villard-de-Lans, Autrans), while further S Le Royans and the Vercors proper are less developed. Here it is mainly forest (Forêt de Lente). Vercors has, since 1970, been part of a nature reserve (1 350 km²) which safeguards agricultural and pastoral activity while promoting rural tourism under controlled conditions. During the last war, the Vercors was the scene of much Resistance activity.

▶ **Grenoble** (→). ▶ **La Tour sans Venin** *(5 min on foot; view★),* one of the "7 Wonders of Dauphiné". Legend has it that soil brought back from the Holy Land keeps this area free of poisonous reptiles. ▶ **Saint-Nizier-du-Moucherotte** (pop. 515) : a balcony over Grenoble and the Alps which can be reached on skis or on foot. Romanesque church★ (12thC). Viewpoint★★. ▶ **Villard-de-Lans★** (pop. 3 320), cradled in pastures and surrounded by forests, a resort which is very popular with children and has an ideal climate. Alpine and cross-country skiing, naturally, but also numerous mountain excursions, including one to the Pas de l'Oeille★★ *(cable-car, then 1 hr on foot).* ▶ **La Balme-de-Rencurel** : right, the dizzy Écouges road★★. ▶ **Grotte du Bournillon** *(1 km left, then 30 min on foot)* and **Grottes de Choranche★** *(2.5 km right),* caves

3. The Vercors massif

with visiting facilities, including the underground lake with astonishing reflections of hollow stalactites ("macaroni"). ▶ **Pont-en-Royans★** (pop. 1 119) : houses★ clinging to the rocks above the River Bourne. Stopover before the famous road through the Petits (Small) and **Grands Goulets★★★,** a narrow defile in the grey rocks. The road emerges suddenly into full daylight on the Plateau de Vercors at **Les Barraques-en-Vercors.** ▶ **Grotte de la Luire** *(left, 5 min on foot)* where the Résistance installed a field hospital in 1944. The wounded were massacred by the Nazis. ▶ Leave the road ahead to the **Rousset Pass★★,** opening on to the southern landscape of the Diois, take the road right to **Vassieux** : National cemetery of Vercors and Resistance museum. ▶ Firs and beeches in the **Lente Forest★★** (68 km²) conceal a chaos of limestone cliffs, riddled with grottos, avens and pot-holes. ▶ Left : the road to the **Bataille Pass★★** (a superb run downhill). The La Machine Pass road leads to **Combe-Laval★★★.** The road clings to the cliff wall 600 m above the spectacular Torrent du Cholet. ▶ **Saint-Jean-en-Royans** (pop. 2 700) : specializing in turned and inlaid wood. ▶ From here, rejoin Pont-en-Royans or reach the N532 Romans to Grenoble road. □

Practical Information _____

Les BARRAQUES-EN-VERCORS, ⊠ 26420, 57 km SW of **Grenoble**.

Hotel :
★★ *Grands Goulets*, ☎ 75.48.22.45, Visa, 30 rm Ⓟ ⫝̸ ⣿ ⣿ closed Oct-Apr, 160. Rest. ♦ ⫝̸ ఉ 55-105.

La CHAPELLE-EN-VERCORS, ⊠ 26420, 62 km SW of **Grenoble**.
ⓘ pl. de l'Hôtel-de-Ville, ☎ 75.48.22.54.   ♥

Hotels :
★★ *Bellier*, ☎ 75.48.20.03, AE DC Visa, 13 rm Ⓟ ⫝̸ ⣿ ⣿ closed 20 Sep-20 Jun, 250. Rest. ♦♦ ♪ ఉ Spec : *poulet aux écrevisses, pintadeau au genièvre*, 120-150.
★ *Nouvel Hôtel*, ☎ 75.48.20.09, 35 rm Ⓟ ⫝̸ ⫝̸ closed 6 Oct-15 Feb, 120. Rest. ♦ 90-160.

⚠ ★★*Municipal* (150 pl), ☎ 75.48.22.54.

CORRENÇON-EN-VERCORS, ⊠ 38250 Villard-de-Lans, 5 km S on the D 215.

Hotel :
★★ *Lièvre Blanc*, Les Mangots, ☎ 76.95.16.79, Euro Visa, 22 rm Ⓟ ⫝̸ ⣿ ⣿ closed Easter-May, Oct-25 Dec, 170. Rest. ♦ ♪ ⫝̸ 85-100.

LANS-EN-VERCORS, ⊠ 38205, 8 km N of **Villard-de-Lans** on the D 531.

Hotel :
★★ *Col de l'Arc* (L.F.), ☎ 76.95.40.08, AE Euro Visa, 22 rm Ⓟ ⣿ ⣿ ♪⧫ closed May, 15 Nov-20 Dec, 200. Rest. ♦ closed Wed (l.s.), 60-120.

SAINT-AIGNAN-EN-VERCORS, ⊠ 26420, 66 km SW of **Grenoble**.

Hotel :
★★ *Le Veymont* (L.F.), pl. de l'Église, ☎ 75.48.20.19, AE DC Euro Visa, 20 rm Ⓟ ⫝̸ ⣿ ♪⧫ closed Nov, 150. Rest. ♦ ♪ ఉ Spec : *poulet aux écrevisses, ravioles du Royans*, 50-110 ; child : 30.

SAINT-NAZAIRE-EN-ROYANS, ⊠ 26190 Saint-Jean-en-Royans, 9 km W.

Restaurant :
● ♦ *Muraz*, ☎ 75.48.40.84, Euro Visa Ⓟ ♪ closed Tue eve and Wed, 9-24 Jun, 29 Sep-28 Oct. Outstanding family-style food : *fricassée de volaille aux écrevisses, feuilleté chaud d'escargots aux cèpes et noix, charlotte aux framboises*, 55-120 ; child : 35.

SAINT-NIZIER-DU-MOUCHEROTTE, ⊠ 38250 Lans-le-Villard, 15 km W of **Grenoble**.
❆ 1162-1900m.
ⓘ ☎ 76.53.40.60.

Hotel :
★★ *Concorde*, ☎ 76.53.42.61, 35 rm Ⓟ ⫝̸ ⣿ ⣿ ⫝̸ closed 1 Nov-15 Dec, 170. Rest. ♦ 60-100.

VILLARD-DE-LANS, ⊠ 38250, 34 km SW of **Grenoble**.
❆ 1050-2170m.
ⓘ pl. Mure-Ravaud, ☎ 76.95.10.38.

Hotels :
● ★★★ *Eterlou*, rte de Grenoble, ☎ 76.95.17.65, 24 rm Ⓟ ⫝̸ ⣿ ♪ ఉ ⫸ ☒ ℘ half pens, closed 10 Apr-15 Jun, 10 Sep-15 Dec, 360. Rest. ♦ ⫝̸ ♪ ⫝̸ 120-220 ; child : 50.
● ★★★ *Paris*, (Mapotel), ☎ 76.95.10.06, 60 rm Ⓟ ⣿ ⣿ ♪ ఉ closed 26 Apr-10 May, 15 Oct-15 Dec, 360. Rest. ♦ ♪ ⫝̸ 80-110.
★★ *Le Pré Fleuri*, rte des Cochettes, ☎ 76.95.10.96, Euro Visa, 18 rm Ⓟ ⫝̸ ⣿ ⣿ closed May, 1 Oct-20 Dec, 230. Rest. ♦ ⫝̸ ♪ ⫝̸ 65-160.
★★ *Villa Primerose*, Les Bains, ☎ 76.95.13.17, 20 rm Ⓟ ⫝̸ ⣿ ℘ half pens (h.s.), closed 3 May-20 Jun, 20 Sep-20 Dec, 360. Rest. ♦ ⫝̸ closed lunch, 60-120.

⚠ ★★★*Font Noir* (200 pl), ☎ 76.95.14.77.

Recommended
Chambres d'hôtes : Les Geymonds, ☎ 76.95.12.77.

VIENNE*

Lyon 30, Grenoble 88, Paris 493 km
pop 29000 ⊠ 38200   A1

Appearances are deceptive ; behind Vienne's grey façade overlooking the river the scenery changes. It is a real pleasure to pursue the narrow streets of the old town in search of times past, when Vienne was one of the major cities of Roman Gaul, and a cradle of the arts under the aegis of its Count-Archbishops.

▶ Don't miss the capitals★ in the nave and the cloister★ (Romanesque 12thC) of the church of **Saint-André-le-Bas** (B1), 9th-12thC, housing the musée d'Art Chrétien (museum of Christian art ; *Apr.-15 Oct., 12 & 2-5 ; Mar., Wed.-Sat., 10-12 & 2-5*) with concerts and a festival of sacred music *(Jun.-Jul).* ▶ The **temple of Augustus and Livia★★** (B2) used to dominate the forum of the Roman town. Built around 25BC, it is remarkably well preserved. ▶ Other interesting classical remains : the portico of the hot baths, with nearby the remains of a temple to the goddess Cybele and a shrine of the Mysteries (today devoted to archaeology). ▶ Backing on to Mont Pipet is a **Roman theatre★** (C2) unearthed in 1922, which has now regained some of its former glory, staging events in the summer such as a jazz festival *(1st 2 weeks in Jun.).* It is one of the largest in Roman Gaul. ▶ **St. Maurice★** (B2 ; formerly a cathedral), unites a 12thC Romanesque nave to a Flamboyant Gothic (14th-15thC) façade in lacy stonework (don't miss the sculpted doorways and the 18thC tomb★ of the Archbishops). ▶ The **museum** (B2) contains collections of Prehistoric and Gallo-Roman remains and some fine Moustiers ceramics★. ▶ **The church of St. Pierre★** (A2), one of the oldest Christian sanctuaries in France (6th-12thC), houses the Musée Lapidaire (Stonework Museum ; *same hours as Christian art museum*).
Also... ▶ The **Pyramide** (A3), which used to decorate the spine of the Roman circus. ▶ **Saint-Romain-en-Gal★** (A1), the commercial and industrial quarter of the ancient city (mosaics★).   ☐

Practical Information _____

VIENNE
ⓘ cours Brillier (A2), ☎ 74.85.12.62.
🚆 (B3), ☎ 74.85.03.17.
🚌 pl. des Allobroges (A3).
Car rental : Avis, 1, rue du 11-Novembre, ☎ 74.85.17.22.

Hotels :
★★★ *Central*, 7, rue de l'Archevêché (B2), ☎ 74.85.18.38, AE Euro Visa, 27 rm Ⓟ ⣿ ఉ 205.

★★★ *Résidence de la Pyramide*, 41, quai Riondet (A3), ☎ 74.53.16.46, AE, 15 rm. Ⓟ ⣿ closed 1 Nov-20 Dec, 260.

★★ *Saint-Maurice*, 18, pl. St-Maurice (A-B2), ☎ 74.85.08.48, 14 rm, closed 25 Déc. and 1 May, 150. Rest. ♦ 40-90.

Restaurant :
● ♦♦♦♦ *La Pyramide*, 14, bd F.-Point (A3), ☎ 74.53.01.96, AE DC ⣿ ఉ closed Feb. The restaurant is up for sale, but the old staff is still on hand serving Guy Thivard's outstanding cuisine, 370-500.

Nearby

BEAUREPAIRE, ⊠ 38270, 30 km SE.
🚆 ☎ 74.84.62.00.

Hotel :
★★ *Fiard*, 23, rue de la République, ☎ 74.84.62.02, AE DC Euro Visa, 18 rm Ⓟ ♪ closed Sun eve and Mon (l.s.), Jan, 250. Rest. ♦♦♦ ♪ ఉ A classic selection of top-quality dishes : *rouelles de lotte au noilly et aux pâtes fraîches, mousseline de truite, nougat glacé aux fruits confits d'Apt*, 95-300.

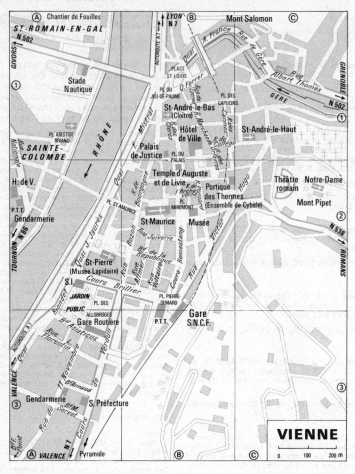

ST-ROMAIN-EN-GAL
Chantier de Fouilles
N 502
GIVORS
① Stade
Nautique
PL. ARISTIDE
BRIAND
SAINTE-
COLOMBE
H. de V.
P.T.T.
Gendarmerie
TOURNON N 86

LYON
N 7
PLACE
ST-LOUIS
PL. DU
JEU-DE-PAUME
St-André-le-Bas
(Cloître)
Hôtel
de Ville
Palais
de Justice
PL. DU
PALAIS
Temple d'Auguste
et de Livie
Portique
des Thermes
(Ensemble de Cybèle)
PL. ST-MAURICE
PL.
MIREMONT
St-Maurice
Musée
St-Pierre
(Musée Lapidaire)
S.I.
JARDIN
PUBLIC
Gare Routière
PL. DES
ALLOBROGES
PL. PIERRE
SEMARD
P.T.T.
Gare
S.N.C.F.
Gendarmerie
S. Préfecture
VALENCE
Pyramide

Mont Salomon
Rue de Gère
GRENOBLE
Rue
Albert Thomas
GÈRE
N 502
①
St-André-le-Haut
Théâtre Notre-Dame
romain
Mont Pipet
②
N 538
ROMANS
③

VIENNE
0   100   200 m

A ★★*Municipal* (50 pl), ☎ 74.84.64.89.

CHONAS-L'AMBALLAN, ⊠ 38121 Reventin-Vaugois, 9 km S on the N 7.

Hotel :
★★ *Domaine de Clairefontaine*, ☎ 74.58.81.52, 18 rm Ⓟ ⟨ ⟩ closed Sun eve (l.s.) and Mon lunch, 8 Dec-1 Feb, 130. Rest. ♦ ⚘ 75-140.

PONT-ÉVÊQUE, ⊠ 38780, 4 km E on the D 502.

Hotel :
★★★ *Midi* (R.S.), pl. de l'Église, ☎ 75.85.90.11, Euro Visa, 17 rm Ⓟ ⟨ ⟩ closed 25 Dec-31 Jan, 230.

Les ROCHES-DE-CONDRIEU, ⊠ 38370, 12 km S.

Hotel :
● ★★ *Bellevue* (L.F.), quai du Rhône, ☎ 74.56.41.42, AE DC Euro, 20 rm Ⓟ ⟨ ⟩ closed Sun eve and Mon eve (l.s.), 16 Feb-13 Mar, 4-14 Aug, 180. Rest. ♦♦ ⟨ ⟩ A place to pause beside the Rhône : *filet de sandre au beurre de ciboulette, turbot braisé au champagne*, 95-180.

SEYSSUEL, ⊠ 38200, 5 km NW.

Hotel :
★★★ *Château des 7 Fontaines*, ☎ 74.85.25.70, AE DC Visa, 15 rm Ⓟ ⟨ ⟩ closed 14 Dec-15 Feb. Sauna, 200. Rest. ♦ ⟨ ⟩ 90-120 ; child : 45.

Franche-Comté

▶ Franche-Comté means "Free County" : the region's long tradition of independence is the fruit of its struggle to retain its personality under successive waves of foreign invasion, but Franche-Comté's independence is combined with a community spirit characterized by the cooperatives set up by dairy farmers and cheesemakers as early as the 13thC. Exploitation of the region's forests too has always been a communual undertaking. The motto of the winegrowers of Arbois in the 19thC — "We are all in charge" — could well stand for the whole region. In the 16thC, Franche-Comté was, along with Flanders and Spain, part of the empire of Holy Roman Emperor Charles the Fifth. It remained attached to the Spanish branch of the Hapsburg family — with a semi-autonomous parliament in Dole — until 1674 when Richelieu reclaimed Franche-Comté for the Sun King, after an arduous six-month campaign and the great siege of Besançon.

Geographically it is really two regions : the high valley of the Saône is wide, gently rolling country with a certain rustic simplicity, while the Jura is wild, untamed and mountainous with torrents of water, forests of black spruces and slopes made for adventurous skiers.

Besançon, birthplace of Victor Hugo and site of a prestigious music festival, has been producing watches since the end of the 17thC, and, despite foreign competition and the need to adapt to new techniques, it is holding its own : in 1980 Besançon workshops and factories produced some 15 million units. Dole is the birthplace of the scientist Louis Pasteur.

Vines have covered the slopes of Revermont since antiquity, and today *A.O.C.* wine is produced in an area covering over 1200 acres. Other local specialties are kirsch, plum brandy and white brandy or *marc*. Franche-Comté is also the home of many excellent cheeses : Comté, Morbier, Vacherin and Cancoillotte. The lakes and rivers of the region are a paradise for fishermen, providing excellent trout, carp and pike and many other smaller fry.

□

 ## Don't miss

★★★ Arc-et-Senans B3, Baume-les-Messieurs A3, Besançon B2, Ronchamp C1.

★★ Dole A3, Goumois Corniche C2, Grand-Combe-Châteleu C3, Hérisson Waterfalls B4, Joux Forest B3, Lison Springs B3, Loue Valley B3, Ornans B2-3, Lake Vouglans A-B4.

★ Arbois B3, Belfort C1, château de Belvoir C2, Champlitte A1, Château-Châlon A3, Dessoubre Valley C2, Esmoulières Plateau C1, Lons-le-Saunier A3-4, Luxeuil-les-Bains B1, Montbenoît B-C3, Morez B4, Neublans A3, Nozeroy B3, Ognon Valley B2, Pesmes B2, Salins-les-Bains B3, the vale of Saône A2, B1-2.

Weekend tips

A quick (half-day) look at Besançon along the Loue Valley with a detour to Morteau and Saut du Doubs and a stopover at Pontarlier. Next day, Nozeroy and Joux Forest, Salins, Arbois (lunch) and Poligny, to Baume-les-Messieurs before climbing back to Dole. Two full days to capture the flavour of the Jura; you will have to come back another time for the northern Franche-Comté.

Farmhouse on the plains

Jura farmhouse

Brief description

Location : *On the Swiss border; the French sector of the Jura and the high plain of the Saône together form most of Franche-Comté.*
Area : *16 271 km².*
Climate : *plentiful lakes and rivers; frequent rain, especially in autumn, but ample sunshine for vine cultivation. Franche-Comté is generally damp and cool; best season, June to September; severe winters, spring sometimes late; mild summers.*
Population : *1 084 000.*
Administration : *Department of the* **Haute-Saône,** *prefecture, Vesoul; Department of* **Territoire de Belfort** *(smallest in France), Prefecture Belfort; Department of* **Doubs,** *Prefecture Besançon; Department of* **Jura,** *Prefecture Lons-le-Saunier.*

 # Brief regional history

BC
Franche-Comté has always occupied a **strategic position** and even the Gallic Sequanii who lived there were frequently obliged to call for outside help against Germanic invasion. An appeal to Julius Caesar resulted in the establishment of a permanent garrison at Vesontio (modern-day Besançon). ● To shake off the Roman yoke the Sequanii made common cause with the Gallic chief Vercingetorix, but met with defeat at Alésia in AD52. Alésia has never been precisely identified, but may have been either at Alaise or Salins in Franche-Comté, or in Burgundy. ● Roads and settlements attest to the **mercantile development** of the region, which lay along the north-south axis of the Roman Empire; Vesontio remained an important military base.

1st-11thC
Two Greek missionaries, Ferréol and Ferjeux, evangelized the region late in the 2ndC. Their martyrdom by the Roman government failed to prevent the spread of Christianity, and Besançon became a bishopric. ● The **Burgundians,** considered by the Romans to be "the most civilized of the Barbarians", established a kingdom extending from Alsace to Provence

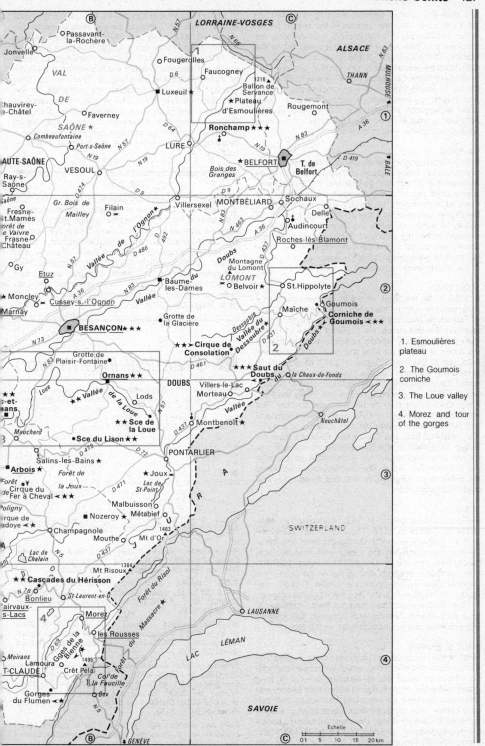

1. Esmoulières plateau

2. The Goumois corniche

3. The Loue valley

4. Morez and tour of the gorges

and from the Jura to Morvan, starting in AD407. At the same time, religious hermits in the region began to live communally in small groups, thus creating the first local monasteries. ● **In 534, Burgundy fell to the Franks.** The conversion of the Frankish King Clovis stimulated the expansion of Christianity, and the Irish missionary monk Columban made his way to Franche-Comté to found monasteries at modern-day Luxeuil and Baume-les-Messieurs. Despite barbarian invasions throughout the 9th and 10thC, the abbeys remained untroubled centres of learning, where many agricultural improvements originated.

9th-13thC
In 843, Charlemagne's empire was divided among his descendants. The allocation to Lothaire of the lands between the Rhine, the Saône and the Rhône was later seized upon by the **German emperors** as the basis of their claims to the territory. In the 10thC, the region was divided : the Jura district formed the county of Burgundy, while the Saône territories were included within the duchy of Burgundy. In 1032, the county was ceded to the German emperor, but imperial control grew progressively weaker as the power of the feudal lords increased.

14th-16thC
In 1384, Philip the Bold, who had received the duchy as a settlement from his father, King John the Good of France, married the heiress to the county and thus **reunited the territories.** He founded a line of Grand Dukes of Burgundy whose power exceeded that of the Kings of France. ● After the death of Charles the Bold, last of the Grand Dukes, in 1477, **King Louis XI seized the Comté.** Fourteen years later, Charles VIII ceded the province to Maximilian, Emperor of Austria who, in 1493, bestowed it on his son Philip the Fair. Philip died young but, by his marriage to Joan the Mad, only daughter of the Spanish rulers Ferdinand and Isabella, left a 6-year-old son, Charles of Austria, who inherited both the Comté and Flanders from his father, ascended to the Spanish throne through his mother, and succeeded his grandfather to become the Emperor Charles V. The Comté prospered under the benevolent rule of Charles, but fared less well under his successors.

17thC
French initiatives begun in 1635 culminated in **conquest by France in 1678.** The Comté has remained part of France ever since. During the long and bitter fighting that preceded the treaty with France, local heros, such as Lacuzon (Jean-Claude Prost, 1607-81) rallied popular strength and came to personify the regional ideal of independence. Under French rule, Besançon replaced Dole as the regional capital. ● The Reformation, preached by Swiss Lutherans, took root around Montbéliard, although Catholicism remained the predominant religion of the territory.

18thC to present
Most of the churches and public buildings in Franche-Comté date from the 18thC, which witnessed concerted efforts to repair the devastating effects of long drawn-out wars. Prosperity increased with peace, and Besançon became an important intellectual and cultural centre. The ancient independent spirit of Comté fostered far-seeing social theorists, including Ledoux (→ Arc-et-Senans), Charles Fourier (1772-1837) and Pierre-Joseph Proudhon (1809-65). The linchpin city

of Belfort, made impregnable by Vauban as demanded by Louis XIV, offered **heroic resistance** to the sieges of 1814, 1815 and 1870. After the disastrous defeat of the French army by the Prussians at Sedan in 1870, 85000 French soldiers managed to reach safety in Switzerland under the protection of the forts at Salins, Joux and Larmont. ● Similarly, the geography of the Jura favoured the activities of the Resistance during WWII. The strategic importance of Besançon and Belfort led to fierce fighting along the Doubs during the Liberation. Today, the region thrives on agricultural and pastoral industries, manufacturing, timber and — to a much lesser extent — tourism.

The Jura

Stretching in an arc from Bugey to Alsace, the Jura is a mountainous region of parallel limestone chains (Monts) running NE/SW enclosing high plateaux that were thrown up by alpine folding during the Tertiary era, and hollowed out by subsequent glacial erosion. The E (Swiss) flank is steep, but the W is gentler and scored by deep valleys (Revermont, Vignoble). Very wet (lakes, springs, and rivers), occupied largely with stock raising and forestry, harsh in winter and temperate in summer, the Jura's highest point is the Crêt de la Neige (alt. 1718 m).

 Practical information

Information : Franche-Comté : *Comité Régional de Tourisme (C.R.T.), 32, rue Charles-Nodier, 25041 Besançon Cedex,* ☎ 81.83.50.47. Doubs : *Association Départementale du Tourisme (A.D.T.), Hôtel du Département, av. de la Gare-d'Eau, 25035 Besançon Cedex,* ☎ 81.81.80.80, ext. 380. Jura : *Comité Départemental du Tourisme jurassien (C.D.T.), 8, av. du 44e-R.I., 39000 Lons-le-Saunier,* ☎ 84.24.19.64 and 84.24.57.70. Haute-Saône : *C.D.T., B.P. 117, 6, rue des Bains, 70000 Vesoul Cedex,* ☎ 84.75.43.66. Territoire de Belfort : *A.D.T., 4, rue de l'Ancien-Théâtre, 90000 Belfort,* ☎ 84.21.27.95. In Paris : *Maison de Franche-Comté, 2, bd de la Madeleine, 75009 Paris,* ☎ (1) 42.66.26.28. Dir. régionale de la Jeunese et des Sports, *10, rue de la Convention, 25030 Besançon Cedex,* ☎ 81.82.16.90. Dir. rég. des Affaires culturelles, *9 bis, rue Charles-Nodier, 25043 Besançon Cedex,* ☎ 81.82.04.89.

Reservations : Loisirs-Accueil (L.A.) Jura and Haute-Saône at the *C.D.T.* L.A. Doubs, *Les Eaux-Vives, 15, av. Édouard-Droz, 25000 Besançon,* ☎ 81.80.38.18.

S.O.S. : Doubs : *SAMU (emergency medical service),* ☎ 81.81.13.12. Jura : *SAMU,* ☎ 15. Haute-Saône : *SAMU,* ☎ 84.76.33.33. Territoire de Belfort, ☎ 84.21.15.15.

Weather forecast : Doubs, ☎ 81.50.47.10. Jura, ☎ 81.50.47.10. Snow conditions : ☎ 84.43.08.10. Haute-Saône, ☎ 84.76.60.60. Territoire de Belfort, ☎ 84.28.26.30.

Farmhouse gîtes and chambres d'hôtes : Doubs : *Relais des Gîtes de France, Office du Tourisme, 25041 Besançon Cedex,* ☎ 81.30.38.18. Jura : *Relais des Gîtes Ruraux du Jura, Service L.A.* Haute-Saône : *L.A.,* ☎ 84.75.43.66. Territoire de Belfort : *Assn. Dép. du Tourisme* ☎ 84.21.27.95.

Fairs and events : Apr : *post card fair in Belfort.* May : *comtoise fair in Besançon; pine-tree festival in Levier; international canoe-kayak rally in Ornans.* Jun : *hill race in*

Echevannes. **Jul** : *Franche-Comté musical encounters* in Arc-et-Senans; *annonciades* (contemporary comtois art) in Pontarlier; *«Brimbelles» festival* in Giromagny. **Aug** : lake festival in Vesoul; *son et lumière* in Château-Chalon and Pesmes. **Sep** : *«biou» festival* in Arbois; *wine and gastronomy fair* in Belfort; *antiques show* in Besançon. **Nov** : book fair and month of the image in Belfort; *international cinema encounters* in Pontarlier.

Rambling and hiking : G.R. tracks 5, 9, 59, 559, 590, and 595 all cross the Franche-Comté. G.R. topoguides. Instructional rambling and hiking courses : *L.A. Jura; L.A. Haute-Saône.* The *A.D.T. du Doubs* publishes a brochure on GRs in the Montbéliard area. Expeditions on foot in the Jura Massif : *Accueil Montagnard,* La Chapelle-des-Bois, 25240 Mouthe, ☎ 81.69.26.19. **Territoire de Belfort :** *S.I.,* Giromagny, ☎ 84.27.14.18.

Cycling holidays : Discover the **Haute-Saône** by bicycle : *L.A. Haute-Saône;* «13 Circuits à Vélo» and «Le Guide du Cyclotourisme du *Doubs»* are extremely detailed brochures published by the *A.D.T. du Doubs.*

River and canal cruises : cruises on the Saône River, the Doubs Canal, the canal linking the Rhône and Rhine rivers. Enq : *C.R.T. Franche-Comté* and *L.A. Haute-Saône;* Groupement pour le Tourisme Fluvial, Chambre régionale de Commerce et d'Industrie du Doubs, 30, av. Carnot, 25043 Besançon, ☎ 81.80.41.11.

Riding holidays : 18 riding centres and 23 centres for horse hire. Riding holidays organized by the *L.A. Jura* and *L.A. Haute-Saône.* List of riding centres and gîtes, centres for horse hire, and Doubs blacksmiths : *A.D.T. du Doubs* and *L.A.*

Technical tourism : *Distillery,* 49, rue des Lavaux, 25300 Pontarlier, ☎ 81.39.04.70. *Salt springs,* S.I. of Salins-les-Bains, 39110, ☎ 84.73.01.34. Visits daily : 9-11 & 2-5:30 Jun-Sep (11:30, 3:30, 4:30 Easter-Jun). *Art Glass manufactury* at Passavount-La Rochère, 70210 Vauvillers, ☎ 84.92.44.44. Visits daily : 2:30-5:30, May-Sep; exhibi-

---

The cheeses of Comté

Comté is an important dairy region (more than 300 000 milk cows) largely relying on the Pie de l'Est *(piebald red and white) and the* Montbéliard *(white flecked with red) breeds. Franche-Comté produces several fine cheeses, of which* **Comté** *is generally acknowledged as the best. Six hundred litres of milk are used for every 50 kg mould of cheese. The milk is partly skimmed, then curdled by heating under pressure; the curd is reheated, stirred, moulded and pressed. It is then matured for 6 months in cellars maintained alternately at 16-18°C and 10-12°C, during which the rind is rubbed with coarse salt. The finished product is solid, with very few holes, unlike its* Emmenthal *and* Gruyère *cousins. The taste is characteristically nutty.*
Morbier is much smaller, requiring only 80 litres of milk per cheese. The initial preparation is similar to that of Comté, but the cheese is drained, cut horizontally, then reformed after the addition of a thin layer of wood charcoal. It is then pressed and matured for 2 months. **Morbier** *can be recognized by the fine black line in the middle of the slice.* **Vacherin,** *an uncooked, very creamy, soft cheese is produced in the Champagnole region.* **Cancoillotte,** *a speciality of the Haute-Saône, is served like cream in a small pot. It is popular for breakfast and is made from pressed curds dried in the cellar, then beaten and mixed with butter and white wine. Processed or fondue cheeses (such as* Crème de Gruyère*) are made industrially in the region around Lons-le-Saunier and Dole.*

Franche-Comté cuisine

Cheese in myriad local varieties rules the regional palate, but charcuterie is also very important. Try the smoked meats and the renowned Morteau sausages known as Jésus. The region is a fisherman's paradise : the abundant lake and river fish (trout, carp, pike, char) are prepared en pauchuse *(with white wine) or* en meurette *(red wine). The chickens of nearby Bresse are prized throughout France, often served with cream sauces or braised* au vin jaune. *In season, game and mushrooms enrich the menu. The gastronomic traditions of the Montbéliard region are similar to those of southern Alsace.*

Jura wines

The slopes of Revermont, facing SSW, were first planted with vines during the Roman era. Cultivation of grapes was spread throughout the Jura during the Middle Ages. Today, vineyards covering more than 1 200 acres produce A.O.C. white, red and rosé wines, including the vin jaune (yellow wines) of Château-Chalon. The five best districts are : **Arbois, Arbois-Pupillin, Côtes du Jura, Étoile** *and* **Château-Chalon.** *The grape harvest is sometimes as late as November for the Savagnin grapes used to make Château-Chalon. High production costs and low yield have made "vin de paille" extremely rare; after a very long fermentation, only 18 litres are produced for every 100 kg of grapes. The wines of the Jura stand natural champagnisation very well. Good years :* 61, 62, 64, 69, 71, 73, 76, 79, 83.
In addition to wines, Franche-Comté makes kirsch (cherry-flavoured liqueur) in the Loue Valley and Fougerolles, plum brandy in Haute-Saône, and marc *(distilled from the skins and fruit left after the grape-pressing) in the vine-growing areas.*

---

tion and sale. Cheese : *Fromagerie jurassienne* in Comté. Pipe-making and diamond-cutting : enq. : *Confrérie des maîtres papiers,* 39200 Saint-Claude, ☎ 84.45.04.02.

Wine guide : *Société de Viticulture du Jura,* av. du 44e-R.I., B.P. 396, 39000 Lons-le-Saunier, ☎ 84.24.21.07, publishes a brochure on wines of the Jura and can provide information.

Golf : Saône-Chevillotte (18 holes).

Winter sports : Enq. : *A.D.T. du Doubs; C.D.T. Jura.* Low-cost package tours *(forfaits)* for cross-country or downhill skiing : *École jurassienne de raid,* Chapelle-des-Bois, 25240 Mouthe, ☎ 81.69.24.87. For all enq. concerning ski centres and schools : *Maison de la Franche-Comté* in **Paris** and *C.R.T. Franche-Comté.* The *Grande Traversée du Jura* is a continuous cross-country track traversing the Massif. Enq. : *A.D.T. du* Doubs and *C.D.T. Jura.* Territoire de Belfort : skiing on the Ballon d'Alsace; enq : *S.M.I.B.A.,* ☎ 84.28.12.01.

Fishing : Numerous fishing associations; enq. : *A.D.T. du Doubs.* **Haute-Saône** : *Féd. dép. de la Pêche,* 12, rue R.-Salengro, 70000 Vesoul, ☎ 84.76.01.74, and *L.A.* **Territoire de Belfort** : *Assn dép. de pêche,* Lepuix-Gy, ☎ 84.29.30.37. **Jura** : *A.D.P.P.,* 5, rue Arney, 39100 Dole, ☎ 84.79.18.19.

Hunting and shooting : Enq. : *Fédérations départementales des chasseurs.* **Haute-Saône** : 5, rue P.-Curie, 70000 Vesoul, ☎ 84.75.24.43. **Territoire de Belfort** : 6, rue Denfert-Rochereau, 90000 Belfort, ☎ 84.22.28.71.

Towns and places ═══════════════

ARBOIS*

Dole 35, Besançon 49, Paris 401 km
pop 4160 ⊠ 39600   B3

The river Cuisance threads a passage among the famous vineyards of the Jura before it reaches picturesque Arbois. This town of winemakers and wine lovers makes an appealing stopover. Many cellars offer visits and tastings.

▶ At the N entry to town, the **family home of Louis Pasteur** (1822-95; inventor of the pasteurization process)★★ is maintained as if the scientist were expected at any moment *(Apr.-15 Jun., 10-12 & 2-5, Sun. 4; 16 Jun.-Oct., 9-12 & 2-6, Sun. 5; closed Tue. and 2nd Sun. of month).* ▶ Near the Place de la Liberté is the **Musée de la Vigne et du Vin** (wine museum) in the cellars of the town hall *(weekends of Assumption and 15 Jun., 3-6; Jul.-22 Sep., daily ex Tue., 3-7).* The **Sarret-de-Grozon Museum** displays furniture, silverware and porcelain in an 18thC mansion *(same hours as wine museum).* ▶ In front of the church of St. Just (along Rue de Faramand and left) view of the towers of old Arbois from the Capucins bridge. ▶ Lookout points at l'**Ermitage** *(D469 then road right)* and le **Tourillon** *(D107 E; orientation chart).*

Nearby

▶ **Reculée des Planches★★** : in the valley bottom are the two springs of the river Cuisance, one of which forms a waterfall at the exit of the **Planches Caverns★** (cave flora and fauna; *9-12 & 2-6:30, Jun.-Aug.; 10-12 & 2-6, Apr., May, Sep.; Sun. in Oct.*); lakes form when the water is high. D469 leads to the **Fer à Cheval** ("horseshoe")★★, a natural **amphitheatre** 200 m above the springs.   ☐

Practical Information ─────────

ARBOIS
ⓘ mairie, ☎ 84.66.07.45.
SNCF ☎ 84.47.50.50.

Hotels :
● ★★ **Le Moulin de la Mère Michelle** (L.F.), Les Planches, ☎ 84.66.08.17, 7 rm 🅿 ← ⚏ ▨ closed Sun eve and Fri lunch, Jan-Feb, 195. Rest. ♦ ᵴ Nearby springs and waterfalls will lull you in this adorable mill house. Private fishing. J.-C. Delavenne at the piano. Spec : *truite au bleu de la cascade, coq au vin jaune et aux morilles.* Superb Arbois wines, 80-150; child : 45.
★★ **Paris**, rue de l'Hôtel-de-Ville, ☎ 84.66.05.67, AE DC Euro Visa, 18 rm 🅿 ⚏ ⚐ closed Mon eve and Wed ex school hols, 15 Nov-15 Mar, 250. Rest. ● ♦♦♦ ᵴ ᵴ In the heart of the Jura mountains, prize-winning chef André Jeunet preserves the tradition of outstanding classic cuisine : *mousseline de brochet, poularde au vin jaune et morilles.* His son, Jean-Paul will astound you with the dishes he prepares with the freshest seasonal ingredients : *ravioles d'écrevisses au jus de ciboulette, flan de langoustines et dés de lapereau, soupe de pêche à la lie de vin mousse cannelle.* Both will help you discover the great wines of Arbois (like the pupillin jaune), and the ripened cheeses of the Comtois region. Wine museum, introduction to wine-tasting, 90-275.

⚐ ★★*Municipal les Vignes* (100 pl), ☎ 84.66.14.12.

Recommended
Guide to wines : at Montigny-les-Arsures, *Lucien Aviet*, wine grower, Caveau de Bacchus ; *Henri Maire*, La Boutière.
♥ pastry : *Hersinger*, 38, Grande-Rue ; pork products : *Breton*, pl. de la Liberté.

┌───┐
│ Don't forget to consult the Practical Holiday Guide: it │
│ can help in solving many problems.   │
└───┘

Nearby

MONT-SOUS-VAUDREY, ⊠ 39380, 17 km NW.
Hotel :
L'Auberge Jurassienne, ☎ 84.81.50.17, Euro Visa, 5 rm 🅿 ᵴ ᵴ half pens (h.s.), closed Wed, 15 Jun-1 Jul, 180. Rest. ♦ ᵴ A pleasant little inn that serves good, simple food : *jambon au pupillin, côtes de veau aux morilles,* 50-105.

ARC-ET-SENANS***

Besançon 37, Lons-le-Saunier 55, Paris 404 km
pop 1300 ⊠ 25610   B3

The architect Claude-Nicolas Ledoux (1736-1806; forerunner of modern city planning) hoped to create an ideal community at **Salines Royales★★★** in **Arc-et-Senans.** The plan was never realized but the beginnings are still visible.

▶ The scheme called for a town built in concentric circles around the salt pans *(salines),* but only the buildings required for salt production were completed (1775). The size and organization of these buildings ranged around the house of the Director suggest the scale of the entire project. Salt water was to be brought by a wooden pipeline from Salins-les-Bains (→), and fuel to be supplied by the Chaux Forest. The venture, never profitable, was abandoned in the 19thC. The Salines Royales of Arc-et-Senans now house an International Centre for Future Studies (colloquia, exhibitions, receptions, shows from the Besançon festival), with an important library (specialized in architecture), and a Salt Museum *(9-12 & 2-6, 5 in winter).* ▶ NE of the salt pans, the **Chaux Forest★★** covers almost 200 km² with oaks, beech, hornbeam, birch and aspen; forest roads lead to Dole (→) and the Doubs Valley.   ☐

Practical Information ─────────

SNCF ☎ 81.86.42.50.

Hotel :
★ **Relais** (L.F.), pl. de l'Eglise, ☎ 81.57.40.60, 14 rm ⚏ ⚐ closed Mon and Sun eve, 3-23 Feb, 2-8 Jun, 20-26 Oct, 100. Rest. ♦ 40-120.

BAUME-LES-DAMES

Besançon 29, Vesoul 48, Paris 444 km
pop 5696 ⊠ 25110   B2

Baume-les-Dames was once an abbey reserved for daughters of the nobility. It was founded in the 7thC on the spot where St. Odile, the patron saint of Alsace (→ Alsace) is said to have sought refuge from her cruel father in the 6thC.

▶ Although badly damaged during WWII, Baume still has several 16th, 17th and 18thC buildings, as well as the abbey church (access via porch in the Place de la République); church of St. Martin, rebuilt in the 17thC, has a Louis XIII altarpiece. The town is a centre of tobacco-pipe manufacturing.

Nearby

▶ **Source Bleue★** : reach the spring by D21 through the Cuisancin Valley, 14 km from Baume via Pont-des-Moulins. ▶ **Glacière Caverns★★** *(19 km S ; Easter-Nov., 9-6, 8 in summer)*; a natural phenomenon preserves ice formations in the cavern all year round. Nearby, 18thC buildings of the monastery of Grâce-Dieu founded in 12thC by the monastic reformer St. Bernard of Clairvaux.   ☐

Practical Information _____

ⓘ mairie, ☎ 81.84.07.13 (h.s.).
SNCF ☎ 81.84.00.25.

Hotels :
★★★ *Château d'As*, ☎ 81.84.00.66, Euro Visa, 10 rm Ⓟ
↝ ⅏ closed Sun eve and Mon (ex Mon hol lunch),
15 Dec-20 Feb, 200. Rest. ◆◆ ♪ Renowned cuisine by a
prize-winning chef. Spec : *foie gras maison en terrine,
goujonnette de sole, poularde de Bresse aux nouilles*,
210-320.

★★ *Central* (L.F.), 3, rue Courvoisier, ☎ 81.84.09.64, Visa,
12 rm Ⓟ ↝ ❦ closed Sun eve (Nov-Mar), 20-30 Oct,
10-31 Jan, 150.

★ *Abbaye*, 8, av. de Verdun, ☎ 81.84.12.13, Visa, 17 rm
Ⓟ ⅏ ᵴ closed Sat eve and Sun (l.s.), 15 Dec-3 Jan, 80.
Rest. ◆ ᵴ 35-60.

⚠ ★*De Lonot* (50 pl), ☎ 81.84.07.13.

BAUME-LES-MESSIEURS★★★

Lons-le-Saunier 17, Dole 54, Paris 424 km
pop 174 ⊠ 39210 Voiteur   A3

In a deep valley : old walls covered with climbing
plants, roofs bowed by time ; flowered cloisters, and
memories of Jean de Watteville, one-time abbot who
was also a brawler, a libertine and, when it suited,
a Muslim.

▶ The **abbey** was founded in the 6thC by the Irish monk
St. Columban (→ Luxeuil) ; a small group from Baume-les-
Messieurs (then Baume-les-Moines) founded the
renowned abbey of Cluny (→ Burgundy) in the 10thC. The
buildings are modest and unadorned. The Romanesque
church★★ has a 15thC façade ; tombstones, Burgundian statuary (15thC), a noteworthy 16thC Flemish **altar-
piece★★** (scenes from the life of Christ). ▶ **Museum of
Crafts of the Jura** in the abbey *(10:30-12:30 & 3-6,
Jul.-15 Sep.;* forge and cooperage). ▶ Natural
amphitheatre of Baume *(D70-E3 and D70-E1) :* **Baume
caves★** *(9-12 & 2-6, 5:30 Sun. and nat. hols.,
15 Mar.-15 Oct.),* several caverns, small lake. Via Baume
to the plateau *(D70 then D4, D471 to right),* lookout over
Baume rocks★★★ from the top of the amphitheatre.   ☐

Practical Information _____

Restaurant :
◆ *Grottes et des Roches*, ☎ 84.44.61.59 Ⓟ ↝ ⅏ ᵴ ♪
closed Wed, Oct-Mar, 50-100.

BELFORT Territory

                                                   C1
In 1871, Belfort surrendered to the Prussians after a
103-day siege. In recognition of the heroic resistance
shown by the townspeople, it was granted the right
to remain French thus becoming the smallest department in France. Today, Belfort is highly industrialized
but the landscapes remain largely unspoilt between
the Jura to the S and the Vosges to the N.

▶ **Malsaucy Lake** *(10 km NW from Belfort),* facing the Ballon d'Alsace heights (→ Alsace), has been developed as
a recreational park (lake shore, sailing, watersports).
▶ **Giromagny**, at the foot of the Vosges, is a centre for
skiing and hiking on the Ballon d'Alsace *(enq. : S.I., tel. :
84.27.14.18).* ▶ **Étueffont** *(15 km NE) :* forge museum with
traditional tools, furniture *(Sun. 2-6 Easter-1 Nov.).* **Rougemont-le-Château :** ruins of a Romanesque priory. **Seigneurie Lake :** shore park. ▶ **Delle** *(SE of Belfort ;* pop.
8 160) : known as the *Petite Sologne ;* like Sundgau just
over the border, many fishing lakes ; 16thC houses. ▶ To
the S, **Beaucourt :** Japy museum (mechanical industry,
watch-making ; *Wed.-Sun 2-5 ex nat. hols.).*   ☐

Practical Information _____

DELLE, ⊠ 90100, 16 km SE of **Belfort**.
ⓘ gare internationale, ☎ 84.36.03.06.
SNCF ☎ 84.36.10.06/84.28.50.50.

Hotel :
★★ *National* (L.F.), 32, av. Gal-de-Gaulle, ☎ 84.36.03.97,
Euro Visa, 14 rm Ⓟ ↝ ⅏ ▱ closed Sun eve and Mon, 160.
Rest. ◆ 75-130.

⚠ ★★*Le Passe-Loup* (150 pl), ☎ 84.36.01.46.

BELFORT*

Besançon 98, Strasbourg 140, Paris 500 km
pop 52700 ⊠ 90000   C1
The city's symbol is a huge sandstone lion carved
by Frédéric Bartholdi (1834-1904), sculptor of New
York's Statue of Liberty. Belfort commands a strategic position between Alsace and Bourgogne, between
the Vosges and the Jura. It is an important centre for
the production of rolling stock, electronic equipment
and other industrial goods.

▶ A system of **fortifications** established by Vauban (military engineer to Louis XIV) proved its worth during three
determined sieges in 1814, 1815 and 1870. The **old town★**
(B2-C2) is organized around the Place de la République *(Trois Sièges* monument by Bartholdi) and the Place
d'Armes on the left bank of the river Savoureuse, which
separates the old town from the new. ▶ Behind the **cathedral of St. Christophe** (C2 ; 18thC wrought iron, wooden
paneling), a recently restored area leads up to the **Châ-
teau★★** (C2 ; *May-Sep., daily 9-12 & 2-7; rest of year
10-12 & 2-5 ex Tue.),* where, on the right of the carpark, is
a path to the **Lion★★★** 22 m long, 11 m high. ▶ The château in the court of honour of the citadel houses the **Art
and History Museum★** : prehistoric artifacts, relief plan of
Belfort, regional art, coins, paintings *(same hours as Château).* ▶ Back toward the town past **Porte de Brisach★**,
erected by Vauban in 1687 (C1).   ☐

Practical Information _____

BELFORT
ⓘ pl. Dr-Corbis (A-B2), ☎ 84.28.12.23.
✈ *Fontaine,* 14 km E, ☎ 84.21.35.35.
SNCF (A3), ☎ 84.28.50.50/84.28.15.14.
▱▱ *C.T.R.B.*, pl. Dr-Corbis, ☎ 84.28.59.02.
Car rental : *Avis,* Fontaine airport ; 21, av. Wilson (A3),
☎ 84.28.45.95.

Hotels :
● ★★★ **Host. du Château Servin**, 9, rue Gal-Négrier (B3),
☎ 84.21.41.85, AE DC Visa, 10 rm Ⓟ ⅏ ↝ closed Fri,
1-28 Aug, 350. Rest. ● ◆◆◆ ♪ The prices are in keep-
with the excellent food. Game in season, fish, shellfish, 180-350.
★★ **Les Capucins**, 20, fg de Montbéliard (A2),
☎ 84.28.04.60, Visa, 35 rm Ⓟ closed Sat-Sun ex Jun-Aug,
20 Dec-11 Jan, 190. Rest. ◆ 65-140.

Restaurant :
◆◆ **Le Pot au Feu**, 27 *bis,* Grand-Rue (C1),
☎ 84.28.57.84, DC Euro Visa ♪ closed Mon and Sun,
1-7 Jan, 1-7 Apr, 1-20 Aug, 180-250.

⚠ ★*Promenades d'Essert* (150 pl), ☎ 84.28.46.56.

Recommended
Baby-sitting : ☎ 84.21.63.29.
Events : *Summer nights at the chateau,* 15 Jun-15 Jul
(theatre, concerts) ; evening concerts, Wed at the Chateau (16 Jul-31 Aug).
♥ salon de thé : *Dame Charlotte,* pl. Grande-Fontaine,
☎ 84.28.18.62.

_____
| Be advised that hotels and restaurants in this Guide |
| have perhaps changed addresses ; prices indicated |
| are also subject to modifications. |
_____

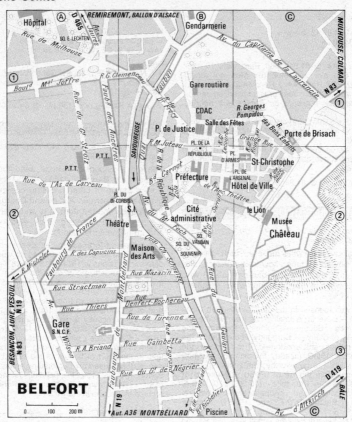

BELFORT

0   100   200 m

Nearby

DANJOUTIN, ⊠ 90400, 3 km S on the N 19 bis.

Restaurant :
● ◆◆ **Le Pot d'Etain**, 4, rue de la République,
☎ 84.28.31.95, Visa ▥ ♪ ᶑ closed Mon, Sat noon, Sun
eve, 2-13 Jan, 6-28 Jul. Roger Clevenot's personalized
cooking will surely surprise you : *gâteau de saumon fumé
et de langoustines, filet de rouget et de homard grillé,*
160-220.

OFFEMONT, ⊠ 90300, 5 km E.

Restaurant :
◆ **Le Sabot d'Annie**, 5, rue A.-Briand, ☎ 84.26.01.71, AE
Euro Visa, closed Sat noon and Sun, 25-31 Jul, 2 wk in
Aug, 140-280.

ChÂteau de BELVOIR

⊠ 25430 Sancey-le-Grand   C2

For seven centuries the lords of Belvoir ruled the plain
from the 12thC château on the Lomont premontory ;
several rooms display furniture and mementos *(10-12
& 2-6:30, daily Jul.-Aug. ; Sun. and nat. hols. Eas-
ter-1 Nov.).* ▶ Market buildings and old houses in the
village.   □

For a complete picture on the gastronomy featured
in the Guide, see p. 8.

BESANÇON★★★

Belfort 98, Dijon 102, Paris 411 km
pop 119600 ⊠ 25000   B2

Besançon used to be a city of watch-makers ; however, since the advent of quartz mechanisms, precision engineering has in part taken the place of the traditional industry. Much of the elegant architecture of
Besançon, abundantly adorned with wrought-iron grillwork, dates from the late 17thC, when Besançon
replaced Dole as capital of the Franche-Comté. The
novelist Victor Hugo (1802-85) was born in Besançon.
The city benefitted during the 16thC from the patronage of Nicolas Granvelle (1486-1550), who rose from
peasant stock to become a doctor of law and chancel-
lor to the Emperor Charles V. The fortune and
power he amassed placed his family among the most
influential in the region.

▶ Besançon has pioneered a traffic control system that
favours pedestrians and the use of public transport.
Leave your car at the Chamars car park *(free, but often
full)* or on the Doubs quays (near the République bridge),
then explore the city on foot or by bus. ▶ The hub of activity is the **Grande-Rue**, which is partly a pedestrian
mall ; nearby, busy market stalls around the **Fine Arts
Museum★★★** (B2), which occupies the former corn
market ; an excellent collection includes paintings by Bellini, Cranach, La Tour, Rubens, Fragonard, Boucher,
Greuze, Ingres, Courbet, David, Goya, Matisse and

Picasso; archaeological finds; interesting watch- and clock-making section *(9:30-12 & 2-6; closed Tue.)*. ▶ Opposite the church of St. Pierre (18thC) are the beautiful façades of the **town hall** (16thC) and the courthouse (Renaissance). ▶ Several mansions from the 16th-18thC stand along the Grande-Rue. ▶ **Granvelle palace**★★ (B2; 16thC) : residence of Nicolas Perrenot de Granvelle (→ above) and of his son Antoine (1517-86), Cardinal-Prime Minister of the Lowlands, Viceroy of Naples, Minister to Philip II of Spain. ▶ **Historical Museum**★ : Charles V tapestry (17thC), mementos of Granvelle, Victor Hugo, Proudhon and Fourier (→ Brief regional history; *9:30-12 & 2-6, closed Tue.)*. Behind the palace is the Granvelle Promenade. ▶ Place Victor-Hugo : birthplaces of the novelist and of the Lumière brothers, Auguste (1862-1954) and Louis (1864-1948) who, in 1895, invented cinematography. ▶ At the end of Grande-Rue : Roman remains including the 2ndC **Porte Noire**★ (Black Gate) in front of the **cathedral of St. Jean** (C3; 12th, 18thC) : with an apse at either end of the nave; Virgin with Saints★ (Fra Bartolomeo, 1512); "the rose of St. John"; 9thC marble; 18thC paintings. ▶ Noteworthy houses in Rues Rivotte and De Pontarlier and Place J.-Cornet (B-C2). ▶ The **citadel**★★★, towering nearly 120 m above the city, was built largely by Vauban (→ Belfort). Its sentry walk provides superb **views**★★. Museums, zoo, aquarium (C3; *Jun.-Sep., 9:15-6; Oct.-May, 9:30-5:15)*. **Comtoise Folk Museum**★★★ : agriculture, crafts, daily life, folklore, furniture, decoration and marionettes; the **Museum of the Resistance and the Deportation** (WWII), and the **Museum of Natural History** occupy neighbouring buildings. The moat has been converted into an **aquarium**. **Also...** ▶ Municipal **library** (B2, facing Granvelle palace) : illuminated manuscripts. ▶ Near the **Prefecture,** 17th and 18thC buildings. ▶ **Battants quarter** (on the right bank of the Doubs) mansions and old houses undergoing restoration. ▶ **Micaud Promenade** (C1). ▶ On the E edge of town, forts offer **splendid views** : Brégille, Chaudanne, Montfaucon, and the lookout at Notre-Dame-de-la-Libération★.

Nearby

▶ **Osselle Caves**★★ *(26 km SW)* : stalactites and stalagmites in several caverns; caves provided refuge for priests during the Revolution *(9-12 & 2-6, Apr.-Oct.; 9-7, Jun.-Sep.)*. ▶ **Courtefontaine :** Romanesque church. □

Practical Information

ℹ 1, pl. de la 1ère-Armée-Française (B1), ☎ 81.80.92.55. ✈ Thise, 7 km NE, ☎ 81.80.40.04. *Agence Air France,* sq. Saint-Amour, 15, rue Proudhon, ☎ 81.81.30.31. **SNCF** (B1), ☎ 81.80.11.58/81.53.50.50. 🚌 9, rue Proudhon (B2). **Car rental :** *Avis,* train station; 7, pl. Flore, ☎ 81.80.91.08.

Hotels :

● ★★ *Gambetta*, 13, rue Gambetta (B2), ☎ 81.82.02.33, AE DC Euro Visa, 26 rm ⬚ & 140.

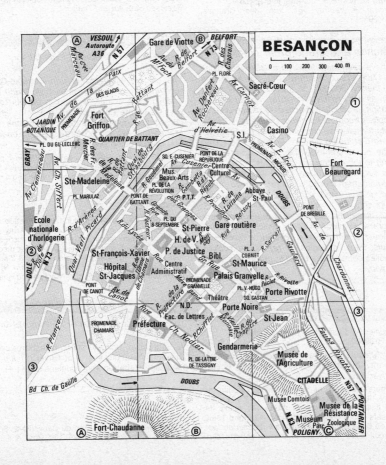

● ★★ **Nord**, 8, rue Moncey (B2), ☎ 81.81.34.56, Tx 361582, AE DC Euro Visa, 44 rm P ⌖ ⅋ 180.
★★ **Franc-Comtois**, 24, rue Proudhon (B2), ☎ 81.83.24.35, AE DC Euro Visa, 22 rm P 167.
★★ **Moncey**, 6, rue Moncey (B2), ☎ 81.81.24.77, AE DC Euro Visa, 25 rm P ⌖ 160.
★★ **Terrass'Hôtel** (L.F.), 38, av. Carnot (B1), ☎ 81.88.03.03, AE DC Euro Visa, 38 rm P closed Sun eve, 155. Rest. ♦ ♪ closed Sun eve, 55-135.
★ **Regina**, 91, Grande-Rue (B2), ☎ 81.81.50.22, Euro Visa, 19 rm P ⌖ closed 22 Dec-3 Jan, 155.

Restaurants :
● ♦♦ **Le Chaland**, prom. Micaud (C2), ☎ 81.80.61.61, AE Euro Visa ♦ ♪ ⅋ closed Sat noon and Sun , Feb, 1-25 Aug. Fresh fish served on a boat moored in the Doubs, 150-300.
♦♦ **Le Chaudanne**, 95, rue de Dole (A2), ☎ 81.52.06.13, Euro Visa ⌖ ♪ ⅋ closed Sat and Sun , eves ex for groups. *Truite au château-chalu, magret de canard à la menthe*, 55-110 ; child : 35.
♦♦ **Poker d'As**, 14, square St-Amour (B2), ☎ 81.81.42.49, closed Mon and Sun eve, 8 Jul-5 Aug, 24 Dec-3 Jan. Spec : fish and seafood, 65-200.
♦♦ **Tour de la Pelote**, 41, quai de Strasbourg (B1), ☎ 81.82.14.58, AE DC Euro Visa ♪ closed Mon, 2-24 Aug. In a 15thC defensive tower, 100-150.

⚓ ★★★★**Plage de Chalezeule** (110 pl), ☎ 81.88.04.26.

Recommended
Baby-sitting : *Service liaison étudiants-entreprises*, ☎ 81.50.26.88 ; C.I.J., ☎ 81.83.20.40.
Guided tours : C.N.M.H.S., Jul-Aug, info at S.I.
♥ tea room : *Vaufrey*, 54, rue des Granges, ☎ 81.81.34.30.

Watches and grandfather clocks

Watches have been manufactured at Besançon since the early 17thC. Two centuries later, the town was producing nearly 300 000 of the 2.5 million made annually in all the French Jura. After regrouping and modernization, production reached 15 million units in 1980, in spite of competition from overseas.
Movements for tall-case clocks made in the Franche-Comté were distributed all over France to be cased locally. The name comtoise (i.e., from Comté) was applied first to the mechanism and later to the whole clock. The second half of the 19thC was the golden age for grandfather clocks : painted, carved, inlaid with wood or encrusted with metal ; pyramidal (the oldest), upright, or — most often — contoured. Behind the glass, the weights and movement were often decorated to match the dials, which were enamelled or laquered with flowers, royalist or revolutionary symbols, imperial eagles or republican cockerels. The belles comtoises are still in production in the Morez region.

CHAMPAGNOLE

Lons-le-Saunier 34, Besançon 71, Paris 426 km
pop 10070 ⊠ 39300   B3
The steel, furniture and toy industries that maintain the prosperity of Champagnole draw their energy from the river Ain.

▶ **Syam** offers a look at the face of industry during the 19thC at the hamlet of Forges *(5 km SE, D127) ;* Empire château in Italian style. **Perte de l'Ain★** *(N)* where the Ain disappears into a crevice, and **Sirod** (12th and 13thC church). S on D279 **Billaude waterfalls★** *(20 min on foot, difficult climb).* D127 continues to the **Langouette Gor-**

ges★ and to the **Malvaux Gorges** formed by the river Saine.   □

Practical Information _____

ℹ hôtel de ville, ☎ 84.52.14.56 (h.s.).
SNCF ☎ 84.52.04.69.

Hotel :
★★ **Parc** (L.F.), 13, rue P.-Cretin, ☎ 84.52.13.20, AE DC Euro Visa, 18 rm P ▨ ⌖ ⅋ closed Sun (l.s.), Nov, 160. Rest. ♦ ⌖ ⅋ 50-120.

Restaurants :
♦♦ **Belle Epoque**, 54, rue du Mal-Foch , ☎ 84.52.28.86, AE DC Euro Visa ⌖ ♪ closed Tue eve and Wed , Nov-Jan, 65-150 ; child : 45.
♦♦ **Taverne de l'Epée**, 2, rue du Pont de l'Epée, ☎ 84.52.03.85, Euro Visa ♪ closed Mon, 7-21 Jan, 45-100 ; child : 25.

CHAMPLITTE*

Dijon 54, Besançon 65, Paris 328 km
pop 1130 ⊠ 70600   A1
Château★ (16th-18thC) with **Museum of Folk Arts and Tradition★★★** ; Spanish-style houses.

▶ The Albert-Demart museum is named after a shepherd who systematically collected articles and artifacts connected with disappearing **rural customs :** reconstructed interiors, furniture, tools, miscellaneous objects *(9-12 & 2-5 or 6 ; closed Sun. am and Tue.).*   □

CHÂTEAU-CHALON*

Lons-le-Saulnier 18, Dole 52, Paris 421 km
pop 156 ⊠ 39210 Voiteur   A3
The sloping vineyards around Château-Chalon are renowned for two fine wines : *vin jaune de garde*, deep gold in colour, is aged in barrels for at least 6 years before being bottled and sold ; *vin de paille* (straw), also golden, is a rare dessert wine made from grapes that are left on straw mats to become overripe before being pressed.

▶ The ramparts and the château are now picturesque ruins ; the **site★★** overlooks the Seille Valley ; treasures of the church include an alabaster panel and a wood carving of Christ.

Nearby

▶ **Cirque de Ladoye** (natural amphitheatre ; *6 km E, D5)★★ :* lookout over a blind valley. ▶ **Arlay** *(12 km W, D120) :* **château** rebuilt in the 18thC ; furnished in Restoration (ca. 1820) style ; park ; ruins of the medieval château overlooking Château-Chalon *(10-12 & 2-6:30 in summer, closed Sun. am).* ▶ **Frontenay** *(7 km N) :* château (12th-18thC ; *10-12 & 2-6, Apr.-Nov.)* among vineyards.   □

CLAIRVAUX-LES-LACS

Lons-le-Saunier 22, Pontarlier 77, Paris 429 km
pop 1430 ⊠ 39130   B4
An attractive holiday spot ; lakeshore beaches at Clairvaux ; aquatic sports at **Étival** *(11 km S D118) ;* the valley of the Ain and Vouglans Lake (→).   □

Practical Information _____

CLAIRVAUX-LES-LACS

Hotel :
★ **Chaumière** (L.F.), 21, rue du Sauveur, ☎ 84.25.81.52, 12 rm P ⌖ ⌖ closed Sun eve, 130. Rest. ♦ ⌖ ♪ 55-90.

Nearby

BONLIEU, ✉ 39130, 11 km NE on the N 78.

Hotels :
★★ *Alpage* (L.F.), RN 78, ☎ 84.25.80.76, 11 rm P ⟨ ⟨ closed Mon, 15 Nov-15 Dec, 140. Rest. ● ♦ Fine typical Jura cooking and decor : *croustade, truite belle comtoise, magret de Barbarie aux airelles*, 75-125.
★★ *Poutre* (L.F.), ☎ 84.25.57.77, AE DC, 10 rm P closed Tue and Wed, 10 Dec-1 Feb, 200. Rest. ● ♦ ሌ M. Moureaux's savoury and authentic cuisine in a beautiful mountain setting : *blancs de volaille aux morilles, filets de truite aux poireaux*. Arbois and Jura wines, nice and cool, 80-250.

DESSOUBRE Valley*

C2

The river Doubs winds among meadows in this wooded valley, passes through a mill-turned-inn *(auberge)* and a saw-mill, eventually reaching a confluence with the Reverotte.

▶ The lookout at **Roche du Prêtre★★★** *(via D41 or D461)* provides the best view of the **Consolation natural amphitheatre★★**, where the Dessoubres River arises. ▶ Back down on D39 via the old convent of Notre-Dame de Consolation (18thC woodwork), follow the river for about 30 km to Saint-Hippolyte (→ Goumois *corniche*). ◻

DOLE**

Dijon 48, Besançon 57, Paris 370 km
pop 27950 ✉ 39100   A3

The Rhône-Rhine canal reflects the red and brown roofs of Dole, clustered around the bell tower of Notre-Dame. Capital of the Comté until superseded by Besançon in 1674, Dole retains much of the past, although it looks ahead to economic and indus-

trial realities. Dole's population is larger than that of Besançon, the department's Prefecture.

▶ From **Place Grévy** (C1) stroll to the **old town★★** : numerous 15th-18thC houses with carved doorways, turrets, courtyards, and wells. ▶ **Church of Notre-Dame★** (B2 ; 16thC) : a stolid exterior concealing broad and airy nave ; 15thC statues, handsome 16thC furniture ; Sainte-Chapelle. ▶ **Rue Pasteur★** : site of the tanner's house where Louis Pasteur (→ box) was born on 27 Dec. 1822 ; museum *(9-12 & 2-6 ; closed Tue. and Oct.)*. ▶ The **hospital★★** : imposing 17thC edifice with balconies, galleries, courtyard, pharmacy. ▶ **Rue des Arènes** (A-B2) : **Museum of Archaeology and Painting** *(9-12 & 2-6 ; closed Tue.)* ; in a blind alley the **Palais de Justice★** (court house) formerly a Cordeliers' Convent (16thC) ; a number of handsome mansions. ▶ **Place aux Fleurs★** : view over the rooftops. ▶ **Rue du Mont-Roland** (A-B2) : **Froissard mansion★★** (courtyard) ; former **Carmelite convent★** with ornate wrought iron. ▶ Rue du Collège-de-l'Arc : a former jesuit **college★★** (1582), now a school (Renaissance porch★ at the entrance to the former chapel). ▶ Faubourg de Chalon *(D973)* : **church of St. Jean** (1964). ◻

Practical Information

ℹ 7, pl. Grévy (C1), ☎ 84.72.11.22.
SNCF (A1), ☎ 84.47.50.50.
🚌 av. A.-Briand (A1).
Car rental : *Avis*, train station, ☎ 84.82.73.03.

Hotels :
★★★ *Grand Hôtel Chandioux*, (Mapotel) 2, rue de Besançon (C1), ☎ 84.79.00.66, Tx 360498, AE DC Euro Visa, 33 rm P 260. Rest. ♦♦ Spec : *ragoût de lotte et écrevisses à l'aligoté blanc*, 130-220.
● ★★ *La Chaumière*, 346, av. du Mal-Juin (off map B2), ☎ 84.79.03.45, Euro Visa, 18 rm P ᠁ ⟨ ♪ ☒ half pens (h.s.), closed Sun, 15-25 Jun, 19 Dec-19 Jan. Modern hotel of traditional style, calm and comfortable, 410. Rest. ● ♦ ♪ ሌ closed Sat and Sun. A former farmhouse at the forest's edge. Classic fare : *filets mignon à la crème de sauge, filet de perche au beurre d'estragon*, 100-180.
★★ *Nouvel Hôtel*, 2, pl. Grévy (C1), ☎ 84.79.12.11, Visa,

DOLE

0   100 m

29 rm P & closed Sun (l.s), 25 Dec-25 Jan, 180. Rest. ♦
♪ & closed Sun, 55-95.

ESMOULIÈRES Plateau*

C1

Circuit *(70 km half-day; see map 1)*

An isolated plateau between the basins of the Saône
and the Moselle at the foot of the blue Vosges mountains. Lakes, wild heaths and woodlands are occasionally punctuated by cultivated fields.

▶ The villagers of **Faucogney-et-la-Mer** (pop. 750) held
out to the last against the forces of Louis XIV. All were put
to the sword in 1674, and the fortified château was razed.
Sheets of zinc protect the gables on the sandstone houses. ▶ Beyond **Mélisey**, the road leaves the **Ognon Valley**
to climb towards **Fresse** (pulpit★ in the church) beside the
river Raddon. Left fork : numerous lookouts before **Bel-
fahy** (alt. 870 m; skiing), where the narrow road descends towards the **Saut de l'Ognon★** and **Servance** (pop.
1 240). ▶ **Croix Pass** (alt. 753 m) : detour to the **Mountain Museum★** in **Château-Lambert**, a typical village of
northern Haute-Saône *(9-12 & 2-6, Easter-1 Nov.;
closed Tue.).* 12 km from the pass, the **Ballon de Servance** (alt. 1 216 m; view★). ▶ After the Mont Fourche
Pass, the emptiness of the plateau is apparent : nothing
but lakes and the single village of **Esmoulières.**   □

The GOUMOIS Corniche**

C2

Circuit *(80 km, full day; see map 2)*

On the high plateaux where Comté cheese is made,
green meadows stretch into dark fir forests. The
Doubs Gorges offer an impressive landscape.

▶ **Maîche** (pop. 4 340), a busy dairy and commercial
centre, good for summer or winter holidays. Near the
church : château where Montalembert (historian and aca-
demician, 1810-70) lived. ▶ The road runs down through
woods to **Saint-Hippolyte** through splendid countryside
dotted with a few old houses, then climbs up the course
of the Doubs, under cliffs. ▶ On the right bank, the rustic
site★ of **Montjoie-le-Château.** ▶ **Vaufrey** : an 18thC château and a fountain★ decorated with lions. ▶ **Glère** still
has traditional houses, unfortunately close to modern
pseudo-chalets. Right to **Indevillers**, typical village surrounded by firs ; beyond, a sawmill. ▶ The **Goumois Cor-
niche★★★** (cliff road) runs above the Doubs Gorges, forming the frontier with Switzerland (bridge of **Goumois** in
a remarkable site★). ▶ **Charmauvillers** : typical Jura hous-

es. ▶ Near **Combe-Saint-Pierre**, S of **Charquemont** :
hikes, and the **Cendrée Belvédère** (lookout)★. ▶ **Échelles de la Mort★★★** : dizzy viewpoint in gorges cut almost
800 m into the plateau *(access via D464, then past the
frontier post [tell the border guards you are not going to
Switzerland] along a road towards the power station of
Refrain; from there 25 min on foot.).*   □

Practical Information ─────────────────

CHARQUEMONT, ⊠ 25410, 6 km SE of **Maîche.**

Hotels :
★★ Poste (L.F.), 6, pl. de l'Hôtel-de-Ville, ☎ 81.44.00.20,
Euro Visa, 32 rm P ▦ ♪ ▭ closed Sun eve, Mon lunch
ex school hols, Nov, 150. Rest. ♦ ♪ 50-75.
Bois de la Biche, rte de la Cendrée, ☎ 81.44.01.82, Visa,
6 rm P ⊰ ▦ ⟍ closed Mon eve, 12 Nov-6 Dec, 130.
Rest. ● ♦ ♪ Regional fare served in a real Comtois
farmhouse : croûte forestière aux morilles, poularde au
champagne, Jura wines, 70-130.

DAMPRICHARD, ⊠ 25450, 7 km E of **Maîche.**

Hotel :
★★ Lion d'Or, 17, pl. Centrale, ☎ 81.44.22.84, DC Euro
Visa, 16 rm P ⊰ ▦ ⟍ ♨ half pens (h.s.), 330. Rest. ♦
♪ closed Sun eve (l.s.), Oct, 40-100; child : 35.

GOUMOIS, ⊠ 25470 Trévillers, 22 km SE of **St-Hippolyte.**

Hotel :
● **★★★ Taillard** (R.S.), ☎ 81.44.20.75, AE DC Euro Visa,
17 rm P ⊰ ▦ ⟍ half pens (h.s.), closed Wed (Mar and
Oct), 12 Nov-15 Mar, 510. Rest. ♦ ⊰ ▨ Paradise for
fishermen. Morilles à la crème double, jambon fumé, foie
gras de canard frais "au torchon", Jura wines, 85-250;
child : 50.

▲ **★★Les Grands Champs** (35 pl), ☎ 81.96.54.53.

MAÎCHE, ⊠ 25120, 60 km from **Belfort.**

Hotel :
★★ Panorama (L.F.), Coteau St-Michel, ☎ 81.64.04.78,
Visa, 32 rm P ⊰ ▦ ⟍ ♪ℯ closed Mon (l.s.) ex school hols,
5 Nov-26 Dec, 165. Rest. ♦ ⊰ ♪ 85-100.

Recommended
Events : horse festival, last Sun of Aug.

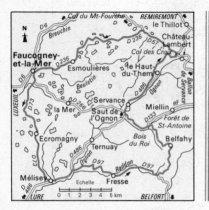

1. Esmoulières plateau

2. Goumois corniche

SAINT-HIPPOLYTE, ⊠ 25190, 50 km from **Belfort.**

Hotel :
★★ **Bellevue** (L.F.), rte de Maîche, ☎ 81.96.51.53, AE DC
Euro Visa, 15 rm P ⫤ ⛄ 160. Rest. ♦ ♪ 40-100 ; child : 25.

GRAY

Besançon 46, Dijon 49, Paris 362 km
pop 8313 ⊠ 70100   A2
Gray sits on the left bank of the Saône, a quiet little
town, and an ideal place to stay if you like the countryside and fishing from river banks.

▶ On the heights, the Renaissance **Hôtel de Ville★** (town
hall), glazed tiles gleaming ; nearby, the **church of Notre-
Dame★** (late Gothic) and **Carmelite chapel** *(weekends
and nat. hols., 4-6).* ▶ Beyond a medieval tower, the **château** (18thC) houses the **Baron-Martin municipal
museum★** : 16th-20thC paintings, engravings★ by Jacques Callot (1592-1635) ; P.-P. Proudhon (1758-1823) :
pastels and drawings★ ; archaeology *(Apr.-Sep., 9-12 &
1-6 ; Oct.-Mar., 9-12 & 2-5 ; closed Tue.).* National Museum
of Esperanto *(Wed. and Sat., 3-6).* ▶ **Autrey-lès-Gray**
(11 km NW) : church frequently remodeled but with
Romanesque choir, handsome statuary.   □

Practical Information _____

🏛 île Sauzé, ☎ 84.65.14.24.   ✔
SNCF ☎ 84.65.22.16.

Hotels :
● ★★★ **Château de Rigny** (R.S.), Rigny, 5 km NE via D
2, ☎ 84.65.25.01, Tx 362926, AE DC Euro Visa, 24 rm
P ⫤ ⅏ ⛄ 🖚 ♪ half pens (h.s.), closed 5-31 Jan, 480.
Rest. ♦♦♦ ⫤ ♪ ⅋ In a 12 acres English park with a river
and pond. Spec : *lapereau au vinaigre de lavande, noisette d'agneau à l'essence de truffe,* 130-200.
● ★★★ **Relais de Nantilly** (R.C.), Nantilly, 5 km W,
☎ 84.65.20.12, AE DC Euro Visa, 11 rm 3 apt P ⅏ 🖚 ♪⁰
closed 20 Oct-1 Apr, 520. Rest. ♦♦ ♪ ⅋ 160-210.
★★ **Bellevue** (L.F.), 1, av. Carnot, ☎ 84.65.47.76, AE DC
Euro Visa, 15 rm P ⫤ ⅏ closed Sat eve and Sun eve (l.s.),
15-31 Dec, 115. Rest. ♦ ⫤ ♪ ⛄ closed Sat and Sun eve
(l.s.) Dec, 50-105 ; child : 30.

🏕 ★★★**Municipal** (100 pl), ☎ 84.65.16.85.

GY

Besançon 31, Vesoul 37, Paris 382 km
pop 985 ⊠ 70700   B2
In the Middle Ages, Gy was the official residence of
the bishops of Besançon to whom the town owes its
château *(15 Jul.-31 Aug., daily 11-12:30 & 3-6 ; rest
of year, weekends only).* **Hôtel de Ville★** (town hall)
in Palladian style ; fountain in the form of a classical
portico ; 18thC neo-Classical **church★.**

Nearby

▶ **Monts de Gy Massif** : hiking trail, Captiot chasm,
expanse of limestone, view. ▶ **Bucey-lès-Gy** *(3 km N)* :
Romanesque church ; town hall and washhouse dating
from 1st Empire (1800-1814). ▶ **Frasne-le-Château**
(9 km NE) : 16thC château built for Cardinal de Granvelle.
                                                                   □

Practical Information _____

Hotel :
Cheval Noir, ☎ 84.32.81.55, 10 rm P ⅏ closed Sun eve
and Mon, 23 Dec-2 Jan, 100. Rest. ♦ 80-130.

┌───┐
│ For the translation of a name of a meat, a fish or a │
│ vegetable, for the composition of a dish or a sauce, │
│ see the Menu Guide in the Practical Holiday Guide ; │
│ it lists the most common culinary terms. │
└───┘

HÉRISSON Falls**
                                                                   B4
At the foot of Aigle peak (alt. 993 m) the Jura presents lakes, waterfalls, and rivers in a pleasant holiday area, with views and walks in all directions.

▶ Follow the course of the Hérisson (a tributary of the
Ain) from **Doucier** by skirting **Lake Chambly** and **Lake Val**
(from car park, 1 hr 15 on foot to Saut-Girard). ▶ **Éven-
tail★★★** *(10 min)* : a 60-m high waterfall ; footbridge to the
top. 300 m ahead left, another footbridge to the **Lacuzon
cave.** ▶ **Grand-Saut waterfall★★** : 60 m in a single fall ;
upstream, **Saut Château-Garnier,** **Saut** (basin), **Saut
de la Forge★.** ▶ 30 min farther to **Saut-Girard,**
leading to **Ilay.**   □

Practical Information _____

DOUCIER, ⊠ 39130 Clairvaux-les-Lacs, 13 km N of **Clairvaux-les-Lacs** on the N 78.

Hotels :
★ **Roux,** ☎ 84.25.71.21, 14 rm P closed Wed (l.s.), Oct,
100. Rest. ♦ ♪ 80-130.
Sarrazine, ☎ 84.25.70.60, Euro Visa, 22 rm P ⅏ closed
Tue eve, Wed (l.s.), 15 Nov-Easter. Rest. ♦ Half-board for
guests only, 55-135 ; child : 40.

ILAY, ⊠ 39150 Saint-Laurent-en-Grandvaux, 10 km NW
of **Saint-Laurent-en-Grandvaux.**

Hotel :
★ **Auberge du Hérisson,** ☎ 84.25.58.18, 14 rm P ⛄ ⅋
pens, closed Wed, 15 Oct-15 Apr, 210. Rest. ♦ Home-
cured pork, trout in Jura cider, 65-95.

JOUX Forest**
                                                                   B3
Fir trunks often more than 50 m high make a cathe-
dral of the Joux Forest, one of the finest in France
(27 km² ; 12 000 trees felled each year). The nearby
forest of Fresse★★ (11.5 km²) is also beautiful. Both
are traversed by marked trails.

▶ The **Route des Sapins** (Fir Road) is signposted from
Equevillon *(D21)* to Villers-sous-Chalamont *(D49, approx.
30 km).* The road passes by the Glacière firs★★, some of
which are 300 years old, to reach an arboretum, then the
Sapin Président★★ (4 m girth, 44 m high, 300 years old).

Nearby

▶ N of **Ilay,** the D75 looks onto **La Motte Lake★, Maclu
Lake** and **Narlay Lake★,** all easily accessible. ▶ N of Doucier, **Chalain Lake★★★** has an attractive recreation centre
(shore, sailing, fishing, aquatic sports ; *tel. : 84.24.29.00*) ;
see it first from the **lookout★★** *(road panel on D39).*   □

Sources du Lison**

(Lison Springs)
                                                                   B3

The Lison runs underground for some distance to
reappear at this enchanting site, easily reached from
the charming village of Nans-sous-Sainte-Anne.

▶ Just beyond the car park, path right to the **Sarrasine cavern★★** *(15 min away, the Lison resurges in wet
weather)* ; 10-min walk away, the main spring bursts out in
a waterfall that forms a lake ; 15 min beyond, **Creux Bil-
lard★,** an impressive chasm. ▶ **Nans-sous-Sainte-Anne** :
very interesting **tool shop★★** with old wooden machinery
powered by the Lison *(Jun.-Sep., daily ex Tue. 10:30-6 ;
rest of year by appt, tel. : 81.53.49.59).* ▶ **Alaise** *(7 km
NW),* said to be the site of the battle where Julius Caesar defeated Vercingetorix (→ Brief regional history).   □

Practical Information ――――――――――――

NANS-SOUS-SAINTE-ANNE, ⊠ 25330 Amancey,
14 km NE of **Salins-les-Bains**.

Hotel :
★ *La Poste* (L.F.), ☎ 81.86.62.57, 11 rm ℗ ≮ ▥ ⌕ ⌘
closed Tue, 3 Nov-1 Feb, 90. Rest. ♦ ≮ 40-105.

LONS-LE-SAUNIER*

Dole 52, Besançon 88, Paris 407 km
pop 21800 ⊠ 39570   A3-4
This peaceful town is the Prefecture of the Jura; it is
also a thermal spa whose waters were appreciated
by the Romans and are still used for the town's
swimming pools. The word *Saunier*, referring to a
salt worker or merchant, reflects the earliest industry
in the town.

▶ **Place de la Liberté :** the clock-tower marks the start of
Rue du Commerce, bordered with 18thC arcades; No. 24
is the birthplace of Claude-Joseph Rouget de Lisle
(1760-1836), composer of the French National Anthem,
the *Marseillaise*. ▶ Hôtel de Ville (town hall) : **museum** of
painting and sculpture *(10-12 & 2-6; closed Tue. and Sat.
am, Sun. am)*; archaeology museum (alpine prehistory;
tel. : 84.47.12.13). Nearby, behind a magnificent wrought-
iron **grille★★**, the 18thC hospital (pharmacy★). ▶ Close to
the Prefecture : **church of St. Désiré★** (Romanesque interior, 18thC vaulting behind a 19thC façade, over an 11thC
crypt). ▶ Attractive gardens on the Chevalerie Promenade
and in the Park des Bains.

Nearby

▶ **Conliège** *(4 km SW)*, among vineyards : beautiful
church (14th-18thC; fine medieval statues). Farther on,
Creux de Revigny. ▶ 5 km N : **château du Pin★★** rebuilt
in the 15thC (square keep). **L'Étoile** *(W, on the other side
of N83)* : recognized for wine; pretty site★ on the hillside,
ruins of a medieval château.   ☐

Practical Information ――――――――――――

LONS-LE-SAUNIER
⌁ (1 Jun-31 Oct), ☎ 84.24.65.01.
ℹ 1, rue Pasteur, ☎ 84.24.20.63.
SNCF ☎ 84.24.01.23/84.47.50.50.
▱▱ av. Thurel.

Hotels :
★★★ *Grand Hôtel de Genève*, 39, rue Jean-Moulin,
☎ 84.24.19.11, 42 rm ℗ ⌘ 300. Rest. ♦ 65-110.
● ★★ *Le Cheval Rouge* (L.F.), 47, rue Lecourbe,
☎ 84.47.20.44, DC Euro Visa, 19 rm ℗ ▥ ⌘ half pens,
closed Sat eve (l.s.), 5-25 Nov, 200. Rest. ● ♦♦ ⌘
closed Tue in Jul-Aug, Sat (l.s) : A pleasant little bastion of
good regional cooking : *ragoût d'escargots au beurre fin,
poulet de Bresse au vin jaune et morilles*, 100-160.

⚘ ★★★★*La Marjorie* (120 pl), ☎ 84.24.26.94.

Nearby

COURLANS, ⊠ 39570 Lons-le-Saunier, 6 km E.

Restaurant :
● ♦♦ *Auberge de Chavannes*, ☎ 84.47.05.52, AE DC
Euro Visa ▥ closed Tue and Wed, 15 Jan-15 Feb,
25 Jun-10 Jul. A limited number of places guarantees
high quality, says Pierre Carpentier : *crème grelette et blinis, pigeons de Bresse en aiguillettes*, Jura cheeses and
wines, 125-250.

CRANCOT, ⊠ 39570 Lons-le-Saunier, 10 km NE.

Hotel :
★ *Belvédère* (L.F.), ☎ 84.48.22.18, 9 rm ℗ ≮ ⌕
closed Sun eve and Mon (l.s.), 1 Jan-2 Feb, 10-20 Oct,
200. Rest. ♦ ⌁ Greenery and absolute peace. *Oreille de
goret farcie de gras-double aux petits lardons chauds, filet
de brochet à l'essence de truffes et beurre blanc*, 65-220.

The LOUE Valley**

                                                         B3
**From the Belvédère du Moine-de-la-Vallée to Arc-et-
Senans** *(approx 100 km full day; see map 3)*

The Loue, one of the most beautiful rivers in the Jura,
springs from the high plateaux. Emerging into the
day after a long journey underground, the river runs
through a valley in which all the landscapes of the
region are found. Here, so the local people say, the
the caverns are haunted.

▶ **Belvédère du Moine★★** overlooks the valley towards
Mouthier and Lods. ▶ **Loue spring★★★** spurts from a
cavern on the flank of a 100-m rock wall to run down the
gorges de Nouailles (view from D67). ▶ Several springs
and waterfalls add to the Loue before it reaches **Mouthier-
Haute-Pierre★**, a village among orchards, half in the valley
and half on a hill (kirsch). Natural History museum *(daily,
8-11:30 & 1:30-5; closed Wed.)*. Mouthier-Haut : old houses and church (15thC; furnishings). ▶ **Lods** (pop. 377;
pronounced *Lô*) : houses on the waterside; view from
the other bank; forges, old mill; 16thC château; **museum
of vines and wine** *(Jul.-Aug., daily ex Tue. 10-12 & 2-6)*.
▶ **Vuillafans** : old houses, ruins, an old bridge. ▶ **Ornans**
(→), then left, chapel of Notre-Dame du Chêne : pilgrimage site. ▶ **Scey-en-Varais** : ruined feudal castle reflected in the river. **Malbrans** *(4 km N)* : 19thC tileworks.
▶ The road skirts the beautiful **château de Cléron★★**
(14th-16thC; *2:30-6, 10 Jul.-20 Aug.*). ▶ Confluence of the
Lison and Loue; Châtillon forges : pretty **sites★**. ▶ **Chenecey-Buillon :** in a loop of the Loue, ruined abbey
and feudal ruins; then road rejoins N83. ▶ **Port-Lesney** (pop. 648), a delightful stopover beside a peaceful stretch of the Loue, very popular with fishermen.
▶ **Arc-et-Senans★★★** (→).   ☐

Practical Information ――――――――――――

LODS, ⊠ 25930, 22 km NW of **Pontarlier**.

Hotel :
★★ *Truite d'Or* (L.F.), ☎ 81.60.95.48, Euro Visa, 14 rm ℗
≮ ▥ ⌕ closed Sun eve Mon ex summer and school hols,
1 Jan-1 Feb, 130. Rest. ♦ ≮ ⌁ Between river and wood,
honest, hearty cooking : *cassolette de morilles, truite au
bleu*, 60-120.

⚘ ★★*Municipal* (60 pl), ☎ 81.62.26.06.

PORT-LESNEY, ⊠ 39340, 8 km SE of **Arc-et-Senans**.

Hotel :
★★ *Parc*, ☎ 84.37.81.41, 15 rm ℗ ≮ ▥ ⌕ ⌘ ⌁ closed
Palm Sun-Easter, 250. Rest. ♦♦ ⌁ 18thC manor, 80-180.

LUXEUIL-LES-BAINS*

Vesoul 28, Belfort 52, Paris 372 km
pop 10530 ⊠ 70300   B1
Luxeuil is a thermal spa (hot radioactive waters, well-
equipped leisure facilities) in an ancient town with
beautiful houses. St. Columban came to Luxeuil from
Ireland in the 6thC to establish one of the first monastic communities in the West.

▶ Around Place St-Pierre and Place St-Martin : pala-
tial former abbot's residence (18thC) now the town hall;
14thC **basilica of St. Pierre** : 16thC choir stalls★; 17thC
organ, cloister★. Renaissance house (supposedly belonged to King François I); **Jouffroy mansion★** (15thC)
opposite the **Hôtel des Échevins★★** (the aldermen's
house), a fortified house of the same period (Jules-Adler
Museum : 19thC paintings and drawings; *2-5:30 ex Tue.*).
▶ At the Municipal Library : **Baumont museum** (historical
archives). ▶ **Baths** : elegant 18thC **façade★★.** ▶ Walks
around **Sept Chevaux Lake.**

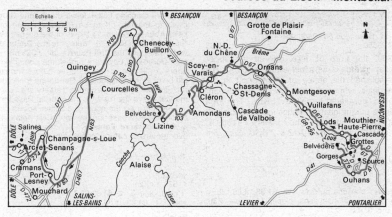

Echelle
0 1 2 3 4 5 km

3. The Loue valley

Nearby

▶ To the N, **Saint-Valbert** : beautiful village washhouse and hermitage *(visits)* in a splendid park (animals). **Fougerolles** (pop. 4 329 ; *9 km*) : kirsch-distilling. Farther on, **Distillery Museum★** *(N57, right on D308)* : houses, workshops, interiors *(daily ex Sun., tel. : 84.49.10.66).* □

Practical Information

LUXEUIL-LES-BAINS
⚓ (1 Apr-30 Nov).
ⓘ 1, rue des Thermes, ☎ 84.40.06.41.
SNCF ☎ 84.40.22.03.

Hotels :
★★★ *Beau Site*, 18, rue Moulinard, ☎ 84.40.14.67, Euro Visa, 44 rm Ⓟ ⪅ ⨇ half pens (h.s.), closed Fri eve and Sat (Nov-Mar), 24-30 Dec. Rest. ♦ ⪅ ⅃ ঌ 65-110.
★ *Ermitage*, 21, rue Marcel-Donjon, ☎ 84.40.15.64, Visa, 25 rm Ⓟ ⨇ ঌ closed Sun eve, 30 Oct-15 Nov, 85. Rest. ♦ ঌ 45-80 ; child : 30.

Restaurant :
♦♦ *Thermes*, 4, rue des Thermes, ☎ 84.40.18.94, DC Euro Visa ⨇ ⅃ ⨳ closed Wed eve and Sun eve, 25 Oct-9 Nov, 45-145.

Ⅺ ★★*Stade Maroselli* (200 pl), ☎ 84.40.02.39.

Nearby

FOUGEROLLES, ⊠ 70220, 9 km N.

Restaurant :
♦ *Au Père Rota*, 8, Grande-Rue, ☎ 84.49.12.11, AE DC Euro Visa ⨇ ⅃ closed Mon and Sun eve ex hols, 23 Feb-9 Mar, 16 Nov-9 Dec, 110-200.

MONTBÉLIARD

Belfort 22, Besançon 82, Paris 483 km
pop 33300 ⊠ 25200   C2

At the heart of the dense industrial development dominated by Peugeot, château Wurtemberg gives a Germanic look to the city. Until 1793, Montbéliard was a free and independent principality, famous at that time for a breed of cattle and for sausage.

▶ **Château★** : museum commemorates native son Georges Cuvier (1769-1832), founder of the study of comparative anatomy and palaeontology. Étienne Oelmichen, a Montbéliard citizen by adoption, made the first helicopter flight on 4 May 1924 at Arbouans. The museum houses a collection of archaeology, 19th-20thC painting *(10-12 &*

2-6 ex Tue.). ▶ **Place St-Martin** : 18thC town hall, Beurnier mansion *(***Museum of Old Montbéliard** : costumes, furniture ; *15 Jun.-Aug., 3-6 ; rest of year by appt, tel. : 81.94.54.11) ;* Temple of St. Martin (18thC Protestant church). ▶ Place Denfert-Rochereau : 16th-17thC market buildings. ▶ Peugeot factories : in business (first as a steel foundry) continuously since 1810 ; entry near the Bonal stadium NE of town *(3-hr visits weekdays 8:30 am ; closed Aug. and Sat. ; tel. : 81.33.12.34).*

Nearby

▶ Church of Sacré-Cœur★★ in **Audincourt** *(6 km SE ; 1951)* : mosaic, stained glass, tapestry designed by the painter Fernand Léger (1881-1955). **Mandeure** *(7 km farther) :* Roman theatre.   □

Practical Information

MONTBÉLIARD
ⓘ 1, rue Mouhot, ☎ 81.94.45.60.
SNCF ☎ 81.94.43.70/81.94.50.50.
Car rental : *Avis*, 31, av. d'Helvétie, ☎ 81.95.16.24.

Hotels :
★★ *Balance*, 40, rue de Belfort, ☎ 81.91.18.54, 41 rm ঌ 140.
★★ *Joffre*, 34 bis, av. du Mal-Joffre, ☎ 81.94.44.64, 30 rm Ⓟ closed Sun (l.s.), 1-15 Aug, 25 Dec-1 Jan, 170.

Restaurant :
♦♦♦ *Tour Henriette*, 59, fg de Besançon, ☎ 81.91.03.24, AE DC Euro Visa ⨇ ⅃ ঌ closed Mon eve , Sun eve and hol eves. Spec : *ris de veau des gourmets, sandre en chemise Arlequin* (h.s.), 100-220.

Recommended
Baby-sitting : *Montbéliard Accueil,* ☎ 81.98.33.61.

Nearby

SOCHAUX, ⊠ 25650, 3 km E.

Restaurant :
♦♦ *Piguet Luc*, 9, rue de Belfort, ☎ 81.95.15.14, AE DC Euro Visa ⨇ ⅃ closed Mon and Sun eve. Prize-winning chef Luc Piguet has transferred his kitchenware to the centre of town, and given them a home with a lovely garden. The food is as good as ever : *raviolis d'escargots sur soupe de champignons sauvages, cuisses de grenouilles à la coque, cul de lapin au thym,* 100-200.

Be advised that hotels and restaurants in this Guide have perhaps changed addresses; prices indicated are also subject to modifications.

MONTBENOÎT*

Pontarlier 14, Besançon 68, Paris 466 km
pop 163 ✉ 25650   B-C3

In the 12thC the Lord of Joux offered the upper Doubs Valley to monks as a penitential offering; the monks established the abbey of Montbenoît in the Val du Saugeais, whose villages formed an independent republic, populated largely by Swiss. The area still preserves unique characteristics including dialect. 12th-16thC church : statuary, choir **stalls★★** (16thC); **cloister★** (15thC; *Jul.-Aug.*, *10-12 & 2-6:30; Sun., pm only).*   □

Practical Information ⎯⎯⎯⎯⎯⎯⎯⎯

Hotel :
★★ Saugeais, Maisons-du-Bois, ☎ 81.38.14.65, Euro Visa, 7 rm 🅿 ⫽ ⌕ ⫻ half pens, closed Mon eve, 230. Rest. ♦ ⫽ ♪ ら 35-90.

MOREY

Vesoul 38, Langres 42, Paris 336 km
✉ 70500 Jussey   A1

A peaceful village on the flank of La Roche (view★★) with a leisure park *(tel. : 84.91.02.14).*

▶ **Chauvirey-le-Châtel** *(10 km N)* : 15thC chapel of St. Hubert (carved stone altarpiece); church (16thC altarpiece).   □

MOREZ

Lons-le-Saunier 58, Besançon 86, Paris 459 km
pop 6999 ✉ 39400   B4

Tour of the Gorges *(approx 68 km, half-day; see map 4)*
A country of high plateaux, deep gorges, hidden valleys.

▶ **Morez** stretches out in a narrow gorge along the Bienne; production of cheese (museum, *enq. : S.I.*), watches and clocks. Jourdain Museum *(Thu., Fri.).*

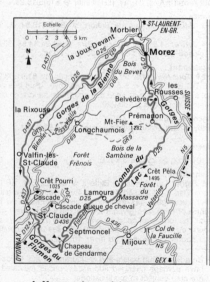

4. Morez and tour of the gorges

▶Before reaching Lézat, leave the **Bienne Gorges★** and climb to the turn-off to **La Rixouse** : road on right to **Lake Abbaye** *(12 km).* ▶Views of the gorges before your reach **Saint-Claude** (→) : detour to the **Queue de Cheval water-fall★** and the **Crêt Pourri★** (alt. 1 025 m). ▶The **Flumen Gorges★** : beyond a tunnel, the *corniche* (cliff road) offers a glimpse of the waterfall before forming a hairpin bend at the **Chapeau de Gendarme** (policeman's cap) rock formation dating from the Tertiary era. ▶After **Septmoncel**, leave the road for the Faucille Pass on the right. ▶**Lamoura** : on the edge of a winter sports plateau just before the lake pass; on the right, **Crêt Pela** (alt. 1 495 m) in the **Massacre Forest★**. ▶ After **Prémanon**, lookout over the Arcets natural amphiteatre.   □

Practical Information ⎯⎯⎯⎯⎯⎯⎯⎯

MOREZ
🜨 830-1360m.
ⓘ pl. J.-Jaurès, ☎ 84.33.08.73.
SNCF ☎ 84.33.01.33.

Hotel :
★★ Poste, 1, rue du Dr-Regad, ☎ 84.33.11.03, AE DC Euro Visa, 45 rm 🅿 ⑭ ⌕ ら closed 25 Nov-25 Dec, 175. Rest. ♦♦ ら closed Mon. Successful use of fine ingredients : *jambon de morteau gratiné, suprême de volaille aux morilles et gyromitres,* 60-150.

Nearby

LAMOURA ✉ 39310 Septmoncel, 16 km W of **Saint-Claude.**

Hotel :
★★ La Spatule (L.F.), ☎ 84.41.20.23, Visa, 25 rm 🅿 ⫽ ⌕ closed 30 Apr-15 Jun, 1 Oct-15 Dec, 135. Rest. ♦ ⫽ ♪ ⫻ 60-120.

MORTEAU

Pontarlier 31, Besançon 67, Paris 477 km
pop 6699 ✉ 25500   C3

Morteau is a relatively new town rebuilt during the 19thC after a disastrous fire. Numerous watchmakers; visits to the bell foundry (Rue Louhière, *weekdays 9-12 & 2-4:30; closed 15 Jul.-15 Aug.; tel. : 81.67.04.08).*

Nearby

▶ Upstream, the Doubs runs through the Coin de la Roche pass *(D437)* at the foot of the village of **Grand-Combe-Châteleu★★**, which has many traditional *tué* houses; church, Baroque altarpieces. ▶ The **Doubs Gorges★★** : downstream from Morteau, **Villers-le-Lac** : watch collection at the Hôtel de France. Take a boat to explore the **Saut** (waterfall) **du Doubs★★★** beyond **Lake Chaillexon★★**, or drive *(follow road signs; 25 min on foot).*   □

Practical Information ⎯⎯⎯⎯⎯⎯⎯⎯

MORTEAU
ⓘ pl. de la Gare, ☎ 81.67.18.53 (h.s.); mairie, ☎ 81.67.14.78.
SNCF ☎ 81.53.50.50.

Hotel :
★★ Guimbarde (L.F.), 10, pl. Carnot, ☎ 81.67.14.12, 20 rm 🅿 ⌕ 140. Rest. ♦ closed Mon noon ex Aug, 50-110.

Nearby

GRAND-COMBE-CHÂTELEU, ✉ 25570, 3 km SE on D437.

Restaurant :
♦♦ **Auberge de la Roche**, ☎ 81.68.80.05, Euro Visa ♪ ら closed Mon and Sun eve, 5-26 Jan, 8-15 Jun, 7-14 Sep, 100-160.

VILLERS-LE-LAC, ⊠ 25130, 6 km W.
⌇ 1100-1290m.
ⓘ rue Bercot, ☎ 81.43.00.98 (h.s.).

Hotel :
★★ *France* (L.F.), 8, pl. M.-Cupillard, ☎ 81.68.00.06, AE
DC Euro Visa, 14 rm Ⓟ ⌇ ♪ closed Sun eve and Mon,
31 Oct-1 Feb, 220. Rest. ● ♦♦ ♪ Beautiful cuisine of the
Franche-Comté : *morteau grillé, feuilleté de ris de veau
aux nouilles, cassolette d'escargots au vin pétillant du
Jura*, 100-150.

Å ★★*Saut du Doubs* (70 pl), ☎ 81.43.04.97.

NEUBLANS*

Dole 30, Chalon-sur-Saône 42, Paris 353 km
pop 383 ⊠ 39120 Chaussin   A3

The **château de Neublans** was built for an 18thC president of the Parliament of Franche-Comté ; the stables are almost as beautiful as the house *(ext. visits
only)*.   □

NOZEROY*

Pontarlier 33, Lons-le-Saunier 51, Paris 443 km
pop 452 ⊠ 39250   B3

Nozeroy is a former stronghold in the middle of an
unspoilt plateau crossed by the Serpentine River. Two
gateways and part of the ramparts of the 16thC château des Chalon, ruined in the Revolution, still attest
to its former grandeur. ▶ 16thC church ; old houses
in the Grand'Rue.

Nearby

▶ **Mièges** *(2 km N)* : 16th-17thC church, once part of a
priory ; rich furnishings, Flamboyant Gothic chapel. ▶ To
the S, Serpentine waterfalls and the **Source de l'Ain**★
(paths from D283).   □

OGNON Valley*

                                                       B2
From Lure to Pesmes *(approx 120 km, full day)*
The river Ognon runs down from the Vosges mountains to irrigate a large part of the Franche-Comté,
and forms the frontier between the Haut-Saône and
the Doubs departments for two-thirds of its course.
The pleasant valley is ideal for exploring on foot or
by bicycle.
▶ **Lure.** ▶ **Villersexel** : 19thC château *(weekdays ex Mon.,
3-5 ; Sat., Sun., 2:30-6 ;* furniture, history). To the W, ruined priory of **Marast** (12thC) and feudal fortress of **Oricourt.** ▶ **Montbozon** : 16thC château. ▶ W of the valley, 17thC châteaux of **Bellevaux** (D209) and **Sorans**
(N57). ▶ Pretty 16thC château at **Buthiers.** ▶ **Voray-sur-
l'Ognon** : large **church** with cupola, late 18thC. ▶ **Etuz** :
colonnaded village washhouse (18thC). ▶ **Moncley**★★ :
château (18thC) is perhaps the most beautiful in Franche-Comté, surrounded by trees, convex façade towards
the courtyard, concave to the garden side *(Sat. and
Sun. 2:30-6:30, 15 Apr.-15 Sep. ;* furniture, wallpapers★*).*
▶ **Marnay** : old houses near the fortified château and
the church (15th-16thC ; statuary). **Acey abbey** (founded
12thC, rebuilt 18th) a Cistercian centre for Gregorian
chant. ▶ **Malans** : a feudal fortified farmstead that assumed its present aspect in the 16th and 19thC ; 2nd
Empire (ca. 1850) furniture *(3-5 ex Tue., 15 Jun.-15 Sep.).*
▶ **Pesmes**★ : a splendid site over the river where ramparts and château recreate the past ; church★
(13th-14thC) : furnishings, fine statuary ; Renaissance
Andelot chapel★ in marble. An attractive setting, with
excellent facilities for summer holidays.   □

AUBIGNEY, ⊠ 70140 Pesmes, 7 km N of **Pesmes**.

Hotel :
★★ *Auberge du Vieux Moulin* (C.H.), ☎ 84.31.21.16, AE
DC, 7 rm Ⓟ ⋒ ⌖ closed Jan-Feb, 250. Rest. ● ♦♦ ♪
The Mirbey sisters (A.R.C.) uphold the traditon of savoury
"cuisine de femmes" : *lapereau en gelée, œufs en meu-
rette.* Desserts by Babeth, 155-300.

CUSSEY-SUR-L'OGNON, ⊠ 25870, 16 km NE of **Marnay.**

Hotel :
★★ *Vieille Auberge,* ☎ 81.57.78.35, Euro Visa, 8 rm Ⓟ ⌖
closed Mon eve and Sun eve, 145. Rest. ● ♦♦ ♪ Simple
fare in a village of the Franche-Comté : *saumon au gros
sel, croûte aux morilles, entrecôte grand-mère*, 70-150.

ÉTUZ, ⊠ 70150 Marnay, 15 km NE of **Marnay.**

Restaurant :
● ♦♦ *La Sablière,* rte de Cussey-sur-l'Ognon,
☎ 81.57.78.50, AE DC Euro Visa Ⓟ ⋒ ⌖ ⊡ closed
Thu and Sun eve, 16-21 Feb, 24 Aug-16 Sep. Traditional
dishes of the Jura : *truite belle comtoise, coq au vin,* game
in season, 85-190.

PESMES, ⊠ 70140, 24 km from **Dole.**
ⓘ mairie, ☎ 84.31.22.16/84.31.20.32.   ♥

Hotel :
★★ *France* (L.F.), 36, rue Vannoise, ☎ 84.31.20.05, Euro
Visa, 10 rm Ⓟ ⌇ ⋒ ⌖ ♨ closed 15 Nov-8 Dec, 100.
Rest. ♦ ⌖ ⌂ 50-100.

VILLERSEXEL, ⊠ 70110, 26 km from **Vesoul.**

Hotels :
★★ *La Terrasse* (L.F.), ☎ 84.20.52.11, Euro Visa, 16 rm
Ⓟ ⋒ ⌖ closed Fri eve and Sun eve (l.s.), 19 Dec-3 Jan,
150. Rest. ♦ ⌖ 45-100.
★ *Commerce* (L.F.), 1, rue du 13-Septembre-1944,
☎ 84.20.50.50, Euro Visa, 14 rm Ⓟ ⌖ half pens, closed
Mon eve, 1-15 Jan, 4-17 Oct, 145. Rest. ♦ ♪ 40-110 ;
child : 30.

Å ★★*Du Chapeau Chinois* (55 pl), ☎ 84.43.04.97.

ORNANS**

Besançon 26, Pontarlier 34, Paris 436 km
pop 4234 ⊠ 25290   B2-3

Home town of the painter Gustave Courbet who found
much of his inspiration there (museum in his birthplace, *10-12 & 2-6 Apr.-Nov. ; closed Tue. the rest of
year).* The wooden balconies of the houses overhang
the river Loue (view★★ from the Grand Pont), which
broadens a little farther into a pond called the Miroir.
The village is the tourist centre of the valley, but has
kept a simple rustic charm ; choir stalls and 18thC
altarpiece in the church.

Nearby

▶ Via the Puits Noir ravine *(D67 then right)* to the **Grotte
de Plaisir-Fontaine** (cavern). ▶ Farther N *(D67 and D112)*,
Foucherans : rural museum *(Jul.-Sep., daily 2-6 ; rest of
year by appt, tel. 81.86.73.20) ;* and **Trépot** : old cheese
dairy★ *(2-6, Jul.-15 Sep.).* ▶ **Poudrey chasm** *(14 km by
D492)* : mineral formations, subterranean river, immense
subterranean hall (600 m in circumference, 110 m deep)
*(May-Sep., 8:30-12 & 1:30-7 ; Mar., Apr., Oct., Nov., 9-12 &
2-6 ex Wed.).*   □

ORNANS
ⓘ ☎ 81.62.21.50.

Å ★★★*Le Chanet* (70 pl), ☎ 81.62.23.44.

Recommended
Events : *secondhand sale,* in Jul.

Nearby

BONNEVAUX-LE-PRIEURÉ, ⊠ 25660 Saône, 6 km on D67.

Hotel :
● ★★★ *Moulin du Prieuré*, (I.L.A., C.H.), ☎ 81.59.21.47, AE DC Euro Visa, 8 rm P ≪ ∰ ⌕ ♪ ও closed 15 Nov-15 Mar, 250. Rest. ● ♦♦ ♪ ও Spec : *millefeuille de la mer, filet de canard gavé des Landes, terrine de fruits en sauce*, 100-250 ; child : 45.

POLIGNY

Lons-le-Saunier 28, Besançon 60, Paris 403 km
pop 5182 ⊠ 39800   A-B3

Poligny is a wine-producing centre located in a blind valley *(reculée)* cutting into the main plateau of the Jura. It is also the acknowledged centre of the Comté cheese industry.

▶ Infirmary *(Hôtel-Dieu)* and 17thC houses around the **church of St. Hippolyte** (15th-16thC) : fine collection of Burgundian statues, 15thC altarpiece, 18thC wood paneling. ▶ **National Dairy Industry School** (Place du Champ-de-Foire) fosters progress in the regional industry. ▶ Near Champagnole, N5 offers views of the **Culée de Vaux** behind Poligny.   □

Practical Information _____

POLIGNY
ⓘ Grande-Rue, ☎ 84.37.24.21 (h.s.).
▦▦▦▦ ☎ 84.37.20.01.

Hotel :
● ★★ *Host. La Vallée Heureuse* (L.F.), rte de Genève, RN 5, ☎ 84.37.12.13, AE DC Visa, 10 rm P ≪ ⌕ closed Wed, Thu lunch ex school hols, 10-20 Jun, 10-30 Oct, 200. Rest. ● ♦♦ ≪ ♪ For lovers of peace and simple food, 75-200.

Nearby

PASSENANS, ⊠ 39230 Sellières, 11 km SW on N 83.

Hotel :
● ★★ *Domaine Touristique du Revermont*, (R.S., L.F.), ☎ 84.44.61.02, Visa, 28 rm P ≪ ∰ ⌕ ♪ ও ⌇ ☐ ♪ half pens (h.s.) closed Sun eve and Mon (l.s.), Jan-Feb, 390. Rest. ♦ ≪ ♪ ও ⌇ Perfect peace and comfort in a park setting. *Suprême de volaille au vin jaune*, 75-160 ; child : 40.

PONTARLIER

Besançon 58, Lons-le-Saunier 77, Paris 454 km
pop 18800 ⊠ 25300   B3

Pontarlier is a commercial and holiday centre of the upper Doubs. The surrounding countryside is more interesting than the town itself, which was rebuilt in the 18thC (commemorative arch) ; statuary in the church of St. Bénigne ; municipal museum *(weekdays, 10-12 & 2-6, week-ends 2-6)* : Franche-Comté painting, archaeology.

Nearby

▶ **Entreportes Pass** *(D47, E)* : rocks, meadows and firs ; a popular place for a stroll. ▶ **Fort du Larmont** ; **château de Joux★★** *(Arms museum ; Apr.-Oct., 10-12 & 2-5 ; Jul.-Aug., 9-12 & 2-6)* rebuilt by Vauban ; Toussaint Louverture (1743-1803), who led the slaves of Santo Domingo in their struggle for freedom, died here, where he had been imprisoned on the personal orders of Napoleon. The fort overlooks the 200-m deep valley of **La Cluse-et-Mijoux★★**. ▶ Recreation facilities on **Saint-Point Lake**, and along the Doubs, especially at **Malbuisson**. ▶ **Métabief, Les Hôpitaux-Neufs** and **Jougne** *(21 km S)* are winter sports centres near Mont d'Or (alt. 1463 m).   □

Practical Information _____

PONTARLIER
ⓘ Hôtel de Ville, ☎ 81.46.48.33.
▦▦▦▦ ☎ 81.53.50.50.
Car rental : *Avis*, train station.

Hotels :
★★★ *Commerce*, 18, rue du Dr-Grenier, ☎ 81.39.04.09, Euro Visa, 30 rm P ∰ ⌕ ও half pens (h.s.), closed 5-20 Jan, 370. Rest. ♦ closed Mon noon and Sun eve (l.s.), 70-100.
★★ *Grand Hôtel de la Poste*, 55, rue de la République, ☎ 81.39.18.12, Euro Visa, 21 rm P 200.
★ *Morteau*, 26, rue J.-d'Arc, ☎ 81.39.14.83, Visa, 19 rm P ⌦ closed Sat eve , Sun (l.s.), Mar, Jun, 15 Sep-7 Oct, 110. Rest. ♦ ♪ closed Sat eve and Sun, 40-80.

Nearby

Les HOPITÂUX-NEUFS, ⊠ 25370, 3 km E of **Métabief**.
ⓘ ☎ 81.49.13.81.

Hotel :
★★ *Robbe* (L.F.), ☎ 81.49.11.05, Euro Visa, 20 rm P ∰ half pens (h.s.), 285. Rest. ♦ ≪ closed 1 May-25 Jun, 10 Sep-15 Dec, 50-70.

JOUGNE, ⊠ 25370 Les Hôpitaux-Neufs, 3 km S of **Métabief**.
ⓘ mairie, ☎ 81.49.11.75.

Hotels :
★★ *Bonjour*, ☎ 81.49.10.45, Visa, 18 rm ≪ ⌕ ⌇ ♠ ⌦ closed 8 Apr-8 Jun, 15 Sep-18 Dec, 150. Rest. ♦ ≪ ও 50-100 ; child : 40.
★★ *Deux Saisons*, ☎ 81.49.00.04, DC Visa, 21 rm P ≪ ∰ ⌕ ও pens, closed 26 Apr-1 Jun, 1 Nov-18 Dec, 155. Rest. ♦ ≪ ⌦ 50-95.

MALBUISSON, ⊠ 25160, 16 km.
⌇ 900-1000m.
ⓘ ☎ 81.69.31.21.

Hotels :
★★★ *Le Lac*, ☎ 81.69.34.80, Tx 360713, DC Euro Visa, 55 rm P ≪ ∰ half pens (h.s.), closed ex weekends, 17 Nov-18 Dec, 345. Rest. ♦♦ ≪ ও 60-150 ; child : 45.
★★★ *Les Terrasses* (L.F.), ☎ 81.69.30.24, AE DC Euro Visa, 23 rm P ≪ ⌕ ⌦ closed Mon (l.s.), 10 Nov-20 Jan, 200. Rest. ♦♦ ≪ ⌦ 85-130.
★★ *Le Bellevue*, ☎ 81.69.30.89, AE DC Visa, 12 rm P ∰ ⌕ closed Sun eve and Mon, 3-31 Jan, 15-30 Apr, 150. Rest. ♦ ≪ ♪ ও Spec : *suprême de pintadeaux aux morilles*, Jura wines, 150-200.
★ *Auberge de la Poste* (L.F.), ☎ 81.69.31.72, Euro Visa, 9 rm P ⌕ closed Tue (l.s.), 1-12 May, 11 Nov-20 Dec, 120. Rest. ♦ ≪ ও 50-100.

⛺ ★★★*Les Fauvettes* (300 pl) ☎ 81.69.31.50 ; at Saint-Point, 6 km, ★★*Municipal* (80 pl), ☎ 81.89.40.18.

MÉTABIEF, ⊠ 25370 Les Hôpitaux-Neufs, 16 km.

Hotel :
★ *Etoile des Neiges*, 4, rue du Village, ☎ 81.49.11.21, 15 rm P ≪ ∰ ⌕ ⌦ closed May, Nov, 135. Rest. ♦ *Le Bief-Rouge* ♪ 50-120.

MOUTHE, ⊠ 25240, 31 km S.

Hotel :
★★ *Le Castel Blanc* (L.F.), Chatelblanc, ☎ 81.69.24.56, 11 rm P ≪ ∰ ⌕ ♪ half pens (h.s.), closed 15 Apr-30 Jun, 1 Oct-15 Dec, 190. Rest. ♦ ≪ ♪ ও 55-120.

⛺ ★★*Source du Doubs* (50 pl), ☎ 81.69.23.57.

Recommended
Sports : *ski school*, ☎ 81.69.22.64, cross country and alpine ; at La Chapelle-des-Bois, *cross-country ski school*, ☎ 81.69.26.19.

OYE-ET-PALLET, ⊠ 25160 Malbuisson, 7 km S on D 437.

Hotels :
★★ *Parnet* (L.F.), ☎ 81.89.42.03, Visa, 18 rm P ≪ ∰ ⌕

 closed Sun eve and Mon, 12-30 Jan, 17-27 Nov, 210.
Rest. ♦ ⟨ ⫽ ⑆ ⑉ 70-160.
★★ *Riant-Séjour* (L.F.), ☎ 81.89.42.03, 18 rm Ⓟ ⟨ ⑱ ⑉
closed Sun eve and Mon, 1-15 Oct, 3 Dec-3 Jan, 220.
Rest. ♦♦ ⫽ 70-150.

The REVERMONT Region

A4

As you look over the plain of Bresse towards distant Burgundy, pastures gradually turn into vineyards. Here, on the borders of the Comté, S of Lons-le-Saunier, D59, D10, then D117 thread through a historic landscape.

► From **Montaigu**, view★★ over Lons and the surrounding area; house of Rouget de Lisle (→ Lons-le-Saunier). Another remarkable view★★ at **La Croix-Rochette** *(9 km farther, on right)*. ► Right again, ruins of the fortified château in **Présilly**. ► **Orgelet** and **Arinthod** : small market towns with arcade houses. ► **Saint-Hymetière** : **Romanesque church**★★ on the W side of the village.► W to the Suran Valley : **Montfleur** (17thC château, former medieval stronghold).► **Andelot-lès-Saint-Amour** : 15th-16thC château.► **Gigny** : 10thC **Romanesque church**★, remains of a Cluniac abbey. ► **Cressia**★ : 15thC château in an old town, picturesque but less well-situated than **Saint-Laurent-la-Roche** (view★★). ☐

Practical Information

ARINTHOD, ⊠ 39240, 37 km S of **Lons-le-Saunier**.
ⓘ mairie, ☎ 84.48.00.67.

Hotel :
★ *Tour*, ☎ 84.48.00.05, 14 rm Ⓟ ⑆ 146. Rest. ♦ 45-90.

SAINT-AMOUR, ⊠ 39160, 33 km SE of **Lons-le-Saunier**.
ⓘ pl. de la Chevalerie, ☎ 84.48.76.69 (h.s.); mairie,
☎ 84.48.74.77.

Hotel :
● ★★ *Alliance*, ☎ 84.48.74.94, DC Visa, 16 rm Ⓟ ⑱
closed Sun eve and Mon (l.s.). Handsome 17thC dwelling,
140. Rest. ♦♦ 40-100.

Ⓐ ★★*Municipal* (70 pl), ☎ 84.48.71.68.

RONCHAMP***

Belfort 21, Vesoul 43, Paris 492 km
pop 3139 ⊠ 70250   C1

The **chapel of Notre-Dame du Haut de Ronchamp**★★, although dedicated to peace, has fallen victim to several wars. It was most recently rebuilt in 1955 by the architect Le Corbusier (1887-1965) who created a major work of art here.

► The design of the chapel unites elegance, functional aptitude (external pulpit for pilgrims) and technical expertise (concrete roof shell) to make a beautiful place of meditation *(9-8, Apr.-Oct.; 10-4, Nov.-Mar.).* ► In the village, where coal was mined until 1958, the **Maison de la Mine**★ (mining museum, arts centre; *3-6, May-Sep.*).   ☐

Practical Information

ⓘ ☎ 84.20.64.70.
SNCF ☎ 84.20.60.46.

Hotel :
★★★ *Ronchamp*, 1, rue Neuve, ☎ 84.20.60.35, Euro Visa,
21 rm Ⓟ ⟨ ⑱ ⬙ ⑉ closed Sun eve (l.s.), 15 Dec-25 Jan,
155.

In preparing for your trip, consult the pages pertaining to the regions. You will find there the description of the region you wish to visit, as well as a list of sites that must be seen, a brief history and practical information.

Les ROUSSES

Geneva 47, Lons-le-Saunier 66, Paris 470 km
pop 2573 ⊠ 39220   B4

A winter sports resort that is also a pleasant spot in summer on a 1100-m high plateau. Fine view from the church; walks, especially towards the fort (19thC), the **Rousses Lake**★ and the Risoux Forest (partly in Switzerland).   ☐

Practical Information

⚡ 1120-1680m.
ⓘ pl. Pasteur, ☎ 84.60.02.55.

Hotels :
★★★ *France*, 323, rue Pasteur, ☎ 84.60.01.45, 34 rm Ⓟ
⑱ closed 1-25 Jun, 1 Nov-17 Dec, 240. Rest. ● ♦♦
⫽ Light, inventive fare for food-loving skiers : *ravioles d'escargots, volailles de Bresse*, Jura wines, 100-160.
★★ *Auberge du Vivier* (L.F.), 70, rte du Vivier, Bois d'Amont, 10 km NE, ☎ 84.60.93.00, AE Euro Visa, 12 rm Ⓟ ⑱ ⬙ pens, half pens, closed 4-30 Apr, 1 Oct-5 Dec, 220. Rest. ♦ ⟨ 80-150.
★★ *Le Chamois*, ☎ 84.60.01.48, Visa, 12 rm Ⓟ ⬙ pens, closed May-Oct, 400. Rest. ♦ ⟨ 50-100.
★★ *Relais des Gentianes* (L.F.), ☎ 84.60.50.64, AE DC Euro Visa, 14 rm Ⓟ ⑱ 160. Rest. ● ♦ Hearty classic cuisine, 80-140.

Ⓐ ★★*Les Monts Jura* (70 pl), ☎ 84.60.01.63.

SAINT-CLAUDE

Lons-le-Saunier 60, Geneva 61, Paris 467 km
pop 14100 ⊠ 39200   B4

Saint-Claude lies along a terrace★ between the Bienne Gorges and Tacon. Diamond-cutting and pipe-making are the main industrial activities.

► **Cathedral**★ : 14th-15thC with 18thC façade; vestige of a famous abbey with noteworthy choir stalls★★ and altarpiece★. ► **Pipes exhibition** *(left of cathedral; 9:30-11:30 & 2-6:30, Jun.-Sep.)*; **display of precious stones** *(next door, same hours).* ► Nearby, **church of Saint-Lupicin**★ *(12 km W)*; **chapel of Saint-Romain** *(view over the Bièvre Valley; 15 km W).*   ☐

Tobacco pipes

The use of tobacco pipes spread throughout France with tobacco, imported from the New World, beginning in the 16thC and achieving wide popularity by the 18thC. Since 1854, craftsmen at Saint-Claude have turned stems and bowls of briar-root imported from the Mediterranean basin. Measurement, rough-cutting, drilling, trueing, counter-sinking and grinding are the major manufacturing operations in the production of 3 million pipes per year.

Practical Information

SAINT-CLAUDE
ⓘ 1, av. de Belfort, ☎ 84.45.34.24.
SNCF ☎ 84.45.03.05.

Hotels :
★★ *Au Retour de la Chasse* (L.F.), Villard-Saint-Sauveur, 5 km S., ☎ 84.45.44.44, AE DC Euro Visa, 14 rm Ⓟ ⟨ ⑱ ⬙ ⯑ closed Sun eve and Mon, 26 Apr-6 Jun, 160. Rest. ♦ ⫽ Copious regional fare : *mousse de saumon frais, escalope jurassienne, poularde au côte du jura*, 55-150.
★★ *Saint-Hubert*, 3, pl. St-Hubert, ☎ 84.45.10.70, 30 rm Ⓟ closed 15-31 Dec, 150.

Nearby

Le MARTINET, ⊠ 39200 Saint-Claude, 3 km S.

Hotel :
● ★★ *Joly* (L.F.), ☎ 84.45.12.36, Visa, 16 rm ℙ ≼ ⋘ ⬟
⬚ closed Sun eve and Mon (l.s.), Nov-Jan, 180. Rest. ◆◆
≼ ♪ ⬟ ⬚ Nice, quiet establishment; the cooking is tame,
but well done. Spec : *soufflé de brochet au coulis d'écrevisses, coq au vin jaune d'Arbois*, 80-150.

SAINT-LAURENT-EN-GRANDVAUX

Lons-le-Saunier 46, Pontarlier 60, Paris 448 km
pop 1813 ⊠ 39150
B4

Saint-Laurent (alt. 908 m) is the main settlement of
the Grandvaux plateau; zinc has replaced the wood-
en panels that used to protect the houses from the
weather. In times gone by, the *rouliers* used to leave
here in the autumn to carry local products all over
France on their carts; in the spring they returned to
work on the land.

▶ Saint-Laurent is a base for exploring the wooded mountains of the Crête de la Joux-Devant, the Mont Noir Forest
and the Pic de l'Aigle (→ Hérisson Falls). ▶ Lake Abbaye
(7 km SW) : private property; aquatic sports for a fee.
▶ 9 km on the other side of the Savine Pass (alt. 991 m),
Morbier which gave its name to a cheese now produced at Morez (→).   ⬚

Practical Information _____

Hotel :
★★★★ *Moulin des Truites Bleues* (C.H.), ☎ 84.60.83.03,
Tx 360443, AE DC Visa, 20 rm ℙ ≼ ⋘ ⬟ ♪ 400. Rest. ◆◆
≼ ♪ Spec : *filet de bœuf à la jurassienne*, 105-200.

⚐ ★★*Champ-de-Mars* (100 pl), ☎ 84.60.87.21.

SALINS-LES-BAINS*

Besançon 45, Lons-le-Saunier 52, Paris 411 km
pop 4180 ⊠ 39110
B3

On the right bank of the river Furieuse and, until the
19thC, deriving its prosperity from salt. Salt production in turn gave rise to a wood industry. The town's
prosperity was defended by the Belin and Saint-
André★ forts, the remains of which are visible. The
warm springs (spa) and pleasant surroundings attract
tourists.

▶ To the E, church of St. Anatoile (13thC Cistercian
Gothic) overlooks the town. ▶ The main monuments are
the Hôtel de Ville (town hall, 18thC), chapel of Notre-
Dame-la-Libératrice (17thC) and the infirmary (17thC); **salt
springs★★★** comparable to those at Arc-et-Senans (→)
(9-12 & 2-6 year round) : 12thC galleries; old boilers and
machinery. ▶ Pretty villages of **Aresches, Fonteny** and
Cernans *(SE)*.   ⬚

The vale of SAÔNE*

A2, B1-2

The river Saône winds through a wooded valley below
the Vosges, where glazed tiles gleam on square-
topped bell towers. The water still serves 18thC washhouses in agricultural villages, which date largely from
the reconstruction following the 30 Years' War (18thC).
From north to south :

▶ At **Passavant-la-Rochère** : the oldest glass-blowing
works in France, founded in 1475 and still in use *(2:30-6,
May-Oct.; closed Sun. and Aug.)*. ▶ **Jonvelle** : archaeological and agricultural museum near the Roman baths *(2-6
daily, Jul.-15 Sep.; Sun., nat. hols. rest of year)*; remains
of a 15thC château and 12th-16thC church with Renais-

sance doorway; bridge. **Jussey** (pop. 2 180), on the
Amance : 18thC church and fountains. **Noroy-les-Jussey :**
archaeological excavations. **Blondefontaine** *(6 km NW)* :
18thC octagonal church. ▶ **Faverney** (pop. 1 116) :
entombment of Christ (15thC) in the church, formerly part
of an abbey : Romanesque nave, 13thC porch, Flamboyant Gothic choir, apse. **Saint-Rémy** *(N) :* regional hospital in the 18thC château. ▶ **Port-sur-Saône** (pop. 2 650) :
best stopover in the Saône Valley, good leisure facilities. ▶ 18thC churches at **Scey-sur-Saône** and **Rupt-sur-
Saône** (medieval keep). ▶ **Ray-sur-Saône** : 17 th-18thC
château in a park (furniture, weapons; *ext. visit only*);
church with 16thC furnishings. ▶ SE of **Fresne-Saint-
Mamès** (recreation area) : former abbey de La Charité
(Louis XVI château); village of **Fondremand** : keep, old
houses, 12th-14thC church. ▶ **Gray** (→).   ⬚

Practical Information _____

COMBEAUFONTAINE, ⊠ 70120, 12 km W of **Port-sur-
Saône** on the N 19.

Hotel :
★★ *Balcon* (L.F.), rte de Paris, ☎ 84.92.11.13, 26 rm ℙ
⋘ ⬚ closed Sun eve and Mon (l.s.), 26 Dec-15 Jan, 150.
Rest. ◆◆ ♪ 65-160.

PORT-SUR-SAÔNE, ⊠ 70170, 12 km from **Vesoul.**
ⓘ mairie, ☎ 84.91.50.18.
SNCF ☎ 84.91.50.50.

Hotel :
★ *Pomme d'Or* (L.F.), 1, rue St-Valère, ☎ 84.91.52.66,
Euro Visa, 9 rm ℙ ≼ closed Mon eve, 22 Aug-15 Sep,
100. Rest. ◆ ♪ closed Mon, 55-80.

Restaurant :
◆◆◆ *Château de Vauchoux*, (I.L.A.), rte de la Vallée-de-
la-Saône, à 3 km, ☎ 84.91.53.55, Tx 361476, AE DC Euro
Visa ≼ ⋘ ♪ ⬚ ⬚ closed Mon and Tue , Feb. Tennis court.
Louis XV, used to visit here. He would surely approve of
the quality fish and shellfish served in the dining-room.
Fine cellar, 140-350.

⚐ ★★★*Municipal* (130 pl), ☎ 84.91.51.32.

VESOUL

Besançon 47, Belfort 64, Paris 450 km
pop 20200 ⊠ 70000
B1

Vesoul, around the curve of La Motte (panorama★)
the Prefecture of Haute-Saône, blends thriving
modern industry with an old town.

▶ Old houses and mansions grouped around the **church
of St. Georges** (Classical style with cupola, 18thC; furnishings, 16thC statues) in a new pedestrian precinct.
▶ Rue des Ursulines, **G. Garret Museum** *(daily ex Tue.
2-6)* : local archaeology, paintings. ▶ Former hospital
(17thC) and fortified medieval gateway to the N.

Nearby

▶ W, **Lake Vaivre;** Roman camp of Cita; then *(12 km by
D13, left)* the **Baignes forges** (18thC). ▶ S, the Rocher de
la Baume and the Solborde Grotto. ▶ On a promontory,
château de Filain (15th-16thC) : handsome Renaissance
interiors (overmantels; *14 Jul.-Aug., daily 10-12 & 2-7;
Easter-Oct., Sat., Sun.*).   ⬚

Practical Information _____

ⓘ rue des Bains, ☎ 84.75.43.66.
SNCF ☎ 84.76.50.50.
🚌 pl. de la Gare, ☎ 84.76.05.44.
Car rental : *Avis*, 4, bd des Alliés, ☎ 84.76.18.48.

Hotels :
★★★ *Nord*, 5, rue de l'Aigle-Noir, ☎ 84.75.02.56, AE DC
Euro Visa, 36 rm ℙ ♪ ⬟ 170. Rest. ◆◆ ♪ ⬟ 80-150;
child : 35.

★★★ *Relais*, Rocade Ouest, N 19, rte de Paris,
☎ 84.76.42.42, AE DC Euro Visa, 24 rm ℙ ≼ ⋘ ⬟ closed

Sat and Sun in winter, 20 Dec-11 Jan, 200. Rest. ♦ ⍉
& 75-200.
** *Lion*, 4, pl. de la République, ☎ 84.76.54.44, 19 rm ℗
⌕ 175.

Recommended
Events : *horse racing*, at "Le Sabot", early Aug.

Lake VOUGLANS**

A-B4

The Ain was dammed in 1968 to form the third-largest reservoir in France (32 km long, 16 km²). The steep, wooded banks have been left in their natural state, except where two aquatic sports centres have been established.

▶ **La Pyle Bridge** *(D470; 2 km NW)* : pilgrim church of **St. Christophe** (12th-15thC), view over the N of the lake *(take D301 right).* ▶ **Maisod** : near château, a path above the lake. Farther on, the **Regardoir belvédère**★★ (lookout). ▶ S of the lake : view of the dam, 103 m high and 420 m wide ; the power station produces 235 million kWh per year. □

Ile-de-France

▶ When we think of a region, we think of a place united by geography or history, with its own special language and customs. The Ile-de-France is an exception to the rule, since its history, customs and language have merged with those of Paris, and spread throughout the whole country. The destiny of France was played out in the Ile-de-France, in the magnificent châteaux of Fontainebleau, Compiègne, Provins, Chantilly, Saint-Germain and Versailles. This "garden of the kings" is, in fact, made up of many smaller regions whose names — Valois, Beauvaisis, Vexin, Brie, Gatinais, Hurepoix — irresistibly evoke royal banners and the pageantry of past years. Despite urban sprawl and agricultural uniformity, they still retain much of their individuality.

Square bell-towers in gentle valleys under the everchanging sky, white silos on endless plains of wheat : subtle and harmonious countrysides painted and praised by Racine, La Fontaine, Corot and all the landscape painters. The region is a living museum : Gothic art was born here and there are hundreds of beautiful churches and cathedrals. Ile-de-France was populated early, and its clergy benefitted from the generosity of the great lords and the royal family. The magnificent châteaux of Chantilly, Fontainebleau and Versailles with its magnificent royal apartments and gardens, bring the history of France to life again. The cathedral of Chartres dominates the flat wheat-covered plains of Beauce and the mediaeval town at its feet. Its stained glass windows mark the apogee of an art which has never yet been transcended, nor even equalled.

Thanks to the royal penchant for hunting, Paris is surrounded by forests : Fontainebleau, Compiègne, Saint-Germain-en-Laye, which attract Parisians by the thousands every weekend. There are interesting walks and hundreds of little paths where lovers of all ages stroll down leafy avenues and breathe in the freshness of these green retreats from the big city. ☐

Don't miss

★★★ Chantilly C1, Chartres A3, Compiègne Forest C-D1, Écouen C2, Fontainebleau C3-4, Fontainebleau Forest C4, Vaux-le-Vicomte C3, Versailles B2.

★★Compiègne D1, Montfort-l'Amaury B3, Provins D3, Rambouillet Forest B3, Royaumont C2, Saint-Germain-en-Laye B2, Senlis C1, The Vexin Region B1-2.

★ Anet A2, Auvers-sur-Oise C2, Beauvais B1, Châteaudun A4, Château-Landon C4, Chevreuse Valley B3, Clermont C1, Crépy-en-Valois D1, Dourdan B3, Enghien C2, Étampes C3, Ferrières C2, Gallardon A3, Grand-Morin Valley C-D2, Illiers-Combray A4, Jouarre D2, Maintenon B3, Marly-le-Roi B2, Meaux D2, Milly-la-Forêt C4, Moret-sur-Loing D4, Noyon D1, Pierrefonds C-D1, Rambouillet B3, Saint-Germain Forest B2, Seine Valley C3-D4.

Weekend tips

Start your "17th Century Weekend" with a trip to Port-Royal. Lunch in the Chevreuse Valley and end the day at Vaux-le-Vicomte (candle-light tour on summer Saturdays). Versailles is an inexhaustible treasure-house; spend Sunday there. In the town you will find numerous good restaurants. In summer see the "Grandes Eaux" fountain displays.

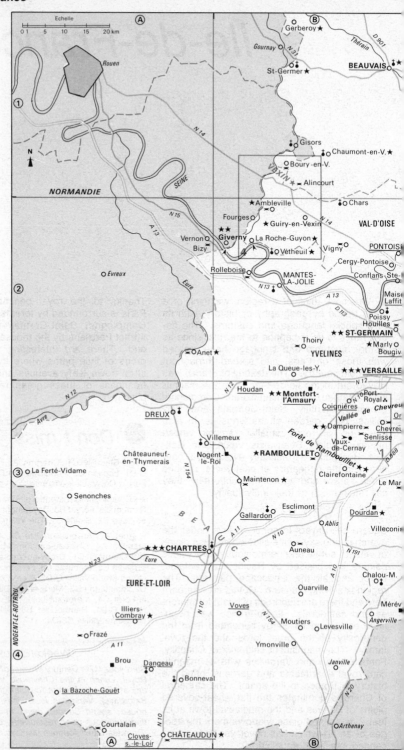

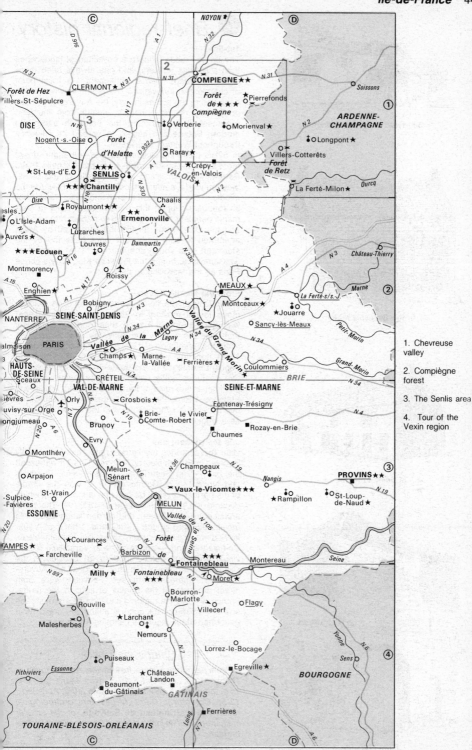

1. Chevreuse valley

2. Compiègne forest

3. The Senlis area

4. Tour of the Vexin region

Courtyard and out-buildings

In the Beauvais region

In Seine-et-Marne

Farm entrance

 Brief regional history

1st-5thC

The Ile-de-France is more a collection of landscapes than a definite territory, and has always been more of a crossroads than a settlement : a focal point of change and innovation. The population has never been tied to the soil as in, say, the Auvergne, Corsica or Brittany. ● Nevertheless, wealth from the land progressively transformed the **Frankish state** into **modern France** and helped to spread its influence throughout Western civilisation.

In 52BC Labienus, Julius Caesar's lieutenant, drove the Parisii (a Gaulish tribe) from the Grenelle Plain. Retreating to an island in the middle of the Seine, they founded a settlement called **Lutetia.** Towards the middle of the 4thC, this became known as Paris, after its founders. During this period, the **Franks** (a Germanic people) colonised the area between the Marne and the Oise rivers. In 451 the Huns, led by Attila, attempted to take Paris, but were deflected by the statecraft of a young shepherdess, later revered as St. Geneviève. In 508 the Frankish King **Clovis** chose Paris as the Merovingian capital.

From the Middle Ages...

The duchy of the Ile-de-France became an autonomous feudal territory in 987, when **Hugues Capet** was elected King of France, thus founding a dynasty that ruled the country with only one brief interruption (from the Revolution of 1789 to the end of the Empire, 1814) until the middle of the 19thC. ● The independent existence of the Ile-de-France continued for two centuries while reluctant vassals were brought into line, as the ruins of **feudal keeps** (e.g. Montlhéry, Étampes, Dreux, Pierrefonds) attest. In the 13thC, the duchy became synonymous with the French kingdom as a whole.

...to the present day

Over the centuries the Ile-de-France has been vitally involved in French history. ● In the 12thC it witnessed the birth — at Saint-Denis, Paris, Senlis, Beauvais and Noyon — of **Gothic art.** ● It was the cradle of the northern French tongue (the *langue d'oïl*), which became the official language in 1537. ● The great architecture of châteaux and garden landscapes was developed here in the 17thC and 18thC, at Vaux-le-Vicomte, Saint-Germain, Chantilly, Fontainebleau, Compiègne, and — above all — at Versailles. ● The visual revolution behind modern art evolved in the villages of Barbizon, Argenteuil, Bougival and Auvers-sur-Oise; Impressionism and Fauvism were both direct products of the quality of light in the Ile-de-France. ● Only the region's situation as a crossroads and a melting-pot for cultural influences could have generated these vigorous historical movements.

Safaris start here

African big game roams free in the reserve park at **Thoiry** *(10-6, Apr.-Oct.; 10-5, Nov.-Mar.), as well as in the wooded park at* **Saint-Vrain** *(10-6, Apr.-Sep.; 12-5, Oct.-Mar.). Don't forget the ornithological reserve at the* **Château de Sauvage**, *or the smaller indigenous wildlife in the forest of Rambouillet at* **Clairefontaine.**

● *Practical information*

Information : Ile-de-France : *Comité Régional de Tourisme (C.R.T.),* 137, rue de l'Université, 75007 Paris, ☎ (1) 47.53.79.93. **Essonne :** *Comité Départemental du Tourisme (C.D.T.),* Immeuble Bineaux Evry II, 523, les Terrasses de l'Agora, 91000 Evry, ☎ (1) 64.97.35.13. **Eure-et-Loir :** *C.D.T.,* 19, pl. des Épars, B.P. 67, 28000 Chartres, ☎ 37.21.39.99. **Oise :** *C.D.T.,* 1, rue Villiers-de-L'Isle-Adam, B.P. 222, 60008 Beauvais Cedex, ☎ (1) 44.45.82.12. **Seine-et-Marne :** *C.D.T.,* château Soubiran, av. H.-Barbusse, 77190 Dammarie-les-Lys, ☎ (1) 64.37.19.36. **Val-d'Oise :** *C.D.T.* 2, av. du Parc, le Campus, 95000 Cergy-Pontoise, ☎ (1) 34.43.30.30. **Yvelines :** *C.D.T.,* Hôtel du Dpt, 2, pl. André-Mignot, 78012 Versaille Cedex, ☎ 39.02.78.78, ext 3122. **Oise :** rue Villiers-de-l'Ile-Adam, 60000 Beauvais, ☎ 44.45.13.82. *Dir. rég. de la Jeunesse et des Sports,* 6-8, rue Eugène-Oudiné, 75013 Paris, ☎ (1) 45.84.12.05. *Dir. rég. des Affaires culturelles,* Grand Palais, porte C, av. Franklin-D.-Roosevelt, 75008 Paris, ☎ (1) 42.25.11.40.

S.O.S. : Eure-et-Loir : *SAMU* (Emergency Medical Service), ☎ 17. *Poisoning Emergency Centre* (Tours), ☎ 47.66.15.15. **Oise** and **Essonne :** *SAMU,* ☎ 17. **Val-d'Oise :** *SAMU,* ☎ 15. *Poisoning Emergency Centre* (Paris) : **Oise, Essonne, Val-d'Oise, Yvelines, Seine-et-Marne,** ☎ (1) 42.05.63.29.

Weather forecast : Essonne : ☎ (1) 60.84.65.81. **Eure-et-Loir :** ☎ 37.21.28.24. **Oise :** ☎ 44.45.27.90. **Seine-et-Marne :** ☎ 64.37.14.29. **Val-d'Oise :** ☎ (1) 30.31.23.39. **Yvelines :** ☎ (1) 36.32.29.98.

Farmhouse gites and chambres d'hôtes : *Gîtoise, Relais dép. des Gîtes ruraux de l'Oise,* B.P. 222, 60008 Beauvais Cedex, ☎ 44.48.16.87. *Relais dép. des Gîtes ruraux de Seine-et-Marne :* C.D.T. Seine-et-Marne. *Relais dép. des Gîtes ruraux d'Eure-et-Loir,* Loisirs-Accueil Eure-et-Loire, at the *C.D.T.;* Yvelines at the *C.D.T.;* Essonne at the *C.D.T.*

Camping car rental : Eure-et-Loir : *Auto Sport* 28, route du Houdan, 28210 Faverolles, ☎ 37.51.90.66. **Oise :** *Icare,* R.N. 16, Couffry, 60290 Rantigny, ☎ 44.73.33.86. **Seine-et-Marne :** *G.S.O. Loisirs,* 77330 Ozoir-la-Ferrière, ☎ (1) 60.28.04.00. **Yvelines :** *Fernand Criton International,* La Maison Blanche, 78121 Crespières, ☎ (1) 30.56.51.51. **Essonne :** *Palmas Location,* 274, rue de Paris, 91120 Palaiseau, ☎ (1) 60.14.45.45. **Val-d'Oise :** *Citer,* 117-121, bd Jean-Allemane, 95100 Argenteuil, ☎ (1) 49.80.37.73.

Festivals and events : Apr : *Auturae musicae concerts* in Dreux; *wine and cheese fair* in Coulommiers. **May :** *Ile-de-France festival* (concerts, events in châteaux, gardens); *lily-of-the-valley festival* in Fontainebleau; **May-Jun :** *music festivals* in Fontainebleau, Meaux, Provins; le Perche, Royaumont; *architecture and jazz festivals* in Fontainebleau. **Jun :** *music festival* in Blandy-les-Tours; *festivals* in Versailles; *boatmen's pardon* in Conflans-Sainte-Honorine; *mediaeval week* in Moret-sur-Loing; *mediaeval games and book fair* in Provins; *rose festival* in Brie-Comte-Robert; *daisy festival* in Le Vésinet. **Jul :** *summer festival* in Chartres; *fête des Loges* in Saint-Germain-en-Laye; *old-fashioned threshing* in Saint-Victor-de-Buthon. **Aug :** *organ recitals* in Chartres cathedral; *harvest festival* in Provins. **Sep :** *night festivals* in Versailles; *international cello festival* in Nemours; *September rendez-vous* in Senlis; *tomato fair* in Montlhéry; *bean fair* in Arpajon; *carrot festival* in Croissy-sur-Seine. **Oct :** *riding festival* in Rambouillet; *Paris-Versailles foot race.* **Nov :** *humour festival in Meaux.* **Dec :** *annual poultry competition* in Égreville.

Rambling : GR 1, 2, 11, 12, 13, 14, 14A, 22, 26, 32, 35, 111, 122, 123 cross the Ile-de-France region. *Topoguides* nos 1, 2, 11, 111, 12, 13, 14A, 14, 32, 35. *I.G.N. maps*

The glory of the cathedrals

Gothic art was sired by invention out of necessity. The need was for larger and lighter churches to accommodate growing populations and to exalt the faith. The invention was the ogive vault, which redistributed the thrust of the classic Romanesque vault, enabling windows and openings to be more easily introduced. This new architectural technique made its first timid appearance in France at Morienval around 1125, in the wake of early developments in Lombardy and England. The architects of the Ile-de-France initiated the series of great cathedrals that were to symbolise the enthusiastic faith of the Middle Ages. All the arts were involved in this creative explosion : Gothic sculpture appeared at Chartres in 1145 and was perfected at Senlis with the invention of the statue column; Chartres alone demonstrates that stained glass achieved its most brilliant expression in the Gothic era : the blues have never been reproduced or repeated elsewhere.

Ile-de-France : a painter's landscape

The Ile-de-France assumed an important place in the history of painting at the beginning of the 19thC, when the landscape was finally recognised as a fit subject in its own right, rather than a mere backdrop. In 1830, at the age of 34, Camille Corot moved to Barbizon and set up his easel in the forest of Fontainebleau. He was fascinated by the light filtering through the woods, and by the lakes of Ville-d'Avray and Mortefontaine. The artists who followed — Rousseau, Diaz, Ziem, Troyon, and Millet — eventually became known as the Barbizon School. In 1871 Cézanne and Pissarro settled in Pontoise; Renoir, Monet, Sisley and Degas worked in Louveciennes and Argenteuil. The landscape movement lasted 10 years, until Cézanne left for Provence and Renoir for Algeria and Italy; Sisley moved to Moret and Monet to Giverny. Sixty years after Corot led the way into the Ile-de-France, Van Gogh committed suicide in front of his easel at Auvers-sur-Oise. Painting had entered the 20th century.

Facts and figures

The Ile-de-France described here for visitors is not identical with the administrative region of that name : strictly speaking the Oise belongs to Picardy, Eure-et-Loir to the centre; only Essonne, Seine-et-Marne and Yvelines, together with Paris and its peripheral departments, fall within the administrative boundaries of the Ile-de-France.
Essonne : 1820 km², pop. 997 522 (543/km²). Prefecture : Évry.
Yvelines : 2284 km², pop. 1 211 521 (524/km²). Prefecture : Versailles.
Seine-et-Marne : 5915 km², pop. 901 593 (150/km²). Prefecture : Melun.
Oise : 5857 km², pop. 675 172 (103/km²). Prefecture : Beauvais.
Eure-et-Loir : 5879 km², pop. 370 952 (63/km²). Prefecture : Chartres.

n°s 401 (Fontainebleau), 402 (Rambouillet), 403 (Compiègne), 404 (Chantilly), 418 (Val-d'Oise), 413, 419. Brochures suggesting various ramble roads are published by the Essonne, Oise, Seine-et-Marne and Yvelines *C.D.T.*, and the *Assn dép. de Tourisme pédestre d'Eure-et-Loir*, at the *C.D.T. Délégation régionale de l'Ile-de-France des Sentiers et de la Randonnée pédestre*, 64, rue de Gergovie, 75014 Paris, ☎ (1) 45.45.31.02.

Riding holidays : A.R.T.E.I.F. : *Association Régionale de Tourisme Equestre de l'Ile-de-France*, 15, rue de Bruxelles, 75009 Paris, ☎ (1) 48.74.53.15. **Eure-et-Loir** : *Assn Randonneurs équestres*, M. Chary, château Javersy, 28300 Coltainville, ☎ 37.31.69.64. **Oise** : *C.D.T. Equestre de l'Oise*, ☎ 44.45.82.12. Week-end outings on donkeys, enq. and reservations : M. Bonnard, 60138 Chiry-Ourscamp, ☎ 44.76.98.29.

Horse-drawn holidays : *Assn d'attelage*, M. Decourty, Villars, Châtillon-en-Dunois, 28290 Arrou. *Le Clermontel*, RN 31, Agnetz, 60600 Clermont, ☎ 44.50.09.90.

Cycling holidays : the S.N.C.F. publishes a brochure "16 Promenades à vélo en Yvelines, Eure, Eure-et-Loir, Oise avec parcours d'approche en train", which suggests interesting roads. Enq. : ☎ (1) 42.61.50.50. *R.E.R.* bicycle hire in Saint-Germain-en-Laye. *S.N.C.F.* bicycle hire in Chartres, Dreux, Esbly, Fontainebleau, Gretz-Armainvilliers, La Ferté-sous-Jouarre, La Loupe, Maintenon, Nogent-le-Rotrou, Rambouillet, Ballancourt, Dourdan, Étampes, Montsoult, Pontoise, *Comité Départemental de cyclotourisme*, 11, rue de Mignières, 28360 Dammarie. The *Comité régional de Tourisme et des Loisirs* and the *Bicy-Club de France* publish a booklet of 10 roads in the Ile-de-France region. The **Yvelines, Essonne, Eure-et-Loir** and **Oise** *C.D.T.* have organised touristic cycling itineraries.

River and canal cruises : *Péniche Amour*, 77920 Samoissur-Seine, ☎ (1) 64.24.66.99. Canal cruises : *Quiztour*, 19, rue d'Athènes, 75009 Paris, ☎ (1) 48.74.75.30. *B.N.A.L.*, B.P. 27, 60150 Longueil-Annel, ☎ 44.76.18.80. *Vedettes du Val de Seine*, 5, quai du Loing, 77670 Saint-Mammes, ☎ 60.70.52.73.

Technical tourism : **Yvelines** : *Renault* in Flins, ☎ 34.74.72.72; *Talbot* in Poissy, ☎ 39.65.40.00; *Rochas* Perfumes in Poissy, ☎ 30.74.92.92; *C.V.S. Radio* in Versailles, ☎ 30.21.44.44; *Automatic postal sorting centre* in Trappes, ☎ 30.43.81.37.

Handicraft courses : leather-work and tanning in Combres; weaving, painting on silk in Rebais, Samoissur-Seine, Héricy; enq. : *C.D.T. Seine-et-Marne*.

Other courses : introduction to theatre and video : *Forum de la Madeleine*, mail J.-Dunois, 28000 Chartres, ☎ 37.35.08.83; Video programming and audio-visual, *Crear*, near Chantilly (*C.D.T. Oise*); introduction to horse-back-riding : *Centre équestre du Carillon*, rue de la Vallée-de-l'Eure, 28600 Luisant, ☎ 37.34.74.24; *Centre équestre de Recloses-Fontainebleau* (*C.D.T. Seine-et-Marne*); other centres : *C.D.T. Eure-et-Loir;* introduction to nature : *Atelier Vert*, 77300 Fontainebleau, ☎ 60.72.38.92; courses in cooking, programming, music, enq. : *C.D.T. Oise*.

Archery courses : Enq. at Eure-et-Loire *L.A.*

Leisure centers : Amusement parks : *la Vallée des Peaux-Rouges* (Red-skin Valley), N. of Senlis, at Fleurines, ☎ 44.54.10.66. *Mer de sable* at Ermenonville, ☎ 44.54.00.96. Zoological and recreation park at Thoiry, ☎ 34.87.40.67. *Mirapolis* amusement park in Cergy-Pontoise, ☎ 34.22.11.11.

Golf : Bertichères (9 holes), Bois-le-Roi (6), Brétigny (9), Chaumont-en-Vexin (18), Chantilly (9, 18), Compiègne (18), Le Coudray (9, 18), Chevry (9), Fontainebleau (18), Fourqueux (3 × 9), Lamorlaye (9, 18), Mortefontaine (18), Ormesson (18), Ozoir-la-Ferrière (9, 18), Plaisir (9), Le Prieuré à Sailly (18), Rochefort (18), Saint-Germain-en-Laye (18), Saint-Nom-la-Bretèche (18), Saint-Quentin-en-Yvelines (18), Seraincourt (18), Torcy-Vaires-Saint-Rémy-de-la-Vame, Versailles (18), Vilennes (18), Villeray (18).

Aquatic sports : numerous aquatic centres. Enq. : *Ligue régionale de Voile*, M. Devesa, B.P. 5, Le Mesnil-le-Roi, 78600 Maison-Laffitte, ☎ (1) 39.62.93.53, and *C.D.T.* In the Oise, wind-surfing is allowed on the stretches of water of Canada, Beauvais, Therdonne, Saint-Leu-d'Esserent and Verberie. List of expanses of water available from *C.D.T.* Sailing week-ends organized by the *Association Percheronne d'Activités Nautiques;* enq. : *L.A.* Eure-et-Loir.

Forests

The numerous forests around Paris owe their existence to the royal predilection for hunting. The forests were formerly maintained as game reserves and most still shelter a large number and variety of game birds and animals. The best-known forests are Fontainebleau, Compiègne, Rambouillet and Chantilly, but the Oise, Ermenonville, L'Isle-Adam, Carnelle, Villers-Cotterêts, Halatte, Dreux-Anet, and Hez-Froidmont are pleasant diversions. Foresters from the Office National des Forêts (O.N.F.) will willingly guide you. The forests deserve their title of poumons verts (green lungs) : over a year 1 ha (2.5 acres) of beech filters 80 tons of dust (vs. 30 tons for the same area of spruce).

Canoeing, kayak : *Club Bonnevalais*, Moulin du Pont leisure centre, 28800 Bonneval, ☎ 37.47.48.59 or 37.47.56.14. *Piscine des Vauroux*, 28300 Mainvilliers, ☎ 37.21.68.90. Courses offered by the *L.A.* Eure-et-Loir.

Climbing : most of the climbing roads are in La Ferté-Alais region, Fontainebleau Forest, the massif des Trois-Pignons, and the area from Malesherbes to Nemours. Group excursions, discovery and beginners' courses, are organised by the *Club Alpin Français, Touring Club de France, F.S.G.T.*, 31, av. C.-Vellefaux, 75010 Paris, ☎ (1) 42.01.82.00, and the *Groupe Universitaire de Montagne*, 12, rue du Moulin-Vert, 75014 Paris, ☎ (1) 45.43.48.37.

Flying, gliding and ballooning : *Assn. aéronautique de Coulommiers*, 6, av. C.-Bernard, 77320 La Ferté-Gaucher. *Assn. aéronautique de Meaux*, aérodrome Coulmiers-Voisins, 77120 Coulommiers; *Centre de vol à voile de Fontainebleau*, aérodrome de Moret-Episy, 77250 Moret-sur-Loing. Glider : *Bruno Bonnevaux*. Old planes : Cerny-La Ferté-Allais. *Centre aéronautique de Beynes* and the *Centre de jeunesse fédéral de vol à voile de la Région parisienne*, aérodrome, 78650 Beynes. *Assn. aéronautique du Val-d'Essonne*, B.P. 31, 91490 Milly-la-Forêt. *Assn. aéronautique du Val-d'Oise*, aérodrome de Chérence, 95510 Vétheuil. *Centre de parachutisme sportif Paris-Ile-de-France*, 77320 La Ferté-Gaucher. Aéroclub de Chartres, ☎ 37.34.43.48; Baineau Armenonville, ☎ 37.31.40.26.

Fishing : *Féd. dép. des Assn. de Pêche et de Pisciculture*, **Seine-et-Marne** : 13, rue des Fossés, 77000 Melun, ☎ 64.39.03.08. **Yvelines** : 19, rue du Dr-Roux, 78520 Limay, ☎ (1) 34.77.58.90. **Eure-et-Loir** : M. Seigneuret, 11, rue des Demoiselles, 28200 Châteaudun, ☎ 37.45.42.40. **Oise** : 10, rue Pasteur, 60200 Compiègne, ☎ (1) 44.40.46.41. **Val-d'Oise** : 19, rue des Coteaux, 95300 Pontoise, ☎ (1) 30.38.39.33. **Essonne** : 10, rue de la Tuilerie, 91100 Corbeil-Essonne, ☎ (1) 60.75.14.63. *Plaisance sur Seine*, chemin de la Varenne, 77870 Vulaines-sur-Seine, ☎ 64.23.71.87; you may have your trout or salmon catch prepared at the adjoining restaurant.

Hunting and shooting : *Féd. dép. des Chasseurs d'Eure-et-Loir : maison de l'Agriculture*, 28000 Chartres, ☎ 37.34.52.09. *Féd. Interdép. des chasseurs des Yvelines*, 16, rue Vignon, 75009 Paris, ☎ (1) 47.42.91.53.

Towns and places

ANET*

Dreux 16, Chartres 50, Paris 80 km
pop 2430 ⊠ 28260   A2

The damaged but still majestic late Renaissance **château★** of Diane de Poitiers (1499-1566 ; Henri II's mistress) was the crowning achievement of the architect Philibert Delorme. The most distinguished artists of the time, including Cellini and Goujon, contributed to the decoration. ▶ The one remaining wing was much modified during the 17thC, as was the funerary chapel★ *(Apr.-Oct., 2:30-6:30; Sun. and hols. 10-11:30 & 2:30-6:30; Nov.-Mar., Sat. pm, Sun.; closed Tue.).*

Eure Valley *(22 km from Anet to Dreux).*

▶ **Ezy-sur-Eure** : Gothic bridge. ▶ **Château de Sorel** (ruins) : Renaissance doorway. ▶ On the other bank of the river : disused 12thC abbey of **Breuil-Benoist** in light, golden stone, standing in a huge clearing; Louis XIII abbey manor *(visits on request).* ▶ **Saint-Georges-Motel** : château (also Louis XIII ; *no visitors*) hidden in parkland. ▶ **Louye** : church and château.   □

Practical Information ─────────────
ANET

Hotel :
★ *Auberge de la Rose* (L.F.), 6, rue Ch.-Lechevrel, ☎ 37.41.90.64, Visa, 6 rm ⌕ 100. Rest. ♦♦ ⸴ ⌕ closed Mon, Thu, Sun eve , Feb and Aug, 70-150.

Nearby
BERCHÈRES-SUR-VESGRES, ⊠ 28560, 8 km E.

Hotel :
● ★★★★(L) *Château de Berchères*, (C.H., R.S.), 18, rue du Château, ☎ 37.82.07.21, Tx 780684, AE DC Euro Visa, 32 rm ℗ ⸕ ⌘ ⚲ ⸴ ᠵ closed Aug, 24 Dec-1 Jan. Château Louis XV, 420. Rest. ♦♦ ⸴ ᠵ Spec : *filet de sole Berchères*, 145-215.

ÉZY-SUR-EURE, ⊠ 27530, 2 km NW.

Restaurant :
● ♦♦ *Maître Corbeau*, pl. du Marché, ☎ 37.64.73.29, AE DC Euro Visa ℗ ⌘ ᠵ ⸜ closed Tue eve and Wed, 6 Jan-4 Feb. The garden is a delight in fine weather, but all year round, the tables are prettily laid and the service is refined. Cooking with character : *canard sauvage aux chanterelles*, 175-210.

ARPAJON

Etampes 19, Paris 22, Rambouillet 41 km
pop 8000 ⊠ 91290   C3

Heart of the French bean-growing country, marred by traffic, but with beautiful 17thC **covered market;** market-day Friday.

Nearby
▶ **Semouille Valley**
▶ **Arpajon.** ▶ **Montlhéry** : famous race track. Fine view from the **Tour de Montlhéry** *(Easter-Oct., 10-12 & 2-6, 4:30 off season; closed Thu., Fri.);* old quarter : 15thC Baudry gate. ▶ **Longpont-sur-Orge** : basilica★ (12th-13thC). ▶ **Château de Marcoussis** : keep, foundations. ▶ **Château de St-Jean-de-Beauregard★** (Louis XIII ; *15 Mar.-15 Nov., Sun. and hols., 2-6*) : 17thC vegetable garden. ▶ **Courson** *(9 km W)* : château originally built by Guillaume de Lamoignon. Gardens★ repre-

sent the French idea of an English park *(15 Mar.-15 Nov., 2-6 Sun. and hols.).*

Remarde Valley★ *(26 km from Arpajon to Saint-Arnoult).*

▶ Winds among rustic villages and elegant châteaux W of **Arpajon.** ▶ **Château du Marais★** : Louis XVI structure fronted by a mirror-like lake *(15 Mar.-15 Nov., Sun. and nat. hols., 2-6:30).* ▶ **Saint Cyr-sous-Dourdan** : fortified farmhouse and 13thC church. ▶ **Rochefort-en-Yvelines**, on a hillside : old houses, town hall in 18thC prison. Château (1900), copy of the Palace of the Legion of Honour in Paris. ▶ **Saint-Arnoult** : Romanesque church modified in 15thC ; panelled vaulting ; murals. ▶ Dourdan road runs through an oak forest.   □

AUVERS-SUR-OISE*

Pontoise 7, Paris 22, Beauvais 49 km
pop 5700 ⊠ 95430   C2

A pretty town on a slope above the river Oise, forever associated with the Dutch Impressionist painter Vincent Van Gogh (1853-90) : the room where he died ; in the cemetery, his tomb next to that of his brother Theo ; monument by Zadkine ; the church *(painted by Van Gogh)* mingles Gothic and Renaissance styles (12th, 13th, 16thC).   □

BARBIZON

Fontainebleau 10, Etampes 40, Paris 60 km
pop 1270 ⊠ 77630   C3

Village in the forest of Fontainebleau (→), once fashionable among the followers of the landscape painters Théodore Rousseau (1812-67) and Jean-François Millet (1814-75) who used to gather at the **Auberge du Père Ganne.** Unfortunately, the village is now over-commercialised but the Auberge (now a museum : *Apr.-Oct., 10-5:30 ex Tue.)* and Millet's former studio are worth a visit ; small museum in converted barn (formerly Rousseau's *atelier*). The artists' tombs are at **Chailly-en-Bière.**   □

Practical Information ─────────────
BARBIZON
🛈 41, rue Grande, ☎ (1) 60.66.41.87.

Hotels :
● ★★★★(L) *Bas Bréau* (R.C.), 22, rue Grande, ☎ (1) 60.66.40.05, Tx 690953, AE Euro Visa, 12 rm 7 apt ℗ ⸕ ⌘ ⚲ ᠵ closed 1 Jan-15 Feb. Magnificent garden setting, 950. Rest. ● ♦♦♦♦ ⸕ ⚲ An excellent place for a gastronomic summit meeting : *sole de petit bateau, poulet fermier en vessie*, 500.
● ★★★ *La Clé d'Or* (C.H.), 73, Grande Rue, ☎ (1) 60.66.40.96, Tx 692131, 15 rm ℗ ⌘ ⚲ closed Mon eve and Sun eve, 15 Nov-15 Dec, 200. Rest. ♦♦ ᠵ ⚲ Spec : house-smoked salmon, 130-250 ; child : 90.
★★★ *Les Pléiades*, 21, rue Grande, ☎ (1) 60.66.40.25, Tx 692131, 18 rm ℗ ⌘ ⚲ closed Feb, 240. Rest. ♦♦ ᠵ R. Karampournis has successfully salvaged this fine house : *homard et ris de veau au flan d'asperges*. Round-table dinners held monthly, 115-155.
● ★★ *Les Alouettes*, 4, rue A.-Barrye, ☎ (1) 60.66.41.98, Tx 692131, 23 rm ℗ ⸕ ⌘ ᠵ 190. Rest. ♦ ⸴ ᠵ 125-225 ; child : 75.

Restaurants :
♦♦♦ *Grand Veneur*, N 7, at the edge of the forest,

☎ (1) 60.66.40.44 Ⓟ closed Wed eve and Thu, Aug. Food spit-roasted before your eyes, 220-310.
◆◆ *Bistrot du Musée*, 86, Grande-Rue, ☎ (1) 60.66.41.71 ⚌ closed Mon and Tue, 1 Jan-1 Mar. A favourite gathering spot for singers, with a dinner-show every Thu, 75-100.
◆ *La Broche de Barbizon*, RN 7, ☎ (1) 60.66.40.76 Ⓟ closed Wed eve and Thu, 6-30 Jan. Spit-roasted ham and chicken, 80-120.
◆ *Le Relais de Barbizon*, 2, av. Ch.-de-Gaulle, ☎ (1) 60.66.40.28, Visa ⚌ ♪ closed Tue and Wed, 18-29 Aug, 23 Dec-8 Jan, 88-135.

Nearby

ARBONNE, ⊠ 77630 Barbizon, 5 km S.

Restaurant :
◆◆ *Le Petit Corne Biche*, 417, rue de la Libération, ☎ (1) 60.66.26.34, Visa ✦ ⚌ ♪ ٹ closed Tue and Wed, 17-27 Feb, 15 Aug-7 Sep. Spec : *ris de veau, saumon frais au citron vert*, 80-150.

CHAILLY-EN-BIÈRE, ⊠ 77960, 1 km N.

Restaurants :
◆◆ *Auberge de l'Empereur*, 27, rte de Paris ☎ (1) 60.66.43.38, AE DC Euro Visa Ⓟ ⚌ ⚲ ٹ closed Wed eve, Thu, Sun eve, 20 Jan-20 Feb, 17-25 Sep. Spec : *ragoût de fraise de veau aux pleurotes*, 70-200.
◆◆ *Auberge Le Chalet du Moulin*, N 7, ☎ (1) 60.66.43.42, AE Euro Visa Ⓟ ✦ ⚌ ⚲ ♪ ٹ closed Mon eve and Tue. Grills and roasts from the fireplace served in a lovely setting of greenery, 235.

The BEAUCE Plain

B4

The wide horizons of the Beauce plain roughly correspond to the Midwest cornbelt in the USA, with mechanised farming, straggling villages here and there (the Beauce was never densely populated) and occasional fortified farmsteads. Although wheat silos have replaced windmills, a few mills are still valued for their beauty and as reminders of an earlier way of life.

Around the windmills of Beauce *(130 km approx, full day)*

▶ Chartres (→). ▶ Moulin de Maisons : mill closed to visitors. ▶ Denonville fortress : rebuilt 16thC *(2-6, Jul.-Sep. ex Tue.).* ▶ Ouarville : 14thC mill *(Sat. and Sun. pm May-Sep. on request; tel. : 37.99.56.49).* ▶ Levesville-la-Chenard : 15thC mill *(pm on request; tel. : 37.47.59.97).* ▶ Moutiers-en-Beauce : working mill *(pm on request; tel. : 37.47.56.97).* ▶ Between the mills at Ymonville and Bazoche *(daily on request; tel. : 37.99.78.72)* : Villeprévost château *(S of D927),* a fine example of a gentleman's 18thC country house; small regional museum *(Jun.-Sep., 10-12 & 2-6:30, Sat. and nat. hols.; 2-6:30 Sun.).* ▶ Bois-de-Feugères : mill under repair *(tel. : 37.47.56.97).* ☐

BEAUVAIS*

Amiens 60, Rouen 80, Paris 76 km
pop 54000 ⊠ 60000
B1
Bombardments in 1940 virtually destroyed this mediaeval town. The airy cathedral★★ (loftiest choir in the world) was spared, even though the organ was wrecked by a direct hit. This was one of the most ambitious of Gothic cathedrals. The Gothic style here reached both its greatest beauty and its technical limits. Successive bishops struggled in vain for four centuries to complete the building, but were thwarted by lack of funds and structural collapses.

▶ Choir★ (13th-19thC) : the highest ever built (48m vaults), is supported by gigantic double flying buttresses; transept (finished in 16thC) : adorned with carvings★ by

Jean le Pot, *ca.* 1530. Tree of Jesse★ (genealogy of Christ) in N window (16thC). Astronomical clock (1868) copied from one in Strasbourg; 15th-16thC cloister; the lower transept (the original cathedral) dates from before the 10thC. ▶ At the extreme E end of the cathedral is the **National Gallery of Tapestry and Textile Arts** *(9:30-11:30 & 2-6, 10-11:30 & 2:30-4:30 off season; closed Mon. and nat. hols.),* exhibition of French tapestry from 15thC to present day. The Beauvais tapestry works, established by Jean-Baptiste Colbert (1619-83; Louis XIV's minister of finance), achieved their finest hour with designs by the painter Jean-Baptiste Oudry (1686-1755). In 1939 the workshops were evacuated to the Gobelins textile works in Paris, where they have remained ever since (temporary exhibitions). ▶ Former Episcopal Palace★ (late Gothic) : **museum** : statuary in stone and wood; paintings by Antoine Caron (1521-99) and Quentin Varin (1590-1634); Italian paintings; ceramics, regional archaeology, *art nouveau* and contemporary art *(10-12 & 2-6 ex Tue. and nat. hols.).* ▶ **Church of St. Étienne**, also built over several centuries : Romanesque nave, Flamboyant Gothic choir, 16th-18thC tower; interesting carvings at the N end; Renaissance statues and stained glass★★.

Also... ▶ Hôtel de Ville : 18thC façade. ▶ Voisinlieu : **Maladrerie St. Lazare** (former leper hospital) : **Marissel** : beautiful church (12thC bell-tower, 13thC choir, 16thC nave). ▶ On the last Sunday in June Beauvais commemorates the local heroine Jeanne Hachette who in 1472 led the resistance against the siege by Charles the Bold, Duke of Burgundy *(following Mon. is a holiday; museums closed).*

Nearby

▶ Churches at **Alonne** *(4 km S),* **Therdonne** *(5 km SW),* **Jouy-sous-Thelle★** *(17 km SW).* ▶ **Tillard** : quaint village. ▶ Milly-sur-Thérain : **château de Troissereux** *(Apr.-Nov., Sat. and Sun. pm).*

Drive through the Bray region★ *(65 km)*

▶ **Bray** is a patchwork of shady pastures in the midst of a wheat-growing plain. The area seems to have been lifted out of Normandy and transplanted to the Beauce, where it is kept green by the *river Thérain* (good angling; bordered by picturesque villages). ▶ **Beauvais.** ▶ **Gerberoy★** : formerly a walled town, now a delightful village of half-timbered houses covered with roses : 15thC church; 18thC town hall; terraced gardens★. ▶ **Saint-Germer-de-Fly★** : church of great architectural interest, transitional between Romanesque and Gothic (17thC façade and 18thC bell tower). Group of eight stone figures★ (17thC); the Gothic Sainte Chapelle is similar to the chapel of the same name in Paris. *(son et lumière the 1st Sat. Jun.-Sep.; musical week in Aug.).* ▶ Road to Beauvais : excellent views of the region. At **La Chapelle-aux-Pots** (museum : *4-7 Tue., Fri.; 10-12 Wed., Thu.),* **Armentières** and **Saint-Germain-la-Poterie**, potters continue the old local tradition. ☐

Practical Information

BEAUVAIS
ⓘ 6, rue Malherbe, ☎ 44.45.08.18; 1, rue St-Pierre, ☎ 44.45.25.26 (h.s.).
✈ Tillé, 4 km NE, ☎ 44.45.01.06.
SNCF ☎ 44.45.91.11.
🚌 rue du Warge, ☎ 44.48.08.47.
Car rental : *Avis*, 16, pl. des Halles, ☎ 44.45.03.04.

Hotels :
● ★★★ *Chenal*, (Inter-Hôtel), 63, bd du Gal-de-Gaulle, ☎ 44.45.03.55, Tx 145223, AE DC Euro Visa, 29 rm Ⓟ ⚌ ♪ films on video cassette shown nightly, 265.
★★ *La Résidence*, 24, rue Louis-Borel, ☎ 44.48.30.98, Euro Visa, 24 rm Ⓟ ⚲ closed Sun eve, 120.
★★ *Palais*, 9, rue St-Nicolas, ☎ 44.45.12.58, Euro Visa, 15 rm Ⓟ ⚲ ٹ 150.
★ *Normandie*, 20, rue de la Taillerie, ☎ 44.45.07.61, Visa, 12 rm Ⓟ closed Wed, 23 Dec-1 Feb, 150. Rest. ◆ ♪ Simple and good, 65-130.

Restaurant :
♦ *La Crémaillère*, 1, rue Gui-Patin, ☎ 44.45.03.13, Visa
🅿 ⌕ ♪ closed Tue eve and Wed ex advance reservation.
Spec : *ficelle picarde, tripes au cidre*. Terrace dining in
summer, 86-180.

⚊ ★★*Municipal* (100 pl), ☎ 44.02.00.22.

Recommended
Events : *fête de Jeanne Hachette*, last we in June.
Guided tours : *C.N.M.H.S.*, Sun May-Nov. Info S.I.

Nearby

FRAMICOURT, ⊠ 60430 Noailles, 16 km SE.

Restaurant :
♦♦ *Manoir de Framicourt*, ☎ 44.03.30.16, AE DC Euro
Visa ▦ ⌕ ♪ closed Wed, 26-31 Dec. Evenings by reservation. A little 17th-C manor house set in the greenery. An
enjoyable stop, with fine food and a well-stocked cellar :
flamiche, ris de veau au cidre, 110-250.

SAINT-GERMER-DE-FLY, ⊠ 60850, 24 km SE.

Restaurant :
♦ *Auberge de l'Abbaye*, 5, pl. de l'Abbaye,
☎ 44.82.50.73, Euro Visa 🅿 ▦ ⌕ ♪ ⟁ ⚘ closed Tue
eve and Wed , and Sun eve (ex reservation), 5-25 Jan,
17 Aug-2 Sep. Across from the abbey. Simple, faultless
cuisine prepared by B. Leclerc : *feuilleté de grenouilles et
escargots, blanquette dieppoise, coq au vin*, 87-180.

BIÈVRE Valley

C3

The valley has managed to keep its rural character
despite urban encroachment. Rustic villages, churches and châteaux seem oddly out of place in a
20thC environment.

▶ **Bièvres :** National Photography Museum★ *(9-12:30 &
1:30-6)*. ▶ **Jouy-en-Josas,** beautiful statue of the Virgin in
the 13th-16thC church ; **Oberkampf Museum★,** manufacture of *toiles de Jouy* (printed textiles). **Fondation Cartier,**
contemporary art centre in 19thC English garden *(daily ex
Mon., 11-7)*; houses of Juliette Drouet (Victor Hugo's mistress) and Léon Blum (1870-1952 ; French prime minister
1936-37). ▶ **Buc Aqueduct :** built to supply Versailles.

▶ Artificial lakes (near the sources of the river Bièvre) with
fishing and sailing facilities.   □

Practical Information ────────────

JOUY-EN-JOSAS, ⊠ 78350.

Restaurant :
● ♦♦♦ *Fondation Cartier*, 3, rue de la Manufacture,
☎ 39.56.46.46, Tx 699124, AE DC Euro Visa ≾ ▦ ⚘
closed Mon and eves. In this temple of contemporary art,
the arts of the table are not neglected. Young Olivier Richy
cooks, surrounded by the works of César. Good, light
cuisine : *raviolis de saumon, pistou et tomates, loup à la
graine de moutarde, filet de bœuf*. Cafeteria in the
park, 85-250.

CARNELLE Forest

C2

▶ On the E edge of the forest, **Viarmes :** church
(12th, 13th, 19thC) ; **Asnières-sur-Oise :** town hall château (18thC), charming church (12th-13thC). ▶ Interesting church at **Beaumont-sur-Oise** (12th-16thC) *11-6 Sat.,
Sun. and hols. ; 15 Mar.-15 Nov., 2-6 weekdays)*. ▶ More
lovely churches at **Belloy-en-France** (14th-16thC) S of
Viarmes, and at **Champagne-sur-Oise** (13th-16thC).   □

CHANTILLY★★★

Paris 48, Beauvais 50, Amiens 91 km
pop 10200 ⊠ 60500   C1

Chantilly, historically the seat of the Princes de
Condé (princes of the royal blood, descended through
Charles de Bourbon from a younger son of St. Louis),
has two great attractions : the château, in a park on
the edge of one of the great forests of France, and
the race-course, created by the horse-crazy dandies
of the last century.
The thoroughbred horse has reigned supreme ever
since in this blue-blooded town : 3 000 thoroughbreds
train here each year for many world-renowned races,
including the Prix de Diane and the Prix de l'Arc de
Triomphe. The 18thC **stables★★** have now become
the **Living Museum of the Horse★** ; they are more
sumptuous than most human dwellings, which may

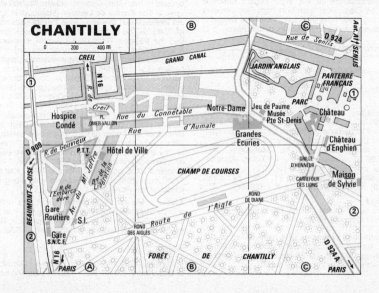

be less astonishing when you remember that at least one Prince de Condé expressed a desire to be reincarnated as a horse! A must for horse-lovers *(10:30-5:30, 2-4:30 in winter, week-end 10:30-5:30; closed Tue.; dressage in costume).*

▶ The great chef Vatel committed suicide when Louis XIV dined at the **château de Chantilly** and the fish arrived too late to be served. Today the château houses a **collection** of masterpieces★★★ that are displayed in the old-fashioned style preferred by the 19thC owner, the Duc d'Aumale (1822-97). This son of King Louis-Philippe bankrupted himself in his efforts to restore Chantilly to its former splendour, and finally donated the château and its works of art to the Institut de France.

The major Italian painters are represented, together with France's Poussin, Delacroix, and Ingres, and the Flemish Masters. Jewels of the collection include the Fouquet miniatures, the 16thC Clouet portraits and unique illuminated manuscripts *(10-6, Apr-Sep; 10:30-5, Oct-Mar; closed Tue.* ▶ Two great houses were built on the site by Anne de Montmorency (1493-1567; male, despite his name), Constable of France and brilliant soldier who developed his taste as a patron of the arts during a sojourn in Italy. However, only the smaller (built ca. 1560 by Jean Bullivant) survived the Revolution; the larger was rebuilt during the 19thC by the Duc d'Aumale. ▶ The park includes French gardens by André Le Nôtre (1630-1700), English gardens, the Maison de Sylvie; pretty 17thC forerunner of the Trianon (→ Versailles), and the Jeu de Paume, once a covered tennis court (concerts).

▶ Chantilly is an **elegant town**, with grand mansions and handsome houses lining the broad avenues, and bridle paths cut through the town.

Chantilly Forest★★

▶ Chantilly, Halatte and Ermenonville form an almost continuous forest. Chantilly alone covers 63 km², painstakingly planted and laid out for deer hunting by its princely owners. Lily-of-the-valley still grows wild under oak, beech, lime and pine. Most of the roads are closed to cars, but three GR trails cross the forest : GR11 (from Maison de Sylvie to Senlis, *approx 3 hr); GR 12* (from Commelles Pond★ to Halatte Forest, *3 hr*); and GR 1 (from Luzarches to Ermenonville, *6 hr*). ▶ Forest guides : *ask at the SI.*

Nearby

▶ **Saint-Leu-d'Esserent** (6 km W) : superb church★ overlooking the Oise, clear transition from Romanesque to Gothic. Pretty view from the cloister★ of the Benedictine priory. Leisure centre on the banks of the Oise. □

Practical Information _____

CHANTILLY
ⓘ av. du Mal-Joffre (A2), ☎ (1) 44.57.08.58.
SNCF (A2), ☎ (1) 44.57.00.77/(1) 44.57.57.61.
🚌 *next to station.*

Restaurants :
● ◆◆ *Tipperary,* 6, av. du Mal-Joffre (A2), ☎ (1) 44.57.00.48, AE DC Euro Visa 🅿 ♪ ♿ Brice Auriault applies culinary techniques taught him by Jean Delaveyne, the "wizard of Bougival". Regional specialities, 95-150.
◆◆ *Relais de Condé,* 42, av. Mal-Joffre (A2), ☎ (1) 44.57.05.75 ⦿ closed Mon, 1-30 Jan. A distinguished table. Interesting wine list, 150-275.
◆ *Relais du Coq Chantant,* 21, rte de Creil, ☎ (1) 44.57.01.28, AE DC Euro Visa 🅿 ♪ 125-245.

Recommended
Hippodrome : *horse racing* (Jockey Club, Prix de Diane; in Jun). Grande Semaine de Chantilly.

> For the translation of a name of a meat, a fish or a vegetable, for the composition of a dish or a sauce, see the Menu Guide in the Practical Holiday Guide; it lists the most common culinary terms.

Nearby

GOUVIEUX, ⊠ 60270, 3 km E.

Hotels :
● ★★★ *Château de la Tour,* ☎ (1) 44.57.07.39, AE Euro Visa, 15 rm 🅿 ♦ ⦿ ⚲ ⤴ closed 27 Jul-11 Aug, 260. Rest. ◆◆ ♦ ♪ ♿ closed 15 Jul-11 Aug, 80-150.
● ★ *Pavillon St-Hubert,* Chemin du Marisy, ☎ (1) 44.57.07.04, AE DC Visa, 23 rm 🅿 ♦ ⦿ ⚲ 🦀 ⤴ 200. Rest. ♦ ♦ ♪ ♿ 110-150; child : 60.

LAMORLAY, ⊠ 60260, 5 km S.

Hotel :
● ★★ *Hostellerie du Lys,* 7ème av., Rond-Point de la Reine, ☎ (1) 44.21.26.19, Tx 150298, AE DC Euro Visa, 35 rm 🅿 ⦿ ⚲ ♪ 240. Rest. ◆◆ ♪ 115-160.

RANTIGNY, ⊠ 60290, 20 km N.

Hotel :
★★ *Le Chalet Normand,* 10, pl. de la Gare, ☎ (1) 44.73.33.16, 12 rm 🅿 150.

CHARTRES★★★

Orléans 73, Paris 90, Le Mans 116 km
pop 39250 ⊠ 28000   A3

The cathedral of Chartres soars clear, sharp and immense from the surrounding plains of wheat. The mediaeval upper town clusters around the cathedral, while the lower town with its hump-backed bridges stretches along the banks of the Eure.

▶ The **cathedral★★★** (B2) is a perfect example of a pilgrim church. The structure was built over a period of only 30 years (1194-1225) and the architectural style is consequently uniform. Only the façade dates from the 12thC; the **Royal Doorway★★★** (1145-1155), which depicts Christ in glory, marks a transition from Romanesque to Gothic style. The two **side porches★★★** were not in the original plans; the N porch (ca. 1200-1225) shows Old Testament figures, and the S porch (1224-1250) represents New Testament themes. Two **towers** frame the façade : the Clocher Neuf (new bell-tower, left) is actually the older, but its spire was only added in the 16thC. The recently-restored **stained glass★★★** provides one of the most complete examples of this 13thC art. The 14thC **choir screen** of carved stone can be seen in the treasure room★. 9th and 10thC crypts beneath the side aisles. The SI is housed in the 13thC Canons' House *(maison des chanoines).* ▶ The **Enclos de Loëns★** (storehouse) now houses the **International Stained Glass Centre** (exhibitions; *10-6 ex Tue.).* ▶ The Bishop's Garden overlooks the Eure Valley; the Palace★ (14th-19thC) is now a **museum** *(10-12 & 2-5; closed Tue., Sun. am off season)* : 16thC Flemish tapestries; 14thC Limoges enamel★; paintings (Ste. Lucie★ by Zurbàran, Molière by Mignard). Regional museum; The Vlaminck Donation; contemporary art exhibitions. ▶ **Upper town★** : numerous old houses (B2) : Maison du Saumon (15thC), Queen Bertha's staircase (16thC), Hôtel de la Caige (15thC), church of St. Aignan (16thC), Hôtel de Ville (17thC), Renaissance house of Claude Huvé, doctor to Henri II. ▶ **Lower town** : the **church of St. André** (B1; 12thC) partly destroyed in the 19thC; now disused; formerly the church of the craftsmen of Chartres (concerts). ▶ **Church of St. Pierre★** (C3) : part of a Benedictine abbey from 1700 to 1709; 11thC tower; 12th and 13thC additions; 14th and 16thC stained glass★, 17thC convent buildings. Pleasant walk along the **Eure★** (boats at the *Pont de la Courtille).*

Also... ▶ **Maison Picassiette★** decorated with colourful shards of porcelain (primitive painting, 22, rue du Repos, *10-12 & 2-5:30 ex Mon., Tue. in season).* ▶ **Gardens of the Horticultural Society** N of the town *(8-7:30, Apr.-Oct.).*

Nearby

▶ **Meslay** *(6 km SW)* : church (frescos : *Danse Macabre).*
▶ **Gallardon★** *(20 km NE)* : 12thC keep, known locally as

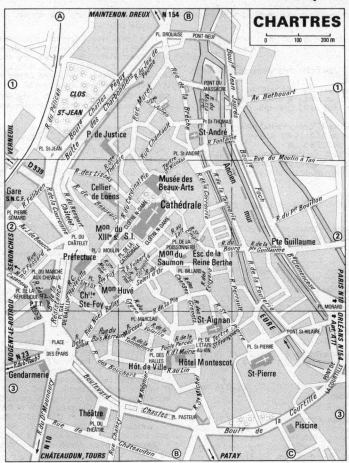

CHARTRES
0   100   200 m

"the shoulder"; old houses including one with carved wooden facings (15thC); 13thC church★. ▶ **Auneau** *(25 km E)* : typical village of the region; 14thC castle★ with 11thC keep.

Along the Eure Valley★ between Chartres and Dreux *(43 km; 2-3 hr).*

▶ **Jouy** : interesting church doorway (13thC). ▶ **Saint-Piat** : mill; sarcophagus★ (5thC) in the 16thC church. ▶ **Maintenon★** : château★ (12th, 16th, 17thC) that belonged to the Marquise de Maintenon (1615-1719), secretly married to Louis XIV soon after the death of his first wife; attractive canal setting. *(Apr.-Oct., 2-6; Sun. and nat. hols. 10-12 & 2-6; off season, Sat. and Sun. pm)*; Chinese wallpaper★ in the reception rooms. ▶ The Eure branches out at **Nogent-le-Roi** : 16thC houses; Flamboyant Gothic and Renaissance church. On the other bank : former abbey of **Coulombs**; mill. ▶ **Dreux** (→). □

Practical Information _____

CHARTRES
ℹ 7, cloître Notre-Dame (B2), ☎ 37.21.54.03.
SNCF (A2), ☎ 37.28.50.50/37.28.42.61.
🚌 next to the station (A2), ☎ 37.31.30.35.
Car rental : *Avis*, 36, av. du mal Leclerc-à-Luce, ☎ 37.28.37.37.

Hotels :
● ★★★ *Grand Monarque*, (Mapotel), 22, pl. des Epars (A3), ☎ 37.21.00.72, Tx 760777, AE DC Euro Visa, 46 rm 🅿 ♨ 🏡 350. Rest. ♦♦♦ What shame that the food is not equal to the fabulous wine list and the cordial welcome extended by Georges Jallerat and his staff, 175-255.
★★ *Jehan de Beauce*, 19, av. J.-de-Beauce (A2), ☎ 37.21.01.41, Euro Visa, 46 rm, closed 21 Dec-11 Jan, 180.
★★ *Ouest*, 3, pl.-Sémard (A2), ☎ 37.21.43.27, 29 rm, 115.
★★ *Poste* (L.F.), 3, rue du Gal-Kœnig (A2), ☎ 37.21.04.27, Tx 760533, AE DC Euro Visa, 60 rm 🅿 ≼ ♪ 180. Rest. ♦ ♪ ๕ 70-130 ; child : 40.

Restaurants :
♦♦♦ *Le Buisson Ardent*, 10, rue au Lait (B2), ☎ 37.34.04.66, AE DC Visa 🅿 ♪ closed Tue eve, Wed, Sun eve. Pleasant setting. Spec : *salade tiède de raie à l'huile d'olive, saumon fumé*, 70-145.
● ♦♦ *La Vieille Maison*, 5, rue au Lait (B2), ☎ 37.34.10.67, AE DC Euro Visa, closed Mon and Sun eve. Old establishment, youthful cuisine : *saumon rôti au chou vert, flan d'asperges*, 150-300.
♦♦ *Henri IV*, 31, rue du Soleil-d'Or, ☎ 37.36.01.55, AE DC ≼ closed Mon eve and Tue , Feb. Contemporary culinary classics : *pot-au-feu de lotte, foie gras de canard aux pommes*. Wonderful cellar, 155-250.

♦ ***Normand***, 24, pl. des Epars (A3), ☎ 37.21.04.38, closed Mon, 65-120.

⛺ ★★★*Bords de l'Eure*, rue de Launay (250 pl), ☎ 37.28.79.43.

Recommended
Auction house : 7, rue Collin-d'Harleville, ☎ 37.36.04.33, auction every Sun.
Events : *Antiques fair*, late Oct; *stained glass exhibit*, Centre international du vitrail, ☎ 37.21.54.03, Jun-Sep.
Guided tours : ☎ 37.21.54.03, Cathedral. Old town (audio-guide). Info S.I.
Handicrafts : *Ateliers F. Lorin, master glass worker*, 46, rue de la Tannerie, ☎ 37.34.00.42; *Ateliers P. Millous*, 10, rue des Chaises, ☎ 37.28.62.28.
Night-clubs : *Lido Club*, av. Marcel Proust, ☎ 37.34.41.41.
Youth hostel : 23, av. Neigre, ☎ 37.34.27.64.
♥ candy : *Bazille*, 15, rue de la Pie.

Nearby

CHÂTEAUNEUF-EN-THYMERAIS, ⊠ 28170, 25 km NW.

Hotel :
★★ ***Ecritoire***, 43, rue de Dreux, ☎ 37.51.60.57, 5 rm 🅿 closed Tue, 22 Jan-9 Feb, 22 Aug-7 Sep, 180. Rest. ♦♦ ♪ 18th-C coach house, 90-250.

Restaurants :
♦♦ ***Saint-Jean***, Saint-Jean-de-Rebervilliers, ☎ 37.51.62.83, AE DC Euro Visa ♪ closed Thu eve and Fri, 19 Feb-20 Mar, 10-26 Sep, 130-200.
♦ ***Relais d'Aligre***, 25, rue Jean-Moulin, ☎ 37.51.69.59, Euro Visa ♪ ♿ closed Mon and Thu eve, 12 Jan-2 Feb, 31 Aug-23 Sep, 70-130.

SAINT-PREST, ⊠ 28300 Mainvilliers, 6 km N.

Hotel :
★★★ ***Manoir du Palomino***, ☎ 37.22.27.27, AE DC Euro Visa, 14 rm 🅿 ♪ ♿ 300. Rest. ♦ ♪ ♿ closed Mon, 160-235; child : 50.

SAINT-SYMPHORIEN-LE-CHÂTEAU, ⊠ 28700 Auneau, 6 km W of **Gallardon**.

Hotel :
● ★★★★(L) ***Château d'Esclimont*** (R.C.), ☎ 37.31.15.15, Tx 780560, Visa, 54 rm 🅿 ♪ 60-ha park, musical evenings, 820. Rest. ● ♦♦♦ ♪ ♿ An enchanting decor for a talented young chef : *fleur de courgettes mousseline de langoustines*, 225-310.

THIVARS, ⊠ 28630, 9 km S.

Restaurant :
● ♦♦ ***La Sellerie***, 48, rue Nationale, ☎ 37.26.41.59, Euro Visa 🅿 ♪ closed Mon eve and Tue , Sun eve (Mar-Nov), 6-18 Jan, 3-25 Aug. Good cooking in the heart of the Beauce region : *tête de veau beauceronne, mille-feuilles de ris de veau aux aubergines*, 100-250.

VOVES, ⊠ 28150, 24 km SE.

Hotels :
● ★★ ***Au Quai Fleuri*** (L.F.), 15, rue Texier-Gallas, ☎ 37.99.11.20, Tx 783373, AE Euro Visa, 15 rm 🅿 closed Fri eve (l.s.) and Sun eve, 8-16 Aug, 12 Dec-12 Jan, 230. Rest. ♦ ♪ ♿ Nostalgic charm. Chadorge's excellent food : *feuilleté d'escargot, magret aux morilles. Vins gris meunier de l'Orléanais saumur.* Carriage rides, play area, fireworks, cartoons, video, 50-150; child : 35.
Aux Trois Rois (L.F.), 4, rue des Trois-Rois, ☎ 37.99.00.88, Visa, 7 rm, closed 2-9 Mar, 75. Rest. ● ♦♦ ♪ closed Tue eve and Wed. Weddings and banquets are traditional here : *magret de canard au poivre vert, escalope de saumon crème d'oseille*, 65-120.

CHÂTEAU-LANDON*

Nemours 15, Montargis 18, Paris 95 km
pop 3011 ⊠ 77570 C4

Overlooking the Fusain Valley. A signposted circuit leads past the sentry-walk *(terrasse des larris)*, the Madeleine Tower and the former *château-mairie* (municipal offices).

▶ The psychiatric hospital was once an abbey (14th-16thC); beneath the ruins of the abbey church is an older church (11thC) with murals. The church of Notre-Dame was built in the 10th-14thC. In the centre of town, a Romanesque tower; former Mint. Lovely view down the Loing Valley (→) from the sentry-walk.

Also... ▶ On the other side of the Loing and the N7, ruins of the colossal 13thC château of **Mez-le-Maréchal★**. □

CHÂTEAUDUN*

Orléans 48, Tours 95, Paris 132 km
pop 16000 ⊠ 28200 A4

A defensive site on a spur formed by the river Loir, reinforced by a feudal château★★ whose foundations plunge sheer to the bottom of the valley.

▶ 12thC **keep** with 15thC timberwork; Flamboyant Gothic Saint Chapelle with statuary★★ carved in the Loire Valley (late 15thC); main building 15thC with 16thC return wing; kitchens★; tapestries★; *(9:30-11:45 & 2-6, 23 Mar.-Oct.; 10-11:45 & 2-4, Nov.-22 Mar.).* ▶ Near the ramparts, Romanesque **church of the Madeleine★.** ▶ To the E, the **church of St. Valérien★** (late 12thC), vaulting 12thC, bell-tower late 15thC. ▶ Cemetery : façade of 16thC church. ▶ On the opposite bank of the Loir, **church of St. Jean** (11th, 12th, 15thC). ▶ Houses in the old town rebuilt by Jules Hardouin-Mansart (1647-1708, grandson of the renowned architect François Mansart).

Nearby

▶ **Mémillon** *(10 km N)* : three châteaux along the Loir, the most important dating from the Second Empire (Napoléon III, 1852-70). ▶ **Bonneval** *(14 km on Chartres road)* : 13thC bridge; 12th-15thC abbey, now a psychiatric hospital; church; Gothic houses; local museum. ▶ **Alluyes** *(7 km NW from Bonneval)* : 16thC church with Romanesque apse and Gothic paintings; feudal castle with Renaissance additions. ▶ **Dangeau** *(9 km W from Bonneval)* : fine Romanesque church (15th-16thC statues); bridge. ▶ **Courtalain,** along the river Yerre; Renaissance château built in 1483 on the site of a mediaeval fortress. ▶ **Cloyes-sur-le-Loir,** chapel of Yron, Romanesque frescos. □

Practical Information

CHÂTEAUDUN
ℹ 1, rue de Luynes, ☎ 37.45.22.46.
SNCF ☎ 37.45.00.54/37.45.15.15.

Hotels :
★★ ***Beauce***, 50, rue de Jallans, ☎ 37.45.14.75, Euro Visa, 24 rm 🅿 closed Sun eve (l.s.), 23 Dec-23 Jan, 190.
★ ***Rose*** (L.F.), 12, rue Lambert-Licors, ☎ 37.45.21.83, DC Visa, 8 rm, half pens (h.s.), closed Sun eve and Mon, Dec, 150. Rest. ♦♦ ♪ ♿ Spec : *gourmandise de volaille, 75-200.*

Restaurants :
♦♦ ***Caveau des Fouleurs***, 33, rue des Fouleries, ☎ 37.45.23.72, AE DC Euro Visa ♪ closed Mon and Sun eve, 15 Feb-1 Mar, 15 Aug-1 Sep, 80-150; child : 50.
● ♦ ***La Licorne***, 6, pl. du 18-Octobre, ☎ 37.45.32.32, Euro Visa ♪ ♿ closed Tue eve and Wed, 10-20 Jun, 28 Sep-7 Oct, 21 Dec-20 Jan. Cuisine by a pro in a peaceful setting : *salade Licorne, filet de bœuf au roquefort*, 50-120.

⛺ ★★*Municipal* (100 pl), ☎ 37.45.05.34.

Nearby

CLOYES-SUR-LE-LOIR, ⊠ 28220, 12 km SW.

Hotel :
★★★ ***Hostellerie Saint-Jacques***, 35, rue Nationale, ☎ 37.98.40.08, DC Visa, 21 rm 🅿 closed Sun eve and Mon ex Jul-Aug, 15 Nov-1 Feb, 200. Rest. ● ♦♦♦ ♿

In his attractive former post-house, Simon Le Bras makes time stand still : *charlotte d'asperges au jus de langoustines, filet de Saint-Pierre aux courgettes sauce framboise*, 135-230.

⚖ ★★★*Parc de loisirs* (100 pl), ☎ 37.98.60.63.

DANGEAU, ⊠ 28160 Brou, 18 km N.

Hotel :
★★★ *Relais de Poste Saint-Jacques*, 8, pl. de l'Eglise, ☎ 37.98.97.12, Visa, 10 rm Rest. ● ♦♦ ♪ closed Tue eve and Wed eve. This coaching inn dates from 1515, but François Morgillo's cuisine is resolutely modern : *saumon à la crème de moutarde, magret de canard d'entre Beauce et Perche, (cidre et maïs)*, 140-220.

MARBOUÉ, ⊠ 28200 Châteaudun, 7 km N.

Restaurant :
● ♦♦ *Château des Coudreaux*, ☎ 37.45.53.78, AE DC Euro Visa ⫞ ⑳ ♪ ⚹ closed Sun eve , Feb. A marvel of tasteful simplicity : *trois petits feuilletés des Coudreaux, turbotin braisé au vouvray, filet de bœuf au chinon et à la moelle*, 95-240.

CHEVREUSE Valley*

B3
Round trip starting at Saint-Quentin-en-Yvelines *(approx 35 km ; half day ; see map 1)*

Wooded slopes in the upper Yvette Valley, villages, châteaux and historic remnants of a period of religious and political confusion.

▶ **Saint-Quentin-en-Yvelines** : the former house of the **Commandery of Villedieu** (Knights Templars) has been converted into a cultural and information centre. ▶ **Le Mesnil-Saint-Denis** : château de Montmort (16thC), now the Town Hall ; park. ▶ **Dampierre★★** : 17thC château built by Hardouin-Mansart for the Duc de Luynes *(2-6 ex Tue., Apr.-15 Oct.)*; gardens★ (André Le Nôtre) irrigated by the river Yvette ; festival hall *(Salle des Fêtes)★* decorated by the painter Ingres. ▶ **17 Bends** *(tournants)* Road★ climbs to Port-Royal. ▶ **Senlisse** : château ; church on the hillside above a stream. ▶ To the W, **Vaux-de-Cernay★** : lakes and a "sea" of sand, one of the best-known sites in

the vicinity of Paris. Walk from the Moulin des Roches to the former Cistercian abbey. ▶ **Château de Breteuil** (Louis XIII style); wax museum recalls celebrities who stayed here in the 19thC ; park★ (birdlife ; *daily 2-5:30 or 6 and 11-12:30 Sun. and nat. hols.* ; park open from *10 am*). ▶ **Chevreuse** : church (12th-17thC) ; feudal keep (La Madeleine, 12thC). Racine Road *(signposted, 5km)* leads to ▶ **Port-Royal★** *(pm only, 3 persons min. ; closed Tue.)* : the abbey, once a hotbed of political intrigue and religious dissension, was suppressed by royal command in 1710. Bones exhumed from the nuns' cemetery during the dissolution were tossed into a common pit ; a granite monument near the church of **Saint-Lambert-des-Bois★** marks the spot. ▶ The **Granges National Museum,** in the former school building *(Petites Écoles)*, provides an insight into the importance of Jansenism (a 17thC religious movement) in the development of French religious thought *(10-11:30 & 2-5:30 ; closed Mon., Tue. and nat. hols.)*. ▶ **Magny-les-Hameaux** : the church is adorned with the tombstones from the desecrated abbey. ☐

Practical Information ———————————————

CHÂTEAUFORT, ⊠ 78530, 8 km NE of **Chevreuse**.

Restaurant :
● ♦♦♦ *La Belle Epoque*, 10, pl. de la Mairie, ☎ (1) 39.56.21.66, AE DC Visa ⫞ ⑳ ⚹ closed Mon and Sun eve, 12 Aug-12 Sep, 22 Dec-6 Jan. In his handsome turn-of-the-century 1900 decor, Michel Peignaud, a headstrong, mustachioed native of Berry has made some changes, and added some new creations inspired by exotic cuisines, e.g. : ikebana of salmon with chervil. But France is well represented too : *tête de veau, homard breton à toute vapeur, Saint-Pierre comme dans le passé*. Cheese ripened by Eugène, 250-310.

CHEVREUSE, ⊠ 78460, 16 km SW of **Versailles**.

Hotel :
La Puszta, (Hungarian inn), carrefour St-Laurent, ☎ (1) 34.61.18.35, AE Visa, 5 rm Ⓟ ⫞ ⑳ ⚹ ♿ closed Mon eve and Tue, 350. Rest. ♦♦ 120-170.

Restaurant :
♦ *Lou Basquou*, 18, rte Madeleine, ☎ (1) 30.52.15.77 ⫞ closed Wed eve and Thu, 16 Aug-7 Sep. Spec : *chipirons*, 100-200.

GIF-SUR-YVETTE, ⊠ 91190, 7 km E of **Chevreuse**.

Restaurant :
● ♦ *Bœuf à Six Pattes*, N 118, exit Centre Universitaire (C.D. 128), ☎ (1) 60.19.29.60, Euro Visa ⫞ ⑳ ♪ ♿ Decorator Slavik has hung steers from the ceiling ; beef is what you'll find on your plate as well, beautifully grilled, 70-140.

SAINT-RÉMY-LES-CHEVREUSE, ⊠ 78470, 3 km E of **Chevreuse**.

Restaurant :
♦♦♦ *La Cressonnière*, 46, rte de Port-Royal, ☎ (1) 30.52.00.41, AE DC Visa ⑳ ♪ ♿ closed Tue and Wed , Feb school hols. Fine food, 6 recommended fixed meals, 150-330.

SENLISSE, ⊠ 78720 Dampierre, 3 km S of **Dampierre**.

Hotels :
★★★ *Auberge Le Pont Hardi*, 1, rue du Couvent, ☎ (1) 30.52.50.78, DC Visa, 5 rm Ⓟ ⫞ ⑳ ⚹ closed Tue eve , Wed, Feb school hols, 1-15 Aug, 320. Rest. ♦♦♦ ⫞ ♪ ♿ Spec : *millefeuille de langouste, blanc de turbot*, 165-270.
★★ *Le Gros Marronnier*, 3, pl. de l'Eglise, ☎ (1) 30.52.51.69, AE Visa, 14 rm Ⓟ ⫞ ⑳ ⚹ 250. Rest. ♦♦ Spec : *tartare de saumon à la menthe fraîche*, 150-180.

In preparing for your trip, consult the pages pertaining to the regions. You will find there the description of the region you wish to visit, as well as a list of sites that must be seen, a brief history and practical information.

1. Chevreuse valley

CLERMONT*

Beauvais 26, Amiens 66, Paris 77 km
pop 8700 ⊠ 60600   C1

A hill, a river, forests all around. ▶ Remarkable 14thC Hôtel de Ville★ (restored 19thC). Church★ (14thC, remodelled 15th and 16thC) : 16thC sepulchre, stained glass, organs (15th-16thC).

Nearby

▶ The **forest of Hez**★ stretches W across the plateau with more than 4 000 acres of beech and oak. Marsh and Riding Habit Museum at **Sacy-le-Grand** *(Sun., 2-6)*. ▶ To the W, **Agnetz** : church (12th-16thC); S, **Cambronne-lès-Clermont** : 12th-13thC church; SW, **Bury** : church (11th-13thC). In the N, facing Picardy, are the abbey church (13thC) and the farm buildings of **Saint-Martin-aux-Bois**★. ▶ S, **Neuilly-sous-Clermont** : 14thC house and chapel of the Knights Templars, Renaissance residence *(visit on prior request, 1 May-15 Oct.).* ▶ 18thC **château de Verderonne** houses a Magic Museum *(3-7, Sat. and Sun., 15 Apr.-15 Oct., and by appt.).* ☐

COMPIÈGNE**

Beauvais 57, Amiens 76, Paris 82 km
pop 43300 ⊠ 60200   D1

Compiègne was a country retreat for French rulers from the earliest Capets to Napoleon III. The 18thC **château**★ built by Jacques and Jacques-Ange Gabriel (father and son architects to Louis XV) is a treasury of 1st and 2nd Empire art and design (grand apartments); **Musée de la Voiture**★ will delight car enthusiasts *(9:30-11:15 & 1:30-4:30, closed Tue. and nat. hols.).* ▶ The **Allée des Beaux Monts**★ leads from the **park**★ to the forest (→).

▶ **Hôtel de Ville** (B2 ; late Gothic, restored) : historical statuettes★ *(9-12 & 2-5 or 6, ex Mon.);* carillon in the façade. ▶ **Cloister of St. Corneille** (14thC). ▶ **Vivenel Museum** (A2) in 18thC mansion : Greek vases★, statues, enamels *(9-12 & 2-5 or 6 ex Tue. and nat. hols.).* ▶ Rue des Lombards (B2) : gabled house (16thC); 18thC covered market designed by Nicolas Ledoux (foremost neo-Classical architect, 1736-1806); 17th and 18thC mansions; stud farm *(haras)* designed by Gabriel.

Nearby

▶ **Château du Plessis-Brion**★, 16thC pink and black patterned *(1 Jul.-15 Aug.),* between the river Oise and the Laigue Forest. ▶ Ruins of **Ste-Croix d'Offémont Priory :** church of **Saint-Crépin-aux-Bois** (early 17thC). ☐

Practical Information

COMPIÈGNE
ⓘ pl. de l'Hôtel de Ville (B2), ☎ 44.40.01.00.
SNCF (B1), ☎ 44.83.36.36/44.83.37.55.
🚌 across from the station (B1).

Hotels :
● ★★★ **Harlay**, 3, rue de Harlay (B1), ☎ 44.23.01.50, AE DC Euro Visa, 21 rm ℗ ⛄ closed 21 Dec-6 Jan, 255.
● ★★ **Royal-Lieu**, 9, rue de Senlis (off map A3), ☎ 44.20.10.24, AE DC Euro Visa, 18 rm ℗ ⚨ ♨ ⚕ 260. Rest. ♦♦ 160-230.

Restaurant :
♦♦ **Auberge des Etangs du Buissonnet**, 825, rue des Vineux, Choisy-au-Bac 5 km NE, ☎ 44.40.17.41, Euro Visa ℗ ⛄ ⚨ ⚕ ♪ closed Mon and Sun eve. Spec : *filet de bœuf Gascon, andouillettes du pays*, 145-200.

⚐ ★★*Hippodrome* (100 pl), ☎ (1) 44.20.28.58.

Recommended
♥ *Salle des Ventes*, 18, rue des Cordeliers (B2), ☎ 44.40.06.16.

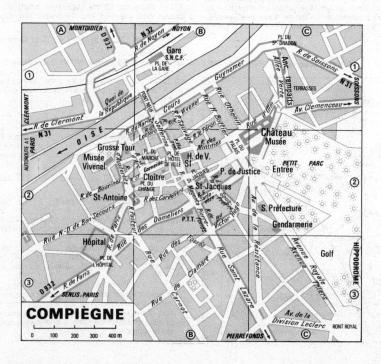

COMPIÈGNE

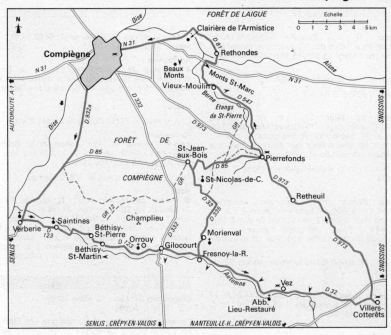

2. Compiègne forest

Nearby

ÉLINCOURT-SAINTE-MARGUERITE, ⊠ 60157, 15 km S on the D 142.

Hotel :
★★★ *Château de Bellinglise*, ☎ 44.76.04.76, Tx 155048, AE DC Euro Visa, 55 rm P ≼ ♨ ♧ ♪ ✼ ⚲ closed Sun eve, 360. Rest. ♦♦ ≼ ♪ ✼ 85-150.

COMPIÈGNE Forest***

C-D1
Down the Automne Valley through the forest of Compiègne *(approx 80 km, can be combined with Halatte → Senlis excursion; see map 2)*
Compiègne Forest is among the largest and most beautiful in France, 220 km² including the forests of Laigue, Ourscamps, and the 130 km² of Villers-Cotterêts; fringed by hills providing splendid views (especially to the N), cut by gorges and watered by numerous streams and ponds. The E forest is the most interesting for walkers; marked trails.

► **Compiègne** (→). ► The Automne Valley★ runs between the Halatte and Retz forests; the road follows the river. ► **Verberie** : church (13th-15thC), doorway with beautiful carved Virgin. ► **Saintines** : church with double nave, Romanesque spire, 15thC doorway and polychrome statues. ► Twin villages, contrasting churches : **Béthisy-Saint-Pierre** (Romanesque church rebuilt 16thC, former priory 14th-16thC) and **Béthisy-Saint-Martin** (13thC church). ► **Orrouy** : fine Romanesque bell-tower and remarkable Renaissance stained glass; 16thC manor. ► **Champlieu** : Gallo-Roman ruins. ► **Gilocourt** : 13th and 15thC church. ► **Fresnoy-la-Rivière** (13th-15thC church) : on the edge of deep countryside again. ► **Morienval★★** : three bell-towers and the finest Romanesque church in Ile-

de-France; in the ambulatory an unknown mason raised the first Gothic vaults in the region; choir stalls; 15thC Christ.
► From Morienval to Pierrefonds : forest road past the ruined priory of St-Nicolas-de-Courson, and one of the prettiest villages in the forest, **Saint-Jean-aux-Bois★** born from a 13thC Benedictine abbey. ► **Lieu-Restauré :** the abbey rising from the ruins was rebuilt in 16thC (hence the name, meaning "restored place"). ► **Vez**, with 14thC keep : once the capital of the ancient county of Valois; 12th-13thC church, l6thC timberwork, 17thC wood panelling, view. ► **Largny-sur-Automne** (fine 12thC church with 16thC porch) is the last village in the valley before the broad fields of Villers-Cotterêts (→) and the Champenois. ► **Pierrefonds★** : rises out of the woods by the lake, its colossal walls looking like a stage set. The restoration by the 19thC architect Eugène Viollet-le-Duc has been much criticized, but gives an idea of late feudal architecture, designed for both military and residential needs. Delightful for children of all ages. *(10-1:45 & 2-5:45, Apr.-Oct.; 4, Oct.-Mar.; closed Tue., Wed.).* ► **Etangs de Saint-Pierre** (lakes) near **Vieux-Moulin.** ► The avenue of **Beaux Monts★** was laid out by Napoleon to remind his second wife Marie-Louise, Archduchess of Austria, of her childhood home, Schönbrunn Palace in Vienna. ► The 1918 Armistice was signed in a clearing near **Rethondes** by Maréchal Foch; the railway wagon where this historic document was signed was taken to Germany in 1940 but has since been reproduced (museum : *8-12 & 1:30-6:30, Mar.-11 Nov; 9-12 & 2-5:30 ex Tue., 12 Nov.- Feb.).* □

Practical Information

MORIENVAL, ⊠ 60127, 10 km S.

Hotel :
★ *Auberge du Bon Accueil* (L.F.), carrefour de Vaudrampont, ☎ 44.42.84.04, Visa, 7 rm P ≼ ♨ closed Mon eve and Tue, Feb, 15-30 Aug, 175. Rest. ♦ ≼ ♪ ♿ 120-220.

PIERREFONDS, ⊠ 60350, 14 km SE.

Hotel :

★ **Etrangers**, 10, rue Beaudon, Cuise-la-Motte, ☎ 44.42.80.18, Visa, 16 rm Ⓟ ≼ ▩ half pens, closed Sun eve and Mon (Nov-Mar), 15 Jan-15 Feb, 270. Rest. ♦ ≼ ♪ 45-180.

△ ★★*Batigny* (50 pl), ☎ (1) 44.42.80.83.

RETHONDES, ⊠ 60153, 9 km NE.

Restaurant :

♦♦ **Auberge du Pont**, 21, rue du Mal-Foch, ☎ 44.85.60.24, Visa ≼ ▩ ⅋ closed Mon and Tue, 28 Feb-5 Mar, 30 Sep-5 Oct. A fine place to pause : *salade de filets de sole grillées aux épinards crus, foie chaud de canard aux airelles et framboises*, 118-250.

SAINT-JEAN-AUX-BOIS, ⊠ 60350 Cuise-la-Motte, 6 km W of **Pierrefonds**.

Hotel :

● ★★★ **La Bonne Idée**, rue des Meuniers, ☎ 44.42.84.09, Tx 155026, AE Euro Visa, 24 rm Ⓟ ≼ ▩ ⊾ closed Tue and Wed lunch, 12 Jan-13 Feb, 24 Aug-5 Sep, 250. Rest. ♦♦♦ ♪ Spec : *cassolette d'escargots, foie gras frais, aiguillette de canette à la fleur de moutarde*, 190-250.

VIEUX-MOULIN, ⊠ 60350 Cuise-la-Motte, 10 km SE on the N 973 D 14.

Restaurant :

♦♦♦ *Auberge du Daguet*, 25, rue St-Jean, ☎ 44.85.60.72 ≼ ♪ ⅄ closed Wed , Feb school hols, 1-15 Jul. Fine 17th-C dwelling, 80-180 ; child : 50.

CONFLANS-SAINTE-HONORINE

Pontoise 8, Paris 30, Mantes 40 km
pop 29000 ⊠ 78700   B2

At the confluence ("conflans") of the Seine and the Oise, an important port for barges and lighters ; the town's social services are based in the converted barge *Je sers* ("I serve") ; there is a school for bargees' children and a chapel where a special service with procession is held in late June.

▶ **Musée de la Batellerie** (boating and barge museum ; *weekdays ex Tue am, 9-12 & 2-6 ; summer, daily 3-6 ; winter, weekends, 2-5).* ▶ Church of St. Maclou, 11th-13thC.

Also... ▶ **Andrésy** *(2.5 km SW) :* church (Romanesque Gothic) ; 16thC stained glass.   □

Practical Information

ⓘ 23, rue M.-Berteaux, ☎ (1) 39.72.66.91.
SNCF ☎ (1) 39.19.90.47.

Restaurant :

♦ **Au Bord de l'Eau**, 15, quai des Martyrs, ☎ (1) 39.72.86.51 ≼ ♪ ⊾ closed Mon , eves ex Wed and Sat, 9-15 Mar, 3-28 Aug, 100-140.

COULOMMIERS

Meaux 29, Paris 60, Sens 77 km
pop 12250 ⊠ 77120   D2

Coulommiers cheese is no longer made in the town itself ; however, the marketplace, the Rues Beaurepaire, de la Récherie, Bertrand-Flornoy and the old Rue de Melun remain the hub of activity.

▶ Municipal Park : remains of the **château des Longueville,** by Salomon de Brosse (1571-1624, architect of the Luxembourg Palace in Paris), situated between two arms of the Morin. Small municipal and regional museum in the chapel *(Sat. and Sun. pm in summer).* ▶ In the upper town, a former **Templars Commandery** houses numerous exhibitions and provides archaeological interest.   □

Practical Information

COULOMMIERS
ⓘ 11, rue du Gal-de-Gaulle, ☎ (1) 64.03.51.91.
SNCF ☎ (1) 64.03.01.61.

Restaurant :

♦ **Auberge de Montapeine**, 72, av. de Strasbourg, ☎ (1) 64.03.09.16, AE Euro Visa ▩ closed Mon, Wed eve, Sun eve, 15 Aug-8 Sep. Périgourdine specialties, 45-100.

Nearby

CHAUFFRY, ⊠ 77169 Boissy-le-Châtel, 8 km E.

Restaurant :

♦♦♦♦ **Taverne du Pot d'Etain**, 115, Grande Rue, ☎ (1) 64.20.42.08, AE Visa Ⓟ ▩ ♪ closed Mon eve and Tue, 15 Jan-15 Feb, 190-250.

FONTENAY-TRÉSIGNY, ⊠ 77610, 23 km.

Hotel :

● ★★★★ **Le Manoir** (R.C.), D 402, ☎ 64.25.91.17, Tx 690635, AE DC Euro Visa, 14 rm Ⓟ ▩ ⊾ ♪ ⅄ closed Tue, 1 Jan-10 Apr, 15 Nov-31 Dec, 570. Rest. ● ♦♦ ♪ closed Tue. A former huntsman's rendez-vous with Anglo-Norman charm. A fine place to eat : *saumon sauvage mariné à la suédoise, filet mignon à la moutarde de Meaux, aiguillette de canard au miel*, 120-220.

CRÉPY-EN-VALOIS*

Compiègne 24, Laon 68, Paris 70 km
pop 12280 ⊠ 60800   D1

Between the forests of Compiègne and Retz, Crépy-en-Valois retains reminders of its heyday as the former principal city of the Valois (Place Gambetta : sculpted façades, turrets, pediments).

▶ **Church of St. Denis** (12th and 16thC, restored). ▶ The former **Abbey of St. Arnould** dates from the 11thC, crypt 12thC, cloister 14thC. ▶ The fortress du **Château Royal** is now the **Archery Museum★,** honoring a tradition that still flourishes in the region ; the museum also contains religious images rescued from defunct or destroyed churches throughout the Valois *(10-12 & 2-6, Apr.-11 Nov. ; Sun., 10-12 & 3-7 ; closed Tue.).*

Also... ▶ 12thC façade of the **church of St. Thomas** (named for the martyred English Archbishop Saint Thomas-à-Becket).   □

Practical Information

SNCF ☎ 44.87.14.11/44.87.16.44.

Hotel :

★★ **Relais du Valois**, 2, pl. de Paon, ☎ 44.59.11.21, 14 rm Ⓟ closed Sun eve and Mon (l.s.), Feb, 150. Rest. ♦ Spec : *poissons (ragoût frais de la mer), pigeonneau à la valoise*, 65-120.

DOURDAN*

Etampes 18, Chartres 42, Paris 55 km
pop 8057 ⊠ 91410   B3

Capital of the **Hurepoix** region, traditionally one of the market gardens of Paris.

▶ **Place du Marché-aux-Grains★** : keep dating from Philippe Auguste (1125-1223) ; salt barn, now a museum *(10-12 & 2-6 ex Mon., Tue.) ;* church (12th-13thC, spires 17thC), 17thC covered market, 17th and 18thC mansions.

Nearby

▶ The Orge Valley divides the **Dourdan Forest** into two parts : the forests of St. Arnoult in the N and Ouye in the S. ▶ **Ouye** : former abbey *(3 km S) ;* moated **château de Sainte-Mesme** (17thC). ▶ **Château de Villeconin★** *(10 km E)* built by a Scots veteran of the Hundred Years' War ; transformed in the 17thC *(Jun.-Jul., 2-6:30 Sun. and nat.*

hols., daily in Aug.). ▶ **Saint Sulpice-de-Favières★** *(5 km from Villeconin)* : one of the prettiest churches in Ile-de-France. ☐

Practical Information _____

ℹ pl. Gal-de-Gaulle, ☎ (1) 64.59.86.97.
SNCF ☎ (1) 64.59.70.46, R.E.R. (ligne C), ☎ (1) 64.59.70.46.

Hotel :
● ★★★★ *Blanche de Castille*, pl. des Halles, ☎ (1) 64.59.68.92, Tx 690902, AE DC Visa, 40 rm Ⓟ 〰️ 280. Rest. ● ◆◆◆ ♪ Excellent value, enjoyable food : *poisson fine marée, ragoût ris et rognons*, 200-250.

⚠ ★★★*Les Petits Prés* (150 pl), ☎ (1) 64.92.80.75.

DREUX

Chartres 35, Paris 82, Rouen 97 km
pop 33760 ⊠ 28100   A3

The old town seems unaware of development that has made it the region's most important industrial centre. ▶ The church★ and the belfry★ are the work of two architects from the local Métezeau family (16thC); however, the ▶ Chapelle Royale of the royal Orléans family is much better known; the funerary chapel is a showcase of 19thC academic statuary *(9-12 & 2-dusk).* ▶ Drouais Museum *(2-5, Wed., Sat., Sun.).*
☐

Practical Information _____

DREUX
ℹ 4, rue Porte-Chartraine, ☎ 37.46.01.73.
SNCF ☎ 37.28.50.50/37.50.15.51.
Car rental : Avis, 3, rue des Embûches, ☎ 37.46.23.58.

Hotel :
● ★★ *Auberge Normande* (L.F.), 6, pl. Métezeau, ☎ 37.50.02.03, AE Euro Visa, 16 rm Ⓟ ⌖ closed Sun eve and Mon, 20 Dec-6 Jan, 160. Rest. ◆ 75-110.

Recommended
Youth hostel : 19, rue Pastre, ☎ 37.42.09.58.

Nearby

CHERISY, ⊠ 28500 Vernouillet, 2 km E.

Restaurant :
◆ *Le Vallon de Cherisy*, 12, rte de Paris, ☎ 37.43.70.08 ⌖ 〰️ ♪ closed Wed, 130-170.

SAINTE-GEMME, ⊠ 28500, 3 km E of **Moronval**.

Restaurant :
◆◆ *L'Escapade*, pl. Ch.-Jouves, ☎ 37.43.72.05, Visa Ⓟ 〰️ ♪ closed Mon and Sun eve, 15 Feb-1 Mar. Spec : *escargots au chèvre chaud, ris de veau impérial*, 130-220.

VERNOUILLET, ⊠ 28500, 2 km SW.

Hotel :
★ *Auberge de la Vallée Verte* (L.F.), 6, rue Lucien-Dupuis, ☎ 37.46.04.04, Visa, 12 rm, pens, closed Fri eve, Sun eve, Mon and Aug, 25 Dec-2 Jan, 220. Rest. ◆◆ ♪ 85-140.

Restaurant :
◆◆ *Aquaparc*, 28, rue Etienne-Malassis, Ecluzelles, ☎ 37.43.74.75, AE DC Euro Visa ⌖ 〰️ ♪ & closed Tue eve and Wed, 17 Feb-11 Mar. Spec : *paupiette de barbue à la mousse de rascasse*, 100-190.

ÉCOUEN★★★

Enghien 8, Chantilly 22, Paris 25 km
pop 4390 ⊠ 95440   C2

The sumptuous château of Anne de Montmorency (→ Chantilly) is one of the most important buildings

of the 16thC (1538-1555); now the **National Renaissance Museum★★★**. Twenty restored rooms display collections formerly in the Cluny Museum in Paris *(9:45-12:45 & 2-5:15; closed Tue.; free of charge Wed.).* Painted overmantels in the style of Fontainebleau; tapestry depicting David and Bathsheba★★; ceramic flooring by Abaquesne; enamels by Léonard Limosin; sculptures by della Robbia, Goujon and others; park and panorama★.

▶ **Saint-Acceul** and **Le Mesnil-Aubry** *(4 km N)* : stained glass in the parish churches.   ☐

ENGHIEN★

Pontoise 20, Paris 18, Chantilly 32 km
pop 9740 ⊠ 95880   C2

Lake surrounded by greenery, pedal boats, casino and rococo villas : all the charm of a turn-of-the-century spa only a short drive from Paris.   ☐

Practical Information _____

♨ (15 Mar-31 Dec).
ℹ 2, bd Cotte, ☎ (1) 34.12.41.15.
SNCF ☎ (1) 39.64.05.45/(1) 39.64.62.04.

Hotels :
★★★★(L) *Le Grand Hôtel*, 85, rue Gal-de-Gaulle, ☎ (1) 34.12.80.00, Tx 697842, AE DC Visa, 51 rm Ⓟ ⌖ 〰️ ⊡ 445. Rest. ◆◆ ⌖ ♪ & 125-220.
★★ *Villa Marie-Louise*, 49, rue de Malleville, ☎ (1) 39.64.82.21, 22 rm 〰️ ⊛ 190.

Restaurant :
● ◆◆◆ *Duc d'Enghien*, 3, av. de Ceinture, au casino, ☎ (1) 34.12.90.00 ⌖ & closed Mon and Sun eve Jan. Pierre Ducis, the energetic owner of the Duc d'Enghien (who's still waiting for his roulette table to arrive), has persuaded Michel Kéréver and his wife, Nelly (manager of the Grand Hôtel) to settle down here, much to the glee of the patrons and spa-goers who frequent this resort. Even if you're bound to diet, the light, inventive and savoury cuisine will please you : *langoustines rôties au gingembre, fanes de celeri frites, pigeon rôti aux lentilles, oignons blancs et lardons*. Fine cellar, 300-350.

Recommended
Casino : 3, av. de Ceinture, ☎ (1) 34.12.90.00.

ÉTAMPES★

Evry 37, Paris 51, Chartres 61 km
pop 19503 ⊠ 91150   C3

This large town on the edge of the Beauce plain hides treasures worthy of an Italian Renaissance city-state behind its somewhat suburban façade, including several Gothic churches and the Renaissance mansions of successive royal mistresses. ▶ **Church of St. Basile** : Romanesque façade from the 15th-16thC (*bas-reliefs* illustrating the life of Christ); Renaissance house opposite. ▶ **Notre-Dame-du-Fort** (end 12thC) : doorway reminiscent of Chartres, Romanesque capitals, 16thC stained glass, 11thC crypt. ▶ Numerous Renaissance mansions around the town hall (1514); local museum *(2-5 weekdays, 3-6 Sun. and hols.; closed Tue.).* ▶ **Guinette Tower**; 12thC royal keep with four watch-turrets, at the top of the town. ▶ Down the main street : **St. Gilles Church** has a Romanesque façade with Gothic nave and bell-tower, 15th-16thC side aisles. ▶ **Church of St. Martin** (12th-16thC) has a leaning tower.

Also... ▶ **Farcheville★** : imposing 13thC **fortified château** *(7 km E; no visitors).*

Round trip S of Étampes *(42 km approx)*

▶ The **Juine** and its tributary, the **Chalouette★**, cut through the golden plain of Beauce. ▶ **Méréville** : lake fed by the Juine; 18thC park, partly subdivided. Near the station and the covered market is Cook's Column, all that remains of the statuary commissioned by Jean-Joseph de Laborde (finance minister to Louis XVI), 18thC proprietor of the Renaissance château. The rest of the sculpture is now at Jeurre (→ below). ▶ **Chalou-Moulineux** : the source of the Chalouette river (fontaine Ste. Apolline); the 12thC church was a dependency of the neighbouring Templar's Commandery. ▶ **Moulineux** : lake reflecting the ruined 12thC church. ▶ **Chalo-Saint-Mars** : 11thC church, much remodelled. ▶ Return road to Étampes bordered by green fields.

Round trip N of Étampes *(60 km approx)*

▶ The **Juine Valley★** abounds with châteaux. ▶ **Morigny** : Abbot's Palace (18thC) and 12thC church★. ▶ Fortified farmhouse (now a hotel) at **Villemartin**. ▶ **Jeurre★** : park with statuary★ from Méréville (→ above; *visits at 10, 3*). ▶ On the opposite bank : **château de Chamarande★** and park by Mansart and Le Nôtre *(park visit only)*. ▶ **Gillevoisin** : château comprises three 17thC buildings. ▶ **Lardy** : the river flows through the town hall park. ▶ One of the largest dovecotes in France at the **château de Mesnil-Voisin**, a severe Louis XIII building *(2-6, Sun.)*. ▶ **Saint-Vrain** : where Mme. du Barry, Louis XV's mistress, was banished on his death; 325-acre safari park with African fauna *(Mar.-Nov., 10-6 daily)*. ▶ Junction of the Juine and Essonne rivers; popular with anglers and hunters. ▶ **Ballancourt** : château du **Grand Saussaye**, two 17thC buildings face-to-face *(2-5 Sun., 15 Mar.-15 Oct.)*. ▶ **La Ferté-Alais** : one of the earliest Gothic churches in the region. ▶ Follow the road along the right bank. ▶ **Boutigny-sur-Essonne**; another 12thC church, a mill and the château de Belesbat (17thC; now a hotel-restaurant); the river runs through cress beds, a regional speciality. ▶ Return to Étampes through the last stretch of Fontainebleau Forest; view of the imposing walls of **Farcheville★**. □

Practical Information

Nearby

MORIGNY, ⊠ 91150, 10 km NE.

Hotel :
● ★★★ **Hostellerie de Villemartin** (C.H.), ☎ (1) 64.94.63.54, AE Visa, 14 rm 🅿 ⧫ ⧫ ﹌ ♪ ⁄° closed Sun eve and Mon, Aug, 20 Dec-6 Jan, 210. Rest. ♦♦ ⧫ ♫ Peace and a pleasant change of scene in a 17-ha park, 90-200.

Melun 25, Paris 34, Versailles 38 km
pop 29578 ⊠ 91000   C3

Practical Information

ÉVRY
ℹ️ pl. de l'Agora, ☎ (1) 60.77.36.98.
SNCF ☎ (1) 60.77.31.34.

Nearby
Le COUDRAY-MONTCEAUX, ⊠ 91830, 7 km.

Restaurant :
♦ **Auberge du Barrage**, 40, Voie-de-Seine, ☎ 64.93.81.16, AE DC Visa ⧫ ♪ closed Mon and Sun eve , 1st week in Mar, 1-21 Oct, 120-280.

GRIGNY, ⊠ 91350, 4 km NW.

Hotel :
★★★ **Château du Clotay**, (I.L.A., C.H.), 8, rue du Port, ☎ (1) 69.06.89.70, AE DC Visa, 10 rm 🅿 ⧫ ▦ ﹌ ᓂ ⧫ ⌂ ⁄° closed Sun eve , Mon, Feb school hols, 450. Rest. ♦♦♦ ⧫ ♪ ⧫ A total change of scene just a few minutes from the capital; opulent, generous cuisine by A.Christian, 140-300; child : 100.

VILLIERS, ⊠ 91120 Villebon-sur-Yvette, 4 km of **Longjumeau**.

Restaurant :
♦♦ **Le Jardin de Villiers**, 34, rue de Saulx-les-Chartreux, ☎ 60.10.16.32, Visa 🅿 ▦ ♪ closed Mon and Sun eve, 10-20 Aug. A pleasant terrace in the country is the setting for Patrick Troquenet's youthful cuisine : *hure de saumon au citron vert, cassoulet de morue fraîche, palette de boeuf à la marinade*, 55-120.

Meaux 23, Paris 25, Melun 34 km
pop 1340 ⊠ 77164   C2
An astonishing steel-and-glass structure in Renaissance style built in 1859 by Joseph Paxton (English architect, 1801-65) for the financier James de Rothschild; scene of magnificent entertainments and also of negotiations that led to the Franco-Prussian Armistice of 1871. Louis XVI-Impératrice decoration★ by the painter Eugène Lami (1800-90); English park★ *(May-Sep., 2-7 ex Mon., Tue.; Oct.-Apr.; Sun. 2-5, groups on request).* □

Melun 16, Paris 65, Orléans 88 km
pop 18750 ⊠ 77300   C3-4
The **château★★★** was built for the kings of France, who hunted deer, boar, wolf and other game in the forest. François I built the original hunting lodge, but his successors in turn transformed it to suit contemporary tastes : Francois I's gallery, Henri II's ballroom, the apartments of the three queen mothers (Catherine and Marie de Medicis and Anne of Austria), the throne room (Louis XIII ceiling), Madame de Maintenon's apartments, the Louis XV wing, Marie-Antoinette's boudoir. Napoleon refurnished many of the salons; the courtyard with the famous horseshoe staircase is also known as *«la Cour des Adieux»* (the farewell courtyard), for it was here that Napoleon bade farewell to his men when he abdicated in 1814. Forty years later, Napoleon III added a charming theater.

Like Versailles at a later date, Fontainebleau created a decorative style of its own. The first school of Fontainebleau, as the earlier style is known, was influenced by Mannerist tastes introduced by the Italian artists — Il Primaticcio, Rosso, Cellini, to name only three — whom François commissioned to adorn his residence. This style was supplanted by the work of the Flemish craftsmen who, during the reign of Henri IV, inspired the second Fontainebleau school. ▶ Garden of Diana — named for the central statue of the Goddess Diana : **gardens★** arranged in the manner of an English park to the E, and in the formal French style to the W *(visits : gardens and park, sunrise to sunset; château : 9:30-12 & 2-5 ex Tue.).*
Also... ▶ **Napoleonic Museum** *(10-12 & 2-5 ex Sun., Mon.; closed Sep., nat. hols.).* ▶ Le Vieux Logis, ravishing Ile-de-France house opposite park *(10-12 & 2-4, Apr.-Sep. ex Sun.).* ▶ **Avon church★** (12th-16thC). □

Practical Information

FONTAINEBLEAU
ℹ️ 31, pl. Bonaparte (B-C2), ☎ (1) 64.22.25.68.
SNCF ☎ (1) 64.22.39.82.
Car rental : *Avis*, 185, rue Grande (C2), ☎ (1) 64.22.49.65.

Hotels :
● ★★★★(L) **L'Aigle Noir**, (Mapotel), 27, pl. Napoléon-Bonaparte, ☎ (1) 64.22.32.65, Tx 600080, AE DC Euro Visa, 30 rm 🅿 ⧫ 🐎 785. Rest. ● ♦♦♦ ♪ Delightful classic cuisine, 180-350.

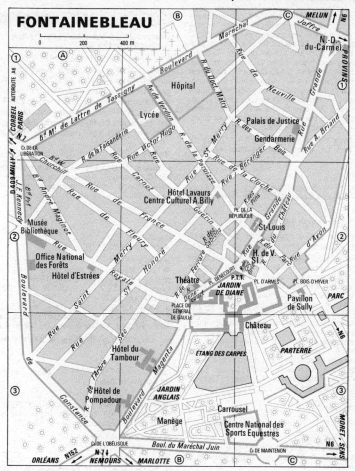

FONTAINEBLEAU

0   200   400 m

Legris et Parc, 36, rue du Parc (C2), ☎ (1) 64.22.24.24, Euro Visa, 30 rm ▥ ♨ closed 21 Dec-25 Jan, 230. Rest. ♦♦ ≼ closed Sun eve (l.s.), 75-140.

★★ Londres, 1, pl. du Gal-de-Gaulle (B2-3), ☎ (1) 64.22.20.21, AE Euro Visa, 22 rm Ⓟ ≼ closed 20 Dec-1 Feb, 240. Rest. ♦♦ ≼ 85-230.

★★ Toulouse, 183, Rue-Grande (C1), ☎ (1) 64.22.22.73, Visa, 18 rm Ⓟ closed 20 Dec-20 Jan, 128.

Restaurants :

♦♦ ***Chez Arrighi***, 53, rue de France (Ile de Beauté) (A-B2), ☎ (1) 64.22.29.43, AE DC Euro Visa ♪ 75-120.

♦♦ ***Le Filet de Sole***, 5, rue du Coq-Gris (C2), ☎ (1) 64.22.25.05, AE DC Euro Visa ♨ closed Tue and Wed , Jul. In a venerable residence, 100-150.

♦♦ ***Le François-1er***, 3, rue Royale (A2), ☎ (1) 64.22.24.68, AE DC Euro Visa Ⓟ ≼ ▥ ♪ closed Thu (l.s.), 5-31 Jan, 110-300 ; child : 50.

Recommended

♥ pastry : *Le Délice Impérial*, 1, rue-Grande, ☎ 64.22.20.70.

> On the maps, a town's name underlined <u>Saulieu</u> means that the locality possesses at least one recommended establishment (blue or red point).

Nearby

BROLLES, ✉ 77590 Bois-le-Roi, 12 km N.

Hotel :

★★ Forêt, 67, av. Alfred-Roll, ☎ (1) 60.69.64.64, Visa, 23 rm Ⓟ ▥ ♨ half pens, 295. Rest. ♦♦ ♪ Spec : *ragoût de Saint-Jacques aux truffes, terrine d'anguille au poivre vert*, 85-180.

FONTAINEBLEAU Forest

C4

The 170 km² forest of Fontainebleau has been a renowned hunting ground since the Middle Ages when it was known as Bière. Dramatic rocks, lush vegetation and abundant wildlife attract thousands of nature-lovers, archaeologists, rock-climbers and hikers every week. Newcomers can find a guide at the Office National des Forêts, 217 Rue Grande, Fontainebleau.

Oak is found most often, followed by beech, hornbeam, alder and pine. Long, broken sandstone ridges have a total of about 40 km² and end in bare spurs and plateaux. Depressions are called *gorges, vallées* or *plaines*, according to size. Many of the rocky outcrops contain caves with markings that provoke endless debate among archaeologists. Paths were first marked out in the 19thC when enthusiasm was at its height for the natural landscape beloved by the Barbizon school painters. Today a network of walking and bridle paths is in constant use, and four "quiet zones" have been created. The **forest paths** are marked in blue, the GR in red/white; don't confuse these signs with the orientation marks painted on the rocks for climbers. Among the most famous sites : Denecourt Tower (named for one of the first 19thC enthusiasts), La Solle (above the racecourse), Apremont Gorges near Barbizon (→) and the Franchard Gorges.

Also... ▶ Les Trois Pignons near Milly (→), Chaos de Nemours (→) and La Dame Jehanne near Larchant (→ Nemours). □

GRAND-MORIN Valley*

C-D2

From Lagny to Coulommiers (45 km approx)

The Brie plateau is picturesque valley country with lush vegetation, apple orchards, streams and villages.

▶ **Lagny-sur-Marne** (pop. 18 000), and old fortified town, now part of the new town of **Marne-la-Vallée** : gabled houses in the 15thC covered market, Place de la Fontaine (12thC fountain and Flamboyant Gothic church), and Notre-Dame-des-Ardents★ (unfinished 13thC abbey church). Local museum *(2-6 Wed.-Sun).* ▶ **Coupvray** is a traditional Brie village, birthplace of Louis Braille (1809-52), the harness-maker's son who, although blind himself from the age of three, invented the alphabet fot the blind. **Museum★** *(10-12 & 2-6 ex Tue).* ▶ **La Chapelle-sur-Crécy** : elegant 13thC Gothic collegiate church★. ▶ **Crécy-la-Chapelle★**, a fortified island town encircled by the Morin. A pleasant road continues along the left bank as far as **Coulommiers** (→), through **Tigeaux** and **Guérard**, in a bend of the river. □

Practical Information ————

CRÉCY-LA-CHAPELLE, ⊠ 77580, 15 km S of **Meaux**.

Restaurant :
♦♦♦ *Auberge du Moulin*, ☎ (1) 64.36.99.89 P 〈 ⅏ ⚲ closed Tue eve and Wed. Savoury seasonal cuisine in a pretty mill house, 150.

HOUDAN*

Dreux 21, Versailles 41, Paris 63 km
pop 2975 ⊠ 78550   B3

When Houdan was a staging post for the army, the wood-fronted houses along the two streets leading to the **church★** were mostly inns. The church, a superb mixture of Flamboyant Gothic and Renaissance styles, has an amusing 16thC fresco. 12thC keep, washhouses on the Vesgre and the Opton rivers. □

Practical Information ————

SNCF ☎ 36.46.60.58.

Restaurant :
● ♦♦♦♦ *La Poularde*, (Pierre et Sylvain Vandenameele), N 12, 24, av. République, ☎ (1) 30.59.60.50, AE Visa P ⅏ ⚲ ♪ closed 10-20 Feb. The house was pleasant enough before, but since change is now the fashion, father and son have followed the trend. Result : a comfortable new decor where you can enjoy the same delicious 'classic or modern' cuisine : *tourte houdannaise, poulette en aumonière truffée, morue fraîche aux pleurotes*, 180-250.

Recommended
Events : *foire Saint-Matthieu*, end Sep.

ILLIERS-COMBRAY*

Chartres 25, Le Mans 95, Paris 118 km
pop 3450 ⊠ 28120   A4

The writer Marcel Proust (1871-1922) spent his childhood holidays at Illiers with his Aunt Léonie (museum★, *visits at 3, 4 ex Tue.*), and devotees of his great novel *Remembrance of Things Past* come here to discover Combray, the Vivonne (the Loir), the Pré-Catelan, St. Hilaire (church of St. Jacques, 14thC, with painted wood barrel-vault) and the famous *madeleine* cakes from the local bakery, the *Pâtisserie Benoist*.

Nearby

▶ **Brou★** : old market town between Beauce and Perche; 16thC houses. ▶ Renaissance church at **Yèvres** (wood panelling and French Classical furniture). ▶ **Chateau de Frazé** (15thC, much restored; *open Sun. and nat. hols.*). □

Practical Information ————

ILLIERS-COMBRAY
SNCF ☎ 37.22.01.51.

Hotels :
● ★★ *Moulin de Montjouvin* (L.F.), rte de Brou, ☎ 37.24.32.32, DC Euro Visa, 19 rm P 〈 ⅏ ⚲ ♪ closed Wed, 27 Jul-11 Aug, 20 Dec-20 Jan, 160. Rest. ♦ 〈 ♪ 60-195; child : 40.
★ *Gare* (L.F.), pl. de la Gare, ☎ 37.24.04.21, AE DC Euro Visa, 8 rm P ⚲ closed Mon eve and Sun eve, 20 Aug-7 Sep, 20 Dec-7 Jan, 145. Rest. ♦ 〈 45-120.
⚴ ★★*de Montjouvin* (30 pl), ☎ 37.24.03.04.

Nearby

La BAZOCHE-GOUET, ⊠ 28330 Authon-du-Perche, 20 km SW of **Brou**.

Restaurant :
● ♦ *L'Etoile*, 58, rue J.-Moulin, ☎ 37.49.30.64, Visa P ⚲ ♪ closed Wed. With room and bicycle rental. Excellent value at this pleasant stopover, 55-120.

BROU, ⊠ 28160, 13 km SW.
SNCF ☎ 37.47.00.17.

Hotel :
★ *Plat d'Etain*, 15, pl. des Halles, ☎ 37.47.03.98, 18 rm P ⚲ ✆ closed Sun eve (l.s.), 1 Feb-5 Mar, 190. Rest. ♦ 70-95.

Restaurant :
♦ *La Clé des Champs*, Unverre, 7 km NW, ☎ 37.97.20.36 P 〈 ⅏ ⚲ ⚲ closed eves ex Sat, Tue lunch, 1-8 Feb, 15-22 Apr, 15-30 Jul, 50-150.

L' ISLE-ADAM

Pontoise 13, Chantilly 23, Paris 39 km
pop 9480 ⊠ 95290   C2

On the Oise, riverbank recreation area; Cabouillet Bridge; Renaissance church; a forest of oak and limetrees. Hilly to the E; pleasant churches at **Presles** (12th-16thC) and **Maffliers** (16thC). □

JOUARRE*

Meaux 20, Coulommiers 34, Paris 73 km
pop 2704 ⊠ 77640   D2

Jouarre looks down from the Brie plateau to the Petit Morin, melting into the Marne. The road, dating from the Revolution, divides the buildings of the Benedictine abbey★.

▶ On one side is the parish church (16thC; remarkable sculptures) and the **Mérovingian crypt** built of Gallo-

Roman material (tombs★★ of the founders); on the other side is the Romanesque tower of the abbey church, three superimposed units vaulted in the 16thC, where memorabilia from the abbey are on display *(weekdays 10-12 & 2-6, 5 in winter; Sun. opens at 11; closed Tue.).*

Petit Morin Valley★ *(50 km approx)*

▶ **Jouarre.** ▶ The road runs up the central plateau of dairy-farming Brie until it reaches **Rebais**, on Gargantua Hill (view) : 12thC church and abbey buildings (17thC). ▶ Detour to **Doue** to see the Gothic choir and 14thC stained glass. ▶ The imposing church at **Verdelot** (15th-16thC) is dedicated to St. Crispin, patron saint of shoemakers (15thC statuettes). ▶ Frescos in the 13th-14thC church at **Bellot.** ▶ Return along the right bank via **Saint-Cyr-sur-Morin** : the writer Pierre MacOrlan (1882-1970) lived here from 1924 until his death; (museum; *pm*); church 12th, 14th and 16thC.   □

Practical Information _____

JOUARRE

Hotel :
★ **Plat d'Etain** (L.F.), 6, pl. A.-Tinchant, ☎ (1) 60.22.06.07, 14 rm Ⓟ closed Sun eve and Mon, 15 Feb-1 Mar, 180. Rest. ◆ 120-210.

Nearby

La FERTÉ-SOUS-JOUARRE, ⊠ 77260, 3 km N.

Restaurant :
● ◆◆◆◆ *Auberge de Condé*, 1, av. de Montmirail, ☎ (1) 60.22.00.07, AE DC Euro Visa Ⓟ ♪ closed Mon eve and Tue , Feb school hols. Much to his parents' satisfaction, Pascal Tingaud has decided to go solo : *salade de langoustines au foie de canard, navarin de la mer, tournedos au bouzy.* All (or nearly all) the great Champagnes, 250-400; child : 70.

MERY-SUR-MARNE, ⊠ 77440 Lizy-sur-Ourcq, 11 km NE.

Hotel :
★★ *Le Château Marysien* (L.F.), ☎ (1) 60.01.71.30, 10 rm Ⓟ ⅏ closed Sun eve and Mon, Feb, 180. Rest. ◆◆ 75-150.

NANTEUIL-SUR-MARNE, ⊠ 77730 Saâcy-sur-Marne, 13 km NE.

Hotel :
Auberge du Lion d'Or, 2, rue du Bac, ☎ 60.23.62.21, Euro Visa, 12 rm Ⓟ ♣ ⅏ ⌕ closed Sun eve , Feb. Rest. ◆ ⅋ ♪ 55-130.

MANTES-LA-JOLIE

Versailles 44, Paris 60, Rouen 81 km
pop 43585 ⊠ 78200   B2

This town no longer lives up to its name ("Pretty Mantes") : WWII left little of its former beauty, and the banks of the Seine, polluted and concrete-laden, offer little to attract walkers. Nevertheless the **collegiate church★★**, twin of Notre-Dame of Paris, is an important example of Gothic art.

▶ Central doorway; chapel of Navarre (14thC); statuettes of the four royal foundresses. ▶ Hôtel-Dieu (18thC; hospital). ▶ Saint-Maclou Tower. ▶ Maximilian Luce museum (work of local landscape painter; *2-5:30 ex Tue.*). ▶ Pont de Limay (12thC bridge). ▶ **Gassicourt** (2 km W) : Romanesque church (12th-13thC) with 13thC stained glass. ▶ Limay : 11th-13thC church, statues★.

Nearby

▶ **Rosny** : to the W, the Château de Sully (16th-19thC), neo-Classical almshouse; and Singer sewing-machine factory. ▶ To the S, Vaucouleurs Valley : châteaux of **Rosay** (17thC) and **Septeuil** (18thC). ▶ **Mauldre Valley** :

12thC church; **château d'Épône** (18thC). ▶ **Maule** : château (Louis XIII) and Romanesque-Renaissance church.

Valleys of the Vexin★ *(65 km approx, half-day)*

Every village has a pretty church and/or a château. ▶ **Mantes.** ▶ The route climbs N on the plateau of Arthies (views). ▶ Romanesque church at **Fontenay-Saint-Père**; pink and white château at **Le Mesnil.** ▶ **Arthies** : fortress with dovecote. ▶ In July, detour via the **château de Maudétour** (18thC, unfinished). ▶ **Guiry-en-Vexin★** : classical 17thC château where J. de Maistre (1753-1821 ; Catholic political theorist) lived. Local archaeology museum *(tel. : (1) 34.67.40.31 or 37.04.31.73).* Renaissance church. ▶ Another 17th-18thC château at **Gadancourt**; church with Romanesque bell tower. ▶ **Avernes**, by the source of the river Aubette : 13th and 18thC church. ▶ **Thémericourt** : lovely site, 17thC château and 13thC church. ▶ **Château de Vigny** (Renaissance, 19thC; *Mar.-Nov., Sat.-Mon. and hols.*), ancestral home of the poet Alfred de Vigny (1797-1863). Nearby, château de **Grizy** *(Aug., pm).* ▶ **Longuesse** : Romanesque church, remodelled in 17thC. ▶ **Château de Villette★**, designed by Hardouin-Mansart (1667). The philosopher and encyclopaedist Condorcet (1743-94) lived here *(Sun. and nat. hols., 3-6).* ▶ **Meulan** : a yachting centre on the Seine. ▶ Return along the **Montcient Valley** in the shadow of the 12th-13thC church spires of **Gaillon-sur-Montcient**.   □

Practical Information _____

MANTES-LA-JOLIE
ⓘ pl. Jean-XXIII, ☎ (1) 34.47.10.30.
SNCF ☎ (1) 34.77.55.14/(1) 30.92.45.16.
Car rental : *Avis*, 78, av. Franklin-Roosevelt, ☎ 30.94.44.44.

Restaurant :
◆◆◆ *La Feuilleraie*, 4, rue Wilson, Follainville, ☎ (1) 34.77.17.66, Euro Visa ⅋ ⅏ closed Mon and Tue, 3-28 Aug. Spec : *ris et rognons de veau aux champignons,* 250-300.

Nearby

BONNIÈRES, ⊠ 78270, 12 km NW.

Restaurant :
◆◆ *Hostellerie du Bon Accueil*, rte de Vernon, RN 15, ☎ (1) 30.93.01.00 ♪ ♧ closed Tue eve and Wed , Feb shool hols, Aug. Spec. : *nage de coquille St-Jacques aux herbes fraîches, sabayon aux fruits rouges,* 260-290.

ROLLEBOISE, ⊠ 78270 Bonnières, 9 km W.

Hotel :
● ★★★ *Château de la Corniche*, (C.H., R.S.), 5, rte de la Corniche, ☎ (1) 30.93.21.24, Tx 695544, 30 rm Ⓟ ⅏ ☒ ♪° half pens, closed Sun eve and Mon (l.s.), Mar-Apr, 420. Rest. ◆◆◆ ⅋ ♪ ♧ Spec : *montgolfière de homards, truite de mer à la normande, foie gras au naturel,* 190-350.

MARLY-LE-ROI*

Saint-Germain-en-Laye 4, Versailles 9, Paris 27 km
pop 17300 ⊠ 78160   B2

The hillside town of Marly once looked down on the 13 pavilions built by Mansart to provide a country retreat for Louis XIV. The pavilions have long since gone, but the grounds have been preserved.

▶ The **park★** plunges down to the Seine; the horse-pond was formerly adorned by the Girardon statues of horses now to be seen in Paris at the junction of the Champs-Elysées and the Place de la Concorde. Near the royal gate, an **outdoor museum** records the history of the village and the estate *(2-6 ex Mon., Tue. and nat. hols.)*. Artists such as Sisley, Maillol and Vuillard flocked to Marly in the late 19thC and early 20thC. ▶ The church of St. Vigor is by Mansart. ▶ 18thC mansions around the town hall and the royal kennels. ▶ **Port-Marly** : Villa Monte-Cristo, the

Oriental-Gothic folly where the novelist Alexandre Dumas the elder (1802-70) lived.

Nearby

▶ **Louveciennes** : another aristocratic retreat : 13thC church; 18thC château; Mme. du Barry's pavilion (designed by Ledoux). ▶ **Forest of Marly** : 20 km² of oak, beech and chestnut with many roe deer; explore it along GR1.　　□

Practical Information _____

MARLY-LE-ROI
🄸 pl. du Gal-de-Gaulle, ☎ (1) 39.58.73.00.
SNCF ☎ (1) 39.58.51.90.

Hotel :
★★★ *Auberge Henri IV*, 5, pl. de l'Abreuvoir, ☎ (1) 39.58.47.61, AE, 8 rm 🄿 ⌇ 🔊 ♪ 🔥 🏖 closed Feb school hols, 31 Jul-31 Aug, 250. Rest. ◆◆ ⌇ 🔥 🏖 closed Wed eve and Sun eve. Spec : *turbot au champagne, ris de veau en papillote*, 125-160.

Nearby

LOUVECIENNES, ✉ 78430, 2 km E.

Restaurant :
◆◆ *Aux Chandelles*, 12, pl. de l'Eglise, ☎ (1) 39.69.08.40, AE Visa ⌇ 🔊 ♪ closed Wed, Sat noon, Sun eve, 120-180.

MARNE Valley

C2

The area between Nogent and Lagny has still retained its rustic character; the river is dotted with islands, and a canal runs beneath rows of poplars. Parks and a leisure centre are still under construction for the new town of Marne-la-Vallée.

▶ Mme. de Pompadour lived at the **Château de Champs**★ (18thC; *10-12 & 2-6, 4:30 in winter*). ▶ See the Menier chocolate factory★ (designed by Gustav Eiffel, 1832-1923) and workers' accommodation at **Noisiel**; a valuable reminder of 19thC industrial architecture and workforce organisation. ▶ **Guermantes**★ : château, evoking Proust's masterpiece; 18thC décor *(2-6, Sat., Sun. and nat. hols., 15 Mar.-15 Nov.)*.　　□

Practical Information _____

GUERMANTES, ✉ 77400 Lagny, 4 km W of **Marne-la-Vallée**.

Restaurant :
◆ *Relais de Guermantes*, pl. de l'Eglise, ☎ (1) 64.30.13.03, Visa 🔊 closed Tue eve and Wed, Aug, 100-150.

MEAUX*

Paris 53, Melun 57, Reims 96 km
pop 45875 ✉ 77100　　　　　　　　　　D2

This market town in a loop of the Marne is renowned for Brie and Bossuet : Brie de Meaux is the local variety of the cheese; the celebrated bishop of Meaux, the writer and orator Bossuet (1627-1704), was tutor to the Dauphin (later Louis XV), and a leading 17thC intellectual.

▶ The Gothic cathedral★ (end 12th-16thC) is connected to the chapterhouse (13thC; covered staircase 16thC). ▶ The former episcopal palace★ (12th, 17thC) squares off the courtyard; Bossuet Museum (personal effects, writings) and Briard Museum (the Brie region; *10-12 & 2-6, closed Tue. and nat. hols.*); garden in the form of a bishop's mitre by Le Nôtre; Bossuet's study *(historical spectacle in summer)*.

Nearby

▶ **Trilport** *(5 km E)* : riverside recreation area. **Montceaux-lès-Meaux** *(8.5 km E)* : ruins of Catherine de Médicis' château★ in park (*visit on request*, ☎ *(1) 64.35.93.03*).　　□

Practical Information _____

MEAUX
🄸 2, rue Notre-Dame, ☎ (1) 64.33.02.26.
SNCF ☎ (1) 64.33.11.36/(1) 64.34.06.14.
Car rental : *Avis*, 113, av. Foch, ☎ 64.34.59.87/ 64.34.48.04.

Recommended
♥ at Mareuil-les-Meaux, brie : *Caves d'affinage A. Berton*, La Grande Madeleine, ☎ 64.34.69.72.

Nearby

ARMENTIÈRES-EN-BRIE, ✉ 77440 Lizy-sur-Ourcq, 9 km NE.

Hotel :
Auberge du Poisson Couronné, 7, rue de Meaux, ☎ (1) 64.35.50.85, AE Visa, 12 rm 🔊 closed Nov-Jan, 180. Rest. ◆◆◆ A former boatmen's inn. Spec : *confit de lotte aux amandes, émincé de bœuf au coulis landais*, 130-225.

CLAYE-SOUILLY, ✉ 77410, 15 km W.

Restaurant :
◆◆ *La Grillade*, 19, rue J.-Jaurès, ☎ (1) 60.26.00.68, AE Euro Visa ♪ 🏖 closed Mon eve and Sun eve, Feb, 14 Aug-14 Sep. Spec : *délice de morilles à la ciboulette*, 130-220.

SANCY-LES-MEAUX, ✉ 77580 Crépy-la-Chapelle, 13 km S.

Hotel :
● ★★★ *La Catounière* (C.H.), 1, rue de l'Eglise, ☎ (1) 60.25.71.74, AE DC Euro Visa, 11 rm 🄿 ⌇ 🔊 🔥 🄵 🐕 close, closed 17 Aug-1 Sep, 11 Sep-1 Dec, 720. Rest. ◆◆ ⌇ 🔥 A handsome 18th-C residence. Spec : *foie gras de canard maison, émincé de rognon de veau moutarde de Meaux*, 180-250; child : 80.

VARREDDES, ✉ 77910, 8 km NE.

Hotel :
★★★ *Auberge du Cheval Blanc*, ☎ 64.33.18.03, AE DC Visa, 10 rm 🄿 🔊 closed Sun eve and Mon, Aug, 200. Rest. ◆◆ ♪ 🏖 150-220.

Restaurant :
◆◆ *Auberge du Petit Matin*, 7, rue d'Orsay, ☎ 64.33.18.12, AE Euro Visa 🔊 ♪ 🏖 closed Tue eve, Wed, Thu eve, 11 Feb-6 Mar, 15-31 Jul, 100-160.

MELUN

Meaux 57, Paris 57, Sens 66 km
pop 36220 ✉ 77000　　　　　　　　　　C3

Melun, like Paris, grew from an island in the Seine into an important industrial centre.

▶ On the right bank, **St. Aspais Church** (late Gothic, 16thC). ▶ On the island, next to the prison, the **church of Notre-Dame** (Romanesque, much restored); Vicomté Mansion, Quai de la Courtille : small museum with 19thC landscapes *(10-12 & 2-6; closed Tue., Sun. and nat. hols.)*.

Nearby

▶ Ruins of the **abbey of Lys** *(3 km SW)*, founded by Blanche de Castille (1188-1252, wife of Louis VIII and mother of Louis IX (St. Louis). ▶ 18thC château at **Vaux-le-Pénil**★ *(2 km on Chartrettes road)*; now a museum of Surrealist art (Dali, de Chirico; *usually open Sun. pm; tel. 60.68.61.33)*. ▶ 11 km into the Brie plain is the **château de Blandy**, an interesting example of feudal architecture (14th, 16th-17thC; *9-12 & 2-6, 7 Sat., Sun.; Nov.-Apr. by* appt.). ▶ Gothic church at **Champeaux★** *(11 km NE)* : amusing choir stalls. □

Practical Information

MELUN
ℹ angle av. Thiers et av. Gallieni, ☎ (1) 64.37.11.31.
ЅＮＣＦ ☎ (1) 64.37.15.91/(1) 64.39.18.23.
Car rental : *Avis*, 8, av. du Gal Patton, ☎ 64.52.71.72.

Hotel :
★★★ *Grand Monarque Concorde*, rte de Fontainebleau, ☎ (1) 64.39.04.40, Tx 690140, AE DC Euro Visa, 50 rm 🅿 ⌣ ⌘ ◁ ♪ ⚘ ♿ ⊡ 370. Rest. ♦♦ ♪ Spec : *dos de saumon rôti à la crème d'artichauts, jambonnette de lapereau à la fleur de moutarde*, 145-220.

Restaurant :
♦♦ *Auberge Vaugrain*, 1, rue de la Vannerie, ☎ (1) 64.52.08.23, AE Euro Visa ♪ closed Mon and Sun eve. F. Desroys du Roure serves contemporary cuisine in a 16th-C house : fish, oysters and shellfish, dessert buffet, 180-250.

Nearby

BRIE-COMTE-ROBERT, ✉ 77170, 18 km NW.

Restaurant :
♦ *La Grâce de Dieu*, 45, rue Gal-Leclerc, ☎ 64.05.00.76, Visa ⌀ closed Wed and Sun eve , Aug. Spec : *coq au vin, filet au poivre, civet de lièvre*, 75-150.

PRINGY, ✉ 77310, 6 km SW.

Restaurant :
♦♦ *Auberge du Bas-Pringy*, 20, av. de Fontainebleau, ☎ (1) 60.65.57.75, AE DC Euro Visa ⌀ ♪ ♿ closed Mon eve and Tue, 23 Feb-4 Mar, 27 Jul-27 Aug. Spec : *cassolette d'escargots de Bourgogne fenouillarde, noix de ris braisées aux pleurotes fraîches à la crème*, 50-180 ; child : 40.

VARENNES-JARCY, ✉ 91480, 22 km.

Restaurant :
♦ *Auberge du Moulin de Jarcy*, 50, rue Boieldieu, ☎ 69.00.89.20, Visa 🅿 ⌣ ⌀ ♫ 5 rm, closed Wed and Thu, 70-150.

MILLY-LA-FORÊT*

Fontainebleau 20, Paris 62, Orléans 76 km
pop 3795 ✉ 91490   C4
Milly lies in a basin on the edge of the forest of Fontainebleau, where the river École waters cress beds and fields of medicinal plants. The decorations by Cocteau (1959) in the chapel of **St-Blaise-des-Simples** were inspired by this local speciality of "simples" or medicinal herbs *(Easter-1 Nov., daily ex Tue. ; winter, Sat. and Sun., 10-12 & 2-6)*. 15thC **marketplace★**.

Nearby

▶ **Massif des Trois Pignons★★** : among the most dramatic in Fontainebleau Forest. ▶ **Château de Courances** *(10 km NE)* : surrounded by a magnificent water-garden★★ *(Apr.-Nov., 2-6:30, Sat., Sun., and nat. hols.)*. □

Practical Information

Restaurant :
● ♦♦♦ *Le Moustier*, 41 bis, rue Langlois, ☎ 64.98.92.52, closed Mon and Tue, 19 Aug-9 Sep, 22 Dec-6 Jan. In his fine 14th-C chapel, chef Gauthier serves discreet, classic cuisine. Portions are pretty discreet too - how about a more generous hand, chef? Langoustines sautées aux girolles, canard aux pêches, 140-300.

△ ★★★*La Musardière* (120 pl), ☎ (1) 64.24.52.03.
Recommended
♥ at Soisy-sur-Ecole, art glass : ☎ (1) 64.99.00.03.

MONTEREAU-FAULT-YONNE

Fontainebleau 22, Melun 30, Paris 90 km
pop 19557 ✉ 77130   D4
At the junction of the Seine and the Yonne ; church of Notre-Dame and St-Loup (14th-16thC) ; priory of St-Martin (11thC) ; prehistoric site at Pincevent on the Varennes road. **Faience Museum** in former post-office *(Jun.-14 Sep., 2-6 daily ex Tue. ; rest of year, weekends only)*. □

MONTFORT-L'AMAURY**

Versailles 28, Dreux 40, Paris 50 km
pop 2675 ✉ 78490   B3
At the edge of Rambouillet Forest (→) : rather self-consciously picturesque, with tiled roofs and cobbled streets.

▶ Old ramparts ; ruins of the Montfort keep (11thC) ; tower of Anne de Bretagne (15thC). ▶ Church of St. Pierre (end 15th-17thC ; Renaissance stained glass). ▶ Former **charnel-house★** (1584-1608). ▶ Ravel Museum : the composer Maurice Ravel lived here 1921-37 *(9-11:30 & 2:30-5:30 or 6, Sat., Sun. and nat. hols. ; Mon., Wed., Thu. : pm)*.

The Forest of Rambouillet

▶ GR1 from Neauphle to Saint-Léger goes past Ravel's house to the lake near the Baudet Gate ; a cycle path runs to Rambouillet (→) past the prettiest **lakes** in the forest. Views of châteaux : ▶ SE, **Les Mesnuls** (16th-18thC), now a hospital and training centre for physically-handicapped children ; ▶ **La Mormaire**, (Louis XIII style ; *4 km SW*) ; ▶ **Château du Rouvray** W of Saint-Léger ; ▶ **Château de Neuville** (16thC), at **Gambais**. ▶ **Parc zoologique de Thoiry** : 21 species and more than 100 herbivores and African birds in partial liberty *(10-5 in winter, 6 in summer)*. □

Practical Information

MONTFORT-L'AMAURY
ЅＮＣＦ ☎ (1) 34.86.00.56.

Restaurants :
● ♦♦♦ *Les Préjugés*, 18, pl. R.-Brault, ☎ (1) 34.86.92.65, AE DC Visa ⌣ ♿ closed Tue, 5 Jan-12 Feb. A garden and lovely bouquets set the stage for the delicate cuisine of a young Cambodian chef. 'Eclectic' fixed meal, 175-380.
♦♦ *Chez Nous*, 22, rue de Paris, ☎ (1) 34.86.01.62, AE DC Visa ♪ closed Mon and Sun eve , Oct. Seasonal cooking : *sauté de gigot à l'ail doux, chavignol sur fondue de poireaux au sancerre, gratin de framboises*, 120-210.

Nearby

Les MESNULS, ✉ 78490, 3 km SE.

Restaurant :
♦♦♦ *La Toque Blanche*, 12, Grande-Rue, ☎ (1) 34.86.05.55, AE Visa ⌀ closed Mon and Sun eve , Aug and Xmas. Spec : *marmite de canard sauce poivrade*, 240-320.

PONTCHARTRAIN, ✉ 78760, 9 km NE.

Hotel :
★★★★ *Auberge de la Dauberie* (C.H.), Les Mousseaux, ☎ (1) 34.87.80.57, AE DC Euro Visa, 10 rm 🅿 ⌀ ⌣ closed Mon, Tue (l.s.), 12 Jan-12 Mar, 420. Rest. ♦♦♦ 220-320.

Restaurants :
● ♦♦♦ *L'Aubergade*, RN 12, ☎ (1) 34.89.02.63, Visa ⌣ ⌀ closed Tue eve and Wed, 27 Jul-28 Aug. In Lucien

Ogier's fine house, son-in-law Jean Bordier upholds tradition : *gratin de queues d'écrevisses*, excellent array of Burgundies, 250-300.
♦♦♦ **Chez Sam**, 87, rte du Pontel, RN 12, ☎ (1) 34.89.02.05, AE DC Visa ⟶ ♪ closed Mon eve and Tue, 20 Jan-1 Mar, 150-250; child : 80.

La QUEUE-EN-YVELINES, ⊠ 78890, 5 km NW.

Restaurant :
♦♦ **Auberge de la Malvina**, lieu-dit La Haute Perruche, Garancières, ☎ 34.86.45.76, Visa ⟶ ♪ closed Wed eve and Thu ex hols, 3-27 Nov. The tranquillity of a blooming summer garden, a crackling fire in winter. Spec : *filet de boeuf Soraya, gâteau de courgettes*, 145-220.

SAINTE-APOLLINE, ⊠ 78370 Plaisir, 13 km NE.

Restaurant :
♦♦ **Maison des Bois**, rte de Pontchartrain, ☎ (1) 30.54.23.17, Visa ⟶ closed Thu and Sun eve , Feb school hols, 30 Jul-5 Sep. Spec : *ris de veau aux écrevisses*, 130-210.

THOIRY, ⊠ 78770, 12 km N.

Hotel :
★★★ **Etoile**, 38, rue de la Porte-St-Martin, ☎ (1) 34.87.40.21, AE DC Euro Visa, 12 rm ⟶ ⟶ closed Mon and Jan, 145. Rest. ♦♦ ♪ 60-150.

MONTMORENCY

Enghien 3, Paris 22, Pontoise 24 km
pop 20830 ⊠ 95160   C2
A quiet residential town on a hill SE of the forest, once the fief of the Montmorencys, one of the great families of Old France. The philosopher Jean-Jacques Rousseau stayed here; it was a fashionable resort during the Second Empire (mid-19thC).
► Hôtel de Ville (end of 18thC). ► Flamboyant Gothic-Renaissance church (stained glass★). ► Rousseau Museum *(2-6 ex Mon.)*.

Nearby

► SW, **Taverny** church★ : many sculptures★; Renaissance altar piece; four statues of the Virgin; 16thC crucifix; wood panelling. Former priory *(Sat., Sun., in summer)*.   □

MORET-SUR-LOING*

Fontainebleau 10, Sens 43, Paris 77 km
pop 3555 ⊠ 77250   D4
A favourite of Impressionist painters.
► 14thC gates in town wall. ► François I house in Hôtel de Ville courtyard; ► 15th-16thC house in Rue Grande; ► 13th-15thC church; ► 15thC main building of Bon St-Jacques almshouse; ► damaged 12th-17thC keep *(2:30-6:30, Sat., Sun. and nat. hols., Easter-Oct.)*; ► House of Alfred Sisley (1839-99), English Impressionist; ► Clemenceau museum on the other side of the Loing Bridge★ *(Sat. and Sun. pm)*.
Also... view over the town from Montigny road, ► **Saint-Mammès** : excursions on the Seine. Leave from the right bank quay. ► Lakes to the S (→ Nemours). ► Summer festival *(every Sat.)* : local history depicted by costumed townspeople. ► Try the **sucres d'orge** (barley sugar) originally made by local nuns and still a thriving cottage industry in Moret.

Down the valley of the Loing★ *(40 km approx, half day)*

► Sisley's favourite river runs along the edge of the forest parallel to a poplar-lined canal, through a series of charming villages. ► On the left bank, **Montigny** is crowned by the massive bell-tower of its 11th-16thC church. ► **Bourron-Marlotte**, turn-of-the-century villas in the forest *(W)*, a second Barbizon (→) for Romantic and Impressionist

painters; attractive Louis XIII château *(25 Mar.-1 Nov., 2-6 Sat., Sun. and nat. hols.; groups all year ex Mon., on request, tel. 64.45.79.03)*. ► The best view of **Grez-sur-Loing** is from the other bank, near **Montcourt** : mossy 15thC bridge, 12thC keep and 12th-13thC church among thickets. ► At **Fromonville**, the canal joins the river to form a sort of peninsula. To one side is a small Romanesque church. ► The other side of **Nemours** (→) : massive rock outcrops in the woods. ► **Portonville** and **Glandelles** : mills, then scattered islets. ► **Souppes-sur-Loing** : lake and Romanesque church (13thC). ► **Château-Landon**★ (→).   □

Practical Information ————————————————

MORET-SUR-LOING
ⓘ pl. Samois, ☎ (1) 60.70.41.66 (h.s.).
SNCF ☎ (1) 64.24.82.47.

Hotel :
★★ **Auberge de la Terrasse**, 40, rue de la Pêcherie, ☎ (1) 60.70.51.03, DC Visa, 20 rm ⟶ closed Sun eve and Mon, 15 Dec-15 Jan, 200. Rest. ♦ 70-150.

Nearby

La GENEVRAYE, ⊠ 77690 Montigny, 10 km SW.

Restaurant :
♦♦ **L'Auberge de la Genevraye**, ☎ 64.45.83.99 ⟶ ♿ closed Mon eve and Tue, 25 Feb-12 Mar, 9 Sep-1 Oct, 70-130.

NEMOURS

Melun 32, Paris 80, Orléans 87 km
pop 11675 ⊠ 77140   C4
A waterside clearing around a feudal château and a church, between the river Loing and the canal.
► 16thC church of St. Jean-Baptiste : noteworthy radiating chapels; 12th-13th and 15thC château *(10-12 & 2-5 ex Tue.)*. ► In the forest, **Museum of Prehistoric Ile-de-France★★** *(Sens road, 10-12 & 2-5 ex Tue. and nat. hols.)*. ► **Rochers Gréau Park★**, 70 acres of rocky forest.

Nearby

► **Larchant★** *(8 km NW)* : a charming village in the Commanderie Woods★, part of the forest of Fontainebleau (→). Remains of the pilgrim church★ of St. Mathurin ("for the healing of madmen and fallen women"); various styles from late Romanesque to Gothic; 14thC doorway★ , 15thC statues★. ► The wood N of Larchant hides the largest rock outcrop in the forest, including **La Dame Jehanne★**, the highest rock in the vicinity of Paris. ► **Egreville★**, picturesque village *(19 km SE)* : 16thC market; 13th-15thC church; 16thC barn and 16th-17thC château once owned by the opera composer Jules Massenet (1842-1912).

Along the valleys of the Lunain and the Orvanne★ *(65 km approx)*

The two rivers spread out into lakes before mingling with the Loing. ► **Nemours**. ► **Paley** : a gabled bell-tower. ► **Lorrez-le-Bocage** : the Lunain empties into the moat of à theatrical 16thC château; 13thC church. ► Church and tithe barn at **Chéroy**. ► Take the fork to **Vallery** : unfinished Renaissance château★. ► The Orvanne runs past the foot of the **Manor of Diant**. ► **Chevry** : Louis XIII château. ► Mill-hotel at **Flagy** : an ideal stop. ► **Château Saint-Ange** : once the residence of the Duchess of Étampes, François I's mistress. ► **Villecerf** : a last look at the Orvanne and the **Moret Lakes★** (→).   □

Practical Information ————————————————

NEMOURS
ⓘ 17, rue des Tanneurs, ☎ (1) 64.28.03.95.
SNCF ☎ (1) 64.28.00.23.

Hotels :
★★ **Ecu de France**, 3, rue de Paris, ☎ (1) 64.28.11.54, 28 rm P closed 2 wk at Xmas, 195. Rest. ◆◆ ♪ 70-120.
★★ **Saint-Pierre**, 10-12, av. Carnot, ☎ (1) 64.28.01.57, Euro Visa, 25 rm P closed 1-15 Mar, 1-15 Oct, 160.

⚹ ★★★A.C.C.F. (119 pl), ☎ (1) 64.28.10.62.

Nearby

BAGNEAUX-SUR-LOING, ⊠ 77167, 5 km S.

Restaurants :
◆◆ **Poisson Doré**, 51, rte de Glandelles, ☎ (1) 64.28.07.03, Visa ♨ ♪ 5 rm, closed Tue eve and Wed. In summer, service on the banks of the Loing. Spec : ris de veau lyonnaise, 70-145.
◆ **Les Marronniers**, 59, rte de Glandelles, ☎ (1) 64.28.07.04, Visa ⟨ ♪ ⚹ closed Tue eve and Wed, 1-22 Aug. Spec : escalope de saumon à l'oseille toast chaud, 70-200.

FLAGY, ⊠ 77156 Thoury-Férottes, 12 km SE.

Hotel :
● ★★★ **Moulin**, 2, rue du Moulin, ☎ (1) 60.96.67.89, AE DC Visa, 10 rm P ⟨ ♨ ⚹ closed Sun eve and Mon, 13-25 Sep, 18 Dec-22 Jan, 165. Rest. ● ◆◆ ⟨ ♪ ⚹ Candlelight and firelight in a 13th-C mill : rillettes aux deux saumons, magret de canard aux baies de cassis, 80-160.

NOGENT-LE-ROTROU

Chartres 54, Le Mans 71, Paris 147 km
pop 13200 ⊠ 28400   A4
This principal town of the Perche region is an important agricultural market and industrial centre.
▶ The old town, rebuilt in the 15thC, possesses numerous Flamboyant Gothic and Renaissance buildings.
▶ 11th-12thC château, now the **Perche museum** (regional ethnology; 10-12 & 2-6, 5 off season; closed Tue.).
▶ Church of Notre-Dame (13th-14thC, much restored) : former chapel of the 17thC Hôtel-Dieu (hospital); tomb of Sully (1559-1641; minister to Henri IV) and his wife. ▶ Old houses in Rues Bourg-le-Comte and St-Laurent. ▶ Churches of St-Laurent (15th-16thC) and St-Hilaire (same era, 13thC choir). ▶ Nearby : **Cloche Valley★**, NE.   □

Practical Information _____

NOGENT-LE-ROTROU
ℹ rue Gouverneur, ☎ 37.52.22.16.
SNCF ☎ 37.52.10.26.

Hotels :
★★ **Le Dauphin**, 39, rue Villette-Gâté, ☎ 37.52.17.30, Euro Visa, 26 rm P ♨ ⚹ closed Sun eve and Mon (Mar, Oct-Nov), 1 Dec-1 Mar, 200. Rest. ◆◆ Salade du pêcheur, turbot petits légumes, jambonneau confit, 70-180.
★★ **Lion d'Or** (L.F.), 28, pl. St-Pol, ☎ 37.52.01.60, Euro Visa, 14 rm P ♨ ❀ half pens (h.s.), closed Sun eve and Mon, 1-15 Jan, 5-20 Aug, 200. Rest. ◆ ♪ ⚹ ❀ 60-180.

Recommended
♥ pastry : Cosse, 35, rue Villette-Gâté.

Nearby

VILLERAY, ⊠ 61110 Condeau, 11 km.

Hotel :
★★★★ **Moulin de Villeray** (R.C.), ☎ 33.73.30.22, Tx 171779, AE DC Euro Visa, 10 rm P ♨ half pens (h.s.), closed Tue, Wed lunch, 30 Nov-1 Feb, 1250. Rest. ◆◆◆ ♪ ⚹ 200-280.

NOYON*

Amiens 60, Reims 98, Paris 106 km
pop 14850 ⊠ 60400   D1
This industrial centre between canals that run parallel to the Oise River retains numerous monuments

despite widespread destruction during WWII. **Cathedral★** : one of the first in the Gothic style (1145-1200), still surrounded by dependencies (chapterhouse, 16thC library and 13thC cloister).
▶ Noyonnais museum in the Renaissance episcopal palace (10-12 & 2-5 or 6 ex Tue.). ▶ Restored Renaissance Hôtel de Ville. ▶ The religious reformer Jean Calvin, born here in 1509, is commemorated by a museum (Apr.-Nov., 10-12 & 2:30-5 ex Tue.). Municipal Museum of Noyonnais (daily ex. Tue., 10-12 & 2-5 or 6).
Also... ▶ Ruined **Abbey of Ourscamps★★** (12th-13thC); Salle des Morts★ (13thC infirmary) is now a chapel; 18thC building. ▶ Franco-American museum in the **Château de Blérancourt** (14 km SE; tel. 23.39.60.16).   □

Practical Information _____

ℹ 1, pl. de l'Hôtel-de-Ville, ☎ 44.44.02.97.
SNCF ☎ 44.44.00.61.

Hotel :
★★ **Saint-Eloi**, 81, bd Carnot, ☎ 44.44.01.49, 31 rm P closed Sun eve, 155. Rest. ◆ ♪ 65-180.

Restaurants :
◆ **Auberge de Crisolles**, Crisolles, D 932, ☎ 44.09.02.32, Euro Visa ⟨ ♨ ♪ closed Wed and Sun eve, 85-140.
◆ **Dame Journe**, 2-4, bd Mony, ☎ 44.44.01.33, AE Euro Visa ♪ ⚹ closed Mon eve. Outstanding value : lard de jambon cru d'Alsace, pleurotes du pays, côtes de bœuf Villette, 85-170.

ORSAY

Palaiseau 7, Versailles 16, Paris 27 km
pop 14071 ⊠ 91400   B2

Restaurant :
● ◆◆ **Le Boudin Sauvage**, 6, rue de Versailles, ☎ (1) 69.28.42.93, AE DC Euro Visa ♨ ⚹ closed Sat and Sun , eves ex Tue and Fri, 30 Jul-1 Sep. Don't neglect to book ahead to sample Anne-Marie de Gennes's savoury seasonal specialties, served in the dining room or the garden : boudin sauvage, magret de canard aux trois chutneys and the star of her menu, fresh fish, 210-250.

POISSY

Pontoise 17, Paris 28, Mantes 30 km
pop 36550 ⊠ 78300   B2
The town was a royal residence until the 15thC. St. Louis (Louis IX), who was born here, instituted a cattle market that eventually became the biggest in France. The town is now largely supported by the motor industry.
▶ Church of Notre-Dame (12thC) : Romanesque belltowers, remodelled in 13th, 15th, and 16thC; restored by Viollet-le-Duc (19thC). St. Louis may have been baptised in the font in 1215; 16thC Burial of Christ, statue.
▶ Abbey of Poissy : 14thC building flanked by towers at the entrance; inside : **Toy Museum★** (9:30-12 & 2-5:30 ex Mon., Tue. and nat. hols.). ▶ **Villa Savoye★** in the school grounds, designed by the architect Le Corbusier in 1930 (enq. : S.I.).

Practical Information _____

ℹ 132, rue du Gal-de-Gaulle, ☎ (1) 30.74.60.65.
SNCF ☎ (1) 30.74.17.06.
Car rental : Avis, 45bis, bd Gambetta, ☎ 39.11.90.08.

Restaurant :
◆◆ **L'Esturgeon**, 6, cours du 14-Juillet, ☎ (1) 39.65.00.04, AE DC Visa ⟨ ♪ closed Thu, 1-9 Jan, 1-31 Aug. Spec : foie gras de canard, caneton aux cerises, trois poissons au pistil de safran. On the banks of the Seine, 120-250.

PONTOISE

Paris 36, Mantes 40, Rouen 90 km
pop 29400 ⊠ 95300   B2

This ancient stronghold of the Vexin retains its historic charm despite WWII damage and recent urban development nearby. The lower town, along the banks of the Oise, is crowned by the red roofs of houses built by generations of craftsmen. Kings of France who visited Pontoise endowed it with monuments.

► Church of Notre-Dame (late 16thC, statues 13thC). ► **Church of St-Maclou** : primitive Gothic choir (ca. 1140); nave and façade date from 15thC; Renaissance side aisles (see 16thC *Burial of Christ;* windows). ► The **Tavet-Delacour Museum** in a turreted mansion dating from the late Gothic period : 16th-18thC sculpture in wood and stone, drawings, Freundlich Collection (works of Otto Freundlich, 1878-1943, and others : *10-12 & 2-6; ex Tue. and nat. hols.).* **Pissarro Museum** *(2-6 ex Mon., Tue. and nat. hols.).*

Along the Viosne Valley *(approx 40 km)*

The river's green banks are marked out by old mills, and every village boasts a church that deserves more than a casual glance; an area popular with weekend cyclists. ► **Pontoise.** ► **Montgeroult** : Classical château *(5 Jul.- -10 Aug. and 20 Aug.-10 Oct. ex Thu., Fri.)* and 13thC church. Opposite, **Courcelles** (Louis XIII manor) by the riverside. ► Three churches you should see : **Santeuil★** (Romanesque), **Nucourt★** (Renaissance; 15th-16thC statues), and **Chars★** : Romanesque façade, Gothic choir, Renaissance tower. ► Return via **Marines** (interesting Renaissance doorway); **Moussy** (16thC château, *1 May-15 Oct.*); **Cormeilles-en-Vexin** (12th, 13th, 16thC church).   ☐

Practical Information _____

PONTOISE
ⓘ 6, pl. Petit-Martroy, ☎ (1) 30.38.24.45.
SNCF ☎ (1) 30.32.45.45.
Car rental : Avis, 27, rue du Gal Leclerc, ☎ 30.37.37.37.

Restaurant :
● ♦♦ *Jardin des Lavandières*, 28, rue de Rouen, ☎ (1) 30.38.25.55, Visa, closed Sat noon and Sun , hols, 17-28 Apr, 31 Jul-25 Aug, 24 Dec-5 Jan. It's a lively, refreshing spot with the added attraction of J.-L. Decout's cooking. *Foie gras chaud compote d'oignons, rognon de veau goutte de sang, turbot fondue de poireaux,* 220-250.

Nearby

CORMEILLES-EN-VEXIN, ⊠ 95830, 10 km NW.

Restaurant :
● ♦♦ *Relais Sainte-Jeanne*, rte de Dieppe, D 915, ☎ 34.66.61.56, AE DC Visa ⌂ ♪ closed Mon , Sun eve, Feb school hols, 2-25 Aug. *Grande cuisine* is a tradition in the Cagna family. *Saumon poêlé poivre noir et gros sel, suprême de pintade en chemise,* 250-300.

OSNY, ⊠ 95520, 2 km W.

Restaurant :
♦♦ *Le Moulin de la Renardière*, rue du Grand-Moulin, ☎ (1) 30.30.21.13, AE DC Euro Visa ⌂ ⌂ ♪ closed Mon and Sun eve, 8-31 Aug, 160-210.

PROVINS**

Melun 48, Troyes 76, Paris 90 km
pop 12680 ⊠ 77160   D3

This "town of roses" rising, like Chartres, from fields of corn, is a superb, yet little-known relic of the Middle Ages. The 12th-13thC ramparts of the upper town, worthy of the renowned walled city of Carcassonne, enclose exceptional buildings, charming cottages and

gardens spilling over with roses. Mediaeval gables and Renaissance doorways recall the days when Provins was the third-largest town in France and merchants from all over Europe flocked to the twice-yearly Foires de Champagne (regional fairs) : tour of the monuments *(9 :30-12 & 2-6 ex 25 Dec., 1 Jan.).*

► Upper town : Rue St-Thibault (B1); the Hôtel-Dieu (old infirmary) has a 13thC doorway, a Renaissance stone altarpiece and 13thC font. N° 16 : entrance to the vaulted and ornamented **underground passages★** that run beneath the infirmary *(2-6, Sun. and nat. hols., Easter-1 Nov.);* N° 18 : 16thC house; N° 50 : remains of 12thC birthplace of St. Thibault. ► **Church of St. Quiriace** : choir★ (late 12thC), transept and nave 13thC (remodelled), fine N (12thC) and S (13thC) doorways. ► **Caesar's Tower** *(Tour César)★* is a 44 m-high landmark dating from the 12thC; the base was added by English soldiers during the Hundred Years' War (14thC); 17thC roofs (timberwork and sentry walk★). ► Rue du Palais : Romanesque house. ► Tithe barn★ (end 12thC). ► The best-preserved **ramparts** run between the St-Jean and Jouy gates. ► St. Thibault's ramp leads to the **lower town.** ► To the S, 13thC mansions of Vauluisant and Croix d'Or. ► In the N, Ste-Croix church (B1; 12thC nave, 16thC choir); **church of St-Ayoul** (C2), a former Benedictine abbey church : 12thC, much rebuilt especially in the 16thC. Romanesque doorway (damaged), 16thC statues, 17thC woodwork. ► Tower of Notre-Dame-du-Val : sole remnant of a 16thC collegiate church.

Nearby

► Some of the most beautiful churches in France are hidden in the green countryside around Provins. ► **Saint-Loup-de-Naud★** *(8 km SW)* : rivals Provins from its walled hilltop; Benedictine church with superb doorway★★ (11th-12thC). ► Detour to the fortress of **Sigy** (15th-17thC; *visit by written request) en route* to the fortified town of **Donnemarie-Dontilly** *(18 km SW)* : early 13thC church★ , cemetery with 16thC wooden gallery. ► SW of Donnemarie : imposing Cistercian abbey of **Preuilly** with attached farm. ► **Rampillon★** : 13th-14thC church, once a Commandery of the Knights Templar; only one tower remains, but the Twelve Apostles still await the Judgement Day★★. ► **Nangis**, former stronghold on the Champagne fair route : fortress (transformed) and Gothic church. ► Before returning to Provins, visit the 17thC **Chaix mill★** at Gastines, N of Nangis *(tel. : 60.68.71.73).* ► **La Bassée plain★** between Bray and Nogent.   ☐

Practical Information _____

PROVINS
ⓘ tour César (A1), ☎ (1) 64.00.16.65.
SNCF (C3), ☎ (1) 64.00.01.95.

Hotel :
★★ *Croix d'Or*, 1, rue des Capucins (B2), ☎ (1) 64.00.01.96, AE DC Euro Visa, 7 rm ℗ closed Sun eve and Mon, 1-13 Aug, 160. Rest. ♦ ♪ 70-170.

Restaurant :
● ♦ *Aux Vieux Remparts*, 3, rue Couverte (A1), ☎ (1) 64.00.02.89, AE Visa ⌂ ♪ closed Tue eve and Wed, 24 Feb-12 Mar, 7-30 Sep. Country charm and local cooking, 60-180.

Recommended
♥ pastry-candy : Guy Pelé, 5, pl. du Mal-Leclerc, rose jelly.

Nearby

LIZINES, ⊠ 77650 Longueville, 10 km SW.

Restaurant :
♦♦ *Auberge Saint-Georges*, 2, rue Saint-Georges, ☎ (1) 60.67.32.48, closed Wed , eves ex Sat, 15-31 Jan, 15-30 Sep, 45-120.

NANGIS, ⊠ 77370, 22 km W.
ⓘ mairie, ☎ (1) 64.08.00.50.
SNCF ☎ (1) 64.08.00.68.

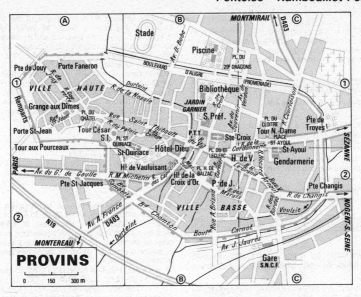

PROVINS

0   150   300 m

Hotel :
★★ *Le Dauphin*, 14, rue du Dauphin, ☎ (1) 64.08.03.57, AE Visa, 12 rm 🅿 🔒 closed Sun eve, 22 Dec-3 Jan, 140. Rest. ● ◆◆ ♪ In a Napoleonic-era coach inn, seafood and local ingredients : *blanquette de turbot, poulet de grain*, 65-150.

NOYEN-SUR-SEINE, ✉ 77114 Gouaix, 18 km S.

Hotel :
★★ *Host. du Port Montain* (L.F.), ☎ (1) 64.01.81.05, Euro Visa, 9 rm 🅿 ≼ 🎰 🔒 ₲ closed Sun eve ex hols, 13 Jan-3 Feb, 2-17 Nov, 155. Rest. ◆ ≼ ♪ ₲ closed Mon ex hols, 85-190.

RAMBOUILLET*

Chartres 41, Paris 52, Mantes 70 km
pop 22500 ✉ 78120   B3

The **château**★ (mostly 18thC) has often been rebuilt, but the round tower where François I died can still be seen. Louis XVI here established Marie-Antoinette's dairy, the **English gardens** and an experimental farm that was the forerunner of the modern-day sheepfolds of the **Bergerie Nationale**★, where you can see the renowned merino stud★ *(10-12 & 2-6, 5 out of season; closed Tue., Wed.).* **Rambolitrain Museum :** railway history with 4 000 model trains and toys (4, pl. Jeanne-d'Arc; *daily ex Mon., Tue., 10-12 & 2-5:30).*   ☐

Practical Information _____
RAMBOUILLET
ⓘ ☎ (1) 34.83.31.21.
Ⓢ Ⓝ Ⓒ Ⓕ ☎ (1) 34.83.84.45.
Car rental : Avis, 4, Pl. de la Gare, ☎ 34.83.35.36.

Hotels :
Villa Marinette (L.F.), 20, av. du Gal-de-Gaulle, Gazeran, ☎ (1) 34.83.19.01, AE DC Visa, 6 rm 🅿 🐾 closed Tue eve , Wed, Feb school hols, 19 Aug-15 Sep, 160. Rest. ◆◆ ₲ 60-150.

Restaurants :
● ◆◆ *Auberge de l'Etoile*, 89, rue Charles De Gaulle, St

Arnou en Yvelines, ☎ 30.41.20.30 Visa closed Mon. and Sun. eve. A likable little eatery not far from Paris, yet with a country atmosphere, 70-120.
◆◆ *Rendez-vous de Chasse*, 30, av. du Gal-de-Gaulle, Gazeran, ☎ (1) 34.83.81.49, Visa 🎰 closed Mon eve and Tue eve. Southwestern specialties, 150-200.

🛆 ★★★*Le Pont Hardi* (65 pl), ☎ (1) 30.41.13.81.

Nearby

Les BRÉVIAIRES, ✉ 78610 Le Perray-en-Yvelines, 8 km NW.

Restaurant :
◆◆ *Auberge des Bréviaires*, ☎ (1) 34.84.98.47, AE Visa 🎰 ♪ closed Wed eve and Thu, 20 Feb-15 Mar. Spec : *lotte à la marseillaise, gratin aux pommes*, 145-220.

Les CHAISES, ✉ 78120 Raizeux, 11 km W.

Restaurant :
◆◆ *Maison des Champs*, ☎ (1) 34.83.50.19, AE Euro Visa ₲ closed Mon eve, Tue eve, Wed , Feb and Aug. Reserve, 180-230.

SAINT-LÉGER-EN-YVELINES, ✉ 78610 Le Perray-en-Yvelines, 5 km N.

Hotel :
★★★ *La Belle Aventure*, 8, rue de la Croix-Blanche, ☎ (1) 34.86.31.35, 13 rm 🅿 🎰 🔒 ♪ pens, closed Sun eve and Mon, 15 Aug-3 Sep, 22-26 Dec, 600. Rest. ◆ ♪ Spec : *poêlon de praires aux poivres, pintade au champagne*, 115-150.

RAMBOUILLET Forest**

                                                        B3

A royal hunting preserve where packs still hunt; abundant growth of oak, birch and beech, with good access; many streams and ponds★.

▶ GR1 runs right through the forest, and two cycle trails run from Rambouillet to Montfort-l'Amaury (→) and from Montfort to Saint-Léger-en-Yvelines. The forest population of wild boar, red deer and roe deer can be seen in the animal park at **Clairefontaine** *(pm, all day Sun. ; closed Mon. and May-Jun.).*

Nearby

▶ **Épernon** *(13 km)* : timber-framed houses, church in Beauce Gothic, 12thC cellars. ▶ **Château de Sauvage★** : ornithological reserve and deer park *(6 km from Épernon)*. ▶ **Le Perray-en-Yvelines** : stud farm. □

ROYAUMONT**

Paris 44, Beauvais 54, Amiens 94 km

C2

The abbey, founded by Saint Louis when he was only 12, became one of the richest in the Ile-de-France *(daily ex Tue.)*; it is now a cultural centre (concerts★).
▶ Abbey church : 13thC remnants among woods and lakes; Gothic cloister★★ and refectory★★ ; 18thC abbot's palace built by Ledoux.
Also... ▶ Romanesque, Gothic and Renaissance church at **Luzarches** *(5 km S)*. □

SAINT-GERMAIN Forest*

B2

Although intersected by major roads, this 40 km² forest in a bend of the Seine has well-planned walking trails.
▶ **Château du Val** *(3 km NE)*, designed by Mansart (1669).
▶ **Maisons-Laffitte** *(9 km NE)* : a dormitory town centred on a race-course; Mansart's best-known château★, a model of 17thC architecture *(9-12 & 2-6 ex Tue. and Sun. am)*. □

Practical Information ――――――――――――――――

MAISONS-LAFFITTE, ⊠ 78600, 18 km S of **Pontoise**.
SNCF ☎ (1) 39.62.02.53.

Restaurants :
● ◆◆◆◆ *La Vieille Fontaine*, 8, av. Grétry, ☎ (1) 39.62.01.78, AE DC Euro Visa 🗲 ⚜ ♪ closed Mon and Sun, 3 Aug-4 Sep. Lots is going on in the lovely Second-Empire house where Manon Letourneur and François Clerc preside : she has fitted up the first floor with a little dining room, and he has created a catering division alongside his efforts for the Fontaine's patrons : *foie de veau aux morilles, cuisses de grenouilles "à la coque", grands desserts.* Great cellar, 280-500.
● ◆◆◆ *Le Tastevin*, 9, av. Egle, ☎ (1) 39.62.11.67 ⚜ closed Mon eve and Tue , Feb, 16 Aug-10 Sep. M. Blanchet offers fine, seasonal specialties : *filet de sandre rôti à l'échalote, escalope de foie gras chaud au vinaigre de cidre,* 260-360.
◆◆ *Le Laffitte*, 5, av. de St-Germain, ☎ (1) 39.62.01.53, AE Euro Visa, closed Tue eve, Wed, Sun eve , Aug. Spec : fish, 200-250.
△ ★★★★Airotel International (200 pl), ☎ (1) 39.12.21.91.

SAINT-GERMAIN-EN-LAYE**

Paris 21, Mantes 34, Dreux 70 km
pop 40830 ⊠ 78100   B2
The epitome of an affluent residential town : an old château in the forest, good air, fast trains to Paris *(40 min by RER regional express network)*.
▶ The **château** was one of the principal royal residences; many aristocratic 17th and 18thC mansions are still in evidence nearby. The château was rebuilt by François I and restored under Napoleon III; 14thC keep, and Sainte Chapelle★ from the reign of St. Louis. **National Antiquities Museum★★** : artifacts from Prehistoric (Brassempouy Venus★★), Celtic (Antreville helmet★, Bourray deity★), Gallo-Roman (statue of Mercury from Lezoux★, candelabrum from Bavai★, mosaic from St-Romain★), and Merovingian eras *(9:45-12 & 1:30-5 ex Tue.)*. ▶ **Terrace** designed by Le Nôtre overlooking the Seine (view★); the

Henri IV pavilion, S, is a remnant of the château where Louis XIV was born. ▶ Classical church (1776). ▶ In the Arts garden, sculpture by Lobo and **museum** : 16th-17thC satirical Flemish paintings (*The Conjuror* by Hieronymous Bosch); drawings; medicine chest that belonged to Mme. de Montespan (1641-1707), Louis XIV's mistress *(closed for renovation)*. ▶ Almshouse★, founded by Mme. de Montespan, where Maurice Denis (1870-1943) lived; now the **Prieuré Museum★**, displaying the works of the Symbolist school and the Nabis; Maurice Denis studio *(10:30-5:30, ex Mon., Tue. and nat. hols)*; monument to Debussy by Maillol. □

Practical Information ――――――――――――――――

SAINT-GERMAIN-EN-LAYE
ⓘ 1 bis, rue de la République (A2), ☎ (1) 34.51.05.12.
SNCF ☎ (1) 39.73.37.38 ; *R.E.R. station, line A* (B2),
☎ (1) 34.51.02.82.

Hotels :
● ★★★★(L) *Cazaudehore et la Forestière* (R.C.), 1, av. du Pdt-Kennedy (B1), ☎ (1) 39.73.36.60, Tx 696055, Euro Visa, 30 rm 🅿 ⚜ ⚘ ♪ 560. Rest. ● ◆◆◆ ♪ & closed Mon ex for hotel patrons. An enchanting stopover on the edge of the forest : *foie gras de canard, étuvée de lotte à la crème d'oignons, panaché de confits paysan pommes landaises,* 320-400.
● ★★★★(L) *Pavillon Henri IV*, (I.L.A.), 21, rue Thiers (C2), ☎ (1) 34.51.62.62, Tx 695822, AE DC Euro Visa, 42 rm 🅿 🗲 ⚜ ⚘ The birthplace of Louis XIV, 1100. Rest. ● ◆◆◆ A shrine to *pommes soufflées* and Béarnaise sauce, 220-450.
★★ *Le Cèdre*, 7, rue d'Alsace (A1-2), ☎ (1) 34.51.84.35, 31 rm ⚜ ⚘ 🕊 closed 31 Jan-5 Mar, 220. Rest. ◆ ⚘ 90-140.

Restaurant :
◆ *"7 Rue des Coches"*, 7, rue des Coches (A-B3), ☎ (1) 39.73.66.40, AE DC Euro Visa ♪ closed Mon and Sun eve, 3-25 Aug. Young people who deserve encouragement. Menu inspired by that of the château de la Jonchère, 100-250.

Recommended
Events : *concert*, every Sun at kiosk on the château terrace; *fête des Loges*, amusement fair ; mid-Jul to mid-Aug.
♥ pastry-catering-ice cream : *Dumas Sibenaler*, 21, rue du Vieux-Marché, ☎ (1) 34.51.02.07.

Nearby

ORGEVAL, ⊠ 78630, 8 km NW.

Hotel :
● ★★★★ *Moulin d'Orgeval*, rue de l'Abbaye, ☎ (1) 39.75.85.74, AE Visa, 14 rm 🅿 🗲 ⚜ ♪ ⚘ 600. Rest. ◆◆ 🗲 ♪ & closed Sun eve (l.s.). Spec : *terrine de foies de volailles, gigot au gratin dauphinois,* 150-180 ; child : 100.

Le VÉSINET, ⊠ 78110, 3 km E.

Hotel :
★★★ *Les Ibis*, Ile du Grand-Lac, ☎ (1) 39.52.17.41, AE DC Euro Visa, 20 rm 🅿 🗲 ⚜ ⚘ closed 6 Jul-6 Sep. On an island, 265. Rest. ◆◆ 🗲 170-205 ; child : 70.

SEINE Valley*

C3-D

Excursion *(30 km approx from Moret to Melun)*
Between Moret (→) and Melun (→) the Seine takes on a festive air and the villages on the forested banks look like turn-of-the-century shore resorts.
▶ **Moret.** ▶ **Thomery★**, reminiscent of the Midi : vineyards everywhere; large low church (12th-14thC); 17thC château. ▶ **Samoreau**, between the forest and the Brie plain. ▶ **Héricy** : green islets in the Seine ; charming church with four gables on the bell-tower, typical of Brie. ▶ **Fontaine-**

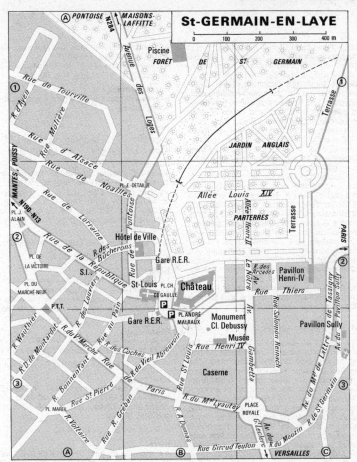

C1

le-Port : similar bell-tower. ► After **Melun** (→) : regatta waters around **Seine-Port** and **Morsang-sur-Seine.** ☐

SENLIS***

Meaux 38, Paris 51, Amiens 100 km
pop 15280 ⊠ 60300   C1

Senlis is a quiet country town where life goes on behind imposing Renaissance and neo-Classical doorways. The town is charming rather than spectacular, although it contains a famous cathedral and Gallo-Roman fortifications with 16 towers.

► **Cathedral★★** (B1) : the first in a chain of churches dedicated to the Virgin; the history of Gothic architecture in the Ile-de-France is evident in this 12th to 16thC construction. The airy 13thC spire★ was often copied; the central doorway★ was the first to be entirely dedicated to the Virgin Mary (end of 12thC); the lateral doorways★ are in Flamboyant Gothic; Flamboyant carvings behind the façades; chapel of the Blessed Sacrament (actually a tiny pre-Romanesque church) with 15thC frescos; 14thC chapterhouse with interesting capitals; 14th-15thC statuary. ► In the square, 13th-16thC episcopal palace which now contains the **Museum of Art and Archaeology** *(10-12 & 2-6, 5 from Oct.-Mar.; closed Tue. and Wed. am)*,

16th-18thC houses. ► Cathedral parvis : Hôtel de Vermandois, now a museum of fine arts *(same hours as above)*. ► S, Place St-Frambourg : 12th-13thC church has become a concert auditorium named after renowned pianist Gyorgy Cziffra *(concerts Sat., Sun. pm. Apr.-Oct.)*. ► Church of St. Pierre (12th, 13th and 16thC); E, library (18thC). ► On the other side of the parvis : 16thC House of the Three Pots (16thC) and the Château de Saint Louis (13th-14th, 18thC), now a **hunting museum★ (Musée de la Vénerie;** *10-12 & 2-6, 5, Oct. to Mar.; closed Tue. and Wed. am)*. ► View of the château and the Gallo-Roman wall from Rue du Chat-Haret (B1). ► Numerous old houses, especially Rue du Chatel, Rue de la Treille, Place Gérard-de-Nerval (A1), Rue de Beauvais, Rue Vieille-de-Paris (hôtel de ville 1495).

Also... ► **Gallo-Roman arena,** W *(9-6)*. ► **Abbey de La Victoire★,** commemorating Philippe Auguste's victory over Flemish forces at Bouvines (1214). ► Direct road to Mortefontaine (→) through the forest★.

Round trip S of Senlis *(55 km, approx half day)*

► **Senlis.** ► The **forest of Ermenonville★★** has many attractions : lily-of-the-valley growing wild in the spring, play areas for children, picturesque ruins, a museum and parks with reminders of J.-J. Rousseau and the poet Gérard de Nerval (1808-55). ► **Montépilloy :** 12thC fortress on a hilltop. ▶ **Fourcharet** : 13thC monastery barn in a perfect state of preservation. ▶ The ruins of the **Abbaye de Châalis★** (13thC) are overgrown and a roost for birds; frescos in the abbey chapel are attributed to Il Primaticcio; 18thC buildings by Aubert (architect of the Chantilly stables) house the superb **Jacquemart-André collections★★** : Egyptian and Roman antiquities, mediaeval sculptures, two paintings by Giotto, and Italian Renaissance art (rose garden, *1:30-6, Mon., Wed., Sat., Sun., Mar.-Nov.; park★ daily ex Tue.*). ▶ The **Mer de Sable** (literally, "sea of sand"), opposite, is a very popular fine-weather leisure area. ▶ Less crowded in **Ermenonville** : the **Desert★** (a sandy tract) or the Marquis de Girardin's park, a splendid example of a garden from the Romantic era, dedicated to J.-J. Rousseau and his ideals of Nature, and ornamented with follies (*daily 10-6, Apr.-Sep.; 1:30-5 rest of year*). ▶ The mystical writer and poet Gérard de Nerval spent his childhood first at Loisy and then at **Mortefontaine** with an uncle, while his parents followed Napoleon's Grande Armée across Europe. Nerval's novel *Sylvie* seems to come to life in the still-wild **Thève Valley★.** ▶ **Vallière park** : another of the Romantic gardens so much admired in the 18thC; glimpses of it among mist-shrouded lakes from GR1. ▶ A delightful road overlooks the **Commelles Ponds★** in the forest of Chantilly (→). ▶ The hunt used to meet at the 19thC Château de la Reine Blanche. ▶ The forest road★ is the best approach to Chantilly : see the châteaux, the vast stables, the lakes and the racecourse at a single glance.

Round trip N of Senlis *(40 km approx, 2-3 hr)*

▶ **Senlis.** ▶ The **forest of Halatte★** together with the forests of Chantilly★, Pontarmé and Ermenonville formed the great princely hunting ground of the Guise Forest. The tradition lives on, and *la chasse à courre* (literally, "hunting in pursuit", i.e. not waiting for driven game) is still practised in the Valois (→), as is the ancient art of archery. ▶ **Raray★** : visit the Italian park (*15 Mar.-15 Nov., Sat. and Sun. pm*). Renaissance château (remodelled in 18thC); remarkable sculpture and carved hunting scenes; location for Cocteau's film *Beauty and the Beast*. 15th-16thC church and Renaissance manor in the village. ▶ The wide plain is succeeded by valleys and villages with appealing churches. ▶ **Saint-Vaast-de-Longmont,** 12thC spire, 16thC doorway. ▶ **Rhuis★** : three-story bell-tower and early ogive vaulting. ▶ **Montcel Abbey★** (14th, 17thC; *daily ex Tue. and Fri., 9-12 & 2-6*). ▶ From Montcel to **Fleurines** (Hoffmann'Land amusement park); road through deep forest. ▶ Ruined priory of St. Christophe, where Nature has clearly won over Art. ▶ **Verneuil-en-Halatte** : Graffiti studio; collection of casts (*Sat., Sun. 10-12 & 3-7*). ☐

Practical Information _____

SENLIS
ⅈ hôtel des Trois-Pots, pl. du Parvis-Notre-Dame (B1), ☎ 44.53.06.40.
SNCF ☎ 44.53.00.06.

Hotels :
● **★★ Hostellerie de la Porte Bellon** (L.F.), 51, rue Bellon (C2), ☎ 44.53.03.05, 19 rm Ⓟ ⏆ ❀ closed Fri (l.s.), 20 Dec-20 Jan, 220. Rest. ◆◆ 120-210.
★ **Auberge de Fontaine** (L.F.), 22, Grand'Rue, Fontaine Châalis, ☎ 44.54.20.22, AE, 7 rm ⏆ ◑ ❀ closed Tue eve and Wed, 15 Jan-15 Feb, 180. Rest. ◆ ♪ ❖ ❀ 85-190.

Restaurants :
◆◆ **Le Formanoir**, 17, rue du Châtel (B1), ☎ 44.53.04.39, Euro Visa ♪ A former covent, dating from the 16thC. Bistro closed Sun, 180-220.
◆ **Auberge de la Mitonnée**, 93, rue du Moulin-St-Tron, ☎ 44.53.10.05, Visa, closed Mon eve and Sun eve, 17-31 Aug, 90-220.
◆ **Le Vert Galant**, 15, pl. Henri-IV (B1-2), ☎ 44.53.60.15,

AE Visa ⏆ ♪ closed Mon and Sun eve , Feb school hols, 1 May, 10-25 Aug, 85-200.
◆ **Les Remparts**, 37, pl. de la Halle (B2), ☎ 44.53.58.59, AE Euro Visa ❖ ♪ closed Tue, 80-250.

Recommended
Events : *concerts at the Franz Liszt auditorium*, St-Frombourg church.

Nearby
ERMENONVILLE, ⊠ 60440, 14 km S.
ⅈ parc J.-J.-Rousseau, ☎ 44.54.01.58.
Hotels :
★★★ **Le Prieuré**, chevet de l'église, ☎ 44.54.00.44, Tx 145110, AE DC Euro Visa, 10 rm Ⓟ ⏆ 340.
★ **La Croix d'Or** (L.F.), 2, rue Prince-Radziwill, ☎ 44.54.00.04, Euro Visa, 11 rm Ⓟ ❖ ⏆ closed Mon, 15 Dec-7 Feb, 105. Rest. ◆◆ ♪ ◑ Spec : *raviolis d'escargots, navarin d'agneau et sa terrine de légumes*, 80-180; child : 45.

⚘ ★★J.-J. Rousseau (200 pl), ☎ 44.54.00.08.

FLEURINES, ⊠ 60700, 7 km N.
Hotel :
Le Vieux Logis, 105, rue de Paris, ☎ 44.54.10.13, AE DC Visa, 4 rm Ⓟ ⏆ closed Sun eve and Mon. Rest. ◆◆ ❖ ♪ ◑ An enjoyable stopover run by the Nivet family : *Saint-Pierre grillé aux noix, terrine de lapin, rognon de veau Gaël*, 125-260.

Restaurant :
◆ **Auberge de la Biche au Bois**, 27, rue de Paris, ☎ 44.54.10.04, Euro, closed Tue eve and Wed, 100.

NOGENT-SUR-OISE, ⊠ 60100 Creil, 15 km NW of Senlis.
Hotel :
★★★ **Le Sarcus**, (Inter-Hôtel), 7, rue Chateaubriand, ☎ 44.74.01.31, Tx 150047, AE DC Euro Visa, 62 rm Ⓟ ⏆ closed 27 Jul-23 Aug, 260. Rest. ◆ ❖ ♪ ◑ closed Sat noon and Sun, 90-160.

PLAILLY, ⊠ 60128, 15 km S.
Hotel :
★★ **Auberge du Petit Cheval d'Or** (L.F.), 48, rue de Paris, ☎ 44.54.36.33, Tx 150176, AE DC Euro Visa, 20 rm Ⓟ ❖ ⏆ ◔ ◑ 260. Rest. ◆ ♪ ◑ 95-200.

VER-SUR-LAUNETTE, ⊠ 60520, 2 km S of Ermenonville.
Restaurant :
● ◆ **Le Rabelais**, pl. de l'Eglise, ☎ 44.54.01.70, AE Euro Visa ♪ closed Mon eve and Wed, 17 Aug-3 Sep, 2-26 Nov. Spec : *feuilleté d'escargots aux champignons de Soissons, brie de Meaux*, 80-190.

SENONCHES

Dreux 35, Mortagne 42, Paris 120 km
pop 3410 ⊠ 28250   A3

▶ 15th-17thC château flanked by square 12thC keep, deep in the forest; 15thC church. ▶ Oak woods★ dotted with ponds to the NW; a paradise for mushroom-pickers. The woods continue into Montecot and Champrond woods.

Nearby
▶ **Thymerais** : a small region between Beauce and Perche, ideal for cyclists. ▶ **La Ferté-Vidame** (*12 km W*) : the ancient château of St.-Simon has long since disappeared; the "new" one (18thC) is now in ruins; 17thC church. ▶ **Pontgouin** : on the edge of the Eure (*20 km SE*) : 16thC château, Romanesque and Gothic church, canal locks★ designed by the engineer Sebastien Vauban (1633-1707). ▶ **Courville** (*7 km SE of Pontgouin*) : 16thC

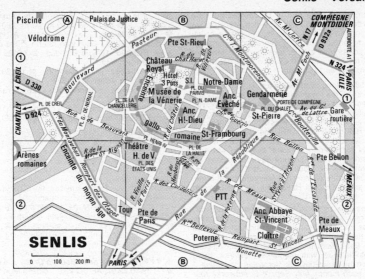

church; wooden barrel-vault; altarpiece★ and **château de Blanville,** Louis XIII style *(visits on request).* ▶ **Tillières** *(21 km N)* : Romanesque church. ▶ **Château de Maillebois** *(12 km NE)* defended by the fortified farmstead at **Rouvray** *(visits on request, 15 Apr.-15 Sep.).* ☐

Practical Information _____

SENONCHES

Hotel :
★ *La Forêt* (L.F.), pl. du Champ-de-Foire, ☎ 37.37.78.50, Visa, 14 rm 🅿 ▨ 🗘 half pens (h.s.), closed Thu, Feb, 160. Rest. ♦ ⚘ & 55-170.

Nearby
La LOUPE, ☒ 28240, 11 km S.

Hotel :
★ *Chêne Doré* (L.F.), 12, pl. de l'Hôtel-de-Ville, ☎ 37.81.06.71, AE DC, 14 rm 🅿 closed Sun eve and Mon, 28 Jul-13 Aug, 23 Dec-20 Jan, 150. Rest. ♦♦ ♪ & Spec : *escalope de foie gras chaude "percheronne", noix de porc au cidre et miel,* 45-140; child : 25.

THÉRAIN Valley

B-C1
From Creil to Beauvais *(45 km)*

The river Thérain meanders through Corot country between Creil and Beauvais; almost every village church hides a masterpiece. **Creil** itself is an important industrial centre in the valley of the Oise.
Don't miss the **Gallé-Juillet Museum★,** a late 18thC house built on the ogival basement of the former château; original decor (ceramics, delft-ware, porcelain; *winter : 1-5; summer : 1:30-5:30 ex Tue.).* Take the right bank from **Cramoisy** to **Mello** : 18thC château and Renaissance church. ▶ **Bury** : church (transitional Romanesque-Gothic). ▶ **Villers-Saint-Sépulcre** : superb Burial of Christ★ in polychrome stone in the church. ▶ A forest road cuts through the **Hez woods** (beech) to Clermont (→). ☐

> If you enjoy sports, consult the pages pertaining to the regions; there you will find addresses for practicing your favorite sport.

Practical Information _____

CREIL, ☒ 60100, 13 km NW of **Senlis.**

Restaurant :
♦ *La Petite Alsace,* 8, rue Brobeil, ☎ 44.55.28.89, Euro Visa ♪ closed Mon, Sat noon, Sun eve, Aug, 24 Dec-1 Jan, 80-150.

VAUX-LE-VICOMTE★★★

☒ 77950 Maincy   C3

This splendid château was built by the celebrated 17thC architects Le Brun, Le Vau and Le Nôtre for Nicolas Fouquet (1615-80; minister of finance under Louis XIV). Not to be outdone, the king employed the same architects to build Versailles, first exiling the over-reaching Fouquet to Brittany before condemning him to life imprisonment. Following extensive renovation, three floors are now open for visits *(Mar.-1 Nov., daily 10-1 & 2-6; winter, weekends only, 2-5; closed Jan.; visits by candlelight 1st, 3rd Sat. of month).* The **gardens★★,** relaid from Le Nôtre's drawings and now replanned each year, maintain the splendour of the *Grand Siècle (fountains play 2nd and 4th Sat., 3-6, Jun.-Sep.).* ☐

VERSAILLES★★★

Paris 23, Chartres 68, Orléans 120 km
pop 95240 ☒ 78000   B2

Imitated, praised and debated (Is it neo-Classical or Baroque?), Versailles is a unique expression of the vitality of French art during the 17th-18thC. Decoration ranges from the grandiose Louis XIV *Grands Appartements* to the grace of the Louis XV and Louis XVI *Petits Appartements.* The gardens are simply unrivalled. Four million visitors annually pass through the palace and grounds.
▶ Louis XIV took up residence at Versailles in May 1682 before construction was completed, while Mansart was still overseeing 36,000 labourers and soldiers. Ten thousand residents crowded into the buildings, not counting the servants. The pomp and circumstance which attract-

ed awed attention from the rest of Europe did not hide the reverse side of the coin : overcrowding, disorganisation encouraging intrigues of all sorts, the palace so filthy that the air often became unbearable. Fortunately, the king and court could always take the air at Marly or another royal retreat *(9:45-5:30 ex Mon. and nat. hols.; park daily from sunrise to sunset)*.

▶ **W façade**, 580 m long overlooking the park. The central section that housed the royal family projects in front of the wings; the leading sculptors of the period were employed here. ▶ The **château** itself can be visited in four stages : (1) Chapel★★★ (1689-1710); Grands Appartements★★★ including the Hall of Mirrors *(Salle des Glaces)* and the Salon d'Hercule *(no guides)*; (2) the King's apartments and the Louis XV interiors *(guided tour)*; (3) Museum of French History, 15thC to present day *(no guides)*; (4) Petits Appartements★★★ (Louis XV, Louis XVI and Marie-Antoinette), apartments of Mme. de Maintenon and Mme. du Barry★★, and the Opéra Royal★★★ *(lecture-tours at various times; tel 39.50.58.32)*.

▶ The **gardens**★★★ by Le Nôtre are classic French formal gardens (derived from Italian design theory); geometric flower-beds and fountains (by Le Brun and Mignard) are in perfect harmony with the architecture of the palace. The **Grandes Eaux**, with an hour-long fountain display, and the **Fêtes de Nuit**, with nighttime fireworks, bring back a little of the great days at Versailles *(fountains 2 or 3 Sundays each month, May-Sep., 4-5; fireworks four times each summer, enq. : SI)*. In the **park**★ *(open to cars)* the **Grand Canal**★ leads the eye towards the horizon.

▶ The **Grand Trianon**★★ *(on your right in the park as you leave the château)* built by Mansart in 1687; Louis XIV used to seek rest here : façades in white and pink marble; Empire-style decoration dating from Napoleon, who used to stay here *(no guides; guided tour on request Sat. and Sun. in summer)*. ▶ The **Petit Trianon**★★ (1768) : built by Gabriel, decorated by Guibert for Louis XV and Mme. de Pompadour; favourite residence of Marie-Antoinette, who commissioned the Anglo-Chinese gardens★★ and had built the make-believe rustic hamlet *(2-5 or 6 ex Sat.-Mon., hols.; check by phone, 39.50.58.32)*.

The town

Versailles grew up as a dependency of the château, around three avenues radiating from the Place d'Armes where the Grandes et Petites Écuries (stables) are located. Built by Mansart in 1685 and recently restored, the Petites Écuries now house the National School of Architecture, Motorcar Museum and Museum of Ancient Monuments. ▶ The old town evokes the 18th and 19thC; the heart of the N section is the **church of Notre-Dame**, the oldest in Versailles (1658, by Hardouin-Mansart). ▶ **Lambinet Museum** of local history, especially 18thC *(2-6 ex Mon., nat. hols.)*. ▶ The S section of Versailles housed government ministries in the 18thC; the **Salle du Jeu de Paume** (tennis court), restored to its 1789 condition, will shortly be open to the public. The **St. Louis Cathedral** (1754) overlooks the former palace kitchen garden (now the National Horticultural School) and the courtyards of the **Carrés St-Louis**★ (18thC commercial development). ▶ The **Arboretum de Chèvreloup**★ near Roquencourt is an annex of the Jardin des Plantes in Paris *(10 and 2:30, Sat.)*.

Practical Information _____

VERSAILLES
ⅈ 7, rue des Réservoirs, ☎ (1) 39.50.36.22.
SNCF R.E.R. ligne C and S.N.C.F., ☎ (1) 30.64.50.50.
🚌 pl. Lyautey, ☎ (1) 39.50.45.55.
Car-rental : Avis, 146, av. du Gal-Leclerc, ☎ 30.24.34.56.

Hotels :
● ★★★★(L) **Trianon Palace**, 1, bd de la Reine, ☎ (1) 39.50.34.12, Tx 698863, AE DC Euro Visa, 130 rm Ⓟ 🅿 🔎 🏃 816. Rest. ♦♦♦ ₺ 🍴 Jean-Jacques Mathou has brought a new spirit to the kitchen : *terrine fondante*

de pigeon au foie gras, paupiette de saumon au fumet d'huîtres, noix de ris de veau au porto, 200-250.
● ★★★ **Bellevue**, 12, av. de Sceaux, ☎ (1) 39.50.13.41, Tx 695613, AE DC Euro Visa, 25 rm Ⓟ 🔎 ₺ 233.
★★★ **Richaud**, 16, rue Richaud, ☎ (1) 39.50.10.42, DC Visa, 39 rm Ⓟ 245.
★★★ **Versailles**, 7, rue Ste-Anne, ☎ (1) 39.50.64.65, AE DC Euro Visa, 48 rm Ⓟ 🔎 320.
● ★★ **Home Saint-Louis**, 28, rue St-Louis, ☎ (1) 39.50.23.55, 27 rm 🔎 ₺ 180.
★★ **Angleterre**, 2 bis, rue de Fontenay, ☎ (1) 39.51.43.50, Tx 696388, AE Visa, 20 rm 🍴 🔎 ₺ 🍴 220.

Restaurants :
● ♦♦♦♦ **Les Trois Marches**, 3, rue Colbert, ☎ (1) 39.50.13.21, AE DC Euro Visa 🔎 🍴 🎵 closed Mon and Sun, 18 Jan-2 Feb. You'll have to climb high to gain access to the Royal House of Gérard Vié (the Duc de Gramont's former mansion) after stationing your carriage near the statue of his neighbour, the Sun King. The subtle cooking is worthy of the surroundings : *flan de foie gras aux huîtres, galette de turbot pommes de terre, crustacés au jus de carottes*. Fabulous *cassoulet sous filet de vinaigre*. A selection of coffees. Great wines. Open fire on winter evenings; in the summer the garden bears comparison with the "Field of the Cloth of Gold". Powdered wigs are not compulsory, 200-550.
● ♦♦♦ **Rôtisserie de la Boule d'Or**, 25, rue du Mal-Foch, ☎ (1) 39.50.22.97, AE DC Visa 🎵 closed Mon and Sun eve. At Versailles's oldest inn, everything is 'period' including the food by M. Saillard and chef J.-C. Aubry : *sole à la sauce aux Rois de Vincent de La Chapelle, haricot de mouton, filet de bœuf au beurre d'oursins*. Dishes created by the Sun Kin's master chefs, 155-270.
● ♦♦ **Le Potager du Roy**, 1, rue au Mal-Joffre, ☎ (1) 39.50.35.34, Visa 🎵 closed Mon and Sun. The simple annex of the elegant Trois Marches serves delicious dishes like *assiette de truite de mer crue en marinade, gâteau de foies blonds, sauce homard*, 85-180.
● ♦♦ **Rescatore**, 27, av. de Saint-Cloud, ☎ (1) 39.50.23.60, AE Visa 🎵 ₺ closed Sat noon and Sun. In his boat-cum-restaurant, M. Bagot does wonderful things with seafood. Alas, it doesn't come cheap : *cassoulet de poissons*, 190-280.
♦ **Bistro de la Mer**, 1, av. de St-Cloud, ☎ (1) 39.50.42.26, AE DC Visa 🔎 🎵 90-180.
♦ **Bistro des Halles**, 4, rue au Pain, ☎ (1) 39.50.31.19, AE DC Visa 🔎 🍴 🎵 60-160.

△ ★★Municipal (160 pl), ☎ (1) 39.51.23.61.

Recommended
Auction house : *hôtel Chevaux-Légers*, Pas. des Antiquaires, 10, rue Rameau, ☎ (1) 39.53.84.96, open Fri-Sun 10am-7pm.
Events : *festival de Versailles*, info théâtre Montpensier, ☎ (1) 39.50.71.18, May-Jun and Sep.
♥ antiques, folk art : *Le Grenier*, 7, pl. St-Louis, ☎ (1) 39.51.71.70; pastry : *tea room Guinon*, 60, rue de la Paroisse, ☎ (1) 39.50.01.84.

Nearby

BOUGIVAL, ✉ 78380, 7 km.

Hotel :
★★★★ **Château de la Jonchère**, 10, côte de la Jonchère, ☎ (1) 39.18.57.03, Tx 199491, AE Euro Visa, 48 rm 🍴 800. Rest. ♦♦♦♦ 🔎 ₺ closed Mon and Sun eve. Enjoyable fare cooked by Cyril Corbel : *salade de raie à l'huile de noisette, curry de coq et de moules de Bouchot sur des de céléris*, 200-350♦♦ **Les Années 30** A wine bar set in a spacious greenhouse, serving daily specials, caviar, salmon, wines by the glass, 90-160.

Restaurants :
● ♦♦♦♦ **Le Camélia**, 7, quai G.-Clemenceau, ☎ (1) 39.69.03.02, AE DC Visa 🎵 🍴 🍴 closed Mon and Sun eve. Jean Delaveyne, the 'wizard of Bougival', as his colleagues call him, has been named president of the *Chambre Syndicale de la Haute Cuisine Française*. Our warmest congratulations go out to the pillar of our chefs'

panel. We are glad to note that his new position will not take Delaveyne out of the kitchen, where he will continue to practice the grand art of French cuisine, of which he is a past master. Sample his *terrines friandes (canard, perdreau, grive), blanquette d'agneau Ile-de-France aux fèves et champignons, soyeux d'agneau, pied de cochon en daube...* etc. Yvonne and Guy welcome the guests, while the cellar and dining room are supervised by members of the family. Next door, the annex, L'Huître et la Tarte, offers foies gras, caviar, an oyster bar, wine by the glass, and a selection of gourmet groceries and take-out foods. Upstairs, a de luxe quick- service restaurant, 200.
♦♦♦♦ *Coq Hardi*, 16, quai Rennequin-Snalem, ☎ (1) 39.69.01.43, AE DC Euro Visa ⫽ ⅏ closed Tue eve (Nov-Mar) and Wed 15 Jan-15 Feb. Enchanting setting with cascading hydrangeas. High prices, 250-400.

Le CHESNAY, ⊠ 78150, 3 km N.

Restaurant :
☎ *La Rapière*, 31, rue du Col-de-Bange, ☎ (1) 39.54.14.25, AE Euro Visa ♪ closed Sun and Aug, 90-120.

COIGNIÈRES, ⊠ 78310 Maurepas, 18 km SW.

Restaurants :
♦♦♦ *Auberge d'Angèle*, 296, RN 10, ☎ (1) 30.50.58.23, AE DC Euro Visa Ⓟ ⅏ ⚲ ♪ closed Sun eve. Spec : *ragoût de langouste au poivre rose, filet de bœuf en chevreuil, soufflé à la liqueur de chocolat*, 200-270.
♦♦♦ *Capucin Gourmand*, 170, RN 10, ☎ (1) 30.50.30.06, AE DC Euro Visa ⅏ ♪ ⚭ Spec : *velouté d'huîtres et de moules en feuilleté, turbot soufflé au champagne, tournedos Capucin*, 200.
● ♦ *Saint-Georges*, 30, RN 10, ☎ (1) 30.50.10.23, Euro Visa closed Sat noon and Sun eve, Aug, 100-150.

GUYANCOURT, ⊠ 78280, 5 km S.

Restaurant :
♦ *Lac Hong*, rte de la Minière, ☎ (1) 30.44.03.71 Ⓟ ⫽ ⚲ closed Wed, 5 Aug-1 Oct. Facing the ponds of la Minière, a fine place for excellent Vietnamese specialties prepared by M. Tung : *pintadau désossé farci au riz et aux champignons parfumés, canette à la prune*, Peking duck, 50-80.

SAINT-CYR-L'ÉCOLE, ⊠ 78210, 5 km W.

Hotel :
● ★★ *Aérotel* (R.S.), 88, rue Dr-Vaillant, ☎ (1) 30.45.07.44, Tx 698160, 26 rm Ⓟ ⅏ ⚲ ♪ ৬ 230.

The VEXIN Region**

B1-2
Through the Vexin★ *(80 km approx, full day)*
The Vexin abounds in rich agricultural land and wealthy farms, vineyards along the Seine, and wooded hills ; stone spires of numerous Romanesque church-es break the skyline. Many of the churches were remodelled during the Renaissance (→ Mantes).

► **Vétheuil★** looks like a fishing village, with narrow streets leading down to the water ; church with early Gothic choir and pre-Renaissance nave and façade. ► A sudden bend in the river downstream **(Lavacourt Pool)**, often inspired the Impressionist Claude Monet. The chalky banks that enclose the Seine are honeycombed by caves, many of which have been made into attractive dwellings. ► **Haute-Isle** : a village of "troglodyte" weekend cottages ; there is even a cave-church in the cliff. ► **La Roche-Guyon★** : château built partly into the cliff-face with 13th keep ; main building 13th to 18thC ; stables worthy of Chantilly (→). 14th-15thC church ; town hall in the former covered market (18thC) ; yachting centre. ► Continue to **Giverny**, Monet's renovated house★ and replanted gardens★★ : enchanting whatever the time of year *(10-6, Apr.-Oct.)*. The Moulin de **Fourges** : on the banks of the **Epte** where the Plantagenêts (once the royal house of England) had their châteaux ; an ideal base for exploring the Vexin. ► **Beaudémont** and **Berthenonville** : ruined châteaux. ► In 911 the treaty of **Saint-Clair-sur-Epte** defined the boundaries of Normandy, the region named for the invading Norsemen who had settled there. ► **Dangu** : Gothic and Renaissance church ; 16th-17thC statues of the Twelve Apostles ; stud-farm. ► **Boury-en-Vexin** : château by Hardouin-Mansart *(Jul.-Aug., daily ex Tue., 2:30-6:30 ; Sat., Sun., Easter-15 Oct.)*. ► Churches at **Montjavoult, Parnes** (Romanesque) and **Saint-Gervais★** with magnificent Renaissance doorways. ► The **château d'Alincourt**, bristling with towers and turrets, is a medley of styles from the 15th to 17thC. ► **Magny-en-Vexin** : the church, like most of those in the region, veers between late Gothic and early Renaissance. ► **Wy** : château de **Maudéjour** *(2-6 daily)*, and mediaeval forge and tool museum★ *(9-12 & 2-6:30 ex Sun. am)*. ► **Omerville★** : classified site includes 15thC farm and church. ► **Amble-ville** : château with two beautiful gardens and two façades, one Renaissance, the other neo-Classical. ► **Villarceaux** : delightful water-garden ; Renaissance manor ; 18thC château. ► The hilltop road★ ends the trip with views over the Epte and Aubette valleys and the keep at La Roche-Guyon. □

Practical Information

VÉTHEUIL, ⊠ 95510, 9 km N of **Mantes-la-Jolie**.

Hotel :
★★ *Hostellerie St-Denis* (R.S.), rue des Cabarets, Chérence, ☎ (1) 34.78.15.02, AE Visa, 6 rm Ⓟ ⅏ ⚲ ৬ closed Tue eve ex reservation, Mar, 230. Rest. ♦ ⫽ ♪ ৬ 115-190 ; child : 60.

Recommended
Events : *onion fair*, 1st Wed in Dec.

Languedoc-Roussillon

▶ A region of many personalities, set between the peaks of the Cévennes and the Pyrénées, and the blue Mediterranean, with plains and mountains, plateaus and thriving cities. Languedoc-Roussillon is studded with vineyards and salty marshlands, and a wealth of Romanesque buildings, all imbued with the spirit of the South : Catalan and *langue d'Oc* traditions with their special lifestyles, their deep religious feeling and their passion for rugby and bull-fighting.

Carcassonne is a city whose past is so strong that it almost overpowers the present. It is, in fact, two villages, one made up of the acropolis and its fortifications, restored by Viollet-le-Duc, and the other, lower, on the left bank of the Aude. Montpellier is a university town a few kilometres from the sea. France's first medical colleges were established there in the year 1000 after contact with the learned Orient, and, in 1289, Pope Nicholas IV created the University of Montpellier. Today the Medical Faculty of Montpellier shares with the Paris Faculty the distinction of being the leading medical university in France. The old part of Perpignan has barely changed since the 18th century, but the dynamism and prosperity of this Catalan town with its festivals and processions and its bustling produce markets and wine trade mark it as belonging very much to the living present.

Almost the whole of the low country is covered with vineyards, but recently the risks of over-production and foreign competition have stimulated local farmers to diversify their crops. Now fruit trees and market-gardens are slowly invading the irrigated parts of the Aude Valley.

Cooking is Provençal, characterized by garlic and olive oil, with delicious sausages and smoked hams, *foie gras* and truffles. The region produces delicious pastries and sweetmeats made from almond paste and flavoured with aniseed, pistachio and orange-flower water.

Don't miss

★★★ Canigou Massif A3, Carcassonne A2, Montpellier C1.

★★ Espinouse Range B1, Hérault Valley C1, Narbonne B2, Perpignan B3, Pézenas C1, the Razès Region A2-3, Côte Vermeille B3.

★ Agde C2, Amélie-les-Bains B3, Béziers B2, the Cerdagne Region A3, Céret B3, Ganges C1, La Grande-Motte C1, Minerve and the Minervois Region B2, Montagne Noire A2, Mont-Louis A3, Saint-Martin-de-Londres C1, Sète C2.

Weekend tips

The first day will take you from Montpellier, Sète or Béziers into the Hérault Valley; lunch at Ganges; then through the Vis Valley and the natural mountain amphitheatre at Navacelles to Lodève (stopover). Up the Orb Valley on the second day to the Espinouse Range (lunch at Lamalou or Saint-Pons) and the Montagne Noire, before arriving at Carcassonne. Another suggestion : from Narbonne, go right up the valley of the Aude and lunch at Carcassonne; after Quillan, a stopover at Font-Romeu. On day two, after an excursion into Cerdagne, turn back through Conflent towards Perpignan; lunch at Villefranche, then Saint-Michel-de-Cuxa or Saint-Martin-du-Canigou.

Catalan house

● *Brief regional history*

The beginning

450 000 years separate us from **Tautavel Man,** the first known inhabitant of the Pyrénées, some of whose bones were found at Tautavel in the Eastern Pyrénées. ● During the **Neolithic Age,** farming settlements developed along the coastal fringe. The numerous **megaliths** in the region date from that period. ● During the 8th-7thC BC (Iron Age), successive waves of migration prompted the inhabitants already settled to construct strongpoints, such as at Ensérune, on easily-defended heights. At about the same

Facts and figures

Location : *on the Mediterranean coast, between the Rhône delta and the Spanish frontier, and including the southern face of the Cévennes Massif and the eastern Pyrénées.*
Area : *16 431 km².*
Climate : *Summer temperatures are high along the Eastern Pyrénées and the Mediterranean coast : Perpignan shares the national mean temperature record with Corsica. The area is exceptionally sunny (notably around Font-Romeu and the Cerdagne region). Winters are extremely mild in the lower Pyrénées valleys. Spring comes early in the Corbières region, which has a milder climate than the coastal regions, especially when the cold Tramontane mountain wind is blowing. Further inland, winters are harsh in the Cévennes and the lower tip of the Massif Central; summer here is also cooler than elsewhere. Although there is comparatively little rainfall in the region as a whole, mountain storms occasionally produce disastrous effects.*
Population : *1 321 740 inhabitants, mainly concentrated in the coastal towns.*
Administration : Aude *Department, Prefecture : Carcassonne;* **Hérault** *Department, Prefecture : Montpellier;* **Pyrénées-Orientales** *Department, Prefecture : Perpignan.*

Hérault region mountain house

period, Greek navigators founded several **coastal trading stations,** including Agde. ● **Celts** settled the region in the 4thC BC.

1stC BC - 8thC AD

The Romans arrived in the province of Narbonne in the 2ndC BC; they established colonies of military veterans at Narbonne, Béziers and Carcassonne. ● The region thrived under the **Pax Romana** but, like most of Gaul, eventually succumbed to **Barbarian invasion.** Nevertheless much of Latin culture was maintained during a century of **Visigoth** rule. ● Arabs invading from Spanish strongholds in AD 719 held a substantial territory, including Narbonne and Carcassonne, for the next 40 years.

8th-13thC

The 8thC **Empire of Charlemagne** brought a brief stability, although the nature of the landscape, as much as that of the people, fostered feudal rivalry and separatism. ● Wealth from trade combined with the literary flowering of the **langue d'oc** (the regional tongue supplanted by the *langue d'oïl*, which a Royal decree designated as the official French language in 1539) encouraged the founding of universities at Toulouse and Montpellier. Many towns and villages also prospered as way-stations on the pilgrimage routes to Santiago de Compostela in Spain. ● The independent spirit of the Languedoc was expressed in a persistent religious movement, **Catharism,** a branch of the Albigensian heresy whose basic tenet proposed that man

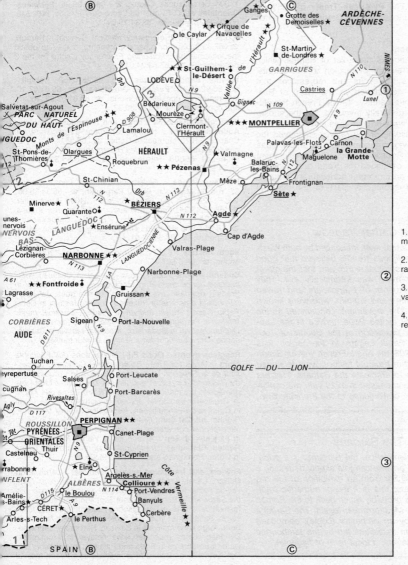

1. The Canigou massif

2. The Espinouse range

3. The Hérault valley

4. The Razès region

and the material world were the antithesis of the deity and, hence, inherently base. The movement was ruthlessly suppressed, largely under the leadership of the Anglo-French Simon de Montfort (1208-65), who rooted the heretics out of every mountain stronghold. Despite the savage eradication of the Cathars, religious dissidence persisted in the region.

13th-17thC
In 1258, the King of France ceded the sovereignty of Catalonia and the Roussillon to the Spanish House of Aragon. ● Resentment of Spanish rule, together with widespread adoption of the **Protestant Reformation,** brought sustained civil unrest, which was quelled only with the personal intervention of Louis XIII of France. ● In the wake of a general revolt against the Spanish government, French troops occupied the entire area from 1642. The **Pyrénées Treaty** of 1659 restored Roussillon, together with Cerdagne, to French rule.

17thC to the present
The 1685 Revocation of the Edict of Nantes, which had guaranteed freedom of religion to Protestants, opened the doors to revolts and repressions that caused as much devastation as the Wars of Religion of the previous century. ● The French **Revolution** of 1789 was generally favoured, but the subsequent Napoleonic wars drained men and money. ● In the 19thC, the building of the railway stimulated the economy by providing access to the many spas in the Languedoc-Roussillon. Industrial development and **tourism** have continued the trend to prosperity, and the region is an important agricultural producer, accounting for a substantial part of the national **wine output.**

The Cathar tragedy
Adherents of the Cathar sect, influenced by both Western and Eastern religious trends, believed that good resided only in the spiritual world, and that the material world, hence man, was intrinsically evil. They rejected the sacraments of Catholicism and raised a clergy of both men and women, who were known as the "Perfects". The movement, condemned as the Albigensian heresy by the Pope, thrived in the Languedoc under the protection of the Counts of Toulouse. After the Papal Legate to the region was assassinated in 1208, the Anglo-French warrior Simon de Montfort (→ Brief regional history) was delegated to lead a crusade to eradicate the Cathars. This era of religious upheaval ceased in 1229 with the capitulation of the Count of Toulouse to the French crown.

The Sardana
A traditional Catalan dance, the Sardana, is a popular event in which anyone can join simply by finding a place in the circle. Far from an exhibition of folklore kept up for tourists, this is a living, authentic tradition whose origins probably reach back to the Roman occupation of the Mediterranean basin. The Sardana is accompanied by an orchestra (cobla), composed generally of eleven musicians led by the tambourine and the strident flaveol, a local form of flageolet.

● *Practical information*

Information : Languedoc-Roussillon : *Comité Régional du Tourisme (C.R.T.),* 12, rue Foch, 34000 Montpellier, ☎ 67.60.55.42; **Aude :** *Comité Départemental du Tourisme (C.D.T.),* 39, bd Barbès, 11012 Carcassonne Cedex, ☎ 68.71.30.09; **Hérault :** *C.D.T.,* pl. Godechot, 34000 Montpellier, ☎ 67.54.20.66; **Pyrénées-Orientales :** *C.D.T.,* quai de Lattre-de-Tassigny, 66005 Perpignan Cedex, ☎ 68.34.29.94. In **Paris :** *Maison des Pyrénées,* 15, rue Saint-Augustin, 75009, ☎ (1) 42.61.58.18. *Dir. régionale de la Jeunesse et des Sports,* 200, av. du Père-Soulas, 34064 Montpellier Cedex, ☎ 67.63.09.09. *Dir. rég. des Affaires culturelles,* 5, rue Salle-l'Évêque, 34000 Montpellier, ☎ 67.60.66.31.

Reservations : Aude : *Loisirs-Accueil,* 39, bd Barbès, 11004 Carcassonne Cedex, ☎ 68.47.09.06. **Pyrénées-Orientales :** *C.D.T.,* quai de Lattre-de-Tassigny, B.P. 540, 66005 Perpignan, ☎ 68.34.29.94.

S.O.S. : *SAMU* (Emergency Medical Service) : **Hérault,** ☎ 67.63.00.00. For other departments, dial 17 to obtain the local number; *Poisoning Emergency Centre* for the 3 departments, ☎ 67.63.24.01.

Weather forecast : Aude : ☎ 68.25.10.58; **Hérault :** ☎ 66.92.62.12; **Pyrénées-Orientales :** ☎ 68.61.07.10. Information on coastal conditions : ☎ 68.61.03.92; mountain conditions : ☎ 68.61.30.32.

Rural gîte, chambres d'hôtes and farmhouse camping : Aude, see *C.D.T.;* **Hérault,** *Chambre d'Agriculture,* pl. Chaptal, 34076 Montpellier Cedex, ☎ 67.58.09.90; **Pyrénées-Orientales,** *Comité de l'Habitat rural,* 30, rue P.-Bretonneau, 66000 Perpignan, ☎ 68.55.33.55 and 68.34.55.06.

Holiday villages : *Fédération catalane Léo Lagrange,* 32, rue du Mal-Foch, 66000 Perpignan, ☎ 68.34.38.96; *V.V.F.,* 22, rue du Grand-St-Jean, 34000 Montpellier, ☎ 67.92.45.94; *Fédération audoise des œuvres laïques,* B.P. 24, rue A.-Marty, 11000 Carcassonne, ☎ 68.25.51.66; **Hérault :** 40, rue du Fg-St-Jaumes, 34000 Montpellier, ☎ 67.54.07.01.

Youth hostels : *F.J.T.,* 3A, rue du Capitole, 11000 Narbonne, ☎ 68.32.07.15.

Cultural events : Jul : *music festival* in Béziers; *international dance festival* in Montpellier; *cinema festival* in Prades; *dramatic arts festival* in Marsillargues. **Jul-Aug :** *mirondella dels arts* in Pézenas; *theatre festival* in Sète; *Pablo Casals music festival* in Prades; *classical music festival* in Perpignan. **Aug :** *classical music festival* in Hix; *Occitan festival* in Bédarieux; *medieval festival* in Carcassonne. **Oct :** *bullfight films festival,* in Montpellier.

Religious events : Good Fri : *processions des Pénitents Noirs* in Arles-sur-Tech, Bouleternère, Collioure; *procession de la Sanch* in Perpignan. **Easter Sun :** *processions du Ressuscité* in Céret and Ille-sur-Têt. **Easter Mon :** *pilgrimage to the marine cemetery* of Notre-Dame des Auzils in Gruissan; *traditional aplech* at Notre-Dame de Laval in Caudies-de-Fenouillèdes. **Ascension :** *votive festival* in Gignac. **Jul, 2st Sun :** *Grand Pardon de St-Pierre* in Sète; *international conference on religious history of the Midi,* in Farjeaux. **8 Sep :** *Aplech de la Vierge Noire* in Font-Romeu. **Christmas :** *traditional vocal music of the Goigs* in Céret, Perpignan and Prats-de-Mollo.

Folklore and traditional events : Feb-Mar : *carnivals* in Quillan, Céret, Argelès, Perpignan, Trouillas; *bear festivals* in Prats-de-Mollo. **Jun :** *festival de la Saint-Jean and the Sardanes* in Perpignan (until Sep) and Montauriol. **Jul :** *festival de la Cité* in Carcassonne; *international folk festival* in Saint-Pons; *national water tournament festival* in Sète. **Aug :** *wine festivals* in Saissac, Narbonne, Lagrasse, Sérignan, Elne; *muscatel wine festival* in Frontignan; *water tournaments* in Agde and Palavas; *international folk faïr* in Amélie-les-Bains; *féria* in Béziers; *sardane festival* in Céret. **Sep** : *wine festival* in Bram. **Oct** : *new wine festival* in Béziers ; *chestnut festival* in Saint-Pons ; *wine and produce festival* in Perpignan.

Fairs and markets : **Apr** : *antique fairs* in Montpellier and Perpignan. **Jun** : *gastronomy fair* in Castelnaudary. **Jul** : *bric-à-brac and second-hand cars* in Narbonne. **Oct** : *international vine and wine fair* in Montpellier. **Nov** : *St. Martin's fair* in Perpignan.

Nature parks : *parc naturel du Haut-Languedoc*, 12, rue du Cloître, 34220 Saint-Pons, ☎ 67.97.02.10.

Rambling and hiking : *topoguides* G.R. 36, 6, 7/74, 71, 77, 10. *Féd. Audoise de Tourisme de Randonnée*, 70, rue Aimé-Ramon, 11000 Carcassonne, ☎ 68.47.09.06. M. Ségui, *Assn. de Tourisme de Randonnée Languedoc-Roussillon (A.T.R.),* 14, rue des Logis, Loupian, 34140 Mèze, ☎ 67.43.82.50 and *l'Air du Sud*, Christian Fontugne, mountain guide, B.P. 9124, 34042 Montpellier Cedex, ☎ 67.64.51.76 ; *Club Alpin Français (C.A.F.),* 4, rue de l'Académie, 66000 Perpignan. *C.I.M.E.S.*, 3, sq. Balagué, 09200 Saint-Girons, ☎ 61.66.40.10. Also consult *Guides des Hauts Cantons*, 34390 Olargues, ☎ 67.97.71.27.

Cycling holidays : *Ligue du Languedoc-Roussillon,* M. Coupet, 24, av. de Figuerolles, 34000 Montpellier. Roussillon discovery : enq. : *O.T.,* Argelès-sur-Mer, ☎ 68.81.15.85.

Riding holidays : *Assn. Régionale pour le Tourisme Équestre et l'Équitation en Languedoc-Roussillon (A.T.E.C.R.E.L.),* M. Ségui, 14, rue des Logis, Loupian, 34140 Mèze, ☎ 67.43.82.50. Also : *L.A. Aude* and *C.D.T.*

Scenic railways : Hérault : *funiculaire de la grotte des Demoiselles*, 3, rue Maguelonne, 34000 Montpellier, ☎ 67.72.74.12, daily and evenings, 10 Jul-31 Aug. **Pyrénées-Orientales** : The Cerdagne-Villefranche-La Tour-de-Carol line, S.N.C.F., Perpignan, ☎ 68.54.50.50, and S.N.C.F. Villefranche-de-Conflent, ☎ 68.05.60.01. **Aude** : Narbonne-Bize-Minervois line, *Assn. des amis de la 141R1126,* ☎ 68.46.82.53.

River and canal cruises : on the Midi canal, from Castelnaudary to Thau Lagoon, on the Rhône canal in Sète and the lateral canal of the Garonne. For boat hire, enq. at : *Beaver Fleet,* port Cassafières, 34420 Portiragnes, ☎ 67.90.91.70 ; *Blue Line,* Grand Bassin, B.P. 21, 11400 Castelnaudary, ☎ 68.23.17.51, or 3, quai Sud-Ouest, 34340 Marseillan, ☎ 67.77.21.59. *Flot'home,* B.P. 151, 34300 Agde, ☎ 67.94.94.20. *Fluvia promenades*, 7, quai du Chapitre, 34300 Agde, ☎ 67.94.08.79. *Lo Pais,* 18, rue Dom-Vaissette, 34000 Montpellier, ☎ 67.58.77.58.

Technical tourism : *Chocolaterie Cantalou*, rte de Thuir-Orle, 66000 Perpignan, ☎ 68.85.11.22 : group visits 15 Jul-31 Aug, 2:30-5:30 ; rest of year, Wed 3. *Cusenier,* 6, bd Violet, 66300 Thuir, ☎ 68.53.05.42 : Easter-Oct, 8:30-11:45 & 2:30-5:45.

Handicraft courses : Hérault : fine book-binding, decoration of paper, book restoration, enq. : *O.T.,* 34300 Cap d'Agde, ☎ 67.26.58.58 ; ceramies, enq. : *Ceracap SARL,* la Bergerie, 4, av. de Cassiopée, 34300 Cap d'Agde, ☎ 67.26.86.52. **Pyrénées-Orientales** : macramé, pottery, enq. : *Host. "le Coffret",* la Preste, 66230 Prats-de-Mollo, ☎ 68.39.71.02, and *Ateliers d'art de Juyols,* 663760 Olette, ☎ 68.97.03.22.

Other courses : Medieval archaeology (15 days), 42, rue Victor-Hugo, 11000 Carcassonne, the *Institut Méditerranéen d'Initiation à la Culture Française,* B.P. 6039, 34030 Montpellier Cedex, proposes courses for foreigners in French language and civilisation.

Wine guide : courses in oenology, enq. : *Syndicat du cru minervois,* bd L.-Bazin, 34210 Olonzac, ☎ 67.91.21.66. *Comité interprofessionnel des vins de Fitou, Corbières et Minervois et des coteaux occitans,* RN 113, 11200 Lézignan-Corbières, ☎ 68.27.03.64.

Leisure centres : *Aqualand,* Cap d'Agde, 34300 Agde, ☎ 67.26.71.09 (end May-end Sep) ; *Aquacity,* Saint-Cyprien.

Regional wines

The vine is omnipresent in the Languedoc-Roussillon, starting at Fenouillèdes or the middle of the Aude Valley. In most districts, cooperatives encourage quality improvement and assist in the distribution of wine. Production in the Languedoc-Roussillon amounts to about 60 % of total national output. The wines are as varied as the landscape : red from Hérault, the Minervois and Corbières ; whites from Narbonne ; sparkling white known as blanquette from Limoux ; dessert wine (Muscat de Frontignan) ; and apéritifs such as the sweet wine of Banyuls. To lessen regional economic dependence on wine and problems of overproduction, efforts have been made during the past 20 years to return to a more diversified agriculture. Fruit orchards and market gardens have been established, especially in the irrigated areas of the lower Aude Valley.

The table

The food of Languedoc and Roussillon is essentially the cuisine of the Midi. The regional dishes are quite similar to those of neighbouring Provence. The staple ingredients are olive oil and garlic enlivened by aromatic herbs from the stony heath of the garrigue, and the plentiful regional wine. Mutton and lamb are the most common meats on the chalky plateaus and narrow valleys of the causse ; charcuterie is also important, particularly the sausages and smoked ham that are essential ingredients of the cassoulet of Castelnaudary. Specialities include foie gras, turkey pâtés, and other preparations flavoured with the rare truffle. In season, game from the garrigue is much sought after. Snails are often prepared en cargolade, that is, grilled over vine cuttings. Fish is popular along the coast : anglerfish is frequently included in the fish soup (bourride) of Sète and the fish stew (boulinade) of Roussillon. Mussels and oysters are cultivated in the Thau Lagoon. The region has relatively few cheeses, although the bleu des Causses (made from cow's milk) is widely known. The local pastries and sweets are often based on almond paste flavoured with aniseed, pistachio or orange-flower water.

Children : tennis and football coaching : Grand Stade, 66750 Saint-Cyprien, ☎ 68.21.24.21. For winter sports, contact : *Assn. Loisirs Montagne*, 1, rue Morse, 34500 Béziers, and *Comité Dép. UFOLEP*, Maison des Sports, 34100 Montpellier, ☎ 67.54.02.02 ; *A.D.P.E.P.,* 24, rue Émile-Zola, 66000 Perpignan, ☎ 68.34.21.37. Stays on mountain farms, enq. : *L.A. Aude.*

Canoeing : *Ligue Régionale*, moulin de Tarassac, 34390 Mons-la-Trivalle, ☎ 67.97.74.64, and C.D.T.

Water skiing : enq. : C.D.T.

Sailing and wind-surfing : *Ligue Régionale Languedoc-Roussillon*, 33, rue des Deux-Ponts, 34000 Montpellier. Courses, enq. : C.D.T.

Diving : *Ligue Régionale Languedoc-Roussillon*, 6, rue Dautezac, 31300 Toulouse. *Club International* in Collioure, ☎ 68.82.06.34. *Redris Club* in Banyuls, ☎ 68.38.31.66. *Les Corailluiers* in Argelès, ☎ 68.81.16.33.

Motorcycling : enduro, trail-bikes and scrambling in Amélie-les-Bains, M. Fernandez, ☎ 68.39.04.34, and *Moto-club de Corbère-les-Cabanes,* ☎ 68.52.72.29.

Golf : Perpignan-Saint-Cyprien (18 and 9 holes), La Grande-Motte (18).

Potholing and spelunking : Languedoc-Roussillon is an ideal potholing region which abounds in caves. *Assn. Entente Spéléo du Roussillon,* 4, rue Mailly, 66000 Perpignan; *Spéléo-Club Alpin,* rue de Substantion, 34000 Montpellier.

Climbing : *Compagnie des Guides du Languedoc-Roussillon (C.I.J),* impasse Petite-Corraterie, 34000 Montpellier, ☎ 67.72.16.19 and 67.27.54.10. Courses, enq. : *C.D.T.*

Winter sports : cross-country skiing in the parc du Haut-Languedoc. Sports activities, 34390 Mons-la-Trivalle, ☎ 67.97.72.85. Also Font-Romeu, ☎ 68.30.02.74; at the *Maison de la montagne* in Matemale, ☎ 68.04.41.48; by the *Groupe Excursionniste Pyrénéen,* 66360 Mantet, ☎ 68.05.54.90, and in Valcevollère, ☎ 68.04.52.33; *Club Alpin* (mountaineering club) branches in Perpignan, Prades, Canigou and Carcassonne. Also *C.I.M.E.S.,* 3, sq. Balagué, 09200 Saint-Girons, ☎ 61.66.40.10.

Hang-gliding : **Aude** and **Pyrénées-Orientales** : *Delta-Club,* 28, rue Armand-Izarn, 66000 Perpignan, ☎ 63.67.26.72. *Ailes catalanes,* 3, av. Boulès, 66170 Millas, ☎ 68.57.19.49.

Parachuting : *Centre-école du Roussillon,* B.P. 4, 66000 Salses, ☎ 68.89.20.60 or 68.83.04.80; upward parachuting, plage des Elmes, 66650 Banyuls-sur-Mer, ☎ 68.88.33.43.

Hunting and shooting : *Ligue Régionale Languedoc-Roussillon,* 12, rue Maury, 34000 Montpellier, ☎ 67.92.95.86, and *Féd. Dép. de la Chasse des Pyrénées-Orientales,* 7, pl. Paul-Bert, Lot. Porte d'Espagne, 66000 Perpignan, ☎ 68.56.70.55.

Fishing : *Halieutique interdépartementale,* mas de Carles-Octon, 34800 Clermont-l'Hérault, ☎ 67.96.11.35. **Aude** : *Féd. Dép. de Pêche et Pisciculture,* 32, rue de Mazagran, 11000 Carcassonne, ☎ 68.25.16.03. **Pyrénées-Orientales** : *Féd. de Pêche,* H.L.M. Victor-Dalbiez, 66000 Perpignan, ☎ 68.56.93.70.

Towns and places

AGDE*

Béziers 22, Montpellier 58, Paris 815 km
pop 13107 ⊠ 34300   C2

Agde, on the bank of a branch canal from the Hérault, seems far removed from the coast, suspended between an ancient past and the modern seasonal influxes of holiday-makers. The port has seen better days; it was founded as an outpost of the Greek colony of Marseilles.

▶ **Church of St. Étienne★** : Romanesque, formerly a fortified cathedral; barrel-vaulted interior; 17thC furnishings.
▶ **Agde Museum** : near Place Gambetta, in a mansion (5, Rue de la Fraternité; *10-12 & 2-6 ex Tue.*) : ethnography and regional archaeology, scale model boats.

Nearby

▶ **Cap d'Agde** *(7 km SE) :* tourist area on a volcanic promontory; the pier was part of an 18thC scheme to link the cape to the fortified islet of Brescou; marina, aquatic sports, *Aqualand* leisure park, amusement park, fishing, sea trips (glass-bottomed boat and water bus serving the beaches, seminar centre, naturism. Graspa Museum *(daily ex Mon., 10-12 & 3-6)* : finds by local underwater archaeologists. ▶ On either side of the mouth of the Hérault *(4 km S),* beaches at **Grau d'Agde** and **La Tamarissière** (naturism). ▶ **Vias** *(4 km) :* 14thC church. **Cassafières Port** *(9 km farther),* on the Midi Canal : houseboats for rent. ☐

Practical Information ─────────────────

AGDE
ⓘ rue L.-Bages, ☎ 67.94.29.68/67.94.25.86.
SNCF ☎ 67.62.50.50.

Hotels :
● ★★★ *La Tamarissière,* (I.L.A., L.F), 21, quai Th.-Cornu, La Tamarissière, ☎ 67.94.20.87, Tx 490225, 35 rm Ⓟ ≪ ♨ ⌕ closed 15 Dec-15 Mar, 300. Rest. ● ◆◆◆ ≪ closed Mon and Sun eve in spring and autumn. In his nicely kept family hotel, Nicolas Albano, a gifted, good-humored chef, carries on as the third generation in a line of native Languedoc chefs. On the banks of the Hérault river and close to the beach, the restaurant boasts fabulous fresh fish : *mouclade* of Bouzigues mussels, *salade de piments doux aux crevettes royales, bourride de baudroie.* Excellent wines, 80-250.
★ *Bon Repos,* 15, rue Rabelais, ☎ 67.94.16.26, Euro Visa, 15 rm ≪ ⌕ 120.

Restaurant :
◆◆ *Jardin de l'Amandier,* 2, pl. de la Mairie, ☎ 67.21.11.86 ≪ ♨ ⌕ Pleasant garden and indoor patio. Fresh fish, 70-150.

⚲ ★★★★*Domaine des Champs Blancs* (103 pl), ☎ 67.94.23.42; ★★★*International* (416 pl), ☎ 67.94.12.83; ★★★*L'Escale* (128 pl), ☎ 67.21.21.09; ★★★*La Clape* (450 pl), ☎ 67.26.41.32; ★★★*Lou Rouquet* (66 pl), ☎ 67.94.21.82.

Recommended
Guide to wines : *coopérative du Pinet,* ☎ 67.77.03.10; at Pinet, CP 34850, 10 km NE, *Claude Gaujal,* domaine de Pinet, ☎ 67.77.02.12, wine sold.

Nearby

Le cap d' AGDE, ⊠ 34300, 5 km SE.
ⓘ ☎ 67.26.00.97; ☎ 67.26.38.58.

Hotels :
★★★ *Golfe,* (I.L.A.), île des Loisirs, ☎ 67.26.87.03, Tx 480709, AE DC Visa, 50 rm Ⓟ ≪ ♨ ⌕ ♨ ⌕ closed 1 Dec-20 Mar, 395. Rest. ◆ *Lassevaine* ≪ ⌕ ⌕ Fish and regional cuisine, 90-190.
★★★ *La Voile d'Or,* pl. du Globe, ☎ 67.26.30.18, Tx 480982, AE DC Euro Visa, 20 rm Ⓟ ≪ ♨ ⌕ closed 1 Dec-1 Feb, 300.
★★★ *Saint-Clair,* (Mapotel), pl. St-Clair, ☎ 67.26.36.44, Tx 480464, AE DC Euro Visa, 82 rm Ⓟ ⌕ ⌕ closed 4 Nov-20 Mar. Handsome Art-Deco dining-room, private dining-room, 305. Rest. ● ◆◆ *Les Trois Sergents,* closed 15 Nov-1 Mar. Delicious food, 115-220.

Restaurants :
◆◆ *Le Pétoulet,* pl. St-Clair, ☎ 67.26.00.70, AE Visa ≪ ⌕ & *Foie de canard maison, huîtres gratinées, navarin de homard aux légumes,* 65-170.
◆ *Brasero,* Port-Richelieu II, ☎ 67.26.24.75 Ⓟ ≪ ⌕ & closed Tue (Oct-Apr), 6 Jan-27 Feb. *Moules farcies aux pâtes fraîches,* 80-120.

Recommended
Marina : *1800 pl.,* ☎ 67.26.00.20.

FLORENSAC, ⊠ 34510, 10 km N.

Hotel :
★★ *Léonce,* 8, pl. de la République, ☎ 67.77.03.05, AE DC Visa, 18 rm ♨ ⌕ closed Sun eve and Mon, Feb school hols., 14 Sep-7 Oct, 160. Rest. ● ◆◆ ⌕ Talented G.C Fabre (trained by Maximin) is brimming with ideas. We hope he will soon have the chance to carry them out and dazzle us with his light, inventive cuisine. *Terrine de*

lapereau, mousseline de morue, rôti de Saint-Jacques et lotte aux asperges, daube d'agneau, nougat glacé. Pleasant Fougères and other local wines, 110-200.

AMÉLIE-LES-BAINS*

Perpignan 32, Prades 60, Paris 944 km
pop 3713 ⊠ 66110   B3

Spa with 20 springs rich in sulphur and sodium. The site was a thermal resort in Roman times, as evidenced by the Roman paving in a restored pool; favoured as a winter resort for the dry even climate.

Nearby

▶ **Palalda**★ *(1.5 km NE)* : a Catalan village on the mountainside above Amélie ; 10thC church ; two towers remaining from the castle ; Postal Museum *(tel. 68.39.01.98).* Higher up, the **Ample Gorges.** ▶ **Montbolo** *(6 km NW)* : Romanesque church in a village above the Tech Valley. ▶ **Montalba** *(8 km SE)* via the **Mondony Gorges**★ : from there a 3-hr hike on GR10 to **France Rock** (alt. 1 450 m) : view★ of both sides of the frontier. ▶ **Arles-sur-Tech** *(4 km SW)* : commercial centre of the Vallespir, in an old town wound around the 11th-12thC **Romanesque abbey**★ (sculpted façade, 17thC reredos, 13thC cloister). Farther still, D3 climbs through the **Guéra Gorges**★ (chestnut forest) to **Saint-Laurent-de-Cerdans**★ and **Coustouges** *(24 km from Amélie-les-Bains)*; on a spur between the basins of the Tech and the Muga, Romanesque church built in 1147.   □

Practical Information

AMÉLIE-LES-BAINS
♨ ☎ 68.39.01.00, (all year ex 25 Dec-10 Jan).
🛈 pl. de la République, ☎ 68.39.01.98.
🚒 ☎ 68.39.00.90.

Hotels :
★★★ *Reine Amélie*, 30, bd de la Petite-Provence, ☎ 68.39.04.38, 69 rm P ᄽ 260. Rest. ♦♦ ♪ 120-160.
★★ *Castel Emeraude* (R.S.), rte de la Corniche, ☎ 68.39.02.83, Visa, 31 rm P ᄽ ₩₩ ᄼ half pens (h.s.), closed 1 Dec-31 Jan, 410. Rest. ♦ ᄼ 65-185.
★★ *Ensoleillade* (L.F.), 70, rue J.-Coste, ☎ 68.39.06.20, 19 rm P ᄽ ₩₩ closed 30 Nov-1 Apr, 145.
★ *Central*, 14, av. du Vallespir, ☎ 68.39.05.49, Visa, 21 rm, pens, closed 20 Dec-20 Jan, 270. Rest. ♦ 55-80.

Restaurant :
♦♦ *Auberge Saint-Michel*, La Bastide, ☎ 68.39.41.49 ᄽ ₩₩ ᄽ 95-145.

▲ ★★*Gaou* (170 pl), ☎ 68.39.19.19.

Nearby

ARLES-SUR-TECH, ⊠ 66150, 4 km SW.
🛈 ☎ 68.39.11.99.

Hotel :
★★ *Les Glycines* (L.F.), ☎ 69.39.10.09, Euro Visa, 34 rm P ₩₩ ᄼ closed Dec, Jan, 170. Rest. ♦ ♪ ᄼ closed Mon, 65-160 ; child : 50.

▲ ★★★*La Rive* (100 pl), ☎ 68.39.15.54 ; ★★★*Vallespir* (100 pl), ☎ 68.39.05.03 ; ★★*Riuferrer* (150 pl), ☎ 68.39.11.06.

BÉZIERS*

Montpellier 67, Perpignan 93, Paris 825 km
pop 90000 ⊠ 34500   B2

Founded as the Roman colony of *Julia Septimania Biterae*, Béziers is on the edge of a plateau overlooking the left bank of the river Orb. The city is the centre for the wine, spirits and related industries of the Languedoc. To understand the true character of the Midi, try to spend an evening at Béziers following a rugby final.

▶ **Allées Paul-Riquet** (B-C2-3) : a network of narrow streets leading off the main thoroughfare and centred on a statue of Pierre-Paul Riquet, Baron de Bonrépos (1604-80), a local landowner who conceived and executed the Midi Canal that links the Mediterranean to the Atlantic by way of the river Garonne. The Allées lead to **Plateau des Poètes** (C3-4) : public gardens. ▶ To W, medieval streets : **Rue du Quatre-Septembre** *(pedestrians only)* crosses in front of the **Penitents' Church** (Flamboyant Gothic doorway) and leads to Place Gabriel-Péri and the 18thC **town hall.** ▶ **Cathedral of St. Nazaire** (A3) : rebuilt during the 13th-14thC following the Albigensian Crusade, when the town was sacked (1209) ; statuary museum in the **cloister ; view** over the Orb Valley. ▶ **Fine Arts Museum** (Fayet Museum)★ in the Fabrégat Mansion (A3 ; 16th-20thC paintings, Greek vases ; *daily ex Sun. am and Mon., 9-12 & 2-6).* ▶ In the former Dominican church, **Museum of the Old Biterrois** (a Biterrois is an inhabitant of Béziers) **and of Wine**★ (A3, 7 Rue Massol ; *daily ex Mon., 9-12 & 2-6)* : regional costumes ; underwater archaeological finds from near Agde. ▶ **Rue des Canterelles,** lined with ancient houses, leads to the 13thC **Pont Vieux** (Old Bridge ; A3). **Church of St. Jacques** (B4) : 12thC apse ; terraces offer a view over the cathedral and the numerous Orb bridges, including the aqueduct that carries the Midi Canal.
Also... ▶ **Natural History Museum** (15 Place Pierre-Sémard, A2, *open 2-5 ex Sat. and Sun.).* ▶ **Church of la Madeleine** (B2) : Romanesque, last and vain refuge during the massacre of 1209. ▶ **Basilica of St. Aphrodise** (B1) : pre-Romanesque origins, a cathedral until 760.

Nearby

▶ On the SW edge of the town, the **locks** of **Fonséranes** compensate for the 25-m difference between the levels of the aqueduct and the Orb. ▶ **Ensérune**★ *(12 km SW)* : a fortified hill-top town occupied between the 6thC BC and 1stC AD by Celtiberians *(open year-round)*; view★ over the ancient **Montady Pool,** drained during the 13thC ; **Museum** : reconstructed burial sites ; Greek vases *(daily ex Tue.).* ▶ **Nissan-lez-Ensérune** *(3 km S)* : 14thC church : archaeological museum. ▶ **Valras-Plage** *(15 km SE)* : at the mouth of the Orb, a fishing port and marina : aquatic sports ; view from the 7 km-long beach extends from Cap d'Agde to the Canigou Massif.   □

Practical Information

BÉZIERS
🛈 27, rue du 4-Septembre (B2), ☎ 67.49.24.19.
✈ *Béziers-Vias,* 15 km E, ☎ 67.94.02.80.
SNCF (C4), ☎ 67.62.50.50.
Car rental : Avis, train station ; 18, bd. de Verdun (B-C4), ☎ 67.28.65.44/67.28.55.88.

Hotels :
★★★ *Europe*, 87, av. Pdt-Wilson (C3), ☎ 67.76.08.97, Tx 490064, AE DC Euro Visa, 30 rm P 380.
★★★ *Grand Hôtel du Nord*, 15, pl. Jean-Jaurès, ☎ 67.28.34.09, Visa, 42 rm P 200.
★★★ *Midi*, (Inter-Hôtel), 13, rue de la Coquille (B2), ☎ 67.49.13.43, Tx 490608, AE DC Euro Visa, 31 rm, closed 15 Nov-1 Dec, 250. Rest. ♦♦ *La Rascasse* ♪ ᄼ closed Sat noon and Sun. Spec : fish 70-150 ; child : 50.
● ★★ *L'Ambassade*, 22, bd de Verdun, ☎ 67.76.06.24, AE DC Euro Visa, 15 rm, half pens (h.s.), closed Sat lunch, 390. Rest. ♦♦ ♪ P. Seguin offers appealing dishes like *duo de bar aux asperges, mignon de lièvre à l'écarlate.* Accent on wines (extensive selection, reasonably priced). Fruit-flavoured apéritif wines (orange, walnut, peach, quince, etc...). Wine-and-cheese combinations, especially the more interesting examples, are overpriced, 100-210 ; child : 60.
★★ *Poètes*, 80, allées P.-Riquet (B2), ☎ 67.76.38.66, Tx 490206, Euro Visa, 14 rm P ᄽ ᄿ ♨ 165.
★★ *Splendid*, 24, av. du 22-Août (B2), ☎ 67.28.23.82, Euro Visa, 26 rm P 130.

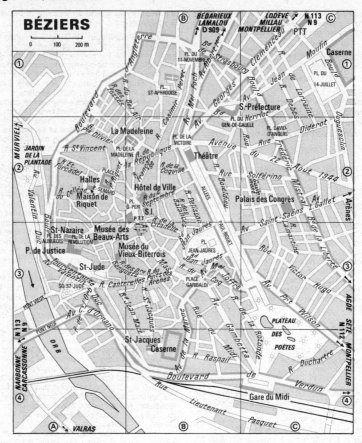

BÉZIERS

0   100   200 m

Restaurants :

● ◆◆◆ *L'Olivier*, 12, rue Boïeldieu (B2), ☎ 67.28.86.64, AE DC Euro Visa ♪ closed Mon noon and Sun eve ex Jul-Aug. Some effort is needed if the reputation is to be retained... 140-220.

● ◆◆ *Le Jardin*, 37, av. Jean-Moulin, ☎ 67.36.41.31, AE Visa ♪ closed Mon and Sun eve , Sat-Sun lunch and Mon (l.s.), 15 Feb-2 Mar, 18 Oct-2 Nov. Two young brothers with excellent culinary credentials (Maximin, Witzigmann). Spec : *ravioles de palourdes, tresse de sole au basilic.* Cellar rich in local wines and Bordeaux, 85-150.

● ◆◆ *Le Framboisier*, 33, av. Pdt-Wilson, ☎ 67.62.62.57, DC Visa ♪ closed Mon and Sun eve, 15-28 Feb, 17 Aug-1 Sep. Excellent cuisine, a wide choice of fresh fish prepared by Angel Yagues, 90-170.

◆ *Le Gourmandin*, 34, av. A.-Mas, ☎ 67.28.39.18, AE DC Visa ♪ & closed Mon and Sun eve. Spec : *Saint-Pierre en feuilletage, noix de Saint-Jacques et palourde,* smoked salmon, 80-180.

Nearby

POILHES-LA-ROMAINE, ✉ 34310 Capestang, 15 km S.

Restaurant :

● ◆◆◆ *La Tour Sarrasine*, ☎ 67.93.41.31, Euro Visa ⩔ ♪ closed Mon and Sun eve, 12 Jan-27 Feb. On the banks of the Canal du Midi, a pleasant view and good food at an up-and-coming eatery. *Quenelles d'asperges à la crème de homard* (in season), *magret au coulis de cèpes, feuil-*

leté de saumon à l'oseille. Local wines and great Bordeaux, 150-210.

VALRAS-PLAGE, ✉ 34350, 15 km SE.
ℹ pl. Cassin, ☎ 67.32.36.04.

Hotels :

★★★ *Mira-Mar*, bd Front-de-Mer (Jean-Moulin), ☎ 67.32.00.31, AE Euro Visa, 52 rm Ⓟ ⩔ closed Oct-Mar, 265. Rest. ◆◆ ♪ 70-160 ; child : 20.

★★ *La Plage* (L.F.), 3, Bd Saint-Saëns, ☎ 67.32.08.37, Euro Visa, 20 rm, half pens (h.s.), 380. Rest. ◆ ♪ & 60-120 ; child : 35.

▲ ★★★★*La Yole* (1000 pl), ☎ 67.37.33.87 ; ★★★*Méditerranée* (300 pl), ☎ 67.37.34.29 ; ★★*Le Port* (50 pl), ☎ 67.32.33.86 ; ★★*Valras* (333 pl), ☎ 67.37.31.31.

VILLENEUVE-LES-BÉZIERS, ✉ 34420, 5 km E on the A 9.

Restaurant :

● ◆◆ *L'Ecluse*, rte de Sète, ☎ 67.62.11.02, AE Euro Visa ⩔ ౸౸౸ closed Mon and Sun eve. A delightful place to stay near the canal, with equally delightful food and desserts, 65-150.

> In preparing for your trip, consult the pages pertaining to the regions. You will find there the description of the region you wish to visit, as well as a list of sites that must be seen, a brief history and practical information.

The CANIGOU Massif***

A3
2-day tour starting from Prades *(approx 180 km; see map 1)*

Standing as a sentinel before the eastern Pyrénées, the Canigou Massif is visible from far away, especially from the coast. Snow is present practically year-round in the high country. The mountain rises behind the high hills of Aspres, which are covered in Mediterranean vegetation but cleared for vineyards in the Roussillon. Attractive villages dotted along the route and a wealth of ancient churches mark the way, most originating in Carolingian times. Regional pre-Romanesque and Romanesque sculpture reached a peak around Canigou.

▶ **Prades** (→). ▶ **Saint-Michel-de-Cuxa**★★★ : the monastery, founded in 878, was a religious centre that reached its zenith during the 11th-12thC. Two galleries of the cloister (capitals★) have been reconstructed next to the church, which was consecrated in the late 10thC. Many elements of the original cloister are now incorporated in the Cloisters Museum (part of the Metropolitan Museum of Art) in New York. In 1965, Benedictine monks from the abbey of Montserrat in Spain resumed monastic life at

Saint-Michel *(daily 9:30-11:30 & 2-6, Sun. 9:30-11 & 2-6)*. ▶ **Corneilla-de-Conflent** : well-preserved Romanesque church★ with wrought-iron on the doors, carved reredos of 1345. ▶ **Canalettes Caverns** *(10-min walk from the car park; visit takes approx. 45 min; daily 10-12 & 1:30-6)*. **Grands Canalettes Caverns** *(in season, 9:30-6:30 daily; off season, tel. 68.96.31.17)*. ▶ **Villefranche-de-Conflent**★ : dominated by a citadel; **ramparts** *(daily 9-12 & 2-6)*. The streets within the walls *(pedestrians only)* recreate a medieval atmosphere with houses from the 15th, 16th and 17thC. **Church** (11th-12thC) : interesting artwork★, including a 14thC Recumbent Christ. ▶ **Fuilla** : church with three naves is one of the oldest examples of Romanesque in the Roussillon. ▶ **Sahorre** : Romanesque church★ (apse, bell tower). ▶ **Vernet-les-Bains,** deep in a valley; a spa, summer resort and popular excursion area; thermal springs rich in sodium and sulphur; casino. **Vieux Vernet** : Romanesque Church, ancient château. ▶ **Saint-Martin-du-Canigou**★★ *(45-min walk from neighbouring Casteil, or by jeep from Vernet)* : 1065 m above sea-level on a peak above precipices; founded in the early 11thC; the church and square bell tower have been ably restored in the 20thC; cloister (modernised) has beautiful carved capitals★ *(daily at 11, 2, 3, 4 and 5; be present 15 min before)*. ▶ **Goa** : a medieval watchtower 90 min from Casteil; view★. ▶ **La Preste** (alt. 1 130 m) : alka-

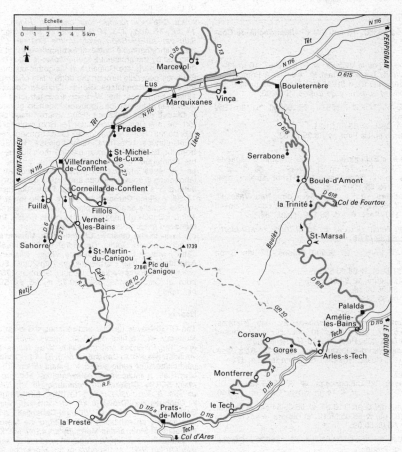

1. The Canigou massif

line, sulphur-bearing, radioactive springs in an extensive bathing establishment on a beautiful site; a good centre for day trips into the mountains, especially towards the **Costabonne Peak** (alt. 2 465 m; view★). ▶ **Prats-de-Mollo** : well-kept square, ramparts and 17thC church, dominated by Fort La Garde, with a 13thC tower. Trips into the mountains might include the **Mir Tower** (*2 hr SW;* 13thC watchtower) and the **Coral Hermitage** (*2 hr 30 S*) rebuilt 17thC; views★. ▶ Beyond the **Baillanouse Pass** reach Arles direct via the **Pas de Loup** or detour through **Montferrer** (Romanesque church; view★ over the Vallespir and Canigou) and the **Fou Gorges★** : in places no wider than 1 m (*entrance fee to a wooden footbridge, Easter-end Sep. 9-6).* ▶ **Arles-sur-Tech, Amélie-les-Bains** (→). ▶ **Prunet-et-Belpuig** : in the heart of the Aspres, **church of the Trinity** (Romanesque) with 12thC wood Christ; 30 min to the ruined **château de Belpuig** (view★) and the **Fourtou Pass.** ▶ **Boule-d'Amont** : beautiful apse in the Romanesque church. ▶ **Serrabone** : priory★, 11th-12thC Romanesque gallery along the S side; sculpted marble pulpit separating the nave from the choir (*closed Tue.).* ▶ **Bouleternère** : steep streets up to the church in a village built of brick and pebble. ▶ **Vinça** : orchard (peaches) centre beside the river Têt; Romanesque wrought iron in the church. ▶ **Marcevol** : priory, fortified church from the 12thC (*daily 3-7);* Romanesque church in the nearby village (mostly in ruins). ▶ **Eus★** : typical fortified Roussillon village, crowned by a church astride a series of arcades, vaulted passages and stairways : Romanesque chapel in the cemetery.   ☐

Practical Information ⎯⎯⎯⎯⎯⎯⎯⎯⎯⎯⎯

OLETTE, ⊠ 66360, 10 km SW of **Villefranche-de-Conflant.**

Hotel :
★ *Fontaine,* pl. de la Victoire, ☎ 68.97.03.67, 10 rm 🅿️◳ ᴧ closed Wed, Jan, 120. Rest. ● ◆◆ ⅃ ᴧ A French chef who has returned from the U.S.A. *Magret de canard aux figues, homard au beurre de truffes,* 100-200.

PRATS-DE-MOLLO-LA-PRESTE, ⊠ 66230, 61 km SW of Perpignan.
⚘ (1 Apr-1 Dec), ☎ 68.57.21.21.
ⓘ foyer rural, pl. Le Firal, ☎ 68.39.70.83.

Hotels :
★★★ *Park d'Estamarius,* by the bridge d'Espagne, ☎ 68.39.70.04, DC, 78 rm 🅿️ ∻ ᴧ ⅃ ⚘ ᴧ ⊠ ⅌ half pens (h.s.), closed Nov-Apr. Trout stream, 290. Rest. ◆◆ ∻ ᴧ 55-100; child : 35.
★★ *Touristes* (L.F.), 1, av. du Haut-Vallespir, ☎ 68.39.72.12, AE DC Euro Visa, 44 rm 🅿️ ∻ ⚿ ᴧ closed Nov-Mar, 180. Rest. ◆ ᴧ 60-130; child : 35.

▵ ★★*Can Nadal* (85 pl), ☎ 68.39.70.89; ★★*St-Martin* (75 pl), ☎ 68.39.73.08.

VERNET-LES-BAINS, ⊠ 66500 Prades, 12 km S on the Prades.
⚘ (1 Jan-31 Dec), ☎ 68.05.52.24.
ⓘ 1 sq. Mal-Joffre, ☎ 68.05.55.35.
SNCF ☎ 68.96.09.18.
⎘ ☎ 68.05.52.24.

Hotels :
★★★ *Comte Guifred du Conflent,* av. des Thermes, ☎ 68.05.51.37, DC Visa, 10 rm 🅿️ ⚿ ⅃ closed 26 Oct-15 Dec, 235. Rest. ◆ ⅃ 70-100; child : 35.
★★ *Princess,* rue des Lavandières, ☎ 68.05.56.22, Visa, 23 rm 🅿️ ∻ᴧ closed Nov-Mar. Solarium terrace, 170.

Restaurant :
◆◆ *Thalassa,* bd Clemenceau, ☎ 68.05.55.42, AE DC Euro Visa 🅿️ ∻ ⚿ ᴧ ⅃ ⚘ 14 rm, closed Dec-Feb, 70-140.

▵ ★★*Camp del Bosc* (110 pl), ☎ 68.05.54.54; at Casteil, ★★*Cady* (83 pl), ☎ 68.05.56.12; at Sahore, ★★*Fontanelle* (50 pl), ☎ 68.05.56.09.

VILLEFRANCHE-DE-CONFLENT, ⊠ 66500 Prades, 6 km SW of **Prades.**
ⓘ pl. de la Mairie, ☎ 68.96.10.78.

SNCF ☎ 68.96.09.18.

Hotels :
★★ *Auberge du Cèdre* (L.F.), domaine Ste-Eulalie, ☎ 68.96.37.37, AE DC Euro Visa, 10 rm 🅿️ ∻ ⚿ ᴧ ᴧ closed Tue eve and Wed, 5 Jan-8 Feb, 200. Rest. ◆◆ ∻ ⅃ ᴧ 85-120.
★★ *Vauban,* 5, pl. de l'Eglise, ☎ 68.96.18.03, Euro Visa, 16 rm 🅿️ ∻ ᴧ 130.

Restaurant :
◆◆ *Au Grill,* 81, rue St-Jean,, ☎ 68.96.17.65, Euro Visa ⅃ closed Mon and Sun eve, 11 Nov-10 Jan. Catalan specialities, 60-130; child : 35.

CARCASSONNE***

Narbonne 61, Perpignan 113, Paris 907 km
pop 41153 ⊠ 11000   A2

Carcassonne is an intact walled city whose turbulent history in no way detracts from its modern status as the commercial centre of the region. The upper town is enclosed within double walls (an exceptional example of medieval fortification), whereas the lower is a more recent grid of roads and houses on the left bank of the Aude. Carcassonne suffered severely during the Albigensian Crusade at the beginning of the 13thC.

▶ **La Cité★★★** (*guided tour daily ex. 1 Jan., 1 May, 14 Jul., 15 Aug., 1 & 11 Nov. and 25 Dec.; night visits, 9:30 pm Jul.-15 Sep.; apply to the Château Comtal*) : the most remarkable medieval **fortifications★★** in Europe, restored by the architect Eugène Viollet-le-Duc (1814-79); the oldest parts are Roman and Visigothic constructions. Entrance generally through the double line of ramparts by the **Porte Narbonnaise★** (E3). ▶ **Château Comtal★** (E3; 12thC) reinforces the W flank (reconstructed wooden outworks); museum of stonework open to guided tours. ▶ **Church of St. Nazaire★** (E3) : where Simon de Montfort, the anti-Catharist crusader (→ Brief regional history) was buried; Romanesque nave, 13thC transept and choir, 14thC statues, 14th-16thC stained glass★. The 360° view from the **St. Nazaire Tower** (behind the church) takes in the Montagne Noire and the Pyrénées. ▶ The visit to La Cité ends with a stroll through the medieval streets (abounding in souvenir shops and outlets for regional products) and a tour of the **ramparts.** Fireworks display on 14 Jul. ▶ **Place Carnot** (E2) : centre of the **lower town,** a market square shaded by plane trees and adorned with 18thC fountain of Neptune. ▶ Along the E side, **Rue Clemenceau** (*pedestrians only*), which runs from one end of the town to the other. ▶ **Church of St. Vincent★** (C1) : 14thC Southern Gothic. **Cathedral of St. Michel** (C2) : 13thC, with a 14thC polychrome Virgin; treasury; **Fine Arts Museum** (C2) : archaeology, 16th-20thC European painting, including works by Jacques Gamelin (1738-1803) born at Carcassonne (*daily 10-12 & 2-6 ex Sun. and nat. hols.).*

Nearby

The GR36 leaves La Cité and reaches the crest of **Alric Mountain** with a hike of 2-3 hr. (view★ over the Corbières, the Pyrénées and the valley N as far as the Cévennes); descent to **Capendu** (*16 km E*) : 14thC church, ruined château of same period. ▶ **Palaja** (*5 km SE*) : in the town hall, a museum of palaeontology and pre-history (*daily 5-7).* ▶ **Château de Pennautier** (*6 km NW; daily ex Tue. & Sun., Jul.-Oct.*) : 17th-18thC furnishings; park. ▶ **Conques-sur-l'Orbiel** (*8 km N*) : fortified village with Gothic church. ▶ 5 km NE, **Villarzel-Cabardès** : in the former school, an exhibition of finds from the Merovingian cemetery of Mourral-des-Morts (*by appt; tel. 68.77.02.11).* ▶ **Villegailhenc** (*9 km N*) : regional produce on sale. **Aragon** (*10 km NW*) : at the edge of the Montagne Noire, in a strategic position around a church and 12thC château.☐

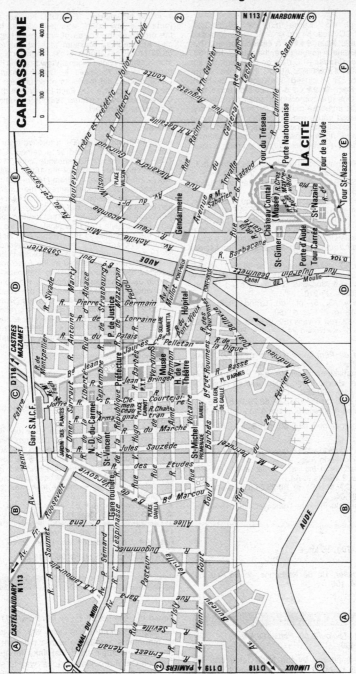

Practical Information

CARCASSONNE
ⓘ bd Camille-Pelletan (C2), ☎ 68.25.07.04/68.25.41.32.
✈ *Carcassonne-Salvaza*, 3 km W, ☎ 68.47.14.50.

SNCF (C1), ☎ 68.47.50.50.

bd Sabatier (D1), ☎ 68.25.12.74.

Car rental : *Avis*, 52, rue A.-Marty, ☎ 68.25.05.84.

Hotels :

★★★★ *Cité*, pl. de l'Eglise (E3), ☎ 68.25.03.34, Tx 500829, AE DC Visa, 54 rm P ⊱ ▨ ⌕ ♪ ♿ closed 17 Oct-20 Apr, 620. Rest. ♦♦♦ ⊱ ♿ closed Mon and Tue noon. Elegant cuisine in keeping with the setting, 135-180.

★★★★ *Domaine d'Auriac* (R.C.), rte de St-Hilaire, 3.5 km S., ☎ 68.25.72.22, Tx 500385, AE DC Euro Visa, 23 rm P ⊱ ▨ ⌕ ♪ ♿ ⊡ ♪° closed Sun (Oct-May ex hols), 15-31 Jan, 500. Rest. ● ♦♦ ⊱ ♪ ♿ closed Mon noon , Sun eve (Oct-May). Only the twittering of small birds breaks the silence of this immense park set in the wine country. The owner's special house wine and other local vintages accompany this excellent, generously apportioned fare : *cassoulet au confit maison, pilon de riz brun, canard à la Gaston Bonheur, écrevisses sautées à l'huile d'olive,* 185-300.

★★★ *Donjon*, (Mapotel), 2, rue du Comte Roger (E3), ☎ 68.71.08.80, Tx 505012, AE DC Euro Visa, 36 rm P ⊱ ▨ ⌕ ♪ ♿ 255. Rest. ♦♦ ♪ closed Wed and lunch, 90-150 ; child : 50.

★★★ *Logis de Trencavel* (L.F.), 290, av. du Gal-Leclerc, 3 km E. (off map F3), ☎ 68.71.09.53, AE DC Euro Visa, 12 rm P ▨ ♪ closed Wed, 10 Jan-10 Feb, 170. Rest. ● ♦♦♦ ♪ Award winning chef J.-C. Rodriguez produces hearty, satisfying classics like : *cassoulet languedocien, salade de truffes, confits* and *anguilles en salade.* Local wines, 110-230.

★★★ *Monségur*, 27, allée d'Iéna (B2), ☎ 68.25.31.41, AE DC Euro Visa, 21 rm P closed 1-15 Jan, 290. Rest. ♦♦ *Languedoc* ♪ closed Mon and Sun eve (l.s.), 1-15 Jan. Regional specialities, 95-210.

● ★★ *Remparts*, 3, 5, pl. du Grand Puits (E3), ☎ 68.71.27.72, 18 rm P ⊱ ▨ ♿ 180.

★★ *Pont Vieux*, 32, rue Trivalle (E2-3), ☎ 68.25.24.99, AE Visa, 15 rm P ⊱ ▨ ⌕ closed 24 Dec-Jan, 200.

Restaurants :

● ♦♦ *Auberge du Pont-Levis* (E3), ☎ 68.25.55.23, AE DC Euro Visa P ▨ ⌕ ♪ ∜ closed Mon and Sun eve. Comfortable establishment, where the Pautard family serves generous, classic food : *pigeon rôti en croûte de sel, purée d'ail, sole,* 100-250.

♦♦ *Crémade*, 1, rue du Plô (E3), ☎ 68.25.16.64, AE DC Euro Visa ♪ closed Mon and Sun eve (l.s.) , Jan, 60-120.

⚠ ★★*Stade Albert Domec* (200 pl), ☎ 68.25.11.77.

Recommended
Bicycle-rental : *Bourronnet*, 12 bis, rue Auguste-Comte, ☎ 68.25.66.64, closed in Aug.
Events : *illuminations in the cité*, 14 Jul at 10 : 30 pm ; *medieval fair*, 1st 2 weeks in Aug.
Guided tours : *C.N.M.H.S.*, ☎ 68.25.04.65 ; *dépôt lapidaire* ☎ 68.25.07.04.
Youth hostel : rue du Vicomte-Trencavel, cité médiévale, ☎ 68.25.23.16.

Nearby

CAPENDU, ⊠ 11700, 16 km E.

Hotel :
★★ *Top du Roulier*, rte de Narbonne, ☎ 68.79.02.60, Visa, 27 rm P ∜ 150.

CASTELNAUDARY

Carcassonne 41, Toulouse 59, Paris 768 km
pop 10750 ⊠ 11400   A2

Castelnaudary is served by the Midi Canal and the railway, as well as by N113 and A61, which bypass the town centre. The former capital of Lauragais, strategically placed on the road from the Mediterranean towards Toulouse, has often been bitterly contested. This city is renowned for the local speciality of *cassoulet*, a savoury stew of several kinds of meat baked with beans in the oven. The Foreign Legion maintains a barracks here.

▶ In the **old quarter**, 16th-18thC houses ; the **Présidial**, formerly a law court, was built during the 16thC on the orders of the Queen of France, Catherine de Médicis ; **Archaeology Museum** *(ask at the town hall, tel. 68.23.11.16).* ▶ **Church of St. Michel :** 13th-14thC, restored 18thC ; choir ; organs. View from the nearby terrace garden to the Pyrénées. ▶ **Grand Bassin** on the Midi Canal, feeding the five locks of Saint-Roch : also a base for pleasure-craft. ▶ On Pech Hill *(N side of town)*, 17thC **Cugarel windmill** (restored 1962) in operation up to 1919 *(ask at the town hall).*

Nearby

▶ **Saint-Papoul** *(8 km NE)* : a fortified town with a Benedictine abbey that served as a cathedral from 1317 to 1790 ; 16thC nave, Romanesque choir, 14thC cloister. Former episcopal palace of the 16thC. **Château de Ferrals** *(3 km farther on).* ▶ **Bram** *(16 km SE)* : Roman town of *Eburomagus*, market centre of the Lauragais, in concentric circles around the church ; archaeological exhibition at the town hall *(closed Sat., Sun.).* ▶ **Montréal** *(23 km SE)*, on an isolated hill-top : 14thC fortified church in meridional Gothic style (18thC organs) ; from the belfry, view★ from the Cévennes to the Pyrénées. ▶ **Notre-Dame-de-Prouille** *(17 km SE)* : monastery founded in 1206 by St. Dominic (founder of the Dominican Order of Preachers) ; the church, destroyed in the Revolution, has been replaced by a mediocre building. **Fanjeaux** *(3.5 km on)* : *Fanum Jovis* (temple of Jupiter) to the Romans ; stronghold where St. Dominic lived and preached in the early 13thC ; 13th-14thC Dominican convent *(visits by request, tel. 68.24.70.16).* Church of St. Marie : rebuilt in the late 13thC in Languedoc Gothic style *(visit to the treasury by appt., tel. 68.24.70.05)* ; view★. ▶ **Salles-sur-l'Hers** *(20 km W)*, in a valley known as the **Piège** (the trap) with several châteaux of which the most recent (17thC) offers a misleadingly medieval appearance.   ▫

Practical Information _____

🛈 cour de la République, ☎ 68.23.05.73.
SNCF ☎ 68.23.29.56.
🚌 cour de la République, ☎ 68.23.04.85.

Hotels :

★★★ *Les Palmes*, (Mapotel) 10, rue du Mal-Foch, ☎ 68.23.03.10, Tx 500372, AE DC Euro Visa, 20 rm P ♪ closed 15-30 Jan, 250. Rest. ♦♦ ♪ ♿ 70-130.

★★ *Fourcade*, 14, rue des Carmes, ☎ 68.23.02.08, AE DC Euro Visa, 14 rm P closed Tue eve , Wed, 23 Jan-2 Mar, 95. Rest. ● ♦♦ ♿ Memorable cassoulet, but Michel Chabit also makes an excellent *foie gras* of goose (or duck), 55-170.

★ *Languedoc* (L.F.), 33, rue du Gal-Dejean, ☎ 68.23.16.78, AE Visa, 14 rm ▨ ♿ 110.

★ *Les Jardins de Bellondrade*, (formely L'Auberge), RN 113, ☎ 68.23.13.04, AE DC Visa, 6 rm P ⌕ ♿ ∜ 100. Rest. ♦♦ ♪ ♿ ∜ closed Mon noon, 50-80.

⚠ ★★*Municipal* (35 pl), ☎ 68.23.11.23.

The CERDAGNE Valley*

                                                                        A3

Round trip *(approx 50 km by D618 and N116)*

Cerdagne is an attractive valley with views and majestic mountains, combined with a pleasant way of life. The little mountain train that links Mont-Louis to La Tour-de-Carol provides an ideal way to see the landscape in the spring encircled by mountains still white with snow, and budding fruit trees and cattle farms stretching into the distance.

▶ **Mont-Louis** (→). ▶ **Superbloquère**, S of D618 (alt. 1 780 m) a health resort composed of villas in a forest of larch, pine and fir. ▶ **Pyrénées 2000** *(N of D618)* : a winter sports resort offering night skiing on the plain of Serrat de l'Ours. ▶ **Calvaire de Font-Romeu** : view★★ over the Sègre Valley towards Spain. ▶ **Hermitage de Font-Romeu** : near a spring that once attracted pilgrims (*romeu* in dialect); chapel with Baroque decoration; buildings from the 18thC. ▶ **Font-Romeu★** (alt. 1 800 m) : winter sports, health resort for children with respiratory diseases, faces full S; averages 3 000 hr of sun per year; 30 km of ski-slopes, numerous ski-lifts; 100 km² of forest; about 70 km of marked trails. ▶ Near the neighbouring resort of **Odeillo★** : solar furnace (installed in 1969) with a power of 1 000 kW thermal, achieving temperatures above 3 500 ºC. ▶ From **Targassonne★**, a road to Thémis : most powerful solar generating station in the world (2.5 megawatts), inaugurated in 1983; it is equipped with 200 heliostats that adjust the power level and focus light on the giant receptor at the top of an 80-m tower *(temporarily closed)*. ▶ Descend to the bottom of the valley via the **chaos** (gorge) **de Targassonne★** : granite rock formation; views★. ▶ Church of **Ur**, consecrated in 953 : a Romanesque trefoil apse and decorated interior. Beyond **Enveigt** *(3 km W)*, the Carol Valley ascends the Puymorens Pass (→ Midi Toulousain, Pyrénées). ▶ **Bourg-Madame** : on the Spanish frontier, 4 km from the health resort of **Osséja**; from here walkers can climb to Mont-Louis by GR E4. ▶ From **Saillagouse** (lapidary workshop, jewel mounting) to **Llo★** *(2 km E)* : a remarkable site at the entrance to the **Sègre Gorges**; or to **Estavar** *(4 km W)* : Romanesque 12thC church (murals) on the edge of the Spanish enclave of **Llivia**. ▶ After crossing the **Perche Pass** (alt. 1 579 m; view★) return to Mont-Louis. □

Practical Information _____

BOURG-MADAME, ⊠ 66760, 9 km SW of **Saillagouse** on the N 116.
ⓘ ☎ 68.04.55.35/68.04.52.41.

Hotel :
★★ *Célisol*, 1, av. des Guinguettes, ☎ 68.04.53.70, Visa, 14 rm 🅿 ≮ 180.

⚠ ★★★*Meya-Jean* (60 pl), ☎ 68.04.51.76; ★★*Le Mas-Piques* (100 pl), ☎ 68.04.62.11.

ENVEIGT, ⊠ 66800 Saillagouse, 7 km NW of **Bourg-Madame**.

Hotel :
★★ *Transpyrénéen*, (L.F. Inter-Hôtel), ☎ 68.04.81.05, 40 rm 🅿 ₩ ⚄ closed June, 1 Oct-15 Dec, 180. Rest. ♦ ⚹ 60-160.

⚠ ★★★*Robinson* (166 pl), ☎ 68.04.80.38.

EYNE, ⊠ 66800, 7 km E on the Llo (D 33).

Hotel :
★★ *Roc Blanc*, ☎ 68.04.72.72, AE Visa, 23 rm 🅿 ≮ ⚄ closed 15 Apr-20 Jun, 10 Sep-1 Dec, 180. Rest. ♦♦ ≮ ♪ 55-80.

FONT-ROMEU, ⊠ 66120, 45 km SW on the Prades. ⚡ 1800-2250m.
ⓘ av. E.-Brousse, ☎ 68.30.02.74.
𝘚𝘕𝘊𝘍 ☎ 68.30.03.12.
🚌 ☎ 68.30.01.28.

Hotels :
★★★ *Cîmes* (L.F.), rue des Ecureuils, ☎ 68.30.07.45, Tx 500802, Euro Visa, 23 rm 🅿 ≮ closed 25 Apr-1 Jul, 15 Sep-20 Dec, 240.
★★ *Carlit* (L.F.), ☎ 68.30.07.45, Tx 500802, Euro Visa, 58 rm ≮ ♪ ⚘ closed 25 Apr-1 Jun, 30 Sep-20 Dec, 240. Rest. ♦ 70-120.
★★ *Clair Soleil*, av. F.-Arago, rte d'Odeillo, ☎ 68.30.13.65, Euro Visa, 31 rm 🅿 ≮ ₩ ⚄ ♪ closed 5 May-10 Jun, 15 Oct-15 Dec, 160. Rest. ♦ ≮ ♪ ⚘ 75-100.
★★ *Le Grand-Tétras*, av. E.-Brousse, ☎ 68.30.01.20, Tx 500802, AE DC Euro Visa, 36 rm 🅿 ♪ ⚴ ⚅ closed 15 May-15 Jun, 15 Nov-15 Dec, 190.
★★ *Pyrénées*, pl. des Pyrénées, ☎ 68.30.01.49, AE, 37 rm ≮ ⚄ ♪ ⚴ closed 5 May-1 Jun, 5 Nov-10 Dec, 185. Rest. ♦ ≮ ♪ 70-100; child : 35.
★★ *Romarin*, av. F.-Arago, Odeillo, ☎ 68.30.09.66, AE Visa, 16 rm 🅿 ≮ ₩ ⚄ half pens (h.s.), closed

31 May-15 Jun, 31 Oct-15 Dec, 325. Rest. ♦ ≮ ♪ ⚘ 70-120.
★★ *Y Sem Bé*, rue des Ecureuils, ☎ 68.30.00.54, Visa, 28 rm 🅿 ≮ ₩ ⚄ ♪ half pens (h.s.), closed 20 Apr-1 Jun, 20 Sep-15 Dec, 200. Rest. ♦ ≮ ♪ ⚘ closed 20 Apr-1 Jun, 80-130.

Restaurant :
♦♦ *La Potinière*, rue E.-Brousse, ☎ 68.30.11.56, AE DC Euro Visa ≮ ♪ ⚄ closed Tue (l.s.), 2 May-20 Jun, 10 Oct-15 Dec, 70-160; child : 40.

⚠ ★*Le Menhir* (200 pl), ☎ 68.30.09.32.

Recommended
Baby-sitting : info S.I.

LLO, ⊠ 66800, 2 km SE of **Saillagouse**.

Hotel :
★★★ *Auberge Atalaya*, (R.S., C.H.), ☎ 68.04.70.04, 9 rm 🅿 ≮ ₩ ⚄ closed 5 Nov-20 Dec, 300. Rest. ♦♦ closed Mon and Tue noon. Good mountain cooking, 100-175.

⚠ ★★★*Cerdan* (50 pl), ☎ 68.04.70.46; ★★*Segré* (80 pl), ☎ 68.04.74.72.

Recommended
Youth hostel : rte d'Estavar, ☎ 68.04.71.69.

SAILLAGOUSE, ⊠ 66800, 9 km NW of **Bourg-Madame**.
ⓘ mairie, ☎ 68.04.72.89 (h.s.).
𝘚𝘕𝘊𝘍 ☎ 68.04.72.88.

Hotels :
★★ *Planes*, (The old Cerdan house), pl. de Cerdagne, ☎ 68.04.72.08, Visa, 20 rm 🅿 ≮ ₩ ⚅ half pens (h.s.), closed 15 Oct-15 Dec, 340. Rest. ♦♦ 65-135; child : 40.
★★ *Planotel*, rue du Torrent, ☎ 68.04.72.08, Visa, 20 rm 🅿 ≮ ₩ ⚄ closed ex school hols, 15 Oct-15 Dec, 180.

TARGASSONNE, ⊠ 66120 Font-Romeu, 4 km W of **Font-Romeu**.

Hotel :
★ *La Tourane*, ☎ 68.30.15.03, 25 rm 🅿 ≮ ⚄ half pens, closed 15 Nov-15 Dec, 280. Rest. ♦♦ ≮ 55-90.

CÉRET*

Perpignan 31, Prades 55, Paris 938 km
pop 6798 ⊠ 66400   B3

A centre of Catalan culture, where avant-garde artists and adherents of Cubism gathered around the composer Déodat de Séverac (1873-1921) and the Catalan sculptor Manolo (1872-1945) in the early years of the century. Céret is also an important agricultural centre, especially for the cultivation of cherries and grapes. The Easter Sunday procession, the Sardane dance festival *(last Sun. in Aug.)* and the September bull races show that Catalan traditions are thriving.

▶ In the old town, 18thC **church** with three cupolas and a 14thC portal. This quarter is a series of courtyards shaded by plane trees marking the lines of the ancient ramparts, whose French and Spanish gates still stand. ▶ Place Pablo-Picasso : former convent of St. Thérèse, now the **Catalan Cultural Centre** with a museum, theatre and dance group *(summer, 10-12 & 2-6 ex Sun.)*; next door is the **St-Roch Crafts Centre**. ▶ **Museum of Modern Art★** : Cubist paintings *(10-12 & 2-5, 3-7 in Jul., Aug.; closed Tue)*. ▶ Place de la **Résistance** (not far from the bullring) : the **Toreador Monument** designed after a statuette by Manolo.

Nearby

▶ **Fontfrède Peak** *(12 km S)* : one of the most entrancing sites★ in the region. ▶ Bridge of 1340 *(1.5 km N of town centre, near D115)* : restored in the 18thC. ▶ **Château d'Aubiry** : turn off D115 to visit the wine cooperative *(3 km NE; daily ex Sun., Mon.)* ▶ **Le Boulou** *(9 km NE)* : church with Romanesque doorway and 17thC altarpiece; thence to **Le Perthus Road** via **Les Bains-du-Boulou** :

spa (sodium bicarbonate) specialising in treatment of liver complaints; church of **Saint-Martin-de-Fenollar★** (11th-12thC, with 12th-13thC paintings), and **L'Écluse** (remains of Roman fortifications, ruins of medieval château, Romanesque church). ▶ **Le Perthus** *(14 km SE)* : a village astride a spur of the same name (alt. 290 m) between France and Spain; on the path of the Carthaginian general Hannibal who crossed the Alps with elephants in 218 BC. From here, a small road climbs *(13 km E)* to the **Ouillat Pass** (936 m), continuing to **Trois Termes Peak** (alt. 1 130 m) : views★★.   ☐

Practical Information _____

CÉRET
ⓘ av. G.-Clemenceau, ☎ 68.87.00.53.
SNCF ☎ 68.87.00.14.

Hotels :
★★★ *La Terrasse au Soleil* (R.S.), rte de Fontfrède, ☎ 68.87.01.94, Visa, 18 rm Ⓟ ⫶ ⌂ ⌕ ⅋ ▤ closed 12 Nov-21 Mar, 310. Rest. ◆◆ ♪ & closed Mon and Tue noon, 150-180.
★★ *Arcades*, 1, pl. Picasso, ☎ 68.87.12.30, AE DC Euro, 26 rm Ⓟ ⫶ ⅋ closed 15-30 Nov, 150.
★★ *Châtaigneraie*, rte de Fontfrède, 2 km W, ☎ 68.87.03.19, 8 rm Ⓟ ⫶ ⌂ ⅋ ⫶ ▤ closed 1 Oct-14 May, 300. Rest. ◆ ⫶ ♪ ⅋ closed Sun and lunch, 170.

Restaurant :
◆◆ *La Ferme de Céret*, 15, bd G.-Clemenceau, ☎ 68.87.07.91, Euro Visa ⌂ ♪ closed Mon and Sun eve, 20 Dec-5 Feb, 55-75.

⊼ ★★★*Saint-Georges* (60 pl), ☎ 68.87.03.73 ; ★★*Bosquet de Nogarède* (132 pl), ☎ 68.87.26.72.

Recommended
Farmhouse-inn : at Oms, *Mas Cantuern*, ☎ 68.39.41.90, spec : *civet de sanglier.*

Nearby

Le BOULOU, ✉ 66160, 9 km NE.
⚓ (10 Apr-31 Oct), ☎ 68.83.01.17.
ⓘ pl. de la Mairie, ☎ 68.83.36.32.
SNCF ☎ 68.83.15.51.
▭▱▭ pl. de la République, ☎ 68.83.15.59.

Hotels :
★★★ *Relais des Chartreuses*, (I.L.A.), à 4.5 km, rte d'Argelès-sur-Mer, ☎ 68.83.15.88, 10 rm Ⓟ ⌂ ⌕ & ⅋ ▤ ½ half pens (h.s.), 720. Rest. ◆ ♪ & closed Mon. Reserve in winter. Moroccan and French cuisine, 220.
● ★★ *Grillon d'Or*, (Inter-Hôtel), 40, rue de la République, ☎ 68.83.03.60, 40 rm Ⓟ ⌕ ▤ closed 15 Jan-1 Mar, 170. Rest. ◆ 50-130.

⊼ ★★*Le Mas LLinas* (100 pl), ☎ 68.83.25.46.

Recommended
Casino : rte du Perthus, ☎ 68.83.02.81. Rest.

The ESPINOUSE Range**

B1

Round trip *(approx 170 km, full day ; see map 2)*

The Espinouse (prickly) Range is a granite crest linking Larzac (→ Rouergue-Albigeois) and the Montagne Noire (→). The S face, with torrential streams and steep rocks, is covered with prickly maquis (hence the name) that, lower down, yields first to chestnut trees then to olive groves. The more humid N face is pastureland. The Orb and Agout valleys demonstrate the difference in terrain. The Haut-Languedoc Nature Park includes part of the range.

▶ **Lamalou-les-Bains :** hot springs★ with temperatures from 16° to 50° C beside the river Bitoulet; church of **St-Pierre-de-Rhèdes** contains fine Romanesque murals *(Jun.-Sep., Sun. at 5 ; rest of year, enq. : tel. :*

67.95.62.60); lookout point at **Notre-Dame-de-Capimont** *(approx. 50-min climb)* or **château de Saint-Michel** *(approx. 2hr SE)*. ▶ Near the confluence of the Jaur and the Orb, you can go down the **Orb Gorges** (Saint-Chinian) or up the **Héric Gorges** : view of Mons-la-Trivalle. ▶ **O-largues** : on a promontory in a bend of the Jaur and dominated by a square tower; 15thC bridge. ▶ **Saint-Pons-de-Thomières** : near the source of the Jaur (site★) in a natural mountain amphitheatre; the **Haut-Languedoc Nature Park** is based here. The **church**, first an abbey, then a cathedral until the Revolution, is one of the most imposing fortified churches in the Languedoc; the choir was destroyed when the existing façade was built in the 18thC. Several 15th-17thC houses; archaeological museum in the former Chapel of the Penitents. ▶ **Devèze Cavern★** : discovered in 1886 *(open year-round)*. ▶ **Labastide-Rouairoux** : textile production centre of the Tarn region. ▶ **Raviège Reservoir** : a dam on the Agout, with a road alongside the lake. ▶ **La Salvetat-sur-Agout :** centre for cattle raising and cereal cultivation on the N face of the Espinouse. ▶ Detour via **Saut de Vésole** (view★) at the foot of a dam of the same name. ▶ Panorama from the **Espinouse** summit (alt. 1 125 m). ▶ **Douch** *(2.5 km SW of D180)* : Natural History Museum *(Jun.-Sep.)*; point of departure for a climb *(approx. 40 min)* up **Mont Carroux★** : lookout over much of the Languedoc and the Pyrénées; below, the **Héric Gorges.** ▶ E, a path crosses the **Écrivains Combattants** (soldier-writers) **Forest :** pines and firs planted from 1931 onwards in memory of writers who died in WWI. ▶ **Saint-Gervais-sur-Mare :** village and excursion centre; geology and regional history museum. ▶ A little off the route, **Boussagues**, now a village, formerly a stronghold. ▶ **Bédarieux**, near bauxite mines : 15th-16thC church, cultural centre on Avenue Abbé-Tarroux (regional artists ; *daily pm Jun.-Oct.*).   ☐

Practical Information _____

BÉDARIEUX, ✉ 34600, 9 km NE of **Lamalou-les-Bains**.
ⓘ rue St-Alexandre, ☎ 67.95.08.79.
SNCF ☎ 67.95.02.92.

Hotel :
★★ *Moderne*, 64, av. Jean-Jaurès, rte de St-Pons, ☎ 67.95.01.52, AE DC Euro Visa, 28 rm Ⓟ ⫶ closed 10 Dec-20 Jan, 160.

⊼ at Aires, ★★*Camp de Gatinie*, 6 km W on D 160 (103 pl), ☎ 67.95.60.81.

Recommended
Farmhouse-inn : at La tour-sur-Orb 6 km on D 157, *Mas de Riols*, ☎ 67.23.10.53, a gîte-rural accepting up to 20 guests.

LAMALOU-LES-BAINS, ✉ 34240, 39 km N of **Béziers**.
⚓ ☎ 67.95.22.40.
ⓘ 24, av. Charcot, ☎ 67.95.64.17.

Hotels :
★★ *Belleville*, 1, av. Charcot, ☎ 67.95.61.09, Euro Visa, 44 rm Ⓟ ⫶ ⌂ ⌕ & ▤ 140. Rest. ◆ ⫶ ♪ & 40-110.
★★ *Grand Hôtel Mas* (L.F.), 25, av. Charcot, ☎ 67.95.62.22, DC Euro Visa, 40 rm Ⓟ ⫶ ⌂ ⅋ ♪° closed 2 Jan-26 Feb, 160. Rest. ◆◆ ⫶ ♪ & 45-150.

⊼ ★★*Muni* (100 pl), ☎ 67.95.26.89.

OLARGUES, ✉ 34390, 18 km SW of **Lamalou-les-Bains**.
ⓘ rue de la Place, ☎ 67.97.71.26 (h.s.).

Hotels :
● ★★ *Domaine de Rieumégé* (R.S.), rte de Saint-Pons, ☎ 67.97.73.99, Visa, 11 rm Ⓟ ⫶ ⌂ ⌕ ▤ ♪° half pens (h.s.), closed lunch ex Sun, 1 Oct-15 May, 515. Rest. ◆ ⫶ ♪ 110-185 ; child : 50.
Laissac, av. de la Gare, ☎ 67.97.70.89, Euro Visa, 14 rm ⅋ half pens (h.s.), closed Oct-Mar, 207. Rest. ◆ ⅋ 50-90.

SAINT-PONS-DE-THOMIÈRES, ✉ 34220, 51 km NW of **Béziers**.
ⓘ pl. du Foirail, ☎ 67.97.06.65 (h.s.).

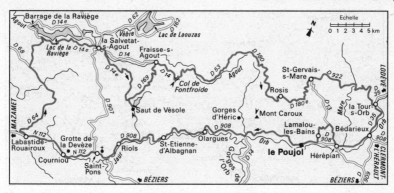

2. The Espinouse range

Hotel :
★★★ *Château de Ponderach* (R.C.), rte de Narbonne, ☎ 67.97.02.57, AE DC Euro Visa, 12 rm, closed 15 Oct-1 Apr, 350. Rest. ♦♦♦ Spec : *mousse de poireaux truffée, sole en croûte,* 150-230.

La SALVETAT-SUR-AGOUT, ⊠ 34330, 21 km NW of **Saint-Pons-de-Thomières.**
🛈 ☎ 67.97.64.44.

Hotel :
★ *Cros,* rte de Lacaune, ☎ 67.97.60.21, 23 rm ⓟ ⚸ ⚏ closed Mon (l.s.), 31 Oct-1 May, 120. Rest. ♦ Very good value, 50-130.

⚠ ★★★*Goudal* (100 pl), ☎ 67.97.60.44 ; ★★*Bouldouires* (100 pl), ☎ 67.97.62.30 ; ★★*La Blaquière* (60 pl), ☎ 67.97.61.29.

Le SOULIE, ⊠ 34330, 10 km S on the D 150.

Restaurant :
♦♦ *Moulin de Vergougniac,* ☎ 67.97.05.62, Euro Visa, closed Mon eve and Tue, 1 Jan-15 Mar, 90-130.

GANGES*

Montpellier 45, Nîmes 64, Paris 757 km
pop 3533 ⊠ 34190   C1

At the junction of several mountain valleys (Hérault, Rieutord, Vis), Ganges is one of the gates to the Cévennes. From the 17thC until the advent of synthetic fibres, the town thrived from the manufacture of silk stockings. The hosiery industry — now based on modern textile and chemical production — continues to be the mainstay of Ganges.

Nearby

▶ From Ganges, go down the **Hérault Valley** (→) or go up (defile★) to reach the **Vis Valley★** overshadowed on the left by the limestone chain of **Séranne** (alt. 953 m) : view★ over the gorges★ from roads winding up to Saint-Maurice-Navacelles. ▶ Best view of the **natural amphitheatre of Navacelles★★** is from La Baume-Auriol, a farming settlement on the edge of the plateau. ▶ In a depression *(approx 33 km from Ganges)* formed by a loop in the river, **Navacelles :** hamlet and waterfall★. A 2hr hike up the Vis Valley to the **Vissec amphitheatre★** ; or a drive via the village of Blandas (views★).   □

Practical Information _____

🛈 plan des Ormeaux, ☎ 67.73.84.79.
SNCF ☎ 67.73.68.58.

Hotel :
★ *Aux Caves de l'Hérault* (L.F.), 14, av. Jeu-de-Ballon, ☎ 67.73.81.09, Euro Visa, 14 rm ⚸ ⚏ closed Fri eve and Sat, 30 Nov-1 Feb, 105. Rest. ♦ ♪ closed Fri eve and Sat, 30 Nov-1 Feb, 50-100.

Recommended
Farmhouse-inn : at St-Bauzille-de-Putois, *Mas de Coulet,* 8 km on D 986, ☎ 67.73.74.18, with 2 5-pers gîtes.

The HÉRAULT Valley**

                                                  C1

Round trip from Lodève *(approx 180 km, full day; see map 3)*

On the verge of the Larzac plateau and the scrubland marking the hinterland of Montpellier. The softer rocks have been eroded by subterranean rivers and weathered into an unusually beautiful landscape. Man's traces are apparent in the form of Romanesque buildings.

▶ **Lodève** (→). ▶ Priory of **Saint-Michel-de-Grandmont :** just off the route, an 11th-12thC building in an extensive park with prehistoric megaliths and ancient statues *(daily pm ex Mon., 15 Jun.-15 Sep. ; Sun. and nat. hols. pm, 15 Mar.-14 Jun. and 15 Sep.-31 Oct.).* ▶ **Saint-Jean-de-Buèges :** hike from here down the Buège Gorges. ▶ **Brissac★ :** a mountain village crowned by a ruined 16thC château. Between Brissac and Cazilhac, walk to the **Rubanel Abyss,** a sinkhole more than 100 m deep. ▶ **Cazilhac :** 12th-16thC château *(visits pm).* ▶ **Ganges** (→). ▶ At the exit of a pass between high white cliffs, access to the **Demoiselles Grotto★★,** a pothole in the Thaurac plateau discovered in 1770 *(daily).* ▶ Romanesque chapel of **Saint-Étienne-d'Essensac :** a site typical of the banks of the Hérault. ▶ From the hamlet of **Moscla,** follow the **Arcs Ravine** hollowed out by the Lamalou and running under several natural bridges *(approx 1hr).* ▶ **Saint-Martin-de-Londres** (→). ▶ After leaving the valley, the road rejoins the **Hérault Gorges★,** with chalky walls typical of the Midi region. ▶ **Saint-Guilhem-le-Désert★★ :** beautiful village squeezed into the narrow Verdus Gorge. **Romanesque church★★,** built to house a supposed fragment of Christ's cross, is a fine example of Languedoc Romanesque (apse★★, statues of Apostles, 12thC altar, remains of cloister). Walk up the **Verdus Gorges** to the **amphitheatre of Infernet★** surrounded by steep cliffs, or visit the **Baume-Cellier Cavern.** ▶ Downstream from Saint-Guilhem, the route crosses the natural basin of the **Foux de Clamouse** ("the bawling fountain"), which cascades into the bed of the Hérault, outlet of a subterranean network draining the waters from the Larzac plateau. The **Clamouse Cavern★★ :** mineral formations *(daily).*

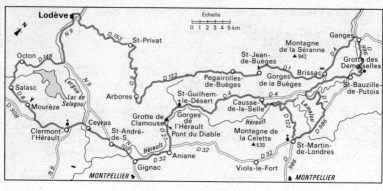

3. The Hérault valley

▶ **Gignac** : fortified city, parts of whose ramparts and a 13thC keep survive; view★ from the 17thC chapel of **Notre-Dame-de-Grace.** ▶ **Clermont-l'Hérault** : once protected by the keep now in ruins; old houses; fortified 14thC church. ▶ **Villeneuvette★** : a weaving town with a 17thC appearance. ▶ **Mourèze amphitheatre★** : rocky wilderness surrounding the village of **Mourèze.** ▶ **Salasc** : museum of folk arts and traditions of the Lodève. ▶ Above **Octon** (ruins of the 15thC château de Lauzières), the road follows the **Salagou Dam** (8 km²; aquatic sports; fishing). ☐

Practical Information

CLERMONT-L'HÉRAULT, ⊠ 34800, 41 km W of **Montpellier.**
ⓘ rue René-Gosse, ☎ 67.96.23.86 (h.s.). 🕊
 ☎ 67.96.04.01.

Hotels :
★★ *Sarac*, rte de Nébian, ☎ 67.96.06.81, 22 rm ℗ ⫽ ⅋
closed Sat-Sun (1st Oct-1st Mar), 15 Dec-15 Jan, 135.
★ *Terminus*, 11, allées Roger-Salengro, ☎ 67.96.10.66,
AE Euro Visa, 32 rm ℗ ◔ 125. Rest. ♦ 75-100.

▲ ★★*Lac du Salagou* (300 pl), ☎ 67.96.06.18; at Canet,
5 km, ★★*Les Rivières* (66 pl), ☎ 67.96.75.53.

Recommended
Farmhouse-inn : at Salasc, 15 km W D 8, *Vallée du Salagou*, ☎ 67.96.15.62. Goat-cheese specialties; cheese for sale.
▼ grape candy : *M. Boudet*, ☎ 67.96.38.31.

GIGNAC, ⊠ 34150, 30 km NW of **Montpellier.**
ⓘ pl. du Gal-Claparède, ☎ 67.57.58.83.

Hotels :
★★ *Capion*, 3, bd de l'Esplanade, ☎ 67.57.50.83, AE DC Euro Visa, 8 rm ℗ half pens (h.s.), closed Sun eve and Mon (l.s.), Feb, 580. Rest. ♦♦ ♪ Market cuisine that's traditional and tasty, 135-240; child : 45.
Commerce, 1, bd Pasteur, ☎ 67.57.50.97, 17 rm ℗
half pens (h.s.), closed Sun, Jan, 320. Rest. ♦ 70.

MOURÈZE, ⊠ 34800 Clermont-l'Hérault, 8 km E of **Clermont-l'Hérault** on D 8.

Hotel :
♦ *Les Hauts de Mourèze*, ☎ 67.96.04.84, 10 rm ℗ ⫽ ⟨⟩
◔ ⅋ ▭ closed 15 Oct-29 Mar, 160.

SAINT-GUILHEM-LE-DÉSERT, ⊠ 34150 Gignac, 13 km N of **Gignac** on the D 27.

Hotel :
Fonzès, 2, av. St-Benoît d'Amane, ☎ 67.57.72.01, 12 rm
℗ ⫽ ⟨⟩ ⅋ closed 15 Nov-15 Mar, 130. Rest. ♦ ⫽
⅋ 65-100.

LEUCATE

Perpignan 34, Narbonne 37, Paris 883 km
pop 1968 ⊠ 11370   B3

ⓘ ☎ 68.40.91.31 (h.s.).
ⓢⓝⓒⓕ ☎ 68.45.70.01.

Hotels :
★★ *La Plage*, La Franqui-Plage, 7 km N, ☎ 68.45.70.23,
32 rm ℗ ⫽ ⸰⸰⸰ pens (h.s.), closed 1 Oct-1 May, 360.
Rest. ♦♦ ♪ 55-85.
★ *Côte Rêvée*, bd du Front-de-Mer, ☎ 68.40.00.68, Visa,
11 rm ℗ ⫽ ⟨⟩ half pens (h.s.), closed Jan-May, 300.
Rest. ♦ ⫽ ♪ ◔ 65-120.

▲ ★★★*camping naturiste Ulysse* (142 pl), ☎ 68.40.93.94 ;
★★★*Rives des Corbières* (275 pl), ☎ 68.40.90.31 ; ★★*Cap Leucate* (450 pl), ☎ 68.40.01.37 ; ★★*Domino* (33 pl),
☎ 68.45.70.12.

LODÈVE

Montpellier 54, Béziers 64, Paris 815 km
pop 8378 ⊠ 34700   B1

At the junction of the Roman road and muletracks, and hemmed in on a terrace overlooking old factories on the riverbank, Lodève seems to hover between its prosperous wood-working, paper-making and weaving past, and an uncertain industrial future to be derived from the recent discovery of uranium nearby. The town used to hold a monopoly on the manufacture of military uniforms. Today a workshop reproduces antique furniture for the Mobilier National (French equivalent of the National Trust).

▶ The dark, narrow streets and grey houses built of stone and basalt are enlivened by carriage doors and wrought-iron balconies. ▶ **Church of St. Fulcran** : fortified, 14thC (18thC furnishings, 15th-18thC cloister); a cathedral until 1790. The 18thC bishop's palace is now the town hall. The gothic Montifort bridge straddles the Soulandres River, beneath the church. ▶ In the former Carmelite chapel (3, bd de Fumel), the **Jacques-Audibert Museum** maintains exhibits on geology and prehistory.

Nearby

▶ **Gourgas amphitheatre★** known as the Bout-du-Monde (World's End) : a craggy wooded site *(9 km NE)*. S of D25, the **forest of Parlatges.** ▶ **Pas-de-l'Escalette** : the name refers to wooden stairways that formerly marked a passage along the edge of the plateau (view★ over the Lergue Valley). Le Caylar *(19 km N)*, at the foot of a rockfall : modern church with 14thC altarpiece. ▶ W by the

Baraque-de-Bral Pass to **Lunas** *(15 km)*. ▶ From **Le Bousquet-d'Orb** *(17 km)* down the **Orb Valley** towards **Bédarieux** (→ Espinouse Range), or up the valley to the **Avène Reservoir**, passing **Joncels Abbey** and the **château de Cazilhac**, built as the valley's main defense in the 13thC, rebuilt during the Renaissance; terraced gardens *(daily pm; closed Tue.-Thu., ex nat. hols., 10 Jul.-20 Sep.)*. Winding **Orb Gorges★**; thermal spring at **Bains-d'Avène**. ☐

Practical Information _____

LODÈVE
ⓘ 7, pl. de la République, ☎ 67.44.07.56.

Hotels :
★★ *La Croix Blanche*, 6, av. de Fumel, ☎ 67.44.10.87, 32 rm Ⓟ ⟐ closed 1 Dec-1 Apr, 150. Rest. ♦ closed lunch, 40-90.
★★ *Nord*, 18, bd de la Liberté, ☎ 67.44.10.08, AE Euro Visa, 19 rm Ⓟ ⟐ closed Sat, Nov, 160. Rest. ♦ ♪ 40-140.

Nearby
LUNAS, ⊠ 34650, 15 km SW.

Restaurant :
♦ *Le Manoir de Gravezon*, ☎ 67.23.81.58, Visa ⟐ ⟐ ♪ closed Mon eve and Tue (l.s.), 15 Nov-31 May, 65-130; child : 40.

MINERVE and the MINERVOIS*

Montpellier 134, Béziers 45, Paris 791 km
pop 112 ⊠ 34210 Olonzac   B2
In a landscape of chalky rocks, Minerve has lent its name to the whole calcareous region of the Cévennes foothills, scored with canyons hollowed by the rivers Cesse, Argent-Double and Clamoux. Wines from the regional vineyards are widely appreciated.
▶ In the once-fortified **village★** (ruins of 11th-13thC château), you can visit the little **Romanesque church** (rare altar of 465) and the **Prehistorical and Cathar Memorial Museum** (recalls the dramatic passage of Simon de Montfort through the region in 1210 → box). ▶ Go round the spur on which the village is built to see the two **natural tunnels** dug by the river Cesse *(direct access in summer when the river bed is dry)*.

Tour of the Minervois Region★★ *(approx 90 km)*
▶ **Bize-Minervois** *(17 km SE)* : a village on the edge of the plain, overlooked by the ruined tower of Boussecos. ▶ At the entry to **Mailhac** *(5 km SW of Bize)* : the archaeological depository *(Sun. pm by appt. : tel. 68.46.14.05)* with the results of the diggings at the *oppidum* (fortified hilltop) of Cayla. ▶ At **Olonzac** *(9 km W of Mailhac)*, centre of the Minervois wine industry, there is a small archaeological museum *(tel. 68.91.20.33)*. ▶ Go through **Pépieux** *(5 km W of Olonzac)*, formerly fortified, and now a wine growing town and **Azille** *(3 km SW of Pépieux)*; 14thC church) to reach **Rieux-Minervois** *(6 km W from Azille)* : curious Romanesque church with a heptagonal ground plan; 3 km S : the prehistoric **covered road** of **Saint-Eugène**. ▶ **Laure-Minervois** *(6 km SW of Rieux)* : one of the centres of the Minervois wine industry (traces of fortifications). ▶ **Caunes-Minervois** *(9 km N of Laure)* at the entrance to the **Argent-Double Gorges★** : an ancient Benedictine abbey in Romano-Gothic style, several well-restored houses of 16th-17thC; nearby, red and rose marble quarries and the hermitage of Notre-Dame-de-Cros. ▶ Return towards Minerve via **Félines-Minervois** *(8 km E of Caunes)* : small archeological museum : *M. Marty, tel. 68.91.41.79)* and the **La Cesse Gorges★**. ☐

For the translation of a name of a meat, a fish or a vegetable, for the composition of a dish or a sauce, see the Menu Guide in the Practical Holiday Guide; it lists the most common culinary terms.

Practical Information _____

Nearby

PEYRIAC-MINERVOIS, ⊠ 11160 Caunes, 20 km SW.

Hotel :
★★★ *Château de Violet*, (R.S., C.H.), rte de Pépieux, ☎ 68.78.10.42, AE DC Euro Visa, 15 rm Ⓟ ⟐ ⟐ ⟐ ☐ closed Nov-May, 375. Rest. ♦♦ ⟐ ♪ ⟐ 135-220.

Recommended
Farmhouse-inn : *Domaine du Bois Bas*, ☎ 67.97.14.95, table d'hôte, camp sites and poultry for sale.

MONT-LOUIS*

Prades 36, Perpignan 79, Paris 991 km
pop 239 ⊠ 66210   A3
Mont-Louis was built as a stronghold by Louis XIV's engineer Vauban to maintain peace in the Pyrénées. It is located at 1 600 m altitude on a narrow plateau between the Perche and Quillaine passes, in a strategic position for controlling the valleys of the Sègre (→ Cerdagne), the Têt (Conflent) and the Aude (Capcir).
▶ **Citadel** : a classically regular construction; 1736 **church** with late 16thC crucifix. Visits also to the experimental **solar furnace**, which was used from 1952 to 1967 *(daily 9-12 & 2-5)*. ▶ Outside the fortified enclosure, monument to General Dagobert, an expert in mountain warfare, who repulsed a Spanish invasion of the Roussillon in 1793.

Nearby
▶ **Planès** *(6 km S)* : 11th-12thC **church★** with three apses in an unusual triangular design. ▶ **Lake Bouillouses** *(14 km NW by a forest road)* : alt. 2 015 m. A 13 million m^3 reservoir that regulates the flow of the Têt in summer; ski centre linked to the Domaine de Font-Romeu (→ Cerdagne); numerous forest walks. The lake is surrounded by mountains★ ending to the W at **Carlit Peak** (alt. 2 291 m; *4hr climb, guide advisable;* panorama★★). ▶ **Thuès-les-Bains** *(17 km E)* : 42 alkaline, silicate and sulphur-bearing springs in the enclosed Têt Valley. From **Thuès-entre-Vals** farther upstream, a path up the **Carança Gorges** to a lake of the same name (alt. 2 265 m; approx. 5 hr 30). ▶ From Mont-Louis to **Villefranche-de-Conflent** (→ Canigou Massif), take the mountain train from La Tour-de-Carol-Perpignan across the Têt Valley (Gisclard bridge and Séjourné viaduct).

The upper Aude Valley★★ *(57 km N)*
▶ By **La Llagonne** (cross-country skiing; 12thC painted wood crucifix in church) and the **Quillaine Pass** (alt. 1 715 m; view★) to the **Capcir★, upper basin of the Aude.** ▶ At the foot of **Aude Rock** (alt. 2 377 m) and other peaks that are under snow 7-8 months of the year, a winter sports resort and the village of **Les Angles** (alt. 1 600 m) above the Matemale reservoir (3 km^2). ▶ Winter sports also around **Formiguères**, former capital of Capcir. ▶ Leaving the Aude Valley, visit the ruins of the château of **Quérigut**, then rejoin the Aude at **Usson-les-Bains** (sulphurous and arsenical waters) below the ruins of a château that once controlled the confluence of the Aude and the Bruyante. ▶ Nearby, "potholing and spelunking safaris" in **Laguzon Cavern** *(full day; max. 10 persons; equipment provided : Jul.-Aug. by appt. with M. Bataillon at Usson, tel. 68.20.40.33)*. Finally, via the **Aude Gorges★** and the **Saint-Georges Defile★**, framed by wooded hillsides, to Axat, at the gates of the Pierre-Lys Pass (→ Razès). ☐

Practical Information _____

MONT-LOUIS
ⓘ ☎ 68.04.21.97.

Nearby

Les ANGLES, ⊠ 66210, 13 km W.
⌇ 1600-2400m.
ⓘ La Matté, ☎ 68.04.42.04.

Hotel :
★★ **Llaret**, av. de Balcère, ☎ 68.04.42.02, 28 rm Ⓟ ⫟ ⚲
closed 3rd May-1st Jun, Oct-Nov, 150. Rest. ◆ 60-110.

Restaurant :
◆◆ **La Ramballade**, rue de la Ramballade, ☎ 68.04.43.48,
AE Visa ⫟ ♪ closed Mon and Sun eve (l.s.) May-Jun, 1st
Oct-15 Dec, 70-165.

La LLAGONE, ⊠ 66210, 3 km N.

Hotel :
★ **Commerce**, ☎ 68.04.22.04, Visa, 30 rm Ⓟ ⫟ ⊞ ⚲ ⋙
♪ closed 4 May-6 Jun, 27 Sep-19 Dec, 130. Rest. ◆◆ ⫟
♪ ⚶ 60-130.

MONTAGNE NOIRE*

(Black Mountain)
A2

Round trip from Saissac *(approx 120 km, full day)*

Between Mazamet and Carcassonne, the broad plateau of the Montagne Noire culminates abruptly at
Nore Peak (alt. 1210 m). The N face, towards the
Tarn and the Haut-Languedoc National Park, is more
humid and forested with beech, spruce, oak and fir.
The mountain descends even more abruptly towards
the Aude, in the broad terraces of the historic
Cabardès region, with numerous vestiges of the Middle Ages.

▶ **Saissac** : a medieval city, and a good departure
point for excursions : remains of 15th-16thC fortifications
below; the 12thC tower in the village is now the **Museum
of Old-Time Crafts of Montagne Noire** *(daily Jul.-15 Sep.,
11-12 & 3-6; off season ask at the town hall,
tel. 68.24.40.22);* view★ to NE of the town. ▶ **Villelongue
Abbey** *(8 km S)* : on the banks of the Vernassonne, ruined
13thC church occupied by a farm. **Montolieu** *(4 km E) :* a
township of several thousand inhabitants in the 17thC, as
the large church suggests. ▶ **Salsigne** *(16 km E) :* gold
(or) still to be found in the region gives its name to the
nearby river Orbiel. ▶ Continuing E, on the left, access to
the **lookout**★ of the **châteaux de Lastours** : village under-
neath a huge rock on whose four peaks stand the ruins
known as Cabaret, Régine Tower, Surdespine and Quer-
tinheux. ▶ **Limousis Cavern**★ *(7 km E) :* mineral formations *(daily Jun.-Oct.; rest of year, Sun. and nat. hols.
pm by appt.; tel. M. Montagné 68.77.12.65).* ▶ Through
the **Clamoux Gorges**★ N to the mountain village of **Pradelles-Cabardès** (view★). ▶ **Mas-Cabardès** *(11 km SW
from Pradelles)* : below medieval ruins ; beyond, ruins of
the 16thC **church of Saint-Pierre-de-Vals** and the fortress
of **Miraval-Cabardès** in the upper valley of the Orbiel. ▶ S
of **Martys**, a small health resort called **Cuxac-Cabardès**.
▶ From here NW via **Fontiers-Cabardès** (view over the
Corbières and the Pyrénées) to the **Alzeau Basin** designed by Riquet (→ **Sète**) to feed the Midi Canal over the
verge of Naurouze ; a road runs along the channel as far
as the Saint-Ferréol Basin (→ **Midi Toulousain-Pyrénées**).
Cross the **Ramondens Forest** and skirt the **Lampy Reservoir** to arrive at **Saissac** by D4, passing close to the menhir called the **Pierre Levée** (raised stone) **of Picaret**.   ☐

Practical Information _____

SAISSAC, ⊠ 11310, 22 km NE of **Castelnaudary**.

Hotel :
★★ **Castel de Villemagne** (C.H.), on D 103, 7 km,
☎ 68.60.22.95, Visa, 7 rm ⫟ ⚲ closed 31 Oct-31 Mar. ex
reservation, 285. Rest. ◆◆ ♪ closed Mon noon, 80-180 ;
child : 35.

⚘ ★★★**V.A.L.** (94 pl), ☎ 68.24.42.98.

MONTPELLIER***

Nîmes 51, Béziers 93, Paris 761 km
pop 201067 ⊠ 34000   C1

The settlement, about 10 km from the coast, began as
a trading post on the spice route from the Near East,
and later prospered as a stopover on the pilgrimage
route to Santiago de Compostela. Cloth was traded
in the city, and the university and renowned medical school were founded in the 13thC. The handsome appearance of Montpellier is due in large part to
extensive building and development during the 18thC.
The prosperous 19thC wine trade was checked by
the vine-louse phylloxera, which devastated French
vineyards. Re-establishment of French vines on resistant American root stocks put the wine growers back
in business by the mid-20thC. Montpellier today is a
dynamic regional capital.

▶ **Place de la Comédie** (C3), with the 18thC fountain of
the Three Graces, is the main meeting place. From the
19thC **theatre** (Comédie) at the S end, the place is prolonged N by the **Esplanade** and the Champ de Mars garden
at the foot of the 17thC citadel, and NE *(direct pedestrian
access)* by the new commercial and administrative quarter of **Le Polygone** (hotels, shopping arcades, department
stores, town hall). ▶ From the Place, **Rue de la Loge** (C3)
joins **Rue Foch** near the Prefecture (B2), forming the main
axis through the old city. ▶ The street passes under
the 1691 **Arc de Triomphe** (commemorating victories
of Louis XIV) to reach the **Peyrou Promenade**★ (A2) :
17th-18thC terraces shaded by plane trees around reflecting pools : views to the mountains ; the 18thC aqueduct
ends in canals that lead to the handsome water-tower of
the same era. ▶ The **old town**★★ is divided by the central axis, which was laid out in the 19thC. From medieval
beginnings, it was progressively transformed during the
17th-18thC. Mansions, often hidden behind austere carriage entrances, are open to discovery by enquiring
pedestrians *(plan from the TO).* The 17thC buildings show
marked Italian influence, with central courtyards, monumental staircases and galleries on the first floors. The
more "frivolous" buildings of the following century are
adorned with wrought-iron balconies and carving. ▶ S of
the major transverse axis, the commercial sector is pierced
by **Rue de l'Argenterie** and **Grand'Rue-Jean-Moulin**,
both now pedestrian precincts ; at the crossroads (B3), the
1757 **St. Côme Mansion**★, formerly the College of Sur-
geons. ▶ From Rue de la Loge, **Rue des Trésoriers-
de-France** runs through an equally lively sector (C1-2 :
at No. 5, the 17thC **Lunaret Mansion** is the office of the
archaeological society) to the **Place Pétrarque** (C2), where
a university for senior citizens is maintained in the Nicolas Mansion (No. 2), together with the **Fougau Regional Museum** (ethnography, Occitanian library ; *Wed., Thu.
3-6:30*). Farther on, the former University quarter has
become more residential with the passage of time. ▶ The
Faculty of Medicine (B1-2) since 1795 has occupied the
restored 16thC Abbey of St. Benoit; here too, **Atger
Museum** : 17th-18thC Italian and French drawings *(closed
Sat., Sun. and Aug.);* the former abbey church, now the
cathedral of St. Pierre, has a 14thC nave and porch but
was clumsily restored in the 17th and 19thC. ▶ From the
other side of Boulevard Henri-IV (beside which stands the
Pins Tower, a vestige of the medieval fortifications) the
Botanical Gardens★ (Jardin des Plantes), the oldest in
France, founded in 1593. ▶ **Fabre Museum**★★ (C2 ; enter
from Boulevard Sarrail ; *daily ex Mon., 9-12 & 2-5 or 5:30)*
occupies part of the former Jesuit College (18thC); fine
art including paintings ranging from regional Primitives to
the 20thC, notably important 19thC works. Nearby in Rue
Montpelliéret, **Cabrières-Sabatier d'Espeyran Mansion** :
museum of 18th and 19thC decorative arts *(guided tours
Wed., Sat.).*

The arrow (→) is a reference to another entry.

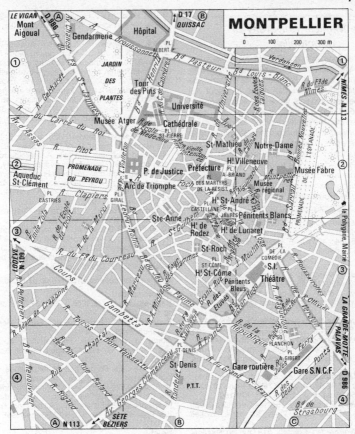

Nearby

▶ The **University of Montpellier** is now relocated outside the old town; in the new sector, N : accommodation, the stadium, several scientific institutes and clinics, as well as the zoo. ▶ On the edge of town, follies built as country retreats by wealthy citizens during the 17th and 18thC : **châteaux★ de la Piscine** *(3 km W,* formal French park*)*; **de la Mosson** *(5 km W,* 1723*)*; **de l'Engarran** *(6 km SW,* formal French park*)*; **d'O** *(4 km NW,* beautiful garden*)*; **d'Assas** *(12 km N,* built next to a Romanesque church*; Sat., Sun. pm, Easter-mid-Oct.);* **de Flaugergues** *(3 km E near the E motorway,* French and English gardens with Mediterranean trees; furnishings; wine tastings; *daily pm ex Mon., 15 May-15 Sep., tel. : 67.65.51.72);* **de la Mogère** *(4 km E,* park; *daily pm, Easter-15 Oct., Wed., Sat., Sun. and nat. hols. pm, 15 Oct.-Easter.).* ▶ **Castries** *(12 km NE) :* the most beautiful **château★** in the region; built in 1565, it was remodeled in the 17thC to house the Languedoc regional government; furniture; parkland designed by Le Notre (→ Île-de-France : Versailles) and fed by a 27-km aqueduct *(daily ex Mon. and nat. hols., Apr.-15 Dec.; Sat. and Sun. pm, 15 Jan.-Mar.).* ▶ **Château d'Agnac** *(12 km S the other side of Fabrègues) :* the Mediterranean Institute for Introduction to French Culture (courses for foreigners). ▶ **Lattès** *(5 km S) :* originally the maritime port for the city, but supplanted by Marseilles at the end of the 15thC and disused since the 17thC; Romanesque church with sculpted grotesques on the façade. ▶ **Maguelonne Abbey** *(16 km via Palavas) :* a fortified

bishopric from Merovingian times until the see was transferred to Montpellier; 11thC church★ (doorway of 1178) on an isolated hilltop surrounded by lakes. ▶ Farther E, **Lake Mauguio** : fishing and waterfowl hunting. ▶ This lake separates the true coastline from the tourist area that stretches as far as the lakes of the Camargue (18-km beach). From W to E, successively : **Palavas-les-Flots,** the seaside resort of Montpellier (not attractive) and a fishing port (Museum of Old Palavas and Underwater Archaeology; *daily pm ex Thu., Jun.-Sep.);* **Carnon-Plage** : sparkling new marina, but hardly more attractive than Palavas; **La Grande-Motte★,** best-known of Languedoc seaside resorts, is a successful example of contemporary town planning, with 52-acre marina and the commercial centre of Point Zero; **Le Grau-du-Roi** and **Port-Camargues** : marinas and yacht harbours. ▶ **Lunel** *(22 km NE) :* at the entry to the Camargue, wine centre (Muscat); public gardens. ▶ **Château de Marsillargues** *(4 km SE) :* in Renaissance style, with Paul Pastre museum of geology, archaeology, ethnology, fine arts *(pm daily ex Sun.).* □

Practical Information _____

MONTPELLIER
ℹ️ 6, rue Maguelone (C3), ☎ 67.58.26.04; train station (C4), ☎ 67.92.90.03.
✈ *Montpellier-Fréjorgues,* 6 km SE, ☎ 67.65.60.65. *Air France* office, Fréjorgues airport, ☎ 67.65.43.43; 6, rue Boussairolles, ☎ 67.58.81.94.
SNCF (C4), ☎ 67.58.50.50.

The Medical University of Montpellier

Medieval connections with the East through the spice trade enabled Montpellier to attract learned men who brought with them medical knowledge far in advance of what was then known in the West. In about AD 1000 formal medical schools were first established in the city. Grouped into a single faculty in 1221, they were confirmed as the University of Montpellier in 1289 by Pope Nicolas IV. Montpellier still rivals Paris in the brilliance of its medical school. The University maintains a standard of intellectual activity in Montpellier, while also fostering the turbulent spirit of youth and enquiry characteristic of university towns. Many of the most distinguished scientists of France have been educated at Montpellier.

---

rue Jules-Ferry (C4), ☎ 67.92.01.43.
Car rental : *Avis*, train station (C4), 12 bis, rue J.-Ferry (C4), ☎ 67.64.61.84; 49, rue F.-Bazille, ☎ 67.65.15.19; airport ☎ 67.65.57.56.

Hotels :
★★★★ **Métropole**, (Mapotel), 3, rue du Clos-René (C3), ☎ 67.58.11.22, Tx 480410, AE DC Euro Visa, 92 rm P̄ 🕮
⚲ ♪ 🐎 610. Rest. ♦♦♦ ♪ ⚹ Spec : *turbot aux huîtres sauce iodée, éminçé de pintadeau à l'infusion de thé vert*, 150-230.
● ★★★ **Demeure des Brousses**, rte de Vauguières, 4 km E., ☎ 67.65.77.66, AE DC, 17 rm P̄ ⚶ 🕮 ⚲ closed Jan, 300. Rest. ● ♦♦ **L'Orangerie** ⚶ ♪ Peace and solitude in the countryside, plus Michel Loustau's opulent *sole aux palourdes, filet de boeuf aux truffes*, Languedoc wines, 130-200.
● ★★★ **Les Réganeas**, rte de Palavas, Lattes, 6 km (off map C4), ☎ 67.92.52.18, AE DC Euro Visa, 20 rm P̄ 🕮 ♪ ⚹ 🖃 ✎ 260. Rest. ● ♪ closed Sun, 120-180.
● ★★★ **Noailles**, 2, rue des Ecoles-Centrales (C2), ☎ 67.60.49.80, AE DC Euro Visa, 30 rm ⚲ closed 18 Dec-11 Jan, 270.
★★★ **Altéa Polygone**, (ex Frantel), 218, av. du Bastion-Ventadour, Le Polygone (off map C2), ☎ 67.64.65.66, Tx 480362, AE DC Euro Visa, 116 rm P̄ ⚶ ♪ 🐎 ⚹ 405. Rest. ● ♦♦ **Lou Païrol** ♪ closed Sat noon and Sun noon, Sun eve (l.s.), 20 Dec-5 Jan. Original creations by Serge Mignot : *persillé de langouste, ris de veau, filet de bœuf au parfum de pélardon*. Local wines, 115-250.
★★★ **George V**, (Inter-Hôtel), 42, av. Saint-Lazare (C1), ☎ 67.72.35.91, Tx 480953, AE DC Euro Visa, 39 rm P̄ ⚲ ♪ 250.
★★★ **Grand Hôtel du Midi**, 22, bd V.-Hugo (C3), ☎ 67.92.69.61, Tx 490752, AE DC Euro Visa, 50 rm 🕮 ⚲ ♪ 280.
★★ **L' Hôtel**, (Inter-Hôtel), 8, rue Jules-Ferry (C4), ☎ 67.58.88.75, Tx 490105, AE DC Euro Visa, 55 rm, 170.
★★ **Les Myrtes**, 5, av. Leyris (off map A4), ☎ 67.42.60.11, Visa, 31 rm 🕮 ⚹ ⚶ 🗏 closed Feb, 165.
★★ **Parc**, 8, rue Achille-Bégé (off map A1), ☎ 67.41.16.49, Visa, 19 rm P̄ 🕮 ⚲ 180.

Restaurants :
● ♦♦♦ **Janus**, 11, rue Aristide-Ollivier (C3), ☎ 67.58.15.61, AE DC Visa ♪ closed Sun, 15 Jul-20 Aug. François Lucena trained with A. Daguin and worked in Samatan, the foie gras capital. He knows his stuff! Assisted by son Christophe and his wife (in charge of service), he offers a menu modified monthly in tune with the seasons, 90-250.
● ♦♦ **Le Chandelier**, 3, rue Leenhardt (B4), ☎ 67.92.61.62, AE DC Visa ♪ closed Mon noon and Sun, Feb school hols, 1-21 Aug. J.-M. Forest and Gilbert Furlan form a perfect partnership, for their patrons' pleasure : *ragoût de langoustes aux herbes et lasagnes, magret aux échalotes*, 105-260.
● ♦♦ **Isadora**, 6, rue du Petit-Scel (B2), ☎ 67.66.25.23,

AE DC Euro Visa ♪ closed Sat noon and Sun. Enjoyable atmosphere in lovely 17th-C vaulted cellar. Good, simple food, 95-180.
● ♦♦ **L'Olivier**, 12, rue Aristide-Ollivier (C3), ☎ 67.92.86.28, AE DC Visa, closed Mon , Sun and hols, 20 Jul-20 Aug. A menu of savoury specialities conceived by Michel Breton at prices designed to please : *tarte fine de rougets aux moules de Bouzigues, fricassée de filets de soles aux palourdes, agneau farçi aux herbes*, 75-170.
● ♦♦ **Ong Dam**, 3, rue des Multipliants, ☎ 67.60.45.54 ♪ closed lunch and Sun, 19 Jul-18 Aug, 20-31 Dec. A Vietnamise restaurant-bar that has to turn people away. Reserve, 80-120.
♦♦ **La Réserve Rimbaud**, 820, av. de St-Maur, quartier des Aubes (off map C1), ☎ 67.72.52.53, AE DC Visa ⚶ 🕮 ✎ closed Mon and Sun eve. A riverside terrace that's a local institution. Jean Tarrit avoids novelty, but 'tis tasty withal : *gigot de mer aux herbes de la garrigue*, 180-210.
● ♦ **Louvre**, 2, rue de la Vieille (B3), ☎ 67.60.59.37, DC Euro Visa ♪ ⚹ closed Mon and Sun, 1-15 May, 15 Oct-1 Nov, 80-160.
♦ **Chez Marceau**, 7, pl. de la Chapelle-Neuve (C1), ☎ 67.66.08.09, AE Euro Visa ⚶ 🕮 ♪ closed Sun, 10-20 Feb, 23 Dec-6 Jan. For salad lunches, 45-85.
♦ **Dolce Vita**, 6, rue Henri-René (C4), ☎ 67.64.40.90, AE DC Visa ♪ closed Sat noon and Sun noon , Jul-Aug. Heart-warming Italian food : *spaghetti aux fruits de mer, foie de veau vénitienne*. Open late, 80-120.

⚱ ★★★**Montaubérou** (136 pl), ☎ 67.65.40.60.

Recommended
Baby-sitting : AGEM, ☎ 67.60.57.23; CROUS, ☎ 67.63.57.93.
Events : *Music festival*, Radio-France-Montpellier (mid-Jun-early Aug).
Guide to wines : *Le Tire-Bouchon*, 2, pl. Jean-Jaurès, Pleasant wine bar. Tables on the square in summer,100-150.
♥ cheese : *Le Buron*, galerie marchande du Polygone; confectionery : *Réglisse Deleuze*, rte de Toulouse, ☎ 67.42.50.68; exotic and gourmet groceries : *Pinto*, 14, rue de l'Argenterie; ice cream : *Jardin des glaces*, sur l'Esplanade, 25, bd Sarrail; *Sorbets de Fréjorgues*, Z.I. des Prés d'Arène, ☎ 67.58.72.98, only Sat.

Nearby

CASTRIES, ⊠ 34160, 13 km NE.

Restaurant :
● ♦♦ **L'Art du Feu**, 13, av. du 8-Mai-1945, ☎ 67.70.05.97, AE DC Euro Visa ♪ ✎ closed Tue eve and Wed , Feb school hols and Aug. Simple, inexpensive food, 65-140; child : 40.

La GRANDE-MOTTE, ⊠ 34280, 20 km SE.
ⓘ pl. du 1er-Octobre, ☎ 67.56.62.62.

Hotel :
★★ **Europe**, (Inter-Hôtel), ☎ 67.56.62.60, Visa, 34 rm P̄ ⚲ 🗏 🖃 closed 15 Oct-24 Mar, 260.

Restaurant :
♦♦♦ **Alexandre-Amirauté**, esplanade de la Capitainerie, ☎ 67.56.63.63, Euro Visa ⚶ 🕮 ♪ ✎ closed Mon and Sun eve (l.s.) , Nov school hols, 6 Jan-14 Feb. Spec : *cassolette d'huîtres au beurre de truffe, quenelle de rascasse sauce aux Favouilles*, 150-220; child : 60.

⚱ ★★★★**Garden** (237 pl), ☎ 67.56.50.09; ★★★★**L'Or** (300 pl), ☎ 67.56.52.10; ★★★★**Lorraine-Aquitaine** (240 pl), ☎ 67.56.50.41; ★★★★**Lous Pibons** (200 pl), ☎ 67.56.50.08.

Recommended
Marina : ☎ 67.56.50.06, 1200 pl.

Le GRAU-DU-ROI, ⊠ 30240, 26 km SE.
ⓘ bd du Front-de-Mer, ☎ 66.51.67.70.
▮SNCF▮ ☎ 66.51.40.93.

Hotels :
★★ **Les Acacias**, 21, rue de l'Egalité, ☎ 66.51.40.86, 27 rm 🕮 ✎ closed 30 Oct-22 Mar, 180. Rest. ♦ 55-125.

★★ *Plage*, 3, bd du Front-de-Mer, ☎ 66.51.40.22, Euro Visa, 19 rm, closed 1 Nov-15 Mar, 150. Rest. ◆ 50-150.

▲ ★★★★*Abri de Camargue* (300 pl), ☎ 66.51.54.83; ★★★★*L'Eden* (400 pl), ☎ 66.51.49.81; ★★★★*Le Boucanet* (436 pl), ☎ 66.51.41.48.

LUNEL, ⊠ 34400, 25 km NE.
Ⓘ pl. des Martyrs-de-la-Résistance, ☎ 67.71.01.37.
SNCF ☎ 67.71.11.90.

Hotel :
★★ *Le Palais*, 12, av. de-Lattre-de-Tassigny, ☎ 67.71.11.39, 26 rm Ⓟ ⬙ ₩ ♪ half pens (h.s.), closed Sun eve and Mon lunch, 15 Dec-15 Jan, 300. Rest. ◆ ♪ ⭑ Quality is traditional at this former coaching inn, 50-110.

▲ ★★★*Bon Port* (115 pl), ☎ 66.71.15.65; ★★*Municipal* (100 pl), ☎ 66.71.18.70; ★★*Pont de Lunel* (44 pl), ☎ 66.71.10.22.

PALAVAS-LES-FLOTS, ⊠ 34250, 12 km S.
Ⓘ hôtel-de-ville, ☎ 67.68.02.34.

Hotels :
★★★ *Amérique*, av. F.-Fabrège, ☎ 67.68.04.39, 37 rm Ⓟ ⭑ ⊟ closed 17 Dec-3 Jan, 170.
★★ *Brasilia*, 10, bd Mal-Joffre, ☎ 67.68.00.68, AE DC Euro Visa, 22 rm Ⓟ ⬙ 195.
★★ *Languedoc*, 4, rue Carrière, ☎ 67.68.03.45, Euro Visa, 21 rm ⬙ ⬗ closed Dec-Jan, 160.

Restaurants :
◆◆ *Maison de l'Huître*, 3, av. Foch, ☎ 67.68.09.85, AE DC Euro Visa ⬙ ₩ ⭑ closed Wed, 22 Dec-26 Jan. Shellfish, fish, 60-200.
◆◆ *Sphinx*, quai P.-Cunq, ☎ 67.68.00.21, AE DC Euro Visa ♪ closed 15 Dec-25 Jan. Bouillabaisse, fish, 200-250.

▲ ★★★*Palavas* (500 pl), ☎ 67.68.01.28; ★★★*Roquilles* (792 pl), ☎ 67.68.03.47; ★★★*Saint-Maurice* (150 pl), ☎ 67.68.99.61; ★★*Montpellier-Plage* (730 pl), ☎ 67.68.00.91.

Recommended
Marina : ☎ 67.68.00.90, 610 pl.

PORT-CAMARGUE, ⊠ 30240 Le Grau-du-Roi, 3 km S of Le Grau-du-Roi.

Hotel :
● ★★ *Le Spinaker*, pointe du Môle, ☎ 66.51.54.93, Euro Visa, 20 rm Ⓟ ⬙ ₩ ⬗ ⭑ ⊟ half pens (h.s.), closed Sun eve and Mon (l.s.), 11 Jan-18 Feb, 11-28 Nov, 445. Rest. ◆◆ ⬙ ⭑ Spec : *raviolis de langoustines en crème de nage, paupiettes de sole à la crème d'échalote et tomate*, 170-200; child : 60.

Recommended
Marina : ☎ 66.51.43.09, 4300 pl.

NARBONNE★★

Béziers 27, Carcassonne 61, Paris 849 km
pop 42657 ⊠ 11100   B2

In succession, a Roman, Visigothic and Arab city, essentially Mediterranean. The site is divided by the canalized Robine River. The old town, with its tortuous, narrow streets and medieval monuments is girded by shady boulevards that are most lively at midday and in the evening, when the residents like to spend an hour or two on the café terraces.

▶ In the centre of town, the former **Archbishop's Palace** (B2), now the **town hall** and **museums★★** *(daily; closed Mon., Oct.-15 May)*. The **Gilles-Aycelin Keep** was built in the 13thC on Roman foundations; view over the town *(daily Jul.-Sep.)*. In the inner courtyard, the **Archaeological Museum★** (prehistory through Early Christian); on 2nd floor (Classical staircase), **Fine Arts Museum** and the Archbishop's **Apartments★** fitted out in the 17thC *(10-11:50 & 2-5:15 or 6; closed Mon. off season)*. ▶ Leading from the Palace courtyard, the **Passage de l'Ancre**, facing the **Madeleine Courtyard** where the apse of the

cathedral can be seen. At the end of the passage (marked by the anchor that gives the alley its name), cross the 13thC cloister directly into the choir of the **cathedral of St. Just★** (B2). The choir was constructed between 1272 and 1310 in the Gothic tradition of northern France, but the church was never finished (treasury with 15thC Flemish tapestry depicting the Creation★). ▶ N from the cathedral, near the TO, the **Maison Vigneronne** (wine museum; exhibitions), occupying a 17thC powder magazine. ▶ In the maze-like old city, **Place Bistan** (B-C2) marks the site of the Roman capital and forum, which can be picked out, with the aid of an explanatory plan, from a few fragments of architecture. **Church of St. Sébastien** (C2), 15th-17thC, built on the presumed birthplace of this early Christian martyr. ▶ Rue Rouget-de-l'Isle, **Horreum** (B2) : an underground warehouse built by the Romans in the 1stC AD. ▶ Along **Rue Droite** (B2) return to the Place de l'Hôtel-de-Ville; the street continues as the pedestrian **Rue du Pont-des-Marchands** and crosses the river Robine by the ancient Roman bridge, of which one arch still stands. View of the old bridge, as well as of the principal medieval monuments, from the alleys of Cours Mirabeau (B3).
Also... ▶ In the S part of the city, 12th-13thC **church of Notre-Dame-de-Lamourguier** (B3), now a Sculpture and Stonework Museum of Gallo-Roman and Early Christian antiquities. **Basilica of St. Paul-Serge** (A3) : 12th-13thC, next to an Early Christian cemetery. Nearby in Rue de l'Hôtel-Dieu, the 16thC **Maison des Trois Nourrices** (house of the three wet-nurses), facetiously named for the amply endowed caryatids on the façade.

Nearby

▶ The **Montagne de la Clape** : a chalky outcropping, covered in vineyards on the lower slopes, separates Narbonne from the sea. To the S, **Gruissan** *(15 km)* : charming village★ on a peninsula extending into the lagoons and overlooked by a ruined tower; tourist development at **Gruissan Beach**, with weekend houses perched on stilts, as well as hotels, restaurants, shops and marina. Chapel of **Notre-Dame-des-Auzils** (view★) next to a sailors' cemetery (numerous *ex-votos* left by sailors). Farther N, the seaside resorts of **Narbonne-Plage** and **Saint-Pierre-sur-Mer**, with the l'**Œil Doux Chasm** *(1.5 km N, then foot path for 500 m)*. At the mouth of the Aude *(23 km NE)*, the fishing village of **Cabannes-de-Fleury**. ▶ **Ouveillan** *(approx. 4.5 km SE; 14 km N)* : 11th-12thC church; remains of a 13thC moated grange, which was a dependency of Fontfroide Abbey. ▶ **Lézignan-Corbières** *(21 km W)*, on the edge of the Corbières and the Minervois : Museum of Vines and Wine (3, Rue Turgot : wine-tastings *daily*). ▶ **Fabrezan** *(9 km SW of Lézignan)* : memorial museum named for Charles Cros, a local intellectual, poet and photographer *(daily ex Sat., Sun. and nat. hols.)*. ▶ **Lagrasse★** *(approx. 10 km)*, a medieval village, formerly fortified and ably restored : 14thC church of St. Michel, 15th-18thC houses, cobbled streets, artists' studios. Over a hump-backed bridge (1308) to the **abbey★** founded under Charlemagne, whose successive constructions date from the 10th to the 18thC; now maintained by a Byzantine Catholic religious community, which is restoring it *(visits daily ex Sun. am and religious hols.)*. ▶ Between Lagrasse and Narbonne *(41 km)*, cross the river Nielle at **Saint-Laurent. Château de Gaussan** : 13thC, formerly a property of Fontfroide abbey (wine-tasting). A narrow road on the right *(2 km)* leads to **Fontfroide Abbey★★** situated at the entrance to deep ravines *(visits daily; closed Tue., Oct.-Mar.)* : 12th-13thC cloister and chapterhouse, and various monastic buildings (most recent, 17thC); some of the most beautiful Cistercian architecture in the Midi. ▶ Beside Lake Bages and Sigean, **Peyriac-de-Mer** *(13 km S of Narbonne)* : museum of ornithological specimens from the lake and artifacts excavated from the neighbouring *oppidum* (hill-fort) of Moulin *(visits by appt. : M. Jouas, tel. 68.32.50.45 or M. Fabre, tel. 68.32.37.43)*. ▶ Beyond, **Sigean Safari Park★** *(visits daily by car)*. ▶ Near **Portel-des-Corbières** *(17 km S)* : the ruined church of **Notre-Dame-des-Oubliels** (under restoration). ▶ **Sigean** *(21 km)* : archaeological museum of Corbières

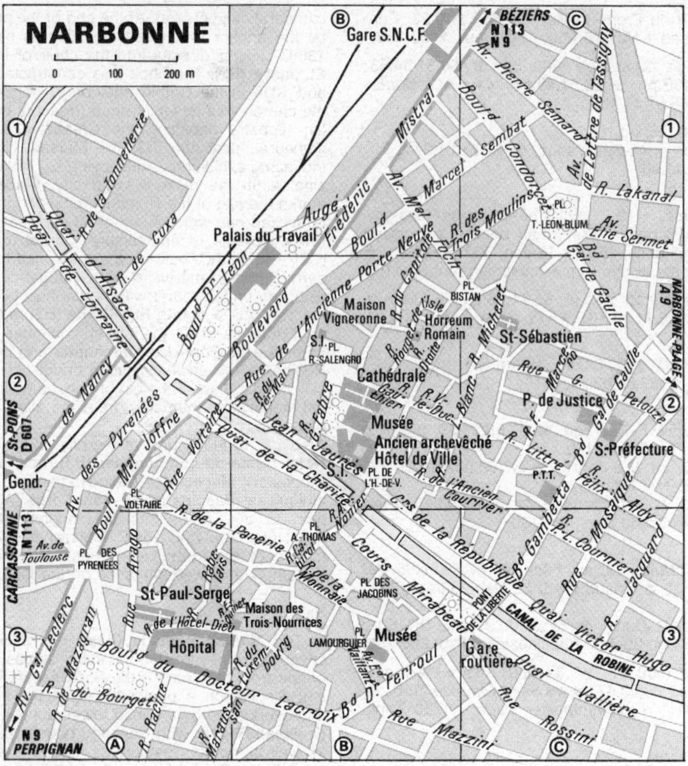
NARBONNE
0
100
200 m
Gare S.N.C.F.
BÉZIERS
N 113
N 9
Av. Pierre Sémard
Av. de Lattre de Tassigny
Boul.d Condorcet
Boul.d Marcel Sembat
Av. Mal Foch
Frédéric Mistral
R. Lakanal
PL. T.-LÉON-BLUM
Av. Elie Sermet
Bd Gal de Gaulle
NARBONNE-PLAGE
A 9
R. des Trois Moulins
Quai de Lorraine
R. de la Tonnellerie
R. de Cuxa
R. d'Alsace
Palais du Travail
Boul.d Dr Léon
Boulevard
Augé
Boul.d de l'Ancienne Porte Neuve
R. du Capitole
Maison Vigneronne
R. Rouget de l'Isle
Horreum Romain
PL. BISTAN
R. Michelet
St-Sébastien
S.I.
PL. R.-SALENGRO
Cathédrale
R. Droite
R. V.-le-Duc
R. Gauthier
R. L. Blanc
Rue Marcel G.
P. de Justice
Pelouze
Bd Gal de Gaulle
Musée
Ancien archevêché
Hôtel de Ville
S.I.
PL. DE L'H.-DE-V.
R. de l'Ancien Courrier
R. Littré
R. F. Félix Aldy
S-Préfecture
P.T.T.
Bd Gambetta
Rue Mosaïque
R. P.-L. Courrier
R. Jacquard
R. de Nancy
Av. des Pyrénées
Boul.d Mal Joffre
Rue Voltaire
Rue de l'Ancien
R. Fabre
Jean Jaurès
Quai de la Charité
ST-PONS
D 607
Gend.
PL. VOLTAIRE
R. de la Parerie
PL. A.-THOMAS
R. A. Nonier
Crs de la République
CARCASSONNE
N 113
Av. de Toulouse
PL. DES PYRÉNÉES
R. Arago
R. Rabelais
R. de la Monnaie
Cours Mirabeau
PL. DES JACOBINS
PONT DE LA LIBERTÉ
Quai Victor Hugo
CANAL DE LA ROBINE
St-Paul-Serge
Maison des Trois-Nourrices
R. de l'Hôtel-Dieu
Hôpital
R. du Luxembourg
PL. LAMOURGUIER
Musée
Gare routière
Av. Gal Leclerc
R. de Mazagran
Boul.d du Docteur Lacroix
Bd Dr Ferroul
Quai Vallière
R. du Bourget
R. Racine
R. Marcaussan
Rue Mazzini
Rue Rossini
N 9
PERPIGNAN

displaying ceramics from the Pech Maho *oppidum* (64 Grande-Rue, *by appt., tel. 68.48.20.04*). ▶ **Port-La-Nouvelle** *(30 km)*, founded in 1820 as a maritime port for the Midi-Toulousain region; today both a port and an industrial centre (salt pans, cement works, oil storage, heavy cargo, shipping, fishing) as well as a seaside resort stretching along a beautiful sandy beach. □

Practical Information

NARBONNE

ℹ pl. R.-Salengro (B2), ☎ 66.65.15.60.
SNCF (B1), ☎ 68.62.50.50.
🚌 quai Vallière (C3), ☎ 68.32.07.60.
Car rental : *Avis*, train station (B1); 21, bd M.-Sembat (B-C1), ☎ 68.32.43.36.

Hotels :

● ★★★ ***La Résidence***, 6, rue du 1er-Mai (B2), ☎ 68.32.19.41, Tx 500441, AE Euro Visa, 26 rm 🅿 closed 4 Jan-8 Feb, 250.

★★★ ***Languedoc***, (Mapotel), 22, bd Gambetta (C3), ☎ 68.65.14.74, Tx 505167, AE DC Euro Visa, 45 rm 🅿 ♿ 220. Rest. ♦♦ ♪ ♿ closed Fri eve and Sat (l.s.), 1 Jan-2 Feb, 60-160.

★★ ***France***, 6, rue Rossini (C3), ☎ 68.32.09.75, Visa, 16 rm 🅿 160.

Restaurants :

● ♦♦♦ ***Le Réverbère***, 4, pl. des Jacobins (B3), ☎ 68.32.29.18, AE DC Visa ♪ closed Mon , Sun eve and Feb. Claude Giraud's *"menu dégustation"* resists bot passing trends and inflation. His four choices of lobster *(pinces, rouelles, ravioles* and *"habit de choux verts")* are unforgettable, and like his other dishes show off his impressive talent : *bonbon de foie gras à l'aigre doux de miel d'acacia, filet de sole au jus de veau, canette mi-sauvage rôtie*. Corbière and Minervois wines. Tea and coffee selection, 145-280.

● ♦♦ ***Alsace***, 2, av. Pierre-Semard (C1), ☎ 68.65.10.24, AE DC Euro Visa ♪ ♿ closed Mon eve and Tue, 17 Nov-17 Dec. The Sinfreu family all join in preparing seafood specialties : *ragoût de palourdes Tante Julie, salade chaude de fruits de mer, huîtres chaudes Narbonnaise*, 60-190.

Recommended

♥ pastries : *Louvel*, 8, rue du Pont-des-Marchands, ☎ 68.32.03.47.

Nearby

FONTJONCOUSE, ✉ 11360, 27 km W.

Restaurant :

● ♦♦ ***Auberge du Vieux Puits***, ☎ 68.44.04.34 ♪ ♿ closed Wed. Thanks to David Moreno, here's a new restaurant that people will be talking about : *civet de homard au rancio, filet de veau aux champignons*, 60-165 ; child : 25.

GRUISSAN, ✉ 11430, 14 km SE.
ℹ bd Pech-Meynaud, ☎ 68.49.03.25.

Hotel :

★★ ***Le Corail*** (L.F.), quai du Ponnant, ☎ 68.49.04.43, Visa, 32 rm 🅿 half pens (h.s.), closed Nov-Feb, 205. Rest. ♦ ♪ ♿ Well situated near the port. Cordial welcome. Decent food, 70-110.

Restaurant :

● ♦♦ ***Le Chebek***, bd P.-Meynaud, quai d'Honneur et Levant, ☎ 68.49.02.58, AE DC Euro Visa ♪ closed Mon and Sun eve (ex Jul-Aug), Jan-Feb. The Sanyas family serves an array of fish and seafood near the pleasure port : *civet de homard, langouste au rancio*, 80-150.

⚑ ★★★*Les Ayguades* (400 pl), ☎ 68.49.81.59 ; ★★*Municipal* (200 pl), ☎ 68.49.07.22 ; ★★*Pech-Rouge* (255 pl), ☎ 68.49.80.88.

Recommended
Events : *fisherman's feast on St Peter's day*, 27, 29 Jun. ♥ smoked fish : ☎ 68.49.05.00, follow the signs as you enter the town.

LÉZIGNAN-CORBIÈRES, ⊠ 11200, 21 km W.
🛈 sq. Marcellin-Albert, ☎ 68.27.05.42.

Hotel :
★★ *Tassigny*, pl. de-Lattre-de-Tassigny, ☎ 68.27.11.51, Visa, 16 rm 🅿 ⌕ closed Sun eve, 15-30 Sep, 170. Rest. ♦ closed Mon and Sun eve, 60-210.

NARBONNE-PLAGE, ⊠ 11100 Narbonne, 13 km E.

⚑ ★★★★*La Falaise* (461 pl), ☎ 68.49.80.77 ; ★★★★*La Nautique* (395 pl), ☎ 68.90.48.19 ; ★★★*Languedoc* (170 pl), ☎ 68.65.24.65 ; ★★★*Mimosas* (160 pl), ☎ 68.49.03.72 ; ★★★*Soleil d'Or* (212 pl), ☎ 68.49.86.21 ; ★★*Roches Grises* (130 pl), ☎ 68.41.75.41 ; ★★*Saint-Solvayre* (100 pl), ☎ 68.32.08.19.

ORNAISONS, ⊠ 11200 Lézignan-Corbières, 8 km E.

Hotel :
★★★ *Relais du Val d'Orbieu*, (R.S., C.H.), D 24, ☎ 68.27.10.27, AE DC Visa, 16 rm 🅿 ⌕ ▩ ⌘ 🐎 ⅃ 🖾 half pens (h.s.), 850. Rest. ● ♦♦ ⌕ ⅃ ⅃ In the middle of Corbières wine country, a peaceful gourmet stopover : *turbot rôti au vin rouge des Corbières, escalope de canard en foie gras, soupe de kiwis au zeste de citron vert*, 95-250 ; child : 50.

PORT-LA-NOUVELLE, ⊠ 11210, 30 km S.

Hotel :
★★★ *Méditerranée*, (Mapotel, L.F.), bd St-Charles, ☎ 68.48.03.08, Tx 500712, AE DC Euro Visa, 31 rm 🅿 ⅃ half pens (h.s.), closed 5 Jan-5 Feb, 540. Rest. ♦♦ ⅃ ⅃ closed Mon noon and Sun eve (l.s.). Regional cuisine, 55-160.

⚑ ★★★*Cap du Roc* (109 pl), ☎ 68.48.00.98 ; ★★★*Côte Vermeille* (334 pl), ☎ 68.48.05.80.

Recommended
Leisure activities : *La Tramontane*, ☎ 68.65.15.60, the ponds and canal of the Robine. Info at S.I.

SAINT-PIERRE-SUR-MER, ⊠ 11560, 18 km E.

Restaurant :
♦ *La Floride*, 1, pl. du Port, ☎ 68.49.81.31, Euro Visa ⌕ ⅃ ⌘ closed 31 Oct-1 Mar, 70-160 ; child : 50.

SIGEAN, ⊠ 11130, 21 km S.

Hotel :
★★★ *Château de Villefalse* (C.H.), rte de Narbonne, ☎ 68.48.21.53, 19 rm 🅿 ▨ ⌕ 🖾 closed Tue and Wed lunch (l.s.), 1 Nov-28 Feb, 300. Rest. ♦♦ ⅃ Painstakingly prepared food, 120-200.

⚑ ★★★*Les Kakis* (65 pl), ☎ 68.48.20.68 ; ★★*Municipal* (380 pl), ☎ 68.48.43.68.

PERPIGNAN★★

Béziers 93, Carcassonne 113, Paris 909 km
pop 120000 ⊠ 66000   B3

The city proudly proclaims its Catalan identity as "Perpinya" on roadsigns at the entrance to town. Built on a plain between a fortified hilltop and the Têt Valley, it was the former capital of the Kingdom of Majorca and stronghold of the Roussillon. The old town has changed little since the 18thC, but Perpignan is not a museum town. The vitality of bustling streets and markets attests to the prosperous fruit, vegetable and wine trades that provide the main local livelihood. The

Catalan spirit is kept alive by festivals in the town. The Sardana is danced at the Place de la Loge twice a week in summer. The Good Friday processions of penitents resemble their Spanish counterparts.

▶ The river Basse runs between the flowered banks of a canal to cross **Place Arago** (A-B2), the central square, and leads eventually to the **Castillet★** (B1), the handsome fortified gateway built in about 1370 and transformed into a fortress a century later. The gateway is now the **Casa Pairal**, a museum of Catalan folk arts and traditions *(daily ex Tue. and nat. hols.; 9:30-12 & 2:30-7 in summer, 9-12 & 2-6 rest of year)*; view from the terraces. ▶ **Place de la Loge★** (B2) : adorned with a statue of Venus by Maillol ; the Place is named for the beautiful Gothic building called the **Loge de Mer**, built in 1388 to serve as the muncipal commodity exchange (Bourse). The **Hôtel de Ville** (town hall) next door was rebuilt during the 16th-17thC ; in the courtyard, a statue by Maillol representing the Mediterranean. ▶ **Cathedral of St. Jean** (B1) : built between 1324 and 1507, one of the largest examples of Meridional Gothic architecture ; the exterior is undistinguished, but the interior is paved with Pyrenean marble and decorated with superb altarpieces★, of which the most interesting are those of the main altar (1620), St. Peter (left apse, 15thC) and the Virgin (right apse, ca. 1500). Through the S door into a chapel where a crucifix, revered as the **Devout Christ★★** (German, early 14thC) is kept. ▶ No. 16 Rue de l'Ange, in the 17thC Lazerme Mansion, the **Fine Arts Museum★** (B2, *closed Tue. and nat. hols.*) : works by the 17thC Perpignan painter Hyacinthe Rigaud, as well as modern paintings and Catalan ceramics. ▶ The **citadel** (B3 ; entry facing Avenue G.-Brutus ; *closed Tue.*) : fortifications built by Louis XI of France, Charles V and Philip II of Spain enclosing the former 13th-14thC **Palace of the Kings of Majorca★** ; in the Court of Honour, the loggia and "Paradise Gallery" framing the two-storey chapel ; exhibitions in the Majorca Hall *(daily ex Tue., nat. hols.)*. **Also...** ▶ **Platanes Promenade** (B1) : designed for strolling, and leading to the **Congress Palace**, with extensive gardens remarkable for their varied vegetation. ▶ **St. Jacques Church** (C2) : 14th-18thC, with altarpiece of Notre-Dame-de-l'Espérance (late 15thC), and Chapel of La Sanch (Precious Blood) supported by the brotherhood that organizes the Good Friday procession (Cross of Dishonour, representing the various stages of Christ's Passion, in the cloister). Behind the church, the **garden of La Miranda** on the remains of medieval fortifications. ▶ In the suburb of Saint-Godérique *(1.5 km SE)* is the **Mas St. Vicens** : cultural centre in an old house decorated by the contemporary tapestry designer Jean Lurçat ; exhibitions and sale of contemporary ceramics and tapestries.

Nearby

▶ **Château-Roussillon** *(6 km E)* : founded in 7thC BC on the road to Le Perthus and superseded by Perpignan in the 10thC AD ; archaeological excavations. ▶ **Cabestany** *(5 km SE)* : church with Romanesque tympanum★ depicting the sleeping Virgin. ▶ **Saint-Cyprien-Plage** *(17 km SE)* : together with **Canet-en-Roussillon** *(13 km E)* is the southernmost point of the development of the Languedoc-Roussillon coast ; separated by 9 km of fine sandy beach, both towns have marinas ; parks. ▶ **Port-Barcarès** and **Port-Leucate** *(15 km N, 25 km NE ; Aquacity)* : twin resorts that offer numerous diversions ; marinas ; activities both on the sea front and around Lake Leucate, beyond which the Canigou Massif is visible. **Port-Barcarès** : a seawater treatment centre ; casino-nightclub on the steamboat *Lydia* ; marine zoo ; oyster beds along road to **Leucate**. ▶ **Fort de Salses★** *(16 km N)* : a model of 16thC military architecture built by the Spaniards to defend the entry to the Roussillon *(visits daily)*. ▶ **Rivesaltes** *(9 km N)* : birthplace of the WWI military leader Marshal Joffre (1852-1931) ; renowned for Muscat wines (wine-cellars, cooperative), garden produce and apricots. ▶ **Espira-de-l'Agly** *(3 km W)* : Romanesque church with nave ending in twin apses encompassed by a single massive piece of stonework. ▶ **Estagel** *(13 km farther)* : the birthplace of the physician and politician François Arago (1786-1853).

► 14 km W of Rivesaltes, at Cases-de-Pène, **château de Jau★** : modern painting exhibitions *(summer)*. ► **Millas** *(14 km S of Estagel)* : reached via the Bataille Pass, base also for the **Hermitage of Força-Réal** : view★ over the Têt Valley and the Canigou. **Château de Corbère**, built in the 11thC on a promontory *(6 km from Millas)*; **Castelnou★** *(8 km SE)* : fortified village on a foothill of the Aspres, which is crowned by a 10thC fortress (restored 1875). ► **Thuir** *(5 km NE of Castelnou, 13 km SW of Perpignan)* : visits to the Celliers des Aspres (wine museum). ► Priory of **Monastir-del-Camp★** *(11 km SE)*, believed to have been founded by Charlemagne : 11thC church with 12thC W door and early-14thC cloister. ► **Brouilla** *(8 km SE)*: Romanesque church with trefoil choir. ► **Saint-Génis-des-Fontaines** *(S of Tech; 3 km from Brouilla)* : church with figured Romanesque lintel datable, by an inscription, to 1020; most of the cloister has been removed to the Philadelphia Museum of Art in the U.S. ► **Elne** *(10 km NE of Saint-Génis, 14 km S of Perpignan)*, a bishopric from 577 to 1602; upper town partly surrounded by ancient ramparts that are still flanked by towers. 11th-12thC **church★**, formerly a cathedral; the cloister★★ (12th-14thC) is considered one of the most beautiful in France; the S gallery, a masterpiece of sculpture of the Roussillon school *(daily ex Sun. off season)*. Small historical museum in chapter room. ☐

Holy week

Holy Week in Roussillon is celebrated almost as fervently as in neighbouring Spain. After the good cheer of Palm Sunday (processions with palm branches), on Wednesday the ceremonies assume a funereal character. The procession at Perpignan is the most remarkable, although impressive Good Friday processions are also held at Arles-sur-Tech, Bouleternères, Bompas and Collioure. Organized since 1416 by the Confrérie de la Sanch (Brotherhood of the Blood), the procession winds through the streets from the church of St. Jacques to the cathedral of St. Jean. At the head, the Regidor, a red-robed Penitent, wears the traditional hood of persons condemned to death; he is followed by Penitents in black, displaying the misteris, wax and wood figures representing the various personages of the Passion, and carrying the Croix des Outrages, a cross adorned with all the instruments of the Passion, but without the Christ. Interesting Easter Day processions, representing Christ's Resurrection, are held at Ille-sur-Têt and Céret.

Practical Information _____

PERPIGNAN
ⓘ quai de Lattre-de-Tassigny (A2), ☎ 68.34.29.94. Palais des Congrès, pl. Armand-Lanoux (C1), ☎ 68.34.13.13.
✈ Perpignan-Rivesaltes, 6 km N, ☎ 68.61.28.98. *Air France* office, 66, av. du Gal-de-Gaulle, ☎ 68.35.58.58.
SNCF (off map A2), ☎ 68.55.50.50.
🚌 2, bd St-Assiscle.

Car rental : *Avis*, Airport; 13, bd du Conflent, ☎ 68.34.26.71; train station.

Hotels :
★★★ **Loge**, pl. de la Loge (B2), ☎ 68.34.41.02, AE DC Euro Visa, 29 rm ⌂ 230.
★★★ **Mas des Arcades**, av. d'Espagne (off map A1), ☎ 68.85.11.11, Tx 500176, Euro Visa, 128 rm ℗ ⌂ ⌂ ✦

⬧ ⚭ ▦ ⚲ closed 21 Dec-10 Jan, 230. Rest. ♦ ♪ ⬧
⚭ 95-160.

★★★ **Park**, 8, bd J.-Bourrat (C1), ☎ 68.35.14.14, AE DC
Euro Visa, 67 rm Ⓟ 270. Rest. ● ♦♦ **Le Chapon Fin**,
closed Sat eve and Sun, 8-31 Aug, 20 Dec-6 Jan. One of the
finest tables in the city...indeed in all the Catalan region :
*ris de veau au rancio, légumes confits aux anchois, lape-
reau aux oignons.* Local wines, 85-230.

★★★ **Windsor**, (Inter-Hôtel), 8, bd Wilson (B1),
☎ 68.51.18.65, Euro Visa, 57 rm ⚒ closed 1-15 Feb, 295.

● ★★ **Athéna**, 1, rue Queya (B2), ☎ 68.34.37.63, AE DC
Euro Visa, 37 rm Ⓟ ▦ ⚒ ▦ 160.

★★ **Le Majorca**, 2, rue Font-Froide (B1), ☎ 68.34.57.57,
61 rm ⚒ closed 15 Dec-15 Jan, 175. Rest. ♦♦ closed
Mon eve and Wed noon, 15 Dec-23 Jan, 70-120.

★★ **Poste et Perdrix**, 6, rue Fabriques-Nabot (B2),
☎ 68.34.42.53, 39 rm, closed 15 Jan-15 Feb, 170. Rest. ♦
closed Mon and Sun eve, 70-130.

Restaurants :

● ♦♦ **Delcros**, 63, av. du Gal-Leclerc (A1),
☎ 68.34.96.05, Euro Visa, closed Mon and Sun (l.s.), Mon
and Sun eve (h.s.), 1-15 Jul. Henri Delcros carried his pots
for and wide before settling here, as his technique and
expertise prove : *consommé de crustacés aux raviolis de
homard, filets de sole en civet aux poireaux et champignons, panaché au chocolat,* 165-250.

● ♦♦ **François Villon**, 1, rue du Four-Saint-Jean,
☎ 68.51.18.43, closed Mon and Sun, 14 Jul-15 Aug.
Pierre Chareton's lovely, delicious cuisine, served here in
Catalan country : *escalope de foie de canard au vinaigre
de Gamay, gratin de noix de coquilles Saint-Jacques aux
noisettes et champignons de saison,* 140-250.

● ♦♦ **Le Festin de Pierre**, 7, rue du Théâtre (B2),
☎ 68.51.28.74, AE DC Visa ♪ closed Tue eve , Wed and
Feb. And a feast is indeed awaiting you, capably prepared by Michel Bellaton. *Roulé de soles aux girolles, panache de la mer,* 120-220.

● ♦♦ **Le Vauban**, 29, quai Vauban (B2), ☎ 68.51.05.10,
AE DC Visa ⚘ ♪ closed Sun. Other brasseries should take
a lesson in quality and freshness from the good, simple
food served here (à la carte only). Wine bar, 150-150.

♦♦ **La Serre**, 2bis, rue Dagobert (A2-3), ☎ 68.34.33.02,
AE DC Euro Visa ♪ closed Sun. Spec : *gambas à la provençale, lotte à la settoise,* 90-150.

♦♦ **Les Antiquaires**, pl. Després (B2), ☎ 68.34.06.58,
AE DC Euro Visa ♪ closed Mon noon and Sun, 1-20 Jul.
Spec : *terrine de saumon frais, turbot au champagne,
pigeon à la purée d'ail,* 110-170.

♦♦ **Pizzeria Luigi**, 11, quai Batlo (B1), ☎ 68.35.15.56,
AE DC Euro Visa ▦ ♪ closed Mon eve, Tue, Wed,
20 Dec-5 Jan. Hard to find a better pizza. The rest is tasty
too, and affordably priced, 80-100.

♦ **Le Palmarium**, pl. Arago, ☎ 68.34.51.31, Euro Visa,
30-70.

⚠ ★★*Catalan* (80 pl), ☎ 68.63.16.92 ; ★★*La Garrigole*
(22 pl), ☎ 68.54.66.10.

Recommended
Youth hostel : av. de Grande-Bretagne (A1),
☎ 68.34.63.32.

Nearby

CANET-PLAGE, ⊠ 66140, 13 km E.
ⓘ pl. de la Méditerranée, ☎ 68.80.20.65/68.73.25.20.

Hotels :

★★★ **Sables**, (Inter-Hôtel), 25, rue de la Vallée-du-Rhône,
☎ 68.80.23.63, AE DC Euro Visa, 41 rm Ⓟ ▦ ⚒ ▦ 200.

★★ **Athaéa**, (Mapotel), 120, prom. de la Côte-Vermeille,
☎ 68.80.28.59, Euro Visa, 48 rm Ⓟ ⚘ ⚒ closed Nov-
Mar, 305.

★★ **Font-le-Patio**, 71, bd Tixador, ☎ 68.80.31.04, 70 rm
Ⓟ ⚘ ⚭ half pens (h.s.), closed Nov-Mar, 300. Rest. ♦
⚘ 50-120.

★★ **L'Aquarius**, 40, av. du Roussillon, ☎ 68.80.25.48,
40 rm Ⓟ ▦ ⚭ ▦ half pens (h.s.), closed Oct-Mar, 400.
Rest. ♦ ⚭ 70-115.

★★ **Le Clos des Pins**, 34, av. du Roussillon,

☎ 68.80.32.63, AE DC Ⓟ ⚘ ▦ ⚒ ⚭ half pens, closed
Oct-Apr, 480. Rest. ♦ 70-130.

⚠ ★★★★*Ma Prairie* (260 pl), ☎ 68.80.24.70 ; 9
grounds★★★ ; 4 grounds★★.

CASTELNOU, ⊠ 66300 Thuir, 17 km SW.

Restaurant :
♦ **L'Hostal**, ☎ 68.53.45.42 ⚘ ▦ closed Mon and Wed eve,
3 Jan-15 Mar, 75-140.

PORT-BARCARÈS, ⊠ 66420, 21 km NE.
ⓘ Front-de-Mer, ☎ 68.86.16.56/68.86.10.50 ; and the
Suisse and Bordeaux shopping centre, ☎ 68.86.18.23.

Hotels :

★★★ **Lydia Playa**, (P.L.M.), la Grande-Plage,
☎ 68.86.25.25, AE Visa, 192 rm Ⓟ ⚘ ▦ ▦ ⚲ closed
30 Sep-20 Apr, 480. Rest. ♦♦ 90-120.

★★ **Casa Blanca**, 6, bd de la Côte-Vermeille,
☎ 68.86.13.18, Visa, 20 rm Ⓟ ⚘ ⚒ closed 1 Nov-15 Feb,
200.

★★ **Helios**, (Inter-Hôtel), av. Thalassa, Cap-de-Front,
☎ 68.86.32.82, Euro Visa, 50 rm Ⓟ ⚘ ♪ ⬧ ▦ ⚲ ✈ 355.
Rest. ♦ **Antinéa** ♪ ⚭ 70-110 ; child : 30.

⚠ ★★★★*Le Paris* (200 pl), ☎ 68.86.15.50 ; ★★★*Tamaris*
(330 pl), ☎ 68.86.08.18.

RIVESALTES, ⊠ 66600, 10 km N.
ⓘ ☎ 68.64.04.04.
✈ Perpignan-Rivesaltes, 4 km S, ☎ 68.61.22.24.
SNCF ☎ 68.64.09.54.

Hotels :

★★ **Alta-Riba**, av. de la Gare, ☎ 68.64.01.17, Visa, 54 rm
Ⓟ ⚘ ⚭ closed 15 Dec-15 Jan, 180. Rest. ♦ ♪ closed Mon
noon, Fri eve, Sun eve, 55-130.

★ **Debèze**, 11, rue Armand-Barbès, ☎ 68.64.05.88, AE
DC Euro Visa, 16 rm Ⓟ ⚒ 130.

SAINT-CYPRIEN, ⊠ 66750, 15 km SE.
ⓘ quai A.-Rimbaud, ☎ 68.21.01.33 ; and quai de la Pêche,
☎ 68.21.08.14.

Hotel :

★★ **Belvédère**, rue P.-Benoît, ☎ 68.21.05.93, 30 rm Ⓟ ⚘
⚒ closed Oct-May, 210. Rest. ♦ 60-150.

⚠ ★★★★*Cala Gogo* (500 pl), ☎ 68.21.07.12 ; ★★★*Bosc
d'En Roug* (660 pl), ☎ 68.21.11.82 ; 4 terrains.

SAINT-CYPRIEN-PLAGE, ⊠ 66750 Saint-Cyprien, 3 km
from **Saint-Cyprien**.

Hotels :

● ★★★ **Le Mas d'Huston**, Golf de Saint-Cyprien,
☎ 68.21.01.71, Tx 500834, AE DC Euro Visa, 50 rm
Ⓟ ⚘ ▦ ♪ ⚲ ✈ half pens (h.s.), closed Feb,
23 Nov-13 Dec, 700. Rest. ● ♦♦ ⚘ ♪ ⚭ Golf is all the
rage, and so is the light tasty cuisine of the Mas directed
by M. Guillaumou, a chef on a par with the best : *homard
au four, pot-au-feu aux trois confits, pigeonneau en feuille
de chou cuit à la cocotte,* 105-250.

★★ **La Lagune**, Les Capellans, ☎ 68.21.24.24, Visa,
36 rm Ⓟ ⚘ ♪ ⬧ ▦ ⚲ closed 30 Oct-30 Mar, 250.
Rest. ♦ ⚘ ♪ ⬧ ⚭ 60-130.

PÉZENAS**

Béziers 23, Montpellier 50, Paris 809 km
pop 8051 ⊠ 34120   C1

Pézenas used to be the site of three annual fairs that
attracted traders from all over Europe. The city played
an important political role between the 15th and 17thC
as the seat of the Languedoc regional government. The
Montmorencys, royal governors of the province,
and later, Armand de Bourbon, Prince de Conti, made
Pézenas into a cultural haven that attracted artists
and writers. The playwright Molière (1622-73) spent
several extended periods at Pézenas as "Actor to His
Serene Highness the Prince de Conti". Many man-

sions have survived from that era *(arrowed itinerary in the old town)*. Pézenas offers a wealth of cultural and theatrical activities, especially during the Arts Festival (Mirondela dels arts; *Jul.-Aug.*).

▶ At the foot of the hill crowned by Château Montmorency, a pedestrian precinct is the heart of the **old town★★**, centred on the Place Gambetta. Renaissance **Consulaire Mansion** (1693 belfry); nearby, the **Vulliod-St. Germain Museum** (3 Rue Albert-Paul-Alliés; *daily ex Mon. and Tue.; mementoes of old Pézenas and Molière's day)*. ▶ At the entrance to Rue F.-Oustrin, the TO is in the house where Molière lodged. Farther on, the 15thC **Lacoste Mansion★**, where Louis XIV stayed; exhibitions in the stables. ▶ Facing the 17thC **church of St. Jean**, the 16thC Commandery of the Order of St. John of Jerusalem (Knights-Templar). ▶ Along **Rue de la Foire**, bordered by beautiful houses, and Rue Émile-Zola, the medieval Jewish quarter. ▶ From there via the gate of the Consulaire Prison to **Cours Jean-Jaurès**, laid out in 1627 (interesting houses) at the edge of the medieval town. ▶ Beyond, the 17thC sections of the town also contain interesting houses, especially **Rue de Conti** : No. 36, **Alfonce Mansion★**; see the rear courtyard★ with two-tiered loggias (concerts and theatrical performances in the summer); also, the **Hostellerie du Griffon d'Or**, courtyard of an inn typical of the period.

Nearby

▶ **Saint-Thibéry** *(8 km S)* : in a volcanic basalt amphitheatre, a 15th-16thC abbey church; close by, ruins of a **Roman bridge** mark the path of the *Via Domitiana* (ancient Roman highway) over the Hérault. ▶ **Montagnac** *(6 km E)* : also an important medieval market; Gothic church. **Lavagnac** *(3 km N)* : 17thC château surrounded by medieval turrets. ▶ **Valmargne★** *(7 km E)* : 13th-14thC Cistercian **abbey** church and cloister★; 17thC main buildings *(pm daily ex Tue., 15 Jun.-15 Sep.; Sun. and nat. hols. pm rest of year)*; site. ☐

Practical Information _____

⃞ pl. Gambetta, ☎ 67.98.11.82.

Hotel :
★★ **Genieys** (L.F.), 9, av. A.-Briand, ☎ 67.98.13.99, AE DC Euro Visa, 20 rm ℙ ∰ half pens (h.s.), closed Sun eve and Mon, 3-25 Nov, 200. Rest. ♦ ♪ Good small menu, 55-160.

Recommended
Guide to wines : *Château de Saint-Ferréol*, ☎ 67.98.23.80, Comte d'Ormesson; at Paulhan CP 34230, 10 km N, *Château de la Condamine-Bertrand*, ☎ 67.24.46.01, M. Jany (white wines).

PRADES

Perpignan 43, Andorre-la-Vieille 123, Paris 954 km
pop 6524 ⊠ 66500   A3
Formerly the main centre of the Conflent region, this town paved with pink marble grew around a Gothic church (Romanesque bell-tower in Lombard style; 17thC altarpiece). Setting for the annual Pablo Casals Festival (named for the revered Catalan cellist, 1876-1973); an excellent starting point for climbing Canigou Peak.

Nearby

▶ **Canigou Peak★★** (try to spend 2 days, sleeping at the Chalet des Cortalets), reached by a difficult, winding forest road *(jeeps for hire at Prades, tel. 68.96.53.38 or Vernet-les-Bains, Villacecque garage, tel. 68.05.51.14)* to 27 km beyond **Cortalets** (alt. 2 200 m; view★), then another 1 hr 45 hike to the summit (alt. 2 785 m; astounding panorama★★); go down directly to Vernet-les-Bains via the **Escale de l'Ours★**. ▶ **Conat** *(6 km W)* : at the entrance to the wild Nohèdes Valley, Romanesque church

perched on one hilltop and the modest village on its neighbour. ▶ **Moligt-les-Bains** *(8 km NW)* : thermal springs (sulphur, soda, radioactive waters for the treatment of skin and eye, ear and throat ailments) in the Castillane Gorges; fishing and hunting on the mountain add to resort attractions. ☐

Practical Information _____

Nearby

MOLITG-LES-BAINS, ⊠ 66500 Prades, 8 km NW.
⌖ ☎ 68.05.00.50.
⃞ ☎ 68.96.27.58.

Hotel :
★★★★(L) **Château de Riell** (R.C.), ☎ 68.05.04.40, Tx 500705, AE Visa, 21 rm ℙ ⊰ ∰ ⚲ ♪ ☐ ⁓ closed 3 Nov-1 Apr. In the château's setting, a private club : "Les Oubliettes", 750. Rest. ♦♦♦ ⊰ ♪ ⊗ A refined decor enhances this neo-gothic château. The menu is sumptuous indeed : *filet de sandre à la moelle, mitonnée de joue de porc aux petits oignons*, good wines, 280-375; child : 200.

QUILLAN

Carcassonne 51, Perpignan 74, Paris 961 km
pop 4459 ⊠ 11500   A2-3
An industrial centre (for the manufacture of laminated surfaces), Quillan is an excellent base for exploring the Corbières and the Aude Valley.
▶ At the foot of medieval ruins, town hall in the 18thC **Espezel Mansion**.

Nearby

▶ SE of the town, an interesting drive through the **Fanges Forest★** above the **Pierre-Lys Gorges** (→ Razès) among fir trees growing at the 1 000 m mark. ▶ Along D613 and the **Sault Plateau** or from **Axat** *(11 km S)* to the **valley of the Rebenty★**; upstream of Joucou, the **Joucou Defiles★** (road tunnels), **Able** (Moulin d'Able electric power station) and **Niort** (or Sault). ▶ Across the **Portel Pass** (alt. 601 m; view) and through **Nébias** *(9 km W)* : museum of hunting *(daily Jul.-Aug.; pm Sun. and nat. hols. by appt. out of season, tel. 68.20.06.13, town hall)*; then to **Puivert**, below the ruins of a 12th-13thC **château** *(passable road from D121)*, one of the most easily accessible Corbières châteaux, once the haunt of troubadours (→ Provence). From the aviation base at Puivert you can take an air excursion over the Cathar châteaux. ▶ **Chalabre** *(8 km N of Puivert)* : social and cultural centre at Les Cèdres; various sporting activities. ☐

Practical Information _____

QUILLAN
⃞ pl. de la Gare, ☎ 68.20.07.78.   ♥
ɪɴᴄꜰ ☎ 68.20.05.63.

Hotels :
★★★ **La Chaumière**, (L.F., Inter-Hôtel), 25, bd Ch.-Gaulle, ☎ 68.20.17.90, Euro Visa, 37 rm ℙ ⊰ ∰ closed Fri eve and Sat lunch, 1 Nov-20 Dec, 200. Rest. ♦♦ ⊰ 55-150.
★★ **Cartier**, (France-Acceuil), 31, bd Ch.-de-Gaulle, ☎ 68.20.05.14, Euro Visa, 35 rm ℙ closed 15 Dec-16 Mar, 180. Rest. ♦ *Les Trois Quilles* ♪ ♧ closed Sat (l.s.), 55-105; child : 35.
★★ **La Pierre-Lys**, rte de Carcassonne, ☎ 68.20.08.65, 20 rm ℙ ∰ pens (h.s.), closed 15 Nov-15 Dec, 330. Rest. ♦♦ ⊰ ⊗ Spec : *confit d'oie maison, omelette aux truffes*, 45-115.

⚑ ★★★*Les Sapinettes* (100 pl), ☎ 68.20.13.52.

> For the translation of a name of a meat, a fish or a vegetable, for the composition of a dish or a sauce, see the Menu Guide in the Practical Holiday Guide; it lists the most common culinary terms.

Nearby

BELCAIRE, ⊠ 11340 Espezel, 27 km SW.

Hotel :
★ *Bayle* (L.F.), ☎ 68.20.31.05, Euro Visa, 16 rm ℗ ▥ ⬥
closed Fri eve and Sat lunch (l.s.), 3 Nov-13 Dec, 150.
Rest. ♦ ⬥ Regional cuisine, 55-140.

The RAZÈS Region**

A2-3

Round trip *(approx 150 km, full day)*
In the central Aude Valley, where the western buttresses of the Corbières meet the Pyrénées and encom-
pass the Fenouillèdes (upper Agly Valley), Razès is a
region of contrasts. The Pierre-Lys and Galamus Gorges, which carve a passage between the forested
limestone crests, contrast with neat vineyard valleys
producing *blanquette de Limoux* (→ box). This Roman
settlement of *Rhedae* was succeeded as regional
capital by Rennes-le-Château, whereas in the 14thC,
Alet became the episcopal see; on every peak stand
the remains of the apparently inaccessible châteaux
that formerly defended the region.

▶ **Quillan** (→). ▶ **Couiza :** at the exit from town, near
the Aude, the one-time château of the dukes of Joyeuse
is today a seminar and convention centre; the medieval
appearance is tempered by Renaissance elements (courtyard). ▶ **Alet-les-Bains★ :** best approach to the medieval township is along the Saint-Salvayre road; church of
Notre-Dame, first an abbey then a cathedral, was destroyed during the 16thC Wars of Religion; visit the **ruins**
(daily ex Sun.; key at the neighbouring tobacconist); the
church of St. André was built in the 16thC in meridional
Gothic. The Place de la République, with its half-timbered
houses, has the appearance of a theatre set. The former
convent buildings are now partly occupied by a thermal
spa. ▶ Farther on, the road enters a craggy **defile** known
as the **Étroit-d'Alet★**, then runs into the fertile basin
where the *blanquettes de Limoux* are produced (visits
to cellars, including the producers cooperative, on the
Alaigne road). ▶ **Limoux :** the centre of activity is the
Place de la République, surrounded by arcaded houses;
nearby, the 14th-16thC church of St. Martin has a Romanesque doorway. On the Avenue de Tivoli (fortifications W
of the town) is the **Petiet Museum,** late-19thC decorative
arts *(daily ex Mon. Jul.-Aug., or by appt. at the mayor's
office, tel. 68.31.01.16).* ▶ A miraculous spring was the
origin of the church of **Notre-Dame-de-Marceille** (pilgrimage site, 17th-18thC interior decoration). ▶ Among
vineyards, the fortified church of St. Hilaire : transition between Romanesque and Gothic styles (early 13thC;
14thC cloister). ▶ **Saint-Polycarpe :** 11th-14thC abbey
church, also fortified. ▶ **Arques Keep★** (24 m high,
13th-14thC), one of the best-preserved in the region
(Jun.-Aug., tel. 68.74.03.37). ▶ At the crossroads of D14
and 613, the barely-discernible ruins of **château de Blanche-
fort** (view★). ▶ **Rennes-les-Bains :** a spa in **Sals Gorges.** ▶ **Galamus Gorges★★ :** linking the Agly to the
Fenouillèdes (lookout at the chapel of St. Antoine; *15 min
on foot).* ▶ Downstream from **Saint-Paul-de-Fenouillet,**
the Agly runs through the **Clue de la Fou.** ▶ S of **Caudiès-
de-Fenouillèdes,** marking the W boundary of the Roussillon vineyards, the chapel of **Notre-Dame-de-Laval** stands
at the entry to **Saint-Jaume Gorge** (ruins of several
fortresses, picturesque village of **Fenouillet**). ▶ Above
Lapradelles-Puilaurens *(4.5 km S by narrow road, then
15-min walk)* : on a crag, the ruined **château de Puylau-
rens★** (11th-13thC). ▶ The Aude Valley runs downstream
from Quillan into a deep wooded gorge called the **Pierre-
Lys Defile★★.**   □

Practical Information ───────────────

ALET-LES-BAINS, ⊠ 11580 Limoux, 8 km S of **Limoux.**
♨ ☎ 68.69.90.27, (Jun-Sep).

ℹ ☎ 68.69.92.94.
🚂 ☎ 68.31.02.17.

Hotel :
★ *Evêché* (L.F.), av. N.-Pavillon, ☎ 68.69.90.25, 35 rm,
closed 30 Sep-1 Apr, 170. Rest. ♦ ⬥ 50-150♦ 50-150.

LIMOUX, ⊠ 11300, 24 km SW of **Carcassonne.**
ℹ prom. du Tivoli, ☎ 68.31.11.82 (h.s.).
🚂 ☎ 68.31.02.17.

Hotels :
★★ *Mauzac*, av. C.-Bouche, ☎ 68.31.12.77, AE DC Euro
Visa, 21 rm ℗ ⬥ 1500.
★★ *Moderne et Pigeon* (L.F.), 1, pl. Gal-Leclerc,
☎ 68.31.00.25, AE DC Euro Visa, 26 rm ℗ half pens (h.s.),
closed 15 Dec-15 Jan, 480. Rest. ♦ ♪ ໒ closed Mon (l.s.),
Mon lunch ex Jul-Aug, 60-150.

Restaurant :
♦♦ *Maison de la Blanquette*, prom. du Tivoli,
☎ 68.31.01.63, Euro Visa ⬥ ♪ ໒ closed Wed eve , Oct.
Savoury regional specialities : *gras double languedocien,
cassoulet au confit fait maison,* 60-100.

Å ★★*Du Breuil* (50 pl), ☎ 68.31.13.63.

Recommended
Guide to wines : *Antech*, domaine de Flassian,
☎ 68.31.15.88, sparkling wine; *Claudevel*, rte de Carcassonne, ☎ 68.31.02.45, sparkling wine; *Guinot*, chemin de
la Ronde, ☎ 68.31.01.53, sparkling wine.

RENNES-LES-BAINS, ⊠ 11190, 9 km SE of **Couiza.**
♨ (1 Apr-13 Nov), ☎ 68.69.87.01.
ℹ ☎ 68.69.88.04 ; mairie, ☎ 68.69.87.95.

Hotel :
★★ *France* (L.F.), ☎ 68.69.87.03, Visa, 25 rm ℗ ⬥ ⬥ ໒
pens (h.s.), closed Wed, 220. Rest. ♦ ໒ 50-100.

Å ★★*La Bernède* (50 pl), ☎ 68.69.86.49.

SAINT-CHINIAN

Béziers 28, Perpignan 44, Paris 800 km
pop 1735 ⊠ 34360   B1-2

Saint-Chinian, at the mouth of the Nouvre★, hemmed
in by high, coppery cliffs, lends its name to a red wine.

Nearby

▶ **Villespassans** *(9 km SW) :* museum of mineralogy and
archaeology in the town hall *(tel. 68.38.04.53).* ▶ **Cruzy**
(13 km S) : museum of prehistory, Gallo-Roman era *(con-
tact M. Fages, tel. 67.89.41.79).* ▶ **Quarante** *(2.5 km SE of
Cruzy) :* statuary museum near the 10th-11thC Roman-
esque church. ▶ **Abbey of Fontcaude** *(10 km E; daily ex
Mon.) :* abbey founded by the Premonstratensian Order
(White Canons) in the 12thC, ruined in 1560 during the
Wars of Religion. ▶ From *Cessenon (9 km NE)* to the vil-
lage of **Roquebrun★** (dessert wines), then continue up the
Orb Gorges★ towards Lamalou-les-Bains (→ Espinouse
Range).   □

SAINT-MARTIN-DE-LONDRES*

Montpellier 25, Nîmes 62, Paris 786 km
pop 1065 ⊠ 34380   C1

A large village★ on the road from Montpellier to
Ganges. The lower village, around the bell-tower and
the fountain, suffers a little from being near a main
road, but as you climb towards the centre of the village you discover a rare site that time seems to have
passed by. The houses form a barrier around the
church★, which is a typical example of early Languedoc Romanesque.

┌───┐
│ Send us your comments and suggestions; we will │
│ use them in the next edition.   │
└───┘

Nearby

▶ **Viols-le-Fort** *(6 km S)* : archaeological museum. ▶ **Les Matelles** *(12 km SE)*, just off D986 : museum of the University of Montpellier's Centre for Prehistoric Studies; the region is rich in neolithic traces, dolmens and Gallic hillforts. ▶ **Saint-Loup-Peak** can be reached by GR60 from Saint-Martin *(or in less than 3hr walk from Cazevielle, 8 km SE)*; at 658 m, the highest point in the region; view★★ over the Cévennes, the Garrigue, the Camargue, the Pyrénées and the sea. Beyond, ruined **château de Monferrand**, formerly a dependency of Maguelonne Abbey (→ Montpellier) with a view from a height of 410 m★. ▶ **Notre-Dame-de-Londres** *(7 km NE)* : 15thC **château**, with Renaissance furnishings and paintings *(daily pm Jul.-Sep.; pm Sun. and nat. hols., rest of year)*. □

Practical Information ───────────────

[i] ☎ 67.55.03.99.

Hotel :
★★★ *La Crèche*, rte de Frouzet, 5 km on the D 122, ☎ 67.55.00.04, 7 rm ℙ ⬚ ⬚ ⬚ ◹ ⬚ ⬚ closed Mon and Tue in winter, 1 Feb-1 Mar, 230. Rest. ● ◆◆ The sheephold dates from the 15thC, the view is unimpeded... chef G. Rousset and son produce modern food for a contemporary clientele : *huîtres de Thau en omelettes, paupiettes de sole au caviar*, and lamb, hams, 160-230.

SÈTE*

Montpellier 34, Béziers 53, Paris 791 km
pop 39545 ⊠ 34200   C2

Between the lake, the sea and Mont Saint-Clair, Sète is the major fishing port of the Mediterranean and the second commercial port after Marseilles, developed as a result of the Midi Canal. In the background of the picturesque waterfront, cranes, warehouses and reservoirs, and the pervasive smell of oil suggest the extent of recent industrial expansion in the town.

▶ At the foot of Mont Saint-Clair, the **Sète Canal** (B3) is bordered by Résistance Quay and Général-Durand Quay, where fishing-boats and fish restaurants draw crowds. Rue Général-de-Gaulle *(pedestrians only)* runs into the oldest quarter, near the 17thC **church of St. Louis** (B3), surmounted by a statue of the Virgin. ▶ At the end of Général-Durand Quay is the fish market, and beyond it the **St. Louis Breakwater** (B-C4), which protects the port and the training center for the America's cup (Marc Pajot), and provides a view back over the whole town. ▶ Farther S, 17thC **Fort Saint-Pierre** is cut off from the mountain by the Route de Corniche (cliff road). Today the Fort is occupied by the Theatre of the Sea. ▶ St. Charles Cemetery is a little below the sailors' cemetery (**Cimetière Marin**; A-B4), immortalized by the poet Paul Valéry (1871-1945) and where he himself is buried. The musician Georges Brassens (d. 1982) is buried 3 km farther on in the new cemetery facing the Thau Lagoon. ▶ Just above the Cimetière Marin is the **Paul Valéry Museum★** *(daily ex Tue., nat. hols., 10-12 & 2-6 or 7)* : art, archaeology, history; exhibits on water jousting (→ box) and on Valéry and Brassens. ▶ Higher still, **Fort Richelieu**, continuing *(2 km, tiring walk)* to the summit of **Mont Saint-Clair** (pilgrimage chapel), covered with weekend cottages. View of the Garrigues, the Cévennes, the Canigou Massif and the Mediterranean. ▶ Beyond the railway station (C1), **Pointe Courte**, the fishermen's quarter. ▶ To the W, the seaside resort and tourist *quartier* of the Corniche opens onto the Quilles marina and the beach-stretching toward Agde.

Nearby

▶ **Frontignan** *(7 km NE)* : excellent muscat wine and plenty of opportunities to try it. Fortified **church of St. Paul**; at No. 4 Rue Lucien-Salette, **Municipal Museum** (prehistory, Middle Ages, local economy); on the edge of town, a huge oil refinery.

Tour of Thau Lagoon★ *(approx 50 km)*

▶ Cross the industrial zone of Sète-Balaruc to reach **Balaruc-les-Bains**, a thermal spring dating from Roman times (casino) projecting into the Thau Lagoon, and the vine-growing village of **Balaruc-le-Vieux**. ▶ From **Gigean** *(6 km NE)*, a 3-km hike to **Saint-Félix-de-Monceau**, a ruined Benedictine abbey founded in the 11thC and abandoned in the 16thC; now maintained by an association for the aid of handicapped children *(open daily)*. ▶ **Bouzigues** : renowned for the oysters and mussels that since WWII have been raised commercially on the N shore of the Thau Lagoon. ▶ **Loupian** : set back from the coast, a vine-growing village with a Romanesque church from the 11th-12thC. ▶ **Mèze**, at the very edge of the lagoon, divided between grape-growing and shellfish-raising; the commercial centre of Thau. ▶ Finally, **Marseillan** and **Marseillan-Plage** (beach), whence you return to Sète along the sand spit separating the lagoon from the Mediterranean; salt-pans, vineyards, campsites, coast road and magnificent beach. □

───────────────────────────

Water jousting

The tradition of water jousting (les joutes) stretches back to the founding of Sète in the 17thC. Jousts are held during the latter 2 weeks of August. Two boats, each with 10 rowers and a pair of musicians who play the 300-year-old jousting song, are equipped with projecting prows on which the jousters stand, each armed with lance and shield. The uproarious game consists of manœuvering until one of the jousters can land a blow to topple his adversary into the water. Mementoes of past jousts are to be seen in the Museum of Sète. This form of jousting is also practised at Agde, but the water tournaments of Sète are better known.

───────────────────────────

Practical Information ───────────────

SÈTE
[i] 22, 60 Grand Rue Mario Roustan (B3), ☎ 67.74.73.00.
SNCF (C1), ☎ 67.58.50.50.
⚓ *C.N.C.M.*, 4, quai d'Alger (C3), ☎ 67.74.70.55.
Car rental : Avis, 5, rue Longuyon (C1), ☎ 67.74.60.76; train station (C1).

Hotels :
★★★ *Impérial*, (Mapotel), pl. Ed-Herriot, La Corniche (off map A1), ☎ 67.53.28.32, Tx 480046, AE DC Euro Visa, 43 rm ℙ ⬚ ⬚ 410.
★★★ *Le Grand Hôtel*, 17, quai de Tassigny, ☎ 67.74.71.77, Tx 480225, AE DC Euro Visa, 51 rm ℙ ⬚ ⬚ ♪ closed 22 Dec-1 Jan, 275. Rest. ◆◆ 80-150.
★★ *La Joie des Sables*, beach of la Corniche (off map A1), ☎ 67.53.11.76, AE DC Euro Visa, 35 rm ℙ ⬚ ⬚ ⬚ 240.
★★ *Orque Bleue*, 10, quai Aspirant-Herber (C3), ☎ 67.74.72.13, AE DC Visa, 30 rm ⬚ ⬚ closed 10 Jan-20 Mar, 190.
★★ *Régina*, 6, bd Danielle-Casanova (A1), ☎ 67.74.31.41, Visa, 20 rm ℙ ⬚ closed 10 Nov-20 Dec, 205.

Restaurants :
● ◆◆ *La Palangrotte*, 1, rampe Paul-Valéry (B2), ☎ 67.74.80.35, AE DC Euro Visa ⬚ ⬚ closed Mon and Sun eve (l.s.), 10 Nov-10 Dec. Goodness, what fresh fish! Alain Geminignam serves it in what looks like a stage set for a Mediterranean musical. Spec : *huîtres et moules de l'étang de Thau*, 75-200.
◆ *Alsacien*, 25, rue P.-Sémard (C2), ☎ 67.74.77.94, Visa ♪ ⬚ ⬚ closed Mon and Sun eve, 10 Jun-10 Jul, 22 Dec-3 Jan. Homesick for Strasbourg? Come here to sample the *quiche, choucroute*, 75-150.
◆ *Le Jacques-Cœur*, 17, rue P.-Valéry (B2), ☎ 67.74.33.70, AE DC Visa ℙ ⬚ ♪ ⬚ closed Sun,

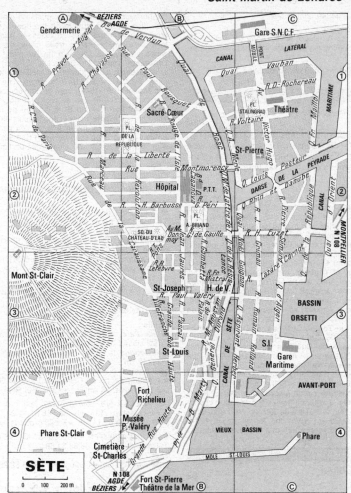

24 Dec-4 Jan. Heartwarming food : *loup à la tahitienne, moules farcies, bourride à la Sétoise, rougets à la moëlle,* 130-250.

⚐ ★★★★*Castellas* (896 pl), ☎ 67.53.26.24 ; 4 terrains.

Recommended
Marina : 220 pl., ☎ 67.74.98.97.
♥ pastry : *Cappucchi*, 9, av. V.-Hugo, ☎ 67.74.57.27.

Nearby

BALARUC-LES-BAINS, ⊠ 34540, 5 km N.
⚕ (14 Feb-17 Dec), ☎ 67.48.51.02.
ⓘ av. des Nouveaux-Thermes, ☎ 67.48.50.07.

Hotel :
★★ *Grand Hôtel Azur*, 2, av. du Port, ☎ 67.48.50.26, 16 rm, half pens (h.s.), closed 1 Dec-15 Mar, 300.

Restaurant :
♦♦ *Martinez*, 2, rue M.-Clavel, ☎ 67.48.50.22 ≼ ⚘ ⚘ & ⚭ closed Mon and Sun eve (l.s.), 15 Jan-15 Mar, 70-150.

⚐ ★★★*Mas du Padre* (112 pl), ☎ 67.48.53.41 ; ★★*Chemin des Bains* (152 pl), ☎ 67.48.51.48 ; ★★*Pech d'Ay* (163 pl), ☎ 67.48.50.34.

BOUZIGUES, ⊠ 34140, 15 km NW.

Hotel :
★★★ *Côte Bleue*, ☎ 67.78.31.42, Euro Visa, 32 rm ℗ ≼ ₪ ⚲ ⊠ closed Feb, 275. Rest. ♦ ≼ closed Tue eve and Wed ex summer, Sun eve, Mon (h.s.). Be sure to reserve a table if you want to sample M. Archambaud's famous oysters and mussels, 130-180.

FRONTIGNAN, ⊠ 34110, 7 km NE on the N 112.
ⓘ ☎ 67.48.33.94.

Hotel :
★★★ *Balajan*, (Inter-Hôtel), RN 112, Vic-la-Gardiale, ☎ 67.48.13.99, Visa, 21 rm ℗ ≼ ₪ & half pens (h.s.), closed 6 Feb-6 Mar, 26 Dec-3 Jan, 415. Rest. ♦♦ ≼ ⚘ closed Mon noon, 55-130 ; child : 50.

Restaurant :
♦♦ *La Rascasse*, 27, quai Gal-Durand, La Marine, ☎ 67.74.38.46, AE DC Visa ≼ ₪ closed 25 Nov-25 Dec. Spéc. : *plateau de coquillages*, 65-130.

Recommended
♥ Muscat : *wine cooperative*, ☎ 67.48.12.26.

MARSEILLAN, ⊠ 34340, 26 km NW.
Restaurant :
♦♦ *Le Glacier*, bd V.-Hugo, ☎ 67.77.22.04, Visa ♪ ⍩
closed Mon. For luminously fresh shellfish and bistro atmosphere, 90-210.

⩘ ★★★★*Les Sirènes* (600 pl), ☎ 67.94.15.12.

TUCHAN

Perpignan 36, Narbonne 90, Paris 939 km
pop 814 ⊠ 11350   B2-3
At the intersection of the roads across the Corbières, at the foot of Tauch Mountain, Tuchan is a busy wine centre in the official wine district of Fitou; the village of the same name is situated near the coast.

Nearby

▶ 3 km E, overlooking the vineyards is the ruined 12thC **château d'Aguilar**, which during the Middles Ages kept watch over the Spanish frontier; the château was abandoned when the frontier was moved to its present position in the 17thC. ▶ Along D12 to **Vingrau** *(10 km SE)* in the Eastern Pyrénées, then to the **Caune de l'Arago** (cavern; *guided tours in Jul.-Aug.*), where the remains of Tautavel Man dating from 450 000-400 000BC were discovered. Above the village of **Tautavel**, the Museum of Prehistory displays important finds excavated on the site *(daily ex Tue., 1 Jan., Easter Mon., Whitsun, 1 May, 25 Dec.)*; ruined 11thC château, and Cooperative of the Maître Vignerons (Master Wine Makers) of Tautavel. ▶ **Château de Padern** *(8 km SW)* in ruins; once the stronghold at the entrance to the **Torgan Gorges★**. ▶ From **Cucugnan** *(13 km)* climb to the **Grau de Maury** (view★) and the 13th-14thC **château de Quéribus** built on a crag after the Albigensian Crusade. ▶ Above **Duilhac** *(17 km)*, the 11th-12thC **château★ de Peyrepertuse** *(20 min on foot)* with the château of San-Jordy forms a defensive fortification on the same rocky crest 800 m higher up; view★; the path completes the circuit *(approx 1 hr 30)*. ▶ **Rouffiac des Corbières** *(2 km)* : château; Romanesque church modified in the 14thC. ▶ **Termes** *(30 km NW)* and **Villerouge-Termenès** *(28 km NW)* : the former has a 12thC keep; the latter is the very picture of a medieval village. ☐

La Côte VERMEILLE**
(The Gilded Coast)
                                                        B3

Itinerary Argelès-sur-Mer to the Spanish frontier *(approx 30 km, half-day)*
Coastal Roussillon between Argelès and Cerbère, with a rapid succession of creeks, cliffs and ports, is known as the Gilded Coast (Côte Vermeille). The name seems particularly appropriate at sunset, when the light enhances the ochre shades of the predominant schist. Béar, Abeille, Rederis and Cerbère are forelands offering lookouts along the route. The traditional nighttime fishing by lamplight has declined in recent years.

▶ **Argelès-sur-Mer** : behind crumbling ramparts, a typical village of the plain; 14thC Gothic church. ▶ **Argelès-Plage** *(3 km on)* : a busy seaside resort. ▶ **Collioure** : attractive site and historical charm for an important tourist centre; typical Mediterranean medieval **fortified city★**, with a port overlooked by a **royal château** (12th, 14th, 17thC); museum of folk arts and traditions of the Roussillon). Many painters, including Pablo Picasso and Henri Matisse, have been attracted by the exceptionally brilliant light and colour. The tower of the 17thC church formerly served as a lighthouse; the **church** altarpiece★ is considered a masterpiece of Catalan Baroque. ▶ **Port-Vendres** *(Porta Veneris* : "gate of Venus" for the Romans), fortified by the military engineer Sébastien Vauban (1633-1707), still looks like a simple fishing port, even if

the harbour is taken over by pleasure craft. At the quayside, fish are sold straight off the boat at the end of the afternoon near the terraced cafés. ▶ **Banyuls-sur-Mer :** in a bay★ where orange trees grow, reputed for sweet wines (audiovisual display in the Templars' cellars). **Arago Laboratory** (part of the University of Paris) : marine biological research and aquarium of Mediterranean specimens *(daily 9-12 & 2-6:30, 10 in season)*. The sculptor Aristide Maillol (1861-1944), born in Banyuls, created the War Memorial on the Ile-Grosse rock; his grave at the **Métairie Maillol** (farm; *4 km S*) is marked by his bronze The Thinker. ▶ **Cerbère** : last French resort on the coast in a deep bay ringed by mountains. ▶ You can return by the **Balcon de Madeloc** road between Banyuls and Collioure, with view★ through the vineyards, particularly from the 14thC Madeloc Tower. ☐

Practical Information ——————————

ARGELÈS-PLAGE, ⊠ 66700 Argelès-sur-Mer, 3 km E.
Hotels :
● ★★★ *Lido*, (Inter-Hôtel), bd de la Mer, ☎ 68.81.10.32, Tx 505220, Euro Visa, 65 rm ℙ � ⌂⌂⌂ ⊟ closed 1 Oct-15 May, 400. Rest. ♦♦ ♪ 70-130.
★★ *Marbella*, allée des Palmiers, ☎ 68.81.12.24, 37 rm, closed 15 Sep-24 May, 200.
★ *Solarium*, 9, av. du Vallespir, ☎ 68.81.10.74, 18 rm ⍨ ⍩ half pens (h.s.), closed 30 Sep-1 May, 300. Rest. ♦ 60-120.

ARGELÈS-SUR-MER, ⊠ 66700, 21 km S of **Perpignan.**
ⓘ pl. des Arènes, ☎ 68.81.15.85.
𝗦𝗡𝗖𝗙 ☎ 68.81.02.00.
Hotels :
● ★★ *Parc*, ☎ 68.81.05.52, AE DC Euro Visa, 23 rm ⌂⌂⌂ ⍨ ⊟ closed 30 Sep-1 Jun, 200.
★★ *Cottage* (L.F.), 21, rue A.-Rimbaud, ☎ 68.81.07.33, Visa, 12 rm ℙ � ⌂⌂⌂ ⍨ ♪ half pens (h.s.), closed Oct-Mar, 350. Rest. ♦ � ♪ Regional dishes, 75-95; child : 30.
★★ *Mouettes*, rte de Collioure, 3 km, ☎ 68.81.21.69, AE DC Euro Visa, 23 rm ℙ � ⌂⌂⌂ ⊟ 250. Rest. ♦♦ 90-120.
⩘ ★★★★*Arbre Blanc* (132 pl), ☎ 68.81.26.49; ★★★★*Licorne* (137 pl), ☎ 68.81.15.24; ★★★★*Sirène* (750 pl), ☎ 68.81.14.48; ★★★*28 grounds*; ★★*80 grounds*.

BANYULS-SUR-MER, ⊠ 66650, 37 km SE of **Perpignan.**
ⓘ Hôtel de Ville, ☎ 68.88.31.58.
𝗦𝗡𝗖𝗙 ☎ 68.88.30.64.
⛟ av. du Gal-de-Gaulle, ☎ 68.88.32.26.
Hotels :
★★★ *Catalan*, rte de Cerbère, ☎ 68.88.02.80, Tx 500575, AE DC Euro Visa, 36 rm ℙ � ⌂⌂⌂ ⍨ ⊟ ⍩ closed 15 Oct-1 Apr, 340. Rest. ♦ 70-160.
★★ *Les Elmes*, plage des Elmes, ☎ 68.88.03.12, AE Euro Visa, 21 rm ℙ � & ⍩ half pens (h.s.), closed 1 Nov-20 Mar, 450. Rest. ♦♦ � & ⍩ Spec : *baudroie en fricassée aux poireaux confits, coques de seiches et sa julienne de légumes*, 60-100.

Restaurant :
♦♦ *Le Sardinal*, pl. Paul-Reig, ☎ 68.88.30.07, Euro Visa � ♪ & closed Mon and Sun eve (l.s.), 2-24 Jan, 12-29 Oct. Spec : *foie au vinaigre de Banyuls, marmite de filets de poissons*, 65-180; child : 30.

⩘ ★★★*Le Stade* (33 pl), ☎ 68.88.31.70; ★★*Municipal* (80 pl), ☎ 68.88.32.13.

Recommended
Guide to wines : *G.I.C.B.*, Mas Reig, rte des Crètes, ☎ 68.88.31.59, daily 9am-7pm, cellar tours.

CERBÈRE, ⊠ 66290, 47 km SE of **Perpignan.**
ⓘ 1, av. de la Côte-Vermeille, ☎ 68.88.42.36.
𝗦𝗡𝗖𝗙 ☎ 68.88.40.20/68.88.41.32.
Hotel :
★★ *La Dorade*, av. du Gal-de-Gaulle, ☎ 68.88.41.93, Euro Visa, 25 rm ⍨ half pens (l.s.), 15 Oct-20 Mar, 300. Rest. ♦♦ ♪ & Spec : *terrine de poisson au poivre vert, civet de lotte, bouillabaisse*, 55-130.

⚞ ★★*Plage del Sorell* (80 pl), ☎ 68.38.41.64.

COLLIOURE, ✉ 66190, 27 km SE of **Perpignan.**
ⓘ av. C.-Pelletan, ☎ 68.82.15.47.
▰▰▰ ☎ 68.82.05.89.
▰▰▰ ☎ 68.82.18.83.

Hotels :
★★★ ***Casa Pairal*** (R.S.), imp. des Palmiers,
☎ 68.82.05.81, Tx 505220, 26 rm Ⓟ ░░░ ⚲ ▣ closed
30 Oct-30 Mar, 220.
★★★ *La Frégate*, 24, quai de l'Amirauté, ☎ 68.82.06.05,
Tx 505072, Visa, 24 rm, closed 12 Nov-28 Feb, 220.
Rest. ● ◆◆ Regional dishes get top billing. The other
more classic fare is less interesting. They should try hard-
er : *salade de poissons crus, terrine de ratatouille aux
anchois*, 100-180.
★★ ***Caranques***, rte de Port-Vendres, ☎ 68.82.06.68,
16 rm Ⓟ ░░░ ⚲ ⚯ half pens (h.s.), closed 10 Oct-1 Apr.
Direct access to the sea, 400. Rest. ◆ ⚕ ⚯ closed
1 Jun-30 Sep.
★★ ***Le Bon Port***, rte de Port-Vendres, ☎ 68.82.06.08,
22 rm Ⓟ ░░░ half pens (h.s.), closed 15 Oct-Easter, 400.
Rest. ◆ An enchanting view of Collioure, 60-140.
★★ ***Les Templiers***, 12, quai de l'Amirauté, ☎ 68.82.05.58,
Visa, 52 rm ⚕ half pens (h.s.), closed 5 Jan-1 Apr,
3 Nov-20 Dec, 420. Rest. ◆ ⚕ closed Mon and Sun
eve, 75-180.
● ★ ***La Bona Casa***, 10, av. de la République,
☎ 68.82.06.62, Visa, 8 rm, closed Wed, Thu lunch,
15 Oct-15 Mar, 110. Rest. ◆ ♪ ⚳ 85-220.

Restaurants :
● ◆◆◆ *La Balette*, rte de Port-Vendres, ☎ 68.82.05.07,
Visa Ⓟ ⚕ ░░░ ♪ closed Mon and Sun eve (l.s.), 7 Jan-7 Feb.
In this stupendous setting, enjoy a *fricassé de homard au
vieux Banyuls* or *une blanquette de sole aux coques avec
son flan de fenouil*. Good desserts, 90-250.
◆◆ *La Bodega*, 6, rue de la République, ☎ 68.82.05.60,
closed Mon eve and Tue, 8 Nov-24 Dec. You will find
bouillabaisse or fish on the menu, in this former wine storehouse, 85-240.
◆ *Le Chiberta*, 18, av. du Gal-de-Gaulle, ☎ 68.82.06.60,
Visa ♪ closed Mon eve and Tue (Apr-Jun), Oct-Apr,
55-105 ; child : 30.

⚞ ★★*Amandiers* (92 pl), ☎ 68.81.14.69 ; ★★*Girelle*
(65 pl), ☎ 68.81.25.56.

Recommended
♥ *Boutique du Port*, pl. de la République, genuine Cata-
lan espadrilles for dancing the sardane ; local products :
Roque, 40, rue de la Démocratie, ☎ 68.82.04.99 ; pastry :
Bartissol, rte de Port-Vendres.

PORT-VENDRES, ✉ 66660, 31 km SE of **Perpignan.**
ⓘ quai Forgas, ☎ 68.82.07.54.
▰▰▰ ☎ 68.82.00.42.

Hotel :
★★ ***Tamarins***, plage des Tamarins, ☎ 68.82.01.24, AE DC
Euro Visa, 35 rm Ⓟ ⚕ ░░░ ⚲ closed 15 Oct-5 Mar, 220.
Rest. ◆ 70-100.

Limousin

▶ Land of trees and water — this slightly hackneyed phrase sums up the two outstanding characteristics of Limousin. Water everywhere you look, welling up from thousands of springs, carving out valleys and gorges in its path towards the Loire or the Garonne rivers, irrigating sloping meadows dotted with reservoirs and strings of tranquil mirror-smooth lakes reflecting the sky. Here and there the hiss of the turbines gives way to the creaking of an old moss-covered waterwheel, or the tuneful murmurs of waterfalls and ancient wishing wells reputed to cure a whole host of human ills. Limousin is also a region of trees, thickets, and dense groves, narrow roads bordered with hedgerows and great stands of beeches, oaks and chestnut trees.

The gorges of the Dordogne and Maronne rivers, with their views of high-growing patches of purple heather and yellow broom, welcome the citydweller thirsty for greenery, for Limousin is a mosaic of green : the soft velvety green of its meadows, the sharper green of newly-cut grass, and the deep green of its dense forests, interspersed with the translucent green of fern fronds. Far from the madding crowd the visitor can find a warm welcome at country guesthouses, and wander for a whole day along country tracks without meeting another tourist.

But Limousin has other charms besides rural pleasures. The town of Aubusson, former site of the Royal Tapestry Works, Limoges with its fine porcelain and the ruins of the Saint-Martial Abbey, the Château Pompadour, converted into a stud-farm after the death of the famous Marquise de Pompadour, and the holiday town of Bort-les-Orgues nestling under its high dam and vast man-made lake, all bear out the local

tourist board slogan "a discovery awaits you at the end of every path". The local people have another saying — "chabatz d'entrar", or "have done with entering" — another way of bidding you to make yourself at home. ☐

Facts and figures

Location : in the heart of France, between the Massif Central and the Atlantic coast.
Area : 16 932 km²
Climate : influenced by the Atlantic (W and SW winds) and relatively mild except in the East (Plateau de Mille-vaches), which is more continental.
Population : 378 726
Administration : **Corrèze** Department, Prefecture : Tulle. **Creuse** Department, Prefecture : Guéret. **Haute-Vienne** Department, Prefecture : Limoges.

 Don't miss

★★★ Bort-les-Orgues B2, Dordogne Gorges B2.

★★Collonges-la-Rouge B3, Vassivière Lake B2.

★ Argentat B3, Beaulieu-sur-Dordogne B3, Le Dorat A1, Limoges A1, Moutier-d'Ahun B1, Pompadour A2, Uzerche A2.

Weekend tips

Enjoy the Saturday morning bustle in Brive-la-Gaillarde (and its market), before lunching early at a speciality restaurant in Varetz; along the valley of the Corrèze, via Tulle to Argentat (stopover). The trip round the Dordogne and Maronne gorges will make a pleasant Sunday morning; after lunch, perhaps at Beaulieu-sur-Dordogne, return to Brive via Collonges-la-Rouge and Turenne.

Brief regional history

Before the Roman conquest
The Limousin is a **plentiful source of neolithic
remains**, even if they are not as spectacular as those
in neighbouring Périgord. ● The native population —
the Lemovici *—* developed from the amalgamation of
Ligurian, Iberian and Celtic immigrants.

52BC-10thC
The Limousin was part of the Roman province of
Aquitaine, and suffered badly during the barbarian
invasions which followed the collapse of the Roman
Empire. The region was not secured and consolidated
until the 7thC, in the reign of King Dagobert. ● Subsequently, the relative isolation of the region left it more
or less untouched by the great political upheavals of
the period; its peaceful existence favoured the spread
of **abbeys and monasteries.**

10th-14thC
Around the 10thC, the Limousin was **divided into
feudal fiefs,** Vicomtés, Seigneuries, or Baronnies, all
more or less independent. ● Still part of Aquitaine,
Limousin became English after the marriage of Eleanor (1152) to Henry II Plantagenêt. ● It was not definitively reclaimed for France until the reign of Charles V
(1374). Even then, it remained a **frontier region**
between **northern** and **southern** France, between the
"Langue d'Oïl" (the culture and language of the North,
with written laws) and the "Langue d'Oc" (the culture
and language of the South, with laws based on custom).

15th-18thC
Limousin was **annexed to the Royal Estate by
Henri IV** in 1607, and there were a number of revolts
in 1636 and 1637 provoked by Cardinal Richelieu's
centralization policy. ● Between 1730 and 1774, the
administrators (Intendants) of the province had more
flexible policies and were concerned for the economic
future of the region (road-building, introduction of the
potato, development of porcelain, and popularisation
of tapestries).

Practical information

Information : *Délégation régionale au tourisme* and
Comité Régional de Tourisme (C.R.T.), 8, cours Bugeaud,
87000 Limoges, ☎ 55.79.57.12. **Corrèze** : *C.D.T., Maison
du tourisme,* quai Baluze, 19000 Tulle, ☎ 55.26.46.88.
Creuse : *C.D.T.,* 43, pl. Bonnyaud, 23000 Guéret,
☎ 55.52.33.00. **Haute-Vienne** : *Union touristique-C.D.T.,*
4, pl. Denis-Dussoubs, 87000 Limoge, ☎ 55.79.04.04. **In
Paris** : *Maison du Limousin,* 18, bd Haussmann, 75009
Paris, ☎ 47.70.32.63. *Dir. rég. de la Jeunesse et des
Sports,* cité administrative, place Blanqui, 87031 Limoges Cedex, ☎ 55.33.50.50. *Dir. rég. des Affaires culturelles,* 2 *ter,* rue Haute-Comédie, 87000 Limoges,
☎ 55.34.38.00.

Reservations : *Loisirs-accueil (L.A.)* **Haute-Vienne** at
C.D.T., **Corrèze,** quai Baluze, 19000 Tulle, ☎ 55.26.46.88.
Creuse, 43, pl. Bonnyaud, 23000 Guéret, ☎ 55.52.33.00.

S.O.S. : **Corrèze** : *SAMU (emergency medical service),*
☎ 55.26.00.00. **Creuse** : ☎ 17. **Haute-Vienne** : *SAMU,*
☎ 55.33.33. *Poisoning Emergency Centre :* **Corrèze** :

☎ 56.96.40.80 and 73.91.96.96. **Creuse** : ☎ 73.91.96.96.
Haute-Vienne : ☎ 56.96.40.80.

Weather forecast : **Corrèze** : ☎ 55.26.29.99. **Creuse** :
☎ 55.52.52.52. **Haute-Vienne** : ☎ 55.06.06.06.

**Farmhouse gîtes, chambres d'hôtes, gîtes for children,
farmhouse camping** : enq. at the *C.R.T.* and *relais départ.*
Corrèze : 36, av. du Gal-de-Gaulle, 19000 Tulle, ☎
55.20.24.54. **Creuse** : 1, rue Martinet, 23000 Guéret,
☎ 55.52.55.75. **Haute-Vienne** : at *C.D.T.*

Holiday villages : reservations at *L.A., C.D.T.* and *C.R.T.;
Vacances Auvergne-Limousin,* 31, rue E.-Gilbert, 63038
Clermont-Ferrand Cedex, ☎ 73.93.08.75. *Vacances Pro-
motion,* 52, rue du Dr-Finlay, 75015 Paris, ☎ 45.71.31.30.

Limousin cuisine

*As a starter, there is a marvelous soup called Bré-
jaude, eaten with rye bread, and so thick with cabbage and other vegetables that your spoon will stand
up in it. Charcuterie (pork products) occupies an
important place : saucisses, andouille (chitterling sausage), boudin (blood sausage) with chestnuts, not for-
getting the grillons (pork crackling) prepared when the
lard is rendered. Traditional dishes include a variety of
stews, slowly simmered on the kitchen fire, and
sauced dishes, accompanied by chestnuts or rye pancakes (galettes, galetons in Haute-Vienne and tourtons
in the Corrèze); also try the potée (cabbage stew) and
the cassoulet (pork and beans). The beef of the region
is extremely tender and full of flavour. There are few
cheeses apart from the Brach, a cousin of the Roquefort, since cattle breeding is mostly for meat. Desserts
include thick home-made cakes : clafoutis with cherries, flaugnarde with apples, galette Corrézienne, and
the almond cake of the Creuse.*

Festival and events : early May : *choral and orchestral
performances* in Limoges; *spring festival* in Davignac.
Jun : *departmental music festival* in Aubusson. **Jun-Jul** :
Jean Giraudoux theatre, dance and music festival in Bellac. **Jul** : *vieux Chénérailles medieval festival;* Guéret *festival; international accordion festival* in Tulle (first two
weeks). **Jul-Aug** : *music festivals* at St-Léonard Collegiate Church in Aubazine, in Beaulieu-sur-Dordogne, Saint-
Robert, Saint-Sétiers, Sédières, Turenne, Ussel and
Uzerche; *international folklore festival* in Brive; *fortnight
of popular arts and traditions* in Davignac and in Ségur-
le-Château; Vassivière *festival; biennal international enamels festival* in Limoges. **Aug** : *international folklore festival* in Felletin. **End Sep** : *comedy convention* at Saint-
Just-le-Martel. **Early Oct** : *francophone festival* in Limoges; *festival of concerts* in the Tulle cloister.

Exhibitions and trade fairs : early Jan : *Foire des Rois :*
sale of *foies gras* and truffles in Brive. **Apr** : *goat fair* in
Aubazine. **May** : *horse fair* in Chénérailles; *foire de la St-
Loup* in Limoges. **Jun** : *ham day* in Saint-Mathieu; *wool
fair* in Chénérailles. **Jul** : *second-hand and bric-à-brac
fairs* in Argentat, Aubazine, Chénérailles and Objat;
cheese days in Pageas and *cheese fair* in Aubusson.
Aug : *sheep fair* in Féniers. **Sep** : *Limousin cattle breeding
- international days, pig fair* in Bonnat. **Oct** : *horse fair* in
Chénérailles; *chestnut fair* in Dournazac; *mushroom festival* in Aubusson. **Nov** : *book fair* in Brive (2nd weekend);
antique fair in Vigeois (last Sun). **Dec** : *turkey fair* in Chénérailles and Chambon-sur-Voueize.

Folklore festivals : Jun : «*Bonnes Fontaines*» *folklore festival* in Cussac. **Jul** : *coronation of the King and ring race*
in Saint-Léonard-de-Noblat. **Aug** : *cattle breeding festival*
in Brive (last weekend); *fair, goat competition and craft
fair* in Meymac. **Oct** : *Fête de Notre-Dame des petits
ventres* in Limoges.

Rambling and hiking : the region is crossed by GRs 33, 4, 41, 44, 46, 440 and 480 (topoguides and GR of the Aygurande region). **Corrèze :** a topoguide of short rambles is available at the *C.D.T.;* possible rambles with mules. **Creuse :** three remarkable brochures, *Itinéraires pédestres de petite randonnée,* containing indications and descriptions of short hikes and rambles. **Haute-Vienne :** the *C.D.T.* publishes *Fiches-circuits pédestres* (leaflets on walking routes).

Cycling holidays : excursions, bicycle rambles : enq. at *L.A.* and *C.D.T.*

Riding holidays : enq. and lists of riding centres : *C.D.T.* Courses and excursions : bookings at the *L.A.*

NW of Limoges

Technical tourism : Creuse : reproductions of antique tapestries, tapestry manufacture ; enq. at *S.I.* in Aubusson, ☎ 55.66.32.12. For porcelain and enamel workshops, info at Limoges *S.I.* or *C.D.T.* **Corrèze :** for a tour of dams, enq. at *C.D.T.*

Handicraft courses : Creuse : weaving, enq. : *L.A.* **Corrèze :** pottery, lace-making, wood-carving, info at *C.D.T.* and *L.A.* **Haute-Vienne :** painting on porcelain, enamel-work, pottery and crafting of stringed instruments *(lutherie).* Enq. at *C.D.T.*

Other courses : weekend courses in regional cooking for beginners, weekend courses in *cuisine du terroir* (preparation of *foie gras, conserves d'oie),* etc. : enrollments at the *C.D.T.* **Corrèze** and *L.A.* **Creuse.**

Children : Numerous gîtes for children, proposing specific activities (walks, cycling, etc.). Info at *L.A.* Other enq. at the *relais départ. des gîtes ruraux. Fishing course, enq. at L.A.* **Creuse.**

Aquatic sports : enq. at *C.D.T.* for a list of available water areas and numerous possibilities for aquatic sports.

Canoeing : centres in Anzème, Aubusson, Vassivière-en-Limousin, Guéret, Argentat-sur-Dordogne, Beaulieu-sur-Dordogne, Brivezac, Marcillac-la-Croisille, Saint-Priest-de-Gimel, Tulle, Uzerche, Bufat, Servières-le-Château,

1. The Dordogne gorges

2. Vassivière lake

Voutezac. Enq. at the *C.D.T.; Kayak-club Marchois*, ☎ 53.52.74.77.

Golf : Aubazine (9 holes), Neuvic (18 holes), Limoges (18 holes).

Cross-country skiing : at Bonnefond, Saint-Setiers. Info on outings at the *C.D.T.* Corrèze. **Creuse :** Pigerolles, enq. : *S.I.M.I.V.A.*, ☎ 55.69.20.45.

Hunting and shooting : enq. at the *Féd. dép. des chasseurs : * **Corrèze :** 1, av. W.-Churchill, 19000 Tulle, ☎ 55.20.08.85. **Creuse :** av. Sénatorie, 23000 Guéret,

☎ 55.52.17.31. **Haute-Vienne :** 43, rue St-Paul, 87000 Limoges, ☎ 55.79.12.62.

Fishing : the region abounds in pure, rapid rivers and streams. Enq. at the *Féd. dép. des A.P.P. :* **Corrèze :** 12, quai de Rigny, 19000 Tulle, ☎ 55.26.11.55. **Creuse :** *Maison de La Pêche*, 60 *bis*, av. L.-Laroche, 23000 Guéret, ☎ 55.52.24.70. **Haute-Vienne :** 7, rue Banc-Léger, 87000 Limoges, ☎ 55.34.35.89. Fly fishing : enq. and bookings at the *S.L.A.* Creuse, Corrèze and Haute-Vienne.

Towns and places

ARGENTAT*

Tulle 30, Aurillac 54, Paris 513 km
pop 3424 ⊠ 19400　　　　　　　　　　　　　　**B3**

The old stone bridge crossing the Dordogne has a view over this ancient town which would delight any painter : the ragged lines of low, wooden-porched houses along the quay, the circle of pointed stone or slate roofs, studded with windows, turrets and pepper-pot towers.

▶ 500 m E and 500 m S, the Raz and Bac châteaux (dove-cote and chapel) are beautiful examples of Limousin architecture. ▶ SW, the **puy du Tour** (408 m) offers an exciting panorama.

Nearby

▶ 4.5 km SW : see the murals in the church at **Monceaux★**. ▶ The church in **Saint-Chamant** *(6 km NW)* has a 15thC wooden-galleried bell tower and a Romanesque doorway ; from here, continue to the waterfalls at Murel, to **Albussac** (11thC church) and to the **Roche de Vic★** (636 m peak ; panorama ★).

Round the Dordogne and Maronne Gorges★★★ *(60 km ; approx 2hr30 ; see map 1)*

▶ **Argentat.** ▶ Enjoyable drive along the left bank of the Dordogne, reflecting the 14thC **château de Gibanel** ; farther on, see the wall belfry of the Romanesque church at **Glény.** ▶ The 85 m high dam at **Chastang** turns the Dordogne into a lake 30 km long ; panorama★ from the viewing area close by. ▶ **Servières-le-Château** is a former stronghold with stone-roofed houses nicely set over the gorges of the Glane. ▶ **Saint-Privat :** 13th-16thC church with broad square tower. ▶ From Saint-Julien-aux-Bois,

drive down to **Saint-Cirgues-la-Loutre** ; you come out high above the **Maronne gorges★.** ▶ The **Tours de Merle★** (11th-18thC) were once a fortress in joint ownership ; hence the two keeps! *(Jun.-Sep., 10-1 & 2-7; son et lumière show Jun.-mid-Sep.).*　　　　　　　　□

Practical Information

ⓘ av. Pasteur, ☎ 55.28.10.91 (l.s.) ; ☎ 55.28.16.05 (h.s.).

Hotels :

★★ **Gilbert** (L.F.), av. J.-Vachal, ☎ 55.28.01.62, AE DC Euro Visa, 30 rm Ⓟ ⚏ ⚲ 🛁 half pens (h.s.), closed 1 Dec-1 Mar, 320. Rest. ● ◆◆ closed Sat (l.s.), Generous, varied and tasty, 60-130 ; child : 30.

★ **Fouillade**, 11, pl. Gambetta, ☎ 55.28.10.17, 30 rm Ⓟ ⚏ closed 4 Nov-5 Dec, 140. Rest. ◆ closed Mon (15 Oct-15 May ex school hols). Country setting and pleasant service. Auvergnal home-style cooking, 50-140.

⚠ ★★*Le Longour* (60 pl), ☎ 55.28.13.84.

Recommended

Events : fair, 1st and 3rd Thu of the month.
Farmhouse-gîte : *Moulin Bas*, ☎ 55.28.00.25, fishing.

AUBUSSON

Guéret 42, Clermont-Ferrand 93, Paris 382 km
pop 6153 ⊠ 23200　　　　　　　　　　　　　　**B1**

Famous for its tapestry workshops since the 16thC. Tapestry is everywhere : galleries, exhibitions, workshops, and street names.

▶ On the left bank, visit the **École Nationale d'Art Décoratif** *(Jul.-Sep., 9-12 & 2-5 ex Sat. pm, Sun. and nat. hols.)*, and the **tapestry museum** (Centre Culturel et Artistique Jean Lurçat ; *daily ex Tue. am*). ▶ On the right bank, see the **Maison des Vallenet** (16thC mansion), the **Hôtel de Ville** (exhibitions in summer) and near by, the **Maison du Vieux Tapissier★** (16thC ; old tapestry workshop ; local history ; *15 Jun.-10 Sep., 9:30-12 & 2-6:30*). ▶ From the church (large 1770 tapestry), climb up to the château ruins (panorama★).

Nearby

▶ **Felletin** *(11 km S) :* bell tower★ (1451) on the 12th-15thC church of Le Moutier ; Flamboyant doorway. This town has always been the rival of Aubusson : several workshops, exhibitions *(Jul.-15 Sep.)* in the former church of Notre-Dame du Château (15thC, wooden shingled bell tower) ; 12thC lantern of the dead in the cemetery ; handsome medieval bridge and old houses. ▶ **Saint-Maixant :** 12thC church and 14thC castle, roofed with chestnut shingles ; beautiful park. ▶ Near **Saint-Michel-de-Veisse** *(10 km W)*, the Borne Chapel (early 16thC), has a lovely stained-glass window (1552, The Tree of Jesse) and a 17thC tapestry. 8 km SW from here, near **Vallière** (13th-15thC church) is the château Villeneuve (16th-18thC). ▶ Below Aubusson, a trip could be made along the **Creuse Valley★** : part-Romanesque churches in

1. The Dordogne gorges

Aileyrat (12thC), **La Rochette** (12th-15thC) and, off to one side, **Saint-Médard** (11thC, fortified 14thC). □

Tapestries

Although Aubusson tapestries have never been as exquisite as those of the Netherlands, the industry has flourished here since the 16thC, and was probably established as early as the 14thC. During the reign of Louis XIV (17thC), the workshops at Aubusson were elevated to the status of Manufactures Royales (Royal workshops). The abundant output of the 17th and 18thC led to a loss of originality. Designs were frequently copied from paintings and repetition of the same designs brought a decline in creativity. In the '30s, Madame Cuttoli commissioned Aubusson tapestries based on contemporary paintings. In 1937, Jean Lurçat reduced the number of colours in use and created original designs better adapted to weaving techniques. He has been followed by Gromaire, Picart le Doux, Saint-Saëns, Dom Robert and many others who have contributed to the revival of what is now a contemporary form of artistic expression.

Practical Information

ℹ rue Vieille, ☎ 55.66.32.12 (h.s.).
SNCF ☎ 55.66.13.28.
🚌 av. des Lissiers, ☎ 55.66.20.32.

Hotels :
★★ **La Seiglière** (L.F.), vallée du Léonardet, ☎ 55.66.37.22, Tx 790073, Visa, 42 rm 🅿 🍴 🐕 ♪ ⛄ 🏊 🎾 half pens (h.s.), closed 1 Dec-1 Mar. Private pond, 380. Rest. ♦♦ 🍴 ♪ ⛄ 80-180.
★★ **Le France** (L.F.), 6, rue des Déportés, ☎ 55.66.10.22, AE DC Euro Visa, 23 rm 🅿 half pens (h.s.), closed Sun eve and Mon (l.s.) ex Easter, 390. Rest. ♦♦ ♪ Traditional local specialities, 75-120.
🅰 ★★★*La Croix Blanche* (95 pl), ☎ 55.66.18.00.

Recommended
Events : *sausage and fondue festival*, every two years, beginning of Sept.
♥ pastry : *La Noisetine*, 11, rue Franche, ☎ 55.66.18.21, spec : *noisette aubussonnaise*.

BEAULIEU-SUR-DORDOGNE*

Tulle 40, Aurillac 65, Paris 523 km
pop 1603 ⊠ 19120 B3

On the edge of one of the most beautiful rivers in France, this little city has a famous 12thC **abbey church**, a fine example of Limousin Romanesque art.

▶ The impact of the carved tympanum★★ over the main doorway (a Last Judgement, reminiscent of the one at Moissac) tends to distract from the church itself. The nave has large side-aisles with galleries like those in the Auvergne region ; see the ambulatory and radiating chapels ; don't miss the treasure room★ (12thC Virgin in silvered wood, 10thC reliquary, enameled 13thC shrine). ▶ Charming old houses around the church, including one from the Renaissance. ▶ By the Dordogne, there is a picturesque chapel with 12thC wall-belfry.

Nearby
▶ **Queyssac-les-Vignes** *(9 km WSW)* : fine view of the Dordogne from the tower of an ancient château. From here, proceed to **Curemonte** (12thC church with 16thC cross outside, massive castle with keep and square towers), on a spur above the Sourdoire ; on to **Puy d'Arnac** (panorama★ from the church terrace). ▶ To the E is **Reygade** *(13 km, D41)* : 15thC Burial of Christ★

in polychrome stone (cemetery chapel) ; 8 km farther on : **Mercœur**, with an old Gothic church roofed with stone tiles. From here you can reach **Argentat** by **La Chapelle-Saint-Géraud** (part-Romanesque church) and come back on the right bank of the Dordogne. □

Practical Information

ℹ pl. Marbot, ☎ 55.91.09.94. ♥

Hotels :
★★★ *Le Turenne*, 1, bd St-Rodolphe, ☎ 55.91.10.16, AE DC Euro Visa, 21 rm ⚿ closed 30 Sep-10 May, 155. Rest. ♦ ⛄ 70.
★★ *Central Hôtel Fournié* (L.F.), 4, pl. du Champ-de-Mars, ☎ 55.91.01.34, 32 rm 🅿 ⚿ ⛄ pens (h.s.), closed 15 Nov-15 Mar, 380. Rest. ● ♦♦ ⛄ Located in a large provincial house : *grilled pork, confit de lapin aux girolles*, 70-150.

BELLAC

Limoges 41, Guéret 74, Paris 360 km
pop 5465 ⊠ 87300 A1

On the edge of the Limousin and Poitou regions, the tall granite houses of Bellac give the town an austere look, its quiet narrow streets overlooking the steep banks of the Vincou.

▶ The birthplace of playwright Jean Giraudoux (1882-1944) now houses a cultural centre, and the Hôtel de Ville is in a small château flanked by corbelled turrets. ▶ Pretty view from the **church terrace** (two naves, one Romanesque, the other Gothic) ; 12thC shrine★ in worked copper with champlevé enamels.

Circuit on the edge of Limousin and Poitou regions *(65 km ; 1/2 day)* ▶ Bellac. ▶ Take the D675 N. ▶ **Le Dorat**★ has a remarkable 12thC Romanesque church★★ with 60m octagonal bell tower. The interior is surprisingly high and the choir full of light. 11thC crypt ; treasure room. Remains of 15thC ramparts and machicolated gateway *(son et lumière show in Aug, res. S.I.)* ; 5 km NW is **Oradour-Saint-Genest** with its lantern of the dead ; not far away in a romantic setting is the fortified mill of Riveillerie. ▶ At **Magnac-Laval** the 12thC restored church houses the relics of Saint-Maximin. They are carried in a procession 50 km long on Pentecost Monday. Also visit there the hospital's chapel and park, remodeled into a lapidary museum. ▶ **Châteauponsac** *(21 km E)* has a 15thC gateway and a church (12th-15thC) with a choir opening on the side-aisles through elegant arches★ ; local history museum in former 15thC priory ; attractive old-fashioned houses ; view★ over the city from the bridge (1609). ▶ There is a Romanesque church (12th-13thC, fortified 14thC) and lantern of the dead (12thC) in **Rancon**, as well as a small archaeological collection at the town hall.

Monts de Blond *(10 km S)*
▶ On the border between upper Limousin and the Poitou region lies this small mountain range of 500 m. It offers a number of beautiful views. ▶ At **Blond** can be seen a Romanesque church fortified in the 16thC. ▶ **Mortemart**, with its timbered marketplace and old freestone houses, château ruins, old convents and church featuring 15thC pews, is an attractive stopover. □

Practical Information

ℹ 1 bis, rue Jouvet, ☎ 55.68.12.79. ♥
SNCF ☎ 55.68.00.07.

Hotels :
★★ *Les Châtaigniers*, rte de Poitiers, 3 km W, ☎ 55.68.14.82, Euro Visa, 27 rm 🅿 ⚿ ⬜ closed Fri eve and Sun eve, Sat (l.s.), Nov, 250. Rest. ♦ 70-200.
★ *Central* (L.F.), 7, av. Denfert-Rochereau, ☎ 55.68.00.34,, 15 rm 🅿 closed Sun eve and Mon, 15 Sep-10 Oct. Rest. ♦

⛺ ★★*Les Rochettes* (100 pl), ☎ 55.68.13.27.

Recommended

Tables d'hôtes : at Blanzac, *Rouffignac*, ☎ 55.68.03.38; at Blond, *la Plaine*, ☎ 55.68.82.57; at Cieux, CP 87520, *Les Hauts de Boscartus*, ☎ 55.03.30.63; at Peyrat de Bellac, CP 87520, *Montmartre*, ☎ 55.68.14.37.

BORT-LES-ORGUES***

Tulle 71, Aurillac 86, Paris 470 km
pop 4950 ✉ 19110 B2

At the border of Limousin and Auvergne, once renowned for its tanneries. Now a popular holiday resort in superb surroundings.

▶ 12th-14thC church, formerly fortified. ▶ The famous **Orgues★** can be reached from the hamlet of Chantéry *(2.5 km SW)*; they are enormous phonolithic columns 8-10 m in diameter and 80-97 m high, separated by fissures created when the prehistoric lava cooled. The plateau at the top (alt. 769 m) can be reached by car (view★). ▶ N of the town is the **Bort Dam★,** 120 m high, forming an 18-km lake on the Dordogne (boating); by the lake, see the five round towers of the **château de Val★** (15thC; *9-12 & 2-6; closed 2 Nov.-15 Dec. and Tue.*).

Dordogne Gorges, from Bort to the Barrage de l'Aigle *(83 km; approx 3hr)*

▶ Leave Bort by the Meymac road, which runs close to the château de Pierrefitte (15thC), and fork left towards the site★ of **Saint-Nazaire** *(1/4hr on foot)*, a promontory above the junction of the Dordogne and the Diège; a long detour is subsequently necessary to get round the gorge. ▶ Near **Liginiac** (12thC ironwork on the church door) go to see the **Marèges Dam★** before moving on to the one at Neuvic-d'Ussel. ▶ At **Neuvic-d'Ussel,** 12th-15thC church, remains of fortifications, Henri Queuille Museum (dedicated to this famous radical thinker and to the Resistance; ethnography collection). ▶ Small Romanesque church in **Sérandon;** here join the **Route Touristique des Ajustants★,** running down into the gorge of the Dordogne and along the right bank. ▶ After **Saint-Projet** (site★, suspended **bridge** between two little tunnels), the Labion Gorge leads on to Mauriac. ▶ At La Besse, D105 *(on the left)* runs back to the Dordogne at the **Barrage de l'Aigle★** (dam, 90 m high). ▶ Return to Bort via Mauriac (→ Auvergne). □

Practical Information

ℹ pl. Marmontel, ☎ 55.96.02.49.
SNCF ☎ 55.96.71.19.

Hotel :

★★ ***Central*** (L.F.), 65, av. de la Gare, ☎ 55.96.74.82, Tx 580106, Euro Visa, 25 rm Ⓟ closed Sun eve and Mon (l.s.), 10 Jan-10 Mar, 185. Rest. ♦ ♪ A friendly reception and enjoyable food at moderate prices (reserve), 75-160.

⛺ ★★★*Aubazines* (55 pl), ☎ 55.96.00.29; ★★*Beau Soleil* (200 pl), ☎ 55.96.00.31.

Recommended

Bicycle-rental : *M. Combe*, 82, av. Gambetta, ☎ 55.96.02.83, from Jun to Sep.
Events : *fair*, the 2nd and 4th Tue of each month, Wed of Holy Week, Sat before Holy Cross Sun.

BOURGANEUF

Guéret 33, Limoges 49, Paris 387 km
pop 4030 ✉ 23400 B1

The Tour Zizim (named after an Ottoman prince detained there) is one of the three towers of a former Hospitallers' castle (15thC); superb timber-work★; small museum *(daily 15 Jul.-1 Sep.; Sun. and nat. hols. Apr.-Jul.)*; 12th-15thC church; at the Hôtel de Ville, 18thC Aubusson tapestry★ *(closed Sat., Sun. and national hols.)*; another small museum in the Chapelle de l'Arrier (17thC).

Nearby

▶ At **Pontarion** *(10 km NE)*, a lovely 15thC château; to the S, on Martinèche hill (574 m high) can be seen enormous, strangely-shaped boulders, one of which is known as Roche-aux-neuf-gradins. □

Practical Information

BOURGANEUF
ℹ à la mairie, ☎ 55.64.07.61.
SNCF ☎ 55.64.00.04.
🚌 ☎ 55.64.00.27.

Hotel :

★★ ***Commerce*** (L.F.), 12, rue de Verdun, ☎ 55.64.14.55, 16 rm ♪ closed Sun eve and Mon ex hols and h.s., 22 Dec-15 Feb. Rest. ♦ ♪ Standard family cuisine, 55-130.

Recommended

♥ pastry : *Lenoir*, 21, rue Zizim, ☎ 55.64.06.82, spec : *pâté de champignons creusois*.

Nearby

SAINT-GEORGES-LA-POUGE, ✉ 23250 Pontarion, 12 km E of **Pontarion**.

Hotel :

● ★ ***Domaine des Mouillères***, ☎ 55.66.60.64, AE, 7 rm Ⓟ ⚘ ⚘ ♨ ♿ closed 1 Oct-1 Apr, 200. Rest. ♦ ⚘ ♪ ♿ A warm and cosy old residence in wooded farmland. The savoury, if not overly original cuisine is for guests only, 90.

SAINT-MOREIL, ✉ 23400 Bourganeuf, 13 km SW on the D941-D22.

Hotel :

● ★★ ***Moulin de Montalétang***, (R.S., L.F.), ☎ 55.54.92.72, Euro Visa, 14 rm Ⓟ ⚘ ⚘ ♨ ♿ closed 30 Oct-15 Mar, 200. Rest. ♦♦ ⚘ ♿ ⚘ Agreeably situated in a former flour mill, 85-150.

BOUSSAC

Montluçon 34, Guéret 41, Paris 337 km
pop 1868 ✉ 23600 B1

The 15th-16thC **château★** stands above the confluence of the Petite Creuse and Béroux rivers, a long tall building with brown roofs flanked by towers. Writer George Sand found it "charmingly simple".

▶ Large medieval rooms and small 18thC apartments, displaying ancient tapestries; every year there is an exhibition of the work of a contemporary artist *(daily 9-12 & 2-7;* good view of the castle from the bridge over the Petite Creuse). ▶ Remains of ramparts and old turretted houses. ▶ In **Boussac-Bourg,** two Romanesque churches; Notre-Dame has kept some of its 12thC frescos.

Nearby

▶ 5 km S, at the top of a hill (595 m high; view★) the rocky outcrops★ of **Pierres Jaumâtres;** 5 km farther on, **Toulx-Sainte-Croix** is well situated on a hill for a panoramic view from one of its towers *(entrance fee)*; also a small Romanesque church now separate from its massive, shingled bell tower contains sarcophagus and relics from the past. ▶ **Lavaufranche** *(6 km SE)* : former commandery★, first belonging to the Templars, then to the Hospitaliers. 12thC keep, 12th-13thC chapel (remains of frescos), 15thC castle and outbuildings (Musée d'Arts et Traditions Populaires - folk art museum; tapestries; *2-6, daily Jul.-Aug.; Sun. only : May, Jun., Sep., Oct.*). □

Practical Information

ℹ château, ☎ 55.65.07.62.
SNCF ☎ 55.65.00.97.

Hotels :

★ **Bœuf Couronné** (L.F.), pl. de l'Hôtel-de-ville, ☎ 55.65.15.92, DC Visa, 11 rm ℗ ░ ⌕ closed Mon, 10 Jan-1 Feb, 130. Rest. ♦ 40-120.

Relais Creusois, rte de la Châtre, ☎ 55.65.02.20, Visa, 4 rm ≮ ⌕ closed in winter, 90. Rest. ♦ ≮ ♪ closed Tue eve and Wed (l.s.). Spec : *nage de turbot à la badiane et à l'orange, pigeonneau du prieuré à l'ail*, 80-200.

Recommended
♥ pastry : *Aux Délices*, rue Martin-Nadau, ☎ 55.65.02.05.

BRIVE-LA-GAILLARDE

Tulle 29, Limoges 96, Paris 493 km
pop 54032 ⊠ 19100   A2-3

There is a southern feel to the market in Brive, with its piles of fruit and vegetables grown in this fertile valley. Because it is so near Périgord, you also find truffles, *cèpes* (mushrooms), *foie gras* and other temptations.

▶ The much-restored 12th-14thC **church** lies in the heart of the old town (see the treasure-room). The streets radiate out to the shady boulevard following the lines of the former ramparts ; S of the church, charming 15th-16thC turreted houses. ▶ A 16thC mansion is now the **Ernest-Rupin Museum** (regional history and art ; *10-12 & 2-5 or 6, closed Sun. and nat. hols.*). Close by, the charming Renaissance **Hôtel de Labenche**★ (courtyard). In Rue Charles Teyssier, 13th-15thC houses. The Town Hall is now installed in the 17thC buildings★ of a former religious and political movement known as the Doctrinaires. **Edmond-Michelet Museum** (Rue Champanatier ; *10-12 & 2-6, closed Sun.* ; WWII Resistance and Deportation).

Nearby

▶ **Valley of the Corrèze**★ : pretty route to Tulle *(29 km)* ; detour via **Aubazine** to see the Cistercian abbey church★★ (12thC ; inside, 12thC stained-glass, beautiful 12thC decorated oak cupboard with arcatures ; 13thC Gothic tomb of St. Etienne★★) ; in the abbey buildings (16th-18thC), Romanesque chapter *(1 Jun.-15 Sep., pm daily, ex Mon. 2-5:30 ; off-season, Sat., Sun. pm).* From here, go up the Puy de Pauliac (alt. 520 m ; panorama★ ; *drive, then 10 min on foot*). ▶ **Vézère Gorges** and the peak of **Puy d'Yssandon** *(NW ; 75 km ; approx 2hr30)* : drive first to **Donzenac**, a picturesque country town on the banks of the Maumont ; turreted houses. In **Alassac**, see the impressive bell tower keep of the 12thC church. A Gothic bridge crosses the Vézère where it leaves the Gorges, between the château de Lasteyrie (19thC, left bank) and the **château du Saillant**. From **Objat**, N to **Saint-Bonnet-la-Rivière** (circular Romanesque church copied from the Holy Sepulchre in Jerusalem) reach **Saint-Robert**, to the SE ; (fine Romanesque choir in the church) and continue to the **Puy d'Yssandon** (355 m peak ; château ruins). □

Practical Information _____

BRIVE-LA-GAILLARDE
ℹ pl. du 14-Juillet, ☎ 55.24.08.80.
✈ *Laroche*, 5 km W, ☎ 55.87.32.94.
ﲓ ☎ 55.23.50.50.
🚌 10, av. du Mal-Leclerc, ☎ 55.24.29.93.

Car rental : Avis, 56, av. J.-Jaurès, ☎ 55.87.02.23 ; 19, av. P.-Sémard, ☎ 55.87.15.02.

Hotels :
★★★ **Chapon Fin**, 1, pl. de Lattre-de-Tassigny, ☎ 55.74.23.40, Tx 580645, AE DC Euro Visa, 30 rm ℗ ░ ♪ ﳝ 200. Rest. ♦♦ ♪ 70-120.
★★★ **Le Quercy**, 8 bis, quai Tourny, ☎ 55.74.09.26, AE DC Euro Visa, 80 rm ℗ & ⅌ closed 18 Dec-14 Jan, 160.
● ★★ **La Crémaillère** (L.F.), 53, av. de Paris, ☎ 55.74.32.47, AE Visa, 10 rm ⅌ closed Mon eve and Sun eve, 15 Jan-15 Feb, 160. Rest. ● ♦♦♦ ⅌ closed Sun eve. At the market in Brive-la-Gaillarde and in the region at large "Charlou" Reynal is known as a careful

buyer of quality produce. The citizens of Brive approve of his frank, hearty cooking, as solid as the local rugby team, yet as light as the ball they toss about. Dear readers, seek out this straightforward cook who is also a member of our culinary judging panel. Whether indoors or on the little patio in summer, you'll enjoy his seasonal specialities : *salade de haricots verts et girolles, œufs aux truffes, cèpes, choux farci, gaspacho à la coriandre, confit, foie gras*. Good wines, 60-200.
★★ **Urbis**, 32, rue Marcellin-Roche, ☎ 55.74.34.70, Tx 590195, Visa, 55 rm ℗ ≮ ⌕ 210.

Restaurant :
● ♦♦ **La Belle Epoque**, 27, av. J.-Jaurès (A3), ☎ 55.74.08.75, Euro Visa ♪ closed Tue, 1-15 Feb, 1-8 Sep. Everything here sparkles, just like the luminously fresh fish cooked with a light hand by Thierry Charonnet, 100-250.

⚘ ★★**des Iles** (93 pl), ☎ 55.24.34.75.

Recommended
Bicycle-rental : M. *Vergne*, 30, av. de Paris, ☎ 55.24.08.51.
Events : *secondhand sale*, rue Cap.-Gallinat, 1st and 3rd Tue of each month (am).
Youth hostel : 56, av. Mal-Bugeaud, ☎ 55.24.34.00.
♥ Auction house : M. *Galatry*, rue Gambetta ; liqueurs, mustards : *Epicerie Denoix*, 9, bd du Mal-Lyautey, ☎ 55.74.34.27 ; mushrooms : *Monteil et fils*, Z.I. Cana Est, ☎ 55.88.00.73 ; pork products : *Jardel*, av. E.-Zola.

Nearby

AUBAZINE, ⊠ 19190 Beynat, 15 km E.
ﲓ ☎ 55.25.70.07.

Hotels :
★ **Le Saut de la Bergère** (L.F.), ☎ 55.25.74.09, 10 rm ℗ ≮ ░ ⌕ 105. Rest. ♦ ≮ ♪ 60-75 ; child : 35.
★ **Tour**, ☎ 55.25.71.17, Visa, 24 rm ℗ ⌕ closed Sun eve and Mon lunch, 26 Jan-23 Feb, 135. Rest. ♦ 65-140.

⚘ ★★★*Centre de tourisme du Coiroux* (143 pl), ☎ 55.27.21.96.

OBJAT, ⊠ 19130, 20 km NW.

Hotel :
Pré Fleuri, ☎ 55.25.83.92, 7 rm ℗ ░ ⅊ closed Mon, 10-25 Jan, 110. Rest. ● ♦♦ A pleasant little outpost of regional cuisine : *tourin à l'ail, soupe aux truffes, fricassée de cèpes*, 130-220.

USSAC, ⊠ 19270 Donzenac, 5 km N on the N20 ; D57.

Hotel :
★★ **Auberge Saint-Jean** (L.F.), ☎ 55.88.30.20, 13 rm ⌕ half pens, 320. Rest. ♦ ♪ closed Fri eve, 50-150 ; child : 35.

VARETZ, ⊠ 19240 Allassac, 10 km NW on the D152.

Hotel :
● ★★★★ **Castel Novel** (R.C.), ☎ 55.85.00.01, Tx 590065, AE DC Euro Visa, 38 rm ℗ ≮ ░ ⌕ ﳝ ⅂ ✓ closed 30 Oct-1 May, 570. Rest. ● ♦♦♦ ≮ Time cannot lessen the charm of this fine Castel, so dear to the heart of the writer Colette, who shares her centennial wih the handsome old oaks in this park. Christine and Albert Parveaux assure your comfort, while Jean-Pierre Faucher draws on local gastronomic riches to dazzle your appetite : *œuf poché au jus de truffe, quasi de veau au miel et carottes braisées marrons de Corrèze : glace et mousse*. Cahors, Bergerac, Pécharmant, 165-280.

CHÂLUS

Limoges 36, Angoulême 77, Paris 432 km
pop 2094 ⊠ 87230   A2

The hills around Châlus are still frequented by *feuillardiers*, the men who prepare the chestnut slats used in barrel-making (these barrels give Cognac its amber colour). The wood is also used for furniture manufacture.

▶ Châlus is built around a sloping square and a circular 13thC keep. Across the Tardoire river there is an older **keep**, the remains of the **château de Châlus-Chabrol** where Richard the Lion-Hearted was mortally wounded in 1199. ▶ Close by is the **Musée des Feuillardiers**, a museum in a 13thC building *(15-30 Jun., 1-15 Sep., Sun. and nat. hols; Jul.-Aug. daily 10-12 & 2-6)*.

Nearby

▶ **Les Cars** *(8.5 km E, D15)* is a small village surrounded by château ruins, which give it a warlike aspect. **Lastours**, 6.5 km SE, is also dominated by ruins. ▶ 6.5 km SW will lead you to the Romanesque church (cornice★) of **Dournazac**; 4 km more on the Nontron route and you will discover the "Sleeping Beauty" quality of the Lamberty château (16th-19thC). ▶ There is a magnificent 12th-14thC fortress★ at **Montbrun** *(daily 9-12 & 2-5 or 7)*. ▶ The summit of **Puyconnieux** (496 m high) holds a panoramic view of the region. ▶ The **château de Brie**★ (16thC; *Apr.-Sep., Sun. and nat. hols. 2-4*) has a fine collection of Louis XVI furniture. ☐

COLLONGES-LA-ROUGE**

Brive 21, Tulle 45, Paris 513 km
pop 379 ☒ 19500 Meyssac   B3
No electricity cables, no telegraph poles and no cars *(Jun.-15 Sep.)*; 15th-17thC houses built in red sandstone (hence the name); manors, towers, pepper-pot chimneys, corbeled turrets, the town gate, a charming covered market with a communal oven, and roofs of slate or stone; all these features make Collonges-la-Rouge the prettiest village in Limousin.

▶ 11th-15thC **church** with tympanum showing the Ascension. Next to it is the **chapel of the penitents** (exhibitions).

Round the Corrèze Plateau *(50-70 km; approx 2hr30)*

▶ **Collonges**. ▶ Drive to **Meyssac**, another town in red sandstone, full of old houses : 12thC church; pottery workshop. ▶ The handsome Romanesque doorway★ of the church in **Saillac** is protected by a narthex. ▶ **Turenne**★ is built entirely in white limestone; until the 18thC, it was an independent Limousin Vicomté; numerous 15th and 16thC houses and a huge church (end of 16thC) on the slopes of the hill below the castle ruins★ (14thC square tower, 13thC round tower; *daily 9-12 & 2-7, Mar.-15 Nov.; Sun. 2-5, 16 Nov.-Feb.)*; 1 km S : château de Linoir (15thC); 5 km N : exhibition of contemporary ceramics in the outbuildings of the **château de Lacoste** (13th-15thC; *daily, pm)*. ▶ On the road to Noailles, **Grotte de La Fage** (cave; *school holidays : 10-7 daily)*. ▶ At **Noailles**, 15th-18thC château, home of a famous French family, next to a Romanesque-Gothic church (12th-13thC); 1 km N, a valley hides the **grottes de Lamoureux**, caves dug into soft sandstone ages ago; inhabited in the Middle Ages, they are now considered significant troglodyte villages. ▶ To get to Brive (→), loop by **Lissac** and lovely Causse Lake.

Practical Information _____

Hotel :
★★ **Relais de Saint-Jacques de Compostelle**, ☎ 55.25.41.02, AE Euro Visa, 12 rm 🅿 ⌖ ⋙ ⌕ closed Tue eve and Wed, 1 Dec-1 Feb, 190. Rest. ♦ ⌖ ♪ A terrace garden is the setting for J.-P. Castera's heartfelt cuisine, 65-120; child : 40.

For the translation of a name of a meat, a fish or a vegetable, for the composition of a dish or a sauce, see the Menu Guide in the Practical Holiday Guide; it lists the most common culinary terms.

ÉVAUX-LES-BAINS

Montluçon 25, Guéret 52, Paris 345 km
pop 1906 ☒ 23110   B1
This little spa on a granite plateau is a good base for exploring the upper valleys of the Cher and the Tardes. 11th-13thC gate-tower on the church.

Nearby

▶ **Viaduc de Tardes**★ *(2 km NW)*, built 92 m above the river by Eiffel in 1884. ▶ Further upstream, **Chambon-sur-Voueize** has one of the most beautiful Romanesque churches★ in the Limousin (11th-12thC, stalls, enclosures and woodwork from the 17thC; reliquary bust★ of Saint Valérie, 15thC); medieval hump-backed bridge; N of the city are the Voueize Gorges towered over by the ruins of a château which supposedly belonged to Bluebeard. ▶ 15.5 km N, the **Rochebut Dam** on the River Cher. ▶ 17 km S is the commercial center of **Auzances**. It features a large market *(Tue.)*, Romanesque and Gothic church decorated with contemporary frescoes by N. Greschny, a 17thC turreted house on the square, and a small archaeological museum in the Sainte-Marguerite chapel (17thC). ▶ 10 km SE of Auzances, follow attractive well-marked paths in the **Drouille Forest**; 15 km SW near the Aubusson route is the church of **Lupersat** and its unusual cornices; at **Rougnat** *(3 km N of Auzances)* can be seen elegant woodwork and Italian paintings from the 18thC. ☐

Practical Information _____

ÉVAUX-LES-BAINS
⚓ (1 Apr-21 Oct), ☎ 55.65.51.77.
ⓘ pl. de l'Eglise, ☎ 55.65.50.90.
SNCF ☎ 55.65.51.38.

Hotels :
★★ **Grand Hôtel Thermal** (L.F.), ☎ 55.65.50.01, 77 rm 🅿 ⋙ ⌕ ⊡ ⌁ closed 20 Oct-31 Mar, 160. Rest. ♦ ⌖ 🏊 50-145.
★ **Chardonnet** (L.F.), 18, rue de l'Hôtel-de-Ville, ☎ 55.65.51.78, Euro Visa, 28 rm 🅿 ⋙ ⌕ pens (h.s.), closed 1 Jan-15 Mar, 310. Rest. ♦ ⌖ ⌕ 🏊 50-70; child : 35.
⚐ ★*Ouche de Budelle* (40 pl), ☎ 55.65.50.20.

Nearby

CHAMBON-SUR-VOUEIZE, ☒ 23170 Evaux-les-Bains, 6 km W.

Hotel :
★★ **Les Estonneries** (L.F.), ☎ 55.82.14.66, DC Visa, 10 rm 🅿 ⌖ ⋙ ⌕ ♪ closed Mon, 22 Dec-28 Mar, 175. Rest. ♦ ⌖ ♪ ⌁ 🏊 155; child : 30.

Mont GARGAN

                                                             B2
From a 731 m high ridge between the Loire and Garonne basins can be seen a mixed panorama of woods and pastureland dotted with towns and farms.

Nearby

▶ From Saint-Vitte and **Curzac** (charming 15thC château) you can reach **Saint-Germain-les-Belles** : fortified church★ (1376) with a stairway leading to the rampart-walk; 6 km W of here, on the N20, are the stained-glass windows of the 15thC church of **Magnac-Bourg**. ☐

Practical Information _____

MAGNAC-BOURG, ☒ 87380 Saint-Germain-les-Belles, 30 km SE of **Limoges** on the N 20.

Hotels :
★★ **Auberge de l'Etang** (L.F.), ☎ 55.00.81.37, 15 rm 🅿 ⌕ closed Sun eve and Mon (l.s.), 10 Feb-10 Mar, 20-26 Oct,

150. Rest. ♦ ♪ closed Mon and Sun eve (l.s.). Spec : *foie d'oie frais au sauternes, confit de canard aux marrons*, 50-160.
★★ *Midi* (L.F.), ☎ 55.00.80.13, 13 rm P 🏨 half pens (h.s.), closed Mon (l.s.) and hols, 15 Jan-15 Feb, 15-30 Nov, 360. Rest. ♦ ♪ 65-160.

Restaurant :
♦♦ *Tison d'Or*, ☎ 55.71.84.78, AE DC Euro Visa, 10 rm, closed Tue and Sun eve (l.s.), 50-100.

⚠ ★★★*Les Ecureuils* (30 pl), ☎ 55.00.80.28.

GUÉRET

Châteauroux 89, Limoges 90, Paris 354 km
pop 16621 ⊠ 23000   B1

Close to the valley of the Creuse, bordered by wooded hills to the S. Capital of the Creuse Department.

▶ Next to the Prefecture is the **Hôtel des Moneyroux**★ (15th-16thC Gothic). ▶ Almost opposite, the Grande-Rue leads to the heart of **Old Guéret**; picturesque market in the Place Piquerelle *(Thu., Sat.)*. ▶ S of the town, in a public garden, is a former 18thC convent, enlarged in 1905 and now housing the **museum** *(10-12 & 2-5:30 or 6:30; closed Tue.)* : Limousin enamels★★, ceramics★ (including Chinese), tapestries, antiques, etc.

Nearby

▶ **Maupuy Summit** *(3 km SW; 685 m alt.; view★)*. ▶ **Chabrières Forest** *(3 km S)* has many marked paths winding among blocks of granite. ▶ **Sainte-Feyre** *(7 km SE)* : 18thC château; 2 km further : charming Romanesque church at **La Saunière**; 1 km from the village, **château du Théret** (15th-16thC) roofed with chestnut shingles; further on *(4 km)*, is the château de Beaumont (17th-18thC). From here, proceed through **Chaumeix** (regional house with reproduction of a 19thC interior; old tools). ▶ **Glenic** *(7.5 km NE)* has a small fortified church (11th-15thC, frescoes) perched above the Creuse River (threatened by dam improvements upstream); for a short while you can follow the valley▶ to go 12 km to **Bonnat** (fortified church) and **Malval** (granite Romanesque church and ruins), above the Petite Creuse (old mill). From here, go SE to **Bourg d'Hem** (view★ from the church square, 12thC), then to **Anzème** (another beautiful view★ on the Creuse) from where you can loop SW through **Saint-Vaury** (15thC bas-relief in the church and a walk to the Puy des Trois Cornes★) on the way back to Guéret, to Moutier d'Ahun (→).   ☐

Practical Information _____

ℹ av. Ch.-de-Gaulle, ☎ 55.52.14.29.
SNCF ☎ 55.52.50.50.
🚌 av. du Dr-Brézard, ☎ 55.52.46.44.

Hotels :
★★ *Auclair* (L.F.), 19, av. de la Sénatorerie, ☎ 55.52.01.26, AE DC Euro Visa, 33 rm P 🏨 ⚲ ♪ closed 15 Jan-15 Feb, 165. Rest. ♦♦ closed Mon noon and Sun eve, 55-165.
★★ *Le Moulin Noyé* (L.F.), Glénic, rte de Paris, 9 km, ☎ 55.52.09.11, Visa, 33 rm P 🏨 ⚲ ♪ 145. Rest. ♦ ⚱ ♪ 45-150.
★ *L'Univers*, 8, rue de l'Ancienne-Mairie, ☎ 55.52.02.03, Euro Visa, 7 rm ⚲ ≋ pens, closed Mon, 30 Jul-12 Aug, 190. Rest. ● ♦ closed Mon. Local fare, warm welcome, 45-100.

⚠ ★★★*Pommeil* (103 pl), ☎ 55.52.07.02.

Recommended
♥ pastry : *Villechalane-Sionneau*, 1, pl. Bonnyaud, ☎ 55.52.53.31, spec : *creusois*, chocolates, bread baked in a wood-fired oven.

┌───┐
│ Looking for a locality? Consult the index at the back │
│ of the book. │
└───┘

LIMOGES*

Poitiers 119, Bordeaux 220, Paris 396 km
pop 144082 ⊠ 87000   A1

Limoges, the capital of the French porcelain industry, is too little known. In addition to the attraction of the town itself, the surrounding countryside is delightful.

▶ Parking in the Place de la République (B2); two steps away is the **crypt of St. Martial**★ (4th-9thC), the only remains of a once-famous abbey *(Jul.-Sep. 9:30-12 & 2:30-6)*. ▶ Opposite **St. Pierre du Queyroix** (12th-16thC; handsome tower★; interesting statues) is a marvelous 1900 building entirely covered with porcelain tiling. ▶ Through the pedestrian Rue du Consulat (see the **Cour du Temple**★ at N°22, surrounded by 16thC half-timbered buildings), go to the Place des Bancs (market★), and up to the **Rue de la Boucherie**★ (B2-3). This is the heart of a picturesque district of half-timbered houses; at N°36, visit the **Maison Traditionnelle de la Boucherie** (17thC butcher's house and traditional shop). ▶ Through the Place de la Motte (note ceramic frieze under the cornice of the market building) to the Place d'Aine; behind the Palace of Justice is the beautiful **Jardin d'Orsay**★ (A2; *9-7* 18thC garden; remains of Roman arena). ▶ See the **Musée National Adrien Dubouché**★★ : splendid collection of Limousin, French, European and Asian ceramics (10000 pieces; *10-12 & 1:30-5, closed Tue.*). ▶ The bell tower★ of **St. Michel-des-Lions** (B2; 14th-16thC) is very elegant; N of the church, the **Place du Présidial** is lined with fine buildings (17th-18thC; half-timbered houses); see the **Maison Limousine de la Vie Populaire**. ▶ Overlooking the right bank of the Vienne river is the former episcopal town known as the Cité, with old houses grouped around the **cathedral**★ (C2; 12th-16thC, flanked by a bell tower copied by many other churches in the Limousin). Enter by the Flamboyant N doorway★; inside, 16thC stained glass, Renaissance choir-screen★, 14th and 16thC tombs. ▶ In the middle of the **Jardin de l'Evêché** (18thC bishop's garden, C3; *9-7*), is the **museum**, with its well-known collection of Limousin enamels★★ *(10-11:45 & 2-5:45, Jul.-Sep.; Oct.-Jun., 10-11:45-2:4:45, closed Tue. except Jul.-Sep.)*. ▶ From the chevet of the cathedral the **quartier de l'Abbessaille's** ancient houses slope down towards the Vienne and the 13thC **St. Etienne bridge**★ (C2-3).

Nearby

▶ **Limoges.** ▶ Follow the Périgueux route N21 for 6 km and turn left. ▶ **Solignac**★ : where St. Eloi founded an abbey in 632; Romanesque abbey church★★ (1143), in Périgord style with cupolas over the nave; fine 15thC stalls. ▶ At **Vigen**, 11th-12thC church. ▶ Torn down in 1593, the **château de Chalusset** (12th-13thC) is situated on a promontory overlooking the Briance *(20 min on foot)*. Lovely old houses are in the upper reaches of **Pierre-Buffière;** exhibition in the historical house on Rue Dupuytren. ▶ From here, return by way of **Saint-Hilaire-Bonneval, Eyjeaux** and **Feytiat** (13thC churches).

Round trip of the Ambazac mountains and the Taurion Valley *(133 km; full day)*

▶ From Limoges, follow the N20 N to **La Crouzille**, once well known for its uranium mines. **Compreignac** *(6 km W)* : 12th-15thC church★ is one of the most complete examples of Limousin fortified religious architecture. ▶ The **St. Sylvestre church** has two reliquaries★ (13th and 15thC) from the treasures of the neighbouring **Abbey of Grandmont**, which is now only a heap of ruins near two small lakes★ dug by the monks. ▶ Towards the NW, beyond **Razès**, the artificial **lake of Saint-Pardoux** *(15 km from Saint-Sylvestre)* has been made into a leisure centre. ▶ In **Saint-Léger-la-Montagne** *(7 km NE of Saint-Sylvestre)* : 12th-15thC church; 3 km S at the foot of the **Puy de Sauvagnac** (alt. 701 m; *1hr round trip on foot;* panorama★) is the hamlet of **Sauvagnac**, with a 12th-15thC church★ *(guided tours in summer)*. ▶ Further N, **Saint-Sulpice-Laurière** : 12th-13thC church built around an 11thC keep. ▶ At **Saint-Goussaud**, SE, there is a statue of the saint in

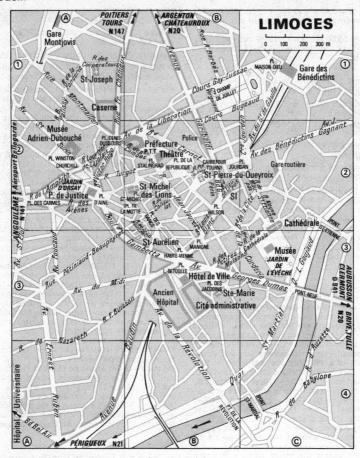

the village church; it is full of holes, as young unmarried villagers stick pins in the statue in the hope that their patron saint will help them find a partner; lantern of the dead; small archaeology and folklore museum; 1.5 km SE is the **Puy de Jouer** (697 m peak; panorama) on which is the smallest Roman theatre known. ▶ **Châtelux-le-Marcheix★** is built on a promontory above the Taurion river. ▶ 16thC frescos in the church (12th-16thC) of **Saint-Martin-Saint-Catherine**. ▶ After **Les Billanges** (precious metalwork in the church), cross the Taurion by the **Pont du Dognon** (bridge; site★), and again at **Saint-Martin-Terressus** (view★ over the gorges). ▶ **Ambazac**: 12th-15thC church with two more magnificent pieces from the treasure of the Abbey of Grandmont, a 12thC shrine★★ and a dalmatic (11thC). ▫

Practical Information _____

LIMOGES

ⓘ bd de Fleurus (B2), ☎ 55.34.46.87, closed Sun (l.s.).
✈ Limoges-Bellegarde, 10 km NW, ☎ 55.00.10.37.
🚄 (C1), ☎ 55.77.58.11/55.01.50.50.
🚌 9, rue Charles-Gide (C2), ☎ 55.34.47.77.
Car rental : Avis, 5, bd de Fleurus (B2), ☎ 55.33.36.37.

Hotels :
★★★ Richelieu, 40, av. Baudin (B3), ☎ 55.34.22.82, 27 rm
Ⓟ ▥ 170.
★★ Orléans Lion d'Or, (France-Accueil), 9-11, cours Jour-

Porcelain

This hard and translucent ceramic, made by the Chinese from the clay deposits of Kao Ling, was known and admired in Europe in the 16thC. The Italians, under the Medicis, and the French ceramicists of Rouen and Saint-Cloud, towards the end of 17thC succeeded in making an artificial "soft paste" porcelain. Finally, a kaolin deposit was discovered near Meissen and the secret was sold to the manufacturers of Sèvres in 1761. Exhaustive search led to the discovery of another deposit at Saint-Yrieix in 1765, when Turgot, Intendant (administrator) of Limousin, encouraged the further development of the French porcelain industry. The paste from which porcelain is made is a mixture of kaolin, quartz and feldspar, which is slowly dried and then given an initial firing at 950-980°C; this is the "biscuit". It is then covered with liquid enamel and refired at 1400°, to vitrify the paste. Finally, decoration is applied, and fired between 800-950°; these are the principal stages of a process involving some thirty operations.

dan (B2), ☎ 55.77.49.71, Tx 580011, AE DC Euro Visa, 42 rm, closed 21 Dec-6 Jan, 145.

Restaurants :
◆◆ *Cantaut*, 10, rue Rafilhoux (B2), ☎ 55.33.34.68, AE DC, closed Sun (Sep-Jun). Gourmet cooking. Spec : *choux farcis à la mousse de truite, crème de cèpes*. Very good wines, 100-175.
◆◆ *Le Versailles*, 20, pl. d'Aine (A2), ☎ 55.34.13.39, Visa, closed Mon and Sun eve, 3-17 Feb, 5-26 Jun. The town's top brasserie. Quality, low prices and good Limousin meat, 110-140.
◆◆ *Les Petits Ventres*, 20, rue de la Boucherie (B2-3), ☎ 55.33.34.02, AE Euro Visa ⑩ ♪ closed Mon noon and Sun, 1-15 Jul. Spec : *turbot aux pâtes fraîches, confit de canard aux cèpes*, 75-200.

⚓ *Vallée de l'Aurence* (190 pl), ☎ 55.38.49.43.

Recommended
Baby-sitting : *C.R.O.U.S.*, ☎ 55.01.46.12.
♥ dolls : *Mme Sagnat*, 86, av. Garibaldi, ☎ 55.77.69.29; paintings : *Galerie Corot*, marché Brousseau, pictures, sculptures, decorative objects; stained glass : *Galerie du Bouvier*, 18, rue de la Boucherie, ☎ 55.34.65.64.

Nearby

BEAUNE-LES-MINES, ✉ 87830, 9 km N.

Hotel :
★★ *La Résidence*, RN 20, ☎ 55.39.90.47, Euro Visa, 20 rm Ⓟ ⑩ ❀ closed Sun eve and Sat, 15 Jan-15 Feb, 30 Aug-10 Sep, 180. Rest. ◆ 80-150; child : 30.

NIEUL, ✉ 87510, 12 km NW on the N 147.

Hotel :
● ★★★ *La Chapelle St-Martin* (R.C.), ☎ 55.75.80.17, Visa, 12 rm Ⓟ ⋖ ⑩ ⚘ ♪ ᕫ ⌀ closed Mon, Jan-Feb, 500. Rest. ◆◆◆ ⋖ ♪ ᕫ ❀ 160-240.

SAINT-LAURENT-LES-ÉGLISES, ✉ 87340 La Jonchère, 25 km N.

Hotel :
★★ *Le Rallye* (L.F.), Pont-du-Dognon, ☎ 55.56.56.11, Euro Visa, 20 rm Ⓟ ⋖ ⑩ ⚘ closed Mon ex for guests, 1 Nov-1 Apr, 170. Rest. ◆ ⋖ ♪ ᕫ ❀ 60-120.

SÉREILHAC, ✉ 87620, 23 km W on the N 21.

Hotel :
★★ *La Meule* (L.F.), RN 21, ☎ 55.39.10.08, 10 rm Ⓟ ⋖ ⑩ ⚘ 200. Rest. ◆◆ An attractive inn between Limoges and the gateway to Périgord, with a view of the countryside that enhances Nicole Jouhaud's cuisine : *délice du fumoir norvégien, aiguillettes de saumon sauvage en coussin d'air beurre blanc, soyeux de lapereau en chemise*, 80-350.

SOLIGNAC, ✉ 87110, 12 km S.
ⓢⓃⒸⒻ Solignac-le-Vigen (A2), ☎ 55.00.50.21.

Hotel :
★ *Auberge du Pont Rompu* (L.F.), ☎ 55.00.51.38, 7 rm Ⓟ closed 24 Oct-27 Nov, 140. Rest. ◆ closed Sun, 45-75.

Restaurant :
◆◆ *Domaine de Pradepont*, ☎ 55.00.50.40 ⋖ ⑩ ♪ closed Sun eve and hols at 6pm, 100-150; child : 50.

MILLEVACHES Plateau

B2
Despite its name, this doesn't mean "plateau of the thousand cows"! The name is of Celtic origin, indicating the presence of many streams : the rock and soil formations act as a water reservoir. The bare landscape has a beauty all of its own, with marvelous views, especially when the heather is in bloom.

▶ In the heart of the plateau the village of **Millevaches** (pop. 79) still has a number of thatched houses. ▶ N of the village *(3.5 km and 20 min. on foot)* the **signal d'Andouze**

(alt. 954 m) offers a wonderful view; 7 km NW the pretty town of **Peyrelevade** with its slate roofs nestles against numerous lakes. ▶ 9 km SW are the Gallo-Roman ruins of **Cars**.

The MONEDIÈRES Massif

B2
The Monedières look like mountains from the S and molehills from the N. They offer a marvelous view over the Limousin, with its black forest land and purple heather.

▶ **Treignac**★ : at the foot of the Massif, on the left bank of the Vézère; Gothic bridge; 15thC church; Marc Sangnier Museum (folk art; *closed Sun.*). ▶ From here to **Lestards** (12th-13thC church), after the intersection, a magnificent view★ to the S and E from the cross (alt. 854 m). ▶ The **Suc au May** (911 m high; landmark indicator, 360° view★) can be reached by car. ▶ Narrow twisting roads go past Chauzeix and Freysselines to **Chaumeil**, a charming town of granite houses; in the church : 17thC altarpiece and wooden statue of St Jacques le Majeur, a reminder that Chaumeil was a stop on the pilgrimage route to Compostela; panorama from TV relay tower. ☐

Practical Information _____

TREIGNAC, ✉ 19260, 14 km N of **Tulle**.

Hotel :
★ *Lac* (L.F.), Les Bariousses, 4 km by D 940, ☎ 55.98.00.44, 20 rm Ⓟ ⋖ ⚖ closed Wed, 30 Oct-15 Mar, 90. Rest. ◆ ⋖ 50-100.

Recommended
♥ pork products (blood sausage) : *Navaud*.

MOUTIER-D'AHUN*

Guéret 20, Limoges 80, Paris 364 km
pop 234 ✉ 23150 Ahun   B1
Only the Flamboyant doorway and the Romanesque choir and transept remain of the abbey church. See the remarkable **woodwork**★★ (17thC enclosures, stalls, paneling, altarpiece and lectern; *9-12 & 2-7*). 14thC bridge over the Creuse.

Nearby

▶ **Ahun** *(2 km SW)* was an important town in Gallo-Roman days; in the Middle Ages money was minted here; partially Romanesque church (apse★; 10thC crypt). ▶ 12 km E : **Chénérailles**, a charming medieval town; bas-relief★ of 1300 in the church; in a lovely setting of lakes, woodland and châteaux, especially the château Villemonteix, fortified in the 15thC *(Jun.-Oct. 10-12 & 2-7*, summer tapestry exhibition). ☐

Practical Information _____

Recommended
Holiday villages : at Ahun, PC 23150, *le Moulin du Comte*, ☎ 55.62.53.75, on the banks of the Grande Creuse.

POMPADOUR*

Brive 52, Limoges 59, Paris 455 km
pop 1474 ✉ 19230 Arnac-Pompadour   A2
The famous Marquise de Pompadour hardly ever visited the château here, given to her by Louis XV when she received her title in 1745. After her death, the king repurchased the estate and created the stud-farm which still bears her name.

▶ The **château** (18thC façade between machicolated 15thC towers) has terraces which are open to visitors *(9-12 & 2-6; closed pm on race-days)*. ▶ The **stud** breeds Anglo-Arabs *(weekdays 2:30-5; Sun. and nat. hols. 10-11:30 & 2:30-5; closed 21 Feb.-15 Jul.);* horse shows and races in summer. □

Practical Information ───────────

⚑ Mairie, ☎ 55.73.30.43.
SNCF ☎ 55.73.93.45.

Hotel :
★★ **Auberge de la Marquise** (L.F.), av. des Ecuyers, ☎ 55.73.33.98, AE DC Euro Visa, 12 rm 🅿 🕓 ⊘ closed Tue (l.s.), 3 Nov-1 May, 200. Rest. ♦ Spec : *foie gras chaud aux airelles, aiguillettes de canard aux girolles,* 75-200.

Recommended
Riding center : *La Jumenterie,* ☎ 55.73.33.78.

SAINT-JUNIEN

Limoges 30, Angoulême 73, Paris 434 km
pop 11194 ⊠ 87200   A1

On the heights of the right bank of the Vienne, facing S, Saint-Junien has a tradition of glove-making that dates from the Middle Ages, now supplemented by the production of leatherwear.

▶ A circular boulevard follows the line of the old ramparts around the centre of town (14thC houses). 11th-13thC **church★** : tomb of St. Junien★★, masterpiece of 12thC sculpture; other sculptures★, remains of 12th-13thC frescos; interesting statues. ▶ Near the 13thC **bridge★**, is the chapel of Notre-Dame-du-Pont (15thC, with charming 13thC statue of the Virgin).

Nearby
▶ **Valley of the Glane★** : see the *site Corot* which inspired the great painter *(1 km N and 15-min round trip on foot).* ▶ 15thC **château de Rochebrune** *(10 km W; Palm Sun.-11 Nov., 2-6; Jul.-Sep. 15:10-12 & 2-6; closed Tue. except Jul.-Aug.)* : Empire furniture and memorabilia. ▶ From here you can reach **Chassenon** : significant Gallo-Roman ruins (baths, temple, theatre; *Jul.-Sep. 15, 9 or 10-12 & 2-6 or 7).* **Rochechouart** : view★ from a high hill. Old houses, tower, ramparts and a large late-15thC château★ (17thC façades), with museum; 16thC frescos★ in one of the rooms *(in season, 10-11:30 & 2:30-5:30);* 12th-13thC church in neighbouring village of **Bienac;** walks in the Rochechouart Forest. ▶ **Oradour-sur-Glane** *(13 km NE of Saint-Junien)* : in June 1944, 642 people including 247 children (the entire population of the village), were massacred by the Nazi SS; burned remains of the old village. ▶ You can get back to Saint-Junien by way of **Saint-Victurnien;** see the church, whose two naves (12th-14thC) shelter an ornately-painted 15thC altarpiece. □

Practical Information ───────────

⚑ pl. du Champ-de-Foire, ☎ 55.02.17.93 (h.s.).   ♥
SNCF ☎ 55.02.10.25.

Hotel :
★★ **Relais de Comodoliac,** 22, av. Sadi-Carnot, ☎ 55.02.27.26, 28 rm 🅿 ⱬ 190. Rest. ♦ ♪ 60-150.
⚐ ★★*Municipal* (90 pl), ☎ 55.02.34.86.

Recommended
Chambres d'hôtes : *Le Goth,* ☎ 55.09.80.77, fishing.
Events : *fair,* 3rd Sat of each month.
Youth hostel : 13, rue St-Amand, ☎ 55.02.22.79.

───────────────────────────
In preparing for your trip, consult the pages pertaining to the regions. You will find there the description of the region you wish to visit, as well as a list of sites that must be seen, a brief history and practical information.
───────────────────────────

SAINT-YRIEIX-LA-PERCHE

Limoges 40, Brive 62, Paris 436 km
pop 8037 ⊠ 87500   A2

This is the town that made the fortune of Limoges. At nearby Marcignac *(4 km E),* the first kaolin deposits were discovered in 1765.

▶ The **collegiate church,** or Moûstier★ (13thC), has a sturdy 12thC gate-tower; see the treasure room★. ▶ Close at hand is the Plô Tower (1243). ▶ **Les Palloux :** porcelain museum, near the Arfeuille lake.

Nearby
▶ **Le Chalard** *(8 km NW)* : almost intact 12thC priory; (interesting church furniture); unusual medieval cemetery and a few old houses; Romanesque priory ruins at **Ladignac-le-Long** *(4 km N).* ▶ At **Coussac-Bonneval★** *(11 km E)* : 12thC lantern of the dead and imposing château (14th-18thC; furniture and tapestries of 16th-18thC; *Sat. and Sun. 2-6:30).* □

Practical Information ───────────

Nearby

COUSSAC-BONNEVAL, ⊠ 87500, 11 km NE.

Hotel :
★★ **Voyageurs** (L.F.), ☎ 55.75.20.24, Euro Visa, 12 rm 🅿 ⱬ 🕓 closed Sun eve and Mon (l.s.), 8-30 Jan, 150. Rest. ♦♦ ₲ Good traditional food, 60-150.

La ROCHE-L'ABEILLE, ⊠ 87800 Nexon, 12 km N on the D 704.

Hotel :
★★★ **Moulin de la Gorce,** ☎ 55.00.70.66, AE DC Visa, 9 rm 🅿 ⱬ 🕓 closed Sun eve and Mon (l.s.), 20 Jan-15 Feb, 20 Nov-5 Dec, 360. Rest. ● ♦♦ In a restored 16th-C mill : *lièvre à la royale aux cèpes,* in season, 200-300.

La SOUTERRAINE

Guéret 34, Bellac 40, Paris 341 km
pop 5850 ⊠ 23300   A1

This town got its name (meaning "underground") from a very old crypt beneath the church, communicating with an even older burial vault, possibly Gallo-Roman; the church itself is Romanesque, but was over-restored in the 19thC. Interesting 15thC city gate.

Nearby
▶ **Bridjers** tower *(2 km W),* enormous 14thC cylindrical castle-keep. ▶ 6 km N, **Saint-Agnant-de-Versillat.** Romanesque church and lantern of the dead (12thC); 4 km from here is **Saint-Germain-Beaupré** : castle★ (16th-17thC, well-restored; *Jul.-Sep., Sat., Sun., Tue., 9-12 & 2-6);* farther N, don't miss the gorges de la Creuse★. You can get back to La Souterraine by **Maison-Feyne** (11thC church) and **Le Grand-Bourg,** which has a 13thC church and is surrounded by castles on the edge of the Gartempe river; 5 km S, **Bénévent-l'Abbaye** has a remarkable Romanesque church★ (12thC, much restored); walk to Puy de Goth (541 m peak; panorama★); ▶ To the SW, **Fromental** castle : the main section of this Romanesque structure is dominated by a square keep (14thC) and surrounded by a moat *(ext. only, 15 Jun.-15 Sep.).* □

Practical Information ───────────

Nearby

DUN-LE-PALESTEL, ⊠ 23800, 18 km NE.
⚑ rue des Sabots, ☎ 55.89.00.75; mairie, ☎ 55.89.01.30.

Hotel :
★ **Joly** (L.F.), ☎ 55.89.00.23, Visa, 15 rm 🅿 ⊘ closed Mon eve , Feb, 110. Rest. ♦♦ ♪ ⊘ 50-165.

△ ★★*Forêt* (60 pl), ☎ 55.89.01.30.

Recommended
♥ pastry : *M. Delorme*, ☎ 55.89.09.70, spec : *creusois, croquets aux amandes.*

TULLE

Aurillac 84, Limoges 88, Paris 483 km
pop 20642 ⊠ 19000   B2
A long string of houses at the bottom of the narrow picturesque valley of the Corrèze.

▶ The 12thC **cathedral★** with its single nave is a very elegant building overlooked by a 75 m bell tower★ (12th-14thC). ▶ In the cloister★ and the chapter room (remains of 14thC frescos) is the **André-Mazeyrie Museum** (archaeology and art; *9:30 or 10-12 & 2 or 2:30-5 or 6, closed Tue.*). ▶ Opposite the cathedral, the 16thC **Maison de Loyac★** stands on the edge of the old quarter of the town. ▶ **Resistance and Deportation Museum :** document center, open to visitors (2 quai E.-Perrier, *tel. 55.26.24.36*). ▶ On the opposite side of town is the **Manufacture Nationale d'Armes** (fine collection of weapons; *groups only, by previous request, tel. 55.20.10.09*).

Nearby

▶ The church at **Saint-Fortunade** *(9 km S)* has a 12thC choir and houses a beautiful 15thC bust reliquary★; 15thC castle, much restored. ▶ The church at **Naves** contains a beautiful 12thC altarpiece. ▶ *14 km NE :* **Gimel-les-Cascades** is set in a magnificent site★★ in the gorge of the Montane river, which, upstream, breaks into a series of waterfalls (143 m total height; view★ from Vuillier Park, *open Mar.-Nov.*); ruins of 16thC château; superb collection in the treasure room★ of the church; 9 km E of Gimel is **Clergoux** near the artificial lake of La Valette. From here, visit the Renaissance **château de Sédières** (14th-16thC; ethnography museum; *Jul.-Aug., 10-12 & 2-7, closed Tue.*). 38 km NE, on a steep-walled promontory are the proud ruins of the **château de Ventadour★** (12thC).   □

Practical Information _____

TULLE
ⓘ quai Baluze, ☎ 55.26.59.61, closed Mon and Sun (l.s.).
SNCF ☎ 55.20.22.54.
▨▨ covered market, at the train station, ☎ 55.20.18.45.

Hotels :
★★★ *Limouzi*, 16, quai de la République, ☎ 55.26.42.00, AE DC Euro Visa, 50 rm 🅿 150. Rest. ● ◆◆ *Ventadour* ♪ ♿ closed Sun (Oct-Mar). Outstanding food : *escalope de truite saumonée soufflée à la vapeur, tournedos d'agneau au beurre d'herbes*, 110-200.
★★ *Farjounel* (L.F.), 25, av. de la Gare, ☎ 55.20.04.04, Visa, 14 rm 🅿 half pens, closed 1-15 Sep, 300. Rest. ◆ ♪ 60-80.
★★ *La Toque Blanche*, 29, rue J.-Jaurès, ☎ 55.26.75.41, AE Visa, 10 rm 🅿 closed Sun eve (l.s.) and hols, 10-30 Jan, 120. Rest. ◆◆ ♪ Friendly welcome. Fine traditional fare : *tête de veau à l'ancienne, civet de lapin au cahors*, 65-200.
★★ *Royal*, 70, av. V.-Hugo, ☎ 55.20.04.52, AE DC Euro Visa, 14 rm 🅿 150.

Restaurant :
◆ *Le Central*, 32, rue J.-Jaurès, ☎ 55.26.24.46, Visa, closed Sat and Sun eve, 20 Jul-17 Aug, 90-170.

△ ★★★*Bourbacoup* (58 pl), ☎ 55.26.75.97.

Nearby

SAINT-MARTIN-LA-MÉANNE, ⊠ 19320 Marcillac-La-Croisille, 30 km SE.

Hotel :
★ *Les Voyageurs* (L.F.), ☎ 55.29.11.53, 19 rm 🅿 ▨▨ ♿ closed Sun eve, 1-15 Feb, 15-30 Nov. Rest. ◆ ♿ 45-140; child : 35.

USSEL

Tulle 60, Clermont-Ferrand 86, Paris 439 km
pop 12252 ⊠ 19200   B2
This old town at the top of a hill is a network of narrow streets with turreted 15th and 16thC houses. See the **Hôtel de Ventadour★**, an elegant building in spite of the rugged granite from which it is built. In front of the school is a large Roman eagle★. N° 12 Rue Michelet houses the craft collections of the **Musée du Pays d'Ussel** (regional museum; *Jul.-Aug., 10-12 & 3-7*); the art and ethnography collections are in the **chapel of the Pénitents Blancs** in Rue Pasteur *(same hours)*. The street leads up to the **chapel of Notre-Dame de la Chabanne** (1640; *10 min;* panorama★). ▶ At **Neric-d'Ussel,** museum of the Resistance *(Jul.-Aug.; 10-12 & 3-7)*.

Nearby

▶ **Saint-Angel** *(9 km SW)* has a former priory and 12th-14thC granite church, 14thC chapter room and 15thC tower. ▶ 8 km NW, **Meymac :** at the foot of the Plateau de Millevaches. Here you can see the church★ of a former Benedictine abbey, a pretty wooden covered market on granite pillars and a 15thC belfry; on the top floor of the abbey is the Marius-Vazeilles Museum (local collections; *Jul.-Aug., daily ex Tue., 10:30-12 & 3:30-6:30; May-Jun. and Sep.-15 Oct., Sat., Sun. and nat. hols. 3-5*).   □

Practical Information _____

USSEL
ⓘ pl. Voltaire, ☎ 55.72.11.50; 2, bd de la Prade, ☎ 55.96.11.32, closed Sat and Sun (l.s.).
SNCF ☎ 55.96.14.89/55.96.24.83.

Hotel :
★★ *Les Gravades*, Saint-Dézery, RN 89, 4 km, ☎ 55.72.21.53, Visa, 20 rm 🅿 ▨▨ ♿ 280. Rest. ● ◆◆ ♪ closed Fri eve and Sat noon. Surrounded by greenery. Beautifully prepared food : *salade auvergnate, papillotes de truite aux cèpes*, 70-150.

△ ★★★*Le Ponty* (140 pl), ☎ 55.72.30.05.

Recommended
Bicycle-rental : *M. Malves*, 7, bd V.-Hugo, ☎ 55.72.10.27; *M. Bourdain*, 2, pl. Victoire, ☎ 55.95.25.76.
Farmhouse-gîte : *La Grange du Bos*, ☎ 55.72.15.68, camping ; at Saint-Etienne-aux-Clos, 19200, *Les Couderches*, 15 km from Ussel via RN 89 and RD 27, ☎ 55.94.51.40, camping, farm produce for sale.
Youth hostel : rue Pasteur, ☎ 55.96.13.17.

Nearby

MEYMAC, ⊠ 19250, 52 km NE of **Tulle.**
ⓘ pl. Bucher, ☎ 55.95.18.43 (h.s.).   ♥
SNCF ☎ 55.95.11.69.

Recommended
Farmhouse-inn : at Lestrade, 8 km, ☎ 55.95.19.30, closed Mon-Thu. in winter. Spec : crabs, stuffed cabbage, poultry and young lamb.

UZERCHE*

Tulle 31, Limoges 56, Paris 452 km
pop 3185 ⊠ 19140   A2
Built on a promontory in a loop of the Vézère, Uzerche is a ravishing town with an unusual number of elegant turreted 15th-16thC houses.

▶ Superb **view★** of the town, especially at sunrise, from the Eymoutiers road. ▶ Enter the town from the S via Place Marie-Colein, the Rue Porte-Barachaude (old houses) and the **Porte Bécharie★** (14thC town gate). ▶ The church of **St. Pierre★** is a handsome 12thC Romanesque building with 11thC crypt and an attractive Limousin bell tower.

Nearby

▶ At **Vigeois** *(9 km SW),* part-Romanesque church with decorated cornices on the exterior apse and medieval bridge. ▶ **Chamboulive** *(16 km E)* : church with 14thC portal and Romanesque bell tower.   □

Practical Information _____

ⓘ pl. Lunade, ☎ 55.73.15.71 (h.s.).
SNCF ☎ 55.73.25.49.

Hotel :
★★ *Tessier,* rue du Pont Turgot, ☎ 55.73.10.05, Euro Visa, 17 rm Ⓟ ≼ closed Wed eve, 15 Nov-28 Mar, 140. Rest. ♦ closed Wed ex Aug-Sep, 84-120.

Å ★*La Minoterie* (33 pl), ☎ 55.73.17.00.

VASSIVIÈRE Lake**

Limoges 56, Guéret 60, Paris 413 km
✉ 87470 Peyrat-le-Château   B2

From Saint-Léonard-de-Noblat to the lake *(70 km; leisurely half-day)*
A 10 km^2 artificial lake created in 1952 by damming the Maulde river. Hydro-electric generating stations downstream. The lake is remarkably well-equipped and is one of the largest leisure centres in the Limousin, popular with nature lovers as well as with sports enthusiasts.

▶ **Saint-Léonard-de-Noblat**★ (pop. 5 318) has a medieval air, with its numerous old houses (including one 13thC Gothic house) and 11th-12thC church★ (remodeled, fine Limousin bell tower★), 15thC stalls. ▶ The ruins of the **Prieuré de l'Artige** (1165 ; site★) overlook the confluence of the Vienne and Maulde rivers. ▶ Formerly wild and capricious, the Maulde has been equipped upstream by 8 dams, transforming it into a calm and stepped river which, followed rather closely by this route, offers some attractive views. ▶ At **Peyrat-le-Château** see the tall square tower (12thC) of the old castle (15thC); 10 km S, **Eymoutiers** : 15thC choir lit by 15 stained-glass windows★ (15th-16thC) in the church; treasure-room. ▶ Scenic route round **Vassivière Lake** ; the water is said to be extremely pure. ▶ S of the lake, walks in the Feuillade Forest★. ▶ E of the lake is **Gentioux** : extremely moving monument to the war dead, a Limousin child raising his fist and cursing the war...   □

Practical Information _____

VASSIVIÈRE Lake

Hotels :
● ★★★ *La Caravelle* (L.F.), ☎ 55.69.40.97, Visa, 22 rm Ⓟ ≼ ♨ ♙ ♿ half pens, closed 1 Jan-4 Mar, 500. Rest. ♦♦ ≼ ♿ 130-150.   ♥
★★ *Au Golf du Limousin* (L.F.), Auphelle, ☎ 55.69.41.34, 18 rm Ⓟ ≼ ♨ ♿ half pens (h.s.), closed Wed, 30 Oct-1 Mar, 400. Rest. ♦ ♪ 60.

Å ★★*Le Moulin de l'Eau* (60 pl), ☎ 55.69.41.01 ; ★★*Les Peyrades d'Auphelle* (135 pl), ☎ 55.69.41.32.

Nearby

SAINT-LÉONARD-DE-NOBLAT, ✉ 87400, 37 km NE.
ⓘ ☎ 85.56.25.06.
SNCF ☎ 55.56.00.09.

Hotels :
★★ *Grand Saint-Léonard,* rte de Clermont, ☎ 55.56.18.18, AE DC Euro Visa, 14 rm Ⓟ closed Mon, Tue lunch, 15 Dec-15 Jan, 130. Rest. ♦ ♪ ♽ 180-220.
● ★ *Beau Site* (L.F.), ☎ 55.56.00.56, 11 rm Ⓟ ♨ ♿ half pens, closed Fri eve , Mon lunch, Sat lunch (l.s.), 14 Feb-3 Mar, 26 Oct-6 Nov, 300. Rest. ♦ An old-fashioned atmosphere. Pond fishing possible, 50-80.
★ *Modern'Hôtel* (L.F.), 6, bd Adrien-Pressemanne, ☎ 55.56.00.25, Euro Visa, 8 rm ♿ half pens (h.s.), closed Sun eve and Mon ex Jul-Sep, 1 Feb-3 Mar, 13-20 Oct, 325. Rest. ♦ ♪ A cordial welcome, 130-160.

Å ★★*Parc de Vacances de Beaufort* (100 pl), ☎ 55.56.02.79.

Recommended
Rural-gîte : *Le Chalet,* ☎ 55.56.15.05, camping, tennis, hiking.

Lorraine, Vosges

▶ Battlefields and garrison towns, countryside blackened by industrial smoke and dust, cloudy skies, cold and taciturn people — these are only some of the unjust and unflattering clichés applied to a region which deserves far better. Because of its geographical location Lorraine was the site of some of the fiercest battles of both World Wars, and is still the centre of heavy industry in France. Ever since the time of Joan of Arc, born in the little town now known as Domrémy-la-Pucelle, the inhabitants of Lorraine have earned a reputation for their devotion to the nation and their willingness to work hard for its sake.

And yet Lorraine's country castles and churches, the superb cathedral of Metz, one of the best examples of Gothic architecture in Europe, and the gracious proportions of the Place Stanislas in Nancy, can hold their own against any rival. Lorraine was the cradle of many of the industrial arts in the early 18th century and is still justly renowned for its fine glassware, crystal and earthenware, which attract tourists in search of the painstaking excellence of master craftsmen. The Lunéville château, impregnated with the memory of Stanislas, ex-king of Poland and father-in-law of Louis XV, is an interesting variant on the theme of Versailles. The good Stanislas is reputed to have invented the original *rhum baba* — still a Lorraine speciality — while one of his female cooks is credited with the invention of the ubiquitous *madeleine* cake.

But perhaps the greatest charm of this region lies in its green countryside, its thick forests alternating with ploughed fields and meadows, the famous thermal stations of Bains-les-Bains and Contrexéville, and the peace and tranquillity of Lorraine's national park, created to provide the hardworking population with easy access to nature. The Vosges forest too is another inexhaustible source of pleasure for hikers and weekend walkers. The region also has another source of natural wealth in its inhabitants who, despite the harsh and often bitter destiny of their native land, can offer the tourist eager to communicate with his fellow man, a gift of solid friendship and a tradition of human solidarity. ☐

Don't miss

★★★ Metz B2, Nancy B2-3.

★★ Gérardmer C4, Lunéville C3, Toul B3.

★ The Argonne Region A1-2, Bar-le-Duc A2, Domrémy-la-Pucelle A3, Épinal B-C4, Liverdun B2, Montmédy A1, Pont-à-Mousson B2, Remiremont C4, Saint-Dié C3, Saint-Mihiel A2, Saulx Valley A3, Sion-Vaudémont Hill B3, Verdun A3, Vittel B4.

Weekend Tips

The simplest weekend if you've never visited the area : 1 day each in Nancy and Metz (the towns are 60 km apart and barely 3 hr from Paris by train).
Or else : Friday night, Paris to Épinal; Saturday, Épinal to Remiremont, Plombières, Vittel; Sunday, Vittel to Sion, Haroué, Lunéville, Nancy.
Another choice : 1 day in Metz and the 2nd in the nature reserve (Pont-à-Mousson, Rupt de Mad Valley, Hattonchâtel, Saint-Mihiel); return to Paris via Bar-le-Duc (2hr by train).

Farmhouse in the Metz region

Vosges farmhouse

Bar-le-Duc region

● *Brief regional history*

Prehistory and Roman times
When the Romans invaded Lorraine they found it inhabited by two Celtic peoples centred mainly around modern-day Metz and Toul. ● Here and there, iron was already being smelted, salt mines were in production, and trade was growing with Belgium and Burgundy. The Roman organization of roads and cities encouraged economic development.

6th-10thC
A territory now roughly corresponding to Lorraine was allotted to Thierri, one of the four sons of Clovis, King of the Franks, in the 6thC. The early capital of Reims was superseded by Metz; the country prospered. In the 8thC, the Emperor Charlemagne often visited **Austrasia,** as it was then designated, stopping at Metz, Remiremont, Thionville and other cities. **Lothaire II,** 9thC King of the Franks, lent his name to the region extending from the upper Saône to the mouth of the Rhine; "Lorraine" is derived from Lotharingia (*lotharii regnum* = Lothar's kingdom). A Duchy corresponding more or less to modern-day Lorraine was created during the 10thC reign of the Holy Roman Emperor Otto I.

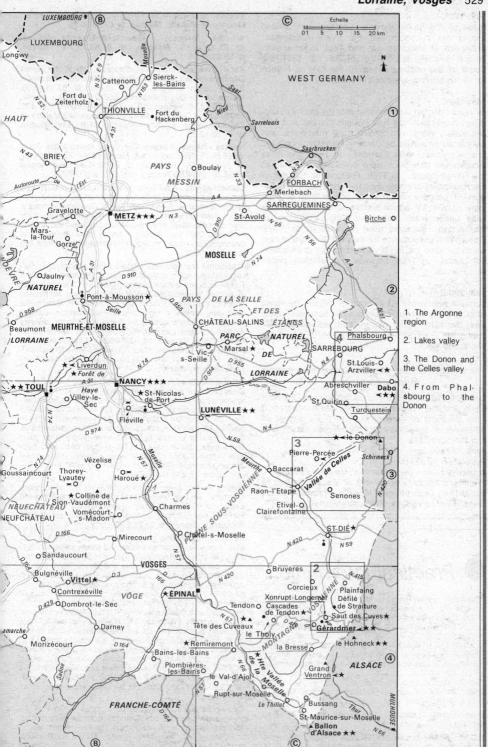

1. The Argonne region

2. Lakes valley

3. The Donon and the Celles valley

4. From Phalsbourg to the Donon

10th-14thC
Ruled by the Saxon dynasty, Lorraine was divided among the dukedom and the three independent bishoprics of Metz, Verdun and Toul, together with several counties, led by that of Bar. In 1301, the Count of Bar became vassal of the King of France for all his territory west of the Meuse.

14th-18thC
50 years later Bar was reunited with the Duchy of Lorraine; but France still had designs on this rich border state. Wars with Spain, royal marriages, and skirmishes provoked by Cardinal Richelieu increased France's control over Lorraine. In 1648, the three independent bishoprics were definitively attached to the French crown. In 1738, François III, founder of the Habsbourg-Lorraine dynasty, abdicated the dukedom of Lorraine in order to accept that of Tuscany. Louis XV appointed his father-in-law, **Stanislas Leszczynski**, dethroned King of Poland, to fill the gap. Stanislas ruled benevolently as Royal Governor of the province for the next 30 years, during which he used the funds allotted to him to embellish the capital. In 1766, Lorraine was officially united with France.

18th-20thC
Lorraine has remained a focus of dispute by virtue of its strategic but vulnerable position between France and Germany. The region suffered extensively during the Franco-Prussian War of 1870-71 and the two World Wars.

Brief description

Location : NE corner of France between the Parisian basin and the Vosges mountains, which separate it from the Plain of Alsace; the rivers are almost all tributaries of the Meuse and the Moselle, which flow into the North Sea.
Area : 23 700 km²
Population : 2 331 000
Administration : Department of **Meurthe-et-Moselle**, Prefecture Nancy; Department of **Meuse**, Prefecture Bar-le-Duc; Department of **Moselle**, Prefecture Metz; Department of **Vosges**, Prefecture Épinal.

● Practical information

Information : **Meurthe-et-Moselle** : Association Départementale du Tourisme (A.D.T.), 1, rue Mably, B.P. 65, 54002 Nancy, ☎ 83.35.56.56. **Meuse** : C.D.T., Préfecture, 55012 Bar-le-Duc, ☎ 29.79.48.10. **Moselle** : O.D.T., Hôtel du Dép., B.P. 1096, 57036 Metz Cedex 1, ☎ 87.32.11.11. **Vosges** : C.D.T., rue Gilbert, B.P. 332, 88008 Épinal Cedex, ☎ 29.82.49.93. In **Paris** : Maison de l'Alsace et des Vosges, 39, av. des Champs-Élysées, ☎ (1) 42.56.15.94. Dir. régionale de la Jeunesse et des Sports, 13, rue de Mainvaux, 54130 Saint-Max, ☎ 83.21.40.74. Dir. rég. des Affaires culturelles, 10-12, pl. Saint-Étienne, 57000 Metz, ☎ 87.75.22.77.

Reservations : **Meuse** : Préfecture, ☎ 29.79.48.10, ext. 471.

S.O.S. : SAMU (Emergency Medical Service) : **Meurthe-et-Moselle**, ☎ 83.32.85.79. **Moselle**, ☎ 87.62.27.11.

Vosges, ☎ 29.34.34.34. Poisoning Emergency Centre : **Meurthe-et-Moselle, Moselle**, ☎ 83.32.36.36.

Weather forecast : **Meurthe-et-Moselle, Meuse**, ☎ 83.29.49.15. **Moselle**, ☎ 87.63.13.73. **Vosges**, ☎ 29.35.15.15.

Rural gîtes and chambres d'hôtes : enq at the Relais Départementaux des Gîtes Ruraux; **Meurthe-et-Moselle**, 5, rue de la Vologne, 54520 Laxou, ☎ 83.96.49.58. **Meuse** : Hôtel du Département, 55012 Bar-le-Duc Cedex, ☎ 29.79.48.10. **Vosges** : 13, rue Aristide-Briand, B.P. 405, 88010 Épinal Cedex, ☎ 29.35.50.34. **Moselle** : Maison de l'Agriculture, 64, av. André-Malraux, 57045 Metz Cedex, ☎ 87.63.13.25.

Holiday villages : **Vosges**, Corcireux, domaine des Bans, ☎ 29.50.67.42. Vittel : Club Mediterranée, Grand Hôtel, ☎ 29.08.10.56; Ermitage, ☎ 29.08.16.89, and Nouvel Hôtel, ☎ 29.08.35.36; lists at C.D.T. and O.T.S.I.

Cultural events : **Apr** : science-fiction festival in Metz. **End Jun** : cultural festival (music) in Fénétrange; international image festival in Épinal. **Jun-Aug** : Concerts in Nancy. **Jul** : Jean d'Heures soirées in Lisle-en-Rigault; summer dance festival in Pont-à-Mousson. **Sep** : art festival in Nancy. **Oct** : jazz festival in Nancy. **Nov** : international contemporary music festival and international super-8 film festival in Metz.

Traditional festivals and folklore : **Feb** : carnaval in Sarreguemines. **Apr** : daffodil festival in Gérardmer (only if Easter hols are before 25 Apr); fête des Champs-Golots in Épinal, Wed before Easter (children float illuminated boats in the gutters). **Jun** : fête et tradition in Manonville. **Jul** : wine festival in Vigneulles-lès-Hattonchâtel; cottage cheese and rural traditions festival in Sarrebourg; bilberry festival in Dabo; festival in Bitche. **Aug** : Féerie Lumineuse (light display) on Gérardmer Lake the 14th); plum festival in Darney, Metz, Vigneulles-lès-Hattonchâtel. **Nov** : Saint-Hubert festival in Nancy. **Dec** : Saint-Nicholas festivals everywhere.

Fairs, exhibitions and markets : **Mar** : spring fair in Bar-le-Duc; gastrolor and "journalists' iron frying pan" in Metz; spinamalt fair in Épinal. **Apr** : antique dealers' salon, minerals market in Nancy; handicrafts fair in Saint-Nicolas-de-Port; old paper fair in Bar-le-Duc. **Jun** : international fair in Nancy. **Jul** : horse festival in Vigneulles-lès-Hattonchâtel. **Sep** : Expo in Verdun; bilberry festival (every other year) and antique dealer's salon in Bar-le-Duc. **Oct** : Jazz Festival in Nancy. **Nov** : antique dealers' salon, international aviculture exhibition in Metz; ornithology exhibition in Épinal; autumn fair in Bar-le-Duc.

Nature parks : parc naturel régional de Lorraine, headquarters : 10, rue Émile-Cavalier, 54703 Pont-à-Mousson Cedex, ☎ 83.81.11.91. Parc naturel régional des Vosges du Nord, headquarters : château de la Petite-Pierre, 67290 Wingen-sur-Moder, ☎ 88.70.44.30.

Rambling and hiking : topoguides G.R.5, 7, 14/141, 53. Enq. concerning indicated trails and forest walks : C.R.T. Lorraine-Vosges, Assn. parc naturel régional de Lorraine, Assn. parc naturel régional des Vosges du Nord, O.T.S.I. de la Montagne, which publishes local maps and guides, and Assn. des Accompagnateurs de Moyenne Montagne, ☎ 29.63.17.50. Signposted trails : list can be obtained from Vita, 1, rue Vernet, 75008 Paris, ☎ 47.23.72.02. Enq. concerning shelters : local SI, Club Pédestre Vosgien, M.J.C., rue de Fontenay, 54000 Nancy, ☎ 83.32.14.55, and Amis de la Nature, 28, rue des Soupirs, 88000 Épinal, ☎ 29.82.37.63. Grande Traversée des Vosges (major trail across the Vosges Mountains) : M. André Richard, Remiremont, ☎ 29.62.13.41. Also health walks (forest trails), rambles and hiking from Gérardmer; enq. Hautes-Vosges Randonnées Loisirs, B.P. 8, 88400 Xonrupt-Longemer, ☎ 29.63.00.54 and 29.63.15.30 (also snow-shoe treks in winter).

Cycling holidays : numerous possibilities — Tour of the Vosges, Randonnée des Grandes Sources (excursions) and proficiency certificate for the Hautes-Vosges, enq. : M. Carsani, 41, rue de la Xanée, 88200 Remiremont, ☎ 29.62.51.54, and local bicycle dealers. The Comité *dép. Meurthe-et-Moselle* publishes a brochure listing itineraries, ☎ 83.72.63.83.

Riding holidays : list of riding centres can be obtained from the *Assn. Régionale de Tourisme Équestre*

Cuisine in Lorraine

In Lorraine, grandfathers traditionally ask : "Who do you love best, Maman or Papa?" The traditional teasing answers : "I love bacon best!" People in Lorraine love bacon; they are also very fond of cream and butter and eggs. That's how they invented the quiche (whose original name, which nobody uses any more, is fiouse). *Depending where you are, the tart may be enlivened with mushrooms, chives, onions or any of a dozen additions. The* migaine *is often poured into other kinds of pastry delicacies through a hole in the crust during the baking. A regional speciality is the tourte, a pie made with short pastry enclosing a mixture of roughly equal parts of minced pork and veal, marinated overnight with red wine, onions, parsley and other seasonings. Bacon is an indispensable ingredient in potée Lorraine, a stew that, like many other local recipes, is hearty but not as heavy as you might suppose.*

Pike, perch, freshwater crayfish, trout and frogs all contribute to the tastes and textures of the table, while poultry and game also have their place. Cheeses are not outstanding, which is disappointing when you consider that Lorraine is the largest French cheese-producing region by tonnage. To finish the meal, sample a tart or an eau-de-vie flavoured with brimbelles *(currants) or golden* mirabelle *plums.*

Just desserts

The rhum baba, a yeast-cake steeped in rum syrup, was supposedly invented by ex-King Stanislas at Lunéville. Sweet delicacies are extremely popular in Lorraine : chocolate thistles (chardons), candy pebbles (cailloux) in the Vosges, truffles (truffes) and "little nothings" (nonettes); small butter cakes (madeleines) from Commercy, hard candies (dragées) in Verdun, fondants (bergamotes) and macaroons (macarons) from Nancy, and the seedless preserves of whole red currants from Bar-le-Duc.

Beer, wine and spirits

Not long ago, almost every regional town had its own brewery and there were great brews to be discovered. In recent years, take-overs, amalgamations and closures have reduced the brewing industry to a few vast factories whose beer is consistent but little else. Wines from the Côtes de Toul — rosé, called "grey" (gris) locally — and the Côtes de Moselle near Metz (white) are dry, fruity and perfumed, delicate and fine.If you are not driving, try an eau-de-vie, one of the fruit-flavoured spirits that rival those of Alsace and Haute-Saône : cherry (kirsch), raspberry (framboise), purple plum (quetsche), sloe (prunelle), bilberry (myrtille), pear (poire) and especially the little golden mirabelle *plum with its incomparable perfume.*

Lorrain, 10, Grande-Rue, 54380 Autreville-sur-Moselle, ☎ 83.24.90.72. Excursions and stays : *ARDACETTE,* Chambre d'agriculture, 55000 Bar-le-Duc, ☎ 29.79.44.66. Horse-drawn wagons : *Centre de tourisme équestre,* Biancourt-sur-Orge, 55290 Montiers-sur-Saulx, ☎ 29.75.34.26; les Éparges, 55160 Fresnes-en-Woëvre, ☎ 29.87.35.69, and *Le Relais des Écuries du Château,* 55260 Thillombois, ☎ 29.75.00.94. Tour of the Vosges on horseback, enq. : *C.D.T. Vosges.*

Scenic railways : Moselle : *Association du Chemin de Fer Touristique d'Abreschviller,* ☎ 87.03.70.09. From Easter to early Oct, 1 service on Sat, 6 services on Sun and nat hols, special supplementary services Jul-Aug, Mon-Sat and on request all year round. *Vallée de la Larnes,* from Vigy to Hombourg-Budange, 26 Apr-15 Oct, Sat, Sun and hols; enq. : ☎ 87.63.56.01 and 83.49.07.64; reserv. : 82.56.22.78. **Vosges :** *Rabodeau,* gare de Sénones, ☎ 29.57.60.32. Organizer : M. Jean Hubert, at Yutz, ☎ 82.56.07.87. Services on Sat, Sun and nat hols, Jun-Sep. Trains can be reserved for groups and special outings.

Technical tourism : Crystal : *Vannes-le-Châtel,* ☎ 83.25.41.01 and 83.25.45.93 (May : visit to manufacture of Sèvres crystal); *Ateliers Daum,* rue des Cristalleries, 54000 Nancy, ☎ 83.32.14.55 and 83.36.44.01; *Cristallerie Saint-Louis-lès-Bitche,* ☎ 87.06.40.04; *Valcrystal,* ☎ 87.25.11.33. *Imagerie Pellerin,* 42 bis, quai de Digneville, 88000 Épinal, ☎ 29.34.21.87 (ex Sun) and museum (10-12 & 2-6 ex Tue, nat hols). Faience and enamels : manufacture of "cloisonnés", enq. : *S.I.,* Longwy, ☎ 82.24.27.17 and 82.24.58.20. Brewery : *Brasserie Amos,* 29, rue Maugier, 57000 Metz, ☎ 87.68.58.12 (visits by appt). Also, visits to textile mills, forests, granite quarries, enq. : *O.T.,* Gérardmer, ☎ 29.63.08.74.

River and canal cruises : *Meuse Nautic,* Dun-sur-Meuse, ☎ 29.80.94.17, and *Navilor,* 55100 Verdun, ☎ 29.86.56.22; **Meurthe-et-Moselle :** cruises on the Moselle and canals : 2, rue Victor, 54000 Nancy, ☎ 83.37.32.25. The brochure *Pratique du tourisme fluvial en Lorraine* gives full info., available from *C.R.T.* and *C.D.T.*

Instructional courses : photography, pottery, weaving, Vosges spinet, folk dancing, guitar, enq. : *Maison de la culture,* 1, bd Saint-Dié, 88400 Gérardmer, ☎ 29.63.11.96 (early Jul-mid-Aug) and Bar-le-Duc, ☎ 29.79.48.55. Organ academy (7-20 Jul) : interpretation, accompaniment, musical analysis, enq. : Pasteur Marc Goez, 16, rue du Maréchal-Foch, 88100 Saint-Dié. Moselle, in Bitche : tennis, painting, yoga, riding. Pottery : *Action culturelle,* Ligny-en-Barrois, ☎ 29.78.08.48. Spinet-making, painting on wood : *Relais Rencontre,* Vilosnes, ☎ 29.85.82.87.

Children : farmhouse holidays, see *Relais dép. des gîtes ruraux.* Nature and environmental courses : *Assn du Vieux-Châtel,* 88330 Châtel-sur-Moselle, ☎ 29.67.14.18 and 29.66.90.14 : *Chantier REMPART du Vieux-Châtel,* rue des Capucines, 88330 Châtel-sur-Moselle. *C.P.I.E.,* Bonzée, 55160 Fresnes-en-Woëvre, ☎ 29.87.36.65, and in the *maisons du parc.* Handicrafts, discovery of the rural world : *Foyer rural,* Saint-Maurice-sous-les-Côtes, 55210 Vigneulles-lès-Hattonchâtel, ☎ 29.89.38.95, and *M.J.C.,* Beaumont, 54470 Thiaucourt, ☎ 83.52.23.01. *Relais Rencontre,* Vilosnes, ☎ 29.85.82.87. Courses, riding, computers, sailing, etc. : *Base du Lac de Madine. Centre permanent de classes de découverte,* Beaulieu-en-Argonne, ☎ 29.70.72.83.

Water skiing : Meurthe-et-Moselle : Fontenoy, ☎ 83.43.60.70; Pont-à-Mousson, ☎ 83.82.12.98. **Meuse :** Madine Lake, ☎ 29.89.32.50; Dun-sur-Meuse, ☎ 29.80.90.38; Saint-Mihiel, ☎ 29.89.03.59; Bonzée, ☎ 29.87.31.98; **Moselle :** Metz-Campagne, ☎ 87.75.65.21, and Thionville-Sierck, ☎ 82.53.33.18.

Diving : Meuse : Madine Lake, ☎ 29.89.32.50; Contrisson and Mouzay, ☎ 29.79.48.55, ext. 321; Sommedieue, ☎ 29.87.60.45. **Moselle :** diving is possible in all the larger stretches of water (→ Sailing). **Vosges** : Corbeaux Lake, ☎ 29.61.11.29.

Sailing and wind-surfing : sailing circuit in Moselle (100 km); enq *Dir Dép. de la Jeunesse et des Sports,* 57036 Metz, ☎ 87.75.41.55. *Centre-École,* Madine Lake, ☎ 29.89.03.59. **Meuse** : *Dir. Dép. Jeunesse et Sports,* ☎ 29.79.48.55; centres at Messein, ☎ 83.47.22.21 (town hall), Pont-à-Mousson, ☎ 83.81.10.76. **Moselle** : school at Mittersheim, ☎ 87.07.67.82.

Rowing : Madine Lake, ☎ 29.89.32.50; Dun-sur-Meuse, ☎ 29.80.90.38; Saint-Mihiel, ☎ 29.89.15.11; Bonzé-en-Woëre, ☎ 29.87.31.98; Thionville-Sierck, ☎ 82.53.33.18; Château-Salins, ☎ 87.92.10.07; Bitche, ☎ 87.06.00.13; on the lakes of the Maginot Line, ☎ 87.09.60.01; Dabo, ☎ 87.03.11.82; Gérardmer Lake, ☎ 29.63.08.74; Toul, ☎ 88.64.35.00 and *Maison de l'aviron,* ☎ 83.64.39.57.

Canoe-kayak : *Comité de Canoë-Kayak,* 18, rue de Champagne, 55800 Revigny-sur-Ornain, ☎ 29.70.61.95. **Assn** *Golbéenne Sports et Loisirs Canoë-Kayak,* 8, rue d'Épinal, 88190 Golbey, ☎ 29.34.34.62 and *C.D.T.* **Moselle** : at Bitche, ponds along the Maginot Line, Sarrebourg.

Climbing-mountaineering : instructional courses, excursions, climbing school : *Club Alpin Français,* 5, rue Saint-Julien, 54000 Nancy, ☎ 83.32.37.73, and *O.T.* in Gérardmer, ☎ 29.63.08.74, La Bresse, ☎ 29.61.11.29. *Relais Rencontre,* Vilosnes, ☎ 29.85.82.87. *Centre départemental de Plein air,* Saint-Mihiel, ☎ 29.89.03.59.

Skiing : most ski resorts are in the Vosges Mts, offering cross-country, down-hill skiing, or Nordic-style ski-treks. Enq : **Vosges** : 13, rue A.-Briand, 88000 Épinal, ☎ 29.35.50.34; *Centre-École de Longemer,* ☎ 29.63.10.76. *Centre-École (cross-country) des Bas-Rupts,* 88400 Gérardmer, ☎ 29.63.12.06 (high season), 29.63.13.87 (low season). **Meurthe-et-Moselle** : *Club Vosgien,* rue de Fontenay, 54000 Nancy, ☎ 83.32.80.52. Ski jump in Bussang, *T.O.,* ☎ 29.61.50.37.

Flying, gliding, parachuting, ballooning : *Base de Marville,* ☎ 82.26.63.62; *Hauts de Chée,* ☎ 29.75.72.75. Numerous air clubs for gliding : *Aéro-Club (A.C.) de l'Est,* ☎ 83.29.43.63 and 83.29.34.58; *A.C. de Blainville,* ☎ 83.29.50.42; *A.C. de Haute-Moselle,* ☎ 83.47.33.54, *Ailes Mosellanes,* 57000 Metz, B.P. 701, *A.C. de Sarrebourg;* Dieuze, Sarreguemines and Thionville : enq. *S.I.* and *T.O.* Parachuting : *A.C. de Doncourt,* ☎ 83.29.58.78, *Ailes Mosellanes* (→ above). Flights in light aircraft, beginners' courses and first flights at all air clubs. Hang gliding : Thionville : *A.C. de Basse-Moselle,* Thionville-Yutz Airfield and *A.C. de Sud-Meusien,* ☎ 29.79.23.72 or 29.78.56.06; Plagny-la-Blanche-Côte, ☎ 29.89.46.67. Ballooning : *A.C. de la Mortagne,* ☎ 83.73.27.21, *A.C. Bassin de Briey,* ☎ 83.29.58.78, and Lorraine Aéronautic Club, ☎ 29.36.31.85.

Hunting and shooting : *Féd. Dép. :* **Meurthe-et-Moselle** : 1, rue St-Dizier, 54000 Nancy, ☎ 83.32.33.21. **Meuse** : 4, rue Henri-Dunant, 55000 Bar-le-Duc, ☎ 29.79.03.31. **Moselle** : 2, rue Chèvremont, 57000 Metz, ☎ 87.75.11.74. **Vosges** : 11, rue Charlet, 88000 Épinal, ☎ 29.31.10.74.

Fishing : enq at *Féd. Dép. de la Pêche.* **Meuse** : 2, rue Saint-Maur, 55100 Verdun, ☎ 29.86.15.70. **Moselle** : 5, rue de la Monnaie, 57580 Remilly, ☎ 87.64.60.72. **Vosges** : 18, av. du Mal-de-Lattre-de-Tassigny, 88000 Épinal, ☎ 29.35.08.89.

Salt

From time immemorial Lorraine has been a major centre of salt production in France. Traces of large salt mines dating from prehistoric times have been found in Saulnois (→ Marsal). Today, Lorraine remains responsible for half the national production. In the 19thC, the availability of salt deposits encouraged the development of chemical industries (e. g., chlorine, bicarbonate of soda), which were established mostly between Nancy and Lunéville.

Golf : Bitche (open for practice; in 1988, 18 holes); Combles (9 km from Bar-le-Duc, 9 holes); Cherisey (9), Épinal (9), Madine (2 × 9), Nancy (18), Vittel (18, 9).

 Towns and places

From Clermont to Beaulieu *(approx 90-120 km, half-day; see map 1)*

Rising 100m from the plains, this wooded massif separating Lorraine from Champagne was an important strategic area during WWI.

► **Clermont-en-Argonne** (pop. 1 810) : overlooking the Aire Valley (view★ from the terrace of the 16thC church), on the site of the château, chapel with 16thC Holy Sepulchre; orientation chart. ► near Rarécourt **fortified house of the Valley** (17th-18thC; *6 km S, Jul.-Aug. 9-12 & 2-6:30;* collection of regional ceramics★). ► Only shell-holes mark the spot where the village of **Vauquois** once stood. Like many hill sites, this was the scene of bitter fighting during WWI, as vast cemeteries attest; similarly with **Côte 304** (Hill no. 304, across from Mort-Homme, 11.5 km E) and **Montfaucon Crest** (American Memorial, *234 steps,* view★). ► **Varennes-en-Argonnes** : where Louis XVI was arrested during his flight from Paris on 21 June 1791; also the scene of wartime carnage. Argonne Museum *(daily ex Tue.; Jul.-Sep., 10-12 & 2-6; rest of year, 2:30 & 5:30).* ► Along the Haute-Argonne, a quick detour via the former Cistercian **abbey of Lachalade** (14thC church, 17thC buildings), back to Islettes and up the Biesme Valley. ► **Hermitage of**

Saint-Rouin : chapel★ (1955), one of the prettiest sights of Argonne, near a string of lakes. ► **Beaulieu★** on a crest, a neat little village with a 13thC wine press. □

Practical Information

CLERMONT-EN-ARGONNE, ⊠ 55120, 30 km W of **Verdun.**

Hotel :
Bellevue (L.F.), rue de la Libération, ☎ 29.87.41.02, AE DC Euro Visa, 16 rm Ⓟ ⊰ ◍ closed Wed, 15-28 Feb, 22 Dec-15 Jan, 100. Rest. ♦♦ ⊰ Spec : *terrine de foies de volailles, truite Belle Lorraine, lotte à l'oseille,* 55-125; child : 30.

FUTEAU, ⊠ 55120, 10 km SW of **Clermont-en-Argonne.**

Hotel :
★★ *L'Orée du Bois* (L.F.), ☎ 29.88.28.41, Euro Visa, 10 rm Ⓟ ⊰ ⌂ ⬥ closed Jan, 210. Rest. ♦♦ ⊰ ♪ 10 rm, closed Tue and Sun eve, 60-180.

1. The Argonne region

BACCARAT

Epinal 43, Nancy 55, Paris 351 km
pop 5437 ⊠ 54120   C3
On the edge of the Vosges mountains, where the fir-covered slopes become steeper and sandstone is the favoured building material.
▶ Next door to the renowned **Baccarat crystalworks** founded in 1764, the **Crystal Museum**★ explains the production processes; many splendid examples *(Apr., Sun., 2-6; May-15 Jun, weekends 2-6; 16 Jun.-15 Jul. daily 2-6:30; 16 Jul.-15 Sept. daily 10-12 & 2-6:30, Sun., Tue. am; 16-30 Sep. daily 2-6; 1-15 Oct., Sun. 2-6).* ▶ **Church** (1957) with steeple belfry 70m high, and crystal windows★ mounted in sculpted concrete.   □

Practical Information ─────────────

BACCARAT
ⓘ résidence du Centre, ☎ 83.75.13.37.
SNCF ☎ 83.75.10.39.

Recommended
Farmhouse-inn : *Ferme de Prébois*, 2, rte de Bayon, ☎ 83.75.13.75, Table d'hôte. Spec : *quiche lorraine, poulet aux raisins, pastourelle..*
♥ *Cie des Cristalleries de Baccarat*, rue des Cristalleries, ☎ 83.75.12.47.

┌───┐
│ If you enjoy sports, consult the pages pertaining to │
│ the regions; there you will find addresses for prac- │
│ ticing your favorite sport.   │
└───┘

Nearby
RAON-L'ÉTAPE , ⊠ 88110, 9 km SE.
Hotel :
★★ *Eau Vive* (L.F.), rue J.-B.-Demenge, ☎ 29.41.44.68, Visa, 12 rm ℗ ⚌ ⚘ closed Wed, 160.

BAINS-LES-BAINS

Epinal 30, Vesoul 50, Paris 359 km
pop 1792 ⊠ 88240   B4
A spa in the middle of the woods with 16 springs whose supposed curative properties were known to the Romans; village atmosphere; the "Bain Romain" (Roman bath) is a delightful specimen of 19thC spa architecture.
▶ Numerous walks in the surrounding woods dotted with ponds : **Fontaines Chaudes** *(7 km W)*, **Noirmont** *(8 km E;* view as far as the Juras), **Uzemain** *(12 km N;* zoo amusement park), **Fontenoy-le-Château** *(7 km SW;* small embroidery museum in town hall, *May-Sep., Tue. and Fri. pm).*   □

Practical Information ─────────────

♨ 1, av. du Dr-Matthieu, ☎ 29.36.32.04.
ⓘ pl. du Bain-Romain, ☎ 29.36.31.75.
SNCF ☎ 29.36.30.22.

Hotel :
★★ *La Poste*, 11, rue de Verdun, ☎ 29.36.31.01, 30 rm ⚘ pens (h.s.), closed Sat and Sun, 400. Rest. ♦ ⚘ 58-170.

▲ ★★*Les Pins* (50 pl), ☎ 29.36.33.51.

BAR-LE-DUC*

Verdun 57, Nancy 85, Paris 229 km
pop 20029 ⊠ 55000   A2
Former capital of a duchy split between the rulers of France and Germany; now an important market town in the heart of dairy country; Europe's largest cheese depot.
▶ **Place Saint-Pierre**★ : in the upper town, surrounded by 14th-17thC mansions; law courts (Palais de Justice); **church of St. Etienne**★ (14th-16thC Gothic) displaying the skeletal figure★★ sculpted by Ligier Richier (1500-67) at the request of René de Châlon, prince of Orange who, killed in battle in 1545, left precise instructions that his memorial should represent a body that had lain 3 years in the tomb. 16th-18thC façades in the neighbouring streets, especially Rue des Ducs-de-Bar (no. 75, 14thC winepress in the courtyard). ▶ **Château Neuf** (16th-17thC) with a view★ over the old town, a local **museum** *(Jun.-15 Sep.; daily ex Tue., 2-6; 16 Sep.-May, Wed., Sat., Sun., 3-6).* ▶ Former **Collège Gilles-de-Trèves** (Renaissance courtyard★) : towards the lower town. ▶ Rue du Bourg : 16th-18thC houses. ▶ **Church of St. Antoine** : 14th-15thC frescos. ▶ On the left bank of the Ornain, **church of Notre-Dame,** building mostly 13th-14thC; 16thC sculpture of Christ★.

Upper Ornain Valley, from Bar-le-Duc to Domrémy *(62 km)*

▶ **Bar-le-Duc.** ▶ Diversified light industry has not changed the agricultural nature of the countryside. ▶ View★ over the valley from the **Tannois** lookout *(belvédère).* ▶ **Ligny-en-Barrois,** centre of the French lens-making industry : 13th-17thC church with interesting pulpit★, statuary; museum of the Luxembourg Tower (12th-14thC.): local archaeology *(May-Sep., 2-6; Jul.-Aug., 10-12 & 2-6; closed Tue.).* ▶ **Saint-Amand** : Gallo-Roman excavations *(open Aug.).* ▶ **Bonnet** *(4.5 km from Houdelaincourt)* : 12th-14thC church; polychrome recumbent effigy of Saint Florentin, damaged but interesting paintings of his miracles. ▶ **Gondrecourt-le-Château** : 14thC tower next to old building housing a Horse Museum.   □

Practical Information _____

ℹ hôtel de ville, ☎ 29.79.11.13.
SNCF ☎ 29.79.21.98.
🚏 pl. Reggio, ☎ 29.79.34.35.
Car rental : *Avis*, Saint-Dizier train station.

Hotels :
★★★ *Ducs*, parc Bradfer, ☎ 29.79.32.66, 26 rm P ▨ ⌕ 240. Rest. ♦ ♪ 60-210.
★★ *Auberge de la Source* (L.F.), Tremont-sur-Saulx, ☎ 29.75.45.22, Euro Visa, 16 rm P ≼ ▨ ⌕ closed Sun eve and Mon, 14-28 Feb, 2-24 Aug, 180. Rest. ♦ ♪ ⅙ ❦ 120-210.

Restaurants :
● ♦♦ *La Meuse Gourmande*, 1, rue François-de-Guise, ☎ 29.79.28.40 P ≼ ▨ ⌕ ♪ ⅙ closed Mon and Sun eve. In the old town, a former monastery is now a gourmet restaurant featuring regional cuisine by J.-L. Chrétien : *potau-feu de lotte, blanquette d'escargots*, local desserts, 145-170.
♦♦ *Le Château de Tannois*, Tannois, 7 km dir. Nancy, ☎ 29.79.15.70, AE P ≼ ▨ ⌕ ♪ ❦ closed Mon and Sun eve, Aug. Chambres d'hôte. Spec : poached marinated salmon, *confit, terrine de légumes, foie gras de canard*, 130-200.

Recommended
Farmhouse-inn : at Vilotte-sur-Aire, *Colombier*, 55260 Pierrefitte-sur-Aire, ☎ 29.70.00.19.
♥ *Auction house*, 40, quai V.-Hugo, ☎ 29.79.20.64 ; currant jam : *Aux Ducs de Bar*, 72, bd de la Rochelle, ☎ 29.79.01.38 ; pub : *Le Shannon*, 5, rue Arras, ☎ 29.79.38.68, open til 3am ; tea room : *Le Madizan*, 7, rue Dufour, ☎ 29.76.35.14, open 11am-3am.

BUSSANG

Belfort 43, Epinal 50, Paris 410 km
pop 1920 ▨ 88540   C4
Among mountains near the source of the Moselle, where the Théâtre du Peuple (People's Theatre) was founded in 1895 ; open-air stage where performances are given by the local people *(Sat., Sun. in Aug.)*.

Nearby
▶ The Route du Col 4 km E to the source of the Moselle. A narrow forest track climbs to the **Petit Drumont** *(5-km drive then 15 min on foot;* alt. 1 200 m ; splendid view★). ▶ Down the **Moselle Valley★** via **Saint-Maurice** (climb to Tête des Perches, *11 km;* alt. 1 224m ; view ; or the Ballon d'Alsace★★, *9.5 km;* → Alsace) and **Le Thillot** (side trip to the Ballon de Servance, *1.5-km drive then 10 min on foot,* alt. 1 216 m, superb view★).   ☐

Practical Information _____

BUSSANG
✆ 641-1220m.
ℹ 7, rue d'Alsace, ☎ 29.61.50.37.
SNCF ☎ 29.61.50.21.

Hotels :
★★ *Le Tremplin* (L.F.), 8, rue du 3e-R.T.A., ☎ 29.61.50.30, AE DC Euro Visa, 20 rm P ≼ 🐎 ❦ closed Mon ex school and public hols, 30 Sep-30 Oct, 140. Rest. ♦ ♪ ⅙ 50-100 ; child : 35.
★★ *Sources* (L.F.), 12, rte des Sources, D 89, ☎ 29.61.51.94, Visa, 9 rm P ≼ ▨ ⌕ ❦ half pens (h.s.). Gym, UVA solarium, 320. Rest. ♦♦ ≼ ❦ 55-135 ; child : 40.

△ ★★*Deux-Rivières* (35 pl), ☎ 29.61.50.36 ; ★★*Larcenaire* (58 pl), ☎ 29.61.51.74.

Nearby

SAINT-MAURICE-SUR-MOSELLE, ▨ 88560, 5 km SW.
✆ 560-1250m.

ℹ pl. du 2-Oct. 1944, ☎ 29.25.12.34 ; mairie, ☎ 29.25.11.21.

Hotels :
★★★ *Relais des Ballons*, rte Benelux-Bâle, ☎ 29.25.11.09, 17 rm P ▨ ⌕ closed Mon lunch, 7-21 Oct, 200. Rest. ♦ *L'Auberge*, 80-130.
★★ *Au Pied des Ballons*, 1, rte du Ballon, ☎ 29.25.12.54, Euro Visa, 12 rm P ≼ ▨ ⌕ 🐎 ♪° closed 10-30 Nov, 165. Rest. ♦ closed Mon noon, 50-90.

△ ★★★*Les Deux Ballons* (130 pl), ☎ 29.25.11.26.

Le THILLOT, ▨ 88160, 10 km W.
ℹ mairie, ☎ 29.25.00.59.
SNCF ☎ 29.25.00.67.

Hotel :
★★ *Le Perce-Neige* (L.F.), Col-des-Croix, ☎ 29.25.02.63, AE DC, 20 rm P ≼ ▨ ⌕ closed 11 Nov-20 Dec, 160. Rest. ♦ ⅙ 60-90.

Recommended
Farmhouse-gîte : at Chapelle des Vées, *Le Prey*, 3 km on N 486, skiing (Alpine and cross-country).
Special children : at Ménil 2 km N, *H. Divoux*, Colline des Granges, ☎ 29.25.03.00, Goats, geese, ducks. Cross-country skiing lessons.

CHARMES

Epinal 26, Nancy 44, Paris 324 km
pop 5457 ▨ 88130   B3
On the banks of the Moselle, a small town whose reconstruction after WWII did not affect its charm. 15thC church, 16thC chapel. Monument de Lorraine *(3.5 km SW)* : valley view★.

Nearby
▶ 9km E, **Portieux** glassworks *(visit Tue., Fri. 9-12 ; closed 1 month in summer)*. ▶ **Châtel-sur-Moselle** *(11 km SE)* : ruins of 15thC fortress razed by Louis XIV, currently being restored ; underground passages and small museum *(Sat., Sun. and hols., 3-6,Mar.-Oct.)*.   ☐

Practical Information _____

ℹ mairie, ☎ 29.32.85.85.

Hotels :
★ *Central* (L.F.), 4, rue des Capucins, ☎ 29.38.02.40, 10 rm P ▨ closed Mon eve and Sun eve, 15-30 Jan, 10-24 Nov, 160. Rest. ♦♦ ♪ 60-180.
★ *Dancourt* (L.F.), 6, pl. Hôtel-de-Ville, ☎ 29.38.03.09, Euro Visa, 10 rm P ▨ closed Sun eve and Mon, 1-15 Jan, 1-15 Jul, 140. Rest. ♦ ♪ Spec : *millefeuille de coquilles Saint-Jacques au vermouth, noisettes d'agneau aux cinq* baies, 60-160.

△ *Municipal* (70 pl), ☎ 29.32.85.85.

COMMERCY

Bar-le-Duc 38, Verdun 53, Paris 267 km
pop 7958 ▨ 55200   A2
When Stanislas Leszczynski governed Lorraine in the 18thC (→ Brief regional history), his cook, it is said, invented the widely-appreciated little cakes known as *madeleines de Commercy*.

▶ **Château★** (18thC), destroyed by fire in 1944 and rebuilt, now houses municipal offices ; museum with small but choice display (ivories, ceramics ; *16 Jul.-2 Sep., 4 pm daily ex Tue. ; Sun. 3, 4:30)*. ▶ 9 km S, **Void** : small 17thC covered market, remains of 14th-15thC château.   ☐

Looking for a locality? Consult the index at the back of the book.

CONTREXÉVILLE

Epinal 48, Nancy 76, Paris 329 km
pop 4582 ⊠ 88140   B4

A well-known spa in a peaceful, wooded valley near Vittel (→).

▶ **Bulgnéville** *(6.5 km W)* produces several cheeses including Munster; 16thC entombment of Christ in the church; small museum. 7 km SW of there, **Saint-Ouen-lès-Parey** : small 17thC château hidden in foliage; church (part Romanesque).

Forest of Darney, from Contrexéville to Vittel *(approx 100 km, half-day)*

▶ **Contrexéville.** ▶ Through **Dombrot-le-Sec** (14thC statue of the Virgin, 16thC Sainte Anne, 18thC wrought iron) to **Viviers-le-Gras** (pretty fountains), then follow the winding road at the foot of the hills. ▶ **Morizécourt** : 17thC Benedictine priory *(daily ex Tue. and Fri. 2-5 in Jul.; Sat. and Sun., Aug.-Sep.).* ▶ **Sérécourt** : fortified church; mink farm. Through **Flabémont Forest** (18thC portal and ruined cloister 2 km SW of Tignicourt) to ▶ **Monthureux-sur-Saône** : church with 16thC entombment of Christ showing Rhenish influence. ▶ **Bleurville** : small 11th-14thC church, long over a barn, built over an 11thC crypt *(daily 2-7).* ▶ Return to Monthureux, then via Claudon to **Droiteval** : Romanesque church on the magnificent site of a Cistercian abbey. ▶ Detour to **Cristallerie de la Rochère** (→ Franche-Comté) and through the forest to ▶ **Darney** where the state of Czechoslovakia was officially proclaimed at a meeting between the French Prime Minister Poincaré and the Czech Masaryk in 1918 (monument; museum in 18thC town hall). ▶ A short detour to see the **château de Lichecourt** (18thC) then on to **Relanges** : Romanesque church★ in the style of Cluny (11thC, 16thC nave). ▶ Via the **Chèvre Roche** vale★ to **Saint-Baslemont** : 16th-18thC château illustrating development from fortress to elegant residence. ▶ **Thuillières** : austere 18thC château *(Aug. : Sat.-Mon., 2:30-7).* ▶ **Vittel** (→).   ☐

Practical Information

♨ ☎ 29.08.03.24, (May-Sep).
ⓘ spa galleries, ☎ 29.08.08.68; mairie, ☎ 29.08.09.35.
SNCF ☎ 29.08.01.42.

Hotels :
● ★★★ *Etablissement*, Cour d'honneur, ☎ 29.08.17.30, AE DC Visa, 29 rm Ⓟ ≮ ⸬ closed 18 Sep-5 May, 280. Rest. ♦♦ ≮ ồ 115-140.
★★★ *Souveraine*, parc thermal (spa), ☎ 29.08.09.59, AE DC Euro Visa, 31 rm Ⓟ ⸬ closed 18 Sep-5 May. Built for the Shah of Persia in 1905, 280.
★★ *France*, 58, rue du Roi-Stanislas, ☎ 29.08.04.13, Visa, 40 rm Ⓟ ⸰ pens (h.s.), closed Mon, 1-29 Jan, 430. Rest. ♦ ⸰ ồ 60-120.

⚠ ★★★*Municipal* (80 pl), ☎ 29.08.15.06.

DOMRÉMY-LA-PUCELLE*

Nancy 57, Bar-le-Duc 62, Paris 443 km
pop 205 ⊠ 88300 Neufchâteau   A3

The most famous village in Lorraine, among wooded hills overlooking the Meuse Valley.

▶ **Joan of Arc's birthplace** (maison de Jeanne d'Arc; *daily 8-12:30 & 1:30-7, Apr.-12 Oct.; 9-12 & 2-5 ex Tue., rest of year).* Typical well-to-do 15thC peasant's house; the museum traces Joan's life (1412-31) and heroic career. ▶ Church : 12thC font where Joan was christened. ▶ Basilica (1891-1926) at **Bois-Chesnu**, where Joan heard her voices; a popular place of pilgrimage; view★ over the valley.

To Vaucouleurs *(22 km N)*

▶ **Goussaincourt** : in the outbuildings of the 16th-18thC château, a museum of peasant life and crafts exhibition. ▶ **Montbras** : château★ (1600) with superb Renaissance façade. ▶ **Sepvigny** : 15thC fortified church; 500 m away, Vieux Astre chapel (12thC; remains of 15thC frescos).   ☐

Joan of Arc

Joan of Arc was born in the village of Domrémy on 6 January 1412. At the age of 13, by now a shepherdess, Joan began to hear voices (St. Michael, St. Catherine, St. Margaret) urging her to drive the English out of France and to have the Dauphin crowned King at Reims. Joan kept quiet for 3 years but eventually confided in her uncle, who accompanied her to an audience with Robert de Baudricourt, the royal governor at Vaucouleurs. Undeterred by Baudricourt's incredulous dismissal (he threatened to box her ears and have her exorcised), Joan managed by her sincerity to win support among the people of the region. They gave the girl a horse and equipment, and Baudricourt, won over by her determination, supplied an escort of six men. On 23 February 1429, to the acclamations of the townsfolk, 17-year-old Joan rode out of Vaucouleurs to seek the Dauphin at Chinon. She never saw her native Lorraine again.

DUN-SUR-MEUSE

Verdun 33, Sedan 47, Paris 275 km
pop 749 ⊠ 55110   A1

A country town, formerly fortified, on a hill 80m above the river; 14thC church with a martial appearance.

▶ **Mont-devant-Sassey** *(6 km N)* : 11th-12thC Romanesque church★ showing Rhenish influence, porch★, 11th-16thC statuary, crypt. ▶ **Stenay** *(13 km N),* another fortified town, now a centre of light industry; a few 17th-18thC houses. Museum of the Stenay Region (archaeology, folk arts and traditions; *10-12 & 2-6, May-Sep.).*   ☐

Practical Information

DUN-SUR-MEUSE
ⓘ mairie, ☎ 29.80.90.55.   ♥

Hotel :
★★ *Commerce* (L.F.), pl. du Monument, ☎ 29.80.90.25, DC Euro Visa, 11 rm Ⓟ pens, closed Mon, 25 Dec-1 Feb, 350. Rest. ♦ ⸰ ồ 50-115.

⚠ ★★*Lac Vert* (110 pl), ☎ 29.80.90.38.

Nearby

INOR, ⊠ 55700, 7 km N.

Hotel :
★★ *Faisan Doré* (L.F.), rue de l'Écluse, ☎ 29.80.35.45, Euro Visa, 13 rm Ⓟ ⸬ ⸰ ⸙ closed Fri eve (Oct-Apr), 155. Rest. ● ♦♦ closed Fri noon. On the banks of the Meuse, good, fresh cooking : *sanglier aux morilles, canard aux mirabelles*, 40-150.

ÉPINAL*

Nancy 70, Vesoul 85, Paris 360 km
pop 40954 ⊠ 88000   B-C4

Images d'Épinal, brightly-coloured pictures on patriotic, pious or moralistic themes, were distributed throughout France by peddlers during the 18th and 19thC.

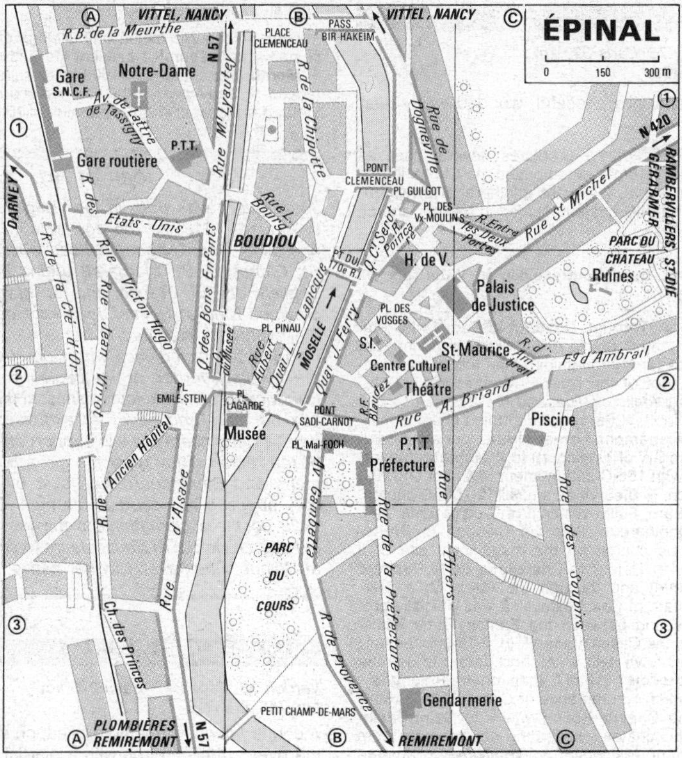

▶ **Museum** (B2) : paintings (including 17thC works by Georges de la Tour and Rembrandt) and an exceptional collection of popular art from the 16thC to the present day *(daily ex Tue. and nat. hols., 10-12 & 2-6 or 5, Oct.-Mar.)*. ▶ **Imagerie Pellerin** (42 *bis* quai de Dogneville, *via B1*), exhibition and sale of popular art *(8:30-12 & 2-6:30 ex nat. hols.)*. ▶ Near the Place des Vosges (B2; arcades, old houses) : 13th-14thC **basilica of St. Maurice;** 11thC tower, reinforced 13thC; late Romanesque and regional Gothic. **Also...** ▶ **Church of Notre-Dame** (A1; 1958) : door with enamelled panels; stained glass★. Library and Rose Garden on left bank of the Moselle *(via B1)*.

Nearby

▶ Numerous walks in neighbouring forests *(signposted trails)*. ▶ **Bouzey Lake** *(8 km W)* : aquatic centre in pretty surroundings. □

Practical Information

ⓘ 13, rue de la Comédie (B2), ☎ 29.82.53.32.
✈ *Épinal-Mirecourt*, 40 km NW, ☎ 29.37.01.99.
SNCF ☎ 29.82.50.50.
🚌 pl. de la Gare (A1), ☎ 29.82.54.82.
Car rental : *Avis*, train station; 47, rue de Nancy, ☎ 29.82.26.25.

Hotels :

★★★ ***Ducs de Lorraine***, 16, quai du Colonel-Sérot (B1), ☎ 29.34.35.20, Visa, 10 rm Ⓟ closed Sun eve and Mon, 15 Jul-15 Aug, 250. Rest. ♦♦♦ ♪ Spec : *oeufs de caille aux morilles et foie d'oie, filet de boeuf canaille*, 85-220.

★★ ***Le Colombier***, (Inter-Hôtel), 104, fg d'Ambrail (C2), ☎ 29.35.50.05, Tx 960141, AE DC Euro Visa, 32 rm Ⓟ closed 18 Jul-10 Aug, 23 Dec-4 Jan, 245.

★★ ***Mercure***, 13, pl. Stein (A2), ☎ 29.35.18.68, Tx 960277, AE DC Euro Visa, 45 rm Ⓟ ♪ ♿ half pens (h.s.), 660. Rest. ♦♦ ***Mouton Blanc*** ♪ ♿ *Saumon mariné à l'huile de gingembre, foie de veau poêlé à la framboise*, 75-200; child : 35.

Restaurant :

● ♦♦ ***Les Abbesses***, 23, rue de la Louvière, ☎ 29.82.53.69, AE Visa Ⓟ ♪ ♿ closed Tue and Sun eve. J.-C. Aiguier now serves his succulent specialties to the inhabitants of Épinal : *foie gras, pieds de porc farcis, feuilleté de sole et lotte aux écrevisses à l'oignon croquant*, 155-270.

FORBACH

Sarreguemines 20, Metz 60, Paris 384 km
pop 27321 ✉ 57600 C1

ⓘ hôtel de ville, ☎ 87.85.02.43.
SNCF ☎ 87.85.50.50.

Hotel :

★★ ***Berg***, 50, av. St-Rémy, ☎ 87.85.09.12, 21 rm Ⓟ ♪ 145.

Restaurant :

● ♦ ***Chez Lucullus***, 35, rue de Verdun, ☎ 87.87.62.40, Visa ♪ closed Mon eve, Tue eve, Sun eve, 55-130.

GÉRARDMER**

Saint-Dié 30, Epinal 44, Paris 404 km
pop 9647 ✉ 88400 C4

The oldest tourist office in France was founded here in July 1875; pure air and superb countryside (lake,

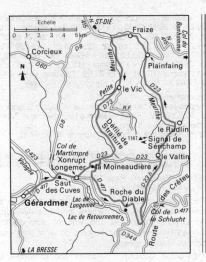

2. Lakes valley

meadows, woods, mountains) make it a pleasant year-round resort where the traditional production of fine linens continues. ▶ Delightful walks by the lake. ▶ In town, **Forestry Museum** (6 Rue du 152ᵉ-RI); **Vosges Regional Craftshop** (Pl. de l'Église). ▶ More than 300km of marked trails in the forest.

Vallée des Lacs (the valley of lakes) and the upper Meurthe region *(round trip approx 70km, half-day, see map 2).*

▶ **Gérardmer.** ▶ **Saut-des-Cuves**★ : waterfall. ▶ 2 km beyond **Xonrupt-Longemer**, a road on the right leads to **Moineaudière** (site★) : exhibition and sale of cacti, fossils and minerals★. ▶ One-way road leads to D417 running above the Vallée des Lacs : view★★ over **Lakes Retournemer** and **Longemer** from the **Roche du Diable** (devil's rock)★ : exhibition of minerals *(Jun.-Sep.).* ▶ From **Le Collet** *(2 km from the Schlucht Pass★)* : excursions to **Hohneck**★★ and the Alpine Garden at Haut-Chitelet (→ Alsace). Return by the Meurthe Valley. Just before Rudlin : the **Rudlin Waterfall** *(45-min walk there and back).* ▶ **Plainfaing** and **Fraize** : up the **Petite Meurthe Valley.** ▶ From Vic : forest track to the **Sérichamp Signal** (alt. 1 147 m ; panorama★★). ▶ **Defile de Straiture** : valley narrows and, in summer, the river disappears under the tumbled rocks.

Towards Épinal

▶ **Liézey** *(10 km)* : craftshop (exhibition, sale ; *Sun. and school hols., 3-6 ; closed Jan.-Mar.).* ▶ After **Le Tholy** : great and small **Tendon** waterfalls★. ▶ On the banks of the Vologne, **Champ-le-Duc** : early-12thC church★ replaces one built by Charlemagne.

Tétras road, from Gérardmer to Bussang *(approx 40 km).*

▶ **La Bresse** *(14 km S of Gérardmer)* : important winter sports resort ; the road cuts through 100 km² of forest inhabited by red and roe deer, wild boar, woodgrouse and other game. ▶ **Lake Corbeaux** : walled in granite. Proceed to La Vierge pass and, by the forest roads, one arrives at the foot of **Grand Ventron**★ (alt. 1 202 m ; *10 min on foot;* view★). ▶ From La Chaume, get back on the road which, starting at **Ventron**, climbs towards the Oderen Pass. ▶ Before arriving at the summit, turn right on a small road which leads to the Page Pass, then back down towards Bussang (→).

Practical Information _____

GÉRARDMER
☎ 666-1113m.
ⓘ pl. des Déportés, ☎ 29.63.08.74.
SNCF ☎ 29.63.08.76.

Hotels :
★★★ *Bragard*, pl. du Tilleul, ☎ 29.63.06.31, Tx 960964, AE DC Euro Visa, 61 rm 🄿 ⁂ ♨ ▥ 330. Rest. ♦♦♦ ⁂ ♪ 80-160 ; child : 45.
★★★ *La Réserve*, facing the lake, ☎ 29.63.21.60, Tx 961509, AE DC Euro Visa, 32 rm 🄿 ⁂ ♨ ♪ ⁂ closed 15 Nov-20 Dec, 180. Rest. ●● ⁂ ♪ Spec : *cailles en cocotte aux fondants d'échalotes, jambon de montagne braisé sauce crème au vin d'Alsace,* 80-125.
● ★★ *Chalet du Lac* (L.F.), on the right bank of the lake, D 417, ☎ 29.63.38.76, Visa, 11 rm 🄿 ⁂ ♨ closed Fri (l.s.), 1 Oct-1 Nov, 170. Rest. ♦ ⁂ ♪ ♨ 80-130.
● ★★ *Relais de la Mauselaine* (L.F.), La Rayée, ☎ 29.63.05.74, Visa, 15 rm 🄿 ⁂ ♨ ✇ closed 1 Oct-15 Dec, 15-31 Mar. At the foot of the slopes, 210. Rest. ● ♦ ♪ 50-140.
★★ *La Bonne Auberge de Martimprey*, Col de Martimprey, 3 km dir. Saint-Dié, ☎ 29.63.19.08, Tx 961408, AE DC Euro Visa, 14 rm 🄿 ⁂ ♨ closed Tue eve and Wed (l.s.), 5 Nov-15 Dec, 180. Rest. ♦ ♪ 55-100.
★★ *La Paix* (L.F.), facing the lake, ☎ 29.63.38.78, AE Euro Visa, 21 rm 🄿 ⁂ ♨ ✇ 210. Rest. ♦ ●● ⁂ ♪ ♨ Award-winning chef Gérard Lagrange offers contemporary comfort and luscious food along with old-fashioned charm : *matelote d'escargots aux poireaux, pot-au-feu du pêcheur, civet de marcassin au chou rouge.* High-class wines, 65-170.
★★ *Lac Hôtel*, esplanade du Lac, facing the lake, ☎ 29.63.38.23, 41 rm 🄿 ⁂ ♨ closed 30 Sep-20 Apr, 200. Rest. ♦ ✇ 45-200.
★★ *Parc* (L.F.), 12-14, av. de la Ville-de-Vichy, ☎ 29.63.32.43, Tx 961408, Euro Visa, 38 rm 🄿 ⁂ ♨ half pens (h.s.), closed Oct-Easter ex Feb school hols, 300. Rest. ♦ ⁂ ♪ 55-85.
★★ *Viry*, pl. des Déportés, ☎ 29.63.02.41, Tx 961408, AE DC Euro Visa, 18 rm 🄿 ♨ ⁂ ⁂ pens, half pens (h.s.), 390. Rest. ♦ ⁂ ♪ *L'Aubergade* ♪ ⏚ closed Sat eve (l.s.), 55-130 ; child : 45.
★ *Auberge de Lorraine* (L.F.), 44, bd de St-Dié, ☎ 29.63.09.82, Euro Visa, 8 rm 🄿 ⁂ ♨ ✇ closed Sun eve and Wed (l.s.), 15 Nov-15 Dec, 120. Rest. ●● ⏚ 45-100 ; child : 40.
⚑ ★★★★*Ramberchamp* (266 pl), ☎ 29.63.03.82 ; ★★*Bas-Rupts* (50 pl), ☎ 29.63.37.15 ; ★★*Granges Bas* (100 pl), ☎ 29.63.12.03 ; ★★*Myrtilles* (65 pl), ☎ 29.63.21.38 ; ★★*Ruisseaux* (70 pl), ☎ 29.63.13.06 ; ★★*Sapins* (70 pl), ☎ 29.63.15.01 ; ☎ 29.25.41.29.

Nearby

Les BAS-RUPTS, 4 km S on the D 486.

Hotel :
● ★★★ *Hostellerie des Bas-Rupts, Chalet Fleuri* (R.S.), ☎ 29.63.09.25, Tx 960992, AE DC Visa, 26 rm 🄿 ⁂ ♨ ♪° half pens (h.s.), 680. Rest. ●● ⁂ ♪ Light cuisine by M. Philippe in an elegant mountain chalet. Reserve. *Pot-au-feu de la mer, feuilleté de soles.* 100-220 ; child : 55.

Restaurant :
♦♦ *A La Belle Marée*, ☎ 29.63.06.83, AE DC Euro Visa 🄿 ⁂ ♨ ✇ closed Mon and Sun eve, 45-150 ; child : 30.

La BRESSE, ✉ 88250, 14 km S.
☎ 630-1350m.
ⓘ 21, quai Iranées, ☎ 29.25.41.29.

Hotels :
● ★★★ *Résidence des vallées* (L.F.), 31, rue Paul-Claudel, ☎ 29.25.41.39, Tx 960573, AE DC Euro Visa, 54 rm 60 apt 🄿 ⁂ ♨ ♪ ⁂ ⏚ ▥ ♪° half pens (h.s.), body-building gym, sauna, 520. Rest. ♦ ⁂ ♪ ⏚ 70-100 ; child : 40.
★ *Lac des Corbeaux* (L.F.), 103, rue du Hohneck, ☎ 29.25.41.17, DC Euro Visa, 17 rm 🄿 ⁂ ♨ ✇ 120. Rest. ♦ ⁂ ♪ ⏚ 40-100.

Auberge du Pêcheur (L.F.), La Vologne, ☎ 29.25.43.86, AE DC Euro Visa, 5 rm ℙ ≼ ⋘ ⌕ closed Tue eve and Wed, 25 Jun-7 Jul, 1-15 Dec, 95. Rest. ♦ ≼ ♪ 35-100.

⚠ ★★*Les Ecorces* (150 pl), ☎ 29.25.41.29.

Recommended
Farmhouse-inn : *La Retelere*, ☎ 29.25.52.10, lodging in summer only; appetizing food, local products for sale.

PLAINFAING, ⊠ 88230 Fraize, 24 km NE.

Hotel :
★★ **Relais Vosges-Alsace** (L.F.), Col du Bonhomme, ☎ 29.50.32.61, AE DC Euro Visa, 13 rm ℙ closed 2 Nov-2 Dec. In the heart of the Vosgian forest, 170. Rest. ♦ ≼ 45-110.

Recommended
Farmhouse-gîte : *F. Pierron*, near the Col de Bonne-Fontaine, 2 km NW on D 11, ☎ 29.61.80.45, camping, fishing; at Mandray, 10 km N, *domaine du Grand Maly*, ☎ 29.58.01.74 Horseback riding and fishing, food items for sale.
Farmhouse-inn : *les Grands Prés*, ☎ 29.50.41.66. Spec : *terrines, pâté lorrain*, poultry, raspberry tarts, plums, *foie gras and confits* (in autumn).

Le THOLY, ⊠ 88530, 10 km W.
ⓘ mairie, ☎ 29.61.81.18.

Hotels :
★★ **Gérard** (L.F.), pl. Gal-Leclerc, ☎ 29.61.81.07, Tx 961408, AE DC Euro Visa, 23 rm ℙ ≼ ⋘ ⌕ 🐎 half pens, closed Sep-Oct, 170. Rest. ♦ ≼ ♪ 55-110.
★★ **La Grande Cascade** (L.F.), 24, rte du Col de Bonnefontaine, ☎ 29.33.21.08, Tx 961408, AE DC Euro Visa, 21 rm ℙ ≼ ⋘ ⌕ ঌ closed 26 Oct-8 Dec, 95. Rest. ♦ ≼ ♪ ঌ 55-160 ; child : 35.

⚠ ★★★★*De Noir Rupt* (35 pl), ☎ 29.61.81.27.

Recommended
Farmhouse-inn : at Bouvacôte, *F. Maxant*, 3 km E on D 417, ☎ 29.61.84.82.

VENTRON, ⊠ 88310 Cornimont, 26 km S.
♒ 630-1100m.
ⓘ ☎ 29.25.07.02.

Hotels :
● ★★★ **Les Buttes**, Ermitage Frère Joseph, dir. Col d'Oderen, ☎ 29.24.18.09, Euro Visa, 30 rm ℙ ≼ ⋘ ⌕ ♪ 🐎 ঌ ▭ ☞ pens, closed 15 Nov-20 Dec. At the foot of the slopes, 300. Rest. ♦ ♪ ঌ 🐎 95-130 ; child : 50.
★★ **Ermitage** (L.F.), annex of *Les Buttes*, ☎ 29.24.18.09, Euro Visa, 60 rm ℙ ≼ ⋘ ⌕ 🐎 ঌ ▭ ☞ closed 15 Oct-15 Nov, 260. Rest. ♦ 65-100.

Recommended
Farmhouse-inn : *La Zimette*, Rupt du Moulin, ☎ 29.24.18.20, Spec : *terrine maison, coq au riesling*. Ski, fishing, tennis. Recommended stopover ; *La Chaume du Grand Ventron*, alt. 1 200 m, ☎ 29.25.52.53, Spec : *fumé de Laboyaure, omelette des Chaumes, saucisse fumée aux tofayes*. Recommended stopover.

XONRUPT-LONGEMER, ⊠ 88400 Gérardmer, 2 km E.
♒ 700-1225m.
ⓘ Gérardmer, ☎ 29.63.08.74.

Hotels :
● ★★★ **Le Collet** (L.F.), 2 km from the Col de la Schlurcht, ☎ 29.63.11.43, Tx 961408, AE DC Euro Visa, 25 rm ℙ ≼ ⌕ 🐎 ঌ half pens (h.s.), closed 6-16 Apr, 12-17 Nov, 470.
★★★ **Saut des Cuves**, au pont Saut-des-Cuves, ☎ 29.63.30.46, 27 rm ℙ ≼ ⌕ closed 15 Nov-15 Dec, 240. Rest. ♦ ♪ 55-105.
★★ **La Vallée**, rte de la Schlurcht, ☎ 29.63.37.01, 12 rm ℙ ≼ ⌕ closed Nov, 130. Rest. ♦ Family atmosphere. Spec : *truite au bleu, tourte vosgienne*, luscious tarts, 40-70.
★★ **Lac de Longemer** (L.F.), 100, rue Longemer, ☎ 29.63.37.21, 18 rm ℙ ≼ ⋘ closed 15 Nov-15 Dec, 200. Rest. ♦ ♪ 50-170.

⚠ ★★*Belle Vue* (35 pl), ☎ 29.63.13.30 ; ★★*Chaumière* (35 pl), ☎ 29.63.13.30 ; ★★*Domaine de Longemer* (210 pl), ☎ 29.63.07.30 ; ★★*Eau Vive* (42 pl), ☎ 29.63.07.37 ; ★★*Jonquilles* (220 pl), ☎ 29.63.34.01 ; ★★*Les Pergis* (70 pl), ☎ 29.63.20.36 ; ★★*Orée du Bois* (40 pl), ☎ 29.63.29.82 ; ★★*Sorbiers* (33 pl), ☎ 29.63.36.04 ; ★★*Vologne* (70 pl), ☎ 29.63.06.57 ; *Verte Vallée* (90 pl), ☎ 29.63.24.77.

Recommended
Farmhouse-inn : at Balveurche, rte du col de la Schlurcht, ☎ 29.63.26.02, Spec : sauerkraut, pies and Munster cheese for sale. Skiing.
Youth hostel : *la Roche du Page*, ☎ 29.63.07.17.

LONGWY

Metz 65, Verdun 66, Paris 332 km
pop 17482 ⊠ 54400   B1

The second-largest steel production centre in Lorraine is at Longwy-Bas, where immense mills crowd the Chiers Valley. At the ancient stronghold of Longwy-Haut, trees and flowers do what they can to improve the landscape.

▶ **Regional Museum** : ceramics and enamels★ from Longwy. ▶ Lookout offers spectacular views of the valley at night. ▶ N, in Longwy-Haut, **Mont-Saint-Martin** : Romanesque church★ (12thC ; disused). ▶ At the SW exit from town, the **Chiers Valley** regains a country look ; large Renaissance château (1572 ; *15 Jul.-31 Aug., 2-6*) at **Cons-la-Grandville**. A bit further, on the plateau, the **fort de Fermont**, part of the Maginot Line (*Apr.-Sep., daily 1:30-5 ; Sat., Sun. in Oct. ; Sun., Nov.-Mar.*).   □

Practical Information _____

LONGWY
ⓘ ☎ 82.24.27.17.
𝘚𝘕𝘊𝘍 ☎ 82.24.50.50.
🚌 ☎ 82.24.37.08.

Nearby
BEUVEILLE, ⊠ 54620 Pierrepont, 8 km SE on D 18.
Restaurant :
♦♦ **La Grillade**, ☎ 82.89.75.06, Visa ⌀ closed Mon eve and Tue , Feb, 20 Dec-3 Jan. Nice little inn, 60-160.

LONGUYON, ⊠ 54260, 18 km SW.
𝘚𝘕𝘊𝘍 ☎ 82.39.42.57.

Hotel :
★★ **Lorraine**, (I.L.A.), pl. de la Gare, ☎ 82.26.50.07, AE DC Euro Visa, 15 rm ℙ closed Mon, 6 Jan-4 Feb, 160. Rest. ● ♦♦ **Le Mas** ♪ A top *sommelier de France*, G. Tisserant serves seasonal dishes : *langoustine en feuilleté à la julienne de légumes*. Great and simple wines, 80-220.

LORRAINE Nature Park

A-B2
185 km² of nature park, created in 1974 to improve the quality of life in major urban areas and to encourage agricultural development.

Western zone
▶ From the Meuse to the Moselle, including the Côtes de Meuse : scene of heavy fighting in 1914-18 ; the Plain of Woëvre, covered with lakes and forests ; the Côtes de Moselle (numerous small valleys, → Pont-à-Mousson and Metz). ▶ **Butte de Montsec★** : American memorial to the fallen (1918) ; view over Lake Madine : recreation centre. ▶ Follow the road at the foot of the slopes, where plum orchards replace vineyards. ▶ N of **Heudicourt : bird sanctuary★** (*15 Jun.-15 Sep., 9-8, Tue. 2-8 ; 15 Mar.-14 Jun. and 16 Sep.-15 Nov., 2-6 Mon.-Sat., 10-6 Sun., nat. hols. and school hols.*). ▶ **Hattonchâ-**

tel★ : 14thC church with Renaissance altarpiece★ ; château completely rebuilt (in "Walt Disney Gothic") during the 1920s by an American donor *(daily, 9-12 & 2-5 or 7; closed Nov.-Easter);* Louise Cottin Museum (painter, 1907-74). ▶ **Hannonville** : Museum of Rural Arts and Traditions★ (19thC life in the region; *2-6, closed Tue., Fri.; Thu., Sat. 9-12 & 2-6).*

Eastern zone

▶ Forest and lakes (now recreation areas) between Château-Salins and Sarrebourg. ▶ **Vic-sur-Seille** : a few old houses, including the 1456 Mint *(Jul.-15 Sep., Wed-Sun., 9-12 & 2-6);* gate and towers of 13thC château. ▶ **Marsal**★ : salt was mined here in prehistoric times; Salt Museum★ *(Thu.-Sat., 9-12 & 2-6; Sun., Mon., Wed., pm only; closed Jan., Feb.).* ▶ **Tarquimpol,** on the edge of Lake Lindre : church with round bell tower; 1.5 km farther, château (16th-18thC) d'Alteville. ▶ **Vision-de-Sainte-Croix Park** near Stock Lake *(daily ex Mon. from 10 am., Apr.-Nov., tel. 87.03.92.05).* ▶ **Fénétrange** *(E of park)* : small medieval town where a nightwatchman still makes the rounds *(May-Sep., 9 and 10pm);* old houses, remains of fortifications (15th-16thC door); château (15thC), now Museum of Folk Arts and Traditions. ▶ **Munster** *(N of park, near Albestroff)* : 13th-14thC church★ in pure Gothic style. ☐

Practical Information ─────────────

BOUCONVILLE-SUR-MADT, ⊠ 55300 Saint-Mihiel.

Restaurant :
◆◆ *Deux Cheminées,* ☎ 29.90.42.79, closed Mon eve and Tue , Feb hols, 1-15 Sep. Spec : *turbotin à l'anchois au pistil de safran, agneau aux fèves et purée d'ail.* Cooked over a wood fire, 90-180.

HEUDICOURT, ⊠ 55210 Vigneulles-lès-Hattonchâtel.

Hotel :
★★ *Lac de Madine* (L.F.), ☎ 29.89.34.80, AE Euro Visa, 30 rm ℗ ⚜ ⚑ ㉓ closed Mon, Jan, Feb, 170. Rest. ◆ ♪ ㉓ 50-110.

⚐ ★★*Les Aires* (100 pl), ☎ 29.86.56.76 ; ★★*Les Passoms* (201 pl), ☎ 29.89.36.08.

LUNÉVILLE**

Nancy 30, Metz 93, Paris 326 km
pop 23231 ⊠ *54300* C3

The 18thC philosopher Voltaire called this town "the Versailles of Lorraine" in honour of brilliant evenings at the court of Duke Leopold and later of Stanislas Leszczynski.

▶ **Château**★★★ (started in 1702; restored after WWII) laid out like Versailles ; unfortunately, the interior decoration has completely disappeared. ▶ **Museum** : local ceramics★, history of the local garrison *(9-12 & 2-5 or 6 daily ex Tue.).* ▶ **Promenade des Bosquets** : large garden in French style *(son et lumière* spectacle 'Le Grand Carrousel' ; *Fri, Sat., Sun., 29 Jun.-16 Sep.).* ▶ **Motorcycle Museum** *(9-12 & 2-6 daily ex Mon. and nat. hols).* ▶ **Church of St. Jacques**★ (1745 ; Regency woodwork★) : a perfect example of Rococo style. ☐

Practical Information ─────────────

LUNÉVILLE
ⓘ pl. du château, ☎ 83.74.60.70.

Hotels :
● ★★ *Le Voltaire,* 8, av. Voltaire, ☎ 83.74.07.09, AE DC Euro Visa, 10 rm ℗ ⚜ ⚑ 120. Rest. ◆◆ ♪ ㉓ closed Mon and Sun eve, 70-180.
● *Château d'Adoménil,* Rehainviller, 3 km S on D 31, ☎ 83.74.04.81, AE DC Euro Visa, 5 rm ℗ ≼ ⚜ ⚑ closed Sun eve and Mon, 15 Jan-15 Feb, 500. Rest. ● ◆◆◆ ≼ ♪ An elegant and comfortable stopover not to be

missed. Excellent food : *noisettes d'agneau échalotes confites, homard au meursault,* 160-260.

Restaurant :
◆◆ *Georges de la Tour,* 18, rue de Lorraine, ☎ 83.73.44.04 ⚜ ♪ closed Tue eve and Wed , Feb school hols, 15-31 Aug. Spec : fish, game (in season), 70-140.

Nearby

LAMATH, ⊠ 54300 Lunéville, 7 km S.

Restaurant :
◆ *Auberge de la Mortagne,* rte de Bayon, ☎ 83.73.06.85, AE DC Euro Visa ⚜ ♪ ㉓ closed Wed and Sun eve, 15 Jul-4 Aug. Spec : *salade de girolles tièdes au foie gras, filet de sandre au pinot noir,* 90-160.

METZ***

Nancy 57, Strasbourg 162, Paris 330 km
pop 118502 ⊠ *57000* B2

Metz, an important commercial town since the Middle Ages and now 3hr from Paris by motorway, is the capital of the region and seat of the university. On the edge of the industrialized valley of Thionville, it was annexed to Germany between 1871 and 1918. Rebuilding, restoration and development have continued since the end of WWI.

▶ **Cathedral of St-Etienne**★★★ (B2 ; Gothic) : 13th-14thC structure of golden sandstone ; the uniformity of the architecture gives it particular distinction ; the elevations of the E end, the Mutte tower (facing the Place d'Armes) and the nave (42-m vaulting) are superb ; the glowing stained glass★★★ (6500 m² in area) dates from the 13th, 15th and 16thC ; panels designed by the 20thC artists Marc Chagall, Roger Bissière and Jacques Villon have been installed ; museum of religious sculpture in the crypt (16thC entombment of Christ★). ▶ The Classical **Hôtel de Ville** (town hall) dates from the 18thC. ▶ **Museum of Art and History**★★ (B1-2 ; *daily ex Tue., 9-12 & 2-5 or 6)* : in buildings incorporating ancient Roman baths and 15thC grainstore ; well-organized museum with important archaeological and medieval collections ; fine arts ; military section. ▶ S of the cathedral : covered market (an episcopal palace begun in 1785 and never finished) past streets leading to the **Place St-Louis** : medieval arcades, 14th-16thC houses with sturdy stone buttresses. ▶ **Church of St-Martin** (B3 ; 13th-15thC) : on the Roman rampart. ▶ **Esplanade** (A2)★, bordered N by the 18thC law court (palais de justice), offers a pleasant stroll overlooking the Moselle. ▶ **Church of St. Pierre-aux-Nonnains**★, reputedly the oldest in France, occupying a 4thC Roman basilica that was divided into three naves in the 10thC ; octagonal Templar's chapel (12thC). ▶ Governor's Palace (Palais du Gouverneur, A3) : one of numerous neo-Renaissance buildings erected by the Germans in about 1900 ; the area near the station (B3) has many such structures ; the **station**★ itself was inspired by Rhenish Romanesque architecture. Note Kaiser Wilhelm II portrayed as Charlemagne in stained glass. ▶ **St. Maximin** (C2), near the banks of the Seille, partly 12thC ; modern stained glass by Jean Cocteau (1974). **St. Eucaire** : 12th-15thC ; interesting interior. Remains of 13th-15thC ramparts including the **German Gate** (porte des Allemands)★, heavily fortified.
Also... ▶ **Theatre**★ (B1-2) : elegant structure (1806) next to the police HQ. ▶ Modern **church of Ste. Thérèse** (off A2 ; 1938-54) : stained glass by N. Untersteller. ▶ In the S suburb, **fort de Queuleu,** Deportation memorial *(2-4 or 5, Mon. and 1st Sun. of month, Apr.-Oct.).*

Nearby

▶ **Scy-Chazelles** *(5 km W)* : the house of the statesman Robert Schuman (1886-1963), "father of Modern Europe" *(Apr.-Oct., Sun. and nat. hols. 2-6).* Schuman's tomb is in the fortified church. ▶ **Rozérieulles** *(3 km on)* : 15thC church, old houses, view★ over Metz. ▶ Road up the left

bank★ of the Moselle : view of Roman aqueduct at **Jouy-aux-Arches**; narrow road right to **Gorze** (site★) : old town clustered around an abbey, 17thC buildings, late 12thC church with Romanesque exterior, Gothic interior; small museum of the Gorze region *(Mar.-Oct., Sun., hols.)*. ► Lorraine Nature Park (→) : excursion to the **Rupt de Mad Valley**, via **Waville** (13thC church) as far as **Jaulny**, with 16th-18thC château *(Apr.-Dec. daily 2-6)*. ► **Sillegny** *(16 km S)* : 13th-15thC church with frescos from 1540. □

Practical Information _____

METZ

⚑ pl. d'Armes (B2), ☎ 87.75.65.21.

✈ Metz-Frescaty, 6 km SW, ☎ 87.65.41.11. *Air France office*, 29, rue de la Chèvre, ☎ 87.74.33.10.

SNCF (B3), ☎ 87.63.50.50.

🚌 pl. Coislin (C2-3), ☎ 87.75.26.62.

Car rental : *Avis*, train station; 23, rue Lafayette, ☎ 87.63.21.21.

Hotels :

★★★ **Altéa St-Thiébault** (ex Frantel), 29, pl. St-Thiébault (B3), ☎ 87.36.17.69, Tx 930417, AE DC Euro Visa, 112 rm ℙ ♨ ⚓ ♿ ♿ 370. Rest. ♦♦ *Les Quatres Saisons* ♪ ♿ closed Sat noon and Sun, 20 Dec-3 Jan. Quality food, 70-180.

★★★ **Royal Concorde**, 23, av. Foch (B3), ☎ 87.66.81.11, 73 rm ℙ 400. Rest. ♦ *Le Caveau* ♪ 130-210.

★★ **Central Urbis** (Ibis), 3 *bis*, rue Vauban (B3), ☎ 87.75.53.43, Tx 930281, Euro Visa, 72 rm ♪ ♨ 245.

★★ **Grand Hôtel de Metz**, 3, rue des Clercs (B2), ☎ 87.36.16.33, Visa, 57 rm ℙ ♿ ♿ 190.

Restaurants :

♦♦♦ *La Ville de Lyon*, 7, rue des Piques (B2), ☎ 87.36.07.01, AE DC Euro Visa ♪ ♿ closed Sun eve, 28 Jul-24 Aug. A traditional restaurant with a superb "à la carte" selection : confit de canard, crêpes Suzette, 85-180.

● ♦♦ *La Dinanderie*, 2, rue de Paris (A1), ☎ 87.30.14.40, AE Visa ♪ ♿ closed Mon and Sun , Feb school hols, 8-25 Aug, 24 Dec-2 Jan. Lightness and creativity are chef Regorgi's hallmarks : pot-au-feu de caille, blanc de turbot, 110-300.

● ♦♦ *Roches*, 25-29, rue des Roches (B2), ☎ 87.74.06.51, AE DC Euro Visa ♦ ♪ closed Sun eve. Excellent seasonal cuisine, 110-200.

♦♦ *La Goulue*, 24, pl. St-Simplice (C2), AE Euro Visa ♪ ♿ closed Mon and Sun. Market cuisine and turn-of-the-century decor, 190-230.

♦ *Loyon*, 22, pl. Saint-Simplice (C2), ☎ 87.37.32.81, AE DC Euro Visa ♪ ♿ closed Mon and Sun eve, 135-220.

⚠ ★★★★*de Metz* (150 pl), ☎ 87.32.42.49.

Recommended
Events : *mirabelle plum festival,* late Aug, early Sep.
Market : *flea maket,* 1st and 3rd Sat of every month. In Oct and Nov : 3rd Sun.
♥ chocolates : *Pierre Koenig,* 11, rue Pasteur.

Nearby

COURCELLES-CHAUSSY, ⊠ 57530, 13 km NE on D 954.

Restaurant :
♦♦ *Auberge de Mazagran,* rte de Boulay, par D 954, ☎ 87.76.62.47, AE Visa ⅏ ♪ ♿ ✵ closed Tue eve and Wed, 16 Aug-11 Sep. Spec : *cassolette d'escargots à l'anis, filet de sole Valery, mignon de veau Marie Galante,* 75-150.

GORZE, ⊠ 57130 Ars-sur-Moselle, 20 km SW.

Hotel :
★ *Lion d'Or* (L.F.), 105, rue du Commerce, ☎ 87.52.00.90, DC Euro Visa, 10 rm 🅟 ⅏ ⚓ closed Mon, 14-24 Feb, 115. Rest. ♦♦ ⚶ ♪ Spec : *filet de truite à la moëlle de bœuf et pinot rouge, gâteau de lapereau en gelée,* 90-150 ; child : 50.

HAGONDANGE, ⊠ 57300, 17 km.

Restaurant :
♦♦ *Meligner,* 69, rue de la Gare, ☎ 87.71.47.53, AE DC Euro Visa ♪ closed Sat , Aug. Spec : *cochon de lait en gelée, saucisson de St-Jacques au basilic,* 60-125.

MONTMÉDY*

Verdun 48, Charleville 64, Paris 258 km
pop 2324 ⊠ 55600   A1

This citadel, successively Burgundian, Austrian and Spanish before finally being taken by the 19-year-old Louis XIV (1657), sits atop a promontory above a meandre in the Chiers.

▶ **Upper town★ :** typical 17thC fortifications ; tour the ramparts, moats (now dry) and underground passages *(directional arrows)* starting at the barracks (SI ; small museum ; daily 9:30-6 Mar.-Oct.).* ▶ **Lower town** : Bastien Lepage (local painter) museum in the town hall.

Nearby

▶ **Avioth** *(8 km N)* : flamboyant Gothic basilica★★ (12th-14thC), site of pilgrimage every 16 July ; Gothic and Renaissance furnishings★, 14thC stained glass ; the Récevrisse (receptacle)★, a small Gothic structure in front of the church, is where pilgrims used to leave offerings. ▶ **Fort** at Villy-la-Ferté *(19 km W)* : W end of the Maginot Line, the defensive barrier erected between the two World Wars to protect French territory from invasion from the E and named after Minister of War André Maginot (1877-1932 ; *1:30-4:30, Palm Sun.-Oct., Sun. and nat. hols. ; daily Jul.-Aug.)* ; 5,5 km SE of fort, **Saint-Walfroy Hermitage** (view★ ; small museum.) ▶ To the S, pretty drive through the **Loison Valley** ; follow the D110 past a former fortified house (now a farm) to **Louppy-sur-Loison** : ruins of a fortified château (13th-14thC) ; vast, sumptuous Renaissance château★ *(Jul.-Sep., 1:30-6 ex Tue.)*. ▶ **Marville** *(12 km SE)* prospered from the leather and cloth industries in the 16thC ; unusually large number of 16th-17thC houses with carved façades ; 11th-12thC chapel *(often closed)*; cemetery, a "museum" of 14th-17thC funerary sculpture.   ☐

NANCY***

Metz 57, Strasbourg 145, Paris 294 km
pop 99307 ⊠ 54000   B2-3

A town proud of its history, from the dukes who made it their capital, to Stanislas Leszczynski who made it elegant. Now an important industrial and university town, Nancy has not forgotten its artistic heritage, apparent in the Art Nouveau façades of the buildings and in the Jazz Festival.

▶ **Place Stanislas★★★** (B2) : a magnificent mid-18thC architectural achievement created for Stanislas Leszczynski by Emmanuel Héré, a local architect ; fountains★ by Guibal, a Nîmes sculptor ; Jean Lamour, a local craftsman, wrought the gates of gilt iron★★ as well as the baluster of the town hall (hôtel de ville) staircase★ *(audio-guided visits of the reception rooms, evenings 15 Jun.-15 Sep.)*. ▶ **Fine Arts Museum** : Italian works, French Classical and contemporary paintings *(10-12 & 2-6, closed Mon. am, Tue. and nat. hols.)*. ▶ Place Stanislas is linked to **Place de la Carrière** (B1) by a triumphal arch in honour of Louis XV. Former ducal château (16thC), now the **Museum of Lorraine** (B1 ; *10-12 & 2-5 or 6, closed Tue. and nat. hols.)*. ▶ **Cordeliers' church** : tombs of the dukes of Lorraine ; recumbent effigy★ of Philippe de Gueldre (mid 16thC ; *same hours)*. **Museum of Folk Arts and Traditions** *(daily ex Mon. 10-12 & 2-5 or 6)*. ▶ 16th and 17thC mansions, some in poor repair, in neighbouring streets. ▶ Grande Rue, main street of the old town, leads to the **Craffe Gateway** (14th-15thC), now a museum of religious sculpture *(15 Jun.-15 Sep., 10-12 & 2-6, closed Tue.)*. ▶ Walk back to the town centre through the 60-acre plant nursery **(La Pépinière)**. ▶ At the entrance to the **Botanical Gardens** (C1) is the **Zoological Museum** : the tropical aquarium★ is unique in France *(2-6 ; closed Tue. ex Jul.-Aug. and school hols.)*. ▶ Through the Place d'Alliance to the Classical **cathedral** (C2) : treasury★ *(visits by request)*. Also... ▶ **Church of Notre-Dame-de-Bonsecours,** Avenue de Strasbourg (via C3) : 18thC tomb of Stanislas Leszczynski ; **Museum of the School of Nancy★★** (36 Rue du Sergent-Blandan, via Avenue Foch, A3 ; *10-12 & 2-5 or 6 ; closed Tue.)* : major contributions by local artists to the Art Nouveau movement. Several houses exemplify the style ; ask for addresses at the museum. **Cristalleries Daum** (Rue des Cristalleries via C1) : crystal-works *(weekday am, pm Sat. and Sun.)*; **Museum of Ironwork★** (at Jarville) : metallurgy since prehistoric times *(2-5 or 6 ex Tue.)*.

Nearby

▶ **Château de Fléville** *(8 km S on B33 and 1 km left)* : Renaissance building with 12thC keep *(Apr.-Oct., Sat., Sun. and nat. hols., 1-7 ; Jul.-Aug., 2-6 daily)*. ▶ **Chartreuse de Bosserville** *(8 km E)* : 17th-18thC convent buildings. Farther on, **Saint-Nicolas-de-Port** : flamboyant Gothic (late 15th-early 16thC) basilica★ : large size emphasizes the importance of pilgrimages to the relic (a finger preserved here) of the patron saint of Lorraine ; early 16thC stained glass ; treasury. ▶ **Haye Forest★** *(10 km W on N4)* : zoo★ (mostly local varieties ; *9-12 & 2-sunset)*; Automobile Museum *(Jul.-Sep., Wed., Sat.-Sun., 2-6:30)*. ▶ **Liverdun★** *(15 km NW)*, on a hill in a bend of the Moselle : 16thC gate, late 12thC church.   ☐

Practical Information _____

NANCY
ⓘ pl. Stanislas (B2), ☎ 83.35.22.41.
✈ Nancy-Essey, 4 km NE, ☎ 83.21.56.90. *Air France office,* 11, pl. Stanislas, ☎ 83.35.05.03.
🚄 3, pl. Thiers (A2), ☎ 83.56.50.50.
🚌 14, pl. Colonel-Driant (C2), ☎ 83.32.23.58 ; 56, pl. Mgr-Ruch (C2), ☎ 83.32.34.20.
Car rental : *Avis,* train station ; 21, pl. des Vosges (C3), ☎ 83.36.72.97 ; Les Thiers, pl. de la Gare (A2), ☎ 83.35.40.61.

Hotels :
● ★★★★ *Grand Hôtel de la Reine* (R.C.), 2, pl. Stanislas (B2), ☎ 83.35.03.01, Tx 960367, AE DC Euro Visa, 52 rm 2 apt. One of France's most beautiful hotels on a famous square, 550. Rest. ● ♦♦♦ ⚶ People are talking about chef Jary, a disciple of Paul Bocuse, 140-280.
★★★ *Altéa Thiers* (ex Frantel), 11, rue Poincaré (A-B2), ☎ 83.35.61.01, 112 rm 🅟 400. Rest. ♦♦ ♪ closed Sat noon, Sun and hols, 14 Jul-1 Sep. Spec : *chausson de brouet*

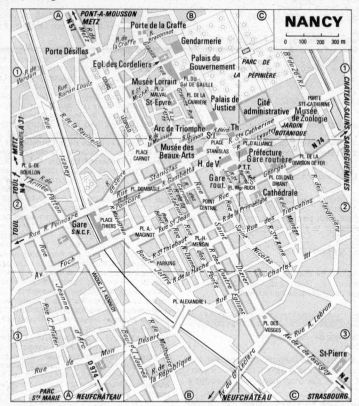

de Saint-Pierre aux radis, mignon de bœuf poêlé au vin, 110-170.
★★★ **Astoria-Albert 1er**, 3, rue de l'Armée-Patton (A2), ☎ 83.40.31.24, Tx 850895, AE DC Euro Visa, 136 rm P ▥ ⌂ ♪ ⴺ 235.
● ★★ **Le Stanislas**, 22, rue Ste-Catherine (C1), ☎ 83.37.23.88, 16 rm P ⌂ 185.

Restaurants :
● ♦♦♦ **Capucin Gourmand**, 31, rue Gambetta (B2), ☎ 83.35.26.98, AE Visa ♪ closed Mon and Sun eve, 1-20 Aug. In his authentic 1929 "modern-style" decor, traditionalist Gérard Veissière champions the food of his native Lorraine and quality service : foie gras, œufs brouillés en feuilleté aux poireaux et lardons, trilogie de la mer. Luscious pastries. Tastings in a century-old wine cellar, 140-350.
♦♦♦ **Le Goéland**, 27, rue des Ponts (B2), ☎ 83.35.17.25, AE DC Visa ♪ closed Mon noon and Sun. Spec : fish and seafood, 110-250.
● ♦♦ **Gentilhommière**, 29, rue des Maréchaux (B1), ☎ 83.32.26.44, Euro Visa ▥ ♪ ⴺ closed Sat , Sun, Feb school hols, 8-31 Aug. Victor Hugo's paternal forebears dwelt here and would doubtless have appreciated the fine cooking that goes on here today : foie gras frais de canard, filets de sole à la vapeur et aux épices, rognon de veau à la moutarde, 130-250.
♦♦ **Le Gastrolâtre**, 39, rue des Maréchaux (B1-2), ☎ 83.35.07.97 ▥ ♪ closed Mon and Sun, 1-8 Jan, 20 Mar-8 Apr, 8-30 Sep. P. Tanesy creates light, enjoyable fare in a pretty turn-of the century decor : cervelas de grenouille, chou farci aux langoustines, lobster and oysters, 150-235.
♦♦ **Le Wagon**, 57, rue des Chaligny (off map C2),

☎ 83.32.32.16, Visa ♪ closed Sat, Sun and hols, 11 Jul-9 Aug. A nostalgic setting of wood and real brass (1927) for this railway restaurant situated in a shopping centre, 100-140.
♦ **Au Bon Accueil**, 1, rue de Liehel, Richardménil, RN 57, 14 km, ☎ 83.54.62.10, AE DC Euro Visa ♦ ⴺ closed Wed eve and Thu, 27 Feb-13 Mar, 31 Jul-22 Aug, 80-130.
♦ **Les Trois Marches**, 2 bis, rue St-Léon (A2), ☎ 83.41.33.00, Visa ♪ closed Sun, 75-130.
♦ **Nouveaux Abattoirs**, 4, bd d'Austrasie (C1), ☎ 83.35.46.25, closed Sat , Sun and hols, 25 Jul-23 Aug. For meat-eaters, 45-130.

▲ at Villers-lès-Nancy, ★★Municipal (500 pl), ☎ 83.27.18.28.

Recommended
♥ auction house : 107, rue du Sergent-Blandan (off map), ☎ 83.28.13.31 ; 23, rue Gustave-Simon (B1-2), ☎ 83.32.00.76 ; chocolates : Lalonde, 59, rue St-Dizier (B1) ; foie gras and gourmet pork products : Caraux-Caderlet, 52, rue Stanislas (B2) ; macaroons and candies : Maison Aptel, 21, rue Gambetta (B2).

Nearby

BOUXIÈRES-AUX-CHÊNES, ✉ 54770, 13 km N on D 913.

Restaurant :
♦♦ **La Fine Aiguille**, 6, rue Nationale, ☎ 83.31.10.01 ♪ ⴺ closed Mon and Sun eve. Regional fare : salade d'anguille au vinaigre de framboise, estouffade de poissons fins, smoked fish, 150-200.

CHAVIGNY, ⊠ 54230, 10 km SW.

Restaurant :
♦♦ *Auberge de la Forestière*, ☎ 83.47.26.32, AE DC Euro Visa Ⓟ ⟨ ▒▒ ♪ ✕ closed Mon and Sun eve, 2-16 Mar, 17 Aug-5 Sep. The all-season panoramic terrace is a pleasant place indeed to enjoy André Morissot's delicious cuisine : fish and shellfish (in winter), game in season, *pigeon au melon et Sauternes*, 120-270.

FLAVIGNY-SUR-MOSELLE, ⊠ 54630, 15 km S.

Restaurant :
♦♦ *Le Prieuré*, 3, rue du Prieuré, ☎ 83.26.70.45, AE DC Euro Visa ⟨ ▒▒ ⅋ ✕ closed Wed and Sun eve , Feb school hols, 1 Nov, 25 Aug-5 Sep. Spec : *crêpe de sandre fumé à la minute beurre ciboulette, viennoise de turbot, noisette de lotte au bacon et vinaigre d'échalote, mignon de porc à la mirabelle*, 100-250.

LIVERDUN, ⊠ 54460, 16 km NW.
𝗦𝗡𝗖𝗙 ☎ 83.24.47.87.

Hotel :
★★★ *Hostellerie Les Vannes* (R.C.), 3, rue Porte-Haute, ☎ 83.24.46.01, AE DC Visa, 11 rm Ⓟ ⟨ ▒▒ ⅋ ✕ closed hols, Feb. Rest. ● ♦♦ ⟨ ♪ ⅋ The current young chef is trying hard : *émincé d'agneau à la graine de moutarde, duo de rouget et rascasse au citron vert confit*, 155-345.

Restaurant :
♦♦ *Golf Val Fleuri*, rte de Villey-St-Étienne, ☎ 83.24.53.54, Euro Visa ⟨ ▒▒ ♪ ⅋ closed Wed ex summer, 2 Jan-1 Feb. Miniature golf. Spec : *marmite du tripier au vin rouge de Toul, assiette du pêcheur au beurre blanc*, 115-180.

⚐ ★★★*Municipal* (166 pl), ☎ 83.24.43.78.

NEUFCHÂTEAU

Chaumont 56, Epinal 74, Paris 301 km
pop 9086 ⊠ 88300   B3

Rulership of the town was hotly disputed during the Middle Ages by the dukes of Champagne and Lorraine.

▶ On the hill where the ducal château used to stand, the **church of St. Nicolas** (12th-13thC) has two storeys to fit the steep slope; it houses a holy sepulchre★ with a group of nine figures (15thC Swabian). ▶ **Church of St. Christophe** (12th-15thC) : Burgundian portal; baptismal chapel (unusual 15thC vaulting). ▶ Renaissance town hall (Hôtel de Ville, 1597) : fine Italian staircase.

Nearby

▶ **Grand**★ *(23 km W)* : despite its name, a small village; excavations (continuing for the past century) of a Roman town, including a large amphitheatre *(daily 9-12 & 2-7, 5 in winter)*; basilica has the largest mosaic★★ in France *(daily Apr.-11 Nov.; Sat. and Sun. rest of year)*; 15thC church. ▶ Returning to Neufchâteau, detour via **Liffol-le-Grand** (archaeological museum in town hall; Aug.). ▶ 7 km N, **Coussey** : church (partially Romanesque); go via Frébécourt at the foot of **château de Bourlémont** (15th-16th, 19thC), return through **Saint-Élophe** (11th-16thC church; furniture). ▶ **Pompierre** *(11.5 km S)* : church with Romanesque doorway★ (12thC), naive but lively sculpture. ▶ 15 km SE, **Beaufremont** : remains of 13thC château; view. ▶ **Sandaucourt** *(11 km E)* : charming 17thC country château with four angled towers *(15 Mar.-15 Oct., Sat., Sun. 5 pm)*; chapel now museum of liturgical art.   ☐

Practical Information ─────────────

🄸 mairie, ☎ 29.94.14.75; 48, av. Gal-de-Gaulle, ☎ 29.94.06.95.
𝗦𝗡𝗖𝗙 ☎ 29.94.19.22.

Hotel :
★★ *Saint-Christophe*, rte de Dijon, ☎ 29.94.16.28, Euro Visa, 34 rm Ⓟ 200. Rest. ♦ 55-130.

PLOMBIÈRES-LES-BAINS

Epinal 30, Verdun 48, Paris 380 km
pop 2298 ⊠ 88370   B-C4

Typical 18th-19thC spa in a deep valley framed by forests.

▶ Street names constitute a directory of famous invalids who have taken the waters at the 30 warm springs; **Bain** *(bath)* **Stanislas** (1736; underground, *visits 3pm Tue., Wed., Sat., May-Sep.)*; **Bain Romain**; **Bain National** (Napoleonic era façade, pre-1814); **Thermes** (warm baths) **Napoleon** were built during the Second Empire (ca. 1855). ▶ Maison des Arcades (1761; SI). ▶ **Louis Français Museum** : Barbizon school painter (→ Ile-de-France) and his associates *(2-6 ex Tue., May-Sep.)*. ▶ National Park.

Nearby

▶ **Fontaine Stanislas** *(4 km SW)* : in beech woods. ▶ **Val d'Ajol** *(12 km SE)* : pretty drives in the Roches Valley (Faymont Falls) and to Géhard Falls. ▶ To the SW, the Augronne and Semouse valleys.   ☐

Practical Information ─────────────

PLOMBIÈRES-LES-BAINS
♨ ☎ 29.66.02.17 (May-Nov).   ♥
🄸 rue Stanislas, ☎ 29.66.01.30.
𝗦𝗡𝗖𝗙 ☎ 29.66.00.29.

Hotels :
★★★ *Grand Hôtel*, 2, av. des États-Unis, ☎ 29.66.00.03, 115 rm Ⓟ ▒▒ ⟍ ✕ closed Oct-Apr, 220.
● ★★ *La Fontaine Stanislas*, ☎ 29.66.01.53, 19 rm Ⓟ ⟨ ▒▒ ⟍ half pens (h.s.), closed Oct-May, 375. Rest. ♦♦ ⟨ ✕ Jacqueline Lemercier and her son Michel spoil you, 60-125.
★★ *Rosiers* (L.F.), av. Val-d'Ajol, ☎ 29.66.02.66, DC, 22 rm Ⓟ ▒▒ ⟍ closed Nov-Easter, 170. Rest. ♦ ✕ 50-120.
★ *Touring* (L.F.), av. Louis-Français, ☎ 29.66.00.70, Visa, 23 rm Ⓟ ⟨ closed Nov-Apr, 140. Rest. ♦ closed 25 Nov-1 Jan, 50-85.

⚐ at Ruaux, 4 km W, ★★*Municipal* (50 pl), ☎ 29.66.00.71.

Recommended
Farmhouse-gîte : at 1,5 km, *les Cinq-Sols*, ☎ 29.66.03.46, farmhouse inn, farm produce for sale ; at la Crousette (3 km), *Etang des Prêtres*, ☎ 29.66.03.84.
Leisure activities : *Club aérostatique de Lorraine*, ☎ 29.36.31.85. Ballooning.
♥ embroidery : *maison Dié*, rue du Chevalier-de-Boufflers; tutti-frutti ice cream : *chez Pierre Brunello*, 15, rue Liétard, ☎ 29.66.01.52.

Nearby

Le VAL-D'AJOL, ⊠ 88340, 12 km S.
🄸 2, rue du Devau, ☎ 29.30.66.69.

Hotel :
★★ *La Résidence* (L.F.), 5, rue des Mousses, ☎ 29.30.68.52, Tx 960573, AE DC Euro Visa, 60 rm Ⓟ ⟨ ▒▒ ⟍ ⅋ closed 15 Nov-15 Dec, 160. Rest. ♦ ⟨ ♪ ⅋ ✕ 45-85 ; child : 35.

Recommended
Farmhouse-gîte : *Saint-Vallier*, les Haies, vallée de Girmont, ☎ 29.30.62.77, spec : *omelette au lard, jambon de montagne* and *andouille du Val d'Ajol*.

PONT-A-MOUSSON*

Nancy 31, Metz 32, Paris 325 km
pop 15746 ⊠ 54700   B2

The name is recognized throughout France on drainpipes and manhole covers.

▶ Place Duroc : surrounded by 16th-18thC **arcaded houses**, the town centre. ▶ On the right bank, the 15th-16thC

church of St. Martin : late 15thC entombment of Christ. Opposite, the Jesuit College (restored) : an important 16thC university, transferred to Nancy in 1768. ▶ The **Premonstratensian** (Prémontrés) **abbey★** : 18thC monastery just to the N, now a cultural centre and the site of international meetings for the plastic arts, music, theatre and contemporary dance *(8-12 & 2-6; closed 20 Dec.-19 Jan.)*; Baroque church with three naves, wrought-iron baluster★ in the abbey.

Nearby

▶ E *(20 min on foot, 7 km by road)*, **butte de Mousson** : château ruins, view★ over the Moselle Valley. ▶ **Dieulouard** *(7 km S)* : church (1504), two 15thC statues of the Virgin; from here make a short excursion to **Little Switzerland of Lorraine** (petite Suisse Lorraine) through the Esch Valley : châteaux at Pierrefort (15thC, now a farm) and Manonville (16th-17thC). ▶ 13 km N, overlooking the valley, ruins of château de **Prény** (13th-14thC). □

Practical Information ———————

PONT-A-MOUSSON

ⓘ 52, pl. Duroc, ☎ 83.81.06.90.

SNCF ☎ 83.56.50.50.

Hotel :

★ *Poste*, 42 bis, rue V.-Hugo, ☎ 83.81.01.16, Euro Visa, 24 rm Ⓟ closed Sun, 20 Dec-10 Jan, 250. Rest. ♦ ♪ 65-150.

Nearby

BELLEVILLE, ✉ 54940, 13 km S.

Restaurants :

● ♦♦ *Bistroquet*, ☎ 83.24.90.12, AE DC Euro Visa, closed Mon, Sat noon, Sun eve , Aug, 21 Dec-2 Jan. You must reserve to enjoy Mme Ponsard's exceptional cooking : *foie gras, rognons de veau au bouzy, tarte aux poires*, 260-360.

♦ *La Moselle*, facing the station, ☎ 83.24.91.44, AE Euro Visa ♪ closed Tue eve and Wed, 11-25 Feb, 19 Aug-3 Sep. Fine array of fish, *nougat glacé à la bergamote*, 100-200.

REMIREMONT*

Epinal 27, Vesoul 64, Paris 414 km
pop 10860 ✉ 88200   C4

A busy textile centre, once the site of an abbey for noble ladies that was as exclusive as it was independent.

▶ The main street (renamed Rue du General-de-Gaulle) : more than 200m of 18thC arcades. ▶ **Charles-de-Bruyères Museum** *(10-12 & 2-5, 6 ex Tue. and nat. hols)* : regional life and history. **Charles-Friry Museum** : history of the abbey, fine arts *(2-6 ex Tue.)*. ▶ **Abbey church** (13thC, restored 18thC) has an 11thC crypt. Hôtel de Ville (town hall), adjacent, the former abbess's residence (1752). Nearby, 17th-18thC houses where the ladies of the abbey (canonesses) lived independently without the restraints of vows. □

Practical Information ———————

REMIREMONT

ⓘ 2, pl. H.-Utard, ☎ 29.62.23.70.

SNCF ☎ 29.62.54.87.

Hotel :

★★ *Les Chanoinesses* (Inter-Hôtel), 14-16, fg du Val-d'Ajol, ☎ 29.62.27.46, Tx 960277, AE DC Euro Visa, 30 rm Ⓟ 220. Rest. ♦♦ ♪ ⅋ 85-110.

Recommended

♥ *Charcuterie Claude Thiébaut*, across from the statue of the Volunteer : raw ham, dried beef; *Pâtisserie B. Thinws*, under the Arcades : local specialties; cloth : *Toile des Vosges*, 14, rue de la Courtine.

Nearby

SAINT-NABORD, ✉ 88200 Remiremont, 5 km NE.

Hotel :

★★ *Relais de Belcour* (L.F.), 3, rue Turenne, ☎ 29.62.25.31, Visa, 18 rm Ⓟ ⅏ ⚲ ⅋ closed Sun and Sat (l.s.), 25 Dec-1 Jan, 165. Rest. ♦ 45-70.

SAINT-DIÉ*

Epinal 50, Strasbourg 90, Paris 460 km
pop 24816 ✉ 88100   C3

This city calls itself "America's godmother," since, in 1507, the first book calling the New World by the name of America was printed here. The pink sandstone buildings were reconstructed after WWII.

▶ **Cathedral** : Classical façade covers a typically Rhenish-Romanesque structure (12thC); the 16thC choir shows the influence of Champagne. A flamboyant Gothic **cloister★** links it with the **Church of Notre-Dame★** (12thC), also Romanesque, from the same source. ▶ Behind, **museum** of Everyday Life in the Vosges mountains *(2-7 ex Mon.)*. ▶ Quai du Torrent *(N)* : factory designed by Le Corbusier (1946). ▶ Moyo-dé-Soyotte at **Le Faing de Sainte-Marguerite** *(2 km S, N415)* : a renovated farm illustrating rural crafts and life.

Nearby

▶ Excavations of **La Bure Celtic camp** *(6 km N then 25 min on foot)*; view★. ▶ Trips by car or on foot to the wooded mountains which offer fine views. □

Practical Information ———————

ⓘ 32, rue Thiers, ☎ 29.56.17.62.

SNCF ☎ 29.56.10.00.

▦ pl. des Déportés, ☎ 29.56.18.65.

Hotels :

★★ *France*, 1, rue Dauphine, ☎ 29.56.32.61, AE DC Euro Visa, 11 rm Ⓟ ⅋ 200.

★★ *Vosges et Commerce*, 53-57, rue Thiers, ☎ 29.56.16.21, AE DC Euro Visa, 29 rm Ⓟ ⚲ 220.

Restaurant :

● ♦ *Le Tétras*, 4, rue d'Hellieule, ☎ 29.56.10.12 ♪ ⅋ closed Sat noon. Rib-sticking meals : game in season, *tarte au miel et amandes*, 75-140.

SAINT-MIHIEL*

Bar-le-Duc 33, Metz 66, Paris 303 km
pop 5555 ✉ 55300   A2

On the banks of the Meuse, seat of an important abbey from Carolingian times, later a 14thC regional capital.

▶ Birthplace of the sculptor Ligier Richier (1507-67), whose works are the principal attractions in local churches : Fainting Virgin supported by Saint-John★ in **St. Michel** (rebuilt 17thC, 16th-18thC furnishings). The neighbouring **abbey★**, rebuilt at the same time, now houses the municipal offices, Court and Library★. **Church of St-Étienne** : Holy Sepulchre★★ (16thC). ▶ Old houses. ▶ N : cliffs (view★ over the valley). □

Practical Information ———————

Restaurant :

♦ *Relais des Deux Cheminées*, Bouconville-sur-Madt, ☎ 29.90.42.79, AE Euro Visa ♪ ⅋ closed Mon eve and Tue , Feb school hols, 95-250.

Be advised that hotels and restaurants in this Guide have perhaps changed addresses; prices indicated are also subject to modifications.

SARREBOURG

Strasbourg 70, Nancy 74, Paris 426 km
pop 15139 ⊠ 57400 C2

On the edge of the Lorraine plateau, abutting the outcrops of the Vosges which supplied the pink sandstone for its houses.

▶ **Chapel of the Cordeliers** (13thC) : façade illuminated by a modern stained-glass window★ (Chagall). ▶ **Regional Museum of Sarrebourg** (13 Ave. de France; *8-12 & 2-6 ex Tue.; closed Sun. am out of season)* 16thC ceramics★.

Nearby

▶ **Saint-Ulrich** *(4 km NW)* : Gallo-Roman villa *(closed for repairs).* ▶ **Réding** *(3.5 km E)* : 13thC frescos in chapel of Ste. Agathe. ▶ **Phalsbourg** *(16 km E)* : 16thC fortified square; museum of local military history and art on the Place d'Armes *(apply to the Mayor's office; 15 Mar.-Oct., 2-5; Sun. and nat. hols., 10-12, Wed. and Sat., 9-11).* Veralor crystal-works.

From Phalsbourg to the Donon *(67 km, half-day)*

▶ **Phalsbourg.** Enter the narrow Zorn Valley at **Lutzelbourg**★ overlooked by a ruined 12thC château on a spur (view★). ▶ A few kilometres upstream, the spectacular barge lift at **Saint-Louis-Artzviller**★ cuts out 17 locks *(visit by boat daily Mar.-Nov.).* ▶ **Rocher** (rock) **de Dabo**★★ (alt. 664 m) provides a superb view that can hardly be bettered — even by climbing the tower. ▶ Just off the road, **Niderviller** and **Vallerysthal** have been producing fine crystal and ceramics since the 18thC. ▶ A little steam train offers trips through the forest at **Abreschviller** in a pretty valley watered by the Sarre-Rouge *(Sun. and nat. hols. in Apr., plus Sat. in May, Jun., Sep.; daily, Jul.-Aug.).* ▶ 18thC abbey church at **Saint-Quirin** is topped by a triple onion dome; from **Turquestein-Blancrupt** down the Sarre-Blanche Valley to ascend to the Donon. □

Practical Information

SARREBOURG
ℹ chapelle des Cordeliers, ☎ 87.03.11.82.
SNCF ☎ 87.03.50.50.

Hotel :
★★ ***France*** (L.F.), 3, av. de France, ☎ 87.03.21.47, Euro Visa, 52 rm Ⓟ ♿ 205. Rest. ♦ ♪ closed Sat, 15-28 Feb. Le Saravis grill is open in winter, 45-115.

Restaurant :
♦♦ ***Mathis***, 7, rue Gambetta, ☎ 87.03.21.67, AE DC Euro Visa ♪ closed Mon and Sun eve. Spec : *fondue de légumes aux ris de veau*, 130-200.

Nearby

ABRESCHVILLER, ⊠ 57560, 25 km SE.
ℹ mairie, ☎ 87.03.70.32.
SNCF ☎ 87.03.70.28.

Hotel :
★★ ***Cigognes*** (L.F.), 92, rue Jordy, ☎ 87.03.70.09, Tx 861472, AE DC Visa, 29 rm Ⓟ ♨ ⊡ 180. Rest. ♦♦ 70-130; child : 40.

DABO, ⊠ 57850, 21 km SE.
ℹ 19, pl. de l'Église, ☎ 87.07.47.51.

Hotel :
★ ***Belle-Vue***, 30, rue St-Léon-IX, ☎ 87.08.40.21, Euro Visa, 15 rm Ⓟ ⚘ ⛱ ✈ half pens, closed Tue eve , Wed. (Oct-Mar), 10 Jan-1 Feb, 330. Rest. ♦ ⚘ ♪ ♿ ✈ 60-165; child : 40.

Restaurant :
♦♦ ***Au Rocher***, ☎ 87.07.40.14 ⚘ ♪ ✈ closed Oct-Mar. Spec : *choucroute aux morilles*, 80-250.

LUTZELBOURG, ⊠ 57820, 20 km E.

Hotel :
★ ***Vosges***, 149, rue Ackermann, ☎ 87.25.30.09, 22 rm Ⓟ ♨ 🚴 closed 13 Jan-15 Mar, 120. Rest. ♦♦ 40-100; child : 35.

PHALSBOURG, ⊠ 57370, 16 km E.

Hotel :
★★ ***Erckmann-Chatrian***, 14, pl. d'Armes, ☎ 87.24.31.33, AE DC Euro Visa, 18 rm Ⓟ ⚘ ♪ ♿ 180. Rest. ● ♦ ⚘ ♪ ♿ closed Mon and Tue noon. A happy blend of classic and modern cuisine, 45-150; child : 25.

Restaurant :
● ♦♦ ***Au Soldat de l'An II***, 1, rte de Saverne, ☎ 87.24.16.16, Visa ⚘ ♨ ♪ closed 6 Jan-2 Feb. Very pretty decor, and G. Schmitt's savoury cuisine : *sandre Paul Haeberlin, filet de biche en saison*, 125-250; child : 50.

TURQUESTEIN-BLANCRUPT, ⊠ 57560 Abreschviller, 35 km SE.

Hotel :
● ★★ ***Kiboki***, (L.F., R.S.), ☎ 87.08.60.65, Visa, 15 rm Ⓟ ⚘ ♨ ⛱ ♪ ♿ ✈ 🎾 half pens (h.s.), closed Tue, 1 Feb-1 Mar, 20-27 Dec, 400. Rest. ♦ ⚘ ♪ ♿ ✈ 80-150.

SARREGUEMINES

Metz 69, Strasbourg 104, Paris 304 km
pop 25178 ⊠ 57200 C1-2

Separated from Germany by the river Sarre and famous for ceramics.

▶ Unique collection of ceramics★ from 18thC to present day in the town hall museum *(2-6 ex Tue., and Wed. 9-12).* ▶ Nearby, very old kiln.

Nearby

▶ **Frauenberg** *(6 km NE)* : ruined château (14thC). ▶ **Zetting** *(7 km SE)* : 15th-16thC church; round Romanesque bell tower; stained glass; furnishings. ▶ **Heckenransbach** *(9 km SW)* : fortified cylindrical bell tower★ (10thC). ▶ **Bliesbruck** : Gallo-Roman excavations *(guided tour).* □

Practical Information

SARREGUEMINES
ℹ rue de la Poste, ☎ 87.98.52.32.

Hotel :
★★★ ***Alsace***, (Mapotel), 10, rue Poincaré, ☎ 87.98.44.32, Tx 860582, AE DC Euro Visa, 28 rm Ⓟ ⛱ ♪ ♿ ✈ closed Good Fri and Xmas eve, 255. Rest. ♦♦♦ ***Ducs de Lorraine*** ♪ ✈ Lightened traditional fare, 115-200.

Restaurants :
♦♦♦ ***Vieux Moulin***, 135, rue de France, ☎ 87.98.22.59, AE DC Euro Visa ⚘ ♪ closed Tue and Wed, 15 Aug-8 Sep. By the riverside. Spec : *truite au riesling, filet de sole au gewurtztraminer, ballotine de canard au foie gras*, 115-220.
● ♦♦ ***Auberge St-Walfrid***, 58, rue de Grosbliederstroff, ☎ 87.98.43.75, Visa ♨ closed Mon and Sun, Jan, Aug. A pleasant stopover, delicious seasonal cuisine, 115-280.

Nearby

SAINT-AVOLD, ⊠ 57500, 28 km E.
ℹ mairie, ☎ 87.91.10.07.
SNCF ☎ 87.91.17.27.

Restaurant :
● ♦♦ ***Le Neptune***, stade nautique, ☎ 87.92.27.90, Visa ♨ ♿ ✈ closed Mon, Sat noon, Sun eve, 2-9 Jan, 15 Aug-15 Sep. Spec : *saumon au pot-au-feu, poëlon aux 3 poissons*, 140-250.

> For the translation of a name of a meat, a fish or a vegetable, for the composition of a dish or a sauce, see the Menu Guide in the Practical Holiday Guide; it lists the most common culinary terms.

SAULX Valley*

A3
Stainville to Mognéville and Bar-le-Duc *(41 km, approx 2hr)*

Neat stone houses alongside a tributary of the Marne that has provided power for local industries since the Middle Ages.

▶ **Stainville** : 16thC château. ▶ **Bazincourt** *(6 km)* : château (1534 ; *Sun. and nat. hols. pm in Jul., last 2 wks of Aug. and Sep.; pm daily first 2 wks Aug. and Sep).* ▶ **Rupt-aux-Nonnains** : pretty stone bridge (1775). ▶ **Haironville** : two châteaux almost face-to-face, La Varenne★ (16thC; *15 Jul.-1 Sep., 10-12 & 2-5)* in a beautiful park, and La Forge (1735). ▶ **Ville-sur-Saulx** : paper mills, now disused, were active in 1348; château (1555) and outbuildings *(Whitsun-Aug., Thu.-Sun., 2-4:30).* ▶ Beyond **Lisle-en-Rigault,** the road skirts the park of the **château de Jean d'Heurs★** (18thC, restored 19thC, *visits summer by appt., tel. 29.71.30.52).* ▶ **Couvonges** : Romanesque church★ (11th-13thC) with overhanging roof. ▶ **Mognéville** : church (13th-15thC) with magnificent 15thC carved wood altarpiece★. ▶ Return to Bar-le-Duc along the same road as far as **Beurey** then via **Trémont-sur-Saulx.** □

Practical Information _____

BAZINCOURT, ⊠ 55000 Bar-le-Duc, 14 km S of **Bar-le-Duc.**

Restaurant :
♦ *Auberge des Chasseurs,* ☎ 29.78.60.48 ⑩ closed Wed, Sep, 80-100.

STAINVILLE, ⊠ 55500 Ligny-en-Barrois, 19 km S of **Bar-le-Duc.**

Restaurant :
● ♦ *La Petite Auberge,* ☎ 29.78.60.10, AE DC Euro Visa ♪ closed Mon and Sun eve, 23 Jul-13 Aug. Pleasant stopover, classic cuisine : *truite aux herbes, filet de bœuf aux morilles,* 80-120.

TRÉMONT-SUR-SAULX, ⊠ 55000 Bar-le-Duc, 10 km SW of **Bar-le-Duc.**

Hotel :
● ★★ *Auberge de la Source* (L.F.), ☎ 29.75.45.22, 16 rm ℗ ⬙ ⬙ closed Sun eve and Mon, 14-28 Feb, 2-24 Aug, 180. Rest. ♦ ♪ ὴ ⬙ 80-160.

SENONES

Epinal 70, Strasbourg 51, Paris 436 km
pop 3506 ⊠ 88210   C3
The 18thC capital of the principality of Salm, which Voltaire said a snail could walk around in one day. The town grew up around a Benedictine abbey, today occupied by a textile factory.

▶ **Château** of the Princes of Salm, **abbey** and town hall form a fine if austere 18thC architectural group; at the foot of the abbey staircase★ is a small **museum** of local history ; in summer *(Sun. 11:30 am),* re-enactment in period costume of the changing of the guard.

Round trip of the Donon and the Celles Valley *(approx 80 km, half-day)*

▶ **Senones.** ▶ The road runs up the Rabodeau Valley into the forest; pretty drive to the Donon pass★ (→ Alsace) then down to Raon-l'Étape. ▶ **The Plaine Valley** (also known as Celles Valley) has magnificent fir forests on the slopes. ▶ From **Vexaincourt,** charming drive to **Maix Lake.** ▶ The sawmill *(scierie)* at **Hallière** *(open in summer)* continues a traditional valley trade. ▶ From **Celles-sur-Plaine** up to **Pierre-Percée** at the foot of a ruined 11thC château (view★). ▶ Beyond the lake, which supplies part of the needs of the French electricity company, the road joins the Meurthe Valley at Raon-l'Étape. ▶ **Étival-Claire-fontaine** : 12thC abbey ; tourist train to Senones.

▶ **Moyenmoutier** (between Étival and Senones) : beautiful 18thC church (choir stalls). □

SION-VAUDEMONT Hill*

B3
Limestone crescent emerging from flat, rich earth. One end of the crescent is the site of a very old pilgrimage to the Virgin ; at the other is the ruined château of the counts of Vaudémont, dukes of Lorraine.

▶ **Views** over the countryside from the orientation chart behind the convent (archaeological and missionary museum). ▶ Signal de Vaudémont *(3 km S)* : another orientation chart and view. ▶ **Vaudémont** : ruined 11thC fortress.

Nearby

▶ **Thorey-Lyautey** *(6 km W)* : château built in 1928, currently being converted to a museum. ▶ **Vézelise** *(8 km N)* : 16thC houses, church with Renaissance stained glass, covered markets (1599). ▶ **Haroué** *(11 km NE)* : château★ of the princes of Beauvau-Craon, one of the masterpieces of 18thC architecture in Lorraine *(15 Mar.-15 Nov., 2-6).* ▶ **Mirecourt** *(17 km S),* famous for skilled musical-instrument makers (museum in the municipal offices, *Mon.-Fri., 9-12 & 2-5);* covered markets contemporary with those at Vézelise; the bell tower of the church (13th-15thC) is shut in by houses. □

THIONVILLE

Metz 29, Verdun 87, Paris 340 km
pop 41448 ⊠ 57100   B1
Capital of a vast industrial agglomeration stretching along the Moselle to Metz and invading neighbouring valleys, this iron- and steel-working city was hard hit by the early-1980s steel crisis.

▶ Thionville, a favourite residence of Charlemagne, later became an important fortress. Still evident are 16thC arcaded houses, bastions, a bell tower and the **Tour aux Puces★** (tower of fleas, so-called from a grisly legend about a princess, captive in the tower, who was bitten to death; 11th-12thC; local history museum, *2-6 ex Mon.).* ▶ **Château de la Grange★** at the N exit from town (furniture★ ; *2:30-5:30; daily in Aug.; Sat., Sun. rest of year).* ▶ NW, **fort de Guentrange,** brick German construction (1899) to be transformed into a museum *(ext. visit).*

Nearby

▶ You can visit several sectors of the Maginot Line : **Zeiterholz** *(9 km NW, near Entrange; 1st and 3rd Sun. May-Sep., 2-5:30);* **Immerhof** *(near Hettange-Grande, 2nd and 4th Sun.);* **Hackenberg★** *(20 km, near Veckring)* the largest *(Sat., Sun. from 2 pm).* ▶ **Rodemack** *(15 km N)* : remains of 14thC ramparts★ and a Baillif's House *(Sep.-Jun., daily ex Mon., 3-7);* **Roussy-le-Bourg** : two large châteaux (14th and 18thC) and further N, the château de Praisch (17thC, park). ▶ **Sierck-les-Bains** : where the river Moselle narrows into a gorge; ruined 11thC château high on the rocks *(9:30-12 & 1:30-7; closed Mon. am;* view★); 8 km further NE, **Meinsberg** : imposing ruins of 15th-17thC château. ▶ **Vitry-sur-Orne** *(11 km SW)* : Clouange zoo. □

Practical Information _____

THIONVILLE
ℹ 16, rue du Vieux-Collège, ☎ 82.53.33.18.
SNCF ☎ 82.56.50.50.
⊞ pl. du Luxembourg, ☎ 82.53.84.75.
Car rental : *Avis,* train station; 12, av. de la Libération, ☎ 82.34.09.22.

Hotels :
★★★ *L'Horizon* (R.C.), 50, rte du Crève-Cœur, ☎ 82.88.53.65, Tx 860870, AE DC Visa, 13 rm ℗ ⬙ ⑩

♪ ♿ closed 25 Dec-15 Feb, 390. Rest. ♦♦ ⸸ ♿ closed Sat noon, 20 Dec-15 Feb, 140-200.
★★ **Aux Portes de France** (L.F.), 1, pl. du Gal-Patton, ☎ 82.53.30.01, AE DC Visa, 21 rm Ⓟ ⚲ ⚯ closed Sat eve, 1-24 Aug, 150.
★★ **Concorde**, 6, pl. du Luxembourg, ☎ 82.53.83.18, Tx 861338, AE Euro Visa, 25 rm Ⓟ ⸸ 220. Rest. ● ♦♦ ⸸ ♪ closed Sun eve, 27 Jul-26 Aug. High in the sky, with the Moselle flowing below. Spec : *ravioles de langoustines, boudin de pieds de porc*, 145-200.

Restaurant :
♦♦ **Auberge du Crève-Cœur**, ☎ 82.88.50.52, AE DC Euro Visa ⸸ ♪ closed Mon eve and Sun eve. Since 1899, wine growers have appreciated the good cooking featured here : *porcelet en gelée, foie de veau aux petits oignons, caroline aux myrtilles*, 85-135.

Nearby

SIERCK-LES-BAINS, ✉ 57480, 18 km NE.

Hotel :
★ **Central**, 6, quai des Ducs-de-Lorraine, ☎ 82.83.71.14, 14 rm Ⓟ ⸸ closed Fri, 26 Aug-14 Sep, 110. Rest. ♦ ♪ 40-130.

Restaurant :
● ♦♦ **La Vénerie**, 10, rue de la Porte de Trêves, ☎ 82.83.72.41, AE DC ⸸ ⚲ ♿ closed Mon and Wed eve, 20 Jan-1 Mar. Holds a high reputation among the local frontier folk for its excellent cuisine : *gratin de cuisses de grenouilles, foie gras d'oie au torchon, civet de canard*, 115-230.

⚠ ★★*Municipal* (100 pl), ☎ 82.83.82.15.

TOUL**

Nancy 24, Bar-le-Duc 61, Paris 270 km
pop 17752 ✉ 54200   B3
Overflowing 17thC fortifications, this ancient episcopal seat stretches along the Moselle, which is in the course of being "depolluted" to meet European standards.

The **cathedral**★★ (13th-14thC) : Gothic style of Champagne with flamboyant Gothic façade★★ (late 15thC); view from the cloister★. The cathedral symbolized the town's historic independence as one of the Three Bishoprics (→ Brief regional history) that existed outside the jurisdiction of either Lorraine or France until 1648.
▶ **Church of St. Gengoult**★ (13th-15thC) : close in style to the cathedral but with an even more elegant 16thC cloister. ▶ In the former infirmary (Maison Dieu, 16th-17thC) the local **museum** is currently undergoing restoration.

Nearby

▶ **Blénod-lès-Toul** *(9 km S)* : church was a Renaissance covered market (1509; tomb★ of the founder) in the courtyard of the former château of the bishops of Toul; 2 km S, château de **Tuméjus** (16th-18thC). ▶ **Pierre-la-Treiche** *(8 km E)* : picnic spot on the banks of the Moselle. ▶ 11 km E, **Villey-le-Sec** : interesting fort (end 19thC; *May-Sep., Sun, nat. hols. at 3*). ▶ **Bruley** *(6 km NW)*, with its neighbours, among the last vine-growing areas of central Lorraine; they produce "Gris de Toul", a very dry white wine. ▶ **Écrouves** : 12th-13thC Romanesque church.   □

Practical Information ———————

ℹ parvis de la Cathédrale, ☎ 83.64.11.69.
SNCF ☎ 83.43.10.30.
🚌 ☎ 83.43.01.29.

Hotel :
★★ **Europe**, 35, av. V.-Hugo, ☎ 83.43.00.10, 21 rm Ⓟ closed 1-15 Feb, 180.

Restaurants :
● ♦♦ **Dauphin**, rte de Villey-Saint-Étienne,

☎ 83.43.13.46, Euro Visa ⚲ ♿ closed Mon and Sun eve, 1-15 Aug. An elegant stopover with fine cuisine by C. Vohmann : *foie gras aux mirabelles séchées, turbot aux côtes de Toul*, local wines, 130-250.
♦♦ **Belle Epoque**, 31, av. V.-Hugo, ☎ 83.43.23.71, Euro Visa ♪ ♿ ⚯ closed Sat and Sun, 15 Feb-2 Mar, 13 Aug-3 Sep. Spec : *escalope de lotte à la ciboulette et nouilles fraîches, escalope de sandre et turbot à la petite sauce d'herbes, panaché des cinq poissons à la vapeur*, good desserts, 75-145.

Recommended
Guide to wines : *Gabriel Demange*, 4, rue du Chêne, ☎ 83.43.20.96 : Toul's noted *vin gris*.

VAUCOULEURS

Commercy 20, Nancy 46, Paris 278 km
pop 2511 ✉ 55140   A3
Little remains of the château where Robert de Baudricourt, royal governor of the region, dismissed Joan of Arc after threatening to box her ears. The chapel still stands (rebuilt in 1924, except for the 13thC crypt).

▶ The **French Gateway** (La Porte de France), where Joan set out for Chinon, was rebuilt in the 17thC; a few other towers remain from the old ramparts. ▶ 18thC church. ▶ **Johannique museum,** Place de la Mairie with Joan of Arc room ; Joan prayed in front of the image of Christ (then in a country chapel) before setting out on her mission in 1429. *(Jul.-Aug., 9-12 & 2-6; on request from the town hall rest of year).* ▶ **Gombervaux** *(4 km farther) :* ruins of 14thC feudal **château** with gate keep.   □

Practical Information ———————

Nearby

HOUDELAINCOURT, ✉ 55248 Gondrecourt-Le-Château, 17 km SW.

Hotel :
★★ **Auberge du Père Louis** (L.F.), ☎ 29.89.64.14, AE DC Euro Visa, 8 rm Ⓟ ⚲ ♪ ⚯ ✎ closed Sun eve and Mon, 3-10 Aug, 24 Dec-1 Jan, 170. Rest. ♦ ♪ Spec : *blanc de turbot au beurre de pamplemousse, escalope de ris de veau aux truffes*, 70-200.

VERDUN*

Metz 78, Reims 120, Paris 261 km
pop 24120 ✉ 55100   A2
This name is forever-written on the blackest pages of history, even though German and French troops alike showed heroic courage and self-denial. The successive battles from Feb. 1916 to Oct. 1917 killed more than 800 000 men.

▶ **Cathedral**★ (11th-12thC, frequently restored) at the top of the town : Rhenish-Romanesque (Romanesque crypt; flamboyant Gothic cloister★; treasury). Next door, 18thC bishop's residence. ▶ Renaissance **Hôtel de la Princerie** (residence of the clergyman second in importance to the bishop)★ : museum *(May-Sep., 10-12 & 2-6; closed Tue.).* ▶ Administrative offices and law courts are in a 17thC abbey. ▶ **Porte Chaussée**, facing the bridge over the Meuse, a vestige of the 14thC ramparts. ▶ On the right bank, Town Hall (1623). ▶ The **Citadel,** which stands on top of 7 km of underground tunnels, has been turned into a War Museum *(8-12 & 2-5 or 7 according to the season; closed 15 Dec.-28 Feb.).*

Battlefield of Vaux-Douaumont *(marked tour of 31 km; forts open 10-12 & 2-5:30 off season, 9-6 in season)*

Leave Verdun by the Étain road *(N3)* then take the left fork to **Fort-de-Vaux.** ▶ Through Fort-de-Souville (destroyed) you reach the site of Fleury, a village completely destroyed *(memorial museum closed 15 Dec.-15 Jan.).* ▶ Passing alongside the **National Cemetery** (Cimetière National; 15 000 graves) to **Fort-de-Douaumont** above the site of a lost village of the same name. ► Return to the **Ossuaire de Douamont**, last resting-place for 130 000 unidentified soldiers *(open all year)*. ► **The Bayonet Trench** (La tranchée des Baïonnettes), where two entire infantry companies were buried alive during fierce bombardment. Back to Bras-sur-Meuse, thence to Verdun.

Nearby

► **Dugny-sur-Meuse** *(8 km S)* : Romanesque church, bell tower crowned with a wooden gallery. ► **Génicourt** *(10 km upstream on the other bank)* : church with fortified bell tower; 16thC furnishings, frescos and stained glass. ► **Étain** *(20 km NE)*, entirely rebuilt after 1918, still has a 14th-15thC church with flamboyant Gothic choir★★ (modern stained glass★). ◻

Practical Information ————————

VERDUN
ⓘ pl. de la Nation, ☎ 29.84.18.85.
SNCF ☎ 29.86.18.97.
pl. Vauban, ☎ 29.86.02.71.

Hotels :
● ★★★ *Coq Hardi*, 8, av. de la Victoire, ☎ 29.86.36.36, Tx 860464, AE Euro Visa, 39 rm, closed 23 Dec-1 Feb, 280. Rest. ◆◆ ⅋ closed Wed. Spec : *terrine d'écrevisses au sabayon rose, canard au vinaigre de framboises, mirabelles flambées au caramel*, 135-300.
★★★ *Bellevue*, 1, rd-pt du Mal-de-Lattre-de-Tassigny, ☎ 29.84.39.41, 72 rm ℗ ⌂ ⅋ closed 15 Oct-1 Apr, 320. Rest. ◆ 85-150.
★★ *La Poste*, 8, av. de Douaumont, ☎ 29.86.03.90, Visa, 23 rm ⌂ closed 20 Jan-20 Feb, 85. Rest. ◆◆ *La Pergola* Interesting spot. Spec : *coquilles Saint-Jacques au vermouth, tournedos aux morilles*, 65-110.

Recommended
♥ Jordan almonds : *Braquier*, ☎ 29.84.30.00, At Coulmier, tours of the candy factory.

Nearby

DAMVILLERS, ⊠ 55150, 26 km.

Hotel :
★ *Le Rallye* (L.F.), ☎ 29.88.01.45, AE Visa, 11 rm ℗ ⌂ pens, half pens, 280. Rest. ◆ 50-100.

ÉTAIN, ⊠ 55400, 20 km NE.

Hotel :
★ *Sirène* (L.F.), 22, rue Prud'homme-Havette, ☎ 29.87.10.32, Euro Visa, 30 rm ℗ ⌂ ⅋ closed 23 Dec-1 Feb, 130. Rest. ◆ closed Mon, 50-100.

ISSONCOURT, ⊠ 55220, 24 km S.

Hotel :
★★ *Relais de la Voie Sacrée* (L.F.), ☎ 29.70.70.46, Euro Visa, 7 rm ℗ ⌂ ⌂ closed Mon, 21 Dec-31 Jan, 135. Rest. ◆ ⅋ ♿ closed Mon and Sun eve (Nov-Mar), 60-150; child : 35.

SENON, ⊠ 55230 Spincourt, 30 km NE.

Restaurant :
● ◆◆ *La Tourtière*, ☎ 29.85.98.30, Euro Visa ⌂ ⅋ ♿ closed Tue eve and Wed. In her lovely 1752 house, Marie-

Laure Becq-Moreau upholds the tradition of true Lorraine cookery : *tourte aux grenouilles, lapereau aux girolles, verger lorrain*. Very old vintage Burgundies and Bordeaux. The attractive antiques hanging on the walls are for sale, 120-250; child : 35.

VITTEL*

Epinal 43, Nancy 70, Paris 334 km
pop 6440 ⊠ 88800   B4
A renowned resort created in 1854 for the treatment of metabolic disorders, including liver and kidney ailments, by a lawyer from Toulouse. It is now a popular centre for rest and relaxation, notably among top-class athletes; parks, golf, race-course, country walks.

► Church of St. Rémy : 12thC, remodeled 15th-16thC.
► **Water-bottling factory** : almost 3.5 million bottles daily *(visits 9-11 & 2-4; closed Sat., Sun., and nat. hols.)*.

Nearby

► 3 km NE, **Mont Saint-Jean** (alt. 435 m) : view★; 6 km further, **Domjulien** : church (15th, 16thC sculpture).
► Excursions on foot or by car among the woods and lakes of the Faucille mountains. ◻

Practical Information ————————

VITTEL
⌘ ☎ 29.08.00.00.
ⓘ palais des Congrès, ☎ 29.08.12.72.
SNCF ☎ 29.08.02.24.

Hotels :
★★★ *Angleterre*, rue de Charmey, ☎ 29.08.08.42, AE DC Euro Visa, 62 rm ℗ ⌂ ♿ closed 15 Dec-15 Jan, 250. Rest. ◆ ⅋ ♿ 90-120.
★★★ *l'Aubergade*, 265, av. des Tilleuls, ☎ 29.08.04.39, AE Visa, 9 rm ℗ ⅋ ⌂ ♿ 380. Rest. ◆◆ ⅋ ♿ Light fare for spa-goers and others, 110-250.
★★ *Beauséjour*, 160, av. des Tilleuls, ☎ 29.08.09.34, Euro Visa, 37 rm ℗ ⌂ ⌂ closed 1 Oct-15 Apr, 200. Rest. ◆ ⅋ ♿ 70-135.
★★ *Castel Fleuri*, rue de Metz, rue Jeanne-d'Arc, ☎ 29.08.05.20, 42 rm ℗ ⌂ ⌂ closed 22 Sep-19 May, 230. Rest. ◆ 75-90.
★★ *L'Orée du Bois*, Hippodrome entrance, autoroute A 31, exit Chatenais, ☎ 29.08.13.51, Tx 960573, AE Visa, 38 rm ℗ ⅋ ⌂ ⌂ ⅋ ⁄° 185. Rest. ◆ ⅋ closed Sun eve (l.s.), 50-100.
★★ *Le Chalet* (L.F.), 6, av. G.-Clemenceau, ☎ 29.08.07.21, 10 rm ℗ ⌂ closed Sat (l.s.), 1 wk in Jan, Nov, 105. Rest. ◆ closed Sun eve. Spec : *soufflé chaud à la mirabelle*, 70-150.

⚑ ★★★*Municipal* (130 pl), ☎ 29.08.02.71; .

Nearby

ROUVRES-EN-XAINTOIS, ⊠ 88500 Mirecourt, 10 km N.

Hotel :
★★ *Burnel* (L.F.), ☎ 29.65.64.10, Euro Visa, 8 rm ℗ ⌂ half pens (h.s.), closed Sun eve (l.s.), 20-31 Dec, 275. Rest. ◆ ⅋ 105-140; child : 35.

Lyonnais, Bresse

▶ The city of Lyon, with a population second only to Paris — and thanks to the TGV or High-Speed train, a mere two hours from the capital — has dominated life and landscape in this region since the Roman conquest of Gaul. Its influence is felt far beyond the borders of the three *départements* described in this chapter and the relatively new name of "Lyonnais" covers an enormous disparity of natural regions, historical identities and economic development.

To the east is the department of Ain, made up of a number of smaller regions which were attached to the House of Savoy before coming under the sway of the Kings of France in the 17th century. To the west, the Forez region has flourished for over one hundred years in the shadow of the enormous industrial and economic complex of Saint-Étienne. To the north is Beaujolais, still living on the excellent tradition and reputation of its vineyards, where every year around October the new wine is bottled and sent to restaurants and wine cellars all over the world. To the south are the Pilat Mountains marking the northern border of Vivarais.

And yet, despite this seeming disparity, the city of Lyon, city of rivers, provides a link forging the parts into a single whole, adding the human dimension and retaining its links with the industrial empire of bygone days. Lyon, whose cooking is reputedly the finest in France and, many would claim, the world, is full of surprises for the tourist. It may have lost its silkweavers and the army of small craftsmen chased out by the factory owners after the bloody uprisings

of the early 19th century, but it has kept its old panoramas and invented new ones. The enterprising tourist will discover the old Roman town of *Lugdunum* beneath its modern trappings, and by wandering through its streets and visiting its many museums, will be able to enjoy the busy cultural life of a city which has been an important crossroads of civilization for some 2000 years. □

Don't miss

★★★ Lyon B2.

★★ La Bastié-d'Urfé A2, Beaujolais Region A-B1, Bourg-en-Bresse B1, Charlieu A1, Pérouges B2.

★ Ambierle A1, Bresse Region B1, Dombes Region B1-2, Ferney-Voltaire C1, Grangent A3, Montbrison A2, Mont-d'Or Lyonnais B2, Nantua C1, Mont Pilat A-B3, Saint-Bonnet-le-Château A3, Trévoux B2, Yzeron A2.

Weekend tips

Lyon, 2 hrs by TGV (Train Grande Vitesse : high-speed train) from Paris. First day, city tour : Fourvière and the old city (morning); a museum or two and a stroll through the passageways (traboules) of Lyon (afternoon); a visit to Tête d'Or Park (evening). Second day : half-day or day trip to Mont-d'Or and Rochetaillée; or Beaujolais, Bresse, or Dombes and Pérouges. From the Saint-Étienne region : visit Forez Plain or drive to Mont Pilat. At Divonne or in the Gex area : Faucille Pass, Valserine and Valromey (preferably between May and late Oct.). On any trip, plan to dine at one of the superb regional restaurants.

● *Brief regional history*

6thC BC-4thC AD
The valley had known at least 2000 years of human habitation and trade **(the tin and amber road)** before the first Roman colonists settled at *Lugdunum* (Lyon) in 43 BC. The site was a convenient centre for the administration of the **Roman colonies;** a road network spread, and the city was made the capital of Gaul in 16 BC. ● The population soon reached 100000. **Early Christians** sought protection at Lyon in 177, but many of them were martyred : in AD 197, the victory of Septimus Severus over Albinus brought about the destruction of the city and the massacre of its 18000 inhabitants. During the reign of the Roman Emperor Diocletian (284-305), Lugdunum was eclipsed in political importance by Arles, Trier and Vienne.

5th-14thC
At the dissolution of Charlemagne's Frankish Empire, the region of Lyonnais was incorporated into the kingdom of Provence, and later integrated, along with Burgundy, into the Holy Roman Empire. The establishment of church buildings affiliated with Cluny Abbey caused Romanesque art to flourish in the region. ● Lyon continued to expand as an important **trading centre;** the townspeople resisted attempts by the Church to interfere in commerce, and banded together to form the first municipality (1240) in France, which received the formal **protection of the French Crown** in 1275.

15th-16thC
At the beginning of the 15thC, refugees from civil wars in the Italian city republics fled to Lyon, where they introduced the **silk industry.** When, in 1463, Louis XI granted Lyon the privilege of four free fairs per year, **Florentine merchant bankers** opened branches of their Geneva operations at Lyon in 1466, and **Germain printers** set up shop on Rue Mercière in 1473. ● By the 16thC Lyon had outdistanced Paris in wealth and population; the city stock market — the oldest in France — was opened in 1506, by which time more than 100 publishers were in business. The Protestant **Reformation** found ready acceptance. ● In this independent atmosphere occurred the first recorded **workers' strike** — by printers in 1539-1542. Protestants began to suffer reprisals during the 1540s, and many were forced to flee to Geneva and other sympathetic refuges in 1551.

17th-18thC
The first workers' organizations were formed at the Lyon silk mills in the 18thC. **Coal mines** were put into commercial production in the **Saint-Étienne area** in 1759. ● From the eve of the Revolution onwards, invention and innovation were flourishing in the Lyonnais region : the first balloon ascent was made at Les Brotteaux in 1784, shortly after the *pyroscaphe* — precursor of the steamship — had been successfully launched on the Rhône.

19thC-present
Invention and industry continued to thrive with Joseph-Marie Jacquard's loom of 1804, based on the same punched-card principal used in computers today. The Jacquard loom revolutionized textile weaving (and

hence the clothing and related industries) throughout the world. Violent workers' revolts in the 1830s led many mill-owners to abandon mechanized city plants and re-establish weaving centers in the countryside where labour was plentiful and cheap. ● Metalworking thrived by virtue of the ample fuel supply in the Saint-Étienne region. ● During WWII, Lyon was the "capital" of the Resistance movement.

House in the Beaujolais region

House in the Bresse region

Farmhouse in the Dombes region

Facts and Figures

Location : *an artificial designation for the region between Auvergne and the Jura Mountains, the Lyonnais region straddles a swath cut by the River Rhône. The three administrative areas (départements) are : Eastern and Western Loire (4 800 km², corresponding to the former designation of Forez; Rhône, the country's smallest department (3 215 km²) after Paris, and Ain (5 836 km²), a mosaic of small landholdings.*

Climate : *Mediterranean in the Beaujolais and Bresse; in low-lying areas and around Lyon, fog and overcast skies are common. The forested mountains have wet, brisk weather, harsh in winter on Mont Pilat and in the upper reaches of the Jura — which may have snow until May.*

Population : *Ain, 429 300; Loire, 747 600; Rhône, 1 464 300. Density : 192/km² — among the highest in France, with the urban population more than 50% of the total.*

The Lyon-Saint-Étienne Region extends from Firminy in the west to the confluence of the Rhône and the Ain in the east; 90% of the region's population — more than 2.64 million — lives in this urban band.

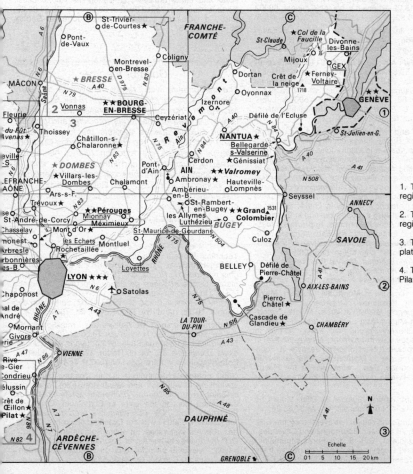

1. The Beaujolais region

2. The Bresse region

3. The Dombes plateau

4. Tour of Mont Pilat

Practical information

Information : *Comité Régional de Tourisme (C.R.T.)*, 5, pl. de la Baleine, 69005 Lyon, ☎ 78.42.50.04. C.D.T. **Rhône** : *Comité Départemental de Tourisme (C.D.T.)*, 69214 Lyon Cedex 2, ☎ 78.42.25.75 ; **Loire** : *C.D.T.*, 5, pl. Jean-Jaurès, 42021 Saint-Étienne Cedex 1, ☎ 77.33.15.39 ; **Ain** : *C.D.T.*, 34, rue du Gal-Delestraint, 01002 Bourg-en-Bresse Cedex, ☎ 74.21.95.00. — *U.D.S.I.* du Rhône and *T.O.* Lyon-Communauté, pavillon du Tourisme, pl. Bellecour, 69002 Lyon, ☎ 78.42.25.75. *Dir. régionale de la Jeunesse et des Sports*, 51, rue du Pensionnat, 69422 Lyon Cedex 3, ☎ 78.60.70.91. *Dir. rég. des Affaires culturelles*, 23, rue Roger-Radisson, 69322 Lyon Cedex, ☎ 78.25.29.72.

Bookings : *Loisirs-Accueil Loire* and *Loisirs-Accueil Ain*, enq. : *C.D.T.*

S.O.S. : *SAMU* (Emergency Medical Service), ☎ 78.54.51.55 ; *Poisoning Emergency Centre*, ☎ 78.54.14.14.

Weather forecast : **Ain**, ☎ 74.38.21.58 ; **Loire**, ☎ 77.55.44.44 ; **Rhône**, ☎ 78.26.73.74. *Snow conditions*, ☎ (1) 42.66.54.26.

Rural gîtes : enq. at the *Relais départementaux*. **Ain** : 1, pl. Clemenceau, 01000 Bourg-en-Bresse, ☎ 74.23.61.96. **Loire** : 43, av. Albert-Raimond, 42272 Saint-Priest-en-Jarez, ☎ 77.79.15.22. **Rhône** : 4 bis, pl. Gensoul, 69002 Lyon, ☎ 78.42.65.92.

Holiday villages : in the Monts du Lyonnais at Saint-Martin-en-Haut ; **Ain** : Saint-Germain-de-Joux, Hotonnes, Lelex, Thoissy ; **Loire** : Chalmazel, Saint-Jean-la-Vêtre.

Camping-car rental : **Ain** : *Loca Loisirs*, 01130 Saint-Jean-de-Gonville, ☎ 50.59.42.86 ; *Mionnay Loisirs*, RN 83, 01190 Mionnay, ☎ 78.91.82.31. **Loire** : *Loisirs système location*, 4, rue Saunerie, 42110 Feurs, ☎ 77.26.20.67. **Rhône** : *Mapi*, 85, cours Gambetta, 69003 Lyon, ☎ 78.60.32.86 ; *L. Paget Autos*, 11, rue d'Inkermann, 69100 Villeurbanne, ☎ 78.24.52.11.

Sporting, cultural and religious events : **end Jan** : *grande traversée du Haut Bugey* (cross-country ski race at Le Poizat) ; *"la Vague" festival* in Villefranche-sur-Saône (last Sun). **Mar** : *auto rally* Lyon-Charbonnières. **May** : *cultural, folkloric and sporting festival* in Lyon ; *medieval festival* in Villerest. **Jun** : *festival* in Villeurbanne ; *Val-Grangent live spectacle* in Saint-Victor-sur-Loire ; *international children's theatre festival* in Lyon. **Jul** : *cycling days* at the Col (pass) de la République ; *historical festival* in Lhuis ; *festival* in Divonne-les-Bains. **Jul-Aug** : *aquatic jousting* in Condrieu. **4 Aug** : *pilgrimage* in Ars-sur-Formans. **Sep** : *music festival* at the Abbaye d'Ambronnay ; *mechanical music festival* in Oingt ; *folklore and historical festival* in Vieu-en-Valmorey ; *vine-growers' pilgrimage* (the 8th) to Mont Brouilly. **Nov** : *cinémathèque festival* (the 1st) in Lyon. **Dec** : *illumination in honor of the Virgin* in Lyon ; *lantern procession and midnight Mass* in Pérouges.

Festivals : **Apr** : *egg race* in Montrottier (Easter). **May** : *cherry festival* in Bessenay ; *strawberry festival* in Courzieu. **Jul** : *peach festival* in Arse, Millery ; *woodcutters' festival* in Mijoux. **Aug** : *chicken festival* in Beny ; *hay harvest* in Chezery Forens ; *old trades festival* in Crémeaux ; *rummage sale* in Leyment ; *bilberry festival* in Souvin. **Sep** : *groasse* (boiled chicken) *festival* in Fourneaux. **Oct** : *fourme day* in Montbrison ; *wine festival* in Saint-Trivier-de-Courtes. **Dec** : *wine sale* at the Hospices in Beaujeu ; *2-bottles competition* in Villefranche-sur-Saône.

Nature parks : *parc naturel régional du Pilat*, Moulin de Virieu, 2, rue Benäy, 42410 Pélussin, ☎ 74.87.65.24.

Rambling and hiking : the region is traversed by the G.R. trails 32, 7, 72, 73, 76 between Bourgogne and Cévennes ; 760 (tour of Beaujolais) ; G.R. 3, the Forez Mountains ; G.R. 59 (Bresse and Bugey) ; G.R. 9 and alternative trails (*G.T.J. :* major crossing of the Jura ; 200 km ; *G.T.A. :*

major Alpine crossing, from the Rhône to the Riviera). Rambling and hiking programs are organized by the *Ligue du Lyonnais*, 43, bd L.-Guérin, Vénissieux, *Assn. des groupes de randonneurs de la Loire* (at the *C.D.T.*), the *Comité départ. de tourisme pédestre du Rhône (C.D.T.)*. Also see the *Féd. de Moyenne-Montagne*, 4, Grande-Rue-de-la-Guillotière, 69007 Lyon, ☎ 78.72.02.69.

Scenic railways : *Commelle-Vernay belvedere*, 42370 Renaison, ☎ 77.70.62.40 or 77.66.84.64 (M. Heitz).

Riding holidays : *A.R.A.T.E.*, M. Buriane, 46, rue Léon-Lamazière, 42118 Saint-Étienne ; main office : 4, rue André-Malraux. *F.E.F., Ligue Rhône-Alpes*, 28, pl. Bellecour, 69001 Lyon, ☎ 78.37.33.68.

Horse-drawn holidays : departure from Sainte-Catherine (Lyonnais mountains), ☎ 78.81.81.94 ; in the **Ain**, in Ceyzériat : Cheval-Bugey, ☎ 74.30.01.21. Equestrian farm at Malagretaz, ☎ 74.30.81.19.

Cycling holidays : *Fédération française de cyclotourisme* : *Ligue du Lyonnais*, 49, rue Pasteur, 69300 Caluire ; *Ligue du Forez*, 11, rés. Fontquentin, Roanne ; *C.D.T.* Bourg-en-Bresse. Excursions organized in the Pilat region (*C.D.T.*), in Saint-Étienne, and *maison du Parc*, in Pélussin), the Beaujolais area (leaving from Villefranche) ; cycle tour of the **Loire** : M. Frasse, Pouilly-sous-Charlieu ; in the **Ain** : *Cyclo-Bressan* (train + vélo) at the Montbrison and Villars-les-Dombes railway stations.

River and canal cruises : cruise on the Rhône canal, *Portout Plaisance*, 73310 Portout Chanaz, ☎ 79.54.29.25, and *la Galiotte*, 69400 Villefranche-sur-Saône, ☎ 74.62.28.75.

Guignol theatre

The marionnette was created at Lyon in the early 19thC by Laurent Mourguet (1769-1841). Guignol — Mr. Punch French-style — embodies the canut, the Lyons silk weaver. Bantering, mocking and philosophical, Guignol theatre projects the local workers' slang, outlook, dress and character. Among Guignol's principal partners are Madelon (Judy), his stingy, screechy, quarrelsome and intractable wife, and his friend Gnafron, always the tipsy, mawkishly sentimental, pompous moralizer. The Guignol presentations make much of local and national politicians as well as other public figures.

Technical tourism : river development, visits to completed projets daily ex Sat, Sun, hols, 8-12 & 2-5 ; *la Compagnie nationale du Rhône*, ☎ 78.29.94.31. Nuclear power plant : *Centre nucléaire de Bugey*, Électricité de France (E.D.F.) in Saint-Vulbas, ☎ 74.34.12.34. *Société française Martine et Rossi* in Culoz, ☎ 79.87.01.60 ; La Maison des Canuts, 10-12, rue d'Ivry, 69004 Lyon, ☎ 78.28.62.04.

Handicrafts courses : *les Ateliers des Trois Soleils*, 75, rue Eugène-Pons, 69004 Lyon, ☎ 78.28.34.30 ; *les Mains Enchantées*, 58 bis, rue Stala, 69002 Lyon ; *Ateliers éducatifs et culturels*, 16, rue du Raisin, 42000 Saint-Étienne. Pottery courses in Pérouges ; enq : *C.D.T. Ain*.

Other courses : ornithology in the Dombes (summer) ; spelunking in Jujurieux and Menthières (Ain) ; ethnology in Saint-Trivier-de-Courtes (*Université rurale bressane*) ; excavation sites in the Loire at Châtelneuf, Chambles, Essertines, enq : *Dir. des antiquités préhistoriques*, 28, rue Radison, 69005 Lyon ; for Lyon and environs : *Dir. rég. des Affaires culturelles* ; at Saint-Romain-en-Gal, enq. : *O.T.* in Vienne ; in the Ain at Jujurieux (château de Chenavel) ; "weekend pain au cœur du vignoble du Cerdon", *Assn. pays du Cerdon*, ☎ 74.39.95.42.

Lyon regional cuisine

From Lyon to Bresse and Bugey by way of the Dombes, food is an art and a science. The raw materials are superb : poultry, butter, cheese, freshwater fish, mushrooms, and wine.
Traditional regional cooking does not tamper with basic flavour. As the French say, "Let things taste as they are." François Rabelais (ca. 1490-1553), author and physician at the Lyon hospital (Hôtel-Dieu), acknowledged the region's culinary traditions in his exuberant satirical chronicles of sensory pleasure.
The city of Lyon alone has about 30 renowned restaurants. The Dombes area, the Rhône Valley and Forez boast many others of international repute. Gastronomic tours are organized by TO at Vienne, Pérouges and Saint-André-de-Corcy. Regional homestyle dishes include the sausages known as rosette and Jésus, potted pork (cru) and pâté in pastry crust; salads made with the mushroom known as pied de mouton (sheep's foot), with dandelion, sippets and herring, or with dandelion and coddled eggs; poached mousse of pike (quenelles de brochet) with a hot butter sauce; tripe known as "sapper's apron" (tablier de sapeur); pig's tail; "chicken in half-mourning" with slices of truffle under the skin; cardoons with marrow; and sundry tasty snacks taken at any time of day with a glass of Beaujolais. Specialities of Forez and Bugey include freshwater crayfish (écrevisse), duck braised in red wine, and roast game.

Wine guide : *Syndicat des vins de Bugey,* 01300 Belley, ☎ 79.81.30.17; *Union interprofessionnelle des vins du Beaujolais,* 210, bd Vermoul, 69400 Villefranche-sur-Saône, ☎ 74.65.45.55.

Leisure centres : *parc et réserve ornithologique* (bird sanctuary) *de la Dombes,* 01330 Villars-les-Dombes, ☎ 74.98.05.54; *base de plein air* (open-air centre) *de Montrevel,* 01340 Montrevel-en-Bresse, ☎ 74.30.80.52.

Young people : *Direction départementale de la Jeunesse et des Sports* or the *Centre régional informations jeunesse,* 9, quai des Célestins, 69000 Lyon, ☎ 78.37.15.28.

Canoeing : *Féd. française,* 17, rte de Vienne, 69007 Lyon, ☎ 78.61.28.06; *Ligue du Lyonnais,* 56, rue du Perron,

69600 Oullins; *Comité départ.* : **Ain**, based at Longeville-Ambronay, 01500 Ambérieu-en-Bugey; trip on the Ain River, enq. at *C.D.T.*

Golf : Rhône : Villette-d'Anthon (Golf-Club des Iles de Lyon; 27 holes), Saint-Symphorien-d'Ozon (9), Villars-les-Dombes (15); **Ain :** Divonne-les-Bains (18); Crottet (15). **Loire :** Gaintilleux (18), Champlong (9).

Potholing and spelunking : in particular, in the Colomby-de-Gex, Bugey and Revermont chasms **(Ain)**; *Departmental Committees :* 29, rue Michelet, Oyonnax; and *Maison des Sociétés, Bourg-en-Bresse;* **Rhône,** 28, quai Saint-Vincent, 69001 Lyon, at the *Féd. Nat. de spéléologie,* ☎ 78.39.43.30; M. Krupa Daniel, 16, rue du Cimetière, 42000 Saint-Étienne.

Climbing, mountaineering : especially in the **Ain** (Revermont, Bugey, Valserine) : *Maison des Sociétés,* bd Juliot-Curie, 01000 Bourg-en-Bresse, ☎ 74.23.29.43, *M.J.C.* de Bellegarde, ☎ 50.48.13.31. Climbing section of the *C.A.F. :* 38, rue Thomassin, 69002 Lyon; 26, rue Marengo, Saint-Étienne; 1, montée de l'Abbaye, 01130 Nantua, ☎ 74.76.52.58.

Skiing : Ain : 15 fully-equipped resorts, 900 km of cross-country ski trails : enq. *C.D.T.* and *Assn. Départementale du ski de fond de l'Ain.* **Loire :** *Assn. dép. pour le développement du ski nordique,* M. Charrondière, Les Noës, 42370 Renaison; *Comité Forez de la F.F.S.,* 2, rue Étienne-Dolet, 42000 Saint-Étienne, ☎ 77.32.42.53.

Flying, gliding, hang-gliding : *Union des aéroclubs Rhône-Alpes,* aérodrome de Lyon-Bron, ☎ 78.26.81.09. *Assn. aéronautique de Bellegarde,* ☎ 50.77.90.83. Hang-gliding : *Club du Rhône,* 66, chemin du Boisset, 69600 Oullins; *Assn. de Vol libre,* 01130 Nantua; *Club du Pays gessien,* 01170 Gex; *Université-Club,* 34, rue Francis-Baulier, 42000 Saint-Étienne.

Hunting and shooting : *Fédération de chasseurs :* **Ain,** 57, rue de la République, 01000 Bourg-en-Bresse, ☎ 74.22.25.02; **Loire,** 8, pl. de l'Hôtel-de-Ville, 42000 Saint-Étienne, ☎ 77.25.25.96; **Rhône,** 11, rue Childebert, 69002 Lyon, ☎ 78.42.69.09.

Fishing : numerous stretches of water, 1st category for fishing : rivers in Ain (trout, granyling); the thousand lakes of the Astrée region (Forez) in the 1st or 2nd category; organized fishing holidays (Saint-Paul-de-Varax). *Departmental Federations* of fishing associations, **Ain :** 10, allée de Challes, 01000 Bourg-en-Bresse, ☎ 74.22.38.38; **Rhône,** 10, quai Augagneur, 69003 Lyon, ☎ 78.60.81.05; **Loire,** 2, rue d'Arcole, Saint-Étienne, ☎ 77.32.14.99. In the **Rhône :** *Féd. des groupements de pêcheurs sportifs* (fishing competition in the Ain River), 5, rue Jules-Verne, 69740 Genas.

Towns and places

AMBÉRIEU-EN-BUGEY

Pérouges 14, Bourg-en-Bresse 29, Paris 456 km
pop 10470 ⊠ 01500   B2

A small town beneath Mont Luisandre *(NE)* amid countryside popular with anglers for trout and grayling.

Nearby

▶ **Ambronay** *(4 km N)* : Benedictine abbey with Gothic cloister★ *(closed Sun., Jul.-Aug. & Mon. rest of year),* monks' cells, gargoyle-emblazoned door (13thC). ▶ E on a ridge of **Mt Luisandre** (alt. 809 m, panorama★), 13th-16thC **château des Allymes**, fortress, later home of the counts of Savoy. ▶ **Saint-Sorlin-en-Bugey** *(S via Lagnieu, near the Rhône),* "city of roses" : Romanesque and Gothic church of the Madeleine (15thC fresco; summer concerts).   □

AMBIERLE*

Roanne 18, Vichy 52, Paris 375 km
pop 1596 ⊠ 42820   A1

Among the Roanne vineyards, a hillside market town around a Gothic church★; in the valley, one of the best provincial museums of folk arts and traditions★★.

▶ Church : **stained-glass windows★**, Gothic choir stalls, 15thC Burgundian-Flemish School triptych depicting **Christ's Passion★.** ▶ **Forez Regional Museum :** Alice-Tavern *(10-12 & 2-5, 6 or 7 according to season; closed Tue. ex Jun.-Aug.),* reconstructed 18th and 19thC interiors★★.

Don't forget to consult the Practical Holiday Guide: it can help in solving many problems.

Roanne Region

▶ **Saint-Haon-le-Châtel** *(S)* : walled market town★ (12th-15thC); ramparts, clock tower, gate, former hospital, church, 15thC château, Renaissance house, wine cellar *(open Sun. pm)*. ▶ **Renaison** *(2 km E)* : château de Boisy (15th-16thC). Follow the Renaison Valley to Tache Dam *(6 km)*. ▶ **Saint-André-d'Apchon** : Renaissance stained glass in church (12th-15thC); château des d'Albon (Renaissance). ▶ **Saint-Alban-les-Eaux** : mineral springs. ▶ **Lentigny** (pop. 1311). ▶ **Crozet★** *(N)* : walled market town; Romanesque keep : panorama; houses, some timbered; local history museum. ▶ **La Pacaudière** *(1 km)* : 16thC houses. ▶ Via the Paris road, spa at **Sail-les-Bains** (treatment of skin diseases). ☐

Practical Information

Nearby

LENTIGNY, ⊠ 42128, 9 km SW on the D 53.

Hotel :
★★★ *Ferme Napoléon*, Le Ruizor, ☎ 77.63.11.11, 7 rm ℙ ▒ closed Sun eve and Mon, 15-31 Aug, 210. Rest. ◆◆ ♪ Rich, classic cooking. *Foie gras*, lobster, fine meat, 160-300.

RENAISON, ⊠ 42370, 7 km S.

Hotel :
★ *Jacques Cœur* (L.F.), 15, rue de Roanne, ☎ 77.64.25.34, AE DC Visa, 10 rm ℙ closed Sun eve, Mon and Feb, 115. Rest. ◆ 60-190.

SAIL-LES-BAINS, ⊠ 42310 La Pacaudière, 16 km N. ⅃ (15 May-30 Sep), ☎ 77.64.30.81.

Hotel :
● ★★ *Grand Hôtel*, parc de l'établissement thermal, ☎ 77.64.30.81, 32 rm ℙ ⟨ ▒ ⊙ ♪⁰ closed 1 Oct-15 May, 240. Rest. ◆ 50-130.

△ ★★*Municipal* (70 pl), ☎ 77.64.30.85.

SAINT-ANDRÉ D'APCHON, ⊠ 42370 Renaison, 3 km S of **Renaison** on the D 8.

Hotel :
Le Lion d'Or, pl. de la Mairie, ☎ 77.65.81.53, Visa, 7 rm ℙ closed Mon eve and Sun eve, 5-30 Jan, 15-26 Jul, 130. Rest. ◆ ♪ Interesting fixed-price meals by a chef who worked with Bocuse and Alain Chapel. Spec : *goujonettes de sole au piment doux*, 70-180.

L'ARBRESLE

Lyon 25, Roanne 61, Paris 457 km
pop 4909 ⊠ 69210   B2

In one of the Brévenne valleys, this industrial centre preserves vestiges of the Savigny monks' buildings (→ below).

▶ 13th-16thC church (Gothic stained glass); Renaissance houses; 11thC château ruins. ▶ Historical museum (Rue P.-Sémard : *Sun. pm*). ▶ **La Tourette Convent**★★ *(1 km S via Éveux)*, designed by the architect Le Corbusier (1887-1965) for Dominican nuns (1957-59 : *drive-through private park ; Sun. visits to church, weekdays on written request*).

Nearby

▶ By the Tarare road, **Bully** : 14thC-Renaissance castle and ramparts.
▶ S by N 89, **Saint-Bel** : 12thC ruins. ▶ **Saint-Pierre-la-Palud** : mining museum *(Mar.-Nov., Sat., Sun, hols., 2-6)*.
▶ **Savigny** *(2 km W)* : museum of medieval architecture.
▶ **Nuelles** *(N)* : two churches, one Romanesque, the other (more interesting) Gothic (outside staircases).
▶ E by the Lyon road : lookout *(3 km, left)*. ▶ **Lentilly.** ▶ **Charbonnières-les-Bains** *(15 km)* : attractive thermal spa (park), centre for rheumatology, traumatology and cardiac rehabilitation. ▶ N, **Dardilly** (pop. 5111) : museum

open daily in the house where Jean-Baptiste Vianney, a priest from Ars (→ Trévoux), was born in 1786. ▶ **Écully** (pop. 18467). ☐

Practical Information

L' ARBRESLE
ⅈ ☎ 74.01.48.87; mairie : pl. de la République, ☎ 74.01.12.44.
SNCF ☎ 74.01.02.06.

Hotel :
★ *Le Lion d'Or*, 4, rue Centrale, ☎ 74.01.00.16, 12 rm ℙ 150. Rest. ◆ 40-70.

Restaurant :
◆ *Le Vieux Four*, RN 7, Bully, ☎ 74.01.02.67, AE Euro Visa ⟨ ▒ ♪ closed Mon, 5-30 Jan, 50-90; child : 40.

△ ★★★*Municipal* (100 pl), ☎ 77.01.11.50.

CHARBONNIÈRES-LES-BAINS, ⊠ 69260, 18 km SE. ⅃ All year.
ⅈ parc thermal, ☎ 78.87.05.21.
SNCF ☎ 78.92.17.28.

Hotels :
★★★ *Thermes*, parc thermal, ☎ 78.87.12.33, Tx 375528, AE DC Euro Visa, 50 rm ℙ ▒ 𝄐 300. Rest. ◆ Spec : *aiguillettes de lapereau à la feuille de thym*, 80-180.
● ★★ *Le Beaulieu*, 19, av. Gal-de-Gaulle, ☎ 78.87.12.04, AE DC Euro Visa, 45 rm ℙ ⟨ 160.

Restaurant :
● ◆ *Gigandon*, 5, av. Gal-de-Gaulle, ☎ 78.87.15.51, AE Visa, closed Mon eve and Sun eve, Aug. A calm, relaxing setting and good food, 100-150.

Recommended
♥ casino : rue du casino, ☎ 78.87.02.70.

CHASSELAY, ⊠ 69380 Lozanne, 10 km W.

Restaurant :
● ◆◆ *Lassausaie*, rue Bellecize, ☎ 78.47.62.59, AE DC Euro Visa ⟨ closed Tue eve and Wed, 15-28 Feb, Aug. Cooking here is a family affair : *foie gras chaud aux poires, volaille sautée à l'ail confit, râble de lapin au vinaigre de framboise*. Rhône Valley wines, 90-160.

DARDILLY, ⊠ 69570, 14 km E.

Restaurant :
◆◆ *Le Panorama*, 2, pl. Gal-Brosset, ☎ 78.47.40.19, AE Visa ⟨ ▒ closed Mon eve, Tue, Sun eve , Feb, Jul. Spec : veal kidneys, marinated salmon, 165-250.

△ ★★★★*Porte de Lyon* (150 pl), ☎ 78.35.64.55.

La BASTIÉ-D'URFÉ★★

A2

Just beyond the **Astrée lakes region**, and at the foot of the Madeleine Peaks (**Pierre-sur-Haute** panorama★), the medieval castle, renovated in Italian Renaissance style during the 16thC, is the architectural jewel of Forez.

▶ Guided tour *(9:30-11:30 & 2:30-6:30 ex Tue. ; tel. 77.97.54.68)*; courtyard with **equestrian gallery**; painted chapel; "honeycombed" sleeping quarters; "nymphs' grotto". ▶ Gazebo *(pavillon d'amour)* : Renaissance-style round temple in adjacent grounds.

The Astrée region

▶ **Boen** *(7 km NE)* : 18thC château. ▶ **Pommiers★** *(12 km N of Boen)*, medieval fortified town : fortified priory, Romanesque church, 15th-16thC frescos, local history museum on the ramparts. ▶ **Saint-Germain-Laval** *(4 km from Pommiers)* : Gothic/Renaissance houses ; museum in town hall. ▶ **Sail-sous-Couzan** : overlooked by ruined **château de Couzan**★ on a 450-m peak. ▶ **Montverdun** *(S)* : 12th-16thC church on an isolated volcanic ridge. ▶ **Chalain-d'Uzore** : 14th-16thC castle, formal gardens

(1 Apr.-1 Nov., 8-12 & 2-6). ▶ **Champdieu** *(3 km farther)* : ramparts, church (fortified 14thC)★ of Romanesque priory (13thC nave, crypt, cloister). ☐

Practical Information ───────────────────

SAINT-GERMAIN-LAVAL, ⊠ 42260, 12 km N of **Boën-sur-Lignon**.

Recommended
Farmhouse-inn : at Saint-Georges-en-Couzan, *Le Vieux Moulin*, Veaux, ☎ 77.24.23.32 ; *Le Mazet*, ☎ 77.24.80.95, pork products from the farm, patcha and fruit pies.
Guide to wines : *cave coopérative des Côtes du Forez*, ☎ 77.24.00.12, D8.

The BEAUJOLAIS Region**

A-B1
260 km round-trip from Lyon *(at least a full day ; see map 1)*

Vineyards, pastures and forests in countryside traced by tributaries of the River Saône. Essentially mountain country isolated by two large valleys (the Loire in the W), Beaujolais has remained essentially rural with three distinct natural regions : the granite peaks crowned by **Mont Saint-Rigaud** (alt. 1 012 m), where forestry is the staple industry ; E, between 500 m and 200 m above sea-level, the compact **vineyard area** 8 km across (in the N section, the major growths of Juliénas, Chénas, Fleurie) and, around, especially to the S, Beaujolais-Villages ; finally, the chalky soil called **pierres dorées** (golden stones), where pastures turn into vineyards at the elevations that suit the vines.

▶ **Lyon** (→). ▶ **Dardilly** (→ L'Arbresle) and the Azergues Valley★. ▶ **Civrieux-d'Azergues**. ▶ N, **Chazay★**,

1. The Beaujolais region

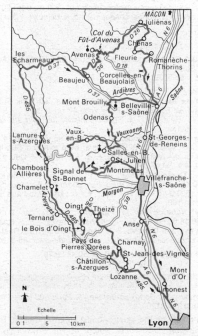

at the gateway to the *pierres dorées* : medieval ramparts (Baboon Gateway) ; Rural Architecture Museum. ▶ **Lozanne** (pop. 1 704) : N, château de Gage, valley watchtower. ▶ **Châtillon-d'Azergues★**, on a hillock next to a Romanesque castle : two 10thC chapels, one with a painting by Hippolyte Flandrin (→ Lyon). ▶ **Charnay** *(3 km N)* : fortified castle ; mullioned windows ; Romanesque church. ▶ **Alix** *(3 km farther)* : Romanesque church façade ; feudal château de Marzé. ▶ **Le Bois-d'Oingt** (pop. 1 465) : château de Tanay (15thC). ▶ **Bagnols** *(SE)* : porticoed houses, Romanesque church, Gothic château fireplace. ▶ **Theizé** : concerts in the church ; manor-houses ; museum in Clos de la Platelière. ▶ **Oingt★** : ruins of fortress. ▶ **Ternand★**, right bank of the Azergues *(36 km from Lyon)*, Gaulish fortified town on a promontory ; medieval village (historic site★) ; church fresco★, 6thC crypt ; château of the count-archbishops of Lyon (view from Tarare Peaks road). ▶ **Saint-Vérand** : two Gothic châteaux, one restored by the architect Eugène Viollet-le-Duc (1814-79), in a park★. ▶ **Sainte-Paule** : medieval church. ▶ **Létra** : castle ruins. ▶ **Chamelet** : fortified market town on the edge of vineyards and pastures. ▶ **Chambost** : Gothic church. ▶ **Lamure-sur-Azergues** (pop. 1 065) : W, château de Pramenoux (15th-18thC). ▶ **Écharmeaux Pass** (alt. 720 m) : at Poule-les-Écharmeaux, in a pine forest (hiking and rambling trails). ▶ **Chénelette** : at the foot of **Mont Tourvéon** (alt. 953 m, panorama). ▶ **Beaujeu★** (pop. 2 013) : old houses ; temple of Bacchus (wine-tastings) ; folk art **museum** (19thC dolls, reconstruction of an interior ; *Easter-1 Nov., closed Tue. & am in winter).* ▶ **Fût d'Avenas Pass** (alt. 762 m) : vineyard panorama★. ▶ **Avenas** : Carolingian altar★ in modest church. ▶ Down to the valley via Chiroubles and the Saint-Amour and Moulin-à-Vent **vineyards** ; Romanesque churches at **Juliénas** (cellars, tithe barn), **Chénas** and **Fleurie**. ▶ **Romanèche-Thorins** : zoo *(daily)* and Trades Museum *(Sun. and hols. ; Easter-1 Nov.).* ▶ **Château de Corcelles** : 16th-17thC *(Sat., Sun.).* ▶ **Belleville-sur-Saône** (pop. 6 580) : 12thC walled enclave *(bastide)* of the lords of Beaujeu ; old pharmacy. ▶ **Mont Brouilly** : vineyard panorama★ from summit (alt. 485 m). ▶ **Odenas** : château de **La Chaize** *(1 km away)* built by Mansart, formal gardens by Le Nôtre (the foremost designer of the 17thC, → Ile-de-France, Versailles) *(temporarily closed).* ▶ **Blaceret**. ▶ **Salles** : Romanesque cloister★ in former priory. ▶ **Saint-Bonnet Pass** (alt. 660 m) : panorama★ reached by hill paths. ▶ **Château de Montmelas** : 19thC restoration by Viollet-le-Duc. ▶ **Saint-Julien** : museum in the house of Claude Bernard *(closed Mon.).* ▶ **Villefranche-sur-Saône** (→). ▶ 6 km on, **Anse** (pop. 3 745) : site occupied by Celts and Romans (archaeological excavations, → Lyon, Fourvière museum) ; small museum in town hall. ▶ Return to Lyon via Limonest (→ Mont d'Or). ☐

Practical Information ───────────────────

ANSE, ⊠ 69480, 6 km S of **Villefranche**.
ℹ️ mairie, ☎ 74.67.03.84.

Hotel :
★★ *Saint-Romain* (L.F.), rte de Graves, ☎ 74.68.05.89, Tx 310514, AE DC Euro Visa, 23 rm 🅿 ▥ ♫ pens. Renovated farmhouse, 440. Rest. ♦ ≤ ♪ ♨ closed Sun eve , Nov.-Apr. Spec : *tartare d'escargots et Saint-Jacques, turbotin au beurre de morilles*, 60-140.

BEAUJEU, ⊠ 69430, 26 km of **Villefranche**.
ℹ️ mairie, ☎ 74.04.80.84.

Hotel :
★ *Anne de Beaujeu* (L.F.), 28, rue de la République, ☎ 74.04.87.58, 7 rm 🅿 ▥ ♨ half pens (h.s.), closed Sun eve and Mon, 15-22 Jun, 21 Dec-20 Jan, 130. Rest. ♦ ♪ 65-100.

Recommended
Guide to wines : *le Temple de Bacchus*, ☎ 74.04.81.18, wine auction for the hospices, 2nd Sun of Dec.
♥ regional products, exhibit : *Maison de Pays de Beaujeu*.

BELLEVILLE-SUR-SAÔNE, ⊠ 69220, 25 km SW of **Mâcon.**
[i] 50, rue de la République, ☎ 74.66.21.00.
SNCF ☎ 74.66.32.11.

Hotels :
★★★ *Château de Pizay* (R.S.), Saint-Jean-d'Ardières, ☎ 74.66.51.41, Tx 305772, AE DC Visa, 34 rm [P] ⚫ ◱ ♨ ☐ ♪⁰ 370. Rest. ♦♦ 150-250; child : 80.
★ *Le Beaujolais*, 40, rue du Mal-Foch, St-Jean-d'Ardières, ☎ 74.66.05.31, Euro Visa, 10 rm [P] ☜ closed Tue eve and Wed, 1-28 Dec. Rest. ● ♦♦ ☜ One of Georges Blanc's favourites : frogs legs, crayfish, *coq au vin*, *andouillettes*. Appealing wines, 70-160.

BLACERET, ⊠ 69830 Saint-Georges-de-Reneins, 2 km E of **Salles.**

Restaurant :
♦♦ *Beaujolais*, ☎ 74.67.54.75, AE DC Euro Visa, closed Mon and Tue , Feb, 75-150.

Le BOIS-D'OINGT, ⊠ 69620, 19 km N of **L'Arbresle.**
SNCF ☎ 74.71.76.69/64.71.60.53.

Restaurant :
♦ *France*, ☎ 74.71.60.61 [P] ☜ ◱ ♨ closed Wed, 1-25 Aug, 45-120.

Recommended
Guide to wines : *Terrasse des Pierres-Dorées*, tastings in the wine cellar (wkends and hols).

CHÉNAS, ⊠ 69840 Juliénas, 19 km SW of **Mâcon.**

Restaurant :
♦♦ *Daniel Robin*, Les Deschamps, ☎ 85.36.72.67, Tx 351004, AE DC Euro Visa ⚫ ⚫ ◱ closed Wed , eves ex Sat, 1 Feb-1 Mar, 5-12 Aug, 145-225.

Recommended
Guide to wines : *Château de Chénas*, ☎ 74.04.11.91, cellar tour.

FLEURIE-EN-BEAUJOLAIS, ⊠ 69820, 21 km SW of **Mâcon.**

Restaurant :
● ♦♦ *Auberge du Cep*, pl. de l'Église, ☎ 74.04.10.77, AE Euro Visa [P] ⚫ closed Mon and Sun eve , Dec. Food served in the garden. Spec : *mousseline chaude de sandre*, 200-300.

⚠ ★★★*Grappe Fleurie* (50 pl), ☎ 74.69.80.07.

Recommended
Guide to wines : *cave coop. des grands vins de Fleurie*, ☎ 74.04.11.70, daily.

JULIÉNAS, ⊠ 69840, 17 km SW of **Mâcon.**

Hotels :
★ *Chez la Rose*, Le Bourg, ☎ 74.04.41.20, Euro Visa, 12 rm [P] ◱ ☜ closed Tue, 8-16 Jan, 85. Rest. ♦ ◱ ☜ 60-100.
★ *Le Coq au Vin*, ☎ 74.04.41.98, AE Euro Visa, 7 rm [P] ◱ closed Wed and Thu lunch in winter, 15 Jan-15 Feb, 90. Rest. ♦ ☜ ◱ Terrace dining, 45-95.

Recommended
Guide to wines : at Château-du-Bois-de-la-Salle, *cellier de la Vieille Église*, ☎ 74.04.42.61, Beaujolais wines.

QUINCIÉ, ⊠ 69430 Beaujeu, 6 km from **Beaujeu.**

Hotel :
★★ *Le Mont Brouilly* (L.F.), Le Pont des Samsons, ☎ 74.04.33.73, AE Euro Visa, 26 rm [P] ☜ ◱ ◱ closed Mon eve and Sun eve (Dec-Mar), 1-15 Feb, 180. Rest. ♦ ☜ ◱ 70-120.

SALLES-EN-BEAUJOLAIS, ⊠ 69830 Saint-Georges-de-Reneins, 12 km NW of **Villefranche.**

Hotel :
● ★★★ *Hostellerie Saint-Vincent*, ☎ 74.67.55.00, Tx 375777, AE DC Euro Visa, 28 rm [P] ☜ ⚫ ♪ ☐ ♪⁰ closed Mon eve and Sun eve , Feb, 195. Rest. ♦ ☜ ♪ ◱ 85-140; child : 50.

Restaurant :
♦♦ *La Benoîte*, ☎ 74.67.52.93, AE Euro Visa [P] ⚫ ◱ ◱ closed Wed, 4-20 Feb, 26 Jul-15 Aug, 50-95.

Recommended
Guide to wines : *La Tassée du Chapitre*, Beaujolais tastings at wine cellar.

BELLEGARDE-SUR-VALSERINE

Nantua 18, Annecy 41, Paris 508 km
pop 11787 ⊠ 01200   C1

An industrial centre at the confluence of the Rhône and Valserine rivers, overshadowed to the N by the **Grand Crêt d'Eau** (alt. 1 624 m); panorama★★ over Mont Blanc (Alps) and Lake Léman (Switzerland), Lakes Annecy and Bourget (Savoy); trail *(4-hr hike one-way)*.

Nearby

▶ S by D25 and Billiat : **Génissiat Dam**★ *(14 km)*, France's largest hydroelectric station (1.8 million kWh) after Donzère-Mondragon *(no visits)*. ▶ E towards Gex (→) and Geneva, the **Écluse Defile**★ *(10 km)*. ▶ W towards Valromey (→ Hauteville-Lompnès), the road climbs the E rim (view★) from the **Retord Plateau** (alt. 1 200-1 300 m); S, **Crêt du Nu** (alt. 1 351 m). ▶ N via N84 toward Nantua (→) : **Perte** (disappearance) of the River **Valserine**★ *(3 km)*. ▶ Beginning at Châtillon-de-Michaille *(5 km)*, the road overlooks the gorge and River Sémine to *(12 km)* **Saint-Germain-de-Joux.** ▶ From there, N via **Giron** (winter sports resort), **Fauconnière**★ (natural amphitheatre) and, via Belleydoux, Orval combe.

Valserine Valley from Bellegarde to Mijoux *(37 km, D991)*

▶ **Pont-de-Pierres** : 80-m arched bridge. ▶ **Chalam Crest**★ (alt. 545 m) : looking on to **Chezery-Forens** (17thC church, abbey buildings). ▶ The road climbs beyond **Sous-Balme Defile**★ ; to the right, the **Jura Crest** (over 1 700 m) : Reculet, Crêt de la Neige and, N, Colomby-de-Gex and Mont-Rond (→ Gex; *more than 3 hr climb*); views★★. ▶ **Lelex** : winter resort (alt. 900 m, pop. 203) ; semiprecious stones, cheesemaking. ▶ **Mijoux** (→ Gex).

Practical Information _____

[i] rue de la République, ☎ 50.48.03.56, closed Mon and Sun.
SNCF ☎ 50.48.04.74.

Hotels :
● ★★★ *Le Fartoret*, (R.S., L.F.), Eloise, left bank of the Rhône, ☎ 50.48.07.18, Euro Visa, 42 rm [P] ☜ ⚫ ◱ ◱ ☐ ♪⁰ 195. Rest. ♦♦ ☜ ◱ Spec : *compote de lapin aux herbes*, 75-180.
★★★ *La Belle Epoque*, 10, pl. Gambetta, ☎ 50.48.14.46, AE Euro Visa, 10 rm [P] ♪ closed Mon eve and Sun eve (l.s.) for the restaurant only, 5-25 Jul, 15 Nov-5 Dec, 130. Rest. ♦♦ ♪ 110-200.
★★ *Central-Colonne* (L.F.), 1, rue J.-Bertola, ☎ 50.48.10.45, AE DC Euro Visa, 30 rm [P] ♪ ◱ closed Sun eve, 15 Oct-15 Nov, 170. Rest. ♦ ♪ ◱ closed Mon and Sun eve, 60-100.
● ★ *Auberge de la Fontaine*, Ochiaz, par D 99, ☎ 50.48.00.66, AE DC Euro Visa, 7 rm [P] ⚫ ◱ closed Mon eve and Sun eve, 3-30 Jan, 24-30 Jun, 105. Rest. ♦ Spec : *quenelle de brochet, volaille demi-deuil*, 65-210.

⚠ ★★★★*Crêt d'Eau* (70 pl), ☎ 50.48.23.70.

BELLEY

Chambéry 36, Bourg-en-Bresse 75, Paris 502 km
pop 8372 ⊠ 01300   C2

Birthplace of the gastronomist Jean-Anthelme Brillat-Savarin (1755-1826), author of *The Physiology of*

Taste (1825), still considered the gourmet's bible. The poet Alphonse Lamartine (1790-1869) attended secondary school in Belley.

▶ Cathedral finished in the 19thC : Gothic choir and transepts. Bishop's palace (late 18thC). Brillat-Savarin's birthplace (62 Grande-Rue). ▶ Seminary museum, Rue Sainte-Marie.

Nearby

▶ Bugey vineyards ; tasting cellars. ▶ **Pierre-Châtel Defile★** *(8 km, S),* cut by the Rhône, site of a namesake medieval fortress enlarged in the 19thC. ▶ Road follows the **Bugey Peaks** (alt. 700-1 000 m) : château de Peyrieu ; ruined château de Cordon. ▶ **Glandieu Waterfall★.** ▶ **Château de Groslée.** ▶ **Lhuis★,** overlooking the Rhône : Gallo-Roman traces ; church with Romanesque apse. ▶ W, via Saint-Germain-les-Paroisses *(7 km) :* ruins of **château de Beauretour.** ▶ **Massignieu Lake** *(6 km E),* leisure centre. □

Practical Information _____

BELLEY
ⓘ pl. de la Victoire, ☎ 79.81.16.16 ; Hôtel de ville, ☎ 79.81.29.06.

Recommended
Farmhouse-inn : at Boissieu, 4 km, *l'Auberge,* ☎ 79.81.35.74, Spec : *coq au vin, gigot* ; at Ordonnaz, 19 km NW on D32, ☎ 79.36.42.39.
Guide to wines : *syndicat des vins du Bugey,* bd du 133e-R.-I., ☎ 79.81.30.17 ; at Flaxieu, 10 km N, *M. Crussy,* wine grower.
♥ brandies and liqueurs : *Distillerie de l'Etoile,* 44, rue Ste-Marie.

Nearby

BENONCES, ✉ 01470 Serrières-de-Briord, 28 km NW.

Hotel :
★★ *Auberge de la Terrasse* (L.F.), ☎ 74.36.73.56, Euro Visa, 9 rm ℗ ⏃ △ closed 2 Jan-20 Mar, 180. Rest. ♦ ♪ closed Mon, 50-120.

Lyon 62, Lons-le-Saunier 62, Paris 427 km
pop 43675 ✉ 01000   B1
A gourmet's delight, as well as an art and architecture centre of the first order, thanks to the church and monastery of **Brou★★** (C2).

▶ Church (1505-1536), among the finest examples of Flamboyant Gothic : choir **rood-screen★** : choir stalls★, Renaissance stained glass ; sculpted **tombs★** ; altarpiece (Flemish Renaissance : Seven Joys of the Virgin★). ▶ **Ain Museum★★★** : in the three monastery cloisters regional folk art and traditions, reconstructed interiors *(Oct.-Mar., 9-12 & 2-5, 6:30, Apr-Sep.).* □

Practical Information _____

ⓘ 6, av. Alsace-Lorraine, ☎ 74.22.49.40 ; bd de Brou, ☎ 74.22.27.76 (h.s.).
SNCF ☎ 74.21.50.50.
Car rental : *Avis,* train station (A2) ; 2, bd. E.-Herriot (B1), ☎ 74.22.29.58.

Hotels :
● ★★★ *Prieuré,* 49-51, bd de Brou (C2), ☎ 74.22.44.60, AE DC Visa, 14 rm 1 apt ℗ ⏃ ▨ △ ♿ 350.
★★★ *Logis de Brou,* 132, bd de Brou (C2), ☎ 74.22.11.55, AE DC Visa, 30 rm ℗ ▨ 230.
★★ *Ariane,* bd Kennedy (off map C1), ☎ 74.22.50.88, Euro Visa, 30 rm ℗ ▨ △ ♪ ♿ ▨ closed 22 Dec-5 Jan, 250. Rest. ♦ ♪ ♿ closed Sun and lunch, 80-120.
★★ *Chantecler,* (R.S., Mapotel), 10, av. de Bad-Kreuznach (off map C1), ☎ 74.22.44.88, Tx 380468, AE DC Euro Visa, 28 rm ℗ ▨ △ 205. Rest. ♦ ♪ ⁑ 100-140.
★★ *Mail,* 46, av. du Mail, ☎ 74.21.00.26, DC Visa, 11 rm ℗ ▨ closed Sun eve and Mon, 6-21 Jul, 21 Dec-12 Jan, 140. Rest. ♦♦ ♿ 90-180.
★★ *Terminus,* (France-Accueil), 19, rue A.-Baudin (A2), ☎ 74.21.01.21, Tx 380844, AE DC Euro Visa, 50 rm ℗ ▨ ♪ 245. Rest. ♦ *l'Albatros* ⁂ ♪ closed Sat noon, 26 Dec-10 Jan, 70-140 ; child : 40.
★ *Revermont,* 19, rue Charles-Robin, ☎ 74.22.66.53, Visa, 15 rm, closed Sun, 100. Rest. ♦♦ Simple, good and cheap, 45-110.

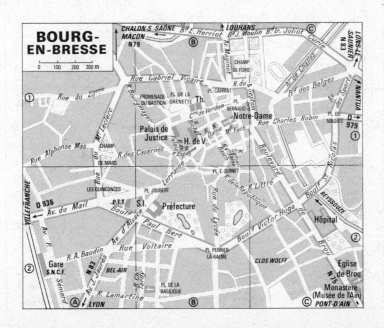

Restaurants :
● ♦♦♦ *Auberge Bressane*, 166, bd de Brou (C2), ☎ 74.22.22.68, AE Euro Visa ⚜ ﷽ ᶦ Wonderful Bresse poultry with all the trimmings. *Emincé de turbot à la vinaigrette de truffes, ragoût de homard*, 115-230.
♦♦ *Brasserie du Français*, 7, av. Alsace-Lorraine (B2), ☎ 74.22.55.14, AE Euro Visa ﷽ ♪ ᶦ closed Sat eve and Sun, 10-31 Aug, 20-31 Dec, 80-140.
♦ *Brasserie du Théâtre*, 1, rue Paul-Pioda, ☎ 74.23.35.72, Euro Visa ♪ ᶦ 52-100.

▲ ★★★★*Challes* (125 pl), ☎ 74.22.27.79.

Recommended
Youth hostel : *Alatsa*, Centre Culturel, ☎ 74.22.03.53.

The BRESSE Region*

B1
"Saracen chimneys route" *(approx. 130 km NNW of Bourg; full day; information at O.T. in Bourg and S.I. in Saint-Trivier-de-Courtes; see map 2)*

Mixed forest and pastureland, renowned for blue cheese *(visits to cheese factories)* and chicken. Bresse was placed under the crown by Henri IV in 1601. Many of the regional **timber-built farmsteads** date back to that era. The chimneys of these farmsteads — ornamented in Mediterranean style and known as "Saracen" chimneys to the local people — are a distinctive feature of the landscape.

▶ Leave Bourg via N83; at **Saint-Étienne-du-Bois** *(12 km)* take the first road E through Treffort Wood. ▶ **Treffort-Cuisiat :** Gothic church (furnishings); 15th-16thC houses; covered market. ▶ **Cuisiat :** chapel of Notre-Dame-de-Montfort (13th-14thC). ▶ **Meillonas** *(S)* : pottery centre (18thC). ▶ **Verjon :** church partly Renaissance (unusual for Ain), 17thC triptych. ▶ **Coligny :** 15th-16thC church.

▶ **Courtes** *(18 km from Coligny)* : forest farm★ (Romanesque-style square chimney hood, folklore museum). ▶ **Vernoux** *(N)* : Grand Colombier farms. ▶ **Saint-Trivier-de-Courtes★** *(guided tours, ask at the SI)*, farms at Tremblay (three-storeyd chimney) and Grandval (Romanesque-style chimney hood). ▶ **Pont-de-Vaux** (pop. 2 050) : Chintreuil Museum (paintings by a student of the 19thC landscape painter Camille Corot); Gothic church; Baroque school façade; medieval and Renaissance houses. ▶ **Reyssousse :** chimney topped by brick cross at Reyssousse Farm. ▶ **Chevroux :** Mont Farm (exterior staircase); Bourlière Farm (16thC chimney hood). ▶ Via Bâgé-le-Châtel, **Saint-André-de-Bâgé :** 11thC Romanesque church, octagonal bell tower. ▶ **Pont-de-Veyle :** two towers from old fortifications; old houses; château. ▶ **Saint-Cyr-sur-Menthon :** N, Planons Farm★ (wooden gallery, fireplace, furnishings). ▶ From Bourg on N79 : **Logis-Neuf** *(N*, Confrançon). ▶ **Vonnas** *(5 km SE; pop. 2 500)*. ▶ **Montrevel-en-Bresse** *(NE; pop. 2 000)* recreation area 1 km W; Sougey Farm★★ (one of the finest Bressan interiors in the region). ▶ **Foissiat :** Tiret Farm (brick chimney rebuilt early 20thC). ▶ Return to Bourg via Viriat (church). □

Practical Information _____

COLIGNY, ✉ 01270, 21 km N of **Bourg**.
ᶦ ☎ 74.30.10.97.

Restaurant :
● ♦♦ *Au Petit Relais*, Grande-rue, ☎ 74.30.10.07, AE DC Euro Visa ﷽ ♪ closed Tue eve and Wed , Feb school hols, 10-26 Jun. J. Guy serves, among other things, beautifully cooked fresh fish, 80-220.

CONFRANÇON, ✉ 01130 Polliat, 15 km W of **Bourg**.

Hotel :
★★★ *Auberge la Sarrasine* (R.S.), Logis-Neuf, ☎ 85.30.25.65, Tx 375830, Euro Visa, 10 rm ℗ ﷽ ⚐ ᶦ ⊠

2. The Bresse region

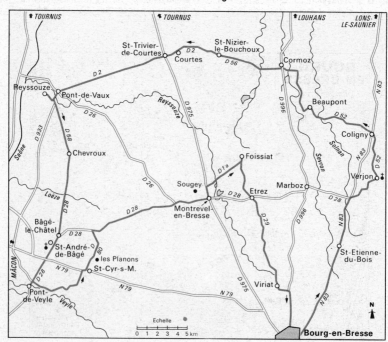

Echelle
0 1 2 3 4 5 km

N

closed Wed and Thu lunch, 320. Rest. ♦♦
♪ ᵫ 150-200.

PONT-DE-VAUX, ⊠ 01190, 38 km NW of **Bourg**.
🄸 2, rue du Mal-de-Lattre, ☎ 85.30.30.02 (h.s.).

Hotels :
★★ *Commerce*, 5, pl. Joubert, ☎ 85.30.30.56, AE DC
Euro Visa, 11 rm 🄿 closed Tue, Wed, 9-23 Jun,
16 Nov-12 Dec, 180. Rest. ♦♦ 80-140.
★★ *Le Joubert*, (ex La Reconnaissance), 9, pl. Joubert,
☎ 85.30.30.55, AE DC Euro Visa, 16 rm 🄿 closed Sun eve
and Mon, 5-22 Jan, 180. Rest. ♦ 65-150.
★★ *Le Raisin*, ☎ 85.30.30.97, AE DC, 7 rm 🄿 ⌘ closed
Sun eve and Mon, 1 Jan-6 Feb, 140. Rest. ♦ ᵫ 60-170.

⅄ ★★★*Les Peupliers* (160 pl), ☎ 85.37.31.01.

REPLONGES, ⊠ 01750, 13 km S.

Hotel :
★★★★ *La Huchette*, N79, ☎ 85.31.03.55, Tx 800787, AE
DC Euro Visa, 14 rm 🄿 ≪ ∭ ◿ ᵫ 🖻 ◢ closed
5 Nov-15 Dec, 420. Rest. ♦♦ ≪ ᵫ Country charm and
quiet. *Escargots crème de cresson, turbotin sauce musca-*
det, canard aux cerises, poularde à l'ancienne, 135-250.

VILLEMOTIER, ⊠ 01270, 21 km S of **Bourg**.

Hotel :
★★ *Le Solnan* (L.F.), Moulins-des-Ponts, ☎ 74.51.50.78,
AE DC Euro Visa, 20 rm 🄿 ≪ ∭ closed Sun eve and Mon
(l.s.), 2-30 Jan, 170. Rest. ♦ ♪ ᵫ Spec : *feuilleté de gre-*
nouilles aux herbes, 85-210.

VONNAS, ⊠ 01540, 24 km W of **Bourg**.

Hotel :
● ★★★★ *Georges Blanc* (R.C.), ☎ 74.50.00.10,
Tx 380776, AE DC Euro Visa, 30 rm 🄿 ≪ ∭ ◿ 🖻 ◢
◿ closed 2 Jan-14 Feb, 800. Rest. ● ♦♦♦♦ ≪ ᵫ closed
Wed and Thu ex Thu eve in season. Neither Jean-Louis
Blanc the founder, nor Adolphe Blanc and his wife Elisa
(later to become the famous "Mère Blanc"), nor Paulette,
mother of the present owner, would recognize the old
(1872) family inn near the Vonnas fair grounds. Since 1965
Georges Blanc and his wife, Jacqueline, have transformed the place into an enchanting destination, surely
one of the most delightful and blooming in all of France.
His forebears would be happy and proud, because Georges Blanc respects the same solid culinary traditions —
grenouilles sautées, Bresse poultry *grand'mère Blanc à*
la crème — while creating wonderful contemporary dishes
as well : *bar marinière au vin d'Aze, crêpe parmentière*
au saumon et caviar, pigeon de Bresse en cocotte, petits
chèvres du Mâconnais. Sumptuous pastries and frozen
desserts. The cellar holds some 90,000 bottles, representing 1 200 different appellations, something of a record!
Charming rooms for a restful stay, 270-350.

⅄ ★★★★*Municipal* (50 pl), ☎ 74.50.02.75.

CEYZERIAT

Bourg-en-Bresse 8, Nantua 32, Paris 435 km
pop 1982 ⊠ 01250   B1

Base for hiking excursions at the foot of the Rèver-
mont foothills of the Jura.

Revermont and the Ain Gorges *(E, about 95 km, 5-hr*
round trip)

▶ Via **Hautecourt-Romanèche** *(10 km) :* view from **Haute-**
court peak over Allemant Lake and Dam. ▶ N, via **Cize**,
follow D59b ridge road (views). ▶ At **Thoirette**, cross to
the left bank and climb towards **Coiselet Dam.** ▶ Return
to D18 and head for Nantua, passing by **Oignin** reservoir
(at upper end, Charmine Falls). ▶ **Izernore** : Gallo-Roman
excavations with three columns from the temple of *Izarno-*
durum ; museum in village. ▶ Return to Ceyzériat via **Ber-**
thiand Pass (views) and the landmarks visible from **Ser-**
rières bridge over the Ain.   □

Hotels :
★★ *Mont-July* (L.F.), ☎ 74.30.00.12, 19 rm 🄿 ≪ ∭ ◿
closed Thu eve (l.s.), 30 Oct-2 Mar, 180. Rest. ♦ 60-130.
★ *Balcon* (L.F.), rue Jérôme-Lalande, ☎ 74.30.00.16,
10 rm 🄿 ♪ half pens (h.s.), closed Mon eve and Sun eve,
15 Nov-21 Dec, 180. Rest. ♦ ♪ 60-160.

Restaurant :
♦♦♦ *La petite auberge*, Saint-Just, ☎ 74.22.30.04, Visa
🄿 ∭ ◿ ♪ ᵫ closed Mon eve and Tue, 12 Jan-12 Feb,
95-150.

CHARLIEU**

Roanne 19, Mâcon 77, Paris 405 km
pop 4380 ⊠ 42190   A1

Romanesque Benedictine **abbey** ruins : 15thC **clois-**
ter, chapter house, **narthex** and **portal★** (a masterpiece of 12thC Burgundian sculpture ; *mid.-Jun.-Sep.,*
9-12 & 2-7 ; Apr.-mid-Jun., closed Tue. ; Oct.-Nov. and
Feb.-Mar., closed Tue. and Wed.). Painted Renaissance choir stalls can be seen in the parish church.

▶ Upstairs, stonework museum : **ornamentation** from the
abbey. ▶ Ancillary buildings (15thC, Renaissance) are private property *(no visits).* ▶ 500 m from abbey, former **Cor-**
deliers' convent : 14th-15thC cloister★. ▶ Gothic houses
in town.

Nearby

▶ N, to see the Brion Romanesque churches (→ Burgundy). ▶ 5 km W, via **Pouilly-sous-Charlieu** (pop. 2 973).
▶ **La Bénisson-Dieu★** *(5 km farther) :* abbey church
(12thC nave, 15thC bell tower, glazed-tile roof).   □

🄸 rue A.-Farinet, ☎ 77.60.12.42 (h.s.).

Hotel :
★★ *Relais de l'Abbaye* (L.F.), Le Pont-de-Pierre,
☎ 77.60.00.88, Tx 307599, AE DC Euro Visa, 27 rm 🄿 ≪
∭ ◿ ♪ ᵫ 185. Rest. ♦ ≪ ♪ ᵫ Fish cookery : *soufflé de carpe*
au vert, loup beurre blanc, 80-165 ; child : 50.

⅄ ★★★*Municipal* (100 pl), ☎ 77.60.09.47.

DIVONNE-LES-BAINS

Geneva 19, Nantua 65, Paris 506 km
pop 4783 ⊠ 01220   C1

Cold-water mineral springs used to treat nervous
disorders.

▶ Spa situated at the feet of the highest peaks in Jura (the
Crêt d'eau, the Crêt de la neige, 1 723 m) in a 74-acre **park**
with recreational facilities, including golf, casino, lake.   □

⚕ ☎ 50.20.05.70, (all year).
🄸 pl. des Bains, ☎ 50.20.01.22.
SNCF ☎ 50.20.07.27.

Hotels :
● ★★★★ *Château de Divonne* (R.C.), rte de Gex,
☎ 50.20.00.32, Tx 309033, Visa, 23 rm 5 apt 🄿 ≪ ∭ ◿
closed 6 Jan-15 Mar, 680. Rest. ● ♦♦♦ ≪ ♪ Despite his
youth, talented Guy Martin (a pupil of Troisgros and
Robuchon) manages both to fulfill his culinary duties and
to direct this venerable establishment. Spéc. : *minute de*
cabillaud, ris de veau pané, soufflé glacé. The spa patrons
are happy as clams, 195-280 ; child : 85.
★★★★ *Les Grands Hôtels* ≪ 50.20.06.63, Tx 385716,
AE DC Euro Visa, 145 rm 🄿 ≪ ∭ ◿ ⚷ 🖻 ◿ ◢ 600.
Rest. ♦♦ ≪ 200-300 ; child : 80.
● ★★ *Bellevue* (L.F.), rte d'Arbère, ☎ 50.20.02.16, AE
DC Euro Visa, 16 rm 🄿 ≪ ∭ pens (h.s.), closed

2 Jan-5 Mar, 600. Rest. ♦ *Marquis* ⟨ ♪ ♨ closed Mon and Tue noon, 115-250.
★★ *Le Divona*, 3, rue de Genève, ☎ 50.20.00.91, Visa, 22 rm Ⓟ closed 1 Dec-4 Jan, 150.
★★ *Les Coccinelles*, rte de Lausanne, ☎ 50.20.06.96, Euro Visa, 22 rm Ⓟ ♨ ≈ closed 24 Dec-24 Jan, 180.
★★ *Mont-Blanc* (L.F.), rte de Grilly, ☎ 50.20.12.54, 18 rm Ⓟ ⟨ ♨ ≈ ♪° pens (h.s.), closed 1 Nov-1 Apr, 560. Rest. ♦ closed eves, 120-160.

Recommended
Casino : ☎ 50.20.06.63, and 50.20.08.44.
Farmhouse-inn : at Vesancy 3 km SW, *la Colombette*, ☎ 50.41.64.17. Spec : *foie gras, confits, magrets.*

The DOMBES Plateau*

B1-2
Starting from Villars-les-Dombes (→ *below*); *see map 3*, from Bourg (→) or from Trévoux (→).

A plateau dotted with ponds, popular with waterfowl hunters and anglers; also a preserve for migrating birds, including grey and tufted heron, duck, the barnacle goose, coot and buzzard.

▶ **Villars-les-Dombes** (pop. 2 832) : ruined Romanesque castle; 14th-15thC church. 1 km S, 54-acre **bird sanctuary★★** (*daily*) next to a 515-acre preserve closed to the public; more than 2 000 animals and birds of 400 species, including all indigenous species of the Dombes and tropical birds; aquarium, vivarium. ▶ **Chalamont** *(14 km E) :* sandy moors and reeds at the foot of the highest peak in the Dombes (alt. 334 m, view); Gothic houses, Plantay "tower". ▶ **Meximieux, Pérouges** (→). ▶ Toward Lyon, **Montluel★** (pop. 5 604), fortified city : ramparts, cloister, old streets, 15th-17thC mansions; Notre-Dame-des-

Marais collegiate church; chapel of St. Barthélemy (13thC); hospital apothecary (painted ceiling). ▶ **Miribel** (pop. 7 111). ▶ **Les Échets.** ▶ **Mionnay.** ▶ **Saint-André-de-Corcy.** ▶ **Trévoux;** Ars-sur-Formans, Jassans-Riottier (→ Trévoux). ▶ **Châtillon-sur-Chalaronne★** (pop. 2 687), floral town : ramparts (Villars Gateway); 15thC covered market; 11thC castle ruins. ▶ **Saint-Paul-de-Varax** *(14 km from Villars) :* Romanesque church (sculpted doorways★); Jourdan Museum of painting. ▶ Return to Villars via Notre-Dame-des-Dombes Abbey. □

Practical Information

CHÂTILLON-SUR-CHALARONNE, ⊠ 01400, 24 km SW of **Bourg.**
ⓘ Champ-de-foire, ☎ 74.55.02.27 (h.s.). ♥

Hotels :
★★★ *Au Chevalier Norbert*, 32, av. Clément-Desormes, ☎ 74.55.02.22, AE DC Euro Visa, 34 rm Ⓟ ♿ 200. Rest. ♦♦ ⟨ ♪ ♿ closed Mon (l.s.) Oct-May, 2 Jan-2 Feb. Spec : *mousseline de saumon aux cuisses de grenouilles, millefeuille de pigeon au jus de truffes,* 100-200 ; child : 65.
★★ *Tour*, pl. de la République, ☎ 74.55.05.12, Visa, 12 rm Ⓟ closed Sun eve and Wed (l.s.), 10 Feb-15 Mar, 150. Rest. ♦ 75-150.

Restaurant :
♦♦ *Auberge de Montessuy*, rte de Marlieux, 1 km S.-E., ☎ 74.55.05.14, Euro Visa ⟨ ♨ ♪ closed Mon eve and Tue, 27 Sep-6 Oct, 1 Nov-31 Dec. Spec : *mousse de truite et croustade de ris de veau aux morilles,* 80-100 ; child : 40.

Å ★★★★*Le Vieux Moulin* (16 pl), ☎ 74.55.04.79.

Les **ÉCHETS,** ⊠ 01700, 16 km NE of **Lyon.**

Hotels :
★★★ *Douillé*, RN 83, ☎ 78.91.80.05, AE Euro Visa, 8 rm

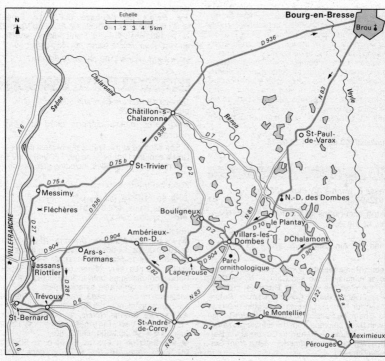

3. The Dombes plateau

P ⌨ ♪ closed Mon eve and Tue, 14-28 Feb, 4-21 Aug, 245. Rest. ♦♦♦ ♪ & Spec : *fricassée de volaille à la crème*, 140-250.

★★★ *Le Sarto*, rte de Bourg, ☎ 78.91.80.02, Tx 305141, Euro Visa, 13 rm P ⌨ ⌨ ♪ closed Sun eve and Mon, 190. Rest. ♦♦♦ ⌨ ♪ 200-250 ; child : 80.

★★ *Marguin*, rte de Strasbourg, N 83, ☎ 78.91.80.04, AE DC Euro Visa, 9 rm P ⌨ ♪ ♨ closed Tue eve and Wed, 2-16 Jan, 2-11 Sep, 190. Rest. ● ♦♦♦ ⌨ ♪ & A fortunate disciple of Bocuse, Jacques Marguin cooks with sure talent, backed up by his wife : *mousseline de grenouilles, pintadeau au citron vert, volaille à la crème*. Excellent, extensive selection of Burgundies, 110-200.

MARLIEUX, ✉ 01240 Saint-Paul-de-Varax, 9 km NW of Villars-les-Dombes on the N38 and D7.

Hotel :
★ *Lion d'Or* (L.F.), ☎ 74.42.85.15, Visa, 8 rm P ♨ closed Sun eve and Mon, Feb school hols, 160. Rest. ♦ ♪ 80-160.

Restaurant :
● ♦ *Entre Chasse et Pêche*, ☎ 74.42.86.02 & ♨ closed Tue eve and Wed noon, 15 Sep-1 Oct. A former Bocuse assistant is now out on his own, cooking up hearty regional fare, 60-200.

MIONNAY, ✉ 01390 Saint-André-de-Corcy, 19 km NE of Lyon.

Hotel :
★★★★(L) *Alain Chapel* (R.C.), ☎ 78.91.82.02, Tx 305605, AE DC Euro Visa, 13 rm P ⌨ closed Mon and Tue lunch ex hols, 550. Rest. ● ♦♦♦♦ One really ought to bow one's head in reverent silence upon entering this gastronomic temple. Although he would never lay claim to the epithet, Alain Chapel is truly a poet (a special prize should be devised just for him). The precise low-key descriptions on his *carte* will never lead you astray.Trust them : *bouillon de champignons comme un "capuccino", écrevisses au cerfeuil, délicate gelée au vin rouge, bœuf à la cuiller et vinaigrette, côte de veau en cocotte*. Then a few farmhouse cheeses, some desserts and sweets...You'll swear that a dream has become reality at your table, 350-450.

MONTLUEL, ✉ 01120, 44 km SW of Bourg.
ℹ pl. des Augustins, ☎ 78.06.20.46.
SNCF ☎ 78.58.01.21.

Hotels :
★★ *Chez Nous* (L.F.), Sainte-Croix, 5 km N on D 61, ☎ 78.06.17.92, Euro Visa, 16 rm P ⌨ ⌨ closed Sun eve and Fri, 1 Feb-1 Mar, 15-24 Aug, 150. Rest. ♦ 70-120 ; child : 40.

★★ *Le Petit Casset*, La Boisse (RN 84), ☎ 78.06.21.33, Visa, 10 rm P ⌨ ⌨ & 220.

SAINT-ANDRÉ-DE-CORCY, ✉ 01390, 24 km N of Lyon.
SNCF ☎ 78.81.11.62.

Hotel :
★★★ *Manoir des Dombes*, Saint-Marcel (3 km N), ☎ 72.26.13.37, 18 rm P ⌨ ⌨ 300.

VILLARS-LES-DOMBES, ✉ 01330, 28 km SW of Bourg.
ℹ ☎ 74.98.06.29 (h.s.).

Restaurant :
● ♦♦ *Auberge des Chasseurs*, Bouligneux, 3 km N, ☎ 74.98.10.02, Visa ⌨ & closed Tue eve and Wed, Feb, 15 Aug-1 Sep. A recommended stopping place : *panaché de poissons, canard sauvage aux petits navets*, 140-250.

⚓ ★★★★*Les Autières* (240 pl), ☎ 74.98.00.21.

Recommended
♥ *Maison artisanat et tourisme de l'Ain*, ☎ 74.98.05.90, at the entrance to the ornithological park ; pastry : *Paul Kœrberlé*.

Looking for a locality? Consult the index at the back of the book.

Saint-Etienne 38, Lyon 68, Paris 431 km
pop 8108 ✉ 42110   A2
A Gallo-Roman city on a strategic crossroads.

▶ Gothic church, ornamented portals (Renaissance panels). ▶ **Gallo-Roman Museum★**, Assier Park : reconstructed villa (mosaics ; *2-6*).

Nearby

▶ **Bussières** *(12 km)* : interesting weaving museum *(guided visit, tel. 77.28.33.95)*. ▶ N, via **Balbigny** (pop. 2 469), **Saint-Marcel-de-Félines** *(17 km)* : 16thC château, rooms decorated with paintings *(22 Apr.-1 Nov., Sun., Mon., hols. 2-6, daily)*. ▶ **Panissières** *(15 km NE; pop. 2 944)* : base for mountain hikes. ▶ **Montrond-les-Bains** *(11 km S; pop. 3 194)* : mineral-water spa : 11th-16thC castle ruins *(Jul.-Aug., Sat., Sun., hols., 2-6)*; Renaissance church. ☐

Practical Information _____

FEURS
ℹ pl. Antonin-Drivet, ☎ 77.26.05.27 ; château d'Assier, ☎ 77.26.05.27 (h.s.).
SNCF ☎ 77.26.04.56.

Hotels :
★★ *L'Astrée*, 2, chemin du Bout-du-Monde, ☎ 77.26.54.66, 16 rm P closed Sun eve, 160.
Commerce, 2, rue de la Loire, ☎ 77.26.05.87, AE Visa, 11 rm P closed Tue eve and Wed, 1-12 Feb, 15-22 Jun, 190. Rest. ♦ ♪ 95-120.

Restaurants :
♦♦♦ *Le Chapeau Rouge*, 21, rue de Verdun, ☎ 77.26.02.56, AE DC Euro Visa ⌨ & closed Tue eve and Wed. Spec : *terrine de crustacés, cassolette de ris de veau aux morilles*, 60-150.
♦♦ *La Boule d'Or*, 42, rte de Lyon, ☎ 77.26.20.68, Visa ⌨ closed Mon and Sun eve, 19 Jan-6 Feb, 16 Aug-3 Sep, 50-130.

⚓ ★★★*Municipal* (380 pl), ☎ 77.26.43.41.

Recommended
Bicycle rental : 3, pl. Geoffroy-Guichard.

Nearby

MONTROND-LES-BAINS, ✉ 42210, 11 km S.
⚕ (15 May-1 Oct), ☎ 77.54.40.04.
ℹ mairie, ☎ 77.54.40.04/77.94.67.74.
SNCF ☎ 77.54.42.65.

Hotel :
★★★ *Hostellerie La Poularde* (R.C.), ☎ 77.54.40.06, AE DC Euro Visa, 14 rm P closed Mon eve and Tue, 2-16 Jan, 250. Rest. ● ♦♦♦ ♪ & A local institution. Hearty and good, 135-320.

Restaurant :
♦♦ *Le Vieux Logis*, 4, rte de Lyon, ☎ 77.54.27.71 ♪ closed Mon and Sun eve, 1-15 Feb, 15-30 Jun. Fixed-price meals only, 70-190.

Recommended
Casino : ☎ 77.54.41.13.

SAINT-GALMIER, ✉ 42330, 15 km S.

Restaurant :
♦ *Auberge du Parc*, 5, bd Dr-Cousin, ☎ 77.54.01.57, AE Euro Visa, closed Wed, 1-25 Oct, 60-150 ; child : 50.

In preparing for your trip, consult the pages pertaining to the regions. You will find there the description of the region you wish to visit, as well as a list of sites that must be seen, a brief history and practical information.

FIRMINY

Saint-Etienne 12, Le Puy 66, Paris 531 km
pop 24356 ⊠ 42700   A3
Important industrial centre.

▶ **Firminy-Vert** complex★, collaborative project by the architect Le Corbusier (1887-1965) : cultural centre, apartment building, pool, two stadiums and a church.

Nearby

▶ E, **Feugerolles** : feudal château★. ▶ **Unieux** *(NW; pop. 8 309 at Le Pertuiset)* : view★ from suspension bridge. S, **château de Cornillon**★ with 13th-16thC church, on a rock at a bend in the River Loire. ▶ **Château des Bruneaux** (16th-18thC) : paneling, paintings *(24 Mar.-30 Sep., Sat., Sun., hols., 2-6:30).*   □

Practical Information _____

SNCF ☎ 77.56.12.37.

Hotels :
★★★ *Firm'Hôtel*, 37, rue J.-Jaurès, ☎ 77.56.08.99, 22 rm, 170. Rest. ♦ closed Sun eve, 1-20 Aug, 50-90.
★★★ *Le Pavillon* (C.H.), 4, av. de la Gare, ☎ 77.56.91.11, AE DC Euro Visa, 22 rm ℗ 210. Rest. ♦♦ ♿ closed Mon and Sun eve. Renowned cellar, 60-190.

Restaurant :
♦ *La Réserve*, 8, rue de la Gampille, La Tardive, ☎ 77.56.01.45, AE DC Visa ▨▨ 90-150.

Recommended
Youth hostel : Le Pertuiset, 5 km NE, ☎ 77.35.72.94.

GEX

Geneva 17, Nantua 57, Paris 498 km
pop 4869 ⊠ 01170   C1
Summer resort (alt. 600 m) with views★ toward Geneva and the Alps ; English-style garden★.

▶ W, **Le Pailly** (alt. 1 200 m) : winter sports and summer recreation centre ; view★. ▶ **Col de la Faucille** (pass ; *12 km N, via N5)* : winter sports centre (alt. 1 328 m) ; view to Mont Blanc. ▶ **Mont-Rond** *(3 km SW; alt. 1 540 m)* : cable car ; orientation table. **Colomby-de-Gex** *(8 km farther;* alt. 1 691 m), overlooking countryside ; walking trails over pasturelands. ▶ Beyond the pass *(3 km),* Valserine Gorge, source of river of same name ; in Valserine Valley, **Mijoux** (winter-sports centre), as at **Lélex.** ▶ E, Divonneles-Bains *(→)*. ▶ S, via the Geneva road, **Ferney-Voltaire**★ *(10 km;* pop. 6 400) : village around the château where the philosopher Voltaire (1694-1778) spent his last 18 years before dying during a triumphal visit to Paris in 1778 : memorabilia, portrait by Quentin de la Tour *(Jul.-Aug., Sat. pm)*. ▶ SW toward Bellegarde, **Echenevex :** winter-sports centre ; 11 km farther : **Saint-Genis-Pouilly** (pop. 4 655).   □

Practical Information _____

GEX
ℹ rue A.-Reverchon, ☎ 50.41.35.85.

Hotels :
★★★ *Auberge des Chasseurs*, Echenevex, 4 km S, ☎ 50.41.54.07, 11 rm ℗ ⦅ ▨▨ ⚲ ▱ closed Sun eve and Mon ex Jul-Aug, 3 Nov-1 May, 240. Rest. ♦♦ ♪ ♿ 90-200.
★★ *Parc*, av. des Alpes, ☎ 50.41.50.18, Visa, 20 rm ℗ ▨▨ ❄ pens (h.s.), closed Sun eve and Mon, 15 Nov-1 Feb, 240. Rest. ♦ ♪ 110-235.

Restaurant :
♦♦ *Auberge Gessienne*, Chevry, 7 km S on D 84, ☎ 50.41.01.67 ℗ ▨▨ ♿ closed Mon and Sun, 16 Feb-3 Apr, 4-27 Aug. Converted farmhouse. Savoury food : *quenelles*

de brochet, gratin de queues d'écrevisses, gratin dauphinois, good wines, 85-150.

Recommended
Youth hostel : 482, rte de l'Etraz, ☎ 50.41.55.80.

Nearby

Le **COL DE LA FAUCILLE**, ⊠ 01170, 11 km NW.

Hotel :
★★ *La Couronne*, ☎ 50.41.32.65, Euro Visa, 24 rm ℗ ⦅ ▨▨ ⚲ closed 15 Apr-15 May, 15 Nov-15 Dec, 160. Rest. ♦ ⦅ ♿ 70-100 ; child : 35.

FERNEY-VOLTAIRE, ⊠ 01210, 10 km S.

Hotels :
★★★★ *Pullman Ferney Genève* (ex Frantel), av. du Jura, ☎ 50.40.77.90, Tx 309071, AE DC Euro Visa, 122 rm ℗ ⦅ ⚲ ♪ ♿ 410. Rest. ♦♦ ♪ ❄ Regional specialties and local seasonal products, 55-180.
★ *Bellevue*, 5, rue de Gex, ☎ 50.40.58.68, 12 rm ▨▨ ❄ closed Sun eve and Sat, 15 Oct-15 Nov, 150. Rest. ♦ ❄ 50-105.

Restaurant :
● ♦♦♦ *Le Pirate*, av. de Genève, ☎ 50.40.63.52, AE DC Euro Visa ℗ ▨▨ closed Mon noon and Sun, 12 Jul-2 Aug, 20 Dec-3 Jan. Don't be put off by the name, this restaurant serves fine food. Try the fish ; sampling menu available, 160-250.

MIJOUX, ⊠ 01410 Chézery-Forens, 19 km NW.

Hotels :
● ★★★ *La Mainaz* (R.S.), ☎ 50.41.31.10, Tx 309501, AE DC Euro Visa, 25 rm ℗ ⦅ ▨▨ ⚲ ♿ closed 15 Jun-1 Jul, 1 Nov-18 Dec, 235. Rest. ♦ ⦅ ❄ 90-180.
● ★★ *Crêt de la Neige*, Lelex, 8 km from Mijoux, ☎ 50.20.90.15, Euro Visa ℗ ⦅ ▨▨ ♪⊙ pens (h.s.), closed 10 Sep-20 Dec, 15 Apr-29 Jun, 395. Rest. ♦ ⦅ ♪ ❄ 60-130.
★★ *Les Egravines*, ☎ 50.41.30.65, Visa, 16 rm ℗ ⦅ ⚲ ♪ ❄ pens (h.s.), closed 10 Apr-30 Jun, 31 Aug-20 Dec, 495. Rest. ♦ ⦅ ♪ 70-110.

SAINT-JEAN-DE-GONVILLE, ⊠ 01630 Saint-Genis-Pouilly, 15 km.

Hotel :
★ *Demornex* (L.F.), ☎ 50.56.35.34, AE DC Euro Visa, 10 rm ℗ ⦅ ▨▨ pens, closed Mon eve and Sun eve, 8-31 Jan, 1-15 Jul, 180. Rest. ● ♦♦ ⦅ ♪ ♿ Appetizing food in a bucolic setting. Crayfish (ex in spring), Bresse poultry, Bugey wines, 100-220.

GIVORS

Vienne 12, Lyon 22, Paris 485 km
pop 20554 ⊠ 69700   B2

SNCF ☎ 78.73.02.17/78.73.06.46/78.73.05.48.

Hotel :
★★ *Gare*, 6, pl. Pasteur, ☎ 78.73.02.42, 14 rm ℗ closed Sun eve, 130.

Restaurant :
♦♦ *Camerano*, 35, rte Nationale, Loire-sur-Saône 4 km S.-E., ☎ 78.73.20.07, Euro Visa ℗ ⦅ ♿ closed Mon and Sun eve , Aug. Spec : *matelote d'anguilles, lavaret à la crème,* 75-150.

Nearby

GRIGNY, ⊠ 69520, 2 km N.

Hotel :
● ★★★ *Les Sources* (R.S.), 43, rue A.-Sabatier, ☎ 78.73.05.61, Tx 305694, Euro Visa, 10 rm ℗ ⦅ ▨▨ ⚲ closed Jan-Feb, 280. Rest. ♦♦ closed Mon and Sun eve (l.s.), 95-180.

SAINTE COLOMBE, ⊠ 69560, 12 km SE.

Restaurant :
♦♦ *Le Gallo-Romain*, RN 86, Saint-Romain-en-Gal, ☎ 74.53.19.72, AE DC Visa 𝖯 ⬝⬝ ; ᕔ closed Mon and Sun eve ex hols, 80-170.

GRANGENT*

Round trip from Saint-Étienne *(55 km, approx. 2 hr)*   A3

Feudal site, today on the edge of the 23-km long reservoir created by the **Loire Gorges Dam★**.

► **Saint-Étienne** (→). ► S via the left bank, road left toward **Essalois** : 12thC **château**, view from 150 m above the river. ► **Chambles** : view★ from Romanesque church tower (flanked by a round keep). ► **Le Pertuiset** : atmosphere of popular country pastimes (→ Firminy). ► Via the right bank, **Saint-Victor-sur-Loire** : site★ ; swimming, boating ; Romanesque church ; château rebuilt in Renaissance style (cultural centre, concerts). ► 5 km N, **Saint-Just-Saint-Rambert** (pop. 10 646) : Saint-Rambert, ruined ramparts ; Renaissance houses ; Romanesque church★ with two bell towers (Carolingian, Romanesque) ; regional museum *(pm Sat., Sun., hols.)*.   ☐

Practical Information ─────────────

ANDRÉZIEUX-BOUTHÉON, ⊠ 42160, 9 km N.
SNCF ☎ 77.55.04.46.

Recommended
Farmhouse-inn : at Cordeyron, *La Bergerie*, ☎ 77.52.38.19 ; at Saint-Just-Saint-Rambert, *les Faux*, 3 km S, ☎ 77.23.01.58.

HAUTEVILLE-LOMPNÈS

Belley 33, Bourg-en-Bresse 52, Paris 479 km
pop 4905 ⊠ 01110   C1

Summer resort at alt. 800 m in the heart of Bugey ; well known for climate (rest centres, functional re-education).

Round trips from Haut-Bugey and Valromey★★ *(68 km, at least a half-day)*

► SW on D21, **Albarine Gorges★** ; 4 km, Charabotte Waterfall ; **cliffs** rising 500 m above the road. ► At Tenay, take the Chambéry road left : **Cluse des Hôpitaux★★** (gorge) ; ruined feudal château de Rossillon. ► **Virieu-le-Grand** : château ruins. ► **Artemare** : continue left towards **Valromey★★** ; alpine flora. **Cerveyrieu Waterfall★** and cross-country skiing in winter ; on left, Luthézieu. ► **Ruffieu** (alt. 730 m) : attractive scenery ; via **Rochette Pass** (alt. 1 119 m ; view★★ to Mont Blanc) to Hauteville.   ☐

Practical Information ─────────────

HAUTEVILLE-LOMPNÈS
⌇ 850-1195m.
ⓘ mairie, ☎ 74.35.39.73.

Hotel :
★★ *La Chapelle* (L.F.), rue de la Chapelle, ☎ 74.35.20.11, Euro Visa, 20 rm 𝖯 ⬝⬝ ᕔ closed Wed eve, 26 Oct-6 Nov, 140. Rest. ♦ ᕔ 70-145.

Nearby

LUTHÉZIEU, ⊠ 01260 Champagne, 15 km SE of **Artemare**.

Hotel :
● ★★ *Vieux Tilleul* (L.F.), ☎ 74.87.64.51, AE Euro Visa, 12 rm 𝖯 ⬝ ⬝⬝ ᕔ closed Tue eve and Wed eve Jan, 125. Rest. ♦ 65-140.

LYON***

Chambéry 98, Grenoble 104, Paris 463 km
pop 418476 ⊠ 69001 à 69009 (arrondissements)   B2

Two rivers, one calm, the other spirited ; two hills, Fourvière "begging", and La Croix-Rousse "working" — according to the French historian Jules Michelet (1798-1874). Ever since Man came to live here 600 years before the Roman occupation (→ *Brief regional history*), the territory has been expanded by means of the rivers. In the High Middle Ages, the Saône and Rhône converged slightly W of the present Place des Terreaux, which explains the original Celtic name of *Condate* (confluence). Canabae, one of the two islands to the S, was already inhabited when, in 43BC, Julius Caesar's officers founded *Lugdunum* on the summit of the western hill. The high ground was gradually abandoned in the 3rd and 4thC in favour of the Ile Saint-Jean below, now the site of "Old Lyon". A merchant colony flourished between the two rivers, alongside one of the oldest religious foundations in the country — the abbey of St. Martin, known as Ainay since the 11thC. The history of Lyon can be traced in the present city layout : the original settlement W to E in Fourvière ; the medieval and Renaissance city on the right bank of the Saône ; 17th-18thC development between the rivers ; and Croix-Rousse, dating from the 19thC, on the left bank of the Rhône and within the industrial suburbs that are home to two-thirds of the area's residents. Eighty-five percent of the city's annual total of 5 million visitors are not tourists ; they come for the range of events held all year round at Eurexpo, Lyon's new centre for exhibitions at Chassieu *(6 km)*.

Old Lyon★★ AB2-3 and A4

► From **Place Bellecour** cross **Bonaparte Bridge** (B3) opposite the eastern end of the cathedral of St. Jean. ► Enter Old Lyon, the most extensive (61 acres) grouping of 15thC and Renaissance buildings in France. ► Avenue Adolphe-Max, in the same direction as the bridge, towards the **St-Jean Quarter**, restored, together with the neighbouring districts, some years ago and now closed to vehicles. ► Former archbishop's palace, now the municipal library ; at the end of the street, cable-car station. ► **Manécanterie** (former house of the cathedral cantors) : early Romanesque frieze-ornamented façade ; first floor, cathedral treasury *(entry from the cathedral)* : medieval Limoges enamels, ivory, 12thC Byzantine works of art. ► **St. Jean Cathedral★** (A3), formerly the Seat of the Primate (chief bishop) of Gaul : Romanesque ; façade finished in Flamboyant Gothic ; portals with 368 15thC sculpted insets. In the nave, four 32-m-high vaulted bays ; decoration★ in choir, apse and side chapels (chapel of the Bourbons ; chapel of the Annunciation) ; stained glass★, much of it 13thC (apse) ; in left transept, 17thC astronomical clock★★. ► On the N side, **excavation** of primitive church★. ► S of cathedral, **St-Georges Quarter★** : Place de la Trinité dominated by **Café du Soleil**, a former convent later used for *Guignol* (Punch and Judy) performances. Enter at No. 2 Rue St. Georges to reach oval courtyard★ of the Maison du Soleil ; proceed by the signposted passageways *(traboules)* to Gourguillon. ► **Rue St-Georges** (A3) : shop signs, Gothic windows, artisans' workshops here and in adjacent Rue du Doyenné (interesting courtyard at No. 32). ► **Rue St-Jean** (A3, *N*) : medieval thoroughfare ; No. 37, Chamarrier Mansion. ► Farther, **law courts** with 19thC colonnade★, opening on to Saône Quay. ► **Viste Mansion** (Nos. 29-27) : Gothic portal. ► Passageway at No. 19 links to Rue des Trois-Marie (Renaissance houses). ► **Place de la Baleine** : No. 5, HQ for the Old Lyon Urban Renewal Association. ► No. 24 Rue St-Jean, Laurencin Mansion *traboule* joins up with No. 1 Rue du Bœuf. ► **Place du Gouvernement** : Gothic

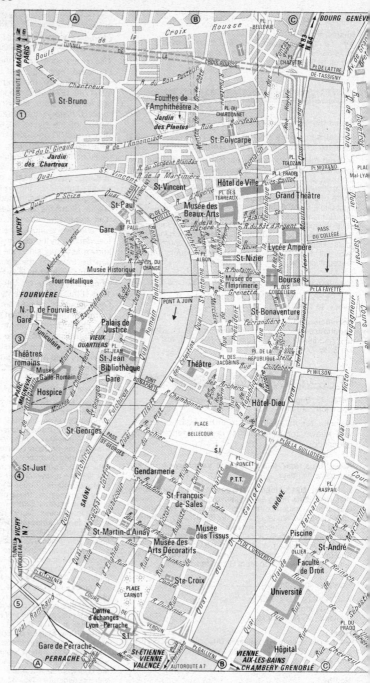

façade, Governors' Assembly; upstairs, raised courtyard, gallery★, covered well. ▶ No. 11 Rue St-Jean : Gothic courtyard, passageway and ornamented door★. ▶ **Place du Change** (B2) : Renaissance drapery market; 18thC gallery. Opposite, **Thomassin Mansion** : enter through court-yard★. ▶ **Rue Lainerie** : staircase at No. 18; **Mayet-de-Beauvoir Mansion★** (No. 14) : Gothic façade. ▶ **Place St-Paul** (A2) : Laurent Mourguet, creator of Guignol, grew up at No. 2 (→ box). ▶ **St. Paul church :** octagonal lantern tower; Flamboyant Gothic chapel; sculpted animals

at E end ; frieze depicting angel-musicians (3rd chapel on right). ▶ Return to St. Jean via **Rue de la Juiverie** (A2) : No. 4, **Paterin Mansion** (or Henri IV House) : staircase, galleries, arcades. ▶ No. 8 **Buillioud Mansion** : gallery on squinches★, a major architectural expression of the

Renaissance. ▶ Nos. 22-23, Dugas Mansion (Lion House). ▶ At intersection with Rue de la Loge, **montée du Change** (stairway) ; view★. ▶ **Rue de Gadagne** : No. 12, mansion of same name with **historical museum**, **Édouard-Herriot Museum** and **Marionette Museum★** (entrance at No. 14,

10:45-6; closed Tue.) : worldwide theatres★, including Mourguet's. ▶ **Place du Petit-Collège** (Garillan steps). ▶ **Rue du Bœuf** (A3; *traboule* at No. 1) : No. 19, **L'Outarde d'Or** (famous "golden bustard" shop sign); No. 16, passage to **Crible House★★** (17thC); turreted staircase. ▶ At **corner of Rue de la Bombarde** (restored Renaissance covered staircase★), sculpture of bull (the *bœuf* of the street). ▶ Place St-Jean : cable-car.

Fourvière★ A3

▶ **Basilica parvis**, 130 m above Old Lyon; on the site of a Romanesque church, the 1870 edifice overlooks the city. ▶ Access to the **basilica** via 300 steps; orientation table *(daily Mar.-Oct.; Sat., Sun. rest of year)*; **view★** over Lyon, the Auvergne region, the Alps from Mont Blanc to Ventoux in clear weather. ▶ **View★★** from left terrace of church, site of the first forum of the Roman city of Lugdunum. ▶ **Gallo-Roman Museum★★**, 17 Rue Cléberg : *(9:30-12 & 2-6; closed Mon., Tue.; optional guided tours)* built in 1975 on the hillside site of Lugdunum, chronicles regional history from the Neolithic Era to the High Middle Ages; Gallo-Roman inscriptions, Gallic calendar from Coligny, the Claudian tablet★★ (plea presented by the Emperor Claudius to the Roman Senate), epitaphs, treasures from Vernaison, Crémieu, La-Côte-Saint-André, statuary★, sarcophagi, everyday objects, restored **mosaic★★★**. ▶ From museum windows, the Roman **theatre★★ excavations** are visible (entrance at 6 Rue de l'Antiquaille ; *in season, Mon.-Fri., 8-12 & 2-6, Sat. 9-11:45 & 3-6, Sun. 3-6; off season, 8-12 & 2-5, closed Sat., Sun.*). ▶ The **Grand Théâtre** : the oldest in France (15BC) and one of the largest (10 500 spectators after enlargement under the Emperor Hadrian); access by a side staircase (view★), where Roman paving (about 80 m) slopes towards the Odeon. ▶ Right, site of the ruined **Temple of Cybele** (most important in the Roman world), among other finds. ▶ The **Odeon★** (capacity 3 000) : an auditorium dating from the same period as the Temple; restored paving★. ▶ The ancient city grew up on the plateau; early ruins abound in the **St. Just Quarter** around **St. Irénée Church** (5thC crypt) and at Choullans, where the aqueducts (→ Mornant) that provided city water for 300 years terminated. ▶ Return via the Quai de la Saône through the **Duchère Quarter** : view; Firemen's Museum *(Wed., Sat. am; closed Aug.)*.

The Museums of the Presqu'île★★★ BC2-3-4

▶ Europe's largest pedestrian mall (2 km between Perrache Station and the Town Hall) parallels the *Métro* (underground transport) line and simplifies visits to central Lyon. ▶ At the SE corner of **Place Bellecour** (B4; TO), the tower of the former Charité Church overlooks flower stalls along **Rue de la Charité**. ▶ No. 30, **Decorative Arts Museum★★** (B5; *10-12 & 2-5:30 ex Mon., Sun.; ticket includes visit to Textile Museum*) : more than 200 exceptional works in furnished rooms on three floors (goldsmiths' work, porcelain, pendulum clocks). ▶ No. 34, **Historical Museum of Textiles★★★** (Villeroy Mansion; *same hours as Decorative Arts Museum*) : Coptic tapestries, weaving from 4thC Egypt up to contemporary fabrics from Lyon; Byzantine and Persian textiles, Oriental carpets, 18thC furnishing silks, Japanese screens, Chinese costumes, Italian and Spanish cloth. ▶ Rue des Remparts-d'Ainay crosses **Rue Auguste-Comte** (antiques), then **Rue Victor-Hugo**, a pedestrian precinct. ▶ At the S end, **Perrache Trade Centre** (A1), a controversial modern building. ▶ **Ainay★** (A4) : restored Carolingian church with Romanesque features remaining from a monastery founded in the 6thC, active until the 18thC; gate tower, side tympanum, capitals. ▶ **Saône quays** : view of Old Lyon and Fourvière. ▶ Via the Célestins Theatre (B3; 19thC), **Place des Jacobins** and Rue Mercière to **St. Nizier★** (B2) : townspeople's church; 15thC tower (another 19thC); Flamboyant Gothic interior; Virgin and Child by the sculptor Antoine Coysevox (1640-1720), born in Lyon. ▶ **Place des Terreaux** (B2) : fountain★ by Frédéric Bartholdi, 19thC sculptor of New York's Statue of Liberty; **Town Hall** (façade clock tower; 18thC interior decoration). **St. Pierre Palace** : for-

mer abbey; 18thC **cloister★**, statuary★ by Auguste Rodin, Aristide Maillol and Antoine Bourdelle, now the **Fine Arts Museum★★★** *(10:45-6; closed Tue.)*, most important museum in France, after the Louvre in Paris, for late 19thC and 20thC art; French art; also important Italian, Spanish, Flemish and Dutch works. ▶ S towards Bellecour, parallel streets : **Rue de la République** (pedestrian street) and Rue du Président-Herriot (luxury shopping); opposite the Commercial Building and the **Stock Exchange** *(Bourse, C3)*, Rue de la **Poulaillerie**, No. 13, Printing and Banking Museum★ (Couronne Mansion; Gothic courtyard★; *9:30-12 & 2-6; closed Mon., Tue.*) : important industries in Lyon since the Renaissance (the first book printed in French rolled off the press of Barthélemy Buyer, Rue Mercière, in 1476). ▶ **Place des Cordeliers** : church of St. Bonaventure : Gothic; 17thC Aubusson tapestries. ▶ **Hospital** *(Hôtel-Dieu; 1741; C3-4)* : 325-m façade on the Rhône, now the **Public Hospice Museum★★**, entrance, Place de l'Hôpital *(1:30-5:30, closed weekends and hols.)* : history of city hospitals and medicine through works of art and objects for the most part from the demolished Hôpital de la Charité : tapestries, Flemish and Italian primitive paintings, pharmacy jars, 17th-18thC woodwork, Louis XIII **pharmacy★**, exhibition on the history of the medical profession at Lyon.

The passageways of Lyon

The traboules, *covered passageways giving access from one street to another through courtyards and buildings, are a unique feature of Lyon. No fewer than 100 honeycomb the Old City and the slopes of Croix-Rousse. The entrance to a* traboule *often is hidden behind a building doorway. During the last century certain* traboules *were the scene of violent uprisings by workers* (canuts) *from the silk mills.*

La Croix-Rousse BC1-2

▶ **Place des Terreaux** (B2) : at No. 6, enter the *traboule* running to the church of St. Polycarpe (17thC), through courtyards and buildings. ▶ **Place Sathonay**, near the site of the Gallic settlement of *Condate;* farther on, **Trois-Gaules Amphitheatre**, site of early Christian martyrdoms; excavations at the Botanical Garden (B1). ▶ Rue de l'Annonciade to **Place Rouville** (A2) : view. ▶ **Church of St. Bruno** : Baroque architecture and decoration★ (18thC). ▶ Boulevard de la **Croix-Rousse** towards square of same name *(direct by Métro from Town Hall)* : centre of activity for quarter. ▶ N by Rue du Mail to **Rue d'Ivry** (second on right) : **Maison des Canuts** (No. 10), two facing buildings housing a workshop and the *Cooptis* (Weavers' Cooperative) display *(closed Sun.);* Lyon supported 15 000 weavers *(canuts)* in 1930, today only 300 maintain the trade and all belong to this workers' cooperative. ▶ E, Blvd. de la Croix-Rousse ends at **Place Bellevue** : boulder left from the last Ice Age. ▶ Go back down towards Place des Terreaux by **Rue des Fantasques** (C1, views★); or from St. Sébastien stairway to the right of **Place Colbert,** go in at No. 9 to stroll by *traboule* right to the Place de la Comédie.

Left Bank of the Rhône DE-1 *(drive)*

▶ N of the **Les Brotteaux Quarter**, **Guimet Museum★** (D1; 28 Blvd. des Belges; *closed Mon., Tue. and am daily).* ▶ **Tête d'Or Park** (E1, entrance N of D1) : 350 acres of trees centuries old, lake with islands, zoo, botanical garden, 19-acre **rose garden.**) ▶ **Villeurbanne** (pop. 118 330; E of Brotteaux railway station, H3) : **Place de la Libération** built in 1934; new **Modern Art Museum** (11 Rue du Dr-Dollard, *pm. ex Tue.*). ▶ **La Part-Dieu** (E3-4) : view★★ from tower of Crédit Lyonnais; pedestrian walkways, fountains; Maurice Ravel **auditorium★**; commercial centre, library, radio & television broadcasting centre. ▶ **Medical Quarter** *(1 km S of Guillotière Bridge, C5)* :

Édouard Herriot Hospital designed by Tony Garnier. ► **Vénissieux** (pop. 64 982; *SSE of map*) : Motor Museum at Berliet factory. ► **Gerland** *(2 km S of map)* : modern architectural development.

Nearby

► **Saint-Rambert** *(5 km N)*, on a mid-river island, site of **L'Ile Barbe**, former abbey; 12thC bell tower remaining; Renaissance pavilion; boat trips (Saint-Rambert Port). ► **Fontaines-sur-Saône** *(12 km N; pop. 7 129)*. ► **Roche-taillée-sur-Saône★** *(2-km climb)* : fortress★ (restored in the 19thC) of the count-archbishops of Lyon, now a unique Motor Museum★★ *(daily 8-12 & 2-6 or 7)*. ☐

Guignol theatre

The marionette was created at Lyon in the early 19thC by Laurent Mourguet (1769-1841). Guignol — Mr. Punch French-style — embodies the canut, the Lyon silk weaver. Bantering, mocking and philosophical, Guignol theatre projects the local workers' slang, outlook, dress and character. Among Guignol's principal partners are Madelon (Judy), his stingy, screechy, quarrelsome and intractable wife, and his friend Gnafron, always the tipsy, mawkishly sentimental, pompous moralizer. The Guignol presentations make much of local and national politicians as well as other public figures.

Practical Information _____

LYON
ⓘ pl. Bellecour (B4), ☎ 78.42.25.75.
✈ Lyon-Bron, ☎ 78.26.81.09; *Satolas*, 25 km E, ☎ 78.71.92.21. Air France office, 17, rue V.-Hugo, 69002 (B4), ☎ 78.92.48.11; Satolas airport, ☎ 78.71.96.20; 10, quai J.-Courmont, 69002 (C3), ☎ 78.92.48.10.
SNCF Perrache and Part-Dieu (F3), ☎ 78.92.50.50/ 78.92.10.70.
🚌 *Centre d'échanges de Perrache*, ☎ 78.42.27.39.
Car rental : *Avis*, 40, rue de la Villette, 69003, ☎ 72.33.99.14; 17-21, bd E.-Deruelle, 69003 (E3), ☎ 78.60.36.20; 72, rue d'Heyrieux, Saint-Priest 69800, ☎ 78.20.45.50; la Part-Dieu train station, 69003, ☎ 72.33.37.19; 11, bd Novy-Jicin, (Z.I.), Vénissieux 69200, ☎ 72.50.56.00; Perrache train station 69002, ☎ 78.37.14.23; 8, rte de Vienne, 69007; Satolas airport, 69125, ☎ 78.71.95.25; 385, rue Garibaldi, 69007, ☎ 78.58.33.44.

Hotels :
Bellecour-Terreaux (69001 et 69002) :
★★★★(L) *Sofitel*, 20, quai Gailleton (B4), ☎ 78.42.72.50, Tx 330225, AE DC Euro Visa, 200 rm Ⓟ ♦ ♪ & 880. Rest. ● ♦♦♦ *Les Trois-Dômes* ⑂ ♪ & ⑳ Delectable food by Guy Girard, pupil of chef Alix, classic gourmet dishes, 200-340.
● ★★★ *Carlton*, (Mapotel), 4, rue Jussieu (C3), ☎ 78.42.56.51, AE DC Euro Visa, 87 rm Ⓟ ♪ 🏡 335.
● ★★★ *Royal*, (Mapotel), 20, pl. Bellecour (B4), ☎ 78.37.57.31, Tx 310785, AE DC Euro Visa, 90 rm Ⓟ ⑂ ⑳ ⚲ ♪ 345. Rest. ♦ ♪ & 80-95.
★★ *Globe et Cecil*, (Inter-Hôtel), 21, rue Gasparin (B3), ☎ 78.42.58.95, 65 rm, 225.
★★ *Moderne*, 15, rue Dubois (B3), ☎ 78.42.21.83, Visa, 31 rm Ⓟ & 180.
★ *Saint-Vincent*, 9, rue Pareille, ☎ 78.28.67.97, Euro Visa, 30 rm, 130.
Croix-Rousse (69004) :
★★★ *Lyon Métropole*, 85, quai Joseph-Gillet (A1), ☎ 78.29.20.20, Tx 380198, AE DC Euro Visa, 119 rm Ⓟ ⑂ ♪ 🏡 & ☐ ⑳ 320. Rest. ♦♦♦ *Les Eaux-Vives - le Grill de Lyon* In this new sports complex, the kitchens are overseen by Lyon's chefs Bourillot and Nandron, 80-120.
La Part-Dieu (69003) :

★★★★ *Pullman-Part-Dieu*, (ex Frantel), 129, rue Servient (E3), ☎ 78.62.94.12, Tx 380088, AE DC Euro Visa, 245 rm Ⓟ ⑂ ♪ 🏡 & 620. Rest. ● ♦♦♦ *L'Arc-en-Ciel*, closed Mon noon and Sun, 11 Jul-18 Aug. On the 32nd floor, gastronomy in the clouds. High-flying Lyonnais specialties by Francis Galabert : *brouet de langouste en chaudfroid, minute de loup à la fleur de thym*, 165-200; child : 40.
★★★★(L) *Lyon Atlas*, 29, rue de Bonnel (E3), ☎ 72.61.90.90, Tx 330703, 159 rm Ⓟ Very high standards of comfort in American-style (double and single rooms) : rooms for the businesswoman, rooms with computers, nonsmoking floor, sauna. Steam room, jacuzzi, boutiques, piano-bar. 900. Rest. ♦♦ *Nouvelle Orléans*. Cajun specialties 250.
(69005) :
● ★★★★(L) *Cour des Loges*, 24, rue du Boeuf (A3), ☎ 78.42.75.75, Tx 330831, AE DC Euro Visa, 63 rm Ⓟ ⑂ ᨆ ⚲ ☐ Renaissance-style, contemporary furniture, jacuzzi, sauna, 1200. Rest. ♦♦♦♦ In a historic setting in the heart of old Lyon, a totally successful renovation : hot springs, gardens, terraces and a restaurant with food supplied by P. Chavent of the nearby *Tour Rose*. Tasting cellar, 200-400.
Les Brotteaux (69006) :
★★★ *Le Roosevelt*, 25, rue Bossuet (D3), ☎ 78.52.35.67, Tx 300295, AE DC Euro Visa, 90 rm Ⓟ ⚲ ♪ 320. Rest. ♦ *Room Service*, 70-150.
Monchat-Montplaisir (69008) :
★★★ *Lyon-Est*, 104, rte de Genas (off map F4), ☎ 78.54.64.53, 42 rm Ⓟ 210.
★★ *Maréchal Foch*, 59, av. Mar.-Foch (D1), ☎ 78.89.14.01, 15 rm ⚲ closed 1-21 Aug, 160.
Perrache (69002) :
★★★ *Le Charlemagne*, 23, cours Charlemagne (A5), ☎ 78.92.81.61, 120 rm Ⓟ ᨆ 270. Rest. ♦ closed Sat and Sun eve , Aug, 80-150.
★★★ *Terminus*, (Frantour), 12, cours de Verdun (A5), ☎ 78.37.58.11, Tx 330500, 140 rm Ⓟ 🏡 480. Rest. ♦ & closed Sat and Sun, 80-160.
Préfecture-Guillotière (69003, 69007) :
★★★ *Columbia*, 8, pl. A.-Briand, 69003 (D5), ☎ 78.60.54.65, Tx 330949, AE DC Euro Visa, 66 rm Ⓟ ⚲ 200.
★★★ *Helder et de l'Institut*, 38, rue de Marseille, 69007 (C5), ☎ 78.72.09.39, Tx 306411, AE DC Euro Visa, 110 rm Ⓟ & 200.

Restaurants :
Centre :
● ♦♦♦♦ *Léon de Lyon*, 1, rue Pleney (B2), 69001, ☎ 78.28.11.33, Euro Visa, closed Mon noon and Sun, 23 Dec-8 Jan. "Fill your cellar with Beaujolais, joy and peace will come your way." G.-Dubœuf's wines are a perfect illustration of that adage. And since chef J.P.-Lacombe is a prudent man and an excellent cook, he'll make sure you don't wither away with hunger in his friendly Lyonnais bistro. Great, inspired cooking. Lyonnais dishes of course : *les lyonnaiseries, salades, saucisson chaud, gras double*, and also : *la terrine de langoustines, la salade d'herbes nouvelles, le sauté de gigot d'agneau*, and cheeses from la Mère Richard, 180-250.
● ♦♦♦ *Bourillot*, 8, pl. des Célestins (B3), 69002, ☎ 78.37.38.64, AE DC Visa ♪ & closed Sun, 28 Jun-28 Jul, 24 Dec-20 Jan. Excellent value is what prize-winning chef C. Bourillot delivers : *salade de crustacés à l'huile de noix, ragoût de ris de veau et rognons*, 180-260.
● ♦♦♦ *Henry*, 27, rue de la Martinière (B2), 69001, ☎ 78.28.26.08, AE DC Euro Visa, closed Mon and Sat eve. Light, modern fare by P. Belladonne : *salade de homard breton aux pousses d'épinards, mousse de pigeon de Bresse*, 120-300.
● ♦♦♦ *La Tour Rose*, 16, rue du Bœuf (A3), 69005, ☎ 78.37.25.90, AE DC Visa, closed Sun. An impressive display of flavours and lightness orchestrated by M. Chavent : *foie de canard chaud au cerfeuil, langoustines rôties à la crème d'asperges*. Sublime cellar, wine bar across the street, 180-300.
● ♦♦♦ *Nandron*, 26, quai Jean-Moulin (C2), 69002, ☎ 78.42.10.26, AE DC Euro Visa ⑂ ♪ closed Fri eve

and Sat, 25 Jul-23 Aug. An institution on the quais of the Rhône. Classic Lyonnais cooking and contemporary creations : *quenelles de brochet, ris de veau aux truffes,* 150-300.

● ◆◆◆ **Pierre Orsi**, 3, pl. Kléber (D2), 69006, ☎ 78.89.57.68, Tx 305965, AE Euro Visa ♪ ᚼ closed Sat and Sun June-Sep, 2 Aug-2 Sep. A fine old Lyonnais tradition : narket cuisine by the masterly hand of P. Orsi. Generous local dishes, greens, meats and grills, cheeses from Mme Richard, luscious desserts and a quality cellar, 180-350.

● ◆◆◆ **Vettard**, 7, pl. Bellecour (B4), 69002, ☎ 78.42.07.59, AE DC Visa ᚼ closed Sun, 30 Jul-30 Aug. Edouard Herriot's preferred Lyonnais hangout. J. Vettard has freshened up the interior and the cuisine : *loup raidi à l'huile de basilic et vinaigre de xérès, quenelle de brochet Bellecour,* 200-330.

◆◆◆ **Commanderie des Antonins**, 30, quai Saint-Antoine (B2-3), 69002, ☎ 78.37.19.21, closed hols. Old-fashioned hearth-cooked specialties in a magnificent 13thC chapter room, 110-250.

◆◆◆ **Les Fantasques**, 47, rue de la Bourse (C2), 69002, ☎ 78.37.36.58, AE Visa ᚼ closed 8-24 Aug, 180-250.

● ◆◆ **Chez Gervais**, 42, rue P.-Corneille (D2), 69002, ☎ 78.52.19.13, AE DC Visa ♪ closed Sat noon and Sun , Jul. Inventive and classic dishes by Gervais Lescuyer : *gratin d'écrevisses, volailles au vinaigre,* 100-180.

● ◆◆ **Daniel et Denise**, 2, rue Tupin (B3), 69002, ☎ 78.37.49.98, AE DC Visa ♪ closed Mon noon and Sun Aug. Just a few tables, traditional cooking : *terrine de homard, soufflé de turbotin florentine, filet d'agneau en croûte,* 120-300.

● ◆◆ **Garioud**, 14, rue du Palais-Grillet (C3), 69003, ☎ 78.37.04.71, AE Euro Visa ♪ closed Sat noon and Sun. An alumnus of the Bocuse kitchen who has settled down just a few miles away. Fine menu : *escargots en pot, filets de sole pochés,* 100-160.

● ◆◆ **La Mère Brazier**, 12, rue Royale (C1), 69001, ☎ 78.28.15.49, AE DC Euro Visa, closed Sat noon and Sun , Aug. For all those who fondly remember the famous "mère" of Lyon, the family still carries on the tradition : *fonds d'artichauts au foie gras, poularde de Bresse,* 200-300.

● ◆◆ **La Voûte-Chez Léa**, 11, pl. Antonin-Gourju (B3), 69002, ☎ 78.42.01.33, AE DC, closed Sun, 4-28 Jul. Trained by Léa herself, P. Ravatel has made no changes here : *tablier de sapeur, poulet au vinaigre de vin vieux, quenelles Mère Léa,* 80-120.

● ◆◆ **Le Gourmandin**, 156, rue P.-Bert (E4), 69003, ☎ 78.62.78.77, AE DC Visa, closed Sat and Sun and hols, 8-22 Aug. Led by a disciple of Paul Bocuse, Daniel Abattu, the kitchen turns out savoury market cuisine : *fricassée de champignons, paillard de veau,* 115-280.

● ◆◆ **Le Bistrot de Lyon**, 64, rue Mercière (B3), 69002, ☎ 78.37.00.62, Euro Visa, closed Sun, 23 Dec-8 Jan. A 1900-style interior and Lyonnais specialties by J.-P. Lacombe et J.-C. Caro. Next door, the *Bar du Bistrot* is open eves except Sun, 170-230.

● ◆◆ **Le Bouchon aux Vins**, 62, rue Mercière (B3), 69002, ☎ 78.42.88.90 Tradition, quality and good humour are the trademarks of J.C.-Caro and J.P.-Lacombe in their latest creation. In summer, it's almost St Tropez. Wine by the glass and bottles from an exceptional cellar. Good quality restaurant with rapid service, 150.

◆◆ **Industrie**, 96, cours du Dr-Long, 69003, ☎ 78.53.27.05, closed Sat and Sun , Aug. A few tables well served by André Perez : *foie gras chaud de canard aux pruneaux, pigeon farci, ris de veau aux truffes,* splendid menu, 200-250.

◆◆ **Le Passage**, 8, rue du Plâtre (B4), 69001, ☎ 78.28.11.16, Euro Visa ♪ closed Sat noon and Sun , hols, 130-200.

◆ **Chevallan**, 40, rue Sergent-Blandan (B2), 69001, ☎ 78.28.19.83, Visa ♪ closed Tue and Wed, 15-25 Feb, 1-30 Sep, 75-160.

◆ **Le Val d'Isère**, 64, rue Bonnel (E3), 69003, ☎ 78.71.09.39 ♪ closed Sun , Jul. Across from the Part-Dieu food markets is the "mâchon" (Lyonnais light lunch) favoured by Bocuse and his chums, 80-110.

Perrache :
◆ **Le Pasteur**, 83, quai Perrache (B5), 69002, ☎ 78.37.01.04, closed Sat and Sun, Aug. A different fixed-price meal every day, 80-130.

◆ **Savoy**, 50, rue de la République (C2-3), 69002, ☎ 78.37.69.25 ♪ One of Lyon's last great brasseries, 60-160.

Rive gauche :
● ◆◆◆ **Roger Roucou-Mère Guy**, 35, quai J.-J. Rousseau (off map A5), 69350, ☎ 78.51.65.37, Tx 310241, AE DC Visa ⌀ 🎖 closed Mon and Sun eve , Feb school hols, Aug. Consistent quality is the key word here : *foie gras d'oie des Landes au naturel, gratin de queues d'écrevisses,* 160-320.

◆◆◆ **Cazenove**, 75, rue Boileau (D1-2), 69006, ☎ 78.89.82.92, Tx 305965, AE Euro Visa ♪ ᚼ closed Sat and Sun, 2 Aug-2 Sep, 170-250.

● ◆◆ **Fédora**, 249, rue M.-Mérieux (off map B5), 69007, ☎ 78.69.46.26, AE DC Euro Visa ♪ closed Sat noon and Sun. D. Judeau is a young chef who is proving to be a master of fish cookery : *charcuterie de la mer, homard à l'oseille,* 95-350.

● ◆◆ **Le Quatre Saisons**, 15, rue Sully (D-E1), 69006, ☎ 78.93.76.07, AE DC Visa ♪ closed Sat noon and Sun , wkends in Jun, Jul, Aug. Trained by Paul Bocuse, Lucien Bertoli learned the master's lessons well : *noix de coquilles Saint-Jacques à la coque, rognons de veau cuits dans leur graisse en aigre-doux,* 260-350.

◆◆ **La Pastourelle**, 51, rue Tête-d'or (E2), 69006, ☎ 78.24.90.89, AE DC Visa ♪ 🎖 closed Sat noon and Sun, 31 Jul-1 Sep, 100-145.

● ◆ **Chez Rose**, 4, rue Rabelais (D3), 69003, ☎ 78.60.57.25, AE DC Euro Visa 🎖 closed Sun, 11-17 Aug. Here's the place for good Lyonnais dishes : *lyonnaiseries, pavé de cabillaud aux poireaux, lotte de rivière meunière,* 85-175.

◆ **Carron**, 65, bd Vivier-Merle (F3), 69003, ☎ 78.60.87.13 ♪ closed Sat eve and Sun, 5 Jul-5 Aug. Traditional, generous, tasty Lyonnais specialties, focus on fish, 80-130.

◆ **La bonne Auberge "Chez Jo"**, 48, av. Félix-Faure (E-F4), 69003, ☎ 78.60.00.57, AE DC Visa, closed Sat eve and Sun, 2-30 Aug, 150.

Bouchons :
◆ **Café des Fédérations**, 8, rue Major-Martin, 69001, ☎ 78.28.26.00, 70-90.
◆ **Chez Sylvain**, 4, rue Tupin (B3), 69002, 40-70.
◆ **Club du Vieux Lyon**, 4, quai R.-Rolland (B3), 69001, ☎ 78.42.28.52, 40-70.
◆ **Dussaud**, 12, rue Pizay, 69001, ☎ 78.28.10.94, 40-70.
◆ **Le Mintonné**, 26, rue Tronchet (D-E1), 69006, ☎ 78.89.36.71, Euro Visa ♪ ᚼ closed Sat and Sun , hols, 1-11 Apr, 7-17 Aug. A true Lyonnais *bouchon* serving good, hearty fare by Micheline Danné. Beaujolais by the pitcher, 65-100.
◆ **Saint-Antoine**, 4, rue Tupin (B3), 69002, ☎ 78.37.01.35, 40-70.

Recommended
Baby-sitting : *S.O.S. urgence maman,* ☎ 78.37.75.43.
Events : *city lights,* 8 Dec ; *curio fair,* 5, pl. de la Baleine, 69005, ☎ 78.37.16.04, late May, renaissance of old Lyon in the Saint-Jean district; at Chassieu, 69683, Eurexpo, ☎ 72.22.33.44, last 2 wks in Mar.
Guided tours : *C.N.M.H.S.,* daily 1 Jul-15 Sep ex Sun, bus tour of city ; *gallo-romain museum and guide service,* 5, pl. Saint-Jean (S.I.), ☎ 78.42.25.75, Wed am : Old Lyon ; City hall district; Croix-Rousse ; archeological sites, info S.I.
Leisure activities : *Hexatour,* 3, rue de l'Arbre-Sec, ☎ 78.36.33.15, river-boats ; *France Croisières fluviales,* 4, quai Rambaud, 69002, ☎ 78.37.42.66, tours with commentary : Lyon between the Saône and Rhone, daily at 9am and 2pm (3-hour cruise); *bateau Hermes,* quai Claude-Bernard, 69007, ☎ 78.58.36.34, boarding daily at pont de l'Université. Good restaurant ; many concerts halls, auditoriums, puppet shows (info : C.D.T.
♥ antiques : between Bellecour and Perrache, rues A.-Comte and V.-Hugo; bakery : *L. Mano,* 92, Grande-rue-de-la-Guillotière, 69003 ; caterers : *Bocuse-Bernachon,* 49, rue de Sèze, 69006 ; cheese : *Renée Richard,* Hal-

les, 102, cours La Fayette, ☎ 78.62.30.78 ; market : *de la création*, quai R.-Rolland, 69005, every Sun morning ; pastries-chocolates : *Casati*, 31, rue Ferrandière, 69002 ; *Pignol*, 17, rue E.-Zola, 69002, ☎ 78.37.30.67 ; *Bernachon*, 42, cours F.-Roosevelt, 69006 ; pork products : *Sibilia*, Halles de Lyon, 102, cours Lafayette, ☎ 78.62.36.28 ; *Reynon*, 18, rue des Archers, ☎ 78.37.39.08 ; *René Besson et Fils*, Halles, 66, rue Bonnel, ☎ 78.62.66.10 ; silks : *Clarence*, 24, rue des Archers ; *Maison des Canuts-Cooptis*, La Croix-Rousse, 10, rue d'Ivry ; *Nuance*, 4, rue Childebert ; *Moriss*, rue de l'Ancienne-Préfecture ; *Bloch-Lazarus*, 54, rue du Pdt-Herriot ; take-out food : *Frédérique et Claude Rolle*, Halle de Lyon, 69003, fresh salmon smoked in front of the client ; *Le Comptoir du Bœuf*, pl. Neuve-Saint-Jean, 69005, cooked dishes and ingredients by Chavent ; *les Halles de La Part-Dieu*, all the best food markets.

Nearby

BRON, ✉ 69500, 10 km E from exit N6.

Hotels :
★★★ *Dau-Ly*, 28, rue de Prévieux, ☎ 78.26.04.37, AE Visa, 22 rm Ⓟ ⚏ ♪ 220.
★★ *Lyon-Bron*, 7, rue des Essarts, ☎ 78.74.24.73, Visa, 40 rm Ⓟ ⚏ ♿ 200.

CALUIRE, ✉ 69300, 2 km N.

Restaurant :
♦♦♦ *Auberge de Fond-Rose*, 23, quai Clemenceau, ☎ 78.29.34.61 ⚏ closed Sun eve and Mon in winter, Feb. Lovely summer terrace. Classic cuisine : *homard grillé, carré d'agneau*, 150-300.

CHAMPAGNE-AU-MONT-D'OR, ✉ 69410, 7 km NW.

Restaurant :
♦♦ *Les Grillons*, 18, rue Dominique-Vincent, ☎ 78.35.04.78, AE DC Euro Visa ⚏ ♪ closed Mon and Sun eve , Mar, Nov, 100-180.

COLLONGES-AU-MONT-D'OR, ✉ 69660, 9 km N on D 433.

Restaurant :
● ♦♦♦♦ *Paul Bocuse*, pl. d'Illhaeusern, ☎ 78.22.01.40, Tx 375382, AE DC Visa Paul Bocuse, commander-in-chief of the "Grande Cuisine Française", chef Roger Jaloux assisted by Christian Bouvarel who's in charge of the stoves, chef Jean Fleury, who oversees the computer and general organization, as well as the 60-strong staff, all welcome you to their lovely 17thC inn beside the Saône. Nothing new can be said about the "Pope of Gourmandise", but no one can say enough. The many patrons who take the TGV just to partake of this divine cuisine can't be wrong : *soupe aux truffes V.G.E., loup en croûte, volaille de Bresse, saumon frais mariné rôti sur sa peau*, fresh and ripened cheeses from la Mère Richard, the boss's special Beaujolais and all the cellar's fabulous vintages. Next door at the abbaye Limonaires, circus music and confetti to help the party mood along, 280-500 ; child : 45.

FONTAINES-SUR-SAÔNE, ✉ 69270 on left bank, 8 km N.

Hotel :
★ *Terrasse*, 12, quai Simon, ☎ 78.22.36.86, 11 rm Ⓟ ⚏ 160. Rest. ♦ closed Aug, 80-130.

MEYZIEU, ✉ 69330, 8 km E of **Villeurbanne**.

Hotels :
● ★★★ *La Régence*, 35, rue Saulnier, ☎ 78.31.40.04, 19 rm, closed Aug, 250. Rest. ♦ ♪ 55-170.
★★ *Le Mont Joyeux* (L.F.), av. V.-Hugo, ☎ 78.04.21.32, AE DC Euro Visa, 20 rm Ⓟ ⚏ ⚏ ♪ ♿ 200. Rest. ♦♦ ♪ closed Mon and Sun eve, 56-180.

MIONS, ✉ 69780, 14 km SE.

Hotel :
★★ *Parc*, 30, av. de la Libération, ☎ 78.20.16.41, 20 rm, closed Sun eve , hol eves, Aug, 160. Rest. ♦♦ 80-130.

RILLIEUX-LA-PAPE, ✉ 69140, 7 km NE.

Restaurant :
● ♦♦ *Larivoire*, Chemin des Iles, ☎ 78.88.50.92, AE DC Visa ⚏ closed Mon eve and Tue, 1-25 Feb, 1-8 Sep. The fashionable meeting-place for Lyonnais loath to go far afield. In the kitchen, B. Constantin, formerly with Paul Bocuse : *huîtres chaudes, œuf cocotte aux langoustines et aux truffes, fricassée de volaille au vinaigre*, 130-260.

ROCHETAILLÉE-SUR-SAÔNE, ✉ 69270 Fontaines-sur-Saône, 2 km NE of **Fontaines-sur-Saône**.

Hotel :
★ *Paris* (L.F.), 2, rue Henri-Bouchard, ☎ 78.22.33.62, 8 rm Ⓟ ⚏ ⚏ ⚏ 170. Rest. ♦♦ Spec : *quenelles de fruits de mer*, 60-160.

SAINT-PRIEST, ✉ 69800, 11 km SE.

Hotel :
★★ *Central*, 18, rue A.-Briand, ☎ 78.20.26.62, 22 rm Ⓟ closed Sun eve, 4-24 Aug, 120.

SAINTE-FOY-LÈS-LYON, ✉ 69110, 6 km SW.

Hotel :
★★ *Les Provinces*, 10, pl. Saint-Luc, ☎ 78.25.01.55, 14 rm, 155.

SÉRÉZIN-DU-RHÔNE, ✉ 69360, 15 km S.

Hotel :
★★ *La Bourbonnaise* (L.F.), 45, av. du Dauphiné, ☎ 78.02.80.58, AE DC Euro Visa, 36 rm Ⓟ ⚏ ⚏ ♪ 185. Rest. ♦ ⚏ ♪ ♿ 80-140 ; child : 35.

TASSIN-LA-DEMI-LUNE, ✉ 69160 suburb W.

Restaurants :
♦♦ *Le Chateaubriand*, 12, av. Mal-Foch, ☎ 78.34.15.64, AE DC Euro Visa ⚏ closed Wed eve, Sat, Sun eve, 1 Aug-2 Sep. Fine food in a large house surrounded by a handsome park. Weddings and banquets, 75-200.
♦♦ *Les Tilleuls*, 146, av. Charles-de-Gaulle, ☎ 78.34.19.58, AE Visa ♪ closed Mon and Sun eve , Feb school hols, 15-26 Aug. Excellent cooking by R. Leschelet : *salade de ris d'agneau, assiette du pêcheur au basilic, pigeonneau de Bresse en cocotte*, 85-170.

VILLEURBANNE, ✉ 69100.

Hotels :
★★ *Athéna-Tolstoï*, 90, cours Tolstoï, ☎ 78.68.81.21, 140 rm Ⓟ 180. Rest. ♦ closed Sat and Sun, 65-125.
★★ *Athéna-Zola*, 163, cours E.-Zola, ☎ 78.85.32.33, 100 rm Ⓟ 180. Rest. ♦ closed Sat and Sun, 65-125.
★★ *Congrès*, pl. du Cdt-Rivière, ☎ 78.89.81.10, 132 rm Ⓟ 230. Rest. ♦ closed Sun, 150-240.

Recommended
♥ antiques : *Brocante Stalingrad*, 115, bd de Stalingrad, Thu, Sat, Sun.

The MONT-D'OR LYONNAIS*

B2

Round trip from Lyon *(55 km, approx 3 hr)*

▶ **Lyon** (→). ▶ Paris road. ▶ **Champagne-au-Mont-d'Or** : on the right by a footpath over the hills, **Saint-Didier**, a large village : two châteaux, one Renaissance, the other with Henri II courtyard. ▶ **Limonest** (pop. 2 244) on mountainside ; footpaths begin at alt. 400 m ; village nature museum. ▶ Head towards Mont Verdun. On the right after 4 km, **Saint-Fortunat**. Climbing towards the pass : right, 18thC château de la Barollière. ▶ **Mont Verdun** (alt. 625 m) French Army base *(no visits)*; **view** from pass. ▶ **Poleymieux** (alt. 500 m ; pop. 1 364) : museum of folk arts and crafts *(closed Mon.)*. N, **Croix-Rampeau** road *(1.5 km)* : orientation table (alt. 463 m); **view**★ (clear weather) from Meije to Puy de Dôme. S, **Electricity Museum** *(closed Tue.)* in the birthplace of André-Marie Ampère, with 18 visitor-operated basic electrical experiments. ▶ In the valley, **Albigny-sur-Saône** *(8 km ; pop. 2 653)*. ▶ **Mont Thou** (alt. 609 m) : views, summit closed to public. ▶ Below, near the Saône, **Couzon** (pop. 2 476) : church with 12thC bell tower; quarries for the Lyon building stone. ▶ **Mont Cindre** (alt. 469 m) : television relay tower; 14thC hermitage; view★ from adjacent terraces of the Saône entering Lyon 300 m below. ▶ **Saint-Cyr** (pop. 4 914) : 13thC château tower; Lyon Regional Museum of Criminology (at the police academy; *written requests in advance*). ▶ **Saint-Rambert** (→ Rochetaillée-sur-Saône). □

Practical Information _____

ALBIGNY-SUR-SAÔNE, ⊠ 69250 right bank, upstream.

Restaurant :
◆ *Les Isles*, 1, av. Gal-de-Gaulle, ☎ 78.91.30.88 ⑴ ♪ closed Mon eve and Tue. Spec : game in season, *lotte à l'armoricaine*, 60-140.

COUZON-AU-MONT-D'OR, ⊠ 69270 Fontaines-sur-Saône, on the right bank.

Hotel :
★ *Les Tonnelles*, 26, rue Gabriel-Péri, ☎ 78.22.17.05, Visa, 8 rm P ⑴ ⎯ 100. Rest. ◆ ♪ closed Sat noon, 85-170.

LIMONEST, ⊠ 69760, 13 km NW of **Lyon**.

Hotel :
★ *Puy d'Or* (L.F.), 25, rte du Puy d'Or, 3 km S on D 42, ☎ 78.35.12.20, Euro Visa, 7 rm P ⋌ ⑴ closed Tue eve and Wed, 5-31 Oct, 140. Rest. ◆ 80-150.

Le MONT CINDRE, ⊠ 69450 Saint Cyr-au-Mont-d'Or, 14 km N of **Lyon**.

Restaurant :
◆◆ *Ermitage*, ☎ 78.47.20.96, AE Euro Visa ⋌ ⑴ ⎯ closed Tue and Wed, 4 Jan-1 Mar, 80-200; child : 65.

MONTBRISON*

Saint-Etienne 36, Lyon 95, Paris 456 km
pop 13650 ⊠ 42600   A2

Once the principal town of the Loire and capital of the Lords of Forez, who surveyed the city from their château situated on a volcanic outcrop.

▶ On the circular road along the former ramparts, **Barrière Tower** (also known as Baron-des-Adrets). ▶ Gothic **collegiate church** of Notre-Dame-d'Espérance★ (13th-15thC). ▶ At the E end, the Chamber of Diana, late 13thC Gothic vaulting, poorly restored in the 19thC; adjoining museum *(10-12 & 2-5, 6, Jun.-Sep.; closed Tue.)* of Gallo-Roman archaeology (city gate panels), medieval sculpture. ▶ Town Hall in former Cordeliers' Convent (15th-18thC); law courts in former Visitation Convent (18thC). ▶ **Old houses** (some 15thC) around modern church of St. Pierre. ▶ **Musée de la Poupée★** (Doll Museum) and **Allard Museum** of mineralogy, ornithology *(2:30-6).*

Nearby

▶ S, **Moingt** : Romanesque church; Gallo-Roman excavations. ▶ By the Saint-Étienne road, **Saint-Roman-le-Puy** *(8.5 km;* pop. 2 423) : a basalt peak (panorama★) supporting a fortified priory (Romanesque and 15thC church; fresco fragments, 10thC nave, crypt★). ▶ **Sury-le-Comtal** *(12 km;* pop. 4 207) : 18thC château★ (woodwork, fireplaces, ceilings; *Easter-15 Oct., Sun., Mon. and hols., 2-6).* N, **Motor Museum** : 50 models of 1930-37.   □

Practical Information _____

ⓘ pl. de l'Hôtel-de-Ville, ☎ 77.96.18.18.

Hotels :
★★ *L'Escale* (L.F.), 27, rue de la République, ☎ 77.58.17.77, 18 rm P 150. Rest. ◆ closed Sun eve, 45-60.
★★ *Lion d'Or* (L.F.), 14, quai des Eaux-Minérales, ☎ 77.58.34.66, DC Euro Visa, 14 rm P ⋌ ⎯ closed Sun eve , Mon, Feb school hols, 31 Aug-15 Sep, 175. Rest. ◆◆ 100-180.

MORNANT

Lyon 23, Saint-Etienne 35, Paris 482 km
pop 3463 ⊠ 69440   B2

In a small valley broached by the 30-arch Roman **aqueduct★** serving Lyon; ruins visible around Orliénas and Beaunant, among other sites; N of Mornant, a single arch remains from huge bridge. Gothic church : woodwork; 15thC Madonna in priory. ▶ **Riverie★** *(8 km NW)*, medieval market town on promontory : site★; crafts centre.   □

Practical Information _____

Hotel :
★★ *Poste* (L.F.), 5, pl. de la Liberté, ☎ 78.44.00.40, Visa, 12 rm P ⑴ 150. Rest. ◆ closed Sun and Mon eve (l.s.), 55-145.

NANTUA*

Bourg-en-Bresse 56, Lyon 96, Paris 483 km
pop 3639 ⊠ 01130   C1

Ancient lookout at a mountain pass, on a 3-km-long lake, Nantua was a religious centre before it became a summer resort and a centre of gastronomy.

▶ **Church** : Romanesque; doorway★; interior, Renaissance altar, woodwork, painting by Eugène Delacroix, Martyrdom of St. Sebastian★. ▶ S *(2-hr walk round trip)*, view from **Mont D'Ain★** (alt. 1 127 m) to the fir-covered lakeshore *(500 m)*, large leisure centre.

Nearby

▶ E, the Geneva road through the **Cluse★** follows the N shore of **Lake Sylans** (ancient glaciers) for 2 km. ▶ Left on D95, via Charix, **Lake Genin** *(16 km from Nantua)* : site★ (alt. 830 m). ▶ N via the Saint-Claude road, **Oyonnax** *(16 km;* pop. 22 804) : comb and eyeglass manufacturing, reorganized since WWII for plastics manufacture *(plant visits);* Museum of Combs and Plastics *(10-12 & 3-6, Jul.-Aug.; closed Sun., hols; 2-5 Tue., Sat. rest of year).* 8 km farther, **Dortan**, the capital of chess in a pass below a ruined château; boxwood artisans' workshops. ▶ SW by the Lyon road, **Cerdon Caverns** *(23 km)* : handsome entrance to 800-m walk. ▶ Vineyard producing Cerdon, a sparkling rosé wine.

Practical Information _____

ⓘ 2, rue du Dr-Mercier, ☎ 74.75.00.05 (h.s.).   ♥

Hotels :
★★★ *France*, 44, rue du Dr-Emile-Mercier, ☎ 74.75.00.55, AE DC Euro Visa, 19 rm P ⑴ closed Fri, 1 Nov-20 Dec, 275. Rest. ● ◆◆◆ Gilbert Le Tort, former sommelier at the *Plaza*, is an added strength here. He oversees the very fine wine list. Good traditional Bresse regional fare, 105-180.
★★ *Embarcadère* (L.F.), av. du Lac, ☎ 74.75.22.88, Euro Visa, 50 rm P ⋌ ⑴ ⎯ closed Mon, 28 Apr-4 May, 20 Dec-20 Jan, 220. Rest. ◆ ⋌ ⌘ 85-150.
⚠ ★★★★*Le Signal* (80 pl), ☎ 74.75.02.09.

Nearby

ÉCHALLON, ⊠ 01490 Saint-Germain-de-Joux, 5 km N on the D 55.

Hotel :
★ *Auberge de la Semine*, ☎ 74.76.48.75, Euro Visa, 11 rm P ⑴ ⎯ closed Sun eve and Mon, 10 Nov-20 Dec, 90. Rest. ◆ ♪ Likable mountain inn with beams and rough-hewn stone : *soufflé de truite sauce écrevisse, filet de bœuf aux morilles, filets de Perche au noilly*. Savoy wines, 40-95.

OYONNAX, ⊠ 01100, 16 km N.
ⓘ 83, rue A.-France, ☎ 74.73.58.13.
Car rental : *Avis*, 53, rue Castellion (Garage Opel),
☎ 74.77.26.96.
Hotel :
★★ *Buffard* (L.F.), pl. de l'Église, ☎ 74.77.86.01, 28 rm
≼ ⋘ ♪ 150. Rest. ♦ ♪ closed Fri eve, Sat, Sun eve,
15 Jul-15 Aug, 60-100.

NOIRÉTABLE

Roanne 47, Saint-Etienne 80, Paris 413 km
pop 1998 ⊠ 42440   A2
On the border of Forez and the Livradois, medium-
altitude (700 m) resort. Attracts hikers and anglers for
trout. Gothic church.

Nearby

▶ **Notre-Dame-de-l'Ermitage** (*7 km SW; alt.* 1 100 m) :
site. ▶ **Cervières★** (*3 km N*), ancient market town : ruined ramparts ; Renaissance houses ; 15th-16thC church ;
linden tree. ▶ Via Champoly (*10 km NE*), ruined **château
d'Urfé★** (*1-hr walk; alt.* 936 m) : view of Alps in clear
weather. ▶ **Saint-Just-en-Chevalet** (*18 km; pop.* 1 798)
in Aix Valley : ruined castle ; 15thC church on knoll. ▶ S,
D101 passes through Ermitage Woods and Loge Pass
(alt. 1 243 m) before entering the **Forez Peaks.**▶ **Chalmazel** (*28 km; pop.* 670), winter sports resort (alt. 867 m) :
13th-16thC château (*school hols. : daily, 10-12 & 2-6;
closed Nov.-Easter*). ▶ Via **Béal Pass★** (alt. 1 390 m;
10 km W) and the high Forez Peaks road, **Pierre-sur-
Haute★** (alt. 1 634 m; *1h30 walk*) : panorama★★. ▶ Via
N89 from Saint-Étienne, **Hôpital-sous-Rochefort** (*21 km*) :
12th-16thC church, ruins of fortified priory (15th-16thC).
Close by, to the W, **Saint-Laurent-Rochefort** : Gothic
church, castle and 12thC chapel on a cliff.   □

Practical Information
NOIRÉTABLE
ⓘ ☎ 77.24.70.12.
SNCF ☎ 77.24.72.49.

Restaurant :
♦♦ *L'Aquarium*, RN 89, Saint-Julien-la-Vêtre,
☎ 77.97.85.26, Euro Visa, closed Mon, 1-15 Dec, 60-100 ;
child : 25.

Recommended
Farmhouse-inn : *Les Sapins*, Cervières, 5 km N,
☎ 77.24.71.94, *patcha, truite aux amandes, potée.*

Nearby

SAINT-JUST-EN-CHEVALET, ⊠ 42430, 18 km NE.
ⓘ mairie, ☎ 77.65.00.62.

Hotel :
★ *Poste* (L.F.), rte de Thiers, ☎ 77.65.01.42, DC Visa,
15 rm Ⓟ ⋤ closed Tue eve, 15-28 Feb, 15-30 Oct, 155.
Rest. ♦ 50-85.

PÉROUGES★★

Bourg-en-Bresse 37, Lyon 39, Paris 455 km
pop 658 ⊠ 01800 Meximieux   B2
This medieval village of weavers, situated 70 m above
the plain, has been completely restored since 1911
and has provided the scenery for numerous films. A
fortified city with houses built up to the ramparts, fortified church, palace, 15th-16thC craftsmens'
workshops along **Rue des Rondes★** and the central square.

▶ Avoid the summer tourist peak and Sun. ▶ **Place du
Tilleul** : Museum of Folk Arts and Traditions ; the weaver's workshop reflects the time when hemp was the only
regional crop (*closed Wed.*).

Nearby

▶ **Meximieux** (*2 km E; pop.* 4 254) : sculpted choir stalls
in church ; château du Monteiller (restored 11thC keep).
▶ **Saint-Maurice-de-Gourdans** (*13 km S; pop.* 1 157) :
Gothic paintings in church nave. ▶ 20 km S via D65,
Loyettes (pop. 1 178).   □

Practical Information
PÉROUGES

Hotel :
● ★★★★ *Vieux-Pérouges*, pl. du Tilleul, ☎ 74.61.00.88,
Visa, 28 rm Ⓟ ≼ ⋘ ⋤ closed Wed and Thu lunch (l.s.). 13thC
Bressan inn. Attentive service, 450. Rest. ♦♦ 145-250.

Nearby
LOYETTES, ⊠ 01980, 16 km S of **Meximieux.**

Restaurant :
● ♦♦ *La Terrasse*, ☎ 78.32.70.13, AE Visa, closed Mon
and Sun eve, 15 Feb-11 Mar. A favourite gathering spot
for Lyonnais natives who appreciate the excellent seasonal cuisine of G. Antonin : *petite pêche bretonne, courgettes frites*, 90-220.

MEXIMIEUX, ⊠ 01800, 2 km E.

Hotel :
★★ *Claude Lutz* (L.F.), 17, rue de Lyon, ☎ 74.61.06.78,
AE Visa, 16 rm Ⓟ ⋘ closed Sun eve and Mon, 15-24 Jul,
19 Oct-10 Nov, 170. Rest. ♦♦ Claude Lutz is a talented
alumnus of the Bocuse kitchen : *cassolette de grenouilles
au chardonnay, civet de turbot au gamay, pavé de charolais au gamay*, 105-180 ; child : 60.

SAINT-MAURICE-DE-GOURDANS, ⊠ 01800 Meximieux,
12 km SE.

Hotel :
● ★★ *Relais Saint-Maurice*, rte de Meximieux,
☎ 74.61.81.45, AE Visa, 10 rm, closed Fri and Sat lunch,
1-25 Jan, 1-15 Sep, 180. Rest. ♦ ♪ 75-120.

Mont PILAT★

                                                         A-B3
Like a pyramid rising sharply 1 000 m above the Gier
and the Rhône, Mont Pilat, with massive crests (*chi-
rats*) at about 1 400 m, supports a naturally wooded
regional park — ash, chestnut, beech and pine —
with few pastures. 200 km of rivers and streams flow
off the mountain, which is a haven for wildlife including boar, fox, civet and deer, predatory birds and
butterflies. Designated a nature park in 1974 (600 km^2
including 280 km^2 coniferous forest), Mont Pilat, with
ski slopes and 300 km of hiking trails, is the open-air
playground for Lyon-Saint-Étienne.

From Saint-Étienne to the Rhône Valley

▶ **Via Le Bessat and Pélussin** (*57 km*) : **Rochetaillée**
(→ Saint-Étienne). ▶ **Le Bessat** (pop. 214) : mountain
resort. ▶ After the Chambouret Cross, left 7 km to **Pilat
Farmstead** : view of Perdrix Crest (alt. 1 434 m).▶ **Œillon
Crest Pass** : orientation table at summit★ (alt. 1 365 m ;
1-hr round trip). ▶ **Pélussin** (pop. 2 930), lookout over the
Rhône Valley : old town ; disused mill (Virieu). ▶ N, **Saint-
Croix-en-Jarez** : 13thC charterhouse abandoned at the
French Revolution. ▶ **Chavanay** : 10 km E on the Rhône ;
pop. 1 858. ▶ N, **Condrieu** (pop. 3 158) : old houses ;
river port ; Croix-Regis zoo (*2 km upriver*); renowned
vineyards.

▶ **By Col de la République** (pass, alt. 1 145 m) **and
Bourg-Argental** (*65 km*). ▶ Detour via **Saint-Genest-Mali-
faux** (pop. 2 384) : cottage industry of braid trimmings.
Marlhes : folk arts and traditions in the Eau and Béate
Houses (*14 Jul.-15 Sep., Sun. and hols., 3-6:30*).▶ **Saint-
Sauveur-en-Rue** : Vialle gateway ; church (Descent from

the Cross); fortified house in **Rue.** ▶ **Bourg-Argental** (pop. 3302) : Town Hall in feudal château; church with Romanesque portal. ▶ **Saint-Julien-Molin-Molette** : megalith. ▶ **Malleval** : medieval village★ on a crag above gorges, waterfall. □

Practical Information

LE BESSAT, ✉ 42660 Saint-Genest-Malifaux, 18 km SE of **Saint-Etienne.**
1170-1430m.
ℹ ☎ 77.20.40.61.

Hotel :
★★ ***France*** (L.F.), ☎ 77.20.40.99, DC Euro Visa, 30 rm Ⓟ closed, New Year's Day, 1-15 Apr, 1-30 Sep, 25 Dec, 130. Rest. ♦ 40-100.

BOURG-ARGENTAL, ✉ 42220, 28 km SE of **Saint-Etienne.**
ℹ rue de la République (e.s.) et mairie, ☎ 77.39.60.40.

Hotel :
★★ ***France*** (L.F.), pl. du 11-Novembre, ☎ 77.39.60.28, Visa, 10 rm Ⓟ closed Sun eve (l.s.) , Mon and Feb, 160. Rest. ♦ 100-160.

CHAVANAY, ✉ 42410 Pélussin, 7 km SW of **Condrieu.**

Restaurant :
♦♦ ***Alain Charles***, RN 86, ☎ 74.87.23.02, Euro Visa ♿ closed Mon and Sun eve. Spec : *fricassée de volailles, pâté chaud de canard sauce truffes, loup sur lit de poireaux, 65-150.*

CONDRIEU, ✉ 69420, 11 km SW of **Vienne.**
ℹ pl. du Marché, ☎ 78.85.53.48.

Hotel :
● ★★★★ ***Beau Rivage*** (R.C.), 2, rue du Beau-Rivage, ☎ 74.59.52.24, Tx 308946, AE DC Euro Visa, 26 rm Ⓟ half pens (h.s.), closed 5 Jan-15 Feb, 1110. Rest. ● ♦♦♦ ♿ Its a well-know fact that lovers are eternally young (at heart, anyway). Paulette Castaing, a lover of fine cuisine, has spent Lord-knows-how-many hours at her stove, fixing wonderful traditional dishes for her faithful clientèle. Spec : *sandre à la côte rôtie, foie gras à l'embeurrée de choux*, 200-400.

⛺ ★★★*Belle Rive* (180 pl), ☎ 77.59.51.08.

SAINT-PIERRE-DE-BOEUF, ✉ 42410 Pélussin, 12 km SW of **Chavanay.**

Restaurant :
♦ ***La Diligence***, RN 86, ☎ 74.87.12.19, AE Visa, closed Mon and Sun eve, 15-30 Jul, 80-170.

PONT-D'AIN

Bourg-en-Bresse 19, Nantua 35, Paris 446 km
pop 2224 ✉ 01160 B1

The most frequented part of the valley (popular with trout and grayling anglers), where the Dombes and Bugey meet, Pont-d'Ain lies below the ruined 15thC château where Louise de Savoie (mother of François I) was born; Renaissance staircase; grounds.

Nearby

▶ 6 km E, **Jujurieux,** a town of 15 châteaux, including the château de la Tour des Échelles, French gardens★ *(Sat., Sun., Jul.-Sep.).* ▶ Via the Nantua road, **Poncin** *(8 km;* pop. 1204) : 13thC castle; on the right bank of the Ain, Colombière Cavern. ▶ Farther on, via the Veyron Valley and S, **Préau Pass★** and ruined château de Châtillon.□

Practical Information

ℹ 17, rue St-Exupéry, ☎ 74.39.05.84 (h.s.).

Hotel :
★★ ***Alliés*** (L.F.), 1, rue Brillat-Savarin, ☎ 74.39.00.09, Euro Visa, 18 rm Ⓟ closed Thu and Fri lunch, 9-15 Jun, 22 Dec-18 Jan, 155. Rest. ♦ 80-120.

⛺ ★★★*Municipal* (250 pl), ☎ 74.39.05.23.

ROANNE

Vichy 74, Lyon 86, Paris 392 km
pop 49638 ✉ 42300 A1

A one-time Loire River port superseded in the 19thC by the canal to Briare, Roanne has a new 30 km-long reservoir available for boating or viewing from the scenic railway along its edge. The city is an industrial centre for metallurgy, armaments, tyres and textiles, with an equal reputation for fine food.

▶ 200 m from the Town Hall, **Joseph Déchelette Museum** (Rue Anatole-France, *10-12 & 2-6; closed Tue.*) : archaeology, painting, regional ceramics. ▶ Saint-Étienne Church : Renaissance stained glass, near ruined 11thC keep. ▶ Surrounding area abounds in Gallic and Gallo-Roman sites.

Nearby

▶ Via N7 from Lyon : l'**Hôpital-sur-Rhins** *(10 km).* ▶ **Saint-Symphorien-de-Lay** : 15thC church, Renaissance woodwork★; summer exhibits at 17thC Mansardes House. ▶ Climb to **Pin-Bouchain Pass** (alt. 764 m); S via back roads, 27 km from Roanne, **château de l'Aubépin★** (Gothic and Renaissance; *access to park only*). □

Practical Information

ROANNE
ℹ cours de la République, ☎ 77.71.51.77/77.71.25.01.
✈ *Roanne-Saint-Léger*, ☎ 77.66.83.55.
SNCF ☎ 77.71.25.01/77.71.11.46.
🚌 ☎ 77.72.28.66.
Car rental : *Avis*, 16, bd J.-Ferry, ☎ 77.71.84.95; train station.

Hotels :
● ★★★★ ***Troisgros*** (R.C.), pl. de la Gare, ☎ 77.71.66.97, Tx 307507, AE DC Euro Visa, 24 rm Ⓟ ♿ closed Tue and Wed lunch, 2-29 Jan, 4-19 Aug, 500. Rest. ● ♦♦♦♦ ♿ Pierre Troisgros remains firm in his resolve not to move to the country, despite advice to the contrary. But he has added a gloriously green hanging garden to his property across from the train station, an event duly noted and celebrated by his peers. It won't be long before the vines (grape vines, that is) begin to flower. Michel Troisgros has brought a youthful new outlook to the kitchen. A memorable dining experience is assured with brand-new creations alongside traditional favourites : *salade multicolore aux crabes dormeurs, sifflets de sole à l'écrasée de pommes de terre, émincé de rognons au citron saumuré, flan meringué "Jasmina"*. And the great Burgundies, of course, as well as more modest house wines (côte Roannaise, Beaujolais) not to mention the cheeses, the cigar selection, and the staff's smiling warmth. To show you're in the know, ask chef Pierre where to find the first hole, the pool and the heliport, 240-400.
★★★ ***Grand Hôtel***, (Inter-Hôtel), cours de la République, ☎ 77.71.48.82, AE DC Euro Visa, 35 rm Ⓟ closed 23 Dec-5 Jan, 280.
★★ ***Le Marcassin*** (L.F.), Riorges, 3 km W via D 31, ☎ 77.71.30.18, AE Visa, 10 rm Ⓟ closed Sat, Feb school hols, 10-20 Aug, 120. Rest. ● ♦♦ ♪ ♿ J. Farge and son Pierre man the kitchens : *salade de langoustines, noisettes d'agneau à la crème de thym*, 55-150.
★★ ***Terminus***, 13, cours de la République, ☎ 77.71.79.69, Tx 900394, 51 rm Ⓟ ♿ 175.

Restaurants :
● ♦♦ ***Côté Jardin***, 10, rue Benoît-Malon, ☎ 77.72.81.88, Visa ♪ ♿ closed Sat noon and Sun. In a garden setting, Pierre Gaillard cooks in an original, inventive mode, and the prices are very attractive : *bisquebouille de filets de poissons aux spaghettis de courgettes, salade tiède*

d'aiguillettes de caneton aux morilles, granité de citron vert à l'alcool de gingembre, 75-150.

♦♦ **L'Astrée**, 17bis, cours de la République, ☎ 77.72.74.22, AE DC Visa ♪ closed Sat eve and Sun, 17-31 Aug, 22 Dec-5 Jan. Spec : *paupiettes d'huîtres au saumon fumé, râble de lièvre aux figues fraîches*, 80-250.

♦♦ **Taverne Alsacienne**, 2, pl. de la Paix, ☎ 77.71.21.14 ⟲ ♪ closed Mon, 27 Apr-21 May, 15-28 Oct, 50-110.

▲ ★★★*Municipal* (80 pl), ☎ 77.71.67.53.

Recommended

♥ chocolates : *Pralus*, 8, rue Ch.-de-Gaulle; *Paul Christophe*, 56, rue Ch.-de-Gaulle.

Nearby

Le COTEAU, ⊠ 42120 on the right bank.

Restaurant :

● ♦ **Auberge Costelloise**, 2, av. de la Libération, ☎ 77.68.12.71, Visa ⟨ & closed Mon and Sun , Feb school hols, 20 Jul-20 Aug. Daniel Alex offers well-conceived, varied fixed-price meals : *millefeuille de foie gras aux pommes et au céleri, saumon à la croqu'au sel*, 90-200.

L'HÔPITAL-SUR-RHINS, ⊠ 42132 Saint-Cyr-de-Favières, 10 km S on the D 43.

Hotel :

★★ **Le Favières** (L.F.), ☎ 77.64.80.30, Visa, 16 rm ℗ ⟲ closed Fri eve and Sat, 2 Jan-2 Feb, 155. Rest. ♦♦ ♪ Spec : *compote de lapereau à l'ancienne, noix de St-Jacques à la vapeur de safran*. Appealing and affordable fixed-price meals, 60-170.

SAINT-GERMAIN-LESPINASSE, ⊠ 42640, 12 km NW.

Hotel :

★★★ **Relais de Roanne**, (France-Accueil), RN 7, ☎ 77.71.97.35, Tx 307554, AE DC Euro Visa, 30 rm ℗ ⟲ ⟲ ⟲ ♪ & 195. Rest. ● ♦♦ ⟨ ♪ &*filet de turbot au beurre de caviar, magret de canard aux mangues et citron vert*, 60-200.

SAINT-BONNET-LE-CHÂTEAU*

Saint-Etienne 35, Le Puy 65, Paris 499 km
pop 2089 ⊠ 42380   A3

A lace-making town, formerly fortified, some walls still intact; 16thC double gate. ▶ View★ over Forez Plain and the Lyonnais mountains. ▶ Gothic and Renaissance houses. ▶ Collegiate church (15th-16thC) : Renaissance doorway, Gothic fresco in crypt; mummified remains. ▶ Hospital chapel : Baroque furnishings, altarpiece. ▶ **Usson-en-Forez** (13 km SW; pop. 1358) : summer resort (alt. 944 m), angling; 15thC church with three naves.   □

SAINT-ÉTIENNE

Lyon 59, Le Puy 78, Paris 522 km
pop 206688 ⊠ 42000   A2-3

At the foot of Mt. Pilat (→) on a slope ranging from 700 to 500 m alt., crossed by the high Furan Valley, Saint-Étienne started to grow in the 16thC; industry has continued to expand for the past 150 years in metallurgy, arms, tools and milling machinery. A "green city", Saint-Étienne enjoys 2000 hours of sunshine annually (more than half the year) and an active cultural life.

▶ The N-S road (6 km) leads to the **Town Hall** (square★) and historic quarter (medieval church, restored in the 19thC), around the **Place du Peuple** (B3), bright with flower-stalls. ▶ S, the **Palais des Arts** houses the Museum of Art and Industry★★ and the Mining Museum★ : zoology, weaving, armour, contemporary painting★, sculpture, prints, drawings (10-12 & 2-5; closed Tue. and Wed. am).

▶ Museum of Old Saint-Étienne (No. 13 Rue Gambetta; B3). ▶ Near the Palais des Arts, **Jardin des Plantes** (Botanical Garden; C3) : view from terraces of Cultural Centre. ▶ Return by way of the Town Hall and Arms Museum (19 Rue J.-C.-Tissot, B2; visit by appt. only).

Nearby

▶ **Rochetaillée** (7 km E), old village overlooking (alt. 800 m) the Furan Valley; **Gouffre d'Enfer**, lake created by 50-m-high dam spillway. ▶ **Valley of the Gier** (E) : Saint-Chamond (12 km; pop. 40571) : naval shipyards (closed Sat., Sun.); ruins of Roman aqueduct; 9thC feudal castle. ▶ **Rive-de-Gier** (22 km; pop. 15850) : glassworks (visits).   □

Practical Information _____

SAINT-ÉTIENNE

ℹ 12, rue Gérentet (B2), ☎ 77.25.12.14; 5, pl. Jean-Jaurès, ☎ 77.33.15.39.
✈ 15 km NW, ☎ 77.55.03.91/77.36.54.79. Air France office, 29, av. de la Libération, ☎ 77.33.03.03.
SNCF (A3), ☎ 77.37.50.50/77.32.43.79.
Car rental : Avis, train station (A3); 140, rue A.-Durafour (off map B3), ☎ 77.80.33.13; 27, av. Denfert-Rochereau (C2), ☎ 77.32.09.61; Airport.

Hotels :

★★★ **Altéa Parc de l'Europe**, (ex Frantel), rue de Wuppertal (off map C3), ☎ 77.25.22.75, Tx 300050, AE DC Euro Visa, 120 rm ℗ ⟲ ⋇ & 300. Rest. ♦♦♦ **La Ribaudière** ⟨ ♪ & closed Sat noon and Sun, 24 Dec-2 Jan, 115-200; child : 50.

★★★ **Astoria**, rue Henri-Dechaud (off map C3), ☎ 77.25.09.56, Tx 330949, AE DC Euro Visa, 33 rm ℗ ⟨ ⟲ ⟲ ♪ 195.

★★★ **Midi**, 19, bd Pasteur (off map A3), ☎ 77.57.32.55, Tx 300012, AE DC Euro Visa, 27 rm ℗ closed Aug, 225.

★★★ **Terminus du Forez**, (France-Accueil), 31, av. Denfert-Rochereau (C2), ☎ 77.32.48.47, Tx 333680, AE DC Euro Visa, 66 rm ℗ ♪ 200. Rest. ♦ ♪ closed Sun, 65-120.

★★ **Arts**, 11, rue Gambetta (B3), ☎ 77.32.42.11, Euro Visa, 63 rm ℗ ⟲ closed Aug, 120.

★★ **Cheval Noir**, 11, rue F.-Gillet (B2), ☎ 77.33.41.72, AE DC Euro Visa, 46 rm, 115.

★★ **Touring Continental**, 10, rue F.-Gillet (B2), ☎ 77.32.58.43, 25 rm ℗ ⟲ 150.

Restaurants :

● ♦♦♦ *Pierre Gagnaire*, 3, rue Georges-Teissier (A3), ☎ 77.37.57.93, AE DC Visa ♪ & closed Mon and Sun, Feb school hols, 2 wks in Aug. Pierre Gagnaire's progressive cuisine is in the forefront of French gastronomy today. Bright, sunny decor. Spec : *poêlée de clams au jus de persil, tranche de saumon d'Ecosse, tempura de langoustines aux pommes de terre, crépinette de pintade à la sauge, canard rôti entier*. Superb desserts and splendid Rhône wines, 160-350; child : 70.

♦♦ *Le Clos des Lilas*, 28, rue Virgile (off map C3), ☎ 77.25.28.13, AE DC Euro Visa ⟨ closed Mon and Sun eve , Aug, 105-160.

♦♦ *Le Monte-Carlo*, 19 bis, cours V.-Hugo (B3), ☎ 77.32.43.63, AE DC Visa ♪ 90-200.

Nearby

L'HORME, ⊠ 42152, 12 km.

Hotel :

★★ *Vulcain*, 1, rue du Puits-Gillier, ☎ 77.22.17.11, Tx 370425, AE DC Euro Visa, 30 rm ℗ ⟲ ♪ & 160.

RIVE-DE-GIER, ⊠ 42800, 22 km NE.
SNCF ☎ 77.75.00.20.

Hotels :

★★★★ *La Renaissance*, 41, rue A.-Marrel, ☎ 77.75.04.31, AE DC Euro Visa, 10 rm ℗ ⟨ ⟲ ⟲ 240. Rest. ● ♦♦ ⟨ ♪ & Chef Gilbert Laurent's talented lieutenant is now on his own, preparing superior cuisine. Original specialties. Côtes du Rhône wines, 105-330; child : 70.

★ *Au Feu de Bois*, Le Sardon, Génilac, ☎ 77.75.61.70,

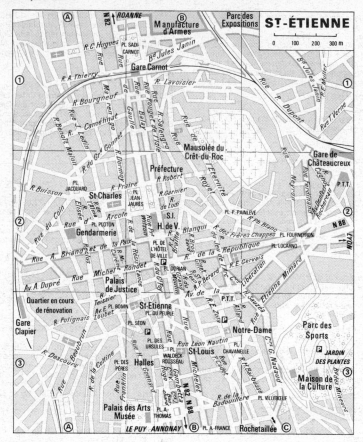

St-Étienne map with scale 0 100 200 300 m

Visa, 11 rm P closed Sat, New Year's Day, 10-31 Aug, 25 Dec, 170. Rest. ♦♦ 45-120.

SAINT-CHAMOND, ⊠ 42400, 12 km E.
SNCF ☎ 77.22.02.28.

Recommended
Farmhouse-inn : at Saint-Paul-en-Jarez, *les Grillons,* ☎ 77.22.25.19, *soufflé de foies de volaille aux quenelles, gratin maison.*

SAINT-PRIEST-EN-JAREZ, ⊠ 42270, 4 km N.

Restaurant :
♦♦♦ **Le Clos Fleuri,** 76, av. A.-Raimond, ☎ 77.74.63.24, AE DC Euro Visa ⊞ ♪ & ♨ closed Mon eve and Sun eve, Feb school hols,, 110-250 ; child : 80.

TARARE

Roanne 43, Lyon 43, Paris 468 km
pop 10935 ⊠ 69170   A2

43 km from Lyon, weavers' houses line the main street of a town that flourished in the late 18thC by making muslin and cotton goods ; Tarare still thrives from the manufacture of curtain materials and synthetics.

▶ Commercial Court in a 17thC Capuchin friary ; textile and natural sciences museums *(temporarily closed);* 16thC tower. ▶ Hikes among the woods, streams and

waterfalls of the nearby mountains. Every five years (those ending in 0 and 5) : fête de la Mousseline.

Nearby

▶ **Pontcharra-sur-Turdine** *(6 km E ; pop.* 1 833), silk centre. ▶ S, picturesque **Toranchin Valley★ ;** SE, Clévy : Gothic chapel ; pilgrimage site. ▶ **Saint-Loup,** village of flowers.

Tarare Peaks *(N via D8)*

▶ **Sauvage Pass** *(8 km ; alt.* 723 m). ▶ **Amplepuis** (pop. 5 055), formerly an important textile centre : sewing-machine museum ; castle ruins (tower built in the year 1 000) ; Roman bridge. ▶ NW, **Saint-Victor-sur-Rhins★** *(6 km) :* partly Romanesque church. ▶ E, Pilon Pass, **Ronne :** cromlech (prehistoric stone monoliths encircling a mound) ; menhir (single stone megalith) adapted to Christian devotion. ▶ NE, **Cublize :** echo phenomenon in church. ▶ From Amplepuis to Cours, "Pines Road". ▶ **Thizy★** (alt. 560 m ; pop. 3 699, 3 200 at Bourg-de-Thizy), a textile centre in the 18thC ; tile-roofed village on a **promontory★** overlooking Trambouze Valley (view★) : medieval quarter, 11thC church decorated with frescos ; château once occupied by Mme. Roland (1754-93), a member of the moderate republican party (Gironde) during the Revolutionary period, to whom is attributed the cry : "Oh liberty ! What crimes are committed in thy name !" ▶ **Cours-la-Ville** (pop. 5 095 ; alt. 560 m), formerly a centre for manufacturing cotton bedspreads.   □

Practical Information ——————————

TARARE
ℹ 6, pl. de la Madeleine, ☎ 74.63.06.65.
SNCF ☎ 74.63.01.81.

Hotels :
★★ *Europe*, 17, rue de la République, ☎ 74.63.02.81, AE
Euro Visa, 20 rm Ⓟ closed Sun eve and Mon, 140.
Rest. ♦ 70-130.
★★ *Git'otel* (L.F.), R.N. 7, ☎ 74.63.44.01, Tx 330929, AE
DC Euro Visa, 35 rm Ⓟ ⅏ ⚒ ⴵ 210. Rest. ♦♦ *La Grange
Cléard* ⴵ closed Sun, 45-90.

Restaurant :
● ♦♦ *Jean Brouilly*, 3 ter, rue de Paris, ☎ 74.63.24.56,
AE DC Visa closed Mon and Sun , Feb school hols,
3-18 Aug. With a name like that, how could the chef be
anything but an excellent cook? Spec : *lapin à la gelée de
roquette, rouget aux deux foies, nounou d'agneau braisé
aux légumes concassés*, 120-190 ; child : 60.

Nearby

Le **CERGNE**, ✉ 42460 Cuinzier, 4 km N of **Cours-la-Ville**.

Hotel :
★ *Le Bel'Vue* (L.F.), av. du Bourg, ☎ 74.89.77.56, AE
Visa, 8 rm Ⓟ ⅏ ⚒ ♪ 140. Rest. ♦♦ ⟜ ♪ ⴵ closed Mon and
Sun eve. Spec : *beignets de foie gras, poissons croûte de
gros sel, pièce de bœuf à la moelle*, 70-180 ; child : 50.

PONTCHARRA-SUR-TURDINE, ✉ 69490, 6 km E.

Hotel :
★★ *France*, 27, rue Michelet, ☎ 74.05.72.97, 12 rm Ⓟ
closed Nov, 180. Rest. ♦ closed Wed (l.s.), 80-130.

⚐ ★★★*Municipal* (40 pl), ☎ 74.63.26.80.

THIZY, ✉ 69240, 27 km NE.
ℹ 28, rue Jean-Jaurès, ☎ 74.64.03.84.

Hotel :
★★ *La Musardière*, 12, rue du Bois-Sémé, ☎ 74.64.03.15,
Euro Visa, 11 rm Ⓟ ⅏ ⚒ closed Sun eve and Mon lunch,
15 Dec-15 Jan, 140. Rest. ♦ 70-150.

Recommended
♥ liqueurs : Croizet.

VIOLAY, ✉ 42780, 11 km SE of **Pontcharra-sur-Turdine**.

Hotel :
★★ *Poirier* (L.F.), pl. de l'Église, ☎ 74.63.91.01, AE DC
Euro Visa, 15 rm ⚒ ⅏ closed Feb, 160. Rest. ♦ ♪ closed
Sat, 60-110.

TRÉVOUX*

Lyon 28, Bourg-en-Bresse 51, Paris 448 km
pop 5055 ✉ 01600   B2
Former capital of the principality of Dombes, a pleasure-craft port on the river Saône.

▶ Medieval streets ; mansions facing the river ; **Government Palace**. ▶ Old **pharmacy** in hospital grounds.
▶ Town Hall ▶ historical **museum-library** (Trévoux newspaper collection★ ; Jesuit dictionary. ▶ 11th-12thC **fortified castle** : view from octagonal tower.

Nearby

▶ **Ars-sur-Formans** *(9 km NE)* : pilgrimages to the former presbytery of a popular priest, Jean-Baptiste Vianney (1786-1859, canonized 1925) : basilica *(Mar.-Sep.)*.
▶ Toward Ambérieux (rose gardens), road crosses the
TGV high-speed train line.

Saône Valley, upstream

▶ **Saint-Bernard** : château belonged to the painter Maurice Utrillo. ▶ **Jassans-Riottier** (3 380) : Romanesque
church. ▶ Via Fareins *(14 km)*, 17thC **château de Fléchères**★ in a deer park *(Sat., Sun., hols., Jul.-Sep.)*. ▶ **Mont-**

merle-sur-Saône *(21 km ;* pop. 2 023). ▶ **Thoissey** *(35 km ;*
pop. 1 421) : old pharmacy in former hospital.   ☐

Practical Information ——————————

TRÉVOUX
ℹ 26, Grande-Rue, ☎ 74.00.17.46.
SNCF ☎ 74.00.08.18.

Hotel :
★ *Gare* (L.F.), ☎ 74.00.12.42, Visa, 7 rm ⅏ ⅏ closed
Mon eve and Tue, Jul, 120. Rest. ♦ 70-120.

⚐ ★★★★*La Petite Saône* (200 pl), ☎ 74.00.14.16.

Nearby

ARS-SUR-FORMANS, ✉ 01480 Jassans-Riottier, 9 km N.E.
ℹ mairie, ☎ 74.00.71.84.

Hotel :
★★ *Régina* (L.F.), ☎ 74.00.73.67, Tx 305767, Euro Visa,
31 rm Ⓟ ⚒ ⅏ closed 15 Nov-15 Mar, 160. Rest. ♦ ⴵ 60.

Recommended
Events : *son et lumière*, Jul-Sep.

JASSANS-RIOTTIER, ✉ 01480, 6 km N.

Restaurant :
♦ *Auberge Bressane*, rue de l'Octroi, Beauregard,
☎ 74.60.93.92, Visa ⟜ ⅏ closed Tue eve and Wed,
60-180.

⚐ ★★★*Ideal Camping* (400 pl), ☎ 74.65.95.44.

MONTMERLE-SUR-SAÔNE, ✉ 01090, 15 km N.

Hotel :
★★ *Castel de Valrose*, 12, bd de la République,
☎ 74.69.30.52, Visa, 7 rm ⅏ ⚒ half pens (h.s.), closed
Sun eve and Mon, 4 Jan-3 Feb, 650. Rest. ♦♦ ♪ Spec :
*ragoût de queues d'écrevisses, noix de ris de veau en
papillotes, filet de loup au coulis d'épinards*, 115-250.

⚐ ★★★★*Municipal* (440 pl), ☎ 74.69.34.40.

THOISSEY, ✉ 01140, 35 km.

Hotel :
● ★★★★ *Chapon Fin* (R.C.), ☎ 74.04.04.74, 25 rm Ⓟ ⅏
⚒ 350. Rest. ● ♦♦ closed Tue (l.s.), 7 Jan-7 Feb. The
culinary crossroads of the Bresse, Beaujolais and Dombes regions : *fricassée de volailles aux morilles à la
crème, crêpes Parmentier*, 175-250.

⚐ ★★★★*Plage* (440 pl), ☎ 74.04.02.97.

VILLEFRANCHE-SUR-SAÔNE

Lyon 31, Mâcon 41, Paris 436 km
pop 29066 ✉ 69400   B1-2
Walled town founded in the 12thC by the lords of
Beaujeu ; 15thC capital of Beaujolais (→), today a
centre for the cotton industry and the wine trade.

▶ **Rue Nationale** *(N6)* bordered for 3 km by **14th-16thC
houses** : Nos. 83, 142, 144, 196 (Renaissance, former
Town Hall), 202, 793, 831 (former prison). ▶ Church
12th-16thC.   ☐

Practical Information ——————————

VILLEFRANCHE-SUR-SAÔNE
ℹ 290, rue de Thizy, ☎ 74.68.05.18.
SNCF 113, pl. de la Gare, ☎ 74.65.27.16.
Car rental : Avis, 83, rue P.-Berthier, ☎ 74.68.08.43.

Hotels :
★★★★ *Château de Chervinges* (C.H.), Chervinges Gleize,
3 km (dir. Roanne), ☎ 74.65.29.76, Tx 380772, AE DC
Euro Visa, 17 rm Ⓟ ⟜ ⚒ ⅏ ⚒ ☐ ♪ closed 2 Jan-28 Feb,
1200. Rest. ♦♦ ⅏ closed Mon and Sun eve (l.s.). Spec :
*noisettes de grenouilles à la crème de ciboulette, aiguil-
lettes de canard sauce bigarade*, 150-275.
★★★ *Plaisance*, 96, av. de la Libération, ☎ 74.65.33.52,
Tx 375746, AE DC Euro Visa, 68 rm Ⓟ ♪ closed

24 Dec-2 Jan, 240. Rest. ♦ ♪ ᕕ closed Sun, 15 Dec-2 Jan, 70-200.
★★ *Paris-Nice*, 573, rue d'Anse, ☎ 74.65.36.95, 12 rm Ⓟ closed Sun and year-end hols, 120.
★ *Bourgogne*, 91, rue Stalingrad, ☎ 74.65.06.42, AE Euro Visa, 18 rm, 125.

Restaurants :
♦♦♦ *Auberge du Faisan Doré*, Le Pont-de-Beauregard, 2 km N, ☎ 74.65.01.66, AE DC Euro Visa Ⓟ ⚏ ♪ closed Mon and Sun eve, Aug, 160-200.
♦♦ *Fontaine Bleue*, 18, rue Jean-Moulin, ☎ 74.68.10.37, Tx 375746, AE Euro Visa Ⓟ ᕦ ♪ ᕕ closed Sun, 15 Dec-6 Jan. Spec : *éventail de langouste et foie gras, turbotin poché à la verveine, magret de canard au vinaigre de framboise*, 75-180.

⏶ ★★★*Municipal* (125 pl), ☎ 74.65.33.48.

Recommended
Guide to wines : *Union Inter-prof. des Vins du Beaujolais*, 210, bd Vermorel, ☎ 74.65.45.55.

Nearby

BEAUREGARD, ⊠ 01480 Jassans-Riottier, 3 km NE on the D 44.

Restaurant :
♦♦ *Auberge Bressane*, rue de l'Octroi, ☎ 74.60.93.92, Euro Visa Ⓟ ᕦ ⚏ ᕕ closed Tue eve and Wed, 25 Nov-17 Dec. Shady, blooming terrace overlooking the river. Spec : *tournedos aux morilles, mousseline froide de saumon et Saint-Jacques*, 60-160 ; child : 30.

YZERON*

Lyon 28, Saint-Etienne 52, Paris 483 km
pop 590 ⊠ 69510 Thurins   A2
Small resort at medium altitude (700 m) on a crag (orientation map behind church ; excursions ; mountain-climbing) ; during the 19thC, an important production centre for velvet (150 looms in a village of 800 people). **Châteauvieux** *(2.5 km)* : farms, megaliths, ruined Roman aqueduct.

Lyonnais Mountains

▶ **Luère Pass** *(10 km NE ;* alt. 714 m) : view★. ▶ Below, **Pollionnay**★ (pop. 1 088) : 15thC fortified house, Renaissance church, square tower on Romanesque château *(exhibitions in summer)*. ▶ W via Duerne *(8 km)*, at alt. 830 m, **Sainte-Foy-l'Argentière** *(15 km ;* pop. 1 188) in Brévennes Valley★. ▶ Farther N, **Haute-Rivoire**★, old village. ▶ S, **Saint-Martin-en-Haut** *(8 km ;* alt. 736 m ; pop. 2 969) : traces of Roman roads, ruined château de Rollefort *(1.5 km)*. ▶ **St. André Peak** *(5 km farther,* alt. 937 m, *footpath)* : highest point in the Lyonnais Mountains (panorama). □

Maine, Anjou

Unlike their counterparts in Touraine, the stately manors and châteaux of the Anjou region have deserted the banks of the River Loire to hide away instead in the countryside around Angers, in romantic parks or melancholy splendour beside the region's tiny lakes. At the château du Lude on summer evenings, jousting matches, pavanes and minuets illuminated by a thousand lights bring the past to life again; during the day the tourist can confirm Maine's claim to possess the largest number of inhabited châteaux and manorhouses in France, as he peers down country lanes to discover signs of life.

But alongside this past, full of historical associations and imaginary deeds of valor, there is another more concrete reality — the countryside itself and its regional differences : the Loire Valley full of orchards and flower gardens, the sunny charm of local vineyards and dark brooding stretches of mushroom beds. The vineyards of Layon produce wine as mild as the landscape itself, before giving way to the bristling hedgerows and narrow paths of Mauges and Le Choletais where Royalist and Republican armies laid bloody ambushes for each other in the days of the Revolution. Further on is the Vendée, a landscape of heather and gorse, alternating with rich meadowland and peacefully grazing herds of cattle.

The town of Anjou on the Maine River is famous for its produce market — fruit, vegetables and local wine — and boasts possession of the Apocalypse tapestry, woven between 1373 and 1380, as well as a museum displaying its modern counterpart, Jean Lurçat's Song of the World, woven from the master's sketches between 1957 and 1966.

To the north, between Brittany and Normandy, the Maine region has all the charm of the traditional French countryside : thick groves alternating with wheat fields and dark pine forests. Black and white cows and plump piglets forage peacefully in the shade of apple trees in bloom. With its signposted tracks and country roads, and its miles of tranquil waterways and locks, Maine is perfect for tourists who are allergic to crowds. □

● Don't miss

★★★ Angers A3, Fontevraud-l'Abbaye B4, Le Mans B2, Saumur B3.

★★ Bercé Forest C2, Évron B1.

★ The Alpes Mancelles B1, the Angevine Corniche A3, Bazouges-sur-le-Loir B2-3, Champtoceaux A3, Château-Gontier A2, La Flèche B2, Laval A1, Le Lude B2-3, Valley of the Mayenne A1, Montreuil-Bellay B4, Montsoreau B4, Saint-Calais C2, Saint-Florent-le-Vieil A3, Segré A2.

Weekend tips

From Angers there are two outstanding tours which take in most of the region. The first (the Loire and the Coteaux de Layon) takes you up the Loire to the white town of Montsoreau, a good place for lunch before going on to Fontevraud and Montreuil-Bellay along the minor roads of the Layon Valley.
The second circuit covers the area of Haute (Upper) Maine; from Angers to Sablé (→), via the famous château of Plessis-Bourré (→ Angers). From Sablé, the country roads pass by hidden manor-houses and secluded villages; Asnières-sur-Vègre, Malicorne (lunch), Gallerande, etc.

Maine farmhouse

House in Anjou

Tufa built house

● *Brief regional history*

Up to the Roman Conquest
Traditionally, the first men in Maine and Anjou are supposed to have appeared in the **Palaeolithic** (Saulges Caves) and **Neolithic** periods respectively. ● Maine and Anjou, corresponding to the Gallic regions of *Aulerques* and *Andécaves*, enter history with Caesar's conquests. ● From this point on, **Vindinium** (Le Mans) and **Noviodunum** (Jublains) became important crossroads, while Angers — former capital of the Andécaves — developed into **Juliomagus,** a substantial Roman city with heated baths, a theatre and an amphitheatre.

9th-11thC
During the 9thC century, Maine and Anjou were invaded by the **Normans** and the **Bretons.** ● During the second half of the 9thC, the **Count of Angers,** Robert the Strong, fought off the Normans and bequeathed the County of Angers to his son Robert, briefly king of France. He in turn installed a viscount, **Ingelger,** who founded the first Angevin dynasty. Maine too became a hereditary county in 955 (Hugues 1st), but its

overlordship was disputed by the Dukes of Normandy and the Counts of Anjou. ● The greatest of the region's medieval overlords was without doubt **Fulk Nerra** (970-1040), who waged unremitting war on his neighbours well into his old age. With his son **Geoffroi Martel,** he extended Anjou to cover Mauges (→ Cholet), Saumur, part of Touraine, Vendôme and Maine. He is reputed to have been violent, greedy, ambitious

and unscrupulous, with sudden accessions of Christian humility (leading him on one occasion to make a penitential pilgrimage to Jerusalem) and to shower churches and convents with endowments. He built some twenty fortresses in Anjou and Touraine.

12th-14thC

Marriages and alliances played an essential role in the ascent of the House of Anjou. One of its sons, **Geoffroi V the Handsome** (1113-51), who carried a sprig of broom in his hat *(genêt, hence plante à genêt),* married Matilda, daughter of Henry I of England. Their descendants took the name of Plantagenêt, and the son, Henry, married Eleanor of Aquitaine in 1152. Two years later, he acceded to the throne of England as Henry II Plantagenêt. ● Anjou then became part

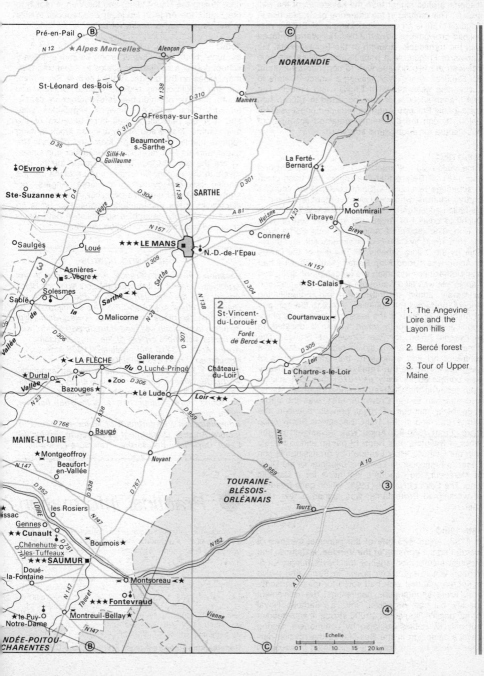

1. The Angevine Loire and the Layon hills

2. Bercé forest

3. Tour of Upper Maine

of an empire which included England, Normandy, Brittany, Aquitaine and Gascony. ● The 12thC was also the great epoch of **Angevin architecture** (church at Cunault, abbey of Fontevraud). In 1130, the first ogive vault appeared in the tower of St. Aubin at Angers. Angevin ingenuity was to devise a new approach to the problem of vaulted structures, the domed **Angevin** (or Plantagenêt) **vault**, with the keystone of the diagonal arches higher than the keystones of the wall arches. The vaulting in the cathedral of St. Maurice in Angers (1150) is an excellent example. ● But the vassal had grown more powerful than his overlord; faced with the formidable strength of the Plantagenêts, the Capets of France cut a poor figure. Political struggle between the two houses was to continue throughout the Hundred Years' War, leaving a legacy of strife to succeeding generations of English and French. The first French success of note occurred in 1205, when the capable **Philippe Auguste** regained possession of Anjou, though the suzerainty remained an object of hot dispute for a long time afterward.

15th-17thC
Thus, Anjou did not enter the French camp for good until 1481. ● Before that, the region had been given in appanage by Louis IX (Saint Louis) to his younger brother **Charles**, who was however more interested in his Italian adventures. Subsequently it was given as a Duchy to Louis I of Anjou, the younger son of Jean le Bon. The crown of Anjou was thus borne from the 13th-15thC by Capets of direct descent, and thereafter by the Valois dynasty. ● The last of the Dukes of Anjou was **"Good King René"** (1409-80), who had many other titles including the kingships of Sicily and Naples. He was also Count of Provence and, although extremely active in improving and embellishing Angers, preferred the sunshine of Aix to the soft airs of Anjou — or such is the reason given for his philosophical retreat south when Louis XI decided to repossess Anjou for the Crown of France. The dynasty of Valois-Anjou did in fact make Angers a centre of art and education; the famous series of hangings known as the **Tapisseries de l'Apocalypse** was completed as early as 1376; they can still be seen today in the Château of Angers (→). ● Maine, also attached to the Crown in 1481, was the appanage of a number of royal princes between the 16th-17thC, and in the 18thC became a Duchy once more. From 1560-98, Anjou was devastated by the **Wars of Religion**, until **Henri IV** put an end to trouble with the Catholic "Holy League", by promising his son César to Françoise de Lorraine, daughter of the Duke of Mercoeur, the League's last hope for a Catholic king. The Edict of Nantes (1598), which gave freedom of worship to Protestants, was signed a few days later.

18th-19thC
In 1793, Anjou was one of the principal theatres of war during the **uprising of the Vendée**, a Catholic and Royalist insurrection against the Revolutionary Convention which had taken power in Paris, and which in February of that year had voted for mass conscription. From spontaneous beginnings, the movement quickly became organized into a "Catholic Royal Army" (the Whites) some 40 000 strong. It was headed not only by nobles but also by commoners. During Laval's campaign in the Bas-Maine, the royalist partisans were for the first time nicknamed **"Chouans"**,

from the call of the tawny owl *(le chat-huant)* which they adopted as a rallying cry. After capturing a number of towns (including Angers) in surprise attacks, the Whites were defeated by the Republican armies (the Blues) at Cholet, Le Mans and Savenay (Dec. 1793). Guerilla resistance continued until the offensive launched by Hoche in 1796. ● After losing the Mayenne region in the North (Bas-Maine; Sarthe constituting the Haut-Maine) and the Vienne region to the South, the Angevin kingdom was reduced in size to the department of **Maine-et-Loire.**

20thC
In June 1940, the Cadets from Saumur's military school put up a spirited resistance to advancing German troops on the bridges of the Loire. ● Since then, like the neighbouring regions around Orléans and Tours, the Vale of Anjou has settled into more peaceful agricultural activities; flowers, vegetables, wine and fruit do particularly well here because of the mild climate. Maine and Anjou are also stock farming regions (cattle, pigs, sheep, goats and poultry). The cattle markets — Craon, Château-Gontier and Cholet — are the principal points of assembly for the little towns in the region. ● Angers and Le Mans are the leading industrial centres of the area; Angers, formerly a slate and umbrella producer, has now added electronics to its manufacturing capacities, while Le Mans is, suitably enough, a specialist in both insurance and automobile production (Renault).

Facts and figures

Location : *in western France, Anjou is joined to the Armorican Massif to the west ("Anjou Noir", or Black Anjou) and the Parisian Basin in the east ("Anjou Blanc", or White Anjou, and the Vale of Anjou). A distinction is also made between Bas (lower) Maine with its heavy Armorican soil, and Haut (upper) Maine, with its lighter soil more typical of the Parisian Basin.*
Area : *Anjou : 7 218 km²; Maine : 11 456 km².*
Population : *1 451 873 inhabitants.*
Climate : *The Vale (Val) of Anjou has an especially warm, dry climate, ideal for delicate crops. Mediterranean plants, such as magnolias and palm trees are to be found here. Maine has a somewhat harsher, moist climate.*
Administration : *Department of Maine-et-Loire, Prefecture Angers. Department of Mayenne, Prefecture Laval. Department of Sarthe, Prefecture Le Mans.*

 Practical information

Information : *Comité Régional du Tourisme (C.R.T.) Pays de Loire*, pl. du Commerce, 44000 Nantes, ☎ 40.48.15.45 or 40.48.24.20. **Maine-et-Loire :** *Comité Départemental du Tourisme (C.D.T.)*, B.P. 2148, pl. Kennedy, 49021 Angers Cedex, ☎ 41.88.23.85. **Mayenne :** *C.D.T.*, 84, av. R.-Burron, 53000 Laval, ☎ 43.53.18.18. **Sarthe :** *C.D.T.* and *D.D.T.*, Hôtel du Département, 2, rue des Maillets, 72040 Le Mans Cedex, ☎ 43.81.72.72. *Dir. régionale de la Jeunesse et des Sports*, château de l'Éraudière, chemin de l'Éraudière, B.P. 936, 44075 Nantes Cedex, ☎ 40.49.41.24. *Dir. rég. des Affaires culturelles*, 2, allée du Cdt-Charcot, 44035 Nantes Cedex, ☎ 40.29.32.55.

Reservations : *Loisirs-Accueil Mayenne, see C.D.T.*

S.O.S. : Maine-et-Loire : *S.A.M.U.* (Emergency Medical Service), ☎ 41.48.44.22. **Sarthe :** *S.A.M.U.,* ☎ 43.23.23.23. *Poisoning emergency centre :* Angers, ☎ 41.48.21.21.

Weather forecast : Maine-et-Loire, ☎ 41.43.66.66. **Mayenne,** ☎ 43.53.43.82. **Sarthe,** ☎ 43.72.02.02.

Farmhouse gîtes and chambres d'hôtes : *Relais départementaux des Gîtes ruraux :* cf. *C.D.T.*

Holiday villages : Maine-et-Loire : La Pommeraye, **Mayenne :** *V.V.F.,* Sainte-Suzanne, ☎ 43.01.40.76.

Camping car rental : Maine-et-Loire, *ELS,* 169, rue de Lorraine, 49300 Cholet, ☎ 41.62.41.42. **Sarthe :** *Loire Evasion,* 1, bd Pasteur, 42700 Allonnes, ☎ 43.80.43.59.

Cultural, folklore and sporting events : Mar : *prytannées* in La Flèche ; *fête des lances* (historical pageant) in Champagne. **Apr :** *motorcycle grand prix* in Le Mans. **May :** *music festival* in Laval ; *hunt festival* and *24-hr motorcycle race* in Le Mans. **Jun :** *24-hr auto race* in Le Mans. **Jul :** *Anjou festival* in Angers ; *Lion in wooden shoes* in Lion-d'Angers ; *election of the Duchess of Anjou* in La Ménitré ; *international folklore festival* in La Ferté-Bernard ; *"carrousel du Cadre noir"* (precision horse troops) in Saumur. **Jul-Aug :** *animated son et lumière* in Le Lude ; *festival* in Sablé ; *fête de la Saint-Fiacre* in Château-Gontier. **Sep :** *worldwide music and folklore festival* in Angers ; *dragster races, karting championships* in Le Mans ; *equestrian fortnight* in Saumur ; *horse racing* in Craon. **Oct :** *book festival* and *24-hr truck race* in Le Mans.

Fairs and markets : mid-Feb : *wine fairs* in Chalonnes-sur-Loire, Saumur. **End Mar :** *spring fair* in Le Mans, *meat fair* in Évron. **Sep :** *international medicinal plant market* in Chemille.

Rambling and hiking : topoguides. G.R. 35, 36, 3, 235, 365. Enq at *Délégation dép. de la Féd. Nat. de Randonnée Pédestre :* M. Jenez, rés. des Moulins de l'Huisne, apt. 632, rue des Sablés-d'Or, 72000 Le Mans, ☎ 43.23.25.99, and *C.D.T. Maine-et-Loire.*

Cycling holidays : Circuits organized by the *C.D.T.* along the banks of the Erve, through the Loir Valley and in the Baugeois, with lodgings in chambres d'hôtes. French Railways *(S.N.C.F.),* one of the organizers of this operation, offers a 30 % reduction on certain trains. *Voyages Conseil,* bd de Coubertin, 49000 Angers, ☎ 41.68.19.33.

River and canal cruises : a 250-km network on the Maine, the Mayenne, the Oudon and the Sarthe. Info. : *Service commun de réservation du Bassin de la Maine,* B.P. 2207, 49022 Angers Cedex, ☎ 41.88.99.38. River cruises : *Sablésien,* quai National, 72300 Sablé, ☎ 43.95.14.42. Navigation in flat-bottomed barges : *Brilhaut Plaisance,* 137, rue de Bretagne, 53000 Laval, ☎ 43.81.72.72.

Riding holidays : enq. at *Assn Dép. du Tourisme équestre,* B.P. 852, 49008 Angers Cedex, and *la Poitevinière,* Saumur ; *la Métairie,* Trèves-Cunault, 49350 Gennes, ☎ 41.51.85.25 ; *Forest trails :* office national des forêts, 13, av. Gal-de-Gaulle, 72000 Le Mans, ☎ 43.24.44.70. Horse-hire : *la Groué,* Sillé-le-Guillaume, ☎ 43.20.11.91. Blacksmiths in Lavaré, ☎ 43.93.68.33, and Courtillers, ☎ 43.95.33.02. Brochure at *C.D.T. Sarthe.*

Scenic railways : *Connerré-Plan d'eau de Tuffé-Prévelles-Bonnétable line* (18 km) : M. Blanchard, ☎ 43.28.65.03. M. Terrieux, ☎ 43.21.47.59. M. Lecomte, ☎ 43.29.06.17 ; *train-hire possible. Semur-en-Vallon :* 1st Sun May-end Sep, ☎ 43.93.07.50. *Sillé-le-Guillaume,* around the big lake at Sillé-Plage (20 km), weekends, Easter-Sep, Jul, Aug every day, ☎ 43.97.04.36.

Handicraft courses : pottery in Saint-Jean-sur-Erve, ☎ 43.01.28.23, and Parce-sur-Sarthe, ☎ 43.95.82.60 ; weaving in Ligron, ☎ 43.94.41.54 ; wood-working in Viviers-en-Charnie, ☎ 43.01.45.76 ; wrought iron in Évron, ☎ 43.01.93.48.

Other courses : summer university at the priory of Vivoin (200 places), 1 Jul.-3 Sep. : weaving, flute, cham-

Produce of Maine and Anjou

There is no lack of gastronomic specialities in this region. Various forms of potted meat — rillettes — are produced, especially around Le Mans and Connerré. Rillettes are usually made from pork, but also from goose or rabbit. Le Mans' famous capons are gastronomic rivals of the poulardes — fatted pullets — of La Flèche.

Excellent Reinette apples come from the Sarthe, Montfort-le-Rotrou and Le Mans (the Maine-et-Loire Department is in fact France's leading apple producer).

Freshwater fish — eel, pike, gudgeon — are prepared in typical local style, such as roulade d'anguille (with eel), and various fish pâtés and fried dishes.

The cattle of Maine-Anjou produce very succulent beef, and cul-de-veau à l'angevine is a celebrated regional dish.

The wines of Anjou

Tradition has it that the vineyards of Anjou were introduced by the Gauls. In any case, they have been largely honoured by royalty, and the Plantagenêts, Lords of Anjou and Kings of England, always remained faithful to the wines of their homeland. The whites are made from the Chenin Blanc grape or the Pineau de la Loire, and the reds from the Cabernet Franc and to a lesser extent the Gamay. As for the rosés, they are made principally from Cabernet Franc and Cabernet Sauvignon grapes.

Whites : the wines from the right bank of the Loire (coteau de Savennières) are dry, firm and vigorous, while those from the left bank (crus de Layon) are full-bodied, plump and fruity. The coteaux de l'Aubance are drier than those of Layon with an excellent earthy taste. Among the whites we must also mention the coteaux de Saumur, light and dry, vigorous and perfumed ; some of these wines are transformed into sparkling wine ; the best carry the mention "Tête de cuvée". For a long time the "great" wine of Anjou was the white, but the reds and rosés are now gaining ground.

Among the **rosés** the Rosé d'Anjou is distinguished from the Cabernet d'Anjou, the former being lively and fruity (demi-sec and dry) and the latter, like the Cabernet de Saumur, fine and delicate.

The **reds,** principally coteaux de Saumur ("grand cru": Champigny) are substantial and full-bodied.

ber orchestra, rural discovery, choral singing and direction, classical guitar, theatre ; enq : *Délégation dép. à l'animation culturelle,* hôtel du Département, pl. A.-Briand, 72000 Le Mans, ☎ 43.81.72.72.

Wine guide : *Conseil inter-professionnel des Vins d'Anjou et de Saumur,* 21, bd Foch, 49000 Angers, ☎ 41.87.62.57.

Water skiing : Ingrandes-sur-Loire, ☎ 41.41.40.05. Château-Gontier, on the Mayenne, with a 37-acre stretch of water, ☎ 43.07.97.24. Daon, town hall, ☎ 43.07.14.10.

Sailing, wind-surfing : enq. at *Délégation Dép. de la Jeunesse et des Sports :* **Maine-et-Loire,** Cité administrative, 49043 Angers Cedex, ☎ 41.66.21.32. **Mayenne,** 26, rue Mortier, 53000 Laval, ☎ 43.53.51.81. **Sarthe,** rue Chanzy, 72000 Le Mans, ☎ 43.84.97.84.

Canoeing and Kayaking : Maine lake, ☎ 41.48.57.01; Saumur, ☎ 41.51.03.06; Seiches-sur-Loir, ☎ 41.50.20.27; Laval, ☎ 43.56.08.65; Mayenne, ☎ 43.04.19.37; Daon, ☎ 43.07.14.10; La Flèche, ☎ 43.94.00.26 and see *C.D.T. Sarthe.*

Golf : Arnage-Le Mans (18 holes); Angers-Saint-Jean-des-Mauvrets (9 holes); Laval-Le Jariel (9 holes).

Motoring : advanced courses for race-drivers (auto and motorcycle), enq. : *Automobile-Club de l'Ouest (A.C.O.), Circuit des 24 Heures,* 72040 Le Mans Cedex, ☎ 43.72.50.25.

Mountaineering : *Club Alpin (C.A.F.),* 17, rue Marengo, 72000 Le Mans (excursions in the nearby Mancelles "Alpes").

Hang-gliding : Angers-Avrillé airport, ☎ 41.34.61.57; *Union aéronautique des Mauges,* Cholet, ☎ 41.62.30.43; *aéro-club de Saumur-Terrefort,* ☎ 41.50.20.27 (parachuting); *aérodrome Laval-Entrammes,* ☎ 43.53.71.30.

Hunting and shooting : enq. at the *Féd. dép. des chasseurs.* **Maine-et-Loire** : 9, rue L.-Gain, 49000 Angers, ☎ 41.88.25.04. **Mayenne** : 30, rue Mazagran, 53000 Laval, ☎ 43.53.09.32. **Sarthe** : 1, rue Bruyère, 72000 Le Mans, ☎ 43.82.21.46.

Fishing : enq at the town halls *(mairies),* at the *S.I., C.D.T.,* and at the Maine-et-Loire *Fédération de Pêche et Pisciculture,* 12, rue Grandet, 49000 Angers, ☎ 41.87.57.09. In Laval, special area for handicapped anglers (enq. : *S.I.*).

 Towns and places

The ALPES-MANCELLES*

B1

From Saint-Léonard-des-Bois to Mont des Avaloirs *(20 km, 2 hr).*

The "Alpes Mancelles" turn out to be a mountain area, not very extensive, but wild and charming. Here the Sarthe meanders at its pleasure through deep granite gorges amid gorse and broom.

▶ **Saint-Léonard-des-Bois★** (pop. 512), overlooked by rocky escarpments, on a bend in the river; numerous walks (GR 36 & 36A), especially in the **Vallée de Misère★** *(1hr45 on foot round trip).* ▶ **Saint-Céneri-le-Gérei★** *(D146, 5 km N),* equally appealing with its old bridge and older Romanesque church (14thC fresco★). ▶ **Mont des Avaloirs★** *(D144 for 12.5 km then 2 km right) :* highest point in the W of France (alt. 417 m); a worthwhile complement to this walk is the **Corniche du Pail★** *(leave from Pré-en-Pail, 5 km NW of Mont des Avaloirs),* through the valley of the Mayenne, with views of the Normandy hills. ☐

Practical Information

SAINT-LÉONARD-DES-BOIS, ✉ 72590, 19 km SW of Alençon.
ⓘ mairie, ☎ 43.97.23.75.

Hotel :
★★★ *Touring,* (Mapotel), ☎ 43.97.28.03, AE DC Euro Visa, 53 rm ℙ ⫷ ▩ ⟲ ♿ closed 15 Nov-15 Feb, 225. Rest. ♦♦ ⫷ ♪ ♿ ➰ closed Fri eve and Sat (15 Oct-1 Apr), 15 Nov-15 Feb. Spec : crayfish sauteed in wine 75-200.

⚠ ★★*Municipal* (66 pl), ☎ 43.97.28.10.

ANGERS***

Nantes 89, Poitiers 133, Paris 289 km
pop 141143 ✉ 49000   A3

With its blue roofs and red chimneys, the town of Angers is far friendlier than its formidable fortress of grey crystalline schist would lead you to believe. The capital of Anjou, Angers is also a centre for flowers and for the arts; this tradition dates back to King René of Sicily (1409-80), last and most cultivated of the Counts of Anjou, who had a green thumb and a wide education. Today an important market for the fruits, vegetables and wines of Anjou, Angers is also an industrial centre. Traditional Angevin activities such as slate-quarrying and umbrella manufacture now co-exist with modern electronics and computer facilities.

▶ **Château★★** (B2). This powerful fortress, flanked with 17 huge round towers, was the keystone of a chain of fortifications erected in the 11thC by the famous Fulk Nerra, Count of Anjou, for defense against the neighbouring Count of Blois. Under Saint Louis (Louis IX, 1215-70), the château was rebuil in grey schist on sandstone and granite foundations. Fine **collection of tapestries★★★** (14th-17thC), especially the **"Apocalypse"★★★**, a masterpiece which influenced many later medieval tapestries. The "Apocalypse" is housed in the specially-built Long Gallery (→ box). Other fine tapestries in the Royal Apartments (Logis Royal; Tenture de la Passion★ , end 15thC) and the Governor's Apartments (Logis du Gouverneur; *9:30-12 & 2-6:30 in summer, 10-12 & 2-5:30 in winter).* In the courtyard the chapel of Yolande d'Aragon (15thC, Angevin vaulting★). ▶ Between the château and the cathedral, the old city; narrow, quiet streets, stately doorways. ▶ The two tall steeples of the **Cathedral of St. Maurice** (B-C2; beautiful 12th-13thC Gothic architecture) were rebuilt during the last century. Magnificent doorway decorated with Biblical characters (17thC door leaves) leads to a broad nave (16.38m across, the widest of French cathedral naves), illuminated, left, by rare 12thC stained glass. The heavily-domed vaults are characteristic of Angevin (Anjou) architecture. An astonishing St. Christopher with a dog's head can be made out in the superb stained glass of the choir (13thC); rich treasure-room *(closed Tue.).* ▶ The **Logis Louis Barrault** dates from the same period ; Caesar Borgia (15thC, son of Pope Alexander de Médicis (Henri IV's queen, 1573-1642) stayed here. Today it houses a **Fine Arts Museum** : works of the primitives, canvases from 17th-18thC incl. Watteau, Lancret, Fragonard *(10-12 & 2-5; closed hols.).* In the former Toussaint Abbey, new **David d'Angers Museum** (C3; works of P.-J. David, 1788-1856). ▶ The **St. Aubin Tower** is the belfry of the former abbey; the buildings were reconstructed in the 17thC and now house the Prefecture; magnificently sculpted Romanesque arcades★. ▶ Nearby, the **church of St. Martin** (11th-12thC) marks the site of a Merovingian sanctuary. ▶ A number of pedestrians-only streets with bistros and restaurants are centred around the **Place du Ralliement** (C2). Theatre, department stores and a covered shopping arcade make this the busy heart of the town. ▶ The **Pincé Mansion★** (Hôtel Pincé, C2), Renaissance : two collections are on show here : one of Egyptian, Greek and Roman antiquities, the other, Chinese and Japanese *objets d'art* known as the Turpin de Crissé Museum *(10-12 & 2-6; closed Mon. and nat. hols.).* ▶ Lovers of tapestry will cross the Maine to see the **Jean Lurçat Museum** in the former **Hospital of St. Jean★★** (B1). Built between 1180 and 1210, this is one of the most beautiful buildings of its type in France *(10-12 & 2-6; closed Mon. and nat. hols.).* Under the airy vaulting in the former patients' ward flame the colours of the **Chant du Monde★★** (Song of the World), a magnificent ten-piece tapestry executed at the Gobelins works in Paris (1957-66) from the designs of Jean Lurçat. See also the

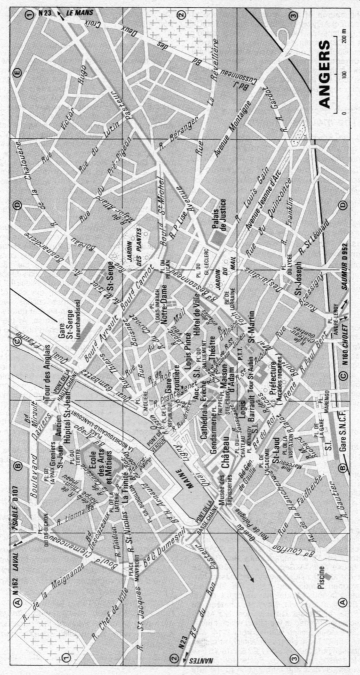

cloister (12thC) and the chapel (13thC). ▶ Formerly the land-owning and aristocratic area of the town; the ancient **abbey of Le Ronceray** (now housing the National School of Arts and Crafts) still has a Romanesque church in Poitevin (Poitiers) style. The **church of La Trinité★** (B1-2), 12thC, was also a dependency of this abbey. ▶ The **Place**

de la Laiterie (B1), center of the Doutre quarter, is an agreeable lace to stroll, among the old 15th-18thC town houses.

The arrow (→) is a reference to another entry.

▶ **Also...** ▶ The **church of St. Serge** (C1) has one of France's most perfect Angevin Gothic choirs (early 13thC). Then there are gardens of which Angers is justly proud : **Jardin du Mail** (D-C2), **Jardin des Plantes★** (D2), **Jardin des Beaux-Arts**, Boulevard du Roi-René, **Arboretum** and the **Parc de la Garenne** overlooking lake St. Nicolas. ▶ W, the **leisure park** on the Lake of Maine (1 km²). ▶ Finally, near the station (B3) the **Parc des Haras** has some interesting exhibition rooms and craft workshops.

The moulins caviers

In addition to the smock-mill, which has a conical wooden roof turning to the wind, and the post-mill, where the entire mill turns, there exists also in Anjou a local variant, in which the post-mill is mounted on a masonry base which is vaulted to make cellars for storage. Its silhouette is easily recognizable : from the stone and earth foundations, a conical tower rises into the sky, carrying the mechanism and the four great sails. Two beams, which also serve as a ladder, are used to turn the mill. Unlikely as it may seem, the moulins-caviers of Anjou are alive and well ; an association, Les Amis des Moulins, sees to their restoration. Several are already back in use. For information (in French) : tel. 41.88.82.23.

Nearby

▶ **Avrillé** *(5 km NW)* is restoring its *moulins caviers* (→ box), typical Angevin windmills ; **château de la Perrière** (17thC). ▶ **Trélazé** *(8 km E)* has covered a good part of the roofs of France with its famous slate. Today the slate is mined underground, but you can visit the old excavations and the see how the "Perreyeux", the old slate miners, lived. Slate (ardoise) museum *(May-Sep., 9-12 & 2-6)*. ▶ **Les Ponts-de-Cé** *(8 km S)* : Musée des Coiffes (Bonnet museum ; *daily Jul.-Aug. 3-6 ; Sep.-Oct., Sat. and Sun.)*.

The châteaux of Anjou *(within 24 km of Angers)*

▶ **Château du Plessis-Macé★** *(13 km NW)* : 15thC, Angevin to the last detail *(10-12 & 2-6:30 Jul.-Sep. ; 1:30-6, Mar.-Jun. and Oct.-Nov. ; closed Dec.-Feb.)*. ▶ **Château du Plessis-Bourré★★** *(17 km N)* : double towers and walls rising from the water in the moat. Built in the 15thC by Jean Bourré, Minister of Finance under Louis XI, as both a fortress and a country seat *(Apr.-Sep., 10-12 & 2-7, 5 rest of year ; closed 15 Nov.-15 Dec., Wed. and Thu. am ex Jul.-Aug.)*. Superb 18thC furniture in the salons and beautiful ceiling★★ (end 15thC) in the Salle des Gardes (Guardroom), painted with humorous and sometimes indecent scenes illustrating proverbs and fables. ▶ **Château de la Hamonière** *(4 km N)*, an elegant 15thC and Renaissance country house *(Jul.-15 Sep., 2-6)*. ▶ **Château de Montgeoffroy★** *(24 km E)* : all elegance and classic harmony, 1775 ; wooden panels and Louis XVI furniture, signed by the most famous cabinet-makers of the period *(9:30-11:30 & 2:30-6:30 Easter-1 Nov.)*. ▶ **Château de Brissac** *(15 km SE)* at **Brissac-Quincé** : just like Montgeoffroy, Brissac has remained in the family which built it, which explains its lived-in feeling. Rebuilt from 1614, with two large round 15thC towers between which stretches a beautiful Renaissance façade *(9:30-11:20 & 2:15-4:15 or 5:45 according to season ; closed Nov.-Easter and Tue. ex Jul.-Sep. ; soirées musicales* and introduction to the arts of the hunt, tel. : *41.91.23.43*). ▶ Saint-Saturnin (D751 ; by appt. tel. 41.91.93.03). ▶ **Château de Serrant★** *(16km SW)* is a true work of the Renaissance although it took three centuries (16th-18thC) to complete it. Its walls of brown schist and white tufa are reflected in the moats and a melancholy lake *(9-11:30 & 2-5:30 Palm Sun.-1 Nov. ; closed Tue. ex Jul.-Aug)*. Staircase★, furniture and 16thC tapestries, tomb of the marquis de Vaubrun (1675). 3 km

SW : a mill in working order *(visits daily in summer and Sun. 2:30-7)*.

Loire - Layon★ *(circuit 177 km, one day, see map 1)*

▶ Gentle curves and peaceful views take the Loire dreamily through Anjou between vineyard and orchard, fringed by smiling villages. This circuit takes us as far as Montsoreau. ▶ **Angers**. ▶ **Le Thoureil★** : the Loire here is an eyefilling expanse of water. En route you may have visited the church of **Saint-Rémy-la-Varenne** (Romanesque apse, Angevin vaulting in the chapel★) or the former **Abbey of Saint-Maur** (6thC). 6 km W of Thoureil is the beautiful **château de Montsabert** (15thC), an echo of Montsoreau (→). ▶ Through **Gennes** (view★ from church of Saint-Eusèbe ; dolmen de la Madeleine★ *1 km S*) you reach **Cunault** : Romanesque church★★ 12thC. Binoculars needed to see details of the marvelous sculptures on the 223 capitals★★ ; 13thC wooden reliquary. ▶ **Chênehutte-les-Tuffeaux** lives up to its name, with gleaming white limestone houses and mushroom beds installed in the cool dark of the quarries. On the other bank : the **château de Boumois** (→ Saumur). ▶ **Saumur** (→). ▶ At **Montsoreau** (→) you leave the Loire. ▶ **Fontevraud-l'Abbaye** (→) has recently recovered much of its ancient dignity. **Montreuil-Bellay** (→). ▶ **Le Puy-Notre-Dame**, whose collegiate buildings are among the most consistent specimens of Angevine architecture of the 13thC. The Virgin's girdle is housed here ; the relic supposedly has the power to alleviate the pains of childbirth. ▶ 9 km N is **Doué-la-Fontaine** (pop. 6 855), the city of roses, sending out several million rose bushes each year. The amphitheatre hewn out of an ancient quarry is the setting in Jul. for the Journée de la Rose. At the gates of the town, other quarries accommodate the **Zoo des Minières** *(8-7, Jul.-15 Sep. ; 9-12:30 & 2-6:30 rest of year)*. **Old trades** *(vieux commerces)* **museum** *(Jul.-Sep., 10-12 & 2-7 ex Mon. am ; 15 May-Jun., closes at 6 and Mon.)*. On the D960, *cavier* mill *(by appt., tel. : 41.59.11.64)*. 6 km NW of Doué-la-Fontaine, at **Louresse-Rochemenier**, a little underground country museum *(daily ex Mon. in summer ; Sat. and Sun. pm in winter)*. ▶ **Layon Valley★** : many picturesque sights, famous wine-producing area. ▶ **Martigné-Briand** is a village of wine growers, specialists in round well-structured whites. ▶ **Thouarcé**, then **Beaulieu-sur-Layon**, where the local cellars welcome visitors and the orientation table *(W exit)* shows you the vineyards of Layon dotted with châteaux. ▶ **Manoir de la Basse-Guerche** (15thC) in a bend of the Layon. ▶ **Corniche Angevine** (→) above the Loire.

The Apocalypse tapestry

This exquisite tapestry was created between 1373-80 by the Parisian weaver Nicolas Bataille from designs by the painter Hennequin de Bruges who drew his inspiration from various illuminated manuscripts of the period. The subject matter closely follows texts of the Apocalypse of St. John, reproduced here and accompanied by photographs. Originally the tapestry (168m by 5m) consisted of seven pieces, each showing a personage of importance followed in two superposed ranks by fourteen scenes with alternate red and blue backgrounds. Four of the personages remain, together with 68 whole scenes and five large fragments.

Practical Information _____

ANGERS

⌷ pl. Kennedy (C2), ☎ 41.88.69.93 ; cour de la Gare (B3), ☎ 41.87.72.50.

✈ Angers-Avrillé, 4 km NW, ☎ 41.34.61.57. *Air France office, Les Halles de la République, pl. Chanlouineau*, ☎ 41.87.60.79.

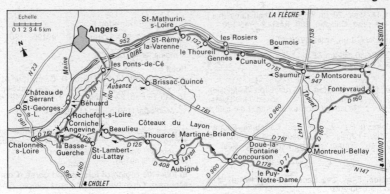

1. The Angevine Loire and the Layon hills

SNCF (B3), ☎ 41.87.76.60/41.80.50.50.
🚌 pl. de la République (B2), ☎ 41.88.59.25.
Car rental : *Avis*, train station ; 13, rue Max-Richard (B3),
☎ 41.88.20.24.

Hotels :
★★★ *Anjou*, (Mapotel), 1, bd Mal-Foch (C3),
☎ 41.88.24.82, Tx 720521, AE DC Euro Visa, 51 rm Ⓟ ♪
260. Rest. ♦♦ *La Salamandre* ♪ ⚘ closed Sun. Good
food, 80-170.
★★★ *France*, 8, pl. de la Gare (B3), ☎ 41.88.49.42,
Tx 720895, AE DC Euro Visa, 57 rm ⚙ 300. Rest. ♦ *Les
Plantagenêts* ♪ ⚙ closed Sat and Sun noon, 70-150.
★★★ *Le Progrès*, (Inter-Hôtel), 26, rue Denis-Papin (B3),
☎ 41.88.10.14, Tx 720982, AE DC Euro Visa, 41 rm ♪ 230.
● ★★ *Iéna*, 27, rue Marceau (B3), ☎ 41.87.52.40,
Tx 720930, Visa, 22 rm ♪ closed 22 Dec-4 Jan, 175.
● ★★ *Le Saint-Julien*, 9, pl. du Ralliement (C2),
☎ 41.88.41.62, Tx 720930, AE Visa, 34 rm, 160.
★ *Le Relais*, 9, rue de la Gare (B3), ☎ 41.88.42.51,
Euro Visa, 16 rm, closed Fri eve, Sat, Mar, Apr, Jul, 110.
Rest. ♦ ♪ 70-100.

Restaurants :
● ♦♦ *Le Quéré*, 9, pl. du Ralliement (C2), ☎ 41.87.64.94,
AE DC Visa ⚘ ♪ closed Fri eve and Sat , Feb school hols,
1-20 Jul. Don't miss the outstanding cuisine prepared by
a former pupil of Joël Robuchon, Paul le Quéré, an able
chef who finds the time to enter culinary competitions to
keep his skills sharp (and his clients happy) : *raviolis de
langoustines, papillon de rouget au confit de courgettes
et olives noires, Saint-Jacques au nid (in season), sauté
minute de filet de bœuf au citron vert et gingembre*. Let
smiling Martine guide you in your choice of Loire Valley
wines, 350.
● ♦♦ *Le Toussaint*, 7, rue Toussaint (B2),
☎ 41.87.46.20, AE DC Euro Visa ♪ ⚘ closed Mon and
Sun , Feb, Aug. Handsome 18thC residence. Loire salmon and eel, 100-250.
● ♦♦ *Le Vert d'Eau*, 9, bd Gaston-Dumesnil (A2),
☎ 41.48.52.31, AE DC Euro Visa ♪ closed Mon Sun eve
and Feb. The dean of this city's restaurants features a
fabulous list of Loire wines. Regional cuisine : *paupiettes
de sandre, ris de veau braisé*, 75-200.
♦♦ *Le Logis*, 17, rue Saint-Laud (C2), ☎ 41.87.44.15 ♪
⚙ closed Sat eve and Sun, 13 Jul-13 Aug. Delicious fish
dishes, 95-220.

⚑ ★★★*Lac de Maine* (165 pl), ☎ 41.73.05.03.

Recommended
Auction house : 12, rue des Arènes, ☎ 41.88.63.89, Sat.
flea market, pl. Imbach (C2).
Guide to wines : *Maison du vin de l'Anjou*, 5 bis, pl. Kennedy (C2), info and tastings.

♥ pork products : *Le Petit St-Antoine*, rue Saint-Aubin
(C3).

Nearby

BRISSAC-QUINCÉ, ☒ 49320, 18 km SE.
ℹ mairie, ☎ 41.91.22.13.

Hotel :
★★ *Le Castel*, 1, rue Louis-Moron, ☎ 41.91.24.74, AE
Visa, 11 rm Ⓟ ⚘ ⚙ closed 12 Feb-1 Mar, 150.

⚑ ★★*Municipal* (35 pl), ☎ 41.91.22.13.

CHAMPIGNÉ, ☒ 49330, 25 km N.

Hotel :
Château des Briottières (I.L.A., C.H.), rte de Sablé,
☎ 41.42.00.02, Tx 720943, 8 rm Ⓟ ⚘ ⚙ closed
15 Nov-15 Feb. On an 18thC estate, 430. Rest. ♦ Table
d'hôtes, 200.

Recommended
Chambres d'hôtes : *Les Briottières*, ☎ 41.42.00.02, dinners, reserve (open 15 Feb-15 Nov).

CHÂTEAUNEUF-SUR-SARTHE, ☒ 49330, 31 km N.
ℹ mairie, ☎ 41.42.10.22.

Hotel :
★★ *Les Ondines*, quai de la Sarthe, ☎ 41.69.84.38, AE
Euro Visa, 30 rm Ⓟ ⚘ 190. Rest. ♦ ♪ 60-140 ; child : 40.

CHEFFES, ☒ 49330 Châteauneuf-sur-Sarthe, 8 km S
of **Châteauneuf**.

Hotel :
● ★★★ *Château de Teildras* (R.C.), on the Juvardeil
road, ☎ 41.42.61.08, Tx 720268, AE DC Euro Visa, 11 rm
Ⓟ ⚘ ⚙ closed 15 Nov-1 Apr. On a 16th-C estate, 740.
Rest. ♦♦ ♪ closed Tue noon. Spec : *sandre à l'oseille,
bar aux petits légumes*, 190-350.

CHÊNEHUTTE-LES-TUFFEAUX, ☒ 49350 Gennes, 8 km
NW of **Saumur**.

Hotel :
● ★★★★ *Le Prieuré* (R.C.), ☎ 41.50.15.31, Tx 720379,
Visa, 37 rm Ⓟ ⚘ ⚙ closed closed Jan-Feb,
700. Rest. ● ♦♦♦ ⚘ ⚙ René Traversac loves beautiful
things. P. Doumerc and J.-N. Lumineau serve fine regional
dishes : *médaillons de lotte aux palourdes et au safran,
confit de lapereau au layon, retour de perche au beurre
rouge*. Good wines, 160-285.

DOUÉ-LA-FONTAINE, ☒ 49700, 41 km SE.
ℹ pl. de l'Hôtel-de-Ville, ☎ 41.59.18.53.

Hotel :
★ *Le Dagobert* (L.F.), 14, pl. du Champ-de-Foire,

☎ 41.59.14.44, Visa, 20 rm ℗ ⚏ ⌕ ♪ half pens (h.s.), closed Fri eve , Sat, Dec-Jan, 280. Rest. ♦ ♪ 45-130.

⚐ ★★*Municipal* (70 pl), ☎ 41.59.14.47.

GENNES, ⊠ 49350, 35 km SE.
ⓘ mairie, ☎ 41.51.81.30.   ♥

Hotels :
● ★★ *Aux Naulets d'Anjou*, 18, rue Croix-de-Mission, ☎ 41.51.81.88, 20 rm ℗ ⚏ ⌕ ⌕ closed Nov-Easter, 210. Rest. ♦ ⌕ ♪ ✲ closed Mon ex Jul-Aug. Low-calorie meals, 60-180.
★★ *La Loire* (L.F.), 9, rue des Cadets-de-Saumur, ☎ 41.51.81.03, 11 rm ℗ ⌕ ⌕ closed Mon eve and Tue, 27 Dec-10 Feb. Former coach house, 200. Rest. ♦ ⌕ 60-160.

Restaurant :
♦ *L'Aubergade*, 7, av. des Cadets, ☎ 41.51.81.07 ℗ ⌕ closed Wed (l.s.), 90-200.

⚐ ★★*District* (170 pl), ☎ 41.51.81.30.

PELLOUAILLES-LES-VIGNES, ⊠ 49112, 7 km NE.

Restaurant :
● ♦♦ *Le Manoir*, 75, rte nationale, ☎ 41.69.57.97, AE DC Euro Visa ⌕ closed Wed , Feb school hols. J. Legeay deserves encouragement for his fine cooking : *anguilles aux savennières, canard au cidre*, 85-180.

SAINT-SYLVAIN-D'ANJOU, ⊠ 49480, 4 km W.

Hotels :
● ★★ *La Fauvelaie* (L.F.), rte de l'Epervière, ☎ 41.43.80.10, 9 rm ℗ ⚏ ⌕ ⌕ 100. Rest. ♦♦ ⌕ ⌕ closed Sun eve, 25-31 Dec, 55-70.
★★ *Auberge d'Eventard* (L.F.), rte de Paris, N 23, ☎ 41.43.74.25, AE DC Euro Visa, 10 rm ℗ ⚏ ✲ closed Mon eve and Sun eve, 2-22 Jan, 9-20 Sep, 150. Rest. ♦♦ ♪ ✲ Spec : *tiède de coquilles Saint-Jacques au vinaigre de xérès*, 80-240.

Restaurant :
● ♦♦ *Le Clafoutis*, rte de Paris, ☎ 41.43.84.71, AE Visa ♪ closed Wed eve, Thu, Sun eve , Feb school hols, Aug. Classic cuisine shows Serge Lebert's appealing style to advantage : steamed river perch, *lapereau à l'ail confit*. Large and attractive selection of Loire wines, 65-150.

The Corniche ANGEVINE*
(The Angers cliff road)   A3

From Angers to Chalonnes-sur-Loire *(29 km, 2 hr)*

SW of Angers between Rochefort and Chalonnes, the road leaves the banks of the Loire to take to the heights along the cliff. The valley of the Loire can now be seen to its full extent. The Loire continues on its way between the islands under the peaceful gaze of little towns and pretty manors, while the manicured slopes of the vineyards promise wines full of character, substance and body.

▶ **Angers** (→); leave by the D111. ▶ **Bouchemaine.**
▶ **Savennières** (church★ part 10thC) remembers its wind-mills : **La Possonnière** still turns *(Sun and nat. hols. Apr.-15 Dec.)* while in the middle of the river, **Béhuard** huddles around the church (15thC) which watched over the sailors on the Loire; doll museum *(tel. 41.54.53.97)*. ▶ Here is **Rochefort-sur-Loire** (pop. 1 819) with watch-towers on its houses; the famous **Corniche Angevine**★ and **La Haie-Longe** (view★). ▶ A brief detour to **Saint-Lam-bert-du-Lattay** and its wine museum *(Apr.-Oct., 10-12 & 2:30-6:30)*. ▶ Finally **Chalonnes-sur-Loire** (pop. 5 358) invites you to stroll along its quays in the old port. ▶ 5 km SW, **Saint-Laurent-de-la-Plaine**, museum of old profes-sions *(9-12 & 2-6, Apr.-Oct.)*.   □

Practical Information _____

ROCHEFORT-SUR-LOIRE, ⊠ 49190, 20 km SW of **Angers**.
ⓘ mairie, ☎ 41.78.70.24.   ♥

Hotel :
★★ *Grand Hôtel* (L.F.), 30, rue R.-Gasnier, ☎ 41.78.70.06, DC Visa, 8 rm ℗ ⚏ ⌕ closed Mon eve and Sun eve (l.s.), 15 Jan-15 Feb, 22-26 Jun, 140. Rest. ♦ ♪ ✲ 90-130.

⚐ *Municipal* (150 pl), ☎ 41.78.70.24.

BAUGÉ and BAUGEOIS region

Angers 38, Tours 68, Paris 260 km
pop 3906 ⊠ 49150   B3

In this little region of forests and gorse (Chandelais★, Monnaie, Chambiers), nothing is simple. The bell to-wers are built in spirals, and they still play with bias bowls, which don't run straight either.

▶ **Baugé**, a peaceful little town with charming old houses. In the château (15thC), museum of weapons and ceram-ics *(Jun.-Sep.; closed Tue.)* and lovely spiral staircase. See also the pharmacy★ in the Hôpital St. Joseph and the famous Croix d'Anjou in the chapel of the Incurables.

Nearby

▶ **Le Vieil-Baugé** *(1.5 km SW)*, **Pontigné** *(5 km E)* and **Mouliherne** *(13.5 km SE)* have spiral, helicoidal or cork-screw bell towers on their beautiful 12th-13thC churches (murals★ in Pontigné). ▶ **Breil** *(25 km SE)* has an operation-al watermill (Moulin au Jau, *3-7 Sat. and Sun.*). ▶ **Beau-fort-en-Vallée** *(15 km SW)*, in the middle of the rich game preserves of the Val d'Anjou, a center of arable farming and flower growing; ruins of a 14th-15thC château; 15th-16thC church with Renaissance bell tower.   □

Practical Information _____

ⓘ mairie, ☎ 41.89.12.12.
SNCF ☎ 41.67.50.50.

Hotels :
★ *Boule d'or*, 4, rue des Cygnes, ☎ 41.89.82.12, 10 rm ℗ ⌕ closed Sun eve and Mon, 15 Jan-15 Feb, 95. Rest. ♦ ♪ 60-90.
● *Château de la Grifferaie*, Echemiré, ☎ 41.89.70.25, AE Visa, 7 rm ℗ ⚏ ⌕ ♪° closed 3 Nov-16 Apr, 450. Rest. ♦ ⌕ ♪ closed Mon, Sun and lunch, 150.

⚐ ★★*Municipal* (100 pl), ☎ 41.89.14.79.

Recommended
Farmhouse-gîte : at Vieil-Baugé, D 61, *Claire Fontaine*, ☎ 41.89.20.74.

BEAUMONT-SUR-SARTHE

Alençon 23, Le Mans 26, Paris 223 km
pop 1938 ⊠ 72170   B1

An old Roman keep, mounting guard over the right bank of the river which twists between the islets. ▶ **La Motte-à-Madame** is a beautiful walk with views★ over the valley.

Nearby

▶ 2.5 km E, ancient Benedictine priory of **Vivoin** (13thC chapter; exhibitions, concerts). ▶ **Fresnay-sur-Sarthe** *(12 km NW; pop. 2 692)*, on a slope overlooking the river : Romanesque church of Notre-Dame (Renaissance main door★). Museum of regional headdresses *(daily, Jul.-Aug.; Sun., Mar.-Jun. and Sep.)* in fortified gateway of château (garden★).   □

_____

Don't forget to consult the Practical Holiday Guide: it can help in solving many problems.

Practical Information _____

BEAUMONT-SUR-SARTHE

Hotel :
★ *Le Chemin de Fer* (L.F.), pl. de la Gare, ☎ 43.97.00.05, Euro Visa, 16 rm ℗ ♨ ♨ closed Mon eve and Sun eve, 9 Feb-3 Mar, 15-31 Oct, 135. Rest. ♦ ♪ 50-90.

⋏ ★★*Val de Sarthe* (66 pl), ☎ 43.97.01.93.

Nearby
FRESNAY-SUR-SARTHE, ⊠ 72130, 12 km NW.
ℹ mairie, ☎ 43.97.23.75.   ♥
SNCF ☎ 43.97.20.33.

Hotel :
★★ *Ronsin* (L.F.), 5, av. Ch.-de-Gaulle, ☎ 43.97.20.10, AE DC Visa, 12 rm ℗ half pens (h.s.), closed Sun eve (l.s.) and Mon lunch, 160. Rest. ♦ Grill-pizzeria, 45-175.

⋏ ★★★*Sans Souci* (100 pl), ☎ 43.97.32.87.

SILLÉ-LE-GUILLAUME, ⊠ 72140, 21 km W.
SNCF ☎ 43.20.10.41.

⋏ ★★★*Les Mollières* (133 pl), ☎ 43.20.16.12.

Recommended
Farmhouse-inn : at Rouez on D 167, *Abbaye de Champagne*, ☎ 43.20.15.74, superb 12th-13thC dwelling. Closed Tue eve and Wed, chambres d'hôtes.

BERCÉ Forest**

C2

Circuit through the Bercé Forest and the valley of the Loir *(93 km, 3 hr; see map 2)*

The oak forests of Bercé are without doubt the most beautiful in France; tall trunks like cathedral pillars accompanied by a few beech trees, in the central and eastern parts of these 54 km² of forest, remnant of the formerly vast forest of Le Mans. The western side is sandier and covered with pines.

▶ **Château-du-Loir** (pop. 589) : you will search in vain for any château here ! ▶ **Vallon de l'Yre**, leading to **Beaumont-Pied-de-Boeuf**, where amateurs of weapons and uniforms will be intrigued by the Sentinelle museum *(Easter-Sep., Sun. pm; 14 Jul.-30 Aug., 2-7 daily).* ▶ **Jupilles**, at the edge of the forest : woodworking crafts *(Easter-30 Jun., 8 Sep.-1 Nov., Sat., Sun. 2:30-6; 1 Jul.-7 Sep., daily ex Mon.).* ▶ **Fontaine de la Coudre** in pretty surroundings. ▶ **Sources de l'Hermitière** among oaks and beeches. ▶ **La Futaie des Clos**★ : magnificent and venerable oaks, some reaching over 40 m in spite of gales. ▶ **Saint-Pierre-de-Lorouër**, via Courdemanche and the valley of the **Étangsort** : green hedges, poplars and willows bordering a pretty river. ▶ At **Vancé** and **Pont-de-Braye** you return to the imperturbable Loir flowing among cow-pastures and meadows. ▶ **Poncé-sur-Loir** : the sculptured vaulting of the Renaissance staircase in the château (1542) is a real marvel; gardens★ and dovecote★ . The ethnographic museum of Maine is located in the château *(10-12 & 2-6; closed Sun. am and Oct.-Easter).* 500 m from the château : the **Moulin de Paillard**, craft centre of Poncé (pottery, glass-blowing, woodwork, weaving, wrought iron; *9-12 & 2-6, closed Sun.).* ▶ **La Chartre-sur-le-Loir** (pop. 1791) produces an excellent white wine, Jasnières, greatly appreciated by Henri IV and many less illustrious connoisseurs.   ☐

Practical Information _____

La CHARTRE-SUR-LE-LOIR, ⊠ 72340.
ℹ 20, rue Carnot, ☎ 43.44.40.04.
SNCF ☎ 43.44.40.42.

Hotels :
★★ *Cheval Blanc* (L.F.), 7, pl. de la République, ☎ 43.44.40.01, Visa, 12 rm ℗ ♨ closed Mon eve and Sun

2. Bercé Forest

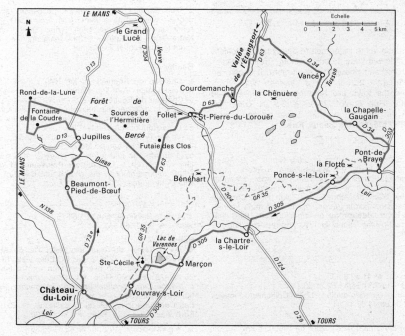

eve (l.s.), 6 Jan-3 Feb. Fishing possible in private pond, 160. Rest. ♦ 50-115.
★★ *France* (L.F.), 20, pl. de la République, ☎ 43.44.40.16, Visa, 30 rm ℗ ▩ ◿ half pens, closed 15 Nov-15 Dec. Fishing possible in private pond, 150. Rest. ♦ ♪ 60-180.
⚑ ★*Vieux Moulin* (100 pl), ☎ 43.44.41.18.

CHÂTEAU-GONTIER*

Laval 30, Angers 46, Paris 284 km
pop 8352 ⊠ 53200   A2
You should come to this old city in Chouan country on Thursdays, when the calf sales are in full swing. Château-Gontier grew up around one of the fortresses built by Fulk Nerra. Its narrow sloping streets and old houses, the quayside on the Mayenne (formerly a port, Château-Gontier is today a *Relais Nautique*) give it great character.
▶ Near the **church of St. Jean** (murals), the **Promenade du Bout-du-Monde**★ overlooks the valley. A former mansion houses the **museum** (antiquities, 17thC Dutch painting, 15thC statue★ of Ste. Marthe ; *daily ex Tue. and Jan.*).
▶ 7km SW, **château de St-Ouen**, 15th-16thC, square tower★ Louis XII style *(no visitors)*.   □

Practical Information ⎯⎯⎯⎯⎯⎯⎯
ℹ️ mairie, ☎ 43.07.07.10.
SNCF ☎ 43.07.10.95.

Hotels :
★★★ *Parc* (L.F.), 46, av. Joffre, ☎ 43.07.28.41, Euro Visa, 23 rm ℗ ≷ ▩ ◿ ♪ ᵒ closed 15 Dec-6 Jan, 200.
★★ *Mirwault*, rte de Mirwault, Bazouges, 1,5 km N, ☎ 43.07.13.17, AE DC Euro Visa, 10 rm ℗ ≷ ◿ closed 1 Jan-15 Feb, 180. Rest. ♦♦ ♪ closed Fri (h.s.) , Fri lunch (Oct-Mar). Spec : *salade de Saint-Jacques et de ris de veau aux cèpes*, 85-200.

⚑ ★★*du Parc* (100 pl), ☎ 43.07.35.60.

CHOLET

Nantes 61, Angers 61, Paris 349 km
pop 56528 ⊠ 49300

Cholet continues to manufacture dainty handkerchiefs side by side with less dated products : from footwear to electronic and pneumatic equipment. It is also an important cattle market. ▶ The Vendéen Wars which destroyed the town are remembered in the Musée Historique (Rue Travot, *10-12 & 2-5 ex Tue., nat. hols.*) in the former town hall. Local painters, ceramics in the **Musée des Beaux Arts.**

Nearby
▶ 4 km SE : leisure centre at **Lake Ribou**. ▶ Between Cholet and the Loire, the **Mauges** form a wooded area of ravines and thicketed valleys. This spot, ideal for ambushes, was the scene of many dramatic episodes during the Wars of Vendée. ▶ 22 km NE : **Chemillé** grows medicinal plants (garden in the Parc de la Mairie). ▶ 19 km NNW : **Beaupréau**, an imposing 15th-18thC château burned by the "Blues" in 1793 and rebuilt during the Restoration.   □

Practical Information ⎯⎯⎯⎯⎯⎯⎯
CHOLET
ℹ️ pl. Rougé, ☎ 41.62.22.35.
SNCF ☎ 41.62.31.35/41.62.31.33.
Car rental : *Avis*, train station ; 17, bd Delhumeau-Plessis, ☎ 41.62.34.88/41.62.14.51.

Hotels :
★★ *Belvédère*, parc des Loisirs de Ribou, 5 km SE. on

the D 20, ☎ 41.62.14.02, 8 rm ℗ ≷ ▩ ◿ closed Sun eve Feb school hols, Aug, 170.
★★ *Europe*, 8, pl. de la Gare, ☎ 41.62.00.97, AE DC Euro Visa, 21 rm ℗ ♪ closed Sat lunch, 180. Rest. ● ♦♦ ♪ 90-250.
★★ *Poste*, 26, bd G.-Richard, ☎ 41.62.07.20, 55 rm ℗ ◿ closed 24 Dec-2 Jan, 210. Rest. ♦♦ ♪ closed Sat eve and Sun, Aug, 26 Jul-18 Aug, 60-130.

Restaurant :
♦♦ *Château de la Tremblaye* (C.H.), rte de La-Roche-sur-Yon, 6 km SW, ☎ 41.58.40.17, Visa ≷ ▩ ♪ closed Mon and Sun eve, 1-22 Aug. Quality cuisine served in a 19th-C château : *blinis de rivière aux écrevisses, aiguillettes et gigot de caneton au vinaigre de framboise*, 55-150.

⚑ ★★★★*Lac de Ribou* (186 pl), ☎ 41.62.47.04.

Recommended
Events : *fair-expo*, late Sep ; *carnival*, mid-Lent.
Farm-gîte : at Longeron 49710, 16 km, *la Roullière*, ☎ 41.46.54.20. A peaceful wooded site. Tennis, horseback riding and river fishing.
♥ pastry-chocolates : *M. Boisliveau*, rue Notre-Dame.

Nearby

NUAILLÉ, ⊠ 49340 Trémentines, 8 km NE.

Hotel :
★★ *Relais des Biches*, (Inter-Hôtel), pl. de l'Église, ☎ 41.62.38.99, Tx 720547, AE DC Euro Visa, 13 rm ℗ ▩ ♪ 🖼 closed Sun, 20 Dec-1 Jan, 210. Rest. ♦♦ ♪ ⅙ ⅋ 70-180.

ÉVRON**

Laval 32, Le Mans 55, Paris 259 km
pop 6774 ⊠ 53600   B1
The basilica of Évron is one of the marvels of the Bas-Maine, an underrated region where it is very pleasant to stroll around the lakes and forests. Évron's Meat Festival *(1st Sun. in Sep.)* renders appropriate homage to its principal activity.
▶ The **Basilica Notre-Dame**★★ possesses a Romanesque tower and nave dating from around AD 1000 ; the remainder is the purest High Gothic ; in the **chapel of Notre-Dame-de-l'Épine**★, 13thC paintings and treasure room (statue★ of Notre-Dame).

Nearby
▶ **Château du Rocher**★ (5 km NW) : the E facade is a masterpiece from the Renaissance *(ext. visits only)*. ▶ **Château de Foulletorte** *(10 km W)* : access as far as the grill to discover this beautiful late-Renaissance building and water-filled moat. ▶ **Sainte-Suzanne**★★ *(7 km SE)*, a delightful little fortified town above the Erve : ramparts, sentry walk, gates and keep are all there, as well as the view★. ▶ **Château de Montecler** *(4 km SW)*, protected by a drawbridge and a vaulted gateway, dates from the time of Henri IV. ▶ **La Chapelle-Rainsouin** *(11 km SW)* : 16thC tombstones★ in the church and Burial of Christ★ with eight figures (1522).   □

Practical Information ⎯⎯⎯⎯⎯⎯⎯
ℹ️ pl. de la Basilique, ☎ 43.01.63.75.   ◖
SNCF ☎ 43.01.60.35.

Hotels :
● ★★★ *Relais du Gué de Selle*, rte de Mayenne, ☎ 43.90.64.05, Tx 722615, AE DC Euro Visa, 18 rm ℗ ≷ ▩ ◿ ♪ᵒ closed Sun eve and Mon ex 15 Jun-15 Jul, 25 Jan-25 Feb, 200. Rest. ♦ ⅙ Spec : *médaillon de lotte à la vapeur de verveine, paupiette de sandre à l'oseille*, 60-160 ; child : 35.
Les Coevrons (L.F.), pl. de la Basilique, ☎ 43.01.62.16, Euro Visa, 6 rm, 120. Rest. ♦ ♪ ⅙ 45-100.

⚑ ★★★*Municipal* (100 pl), ☎ 43.01.65.36 ; .

La FERTÉ-BERNARD

Le Mans 49, Alençon 56, Paris 164 km
pop 10053 ⊠ 72400   C1

Lush meadows with the River Huisne branching crazily through them.
▶ The most interesting thing in La Ferté is the Renaissance choir★★ (1500-96) of **Notre-Dame-des-Marais.** A fortified gateway, old houses (Rues d'Huisne and Carnot) and the market buildings (1536) are also worthy of interest. ▶ 15 km SE, the 15thC **château de Montirail★** *(daily ex Tue., Jul.-15 Sep.; Sun., hols., Mar.-Jun., 16 Sep.-1 Nov.); view.* ▶ 16 km S, **Vibraye** and the forest of the same name (5000 acres) with its well-stocked lakes. ▶ 14 km SW : **Tuffé** with its lake and little tourist train *(Sun. and nat. hols., Jul.-Sep.).*   □

Practical Information _____

La FERTÉ-BERNARD
ℹ mairie, ☎ 43.93.04.42.   ⚑
SNCF ☎ 43.93.00.47.

Hotels :
● ★ **La Perdrix** (L.F.), 2, rue de Paris, ☎ 43.93.00.44, AE DC Visa, 10 rm, closed Tue, 110. Rest. ● ◆ ⬧ 70-150.
★ **Saint-Jean**, 13, rue Robert-Garnier, ☎ 43.93.12.83, 16 rm ℗ ⬥ 160.

⚠ ★★Belle Etoile (66 pl), ☎ 43.93.04.42.

Recommended
Events : *folk festival,* in Jul.

Nearby
VIBRAYE, ⊠ 72320, 16 km S.

Hotels :
★★ **Auberge de la Forêt** (L.F.), 38, rue G.-Goussault, ☎ 43.93.60.07, AE DC Visa, 7 rm ℗ ⬛ ⬥ pens (h.s.), closed Sun eve , Mon ex Jul-Aug, Jan, 450. Rest. ◆ ⬥ 60-180 ; child : 35.
★ **Le Chapeau Rouge** (L.F.), pl. de l'Hôtel-de-Ville, ☎ 43.93.60.02, Euro Visa, 12 rm ℗ ⬥ closed Sun eve, Mon. Rest. ◆ ⬥ 55-180.

⚠ ★★Municipal (85 pl), ☎ 43.93.60.27.

Recommended
Events : *folk festival,* in Jul.

La FLÈCHE*

Le Mans 41, Angers 47, Paris 241 km
pop 16421 ⊠ 72200   B2

Generations of soldiers have passed out of Le Prytanée de La Flèche, the celebrated school for officers' sons ; but this small town is neither rigid nor military in appearance. In a bend in the Loir near a dam and two ancient mills, La Flèche is an important regional market for the fruit producers of Maine ; and, discreetly hidden away, the town's printing presses turn out millions of paperbacks.

▶ Near the bridge (view★) : the much-rebuilt **château des Carmes** (15thC) is now the town hall. ▶ **Le Prytanée★** was formerly a Jesuit college, founded by Henri IV and with Descartes among its alumni. It consists of enormous 17thC buildings and a chapel★ which is a masterpiece of the Baroque *(9:30-12 & 2-5).* ▶ 3.5 km SE at **Tertre-Rouge★** there is a most unusual zoo : its founder, J. Bouillault, is a friend of every animal there, from elephant to crocodile *(9:30-7 in summer ; 10-dusk in winter);* interesting museum on regional fauna.   □

Practical Information _____

ℹ 23, pl. du Marché-au-Blé, ☎ 43.94.02.53 ; maison du Tourisme, ☎ 43.94.49.82.
SNCF ☎ 43.94.00.71.

Hotel :
● ★★★ **Relais Cicéro** (C.H.), 12, bd d'Alger, ☎ 43.94.14.14, Tx 720015, Visa, 20 rm ℗ ⬟ ⬛ ⬥ ⬥ closed Feb, 20 Dec-5 Jan ex conferences, 300. Rest. ● ◆◆ ♪ ⬥ In a fine old 18thC dwelling, 100-150.

⚠ ★★★Municipal (100 pl), ☎ 43.94.55.90 ; *animal park at Tertre Rouge,* open camping, ☎ 43.94.04.55.

FONTEVRAUD-L'ABBAYE***

Tours 61, Angers 69, Paris 306 km
pop 1085 ⊠ 49590   B4

The originality of its architecture, the presence of so much history, and the extraordinary Franco-British dialogue which developed there make Fontevraud one of the high places of Western civilization, another Vézelay (→). Founded in the 11thC by Robert d'Arbrissel, a preacher famous throughout Brittany and Anjou, Fontevraud consisted of five monasteries, of which three still exist : Grand-Moûtier, with the abbey church, St. Benoît, immediately E of the first, and St. Lazare, originally for the sick and leprous. Used as a prison from the time of Napoléon until 1964, Fontevraud is undergoing a rebirth ; currently under restoration, it is now a cultural and convention centre under the aegis of the Historic Monuments Department. It welcomes symposia, organizes concerts, spectacles, exhibitions, courses and activities for young people : studios for arts and crafts, archaeological sites...

▶ The **abbey church★★** is a superb Romanesque building from the first half of 12thC *(9-12 & 2-6:30, Apr.-Sep. ; 10-12 & 2-4, Oct.-Mar.).* In the great single nave, decorated capitals★ adorn the enormous pillars. The Plantagenêts, Counts of Anjou and later Kings of England, greatly favoured the abbey, and many of the family were buried here, including Henry II, his wife Eleanor of Aquitaine, their famous son Richard the Lion-Hearted, and Isabel of Angoulême, wife of his younger brother, King John. Of the effigies of the family, these four are all that remain, magnificent examples of 13thC sculpture★★. ▶ See also the great 16thC cloister, the **chapterhouse** with its 16thC frescos portraying various personalities of the day (restored), the **Romanesque refectory,** vaulted with ogives at the beginning of 16thC, and the famous 12thC **kitchens★★,** with fish-scale tiling and a multitude of chimneys. At the entrance to the abbey is the **church of St. Michel★** (12th-15thC), where numerous works of art from the abbey can be seen (gilt wood altarpiece). To the W, Ste-Catherine chapel, 13thC lantern of the Dead. ▶ The **Musée des Arts et Traditions Fontevristes** recounts the history of the town and its trades (stone-cutters, vintners, lace-makers ; *daily ex Fri., 10-12 & 2-7).*   □

Practical Information _____

ℹ mairie, ☎ 43.51.71.21.

Hotel :
★ **Croix Blanche**, 7, pl. des Plantagenêts, ☎ 41.51.71.11, 19 rm ℗ ⬥ closed 11-30 Nov, 180. Rest. ◆ 40-85.

Restaurants :
● ◆◆ **La Licorne**, 31, rue Robert-d'Arbrissel, ☎ 41.51.72.49, closed 25 Dec-25 Jan. Devoted to regional cooking, this table is on its way up, thanks to owner M. Crinton's painstaking efforts in the dining room, and young Michel Lecomte's cuisine : *panaché de poissons aux petits légumes, étuvée de veau au citron vert, gratin de poires,* local wines, 150-250.
◆ **L'Abbaye**, 8, av. des Roches, ☎ 41.51.71.04 ♪ ⬥ closed Tue eve and Wed, 10 Feb-1 Mar, 6 Oct-1 Nov.

Recommended
Chambres d'hôtes : *Dom. de Mestré,* 5 rm, ☎ 41.51.75.87.

LAVAL*

Angers 73, Rennes 74, Paris 278 km
pop 53766 ⊠ 53000   A1

Mayenne is a region strongly attached to its traditions, but Laval, its capital, has often tended to be nonconformist. Here were born Ambroise Paré (1509-90), often called "the father of modern surgery", Henri Rousseau, the customs officer and renowned naïf painter, Alfred Jarry, precursor of Surrealism, and Alain Gerbault, solo yachtsman. Laval is a pretty town, with its older houses firmly grouped around a solid château on one bank of the Mayenne River, opposite newer buildings on the other side.

▶ Discover the **old town**, with its 16thC houses cantilevered out over the road and its Classical 18thC town mansions; around the **Place de la Trémoille** (B2), stroll along the Rue des Orfèvres, and down the Grande-Rue (house of the **Grand Veneur★**, Renaissance) to the **Pont Vieux** (Old Bridge; 13thC) over the Mayenne. ▶ At the back of the Place is the **Nouveau Château**, now the Law Courts *(Palais de Justice)*, not in fact very new, as it dates from 1540; beautiful Renaissance façade. ▶ The **Vieux Château★**, home of the Counts of Laval, is a severe and forbidding building with an enormous 12thC keep topped by a wooden gallery; very pleasant apartments on the courtyard side, decorated Renaissance style with large richly carved windows *(daily Apr.-mid-Sep.; pm only rest of year; closed Tue.).* ▶ From the ramparts you look over the roofs of the old town; a staircase runs down to the

Romanesque chapel★ (12thC) where the workmanship of the capitals is well worth seeing. ▶ In the main apartvisit the **Salle d'Honneur** (wooden vaulting), with 15thC murals and 14th-16thC regional sculptures; on the ground floor an interesting collection of **naïf paintings**, centred around a work by Douanier Rousseau. ▶ In the keep, 36m high, there is an astonishing **framework of oak and chestnut beams★★**; local historical material, masterpieces by craftsmen and builders of the period. ▶ Excellent view of the château from the **Jardin de la Perrine★** (B3), a terraced garden over the river.

Also... ▶ The **cathedral's** (B2-3). Romanesque nave has been vaulted with primitive ogives (1185); Aubusson tapestries (17thC); at the main altar, an altarpiece in white stone and polychrome marble (1640); large triptych★ of St. John (wooden panels, school of Antwerp 16thC), etc. ▶ Near the cathedral, the 15thC **Beucheresse Gate** is a remnant of Laval's old fortifications. ▶ In the **church of St. Vénérand** (B2), stained glass★ of 1521 showing the Passion. ▶ **Notre-Dame des Cordeliers** (A2): six marble altars★, 17thC. ▶ **St. Martin★** (A2; *closed*): Romanesque, end of 11thC. ▶ To the S (C4), on the banks of the Mayenne, **Notre-Dame d'Avesnières** (11th-12thC): noteworthy apse★. ▶ 2 km N: **Notre-Dame-de-Pritz**, Carolingian origins; murals★ from 11th-16thC and painted 13thC calendar.

Nearby

▶ **Church of Clermont Abbey** (15 km NW): pure lines of Cistercian architecture. ▶ **Château de Montjean** (16 km SW), a ruined lakeside fortress. ▶ **Cossé-le-Vivien** (18 km

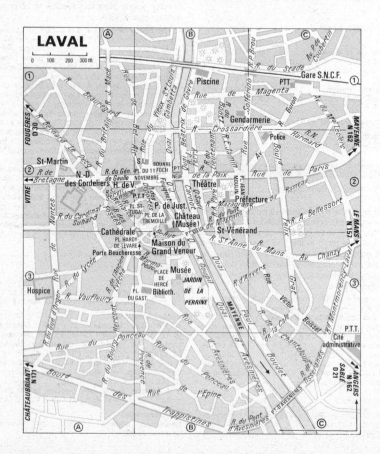

SW) : ceramics and symbolic sculptures by Robert Tatin in the museum *(daily)*. ☐

Practical Information

LAVAL
ℹ pl. du 11-Novembre (B2), ☎ 43.53.09.39.
✗ *Laval-Entrammes-Beausoleil*, ☎ 43.53.73.15.
SNCF (C1), ☎ 43.53.21.50/43.53.35.82.
Car rental : *Avis*, 93, av. R.-Buron (C1-2), ☎ 43.53.07.56.

Hotels :
★★ *L'Impérial Hôtel*, 61, av. Robert-Buron (C1), ☎ 43.53.55.02, AE DC Euro Visa, 33 rm 1 apt ℗ ⟡ ♪ ⅋ closed Aug-Dec, 150.
★ *La Gerbe de Blé*, 83, rue Victor-Boissel (C3), ☎ 43.53.14.10, AE DC Euro Visa, 12 rm, closed Sun eve and Mon, 5-22 Aug, 168. Rest. ● ♦♦ ♪ P. Porter blends regional and classic cuisines : fish and seafood steamed over seaweed, *foie gras chaud à l'hydromel*, Loire Valley wines, 120-220.

Restaurants :
● ♦♦ *Le Bistro de Paris*, 67, rue du Val-de-Mayenne (B2), ☎ 43.56.98.29, Visa ♪ ⅋ ⅋ closed Sat noon and Sun , Feb, Aug. Once upon a time in the West (of France), a prize-winning chef named Guy Lemercier served delicious food at friendly prices. *Foie frais de canard aux raisins, sandre au flan à l'ail, boudin de langoustines.* Sweets, Loire Valley wines, 70-200.
♦♦ *Bellevue La Forêt*, rte de Nantes, ☎ 43.68.03.07, Euro Visa ⟨ ⫿ ♪ & closed Mon and Sun eve. A cool green setting and affordable prices, 80-140 ; child : 25.
♦♦ *La Beucheresse*, 63, Grande-Rue (B3), ☎ 43.53.88.12, AE DC Euro Visa ⫿ ♪ closed Mon and Sun, 1-12 Jan, 10-31 Jul. A 17thC decor in the old town, 60-130.
♦♦ *La Rousine*, 333, rte de Tours (off map C4), ☎ 43.53.03.10, AE Euro Visa ♪ & closed Mon and Sun eve. Likable food, 65-120 ; child : 30.

⚠ at Saint-Pierre-le-Potier, RN 162, ★★*Potier* (42 pl), ☎ 43.53.09.39.

Recommended
Chambres d'hôtes : at l'Huisserie, 9 km on D 112, *Ferme la Véronnière*, 53260 Entrammes, ☎ 43.98.02.96 ; at la Bazouge-de-Chemère, *Ferme du Grand Vaugeron*, 19 km on N 157 and D 152, 53170 Meslay-du-Maine, ☎ 43.01.21.15.

Nearby

ERNÉE, ⊠ 53500, 30 km.

Hotel :
★★ *Relais de Poste* (L.F.), 1, pl. de l'Église, ☎ 43.05.20.33, Tx 730956, Euro Visa, 35 rm ℗ ⫿ & 190. Rest. ♦ closed Sun eve, 60-125.

⚠ ★★★*Municipal* (66 pl), ☎ 43.05.19.90.

LOUÉ

Laval 50, Alençon 61, Paris 228 km
⊠ 72540

Hotel :
● ★★★ *Ricordeau* (R.C.), 13, av. de la Libération, ☎ 43.88.40.03, Tx 722013, AE DC Euro Visa, 22 rm ℗ ⫿ ⟡ closed Jan, 500. Rest. ● ♦♦♦ The Laurent family has restored this famous Sarthes stopover. Gilbert Laurent, a member of our chefs' panel, still displays the talent and enthusiasm that have made him a star in the kitchen. Modest yet demanding, he serves commendable cuisine made from bountiful local produce : famed Loué poultry, *tête de veau Ricordeau, sole de ligne en papillote*. Save room for dessert, especially the "rêve d'enfant sage". Great wines. Gift shop, 190-300.

⚠ ★★*de la Vègre* (35 pl), ☎ 43.27.40.18.
Recommended
Events : *poultry fair*, early Dec.

Le LUDE*

Le Mans 44, Tours 52, Paris 247 km
pop 4895 ⊠ 72800   B2-3
On certain summer nights, the Loir is ablaze with light. On its banks, pavanes and stately minuets are danced, Henri IV caracoles on a snow-white horse, and Mme de Sévigné steps delicately ashore from her barge. The whole town takes part in the glories of an evening on the Loir, in the noble setting of the château and its gardens. The quality of the presentation has contributed largely to the reputation of this little low-roofed town in the Sarthe, a favourite spot for fishermen. Local industry : dairy produce and furniture.

▶ Deep, dry moats protect the **château**★★ and its four enormous towers, though their crenels and machicolations are now no more than decoration. The N façade is Gothic, while the S dates from 1520-30 (François I), with Italian Renaissance medallions and delicate sculptures. Overlooking the Loir, the harmonious Louis XIV façade in white stone unites the two. Take a walk along the terrace above the river *(daily 3-6, Apr.-Sep.)*. ☐

Practical Information

ℹ pl. F.-de-Nicolay (h.s.) ; 8, rue du Bœuf, ☎ 43.94.62.20 (l.s.). ♥

Hotel :
★ *Maine* (L.F.), 24, av. de Saumur, ☎ 43.94.60.54, 24 rm ℗ ⫿ closed Sun eve and Sat (l.s.), 25 Dec-20 Jan, 190.

⚠ ★★★★*Municipal* (400 pl), ☎ 43.94.67.70.

Recommended
Son et lumière : *château du Lude*, ☎ 43.94.62.20, (Fri and Sat, Jun-Sep), a luxurious pageant with 350 actors, 300 fountains and fireworks.

MAMERS

Alençon 25, Le Mans 45, Paris 195 km
pop 6815 ⊠ 72600   C1

ℹ 9, rue Ledru-Rollin, ☎ 43.97.60.63.   ♥

Hotel :
★★ *Bon Laboureur* (L.F.), 1 rue P.-Bert, ☎ 43.97.60.27, AE DC Euro Visa, 10 rm ℗ ♪ 🏃 & closed Fri eve and Sat lunch (l.s.), 14 Feb-1 Mar, 140. Rest. ♦ ♪ & Enjoyable little eatery, 65-125.

⚠ ★★*Municipal* (50 pl), ☎ 43.97.68.30.

Le MANS***

Tours 82, Angers 88, Paris 203 km
pop 150331 ⊠ 72000   B2
The reputation of Le Mans rests on a thrilling 24-hr car race, jars of potted meat *(rillettes)* and delicious apples. It is all too easy to forget that this capital of Maine has seen enough history to be well provided with churches, museums, Gallo-Roman remains, and, of course, a noble cathedral. Fairs, exhibitions, trade and big business in the form of powerful banks, insurance companies and the car industry (Renault) have all combined to make this a city worthy of its past ; and important planning initiatives are under way to make sure that the city's inheritance is not allowed to dwindle.

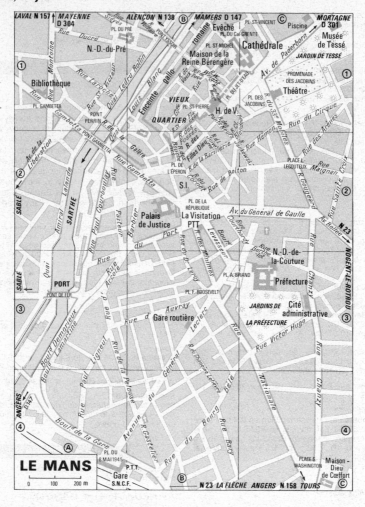

LE MANS

0   100   200 m

> The magnificent **cathedral of St. Julien**★★★ *(8-12 & 2-7)* rises nobly above the **Place des Jacobins** (C1), where the city's Friday market is held. The cathedral's nave and façade are Romanesque (11th-12thC), while the transept and choir are Gothic. On the S side, the statues round the doorway★★ (12thC) recall those of the Royal Door at Chartres. The choir★★★ (1217-54) is a masterpiece of Gothic architecture; superb stained glass★★ (14th-15thC) illuminates the interior; painting★ from the end of the 14thC in the apsidal chapel; in the baptismal chapel, the tombs★★ of Charles IV of Anjou and Guillaume du Bellay (1491-1543, warrior and diplomat).
> Facing the cathedral : restored Renaissance **Grabatoire Mansion**★. ▶ SW of the cathedral : **Vieux Mans** (the old town), with its antique dealers and craftsmen, offers a vivid reminder of the Middle Ages and the Renaissance.
> Many ancient buildings : Rue de la Reine-Bérengère (B1), N° 9, Renaissance house, N° 11-13, **Maison de la Reine Bérengère**, 15thC, devoted to the history, art and popular traditions of Maine; temporary exhibits of arts and crafts from around the world *(9-12 & 2-6 ex Mon.)*.
> Opposite : 15thC **Maison des Deux Amis** (N°s 18-20).
> Nearby : Rue des Chanoines, remains of the **Priory of**

St. Martin (6th-9thC), crypt and artists' workshops *(daily ex Sun., Jul.-15 Sep.)*.
> The **Grande-Rue**, the direct continuation of the Rue de la Reine-Bérengère, is also bordered by fine old houses; see the Maison du Pilier Rouge (16thC), **Maison d'Adam et Eve**★ (N° 69); N°s 86, 108 & 105 are also worth noticing. ▶ The **Gallo-Roman fortress** (3rd-4thC; B1) is one of the marvels of Le Mans; with its eleven towers, the part overlooking the Sarthe is the best preserved. ▶ The **de Tessé Museum**★ (C1) : variety of shows and exhibitions, good paintings *(9-12 & 2-6 ex nat. hols.)*; the star of the show is a large plaque of *champlevé* enamel (c.1150) showing Geoffroi Plantagenêt, ancestor of the Kings of England. Italian primitives are well represented, notably the 14thC school of Siena (Pietro Lorenzetti★); French, Spanish, Flemish and Dutch schools; gallery of contemporary art.

Also... ▶ **Notre-Dame-de-la-Couture** (C3; *8-7 daily*) : former abbey church; note the semicircular★ choir (11thC), the doorway★ (13thC), Virgin★ by Germain Pilon (16thC), the shroud★ of St. Bernard (oriental silk, 6th or 7thC). ▶ **Church of the Visitation**, 1730, dependency of the 18thC convent. ▶ **Notre-Dame-du-Pré** (A-B1) : Romanesque, 11th-12thC. ▶ **Place St-Pierre** (B1), the town hall

of 1760 and the **collegiate church of St-Pierre-la-Cour**
(11th-14thC), now given over to exhibitions *(2-7,
Tue.-Sat.; entry Rue des Fossés-St-Pierre; tel. :
43.84.97.97)* and concerts. ▶ **Church of Ste-Jeanne-
d'Arc**, in the former Coëffort hospital (C4), end of 12thC
(capitals★, beams★).

Nearby

▶ **24-hour race-track** *(6 km S to Automobile Museum).*
Tertre Rouge, Mulsanne and Arnage, famous landmarks
on the course, are household words among motor racing
enthusiasts. Ordinarily open to traffic, the track circuit
measures 13.26 km. The famous day and night race is
held in June. On the D139, at the main entry to the track,
is an underground entrance to the permanent Bugatti circuit (4.24 km, car and motorcycle schools, tests) and
Automobile Museum★★ with 150 vehicles : old cars to
1914, steam, electric and petrol driven cars, racing cars,
the *monstres sacrés* of 1920-49, cars which took part in
the 24 Hours, cycles, motorcycles *(9-12 & 2-7, Easter-15
Oct.; 9-12 & 2-6, 16 Oct.-Easter; closed Tue.).* ▶ The
abbey of l'Épau★ *(4.5 km ESE of Le Mans)*, founded in
1229 by Bérengère (Berengaria), wife of Richard the Lion-
Heart, restored in the 15thC after a fire; chapterhouse,
cellar, kitchen, refectory. The queen's tomb is in the
church, with a 13thC effigy *(9:30-12 & 2-6; closed Thu.
and 15 Sep.-15 Apr.).* Near the abbey : the **Bois de
Changé**, 2.5 km² of leisure park. ▶ **Domaine de Pescheray** *(24 km E)* : agricultural museum, animal park,
"Knowledge of Trees" instructional trail *("Connaissance
des Arbres"; 10-7, Apr.-Oct., closed Mon.; 12-dusk, Wed.,
Sat. & Sun., Nov.-Mar.).* ▶ 21 km N, **Ballon keep**
(11th-15thC). Botanical park *(15 Jul.-Sep., 2:30-6:30).* □

The Le Mans 24-Hour Race

*In 1923 the organizers of the Automobile Club de
l'Ouest, Gustave Singher and Georges Durant, arranged the first of these famous trials for car manufacturers. The first year, the winning car — a Chenard et
Walcker — covered 2,209 km at an average of
92 kph, while the track record was won by a Bentley
(107 kph). Today the famous Hunaudières straight is
taken at over 300 kph, but the noise, the colour, the
lights, the smell and the excitement are still the same.*

Practical Information _____

Le MANS
ℹ 40, pl. de la République (B2), ☎ 43.28.17.22; sq. Jac-
ques-Dubois, ☎ 43.24.84.88.
✈ *Le Mans-Arnage*, 7 km S, ☎ 43.84.00.43.
SNCF (A4), ☎ 43.24.96.10/43.24.74.00/43.24.59.50.
Car rental : *Avis*, train station (A4), ☎ 43.28.56.57 ; 24, rue
du Bourg-Belé (B4), ☎ 43.24.30.50.

Hotels :
★★★ *Chantecler*, 50, rue de la Pelouse (A-B4),
☎ 43.24.58.53, Euro Visa, 36 rm 🅿 🔍 ᕕ 210. Rest. ♦ *La
Feuillantine* ♪ ᕕ closed Sun, 20 Dec-5 Jan, 60-180.
★★★ *Concorde*, 16, av. du Gal-Leclerc (B3),
☎ 43.24.12.30, Tx 720487, AE DC Euro Visa, 68 rm 🅿 ▥
♪ 🎿 375. Rest. ♦♦ ♪ 125-250.
★★★ *Moderne*, 14, rue du Bourg-Belé (B4),
☎ 43.24.79.20, AE DC Euro Visa, 32 rm 🅿 ♪ ᕕ 275.
Rest. ♦♦ ♪ ᕕ 115-250.
● ★★ *La Pommeraie*, rte de l'Éventail, 4 km E on N 23,
☎ 43.85.13.93, 34 rm 🅿 🏃 ▥ 🔍 ᕕ 110.
★★ *L'Escale*, 72, rue Chanzy (C3), ☎ 43.84.55.92, AE DC
Euro Visa, 49 rm 🅿 closed 20 Dec-4 Jan, 150.

Restaurants :
♦♦ *La Grillade*, 1 bis, rue C.-Blondeau (B-C1),
☎ 43.24.21.87, AE Euro Visa ♪ closed Fri eve, Sat noon, Sun
eve, 20-30 Jul, 70-180.
♦ *Le Grenier à Sel*, 26, pl. de l'Éperon (B2),

☎ 43.23.26.30, AE Euro Visa ᕕ closed Mon and Sun eve,
3-24 Aug. Chef André Plunian offers *serpentin de sole et
de saumon à la julienne de poireaux, andouillette en pot-
au-feu, chaud-froid de sorbets à la menthe ciselée et au
chocolat noir*, 100-230.

Recommended
Auction house : rue des Ursulines, ☎ 43.24.47.07.
♥ crafts : *Chambre des Métiers de la Sarthe*, 22, rue
du 33e-Mobiles, ☎ 43.81.41.50; *Emmaüs*, Z.I. nord (rte
d'Alençon), 2, bis rue des Frères-Voisin, ☎ 43.21.30.16;
pastry : *Pasquier*, 33, rue Gambetta, ☎ 43.28.05.37, luscious iced cakes ; pork products : *la Truie qui File*, 25, pl.
de la République, ☎ 43.28.43.36, for their old-fashioned
pork spread.

Nearby

ARNAGE, ✉ 72230, 7 km S on the N23.

Restaurant :
● ♦♦♦ *Auberge des Matfeux*, 289, av. Nationale,
☎ 43.21.10.71, AE DC Euro Visa ⸜ ▥ ♪ ᕕ closed Mon and
Sun eve and hol eves, 2-31 Jan, 15-30 Jul. In his pleasant
restaurant, Alain Souffront admirably prepares ingredients
from a small Sarthois farm : chicken, baby lamb, salads
and garden herbs, 100-260.

BONNETABLE, ✉ 72110, 28 km NE.

Hotel :
★ *Le Lion d'Or*, 1, rue du Gal-Leclerc, ☎ 43.29.30.19,
13 rm 🅿 closed Sun eve and Mon, 1-25 Feb, 110. Rest. ♦
♪ His many years with Jacques Manière taught Michel
Quintreau to make very good and affordable dishes. Incredible 50 and 100 F menus. *Filets de canard au miel, poulet
au vinaigre de cidre*, home-made desserts, 50-130.

CONNERRÉ, ✉ 72160, 25 km E.
ℹ mairie, ☎ 43.89.00.66.
SNCF ☎ 43.29.00.08.

Hotel :
★★ *Saint-Jacques* (L.F.), pl. du Monument, Thorigné-sur-
Due, 4 km SE, ☎ 43.89.95.50, Tx 720410, DC Visa, 10 rm
🅿 ▥ 🔍 ♪ ᕕ closed Sun eve (l.s.) and Mon, 5-31 Jan, 170.
Rest. ♦ ♪ ᕕ 70-200.

Restaurant :
♦♦ *Tante Léonie*, 58, rue de Paris, ☎ 41.89.00.24 ♪
closed Mon eve and Tue, 10 Jan-1 Feb, 70-200.
⏣ ★★*Municipal* (200 pl), ☎ 43.29.00.66.

GUÉCÉLARD, ✉ 72230 Arnage, 16 km SW of **Connerré**.

Restaurant :
♦♦ *Belle Etoile*, N 23, ☎ 43.21.12.02, AE DC Euro Visa ♪
closed Mon, 15 Aug-7 Sep, 70-185.

RUAUDIN, ✉ 72230 Arnage, 5 km SE.

Hotel :
Hippodrome, rte de Tours, ☎ 43.84.29.05, Visa, 10 rm 🅿
⸜ ▥ closed Sat, 90. Rest. ● ♦ *Hunaudières* ♪ A gathering spot for hungry sports aficionados : *rillettes*, fabulous grills with sautéed potatoes, good wines chosen by
owner Maurice Genissel, 50-120.

MAYENNE

Laval 30, Alençon 61, Paris 284 km
pop 14298 ✉ *53100*   A1

The name Mayenne applies to an administrative
department, a small river with many of the aspects of
a mighty torrent, and a quiet town which is rarely in
the news. Perhaps that's why visitors who don't like
tourism come here; Mayenne's principal advantage
is that it has almost no traffic and is ideal for houseboats.

▶ Above the right bank : the **basilica of Notre-Dame**,
(12thC early Gothic) restored after serious damage in

1944. ▶ Remains of ancient château rebuilt in 15thC.
▶ 17thC Hôtel de Ville.

Nearby ˎ

▶ **Lassay** *(19 km NE)* : a real fairy tale fortress★ (15thC)
with five large round towers *(2:30-6:30 in season; son-et-
lumière★ eves every Fri., Sat., May-Sep.)* ▶ **Jublains**
(10 km SE) : Roman fortifications *(closed Tue.).* □

Practical Information ─────────────────

ℹ️ pl. du -9-juin-1944, ☎ 43.04.19.37.   ✦
SNCF ☎ 43.04.11.12.

Hotels :
● ★★ **Grand Hôtel** (L.F.), 2, rue A.-de-Loré,
☎ 43.04.37.35, 29 rm ℗ ⅏ closed 24 Dec-8 Jan, 180.
Rest. ◆ 65-110.
★★ **La Croix Couverte** (L.F.), rte d'Alençon,
☎ 43.04.32.48, AE DC Visa, 11 rm ℗ ≼ ⅏ ♪ closed
25-31 Dec, 150. Rest. ◆◆ ≼ ♪ ఉ closed Sun eve (Oct-Jun),
65-150; child : 40.

⚐ ★★*Municipal* (100 pl), ☎ 43.04.21.01.

Recommended
Chambres d'hôtes : *ferme Grappay,* at Brécé, 20 km NW
on N 12 and D 5, 53120 Goron, ☎ 43.04.63.65.

Valley of the MAYENNE*

A1
From Laval to Angers *(115 km, half-day)*
There are forty locks between Laval and Angers,
which makes it a poor river for commercial traffic
but excellent for pleasure craft; and the same may be
said for the whole of the Maine basin. The Mayenne
is quite different from the Sarthe and the Loir; it has
dug its bed in the last schistic outcrop from the Armorican Massif, with banks steep enough to ˒prevent
towns or villages from springing up along its edges.
Bas-Maine, which the Mayenne waters from N to S,
was formerly the poor country of the Chouan insur-
rectionists, nothing but heath and scrub. Today, lush
meadows and forage crops feed the area's pigs
and cattle.

▶ **Laval** (→) ▶ **La Trappe du Port-du-Salut** is the home of
the famous cheese of the same name, made today in a
dairy next to the abbey. ▶ **Château-Gontier** (→). ▶ Several handsome manor-houses standing well back from the
river : **Escoubière Manor** (16thC); **château du Percher,**
between Gothic and Renaissance; **château du Bois-Mauboucher** (15th-17thC) next to a lake. ▶ **Le Lion-d'Angers**
(pop. 2775) occupies a picturesque site on the right bank
of the Oudon; see the church of St. Martin (11thC nave,
15thC paintings). Le Lion is known for horse-breeding;
1 km E, the **National Stud of l'Isle Briand** is open to visitors *(2-5).* ▶ **Le Plessis-Macé** (→ Angers). □

Practical Information ─────────────────

Le LION-D'ANGERS, ⊠ 49220, 22 km NW of **Angers.**
ℹ️ mairie, ☎ 41.91.30.16; 14, pl. du Champ-de-Foire,
☎ 41.91.83.19 (h.s.).   ✦

Hotel :
★ *Voyageurs,* ☎ 41.95.30.08, 13 rm ℗ closed Sun eve ex
Jul-Sep, 15 Jan-10 Feb, 1-25 Oct, 160. Rest. ◆ closed
Sun eve (l.s.), 40-130.

⚐ ★★*Municipal* (100 pl), ☎ 41.91.31.56.

MONTREUIL-BELLAY*

Angers 53, Poitiers 80, Paris 315 km
pop 4331 ⊠ 49260   B4
One of the most picturesque sites in Anjou, on a little
hill above the right bank of the Thonon. Two fortified

gateways and part of the ramparts still surround
the town.

▶ They say that the fearless Duchess of Longueville
(1619-79), sister of the Grand Condé (Louis II de Bourbon,
the brilliant general), rode her horse up the staircase of
the **château**★; the edifice in question was a rugged fortress in the 11thC, metamorphosed during the 15thC into
a superb residence. Remarkable **kitchen**★ with a central
hearth *(10-12 & 2-6, Apr.-Oct.; 10-12 & 2:30-6:30, Jul. &
Aug.; closed Tue.).* ▶ At the foot of the château, remains
of the Nobis Priory (12th, 14th & 17thC). ▶ On the edge of
the forest of Cizay, the **abbey of Asnières** *(8 km N)* is
in ruins, but the choir★★ of the church (1210-20) is one of
the most perfect specimens of 13thC Angevin Gothic
(10-12 & 2-6, Jul.-Aug.; closed Tue.). □

Practical Information ─────────────────

ℹ️ mairie, ☎ 41.52.33.86.
SNCF ☎ 41.67.50.50.

Hotel :
● ★ **Splendid** (L.F.), rue du Dr-Gaudrez, ☎ 41.52.30.21,
Euro Visa, 40 rm ℗ ≼ ⅏ ⌖ ☞ ⊡ half pens (h.s.), closed
Sun eve (l.s.), 15-25 Jan, 350. Rest. ◆ ♪ ☞ 50-160.

Restaurant :
◆◆ **Porte Saint-Jean,** 432, rue Nationale, ☎ 41.52.30.41,
Visa ♪ ఉ closed Mon and Tue , Feb, 15-30 Nov. The chef
is inspired by the market and the seasons : *boudin de brochet, assiette du pêcheur du val,* 110-250.

⚐ ★★★*Airotel des Nobis* (100 pl), ☎ 41.52.33.66.

MONTSOREAU*

Tours 56, Angers 64, Paris 301 km
pop 454 ⊠ 49730   B4
On the edge of Anjou and Touraine, the epitome of
the discreet Loire town. Nothing is missing : the white
wine (coteaux de Saumur) is full and perfumed, and
the château overlooks the river.

▶ The **château**★ (15thC) was the earliest in Anjou to
evolve from the medieval fortress to a more courtly residence; Grand Staircase★; *Goums* museum (North African
tribal levies in the French Army; *9-12 & 2-7, Apr.-Sep.;
9-12 & 2-5, Oct.-Mar.; closed Tue.).* ▶ 2.5 km NW : **Moulin
de la Herpinière** (mill) at Turquant *(15 Mar.-15 Oct.; closed Mon. ex Jul. & Aug.).* □

Practical Information ─────────────────

ℹ️ mairie, ☎ 41.51.70.22.

Hotel :
● ★★ **Diane de Méridor-Le Bussy** (L.F.), quai Philippe-
de-Commynes, ☎ 41.51.70.18, Visa, 19 rm ℗ ≼ ⅏ ⌖ ఉ
closed Mon eve and Tue ex Jul-Aug, 15 Dec-31 Jan, 210.
Rest. ◆◆ ≼ ఉ **Spec** : *sandre au beurre blanc, soufflé aux
framboises,* 75-120; child : 50.

⚐ ★★*de l'Isle verte* (160 pl), ☎ 41.51.76.60.

Recommended
Rural-gîte : *Château de Parnay,* ☎ 41.38.10.85, pool, tennis, fishing 500 m away.

SABLÉ-SUR-SARTHE

Laval 42, Le Mans 48, Paris 252 km
pop 12721 ⊠ 72300   B2
An imposing château in severely Classical style
overlooks this modest town, which has given its name
to a famous form of biscuit *(sablés).* The town occupies both banks of the Sarthe. In the Island Quarter *(Quartier de l'Ile),* see the church of Notre-Dame (1891); 15th-16thC stained glass. Pleasant gardens
above the river.

Exploring the Haut-Maine, trip from Sablé-sur-Sarthe to Durtal *(96 km, half-day)*

▶ The Sarthe and the Loir (→ Bercé Forest) meander peacefully through the pastureland of the Haut-Maine in the department of the Sarthe, a landscape full of woods and meadows, with little-known villages and hidden manors. ▶ **Solesmes :** Benedictine abbey, rebuilt in 1833, on the banks of the Sarthe; source of a world-famous series of Gregorian Chant recordings. See especially the **Saints of Solesmes★★**, marvelous sculptures of 15th-16thC in the partially Romanesque church *(Gregorian chant, Mass sung 9:45, vespers 5 pm).* ▶ **Asnières-sur-Vègre★ :** an old bridge over the river, Romanesque church (11thC; murals★ 13th-14thC) and a romantic setting among the greenery; a charming village. 2.5 km NW : **château de Verdelles★**, 1490, has come down through the centuries unchanged *(by appt., tel. : 43.71.53.59).* ▶ **Parcé-sur-Sarthe :** see the great mill on the dam. ▶ **Malicorne-sur-Sarthe** (pop. 1773) : Madame de Sévigné (1626-96; renowned chronicler of the era) praised the charm of its château (17thC), but this small town is best known for its pottery *(guided tour of workshops and museum Easter-Sep., 8-12 & 2-6; closed Sun.).* ▶ **Saint-Jean-de-la-Motte.** ▶ **Luché-Pringé** (pop. 1433), on the right bank of the Loir; see the Plantagenêt (Angevin) choir★★ (13thC) and the Pietà★ (1500) in the church. ▶ 3 km NW : charming **manor of Vénevelles** (16th-17thC). ▶ 10 km SE : **château du Lude** (→). ▶ **Château de Gallerande★** (15thC), easily seen from the road *(no visitors)* in a romantic park with peacocks. ▶ **La Flèche** (→). ▶ **Bazouges-sur-le-Loir★** (pop. 1313) : from the bridge over the river, the old washhouses, the 16thC château and the mill make a charming picture. ▶ **Durtal**, a peaceful town on the Loir : waterfront, mills, 15th-17thC château. S : **Chambiers Forest** (13 km² of oak and pine), pleasant walks. □

Practical Information ⸻

Nearby

BAZOUGES-SUR-LE-LOIR, ⊠ 72200 La Flèche, 7 km W of **La Flèche.**

Restaurant :
♦♦ *Croissant*, ☎ 43.45.32.08, closed Mon and Sun eve, 5-31 Jan, 70-120.

⚓ ★★*Municipal* (53 pl), ☎ 43.94.30.20.

DURTAL, ⊠ 49430, 13 km W of **La Flèche.**
ℹ mairie, ☎ 41.80.10.24. ✦

Restaurant :
● ♦ *La Boule d'Or*, 19, av. d´Angers, ☎ 41.76.30.20, Euro Visa ⚆ ♪ ௲ closed Wed, 3-13 Mar, 11 Aug-4 Sep. Excellent value. Spec : *foie gras frais de canard maison, saumon à l'oseille beurre blanc*, 45-150.

⚓ ★★★*Municipal* (150 pl), ☎ 41.80.11.80.

LUCHÉ-PRINGÉ, ⊠ 72800 Le Lude, 10 km NW.

Hotel :
● ♦ ★★ *Le Port des Roches* (L.F.), 2 km on D 214, ☎ 43.45.44.48, DC Euro Visa, 15 rm ℗ ⚆ ௲ ⚘ closed Sun eve and Mon, 150. Rest. ♦ ♪ 65-95.

MALICORNE-SUR-SARTHE, ⊠ 72270, 32 km SW of **Le Mans.**

Restaurant :
♦ *Petite Auberge*, 5, pl. Du Guesclin, ☎ 43.94.80.52, Euro Visa ♪ closed Mon. Spec : *huîtres chaudes, foie de canard à l'armagnac*, 65-100.

⚓ ★★*Municipal* (83 pl), ☎ 43.94.80.14.

SAINT-DENIS-D'ANJOU, ⊠ 53290 Grêz-en-Bouère, 10 km SW.

Restaurant :
♦♦ *Roi René*, 4, Grande-Rue, ☎ 43.70.52.30, DC Euro Visa ⚆ ♪ ௲ closed Tue eve and Wed, 20 Jan-3 Mar, 65-140; child : 30.

SAULGES, ⊠ 53340 Ballée, 20 km NW.

Hotel :
● ★★ *L'Ermitage* (L.F.), Le Bourg, ☎ 43.01.22.28, Euro Visa, 22 rm ℗ ⚆ ⚆ ௲ ♪ ℘ closed Sun eve , Mon (ex 15 May-30 Sep), Feb, 130. Rest. ♦♦ ♪ Carefully prepared food, 75-145.

⚓ ★★*Municipal* (35 pl), ☎ 43.01.22.23.

SOLESMES, ⊠ 72300 Sablé-sur-Sarthe, 3 km NE.

Hotel :
★★★ *Grand Hôtel* (France-Accueil), 16, pl. Dom Guéranger, ☎ 43.95.45.10, Tx 722903, AE DC Euro Visa, 30 rm ⚆ ௲ closed Feb, 220. Rest. ♦♦ Spec : *salade de saumon sauvage au citron, petits choux farcis aux langoustines, pot-au-feu de volailles*, 85-250; child : 35.

SAINT-CALAIS*

Le Mans 45, Blois 64, Paris 186 km
pop 4779 ⊠ 72120   C2

The River Anille (it means 'tendril') twines prettily past the moss-covered stones and flowered gardens of this important agricultural market town on the edges of Maine and the Vendômois.

▶ The **church of Notre-Dame :** handsome Renaissance façade★ (1522). ▶ Ruins of 11thC château on the hill. ▶ 11 km S : **château de Courtanvaux**, 15th-16thC, restored in 1815 *(free entry to the park ; tours daily ex Tue. at 10, 11, 2, 3, 4, 5, 6, May-Sep.; Sun. and nat. hols., Oct.-Apr.; in season, art exhibitions, theatre and music).* □

Practical Information ⸻

ℹ rue Ch.-Garnier, ☎ 43.35.00.36. ✦

Hotel :
★ *Angleterre*, 9, rue du Guichet, ☎ 43.35.00.43, Visa, 13 rm ℗ closed Sun eve and Mon, 9-22 Jun, 24 Dec-11 Jan, 130. Rest. ♦ Good regional table, 55-100.

⚓ ★★*du Lac* (100 pl), ☎ 43.35.04.81.

Recommended
Events : *folk festival*, in Sep; *apple turnover festival*, 1st weekend in Sep.

SAINT-FLORENT-LE-VIEIL*

Angers 42, Nantes 57, Paris 330 km
pop 2560 ⊠ 49410   A3

On a hill above the Loire the bell tower stands like a signpost, with old stone houses descending to the quays. Two leaders of the Vendéen insurrection are buried here : Bonchamp, in the church with a splendid **tomb★** sculpted by David d'Angers, and Jacques Cathelineau. Magnificent view of the Loire from the esplanade in front of the church.

Nearby

▶ **Château de la Bourgonnière** *(5.5 km W)* : an enormous park surrounds this 19thC château; superb Renaissance chapel★ (Christ in Majesty★). ▶ **Champtoceaux★** *(21 km W;* pop. 1252) : wonderful site, and the Promenade de Champalud★★, a long terrace overhanging the Loire, is one of the principal sights of Anjou. The local white wine has considerable merit. ▶ **Liré** *(12 km W),* birthplace of poet Joachim du Bellay, "the French Ovid" (1522-60) ; little museum devoted to him in the village *(closed Mon.).* □

Practical Information ⸻

SAINT-FLORENT-LE-VIEIL
ℹ mairie, ☎ 41.78.50.39. ✦

Hotel :
★ *Gabelle* (L.F.), ☎ 41.78.50.19, AE DC Euro Visa, 17 rm

P ⧖ ⟁ closed 28 Oct-3 Nov, 23 Dec-3 Jan, 100. Rest. ◆
⧖ ⟁ closed Sun eve (l.s.), 50-120.

Nearby

CHAMPTOCEAUX, ⊠ 49270 Saint-Laurent, 20 km W.
Ⓘ mairie, ☎ 40.83.52.31.

Hotel :
★★ *Côte* (L.F.), 2, rue du Dr-Giffard, ☎ 40.83.50.39, Euro
Visa, 28 rm P ⟁ ⟁ 170. Rest. ◆ closed Fri eve and Sat
(l.s.), Oct-Mar, 50-165.

Restaurant :
● ◆◆ *Auberge de la Forge*, 1 bis, pl. des Piliers,
☎ 40.83.56.23, AE DC Euro Visa ⧖ ⟁ ♪ closed Tue eve,
Wed, Sun eve, Feb school hols, 30 Jun-8 Jul, 13-28 Oct.
Paul Pauvert serves his generous cuisine in a pretty
decor : *brochet beurre blanc*, 80-200.

INGRANDES-SUR-LOIRE, ⊠ 49170 Saint-Georges,
9 km NE.

Restaurant :
◆ *Chez Baudoin*, Mesnil-en-Vallée, ☎ 41.39.20.25 ⧖
Reserve, 70-140.

SAUMUR★★★

Angers 52, Tours 66, Paris 300 km
pop 33953 ⊠ 49400   B3

"The pearl of Anjou" owes its renown in great part
to the horse : the famous Cadre Noir cavalry school,
renowned throughout the equestrian world, is based
here, and has schooled generations of horsemen and
their mounts. The town has other claims to fame,
however : its white wines, vigorous and perfumed, the
mushrooms of the area and, perhaps least known of
all, its carnival mask factory, which exports laughter
all over Europe.

▶ The **château** (C3) rises proudly over the grey slate roofs
and the light-filled landscape of the Loire. Rebuilt at the
end of the 14thC and remodeled a number of times since,
it has four towers at the corners crowned with machicolations *(daily 9-6:30, Jul.-Sep.; 9-11:30 & 2-6 Apr.-Jun. and
Oct.; 9:30-11:30 & 2-6 ex Tue., Nov.-Mar.; Jul. and Aug.,
evening tours 8:30-10:30).* ▶ As its name indicates, the
Tour du Guet (watchtower) has a splendid outlook over

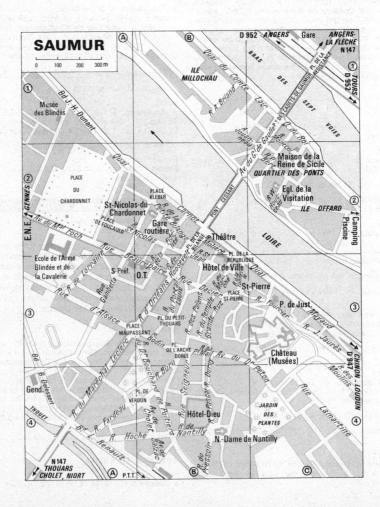

the valleys of the Loire and the Thouet. ▶ There are two museums in the château : the **Decorative Arts Museum** occupies the first floor of the two restored wings. Beautiful collections of *objets d'art* from the Middle Ages and the Renaissance (chests, enamels, tapestries; the Bal des Sauvages, c.1500) and a rare collection of 17th-18thC ceramics (Delft, Rouen★, Nevers, Moustiers) and French porcelains. On the second floor, the **Museum of the Horse★** traces the history of equitation in France and abroad; collections★ of saddles, bits, stirrups, etc. ▶ On leaving the château, there is a pleasant walk along the hilltop **Rue des Moulins** (C4). ▶ The **church of Notre-Dame de Nantilly** (B4) is a fine Romanesque building (12thC), both powerful and severe; it houses a remarkable collection of tapestries★★ (16th-17thC) from the Loire, Tournai, Flanders, Brussels and Aubusson; note particularly the Tree of Jesse★ (N transept). ▶ **Cavalry Museum** (A2-3) displays the history of the famous French cavalry officers' training school, founded in 1768. The school now teaches the tactics and strategy of tank warfare *(visit on request)*. In 1972 the École Nationale d'Equitation (National Riding School) was founded in the Terrefort woods where the celebrated **Cadre Noir** has its headquarters *(guided visits daily at 3, Apr.-Oct.)*. Don't miss the renowned equestrian and mechanized tattoo in the **Place du Chardonnet** (A2; end Jul.). ▶ The **Musée des Blindés** (tank museum; A1) includes some 150 vehicles of French and foreign origin, from the Renault tank of 1918 to modern armoured vehicles, including the dreaded Panzers of WWII. *(9-11:30 & 2-5:30)*.

Also... ▶ The **Hôtel de Ville** (town hall; B3), a Gothic construction fortified at the beginning of the 16thC and including the charming 13thC chapel of St. Jean. ▶ **Church of St. Pierre★** (B-C3) : Angevin Gothic, 12th-13thC; 16thC tapestries★. ▶ **Chapel of Notre-Dame-des-Ardillers** (A1), 17thC, fronted by an enormous 20.6 m diam. rotunda. ▶ **Jardin des Plantes** (Botanical Gardens; B-C4) : flowered steps and terraces of vines across the hillside (view). ▶ **Pont des Cadets-de-Saumur** (bridge, C1; inscription) commemorates the heroic defense of the bridges on the Loire by the cadets of the Cavalry school, which held up the German advance for three days.

Nearby

▶ **Château de Boumois★** *(6.5 km NW)*, mid-way between Gothic and Renaissance, built in tufa (end 15th-early 16thC); collections of weapons, dovecote *(10-12 & 2-6, Palm Sun.-1 Nov.; 10-6:30, Jul.-Aug.; closed Tue.)*. ▶ **Saint-Hilaire-Saint-Florent** *(2 km NW)* : Mushroom Museum *(10-12 & 2-6, 15 Mar.-15 Nov.)*. ☐

Practical Information

SAUMUR
ℹ 5, rue Beaurepaire (A-B3), ☎ 41.51.03.06.
SNCF av. David-d'Angers (C1), ☎ 41.67.50.50.
🚌 pl. St-Nicolas (B2), ☎ 41.51.27.29.
Car rental : *Avis*, train station (C1); 5, rue de Rouen (C1), ☎ 41.67.48.68.

Hotels :
● ★★ **Anne d'Anjou**, 32-33, quai Mayaud (C3), ☎ 41.67.30.30, AE Euro Visa, 50 rm Ⓟ ≼ ▩ ⚸ ♪ ⛟ ⚡ closed 23 Dec-3 Jan, 150.
★★ **Roi René**, 94, av. du Gal-de-Gaulle (B-C2), ☎ 41.67.45.30, AE DC Euro Visa, 28 rm Ⓟ ≼ ♪ ⚡ closed 20 Dec-15 Jan, 240. Rest. ♦ ≼ ♪ ⚡ closed Sat noon, 65-120; child : 55.

▲ ★★★*Municipal* (150 pl), ☎ 41.50.45.00.

Recommended
Farmhouse-gîte : *La Poitevinière*, 8 km N on N 147, 49680 Neuillé, ☎ 41.52.55.08, equestrian centre with 3 ch. d'hôtes, restaurant. Riding on premises, pool.

Nearby

Les ROSIERS-SUR-LOIRE, ✉ 49350 Gennes, 15 km.
ℹ mairie, ☎ 41.51.80.04. ⚑

Hotels :
★★★ **Jeanne de Laval**, 54, rue Nationale, ☎ 41.51.80.17, 15 rm Ⓟ ▩ ⚸ ♪ ⛟ closed Sun eve and Mon ex hols (l.s.), 4-12 Mar, 20 Nov-28 Dec, 260. Rest. ● ♦♦♦ Albert Augereau's famous *beurre blanc*, prepared by his son Michel, is a delicious accompaniment to Loire river fish. Anjou wines, 140-250.
● ★ **Val de Loire** (L.F.), pl. de l'Église, ☎ 41.51.80.30, 11 rm ▩ ⚸ closed Sun eve and Mon (l.s.), 1-28 Oct, 150. Rest. ♦ ♪ Regional fare, 80-135.

Restaurant :
● ♦♦ **La Toque Blanche**, 2, rue Quarte, ☎ 41.51.80.75 ♪ closed Tue eve and Wed, 10 Feb-1 Mar, 25 Aug-4 Sep. Three varied and inspired fixed-price menus. Spec : *gâteau de brochet beurre blanc*, 90-130.

▲ ★★*District* (100 pl), ☎ 41.51.80.04.

SEGRÉ*

Angers 36, Laval 50, Paris 305 km
pop 7416 ✉ 49500 A2

An old stone bridge spans the Oudon and, with the quays and a few houses of character, lends a great deal of charm to this unassuming regional capital. The area specializes in stock raising and multiple crop farming in enclosed fields.

Nearby

▶ **Château de la Lorie** (17th-18thC; *Jul.-15 Sep., 3-6 ex Tue.*). ▶ **Château de Bouillé-Thévalle** (15thC; *May-Sep., 2:30-7).* ▶ **Château de Mortiercrolles★** *(10 km N)*, built at the end of 15thC *(2:30-5:30 ex Tue., Jul.-Aug.).* ▶ **Craon** *(20 km N)* has a beautiful late 18thC château in white stone *(garden and park, 9-5 or 7 according to season)*. ▶ **Château de Raguin** *(8.5 km S)* : early 17thC *(May-Sep.).* ▶ Fortified château de **Pouancé** *(25 km W; Jul.-Aug., 9:30-12 & 2-6).* ▶ Mill-lovers should go to see the **moulin d'Angrie**, still turning *(18 km SW; Sat. and Sun.)* and the mill at **Challain-la-Potherie** which is also in running order *(16 km SW; mill 2 km SW of the village; Sat. pm, Jun.-15 Sep.).* ☐

Practical Information

Nearby

CRAON, ✉ 53400, 20 km N.
ℹ rue Pantigny, ☎ 43.06.14.33.
SNCF ☎ 43.06.14.33.

Hotel :
Château de Craon, ☎ 43.06.11.02, 5 rm ▩ ⚸ ⛟ 🄿 closed 15 Sep-15 Jun. 18thC castle setting in a park, 600.

Restaurant :
♦♦ *Ancre d'Or*, 2, av. de la Prom. Ch.-de-Gaulle, ☎ 43.06.14.11, closed Mon eve, Tue eve, Sun eve (l.s.), 50-160.

Recommended
Farmhouse-inn : at 2.5 km, *La Borderie*, ☎ 43.06.26.67, closed Wed and 23-29 Dec. Pork products, *galettes*, *crêpes*. Reserve weekends.

POUANCÉ, ✉ 49420, 24 km W.
ℹ mairie, ☎ 41.92.45.86. ⚑

Hotel :
★★ *Cheval Blanc*, rte de Segré, ☎ 41.92.41.16, Euro Visa, 14 rm Ⓟ closed 15 Jan-10 Feb, 140. Rest. ♦ closed Mon (l.s.), 70-130.

▲ ★★*Municipal* (50 pl), ☎ 41.92.43.97.

Midi Toulousain, Pyrénées

▶ The Garonne runs its course between the lush Armagnac and the outwardly austere Ariège regions. Here, cliffs and peaks rise up abruptly above green valleys, serving as foundation stones for look-out castles and churches echoing the untamed color of the surrounding stone.

Traces of human society dating back as far as 300,0000 or 400,000 years have been discovered in Haute-Garonne, and on the walls of the famous Ariège caves are paintings done by Paleolithic hunters. Many centuries later the caves provided welcome shelter for people fleeing the violence of the Wars of Religion and the Cathar tragedy. Other traces of prehistoric art have been found here, too — animals sculpted from deer antlers, clay figurines and, at the end of the Paleolithic area, the beginnings of a geometrical and abstract art with in some places stylized human figures.

In the 12th and 13th centuries, the troubadours sang the joys of courtly love in the *Langue d'Oc* (the southern French tongue), beginning a transformation of the unsophisticated habits of the day into something finer and more poetic. But the Albigensian crusades sounded the deathknell for this form of literary expression and the troubadours and their language died out.

Where the Garonne makes a final hair-pin turn and chooses the Atlantic coast, midway between the Atlantic and the Mediterranean is Toulouse, whose extraordinary location has proved its fortune. The "pink city," so named after the color of its brick, is an economic and intellectual capital whose dynamism and char-acter make it the natural capital of the whole region between the Pyrénées and the foothills of the Massif central. Once the capital of the Haut-Languedoc kingdom, it is now the spokesman for the *Langue d'Oc* culture and works hand in hand with its sister cities to revive the language and literature of this second branch of French culture and civilization. ☐

 Don't miss

★★★ Saint-Bertrand-de-Comminges A3, Toulouse C2.

★★ Auch A1-2, Bagnères-de-Luchon A3.

★ Ax-les-Thermes C3-4, les Bastides d'Armagnac A1-2, Condom A1, The Upper Couserans Valleys B3, Foix C3, Gimont B1-2, Lectoure B1, Martres-Tolosane B2, Mirepoix C3, Montrejeau A3.

Weekend Tips

Starting from Saint-Gaudens, the first day will cover from Montmaurain to Aurignac, Martres-Tolosanne and Salies-du-Salat (lunch); continue via Saint-Girons and the Gorges de Ribaouto to the valley of Bethmane and Castillon-en-Couserans; stop here for the night. The next day, visit Saint-Béat, lunch at Luchon and on to Saint-Bertrand-de-Comminges and Montréjeau.
From Foix, there is a different route running through Tarascon-sur-Ariège and the Grotte de Niaux, Vicdessos, Aulus-les-Bains and Masat, where you have lunch. Take the road to Verte, the Bastide-de-Sérou and the Mas-d'Azil; stopover at Foix, Varilhes or Saint-Jean-de-Verges. Return to Toulouse through Lavelanet, Montségur, Bélesta, Mirepoix (lunch) and Villefranche-de-Lauragais.

House in the Gers region

Toulousain farm

Sauvetés, castelnaux and bastides

The first sauvetés appeared in the 11thC. They were little communities founded by religious orders to clear the land and bring it under cultivation. At almost the same period, the castelnaux began to spring up near the feudal castles, creating another form of agricultural township. The bastides were introduced into the region in the 13thC to reassemble and control the population after the Albigensian Crusades and the extermination of the Catharist heretics had "purged" the region (first half of 13thC - p. 652); two successive kings, Philippe III and IV, followed this policy, aided by a number of feudal lords and princes of the Church. Many of these bastides were symbolically sponsored by important cities throughout Christendom, hence the names : Barcelone, Boulogne, Cologne, Grenade, Fleurance, Plaisance, Valence... and even Montréal, which has no connection with its Canadian counterpart.

Simple mountain house ("maison-bloc")

 Brief regional history

From Earliest Times to Rome

The earliest traces of man so far discovered (near Montmaurin, in the Haute-Garonne) go back some 300 to 400 000 years. The caves of the Ariège region (Niaux, Gargas...) still have paintings by **palaeolithic hunters** on their walls and one of these grottoes, at

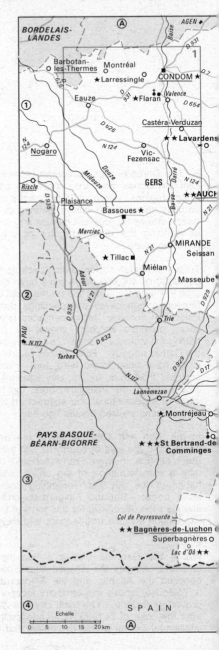

the foot of the Pyrénées, has given its name to a stage of the Upper Palaeolithic period known as Aurignacian, while another has enabled palaeontologists to situate the beginnings of the Mesolithic (Azilian) period. ● Much later we find peoples of Ligurian stock inhabiting the region and finally, about 600 B.C., settlers of the Iberian race. Later still, a people known as the **Volques Tectosages** moved into the territory between the Garonne and Rhone rivers and founded the citadel of Toulouse which soon con-

trolled the area economically. It passed under Roman domination between 120 and 115 B.C.

From 100 B.C. to 700 A.D.
After campaigning in Spain, Pompey gathered a mountain people called the Garunni around the citadel of *Lugdunum Convenarum*, later to become Saint-Bertrand-de-Comminges. ● **Gallo-Roman civilisation** flourished in the upper valley of the Garonne and on a line running from the Atlantic to the Mediterranean

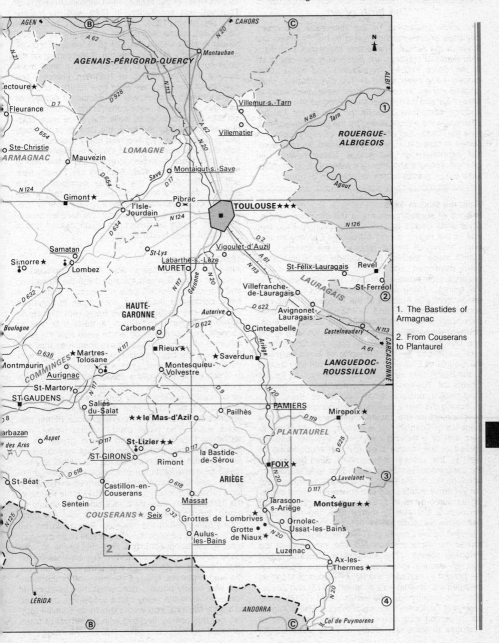

1. The Bastides of Armagnac

2. From Couserans to Plantaurel

while Toulouse became the capital of a region on which several routes converged. ● The countryside was divided into large estates which are now the sites of towns such as Martres Tolosane, Montmaurin and Séviac. ● The Visigoths were next to arrive making Toulouse their capital and settling in the region until they were defeated by the Frankish king, Clovis, near Poitiers. In 585 *Lugdunum Convenarum* was destroyed by the Burgundians.

The birth of art

The most interesting of the numerous prehistoric paintings and engravings found in the Pyrénées are those in the Ariège. These first expressions of mankind's artistic instincts are particularly well-displayed in the caves at Les Trois-Frères and Niaux. Clay models have been found at Tuc d'Audoubert, while animals carved in reindeer horn were discovered at Mas-d'Azil and many other sites. Progressive changes in living conditions towards the end of the Palaeolithic era were accompanied by the development of a new geometric and abstract style of expression, enriched at Mas-d'Azil by stylised human figures. Pictorial expression in the Ariège Valley reflects the changes brought about by new technology in the Neolithic era, in particular the introduction of pottery.

From the 8thC to 1229

In spite of spreading slowly in the mountain valleys, Christianity began to play an increasingly important role in the region during a troubled Carolingian and post-Carolingian period (abbeys were founded, the 10thC roads leading to Santiago de Compostela were developed and during the 11th and 12thC religious communities, known as sauvetés, came into being). Along with the ever-present threat of an attack from the Arabs and the Normans, there was economic stagnation and — thanks to Franco-Spanish rivalries — the **proliferation** of a number of **independent democratic states** of which Andorra is the only one left today. While the county of Comminges was surpassed by the bishopric of Saint-Bertrand, the Counts of Foix kept their power until they moved to the Béarn after inheriting that territory. As for the Counts of Toulouse, the Raymonds, they held a predominant position from the 9th to the 13thC. ● Among the many factors which contributed to the development of the region must be mentioned the influence of Spanish-Arabic culture, that of Italian traders and of a thriving commerce, together with the spread of the **langue d'oc** (by the troubadours) as well as the cultural influence of Saint-Sernin and the Languedoc-Roman school. This renaissance irritated, no doubt, the Capetian central government still not yet firmly established and concerned about ensuring its authority over a 'South' too 'liberated'. ● At the end of the 12thC, shortly after the Council of Saint-Félix-de-Lauragais (1167), the Cathar 'heresy', tolerated by the Counts of Toulouse, began to spread across the plane towards Albi and into parts of the Pyrenees valleys. The **Albigensian Crusade** (1209) was an excuse to subdue a rebellious South, on the pretext of restoring the faith. Simon de Montfort defeated the southerners at Muret (1213) and devastated the countryside and at his death (1218), while besieging Toulouse, the King of France, Phillip Augustus in person took command, forcing the Count of Toulouse to surrender (treaty of Paris-Meaux 1229)

and **incorporating the Languedoc into the French kingdom.** Later, Alphonse of Poitiers, brother of Saint-Louis, married the heiress of the Counts of Toulouse.

13th and 14thC

In order to strengthen the hand of the French crown, Saint Dominic was encouraged (1216) to found settlements of his Order of the Preaching Friars (known as Jacobins) in the region, the Catholic University of Toulouse was established in 1229, and the Inquisition set up in 1234. As for the last bastion of Cathar resistance, Monségur, it was forced to surrender in 1244 after a siege of 10 months. Throughout this period we also see the development of the Southern Gothic style of architecture, a style more austere than the Gothic of Northern France. The majority of the churches were now fortified and built in brick (which is cheaper). In addition a number of **bastides**, or fortlets, were constructed according to a set plan. Surrounded by walls, they were really colonies established by the King, the Church or the local feudal power and they received many preferences to help them develop trade and attract residents. ● The number of these bastides increased still further during the **Hundred Years War,** both on the French side and on that part of the country occupied by the English. Many of these last were in Gascony where foreign occupation had inflicted a severe blow to Toulouse trade. As a consequence, the Mediterranean-Pyrénées region became once again divided into a number of small feudal kingdoms.

16thC to our times

After the Hundred Years' War, France continued its policy of unification and towards 1500 the Armagnac and Comminge regions were recovered. With peace back, commerce flourished once again in Toulouse especially the pastel blue dye trade with exports to Antwerp, England and Spain, a trade that was to become the foundation on which were built the large fortunes of many families whose mansions may still be seen in the city. Agriculture developed, too, with the introduction of metayage, a system of land tenure in which the farmer paid a proportion of the produce to the owner. ● After 1560, however, these sources of wealth were abruptly cut off when pastel was superseded by indigo blue dye brought over from America and also by the consequences of the religious wars. The woad plant, yielding pastel, was abandoned and **wheat and maize** grown in its place. This new undertaking was not very successful — except for a period during the 18thC at Auch under the remarkable administration of Antoine d'Etigny — and the introduction of the free exchange of farm produce throughout the country, in the middle of the 19thC, finally brought it to a close. It should be noted, too, that the governing class was not particularly interested in the Industrial Revolution nor did Paris seem to be especially favourable to its development in the Languedoc (the first railway-line to Toulouse was not opened till 1884). The inevitable result of the decline of agriculture was a mass exodus from the land. ● In the Ariège-Pyrénées district the situation was hardly better. Iron, which had been mined for centuries in the valley of the Vicdessos, continued to supply the local iron-works known as 'Catalan forges', but this activity declined with the arrival of blast-furnaces running on coke (1870). Aluminium replaced iron when the mines were finally closed (Rancié 1931) and water-power was also much used. ● In the Toulouse region it became necessary to bring in foreign hands (mostly Italians) to work on the farms and, since the war, agriculture is once again flourishing. A large number of Algerian colonists returned to France, after that country obtained independence, and many of them were able to settle in the region and start up new industries. The renown of Toulouse today extends well beyond the Midi.

Facts and figures

Location : *the central portion of the Pyrénées, the upper valley of the Garonne and the valleys that fan out from the plateau of Lannemezan to the Gers.*
Area : *17 456 km²*
Climate : *A variety of micro-climatic conditions; the numerous valleys each have differing degrees of sunshine and exposure to prevailing winds, which come from the Atlantic; in autumn, the south-easterly Autan is strongly felt in the middle valley of the Garonne. Winters can be colder and dryer than in the Paris region.*
Population : *approx 1 189 000.*
Administration : *the three departments belong to the Midi-Pyrénées economic region.* **Ariège,** *Prefecture :* **Foix.** **Haute-Garonne,** *Prefecture :* **Toulouse.** **Gers,** *Prefecture : Auch.*

 Practical information

Information : Midi-Pyrénées : *délégation régionale au tourisme (D.R.T.),* 12, rue Salambô, B.P. 2166, 31022 Toulouse Cedex, ☎ 61.47.11.12. **Ariège** : *comité départemental du tourisme* d'Ariège-Pyrénées *(C.D.T.),* 14, rue Lazéma, 09000 Foix, ☎ 61.65.29.00 ; **Haute-Garonne,** *C.D.T.,* administrative centre, 31, rue de Metz, 31066 Toulouse, ☎ 61.33.43.69. **Gers** : *C.D.T.,* B.P. 69, 32000 Auch, ☎ 62.05.37.02. In **Paris** : *maison du Gers et de l'Armagnac,* 16-18, bd Haussmann, 75009, ☎ 47.70.39.61 ; *maison des Pyrénées,* 15, rue St-Augustin, 75002, ☎ 42.61.58.18. In **Lille** : *maison de Midi-Pyrénées,* 57-59, rue Faidherbe, 59800, ☎ 20.06.15.06. *Dir. rég. de la jeunesse et des sports,* 44, rue des Couteliers, 31072 Toulouse Cedex, ☎ 61.25.60.13. *Dir. des affaires culturelles,* 56, rue du Taur, 31000 Toulouse, ☎ 61.23.20.39.

Reservations : **Haute-Garonne** : *Loisirs-Accueil (L.A.),* pl. Dupuy, 31066 Toulouse, ☎ 61.62.42.62. **Gers,** *maison des agriculteurs,* rte de Mirande, 32003 Auch Cedex, ☎ 62.63.16.55. *Loisirs-Accueil-Ariège,* 14, rue Lazéma, 09000 Foix, ☎ 61.65.01.15.

S.O.S. : **Ariège** : ☎ 17. **Haute-Garonne** : ☎ 61.49.33.33. **Gers** : *S.A.M.U.,* emergency medical service, ☎ 62.05.33.33. emergency poisoning centre, Toulouse, ☎ 61.49.33.33.

Weather forecast : **Ariège** : ☎ 61.66.28.22. **Haute-Garonne** : ☎ 61.71.02.76. **Gers** : ☎ 62.63.07.22.

Rural gîtes and chambres d'hôtes : *relais départementaux,* **Ariège** : *association des gîtes de France,* 14, rue Lazéma, 09000 Foix, ☎ 61.65.01.15. **Haute-Garonne** : 31, rue de Metz, 31066 Toulouse, ☎ 61.33.43.44. **Gers** : *chambre d'agriculture,* rte de Tarbes, 32003 Auch Cedex, ☎ 62.05.36.36, poste 395-390.

Holiday villages : **Ariège** : La Souteille-de-Lannes, 09140 Seix, ☎ 61.66.85.40 ; Les Soulades-Le Pla, 09460 Quérigot, ☎ 68.20.42.23 ; *V.V.F.,* 09310 Les Cabannes,

☎ 61.64.77.67 ; *village de gîtes du Biros Sentein,* 09800 Castillon, ☎ 61.65.01.15. **Haute-Garonne** : village du Boulogne-sur-Gesse, ☎ 61.88.20.38 ; La Tounis, 31200 Cazères, ☎ 61.97.01.28 ; village de l'Isle-en-Dodon, ☎ 61.94.00.28 (town hall). **Gers** : *village de gîtes familiaux* de Mielan, ☎ 62.67.51.76 ; villages de Mauvezin, ☎ 62.06.81.45, Condom, ☎ 62.28.24.88.

Camping-car rental : **Haute-Garonne** : *Lexa,* commercial center of Gros, avenue de Carrieu, 31094 Toulouse Cedex, ☎ 61.40.31.67 ; *Sud-Ouest car,* EKS, 165, route de Paris, 31100 Fenouillet, ☎ 61.70.00.32.

Festivals : **May** : *journées intercontemporaines (concerts by contemporary music ensemble)* in Auch, spring festival of popular arts and traditions in Launac. **May-Jun** : *festival d'Auch et de Gascogne, rencontres sans paroles* in Auch, Grand Fénétra in Toulouse. **Jun** : *documentary film festival* in Luchon, *week of organ music* in Toulouse, *journées Gasconnes* in Valence-sur-Baïse, *fireworks festival* in Auch. **Jul** : *théâtre en pays d'Auch, musical evenings* in Armagnac, *theatre and concerts* at Flaran Abbey. *International festival (classical music)* in St. Lizier. **Jul-Aug** : *festival de Messidor* at Vendémiaire ; *music festival* in St-Bertrand-de-Comminges. **Sep** : *international history conferences,* in Valence-sur-Baïse and Lectoure. **Nov** : *festival de piano aux Jacobins* in Toulouse.

Religious event : **Christmas** in Vals, in the Carolingian stone church, with a real manger, Occitan Christmas.

Local festivals and folklore : **Apr** : *flower festival* in Fourcès. **May** : *flower festival* in Mazères, *festival de Bandas y Penas,* in Condom. **Jun** : *fête des brandons (torch festival)* in Luchon. **Jul** : *journées médiévales de Gaston Phœbus* in Foix, *folk festival* in La Bastide-de-Sérou, *popular and artistic festivals* in Luchon, *mediaeval pageant* in Mirepoix. **Aug** : *Sentein folk festival, festival international d'art populaire* in Geix, *flower festival* in Luchon, *annual folk festival* in Montréjeau ; «jazz in Marciac» in Marciac. **Sep** : *festival of Foix.*

Fairs and markets : **Apr-May** : *Toulouse fair and foire au salé (salted goods); fair-exhibition* in Auch ; *fair-exhibition* from Ariège to St. Girons. **Jun** : *foire aux eaux-de-vie d'Armagnac (Armagnac brandy fair)* and, in **Aug,** animal fair in Eauze. **Oct** : *automobile show, garlic fair* and, in **Nov,** exhibition organised by the Toulouse antique dealers.

Sporting events : **Easter** : *Grand Prix automobile* (F2) in Nogaro. **Whitsun (Pentecost)** : *Grandes Corridas* in Vic-Fézensac (bull-fights). **Aug** : *horse races* in Nogaro.

Rambling and hiking : topoguides, G.R. 65, 652, 653 (Santiago de Compostela "St-Jacques-de-Compostelle" pilgrimage route), 7, 10. Enq. : *délégation régionale Midi-Pyrénées-Sud de la F.F.R.P.,* M.G. Ville, 11, rte de Grenade, 31700 Blagnac ; *comité dép. de R.P.,* 14, rue Lazéma, 09000 Foix, ☎ 61.65.29.00. **C.I.M.E.S.** : *délégation dép.* **Ariège** : B.P. 09200 Saint-Girons, ☎ 61.66.40.10. **Haute-Garonne** : M. Évrard, rés. les Ormes, bât. G3, 31320 Castanet-Tolosan, ☎ 61.81.77.69. **Gers** : *délégation des sentiers G.R.,* 32700 Lectoure, ☎ 62.68.76.98, and château de Saint-Cricq, 32100 Auch, ☎ 62.05.27.17.

Cycling holidays : *féd. française de cyclotourisme, Ligue des Pyrénées,* 1, allée de l'Estérel, 31770 Colomiers, ☎ 61.78.77.29.

Riding holidays : *Transpyrénéenne* and *Grande Traversée ("great crossing") des Pyrénées* : enq. at C.I.M.E.S. and *maison des Pyrénées.* Chevauchée des Deux-Mers : enq. and enrollments *Loisirs-Accueil* in Gers. *L'Armagnac en roulotte : les attelages d'Armagnac,* domaine de Cézaou, 47170 Mézin, ☎ 53.65.70.61. **Ariège** : *Adatel,* 32, av. du Gal de Gaulle, B.P. 53, 09000 Foix, ☎ 61.65.20.00.

Technical tourism : **Ariège** : *Talcs de Luzenac,* 09250 Luzenac, ☎ 61.64.48.01 : visit to chalk quarries by permission (20 Oct.-10 May). *Painting,* Z.I. 09100 Pamiers, ☎ 61.67.07.40, call 48 hrs. in advance. **Haute-Garonne** : *space center* of Toulouse, 18, av. E.-Belin, 31055 Toulouse Cedex, ☎ 61.27.31.31, give one month notice.

Toulousaine cuisine

Toulouse lies at the heart of the largest of the original French Provinces. Cassoulet, plain or fancy, is the traditional dish. There are numerous different recipes. Don't forget to try the famous Saucisse de Toulouse, made from coarse cut saddle of pork. Goose in all its forms is one of the star turns : foie gras, magrets (breasts of goose or duck) and confits (meat cooked and preserved in its own fat). Duck and truffles are also popular - truffles, like wine, have good and bad years. Lots of poultry and game in season : thrush, partridge, wood-pigeon, hare, and more rarely, ortolans. Of course, the white beans are excellent. The ewe's-milk cheeses are no less admirable.

Armagnac

Approximately 350 km² of vineyard stretch across the north and west of the Gers and overflow into the Departments of the Lot-et-Garonne and the Landes. Production from Bas Armagnac (110 km²) is considered superior by connoisseurs; next come Ténarèze (110 km² in the heart of the region) and Haut Armagnac.
Armagnac is distilled from an indifferent local white wine. However, only wine made from specified varieties of grape (Folle Blanche, Jurançon and St. Emilion) may be distilled. The characteristic golden colour comes from prolonged aging in oak barrels. Armagnac can be drunk after four years in the barrel, but eight or ten years are required to give it a smooth yet vigorous fullness.

Gers : *Ducs de Gascogne,* 32200 Gimont, ☎ 62.67.72.95, *(foie gras museum)* : visits by request at 9:30 am or 2:30 pm in groups for half-hour tour; free tastings. *Armagnac-Samalens,* Laujuzan, 32110 Nogaro, ☎ 62.09.14.88. Tours of the distillery, casks and bottling room with free tasting. Daily 8:30-12 & 2:30-6:30, closed Sun. and nat. hols.

Handicraft courses : Ariège : walks on foot or on horseback, cross-country ski excursions and downhill skiing, crafts : enq and enrolments bookings at *L.A. Ariège-Pyrénées.* Gold prospecting from Jun. to Sep.; enq at Chamber of Commerce, 21, allée de Villote, 09000 Foix, ☎ 61.65.30.30. **Haute-Garonne :** photography courses, fine and applied arts, spelunking, canoe-kayak, ballooning, car driving, hang-gliding, customs and nature, archaeological digs at Séviac, enq. and enrollments : *Loisirs-Accueil* and *S.I.* Auch.

Aquatic sports : Sailing : *Ligue Midi-Pyrénées,* 54, rue des Sept-Troubadours, 31000 Toulouse, ☎ 61.62.19.65. Water skiing : *Ligue Midi-Pyrénées,* 17, rue Daydé, 31200 Toulouse, ☎ 61.23.92.48.

Diving : *groupe d'activités sous-marines,* 6 bis, rue Kennedy, 31000 Toulouse, ☎ 61.78.64.64, and *féd. franç. d'études et sports sous-marins : comité régional,* 6, rue d'Autezac, 31000 Toulouse, ☎ 61.42.17.64.

Canoeing : *comité dép. de Haute-Garonne,* 54, rue des Sept-Troubadours, 31000 Toulouse, ☎ 61.41.08.48, and *ligue régionale,* 4, rue du Château-de-l'Hers, ☎ 61.20.13.96; Canoeing section, A.S.P.T.T. Ariège, 09000 Foix, ☎ 61.65.05.06, and *C.I.M.E.S.*

Golf : Luchon (9 holes); Toulouse-Palmola (18 holes); Golf-club de Toulouse (18 holes); L'Isle-Jourdain (9 holes); la Bastide-de-Serrou (9 holes).

Potholing-spelunking : Ariège : *comité dép. de spéléo,* M. Christian Billiard, «Clarac» Boulon, 09000 Foix. **Haute-Garonne :** *comité dép.,* 54, rue des Sept-Troubadours, 31000 Toulouse. *Maison des Gouffres,* Herran-Labaderque.

Winter sports : *comité régional Pyrénées-Est,* 1, rue de la Charité, 31000 Toulouse, ☎ 61.62.89.25; *Pyrénées club de France,* 29, rue du Taur, 31000 Toulouse, ☎ 61.21.11.44. There are five ski stations (Axbonascie-Le-Saguet, Guzet-neige, Ascou-Pailhères, Mijanès-Latrabe, Les Monts d'Olme) where the major activities are Alpine-style skiing, cross-country skiing and nature-discovery hikes on snow-shoes : foyers of Prades-Montaillou, Trois Seigneurs in Massat, Manupied in Bosc (Barguillère Valley) and A.D.E.P.A.N.A. (Biros Valley) in Ariège, from the Larboust Valley to Haute-Garonne. Enq. : *A.D.S.F.A. au C.D.T. Ariège,* ☎ 61.65.29.00. *Club Alpin* (C.A.F.), M. Brionne, 8, chemin de Caussou, 09000 Montgaillard, ☎ 61.65.38.65, and *U.C.P.A.* 40, rue de la Concorde, 31000 Toulouse, ☎ 61.62.63.18.

Hang-gliding : *Aigles de Cabaillère,* 17, rue Bayle, 09000 Foix, ☎ 61.65.01.73.

Parachuting : *Ligue des Pyrénées* (F.F.P.), 87, rte de Narbonne, 31400 Toulouse, ☎ 61.53.74.06.

Gliding : air-clubs in Saint-Girons-Antichan, ☎ 61.66.11.00, and Pamiers, ☎ 61.68.60.60, for gliding, light aircraft, for beginners and first flights, contact M. Andriou in the Haute-Garonne, 6, pl. Gilbert-Privat, 31100 Toulouse, ☎ 61.40.51.82.

Hunting and shooting : Ariège : *féd. dép.,* 50, av. Gal-Leclerc, 09000 Foix, ☎ 61.65.04.02. Game : quail, hare, boar and wild goat. To organise full- or half-day hunting, contact *Sologne Ariégeoise,* Montégut-Plantaurel, 09210 Varilhes, ☎ 61.92.24.12. **Haute-Garonne :** *féd. dép.,* 2, rue Jolimont, 31000 Toulouse, ☎ 61.48.49.66. Enq. in **Gers** at *Loisirs-Accueil* which organises week-end pigeon hunts.

Fishing : Ariège : *féd. dép. des assn. de pêche et de pisciculture,* 26, av. de Barcelone, 09000 Foix, ☎ 61.65.12.62. **Haute-Garonne :** *assn. pêche et pisciculture,* 5, pl. Wilson, 31000 Toulouse, ☎ 61.21.18.65, *Club Français des pêcheurs à la mouche,* quartier la Fount, 31130 Balma, ☎ 61.24.27.81. **Gers :** *féd. dép. des assn. pêche et pisciculture,* 75, bd Sadi-Carnot, 32000 Auch, ☎ 62.05.15.95.

 Towns and places

AUCH⋆⋆

Agen 71, Toulouse 81, Paris 797 km
pop 25540 ⊠ 32000   A1-2

The interesting part of this old town is on the hill overlooking the Gers. Here you will find the Hôtel de

Ville, the Allées d'Étigny, the cathedral, shops selling regional produce, and Daguin, one of the best gastronomic addresses in the region.

▶ The **cathedral**⋆ (B1) has a late 17thC French-Classical façade (fine wrought iron gates), but is in fact a Gothic 15th-16thC building; exceptional stained glass⋆, most-

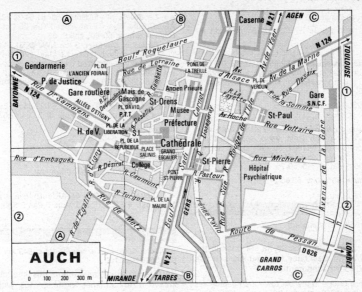

ly by Arnaud de Moles, ca. 1513. Carved stalls★★ in the choir, from 1520-30.▶ North of the cathedral is the former archbishop's residence, a fine 18thC mansion now occupied by the **Prefecture**. The Tourist Office is located in a handsome 15thC brick and timber house on the corner of the Rue Dessoles (B1), a pedestrians-only shopping street running into the old town.▶ **The Escalier Monumental** (staircase, 1863; statue of d'Artagnan) runs down to the river. Nearby is the network of narrow, steeply-sloping mediaeval streets known as **"pousterles"**.▶ **Art and archaeology museum** in a former Dominican chapel, Rue Daumesnil (B1; mediaeval antiques, paintings, Gascon ethnography, religious art from South America and fine collection of Peruvian vases; *10-12 & 2-8, or 4:00 out of season, closed Sun., Mon. and nat. hols. out of season*).▶ Return to the town centre along Rue Gambetta, a busy shopping street (B1), running past the **Maison de Gascogne** in an old 18thC covered market (regional produce in the summer) and ending at the **Town Hall** (1770) and the promenade at **allées d'Etigny** (named after one of the region's best administrators in the 18thC).▶ Rue Pagodéontés, **Resistance Museum** (*Wed.-Fri., 2:30-4:30*).

Nearby

▶ 4 km E, mediaeval **Saint-Cricq château**, restored for seminars and conventions; 11 km farther on, **Marsan** château (18thC).▶ **Pessan** *(6 km SE)* abbey remains, hill-top town, interesting houses. **Castelnau-Barbarens** *(15 km)*, fortified by the counts of Astarac, view of Midi peak to Bigorre from the church.▶ 19 km S, meat market at **Seissan**, and 25 km farther is **Masseube**, 13thC blockhouse. From here you can reach *(9 km approx)* the reservoir of Astarac dam (water sports) and the 14th-15thC Gontaut-Biron château and 15thC church (14thC altarpiece) of **Saint-Blancard**.▶ 20 km NW is one of the most picturesque châteaux in Gascony, in Lavardens. ☐

Practical Information

AUCH
ⓘ pl. de la Cathédrale (B1), ☎ 62.05.22.89.
✈ *Auch-Lamothe*, 5 km N, ☎ 62.63.03.89.
SNCF (C1), ☎ 62.05.60.95.
🚌 cité administrative (A1), ☎ 62.05.76.37.

Hotels :
● ★★★ *France*, pl. de la Libération (A1), ☎ 62.05.00.44,

Tx 520474, AE DC Euro Visa, 29 rm Ⓟ Rooms decorated by Jo Daguin, 350. Rest. ● ◆◆◆ *Daguin* ♪ closed Mon and Sun eve, 2 Jan-2 Feb. Jocelyne Daguin has infused a new life into this fine old dwelling. In the kitchen, André, (the d'Artagnan of the Gascon culinary musketeers), and his son Arnaud, cook savoury delights with a regional accent : *table d'hôtes de l'oie, du canard et des denrées de Gascogne (foie, magrets de canard confits)*. Succulent meat and poultry : ribs of Bazas beef and, on occasion, bull. Wines both grand and modest : colombard, Bouchy discovered by Daguin himself. Rare Armagnac. Epic breakfasts. Wine and a two-day course given from Oct to Apr; a course on farm produce. Pastis, brandies, 275-350◆◆ *Le Neuvième* ♪ Friendly little bistro-bar. Simple, heathful food, quick service till midnight : *faux filet, brochette de cœur, garbure*, 120-135◆ *Côté Jardin* ♪ closed Nov-Apr. Fresh, sunny food served on a tiny terrace. Salads, pâtés, grilled meat, and fish, 170.
★★★ *Robinson*, rte de Tarbes, 3 km S, ☎ 62.05.02.83, Euro Visa, 26 rm Ⓟ ₩ 🍴 160.
★★ *Paupiné*, 5, av. de la Marne (C1), ☎ 62.05.26.81, Euro Visa, 32 rm Ⓟ ⅍ closed 20 Dec-10 Jan, 200. Rest. ◆◆ ⅍ 70-120.
★ *Paris*, 38, av. de la Marne (C1), ☎ 62.63.26.22, Visa, 22 rm Ⓟ ⅍ closed Nov, 120. Rest. ◆ ♪ closed Sun eve, 45-90.

Restaurant :

◆◆ *Claude Laffitte*, 38, rue Dessoles (B1), ☎ 62.05.04.18, AE DC Euro Visa ⅍ ♪ closed Mon and Sun eve (l.s.). Gascon inn. Local products, bar, modest fixed-price meals, 75-210.

Recommended

Baby-sitting : info at the *S.I.*
Events : *organ festival at the cathedral*, in Jun.
Guided tours : info at *S.I.*
Market : Wed am, Thu, Sat.
Night-clubs : *L'Aventure*, 11, av. de la Marne (C1), ☎ 62.63.26.05.
♥ foie gras, Armagnacs, spiced fruits : *Caves de l'Hôtel de France*, pl. de la Libération (A1); foie gras, Armagnacs, spiced fruits : *Maison de la Gascogne*, rue Gambetta (B1); Gascon dollars : *Caperan*, 8, rue d'Etigny (A2), ☎ 62.05.07.69; pork products : *Claude Laffitte*, 34, rue Dessoles (B1); *Les Trois Mousquetaires*, 10, rue Dessoles (B1), ☎ 62.05.33.66.

Nearby

SAINTE-CHRISTIE-D'AUCH, ⊠ 32390, 13 km N on the N 21.

Restaurant :
● ♦♦ *Relais de Cardeneau*, ☎ 62.65.51.80, AE DC Euro Visa, closed Mon. Way out in the country, quality cooking with a feminine touch : *cassoulet de morue, fricassée de pintade*, 60-120.

SEISSAN, ⊠ 32260, 19 km S.

Hotels :
★★ *Samaran*, rue du Marché, ☎ 62.66.20.32, Euro Visa, 6 rm P ⚲ closed Mon, Sep. Rest. ♦♦ ⬥ Spec : *foie gras au naturel, magrets aux pommes*, 60-120 ; child : 35.
★ *Pyrénées*, pl. Carnot, ☎ 62.66.20.35, 7 rm P ⬚ ⚲ closed Mon, 105. Rest. ♦ ♪ ⬥ 50-75.

⚐ ★★★*Laverdure* (85 pl), ☎ 62.66.21.76.

AX-LES-THERMES*

Foix 42, Quillan 53, Paris 834 km
pop 1510 ⊠ 09110   C3

This spa and winter sports centre is set back in the mountains and is an ideal base for excursions. It has 60 springs and four health centres.

▶ Near the Breilh bridge in the old town the **hospice** still has its chapel from 1260 ; nearby, the "lepers' basin" is a reminder of the era of Saint Louis, when Ax attracted Crusaders who had caught leprosy in Palestine. City walkways (allées du Couloubret) in front of the casino.

Nearby

▶ Up a winding road to the **Plateau du Bonascre** *(8 km SW)* and the ski centre of **Ax-1400** ; cable-car to the plateau du Saquet (alt. 2 030 m), where you can climb the **Tute de l'Ours** (2 255 m ; panorama★★). Cable-car down the valley returning to Ax by the narrow valley of Défilé du Berduquet. ▶ Higher up through the valley of the Ariège at 1 436 m is **l'Hospitalet-Près-l'Andorre**, another winter sports and mountain resort (1 436 m high). Further on in the Pyrénées Orientales, you come to the **Puymorens Pass** (alt. 1 915 m ; winter sports) on the mountain ridge which runs from the Atlantic to the Mediterranean. From here, you can go down towards the **Cerdagne** (→ Languedoc-Roussillon) or through the **Pas de la Case** (alt. 2 085 m ; winter sports) : here a bridge crosses the Ariège, which marks the frontier with the **Principality of Andorra**. The Ariège rises in a lake : **Font Nègre** *(30 min on foot)*. ▶ East of Ax-les-Thermes is the **Orlu Valley** (43 km² nature reserve ; site of the Orlu gorge, and the Cascade (waterfall) of Nioles★, 300 m high). Access from here to the delightful site of the **Naguilles dam★** (alt. 1 864 m) and the En Beys mountain refuge, base camp for a number of guided expeditions in the mountains. ▶ **Ascou-Pailhères** : winter-sports resort 11 km E (alt. 1 500 m), in the Lauze valley. ▶ Go through the **Chioula Pass** *(10 km N ; alt. 1 430 m ; good view★* from the Signal de Chioula, *10 min,* alt. 1 507 m) and the **Marmare Pass** (alt. 1 360 m), to reach the **Route des Corniches★** (cliffroad) and **Lordat** *(29 km)*, Roman church and château-fort ruins from 13thC, where the road runs up to the **Talc quarries at Trimouns★** *(12 km)*, the largest in the world *(every pm ex Sun., Jul.-Aug. ; by appointment for groups, tel. 61.64.48.01).* ☐

Practical Information —————————————

AX-LES-THERMES
♨ ☎ 61.64.24.83.
ᯤ 720-2300m.
ⓘ av. Delcassé, ☎ 61.64.20.64.
𝗦𝗡𝗖𝗙 ☎ 61.64.20.72.

Hotels :
★★★ *Royal Thermal*, (Mapotel), espl. du Couloubret, ☎ 61.64.22.51, Tx 530955, AE DC Euro Visa, 68 rm P ⚞ ♪ ⬚ 295. Rest. ♦ ⚞ ♪ 80-100.

★★ *Le Breilh*, pl. du Breilh, ☎ 61.64.24.29, Tx 530806, AE DC Euro Visa, 31 rm, closed Tue, 25 Oct-15 Dec, 120. Rest. ♦ *Snack*, 50-80 ; child : 35.
★★ *Perles et Castelet*, 3 km NW, ☎ 61.64.24.52, 28 rm P ⚞ ⚿ ⚲ closed 1 Dec-12 May, 170. Rest. ♦♦ ♪ ⬔ closed Tue eve and Wed ex school hols, 60-180.
★★ *Sicre et d'Espagne*, 2, av. du Dr-Gomma, ☎ 61.64.22.95, Visa, 68 rm ⚿ closed Nov-Jan, 200. Rest. ♦ ⚞ ⬥ 50-95.

⚐ ★★*En Rameil* (60 pl), ☎ 61.64.22.85 ; at Luzenac, 8 km NW, ★★★*Le Castella* (100 pl), ☎ 61.64.47.53.

Recommended
Casino : ☎ 61.64.20.20.

Nearby

UNAC, ⊠ 09250 Luzenac, 9 km NW.

Hotel :
★ *L'Oustal*, ☎ 61.64.48.44, AE Euro Visa, 4 rm ⚞ ⚿ ⚲ ♪ 100. Rest. ♦♦ ⚞ ♪ closed Mon, 5 Jan-5 Feb, 115-150.

BAGNÈRES-DE-LUCHON**

Saint-Gaudens 46, Tarbes 89, Paris 843 km
pop 3600 ⊠ 31100   A3

Referred to simply as **Luchon,** this little town was well known in Roman times for its springs. Within reach of Toulouse, it is an important Pyrenean tourist centre, a spa, winter resort and mountaineering rendez-vous, with excellent facilities at Superbagnères.

▶ The **Allées d'Étigny** with their cafés and restaurants are the heart of the town's social life. At N18 is the 18thC **Château Laffont-Lassalle** ; *T.O.* and **Luchon Regional Museum** (Musée du Pays de Luchon ; history, ethnography ; relief map of the Pyrénées). At the far end of the Allées is the lovely **Quinconces Park★** where you will find the spa, built (1848) on the site of the Roman baths, with vaporarium, the Lepape Springs and pump room.

Nearby

▶ **Superbagnères** *(19 km SW on D46)* : marvellous view★ from (alt. 1 800 m) of the mountain chain, from the Crabère in the east, to the Arbizon in the west, including the Massif de la Maladeta. Down below : the **Lys Valley★,** which actually means "valley of the avalanches" (Lis) is a wooded valley leading to the Cascade (waterfall), the Gouffre (chasm) and the **cirque d'Enfer★** (natural amphitheatre). ▶ Along the **valley of La Pique★** you come to the **Hospice de France** *(10.5 km ;* alt. 1 360 m site★) near the Cascade du Parisien ; excursions to the Port de Vénasque (alt. 2 448 m), superb views★★ over the Spanish border to the **Pic d'Aneto** (alt. 3 404 m), the highest peak in the Pyrénées and on Spanish territory. ▶ Finally the **One Valley** is the north-west passage to the **Oueil Valley★** (you can climb Mont Né★ to Bordères lake★), and to the **Larboust Valley★** (**Saint-Aventin**, village with charming Romanesque church) and to the **Val d'Oô★.** From here, you arrive at the Val d'Astau (valley) and climb on foot to the **Lake Oô★★** surrounded on all sides by jagged peaks ; the Lake Espingo empties into it in a 273 m waterfall. The Peyresourde Pass (alt. 1 570 m) leads to the Aure Valley (→ Basque Country, Béarn, Bigorre). ☐

Practical Information —————————————

BAGNÈRES-DE-LUCHON
♨ (1 Apr-20 Oct), ☎ 61.79.03.88.
ⓘ 18, allées d'Étigny, ☎ 61.79.21.21.
𝗦𝗡𝗖𝗙 ☎ 61.79.00.85/61.79.03.36.

Hotels :
★★★ *Corneille*, 5, av. A.-Dumas, ☎ 61.79.36.22, 58 rm P ⚞ ⚲ ⬚ closed 20 Oct-1 Apr, 350. Rest. ♦ 60-190.
● ★★ *Loisirotel*, 29, allées d'Étigny, ☎ 61.79.00.40, AE DC Euro Visa, 60 rm P ⚞ ⚿ ⚲ ♪ ⚶ ⬚ closed 10 Oct-24 Apr, 235. Rest. ♦♦ 65-130 ; child : 40.

⚠ ★★*Beauregard* (133 pl), ☎ 61.79.30.74; ★★*Val de l'Air* (80 pl), ☎ 61.79.10.02; at Montauban-de-Luchon, ★★★*la Lalette*, (270 pl), ☎ 61.79.00.38.

Nearby

BOURG-D'OUEIL, ✉ 31110, 14 km.

Hotel :
★ *Le Sapin Fleuri*, ☎ 61.79.21.90, 22 rm 🅿 ⬠ ◔ ♪ pens, closed 30 Apr-15 May, 20 Oct-20 Dec, 170. Rest. ♦ ⬠ ♪ ᕑ ⌾ 65-110.

The BASTIDES of ARMAGNAC*

A1-2

Round trip *(approx 300 km, 2 days; see map 1)*

Solid fortified towns with covered markets and arcades, unpretentious country châteaux, little churches; all hidden in the soft countryside of the Gers. Spring is the ideal season for visiting this charming region, unless you prefer the colours of autumn, when the vineyards are a blaze of russet.

▶ **Condom** (→). ▶ **Valence-sur-Baïse**, a 13thC *bastide* (→ p. 793) which still has its old church (14thC) and its arcaded square. The church at **Flaran**★ is more interesting, with chapter and cloister of the former Cistercian abbey, founded in the 12thC. Nearby, numerous Gascon **châteaux** in ruins. ▶ **Cassaigne** is today a centre of Armagnac production; the bishops of Condom formerly had their country residence in the château (traditional kitchen and 18thC Armagnac cellars). ▶ The episcopal residence at **Larressingle**★ is older still, fortified in the 13thC, but today a peaceful and charming little village, the size of a pocket handkerchief (sale of Armagnac and Gascon produce). ▶ The little *bastide of* **Fourcès**★ was an 11thC stronghold; it is built in concentric circles round a tiny village square (15thC castle). ▶ **Montréal** was founded in 1255; the **Gallo-Roman villa of Séviac** and the mosaics discovered there *(every day in summer; guided tours, tel. 62.28.43.18)* are reminders of the importance of northern Armagnac in Roman days. ▶ **Éauze**, on a hill overlooking

the Gélise, was the most important Gallo-Roman town in its district, eventually becoming a bishopric. The southern Gothic cathedral was built at the end of the 15thC. On the arcaded square is a house known as the Maison de Jeanne d'Albret (Henri IV's mother). Armagnac production; equestrian centre. ▶ Between **Castelmore** (supposed birth place of Dumas' hero d'Artagnan) and Lupiac, there is an old windmill on the Ténarèze hills which has been restored; view. ▶ The **Aignan** church possesses a simple, but lovely, Roman doorway. ▶ Coming from Fustérouau, there is an excellent view of the **château de Termes d'Armagnac**, a tall keep (36 m high, 14thC) overlooking the valley of the Adour. The Romanesque church of **Tasque** has an 11thC doorway. ▶ The *bastide* of **Plaisance** is a peaceful town in the centre of the plain. ▶ **Beaumarchès**, another *bastide*, (solid bell-tower with 16thC stone carving) is higher up; the road continues along a ridge with good views. ▶ **Marciac** is a characteristic late 13thC bastide; near the arcaded square, you can see the high bell-tower (70 m) of the southern Gothic church (14th-16thC) and another bell-tower belonging to a disaffected convent. 80-acre lake for aquatic sports. ▶ Through **Villecomtal** to the **Puntous de Laguian**, view★ of the Pyrénées. ▶ **Miélan**, former *bastide*, not far from a dammed lake on the Osse. ▶ The little village of **Tillac**★, older than the *bastides* is built on both sides of a short central street closed by two gates. ▶ **Bassoues**★ has one of the most beautiful keeps★ in the Gers (14thC; 38 m) overlooking the remains of a castle belonging to the former bishops of Auch. Don't miss the central square where the houses with their wooden arcades front an old covered market spanning the road. The 14th-15thC church still contains the holy-water basin of the outcast descendants of lepers. Saint-Fris basilica over Carolingian crypt. ▶ The attractive little town of **Montesquiou** is built on a promontory overlooking the Osse (remains of 13th-14thC fortifications). ▶ **Isle-de-Noé** is a little fishing centre at the junction of the Grande and Petite Baïse (17thC château). ▶ **Barran :** remnants of fortifications and unusual spiral bell-tower on the 15thC church (note stalls of same period in the choir). Arcades and woodbuilt covered market. ▶ Farther on, the 14th-17thC château, part brick, of **Mazères**. ▶ Nearby is the remarkable site of the **Biran**★ village ramparts. ▶ **Jégun :** Romanesque-Gothic church. ▶ **Lavardens**★★ : a fortified village dramatically situated on a spur with a large 17thC château. ▶ **Castéra-Verduzan** is a small spa specialising in mouth and gum ailments. ▶ The Monluc château near **Saint-Puy** was a fencing capital of the region. ▶ **La Sauvetat :** church with 13thC doorway, tower. ▶ **Terraube :** 14thC fortified village; fine château from a later period. ▶ On the top of a hill is **Marsolan**, where the Viscounts of Lomagne built a castle in the 11thC. ▶ The collegiate church★ of **La Romieu** was built in 1317 on the pilgrim *(roumiou)* road to Compostela. It had its own fortified wall around the church, flanked by two towers with a fine 14thC cloister, which formerly had two floors. ▶ On the way back to Condom you can loop past the Renaissance castle of **Maridac**. ☐

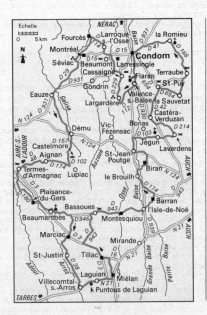

1. The Bastides of Armagnac

Practical Information

BASSOUES, ✉ 32320 Montesquiou, 35 km W of **Auch**.

Hotel :
★ *Donjon*, ☎ 62.64.90.04, 8 rm 🅿 ⬠ ♪ closed Feb, 100. Rest. ♦♦ ♪ closed Sat, 40-100; child : 25.

CASTÉRA-VERDUZAN, ✉ 32410 Valence-sur-Baïse, 7 km SE.
⚓ (1 May-31 Oct), ☎ 62.28.53.41.
ⓘ ☎ 62.68.10.66 (h.s.).

Hotel :
★★ *Ténarèze*, ☎ 62.68.10.22, AE DC Euro Visa, 22 rm 🅿 ⬠ ⬠ closed Feb, 135. Rest. ♦♦ *Florida* ♪ ᕑ closed Mon and Sun eve (l.s.). Family atmosphere and food. *Foie frais aux fruits, ris de veau.* Terrace dining, 55-140.

⚐ ★*Les Thermes* (20 pl), ☎ 62.68.13.41.

EAUZE, ⊠ 32800, 52 km NW of **Auch**.
ⓘ pl. de la Mairie, ☎ 62.09.85.62.
SNCF ☎ 62.09.82.59.

Hotel :
L'Armagnac, 1, bd St-Blancat, ☎ 62.09.88.11, Euro Visa,
14 rm, closed 1-15 Mar, 90. Rest. ♦ 50-90.

⚐ ★★*Pouy Plage* (20 pl), ☎ 62.09.86.00.

Recommended
Events : *operetta festival*, in Aug.
♥ floc de Gascogne (local dessert) : *Marquis de Caussade*, rte de Cazaubon, son et lumière in the chai (wine
storehouse) 1 Jul-15 Sept; *Chevalier Gascon*, 60, rte de
Nogaro; *Syndicat des Producteurs*, 9, pl. d'Armagnac.

GONDRIN, ⊠ 32330, 12 km NE of **Eauze**.

Hotel :
★ *Le Pardaillan*, rue Nationale, ☎ 62.29.12.06, Euro Visa,
20 rm ⫞ ◎ ⁀ On the edge of the Gondrin pond (swimming), 120. Rest. ♦ ⫞ ♫ Friendly reception. Regional
fare, 40-100.

L' ISLE-DE-NOÉ, ⊠ 32300 Mirande, 9 km N of **Mirande**.

Hotel :
★ *Auberge de Gascogne*, rue du Pdt-Wilson,
☎ 62.64.17.05, Visa, 7 rm ◎ closed Wed, 3-10 Jul,
2 Nov-1 Dec, 120. Rest. ♦ ♫ ◎ 50.

MANCIET, ⊠ 32370, 10 km SW of **Eauze**.

Hotel :
★★ *La Bonne Auberge*, ☎ 62.08.50.04, AE DC Euro Visa,
13 rm P ◎ ♫ half pens, closed Sun eve and Mon, Dec,
180. Rest. ♦♦ ♫ 60-200.

MIÉLAN, ⊠ 32170, 34 km NE of **Tarbes**.

Hotel :
★★ *Lac de Miélan*, N 21, ☎ 62.67.51.59, Visa, 30 rm P ⫞
◎ ⟍ ♫ ♣ ₺ ⁀ 155. Rest. ♦ ⫞ ♣ ₺ 57-120; child : 30.

⚐ ★★★*Lac* (70 pl), ☎ 62.67.51.76.

MONTRÉAL, ⊠ 32250, 10 km W of **Larressingle**.
ⓘ pl. de l'Hôtel-de-Ville, ☎ 62.28.43.18.

Restaurants :
♦♦ *Gare*, 3 km S. on D 29, ☎ 62.28.43.37, AE DC Euro
Visa P ◎ ⟍ ♫ 5 rm, closed Thu eve and Fri (l.s.),
5-31 Jan. Set in a former train station. Spec : *garbure gasconne, salmis de palombes, poulet grillé à l'échalote* and
honest regional fare, 70-110.
♦ *Chez Simone*, ☎ 62.28.44.40, AE DC Euro Visa P ⟍ ♫
55-120; child : 35.

PARLEBOSCQ, ⊠ 40310, 16 km NW of **Eauze**.

Restaurant :
● ♦♦ *Le Hay*, ☎ 58.44.32.10, Visa P ◎ ⟍ ♫ closed
Mon, 2 Jan-12 Mar. Delicious cooking by Alain Ponty,
a young chef who deserves encouragement. Honest prices : *terrine de foie gras des Landes, raviolis de petits
gris éclairés de leur gâteau d'ortie*, 100-180; child : 70.

PLAISANCE, ⊠ 32160, 13 km SE of **Riscle**.
ⓘ 4, rue Ste-Quitterie, ☎ 62.69.44.69.

Hotel :
★★ *Ripa Alta* (L.F.), pl. de l'Eglise, ☎ 62.69.30.43, AE
DC Euro Visa, 15 rm P closed Sun eve , Nov, 180.
Rest. ● ♦♦ ♫ closed Mon and Sun eve. One of the best
restaurants in the southwest, run by the imaginative M.
Coscuella, who cooks in harmony with the seasons and
the market's bounty : *poulet à l'armagnac, pibales*. Fine
cellar, 70-210; child : 35.

⚐ ★★*L'Arros* (33 pl), ☎ 62.69.30.28.

Recommended
Events : at Marciac, 14 km, *jazz festival*, 15 Aug.

VALENCE-SUR-BAISE, ⊠ 32310, 8 km S of **Condom**.

Hotel :
★★ *Ferme de Flaran*, rte de Condom, ☎ 62.28.58.22, AE

Euro Visa, 15 rm P ◎ ⟍ ⊠ closed Sun eve and Mon,
12 Nov-5 Dec, 190. Rest. ♦♦ ♫ ₺ Good regional cooking, 75-180.

CONDOM*

Agen 40, Auch 44, Paris 740 km
pop 7840 ⊠ 32100   A1

This town has clustered up around its abbey-turned-
cathedral since mediaeval times. Condom is now a
vigorous agricultural market town, with a brisk trade
in Armagnac.

▶ The old **cathedral**★ in the town centre was rebuilt at
the beginning of the 16thC (Flamboyant doorway, cloister and 18thC furniture). ▶ In the outbuildings of the former bishop's residence is the small but interesting **Armagnac Museum** *(daily ex Sun., and Mon. and nat. hols. out
of season)*. ▶ Strolling around the old town, you will find
a number of handsome 17th and 18thC houses.

Nearby

▶ See **Pouypardin** château, one of many in the region,
built from the 13th-16thC.   □

Practical Information _____

ⓘ pl. Bossuet, ☎ 62.28.00.80.
SNCF ☎ 62.28.15.36.

Hotels :
★★ *Continental*, 20, av. du Mal-Foch, ☎ 62.28.00.58,
Visa, 20 rm ◎ ⟍ closed Mon eve (l.s.) , Dec, 100.
★★ *Table des Cordeliers* (R.S.), 11, rue des Cordeliers, ☎ 62.28.03.68, DC Euro Visa, 21 rm P ◎
closed Mon (l.s.), 150. Rest. ● ♦♦♦ closed 1 Nov-1 Mar. In
an enchanting decor, top-quality regional fare : *saumon
mariné au citron vert, escalope de foie chaud au fruit de
saison, aiguillette de caneton aux airelles*, 95-155; child :
60.

⚐ ★★★*Municipal* (75 pl), ☎ 62.28.17.32.

Recommended
Events : *Bandas festival*, in Aug.
Guide to wines : *Château de Cassaigne*, 6.5 km SW,
Armagnac, tour of storehouse.
♥ foie gras, magret, confits : *château de Roquebère*, rte
de Nérac.

The Upper COUSERANS Valleys*

                                                          B3

The Couserans, a historically rich area traditionally
covering eighteen valleys, runs up to the Spanish
border. This charming maze of valleys can be explored by a network of ancient paths. Castillon-en-Couserans (former capital of the area), Oust and Aulus-
les-Bains are good starting points (→ From Couserans to Plantaurel).

▶ **Sentein**, at the foot of the Crabère (alt. 2629 m) and
Maubermé (alt. 2880 m) peaks, has a fortified Romanesque church decorated with frescoes.▶ The **Riberot Valley**, edged by the Bordes forest, leads to the **Massif du
Valier reserve** (88 km²; panorama from the top of the
mountain, alt. 2838 m). ▶ Along the **Haut Salat Valley★**,
past Conflens, you come to the **Pause Pass**, (views★)
and to the tungsten **mines** at Salau; 11thC Romanesque
church in the village. ▶ The **Ustou Valley★**, one of
the most interesting, branches off the Salat Valley at the
foot of the ruins of the **château de Lagarde**; traditional
cheese-making.   □

For the translation of a name of a meat, a fish or a
vegetable, for the composition of a dish or a sauce,
see the Menu Guide in the Practical Holiday Guide;
it lists the most common culinary terms.

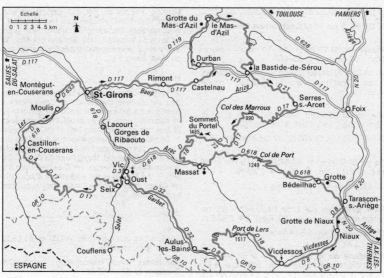

2. From Couserans to Plantaurel

From COUSERANS to PLANTAUREL

B-C3

Round trip *(approx 240 km, 2 to 2 1/2 days : see map 2)*

The foot-hills of the Pyrénées, with their wooded cover and uneven terrain, promise delightful discoveries. Since prehistoric times men have lived in these mountains, where there are numerous caves containing traces of sophisticated symbolic and figurative art. The caves at Niaux and Mas d'Azil, open to visitors, are in this respect the most important in the region.

▶ **Saint-Girons** (→). ▶ **Rimont** is a former 13thC *bastide*, rebuilt after WWII; monument to the Martyrs of the Resistance. ▶ Near **Durban** are the impressive ruins of **Saint-Barthélemy château** (12th, 13th and 15thC). ▶ The **caves of Mas d'Azil**★★ are among the most beautiful in the Pyrénées. They were inhabited during the Upper Palaeolithic period, 40 000 to 10 000 BC; prehistoric collection in the cave, prehistory museum close by; reproductions and photographs of the wall paintings *(daily Jul.-Sep.; Sun. and nat. hols. and daily pm Apr.-Jun.)*. The village was an early seat of Protestantism; the church was restored in the 18thC; several typical houses. ▶ **La Bastide-de-Sérou** was founded in 1254 : 15thC church and castle ruins from the Louis XIII period. ▶ **Serres-sur-Arget** lies in the heart of the valley of the Barguillère (or Arget) where the **Route Verte**★ runs up to the **Marrous Pass**★ (alt. 990 m). Past the foot of the **Tour Laffont**, a former lookout post with a view★ over the Pyrénées, to the top of **Portel** (alt. 1 485 m; similar view★) and the road to the Crouzette (alt. 1 240 m). ▶ Run down through the **valley of the Arac**, a winding defile★ lined with red rocks. ▶ **Massat** : 17thC church and chapel of Ave Maria (16thC). ▶ The **Port Pass**★ (alt. 1 250 m) leads to the Saurat Valley. The caves at **Bédeilhac** were also inhabited in prehistoric times : 14 000 year-old paintings and rock carvings; the lower cave has revealed numerous worked flints and clay models *(daily Jul.-10 Sep., visits every 30 min, 10-11:30 & 2-6; Easter-Jun. and early Sep.-early Oct., at 3 pm and 4:30 ex Tue.)*. ▶ **Tarascon-sur-Ariège**, set between high mountains, is the industrial centre of the val-

ley (electro-metallurgy). The church was rebuilt in 17thC; 14thC doorway. The **caves of Lombrives**★★, 3.5 km SE, are, at more than 17 km deep, the largest in Europe and the most visited; fine rock formations; underground lake *(10-12 & 2-5, Palm Sun.-31 May, 30 Sep.-31 Oct., daily 10-5, Jun.-Sep.)*. Further on, you come to the hot spa of **Ornolac-Ussat-les-Bains**; here the water emerges at 38°C. ▶ At the entrance to **Niaux** is the Musée Paysan (farmers' museum; *daily 10-6 Easter holidays and Jun.-Sep.)* : tools and everyday objects from the old days in the area. **Niaux caves**★ *(daily Jul.-Sep., visits every 45 min, tel. 61.05.85.10; Oct.-Jun., daily at 11, 3 and 4:30; 20 people max per visit)*. Magdalenian era drawings★ (10-14 000 BC). On the opposite side of the valley, the cave of **La Vache Alliat** was also inhabited during the same period *(daily Jul.-Sep., visits every 30 min 10-11:30 & 2-6; Easter-Jun. and early Sep.-early Oct., daily ex Tue. at 3:30 and 5 pm)*. ▶ Miglos castle ruins, 14thC square castle-keep above **Capoulet**. ▶ Industrial area of **Vicdessos** and **Auzat** (aluminium) at the foot of Montcalm; ruins of the château of Montréal. ▶ Across the Port de Lers and the Agnès Pass : mountain **valley of the Garbet**★. ▶ At **Aulus-les-Bains** (spa with calcium, iron and sulphate waters; new treatment buildings 1983) : facilities for excursions on foot and horse-back into the mountains; craft workshops; see the Cascade d'Arse nearby. ▶ The **Ercé** chapel was built in the 11thC near the village of **Cominac**. ▶ Coffered ceiling in 12thC Romanesque church at **Vic**, close to **Oust**. ▶ Beyond **Seix**, the road climbs to the Core Pass (alt. 1 395 m), descent into the **Bethmale Valley**★. The church at **Ayet**, close by, has beautiful woodwork. ▶ 12thC Saint-Pierre church in **Ourjout** near Bordes-sur-Lez and 13thC chapel in **Aubignac**. ▶ See the Romanesque chapel of calvary★ (12th-13thC) at **Castillon-en-Couserans**; the château of Coumes is open in summer by appointment. ▶ The church of Notre-Dame de Tanesaygues at **Audressein** is decorated with 15th-16thC frescos; visit the clog maker. ▶ In the Luzenac hamlet of **Moulis** is a Romanesque church. ▶ 13thC castle-keep in the château de **Montégut-en-Couserans**. □

Looking for a locality? Consult the index at the back of the book.

Practical Information ⎯⎯⎯⎯⎯⎯⎯⎯⎯⎯⎯⎯⎯⎯

ARGEIN, ✉ 09800, 4 km W of **Castillon-en-Couserans**.

Hotel :
★★ *La Terrasse*, ☎ 61.96.70.11, AE, 10 rm ⇇ ◿ closed 30 Sep-1 Mar, 150. Rest. ♦ ♿ 55-120.

AULUS-LES-BAINS, ✉ 09140, 33 km SE of **Saint-Girons**.
ⓘ allée des Thermes, ☎ 61.66.94.59; mairie, ☎ 61.66.93.55.

Hotel :
● ★ *France*, ☎ 61.96.00.90, Visa, 30 rm ℙ ⇇ ⦀ ◿ closed 15 Oct-15 Dec, 150. Rest. ♦ ☏ 70-150.

La BASTIDE-DE-SÉROU, ✉ 09240, 17 km NW of **Foix**.

Hotel :
★ *Ferré*, rte de St-Girons, ☎ 61.64.50.26, 10 rm ◿ ☏ closed Mon (l.s.), 2-15 Jan, 70. Rest. ♦ ♪ 40-180.

MASSAT, ✉ 09320, 17 km SW of **Foix**.

Hotel :
● ★★★ *Trois Seigneurs* (L.F.), ☎ 61.96.95.89, 25 rm, closed Nov-Mar (ex school hols), 190. Rest. ♦♦ ♪ 50-200.

OUST, ✉ 09140 Seix, 2 km NE of **Seix**.

Hotel :
● ★★★ *Hostellerie de la Poste*, Seix, ☎ 61.66.86.33, 28 rm ℙ ⇇ ⦀ ♪ ▣ closed 1 Nov-1 May, 200. Rest. ♦♦ ♪
Spec : *pigeon à la crème d'ail, papillote de saumon aux cèpes, desserts*. Fine cellar, 75-210.

RIMONT, ✉ 09420, 12 km E of **Saint-Girons**.

Hotel :
Bon Accueil, ☎ 61.96.30.70, Visa, 11 rm ℙ ◿ ☏ 80. Rest. ♦♦ ♪ ☏ Generous, savoury food, 45-100; child : 20.

TARASCON-SUR-ARIÈGE, ✉ 09400, 16 km S of **Foix**.
ⓘ av. V.-Pilhes, ☎ 61.05.63.46.
▩ ☎ 61.05.62.61.

Hotel :
★★ *Poste* (L.F.), 16, av. V.-Pilhes, ☎ 61.05.60.41, 30 rm ⇇ ⦀ 170. Rest. ♦ ♪ 60-90.

⚓ ★★*Pré Lombard* (100 pl), ☎ 61.64.61.94.

USSAT-LES-BAINS, ✉ 09400 Tarascon-sur-Ariège, 4 km S of **Tarascon** on the 61056362.

Hotels :
★★ *Parc*, ☎ 61.05.74.74, AE Euro Visa, 60 rm ℙ ⦀ ◿ ♪ ☏ closed 31 Oct-1 Apr, 175. Rest. ♦ ♪ ☏ 65-130.
★ *Palmiers* (L.F.), Ornolac, RN 20, ☎ 61.05.62.02, AE DC, 11 rm ℙ ⇇ ⦀ closed 1 Oct-1 Apr, 75.

FOIX*

Carcassonne 81, Toulouse 83, Paris 792 km
pop 10060 ✉ 09000   C3

Whether you are coming from Toulouse, Saint-Girons, or Ax-les-Thermes, Foix looks like an enormous rock bristling with towers, at the foot of which run the Ariège and the Arget rivers. The annual "Journées Médiévales" are held in July (historic parade and mediaeval spectacle, market, craftsmen; one week duration) — the best time to buy regional products and craftwork.

▶ There are two bridges across the Ariège linking the N20 with the heart of the town. The **château**★ **des Comtes de Foix** (A2; *daily ex the first Mon. in Sep., tel. 61.65.56.05*) has three towers, of which the most conspicuous is the 42m high 15thC keep. At its foot, the **Ariège museum** exhibits prehistory, history and ethnography collections; view★ from the centre tower *(daily, 1 May-30 Sep., 10-12 & 2-6:30; 1 Oct.-30 Apr., 10-12 & 2-6).* ▶ The **church of St. Volusien** (B2) presently being restored, has undergone numerous transformations (11th-14th-17thC). Fine presbytery visible from the other bank of the Ariège. ▶ In the

twisting streets of the old city, there are many timbered 15th-16thC houses and two beautiful (19thC) covered markets, well-restored, where fresh produce is sold : halle de St-Volusien : *1st, 3rd and 5th Mon. of the month, every Wed. and Fri.* and a poultry market (near the Hôtel de Ville, *every Fri.*).

Nearby

▶ To the north, **Vernajoul** *(2.5 km;* Romanesque church) and the **underground river of Labouiche**★ *(5 km);* this river can be explored for 3 800 m (boat trip 1 500 m; *daily in summer, enq. tel. 61.65.04.11*). **Saint-Jean-de-Verges** *(6 km)* has an interesting little 12thC Romanesque church. ▶ To the south : **Montgaillard** *(4.5 km);* at the foot of the *Pain de Sucre* (Sugarloaf Hill) is a ruined château. 8 km farther on is the old 13thC **Pont du Diable** (Devil's Bridge) across the river Ariège, on the road from Foix to Tarascon. ▶ 14 km SE is the pilgrimage chapel of Notre Dame de Celles, built after the Virgin Mary supposedly appeared here in 1686.   □

Practical Information ⎯⎯⎯⎯⎯⎯⎯⎯⎯⎯⎯⎯⎯⎯

FOIX
ⓘ 45, cours Gabriel-Fauré (A-B3), ☎ 61.65.12.12.
▩ (B1), ☎ 61.65.27.00.

Car rental : *Avis*, train station; Garage Citroën, RN 20 Peysales ☎ 61.65.50.66.

Hotels :
★★★ *Pyrène*, Le Vignoble, ☎ 61.65.48.66, Euro Visa, 12 rm ℙ ⇇ ♿ ▣ ♪° closed 20 Dec-5 Jan, 170.
● ★★ *Audoye Lons* (L.F.), 4, pl. G.-Duthil (C2), ☎ 61.65.52.44, AE DC Euro Visa, 35 rm ⇇ closed Dec-Jan, 160. Rest. ♦♦ ⇇ ♪ closed Sat (l.s.), 50-130.
★★ *Le Couloumié*, lac de Labarthe, ☎ 61.02.72.20, AE Euro Visa, 20 rm ℙ ⇇ ⦀ ◿ 180. Rest. ♦ ⇇ ♪ 60-160; child : 35.

Restaurants :
♦♦ *Le Phœbus*, 3, cours Irénée-Cros (B1-2), ☎ 61.65.10.42, Euro Visa ⇇ ♪ ♿ closed Mon. Fish specialties, 60-140.
♦ *Le Médiéval*, 42, rue des Chapeliers (B2), ☎ 61.02.81.50, Euro Visa ⇇ ♪ ♿ closed Wed, Sat noon, Sun eve, 55-140; child : 40.

⚓ ★★*Municipal* (300 pl), ☎ 61.65.11.58.

Recommended
Farmhouse-gîte : *Cantegril*, St-Martin-de-Caralp, 7 km NW, ☎ 61.65.15.43.
Leisure activities : *trout fishing.*
Nightclubs : *L'Invaders*, Serres-sur-Anget 10 km SE, ☎ 61.65.14.07.
Sports : *horse riding.*
♥ antiques : *Foix*, 23, rue la Faurie; bakery : *Hébrard*, 18, rue la Faurie; pork products : *Rouch*, pl. St-Volusien.

Nearby

SAINT-PAUL-DE-JARRAT, ✉ 09260, 7 km S on the N20, D117.

Hotel :
● ★★ *La Charmille* (L.F.), ☎ 61.64.17.03, Euro Visa, 10 rm ℙ ⇇ ⦀ ☏ closed Mon, 20 Sep-5 Oct, 20 Dec-1 Feb, 135. Rest. ♦♦ 45-110.

GIMONT*

Auch 26, Toulouse 53, Paris 732 km
pop 2950 ✉ 32200   B1-2

The high street in Gimont runs through a wooden covered market; this ancient *bastide* was founded in 1322; *foie gras* is a local speciality.

▶ Not far from the 15th-16thC covered market is a **church** built in 1704. ▶ On the opposite bank of the Gimone river, **Cahuzac** suburb contains an early 16thC Gothic chapel;

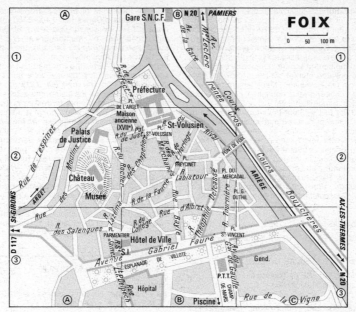

1 km upstream are the ruins of 12thC Cistercian **Gimont Abbey.**

Nearby

Mauvezin *(13 km N)* is proud of its town square, larger than the Capitole in Toulouse (covered market and arcades). Not far from here is a church with a Gothic bell tower and unusual 15th-18thC furniture and a lovely view of Arrats Valley from the upper terrace. ▶ The former *bastide* at **Cologne** *(7 km from Mauvezin)* has a similar arcaded square round a central 14thC market. Between Cologne and L'Isle-Jourdain *(10 km E from Gimont)* is the St. Cricq Lake (aquatic sports); another lake at **L'Isle-Jourdain** itself. Also the arcaded square, covered market, the 15thC castle tower and the collegiate church (1785). ▶ Near **Cazaux-Savès** *(13 km SE of Gimont)* is the 16th-18thC **château de Caumont** *(for visits, tel. : 62.62.37.01).*   □

Practical Information _____

GIMONT

Hotel :
● ★★★ *Château de Larroque* (R.C.), rte de Toulouse, ☎ 62.67.77.44, Tx 531135, AE DC Visa, 15 rm 🅿 ⚹ 🎿 🔝 ♨ closed Jan, 310. Rest. ● ♦♦♦ ♪ 130-240; child : 60.

⚠ ★★*Municipal* (50 pl), ☎ 62.67.70.02.

Recommended
Events : *salted meat fair,* 1st Wed of Lent.
Farmhouse-inn : *En Sarrade,* ☎ 62.67.76.14, Spec : *poule farcie, palombes forestières.*
♥ foie gras : *Ducs de Gascogne,* rte de Mauvezin ; pastry-chocolates : *Urraca,* pl. Saint-Eloi ; pork products : *Ghiesni,* 2, pl. Saint-Eloi, ☎ 62.67.72.92.

Nearby

L' ISLE-JOURDAIN, ✉ 32600, 10 km E.
ℹ mairie, ☎ 62.07.14.39 ; Maison du Lac, ☎ 62.07.25.57 (h.s.).

Hotel :
★★★ *Lac,* 1 km W on N 124, ☎ 62.07.03.91, 25 rm 🅿 ⚹ 🎿 🔝 closed Mon, Jan, 190. Rest. ♦♦ Spec : *foie frais aux pommes,* 50-170.

⚠ ★★*Municipal* (53 pl), ☎ 62.07.14.39.

Recommended
♥ salt-cured meats : *La Tuilerie de Monseigneur* (J. Moudenc).

MAUVEZIN, ✉ 32120, 13 km N.

Restaurant :
♦♦ *La Rapière,* rue des Justices, ☎ 62.06.80.08, AE DC Euro Visa ♪ ♿ ♨ closed Tue eve and Wed , Oct. Good, earthy cooking. Reserve, 70-130 ; child : 35.

⚠ ★★*Municipal* (50 pl), ☎ 62.06.81.45.

MONTAIGUT-SUR-SAVE, ✉ 31530 Lévignac, 15 km NE of **L'Isle-Jourdain.**

Hotel :
● ★★ *Le Ratelier,* rte de l'Isle-Jourdain, ☎ 62.85.43.36, AE DC Euro Visa, 13 rm 🅿 🎿 🔝 200. Rest. ♦ ♪ closed Tue. An enjoyable stop, 80-120 ; child : 55.

The LAURAGAIS Region

C2

The Lauragais, between the Massif Central and the Pyrénées, is where Aquitaine meets the Midi. In spite of its low altitude (190 m) the watershed at Narouze (Aude) between the Mediterranean and Aquitaine basins is marked by distinct changes in vegetation. This is where the Canal du Midi is joined by the feeder canal from the Bassin de St. Ferréol (memorial to Riquet, the canal engineer).

▶ **Avignonet-Lauragais,** near the canal and close to three well-stocked lakes, has a 14thC church ; Paul Riquet centre can be reached by the rest area of **Port Lauragais** (A61), the Midi Canal and the RN113. There one follows the history of the Midi Canal and a sculpture fountain which illustrates the system of water supply. Permanent and temporary exhibitions and audiovisual displays complete this. The church at **Baziège** was fortified in the 14thC; Lastours castle (early 16thC) is surrounded by a moat *(furniture; visits in the afternoon).* ▶ **Revel** (winter resort); a former *bastide* (1342), now a food production and craftwork centre (furniture, marquetry; workshop visits). Arcades around the central square; temporary exhibitions are held in the covered market, which is crowned by a tower dating from the Revolution. Many leisure facilities : fishing, sailing, canoe/kayak, equitation, cycling, potholing, spelunking, hang-gliding, etc. (large artificial lake at Saint-Ferréol *(3 km SE).* ▶ **Saint-Félix-Lauragais,** charming site : 14thC church, covered market and old streets clustered inside the remains of the fortifications; 12th-13thC castle with 14thC keep *(open daily ex Wed.);* artificial lake at Enclas. ▶ **Saint-Paulet** (between Saint-Félix and Avignet); castle altered in 16th and 18thC, and nearby **Montmaur** also contains a mediaeval château modified during the Renaissance. **Villefranche-de-Lauragais,** 12thC *bastide,* 13th-14thC Southern Gothic church with wall-belfry. *Cassoulet* (pork and bean stew) is a local speciality.   □

Practical Information ―――――――――――――

PORT-LAURAGAIS, ⊠ 31290, 10 km SE of **Villefranche.**

Restaurant :
◆ *La Dinnée,* ☎ 61.27.14.50, AE DC Euro Visa ⍒ 70-100.

REVEL, ⊠ 31250, 53 km SE of **Toulouse.**
ⓘ pl. Ph.-de-Valois, ☎ 61.83.50.06.

Hotel :
★★ *Hostellerie du Lac,* (Inter-Hôtel), Saint-Férréol, ☎ 61.27.66.55, AE DC Euro Visa, 35 rm Ⓟ ⍒ ⑭ ⍤ ♪ closed Sun eve (l.s.), 23 Dec-4 Jan. On the shore of Lake Saint-Ferréol, 180. Rest. ◆ ⍒ ⛊ 55-120; child ; 30.

Restaurant :
◆◆ *Lauragais,* av. de Castelnaudary, ☎ 61.83.51.22 ⑭ Earthy food in a rustic setting. Spec : *foie gras à l'ancienne, cassoulet au confit d'oie,* 120-210.

Recommended
♥ at Durfort, 4 km from Sorèze, copperware : *M. Bonnafous,* 81540 Sorèze.

SAINT-FÉLIX-LAURAGAIS, ⊠ 31540, 10 km W of **Revel.**
ⓘ ☎ 61.83.01.71.

Hotel :
★★★ *Poids Public,* ☎ 61.83.00.20, AE Euro Visa, 13 rm Ⓟ ⍒ ⑭ ⍤ half pens (h.s.), closed Sun eve (15 Oct-15 Mar), 6 Jan-7 Feb, 185. Rest. ◆ ⍒ ♪ A gastronomic stopover not to be missed. B.Augé is an exemplary cook : *jambon de sanglier, civet d'anguille.* Regional wines, 45-180.

VILLEFRANCHE-DE-LAURAGAIS, ⊠ 31290, 33 km SE of **Toulouse.**
▆▆▆ ☎ 61.81.60.29.

Hotel :
★★ *France,* 106, rue de la République, ☎ 61.81.62.17, Tx 530955, AE DC Euro Visa, 19 rm Ⓟ closed Mon, 19 Jan-3 Feb, 6-27 Jul, 110. Rest. ◆ 50-110.

LAVELANET

Foix 27, Carcassonne 66, Paris 814 km
pop 8430 ⊠ 09300   C3

On the Cathar pilgrimage road to Montségur, this former capital of the Olmes area is a lively little textile town. A textile museum has just opened here *(Jun.-Sep., 2-7).*

▶ 16thC **church** and an interesting view (from the centre square) of Montségur and its surrounding snowy peaks.

Nearby

9 km W on a rocky outcrop are the remains of the **château de Roquefixade** (12th-13thC); a heliograph (light signal) system made it possible to communicate from here

with the fortresses of Montgaillard, Montségur and Puivert. ▶ **Monts d'Olmes** (alt. 1 400-2 100 m) winter sports resort *(21 km SW; season Dec.-Mar.);* St. Barthélemy Peak (alt. 2 348 m). ▶ **Montségur★★** *(12 km S; difficult 30 min climb from the carpark);* the last stronghold of the Cathar religious movement, finally captured after a ten month siege in 1244; the 210 men and women who refused to renounce their "heresy" were burnt alive... Exceptional view★ from the ruins (alt. 1 215 m). Oddly enough, they show none of the usual characteristics of military architecture found in other fortresses in the region. In the little tile-roofed village below, there is a small archaeological and prehistory museum *(near the town hall; daily May-Sep. or by appt. tel. 61.01.10.27).* ▶ Further on, through the **Gorges du Lasset, Fougax-et-Barrineuf** (access road to the **Gorges de la Frau★**) and past the intermittent fountain at **Fontestorbes,** the road runs down to **Bélesta** "world capital of natural horn combs". Walks in the forest of Bélesta; 1.5 km on the Puivert route brings you to the pilgrimage chapel of **Notre-Dame-du-Val d'Amour.** ▶ Down in the **valley of the Hers, L'Aiguillon** and **La Bastide-sur-l'Hers** also specialise in horn comb production; visit the premises of Laffont de La Bastide *(15 people max.; tel. 61.01.11.01).* 5 km N of Lavelanet is the 16thC Saint-Roch chapel at **Larogues-d'Olmes.**   □

Practical Information ―――――――――――――

ⓘ foyer municipal, ☎ 61.01.22.20.

Hotel :
★★★ *Espagne,* 20, rue J.-Jaurès, ☎ 61.01.00.78, 23 rm ▭ 165. Rest. ◆ ♪ 50-120.

Recommended
Events : *lectures,* info. : l'occitadelle, ☎ 61.01.21.77, slide shows with commentary on the Cathares.

LECTOURE*

Condom 23, Agen 36, Paris 762 km
pop 4420 ⊠ 32700   B1

To see Lectoure at its best, you should come from Fleurance; the old houses seem to huddle inside their mediaeval protective walls.

▶ From the **Promenade du Bastion★,** you can see most of the Pyrénées in fine weather. ▶ The former **cathedral** (it was demoted to church during the Revolution) combines Southern Gothic (13thC nave) with Northern Gothic (14thC choir). The bishop's palace (16th-18thC) is today the **town hall** : portraits of great men born in the region; **Antiquities Museum★** *(daily).* In 1540, 3rd-4thC altars for ritual bull sacrifices were discovered on the site of the cathedral choir; local excavations have produced many remains from Gallo-Roman civilisation in the northern Gers.

Nearby

▶ Artificial lake at **Trois Vallées** *(3 km SE).* ▶ **Miradoux** *(15 km NE)* fortified town with 13thC church; 4.5 km farther, castle and Lahitte eco-museum at **Flamarens.** ▶ The 13thC **château de Gramont★** *(14 km E in the Lot-et-Garonne; daily ex Tue. Apr.-Oct.; closed mornings Apr.-Jun. and 16 Sep.-Oct.),* was remodelled in the Renaissance; furniture and terraced gardens. ▶ **Saint-Clar** *(15 km SE)* : an elegant Gascon *bastide;* remains of a 16thC château of the kings of Navarre and another (17thC) belonging to the bishops of Lectoure; sale of regional produce. ▶ 3 km SE above the valley of the Arratz is the 13thC **château d'Avezan,** rebuilt in 17thC *(daily 10-6, guided tours in summer).* ▶ **Fleurance** *(11 km SE)* : a *bastide* founded in 1280; 14th-15thC church in Southern Gothic, with three fine 16thC stained glass windows★ by Arnaud de Moles, not far from the town square (arcades, covered market in stone). ▶ **Château de Terraube** *(9 km, afternoons in season).*   □

Practical Information

LECTOURE

Hotel :
★★ *Bastard*, rue Lagrange, ☎ 62.68.82.44, Euro Visa, 30 rm P ⬩ ⬩ ⬩ ♪ closed Feb. 18th-C manor house, 185. Rest. ♦ ⬩ ♪ 55-130; child : 40.

Restaurant :
♦♦ *Les Bouviers*, 8, rue Montebello, ☎ 62.68.71.69 ♪ closed Tue , Feb. Spec : *jambonnette de volaille au coulis de langoustine*, 75-230.

Nearby

FLEURANCE, ⊠ 32500, 11 km SE.
ℹ mairie, ☎ 62.06.10.01.
SNCF ☎ 62.06.10.92.

Hotels :
★★★ *Le Fleurance*, rte d'Agen, ☎ 62.06.14.85, AE DC Euro Visa, 25 rm P ⬩ ⬩ closed 15 Dec-15 Jan, 230.
★★ *Le Relais*, rte d'Auch, ☎ 62.06.05.08, 25 rm P closed 20 Jan-15 Feb, 145.

Restaurant :
♦♦ *Cusinato*, rte d'Agen, ☎ 62.06.07.70, AE DC Euro Visa ⬩ ⬩ ♪ closed Mon and Sun eve (l.s.), 15 Dec-15 Jan. The felicitously named Bernard Cusinato prepares local specialties like : *pot-au-feu de canard gras aux petits légumes, pain perdu au Grand Marnier*, 60-200.

LOMBEZ

Auch 38, Toulouse 50, Paris 731 km
pop 1240 ⊠ 32220   B2
Lombez, like Lectoure, was formerly a bishopric, which explains the large cathedral in so small a village.

▶ This fine brick 14th-15thC church has a fortress-like appearance relieved only by the elegant five-storied octagonal bell-tower in Toulousain style; old stained-glass and fine recumbent Christ from a 15th-16thC Burial of Christ; treasure room.

Nearby

▶ 3 km NE of Lombez is **Samatan**, an agricultural centre of some importance (market). ▶ Romanesque church *(14 km NW)* at **Saramon**. ▶ **Saint-Christophe chapel** *(7 km NW;* view), pilgrimage for motorists. ▶ **Simorre** *(17 km SW)* has the most beautiful fortified church★ in Gascony (14thC; stalls and stained glass 16thC). ▶ **L'Isle-en-Dodon** *(14 km S,* in the Haute Garonne) is a winter and country-holiday resort (equitation, cycling holidays, fishing and shooting); 14thC church, automobile museum *(closed Mon.).*   □

Practical Information

Nearby

SAMATAN, ⊠ 32130, 3 km NE.

Hotel :
★ *Maigné*, ☎ 62.62.30.24, 15 rm P ⬩ ⬩ closed 20 Sep-20 Oct, 85. Rest. ● ♦♦ Wonderful regional fare : *foie gras, cassoulet* 65-180.

Recommended
Market : *fatted ducks and geese*, 11 Nov, antiques, cooking contests.

MIRANDE

Auch 25, Toulouse 103, Paris 793 km
pop 4150 ⊠ 32300   A2
A *bastide* founded in 1285 with central square and streets laid out on a grid pattern; one of the most typical in SW France.

▶ Near the arcaded **square**, the 15thC fortified **church** has an unusual bell-tower straddling the street. ▶ Beside it, **museum** *(daily; if closed, apply to SI next door)* : collection of minor masters, from Italian primitives to 19thC French painters, old ceramics and Gascon glazed pottery.   □

Practical Information

ℹ 13, rue de l'Evêché, ☎ 62.66.68.10.

Hotel :
★★ *Europ'Hôtel Maupas*, 2, av. d'Etigny, ☎ 62.66.51.42, Euro, 20 rm P ⬩ ⬩ closed Sat (l.s.), 130. Rest. ♦♦ ⬩ 60-110; child : 40.

⚠ ★★★*Ile du Pont* (100 pl), ☎ 62.66.64.11.

Recommended
Market : *fatted ducks and geese.*
♥ *Les Producteurs Gascons*, rte d'Auch, foie gras and confits.

MIREPOIX*

Foix 34, Carcassonne 47, Paris 796 km
pop 3580 ⊠ 09500   C3
This 13thC *bastide* is straight out of the Middle Ages, with its regular street plan and houses almost intact. Market days are Thursday and Saturday; picturesque cattle market on the second and fourth Monday each month. Mediaeval Week in July.

▶ The half-timbered houses on the **Place Centrale** are built over one of the largest arcaded squares in the Midi Toulousain. ▶ The **cathedral** was begun in the 13thC, but the present vaulting dates from 1867; the 60 m bell-tower is a prominent landmark. ▶ The **Tour Ste. Foy** is a remnant of the 12th-13thC fortress of Lévis-Mirepoix. ▶ To this family also belonged the **Lagarde château** *(8 km SE)*, rebuilt in the 18thC over a 13thC structure, as well as the **château de Caudeval** *(9 km E* in the Aude, dating from 12th, 16th and 17thC); museum : artillery and Roman remains *(daily mid-Jul.-end Aug.).*   □

Practical Information

Hotel :
★★ *Le Commerce* (L.F.), cours du Dr-Chabaud, ☎ 61.68.10.29, Euro Visa, 32 rm P ⬩ ⬩ pens (h.s.), closed Jan, 2-18 Oct, 320. Rest. ♦ ⬩ closed Sat (l.s.), 50-110.

⚠ ★★*Municipal* (64 pl), ☎ 61.68.10.47.

Recommended
Farmhouse-gîte : *Mazerette*, ☎ 61.68.15.25, horse riding, lake, hiking, cycling, tennis, and swimming pool.

MURET

Toulouse 21, Auch 75, Paris 729 km
pop 16190 ⊠ 31600   B-C2
Once the administrative capital of Comminges, Muret is now part of the Toulouse sector; a late reprisal, perhaps, for the 1213 defeat of Count Raymond VI by Simon de Montfort during the crusade against the Albigeois.

▶ A statue of Icarus by Landowski is a reminder that this city, the center of a flying-club, was the home of one of aviation's pioneers : Clément Ader (1841-1925). ▶ 12thC Romanesque **church** witth crypt, Toulousain bell-tower from Gothic period.   □

In preparing for your trip, consult the pages pertaining to the regions. You will find there the description of the region you wish to visit, as well as a list of sites that must be seen, a brief history and practical information.

NOGARO

Mont-de-Marsan 42, Auch 62, Paris 747 km
pop 2400 ⊠ 32110   A1

Nogaro is well known to sports enthusiasts : in spring and autumn numerous motorcycle and car races are held on the Circuit Paul-Armagnac. Hang-gliding is also popular. ▶ 12thC collegiate church (doorway).

Nearby

▶ 14thC church at **Riscle** *(14 km S, summer resort).*
▶ **Barbotan-les-Thermes,** 26 km N, is a spa (calcium, magnesium and sulphur waters; *season Apr-Nov)* specialising in the treatment of rheumatism and circulatory disorders. Fishing, *Courses Landaises* (dodging a charging heifer by skillful footwork) and wood-pigeon *(palombe)* shooting are among the favourite activities; lovely park; a fortified gateway forms the porch of the Romanesque church.   ☐

Hotel :
★ *Dubroca*, 11, rue d'Artagnan, ☎ 62.09.01.03, Euro Visa, 12 rm Ⓟ 𝄞 ♪ closed Fri eve , Sat and Sun (l.s.), 19 Dec-5 Jan, 105. Rest. ♦ ♪ ら 50-95.

Recommended
Events : *grand prix motor race*, Easter.

Nearby
BARBOTAN-LES-THERMES, ⊠ 32150, 26 km N.
⚓ (1 Feb-20 Dec), ☎ 62.69.52.09.   ♥
ⓘ pl. d'Armagnac, ☎ 62.69.52.13.

Hotels :
★★★ *Bastide Gasconne* (R.C.),   ☎   62.69.52.09, Tx 521009, AE, 43 rm ▭ 🏊 closed 31 Oct-1 Apr, 420. Rest. ♦♦♦ Spec : *fricassée d'escargots, pintadeau au lard fumé et au margaux, crêpes fourrées à l'armagnac.* Outstanding cellar, 180-250.
● ★★ *Cante Grit*, av. des Thermes, ☎ 62.69.52.12, AE Visa, 23 rm Ⓟ 𝄞 ♪ closed 1 Nov-15 Apr, 245. Rest. ♦♦ ♪ ☀ 85-140.
★★ *Château de Bégué* (R.S.), 2 km SW, ☎ 62.69.50.08, 20 rm 15 apt Ⓟ 𝄞 𝄞 ⚘ ▭ closed 15 Oct-1 May, 260. Rest. ♦ 105-150.
★★ *Résidence Les Mousquetaires*, rue de la Tour, ☎ 62.69.52.09, 50 rm Ⓟ 𝄞 ⚘ ら closed Jan, 21-31 Dec, 190.

⚠ ★★★*l'Uby* (200 pl), ☎ 62.09.53.91.

Recommended
♥ at Labastide-d'Armagnac, Armagnac, liqueurs, foie gras : *Château-Garreau*, ☎ 58.44.81.08.

CAZAUBON, ⊠ 32150, 3 km SW.

Hotel :
★★★ *Château Bellevue*, rue J.-Cappin, ☎ 62.09.51.95, Tx 521429, AE DC, 26 rm Ⓟ 𝄞 𝄞 ⚘ ▭ closed 30 Nov-1 Mar, 255. Rest. ♦ ♪ 100-160.

LUPPÉ-VIOLLES, ⊠ 32110 Nogaro, 9 km SW on the N 124.

Hotel :
● ★★★ *Relais de l'Armagnac*, ☎ 62.08.95.22, AE Euro Visa, 10 rm Ⓟ 𝄞 ♪ 🐎 ☀ closed Sun eve and Mon ex Jun-Sep, 2 Jan-7 Feb, 220. Rest. ● ♦♦ 𝄞 ♪ ら 🌿 Highly rated regional cooking, 60-180.

SÉGOS, ⊠ 32400 Riscle, 18 km W.

Hotel :
★★★★ *Domaine du Bassibé* (R.C.), ☎ 62.09.46.71, Tx 531918, AE DC Euro Visa, 9 rm Ⓟ 𝄞 𝄞 ⚘ ら 🏊 half pens (h.s.), closed 2 Nov-19 Apr, 900. Rest. ● ♦♦♦ ♪ Excellent regional fare in the traditional mould : *confit aux cèpes, tripes de mouton à l'armagnac*, 160-220.

PAMIERS

Foix 19, Toulouse 64, Paris 773 km
pop 15190 ⊠ 09100   C3

The town was named by the Count of Foix on his return from the Crusades (12thC), in memory of Apamea on the banks of the Orontes, where he acquired a number of holy relics. Pamiers is today the major commercial and industrial centre of the department. The paper and cardboard-making centres are open to the public *(daily except Sat. and Sun., maximum 8 people).*

▶ One of the castles of the Counts of Foix used to stand on the **Butte du Castella;** view★ over the Pyrénées and the plain of Toulouse. ▶ The **cathedral of St. Antonin,** remodelled in the 18thC, has a 12thC doorway and a 14thC Toulousain bell-tower. ▶ The church of **Notre-Dame-du-Camp** was also rebuilt (17th-18thC) and has preserved an imposing 14thC fortified façade.

Nearby

▶ **Varilhes** *(9 km S;* country holidays), where the valley of the Ariège widens out, has numerous old half-timbered houses. ▶ **Vals** *(13 km E)* has an unusual church built into the rock; it dates from Carolingian times (8th-10thC) and is decorated with 11thC Romanesque frescos; small archaeological museum in a neighbouring house. ▶ The **château de Gaudiès** *(13 km NE)* was completed in the late 13thC but modified in 17th-18thC *(daily May-Aug).* ▶ 15thC church in the fortified town of **Montaut,** on an isolated hill *(9 km N).* ▶ **La Bastide-de-Mazères** *(17 km NE)* was built to a grid pattern in 1252 and still has its old covered market where, each December, the best goose and duck *foie gras* are judged. Annual *fête des fleurs* (flower festival) at the end of May. ▶ **Saverdun** *(13 km N)* was one of the key towns of the County of Foix in the 12thC and a centre of the Reformation during the Wars of Religion (second half of the 16thC). The upper town was formerly defended by a feudal castle (Tour Gaston Phoebus; view) while the lower town was surrounded by defensive walls. Regional information and sale of produce (food and crafts) at the Maison de l'Ariège. ▶ 34 km NW, Gothic church with Romanesque doorway, 14thC brick houses and lovely Biac park in **Lézat-sur-Lèze.** ▶ The old fortified town of **Saint-Ybars** *(29 km NW)* has a lively poultry market on the fourth Wednesday of each month. ▶ **Le Fossat** (27 km NW) still has its mediaeval character, and it is equally apparent at the fortified village *(4 km farther)* of **Carla-Bayle,** once a Protestant stronghold. ▶ Interesting churches at **La-Bastide-de-Besplas** *(37 km NW :* paintings, sculptures, mosaics, stained glass) and at **Daumazan** *(33 km NW;* Romanesque apse raised at a later date). ▶ **Pailhes castle** *(17 km W),* now in ruins, was visited by Henry IV of Navarre.   ☐

Practical Information _____

ⓘ pl. du Mercadal, ☎ 61.67.04.22.
SNCF ☎ 61.67.00.85.

Hotels :
● ★★ *France* (L.F.), 5, cours Rambaud, ☎ 61.60.20.88, Visa, 32 rm Ⓟ 𝄞 ⚘ closed Sun (l.s.), 25 Dec-5 Jan, 120. Rest. ♦ 65-120.
★★ *Parc* (L.F.), 12, rue Piconnières, ☎ 61.67.02.58, Visa, 12 rm, closed Mon, Nov, 150. Rest. ♦ 60-110.

⚠ ★★*Municipal* (100 pl), ☎ 61.67.12.24 ; at Varilhes, 9 km S, ★★*Municipal* (100 pl), ☎ 61.60.71.17.

Recommended
Leisure activities : at Lézat-sur-lèze, *Musée de l'outil*, 28, av. des Pyrénées, ☎ 61.69.14.35, open 1 Apr-15 Nov 2pm-7pm daily, Sun : 3pm-7pm.
♥ candy : *Laurent*, 28, rue des Jacobins, ☎ 61.67.01.65, for their *marquisettes*.

ST-BERTRAND-DE-COMMINGES***

Saint-Gaudens 17, Tarbes 61, Paris 816 km
pop 230 ⊠ 31510   A3
On an isolated knoll overlooking the valley of the
Garonne. Archaeological research and the existing
historic monuments combine to make this little town
the most renowned art and history site in the central Pyrénées.
▶ The **cathedral of St. Marie★**, in the heart of the upper
town, was built in several stages : 11th-12thC nave with
bell-tower keep and Romanesque doorway ; 14th-15thC
choir and rich **furnishings★★** (note the Renaissance stained glass, the choir-screen, the stalls, the 15thC bishops'
tombs, the mausoleum of St. Bertrand (15thC), the
curiously positioned organs and the 16thC Flemish tapestries) ; treasure room★ in the former chapter, and clois-
ter★ with one Gothic and three Romanesque galleries.
▶ Don't miss the **Gallo-Roman museum★** *(closed in '87
for restoration)* in the former Benedictine (Olivetan) chapel. Numerous 15th-16thC houses within the upper town.
▶ The **lower town★**, sacked by the Vandals in 408, is built
on the site of the Gallo-Roman town of *Lugdunum Convenarum ;* excavations have revealed the remains of the
theatre, the forum, the baths, a Roman basilica, and a
4thC Christian basilica. ▶ 2 km away, on the banks on
the Garonne, **Valcabrère** was built in the late Middle Ages
using material from the ruins of the Gallo-Roman city ; the
church of St. Just★, somewhat apart from the town, was
the first cathedral of the diocese of Comminges (rebuilt in
the 11th-12thC).

Nearby

▶ The **Gargas Caves** *(6 km NW,* Hautes Pyrénées, enq. :
62.39.72.07) are famous for their rock formations and a
large number of prehistoric hand prints ; these show
hands missing parts of one or two fingers ; their signifi-
cance is unknown. ▶ **Barbazan** *(5 km E)* is a spa with calcium sulphate waters *(season May-Sep.) ;* beautiful park★,
small natural lake, fishing and walks in the mountains.
▶ **Mauléon-Barousse** *(10 km S,* Haute Pyrénées) is
the former capital of la Barousse : historic chapel and,
nearby, the Saoule chasm. ▶ 13 km S, **Saléchon,** Romanesque chapel in the cemetery. ▶ **Saint-Béat** (where
stands the house which gave E. Rostand the inspiration
for the balcony scene between Cyrano de Bergerac and
Roxane, *20 km S)*, is a pleasant resort (trout fishing and
mountain hikes), built on both banks of the Garonne with
a marble bridge in the middle (marble and onyx quarries nearby, from which certain sections of Versailles originated). Pretty Romanesque church reconstructed by
the Beaux-Arts : treasury★ (tympanum) and ruins of
14th-15thC castle (view). The chair-lift at Mourtis *(10 km
E)* goes to the top of the **Tuc de l'Étang** (alt. 1 860 m)
with a view★ of the central Pyrénées.   ☐

Practical Information

SAINT-BERTRAND-DE-COMMINGES
ℹ ☎ 61.88.37.07.

Hotel :
★ *Comminges* (L.F.), ☎ 61.88.31.43, 12 rm Ⓟ ∦ ✵ closed
Nov-Easter, 180. Rest . ♦ ✵ closed eves, 70-140.

Nearby

BARBAZAN, ⊠ 31510, 5 km E.
ℹ ☎ 61.88.35.64.

Hotels :
★★★ *L'Aristou* (L.F.), rte de Sauveterre, ☎ 61.88.30.67,
AE DC Euro Visa, 8 rm Ⓟ ∦ ᎅ ♪ & 250. Rest. ♦♦ ∦ ♪
& 75-200 ; child : 50.
★★ *Panoramique* (R.S.), hameau de Burs, ☎ 61.88.35.23,
Visa, 20 rm Ⓟ ∦ ᎅ ᎁ closed in winter, 180. Rest. ♦
closed Mon (l.s.). A comfortable hotel in a green setting with
a view of the Pyrénées ; delicious food too : *foie gras au
torchon, délices de sole à l'oseille, côte de boeuf,* 80-130.

⅄ ★★*Es Pibous* (66 pl), ☎ 61.88.31.42.

CIERP-GAUD, ⊠ 31440 Saint-Béat, 5 km W of **Saint-Béat.**

Hotels :
★ *Pyrénées*, pl. des Ecoles, ☎ 61.79.50.12, 15 rm Ⓟ ∦ ᐃ
closed 2 Nov-20 Dec, 80.
La Bonne Auberge, ☎ 61.79.54.47, 5 rm Ⓟ ∦ ᐃ half pens,
closed 15-30 Sep, 240. Rest. ♦ 80-160.

SAUVETERRE-DE-COMMINGES, ⊠ 31510 Barbazan,
4 km E of **Barbazan.**

Hotel :
● ★★★ *Hostellerie des Sept Molles* (R.C.), hameau de
Gesset, ☎ 61.88.30.87, AE DC Euro Visa, 19 rm Ⓟ ∦ ᎅ
ᐃ ▭ ⌀ closed 25 Oct-15 Mar, 360. Rest. ♦♦♦ ♪ Traditional gastronomy. Spec : *foie gras frais aux myrtilles,
saumon aux pousses d'asperges, sabayon de juraçon.*
Reserve, 140-200.

SAINT-GAUDENS

Tarbes 65, Toulouse 90, Paris 797 km
pop 12229 ⊠ 31800   B3
Saint-Gaudens is built on a hillside overlooking the
Garonne. Industrial activity includes gas production
from the St. Marcet field and the manufacture of
paper pulp. Tourist and leisure activities : shooting,
fishing and horse riding. Artificial lake. Calf sale every
Thursday (the local breed is milky white).

▶ 11th-12thC **church** modelled on St. Sernin in Toulouse.
The largest carillon of the Midi-Pyrénées and tapestries of
Aubusson of 18thC. Behind it is the *S.I.* and the **museum**
(closed) with prehistory, history, religious art and ethnog-
raphy collections. View★ over some 180 km of the
Pyrénées from **Boulevard Jean-Bepmale. Comminges
Museum :** local folklore *(daily ex Sun. 8:30-12 & 2-6).*

Nearby

▶ The **Caoue chapel** was built on Rue Père-Marie-Antoine,
on the spot where the shepherd Gaudens was decapitat-
ed. ▶ Ruins of Gallo-Romanesque villa 3 km SW, at
Valentine. ▶ **Montréjeau★** *(14 km W)* : a 13thC *bastide*
founded by King Philippe III in 1272. Situated at the junction of the Neste and the Garonne (view★), it has become
a tourist and resort town ; international folklore festival the
week of 15 Aug. ▶ 18 km NW, noteworthy remains of the
Gallo-Roman villa Montmaurin★ (4thC ; museum ; *closed
Tue. and Wed.).* From here you can reach the **Save gorges** and *(9 km)* the former *bastide* at **Boulogne-sur-Gesse**
(13thC ; 15thC church ; arcaded square) which is now a
holiday town (artificial lake). ▶ 8 km S is the former spa
of **Encausse-les-Thermes.** ▶ **Aspet** *(15 km SE)* (Saracen
tower, Henri IV fountain) : a pleasant town set among
wooded valleys (mediaeval tower, music festival in July) ;
mountain walks to the caves (incl. that of Gouillon) and
the **Portet d'Aspet** (pass at 1 069 m ; view★).   ☐

Practical Information

SAINT-GAUDENS
ℹ Mas-St-Pierre, ☎ 61.89.15.99.
🚈 ☎ 61.89.16.07.

Car rental : *Avis,* 10, bd Charles-de-Gaulle,
☎ 61.95.33.50 ; train station.

Hotels :
★★★ *Cèdres*, Villeneuve-de-Rivière, ☎ 61.89.36.00, 20 rm
Ⓟ ∦ ᎅ ᐃ ♪ ⌀ pens (h.s.), 800. Rest. ♦♦♦ ∦ ♪ & In Mme
de Montespan's former manor house, trust André Clausse
and his scrumptious creations, 95-150.
★★ *Commerce*, av. de Boulogne, ☎ 61.89.44.77, AE DC
Euro Visa, 54 rm Ⓟ ✵ closed 15 Dec-2 Feb, 150.
Rest. ♦ 60-120.
★★ *Esplanade* (L.F.), 7, pl. du Mas-St-Pierre,
☎ 61.89.15.90, 12 rm Ⓟ ∦ ᐃ 100.
⅄ ★★★*Belvédère* (96 pl), ☎ 61.89.15.76.

Nearby

ENCAUSSE-LES-THERMES, ⊠ 31160, 11 km S.

Hotel :
★ *Aux Marronniers*, ☎ 61.89.17.12, 11 rm ℙ ▦ ⌕ pens (h.s.), closed Sun eve and Mon (l.s.), 4 Jan-3 Feb, 300. Rest. ◆ ♿ 50-90.

MONTREJEAU, ⊠ 31210, 14 km W.
ⓘ pl. Valentin-Abeille, ☎ 61.95.80.22; mairie, ☎ 61.95.84.17.
SNCF ☎ 61.95.80.29.

Hotel :
★★ *Lecler*, (Inter-Hôtel), 4, av. de St-Gaudens, ☎ 61.95.80.43, Euro Visa, 22 rm ℙ ⧳ ▦ ⌕ ♪ closed 6 Jan-15 Feb, 120. Rest. ♪ closed Mon, 60-100.

▲ ★★*Hortensias* (33 pl), ☎ 61.95.80.22; ★★*Midi-Pyrénées* (100 pl), ☎ 61.95.86.79.

SAINT-GIRONS

Foix 44, Toulouse 91, Paris 800 km
pop 7720 ⊠ 09200   B3

A little market town at the junction of a number of roads and valleys, seat of the local administration.

▶ The **church of St. Valier** has a crenellated wall-belfry over its façade; 16thC bridge near the church of St. Girons, named after a martyr put to death by the Visigoths. Visit to the cheese-producers Faup and Temp Lait *(every am ex Sat. and Sun.).* ▶ **Saint-Lizier★★** *(2 km N;* festival of classical music in Sep.) is the Gallo-Roman city of *Lugdunum Consaranorum;* the capital of Couserans in the Middle Ages (remains of fortifications). The 12thC cathedral, with 14thC ogive vaulting and a Toulousain bell-tower, is decorated with 12th and 14thC frescos; the cloister★ (end 12thC) had an additional story added in 15thC; treasure room★ *(daily 15 Jun.-15 Sep., 10-12 & 2:30-6:30, tel. 61.66.16.22).* **Notre-Dame-du-Siège**, in the upper town, is also a cathedral; 12thC chapter, fine view of the Pyrénées. Old half-timbered houses in the narrow streets. ▶ **Montjoie-Volvestre★** *(2.5 km NE),* fortified 14thC village. ▶ Above the town are the **gorges of Ribaouto★.**   ▢

Practical Information ―――――――――――――

SAINT-GIRONS
ⓘ pl. A.-Sentein, ☎ 61.66.14.11.
SNCF ☎ 61.66.01.13.

Hotels :
● ★★★ *Eychenne*, (Mapotel), 8, av. P.-Laffont, ☎ 61.66.20.55, Tx 521273, AE DC Euro Visa, 48 rm ℙ ⧳ ▦ ⌕ closed 20 Dec-31 Jan, 300. Rest. ● ◆◆◆ ♿ Good regional cuisine served in a former coach house : *foie de canard aux raisins, confit de canard aux cèpes, soufflé au grand marnier,* 80-205.
★★★ *La Truite Dorée* (L.F.), 28, av. de la Résistance, ☎ 61.66.16.89, AE DC Euro Visa, 15 rm ℙ ⧳ ▦ half pens (h.s.), closed 15 Oct-30 Nov, 340. Rest. ◆ ⧳ ♿ A family-run inn with an appetizing menu. Spec : *foie gras aux pruneaux, confits, magrets, cailles aux cerises,* 70-150.
★★ *France*, 4, pl. des Poilus, ☎ 61.66.00.23, AE Visa, 21 rm ℙ ⌕ ⌖ closed Sun eve, 10-30 Nov, 110. Rest. ◆◆ ⌖ 55-150.

Nearby

LORP-SENTARAILLE, ⊠ 09190 Saint-Lizier, 5 km NW.

Hotel :
★★ *Horizon 117* (L.F.), ☎ 61.66.26.80, AE DC Visa, 20 rm ℙ ▦ closed Sun eve, 15 Oct-1 Nov, 200. Rest. ◆◆ ♪ 55-135.

On the maps, a town's name underlined <u>Saulieu</u> means that the locality possesses at least one recommended establishment (blue or red point).

SAINT-MARTORY

Saint-Gaudens 19, Toulouse 76, Paris 778 km
pop 1170 ⊠ 31360   B2-3

A little town on the Garonne on the site of a Gallo-Roman city. ▶ An 18thC bridge links the town to the suburb on the right bank, by the **château de Montpezat** (15th-16thC; restored).

Nearby

▶ 5 km W, remains of the former abbey of **Bonnefont**; parts of the cloister are in Saint-Martory; the remainder grace the Cloisters Museum in New York; on the site, you will see parts of the wall, the dovecote and a 16thC door.
▶ The spa at **Salies-du-Salat** *(6 km S; season May-Sep.)* is characterised by extremely salty water gushing from a cristalline salt deposit 200 m down. The town is built at the foot of a hill on which are the ruins of the castle of the Counts of Comminges (11th-13thC). **Montsaurès** *(2 km),* Templars' commandery. From here, you can go up the **Arbas Valley** and, beyond Labaderque *(23 km),* on foot to the **Gouffre (chasm) de la Henne Morte,** 446 m deep.
▶ Through the transverse valley of **Boussens** (menhirs at **Mancioux,** *4.5 km)* to **Martres-Tolosane★** *(10 km)* is the site of some Gallo-Roman villas, including the villa of Chiragan (2ndC); 1309 church with Toulousain bell-tower. The circular layout of this little mediaeval city (14thC Gothic church), is especially interesting. Handworked ceramics, produced since the 18thC (visit studios). ▶ **Alan** *(8 km NW from Martres-Tolosane),* with château of the bishops of Comminges (famous carving of a cow over the door to the staircase tower). ▶ **Aurignac** *(5 km W from Alan, 12 km NW from Saint-Martory)* gave its name to the prehistoric Aurignacian period; Cro-magnon man lived in these regions some 30 000 years ago; prehistory museum *(daily, Jul.-Aug.; or by appt. with the town hall, tel. 61.19.90.08);* view★ from the ruins of a keep (ca. 1240) on a neighbouring rock. ▶ Gallo-Roman thermal baths discovered in 1957 at **Montoulieu** (Arezac residence) between Aurignac and Alan. ▶ **Rieux-Volvestre** *(31 km NE from Saint-Martory)* in a bend of the Arize, is a former episcopal city which is now a holiday resort; 13th-14thC cathedral (Toulousain bell-tower and remarkable bishop's treasury★); brick houses from the 15th, 16th and 17thC; *fête of the Papagaï* (archery contests) on first Sun. in May.   ▢

Practical Information ―――――――――――――

Nearby

AURIGNAC, ⊠ 31420, 12 km NW.
ⓘ ☎ 61.98.90.08.

Hotel :
★★ *Le Cerf Blanc*, rue St-Michel, ☎ 61.98.95.76, AE DC Visa, 11 rm ℙ ⧳ ▦ ♪ closed Mon, 185. Rest. ● ◆ ⧳ ♪ The Picards take good care of you in their lovely home. Seasonal cuisine, 65-250.

BOUSSENS, ⊠ 31360 Saint-Martory, 5 km SW.

Hotel :
★★ *Lac*, ☎ 61.90.01.85, AE Visa, 12 rm ℙ ⧳ ▦ ⌕ closed Jan-Feb, 150. Rest. ◆◆ ♪ closed Sun eve (l.s.). Little family-run eatery, 50-160.

MARTRES-TOLOSANE, ⊠ 31220 Cazères-sur-Garonne, 14 km NE.

Hotel :
★★ *Castet*, rue de la Gare, ☎ 61.90.80.20, Euro Visa, 15 rm ▦ ☒ closed Oct, 130. Rest. ◆ closed Mon. Spec : *foie frais aux pommes et queues d'écrevisses,* 50-150.

▲ ★★★*Le Moulin* (50 pl), ☎ 61.90.86.41.

SALIES-DU-SALAT, ⊠ 31260, 6 km S.
ⓘ bd J.-Jaurès et mairie, ☎ 61.90.53.93 (h.s.).

Hotel :
● ★★ *Grand Hôtel* (L.F.), 3, av. de la Gare,

☎ 61.90.56.43, 26 rm Ⓟ ♨ ⌕ ⌘ closed 16 Sep-1 Jun, 110. Rest. ♦ ♪ ⌘ 50-95; child : 30.

TOULOUSE***

Auch 78, Foix 83, Paris 709 km
pop 354290 ⊠ 31000   C2

Toulouse has developed in concentric circles around its site on a wide bend in the Garonne. The Roman *castrum* and the city of the Visigoths gave way to the towns of the Middle Ages and the Renaissance, later enclosed by a circle of boulevards; around these grew new rings, outlined by the Canal du Midi and the motorways. More recently still, new towns such as Le Mirail and Colomiers have sprung up on the out-skirts. During the periods of the city's greatest histori-cal importance (12th, 13th, 16th and 18thC), Toulouse was enriched by the construction of many remarkable buildings. After a quiescent period in the 19thC, Tou-louse has achieved a place in the front rank of French cities during the second half of the 20thC. The intel-lectual impetus of the university (founded in 1229) has burgeoned not only in scientific research but in its industrial application (aerospace, electronics, data processing, chemistry, biology, agronomy, etc.), while the artistic traditions of the town have been reborn in the creation of a number of art and music festivals; Toulouse now shares with Bordeaux the blossoming of the Great Southwest. It is lively and animated in the evenings.

▶ The **Place du Capitole★** (D2; cafés, restaurants and famous bookshops) is the living heart of the town. One side of the Place is bordered by the **Capitole★★** (1750-53) which was the assembly hall of the municipal magistrates *(Capitouls)* and today houses the city's administrative of-fices, together with one of France's most renowned thea-tres *(to visit the historic parts of the building ex Tue., Sat., Sun. and nat. hols. tel. 61.22.29.22, ext 3412)*. Behind the Capitole building is the **keep** (D2), which formed part of the Capitole itself in the 16thC. It now houses the Tourist Office; pleasant gardens. ▶ The church of **Notre-Dame-du-Taur** (D2) was built in the 14thC in Southern Gothic style; its fortified façade has a wall-belfry which inspired many churches throughout the Midi. ▶ The **basilica of St. Sernin★★** (an important stop on the road to Santiago de Compostela; D1-2; 11th-12thC) is dedicated to the saint who evangelized Toulouse, becoming its first bishop in the 3rdC. It is the church of a former Benedictine abbey and is 115 m long: during the Romanesque period only Cluny (in Burgundy) was larger. See the chevet★ with its radiating chapels, the 12th-13thC spire★ which was the model for so many "Toulousain" bell towers, and the Romanesque Miégeville gate★ facing the Rue du Taur. Inside, note the 11thC altar, the stalls (1670) and the tomb of St. Sernin, in an 18thC sculptural setting. ▶ On the square the **Saint-Raymond Museum**, in a former 16thC college, specializes in archaeology from prehistory to the Carolingian period *(10-12 & 2-6, closed Tue., Sun. am and nat. hols.)*. ▶ The **Jacobins convent★★** *(Couvent des Jacobins; C3; daily ex Sun. am;* music festival in summer) was founded by St. Dominique to counteract the Cathar heresy. It has been recently restored. Note the double nave (13th-14thC) and the palm leaf-ribbed vaulting; see the cloister, the chapter, and the chapel of St. Antonin (decorated with 14thC frescos). The bell tower (no spire) of 1294 is considered one of the most perfect examples of Toulousain Gothic. Reliquary containing the remains of Saint Thomas Aquinas, brought back from Italy in the 14thC. ▶ The church of **Notre-Dame-de-la-Daurade** (C3), rebuilt in the 18thC, takes its name from the gilded mosaics which decorated the original 5thC sanctuary; many column capitals from the Romanesque building are exhibited in the Augustins museum. ▶ **Notre-Dame-de-la-Dalbade** (D4) is a fine specimen of Southern Gothic (16thC; the enamelled terra-cotta tympanum on the

façade dates from 1878). The church takes its name from the lime rendering which was used for the walls of the first church on this site. ▶ The **old quarter★★** to the S of the Capitole has hardly changed since wealthy merchants in the dye and grain trades built magnificent brick houses here between the 16th and 18thC; **Hôtel de Berrins** (16thC) Rue Gambetta; **Hôtel d'Assézat★** (D3; 1555; Museum of Medecine; *open Tue., 10-12 & 2-6)*, Rue de Metz; **Hôtel de Clary** and **Hôtel des Chevaliers de Malte, Hôtel de Pierre** two fine mansions standing in the Rue de la Dalbade (D4); **Maison Calas**, 50 Rue des Filatiers (D4; *visit on request, tel. 61.53.14.00, for public open-days enq. TO);* in the **Hôtel du May** (16th-17thC), 7 Rue du May : **Museum of Old Toulouse★** (D3; *Musée du Vieux-Toulouse; Thu. pm Mar.-May and Oct.-Nov.; 3-6 ex Sun. Jun.-Sep.).* Don't miss the antique dealers' quarter around la Daurade, or the regional craftshop, 42 Rue Pharaon (D4). The Rue de Metz and the Place d'Esquirol (D3) run through the heart of the old town from the river; the Rues des Filatiers, des Changes and St-Rome run into the Place du Capitole, and are pedestrian precincts. ▶ The **Rue d'Alsace-Lorraine** (D2-3) was constructed in the last century between the Capitole and the **Place du Prési-dent-Wilson** (D-E2) with its surrounding cafés. ▶ Further to the SE, the **Place Occitane** (E3) is the centre of a newly renovated area (hotels, restaurants, boutiques, lively in summer). ▶ The **Augustins Museum★★** (D3; 21 Rue de Metz, *daily 10-12 & 2-6 ex Sun. am and Tue.; Wed. pm till 10)*, in the former convent of that order, displays rich collections of sculpture from palaeochristian times to the present day (Romanesque capitals★), 16th to 19thC paint-ings and a recent organ (concerts in the church). ▶ The cathedral of **St. Étienne★** (E3) was built in two parts on different axes between the 12th and 15thC. There are a number of antique shops in the vicinity, and also the oldest house in Toulouse (13thC, 15 Rue Croix-Baragnon, D-E3). ▶ **Paul Dupuy museum**, 13 Rue de la Pleau (D4) : collection of applied art from the Middle Ages to the pres-ent *(tel. : 61.22.21.83).* Beautiful view from the New Gal-leries terrace.

Nearby

▶ **Bordettes zoological park**, 14 km SW from Plaisance-du-Touch. ▶ **Pibrac** *(17 km W) :* medieval church with wall belfry and 1967 basilica (pilgrimage in honor of Germaine Cousin, who lived here in the 17thC); 1540 Renaissance château. ▶ Approx 15 km beyond is the **Bouconne forest** (20 km²). ▶ **Grenade** *(27 km NW),* bastide from 1290; 14thC basilica with Toulousain bell tower and covered markets (16thC). ▶ **Villemur-sur-Tarn** *(33 km N) :* royal granaries★ (16thC) in the middle of an irrigation pilot scheme covering 30 km²; sailing, walks along the banks of the Tarn; vineyards.   ▢

Practical Information

TOULOUSE
🏛 donjon du Capitole (D2), ☎ 61.23.32.00.
✈ *Toulouse-Blagnac,* 7 km W, ☎ 61.71.11.14. Air France office, Blagnac airport, ☎ 61.71.40.00; 2, bd de Stras-bourg (D1-2), ☎ 61.62.84.04.
SNCF (F1), ☎ 61.63.11.88/61.62.85.44.
🚌 68, rue P.-Sémard (E1), ☎ 61.48.71.84.
Car rental : *Avis,* airport, ☎ 61.30.04.94; train station (F1); 45, rue Bayard (E1), ☎ 61.62.50.40.

Hotels :
● **★★★ *Grand Hôtel de l'Opéra*,** 1, pl. du Capitole (D2), ☎ 61.21.82.66, Tx 521998, AE DC Euro Visa, 49 rm ♨ ⌕ ♪ 🖾 520. Rest. ● ♦♦♦ *Les Jardins de l'Opéra* ⟨ ♪ closed Sun, 14-21 Aug. Dominique Toulousy's talent and creativity are raising him to the first rank of chefs. Smiling Maryse oversees the well-stocked cellar. *Salade de lar-dons de peau de canard, raviolis de foie gras, salade de coques au citron et coriandre, canette aux deux cuis-sons, 150-270.*

★★★ *Airport,* 176, rte de Bayonne, Saint-Martin-du-Touch, 6 km W (off map A4), ☎ 61.49.68.78, 48 rm Ⓟ ⌕ 240.

★★★ *Diane*, 3, rte de Saint-Simon, Le Mirail (off map A5),

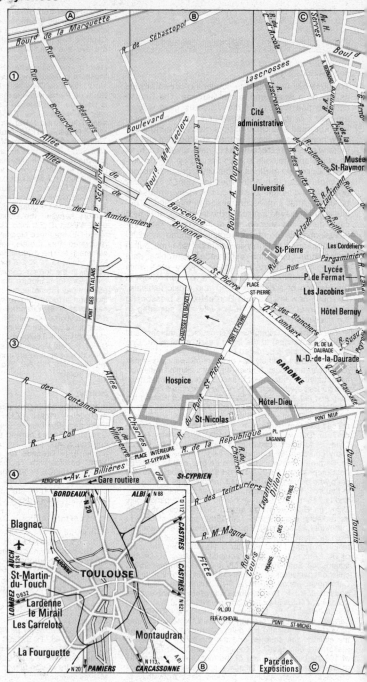

☎ 61.07.59.52, Tx 530518, AE DC Euro Visa, 35 rm ℗ ≼
▨ ♨ ▤ ⋌ 300. Rest. ♦♦♦ *Le Saint-Simon* ≼ ≀ ⌘
closed Sat noon and Sun. Spec : *feuilleté de foie frais
aux huîtres, ravioles de Saint-Jacques et saumon, assiette*

de magret fumé et de foie de canard, 120-180.
★★★ *La Caravelle*, (Mapotel), 62, rue Raymond-IV (E1),
☎ 61.62.70.65, Tx 530438, AE DC Euro Visa, 32 rm ℗
♨ 320.

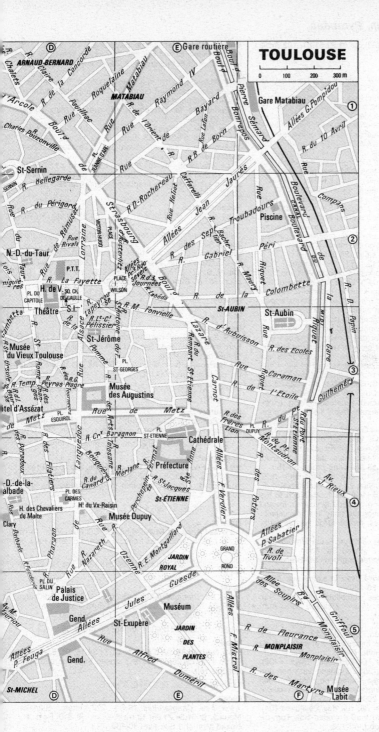

TOULOUSE

0   100   200   300 m

★★★ **Progrès** (Inter-Hôtel), 10, rue Rivals (D2), ☎ 61.23.21.28, Visa, 33 rm ⓟ ◿ 230.

★★ **Arnaud Bernard**, 33, pl. des Tiercerettes (D1), ☎ 61.21.37.64, Tx 530955, Visa, 21 rm ◿ 185.

★★ **Bordeaux**, 4, bd Bonrepos (F1), ☎ 61.62.41.09, DC Euro Visa, 22 rm ⓟ ≶ 140. Rest. ◆ closed Jun-Oct. Grill, 55-80.

★★ **Capoul**, 13, pl. Wilson (E2), ☎ 61.21.51.87, 105 rm Ⓟ 200. Rest. ♦ 55-165.

Restaurants :

● ♦♦♦♦ **Vanel**, 22, rue Maurice-Fonvielle (E3), ☎ 61.21.51.82, AE Euro Visa, closed Mon noon and Sun, 1 Aug-1 Sep. Lucien Vanel has loads of character, all of it good : no background music here! he affirms. Unless of course one of the diners decides to lift his voice in song! Character marks his fine, generous cuisine, always inventive, with its roots in the Quercy region : *omelettes aux cèpes, aux truffes, confit d'oie à l'oseille et d'autres traditionnels, brandade de morue, compote de lapin, civet de pied de cochon aux oignons tendres et huîtres.* An abundance of desserts, coffees, teas, herb teas, fruit brandies, Cognacs, Armagnacs. No fewer than 17 wines under 80F, and always a surprising bottle of the month, 200-300.

● ♦♦♦ **Belle Epoque**, 3, rue Pargaminières (C2), ☎ 61.23.22.12, AE DC Visa ♪ closed Sat noon and Sun and hols, 24 Dec-2 Jan. Ever the creative chef, P. Roudgé will astonish and delight you : *sole de ligne en goujonnette, ravioles de truffes au céleri, magret de canard.* Calorie counts are recorded on the menu. It's up to you to decide to splurge or play it safe! 125-250.

● ♦♦♦ **Chez Emile**, 13, pl. St-Georges (E3), ☎ 61.21.05.56, AE DC Euro Visa ♪ closed Mon and Sun, 2 wks in Aug, 23 Dec-6 Jan. F. Ferrier is a master of fish cookery with over 200 recipes in his repertoire : *salade tiède de la mer, blanquette marine aux pointes d'asperges.* For tradition's sake, an excellent *cassoulet,* 85-180.

● ♦♦♦ **Darroze**, 19, rue Castellane (E2), ☎ 61.62.34.70, AE DC Visa ೬ ⅋ closed Sat noon and Sun, 21 Feb-1 Mar, 18 Jul-9 Aug. The entire Darroze family contributes with great success to the greater glory of regional Landes cuisine : *délice de salade au foie gras, foie gras frais aux raisins,* game (in season). Extensive list of Bordeaux vintages, handsome collection of Armagnacs, 125-230.

● ♦♦♦ **Ubu Club**, 16, rue St-Rome (D3), ☎ 61.23.26.75, AE DC Visa ♪ closed Sun. Open till 2 am, this is the 'in' place for the fashionable crowd. Subdued lighting, excellent food : grilled or poached fresh fish, *foie gras, magrets,* 180-220.

● ♦♦ **Aquarius**, 10, bd de la Gare (F2-3), ☎ 61.34.84.10, Visa ⅏ ♪ ⌧ closed Sun eve. With Patrick Lannes' light, low-calorie cooking, no one need worry about regaining the weight lost at Michel Narbonne's chic fitness club. The prettiest girls in Toulouse are living proof, 55-150.

● ♦♦ **Bouchon Lyonnais**, 13, rue de l'Industrie (E2), ☎ 61.62.97.43, AE DC Euro Visa ♪ In his likable bistro, L. Orsi upholds the tradition of Lyonnais food, much to the delight of the local population : *salade lyonnaise, magret de canard grillé,* not to mention the tasty fish specialties : *mérou au coulis d'écrevisses, turbot citron vert et estragon,* 90-170.

● ♦♦ **La Marmite en Folie**, 28, rue Paul-Painlevé (B5), ☎ 61.42.77.86, Visa ⅋ ⅏ ♪ closed Sat noon and Sun. Much to the satisfaction of his patrons, M. Brandolin's cooking gets more expert all the time : *flan d'épinard aux langoustines, mérou grillé avec la sauce aux pistils de safran, filet de caneton,* 85-180.

♦♦ **Belvédère**, 11, bd des Récollets (off map D5), ☎ 61.52.63.73, AE DC Euro Visa ⅋ ♪ closed Sun , Aug. Good regional fare, 100-190.

♦♦ **Le Cassoulet**, 40, rue Peyrolières (C3), ☎ 61.21.18.99, closed Mon, 2-10 Jul, 24 Dec-4 Jan. Spec : *mousse de maïs aux moules, le vrai cassoulet au confit d'oie, les pruneaux bidia,* 70-90.

♦♦ **Le Sarran**, 9, rue G.-Péri (off map E-D2), ☎ 61.62.70.44, AE Euro Visa ♪ closed Sat noon and Sun, 1-20 Aug, 25 Dec. Spec : *salade de pâtes fraîches aux crustacés, matelote d'anguilles aux poireaux, cassoulet aux haricots tarbais,* 80-200.

♦♦ **Rôtisserie des Carmes**, 38, rue des Polinaires (D4), ☎ 61.52.73.82, AE DC Euro Visa ♪ closed Sat. Turn-of-the-century setting. Good food, 60-120.

● ♦ **Chrisflor**, 26, av. de Saint-Exupéry (E5), ☎ 61.53.12.86, Visa ♪ closed Mon eve, Sat noon, Sun, 1-26 Aug. Delicious food with a feminine touch by P. Pezet : *soupe de langoustines au foie gras, turbotin aux courgettes braisées,* 100-130.

● ♦ **Le Colombier**, 4, rue Bayard (E1), ☎ 61.62.40.05, AE Euro Visa, closed Sat and Sun , 1 wk Xmas and Easter, 1-21 Aug. For lovers of G. Zasso's authentic *cassoulet,* 90.

● ♦ **Maréchale**, 18, rue Mage (D3), ☎ 61.52.21.16 ♪ closed Mon noon, Sat noon, Sun. An astonishing, oft-renewed fixed-price offering, 85-120.

♦ **Bistrot de la Maréchale**, 47, rue de Metz (D-E3), ☎ 61.21.78.69, 50-100.

♦ **La Belle Chaurienne**, Canal de Brienne, pl. Héraclès (A2), ☎ 61.21.23.85, Euro Visa ♪ closed Sat noon, 15 Aug-1 Sep. Once a riverboat, now a restaurant. Spec : *cassoulet,* 120-150.

♦ **La Braisière**, 42, rue Pharaon (D4), ☎ 61.52.37.13, Visa, closed Sat noon and Sun. Warm, plush atmosphere around a country-style fireplace : *moules farcies, côte de bœuf,* 80-140.

Recommended
Baby-sitting : *CROUS,* ☎ 61.21.29.66; *CRIJ,* ☎ 61.21.20.20.
Guided tours : Guided tours of the city and region from Jun to Sep. Info S.I.
Nightclubs : *L'Ubu,* 16, rue St-Rome, ☎ 61.23.26.75.
♥ *Crafts,* 42, rue Pharaon, ☎ 61.52.49.96; cheese : *Xavier,* 6, pl. V.-Hugo, ☎ 61.21.53.26; *Le Coup de Torchon,* 22, pl. Dupuy, ☎ 61.63.76.40.

Nearby

BLAGNAC, ✉ 31700, 6 km NW.

Restaurants :
♦♦♦ **Pujol**, 21, av. du Gal-Compans, ☎ 61.71.13.58, DC Euro Visa ⅏ ♪ closed Sat and Sun eve. For connaisseurs of *foie gras,* 200-230.
♦♦ **Horizon**, airport, ☎ 61.30.02.75, AE DC Visa ⅋ ♪ Earthy regional fare, 100-130.

LABARTHE-SUR-LÈZE, ✉ 31120 Portet-sur-Garonne, 15 km W.

Restaurant :
♦ **Le Poêlon**, ☎ 61.08.68.49, Visa ⅏ ♪ ⅋ closed Mon and Sun eve. Market-fresh produce in season, 100-170.

LACOURTENSOURT, ✉ 31140 Aucamville, 8 km N.

Restaurant :
♦♦ **La Feuilleraie**, 5, rte de Paris, ☎ 61.70.16.01, Tx 530879, AE DC Euro Visa ⅏ ♪ ⌧ Spec : *fricassée de poularde aux cèpes, ballotine de pintade au foie gras,* 70-150.

MONTRABE, ✉ 31130, 6 km E.

Hotel :
★★★ **Val Rose**, ☎ 61.84.76.58, AE DC Euro Visa, 14 rm Ⓟ ⅏ ೬ ⌧ Century-old trees; a nightclub, 270. Rest. ♦ 70-150.

RAMONVILLE-SAINT-AGNE, ✉ 31520, 7 km SE on the N 113.

Hotel :
★★★ **La Chaumière**, (Inter-Hôtel), 102, av. Tolosane, ☎ 61.73.02.02, Tx 520646, AE DC Euro Visa, 43 rm Ⓟ ⅏ ۩ ♪ ೬ 260. Rest. ♦ ♪ 65-200; child : 50.

SAINT-JEAN, ✉ 31240, 4 km NE on the N 88.

Hotel :
★★★ **Horizon 88**, rte d'Albi, ☎ 61.74.34.15, DC Euro Visa, 38 rm Ⓟ ⅏ ⌧ 250. Rest. ♦ ♪ closed Sat noon and Sun , Feb, 60-160.

TOURNEFEUILLE, ✉ 31170, 9 km E.

Hotel :
★★★ **Les Chanterelles** (R.S.), 277, chem. Ramelet-Moundi, ☎ 61.86.21.86, 10 rm Ⓟ ⅏ ۩ ⅋ 310. Rest. ♦ ♪ closed Mon and Sun eve, 90-130.

VIGOULET-D'AUZIL, ✉ 31320, 12 km SW.

Restaurant :
● ♦♦♦ **Tournebride**, ☎ 61.73.34.49, AE DC Visa ⅋ ⅏ ♪ closed Mon and Sun eve , Jan, 10-25 Aug. The stunning

view of the Pyrénées is just one more reason to enjoy the warm, family-style, welcome and delicious food provided by the Nonys. A happy blend of classic and seasonal cuisine : *émincés de veau, steak au pot, perdreau en croûte.* Fine wines, Armagnacs, 160-220.

VILLEMUR-SUR-TARN, ⊠ 31340, 24 km N.

Hotel :
● ★★ *Villa des Pins*, Vacquiers, ☎ 61.84.96.04, AE DC, 15 rm Ⓟ ⊰ ⋘ ⟁ ⅍ closed Sun eve and Mon, 150. Rest. ♦ ⊰ ♪ 55-100.

Restaurant :
● ♦ *Auberge de la Braise*, Villematier, ☎ 61.35.35.64, AE DC Euro Visa ⋘ ♪ ⅙ closed Mon, Tue, Sun eve, 15-31 Jan, 15 Jul-14 Aug. At their renovated farmhouse, the Bertins treat the patrons to *foie gras frais au verjus truffé, homard au langouste sauce de la braise, petits cailloux de Villematier*, 95-250.

> If you enjoy sports, consult the pages pertaining to the regions; there you will find addresses for practicing your favorite sport.

VIC-FEZENSAC

Auch 30, Agen 68, Paris 768 km
pop 3990 ⊠ 32190   A1

A small vacation centre in the Osse Valley, famed for its bullfights ; festivals in May.

▶ The **church,** altered in the 15thC, has a Romanesque apse ; nearby, wedged between the houses, a 14thC fortified building ; handsome *Assumption* in the **hospital chapel;** 2 km N at **Marambat :** ruined chateau and remains of rampart.   □

Practical Information _____

Hotel :
● ★ *Le d'Artagnan* (L.F.), 3, cours Delom, ☎ 62.06.31.37, 10 rm Ⓟ ♪ 85. Rest. ♦ ♪ ⅙ Gascon cuisine, 45-150 ; child : 25.

⚠ ★★*Municipal* (33 pl), ☎ 62.06.30.08.

Recommended
Events : *feria and corrida* (bull run), Pentecost.

Normandy

Normandy is no longer the home of the Norsemen, those blond, blue-eyed Vikings who roamed the world in wooden-prowed boats, although their descendants continue to wrest a living from the sea. The sea plays an important role in this region, with its 600 km of coastline, beaches and cliffs framing the vast estuary of the Seine.

Normandy, shaped by history and geography into a single cultural entity, is an intensely agricultural region, with medium-sized farms scattered throughout a landscape of alternating forest and meadow land, with fruitful orchards and excellent dairy produce. It is also the historic land of the great abbeys and châteaux, the manor-houses described by novelists such as Flaubert and Maupassant, the seascapes of Boudin and Monet's vision of the Rouen cathedral metamorphosed by light. This is a Normandy to discover and explore, with its inviting seaside or country beauty spots sitting calmly side by side with the economic bustle and dynamism of its two capitals — Rouen and Caen — and the industrial and port complex of Le Havre-Rouen.

Peasant women in lace headdresses on their way to the village market, and the once-common Percheron horses, are now very rarely glimpsed. But, although the personality of Normandy may be more muted than that of Brittany or Alsace, you can sense behind the tranquil façade of everyday life what it means to belong in Normandy, what it means to belong to a single community on a single land, a unity enriched and softened by the age-old generosity of its inhabitants. Fishing villages, traces of the Viking past in the Cotentin peninsula, the quaint half-timbered houses of the Auge region, the American Film Festival and summer casino in fashionable Deauville — all make up the rich mosaic of Normandy, while to the extreme west, Mont-Saint-Michel rises up out of the flat salty marshlands of the bay, bearing the heavy crown of its medieval abbey and its streets thronged since the 11th century with pilgrims, merchants and sightseers. □

Don't miss

★★★ Auge Region C2, Caen B2, D-Day Landing Beaches A-B2, Honfleur C2, Mont-Saint-Michel A3, Rouen D2, lower Seine Valley C-D2.

★★ Alençon C3-4, Bayeux B2, the Cotentin Coast A1-2, Étretat C1, the Suisse Normande B2-3.

★ Les Andelys D2, Argentan C3, Bagnoles-de-l'Orne B3, Barfleur A1, Bernay C2, Cherbourg A1, Coutances A2, Deauville C2, Dieppe D1, Évreux D2, Falaise B3, Fécamp C1, Gisors D2, Granville A3, Le Havre C2, Lisieux C2, Neubourg Plateau D2, Orbec C2-3, Ouche Region D2, Perche Region C3-4, Pont-Audemer C2, Les Quatre Vallées D2, Tancarville C2, Valognes A1-2, Vernon D2.

Weekend tips

Two days in Normandy : Les Andelys, Rouen, Honfleur, Deauville, Caen (stopover), the D-Day Landing Beaches, Mont-Saint-Michel and Alençon. It can be done, but it's better not to be too ambitious. Start with a quick visit to Rouen and the valley of the Seine; stop-over in Le Havre. Next day : Étretat, Fécamp, Rouen. Alternatively, still starting from Rouen : Marais Vernier, Honfleur, Deauville (stop-over), the Auge region, Caen. Starting from Alençon : the Argentan region, the Suisse Normande (stop-over), Caen ; alternatively Perche, the Ouche region (stop-over), Neubourg, Évreux, Vernon, the valley of the Seine, Rouen.

● *Brief regional history*

Up to the Roman era

Little is known about the pre-Stone Age inhabitants of the Normandy region. ● During the **Bronze Age,** trade relations were established with the British Isles (tin from Cornwall, gold from Ireland). ● In the **Iron Age,** the Celtic Gauls enter history; the Unelli tribe

was defeated by one of Caesar's lieutenants in 56BC. The "Pax Romana", established at the beginning of the Christian era, led to the emergence of prosperous Gallo-Roman cities, among them *Juliobona* — present-day Lillebonne. Large agricultural estates were developed at this period.

3rd-10thC

In the 3rd century a separate northwestern Roman province was created which included present-day

Normandy. Its capital was at *Rotomagus* (Rouen). As early as 260, Rouen was the seat of the first Norman bishopric. ● During the centuries that followed, the Franks got the upper hand of other invaders. ● With the foundation of the **first Norman abbeys,** the land began to be cleared for agriculture. The succeeding Merovingian and Carolingian dynasties continued this policy, and the abbeys became important cultural centres. ● **From 820 on, Vikings from Denmark** and Norway began their raids.

911-1204
By the 10thC, the new invaders were strong enough to force the Frankish King Charles to acknowledge the Viking Rollo's overlordship of Normandy; he received the title of Duke, and agreed to be baptized (**Treaty of Saint-Clair-sur-Epte,** 911). In 1066, Duke William successfully asserted his claim to the English throne. ● In Normandy itself Benedictine and Cistercian monks reformed the Norman abbeys and perfected Norman Romanesque architecture during the 11th

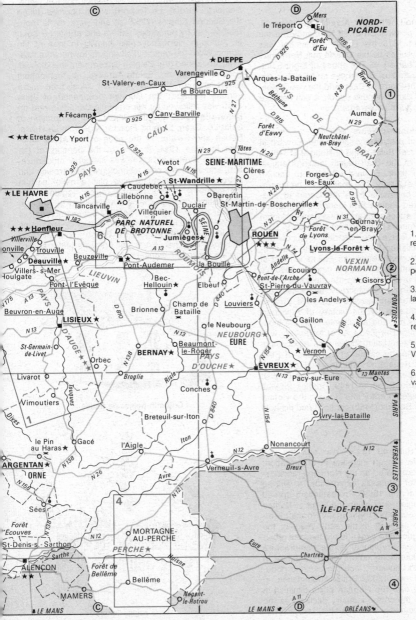

1. The Auge region

2. The Cotentin peninsula

3. The D-Day landing beaches

4. The Perche region

5. Les Quatre Vallées

6. Lower Seine valley

and 12thC. The Abbaye aux Hommes in Caen, founded by William, is the prototype of this style. Henry II, Duke of Normandy and son of Geoffroy V of Anjou, succeeded to the throne in 1154, and married Eleanor of Aquitaine after Louis VII of France repudiated her. The English Crown thus acquired its vast land holdings which stretched from the borders of Brittany to the Pyrénées. These possessions were later bitterly disputed, both legally and by force, during the period of the Hundred Years' War (14th-15thC).

1204-1346

During this period, Philippe Auguste (Philippe II, 1180-1223) won possession of all Normandy but the Channel Isles. In 1315 the Rouen Parliament was given special privileges by the **Charte aux Normands** (The Normans' Charter). ● The abbey of Mont-Saint-Michel, the cathedrals of Coutances and Bayeux, the bell tower of Saint-Pierre at Caen and the new cathedral at Rouen all date from this epoch, a rich heritage of Gothic architectural achievement.

1346-1450 The Hundred Years' War

After a number of preliminary skirmishes, Edward III landed his troops at Saint-Vaast-la-Hougue (1346), a few miles north of the Utah beach landings almost exactly 600 year later. Edward went on to win an important victory at Crécy. Ten years later, he inherited the Cotentin peninsula from the Count of Harcourt, and captured Jean le Bon (John the Good, one of France's least-successful and least-popular kings) at the battle of Poitiers, holding him prisoner in London. ● In 1364, Jean's son, Charles V, succeeded him, and re-established French influence in the strategic but unruly Norman region, as well as in most of the centre and Southwest. After his death in 1380 his successors were unable to keep the dukedom out of the hands of the English aristocracy, themselves descendants of the Norman invaders of England. **English rule was consolidated** by the victory of Agincourt under Henry V (1415), and an alliance with the independant dukedom of Burgundy. All of Normandy with the exception of Mont-Saint-Michel was reoccupied, and Rouen became the capital of the Duke of Bedford, the English Regent. ● With the resurgence of French national spirit under Joan of Arc, the English were forced to retreat and, in 1449, Charles VII was able to make a solemn entry into Rouen; **the victory of Formigny** near Bayeux (1450) consolidated his hold on Normandy.

1469-18thC

The end of the Hundred Years' War saw the rise of the bourgeoisie and an increase in urbanization. ● Norman ports prospered as the Normans rediscovered their taste for overseas exploration. ● During the second half of the 16thC Protestantism spread throughout the region, and when the Edict of Nantes was revoked by Louis XIV (1685), many Norman Protestants went into exile. ● In the early years of the 18thC, Norman agriculture expanded to feed the growing Paris population; traditional **textile manufacture** gave way to a flourishing cotton goods industry in Rouen, Elbeuf and Louviers; **lace** too became popular (Argentan). From 1763, British domination in Canada and India saw the Norman ports diminish in importance, while the cotton industry declined as the British textile production was industrialized. ● Nor-

mandy held aloof from the French Revolution, giving little support to either revolutionaries or royalists.

19thC to the present day

In the early 19thC, the British naval blockade against Napoléon paralyzed the Norman ports, but the **textile industry found profitable domestic markets.** ● In 1843, the Paris-Rouen railway was inaugurated; Paris-Cherbourg followed in 1858; the first steamship line to the United States had begun in Cherbourg in 1847. The railway contributed largely to the development of the **resort towns** on the Normandy coast (Dieppe, Deauville, Étretat, Le Tréport), which boomed during the Second Empire (1852-70) and were made more famous still by numerous writers and artists (→ box). ● Although Normandy paid heavily in loss of life during WWI, the region itself and its towns were relatively unharmed (the Belgian Government-in-exile was accommodated in Sainte-Adresse, a fashionable resort area of Le Havre). WWII caused far more serious damage; the German occupation of June 1940 was followed by the dramatic **Canadian raid on Dieppe in 1942,** and the almost total destruction of Saint-Lô, Caen, Lisieux, Falaise, Argentan, Le Havre, Rouen and Évreux as the price of the **Allied landings in June 1944.** ● One of the benefits of the subsequent reconstruction was industrial modernization, and intensive new technologies (electronics and petrochemical industries) now play a major part in the economy of this historic region, together with new energy sources (Seine-Maritime and La Manche nuclear power stations). The 1984 commemoration of the WWII Allied landings saw the visit of United States President Ronald Reagan, the British Prime Minister, Margaret Thatcher, President François Mitterrand of France and other dignitaries.

Cotentin peninsula house

Auge region house

Fortified house in the Perche region

The abbeys of Normandy

The oldest of the many abbeys in Normandy date back to the 6th and 7thC. Mont-Saint-Michel in fact was founded in 708. A spate of building occurred in the 11th and 12thC; William the Conqueror and his wife Matilda are credited with some 30 foundations. Some abbeys, such as Jumièges and Hambye, are picturesque ruins, whereas others, such as Saint-Evroult, have almost disappeared. Many were remodeled in the 17thC (Bernay, Le Bec-Hellouin, Saint-Wandrille), or completely rebuilt in the 19thC (La Grande Trappe). Some abbey churches are as big as cathedrals (Fécamp, the Abbaye aux Hommes at Caen). The earliest abbeys were models of Norman Romanesque art and architecture, which spread to England during the English occupation of Western France. The style was transformed in the late 12thC by the development of the ogival vault, which gave rise to the Gothic style.

Facts and figures

Location : *Normandy is bordered on the North and West by the English Channel; it extends inland from the edge of the granite massif of Brittany to the limestone region around Paris.*
Area : *29 896 km².*
Climate : *moist, temperate climate; summer and winter temperatures differ relatively little, but more on the coast than inland. Frequent rain provides luxuriant vegetation. The area is never very cold in winter, but the swimming season rarely extends beyond Jun.-Sep.*
Population : *approx 3 008 000; more than one-third in the Department of Seine-Maritime.*
Administration : *includes the two economic regions of Haute (upper) Normandie (Departments of **Eure**, prefecture : Évreux and **Seine-Maritime**, prefecture : Rouen) and Basse (lower) Normandie (Departments of **Calvados**, prefecture : Caen, **Manche**, prefecture : Saint-Lô and **Orne**, prefecture : Alençon).*

● Practical information

Information : *Comité Inter-régional de Tourisme (C.I.T)*, 46, av. Foch, bât. E, 27000 Évreux, ☎ 32.31.03.03. **Calvados :** *Comité Départemental de Tourisme (C.D.T.)*, pl. du Canada, 14000 Caen, ☎ 31.86.53.30. **Eure :** *C.D.T.*, Chambre de Commerce, 35, rue du Dr-Oursel, 27000 Évreux, ☎ 32.38.21.61. **Manche :** *Office Départemental de Tourisme (O.D.T.)*, préfecture, B.P. 419, 50009 Saint-Lô, ☎ 33.57.52.80. **Orne :** *C.D.T.*, 60, rue St-Blaise, B.P. 50, 61002 Alençon Cedex, ☎ 33.26.18.71. **Seine-Maritime :** *C.D.T.*, B.P. 666, 76008 Rouen Cedex, ☎ 35.88.61.32. *Dir. régionale de la Jeunesse et des Sports*, 151-153, rue de La Délivrance, 14000 Caen, ☎ 31.91.62.15, and Immeuble Normandie II, 55, rue Amiral-Cécille, 76045 Rouen Cedex, ☎ 35.73.09.70. *Dir. rég. des Affaires culturelles*, Maison des Quatrans, 25, rue de Goële, B.P. 222, 14051 Caen Cedex, ☎ 31.86.37.10 and Cité administrative, rue Saint-Sever, 76037 Rouen Cedex, ☎ 35.63.40.36.

S.O.S. : Calvados, ☎ 15; **Eure :** *SAMU* (Emergency Medical Service), ☎ 15; **Orne :** *SAMU Alençon*, ☎ 33.26.65.65. **Manche :** *S.A.M.U.*, ☎ 33.06.33.15; **Seine-Maritime,** ☎ 15. Poisoning Emergency Centre : Rennes, ☎ 99.59.22.22; Rouen, ☎ 35.88.44.22.

Weather forecast : Calvados : Deauville-Saint-Gatien, ☎ 31.88.84.22; **Eure,** ☎ 32.39.20.96; **Manche,** ☎ 33.44.45.00; **Orne,** ☎ 33.29.37.97. **Seine-Maritime,** ☎ 35.21.04.19; Marine and coastal forecast, ☎ 35.21.16.11; **Manche-Haute-Normandie,** ☎ 35.80.22.48.

Gîtes ruraux and chambres d'hotes : gîtes d'étapes for hikers, gîtes d'enfants : enq. at the *Relais Départementaux des Gîtes Ruraux :* **Calvados,** 4, promenade de Mme-de-Sévigné, 14039 Caen Cedex, ☎ 31.84.47.19. **Eure,** 5, rue de la Petite-Cité, 27000 Évreux, ☎ 32.39.53.38. **Manche,** préfecture, 50009 Saint-Lô, ☎ 33.57.52.80; gîte villages at Bellefontaine, Moidrey, Saint-Jean-de-la-Rivière, Saint-Laurent-de-Terregatte and Ver. **Orne,** 60, rue St-Blaise, B.P. 50, 61002 Alençon Cedex, ☎ 33.26.18.71. **Seine-Maritime,** Chambre d'Agriculture, chemin de la Brétèque, B.P. 59, 76232 Bois-Guillaume, ☎ 35.60.73.34.

Holiday villages : Calvados : Branville, Colleville-sur-Mer, Grandcamp-Maisy, Lion-sur-Mer; **Manche :** Blainville-sur-Mer, Portbail; **Orne :** Vimoutiers; **Seine-Maritime :** Criel-sur-Mer, Forges-les-Eaux, Val-de-Saône, Veules-les-Roses, Yport. Enq. : *C.D.T.*

Camping-car hire : Seine-Maritime : *Picard S.A.*, B.P. 551B, 76370 Neuville-Dieppe, ☎ 36.84.21.01.

Cultural and sporting events : Apr : *24-hr speedboat races* in Rouen. **May :** *Norman festival* in Étretat; *sea days* in Le Havre; *international regattas* in Cherbourg. **May-Jun :** *"l'Eure in flower"; international chamber music festival* in Saint-Pierre; *summer festival* in Seine-Maritime. **Jun :** *balloon day* in Balleroy. **Jul :** *international folklore festival* in Domfront; *bridge festival* in Deauville; *festival* in Bagnoles-de-l'Orne; *music festival* at Mont-Saint-Michel. **Jul-Aug :** *horse racing* in Deauville. **Aug :** *organ recitals* at St-Maclou in Rouen; *sea and painting festival* in Yport; *Mitouries festival* in Dieppe. **Sep :** *American film festival* in Deauville; *mycology days* in Bellême; *horse racing* at Haras-du-Pin.

Exhibitions and trade fairs : Mar : *spring fair* in Caen. **May :** *fair* in Rouen; *gastronomic fair* in Cherbourg; *antiques fair* at the château de Bizy (Eure). **Jun :** *antiques and bric-à-brac fair* in Caen. **Oct :** *antiques fair* in Cherbourg; *apple fair* in Pont-d'Ouilly. **Nov :** *herring fair* in Dieppe; *cider festival* in Beuvron-en-Auge. **Dec :** *Saint-Nicholas fair* in Évreux.

Pilgrimages : Whitsun : *procession of the Brotherhoods of Charity* in Bernay; *sailors' pilgrimage* to Notre-Dame-de-Grâce in Honfleur; *charitons festival* in Préaux. **May :** *Joan of Arc festival* in Rouen. **Jun :** *Trinity festival, pilgrimage* to Mont-Saint-Michel. **Sep :** *Saint Thérèse festival* in Lisieux.

Norman gastronomy

Normandy is in the fortunate position of having ample agricultural resources as well as access to the sea. Normandy butter is widely appreciated, as is crème fraîche (clotted cream). Thirty-two different varieties of cheese are produced on Norman farms. The local beef is particularly tender, and the salt meadows (prés-salés) are ideal for raising succulent lamb. In the kitchen, preparations Norman-style (à la Normande) imply the use of cream either alone or blended with cider or calvados (apple brandy from the Calvados region). Andouilles de Vire (chitterling sausage), tripes à la mode de Caen (tripe braised in cider), poulet Vallée d'Auge (chicken cooked with onions, cider or calvados, and cream), canard à la Rouennaise (duck in its own juices) and Mont-Saint-Michel's omelette de la Mère Poulard (soufflé omelette) are other specialities. Numerous varieties of fish (especially sole), are caught along the coast, and small grey shrimp at Honfleur.

Nature parks : Parc naturel régional de Brotonne : Maison du Parc, 2, Rond-Point Marbec, 76580 Le Trait, ☎ 35.37.23.16. Parc naturel régional Normandie-Maine : Maison du Parc, Ferme du Chapître, B.P. 05, 61320 Carrouges, ☎ 33.27.21.15.

Rambling and hiking : the region is traversed by the G.R. 2, 21, 22 bis, 23, 25, 211, 221, 223 and 225. Topoguides are available for the G.R.21/211/212, 22, 22/22b, 221/221 A and B, 22, 223 and 26. Comité Départemental de la Randonnée Pédestre de Seine-Maritime, B.P. 666, 76008 Rouen Cedex.

Riding holidays : Association Régionale de Tourisme Équestre (A.R.T.E.) de Haute-Normandie, M. Stlez, rue P.-et-M.-Curie, 76480 Duclair, ☎ 35.37.52.64. A.R.T.E. de Basse-Normandie, 6, prom. de Mme-de-Sévigné, 14039 Caen Cedex, ☎ 31.84.47.19. Various excursions organized by Centre équestre de la Caboche, 50650 Hambye, ☎ 33.61.42.62; C.D.T. Équestre de l'Eure, 27190 Conches, ☎ 32.30.22.56.

Holidays in horse-drawn caravans : departure from Tessé-la-Madeleine near Bagnoles-de-l'Orne; enq. : Jean Dinard, B.P. 6, Tessé-la-Madeleine, 61140 Bagnoles-de-l'Orne, ☎ 33.37.00.56. Les Roulottes du Valdoré, rte de

The horses of Normandy

Organized horse-breeding in Normandy dates back to the 14thC, when Philippe VI de Valois founded a stud near Domfront. In 1665, Jean-Baptiste Colbert (Louis XIV's Prime Minister) centralized the management of the national studs in Normandy and encouraged the development of sires. Later, trotters were bred to accommodate the demands of racing enthusiasts. Draught-horses, notably the powerful Percheron, have almost disappeared since the advent of mechanization on roads and farms. The Japanese, however, are interested in developing a Percheron cross to improve trotting breeds. The national studs (haras) at Saint-Lô and Le Pin maintain some 200 and 80 stallions, respectively. Horse-breeding is particularly widespread in Orne and Calvados. The racing year in Normandy is crowned by the Grand Prix de Deauville. Race-meetings are held frequently at Caen, Lisieux, Rouen, Argentan, Saint-Lô, and Graignes, among other centres.

Manerbe, 14340 Cambremer, ☎ 31.31.14.97. M. de Cressac, manoir d'Auvillars, Hotot-en-Auge, ☎ 31.79.28.86. Excursions in horse-drawn buggies, enq. : M. de Bellaigne de Bughas, Château de Vaumicel, 14115 Vierville-sur-Mer, ☎ 31.22.40.06. Seine-Maritime : M. Dubreuil, Ferme des Loisirs-Mauquenchy, ☎ 35.90.58.22.

Cycling holidays : S.N.C.F. "Train-Vélo" service : 9 stations in Normandy : Bayeux, Caen, Lisieux and Vire (14); Bueil, Vernon (27); Granville, Pontorson, Villedieu-les-Poêles (50); Argentan (61); Dieppe, Le Tréport (76). Bicycle and scooter hire : Free way, 21, rue des Bonnetiers, 76000 Rouen, ☎ 35.70.04.04 (mid-Apr.-mid-Oct.). **Seine-Maritime :** Comité dép. de la fédération française de cyclotourisme, M. Poincelet, 3, cavée Haize, 76310 Sainte Adresse, ☎ 35.46.22.45.

Handicraft courses : Calvados : lace-making with a spindle, polished tapestry work in Bayeux, pottery in Brucourt, wool-spinning in Marolles, weaving at Saint-Laurent-du-Mont, Villy-Bocage, photo at Bougy. **Eure :** weaving and tapestry-making in Saint-Denis-le-Ferment near Gisors; weaving, pottery, torchis at the Maison des métiers in Bourneville near Pont-Audemer, pottery in Muids. **Manche :** the workshops of Val de Saire; courses in manual and technical work at Cherbourg and Saint-Pierre-Église. **Orne :** furniture restoration in Mortrée. **Seine-Maritime :** ornamental gardening in Dieppe, wood sculpture in Rouen, marionettes in Saint-Romain-de-Colbosc. Enq. at the C.D.T.

Other courses : prehistoric excavations in **Calvados, Eure, Manche, Orne** and **Seine-Maritime;** info from Direction des antiquités préhistoriques de Haute-Normandie, cité administrative St-Sever, 76032 Rouen Cedex, ☎ 35.63.40.36; and de Basse-Normandie, 22, rue Jean-Eudes, Caen, ☎ 31.85.51.26.

Golf : Agon-Coutainville (9 holes), Brehal (9), Bagnoles-de-l'Orne (9), Cabourg (18), Cherbourg (9), Deauville (18), Dieppe (18), Étretat (18), Fontenay-sur-Mer (9), Granville (18), Le Havre (18), Houlgate (9), Rouen (18), Le Vadreuil (18). For beginners : Centre d'initiation au golf, château du Champ-de-Bataille, 27110 Le Neubourg, ☎ 32.35.27.66.

Aquatic sports : enq. at the C.D.T. and T.O. Sailboat stays at the Centre Régional de Nautisme de Granville, B.P. 124, 50400 Granville, ☎ 33.50.18.95. Boats for hire for holiday cruises, Lesjesqueux Voile, 3, rue Clément-Desmaisons, 50400 Granville, ☎ 33.50.18.97.

Canoeing : Calvados : Comité Départemental Stade Nautique, av. Albert-Sorel, 14000 Caen, ☎ 31.86.04.12. **Eure :** Direction de la Jeunesse et des Sports, Cité administrative, 27023 Évreux, ☎ 32.39.52.09. **Manche :** Association sportive Elle et Vire at Condé-sur-Vire; Club Nautique of Carentan; Loisir et Tourisme at Hambye; Loisir et Plein Air at Saint-Hilaire-du-Harcouët; Centre régional de nautisme at Granville; Club de Kayak de mer du Nord-Cotentin.

Potholing and spelunking : quarries in Caumont, Thuit caves (Eure). Enq. : Comité de spéléologie, ☎ 32.38.53.58.

Climbing : rock-climbing in the parks in Suisse normande (Clécy), enq. : C.A.F., 13, rue Jacques-Durandas, 14000 Caen, ☎ 31.93.07.23; in the **Eure** region, near Les Andelys and on the Deux-Amants coast, enq. : C.A.F., 190, rue Beauvoisine, 76000 Rouen, ☎ 35.71.21.97.

Flying, gliding and parachuting : gliding at the Caen-Carpiquet aéroclub, ☎ 31.73.12.00; on the Eraine mountains in Falaise, ☎ 31.90.06.54; at the Jean-Mermoz aéroclub in Clécy, ☎ 31.69.07.21. Parachuting in Évreux, Aéro-club de l'Eure, Fauville, ☎ 32.33.13.86; in Dieppe, Parachute-Club, Saint-Aubin-sur-Scie, ☎ 35.84.81.97; in the Cotentin region : Cherbourg, Lessay, Saint-Lô, Granville and Avranches airclubs; in the **Seine-Maritime** region : Boos, Dieppe, Eu, Le Havre, Rouen, Saint-Romain-de-Colbosc, Saint-Valéry-en-Caux, Yvetot airclubs. Deltaplane : Blangy sur Bresle, ☎ 35.93.63.50.

Hunting and shooting : Fédération Départementale des Chasseurs : **Calvados :** rue des Compagnons, la Folie-

Couvrechef, 14000 Caen, ☎ 31.95.41.74. **Eure** : 32, rue Politzer, 27000 Évreux, ☎ 32.33.09.76. **Seine-Maritime** : 216, rte de Neufchâtel, 76420 Bihorel, ☎ 35.60.35.97.

Fishing : *Fédération Départementale des Associations de Pêche et de Pisciculture* : **Calvados** : 120, bd Mal-Leclerc,

14300 Caen. ☎ 31.86.06.97. **Eure** : 34, pl. Louis-Gillain, 27500 Pont-Audemer, ☎ 32.41.04.47. **Manche** : 24, rue de la République, 50120 Equeurdreville-Hainneville, ☎ 33.53.25.63. **Orne** : 8, rue du Collège, 61000 Alençon, ☎ 34.26.10.66. **Seine-Maritime** : *la Belle Gaule de Rouen et de Normandie*, M. Beaulès, rue Louis-Brune, 76000 Rouen.

● *Towns and places*

ALENÇON**

Laval 90, Chartres 115, Paris 191 km
pop 32530 ⊠ 61000   C3-4

Commercial and administrative centre of the rich Sarthe countryside, this lace-making town retains the aristocratic air of a one-time ducal city; now also an important centre for the manufacture of household appliances.

▶ Across from the **Prefecture**★ (B1; 1630) is the Rue St-Blaise ending in a pedestrian precinct by the **church of Notre-Dame**★ (B2; 16thC porch★). The neighbouring 15thC Maison d'Ozé houses the SI. Rue du Pont-Neuf (B2) : lace-making school (École Dentellière, *visits*). ▶ Church of St. Léonard (B2), Flamboyant Gothic, the centre of **old Alençon.** ▶ Place Foch (A-B2) : the 1783 Hôtel de Ville (town hall) stands near the 14th-15thC Château des Ducs. The **Musée des Beaux-Arts et de la Dentelle**★ (Fine-Arts and Lace-making Museum, A1; *closed Mon.*) is installed in the former Jesuits' college (1620).

Nearby

▶ **Saint-Céneri-le-Gérei**★ *(14 km SW)*, on the edge of the "Alpes Mancelles" (hills, really) in a loop of the Sarthe : 14thC frescos in the Romanesque church. ▶ **Perseigne Forest** (50 km², *SW*) and **Écouves Forest** (75 km², *NW*) are both part of the Normandy-Maine Nature Park ; both shelter red and roe deer and wild boar. ▶ **Sées** *(22 km N)*, seat of a bishopric : 13th-14thC Gothic cathedral★★ (14th-15thC stained glass★, 19thC spires); museum of sacred art; episcopal palace (1778); remains of the 18thC **abbey of Notre-Dame-de-la-Place.**   □

Practical Information _____

ALENÇON
ℹ Maison d'Ozé, pl. Lamagdelaine (B2), ☎ 33.26.11.36.
SNCF (C1), ☎ 33.29.38.37.
Car rental : *Avis*, 45, rue de Paris (C1), ☎ 33.29.40.67.

Hotels :
● ★★★ *Grand Cerf*, 21, rue St-Blaise (B1), ☎ 33.26.00.51, Tx 170296, AE Euro Visa, 33 rm Ⓟ ≼ ▒▒▒

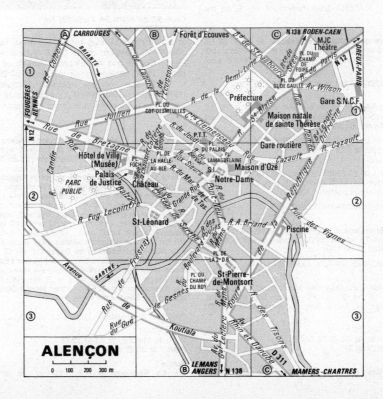

ALENÇON
0   100   200   300 m

Lace-making

The fashion for lace became a craze in the latter half of the 16thC with the widespread importation of lace from Venice. The Prime Minister, Jean-Baptiste Colbert, decided to counter the drain of funds by creating a French lace industry. In 1665 Alençon began lace production on an industrial scale. In the 18thC, an Alençon lace-maker, Mme. La Perrière, perfected a pattern that consisted of a network of very fine hexagonal stitches scattered with tiny flowers. The 19thC gave rise to the exaggerated lace headdresses, or Normandy bonnets, worn by well-to-do farmers' wives and townswomen at festivals. Alençon, Argentan and Bayeux still maintain the lace-making tradition; craft courses are available in Bayeux.

⚲ ♪ � closed closed Sun (l.s.), 15 Dec-15 Jan, 14-21 Jul, 250. Rest. ◆◆ ♪ ㅊ closed (l.s.), 60-110.
★★ **Le Chapeau Rouge**, 1-3, bd Duchamp (A1), ☎ 33.26.20.23, Visa, 16 rm ℗ ▩ ㅊ 150.

Restaurant :
◆◆ **Au Petit Vatel**, 72, pl. du Cdt-Desmeulles (B1), ☎ 33.26.23.78, AE DC Euro Visa ♪ closed Wed and Sun eve , Feb, 15-31 Aug, 100-220 ; child : 60.

⚖ ★★★*de Guéramé* (75 pl), ☎ 33.26.34.95.

Recommended
Events : *September music festival.*
Youth hostel : at Damigny PC 61250, 3 km N, ☎ 33.29.00.48, Annex of Saint-Céneri-le-Gérei, same tel.
♥ pastry : *Augnet*, 39, Grande-Rue (B2), ☎ 33.26.00.47.

Nearby

ARCONNAY, ✉ 72610 Saint-Paterne, 4 km S on the N 138.

Hotel :
★ *Hostellerie du Château de Maleffre*, ☎ 33.31.82.78, Euro Visa, 13 rm ℗ ≼ ▩ ⚲ ⚖ closed 20 Dec-6 Jan, 190. Rest. ◆ ≼ ⚖ closed Fri, Sat, Sun. Meals for residents, 115.

GACÉ, ✉ 61230, 24 km N of **Sées** on the N 138.

Hotel :
★★ **Le Morphée**, 2, rue de Lisieux, ☎ 33.35.51.01, AE Visa, 10 rm ℗ ≼ ▩ ⚲ closed 4 Jan-15 Feb. Splendid 19th-C residence, French billiards, 200.

Le MÊLE-SUR-SARTHE, ✉ 61170, 22 km NE.
ⓘ pl. du Marché, ☎ 31.27.60.54.   ♥

Hotel :
★ *Poste* (L.F.), ☎ 33.27.60.13, Euro Visa, 19 rm ≼ ▩ ⚲ ♪ closed Sun eve and Mon lunch, 1-15 Feb, 1-15 Oct, 165. Rest. ◆ ♪ Generous portions, 50-100.

SAINT-DENIS-SUR-SARTHON, ✉ 61420.

Hotel :
● ★★ **La Faïencerie** (C.H.), ☎ 33.27.30.16, 18 rm ℗ ▩ closed 15 Nov-15 Apr. A royal porcelain works in a 3-ha park, 200. Rest. ◆ 80-120.

SAINT-PIERRE-DES-NIDS, ✉ 53370, 27 km W.

Hotel :
★ *Le Dauphin* (L.F.), rue des Moulins, ☎ 43.03.52.12, Euro Visa, 10 rm ℗ ▩ ⚲ closed Tue eve, Wed, 13 Feb-5 Mar, 21 Aug-5 Sep, 85. Rest. ◆ ㅊ 65-190 ; child : 30.

SÉES, ✉ 61500, 22 km N.
ⓘ Hôtel de ville, ☎ 33.28.74.79 (h.s.).
▦▦ ☎ 33.27.80.37.

Hotel :
★ *Cheval Blanc* (L.F.), 1, pl. St-Pierre, ☎ 33.27.80.48,

Visa, 9 rm ℗ ⚲ closed closed Fri and Sat (l.s.), 1-10 Mar, 18 Oct-9 Nov, 70. Rest. ◆ ♪ ㅊ ⚲ 55-95 ; child : 40.

⚖ ★★*Le Clos Normand* (33 pl), ☎ 33.27.98.08.
Recommended
Son et lumière : at the cathedral (h.s.).

Les ANDELYS*

Rouen 39, Beauvais 63, Paris 72 km
pop 8210 ✉ 27700   D2
The town includes **Grand Andely** (church of Notre-Dame★, 12th-15thC, with Renaissance organ-casing) and **Petit Andely.**

▶ Church of St. Sauveur★ (11thC) with 14thC wooden porch ; Hospice St. Jacques (infirmary) ; 1784 dome.
▶ **Château Gaillard★★** : an exceptional view★ over the Seine ; the fortress, once the pride of the 12thC English King Richard the Lion-Heart, was captured by Philippe Auguste in 1204 ; it is now in ruins *(daily ex Tue. and Wed. am).* ▶ **Muids** *(10 km SW)* : pottery centre. ▶ **Ecouis** *(8 km N)* : church (1313) ; 14th-15thC religious sculpture★).   □

Practical Information _____

ⓘ rue Philippe-Auguste, ☎ 32.54.41.93.

Hotels :
★ **Le Normandie**, 1, rue Grande, ☎ 32.54.10.52, Visa, 11 rm ℗ ≼ ▩ ⚲ closed Wed eve and Thu, 4 Dec-4 Jan, 160. Rest. ◆ ≼ 80-130.
★ **Paris**, 10, av. de la République, ☎ 32.54.00.33, Euro Visa, 8 rm ℗ ▩ closed Wed, Feb, 80. Rest. ◆ ♪ 45-110.

⚖ ★★★*L'Ile des Trois Rois* (100 pl), ☎ 32.54.23.79.

ARGENTAN*

Caen 57, Le Mans 94, Paris 195 km
pop 18000 ✉ 61200   C3
In a rich cattle-farming region, the town was rebuilt after WWII. Remains of the 14thC château and 12thC keep ; Gothic and Renaissance church of St. Germain ; 16thC stained glass in church of St. Martin.
▶ Birthplace of the painter Fernand Léger (1881-1955). ▶ Benedictine abbey (2 Rue de l'Abbaye) where the nuns make lace *(point d'Argentan).*

Nearby

▶ Numerous **châteaux** and **manor-houses★★** from various periods : **Commeaux** *(8 km NW)* with a 16thC manor *(daily, Jul.-15 Aug.);* **Chambois** *(12 km NE)* : ruins of 12thC keep and nearby, château d'**Aubry-en-Exmes** (Louis XIII style) ; Renaissance manor at **Argentelles** near Exmes *(16 km E);* elegant Louis XIV château at **Bourg-Saint-Léonard** ; 15 km E, the **château du Pin★** (1728), site of a stud-farm founded in 1714 *(free guided tours ; harness horse demonstrations every Thu. at 3, end May-end Sep. ; racing Sep.-Oct.);* 12 km SE on D240, château de **Médavy**, rebuilt 18thC *(daily, 14 Jul.-Sep.);* near Mortrée *(16 km SE),* the graceful **château d'O★** *(closed Tue. ; am only Nov.-Apr.);* **château du Sassy** *(12 km S)* : terraced gardens *(pm, Palm Sun.-1 Nov.),* not far from **Saint-Christophe-le-Jajolet** where drivers can have their cars blessed *(pilgrimage last Sun. in Jul.).* ▶ 9 km SW, **Ecouché** : Renaissance church★ ; 5 km further, **Mesnil-Glaise** : pleasant site in a bend of the Orne.

Practical Information _____

ARGENTAN
ⓘ pl. du Marché, ☎ 33.67.12.48.
▦▦ ☎ 33.67.50.50/33.67.20.86.

Hotels :
★★ **La Renaissance** (L.F.), 20, av. de la 2e-D.-B.,

☎ 33.36.14.20, AE DC Visa, 15 rm Ⓟ 180. Rest. ◆◆ *La Marmite* ♪ Warm reception, 75-165; child : 45.
★ *Donjon*, 3, rue de l'Hôtel-de-Ville, ☎ 33.67.03.76, 17 rm Ⓟ ⌕ ⚹ closed Mon lunch and Sun eve, 15 Sep-15 Oct, 120. Rest. ◆ 45-90.

Nearby

MORTRÉE, ⊠ 61500 Sées, 15 km.

Hotel :
● ★ *La Ferme d'O*, ☎ 33.35.35.27, Euro Visa ⧖ ♨ ⌕ ♿ closed Tue and Sun eve (l.s.), Tue lunch (h.s.), 5 Jan-25 Feb. A 12th-C Commander's residence, 90-180.

The AUGE Region***

C2
From Deauville to Cabourg *(approx 180 km, full day; see map 1)*

This is picture-book Normandy : the coast is dotted with attractive towns (Cabourg, Deauville-Trouville, Honfleur), while inland, contented cows provide milk for Camembert, Pont-l'Évêque and Livarot cheeses; where apple blossoms in May enchant the eye. The Auge region includes the valleys of the Dives, the Vie

1. The Auge region

and the Touques. Wood is the usual building material for farmsteads★ and manor-houses★.

▶ **Deauville** (→). ▶ **Touques** : wooden houses, the manor of **Mentry** (stud farm) and, further, ruins of the feudal château de **Bonneville** *(Apr.-Oct., pm Sat., Sun. and nat. hols.).* ▶ **Canapville** : 15thC rustic manor-house. ▶ After the manor at Glatigny (wood and stone, 16th-17thC), **Beaumont-en-Auge** : viewpoint★, timbered houses overlooking the Touques Valley. ▶ **Pont-l'Évêque** : a superb cheese named after the town is made in the surrounding villages; Flamboyant Gothic church of St. Michel; Montpensier and de Brilly mansions (17th, 18thC); half-timbered houses. ▶ After **Pierrefitte-en-Auge** (13thC church), picturesque valley of Saint-Hymer. ▶ The church at **Quilly-le-Vicomte**, its foundations dating from the 10thC, is one of the oldest in Normandy. ▶ **Lisieux** (→). ▶ Detour to the **château de Mesnil-Guillaume★** : barely visible from the road but a superb example of Louis XIII architecture *(no visits)*; rejoin the Touques Valley at the **château de Saint-Germain-de-Livet★★** : the towers and ramparts of this 15th-16thC castle rise from the water like a checkerboard of stone and glazed brick; the courtyard façades are half-timbered (furnishings, frescos; *closed 15 Dec.-end Jan. and Tue.).* ▶ **Château de Fervaques** : historic but less romantic; the writer Chateaubriand (1768-1848) used to stay here *(ext. visit only).* ▶ Leave the Touques Valley at **Moutiers-Hubert (Chiffretot** Manor, 17thC) and drive past **Bellou Manor★** (17thC, half-timbered). Near **Lisores**, Bougonnière farm *(ferme),* with a small Fernand Léger Museum *(May-Sep., daily 10-12 & 2-6 ex Wed.; Oct.-Apr., Sat., Sun. and nat. hols).* ▶ **Vimoutiers**, Place de la Mairie : statue of Marie Harel, a local farmwoman who perfected the making of Camembert cheese. ▶ **Camembert** : in the late 19thC, Marie Harel made her cheese at the Beaumoncel farm. ▶ **Livarot**, on the Vie, lends its name to another well-known cheese; also a major butter producer *(visits of cheese-making).* ▶ **Coupesarte** : 16thC timber-built manor-house★. **Grandchamp** : unusually tall half-timbered building. **Le Mesnil-Manger** : Coin Manor (15th-16thC). ▶ **Crèvecoeur-en-Auge,** a fortified site from the 11thC; restoration undertaken by the industrialist Schlumberger family; includes museums of Norman Architecture and Petroleum Research *(Apr.-Jun. and Sep., closed Wed.; Feb., Mar., Oct., Nov., Sat. and Sun.; open daily, 12-8, Jul.-Aug.; closed Dec. and Jan.).* ▶ Beyond the ruins of the former **Val Richer abbey,** the Classical 17thC **château de la Roque-Baignard.** ▶ **Cambremer,** the heart of cider country; visits to farms displaying the sign *"cru* (crop) *de Cambremer".* ▶ Important stud farm at the **château de Victot★** (16thC). ▶ **Beuvron-en-Auge★** : craft-centre; historic village (Place de la Halle) sometimes called "the cider capital" (festival in Nov.). **Clermont-en-Auge** : view★ over the Auge Valley. **Cricqueville-en-Auge** : château (1584). ▶ You reach the coast at Dives-sur-Mer and Cabourg. ☐

Practical Information

BEUVRON-EN-AUGE, ⊠ 14430, 13 km S of **Dives-sur-Mer.**

Restaurant :
● ◆◆ *Le Pavé d'Auge*, ☎ 31.79.26.71, DC Visa Ⓟ ⧖ ♪ ♿ closed Mon eve and Tue (l.s.), 15 Jan-15 Mar. This fairytale setting is the scene of Odile Engel's culinary magic : sole, homard, poulet, crème au cidre, 125-200.

Le BREUIL-EN-AUGE, ⊠ 14130 Pont-l'Eveque, 8 km S of **Pont-l'Eveque.**

Restaurant :
● ◆◆ *Auberge du Dauphin*, ☎ 31.65.08.11, Visa ♪ ⚹ closed Tue eve and Wed, 30 Sep-28 Oct. An authentic Norman inn, a favourite with Deauville's gourmets : sauté de spaghettis aux cèpes, fleurs de courgettes farcies au homard, escalope de foie gras de canard poêlée aux échalotes confites, 80-250.

CORMEILLES, ⊠ 27260, 12 km SE of **Pont-L'Evêque.**

Hotel :
● ★ *Auberge du Président*, 70, rue de l'Abbaye,

☎ 32.57.80.37, 14 rm ≮ ♨ ⌕ 95. Rest. ♦♦ ♪ ᖴ Spec : *sole farcie Hermitage, omelette aux girolles*, 50-150.

Recommended
Events : *Concerts*, at the church of St Mélier, mid-Aug.

LIVAROT, ✉ 14410, 18 km S of **Lisieux**.
Ⅱ ☎ 31.63.53.19.

Hotel :
★★ *Vivier* (L.F.), pl. de la Mairie, ☎ 31.63.50.29, Euro Visa, 11 rm Ⓟ ♨ half pens (h.s.), closed Mon ex hols, 1-7 Oct, 20 Dec-25 Jan, 250. Rest. ♦ closed Sun eve (l.s.) and Mon, 50-110.

Recommended
Guide to wines : *Cidrerie du Calvados*, ☎ 31.63.50.53.
♥ cheese dairy : *Graindorge*, ☎ 31.63.50.02.

PONT-L'ÉVÊQUE, ✉ 14130, 11 km SE of **Deauville**.
Ⅱ mairie, ☎ 31.64.12.77.
🚄 ☎ 31.64.10.69.

Hotel :
★★ *Le Lion d'Or*, 8, pl. du Calvaire, ☎ 31.65.01.55, DC Euro Visa, 30 rm Ⓟ ≮ ⌕ ᖴ 210. Rest. ♦ ≮ 95-150; child : 40.

Restaurants :
♦♦ *Auberge de la Touques*, pl. de l'Eglise, ☎ 31.64.01.69, Euro Visa ≮ ♪ closed Mon eve and Tue , 15 Nov-31 Dec. Spec : *flan de homard, barbue aux pommes*, 85-145.
♦♦ *L'Aéroport*, ☎ 31.88.38.75, AE DC Euro Visa ≮ ♪ closed Tue eve and Wed, 15 Jan-1 Mar, 80-130.

⚠ ★★★*Cour de France* (333 pl), ☎ 31.64.17.38.

Recommended
♥ Calvados : *Le Père Magloire*, Ets Debrisse-Dulac, ☎ 31.64.12.87; at Bonneville-la-Louvet, 10 km, ☎ 31.64.75.11, farm produce, cider, Calvados; at Bizouard-du-Breuil, chocolates, candies; at Pierrefitte-en-Auge, 5 km S, *Auberge des deux Tonneaux*, Norman-style snacks.

QUETTEVILLE, ✉ 14130 Pont-L'Evêque, 10 km NE of **Pont-l'Evêque**.

Hotel :
★★ *Auberge de la Hauquerie* (L.F.), rte de Pont-l'Eveque, ☎ 31.64.14.46, Visa, 8 rm ≮ ♨ ⌕ half pens (h.s.), closed Thu ex hols and Aug, 6 Jan-15 Feb, 10-30 Dec, 500. Rest. ♦♦♦ ≮ ᖴ In the peaceful green Normandy countryside, Mme Carlos Lombard serves her excellent, personalized cooking to a growing number of fans, 80-150; child : 60.

SAINT-MARTIN-AUX-CHARTRAINS, ✉ 14130 Pont-l'Evêque, 3 km N of **Pont-l'Evêque**.

Hotel :
★ *Auberge de la Truite* (L.F.), ☎ 31.65.21.64, AE DC Visa, 7 rm Ⓟ ≮ ♨ closed Wed eve and Thu, Feb, 100. Rest. ● ♦♦ ♪ ᖴ Chef J.-M. Lebon's cooking is as good as his name implies : *crêpes de langoustines, florentins d'huîtres, duo de pigeon et caille*, 75-230.

BAGNOLES-DE-L'ORNE*

Alençon 48, Laval 61, Paris 233 km
pop 780 ✉ 61140   B3

One of the major spas in western France, situated in the valley of the river Vée. Casino on the lake and, in the middle of the warm springs park (Parc Thermal), a rocky gorge covered with fir trees.

Nearby

▶ **Andaines Forest**, (40 km²), ideal area for walking, riding, cycling or driving. ▶ 3 km S, 16th-18thC château de Conterne ; 8 km SE, château de **Monceaux** (French gardens). ▶ After **La Ferté-Macé** *(6 km ;* small museum in town hall), **Carrouges** *(23 km E)* : fine 15th-17thC château★ *(closed Tue. ;* antique furnishings). On the edge of

the estate, a 15thC house in the Normandy-Maine Nature Park★★ HQ : the 234 km² park includes the forests of Andaines, Écouves (in the Orne Department) Perseigne, and Sillé (in the Sarthe Department) ; numerous recreational facilities, including cross-country hikes, horse riding, rock climbing, canoeing, kayaking, sailing. ▶ **Domfront** *(19 km W)* : view★ from the ruins of the 11thC keep, surrounded by a fine park ; below, the church of Notre-Dame-sur-l'Eau (11thC). ▶ 9 km NW of Domfront, **Lonlay-l'Abbaye** : 11th-15thC abbey church ; nearby, many 15th-18thC manor-houses.   ⬜

Practical Information _____

BAGNOLES-DE-L'ORNE
⚓ (1 Apr-30 Sep).
Ⅱ pl. de la Gare, ☎ 33.37.05.84 (h.s.).
🚄 ☎ 33.37.80.04.

Hotels :
● ★★★ *Lutetia* (C.H.), pl. du Gal-de-Gaulle, ☎ 33.37.94.77, AE DC Visa, 34 rm Ⓟ ♨ ⌕ ᖴ closed 30 Oct-1 Apr, 230. Rest. ♦♦ *Reine Astrid* ⁂ 85-180.
★★★ *Bois Joli*, 12, av. Philippe-du-Rozier, ☎ 33.37.92.77, Tx 171782, AE DC Euro Visa, 20 rm Ⓟ ♨ ⌕ ⁂ closed 15 Oct-1 Apr. Pretty rooms, 280. Rest. ♦ ⁂ closed Wed and Sun eve. Spec : *sole soufflée au champagne*, 130-150; child : 50.
★★★ *Capricorne*, allée Montjoie, ☎ 33.37.96.99, Tx 175525, AE DC Euro Visa, 24 rm Ⓟ ♨ ⌕ ♪ ⁂ closed 3 Oct-1 Apr, 320. Rest. ♦♦ ♪ ⁂ closed lunch. Dinner for guests only, 90-150.
★★★ *Le Manoir du Lys* (R.S.), rte de Juvigny, ☎ 33.37.80.69, Tx 170525, AE Euro Visa, 13 rm Ⓟ ♨ ⌕ ♪ ⁂ closed Mon eve and Tue, 1 Jan-15 Mar, 320. Rest. ♦ ≮ ᖴ ⌕ ⁂ The Quinton family's delightful inn set in the forest, 87-250.
★★ *Le Grand Veneur*, 6, pl. de la République, ☎ 33.37.86.79, 23 rm Ⓟ ♨ closed 15 Oct-15 Apr. Family atmosphere, 192. Rest. ♦ 70-135; child : 40.

⚠ ★★★*de la Vée* (133 pl), ☎ 33.37.25.36.

Recommended
Casino : ☎ 33.37.01.88, 1 May - 30 Sep.
Leisure activities : *Manoir du Lys*, rte de Juvigny, ☎ 33.37.80.69. Mushrooming weekends (mid Sep-late Oct).

Nearby

CARROUGES, ✉ 61320, 22 km E.
Ⅱ hôtel de ville, ☎ 33.27.20.38/33.27.20.49.

Hotel :
★ *Saint-Pierre* (L.F.), pl. de la Mairie, ☎ 33.27.20.02, Euro Visa, 7 rm Ⓟ ♨ ⌕ ♪ closed Tue and Wed, Feb, 24-31 Dec, 143. Rest. ♦ ♪ There's a tea room too, 52-125.

DOMFRONT, ✉ 61700, 18 km W.
Ⅱ rue Fossés-Plissons, ☎ 33.38.53.27 (h.s.).
🚄 ☎ 33.38.65.10.

Hotel :
★★ *Poste* (L.F.), 15, rue Mal.-Foch, ☎ 33.38.51.00, 29 rm Ⓟ closed Sun eve and Mon (l.s.), 15 Jan-25 Feb, 170. Rest. ♦ 60-160.

Recommended
Events : *international folklore festival*, in Jul.

BAYEUX**

Caen 27, Cherbourg 92, Paris 268 km
pop 15240 ✉ 14400   B2

The fame of the tapestry (in fact an embroidery) tends to make one forget that Bayeux is charming in its own right.

▶ **Cathedral of Notre-Dame★★** (B2), a fine example of Norman Gothic (13thC) : two towers on the façade, 15thC lantern tower★ topped in the 19thC. ▶ The former episcopal buildings (B2) are now occupied by the town hall, the

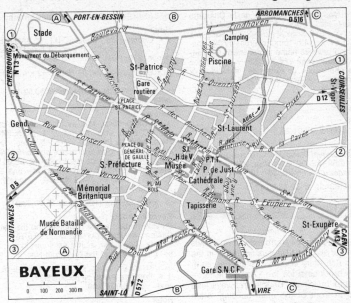

BAYEUX

0   100   200   300 m

Law Courts (Palais de Justice; ceiling from the Renaissance chapel), and the **Baron-Gérard Museum★** (paintings ranging from Italian Primitives to Impressionists and local artists; lace and decorative arts; *16 Mar.-14 May, 9-12:30 & 2-6:30; 15 May-15 Sep., 9-7; 16 Sep.-15 Mar., 9:30-12:30 & 2-6).* ► Centre Culturel Guillaume le Conquérant (B2-3) houses the **Bayeux Tapestry** (linen)★★★ *(same hours as the museum)*, once wrongly attributed to William's consort Queen Matilda. Fifty-eight scenes covering a length of 70 m tell the story of William's conquest of England in 1066; the embroidery was done in about 1077 in England. ► In the **Hôtel du Doyen** (B2), diocesan museum of religious art and lace work-shop *(open daily in summer, closed Sun. rest of year).* ► Old houses★ in the town centre. ► Place aux Pommes (B2) : on one side of the river Aure (good view) is the Centre Normand de la Dentelle au Fuseau (bobbin lace centre; *closed Sun. in summer, Sun. and Mon. rest of year);* on the other, Ateliers de l'Horloge (weaving, lace-making).
Also... ► **Memorial museum** of the battle of Normandy★ (Musée Mémorial de la Bataille de Normandie; A3; *10-12:30 & 2-6:30, Mar.-May, Sep., Oct.; 9:30-7, Jun.-Aug.; weekends 10:30-12:30 & 2-6:30, Nov.-Feb.).* ► S of town, **Saint-Loup-Hors** : 12th-14thC church. ► **Saint-Vigor-le-Grand** (C1) : remains of 13thC priory.   □

Practical Information ─────────────

ⓘ 1, rue des Cuisiniers (B2), ☎ 31.92.16.26.
SNCF (B3), ☎ 31.92.80.50.
🚌 pl. St-Patrice (A1); pl. de la Gare (A1).

Hotels :
● ★★★ **Lion d'Or** (R.S.), 71, rue St-Jean (B2), ☎ 31.92.06.90, Tx 171143, AE DC Visa, 30 rm 🅿 ⌂ half pens (h.s.), closed 20 Dec-20 Jan. A large, handsome inn founded in 1770, 560. Rest.● ♦♦ ♪ ♨ A peaceful stop in the centre of town, for good Norman cooking : *andouille chaude à la Bovary, fricassée de poulet Normandie, grenadin au Pommeau,* 112-200; child : 65.
● ★★ **Argouges**, (I.L.A., C.H.), 21, rue St-Patrice (A1-2), ☎ 31.92.88.86, Tx 170234, AE DC Euro Visa, 25 rm 🅿 ⌂ ♪ 18th-C town house, 200.
★★ **Le Bayeux**, 9, rue Tardif (B2), ☎ 31.92.70.08, AE Visa, 30 rm 🅿 ⌂ ♿ closed 20 Dec-1 Feb, 210.
★★ **Manoir du Chêne** (C.H.), Nonant, ☎ 31.92.58.81,

The Bayeux tapestry

Locally known as "La Telle du Conquest" (the conquest cloth), the Bayeux Tapestry is an embroidery of woolen threads on a linen ground, 69.55 m long and 50 to 55 cm wide. The sequence of 58 scenes relates the history of the Norman conquest of England from the decision of the childless English king, Edward the Confessor, to name his cousin William, Duke of Normandy, as his heir, through the broken oath of loyalty by William's English rival Harold, to William's victory over Harold at Hastings on 14 October 1066. The scenes are bordered by a frieze of animals and fabulous beasts, the whole providing an incomparable document of medieval warfare, costume and social organization. The embroidery is Saxon work, dating from about 1077.

Tx 171777, Visa, 16 rm 🅿 ⌂ ⌂ ♿ 🖂 half pens, closed Nov-Mar, 555. Rest. ♦ ⌂ ♿ ♨ closed Mon and Tue-Fri eve, 85-120.

⚠ ★★★*Municipal* (150 pl), ☎ 31.92.08.43.

Recommended
Bicycle-rental : *Family Home,* 39, rue du Gal-de-Dais, ☎ 31.92.15.22, and at the train station.
Events : *horse festival,* in Jun.
Youth hostel : 39, rue du Gal-de-Dais, ☎ 31.92.15.22.

BERNAY*

Rouen 58, Alençon 87, Paris 150 km
pop 10950 ✉ 27300   C2

An important cattle-rearing centre and market town that originally developed around an 11thC abbey.

► Next to the abbey **church★**, the *logis* (17thC) houses a museum of ceramics, furniture, paintings *(closed Tue. and am low-season ex Wed.);* it overlooks a public garden.
► Half-timbered **houses★** in many streets, especially

Rue G.-Folloppe; No. 15 is the Musée de la Charrette (museum of daily life in the 19thC; *closed Mon.*).
▶ **Plasnes** *(6 km N)* : ornithological park *(Sat. & Sun. pm).*
▶ **Broglie** *(11 km SW)* : 14th-16thC church; 17thC château of family which gave its name to the town; **Charentonne Valley.** ▶ **Beaumesnil** *(14 km SE)* : one of the finest Louis XIII châteaux★ in existence; exhibition of book-binding from 16thC on *(May-Sep. 2:30-6 Fri.-Mon).* □

Practical Information _____
[i] ☎ 32.43.32.08.
[SNCF] ☎ 32.43.17.11/32.43.01.25.

Hotel :
★ **Angleterre et du Cheval Blanc** (L.F.), 10, rue du Gal-de-Gaulle, ☎ 32.43.12.59, AE DC Euro Visa, 23 rm [P] [♨] [Ⓛ] 140. Rest. ♦ *Pintadeau financière*, 80-170.

△ ★★★Municipal (83 pl), ☎ 32.43.30.47.

The BESSIN Region

A2

W of Caen lies the traditional Normandy of meadows and hedges with the spires of Bayeux cathedral in the distance. This is rich dairy country; Isigny has been famous for dairy produce since the 17thC. The farmsteads are beautiful buildings : double archways lead into a courtyard in front of the main building, often dating from the 15th or 16thC, and sometimes flanked by a tower. The subsoil of the southern Bessin is granitic. The English Channel *(la Manche)* coast is a wall of limestone cliffs broken by small coves that shelter little ports (→ D-Day Landing Beaches). □

The BRAY Region

D1

This low-lying, cattle-farming area between the plateaux of Picardy, the Caux region and the Vexin is the "dairy of Paris".

▶ **Aumale**, on the right bank of the Bresle : church (fine vaulting reminiscent of Picardy); picturesque Auberge du Mouton Gras (inn). ▶ **Forges-les-Eaux** is a spa launched by Louis XIII (1601-43), his wife Anne of Austria and Cardinal Richelieu; three springs are named after them. In the park, museum of model horse-drawn carriages *(pm in season).* The ceramics museum (Musée de la Faïence) in the town hall *(daily 10-11:30 & 2-5 ex Mon., hols.)* illustrates local production up to the 19thC; 7.5 km NW : ruins of **Beaubec Abbey** (founded 1128). ▶ **Foucamont** : 20thC church and nearby, ruins of 12thC abbey; 4 km SE, **Saint-Léger-aux-Bois.** ▶ **Gournay-en-Bray** : church of St-Hildevert (Romanesque, Gothic). ▶ 7 km SW, typical village of **Bézancourt.** ▶ **Neufchâtel-en-Bray**, know for its cheese *(bondon);* the town was rebuilt after WWII; church of Notre-Dame (13th-16thC); J. B. Mathon and A. Durand museum in a 16thC house (folk art; *pm in season, Sat. and Sun. out of season).* ▶ **Mesnières-en-Bray** *(5 km NW)* : Renaissance château★ *(Sat. and Sun. pm).* ▶ **Saint-Saëns** is a good starting point for exploring the **Varenne-Valley**★ or the 65 km² **Eawy Forest**★ (beech). □

Practical Information _____
AUMALE, ⊠ 76390, 26 km E of **Neufchâtel-en-Bray.**
[i] mairie, ☎ 35.93.41.68.   💘

Hotel :
★★ **Le Dauphin**, 27, rue St-Lazare, ☎ 35.93.41.92, AE Visa, 10 rm [P] [♨] closed Sat eve and Sun ex hols, 20 Dec-26 Jan. 15 Jul, 15 Sep, 160. Rest. ♦ ♪ ♨ 55-160.

△ ★Municipal (60 pl).

Recommended
Bicycle-rental : info. S.I.

BÉZANCOURT, ⊠ 76220 Gournay-en-Bray.

Hotel :
★★ **Château du Landel** (C.H.), ☎ 35.90.16.01, 17 rm [P] [♨] [ₘ] [Ⓛ] ✗ closed Sun eve, 15 Dec-15 Mar. 18th-C residence, 240. Rest. ♦♦ ♨ ♨ 85-150.

FORGES-LES-EAUX, ⊠ 76440, 42 km of **Rouen.**
♨.   💘
[i] parc de l'Hôtel-de-ville, ☎ 35.90.52.10.
[SNCF] ☎ 35.90.50.45.

Hotels :
★★★ **Continental**, 110, av. des Sources, ☎ 35.09.80.12, AE DC Euro Visa, 49 rm [P] [♨] [ₘ] ♨ ❀ [Ⓛ] ✗ 200. Rest. ♦♦♦ **Le Cardinal** ♨ ♨ ♨ Spec : *feuilleté picard, brochettes de lotte, tournedos au Neufchâtel*, 120-210. **Paix** (L.F.), 17, rue de Neufchâtel, ☎ 35.90.51.22, AE DC Euro Visa, 5 rm [P] closed Mon eve and Sun eve (l.s.), 15 Dec-15 Jan, 95. Rest. ♦ Spec : *médaillon de saumon fumé*, 55-150.

△ ★★La Minière (120 pl), ☎ 35.90.53.91.

Recommended
Bicycle-rental : at the campsite and the train station.
Casino : av. des Sources, ☎ 35.90.52.67.
Events : horse fair, in Jul; Art show, in Jul; *"Golden Voices" tournament*, at the Casino in Nov.

GOURNAY-EN-BRAY, ⊠ 76220, 30 km E of **Beauvais.**
[i] 4, Porte-de-Paris, ☎ 35.90.28.34.
[SNCF] ☎ 35.90.00.09.

Hotel :
★★ **Le Cygne**, (Inter-Hôtel), 20, rue Notre-Dame, ☎ 35.90.27.80, AE DC Euro Visa, 30 rm [P] [♨] ♨ ♨ ♨ 200.

CAEN★★★

Cherbourg 120, Le Mans 151, Paris 240 km
pop 117120 ⊠ 14000   B2
The capital of Lower Normandy was rebuilt in a few decades after WWII, which miraculously spared its ancient churches. Today, the favourite city of William the Conqueror is a thriving industrial centre. The Orne canal provides access to the sea for the shipment of goods.

▶ **Castle**★★ (B1; founded by William the Conqueror) : wartime destruction exposed the medieval walls. From flowered terraces, views★ over the town and the Maison des Quatrans★ (14th-16thC). The base of the 12thC keep has also been exposed. ▶ The chapel of St. Georges (12th-15thC; Caen Battle Memorial); the Échiquier de Normandie (14thC; formerly the great hall of the ducal palace) and the former Governor's Residence (17th-18thC) have been restored. The Residence houses the **Normandy Museum**★★ (history and ethnography; *daily ex Tue. and nat. hols.*); **Fine Arts Museum**★★ (Musée des Beaux Arts; *same hours*); Italian and Flemish Primitives to 19thC paintings, in a modern building. ▶ **Church of St. Pierre**★★ (B2) : the 78-m spire (rebuilt after 1944) was the model for many Breton and Norman bell towers; Renaissance apse; the **Hôtel d'Escoville**★ (mansion) is of the same period (B2; TO). ▶ Rue St-Jean leads to the Flamboyant Gothic church of St. Jean (15thC; C2); Boulevard Maréchal-Leclerc (C2), at the centre of the rebuilt sector, is the busiest street (pedestrian zone). To the W, **Rue St-Pierre** (church of St. Sauveur) is the S boundary of the St. Sauveur quarter (fine 13thC buildings on the square of the same name); it leads to the **Abbaye aux Hommes**★★ (A2; founded by William the Conqueror); the abbey church of St. Étienne★★ is a fine example of Norman Romanesque, with two bell towers on the façade and a beautiful apse; the gardens around the chevet (E end) enhance the 18thC buildings; in the **Hôtel de Ville** (town hall), Nature Museum★ *(guided visits daily).* Opposite, ruins of the Old St. Étienne (13th-16thC). **Also...** ▶ **Abbaye aux Dames**★ (C1), founded by Queen Matilda in 1062; the church of La Trinité★ (11th, 12thC,

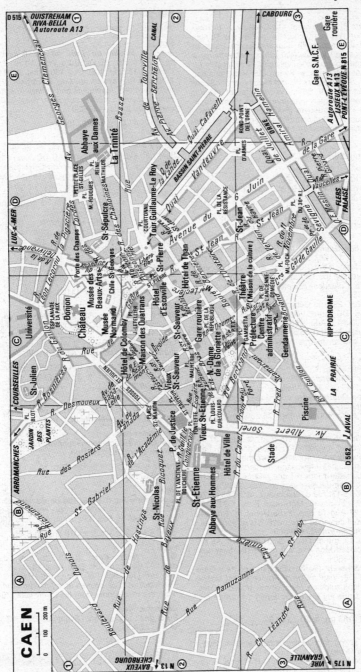

remodeled 19th) rivals that of the Abbaye aux Hommes. The convent buildings, administrative centre for Lower Normandy have been admirably restored *(visits daily at 3, 4, Sat. at 10, 11; closed Sun.).*

Nearby

▶ **Troarn** *(18 km E)* : remains of 11thC abbey. ▶ **Norrey-en-Bessin** *(13 km W)* : 13thC church★. ▶ **Tilly-sur-Seulles** *(20 km W),* rebuilt since WWII; museum of the Battle of Tilly in the chapel of the Vale *(Sat., Sun., nat. hols. pm).* ▶ **Villers-Bocage** *(26 km SW)* : lively cattle market *(Wed.);* leisure centre at Cahagnes. ▶ 24 km SE, 18thC château de **Canon** *(Sat., Sun., Easter-Jul., pm in summer).* ▶ **Saint-Pierre-sur-Dives** *(31 km SE)* : country market *(Mon.);* Gothic church and chapter, conservatory of cheese techniques. Château at **Vendeuvre** *(6 km farther S)* : 18thC; international museum of miniature furniture★ and masterpieces by guild craftsmen in the orangery *(pm Jun.-15 Sep.).* ☐

Practical Information _____

CAEN

ⓘ pl. St-Pierre (C2), ☎ 31.86.27.65.
✈ *Caen-Carpiquet,* 6 km W, ☎ 31.73.18.00. *Air France office,* 143, rue St-Jean, ☎ 31.85.41.26.
SNCF ☎ 31.83.50.50/31.82.13.31.
Car rental : *Avis,* 44, pl. de la Gare (E3), ☎ 31.84.73.80/31.84.61.59 ; train station (E3).

Hotels :

★★★★ *Relais des Gourmets,* 13-15, rue de Geôle (C2), ☎ 31.86.06.01, Tx 171657, AE DC Euro Visa, 32 rm 🅿 ≪ ⚏ ⚐ ♨ 280. Rest. ♦♦ ≪ ♪ ₺ closed Sun eve. Excellent food served forth by the Legras clan : *rognon de veau flambé au vieux Calvados, assiette de quatre poissons au Noilly,* 150-250.
★★★ *Le Dauphin,* 29, rue Gémare (B2), ☎ 31.86.22.26, Tx 171707, AE DC Euro Visa, 21 rm 🅿 ⚐ closed 14-23 Feb, 15 Jul-11 Aug, 255. Rest. ● ♦♦♦ closed Sat. Light, unfussy fare prepared by Robert Chabredier : *filet de barbue calville, huîtres frémies au beurre rouge,* 75-250.
★★★ *Malherbe,* pl. Foch (D3), ☎ 31.84.40.06, Tx 170555, AE DC Euro Visa, 45 rm 🅿 ≪ ⚏ ♪ ₺ 245.
★★★ *Moderne* **(Mapotel),** 116, bd Mal-Leclerc (C2), ☎ 31.86.04.23, AE DC Euro Visa, 57 rm 🅿 ♪ 🐎 360. Rest. ● ♦♦ *Les Quatre Vents* ♪ ₺ closed Sun eve (15 Oct-15 Mar). The city's most elegant eatery. Good food : *blanc de turbot à la crème d'huîtres,* 75-200 ; child : 38.

Restaurants :

● ♦♦♦ *Echevins,* 36, rue Ecuyère (B2), ☎ 31.86.37.44, AE DC Euro Visa ♪ closed Mon noon and Sun Feb, 28 Jun-14 Jul. Two types of cooking share the bill : classic cuisine with rich sauces *(saucisson de canard aux lentilles),* and light, modern fare like the *millefeuille de saumon au cerfeuil, Saint-Jacques aux endives,* 135-230.
● ♦♦ *Bourride,* 15-17, rue du Vaugueux, ☎ 31.93.50.76, AE DC Visa ⚏ ♪ closed Mon and Sun, 5-21 Jan, 28 Apr-5 May, 26 Aug-13 Sep. Expert chef M. Bruneau offers a short, well-designed menu with lots of surprises : raw fish, *papillote de truffes,* 150-300.
● ♦♦ *L'Ecaille,* 13, rue de Géole, ☎ 31.86.49.10, AE DC Euro Visa ≪ ♪ closed Mon and Sat noon. The best seafood in Caen, 115-150.
● ♦♦ *Relais Normandy,* (Buffet de la gare), pl. de la Gare (E3), ☎ 31.82.24.58, Visa ♪ One of France's best station buffets, with a long tradition of quality at honest prices, run for 20 years now by the Piniac family : Norman cuisine, 65-150.

⚠ ★★*Municipal* (133 pl), ☎ 31.73.60.92.

Recommended
Events : Mar : *spring fair.* June : *antiques show.* Sep : *Caen fair, horse racing.*
Guided tours : lecturers from the C.N.M.H.S., info. S.I.
♥ Chocolates, candy : *Hotot,* 13, rue Saint-Pierre; chocolates, candy : *Charlotte Corday,* 114, rue Saint-Jean; *Témoins,* 69, rue Saint-Pierre.

Be advised that hotels and restaurants in this Guide have perhaps changed addresses; prices indicated are also subject to modifications.

Nearby

BAVENT, ⊠ 14860, 17 km from **Caen.**

Hotel :
★★ *Le Moulin du Pré,* rte de Gonneville-en-Auge, ☎ 31.78.83.68, AE DC Euro Visa, 10 rm 🅿 ≪ ⚏ ⚐ 🐎 closed 1-15 Mar, 1-31 Oct, 180. Rest. ● ♦♦ ♪ ₺ closed Mon and Sun eve ex Jul-Aug. Let's hear it for the country, farm-fresh ingredients and Jocelyne Holtz's light, delicious cooking : *moules coque au fenouil, flan de turbot, canette au citron,* 160-220.

BÉNOUVILLE, ⊠ 14970, 10 km.

Hotel :
● ★★★ *Manoir d'Hastings,* 18, av. de la Côte-de-Nacre, ☎ 31.44.62.43, Tx 171144, AE DC Visa, 11 rm 🅿 ⚏ ⚐ 650. Rest. ● ♦♦♦♦ ≪ The 7th-C Norman priory keeps a benevolent eye on the Pegasus Bridge which made history on June 6 1944. 11 bed-sitting rooms, prettily decorated by Aline Scaviner provide many of those little extras (towel-warmers, basket of fruits) often neglected elsewhere. Husband Claude mans the stove, making the most of Normandy's fine raw materials (thick cream, cider, Calvados, apples) and striving for ever-more-spectacular culinary "coups" : *terrine de sardines fraîches, moules grillées, festival de homard et de langouste (braisée "Adrienne"), jambon au cidre.* Ask for his unctuous rendition of tripe. *Truffes au Calvados.* Regional and homemade specialities on sale in the boutique, 140-230.

FLEURY-SUR-ORNE, ⊠ 14123, 5 km S.

Restaurant :
● ♦♦ *Auberge de l'Ile Enchantée,* 1, rue Saint-André, ☎ 31.52.15.52, AE DC Visa 🅿 ≪ ⚐ ♪ closed Mon and Sun eve, 15 Feb-2 Mar, 27 Jul-25 Aug. Jean-Claude Blaize loves fish and prepares it with talent. *Barbue au cidre, matelote de poissons du pays,* 90-180.

SAINT-PIERRE-SUR-DIVES, ⊠ 14170, 31 km.
ⓘ 17, rue St-Benoît, ☎ 31.90.81.68 (h.s.).
SNCF ☎ 31.20.74.01.

Hotel :
★ *Gare,* 47, bd Colas, ☎ 31.20.74.22, Visa, 18 rm 🅿 ⚏ 60. Rest. ♦ *Le relais fleuri* ♪ 40-120.

Recommended
Events : *dressage competition,* in Jun.
Market : *rural market,* Mon.

TILLY-SUR-SEULLES, ⊠ 14250, 20 km W.
ⓘ ☎ 31.77.16.14.

Hotel :
★ *Jeanne-d'Arc* (L.F.), 2, rue de Bayeux, ☎ 31.80.80.13, AE Euro Visa, 14 rm 🅿 ≪ ⚏ ⚐ 🐎 closed Sun eve and Mon, 15 Jan-15 Feb, 130. Rest. ♦ ♪ 55-100.

VILLERS-BOCAGE, ⊠ 14310, 26 km SW.

Hotel :
● ★★ *Trois Rois* (L.F.), 2, pl. Jeanne-d'Arc, ☎ 31.77.00.32, AE DC Euro Visa, 14 rm 🅿 ⚏ ⚐ closed Sun eve (Jul-Aug), Feb, Mon, 165. Rest. ● ♦♦ ♪ Ah ! The fabulous tripe cooked up by master chef Henri Martinotti! Warm welcome from his lovely wife, 70-200.

Recommended
Rural gîte : at Caumont-l'Eventé on D 71 (12 km), Craham ☎ 31.77.58.34.

The CAUX Region

C1

A limestone plateau around Le Havre, Rouen and Dieppe, ending at the Channel in a vertical wall of white cliffs. Visited in the 19thC by painters such as Courbet, Boudin, Monet and Corot, these seaside resorts have kept an old-fashioned charm. Inland, valleys and trees protect the fertile farmland. ☐

CHERBOURG*

Caen 120, Rennes 210, Paris 360 km
pop 30110 ⊠ 50100   A1

The best way to arrive at Cherbourg by land is to follow the Avenue de Paris, which seems as if it will run right into the Channel. A huge dyke 3.7 km long protects the beach-front, which includes commercial and passenger ports as well as a military arsenal.

▶ The panorama★ is remarkable from the **Fort du Roule** (B3; Liberation museum; *closed Tue., Oct.-Apr.).* ▶ Near the lively town centre, behind the theatre (B2), are the cultural centre and the **Thomas Henry Museum★** : paintings of the Italian and Dutch schools, portraits by Millet *(closed Tue.).* ▶ The quays along the Bassin du Commerce (commercial port, B2-3) and the outer port lead to the Place de la République (A2); nearby are the church of La Trinité (15thC), the town hall (Hôtel de Ville) and the beach. ▶ At the edge of the **Emmanuel Liais Park★** (A2), created by the naturalist and astronomer (1826-1900), after whom it is named (exotic plants), the Natural History Museum (A1; *closed Tue. and nat. hols., May-15 Sep.; pm rest of year).* ▶ The **Arsenal** (France's first nuclear submarine, *Le Redoutable,* was launched there in 1967) and the military port (A1) are accessible only to French citizens. ▶ **Martinvast** *(6 km SW)* : 19thC château with 11th-12thC keep (park; *Palm Sun.-1 Nov., pm Sat., Sun. and nat. hols.).* ☐

Practical Information

CHERBOURG
🛈 2, quai Alexandre-III (B2), ☎ 33.43.52.02.
✈ *Maupertus,* 12 km E, ☎ 33.22.91.32.
SNCF (B3), ☎ 33.44.31.11/33.20.47.73.
🚌 (B3).
🚢 *Irish Continental Line,* Gare maritime, ☎ 33.44.28.96, to Rosslare (Ireland) Apr-Sep; *Sealink,* Gare maritime, ☎ 33.20.43.38, to Weymouth (Apr-Oct) and Portsmouth year round (Great Britain); *Service maritime Carteret,* Carteret, ☎ 33.54.87.21, to Guernesey in summer; *P.O.* Gare maritime (B1), ☎ 33.44.20.13, to Portsmouth (Great-Britain).
Car rental : *Avis,* train station (B4); 5, av. Carnot (C3), ☎ 33.43.16.00.

Hotels :
★★ *Louvre,* (Inter-Hôtel), 2, rue Henri-Dunant (A1), ☎ 33.53.02.28, Tx 171132, Visa, 42 rm P ♿ closed 24 Dec-1 Jan, 195.
★ *Moderna,* 28, rue de la Mairie (B2), ☎ 33.43.05.30, 24 rm ◔ 115.

Restaurant :
● ♦ **Chez Pain (Rest. Le Plouc),** 59, rue Au-Blé, ☎ 33.53.67.64, Euro ♪ closed Sat noon and Sun, 15 Aug-4 Sep. Authentic rustic decor. Good, straightforward food, 100-180.

Recommended
Boat rental : *Cherbourg Plaisance,* ☎ 33.53.27.34.

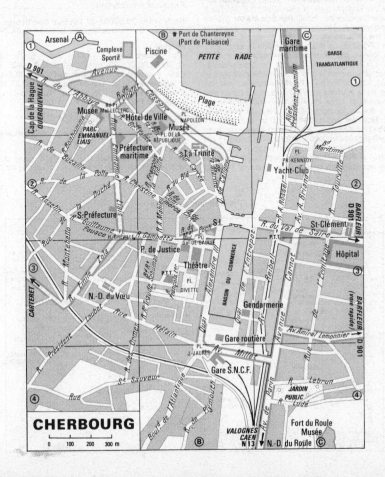

CHERBOURG
0   100   200   300 m

Events : *gastronomic competition*, in May; *international regatta*.
Marina : ☎ 33.53.75.16, (730 pl).
Youth hostel : *social and cultural centre*, 109, av. de Paris, ☎ 33.44.26.31.

Nearby

SAINT-GERMAIN-DES-VAUX, ✉ 50440 Beaumont-Hague, 29 km.

Hotel :
● ★★ *Hostel. l'Erguillère* (L.F.), Port Racine, ☎ 33.52.75.31, 10 rm P ⚡ ⋙ ⌲ & ⚕ half pens (h.s.), closed Sun eve and Mon ex school hols, 15 Nov-15 Mar, 215. Rest. ♦ & closed 1 Oct-15 Mar, 130-150.

The COTENTIN Peninsula**

A1-2
Round trip *(approx 210 km, full day; see map 2)*
The Cotentin Peninsula is where you may still find traces of the Vikings who first settled Normandy. The capes, inlets and headlands rival those of the coast of Brittany; the gentle climate of the Val de Saire favours market gardening. The GR223 follows the coast for part of the way.

▶ **Cherbourg** (→). ▶ **Querqueville** : 10th-11thC Saint-Germain chapel; view. ▶ **Nacqueville** : 16thC **château** surrounded by an English park *(Easter-Oct., 2-5 ex Tue.)*. ▶ After Urville-Nacqueville, 16thC **Dur Écu Manor** *(pm ex Tue.)*. ▶ **Landemer**, a seaside resort charmingly placed at one end of the wild, rocky coast that runs to Cap de la Hague. The GR233 leads to Castel-Vendon Rock (site★). ▶ The D45 follows the **La Hague peninsula★★**. ▶ **Gréville-Hague** : 13thC Virgin in church. ▶ **Omonville-la-Rogue★** : this fishing-port is one of the prettiest villages in the Cotentin; 13thC church. ▶ From **Auderville**, you can drive to **Cap de la Hague★** *(1.5 km N)* and the small port of Goury (view★ of Gros du Raz reef and lighthouse). ▶ Along the coast : **Ecalgrain Bay★**, **Nez de Voidries★** (point) and **Nez de Jobourg★★**; out to sea lies the Channel Island of Alderney. ▶ Jobourg heath supports a nuclear fuel-processing plant (information bureau; *pm 15 Jun.-15 Sep)*. Before **Beaumont**, walk to the lookout *(belvédère)* at **Pierre-Pouquelée** *(approx 20 min from D318; easier access from D403)*; panorama★ of the wild

bay of Vauville and the protected area of the **Mare de Vauville** (barrens). ▶ **Siouville-Hague**, a salt-water therapy centre. ▶ **Diélette**, small port and seaside resort. Flamanville *(2.5 km SW)* : a **nuclear power station** provides electricity for Caen and part of Brittany; viewpoint and information center *(visits, tel. 33.20.10.55)*. The villages of **Flamanville** have maintained their traditional character. The château★ is a fine Classical construction; park★ with palms. ▶ **Bricquebec** : **château** remodeled 14thC; museum in the clock tower *(ask at the town hall)*; keep *(view)*. ▶ To the N, **Notre-Dame-de-Grâce abbey** (Trappist). ▶ **Saint-Martin-le-Hébert** : Cour Manor (16th-17thC) surrounded by moats. ▶ **Valognes** (→). ▶ A detour through **Chiffrevast** and **Montaigu-la-Brisette** (church) brings you to **Val de Saire★** : delightful countryside. ▶ **La Pernelle** : view★ of the whole E coast of the peninsula. ▶ **Saint-Vaast-la-Hougue**, renowned for oysters, faces the Ilot de Tatihou (citadel), linked by a dyke to the fort at La Hougue, built by the 17thC military architect Vauban. ▶ **Réville** : 11thC church and churchyard cemetery. ▶ Pointe de Saire *(2.5 km SE)* : view★. ▶ **Barfleur**, a yachting and fishing port★, formerly the main port for the Cotentin, and once used by Vikings and Anglo-Normans. ▶ **Gatteville-le-Phare** : view★★; from here, you can reach Barfleur point (lighthouse). ▶ **Tocqueville** : family home of Alexis de Tocqueville (1805-59), the author of *Democracy in America;* 15th-18thC château. ▶ **Saint-Pierre-Église** : 18thC château. ▶ **Fermanville** : view★ from Cape Lévy. ▶ **Tourlaville** : 16thC château; park★.   ☐

Practical Information _____

BARFLEUR, ✉ 50760, 27 km E of **Cherbourg**.
ℹ 60, rue St-Thomas-Becket, ☎ 33.54.02.48 (h.s.).

Hotels :
★★ *Phare* (L.F.), 42, rue St-Thomas-Becket, ☎ 33.54.02.07, 20 rm P ⋙ closed 10-25 Mar, 190. Rest. ♦ closed Mon and Sun eve (l.s.), 100-170.
★ *Moderne*, 1, pl. Gal-de-Gaulle, ☎ 33.23.12.44, Euro Visa, 42 rm P ⋙ closed Tue, Wed (Oct-Mar), 15 Jan-15 Feb, 125. Rest. ♦ ⌲ & 55-120.

⚶ ★★*Tamaris* (100 pl), ☎ 33.54.01.58.

BRICQUEBEC, ✉ 50260, 22 km S of **Cherbourg**.

Hotel :
● ★★ *Vieux Château*, (L.F., C.H.), 4, cours du Château, ☎ 33.52.24.49, Visa, 22 rm P ⋙ ⌲ closed 20 Dec-1 Feb.

2. The Cotentin peninsula

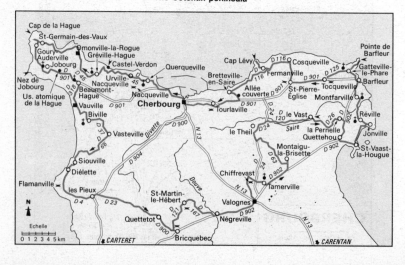

Medieval dwelling, 200. Rest. ♦♦ ♪ Spec : *moules au fumet, rognons de veau au cidre*, 70-140.

SAINT-VAAST-LA-HOUGUE, ⊠ 50500, 30 km E of **Cherbourg**.
ⓘ quai Vauban, ☎ 35.54.41.37 (h.s.); mairie, ☎ 33.54.42.52.

Hotel :
★★ *France* (L.F.), 18, rue Mal-Foch, ☎ 33.54.42.26, DC Euro Visa, 32 rm ░░░ ♪ 🦞 half pens (h.s.), closed Mon, 3 Jan-3 Mar, 200. Rest. ♦♦ *Fuchsias* ♪ ᶑ closed Mon and Tue noon. Spec : *homard au calvados, pâté de lotte sauce gribiche*, 50-150; child : 25.

COUTANCES*

Saint-Lô 27, Avranches 47, Paris 330 km
pop 13440 ⊠ 50200   A2

The original settlement was named for the Roman Emperor Constantine. One corrupted form of the name, "Cotentin", came to include the entire peninsula, whereas a second form was confined to the town. Today, Coutances blends the 20thC and the Middle Ages.

▶ The main churches were built along the major N-S street : St. Nicolas (16thC-17thC); the **cathedral**★★, with its two towers, a masterpiece of 13thC Gothic ; the church of St. Pierre, topped with an octagonal tower. Behind the town hall, the Morinière mansion houses a small museum of ceramics, painting and sculpture *(closed Wed.);* it opens on to the attractive public garden.

Nearby

▶ To the W, around the Sienne estuary : **Regnéville-sur-Mer** *(11 km SW)*, small port and seaside resort ; **Tourville** *(9 km W) :* birthplace and namesake of an unlucky admiral under Louis XIV (Manoir de la Vallée). **Agon-Coutainville** *(12 km W)*, one of the most popular resorts in the region. ▶ **Pirou** *(18 km NW) :* 12thC castle remodeled in the 17thC *(10-6:30 Jul.-Aug.; pm rest of year; closed 15 Dec.-15 Jan.;* in summer, display of modern tapestry, "The Conquest of Puglia and Sicily", inspired by the Bayeux Tapestry). ▶ **Lessay** *(21 km N)* grew around an abbey church founded in 1050 : Romanesque **church**★★ restored after WWII ; an important cattle-market (Foire de la Sainte-Croix) has been held here every Sep. for 1 000 years. ▶ Farther N : **La Haye-du-Puits**, close to **Mont Castre**, a pleasant excursion (view★). **Cerisy-la-Salle** *(14 km E) :* the 17thC **château** is now an international conference centre *(Thu. and Sun. pm, Jul.-Aug.; closed Tue.).* ▶ Ruined **Abbey of Hambye**★ *(22 km SE)*, founded in 1145 ; worth a visit ; conservatory of liturgical ornaments *(closed Wed. out of season).* ▶ **Gavray** *(18 km S)*, dominated by medieval fortress destroyed 17thC; Saint-Luc fair *(Oct.).*   □

Practical Information _____

COUTANCES
ⓘ Les Unelles, ☎ 33.45.17.79.
SNCF ☎ 33.45.17.54.

Hotel :
★★ *Grand Hôtel* (L.F.), pl. de la Gare, ☎ 33.45.06.55, Visa, 28 rm Ⓟ 180. Rest. ♦ ♪ closed Mon, 60-150.

Nearby

COUTAINVILLE, ⊠ 50230, 12 km W.

Hotels :
★★★ *Neptune*, ☎ 33.47.07.66, AE DC Visa, 11 rm ᶑ ᶑ closed 31 Oct-15 Mar, 230.
● ★★ *E. Hardy* (L.F.), pl. du 28-Juillet, ☎ 33.47.04.11, AE DC Euro Visa, 13 rm, half pens (h.s.), closed Mon (l.s.), 7 Jan-8 Feb, 420. Rest. ♦♦ ♪ ⚘ 65-200.

HAMBYE, ⊠ 50650, 22 km SE.

Hotel :
★ *Chevaliers*, Le Bourg, ☎ 33.90.42.09, DC Euro Visa, 6 rm 🦞 half pens (h.s.), closed Sun eve and Mon, Feb, 205. Rest. ♦ ♪ 60-120.

MONTPINCHON, ⊠ 50210 Cerisy-la-Salle, 13 km SE of **Coutances** on the D7 and D27.

Hotel :
● ★★★ *Château de la Salle* (R.C.), ☎ 33.46.95.19, AE DC Visa, 10 rm Ⓟ ░░░ 🦞 half pens (h.s.), closed . 3 Nov-23 Mar, 900. Rest. ● ♦♦ ♪ ⚘ A fine old residence in the heart of the Norman countryside, spec : *millefeuille de Saint-Pierre au beurre de cresson, délice du bois marquis*, 130-240.

TRELLY, ⊠ 50660 Quettreville-sur-Sienne, 12 km SE.

Hotel :
● ★★ *Verte Campagne*, 2 km, ☎ 33.47.65.33, AE Visa, 8 rm Ⓟ ░░░ 🦞 closed Sun eve and Mon (l.s.), 13 Jan-3 Mar. 18th-C farmhouse, 220. Rest. ♦♦♦ 60-180.

DEAUVILLE*

Caen 43, Le Havre 75, Paris 207 km
pop 4770 ⊠ 14800   C2

The horse racing, the *planches* (the famous boardwalk along the seafront) and the proximity to Paris have made Deauville the most popular seaside resort in Normandy.

▶ The **Promenade des Planches** runs the length of the 3-km beach ; **Port-Deauville** (A1) is a marina and yacht harbour at the mouth of the Touques. **Gardens**★, weekend houses and luxury hotels line the **Boulevard Eugène-Cornuché** (A1-2), while on the edge of town are the racecourse and the golf club; elegant houses on the slopes of **Mont Canisy** *(5 km from town centre; view★).*

Deauville to Honfleur *(16 km),* **the flowered coast**

▶ **Trouville** is a less exclusive resort than Deauville; comfortable middle-class houses stand on the hill looking out to sea. Facilities include a casino, a seawater therapy (thalassotherapy) centre and a bustling port. The **Ecological Aquarium**★ features marine reptiles *(daily Apr.-Sep.; pm Oct.-Mar.);* museum at the Villa Montebello (drawings, watercolours, 19thC paintings; *Sat. and Sun. pm, Easter-15 Jun.; daily pm ex Tue. in summer).* ▶ Honfleur (→).

Deauville to Cabourg *(18 km)*

▶ **Bénerville** and **Blonville-sur-Mer**, popular extensions of Deauville beaches. ▶ **Villers-sur-Mer** : invigorating walk along the sea wall. **Houlgate** : approx 2hr drive along the Falaises des Vaches Noires (Black Cow Cliffs)★. ▶ **Butte de Caumont** *(1 km S) :* a column commemorates William the Conqueror's embarkation in 1066 from **Dives-sur-Mer** : 14th-15thC church; 15th-16thC timbered market. ▶ **Cabourg** fans out from the main square, where the Grand Hôtel and the Casino look towards the sea ; turn-of-the century "Norman" country houses.   □

Practical Information _____

DEAUVILLE
ⓘ pl. de la Mairie (A-B3), ☎ 31.88.21.43, closed Sun (l.s.).
✈ *Deauville-St-Gatien*, 7 km E, ☎ 31.88.31.28.
SNCF (C3), ☎ 31.88.28.80/31.88.50.48.
Car rental : *Avis*, train station (C3).

Hotels :
● ★★★★(L) *Normandy*, 38, rue Jean-Mermoz (A-B3), ☎ 31.88.09.21, Tx 170617, AE DC Euro Visa, 325 rm ᶑ ░░░ ☞ 1000. Rest. ● ♦♦♦♦ There's action on the boardwalk. A young, dynamic crew headed by Martha and Lucien Barrière energetically perfect, restore and innovate for the greater pleasure of their guests. For the sportsminded, an indoor pool and health bar. For gourmets, the prestigious La Potinière restaurant, open year round.

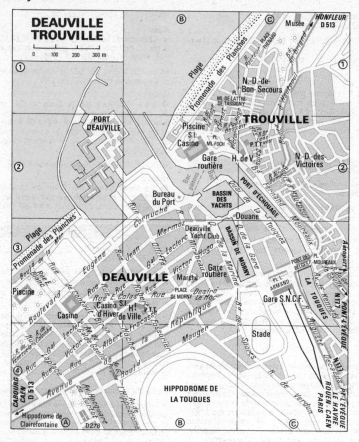

DEAUVILLE TROUVILLE

0 100 200 300 m

Jacques Baise and his team preside in the kitchen, producing light, delicate fare : *cristaux de tomates au saumon et caviar, crème de Meaux, effiloché de raie et joues de turbot* (stingy portion), *beurre de pois frais, canette au beurre de framboises*, local farmhouse cheeses, handsome desserts and splendid wines. Sampling menu for two. Gentlemen must wear ties ; a bit of a bore for summer luncheons, but play along and ask Lucien Barrière to lend you one with the hotel chain's colors. And also : La Table du Normandy (all-day service in summer). Throughout the year, there is a piano-bar, English-style tea with a pastry buffet (daily 3-6pm), brunch and a jazz trio (weekends and holidays). Sampling dinners centered on a fine wine. Low-calorie food available. A varied roster of courses and lessons. Foreign TV channels, 250-350.

● ★★★★(L) *Royal*, bd Cornuché (A3), ☎ 31.88.16.41, Tx 170549, AE DC Euro Visa, 314 rm ℗ ≼ ⬙ ◌ ♨ 𝄞 ▣ ↗ ✔ closed Oct-Mar, 1260. Rest. ● ♦♦♦♦ ≼ 𝄞 ⬙ ☆ Capable, seemingly ubiquitous manager Christian Meunier and his efficient staff are understandably proud of their achievements. If you are feeling flush, there's the Liz Taylor suite, or a costumed dinner with fireworks. Dinner-concerts with classical music. "Dream Weekend" : luxury room, orchid, foie gras, Champagne, 1000 F per person (l.s). "Agatha Christie Weekend" : participate in the unravelling of a mystery, 2995 F. Nor are the children forgotten : Miniroyal Nursery (10) and special children's menus. Giant poolside buffet. Talented Michel Beaujard and his brigade cook up lovely specialties that you can savour in the Etrier, or in the 19th-C setting of the Royal. Splendid

cellar. Piano-bar featuring rare whiskies. Sauna, hairdresser, jeweler. Foreign TV channels,

★★★★(L) *Club 13*, chem. de l'Orgueil, Tourgéville, 4 km, ☎ 31.88.63.40, Tx 171189, AE DC Euro Visa, 25 rm ℗ ≼ ⬙ ◌ 𝄞 ⬙ ▣ ↗ closed 4 Jan-6 Apr. Sauna, UVA, body-building, 800. Rest. ♦♦♦ 𝄞 ☆ 170.

● ★★★ *Golf, Mont Canisy*, 3 km S, ☎ 31.88.75.01, AE DC Euro Visa, 166 rm ℗ ≼ ⬙ ◌ ▣ ↗ ✔ closed 26 Oct-15 Apr, 800. Rest. ♦♦ 𝄞 A real paradise for ever-more-numerous golfers : a charming hotel right on the greens! Pool-side buffet. Excellent food and a club-like atmosphere, 100-150.

● ★★ *L'Aubergade* (L.F.), Canapville, ☎ 31.64.15.63, Euro Visa, 13 rm ℗ ≼ ⬙ ◌ half pens (h.s.), closed Wed, 15 Nov-30 Mar, 460. Rest. ♦ ≼ 𝄞 ☆ 60-150.

★★ *Continental*, 1, rue Désiré-Le-Hoc (B3), ☎ 31.88.21.06, AE DC Visa, 49 rm ℗ closed 15 Nov-15 Mar, 195.

★★ *Hélios*, 10, rue Fossorier (B3), ☎ 31.88.28.26, AE Visa, 44 rm 𝄞 ☆ ✎ ▣ closed 4 Jan-9 Feb, 360.

★★ *Le Trophée*, 81, rue du Gal-Leclerc (B3), ☎ 31.88.45.86, AE DC Euro Visa, 24 rm 𝄞 ☆ ✎ 390. Rest. ● ♦♦ *La Flambée* ≼ 𝄞 ☆ Pleasant Norman-style cooking ignited with a touch of Calvados : *étuvée de homard aux reinettes blondes, escalope de saumon à la moëlle*, 100-200.

Restaurants :

● ♦♦♦ *Les Ambassadeurs*, au Casino, rue E.-Blanc, ☎ 31.88.29.55 ℗ closed 16 Sep-15 Mar. Strong emotions make people hungry, and big winnings deserve a toast. Both eventualities are provided for by C. Girault and his kitchen staff. Classic offerings for dinner only. Galas and parties, weddings, conferences. Catering service, 350-450.

● ♦♦ *Ciro's*, bd des Planches (A3), ☎ 31.88.18.10, Tx 171873, AE DC Visa ⁂ ▥ ♪ Regulars can henceforth enjoy C. Girault's excellent cooking at lunch and dinner all year long : *langoustines rôties aux tagliatelles, fricassée de ris de veau sur feuille d'épinard aux pleurotes*, 160-300.

● ♦♦ *Grill*, Casino d'été, rue E.-Blanc, ☎ 31.88.29.55, 300.

● ♦♦ *La Malibran*, Casino d'hiver, 93, rue E.-Nicolas, ☎ 31.88.29.91 Seafood bar. Oysters to take out or eat on the spot. Wine-tasting dinners (a different wine with each course, with comments by a wine expert).

● ♦♦ *Spinnaker*, 52, rue Mirabeau (B3), ☎ 31.88.24.40, Visa ♪ closed Thu (l.s.) and Wed, 25 Feb-12 Mar, 16-30 Nov. Very good, but terribly slow service. Come on now, speed it up...and how about a smile? : *salade de pâtes aux crabes, langoustines tièdes, bar sauce anisette*, 75-200.

♦♦ *Augusto*, 27, rue Désiré-le-Hoc (B3), ☎ 31.88.34.49, AE DC Euro Visa ▥ ♪ ⅋ closed Mon and Tue (l.s.), 15 Jan-15 Mar. Lobster and more lobster. Stop in at the casino first, or else settle for a sandwich, 130-300.

♦ *Le Bar des Jeux*, Casino d'été, rue E.-Blanc, ☎ 31.88.29.55 From 3 pm until the betting stops, 300.

⚑ ★★★*Clairefontaine*, 5 km S. (260 pl), ☎ 31.88.14.06.

Recommended
Boat rental : at the port, ☎ 31.88.67.32.
Casino : *Casino d'Hiver*, 93, rue E.-Nicolas, ☎ 31.88.29.91, rest. : Le Malibran, dinner only Fri and Sat, 145-300; *Casino d'été*, rue E.-Blanc, (16 Sep-15 Mar), ☎ 31.88.29.55, "Make your bets... but betting makes one hungry, and winning calls for a toast." 3 rest : Ambassadeurs, Le Grill, Le Bar des Jeux.
Events : *Vintage car rally, Paris-Deauville*, in Oct; *American film festival*, in Sep; *yearlings sale*, late Aug; *horse-racing and polo*, in Aug; *world bridge festival*, in Jul.
Marina : *pleasure port*, Port Deauville, ☎ 31.88.56.16, 837 pl.
Night-clubs : *Melody*, 13, rue A.-Fracasse, ☎ 31.88.34.83; *Le Brummel's*, Summer casino. The lovely Roselyne greets the public daily from 1Jul to 15 Sep, and every Fri and Sat year round.
Thalassotherapie : *Centre Biotherm*, bd de la Mer. Hôtels Golf, Normandy et Royal, ☎ 31.98.48.11, cures, exercise and sports.
♥ bar : *Bar du Soleil*, bd des Planches, open from 9am to 6pm, 180. In season until 10.30pm; *Bar de la Mer*, bd des Planches, Focus on fresh seafood. Open from 9am to 6pm, 200.

Nearby

BLONVILLE-SUR-MER, ✉ 14910, 4 km SW.
ℹ allées des Villas, ☎ 31.87.91.14 (h.s.).
🚉 ☎ 31.87.92.24.

Hotels :
★★★ *Grand Hôtel*, (Mapotel), ☎ 31.87.90.54, AE DC Euro Visa, 25 rm ℗ ⁂ ▥ ⚲ 🖵 closed 15 Nov-15 Mar, 600. Rest. ♦♦ *La Brocherie* ⁂ & ⅋ closed Mon eve and Tue. Direct access to the beach, 120-300.
L'Escale, pl. de l'Hôtel-de-Ville, ☎ 31.87.93.56, AE DC Euro Visa, 3 rm ℗ ⁂ ⚲ half pens, closed Mon eve Tue and Wed, 15 Nov-28 Dec, 200. Rest. ♦♦ ⁂ ♪ & 85-150; child : 50.

⚑ ★★★*Lieu Bill* (100 pl), ☎ 31.87.97.27; ★★*Blonville Camping* (400 pl), ☎ 31.87.92.46.

CABOURG, ✉ 14390, 20 km SW.
ℹ Jardins du Casino, ☎ 31.91.01.09.
🚉 *Dives-Cabourg*, ☎ 31.91.00.74.

Hotels :
★★★★(L) *Pullman Grand Hôtel*, (ex Frantel), Jardins du

Casino, ☎ 31.91.01.79, Tx 171364, AE DC Euro Visa, 70 rm ℗ ⁂ ⚲ ♪ 660. Rest. ♦♦♦ *Le Balbec* ⁂ ♪ 140-240.
★★★ *Le Cabourg*, 5, av. de la République, ☎ 31.24.42.55, 7 rm ▥ ⚲ ⅋ closed Oct-Nov, 1 Jan-20 Feb, 10 Mar-10 Apr, 12-21 May, 320.
★★ *Paris*, 39, av. de la Mer, ☎ 31.91.31.34, 24 rm, closed Mon (l.s.), 220.

⚑ ★★★*Camping Plage* (283 pl), ☎ 31.91.05.75; ★★★*La Prairie* (433 pl), ☎ 31.91.03.35; ★★★*Vert Pré* (350 pl), ☎ 31.91.41.68.

Recommended
Casino : ☎ 31.91.11.75.
Events : *antiques show*, mid-Aug; *1000 sails regatta*, in Jul; *William the Conqueror festival*, parade of floats, late Aug.

DIVES-SUR-MER, ✉ 14160, 17 km SW.
🚉 *Dives-Cabourg*, ☎ 31.91.00.74.

Restaurant :
♦♦ *Guillaume le Conquérant*, 2, rue d'Hasting, ☎ 31.91.07.26, AE DC Euro Visa ⁂ ▥ ♪ & closed Tue eve and Wed , Dec. 17th-C half-timbered former coach house. Fish a specialty, 115-180.

⚑ ★★*Tilleuls* (266 pl), ☎ 31.91.25.21.

Recommended
Bicycle-rental : train station, ☎ 31.91.00.74, train + bicycle.

HOULGATE, ✉ 14510, 11 km SW.
ℹ bd des Belges, ☎ 31.91.33.09, closed Sat and Sun; rue d'Axbridge, ☎ 31.91.06.28 (h.s.).
🚉 ☎ 31.91.22.41.

Hotels :
★ *Auberge de la Ferme des Aulnettes*, rte de la Corniche, ☎ 31.91.22.28, 9 rm ℗ ⁂ ▥ ⚲ closed Tue (l.s.), 1-25 Oct, 25 Nov-20 Mar, 135. Rest. ♦ ⁂ & Enjoyable little Norman-style restaurant : *assiette océane sauce ciboulette, myrtillade de magret, goûters*, 100-180.
★ *Ferme du Lieu Marot*, 21, rte de la Vallée, ☎ 31.91.19.44, Visa, 11 rm ℗ ▥ ⚲ half pens, closed Wed, 5-31 Jan, 360. Rest. ♦♦ & Spec : *civet de lapin au cidre*, 85-140.
★ *Hostellerie Normande* (L.F.), 11, rue Emile-Deschanel, ☎ 31.91.22.36, Visa, 10 rm ▥ ⚲ half pens (h.s.), closed Mon eve and Tue, 1 Jan-15 Feb, 185. Rest. ♦♦ ♪ 80-150.

⚑ ★★★★*Falaises*, rte de la Corniche (100 pl), ☎ 31.91.09.66; ★★*Plage* (65 pl), ☎ 31.91.61.25.

Recommended
Bicycle-rental : *Garage Citroen*, ☎ 31.91.53.85.
Boat rental : *sté houlgataise des régates de la Dive*, ☎ 31.91.47.10.
Casino : rue Henri-Dobert, ☎ 31.91.60.94.

SAINT-GATIEN, ✉ 14130 Pont-L'Evêque, 7 km E.

Restaurant :
● ♦♦♦ *L'Aéroport*, ☎ 31.88.38.75, AE DC Euro Visa ⁂ ▥ ♪ & closed Tue eve and Wed, 15 Jan-1 Mar. An aero-club atmosphere, with a crackling fire. Pleasant food, with the focus on fish : *caille en chemise au calvados, blanc de turbot au champagne*, 90-250.

TOUQUES, ✉ 14800 Deauville, 3 km SW of **Trouville**.

Hotels :
★★★ *Amirauté*, (I.L.A.), on N 834, ☎ 31.88.90.62, Tx 171665, AE DC Euro Visa, 121 rm ℗ ⁂ ⚲ 🖵 ♨ 475. Rest. ♦♦ ♪ 130-200.

Restaurants :
● ♦♦ *Le Relais du Haras*, 23, rue Louvel-et-Brières, ☎ 31.88.43.98, AE DC Visa ♪ & closed Tue and Wed, 14 Feb-2 Mar. Where the chic horsey set meets to enjoy gourmet fare, 125-300.
♦♦ *Aux Landiers*, 90-92, rue Louvel-et-Brières, ☎ 31.88.00.39, AE DC Euro Visa ♪ & closed Tue eve and Wed, 90-140.

⛺ ★★★★*Le Haras* (250 pl), ☎ 31.88.44.84.

TROUVILLE-SUR-MER, ⊠ 14360, 2 km N.
ℹ bd Fernand Moureaux (C2), ☎ 31.88.36.19.
✈ *St-Gatien*, 7 km E.
SNCF ☎ 31.88.28.80/31.88.50.48.
Car rental : *Avis* (Voyage Fournier), pl. du Casino, ☎ 31.88.16.73.

Hotels :
● ★★ ***Carmen*** (L.F.), 24, rue Carnot (B2), ☎ 31.88.35.43, AE DC Euro Visa, 16 rm half pens, closed 4 Jan-4 Feb, 400. Rest. ♦♦ ♪ closed Mon eve and Tue. Spec : *huîtres pochées, mousse d'échalote, matelote du Chef*, 60-180 ; child : 40.
★★ ***L'Amiénoise***, 5, rue Bon-Secours (C1), ☎ 31.88.12.23, 12 rm, closed 15 Nov-15 Feb, 180.
★★ ***Reynita***, 29, rue Carnot (B1-2), ☎ 31.88.15.13, AE DC Euro Visa, 27 rm 🅿 closed Jan, 170.

Restaurants :
♦♦♦ ***La Régence***, 132, bd F.-Moureaux (C2), ☎ 31.88.10.71, AE DC Euro Visa ♪ closed Thu (l.s.) , Feb scool hols, 15-29 Dec. Spec : *fruits de mer, poissons*, 105-240.
● ♦♦ ***Le Galatée-Bar des Planches***, on the beach, ☎ 31.88.15.04, Euro Visa ♿ closed Thu ex Jul-Aug, 11 Nov-1 Apr. On the boardwalk, facing the sea, M. Vola serves hearty fare featuring seaweed-steamed fish and creations like *lotte aux morilles, foie de veau tranché épais rôti au four, bar en dauphine*. Excellent value. Relaxed atmosphere and friendly service, 140.
● ♦ ***Les Vapeurs***, 160, bd F.-Moureaux (C2), ☎ 31.88.15.24 ♿ closed Tue eve and Wed, 17 Nov-4 Dec, 5 Jan-6 Feb. Genuine 1950s decor in this seaside institution. Night and day, all year long, the same low prices, food cooked with butter, to your order... Try the live shrimp, the mussels, the fresh fish from Port-en-Bessin. Lively and crowded, 140.

⛺ ★★*Hamel* (100 pl), ☎ 31.88.15.56.

Recommended
Casino : pl. du Mal-Foch, ☎ 31.88.76.09.

VILLERS-SUR-MER, ⊠ 14640, 7 km SW.
ℹ pl. Mermoz, ☎ 31.87.01.18 (h.s.); mairie, ☎ 31.87.00.54.
SNCF ☎ 31.87.40.25.

Recommended
♥ Pork products : *Jacques Blavette*, 18, rue du Gal-de-Gaulle, ☎ 31.87.04.25, Boudins.

VILLERVILLE, ⊠ 14113, 8 km NE.

Hotel :
★★★ ***Manoir du Grand Bec***, ☎ 31.88.09.88, Visa, 10 rm 🅿 ♪ pens, 850. Rest. ♦ ♪ 125-180.

For a complete picture on the gastronomy featured in the Guide, see p. 8.

3. The D-Day landing

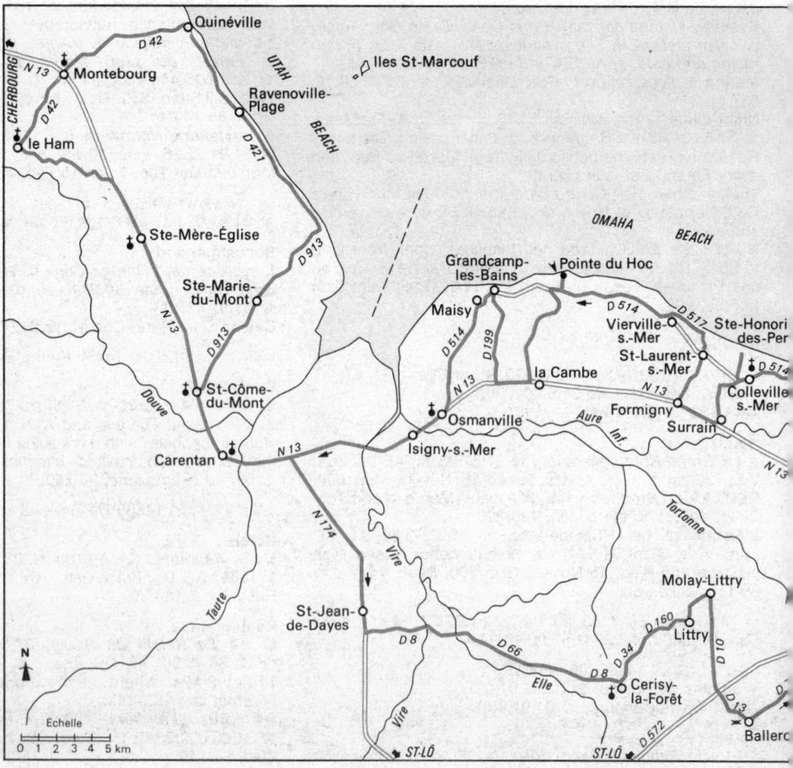

The D-DAY LANDING BEACHES**

Round trip from Caen *(approx 353 km, 2-3 days; see map 3)*

On 6 June 1944, Operation Overlord was launched on Normandy beaches, which were code-named Utah, Omaha, Sword, Juno and Gold. Thousands of soldiers died in the fighting, and many towns were destroyed. The suggested itinerary takes you to the beaches as well as through the quiet, friendly Norman countryside of churches, châteaux and manor-houses.

▶ **Caen** (→). ▶ **Merville-Franceville-Plage** : a long beach runs as far as the mouth of the Orne ; museum of the Melville Battery (artillery) in a former German pillbox *(daily Jun.-Sep.)*. ▶ Between **Ranville** (British cemetery) and **Bénouville** is the Pegasus Bridge over the Orne and its canal ; the double bridge was captured intact on the night of 5-6 June (Paratroop museum ; *daily ex Tue., Apr.-Oct.*). ▶ **Bénouville** : 18thC château by Nicolas Ledoux. ▶ **Ouistreham-Riva-Bella** : 12th-13thC **church** at Ouistreham ; 2-km beach at Riva-Bella ; museum recording the French battalion that liberated the town *(daily Jun.-Oct. ; Sat. and Sun., Palm Sun.-Jun.)*. ▶ **Colleville-Montgomery**, associated with the British Field-Marshal Montgomery (1887-1976), who commanded the 21st Army on D-Day ; his family originated in Normandy. ▶ **Hermanville-sur-Mer**, centre of operations for **Sword Beach**.

▶ **Lion-sur-Mer,** prolongation of family beaches at Riva-Bella and Hermanville ; château with Renaissance pavilion at Haut-Lion. ▶ **Luc-sur-Mer** : beach. ▶ **La Délivrande** : very old pilgrimage to the Virgin (19thC basilica) ; **Langrune** (13thC church★) and **Saint-Aubin-sur-Mer**. ▶ **Bernières-sur-Mer** (12th-14thC church★) and **Courseulles-sur-Mer** : Marvels of the Sea Museum (shellfish) ; the Canadian sector, **Juno Beach** ; the British prime minister Winston Churchill, the commander of the Free French Forces General Charles De Gaulle, and the British monarch King George VI landed between Courseulles and Graye-sur-Mer on 12-16 June 1944 to survey operations. ▶ **Ver-sur-Mer** *(2 km from the coast)* : Romanesque bell tower★ marking the E end of **Gold Beach**. ▶ After **Asnelles-sur-Mer,** panorama★ of the site of Arromanches and the remains of Port Winston where more than 1 000 000 Allied soldiers landed. ▶ **Arromanches**, fishing harbour among the man-made harbours built for the Landings (D-Day museum★). ▶ From **Longues-sur-Mer** (remains of 11thC Sainte-Marie abbey), you can reach the tumbled rocks of Le Chaos★. ▶ **Port-en-Bessin-Huppain**, small fishing harbour in a cove. ▶ **Tour-en-Bessin** : church (14thC choir★). ▶ Other notable churches at **Sainte-Honorine-des-Pertes** (13thC) and **Colleville-sur-Mer** (Romanesque). ▶ Beyond **Colleville-Saint-Laurent, American Cemetery★** (9 385 graves) overlooking **Omaha** beach, one of the most bitterly contested battlefields of 6 Junes 1944. ▶ Detour through **Formigny** 500 years back in history : the French liberated Normandy from the English here in 1450, ending the 100 Years' War. ▶ Between

beaches

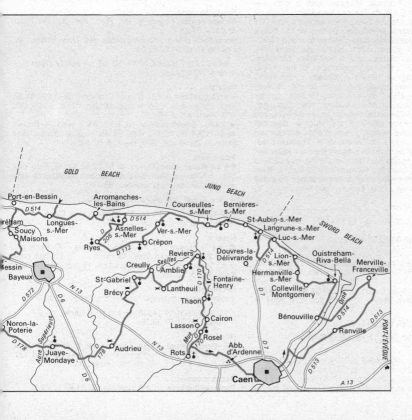

Saint-Laurent and **Vierville-sur-Mer**, the Maritime boulevard★, halfway up the cliffs, returns to Omaha Beach. ▶ After Vierville, **château d'Englesqueville** (17thC). ▶ 15-min walk from the D 514 : **Pointe du Hoc★**, an important German position still kept as it looked after the battle. Detour from here to the dramatically situated German cemetery at **La Cambe** (21 000 graves). ▶ **Grand-camp-Maisy**, a seaside resort and scallop-fishing port. ▶ **Isigny** : dairy produce (milk, cream, butter) and butter-scotch are the specialities here at the edge of rich dairy-farming country (the valleys of the Aure, the Tortonne, the Elle and the Vire). ▶ **Carentan** : Gothic church; milk-processing plant. ▶ **Sainte-Marie-du-Mont** : 11th-15thC church; remains of 15thC castel; **Utah Beach** where American troops also landed; Landing Museum *(daily, Easter-1 Nov. ; Sun. and nat. hols. in winter)*; La Madeleine and the Varreville dunes were the main landing points ; the beach stretches more than 20 km past **Quinéville**. ▶ **Montebourg** : liberation was particularly difficult; the 14thC church was spared in the fighting. ▶ **Sainte-Mère-Église**, one of the main American landings ; the start of the Freedom Road (Voie de la Liberté) is marked by the "O" sign in front of the town hall ; paratroop museum (Musée des Troupes Aéroportées ; *Sun. and nat. hols. in winter ; daily Easter-1 Nov.*). ▶ **Musée de la Ferme du Cotentin** (Farm Museum) set in a typical regional farm *(N 13 ; guest rooms; daily, Jul.-Aug. ; closed Tue. Easter-Jun. and in Sep. ; Sat. and Sun. pm in Oct.).* ▶ **Cerisy-la-Forêt**, on the edge of a large forest (22 km²) : former **abbey church★★** (late 11thC); museum *(Sun. and nat. hols. pm, 15 Mar.-Jul. ; daily ex Sun. am in summer).* ▶ **Molay-Littry** : mining museum★ recalls the creation of a coal mine here in 1743 *(daily ex Wed., Apr.-Oct. ; all day Sun. and pm Tue.-Sat. rest of year)* and milling museum at the Moulin de Marcy *(same hours);* château de Molay *(approx 2.5 km ;* 18thC structure now a hotel). ▶ The **château de Balleroy★★** one of the purest examples of Louis XIII style, built (1626-36) by François Mansart, with a park designed by Le Nôtre *(→ Ile-de-France :* Versailles); Museum of Ballooning *(Mar.-Oct. ex Wed. ;* international balloonists meet in Jun.). ▶ **Noron-la-Poterie** : pottery on the banks of the Drôme. ▶ **Juaye-Mondaye** : abbey founded 13thC, reconstructed 18th (organ, 1741), still in use *(visits pm).* ▶ **Audrieu** : 18thC château now a well-know hotel-restaurant. ▶ **Brécy** : terraced gardens★ at the 17thC château *(Easter-Sep. ex Wed.).* ▶ **Creully** : 12th-16thC fortified castle★ overlooking the valley of the Seulles; **Lantheuil** : noble 17thC château *(Jun.-15 Sep., pm ex Tue., Fri. ; sping and autumn, pm Wed., Sat., Sun., nat. hols.).* ▶ From the Canadian cemetery near **Reviers**, you can go up the pretty valley of the Mue. ▶ Beautiful **château de Fontaine-Henry★** : renaissance with carved decoration *(same hours as Lantheuil).* ▶ **Thaon★** : disused 11thC church in rustic setting on the river Mue ; ask for the key in the house next door. ▶ On the way back to Caen : **Lasson** (dilapidated Renaissance château); **Rots** (12th-15thC church); remains of **Ardenne abbey** (founded 12thC ; 13thC church) divided between two farms. □

Practical Information

ARROMANCHES-LES-BAINS, ⊠ 14117, 30 km NW of **Caen**.
ℹ pl. du Musée, ☎ 31.22.36.45 (h.s.).

Hotels :
★★ **La Marine** (L.F.), quai du Canada, ☎ 31.22.34.19, AE Euro Visa, 23 rm P ≶ closed 15 Nov-15 Feb, 165. Rest. ♦ ≶ ₺ 60-100.
★ **Normandie**, 5, pl. du 6-Juin, ☎ 31.22.34.32, Euro Visa, 21 rm P ≶ half pens, closed 10 Nov-5 Feb, 270. Rest. ♦ ≶ 50-80.

⅄ ★★**Municipal** (166 pl), ☎ 31.22.36.78.

AUDRIEU, ⊠ 14250 Tilly, 12 km SE of **Bayeux**.

Hotel :
★★★★ **Château d'Audrieu** (R.C.), ☎ 31.80.21.52, Tx 171777, Visa, 28 rm P ≶ ⋙ ⚘ ☐ closed 5 Jan-15 Mar. 18th-C château with a 25-ha park, 768. Rest. ● ♦♦♦ ≶ ₺ ⚘ closed Wed and Thu noon. The Livry-Level duo at

the Château, and Alain Cornet in the kitchen make a well-oiled team. Luxurious, refined dining, delicate fare : *salade d'huîtres, caneton au cidre,* great desserts, excellent cellar, 130-255.

CARENTAN, ⊠ 50500, 70 km NW of **Caen**.
ℹ pl. Valnoble, ☎ 33.42.05.87 (h.s.) ; Bureau de tourisme municipal, ☎ 33.42.33.54.
SNCF ☎ 33.42.04.00.

Hotel :
★ **Commerce et de la Gare**, 34, rue du Dr-Caillard, ☎ 33.42.02.00, AE DC Euro Visa, 16 rm P ⋙ closed 1-10 Oct, 22 Dec-22 Jan, 150. Rest. ♦♦ closed Fri and Sun eve in winter, 60-120.

Restaurant :
● ♦♦ **Auberge Normande**, bd de Verdun, ☎ 33.42.02.99, AE DC Visa, closed Mon and Sun eve, 1-15 Feb. Award-winning chef Gérard Bonnefoy (MCF) is one of Normandy's finest cooks, with a penchant for fresh seafood : St-Jacques en feuilles de chou, soupe de langoustines, sole au cidre, 90-200.

⅄ ★★★**Haut Dick** (120 pl), ☎ 33.42.16.89.

Recommended
Marina : ☎ 33.42.24.44, (500 pl).

COURSEULLES-SUR-MER, ⊠ 14470, 18 km NW of **Caen**.
ℹ 54, rue de la Mer, ☎ 31.37.46.80 (h.s.).

Hotels :
★★ **La Belle Aurore** (L.F.), 32, rue du Mal-Foch, ☎ 31.37.46.23, AE DC Visa, 7 rm ≶ ♪ closed Mon (l.s.), Feb, 220. Rest. ♦♦ ≶ ₺ 65-170 ; child : 35.
★★ **La Pêcherie**, 6, pl. du 6-juin, ☎ 31.37.45.84, Tx 171952, AE DC Euro Visa, 6 rm P ≶ closed Jan, 195. Rest. ♦♦♦ ≶ ♪ Seafood, 55-170.

⅄ ★★★★**Champ de Courses** (291 pl), ☎ 31.97.99.26.

Recommended
Bicycle-rental : *garage du Port,* rue du Mal-Foch, ☎ 31.97.97.21.
Horseback riding : *Club hippique des Trois Vallées,* av. Libération, ☎ 31.97.82.04.

GRANDCAMP-MAISY, ⊠ 14450, 57 km NW of **Caen**.
ℹ ☎ 31.22.62.44.

Hotels :
★★ **Duguesclin** (L.F.), 4, quai Crampon, ☎ 31.22.64.22, Visa, 26 rm P ≶ ⚘ ₺ closed 15 Jan-5 Feb, 15-25 Oct, 100. Rest. ♦ ≶ ♪ 45-120.
★ **La Grandcopaise** (L.F.), 84, rue A.-Briand, ☎ 31.22.63.44, AE DC Visa, 18 rm ⚘ pens (h.s.), closed Mon, 20 Dec-5 Jan, 320. Rest. ♦ 40-105.

Restaurant :
♦♦ **La Marée**, quai Chéron, ☎ 31.22.60.55, AE Euro Visa ≶ ⋙ ♪ ₺ closed Mon, 2-31 Jan. Spec : *panaché de lotte et de ris de veau aux morilles,* 65-130.

⅄ ★★**Joncal** (300 pl), ☎ 31.22.61.44.

ISIGNY-SUR-MER, ⊠ 14230, 58 km NW of **Caen**.
ℹ mairie, ☎ 31.21.46.00.

Hotel :
● ★★ **France** (L.F.), 15-17, rue E.-Demagny, ☎ 31.22.00.33, Euro Visa, 19 rm P ⋙ ⚘ ☐ half pens (h.s.), closed Fri eve and Sat lunch, 15 Nov-15 Jan, 380. Rest. ♦ ♪ ₺ 50-160.

Recommended
Youth hostel : *municipal stadium,* ☎ 31.22.00.03.

LUC-SUR-MER, ⊠ 14530, 16 km N of **Caen**.
ℹ mairie, ☎ 31.97.33.25.

Hotel :
★★ **Beau Rivage**, 1, rue Charcot, ☎ 31.96.49.51, Visa, 25 rm P ≶ ⚘ ♪ ⚘ half pens (h.s.), closed 25 Oct-1 Apr, 350. Rest. ♦ ≶ ₺ ⚘ 55-160 ; child : 35.

Recommended
Thalassotherapie : rue Guynemer, ☎ 31.97.32.22.

MERVILLE-FRANCEVILLE-PLAGE, ⊠ 14810, 19 km NE of **Caen**.
ⓘ ☎ 31.24.23.57.

Hotel :
● ★★ *Chez Marion* (L.F.), 10, pl. de la Plage, ☎ 31.24.23.39, AE DC Euro Visa, 18 rm Ⓟ ⪪ ⌕ closed Mon eve and Tue (ex school hols), 5-30 Jan, 6-22 Oct, 185. Rest. ● ◆◆ Freshly caught fish, beautifully prepared : seafood, lobster, turbot, game (in season), 100-280.

⚠ ★★★ *Le Pont du Jour* (150 pl), ☎ 31.91.30.31.

Le MOLAY-LITTRY, ⊠ 14330, 14 km W of **Bayeux**.

Hotel :
★★★ *Château du Molay* (R.S.), (Mapotel), rte d'Isigny, ☎ 31.22.90.82, Tx 171912, AE DC Euro Visa, 38 rm Ⓟ ⪪ ⑾ ⌕ ⅃ ⫘ ⊡ ⁄° closed Dec-Feb, 400. Rest. ◆◆◆ ⪪ ⅋ 140-220.

OUISTREHAM-RIVA-BELLA, ⊠ 14150, 14 km NE of **Caen**.
ⓘ pl. Alfred-Thomas, ☎ 31.97.18.63.

Hotels :
★★ *L'Univers* (L.F.), pl. du Gal-de-Gaulle, ☎ 31.97.12.16, Tx 170352, AE DC Visa, 30 rm Ⓟ ⪪ ⑾ ⅃ half pens (h.s.), closed 3 Dec-3 Jan, 250. Rest. ◆◆ *La Broche d'Argent* ⪪ ⅃ ⅋ Spec : *barbue aux huîtres, coquilles Saint-Jacques au safran*, 95-160.
● ★ *Le Saint-Georges* (L.F.), 51, av. Andry, ☎ 31.97.18.79, Visa, 21 rm Ⓟ ⪪ ⑾ ⌕ pens, closed 15 Dec-1 Feb, 390. Rest. ◆◆ ⪪ ⅃ 55-150.

⚠ ★★★*Les Pommiers* (453 pl), ☎ 31.97.12.66.

Recommended
Bicycle-rental : *Vérel*, ☎ 31.97.19.04.
Boat rental : *Serra Marine*, pleasure port, ☎ 31.97.17.41.
Casino : ☎ 31.97.18.54.
Marina : ☎ 31.97.13.05, 650 pl.

PORT-EN-BESSIN, ⊠ 14520, 36 km NW of **Caen**.

Hotel :
★ *La Marine*, quai Letourneur, ☎ 31.21.70.08, AE DC Euro Visa, 16 rm Ⓟ closed 30 Nov-8 Feb, 150. Rest. ◆ ⪪ ⅃ 70-200.

⚠ ★★*La Prairie* (185 pl), ☎ 31.21.70.06.

Recommended
Farmhouse-inn : at Colleville-sur-Mer, *Loucel* (8 km W on D154), ☎ 31.22.40.95, spec : *pâtés, tarte maison* and cider.

RANVILLE, ⊠ 14860, 12 km NW of **Caen**.

Hotel :
★ *Auberge des Platanes* (L.F.), 12, rue du Gal-de-Gaulle, ☎ 31.78.68.48, 7 rm Ⓟ ⪪ ⑾ ⌕ ⅋ closed 15 Oct-31 Dec, 200. Rest. ◆ ⪪ ⅃ ⅋ 110-150.

⚠ ★★*Relais des Sportifs* (93 pl), ☎ 31.91.29.05.

SAINT-AUBIN-SUR-MER, ⊠ 14750, 18 km NW of **Caen**.
ⓘ rue Pasteur, ☎ 31.97.30.41 (h.s.).

Hotel :
★★ *Le Clos Normand* (L.F.), Prom. Guynemer, ☎ 31.97.30.47, Euro Visa, 30 rm Ⓟ ⪪ ⑾ ⌕ ⅃ half pens (h.s.), closed Oct-Mar. Open All Saints' Day hols (1 Nov), 440. Rest. ◆ ⪪ ⅃ 65-140.

⚠ ★*Municipal* (40 pl), ☎ 31.97.30.24.

VIERVILLE-SUR-MER, ⊠ 14710 Trévières, 50 km NW of **Caen**.
ⓘ mairie, ☎ 31.22.42.66.

Hotel :
★ *Casino*, Trévières, ☎ 31.22.41.02, Visa, 13 rm Ⓟ ⪪ ⌕ closed Dec-Jan, 110. Rest. ◆ ⪪ 60-160.

Recommended
Chambres d'hôtes : at Trévières, *manoir de l'Hormette* (C.A.), 9 km S on D 517 and D 30, ☎ 31.22.51.79, 17thC farmhouse, 180.

DIEPPE*

Rouen 61, Le Havre 105, Paris 200 km
pop 36490 ⊠ 76200   D1

Popular with the English, who cross the channel to shop in the Dieppe supermarkets. The deep harbour has made the city an important port since the Middle Ages. Overtaken by Le Havre, it is still the fifth-largest port in France. 1.5 km of pebble beach ; casino.

▶ The Henri IV and Duquesne quays (B1-2) in the fishing and passenger harbours are the main centres of activity, together with the **Grande Rue** (A2 ; partly pedestrian, market every Sat.), linking the port to the château via the picturesque Place du Puits-Salé. A short distance away are the churches of St. Jacques (A2, 13th-16thC Flamboyant Gothic and Renaissance decoration) and St. Rémy (A2 ; 16th-17thC). ▶ **Château★** (A2 ; *closed Tue. out of season* ; partly 15thC, restored) has an interesting **museum★** of the town's maritime history (16th-17thC pilot maps) and carved ivories★, once a speciality of Dieppe ; also ethnography, archaeology, 19th-20thC paintings. ▶ Panorama★ from the Boulevard de la Mer, above the château. ▶ 2 km W of the town is the War Museum (Musée de la Guerre), commemorating the Canadian Landings in 1942 *(daily ex Mon., Easter-Oct.)*.

Nearby

▶ To the E : **Puys :** small sea side resort ; remains of Gallo-Roman fortress. ▶ Around **Berneval** *(11 km)* the cliffs rise 100 m out of the sea. ▶ Near **Penly** *(15 km)*, a nuclear power station with two reactors is due to be brought on line in 1989-90. ▶ To the W : **Varengeville** *(8 km)*, an elegant resort with beautiful gardens on a wooded plateau ; superb panorama★ from the church and cemetery (stained glass, tomb of the painter Georges Braque, 1882-1962) ; **Parc des Moutiers★**, planted in 1900, with the charm of an English private park *(daily Easter-Dec.)* ; farther off : **Manoir d'Ango** (16thC), beautiful dovecote. ▶ **Sainte-Marguerite-sur-Mer** *(12.5 km)*, a Canadian beach-head in 1942. ▶ **Arques-la-Bataille** *(7 km SE)* : the name ("battle") celebrates a famous victory of Henri IV in 1589 ; remains of a 12thC castle of the dukes of Normandy ; church (16th-17thC) with Renaissance choir-screen★ ; eastwards, State-owned forest. ▶ 17thC **château de Miromesnil** *(6 km SW)*, birthplace of the novelist Guy de Maupassant (1850-93 ; *May-Oct. pm ; ex Tue.*).   ☐

Practical Information ─────────────

DIEPPE
ⓘ bd du Gal-de-Gaulle (B3), ☎ 35.84.11.77.
🚆 (B3), ☎ 35.84.15.00/35.84.28.92.
⚓ *gare maritime* (Sealink), quai Henri-IV (B1-2), ☎ 35.82.24.87, to Newhaven, in 4 hr, all year round.
Car rental : *Avis*, train station (B3), ☎ 35.84.40.84.

Hotels :
★★★ *Aguado*, 30, bd de Verdun (B1-2), ☎ 35.84.27.00, 56 rm Ⓟ ⪪ ⅍ ⅋ 265.
★★★ *La Présidence*, 1, bd de Verdun (B1-2), ☎ 35.84.31.31, AE DC Euro Visa, 89 rm Ⓟ ⪪ ⅃ 340. Rest. ◆◆ *Le Queiros* ⪪ ⅃ Spec : *ris de veau braisé, pot-au-feu en croûte*, fish, 160.
★★ *Relais Gambetta* (L.F.), 95, av. Gambetta (A3), ☎ 35.84.12.91, AE DC Euro Visa, 18 rm Ⓟ ⪪ half pens (h.s.), closed 1-15 Oct, 305. Rest. ◆ ⅃ closed Mon eve and Tue (l.s.), 70-150.

Restaurants :
● ◆◆ *La Mélie*, 2 et 4, Grande-rue-du-Pollet (C2), ☎ 35.84.21.19, AE DC Visa ⅃ closed Mon and Sun eve , Feb. Guy Brachais serves appealing, top-quality regional fare. Fresh and smoked fish, 200.
◆◆ *La Marmite Dieppoise*, 8, rue St-Jean (B2), ☎ 35.84.24.26, Euro Visa ⅃ closed Mon, Thu eve, Sun eve, 21 Jun-5 Jul, 20 Dec-10 Jan. Spec : *choucroute du pêcheur, homard Delphine*, 60-170.
◆ *Le Sully*, 97, quai Henri-IV (B2), ☎ 35.84.23.13, Euro

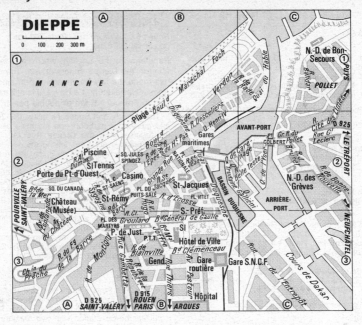

Visa ⚇ ♪ closed Tue eve and Wed, 15 Nov-15 Dec. Meals served on the terrace, 50-100.

⋏ ★★★*Le bois dieu* (35 pl), ☎ 35.83.62.19; ★★★*Vitamin'* (150 pl), ☎ 35.82.11.11; ★★*Pré St-Nicolas* (165 pl), ☎ 35.84.11.39.

Recommended
Casino : 3, bd de Verdun, ☎ 35.82.33.60.
Events : *Mid-August festival, carnival,* 15 Aug; *herring festival,* Nov.
Night-clubs : *Djinn's,* au Casino.
Thalassotherapie : ☎ 35.84.28.67, closed Jan.
Youth hostel : at St-Aubin-sur-Scie, 2 km, rue L.-Fromager-Janval, ☎ 35.84.85.73.
♥ chocolates-candy : *Ratel,* 115, Grande-Rue, ☎ 35.84.22.75.

Nearby

VARENGEVILLE-SUR-MER, ⊠ 76119, 8 km SW.

Hotel :
★★ *La Terrasse,* Vasterival, ☎ 35.85.12.54, 28 rm ℗ ⚐ ⚇
⚐ ⚘ ⚶ half pens (h.s.), closed 1 Oct-15 Mar. In a pine wood, 160. Rest. ♦♦ ⚐ ⚘ 60-100.

ÉVREUX*

Rouen 55, Le Mans 153, Paris 103 km
pop 48744 ⊠ 27000   D2

Capital of the Eure department, although built on the river Iton; rebuilt after WWII; manufacture of electrical equipment and accessories for the automobile industry.
▶ The **cathedral** (B1; 12th-17thC), with a post-war spire, has a rich collection of 13th-16thC stained glass★. Municipal museum★ in the former bishopric dating from 1481 (archaeology, history, ceramics, paintings; *10-12 & 2-5, 6 Sun.; closed Sun. am and Mon.*). Stroll along the ramparts★ by the Iton, between the cathedral and the Tour de l'Horloge (15thC clock tower, 44 m high).

Also... ▶ Former abbey **church of St. Taurin** (11th-15thC; A1) shrine★ of the patron saint with 13thC enamels.

Nearby

▶ **Acquigny**★ *(18 km N on N154)* : Renaissance château, situated at the junction of the Iton and Eure rivers. ▶ **Louviers** *(22 km N),* a former textile centre on the left bank of the Eure : 12th-13thC church of Notre-Dame★ with Flamboyant Gothic porch★; a few half-timbered houses; historical museum, Place Ernest-Thorel *(pm ex Tue.).* ▶ **La Couture-Boussey** *(26 km SE)* : museum of wind instruments and a local tradition of manufacturing recorders, flutes, oboes, clarinets *(pm ex Tue.).* ▶ **Ivry-la-Bataille** *(30 km SE)* : half-timbered houses; **Eure Valley.** ▶ **Pacy-sur-Eure** *(18 km E)* : antique shops, weekend houses. ▶ Near **Miserey** *(7 km E on N13)* : monument commemorating the first balloon-crossing of the Atlantic (Aug. 1978).
                                                            ☐

Practical Information _____

ÉVREUX
🛈 35, rue du Dr-Oursel (A1), ☎ 32.38.21.61.
SNCF (B2), ☎ 32.38.50.50/32.38.53.33.
Car rental : *Avis,* 9, rue P.-Sémard (B2), ☎ 32.39.38.07 ;
train station (B2).

Hotels :
★★★ *Normandie,* 37, rue Ed.-Feray (B1), ☎ 32.33.14.40, Euro Visa, 26 rm ℗ half pens (h.s.), closed Aug and Sun, 250. Rest. ♦♦ ♪ Spec : *feuilleté d'huîtres, fond d'artichaut aux foies blonds, rognons de veau au calvados,* 60-200.
● ★★ *France* (L.F.), 29, rue St-Thomas (A1), ☎ 32.39.09.25, DC Visa, 14 rm ℗ ⚐ ⚇ ⚐ ⚘ closed Sun eve and Mon ex hols, 200. Rest. ♦♦ ⚐ ♪ ⚘ Spec : *langoustines au beurre de carotte, terrine des 4 saisons et coulis de tomates au xérès,* 140-260.

⋏ ★★*Municipal* (100 pl), ☎ 32.39.43.59.

Recommended
Auction house : 29, bis rue Isambard, ☎ 32.33.13.59.
Baby-sitting : *Ecole d'infirmière,* ☎ 32.38.19.16.
Leisure activities : *Maison des jeunes et de la culture,* ☎ 32.39.16.24.

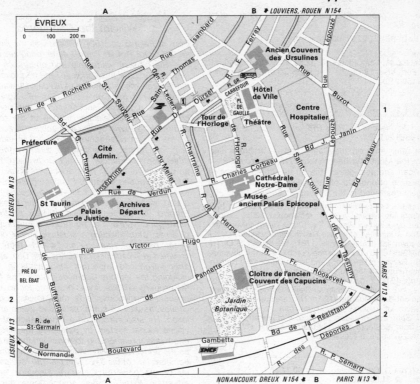

A   B   *♦ LOUVIERS, ROUEN N 154*

A   *NONANCOURT, DREUX N 154 ♦*   B   *PARIS N 13 ♦*

ÉVREUX

Nearby

DOUAINS, ☒ 27120 Pacy-sur-Eure, 6 km NE of **Pacy-sur-Eure** on the D181 et 75.

Hotel :
★★★ *Château de Brécourt* (R.C.), ☎ 32.52.40.50, Tx 172250, AE DC Euro Visa, 24 rm Ⓟ ≼ ▨ ◇ ♪ ⌀ 550. Rest. ● ◆◆◆ ≼ ♪ Warm welcome and modern cuisine in a 16th-C Château from Mrs Saury, Megean (in the kitchen), Travadon (pastry chef). Formal dinners on Friday evening : fresh fish, *filet de bœuf à la moelle*, 150-200.

IVRY-LA-BATAILLE, ☒ 27540, 35 km SE.

Hotel :
● ★★ *Au Grand Saint-Martin* (L.F.), 9, rue d'Ezy, ☎ 32.36.41.39, Visa, 10 rm ⌖ half pens, closed Sun eve and Mon, 350. Rest. ◆ ⅋ closed Jan, 160-170.

Restaurant :
◆◆◆ *Le Moulin d'Ivry*, 10, rue Henri-IV, ☎ 32.36.40.51, AE Visa Ⓟ ≼ ▨ ◇ ♪ ⅋ closed Mon and Sun eve, 26 Jan-27 Feb. Spec : *foie gras de canard, aumônière de la mer*, 120-250.

�† △ ★★★★*Isles* (140 pl), ☎ 32.64.55.77 ; ★★*Détente et Loisirs* (80 pl), ☎ 32.64.02.68.

LOUVIERS, ☒ 27400, 22 km N.
ℹ 10, rue du Mal-Foch, ☎ 32.40.04.41.
Ⓢ ☎ 32.40.01.50.

Hotels :
● ★★★ *Les Saisons*, (I.L.A.), rte des Saisons, Vironvay 1.5 km E, ☎ 32.40.02.56, DC Euro Visa, 15 rm Ⓟ ≼ ▨ ♪ ⅋ ⌖ ⌀ closed Feb, 16-24 Aug, 300. Rest. ◆◆ ≼ ♪ ⅋ closed Mon and Sun eve. Grilled lobster, 85-185.
★★ *La Poste*, 11, rue des 4-Moulins, ☎ 32.40.01.76, AE

Euro Visa, 16 rm, 180. Rest. ◆ ≼ ⅋ closed Mon and Sun eve, 50-140.
★ *Brasserie de Rouen*, 11, pl. Ernest-Thorel, ☎ 32.40.40.02, Euro Visa, 23 rm Ⓟ ◇ closed Sun, 22 Feb-8 Mar, 1-23 Aug, 135. Rest. ◆ 55-70.

Restaurant :
◆◆ *Clos Normand*, 16, rue de la Gare, ☎ 32.40.03.56, Euro Visa, closed Sun. Spec : *terrine de lapin au poivre vert*, 120-210.

PACY-SUR-EURE, ☒ 27120, 18 km E.
ℹ mairie, ☎ 32.36.03.27.
Ⓢ ☎ 32.36.13.03.

Hotel :
★★ *L'Etape*, 1, rue Isambard, ☎ 32.36.12.77, Euro Visa, 10 rm Ⓟ ▨ ◇ ⌖ closed Tue eve and Wed, 2 Jan-1 Feb, 155. Rest. ◆ ≼ ♪ 70-140.

Restaurant :
◆ *La Mère Corbeau*, 1, pl. de la Gare, ☎ 32.36.98.49, Visa Ⓟ ▨ ◇ ♪ closed Tue eve and Wed, 15 Jan-15 Feb. Spec : *foie gras frais de canard maison*, 90-160.

SAINT-PIERRE-DU-VAUVRAY, ☒ 27430, 5 km E of **Louviers.**

Hotel :
● ★★★ *Saint-Pierre*, (R.S., C.H.), 1, chem. des Amoureux, ☎ 32.59.93.29, Visa, 15 rm Ⓟ ≼ ▨ ◇ ⌀ closed 10 Jan-28 Feb, 320. Rest. ◆◆ ≼ ⌖ closed Tue and Wed noon. Spec : *saumon norvégien, méli-mélo de goujonnette de sole au citron vert, crêpes soufflées au grand marnier*, 140-210.

Restaurant :
◆◆ *Le Moulin de Connelles*, D 19, ☎ 32.59.82.54, closed Mon and Sun eve (l.s.), 7-27 Dec. As G. Dupalais wrote

in a local paper : "it's daily recreation!" Prices a bit steep, 300.

Le VAUDREUIL, ⊠ 27100, 27 km N.

Hotel :
★★★ *P.L.M.*, Les Clouets, ☎ 32.59.09.09, Tx 180540, AE DC Euro Visa, 58 rm ⓟ ▥ 🔍 ⚿ Ⴙ ⌧ 〜 320. Rest. ♦♦ 〉♪ 150-210.

FALAISE*

Caen 34, Alençon 67, Paris 216 km
pop 8820 ⊠ 14700   B3

Just after Ante on the Caen road — or better still, from the Mont Myrrha★ lookout *(15 min from C9)* — you can see at a glance the strategic importance of Falaise, a stronghold of the dukes of Normandy and largely destroyed in the fighting of August 1944.

▶ **Castle**★ where William the Conqueror was born in 1027 controls the terrain; a solid, rectangular 12thC keep is linked by a curtain wall to the 13thC Talbot tower *(daily ex Tue. in summer, Mon. and Tue. in winter; closed in Oct.).* The town hall (Hôtel de Ville, 1784), the church of La Trinité (13th-16thC; Renaissance porch★) and the churches of St. Gervais (11th-16thC) and Notre-Dame *(SE; Romanesque)* survived the fighting around the "Falaise pocket" in Aug. 1944. ▶ 9.5 km N, Brèche-au-Diable Gorge and beyond, **Soumont-Saint-Quentin** *(12 km N)* : farm converted into a museum of regional agriculture *(pm in season; Sat. and Sun. out of season; closed in winter).* 2.5 km NE from Soumont, the **château d'Assy**★ (1788) is a perfect example of Classical style.   □

Practical Information _____

ⓘ 32, rue G.-Clemenceau, ☎ 31.90.17.26.
SNCF ☎ 31.90.03.07.
▤ ☎ 31.86.55.30.

Hotels :
★★ *Normandie*, 4, rue Amiral-Courbet, ☎ 31.90.18.26, 28 rm ⓟ 180. Rest. ♦ closed Sun, 50-110.
★ *Commerce* (L.F.), rue de Falaise, Pont-d'Ouilly, ☎ 31.69.80.16, Visa, 15 rm ⓟ 〈 ▥ 🔍 closed Mon eve and Sun eve, 16 Dec-16 Jan, 100. Rest. ♦ ♪ 🔍 45-120.

Restaurant :
♦ *La Fine Fourchette*, 52, rue G.-Clemenceau, ☎ 31.90.08.59, Euro Visa ⓟ ♪ 🔍 closed Tue eve and Wed eve, 8-28 Feb, 1-10 Oct. Specialties of fish and seafood, 55-150.

⚠ ★★★★*du Château* (66 pl), ☎ 31.90.16.55.

FÉCAMP*

Le Havre 40, Rouen 71, Paris 214 km
pop 21700 ⊠ 76400   C1

A Benedictine town twice over : once for the former abbey and once for the Benedictine liqueur originally invented by the monks, rediscovered by Alexandre Legrand and still manufactured at Fécamp. The town no longer maintains a Newfoundland fishing fleet; the main industry today is fish and food processing.

▶ **Church of La Trinité**★★ (B2), 12th-13thC former abbey church the size of a cathedral (Renaissance additions, including the enclosures of the choir chapels); the municipal offices occupy the 18thC abbey buildings. Close by are the ruins of a 10th-11thC castle of the dukes of Normandy. ▶ Rue A.-Legros (B2) : museums and arts centre (fine arts, archaeology, history, folklore; *closed am in winter, and Tue.*). ▶ Just ahead are the **Benedictine Distillery and Museum**★ (A1) with a rich collection of medieval art objects *(daily Easter-11 Nov.; tastings).* ▶ Beyond, the port and church of St-Étienne (B2; Flamboyant

William the Conqueror

Born at Falaise ca. 1027, William was the illegitimate son of Duke Robert I and Arlette, daughter of a furrier. His gifts of leadership and endurance enabled him to overcome this handicap, and he proved one of the great soldier-statesmen of his day. He was a cousin of Edward the Confessor, King of England, who had chosen him as successor. At this period, the crown passed by election to one of the royal line, and the king's own choice was subject to acceptance by the Saxon witangemot, or council of elders. William had further enhanced his claim by forcing the other major contender, Harold Godwinson, to swear an oath in his favour when a shipwreck had enabled the neighbouring Count of Ponthieu (William's vassal) to capture Harold. This oath was subsequently repudiated as having been extracted under threat. When Edward the Confessor died, William proceeded to make good his claim to the throne of England by right of arms; after inflicting a crushing defeat on Harold at the battle of Hastings on 14 Oct. 1066, he was crowned at Westminster on Christmas Day, and thereafter introduced important innovations in England, including the famous Doomsday Book. The first written property census, it was drawn up for taxation purposes, listing woods, fields, mills, towns, houses and castles, as well as cattle, estimated yields and population. He also introduced a modification of the prevailing feudal system by extending the direct sovereign-vassal relationship to minor landholders as well as the principal nobility. William supported the educational system of his day : with his wife Matilda, daughter of the powerful Count of Flanders, he founded some thirty abbeys, among them the Abbaye aux Femmes and the Abbaye aux Hommes in Caen, where he was buried in 1087.

Gothic). On the cliffs N, the chapel of Notre-Dame-du-Salut (B1 ; 13th-14thC ; panorama).

Nearby

▶ Near **Bénouville** *(16 km SW ; GR21),* the cliff valley of Le Curé and the Belval Needle ; at 20 km, the **Falaises** (cliffs) **d'Étretat**★★. Falaise d'Amont : monument and a museum dedicated to the aviators Charles Nungesser (1892-1927) and François Coli (1881-1927) who died in the first attempt to cross the North Atlantic by air (8 May 1927 ; *Sat. and Sun. in spring ; daily in summer).* In town, 12th-13thC church of Notre-Dame. ▶ To the E : the seaside resorts of **Saint-Pierre-en-Port, Les Grandes Dalles** and **Les Petites Dalles** are separated by cliffs★ (GR21). ▶ **Valmont** *(11 km E)* : abbey ruins *(closed Wed. and Sun. ex school hols);* on the hill : 15th-16thC château with 11thC keep *(Sat., Sun. pm and Wed. pm in summer);* recreational area farther on. ▶ **Château de Bailleul**★ *(12 km SE ; daily Easter-1 Nov.)* : Renaissance building (art objects, paintings) in parkland.   □

Practical Information _____

FÉCAMP
ⓘ front de Mer, ☎ 35.29.16.34 ; pl. Bellet (B2), ☎ 35.28.20.51.
SNCF (B1-2), ☎ 35.28.03.11.
Car rental : Avis, 55-57, chem. du Nid-de-Verdier, ☎ 35.28.19.88.

Hotels :
★★ *Angleterre*, 91-95, rue de la Plage (A1), ☎ 35.28.01.60, AE DC Euro Visa, 30 rm ⓟ 〈 🔍 ⚘ closed 20 Dec-5 Jan, 200.
★★ *Auberge de la Rouge* (L.F.), Saint-Léonard, rte de

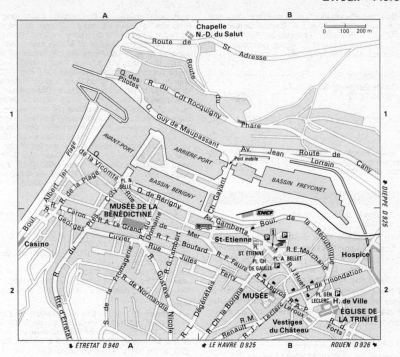

FÉCAMP

Goderville, ☎ 35.28.07.59, AE Euro Visa, 8 rm ℗ ⌂ ♪ ⅃ ♿ closed Sun eve and Mon, 220. Rest. ♦♦ ♪ ♿ 75-200; child : 35.
★★ **La Poste**, 4, av. Gambetta (B2), ☎ 35.29.55.11, Euro Visa, 35 rm ℗ Rest. ♦ ⌂ closed eves ex Jul-Aug, 65.
★ **L'Univers**, 5, pl. St-Etienne (B2), ☎ 35.28.05.88, Visa, 16 rm, 100. Rest. ♦ 80-130.

Restaurants :
♦♦ *Le Maritime*, 2, pl. Nicolas-Selles (A1), ☎ 35.28.21.71 ⅃ Nautical style. Grills, seafood, 65-150 ; child : 40.
♦♦ *Le Viking*, 63, bd Albert-1er (A1-2), ☎ 35.29.22.92, AE DC Euro Visa ⅃ closed Mon. Spec : *poêlée de morue fraîche et son aillade de pommes de terre*, 80-190 ; child : 40.
♦ *Martin*, 18, pl. St-Etienne, ☎ 35.28.23.82, Euro Visa ♿ ⌂ closed Mon and Sun eve, 15 Feb-2 Mar, 1-15 Sep. Spec : *morue fraîche au cidre*, 45-100.

⚐ ★★*Renéville* (350 pl), ☎ 35.28.20.97.

Recommended
Bicycle-rental : at the train station.
Youth hostel : rte du Cdt-Rocquigny, côte de la Vierge, 13, rue de l'Inondation (in summer), ☎ 35.72.06.45.
♥ chocolates : *Porée*, 5, rue A.-P. Leroux, ☎ 35.28.09.22.

Nearby
ÉCRAINVILLE, ⊠ 76110 Goderville, 13 km SE of **Etretat** on the D39, D139.

Hotel :
Château de Diane (C.H.), ☎ 35.27.76.02, 22 rm ℗ ⌂ closed Tue eve, Wed eve, Thu eve ex Aug-Sep, 425.

ÉTRETAT, ⊠ 76790, 17 km SW of **Fécamp**.
ℹ pl. de la Mairie, ☎ 35.27.05.21 (h.s.).

Hotels :
★★★ *Dormy-House*, rte du Havre, ☎ 35.27.07.88, 28 rm

℗ ⅃ ▩ ⌂ half pens (h.s.), closed 6 Nov-1 Apr, 580. Rest. ♦♦ ⅃ ⌂ 105-150.
★★ *Falaises*, 1, bd René-Coty, ☎ 35.27.02.77, 24 rm ⌂ 180.
★★ *Welcome*, 10, av. de Verdun, ☎ 35.27.00.89, Euro Visa, 21 rm ℗ ▩ ⌂ ♿ pens (h.s.), closed Tue eve , Wed, Feb, 295. Rest. ♦♦ ♪ ♿ 70-200.

Restaurant :
♦ *Roches Blanches*, terrasse Eugène-Boudin, ☎ 35.27.07.34 ⌂ closed Wed ,Tue, Thu (l.s), Oct, 5 Jan-5 Feb, 60-135.

⚐ ★★★*Municipal* (120 pl), ☎ 35.27.07.67.

Recommended
Bicycle-rental : filling station Total, av. Georges-V, ☎ 35.27.03.47.
Casino : ☎ 35.27.00.54.
Events : *Norman festival in May.*

FLERS

Argentan 45, Caen 57, Paris 238 km
pop 19405 ⊠ 61100   B3

Once a linen-weaving town that, in the 19thC, turned to processing cotton imported from the United States ; textiles are still an important industry. ▶ **Automobile Museum**, Place Saint-Jean. ▶ **Château★ :** 16th-18thC ; moat ; regional museum of Bocage-Normand, history and ethnography *(Easter-15 Oct. pm).*

Nearby
▶ **Cerisy-Belle-Étoile** *(8 km NW)*, at the foot of Mont de Cerisy (260 m), panorama ; feudal ruins ; rhododendrons in May-Jun.). ▶ 2.5 km E of **Sainte-Honorine-la-Chardonne** *(11 km NE of Flers)* : **château de Saint-Sauveur** (1641 ;

Sat. and Sun. pm, Easter-May; pm in summer; Sun. and nat. hols. in winter; closed Feb.). ► Beyond **Condé-sur-Noireau** *(12 km N of Flers)* : **château de Pontécoulant** (16th-18thC), regional museum (furniture, weapons; *daily ex Tue.; closed in Oct.*) ; fine park. □

Practical Information ────────────

ⓘ pl. du Gal-de-Gaulle, ☎ 33.65.06.75.
SNCF ☎ 33.65.74.79.

Hotel :
★★ *Galion*, 22, rue de la Gare, ☎ 33.64.47.47, Visa, 11 rm, 120.

Restaurant :
◆◆◆ *Le Relais Fleuri*, 115, rue Schnetz, ☎ 33.65.23.89, closed Sat eve and Sun, 20 Jul-20 Aug. Spec : *choucroute du pêcheur*, 200-250.

GISORS*

Beauvais 32, Rouen 58, Paris 70 km
pop 8860 ⊠ 27140   D2

Gisors was one of the most important fortresses on the river Epte, designed to keep a watchful eye on the French Vexin region in the days of the dukes of Normandy. ► Within the **castle**★ walls *(closed 15 Dec.-1 Feb.)*, the 11thC keep towers over the fortifications and gardens *(admission free)*. ► **Church of St. Gervais-St. Protais**★ (13th-16thC), restored after the destruction of 1940 : flamboyant Gothic doorway, Renaissance decoration. □

Practical Information ────────────

ⓘ pl. Carmélites, ☎ 32.55.20.28, closed Tue.
SNCF ☎ 32.55.01.30.

Hotels :
★★★ *Château de la Rapée*, (R.S., C.H.) Bazincourt-sur-Epte, 3.5 km N, ☎ 32.55.11.61, AE DC Visa, 10 rm ℗ ⚍ ⚭ half pens, closed Wed, 15 Jan-1 Mar, 16-30 Aug, 515. Rest. ◆◆ ⚍ ♨ Spec : *terrine de foie gras de canard aux pistaches, gratin d'écrevisses*, 115-220.
★★ *Moderne* (L.F.), pl. de la Gare, ☎ 32.55.23.51, Euro Visa, 33 rm ℗ ♪ ⚭ 225. Rest. ◆ closed Mon and Sun eve, 14 Jul-7 Aug, 20 Dec-7 Jan, 50-200.

GRANVILLE*

Rennes 101, Caen 107, Paris 349 km
pop 15015 ⊠ 50400   A3

A healthy climate and a fine site have made Granville one of Normandy's most popular seaside resorts since the 19thC ; it is also a busy port for commercial, fishing and pleasure craft.

► The **upper town**★ (A1, antique shops) ; the fortifications date from 1720. The Logis du Roi (King's Lodge), behind the Grande Porte, is now the Museum of Old Granville (history, folklore and the sea ; *daily in season ex Tue. ; Wed. pm, Sat. and Sun. rest of year*) ; church of Notre-Dame (A1 ; 15th-18thC) ; Marine Aquarium *(daily, Palm Sunday-1 Nov.)*. ► View★ from the Point of the Roc ; a path► runs down to the port. ► **Historial granvillais**, 39, Rue de Couraye (B1) : wax museum.

Nearby

► **Chausey Islands**★ : more than 300 islets at low tide, fewer than 50 at high tide *(reached from Grande-Île)*, these are the only French islands in the Channel. ► The **Abbey of Lucerne** *(12 km SE)* has buildings dating from 1164 and later, some remodeled in the 17th and 18thC *(daily)*. ► **Champrepus** *(20 km E)* : **zoological park**. ► **Villedieu-les-Poêles** *(28 km E)* : a metalworking tradition revealed in the variety of metal souvenirs and other goods on sale ; bell foundry (13, Rue du Pont-Chignon : 19thC

workshop) ; musée de la Poêlerie ; Lacemaker's house (museum of cooking ware ; Cours du Foyer, *Jun.-15 Sep.*) ; **church of Notre-Dame** : a 15thC dependency of the Order of the Knights of Malta ; every four years in June there is a ceremony for dignitaries of the order (1987), alternating with a flower festival (1989). ► **Carolles-Plage** (beach) and **Carolles-Bourg** *(11 km)* : 12th-13thC church, view★ from Pignon Butor and the Cabane Vauban to the bay of Mont-Saint-Michel. ► **Champeaux** *(15 km)* : view over the bay of Mont-Saint-Michel ; exhibit of local fauna *(Jun.-Sep.)*. ► **Avranches** *(34 km)* : view★ to Mont-Saint-Michel from the Jardin des Plantes★ (botanical garden). The museum in the former episcopal palace, Place St.-Avit, displays precious manuscripts★ (8th-16thC) from Mont-Saint-Michel abbey ; also examples of Norman folklore and crafts *(daily ex Tue., Easter-Sep.)*. The monument to General George Patton (1885-1945) stands in a square that is now United States territory. ► Beyond Avranches, D75 runs beside salt meadows ; views of Mont-Saint-Michel. □

Practical Information ────────────

GRANVILLE
ⓘ 15, rue G.-Clemenceau (B1), ☎ 33.50.02.67.
SNCF (C1), ☎ 33.57.50.50.
🚍 cours Jonville (B2) ; pl. de la Gare (C1), ☎ 33.50.08.99.
Car rental : *Avis,* train station.
⚓ to Chausey and Jersey Islands Oct-May : Wed and Sat ; May-Oct : daily ; info : 33.50.15.56 and 33.50.31.81.

Hotels :
★★★ *Bains*, 19, rue G.- Clemenceau (B1), ☎ 33.50.17.31, Tx 214235, AE DC Euro Visa, 58 rm ⚍ ♪ᵒ ⚭ closed 1 Jan-7 Feb, 230. Rest. ◆◆ *La Potinière* ⚍ ♪ ౬ 75-140.
● ★★ *Normandy Chaumière* (L.F.), 20, rue Paul-Poirier (B1), ☎ 33.50.01.71, AE DC Euro Visa, 7 rm ⚍ ◑ pens (h.s.), closed Tue eve, Wed, Feb school hols, 1-21 Oct, 490. Rest. ◆ ♪ ౬ Spec : *Saint-Jacques aux poireaux, lotte à la fondue normande*, 65-120.

Restaurant :
◆◆ *Le Phare*, 11, rue du Port (A-B1), ☎ 33.50.12.94, AE DC Euro Visa ℗ ⚍ ♪ ౬ closed Wed eve and Thu, 15 Dec-30 Jan. Panoramic sea view. Spec : *andouillette de turbot au beurre blanc, papillote de Saint-Pierre au fenouil*, 60-140 ; child : 35.

Recommended
Events : *carnival,* in spring ; *"pardon" of seamen's guilds,* the Libération : last Sun in Jul.
Guided tours : info. S.I.
Marina : ☎ 33.50.20.06, 800 pl.
♥ fresh lobsters : *Louis Lapie*, 26, rue du Port.

Nearby

AVRANCHES, ⊠ 50300, 33 km SE.
ⓘ rue du Gal-de-Gaulle, ☎ 33.58.00.22.
SNCF ☎ 33.58.00.77.

Hotels :
● ★★ *La Croix d'Or*, 83, rue de la Constitution, ☎ 33.58.04.88, Visa, 30 rm ℗ ▦ ⚭ ౬ closed 15 Nov-15 Mar, 180. Rest. ◆◆ ⚍ ౬ Spec : *rillettes aux deux saumons, lotte aux petits légumes*, 80-160.
★★ *Auberge Saint Michel*, 7, pl. Gal-Patton, ☎ 33.58.01.91, Visa, 22 rm ℗ ▦ half pens (h.s.), closed Sun eve and Mon, 15 Nov-31 Mar, 185. Rest. ◆ Spec : *huîtres de la baie, agneau de pré-salé.* Good value, 60-165.

Recommended
Leisure activities : flight over Mont-Saint-Michel, aéroclub des Grèves du Mont-Saint-Michel, ☎ 33.58.02.91.

BRÉVILLE-SUR-MER, ⊠ 50290 Bréhal, 4 km NE.

Hotels :
★★★ *La Mougine des Moulins à Vent*, dir. Coutances on the D 971, ☎ 33.50.22.41, Euro Visa, 7 rm ℗ ⚍ ⚭ 250.
● ★★ *Auberge des Quatre-Routes* (L.F.), Bréhal, ☎ 33.50.20.10, DC Visa, 7 rm, closed Tue eve and Wed,

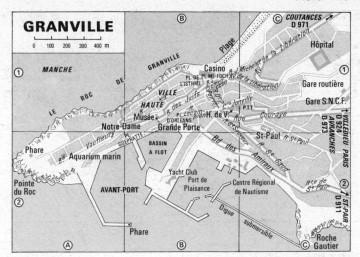

GRANVILLE

0   100   200   300   400 m

1 Jan-2 Apr, 2 Nov-31 Dec, 120. Rest. ♦ ♪ & closed 2-25 Mar, 14-30 Dec, 40-100.

DUCEY, ⊠ 50220, 10 km SE of **Avranches.**

Hotel :
● ★★ *Auberge de la Selune* (L.F.), 2, rue Saint-Germain, ☎ 33.48.53.62, DC Euro Visa, 20 rm Ⓟ ໝ 🅱 half pens (h.s.), closed Mon, 1-25 Dec, 145. Rest. ♦♦ 50-90.

PONTAUBAULT, ⊠ 50220 Ducey, 7 km S of **Avranches.**

Hotel :
● ★★ *Motel des Treize Assiettes* (L.F.), Le-Val-St-Père, ☎ 33.58.14.03, Tx 170537, Visa, 36 rm Ⓟ ໝ △ & closed Wed (l.s.), 15 Nov-15 Mar, 120. Rest. ♦ ♪ & 50-125 ; child : 40.

VILLEDIEU-LES-POÊLES, ⊠ 50800, 28 km E.
ⓘ pl. des Costils, ☎ 33.61.05.69 (h.s.).
SNCF ☎ 33.61.00.30.

Hotel :
● ★★ *Saint-Pierre-et-Saint-Michel* (L.F.), 12, pl. de la République, ☎ 33.61.00.11, 23 rm Ⓟ 🅱 closed 26 Dec-15 Jan, 150. Rest. ♦ ♪ & 40-140.

Restaurant :
♦♦ *Crêperie des Chevaliers*, 6, pl. des Chevaliers-de-Malte, ☎ 33.61.07.94, Euro Visa 🍴 ♪ closed Mon, 15 Nov-15 Jan, 45-70.

⚑ ★★★*Pré de la rose* (100 pl), ☎ 33.61.02.44.

Recommended
Chambres d'hôtes : at Percy, 9.5 km N on the D 999, *le Bois Normand,* ☎ 33.61.23.62.

Le HAVRE*

Rouen 88, Caen 108, Paris 205 km
pop 198760 ⊠ 76600   C2

A lively seaport enhanced by the forest of Montgeon and the hills of Sainte-Adresse, Mont Gaillard and Graville, their natural beauty compensating for the cold 20thC architectural style of Auguste Perret who redesigned the city after WWII. Founded on the Seine estuary in the 16thC by François I, Le Havre is a port second in importance only to Marseilles.

▶ The **Place de l'Hôtel de Ville** (B2 ; 72-m bell tower) is linked by Avenue Foch (A2) to the Ocean Gate (Porte Océane), symbolized by two L-shaped structures that

separate it from the sea. ▶ **Church of St. Joseph★** (A2), an immense building with a bell tower 106 m high ; more attractive from the inside. ▶ The light-filled **André Malraux Fine Arts Museum** has a rich collection of 16th-20thC paintings★ (several works by Boudin, → box ; *closed Tue. and nat. hols.*). ▶ Much of the Natural History Museum has been rehoused in the former courthouse (Palais de Justice, 18thC ; rebuilt on Place du Vieux-Marché at the foot of Rue Notre-Dame ; B3 ; *10-12 & 2-6, closed Tue. and hols.*). ▶ **Cathedral of Notre-Dame** (1574-1630 ; B3), one of the city's oldest monuments. ▶ At Place Gambetta : cultural centre★ **(Espace Culturel Oscar Niemeyer ;** B2, partly underground ; exhibition halls, shopping arcade, theatre ; inaugurated 1981). ▶ The Bassin du Commerce (B2 ; international trade centre, 1982) separates the Bourse (stock exchange) from the Île-Saint-François, formerly the main unloading dock ; 16th-17thC church of St. François and **Old Le Havre Museum** (Musée de l'Ancien Havre ; B2 ; *closed Mon., Tue. and nat. hols.* ; history and navigation).

Also... ▶ Boat trip around the port★ *(Easter-15 Sep. ; embark at the yacht harbour,* A2) including the harbour basins and the François I lock, 400 m long. ▶ **Sainte-Adresse** is an elegant part of town between the beach and the hill, crowned by the chapel of Notre-Dame-des-Flots (view★) ; lookout at Cap de La Hève★. ▶ Archaeological museum in a former priory (11thC nave and transept) in **Graville,** to the E *(closed Mon., Tue.).*

Nearby

▶ **Harfleur** *(6 km E),* a port founded by the Romans, superseded by Le Havre. The areas around the church of St. Martin (15th-16thC ; spire★) and the town hall (Hôtel de Ville, 1650) recall the medieval English occupation of western France ; museum in Harfleur Priory *(10-12 & 3-6, Sun. ; pm ex Mon., Tue. and hols.).* ▶ View★ of the oil refinery and Seine estuary from the terrace of the **château d'Orcher** above Gonfreville *(9 km ; pm ex Tue., Thu., Sat., Jul.-Sep.).* ▶ **Rouelles** : 370-acre leisure park ; 16th, 17thC La Bouteillerie Farm on landscaped site ; 27-acre Arboretum (200 varieties of trees). ▶ 22 km E, **Saint-Jean d'Abbetot** : 12th, 16thC frescos in church. ▶ **Montivilliers** *(11 km NE)* : 11th-15thC abbey church★ *(8-12 & 2-5 ; closed Sun. pm).* ▶ Near **Gommerville** *(24 km on D31),* château de Filières★ (16th-18thC ; *Easter-1 Nov., Wed., Sat., Sun. pm);* park by Le Nôtre. ▶ **Havre-Antifer** *(22 km N),* oil port built in 1973-1975 and protected by a dyke projecting 3500 m from the cliff.   □

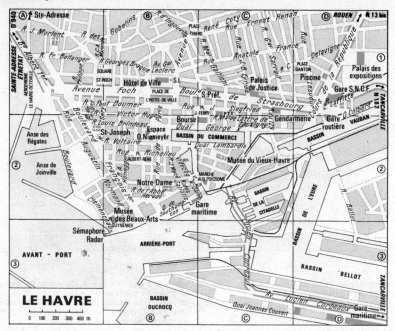

LE HAVRE

0　100　200　300　400 m

Practical Information _____

Le HAVRE
ⓘ pl. de l'Hôtel-de-Ville (B2), ☎ 35.21.22.88, closed
Sun (l.s.).
✈ *Octeville*, 6 km NW, ☎ 35.46.09.81.
SNCF (D1), ☎ 35.43.50.50/35.24.01.76.
🚌 4, rue C.-Laffite (D2), ☎ 35.26.67.23.
⚓ *Irish Continental Line*, rte du Môle Central
(off map D3), ☎ 35.21.55.02, to Rosslare and Cork; *P.O.*,
quai de Southampton (B3), ☎ 35.21.36.50, to Portsmouth.
Car rental : *Avis*, 37, av. du Gal-Archinard, ☎ 35.41.74.11 ;
train station ; 12, rue Magellan (D1), ☎ 35.53.17.20.

Hotels :
★★★ *Bordeaux*, 147, rue Louis-Brindeau (B2),
☎ 35.22.69.44, Tx 190428, AE DC Euro Visa, 31 rm ⊀ ♪
⚘ 330.
★★ *Foch*, 4, rue de Caligny (A1-2), ☎ 35.42.50.69,
Tx 190369, AE Euro Visa, 33 rm ⊀ ᕮ ⚘ 200.
★★ *Monaco*, 16, rue de Paris (B2), ☎ 35.42.21.01, AE DC
Euro Visa, 10 rm ⊀ closed 15 Feb-1 Mar, 1-15 Sep, 205.
Rest. ♦♦ closed Mon ex Jul-Aug and hols. Classic dishes.
Spec : *canard au vinaigre de xérès*, 90-200.
★★ *Parisien*, 1, cours de la République (D1),
☎ 35.25.23.83, Tx 190369, AE DC Euro Visa, 22 rm ℗ ⊀
♪ closed 20 Dec-5 Jan, 220.
★ *Ile de France*, 104, rue Anatole-France (C1),
☎ 35.42.49.29, Euro Visa, 16 rm 🛏 85.
★ *Voltaire*, 14, rue Voltaire (B2), ☎ 35.41.30.91, Visa,
24 rm ℗ ᕮ 120.

Restaurants :
● ♦♦ *La Chaumette*, 17, Rue Racine, ☎ 35.43.66.80, AE
DC Visa, closed Sat and Sun, 17-27 Apr, 7 Aug-1 Sep,
22 Dec-2 Jan. Mouth-watering fish specialties are chalked
up on the board by Christine Frechet in her darling little
eatery, 85-165.
♦♦ *La Manche*, 18, bd Albert-1er (A1), ☎ 35.41.20.13, AE
DC Euro Visa ℗ ⊀ ♪ closed Mon and Sun eve , Jul. A nautical theme is featured here, to clue you about the seafood
specialities : grilled sole with zucchini, shellfish, 105-250.

🌲 ★★★★*Forêt de Montgeon* (266 pl), ☎ 35.46.52.39.

Recommended
Events : *Corso Fleuri*, Sun after 15 Aug ; *international
regatta*, in Jul ; *sea festival*, in May.
Marina : ☎ 33.45.01.35, 130 pl.
Sports : *aéro-club du Havre "Jean Maridor"*,
☎ 35.48.35.91.

Nearby

SAINTE-ADRESSE, ✉ 76310, 3 km NW.

Restaurant :
♦♦♦ *Le Nice Havrais*, 6, pl. Frédéric-Sauvage,
☎ 35.46.14.59, AE Euro Visa ℗ ⊀ ᕮ ᕮ closed Mon eve
and Sun eve , in Aug. Dining room with a sea view. Spec :
*caneton à l'ananas et au pamplemousse, médaillon de
langouste et ris de veau sauce estragon*, 75-225.

HONFLEUR★★★

Le Havre 57, Caen 63, Paris 192 km
pop 8530 ✉ 14600　　　　　　　　　　　　　　　C2

The historic port of Honfleur is clearly centuries older
than Le Havre, on the other side of the Seine estuary.
▶ **Vieux Bassin★★** (old port ; B-C1), lined with houses
of wood and slate ; in front of it, the Lieutenance (C2),
the former governor's residence. **Old Honfleur Museum★**
(Musée du Vieux Honfleur) in the church of St. Étienne
(14th-15thC) and the 16thC house next door (C2 ; ethnography, folk art, local shipping ; *closed weekdays out of
season)*. ▶ The unique church of **St. Catherine★★** (15thC,
B2) was built of wood, except for the foundations, by the
port's master shipwrights at the end of the 100 Years'
War ; two parallel naves ; separate bell tower ; annex of
the **Boudin Museum★**, (B2 ; *closed Tue. and am out of
season ex Sat. and Sun., and in Jan.*) : 60 paintings and
pastels by the painter, plus works by Impressionists and
modern painters who stayed in Honfleur ; Norman costumes and headdresses. ▶ The farm of St. Siméon
(route A. Marais, A1), a meeting place for the Impression-

ists, now a luxury hotel. ▶ View★ from the Côte de Grâce (A1); chapel of Notre-Dame-de-Grâce (1615). ▶ Saint-André-d'Hébertot *(16 km S)* : pleasant moated 17th-18thC château★. □

Practical Information

HONFLEUR
ⓘ 33, cours des Fossés (C3), ☎ 31.89.23.30.
SNCF (off map C3), ☎ 31.89.04.92.
🚗 pl. de la Porte-de-Rouen, ☎ 31.89.28.41.

Hotels :
● ★★★★ *La Ferme Saint-Siméon* (R.C.), rue Adolphe-Marais (A1), ☎ 31.89.23.61, Tx 171031, Euro Visa, 38 rm Ⓟ ⧉ 𝟸 & 🐾 940. Rest. ◆◆◆ ⧉ closed Wed noon , Nov-Mar ex hols. Pricey, erratic cuisine, 180-350.
★★★ *Hostellerie Lechat*, 3, pl. Ste-Catherine (B2), ☎ 31.89.23.85, 26 rm, closed Wed-Thu lunch (l.s.) ex hols, 15 Nov-15 Mar, 330. Rest. ◆◆ closed 15 Nov-15 Mar. Spec : fish, shellfish, 90-200.
★★★ *Le Cheval Blanc*, 2, quai des Passagers (C2), ☎ 31.89.13.49, 35 rm Ⓟ ⧉ 𝟸 half pens, closed 15 Nov-1 Feb, 640. Rest. ◆◆ ⧉ closed Mon. Luxurious Louis-XIII decor in a 15th-C post house, high-quality service and food : *paupiettes de bar aux langoustines, fromages normands*, 160-250.
★★ *Dauphin*, 10, pl. Pierre-Berthelot (B2), ☎ 31.89.15.53, Visa, 30 rm 𝟸 closed 2 Jan-2 Feb, 190.
★ *Ferme de la Grande Cour* (L.F.), Côte de Grâce (off map A2), ☎ 31.89.04.69, AE Visa, 13 rm Ⓟ ⧉ 𝟸 half pens (h.s.), closed Jan, 340. Rest. ◆ 𝟸 closed Wed, 60-120.

Restaurant :
● ◆◆ *L'Absinthe*, 10, quai de la Quarantaine (C2), ☎ 31.89.39.00, AE DC Visa ⧉ & closed Mon eve and Tue ex 1 Jul-15 Sep, 12 Nov-20 Dec. Enjoyable grilled dishes in a 17th-C setting, 105-200.

⚠ ★★★★*La Briquerie*, Equemauville, 3.5 km S (133 pl), ☎ 31.89.28.32.

Recommended
Bicycle-rental : *M. Grégory*, 12, quai Lepaulmier, ☎ 31.89.34.66.
Events : *artists' salon, music festival*, in Jul; *Pentecost : blessing of the sea*, seamen's pilgrimage.
♥ 18 kinds of bread : *La Panetière*, 30, rue Montpensier.

Nearby
BEUZEVILLE, ✉ 27210, 13 km SE.

Hotel :
★★ *Le Cochon d'Or* (L.F.), pl. du Gal-de-Gaulle, ☎ 32.57.70.46, Euro Visa, 23 rm ⧉ half pens, closed Mon eve, 15 Dec-15 Jan, 160. Rest. ◆ Hearty Norman fare, 70-170.

LISIEUX*

Caen 49, Alençon 91, Paris 174 km
pop 25820 ✉ 14100   C2

Lisieux recalls St. Thérèse, a young Carmelite nun (→ Alençon) who lived here; she was canonized in 1927. Formerly a town of great architectural beauty whose half-timbered houses were burnt in 1944, it is now essentially a city of pilgrimage to the cathedral and basilica.

▶ **Cathedral St. Pierre★** (A-B1), a superb example of Norman Gothic (12th-13thC); nearby gilt-decorated law court (Palais de Justice) in a Louis XIII former episcopal palace. ▶ **Church of St. Jacques** (B1, Flamboyant Gothic, 1496-1501). ▶ The pilgrimage to St. Thérèse includes the **chapel of Carmel** (B2) where her relics are venerated, a slide show (diorama de St. Thérèse) and the white basilica (B2; 1954; *son et laser spectacle every eve. at 9:30, 25 May-30 Sep.*). ▶ Her childhood home is at Les Buissonnets *(via B1)*. ▶ **Museum of Old Lisieux** (38, Boulevard Pasteur, A1; *daily ex Tue, 2-6; closed Sat. out of season*) in a handsome 16thC house. ▶ **Orbec★** *(20 km SE)* : numerous old houses★, municipal museum in the

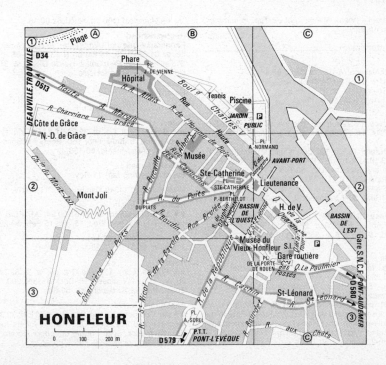

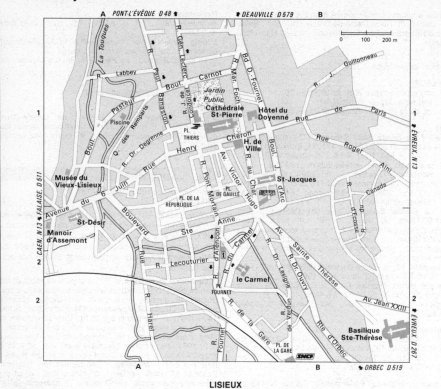

PONT-L'ÉVÊQUE D 48 ↑ ↑ DEAUVILLE D 579 B

0 100 200 m

LISIEUX

old manor-house (Vieux Manoir; *pm ex Tue. in summer;*
Sat. pm rest of year). ☐

Practical Information _____

LISIEUX
ℹ️ 11, rue d'Alençon (A-B2), ☎ 31.62.08.41.
SNCF (B2), ☎ 31.62.00.34/31.62.14.52.
🚌 pl. Thiers (B1), ☎ 31.62.49.95.
Car rental : *Avis*, train station (B2).

Hotels :
● ★★★ *Place*, (Mapotel), 67, rue Henry-Chéron (A-B1),
☎ 31.31.17.44, Tx 171862, AE DC Euro Visa, 33 rm 🅿️ ⏣
⏣ 280.
● ★★ *Bretagne* (L.F.), 30, pl. de la République (A1),
☎ 31.62.09.19, 14 rm 🅿️ closed Feb, 220. Rest. ♦ ♪
closed Mon and Sun eve (l.s.), 50-145.
★★ *La Coupe d'Or* (L.F.), 49, rue Pont-Mortain (A1-2),
☎ 31.31.16.84, AE DC Euro Visa, 18 rm 🅿️ ♪ half pens
(h.s.), 190. Rest. ♦♦ ♪ closed 15 Dec-15 Jan, 50-140;
child : 35.
★★ *Terrasse* (L.F.), 25, av. Sainte-Thérèse (B2),
☎ 31.62.17.65, AE Euro Visa, 17 rm ⏣ ⏣ half pens (h.s.),
closed Wed, 1 Jan-1 Apr, 360. Rest. ♦ ⏣ ♪ ♿ 60-120;
child : 40.

Restaurants :
♦♦ *Ferme du Roy*, 122, bd Herbet-Fournet (B1),
☎ 31.31.33.98, Euro Visa ⏣ ♪ 🏷 closed Mon and Sun
eve, 18 Dec-18 Jan. Spec : *gâteau de sole, foie de veau
aux framboises*, 100-160.
♦♦ *Parc*, 21, bd Herbet-Fournet (B1), ☎ 31.62.08.11, AE
DC Euro Visa ♪ closed Tue eve and Wed, 25 Jan-19 Feb. In the
château's music room, chef Henri Reudet can practice on
the other "piano" : *pavé aux cinq poivres, civet de soles et
d'huîtres*, 80-220; child : 60.

△ ★★*Municipal* (100 pl), ☎ 31.62.00.40.

Recommended
Farmhouse-gite : at Cambremer, *le Bois Hurey*, Leaupar-
tie, ☎ 31.63.01.99, 15 km on N 13 and D 85.
♥ distillery : *du Père Jules*, rte de Dives, ☎ 31.79.20.53,
cider and Calvados for sale.

Nearby

LIEUREY, ✉️ 27560, 28 km E.

Hotel :
★★ *Bras d'Or* (L.F.), ☎ 32.57.91.07, 10 rm 🅿️ ⏣ ⏣ 🏷
closed Mon, 6 Jan-5 Feb, 160. Rest. ♦♦ Spec : fish and
charcoal-grilled meats, 60-150.

Recommended
Events : *herring fair*, 11 Nov.

MANERBE, ✉️ 14340 Cambremer, 7 km NW.

Restaurant :
♦♦ *Le Pot d'Etain*, ☎ 31.61.00.94, AE Euro Visa ⏣ ♪
closed Tue eve and Wed, 15 Jan-15 Feb, 60-200.

ORBEC, ✉️ 14290, 20 km SE.
ℹ️ mairie, ☎ 31.32.73.38.

Hotel :
★★ *France* (L.F.), 152, rue Grande, ☎ 31.32.74.02, Visa,
25 rm 🅿️ ⏣ 🏷 closed 15 Dec-15 Jan, 200. Rest. ♦♦
Spec : *truite à l'orbecquoise*, 60-80.

Restaurant :
♦♦ *Au Caneton*, 32, rue Grande, ☎ 31.32.73.32. Closed
Mon eve and Tue, Feb, Oct. Famed for its food. 17thC
Norman manor. Spec : *gratin de langouste aux épinards,
jambon Michodière*, 220-310.

Recommended

♥ camembert : *Lanquetot*, 8, rue de Vimoutiers, ☎ 31.32.80.02, group tours of the plant; *ferme Nathalie Legros* : chemin des Monts, at the Orbec exit, on the rte de l'Aigle, cider, Calvados, rabbits, berries and cheese for sale, every am ex Sun and Mon; at St-Germain-la-Campagne, Calvados for sale : *Le Buisson*, 27230 Thiberville, 5 km N., ☎ 32.44.71.11.

MONT-SAINT-MICHEL***

Avranches 22, Rennes 66, Paris 370 km
pop 80 ⊠ 50116   A3

The souvenir-sellers who crowd the Grande-Rue right up to the abbey steps continue a tradition begun by the hucksters who accosted pilgrims to Mont-Saint-Michel in the Middle Ages. The architectural beauty and the long history of the fortified abbey draw huge crowds; avoid the high season (mid-summer to early autumn). The monastery was desecrated during the Revolution and converted into a prison during the 19thC. The buildings today are once more maintained in monastic serenity. Salt-meadow lamb and *omelette de la mère Poulard* are the local specialities.

▶ The tour of the **Abbey★★★** *(daily; closed at 4 in winter)* starts with the Romanesque abbey church★★; the first few arches of the nave are missing; Flamboyant Gothic choir, crypt★; magnificent, delicate Gothic cloister with fine coupled columns; *merveille★★* ("marvel"; 1203-28) : three vast Gothic halls one above the other contain the almshouse and storehouse; the guests' hall and knights'

hall; and a refectory on the cloister level; to the W, terraced garden and a few trees. ▶ In the Grande-Rue★, parallel to the **rampart walk★★**, is the 11th-16thC parish church. Two museums : the Historial du Mont and the Musée Historique *(Palm Sun.-15 Oct., 9-6, 8:30-7 in season)* : slide-shows, historic memorabilia, outstanding collection of clock mechanisms. ▶ **Sea Museum** (Musée de la Mer, Rue Principale; more than 200 old boat models). ▶ You can walk around the outside of the Mont in 30 min, but check the times of the tides first.   ☐

Practical Information _____

MONT-SAINT-MICHEL
ⓘ Corps de Garde des Bourgeois, at the entrance to the Mont, ☎ 33.60.14.30 (h.s.).
SNCF ☎ 33.60.00.35.

Hotels :
● ★★★ *Digue* (L.F.), at the dike, 2 km from the Mont, ☎ 33.60.14.02, Tx 170157, AE DC Visa, 35 rm P ⟨ ⋙ ⤳ ⌖ View of the Mont and the bay, 220. Rest. ♦ ⟨ ♪ ♿ ⤳ 55-150; child : 30.
● ★★★ *La Mère Poulard*, ☎ 33.60.14.01, AE DC, 27 rm, half pens (h.s.), closed 12 Nov-14 Feb, 580. Rest. ● ♦♦♦ ⌖ Annette Poulard (1851-1931) would find no reason to worry about her venerable establishment, now open all year long. Jean-Claude Pierpaoli, the energetic manager, has given the place a fresh, new feeling with a new decor, piano-bar, French billiards, etc. In the kitchen (carved out of the rock!) young Jean-Luc Whal (a name to remember) does wonders with the good local produce. Genuine salt-meadow lamb, Couesnon salmon, sole, prawns, lobster, 150-350.

MONT-SAINT-MICHEL

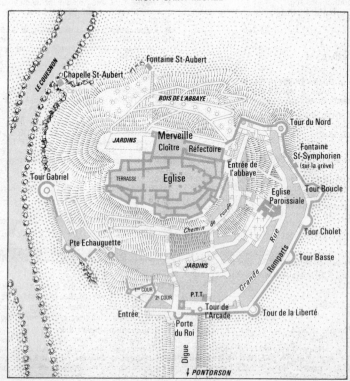

Mont-Saint-Michel Bay

The bay measures 22 km across the mouth from Can-cale to Granville and runs 23 km inland. The rising tide covers the immense stretch of sand at high speed; at low tide, the sea is about 12 km from the shore-line. Efforts have been made since the Middle Ages to reclaim the land. The Dol Marshes were dried out lit-tle by little, and during the last century, attempts were made to repeat the process around Mont-Saint-Michel itself. The unexpected result was a build-up of mud flats in the reclaimed area. The Ministry of the Envi-ronment has studied the site and strenuous efforts are being made to control silting, principally by the destruction of the Roche-Torin dyke, which obstructs the natural flow of the current.

● ★★★ **Les Terrasses Poulard**, ☎ 33.60.14.09, Tx 170197, AE DC Euro Visa, 30 rm ⛄ ▥ 🛆 ♪ half pens (h.s.). Medieval evenings, copper cookware for sale, paint-ings... 640. Rest. ● ♦♦ ⛄ A prettily redone annex to the main restaurant, with a brasserie and oyster bar. Grills and spit-roasted meats done over a wood fire. Magnifi-cent view, 45-150.
★★ **Saint-Aubert** (L.F.), at the end of the dyke, ☎ 33.60.08.74, 27 rm Ⓟ ▥ 🛆 ▩ ⌧ closed Nov-Mar, 195. Rest. ♦ Grill, 90-70; child : 35.

▲ ★★Gué de Beauvoir (30 pl), ☎ 33.60.09.23; at Beau-voir, 4 km S, ★★Mont-Saint-Michel (300 pl), ☎ 33.60.09.33.

Recommended
Events : pilgrimage across the beach, in Jul; *St-Michael's autumn fair,* in Sep; *St-Michael's spring fair,* in May; *festi-val of musical hours,* in Jul-Aug.
Guided tours : *C.N.M.H.S.* (h.s.), info : alms' room, ☎ 33.60.14.14.

Nearby
COURTILS, ⊠ 50220, 9 km.

Hotel :
★★★ **Manoir de la Roche Thorin** (R.S.), ☎ 33.70.96.55, 12 rm Ⓟ ⛄ ▥ 🛆 closed 4 Nov-28 Mar, 290. Rest. ♦ closed Tue and lunch. Spec : salt-meadow lamb, 120-180.

PONTORSON, ⊠ 50170, 9 km S.
ℹ mairie, ☎ 33.60.00.18.
▦ ☎ 33.60.00.35.

Hotel :
● ★★ **Montgomery** (L.F.), 13, rue Couesnon, ☎ 33.60.00.09, Tx 171332, AE DC Euro Visa, 32 rm Ⓟ ▥ 🛆 🛴 half pens (h.s.), closed 15 Oct-12 Apr. Splen-did furnishings in the residence of the Montgomeries, 250. Rest. ♦♦ ⛄ ᵴ Open (l.s.) for groups or banquets. Spec : *choucroute des pêcheurs, carré d'agneau de pré-salé,* 60-190; child : 40.

MONTMARTIN-SUR-MER

Granville 20, Saint-Lô 37, Paris 340 km
pop 871 ⊠ 50590   A2

ℹ mairie, ☎ 33.47.54.54.

Hotels :
★★ **Bon Vieux Temps**, ☎ 33.47.54.44, Visa, 21 rm Ⓟ 🛆 110. Rest. ♦ 45-120; child : 30.
★★ **Plage** (L.F.), Hauteville-sur-Mer, 3 km SW, ☎ 33.47.52.33, 14 rm Ⓟ ⛄ ▥ ▩ 200. Rest. ♦ ♪ closed Tue, 15 Sep-12 Oct. A place to keep in mind. Fresh local products, fish a specialty, 80-250.

Nearby
QUETTREVILLE-SUR-SIENNE, ⊠ 50660, 5 km SE.

Hotel :
★★ **Château de la Tournée** (L.F.), ☎ 33.47.62.91, 10 rm Ⓟ 🛆 ▩ ♪° closed Sun eve and Mon (l.s.), 15 Feb-15 Mar, 15 Sep-15 Oct, 110. Rest. ♦♦ ♪ Spec : marinated salmon, smoked trout, 70-110.

MORTAIN

Avranches 36, Rennes 90, Paris 277 km
pop 3040 ⊠ 50140   B3

Devastated during August 1944, the town was rebuilt with local granite. The site of the town is enhanced by the ravines and waterfalls of the Cance Valley.

► Church of St. Evroult (13thC). ► **Blanche Abbey** (12thC; *1 km N; Sun. pm and daily ex Tue., Jul.-Sep.).* ► Above the town, to the SE, the **chapel of St. Michel** is a lookout point 314 m high★. ► **Mortain Forest** (GR22), part of the Normandy-Maine Nature Park.

Nearby
► **Barenton** *(10 km SE) :* Maison de la pomme et de la poire de la Logeraie (cider museum; *Jul.-Aug., closed Mon.).* ► **Bellefontaine** *(6 km N) :* leisure centre at the Vil-lage Enchanté *(Easter-1 Nov.).* ► **Saint-Michel-de-Mont-joie** *(22 km NW),* in the heart of the granite region; quar-ries, visits; museum *(daily 15 Jun.-15 Oct.; Sat. and Sun. pm, Easter-15 Jun.).*   □

Practical Information ―――――――――――――
MORTAIN
ℹ 1, rue du Bourg-Lopin (h.s.); mairie, ☎ 33.59.00.51. ♥

Hotels :
★★ **Poste**, 1, pl. des Arcades, ☎ 33.59.00.05, 30 rm ⛄ ▩ closed Fri eve and Sat, 20 Dec-1 Feb, 160. Rest. ♦♦ ⛄ ♪ ▩ 60-100.
● ★ **Cascades**, 16, rue du Bassin, ☎ 33.59.00.03, Visa, 13 rm, closed Sun and Mon, 130. Rest. ♦♦ Spec : *ris de veau à la mortainaise, tête de veau sauce gri-biche,* 40-120.

Nearby
SAINT-HILAIRE-DU-HARCOUET, ⊠ 50600, 14 km SW.
ℹ pl. de l'Eglise, ☎ 33.49.15.27; mairie, ☎ 33.49.10.06.

Hotels :
● ★★ **Le Cygne et La Résidence** (L.F.), 67, rue Wal-deck-Rousseau, ☎ 33.49.11.84, AE DC Euro Visa, 45 rm Ⓟ & closed Fri eve and Sat lunch, 15 Dec-15 Jan, 175. Rest. ♦♦ ♪ Spec : *feuilleté forestier aux deux ris, esca-lope de lotte pochée au calvados,* 60-150; child : 35.
★★ **Le Lion d'Or** (L.F.), 120, rue de la République, ☎ 33.49.10.82, 20 rm Ⓟ ▩ closed Sun eve and Mon lunch, 15 Feb-10 Mar, 10-30 Oct, 160. Rest. ♦ ♪ & Spec : *ris de veau à l'ancienne,* 50-100.

Recommended
♥ at Milly, 6.5 km NE, Calvados : *Gilbert,* ☎ 33.49.00.63, sale and tastings.

The NEUBOURG Plateau*

                                                           D2
This plateau between the Risle and Iton rivers, cen-tred on the town of Le Neubourg, is among the richest agricultural areas in upper Normandy; pictur-esque country churches and several fine châteaux.

► **Beaumont-le-Roger** *(8 km SW of Le Neubourg),* a pretty site on the right bank of the Risle : ruins of 13thC priory★; 14th-16thC church of St. Nicolas; **Beau-mont Forest.** ► **Brionne** *(15 km NW of Le Neubourg) :* keep, panorama; the **Maison de Normandie** sells han-dicrafts *(closed Tue., Wed.).* ► **Château du Champ-de-**

Bataille★★ *(4.5 km NW of Le Neubourg)* : early 18thC; furnished rooms; exhibitions *(daily ex Tue., 10:30-7; closed Jan., Feb.)*; also, golf for beginners, cultural events, old-fashioned games and drives in horse-drawn vehicles. ▶ **Harcourt** *(9 km NW of Le Neubourg)* : feudal castle★, horse trials in mid-Jun., 11.5-acre arboretum with exotic trees *(pm, closed Tue. in season, weekdays out of season and Nov.-Mar.)*.   □

Practical Information ⎯⎯⎯⎯⎯⎯⎯⎯⎯⎯⎯⎯

BEAUMONT-LE-ROGER, ⊠ 27170, 13 km SW.
⏻ mairie, ☎ 32.44.23.88.
𝗦𝗡𝗖𝗙 ☎ 32.45.21.03.

Hotel :
● ★★ *Lion d'Or* (L.F.), 91, rue St-Nicolas, ☎ 32.45.48.08, AE Euro Visa, 10 rm Ⓟ ♨ ♫ ⌘ closed Mon eve and Tue, 29 Jul-11 Aug, 22 Dec-21 Jan, 150. Rest. ♦ ♫ ₺ 65-100.

Restaurant :
♦♦ *Le Paris sur Risle*, 12, rue St-Nicolas, ☎ 32.45.22.23, AE Visa ♨ ♫ ₺ closed Mon and Sun eve, 20-25 Jan, 10-22 Mar, 17-23 Dec. Spec : *canard au cidre pommes en l'air, lotte blancs de poireaux*, dessert buffet, 65-130.

Le BEC-HELLOUIN, ⊠ 27800 Brionne, 6 km N of **Brionne.**

Hotel :
● ★★★ *Auberge de l'Abbaye*, ☎ 32.44.86.02, DC Euro Visa, 8 rm Ⓟ ♨ ⌘ half pens (h.s.), closed Mon eve and Tue (l.s.), 12 Jan-27 Feb, 300. Rest. ♦♦♦ Spec : *gratin de homard, médaillons de ris de veau aux morilles*, 100-180.

La RIVIÈRE-THIBOUVILLE, ⊠ 27550 Nassandres, 6 km S of **Brionne.**

Hotel :
● ★★ *Le Soleil d'Or* (L.F.), ☎ 32.45.00.08, Euro Visa, 12 rm Ⓟ ♨ ♨ ⌘ ₺ closed Wed, 25 Jan-10 Mar, 250. Rest. ♦♦ ♫ ₺ Spec : *truite Soleil d'Or*, 70-150; child : 45.

The OUCHE Region*

D2

The land in this forested cattle-raising region is less rich than in the neighbouring areas. The local rivers are the Iton and the Risle.

▶ **L'Aigle**, the "nail and bolt capital", thanks to its long-established main industry; 15th-16thC church of St. Martin with Flamboyant Gothic tower★; "June-44" museum in the Château (1690; designed by Jules Hardouin-Mansart, → Versailles). ▶ **Saint-Évroult-Notre-Dame-du-Bois** *(14 km W)* : remains of 13thC **abbey** next to a pond. ▶ **Breteuil-sur-Iton**, surrounded by water diverted from the river in the 11thC to form a defensive moat; only a few sections of wall are left on the E edge of the forest of Breteuil; **bird sanctuary**. ▶ **Francheville** *(8 km SW)* : Musée de la Ferronnerie (wrought-iron museum *(Sat. and nat. hols. pm, Sun. am)*. ▶ **Conches-en-Ouche**, on a hill in a loop of the river Rouloir : 16thC stained glass★ in the 15th-16thC **church of Ste. Foy**★; public garden in the grounds of the feudal castle; cultural centre (Maison des Richesses de l'Eure, 17thC, half-timbered); the manorhouse (Maison des Seigneurs) now houses a wrought-iron works *(closed Wed.)*. ▶ **Damville** : church of St. Évroult (15th-16thC tower★). ▶ **La Ferrière-sur-Risle** : Gothic church; leisure centre at Risle Valley Park, 2 km away *(Apr.-Sep.)*. ▶ **Verneuil-sur-Avre** at the S limit of the Ouche region, offers strolls on the site of the former ramparts; Flamboyant Gothic tower★ on the church of the Madeleine (16thC); Romanesque church of Notre-Dame, 12thC tower; houses of wood and brick (15th-18thC).   □

Practical Information ⎯⎯⎯⎯⎯⎯⎯⎯⎯⎯⎯⎯

L' AIGLE, ⊠ 61300, 59 km NE of **Alençon.**
⏻ pl. F.-de-Beina, ☎ 33.24.12.40 (h.s.).
𝗦𝗡𝗖𝗙 ☎ 33.24.35.32.

Hotel :
● ★★★ *Dauphin*, (Mapotel), pl. de la Halle,

☎ 33.24.43.12, Tx 170979, AE DC Euro Visa, 24 rm Ⓟ ⌘ 320. Rest. ● ♦♦ ♫ The family takes quality seriously, witness the outstanding food served in this Anglo-Norman-style restaurant. *Saumon poêlé aux laitues, sole normande, canard du pays*, 101-225; child : 54.

Restaurant :
♦♦ *Auberge Saint-Michel*, RN 26, Saint-Michel-Thuboeuf, ☎ 33.24.20.12, Euro Visa Ⓟ ♨ ♫ closed Wed eve and Thu, Feb, 60-120.

⚐ ★★*Municipal* (65 pl) ☎ 33.24.32.79.

BRETEUIL-SUR-ITON, ⊠ 27160, 32 km SW of **Evreux.**
⏻ mairie, ☎ 32.32.82.45.   ⚑

Hotel :
★★★ *Le Mail*, (R.S., C.H.), rue Neuve-de-Bémecourt, ☎ 32.29.81.54, Euro Visa, 13 rm Ⓟ ♨ ⌘ 400. Rest. ♦♦ Spec : *boudin blanc d'écrevisses*, 125-220.

⚐ ★★*Camp Fleuri* (33 pl), ☎ 32.29.76.99.

CONCHES-EN-OUCHE, ⊠ 27190, 18 km SW of **Evreux.**
⏻ ☎ 32.30.23.15.
𝗦𝗡𝗖𝗙 ☎ 32.30.23.17.

Hotel :
★ *La Grand'Mare*, 13, av. Croix-de-Fer, ☎ 32.30.23.30, Visa, 10 rm Ⓟ ♨ ♨ 120. Rest. ♦ ♨ 65-180.

⚐ ★★*Municipal* (100 pl), ☎ 32.30.22.49.

VERNEUIL-SUR-AVRE, ⊠ 27130, 43 km SW of **Evreux.**
⏻ pl. de la Madeleine, ☎ 32.32.17.17.
𝗦𝗡𝗖𝗙 ☎ 32.32.14.90.

Hotels :
● ★★★★ *Hostellerie le Clos* (R.C.), 98, rue de la Ferté-Vidame, ☎ 32.32.21.81, Tx 172770, AE DC Euro Visa, 11 rm Ⓟ ♨ ♨ ₺ closed Mon (Oct-Easter), 15 Dec-31 Jan, 450. Rest. ♦♦ ♫ ♫ ₺ closed Mon. Fish a specialty, 170-250; child : 60.
● ★★ *Saumon* (L.F.), 89, pl. de la Madeleine, ☎ 32.32.02.36, Tx 172770, Euro Visa, 28 rm ₺ 200. Rest. ♦ ♫ Earthy, hearty fare, 65-120.

The PERCHE Region*

C3-4

Round trip *(approx 150 km, full day; see map 4)*

This is the home of the Percheron horse, once eagerly sought for its unique combination of strength and speed, but rare in these days of mechanized farming and transport; meadows, manor-houses, lakes, and large forests of oak and beech pierced by the GR22.

▶ **Mortagne-au-Perche**, a market town in the Percheron hills, which can be seen from the gardens of the town hall; 15th-16thC Flamboyant Gothic church; 12th-16thC city gate (Porte St-Denis) with Percheron museum. ▶ **Forest of Réno-Valdieu** (16 km²) named for a 12thC Carthusian monastery (charterhouse); beech and oak up to 40 m high. ▶ **Chapelle Montligeon** : pilgrimage basilica. ▶ **La Vove** Manor, well-restored 15th-17thC buildings *(Apr.-Oct.)*. ▶ After **Nocé**, pass Courboyer Manor (late 15thC) on the way to **Colonard.** ▶ Drive through the **forest** (24 km²; La Herse lake; view★ of **La Perrière** on the W edge) and down to **Bellême**, where the town clusters around the church and a 15thC fortified gateway. ▶ Château des Feugerets, **Saint-Cyr-la-Rivière** : 17thC terracotta Entombment of Christ in the church; Angenardière Manor and **Sainte-Gauburge** : folk art and traditions at the Musée Percheron in the church *(pm in season)*. ▶ **Rémalard.** ▶ **Monaco Parc** (leisure centre). ▶ **Longny-au-Perche** : 15th-16thC church of St. Martin; chapel of Notre-Dame-de-Pitié★ in the cemetery (Renaissance; sculpture, doorways★). ▶ **Tourouvre** : church with 1892 stained glass commemorating local families who emigrated to Canada in the 17thC. ▶ On the other side of the **forests of Le Perche and La Trappe** (21 km²) : **abbey of La Grande Trappe**, cradle of the strict Cistercian rule

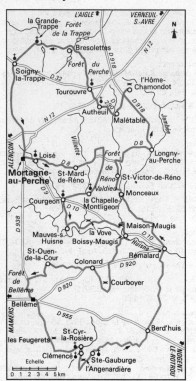

4. The Perche region

(total silence); the monks are better known as Trappists. It was rebuilt in 1884-90; information centre; lakes. □

Practical Information _____

BELLÊME, ⊠ 61130, 41 km SE of **Alençon**.
ⓘ hôtel de ville, ☎ 33.73.02.21. ❦

Hotel :
★ **Boule d'Or**, pl. du Gal-Leclerc, ☎ 33.73.10.32, Visa, 9 rm Ⓟ closed Mon, 70. Rest. ♦ 60-80.

⚠ ★★*Municipal* (25 pl), ☎ 33.73.02.21.

Recommended
Events : *mushroom days*, late Sep.

LONGNY-AU-PERCHE, ⊠ 61290, 56 km NE of **Alençon**.
ⓘ hôtel de ville, ☎ 33.73.65.42.

Hotel :
★ **France** (L.F.), 68, rue de Paris, ☎ 33.73.64.11, Euro Visa, 10 rm Ⓟ closed Sun eve and Mon, 130. Rest. ♦♦ ♪ Spec : smoked salmon, *confit de canard*, 55-170.

Recommended
Events : *national contest, best dish of tripe*, 1 May.

MORTAGNE-AU-PERCHE, ⊠ 61400, 38 km NE of **Alençon**.
ⓘ pl. du Gal-de-Gaulle, ☎ 33.25.04.22 (h.s.).
▦ ☎ 33.25.19.11.

Hotel :
★★ **Tribunal** (L.F.), 4, pl. du Palais, ☎ 33.25.04.77, Euro Visa, 18 rm Ⓟ ▦ ⚸ ♿ 110. Rest. ♦♦ ♪ The charm of a 17th-C house. Spec : *terrine de foie gras maison, smoked*

salmon, *fricassée de volailles au vinaigre*, 55-160; child : 35.

⚠ ★★*Municipal* (30 pl), ☎ 33.25.04.35.

Recommended
Events : *June music festival in Mortagne*; *boudin (blood sausage) festival*, mid-Lent.
♥ smoked boudin : *Charcuterie Maurice Batrel*, 52, pl. du Gal-de-Gaulle, ☎ 33.25.16.43.

TOUROUVRE, ⊠ 61190, 48 km NE of **Alençon**.
ⓘ ☎ 33.25.74.55.

Hotel :
★ **France** (L.F.), 19, rue du 14-Août-44, ☎ 33.25.73.55, DC Euro Visa, 14 rm Ⓟ closed Sun eve and Mon (l.s.), 160. Rest. ♦ ♪ ♿ 45-120; child : 35.

PONT-AUDEMER*

Le Havre 48, Evreux 68, Paris 168 km
pop 10160 ⊠ 27500   C2

Charming town threaded among canal branches of the River Risle. ▶ **Church of St. Ouen★** : 11th-13thC choir, oddly unfinished 15th-16thC nave (Renaissance stained glass★); **half-timbered houses★** in the streets and alleys off the Rue de la République; Canel museum (history, Egyptology, insects; *pm ex Sun.*, *tel. 32.41.08.15*) 17thC Auberge du Vieux Puits★ (inn).

Nearby

▶ **Corneville-sur-Risle** *(6 km E)*, famous due to an operetta by Robert Planquette; carillon of the Hostellerie des Cloches *(daily ex Wed.).* ▶ **Bec-Hellouin★** *(24 km SE)* : abbey built in the 11thC on a tributary of the Risle; desecrated during the Revolution, subsequently reoccupied by Benedictines; 15thC Tower of St. Nicolas and 18thC buildings in a park *(closed Tue.)*; close by, Automobile museum *(Apr.-Nov., closed Tue.)*. ▶ **Bourg-Achard** *(23 km E)* : church (Renaissance stained glass★); fair *(early Sep.)*. □

Practical Information _____

PONT-AUDEMER
ⓘ pl. Maubert, ☎ 32.41.08.21.
▦ ☎ 32.41.01.20.

Hotel :
● ★★ **Vieux Puits**, 6, rue Notre-Dame-du-Pré, ☎ 32.41.01.48, Euro Visa, 14 rm Ⓟ ▦ ⚸ ♿ half pens, closed Mon eve and Tue, 29 Jun-2 Jul, 14 Dec-15 Jan, 295. Rest. ♦♦ ♿ A 17th-C Norman house. Spec : *andouillette de mer grillé au beurre blanc, canard aux cerises griottes*, 140-190.

Restaurant :
♦ **La Frégate**, 4, rue de la Seûle, ☎ 32.41.12.03, AE DC Visa ♪ ♿ closed Tue eve and Wed, 105-180.

Nearby

CAMPIGNY, ⊠ 27500 Pont-Audemer, 3 km S on the D 180.

Hotel :
● ★★★★ **Le Petit Coq aux Champs**, (I.L.A., R.C.), ☎ 32.41.04.19, AE DC Euro Visa, 12 rm Ⓟ ▦ ⚸ ♪ ♿ ▦ half pens, 1540. Rest. ♦♦♦ ♿ ♪ ♿ A Norman cottage. Spec : *saumon à l'unilatéral à la crème d'orties, paleton de barbarie en aiguillettes au cidre*, 180-280; child : 60.

CONTEVILLE, ⊠ 27210 Beuzeville, 10 km NW.

Restaurant :
● ♦♦ **Auberge du Vieux Logis**, ☎ 32.57.60.16, AE DC Euro Visa ♪ closed Wed eve and Thu, 30 Jan-1 Mar, 23-30 Sep. Genuine Norman atmosphere, light and authentic cooking by the owner. *Boudin de pied de porc truffé, caneton*, 200-300.

5. Les Quatre Vallées

Les QUATRE VALLÉES*

D2

Round trip from Lyons-la-Forêt *(approx 162 km, full day; see map 5)*

An attractive excursion through the valleys of the Andelle and its tributaries, the Lieure, the Crevon and the Héron, together with the forest of Lyons and churches, abbeys and châteaux along the way.

► **Lyons-la-Forêt★**, quiet resort in the Lieure Valley : covered market and half-timbered houses ; possibly the most beautiful beech forest (11 km²) in France. In the middle of the forest, the **château de Fleury-la-Forêt** *(Sat., Sun., hols., 2-6)*. ► **Mortemer** : the 12th-13thC Cistercian abbey is in ruins but there is a **museum of monastic life** *(daily 10-6:30)*. ► **Charleval**, 6 km N, near **Perriers-sur-Andelle** : 17thC Trianel Manor in a pretty park *(weekdays, Jul.-Sep.)*. ► Near **Radepont** : ruins of the **Abbey of Fontaine-Guérard★** (13thC ; *pm ex Mon., Mar.-Oct.)* and the former **Levasseur spinning factory** in neo-Gothic Style. ► **La Côte des Deux Amants★** (Two Lovers' Hill) recalls a legend recorded in the 12thC : the king of the region would only let his daughter marry a suitor who could prove his strength by carrying her at a run to the top of the hill. Raoul succeeded, but collapsed and died on reaching the summit ; Caliste, his disappointed burden, immediately perished from grief. View over the junction of the Andelle and the Seine. ► **Pont-de-l'Arche**, on the left bank of the Seine, at the foot of the forest : Flamboyant Gothic church (16thC) ; 1.5 km W, remains of **Bonport Abbey,** founded by Richard the Lion-Heart in 1190. ► **Boos,** near Rouen airport, has a beautiful 16thC dovecote★ with noteworthy brick-work decoration. ► Also in brick, 15th-16thC **château de Martainville★**, houses a museum of Norman folk art *(closed Tue., Wed. and nat. hols.)*. ► **Ry,** famous as the setting of Flaubert's novel *Madame Bovary* (→ box). The Galerie Bovary, in an old cider-mill, uses mechanical figures to illustrate passages from the novel *(Sat., Sun., Mon. and nat. hols., Easter-Oct.)*; carved wooden church porch. ► **Vascœuil** : the historian Jules Michelet (1798-1874) lived in the 14th-16thC château (cultural centre with exhibitions of documents and memorabilia, *Apr.-Oct. ; Sat., Sun. and weekdays pm)*. ► **Bois Héroult** : 18thC château with gardens in the French formal style near the church of **Bosc-Bordel** (Renaissance sculpted wood porch). ► **Forges-les-Eaux** (→ Bray Region).

► **Sigy-en-Bray**, in the upper Andelle Valley : abbey church of 12th, 13th and 18thC. ► **Château de Merval** (17thC) : English park open *(daily ex am in winter)*. □

Practical Information ───────────────

LYONS-LA-FORÊT, ⊠ 27480, 20 km N of **Andelys.**
🅸 mairie, ☎ 32.49.60.87, closed Mon and Sun.

Hotels :

● ★★★ *La Licorne* (L.F.), pl. I.-Benserade, ☎ 32.49.62.02, AE DC Euro Visa, 22 rm 🅿 ⬚ 🔧 ⬚ closed Sun eve and Mon ex May-Sep, 15 Dec-21 Jan, 275. Rest. ♦♦ & ⬚ Spec : *saumon cru à l'aneth au beurre de tomate, rognons de veau aux baies de cassis,* 110-220 ; child : 80.
★★ *Domaine Saint-Paul* (L.F.), rte du Tronquay, ☎ 32.49.60.57, 20 rm 🅿 ⬚ ⬚ 🔧 & ⬚ half pens (h.s.), closed 15 Nov-15 Mar, 460. Rest. ♦♦ & 80-100.
★★ *Le Grand Cerf*, pl. de la Halle, ☎ 32.49.60.44, 10 rm ⬚ 🔧 closed Tue, Wed, 15 Jan-15 Feb, 200. Rest. ♦♦ ♪ 150-190.

⚠ ★★Saint-Paul (40 pl), ☎ 32.49.60.87.

ROUEN***

Évreux 72, Le Havre 88, Paris 140 km
pop 105080 ⊠ 76000   D2

The fourth-largest port in France, with installations stretching almost 20 km downstream on the Seine, it is also a beautiful city. The old quarters have been restored and pedestrian malls have been established. The exceptional grouping of historic monuments and half-timbered houses will make you want to know more about the 10thC Viking Rollo, William the Conqueror, Joan of Arc (→ Lorraine), the poet Pierre Corneille (1606-84), Flaubert (→ box), and other famous people associated with this city. This exceptionally dynamic cultural, and artistic centre only 1hr30 from Paris, has recently built a new administrative complex on the left bank, but the old town remains the historic heart of Rouen.

► The best way to grasp the lay of the land is to view the city from a lookout★★ at Bonsecours (basilica and St. Catherine hill, D4, *3 km SE)*, Canteleu *(4 km W)* or the streets leading to the University at Mont-Saint-Aignan

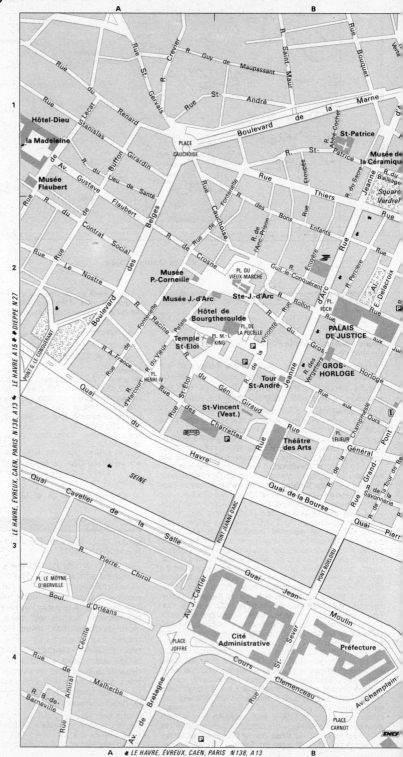

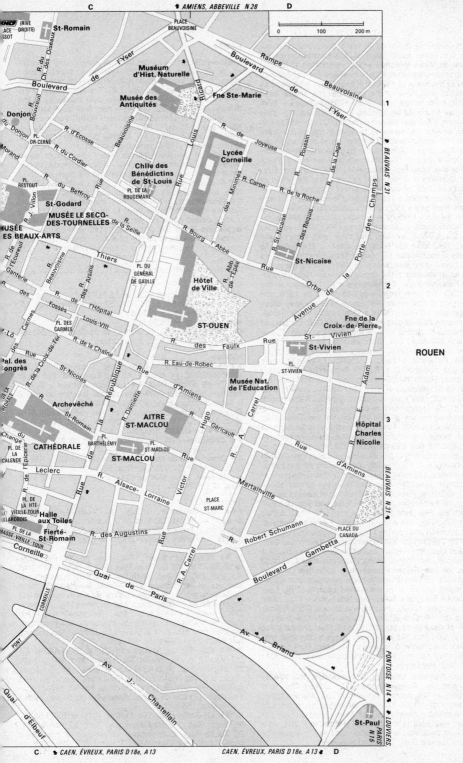

SNCF (RIVE DROITE)
St-Romain

PLACE
BEAUVOISINE

0   100   200 m

Boulevard   Rampe
Rampe de l'Yser   Boulevard   Beauvoisine

Muséum
d'Hist. Naturelle

R. du
Ch. des Oiseaux

R. du

Boulevard   de   l'Yser

Musée des
Antiquités

Fne Ste-Marie

1

Donjon

R. du Donjon
PL
DR-CERNÉ

R. d'Ecosse

R. du Cordier

Beauvoisine

Morand

R. de   Joyeuse

R. de la Cage

BEAUVAIS N 31

Chlle des
Bénédictins
de St-Louis

Lycée
Corneille

R. Caron

R. de la Roche

R. des Requis

Porte   des   Champs

PL
RESTOUT

R. du Beffroy

PL DE LA
ROUGEMARE

R. des Minimes

R. J. Villon

St-Godard

MUSÉE LE SECQ-
DES-TOURNELLES

de la Seille

R. Bourg   l'Abbé

R. St-Nicaise

St-Nicaise

MUSÉE
ES BEAUX-ARTS

R. de
l'Ecureuil

Beauvoisine

Thiers

PL. DU
GÉNÉRAL
DE GAULLE

R. Abb   R. de l'Épée

Rue

Orbe   de   la

2

R. des
Ganterie

R. des Arsins

Hôtel
de Ville

Avenue   St-

Fne de la
Croix-de-Pierre

Fossés

R. de l'Hôpital
Louis-VIII

ST-OUEN

Vivien

Lô

PL DES
CARMES

R. de la Chaîne

R. des   Faulx

St-Vivien

Adam

R. de la Croix-de-Fer

St-Nicolas

Rue

Rue

PL
ST-VIVIEN

ROUEN

al. des
ongrès

R.

République

Rue

d'Amiens

Musée Nat.
de l'Education

Carrel

Hôpital
Charles
Nicolle

3

Archevêché

St-Romain

R. Damiette

AITRE
ST-MACLOU

R. Hugo   Géricault

BEAUVAIS N 31

du
Change

PL DE
LA
CALENDE

PL
BARTHÉLEMY

PL
ST-MACLOU

Rue

Rue   d'Amiens

CATHÉDRALE

ST-MACLOU

Victor

PLACE
ST-MARC

Martainville

PLACE DU
CANADA

Leclerc

R.   Alsace-   Lorraine

PL DE
LA HTE-
VIEILLE TOUR

Halle
aux Toiles

Rue

R. des Augustins   R.   Robert Schumann

Gambetta

PL DE LA
BASSE VIEILLE TOUR

Fierté-
St-Romain

Boulevard

PONTOISE N 14

Corneille

Quai   de   Paris

PONT

Av.   A. Briand

4

Av.   J.   Chastellain

St-Paul

PARIS N 15
LOUVIERS

Quai   d'Elbeuf

or Bois-Guillaume *(5 km N)*. In town, the principal monuments are within easy reach of the central car-parks.
▶ **Place du Vieux Marché**★★ (B2; remodeled 1978-79) : this centuries-old market square is where Joan of Arc was burned at the stake in 1431; the exact spot is marked by a tall cross near the church★ entrance. The church itself (1979) is embellished with 16thC stained glass★★ from the former church of St. Vincent. In the square, No. 33 is the Jeanne d'Arc wax museum *(9:30-6:30; closed Mon. in winter);* several half-timbered façades in the square were restored or reassembled from other areas of town. In the nearby Rue de la Pie (B2) is the birthplace of Pierre Corneille (No. 4 ; *closed Tue., Wed. am and nat. hols.);* Place de la Pucelle, Hôtel Bourgtheroulde (16thC mansion; B2) : in the courtyard is a bas-relief representing the "Field of the Cloth of Gold" where Henry VIII of England and François I of France held a 16thC summit meeting. ▶ The **Rue du Gros Horloge**★★ (B2), a lively pedestrian street, leads through the Gros Horloge★ archway : clock; 1390 belfry; small Renaissance pavilion and Louis XV (18thC) fountain *(Palm Sunday-Oct. ex Tue. and Wed. am).* Nearby, the former 17thC town hall (Hôtel de Ville). ▶ The **Palais de Justice**★★ courthouse (B2; early 16thC), restored to its Gothic beauty after the damage of WWII; during the restoration an interesting 11thC monument with Hebrew graffiti was uncovered. ▶ **Cathedral**★★★ (C3) : begun in the late 12thC, the main fabric was completed by 1250; the Flamboyant Gothic decoration (towers★, façade★) dates from the late 15th-early 16thC; 19thC metal spire. Inside, Renaissance stained glass★, Flamboyant Gothic staircase in N transept; guided tour of the choir★★ *(daily Easter hols. and Jul.-Aug.; Sat., Sun. pm rest of year)* : 16thC stained glass, 13th-16thC funerary monuments. ▶ Opposite the cathedral entrance : former Finance Office★ (1502; C3), now the TO. ▶ Rue St-Romain (C3) takes you to the other Flamboyant Gothic masterpiece of Rouen, the **church of St. Maclou**★★ (C3; 1437-1581) : curved, five-doored porch; lacy spire and stained glass; Renaissance doors in the façade and N doorways. On the square, half-timbered houses. ▶ Rue Martainville, the Aître (cloister) St. Maclou★ (C3), 16th-17thC ossuary, is an oasis of calm. ▶ Interesting strolls through Rue Damiette (antique shops) and the Rue Eau-de-Robec (C3; No. 185, National Museum of Education; *pm ex Mon. and Sun.).* ▶ **Church of St. Ouen**★★ (C-D2) : nearly as imposing as the cathedral, with an outstanding Flamboyant Gothic lantern-tower and stained glass; the town hall is in the former abbey (18thC; C-D2). ▶ Pass by Rue Thiers and instead detour through the pedestrian Rue de l'Hôpital and Rue Ganterie to reach the **Fine Arts Museum** ★★★ (C2; *10-12 & 2-6; closed Tue., Wed. am and nat. hols.)* : Flemish primitives, Italian, Spanish and French 17th-18thC paintings; masterpieces by Caravaggio, Velázquez, Ingres, Delacroix, Géricault and Duchamp-Villon; Impressionists. Close by, at 1 Rue Faucon, the former Hôtel d'Hocqueville★★ (17thC) houses the new **Faïence museum,** a collection including 6000 pieces of French and foreign ceramics and glassware *(same hours).* ▶ In the former church of St. Laurent, the **Le Secq des Tournelles Museum**★★ (C2; *same hours)* displays 12000 wrought-iron objects from Roman times to the 19thC. ▶ Stained glass★ (16th-17thC) in the **church of St. Patrice** (ca. 1535; B1). Rue Jeanne-d'Arc (B-1-2-3) runs from the right bank quays to the train station, near the Jeanne d'Arc tower, the keep, built by King Philippe Auguste in 1207, where Joan was tried (C1; *closed Tue. and Nov.).*

Also... ▶ **Regional Museum of Antiquities, the Middle Ages, and the Renaissance**★ (C1; *closed Thu. and nat. hols.)* in the former convent of St. Marie (1630). ▶ Museum of natural sciences, ethnography, prehistory *(same address; closed Sun. am, Mon., Tue.).* ▶ Gustave Flaubert was born in the hospital (Hôtel-Dieu; A1), now a museum dedicated to the writer and to the history of medicine *(closed Sun., Mon. and nat. hols.).*

Nearby

▶ **Elbeuf** *(20 km S),* former linen-weaving centre : churches of St. Jean and St. Étienne have 16thC stained glass; in the former town hall, Museum of Natural and Local History *(Wed. and Sat. 2-6).* The GR2 leads to the Orival rocks★ *(4 km N;* panorama over the valley of the Seine). ▶ **Clères** *(22 km N)* : zoo and botanical garden around the 15th-19thC château (11thC keep; *closed Nov.-early Mar.).* Nearby, Automobile Museum (1892-1955; *8-6:30 daily).* ▶ **Auffray** *(37 km N) :* 13thC collegiate church (17thC jack-of-the-clock). ▶ 17 km NW : **Barentin,** in the Austreberthe Valley, a veritable street museum (sculpture by Bourdelle, Gromaire, Rodin, et al.); small historical museum *(Sat. pm, Sun., nat. hols.).* ▶ **Yvetot** *(36 km NW),* almost entirely rebuilt; modern stained glass★ in the 1955 church; in the town hall, European and Oriental ivories★ from the Middle Ages to the 19thC *(8:30-11:30 & 1:30-5; closed Mon. am, Sat. pm and Sun.).* ▶ **Allouville-Bellefosse** *(6 km SW of Yvetot)* : 1000 year-old oak tree (chapel), nature museum *(10-12 & 2-7; closed Tue.),* treatment centre for birds, victims of coastal pollution. ☐

Practical Information _____

ROUEN
ℹ pl. de la Cathédrale (C3), ☎ 35.71.41.77.
✈ *Boos,* 11 km SE, ☎ 35.80.22.52. *Air France office,* 15, quai du Havre, ☎ 35.98.24.50.
SNCF (C1), ☎ 35.98.50.50.
Car rental : *Avis,* 13, pl. Joffre, ☎ 35.03.01.11; 24, rue Malouet, ☎ 35.72.77.50; train station.

Hotels :
★★★★(L) *Pullman Albane,* rue Croix-de-Fer (C3), ☎ 35.98.06.98, Tx 180949, AE DC Euro Visa, 125 rm ℙ ♦ ♨ ♿ & 440. Rest. ♦♦ *Le Tournebroche ♪* Spec : *sabayon de chou à l'effeuillée de raie, julienne de sole à la nage de langoustine,* 90-210; child : 40.
● ★★★ *Dieppe,* (Mapotel), pl. Bernard-Tissot (C1), ☎ 35.71.96.00, Tx 180413, AE DC Euro Visa, 44 rm, 315. Rest. ♦♦ *Le Quatre Saisons ♪* 140-210.
★★ *Cathédrale,* 12, rue St-Romain (C3), ☎ 35.71.57.95, 23 rm ♨ 195.
★★ *Grand Hôtel du Nord,* 91, rue du Gros-Horloge (B2-3), ☎ 35.70.41.41, Tx 771938, Visa, 62 rm ℙ ♨ 170.
★★ *Morand,* 1, rue Morand (C1), ☎ 35.71.46.07, AE Euro Visa, 17 rm ♨ 160.

Restaurants :
♦♦♦ *La Couronne,* 31, pl. du Vieux-Marché (B2), ☎ 35.71.40.90, AE DC Visa ♨♨♨ ♪ & closed Sun eve. The oldest inn in France. Spec : *huîtres chaudes aux poireaux confits, tournedos Rossini avec foie gras, soufflé citron vert,* 100-250.
● ♦♦ *Bertrand Warin,* 7-9, rue de la Pie (B2), ☎ 35.89.26.69, AE DC Euro Visa ♪ & closed Mon and Sun eve, 2 Aug-2 Sep, 22-26 Dec. The chef makes excellent use of his training with Michel Guérard. Freshest ingredients go into the light cuisine served in this fine old house with its modern decor and its refreshing greenery. The food varies with the seasons and the markets' bounty : *fricassée de crustacés aux pleurotes, pigeons de Dampierre aux oignons confits, feuillantines aux pêches caramélisées,* 100-250.
● ♦♦ *Gill,* 60, rue St-Nicolas (C2), ☎ 35.71.16.14, AE DC Visa ♪ & ♨ closed Mon noon and Sun , Feb, 23 Aug-13 Sep. A brilliant future ahead for G. Tournadre, a young chef trained at 'Taillevent'. Light, inspired cooking : *raviolis de langoustines au basilic, pigeon à la rouennaise, gratin de poires épicées et de fraises au lait d'amandes,* 155-300.
● ♦♦ *Le Beffroy,* 15, rue Beffroy (C1), ☎ 35.71.55.27, AE Euro Visa ♪ closed Mon and Sun, 22 Feb-9 Mar, 26 Jul-18 Aug. Outstanding cuisine and a handsome house, both thanks to Mme L'Hernault : *foie gras de*

canard chaud, blanc de turbot au beurre de framboises, nougat glacé et son sabayon à la liqueur de noix, 100-250.
● ♦♦ **La Grillade**, 121, rue Jeanne d'Arc, ☎ 35.71.47.01, Euro Visa, closed Sun. As some discerning English patrons put it, this place is 'charming' : neat and tidy and good! *Salade de Neufchâtel, saumon à la menthe, sole normande, côte de veau aux morilles, tarte Tatin,* 49-150.
♦♦ **Dufour**, 67bis, rue St-Nicolas (C2-3), ☎ 35.71.90.62, AE Visa, closed Mon , Sun eve and Aug. Spec : fish, *sole au vieux bordeaux,* 180-200.
♦♦ **Le Réverbère**, 9, pl. de la République (C4), ☎ 35.07.03.14, Visa, closed Sat noon and Sun, 3-23 Aug, 21-27 Dec. Daily specials, 95-190.
♦♦ **Petits Parapluies**, 46, rue Bourg-l'Abbé (D2), ☎ 35.88.55.26, AE Visa ♪ closed Sat noon and Sun, 21 Feb-10 Mar, 1-22 Aug. Remarkable service. Spec : *escalope de foie gras, poêlée de langoustines,* 95-220.
♦ **Pascaline**, 5, rue de la Poterne (B2), ☎ 35.89.67.44, Visa ♪ 45-100 ; child : 30.

Recommended
Bicycle-rental : *Freeway*, 21, rue des Bonnetiers, ☎ 35.70.04.04.
Guide to wines : *Le Bouchon Normand*, pl. du Vieux-Marché, wine bar.
Guided tours : historic districts, museums, port, info S.I.
Night-clubs : *Le King Créole*, 29, bd des Belges, ☎ 35.07.76.20.
♥ chocolates : *Paillard*, 32, rue du Gros-Horloge ; *Granger*, 29, rue du Gal-Leclerc ; pork products : *Hardy*, 22, pl. du Vieux-Marché ; tea room : *Roland*, 78, rue des Carmes ; wine bar : *Le Bouchon Normand*, pl. du vieux-Marché.

Nearby
ELBEUF, ✉ 76500, 20 km S.
ⓘ chambre de commerce, 28, rue Henry, ☎ 35.77.02.16/25.77.03.78.
SNCF ☎ 35.81.02.52.
Car rental : *Avis*, 60,Cours Carnot, ☎ 35.77.45.10.

Hotel :
★ **Nouvel-Hôtel**, 43, rue J.-Jaurès, ☎ 35.81.01.02, Visa, 17 rm P ⅋ closed Sun eve , hols, 1st-10 May, Aug, 130.
Le GRAND-QUÉVILLY, ✉ 76120, 6 km SW.

Hotel :
★★★ **Sorétel**, (France-Accueil), av. des Provinces, ☎ 35.69.63.50, AE DC Euro Visa, 45 rm P 260. Rest. ♦♦ ♪ closed Sat noon and Sun eve, 70-150.
MONTIGNY, ✉ 76380 Canteleu, 8 km W.

Hotel :
★★★ **Atlas**, ☎ 35.36.05.97, AE DC Euro Visa, 22 rm P ⣿ ⚑ 220. Rest. ♦♦ ♪ Spec : *suprême de Saint-Pierre aux morilles, feuilleté de barbue,* 70-130.
PONT-SAINT-PIERRE, ✉ 27360, 21 km SE.

Hotel :
★★★ **La Bonne Marmite** (L.F.), 10, rue René-Raban, ☎ 32.49.70.24, AE DC Euro Visa, 9 rm P ⅋ half pens (h.s.), closed Sun eve (l.s.) , Fri and Sat lunch, 20 Feb-15 Mar, 25 Jul-13 Aug, 490. Rest. ♦ ♪ ᕗ Spec : *pièce de bœuf grillée aux cèpes et aux girolles, suprême de turbot,* 115-200.

Restaurant :
♦♦ **Auberge de l'Andelle**, 27, Grande-Rue, ☎ 32.49.70.18, Euro Visa ᕗ closed Mon, 16-31 Aug. Spec : *matelote d'anguille au cidre, civet de lièvre en saison,* 75-170.
YVETOT, ✉ 76190, 36 km NW.
SNCF ☎ 35.95.08.40.
Car rental : *Avis*, 91 bis, F.-Lechevallier, ☎ 35.95.48.55 ; train station.

Hotel :
★★ **Le Havre**, pl. des Belges, ☎ 35.95.16.77, Euro Visa,

43 rm P 230. Rest. ♦♦ closed Fri eve ex Jul-Aug, Sun, 15 Dec-15 Jan, 65-95.

SAINT-LÔ

Caen 63, Cherbourg 78, Paris 303 km
pop 24790 ✉ 50000   A2
Saint-Lô was almost entirely rebuilt after 1944, but the old ramparts still enclose the town. It is the capital of the Department of La Manche.

▶ Inside the ramparts★ (A1) : administrative district, the Notre-Dame church : 15th-16thC (restored), outdoor pulpit on the left. ▶ Town hall (A-B1) : museum of paintings and 16thC tapestries★ *(daily ex Tue., Jul.-Aug. ; closed am out of season).* ▶ **Stud-farm** (Haras national ; B1) : 200 stallions *(daily 15 Jul.-15 Feb.),* harness-horse display *(10am Thu., 25 Jul.-5 Sep.).*

Nearby
▶ **Canisy** *(8 km SW)* : 16thC château. ▶ **Torigny-sur-Vire** : 16th-17thC château des Matignon, burned in 1944, has been restored *(Easter-Oct., pm ex Sun. ; enq. : town hall).* ▶ **Valley of the Vire★** (GR221) : **Roche de Ham★** *(13 km S),* 100 m above a bend in the river ; picturesque site of **La Chapelle-sur-Vire** (pilgrimage). Not far from here, **Angotière** : 16th-18thC château (site, park, furnishings ; *pm ; closed Tue. and Jul.).*   ☐

Practical Information

SAINT-LÔ
ⓘ 2, rue Havin (B1), ☎ 33.05.02.09.
SNCF (A1), ☎ 33.57.50.50/33.05.11.68.
Car rental : *Avis*, Z.I. Agneaux, ☎ 33.05.18.87.

Hotels :
● ★★ **La Crémaillère**, pl. de la Préfecture (A1), ☎ 33.57.14.68, Euro Visa, 12 rm P ⚑ ♪ ⧉ half pens (h.s.), closed Sat, 15-27 Feb, 15 Oct-1 Nov, 300. Rest. ♦ ♪ ᕗ Spec : seafood, *poêlon de tripes.* Good value, 80-130.
★★ **Le Marignan**, pl. de la Gare (A1), ☎ 33.05.15.15, DC Euro Visa, 18 rm P ⅋ ⚑ closed 7-22 Feb, 180. Rest. ♦♦ ⅋ ♪ Spec : *soupe de petits-gris aux orties, coquilles Saint-Jacques à la coque,* 50-190 ; child : 40.
★★ **Le Terminus** (L.F.), 3, av. Briovère (A1), ☎ 33.05.08.60, Euro Visa, 15 rm P ⅋ ⅋ closed 7 Dec-7 Jan, 110. Rest. ♦ closed Fri eve and Sun, 45-60.
★★ **Les Voyageurs** (L.F.), pl. de la Gare (A1), ☎ 33.05.08.63, AE DC Euro Visa, 15 rm P ⅋ closed Sun eve, 15 Dec-15 Jan, 180. Rest. ♦♦ ♪ closed Mon and Sun eve. Spec : seafood. Good value, 55-120.

Recommended
Sports : *pilots' school*, ☎ 33.57.46.50.

Nearby
MARIGNY, ✉ 50570, 20 km W.

Restaurant :
● ♦♦ **Poste**, ☎ 33.55.11.08, DC Visa, closed Mon and Sun eve, 1-10 Mar, 8-30 Sep. A thousand and one delicious ways to cook oysters and seafood, by Joël Meslin, 85-220.
TESSY-SUR-VIRE, ✉ 50420, 18 km S.

Hotel :
● ★ **France** (L.F.), rue St-Pierre-et-Miquelon, ☎ 33.56.30.01, Euro Visa, 18 rm P ⅋ ⅋ half pens, closed Sun eve (l.s.), 1-15 Feb, 175. Rest. ♦ ♪ Spec : *pintadeau braisé danoise, filets de Saint-Pierre aux herbes,* 50-110 ; child : 40.

If you enjoy sports, consult the pages pertaining to the regions; there you will find addresses for practicing your favorite sport.

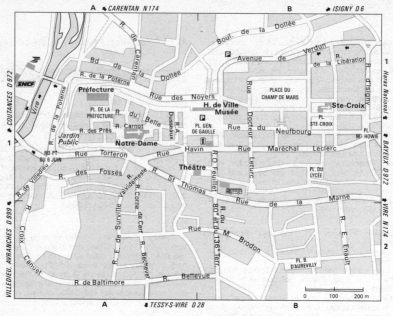

A ↖CARENTAN N174   B   ↗ISIGNY D6

SNCF

Préfecture

PLACE DU
CHAMP DE MARS

Ste-Croix

PL. DE LA
PRÉFECTURE

H. de Ville
Musée

PL. GÉN.
DE GAULLE

PL.
STE-CROIX

R. des Près   R. Carnot   Rue du Neufbourg   PL.
M. HOWIE

Jardin
Public   Notre-Dame   Havin   Rue   Maréchal Leclerc

RD·PT
DU 6 JUIN   Rue   Torteron   Rue   PL. DU
LYCÉE

R.   des   Fossés   Théâtre

R. St Thomas

Rue   de   la   Marne

Rue

PL. B.
D'AUREVILLY

R. de Baltimore   R.   Bellevue

0   100   200 m

A   ↙TESSY-S-VIRE D 28   B

Sᵗ-LÔ

SAINT-VALÉRY-EN-CAUX

Dieppe 32, Rouen 60, Paris 198 km
pop 5810 ⊠ 76460   C1

A fishing and boating harbour, a pebble beach between cliffs, a half-timbered Henri IV house (1540), a little town rebuilt around a chapel dating only from 1963.

Nearby

▶ Just before **Conteville** *(7 km W)*, EDF (Électricité de France) information centre for the **power station of Paluel**, (exhibit on nuclear power; view over the construction site; *call ahead 48hrs; tel. 35.97.36.16).* ▶ **Veulettes-sur-Mer** : seaside resort at the foot of the Câtelier cliff. ▶ **Cany-Barville** *(12 km SW)* : Renaissance church; 18thC covered market and town hall; **château de Cany★** (1646, designed by François Mansart; furniture; *Jul.-Aug.; closed Fri. and 4th Sun. in Jul.).* ▶ **Veules-les-Roses** *(8 km E)*, at the mouth of the smallest non-tributary river in France, the Veule; charming walk along the river and through the streets. Several farms and interesting **villages★** on the Caux plateau : **Blosseville** (stained glass in the church); 17thC châteaux at **La Chapelle-sur-Dun** and **Ermenouville, Canville** and **Bretteville** (half-timbered houses); and **Gruchet-Saint-Siméon.** Luneray *(16 km SE from Saint-Valéry)* : shops; European Traditional Jazz festival *(May-Jun.).* ▶ **Le Bourg-Dun** *(14.5 km E)* : 11th-16thC church★.   □

Practical Information

SAINT-VALÉRY-EN-CAUX
ⓘ pl. de l'Hôtel-de-Ville, ☎ 35.97.00.63.
SNCF ☎ 35.97.08.43.

Hotels :
★★ **Agora**, (PLM), 14, av. Clemenceau, ☎ 35.97.35.48,

Tx 172308, AE DC Euro Visa, 157 rm Ⓟ ≪ ▥ ♪ ♨ ⅙ 250. Rest. ♦ ≪ ♪ ⅙ 65-140 ; child : 50.
★★ **Les Terrasses**, 22, rue Le Peney, ☎ 36.97.11.22, DC Euro Visa, 12 rm Ⓟ ≪ ♨ ♪ closed Tue, 15 Dec-26 Jan, 230. Rest. ♦ ≪ ♪ 75-135.

Restaurant :
♦♦ **Port**, 18, quai d'Amont, ☎ 35.97.08.93, Visa ≪ ♪ closed Mon, Thu eve, Sun eve, 1-15 Sep. Sailor style. Spec : fish, grills, *turbot au basilic*, 110-250.

⚓ ★★*Falaises d'Amont* (133 pl), ☎ 35.97.05.07.

Recommended
Marina : ☎ 35.97.01.30, (600 slips).

Nearby

Le BOURG-DUN, ⊠ 76740, 15 km E.

Hotel :
Auberge du Dun (L.F.), rte de Dieppe, ☎ 35.83.05.84, Visa, 6 rm Ⓟ ♪ ⅙ half pens, closed Sun eve and Mon, 10-28 Feb, 15 Oct-2 Nov, 275. Rest. ● ♦♦ ♪ ⅙ A gifted chef serves excellent food at attractive prices : *grillade du pêcheur en salade, mignardises de la mer à la vapeur d'algues*, 80-200.

CANY-BARVILLE, ⊠ 76450, 12 km S.

Restaurant :
● ♦♦ **Le Manoir de Barville**, hameau de Barville, ☎ 35.97.79.30, Euro Visa ≪ ▥ ♪ 4 rm, closed Mon eve and Tue , Jan. Pleasant cuisine in a delightful little English-style manor house : *mignardise d'œufs au foie gras, aumônière de coquilles Saint-Jacques, pavé de filet*, 80-150.

VEULES-LES-ROSES, ⊠ 76980, 8 km E.

Restaurant :
● ♦♦♦ **Galets**, 3, rue V.-Hugo, ☎ 35.97.61.33, AE Visa ♪ closed Tue eve and Wed , Feb. Gilbert Plaisance is a pleasant chap indeed with a handsome house where he

cooks up lovely dishes like : *assiette de langouste mari-née crème de caviar, dariole de homard et ris de veau truffé en chemise, escalope de turbot sauté aux dés de foie gras et spaghetti de courgettes*, 200-350.

⚑ ★★★*Mouettes*, rte de Sotteville (100 pl), ☎ 35.97.61.98.

VEULETTES-SUR-MER, ⊠ 76450 Cany-Barville, 10 km W.

Hotel :
★★ **Les Frégates** (L.F.), digue Jean-Corruble, ☎ 35.97.51.22, DC Euro Visa, 16 rm P ⋞ pens, 275. Rest. ♦♦ ⋞ ♪ closed Mon noon and Sun eve (l.s.), 22 Dec-5 Jan, 65-190 ; child : 45.

The lower SEINE Valley***

C-D2
Round trip *(approx 235 km, 2 days ; see map 6)*

The Vikings understood the value of the river Seine as a route inland. Since the Middle Ages, it has never lost its importance as a means of transport for the products of agriculture and industry. Industrial devel-opment has not spoilt the countryside. Forests flour-ish at La Lande, Roumare, Mauny, Brotonne (Region-al Park) and the Marais Vernier (polders). Between Rouen and Honfleur, the only two bridges are those of Brotonne and Tancarville at the mouth of the river ; ferry plies the waters at Jumièges.

▶ **Rouen** (→). ▶ Pass quickly through the bland suburbs of Petit and Grand Quevilly to arrive at **Petit-Couronne** and the Maison des Champs bought by the father of the playwright Pierre Corneille so that his delicate son could benefit from country air (memorabilia, furniture, bread oven ; *closed Thu. and Nov.*). ▶ Remains of the 11thC **castle of Robert le Diable** (father of William the Conquer-or) over the village of Moulineaux ; the castle houses a Viking museum *(daily Mar.-Nov. ; Sun. only, rest of year ; closed Jan.)*; view★ of the Seine. ▶ **La Bouille :** stop-over at the foot of the cliffs. ▶ **Jumièges★★,** undoubtedly the most romantic Norman abbey ; founded in the 7thC, rebuilt in the 10thC, now only a splendid ruin ; stone-work museum in the 18thC abbey buildings *(daily ex nat. hols.).* ▶ **Notre-Dame-de-Bliquetuit,** starting point for a trip around **Brotonne Park** *(8 km) :* several half-timbered houses★, including a farm with a dovecote, near the exit towards the Brotonne Bridge★ (1 280 m long ; 1977 ; *toll).* On the other side of the bridge, head towards **Caude-**

bec : church of Notre-Dame★★ (Flamboyant Gothic, noted pipe-organ) and medieval Templar building (Old Caude-bec museum, *Sat. and Sun., Easter-Sep. ; daily, Jul.-Aug.).* ▶ **Saint-Gertrude :** 16thC church, half-timbered houses, watermill. ▶ Drive (site★) to **Villequier :** Victor Hugo museum *(daily ex Tue., 15 Mar.-30 Sep. ; closed Nov. and Jan., Mon., Tue. in winter).* ▶ Between Norville and Saint-Maurice, **château d'Etelan** (late 15thC, restored ; cultural events ; *15 Jul.-end Aug. pm ex Tue.)*; view of the Seine and the Brotonne Forest from the park. A detour through **Notre-Dame-de-Gravenchon** provides views of the val-ley and **Port-Jérôme.** ▶ **Lillebonne :** a theatre remains from the Roman town ; 13thC keep ; local archaeological museum *(pm ex Tue., May-Sep. ; Sun. in winter).* ▶ **Tan-carville★ :** château (14th-18thC) with restaurant, art gal-lery, cabinet-maker's workshop, equestrian centre, and museum. **Tancarville bridge★** (1 410 m long, *toll)* built 20 years before the Brotonne bridge. ▶ Off the Pont-l'Évê-que road, **Saint-Samson-de-la-Roque :** lighthouse, view★ of the Seine estuary as far as Le Havre. ▶ 44 km^2 of marshy plain at the foot of a cliff, drained since the 17thC, bordered by the village of **Marais Vernier★★ :** excep-tionally attractive half-timbered farmsteads, houses and yards (1 May, cattle branding). The road along the dyke, built by 16thC Dutch engineers in the reign of Henri IV, leads to **Quilleboeuf,** once an important river port ; Grande-Rue★ (pedestrian). ▶ The best route to **Saint-Opportune-la-Mare** is along the high, narrow road that provides a view★ of the Marais Vernier and the **Grande-Mare** (bird sanctuary ; mallards). In Saint-Opportune, Maison de la Pomme (apple sales in season) ; the Place de l'Église is also the meeting-place for visits to the Mannevilles Nature Park (go properly equipped to deal with mud, bogs and vipers ; half-day, or full day including the Marais Vernier ; *information from the Brotonne Park Information Office, tel. 32.57.40.41).* ▶ **Vieux-Port★ :** weekend cottages contrast with the farms of the Marais Vernier. ▶ **Bourneville :** the **Musée des Métiers** is a crafts centre (pottery ; courses ; exhibition and sale ; *2-7 ex Mon.).* ▶ Two giant yews★ stand in front of the church at **La Haye-de-Routot;** nearby is a restored bread oven (old utensils, fancy breads ; *pm ex Mon., Jul.-Aug. ; Sat. and Sun., spring and autumn)*; clog-maker's workshop *(pm ex Tue.);* starting point for two footpaths *(6 km and 11 km),* through the regional park. ▶ **Brotonne Forest★** (68 km^2; beech), then Pont de Brotonne. ▶ **Saint-Wandrille :** the abbey★★, founded in the 7thC, is occupied by Benedictines *(Sun. and hols. 11:30, 3 and 4 ; 3 and 4 weekdays);* ruins of 13th-14thC church ; 14th-15thC cloister ; the actual church (noted for Gregorian chant) is a 13thC barn. ▶ **Le Trait,** between the

6. Lower Seine valley

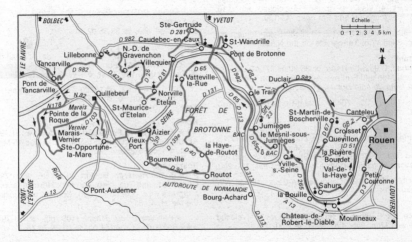

naval shipyards and the thermal power centre at Yainville, HQ of the **Brotonne Nature Park** *(weekdays)*; three different hikes leave from here. The Park★ extends on both sides of the Seine (42 km²) with the aim of protecting the rural environment, cultural heritage, agriculture and crafts of the region. ▶ **Saint-Martin-de-Boscherville** : former **abbey** church of **St. Georges**★★ (12thC) is the finest abbey building left in the valley *(son et lumière, enq. : DT Rouen)*. ▶ **Château de la Rivière-Bourdet** (17thC) and Marbeuf Manor (16thC) via **Sahurs** ; **Croisset** : in the midst of the Rouen harbour installations, an 18thC pavilion remains from Flaubert's estate *(10-12 & 2-6; closed Thu., Fri. am and nat. hols.)*. ☐

Practical Information ────────────────

La **BOUILLE**, ⊠ 76530 Grand-Couronne, 18 km SW of **Rouen**.

Hotel :
● ★★ *Le Saint-Pierre*, pl. du Bateau, ☎ 35.23.80.10, AE DC Visa, 7 rm ℗ ≼ ⅋ closed Tue eve and Wed (Nov-Mar). Rest. ◆◆ ≼ ఉ ⅋ Enjoy the view of the meandering Seine. And enjoy the attractive 100F fixed meal too : *soupe d'huîtres, cervelas de poissons, ravioles de homard, poulet fermière au cidre*, 100-300.

CAUDEBEC-EN-CAUX, ⊠ 76490, 36 km NW of **Rouen**.
ⓘ mairie, ☎ 35.96.11.12. ☙

Hotels :
★★★ *La Marine*, 18, quai Guilbaud, ☎ 35.96.20.11, 33 rm ℗ ≼ ⅋ 260.
★★★ *Manoir de Rétival*, rue St-Clair, ☎ 35.96.11.22, AE DC, 12 rm ℗ ≼ ⅋ closed 30 Nov-1 Feb, 460.
★★ *Le Normandie* (L.F.), 19, quai Guilbaud, ☎ 35.96.25.11, AE Euro Visa, 16 rm ℗ ≼ closed Feb, 165. Rest. ◆◆ ≼ ⅃ closed Sun eve, 50-140.

Recommended
Events : *cider festival*, last wk in Sep or 1st in Oct.

DUCLAIR, ⊠ 76480, 20 km N of **Rouen**.
ⓘ hôtel de ville, ☎ 35.37.50.06.

Restaurant :
● ◆◆◆ *Le Parc*, 721, av. Pdt-Coty, ☎ 35.37.50.31, AE DC Euro Visa ℗ ≼ ⅏ ⅃ closed Mon and Sun eve, 15 Dec-15 Jan. In a pleasant park, the Seine flows at your feet. Excellent, down-to-earth cooking by Pierre Lepatezour : *poêlée d'huîtres et langoustines, gratin de homard thermidor*, 110-220.

NORVILLE, ⊠ 76330, 8 km E of **Lillebonne**.

Hotel :
★ *Auberge de Norville* (L.F.), rue des Ecoles, ☎ 35.39.91.14, Visa, 10 rm ℗ ≼ ⚲ closed Jan, 110. Rest. ◆ ≼ ⅃ closed Fri and Sat noon, 45-130.

SAINT-VIGOR-D'YMONVILLE, ⊠ 76430 Saint-Romain-de-Colbosc, 8 km W of **Tancarville** on the N 182.

Restaurant :
◆◆◆ *Dubuc*, D 982, Le Hode, ☎ 35.20.06.97, AE DC Visa ⅃ ఉ closed Mon and Sun eve, 4-25 Aug. Spec : *salade de homard, filets de sole Dubuc*, 170-250.

TANCARVILLE, ⊠ 76430 Saint-Romain-de-Colbosc, 30 km E of **Le Havre**.

Hotel :
★★ *Marine*, at the foot of the bridge, ☎ 35.39.77.15, 10 rm ℗ ≼ ⅏ ⅋ closed Sun eve , Mon, Feb school hols, 16 Aug-6 Sep, 120. Rest. ◆ ≼ ⅃ ఉ Spec : *filets de sole aux langoustines en habit vert, chaud-froid cauchois*, 120-200.

VILLEQUIER, ⊠ 76490 Caudebec-en-Caux, 40 km NW of **Rouen**.

Hotel :
★ *France*, rue E.-Binet, ☎ 35.56.78.70, 8 rm ℗ ఉ closed Sun eve and Mon, Feb, 120. Rest. ◆ ⅃ 60-120.

La SUISSE NORMANDE★★

B2-3

This oddly-named area (Norman Switzerland) lies to the east of the Bocage region.

Tourist route of the Suisse Normande.
▶ The GR36 follows the Orne between Thury-Harcourt and Putanges. ▶ At **Thury-Harcourt**, ruined château, park and garden of the château d'Harcourt★ *(visit Sun. and nat. hols., Apr.-Jun.; pm daily, Jul.-15 Oct.)*, 2.5 km W, a narrow loop of the river Hom★. ▶ Near Acqueville *(10 km E)* : **château de la Motte** (1660; *park open daily*). ▶ **Clécy**, on a bend in the Orne, the main town in the area; lookouts at Le Pain de Sucre (Sugarloaf Hill, *NE*), L'Eminence *(SW)*, La Croix de la Faverie *(S)* and Butte Saint-Clair *(E)*; Placy Manor (16thC; Antiquities Museum; *pm Jul.-1 Sep., Sun. and nat. hols. out of season)*; "Suisse Normande Miniature", miniature railway museum *(Jun.-mid-Sep.; Sun. pm out of season)*. ▶ Near Condé, **chateau de Pontécoulant** *(closed Mon., Tue. and Oct.)*. ▶ Picturesque sites between **Pont d'Ouilly** and the Rabodanges Dam ; junction of the Rouvre, Oëtre rock★, St. Aubert Gorge, and the lake at **Putanges-Pont-Écrepin**. **Rabodanges** : 17thC château with moats and terraced gardens *(weekdays Jul.-Oct.)*. ☐

Practical Information ────────────────

CLÉCY, ⊠ 14570, 37 km S of **Caen**.
ⓘ mairie, ☎ 31.69.71.47.

Hotels :
★★★ *Hôtellerie du Moulin du Vey* (C.H.), Le Vey, ☎ 31.69.71.08, AE DC Visa, 19 rm ℗ ≼ ⅏ ⅊ noon closed 30 Nov-28 Dec, 330. Rest. ◆◆ ≼ ⅋ closed Fri noon. Spec : *langouste grillée, terrine d'anguille sauce aux câpres*, 95-250.
★★ *Site Normand* (L.F.), rue des Chatelets-Notre-Dame, ☎ 31.69.71.05, AE DC Visa, 12 rm ℗ ≼ ⅊ closed Jan-Feb, 180. Rest. ◆ ⅃ closed Mon (l.s.), 70-155.

⚠ ★★*Moulin du Vey* (100 pl), ☎ 31.69.71.47.

Recommended
Horseback riding : *l'Etrier de la Suisse normande*, le Lande, 3 km S, ☎ 31.69.70.06.

PONT-D'OUILLY, ⊠ 14690, 12 km SE of **Clécy**.
ⓘ ☎ 31.69.80.68.

Hotel :
● ★★ *Auberge Saint-Christophe* (L.F.), D 23, 1.5 km, ☎ 31.69.81.23, AE Euro Visa, 7 rm ℗ ≼ ⅏ ⚲ ⅃ half pens (h.s.), closed Sun eve and Mon (ex Jun-Sep), Feb, Oct, 360. Rest. ◆◆ ≼ ⅃ closed Mon and Sun eve (l.s.), Mon lunch (h.s.), 70-145.

PUTANGES-PONT-ÉCREPIN, ⊠ 61210, 17 km S of **Falaise**.
ⓘ hôtel de ville, ☎ 33.35.02.44.

Hotel :
● ★★ *Lion Verd* (L.F.), pl. de l'Hôtel-de-Ville, ☎ 33.35.01.86, AE Euro Visa, 20 rm ℗ ≼ ⚲ closed 26 Dec-31 Jan, 105. Rest. ◆ ≼ Waterside terrace, 50-120.

THURY-HARCOURT, ⊠ 14220, 26 km S of **Caen**.
ⓘ pl. St-Sauveur, ☎ 31.79.70.45.
🚆 ☎ 31.79.72.48.

Hotel :
★★★ *Relais de la Poste*, Bd du 30-Juin, ☎ 31.79.72.12, AE DC Euro Visa, 11 rm ℗ ⅏ closed 15 Dec-15 Mar, 185. Rest. ◆ ≼ ఉ 95-250.

Restaurant :
◆ *La Bonne Auberge*, Boulon, 10 km NE, ☎ 31.79.37.60, closed Mon and Tue , Sep. Authentic Norman fare : *tripes, teurgoule* (rice cooked in milk), *Norman trout, cider from the barrel*, 40-85.

⚠ ★★★★*Vallée du Traspi* (106 pl), ☎ 31.79.61.80; ★★★*Bords de l'Orne* (70 pl), ☎ 31.79.70.78.

Le TRÉPORT

Dieppe 30, Rouen 91, Paris 170 km
pop 6555 ⊠ 76470   D1

Le Tréport is close enough to Paris to be a convenient seaside resort; the port has recently opened to vessels of large draught.

▶ Port. ▶ Church of St. Jacques, overlooking the port, has a Renaissance doorway and fine hanging keystones.

Nearby

▶ **Mers-les-Bains**, a seaside resort on the other side of the river Bresle. ▶ **Eu** *(4 km SE)*, an old brick town recently restored : former hospital and château of brick and stone, begun in 1578 and restored 19thC *(Apr.-Oct. ex Tue.)*; nearby church of St. Laurent★ (12th-13thC; 15thC Entombment of Christ); college chapel (16thC tombs★; *15 Jun.-15 Sep. and Sun. pm)*. The **Eu Forest** covers 94 km² ; the best part is upstream from **Blangy** along the Bresle Valley.   □

Practical Information _____

Le TRÉPORT
ⓘ esplanade de la plage, ☎ 35.86.05.69, closed Tue and Sun.
𝗦𝗡𝗖𝗙 ☎ 35.86.23.44.

Hotel :
★★ *Picardie*, pl. P.-Sémard, ☎ 35.86.02.22, Euro Visa, 30 rm ℗ ≷ half pens (h.s.), closed Sun eve and Mon (l.s.), 8 Dec-21 Jan, 385. Rest. ♦♦ ⋮ ᕂ ✻ Spec : *médaillon de lotte au coulis d'écrevisses*, 80-200.

Nearby

BLANGY-SUR-BRESLE, ⊠ 76230, 24 km SE.

Hotel :
★ *Auberge de Tivoli*, 1, rte de Neufchâtel, ☎ 35.93.51.16, AE Euro Visa, 14 rm ℗ 130. Rest. ♦ ⋮ closed Sun eve (l.s.), 50-110.

⚠ ★★*Municipal* (36 pl), ☎ 35.93.54.17.

EU, ⊠ 76260, 4 km E.
ⓘ 41, rue Paul-Bignon, ☎ 35.86.04.68.

Hotel :
★★★ *Pavillon Joinville* (R.S.), rte du Tréport, ☎ 35.86.24.03, Tx 172151, AE DC Euro Visa, 19 rm ℗ ≷ ㎞ ⚲ ⌂ ⤴ 345. Rest. ♦♦ *La Ferme Modèle* ≷ ⋮ closed Mon and Sun eve , Jan-Feb, 115-190.

⚠ ★★★*Municipal* (70 pl), ☎ 35.86.20.04.

Recommended
Bicycle-rental : *Roger Mallet*, 19, rue G.-Clemenceau, ☎ 35.86.17.81.

MERS-LES-BAINS, ⊠ 80350, 4 km N.
ⓘ rue J.-Barni, ☎ 35.86.06.14 (h.s.).

Hotel :
★★ *Bellevue*, espl. du Gal-Leclerc, ☎ 35.86.12.89, Euro Visa, 25 rm ≷ ⚲ 150. Rest. ♦ ⋮ closed Mon and Sun eve, 70-110.

⚠ ★★★★*Rompval* (135 pl), ☎ 35.86.25.40 ; ★★*la Falaise* (150 pl), ☎ 35.86.22.14.

VALOGNES*

Cherbourg 20, Saint-Lô 58, Paris 340 km
pop 6960 ⊠ 50700   A1-2

Rebuilt since WWII, Valogne has recovered its prewar aristocratic atmosphere.

▶ 16thC church of St. Malo (rebuilt); old mansions; Beaumont mansion *(daily pm ex Wed., Jul.-15 Sep.)* ; Cider Museum (16thC house, *15 Jun.-30 Sep. ex Wed. and Sun. am)*; museum of spirits *(Eau-de-vie)*

and Old Trades, Hôtel de Thieuville (17th, 19thC). ▶ In the Alleaume suburb *(NE)* : Roman ruins.

Nearby

▶ **Colomby** *(6 km S)* : 13thC church. ▶ **Saint-Sauveur-le-Vicomte** *(15 km S)* : small museum of the writer Barbey d'Aurevilly (1808-89) in the château *(closed Tue.)*; S of town, rebuilt **Benedictine abbey** (pilgrimage). ▶ **Barneville-Carteret** *(30 km SW)* : seaside resort **(Carteret)** with beach; seaside resort at **Barneville** S of the Gerfleur estuary. ▶ 7 km of dunes to **Port-Bail**, a resort and fishing harbour; 11thC church★ with 15thC tower.   □

Practical Information _____

VALOGNES
ⓘ pl. du Château, ☎ 33.40.11.55 (h.s.).
𝗦𝗡𝗖𝗙 ☎ 33.40.10.12.

Hotel :
★ *L'Agriculture* (L.F.), 16, rue Léopold-Delisle, ☎ 33.95.02.02, Euro Visa, 36 rm ℗ ㎞ ⚲ 145. Rest. ♦ ᕂ closed Mon and Sun eve, 1-19 Jan, 29 Jun-6 Jul, 14-30 Sep. Spec : oysters, seafood, *canard au poivre vert*, 45-125 ; child : 25.

Nearby

BARNEVILLE-CARTERET, ⊠ 50270, 30 km SW.
ⓘ pl. du Dr-Auvret, Barneville, ☎ 33.04.90.58 ; av. de la République, Carteret, ☎ 33.53.84.80 (h.s.).
𝗦𝗡𝗖𝗙 *Carteret*, ☎ 33.57.50.50, service in summer Carentan-Carteret.
⛴ *Service maritime Carteret*, ☎ 33.53.87.21, to Channel islands (h.s.).

Hotels :
★★ *Marine* (L.F.), 11, rue de Paris, ☎ 33.53.83.31, DC Euro Visa, 33 rm ℗ ≷ closed 12 Nov-28 Feb, 240. Rest. ♦ ≷ ⋮ closed Mon noon (l.s.). Regional specialities, 130-250.
★★ *Paris* (L.F.), pl. de l'Eglise, ☎ 33.04.90.02, 25 rm ℗ ㎞ ⚲ ᕂ half pens, closed Sun eve and Mon lunch (l.s.), 350. Rest. ♦ ᕂ 45-90.

⚠ ★★*Bocage* (240 pl), ☎ 33.53.86.91 ; ★★*Bosquets*, Barneville beach (240 pl), ☎ 33.54.73.62.

PORT-BAIL, ⊠ 50580, 38 km S.
ⓘ mairie, ☎ 33.04.88.30.

Hotel :
★ *Galiche* (L.F.), 13-15, pl. Ed.-Laquaine, ☎ 33.04.84.18, Euro Visa, 12 rm ℗ ≷ closed Sun eve , Mon (l.s.), Feb, 1-15 Oct, 110. Rest. ♦ 50-150.

⚠ ★★★*Vieux Fort* (100 pl), ☎ 33.54.81.99 ; *V.V.F.*, ☎ 33.04.80.84.

QUINÉVILLE, ⊠ 50310 Montebourg, 15 km E.

Hotel :
★★ *Château de Quinéville*, ☎ 33.21.42.67, 13 rm ℗ ≷ ㎞ ⚲ closed Jan-Mar, 200. Rest. ♦♦ ⋮ 60-110.

VERNON*

Evreux 31, Rouen 63, Paris 82 km
pop 23460 ⊠ 27200   D2

Capital of the Vexin region of Normandy, and too close to Paris to have a truly Norman atmosphere, Vernon is nevertheless a good excursion centre for the Seine, Epte and Eure valleys.

▶ Church of Notre-Dame in the town centre, 13th-14thC building with early-17thC mausoleum; half-timbered houses (15thC) nearby. ▶ Near the Tour des Archives (12thC), wood and stone buildings (15th-17thC) housing the **Poulain Municipal Museum** (paintings, including two by Monet; sculpture and local history ; *pm closed Mon. and nat. hols.)*. ▶ Ruins of a medieval bridge and the château des Tourelles (13thC) at Vernonnet on the other bank. ▶ On the road to Pacy-sur-Eure, **château de Bizy**

(19thC) : stables and outbuildings (18thC) in a park (Napoleonic memorabilia ; *Apr.-Oct. ex Fri.).*

Nearby

▶ Forests of Bizy and Vernon, right bank of the Seine ; walks. ▶ **Giverny** (→ Ile-de-France : Vexin Region). ▶ **Saint-Pierre-de-Bailleul** *(10 km NW)* : pelt-farming *(closed Tue. and Thu.).* ▶ **Gaillon★** *(14 km NW)* : château built by Cardinal d'Amboise (Minister to Louis XII, late 15th-early 16thC) launched the Renaissance style in Normandy ; now in restoration, will house the Upper Normandy Museum ; half-timbered houses near the church. □

Practical Information _____

VERNON
ⓘ passage Pasteur, ☎ 32.51.39.60.
SNCF ☎ 32.51.01.72.
Car rental : *Avis*, 17, av. de Rouen, ☎ 32.51.50.41.

Hotels :
● ★★★ *Evreux*, 11, pl. d'Evreux, ☎ 32.21.16.12, AE DC Euro Visa, 20 rm Ⓟ ♪ 250. Rest. ♦♦ *Le Relais Normand* ♪ & closed Sun , Aug. 150-210.
★★ *Le Strasbourg*, 6, pl. d'Evreux, ☎ 32.51.23.12, Euro Visa, 23 rm Ⓟ closed Sun eve and Mon, 29 Dec-12 Jan, 170. Rest. ♦ ♪ & 65-150.

Restaurant :
● ♦♦ *Au Beau Rivage*, 13, av. Mal-Leclerc, ☎ 32.51.17.27, AE Euro Visa Ⓟ ⅃ & closed Mon and Sun eve, 1-15 Feb, 1-15 Oct. A pleasant place to stop on a weekend drive to Normandy, 100-200 ; child : 60.

⚠ ★★*Fosses Rouges* (82 pl), ☎ 82.51.59.86.

Recommended
Rural-gîte : at Blaru, CP 78270, 8 km S, *"Le But"* Marie-Luce Torrilhon, 17, rue du But, ☎ (1) 34.76.23.09, beginners', advanced lessons, trail riding.
♥ pastry : 45, rue Carnot.

Nearby

CHAMBRAY, ✉ 27120 Pacy-sur-Eure, 18 km SW.

Restaurant :
♦♦ *Le Vol au Vent*, 1, pl. de la Mairie, ☎ 32.36.70.05, DC Euro Visa, closed Mon, Tue noon, Sun eve , Jan. Spec : feuilleté de ris aux morilles, turbot aux huîtres, bourdelot normand, 140-200.

VIRE

Caen 60, Laval 105, Paris 270 km
pop 14540 ✉ 14500 B3

On a beautiful site, the town was badly damaged during WWII, and retains little of its original charm.

▶ Only the Tour de l'Horloge (clock tower ; *Jul.-Aug.*), built on a 13thC fortified gateway and the **church of Notre-Dame** (13th-15thC) are left from historic Vire. ▶ View from Mont Besnard, opposite the château, overlooking the river Vire and a ruined 12thC keep. ▶ Municipal museum *(closed Tue. and nat. hols.).*

Nearby

▶ 7 km SW, Dathée Lake. ▶ 14 km W : **Saint-Sever-Calvados,** on the N edge of **Saint-Sever Forest★** (4174 acres ; wildlife reserve ; signposted trails) : 13thC abbey church, belfry. ▶ 25 km NE, **Cabosse** or **Jurques** zoo (animals in semi-freedom). □

Practical Information _____

VIRE
ⓘ square de la Résistance, ☎ 31.68.00.05.
SNCF ☎ 31.68.04.08.

Hotel :
● ★★ *Cheval Blanc* (L.F.), 2, pl. du 6-Juin-44, ☎ 31.68.00.21, AE DC Euro Visa, 23 rm, closed Fri eve, Sat lunch (15 Sep-1 May), 20 Dec-20 Jan, 200. Rest. ♦♦♦ ♪ Light, refined Norman cooking. Fish is featured, 80-190.

Recommended
♥ tripe : *Michel Ruault*, L'Ecluse, ☎ 31.68.05.78 ; at Saint-Désir-de-Lisieux, 14100, cider, Calvados : *Léon Desfrieches*, ☎ 31.31.17.53.

Nearby

ROULLOURS, ✉ 14500, 3 km SE on the D 524.

Restaurant :
● ♦♦ *Manoir de la Pommeraie*, ☎ 31.68.07.71, AE DC Euro Visa ♪ & closed Sun eve and Mon, Feb, 27 Jul-11 Aug. Georges and Maryse Lesage have settled in new quarters : a pretty 18th-C manor surrounded by a park that boasts century-old trees. Spec : salade de langoustines fraîches, filet de barbue aux poireaux, crème brûlée au Grand Marnier. Great vintage Bordeaux, 99-250.

Picardy

and the North

▶ The North — the name evokes tranquil, misty horizons, meandering rivers and a sky perpetually covered with scudding clouds. Images that can easily suggest monotony. And yet the "flat country" lying between the Paris and the Anglo-Norman basins, and immortalized in the songs of Jacques Brel, includes the most varied regions. The south is characterized by the hard underlying soapstone of the Paris basin where the Artois hills rise 100 or 200 metres up from the plain, and further south still are vast limestone plateaus indented with the green valleys of Vimeu, Ponthieu and Santerre. To the north, beyond the chalky ledges of the Artois peaks with their wooded valleys, the chalk strata sinks deeper under sand and clay to form lower and damper ground — this is the true "flat country" whose only relief is provided by the hills of Flanders. The fertile plateaus of the south with their damp valleys and farmhouses huddled together in villages contrast with the wide northern plains sectioned by groves of trees and hedgerows and dotted with isolated farmhouses. The south is thinly populated along the traditional invasion route from the East. But everywhere are the characteristic windmills adding a touch of poetry and fantasy to the landscape.

Perhaps the best time to visit the Pays du Nord is during one of the many festivals, when the people dance together around wickerwork effigies representing their beloved and legendary "giants"; the Festival of Dunkirk just before Lent and the Festival of Gargantua in Bailleul are among the most important.

The bustling towns and ports of the region — many of which were devastated by the battles of WWII — have their share of famous churches and abbeys, such as the huge cathedral of Amiens, the largest in France, a true masterpiece of Gothic art. Calais, the largest pas-senger port in France, is also noted for its lace industry introduced from England at the beginning of the 19thC. Coal, textiles and steel were the traditional mainstays of the region's economy, and Lille, Roubaix and Valenciennes have for centuries been important manufacturing centres. Slagheaps and colliery lifting gear still mark the land in which Zola set his *Germinal*. Today, the North is — sometimes reluctantly — shedding its smokestack image, and whitecoated technicians and electronics assembly lines are beginning to replace the ruddy glare of blast furnaces seen from the autoroute. □

● Don't miss

★★★ Amiens A-B3, Arras B2, Lille B1.

★★ Authie Valley A-B2, the Avesnois Area C2, Bavay C2, Bergues B1, Boulogne-sur-Mer A1, Canche Valley A-B2, Cassel B1, Douai B2, Montreuil A2, Rue A2, Saint-Omer A1, Saint-Valéry-sur-Somme A2, Somme Valley A2-3.

★ Aire-sur-la-Lys B1, Cambrai B2, Dunkerque B1, Fourmies C2, Valenciennes C2.

Weekend tips

If you approach from the S, first visit the cathedral at Amiens; spend the night in Boulogne (illuminations in the old town). The next day watch the fishermen unloading and sorting fish in the port. Head for Calais along the Côte d'Opale ridge road, over the Boulonnais hills and across two promontories. From Saint-Omer climb towards the typically Flemish town of Cassel, before arriving at Lille. The following day choose between two excursions : through the regional nature reserve of Saint-Amand and the Avesnois, or through the beautiful towns of Douai and Arras to the famous ridges at Vimy and Notre-Dame-de-Lorette (Crêtes du Sacrifice).

Boulonnais region

Avesnois region

Somme region

The giants

Some ninety towns in Picardy and the North field "Giants", immense wickerwork figures which run and dance, propelled by their wearers, on popular feast days. It is impossible to name them all or to work out their family relationships, since these imposing personalities intermarry and have children... Some of the older generation of giants recall men who were remarkable for their prodigious strength or their fabulous exploits, such as "Gayant de Douai", born in 1530, in memory of Jehan Gelon who delivered the people of Douai some four centuries earlier from a band of brigands. Some giants recall legends : Jehan de Calais, or Phynaert and Lydéric of Lille. Finally, the youngsters represent the principal activities of their town, like Cafougnette, the miner from Denai and Batisse, the fisherman from Boulogne. They all appear on religious and public holidays : in Dunkerque, Cassel, Bailleul or Douai, the giants go among their people, retreating to sleep at night to the sound of fanfares, lit by displays of fireworks.

 Brief regional history

1stC BC-3rdC
At the beginning of this period, the population was composed of **Celtic tribes** living in numerous villages; the Romans called the area **Belgium.** From 58 to 57 BC, the Belgian people fought against the invading Roman troops of Caesar's army. Peace was achieved in 54 BC, and cities like Amiens, Arras, Bavay and Boulogne began to grow. ● In 286, the North region was part of **Second Belgium,** with Reims as capital, but this marked the beginning of the Barbaric invasions and the Gallo-Roman towns were forced to surround themselves with fortifications.

4th-6thC
In the 4thC, **Christianity** started to spread throughout the region; during this period, the **Franks** continued their westward expansion, establishing large commu-

nities in the unpopulated northern areas; later this barrier was to define the linguistic frontier between Flemish and French-speaking peoples.

7th-9thC

In the 7thC, N France was part of **Neustrie** (the kingdom of the West); Soissons was its capital. By then, numerous **abbeys** had been founded; as centres of learning and trade, they attracted growing numbers of local inhabitants. ● In the 8thC **Charlemagne** subdivided his kingdom into domains administered by counts. After the **Norman invasions** of the 9thC, the power of these regional landholders increased at the expense of the central royal power; this was the early outline of the feudal system.

10th-12thC

Crowned king in Noyon in 987, **Hugues Capet** ruled over a limited domain surrounded by powerful fiefdoms. As security returned, **agricultural activity** expanded in the North : forest clearances, marsh drainage and more extensive cultivation of wheat. An active **urban upper class** appeared : belfries and ramparts symbolized the liberties won by town councils. A brilliant artistic life developed in the great cities, and **Gothic art** began to spread.

13th-14thC

In 1191, **Philippe Auguste** united Artois to the crown of France; at the battle of Bouvines (1214), he put an end to southward expansion by the Count of Flanders. ● In 1304, **Philippe le Bel** pushed French influence into Flanders itself. At the beginning of the **Hundred Years' War,** the Treaty of Brétigny (1360) gave the victorious English the region around Calais and Ponthieu. ● **Philippe le Hardi,** brother of Charles V and a duke of Burgundy, became Count of Flanders (by marriage) in 1369 and Count of Artois (by inheritance) in 1382, and so created the **unity of northern France.**

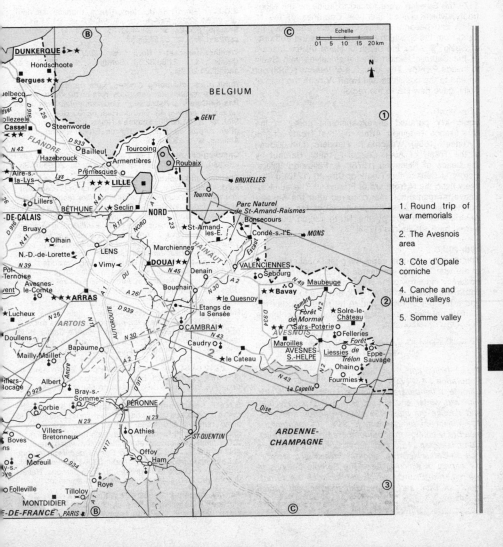

1. Round trip of war memorials

2. The Avesnois area

3. Côte d'Opale corniche

4. Canche and Authie valleys

5. Somme valley

15th-16thC

In 1420, the Treaty of Troyes recognized the rights of the King of England over Picardy and the Boulogne area. After the reconquest led by Joan of Arc, the King of France transferred the sovereignty of these two provinces to the **dukes of Burgundy** (Treaty of Arras, 1435), as a reward for their loyalty. Under the influence of the luxurious court of Burgundy, the towns of Flanders, Artois and Hainaut became centres of artistic achievement. ● **Charles le Téméraire** (the Bold), last Grand Duke of Burgundy, died in 1477. His only daughter married Maximilian of Austria, bringing him all the Burgundian states in her dowry. But **Picardy** was reunited with France under the reign of Louis XI in 1493. ● In the 16thC, the "North Countries" passed from the Austrian Habsburgs to the **Habsburgs of Spain.** ● François I of France, held in check by Charles V of Austria (1529), succeeded in reconquering Calais from the English (1536). During this same period, Protestantism was developing in the North (Calvin was born in 1509 in Noyon), and in 1579 the Spanish were forced to abide by the Mons treaty, which divided the Low Countries of the N, which had become mostly Protestant and independant, from the S, which remained under the authority of Spain. ● After the death of Henri III, the leaders of the Catholic faction allied themselves with Spain to invade Picardy. The armistice of Vervins (1598) put an end to the hostilities and **Henri IV,** with the help of Sully, gave new life to the region.

17th-18thC

Louis XIV pursued an expansionist policy in the N : France regained **Artois** by the Treaty of the Pyrénées (1659), **Wallonia** (S Flanders; Lille, Douai) at the Treaty of Aix-la-Chapelle (1668), **Hainaut** by the peace of Nijmegen (1678). ● Following Villars' victory at Denain, the Treaty of Utrecht (1713) definitively fixed the N **frontiers** of France. ● The administrative reorganization that occurred after the **Revolution** tended to eclipse the **provincial states.** In 1792, Austria tried to occupy the North region but was turned back at Fleurus (1793).

19th-20thC

The discovery of **coal deposits,** near Douai at the end of the 18thC, and in the Pas-de-Calais in 1847, attracted heavy **industry** to the North of France. ● The two **world wars** were particularly destructive in this area, and a number of towns had to be rebuilt. Today the N industrial belt is adapting with courage to changes in energy development.

Facts and figures

Area : *18 803 km².*
Population : *4 477 509.*
Climate : *temperate; prevailing winds W and NW, with wet winter and spring. Summer is usually fine, and despite the inevitable cloudy periods, the average maximum temperature is 21ºC. In autumn the weather is changeable, but temperatures remain mild.*
Administration : *the two departments of **Nord** and **Pas-de-Calais** form a single administrative region, the capital of which is Lille. The **Somme** belongs to the region of Picardy, which also includes the departments of **Oise** and **Aisne,** with the regional capital at Amiens.*

● Practical information

Information : **Nord-Pas-de-Calais** : *Comité Régional de Tourisme (C.R.T.),* 26, pl. Rihour, 59002 Lille Cedex, ☎ 20.57.40.04. *Délégation régionale au tourisme,* pl. Allende, 59650 Villeneuve-d'Ascq, ☎ 20.05.27.28. **Nord** : *Comité Départemental de Tourisme (C.D.T.),* 14, sq. Foch, 59000 Lille, ☎ 20.57.00.61 and 20.57.00.62. **Pas-de-Calais** : *C.D.T.,* 44, Grand-Rue, 62200 Boulogne-sur-Mer, ☎ 21.31.98.58. **Somme** : *C.D.T.,* 21, rue Ernest-Cauvin, 80000 Amiens, ☎ 22.92.26.39. In **Paris** : *Maison du Nord-Pas-de-Calais,* 18, bd Haussmann, 75009, ☎ 47.70.59.62. *Dir. rég. de la Jeunesse et des Sports,* parc de Beauvillé, 80039 Amiens Cedex, ☎ 22.91.88.86, and 7, rue de Thionville, 59800 Lille, ☎ 20.55.95.49. *Dir. rég. des Affaires culturelles,* 5, rue Henry-Daussy, 80044 Amiens Cedex, ☎ 22.91.12.12, and hôtel Scrive, 1, rue du Lombard, 59000 Lille, ☎ 20.06.87.58.

Reservations : *Loisirs-Accueil Somme,* 21, rue Ernest-Cauvin, 80000 Amiens ☎ 22.92.26.39. *Loisirs-Accueil Pas-de-Calais* at the *C.D.T.,* ☎ 21.31.66.80.

S.O.S. : **Nord,** *SAMU* (emergency medical service), ☎ 20.54.22.22; **Pas-de-Calais,** *SAMU,* ☎ 21.71.51.51; **Somme,** *SAMU,* ☎ 22.44.25.25. *Poisoning emergency centre* (Lille), ☎ 20.54.55.56.

Weather forecast : **Nord** : ☎ 20.97.93.11. **Pas-de-Calais** : ☎ 21.55.32.53. **Somme** : ☎ 22.89.44.47 and 22.24.29.95.

Rural gîtes, chambres d'hôtes, farm camping : **Nord** : *Relais départemental des gîtes ruraux du Nord, C.D.T.* **Pas-de-Calais** : *Association départementale des gîtes ruraux de France,* 44, Grande-Rue, 62200 Boulogne-sur-Mer, ☎ 21.31.66.80. **Somme** : *Relais départemental des gîtes ruraux de France,* 21, rue Ernest-Cauvin, 80000 Amiens, ☎ 22.92.36.39.

Camping-car rental : *Lille Caravane,* autoroute A1, exit Lesquin, rue d'Avelin, 59175 Vendeville, ☎ 20.96.07.98.

Festivals and events : **Feb** : *Uischerbende parade in Dunkerque* (mardi gras). **Mar** : *winter carnival in Bailleul.* **Apr** : *international documentary and short film festival in Lille; giants' dance at Cassel* (Easter Mon); *watercress fair in Lécluse.* **May** : *Amiens carnival; tobacco fair in Lille; jazz festival in Amiens.* **Jun** : *fair-exhibition in Amiens; horticulture festival in Amiens; spring cultural festival in Valenciennes.* **Jul** : *fish festival in Boulogne; Opal coast and Picardy coast festivals; summer festival in Somme.* **Aug** : *medieval festival in Boulogne.* **Sep** : *grande braderie* (big jumble, or garage, sale) *in Lille; andouille* (chitterling sausage) *festival in Aire-sur-la-Lys; festival de la Bêtise in Cambrai.* **Nov** : *festival des différences in Amiens.*

Rambling and hiking : **Nord-Pas-de-Calais** : G.R. trails 120, 121, 121A, 122 traverse the region, as does the G.R. of the Thiérache region. *A.D. Rando.* **Pas-de-Calais,** Hôtel de Ville, 62800 Liévin, ☎ 21.20.59.12, and, for the North, enq. at *C.D.T.* **Somme** : *Association des gîtes d'étape de Picardie,* 9, rue Allart, B.P. 0342, 80003 Amiens Cedex, ☎ 22.92.64.64. The Somme Department is traversed by G.R. 123, 124 and 125. Enq. : *Délégation départementale de la F.F.R.P.* G.N.S.G.R., 26, rte de Mareuil, 80250 Ailly-sur-Noye. *S.N.C.F.* : *train + ramble* : during spring and summer, the railroad proposes a number of train trips scheduled to allow rambles and hikes in the Picardy region, with approximately 20 % reductions in train fares. The Somme *C.D.T.* publishes brochures on the region which are available at the *S.I.* and *C.D.T.* The *Comité départemental de la randonnée pédestre,* B.P. 0409, 80004 Amiens Cedex, organizes excursions for groups of 10-25 persons. Reservations required at least three weeks in advance.

Activity centers : *Forest Hill Nauticlub,* avenue de la Marne, 59700 Marcq-en-Barœul, ☎ 20.98.97.97; *Aqualud,* bd de la Mer, 62520 Le Touquet, ☎ 21.05.63.59.

Belfries and bell towers

Originally watchtowers where the city bells were housed, belfries were subsequently used to safeguard maps and treasures. Over the centuries they became symbols of local rights and liberties. Often they were destroyed but always rebuilt; at Arras, Douai and Dunkerque, as in Boulogne, Bergues and Béthune, they overlook huge squares and busy streets. The carillons of the city belfries compete with the bells of neighbouring churches on holidays when both religious and secular peals ring out over the town. The Concerts de Carillons *attract large audiences, especially at Avesnes, Bergues, Douai and Saint-Amand.*

Riding holidays : the **Nord-Pas-de-Calais** region offers 800 km of marked bridle paths. *A.R.T.E. Nord-Pas-de-Calais :* S. Bacquaert, 8, pl. Lis-franc, 59700 Marcq-en-Barœul, ☎ 20.72.56.07, and M. Gayot, 230, pl. Lamartine, 52400 Béthune (ask at *S.I.*). **Somme** : numerous riding clubs (enq. : *Somme S.I.* and *C.D.T.*).

Cycling holidays : *Ligue régionale des Flandres de la fédération française de cyclotourisme,* 77, rue de Soubise, 59140 Dunkerque. *Ligue picarde de cyclotourisme,* M. J.-P. Lavieville, 29, rue Croix-Saint-Firmin, 80000 Amiens, ☎ 22.92.20.08. Bicycle hire : *S.I.*, rue J.-Catelas, 80000 Amiens, ☎ 22.91.79.28.

River cruises : *Assn rég. pour le développement du tourisme fluvial,* 517, av. Marc-Saugnier, 59280 Armentières, ☎ 20.35.29.07.

Technical tourism : many visits possible, by groups and on written request, in Nord-Pas-de-Calais : Dunkerque, Boulogne and Calais harbours, Desvres stoneware, at Montigny (10 km E of Douai), etc.

Handicraft courses : Nord : *Maison de la Thiérache,* 7, rue Maurice-Hédor, 59219 Etroeungt, ☎ 27.61.19.21, offers courses in wrought-iron art and stone sculpture. Handicraft courses in the Mormal region (pottery, weaving, ceramics, and more). Information at the *Syndicat intercommunal de tourisme de l'Ouest avesnois,* hôtel de ville, 59350 Le Quesnoy, ☎ 27.49.12.16. **Somme** : numerous courses in wood, copper, enamels, pewter, stone sculpture, painting, pottery. Enq. at the *C.D.T.* **Pas-de-Calais** : *Maison de l'artisanat,* 62870 Buire-le-Sec, ☎ 21.86.33.73.

Aquatic sports : *Ligue Flandre-Artois de la fédération française de voile,* 16, rue Molière, 62200 Saint-Martin-lès-Boulogne, ☎ 21.31.48.66. *Comité départemental de voile* **(Somme),** M. Gagny, av. du Gal-Leclerc, 80270 Airaines, ☎ 22.26.01.08. Speed-sailing on the extensive Opal Coast beaches are ideal for this sport. Somme speed-sailing clubs at Somme Bay, Marquenterre and Fort-Mahon.

Canoeing and kayaking : enq. at *C.D.T.*

Golf : Nord-Pas-de-Calais : Bondues (9 and 18 holes), Villeneuve-d'Ascq (18 holes), Marcq-en-Barœul (9 holes), Marly (18 holes), Wimereux (18 holes), Neufchâtel-Hardelot (18 holes), Le Touquet (9 holes and two 18 holes). **Somme** : Quervieu (7 km from Amiens) and Nampont-Saint-Martin (2 × 9 holes).

Aerial sports : parachuting : *Centre école régionale de parachutisme du Nord,* 59600 Maubeuge, ☎ 27.68.40.39. U.L.M. : *Assn. valenciennes d'aviation ultra-légère motorisée,* 111, av. Henri-Barbusse, 59770 Marly.

Hunting and shooting : in the **Nord-Pas-de-Calais** region it is possible to hunt on the plains or in the woods, or to shoot waterfowl. Enq. : *Féd. dép. des chasseurs.* **Nord** : 33, bd de la Liberté, B.P. 312, 59026 Lille Cedex, ☎ 20.54.81.90. **Pas-de-Calais** : *la Fosse aux Loups,* rue du Gal-de-Gaulle, B.P. 91, 62223 Saint-Laurent-de-Blangy, ☎ 21.24.23.59. **Somme** : 12, rue de Dijon, 62000 Amiens, ☎ 22.91.28.32.

Fishing : the best fishing areas are in the **Pas-de-Calais** region. Deep-sea fishing : *Comité rég. du Nord, féd. franç. de pêcheurs en mer,* M. Cauchois, 12, rue Namur, 62600 Berche, ☎ 21.09.29.36. For more info : *Fédérations départementales de pêche et de pisciculture.* **Nord** : 10, rue de la Marne, Saint-Souplet, 59360 Le Cateau, ☎ 27.84.09.46. **Pas-de-Calais** : 2, résidence de France, rue É.-Zola, 62400 Béthune, ☎ 21.01.18.21. **Somme** *(C.D.T.* publishes a leaflet listing fishing sites, type of catch and tariffs).

The pleasures of the Northern table

Throughout Picardy and the North you will find fresh fish in abundance and an immense variety of salted and pickled fish : roll-mops, pilchards (sardines), harengs saur (smoke-dried herring) and bouffi (salted and smoked). Lots of crevettes grises (shrimp), coques and moules (cockles and mussels). The eel is king of the area's freshwater fish and is found in many sorts of pâté such as Anguilles au Vert. In recent years a sea plant, the passe-pierre (sea fennel) has become popular in the region. North Sea oysters are excellent. Endives are very common and chicory mixed with coffee is a regional habit. The most typical regional dish is Carbonnade Flamande (beef and onions cooked in beer); and the most original local dish is the Waterzoï (freshwater fish, or chicken, stew). French fries, often served with mussels, can be found everywhere and andouillettes (chitterling sausages) from Armentières, Arras, Cambrai, Douai and elsewhere are particularly delicious.

Windmills

For inhabitants of northern France, windmills symbolize their efforts to make use of the forces of nature, and scores of them are still outined against the sky in Flanders and Artois. Many are near the coast, but few of these still work. They fall into two categories : the pivot mill where the whole structure turns on a vertical shaft to face the wind, and the solid tower in stone or brick where only the roof turns. Windmills can be cylindrical, square or octogonal, built of brick, wood or stone; all create romantic silhouettes across the flat plains of the north.

 # Towns and places

AIRE-SUR-LA-LYS*

Saint-Omer 19, Lille 57, Paris 236 km
pop 10012 ⌧ 62120   B1

In rich and fertile country; some of its streets still keep their 17th-18thC appearance.

▶ **Grand'Place : Hôtel de Ville** (town hall) with classic French belfry and carillon (1717-21). On a corner of the square, the charming Flemish Renaissance **Bail-lage★** (1604; Baillif's Court) formerly housed the city militia. ▶ **Collegiate church of St. Pierre★** is one of the largest Renaissance and Flamboyant Gothic buildings in Flanders : high square tower (18thC); inside : 1663 organ-casing and statue of Our Lady, the city's patron saint. ▶ 17thC Baroque **church of St. Jacques.**   ☐

Practical Information _____

ⓘ mairie, ☎ 21.39.07.22 (h.s.).
SNCF ☎ 21.39.07.09.

Hotels :
● ★★★ *Hostellerie des Trois Mousquetaires,* château de la Redoute, ☎ 21.39.01.11, AE, Euro, Visa, 12 rm. ℙ
⬳ ▩ closed Mon and Sun eve, 20 Dec-20 Jan, 280. Rest.
◆◆ ⬳ ♪ 65-250.
★ *Europ' Hôtel,* 14, Grand'Place, ☎ 21.39.04.32, AE, Euro, Visa, 16 rm. ℙ ⌕ ♒ closed 28 Jun-20 Jul, 80.

⋏ ★★*La Lys,* bassin des Quatre-Faces (44 pl), ☎ 21.39.07.22.

AMIENS***

Arras 63, Boulogne 122, Paris 148 km
pop 131330 ⊠ 80000   A-B3

Amiens is the capital of Picardy and has been a pros-perous textile town since the Middle Ages, with a reputation for fine velvet dating back to the 17thC. At the end of WWII, 60 % of the town was in ruins and has since been extensively rebuilt : the **Tour Perret** (104 m tower; C3) dominating the skyline, the **Maison de la Culture** (cultural center; B2) in a bold mixture of concrete and glass, and the broad univer-sity campus on the edge of town, are all evidence of the town's successful architectural revolution.

▶ In the city centre, **Notre Dame Cathedral★★★** (C2) : 145 m long, 70 m wide at the transept with 43-m high vault-ing, the largest cathedral in France with 126 pillars and a spire reaching 112 m into the sky. This jewel of Gothic art owes its homogeneity to its rapid construction : work began in 1220; the nave was completed in 1236, the choir in 1268 and the building itself (apart from the side-cha-pels (14thC) and the top sections of the towers (14th and 15thC) was erected at the end of the 13thC. On the N side between the Saint-Honoré doorway and the tower of the façade are the six decorated side-chapels and their marvelous statues. The main façade has three great **doorways★** decorated with statues and bas-reliefs★ sculpted between 1225-30; the central door shows Christ surrounded by the Apostles; the statue of "Le Beau Dieu" — Christ in serenity — is the focus of this immense bibli-cal sculpture. Inside the cathedral in its **nave** are the 13thC bronze funeral effigies of the founding bishops. Note the rosette windows decorating the ends of the **tran-sept** (late 13thC). On the S side are two **doorways,** one containing a statue of the Virgin Mary. The **choir** is screened by 18thC grillwork and the 110 stalls★ of the choir (carved oak, 1508-20) are decorated with thousands of realistically-carved figures. In the S ambulatory the choir enclosure★ is decorated with eight groups of figu-res in stone, based on the life of St. Firmin, first bishop of Amiens. Behind the main altar is a fine recumbent effigy (15thC) and the 1628 tomb of a canon (priest) with a famous angel★ sculpted by Nicolas Blasset. A former sacristy (19thC) houses the **treasure room** (*visit by appt.; tel. 22.91.27.31),* containing some thirty sculptures and 12th-13thC goldsmiths' work.

▶ Behind the Palais de Justice (court building; C2-3), the **Hôtel de Berny** (former private mansion; Louis XIII style; no. 36 Rue Victor-Hugo) houses the local Art and Region-al History Museum (*10-12 & 2-6, May-Oct.; closed Mon.; Nov.-Apr., Wed., Sat., Sun.).* ▶ In front of the Palais de Justice are two fine 16thC mansions, side-by-side, the **Logis du Roi** (King's lodgings) and the **Maison du Sagit-taire.** The old **theatre** (late 18thC) in the Rue des Trois-

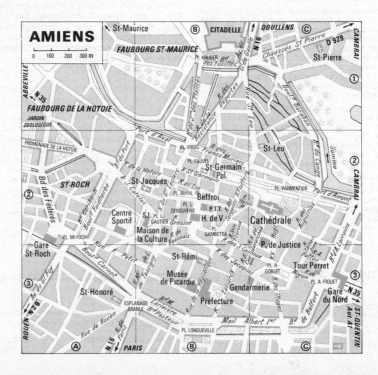

Cailloux (B-C3) has kept its beautiful façade. ▶ In the Rue de la République is the partly-destroyed **church of Saint-Rémy** (B3), containing the Lannoy mausoleums (17thC) and at no. 48 is the **Museum of Picardy★** in a sumptuous Second-Empire building (B3; *10-12 & 2-6, closed Mon.*) : sculptures (Rodin, Bourdelle, Barye) and vast canvases by Puvis de Chavannes ; on the first floor a unique collection of 16thC masterpieces painted on wood★ (votive offerings to the cathedral from the Confraternity of Puy-Notre-Dame) and 18thC French paintings (Chardin, Fragonard, Quentin de la Tour). ▶ Behind the Hôtel de Ville (B2) is the ancient **Bailiff's Court** (1541) which still has its marvelous Renaissance façade. Further N is the 15th and 18thC bell tower. The **church of St. Germain** (B2) has carved Renaissance doors★. At 3 Rue de Condé, an 18thC building houses the **Costume Museum** (B2; *10:30-11:30 & 14:30-16:30, Wed., Fri., Sat. ; visit by appt. tel. 22.92.51.30*). ▶ Beyond the Rue des Francs-Muriers (B2) is the lower town of Saint-Leu flanked by the Somme. Here, beside the new university buildings, you will find picturesque houses grouped around the **church of St. Leu** (C2; 15thC ; 16thC Flamboyant Gothic bell tower). In Place Parmentier (C2), the **waterfront market** still sells regional market-garden produce, formerly brought into town in large black barges. The **market gardens** date from the Middle Ages when the many islands formed by the Somme were first cultivated ; view them from the right bank above **Port d'Amont** (B2).

Visit to a subterranean refuge★★ *(20 km, half day)*

▶ **Bertangles** has a fine stone **château** in French Regency style (1730). The wrought-iron entrance gate★ is decorated with hunting scenes *(15 Jul.-15 Sep., daily).* ▶ **At Villers-Bocage,** the 13th-16thC church contains a Burial of Christ sculpture (16thC). ▶ The mud-walled town of **Naours★** hides the largest network of **subterranean refuges★★** in Picardy. They were used as hiding places during the Normandy invasions of the 9thC, during the Religious Wars and the Thirty Years' War. This subterranean city, developed over the course of centuries, totals 2 km of long rooms, all excavated by hand. The rooms have air shafts reaching the plateau summit 30 m above, and can contain up to 3000 people. Now houses folklore **museum** *(daily).*

Round trip of war memorials★ *(150 km approx, full day ; see map 1)*

▶ **Sains-en-Amiénois** : fine **funeral monument★** (12th-13thC). ▶ **Boves,** at the foot of the hillside, overlooked by remains of 12thC **keep.** ▶ Above **Villers-Bretonneux** is a **memorial** and military cemetery commemorating the 10000 Australian soldiers who died in Picardy

in the spring of 1918. ▶ **Bray-sur-Somme** : the church's massive square bell tower contrasts with the slender lines of the Romanesque choir. ▶ On a bend in the Somme (Curlu), the **belvédère de Vaux★** offers a splendid view of the river and its many green islets. ▶ **Péronne** has kept part of its ancient brick-and-stone **ramparts★** (16th-17thC). The **fortress** is surrounded by a brick bastion ; Charles le Téméraire (Charles the Bold), Duke of Burgundy, held Louis XI of France prisoner here. The Renaissance style town hall houses the **Danicourt Museum** *(visit on request)* : old coins, Gaul and Carolingian jewelry. The **church of St. Jean**, with three naves and flattened chevets, dates from the last Gothic period. ▶ The waters of the Somme and its tributary, the Cologne, create a network of ponds, marshland and small islands covered with market-gardens. ▶ At the exit from **Thiepval** is an immense **memorial** with 16 pillars, bearing the names of 73000 British soldiers who died in this area in WWI. ▶ The trenches in the **memorial park★** between **Hamel** and **Beaumont** have been kept in their original state, illustrating army life in WWI ; a monument representing a caribou commemorates the Newfoundland (Canadian) regiment which fought here in 1916. ▶ **Mailly-Maillet** has a 16thC church with a beautiful Flamboyant Gothic doorway. ▶ **Albert** : the town hall with its Flemish belfry was rebuilt, as was the **basilica Notre-Dame-de-Brebières,** in brick and white stone. The 11thC statue *La Vierge aux Brebis* (The Holy Mother with the lost sheep) is said to have worked miracles and is a frequent object of pilgrimage. ▶ **Corbie** : the former abbey church (16th-18thC) is now the **church of St. Pierre★,** unfortunately reduced to the nave and the façade. Inside : 14th and 15thC statues★, relics. The former **collegiate church of St. Étienne** (11th-13thC) has lost its transept and side aisles but retains a beautiful 13thC doorway dedicated to the Virgin. ▶ **La Neuville** (a suburb, *2 km W*) : the 16thC **church** has a handsome carved tympanum★ over its doorway, representing the Entry of Christ into Jerusalem ; inside, 12thC baptismal fonts. ▶ **Amiens** (→). □

Practical Information ─────────────

AMIENS
ⓘ rue J.-Catelas (B2), ☎ 22.91.79.28/22.92.90.93.
✈ *Air France office,* 2 bis, bd de Belfort (C3), ☎ 22.92.37.39.
SNCF ☎ 22.92.50.50/22.91.95.30.
🚲 rue Vallée, ☎ 22.92.27.03.
Car rental : *Avis,* train station ; 64, rue des Jacobins (B-C3), ☎ 22.92.30.00.

Hotels :
★★★ *Carlton Belfort,* 42, rue de Noyon (C3),

1. Round trip of war memorials

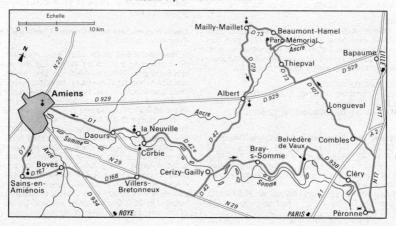

☎ 22.92.26.44, AE DC Euro Visa, 36 rm Ⓟ & ⌘ 260. Rest. ♦♦ & closed Sun eve, 105-175.
★★★ *L' Univers* (Mapotel), 2, rue de Noyon (C3), ☎ 22.91.52.51, Tx 145070, AE DC Euro Visa, 41 rm ▦ ⌘ ♪ ⚬ & 275.
● ★★ *Le Prieuré*, 17, rue Porion (C2), ☎ 22.92.27.67, AE Euro Visa, 11 rm ⚬ ⌘ ♪ ⌘ 145. Rest. ♦♦ ⚬ ♪ A stone's throw from the cathedral, in a 15thC house is a restaurant that is gaining a reputation : fish, trout, shellfish, regional specialities. Cellar stocked with great Bordeaux, 175-260 ; child : 45.

Restaurants :
● ♦♦ *Les Marissons*, 68, rue des Marissons, ☎ 22.92.96.66, Visa ⚬ ♪ closed Mon, Sat noon, Sun eve. In the heart of old Amiens, young Antoine Benoit's talent is inspired by the market's bount : *queue de lotte aux abricots, langues de morue au poivre rose*, 80-200.
♦♦ *Joséphine*, 20, rue Sire-Firmin-Leroux (B2), ☎ 22.91.47.38, Euro Visa ♪ & closed Mon and Sun eve , Feb, 28 Jul-25 Aug. Spec : fish, 115-200.
♦♦ *La Couronne*, 64, rue St-Leu (B-C1), ☎ 22.91.88.57, Visa ♪ closed Sat, 12 Jul-12 Aug. Simple, honest fare at affordable prices : *ballotine de canard, côte de veau crème de laitue, mousse au chocolat*, 75-200.
♦♦ *Le Pré Porus*, 95, rue Voyelles (off map C2), ☎ 22.46.25.03, DC Visa ⚬ ♪ & ⌘ closed Mon eve and Tue, 85-150.
♦ *Le Petit Chef*, 8, rue J.-Catelas (B2), ☎ 22.92.24.23, Visa ⚬ & closed Tue eve and Wed, 5-15 Jan, 15 Jul-6 Aug. The price of the main course determines the price of your meal, 60-130.
♦ *Mermoz*, 7, rue J.-Mermoz (C3), ☎ 22.91.50.63, AE DC Euro Visa ♪ closed Sat and Sun eve , Feb school hols, 24 Dec-2 Jan. Fresh fish stars on this menu, 95-200.

△ ★★*L'Etang Saint-Pierre* (100 pl), ☎ 22.44.54.21.

Recommended
Auction house : 17, rue de la République (B1), ☎ 22.91.54.64.
Boat rental : *Europyachting*, 172, rue Delpech, ☎ 22.95.34.40 ; *Cabruel*, ☎ 22.43.63.41.
Guided tours : enquire at the *S.I.*
Leisure activities : *Maison de la Culture*, pl. Léon Gonthier (B2), ☎ 22.91.83.36, three theatres, exhibition rooms, daily ex Mon noon-9, Sun 1-7.

Nearby

DREUIL-LÈS-AMIENS, ⊠ 80730, 5 km W on the N 235.

Restaurant :
♦♦ *Le Cottage*, 385, av. Pasteur, ☎ 22.43.15.85, Euro Visa ♪ closed Mon eve, Tue eve, Sun eve, 16 Aug-5 Sep, 60-95.

DURY-LÈS-AMIENS, ⊠ 80480, 5 km S on the N 16.

Restaurant :
♦♦ *La Bonne Auberge*, RN 16, ☎ 22.95.03.33, Tx 145861, AE Euro Visa ♪ & ⌘ closed Mon and Sun eve. The setting is rustic, but the food is city-slicker : *pâté d'Amiens, pot-au-feu de poissons, chartreuse de langoustines et filet de sole*, fine cellar, 70-200 ; child : 50.

PÉRONNE, ⊠ 80200, 51 km E.
ⓘ 31, rue St-Fursy (after 3pm), ☎ 22.84.42.38.
⬛⬛⬛ ☎ 22.84.00.35.
Car rental : *Avis*, 26, pl. L.-Daudré, ☎ 22.84.23.16.

Hotels :
★★ *Hostellerie des Remparts* (L.F.), 21, rue Beaubois, ☎ 22.84.38.21, AE DC Euro Visa, 16 rm Ⓟ ▦ ⌘ ♪ half pens (h.s.), 430. Rest. ● ♦♦ ♪ ⌘ closed 3-13 Aug. Michel Drichemont's menu is long and very conservative, but the quality is there : *anguille fumée, ficelle picarde, foie gras maison*, 60-140.
★★ *Saint-Claude*, 42, pl. Louis-Daudré, ☎ 22.84.46.00, AE DC Euro Visa, 37 rm Ⓟ ▦ ♪ half pens (h.s.), 300. Rest. ♦ ♪ 55-160.

Restaurant :
♦♦ *La Quenouille*, 4, av. des Australiens, ☎ 22.84.00.62, AE DC Visa Ⓟ ▦ ⌘ ♪ closed Mon and Sun eve, 95-180.

△ ★★★*Port de Plaisance* (90 pl), ☎ 22.84.19.31.

VILLERS-BOCAGE, ⊠ 80260, 11 km N.

Restaurant :
♦ *Le Bocage*, 13, rue des Charrons, ☎ 22.93.70.94, Euro Visa ▦ ♪ closed Wed, 1 Jul-1 Aug, 70-100.

VILLERS-BRETONNEUX, ⊠ 80380, 17 km E.

Hotel :
★★ *Victoria*, 5, rte de Péronne, ☎ 22.48.02.00, DC Euro Visa, 18 rm Ⓟ ▦ ♪ closed Sun. Grill, 55-100, 140.

ARRAS★★★

Lille 52, Calais 117, Paris 178 km
pop 45364 ⊠ 62000   B2

Arras expanded rapidly after WWII and is today a large modern town. During the Middle Ages it was an important centre of weaving and the cloth trade. In the 17th and 18thC the civic dignitaries built a fine city centre ; its handsome architecture has been carefully preserved.

▶ **The Grand'Place★★★** (C2) and the **Place des Héros★★★** constitute the most perfect example extant of 17th and 18thC Flemish architecture in France. Both are surrounded by tall narrow houses of brick and stone with ornate gables. The street-level arcades are supported on sandstone pillars. Behind the pillars are trap doors leading down to the **cellars** (*les boves*) which are several stories deep and were used as hiding places during various wars. A very colourful market is held each Saturday in both squares. ▶ The **Hôtel de Ville** (B-C2) has a 75-m high **belfry★** (excellent chimes) surmounted by the Lion of Arras. The main building dates from early 16thC but was completely restored after 1918. Guided tour of the underground passages starts in the basement ; display cases from the museum's archaeological section and audiovisual spectacle (20 centuries of history in Arras). ▶ The **cathedral★** (18thC ; B1-2) is a huge building in neo-Classical style. Inside : enormous statues of saints from the Pantheon ; 17thC head of Christ in wood (left arm of the transept) ; fine "Christ Scourged" (wood, 17thC) in the ambulatory. The former 18thC Benedictine abbey of St. Vaast next to the cathedral now houses the **Fine Arts Museum★** (B2 ; *10-12 & 2-5 daily ex Tue.*) : medieval sculpture ; 16th-18thC paintings (triptychs by Bellegambe, 16thC, Northern schools of 18thC) ; 19thC French paintings (Corot, Delacroix, Daubigny, Chassériau). ▶ In the Place du Théâtre opposite the 18thC **theatre** (B2) is the **Ostel des Poissoniers** (Fishermans' Guild Building), a narrow Baroque structure of 1710 decorated with carved sirens and fish.

Les Crêtes du Sacrifice ("Crests of Sacrifice")★★ *(40 km from Arras to Olhain)*
▶ **Mont-Saint-Éloi** *(8 km NW)*, on a strategically-placed hill overlooking the Scarpe Valley, was the scene of violent fighting in 1915 and 1940. On the summit, imposing remains of the famous **abbey**, founded by St. Éloi in the 7thC and rebuilt in the 18thC by the Augustinians. The façade and two towers★ remain of the abbey church ; next to the abbey on the square is the monumental doorway. ▶ **Vimy Ridge** *(8 km NE)* was a key position recaptured in April 1917 by Canadian troops. The 74000 Canadians who died in France are commemorated here, and from the massive **memorial★** there is an extensive view★ over the plain of Lens and its coal mines. To the S, on the wooded slope of the hill, a network of **trenches** has been preserved for visitors. ▶ **Notre-Dame-de-Lorette★★** *(10 km NW of Vimy)* : on this desolate site is a **national cemetery** with 20000 tombs ; eight ossuaries contain the remains of 26,000 unidentified soldiers ; on the first floor of the main **ossuary** between the lantern tower (view) is a

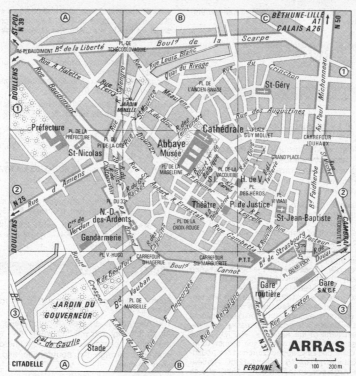

small memorial museum; Roman Byzantine chapel. Below and opposite on the Souchez road is a **museum-diorama of the battlefields** *(Apr.-Nov., daily pm only; Jun.-Aug., 10-6, ex Sun. am).* ▶ **Olhain** *(14 km NW)* : leisure centre in the forest; feudal **château★** (13th-15thC) on a romantic site in the middle of a lake. *(15 Apr.-15 Oct., pm only Sun. and nat. hols.).* □

Practical Information _____

ARRAS

🛈 7, pl. du Mal-Foch (B2), ☎ 21.51.26.95.
SNCF (C3), ☎ 21.73.50.50/21.21.00.42.
🚌 rue du Dr-Brassant (C3), ☎ 21.43.23.42.
Car rental : *Avis*, train station (C3); 6, rue Gambetta (B-C2), ☎ 21.51.69.03.

Hotels :
● ★★★ *L'Univers*, 3, pl. Croix-Rouge (B2), ☎ 21.71.34.01, AE Euro Visa, 36 rm Ⓟ 🏧 🔇 Former monastery, 260. Rest. ♦♦ ⌇ 🍽 65-170.
★★ *Le Chanzy* (L.F.), 8, rue Chanzy (C2), ☎ 21.71.02.02, AE DC Euro Visa, 24 rm Ⓟ 140. Rest. ♦♦ ⌇ One of the finest wine cellars in the land graces this landmark, where the de Troy brothers continue to uphold tradition : *coquilles Saint-Jacques Marco-Polo, filet mariné Mère Jean, coquelet à la bière*, 50-150; child : 25.
★ *Grandes Arcades*, 8, Grand'Place (C2), ☎ 21.23.30.89, AE Euro Visa, 22 rm, closed Sun eve, 120. Rest. ♦ Expect a friendly welcome in this Flemish setting. Delicious food at moderate prices. Spec : *pintadeau aux pêches*, 50-140.

Restaurants :
● ♦♦ *L'Ambassadeur*, Buffet de la gare, pl. Foch (C3), ☎ 21.23.29.80, AE DC Euro Visa ⌇ 👌 🍽 closed Sun eve. One of the most elegant rail station buffets, done in Louis-XVI style, offering traditional and regional fare of excellent

quality. Spec : *harengs à la flamande, sorbet au genièvre*, 110-220.
● ♦♦ *La Faisanderie*, 45, Grand'Place (C2), ☎ 21.48.20.76, AE DC Euro Visa ⌇ closed Mon and Sun eve , Feb school hols, 3-24 Aug. J.-P. Dargent serves brilliantly done regional and seasonal dishes in this historic building : *remoulade de saumon frais, émincé de morue fraîche et vigneaux en Waterzoï, croûte chaude à la compote de fruits frais*, 80-350.
♦♦ *La Rapière*, 44, Grand'Place (C2), ☎ 21.55.09.92, AE DC Euro Visa ⌇ ⌇ closed Wed eve and Sun, 3-30 Aug, 55-100.
♦♦ *Victor Hugo*, 11, pl. V.-Hugo (A2-3), ☎ 21.23.34.96 ⌇ closed Mon and Sun eve , Aug. Seafood, 125-270.
Å ★★*Municipal*, 138, rue du Temple (50 pl), ☎ 21.71.55.06.

Recommended
Guided tours : 2, rue des Jongleurs (B2), ☎ 21.51.36.58, on request, guided tours with commentary by members of the local preservation association.
Market : at the foot of the tower bell, twice a week.
Youth hostel : 59, Grand'Place (C2), ☎ 21.71.07.83.

Nearby
BEAURAINS, ✉ 62217, 3 km S on the N 17.

Restaurant :
♦♦ *L'Auberge*, 31, rue Pierre-Curie, ☎ 21.71.59.30, AE DC Euro Visa ⌇ 👌 closed Sun eve. Good grills, 85-180.

LOUEZ-LES-DUISANS, ✉ 62161, 5 km NW.

Restaurant :
♦ *L'Auberge du Moulin*, 2, rte de Marœuil, ☎ 21.48.68.06, Euro Visa 🏧 ⌇ closed Tue eve, Wed, Sun eve , Feb school hols, 19 Aug-8 Sep, 70-130.

SAINT-NICOLAS-LÈS-ARRAS, ⊠ 62223 Saint-Laurent-Blangy, 1 km NW.

Hotel :
★★★ **Le Régent**, 5, rue Anatole-France, ☎ 21.71.51.09, Visa, 11 rm ℗ ⑳ ◁ ♪ closed Sun eve , Mon ex hols, Aug, 215. Rest. ♦ ♪ 135-230.

AUTHIE Valley**

A-B2

From Doullens to Le Touquet *(110 km approx, full day; see map 4: Canche Valley)*

The Authie River winds through the Picardy plain along a green valley of meadows and marshes, with small woods and cultivated areas near the numerous hamlets. Houses are of brick (sometimes whitewashed), usually with well-stocked flower gardens.

▶ **Doullens** : citadel★ *(Apr.-Sep., Sat., Sun., nat. hols., pm only)* by Vauban surrounding the stone bastions of François I's castle. Hôtel de Ville : early-15thC square **bell tower**; opposite, **church of Notre Dame** with noteworthy stone Burial of Christ (1583); nave of former **church of St. Peter** (13th-15thC). Lombart Museum (Poulbot lithographs; Egyptian and Far Eastern antiquities; *2-5:30 Thu. and Sun.*). ▶ 7 km NW, Lucheux★, on the border between Artois and Picardy : **castle ruins** of the counts of St. Pol (12th-16thC; 13thC Hall of Justice; *daily 9-6*). In the village : 12th-14thC **gate-tower**; 12thC **church** with fine storiated capitals. ▶ **Auxi-le-Château**, in the valley : Flamboyant Gothic **church**; vaulting with remarkable carved keystones. ▶ **Le Boisle** : a traditional basket-weaving centre on the left bank of the Authie. ▶ The D119 runs past the impressive 17thC doorway of the former **Dommartin Abbey**; ruins of 12thC abbey church; 17thC buildings. ▶ **Tortefontaine** *(1 km N)* : pretty 12thC Romanesque church. ▶ **Argoules**, on the left bank : 16thC church and brick manor-house. ▶ Former Cistercian **abbey of Valloires★★** (12thC), close to the Authie Valley : reception room, chapter room, chapel and sacristy have magnificent wood paneling★★ sculpted by Austrian baron J. de Pfaffenhoffen, exiled to France after a duel. The **chapel**, decorated by the same artist, contains lovely wrought-iron work and reclining tomb figures (13thC) in the choir-room *(10-12 & 2:30-6:30 daily, Mar.-Oct.).* ▶ Leaving **Nampont-Saint-Martin**, below the D85E, picturesque 15th-16thC fortified house ; moats filled from the Authie River. ▶ D102 leads to **Fort-Mahon** : miles of beach. ▶ **Berck-sur-Mer** : climate especially suitable for treatment of bone diseases; 13th-16thC **church** in town centre. On the Le Touquet road, Bagatelle Amusement Park (55 acres). ▶ **Saint-Josse**, 10 km NW of Berck : **church** with 15thC choir; 16thC **shrine★** of 5thC hermit St. Josse and triptych illustrating his life. ▶ **Le Touquet** (→ Canche Valley). ☐

Practical Information ——————————

BERCK-SUR-MER, ⊠ 62600, 12 km S of **Le Touquet**.
ⅈ mairie annexe, 5, av. Francis-Tattegrain, ☎ 21.09.50.00.
SNCF ☎ 21.80.50.50.

Hotels :
★★ **La Renaissance** (L.F.), 57, rue Rothschild, ☎ 21.09.05.44, Visa ⑳ ◁ ♪ closed Dec-1 Feb, 180. Rest. ♦ ♪ 60-115 ; child : 30.
★★ **Le Homard Bleu**, 46-48, pl. de l'Entonnoir, ☎ 21.09.04.65, Euro Visa, 18 rm ◁ closed Sun eve and Mon, Feb school hols, 175. Rest. ♦♦ ♪ 60-160.
★★ **Le Marquenterre**, 31, av. F.-Tattegrain, ☎ 21.09.12.13, 40 rm ⑳ ♪ closed 15 Dec-15 Jan, 140. Rest. ♦ ♪ ♪ 60-110.
★ **Banque**, 43, rue Div.-Leclerc, ☎ 21.09.01.09, Visa, 14 rm ◁ ♪ half pens (h.s.), 340. Rest. ♦ ♪ 60-160.

Restaurant :
♦ **Auberge du Bois**, 149, av. Quettier, ☎ 21.09.03.43, AE DC Euro Visa ♪ ◁ closed Wed , 2 Jan-28 Feb. Good simple fare, 63-120.

▲ ★★*Ami-Ami* (153 pl), ☎ 21.09.05.55 ; ★★*Bois Magnier* (310 pl), ☎ 21.09.06.48 ; ★★*International* (180 pl), ☎ 21.09.13.33 ; ★★*L'Alouette* (104 pl), ☎ 21.09.04.64 ; ★★*La Guinguette* (150 pl), ☎ 21.09.04.22.

Recommended
Events : *Speed-sailing competitions*, 6 hours from Berck, late Oct ; *horse races*, 15 Aug.
♥ local sweets : *Aux Sucres Berckois (Mme Matifas)*, 56, rue Carnot, ☎ 21.09.61.30.

DOULLENS, ⊠ 80600, 30 km N of **Amiens**.
ⅈ Le Beffroi, rue du Bourg, ☎ 22.77.04.32.

Hotel :
★ **Aux Bons Enfants** (L.F.), 23, rue d'Arras, ☎ 22.77.06.58, Euro Visa, 8 rm ℗ ⅋ 115. Rest. ♦♦ ♪ ♿ closed Sat, 60-180.

FORT-MAHON-PLAGE, ⊠ 80790, 35 km NW of **Abbeville**.
ⅈ pl. Bacquet, ☎ 22.27.70.75 (h.s.).

Hotel :
★ **Victoria**, pl. Mal-de-Lattre-de-Tassigny, ☎ 22.27.71.05, 17 rm ⑳ closed Sun eve, 105. Rest. ♦ ♪ 55-150.

▲ ★★★*Le Royon* (175 pl), ☎ 22.23.40.30 ; ★★★*Soleil* (100 pl), ☎ 22.27.70.06 ; ★★*Camp de Robinson* (200 pl), ☎ 22.27.71.43.

The AVESNOIS Area**

C2

From Le Quesnoy to Cambrai *(175 km approx, 1 day; see map 2)*

The Avesnois is an area of green fields and hedges. Along the way you will find water mills still turning in the valleys, charming churches, numerous oratories scattered through the countryside and pretty flowered villages.

▶ **Le Quesnoy★★** : 13thC **ramparts★** with leisure centre (including two small lakes) at their foot. The 1585 town hall had a large neo-Classical tower added in 1700 : carillon; concerts. ▶ 2 km E, little 13thC feudal **château de Potelle** with large moats *(exterior visit only).* ▶ **Bavay★★** : slate-roofed houses huddled round the 18thC **Hôtel de Ville**, flanked by a 17thC belfry. This peaceful town was the metropolis of the Gallo-Roman province of Belgium, crossroads for seven major Roman highways. Excavations after WWII revealed the **remains★** of ancient Bagacum (2ndC; small museum with rich collection of daily objects; *weekdays 9-12 & 2-5; closed Tue. ; Sun. and nat. hols. 9:30-12 & 2-7 or 5 out of season).* ▶ 4 km NW, **Bellignies** has a **museum** of objects carved in local marble *(Apr.-Sep. 2-5).* ▶ **Maubeuge**, a major industrial centre in the valley of the Sambre : In the N, the beautiful **Porte de Mons★** (Mons Gate; 1685). On the left bank of the Sambre the **church of St. Pierre** is a remnant of Vauban's fortifications; bell tower with lovely sounding of bells; concerts on Sun. The former chapter of Canonesses (end 17thC) is now a regional **museum** : paintings by Van Dyck and Coypel *(daily, 2-5 or 4 out of season; closed Tue).* The 17thC **Jesuit College** is a fine example of Baroque architecture. By the W wall is a multiple-species **Zoo** *(daily May-Sep. 10-6; Oct.-Apr. 1:30-5).* ▶ **Sars-Poteries** : since the Middle Ages an important earthenware and ceramic centre, turning to glassware in 19thC. Fascinating glass **museum★** *(Musée du Verre; 2-7, Sat., Sun., nat. and school hols.).* ▶ **Felleries** *(3 km S)*, traditionally a barrel-making centre; pleasant **museum** in an old mill *(2:30-6:30 Sun. and nat. hols., Apr.-Jun. and Sep.-Nov. ; daily Jul.-Aug.).* ▶ **Solre-le-Château★** : remarkable collection of old buildings in the town; late-16thC **Hôtel de Ville**; the Gothic **church** (end 16thC) has a turreted gatetower; the spire is topped by an onion dome. Inside : 18thC organ case, 16thC stained glass, treasure room in the sacristy. ▶ **Liessies** on the Greater Helpe River : 16thC **parish church**; 15th-17thC **statues★**; religious artifacts and goldsmiths' work from the former abbey. S of the village : **château de la Motte** (18thC, now a hotel). On

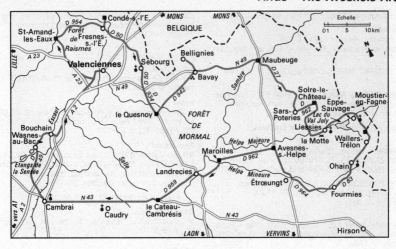

2. The Avesnois area

the other side of Liessies there are good views over the artificial **lake** of **Val Joly.** ▶ **Eppe-Sauvage** has two fine 16thC triptychs in its **church.** ▶ As the valley of the Helpe gets broader, marshes and lakes start to appear. 16thC **priory** at **Moustier-en-Fagne** (*fagne* = marsh). At the entry to the village is a charming 16thC **manor-house** in brick and stone. ▶ Stone houses (because of nearby quarries) at **Wallers-Trélon.** ▶ **Ohain** has a 16thC chapel with a very beautiful wooden statue★ of Christ scourged ; **Trélon** *(3 km N)* is a former glass-making centre ; **Musée du Verre** (Glass Museum) and workshop *(daily Easter-15 Oct.).* ▶ **Fourmies★** became an important textile centre last century. **Ecomusée★★** in a former cotton mill showing the social and working life of the textile workers in 19thC *(daily 9-12 & 2-6 May-Oct.).* A number of lakes in the nearby woods have been converted for leisure use. ▶ **Avesnes-sur-Helpe :** remains of Vauban-style fortifications ; elegant town hall (neo-Classical) ; parish **church of St. Nicolas★** with imposing gate-tower ; inside : beautiful Louis XV altarpieces partially painted by Louis Watteau. ▶ **Maroilles,** on the banks of the Helpe, well known for its cheeses, originally produced by the monks of a Benedictine abbey founded in the 7thC ; this was destroyed in the French Revolution and only the outbuildings exist (17thC tithe barn, or *grange dimière*). ▶ 3 km N, across the Sambre, is the vast **Mormal Forest★,** the largest in the North of France with 22,500 acres ; marked paths and numerous picnic places. ▶ **Le Cateau** is on the boundary between pastoral Avesnois and arable Cambrésis. The former **palace** of the Archbishops of Cambrai is today a **museum★** *(Wed.-Sat. 3-6 ; closed Mon. and Tue. ; Sun. 10-12 & 2-6)* with works by two painters from the region, Auguste Herbin and Henri Matisse (born in Le Cateau, 1869). In the main square the 17thC **Hôtel de Ville** has a charming 1705 bell tower. The **church of St. Martin** (1635) is a good example of Baroque architecture. ▶ **Caudry** has a modern church containing the shrine★ of St. Maxellende. **Cambrai** (→). □

Practical Information

AVESNES-SUR-HELPE, ✉ 59440, 18 km S of **Maubeuge.**
ℹ mairie, ☎ 27.61.11.22.
🚄 ☎ 27.61.10.09.

Restaurants :
● ♦♦ *La Crémaillère*, 26, pl. du Gal-Leclerc, ☎ 27.61.02.30, AE DC Euro Visa ≼ ♪ closed Mon eve and Tue, 3-24 Jan, 1-18 Jul. Cooking is a family affair for J.-L.

and F. Le Laurain : *crépinette de langoustines et saumon, jambonneau de pintade au vinaigre de framboise,* 80-200.
● ♦♦ *Le Carillon*, 12, pl. Leclerc, ☎ 27.61.17.80, AE DC Euro Visa ♪ closed Tue eve and Wed, 15-30 Dec. Michel Lohezil lends a personal touch to food with a strong Breton accent. *Cotriade, homard armoricaine,* 105-150 ; child : 45.
♦♦ *La Grignotière*, 5, av. de la Gare, ☎ 27.61.10.70, closed Mon and Tue eve, 30 Jun-12 Jul, 15-31 Dec. Spec. : fish, 90-140.
● ♦ *Auberge du Châtelet*, Les Haies à Charmes, Dourlers, 4 km N on N 2, ☎ 27.61.06.70, AE DC Visa ≼ ♨ & closed Wed and Sun eve, 2-12 Jan, 15 Aug-15 Sep. The Carlia family's fixed-price offering can't be beat. Spec : *homard aux petits légumes, truite à la Talleyrand,* 80-220.

⚐ ★★*Champ-de-Mars* (40 pl), ☎ 27.61.11.22.

Recommended
Farmhouse-gîte : at Marboux, 8 km W, *Ferme de Foyau*, ☎ 27.61.14.87.

BAVAY, ✉ 59570, 22 km SE of **Valenciennes.**

Restaurant :
♦ *Le Bagacum*, 2, rue d'Audignies, ☎ 27.66.87.00, AE DC Euro Visa ♪ & closed Mon, 1-15 Jan, 1-21 Jul. In this Gallo-Roman town, Pierre Lesne serves enjoyable cuisine from his renovated barn. The accent's on fish, 70-220.

DIMECHAUX, ✉ 59740 Solre-le-Château, 18 km SE of **Maubeuge.**
ℹ mairie, ☎ 27.61.61.14.

Restaurant :
● ♦♦ *La Mère Maury*, rte de Solre, 1.5 km SE on D 27, ☎ 27.67.80.49, AE DC Euro Visa ≼ ♨ ♪ & closed 3-28 Aug. A lovely inn is the setting for D. Versavel's tasty, inventive cuisine : *filets de turbot au basilic, magret de canard aux poires poivrées,* 135-300.

FOURMIES, ✉ 59610, 24 km S of **Solre-le-Château.**
ℹ pl. Verte, ☎ 27.60.40.97, closed Mon and Sun.
🚄 ☎ 27.60.19.55.

Hotel :
★★ *Providence*, 12, rue Verpraet, ☎ 27.60.06.25, 18 rm
ℙ ♨ ⟁ ☜ closed Sat eve and Sun eve , Aug, 150.
Rest. ♦♦ ♪ 50-130.

⋀ ★★*Les Etangs des Moines* (111 pl), ☎ 27.60.04.32.

Recommended
Leisure activities : *theatre*, rue St-Louis.
Market : *mark-down sales*, 1st Sun in Dec and last Sun of Jul.

LIESSIES, ⊠ 59740 Solre-le-Château, 7 km S of **Solre**.

Hotel :
● ★★ **Château de la Motte**, ☎ 27.61.81.94, Euro Visa, 12 rm ℙ ⭠ ▥ 🔥 closed 22 Dec-1 Feb, 140. Rest. ♦ ♪ By advance order only, 70-130.

LOCQUIGNOL, ⊠ 59530, 8 km NW of **Liessies**.

Hotel :
★★★ **Hostellerie de la Touraille** (I.L.A., C.H.), rte de Maroilles, ☎ 27.34.21.21, Tx 810195, DC Visa, 11 rm ℙ ▥ ▥ 🔥 ♪ 250. Rest. ♦♦♦ ⭠ ♪ Fish and shellfish, 150-200.

MAUBEUGE, ⊠ 59600, 39 km SE of **Valenciennes**.
ℹ porte de Bavay, av. du Parc, ☎ 27.62.11.93.
𝑆𝑁𝐶𝐹 ☎ 27.62.30.61.

Hotel :
● ★★ **Grand Hôtel** (L.F.), 1, porte de Paris, ☎ 27.64.63.16, AE DC Euro Visa, 31 rm ℙ 🔥 200. Rest. ♦♦ ♪ 50-190.

⋀ ★★*Municipal* (93 pl), ☎ 27.62.25.48.

Le QUESNOY, ⊠ 59530, 18 km SW of **Valenciennes**.
ℹ mairie, O.T.S.I., Chalet, rte de Ghissignies, ☎ 27.49.12.16.
𝑆𝑁𝐶𝐹 ☎ 27.49.12.10.

Hotel :
★★ **Hostellerie du Parc**, 7, rue V.-Hugo, ☎ 27.49.02.42, Euro Visa, 6 rm ℙ ▥ ▥ ▵ 150. Rest. ● ♦♦ ♪ closed Mon and Sun eve. Regional offerings are highlighted here : *brochette de lotte au whisky, flamiche au maroilles*, 65-110.

⋀ *Municipal du lac Vauban* (180 pl), ☎ 27.49.10.07.

Recommended
Leisure activities : Pont Rouge pond, Lake Vauban (canoeing), Fer à Cheval pond.

SARS-POTERIES, ⊠ 59216, 5 km W of **Solre-le-Château**.

Restaurant :
● ♦♦ **Auberge Fleurie**, 67, rue Gal-de-Gaulle, ☎ 27.61.62.48, AE DC Euro Visa ▥ ♪ closed Mon and Sun eve, 15 Jan-15 Feb, 15-31 Aug. Alain Lequy is an up-and-coming chef who is making a name for himself in his lovely, flowery inn : cold or grilled lobster, *lapin aux pruneaux*, 125-250.

BERGUES**

Dunkerque 8, Lille 65, Paris 283 km
pop 4490 ⊠ 59380   B1
This is one of the most picturesque towns in French Flanders, its numerous canals and neat houses surrounded by powerful-looking fortifications.

▶ There are four gates to the town in the **outer walls★★**; the most beautiful is the **Porte de Cassel★** (17thC; to the S), with the royal sun of Louis XIV in its pediment. From the same period on the N side is the **Couronne d'Hondschoote★**, a large system of defensive works ringed by moats. ▶ In the town centre is a **belfry★** crowned by the Lion of Flanders; pretty carillon (concerts). ▶ Behind St. Martin's church is a 17thC Baroque **Mont-de-Piété**, now the municipal **museum★** : fine collection of 16th and 17thC Flemish paintings, and the celebrated *Joueur de Vielle★* by Georges de la Tour (*daily 10-12 & 2-5; closed Fri.*). In the E quarter, beyond the Hôtel de Ville, are the remains of a former **abbey** : 18thC entry-way, pointed tower (rebuilt 19thC) and 12th-13thC blue tower. ▶ 10 km S, **Esquelbecq** is a typical Flemish country town with its paved main square lined with old houses and its enormous triple-naved church (16thC); the **château★** still looks like a feudal fortress in spite of the wide 17thC win-

dows; nine pepperpot towers, stepped gables, high watchtower and wide moats filled by the Yser River *(2-6, daily, 15 Apr.-15 Oct.).*   □

Practical Information _____

BERGUES
ℹ belfry (in season) and mairie, ☎ 28.68.60.44.   ♥
𝑆𝑁𝐶𝐹 ☎ 28.68.65.77.

Hotel :
★ **Au Tonnelier**, 4, rue du Mont-de-Piété, ☎ 28.68.70.05,, 12 rm ℙ ▵ ▧ closed Fri ex hols, 1-19 Jan, 20 Aug-8 Sep, 185. Rest. ♦ ♪ 🔥 50-110.

Restaurant :
♦♦ **Au Cornet d'Or**, 26, rue Espagnole, ☎ 28.68.66.27 ℙ ♪ closed Mon, 15 Jun-15 Jul. A classified Spanish house. Spec : *crépinettes de saumon frais au cerfeuil, ragoût d'agneau aux pâtes fraîches*, 85-135.

⋀ ★★*Vauban* (90 pl), ☎ 28.68.65.25.

Recommended
♥ chocolates : *Legros*, 9, pl. de la République, ☎ 28.68.66.44.

Nearby

BIERNE, ⊠ 59380.

Restaurant :
♦ **Le Pont Tournant**, ☎ 28.68.61.66, Visa ⭠ ♪ 🔥 closed Thu eve, Fri, Sun eve , Jul. Food served on the terrace, 70-180.

BÉTHUNE

Arras 33, Lille 39, Paris 213 km
pop 26105 ⊠ 62400   B1-2

ℹ 34, Grand'Place, ☎ 21.68.26.29.
𝑆𝑁𝐶𝐹 ☎ 24.57.29.00/21.01.35.35.
Car rental : Avis, train station.

Hotels :
★★ **Bernard et Gare** (L.F.), 3, pl. de la Gare, ☎ 21.57.20.02, DC Euro Visa, 32 rm ℙ ♪ 110. Rest. ♦ ♪ closed Sun eve, 60-160.
★★ **Cordier Claude**, 7, pl. de la Gare, ☎ 21.57.18.04, AE Euro Visa, 20 rm ℙ ▵ 🐎 closed Sat. Rest. ♦ ♪ closed Sat and Sun eve, 60-200.
★★ **Vieux Beffroi**, 48, Grand'Place, ☎ 21.68.15.00, AE DC Euro Visa, 65 rm 🔥 160. Rest. ♦ ♪ 🔥 85-100.

Restaurant :
♦♦ **Au Départ**, 1, pl. de la Gare, ☎ 21.57.18.04, closed Sat eve and Sun eve , Aug. Classic cuisine, 120-210.

Recommended
Riding-gîte : at Saint Venan 62350, *ferme Carvin*, 14 km NW, ☎ 21.54.05.66.

Nearby

BEUVRY, ⊠ 62660, 4 km E.

Hotel :
● ★★ **France II**, RN 41, ☎ 21.57.34.34, Tx 110691, AE DC Euro Visa, 54 rm ℙ ▥ ▵ 264. Rest. ♦♦ ♪ 🔥 Spec : *coquilles Saint-Jacques, poêlon de foie gras*, 90-150.

⋀ ★★*Municipal* (80 pl), ☎ 21.57.02.01.

BRUAY-EN-ARTOIS, ⊠ 62700, 9 km SW.
ℹ pl. de l'Europe, ☎ 21.26.47.46, closed Sat.
𝑆𝑁𝐶𝐹 ☎ 21.26.40.30.

Restaurant :
♦♦ **Le Constant**, pl. du Cercle, ☎ 21.62.32.00 ▥ ♪ closed Mon eve and Sun eve. Pleasant setting. Spec : *salade de magret de canard au foie gras, aiguillettes de canard au sauternes, coquilles Saint-Jacques au goût de mer*, 100-250.

NOEUX-LES-MINES, ⊠ 62290, 6 km S.

Hotel :
★★ *Les Tourterelles* (L.F.), 374, rte Nationale,
☎ 21.66.90.75, Tx 134338, AE DC Euro Visa, 18 rm Ⓟ ▧
◁ ♪ 250. Rest. ♦ ≼ ♪ closed Sat noon, 65-200 ; child : 25.

BOULOGNE-SUR-MER**

Dunkerque 77, Arras 120, Paris 300 km
pop 47650 ⊠ 62200   A1

Julius Caesar set out from here in 55 BC to invade
England ; 17 centuries later Napoléon tried to repeat
the performance. During the last century Boulogne
began to develop a deep-sea fishing fleet and is now
the major French and E.E.C. **fishing port★.** It is also
the leading French fish-processing centre.

▶ The modern port was built on the ruins left after
WWII. In the **upper town★★★** : rectangular medieval ram-
parts★★ with **château** at NE corner. ▶ It is overlooked
by the enormous dome of the **Notre-Dame Basilica** (C2)
built 1827-66 ; inside, in the central chapel is a copy of
the famous wood Notre-Dame statue that was burned
in 1793 ; 11thC Romanesque **crypt** witith painted pillars ;
remnants of 3rdC Roman temple, part of an underground
system of 14 rooms. **Treasure room** of the Basilica. ▶ In
the centre of the upper town : 18thC **Hôtel de Ville** (brick
with stone facing) contrasts with the 12th-13thC square
bell tower (C2). Opposite the town hall, the impressive **Hôtel Desandrouin★,** ca. 1780 in neo-Classical style ;
Napoléon stayed here on several occasions. Nearby is the
former 17th-18thC **Annonciades Convent,** now the Municipal Library. ▶ In the Grande-Rue (B-C2) : at n° 105 is
the house where San Martin (liberator of Chile and Peru)
died. Small **museum** *(closed Sat., Sun. and nat. hols);*
Musée des Beaux-Arts★★ (Fine Arts Museum) at no.
34, housed in a former 18thC seminary : fine collection of
Greek vases★★ and Egyptian antiquities *(9:30-12 & 2-6,*

Wed.-Sun.). Farther down the Grande-Rue, the **church of
St. Nicolas** (B2), 17th-18thC, has a neo-Classical façade.

Côte d'Opale Corniche★★★ (cliff road ; *50 km from Boulogne to Calais ; see map 3)*

▶ **Wimereux** : good view of the port of Boulogne and
the Colonne de la Grande Armée from the seafront dyke.
▶ **Ambleteuse** was once a naval base protected by Fort
Mahon (17thC). ▶ On the left, along the road to Cape
Gris-Nez is a former blockhouse, now a **Museum of the
Atlantic Wall :** military equipment *(daily).* **Cap Gris-Nez★★**
(from the Gaelic 'Craig Ness', rocky cape) ; this is where
the English Channel meets the North Sea. From this windy
promontory 45 m above the waves, you can see the port
of Boulogne *(left),* **Cap Blanc-Nez** *(right)* and the English
coast opposite. ▶ **Audinghen** : fine modern church.
▶ **Wissant,** extensive beach between Gris-Nez and Blanc-
Nez. **Cap Blanc-Nez★★★,** the highest point on the cliffs
(134 m). Sharp winding road with good view★ of the
English cliffs and the coast towards Calais. Below, monument to Latham, who tried in vain to fly the Channel.
▶ **Sangatte** is a proposed starting place for the tunnel
under the Channel. ▶ **Blériot Plage** (beach), named after
Louis Blériot, the first airman to fly the Channel ; he land-
ed in Dover on 25 July 1909. ▶ **Calais** (→).   ▢

Practical Information

BOULOGNE-SUR-MER
ⓘ pl. F.-Sauvage (B2), ☎ 21.31.68.38.
SNCF (C3), ☎ 21.80.50.50/21.80.44.44.
⛴ *Hoverspeed,* (Hoverport Intl.), ☎ 21.30.27.26 ; *P &
O Ferries,* quai Chanzy, ☎ 21.31.78.00 ; *Sealink,* S.N.C.F.,
gare maritime, ☎ 21.30.25.11.
Car rental : *Avis,* train station (C3) ; Hoverport,
☎ 21.83.53.71.

Hotels :
★★ *Lorraine,* 7, pl. de Lorraine (B2), ☎ 21.31.34.78, Euro
Visa, 21 rm Ⓟ ◁ ✀ closed 15 Dec-15 Jan, 170.
● ★ *Plage,* 124, bd Sainte-Beuve (A1), ☎ 21.31.45.35,

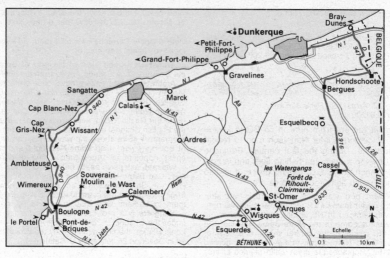

3. Côte d'Opale corniche

Visa, 10 rm Ⓟ ⓕ closed Mon eve and Sun eve, 19 Dec-26 Jan, 105. Rest. ♦ ⓕ ♪ ᵭ 60-130.

Restaurants :
● ♦♦♦ *La Liégeoise*, 10, rue Monsigny (B2), ☎ 21.31.61.15, DC Euro Visa ♪ closed Fri and Sun eve. Interesting little fixed-price meal. Alain Delpierre is a talented disciple of Lilles' Robert Bardot : broiled lobster, *gratin de langoustines*, 90-200.
● ♦♦ *La Matelote*, 80, bd Sainte-Beuve (A1), ☎ 21.30.17.97, Euro Visa ♪ closed Tue and Sun eve, 15-30 Jun, 23 Dec-15 Jan. You needn't break your piggybank to enjoy T. Lestienne's cooking. *Soupe d'huîtres et bigorneaux, dés de gigot d'agneau à la menthe poivrée*, 140-260.

▲ ★★★*Moulin Wibert*, rte de Wimereux (130 pl), ☎ 21.31.40.29.

Recommended
Auction house : 12, rue du Pot-d'Etain, ☎ 21.31.39.51.
Events : *Saint-Nicolas*, 1st Sat of Dec.
Market : food, flowers, pl. Dalton, Wed and Sat am.
Sports : Yacht-Club boulonnais, 234, bd Sainte-Beuve, ☎ 21.31.80.67 ; *Côte d'Opale underwater club*, ☎ 21.31.47.01 ; riding club Boulonnais, ☎ 21.83.32.36.
Youth hostel : 32, rue Porte-Gayole (C3), ☎ 21.31.48.22.

Nearby
COLEMBERT, ⊠ 62142, 18 km E.

Hotel :
★★ *Château des Tourelles* (L.F.), D127, le Wast, ☎ 21.33.34.78, AE DC Euro Visa, 16 rm Ⓟ ⋒ ⚲ ♪ ᵭ 180. Rest. ♦ ♪ ᵭ closed Mon noon, 70-120.

HARDELOT, ⊠ 62152, 15 km.

Hotels :
★★★ *Ecusson*, 443, av. François-1er, ☎ 21.83.71.52, AE DC Euro Visa, 20 rm Ⓟ ♪ closed 15 Nov-15 Dec, 190. Rest. ♦ ♪ ⚘ 80-200 ; child : 25.
★★ *Le Regina*, 185, av. François-1er, ☎ 21.83.81.88, DC, 40 rm Ⓟ ⚲ ᵭ closed 1 Dec-5 Feb, 200. Rest. ♦ ♪ ᵭ ⚘ closed Mon and Sun eve ex Jul-Aug, 68-100.

Restaurant :
♦ *Restaurant du Golf*, 3, av. du golf, ☎ 21.83.71.04, AE DC Euro Visa Ⓟ ⓕ ⋒ ⚲ ♪ closed Tue eve and Wed, 15 Jan-28 Feb. A felicitous blend of golf and good simple fare. Golfers' special, 50-200.

PONT-DE-BRIQUES, ⊠ 62360, 5 km S.
Hotel :
★ *Host. de la Rivière*, 17, rue de la Gare, ☎ 21.32.22.81, Euro Visa, 9 rm Ⓟ ⚲ ⚘ half pens, closed Sun eve and Mon, 1 week in Feb, Aug, 260. Rest. ● ♦♦ ♪ ᵭ An up-and-coming eatery featuring low prices. Spec : *foie gras de canard, goujonnettes de soles à la crème d'orange*, 130-250.

WIMEREUX, ⊠ 62930, 8 km N.
ⓘ pl. Albert-1er and mairie, ☎ 21.83.27.17 (h.s.).
🚃 ☎ 21.32.43.11.

Hotels :
★★★ *Atlantic*, digue de Mer, ☎ 21.32.41.01, Euro Visa, 11 rm Ⓟ ⚲ ♪ ᵭ closed Sun eve, 1 Oct-15 Mar, 220. Rest. ♦♦ ⓕ ♪ ᵭ 145-240 ; child : 80.
★★ *Centre*, 78, rue Carnot, ☎ 21.32.41.08, Euro Visa, 25 rm Ⓟ ⋒ closed 22 Dec-20 Jan, 15-22 Jun, 150. Rest. ♦ ♪ closed Mon. Fish a specialty, 65-150.
★★ *Paul et Virginie*, 19, rue du Gal-de-Gaulle, ☎ 21.32.42.12, AE DC Euro Visa, 18 rm ⚲ ⚘ closed Sun (8 Nov-20 Dec), 20 Dec-25 Jan, 200. Rest. ♦ ♪ ᵭ 65-150.

▲ ★★*Olympic Camping* (110 pl), ☎ 21.32.45.63.

CALAIS

Boulogne 43, Lille 112, Paris 297 km
pop 77000 ⊠ 62100   A1

For centuries Anglo-French rivalry centred around Calais. Today its proximity to England has made it the most important passenger port in France. Largely rebuilt since WWII, Calais has developed an important industrial centre. Lace-making, introduced from England at the beginning of the 19thC, is now complemented by the production of other textiles.

▶ To the N, the **old town** is an island surrounded by canals and harbour basins. The only remnant of its past is the 13thC **watchtower** *(tour de guet)*, used as a lighthouse until 1848, and the **church of Notre-Dame**, begun in 13thC but finished in 16thC under English supervision. This is the only church in France in Perpendicular Gothic, a style developed exclusively in England during the reign of the Tudors.

▶ The **Courgain** quarter : 1848 lighthouse, 58 m high with a marvelous view *(daily, Jul.-Aug.)*; on the other side of the basin is **Fort Risban**, defending the port entry. ▶ In the Rue Richelieu, the **Musée des Beaux Arts et de la Dentelle**★ (Fine Arts and Lace Museum; *10-12 & 2-5 daily; closed Tue.; tel. 21.97.99.00*) : 19th and 20thC sculpture and lace history room on the ground floor; 1st floor, rich collection of paintings especially 16th-19thC Dutch and Flemish schools. ▶ To the S, the **ville neuve** (still called the St. Pierre quarter) was relatively spared from bombardment. **Hôtel de Ville**, built at beginning of 20thC in Flemish Renaissance style, with 75-m belfry (chimes). On the esplanade, the famous **Monument des Bourgeois de Calais**★★, by Rodin, 1895. ▶ Opposite the town hall in St. Pierre park, German blockhouse, now a **War Museum** *(daily, 10:30-5:30 ex Tue., Jun.-Sep. tel. 21.96.62.40).* □

Practical Information ───────────────

CALAIS
ⓘ 12, bd Clemenceau, ☎ 21.96.62.40.
✈ *Calais-Dunkerque*, 8 km E, ☎ 21.96.62.40.
SNCF ☎ 21.96.61.04.
🚌 16, rue Caillette, ☎ 21.36.45.65.
🚢 *Hoverspeed*, Hoverport International, 62226 Calais Cedex, ☎ 21.96.67.10; *Sealink S.N.C.F.*, Terminal Transmanche, ☎ 21.34.55.00; *P.O. Car-Ferries*, Terminal Car-Ferry, 62226 Calais Cedex, ☎ 21.34.41.90.
Car rental : *Avis*, train station; Hoverport, ☎ 21.34.66.51; 36, pl. d'Armes, ☎ 21.34.66.50.

Hotels :
● ★★★ **Meurice**, rue Ed.-Roche, ☎ 21.34.57.03, AE DC Visa, 45 rm ℗ ⚏ ⚲ ⅆ 215. Rest. ◆◆ *La Diligence* ♪ 120-210.
● ★★ **Georges V** (L.F.), 36, rue Royale/7, rue du Duc-de-Guise, ☎ 21.97.68.00, Tx 135159, AE DC Euro Visa, 45 rm, 250. Rest. ◆◆ ♪ closed Sat noon and Sun eve, 27 Dec-7 Jan. Alain Moitel's two restautants sport medieval decors. Classic cuisine and entertainment by "le petit Georges", 60-130.
★★ **Bellevue**, 23-25, pl. d'Armes, ☎ 21.34.53.75, Tx 136702, AE DC Euro Visa, 42 rm ℗ ⚏ 195.
★★ **Richelieu**, 17, rue Richelieu, ☎ 21.34.61.60, AE Euro Visa, 15 rm ℗ ⚏ ⚏ ♪ 165.
★★ **Windsor**, 2, rue Cdt-Bonningue, ☎ 21.34.59.40, AE DC Euro Visa, ℗ ⚲ 150.

Restaurants :
● ◆◆ **Le Channel**, 3, bd de la Résistance, ☎ 21.34.42.30, AE DC Euro Visa ℗ ⚏ ♪ closed Tue and Sun eve, 1-12 Jun, 20 Dec-15 Jan. This handsome, rustic dining room has had a facelift. The Crespo family serves the same quality fare : *pot-au-feu de canard, saumon au champagne, tournedos aux girolles*, 60-200.
◆◆ **La Sole Meunière**, 1, bd de la Résistance, ☎ 21.34.43.01, AE Euro Visa ℗ ⚏ ⅆ ⚏ closed Mon and Sun eve, 22-28 Apr, 28 Oct-3 Nov, 23 Dec-12 Jan, 60-180.

△ ★★*Municipal*, (256 pl), ☎ 21.97.99.00.

Recommended
Casino : *le Touquet's*, 57, rue Royale, ☎ 21.34.64.18.

Nearby

ARDRES, ⊠ 62610, 17 km NW.

Hotels :
● ★★★ **Grand Hôtel Clément** (R.S.), 91, pl. Mal-Leclerc, ☎ 21.82.25.25, AE DC Euro Visa ℗ ⚏ ⚲ ⚏ closed Mon ex hols (l.s.), 15 Jan-15 Feb, 205. Rest. ● ◆◆ ⚏ ⚏ The Coolen family has been pleasing gourmets since 1917. Today, young François, a well-traveled chef, prepares good, modern dishes : *petits choux farcis de langoustines au beurre nantais, paupiettes de ris de veau blanc*, 150-240.
★★ **Le Relais** (L.F.), bd C.-Senlecq, ☎ 21.35.42.00, AE Euro Visa, 11 rm ℗ ⚏ ⚲ ♪ ⚏ closed Tue, 2 Jan-6 Feb, 145. Rest. ◆ ♪ ⅆ Spec : *beignets de filets de daurade*, 60-135.

△ ★★*Vivier*, Bois-en-Ardres (27 pl), ☎ 21.35.45.08.

BRÊMES-LÈS-ARDRES, ⊠ 62610 Ardres.

Hotel :
La Bonne Auberge, 512, rte De Guines, ☎ 21.35.41.09, AE Euro Visa, 7 rm ℗ ⚏ ⚏ closed Sun eve and Mon (ex 15 May-15 Sep), 15 Dec-15 Jan, 100. Rest. ◆ ♪ 55-130.

RECQUES-SUR-HEM, ⊠ 62890 Tournehem-sur-la-Hem, 20 km E.

Hotel :
★★ **Château de Cocove**, (Mapotel), Hameau de Cocove, ☎ 21.82.68.29, Tx 810985, AE DC Euro Visa, 23 rm ℗ ⚏ ⚏ ⚲ ♪ ⚏ 260. Rest. ◆◆ ⚏ ⅆ 80-150.

CAMBRAI*

Lille 64, Amiens 78, Paris 177 km
pop 35270 ⊠ 59400   B2

From a distance the three towers of Cambrai are visible on the right bank of the Escaut : the belfry, the cathedral and the church of St. Géry. Unlike the brick periphery, the centre of town is built of white limestone.

▶ In the Grand'Place, the **Hôtel de Ville** (1786) is crowned by a bell tower on either side of which are two famous mechanical figures, Martin and Martine (1512), who mark the hours by hammering a large bell. To the W, the **church of St. Géry** has a 76-m tower; a neo-Classical building of early 18thC with fine Baroque choirscreen (1635), 18thC woodwork in the choir and a remarkable canvas by Rubens, *The Burial of Christ.* ▶ Further N, former **Beguine convent** (16thC; 24 Rue des Anglaises), remains of ramparts and the ruins of the **château de Selles** (13thC; prisoners' graffiti). ▶ S of the town hall is the Rue de la Victoire : to the right, 15th-18thC **belfry**; in the square farther on, the **Maison Espagnole**★, an old half-timbered house with slate gable (late 15thC; *SI*) and the **chapel of the Grand Séminaire** (1692 : fine Baroque façade). ▶ Opposite, the **cathedral of Notre-Dame** (18thC) is decorated at each end of the transept with *trompe l'œil grisailles* from 1760 ; in the apsidal chapel, fine monument to Fénelon by David d'Angers (1826). ▶ In the Rue de l'Épée is the **municipal museum** (18thC mansion) ; 12th, 16th and 17thC sculpture, 16th and 17thC Dutch and Flemish paintings, 19th and 20thC French paintings *(10-12 & 2-5; closed Tue.).* □

Practical Information ───────────────

CAMBRAI
ⓘ 48, rue de Noyon, ☎ 27.78.26.90/27.42.50.50.
SNCF ☎ 27.81.22.42.
Car rental : *Avis*, 18, av. Michelet, ☎ 27.83.75.11.

Hotels :
★★★ **Beatus**, 718, av. de Paris, ☎ 27.81.52.10, Tx 820211, AE DC Euro Visa, 26 rm ℗ ⚏ ⚏ ⅆ 235.
★★★ **Château de la Motte-Fenelon**, sq. du Château, ☎ 27.83.61.38, Tx 120285, AE DC Euro Visa, 33 rm ℗ ⚏ ⚲ ♪° 230. Rest. ◆◆◆ ♪ closed Sun eve, 95-300.
★★ **Mouton Blanc**, 33, rue Alsace-Lorraine, ☎ 27.81.30.16, Tx 133365, Visa, 32 rm ℗ ⚲ ♪ 155. Rest. ◆ ♪ closed Mon and Sun eve. Quick service, 80-130.

Restaurants :
◆◆ **Aéro Club**, 74, Grande-Rue, Niergnies, 3 km S, ☎ 27.78.11.33, AE DC Euro Visa ℗ ⚏ ⚲ ♪ 60-150.
◆◆ **L'Escargot**, 10, rue Gal-de-Gaulle, ☎ 27.81.24.54, AE Visa ♪ closed Mon ex hols, 15 Dec-15 Jan. Fine, tasty grilled specialities : ribs of beef, *andouillettes de Cambrai*, 60-140.

Nearby

BEAUVOIS-EN-CAMBRESIS, ⊠ 59157, 12 km S.

Restaurant :
◆ **La Buissonnière**, 92, rte nationale, ☎ 27.85.29.97, Euro Visa ℗ ⚏ ⚏ ⚲ ♪ closed Mon and Sun eve, Aug. Spec :

blanc de turbot à l'oseille, ris de veau aux cèpes, crêpes soufflées au coulis de framboises, 75-150.

LIGNY-EN-CAMBRESIS, ⊠ 59191, 10 km SE.

Hotel :
★★★ *Château de Ligny* (R.C.), ☎ 27.85.25.84, Tx 820211, AE DC Euro Visa, 9 rm P ⬕ 🔍 ♪ closed Sun eve (l.s.), Nov-15 Feb. Handsome 13thC and Renaissance château, 450. Rest. ♦♦♦ ♪ ⬧ closed Mon noon and Tue noon (h.s.). Summer meals served in the grand courtyard, 80-200 ; child : 55.

CANCHE Valley★★

A-B2

From Le Touquet to Doullens *(130 km approx, full day ; see map 4)*

The Canche River runs lazily across the Artois plateau, through a countryside of meadows, marshes, peat-bogs and poplar groves.

▶ **Le Touquet,** a seaside-and-health resort at the mouth of the Canche, with elegant villas set back from the seafront among pines and birches. ▶ **Étaples★,** a fishing port with low houses painted in cheerful colours, has been the inspiration of numerous artists. A 17thC salt warehouse is now the archaeological **museum** *(daily, Jul.-15 Sep. ; Wed. and Sun. out of season ; closed Tue.).* ▶ **Montreuil★★,** once a coastal town on the edge of the plateau overlooking the left bank of the Canche. Rebuilt by Vauban (17thC), the 12th-16th and 17thC **citadel★** *(closed Tue.)* and **ramparts★★** are still intact (view). **Church of St. Saulve** (11thC), rebuilt in 13th and 16thC. Flamboyant Gothic **chapel of the Hôtel-Dieu** (hospital) : splendid 17thC furnishings. Opposite Montreuil on the right bank, former **charterhouse of Notre-Dame des Prés** (1314), almost entirely rebuilt in its original style in 1870 by a pupil of the architect Viollet-le-Duc. ▶ **Montcravel** *(5 km N)* : remarkable Flamboyant **church★** : early-16thC storiated capitals. ▶ **Brimeux,** on the right bank : 15th-16thC church with Flamboyant choir and fortified tower with sentry-walk. ▶ **Beauranville** contains some broken walls of the 13thC Lianes château. ▶ Leave the valley at **Aubin-Saint-Vaast** (lovely backward view) for the main road to Hesdin. ▶ **Hesdin★,** founded by Charles V, Holy Roman Emperor in the 16thC ; **Hôtel de Ville★** in former palace of Mary of Hungary (his sister) ; magnificent 1629 bay-window, with 1702 coping ; inside : small museum with Flemish tapestries. 16thC **church of Notre-Dame,** with Baroque furnishings. ▶ **Auchy-lès-Hesdin** *(5 km NW)* : church remodeled in 16th and 17thC ; tombs of the French knights who fell in 1415 at the Battle of **Agincourt.** ▶ **Vieil-Hesdin,** above Hesdin on the right bank, remains of city razed by Charles V *(10 km N).* ▶ Leave the valley at **Conchy** to visit **Flers** *(5 km NE)* : fine Louis XVI **château★**

in brick with stone facings. Remarkable carved keystones to the vaulting in the 15thC chapel. ▶ **Frévent** *(1 km upstream)* : 18thC **château de Cercamp.** ▶ **Avesnes-le-Comte** *(18 km W)* has a beautiful **church★** (15th-16thC), with 12thC choir from an earlier building and a Flamboyant square tower (14th-16thC). ▶ **Doullens** *(15 km S)* : starting point for the trip through the **Authie Valley** (→). □

Practical Information

HESDIN, ⊠ 62140, 35 km NE of **Abbeville.**
ⓘ hôtel de ville, ☎ 21.86.84.76.
SNCF ☎ 21.86.88.21.

Hotel :
★★ *Flandres* (L.F.), 22, rue d'Arras, ☎ 21.86.80.21, Euro Visa, 14 rm P ⬕ 🔍 closed 20 Dec-10 Jan, 210. Rest. ♦ ♪ Good food. Spec : *coq à la bière,* fish, 50-120.

⚠ ★★*Municipal* (140 pl), ☎ 21.86.80.24.

MONTREUIL-SUR-MER, ⊠ 62170, 38 km SE of **Boulogne.**
ⓘ pl. de la Poissonnerie, ☎ 21.06.04.27 (h.s.) ; mairie, ☎ 21.06.01.33. ♥
SNCF ☎ 21.80.50.50.

Hotels :
● ★★★★ *Château de Montreuil* (R.C.), 4, chaussée des Capucins, ☎ 21.81.53.04, Tx 135205, AE DC Euro Visa, 14 rm P ⬕ 🔍 ♪ ♿ ⬧ closed 15 Dec-1 Feb, 420. Rest. ● ♦♦ ♪ ♿ ⬧ closed Thu noon ex Jul-Aug and hols. Pleasant terrace. Orchard and kitchen garden. A charming English garden is the scene of C. Germain's excellent restaurant. A local boy, he trained in London at *Le Gavroche* : *sole à la mâche et citron vert, grillade de lapereau,* 120-300.
Le Darnétal, 1, pl. Darnétal, ☎ 21.06.04.87, AE Euro Visa, 6 rm P ⬕ 🔍 ♪ ♿ closed Mon eve, Tue, 170. Rest. ♦ ⚜ ♪ ♿ 60-120.

Restaurant :
● ♦♦ *Auberge de la Grenouillère,* La Madelaine-sous-Montreuil, ☎ 21.06.07.22, AE DC Visa P ⚜ ⬕ 🔍 ♪ ♿ closed Tue eve and Wed Feb. Foul weather or fair, frogs feature on the bill of fare : *feuilleté, sauté,* any way ...as well as many other good things. Loire Valley wines, 180-190.

⚠ ★★★*Fontaine des Clercs* (76 pl), ☎ 21.06.07.28.

Recommended
Youth hostel : *La Hulotte* (dir. Citadelle), ☎ 21.06.10.83.
♥ chocolates : *Bruno Derick,* 68, Grand'Rue, ☎ 21.86.17.62.

SAINT-AUBIN, ⊠ 62170, 10 km W of **Montreuil.**

Hotel :
★ *Auberge du Cronquelet* (L.F.), rue de Montreuil, ☎ 21.94.60.76, Visa, 8 rm P 🔍 ♪ closed Tue eve and Wed, 130. Rest. ♦ ♪ ♿ In the former village smithy, Clau-

4. Canche and Authie valleys

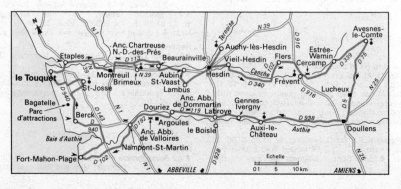

dine Gedolge cooks simple, tasty, inexpensive fare : *lotte à la fondue de poireaux au noilly, ris de veau aux langoustines, aiguillettes de canard au vinaigre de framboises*, 110-150.

Le TOUQUET, ⊠ 62520, 32 km S of **Boulogne.**
ⓘ hôtel de ville, ☎ 21.05.17.55 ; Palais de l'Europe, ☎ 27.05.21.65.
SNCF ☎ 21.80.50.50.
🚌 pl. du Marché-Couvert, ☎ 21.05.22.99.

Hotels :
● ★★★★ (L) *Westminster*, av. du Verger, ☎ 21.05.48.48, Tx 160439, AE DC Euro Visa, 120 rm P ⌁ ♪ closed 11 Nov-15 Mar, 600. Rest. ♦♦ ♪ closed Mon eve and Tue. Classic cuisine by Olivier Dupont in an elegantly renovated setting : *petits choux d'escargot, saumon à la peau, marquise aux chocolats*, 115-180.
★★★ *Côte d'Opale*, 99, bd du Dr-Jules-Pauget, ☎ 21.05.08.11, AE DC Euro Visa, 28 rm ⌁ ♤ ♪ pens (h.s.), closed 11 Nov-15 Mar. ex school hols and wkends until early Jan, 450. Rest. ♦ ♪ ♿ 110-200.
★★★ *Manoir Hôtel*, av. du Golf, 3 km S, ☎ 21.05.20.22, 44 rm P ⌁ ⚓ ♤ ❀ ▱ ♪ᵒ ✓ closed 17 Nov-15 Apr, 520. Rest. ♦♦ ♪ 130-350.
★★ *Plage*, bd de la Mer, ☎ 21.05.03.22, Euro Visa, 29 rm P ⌁ ♪ ❦ closed 15 Nov-15 Mar, 230.
★ *Auberge de la Canche* (L.F.), 3, rte Nationale, Beutin, 10 km, ☎ 21.06.02.75, AE DC Euro Visa, 8 rm P ♨ ♤ half pens (h.s.), closed Mon eve et mar., 15 Nov-15 Dec, 260. Rest. ♦ ♪ 45-100 ; child : 35.

Restaurants :
● ♦♦♦ *Flavio-Club de la Forêt*, 1-2, av. du Verger, ☎ 21.05.10.22, AE DC Euro Visa ♪ closed Wed (l.s.), 15 Nov-28 Feb. The best table on the Opal coast. Flavio keeps a close eye on every aspect of his establishment : lobsters, fish and other delights ; interesting wine cellar, 180-320.
♦♦ *Café des Arts*, 80, rue de Paris, ☎ 21.05.21.55, AE DC Euro Visa, closed Mon and Tue, 1 Jan-7 Feb. Art exhibits, 110-220.
♦♦ *George II*, 187, bd de la Mer, ☎ 21.05.00.68, closed l.s. ex wkend, Wed, 150-350.

Recommended
Casino : *casino des Quatre Saisons*, 26, rue St-Jean, ☎ 21.05.15.53 ; *casino de la Forêt*, pl. de l'Hermitage, ☎ 21.05.08.76 (h.s.).
Farm-gîte : at Cormont, 15 km NE, *ferme du Bout du Haut*, ☎ 21.90.73.29.
Thalassotherapie : *Institut de thalassothérapie*, ☎ 21.05.10.67, sea spa.
♥ chocolates : *"Au Chat Bleu"*, 47 bis, rue St-Jean, ☎ 21.05.03.86.

CASSEL**

Dunkerque 29, Lille 53, Paris 271 km
pop 2220 ⊠ 59670   B1

Above the flat plain of Flanders, Mont Cassel rises 175 m to give a wide view across the country.

▶ In 1914-15, the French forces commander Maréchal Foch made his HQ here, and in 1940, the British army tenaciously defended this strategic position before falling back on Dunkirk. On the top of Mont Cassel is an equestrian statue of Maréchal Foch and a picturesque 18thC wooden **mill★**. Cassel is a charming city with narrow sloping **streets★★** and flights of steps. ▶ In the Grand'Place opposite the town hall is the elegant stone façade of the **Hôtel de la Noble Cour★** ; a fine Renaissance doorway leads into a history-and-folklore museum : parchments, ceramics, Flemish furniture, Louis XV wood paneling *(daily 2-6, Jun.-Sep. ; Sun. only Apr.-May)*. Nearby, the **Hôtel d'Halluin** with fine Louis XVI façade. ▶ The **Collegiate church of Notre-Dame** is a massive triple-naved building in Flemish Gothic.▶ Behind the church is the brick façade of the 17thC **Jesuit chapel.**   □

Practical Information _____

CASSEL
SNCF ☎ 28.42.41.21.

Restaurant :
● ♦♦ *Le Sauvage*, 38, Grand'Place, ☎ 28.42.40.88, AE Euro Visa ⌁ ♨ ♪ closed Mon eve and Tue, Feb. W. Decaestecker's regional fare is served in a rustic dining room : *soupe de homard au cidre et au genièvre, potjevleesch casselois, grillade de canette aux herbes*, 100-250.

Nearby

BAILLEUL, ⊠ 59270, 19 km.
ⓘ des Monts de Flandre, hôtel de ville, ☎ 28.43.07.11.
SNCF ☎ 28.43.08.47.

Hotel :
★ *La Pomme d'Or*, 27, rue d'Ypres, ☎ 28.43.11.01, DC Euro Visa, 7 rm P ♪ closed 1-23 Aug, 120. Rest. ♦ ♪ closed Mon eve and Tue eve. Excellent value, 55-180.

BOESCHEPE, ⊠ 59299, 7 km NW on the D10 and 318.

Hotel :
★ *Mont Noir* (L.F.), ☎ 28.42.51.33, Tx 110672, AE DC Euro Visa, 7 rm P ⌁ ♨ ♤ ♪ closed Fri eve, Jan, 120. Rest. ♦♦ ⌁ ♪ 65-120 ; child : 35.

SAINTE-MARIE-CAPPEL, ⊠ 59670, 3 km.

Restaurant :
● ♦♦ *Au Petit Bruxelles*, ☎ 28.42.44.64, Euro Visa ♨ ♤ ♪ ♿ closed Wed and Sun eve , Feb school hols. Bernard Desnave prepares the fattened ducks of Périgord (*foie gras, magret, confit, rillettes*) and the catch of the day brought in by local fishermen, 200.

Le CROTOY

Abbeville 21, Boulogne 73, Paris 184 km
pop 2351 ⊠ 80550   A2

ⓘ digue J.-Noiret, ☎ 22.27.81.97 (h.s.).

▲ ★★★*Le Pré Fleuri* (70 pl), ☎ 22.27.81.53 ; ★★*la Ferme du Tarteron* (150 pl), ☎ 22.27.80.20 ; ★★*la Prairie* (250 pl), ☎ 22.27.02.65 ; ★★*la Roseraie* (100 pl), ☎ 22.27.80.31.

Nearby

FAVIÈRES, ⊠ 80120, 5 km SE.

Restaurant :
♦ *La Clé des Champs*, pl. des Frères-Caudron, ☎ 22.27.88.00, Visa ⌁ ♪ ♿ closed Mon and Sun eve ex Jul-Aug, 27 Jan-15 Feb, 15-31 Oct, 65-160 ; child : 35.

DOUAI**

Lille 38, Saint-Quentin 65, Paris 193 km
pop 42580 ⊠ 59500   B2

Douai, in the heart of the industrial North, is the capital of the coal country as well as a university town. Its bell tower — immortalized by the painter Corot — has the largest carillon in Europe (62 bells). *Gayant*, the best-known and oldest of the giants of the North, plays a special part in local folklore.

▶ On the Place d'Armes, the beautiful **maison du Dauphin★** *(SI)* typifies the aristocratic appearance of the town in 18thC. Nearby is a famous square **bell tower★★** (late 14thC) crowned by the Lion of Flanders (late 15thC ; *carillons are rung Sat., Sun. and nat. hols.*). **Hôtel de Ville★** (15thC) : Gothic council room, storerooms (still called the Cloth Hall in reference to the 15thC textile industry) and the aldermen's chapel. ▶ Behind the town hall the Rue de l'Université runs in front of the 17thC **Mont-de-Piété** (pawnshop ; fine Classical façade), and leads to the 18thC theatre in Louis XVI style. ▶ Opposite the theatre is the **hôtel d'Aoust** (18thC). ▶ The Rue des Foulons leads back toward the town hall ; note the **hôtel de la Tramerie** in

Louis XIII style. ► On the quays along the River Scarpe, running S-N through the city, is the **Palais de Justice**, formerly the seat of the Parlement de Flandres and rebuilt in the 18thC (façade in Louis XVI style); the great Salle du Parlement★ (1714) is decorated with superb Louis XV paneling. Nearby, **church of St. Pierre** (18thC), large 16th-17thC tower, 18thC organ casing and a series of white marble bas-reliefs. ► W of the town centre on the other side of the Scarpe is a former **charterhouse**, whose 17th-18thC buildings surround a 16thC Flemish Renaissance-style mansion, now a **museum★★** *(10-12 & 2-5; closed Tue.)* : unique collection of Flemish primitives including the famous **polyptych of the Trinity★** (J. Bellegambe, 1510), the Immaculate Conception (1526) and St. Etienne and St. Jacques (Jan Van Scorel, 1541); fine collection of Italian Renaissance canvases (Veronese, Carraccio); 17thC Dutch and Flemish schools, 17th-19thC French schools. In the annex, ceramic and porcelain collections, archaeology and natural history exhibitions.   □

Practical Information _____

ℹ️ bell tower, rue de la Mairie, ☎ 27.87.26.63.
SNCF ☎ 27.88.86.04/24.88.41.27.
Car rental : *Avis*, 136, av. Clémenceau, ☎ 27.88.59.87; train station.

Hotels :
● ★★★ *La Terrasse* (L.F.), 36, Terrasse St-Pierre, ☎ 27.88.70.04, AE Visa, 32 rm 🅿 ◔ ♪ 260. Rest. ● ♦♦♦ ♪ An excellent place to stop. The Hanique family takes good care of guests : *coeur de filet à la fleur de thym, turbotin poëlé*. Fine cellar, 135-280.
★★ *Grand Cerf*, 46, rue St-Jacques, ☎ 27.88.79.60, AE DC Euro Visa, 37 rm 🅿 200. Rest. ♦ closed Sun eve Aug, 70-150.

Restaurant :
● ♦♦ *Au Turbotin*, 9, rue de la Massue, ☎ 27.87.04.16, AE Euro Visa ♪ closed Mon and Sun eve, hol eves, 20 Jul-20 Aug. There's still that unbeatable "seaside" fixed-price meal. Fresh fish is outstanding : *turbotin monseigneur, homard grillé, Saint-Pierre à la crème de tomates*, 70-200.

Recommended
Events : *fêtes de Gayant*, folk processions, concerts, evening bell recitals, 1st 2 weeks of Jul.

DUNKERQUE*

Calais 43, Lille 73, Paris 291 km
pop 73120 ⊠ 59140   B1

Until the 7thC the land now occupied by the town was covered by the sea. It was only in the 11thC that the name of Dunkerque (the French spelling : "church of the dunes") appeared in the archives. Until WWII Dunkirk had kept the appearance of a 17th-18thC Flemish port. Today it is an ultra-modern port whose waterside factories, naval shipyards and high chimneys are totally contemporary.

► Near Place Jean-Bart is a **bell tower★** (15thC) with 48 bells (concerts). Opposite, the 15th-16thC **church of St. Éloi** has a French Classical façade. A central belfry crowns the Flemish Renaissance-style **Hôtel de Ville** built around 1900. ► A little street between **St. Éloi** and the town hall leads to the Place du Général-de-Gaulle and the **Musée des Beaux-Arts** *(10-12 & 2-6; closed Tue)* : ceramics, Dutch and Flemish painting schools (16th-17thC), French schools (17th-19thC). ► On the far side of the town hall is the **port★** (third largest in France) which can be visited by boat (from the Bassin du Commerce, *tel. 20.69.47.14*) or on foot, taking the road to the left which leads over the Trystram and Watier locks as far as the **lighthouse**, lovely view★ of harbour-station. ► From the Place du Minck (fish market) along the fishing docks is the **tour du menteur** (liar's tower : so called because of too many false alerts given by its sentry), the last remaining section of the 14thC ramparts surrounding the town.

A bit farther is **Notre-Dame-des-Dunes chapel** (rebuilt 19thC), which holds a statue of the Virgin Mother worshiped by sailors since the 15thC. ► Beyond the chapel, in a park with modern sculptures, is the **Musée d'Art Contemporain★**, with more than 600 works from 1950-80, particularly César sculptures and canvases from the Cobra movement *(10-7; closed Tue)*. ► On the corner of Av. Faidherbe — a continuation of Avenue des Bains toward **Malo-les-Bains** — and Av. du Casino is the **aquatic museum** *(10-12 & 2-6, closed Tue.)*.

Nearby

► **Gravelines★** *(16 km SW)* : the **fortifications★** inspired by Vauban are perfectly preserved. From the Grand'Place with its belfry you come to the **arsenal**, which now houses art exhibitions. The **church of St. Willibrod** (Flamboyant Gothic with late-Renaissance doorway) contains a magnificent collection of 17thC woodwork (confessionals and organ casings). Next to the church, an unusual 1724 cistern and former Commissariat buildings. ► **Grand-Fort-Philippe** and **Petit-Fort-Philippe** *(2 km NW)* : these two little townships on either side of the Aa River, named after Spain's King Philip II, were rebuilt in Flemish style after WWII, and are now fishing centers and seaside resorts.
          □

_____

Kermesses and carnavals

Traditional festivities are either kermesses (non-religious festivals) or ducasses (Saint's day festivals). Processions and cavalcades, fanfares and chorales play a part in both. The folklore of the region includes giant wickerwork figures and dancing through the streets. The most popular and the most famous carnivals are : Dunkerque and Bailleul (Fête de Gargantua), before Lent; Cassel and Aire-sur-la-Lys set their giants dancing on Easter Mon. Summer carnivals are celebrated nearly everywhere : at Douai the giant Gayant and his family have been feted every July since 1530.

_____

Practical Information _____

DUNKERQUE
ℹ️ belfry, ☎ 28.66.79.21; sea dike, Malo-les-Bains, ☎ 28.63.61.34 (h.s.).
✈ *Calais-Dunkerque*, 28 km SW, ☎ 21.97.90.66.
SNCF ☎ 28.66.50.50.
⚓ *Sally Viking Line*, ☎ 28.68.43.44.
Car rental : *Avis*, train station; 9, rue Belle-Vue, ☎ 28.66.67.95.

Hotels :
★★★ *Borel* (Inter-Hôtel) 6, rue l'Hermitte, ☎ 28.66.51.80, Tx 820050, AE DC Euro Visa, 40 rm ⚔ ◔ 230.
★★★ *Europ'Hôtel*, 13, rue du Leughenaer, ☎ 28.66.29.07, Tx 120084, AE DC Euro Visa, 129 rm 🅿 ♪ 250. Rest. ♦ ♪ ♨ closed Mon and Sun eve and Feb school hols, 15 Aug-7 Sep, 45-120.
★★ *Hirondelle*, 46-48, av. Faidherbe, ☎ 28.63.17.65, Visa, 34 rm, 125. Rest. ♦ ♪ ⚘ closed Mon and Sun eve and Feb school hols, 15 Aug-7 Sep, 45-120.
Au Bon Coin, 49, av. Kleber, Malo-les-Bains, ☎ 28.59.12.63, AE, 5 rm 🅿 ♪ closed 22 Dec-5 Jan, 200. Rest. ♦ ♪ 55-120.

Restaurants :
♦♦ *Le Mareyeur*, 83, rue Henri-Terquem, ☎ 28.66.29.07, Tx 120084, AE DC Euro Visa ♪ ⚔ closed Mon and Sun eve. Seafood and fish. Interesting fixed-price meal, 90-160.
♦ *Richelieu*, Buffet de la Gare, ☎ 28.66.52.13, AE Euro Visa ♪ ⚔ closed Sun eve and hol eves. A great buffet for hungry travelers : *waterzoï de soles, rognons de veau au genièvre*, 110-150.

Nearby

BOURBOURG, ⊠ 59630, 14 km SW.

Restaurant :
♦ **La Gueulardière**, 4, pl. de l'Hôtel-de-Ville, ☎ 28.22.20.97, AE Visa ♪ closed Mon and Sun eve , Aug. P. Philippon's cuisine is a happy discovery : *foie d'oie mariné, saint-pierre au bourbon, ris de veau aux miettes de homard*, 110-200.

TÊTEGHEM, ⊠ 59229, 6 km on the D204.

Restaurant :
● ♦♦♦ **La Meunerie**, 174, rue des Pierres, ☎ 28.26.01.80, Tx 132253, AE DC Euro Visa ﹘ closed Mon and Sun eve, 20 Dec-15 Jan. Fresh local fish, Challans duck, 160-300.

HAM

Saint-Quentin 20, Amiens 67, Paris 135 km
pop 6399 ⊠ 80400   B3
▆▆ ☎ 23.81.00.16.

Hotel :
★ **Valet**, 58, rue de Noyon, ☎ 23.81.10.87, 24 rm ℗ ⌂ closed late Dec, 145. Rest. ♦ ♪ closed Sat and Sun , hols, 50-70.

Restaurant :
● ♦♦ **Le France**, 5, pl. de l'Hôtel-de-Ville, ☎ 23.81.00.22, AE DC Euro Visa ℗ & closed Mon and Sun eve, Feb school hols, Aug. Serious classic cuisine from G. Dumont : *panaché de poissons au beurre bleu, entrecôte au gratin*, 75-150.

HAZEBROUCK

Saint-Omer 22, Lille 42, Paris 239 km
pop 20494 ⊠ 59190   B1
ⓘ hôtel de ville, ☎ 28.41.88.00.
▆▆ ☎ 28.41.94.33.

Hotel :
★★ **Auberge de la Forêt** (L.F.), La Motte-au-Bois, 5 km S, ☎ 28.48.08.78, AE Euro Visa, 14 rm ℗ ﹘ ⌂ closed Sun eve and Mon, 15 Dec-15 Jan, 200. Rest. ♦ ♪ 95-180.

Nearby

LONGUE-CROIX, ⊠ 59190, 8 km NW.

Restaurant :
● ♦ **Auberge de la Longue-Croix**, rte de Staple, ☎ 28.41.93.34 ℗ ✗ closed Mon eve, Tue, Sun eve , hol eve, Dec-Jan, 23 Jun-2 Jul. Just 15 (reserve!) per sitting can savour S. Maertens' short list of specialties : *solettes au cerfeuil, turbot aux artichauts, rognons de veau aux pleurotes*, 120-200.

Recommended
Farm-gîte : *ferme de la Rabaude*, ☎ 28.41.91.28.

LENS

Arras 18, Lille 34, Paris 203 km
pop 38807 ⊠ 62300   B2
▆▆ ☎ 21.28.25.01.

Hotels :
★★ **France**, 2, pl. de la Gare, ☎ 21.28.18.10, AE Euro Visa, 23 rm, closed Sun eve, 125. Rest. ♦ ♪ 50-150 ; child : 30.
★★ **Lutétia**, 29-31, pl. de la République, ☎ 21.28.02.06, AE, 23 rm ℗ ✗ 125.

If you enjoy sports, consult the pages pertaining to the regions; there you will find addresses for practicing your favorite sport.

Nearby

DOUVRIN, ⊠ 62138, 10 km N.

Restaurant :
♦♦ **La Licorne**, 1, pl. Thomas, ☎ 21.79.95.25, Euro Visa ♪ & closed Mon and Sun eve. Lots of creamy, buttery sauces. Good cellar, 50-200 ; child : 35.

LILLE***

Amiens 115, Bruxelles 116, Paris 219 km
pop 168420 ⊠ 59800   B1
In the Middle Ages, the city was surrounded by the River Deule, which is why its name first appears (11thC) as *L'Isle* ("the island"). Once owned by the counts of Flanders, then ruled by the dukes of Burgundy, Lille finally became French in 1667 after nine days of siege by Louis XIV. France replaced the Flemish market, and this prosperous merchant town became the capital of French Flanders. At the beginning of the 19thC, Lille became a busy wool and cotton town ; the textile industry's rapid expansion created an urban proletariat whose wretched conditions were immortalized by Victor Hugo. Since WWII, Lille has been the regional capital of this highly-populated industrial area.

▶ On the Place du Général-de-Gaulle (E2) is a **column** presenting the statue of the "goddess protector" of Lille, commemorating the failed attempt by the Austrians to capture the city in 1792. On the S edge of the place is the **Grand'Garde** (18thC guard house) ; fine façade decorated with trophies. E, the brick-and-stone **ancienne Bourse**★★ (old exchange) ; characteristic 17thC Flemish architecture : 24 houses, side-by-side, forming interior courtyard with covered arcades ; the walls are covered with a luxuriant decoration of caryatids, garlands and medallions. ▶ The Place Rihour (D-E2) just S of Place du Général-de-Gaulle holds a gigantic monument to the dead ; behind it are the ruins (chapel and stepped turret) of **Rihour palace**, the luxurious former residence of the dukes of Burgundy. ▶ To the W, the Baroque **church of St. Étienne** (1696 ; D2). ▶ N of the **Place du Général-de-Gaulle** is the Louis XVI-style **Grand Théatre** (ca. 1910 ; E2) and the **new Bourse** (same period), with 17thC Flemish-style belfry. Opposite the new Bourse is a row of pilastered houses, the Rang de Beauregard, characteristic of late-17thC Lille architecture. ▶ E. **church of St. Maurice**★ (E2) with five naves and ornate 14th-15thC tower ; inside : works by Van Oost (17thC) ; polychrome wood statue (16thC), Christ Scourged. ▶ In the Rue de Paris is the **hospice Gantois** (E3), founded in 15thC and enlarged in 17thC. At the end of the street is the **porte de Paris** (Paris Gate), built in 17thC in honour of Louis XIV. Nearby, the **Hôtel de Ville** (E3), finished in 1933 ; at the base of the 140 m bell tower are sculptures of the two giants of Lille, Phynaert and Lydéric ; fine view from the top *(open Sun. am, Easter-end Sep.)*.

▶ W, Place de la République (D-E3) : **Palais des Beaux-Arts**★★★, one of the richest provincial fine arts museums in France *(9:30-12:30 & 2-5 ; closed Tue. and hols.)* ; all the great schools of painting from Flemish Primitive to Impressionist, in particular 17thC Dutch and Flemish schools. ▶ N of the town centre, **Vieux Lille**★★, the old city, has been under restoration for a number of years : see especially the Rue de la Monnaie (E1) : 17th and 18thC brick-and-stone houses and the **hospice Comtesse**★★, founded in 13thC by Jeanne de Flandres, now the **Musée Régional d'Arts et Traditions Populaires**★ (Folk Art Museum) ; *10-12:30 & 2-5, closed Tue.)* ; kitchen decorated with Delft and Lille tiles, 17thC Flemish furniture, Louis XV paneling. Opposite the main entrance, the 15thC Salle des Malades★ with magnificent boat-shaped timber vaulting is extended by 17thC chapel. ▶ Place Louise-de-Bettignies (E1) : restored Flemish Renaissance houses. Nearby, the unfinished **cathedral Notre-Dame de la Treille** (19th-20thC) ; inside : miraculous statue of the

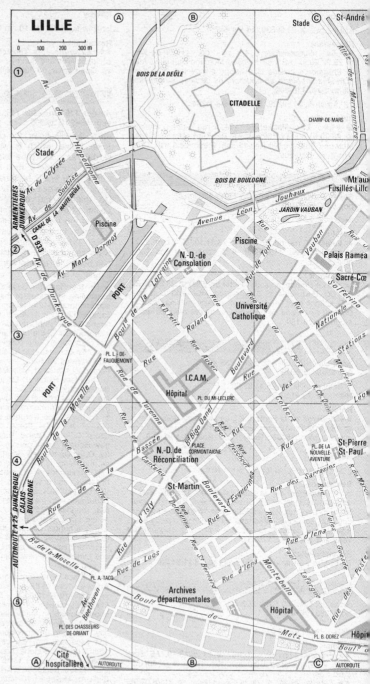

LILLE

0   100   200   300 m

Ⓐ   Ⓑ   Ⓒ   Stade   St-André

① BOIS DE LA DEÛLE

CITADELLE

CHAMP-DE-MARS

Stade

BOIS DE BOULOGNE   Mt aux Fusillés Lille

Jouhaux   JARDIN VAUBAN

② Piscine   Avenue Léon

Piscine   Palais Ramea

N.-D.-de Consolation   Sacré-Cœ

③ Université Catholique

PL. L.-DE-FAUQUEMONT

I.C.A.M.

Hôpital   PL. DU MI-LECLERC

④ N.-D. de Réconciliation   PLACE CORMONTAIGNE   PL. DE LA NOUVELLE AVENTURE   St-Pierre St-Paul

St-Martin

Archives départementales

⑤   Hôpital

PL. A-TACO

PL. DES CHASSEURS-DE-DRIANT

Metz   Hôpi

PL. B-DOREZ

Ⓐ Cité hospitalière   AUTOROUTE   Ⓑ   Ⓒ AUTOROUTE

Treille Virgin, protectress of Lille. ▶ Further W (B-C1) is the **citadel**★★ by Vauban, the largest and best preserved in France *(Sun. pm, guided tours by the SI).* ▶ Near the **church of St. André** (C-D1; 18thC Jesuit-style) at the intersection of Rue Royale and Rue Princesse is the birth-place of Charles de Gaulle (no. 9 Rue Princesse, small **museum**; *10-12 & 2-5, closed Mon. and Tue.*).

The arrow (→) is a reference to another entry.

Nearby

▶ **Villeneuve-d'Ascq** *(8 km E)*, new city formed by the communes of Flers, Annapes and Ascq, home of *cité universitaire scientifique de Lille* : **Musée d'Art Moderne**★★ du Nord *(daily 10-6:30; closed Mon., Tue. and Wed. am)* :

good collection of works from 1900-40, notably canvases by all the great masters of Cubism. ▶ **Seclin**★ *(12 km S)* : **hospital**★ founded in 13thC by Marguerite de Flandres (still in use). The brick-and-stone buildings in Flemish Baroque date from the 17thC with the exception of the *salle des malades* and the chapel (15thC). The parish **church of St. Piat★** (13thC) is built on a Merovingian crypt housing the sarcophagus (3rdC) of St. Piat under a 12thC memorial stone. □

Practical Information _____

LILLE

ⓘ palais Rihour, pl. Rihour (D-E2), ☎ 20.30.81.00.
✈ *Lesquin*, 8 km SE, ☎ 20.95.92.00. *Air France office*, Lesquin airport, ☎ 20.87.53.90; 8-10, rue Jean-Roisin (E2), ☎ 20.57.80.00.
▥▥▥ (E2), ☎ 20.74.50.50/20.06.26.99.
▦▦▦ pl. Buisses (F2), ☎ 20.06.01.33.
Car rental : *Avis*, train station (E2), ☎ 20.06.35.55 ; airport, ☎ 20.87.59.56 ; 125, av. de la République, ☎ 20.06.40.32.

Hotels :
● ★★★ **Carlton** (Mapotel), 3, rue de Paris (E2), ☎ 20.55.24.11, Tx 110400, AE DC Euro Visa, 65 rm 🛏 380.
★★★ **Grand Hôtel Bellevue**, 5, rue Jean-Roisin (E2), ☎ 20.57.45.64, Tx 120790, AE Visa, 80 rm ⪡ 🦞 300.
★★★ **Royal Hôtel**, 2, bd Carnot (E2), ☎ 20.51.05.11, Tx 820575, AE DC Euro Visa, 102 rm Ⓟ ♪ 🦞 ♿ 320.
★★ **L'Univers**, 19, pl. des Reignaux (E2), ☎ 20.06.99.69, AE Euro Visa, 56 rm 🛏 215.
★★ **Monte-Carlo**, 17, pl. des Reignaux (E2), ☎ 20.06.06.93, Euro Visa, 42 rm, 170.
★★ **Strasbourg**, 7, rue Jean-Roisin (E2), ☎ 20.57.05.46, AE DC Visa, 47 rm, 190.

Restaurants :
● ◆◆◆◆ **L'Huîtrière**, 3, rue des Chats-Bossus (E2), ☎ 20.55.43.41, AE DC Euro Visa ♪ ♿ closed Sun eve, 22 Jul-31 Aug. The sea at your table, thanks to Jean Proye, owner of this comfortable restaurant (a former fish store). *Tartare de saumon, terrine de raie*. In season, *poêlée de sole de ligne aux morilles fraîches, blanc de barbue aux jets de houblon* (very rare). All year long, mimolette cheese is featured. Take-out dishes available, 250-300.
● ◆◆◆ **La Devinière**, 61, bd Louis-XIV (F3), ☎ 20.52.74.64, AE DC Visa ♪ closed Sun, 10-25 Aug. B. Waterlot delivers serious, top-quality cuisine : *sauvageon rôti petit jus*, fine cellar, 170-240.
● ◆◆◆ **Le Flambard**, 79, rue d'Angleterre (D1), ☎ 20.51.00.06, AE DC Visa ♪ ♿ closed Mon and Sun eve, 5-11 Jan, 2-31 Aug. In the old section of Lille, painter-chef Robert Bardot is a living contradiction of the dictionary definition of a "flambard" (ostentations with wealth). Bardot lets his table show off instead with treasures like : *œufs coque en tasse à la crème de truffe, raviolis de langoustines dans leur jus huile de crustacés, pigeon rôti rose*. Many vintage wines available, 200-300.
● ◆◆◆ **Le Paris**, 52 bis, rue Esquermoise (D2), ☎ 20.55.29.41, AE DC ♪ ♿ closed Sun eve, Aug. Loïc Martin and chef Gérard Chamoley, go all out to make your stay in Lille a memorable gastronomic experience. *Queues de langoustines au choux-beurre blanc au soja, magret de canard fumé minute sauce jerez et miel, glace au caramel blond, foie gras de canard*. Some venerable vintages at advantageous prices, 170-300.
● ◆◆◆ **Le Restaurant**, 1, pl. Sébastopol (D3), ☎ 20.54.23.13 ♪ closed Sat noon and Sun, 2-19 Jan. Ghislaine Arabian has taken over the kitchen, and the results are quite interesting : at lunch, an enjoyable fixed-price meal with starter, main course, dessert, coffee and sweets for 150F, 130-250 ; child : 45.
◆◆◆ **La Belle Epoque**, 10, rue de Pas (D2), ☎ 20.54.51.28, AE DC Euro Visa ♪ closed Sun eve. Good food : *turbot aux trois légumes, caneton rouennais rôti*, and a very fine wine list, 180-210.
● ◆◆ **Le Hochepot**, 6, rue du Nouveau-Siècle (D2), ☎ 20.54.17.59 ♪ closed Sun eve. Typical Flemish decor. Remarkable selection of coffees and gin, 70-150.
● ◆◆ **Le Varbet**, 2, rue de Pas (D2), ☎ 20.54.81.40, AE DC Visa, closed Mon and Sun hols, 14 Jul-15 Aug, 20 Dec-2 Jan. The quiet, muted atmosphere of this pleasant little restaurant points up the excellent, rich cooking by M. Vartanian : *cassolette d'œufs brouillés aux langoustines, turban de sole à la fricassée de homard*, 115-230.

● ◆◆ **La Petite Taverne**, 9, rue du Plat (E3), ☎ 20.54.79.36, AE Euro Visa ♪ ♿ closed Tue eve and Wed, 16 Jul-14 Aug. In 'Dish Street', Denis Druene dishes out savoury "plats". Seasonal menu, fixed meals (*flamiche, waterzoï*), 65-200.
◆◆ **Charlot II**, 26, bd J.-B.-Lebas (E4), ☎ 20.52.53.38, AE DC Euro Visa ♪ ♿ closed Mon, Sat noon, Sun eve, Aug. Seafood, 90-220.
◆◆ **La Coquille**, 60, rue St-Etienne (D2), ☎ 20.54.29.82, AE Visa ♪ ♿ closed Mon noon and Sun, 1-7 Jan, 1 Aug-1 Sep. 17thC decor, 45-120.
◆◆ **La Provinciale en Ville**, 8, rue des Urbanistes (E1), ☎ 20.06.50.79, AE Visa ♪ closed Mon and Sun eve , Aug. In an 18thC town house, exclusively regional cuisine, 130-150.
◆◆ **Le Compostelle**, 4, rue St-Etienne (D2), ☎ 20.54.02.49, AE DC Euro Visa, closed Sun eve. Enchanting 16thC decor, light cuisine : *turbot au miel et à l'orange, rognons de veau aux baies de genièvre*, 150-300.
◆◆ **Le Gastronome**, 67, rue de l'Hôpital-Militaire (D2), ☎ 20.54.47.43, AE DC Euro Visa ♪ closed Aug. Avant-garde cooking by M. Lescieux : *foie gras d'oie en gelée de roses, magret de canard à la rhubarbe*, take-out foods, 110-150.
◆◆ **Le Lutterbach**, 10, rue Faidherbe (E2), ☎ 20.55.13.74, AE DC Euro Visa ♪ closed 1 Jul-9 Aug. Spec : sauerkraut, fish, 80-190.
◆ **Le Capucin Gourmand**, 138, rue de Wazemmes (E4), ☎ 20.57.23.70, Visa ♪ closed Mon and Sun eve, 4 Aug-4 Sep. Southwestern specialties and seafood. Good value, 60-180.
◆ **Lino**, 1, rue des Trois-Couronnes (E2), ☎ 20.31.12.17 ♪ closed Mon and Sun eve , 15 Aug-15 Sep, 1 wk at Xmas. Italian cuisine, 100-150.

Recommended
Baby-sitting : *C.R.O.U.S*, ☎ 20.56.93.40 ; *C.I.P.E.C.*, ☎ 20.30.60.26 ; *Allô Baby*, ☎ 20.44.19.38.
Events : *Opéra de Lille*, rue des Bons-Enfants, ☎ 20.55.48.61.
Guided tours : *19thC industry*, info. *S.I.*
Market : annual rummage sale, 1st Sun in Sep ; flea-market, Sun eve ; animal market, rue Littré.
Auction house : , 2, rue Ste-Anne, ☎ 20.06.25.81, sale on Mon pm ; 14, rue des Jardins, ☎ 20.06.10.14, sale on Sat pm.
♥ antiques : *Nord Antiquités*, 23-25, rue des Chats-Bossus, ☎ 20.55.03.98 ; pastry and candy : *Meert*, 27, rue Esquermoise, ☎ 20.57.07.44.

Nearby

ARMENTIÈRES, ✉ 59280, 19 km.

Restaurants :
◆◆ **La Petite Auberge**, 4, bd Faidherbe, ☎ 20.77.09.66, AE DC Euro Visa ♪ closed Tue, Sat noon, Sun eve. Good value, 95-155.
◆ **Au Commerce**, 70, rue Nationale, ☎ 20.77.15.03, Visa ♪ closed Wed eve ex Fri, Sat, Aug. Three good menus, 60-120.

Recommended
Leisure activities : *Base des Prés du Hem*, ☎ 20.77.43.99. 272 acres of parkland incl. 108-acre lake.

FACHES-THUMESNIL, ✉ 59155, 5 km S of **Lesquin** airport.

Hotel :
● ★★ **Air Hôtel**, 407, av. Mal-Leclerc, ☎ 20.96.04.39, AE Visa, 13 rm Ⓟ ▥▥▥ 200. Rest. ◆ **Le Pied-de-Cochon** ♪ closed Mon eve and Sun eve, 70-220.

LAMBERSART, ✉ 59130, 3 km NW.

Restaurants :
◆◆ **L'Estaminet**, 67, rue Georges-Boidim, ☎ 20.92.57.63 ♪ closed Sat and eves. Old-fashioned *nouvelle cuisine*, 110-220.
◆◆ **La Laiterie**, 138, av. de l'Hippodrome, ☎ 20.92.79.73,

AE DC Euro Visa ⟨ 🏨 ♪ ᵫ closed Mon and Sun eve. Cooking is a family affair with the Vantours, 100-200.

LOOS-LES-LILLES, ⊠ 59120, 5 km SW.

Restaurant :
♦♦ *L'Enfant Terrible*, 25, rue du Mal-Foch, ☎ 20.07.22.11, Euro 🏨 ♪ ᵫ 150-200.

MARCQ-EN-BARŒUL, ⊠ 59700, 5 km NE.

Restaurants :
● *Le Septentrion*, parc du Château du Vert-Bois, ☎ 20.46.26.98, AE DC Visa ⟨ 🏨 ♪ ᵫ closed Mon, Thu eve, Sun eve. Good value. G. Lelaurain champions earthy, rustic dishes : *potjevleïsh, filet de turbot au pinot noir*, 180-220.
♦♦ *Auberge de la Garenne*, 17, chem. de Ghesles, ☎ 20.46.20.20, AE Euro Visa ⟨ 🏨 ♪ closed Mon, wkday eves, 15-28 Feb, Aug. Three cheers for the Legleyes. Mama in the kitchen, Papa at the bar and cellar, son Marc waiting to greet you at the door. Spec : *chariot de terrines*, game and regional dishes (according to season), *rognons et ris au genièvre*, 70-150.

MARQUETTE, ⊠ 59520 Marquette-lèz-Lille, 5 km N.

Restaurant :
♦ *Auberge de Saint-Arnoult*, 178, rue d'Ypres, ☎ 20.51.69.61, Euro Visa 🏨 ♪ closed Mon, Tue eve, Sat noon, Sun eve, Feb school hols, Aug. A wide choice of fixed meals and a notable cellar, 105-235.

PRÉMESQUES, ⊠ 59840, 10 km W.

Restaurant :
● ♦♦♦ *L'Armorial*, 1055, RN, on D 933, ☎ 20.08.84.24, Tx 136220, AE DC Visa ⟨ 🏨 ♪ closed Tue eve, Wed, Sun eve, 7-31 Jan, 1-15 Aug. The sun shines once more on this handsome house, thanks to Philippe Lepelley's enjoyable, youthful cuisine based on garden produce : *omelette, foie gras et fines herbes*, 180-350.

SECLIN, ⊠ 59113, 12 km S.
SNCF ☎ 20.90.11.54.

Hotels :
★★★ *Au Tournebride*, 59, rue Sadi-Carnot, ☎ 20.90.09.59, 10 rm ℗ closed Sat, 15 Jul-15 Aug, 150. Rest. ♦♦ ♪ Specialties of the Landes region, fish and seafood, 70-150.
★★★ *Auberge du Forgeron* (L.F.), 17, rue Roger-Bourry, ☎ 20.90.09.52, AE Euro Visa, 20 rm ℗ ᵫ closed Sun, 1-21 Aug, 220. Rest. ● ♦♦ ♪ ᵫ Tradition and modernity are the twin poles of this tasty cuisine : *pied de porc farci, paupiette de saumon fumé, marmite du pêcheur*, 75-220.

POIX-DE-PICARDIE

Amiens 28, Beauvais 44, Paris 120 km
pop 2267 ⊠ 80290   A3

🛈 rue St-Denis, ☎ 22.90.08.25 (h.s.); mairie, ☎ 22.90.07.04.
SNCF ☎ 22.90.00.02.

Hotel :
★ *Poste*, 13, pl. de la République, ☎ 22.90.00.33, Visa, 18 rm ℗ 170. Rest. ♦ Spec : *chausson de crabe, confit de canard*, 60-150.

⚐ ★★★*Le Bois des Pêcheurs* (90 pl), ☎ 22.90.11.71.

ROUBAIX

Lille 12, Amiens 127, Paris 230 km
pop 101896 ⊠ 59100   B1

🛈 hôtel de ville, 17, Grand'Place, ☎ 20.70.70.02.
SNCF ☎ 20.73.45.45.
Car rental : Avis, 18, pl. de la Gare, ☎ 20.26.38.36.

Hotel :
★★★ *Altéa le Grand-Hôtel* (ex Grand-Hôtel PLM), 22, av.

J.-B.-Lebas, ☎ 20.73.40.00, Tx 132301, AE DC Euro Visa, 92 rm 🏧 260.

Restaurants :
♦♦♦ *Les Hauts de Barbieux/La Chaudrée*, 31, rue Paul-Lafargue, ☎ 20.26.29.05, Euro Visa 🏨 ♪ closed Mon and Sat noon , eves ex Fri and Sat, 120-260.
● ♦♦ *Le Caribou*, 8, rue Mimerel, ☎ 20.70.87.08, Euro Visa ♪ ⅋ closed Mon eves ex Fri, 12 Jul-30 Aug. Talent and expertise are the keys to the outstanding food served by C. Siesse and his wife; they've made their handsome house a by-word for quality : *rouelle de langouste au céleri, ris de veau aux morilles à la crème, meringues glacées au chocolat chaud*. Exceptional cellar, 160-220.
♦♦ *Chez Charly*, 127, av. J.-B.-Lebas, ☎ 20.70.78.58, Visa ♪ ⅋ closed Sat and eve, 1-25 Aug, 80-170.
♦ *La Calanque*, 58, rue de l'Epeule, ☎ 20.70.79.07, AE DC Visa ♪ closed Mon, Sat noon, Sun, 10 Jul-30 Aug. Fish a specialty, 120-180.

Nearby

CROIX, ⊠ 59170, 2 km W.

Hotel :
★★ *Flandres*, 59, rue Holden, ☎ 20.72.35.01, AE Visa, 31 rm ⚶ closed 7-23 Aug, 160. Rest. ♦ closed Sun, 60-190.

LYS-LES-LANNOY, ⊠ 59390, 5 km SE.

Restaurant :
♦♦ *Auberge de la Marmotte*, 5, rue J.-B.-Lebas, ☎ 20.75.30.95, Euro Visa ♪ closed Tue eve, Wed, Sun eve, 28 Jul-1 Sep. Spec : *filet de sole aux coquilles St-Jacques, grenadin de veau aux morilles*, 75-200.

ROYE

Amiens 42 km
⊠ 80700
SNCF ☎ 22.87.00.12.

Hotel :
★ *Nord* (L.F.), 1, pl. de la République, ☎ 22.87.10.87, Visa, 7 rm ♦, closed 15 Feb-1 Mar, 15 Jul-1 Aug, 160. Rest. ♦ closed Tue eve and Wed, 70-230.

Restaurants :
● ♦♦♦ *La Flamiche*, 20, pl. de l'Hôtel-de-Ville, ☎ 22.87.00.56, AE DC Euro Visa, closed Mon and Sun, 20 Dec-19 Jan. Picardy's great table. Spec : *salade de langoustines aux 3 épinards, raviolis d'anguille de Somme à la crème de poivrons*, 150-330.
♦♦ *La Croix d'Or*, 123, rte de Paris, ☎ 22.87.11.57, AE DC Euro Visa ♪ ᵫ closed Tue eve and Wed, 12-25 Feb, 1-29 Aug. Long and savoury menu of fish and seafood with a nod to carnivores : *steak tartare, andouillette*. Interesting wines, 70-250.

Nearby

MONTDIDIER, ⊠ 80500, 18 km.

Hotel :
★ *Dijon*, 1, pl. du 10-Août-1918, ☎ 22.78.01.35, Euro Visa, 14 rm ℗ ⚶ ♪ closed 2-20 Aug, 26 Dec-20 Jan, 110. Rest. ♦ ♪ closed Mon noon and Sun eve. Spec : *ficelle de canard à l'orange, matelote d'anguille* (in season), 60-100.

RUE**

Abbeville 23, Le Touquet 33, Paris 186 km
pop 3340 ⊠ 80120   A2

Rue was a seaport in the high Middle Ages and is now the principal town of the **Marquenterre area**, a broad coastal plain reclaimed from the sea, between the estuaries of the Somme and the Authie rivers. Its fields and meadows are interspersed with water-filled ditches, lakes and marshes, and provide refuge for many bird species.

▶ Quadrangular 15thC belfry on the **Hôtel de Ville**. On the N side of the parish church is the **St. Esprit Chapel**★★ (15th-16thC), built to house a miraculous crucifix which, according to legend, was discovered at Rue in an abandoned boat from Jerusalem; richly-carved doorway★; inside : marvelously delicate vaulting★ with pendant knobs. Entry from the narthex★ to the two treasure rooms★; upper room decorated with delicately carved biblical scenes; in lower room, vaulting with foliage and animals; early-16thC Virgin and Child. In the **parish church**, rebuilt 19thC, beautiful 16thC oak stalls★. In **Marquenterre** *(7 km W, along coast)* : noteworthy **bird sanctuary**★ *(9:30-6 daily Apr.-Oct.).*   ☐

Practical Information ────────────────

Nearby

CRÉCY-EN-PONTHIEU, ⊠ 80150, 17 km E.

Hotels :
★ **La Maye** (L.F.), 13, rue St-Riquier, ☎ 22.23.54.35, 11 rm ℗ ⫸ closed Mon, Feb, 75. Rest. ♦ 50-100.
Le Canon d'Or, 10, rue du Gal-Leclerc, ☎ 22.23.51.14, 5 rm ℗ ⌕ ⫸ closed Mon eve and Sun eve (l.s.), Jan, 130. Rest. ♦ ♪ ఉ Picardy's specialties : *ficelle picarde*, 45-150.

SAINT-OMER★★

Calais 40, Lille 64, Paris 261 km
pop 15415 ⊠ 62500   A1

This quiet country town on the edge of French Flanders and Artois grew up around the 7thC Benedictine monastery founded by Omer and his companions, who drained, canalized and cultivated the so-called **watergangs**★ (marshes).

▶ On the Place de l'Hôtel de Ville, the old **Bailliage** (bailiff's court) has a fine Louis XVI façade. Going towards the basilica of Notre-Dame, you pass the **Musée d'Histoire Naturelle H. Dupuis**, in a fine 18thC town house *(closed Tue).* ▶ The beautifully proportioned basilica of **Notre-Dame**★★★ has a 13thC choir and transept, 14thC nave and an imposing 15thC tower, decorated with a network of vertical blind arches. Its somber interior contrasts with the magnificent polychrome marble enclosures (17thC) of the side-chapels. This former cathedral is rich in works of art★ : see the astronomical clock of 1558. ▶ E of the basilica is a former **Jesuit collegiate chapel** with a monumental brick façade in the Baroque style. ▶ Nearby, the **library** houses precious manuscripts★ and woodwork from 15thC **Saint-Bernin abbey**. ▶ The Rue des Tribunaux leads from the basilica past the **Palais de Justice** (17thC episcopal palace) to the Place Victor-Hugo : see the monumental doorway of the **hôtel Sandelin** (1777); inside : **Musée des Beaux-Arts**★★ (Fine Arts; *10-12 & 2-6 Wed. & Sun.; Thu. & Fri. am only*); woodwork and furnishings from 18thC; medieval art, including the Cross of St. Bertin★, masterpiece of a 12thC goldsmith's work; collection of Dutch and regional ceramics; paintings from Dutch and Flemish schools of 16th-17thC.

Nearby

▶ **Arques** *(3 km SE)* is well known for its fine crystal ware. The **old boat-lift at Fontinettes** is open to visitors; its construction in 1898 replaced a series of five locks which barges had to pass through on their way from the Aa to the Lys rivers. ▶ The **Benedictine abbey of St. Paul** has been installed for a century in the vast 18thC chateau of **Wisques** *(6 km SW).* ▶ In **Eperlecques Forest** *(15 km NW),* the world's biggest blockhouse was built in 1943-44 to house V2 rockets for the bombardment of England, but never became operational *(Wed., Sat. and Sun. pm, Apr.-mid-Jun. and mid-Sep.-mid-Nov.; daily mid-Jun.-mid-Sep.).*   ☐

Practical Information ────────────────

SAINT-OMER
ⓘ hôtel de ville, ☎ 21.98.40.88; 52, rue Carnot, ☎ 21.38.31.66.
SNCF ☎ 21.38.30.22.

Hotels :
● ★★★ **Le Vert Mesnil** (France-Accueil), rue du Rossignol, Tilques 3 km, ☎ 21.93.28.99, Tx 133360, AE DC Euro Visa, 45 rm ℗ ⫸ ▩ ⌕ ♪ ఉ ⌖ closed Mon lunch, 15 Dec-7 Jan, 240. Rest. ♦♦ ♪ Spec : fish and seafood, 60-200.
★★ **Bretagne** (L.F.), 2, pl. du Vainquai, ☎ 21:38.25.78, Tx 133290, AE DC Euro Visa, 31 rm ℗ ▩ ⌕ closed Sat eve and Sun eve, 2-19 Jan, 230. Rest. ♦♦ ♪ Spec : fish and seafood, 60-200.
★ **La Sapinière** (L.F.), Wisques, ☎ 21.95.14.59, Visa, 9 rm ℗ ⫸ ▩ ⌕ ♪ ఉ closed Sun eve and Mon, 135. Rest. ♦ ⫸ ♪ ఉ 50-80.

Restaurants :
♦♦♦ **La Truye qui File**, 8, rue des Bleuets, ☎ 21.38.41.34, Tx 160600, Visa ♪ ఉ closed Mon and Sun eve, noon. Spec : *cassolette de joues de lotte, cœur de filet aux morilles, nougat glacé au coulis de framboise,* 80-200.
♦ **Cygne**, 8, rue Caventou, ☎ 21.98.20.52, AE Euro Visa ♪ closed Tue and Sat noon, 10-31 Dec, 80-130.

Nearby

LUMBRES, ⊠ 62380, 12 km SW.

Hotel :
★ **Auberge du Moulin de Mombreux**, ☎ 21.39.62.44, AE DC Euro Visa, 6 rm ℗ ⫸ ▩ ⌕ closed Sun eve and Mon, 20 Dec-1 Feb, 130. Rest. ● ♦♦♦ ⫸ ♪ J.-M. Gaudry and his wife have turned this adorable mill into a tranquil stopover for lovers of good food. Fresh, prime foodstuffs star : *blanc de turbot, royale d'asperges aux huîtres à la crème de cerfeuil, paupiette de volaille,* 120-200.

SAINT-POL-SUR-TERNOISE

Arras 34, Boulogne 85, Paris 212 km
pop 6322 ⊠ 62130   B2

ⓘ hôtel de ville, ☎ 21.03.04.98.
SNCF ☎ 21.03.02.55.

Hotel :
★★ **Lion d'Or** (L.F.), 68 and 74, rue d'Hesdin, ☎ 21.03.12.93, Euro Visa, 45 rm ℗ ▩ ⌕ ఉ 150. Rest. ● ♦♦ ♪ closed Sun eve, ex h.s. and school hols. Good regional restaurant between Arras and Montreuil : *escargots frais d'Artois, jambon du pays à l'os braisé aux deux bières, crêpes flambées à la ch'timi,* 65-180; child : 40.

SOMME Valley★★

                                                              A2-3

From Amiens to Saint-Valéry-sur-Somme *(110 km approx, full day)*
The valley of the Somme is very flat and abounds in lakes and water meadows. The numerous branches of the river are well stocked with fish, eels and other freshwater life. Meadows, woods and cultivated fields stretch endlessly.

▶ **Ailly-sur-Somme** clusters around a modern church with a roof in the form of a large sail. ▶ **Picquigny**★, on the left bank of the Somme, nestles under the ruined **château**★ of the Vidames of Amiens. Of the original castle, only the huge 1583 kitchen and the *salle de justice* and its stairway to the prisons remain. Below and opposite is the **collegiate church of St. Martin**, with nave and transept from 13thC and choir and tower of 15thC. ▶ The 18thC buildings of the **Abbaye du Gard** (abbey), founded in the 12thC are undergoing restoration. ▶ **Hangest-sur-Somme** is a little town surrounded by lakes and watercress beds.

In its 12th-16thC church there is 18thC woodwork from the abbey. ▶ 8 km S, **Airaines**★ has a Romanesque church with a baptismal font (11thC) decorated with curious squatting figures. In the other church in the village (Flamboyant Gothic) there is a remarkable 16thC carved Burial of Christ. ▶ **Longpré-les-Corps-Saints** was rebuilt after WWII, but still possesses its doorway★ with carved tympanum of the Assumption and famous relics brought back from the Holy Land at the end of the 12thC. ▶ **Long**, on a hillside overlooking the left bank of the Somme : church with 16thC bell tower ; 18thC château of pink brick and white stone, in a park by the river. ▶ At **Pont-Rémy**, the 15thC château, on an island in the Somme, has been restored in 19thC Romantic Gothic. ▶ **Liercourt** : Flamboyant Gothic church topped by an elegant gabled belfry ; the town is under hillsides fortified in prehistoric times ; this **oppidum du Catelis** was used until the Middle Ages. ▶ **Abbeville**★★, rebuilt around a town hall with a square white stone belfry. **Church of St. Vulfran**★ : fine 16thC Flamboyant Gothic building ; 16thC choir ; beautiful statuary around the three doorways★ ; original 16thC central door★ carved with scenes from the life of the Virgin. In the 13thC belfry and adjoining 15thC building is the **Boucher de Perthes Museum**★ : ornithological and prehistoric collections, local ceramics, medieval sculptures and 16thC paintings *(2-6 ; closed Tue. May-Sep. ; Wed., Sun. and school hols. out of season)*. On the left bank of the Somme at 264 Chaussée d'Hocquet is the **Manufacture Royale des Rames**, built at the beginning of 18thC by the Dutch Van Robais family, who were encouraged by Colbert (Louis XIV's Minister of Finance) to start cloth production in Abbeville. ▶ On the Paris road is the **Château de Bagatelle**★★, built around 1750 by Abraham Van Robais ; period furniture and fine wood paneling inside *(2-6:30 ; closed Tue. Jul.-Sep.)*. ▶ **Saint-Riquier**★★ *(10 km NE)* has an imposing **abbey church**★★ in the best Flamboyant Gothic style ; richly-decorated 17thC façade. Inside : 17thC furnishings in the choir ; splendid Renaissance baptistery in the left transept ; above the sacristy, at the end of the right transept, the abbot's private chapel is now the treasure room★ ; interesting murals on the after-life. The abbey buildings, now a cultural centre, house the **Musée de la Vie Rurale** (Museum of Rural Life : *10-12 & 2-6 daily, Jun.-Sep. ; 2-6, Sat. and Sun., Apr., May and Oct.)*. 16thC **belfry** in the square and, farther on, the early 18thC **Hôtel-Dieu** (hospital), with a richly-decorated chapel★. ▶ **Saint-Valéry-sur-Somme**★★ is a little port at the mouth of the river, with a long shady promenade★ on the dyke along the estuary, giving a good view of the bay. The ramparts of the **upper town**★★ start beyond the lighthouse at the end of the dyke. Inside the fortifications is the **church of St. Martin**★ (14thC) with checkered walls of flint and sandstone (Renaissance triptych in the left nave). ▶ All that remains of the former **abbey of St. Valéry** is the 18thC château down in the valley. On the road linking the higher sections of the village to **Cap Hornu** *(2 km W, view★)* the **chapelle des marins** (sailors' chapel) contains the 1704 tomb of St. Valéry, the founder of the abbey, dead in 622. □

Practical Information ────────────

ABBEVILLE, ⊠ 80100, 45 km NW of **Amiens**.
ⓘ 26, pl. de la Libération, ☎ 22.24.27.92.
SNCF ☎ 22.24.00.25.
Car rental : *Avis*, train station ; 71, av. du Gal-Leclerc, ☎ 22.24.33.00.

Hotels :
★★ *France*, 19, pl. du Pilori, ☎ 22.24.00.42, Tx 150871, AE DC Euro Visa, 77 rm Ⓟ ♪ ċ closed 15 Dec-15 Jan, 155. Rest. ♦ ♪ ċ ⅋ 65-120.
★ *Le Chalet*, 2, av. de la Gare, ☎ 22.24.21.57, 12 rm Ⓟ closed Sun ex hols and h.s., 15 Dec-15 Jan, 125.

Restaurants :
● ♦♦ *L'Escale en Picardie*, 15, rue des Teinturiers, ☎ 22.24.21.51 ♪ ⅋ closed Mon and Sun eve Feb school hols, 9 Aug-4 Sep. Fine, fresh Channel fish prepared by Gérard Perron : home-cured fish, seafood, 90-155.
♦♦ *Auberge de la Corne*, 32, chaussée du Bois,

☎ 22.24.06.34, AE DC Euro Visa ♪ closed Mon, 1-15 Mar, 1-15 Sep. Chef Yves Lematelot has a passion for fresh fish : *panache, lotte au safran, sole aux cèpes*, 75-250.
♦ *Au Chateaubriant*, 3, rue des Lingers, ☎ 22.24.08.23, Euro Visa ⅋ ♪ closed Sun eve, Mon ex hols, Jul, 50-145.

AIRAINES, ⊠ 80270, 28 km NW of **Amiens**.

Restaurant :
♦ *Le Pont d'Hure*, D 936, rte d'Oisemont-Allery, ☎ 22.29.42.10 ⅋ ⍟ ♪ ċ closed wkday eves and Tue lunch, 1-19 Jan, 65-120.

TOURCOING

Roubaix 4, Lille 13, Paris 234 km
pop 97121 ⊠ 59200   B1

ⓘ Grand'Place, ☎ 20.26.89.03.
SNCF ☎ 20.76.30.59.

Restaurants :
● ♦♦ *La Saucière*, 189, bd Gambetta, ☎ 20.26.67.90, Visa ♪ closed Sat noon and Sun, Feb school hols, 1 Aug-9 Sep. Just 20 places for some lucky gourmets. Spec : *turbot rôti, queues de langoustines, saumon mariné au gros sel*, 200-250.
♦ *Le P'tit Bedon*, 5, bd de l'Égalité, ☎ 20.25.00.51, AE Visa, closed Mon, 15-30 Jul, 1-15 Sep. Excellent value, 80-120.

VALENCIENNES*

Lille 51, Bruxelles 102, Paris 206 km
pop 40275 ⊠ 59300   B1

At the heart of the industrialized valley of the Escaut, Valenciennes is the capital of Hainaut and a stronghold which has seen many wars. Over the centuries the town has always had a marked taste for the arts and has been the birthplace of many artists.

▶ Behind a 19thC façade, the **church of St. Géry** has preserved its nave and choir in purest Gothic. On the N side, the **Square Watteau** has a fountain★ in memory of this famous Valenciennois painter, designed in 1827 by Carpeaux, also a native son. ▶ Close by, the **church of St. Nicolas** : pretty 18thC façade ; inside : superb 17thC organ casing. In the adjacent buildings, formerly the **Jesuit College**★, is the **municipal library** with a collection of valuable manuscripts, in particular the *Cantilène de Ste. Eulalie*, one of the first documents written in the French tongue (881). ▶ E of the town centre, along the Bd Watteau is the **municipal museum**★ : 15th-17thC Flemish paintings ; Rubens room ; 18thC Valenciennes painters Watteau and Pater ; 19thC Carpeaux *(10-12 & 2-5 ; closed Tue.)*.

Nearby

▶ **Saint-Amand-les-Eaux**★ *(10 km NW)*, only thermal spa in the region ; on the edge of a large forest, now the **Regional Nature Reserve**★, with marked paths, an ornithological reserve and animal park. There are beautiful remnants of the former Benedictine abbey, notably the elegant Flemish Baroque entrance ; the 17thC **échevinage**★ (town council pavilion), Baroque façade of **abbey church** (ca. 1640), richly-sculpted **tower**★ with lovely chimes (concerts). The tower now houses the municipal **museum** : 18thC ceramics *(Apr.-Sep., daily, 10:30-12:30 ; closed Tue. and am daily, Oct.-Mar.)*. □

Practical Information ────────────

VALENCIENNES
ⓘ 1, rue Askièvre, ☎ 27.46.22.99.
SNCF ☎ 27.46.64.82/27.42.50.50.
🚌 pl. du Hainaut.
Car rental : *Avis*, 15, av. Mal-de-Lattre-de-Tassigny, ☎ 27.46.95.96 ; train station.

Hotels :

★★★ *Grand Hôtel* (Mapotel), 8, pl. de la Gare, ☎ 27.46.32.01, Tx 110701, AE DC Euro Visa, 96 rm, 280. Rest. ◆◆ ♪ Famous for sauerkraut, 70-180.

★★ *Le Bristol*, pl. de la Gare, ☎ 27.46.58.88, 20 rm Ⓟ 165.

Restaurants :

◆◆◆ *Auberge du Bon Fermier*, 64-66, rue de Famars, ☎ 27.46.68.25, AE Euro Visa Ⓟ ≼ ∰ ♪ 10 rm. Regional cuisine served in a historic 17thC coach house. Spec : *goyère valenciennoise, cochon de lait rôti à la broche, sanglier, côte à l'os*, 95-200.

● ◆◆ *L'Alberoi*, Buffet de la Gare, 1, pl. de la Gare, ☎ 27.46.86.30, AE DC Euro Visa Ⓟ ♪ ᨒ closed Sun eve hol eves. In the grand French tradition of railway buffets. F. Benoist keeps an eye on everything : *mignon de bœuf au vin de rully, andouillette de Cambrai grillée, paupiette de bar en habit vert*, 130-300, Brasserie, 50-80.

◆◆ *La Planche à Pain*, 1, rue d'Oultreman, ☎ 27.46.18.28, AE Euro Visa, closed Sat noon and Sun eve. Regional fare, affordably priced, 70-130.

Nearby

QUIÈVRECHAIN, ⊠ 59920, 12 km NE.

Restaurant :

◆◆ *Le Petit Restaurant*, 182, rue J.-Jaurès, ☎ 27.45.43.10, Visa Ⓟ ♪ closed Mon and Aug. The specialty here is fish, 60-90.

RAISMES, ⊠ 59590, 6 km NW.

Restaurant :

◆◆ *La Grignotière*, 6, rue Jean-Jaurès, ☎ 27.36.91.99, AE DC Visa ♪ closed Mon and Sun eve ex hols, Aug. Spec : *blanc de turbotin homardine, foie gras d'oie maison*, 95-150.

SAINT-AMAND-LES-EAUX, ⊠ 59230, 14 km NW.
♨ (1 Mar-15 Dec), ☎ 27.48.50.37.
ⓘ church tower, ☎ 27.48.67.09.
ＳＮＣＦ ☎ 27.48.57.56.

Restaurants :

◆◆ *Auberge de la Forêt*, 92, rte de Valenciennes, ☎ 27.25.51.98, Euro Visa Ⓟ ♪ closed Mon and Sun eve. Spec : game, grills and seafood, 120-250.

◆ *Brasserie Alsacienne*, 23, Grand-Place, ☎ 27.48.50.62, AE DC Visa ♪ closed Mon eve and Sun eve, 15 Jul-13 Aug. Spec : *choucroute au champagne, beignets de lotte sauce rouge, rognons de veau au genièvre*. Interesting wines, 55-100.

⋀ ★★★★*Mont des Bruyères*, A.C.N.F., 806, rue Basly (110 pl), ☎ 27.48.56.87.

SEBOURG, ⊠ 59990 Saultain, 11 km E.

Hotel :

★★ *Jardin Fleuri*, ☎ 27.26.53.44, Euro Visa, 12 rm Ⓟ ∰ ᨓ closed Sun eve, 25 Jan-5 Feb, 15 Aug-9 Sep, 140. Rest. ◆◆ Attractively priced meals, 70-100.

Provence, Côte d'Azur

▶ Astonishing Provence, which juxtaposes the pink flamingoes of the Camargue and the giant reservoirs of industrialized Fos. Old and new mingle harmoniously throughout the region, and technicians at the Cadarache Nuclear Research Center go home at night to thousand-year-old villages perched on the slopes of the Lubéron. Patiently and lovingly, Provence pieces together the puzzle of its past : Mistral and three-holed fipple flute, cowherds and bull-branding, oil presses and medieval trades and crafts. The hilltop villages are coming to life again, grey stone rising up amidst the pinetrees and green oaks. Provence remains true to its origins without compromising its future — a region where life is good, an innovative and inventive culture which keeps one eye on its fascinating past.

The Provence of poets and painters, of Giono, Picasso and Bonnard, still exists — fountains distill eternity under avenues of beechtrees, and lavender still grows in profusion on the high plateau. The Ventoux and Vaucluse mountains are full of honey and truffles, and man-made quarries resemble temples of the gods, abandoned under a sky as blue as that of Greece. The festivals of Aix-en-Provence, Arles and Avignon draw crowds from all over the world to enjoy music and poetry in the perfect climate of the region, or simply to sit in outdoor cafés watching the world go by. Provence's children have dark, laughing faces crowned with unruly black hair, and everywhere you sense the underlying presence of a different culture, once subordinate to the North, but now coming back into its own.

The Côte d'Azur or Riviera, with its palmtrees, beaches and sparkling sea is a favourite holiday spot for French and foreigners alike and, despite its popularity, retains much of its charm and beauty. Tourists stroll along the wide Promenade des Anglais in Nice where the sun shines almost all year round, while Cannes with its luxury hotels in the Croisette, its world-famous film festival and elegant restaurants, forms a sparkling and luxurious façade for the old Roman town of Canois perched on the Sucquet hill behind it. ☐

Don't miss

★★★ Aix-en-Provence B2, Arles A2, Avignon A2, Les Baux-de-Provence A2, the Hyères Islands C3, Sénanque Abbey B2, Le Thoronet Abbey C3, the Grand Canyon of Verdon C2.

★★ The Camargue A2, Cannes D2, the Clues of Haute-Provence D2, the Daluis Gorges C1, the Esterel C-D2, Fontaine-de-Vaucluse A2, Gordes B2, Lubéron Heights B2, Marseille B3, the Maures Massif C3, Menton D2, Monaco D2, Nice and the Riviera D2, Peillon D2, Roya Valley D1, Sainte-Croix Lake C2, Saint-Maximin-la-Sainte-Baume B3, Saint-Paul-de-Vence D2, Saint-Tropez C3, Silvacane Abbey B2, Tinée Valley C-D1, Turini Forest D2, Vaison-la-Romaine A-B1, Vésubie Valley D2, Villeneuve-lès-Avignon A2.

★ Annot C2, Antibes D2, Apt B2, Aups C2, Bormes-les-Mimosas C3, Cagnes-sur-Mer D2, Carpentras A2, Cassis B3, Castellane C2, Cavalaire-sur-Mer C3, Colmars-les-Alpes C1, Cap-Ferrat D2, Grasse D2, Grimaud C3, Lure Mountain B1, Manosque B2, Moustier-Sainte-Marie C2, Napoléon Route C2, Nesque Gorges B2, Orange A1, Peille D2, Peïra-Cava D1-2, Port-Grimaud C3, Ramatuelle C3, Roquebrune-Cap-Martin D2, Roussillon B3, Saint-Rémy-de-Provence A2, Salon-de-Provence A2, Séguret A1, Seillans C2, Sisteron B1, Sospel D2, Tarascon A2, Toulon B3, Tourtour C2, Vence D2, the Ventoux B1, Villefranche-sur-Mer D2.

Weekend tips

Arles on Saturday morning : see the old town and be sure to take in the market in full swing on the Boulevard des Lices. Have lunch in town before heading for Les Baux via Montmajour Abbey. This is the magic triangle of the Alpilles : Les Baux, Glanum and Saint-Rémy, the Provence of Frédéric Mistral (1830-1914), writer and Nobel Prize-winner. Les Baux offers an alluring detour for gourmets. Two possibilities : head for Lubéron (lunch at Cucuron) or go back through Arles to the wide horizons of the Camargue (visit the regional museum of the Camargue, have lunch at Saintes-Maries-de-la-Mer).

● Brief regional history

7thC BC-5thC AD

The Phocean Greeks founded the city of **Massalia** (Marseille) around 600BC, but it was the **Romans** who **developed Provence.** Arles, Fréjus, Glanum and Orange were Roman settlements in the region then called **Provincia,** whose inland areas were renowned for the quality of the olive oil and corn they produced, and whose coastal towns thrived by ship-building.

5th-15thC

After the fall of the Western Roman Empire in 476, Provincia was invaded by Visigoths, Burgundians and

Ostrogoths in rapid succession. Finally, the **Franks peacefully annexed** the region and created a territory of Provence, which was integrated with Burgundy under the administration of counts and viscounts. ● **William the Liberator,** a count who had earned his epithet by recovering a Provençal fort from the Saracens, took the title of *marquis de Provence* in 972 and instituted the first dynasty of the Counts of Provence. ● Provence remained a distinct entity during succeeding centuries, passing by marriage to the **Counts of Catalonia,** and later to the House of Anjou. **Charles du Maine** bequeathed Provence to King Louis XI of France in 1481.

15th-17thC
Under the terms of the **Provençal Constitution,** the two states were to unite on equal terms, and Provence was to retain its rights and privileges. ● The central authorities lost no opportunity to weaken the autonomy of the region and, in fact, since the 16thC, the political history of Provence has been a rearguard action against **administrative centralization.** ● During the 16th and 17thC, the agriculture of Provence changed radically; although sheep and corn remained the basis of the economy, **vineyards** and mulberries spread as the wine and silk industries developed. Land was cleared to accommodate a growing population, and shipbuilding made inroads on the forests. Other important industries were tanning, paper-making, textiles and pottery, including roofing tiles. ● By 1660, **Toulon** was the **largest naval port** in the Mediterranean but in the following century, **Mar-**

1. The Esterel massif

2. The Lubéron heights

3. Maures massif

4. Grand Canyon of Verdon

seille outstripped it, prospering from soap-making and tallow-rendering. In 1720, the Plague struck : Marseille alone lost half its population (38 000 dead) and Provence as a whole lost 100 000 people.

1790 to the present
The political reorganization that followed the French Revolution **eliminated Provence** as an administrative entity; the departments of **Bouches-du-Rhône, Var** and **Basses-Alpes** were created in 1790, and the following year **Vaucluse** was fashioned from the former Papal States; **Alpes-Maritimes** came into being in 1793 and, finally, **Savoy** and **Nice** were **annexed to France in 1860** in exchange for Napoléon III's support for Italian independence. In 1861 France bought Menton and Roquebrune from the Prince of Monaco.
● The opening of the PLM (Paris-Lyon-Marseille) railway, together with the choice of Nice as the favourite winter resort of the English leisure classes towards the end of the 19thC established Provence-Côte d'Azur as one of the most desirable holiday destinations in the world, which it remains today.

Hillside village street

Facts and figures

Situation : N, the Alps of the Dauphiné; E, the Italian frontier; W, the Rhône and the Languedoc; S, the Mediterranean.
Area : 26 135 km².
Climate : Mediterranean, with wide divergencies according to altitude and exposure; heavy rain in spring and autumn; mild winters on the Côte d'Azur; cool nights; hot, dry summers. The dry, cold mistral wind blows down the Rhône Valley as far as Fréjus.
Population : 3 860 139; Alpes-de-Haute-Provence 119 068; Alpes-Maritimes 881 198; Bouches-du-Rhône 1 724 199; Var 708 331; Vaucluse 427 343.
Administration : Department of **Alpes-de-Haute-Provence,** Prefecture Digne; Department of **Alpes-Maritimes,** Prefecture Nice; Department of **Bouches-du-Rhône,** Prefecture Marseille; Department of **Var,** Prefecture Toulon; Department of **Vaucluse,** Prefecture Avignon.

Provençale house

Bories

Southern Europe is strewn with the drystone buildings (5 000-6 000 in Provence alone) that are called bories in Provence, nuraghi in Sardinia, trulli in La Pouille, talayot in the Balearics, casitas in Spain, orris in the Pyrénées, and capitelles in Languedoc. The method of construction, rather than the material, is the distinguishing feature. The borie is usually made of limestone but may be of any suitable rock that can be chipped into flakes. These Stone Age equivalents of log cabins have been built since Neolithic times, with a false roof vault created by corbelling : each circle of stone laid so as to project slightly over the preceding one; at the top, a capstone a little larger than the rest firmly anchors the spiral. Nowadays, bories are used for storing tools or grain, drying lavender, for sheepfolds, country cottages and principal residences. At a few sites, such as Gordes, whole villages have been built of bories.

● *Practical information*

Information : *Comité Régional du Tourisme Provence-Alpes-Côte d'Azur (C.R.T.) :* 22A, rue Louis-Maurel, 13006 Marseille, ☎ 91.37.91.22. *C.R.T. Riviera-Côte d'Azur,* 55, prom. des Anglais, 06000 Nice, ☎ 93.44.50.59. **Alpes-de-Haute-Provence :** *Chambre Départementale du Tourisme (C.D.T.),* Étoile des Alpes, traverse des eaux chaudes, 04000 Digne, ☎ . 92.31.57.29. **Alpes-Maritimes :** *C.D.T.,* same address as *C.R.T. Riviera-Côte d'Azur.* **Bouches-du-Rhône :** *C.D.T.,* 6, rue du Jeune-Anacharsis, 13001 Marseille, ☎ 91.54.92.66. **Var :** *C.D.T.,* 1, bd Foch, B.P. 99, 83303 Draguignan, ☎ 94.68.58.33. **Vaucluse :** *C.D.T.,* pl. Campana, quartier de la Balance, B.P. 147, 84008 Avignon Cedex, ☎ 90.86.43.42. *Dir. régionale de la Jeunesse et des Sports,* 7, av. du Gal-Leclerc, 13331 Marseille Cedex 3, ☎ 91.50.22.23 and 117, rue de France, 06000 Nice, ☎ 93.96.31.00. *Dir. rég. des Affaires culturelles,* 21-23, bd du Roi-René, 13617 Aix-en-Provence Cedex, ☎ 42.27.98.40.

Reservations : *Loisirs-Accueil Bouches-du-Rhône,* domaine du Vergon, 13370 Mallemort, ☎ 90.59.18.05. *Vaucluse-Tourisme-Hébergement,* hall of the Avignon train station; Info, ☎ 90.85.56.68; reservations, ☎ 90.82.05.81.

S.O.S. : Alpes-de-Haute-Provence : ☎ 17. **Alpes-Maritimes :** ☎ 93.92.55.55. **Bouches-du-Rhône :** *SAMU* (emergency medical service) : ☎ 91.49.91.91. **Var :** *SAMU :* ☎ 94.27.07.07. **Vaucluse :** *SAMU :* ☎ 90.88.11.11. *Poisoning Emergency Centre :* Marseille, ☎ 91.75.25.25.

Weather forecast : Alpes-de-Haute-Provence : ☎ 92.64.17.33. **Alpes-Maritimes :** mountain conditions, ☎ 93.21.31.33. **Bouches-du-Rhône :** ☎ 42.09.09.09. **Var :** coastal forecast, ☎ 94.46.90.11; mountain conditions : ☎ 94.64.17.47. **Vaucluse :** ☎ 90.86.55.48 (road conditions), ☎ 90.82.69.00 (snow conditions in winter, schedule of events in summer).

Rural gîtes and chambres d'hôte : enq. at *relais départementaux :* **Alpes-de-Haute-Provence,** ☎ 92.31.52.39, and **Alpes-Maritimes** at the *C.D.T.* **Bouches-du-Rhône :** domaine du Vergon, 13370 Mallemort, ☎ 90.59.18.05. **Var :** 1, bd Foch, 83300 Draguignan, ☎ 94.68.55.43, ext 223. **Vaucluse :** chambre dép. du Tourisme, ☎ 90.85.45.00 and 90.86.43.42.

Camping-car rental : Alpes-Maritimes : *Allage Location,* 14, route de Grenoble, 06200 Nice, ☎ 93.83.27.01. **Bouches-du-Rhône :** *Selg Sarl,* RN7, 13760 Saint-Cannat, ☎ 42.28.23.23. **Vaucluse :** *APTA Location garage Germain,* 56, av. Victor-Hugo, 84400 Apt, ☎ 90.74.10.17.

Holiday villages : numerous in the region. Enq. : *C.D.T.; U.C.P.A.,* 62, rue de la Glacière, 75640 Paris Cedex 13, ☎ (1) 43.36.05.20; *Léo-Lagrange Loisirs,* 19, rue de la Grande-Batelière, 75009 Paris, ☎ 45.23.45.45; *Tourisme et Travail,* 187, quai de Valmy, 75010 Paris, ☎ (1) 42.03.96.16; *O.C.C.A.J.,* 4, bd de la Libération, 13001 Marseille, ☎ 91.48.14.28.

Cultural and sporting events : *bull-fights* in the Camargue and back country, enq : *C.D.T.* **Jan** : *international record and music publications festival* (Midem) in Cannes. **Mar** : *motocross* in l'Isle-sur-La-Sorgue. **Apr** : *hike up Mont Faron* (Toulon); *international tennis open* in Monaco. **May** : *international cartoon festival* in Aix-en-Provence; Apt *music festival; international cinema festival* in Cannes; *motocross* in Sainte-Cécile-les-Vignes and Pernes; *grand prix motorcycle race* in Le Castellet; *formula 1 grand prix* in Monaco; *terre de Provence rally.* **Jun** : *Aix en musique; festival du café-théâtre* in Cannes; *religious music festival* in Nice; *harbour crossing in odd craft* in Marseille; *Cinema Festival* (Lumière brothers' pioneering silent films) in La Ciotat. **Jul** : *Aix international music festival; arts festival* — music, photography, dance — in Arles; *jazz festival* in Antibes-Juan-les-Pins; *international folk festival* at Château-Gombert in Marseille; *Chorégies* (*music festival*) in Orange; *Christian dart festival* in Digne; *festival of early music* in Sénanque-Gordes; *"Nights of the Citadel"* in Sisteron; *New Orleans jazz festival* in Saint-Raphaël; *jazz festival* in Digne; *music festival* in Vaison-la-Romaine; *formula 1 grand prix* in Le Castellet. **Aug** : *dramatic arts festival* in Avignon; Menton *music festival; "musical weeks"* in the Lubéron region; *"musical encounters"* in Saint-Rémy-de-Provence; *piano festival* in La Roque-d'Anthéron. **Sep** : *young cinema festival* in Hyères; *musical autumn* in Digne; *Bol d'Or motorcycle race* in Le Castellet. **Oct** : *"medieval days"* in Brignoles; *VIDCOM (video and communications exhibition)* in Cannes. **Dec** : *international circus festival* in Monaco.

Fairs and folklore : Feb : *plant fair* in Draguignan; *lemon festival* in Menton; *carnival* in Nice; *sea-urchin festival* in Carry-le-Rouet and Sausset. **Mar** : Marseille *international fair; bric-à-brac fair* in Sainte-Maxime; *spring fair* in Grans. **May** : *bric-à-brac fair* in Avignon; *rose festival* in Grasse; **24 and 25** : *pilgrimage of the gypsies* to Les Saintes-Maries-de-la-Mer; *horse fair* in Eyguières. **Jun** : *carreto zamado* (Saracen-style chariot races) in Barbeurane; *olive fair* in Draguignan; *Mediterranean horse show* in Marseille; *broom-flower festival* in Roquebrune-Cap-Martin; *St-Peter's fete* (patron saint of fishermen) in Menton and Toulon. **Jul-Aug** : *santon fair* in Valensole. **Aug** : *lavender festival* in Digne; *jasmine fete* in Grasse. **Sep** :

livestock fair in Salon. **Oct** : *chestnut festival* in Les Mayons. **Dec** : *santon fair* in Marseille, Solliès-ville and Toulon; *shepherds' festival* in Les Baux; *the path of the crèches* in Menton.

National and nature parks : *Parc national du Mercantour,* 23, rue d'Italie, 06000 Nice, ☎ 93.87.86.10; HQ : *Maison du Parc,* La Sapinière, 04000 Barcelonnette, ☎ 92.81.21.31; *Parc national de Port-Cros,* 50, av. Gambetta, 83400 Hyères, ☎ 94.65.32.98. *Parc naturel de la Camargue,* Le Mas de Pont-de-Rousty, 13200 Arles, ☎ 90.97.10.93. Map *I.G.N.* 303. *Parc naturel du Lubéron,* pl. Jean-Jaurès, 84400 Apt, ☎ 90.74.08.55.

Rambling and hiking : the region is traversed by G.R. trails 4, 5, 6, 9, 52, 56, 91, 92, 97 (topoguides). The Didier-Richard maps, 1/50 000 n°s 1, 9, 19 are also very useful (alternative trails and shelters). List of member associations of the Féd. française de la Randonnée pédestre at the *Comité régional P.A.C.A.,* 123, allée des Temps-Perdus, 84300 Cavaillon, ☎ 90.71.26.05. **Alpes-de-Haute-Provence :** *Assn. Dép. des Relais et Itinéraires (A.D.R.I.),* 14, bd V.-Hugo, 04000 Digne, ☎ 92.31.37.70. **Alpes-Maritimes :** *Comité dép. de la Randonnée pédestre,* M. Resse, Villa Taéma, Montaleigne, 06700 Saint-Laurent-du-Var; *Sentiers Amitié Montagne,* 70, bd Perrier, 06110 Le Cannet, ☎ 93.45.16.43. **Bouches-du-Rhône :** *Comité dép. de la Randonnée pédestre,* 16, rue de la Rotonde, 13001 Marseille; *Excursionnistes Marseillais,* 33, allées Léon-Gambetta, 13001 Marseille; *Excursionnistes provençaux,* 8, rue du Littera, 13100 Aix-en-Provence, ☎ 42.21.03.53. **Var :** *Comité dép. du Var de la F.F.R.P.,* 3, imp. Baudin, 83000 Toulon; *Excursionnistes toulonnais,* 26, rue d'Alger, 83000 Toulon. *Assn. Lei Caminaïre,* Le Valat-Seillans, 83440 Fayence, ☎ 94.76.06.04. **Vaucluse :** *Comité départemental,* 63, av. C.-Franck, 84000 Avignon; *Cimes et Sentiers du Haut-Comtat,* Centre culturel À Cœur Joie, av. C.-Geoffrey, 84110 Vaison-la-Romaine. The *C.D.T.* publishes a brochure with map indicating rambling and hiking possibilities in the department.

Leisure centres : *Aquaplash,* av. Mozart, 06600 Antibes, ☎ 93.33.49.49 (Jun-Sep); *Aquacity, Pennes-Mirabeau,* route de Septèmes-les-Vallons, 13170 Les Pennes-Mirabeau, ☎ 91.96.12.13; *Aquatica,* RN98, route de Saint-Tropez, 83600 Fréjus, ☎ 95.52.01.01 (Jun-Sep); *Zygofolis,* rte de Digne and *Castel des deux rois* in Nice, enq : *TO.*

Scenic railways : *Pignes train,* from Nice to Digne, *Chemins de Fer de Provence,* 52, rue Dabray, 06100 Nice, ☎ 93.88.28.56. *Le Petit train de la citadelle,* 04200 Sisteron; enq : *TO,* ☎ 92.61.12.03.

Le train des pignes

From the sea to the mountain, a holiday train takes you 150 km through the valleys and villages between Nice and Digne. Along the Var, through Puget-Théniers and Entrevaux, then across the mountain through Annot, Saint-André-les-Alpes and Barrême, each halt a holiday in itself. Many hikers use the Train des Pignes to reach their base of departure.

Cycling holidays : *Comité dép. de Féd. française de cyclo,* **Var :** 259, chemin rural 133, quartier d'Ouicarde, 83500 La Seyne. **Alpes-de-Haute-Provence :** M. Exubis, 22, av. de St-Véran, La Cassette, 04000 Digne. **Bouches-du-Rhône :** M. Maillet, 15, lotissement de la Trevaresse, 13540 Puyricard, ☎ 42.92.13.41. **Vaucluse :** M. Gouttebaron, 2, rue Lavoisier, 84000 Avignon.

Riding holidays : map 1/50 000 «En Haute-Provence», n°s 14, 19 and 24, Ed. Didier-Richard. **Var** and **Alpes-Maritimes :** *Assn. régionale pour le Tourisme Équestre et l'Équitation de Loisirs,* Arte Proca, 19, bd V.-Hugo, 06130 Grasse, ☎ 93.42.62.98. **Vaucluse, Bouches-du-Rhône, Alpes-de-Haute-Provence :** *Assn. régionale pour le Tou-*

risme équestre, Maison du Docteur, 13810 Eygalières, ☎ 90.95.90.57. **Alpes-Maritimes** : *Comité dép. d'équitation, de randonnées et de raids équestres,* La Jumenterie, route de St-Cézaire, 06460 Saint-Vallier-de-Thies, ☎ 93.42.62.98. **Alpes-de-Haute-Provence** : *A.D.T.E.,* M. Lorion, La Grosse Coasse, 04000 Digne, ☎ 93.31.51.72 and 92.34.71.04. **Bouches-du-Rhône** : *A.D.T.E.,* M. Poitevin, Les Collets-Rouges, 13127 Vitrolles. *Comité dép. d'équitation de randonnée du Var,* 710, av. du Fournas, 83300 Draguignan, ☎ 94.68.30.75. **Vaucluse** : *A.D.T.E.,* M. François, chemin Saint-Julien, 30400 Les Angles, ☎ 90.25.38.91 ; *A.T.M. Voyages,* 15, pl. Castil-Blaze, 84300 Cavaillon, ☎ 90.71.37.66.

Horse-drawn holidays : rentals : M. Moyne, domaine St-Sauveur, 84320 Entraigues, ☎ 90.83.16.26 ; M. Pavon, le Clos des Princes, 84660 Maubec, ☎ 90.71.90.29 and 90.71.70.91.

River cruises : on the Rhône, aboard *le Cygne :* info and reservations, quai de la Ligne, 84000 Avignon, ☎ 66.59.45.08, 1 May-14 Aug and at S.I. ; *Hermès :* info, ☎ 90.82.65.11.

Technical tourism : perfume : *Parfumerie Fragonard,* 20, bd Fragonard, 06130 Grasse, ☎ 93.36.44.65 (daily). Sweets : *Confiserie du Vieux Nice,* quai Papacino, 06300 Nice, ☎ 93.55.43.50 (daily). Roses : *Roseraie Alain-Meilland,* bd du Cap, 06600 Antibes, ☎ 93.61.30.30 (by appt). *Parc international d'activités de Valbonne-Sophia-Antipolis,* 9 km from Antibes (take autoroute A8, exit Antibes ; daily). Glass : *Verrerie de Biot,* 06140 Biot, ☎ 93.65.03.00 (daily ex Sun, hols.). Harbour visit (by appt) : *Port autonome de Marseille,* 23, pl. de la Joliette, 12317 Marseille Cedex 01, ☎ 91.91.90.66.

Handicraft courses : painting, drawing : *Académie internationale d'Été,* villa Paradisio, 21, bd de Cimiez, 06000 Nice, ☎ 93.81.64.06 ; pottery, weaving, spinning : *Centre culturel,* domaine de l'Étoile, 293, av. Pessicart, 06000 Nice, ☎ 93.84.48.12. Wood-working : *L'Escarène,* Assn. Peïra Cava (information centre), ☎ 93.91.57.97. Weaving : O. Miquau, La Gipote, Les Jaisons, 06530 Peymenade, ☎ 93.66.06.13. Wood, earthenware, leather, silk, crafts, etc. : M. Goutelle, palais Couperin, 15, rue Guiglia, 06000 Nice, ☎ 93.88.13.70 ; *Neiges et Merveilles,* 06450 Saint-Dalmas-de-Tende, ☎ 93.04.62.40 ; *C.A.M.A.S.,* 6, av. des Poilus, 06140 Vence, ☎ 93.58.03.01. *A.D.A.C.,* domaine de la Garde, rte de Berre, 13150 Éguilles, ☎ 42.92.43.33. *Arts et creations artisanales,* Mme Mercier, 30, bd Michelet, 13008 Marseille, ☎ 91.77.07.50. *Artisanat Club Mazarin,* 30, rue Cardinale, 13100 Aix-en-Provence, ☎ 42.38.46.60. *A.R.T.I.S.A.R.T.,* 7, bd Mirabeau, 04100 Manosque, ☎ 92.87.56.11. Further enq at *C.D.T.* and *C.R.T.*

Other courses : cooking for beginners : *École du Moulin* (under direction of leading chef Roger Vergé), Moulin de Mougins, Notre-Dame-de-Vie, 06250 Mougins, ☎ 93.75.78.24 ; *Académie niçoise de Cuisine,* restaurant l'Academia, 15, rue A.-Mari, 06300 Nice, ☎ 93.62.35.00. Introduction to gastronomy, info at *C.D.T./S.L.A.* Bouches-du-Rhône. Geology courses (Jul-Sep) at Digne ; info *T.O.*

Wine guide : *Comité interprofessionnel des vins des Côtes de Provence,* 3, av. Jean-Jaurès, 83460 Les Arcs-sur-Argens, ☎ 94.73.33.38.

Youth activities : *Assn. Langues vivantes et Aventures,* Pierrefeu, 06910 Roquestéron, ☎ 93.08.56.15 (language courses, craftwork, excursions). *Vacances Bleues,* 20 bis, av. G.-Clemenceau, 06600 Nice, ☎ 93.88.01.13 (tennis and riding courses). *ARC,* 71, av. des Tuilières, 06800 Cagnes-sur-Mer, ☎ 93.07.28.71 (canoeing). *Aroeven,* Rectorat, 06081 Nice Cedex, ☎ 93.81.45.96 (road from Nice to Digne). *C.I.D.J.,* 4, rue de la Visitation, 13004 Marseille, ☎ 91.49.91.55.

Aquatic sports : numerous marinas and inland stretches of water. Enq at *T.O., C.D.T.* and *Maison de la mer,* RN 559, quartier Robinson, 06210 Mandelieu-la-Napoule, ☎ 93.49.88.77.

Scuba diving : *Centre international de Plongée,* 2, ruelle de Moulins (port), 06000 Nice, ☎ 93.55.59.50. *Féd. de*

Plongée, 24, quai de la Rive-Neuve, 13007 Marseille, ☎ 91.33.99.31.

Canoeing : *Comités dép. :* **Bouches-du-Rhône** : 142, av. J.-Vidal, 13008 Marseille, ☎ 91.73.30.93. **Alpes-Maritimes** : la Vignerette, quartier la Tour, 06700 Saint-Laurent-du-Var, ☎ 93.07.82.15. *Jeunes-Canoë-Kayak d'Avignon,* 66, rue des Tireuses-de-Soie, ☎ 90.87.52.47. **Ligue Alpes-Provence,** ☎ 66.89.83.10. **Alpes-de-Haute-Provence** : *Plein air nature,* 14, bd V.-Hugo, 04000 Digne, ☎ 92.31.37.70. **Vaucluse** : *Base de plein air,* 84800 Fontaine-de-Vaucluse.

Potholing and spelunking : *Délégation régionale Provence-Alpes-Côte d'Azur,* M. Acquaviva, 29, bd Rodocanachi, 13008 Marseille. *Comités dép. :* **Alpes-de-Haute-Provence,** M. Languille, quartier de Trégastel, 04220 Sainte-Tulle, ☎ 92.78.20.89. **Bouches-du-Rhône** : M. Carol, F4, rés. Bayonne, 13800 Istres. **Var** : M. Tainton, Le Pont-d'Arroun, 83110 Sanary. **Vaucluse** : *Soc. de spéléologie d'Avignon,* 67, rue J.-Vernet.

Climbing-mountaineering : *F.F.M.,* 15, av. J.-Médecin, 06000 Nice (list of clubs). *C.A.F. :* same address, ☎ 93.87.75.41, Section Ubaye : mairie, 04400 Barcelonnette, ☎ 92.81.04.73. *Féd. de la Montagne,* 12, rue Notre-Dame, 13007 Marseille. **Vaucluse** : *C.D.T.* and *T.O.*

Provençale cuisine

Unlike the menus touted by tourist-trap restaurants, traditional Provençal cooking has nothing to do with pizza or hamburgers. In Provence, meat is most frequently eaten as a daube, beef braised with garlic, bay or cloves and vegetables. In earlier days, the main meal of the day was often a thick vegetable soup made from fresh vegetables in summer, and dried beans or peas in the winter. The aromatic soupe au pistou is made with summer vegetables and vermicelli, to which is added pistou, a paste of garlic, basil, cheese and olive oil. Vegetables are the traditional staple diet, whether served as gratins, in salads, or stuffed with meat. On the coast, excellent soups and stews are made with rock fish — scorpion fish, gurnard, galinette, sea bream, anglerfish, red mullet, sea dace — which often have more bones than flesh and are therefore unsuitable for grilling or baking. The bouillabaisse — fish in a fragrant emulsion of broth, olive oil and herbs — is the best known of these soups. The bourride is made from white fish only — grey mullet, John Dory, turbot — and served with aïoli, a creamy mayonnaise liberally laced with crushed garlic.

Golf : 18-hole courses in Aix-en-Provence, Les Milles, Antibes-Biot, Cannes-Mougins, La Londe-Valcros, Mandelieu-La Napoule, Peille-Mont-Agel, Saint-Raphaël-Valescure and Valbonne ; 9-hole courses in Sainte-Maxime-Beauvallon and Tende-Vievola.

Gliding : *Ligue du Sud-Est de vol à voile,* M. Gianti, La Collet-de-Christine, 83440 Les Tourettes-Fayence, ☎ 93.20.97.22. *Union aérienne Sisteron-Durance* at Vaumeilh, 04200 Sisteron, ☎ 92.61.27.45.

Parachuting : *Ligue Provence de Parachutisme,* 8, av. Venture, 13006 Marseille, ☎ 91.33.38.69. *Ligue Côte-d'Azur de Parachutisme,* B.P. 8, Le Cannet-des-Maures, 83340 Le Luc, ☎ 94.60.72.83. *Centre inter-clubs,* aérodrome Avignon-Pujant, ☎ 90.25.19.20. Beginners' course at Isola 2000, enq : ☎ 93.23.15.15.

Hang-gliding : *Ligue du vol à voile libre du Sud-Est,* 30, rue Guiglia, 06000 Nice, ☎ 93.88.52.19. *Ligue de Provence,* Le Garagaï, domaine de Roques-Blanches, 13777 Venelles, ☎ 42.57.76.67.

Flying in ultra-light aircraft : *Centre de Provence-Côte d'Azur de vol ultra-léger*, 83129 La Mole, ☎ 94.49.57.71. *Centre national de Formation U.L.M.*, Rustrel, 84400 Apt, ☎ 90.74.30.00.

Winter sports : downhill skiing, ski treks, cross-country skiing : *F.F.M.*, 15, av. J.-Médecin, 06000 Nice. *F.F.S.*, Comité régional de Ski Côte d'Azur, 39, rue Pastorelli, 06000 Nice, ☎ 93.80.65.77. *AGRAM (Assn. des guides et accompagnateurs des Alpes méridionales)* : office in Saint-Martin-Vésubie, ☎ 93.03.21.28, 93.03.20.73 and 166, bd de Cessole, 06000 Nice, ☎ 93.56.73.84 ; Isola 2000, ☎ 93.23.10.50 ; Tende, ☎ 93.04.60.90 ; Saint-Jeannet, ☎ 93.59.53.38 ; Valberg, ☎ 93.02.52.34. For the Haute-Ubaye region, guide office in Barcelonnette, *T.O.*, ☎ 92.81.04.71. Montserein, Montventoux, 84340 Malaucère, ☎ 90.63.49.44.

Hunting and shooting : enq at the *Féd. dép. des chasseurs*, **Alpes-de-Haute-Provence** : 79, bd Gassendi, 04000 Digne, ☎ 92.31.02.43. **Alpes-maritimes** : P.A.L., 7 M.I.N., St-Augustin, 06042 Nice Cedex, ☎ 93.83.82.39. **Bouches-du-Rhône** : quartier Maliverny, 13540 Puyricard, ☎ 42.92.16.75. **Var** : 7, bd G.-Péri, 83300 Draguignan, ☎ 94.68.03.13. **Vaucluse** : rés. Thiers, rue R.-Salengro, 84000 Avignon, ☎ 90.82.51.99.

Fishing : *Féd. dép. de la Pêche*, **Alpes-de-Haute-Provence** : 79, bd Gassendi, 04000 Digne, ☎ 92.31.57.14. **Alpes-Maritimes** : 20, bd V.-Hugo, 06000 Nice, ☎ 93.03.24.09. **Bouches-du-Rhône** : 30, bd de la République, 13100 Aix-en-Provence, ☎ 42.26.59.15. **Var** : B.P. 104, 83170 Brignoles, ☎ 94.69.05.56. **Vaucluse** : 5, Champfleury, 84000 Avignon, ☎ 90.86.62.68.

● *Towns and places*

AIX-EN-PROVENCE★★★

Avignon 75, Nice 176, Paris 753 km
pop 124550 ✉ 13100   B2-3

Aix seems to embody the noblest aspects of Provençal civilization. Much of the architecture is derived from the 17th and 18thC, including 198 mansions built for the regional parliamentary councillors, squares and avenues shaded by plane trees and mossy fountains. In July and August, when the city is given over to an international arts festival, the streets seem to be in a state of permanent celebration. A *pastis* (aniseed-flavoured alcoholic drink) on the terrace of the *Deux Garçons* café is practically a rite of initiation for newcomers.

▶ The **Cours Mirabeau★★** (A-B2) : with attractive cafés and brasseries, bookshops and confectioners, this is one

AIX-EN-PROVENCE

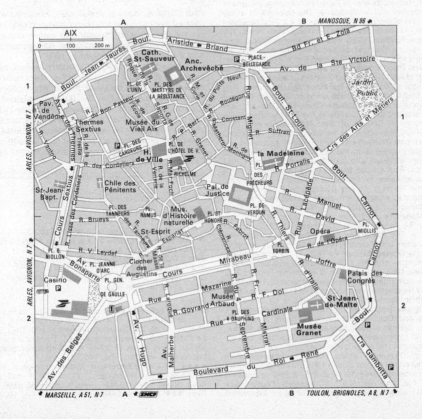

of the great avenues of the world. 17th and 18thC mansions line the avenue; the influence of Italian Baroque is evident : No. 38, **Maurel de Pontevès Mansion★** (1647); No. 55 is the house where the painter Paul Cézanne (1839-1906) spent his childhood. ▶ **Place d'Albertas★★** (A2) : 18thC mansions and a fountain provide a gracious setting for summer concerts. ▶ Nearby, at 6 Rue Espariate, **Boyer d'Éguilles Mansion★** (1675) is a natural history museum *(10-12 & 2-6, closed Sun.).* ▶ **Place Richelme** (A1) : shaded by plane trees, site of the centuries-old morning fruit and vegetable market. ▶ **Place de l'Hôtel-de-Ville** (A1) : flower market *(Tue., Thu., Sat. am).* The 17thC Hôtel de Ville (town hall, courtyard★, Méjanes library, St.-John Perse Foundation *9-12 & 2-5; Sat. 12-5*) stands next to the 16thC **Tour de l'Horloge** (clock tower)★ with four figures representing the seasons. ▶ **Museum of Old Aix★** (A1) in the Estienne de St-Jean Mansion★ *(10-12 & 2-5, 6 in summer; closed Mon. and Feb.).* Next door at No. 17 Rue Gaston-de-Saporta, the **Châteaurenard Mansion★** (1650; monumental staircase★). ▶ Towards the cathedral, **Musée des Tapisseries★** (Tapestry Museum in 17th-18thC Archbishop's palace; display of Beauvais tapestries★ of same period; *10-12 & 2-5, 2:30-6:30 in season; closed Tue., Jan. and some nat. hols.).* The courtyard is the setting for major festival events; gate★. ▶ **St. Sauveur cloister★★** : late-12thC Romanesque. ▶ **Cathedral of St. Sauveur★★** (A1) : decoration and architecture of every period from the 5th to the 18thC are represented; the Gothic building (1285-1350) incorporates the nave of an earlier Romanesque church (S aisle). The panels★ of the door (1510), the 5thC sarcophagus of St. Mître (first bay in right side-aisle) and the Merovingian baptistery★ (second and third bays) are noteworthy, as is the triptych of the **Burning Bush★★★** (1476, right wall of nave) by Nicolas Froment. Typical of Provençal painting at that period, the work includes elements of Flemish Realism as well as Italian Renaissance influences in perspective and landscape. ▶ The cathedral is in the oldest part of the city. The **springs** at Aix (Établissement Thermal, A1) have been in use since Roman times. The **Vendôme Pavilion** (1667) was built as a provincial residence for the Cardinal de Vendôme; the painter Jean-Baptiste Van Loo (1684-1745) lived and worked there (furniture and Provençal works of art, *10-12 & 2-5, 6:30 in season; closed Tue. and last 2 weeks of Jun.).* ▶ Through the streets of Old Aix to the **Place des Prêcheurs** (B1) where fragrant *herbes de Provence* complement the fruit and vegetables in the market★ *(Tue., Thu., Sat. am);* antiques and bric-à-brac stands in the neighbouring Place de Verdun. ▶ **Church of Ste. Marie-Madeleine** (B1; 18th-19thC), interesting for its works of art. The 15thC **Annunciation Triptych★★** (centre panel renowned for the Virgin's smile) is in the left side-aisle. ▶ Return to the Cours Mirabeau and take **Rue du 4-Septembre** (B2) where the **Paul-Arbaud Museum** and Library have much to offer admirers of Provençal ceramics★; documents about the Félibrige Society (founded by Frédéric Mistral and others to preserve Provençal culture) and Provence *(2-5; closed Sun. and nat. hols.).* Nearby, the 18thC **Gaumont Mansion★** at 3 Rue Joseph-Cabassol (A2), now houses the Darius Milhaud Conservatory of Music and Dance. ▶ The **Place des Quatre-Dauphins★** (B2), with old mansions and fountain (1667), an especially attractive square. ▶ **Granet Museum★★** (B2), in the former Priory of the Knights of Malta (1675), displays aristocratic taste of the late 17thC *(10-12 & 2-5, 6 in summer; closed Tue. and nat. hols.);* the Provençal painter Granet (1775-1849) is amply represented; the collection of French works from the 16th to the 19thC includes examples by Clouet, La Tour, Largillière and Ingres (Ingres' **portrait of Granet★★**), Flemish and Dutch works (Rubens, Frans Hals, Rembrandt); German school (**portrait of Sir Thomas More★**, attributed to Mabuse); Italian schools (Guercino, Correggio, Giordano); recently-opened Cézanne room. **Also...** ▶ **Cézanne's studio** (via A1), preserved as it looked when the painter died in 1906 (memorabilia, Centre for Cézanne Studies; *10-12 & 2-5, 2:30-6 in season; closed Tue. and nat. hols.).* ▶ **Vasarely Foundation★** *(4 km W),* an art gallery and study centre for exploration

of the basic preoccupations of the painter Victor Vasarely (b. 1908; *9:30-12:30 & 2-5:30; closed Tue.).*

Nearby

▶ **Oppidum d'Entremont** *(3 km N)* : ruins of the capital of the Celto-Ligurian federation of Salyens *(9-12 & 2-5, 6 in season; closed Tue.).* ▶ **Roquefavour Aqueduct★** *(13.5 km W),* built in 1847 to supply Marseille with water from the Durance. ▶ **Ventabren** *(3.5 km N),* pretty village at the foot of a ruined château.

Mont Sainte-Victoire★★ *(59 km round trip, half-day).*

Sainte-Victoire★★ forms a backdrop to Aix. The mountain is spectacular, the light is beautiful, and it is easy to see why Cézanne was drawn to the site. ▶ **Aix** *(leave via C2);* take the Cézanne Road (D17). ▶ **Le Tholonet** (site★), a favourite excursion for the people of Aix; 18thC château, roads lined with plane trees. ▶ From D17, signposted paths lead towards Sainte-Victoire and the limestone **Cengle plateau,** S of the mountain. ▶ **Puyloubier** : ruins of a medieval château. ▶ **Pourrières.** ▶ Take D23 N then, after 7 km, the Vauvenargues road (D223, D10) down into the upper valley of the Infernet★. ▶ **Château de Vauvenargues** (16th-17thC), isolated on a peak, belonged to Pablo Picasso (1881-1973), who is buried in the garden. ▶ **Les Cabassols** : the easiest path (GR9) to Sainte-Victoire leaves from here; 1hr30 to the priory, then 10 min to the **Croix de Provence★★** (alt. 945 m) where you can see from the Dauphiné Alps across to Esterel. ▶ **Bimont Dam** *(1.2 km left)* : lake reflecting the mountain★; 30 min on foot to the Zola Dam. ▶ D10 runs past the foot of the 16thC **château de Saint-Marc-Jaumegarde.**   □

Cézanne and Aix

Paul Cézanne, born at Aix in 1839, remained a prophet without honour among his contemporaries, including his family, who thought him rather crazy and judged his work as amateur daubs. Recognition came only 2 years before his death in 1906.
He worked in solitude on property owned by his family or in peasant huts rented in the countryside around Aix, where he developed an appreciation for the geometric shapes in the Bibémus quarries, the cube-shaped houses, the heavy mass of Ste-Victoire, and the sharply defined solidity of the landscapes that characterize his work. Ignoring anecdotal detail, this forerunner of abstract art brought forth a fresh vision of the world. His memorabilia are collected in the Pavillon Cézanne at Aix.

Practical Information _____

AIX-EN-PROVENCE
⚓ ✈ 42.26.01.18.
ℹ 2, pl. du Gal-de-Gaulle (A2), ☎ 42.26.02.93.
✈ *Marseille-Marignane, 27 km NW,* ☎ 42.89.90.10. *Air France office,* 2, rue Aude, ☎ 42.26.26.21.
SNCF (A2), ☎ 42.26.02.89/42.27.51.63.
▭▭ rue Lapierre (A2), ☎ 42.27.17.91.
Car rental : *Avis,* 11, cours Gambetta (B2), ☎ 42.21.64.16; train station.

Hotels :
● **★★★★** *Pullman Le Pigonnet* (I.L.A.), 5, av. du Pigonnet (A2), ☎ 42.59.02.90, Tx 410629, AE DC Euro Visa, 50 rm ℗ ⬅ ▥▥ ⬛ 🗐 Charming residence, 500. Rest. ♦♦♦ *Le Patio* ⅃ ♨ ♿ closed Sun eve (h.s.). Traditional cooking, garden dining. From 15 Jul-15 Aug, harp concerts at dinner on Mon, Wed and Sat, 140-220.
★★★★ *Le Mas d'Entremont,* Montée d'Avignon, RN 7, ☎ 42.23.45.32, 16 rm ℗ ⬅ ▥▥ ♨ ⌁ half pens (h.s.), closed 1 Nov-15 Mar. Pretty furnishings; patio, 780. Rest. ♦♦♦ ⅃ ♿ closed Mon noon and Sun eve, 160-220.

● ★★★ *Augustins* (I.L.A.), 3, rue de la Masse (A2), ☎ 42.27.28.59, Tx 441052, AE DC Euro Visa, 29 rm ℗ ∢ ⚏ ◿ ♪ ✆ closed 20 Dec-6 Jan, 400.

● ★★★ *Le Manoir* (R.S.), 8, rue d'Entrecasteaux (A2), ☎ 42.26.27.20, Tx 441489, AE DC Euro Visa, 43 rm ℗ ⚏ ◿ ⅋ closed 15 Jan-15 Feb. Charming historic residence with a 14thC cloister, 225.

★★★ *Caravelle*, 29, bd du Roi-René (B2), ☎ 42.62.53.05, Tx 401015, Euro Visa, 30 rm ℗ 195.

★★★ *Le Nègre-Coste*, 33, cours Mirabeau (A-B2), ☎ 42.27.74.22, Tx 440184, AE DC Euro Visa, 37 rm ℗ ∢ ♪ 350.

★★★ *Mas de la Bertrande* (I.L.A.), Beaurecueil, N 7, towards Nice, ☎ 42.28.90.09, AE DC Visa, 10 rm ℗ ∢ ◿ ☐ closed 15-28 Feb, 260. Rest. ● ♦♦ closed Mon and Sun eve (h.s.). Excellent Provençal-style fare prepared by a lady chef, Elisabeth Gagnaire : *pâtes à l'encre, tian d'agneau, gratin de courgettes*, 150-250 ; child : 65.

★★★ *Résidence Rotonde*, 15, av. des Belges (A2), ☎ 42.26.29.88, AE DC Euro Visa, 42 rm ℗ ♪ closed 20 Dec-5 Jan, 220.

★★ *Cardinal*, 24, rue Cardinale, ☎ 42.38.32.30, AE, 20 rm ◿ & 170.

★★ *Moderne*, 34, av. Victor-Hugo (A2), ☎ 42.26.05.16, AE DC Visa, 22 rm, closed 1-28 Feb, 220.

★★ *Relais Ste-Victoire* (L.F.), ☎ 42.28.94.98, AE Visa, 8 rm ℗ ⚏ ◿ & ☐ ♪ closed Mon eve and Sun eve , Feb, 180. Rest. ● ♦♦ ∢ & Excellent fixed-price meals featuring Provençal specialties, 190-220 ; child : 45.

Restaurants :

● ♦♦ *Aux Semailles*, 15, rue Brueys (A2), ☎ 42.27.23.44 ♪ & closed Mon noon and Sun. An attractive restaurant with three lovely, intimate dining rooms. The food is redolent of Provence : *gâteau de lotte et chapon, mignonnettes de sole au gingembre*, 120-180.

● ♦♦ *Le Clos de la Violette*, 10, av. de la Violette (A1), ☎ 42.23.30.71, AE Visa ⚏ ◿ ⅋ closed Mon noon and Sun, 16 Feb-9 Mar, 1-17 Aug. Spacious garden setting for J.M. Banzo's delicate regional fare : *croûtes de brousse, artichauts barigoule, saumon vapeur*, 150-250.

● ♦♦ *Les Caves Henri IV*, 32, rue Espariat (B2), ☎ 42.26.17.16, AE Euro Visa, closed Mon , Sun eve and Aug. Splendid 16thC vaulted cellars and 20thC cuisine : *vapeur de saumon frais et petits légumes à l'estragon, marquise de chocolat à la menthe fraîche*, 150-200.

♦♦ *La Brocherie*, 5, rue Fernand-Dol (B2), ☎ 42.38.33.21, AE DC Euro Visa ◿ ♪ closed Mon and Sun. A. Barbarant serves up seasonal specialities : *gâteau de lapin en gelée, loup en croûte, bourride, bouillabaisse*, grilled sea bream (if you order in advance), 85-145.

♦♦ *Le Vendôme*, 2 bis, av. Napoléon-Bonaparte (A2), ☎ 42.26.01.00, AE DC Euro Visa ℗ ♪ closed Tue eve and Wed ex Jul-Aug. Pleasant terrace, 165-245.

♦♦ *Puyfond*, 7 km from Rigoulon on the CD 13, ☎ 42.92.13.77 ⚏ ♪ closed Mon eve, Tue eve, Sun eve and lunch ex Sun, 2-23 Feb, 24 Aug-7 Sep. Regional specialties available at this handsome Provençal farmhouse, 110-185.

⚐ ★★★★*Arc-en-ciel* (80 pl), ☎ 42.26.14.28 ; ★★★★*Chantecler* (240 pl), ☎ 42.26.12.98.

Recommended
Casino : pl. Jeanne-d'Arc (A2), ☎ 42.26.30.33.
Guided tours : *C.N.M.H.S*, open day and eve (Jul-15 Sep). Guided tours of châteaux and estates.
Youth hostel : av. Marcel-Pagnol, Jas-de-Bouffan district, ☎ 42.20.15.99.
♥ candy : *Vendôme*, 27 bis, rue du 11-Novembre, ☎ 42.23.42.96. Calissons d'Aix.

Nearby

ÉGUILLES, ⊠ 13510, 11 km W on the D17.

Hotel :
★★★ *Auberge du Belvédère*, Les Landons, ☎ 42.92.52.92, Tx 403521, DC Euro Visa, 39 rm ℗ ∢ ⚏ ◿ & ☐ pens (h.s.), 660. Rest. ♦♦ ∢ & 85-120.

JAS-DE-BOUFFAN, 3 km W on the D10.

Hotel :
★★ *Les Relais Bleus*, bd de la Grande-Thumine, ☎ 42.59.98.01, Tx 441348, Euro Visa, 50 rm ℗ ⚏ ◿ ♪ & closed Sat and Sun lunch, 220. Rest. ♦ ♪ & 60-110.

Restaurant :
♦♦ *Les Nutons*, rte de Berre, ☎ 42.59.55.00, AE Visa ⚏ ♪ closed Wed and Thu noon. Simple, rustic fare : *bouillabaisse, mérou à l'aïoli, guillaumette*, 65-130.

Les MILLES, ⊠ 13290, 10 km W.

Hotel :
★★★ *Le Relais de Saint-Pons*, ☎ 42.24.22.30, AE DC Euro Visa, 7 rm ℗ ⚏ ◿ Hunting, horseback riding on 62 acres, 220. Rest. ♦♦♦ ♪ 125-185 ; child : 40.

ROQUEFAVOUR, ⊠ 13122, 12 km W on the A8 and D64.

Hotel :
★★ *Arquier* (L.F., R.S.), ☎ 42.24.20.45, Visa, 18 rm ℗ ⚏ ◿ & ⅋ pens (h.s.), closed Mon eve and Sun eve (l.s.), Feb. Large riverside park, 530. Rest. ♦♦ & ⅋ Garden dining. Spec : *cassolette de crevettes en croûte*, 100-170.

Castellane 32, Digne 70, Paris 815 km
pop 1062 ⊠ 04240   C2

Known to geologists for sandstone eroded into unusual shapes, which add interest to walks in the vicinity.

▶ **Old town**★ : picturesque (alt. 705 m), with narrow streets, vaulted passages, courtyards with 100-year-old plane trees ; Romanesque church with Renaissance bell tower. ▶ The **Toutes Aures Road**★ leads to **Lake Castillon** (→ Castellane), 19 km SW through the **Clues de Rouaine** and **Vergons.** ▶ **Daluis Gorges**★★ (→) 15 km NW.   □

Practical Information _____

ⓘ pl. du Revely, ☎ 92.83.22.09.

Hotel :
★★ *Grand Hôtel Grac* (L.F.), pl. du Germe, ☎ 92.83.20.02, AE Visa, 20 rm ℗ ⚏ 🏇 closed 30 Nov-15 Mar, 190. Rest. ♦ ♪ Good food. Spec : *filet de marcassin à l'ancienne, cassolette de noix de coquilles Saint-Jacques à la crème*, 60-105.

⚐ ★★*La Ribière* (53 pl), ☎ 92.83.21.44.

Nice 23, Aix-en-Provence 158, Paris 915 km
pop 63248 ⊠ 06600   D2

A superb beach deep in the bay, with all the pleasures of aquatic sports and shore activities. Antibes (*Antipolis* to the Greeks) is an ancient city ; its colourful streets overlook the sea. Like neighbouring Nice, Antibes is a city of flowers, especially roses, which it exports all over Europe.

▶ **Avenue Amiral-de-Grasse**, along the ancient ramparts between sea and town (view★) past the principal monuments. ▶ **Church of the Immaculate Conception** : Romanesque E end and Classical (17thC) fabric. ▶ **Château Grimaldi**, rebuilt in the 16thC ; in 1946, Picasso lived here ; his paintings can be seen in the **Picasso Museum**★ *(8-12 & 3-6, 7 in summer ; closed Tue., nat. hols. and Nov.)*. Drawings, engravings, lithographs and ceramics make up the first-floor display inspired by the Mediterranean. The château also houses archaeology, a painted Descent from the Cross★ (1539) and contemporary art (still life by Nicolas de Staël). ▶ The **Archaeological Museum** displays artifacts from ancient Antipolis *(9-12 & 2-6, 7 in summer ; closed Tue. and Nov.)*.

Nearby

▶ **Marineland** *(4 km N)*, amusement park and marine zoo.
▶ **Biot**★ *(8 km N)*, charming inland hill village; potters, glass-blowers; regional history museum. SE of the village, **Fernand Léger Museum**★★ : works of the painter (1881-1955) who lived at Biot. The collections illustrate Léger's development *(10-12 & 2-5, 2:30-6:30 in summer; closed Tue.)*. ▶ **Sophia-Antipolis** *(8 km NW)* : a sociological research centre where modern architecture is blended with the pines and holm oak of the **Valbonne** plateau.

Cap d'Antibes★ *(12 km round trip)*

▶ On this peninsula separating Antibes from Juan-les-Pins, the privacy of luxurious residences is guarded behind thick screens of vegetation. ▶ Antibes. ▶ **Pointe Bacon** : view of the Nice area. ▶ **Butte de la Garoupe** : lighthouse *(10-12 & 2-5, 6 in season)*; chapel of **Notre-Dame-de-Bon-Port** (13th-16thC), collection of marine *ex-votos*, 14thC icon from Sébastopol. Panorama★★ (orientation chart). ▶ **Thuret Gardens**★ : exotic shrubs and trees acclimatized by the 19thC naturalist for whom the garden is named *(8-12 & 1-5; closed Sat., Sun. and nat. hols.)*. ▶ **Napoléon Museum of the Navy** in a former gun battery with a sea view *(10-12 & 2-5, 3-7 in summer; closed Tue. and Nov.)*. ▶ **Juan-les-Pins** (→). □

Practical Information

ANTIBES
ℹ pl. du Gal-de-Gaulle, ☎ 93.33.95.64.
SNCF ☎ 93.33.63.51.
Car rental : *Avis*, train station; 32, bd Albert-Ier, ☎ 93.34.65.15.

Hotels :

● ★★★ *Royal*, bd du Mal-Leclerc, ☎ 93.34.03.09, AE DC Visa, 43 rm P ⊰ half pens (h.s.), closed Sun eve and Wed, 31 Oct-20 Dec. private beach, 620. Rest. ♦♦ *Le Dauphin* ⊰ ♪ 95-225; child : 40.
★★★ *L'Etoile*, 8, bd James-Wyllie, ☎ 93.61.47.24, Tx 470673, AE DC Euro Visa, 29 rm P ⊰ ♿ closed 16 Jan-28 Feb, 400. Rest. ♦♦ ⊰ ♪ ♿ closed Wed (l.s.), 1 Jan-1 Apr, 80-120; child : 35.
★★★ *Le Mas Djoliba*, 29, av. de Provence, ☎ 93.34.02.48, Tx 461686, AE DC Euro Visa, 14 rm P ▥ ⟁ ⊡ half pens (h.s.). Well situated between the centre of town and the beach, 700. Rest. ♦♦ ⍋ 110.
★★★ *Tananarive*, 763, rte de Nice (N 7), ☎ 93.33.30.00, Tx 470851, AE DC Euro Visa, 50 rm P ⊰ ⟁ ♪ ⊡ ♪° 335.
★★ *Le Caméo*, pl. Nationale, ☎ 93.34.24.17, 10 rm P closed 5 Jan-5 Feb, 200. Rest. ♦♦ closed Tue and Sun eve. Friendly atmosphere. Spec : *sardines fraîches à l'espagnole et soupe au pistou*, 85-120.
★ *Auberge Provençale* (L.F.), 61, pl. Nationale, ☎ 93.34.13.24, AE DC Euro Visa, 6 rm, closed 22 Nov-7 Dec, 240. Rest. ♦♦ ♪ closed Mon. Terrace, attractive furnishings, light, inventive cuisine, 65-180.

Restaurants :

● ♦♦♦♦ *La Bonne Auberge*, N 7, La Brague, ☎ 93.33.36.65, Tx 470989, AE DC Euro Visa ⊰ ▥ ♪ closed Mon eve Jul-Aug, 15 Nov-15 Dec. A temple of classic grand cuisine, 320-420.
♦♦ *L'Ecurie Royale*, 33, rue Vauban, ☎ 93.34.76.20, Euro Visa, closed Mon, Tue noon, Sun eve Mon, Tue lunch, Sun eve (l.s.), 2-11 Jan, Aug. Top-quality ingredients, 145-200.
♦♦ *La Marguerite*, 11, rue Sadi-Carnot, ☎ 93.34.08.27, Visa, closed Mon and Sun eve (l.s.), Mon, Tue lunch (h.s.). Elegant restaurant. Spec : *terrine de pleurotes à la sauce vierge*, 145-270.
♦ *L'Oursin*, 16, rue de la République, ☎ 93.34.13.46, closed Tue eve and Wed, 22 Jul-31 Aug. Fish and shellfish, 60-150.

⚑ ★★★★*Embruns* (50 pl), ☎ 93.33.33.35; ★★★★*Frênes* (110 pl), ☎ 93.33.36.52; ★★★★*Mimosas* (17 pl), ☎ 93.33.52.76; ★★★*Camp Rossignol* (88 pl), ☎ 93.33.56.98.

Recommended

Bicycle rental : *Chez Chenu*, bd Dugommier, ☎ 93.33.89.75; at the station, ☎ 93.33.63.51.
Casino : *California Bowling Club*, rte de Grasse, ☎ 93.33.23.45.
Nightclubs : *la Siesta*, pont de la Blague.
♥ the Provençal market in old Antibes; antique dealers : *J. Gismondi*, Don Quichotte des Remparts.

Nearby

Cap d' ANTIBES, ⊠ 06160 Juan-les-Pins.

Hotels :

★★★★(L) *Grand Hôtel*, bd Kennedy, ☎ 93.61.39.01, Tx 470763, 100 rm P ⊰ ▥ ⟁ ♿ ⍋ ⊡ ♪° closed 1 Oct-4 Dec, 2500. Rest. ♦♦♦ *Cap Eden Roc* ⊰ ♪ ♿ ⍋ 450.
★★★ *Garoupe*, 81, bd Francis-Meilland, ☎ 93.61.54.97, 290 rm P ▥ closed Nov-Feb, 28. Rest. ♦ ♪ ♿ 75-100.
★★★ *La Gardiole*, chem. de la Garoupe, ☎ 93.61.35.03, AE DC Euro Visa, 21 rm ▥ ⟁ ♪ half pens (h.s.), closed 25 Nov-1 Mar. A charming hotel beneath the pines, 500. Rest. ♦♦ ♪ Provençal fare in a Provençal setting, 95-150.
★★ *Antipolis*, (ex Maryland), traverse des Nielles, ☎ 93.61.47.45, AE DC Euro Visa, 26 rm P ▥ ♪ ♿ ⍋ ⊡ closed 1 Nov-15 Feb, 160. Rest. ♦ ♪ ♿ ⍋ Warm, friendly atmosphere and Provençal food, 50-120.

Restaurants :

● ♦♦♦ *Bacon*, bd de Bacon, ☎ 93.61.50.02 ⊰ ▥ ♪ ⍋ closed Mon and Sun eve, 15 Nov-31 Jan. So you think fresh fish can't be had on the Riviera? You're wrong! The Sordello family has plenty, and it can be yours - for a price..., 230-575.
♦♦♦ *Le Cabestan*, 46, bd Garoupe, ☎ 93.61.77.70, AE DC Euro Visa ⊰ ▥ ♿ closed Mon eve and Tue, Jul-Aug Tue only, 15 Oct-1 Apr, 170-280.

BIOT, ⊠ 06410, 7 km N.

Hotel :

★ *Galerie des Arcades*, 16, pl. des Arcades, ☎ 93.65.01.04, AE, 12 rm ⊰ 130. Rest. ● ♦ closed Mon and Sun eve (l.s.), Nov. Friendly café-cum-gallery in a 15thC house where art and gastronomy go well together. Provençal country cooking : *bourride, ris de veau à l'ancienne, aïoli*, 110-140.

Restaurants :

● ♦♦♦ *Auberge du Jarrier*, 30, passage de la Bourgade, ☎ 93.65.11.68, AE DC Euro Visa ▥ ♪ closed Mon eve and Tue (l.s.) Tue, Wed lunch (h.s.), 1-15 Mar, 20 Nov-20 Dec. In an enchanting decor, fresh and varied seasonal fare : *filet de loup à la crème d'huîtres et aux cèpes, aiguillettes de canard au vinaigre de framboise, millefeuille aux poires*, 135-250.
♦♦ *Café de la Poste*, rue St-Sébastien, ☎ 93.65.00.07, closed Wed Dec-Jan. An excellent place to stop in the hills. Spec : *ravioles d'écrevisses cuites dans leur étuvée de légumes*, 120-210.

Recommended

♥ culinary antiques : *Fenouil*, Biot, golfcourse, ☎ 93.65.09.46.

MOUANS-SARTOUX, ⊠ 06370, 12 km NW.

Hotel :

★★ *Le Relais de Sartoux*, 400, rte de Valbonne, ☎ 93.60.10.57, DC Euro Visa, 12 rm P ▥ ⟁ closed Nov, 200. Rest. ♦ ♪ closed Wed ex Jun-Sep, 90-130.

VALBONNE, ⊠ 06560, 18 km NW.
ℹ ☎ 93.42.04.16.

Restaurants :

♦♦ *Cave Saint-Bernardin*, 8, rue des Arcades, ☎ 93.42.03.88 ♪ closed Mon and Sun, 1 Dec-15 Jan. Enjoyable food. Spec : *scampis sauce tartare, feuilleté de lasagnes*, good desserts, 90-150.
♦♦ *Le Val de Cuberte*, rte de Cannes, 1.5 km SW on D 3, ☎ 93.42.01.82, Visa ⊡ closed Mon and Tue (h.s.), Mon and eve. in winter, 12 Nov-22 Dec, 140.

APT*

Avignon 52, Digne 91, Paris 732 km
pop 11560 ⊠ 84400   B2

Between the Lubéron and the Vaucluse, a typical small Provençal town. Ringed by boulevards lined with plane trees, old towers, vestiges of ramparts, fountains, and a colourful and aromatic Saturday morning market. Local industries : crystallized fruit; ochre production.

▶ **Place de la Bouquerie,** beside the Calavon, the centre of town activity.▶ **Church of Ste. Anne,** formerly a cathedral and a record of the city's religious history : 7th and 11thC crypts, Romanesque fabric, chapel of St. Anne with reliquary, treasury, 16thC Italian Annunciation★, 15thC Primitive painting★.▶ **Museum** in an 18thC mansion : archaeology, ceramics (local specialty), chemist's jars★, popular religious art *(9-12 & 2-6, Apr.-Sep.; 10-12 & 2-5, Oct.-Mar.; closed Tue.).*

Nearby

▶ **Roussillon★** *(13 km NW),* gold and red like the surrounding cliffs and ochre quarries.▶ **Rustrel Colorado★** *(10 km NE),* huge ochre quarry; worth the 2hr walk needed to see it all (GR6). ▶ **Canyon d'Oppedette★** *(20 km NE) :* canyon walls up to 120 m high in sight of D201. ▶ **Simiane-la-Rotonde** *(24 km NE),* a hilltop village; the *rotonde* is the keep remaining from a 12th-13thC castle. ▶ **Saignon★** *(4 km S) :* houses cluster 500 m up beside a huge rock; view over Apt; popular site for hikers going to the Claparèdes Plateau; *bories* (→ box).   □

Practical Information _____

APT
ℹ️ pl. de la Bouquerie, ☎ 90.74.03.18.
SNCF ☎ 90.74.00.85.

Hotels :
★★ *Aptois*, 6-8, cours Laure-de-Perret, ☎ 90.74.02.02, 26 rm ⓟ ⌺ closed 15 Feb-15 Mar, 150.
★★ *Le Lubéron*, 17, quai L.-Sagy, ☎ 90.74.12.50, DC Visa, 8 rm ⓟ closed Sun eve and Mon ex Jul-Aug, 15 Dec-15 Jan, 145. Rest. ♦ 95-250.
★★ *Le Ventoux* (L.F.), 67, av. V.-Hugo, ☎ 90.74.07.58, AE DC Euro Visa, 13 rm ⓟ ≼ closed Jan, 160. Rest. ♦♦ 60-120.
★ *Relais de Roquefure* (L.F.), Roquefure, ☎ 90.74.22.80, AE Visa, 17 rm ⓟ ≼ ⌂ closed 15 Nov-15 Dec, 145. Rest. ♦ ≼ closed Tue noon, 70-120; child : 40.

⚠️ ★★*Les Cèdres* (55 pl), ☎ 90.74.14.61.

Recommended
Events : *crafts fair* (Jul-Aug).
Youth hostel : at Saignon (7 km SE), *Regain*, ☎ 90.74.39.34.

Nearby

Le BOISSET, ⊠ 84640 Saint-Martin-de-Castillon, 12 km E.

Hotel :
Auberge du Boisset (L.F.), ☎ 90.75.20.10, 3 rm ⓟ ⌂ ⌂ half pens (h.s.), closed Tue and Wed, 15 Nov-15 Feb. Rest. ♦ ≼ ♪ 110-160.

GARGAS, ⊠ 84400 Apt, 6 km NW.

Restaurant :
♦ *La Grasille*, rte du Perrotet, Saint-Estève, ☎ 90.74.25.40, DC Visa ≼ ⌂ ♪ closed Tue eve (l.s.), Wed, 1-17 Jan, 8-27 Jun. All the hors d'oeuvres you can eat, charcoal-grilled specialties, 70-140.

ROUSSILLON, ⊠ 84220 Gordes, 13 km NW.

Hotels :
● ★★★ *Mas de Garrigon* (R.S.), 2 km N, ☎ 90.05.63.22, AE DC Euro Visa, 8 rm ⓟ ≼ ⌂ ⌂ ⊡ half pens (h.s.), 840. Rest. ♦♦♦ ≼ ♪ ⌾ closed Mon and Sun eve, 16 Nov-27 Dec, 145-270.

★★ *Résidence des Ocres* (L.F.), rte de Gordes, ☎ 90.75.60.50, Euro Visa, 15 rm ⓟ ≼ ⌂ ⌂ closed Feb, 15 Nov-15 Dec, 175.

Restaurants :
● ♦♦ *David*, pl. de la Poste, ☎ 90.05.60.13 ≼ ⌂ ⌂ closed Mon and Tue, 14 Jan-13 Mar. Perfectly classic fare : *feuilleté d'écrevisses, coq en pâte.* Unspoiled view of the cliffs and the valley, 100-200.
♦♦ *La Tarasque*, rue R.-Casteau, ☎ 90.75.63.86, AE DC Euro Visa ♪ closed Wed, 15 Feb-15 Mar, 115-220; child : 50.

⚠️ ★★*Arc-en-Ciel* (35 pl), ☎ 90.75.67.17.

SAINT-MARTIN-DE-CASTILLON, ⊠ 84750, 12 km E.

Restaurant :
♦♦ *La Source*, rte de Viens, ☎ 90.75.21.58, Visa ≼ ⌂ ⌂ closed Mon and Sun eve, 15 Nov-1 Mar. Bird cages adorn the garden. Spec : *canette aux fruits de saison, chevreau au beurre d'amandes*, 160-200.

SAINT-SATURNIN-D'APT, ⊠ 84490, 9 km N on D 943.

Restaurant :
♦♦ *Le Saint-Hubert*, pl. de la Fraternité, ☎ 90.75.42.02 ≼ ♪ closed Mon and Sun eve, 15-28 Feb, 15 Jun-5 Jul. Terrace dining with a view of the Lubéron, 80-220.

ARLES***

Nîmes 30, Marseille 91, Paris 729 km
pop 50772 ⊠ 13200   A2

Arles is a delightful town, alive with traditions centred around the bulls and white horses of the nearby Camargue (→). On the banks of the Rhône, Arles was once the metropolis of Roman Gaul. Today its picturesque streets annually host the Festival of Dance and the International Photography Conventions.

▶ **Boulevard des Lices** (B-C3), the focus of town life, with plane trees, cafés and bustling markets *(Wed., Sat. am).* ▶ **Place de la République** (B2) : the obelisk was originally in the centre of the Roman Circus.▶ **Church of St. Trophime★★** (B2), a synthesis of Romanesque and Classical art, reminiscent of Glanum (→). The richly-ornamented doorway★★ (2nd half of 12thC) contrasts with the simple interior; note the high, exceptionally narrow nave; 1614 Adoration of the Magi (right aisle), French painting in the right transept (late 16thC), and 17thC Annunciation★★ (left transept).▶ **St. Trophime cloister★★** : similar concern with architectural equilibrium and harmonious decoration and carving. The church and cloister make Arles a major landmark in Romanesque art *(9-7, May-Sep. 9-12 & 2-4:30 Dec.; Jan., Feb., Nov., 5:30; Mar., Apr., 6);* the same hours and a single admission ticket cover the city's other monuments and museums. The cloister was built in two stages (12th and 13th-14thC); there are two Romanesque and two Gothic galleries; figures inspired by classical reliefs on the pillars; figured capitals★; museum of religious art in the N gallery; temporary exhibitions in the chapterhouse. ▶ **Town hall★** (B2, late 17thC), incorporating a belfry with a 16thC statue of the Roman god Mars; note the flattened vault★ in the entrance hall and behind, on the Plan de la Cour, the former civic offices (1500) and the Viguier Mansion (1200 and 15thC). ▶ **Museum of Pagan Art★★** *(Musée Lapidaire Païen;* B2) in the former church of Ste. Anne (17thC, Meridional Gothic survival) : Gallo-Roman antiquities excavated around Arles; note, in the nave, the so-called sarcophagus of Phaedra and Hippolytus★ (2nd-3rdC); in the apse, two statues of dancers★ (1stC BC). ▶ **Museum of Christian Art★★** *(Musée Lapidaire Chrétien;* B2), said to be the finest in the world after the Vatican. In a 17thC Jesuit chapel, sarcophagi from the two Early-Christian burial grounds of Alyscamps and St. Genès; a unique display of 4thC Arlesian craftmanship and creativity. Under the museum, entrance to the **cryptoporticus★,** subterranean galleries beneath the forum gates where grain was stored. ▶ **Arlaten Museum★** (B2) in the Castellane-Laval★ mansion,

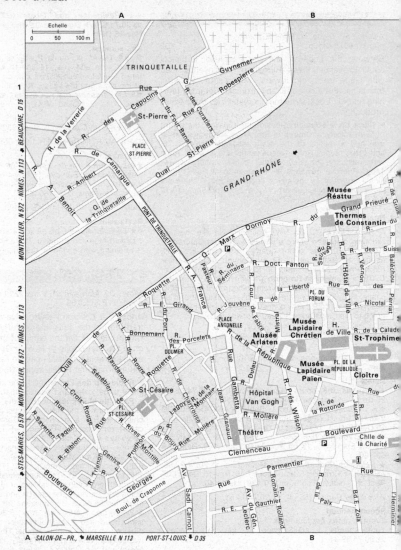

A   *SALON-DE-PR.*, ❧ *MARSEILLE N 113*   *PORT-ST-LOUIS,* ❧ *D 35*   B

early-16thC building; Roman portico★ in the courtyard. Frédéric Mistral created the museum and later enriched it with the money he received for the Nobel Prize in 1904. It examines life in and around Arles : furniture, costumes, festivals, legends, trades, music, the Rhône, the Camargue *(closed Mon. out of season).* ▶ **Roman Theatre★** (C2) : the size alone (seating for 7000 spectators) demonstrates the importance of Arles as a Roman port. It was built during the reign of Augustus (1stC BC). Many of the magnificent decorations are now in the Museum of Pagan Art; a statue known as the Venus of Arles, found here, is now in the Louvre. **Arena★★** (C2), well preserved because, during the Middle Ages, it was converted into a fortress; 200 houses and a church were built in the enclosure. Three 12thC towers remain from the fortification period. The arena, built around AD80, at 136 m by 107 m is slightly larger than the one at Nîmes; it had seating for 25000 spectators. ▶ The **Baths of Constantine** (B1-2)

were originally much larger; the semicircular apse★ enclosed one of the pools. ▶ **Réattu Museum★,** beside the Rhône in the former 14th-16thC priory of the Knights of Malta (B2); in addition to displaying 17th and 18thC works from around Arles, and almost the complete work of Jacques Réattu (1760-1833, local artist), the museum is acquiring contemporary works of art directly connected with the region; room XII contains about 60 **drawings★** by Picasso from early 1971, which he presented to the town; the photographic section includes work by the greatest French and foreign photographers. ▶ The **Alyscamps★** (C3) : for almost 15 centuries, first Pagans, then Christians from around Arles and farther afield looked forward to burial here; coffins accompanied by a sum of money — the *mortellage* or burial fee — were shipped on the Rhône, so great was the spiritual reputation of this necropolis. Today there remains only an alley bordered by tombs leading to the ruined church of **St. Honorat★,** a

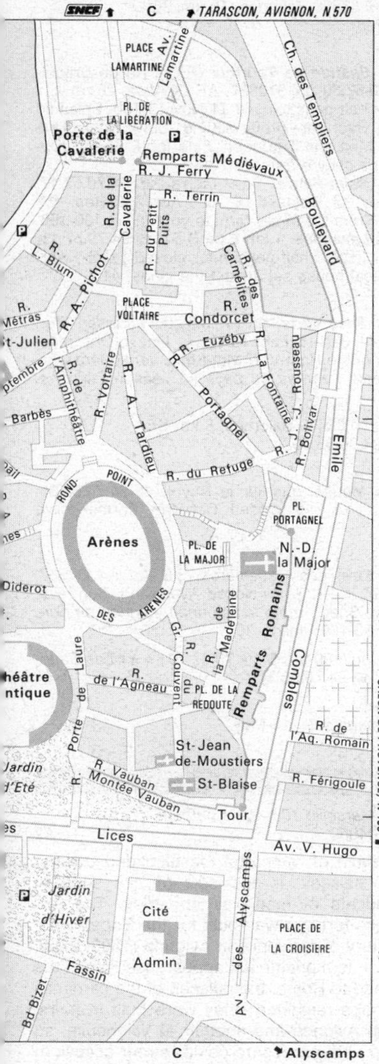

The map on the left shows a street plan of Arles with labels including:

PLACE Av. LAMARTINE
Lamartine
Ch. des Templiers
PL. DE LA LIBERATION
Porte de la P
Cavalerie Remparts Médiévaux
R. J. Ferry
R. de la Cavalerie
R. du Petit Puits
R. Terrin
Boulevard
R. des Carmélites
1
PLACE VOLTAIRE
R. Condorcet
R. des
R. Euzéby
R. La Fontaine
R. A. Pichot
R. A. Blum
R. Métras
St-Julien
-ptembre
R. de l'Amphithéâtre
R. Voltaire
R. A. Tardieu
R. du Refuge
Portagnel
R. de Rousseau
R. Bolivar
Emile
Barbès
Arènes
ROND POINT
PL. PORTAGNEL
PL. DE LA MAJOR
N.-D la Major
Diderot
DES ARENES
de la Madeleine
Remparts Romains
Combles
2
SALON-DE-PROVENCE, N 453 →
théâtre ntique
R. de Laure
Porte de l'Agneau
R. du Couvent
PL. DE LA REDOUTE
R. de l'Aq. Romain
St-Jean-de-Moustiers
Jardin d'Eté
R. Vauban
Montée Vauban
St-Blaise
R. Férigoule
Tour
Lices
Av. V. Hugo
P Jardin d'Hiver
Cité
Admin.
des Alyscamps
PLACE DE LA CROISIERE
3
Fassin
Bd Bizet
Av. des
C
→ Alyscamps

hols.). The unfinished church★ dates from the mid-12thC; only two of the five bays originally planned were built. The crypt★ is built into the hillside; the 12th-13thC cloister★★ is extremely beautiful; commanding keep (1369); the partly underground chapel of St. Pierre★ dates from the foundation of the monastery in the early 11thC. ▶ The small and great **Crau plains** (N and E of Arles), separated by the Alpilles, mark the "sacred triangle", that is the Provence of writers such as Frédéric Mistral and Alphonse Daudet (1840-97). The Petite Crau is cultivated for fruit and vegetables; the Grande Crau, fertile in the N between Arles and Salon, lower down is mostly stones and pebbles from the former delta of the Durance. □

Practical Information

ℹ 35, pl. de la République (B3), ☎ 90.96.29.35.
SNCF (off map C1), ☎ 90.96.43.94.
Car rental : *Avis*, train station; 12 bis, av. V.-Hugo (C3), ☎ 90.96.82.42.

Hotels :
★★★★ *Jules César* (R.C.), 7, bd des Lices (B3), ☎ 90.93.43.20, Tx 400239, AE DC Euro Visa, 60 rm P ⓑ closed 4 Nov-22 Dec. Formerly a Carmelite convent dating from mid-17thC, 600. Rest. ● ♦♦♦ *Lou Marquès* ⓑ Excellent fresh ingredients. Spec : *bouillabaisse de baudroie, anguilles en marinière, bourride du chef*. Good desserts, 175-240.
● ★★★ *Arlatan*, 26, rue du Sauvage (B2), ☎ 90.93.56.66, Tx 441203, AE DC, 46 rm P ⓕ ⁂ ⌂ ♪ Formerly the town house of the counts d'Arlatan de Beaumont, 400.
★★★ *Auberge La Fenière* (R.S.), Raphèle (on N 453, 7.5 km SE), ☎ 90.98.47.44, Tx 441237, AE Euro Visa, 25 rm P ⁑ ⌂ ⓑ Old Provençal farmhouse set in a park, 290. Rest. ♦♦ ⓕ ♪ ⁑ closed Sat noon (l.s.), 1 Nov-20 Dec, 120-180.
★★★ *Les Villages du Soleil*, mas de Véran, quartier Fourchon 2 km S, ☎ 90.96.50.68, Tx 401450, AE DC Visa, 72 rm P ⌂ ⌂ ♪ ⁑ ☐ ♪° half pens (h.s.), closed 1 Jan-1 Feb, 510. Rest. ♦ ♪ ⁑ 95 ; child : 45.
★★★ *Mas de la Chapelle* (C.H.), the little Tarascon road (5 km on D 35), ☎ 90.96.73.43, 15 rm P ⓕ ⁂ ⌂ ☐ ♪° half pens, closed Sun eve (l.s.), Feb. An exceptional setting for a handsome 16thC dwelling, 700. Rest. ♦♦♦ ♪ 140-220.
★★ *La Roseraie*, Pont-de-Crau, 2 km SE on N 113, ☎ 90.96.06.58, 12 rm P ⓕ ⁂ ⌂ ⓑ ⁑ closed 15 Oct-15 Mar, 220.
★★ *Le Cloître*, 18, rue du Cloître (B2), ☎ 90.96.29.50, Visa, 33 rm ⌂ ⁑ closed 15 Nov-15 Mar, 180.
★★ *Lou Gardianoun* (L.F.), 15, rue Noguier (A2), ☎ 90.93.66.28, AE Visa, 20 rm P ⌂ ⁑ half pens (h.s.), closed Sun and Mon lunch, 360. Rest. ♦ ⁑ 75-100.

Restaurants :
● ♦♦ *Le Vaccarès*, pl. du Forum, entrance 9, rue Favorin (B2), 1st floor, ☎ 90.96.06.17 ⁂ closed Mon and Sun ex hols. Personality, balance, lightness and creativity characterize Bernard Dumas' cooking. Spec : *pieds et paquets, estouffade de gigot à l'ancienne, filet de sandre à la poutargue, moules aux herbes*, 150-250.
● ♦ *Chez Bob*, Villeneuve via Arles, 16 km, ☎ 90.97.00.29. Bob likes to light a fire in the hearth while he cooks up good Camarguais dishes. Grills, *pieds-et-paquets, daube*, 150-200.
♦ *Hostellerie des Arènes*, 62, rue du Refuge (C2), ☎ 90.96.13.05, Euro Visa ⁑ closed Wed and Tue eve (l.s.), 20 Jun-1 Jul, 15 Dec-1 Feb. A Provençal setting. Moderate prices, 50-80.

⛺ ★★*Bienheureuse* (70 pl), ☎ 90.98.45.28 ; ★★*City* (100 pl), ☎ 90.93.08.86 ; ★★*Rosiers* (100 pl), ☎ 90.96.02.12.

Recommended
Chambres d'hôtes : *mas du grand Gageron*, ☎ 90.97.00.09.
Guided tours : by the *C.N.M.H.S.* : the preserved sector, Van Gogh tour, Montmajour abbey ; daily (18 Jun-15 Sept), cloister of Saint-Trophime, the Alyscamps, the Roman

Romanesque sanctuary with 5thC origins much reduced from its earlier dimensions; octagonal Romanesque **bell tower★★**, worth a visit.
Also... ▶ The **ramparts** (C2) date in part from the 1stC BC. ▶ **Notre-Dame-de-la-Major** (C2) : Romanesque nave, Gothic choir and apse; 17thC façade. ▶ **St. Jean-du-Moustier** (C2) : Romanesque apse★, and **St. Blaise** (12th-14thC) nearby. ▶ 2 km S of the town centre, near the industrial zone, the drawbridge across the Arles canal at Port-de-Bouc is the re-erected **Pont de Langlois** from Vincent Van Gogh's painting of 1888.

Nearby

▶ **Montmajour Abbey★★** (6 km NE), on a pine-shaded butte overlooking rice fields, the abbey is an anthology of architectural forms from the 11th to the 13thC. Van Gogh made many drawings of the abbey during his stay in Arles (9-12 & 2-5, 6 in season; closed Tue., Nov. and some nat.

arena; the Camargue national park, every other Mon (15 Jul-30 Sep) info and appointments at the *TO*.

AUPS*

Marseille 17, Nice 180, Paris 794 km
pop 1652 ⊠ 83630   C2

Ancient plane trees, old streets, wrought-iron bell towers, fountains, ramparts and gates : Aups is a charming inland Provençal town. The local specialty is honey, and the Midi accent is strong.

▶ **Church of St. Pancrace** : Provençal Gothic with a renaissance doorway. ▶ Chapel of the former Ursuline convent : **Simon Ségal Museum** of modern painting (school of Paris; *10-12 & 3-6 Jun.-15 Sep.)*.

Nearby

▶ Main attractions are the **Grand Canyon du Verdon** (→; *23 km N)* and **Lake Ste. Croix** (→ Moustiers-Sainte-Marie). ▶ The less known **villages of the upper Var** can be explored from Aups. ▶ **Tourtour★** *(10 km SE)* : view★★ over to Saint-Raphaël, old châteaux and regional fossil museum. ▶ **Villecroze** *(8 km SE)*, still medieval; the name refers to the caves dug into the cliffs. ▶ **Salernes** *(10 km S)*, manufacture of hexagonal red floor tiles, called *tomettes*; several fountains. ▶ **Entrecasteaux** *(18 km S)*, medieval, proud of its garden by André Le Nôtre, the 17thC designer of the park of Versailles (→), 17thC château, and the quality of locally-produced rugs and olive oil. ▶ **Carcès** *(26 km S)*, a hillside village and a lake, surrounded by pines, that feeds Toulon. ▶ **Cotignac** *(15 km SW)* : good wine, a beautiful site, a pleasant square. ▶ **Cascade de la Bresque★** *(6 km NE of Cotignac)* waterfall 42 m high.   □

Practical Information ———————————————

AUPS

Hotels :
★★★ *Le Calalou*, Moissac-Bellevue, 5 km on D 9, ☎ 94.70.17.91, Tx 461885, AE DC Euro Visa, 39 rm ℗ ⊱ ⑭ ⚘ ⌂ ⤳ᵒ half pens (h.s.), closed Mon, Jan, 700. Rest. ◆◆ ⊱ ᕫ ♨ 95-200.
★ *Auberge de la Tour*, rue de l'Abbé-Aloïsi, ☎ 94.70.00.30, 24 rm ℗ ⑭ ⚘ Lovely Provençal house and garden, 170. Rest. ◆ ♪ 80-140.

⚠ ★★★*International Camping* (51 pl), ☎ 94.70.06.80; ★★★*Les Prés* (30 pl), ☎ 94.70.00.93.

Recommended
Market : *truffle market*, Thu, Nov-Feb.

Nearby
CARCÈS, ⊠ 83570, 14 km S.

Hotel :
★ *Chez Nous*, 11, rue du Mal-Joffre, ☎ 94.04.50.89, 15 rm ℗ half pens (h.s.), closed 31 Oct-15 Apr, 270. Rest. ◆ ᕫ 60-105.

Recommended
Guide to wines : *La Carcoise*, wine cooperative, 66, av. Ferrandin, ☎ 94.04.53.54.

COTIGNAC, ⊠ 83570 Carcès, 15 km SW.
ⓘ 10, cours Gambetta, ☎ 94.04.61.87.

Hotel :
● ★★★ *Hostellerie Lou Calen*, 1, cours Gambetta, ☎ 94.04.60.40, Tx 400287, AE DC Euro Visa, 16 rm ℗ ⑭ ⚘ ⤳ᵒ half pens (h.s.), closed Nov-Mar, 520. Rest. ● ◆◆ ♪ closed Wed. Remarkable food in an enchanting garden, 85-200.

Recommended
Guide to wines : *Les Vignerons de Cotignac*, ☎ 94.04.60.04. Farm cooperative, closed Sun.

TOURTOUR, ⊠ 83690 Salernes, 10 km SE. ⓘ ☎ 94.70.57.20.

Hotels :
● ★★★★ *La Bastide de Tourtour* (R.C.), rte de Draguignan, ☎ 94.70.57.30, Tx 970827, AE DC Visa, 26 rm ℗ ⊱ ⑭ ⚘ ᕫ ⌂ ⤳ᵒ half pens, closed 11 Nov-15 Feb. Splendid view over the Haut-Var; pretty setting, 1150. Rest. ◆◆◆ ⊱ ♪ ᕫ closed Mon and Tue noon. Fine food. Spec : *rougets, raviolis de chèvre frais*, 140-300.
★★ *Auberge Saint-Pierre*, Saint-Pierre, ☎ 94.70.57.17, 15 rm ℗ ⊱ ⑭ ⚘ ⌂ ⤳ᵒ closed 15 Oct-1 Apr, 250. Rest. ◆◆ ⊱ closed Thu. From the family farm to your table, 130-160.
★★ *Host. des Lavandes*, 1 km E on D 51, ☎ 94.70.57.11, 16 rm ℗ ⊱ ⑭ ⚘ ⌂ ⤳ᵒ half pens (h.s.), closed 1 Oct-1 Apr. Lovely Provençal house set amidst the pines, 415.

Restaurant :
● ◆◆ *Les Chênes verts*, ☎ 94.70.55.06 ⊱ closed Mon and Sun eve, 1 Jan-15 Feb. Reserve. One of the most beautiful sites of the Haut-Var, with fresh, varied fare worthy of the locale : *truffes du pays* (in season), *écrevisses*, 190-250.

VILLECROZE, ⊠ 83690 Salernes, 8 km SE.
ⓘ mairie, ☎ 94.70.63.06.

Hotel :
★★ *Le Vieux Moulin*, quartier le Rayol, ☎ 94.70.63.35, 10 rm ℗ ⊱ ⑭ ⚘ ♨ closed Oct-Mar. Former olive press, 150.

Restaurant :
◆◆ *Au Bien-Etre*, Les Cadenières, 3.5 km on D 557, ☎ 94.70.67.57 ⊱ ⑭ ♪ ᕫ closed Wed and Sun eve, 15 Jan-15 Feb. Spec : *truite saumonnée, mignon de porc aux myrtilles*, 80-180; child : 30.

⚠ ★★★*Le Ruou* (100 pl), ☎ 94.70.67.70; ★★★*Les Cadenières* (80 pl), ☎ 94.70.60.31.

Recommended
Events : *rummage sale*, 15 May.

AVIGNON***

Valence 125, Marseille 100, Paris 690 km
pop 91474 ⊠ 84000   A2

Avignon, a maze of ramparts, machicolated towers, belfries and palaces, is the sort of city seen in ancient woodcuts of medieval tapestries. The formidable palace-fortress was built for the Popes who, during a century of residence in Avignon (1309-1403), gave the town its monumental appearance. When the Popes returned to Rome, the palaces of the cardinals and archbishops remained; they were built in pairs, one palace in Avignon and another at Villeneuve, so that a prelate under pressure could retreat occasionally from the stresses of the Papal court. Famous both for the Pont d'Avignon (the bridge of the song) and for papal history, Avignon today is the setting for an international festival, which is an important annual event in European theatre; the magnificent courtyards and buildings serve as stages for the performances.

▶ **Palais des Papes★★★** (B1) : fortress and palace, a beautiful example of 14thC Gothic. The main fabric is the work of two successive pontiffs, Benedict XII (originally a Cistercian monk) and Clement VI (first a Benedictine). The N part, the Palais Vieux, shows the Cistercian taste for simplicity and austerity, whereas the Palais Neuf to the S, with ogive vaulting instead of simple wooden ceilings, tends to more sumptuous display *(guided tours at fixed times)*. The palace is unfurnished but has beautiful painted murals. **The Requien Museum** (natural history, *9-12 & 2-6, closed Sun., Mon. and nat. hols.)*. ▶ **Palais-Vieux** : Consistory Hall and chapel with frescos★ by Matteo Giovanetti (1348); the Grand Tinel or banqueting hall with frescos by the 14thC Sienese painter Simone Martini, who also decorated the cathedral doorway; the St. Mar-

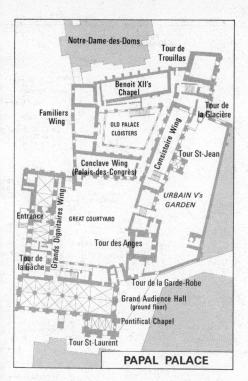

Notre-Dame-des-Doms

Tour de Trouillas

Benoit XII's Chapel

Tour de la Glacière

Familiers Wing

OLD PALACE CLOISTERS

Conclave Wing (Palais-des-Congrès)

Consistoire Wing

Tour St-Jean

URBAIN V's GARDEN

Grands Dignitaires Wing

Entrance

GREAT COURTYARD

Tour des Anges

Tour de la Gâche

Tour de la Garde-Robe

Grand Audience Hall (ground floor)

Pontifical Chapel

Tour St-Laurent

PAPAL PALACE

tial chapel, also with frescos★ by Giovanetti; the Robing Room and the Pope's bedroom★, beautifully painted, and finally the Stag Room★, with frescos★ of rustic and hunting scenes reminiscent of Flemish tapestries. ▶ **Palais-Neuf** : Pontifical chapel★ and Great Audience Chamber★ adorned with frescos depicting the Prophets★ (Giovanetti 1353). ▶ **Place du Palais★** (B1), the heart of the city ▶ **Cathedral of Notre-Dame-des-Doms** (B1), remodeled, is still a good example of Provençal Romanesque (tomb of Pope John XXII★, 1345; 12thC marble throne★). ▶ From the **Rocher** (rock) **des Doms** and its gardens, view over the Rhône, St. Bénézet bridge and the Villeneuve fortifications. ▶ **Petit Palais★** (B1), formerly the Archbishop's residence (14th-15thC), today the setting for paintings, sculptures and other works of art★★ from the Middle Ages and the Renaissance *(9:30-11:30 & 2-6; closed Tue., hols.)*. A major exhibit is the Campana di Cavelli **collection of Italian Primitives★★** (14th-15thC) : Virgin Enthroned, by an anonymous Master (1310); Virgin and Child★★ by Sandro Botticelli; Holy Conversation★★ by Vittore Carpaccio. Among the sculptures : the 15thC tomb of Cardinal de Lagrange★★ is strikingly realistic; recumbent effigy of Antoine de Comps (1495). ▶ **Hôtel des Monnaies★** (the Old Mint), 1619 Italian Baroque, opposite the Papal Palace. ▶ Le Pont d'Avignon of song fame was actually the **Pont St. Bénézet★** (B1) : the Avignonnais in fact used to dance under its arches in restaurants on the midstream Barthelasse Island. Legend has it that the bridge was built by St. Bénézet in the 12thC. Only 4 arches are left out of 22; on the second pier stands the Romanesque and Gothic chapel of St. Nicolas. ▶ The **Place de l'Horloge** (Place Clemenceau, B2) was the Roman forum; a popular meeting place surrounded by cafés and restaurants, it is the scene of much fringe activity during the annual summer festival. Close by, in the **Balance quarter,** well-restored 17thC houses★ and modern buildings well adapted to the surroundings. ▶ The **town hall** (Hôtel de Ville; B2) rebuilt in the last century

(14th-15thC clock tower, where jacks mark the hour); **church of St. Agricol★** (A2), 14th-15thC Gothic building with numerous works of art (near the sacristy, altarpiece★, 1525). ▶ **Calvet Museum★★** (B2) : exhibitions in an 18thC mansion *(10-12 & 2-6; closed Tue. and some nat. hols.)*. Noteworthy exhibits include : 14th-15thC wrought iron★; Greek sculpture (woman arranging her hair★, 4thC BC); paintings from French and other schools (Louis le Nain★, Géricault★, Chassériau★; Corot★ and Manet★); also works by Joseph Vernet (born in Avignon, 1714), Hubert Robert and Soutine. ▶ **Rue des Teinturiers★** (C3), attractive street running along an arm of the Sorgue; you can still see the waterwheels used during the 18th and 19thC in the production of Provençal prints inspired by Indian textiles.

Also... ▶ **Old Avignon** is full of mansions and churches. ▶ **De Crillon Mansion★** (B2; 17thC), one of the most beautiful in the city. ▶ **Fortia de Montréal Mansion** : less ornate, 1637. ▶ In the **chapel★** of the former Jesuit College (1645; Baroque) is the **Lapidary Museum** (B3) : Venus de Pourrières★ and Tarasque de Noves★, a man-eating lion fashioned during the 2nd Iron Age *(9-12 & 2-6; closed Tue. and some nat. hols.)*. ▶ **Church of St. Didier★** (B2), one of the largest Meridional Gothic churches (1359), altarpiece of Notre-Dame-du-Spasme★ (1478), so-called from her anguished expression, first chapel on right; 14thC frescos★, first chapel on left. ▶ **Roure Palace★** (B2) : late-15thC Gothic with delicate Flamboyant Gothic doorway★. ▶ **Church of St. Pierre★** (B2) : Meridional Gothic, Renaissance doors★. ▶ NE, the **Banasterie** quarter : many 17th and 18thC houses. ▶ **Church of St. Symphorien** (C1) : 15th-17thC; 16thC statuary. ▶ **Aubanel Museum** (C1), 7 Place St-Pierre, in a former private mansion, memorabilia of Théodore Aubanel, founder of the Félibrige (printing equipment and rare books from 13thC to present; *guided tours 9-11; closed Sat., Sun., hols. and Aug.)* ▶ **Chapel of the Visitation** (C2) : 1632, fine carving. ▶ **Chapel of the Black Pénitents★** (B1), named for a religious brotherhood; 1739 Baroque architecture with white and gold wood paneling. ▶ Many fine houses in **Rue du Vieux-Sextier** (B-C2, Nos. 10, 20, 22-24 and 33), **Rue Joseph-Vernet** (B2-3, Nos. 58, 64, 83 and 87), **Rue Petite-Fusterie** (B1-2, Nos. 17, 19), **Rue St.-Étienne** (B1, Nos. 17, 18, 22-24). ▶ **Jean Vilar House** (8 Rue de Mons) : theatre library. ▶ **Vouland Museum** (17 Rue Victor-Hugo) : French furniture, regional ceramics, decorative art *(10-1 & 3-6 in summer, Fri. until 8; 2-5 rest of year; closed Sat.-Mon.)*.

Nearby

▶ **Montfavet** *(5 km E)* : 14thC Meridional Gothic church★. ▶ **Châteaurenard** *(10 km S),* with Cavaillon, the most important fruit and vegetable centre in Provence; ruined 14thC feudal château only a few minutes' walk from the church; view★ *(10-12 & 2-6; closed Dec. and Jan.)*.

Villeneuve-lès-Avignon★★ *(2.5 km NW)*

Villeneuve and Avignon, although separated by the River Rhône as well as by administration boundaries, have always had a close, if stormy, relationship. At one time the Pope's entourage maintained country retreats at Villeneuve; today the Avignonnais cross the river to find peace and quiet on the slopes of the Petit Montagné or at Belle-Croix, protected from the *mistral* wind and the morning mists in the valley.

▶ At the head of the St. Bénézet bridge is **Philip the Fair's Tower★** (1293), which was intended to keep Avignon at bay *(10-12:30 & 3-7:30, Apr.-Sep.; 10-12 & 2-5, rest of year; closed Feb.; same hours for other monuments)*. ▶ Access to the tower runs in front of the **Municipal Museum★,** a 17thC mansion housing the **Coronation of the Virgin★★** (1453), a masterpiece by Engerrand Charonton (born c. 1410), a founder of the school of Avignon painters. A copy of the Pietà of Avignon (original in the Louvre, Paris) is attributed to him. ▶ **Church of Notre-Dame** (14thC), with single nave, has 14thC polychrome ivory Virgin★★ in the sacristy; cloister of same period.

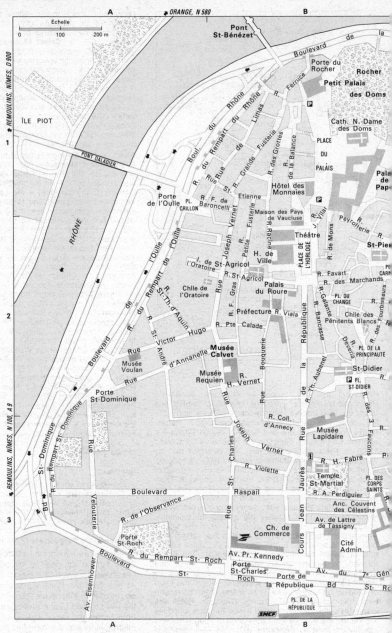

Echelle 0 100 200 m

ORANGE, N 580

Pont St-Bénézet

REMOULINS, NÎMES, D 900

ÎLE PIOT

PONT DALADIER

RHÔNE

Boulevard de la

Porte du Rocher

Rocher

Petit Palais

des Doms

Rhône du Rhône

du Rempart du Rhône

Boul. du Rempart

R. du Rempart

R. Ferruce

R. Limas

R. des Grottes

R. Grande Fusterie

Cath. N.-Dame des Doms

PLACE DU PALAIS

Pala de Pap

Rue de l'Oulle

R. de la Balance

de la Balance

Porte de l'Oulle

PL. CRILLON

R. F. de Baroncelli

R. Etienne

Hôtel des Monnaies

Maison des Pays de Vaucluse

R. Vilar

R. Peyrollerie

R. de Mons

St-Pie

R. des Fourbisseurs

R. des

Rempart de l'Oulle

de l'Oulle

Boul.

Rue

R. Joseph Vernet

R. Petite Fusterie

R. Racine

Théâtre

PLACE DE L'HORLOGE

St-Pie

I. de St-Agricol

l'Oratoire

H. de Ville

R. St-Agricol

R. Favart

R. des Marchands

PE CARN

St-Th-d'Aquin

Chlle de l'Oratoire

R. F. Gras

Palais du Roure

R. Galante

PL. DU CHANGE

de du Rempart

St-Victor

Préfecture

R. Viala

R. Bancasse

Chlle des Pénitents Blancs

R. Viala

Boulevard

Rue

St-André

d'Annanelle

Hugo

R. Pte Calade

R. Bouquerie

R. Th-Aubanel

Devant

PL. DE LA PRINCIPAUTÉ

Musée Calvet

Musée Voulan

Rue

Musée Requien

R. H. Vernet

R. de la

St-Didier

PL. ST-DIDIER

Porte St-Dominique

St-Dominique

R. du Rempart St-Dominique

Rue

R. Coll. d'Annecy

Rue Joseph

R. Charles

Vernet

Rue de

R. des Faucons

Musée Lapidaire

R. H. Fabre

R. Violette

Jaurès

Temple St-Martial

R. A. Perdiguier

PL. DES CORPS SAINTS

Boulevard

Raspail

Rue

Anc. Couvent des Célestins

REMOULINS, NÎMES, N 100, A 9

R. de l'Observance

Porte St-Roch

R. du Rempart St-Roch

Jean

Cours

Av. de Lattre de Tassigny

Ch. de Commerce

Av. Pr. Kennedy

Cité Admin.

Bd

Velouterie

Av. Eisenhower

Boulevard

St-

Porte St-Charles Roch

Porte de la République

Av. du 7e Gén

Bd

St-Ro

PL. DE LA RÉPUBLIQUE

SNCF

▶ **Rue de la République** : Nos. 1, 3 and 53, Cardinals' houses. ▶ **Val de Bénédiction Charterhouse★★** (1356; *9-12 & 2-6:30, closed Tue. and Feb.*), monastery founded by Pope Innocent VI, which in 1973 became the International Centre of Research, Creation and Animation. In the 14thC church is the **mausoleum of Innocent VI★★** (same period); main cloister with the monks' cells; Papal chapel with frescos★ by Matteo Giovanetti (International Summer Conferences take place there parallel to the Avignon Fes-

tival). ▶ **Fort St. André★** *(9-12 & 2-6:30, closed Tue. and Feb.)*, built in the 14thC by order of John the Good and Charles V to watch over Avignon; massive walls and towers, fortified gate★ with two cylindrical towers, a superb example of medieval architecture (inside, graffiti scratched by prisoners, an oven marked out for bread). ▶ **Notre-Dame de Belvezet★**, 12thC Romanesque chapel; the Italian gardens of the former Benedictine abbey make a delightful stroll (view★ over Avignon). ☐

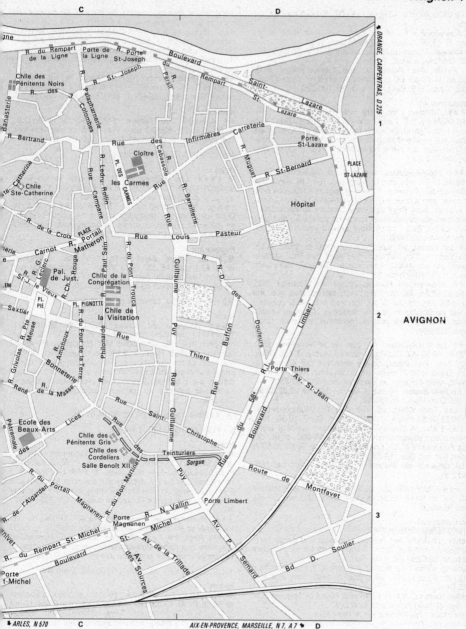

Practical Information

AVIGNON
ℹ 41, cours J.-Jaurès (B3), ☎ 90.82.65.11 ; service hôte-
lier, ☎ 90.82.05.81.
✈ *Avignon-Caumont*, 8 km SE, ☎ 90.31.20.39.
🚆 (B3), ☎ 90.82.62.92/90.82.50.50/90.82.56.29.
Car rental : *Avis*, 29, rte de Montfavet (D3),

☎ 90.87.17.75 ; 34, bd Saint-Roch (B3), ☎ 90.82.26.33 ;
train station.

Hotels :
★★★★ **Europe**, 12, pl. Crillon (A1), ☎ 90.82.66.92,
Tx 431965, AE DC Euro Visa, 53 rm ⌂ ♪ 590. Rest. ♦♦
Vieille Fontaine ♪ closed Sat noon and Sun, 2-23 Jan,
17-24 Aug, 2-9 Nov, 145-200.
★★★ **Midi**, (Inter-Hôtel), 53, rue de la République (B2),

☎ 90.82.15.56, Tx 431074, AE DC Euro Visa, 57 rm
ð 250.
★★ **Angleterre** (L.F.), 29, bd Raspail (B3), ☎ 90.86.34.31,
40 rm ℙ ◊ ⅏ closed 15 Dec-15 Jan, 170.
★★ **Central**, 31, rue de la République (B2), ☎ 90.86.07.81,
Tx 650697, Euro Visa, 29 rm ₩ ◊ 195.
★★ **Palais des Papes**, 1, rue Gérard-Philipe (B1),
☎ 90.86.04.13, AE DC Euro Visa, 30 rm ð ⅏ closed Mon,
1 Dec-1 Jan, 165. Rest. ♦ ≼ ⅃ ð ⅏ 100-230.

Restaurants :
● ♦♦♦ **Brunel**, 46, rue de la Balance (B1),
☎ 90.85.24.83, DC Euro ♪ closed Mon (l.s.) , Sun., Feb
school hols. The whole family gets into the act to produce
a short but excellent list of specialties like : huîtres chaudes gratinées au curry, encornets farcis à la provençale, 130-260.

● ♦♦♦ **Hiély-Lucullus**, 5, rue de la République (B2),
☎ 90.86.17.07, AE, closed Mon and Tue, 16 Jun-3 Jul,
24 Dec-12 Jan. Reserve. P. Hiély proposes a fabulous prix-
fixe meal, with a choice of 12 starters and 12 main courses. Classic, light Provençal fare brought to perfection :
petite marmite du pêcheur, tourte de cailles au foie gras
sauce citron. Red Châteauneuf served young and cool,
by the carafe, 220-450.
♦♦♦ **Le Vernet**, 58, rue J.-Vernet (B2), ☎ 90.86.64.53,
Euro Visa ₩ ♪ closed Sun (Sep-Apr), Jan-Feb. Modern
cuisine in an 18thC townhouse. Several fixed-price
menus, 125-190 ; child : 65.
● ♦♦ **Auberge de France**, 28, pl. de l'Horloge (B2),
☎ 90.82.58.86, AE DC Euro Visa, closed Wed eve and
Thu, 7-28 Jan, 15 Jun-3 Jul. Inspired Provençal cuisine :
moules de Bouzigues farcies, noisettes d'agneau vauclusienne, charlotte au praliné, noisettes au miel. Local
wines, 210-220.

● ♦♦ **Le Saint-Didier**, 41, rue de la Saraillerie (B1),
☎ 90.86.16.50, AE DC Visa ♪ closed Mon and Tue , May,
20-30 Aug. This young couple deserves our encouragement. Good food at moderate prices. Fish fresh from the
market, râble de lapin au citron et au miel, 150-250.
♦♦ **Le Petit Bedon**, 70, rue J.-Vernet (B2), ☎ 90.82.33.98,
AE DC Euro Visa ♪ ð 70-150.
♦♦ **Les Trois Clefs**, 26, rue des Trois-Faucons (B3),
☎ 90.86.51.53, Visa ♪ ⅏ closed Sun, 10-30 Nov,
20 Feb-3 Mar. A flowery little restaurant where a warm
welcome and seasonal fare await you, 95-300 ; child : 60.
♦ **La Fourchette II**, 17, rue Racine (B2), ☎ 90.85.20.93 ð
closed Sat and Sun, 10-25 Jun, 70-90.
♦ **La Grignote du Bistrot**, 1, rue Jean-Vilar, 140-160 ;
child : 35.

△ ★★★★**Pont** (300 pl), ☎ 90.82.63.50 ; ★★★**Bagatelle**
(360 pl), ☎ 90.86.30.39 ; ★★**Les Deux Rhônes** (50 pl),
☎ 90.85.49.70.

Recommended
Bicycle rental : info at S.I.
Events : St-André fair, late Nov ; theatre and dance festi-
val, mid-Jul-mid-Aug. Info : 8 bis, rue de Mons ; Antiques
show, ☎ 90.82.67.08, early Nov.
Guide to wines : Le Bistrot d'Avignon, 1, rue Jean-Vilar
(B1), ☎ 90.86.06.45. Wine bar, closed Sun eve and
1-25 Dec.
Guided tours : C.N.M.H.S., all year round by appointment,
Jul-Sep at fixed times, info at C.D.T.
Night clubs : les Ambassy, rue Bancasse.
♥ Antiques : Dervieux, 11, rue Félix-Gras, ☎ 90.82.14.37,
splendid collection of Provençal faïence ; luscious cakes :
"Brunch", pretty setting ; tea room : Simple Simon, 26, rue
de la Petite-Fusterie (A1), ☎ 90.86.62.70.

Nearby
Les ANGLES, ⊠ 30133, 5 km W.

Hotels :
★★★ **L'Ermitage Meissonnier**, 32, av. de Verdun,
☎ 90.25.41.68, 16 rm ℙ ₩ closed Jan-Mar. Antique decor
and fine Provençal furniture, 200. Rest. ● ♦♦♦ ♪
closed Sun eve (Nov-Mar), Mon ex hols. President of the
"Maîtres Cuisiniers", P.-L. Meissonnier can now devote

more time to that association, for his son, his mother and
his wife are watching over the Ermitage. The outstanding
menu combines fragrant Provençal specialties with the
classics : barigoule tiède d'artichauts, sorbet romarin,
bisque-bouille d'Avignon, châteaubriand en croûte dorée.
Regional wines, the latest Châteauneuf vintage by the
carafe, 180-330.
★★ **Le Petit Manoir** (L.F.), chem. de la Pinède,
☎ 90.25.03.36, 40 rm ℙ ₩ ◊ ♪ ð ⊡ ⅌ half pens (h.s.),
closed Mon lunch, Nov-Dec, 345. Rest. ♦♦ ♪ 55-120.

Restaurant :
♦♦ **Auberge Dou Terraie**, 1125, av. de la 2e-D.B.,
☎ 90.25.49.26, AE DC Euro Visa ₩ ð closed Mon eve,
Tue eve, Wed, 5-14 Jan, 1-20 Jun, 100-170 ; child : 50.

MONTFAVET, ⊠ 84140, 6 km E.

Hotel :
● ★★★★ **Les Frênes** (R.C.), av. des Vertes-Rives,
☎ 90.31.17.93, Tx 431164, AE DC Euro Visa, 17 rm ℙ ≼
₩ ◊ ♪ ð ⊡ half pens (h.s.), closed Nov-Feb. Lovely
setting. Old-fashioned decor, 1225. Rest. ♦♦♦ ≼ ♪ ð
Quiet and comfort, hospitality around the pool. Food with
an Italian lilt : gnocchis verdis au gorgonzola, lapereau à
l'ail doux. Young Châteauneufs, 180-215.

Restaurant :
● ♦ **La Ferme Saint-Pierre**, 1551, av. d'Avignon,
☎ 90.87.12.86, AE DC Euro Visa ₩ ♪ closed Sat and
Sun, 11-19 Apr, 8-30 Aug, 19-27 Dec. Farm-style : terrine
de Saint-Pierre, civet de barcelet, 80-130.

NOVES, ⊠ 13550, 13 km S on the N 571.

Hotel :
★★★★ **Auberge de Noves** (R.C.), ☎ 90.94.19.21,
Tx 431312, AE Euro Visa, 22 rm ℙ ₩ ◊ ♪ ð ⊡ ⅌
half pens (h.s.), closed 3 Jan-5 Mar. Handsome Provençal
farmhouse, 1635. Rest. ● ♦♦♦ ≼ ð closed Wed noon. In
the heart of the Provençal countryside amidst the thyme
and the crickets, the Lalleman family inn provides savoury
dishes like : huîtres gratinées au châteauneuf-du-pape,
salmis de pigeons au gâteau d'échalotes. Fine cellar,
235-365.

△ ★★Belle Laure (70 pl), ☎ 90.94.01.56.

Le PONTET, ⊠ 84130, 3 km NE.

Hotels :
● ★★★ **Agassins** (C.H.), Le Pigeonnier, RN 7,
☎ 90.32.42.91, DC Visa, 26 rm ₩ ◊ ♪ ⊡ ⅏ half pens
(h.s.), closed Jan-Feb, 850. Rest. ● ♦♦♦ **Le Florentin** ♪
⅏ closed Sun (l.s.). A dreamy and delicious stopover just
5 km from Avignon. The Mariani family will make your stay
a happy one. Fragrant Provençal cuisine, 120-205 ; child :
40.
★★★ **Auberge de Cassagne** (I.L.A., R.S.), rte de
Vedenne, ☎ 90.31.04.18, Tx 432997, 14 rm ℙ ₩ ◊ ð ⊡
⅌ 430. Rest. ♦♦ ♪ ð ⅏ Spec : émincé de lapereau et
d'agneau aux petits légumes farcis, tresse de saumon et
de langoustines aux pistils de safran, 165-300 ; child : 90.

VILLENEUVE-LÈS-AVIGNON, ⊠ 30400, 2 km NW.

Hotels :
● ★★★★(L) **Le Prieuré** (R.C.), pl. du Chapitre,
☎ 90.25.18.20, Tx 431042, AE DC Euro Visa, 25 rm 10 apt
ℙ ≼ ₩ ◊ ð ⊡ ♪ ⅏ closed 1 May, 10 Nov-15 Mar. Antique
furnishings in a nicely restored setting, 650. Rest. ♦♦♦ ð
Renowned restaurant. Spec : foie gras de canard, piccata
de lotte au basilic, 180-300.
● ★★★ **La Magnaneraie** (I.L.A.), 37, rue du Camp-de-
Bataille, ☎ 90.25.11.11, Tx 432640, AE DC Euro Visa,
20 rm ℙ ≼ ₩ ◊ ♪ ð ⊡ ⅌ half pens (h.s.). Splendid 15thC
dwelling, 800. Rest. ♦♦ ≼ ♪ ð Spec : noisettes d'agneau
tante Lucie, 130-350 ; child : 70.
● ★★ **L'Atelier** (L.F.), 5, rue de la Foire, ☎ 90.25.01.84,
AE DC Euro Visa, 19 rm ₩ ◊ 16thC residence, 240.
● ★★ **Les Cèdres** (L.F.), 39, bd Pasteur, ☎ 90.25.43.92,
Visa, 25 rm ℙ ₩ ◊ 200. Rest. ♦ **Grill**, closed lunch
and Sun eve, 90-120.
★★ **Coya**, Pont d'Avignon, ☎ 90.25.52.29, AE Visa, 25 rm

P ⸶ ⸶ View of the Papal palace and the Rhône, 190. Rest. ♦ ⸶ ⸶ 80-130.

BANDOL

Toulon 17, Aix-en-Provence 68, Paris 826 km
pop 6713 ⊠ 83150   B3

320 days of sunshine every year, a gentle climate and wooded hills that give shelter from the *mistral*; palms and eucalyptus along the Promenade near the Marina. Bandol is known for red wine. Leisure facilities, including theatre, crafts and exibitions on the tiny Bendor islet a few hundred metres from shore *(boat leaves Bandol on the half-hour).*

▶ **Museum of Wines and Spirits :** 8 000 bottles from 50 countries *(10-12 & 2-6; closed Wed.).*

Nearby

▶ **Sanary-Bandol** *(3 km NE)* : tropical gardens and zoo *(8-12 & 2-6, 7 pm in summer; closed Sun. am and Tue. in winter).* ▶ Above **Le Beausset** *(10 km N),* the Romanesque chapel of **Notre-Dame-du-Vieux-Beausset** (collection of *ex-votos)*; coast view. ▶ To the W of Le Beausset, **Le Castellet** *(10 km N),* fortified village on a rocky outcrop (panorama★ ; Paul Ricard car circuit). ▶ **La Cadière-d'Azur** *(3 km SW of Le Castellet),* wine-making village set back from the coast. ☐

Practical Information _____

BANDOL
ℹ allées Vivien, ☎ 94.29.41.35.
SNCF ☎ 94.29.41.51.
Car rental : Avis, 6, rue du 11-Novembre, ☎ 94.29.40.24 ; train station.

Hotels :
★★★★(L) *Ile Rousse,* (P.L.M.), 17, bd L.-Lumière, ☎ 94.29.46.86, Tx 400372, AE DC Euro Visa, 55 rm P ⸶ ⸶ ⛆ ▤ half pens (h.s.). Private beach. Louis-XV and Louis-XVI decor, 1050. Rest. ♦♦♦ *les Oliviers* ⸶ ♪ ⸶. Terrace dining. Spec : *millefeuille de sole aux morilles,* 150-280.
● ★★★ *Délos Palais,* île de Bendor, ☎ 94.29.42.33, Tx 400383, AE Visa, 55 rm ⸶ ⸛ ⛆ ⸙ ▤ ⸝ 470. Rest. ♦♦ 160.
★★★ *Ker Mocotte* (L.F.), rue Raimu, ☎ 94.29.46.53, 19 rm P ⸶ ⛆ ⸙ closed 20 Oct-1 Feb. Raimu's former villa is now a hotel, 230. Rest. ♦ ♪ 90-120.
★★★ *La Baie,* 62, rue Marçon, ☎ 94.29.40.82, Tx 400479, Euro Visa, 14 rm P ⸶ ⛆ closed 5 Jan-5 Feb, 200.
★★★ *La Réserve,* rte de Sanary, ☎ 94.29.42.71, AE DC Euro Visa, 16 rm P ⸶ half pens (h.s.), 260. Rest. ♦♦ ⸶ ♪ ⸶. closed Sun eve and Mon lunch (Jul-Aug). Spec : *bourride provençale, agneau des Alpilles,* 100-260.
★★★ *Le Provençal,* rue des Ecoles, ☎ 94.29.52.11, Tx 400308, AE DC Euro Visa, 22 rm ♪ pens (h.s.), 600. Rest. ♦♦ ♪ 70-120.
★★ *Splendid* (L.F.), plage de Rénecros, ☎ 94.29.41.61, Tx 400383, AE Visa, 22 rm ⸶ ⸙ half pens (h.s.), closed 10 Feb-15 Mar, 1 Nov-15 Dec, 440. Rest. ♦ ⸶ ♪ ⸙ 100.

Restaurants :
♦♦♦ *Auberge du Port,* 9, allée J.-Moulin, ☎ 94.29.42.63, AE DC Euro Visa ⸶ ⸛ ⛆ ⸶ closed Mon and Sun eve (l.s.). Terrace service. Spec : fish and shellfish, 100-150.
♦ *La Grotte Provençale,* 21, rue Marçon, ☎ 94.29.41.52, closed Tue eve and Wed ex Jul-Aug. Interesting fixed-price meals, 70-130.

▲ ★★*de Capelan* (133 pl), ☎ 94.29.43.92 ; ★★*Vallongue* (90 pl), ☎ 94.29.49.55.

Recommended
Casino : 24, rue de la République, ☎ 94.29.40.88.

For a complete picture on the gastronomy featured in the Guide, see p. 8.

Nearby

Le BEAUSSET, ⊠ 83330, 10 km N.
ℹ mairie, ☎ 94.90.41.39 (h.s.).   ♥

Hotel :
★★ *La Cigalière,* rte du Camp, 1.5 km N on N 8, ☎ 94.98.64.63, Visa, 20 rm 5 apt P ⸶ ⸛ ⛆ ⸶ ▤ ⸝ closed Sun eve (l.s.), 1-15 Feb, 230. Rest. ♦♦ ♪ ⸙ 90.

Restaurant :
♦♦ *L'Estagnon,* 17, bd Chanzy, ☎ 94.98.62.62, AE DC Euro Visa ⸛ ♪ closed Wed, 15 Feb-1 Mar, 15 Nov-1 Dec. A nicely converted former oil press. Spec : *pieds paquets, foie gras frais de canard aux pommes, pâtes vertes aux morilles,* 100-150.

La CADIÈRE-D'AZUR, ⊠ 83740, 9 km N.
ℹ rd-pt R.-Salengro, ☎ 94.29.32.56 (h.s.).

Hotel :
★★★ *Hostellerie Bérard,* av. G.-Péri, ☎ 94.29.31.43, Tx 400509, AE Visa, 40 rm P ⸶ ⸛ ⸙ ▤ half pens (h.s.), closed 30 Oct-8 Dec, 360. Rest. ♦♦ ⸶ ⸙ Spec : *feuilleté de loup sauce champagne, reine de Saba,* 132-250; child : 70.

▲ ★★*la Mallissonne* (250 pl), ☎ 94.29.30.60.

Le CASTELLET, ⊠ 83330 Le Beausset, 10 km N.

Hotel :
★★★ *Castel Lumière,* Le Portail, ☎ 94.32.62.20, AE DC, 5 rm ⸶ ⸛ half pens, closed Tue (l.s.), Nov, 740. Rest. ♦♦ ⸶ ♪ 140-210.

Restaurant :
♦♦ *Lou Mestre Pin,* pl. du Jeu-de-Paume, ☎ 94.90.60.27, Visa ⸛ ♪ ⸶ closed Wed. Good value. Spec : *feuilleté de truite, civet de porcelet à la provençale,* pastries, 66-106.

▲ ★★★*Le Castillon* (150 pl), ☎ 94.90.60.33 ; ★★*Auberge d'Arbois* (135 pl), ☎ 94.90.70.51.

BARCELONNETTE

Gap 69, Briançon 84, Paris 737 km
pop 3314 ⊠ 04400   C1

Barcelonnette is superbly situated among orchards and meadows surrounded by mountains. The name commemorates the Spanish origins of the family that founded this town in the 13thC. Some of the inhabitants, who emigrated to seek their fortune during the 19thC, managed to establish a monopoly on the cloth trade to Mexico. Having prospered, they returned to build magnificent villas that can still be seen on the Avenue de la Libération.

Nearby

▶ **Le Sauze** *(6 km S)* and **Super-Sauze** (alt. 1 700 m) make up a winter sports resort on the N slope of the Fours Pass (alt. 2 314 m). ▶ **Pra-Loup** *(8.5 km SW)* : skiing on the Pégieu slopes (alt. 2 479 m). ▶ Three magnificent **mountain roads**★★ go from Barcelonnette towards the Midi : D908 crosses the **Col d'Allos**★ (pass, alt. 2 240 m), and runs through the high pastures (view★ over the Verdon Valley); D902 runs through the Bachelard Gorges and climbs through the **Col de La Cayolle**★ (alt. 2 327 m) with views over the Var and Bachelard valleys; the third, the highest road in Europe, is the **Route de la Bonette**★★★, beginning at **Jausiers** *(8 km NE)* and climbing through difficult countryside to an altitude of 2 802 m; from here, a 10-min walk to the top of La Bonette (alt. 2 862 m ; magnificent view as far as Pelvoux). ☐

Practical Information _____

BARCELONNETTE
ℹ av. de la Libération, ☎ 92.81.04.71.

Hotels :
★★★ *Grande Epervière,* rte de Gap, ☎ 92.81.00.70, 10 rm

P ≼ ▨ ✇ closed Sun eve eve, 4-30 Jan, 21 Nov-7 Dec.
Rest. ♦ ♪ closed Sun eve , Mon-Fri lunch, 4-30 Jan,
60-130.
★ *L'Aupillon* (L.F.), rte Saint-Pons, ☎ 92.81.01.09, Visa,
7 rm P ≼ ▨ ⌔ half pens (h.s.), closed 1 Nov-1 Dec, 310.
Rest. ♦ ♨ closed Wed eve, 55.

Restaurants :
♦♦ *Le Passe-Montagne*, rte de la Cayolle Uvernet, Uver-
net-Fours, 4 km S on D 902, ☎ 92.81.08.58, AE DC
Euro Visa P ≼ ▨ ⌔ ♪ closed Wed, 20 May-10 Jun,
15 Nov-15 Dec. Spec : *feuillantine de Saint-Jacques aux
morilles, pavé de gigot d'agneau aux échalotes, glace au
miel de pays*, 85-160.
♦ *La Mangeoire*, pl. des 4 Vents, ☎ 92.81.01.61, Euro
Visa ♪ closed Mon and Sun eve, 3 Jan-2 Feb, 10-25 Jun.
Simple, down-to-earth fare, served in a former sheep-
fold, 55-130.
⚐ ★★★*Plan de Barcelonnette* (45 pl), ☎ 92.81.08.11 ;
★★★*Tampico* (80 pl), ☎ 92.81.02.55 ; ★★*Peyra* (50 pl),
☎ 92.81.04.71.

Nearby

PRA-LOUP, ⊠ 04400 Barcelonnette, 9 km SW on the
D902, D109.

Hotels :
★★★ *Les Airelles*, ☎ 92.84.13.24, 20 rm P ≼ ⌔ ✇
closed 1 May-9 Jul, 1 Sep-14 Dec, 260.
★★ *Bergers* (L.F.), ☎ 92.84.14.54, AE, 35 rm P ≼ ⌔ pens
(h.s.), closed 2 May-30 Jun, 1 Sep-15 Dec, 290. Rest. ♦
♪ closed 2 May-15 Dec, 55-130.
★★ *Les Blancs*, Molanès, ☎ 92.84.16.60, Visa, 27 rm P
≼ ▨ ⌔ ♪↣ closed 20 May-10 Jun, 160. Rest. ● ♦♦ This
is Joël Robuchon's choice for a quiet, restful stop. Terrific value. Table d'hôte, take-out food prepared by Pierre
Deliance, 60-150.

Le SAUZE, ⊠ 04400 Barcelonnette, 5 km SE.

Hotels :
★★★ *Alp'Hôtel* (R.S.), Enchastrayes, ☎ 92.81.05.04,
Tx 420437, AE DC Visa, 24 rm 11 apt P ≼ ▨ ⌔ ♪ ▤ pens
(h.s.), closed 1 May-10 Jun, 25 Oct-10 Dec, 330. Rest. ♦
≼ ♪ 55-130.
★★ *Séolanes* (L.F.), ☎ 92.81.05.10, 16 rm P ≼ ▨ ⌔
closed 15 Apr-30 Jun, 1 Sep-15 Dec. Southern exposure
at the foot of the ski-lifts, 140. Rest. ♦ For guests
only, 110-175.
⚐ ★★*La Chaup* (60 pl), ☎ 92.81.02.82.

SUPER-SAUZE, ⊠ 04400 Barcelonnette, 10 km SE on the
D 9A.

Hotels :
★★★ *Le Pyjama*, ☎ 92.81.12.00, DC, 14 rm P ≼ ▨ ⌔
closed 3 May-1 Jul, 30 Sep-20 Dec, 250.
★★ *L'Ourson*, ☎ 92.81.05.21, 20 rm P ≼ ⌔ pens (h.s.),
closed 5 May-30 Jun, 1 Sep-18 Dec, 205. Rest. ♦ ★ Terrace service, 60-80.

BARJOLS

Draguignan 45, Aix-en-Provence 64, Paris 823 km
pop 2016 ⊠ 83670   C2
With fountains playing in shady squares, Barjols epi-
tomizes the Provençal town. The manufacture of tam-
bourines and a three-hole flute, called the *galoubet*,
is traditional here ; the instruments are played at local
festivals. Every 4 years, the *Tripettes* (tripe) Festival, in which an ox is blessed then slaughtered and
roasted for consumption by the townspeople, recalls
pagan and Christian traditions.

Nearby

▶ La Verdière *(17 km NW)*, below a château★ on a spur ;
the old fortress was rebuilt in the 17th-18thC ; plasterwork
decoration, carving *(guided tours 2-5)*.   ▢

Practical Information _____

Hotel :
★ *Pont d'Or*, rue E.-Payan, ☎ 94.77.05.23, Euro Visa,
15 rm P closed 30 Nov-15 Jan, 120. Rest. ♦ closed Mon
and Sun eve (l.s.), 60-130.

Recommended
Events : *tripe festival*, on the feast of St Marcel (Sun nearest 16 Jan).

Les BAUX-DE-PROVENCE★★★

Arles 19, Avignon 30, Paris 718 km
pop 433 ⊠ 13520   A2
The white peaks and olive- and almond-clad valleys
of the Alpilles were the background to the Provençal
"courts of love", where troubadors vied for the prize
of a kiss and a peacock's feather in singing the praises of their lady-loves. At Les Baux-de-Provence, an
immense pile of stone rising above dense scrub is
crowned by a ruined château and ghost town. Right
next door, the still-inhabited village is a living museum
of the Middle Ages.

▶ Enter the town on foot from the car park along the **Rue
Porte-Mage.** The most interesting houses, dating from
the Renaissance, have simple ground floors and first-floor
windows with fluted pilasters clearly inspired by Classical
architecture. ▶ **Manville Mansion★,** now the Town Hall :
1572 Renaissance façade. ▶ **The Brion Mansion** houses
the Louis Jou Foundation (artworks in paper). ▶ The **Por-
celets Mansion** (1569), now the **Museum of Modern Art**
(9:30-12 & 2-6:30, Easter-Oct. ex Wed. in winter). ▶ **Place
St-Vincent★ :** Provençal elms and a 12thC church set in
the rock. ▶ **White Penitents' Chapel,** 17thC cliffside chapel with frescos★ by the Provençal painter Yves Brayer
(b. 1907). ▶ **Rue du Trencat★,** hewn from the rock, leads
to the ghost village and château. ▶ To the right, Tour-de-
Brau Mansion, 14th-15thC house, now the **Archaeological and Lapidary Museum** displaying articles excavated
at the village. ▶ **Views★★** from the S end of the promontory (monument), and then from the 13thC **keep★,** the most
intact part of the château. ▶ **Queen Jeanne's Pavilion★**
(15 min walk W from the village), Renaissance building
that was copied by Mistral for his tomb at Maillane. ▶ **Val
d'Enfer** (Hell Valley) : 30 to 45-min walk NW through the
Vallon de la Fontaine to a gorge full of strangely-shaped
rocks and riddled with caverns. In this fantastic setting,
the **Cathédrale d'Images★** (audiovisual show).

Nearby

▶ **Fontvieille** *(9 km SW) :* the main industry is quarrying
the building stone known as Arles limestone ; to the S
of the town, a small **museum** dedicated to **Daudet,** who
wrote a large part of his humorous sketches of Provençal life, *Lettres de Mon Moulin,* here *(9-12 & 1:30-5:30) ;*
view★ over the Alpilles. ▶ **Saint-Gabriel★** *(6 km N of
Fontvieille) :* 12thC Romanesque **chapel** displaying typical
Provençal taste for the Classical Roman style (façade★,
doorway★).   ▢

Practical Information _____

Les BAUX-DE-PROVENCE
ℹ imp. du Château, ☎ 90.97.34.39.

Hotels :
● ★★★★(L)   *Oustau   de   Baumanière*   (R.C.),
☎ 90.54.33.07, AE DC Euro Visa, 25 rm P ▨ ⌔ ▤ ♪
closed 20 Jan-6 Mar. Provençal farmhouse at the foot of
the château des Baux, 725. Rest. ● ♦♦♦♦ Chef J.-A.
Charial continues to follow his grandfather's advice, with
felicitous results. Naturally grandfather is 89-year-old Raymond Thuillier, the venerable lord of Les Baux. This
enchanted 16thC dwelling is a Provençal paradise. Classic
grand cuisine awaits you : asparagus (in season), *gigot
d'agneau en croûte, mousseline d'artichauts et haricots*

verts du jardin (to keep the bill in bounds). And of course the hearty red Gigondas et Trevallon wines, 400-500.
● ★★★ *Cabro d'Or* (R.C.), Val d'Enfer, ☎ 90.54.33.21, Tx 401810, AE DC Euro Visa, 22 rm 🅿 ▥ 🖾 ,º closed Mon, 16 Nov-19 Dec. Traditional F ovençal farmhouse, 500. Rest. ● ◆◆◆ The slightly more accessible annex of the *Oustau de Baumanière*. All the scents and flavours of Provence, 200-250.
★★★ *Mas d'Aigret*, D 27A, ☎ 90.97.33.54, AE DC Euro Visa, 17 rm 🅿 ⟨ ▥ ⤫ 🖾 half pens (h.s.), closed Thu, 1 Jan-1 Apr. At the foot of the ruins, 470. Rest. ◆ ⟩ & ⌇ Simple food, 95-170.

Restaurant :
◆◆◆ *La Riboto de Taven*, Val d'enfer, ☎ 90.97.34.23, AE DC Euro Visa 🅿 ⟨ ▥ ⟍ ⟩ & closed Mon and Sun eve, 6 Jan-25 Feb. Magnificent setting. Good food. Spec : local mountain lamb 190-220.

Nearby

FONTVIEILLE, ✉ 13990, 8 km W.
ℹ mairie, ☎ 90.97.70.01.

Hotels :
● ★★★★ *La Regalido* (R.C.), rue Frédéric-Mistral, ☎ 90.97.60.22, Tx 441150, 13 rm 🅿 ▥ ⟍ & closed 30 Nov-15 Jan, 650. Rest. ● ◆◆ closed Mon and Tue noon. Reserve. Alphonse Daudet would have loved this picturesque establishment : *gratin de moules, tranche de gigot en casserole et à l'ail*, 150-260.
★★★ *A la Grâce de Dieu*, 90, av. de Tarascon, ☎ 90.97.71.90, AE DC Euro Visa, 10 rm 🅿 ⟨ ▥ ⟍ half pens (h.s.), closed 15 Feb-15 Mar, 550. Rest. ◆◆ ⟩ closed Wed. Bar. Spec : *gratin de queues d'écrevisses, filet de Saint-Pierre au cidre, filet de bœuf aux morilles*, 105-170.
La Tanière, rte de Raphaële, Croix de Jousseaud, ☎ 90.97.61.40, 9 rm 🅿 ⟨ ▥ ⟍ 🖾 closed 25 Nov-15 Mar ex 31 Dec, 155. Rest. ◆ ⟨ ⟩ 45-70.

Restaurant :
◆◆ *Le Patio*, 117, rte du Nord, ☎ 90.97.73.10, Visa ▥ ⟩ & ⌇ closed Tue eve and Wed, 2 Jan-10 Feb. A former sheepfold. Provençal specialties and charcoal-grills, 130-200.

⚏ ★★★*Municipal* (150 pl), ☎ 90.97.78.69.

Recommended
Farmhouse-gîte : *Mas de Suspiron*, ☎ 90.97.30.50. Horseback riding.

Etang de BERRE
(Berre Lagoon)
A-B3

Round trip from Martigues *(112 km, half-day)*
The Berre Lagoon gives a confusing impression of heavy industry and unspoilt nature, modern military installations and Greek fortifications, a large modern airport and a Roman single-span bridge that was a triumph of engineering in its day. In less than half a century, petrochemical development has transformed the area from a fishing and farming economy to one of the key industrial centres of Europe, which serves as a conduit for much of the oil supplied by the Middle East to Switzerland and Germany. Small towns and villages nevertheless preserve their rural charm despite the encroachment of 20thC technology.

▶ **Martigues** (pop. 42 039), a fishing town on the edge of the Étang, now contained within an industrial complex. Martigues is divided by canals into three sections, each of which has a 17thC church. Ferrières *(N bank)* : **museums** in the former Customs House *(Caserne des Douanes ; 10-12 & 2:30-6:30 ex Tue., Jul.-Aug. ; pm ex Mon., Tue. rest of year)* : archaeological and ethnographic collections, Provençal painters including Félix Ziem (1821-1911) and Francis Picabia (1879-1953) ; **Caronte motorway via-**

duct★. ▶ 3.5 km N, the **chapel of Notre-Dame-des-Marins** (view★). ▶ 5 km W, **Port-de-Bouc** (chemical industries) extends on both sides of the Caronte canal, protected by a 17thC fort designed by Vauban, and the oil port of Lavera *(visits by request to the BP Oil Refinery, B.P. 1, 13117 Lavera)*. ▶ On the right, **Saint-Mitre-les-Remparts** : intact 15thC fortifications. ▶ **Saint-Blaise** *(3 km NW)* : **excavations** reveal eight successive layers of human occupation from the 7thC BC to the 14thC. **Chapel of St. Blaise★**, Romanesque 12thC next to a 17thC hermitage. 100 m away, **Greek ramparts★** (3rdC BC) just behind Early Christian vestige ; small museum. ▶ **Istres** (pop. 30 360), between the Lagoon and the Crau plain, has been an aircraft testing ground since before WWI. Old Istre : museum displaying archaeological finds and a reconstructed old-time Provençal kitchen★ *(2:30-6 ex Tue.)*. ▶ **Fos-sur-Mer★** *(10 km S)*, a medieval town (ramparts, Romanesque church, view★) overlooking the metallic industrial landscape. ▶ **La Fossette** *(8 km NW of Fos)* : information centre for the industrial and port complex *(9-12 & 1-5 ; closed Sun. and nat. hols.)*. ▶ **Miramas-le-Vieux**, surrounded by a medieval wall on a rocky plateau (view★). ▶ **Saint-Chamas**. ▶ **Cornillon-Confoux** *(4.5 km NE)*, on a promontory with a fine view of the Lagoon. ▶ Left of the road, **Flavian's Bridge★** (1stC Roman). ▶ 2 km N from the crossroads of D10 and D21 : **Lançon orientation chart★**. ▶ **Vitrolles**, overlooked by a sheer rock, a village enclosed by a large industrial complex. ▶ **Marignane.** □

Practical Information ─────────────

FOS-SUR-MER, ✉ 13270, 10 km S of **Istres**.

Hotel :
★★★ *Camargue* (ex Frantel), rte d'Istres, ☎ 42.05.00.57, Tx 410812, AE DC Euro Visa, 130 rm 🅿 ⟨ ▥ ⟩ ⤫ 🖾 350. Rest. ◆◆ *La Bastidonne* ⟨ ⟩ closed Sat and Sun, 70-170 ; child : 50.

ISTRES, ✉ 13800, 41 km SE on the rte d'Arles.
ℹ allées Jean-Jaurès, ☎ 42.56.91.25.
� ☎ 42.55.01.21/42.56.06.22.

Hotels :
★★★ *Le Mirage*, rue des Anciens-Combattants, ☎ 42.56.02.26, Tx 400983, AE DC Euro Visa, 28 rm 🅿 ▥ ⟍ ⟩ & ⌇ 🖾 250. Rest. ◆◆ ⟩ & ⌇ closed Mon noon and Sat eve , Sat-Sun (l.s.), 60-120 ; child : 35.
★★ *Aystria-Tartugues*, chem. de Tartugues, ☎ 42.56.44.55, 10 rm 🅿 ▥ ⌇ 160.
★ *Le Castellan*, pl. Ste-Catherine, ☎ 42.55.13.09, 17 rm 🅿 ⟍ ⌇ 150.

MARIGNANE, ✉ 13700, 28 km NW of **Marseille**.
ℹ 4, bd Frédéric-Mistral, ☎ 42.09.78.83.
✈ Marseille-Provence, ☎ 42.89.90.10.

Hotel :
★★ *Saint-André*, av. Roland-Corrao, ☎ 42.09.04.11, Euro Visa, 27 rm 🅿 ⟍ ⟩ 200. Rest. ◆ ⟨ ⟩ 60-90 ; child : 35.

Restaurant :
◆◆ *Le Moulin à Huile*, 102, av. Jean-Jaurès, ☎ 42.88.70.59, AE DC Euro Visa ▥ ⟩ ⌇ closed Sat noon and Sun, 10-25 Aug. Spec : fish, 90-110.

⚏ ★★*Le Jai* (128 pl), ☎ 42.09.13.07.

MARTIGUES, ✉ 13500, 15 km S of **Istres**.
ℹ quai Paul-Doumer, ☎ 42.80.30.72.
🚉 ☎ 42.81.40.57.
Car rental : *Avis*, 11, bd L.-Degut, ☎ 42.07.07.96.

Hotel :
★★★ *Saint-Roch*, ancienne rte de Port-de-Bouc, ☎ 42.80.19.73, AE DC Euro Visa, 39 rm 🅿 ⟨ ▥ ⟍ 🖾 Rest. ◆◆ *Le Moulin de Paradis* ⟩ 80-160.

⚏ ★★★*Le Cap* (150 pl), ☎ 42.80.73.02 ; ★★★*Le Mas* (166 pl), ☎ 42.80.70.34 ; ★★7 sites (more than 1300 pl.).

BRIGNOLES

Toulon 50, Marseille 64, Paris 815 km
pop 10894 ⊠ 83170   C3

Brignoles, in the heart of the Var region, has two
faces : a medieval town that makes its living from
regional agricultural produce and, at the foot of the
hill, a new township that has developed as the largest
French centre for the extraction of bauxite (the ore
from which aluminum is derived). Brignoles is also
the marketing centre for wines from the Var and Provence.

▶ **Place Carami :** from this centre of social life, a maze
of alleyways leads uphill to the heart of the old town.
▶ **Church of St. Sauveur :** Meridional Gothic. ▶ **Palace of
the Counts of Provence,** 13thC summer residence of the
provincial rulers, now the **Brignoles Regional Museum :**
sarcophagus of Gayole★, late 2nd-early 3rdC tomb illustrating transition from pagan to Christian symbols, earliest
Christian monument from Gaul ; reconstruction of an
18thC Provençal kitchen★ *(10-12 & 3-5:30 in summer, 5 in
winter ; closed Mon. and Tue. ; if closed, tel. 94.69.00.26,
ext. 247).*

Nearby

▶ The **abbey of La Celle** *(2.5 km SW)* was notorious for
the easy virtue of the nuns, whose habit was nothing
more than a black silk ribbon worn on a dress of the latest
fashion ; a writer of the day declared : "You could only tell
them apart by the colour of their petticoats and the names
of their lovers." The realistic 15thC image of Christ in the
Romanesque church has given rise to a local proverb :
Laï coumo lou bouan Diou de la Cello ("ugly as the Good
Lord of La Celle"). ▶ **Montagne de la Loube★** *(14.5 km
SW to the no-entry road, then 3.5 km on foot, 2hr round
trip) :* limestone rocks in fantastic shapes ; view★★ from
the Alps to the sea.   □

Practical Information ————————

ⓘ pl. Saint-Louis, ☎ 94.69.01.78.
SNCF ☎ 93.69.11.95/94.91.50.50.

Hotels :
★★★ **Le Mas de la Cascade,** 2,5 km S. on D 554,
☎ 94.69.01.49, Euro Visa, 10 rm Ⓟ ⊀ ▦ ⌕ closed Tue eve
(h.s.) and Wed, 25 Jan-25 Feb, 250. Rest. ♦♦ 125-220.
★ **Saint-Louis,** N 7, ☎ 94.69.09.20, Visa, 16 rm Ⓟ ⊀ ▦ ⌕
⊗ 200. Rest. ♦ ⸝ ⅋ ⊗ 60-100 ; child : 50.
⚲ *Municipal* (100 pl), ☎ 94.59.11.86.

CAGNES-SUR-MER*

Nice 13, Cannes 21, Paris 922 km
pop 35426 ⊠ 06800   D2

A landscape of roses and mimosa, dark cypresses
and silvery olive trees bathed in the dazzling Mediterranean light. The painter Auguste Renoir spent
his last days here ; contemporary artists flock to the
annual Cagnes Art Festival. The settlement includes
Le Haut-de-Cagnes, with a medieval château ; Cagnes-
Ville, the modern business centre ; and Le Cros-de-
Cagnes, a fishing port and seaside resort.

▶ **Haut-de-Cagnes,** easily reached on foot by the Bourgade slope *(montée).* ▶ The fortified enclosure dates from
the 13thC. ▶ **Church of St. Pierre :** two naves, one early
Gothic, the other 17thC. ▶ **Château-Museum,** built as a
fortress in the 14thC by Rainier I of Monaco, transformed
into a residence in 1620 ; behind the austere façade, an
elegant arcaded **interior courtyard★★** from the Renaissance. In the 1st floor Festival Hall, the ceiling★, by the
17thC Italian Carlone, is a masterpiece of illusionist painting *(10-12 & 2:30-7, Jul.-Sep. ; 10-12 & 2-6, ex Tue. out of
season ; closed 15 Oct.-15 Nov.).* Exhibitions include the
Olive Museum★, the Suzy Solidor donation★ (40 portraits

of the popular French singer by well-known 20thC painters) ; Museum of Modern Mediterranean Art★ : exhibitions in rotation of works by Chagall, Dufy, Vasarely and
others ; view★ from the tower. ▶ **Notre-Dame de la Protection,** above the valley, 14th-17thC chapel with 16thC
frescos. ▶ **Musée Renoir du Souvenir★** *(follow the signs
E of Cagnes),* at Les Collettes, the property where Renoir
spent his last 12 years. The decoration of the house has
been preserved as Renoir knew it ; paintings in the house,
sculpture in the garden *(10-1 & 2-6).*

Nearby

▶ The **Var Corniche★** (cliff road ; *12 km N on D118)*
leads to the IBM Study and Research Centre (designed
by the architect Marcel Breuer, b. 1902) and *(14 km)* to **La
Gaude,** known for wine ; **Saint-Jeannet** *(3.5 km N of La
Gaude) :* citrus orchards and vineyards on a hillside (site★)
at the foot of a peak called the **Baou** *(1hr on foot, marked
path ;* panorama★★). ▶ **Villeneuve-Loubet** *(3.5 km W of
Cagnes),* overlooked by a medieval château ; Museum of
Culinary Art in the house where the famous chef Auguste
Escoffier (1847-1935) was born *(2-6 ex Mon. and nat.
hols., tel. 93.20.80.51).* ▶ **Marina-Baie des Anges** *(3 km
SW),* yacht harbour with cafés, restaurants and luxurious
buildings in a complex designed by the contemporary
architect André Minangoy.   □

Practical Information ————————

CAGNES-SUR-MER
ⓘ 26, av. Renoir, ☎ 93.20.61.64.
SNCF ☎ 93.20.50.50/93.20.66.11.
Car rental : *Avis,* train station, ☎ 93.34.65.15.

Hotels :
● ★★★ *Cagnard* (R.C.), rue Pontis-Long, ☎ 93.20.73.21,
Tx 462223, AE DC Euro Visa, 19 rm Ⓟ ⊀ ▦ ⌕ closed
Thu lunch, 1-15 Nov, 470. Rest. ♦♦ ⸝ ⅋ closed Thu
noon, 1 Nov-18 Dec. Warm welcome, appealing cui-
sine, 290-340.
★★★ *Motel Horizon,* 111, bd de la Plage, ☎ 93.31.09.95,
AE DC Visa, 44 rm Ⓟ ⊀ closed 5 Nov-15 Dec, 330.
★★ *Beaurivage,* 39, bd de la Plage, ☎ 93.20.16.09, Visa,
21 rm Ⓟ ⊀ ⸝ closed 12-26 Nov, 150. Rest. ♦ ⸝ ⅋ 55-120.
★★ *Les Collettes,* chemin des Collettes, ☎ 93.20.80.66,
13 rm Ⓟ ⊀ ⅋ ⌖ closed 1 Nov-15 Dec, 216.
Auberge du Port, 93, bd de la Plage, ☎ 93.07.25.28, AE
DC Euro Visa, 2 rm 3 apt ⊀ ▦ ☙ closed Wed ex Jul-Aug,
2 Nov-26 Dec, 250. Rest. ♦♦ ⸝ 90-200.

Restaurants :
● ♦♦ *La Réserve (Chez Loulou),* 91, bd de la Plage,
Cros-de-Cagnes, ☎ 93.31.00.17, Euro Visa ⊀ ⅋ closed
Sat and Sun, 26 Jun-1 Sep, 23 Dec-4 Jan. J. Maximin's
favourite place to stop for a friendly, savoury meal. Good,
fresh, down-home fare, 150-200.
♦♦ *Villa du Cros,* bd de la Plage, at the port,
☎ 93.07.57.83 Ⓟ ▦ ⌕ ⅋ closed Sun eve and Mon (l.s.),
Nov, 85-200.
⚲ ★★★★*Oasis* (100 pl), ☎ 93.20.75.67 ; ★★★★*Panora-
mer* (83 pl), ☎ 93.31.16.15 ; ★★★*Camp'Otel du Club*
(40 pl), ☎ 93.20.91.19.

Recommended
Baby-sitting : ☎ 93.61.07.57, available 24 hours a day.
Call between 7:30am and 10pm.

Nearby

Le HAUT-DE-CAGNES, ⊠ 06800.

Restaurants :
♦♦ *Josy-Jo* , 8, pl. du Planastel, ☎ 93.20.68.76, Euro Visa
⊀ ⅋ closed Sun, 15 Dec-15 Jan. A pleasant little place
serving simple, sunny fare : *farcis grand-mère,* 170.
♦ *Peintres,* 71, montée de la Bourgade, ☎ 93.20.83.08,
AE Euro Visa ⊀ ⌕ closed Wed, 100-160.

VILLENEUVE-LOUBET, ⊠ 06270, 2 km W.
ⓘ ☎ 93.20.20.09.

Hotels :
★★★ *Hamotel*, (Inter-Hôtel), les Hameaux du Soleil, ☎ 93.20.86.60, Tx 470623, AE DC Euro Visa, 33 rm 𝕡 ⌇ ◳ ♪ 𝔸 closed 10 Nov-15 Dec, 280.
★★ *Syracuse*, av. de la Batterie, ☎ 93.20.45.09, 27 rm 𝕡 ⌇ ◳ 310.

𝗔 ★★★★*Parc des Maurettes* (116 pl), ☎ 93.20.91.91 ; ★★★★*Vieille Ferme* (47 pl), ☎ 93.33.41.44 ; ★★★*Hippodrome* (72 pl), ☎ 93.20.02.00.

La CAMARGUE**

A2-3
Round trip from Arles *(91 or 134 km, full day)*

The Camargue is a marshy delta that has been preserved largely in its natural state by virtue of decrees in 1928 and 1970 designating the region as a nature park. Extending from Arles (→) between the two arms of the Rhône (Grand Rhône to the E, Petit Rhône W) is a 750 km² alluvial plain. The Camargue stretches westward as far as the Costière de Nîmes (→ Cévennes). The land has been built up by alluvial deposits from the River Rhône, but at the same time eroded by the encroachment of the sea.
In fact, there are two Camargues : a lagoon wilderness and a vast agricultural tract. Protected flora and fauna in the nature park include the *saladelle* (the blue mascot flower of the *gardians*, the cowboys of the Camargue), beaver, badger, heron, flamingo, wild duck and egret. This is also where the cream-coloured Camargue horses (born bay, they lighten in their fourth year) and black bulls are bred.
In the Haute Camargue, sheep-rearing is the traditional livelihood, although it has become less important since drainage and irrigation projects undertaken after WWII have facilitated large-scale agricultural development in the region.

▶ Arles (→). ▶ Take D570 SW (road to Saintes-Maries). ▶ On the left, **mas du Pont de Rousty,** an enormous sheepfold converted into the **Camargue Ecomuseum★** provides a comprehensive introduction to life in the region *(10-12 & 2-6:30 ex Tue., Wed. and some nat. hols.)*; 3.5 km of trails wind among features typical of a Camargue sheep farm. ▶ **L'Albaron** *(right)*, formerly defended by its 13th-16thC tower. ▶ **Aigues-Mortes★★** *(right, 19 km;* → Cévennes). ▶ **Pont de Gau ;** on the shore of Lake Ginès, **Camarguen Museum** (documents, photographs, films ; *9-12 & 3-7, Jul.-Sep.*). Nearby, a **bird sanctuary** *(8 to sunset).* ▶ **Boumian Wax Museum :** dioramas of Camargue life *(10-12 & 2-7).* ▶ **Les Saintes-Maries-de-la-Mer** (*Li Santo* in Provençal), fishing village with vast beaches that attract crowds of summer holidaymakers. The name of the settlement originates from a local legend that Mary Jacob (mother of the apostle James the Less and supposedly the sister of the Virgin), Mary Salome (mother of James the Greater and John), Mary Magdalen and various companions including an Egyptian servant called Sarah, fetched up safely at the site in a boat that had been set adrift from the shore of Palestine. The village is the focus of three huge annual pilgrimages, including the gathering of European Gypsies each May. Girls in Arles costume and *gardians* from the Camargue take part in the colourful celebrations, where *farandoles* are danced, calves are branded and young men brave the bulls. **Church★,** heavily fortified (12th-15thC) with a fresh-water well for use in time of siege. **Baroncelli Museum** recounts Camargue life and traditions *(9-12 & 2-5 or 6 ; closed Wed. and Oct.).* ▶ **Sea dyke** (Digue de Mer ; *15 km, or 30 km as far as Salin-de-Giraud)*, the traditional village promenade (not to the end) of Les Saintes ; boat trips on the Petit Rhône. ▶ Take D85A N ; just before the Cacharel farmstead, the track to Méjanes *(12 km)* offers vantage points for wildlife observation beside the lakes. ▶ Returning to D570, after 14 km take D37 right to **Méjanes.** The farm-

stead *(1.5 km right)* maintains a large herd of bulls (calf-branding, *fêtes taurines*, horses and an electric railway along Lake Vaccarès). ▶ Villeneuve crossroads : return directly to Arles *(left)* or continue via Salin-de-Giraud. The road runs beside **Lake Vaccarès** (views★). ▶ **Salin-de-Giraud,** a late-19thC village founded for harvesting sea-salt. The rows of identical houses bring to mind the housing estates of the industrial North of England. **Plage de Piemançon** *(12 km SE, D36D) :* the vast beach is dangerous for swimming. ▶ Return via D36, past *(600 m on your right)* **château de l'Armellière★** (1607). ☐

Practical Information ──────

Les **SAINTES-MARIES-DE-LA-MER,** ⊠ 13460, 38 km S via **Arles.**
ℹ av. Van-Gogh, ☎ 90.47.82.55.

Hotels :
● ★★★★ *Mas de la Fouque*, rte d'Aigues-Mortes, 4 km, ☎ 90.47.81.02, Tx 403155, AE DC Euro Visa, 13 rm 𝕡 ⌇ ∭ ◳ ♪ ⅋ ☟ half pens (h.s.), closed 2 Nov-28 Mar. A striking natural setting with a view of the Camargue, 1425. Rest. ♦♦♦ ♪ ☟ closed Tue. The catch of the day and grilled meats served poolside, to the strains of gypsy guitars, 185-250.
★★★★ *Auberge Cavalière et Résidence*, rte d'Arles, ☎ 90.47.84.62, Tx 440459, AE DC Euro Visa, 48 rm 𝕡 ⌇ ∭ ◳ ☟ 415. Rest. ● ♦♦♦ ♪ Carefully prepared classics. Spec : *nage de mer aux tellines, taureau gardianne à l'ancienne, filet de rouget*, 90-200.
★★★★ *Pont des Bannes*, rte d'Arles, ☎ 90.47.81.09, Tx 403222, 20 rm 𝕡 ∭ ♪ ☟ closed 2 Jan-1 Apr, 15 Oct-31 Dec. Camargue cowboy cabins converted into bungalows, 400. Rest. ♦♦ ⌇ ☟ 100-180 ; child : 65.
★★★ *Boumian*, rte d'Arles, ☎ 90.47.81.15, Tx 403222, 28 rm 𝕡 ∭ ♪ ☟ ☟ closed 2 Jan-15 Feb, 270. Rest. ♦♦ ♪ ☟ 95-170 ; child : 65.
★★★ *Etrier Camarguais*, (Mapotel), lower Launes road, ☎ 90.47.81.14, Tx 403144, AE DC Euro Visa, 31 rm 𝕡 ∭ ◳ ☟ ⅋ half pens, closed 15 Jan-1 Apr, 685. Rest. ♦♦ ☟ 130-180.
★★★ *Mas des Rièges*, rte de Cacharel, ☎ 90.47.85.07, AE Euro, 14 rm 𝕡 ⌇ ∭ ◳ ⚘ ☟ closed 1 Nov-Easter, 235.
★★★ *Mas Sainte-Hélène*, chemin des Launes, ☎ 90.47.83.29, Tx 403222, 15 rm 𝕡 ⌇ ◳ closed 2 Jan-15 Feb, 335.
★★ *Hostellerie du Pont de Gau* (L.F.), rte d'Arles, ☎ 90.47.81.53, AE Visa, 9 rm 𝕡 ☟ closed Wed, 4 Jan-15 Feb, 135. Rest. ♦♦ ⌇ ☟ Spec : *salade de Saint-Jacques tiède à la vinaigrette de truffes, gambas au noilly, cacharel*, 65-150.

Restaurant :
● ♦♦ *Le Brûleur de Loups*, av. Gilbert-Leroy, ☎ 90.97.83.31, AE ⌇ ∭ ♪ closed Tue eve and Wed, 15 Nov-15 Mar. Light cuisine served in a 1930s decor : *salade d'artichauts et crevettes à l'huile de noix, piccata de veau aux coquilles Saint-Jacques*, 100-200 ; child : 60.

𝗔 ★★★*La Brise* (1600 pl), ☎ 90.47.84.67 ; ★★*Le Large* (350 pl), ☎ 90.97.87.26.

Recommended
Farm-gîte : *Mazet du Maréchal Ferrant*, ☎ 90.97.84.60.
Youth hostel : *former schoolhouse of Pioch-Patet*, ☎ 90.97.85.99.

CANNES**

Nice 34, Toulon 128, Paris 909 km
pop 72787 ⊠ 06400   D2

The face of modern Cannes is glamorous and sophisticated, with luxurious hotels in picture-postcard scenery providing the setting for renowned international festivals of film, music, yachting, and other elements of the good life. Old Cannes (named for the reeds, Latin *cannae*, that abound in the region) was a Roman

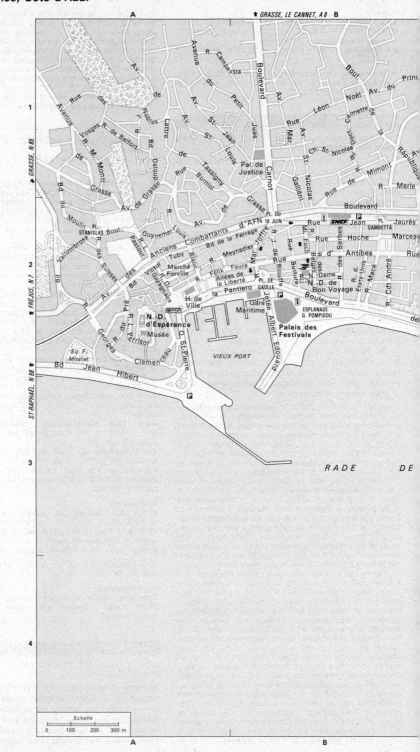

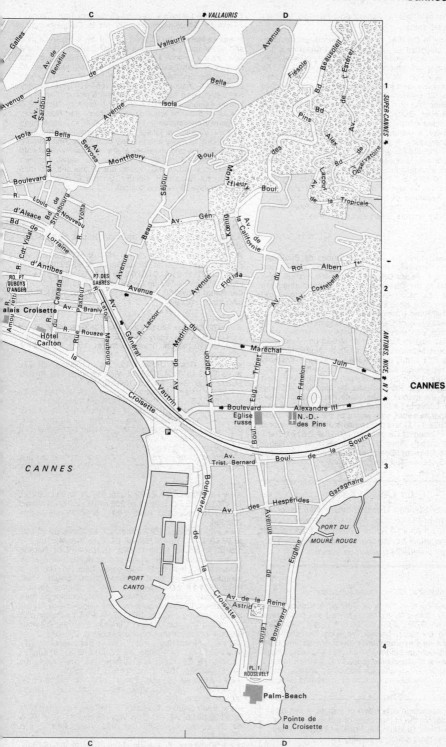

CANNES

CANNES

trading post and later a fishing port strongly fortified against pirate raids.

▶ Everybody in Cannes — whether permanent resident or festival celebrant — heads for the **Croisette★★** (B-C2), the boulevard dividing the beach (partly private) from ranks of hotels, art galleries and exclusive shops. ▶ The **Old Port** (Vieux Port; W, A2) : yachts, fishing boats, flower market, alleyways, and the controversial new ultramodern Festival and Convention Palace. ▶ Farther W, Le Suquet, the **old town** : church of **Notre-Dame-de-l'Espérance** (A2), meridional Gothic with lifelike 15thC statue of St. Anne★; **view★** from the terrace to the left, or from the **Suquet Tower**, a watchtower built against the possibility of Saracen raids. ▶ **Castre Museum★**, in the former château of the abbots of Lérins : superb presentation of Mediterranean archaeology and American, Oriental and African ethnographic collections *(10-12 & 2-5 or 6, Oct.-Jun.; 10-12 & 3-7 in summer; closed Tue. and nat. hols.).* ▶ At the far end of the Blvd. de la Croisette (via D4) is the **headland** of the same name : a cross *(croisette)* used to stand there; **Port Canto**, the **Palm Beach** casino, brilliant flowers, sea views and sunsets.

Nearby

▶ **Le Cannet** *(3 km N)*, linked to Cannes by Boulevard Carnot (B1); the painter Pierre Bonnard (1867-1947) used to stay here. ▶ **Super-Cannes** : along the Avenue Isola Bella (C-D1) to the **Observatory**, with a panorama from the snowy Alps along the Côte d'Azur to Esterel and Italy; in really clear weather, as far as Corsica. ▶ Continue along the **Hill Road** (Chemin des Collines)★ to the **Saint-Antoine Pass** (view of Cannes). ▶ **Mougins★** *(7.5 km N)*, an old village with a renowned restaurant among trees and flowers; next to Autoroute 8, Musée de l'Automobiliste (Motorist Museum; *daily 10-7).* ▶ Notre-Dame de Vie *(2.5 km SE)*, 12thC chapel (site★, view★). ▶ **Vallauris** *(6 km NE)*, an ancient local tradition of pottery was rediscovered in the 1950s by artists such as Édouard Pignon (b. 1905) and Pablo Picasso (who painted the *Man with a Sheep* overlooking the market in the Place Paul-Isnard). A former priory, converted into a château in the 16thC, is now the **municipal museum**, with works by the painter Alberto Magnelli (1888-1971) and prizewinners at the International Biennial Exhibition of Ceramic Art *(10-12 & 2-5; ex Tue.).* The priory chapel, Place de la Libération, is the **National Picasso Museum (Guerre et Paix★**, a 125-m² fresco; *10-12 & 2-5, 2-6 ex Tue. and nat. hols.).*

La Côte d'Azur

The name of Stephen Liégeard means little today. He was a turn-of-the-century poet who wrote a book entitled Côte d'Azur — Azure Coast. *Book and author are long-forgotten, but the title, the world over, instantly conjures up visions of glamorous summer life.*

Tanneron Massif★ *(55-km round trip; 2hr)*

▶ A mimosa-covered hill W of Cannes. ▶ **Cannes** *(Fréjus exit, A1)* : follow N7 to the Logis-de-Paris crossroads, then right on D237, D83 and D37. ▶ **Lake Saint-Cassien.** ▶ To the right, before Tanneron, the **chapel of Notre-Dame de Peygros** (view★ over Grasse and Esterel). ▶ **Auribeau-sur-Siagne★** *(8 km NE)*, charming village. ▶ **Descent★★** to **Mandelieu** (pop. 14 333) which forms a huge seaside resort with **La Napoule;** château de la Napoule : an Orientalized mixture of styles and periods.

For the translation of a name of a meat, a fish or a vegetable, for the composition of a dish or a sauce, see the Menu Guide in the Practical Holiday Guide; it lists the most common culinary terms.

The Iles de Lérins★★ *(regular departures from Cannes; 15 min for Sainte-Marguerite, 30 min for Saint-Honorat).*

▶ **Sainte-Marguerite** *(3.3 km by 950 m)*, a haven of pine and eucalyptus★★ for relaxing after Cannes. The island was once a prison; Fort Royal (1635, remodeled by the ubiquitous 17thC military engineer Vauban) was used to confine the enigmatic "Man in the Iron Mask", who was Louis XIV's prisoner for 16 years (1687-1703); his identity has never been established. Marine Museum : archaeological exhibits *(9:30-12 & 2-6:30 in season, 10:30-12 & 2-4:30 or 5 out of season; closed Mon. and Nov.-Dec.).* ▶ **Saint-Honorat**, only 1.5 km by 400 m; enchanting walk★★ around the island; at the beginning of the 5thC St. Honorat founded a monastery on the site; neo-Romanesque church and museum at the monastery *(9:40-4:40 in summer, 10:40-3:30 in winter).* The earlier fortified monastery★ (6th-15thC), rising out of the sea, still has a beautiful two-storey cloister. On the E point, chapel of La Trinité★ (Byzantine design). □

Practical Information ─────────────

CANNES
ℹ Palais des Congrès, La Croisette (B2), ☎ 93.39.24.53; at the station, ☎ 93.99.19.77.
✈ Nice-Côte d'Azur, 25 km NE, ☎ 93.72.30.30. Air France office, 2, pl. du Gal-de-Gaulle, ☎ 93.39.39.14.
SNCF (B2), ☎ 93.47.01.01/93.99.50.50/93.99.50.51. Ligne des îles de Lérins, ☎ 93.39.11.82.
Car rental : Avis, 69, La Croisette (C2-3), ☎ 93.94.15.86; train station (B2).

Hotels :
★★★★(L) *Carlton*, 58, La Croisette (C2-3), ☎ 93.68.91.68, Tx 470720, AE DC Euro Visa, 355 rm Ⓟ ◈ Magnificent sea view, private beach, nostalgic charm, 1300. Rest. ◆◆◆ 300-450.
★★★★(L) *Grand Hôtel*, 45, La Croisette (B-C2), ☎ 93.38.15.45, Tx 470727, AE Visa, 76 rm Ⓟ ◈ ⊞ Private beach, 1320. Rest. ◆◆ ♪ & 150-230.
★★★★(L) *Gray d'Albion*, 38, rue des Serbes (B2), ☎ 93.68.54.54, Tx 470744, AE DC Euro Visa, 200 rm ◈ ♪ & Private beach, 1250. Rest. ● ◆◆◆ *Gray* & Seekers of the rare and exquisite will be won over by Jacques Chibois. Don't wait to discover this talented protégé of that old wizard, Jean Delaveyne. Chibois's fine kitchen and dining-room staffs are top-notch, as is the knowledgeable sommelier Jean-Pierre Rous : *saumon mariné au gingembre, fricassé de homard aux olives noires, millefeuille de pommes sautées, sauce caramel.* Careful, such feasting isn't cheap, 300-400.
★★★★(L) *Majestic*, 6, La Croisette (B-C2), ☎ 93.68.91.00, Tx 470787, AE DC Euro Visa, 262 rm Ⓟ ◈ ⊞ ⊞ closed 15 Nov-15 Dec, 1380. Rest. ◆◆◆ ♪ & ≈ Private beach, 200-300.
★★★★(L) *Martinez*, (Concorde), 73, La Croisette (C-D3), ☎ 93.68.91.91, Tx 470708, AE DC Euro Visa, 425 rm Ⓟ ♪ & ⊞ ⌐ closed 1 Feb-15 Mar, 15 Nov-18 Dec. Backed by the Concorde hotel chain and energetic manager R. Duvauchelle, this hotel has come back to life as a sumptuous luxury establishment. Private beach, 1100. Rest. ● ◆◆◆ *l'Orangeraie* ♪ & A. Duparc favours a light style of cuisine : *dorade au plat, fondant de foies de volailles.* Excellent desserts. Low-calorie menu. Beach buffet. Cooking lessons, 185-215. ● ◆◆◆ *La Palme d'Or* ◈ ♪ closed Thu and Fri noon. Christian Willer and his team deserve raves for their splendid cooking, 250-400.
★★★★ *Montfleury*, 25, av. Beauséjour (C2), ☎ 93.68.91.50, Tx 470039, AE DC Euro Visa, 181 rm Ⓟ ▦ ◁ ♪ ♣ ⌐ ✗ Set in a 10-acre park overlooking the bay of Cannes, 1000. Rest. ◆◆◆ & 160-250.
★★★ *Athénée*, 6, rue Lecerf (C2), ☎ 93.38.69.54, Tx 470978, AE DC Visa, 15 rm Ⓟ ◁ ♪ closed 30 Nov-25 Jan, 450.
★★★ *Beau Séjour*, (Mapotel), 5, rue des Fauvettes (A2), ☎ 93.39.63.00, AE DC Euro Visa, 46 rm Ⓟ ◈ ▦ ♪ ♣ & ✗ ⊞ closed 2 Nov-15 Dec, 450. Rest. ◆◆◆ ◈ ♪ & 80-120.
★★★ *Embassy*, 6, rue de Bône (C2), ☎ 93.38.79.02,

Tx 470081, AE DC Euro Visa, 60 rm Ⓟ ▥ ◁ ♪ 495.
Rest. ◆◆ ♪ 90-130; child : 100.
★★★ **Paris**, 34, bd d'Alsace (B-C2), ☎ 93.33.30.89,
Tx 470995, DC Euro Visa, 50 rm Ⓟ ▥ ◁ ♪ 🐎 ⊗ ▨
closed 1 Dec-25 Jan, 440.
★★ **Cheval Blanc**, 3, rue Guy-de-Maupassant (A1),
☎ 93.39.88.60, 16 rm ◁ ᕕ closed 31 Oct-30 Nov, 200.
★★ **Modern**, 11, rue des Serbes (B2), ☎ 93.39.09.87,
19 rm Ⓟ ≼ closed 1 Nov-22 Dec, 320.
★★ **Roches Fleuries**, 92, rue G.-Clemenceau (A2),
☎ 93.39.28.78, AE DC Euro Visa, 24 rm Ⓟ ≼ ▥ ◁ ⊗
closed 15 Nov-27 Dec, 175.

Restaurants :
◆◆◆ **Croquant**, 18, bd Jean-Hibert (A2-3), ☎ 93.39.39.79,
AE DC Euro Visa ≼ ♪ closed Mon. Excellent kitchen, quality ingredients. Spec : *fricassée d'escargots aux cèpes,
cuissous de canards en petits confits*, 80-200.
◆◆◆ **Le Rescator**, 7, rue du Mal-Joffre (B2),
☎ 93.39.44.57 ≼ ◁ ♪ closed Mon (l.s.). Light, inventive
cooking with a focus on fresh fish : *salade tiède de rougets, filet de loup, sabayon à l'orange*, 140-280.
● ◆◆ **La Coquille**, 65, rue F.-Faure (A2), ☎ 93.39.26.33
▥ closed 21 Nov-13 Dec. A tiny terrace, where the owner
and his staff extend a friendly welcome. Fresh fish, excellent *bouillabaisse* and *bourride*, 70-170.
● ◆◆ **Les Santons de Provence**, 6, rue du Mal-Joffre (B2), ☎ 93.39.40.91, Euro Visa ◁ ᕕ closed Mon,
18 Nov-22 Dec. The former Reine Pédauque now serves
fragrant southern fare, 115-190.
● ◆◆ **Pompon Rouge**, 4, rue E.-Négrin (A1), closed Mon
and Sun, Nov. No telephone here (terribly chic), so there
is always a bit of a crush and a wait for a table at this
fine restaurant where modish gourmets gather : *foie gras
G. Vié*, delicious daily specials, 170-250.
◆◆ **Au Mal Assis**, 15, quai St-Pierre (A2), ☎ 93.39.13.38,
Euro Visa ◁ ᕕ closed Mon Jan-Mar, 10 Oct-20 Dec. Right
on the port, facing the yachts. Comfortable seats and
fresh fish, 75-180.
◆◆ **Brouette de Grand-Mère**, 9, rue d'Oran (A1),
☎ 93.39.12.10 Ⓟ ≼ closed Sun and lunch, 1-15 Jul,
1 Nov-15 Dec. A nostalgic bistro offering a single fixed
menu and all the wine you can drink, 175.
◆◆ **Caveau "30"**, 45, rue F.-Faure (A-B2), ☎ 93.39.06.33,
AE DC Euro Visa ≼ ♪ A comfortable eatery with a decent
fixed menu and local wines, 85-210.
◆◆ **Embuscade**, 10, rue St-Antoine, Le Suquet (A2),
☎ 93.39.29.00, AE Euro Visa ♪ closed Mon,
15 Nov-27 Dec. Varied set-price meals. Spec : fish
soup, 120-200.
◆◆ **Le Ragtime**, 1, La Croisette (B2), ☎ 93.68.47.10,
Tx 970746, AE DC Euro Visa Ⓟ ▥ ♪ ᕕ closed Sun
(l.s.). American-style piano-bar with a 1920s feel. Open till
2:30am, 105-250.
◆◆ **Mirabelle**, 24, rue St-Antoine (A1), ☎ 93.38.72.75 ♪
closed Tue, 1-26 Dec, 15 Feb-15 Mar. Charming establishment serves sophisticated, light fare and sumptuous
desserts, 250-300.
◆◆ **Plage Ondine**, 15, bd de la Croisette (B-C2),
☎ 93.94.23.15, Visa ≼ closed 3 Nov-20 Dec. Mostly men.
Private beach, 200.
◆◆ **Poêle d'Or**, 23, rue des États-Unis (B2),
☎ 93.39.77.65, AE DC Euro Visa ♪ closed Mon and Tue
noon , Nov. Worth a visit, 130-220.
◆ **Bec Fin**, 12, rue du 24-Août (B2), ☎ 93.38.35.86, AE
DC Visa ♪ ᕕ closed Sat eve and Sun, 25 Dec-24 Jan.
Spec : *daurade grillée au fenouil et petite friture*; deli-
cious, 60-100.
◆ **L'Etagère**, 22, rue Victor-Cousin (B2), ☎ 93.38.27.17,
AE DC Euro Visa ≼ ▥ ♪ ᕕ closed Mon noon and Sun.
Rest.-wine bar. Spec : *queue de bœuf à l'estragon*, 130.
◆ **La Cigale**, 1, rue Florian (B2), ☎ 93.39.65.79, AE DC
Euro Visa ♪ closed Wed , Nov. For the regulars, modest,
tasty, inexpensive food, 70-190.

Recommended
Bicycle rental : *Cycles Remy*, 22, av. des Hespérides and
at the station, ☎ 93.43.44.66 ; 5, rue Alleis, ☎ 93.39.46.15,
all sorts of 2-wheel vehicles for rent.
Casino : *Municipal*, jetée A.-Edouard, ☎ 93.38.12.11 ;

Palm Beach, La Croisette, ☎ 93.43.91.12 ; *Les Fleurs*, 5,
rue des Belges, ☎ 93.68.00.33.
Events : *pleasure boat festival*; *vintage car festival*, in
Sep ; *international theater festival*, in Dec ; *international
folk festival*, in Jul.
Nightclubs : *Galaxy*, Terrasse du Palais des Festivals.
Son et lumière : ☎ 93.39.24.53, Jul, on the islands.
♥ antiques : *M. Jacques Vic*, av. des États-Unis ; bakery :
Martinez, rue Meynadier ; cheese : *Robert Ceneri*, *la
Ferme savoyarde*, 22, rue Meynadier ; chocolates, glazed
fruit : *Maifret*, 31, rue d'Antibes, ☎ 93.39.08.29 ; pastry :
Rohr, 63, rue d'Antibes.

Nearby

MANDELIEU-LA-NAPOULE, ⊠ 06210, 7 km W.
🚹 av. de Cannes, ☎ 93.49.14.39.
𝕊𝕟𝕔𝕗 ☎ 93.49.95.13.

Hotels :
★★★★ **Ermitage du Riou**, (Mapotel), bd H.-Clews,
☎ 93.49.95.56, Tx 470072, AE DC Euro Visa, 42 rm Ⓟ ≼
▥ ◁ ᕕ ▨ Fine Provençal residence across from the
port, 660. Rest. ◆◆ ≼ ᕕ closed 3 Nov-20 Dec, 160-295.
★★ **Sant'Angelo**, 681, av. de la Mer, ☎ 93.49.28.23, 33 rm
Ⓟ ≼ ▥ ◁ ▨ ♪⊗ 245.

Restaurants :
◆◆ **Brocherie II**, at the port, ☎ 93.49.80.73, Visa Ⓟ ≼
closed Mon eve and Tue (l.s.), 3 Jan-3 Feb. A single
fixed-price menu : seafood platter, fish. Excellent value,
150-200.
◆◆ **Lou Castéou**, pl. du Château, ☎ 93.49.95.15, AE
DC Euro Visa ◁ ♪ ᕕ closed Mon eve and Tue,
1 Nov-15 Dec, 70-250.

⚓ ★★★★*L'Argentière* (100 pl), ☎ 93.49.95.04 ; ★★★*Cerisiers* (160 pl), ☎ 93.47.22.25 ; ★★★*Plateau des Chasses* (150 pl), ☎ 93.49.25.93 ; ★★★*Roc Fleuri* (150 pl),
☎ 93.93.08.71.

MOUGINS, ⊠ 06250, 6 km N.

Hotels :
● ★★★★(L) **Moulin de Mougins** (Roger Vergé), quartier Notre-Dame-de-Vie, 2.5 km on D 3, ☎ 93.75.78.24,
Tx 970732, AE DC Visa, 5 rm Ⓟ ◁ ▨ closed
8 Feb-25 Mar, 10 Nov-23 Dec, 1000. Rest. ● ◆◆◆◆ ♪
closed Thu noon , Mon ex Jul-Aug. The Riviera wouldn't
be the same without Mougins. Roger et Denise
Vergé have turned this lovely 16thC mill into a world-
renowned gourmet mecca. The kitchen is capably managed by Serge Chollet, a member of our chefs' panel. The
dishes and menu vary with the seasons, but the food
always has a sunny Provençal lilt : *artichauts Barigoule,
rougets au pistou*, desserts, great wines, boutique...plus
sunshine and cicadas, 440-600.
● ★★★ **Clos des Boyères**, 89, chem. de la Chapelle,
☎ 93.90.01.58, Tx 462462, AE DC Euro Visa, 35 rm Ⓟ ≼
▥ ◁ ♪ ▨ ♪⊗ closed Nov-Jan, 470. Rest. ◆◆ ≼ ♪ closed
Tue, 175.
★★★ **Mas Candille**, bd Rebuffel, ☎ 93.90.00.85,
Tx 462131, AE DC Visa, 23 rm Ⓟ ≼ ▥ ◁ ▨ closed
18 Nov-18 Dec, 7-21 Jan. Pretty terrace gardens, 550.
Rest. ● ◆◆◆ ≼ ◁ ᕕ closed Tue noon and Wed noon,
Tue eve (l.s.). An old Provençal farmhouse with antique
furnishings. C.Taffarello, formerly of the *Moulin de Mougins* mans the kitchen : *courgette fleur, fricassée de lotte
aux pâtes fraîches*, 240-300 ; child : 120.

Restaurants :
● ◆◆◆ **Le Relais à Mougins** (R. C.), pl. de la Mairie,
☎ 93.90.03.47, Tx 462559, Visa, closed Mon and Tue
noon ex Jul-Aug, 15 Nov-15 Mar. Sophisticated food prepared by the staff of André Surmain : fish (salmon, turbot,
monkfish) ; *volaille poêlée au foie gras*, 205-400.
◆◆◆ **Amandier de Mougins**, pl. du Cdt-Lamy,
☎ 93.90.00.91, Tx 970732, AE DC Visa Ⓟ ♪ closed
Wed and Sat noon. Same management as the *Moulin*
next door. Excellent food inspired by R. Vergé. Extraordinary wine list. "Roger Vergé" cooking school, 280-350.
● ◆◆ **Ferme de Mougins**, 10, av. St-Basile,
☎ 93.90.03.74, Tx 970643, AE DC Euro Visa Ⓟ ≼ ▥ ♪

closed Mon and Thu noon, 15 Feb-15 Mar, 15 Nov-15 Dec.
In winter, Henri Sauvenet manages *La Bergerie* in Courchevel. Summer finds him in the fields with flowers and
cicadas. Patrick-Henri Roux features fish and fresh local
produce, 190-350.
● ♦♦ *France*, pl. du village, ☎ 93.90.00.01. Always at
work, often in the kitchen, such is the program of irrepressible Claude Verger (Roger is the other one), who at age
70 has taken to cooking once more : *filet de carpe Bernard Loiseau*, 'menu-carte', 150.
● ♦♦ *Bistrot de Mougins*, pl. du Village, ☎ 93.75.78.34,
Euro Visa, closed Tue and Wed ex Jul-Aug, 1 Dec-20 Jan.
Inexpensive, savoury food and smiling service in this
authentic little bistro. Simple and generous regional fare :
timbale de morue aux épinards, tripes au basilic, 120.
♦♦ *Feu Follet*, pl. du Cdt-Lamy, ☎ 93.90.15.78 ▥ ▨
closed Mon, Sun eve (l.s.), 2-16 Mar, 3-23 Nov, 75-120.

⋀ ★★★*Les Lentisques* (133 pl) ☎ 93.90.00.45.

Le CAP FERRAT*

D2
Round trip *(10 km, 3hr)*.
▸ The Cap Ferrat road leaves the coastal *corniche*
(→ Riviera) at Pont St Jean, 8.5 km NE of Nice. ▸ **Villa-
Museum Île-de-France★**, at the narrowest part of the
peninsula, bequeathed to the Fine Arts Academy in 1934
by Baroness Ephrussi de Rothschild, in magnificent gardens laid out in French, Spanish, Florentine, English and
Japanese styles *(4-6, 3-7 in summer; closed Mon. and
Nov)*. Collections typical of a turn-of-the-century patron of
the arts : furniture, Flemish tapestries ; paintings by Coypel, Fragonard, Hubert Robert ; exceptional French porce-
lains★ (Vincennes, Sèvres, Saxe). ▸ **Saint-Jean-Cap-Ferrat**, a former fishing village, near Nice and Monte-Carlo ;
painting by Jean Cocteau (1889-1973) in the Registry
Office ; **Maurice-Rouvier promenade★** along the shore
to Beaulieu ; **tourist trail★** from the Pointe Saint-Hospice
(45 min). ▸ Complete the tour of the Cap with a visit to the
zoo in the tropical gardens *(9:30-6 ; 9-7 in summer)*, and
the **lighthouse** (view). ☐

Practical Information ─────────────
SAINT-JEAN-CAP-FERRAT, ✉ 06230, 10 km E of **Nice**.
ⓘ 59, av. Denis-Semeria, ☎ 93.01.36.86.

Hotels :
● ★★★★(L) *Grand Hôtel du Cap Ferrat*, bd du Gal-de-
Gaulle, ☎ 93.01.04.54, 66 rm ℗ ≼ ▥ ▨ ▣ ⤴ closed
29 Sep-10 Apr. In a 20-acre park, 2000. Rest. ● ♦♦♦
☜ Dreamy meals poolside or on the terrace. Food full of
character from J.L.Guillon. Buffet for 140 F. Spec : *blanc
de loup au beurre de gingembre*, 230-450.
★★★★(L) *La Voile d'Or*, av. Jean-Mermoz, ☎ 93.01.13.13,
Tx 470317, 50 rm ℗ ≼ ▥ ▨ half pens (h.s.), closed
1 Nov-1 Mar, 2600. Rest. ♦♦♦♦ ≼ ♪ ⌂ A fine table offering
light fare and classic dishes. Spec : *millefeuille de saumon
frais au beurre de cerfeuil, royale de loup St-Jeannoise,
mostèle*, 330-600.
● ★★ *Clair Logis*, allée des Brises, ☎ 93.01.31.01, 16 rm
℗ ▥ ▨ closed 15 Nov-20 Dec, 240.
★★ *Brise Marine*, 58, av. Jean-Mermoz, ☎ 93.76.04.36,
15 rm ≼ ▥ ▨ half pens (h.s.), closed 31 Oct-1 Feb, 566.

Restaurants :
● ♦♦ *Les Hirondelles*, 36, av. J.-Mermoz,
☎ 93.76.04.04, Visa ≼ ⌂ closed Mon and Sun,
30 Oct-1 Mar. All the flavours of Provence at your table
(bouillabaisse, red mulet) compliments of Mme Ventio-
rino, 155-300.
● ♦♦ *L'Abricot*, 7, av. Claude-Vignon, ☎ 93.01.15.53, AE
DC Euro Visa, closed Mon noon and Tue noon , Mon eve
(l.s.), 21 Dec-21 Feb. International specialties : chili con
carne, mimosa, broiled baby chicken, 90-200.
♦♦ *Le Petit Trianon*, 1, bd Gal-de-Gaulle, ☎ 93.01.31.68,
AE DC Euro Visa ≼ ▥ ♪ ☜ closed Wed eve and Thu,
15 Oct-1 Feb. Traditional and regional fare : *mousseline
de rascasse, langouste soufflée à la provençale*, 180-250.
♦♦ *Le Sloop*, Nouveau-port-St-Jean, ☎ 93.01.48.63, AE

DC Visa ≼ ▥ closed Wed and Sun eve (l.s.). Alain and
Régine Therlicoq serve tasty food on their pretty terrace
with a pocket-size garden. Spec : *bouillabaisse de volailles*, Provençal wines, 125-200.
♦♦ *Provençal*, 2, av. Denis-Semeria, ☎ 93.01.30.04, AE
DC Euro Visa ≼ ▥ ♪ ⌂ closed Tue, 5 Nov-28 Dec. Tasty
fish specialties, 160-290.

CARPENTRAS*

Avignon 24, Aix-en-Provence 89, Paris 685 km
pop 25886 ✉ 84200   A2

The former capital of the Papal State *(Comtat)* of
Venaissin remained the property of the popes until
1791 (the Revolution). Numerous monuments ; colourful Friday market ; a caramel candy, called *berlingot*,
is made in the town.

▸ **Hospital** (Hôtel-Dieu ; B2), 18thC building, with a beautiful pharmacy★ decorated with blue and white ceramics
(9-11:30, Mon., Wed., Thu.). ▸ **Cathedral of St. Siffrein**
(B2), late Gothic (1405-1519) ; on the S doorway★ (Flamboyant Gothic), a sculpture known as the *boulo di gari*
(rats gnawing a round object), the meaning of which is
unknown. Fine marble in the chapels★ ; note the stained
glass in the choir (left, primitive 15thC painting★ ; 17thC
organ loft) ; in the treasury, 11thC Limoges enamel cro-
sier. ▸ **Courthouse** (B2, 1640) : façade is a reduced
copy of the façade of the Farnese palace in Rome ; 17thC
interior★. ▸ Festivals are held at the **Place d'Inguimbert**,
where a Roman **triumphal arch** (1stC AD) can be seen.
▸ **Synagogue** (B2), the oldest in France (15thC, rebuilt
18th and 20thC) ; wood paneling, liturgical objects. ▸ **Rue
des Halles★**, an attractive street with covered arcades
(B2). ▸ **Porte** (Gateway) **d'Orange** (B1), sole remnant
of the fortifications built in the latter 14thC. ▸ **Duplessis
Museum** (B2) in an 18thC mansion (paintings) ; same building, **Comtadin Regional Museum** : regional mementos
and artifacts, including bells from herds and flocks that
used to be driven through the town to seasonal pastures
(10-12 & 2-6, 4 in winter ; closed Wed.); and the **Inguimbertine Library** : autograph scores of Johann Sebastian
Bach, Robert Schumann and Johannes Brahms *(9:30-12
& 2:30-7 ex Sat. pm, Sun., and Mon. am)*.
Also... ▸ **Sobirats Museum** (B2) : decorative arts *(hours
as for Duplessis Museum)*. ▸ **Archaeological Museum**
(Musée lapidaire ; B2) : artifacts from the Iron Age to
the Middle Ages *(enq : Inguimbertine Library)*. ▸ **Poetry
Museum** in the Ombrages park *(tel. 90.63.19.49)*.

Nearby

▸ Today the **Comtat Venaissin**, once under Papal authority, is a vast garden, where banks of tall rushes mark out
the irrigation system. Grapes, apples, strawberries, tomatoes and melons ripen in the sun in the shelter of cypresses. ▸ **Château de Tourreau** *(10 km NW)*, 18thC folly ;
interesting *ex-votos* in the chapel. ▸ **Pernes-les-Fontaines**, named for the 33 fountains that ornament its streets
and squares ; Ferrande tower (13thC, murals★) ; 12thC
church of Notre-Dame ; Notre-Dame Gate★ (1548).
▸ **Venasque** *(11 km SE)*, on a spur★ overlooking the
Comtat ; Romanesque church of Notre-Dame with a primitive Crucifixion★ (1498, school of Avignon). Nearby,
the baptistery★ in fact is a little cruciform 11thC church ;
the apparent baptismal font was an imaginative invention
by the 19thC restorers and is at the bottom of the village, Notre-
Dame-de-Vie spiritual centre (17thC chapel) ; Merovingian tombstone.

Practical Information ─────────────
CARPENTRAS
ⓘ 170, allée Jean-Jaurès (B2), ☎ 90.63.00.78.
▦ (B3), ☎ 90.63.02.60.

Hotels :
★★★ *Univers*, pl. A.-Briand (B3), ☎ 90.63.00.05, 25 rm ℗
200. .

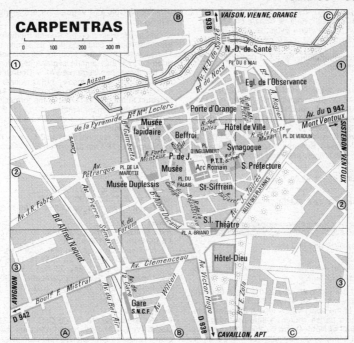

CARPENTRAS

0   100   200   300 m

VAISON, VIENNE, ORANGE

N.-D.-de-Santé

PL. DU 8 MAI

Egl. de l'Observance

Porte d'Orange

Av. du D 942

Mont Ventoux

Musée lapidaire

Beffroi   Hôtel de Ville

PL. DE VERDUN

Synagogue

P. de J.

P.T.T.

Musée   Arc Romain   S. Préfecture

Musée Duplessis   St-Siffrein

S.I.

Théâtre

PL. A.-BRIAND

Hôtel-Dieu

Gare
S.N.C.F.

CAVAILLON, APT

★★ **Fiacre**, 153, rue Vigne (C2), ☎ 90.63.03.15, 19 rm ℗ ▩ ⌕ In an 18thC town house, 160.

Restaurants :
♦ **La Rapière du Comtat**, 47, bd du Nord (B1), ☎ 90.67.20.03, Euro Visa ℗ ⌕ ♪ ♿ closed Mon eve and Sun eve, 20 Dec-31 Jan, 55-110.
♦ **Le Vert Galant**, 12, rue de Clapies (C3), ☎ 90.67.15.50 ℗ ♪ ♿ closed Thu, 1-15 Jul, 24-31 Dec, 60-150.

⚖ ★★**Villemarie** (70 pl), ☎ 90.63.09.55.

Recommended
Guided tours : *C.N.M.H.S.* (Jul-Aug, Tue and Thu), info. S.I.

Nearby

MONTEUX, ⊠ 84170, 4 km SW on the D 942.

Hotel :
★★★ **La Genestière**, rte de Carpentras, ☎ 90.62.27.04, Tx 432770, AE DC Euro Visa, 20 rm ℗ ▩ ⌕ ♪ 🖂 ⌁ half pens (h.s.), 550. Rest. ♦♦ ♪ ♿ 85-180.

Restaurant :
● ♦♦ **Le Saule Pleureur**, Beauregard, 5 km on the rte d'Avignon, ☎ 90.61.01.35, AE Visa ℗ ▩ ⌕ ♪ closed Tue eve and Wed, 1-15 Mar, 15-30 Nov. Michel belongs to the "Sunshine" chain, an apt way to qualify his good seasonal cooking : *pissaladière de loup au beurre de thym, rognons de veau au miel de lavande*, 100-200.

VENASQUE, ⊠ 84210, 11 km SE.

Hotel :
★★ **La Garrigue** (L.F.), rte de Murs, ☎ 94.66.03.40, 10 rm ℗ ▩ ⌕ ♿ closed Wed, 20 Oct-20 Mar, 210.

> In preparing for your trip, consult the pages pertaining to the regions. You will find there the description of the region you wish to visit, as well as a list of sites that must be seen, a brief history and practical information.

CASSIS*

Marseille 23, Toulon 44, Paris 803 km
pop 6318 ⊠ 13260   B3

Pleasure craft outnumber fishing vessels in this port flanked by the Gardiole heights to the W and the Cap Canaille cliffs to the E. The white wine of Cassis is pleasant.

▶ **Archaeological museum** in the mayoral offices *(3-5 Wed., plus Fri. in season).* ▶ La Grande-Mer Beach : the **Promenade des Lombards** gives a good view of the bay. ▶ The main attractions of Cassis are the **Calanques** (inlets) at **Port Miou, Port Pin★** and **En-Vau★★** *(access by boat, 45 min, leave from St. Pierre quay, or on foot, 1hr20 to En-Vau by marked trails)*; a third route by the **Gardiole Pass** *(6 km NW on D559, then narrow road for 3 km; 1hr on foot to En-Vau inlet).* ▶ **Corniche des Crêtes** (Crests Road)★★, tourist road between Cassis and La Ciotat *(19 km SE)* along D41A, following the limestone chain of La Canaille, which falls sheer into the sea (cliffs 400 m high in places). Panoramas from Mont de la Saoupe★★, Cap Canaille★★ and the semaphore★★.   □

Practical Information

ⓘ pl. Baragnon, ☎ 42.01.71.17.
SNCF ☎ 42.01.01.18.

Hotels :
★★★ **Les Jardins du Campanile**, rue Auguste-Favier, ☎ 42.01.84.85, Tx 441390, AE DC Visa, 30 rm ℗ ▩ ⌕ ♿ ▩ 🖂 ♿ closed Nov-Mar, 395. Rest. ♦ ♪ ♿ ▩ 100-180.
★★★ **Les Roches Blanches**, rte des Calanques, ☎ 42.01.09.30, Tx 441287, AE DC Visa, 36 rm ℗ ⌕ ♿ ♿ closed 30 Nov-1 Feb. Large Provençal house overhanging the sea, 320. Rest. ♦ ⌕ ♿ ▩ closed Sat, 150-190.
★★★ **Plage Bestouan**, Plage du Bestouan, ☎ 42.01.05.70, Tx 441287, AE, 29 rm ⌕ ▩ half pens (h.s.), closed 15 Oct-28 May, 250. Rest. ♦♦ ⌕ ♪ 120-150.
★★★ **Rade**, 1, av. des Dardanelles, ☎ 42.01.02.97,

Tx 441287, AE DC Euro Visa, 27 rm ℗ ⊀ ⅏ ⌕ ♪ ▣ closed 15 Nov-1 Mar, 220. Rest. ♦ *Suach*, 80-130.
★★ *Grand Jardin*, 2, rue Pierre-Eydin, ☎ 42.01.70.10, AE DC Euro Visa, 26 rm ℗ ⊀ ⅏ ⌕ ❀ closed 2 Jan-15 Feb, 180.
★★ *Le Golfe*, quai Barthélemy, ☎ 42.01.00.21, 30 rm ℗ ⊀ ⌕ ❀ closed Nov-Mar, 200.

Restaurants :
● ♦♦ *Presqu'île*, quartier Port-Miou, rte des Calanques, ☎ 42.01.03.77, AE DC Euro Visa ℗ ⊀ ⅏ ⌕ ♿ closed Mon and Sun eve ex Jul-Aug, 2 Jan-6 Mar. Tennis. A gourmet's dream, set between sea and sky : raw sea bass, red mullet, stuffed sea bass, 160-220.
♦♦ *Chez Gilbert*, 19, quai des Baux, ☎ 42.01.71.36, AE DC Euro Visa ⊀ closed Sun eve , Tue (l.s.), Tue lunch (h.s.), 30 Nov-15 Feb. Nicely prepared fish, *bouillabaisse*, 150-230.

⚖ ★★*Cigales* (300 pl), ☎ 42.01.71.17.

Recommended
Casino : av. Lerich, ☎ 42.01.78.32.

CASTELLANE*

Digne 54, Grasse 63, Paris 800 km
pop 1460 ⊠ 04120   C2
A typical Provençal town in the shadow of a limestone outcrop 184 m high.

▶ The streets of the old town wind to the Lions Fountain and the 12thC **church of St. Victor**. By the Rue St-Victor, one arrives at the belfry which tops a medieval gate. Behind the modern parish church, a sign-posted path★ leads to the **chapel of Notre-Dame du Roc** having skirted the remains of a 14thC keep dominated by a fine pentagonal tower (ruins of feudal town, view★ over the Napoléon bridge and the Grand Canyon of Verdon).

Nearby

▶ **Senez** *(19 km NW)*, reached by the Route Napoléon (→), which crosses the **Lèques Pass** (alt. 1 146 m, view★) and the spectacular **Clue de Taulanne★** ; Flemish and Aubusson tapestries★ in the former cathedral (Provençal Romanesque, early 13thC).

Round the lakes★★ *(25 km, 1hr)*

▶ N on D955. ▶ At the **Blache Pass**, a little road to Blaron *(D402 on the left)* gives a magnificent view★ over Lake Castillon. ▶ **Castillon Dam** forms a 1 200-acre lake on the Verdon. ▶ Along the Demandolx road (views★★), then D102 *(tricky in places)* to the **Chaudanne Dam**, an electricity generating station.   ▢

Practical Information ─────────────
ℹ rue Nationale, ☎ 92.83.61.14.

Hotels :
★★★ *Commerce*, pl. de l'Église, ☎ 92.83.61.00, AE Euro Visa, 46 rm ℗ ⅏ half pens (h.s.), closed 5 Nov-15 Dec, 230. Rest. ♦ ♪ ❀ 60-100.
★★ *Ma Petite Auberge*, 8, bd de la République, ☎ 92.83.62.06, AE Euro Visa, 18 rm ℗ ⊀ ⌕ closed 15 Oct-15 Mar, 120. Rest. ♦ ♪ closed Wed noon, 55-160.

⚖ ★★★★*International* (80 pl), ☎ 92.83.66.67 ; ★★★★*le Verdon* (421 pl), ☎ 92.83.61.29 ; ★★★*6 sites* (600 pl).

CAVAILLON

Avignon 27, Arles 44, Paris 705 km
pop 20830 ⊠ 84300   A2
Cavaillon is renowned for the quality of the melons grown here. However, the real economic importance of this sleepy-looking town is best understood at the sight of the traffic jam around the gates of the M. I. N. *(Marché d'Intérêt National)* market, where thousands of tons of fruit and vegetables are shipped throughout France.

▶ Ornate decoration on the **Roman triumphal arch** (Place François-Tourel) contrasts with its simple basic form. A 15-min walk from the arch to the **chapel of St. Jacques** (12th-17thC) among cypress and almond trees on the hill above the village (view★). ▶ **Church of St. Véran** : late-12thC five-sided apse★, 14thC cloister★ ; exuberant 17thC decoration in the chapel. ▶ **Archaeological Museum** in the chapel (1755) of the former hospital : prehistory, Gallo-Roman remains *(10-12 & 2-6 in season, 10-12 & 3-5 out of season ; closed Tue).* ▶ **Comtadin Jewish Museum** in the former bakery of the **synagogue★**, 18thC regional art *(10-12 & 2-6 ex Tue.).* ▶ **Regalon Gorges★** *(13.5 km SE, 1hr on foot, inaccessible in wet weather).*   ▢

Practical Information ─────────────
ℹ rue Saunerie, ☎ 90.71.32.01.
SNCF ☎ 90.71.23.98/93.71.04.40.
Car rental : *Avis*, 110, bd Crillon, ☎ 90.71.59.46.

Hotels :
★★★ *Christel*, on the Durance, ☎ 90.71.07.79, Tx 431547, AE DC Euro Visa, 109 rm ℗ ⊀ ⅏ ⌕ ♪ ♿ ▣ ☞ 240. Rest. ♦ ⊀ ♪ ♿ closed Sat noon and Sun noon (l.s.), 95-160.
★★ *Parc*, pl. du Clos, ☎ 90.71.57.78, Euro Visa, 23 rm ℗ ⊀ ⅏ ⌕ closed 25-31 May, 27 Aug-2 Sep, 175.
★★ *Toppin* (L.F.), 70, cours Gambetta, ☎ 90.71.30.42, AE DC Euro Visa, 32 rm ℗ ⅏ 210. Rest. ♦ ♪ 70-150 ; child : 35.

Restaurants :
♦♦ *Fin de Siècle*, 46, pl. du Clos, ☎ 90.71.12.27, DC ♪ closed Wed, 1-21 Sep. Spec : *foie gras, salade de courgettes crues au saumon, feuilleté d'écrevisses*, 90-230.
● ♦ *Nicolet*, 15, pl. Gambetta, ☎ 90.78.01.56, AE DC Euro Visa ℗ ⊀ ♪ ❀ closed Mon and Sun, 10-25 Feb, 1-14 Jul. Everything here is homemade : bread, pastries, *sorbets*, seafood assortment, *noisette d'agneau au caviar d'aubergines*, 120-220.
♦ *Prévôt* (ex *Assiette au Beurre*), 353 av. de Verdun, ☎ 90.71.32.43 ♪ ♿ closed Mon and Sun eve, 9 Jun-1 Jul. Spec : *escalope de foie gras chaud*, 100-215 ; child : 60.

⚖ ★★★*Hippodrome* (150 pl), ☎ 90.71.11.78.

La CIOTAT

Marseille 32, Toulon 37, Paris 806 km
pop 31727 ⊠ 13600   B3
Giant cranes, blue sparks from the arc-welders and the clang of metal-beating are forcible reminders that the town is a naval shipyard in 11 months of the year. To the N, palm trees and villas around the resort area at a beach that holds records for sunshine.

▶ Naval and crafts museum *(Jun.-Sep., 4-7 ; closed Tue., Thu. and Sun.).* ▶ **Church of Notre-Dame-de-l'Assomption**, above the quay : Descent from the Cross (1615). ▶ Excursions to **Ile-Verte** *(30 min by boat from the old port)*, to the **Figuerolles Inlet★** *(1.5 km SW)*, and to the chapel of **Notre-Dame-de-la-Garde** *(2.5 km SW)* : view★ over the bay. ▶ **Les Lesques** *(8 km E)*, family resort ; Tauroentum Museum on the foundations of a Roman villa of the 1stC AD.   ▢

Practical Information ─────────────
ℹ 2, quai Ganteaume, ☎ 42.08.61.32.
SNCF ☎ 42.83.08.63.

Hotels :
★★★ *Ciotel*, corniche du Liouquet, 6 km NE, ☎ 42.83.90.30, Tx 441390, AE DC Visa, 43 rm ℗ ⊀ ⅏ ⌕ ♪ ♿ ❀ ▣ ☞ ♪ closed 15 Nov-1 Mar, 500. Rest. ♦♦ ♿ ❀ closed Mon noon and Sun eve, 145-180 ; child : 50.
★★ *La Rotonde*, 44, bd de la République, ☎ 42.08.67.50, Visa, 32 rm ℗ ❀ 155.

⚠ ★★★*Saint-Jean* (90 pl), ☎ 42.83.13.01; ★★*Castel Joli* (100 pl), ☎ 42.83.50.02; ★★*Sauge* (230 pl), ☎ 42.83.47.65; at Liouquet, ★★*Oliviers* (533 pl), ☎ 42.83.15.04.

COLMARS-LES-ALPES*

Barcelonnette 44, Digne 71, Paris 816 km
pop 314 ⊠ 04370   C1

Forts and ramparts, towers, and walls pierced with loopholes in a mountain setting (alt. 1295 m). **Fort de Savoie★** *(uphill)* and Fort de France *(downhill)* used to guard the town from surprise attack. Today the village represents a style that has hardly changed since the 17thC.

Nearby

▶ Colmars is a good base for exploring the valley of the Verdon (200 km of marked trails; *maps available at SI*), N towards **Allos**, and S to **Lake Castillon** (→ Castellane); near **Beauvezer** *(5.5 km SW)*, hike in the **St. Pierre Gorges★** *(D252 SE then 2hr on foot)*. ▶ From Colmars, a mountain road (D2) SE via the **Champs Pass★** (alt. 2 095 m), **Saint-Martin-d'Entraunes**, to the **Daluis Gorges★★** (→).   □

Practical Information

COLMARS-LES-ALPES
ℹ Hôtel des Postes, ☎ 92.83.41.92.

Hotel :
★★ *Chambois*, ☎ 92.83.43.29, 26 rm Ⓟ ⫶ ₩ ⅋ closed Easter-20 May, 10 Oct-25 Dec, 200. Rest. ♦ ⅋ 90-120.

Nearby

ALLOS, ⊠ 04260, 8 km N.

Hotel :
★ *Altitude 1500*, Le Seignus, 2 km W on D26, ☎ 92.83.01.07, 16 rm Ⓟ ⫶ ₩ ⅋ closed May, Sep-15 Dec, 145. Rest. ♦ ও Reserve, 80-180.

BEAUVEZER, ⊠ 04440, 6 km S.

Hotel :
★★ *Verdon* (L.F.), ☎ 92.83.44.44, 26 rm Ⓟ ⫶ ₩ ⅋ half pens (h.s.), closed 17-26 May, 1 Nov-24 Dec, 130. Rest. ♦ ⅋ 55-140.

DALUIS Gorges**

                                                       C-D1
Round trip from Puget-Théniers *(83 km, half-day)*

Above a white-pebbled river the road crosses red and green ravines and canyons and dives through tunnels to provide astounding views of a unique landscape.

▶ **Puget-Théniers**, an old town★ on the right bank of the Roudoule; church with wooden statuary★ (16th-18thC); in the courtyard, sculpture★ by Aristide Maillol (1861-1944), surrounded by elms and palm trees. ▶ N202 W to **Entrevaux★** : fortified bridge, ramparts, high citadel (views★) in a town straight out of an old engraving; it has hardly changed since the 18thC. Former cathedral (part of the defenses) : works of art, including a 17thC altarpiece★. ▶ D902 right, through **Daluis** into the red schist **gorges★★** where the River Var flows. ▶ **Guillaumes** : ruined château. ▶ **Valberg★** (alt. 1 700 m) : frescos in Notre-Dame-des-Neiges, church dating from WWII. Walk to the **Valberg Cross** *(20 min; view★★)*; road to **Péone** *(8.5 km NW)* in an alpine setting. Valberg is a winter sports resort, like nearby **Beuil★** above the Cians. ▶ The **Cians Gorges★★** : the upper gorge is red schist, the lower, limestone. D28 snakes between them, passing two picturesque villages : **Rigaud** on the right; **Lieuche** among black schist 5 km on the left (the church has a 1479 altarpiece of the Annunciation★ by Louis Bréa). ▶ **Pont de Cians**,

---

bridge at the junction with the Var where D28 rejoins N202. ▶ **Touët-sur-Var★** *(2 km E)*, like a Tibetan village on the rock face, a labyrinth of covered arcades and alleyways, with the river rumbling under the nave of the church.   □

Practical Information

BEUIL, ⊠ 06470 Guillaumes, 7 km E of **Valberg**.
⚐ 1480-2100m.

Hotels :
★ *Les Edelweiss*, ☎ 93.02.30.05, Euro Visa, 24 rm Ⓟ ⫶ pens, half pens (h.s.), closed 15 Nov-15 Dec, 384. Rest. ♦ ⫶ 45-70.
★★ *L'Escapade*, ☎ 93.02.31.27, Euro Visa, 11 rm Ⓟ ⫶ pens (h.s.), 455. Rest. ♦ ⫶ ♪ ও 60-100.

GUILLAUMES, ⊠ 06470, 13 km W of **Valberg**.
ℹ ☎ 93.05.50.13.

Hotel :
Renaissance, ☎ 93.05.50.12, AE, 18 rm Ⓟ ⫶ ও closed 1 Nov-20 Dec, 80. Rest. ♦ ⫶ 65-100.

DIGNE-LES-BAINS

Gap 87, Aix-en-Provence 110, Paris 745 km
pop 16391 ⊠ 04000   C1

Digne : a tourist stopover on the Route Napoléon (→), an excursion centre for the Alps of Provence, a rapidly-expanding thermal spa where you can assuage your rheumatism and respiratory problems, and the centre of the August lavender harvest.

▶ The people of Digne pass their leisure hours under the place trees on **Boulevard Gassendi** (B2; statue of the philosopher Pierre Gassendi, 1592-1655, born in nearby Champtercier). ▶ **Municipal Museum** (C2) : archaeology, mineralogy and paintings (portraits by Franz Pourbus the Younger, 1569-1622; local artists; *10-12 & 2-6; closed Mon.*). Cathedral of Notre-Dame du Bourg★ (B2), 13thC, among Provence's finest Romanesque churches (remains of 14th-16thC mural). ▶ The **Fondation Alexandra David-Neel** (off map, A3), now a Tibetan cultural centre *(guided visits 3 and 5 or by appt. tel. 92.31.32.38)*. Tibetan art shop, festival, courses.

Nearby

▶ **Geological Park** encompasses 760 km^2 around Digne; instructional courses and excursions *(information from the SI)*. ▶ **Courbons★** *(6 km N)* : Romanesque and Gothic church (view★). ▶ Between Durance and Verdon, *clues* (→ Clues of Haute Provence) carved deep into the limestone : **Clues de Barles★** *(16 km N)* and *(35 km N)* **Le Fanget Pass** (view★), leading to **Seyne-les-Alpes**, a winter-sports and summer-holiday centre in a fine mountain site. ▶ **Clue de Chabrières★**, 18 km S of Digne.   □

Practical Information

♨ ☎ 92.31.06.68, closed Mar-Dec.
ℹ Rond-Point (A3), ☎ 92.31.42.73.
🚂 (off map A3), ☎ 92.31.00.67.
🚌 (A3), ☎ 92.31.50.00.
Car rental : Avis, rte de Marseille (Garage Peugeot), ☎ 92.31.06.11.

Hotels :
★★★ *Ermitage Napoléon*, bd Gambetta (off map A3), ☎ 92.31.01.09, AE DC Euro Visa, 59 rm Ⓟ ₩ ⟡ pens (h.s.), closed 3 Nov-15 Mar, 500. Rest. ♦♦ ⫶ ও closed Mon noon and Sat noon, 150.
★★★ *Grand Paris*, 19, bd Thiers (A-B3), ☎ 92.31.11.15, Tx 430605, AE DC, 32 rm 5 apt Ⓟ closed Sun eve and Mon, Jan-Feb. Splendid establishment. Tasteful and comfortable, 300. Rest. ♦♦♦ ♪ Quality fare. Spec : *escalope de truite aux poivrons rouges, mignonette d'agneau*, 180-200.
★★★ *Mistre* (Mapotel) 65, Bd Gassendi (B2),

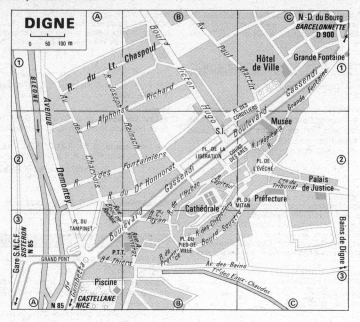

☎ 92.31.00.16, AE Euro Visa, 19 rm Ⓟ closed 10 Dec-10 Jan, 315. Rest. ♦ closed Sat, 120-165.
★★ *Central*, 26, bd Gassendi (B2), ☎ 92.31.31.91, Visa, 22 rm ♪ 130.
★ *Le Petit Saint-Jean*, cours des Ares (B-C2), ☎ 92.31.30.04, 18 rm Ⓟ ⌕ pens, closed 25 Dec-1 Feb, 300. Rest. ♦ 50-120.
▲ *Municipal* (186 pl), ☎ 92.31.04.87.

Recommended
Events : *Lavender festival*, 1st wkend of Aug; *second-hand fair* in Jul-Aug; *fairs and markets*, every Wed and Sat am; *crafts fair* in Jul.
♥ antiques dealer : *Betty Gleize*, 9, bd Gassendi, ☎ 92.31.55.33.

DRAGUIGNAN

Fréjus 29, Toulon 81, Paris 864 km
pop 28194 ✉ 83300   C2
When Baron Haussmann (1809-91), France's greatest town planner, was prefect of the Var Region, he planned the roads and promenades S of the old town that give a spacious perspective to modern Draguignan. In 1974 the prefecture was transferred to Toulon.

▶ **Boulevard Clemenceau** is the main artery. ▶ **Museum,** behind the theatre : local archaeology, ceramics (Moustiers) and 17th-20thC paintings *(9-12 & 2-6; closed Mon., Sun. and nat. hols.)*. The **library,** in the same building, possesses a rare 14thC illuminated manuscript of the great poem of chivalric lore, the *Roman de la Rose.* ▶ Farther on, Place du Marché, with fountains and plane trees, and the self-contained **old town,** where the clock tower (Tour de l'Horloge) has replaced the old keep.

Nearby
▶ **Le Malmont★** *(6 km N)* : panorama and orientation chart. ▶ By the D49 which climbs to Ampus, passing by the restored Romanesque church of Châteaudouble and its ruined château, or by the **Châteaudouble Gorges★** one

arrives at **Comps-sur-Artuby** *(32 km N)* : new buildings spill into the plain; the 13thC chapel of St. André★ looks over the old village from on top of a rock. ▶ 9 km NE of Comps, **Bargème★,** inside a fortified wall at an altitude above 1 000 m. Higher still, château des Pontevès. ▶ Other interesting **villages of the Var★** around Draguignan : **Callas** *(14 km NE),* **Bargemon** *(20 km NE);* **Lorgues** *(13 km SW);* and **Les Arcs** *(10 km S).* ▶ **Chapel of Ste. Roseline** *(4 km NE of Les Arcs),* Provençal Romanesque style ; Baroque altarpiece★ with 16thC Descent from the Cross in high relief ; stained glass.   □

Practical Information ───────────────

DRAGUIGNAN
ⓘ 9, bd Clemenceau, ☎ 94.68.63.30.
SNCF ☎ 94.68.01.13.
Car rental : *Avis*, train station.

Hotels :
★★★ *Col de l'Ange* (Inter-Hôtel), rte de Lorgues, 3 km on D 557, ☎ 94.68.23.01, Tx 970423, Visa, 30 rm Ⓟ ⌕ ⌕⌕ ☒ half pens (h.s.), closed 1 Jan-10 Feb, 320. Rest. ♦♦ 100-150.
★ *Le Dracénois*, 14, rue du Cros, ☎ 94.68.14.57, AE DC Euro Visa, 16 rm Ⓟ ⌕ ♪ closed 4-18 Jan, 125.

▲ ★★*De la Foux* (133 pl), ☎ 94.68.18.27.

Recommended
Events : *international art show* in Jul; *antiques show*, early Feb.
Market : *Flea market*, 1st Sat of the month.
♥ trout, crayfish : *Alain Guiran*, ☎ 94.68.02.55 ; at Seyran, Provençal specialties : *René Eugène*, ☎ 94.68.05.93.

Nearby
AMPUS, ✉ 83111, 14 km NW.

Restaurant :
● ♦ *La Fontaine d'Ampus*, pl. de la Mairie, ☎ 94.70.97.74 ⌕⌕ ♪ closed Mon and Sun eve ex Jul-Aug, 10 Jan-15 Feb.

Les ARCS-SUR-ARGENS, ⊠ 83460, 12 km E.

Hotel :

● ★ *Le Logis du Guetteur*, pl. du Château, ☎ 94.73.30.82, AE DC Euro Visa, 10 rm Ⓟ ⟨ ▨ ⟨ ♪ closed Fri, 15 Nov-15 Dec. An 11thC fortress overlooking the countryside, 160. Rest. ♦ ⟨ ♪ Spec : *petit ragoût d'écrevisses, poularde noire aux dés de langouste*, 55-160.

BARGEMON, ⊠ 83620, 20 km NE.

Restaurant :

● ♦♦ *Maître Blanc*, rue J.-Jaurès, ☎ 94.76.60.24, AE DC Euro Visa ⟨ closed Wed (ex Jul-Aug, open eves). Depending on the chef's inspiration, his mood and his finds at the market : *tourte de civet de lapin, pintade flambée à la fine champagne*, 55-100.

COMPS-SUR-ARTUBY, ⊠ 83840, 32 km N.

Hotel :

★ *Grand Hôtel Bain* (L.F.), ☎ 94.76.90.06, Euro Visa, 17 rm Ⓟ ⟨ ⬥ closed 12 Nov-20 Dec, 140. Rest. ♦ ⟨ 50-135 ; child : 40.

The ESTEREL Massif**

C-D2

Round trip from Saint-Raphaël *(76 km, half-day; see map 1)*

Porphyry eroded into needles, pyramids and ragged chunks against a backdrop of blue sea : Esterel is simply breathtaking. The shoreline is tattered by inlets and deep bays; the road twists and turns through a spectacular landscape between Cannes and Saint-Raphaël.

The forest of umbrella pine, vulnerable to fire and disease, only partly covers the massif; the Forestry Office is attempting to establish more vigorous species such as eucalyptus, holm oak, cork oak and chestnut.

▶ **Saint-Raphaël** (→). ▶ **Le Dramont Beach :** 20 min beyond the camping ground, the Semaphore (panorama★★). ▶ **Agay :** a bay and a wide beach that were known to the Greeks and Romans. ▶ 5.5 km past **Anthéor**, take the forest road left *(red/white barrier)* to the Ours Peak past **Cap Roux Peak** *(marked trail, 2hr*

round trip; view★★) and **Saint-Barthélemy Rock** where the view★ *(30-min round trip)* over the roadstead of Agay is spectacular. ▶ Turn right at the Mourrefrey crossroads. ▶ View★ of the expanse of the bare massif, and another view★★ along the coast to Cannes and the Lérins Islands. ▶ **Notre-Dame Pass** is the starting point for several marked trails, including up the **Ours Peak** *(1hr30 round trip)*, as far as the television transmitter (view★★★ over the sea and the Alps). ▶ Junction with N7, and return along the **Corniche d'Or** among colours that are even more intense at sunset; inlets, bays and resorts on the way : **La Napoule** (→ Cannes); **Théoule-sur-Mer, La Galère and Miramar, Le Trayas.** ▶ From Agay the road leads to **Valescure :** villas behind pine plantations removed from the bustle of Saint-Raphaël. ▶ Another Esterel lookout is **Mont Vinaigre** *(18 km N from Saint-Raphaël through Fréjus; then 30 min round trip).* ▢

Practical Information

THÉOULE-SUR-MER, ⊠ 06590, 10 km SW of **Cannes**. ⓘ pl. du Gal-Bertrand, ☎ 93.49.97.75. **SNCF** ☎ 93.49.96.17.

Hotels :

★★★★ *Villa Anna Guerguy*, La Galère, 2 km via N 98, ☎ 93.75.44.54, 14 rm Ⓟ ⟨ ▨ ⟨ ⬥ closed 1 Oct-10 Feb, 610. Rest. ♦♦ ⟨ ⬥ closed Wed. Agreeably set under the orange trees facing the îles de Lérins. Spec : *langouste, bourride*, 200-300.

★★★ *La Tour de l'Esquillon*, Miramar, ☎ 93.75.41.51, AE DC Euro Visa, 25 rm Ⓟ ⟨ ⟨ closed 10 Oct-1 Mar. Private beach, 600. Rest. ♦ ⟨ 150-210.

★★★ *Saint-Christophe*, 47, av. de Miramar, Miramar, ☎ 93.75.41.36, Tx 470878, AE DC Euro Visa, 40 rm Ⓟ ⟨ ▨ ♪ ☒ half pens (h.s.), closed 1 Nov-10 Apr. Private beach, 800. Rest. ♦♦ ⟨ ♪ 90-165 ; child : 50.

★★ *Corniche d'Or*, 11, bd de l'Esquillon, Miramar, ☎ 93.75.40.12, Visa, 30 rm Ⓟ ⟨ ▨ ⟨ ☒ pens (h.s.), closed Oct-Easter, 520. Rest. ♦ ⟨ 65-120.

FONTAINE-DE-VAUCLUSE**

Carpentras 21, Avignon 30, Paris 705 km
pop 606 ⊠ 84800 L'Isle-sur-la-Sorgue   A2

This is scrub country, between Ventoux and Lubéron, on the Vaucluse plateau. The aromatic *maquis*, composed of numerous plants, and occasional huts and low walls of stone are all that the land has to offer. The soil is worthless for cultivation, but brilliant

1. The Esterel massif

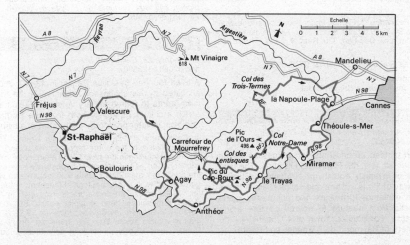

sunshine lights up the fast rivers and streams. Fontaine-de-Vaucluse is watered by the Sorgue and by a spring rising deep from the greenery below a formidable cliff.

▶ **Church of St. Véran,** minor Provençale Romanesque style. Petrach Museum *(undergoing reorganization)* commemorates the Italian poet Petrarch, who lived here from 1337 to 1353). ▶ The **Fontaine Road** climbs up the right bank of the Sorge, fringed with cafés and souvenir shops. On the right, the **Norbert Casteret Museum :** speleology *(9-12 & 2-6 in summer; pm in winter)* and the **Vallis Clausa paper mill★ :** hand-made paper on sale *(9-12:30 & 2-6; Sun. 10:30-12:30 & 2-6; summer 9-7).* ▶ **Musée des Restrictions** (WWII memorabilia; *1-6:30 ex Mon.*). ▶ The **fontaine de Vaucluse★★** is the outlet for a subterranean river draining the water from the limestone plateaus of Vaucluse. In winter and spring the flow reaches 150 000 litres per second; the rest of the year, the water level remains steady at the bottom of a rocky basin.

Nearby
▶ **L'Isle-sur-la-Sorgue,** crisscrossed by branches of the Sorgue : old water-mills; church★, good example of Provençal Baroque (17thC; inside : Assumption★ in gilded wood; paintings★ — 1704-07; in 4th, 5th chapels on left — by Parrocel); Hôtel-Dieu (17thC pharmacy★). ▶ **Le Thor** *(10 km W)* : fine Provençal Romanesque church★ (end 12thC). 2.5 km N of Le Thor, **Thouzon Grotto** *(Easter-Oct., 9-7; rest of year, Sun. 2-6).* □

Practical Information ⎯⎯⎯⎯⎯⎯⎯⎯

FONTAINE-DE-VAUCLUSE
ⓘ pl. de l'Eglise, ☎ 90.20.32.22 (h.s.).

Hotels :
● ★★ *Parc* (L.F.), Les Bourgades, ☎ 90.20.31.57, AE DC Visa, 12 rm Ⓟ ⧏ ⛲ ⌕ closed Wed, 2 Jan-15 Feb, 180. Rest. ◆◆ ⧏ 🕭 70-125.
★★ *Les Sources*, ☎ 90.20.31.84, 12 rm Ⓟ ⧏ ⛲ ⌕ ⚕ closed Mon eve (15 Nov-Apr), Jan, 200. Rest. ◆ ⧏ 50-100.

Restaurant :
◆◆ *Hostellerie du Château*, quartier Petite Place, ☎ 90.20.31.54, DC Euro Visa ⧏ ⛲ closed Tue, 1 Feb-1 Mar, 65-150.

⚹ ★★*Les Prés* (50 pl), ☎ 90.20.32.38.

Recommended
Youth hostel : chemin de la Vignasse, ☎ 90.20.31.65.

Nearby
L' ISLE-SUR-LA-SORGUE, ⊠ 84800, 9 km W.
ⓘ pl. de l'Église, ☎ 90.38.04.78. 👄

Hotel :
★★ *Le Pescadou* (L.F.), Le Pescadou, Le-Partage-des-Eaux, ☎ 90.38.09.69, 10 rm Ⓟ ⧏ ⛲ ⌕ 🕭 half pens, closed Mon eve, Dec-Feb, 320. Rest. ◆ ⧏ 🍴🕭 ⚵ 85-100; child : 35.

⚹ ★★★*La Sorguette* (165 pl), ☎ 90.38.05.71.

Recommended
Events : *festival de la Sorgue* in Jul.

FORCALQUIER

Digne 49, Aix-en-Provence 66, Paris 774 km
pop 3790 ⊠ 04300   B2

The high plateau around Forcalquier runs as far as Lure Mountain (→), the Provençal Olympus. The land abounds in lavender and thyme, truffles and honey but the way of life is austere and solitary; small farms look like miniature fortresses and shepherds guide their flocks from pasture to sparse pasture along dusty tracks. Forcalquier, "town of 4 Queens" — the 4 daughters of Raymond de Béranger and Béatrix de

Savoie all became queens in the 13thC —, slightly larger than other villages in the area, holds monthly fairs *(1st Mon.)* and a weekly market where lambs are the major item of trade.

▶ **Church of Notre-Dame-de-Provence** (orientation table and panorama★) : austere Romanesque lines that set off the Gothic doorway. With a pretty fountain in its forecourt and a covered way which leads to the old Jewish quarter and the synagogue. ▶ **Convent of the Cordeliers★ :** summer exhibitions and concerts (13thC; *May, Jun. 2:30-6:30; Jul., Aug. 10-12 & 2:30-6:30; closed in winter).* ▶ **Museum :** religious art, Provençal furniture and archaeological material *(daily ex weekends, 3-4).* ▶ Attractive houses in the old town (Rues des Cordeliers, du Collège, Béranger, du Palais). ▶ N, **Cemetery★ :** clipped yews.

Nearby
▶ **Notre-Dame-de-Salagon** *(4 km S),* once a priory : Renaissance building and 12thC church (figured★ and Corinthian capitals, *daily 2-6).* ▶ **Château de Sauvan,** at Mane *(5.5 km S; daily 3-6 ex Sat.) :* Classical French 18thC architecture, 100-year-old trees. ▶ **Saint-Michel-l'Observatoire** *(11 km SW) :* observatory★ 2.5 km N of village, established in 1938 *(3pm Wed. and 9:30 1st Sun. of month, Apr.-Sep.).* ▶ **Banon** *(25 km NW) :* tall, narrow houses standing stiffly on the hillside, surrounded by ramparts ; Banon is also the name of a goat cheese, powdered with herb savory, that is delicious with red Gigondas wine. ▶ **Lurs** *(11 km E),* a medieval village where an International Conference on Graphic Arts is held each year. ▶ **Gânagobie Priory★★** *(18 km NE),* on the edge of a plateau covered with holm oak and *maquis* : 12thC Romanesque church; note the doorway★ and mosaics★ of Eastern inspiration in the sanctuary *(9:30-11:30 & 2:30-4:30, 5:30 in season).* View★ over the Durance from the **plateau de Gânagobie.** ▶ **Mées rocks★** *(25 km NE)* resemble a line of stone penitents.   □

Practical Information ⎯⎯⎯⎯⎯⎯⎯⎯

ⓘ pl. Bourguet, ☎ 92.75.10.02.

Hotels :
★★ *Auberge Charembeau*, rte de Niozelles, ☎ 92.75.05.69, 11 rm Ⓟ ⧏ ⛲ ⌕ ⚂ ✈ half pens, closed Nov-Dec, 320. Rest. ◆◆ closed Mon. For hotel patrons only. Spec : *côte de veau aux morilles, ragoût de coquilles Saint-Jacques,* 100.
★★ *Deux Lions* (C.H.,L.F.), 11, pl. du Bourguet, ☎ 92.75.25.30, 18 rm Ⓟ closed Sun eve , Mon am, 2 Jan-15 Feb, 165. Rest. ◆◆◆ closed Mon and Sun eve. Since the 17thC, this authentic coach house has been an excellent stopover. Spec : *sauté de homard aux pâtes, pigeon rôti aux parfums de Provence.* Superb wines, 75-195; child : 45.

FRÉJUS

Draguignan 29, Cannes 40, Paris 874 km
pop 32698 ⊠ 83600   C3

A town founded by Julius Caesar in 49 BC, and later allocated by his successor Augustus in the form of land grants to retired military veterans. Fréjus enjoys a rich architectural legacy both from the Roman era and from its later prosperity as the seat of a bishopric.

▶ **Cathedral★** (C1-2), early Provençal Gothic; Renaissance panels★ in the doors *(apply to the porter),* vigorous ogival vaulting in the nave; 1450 altarpiece★ over the sacristy door. ▶ The octagonal **baptistery★★** dates from the 5thC; the late 12thC **cloister★** is picturesque with its garden and well. ▶ **Archaeological Museum,** in the cloister : Gallo-Roman art and artifacts excavated in Fréjus, including mosaics★, head of Jupiter★ (1stC BC), Diana in Pursuit★ *(baptistery, cloister and museum : 9:30-12 & 2-6, 4:30 in winter; closed Tue. and some nat. hols.).* ▶ The Roman ruins display painstaking construction, but lack

FRÉJUS

0   100   200 m

---

the luxurious features that characterized building in the later days of the Empire. **Amphitheatre★** *(Les Arènes,* A1, *9:30-12 & 2-6, 4 in winter; closed Tue.)* : 114 m by 82 m, held more than 10 000 spectators; **theatre** and **Aqueduct** (C1); **Porte d'Orée** (C2), apparently the remains of the entrance to the public baths.

Nearby

▶ Mementoes of colonial troups stationed at Fréjus : the memorial **Buddhist pagoda** *(2 km N of the centre)* erected by Vietnamese in 1919; and the **Sudanese mosque** *(4 km NW).* ▶ **Zoo** and **Esterel Safari Park** *(5 km N) :* only a windscreen between you and lions. ▶ **Roquebrune Mountain** *(W),* an outcrop of the Maures Massif. From picturesque **Roquebrune-sur-Argens** *(11 km W),* you can drive 1.5 km to the **Convent of Notre-Dame de la Pitié** (view★). The **Roquebrune Rocks** are accessible *(4 km by road then 2hr hike round trip, but the effort is tiring).*   □

Practical Information ———————————

FRÉJUS
ⓘ bd de la Libération, Fréjus-Plage, ☎ 94.51.48.42 (h.s.); pl. du Dr-Calvini (C2), ☎ 94.51.53.87.
✈ Fréjus-Saint-Raphaël, 2 km S, ☎ 94.51.04.07.
SNCF (B2), ☎ 94.51.30.53.

Hotels :
★★ **Auberge du Vieux Four**, 57, rue Grisolle (C2), ☎ 94.51.56.38, AE DC Euro Visa, 8 rm, closed Sun eve and Mon, 20 Sep-20 Oct, 165. Rest. ● ♦♦ ♪ The gentle air of Anjou and the coolness of a vaulted cellar offer relief from the hot Riviera sun : *escalope de saumon frais braisé à l'oseille, foie gras,* Bandol and Côtes-de-Provence, 150-210.
★★ **L'Oasis**, rue Hippolyte-Fabre, Fréjus-Plage, 2 km SE, ☎ 94.51.50.44, 27 rm 🅿 ⋙ 🌣 ⚘ closed Nov-Jan, 170.

Restaurant :
♦♦ **Les Potiers**, 135, rue des Potiers (B2), ☎ 94.51.33.74 ♪ closed Wed noon and Sat noon and Wed (l.s.), 14-26 Feb, 12 Nov-17 Dec. Spec : *marbré de saumon et saint-pierre sauce cresson, ris de veau aux champignons sauvages,* 80-170.

Recommended
Leisure activities : *Aquatica,* ☎ 94.53.58.58, 20-acre park

with a 6000m2 man-made lake; special effects : geysers, rapids, waterfalls, toboggans.
Youth hostel : *domaine de Bellevue, rte de Cannes,* ☎ 94.52.18.75.

Nearby

Les ISSAMBRES-SAN-PEÏRE, ✉ 83380, 13 km.
ⓘ parc des Issambres, ☎ 94.96.92.51.

Hotels :
★★ **La Réserve**, RN 98, ☎ 94.96.90.41, Visa, 8 rm 🅿 ♢ closed 30 Sep-1 Apr, 240. Rest. ♦♦ ♢ closed Wed. Nice little eatery under the pines : *nouilles fraîches au basilic, fondue varoise, filet de bœuf à la provençale,* 105-220; child : 55.
★★ **Le Provençal**, San Peïre, ☎ 94.96.90.49, DC Visa, 28 rm 🅿 ♢ ⋙ ♪ half pens (h.s.), closed Oct-Mar, 510. Rest. ♦ ♢ 95-160.
★ **La Cigale**, Les Calanques-des-Issambres, ☎ 94.96.91.15, Euro Visa, 7 rm 🅿 ♢ ♢ half pens (h.s.), closed Thu (l.s.), 30 Sep-1 Apr, 565. Rest. ♦♦ ♢ ♢ Spec : *bouillabaisse, magret d'oie fumé,* 140-280.
★ **Rodnoï**, San-Peïre-sur-Mer, ☎ 94.96.90.08, 7 rm 🅿 ♢ ⋙ ⚘ half pens, closed 15 Sep-31 Mar, 210. Rest. ♦ 40-80.

GORDES★★

Carpentras 34, Avignon 38, Paris 718 km
pop 1607 ✉ 84220   B2

On an escarpment of the Vaucluse mountains, church and château perched above massed houses and almond trees.

▶ **Château★** (11th-16thC), a feudal fortress lightened by the Renaissance style. Site of the **Vasarely Didactic Museum,** the "personal and subjective" part of the painter's work (→ Aix-en-Provence, Vasarely Foundation; *10-12 & 2-6; closed Tue.).* ▶ Pleasurable stroll through the old town : ramparts, narrow paved streets, vaulted stairways, boutiques, craft workshops. ▶ **Borie village★** *(3.5 km SW) :* restored drystone huts   offering an insight into the life of the peasant families who lived in such dwellings until the early 19thC *(daily 9-sunset).*

Nearby

▶ **Sénanque Abbey★★★** *(4 km N; →).* ▶ **Moulin des Bouillons** *(5 km S)* : stained glass museum★ *(10-12 & 4-6).*
□

Practical Information ⎯⎯⎯⎯⎯⎯⎯⎯

GORDES

Hotels :
● ★★★★ *Domaine de l'Enclos* (R.C.), rte de Sénanque, ☎ 90.72.08.22, Tx 432119, AE, 14 rm ℗ ⫯ ⵌ ⚘ 🖃 ⵂ closed 30 Oct-20 Mar, 610. Rest. ◆◆ ♪ ⵚ closed Mon. All the advantages of a luxury establishment are dispensed at these adorable little cottages set deep in the Lubéron. A dynamic staff in the dining room and kitchen : *charlotte de courgettes et lisettes, escalope de bar braisé aux mousserons,* delicious pastries, 95-180.
★★★★ *Hostellerie du Moulin Blanc,* Les Beaumettes, ☎ 90.72.34.50, AE DC Euro Visa, 18 rm ℗ ⫯ ⵌ ♪ ⵚ 🖃 ⵂ closed Jan-Feb, 445. Rest. ◆◆ ♪ ⵚ ⵚ closed Mon and Tue ex for guests, 140-250.
★★★ *La Mayanelle,* rue de la Combe, ☎ 90.72.00.28, AE DC Euro Visa, 10 rm ⫯ 175. Rest. ● ◆◆ ⫯ closed Tue. Spec : *blanquette de lotte aux petits légumes, pintadeau à la provençale.* Unimpeded view out over the Lubéron, 100-150.
★★★ *Le Gordos,* rte de Cavaillon, ☎ 90.72.00.75, 15 rm ℗ ⫯ ⵌ ⚘ ♪ 🖃 closed 15 Mar-5 Nov, 230.

Nearby

JOUCAS, ⊠ 84220 Gordes, 6 km E on the D2, D102.

Hotels :
● ★★★★ *Hostellerie Le Phébus* (I.L.A., R.C.), rte de Murs, ☎ 90.72.07.04, Tx 650697, AE DC Euro Visa, 16 rm ℗ ⫯ ⵌ ⵚ 🖃 ⵂ half pens (h.s.), closed 15 Nov-15 Mar, 890. Rest. ◆◆ ⵚ Spec : *croustade de coquilles Saint-Jacques aux écrevisses,* 145-200 ; child : 60.
★★★★ *Le Mas des Herbes Blanches* (R.C.), ☎ 90.72.00.74, Tx 432045, AE DC Euro Visa, 14 rm ℗ ⫯ ⵌ ⚘ ♪ 🖃 closed 20 Nov-5 Mar. Facing the Lubéron, a farmhouse set in a ravishing landscape, 620. Rest. ◆◆ ⫯ ♪ ⵚ 180-300.
★★ *Host. des Commandeurs* (L.F.), ☎ 90.72.00.05, Euro Visa, 14 rm ℗ ⵌ ⵂ closed Wed, Feb, 140. Rest. ● ◆ Simple, rustic and good. Spec : *fricassée de volaille au vinaigre, loup au fenouil,* 60-110.
Les Bories, rte de l'Abbaye de Sénanque, ☎ 90.72.00.51, 4 rm ℗ ⫯ ⵚ ⵚ closed Wed, 20 Nov-31 Dec. Rest. ● ◆◆◆ ⫯ ⵚ closed Mon eve, Tue eve, Wed, Sun eve. Book ahead. A little paradise set amid fields of lavender. Inspired cooking : fresh game in season, *bourride de baudroie, nougat glacé au coulis d'abricot,* 170-220.

GRASSE*

Cannes 17, Nice 42, Paris 918 km
pop 38360 ⊠ 06130
D2

At Nice they sell flowers ; the people of Grasse extract and distill the essences to make the flowers live on. The town climbs on ramps and staircases around the top of the natural amphitheatre that surrounds Cannes. Around the town are the fields of flowers that make Grasse the hub of the perfume industry.
▶ **Promenade du Cours** (Cours Honoré-Cresp, A2), the focus of activity in Grasse, terraced over the landscape.
▶ **Museum of Provençal Art and History** (B2), 18thC mansion displaying popular arts and traditions of eastern Provence *(10-12 & 4-5, 6 in summer ; closed Sat. and Nov.).*
▶ **Fragonard Museum** (A2), a beautiful 17thC country house dedicated to the painter Jean-Honoré Fragonard (1732-1806) and his artistic family *(same hours as above) ;* the villa is also a cultural centre ; pretty park. ▶ **Cathedral of Notre-Dame** (B2), early Provençal Gothic ; in the right side-aisle are three paintings★ by Rubens ; altarpiece★ of St. Honorat attributed to Louis Bréa (late 15thC), and Christ Washing the Feet of the Disciples, one of Frago-

nard's rare religious works. ▶ Close by, the **Marine Museum,** mainly dedicated to Admiral Grasse (1722-88), a hero of the American War of Independence who prevented Hood from relieving Cornwallis at Yorktown and landed at Chesapeake Bay to reinforce La Fayette (models★ ; *weekdays, 2:30-5).* ▶ The perfume houses in Grasse are open to visitors. **Maison Fragonard :** international perfume museum at 20 Boulevard Fragonard (B2).

Nearby

▶ **Cabris★** *(6 km W)* : view★ to the sea. 300 m W of the Cabris Cross, a Celtic table stone ; Ligurian remains (summit of the Ondides). ▶ **Saint-Cézaire-sur-Siagne** *(16 km SW),* a feudal village overlooking the Gorges ; orientation chart, view★. **Saint-Cézaire Caverns** *(3 km NE)* : stalactites *(10:30-12 & 2:30-6 in season ; 2:30-5:30 rest of year ; closed Nov.-Mar.).* ▶ 15 km NW through the **Siagne Gorges** to **Mons★,** on a spur : fountains, picturesque streets and a superb view from the Place St-Sébastien.

Around the Loup Gorges★ *(39 km, 3hr)*

▶ **Grasse.** ▶ NE on D2085, then left on 2210. ▶ **Le Bar-sur-Loup** : 16thC château, attractive village ; church with Dance of Death★, remarkable 15thC painting on wood ; also, 15thC doors ; altarpiece★ by Louis Bréa (late 15thC). ▶ D6 to the **Loup Gorges★★** and Courmes Waterfall, a vertical cleft where enormous caverns ("cauldrons") have been hollowed out by the water. ▶ At **Bramafan,** turn left on D3. ▶ **Gourdon★★ :** several artists have chosen to live in this village eyrie above the Gorges. Château (13th-17thC) : a museum, painting collection includes the Legend of St. Ursula★ (school of Cologne, 1500) and *naïf* works including a portrait by Henri Douanier Rousseau (1844-1910) ; *11-1 & 4-7, Jul.-15 Sep. ; 10-12 & 2-7 ex Tue., 16 Sep.-Jun.) ;* gardens★, subalpine flowers. ▶ Return to Grasse by D3 or cross the **Caussols Plateau** by D12 NW.
□

Perfume and patronage

16thC Grasse was a well-established glove-making centre when a fashion arose for perfumed gloves. Abundant flower gardens enabled the city to profit from both sides of the craze. The perfume industry thrived into the 18th and 19thC, and is the mainstay of Grasse today. At first, the flowers were simply distilled. In the mid-18thC, development of the process permitted more thrifty extraction of essences by means of oils and fats. 19thC extraction processes used solvents that could be evaporated to leave a solid residue of perfume and vegetable wax. One ton of jasmine flowers yields 3 kg of an aromatic residue called the concrète. *When oils (60 % of weight) are removed by alcohol treatment, the remaining* absolue de concrète *is the ultimate essence of the flower's perfume.*

Practical Information ⎯⎯⎯⎯⎯⎯⎯⎯

GRASSE
ⓘ pl. Foux (B1), ☎ 93.36.03.56.
🚍 (B1), ☎ 93.36.37.37.

Hotels :
★★ *Bellevue* (L.F.), 14, av. Riou-Blanquet (C1), ☎ 93.36.01.96, 30 rm ⫯ ⵌ closed Nov, 240. Rest. ◆ ♪ ⵚ 60-80.
★★ *Les Arômes* (L.F.), Plan-de-Grasse, 4 km SE on N 85, ☎ 93.70.42.01, Euro Visa, 7 rm ℗ ⫯ ⵚ ♪ ⵚ ⵚ closed Dec-Jan, 160. Rest. ◆◆ ♪ ⵚ closed Sat ex Jul and Aug. Spec : *tournedos au poivre, steak Diane,* 75-150 ; child : 40.
★ *Les Mouliniers* (L.F.), Chemin de Masseboeuf, Plascassier, 6 km SE on D 4, ☎ 93.60.10.37, Visa, 10 rm ℗ ⫯ ⵌ

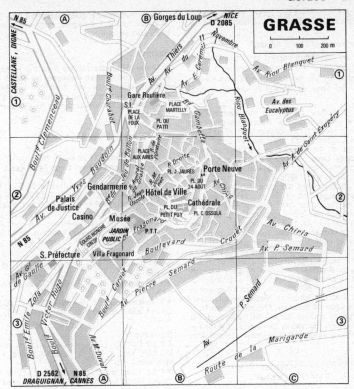

GRASSE

0   100   200 m

△ ♪ pens, half pens (h.s.), closed 15 Dec-15 Jan, 320. Rest. ♦ ⟨ ♪ ᕫ 60-130.

Restaurant :
♦♦ *Chez Pierre*, 3, av. Thiers (B1), ☎ 93.36.12.99, closed Sun eve (1 Oct-1 Jul) and Mon, 15 Jun-15 Jul. Superb pastries, 60-110.

△ ★★★*Pont de la Paoute* (127 pl), ☎ 93.09.11.42.

Nearby

ANDON, ⊠ 06750 Caille, 34 km E.
⌇ 1195-1642m, L'Audibergue.

Hotel :
★ *Hostellerie d'Andon*, ☎ 93.60.45.11, AE Visa, 16 rm ℙ ⟨ ᗰᗰ △ 160. Rest. ♦ ⟨ ♪ 75-95.

Recommended
Farmhouse-inn : *Domaine de Castellaros*, Les Quatre-Chemins-de-Thorenc, ☎ 93.60.00.25, horseback riding.

Le BAR-SUR-LOUP, ⊠ 06620, 9 km NE.

Hotel :
★★★ *Réserve*, pont du Loup, 3 km N, ☎ 93.59.32.81, 15 rm ℙ ⟨ ᗰᗰ ⊡ 240. Rest. ♦ ⟨ 60-160.

△ ★★*Gorges du Loup* (33 pl), ☎ 93.42.45.06.

CABRIS, ⊠ 06820, 5 km W on the D 4.

Hotel :
★★ *L'Horizon* (R.S., L.F.), ☎ 93.60.51.69, AE DC, 19 rm ℙ ⟨ ᗰᗰ △ ✖ half pens, closed 15 Oct-15 Mar, 400. Rest. ♦ ⟨ ✖ closed Wed eve, 75.

MAGAGNOSC, ⊠ 06520, 5 km NE on the D 2085.

Hotel :
Petite Auberge, 105, av. A.-Renoir, ☎ 93.42.75.32, 5 rm

ℙ ⟨ ﾗ pens, closed Wed, Feb school hols, Jul, 370. Rest. ♦ 65-95 ; child : 40.

OPIO, ⊠ 06650 Le Rouret, 7 km E on the D 7.

Hotel :
★ *Mas des Géraniums*, 7, rte de Nice, ☎ 93.77.23.23, 7 rm ℙ ⟨ ᗰᗰ △ closed Oct-Jan, 190. Rest. ♦ closed Sun eve. Spec : *coquelet aux écrevisses*, 90-140.

Recommended
♥ olive oil : *Moulin de Roger Michel*, ☎ 93.77.23.03.

SAINT-VALLIER-DE-THIEY, ⊠ 06460, 12 km NW.

Hotel :
★★ *Hostellerie le Préjoly* (L.F.), ☎ 93.42.60.86, AE DC Euro Visa, 20 rm ℙ ᗰᗰ △ half pens (h.s.), closed Tue, 14 Feb-1 Mar, 15 Dec-15 Jan, 500. Rest. ♦ ⟨ ♪ ᕫ Spec : *poulet cuit dans l'argile, civet de lapereau grand-mère, magret de canard aux cerises*, 80-300.

SPÉRACÈDES, ⊠ 06530 Peymeinade, 8 km W.

Hotel :
La Soleillade, rue des Orangers, ☎ 93.66.11.15, 8 rm ⟨ ᗰᗰ △ half pens (h.s.), closed 30 Oct-15 Mar, 240. Rest. ♦ ᕫ closed Wed noon , Nov. Spec : game, *civet de lapin*, 60-150.

Restaurant :
♦♦ *La Bastide du Clos d'Entoure*, rte de Cabris, ☎ 93.60.53.87 ℙ ⟨ ᗰᗰ △ ♪ closed Wed. Pretty dining room and garden dining too. Spec : *filet de sole aux poireaux, ballotine de canard à la chartreuse*, game, 90-200.

On the maps, a town's name underlined <u>Saulieu</u> means that the locality possesses at least one recommended establishment (blue or red point).

The HAUTE-PROVENCE Clues**

D2

Round trip from Vence *(137 km, full day)*

Clues are narrow passages carved by rivers through the limestone foothills of the Alps ; they create a spectacular landscape in the wild heathland and desert plateaux over an area of about 70 by 30 km N of Grasse.

▶ **Vence** *(→).* ▶ Follow D2 across the **Vence Pass** (extended view★ of the coast). ▶ **Coursegoules** *(1 km to the right),* on a rocky spur : church with altarpiece★ of St. John the Baptist (1500) attributed to Louis Bréa (1458-1523), eldest of the three Bréa painters). ▶ Drive through the **upper Loup Valley★**; Gréolières, at the foot of the Barres-du-Cheiron : Romanesque church with altarpiece of St. Étienne★ (1480) and Virgin and Child★ (14thC). ▶ The road crosses the **Clue de Gréolières★**. ▶ **Gréolières-les-Neiges** (alt. 1 450 m ; *11 km on the right*) : skiing just 1hr by car from Nice. ▶ **Les Quatre-Chemins. Thorenc** *(3 km left)* : rural hotels and villas. ▶ **Bleine Pass★** *(on D5;* alt. 1 439 m), among rocks and firs. ▶ **Clue de St.-Auban★★** : the road winds between cliffs honeycombed with caves. ▶ **Briançonnet** : houses built from the stones of the old Roman town (many inscriptions); altarpiece★ (restored) by Louis Bréa in the church. ▶ **Clue du Riolan★** : the river plunges through a gap. ▶ **Sigale,** a picturesque setting for a stronghold. ▶ **Aiglun★** *(8 km right on D10)* and the **Clue d'Aiglun★,** like a sword-cut in the mountain. ▶ **Roqueteron;** continue on D1 to the **Clue de Bouisse.** The road winds from one hilltop village to another above the valleys of the Bouyon and the Var : **Bouyon★, Le Broc★, Carros★★** and **Gattières,** among vines and olive trees resonant with cicadas.   □

Practical Information ————————————

CARROS, ✉ 06510, 16 km NE of **Vence.**

Hotel :
★★ **Hostellerie Lou Castelet** (L.F.), les Plans de Carros, 4 km SE on D 1, ☎ 93.29.16.66, 14 rm ℙ ⪡ ☐ ♪⁰ closed Mon, 31 Oct-1 Dec, 200. Rest. ♦ ♪ 75-140.

GRÉOLIÈRES, ✉ 06620 Le-Bar-sur-Loup, 26 km NW of **Vence.**
⌘ 1425-1800m.
ⓘ ☎ 93.59.95.16.

Hotel :
★★ **Alpina,** ☎ 93.59.70.19, 9 rm ℙ ⪡ ☐ △ ⅍ half pens (h.s.), closed 15 Apr-1 May, 15 Oct-20 Dec, 600. Rest. ♦ ⅏ closed Thu in summer, 55-90.

HYÈRES

Toulon 18, Aix-en-Provence 99, Paris 857 km
pop 41739 ✉ 83400   C3
Hyères, oldest resort on the Côte d'Azur and a centre for aquatic sports and sailing, is distinguished by flowers and palm trees broad avenues lined with turn-of-the-century buildings, several Moorish-style residences, 35 km of beach, and a good dozen marinas.

▶ **Church of St. Louis★** (B1), 13thC Italianate. ▶ W of Place Clemenceau, a skein of old streets and the market in the **Place Massillon.** ▶ **Place St-Paul** (B1) : lookout★ ; 11th-16thC church with interesting *ex-votos* and a Provençal *crèche.* ▶ In Rue Paradis, an eye-catching (13thC, restored) **Romanesque house★.** ▶ Over the roofs, the crenellated keep and towers of the ruined **château** (A1, 20-min walk from the car park, view★). **Also...** ▶ **Saint-Bernard Park** : Mediterranean flora at the foot of the ruins, view★. ▶ **Municipal Museum** (B2) : archaeology, local painters *(weekdays ex Tue, 10-12 & 3-6, Sat. and Sun. pm only).* ▶ **Notre-Dame de Consolation★** *(3 km S),* built in 1955 by the architect Vaillant, the sculptor Lambert-Rucki and the glazier Gabriel Loir

(view★). ▶ **Olbius Riquier gardens★** (via B2) : 15 acres of palms, dates, eucalyptus, cactus, agave, plus aquatic birds and a small zoo.

Nearby

▶ **Giens Peninsula** *(12 km S to the Fondue Tower),* an island linked to the mainland by roads on a double isthmus divided by salt marshes. ▶ **Giens** is a seaside village with a ruined château (view★★). ▶ The **Fondue Tower** is a departure point for Porquerolles (→ Hyères Islands).   □

Practical Information ————————————

HYÈRES
ⓘ jardins Denis (B1), ☎ 94.65.18.55.
✈ Toulon-Hyères, 4 km S, ☎ 94.57.41.41.
SNCF ☎ 94.57.79.60.
🚌 pl. G.-Clemenceau (B1), ☎ 94.65.21.00.
⚓ ☎ 94.58.21.81. From la Tour Fondue (presqu'île de Giens) to Porquerolles (h.s.), in 30 min, 6 crossings daily ; ☎ 94.57.44.07, from port d'Hyères to Port-Cros, in 30 min, 1 crossing daily in summer, 4 weekly low season.
Car rental : *Avis,* Palyvestre airport, ☎ 94.38.98.02 ; Pont de la Villette, ☎ 94.38.98.02 ; train station.

Hotels :
★★★ **Paris,** 20, av. de Belgique (B1), ☎ 94.65.33.61, 32 rm ⅍ 240.
★★ **Mozart,** 26, av. A.-Denis (C1), ☎ 94.65.09.45, 14 rm ℙ ঌ 145.
★★ **Suisse,** 1, av. A.-Briand (B1), ☎ 94.65.26.68, 25 rm, closed Sat eve and Sun, 18 Dec-10 Jan, 180. Rest. ♦ 40-70.

Restaurants :
♦♦ **Le Delfin's,** pl. Clemenceau (B1), ☎ 94.65.04.27, AE DC Euro Visa ℙ ⪡ ∰ △ closed Sun eve, 1-15 Dec. Fish specialties, 70-150.
♦♦ **Le Tison d'Or,** 1, rue Galliéni (A2), ☎ 94.65.01.37 ♪ closed Mon and Sun eve. Spec : *jambonnette de caneton au vieux bourgogne, œufs pochés en meurette,* 100-160.

⚘ ★★★★2 sites ; ★★★12 sites.

Recommended
♥ vases, jewelry : *Le Lavandin,* 10, rue Portalet, ☎ 94.35.52.86.

Nearby

CARQUEIRANNE, ✉ 83320, 10 km NW.
ⓘ mairie, ☎ 94.58.60.78.

Hotels :
★★ **Plein Sud,** av. du Gal-de-Gaulle, ☎ 94.58.52.86, 17 rm ℙ ⪡ ☐ closed 1 Nov-15 Dec, 195.
★★ **Richiardi,** port des Salettes, ☎ 94.58.50.13, Euro Visa, 10 rm ℙ ⪡ △ closed 3-28 Nov, 230. Rest. ♦ ♪ ঌ 65-100 ; child : 35.
★ **La Réserve,** Port des Salettes, ☎ 94.58.50.02, Euro Visa, 18 rm ⪡ half pens (h.s.), closed 15 Feb-1 Mar, 7 Oct-7 Nov, 300. Rest. ♦ ⪡ ♪ closed Mon, Wed eve, Sun eve, 70-155.

⚘ ★★★★Le Beau Vézé (150 pl), ☎ 94.57.65.30 ; ★★★Les Arbousiers (100 pl), ☎ 94.58.56.56.

GIENS, ✉ 83400, 12 km S on the D 97.

Hotels :
★★★ **Provençal,** pl. St-Pierre, ☎ 94.58.20.09, 50 rm ℙ ∰ ⅍ ☐ ♪⁰ closed 20 Oct-9 Apr. 5-acre park, rooms with terrace or balcony, 350. Rest. ♦♦ ⪡ ♪ ঌ 130-200.
★★★ **Relais du Bon Accueil** (R.S.), ☎ 94.58.20.48, 10 rm ℙ ⪡ ∰ △ ☐ ♪⁰ pens (h.s.), closed 5 Nov-15 Dec, 800. Rest. ♦ ⪡ ♪ 85-120.

Les SALINS-D'HYÈRES, ✉ 83410, 6 km on the N 98.

Hotel :
La vieille Auberge Saint Nicolas, ☎ 94.66.40.01, 11 rm ℙ ∰ Rest. ♦♦♦ closed Mon and Sun eve (l.s.), Jan. Spec : *petits rougets grillés au fenouil,* 250-350.

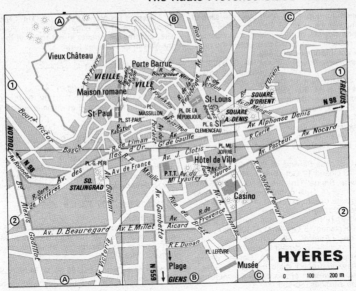

HYÈRES

0   100   200 m

(Hyères Islands)   C3

Greeks and Romans settled on these islands that, during the Renaissance, were known as "the Golden Isles". The archipelago only a short distance from the sophistication of the Côte d'Azur has remained a wild and unspoilt shore forest.

Île de Porquerolles★★★

The westernmost and largest island (7.5 km by 2 km). On the N side, pine, heather and myrtle fringe the beaches. The S shore is steeper, and the interior is a pine forest; delightful strolls with glimpses of the sea. ▶ **Village** on the shore below 16thC Fort Ste-Agathe. Walk to the **lighthouse★** *(2.7 km S)*, the **semaphore★** *(3 km E)*, of to **Grand Langoustier Point★** *(5.5 km W)*.

Île de Port-Cros★★★

Rising 207 m above sea level, where Aleppo pine, eucalyptus, mastic, arbutus, myrtle and heather mingle their scents and colours; you may spot a blue merlin or a peregrine falcon. The island is now a national park, with protection for flora and fauna. ▶ Round the edge of the bay is the village of Port-Cros, with a few colourful houses and an old fort. ▶ Marked trails to various points including **Palu Beach★** *(1hr30 round trip)* along the Botany Trail; **Solitude Valley★** *(1hr20 round trip)*; **Port Man★** *(3hr40)*.

Île de Levant

A narrow, rocky spine, 8 km by 1.2 km, is occupied by a nudist colony at Heliopolis and... the French Navy. □

Practical Information

PORQUEROLLES, ⊠ 83400 Hyères.
🚣 ☎ 94.64.08.04. To Cavalaire, 3 crossings weekly

in season; ☎ 94.57.44.07, to Hyères, 6 crossings weekly in season; ☎ 94.92.96.82, to Toulon; ☎ 94.58.21.81, to presqu'île de Giens, every half-hour (h.s.), 5 crossings daily (l.s.); ☎ 94.71.01.02, to Le Lavandou.

Hotels :
● ★★★ *Mas du Langoustier*, ☎ 94.58.30.09, 48 rm ⊱ ⨝ ⨎ pens (h.s.), 400. Rest. closed 25 Sep-8 May. Magnificent location, 400. Rest. ♦♦ Spec : *feuilleté de loup, bavarois de truite saumonée*, 120-180.
★★ *Relais de la Poste* (L.F.), ☎ 94.58.30.26, 30 rm ⊱ closed Oct-Mar. Warm welcome, 280.
★★ *Sainte-Anne*, ☎ 94.58.30.04, 15 rm ⊱ ⨎ pens, closed 4-14 Jan, 250. Rest. ♦ ♪ 80-180.

Restaurant :
♦♦ *L'Orée du Bois*, rue du Phare, ☎ 94.58.30.57, Visa ⨎ closed Dec-Feb, 100-115.

PORT-CROS, ⊠ 83400 Hyères.
🚣 ☎ 94.57.44.07. To Hyères, 1 crossing daily (h.s.), 4 crossings weekly (l.s.); ☎ 94.64.08.04, to Cavalaire, 1 crossing daily (h.s.); ☎ 94.71.01.02, to Le Lavandou, frequent daily service (h.s.), 4 crossings weekly (l.s.).

Hotel :
● ★★★ *Manoir*, ☎ 94.05.90.52, 24 rm ⊱ ⨎ ⨝ half pens (h.s.), closed 15 Oct-Easter. Reserve far in advance, 860.

Cannes 6, Nice 24, Paris 918 km
pop 12407 ⊠ 06160   D2
For jazz-lovers, the site of a famous festival *(Jul.)*; for summer visitors, a marvelous sandy beach and sophisticated nightlife.   □

Practical Information

ⓘ bd Ch.-Guillaumont, ☎ 93.61.04.98.
SNCF ☎ 93.61.12.40.
Car rental : *Avis*, train station, ☎ 93.34.65.15.

Hotels :
● ★★★★(L) *Juana*, La Pinède, av. Georges-Gallice, ☎ 93.61.08.70, Tx 470778, 45 rm 5 apt Ⓟ ⊱ ⨎ ⨝ ♤ ⨻ ☒ closed 30 Oct-25 Mar, 1430. Rest. ● ♦♦♦ *La Terrasse*

⟨ ♪ ⚓ closed lunch Jul-Aug. Chef Alain Ducasse slipped away to the kitchen of the *Hôtel de Paris* in Monte-Carlo. His successor has not (as of this writing) been named, but François Barrache is determined to maintain the reputation of his fine establishment, 400-500.

★★★★(L) *Belles-Rives*, bd du Littoral, ☎ 93.61.02.79, Tx 470984, AE, 44 rm ⟨ ▨ ⚓ half pens (h.s.), closed 10 Oct-10 Apr. Superb view of the bay, private beach, 2230. Rest. ◆◆◆◆ ⟨ ⚓ ❀ 300-360.

★★★★(L) *Hélios*, 3, av. Dautheville, ☎ 93.61.55.25, Tx 970906, AE DC Visa, 70 rm ℗ ⟨ ⚲ ♪ ⚓ half pens (h.s.), closed 19 Oct-11 Apr, 1420. Rest. ◆◆◆ ♪ ⚓ 180-240.

★★★★ *Beauséjour*, av. Saramartel, ☎ 93.61.07.82, Tx 470673, AE Visa, 30 rm ℗ ⟨ ▨ ⚲ ▢ closed 10 Oct-15 Apr, 660. Rest. ◆◆ ❋ Short menu of cold dishes, 90-175.

★★★ *Mimosas* (R.S.), rue Pauline, ☎ 93.61.04.16, 34 rm ℗ ⟨ ▨ ⚲ ♪ ❀ ▢ closed 12 Oct-15 Apr, 340.

★★★ *Sainte-Valérie*, rue de l'Oratoire, ☎ 93.61.07.15, AE DC Visa, 30 rm ℗ ▨ ⚲ ♪ ⚕ ⚓ half pens (h.s.), closed 15 Oct-15 Mar. Private beach, 620. Rest. ◆◆ ♪ ❀ 90-120.

● ★★ *Le Pré Catelan*, 22, av. des Lauriers, ☎ 93.61.05.11, Visa, 18 rm ℗ ▨ ⚓ half pens (h.s.), 510. Rest. ● ◆ ♪ ⚓ ❀ closed 15 Oct-14 Mar, 105-150.

★★ *Auberge de l'Estérel*, 21, chemin des Iles, ☎ 93.61.08.67, 14 rm ℗ ▨ ⚲ closed 15 Nov-15 Dec, 150. Rest. ● ◆◆ closed Mon and Sun eve. Garden dining. Friendly atmosphere and good value for money. Spec : confit de lapereau au mesclin et aux cerises aigres douces, chartreuse de sardines, 60-180.

★★ *Palais des Congrès*, 4, av. des Palmiers, ☎ 93.61.04.29, AE, 18 rm ℗ ▨ ⚲ ❀ closed Nov-Jan, 250.

★★ *Régence*, 2, av. de l'Amiral-Courbet, ☎ 93.61.09.39, AE DC Visa, 20 rm ▨ pens (h.s.), closed 1 Nov-15 Mar, 420. Rest. ◆ ♪ ⚓ 55-95.

Restaurant :
◆◆ *Bijou Plage*, bd Ch.-Guillaumont, ☎ 93.61.39.07, AE DC Visa ⟨ ▨ ⚲ ♪ closed Mon in winter, 15 Oct-20 Dec, 140-190.

Recommended
Casino : *Eden Beach*, bd Baudoin, ☎ 93.61.00.29.

LAMBESC

Aix-en-Provence 21, Apt 38, Paris 732 km
pop 5353 ⊠ 13410   B2

Restaurant :
◆◆◆ *Moulin de Tante Yvonne*, rue Benjamin-Raspail, ☎ 42.28.02.46, closed Mon, Tue, Sun eve, 15 Jul-31 Aug. Reserve. Former 15thC olive press. Country cooking, 220-360.

Recommended
Rural-gîte : at Rognes, 7 km E on D 15, *Barbebelle*, ☎ 42.50.22.12, in a little 18thC château.

Nearby
MALLEMORT, ⊠ 13370, 15 km NW on the N7-D16.

Hotel :
★★★★ *Moulin de Vernègues*, 9 km, autoroute Senas exit, dir. Aix, ☎ 90.59.12.00, Tx 401645, AE DC Euro Visa, 35 rm ℗ ▨ ⚲ ♪ ⚓ ▢ ⤳ ♪ A splendid park surrounds this former flour mill, 640. Rest. ◆◆◆ ⟨ ⚓ ❀ Gourmet restaurant, 230-250 ; child : 80.

Le LAVANDOU

Toulon 41, Sainte-Maxime 42, Paris 880 km
pop 4275 ⊠ 83980   C3

A yacht harbour and seaside resort, protected by Cap Bénat, with a view across to Port-Cros and Levant islet ; archaeological museum.

▶ **Bormes-les-Mimosas★** *(2 km NW),* like an amphitheatre at the edge of the Dom Forest ; delightful site, picturesque streets in old town. In the background, the **Massif des Maures** (→).   □

Practical Information _____

Le LAVANDOU
ⓘ quai G.-Péri, ☎ 94.71.00.61.
⛴ *Les Iles d'Or*, ☎ 94.71.01.02. To Port-Cros and l'île du Levant, daily service in summer and 3 times weekly in winter.

Hotels :
★★★ *Belle-Vue* (R.S.), Saint-Clair, ☎ 94.71.01.06, Tx 400555, AE Euro Visa, 19 rm ℗ ⟨ ▨ ⚲ ♪ ❀ pens, closed Nov-Mar, 345. Rest. ◆ ⟨ ♪ ❀ 200.

★★ *Beau Rivage*, bd du Front-de-Mer, ☎ 94.71.11.09, DC Visa, 29 rm ℗ ⟨ ▨ ♪ closed 15 Oct-18 Mar, 270.

★★ *L'Escapade*, 1, chem. du Vannier, ☎ 94.71.11.52, 16 rm ℗ ▨ ❀ half pens (h.s.), closed 10 Jan-10 Feb, 15 Nov-15 Dec, 205. Rest. ◆ ♪ 95-130.

Restaurant :
● ◆◆ *Au Vieux-Port*, quai Gabriel-Péri, ☎ 94.71.00.21, AE DC Visa ⟨ closed Tue (l.s.), 12 Jan-12 Mar. Excellent fish. Spec : *filets de rouget, moules fourrées coulis de homard,* 145-320.

⛺ ★★★★*Les Mimosas* (185 pl), ☎ 94.05.82.94 ; ★★★*Pramousquier* (180 pl), ☎ 94.05.83.95.

Nearby

BORMES-LES-MIMOSAS, ⊠ 83230, 5 km NW.
ⓘ rue J.-Aicard, ☎ 94.71.15.17.

Hotels :
● ★★★ *Safari*, rte du Stade, ☎ 94.71.09.83, Tx 404603, AE DC Euro Visa, 33 rm ℗ ⟨ ▨ ⚲ ❀ ▢ ⤳ closed 16 Oct-1 Apr, 370. Rest. ◆ closed noon ex wkends, 70-100.

★★★ *Le Palma*, Le Pré-aux-Bœufs, ☎ 94.71.17.86, Tx 400555, AE DC Euro Visa, 20 rm ℗ ▨ ♪ 290. Rest. ◆◆ ♪ ⚓ closed Mon and Sun eve (l.s.), 1 Nov-15 Dec, 125-250.

Restaurant :
● ◆◆ *La Tonnelle des Délices*, pl. Gambetta, ☎ 94.71.34.84 ⟨ closed wkday lunch ex Apr, 30 Sep-1 Apr. For lovers of fine Provençal cooking, the Gedda brothers give you more : *crabes farcis aux crustacés, pavé de lapereau à la mousse de cèpes.* Attractive fixed-price meals, 120-200.

⛺ ★★★★*Domaine la Favière* (1200 pl), ☎ 94.71.03.12 ; ★★★*Manjastre* (120 pl), ☎ 94.71.03.28 ; ★★*Le Grand Bataillar* (116 pl), ☎ 94.71.08.41 ; numerous ★★ sites.

Recommended
Casino : rue Carnot, ☎ 94.71.15.28.
Market : flea market, 1st Sat of month. In summer, 1st and 3rd Sat of month.

CABASSON, ⊠ 83980 Le Lavandou, 8 km S on D 41.

Hotel :
★★★ *Les Palmiers*, ☎ 94.64.81.94, AE DC Euro Visa, 23 rm ℗ ▨ ⚲ pens, 800. Rest. ◆◆ ♪ ⚓ 100-150.

The LUBÉRON Heights★★

                                                    B2
Through the Lubéron *(74 km from Cavaillon to Céreste ; full day ; see map 2)*

Provençal flora and fauna have maintained their natural equilibrium on the Lubéron Heights, for which reason the whole area is now a regional nature park. The ridge is best explored on foot, along the numerous marked trails ; many villages on both the N and S flanks make good starting points. Although country towns on the S slopes still prosper from their traditional occupations, many smaller villages on the poorer

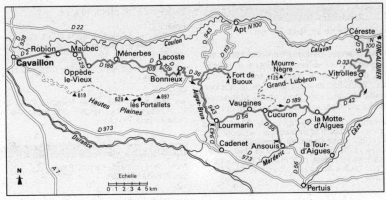

2. The Lubéron heights

N face were abandoned; some are now taking a new lease on life with the summer influx of artists and craftsmen.

▶ **Cavaillon** (→). ▶ **Robion.** ▶ **Maubec.** ▶ **Oppède-le-Vieux★**, an artists' and writers' colony among the ruins. To Mérindol SSE across the Petit Lubéron *(approx. 14 km, 4hr30 by GR6).* ▶ **Ménerbes★**, a citadel on a sheer rock; from here to Mérindol, S across the Petit Lubéron *(approx. 13 km, 4hr30).* **Notre-dame de Lumières** *(7 km NNE of Ménerbes),* a place of pilgrimage; some of the *ex-votos★* in the 17thC chapel are masterpieces of *naïf* art. ▶ **Lacoste** : the imposing ruins of the Marquis de Sade's château frown down. ▶ **Bonnieux★** : from the terrace by the old church, view★ across the Apt; in the new church, four 16thC painted panels★; Rue de la République, Bakery Museum. ▶ **Saint-Symphorien** *(2 km left at the crossroads)* : the slender Romanesque bell tower emerges above the oaks. ▶ 1.5 km father, road right to **Fort de Buoux★** *(path, 1hr30 round trip),* fortified since the 13thC (remains of ramparts and old village, view★). ▶ D943 enters the Lourmarin coomb on the right; this is the only passage through the Lubéron range. ▶ **Lourmarin★** : the château★, part 15thC-part Renaissance, welcomes artists, writers and researchers *(9-11:45 & 2:30-5:45, 4:45 out of season; closed Tue., Oct.-Apr.);* the apartments are decorated with Provençal antiques and ceramics, as well as several 15th-16thC Italian paintings; two monumental fireplaces★. ▶ **Vaugines,** starting point for the N crossing of the Lubéron *(approx. 18 km to Apt, 5hr15, GR9).* ▶ **Cucuron,** model for Daudet's Cucugnan (→ Fontvieille) : Romanesque and Gothic church; remains of château and ramparts; museum of Lubéron archaeology and rural life *(tel. 90.77.25.02).* From Cucuron, a forest trail *(10 km, no cars)* runs to the crest of Grand Lubéron **(Mourre Nègre,** alt. 1125 m, view★★). ▶ **Ansouis★** *(4.5 km SE of Cucuron)* : remains of fortresses and 17thC château *(2:30-6:30 ex Tue.);* extraordinary village museum of village life *(2-6, 7 in summer).* ▶ **Cabrières d'Aigues,** departure point for NNW crossing of the Grand Lubéron *(approx. 12 km, 4hr, GR92).* ▶ **La Motte-d'Aigues.** ▶ **Grambois** *(5 km SE)* : 1519 triptych★ in the church. ▶ **Vitrolles.** ▶ **Céreste.** ▶ **Carluc★** *(3.5 km NE)* : **priory** founded early in the 11thC. ▶ **Reillanne** *(10 km NE of Carluc)* : museum of rustic tools. □

Practical Information

BONNIEUX, ⊠ 84480, 12 km SW of **Apt.**
ⓘ mairie, ☎ 90.75.80.06 (h.s.).

Hotels :
● ★★★ **L'Aiguebrun,** domaine du château de la Tour, 5 km SE on D 36 and D 943, ☎ 90.74.04.14, 8 rm Ⓟ ✦ ⁂ ⌕ closed 15 Nov-15 Mar, 330. Rest. ♦♦ ✦ ♪ closed Mon

noon. A splendid estate blessed with tall old trees. Spec : *figues fraîches à la crème de fenouil,* 150-170.
● ★★★ **Prieuré** (C.H.), ☎ 90.75.80.78, 10 rm ✦ ⁂ ⌕ closed 5 Nov-14 Feb, 345. Rest. ♦♦ closed Wed noon and Tue (summer, lunch only), 5 Nov-14 Feb. Pretty setting : 17thC convent. Good food, 110-135.
⚲ ★**Vallon** (50 pl), ☎ 90.75.86.14.

MÉNERBES, ⊠ 84560, 8 km E of **Bonnieux.**

Hotel :
● ★★★ **Le Roy Soleil** (I.L.A., C.H., R.S.), rte des Beaumettes, ☎ 90.72.25.61, 14 rm Ⓟ ⁂ ⅍ ⌕ ♪ half pens, closed 15 Nov-15 Mar, 710. Rest. ♦♦ ✦ ⅍ ⅋ closed Tue noon. Spec : *magret de canard aux figues fraîches, filet de bœuf sauce foie gras, feuilleté de crabes,* 135-200.

Le LUC

Draguignan 28, Toulon 53, Paris 841 km
pop 6068 ⊠ 83340   C3

ⓘ pl. de Verdun, ☎ 94.60.74.51 (h.s.); mairie, ☎ 94.60.88.21.

Hotels :
★★ **Parc,** 12, rue J.-Jaurès, ☎ 94.60.70.01, AE DC Euro Visa, 12 rm Ⓟ ⁂ closed Mon eve and Tue, 27 Apr-7 May, 16 Nov-16 Dec, 280. Rest. ♦♦ ♪ Spec : *brouillade aux truffes, carré d'agneau,* 135-240.
★ **Mas du Four** (L.F.), Cannet-des-Maures, quartier de la Grande-Bastide, 2.5 km on N 7, ☎ 94.60.74.64, 10 rm Ⓟ ⁂ ⌕ ⅍ ⅌ closed Sun eve and Mon (l.s.), 15 Jan-15 Feb, 210. Rest. ♦ ⅋ 80-140.
⚲ ★★★**Le Provençal** (35 pl), ☎ 94.60.80.50.

Recommended
Market : every Fri.

LURE Moutain*

                                                        B1
The Lure is a 30-km extension of the Ventoux, a spine ending almost sheer above the valley of the Durance. The 1826-m Signal de Lure is the highest point *(15 min on foot, leaving D53/D113, 33 km SW from Sisteron →);* on clear days you can see for 150 km. □

> In preparing for your trip, consult the pages pertaining to the regions. You will find there the description of the region you wish to visit, as well as a list of sites that must be seen, a brief history and practical information.

MANOSQUE*

Aix-en-Provence 53, Digne 58, Paris 772 km
pop 19123 ⊠ 04100
B2

Manosque has changed radically from the 19thC village where sheep were driven through the streets morning and night as they went to and from the hill pastures. With the establishment of a nuclear research centre at Cadarache *(no visitors)*, Manosque has become the principal town in the department.

▶ **Porte Saunerie★**, 14thC gateway to the Rue-Grande (pedestrian zone). ▶ **Church of St. Sauveur** : wrought-iron bell tower★ (1725). **Notre-Dame de Romigier** : Renaissance doorway★ ; 12thC Virgin and Child★ in black wood. ▶ Two pleasant walks : **Mont d'Or** *(1.5 km NE from the town centre)* and **Toutes-Aures Hill**, also called Saint-Pancrace *(2 km SW)*; views.

Nearby

▶ **Valensole Plateau**, E, on the other side of the Durance ; string of attractive villages : **Valensole** *(21 km E)*; **Riez** *(35 km E)*, with 4thC baptistery★, and 35 million year old fossilized wading bird★ in the Provençal Nature Museum *(1 Jul.-15 Sep., 10-12 & 2:30-6:30; rest of year, daily ex Tue., Wed.)*. ▶ Other villages : **Allemagne-en-Provence, Saint-Martin-de-Brômes, Esparron-de-Verdon** (Lake). □

Practical Information _____

MANOSQUE
ⓘ ☎ 92.72.16.00.
SNCF ☎ 92.72.00.60/92.72.08.04.
Car rental : *Avis*, 17, av. J.-Giono, ☎ 92.72.18.18.
Hotels :
★★★ *La Rose de Provence*, rte de Sisteron, ☎ 92.87.56.28, AE Euro Visa, 16 rm P 〈 ﷼ 250. Rest. ♦ 〈 ৬ 100-180.
★★★ *Quintrands*, rte de Volx, ☎ 92.72.08.86, AE DC Euro Visa, 20 rm P ﷼ ৄ ৬ 150. Rest. ♦ ♪ ৬ closed Wed, 15 Dec-15 Jan. Indonesian cuisine, 90-135.

𝐀 ★★★*Municipal* (110 pl), ☎ 92.72.28.08.

Nearby

La FUSTE, ⊠ 04210 Valensole, 7 km E on the D907, D4.
Hotel :
★★★★ *Hostellerie de la Fuste* (R.S.), ☎ 92.72.05.95, AE DC Euro Visa, 10 rm P 〈 ﷼ ৄ pens, half pens, closed Sun eve and Mon (l.s.) ex hols, 6 Jan-20 Feb, 500. Rest. ● ♦♦♦ 〈 ♪ An enchanting terrace under the plane trees. Daniel Jourdan make subtle use of all the culinary riches of Provence : *salade de truites marinées à l'huile d'olive, gratin de fraise de veau*, 160-200.

GRÉOUX-LES-BAINS, ⊠ 04800, 13 km SE.
♨ (1 Feb-23 Dec); ☎ 92.74.22.22.
ⓘ 10, pl. de l'Hôtel-de-Ville, ☎ 92.78.01.08.
Hotels :
★★★ *La Crémaillère*, rte de Riez, ☎ 92.74.22.29, 54 rm P ﷼ ৄ ♪° closed 15 Dec-15 Feb, 260. Rest. ♦♦ ♪ ℘ 120-220.
★★★ *Lou San Peyre*, rte de Riez, ☎ 92.78.01.14, AE DC Euro Visa, 47 rm P 〈 ﷼ ৄ ♪ ৬ ♪° closed 25 Nov-1 Mar, 210. Rest. ♦♦ 〈 ♪ ℘ 75-135.
★★★ *Villa Borghese*, (R.S., Mapotel), av. des Thermes, ☎ 92.78.00.91, Tx 401513, AE DC Euro Visa, 70 rm P 〈 ﷼ ৄ ♪ ▭ ♪° half pens (h.s.), closed Dec-Feb, 630. Rest. ♦♦ ♪ ৬ ℘ 110-200.

𝐀 ★★★*Les Cygnes* (180 pl), ☎ 92.78.08.08; ★★*La Pinède* (76 pl), ☎ 92.78.05.47; ★★*Municipal* (66 pl), ☎ 92.78.00.62.

Recommended
Farmhouse-inn : *la Burlière*, rte de Vinon, ☎ 92.78.00.41. ♥ exhibit of handcrafted objects : in the foyer of the Thermes, figurines, mosaics, etc...

VALENSOLE, ⊠ 04210, 10 km E.
Hotel :
★★ *Piès*, rte de Riez, ☎ 92.74.83.13, Euro Visa, 16 rm P 〈 ﷼ ৄ ৬ closed Wed in winter, 6 Jan-1 Feb, 160. Rest. ♦ 〈 ৬ 60-100 ; child : 45.

VILLENEUVE-DE-HAUTE-PROVENCE, ⊠ 04130, 10 km N on the N96.
Hotel :
★★ *Mas Saint-Yves*, rte de Voex, ☎ 92.78.42.51, 13 rm P ﷼ closed 20 Dec-10 Jan, 200. Rest. ♦♦ A pleasant place to dine, 65-130.

MARSEILLE**

Nice 188, Lyon 315, Paris 778 km
pop 878689 ⊠ 13000
B3

Marseille, founded almost 26 centuries ago by the Greeks, has always seemed to be a sort of autonomous territory involved more with international trade than with life in Provence. In fact, the biggest port in the Mediterranean is more aptly symbolized by the oil refineries at Fos than by the distinctive local accent.

▶ **La Canebière** (C-D2), with hotels, shops and travel agencies that give it the somewhat stereotyped appearance of city main streets, is the shop-window of Marseille. ▶ The **Bourse** (C2), the oldest Chamber of Commerce in France, founded by Henri IV in 1599, now the **Marine Museum**, illustrating the history of the town through its maritime associations (remarkable model ships★; *10-12 & 2:30-6; guided tour Wed. 3 pm; closed Tue.*). Behind the Bourse, the **Marseille Historical Museum★★** : 2000 years of city history, remains of the Greek port★, illustration of daily life long ago, library and exhibition hall *(12-7 ex Sun. and Mon.)*. ▶ The **Old Port★** (Vieux Port; B-C2), the harbour of the Greeks, is today full of pleasure craft. Near the **Port Quay** (17thC town hall façade), the **Roman Docks Museum★** (B2), on the site of ancient warehouses, glazed jars, undersea discoveries *(10-12 & 2-6:30; closed Tue. and Wed. am)*. ▶ The Renaissance **Diamantée Mansion★** houses the **Museum of Old Marseille★** (B2; popular art and traditions, *santons★ ; 10-12 & 2-6:30; closed Tue. and Wed. am)*. ▶ To the rear, the 18thC **public infirmary** (Hôtel-Dieu). ▶ **Church of St. Laurent**, pure Provençal Romanesque (A2), sharing the end of the quay with 17thC **Fort Saint-Jean**, which used to control entry into the Vieux Port. Next to the green and white stonework of the 1893 Romano-Byzantine **cathedral** is the **old cathedral★** (B1), one of the finest examples of Provençal Romanesque art ; ask the porter to show the cherub-adorned chapel of St-Lazare★, the Romanesque altar★ (1175), and the white ceramic bas-relief by Luca della Robbia. ▶ **Old Charity Hospice** (B1), now an exhibition centre, typical of the sumptuous 17thC Baroque style of Pierre Puget (1620-94) ; recent restoration has brought out the rose pink of the stone, especially around the cupola★ in the chapel ; *(10-12 & 2-6:30; closed Tue. and Wed. am)*. ▶ **Basilica of St. Victor** (B3), on the other side of the old port, formerly an abbey ; from outside, the 11thC sanctuary (rebuild several times) looks like a fortress ; inside, 5thC chapel of Notre-Dame-de-Confession, St. Victor's burial crypt, Early Christian inscriptions and sarcophagi from the catacombs *(3-6)*. ▶ From the Canebière, the **Cours Belsunce** and the **Rue d'Aix** (C1-2) run through the North African quarter, a maze of *casbah*-like shops. ▶ **Rue St-Ferréol**, S off the Canebière, is the fashionable street of the city. ▶ **Cantini Museum★** (C-D3), in a late-17thC mansion, ceramics★, nearly 600 pièces of Provençal or Marseillais manufacture (17th-18thC) ; furniture and decorative arts in the salons ; on the upper floors, examples of contemporary art trends : Messagier, Hartung, Vieira da Silva, Germain Richier, Pignon, Adami, César, Saint-Phalle, Télémaque, Monory, among others *(10-12 & 2-6:30; closed Tue. and Wed. am)*. ▶ **Fine Arts Museum★** (D1), in the Longchamp

Palace (1870) : 15th-20thC paintings including Perugino, Carraccio, Rubens (Adoration of the Shepherds★), Pourbus, Ruisdael, Watteau, Tiepolo, David, Ingres, Corot, Courbet, Dufy, Vuillard and two Marseille artists, Pierre Puget, and the great caricaturist Honoré Daumier (1809-79) and a fine collection of African art.

Also... ▶ **Natural History Museum** and aquarium with local and tropical species in the right wing of the palace *(same hours);* behind, the Zoo with school for animal trainers. ▶ **Louis Grobet-Labadié Museum★** (D1), a Marseille art-lover's collection displayed in his 19thC mansion : furniture, tapestries, paintings, musical instruments★, autographed documents of Beethoven and Paganini *(10-12 & 2-6:30; closed Tue. and Wed. am);* a section installed in the Gare de l'Est station at the Marché des Capucins traces the history of public transportation from the omnibus to the métro of today. ▶ **J.-F. Kennedy Corniche★** (by A3), a 5-km drive along the waterfront (views★), leading to Avenue du Prado *(left, at the end of the corniche).* ▶ Immediately on the right, **Borély Park,** an archaeological museum★ in a magnificent setting for Egyptian★ (the-second largest collection after the Louvre) and Mycenaean antiquities, ceramics, 18thC French drawings, statuary *(9:30-12:15 & 1-5:30; closed Tue. and Wed. am).* ▶ From the Prado roundabout, Boulevard Michelet, right, leads *(1 200 m)* to the **Cité Radieuse★,** a residential complex built between 1945 and 1952 by the architect Le Corbusier (1887-1965). ▶ **Notre-Dame-de-la-Garde** (B4), 19thC Romano-Byzantine basilica (gilded Virgin; *ex-votos★*; view★ of the Old Port). ▶ **Port★** : access to terraces from the Place de l'Esplanade (B1 ; *Sun. and nat. hols., the ocean jetty is open to the public*). ▶ Visit by boat to the **château d'If★** *(ask at the Quai des Belges,* C2; *approx. 1hr30 round trip),* the prison built by François I in 1524 and immortalized by Alexandre Dumas in his novel, *The Count of Monte Cristo.* ▶ On another island of the **Frioul Archipelago,** the former **Caroline Hospital,** lazar house and quarantine centre, forms a handsome early-19thC architectural ensemble.

Nearby

▶ By the Ave. Mazargues and the Chemin du Roi, one arrives at the famous **Sormiou, Morgiou** and **Sugiton** calanques. ▶ Four limestone outcrops, the Estaque to the W, the Étoile to the E, and Marseilleveyre and Puget to the S, outline the rim of the Marseille basin. ▶ The **Estaque** shelters a few small resorts popular with the Marseillais : **Carry-le-Rouet** which has kept some of its charm; and, 4 km further W, **Sausset-les-Pins,** a former fishing port. ▶ **Château-Gombert** *(9 km NE),* on the lower slopes of the **Étoile Chain** : museum of popular local arts and traditions *(3-7 in summer, 2-6 in winter, Mon., Sat. and Sun.; guided tours 3 pm Wed. ex school hols.);* in the 18thC church, Raising of Lazarus★. ▶ 2.5-km NW, **Loubière Caverns** *(entrance free, 45 min visit).* ▶ **Allauch** *(13 km NE)* : 16th-17thC church; four 17thC windmills on the esplanade; museum of Old Allauch *(2:30-6, Wed. and Sat., 10-12 & 2:30-6, Sun.).* ▶ **Aubagne** *(17.5 km E)* : HQ and small museum of the French Foreign Legion *(daily ex Mon. 10-12 & 3-7, 6 in winter, Wed., Sat., Sun.).* ▶ The **Marseilleveyre Massif** is a training ground for mountain climbers, but well-marked paths make the summit accessible also to less ambitious hikers. **Callelongue** *(7 km S along the Corniche via A3),* at the end of an inlet *(calanque);* starting point for GR98b to the *calanques.* □

Practical Information _____

MARSEILLE
ℹ️ 4, La Canebière, 13001 (C-D2), ☎ 91.54.91.11.
✈ *Marseille-Provence,* 26 km NW, ☎ 42.89.90.10. *Air France office,* 331, av. du Prado (off map D4), ☎ 91.71.11.00; 14, La Canebière, 13001 (C-D2), ☎ 91.37.38.38; Marignane airport, ☎ 42.89.25.44.
🚆 *St-Charles* (D1), ☎ 91.95.10.00/91.08.50.50/ 91.08.84.12.
🚋 pl. V.-Hugo, 13003 (off map C-D1); ☎ 91.08.16.40.
🚢 quai de la Joliette, 13002 (A1), ☎ 91.91.90.66, to Corsica.

Santons

In the Provençal dialect, santoun means "little saint". These naïf little figures were first produced when the Revolution of 1789 closed the churches. A Marseilles artist evidently had the idea of making terracotta figurines, depicting not only the biblical characters but also the people of the community : shepherds, knife-grinders, blacksmiths, millers, the village simpleton, and so on. Each family could use the figures to make a Nativity scene. A Santons Fair is held at Marseille each December, and the figures are widely exported.

Car rental : Avis, 267, bd National, ☎ 91.50.70.11; train station Saint-Charles (D1), ☎ 91.64.71.00; Marignane airport, ☎ 42.89.02.26; 92, bd Rabatau, ☎ 91.80.12.00.

Hotels :
★★★★(L) *Le Vieux Port* (Sofitel), 36, Bd Ch.-Livon (A3), 13007 ☎ 91.52.90.19, 130 rm � 🅿 ⧏ 🖂 675. Rest. ● ♦ ♦♦ *Les Trois Forts* ⧏ ♪ closed Aug. Serious regional cooking. Spec : *filets de rouget aux deux beurres de poivron, râble de lapereau farci aux écrevisses, nouilles fraîches aux herbes,* 195-200♦ *Le Jardin* Quick service, 130-150.
★★★★ *Beauvau* (I.L.A., PLM), 4, rue Beauvau (C2), 13001, ☎ 94.54.91.00, Tx 401778, AE DC Euro Visa, 72 rm, 550. Rest. ♦ Facing the Vieux Port, the 18thC building has just been freshened up. 1920-style bar, with pianist. Light meals, 500.
★★★★ *Le Petit Nice* (R.C.), anse de Maldormé, corniche J.-F. Kennedy, 13007, ☎ 91.52.14.39, Tx 401565, AE Visa, 18 rm 🅿 ⧏ ⧐ 🖂 closed 2 Jan-8 Feb, 670. Rest. ● ♦♦♦♦ *Passédat* ⧏ ⧐ closed Mon. Papa and Gérard Passedat spare no effort to provide you with creative cuisine influenced by the sun and the beautiful region. *Pistou glacé aux langoustines grillées, homard vapeur, loup à l'huile vierge, canard au mesclin,* 300-500.
★★★★ *Pullman Bourse* (ex Frantel), rue Neuve-Saint-Martin (C1), 13001, ☎ 91.91.91.29, AE DC Euro Visa, 200 rm ⧏ 550. Rest. ● ♦♦ *L'Oursinade,* closed 2-31 Aug. The Lyonnais chef prepares pure-bred Provençal specialties : *feuilleté de côtes bleues parfumées à l'oursin et pousses d'épinard, paupiettes de loup aux algues et fumet d'huîtres,* 160-230.
★★★ *La Résidence Bompard,* 2, rue des Flots-Bleus (off map A3), 13007, ☎ 91.52.10.93, Tx 400430, AE DC, 47 rm 🅿 ⧐ 270.
★★★ *Noailles* (Mapotel), 66, La Canebière (D2), 13001, ☎ 91.54.91.48, Tx 430609, AE DC Euro Visa, 56 rm 🏊 310. Rest. ♦♦♦ ⧏ & In 1937, Charles Trenet made his singing debut in this modernized hotel with an elegant restaurant, 70-250.
★★★ *Palm-Beach* (Concorde), 2, prom. de la Plage, baie du Prado (off map B-C4), 13008, ☎ 91.76.20.00, AE DC Euro Visa, 161 rm 🅿 ⧏ ⧐ 🖂 470. Rest. ♦♦♦ *La Réserve* ♪ Seaside terrace. Excellent fish, 130-300♦ *Les Voiliers* grill, 100-130.
★★ *Européen,* (Inter-Hôtel), 115, rue Paradis (C-D3), 13006, ☎ 91.37.77.20, 43 rm, closed Aug, 190.
★★ *Martini,* 5, bd Gustave-Desplaces (off map D1), ☎ 91.64.11.17, 40 rm 🅿 ⧏ & ⧐ 150.
★★ *New Hotel Astoria,* 10, bd Garibaldi (D2), 13001, ☎ 91.33.33.50, Tx 400430, AE DC Visa, 58 rm ⧐ ⧏ ♪ & ⧐ 260.

Restaurants :
● ♦♦♦ *Aux Mets de Provence,* 18, quai Rive-Neuve (B2-3), 13007, ☎ 91.33.35.38, AE DC ⧏ closed Mon and Sun. Reserve. A museum-restaurant, a veritable institution and shrine to Provençal gastronomy, 220-325.
♦♦♦ *Jambon de Parme,* 67, rue de la Palud (D2-3), 13006, ☎ 91.54.37.98, AE DC Euro Visa, closed Mon and Sun eve, 12 Jul-17 Aug. Italian specialties, fresh fish, charcoal-grilled dishes, 185-250.
● ♦♦ *Calypso,* 3, rue des Catalans (A3), 13007, ☎ 91.52.64.00, Euro Visa ⧏ closed Sun, 1-15 Feb.

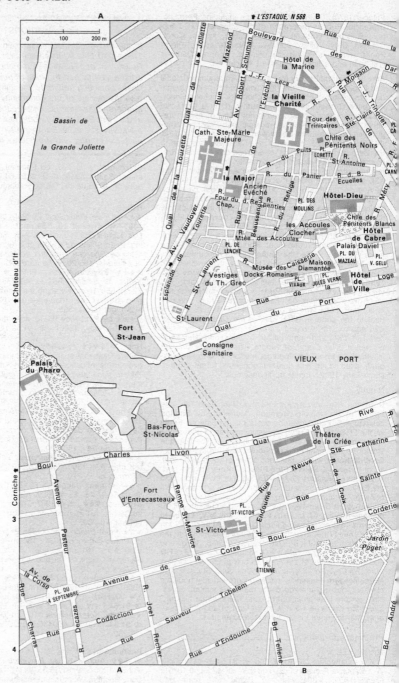

Michel's twin sister. Fresh fish at exaggerated prices, 210-320.

● ◆◆ *Michel-Aux Catalans*, 6, rue des Catalans (A3), 13007, ☎ 91.52.64.22, Visa ≮ closed Wed, 15-31 Dec.

Like the *Calypso* (above), here is a place to eat beautifully done fresh fish : *bourride, bouillabaisse*, shellfish, 250-350.

● ◆◆ *Miramar*, 12, quai du Port (B2), 13002,

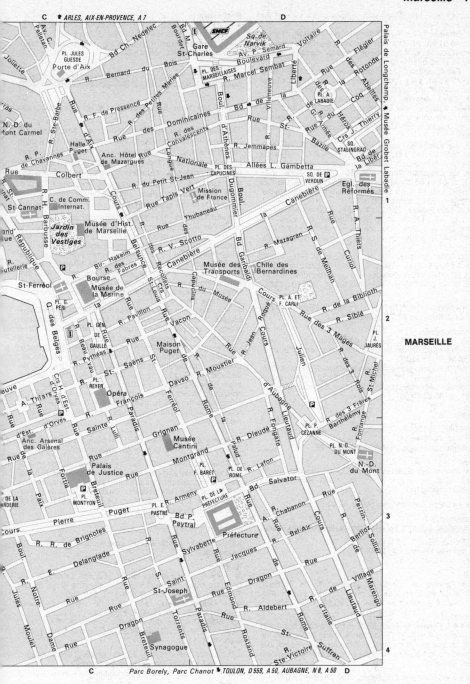

☎ 91.91.10.40, AE DC Euro Visa ⟨ ▒ ♪ & closed Sun, 1-21 Aug, 23 Dec-6 Jan. Facing the Vieux Port, this spot is a classic. Fish get top billing : *bouillabaisse, poissons du Golfe à la croûte de sel, tranche de loup aux flans d'orties*

de mer, crème d'huîtres, 150-220.

● ◆◆ ***Chez Caruso***, 158, quai du Port (B2), 13002,

☎ 91.90.94.04, AE ⟨ ▒ ♪ & closed Mon and Sun eve,

15 Oct-15 Nov. Marseillais atmosphere and a view of the Vieux Port, 140-180.

◆◆ **Patalain**, 66, rue Adolphe-Thiers (D2), 13001, ☎ 91.48.01.69, AE DC Visa ♪ closed Sun and lunch ex reservation, 14 Jul-4 Sep. Spec : *foie de canard maison*, game in season, 135-190.

◆◆ **Tire-Bouchon**, 11, cours Julien (D2), 13006, ☎ 91.42.49.03, Visa ♪ closed Mon and Sun. Turn-of-the-century decor and hearty bourgeois fare, 130-200.

● ◆ **Chez Angèle**, 50, rue Caisserie (B2), 13002, ☎ 91.90.63.35, closed Mon and Sun eve, 15 Jul-15 Aug. Family atmosphere, good humour with a Southern accent : pizza, fresh pasta, *osso buco, pieds paquets*, 65-90.

● ◆ **La Pêcherie**, chem. littoral, 13016, 8 km NW, ☎ 91.46.24.33, DC ⌁ ⏦ ♪ closed Sun eve. The restaurant at the new fishing port features, naturally, fish, 120-200.

● ◆ **Le Chaudron Provençal**, 48, rue Caisserie (B2), 13002 ☎ 91.91.02.37, AE Visa ℗ closed Sat noon and Sun and hols. Lots of fresh fish at relatively affordable prices. Spotlight on local wines, 250-300.

● ◆ **Chez Fonfon**, 140, vallon des Auffes (corniches) (off map A4), 13007, ☎ 91.52.14.38, AE DC Visa ⌁ ⓖ closed Sat and Sun , Oct. An excellent seafood bistro. Fresh fish is grilled over coals or made into *bouillabaisse*, 220-250.

◆ **La Folle Epoque**, 10, pl. F.-Barret (C3-4), 13006, ☎ 91.33.17.26, Euro Visa ♪ ⓖ closed Sat eve and Sun. Hot Lyon-style *charcuterie* served year round. In winter, good home cooking. Art nouveau decor, 95-150 ; child : 35.

⏦ ★★*Bonneveine* (200 pl), ☎ 91.73.26.99 ; ★★*Les Vagues* (200 pl), ☎ 91.73.04.88.

Recommended
Youth hostel : Château de Bois-Luzy, 13012, ☎ 91.49.06.18 ; 47, av. Joseph-Vidal, imp. du Dr-Bonfils, 13008, ☎ 91.73.21.81.
♥ chocolates and calissons : *chocolaterie Puyricard*, 315, corniche Kennedy, 13007, ☎ 91.31.31.32 ; hand-dipped chocolates : *Maurice Mistre*, 45, cours Estienne-d'Orves, 13001, ☎ 91.33.55.00.

Nearby
AUBAGNE, ⊠ 13400, 17 km SE.
SNCF ☎ 42.03.44.84.
Car rental : *Avis*, imp. Ruer, ☎ 42.84.36.06.

Hotel :
★★★ **Manon-des-Sources**, rte d'Eoures, ☎ 42.03.10.31, AE DC Visa, 15 rm ℗ ⌁ ⏦ ⓠ ▭ ♪⌁ 300. Rest. ◆◆ ⌁ ♪ 150-260 ; child : 100.

⏦ ★★★*Claire Fontaine* (66 pl), ☎ 42.03.02.28.

Recommended
♥ Provençal pottery : av. des Goums, tour of workshops.

CARRY-LE-ROUET, ⊠ 13620, 27 km W.
ⓘ 6, bd des Moulins, ☎ 42.45.01.03.
SNCF ☎ 42.45.01.03.

Hotel :
★ **La Tuillière**, av. Draïo de la Mer, rte de Sausset, ☎ 42.45.02.96, Euro Visa, 20 rm ℗ ⌁ ⏦ closed Fri eve, 195. Rest. ◆ ♪ closed Fri in winter, 60-90 ; child : 30.

Restaurant :
● ◆◆◆ **L'Escale**, ☎ 42.45.00.47 ⌁ closed Mon noon and Sun eve in Jul-Aug, 31 Oct-1 Mar. A riot of flowers on the lovely terrace and in the spacious dining room. Spec : *rôti de baudroie aux truffes, casserole de poissons*. Provençal wines, 250-330.

⏦ ★★★★*Caravaning Lou Souleï* (700 pl), ☎ 42.45.05.12.

SAUSSET-LES-PINS, ⊠ 13960, 4 km W of **Carry-le-Rouet.**

Hotel :
★★ **La Plage**, av. Siméon-Gouin, ☎ 42.45.06.31, AE Visa, 11 rm ⏦ ♪ ▭ pens, half pens (h.s.), closed Mon, 480. Rest. ◆ ⌁ ♪ 130-250.

Restaurant :
◆◆ **Les Girelles**, rue Frédéric-Mistral, ☎ 42.45.26.16, Visa ⌁ ⏦ ♪ closed Mon and Sun eve, 2 Jan-1 Mar. Terrace facing the sea. Fresh fish from the grill, attractive fixed-price meal, 105-200 ; child : 50.

MAURES Massif**

C3
Round trip from Saint-Tropez *(126 km, full day ; see map 3)*

The name is derived from the Greek word for dark *(amauros)* and the related Provençal term for a pine forest *(mauro)*. The umbrella pines have fallen victims to fire and disease ; today their place is taken by chestnut and cork-oak. Numerous well-maintained paths and stretches of water, originally designed to prevent forest-fires, offer rambling itineraries far removed from the seasonal traffic-jams of the *corniche*.

► **Saint-Tropez** (→). ► **Cogolin** specializes in the manufacture of briar pipes and wool carpets *(guided tour of the carpet factory, weekdays, 98 Blvd. Louis-Blanc)*. ► **Grimaud★** and, farther up, **La Garde-Freinet**, both with ruined châteaux and superb view★. From **Freinet**, take the **Crest Road★★** *(Route des Crêtes left)*, through beautiful countryside as far as the landmark television relay station, which shares the site★ with a tiny hermitage, **Notre-Dame-des-Anges**, possibly of Merovingian origin, still a pilgrimage site ; view from the Alps almost to Corsica. ► The road runs down the Vaudrèches Valley to **Collobrières**, where the delicious local specialties are chestnut preserve and crystallized fruits ; good white wine. **Charterhouse of La Verne★** *(12 km E ; road in poor repair in places)* : 12th-18thC ruins of brown and green stone merging with the chestnut woods ; kitchens and bakehouse, cloisters ; restaurant in summer). ► Over the **Col de Babaou** (pass) down to the **Col de Gratteloup** (superb drive, views★). ► At the **Col de Caguo-Ven**, take the unmarked asphalt road left, which snakes above the coastline on the **Col du Canadel** ; here continue left *(D27)* towards Cogolin and Saint-Tropez, or turn right to rejoin the Corniche.

Corniche des Maures★ *(26 km from Lavandou to La Croix-Valmer ; 1hr, much longer in summer)*

► Tourist country softened by eucalyptus and mimosas, pinewoods and gardens, sun and sand, windsurfing, water skiing, spectacular sites and views. ► **Le Lavandou** (→) ; **Saint-Clair ; Aiguebelle ; Cavalière** (beach★) ; **Pramousquier ; Canadel-sur-Mer ; Le Rayol** (site★) ; **Cavalaire** (beach★) ; **La Croix-Valmer.** □

Practical Information ―――――――――――

AIGUEBELLE, ⊠ 83980 Le Lavandou, 6 km E of **Le Lavandou.**

Hotels :
● ★★★ **Roches Fleuries**, ☎ 94.71.05.07, Tx 403997, DC Euro Visa, 48 rm ℗ ⌁ ⏦ ▭ half pens (h.s.), closed 15 Oct-16 Apr, 1030. Rest. ◆◆ ⌁ ⏦ 115-160.
★★★ **Grand Pavois**, ☎ 94.05.81.38, 28 rm ℗ closed 15 Oct-15 Mar, 280. Rest. ◆ ♪ 60-120.
★★ **Plage**, 14, rue des Trois-Dauphins, ☎ 94.05.80.74, 52 rm ℗ ⌁ ⏦ ⓠ half pens (h.s.), closed 5 Oct-1 Apr, 465. Rest. ◆ 75-130.

CAVALAIRE-SUR-MER, ⊠ 83240, 14 km S of **Grimaud.**
ⓘ sq. de-Lattre-de-Tassigny, ☎ 94.64.08.28.
⛴ ☎ 94.64.08.04, to Porquerolles, daily service to Port-Cros.

Hotels :
★★★ **Alizés**, prom. de la Mer, ☎ 94.64.09.32, 18 rm ℗ ⌁ half pens (h.s.), closed 15 Nov-20 Dec, 475. Rest. ◆ ⌁ ♪ ⓖ 85-160 ; child : 40.
★★★ **La Pergola**, rue du Port, ☎ 94.64.06.86, DC Visa, 27 rm ℗ ⏦ ⓠ ♪ ⛙ pens, half pens (h.s.), closed

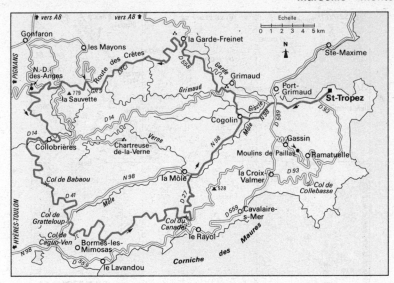

3. Maures massif

4 Jan-5 Feb, 5 Nov-24 Dec, 620. Rest. ♦ ♪ 145-190; child : 75.

🏕 ★★★★*Bonporteau* (240 pl), ☎ 94.64.03.24; ★★★★*La Baie* (480 pl), ☎ 94.64.08.15; ★★★★*La Pinède* (180 pl), ☎ 94.64.11.14; ★★★*Cros du Mouton* (160 pl), ☎ 94.64.10.87.

CAVALIÈRE, ⊠ 83980 Le Lavandou, 8 km E of **Le Lavandou.**

Hotel :
★★★★(L) *Le Club de Cavalière*, plage de Cavalière, ☎ 94.05.80.14, Tx 420317, AE DC Visa, 32 rm 🅿 ≷ 𝕸 ♨ ♒ ♪ ⚓ ⚓ ♒ closed Mon. A pleasant club, open to all, with the added attraction of A. Gigant's cooking : *millefeuille chaud de loup, sabayon verveine, émincé de cigales braisées au blanc de blanc,* 170-300.

COGOLIN, ⊠ 83310, 3 km S of **Grimaud.**
ⓘ pl. de la République, ☎ 94.56.36.52; Marines de Cogolin, ☎ 94.56.03.70.

Hotel :
★★ *Coq'Hôtel*, pl. de la Mairie, ☎ 94.56.12.66, Visa, 18 rm 🅿 closed 1 Nov-2 Jan. Rest. ♦ *Coq'Assis* ♪ ♒ ⚓ closed Wed, 1 Nov-15 Dec, 55-90.

Restaurant :
● *La Ferme du Magnan*, RN 98, ☎ 94.49.57.54 ≷ 𝕸 ♪ closed Tue and wkday noon (h.s.) , Mon-Fri (l.s.), 20 Jan-10 Mar. Rest from the noisy Riviera at the Campanile's farm. The food is healthful, and the grills (done over vine-cuttings) are generous and delicious : mussels, sardines, steaks, 110-180.

La CROIX-VALMER, ⊠ 83420, 6 km NE of **Cavalaire.**

Hotel :
● ★★★ *Les Moulins de Paillas*, plage de Gigaro, ☎ 94.79.71.11, Tx 697987, AE DC, 30 rm 🅿 ≷ 𝕸 ♪ ♨ ⊟ ♒ half pens (h.s.), closed 30 Sep-15 May, 900. Rest. ♦ *Pépé le Pirate* Outside grill, 50-100. ♦♦ *La Brigantine* Excellent cuisine supervised by R.-Guth : *aiguillettes de canard en infusion de vin rouge et mousse de navets, médaillons de lotte au beurre de tomates et gâteau de courgettes,-* 80-180.
● ★★★ *Souleias,* plage de Gigaro, ☎ 94.79.61.91, 48 rm

☐ ♒ Solarium. Stylish and charming, 575. Rest. ♦♦ 140-250.

🏕 ★★★★*Sélection Camping* (240 pl), ☎ 94.79.61.97.

GRIMAUD, ⊠ 83310, 4 km W of **Saint-Tropez.**
ⓘ ☎ 94.43.26.78.

Hotel :
★★★ *Boulangerie*, rte de Collobrières, 3 km W on D 14, ☎ 94.43.23.16, 10 rm 🅿 ≷ 𝕸 ♨ ♪ ⚓ ⊟ ♒ half pens (h.s.), closed 1 Oct-1 Apr, 795. Rest. ♦♦ ≷ ♪ ⚓ 115-145.

Restaurants :
● ♦♦♦ *Les Santons*, rte Nationale, ☎ 94.43.21.02, AE DC Visa, closed Wed noon (l.s.), 15 Oct-15 Mar. Claude Girard, a close friend of Jean Delaveyne, is a very great chef, gifted with tried and true talent. We are glad to welcome him to our chefs' panel for his expertise and virtuosity. His authentic Provençal decor is ravishing (as is Mme Girard) and his delicious cuisine is full of sunny flavours : *terrine de volaille aux herbes, escalopines de bandroie au beurre de basilic, glace au caramel.* Fine wines, 265-350.
♦ *Café de France*, pl. Neuve, ☎ 94.43.20.05, Visa ≷ 𝕸 closed Tue, 1 Nov-2 Feb, 70-120.

🏕 ★★★★*La Plage* (450 pl), ☎ 94.56.31.15; ★★★★*Les Mûres* (700 pl), ☎ 94.56.16.97; ★★★*7 sites* (2400 pl); at Saint-Pons-les-Mûres, ★★★★*Automobile Club de France* (246 pl), ☎ 94.56.30.08.

SAINT-CLAIR, ⊠ 83980 Le Lavandou, 3 km E of **Le Lavandou.**

Hotel :
★★★ *Orangeraie,* plage de St-Clair, RN 559, ☎ 94.71.04.25, AE DC Euro Visa, 20 rm 🅿 ≷ 𝕸 closed 1 Oct-1 May, 350.

MENTON★★

Nice 27, Cannes 63, Paris 963 km
pop 25449 ⊠ 06500   D2
Menton boasts next to no winter, tropical vegetation including orange and lemon trees, and flowers everywhere. The mountains act as a barrier to the prevailing wind and you can tan on beautiful beaches most

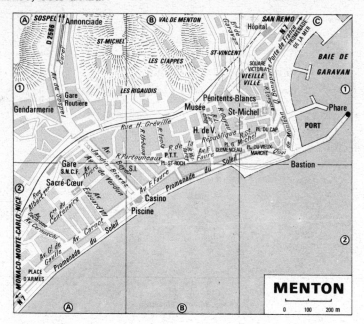

MENTON

0   100   200 m

months of the year. Cultural activities organized by the town range from the Chamber Music Festival to the Biennial International Art Show, not to forget the Lemon Festival, and other delights. The old town is a maze of narrow streets, dark passages, and crooked steps.

▶ Along the sea front, the **Promenade du Soleil★** (A-B2) with cafés, restaurants and shops. ▶ In the fortifications, the **Jean Cocteau Museum★**, arranged according to the artist's instructions with mosaics, tapestries and other works of art *(10-12 & 3-6 in summer, 5:30 in winter; closed Mon., Tue. and nat. hols.).* ▶ From the **Quai Bonaparte** (C1), a monumental stairway leads to the **Parvis★★** and **church of St. Michel★** (Baroque interior, altarpieces★ and organ lofts★). A few steps to the left of the church, **chapel of the Pénitents-Blancs★** adorned with garlands of flowers in stucco; concerts during the chamber music festival. ▶ **Rue St-Michel★** (C1), the Place aux Herbes and the nearby market are all equally irresistible in their charm.

Also... ▶ **Municipal Museum** (B1) : local history, folk arts, and archaeology including the skull of "Menton Man" from the Late Palaeolithic period and female statuettes★ of the same period *(10-12 & 3-6 in summer; 10-12 & 4-5:30 in winter; closed Mon., Tue. and nat. hols.).* ▶ At the **Town Hall**, marriages are celebrated in a registry office★ decorated by Cocteau *(9-12 & 3-6 in summer; 9-12 & 2-6 in winter; closed Sat., Sun. and nat. hols.).* ▶ **Biovès Gardens★** (A1-2) : palm trees, lemon trees, flowers and fountains, *Belle-Epoque* Europe Palace, a cultural centre. ▶ **Carnolès Palace Museum★** (via A2), 18thC former summer residence of the princes of Monaco, now an art museum surrounded by splendid gardens (Italian, French and Flemish paintings; *10-12 & 1-6 in summer, 10-12 & 2-5:30 in winter; closed Mon., Tue. and nat. hols.).* ▶ Above the church of St. Michel, the old **cemetery** : view★. ▶ **Exotic Botanical Gardens★**; **Colombières Gardens★** (via C1).

Nearby

▶ **Gorbio** *(8 km NW),* **Sainte-Agnès** *(11 km NW),* **Castellar** *(7 km N)* : old villages★ among olive and pine trees,

with the charm of Old Provence. ▶ **L'Annonciade** *(5.5 km NNW)* : 17thC monastery among cypress and eucalyptus (view★). ▶ **Sospel★** *(21 km N along D2566)* through the **Carel Valley** and the Castillon Pass in the Alps : old bridge, church with painting of the Virgin by François Bréa (fine example of school of Nice). **Braus Pass★**, SW of Sospel *(22 km to Escarène)* by D2204. Turini Forest★★ *(→)* N of Sospel; and *(25 km)* the Turini Pass via the **Piaon Gorges★** and **Bévera Valley★**. ▶ **Roquebrune-Cap-Martin★** *(5 km W; →* Riviera). □

Practical Information _____

MENTON
ℹ Palais de l'Europe, av. Boyer (A2), ☎ 93.57.57.00.
🚄 (A2), ☎ 93.35.87.89/93.35.36.37.
🚌 av. Sospel (A1), ☎ 93.35.93.60.
⚓ Vieux-Port, quai Napoléon III (C1), ☎ 93.35.51.72, to Monaco.
Car rental : *Avis,* train station (A2); 9, rue V.-Hugo, ☎ 93.35.50.98.

Hotels :
★★★ *Chambord,* 6, av. Boyer (A-B2), ☎ 93.35.94.19, Tx 460000, AE DC, 40 rm 🅿 ♪ 🍴 325.
★★★ *Princess et Richmond,* 617, prom. du Soleil (A2), ☎ 93.35.80.20, Tx 470673, AE DC Euro Visa, 45 rm 🅿 🍴 🐟 closed 4 Nov-20 Dec. Facing the sea, terrace and solarium, 320.
★★ *L'Ermitage,* 30, av. Carnot (A2), ☎ 93.35.77.23, AE Visa, 21 rm 🍴 🕰 200. Rest. ♦♦ *Chez Mireille* ♪ Nice little spot. Spec : *pavé de loup sur confit de blanc de poireaux, caneton de Challans à l'aigre-doux.* 145-200 ; child : 45.
★★ *Stella-Bella,* 850, prom. du Soleil (A2), ☎ 93.35.74.42, Visa, 26 rm 🍴 🛏 pens (h.s.), closed 30 Oct-6 Jan, 460. Rest. ♦ 🛏 🍴 closed Mon, 70-120.
★ *Santons* (L.F.), colline de l'Annonciade (A1), ☎ 93.35.94.10, AE Euro Visa, 10 rm 🅿 🍴 🕰 🛏 half pens, closed 15 Nov-15 Dec, 170. Rest. ♦♦ ♪ A place to keep in mind. Spec : *saumon mariné au basilic, ris de veau aux mousselines de volaille et de champignons,* 90-250.

Restaurants :
● ♦♦ *L'Artisan Gourmand,* 25, rue des Marins, Monti,

5 km N on D 2566, ☎ 93.35.74.21 ♪ closed Sun, 17 Nov-26 Dec. Vegetarian. In old Menton, a whole spectrum of flavours, with fresh young vegetables from the inland hills : *bagna caouda* (basket of raw vegetables with soy sauce), *vol au vent jardinière*, 80-100.
♦♦ *Francine*, 1, quai Bonaparte (C1), ☎ 93.35.80.67, AE DC Euro Visa ♪ closed Mon eve, 16 Nov-23 Dec. One of Menton's few good fish restaurants. Spec : *loup grillé au fenouil, langouste à la normande*, 120-250.
♦♦ *Roc Amadour*, 1, sq. Victoria (C1), ☎ 93.35.76.04, AE DC Euro Visa ≷ ⸙ ♪ ₺ closed Mon, 15 Nov-15 Dec. Simple, traditional fare. Spec : *filet de turbot en marinade de citron au pistou, salade Roc Amadour*, 80-170.
♦ *Chez Germaine*, 46, prom. du Mal-Leclerc (A1), ☎ 93.35.66.90 ⸙ ₺ closed Mon and Sun eve, 15 Jun-15 Jul. Savoury simplicity. Low prices, 140-170.
♦ *Table du Roy*, 31, av. Cernuschi (off map A2), ☎ 93.57.38.38, AE Euro Visa ♪ closed Mon and Sun eve, 120-250.

⚠ ★★*Municipal* (172 pl), ☎ 93.35.81.23 ; ★★*St-Maurice* (50 pl), ☎ 93.35.79.84.

Nearby

CASTILLON, ✉ 06500 Menton, 12 km N on the D2566.

Hotel :
★★★ *La Bergerie*, ☎ 93.04.00.39, 14 rm ℗ ≷ ⸕ closed Oct-Mar, 250. Rest. ♦♦ ≷ ♪ 90-115.

SOSPEL, ✉ 06380, 22 km N.
〈SNCF〉 ☎ 93.04.00.17.

Hotel :
★★ *Etrangers* (L.F.), 7, bd de Verdun, ☎ 93.04.00.09, Tx 970436, Euro Visa, 35 rm ℗ ≷ ⸕ ♪ ⊡ half pens, closed 25 Nov-22 Jan, 440. Rest. ♦ ≷ ♪ ₺ A sympathetic stop in the hills behind Menton, 60-100.

⚠ ★★*Les Merveilles* (66 pl), ☎ 93.04.04.66.

Principality of MONACO★★

Menton 9, Nice 18, Paris 957 km   D2

Although there are no visible frontier posts or Customs, this tiny sovereign State (475 acres) maintains a character of its own, which encompasses casinos, festivals, motor racing, and the rich and tanned at play. Towards the turn of the century, Monte-Carlo emerged as a fashionable resort. Many buildings still reflect the *Belle-Époque;* newer additions are equally stylish but in a different way. Old Monaco sits above Monte-Carlo : a fairy-tale city with Palace and smartly turned-out guards.
▶ *Princely Palace★* (B3), 16th-17thC, with a few medieval vestiges. The changing of the guard takes place on the square daily 5 min before noon; in the Courtyard of Honour★, 16th-17thC frescos; furniture, fine rugs, portraits in the Throne Room and apartments *(Jun.-Sep., 9:30-6:30; 1-15 Oct., 10-5);* **Napoleonic Museum** and **Archives of Monaco** : many personal effects of Napoleon, historic documents of Monaco *(9:30-6:30 in season; 10-11:30 & 2-5:30 out of season; closed Mon.).* ▶ In the Old Town, 1884 neo-Romanesque **cathedral** : paintings of the **School of Nice★**, including Louis Bréa's **St. Nicolas altarpiece★★** (1500) and **Pietà du Curé Teste★.** ▶ Through the **St. Martin Gardens★** (B3) to the **Oceanographic Museum★★,** founded in 1910 by Prince Albert I (aquarium★★, specimens of aquatic fauna; *9 or 9:30-7,9 in Jul.-Aug.);* view★★ from the terrace. ▶ **Historial of the Princes of Monaco** : wax figures depicting the Grimaldi family history *(9-6).* **Chapel of the Miséricorde** : 17thC recumbent Christ★ by the Monegasque artist Bosio. ▶ **La Condamine** (B2, at the foot of the rock, the most luxurious port in the Mediterranean. ▶ **Monte-Carlo** : residential towers, hotel complexes, Congress Auditorium, casinos, the renowned **Hôtel de Paris**, where rubbing the knee of the equestrian statue in the hall is said to bring luck at the casino ; **Museum of Dolls and Automatons★★**

(Avenue Princesse-Grace, C1), a charming mansion designed by Charles Garnier (1825-98, architect of the Paris Opéra) in a rose garden★ (100 19thC working automata, 600 18th-19thC dolls ; *10-12:15 & 2:30-6:30; closed some nat. hols.*).
Also... ▶ **Exotic Gardens★★,** overlooking Fontvieille : 6000 species of semi-desert plants and flowers *(9-6, Oct.-Apr.; 9-7, May-Sep.).* **Observatory Grotto** : rock formations in a cavern inhabited more than 200000 years ago; excavated artifacts in the nearby **Museum of Prehistoric Anthropology★** (A3) include the "Grimaldi Venus" a stone-age statuette.   ☐

Two armed monks

Monaco was settled by Greeks, Romans and even earlier peoples, but current history opened in the 13thC with the advent of the Grimaldi dynasty. At that time, Italy was divided by the rivalry between Guelphs and Ghibellines. In 1297 Francesco Grimaldi, a Guelph, was expelled from Genoa; accompanied by his men disguised as monks, he wrested the fortress of Monaco from Genoese Ghibellines. Francesco failed to hold the fortress, but in 1308 one of his Grimaldi relatives bought the seigneury of Monaco from Genoa. Since then, the Grimaldi arms have featured two monks brandishing swords in honour of the exploits of François La Malice (Francis the Rogue, as he is remembered).

Practical Information ⸻

La CONDAMINE, ✉ 98000.

Hotel :
★★ *Terminus*, 9, av. Prince-Pierre (A3), ☎ 93.30.20.70, 54 rm, 300. Rest. ♦ ♪ closed Sat and Sun noon, 15 Oct-15 Nov, 65-90.

MONTE-CARLO, ✉ 98000.
ⓘ 2a, bd des Moulins (C1), ☎ 93.30.87.01.
〈SNCF〉 (A3), ☎ 93.30.25.53/93.50.60.47/93.30.74.00.
Car rental : *Avis*, 9 av. d'Ostende, ☎ 93.30.17.53; train station.

Hotels :
★★★★(L) *Hermitage*, sq. Beaumarchais (C2), ☎ 93.50.67.31, Tx 479432, AE DC Euro Visa, 260 rm ℗ ≷ ⚑ ⊡ Belle-Epoque decoration. Classified historic monument, 1610. Rest. ♦♦♦♦ *Belle Epoque* ≷ Sumptuous Baroque dining room. Spec : *viennoise de saumon frais au cresson de fontaine, filet d'agneau à la crème et menthe fraîche*, 250-380.
★★★★(L) *Loews Monte-Carlo*, av. des Spélugues (C1-2), ☎ 93.50.65.00, Tx 479435, AE DC Euro Visa, 650 rm ℗ ≷ ⸙ ⚐ ⚑ ₺ ⊡ 1500. Rest. ♦♦♦ *L'Argentin* Excellent grilled meats in a pleasant "hacienda", 250-300. ♦♦♦ *Le Foie Gras* ♪ Traditional fare, 300-450. ♦♦ *La Folie Russe* ♪ ₺ Dinner shows, 320-490. ♦♦ *Le Pistou* ≷ ♪ Provençal specialties, 200-250. ♦ *Le Café de la Mer* ≷ ♪ ₺ Catch of the day and US specialties, 150-180.
★★★★(L) *Mirabeau*, 1-3, av. Princesse-Grace (C1), ☎ 93.25.45.45, Tx 479435, AE DC Euro Visa, 100 rm ℗ ♪ ₺ ⊡ 1050. Rest. ● ♦♦♦ ₺ Savoury food prepared by a pro, Yves Garnier : *poêlée de filets de rouget à l'huile d'olive et basilic sur compotée de fenouil frais, rognon de veau cuit dans sa robe*, 205-350.
★★★★(L) *Paris*, pl. du Casino (C2), ☎ 93.50.80.80, Tx 469925, AE DC Euro Visa, 255 rm ℗ ≷ ⸙ ♪ 1600. Rest. ● ♦♦♦ *Le Louis XIV* Alain Ducasse has just arrived on the scene, with lots of new ideas. Let's 'wait and see!'. ♦♦♦ *Salle Empire* ≷ 250-450. ♦♦ *Le Grill* ≷ closed Mon, 7-22 Jan. Located on the roof with a view of the coast. Disco and cabaret, 200-350.
★★★★ *Beach Plaza*, 22, av. Princesse-Grace (C1),

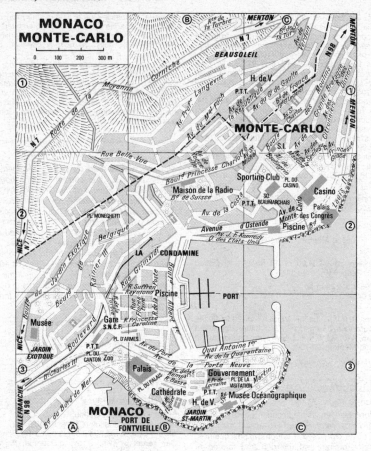

☎ 93.30.98.80, Tx 479617, AE DC Euro Visa, 313 rm ℗ ≮
▨ 🛵 ⅙ ⌷ Splendid view of the sea and Monaco. Private
beach, 1300. Rest. ♦♦♦ ≮ ⅙ ⌷ 130-220.
★★★ *Balmoral*, 12, av. de la Costa (B2), ☎ 93.50.62.37,
Tx 479436, AE DC Euro Visa, 70 rm ≮ ⌷ 500. Rest. ♦♦
⌷ closed Mon and Sun, 1 Nov-1 Dec, 90-150.

Restaurants :
● ♦♦♦ *Dominique Le Stanc*, 18, bd des Moulins (C1),
☎ 93.50.63.37, AE DC Visa, closed Mon, Sat noon, Sun
noon. An uncertain future for young and talented D. Le
Stanc, former pupil of Chapel, Senderens and the Haeberlin brothers. Let's hope all turns out for the best,
210-380.
♦♦♦ *Le Bec Rouge*, 11, av. de Gde-Bretagne (C1),
☎ 93.50.97.48 ♪ closed Jan, Jun. Elegant setting. Spec :
*bavaroise de saumon au basilic, gratin de langouste, pot-
au-feu de la mer*, 170-220.
● ♦♦ *Le Saint-Benoît*, 10 ter, av. de la Costa (B2),
☎ 93.25.02.34, AE DC Euro Visa ≮ ▨ ♪ ⅙ closed Mon,
8-27 Dec. Near the port. Grilled meats and fish get top billing but take note too of the *civette de langouste, pavé de
saumon frais à la crème de menthe*, 120-200.
♦♦ *Rampoldi*, 3, av. des Spélugues (C1-2),
☎ 93.30.70.65, AE DC Euro Visa ♪ closed Nov. Gathering
spot of Monte-Carlo's chic set. Italian food, 170-250.
♦♦ *Toula*, 20, bd de Suisse (B2), ☎ 93.50.02.02, AE DC
Visa ▨ ⅙ closed Mon, 6 Jan-5 Feb. Fine Italian cooking,
good wines, 250-375.
● ♦ *Sam's Place*, 1, av. H.-Dunant (C2), ☎ 93.50.89.33,

AE DC Visa ♪ closed Sun. Likable *brasserie*-style food at
low - for Monte-Carlo! - prices, 80-100.
♦ *Quicksilver*, 1, av. Kennedy (B2), ☎ 93.50.69.39, AE DC
Euro Visa ≮ ♪ ⅙ closed Tue, 6 Jan-1 Feb. Good seafood, 100-210.

Recommended
Casino : pl. du Casino, ☎ 93.50.69.31.
Events : *international firework festival*, Jul-Aug.

MONTE-CARLO BEACH, ⊠ 06190 Roquebrune-Cap-Martin, 3 km NE.

Hotel :
● ★★★★(L) *Monte-Carlo Beach*, av. du Bord-de-Mer,
☎ 93.78.21.40, Tx 479413, AE DC Euro Visa, 46 rm ℗ ≮
⌷ ⌐ ♪ closed 13 Oct-16 Apr. Nostalgic setting for a
splendid view of Monaco and the sea, 1400. Rest. ♦♦ *La
Potinière* ≮ closed 15 Sep-8 Jun, 250-400.

MOUSTIERS-SAINTE-MARIE★

Digne 48, Aix-en-Provence 86, Paris 793 km
pop 575 ⊠ 04360   C2

Beautiful site★ for this town renowned for a ceramic
industry that has flourished since the 17thC.

▶ **Museum of Faïence** (ceramics)★ : superb examples of
local production *(9-12 & 2-7, Jun.-Aug.; 10-12 & 2-6 rest
of year; closed Nov.-Mar.).* ▶ **Church :** Lombard Romanesque bell tower★. **Chapel of Notre-Dame de Beau-
voir★ :** 12th-14thC.

Nearby

▶ **Grand Canyon of Verdon**★★★ (→). ▶ **Lake Sainte-Croix**★★ *(5 km S)*.

Moustiers ceramics

Ceramic glazes known as "Faïence" (after Faenza in Italy where they were invented) were introduced at Moustiers in 1679 by Pierre Clérissy. Legend has it that this son and grandson of potters obtained the secret of a brilliant blue glaze from an itinerant monk. For more than a century thereafter, Moustiers thrived on the process. In the 18thC, high-fired multicoloured glazes copied from Spanish ware gave a further boost to the industry. As fashions changed, the trade declined and, in 1874, died out. The tradition was revived, however, in the 1920s, and flourishes to this day.

Practical Information

ⓘ ☎ 94.74.67.84.

Hotel :
★ *Relais*, ☎ 94.74.66.10, 15 rm, closed 1 Jan-1 Mar, 1-24 Dec, 180. Rest. ♦ 50-100.

Restaurant :
● *Les Santons*, pl. de l'Église, ☎ 92.74.66.48, AE DC Visa ⩽ ♪ closed Mon eve and Tue Mar-June and Sep-Dec, 5 Jan-30 Mar. In a stunning setting, food with the scent of thyme and Provence. Spec : *profiterolle de saumon au beurre blanc, pigeonneau aux deux cuissons à la compote de poireaux*, 130-170.

⚑ ★★★*Saint-Jean* (110 pl), ☎ 92.74.66.85 ; ★★*Le Moulin* (100 pl), ☎ 92.74.66.66 ; ★★*Saint-Clair* (175 pl), ☎ 92.74.67.15.

Route NAPOLÉON*

(Napoléon Road)
C2

This is the route taken by Napoléon in 1815 on his return from exile on the island of Elba, from **Golfe-Juan**, where he disembarked, to Grenoble (→ Dauphiné). Commemorative plaques and monuments at various stopovers mark the route for 180 km through Provence from Golfe-Juan to **Sisteron**★ (→). The main stages are : **Cannes**★★ (→), **Grasse**★ (→), **Castellane**★ (→), and **Digne**★ (→). Superb views from the **Pilon Pass**★★ *(35 km NW of Golf-Juan)* and the **Faye Pass**★★ *(44 km NW of Golfe-Juan)*. ☐

Practical Information

CORPS-LA-SALETTE, ✉ 38970, 40 km NW of **Gap**.
ⓘ rue des Fossés, ☎ 76.30.03.85.

Hotels :
● ★★ *Poste* (L.F.), pl. de la Mairie, ☎ 76.30.00.03, Euro Visa, 14 rm ⩘ ♪ half pens (h.s.), closed 15 Nov-15 Jan, 360. Rest. ● ♦♦ ♪ ఉ A pleasant rustic stopover for G. Delas's good cooking. Spec : *tourte montagnarde, poulet aux écrevisses, gratin dauphinois*, 90-130 ; child : 50.
★★ *Boustigue*, rte de la Salette, 4 km, ☎ 76.30.01.03, 20 rm Ⓟ ⩽ ⩘ ⍁ ⌨ ⍖ closed late Sep-Pentecost ex Feb, 190. Rest. ♦ ⩽ ⍖ 70-130.

Restaurant :
♦ *Tilleul*, rue des Fossés, ☎ 76.30.00.43, closed Sun eve, 1 Nov-16 Dec, 40-75.

GOLFE-JUAN, ✉ 06220 Vallauris, 3 km W of **Juan-les-Pins**.
ⓘ 84, av. de la Liberté, ☎ 93.63.73.12.
▩▩▩ ☎ 93.63.71.58.
🚋 Ligne des îles de Lérins, ☎ 93.63.81.31.

Hotels :
★★★ *Le Petit Trianon*, 18, av. de la Liberté, ☎ 93.63.70.51, 14 rm Ⓟ ⩽ ⍖ closed 20 Oct-20 Mar, 300.
★★★ *Résidence Les Jasmins*, RN 7, ☎ 93.63.80.83, Tx 970935, AE DC Euro Visa, 37 rm Ⓟ ⩘ ♪ ⌗ closed Nov, 305. Rest. ♪ 75-125.
★★ *Beau Soleil* (R.S.), imp. Beau-Soleil, ☎ 93.63.63.63, 30 rm Ⓟ ⍖ ⍁ ⍖ ⌗ closed 15 Oct-15 Mar, 205. Rest. ♦ ♪ ⍖ closed Wed noon, 80.
★★ *Crijansy*, av. Juliette-Adam, ☎ 93.63.84.44 Ⓟ ⍖ ⍁ ⍖ closed 10 Oct-20 Dec, 240. Rest. ♦ 80-150.

Restaurants :
♦♦ *Chez Christiane*, at the port, ☎ 93.63.72.44, AE DC Euro Visa, closed Tue, 15 Nov-15 Dec. Pleasant terrace. Delectable fish, 160-280.
♦♦ *Le Bistrot du Port*, 53, bd des Frères-Roustan, ☎ 93.63.70.64, Visa ⩽ ♪ ⍖ closed Mon and Sun eve (h.s.), 30 Nov-1 Feb. Pretty decor and sprightly cooking, 170-220.
♦♦ *Nounou*, on the beach, ☎ 93.63.71.73, AE DC ⩽ ♪ ఉ closed Thu ex Jul-Aug, 15 Nov-25 Dec. Private beach, 135-260.

LAFFREY, ✉ 38220, 23 km S of **Grenoble**.

Hotel :
★ *Parc* (L.F.), ☎ 76.73.12.98, 11 rm Ⓟ ⩽ ⍖ ⍁ closed Oct, 120. Rest. ♦ ♪ 50-80.

SAINT-FIRMIN, ✉ 05800, 11 km SE.

Hotel :
★★ *Alpes* (L.F.), ☎ 92.55.20.02, AE DC Euro, 30 rm Ⓟ ⍖ ⍖ ⍖ ఉ 120. Rest. ♦ *Chez Gaston* ⩽ ♪ ఉ 50-70 ; child : 35.

⚑ ★★*La Villette* (33 pl), ☎ 92.55.23.55.

VIZILLE, ✉ 38220, 15 km SW of **Grenoble**.
ⓘ pl. du Château, ☎ 76.68.15.16.

Hotel :
★★ *Parc* (L.F.), ☎ 76.68.03.01, 28 rm Ⓟ closed Sun eve, 140.

⚑ ★★★*Bois de Cornage* (130 pl), ☎ 76.68.12.39.

NESQUE Gorges*
B2

17 km E of **Carpentras** (→), D942 climbs to the **gorges**★, their cliffs riddled with caves. At the highest point (734 m) the road passes the **Cire Rock**, a concave cliff-face 400 m high. At the exit from the gorges is **Sault**, between the **Ventoux** (→) and **Lure Mountain** (→). **Albion Plateau** *(7 km SE)* : missile base *(no visitors !)*. ☐

NICE**

Cannes 34, Marseille 188, Paris 834 km
pop 338486 ✉ 06000
D2

Historic site, capital of the Côte d'Azur, and luxurious resort : Nice, a city of French and Italian heritage, is the setting for innumerable carnivals, festivals and exhibitions.

▶ **Place Masséna** (C3), laid out in 1815 in the Italian style, with arcades, gardens, fountains, bronze horses. From Place Masséna, N, department stores on **Avenue Jean-Médecin** (C3), are always busy as is the pedestrian precinct of **Rue Masséna** and **Rue de France** (fish restaurants and pizzerias). ▶ **Promenade des Anglais**★ (A-B3), fringed with gay-90s *(Belle-Époque)* façades of hotels, cafés and restaurants. ▶ **Masséna Museum**★ (B3), late 19thC Italian-style mansion ; Empire-style salons ; primitive Niçois painters★★ (altarpiece of St. Michel, school of Bréa) ; the 16thC Kiss of Peace reliquary★ in enameled silver, Niçois folklore and history, Provençal ceramics, jewels★ *(10-12 & 2-5, Oct.-Apr. ; 9-12 & 3-6, May-Sep. ;*

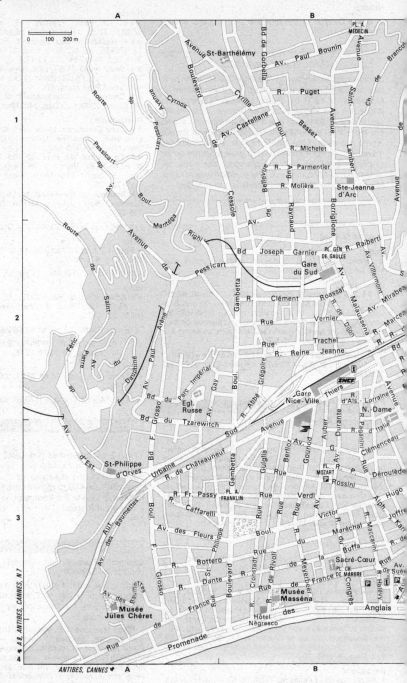

A

B

0 100 200 m

Avenue St-Barthélémy

Bd. de Gorbella

PL. A.
MEDECIN

Av. Paul Bounin

de Brancol

Boulevard

Route de

Avenue Pessicart

Cyrnos

Cyrille

R. Puget

Saint-

Av. Castellane

Boul.

Besset

Avenue

Lambert

Ch. de

Av.

Pessicart

ap.

Av.

Pessicart

Boul.

Mantega

Avenue

Righi

de

Pessicart

R. Michelet

R. Aug. Parmentier

R. Molière

Bellevue

Cessole

Av. de Raynaud

Boriglione

Ste-Jeanne
d'Arc

Avenue

Route de

Saint-

Fénic

ap.

Pierre

Av. du Dauphiné

Av. Paul

Arène

Bd. Joseph Garnier

Gare
du Sud

PL. GEN.
DE GAULLE

R. Raiberti

Av. Villermont

Gambetta

R. Clément

Rue

Roassal

Vernier

R. R. de Diton

R.

Mirabeau

Av. Malaussena

Av. Marcea

Rue

Trachel

R. Reine Jeanne

Bd.

Parc Impérial

Egl.
Russe

Bd. du Tzarewitch

Gay

Av.

Grégoire

Boul.

Gare
Nice-Ville

Thiers

R.
d'Als.-Lorraine

N.-Dame

Av. Durante

Av.

Rue d'Italie

Paganini

Clémenceau

St-Philippe
d'Orves

Bd. F. Grosso

Bd. du Sud

R. Abbé

Avenue

Berlioz

Guigina

Rue

Gounod

Av.

PL.
MOZART

P. Rossini

Dérouléde

Hugo

Urbaine

R. de Châteauneuf

Gambetta

Rue

Rue

Verdi

Alph.

Joffre

R. Fr. Passy

PL. A.
FRANKLIN

Rue

Av.

Victor

R. du Maréchal

R. Maccarini

Karr

Caffarelli

Boul.

Av. des Fleurs

Philippe

Boul.

Rue

la

Buffa

Sacré-Cœur

PL. CR.
DE MARBRE

Av. de Suè

R. Halévy

Aut. des Baumettes

Av. des Baumettes

Bottero

Grosso

Dante

Boulevard

Cronstadt

Rue de Rivoli

de Meyerbeer

Rue

France

Congrès

Musée
Masséna

Anglais

Musée
Jules Chéret

France

Rue

des

Hôtel
Négresco

Rue

Promenade

des

A 8, ANTIBES, CANNES, N 7

B

closed Mon. and hols.). ▶ **Jules-Chéret Fine Arts Museum**★ (A3), built in 1878 in the Italian Renaissance style; paintings by the 18thC brothers Carle and Jean-Baptiste Van Loo (portraits★ of Louis XV and his queen, Maria Leczinska), 17th-18thC French schools; Italian and German primitives; Impressionists; 20thC French painters *(10-12 & 2-5, 3-6 in season; closed Mon. and hols.).* ▶ The **Old Town**★ (Vieille Ville, E4), bustling, colour-

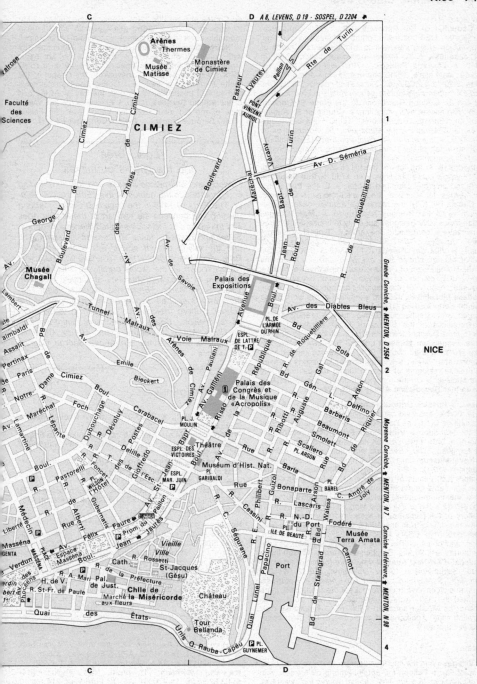

ful, picturesque. ▶ **Church of St. François-de-Paule** (C3), 1733 Niçois Baroque. ▶ **Flower Market** daily on the Cours Saleya (C3) : pedestrian mall with seafood restaurants, boutiques. ▶ **Chapel of la Miséricorde★★**, a 1736 Baroque masterpiece in gold and stucco *(guided tours only)*; 1420 altarpiece of the Virgin of Mercy★ in the sacristy. **Shell Museum** (Galerie de Malacologie), annex of the Natural History Museum : seashells★ from all over the world *(11-1 & 2-7, closed Sun., Mon. and nat. hols.).* ▶ **Cathedral of Ste Réparate** (C3) : 1650 neo-Classical façade, 1730 bell tower, dome of glazed tiles. Inside, a profusion of Baroque stucco and marble. ▶ **Church of St. Jacques★** (C3), former collegiate chapel, built in 1640. ▶ **Lascaris Palace★**, 17thC Genoese style, restored; staircase★, 18thC pharmacy★, folk arts and traditions *(9:30-12 & 2:30-6, 6:30 in season; closed Mon., Tue. and Fri.; open daily during school hols.; guided tours at 10 and 3).* ▶ Along Rue Droite to the **Place St-François** (C3) : fish market every morning. ▶ **Church of St. Augustin** (C3) : Baroque decoration★; 16thC Pietà★ by Louis Bréa. ▶ **Château★★** *(by steps near St. Augustin or by the lift D3 at the end of the Quai des États-Unis)* : almost nothing is left of the fortress, the name now designates the hill; promenade, Italian pines, view★★, ruins of the old cathedral. ▶ At the foot of the hill N, the **Place Garibaldi** (D3) : yellow ochre buildings from 1750. ▶ **Rue Ségurane** (D3) and environs : antique shops. ▶ E, the **Port** (D3) : car ferries for Corsica, boat excursions, restaurants. ▶ **Cimiez Hill** (C1), the residential quarter, called *Cemenelum* when the Romans lived there. ▶ **Marc Chagall Museum★★** (C2), designed specially to house the 17 large canvases★★ comprising the artist's "Biblical Message" *(10-7, Jul.-Sep.; 10-12:30 & 2-5:30, Oct.-Jun.; closed Tue.).* ▶ **Villa des Arènes** (C1; *10-12 & 2:30-6:30, 2-5 out of season; closed Sun. am, Mon. and Nov.),* remains of the Roman town of *Cemenelum,* **amphitheatre, baths★** (2nd-3rdC); display of everyday objects excavated on the site; history of the region (inscriptions, sculpture). **Matisse Museum★** : detailed exhibition of the work of the painter Henri Matisse (1869-1954). ▶ **Convent of Cimiez** : church with "troubadour Gothic" façade (1850); inside, masterpieces of the School of Nice : Virgin of Pity★ (1475) and Descent from the Cross attributed to Antoine Bréa. **Franciscan Museum** : 17thC frescos★ in the oratory *(10-12 & 3-6; closed Sun.);* charming garden with lemon trees; view★. ▶ Nearby, **Cimiez Cemetery** : graves of notable residents of Nice, including the painters Dufy and Matisse. ▶ On the rocky promontory, the **church★** of the former **Benedictine Abbey of St. Pons.**

Also... ▶ **Russian Orthodox Church** (A2) : pink brick, pale grey marble, and vivid ceramic tiles (1912). ▶ **Law School** (Faculté de Droit, Les Baumettes, via A3) : Chagall mosaic on the first floor. ▶ **Vieux-Logis Priory** (A1) : reconstruction of a 14th-16thC interior; kitchen★ *(4-6 summer, 3-5 winter, Wed., Thu., Sat. and first Sun. of each month).* ▶ **Naval Museum** : in 16thC Bellanda Tower (D3), models, weapons *(10-12 & 2-7 Jun.-Sep.).* ▶ **Museum of Natural History** (D3) : casts of mushrooms★ *(9-12 & 2-6; closed Tue.).* ▶ **Terra Amata Museum,** near the port, on the site of a mammoth-hunters' encampment of 400 000 years ago *(10-12 & 2-6 or 7; closed Mon.).* ▶ **Contemporary Art Gallery of the Museums of Nice** : monthly exhibitions of artworks dating from the 1960s to the present *(59 Quai des États-Unis, 10:30-12 & 2-6; closed Sun. am, Mon. and hols.).* ▶ The **Villa Arson** (Nice centre of contemporary art), 20 Ave. Stephen-Liégeard. ▶ **Musée International d'Art Naïf Anatole Jakovsky** (primitive art; château Sainte-Hélène, Ave. Val-Marie, *10-12 & 2-5, Oct.-Apr., 6, May-Sep.; closed Tue., hols.).* ▶ **Acropolis,** arts/music/convention centre, 1 Espl. Kennedy (D2), inaugurated in 1985; Agora, entrance hall with roof which opens; Le Méditerranée, an 1 800-m² multi-purpose hall; bowling alley; Apollon auditorium, one of the most beautiful in Europe.

Nearby

▶ **Villages★★** in the countryside near Nice evoke an older way of life. ▶ **Falicon** *(10 km N),* among olive trees, with **Mont Chauve** *(6.5 km NW, 30-min round trip,* view★★). ▶ **Tourrette-Levens** *(17.5 km N).* ▶ **Aspremont** *(6 km W of Tourrette),* in concentric rings around a château. ▶ **Mont Alban** and **Mont Boron** *(E and NE of Nice, 10 km round trip),* and **Saint-Michel plateau** *(8 km)* : views★ of the coast. ▶ **Contes** *(18 km N),* originally Roman, on a spur among pine and olive; Ste-Madeleine★ altarpiece★ (1525) attributed to François Bréa in the church. ▶ **Châteauneuf-**de-**Contes** *(4.5 km W)* : 11thC Romanesque church; 2 km to ruins of village. ▶ **Berre-des-Alpes** *(27 km N),* on a mountain covered with chestnut woods (site, panorama★). ▶ **Notre-Dame-de-Laghet** *(14 km NE)* : pilgrimage site with collection of *ex-votos.* ▶ **Peillon★★** *(17 km NE)* : straight out of the Middle Ages, a real eyrie on a rock; 15thC frescos★ by Jean Canavesio in the Chapel of the White Penitents. ▶ **Peille★** : Gothic houses, stairways and vaulted passages, views over the bay. ▶ At the end of the **Paillon Gorges★** *(D21),* **L'Escarène** *(25 km NNE)* : view of the old town from the bridge over the Paillon (17thC Baroque church). ▶ **Riviera Corniches★★** (→). □

Louis Bréa
and the Niçois primitives

Frescos and altarpieces in Nice and the surrounding country attest to the genius of this 15thC Niçois painter. The Pietà of 1475 in the church at Cimiez marks a dividing line between the naïf art of the Middle Ages and the advent of the sophisticated Sienese influence. Schematic drapery, facial expression of spirituality, and the telling use of colour are characteristic of Bréa and the other artists (Canavesio, Balaison, Nadal) known as the Niçois primitives. The Masséna Museum at Nice, and churches at Cimiez, Roubion, Villars, Saint-Martin-d'Entraunes, Monaco, Puget-Théniers and Sospel all display brilliant examples of the school. Superb frescos can be seen in the churches at Peillon, Coaraze, Venanson, Saint-Étienne-de-Tinée, Auron, Lucéram, Cians, Roure, Roubion, Valdeblore, Saint-Dalmas, Entraunes, Saorge, Cagnes and Vence.

Practical Information _____

NICE
ⓘ av. Thiers (B2), ☎ 93.87.07.07 ; 5, av. Gustave-V (B3), ☎ 93.87.60.60.
✈ Nice-Côte d'Azur, 7 km SW, ☎ 93.21.30.30. Air France office, at the airport, ☎ 93.72.32.00 ; 7, av. Gustave-V (B3), ☎ 93.21.32.79.
▨ (B2), ☎ 93.88.29.54/93.87.50.50/93.88.89.93.
▨ prom. du Paillon (C3), ☎ 93.85.61.81.
▨ (B3), ☎ 93.89.89.89, to Corsica.
Car rental : Avis, pl. Masséna, 2, av.Phocéens (C3), ☎ 93.80.63.52 ; airport, ☎ 93.21.36.33 ; train station (B2), ☎ 93.87.90.11.

Hotels :

● ★★★★(L) *Negresco,* 37, prom. des Anglais (B4), ☎ 93.88.39.51, Tx 460040, AE DC Euro Visa, 150 rm ≮ ♪ Empire and Napoléon-III decor a classified historic monument, 1550. Rest. ● ♦♦♦♦ *Chantecler* ≮ ♪ & closed Nov. The brilliant winner of our last Hachette Grand Prix, awarded by his peers, Jacques Maximin is a proud and happy chef. He continues to dazzle his patrons with a subtle blend of sunny Niçois cooking and simple, simply great cuisine : *courgettes à la fleur et aux truffes, saumon gros sel, flan de filet d'agneau.* Exceptional dessert menu. Fine cellar, 280-400♦♦ *La Rotonde* ≮ ♪ & Spéc. : *ravioles au fromage, tripes à la Niçoise,* 150-200.

★★★★(L) *Beach Regency,* 223, prom. des Anglais (A4), ☎ 93.83.91.51, Tx 461635, AE DC Euro Visa, 335 rm Ⓟ ≮ ♪ & ▨ 820. Rest. ♦♦♦ *Rendez-Vous* ≮ ♪ & 130-230.

★★★★(L) *Méridien,* 1, prom. des Anglais (B4), ☎ 93.82.25.25, Tx 470361, AE DC Euro Visa, 314 rm ≮ ♪ ▣ ₰ ⌐ 1150. Rest. ♦♦ *L'Estacade* ≮ ♪ 190-230.

★★★★ *La Pérouse,* 11, quai Rauba-Capeu (D4), ☎ 93.62.34.63, Tx 461411, AE DC Euro Visa, 65 rm ≮ ♫ ⌐ ▨ Grill-room and snack-bar in summer, 600.

★★★★ *Park,* 6, av. de Suède (B3), ☎ 93.87.80.25, Tx 970176, AE DC Euro Visa, 145 rm Ⓟ ≮ ♪ ♣ & 565. Rest. ♦♦ ♪ & closed Sun, 110-230.

★★★★ *Westminster* (Concorde), 27, prom. des Anglais (B3-4), ☎ 93.88.29.44, Tx 460872, AE DC Euro Visa, 110 rm ≪ ♪ 900. Rest. ♦♦ *Il Pozzo* ≪ ♪ closed 1 Nov-10 Dec, 160-250♦♦ *Le Farniente* ♪ closed Nov-15 Dec, 140-200.

★★★ *Continental Masséna*, 58, rue Gioffredo (C3), ☎ 93.85.49.25, Tx 470192, AE DC Euro Visa, 116 rm Ⓟ ◪ ♪ 🏊 ♿ 435.

★★★ *Gounod*, 3, rue Gounod (B3), ☎ 93.88.26.20, Tx 461705, AE DC Euro Visa, 50 rm Ⓟ ◪ ♪ 🏊 ▣ 380.

★★★ *L'Oasis*, 23, rue Gounod (B3), ☎ 93.88.12.29, Visa, 41 rm Ⓟ ⅏ ◪ ♪ ♿ 295.

★★★ *La Malmaison* (Mapotel), 48, bd V.-Hugo (B3), ☎ 93.87.62.56, Tx 470410, AE DC Euro Visa, 50 rm ◪ ♪ half pens (h.s.), 610. Rest. ♦♦ ≪ ♪ ♿ 80-150.

★★★ *Midi*, 16, rue Alsace-Lorraine (B2-3), ☎ 93.88.49.17, 40 rm ◪ ♪ ⌘ closed Nov-Jan, 330.

★★★ *Napoléon*, 6, rue Grimaldi (B3), ☎ 93.87.70.07, Tx 460949, AE DC Euro Visa, 80 rm ◪ ♪ 🏊 ♿ 330.

★★ *Alfa*, 30, rue Masséna (C3), ☎ 93.87.88.63, AE DC Euro Visa, 38 rm, 225.

★★ *Crillon*, 44, rue Pastorelli (C3), ☎ 93.85.43.59, 43 rm ⌘ closed 15 Nov-15 Dec, 190.

★★ *Durante*, 16, av. Durante (B3), ☎ 93.88.84.40, 27 rm Ⓟ ⅏ ◪ ♪ closed 30 Oct-1 Dec, 250.

★★ *Flore*, 29, av. Malausséna (B2), ☎ 93.88.01.82, AE, 10 rm ⌘ pens (h.s.), 320. Rest. ♦ 75-95.

★★ *Harvey*, 18, av. de Suède (B3), ☎ 93.88.73.73, AE DC, 58 rm ⌘ closed 1 Nov-1 Feb, 205.

★ *Ann-Margaret*, 1, av. St-Joseph (D2), ☎ 93.96.15.70, AE DC Visa, 29 rm Ⓟ ⅏ ◪ ▣ 175.

★ *Le Gourmet Lorrain*, 7, av. Santa-Fior (B1), ☎ 93.84.90.78, AE Visa, 15 rm ⅏ ◪ ♪ closed Sun eve and Mon, 2-10 Jan, Aug, 150. Rest. ♦♦ ♪ Carefully prepared seasonal cuisine based on the market's bounty, 95-200.

Résidence Hôtel Ulys, 179, prom. des Anglais (A-B4), ☎ 93.96.26.30, Tx 461411, AE DC Euro Visa, 88 rm ≪ ♪ 🏊 ♿ closed Sun eve and Mon, 290. Rest. ♦ ≪ ♪ ♿ closed Mon and Sun eve , Nov, 65-70 ; child : 45.

Restaurants :

♦♦♦ *L'Ane Rouge*, 7, quai des Deux-Emmanuel (D4), ☎ 93.89.49.63 ≪ ◪ ♪ closed Sat and Sun, 14 Jul-1 Sep. Good food. Spec : *huîtres plates au champagne, loup farci au beurre d'écrevisses, Saint-Pierre mascareigne*, 250-350.

● ♦♦ *Gérard Ferri*, 56, bd J.-Jaurès (C3), ☎ 93.80.42.40, Euro Visa ◪ ♪ closed Sat noon and Sun, 1 Jul-15 Aug. Talented chef Ferri is once again *chez lui*, serving a pleasant fixed meal and a top-quality *à la carte* selection : *chartreuse froide de lapereau, chapirons au pistou, tarte légère aux pommes* and lots of other good things, 170-230.

● ♦♦ *Catherine-Hélène Barale*, 39, rue Beaumont (D3), ☎ 93.89.17.94, closed Mon and Sun , Aug. Niçois specialties in a casual setting that's the motto of the lively, everyouthful Catherine-Hélène Barale, in her little eatery filled with antique bric-à-brac : *pissaladière, socca* etc... Lots of atmosphere, 150-200.

● ♦♦ *Le Bistrot d'Antoine*, 26, bd V.-Hugo (B3), ☎ 73.88.49.75 ⅏ ♪ closed Sun. For quality, sincerity and low prices, you can't beat the good local specialities served by A. Villa. Menu gourmand, 80F : starter, fish course, meat course. Daily special or low-calorie menu : 65. A dream, 65-150.

● ♦♦ *Le Florian*, 22, rue Alphonse-Karr (B3), ☎ 93.88.86.60, AE Euro Visa ♪ ♿ closed Mon noon and Sun , Aug. Rush over to taste Cl. Gillon's intelligent cuisine, and give him a bit of encouragement : *queue de bœuf à la confiture d'oignon, flan de Saint-Pierre, râble de lapin aux senteurs de Provence*, 160-270.

♦♦ *Aux Gourmets*, 12, rue Dante (A3), ☎ 93.96.83.53, AE DC Visa ◪ ♪ closed Mon and Sun eve. Classic cuisine, good value, exceptional cellar, 60-150.

♦♦ *Chez les Pêcheurs*, 18, quai des Docks (D3), ☎ 93.89.59.61 ≪ Fish specialties, 180-240.

♦♦ *Coco Beach*, 2, av. Jean-Lorrain (D3), ☎ 93.89.39.26, AE DC Euro Visa ≪ ♪ ♿ ⌘ closed Mon and Sun,

15 Nov-28 Dec. Pricey but good. Outstanding grilled fish and luscious *bouillabaisse*, 300-400.

♦♦ *La Cassole*, 22, av. St-Jean-Baptiste (B3), ☎ 93.85.01.14, AE DC Euro Visa, closed Mon noon, 25 Jul-20 Aug. Périgord specialties, 70-80.

♦♦ *La Rive Gauche*, 27, rue Ribotti (D2-3), ☎ 93.89.16.82, AE Visa, closed Sun , Aug. Simple eatery serving country cooking, 65-130 ; child : 50.

♦♦ *Le Grand Pavois*, 11, rue Meyerbeer (B3), ☎ 93.88.77.42, AE Euro Visa ♪ closed Mon Jul-9 Aug. Savoury seafood, excellent *bouillabaisse*, 160-200.

♦♦ *Nissa Socca*, 5, rue Ste-Réparate (C3), ☎ 93.80.18.35, closed Mon and Sun, 20 May-15 Jun. Robust Niçois cuisine, 100-150.

♦♦ *St-Moritz*, 5, rue du Congrès (B3), ☎ 93.88.54.90, AE Euro Visa ♪ closed Thu, 6 Jan-1 Feb. Mountain atmosphere, 110-250.

● ♦ *La Piscine*, 15, rue Tonduti-de-l'Escarène, ☎ 93.62.58.69, AE Euro Visa ♪ closed Sat noon and Sun noon. For a snack...late at night, 100-150.

♦ *L'Univers*, 54, bd J.-Jaurès, ☎ 93.62.32.22, AE DC Euro Visa ♿ Warm welcome, good food, 160-200.

♦ *La Madonette*, 24, chem. de la Madonette, ☎ 93.86.92.92, closed Mon. Dinner-shows. Folksy atmosphere in the dining room and on stage, 230-300.

♦ *La Merenda*, 4, rue de la Terrasse (C3), closed Mon, Sat eve, Sun , Feb-Aug. Authentic Niçois cuisine, 80-160.

Recommended
Baby-sitting : *Centre Information Jeunesse*, ☎ 93.80.93.93 ; *Alliance culturelle internationale*, ☎ 93.88.23.60.
Bicycle rental : *Moto Rent*, 3, rue Barralis, ☎ 93.88.08.68 ; *Arnaud*, 4, pl. Grimaldi, ☎ 93.87.88.55 ; *Nicea*, 12, rue de Belgique, ☎ 93.82.42.71.
Casino : the famous *Casino Ruhl*, dusted off and restored, has reopened its doors ; 2-4, rue St-Michel, ☎ 93.80.55.70.
Events : *Italian film festival*, Nov-Dec ; *carnival*, Feb.
Market : *flower market*, cours Saleya, 6-5:30pm ex Mon and Sun am.
Amusement park : *Zygofolis*, rte de Digne. Jul-Aug : 10am-midnight ; 1-15 Sep : 10-10 ; rest of year : 10-8.
Night-clubs : *Le Quartz*, 18, rue du Congrès, ☎ 93.88.88.87.
♥ *candied fruit* : *Henri Auer*, 7, rue St-François-de-Paule ; *ice cream* : *l'Entremets*, shopping centre, 15, bd Delfino, ☎ 93.56.06.92 ; *old paintings* : *Galerie Lavantes*, 25, rue de la Place, ☎ 93.88.89.38 ; *olive oil* : *Alziari*, 14, rue St-François-de-Paule.

Nearby

BLAUSASC, ✉ 06440 L'Escarène, 14 km N.

Restaurant :
♦♦ *Logis de la Garde*, ☎ 93.79.51.03 ≪ ◪ ♪ ♿ closed Tue and Wed, 15 Jul-14 Aug. Spec : *stock fish, épaule d'agneau à l'indian curry, civet de sanglier*, 140-220.

La COLLE-SUR-LOUP, ✉ 06480, 19 km.

Hotels :
★★★ *Hostellerie de l'Abbaye*, Le Canadel, rte de Grasse, ☎ 93.32.66.77, Tx 462304, AE DC Visa, 15 rm Ⓟ ⅏ ◪ ♪ ▣ half pens (h.s.), closed 5 Jan-26 Feb. 12thC abbey, 1020. Rest. ♦♦ ♪ closed Tue eve and Wed, 170-220 ; child : 110.

★★★ *Marc Hély* (R.S.), 535, rte de Cagnes, D 6, ☎ 93.22.64.10, AE Euro Visa, 14 rm Ⓟ ≪ ⅏ ♿ closed Nov-Feb. Overlooking Saint-Paul-de-Vence. Pleasant residence, 290.

Restaurants :
♦♦♦ *La Belle Epoque*, rte de Cagnes, ☎ 93.20.10.92, AE DC Visa ◪ ♪ ⌘ closed Mon, 5 Jan-15 Feb. Good food. Spec : *foie gras de canard à l'ail doux, fricassée de poulet au vinaigre de raisins*, 165-250.

♦ *La Strega*, 1260, rte de Cagnes, ☎ 93.22.62.37, Euro Visa ⅏ ♪ closed Mon and Sun eve, 4 Jan-28 Feb, 130-160.

⚕ ★★★*Pinèdes* (70 pl), ☎ 93.32.98.94; ★★★*Vallon Rouge* (27 pl), ☎ 93.32.86.12.

L' ESCARÈNE, ⊠ 06440, 21 km N.
SNCF ☎ 93.79.50.02.

Hotel :
★ *Hostellerie du Castellino*, ☎ 93.79.50.11, Euro Visa, 12 rm ℗ ⬭ ⬭ ⬭ closed Wed. Beautiful location, 170. Rest. ♦ ⬭ Spec : *cassoulet, confit de canard,* 70-140.

LEVENS, ⊠ 06670 Saint-Martin-du-Var, 23 km N.

Hotel :
★★ *Vigneraie*, rte de St-Blaise, ☎ 93.79.70.46, Visa, 18 rm ℗ ⬭ ⬭ ⬭ closed Oct-Jan, 160. Rest. ♦ 60-90.

PEILLON, ⊠ 06440 L'Escarène, 11 km N.

Hotel :
● ★★ *Auberge de la Madone* (L.F.), ☎ 93.79.91.17, 18 rm ℗ ⬭ ⬭ ⬭ ⬭ ⬭ half pens (h.s.), closed Wed, 15 Oct-15 Dec. A pleasant stopover under the olive trees, 270. Rest. ♦♦ ⬭ ⬭ Appetizing local cuisine. Spec : *bouillabaisse en gelée, terrine de foie de volailles à la confiture d'oignons,* 100-250.

SAINT-MARTIN-DU-VAR, ⊠ 06670, 15 km N on the N 202.

Restaurant :
● ♦♦♦ *Auberge de la Belle Route*, RN 202, rte de Digne, ☎ 93.08.10.65, AE DC Visa ⬭ ⬭ closed Mon and Sun eve , Nov school hols, 15 Feb-15 Mar. J.-F Issautier is making a name for himself in his old Provençal inn. The fixed-price meals are most affordable : *feuillantine de loup aux poivrons doux, noisettes d'agneau "Belle Route".* Local wines are priced a little high, 210-350.

SAINT-PANCRACE, ⊠ 84100 Orange, 8 km N on D 914.

Restaurant :
● ♦♦♦ *Rôtisserie de Saint-Pancrace*, 493, rte de Pessicart, ☎ 93.84.43.69, Visa ⬭ ⬭ ⬭ closed Mon ex Jul-Aug, 5 Jan-7 Feb. In the hills behind Nice is this fine family-style inn with a large, shady park : *bouillabaisse en gelée, ravioles au foie gras,* 250-280.

SAINT-ROMANS-DE-BELLET, ⊠ 06200 Nice, 10 km N on the D 714.

Restaurant :
● ♦♦♦ *Auberge de Bellet*, ☎ 93.37.83.84, AE Euro Visa, closed Tue, 15 Jan-30 Feb. Outstanding food in a charming decor, 195-330.

ORANGE*

Avignon 31, Nîmes 55, Paris 660 km
pop 27502 ⊠ 84100   A1

On the motorway S, Orange is the gateway to the Midi, symbolized by the Roman arch at the entrance to the town. Buyers and sellers come from all over Provence to the Thursday market in the Cours Aristide-Briand, redolent with honey from the Ventoux, truffles from Vaison, olives from Nyons, Tricastin lavender, thyme and rosemary, not to mention the fruits of the Comtat. Orange also boasts the best-preserved Roman theatre in existence, which is the setting for the annual international opera festival known as the *Chorégies*.

▶ The **theatre**★★★ (B3) was built in the 1stC BC during the reign of Augustus. The stage wall★★ (Louis XIV called it the "finest wall in the Kingdom") is the only complete one still standing and is classified the 9th monument in the world *(daily 9-6:30 ex performance days ; info TO).* W of the theatre, the forum and temples. ▶ **Municipal Museum** (B3) : Roman stonework, plan★ of the area in AD77, history of Orange, and fine arts including numerous works by the English painter and engraver Sir Frank Brangwyn (1867-1956 ; *8:30-12 & 2-6:30 in summer, 5 in winter).* ▶ Old **Cathedral** (B2) : 12thC Provençal Romanesque remodeled in the 16thC. ▶ **Triumphal Arch**★★ (A1), prob-

ably built in 20BC ; the decoration includes trophies, a frieze of warriors★★, two battle scenes★★, chained captives symbolizing the defeat of the Gauls. ▶ Saint Eutrope hill (B3), a public park (view★) where the château of the Princes of Orange used to be.

Nearby

▶ **Mornas** *(11 km N),* at the foot of a high cliff, plane trees, fortified gates, and a ruined château★. ▶ **Bollène** *(22 km N),* typical Provençal city with plane trees and old houses ; collegiate church of St. Martin (12th-16thC) ; museum (coins, drawings by Picasso and Chagall ; *9-12 & 2-7, Apr.-Sep. ; in winter 3-6, closed Tue.).* ▶ **Sérignan-du-Comtat** *(8 km NE),* where the entomologist Jean-Henri Fabre (1823-1915) lived and studied ; his house and grounds are now a museum *(9-11:30 & 2-4, 6 in summer ; closed Tue. and hols.).* ▶ **Châteauneuf-du-Pape** *(10 km S)* : ruined 14thC château ; the famous local wine is a real "Papal indulgence", especially when well aged. Also see the Musée des vieux outils du vigneron (museum of old winegrower's tools ; *daily ;* wine-tasting). □

Practical Information

ORANGE
ⓘ av. du Gal-de-Gaulle (A3), ☎ 90.34.70.88.
SNCF (C2), ☎ 90.30.14.43.
🚌 av. F.-Mistral (C2), ☎ 90.34.15.59.
Car rental : *Avis,* train station.

Hotels :
★★★ *Arène* (R.S.), pl. de Langes (B2), ☎ 90.34.10.95, Tx 431195, AE DC Euro Visa, 30 rm ℗ ⬭ closed 1 Nov-7 Dec, 200.
★★★ *Louvre et Terminus*, 89, av. F.-Mistral (C2), ☎ 90.34.10.08, Visa, 34 rm ℗ ⬭ ⬭ closed 15 Dec-20 Jan, 240. Rest. ♦♦ ⬭ 70-130.
★★ *Cigaloun*, 4, rue Caristie (B2), ☎ 90.34.10.07, Euro Visa 29 rm ℗ ⬭ 175.
★★ *Le Glacier* (L.F.), 46, cours A.-Briand (A3), ☎ 90.34.02.01, Visa, 29 rm ℗ ⬭ closed Sun eve and Mon lunch (Nov-Easter), 23 Dec-1 Feb, 155.

Restaurants :
♦♦ *Le Pigraillet*, colline St-Eutrope (B3), ☎ 90.34.44.25 ℗ ⬭ ⬭ ⬭ ⬭ closed Mon and Sun eve (l.s.), 6 Jan-10 Feb, 110-240.
♦♦ *Le Provençal*, 27, rue de la République (C2), ☎ 90.34.01.89, Euro Visa ⬭ ⬭ closed Wed. Spec : *filets de sole aux nouilles fraîches, compote de lapereau aux pruneaux, caneton sauvage au gros-plant, croustade d'escargots au vermouth,* 55-150.

⚕ ★★*Saint-Eutrope* (80 pl), ☎ 90.34.09.22 ; *Le Jonquier* (105 pl), ☎ 90.34.19.83.

Recommended
Events : *Chorégies* festival in Jul-Aug.

Nearby
BOLLÈNE, ⊠ 84500, 23 km N.
ⓘ pl. de la Mairie, ☎ 90.30.14.43.
SNCF ☎ 90.30.20.02.

Hotel :
★★ *Mas des Grès*, rte St-Restitut, Les Grès, rue Paul-Valéry, ☎ 90.30.10.79, AE Visa, 13 rm ℗ ⬭ ⬭ closed Mon, Sun eve, Jan, 160. Rest. ♦ 84-129.

⚕ ★★★★*Le Barry* (100 pl), ☎ 90.30.13.20 ; ★★*Le Lez* (70 pl), ☎ 90.30.16.86.

Recommended
Events : *parrot fair* in Jun.

CHÂTEAUNEUF-DU-PAPE, ⊠ 84230, 10 km S.
ⓘ ☎ 90.83.71.08.

Hotels :
● ★★★★ *Château Fines Roches*, 2 km S on D 17, ☎ 90.83.70.23, Euro Visa, 7 rm ℗ ⬭ ⬭ ⬭ ⬭ ⬭ ⬭ half pens (h.s.), closed Mon ex summer, 23 Dec-17 Feb, 900. Rest. ♦♦♦ ⬭ ⬭ closed Mon. A fabulous single

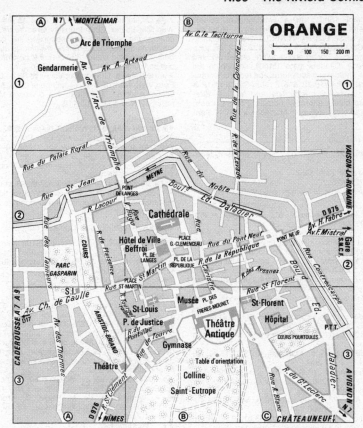

Arc de Triomphe

Av. G. le Taciturne Ⓑ

ORANGE

0 50 100 150 200 m

Gendarmerie

Av. A. Artaud

Av. de l'Arc de Triomphe

①

Rue de la Concorde

①

Rue du Palais Royal

Rue St Jean

MEYNE

PONT DE LANGES

R. Lacour

Rue Hugo

Cathédrale

Boul. Ed. Daladier

Rue du Noble

D 975

Av. H. Fabre

②

R. des Plaisance

R. de Hugo

PLACE G-CLEMENCEAU

Hôtel de Ville
Beffroi

PL. DE LANGES

Rue du Pont Neuf

Rue de la République

PONT NEUF

Av. F. Mistral

Gare S.N.C.F.

②

PARC GASPARIN

PL. DE LA RÉPUBLIQUE

R. de la République

R. Carlotte

R. des Avesnes

Rue Contrescarpe

S.I.

Av. Ch. de Gaulle

PLACE ST-MARTIN

Rue ST-MARTIN

Musée

PL DES FRERES-MOUNET

Rue St-Florent

Boul. Ed.

CADEROUSSE A 7 A 9 D 17

ARISTIDE-BRAND

St-Louis

R. Toursre

Théâtre
Antique

St-Florent

Hôpital

P.T.T.

③

Av. des Thermes

P. de Justice

R. du Pontillac

Rue de Tourre

Gymnase

COURS POURTOULES

Rue du G. Daladier

AVIGNON N 7

③

Théâtre

R. St Clément

Table d'orientation

Colline

Saint-Eutrope

Rue R. Blanc

R. du G. Leclerc

D 976 ↙*NÎMES* Ⓐ

Ⓑ

Ⓒ *CHÂTEAUNEUF!*

---

menu lets you discover Estevenin's delicious regional cuisine, 180.
★★★ **Le Logis d'Arnavel**, rte de Roquemaure, 3 km, ☎ 90.83.73.22, AE Euro Visa, 15 rm 🅿 ⚡ 🎱 ⚲ half pens (h.s.), 420. Rest. ♦ ⚡ ♪ 90-200; child : 50.

Restaurant :
● ♦♦ **La Mule du Pape**, 2, rue de la République, ☎ 90.83.73.30, AE Euro Visa ⚡ closed Mon eve and Tue , eves (15 Nov-15 Feb). The wine country is virtually inside the dining room, and good wine is truly in your glass, to accompany the flavours of the South emanating from this fine cuisine : *caillette vauclusienne, raviole de langoustines, fricassée de volailles au vinaigre,* 75-150 ; child : 40.

Recommended
Guide to wines : cellar tours, lists of growers at *S.I.*

The RIVIERA Corniches**

D2

The *corniche* no longer specifically means the cliff road between Nice and Menton ; nowadays it is also applied to the shore-roads along the Gulf of Genoa. Nevertheless, the three famous *corniche* roads are still there with their fabulous views.
La Grande Corniche★★ *(31 km from Nice to Menton, 2hr30)*
▶ **Nice** *(→, leave by F2 on map).* ▶ **D2564.** ▶ Road to the **Nice Observatory,** built by Garnier *(guided tours, ask at the SI).* ▶ Quatre Chemins Pass. ▶ **Eze lookout** (belvé-

dère) : panorama★★. ▶ **La Turbie,** at the foot of the Tête de Chien, the promontory overlooking Monaco ; spectacular night view ; Niçois Baroque church★ of 1777. Nearby, the Trophy of the Alps★, a monument built by the Romans in 5BC to commemorate the surrender of the Ligurians. It originally stood 50 m high, only 35 m are left ; small museum. ▶ **Le Vistaëro**★★ : view. ▶ **Roquebrune**★ : covered streets, 12thC medieval keep, visits to reconstructed manor-house *(9-12 & 2-7 in summer, 10-12 & 2-5 in winter ex Fri. ; closed Nov.);* streets cut from the rock (Rue Montcollet★); Baroque church façade, shopping arcades, souvenirs, crafts. Walk to Monte-Carlo beach *(1hr30)* along the Le Corbusier promenade★★ on **Cap Martin.** ▶ **Menton** *(→).*

La Moyenne (Middle) Corniche★ *(31 km from Menton to Nice, 1hr30).*

▶ **Menton** *(→).* ▶ N7. Join the Moyenne Corniche at **Cabbé.** ▶ **Beausoleil,** a terrace above Monaco. ▶ **Èze-Village**★ : medieval houses crowded in an extraordinary craggy site★ ; 14thC chapel of the White Penitents (Spanish Smiling Christ, 1258) ; exotic garden with incomparable view *(8 or 9-sunset).* The Frédéric-Nietzsche Path (named after the philosopher, 1844-1900, who lived here for a time) leads to **Èze-sur-Mer** *(25 min).* ▶ **Villefranche Pass** (view of Nice). ▶ **Nice** *(→).*

L'Inférieure (Lower) Corniche★ *(35 km from Nice to Menton, 4hr).*

▶ **Nice** *(→, leave by F4 on map).* ▶ **Villefranche-sur-Mer**★ one of the most beautiful roadsteads in the Mediterranean; still intact 18thC town★ with ancient streets chopped by steps and vaulted passages (see the Rue Obscure★). Chapel of St. Pierre★, (17thC) entirely redecorated by Jean Cocteau in 1957 *(9-12 & 2:30-7 in summer, 4:30 in winter, 6 spring and autumn; closed Fri. and 15 Nov.-15 Dec.).* Citadel★ (late 15thC), containing the Volti Museum★ : numerous sculptures and red-chalk drawings by a local artist *(10-12 & 3-7, Jun.-Sep. ; 11-12 & 2-5, Oct.-May; closed Sun. am, Tue. and Nov.).* ▶ **Èze-sur-Mer.** ▶ **Cap d'Ail** : attractive houses, flowers, trees; Cap d'Ail trail *(30 min);* view★. ▶ **Monaco**★★ (→). ▶ **Menton** (→).   □

Practical Information

BEAULIEU-SUR-MER, ⊠ 06310, 2 km N of **Saint-Jean-Cap-Ferrat.**
ⓘ pl. de la Gare, ☎ 93.01.02.21.
SNCF ☎ 93.01.00.16.
Car rental : Avis, 1, rue G-Clemenceau, ☎ 93.01.00.13.

Hotels :
● ★★★★(L)   *La Réserve*, 5, bd Mal-Leclerc, ☎ 93.01.00.01, Tx 470301, Visa, 50 rm ℗ ⪦ 𝍤 ⌕ ▤ half pens (h.s.), closed 1 Dec-10 Jan, 2500. Rest. ● ◆◆◆ ⪦ ♪ Quality and tradition. Luxurious fare by Gilbert Picard in a century-old Riviera institution, 290-380.
★★★★(L)   *Le Metropole* (R.C.), 15, bd du Mal-Leclerc, ☎ 93.01.00.08, Tx 470304, 53 rm ℗ ⪦ 𝍤 ⌕ half pens, closed 20 Oct-20 Dec, 2500. Rest. ◆◆◆ ⪦ Expensive but top quality. Spec : *court-bouillon de la mer à la crème d'oseille, noisettes d'agneau Saint-Martin, crêpes soufflées Paradis*, 280-350.
★★★★   *Carlton*, 7, av. Edith-Cavell, ☎ 93.01.14.70, Tx 970421, AE DC Euro Visa, 35 rm ℗ ⪦ 𝍤 ⌕ ⌕ ▤ closed 1 Nov-27 Dec, 750. Rest. ◆◆◆ ⌕ & ⅋ closed Tue, 180-200.
★★★   *Comté de Nice*, 25, bd Marinoni, ☎ 93.01.19.70, AE DC Visa, 33 rm ℗ ⪦ ⅋ 300.
★★★   *La Résidence* (R.S.), 9bis, av. Albert-1er, ☎ 93.01.06.02, Tx 470250, AE Euro Visa, 21 rm ℗ ⪦ 𝍤 ♪ 𝍤 & closed Oct-Jan, 530.
★★   *Le Havre Bleu*, 29, bd du Mal-Joffre, ☎ 93.01.01.40, Visa, 22 rm ℗ 𝍤 ⅋ closed Jan, 200.
★   *France*, 1, montée des Orangers, ☎ 93.01.00.92, 16 rm ℗ 𝍤 ⅋ half pens (h.s.), closed 30 Nov-1 Jan, 180.
★   *Select Hôtel*, 1, montée des Myrtes, ☎ 93.01.05.42, 20 rm ⪦ closed 20 Oct-20 Dec, 130.

Restaurants :
◆   *African Queen*, port de Beaulieu, ☎ 93.01.10.85, Tx 462428, AE DC Euro Visa ⪦ & Outstanding seafood, 100-140; child : 40.
◆   *La Pignatelle*, 10, rue Quincenet, ☎ 93.01.03.37, AE Visa ⪦ ♪ closed Wed, 12 Nov-26 Dec. Family-style, 50-100.
◆   *Les Agaves*, 4, rue du Mal-Foch, ☎ 93.01.12.09, Visa, closed Sun eve (l.s.) and Wed, Nov, 80-130.

CAP-D'AIL, ⊠ 06320, 4 km E of **Èze.**

Hotel :
★★   *Miramar*, 126, av. du 3-Septembre, ☎ 93.78.06.60, Visa, 27 rm ℗ ⪦ closed Dec, 160. Rest. ◆ *Chez Eric* ♪ closed Tue. Pizzeria, 40-100.

ÈZE, ⊠ 06360, 12 km NE of **Nice.**
ⓘ mairie, ☎ 93.41.03.03.
SNCF ☎ 93.01.54.34.

Hotels :
● ★★★★(L) *Cap Estel*, bord de mer, ☎ 93.01.50.44, Tx 470305, DC Euro Visa, 48 rm ℗ ⪦ 𝍤 ⌕ ▤ half pens, closed Nov-Jan. Private beach. Park boasts coconut palms, 1775. Rest. ◆◆◆ ⪦ ♪ 260-340.
● ★★★★(L) *Château Eza*, ☎ 93.41.12.24, Tx 470382, AE DC Euro Visa, 7 rm 3 apt ℗ ⪦ 𝍤 ⌕ ♪ closed 2 Nov-10 Apr, 1500. Rest. ● ◆◆◆ ⪦ A new start for Dominique Le Stanc, formerly of Monte Carlo : *tabbouleh de langoustes, daurade à la citronnelle et aux courgettes, pêche blanche rôtie aux pistaches,* 230-500.
★★★★   *Château de la Chèvre d'Or* (R.C.), rue Barri, ☎ 93.41.12.12, Tx 970839, AE DC Euro Visa, 8 rm ⪦ 𝍤 ⌕

♪ 🦩 ▤ closed Dec-Feb, 1075. Rest. ● ◆◆◆ ⪦ ♪ closed Wed Mar-Easter. Sound, quality fare : *huîtres chaudes au champagne, suprême de pigeonneau aux pâtes fraîches enrobées de beurre de truffes, millefeuille aux fraises des bois.* Interesting wines, 300-390. ◆◆ *Le Grill du Château,* pleasant little annex. Grills, 100-250.
★★   *Hermitage*, Grande-Corniche, ☎ 93.41.00.68, AE DC Euro Visa, 14 rm ℗ ⪦ 𝍤 half pens (h.s.). Attractive Provençal stopover, 315. Rest. ◆ ⪦ & closed Mon and Wed noon, 12 Nov-1 Mar, 65-110.

Restaurants :
◆◆ *Le Nid d'Aigle*, 1, rue du Château, ☎ 93.41.19.08, AE ⪦ 𝍤 ♪ closed Thu, 12 Nov-22 Dec. Pretty house, friendly welcome and affordable, flavourful fare, 70-140.
◆ *Cap Roux*, av. de la Liberté, ☎ 93.01.50.17, Euro Visa ⪦ & closed Tue eve (Dec-Feb) and Wed, 15 Oct-1 Dec, 45-140.
◆ *La Bergerie*, Grande Corniche, ☎ 93.41.03.67, Visa ⪦ 𝍤 ♪ closed Wed, 31 Oct-1 Feb. Attractive, flowery terrace that makes the good charcoal-grilled meats and hot *tarte Tatin* taste all the better, 130-180.

⩲ ★★*Nationale*, 7, Gde-Corniche (50 pl), ☎ 93.01.81.64.

ROQUEBRUNE-CAP-MARTIN, ⊠ 06190, 4 km SW of **Menton.**
ⓘ hôtel-de-ville, ☎ 93.35.60.67 ; esplanade Jean-Giono, ☎ 93.57.99.44 (h.s.).
SNCF ☎ 93.35.00.95.

Hotels :
★★★★(L) *Vista Palace*, Grande Corniche, ☎ 93.35.01.50, Tx 461021, AE DC Euro Visa, 70 rm ℗ ⪦ 𝍤 ⌕ ♪ closed 2 Nov-1 Apr, 1200. Rest. ● ◆◆ *Le Vistaero* ⪦ ♪ & ⅋ For people who love the mountains (330m above sea level), beautiful views, calm and comfort... in a natural setting. Spec : *polenta de pigeon, duo d'encornet de pâtes fraîches aux truffes et olives de pays, rosette de langoustines,* 220-500.
★★★ *Alexandra*, 93, av. W.-Churchill, ☎ 93.35.65.45, AE DC Euro Visa, 40 rm ℗ ⪦ ⌕ closed 1 Nov-15 Dec, 360.
★★★ *Victoria et de la Plage*, 7, prom. du Cap, ☎ 93.35.65.90, AE DC Euro Visa, 30 rm ℗ ⪦ closed 1 Nov-1 Feb, 340.
★★   *Westminster* (L.F.), 14, av. Louis-Laurens, ☎ 93.35.00.68, Euro Visa, 31 rm ℗ ⪦ 𝍤 𝍤 half pens (h.s.), closed 2 Jan-15 Feb, 15 Oct-23 Dec, 350. Rest. ◆ ⪦ ♪ & 60-150.
★ *Reine d'Azur*, 29, prom. du Cap-Martin, ☎ 93.35.76.84, 17 rm ℗ ⪦ 𝍤 half pens (h.s.), closed 15 Oct-1 Feb, 305.

Restaurants :
◆◆◆ *L'Hippocampe*, 44, av. W.-Churchill, ☎ 93.35.81.91 ⪦ closed Mon, 2 Jan-1 Feb, 1-25 May, 1 Oct-1 Nov. A superb view of the bay and painstakingly prepared food, 120-260.
◆◆◆   *Le Roquebrune*, 100, Corniche Inférieure, ☎ 93.35.00.16, AE DC Euro Visa ⪦ 𝍤 ♪ closed Wed and Thu noon (l.s.) , lunch (h.s.) ex Fri and we, 5 Nov-5 Dec. Enjoyable terrace. Good ingredients carefully prepared : *bouillabaisse, bourride,* 250-300.
◆◆ *Au Grand Inquisiteur*, 18, rue du Château, ☎ 93.35.05.37, AE ♪ ⅋ closed Mon, 23 Mar-6 Apr, 9 Nov-9 Dec. Reserve. Nice, light food, 100-170.
◆ *Les Lucioles*, 12, av. Raymond-Poincaré, ☎ 93.35.02.19, AE Visa ⪦ ♪ closed Thu and Fri noon, Nov, Mar, 100-170.

⩲ ★★★*Toraca* (40 pl), ☎ 93.35.62.55 ; ★★*Babastrol* (30 pl), ☎ 93.35.74.58.

VILLEFRANCHE-SUR-MER, ⊠ 06230, 4 km NW of **Saint-Jean-Cap-Ferrat.**
ⓘ sq. F.-Binon, ☎ 93.80.73.68.
SNCF ☎ 93.80.71.67.

Hotels :
★★★ *Le Versailles*, bd Princesse-Grace-de-Monaco, ☎ 93.01.89.56, Tx 970433, AE DC Visa, 50 rm ℗ ⪦ ⌕ ♪ ▤ half pens (h.s.), closed 20 Oct-20 Dec, 720. Rest. ● ◆◆ ♪ Cuisine in constant progress. Spec :

salade de langouste aux mangues, escalope de loup sur mousseline d'aubergines, 125-200; child : 75.

★★★ **Les Olivettes**, 17, av. Léopold-II, ☎ 93.01.03.69, AE DC Visa, 17 rm ℙ ≼ ᵐᵐ ⟍ 285.

★★★ **Welcome** (Mapotel, C.H), 1, quai Courbet, ☎ 93.76.76.93, Tx 470281, AE DC Euro Visa, 32 rm ≼ ♪ ढ़ half pens (h.s.), closed 18 Nov-18 Dec. Former 17thC convent, an exceptional site on the harbour, 395. Rest. ♦♦ **Le Saint-Pierre** ≼ ढ़ ॐ Good spot for fish and seafood, 110-230.

★★ **Auberge du Coq Hardi** (L.F.), 8, bd de la Corne-d'Or, ☎ 93.01.71.06, 20 rm ℙ ≼ ᵐᵐ ⟍ ♪ ⌷ half pens (h.s.), closed 5 Nov-10 Dec. A charming little hotel with harbour view, 390. Rest. ♦ ≼ ♪ ढ़ Good, simple cooking, 60-100.

★★ **La Flore** (L.F.), av. Princesse-Grace-de-Monaco, ☎ 93.56.80.29, Euro Visa, 18 rm ℙ ≼ ᵐᵐ ⟍ 🐾 half pens, closed 1 Nov-1 Dec. A magnificent view of the harbour, 375. Rest. ♦ ≼ ♪ closed 1 Nov-15 Dec, 55-130; child : 35.

Restaurants :

● ♦♦♦ **Le Massoury**, av. Léopold-II, ☎ 93.01.93.43, AE DC Visa ≼ ᵐᵐ ॐ closed Wed eve (l.s.) and Wed lunch, 15 Dec-31 Jan. In his stunning Riviera villa with its terrace overlooking the bay, P. Seibt is on his way to fame. Irreproachable service complements consistent cuisine : *Saint-Pierre à la compote de laitue, fricassée de volaille aux concombres et tomates, poire au sabayon de Bandol.* Permanent exhibition of fine paintings, 190-300.

● ♦♦ **Campanette**, 2, rue Baron-de-Brès, ☎ 93.01.79.98, AE Euro Visa ♪ closed Sun, 29 Oct-12 Nov. An adorable little place tucked away in an alley. Fish a specialty. Interesting regional wine list, 100-140.

♦♦ **La Mère Germaine**, 7, quai Courbet, ☎ 93.01.71.39, AE Visa ≼ ᵐᵐ ♪ closed Wed ex May-Sep, 17 Nov-20 Dec. Fish, 130-250.

ROQUEMAURE

Avignon 16, Alès 69, Paris 672 km
pop 4054 ⊠ 30150

Hotel :
★★ **Château de Cubières** (C.H.), rte d'Avignon, ☎ 66.50.14.28, 19 rm ℙ ᵐᵐ ⟍ Handsome 18thC house set in a park, 220. Rest. ♦ closed Tue, 20 Feb-20 Mar, 15-30 Nov, 45-140.

Nearby
SAUVETERRE, ⊠ 30150 Roquemaure, 6 km S.

Hotel :
● ★★ **Varenne**, pl. St-Jean, ☎ 66.82.59.45, 15 rm ℙ ᵐᵐ 130. Rest. ♦ closed Mon and Tue , 1-6 Jan, 1 wk in Feb, 1-8 Nov, 90-175.

Restaurant :
● ♦♦ **La Crémaillère**, ☎ 66.82.55.05, AE Visa ℙ ≼ ᵐᵐ ♪ ढ़ closed Mon eve, Tue eve, Wed , Feb. A lovely country inn. Simple, varied cuisine. Spec : *assiette Crémaillère, filet de bœuf en chemise*, 120-200.

ROYA Valley**

D1
From Sospel to Tende *(40 km, 3hr, plus full day for the Merveilles Valley)*

The Roya Valley attracts kayak enthusiasts ; the principal resources are water power and forestry. The upper valley of the Roya was once a hunting preserve of the King of Italy ; it was attached to France only with the plebiscite of 1947. The old road to Turin also runs through the valley whose gorges open into the Merveilles Valley with its strange prehistoric signs and symbols.

▶ **Sospel**★ (→ Menton). ▶ Along D2204 and over the **Brouis Pass**★, to the Roya between **Breil-sur-Roya** and the **Saorge Gorges**★ : Breil is an appealing village ; 18thC church with 17thC organ case and 1500 altarpiece. In

the Gorges, remarkable bridge of the Nice-Cuneo railway.
▶ **Saorge**★★, village beautifully situated in a' natural amphitheatre. ▶ Road through the red rocks of the **Bergue Gorges**★. ▶ **Saint-Dalmas-de-Tende** : the usual starting point for visiting the **Merveilles Valley**★, site of thousands of Bronze Age engravings (1800-1500 BC). The engravings, made on the rock face with flint or quartz tools, for the most part represent cattle and human figures, and possibly were associated with a bull cult and/or a mountain cult. The trip can be made by hired jeep *(ask at the SI)* or (less easily) in a private car *(10 km W across the Minière Valley, then 3hr on foot to the Refuge des Merveilles, base for the next day's exploration of the valley ; the engravings are difficult to find without a guide. Even in summer, take warm clothing ; up to the end of Jun. and starting again in Oct., snow may cover the engravings).* The valley itself, walled by mountains, carpeted with flowers and dotted with lakes, is beautiful. ▶ **La Brigue** *(2.5 km E of Saint-Dalmas)* : among orchards in the Levens Valley, green schist houses with emblazoned arcades and lintels. Church of St. Martin (12th-13thC) : Lombard Romanesque bell tower, altarpiece of Ste Marthe★ (School of Nice), Nativity★ by Louis Bréa, and Notre-Dame des Neiges★, 1507 triptych. ▶ **Notre-Dame des Fontaines** *(4 km E from La Brigue)* : forceful 15thC frescos★★. ▶ **Tende.** ◻

Practical Information _____

BREIL-SUR-ROYA, ⊠ 06540, 21 km S of **Tende**.
ᔕᑎᑕᖴ ☎ 93.04.40.15. 🚇

Hotel :
★★ **Castel du Roy** (L.F.), rte de Tende, ☎ 93.04.43.66, 15 rm ℙ ᵐᵐ ⟍ 200.

TENDE, ⊠ 06430, 57 km N of **Menton**.
ᔕᑎᑕᖴ ☎ 93.04.65.60.

Hotel :
★ **Centre**, 12, pl. de la République, ☎ 93.04.62.19, AE Euro Visa, 17 rm ℙ ⟍ 110.

ST-MAXIMIN-LA-STE-BAUME**

Aix-en-Provence 43, Marseille 50, Paris 801 km
pop 5552 ⊠ 83470   B3

According to legend, St. Maximin was one of the party that disembarked at Saintes-Maries-de-la-Mer (→ Camargue) ; he was supposedly buried here some 30 years later.

▶ **Basilica of Ste Madeleine**★★ (1295-1532), a blend of soaring Gothic and the simpler, sober Provençal style. Inside, beautiful organ★ by Jean-Esprit Isnard (1773) ; concerts ; Venetian altarpiece of Christ's Passion★ (1520) ; gold-embroidered cope of St. Louis of Anjou (13thC bishop of Toulouse) ; choir screen★ (1691) ; in the crypt, a Gallo-Roman funerary vault of 4th-5thC. ▶ The former **Royal Monastery**★ (13th-15thC), N of the basilica, now the College for Contemporary Exchanges which organizes activities essentially concerned with music. Exquisite 15thC **cloister**★ *(9-11:30 & 2:30-6)*; concerts, recitals, exhibitions in season. ▶ Near the basilica, the town has largely kept its original checkerboard pattern, with here and there small squares and fountains. Rue Colbert : 14thC houses with arcades. ◻

SAINT-RAPHAËL

Cannes 43, Toulon 96, Paris 877 km
pop 24310 ⊠ 83700   C-D3

With Fréjus Bay backed by the magnificent Esterel peaks, the site has been a vacation resort since Roman times.

▶ The seafront promenade and the old port are always lively : palms, restaurants, cafés. ▶ **Templars' Church**, 12thC Provençal Romanesque. ▶ **Archaeological Museum :** Roman artifacts recovered from the sea bed

(10-12 & 3-6 ex Tue. and nat. hols., 15 Jun.-15 Sep.; 11-12 & 2-5 ex Sun. and nat. hols. in winter). ▶ **Saint-Aygulf** *(8 km SW)* : beach fringed by eucalyptus, pine. □

Practical Information ⎯⎯⎯⎯⎯⎯⎯⎯⎯⎯⎯

SAINT-RAPHAËL
ℹ️ pl. de la Gare, ☎ 94.95.16.87.
📠 ☎ 94.95.16.90/94.95.18.91/94.95.13.89.
🚆 pl. de la Gare, ☎ 94.95.24.82.
Car rental : *Avis*, train station; pl. de la Gare, ☎ 94.95.60.42/94.95.61.24.

Hotels :
● ★★★ *Sol E Mar*, Le Dramont, 7 km E on N 98, ☎ 94.95.25.60, 47 rm 🅿 ⸜ ▥ ⚲ 🖵 half pens (h.s.), closed 15 Oct-15 Apr, 390. Rest. ◆◆ ⸜ ⚹ 90-230.
★★★ *Beau-Séjour*, prom. René-Coty, ☎ 94.95.03.75, 38 rm ⸜ closed 1 Nov-20 Mar, 375.
★★ *France*, pl. Galliéni, ☎ 94.95.17.03, 28 rm, closed Sun (l.s), Dec, 210.
★★ *Provençal*, 197, rue de la Garonne, ☎ 94.95.29.35, Visa, 29 rm ⚲ ⚹ 🕸 closed Jan, 170.

Restaurant :
◆◆◆ *La Voile d'Or*, 1, bd du Gal-de-Gaulle, ☎ 94.95.17.04, AE DC Euro Visa ⸜ ♪ closed Tue eve and Wed, 15 Nov-25 Dec. Spec : *bourride raphaéloise, marinade d'anchois*, 130-210.

Recommended
Events : *mimosa festival* in Feb.
Marina : ☎ 94.95.34.30, (1300 empl.).

Nearby

VALESCURE, ✉ 83700 Saint-Raphaël, 5 km NE on D 37.

Hotels :
● ★★★ *Golf de Valescure* (Mapotel), av. Paul-Lhermite, ☎ 94.52.01.57, Tx 461085, AE DC Euro Visa, 40 rm 🅿 ▥ ⚲ 🌲 🏊 ⸜ ⅄ ⚲ J half pens (h.s.), closed 5 Jan-15 Mar, 15 Oct-20 Dec, 685. Rest. ◆◆◆ ⚹ Spec : *galantine de saumon, papillote de rougets de roche, selle d'agneau à la crème d'ail*, 130-180.
★★★ *San Pedro* (C.H.), av. Cl.-Brooke, ☎ 94.52.10.24, 27 rm 🅿 ▥ ⚲ closed 30 Oct-Easter, 450.

SAINT-RÉMY-DE-PROVENCE*

Avignon 21, Arles 25, Paris 709 km
pop 8439 ✉ 13210   A2

Classical ruins, and memories of Frédéric Mistral, the greatest of Provençal poets, who was born and lived in a neighbouring village. More remote yet still-vivid reminders of Nostradamus (1503-66), the physician-astrologer who was born here. Flowers, sun, a fountain, a *pastis* at the café : this is Provence.

▶ The town centre is the **Place de la République.** ▶ **Church** of St. Martin : 14thC bell tower★. ▶ **Alpilles Regional Museum,** N of the church, in the Mistral de Mondragon mansion★ (1550) : folk art and traditions; exhibitions on Mistral and Nostradamus *(Apr.-Oct., 10-12 & 2-6 ex May : Sat., Sun., Mon. and Ascension Day only; in winter, Sat. and Sun., 10-12 & 2-4).* ▶ **Sade Mansion** (15th-16thC) with small archaeological collection : excavations from Glanum; marble portraits of Octavia and Julia★ (wife and daughter, respectively, of the Emperor Augustus). Rue Hoche : birthplace of Nostradamus *(guided tours, every hour).*

Nearby

▶ **Glanum**★★ *(1 km S)*, site of a spring sacred to a healing spirit of the Celto-Ligurians (5thC BC), later a Greek settlement (3rdC BC), then a Roman city. When invading Barbarians destroyed Glanum in the 3rdC, only a mausoleum and memorial arch, known locally today as **Les Antiques,** were left standing. The **Commemorative Arch**★, displaying elements of Greek influence, celebrates the Roman conquest of the Gauls. The **Mausoleum**★★ is somewhat later (1stC AD), built in memory of the two grandsons whom Caesar Augustus had named as his heirs but who died prematurely. ▶ Opposite Les Antiques, an alleyway leads to the **monastery** of **Saint-Paul-de-Mausole**★★, a nursing home where the Impressionist painter Vincent van Gogh (1853-90) spent the final year of his life. Church★ (Romanesque, late 12th, 18thC façade), a scaled-down version of the great Provençal churches; elegant bell tower★ and cloister★. Close by, the **ruins of Glanum** *(9-12 & 2-6; 10-12 & 2-5 out of season; closed Tue.)* : two houses★ from the Greek period, Roman baths, forum, and, right at the S end, the spring★ that gave rise to the town. ▶ **Maillane** *(7 km NW)* : birthplace and home of Frédéric Mistral ; the house he built when he married is now a museum (original décor ; *10-12 & 2-4, 5 in season ; closed Mon.).* ▶ **Mont de la Caume** *(7 km S)* : vast panorama★★ of the Alpilles and Camargue. ▶ **Eygalières**★ *(12 km E)*, the prettiest village in the Alpilles. □

Practical Information ⎯⎯⎯⎯⎯⎯⎯⎯⎯⎯⎯

SAINT-RÉMY-DE-PROVENCE
ℹ️ pl. Jean-Jaurès, ☎ 90.92.05.22.

Hotels :
★★★★ *Château des Alpilles* (C.H.), D 31, ☎ 90.92.03.33, Tx 431487, AE DC Euro Visa, 16 rm 🅿 ▥ ⚲ 🖵 ⅄ closed 12 Nov-20 Mar. A 19thC château once frequented by celebrities, 550. Rest. ◆ Grill by the pool, 85-130.
★★★ *Château de Roussan*, rte de Tarascon, ☎ 90.92.11.63, Visa, 12 rm 🅿 ⸜ ▥ ⚲ 🕸 closed 20 Oct-20 Mar. A 18thC dwelling set in a spacious park, 400.
★★★ *Le Castelet des Alpilles*, 6, pl. Mireille, ☎ 90.92.07.21, AE DC Visa, 20 rm 🅿 ⸜ ⚲ half pens (h.s.), closed 15 Nov-15 Mar, 520. Rest. ◆◆ ⚹ Spec : *bourride marseillaise des pêcheurs, loup de la Méditerranée au pistou*, 65-200.
★★ *Canto Cigalo*, chem. de Canto-Cigalo, ☎ 90.92.14.28, 20 rm 🅿 ⸜ ▥ ⚲ 🕸 closed Nov-Feb. Absolute quiet, 220.
★★ *Chalet Fleuri* (L.F.), 15, av. F.-Mistral, ☎ 90.92.03.62, 12 rm 🅿 ▥ ⚲ closed 1 Nov-15 Mar, 200. Rest. ◆ ♪ Provençal cooking, 75-130.

Restaurant :
◆ *Le Jardin de Frédéric*, 8, bd Gambetta, ☎ 90.92.27.76, AE DC Euro Visa ▥ ♪ closed Tue ex Jul-Aug, 12 Nov-15 Dec. Attractive fixed-price meals, 100-210.

⛺ ★★★*Pégomas* (66 pl), ☎ 90.92.01.21; ★★*Les Platanes* (33 pl), ☎ 90.92.07.63; ★★*Montplaisir* (76 pl), ☎ 90.92.22.70.

Recommended
Rural-gîte : *Montplaisir*, ☎ 90.92.12.91, table d'hôte too.

Nearby

VERQUIÈRES, ✉ 13670 Saint-Andiol, 10 km NE.

Restaurant :
● ◆◆ *Le Coupe Chou*, pl. de l'Église, ☎ 90.95.18.55 ⸜ ▥ ♪ closed Mon and Tue. Just a few tables, served by a young chef deserving of encouragement. Spec : *galantine de gigot d'agneau, flan de lapereau au basilic, petits paquets à la marseillaise*, 130-180.

SAINT-TROPEZ**

Toulon 69, Cannes 75, Paris 878 km
pop 6248 ✉ 83990   C3

Once a paradise for painters (Signac, Matisse, Bonnard, Marquet, Dunoyer de Segonzac) and a writers' retreat (Colette, Maupassant), Saint-Tropez is today the summer haunt of a cosmopolitan mixture of tourists and intelligentsia, whose seasonal hedonism tends to obscure the fact that Saint-Tropez is a seaport whose origins date from time immemorial. "Saint Tropez" himself was probably a Roman officer named Torpes, who was martyred as a Christian under Nero

(Pisa; AD68) and whose headless body, set adrift in a boat, washed up on the shore. Every year, on May 16th and 17th, a procession known as a *bravade* is held to commemorate the saint, whose bust is paraded around the town to the sound of muskets and blunderbusses freely discharged by the *bravadeurs,* the local menfolk dressed in endearingly disparate versions of the traditional French naval uniform. However, St. Torpes was not alone in arriving by sea : corsair raids and Moorish invasions plagued the coastline for centuries, and the seamen of Saint-Tropez were frequently called upon to repel attacks. In 1637 the town fleet routed a force of 21 Spanish galleons, providing the occasion for another *bravade,* held annually on June 15th.

▶ On the heights overlooking the gulf *(E),* the **citadel**★ (14th-16thC) and the **Marine Museum** (models★, marine archaeology; *15 Jun.-15 Sep., 10-6; 16 Sep.-14 Jun., 10-12 & 1-5; closed Thu.).* Splendid view★★ from the keep. ▶ **Annonciade Museum**★★, in an ancient chapel : works of prominent painters who spent time at Saint-Tropez; the view from the windows seems to reflect the paintings (Signac, Van Dongen, Matisse, Derain, Vuillard, Braque, Marquet; *10-12 & 3-7, Jun.-Sep.; 10-12 & 2-6, Oct.-May; closed Tue. and Nov.).*

Nearby

▶ **Beaches :** La **Bouillabaisse** *(1 km W);* **Graniers** *(2 km E);* **Tahiti** *(4 km SE),* leading to **Pampelonne** *(5 km long).* ▶ Chapel of St. Anne *(1 km S),* shaded by umbrella pines; view. ▶ **Ramatuelle**★ *(11 km S),* typical Provençal village, houses huddled at random above vineyards. ▶ **Paillas mills**★ *(moulins; 2 km W)* : panorama★★. ▶ 2.5 km farther, **Gassin**★. ▶ **Les Marines de Cogolin** *(4 km W of Saint-Tropez)* : residential area and marina. ▶ **Port-Grimaud**★ *(6 km W),* built from scratch in 1964, is a "fake" Mediterranean village to which the passage of time has lent a certain authenticity; culverts and canals, narrow streets and colourful "fishermen's houses" add to the effect; less frantic than Saint-Tropez. □

Practical Information

SAINT-TROPEZ
ⓘ quai J.-Jaurès, ☎ 94.97.45.21.
Car rental : *Avis,* 13, bd. L.-Blanc, ☎ 94.97.03.10.

Hotels :

★★★★(L) **Byblos**, av. Paul-Signac, ☎ 94.97.00.04, Tx 470235, AE DC Visa, 107 rm Ⓟ ⊀ ▒ ♪ ⌧ closed 3 Nov-2 Apr. Enchanting Provençal houses clustered in a hotel-village, 1600. Rest. ● ♦♦♦ **La Braiserie** ⊀ ♪ Enjoyable food served poolside, 210-300.
★★★★(L) **Résidence de la Pinède** (R.C.), plage de la Bouillabaisse, ☎ 94.97.04.21, Tx 470489, AE DC Euro Visa, 39 rm Ⓟ ⊀ ▒ ⌕ ♿ ⌧ closed 15 Oct-15 Apr. Private beach, water sports. Spacious rooms, 1600. Rest. ♦♦♦ ⊀ ♪ ♿ 150-300.
● ★★★★ **La Mandarine**, rte de Tahiti, ☎ 94.97.21.00, Tx 970461, AE DC Euro Visa, 42 rm Ⓟ ▒ ⌕ ⌧ closed 1 Jan-9 Apr, 900. Rest. ● ♦ Peace in a green setting. Enjoyable food, regional wines, 180-230.
★★★★ **La Maison Blanche**, pl. des Lices, ☎ 94.97.52.66, AE DC Visa, 8 rm Ⓟ ⌕ ♪ closed 15 Nov-15 Dec, 900.
● ★★★★ **La Tartane**, chem. des Salins, ☎ 94.97.21.23, Visa, 12 rm Ⓟ ⌕ ⌧ closed 10 Nov-15 Mar, 450. Rest. ♦ To escape from the Riviera's sound and fury, 120-180.
● ★★★ **Le Levant**, rte des Salins, ☎ 94.97.33.33, AE DC Visa, 28 rm Ⓟ ▒ ⌕ ⌧ closed 20 Oct-11 Apr, 450. Rest. ♦ 125-190.
● ★★★ **Le Mas de Chastelas**, quartier Bertaud, Gassin, ☎ 94.56.09.11, Tx 462393, AE DC Euro Visa, 31 rm Ⓟ ▒ ⌕ ♪ closed 1 Oct-1 Apr. A former silkworm-breeding house among the vineyards, 700. Rest. ♦♦♦ ⊗ closed 30 Sep-1 May. Lunch : poolside delicious stuffed vegetables (residents only). For dinner, choose from 6 starters

and 6 main courses : *soupe de galinette, rougets à l'étuvée de fèvettes aux olives noires,* 230-300.
● ★★★ **Le Yaca**, 1, bd d'Aumale, ☎ 94.97.11.79, Tx 462140, AE DC Euro Visa, 22 rm 1 apt ⊀ ▒ ♪ ⌧ closed 15 Oct-1 Apr. In old Saint-Tropez, 700. Rest. ♦ ♪ closed 10 Sep-1 Jun, 200-250.
★★★ **La Ponche**, pl. du Revelin, ☎ 94.97.09.29, 23 rm ⊀ closed 15 Oct-30 Apr, 350. Rest. ● ♦♦ ♪ Luxurious and still fashionable. Ordinary food : *petits farcis, blanquette de lotte,* 130-300.
★★★ **Lou Troupelen**, chem. des Vendanges, ☎ 94.97.44.88, DC Visa, 44 rm Ⓟ ⊀ ▒ ⌕ closed 12 Oct-17 Apr, 320.
★★★ **Tahiti Beach**, Le Pinet, ☎ 94.97.18.02, 19 rm Ⓟ ⌕ ⌧ ⤢ closed 31 Oct-1 Apr. Rest. ♦♦ ♪ 120-200.
★★ **La Méditerranée**, 21, bd Louis-Blanc, ☎ 94.97.00.44, AE DC, 13 rm Ⓟ ⊀ ▒ ⌕ half pens (h.s.), closed noon, 20 Oct-10 Mar, 425. Rest. ● ♦ ♪ ⊗ Even here you can still find a pleasant summer garden ; the good food is by Fernand Boix. *Chapons farcis, homard à l'américaine,* 130-180.
★★ **Lou Cagnard**, rue Paul-Roussel, ☎ 94.97.04.24, 19 rm Ⓟ ▒ ⌕ closed 15 Nov-23 Dec, 200.
★★ **Sube-Continental**, at the Port, ☎ 94.97.30.04, Tx 400479, AE DC Euro Visa, 28 rm ⊀ closed 1 Mar-1 Apr, 250. Rest. ♦ ⌕ 70-150.
● **La Bastide de Saint-Tropez**, rte des Carles, ☎ 94.97.58.16, Tx 461516, AE DC Euro Visa, 17 rm Ⓟ ▒ ⌕ ♪ ⌧ closed 5 Jan-15 Feb, 1 Nov-15 Dec, 1200. Rest. ● ♦♦♦ ♪ A cluster of little bungalows is an oasis of quiet just a half-mile from the Place des Lices. Pleasant food, but prices are on the rise, 200-280.
● **La Bastide des Salins**, rte des Salins, ☎ 94.97.24.57, Tx 385587, 12 rm Ⓟ ⊀ ▒ ⌕ ⌧ Hotel residence, 570.

Restaurants :

● ♦♦♦ *Le Chabichou,* av. Foch, ☎ 94.54.80.00, Tx 461051, Visa ▒ ♪ closed 15 Oct-15 May. Summer by the sea, winter in the mountains : that is the secret dream of many vacationers. Irrepressible Michel Rochedy and his supportive wife have nearly realized it. With kitchens at Courchevel and Saint-Tropez , he regales his faithful, demanding patrons with his light, brilliant cuisine (which has earned him a seat on our chefs' panel) : *moules de bouchot en vinaigrette de céleri aux artichauts et champignons des bois, colineau rôti à la crème de laitue, côte de veau au jus simple, casserole de champignons.* Top-flight desserts. Appealing little wines and great vintages too, 220-420.
♦♦♦ **Leï Mouscardins**, rue Portalet, ☎ 94.97.01.53, Visa ⊀ closed 2 Nov-1 Feb. Careful! Things are getting a little lax here. For a 300-400F tab, one expects something more. *Bouillabaisse, chapon farci,* 275-350.
● ♦♦ **Le Bistrot des Lices**, 3, pl. des Lices, ☎ 94.97.29.00, DC Visa ▒ ♪ Formula fixed-price menus. Piano-bar, 160-300.
♦♦ **Chez Nano**, pl. de l'Hôtel-de-Ville, ☎ 94.97.01.66, AE DC Visa, closed Tue, 15 Jan-15 Mar. An institution : to see and be seen, 190-230.
♦♦ **Les Maures (Chez Dédé)**, 4, rue Dr-Boutin, ☎ 94.97.01.50, DC Visa, closed 20 Sep-30 Mar. Pretty setting. Fish and seafood, 120-200.
♦♦ **Lou Pinet**, chemin du Pinet, ☎ 94.97.07.45, AE DC Euro Visa. Poolside or on the terrace, Jo de Salerne serves Provençal cuisine and Seychelles specialties, 140-230.
♦♦ **Lou Revelen**, 4, rue des Remparts, ☎ 94.97.06.34, AE DC Visa ⊀ ♪ closed Sund eve (l.s.), 5 Jan-5 Mar. Regional fare : *bouillabaisse, pâtes fraîches aux langoustines,* 80-130.
● ♦ **La Ramade**, rue du Temple, ☎ 94.97.00.15, Visa ♪ ♿ closed Thu eve , Nov-Easter. Pierrot goes out to fish early in the morning and late at night, then grills his catch over vine-cuttings : *aïoli, bourride,* 130-250.
● ♦ **Café des Arts**, pl. Carnot, ☎ 94.97.02.25 ▒ closed Oct-Easter. Straightforward bistro food, 145.
♦ **Fuchs**, 9, rue des Commerçants, ☎ 94.97.01.25 A *café-tabac* serving great food to a crowd of regulars. Daily specials, fish soup, 100-120.
♦ **L'Escoundu**, 3, rue du Clocher, ☎ 94.54.83.50, closed

15 Oct-15 Mar. Very good value in this simple eatery; tasty dishes prepared by the owner, 80-100.

Recommended
Events : *Bravade des Espagnols*, late Aug-early Sep; *Ste-Anne's fair*, pl. des Lices; *fête de la Bravade*, 16-18 mai; *antiques show*, 26 Jul.
Guide to wines : *wine bar*, 13, rue des Feniers, ☎ 94.97.46.10; *R. Sumeire*, Château Barbeyrolles-Gassin, ☎ 94.56.33.58.
Market : pl. des Lices, Tue and Sat am.
Nightclubs : *L'Aphrodisiaque*, 3, rue Allard, ☎ 94.97.01.15; *Les Caves du Roy*, the fief of Jacqueline Vayssière; *L'Esquinade*, for night-owls; *The Hilarios*, ☎ 94.97.46.10; *Le Papagayo*, run by Régine.
♥ *Sénéquier*, ☎ 94.97.00.90, café by the port; beaches : *Club 55*, ☎ 94.79.80.14; *Tropicana*, ☎ 94.79.83.96; *La Voile Rouge*, ☎ 94.79.84.34; *L'Esquinade*, ☎ 94.79.83.42; *Moorea*, ☎ 94.97.18.17; candy : *Desbrosses*, 29, rue Gambetta, ☎ 94.97.22.36.

Nearby

Les MARINES DE COGOLIN, ⊠ 83310 Cogolin, 5 km W.
ⅱ ☎ 94.56.03.70.

Restaurant :
♦♦ *Port-Diffa*, RN 98, les 3 ponts sur la Giscle, ☎ 94.56.29.07, AE DC ≰ ₩ ♪ ⌘ closed 6 Jan-26 Mar. Moroccan specialties. Interesting fixed-price meal, 130-200.

PORT-GRIMAUD, ⊠ 83310 Cogolin, 6 km W.

Hotel :
★★★★ *Giraglia*, Grand' Rue, ☎ 94.56.31.33, Tx 470494, AE DC Visa, 48 rm ℗ ≰ 🐾 ♪ ⌂ ☒ closed 15 Oct-30 Mar, 1010. Rest. ♦♦ *l'Amphitrite* ≰ ♪ ₺ 205-290.
Recommended
Farmhouse-inn : *La Croix*, rte de Grimaud, ☎ 94.43.21.51.

RAMATUELLE, ⊠ 83350, 10 km S.

Hotels :
● ★★★ *Le Baou* (I.L.A., Mapotel), av. G.-Clemenceau, ☎ 94.79.20.48, Tx 462152, AE DC Euro Visa, 36 rm ℗ ≰ ₩ 🐾 ﾟ⁰ closed 4 Nov-30 Mar, 650. Rest. ♦♦ ≰ ♪ Between the sea and the countryside, a luxurious hotel. Jean-Denis Sénéquier and his wife oversee the prestigious restaurant. Outstanding food by young chef Frérard : *soufflé d'artichauts, rougets juste poêlés, cuisse de lapin farci*, 220-250.
★★★ *La Figuière*, rte de Tahiti, ☎ 94.97.18.21, 42 rm ℗ ≰ ₩ 🐾 ₺ ☒ ﾟ⁰ closed 5 Oct-1 Apr. In the vineyards, 400.
★★★ *Saint-Vincent*, rte de Tahiti, ☎ 94.97.36.90, 16 rm ℗ ≰ ₩ 🐾 ♪ ₺ ☒ closed 3 Nov-12 Apr, 450.
★★ *Les Vieux Moulins*, rte des Plages, ☎ 94.97.17.22, 7 rm ℗ closed 15 Sep-Apr, 420. Rest. ♦♦ closed Wed (Jun) and lunch. Provençal specialties served around the fountain of this old dwelling, 150-200.

Restaurant :
♦♦ *Chez Camille*, quartier de Bonne-Terrasse, ☎ 94.79.80.38 ≰ ₺ closed Tue , Oct-Mar. Spec : *bouillabaisse* and fish, 165-300.

Recommended
Chambres d'hôtes : *l'Amourié*, les Vieux Moulins, ☎ 94.97.22.11, 6 rm, closed 1 Oct-15 May.
♥ beaches : *Tahiti*, ☎ 94.97.28.02.

SAINTE-BAUME Massif**

B3
From Aubagne to Saint-Maximin *(48 km, 3hr)*

"Bauomo" is a Provençal dialect for cave; "Sainte-Baume" is the "holy cavern" where St. Mary Magdalen supposedly repented her misdeeds (→ Les-Saintes-Maries-de-la-Mer, Camargue). The *massif* and green plateau are forested with beech, sycamore, yew, oak and lime, above a carpet of flowers.

▶ **Aubagne** (→ Marseille). ▶ **Gémenos.** ▶ **Saint-Pons Park★**, by the swift river Sauge; nothing remains of the abbey except the Romanesque church. ▶ **Espigoulier Pass** (alt. 728 m) : view of Marseille and the Sainte-Beaume Massif. ▶ **Sainte-Baume Hostelry**, a spiritual retreat open to all, not far from Mary Magdalen's cave. A forest path★★ leads to the cave *(45 min)*, at the foot of a steep escarpment. To reach **Saint-Pilon** (alt. 998 m), go back to the Oratory crossroads; from there, 40 min. At the chapel on the peak, the view★★ makes the climb worthwhile. Many other walks. ▶ **Nans-les-Pins**, summer resort village. ▶ **Saint-Maximin-la-Sainte-Baume** (→). ☐

Practical Information ——————————

GÉMENOS, ⊠ 13420, 6 km E of **Aubagne** on the D 2.

Hotel :
★★★★ *Relais de la Magdeleine* (I.L.A.), rte d'Aix-en-Provence, ☎ 94.82.20.05, Visa, 20 rm ℗ ≰ ₩ 🐾 ♪ half pens (h.s.), closed 15 Jan-15 Mar. An 18thC farmhouse set in a park, 740. Rest. ♦♦ ≰ ♪ 150-220.

Restaurant :
♦♦ *Fer à Cheval*, pl. de la Mairie, ☎ 94.82.21.19, closed Sat eve and Sun eve, 1 Jan, 25 Dec, 100-160.

NANS-LES-PINS, ⊠ 83860, 12 km SW of **Saint-Maximin**.
ⅱ ☎ 94.78.95.91.

Hotel :
● ★★★★ *Domaine de Châteauneuf* (R.C.), ☎ 94.78.90.06, Tx 400747, AE DC Euro Visa, 34 rm ℗ ≰ ₩ 🐾 ♪ ﾟ⁰ ♪ half pens (h.s.), closed 30 Nov-11 Apr, 920. Rest. ♦♦ ♪ ₺ 165-280.
▲ ★★★*Sainte-Baume* (90 pl), ☎ 94.78.92.68.

Le PARC-DE-SAINT-PONS, ⊠ 13420 Gémenos, 3 km E of **Gémenos.**

Hotel :
★★ *Les Salons du Marquis*, vallée de Saint-Pons via D 2, ☎ 42.70.47.64, 12 rm ℗ ≰ ₩ 🐾 closed Tue, Wed, Thu (l.s.), 240. Rest. ♦ ♪ 100-140.

SAINTE-MAXIME

Cannes 61, Toulon 73, Paris 880 km
pop 7364 ⊠ 83120   C3
When the Provençal saints aren't in the mountains, they're on the beaches : Saint-Raphaël, Saint-Tropez and now Sainte-Maxime, a seaside resort facing across the bay to Saint-Tropez.

▶ **Saint-Donat Park** *(10 km N)* : **Museum of Gramophones and Mechanical Music★** with exhibits ranging from Edison's first phonograph to quadraphonic systems *(10-12 & 3-6:30, Easter-15 Oct.).*   ☐

Practical Information ——————————

SAINTE-MAXIME
ⅱ prom. S.-Lozière, ☎ 94.96.19.24.

Hotels :
★★★★ *Golf Hôtel*, Beauvallon, 5 km W on N 98, ☎ 94.96.06.09, 100 rm ℗ ≰ ₩ ﾟ⁰ Private beach, 900. Rest. ♦♦♦ 160-240.
★★★★ *La Belle Aurore*, 4, bd Jean-Moulin, La Croisette, ☎ 94.96.02.45, 17 rm ℗ ≰ ₺ ☒ half pens (h.s.), closed 15 Oct-15 Mar, 650. Rest. ♦♦♦ ≰ ♪ 180-300.
★★★ *Calidianus*, bd Jean-Moulin, ☎ 94.96.23.21, 27 rm ℗ ≰ ₩ 🐾 ♪ ₺ ﾟ⁰ Pleasant setting, 350.
★★★ *Muzelle-Montfleuri*, 4, av. Montfleuri, ☎ 94.96.19.57, 31 rm ℗ ≰ ₩ 🐾 half pens (h.s.), closed 10 Nov-20 Mar, 350. Rest. ♦♦ 100-180; child : 50.
★★ *Auberge des Maures*, 3, rue des Frères-Battaglia, ☎ 94.96.01.92, 10 rm ₩ 🐾 Family atmosphere, warm welcome, 200.
★★ *Le Préconil*, 8, bd A.-Briand, ☎ 94.96.01.73, 19 rm ℗ ₩ closed 31 Oct-15 Mar, 210.
★★ *Marie-Louise*, hameau de Guerrevieille,

☎ 94.96.06.05, 14 rm P ≼ ⋘ ⌇ half pens (h.s.), closed 15 Oct-15 Feb, 460. Rest. ♦ ⌇ ♿ ⋇ Spec : *terrine de crabe, daube à la provençale, civet de porcelet*, 55-140.

Restaurants :
● ♦♦ *L'Esquinade*, at the Port, ☎ 94.96.01.65, DC ≼ ⌇ closed Wed (l.s.), 5 Nov-18 Dec. Nostalgia, *bourride* and kirs, 200-300.
♦♦ *La Gruppi*, av. Gal-de-Gaulle, ☎ 94.96.03.61, Visa ≼ ⌇ closed Mon (l.s.). Facing the sea. Spec : *bouillabaisse des pêcheurs, bourride, loup au champagne*, 140-200.

Recommended
Farmhouse-gîte : *Le Couloubrier*, rte de Plan-de-la-Tour, ☎ 94.96.23.36, camping.

Nearby

Le PLAN-DE-LA-TOUR, ⊠ 83120 Sainte-Maxime, 10 km NW.

Hotel :
★★★ *Ponte Romano*, rte de Grimaud, Préconil, ☎ 94.43.70.56, AE Visa, 10 rm P ≼ ⋘ ⌇ ⛶ ⋏ closed Nov-Mar. Pleasant setting, handsome Provençal house, 400. Rest. ♦♦♦ ⌇ 200-260.

SALON-DE-PROVENCE*

Aix-en-Provence 36, Arles 41, Paris 724 km
pop 35845 ⊠ 13300   A2

Best known for a flying school, Salon is an old merchant town that has prospered with the expansion of the communications network. The town has spread from its original base on the slopes around the château, down across the plain.

▶ **Rue de l'Horloge** runs straight across the old town, from the fountain in the **Place Crousillat** to the château. On the left it passes **Rue Nostradamus**, where the physician-astrologer (→ Saint-Rémy-de-Provence) wrote his prophecies *(daily ex Tue. 10-12 & 3-7)*. ▶ The **Château de l'Emperi★** (12th-16thC) has a noteworthy Courtyard of Honour★ ; exhibitions on French military history from Louis XIV to WWI *(10-12 & 2:30-6:30, 2-6 Oct.-Mar.; closed Tue. and hols.)*. ▶ 13thC **church of St. Michel** (left of the esplanade) : remarkable doorway★ that is part-Gothic (columns, capitals) and part-Romanesque (archivolt, tympanum). ▶ **Rue du Bourg-Neuf** runs down to the machicolated town gate. **Town Hall★** dating from Louis XIV. ▶ 400 m E, **Regional Museum of Salon and Crau**, in an 18thC Provençal mansion (wildlife ; *10-12 & 2-5, weekdays)*. ▶ Collegiate **church of St. Laurent★** *(N of town)* : Provençal Gothic ; in the fourth chapel on the left, the tomb of Nostradamus ; 16thC Virgin★ in alabaster). □

Practical Information —————————

SALON-DE-PROVENCE
ⓘ 56, cours Gimon, ☎ 90.56.27.60.
🚄 ☎ 90.56.01.15/90.56.04.05.

Hotels :
● ★★★★ *Abbaye de Sainte-Croix* (R.C.), rte du Val-de-Cuech, ☎ 90.56.24.55, Tx 401247, AE DC Euro Visa, 24 rm P ≼ ⋘ ⌇ ⌇ ⛶ half pens (h.s.), closed 31 Oct-1 Mar, 1130. Rest. ● ♦♦♦ ≼ ⌇ ♿ ⋇ closed Mon noon. The intelligent menu highlights Yves Sauret's refined dishes : *feuilleté de foie gras de canard, daube de turbot, escalope de loup au basilic*. Provençal wines, 160-400 ; child : 60.
★★ *Midi*, 518, allées de Craponne, ☎ 90.53.34.67, Tx 901056, Euro Visa, 27 rm. P 200. Rest. ⌇ 55-130.
★★ *Vendôme*, 34, rue du Mal-Joffre, ☎ 90.56.01.96, 22 rm P ⋘ 180.

Restaurants :
● ♦♦ *Robin*, 1, bd G.-Clemenceau, ☎ 90.56.06.53, AE DC Euro Visa ⌇ closed Mon and Sun eve. Francis Robin, president of *Cuisiniers du Soleil*, sets a shining example in his Louis-XVI decor : *civet de homard, assiette du pêcheur au safran*, 150-260.

♦♦ *La Brocherie des Cordeliers*, 20, rue d'Hozier, ☎ 90.56.53.42, DC Visa ⌇ ⋇ closed Sat noon and Sun , hols, 1-4 May, 5-19 Jul, 24-26 Dec. Spec : *magret de canard aux myrtilles, sauté de Saint-Jacques à la ciboulette*, 70-160.
♦♦ *Le Craponne*, 146, allées de Craponne, ☎ 90.53.23.92, Visa ⌇ ♿ closed Mon and Sun eve, 1-22 Jul. Pretty interior. Attractive fixed-price meals and a luscious lemon tart, 70-135.

▲ ★★★*Nostradamus* (83 pl), ☎ 90.56.08.36.

Nearby

La BARBEN, ⊠ 13330 Pélissanne, 8 km SE.

Hotel :
★★ *La Touloubre* (R.S., L.F.), ☎ 90.55.16.85, Euro Visa, 17 rm P ⋘ ♿ ⛶ closed Sun eve and Mon, 15-31 Jan, 15-30 Nov, 240. Rest. ♦♦ Interesting fixed-price meals highlighting regional dishes : *jambonnette de volaille au foie gras et morilles*, 100-200.

SANARY-SUR-MER

Toulon 12, Marseille 54, Paris 829 km
pop 11689 ⊠ 83110   B3
A pink and white town protected from the *mistral* by surrounding hills ; palms and sandy beach.

Nearby

▶ The **Gros Cerveau** *(13 km N)* : view★★. ▶ **Ollioules** and **Mont Caume** *(22 km NE)* : flowers, a Romanesque church ; through the **Ollioules Gorges** to **Evenos★**, an old village on a rocky peak. The little road to **Mont Caume** zigzags up to two forts at the peak (alt. 801 m ; view★). ▶ **Ile des Embiez** *(10-min crossing from Le Brusc, 6 km S)*, a sports, cultural and tourist complex developed by Paul Ricard, the *pastis* manufacturer and motor-racing sponsor ; Sea Observatory : aquariums *(9-12 & 2-6 ; closed some nat. hols.)*. ▶ **Notre-Dame-du-Mai★** *(13 km SE)* at **Cap Sicié**, right on the sea (alt. 358 m) ; *ex-votos★* ; view★★. ▶ **Six-Fours-Les Plages** *(5 km SE)* : fort *(2 km N)* overlooking Toulon roads ; collegiate church of St. Pierre : Romanesque and 17thC Gothic ; 16thC painting of the Virgin★ *(Sat. and Sun pm in season ; Sat. only out of season)*. ▶ **Notre-Dame-de-Pépiole★** *(5 km E ; 10th or 11thC)* : a charming site near a wood of pine and cork-oak. □

Practical Information —————————

SANARY-SUR-MER
ⓘ jardins de la Ville, ☎ 94.74.01.04.
🚄 ☎ 94.91.50.50.

Hotels :
★★ *Grand Hôtel des Bains*, av. Estienne-d'Orves, ☎ 94.74.13.47, AE DC Visa, 32 rm P ⋘ ♿ half pens, 420. Rest. ♦ ≼ ⌇ ♿ 80-110.
★★ *Roc Amour*, bd de la Falaise, ☎ 94.74.13.54, 20 rm P ≼ ⋘ ♿ ♿ pens (h.s.), closed 1 Jan-15 Feb, 460. Rest. ♦ ♿ closed Mon. Spec : *poulet aux crustacés*, 70-110.
★★ *Tour*, at the port, ☎ 94.74.10.10, DC Visa, 26 rm . ≼ ⌇ pens (h.s.), closed Dec, 495. Rest. ♦ ≼ ⌇ closed Tue, 90-160.

▲ ★★★*Les Girelles* (220 pl), ☎ 94.74.13.18 ; ★★★*Mogador* (240 pl), ☎ 94.74.10.58 ; ★★★*Val d'Aran* (240 pl), ☎ 94.29.56.16.

Nearby

SIX-FOURS-LES-PLAGES, ⊠ 83140, 4 km E.

Restaurant :
● ♦♦ *Auberge-Saint-Vincent*, pont du Brusc, ☎ 94.25.70.50, AE DC Euro Visa, closed Mon and Sun eve (l.s.). V. Sciré makes laudable efforts for his patrons : shellfish from a saltwater tank, *sole aux trois senteurs de Provence, loup aux olives*. Burgundy and Beaujolais

wines from the Hospices de Beaune and Beaulieu, 95-170.

SEILLANS*

Grasse 31, Castellane 56, Paris 895 km
pop 1609 ⊠ 83440 Fayence   C2

A fortified village on the slopes of Mont Auzières. Charming town, château; enjoyed by the composer Charles Gounod (1758-1823) and the surrealist painter Max Ernst (1891-1976). **Notre-Dame-de-L'Ormeau** *(1 km SE; ask at the SI)* : carved and painted 16thC altarpiece of the Tree of Jesse (geneology of Christ); *ex-votos.*

▶ **Fayence** *(7.5 km SE),* a village of craftsmen on the edge of the Plans de Provence; 18thC neo-Classical church; hang-gliding centre nearby (view★).   ☐

Practical Information _____

SEILLANS

Hotels :
★★★ *Deux Rocs,* pl. Font-d'Amont, ☎ 94.76.87.32, 15 rm ⟨ ░░░ 🛁 closed 1 Nov-21 Mar, 265. Rest. ♦♦ ⟨ ⌘ closed Tue and Thu noon, 100-150.
★★★ *France,* pl. du Thouron, ☎ 94.76.96.10, Tx 970530, 28 rm 🅿 ⟨ ░░░ 🖃 half pens (h.s.), closed Wed (l.s.), 5-25 Jan, 580. Rest. ♦♦ *Clariond* ⟨ ♪ Classic fare : *carré d'agneau à la broche, civet de lapin,* 155-230.

Nearby

FAYENCE, ⊠ 83440, 7 km E.
ⓘ pl. Léon-Roux, ☎ 94.76.20.08.

Hotel :
● ★★★ *Moulin de la Camandoule,* chemin N.-D.-des-Cyprès, 3 km SW on D 19, ☎ 94.76.00.84, DC Visa, 11 rm 🅿 ⟨ ░░░ 🛁 🖃 half pens (h.s.), closed 15 Jan-15 Mar, 15 Nov-15 Dec. A remarkably renovated old oil press, 625. Rest. ♦♦ ⟨ closed Mon (ex Jul-Aug), 5 Jan-31 Mar, 1 Nov-20 Dec, 115-150.

Restaurant :
♦♦ *Le France,* 1, Grande-Rue-du-Château, ☎ 94.76.04.14, Euro Visa ░░░ closed Tue eve and Wed (l.s.), 10 Jan-15 Feb, 15 Nov-20 Dec. Classic dishes : crayfish in season, grilled leg of lamb with herbs. Reasonable prices, 45-150.

⚘ ★★★*Lou Cantaire* (35 pl), ☎ 94.76.23.77 ; at Montauroux, 10 km E, ★★★*Les Chaumettes* (120 pl), ☎ 94.76.43.27.

Recommended
Events : *bric-à-brac sale,* early Aug.

SÉNANQUE Abbey***

B2

In the austere valley of the Sénancole, Cistercian monks built the last of the abbeys know as the "three sisters of Provence" (the other two are Silvacane and Le Thoronet). Sénanque is one of the purest examples of 12thC Cistercian architecture, with elegant lines that would make any further decoration superfluous.

▶ Founded in 1148, Sénanque today is a cultural centre (concerts of ancient music, temporary exhibitions; *10-12 & 4-6, 7 in season).* ▶ Visits to the dormitory, the **cloister★,** the chapterhouse, the monks' hall, and the **church★.** ▶ In the **refectory,** audiovisual introduction to Cistercian life; former kitchens (17thC) present an introduction to Romanesque symbolism. ▶ Farmstead : **museum of the Sahara** *(10-12:30 & 2-7; tel. 90.72.02.05).*   ☐

SILVACANE Abbey**

B2

One of the rare Cistercian foundations not concealed in a forest or solitary valley. The area, however, was never much frequented, isolated as it was in a reed marsh *(silva cannarum =* forest of reeds).

▶ The overall plan is typical of the monasteries of the Order *(10-12 & 2-5, 6 in season; closed Tue. and hols.).* ▶ As at Sénanque and Le Thoronet, the 12th-13thC **church★** is very beautiful. The **cloister** (13thC) is Romanesque but has ogival vaults at three corners.

Nearby

▶ **Cadenet** *(5 km NE)* : church (3rdC baptismal font★). ▶ **Pertuis** *(18 km E)* : vestiges of the Middle Ages (rampart, tower, château); in the church, a 16thC triptych. ▶ **La Tour-d'Aigues** *(6 km NE of Pertuis),* around the ruins of a 16thC château (monumental door★); in the church, painted Christ, 15thC Italian. ▶ **Meyrargues** *(16 km SE)* : medieval château converted into a hotel. ▶ **Peyrolles-en-Provence** *(6 km E),* amid orchards and vineyards : 18thC château, now the town hall. 9 km NE from Peyrolles, the Durance runs through the **Mirabeaux Defile★.** ▶ **Rognes** *(9 km SE)* : quarries; church with collection of carved wooden altarpieces★ (late 15th-18thC).   ☐

Practical Information _____

LAURIS, ⊠ 84360, 18 km W of **Pertuis.**

Hotels :
● ★★ *Auberge du Vieux Pont* (L.F.), ☎ 80.72.85.28, 8 rm 🅿 ⟨ ░░░ 🛁 ⌘ closed Mon. Rest. ♦ ⟨ ♪ 🛁 ⌘ closed Mon and eves (Nov-Feb). Spec : *bouillabaisse,* 60-80.
★★ *La Chaumière* (L.F.), pl. du Portail, ☎ 90.68.01.29, AE DC Euro Visa, 10 rm 🅿 ⟨ ♨ 🛁 half pens (h.s.), closed 5 Jan-20 Feb, 450. Rest. ♦♦ ⟨ ♪ closed Tue and Wed noon. A delicious array of vegetables and local produce prepared by savvy chef Julien Corcinos in a pretty dining room with a view of the Durance River. Provençal and Lubéron wines, 120-175.

MEYRARGUES, ⊠ 13650, 8 km S of **Pertuis.**

Hotel :
● ★★★ *Château de Meyrargues,* ☎ 42.57.50.32, AE DC 14 rm ░░░ 🛁 closed 1 Nov-1 Feb. A fortress overlooking the Durance, 380. Rest. ♦♦♦ closed Mon and Sun eve, 140-250.

PERTUIS, ⊠ 84120, 18 km E.
ⓘ pl. Mirabeau, ☎ 90.79.15.56.
🚅 ☎ 90.79.10.43.

Hotel :
★★★ *Sevan,* (Mapotel), av. de Verdun, ☎ 90.79.19.30, AE DC Euro Visa, 36 rm 🅿 ⟨ ░░░ 🖃 ♪ half pens (h.s.), closed 2 Jan-1 Mar, 575. Rest. ♦♦ ⟨ ♪ ⌘ Spec : *foie gras de canard maison, turbotin braisé au curry, mignonettes d'agneau au chèvre de pays,* 95-160.

⚘ *Municipal* (200 pl), ☎ 90.79.10.98.

SISTERON*

Digne 39, Gap 48, Paris 706 km
pop 6572 ⊠ 04200   B1

Sisteron is the gateway between Provence and the Dauphiné ; flat roofs, a citadel, limestone cliffs eroded over the centuries, and an ageless bridge over the Durance just before the latter widens into a lake.

▶ The **citadel★** (12th-16thC), on a limestone ridge, crowns the site *(8-7, Palm Sunday-1 Nov.; arrowed itinerary);* magnificent view from the top. ▶ **Church of Notre-Dame,** 12thC Provençal Romanesque, with Lombard influences in the doorway and the E end; attractive capitals★ on the pillars in the nave; two French primitive paintings (early 16thC) in the second chapel on the left. Left of the church, an arrowed path leads through the old town.

Nearby

▶ **Vilhosc** *(6 km E)* : remains of 11thC priory ; early meridional Romanesque crypt. ▶ **Château-Arnoux** *(14 km SE)*, above **Lake Escale** on the Durance ; early-16thC château. ▶ Excursions into the Upper **Vançon Valley,** wooded and deserted *(23 km NE, D3).* □

Practical Information _____

SISTERON
ⓘ hôtel de ville, ☎ 92.61.12.03.
𝘚𝘕𝘊𝘍 ☎ 92.61.00.60.

Hotels :
★★★ *Grand Hôtel du Cours*, pl. de l'Église, ☎ 92.61.04.51, AE DC Euro Visa, 44 rm Ⓟ ≼ ⚲ ᶑ closed 15 Nov-15 Mar, 235.
★★ *Chênes* (L.F.), rte de Gap, ☎ 92.61.15.08, Euro Visa, 22 rm Ⓟ ⬚ closed Sun eve (l.s.), 25 Oct-10 Dec, 165. Rest. ♦ Family-style cooking, 60-130 ; child : 48.

⚠ ★★*Municipal* (200 pl), ☎ 92.61.19.69.

Recommended
Events : *nights of the Citadel*, (theatre, dance, music), mid-Jul-mid-Aug.
♥ local sweets : *Canteperdrix*, 32, av. Jean-Jaurès, ☎ 92.61.01.81 ; pork products : *Richard et Badet*, impasse de l'Horloge, ☎ 92.61.13.63. *Pieds et paquets.*

Nearby
CHÂTEAU-ARNOUX, ✉ 04160, 14 km SW.
ⓘ rte Nationale, ☎ 92.64.02.64.

Hotel :
● ★★★★ *La Bonne Etape* (R.C.), chemin du Lac, ☎ 92.64.00.09, Tx 430605, AE DC Euro Visa, 18 rm Ⓟ ≼ ⬚ ♪ closed Sun eve and Mon, 3 Jan-15 Feb, 15-22 Nov. Aubusson tapestry cartoons ; quiet, delightful rooms, 420. Rest. ● ♦♦♦ ≼ ♪ This former coaching inn on the Napoleonic road is indeed a *bonne étape,* a pleasant place to stop over. A smiling welcome from Arlette awaits you. The generous cuisine of Pierre and Jany Gleize is sure to whet your appetite. They take full advantage of the region's fragrant herbs : *jambon et daube d'agneau, omelettes froides à la tapenade, morue fraîche à la Denos Titin, agneau de Sisteron rôti.* Goat and sheep's milk cheeses, olives, oil and local wines, 180-400.

TARASCON*

Arles 18, Avignon 23, Paris 711 km
pop 11024 ✉ 13150   A2

A boundary between Provence and the royal territories of France ; haunt also of the *tarasque,* a mythical monster half-crocodile and half-lion, vanquished by St. Martha (sister of Mary Magdalen → La Camargue) whose presumed relics repose here.

▶ **Château**★★ (completed in the 15thC), poised on a rock rising out of the Rhône, one of the most beautiful feudal buildings in the country ; a frontier post between Tarascon and Beaucaire, outposts of the territories of Provence and France respectively. The crenellated walls and grim exterior hide an interior of great elegance ; the château was both fortress and princely residence *(guided tours at 10, 11, 2, 3 and 4, plus 9 and 5 in season ; closed Tue. and hols.).* The cool interior courtyard★ is surrounded by the graceful Flamboyant Gothic royal lodgings. ▶ The **collegiate church** of **Ste-Marthe**★ (12th-17thC) maintains relics of the saint which have made it a revered site of pilgrimages. The S door★ is Romanesque. Inside, interesting paintings★. Tombs★ of Jean de Cossa (15thC) and St. Marthe (17thC marble mausoleum) in the crypt. ▶ Stroll in **Rue des Halles** (15thC houses) ; see the *Tarasque* at the SI.

Nearby

▶ **Boulbon** *(7 km N),* a rustic hamlet against the tree-covered massif of the **Montagnette,** dominated by a ruined château ; in the cemetery, the 12thC Romanesque **chapel of St. Marcellin**★. ▶ **Abbey of St. Michel-de-Frigolet** *(11.5 km NE),* founded in the 10thC, in the heart of the Montagnette, fragrant with wild thyme ; the abbey is maintained by the Order of White Canons *(guided tours, 9-12 & 2-7).* Only the Romanesque church of St. Michel remains from the old priory ; in the 19thC abbey church, superb woodwork★ frames 14 paintings by Mignard. On sale at the monastery (and concocted in the abbey pharmacy) is the Elixir du Révérend-Père Gaucher, which was immortalized in a novel by Daudet (→ Fontvieille). ▶ **Barbentane** *(15 km NE)* : guarded by two fortified gates, the château★ exemplifies Provençal classicism ; 18thC interior decoration★ *(10-12 & 2-6, Easter-1 Nov. ; closed Wed. ex Jul.-Sep. ; Sun. only in winter, same hours).* □

Practical Information _____

ⓘ av. de la République, ☎ 90.91.03.52.
𝘚𝘕𝘊𝘍 ☎ 90.91.04.82/90.91.08.22.

Hotels :
★★★ *Les Mazets des Roches*, rte de Fontvieille, ☎ 90.91.34.89, AE DC Euro Visa, 24 rm Ⓟ ⬚ ⚲ ♪ ▭ ⤴ closed 15 Oct-15 Apr, 350. Rest. ♦ ≼ ♪ ⫽ closed Thu eve, 90-140 ; child : 65.
★★★ *Provence*, 7, bd V.-Hugo, ☎ 90.91.06.43, AE DC Euro Visa, 11 rm, 190.
★★ *Moderne*, 26, bd Item, ☎ 90.91.01.70, 31 rm Ⓟ 160. Rest. ♦ *Le Mistral,* closed Sat ex groups, 4 Jan-15 Feb. Spec. ♦ *daube provençale,* 50-70.
★★ *Provençal*, 12, cours A.-Briand, ☎ 90.91.11.41, AE Euro Visa, 22 rm Ⓟ closed 1 Nov-15 Mar, 130. Rest. ♦ Regional specialties : *bourride, daube provençale,* 45-105.
★★ *Saint-Jean*, 24, bd V.-Hugo, ☎ 90.91.13.87, AE DC Euro Visa, 12 rm ⫽ closed 15 Dec-15 Jan, 180. Rest. ♦ closed Wed (l.s.). Provençal cuisine. Spec : *terrine de rascasse au poivre rose,* 70-160.

⚠ ★★*Camp Tartarin* (33 pl), ☎ 90.91.04.46 ; ★★*Saint-Gabriel* (44 pl), ☎ 90.91.19.83.

Le THORONET Abbey***

Brignoles 25, Toulon 64, Paris 839 km
pop 819 ✉ 83340 Le Luc   C3

Le Thoronet, third of the "three sisters" (→ Sénanque, Silvacane), is a 12thC example of the 20thC architectural dictum, "Less is more". The perfect proportions, masterly stonework and the use of light, illustrating the principles of the Cistercian Order, more than compensate for the absence of embellishment.

▶ The monastery buildings were erected between 1160 and 1175 ; the clean lines of the Romanesque **church**★ are complemented by the powerful form of the **cloister**★ (access through N aisle). ▶ **Cabasse** *(7 km SW),* hidden in the green Issle Valley : prehistoric menhirs and dolmens ; carved wooden altarpiece★ (1543) in the 16thC church of St. Pons. □

Practical Information _____

Hotel :
Relais de l'Abbaye, Les Bruns, 3 km NW on D 84, ☎ 94.73.87.59, 5 rm Ⓟ ≼ ⬚ ⚲ 280. Rest. ♦♦ ≼ ♪ ᶑ closed Mon eve and Tue. Pleasant setting. Spec : *petit salé roulé séché aux herbes, poulet au citron à la provençale, gâteau aux marrons,* 130-200.

_____

For the translation of a name of a meat, a fish or a vegetable, for the composition of a dish or a sauce, see the Menu Guide in the Practical Holiday Guide ; it lists the most common culinary terms.

TINÉE Valley**

C-D1
From Pont de la Mescla to Saint-Étienne-de-Tinée
(53 km, 4 hr)

The River Tinée rises in the Bonette Pass, site of the highest road in Europe. The valley springs to life each winter with the advent of the skiing season.
▶ **Pont de la Mescla** *(39 km N of Nice on N202).* ▶ D2205 runs along the bottom of the **Mescla Gorges★.** ▶ **La Tour** *(right, 7 km)* : chapel of the White Penitents (1491). ▶ **Clans** *(6.5 km, right)* : church with 12thC frescos, altarpiece of the School of Nice. ▶ **Ilonse★** *(11 km, left; view★).* ▶ **Saint-Sauveur-sur-Tinée**, the valley's shopping centre and departure point for numerous excursions. ▶ 4 km W, road to **Roure★** : 16thC St. Laurent altarpiece★, Niçoise Assumption (1560). ▶ **Roubion★** *(12 km W)* : 12thC ramparts and gates. ▶ **Beuil** *(24 km W; (→ Daluis Gorges).* ▶ D2205 runs through the **Valabres Gorges★.** ▶ **Isola** : Romanesque bell tower, within hearing of the **Louch waterfalls★** (100 m high); 17 km E through the **Chastillon Valley★** to **Isola 2000**, a ski resort in a superb natural amphitheatre; Italy is only 5 km away. ▶ **Saint-Étienne-de-Tinée**, amid pastures and streams, a base for excursions (Lake Rabuons★, *4hr)*; church with Romanesque bell tower★, 15thC frescos in the chapel of St. Sébastien, museum of religious art in the chapel of St. Michel. ▶ **Auron★** *(7 km S; alt.* 1 608 m), the principal winter resort of the Alpes-Maritimes department; **cablecar** from **Las Donnas★** *(closed May, Jun., Oct., Nov.)* : Alpine panorama★★. ▶ **Bonette Peak★★★** *(26 km NW, → Barcelonete).* ☐

Practical Information _____

AURON, ☒ 06660 Saint-Étienne-de-Tinée, 65 km SE of **Barcelonnette**.
✆ 1602-2415m.
ⓘ imm. la Ruade, ☎ 93.23.02.66.

Hotel :
● ★★★ *Pilon*, ☎ 93.23.00.15, 30 rm ℗ ≪ ♨ ☐ closed 15 Apr-25 Jun, 1 Sep-20 Dec. Skating rink, 420. Rest. ♦ ☜ closed lunch (l.s.). In summer, a poolside grill at lunch, 115-200.

ISOLA 2000, ☒ 06420 Saint-Sauveur-de-Tinée, 6 km NE of **Valberg**.
✆ 2000-2603m.
ⓘ maison d'Isola, ☎ 93.02.70.50.

Hotels :
★★★★ *Chastillon*, ☎ 93.23.10.60, Tx 970507, AE DC Euro Visa, 54 rm ℗ ≪ ♨ closed 25 Apr-14 Dec, 1200. Rest. ♦♦ ≪ ♪ 90-150.
★★ *Le Druos*, ☎ 93.23.12.20, Tx 461175, AE Visa, 40 rm ℗ ≪ ♪ ₺ closed 5 May-30 Jun, 15 Sep-15 Dec, 320. Rest. ♦♦ ≪ ♪ ₺ 50-100.

Recommended
Sports : *Club Pascale Paradis*, ☎ 93.23.14.07, Tennis lessons; Delta-plane and horseback-riding lessons, info S.I.

SAINT-ÉTIENNE-DE-TINÉE, ☒ 06660, 58 km SE of **Barcelonnette**.
ⓘ 1, rue des Communes-de-France, ☎ 93.02.41.96 (h.s.). ☝

Hotel :
★ *Pinatelle*, ☎ 93.02.40.36, 12 rm ≪ ﹏ ♨ closed 1 Oct-1 Dec, 110. Rest. ♦ 80-130.

TOULON*

Marseille 64, Nice 153, Paris 839 km
pop 181405 ☒ 83000   B3

See the map p. 762.
Toulon, with its magnificent harbour★★, ranks with Portsmouth, San Diego and Yokohama as one of the world's great naval ports. Although the trim French naval uniform with pomponed beret is no longer man-

datory for sailors on shore leave, the town is steeped in the tradition of the *Royale*, as the French navy is nicknamed. Toulon is ringed by white limestone mountains studded with pine trees. The architecture in the newer quarters is resolutely modern; the old town still holds a daily market★ in the Cours Lafayette.

▶ **Quai Stalingrad** (C3), beside the Old Basin *(Darse Vieille)* : busy cafés isolated from the rest of town by buildings on the Avenue de la République. On the façade of the former town hall, famous Atlantes★ by Puget. ▶ The Maritime Offices mark the beginning of the naval installations. ▶ Near the very handsome monumental gate (formerly the principal entry to the arsenal), the **musée de la Marine★** (Naval Museum, B3) : models★, paintings, figureheads and other reminders of the city's maritime heritage *(10-12 & 1:30-6; closed Tue. and hols.).* ▶ The **Maritime Arsenal** (A-B2), the early hub of Toulon, still a busy naval shipyard. ▶ **Rue d'Alger** (B2), once the hot-spot of old Toulon; the nearby streets are still colourful, although perhaps more restrained than numerous popular songs about Rue d'Alger would suggest. ▶ (C2-3), **Cathedral of Ste Marie** : an odd mixture of Classical (1696 façade) and Romano-Gothic (interesting paintings, including works by Puget, Van Loo, Mignard). ▶ **Cours Lafayette** (C3) : **market★**, "wild thyme, a bit of saffron and a net of figs for five francs..." as a traditional song relates. **Museum of Old Toulon** (No. 69; *3-6 ex Sun.*). ▶ **Church of St. François-de-Paule** : curved Italian Baroque façade (1744); gilded wood statue of the Virgin★ (1660). ▶ **Le Mourillon and Cap Brun** (via D3; *7.5 km round trip).* At the far end of Le Mourillon promontory, the **Royal Tower★** (16thC) : naval museum; panorama★. ▶ **Boulevard Dr-Cunéo** (off D3) leads to the little port of **Mourillon★**, overlooked by the fort of St. Louis★. Farther on, beaches and residential area of Cap Brun.

Also... ▶ **Toulon Museum** (B1-2) : natural history, art, archaeology (Oriental room, paintings by Carraccio, Brueghel, David, Van Loo, Denis, Vlaminck; *10-12 & 2-6; closed nat. hols.).*

Nearby
▶ **Chateauvallon** *(7 km NW)* : arts and cultural centre★ among pines, olive trees and rocks. ▶ **Evenos★** (→ Sanary).

Mont Faron★★ *(18 km-round trip; marked road one-way only; access by cable-car daily ex Mon. am; B1)*

▶ **Mont Faron** : pine woods on a limestone mountain 542 m above Toulon. ▶ On the left, Beaumont Tower : **National Memorial to the WWII landings** in Provence *(9-7 in summer; 9-11:30 & 2-5:30 in winter)*; panorama★★, orientation charts. ▶ Farther on, **Zoo** and **Fort de la Croix-Faron** (view★).

Around the roadstead★ *(la Rade; 1-2hr by boat, leave from Quai Stalingrad, B2; by car, 17 km to Saint-Mandrier, approx 2hr)*

▶ Leave Toulon by A1. ▶ **La Seyne-sur-Mer**, dockyard town; Panoramic Marine Museum (marine fauna and flora; *10-12 & 3-7 in summer; 10-12 & 2-6 in winter; closed Fri., Sat. and Mon. am, Nov.).* ▶ **Fort de Balaguier** : naval museum, galleys and convict hulks; unique view★★ of the roadstead *(10-12 & 3-7 in summer; 10-12 & 2-6 ex Mon. and Tue. in winter).* ▶ **Tamaris** and **Les Sablettes** : seaside resorts. ▶ **Saint-Mandrier** : fishing port, pleasure craft deep in a bay; view★ of the roadstead. ▶ **Cap Sicié** (→ Sanary).   ☐

Practical Information _____

TOULON
ⓘ 8, av. Colbert (C1-2), ☎ 94.22.08.22.
✈ *Toulon-Hyères*, 21 km E, (Le Palyvestre). ☎ 94.57.41.41. *Air France office*, 9, pl. d'Armes, ☎ 94.92.20.50.
〔SNCF〕 (B1), ☎ 94.22.90.00/94.91.50.50/94.22.39.19.

bd P.-Toesca (B1).

🚌 ☎ 94.41.25.76, Regular service to Corsica in season.

Car rental : *Avis*, train station; airport, ☎ 94.38.98.02; Carrefour Léon-Bourgeois (off map D3), ☎ 94.36.20.01.

Hotels :

● ★★★ *Altea Tour Blanche* (ex Frantel), bd Amiral-Vence (off map B1), ☎ 94.24.41.57, Tx 400347, AE DC Euro Visa, 93 rm ℗ ⬦ 🎠 ⬦ 🏖 ⬦ 🖃 A splendid view of Toulon and the port, 420. Rest. ♦♦ ⬦ ♪ 🏖 Regional cuisine, or a fixed-price meal centred on a specific dish : smoked fish assortment, *artichaut barigoule, loup grillé à l'huile d'olive*, 110-200.

★★★ *La Corniche*, 1, littoral F.-Mistral (off map D3), ☎ 94.41.35.12, AE DC Euro Visa, 22 rm ℗ ⬦ 🍴 230. Rest. ♦♦ ⬦ ♪ closed Mon and Sun eve , Feb. Spec : *bouillabaisse, moules neptune*, grilled fish, 80-140.

★★★ *Le Grand Hôtel*, 4, pl. de la Liberté (C2), ☎ 94.22.59.50, Tx 430048, AE DC Euro Visa, 45 rm ℗ 🍴 ♪ 340.

★★ *Europe*, 7 bis, rue de Chabannes (C1-2), ☎ 94.92.37.44, Tx 400479, DC Euro Visa, 29 rm, 150.

★★ *La Résidence*, 18, rue Gimelli (B1), ☎ 94.92.92.81, DC Visa, 27 rm ⬦ 🏖 150.

★★ *Maritima*, 9, rue Gimelli (B1), ☎ 94.92.39.33, 48 rm ⬦ 🏖 130.

Restaurants :

♦♦♦ *Le Lutrin*, 8, littoral F.-Mistral, Le Morillon (off map D3), ☎ 94.42.43.43, AE DC Euro Visa ⬦ ♪ closed Sat. Spec : *foie gras frais de Lutrin, papillote de rascasse sur fond de légumes frais*, 100-250.

♦♦ *La Calanque*, 25, rue Denfert-Rochereau (C2), ☎ 94.92.28.58, AE DC Euro Visa, closed Mon and Sun eve , Feb school hols, 1 wk in Sep. Attractive fixed-price meal. Classic cooking. Spec : *sole soufflée en mousseline, filet de turbot sabayon au fenouil*, 120-210.

♦♦ *La Ferme*, 6, pl. L.-Blanc (C3), ☎ 94.41.43.74, Euro Visa ♪ closed Sun eve , Aug. Spec : *soufflé d'oursins, suprême de turbot au vin du Var*, pastries. The fixed-price meal is a good value, 90-180.

♦♦ *Le Dauphin*, 21 bis, rue Jean-Jaurès (C2), ☎ 94.93.12.07, Visa ♪ closed Sat noon and Sun, 16-23 Feb, 6 Jul-3 Aug. Spec : *saumon mariné huile d'olive, filet de rouget au curry, filet de bœuf aux truffes*, 125-175.

♦♦ *Madeleine*, 7, rue des Tombades (B2), ☎ 94.92.67.85, DC Visa ♪ closed Tue and Wed. Spec : *cassoulet au confit de canard, cassolette de foies de volailles aux girolles*, 85-160.

♦ *Pascal "Chez Mimi"*, 83, av. de la République (B2), ☎ 94.92.79.60, AE DC 🍴 ♪ closed Mon, 90-130.

Recommended

Events : *trade fair* in Oct; *feast of St-Peter* in Jul; *regatta week* in Sep.

Nearby

Les OURSINIERES, 12 km E on the N 559.

Hotel :

● ★★★ *L'Escapade* (I.L.A.), ☎ 94.21.72.76, Euro Visa, 16 rm ℗ ⬦ 🍴 ⬦ 🏊 🖃 400.

La SEYNE-SUR-MER, 🖂 83500, 6 km W.

ⓘ rue L.-Blum, ☎ 94.94.73.09.

SNCF ☎ 94.94.80.07.

Car rental : *Avis*, av. Gagarine, ☎ 94.94.55.47.

Hotel :

★ *Moderne*, 2, rue L.-Blum, ☎ 94.94.86.68, 18 rm ⬦ 190.

⛺ ★★★*Buffalo Parc* (80 pl), ☎ 94.25.22.08; ★★★*L'Union* (35 pl), ☎ 94.94.86.10.

SOLLIÈS-TOUCAS, 🖂 83210 Solliès-Pont, 18 km NE.

Restaurant :

● ♦♦ *Lingousto*, RN 554, ☎ 94.28.90.25, AE DC Visa 🍴 ♪ closed Mon and Sun eve , Mon lunch only (Jul-Aug), 15 Jan-28 Feb. Aromatic Provençal cuisine by Alain Ryon : *mesclun de poisson*, 165-300.

TURINI Forest**

D2

From L'Escarène to the Turini Pass *(26 km, 3hr)*

A complete change of scenery just half an hour's drive from the sea and the palms; 35 km² of chestnut, beech, maple, spruce, and 30-m high larches between the Vésubie and Bévera valleys.

▶ **L'Escarène** (→ Nice). ▶ D2566 to **Lucéram★**, a medieval town on an escarpment between two ravines. Romano-Gothic church, 18thC Italian rococo decoration; altarpiece of St. Marguerite★ (1500) attributed to Louis Bréa; another of St. Antoine★ (1480) attributed to Canevasio; in the treasury★, St. Marguerite and the Dragon★, silver statuette of 1500. ▶ **Chapel of St. Grat** *(1 km S)* and **chapel of Notre-Dame-de-Bon-Cœur** *(2 km NW)* : both with frescos. ▶ **Peïra-Cava★**, year-round resort, view★★. ▶ The road climbs through the Turini Forest★★ to the crossroads at **Turini Pass** (alt. 1 607 m). ▶ **L'Aution★** *(4 km NE)* : memorial to the war dead of 1793 and 1945; **Pointe des Trois-Communes** *(3 km)* : superb view★★. D70 W of the pass to the **Vésubie Valley★★** (→) via the **Sainte-Élisabeth Gorges**. SE, D2566 to **Sospel★** (→ Menton). □

Practical Information

PEÏRA-CAVA, 🖂 06440 L'Escarène, 40 km N of **Nice**.
🎿 1432-1600m.
ⓘ ☎ 94.91.57.22.

Hotel :

★★ *Trois Vallées* (R.S.), col de Turini, 8 km on D 256, ☎ 93.91.57.21, Euro Visa, 22 rm ℗ ⬦ 🏖 ♪ 🎠 closed 15 Nov-15 Dec. A pretty chalet in a wild spot, 240. Rest. ♦♦ ♪ Spec : *crêpes aux champignons, poulet aux écrevisses*, 45-120.

VAISON-LA-ROMAINE**

Carpentras 28, Avignon 47, Paris 67 km
pop 5864 🖂 84110   A1

Four in one : a medieval town on the prehistoric settlement; a modern one on the Roman city. The green waters of the River Ouvèze run under a single-span Roman bridge.

▶ Much of the Roman city is hidden by the modern town; in the **Puymin Quarter** *(9-5, 6 in season)* : the Villa of Messius, once the estate of a well-to-do Roman townsman. Close by, Pompey's Portico, a walled public promenade 52m × 64m. ▶ **Roman Theatre★** (AD20), built against the N hillside. ▶ **Museum** : excavated art and artifacts (marble statues★, head of Venus, athlete crowning himself with laurel wreath★, silver bust of a nobleman★; *same hours as Puymin*). ▶ Along a Roman street to the **Villasse Quarter** : basilica, house where the silver bust was unearthed, House of the Dolphin. ▶ Former **cathedral of Notre-Dame-de-Nazareth★**, an interesting example of Provençal Romanesque; parts (6th-7thC apse★) date from Merovingian times; Romanesque **cloister★** on the N side *(same hours as the Roman monuments; a single admission ticket covers all)*. ▶ **Chapel of St. Quenin★** *(300 m N)* : similar blend of eras; triangular apse from late 12thC. ▶ **Roman bridge** leads to the **medieval town** (13th-14thC); this quarter is gradually being restored. 15thC church; ruins of the 12thC château of the Counts of Toulouse.

Nearby

▶ **Valréas** *(25 km N)*, an administrative anomaly : a section of the Department of Vaucluse surrounded by the Department of Drôme formed as an enclave by Charles VII to prevent further acquisitions of land by the popes at Avignon. 15th-18thC town hall; old houses in the Grande-Rue; 17thC chapel of the White Penitents. Open-air summer theatre festival in the courtyard of the Hôtel de Simiane. ▶ **Richerenches** *(7 km SW)* : 12thC rectangular

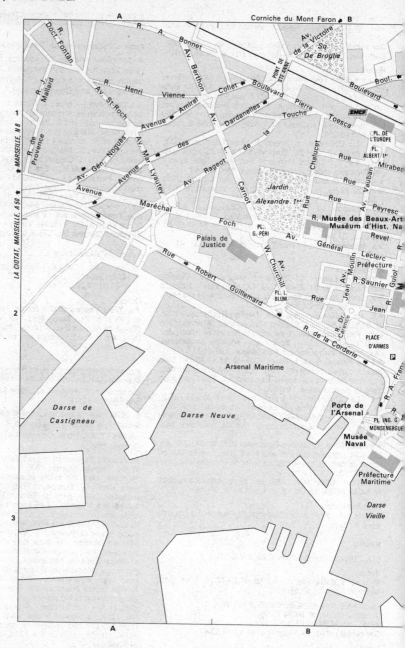

Corniche du Mont Faron

commandery of the Knights-Templar, with fortified towers and walls. ▶ To the S, **Dentelles de Montmirail★**, jagged peaks inviting hikers and rock-climbers. ▶ **Séguret★** *(9 km SW)* attracts artists and craftsmen; 12thC church, steep streets, medieval gates and ramparts. ▶ Farther S, **Gigondas** *(16 km SW)*, source of the full-bodied Côtes-du-Rhône wines of the same name (plenty of opportunities for wine-tasting). ▶ **Notre-Dame d'Aubune★** *(6 km*

S) : 9th-10thC chapel with Romanesque tower inspired by Classical models. □

Practical Information

VAISON-LA-ROMAINE
ⓘ pl. de l'Abbé-Sautel, ☎ 90.36.02.11.
Hotels :
★★★ *Le Beffroi*, rue de l'Evêché, Haute-Ville,

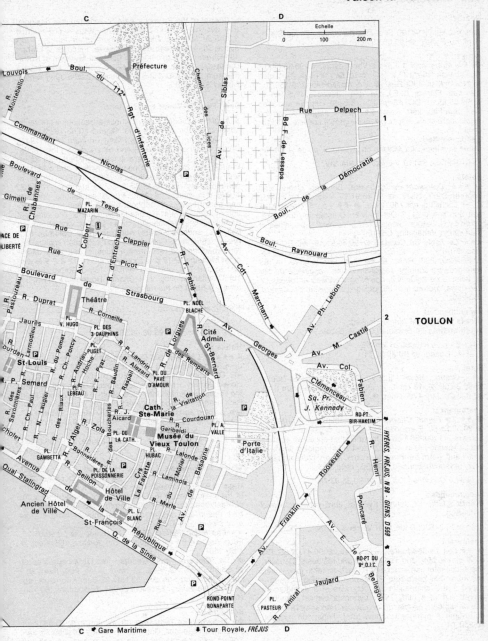

C • Gare Maritime   ↓ Tour Royale, *FRÉJUS*   D

☎ 90.36.04.71, AE DC Euro Visa, 21 rm ℗ ⊰ ⚬⚬⚬ ⚬ closed
11 Nov-15 Dec, 5 Jan-15 Mar, 290. Rest. ● ♦♦ *La Fontaine* ⊰ ♪ ⚬ closed Mon and Tue noon , open Mon in Jul-
Aug. 16thC charm, with a lofty terrace garden and classic
cuisine : *escalope de truite de mer au pistou, filet de bœuf
aux morilles*, 90-150; child : 45.
★★ *Logis du Château* (L.F.), les Hauts de Vaison,
☎ 90.36.09.98, 40 rm ℗ ⊰ ⚬⚬⚬ ⚬ ⊡ ♪ closed
31 Oct-15 Mar, 275. Rest. ♦♦ ♪ 60-125.

★ *Théâtre Romain*, pl. de l'Abbé-Sautel, ☎ 90.36.05.87,
21 rm ℗ ⚬ closed 15 Nov-15 Feb, 150. Rest. ♦ closed
Thu, 65-90.

⚞ ★★*Moulin de César* (140 pl), ☎ 90.36.00.78.

Recommended
Events : *festival*, at the ancient theatre, in Jul.
Guide to wines : at Rasteau, 7.5 km W, *Cave des vigne-
rons*, ☎ 90.46.10.43. Côtes-du-Rhône Villages.

Nearby

GIGONDAS, ✉ 84190 Beaumes-de-Venise, 14 km SW.
🛈 pl. du Portail, ☎ 90.65.85.46 (h.s.).

Hotels :
● ★★ *Montmirail* (L.F.), via Vacqueyras, ☎ 90.65.84.01,
AE DC Visa, 46 rm 🅿 ≼ ⚟ ⚲ ⴺ ☐ half pens (h.s.), closed
15 Nov-1 Mar, 450. Rest. ♦ ≼ ⴺ closed Mon, 90-150.
★★ *Les Florets* (L.F.), rte des Dentelles, 1,5 km E,
☎ 90.65.85.01, DC, 15 rm 🅿 ⚲ closed Tue eve and Wed
(l.s.), Jan-Feb, 200. Rest. ♦♦ Spec : *magret de canard
sauce aigre-doux, escalope de saumon à l'oseille*, 90-140 ;
child : 45.
Recommended
Guide to wines : *La Maison du gigondas*, pl. de la Mairie.

SÉGURET, ✉ 84110 Valréas, 10 km SW.

Hotels :
● ★★★ *Domaine de Cabasse*, between Sablet and
Séguret, D977, N577, ☎ 90.46.91.12, Visa, 10 rm 🅿 ≼ ⚟
⚲ ⅏ ☐ half pens, 750. Rest. ● ♦♦ ≼ ⴺ ⅏ closed Mon
and Sun eve (l.s.), 1 Oct-15 Mar. Outstanding food prepared by N. Latour. Single fixed-price meal. Specialties of
the Comtat Venaissin, 120-160.
★★★ *La Table du Comtat*, ☎ 90.46.91.49, AE DC Euro
Visa, 8 rm 🅿 ≼ ⚟ ⚲ ☐ closed Tue eve and Wed, Feb,
12-25 Nov, 300. Rest. ● ♦♦ ≼ ⴺ ⅏ Reserve. In the
wine-growing country, regional cuisine : *escalope de bar
au velouté de favouilles, noisettes d'agneau enrobées de
foie gras, pot-au-feu de pigeon et cuisse de canard*,
160-250.
Recommended
Events : *Provençal festival* in Aug.
Youth hostel : *Le Bresquet*, rte de Sablet.

VALRÉAS, ✉ 84600, 25 km SE.
🛈 pl. A.-Briand, ☎ 90.35.04.71.

Hotel :
★★ *Grand Hôtel* (L.F.), 28, av. Gal-de-Gaulle,
☎ 90.35.00.26, 18 rm 🅿 ⚟ closed Sat eve and Sun (l.s.),
20 Dec-20 Jan, 170. Rest. ♦ ⁞ 70-100.

Restaurant :
● ♦♦ *La Ferme Champ-Rond*, chemin des Anthelmes,
☎ 90.37.31.68, Euro Visa 🅿 ≼ ⚟ ⚲ ⁞ ⴺ closed Mon and
Sun eve, 11 Jan-28 Feb. A fountain that splashes all summer ; a roaring fire in winter. A festival of regional flavours,
wines and warm Southern welcome. A very pleasant stopover, reasonably priced, 80-150 ; child : 45.

△ ★★*La Coronne* (135 pl), ☎ 90.35.03.78.
Recommended
Events : *Little St John's Eve*, 23 Jun ; theatre festival
in Jul-Aug.

VISAN, ✉ 84820, 9 km S of *Valréas* on the D 976.

Restaurant :
● ♦♦ *Les Troubadours*, Le Château, ☎ 90.41.92.55, DC
ⴺ ⅏ closed Mon and Tue ex hols and residents, Oct-Mar.
The successful partnership of R. Jacquemet in the kitchen
and music-hall performer P. Desportes, settled close to a
ruined 13thC château in the coolness of a dining room
carved out of a cliff. Tasty Lyonnais dishes : *feuillantine de jambon, saucisson beaujolais*. Inexpensive Côtes-
du-Rhône. A marionette show after dinner, on request,
90-250.

VENCE*

Nice 22, Grasse 25, Paris 930 km
pop 13428 ✉ 06140   **D2**

Roses and violets, orange and lemon trees in the
hills 10 km from the sea. A popular year-round resort
sheltered inside medieval walls. Fountains and shady
squares (Place du Peyra★) in the charming old
town★. 11th-18thC cathedral with 15thC satirical carvings on lectern★ and choir stalls★.

▶ **Chapel of the Rosary** (rte de St-Jeannet) was designed
and decorated (1947-51) by Henri Matisse *(10-11:30 &
2:30-5:30 Tue. and Thu. ; open more often Jul.-Sep. ; ask
at the SI).* ▶ **Château des Villeneuve,** Place de la Frêne :
15thC restored, exhibitions. ▶ **Château-Museum of Notre-
Dame-des-Fleurs** *(2.5 km W)* : perfume and liqueur
museum *(10-12:30 & 2-6 in summer ; 2:30-5:30 in winter ;
closed Sun. am).*

Saint-Paul-de-Vence★★ *(3.5 km S)*

▶ A fortified medieval town whose attractions were rediscovered by the painters Paul Signac (1863-1935), Ame-
deo Modigliani (1884-1920), Pierre Bonnard (1867-1947),
Chaim Soutine (1893-1943) and others during the 1920s ;
numerous art galleries have since flourished, and **Saint-
Paul** is now the haunt of painters, writers and entertain-
ers. ▶ **Maeght Foundation**★★ *(NW)*, a living centre of
contemporary art *(10-12:30 & 3-7 in summer ; 10-12:30
& 2:30-6 in winter ; tel. 93.32.81.63) ;* exhibitions, concerts
and performances throughout the year ; important collection of 20thC art★★ exhibited in rotation. ▶ The village of
Saint-Paul is extremely attractive : studios, workshops, art
galleries, antique dealers. **Auberge de la Colombe d'Or**
(Place Général-de-Gaulle) : the art collection makes this
renowned inn and restaurant a museum in itself. ▶ **Municipal Museum** *(9-12 & 3-7 in summer ; 10-12 & 2-6 in winter ; closed Tue. and Sun. am).* ▶ 13thC Gothic church :
18thC Italian painting of St. Charles Borromée★ ; 1740 bell
tower. ▶ **Stroll** on the ramparts.   □

Practical Information _____

VENCE
🛈 pl. Gd-Jardin, ☎ 93.58.06.38.

Hotels :
★★★★(L) *Château du Domaine Saint-Martin* (R.C.), rte
de Coursegoules, via D 2, ☎ 93.58.02.02, Tx 470282,
AE DC Euro Visa, 25 rm 10 apt 🅿 ≼ ⚟ ⚲ ☐ ⅏
closed 20 Nov-1 Mar. Residence overlooking the sea and
the Provençal hinterland, 1300. Rest. ♦♦♦ ≼ closed Wed.
Rich, traditional food : *ragoût de pâtes fraîches aux truf-
fes, carré d'agneau provençale*, tasty wines, 320-400.
★★★ *Diana*, av. des Poilus, ☎ 93.58.28.56, AE DC Visa,
25 rm 🅿 ≼ ⴺ Pretty garden, 240.
★★★ *Le Floréal*, 440, av. Rhin-et-Danube, ☎ 93.58.64.40,
Tx 461613, Visa, 43 rm 🅿 ≼ ⚟ ⁞ ⴺ ☐ closed
30 Oct-1 Mar, 350.
● ★★ *La Roseraie* (L.F.), av. H.-Giraud, ☎ 93.58.02.20,
AE Visa, 9 rm 🅿 ≼ ⚟ ⚲ ⅊ closed Oct-Mar, 220.
Rest. ♦♦ ≼ ⁞ closed Tue and Wed (l.s.). The charm
of the *Belle Epoque* in a former manor-house. Prices are
old-fashioned for the Southwestern specialties : *foie gras
frais chaud aux raisins, salade de magret fumé au foie
gras chaud*, 100-170.
★★ *Les Muscadelles*, 59, av. H.-Giraud, ☎ 93.58.01.25,
Euro Visa, 14 rm ⚟ closed 20 Oct-30 Nov, 165. Rest. ♦
⁞ 60-150.
★ *La Closerie des Genêts*, imp. Marcellin-Maurel,
☎ 93.58.33.25, AE Visa, 11 rm ≼ ⚟ ⚲ 250. Rest. ♦ ≼
closed Mon and Sun eve, 13 Nov-22 Dec. Affordable, appealing little eatery. Excellent *soupe de poissons*, 60-150 ;
child : 40.

Restaurants :
♦♦ *Auberge des Templiers*, 39, av. Joffre, ☎ 93.58.06.05
⚟ closed Mon and Sun eve, 1-10 Jul, 20 Dec-20 Jan.
Spec : *saumon mariné à l'huile de basilic, panaché de
poissons au coulis d'écrevisses*, 95-180.
♦♦ *Château des Arômes*, 2618, rte de Grasse,
☎ 93.58.70.24, AE DC Euro Visa 🅿 ≼ ⚟ ⚲ ⁞ ⴺ closed
Mon eve and Tue, 2 Nov-20 Dec. Herbs and spices used
in an original way : saffron, basil, chives, truffles, rosemary. *Biscuit de homard à la crème de citron vert, mousse
au chocolat à la menthe poivrée*, 100-250.
♦♦ *La Farigoule*, 10, rue Henri-Isnard, ☎ 93.58.01.27 ⚟
⚲ ⴺ closed Fri, 15 Nov-15 Dec. A Provençal inn with a
pleasant garden. Savoury food at low prices, 70-90.

△ ★★★*Domaine de la Bergerie* (310 pl), ☎ 93.58.09.36.

Nearby

SAINT-PAUL-DE-VENCE, ⊠ 06570, 4 km S.
ⓘ Maison Tour, rue Grande, ☎ 93.32.86.95.

Hotels :
★★★★(L) *Mas d'Artigny* (R.C.), chemin des Salettes, ☎ 93.32.84.54, Tx 470601, Visa, 81 rm Ⓟ ≮ ⋘ ⚬ ⌂ ⁓ 1100. Rest. ◆◆◆ ≮ A gourmet table : *marguerite de turbot à la gousse de vanille, bourride de volaille aux zestes d'orange*, 230-300.
● ★★★ *Hameau*, 5, rte de La Colle, ☎ 93.32.80.24, AE Euro Visa, 16 rm Ⓟ ≮ ⋘ closed 15 Nov-15 Feb. A vast garden-orchard against the hillsides, 270.
★★★ *La Colombe d'Or*, ☎ 93.32.80.02, AE DC Euro Visa, 25 rm Ⓟ ≮ ⋘ ⚬ ☀ ⌂ closed 5 Nov-18 Dec, 580. Rest. ◆◆◆ ≮ ⚅ Celebrated for its artistic patrons. Spec : *turbot à la maraîchère, carré d'agneau de Sisteron*, 250.

Restaurant :
◆◆ *Les Oliviers*, rte de La Colle, ☎ 93.32.80.13, AE DC Visa ≮ ⋘ closed Tue (l.s.) , 2 Nov-Feb. A Provençal inn. Spec : *gigot d'agneau à la ficelle, langouste au beurre de corail*, 280.

TOURETTE-SUR-LOUP, ⊠ 06140 Vence, 5 km SE.

Hotels :
★★★ *La Réserve des Gorges du Lion*, Pont-du-Loup, ☎ 93.59.32.81, AE DC Visa, 15 rm Ⓟ ≮ ⋘ ⚬ ⌂ half pens (h.s.), 450. Rest. ◆◆ ≮ ⚅ A pleasant spot for habitués. *Truite meunière aux amandes, truite au bleu*, 60-110.
★★ *Belles Terrasses* (L.F.), 1 km, ☎ 93.59.30.03, 16 rm Ⓟ ≮ ⋘ ⚬ ⚅ 160. Rest. ◆ 55-100.

The VENTOUX**

B1

Round trip from Carpentras *(76 km, full day)*

A varied mountain landscape : olive and holmoak up to 800 m, beech and oak to 1 600 m, then conifers of various sorts — larch, spruce, and cedar of Lebanon★. Good walking country from spring to autumn ; skiing in the winter. At the foot of the mountain, the Côtes de Ventoux yield dry white wines, reds with a full bouquet, fresh rosés.

▶ **Carpentras** (→). ▶ D974 to **Crillon-le-Brave** *(left 2 km)*, former fiefdom of Louis de Crillon (1513-1615), companion-at-arms of Henri IV. ▶ **Bédoin** : church, 14-paneled altarpiece. ▶ Oak, cedar and beech along the mountain road. ▶ **Chalet Reynard** (alt. 1 460 m), a small ski resort at the verge of the forest. ▶ **Tempêtes Pass★** (alt. 1 829 m). ▶ **Ventoux Peak★★** (alt. 1 909 m) : in clear weather you can see the Dauphiné, Provence, the Vivarais and the Cévennes. ▶ **Mont Serein** *(right*, alt. 1 428 m) : another ski centre. ▶ **Lookout on the N slope** : view of the Dentelles de Montmirail★ (→ Vaison-la-Romaine). ▶ **Source** (spring) du Grozeau, then **chapel of the Grozeau** (11th-12thC) : remains of 14thC frescos. ▶ **Malaucène** : 14thC church (18thC organ case★) ; old houses, fountains and washhouses, remains of fortifications. ▶ D938 to **Le Barroux** *(on right)*, below Renaissance château★ (1539) with somewhat feudal appearance. ▶ **Caromb** *(2.5 km on left)* : Côtes-de-Ventoux wines ; 14thC church (15thC School of Avignon triptych) ; ramparts ; wrought-iron belfry★. ▶ **Carpentras** (→). □

Grand Canyon of VERDON***

C2

Round trip from Moustiers-Sainte-Marie *(92 km, full day)*

An axe-blow through the plateau, with sheer cliffs and green waters that appear to stand still ; the grandest of the old-world canyons, running N-S along the alpine folds, turning lower down to run E-W through Provence. Over the 21 km from Rougon to Pont

d'Aiguines, the Verdon has cut a series of gorges 400-700 m in depth with a drop of 146 m and a slope varying from 4° to 14°.

▶ **Moustiers-Sainte-Marie★** (→). ▶ D952 climbs above Lake Sainte-Croix (view★). ▶ **Mayreste Lookout★★**, 150 m right. Lookout at **Ayen Pass** (alt. 200 m). ▶ **La Palud-sur-Verdon** : in the village, take the **Crest** (Crêtes) **Road★★★** right (D23) : succession of extraordinary views. ▶ **Chalet-de-la-Maline** : GR4 starts for Point Sublime *(6hr actual walking time, 8-9hr with halts ; for inexperienced hikers, it is advisable to go with a guide : the walk is demanding, and the weather unpredictable, especially in spring and in periods of heavy rain, but there are memorable sites and views ; only 6 paths are open to the public without danger ; stay on the paths, neither cross nor bathe in the river ; take appropriate footwear, warm clothing, food and torch)*. ▶ Lookouts at **Glacières★★★**, **l'Escalès★★★**. ▶ **Point Sublime★★★**, on the right *(5 min)*, lookout over the entrance to the Grand Canyon. ▶ **Rougon** *(3 km N)*, high up near feudal ruins (view★ of entrance to Canyon). ▶ **Couloir Samson Lookout★** *(1.2 km, right)* : GR4 emerges ; junction of the Baou and the Verdon. ▶ **Trigance**, overlooked by a château now converted into a hotel. ▶ **Balcons de la Mescla★★★** : left bank of the Verdon where it joins the Artuby ; view. ▶ D71 follows the canyon along the **Corniche Sublime★★★**, from one breathtaking view to another ; W, **La Falaise des Cavaliers★★** : restaurant ; site overlooking green waters 300 m below. ▶ The rest of the trip is beautiful : **Baucher Cliff★★**, **Vaumale amphitheatre★★**, ending above **Lake Sainte-Croix★★** (→ Moustiers-Sainte-Marie). □

Practical Information ───────────

AIGUINES, ⊠ 83114 Aups, 16 km N.

Hotel :
★★ *Grand Canyon du Verdon* (L.F.), Falaise des Cavaliers, ☎ 94.76.90.01, 4 rm, half pens (h.s.), closed Wed (Oct), Nov-Mar, 220. Rest. ◆ ≮ ♪ ⚅ 50-120.

La PALUD-SUR-VERDON, ⊠ 04120 Castellane, 20 km SE of **Moustiers-Sainte-Marie**.
ⓘ mairie, ☎ 93.74.68.02.

Hotels :
★★ *Gorges du Verdon* (L.F.), ☎ 92.74.68.26, AE, 35 rm Ⓟ ≮ ⋘ ⚬ half pens (h.s.), closed 30 Sep-10 May, 370. Rest. ◆ ♪ ⚅ Provençal cuisine, 55-130.
★★ *Le Provence* (L.F.), ☎ 92.74.68.88, 15 rm Ⓟ ≮ ⚬ ⚅ half pens (h.s.), closed 12 Nov-11 Apr, 135. Rest. ◆ ⚅ ☀ 55-100 ; child : 30.
⚑ ★★*Municipal* (100 pl), ☎ 93.74.68.02.

ROUGON, ⊠ 04120 Castellane, 8 km E of **La Palud-sur-Verdon**.

Hotel :
★ *Auberge du Point Sublime* (L.F.), ☎ 92.83.60.35, Euro Visa, 14 rm Ⓟ ≮ ⋘ ⚬ ⚅ half pens (h.s.), closed 5 Nov-1 Apr, 130. Rest. ◆ ≮ 45-85.

TRIGANCE, ⊠ 83840 Comps-sur-Artuby, 12 km NW of **Comps**.

Hotel :
★★★ *Château de Trigance* (R.C.), ☎ 94.76.91.18, AE DC Euro Visa, 8 rm Ⓟ ≮ ⚬ half pens, closed 2 Nov-21 Mar. An 11thC fortress at the entrance to the Verdon Gorges, 720. Rest. ◆◆ ♪ closed Wed (l.s.), 190-200.

VÉSUBIE Valley**

D2

From Nice to Saint-Martin-Vésubie *(64 km, full day)*

A trip to the Alpine heartland above Nice : from the sparkling seascape of the Promenade des Anglais to high pastures surrounded by firs, mountains, waterfalls and craggy peaks. The Vésubie Valley is the gateway to the Mercantour National Park (700 km²), one of the richest nature parks in Europe : southern mountain flora, alpine fauna including *chamois, moufflon* (wild sheep), boar, marmot, eagle, Siberian ibex.

▶ **Nice** (→). ▶ N98 SW for 7 km, then N202 up the Var Valley to **Plan-du-Var** *(30 km from Nice)*. ▶ D2565 to the multicoloured walls of the **Vésubie Gorges★**. ▶ **Saint-Jean-la-Rivière.** ▶ **Utelle★** *(9 km left)*, fortified village perched above the Vésubie; church of St. Véran (Gothic) with an Annunciation★ (15thC School of Nice) and a 17thC carved altarpiece of Christ's Passion. 6 km SW from the village is the **panorama of Madonne d'Utelle★★★**, a pilgrimage site since 850. ▶ **Lantosque★**, an old town on a rocky spur blocking the valley. ▶ **Roquebillière**, often rebuilt in the wake of floods and landslides; excursion to the **Gordolasque Valley★★** *(18 km, D171)* : waterfalls, attractive village of Belvédère★. ▶ **Saint-Martin-Vésubie**, an excursion centre in the heart of this Alpine landscape; Rue du Docteur-Cagnoli★ (old houses). ▶ **Le Boréon★** *(8 km N of Saint-Martin)*, surrounded by woods and pastures; waterfall★, departure point for **Mercantour National Park★★**. ▶ **Madonne de Fenestre★** *(13 km NE)*, a magnificent mountain amphitheatre★★. ▶ **Venanson★** *(4.5 km S)* : view; frescos in the chapel of St. Sébastien. ▶ The **Valdeblore Road★** W leads *(25 km)* to the Tinée Valley★★

(→) via **La Colmiane** (winter sports; chairlift to Colmiane Peak, panorama★★); **Saint-Dalmas** (11thC Romanesque church★); **La Bolline** : a cosy summer resort; **Rimplas★** *(2 km right)* on a rock crest. □

Practical Information _____

LANTOSQUE, ⊠ 06450, 45 km N of **Nice**.

Hotels :
★★ *Ancienne Gendarmerie* (L.F.), Le Rivet, D 2565, ☎ 93.03.00.65, AE DC, 10 rm P ⟨ ♨ ⌕ half pens (h.s.), closed Mon lunch, 5 Nov-31 Dec, 550. Rest. ♦♦ ⟨ ♪ ⊗ Fish is a specialty, 105-210.
★★ *Grand Hôtel du Parc*, Bollène-Vésubie, via D 2265, ☎ 93.03.01.01, AE, 42 rm P ⟨ ♨ ⌕ pens (h.s.), closed 15 Oct-Easter, 620. Rest. ♦ ⊗ 65.

SAINT-MARTIN-VÉSUBIE, ⊠ 06450 Lantosque, 59 km E of **Valberg**.
ⓘ pl. Félix-Faure, ☎ 93.03.21.28 (h.s.).

Hotel :
★★ *Bonne Auberge*, allée de Verdun, ☎ 93.03.20.49, 33 rm P ♨ ⌕ closed 4 Nov-24 Dec, 150. Rest. ♦ ⊗ closed Wed (Oct-May), 80-100.

Rouergue, Albigeois

▶ Here the last foothills of the Massif Central roll gently to a stop. The Midi is just a stone's throw away. The whole region is characterized by the contrast between north and south, the cool greenness of the highlands mingling with a light that is already Mediterranean. Two regions in fact, with striking similarities and just as many differences : the accent of Auvergne and the singing tone of the South — rural Aveyron and industrial Tarn. Their histories are dissimilar too : "poor and pious Rouergue" has always been the land of tradition, while the Albigeois region has cradled all the major religious heresies and the great movements of the working class.

And yet these green countries of southern France share the same astonishing landscape of rocky, limestone plateaus known as *causses*, ryefields and gorges dotted with rivers, lakes and ponds. A landscape of many contrasts, from the dry and arid *causse* to sunny valleys, from sheep to vineyards, from red and black gorges to melancholy swamps. The architecture of the region shows the same diversity : the Middle Ages have left their mark and their masterpieces, from the abbey of Conques to the cathedral of Albi, and each village has some treasure to show, something to offer the visitor in search of the past — Cordes, perched on a hilltop overlooking the Cérou Valley, offers its Gothic houses in a perfect state of repair, and its 13thC church. The windswept, stony plains of Larzac with isolated flocks of sheep and lonely shepherds is the home of Roquefort cheese, set amidst a landscape of magnificent rugged peaks with the twisted shapes of ruined castles. It is also a land of archaeological treasures — prehistoric dolmens and menhirs —

fortified farmhouses and look-out points. The leather industry of Millau, now fallen on hard times, once sent luxury gloves all around the world ; Laguiole, set in the high pasturelands of the Aubrac mountains, still possesses a knife industry — Laguiole knives are hand-made, each one unique, solid, sturdy and beautiful to look at.

Today the region offers all kinds of holiday activities — pottery, weaving, ceramics, video, dance, trekking. Each year there are new courses to take, with villages and craftsmen outdoing each other to create new and exciting formulas. □

 ## Don't miss

★★★ Albi A3, Aubrac mountains C1, Conques B1, Cordes A3, Larzac plateau C3.

★★ Dourbie Gorges C3, Espalion B1-2, Lot Gorges, Lot Valley B1, Montpellier-le-Vieux C2, Najac A2, Sauveterre-de-Rouergue B2, Sidobre and the Laucaune mountains B4, Sylvanès C3, Villefranche-de-Rouergue A2.

★ Ambialet B3, Brousse-le-Château B3, Castres B4, the Comtal plateau B2, Entraygues B1, Estaing B1, Gaillac A3, Nant C3, Peyrusse-le-Roc A2, Rodez B2, Roquefort-sur-Soulzon C3, Saint-Sernin-sur-Rance B3, the Tarn Valley B3, the Truyère Gorges B1.

Weekend tips

The decision is simple : from Albi to Conques, through Cordes, Najac, Villefranche-de-Rouergue, Villeneuve and Peyrusse-le-Roc, with a choice between two fine restaurants : the Grand-Écuyer at Cordes, and La Charmille at Villefranche.

House in Rouergue

House on the causse

● *Brief regional history*

Prehistory to Roman era
Neolithic herdsmen and farmers left numerous menhirs and dolmens (→ Brittany, Menhirs/Dolmens) in the region (→ Occitania, Midi-Toulousain). ● Since the time when the settlement now known as Rodez was the capital of the Celtic **Ruteni,** the Rouergue has kept the same outline, enclosing three different climates, three types of terrain and agriculture appropriate to each. The Romans incorporated the Albigeois district into the administrative region of Narbonne. Millau became an important pottery centre during the **Gallo-Roman period.**

10thC
The great **Benedictine abbeys** of Conques, Nant and Saint-Antonin played a major role in the development of the area; many villages grew around priories affiliated with one or other of these abbeys. The townships of Espalion and Estaing prospered alongside bridges on the pilgrim road to **Conques.**

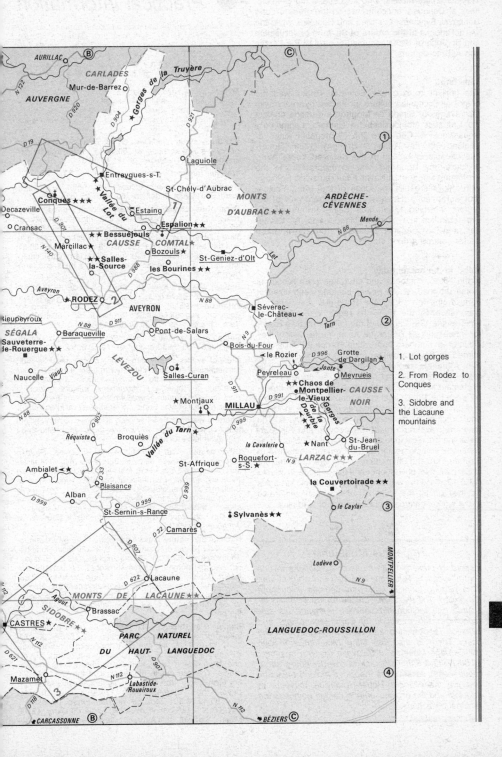

1. Lot gorges

2. From Rodez to Conques

3. Sidobre and the Lacaune mountains

12thC

The **Cistercian monks,** who succeeded the Benedictines at Conques, concentrated on the areas around Bonneval, Sylvanès, Loc-Dieu and Beaulieu, while the warrior-monks of the orders of St. John of Jerusalem and St. John of Malta assumed control of the Larzac and Aubrac regions.

13th-16thC

The brilliant court of the Count of Rodez was the centre of Occitanian culture, protected by treaty from the ravages of Simon de Montfort's crusade against the Catharist Albigensians (→ Cathars, Languedoc-Roussillon). ● Ceded to the Plantagenêt kings of England with the Treaty of Brétigny (1360), Rouergue became embroiled in the **Hundred Years' War.** ● Later, the Rouergue was incorporated into the Protestant kingdom of Navarre but remained Catholic, with little interest in the ideas of the 16thC Protestant Reformation. However, the southern part of the region, including Millau and Saint-Affrique elected **Protestantism** just as the Albigeois and the Cévennes, and thus became estranged from the northern sector centred around Rodez.

16thC to the present day

In the 15thC, châteaux and churches were rebuilt as peace returned. ● As power became centralized in Paris during the 16thC, the Rouergue diminished in importance. By the 19thC the region was a backwater. The late 19thC arrival of the railway made it easier for inhabitants of Rouergue to emigrate, which they did in great numbers both within France (to Paris) and abroad (to South America).
The **Albigeois region,** farther S, fared differently thanks to its traditional crafts and by the efforts of Protestant industrialists who had built up local **industry** since the 18thC: coal at Carmaux, cloth at Castres, processing sheepskins at Mazamet, tanning at Millau and Graulhet, all of which thrive to this day. ● The **industrial revolution** made Decazeville and Albi-Carmaux the principal industrial centres of the Midi. They were later complemented by the Creusot steelworks at Saut-du-Tarn and Saint-Juéry. In the late 19thC the socialist politician, philosopher and historian **Jean Jaurès** (1859-1914) led the workers in a series of epic struggles for their rights; the strike of 1896 is commemorated at the worker-controlled glass factory of Carmaux.

Rouergue Museums

Instead of presenting its museum collections in one central location, Rouergue has had the original idea of dispersing them in traditional settings throughout the region. The two major museums are at Salles-la-Source (the relationship between man and his surroundings; the evolution of early technology) and Espalion (society and attitudes; traditions from the past). There is also the Mine Museum at Aubin, the Carriage Museum at Salmiech (daily in summer; 10:30-12:30 & 3:30-6:30; ask at café Delbourg about group visits). At Millau is the glove-making museum, and the independent Upper-Rouergue museum at Laguiole and the eco-museum in Larzac complete the regional collections.

 Practical information

Information : Haute Garonne : *Comité Régional de Tourisme (C.R.T.),* 12, rue Salambô, 31200 Toulouse, ☎ 61.47.11.12. **Aveyron :** *Comité Départemental de Tourisme (C.D.T.),* 33, av. V.-Hugo, 12000 Rodez, ☎ 65.68.11.43. **Tarn :** *C.D.T.,* hôtel du département. 81014 Aibi Cedex, ☎ 63.54.65.25. In **Paris :** *Maison du Tarn,* 34, av. de Villiers, 75017, ☎ (1) 47.66.55.80 ; *Maison de l'Aveyron,* 46, rue Berger, 75001, ☎ (1) 42.36.84.63 ; *Dir. rég. jeunesse et sports,* 46, rue des Couteliers, 31068 Toulouse Cedex, ☎ 61.25.60.13 ; *Dir. des affaires culturelles,* 56, rue du Taur, 31069 Toulouse Cedex, ☎ 61.23.20.39.

S.O.S. : Aveyron : *S.M.U.R.,* ☎ 18. **Tarn :** *S.A.M.U. (emergency medical service),* ☎ 63.47.15.15. Emergency poisoning centre (Toulouse), ☎ 61.49.33.33.

Weather forecast : Aveyron : ☎ 65.60.05.33.

Reservations : *Loisirs-Accueil Tarn,* hôtel du département, 81014 Albi Cedex, ☎ 63.54.65.25, ext. 508.

Rural gîtes, chambres d'hôtes, children's gîtes : Aveyron : *A.P.A.T.A.R.* (reservation and information service), 56, bd du 122e R.I.,12006 Rodez Cedex, ☎ 65.68.11.38. **Tarn :** *l'Assn. Tarnaise de tourisme en espace rural,* maison des agriculteurs, B.P. 89, 81003 Albi, ☎ 63.54.39.81, publishes a guide which lists rural gîtes, farmhouse camping, farms with riding facilities, children's gîtes and farmhouse-inns.

Holiday villages : Aveyron : Entraygues, ☎ 65.44.53.31 ; Espalion, ☎ 65.44.02.15 ; Mergieux, ☎ 65.65.70.47 ; Villefranche-de-Panat, ☎ 71.09.58.09 (number good for Espalion) and 65.46.58.31 ; Brommat, ☎ 65.66.08.21. **Tarn :** Brassac, ☎ 71.09.58.09 and 63.50.01.37.

Camping-car rental : Tarn, *Solocatel,* 112, route de Béziers, 81100 Valdurengue, ☎ 63.50.50.42.

Cultural events : early Jun : *photography week* in Albi ; *music festival* in Rodez. **Jul :** *theatre festival* in Albi ; *music festival* in Cordes. **Aug :** *Rouergue music festival* in Villefranche-de-Rouergue ; *international folklore festival* in Pont-de-Salars ; *international amateur cinema festival* and *music festival* in Albi. **Sep :** *J. S. Bach festival* in Mazamet.

Sporting events : Feb : *Aubrac 50* (cross-country skiing) **last weekend in Sep :** *100 km (on foot),* Millau. **Mid-Sep :** *Albi automobile Grand Prix.*

Other events : Jun : *hunting festival* in Lavaur ; *St-Jean festivals* in numerous districts. **Jul :** *wine festival* in Lisle-sur-Tarn ; *grand fauconnier festival* in Cordes. **Aug :** *grain threshing festival* in La Salvetat-Peyralès ; *wine festival* in Gaillac (2nd Sun) ; *fouace festival* in Najac ; *pink garlic fair* in Lautrec ; *summer festival* in Salles-Curan ; *mineral show* in Millau. **Sep :** *horse fair* in Montredon-Labessonnie. **Oct :** *chestnut and sweet cider festival* in Sauveterre ; *antiques fair* in Albi.

National and nature parks : *parc naturel du Haut-Languedoc,* enq : 13, rue du Cloître, B.P. 9, 34220 Saint-Pons-de-Thomières, ☎ 63.97.02.10 ; *maisons du parc* in : Brassac-sur-Agout, Dourgne, Fraisse-sur-Agout, La Salvetat-sur-Agout, Montredon-Labessonnie, Murat-sur-Vèbre, Rieu-Montagné, Roquebrun, Saint-Gervais-sur-Mare, Sorèze et Vabre. *Relais du parc,* hôtel de ville, 81260 Brassac, ☎ 63.74.01.29, and at the *S.I.* situated on the outskirts of the park.

Rambling and hiking : the G.R. 6, 65 (path traditionally taken for Santiago-de-Compostela), 62, 62 A, 36, 71, 71 A, 71 B, 71 C, 46, 416, 763 (topoguides) run through the region. The *C.D.T. Tarn* publishes a brochure "Up hill and down dale in Tarn", with outing descriptions and diagrams. You can obtain this booklet in the *O.T.* and *S.I.* For further enq. : *féd. interdépartementale des sentiers de pays,* bd Clemenceau, 12400 Saint-Affrique, ☎ 65.49.30.50 ; *féd. de la randonnée pédestre : C.N.S.G.R. - Délégation Aveyron,* 1, rue du Barry, 12100 Millau ; *Sentiers de l'Aubrac : Assn. rencontre randon-*

née Soulages-Bonneval, 12210 Laguiole; Sentier des 3 Vallées-Decazeville : *Assn. les randonneurs du bassin,* B.P. 25, 12300 Decazeville. A brochure of *C.D.T. Aveyron* also lists numerous paths.

Scenic railways : *chemin de fer touristique du Tarn,* in Saint-Lieux-lès-Lavaur (81), Easter-Oct, Sun and nat hols; Sat-Mon, 14 Jul-31 Aug. Enq. : *A.C.O.V.A.,* B.P. 2040, 31018 Toulouse Cedex, ☎ 61.47.44.52.

Cycling holidays : 7-day tour of **Aveyron.** Enq. at the *Aveyron C.D.T.* and *O.T.; Assn. pour la promotion du cyclisme en Aveyron,* Lédergues, 12170 Réquista, ☎ 65.70.21.19. For the **Tarn,** enq. : 63.47.30.00, ext. 32.24.

Riding holidays : Many riding centres : all kinds of riding (courses, rambles, excursions, specialization : grooming, harnessing, jumping). Info : *chambre d'agriculture,* 50, bd du 122e R.I., 12006 Rodez Cedex, ☎ 65.68.11.38 ; *C.D.T. Tarn* and *A.D.T.E. maison de l'élevage,* La Milliasolle, B.P. 102, 81003 Albi, ☎ 63.54.39.81.

Technical tourism : *Alric* (tannery) at Millau, 11, rue de la Saunerie, by appt, ☎ 65.60.53.12. *Verrerie* (glass-making) *ouvrière d'Albi,* 146, av. Dembourg, ☎ 63.60.75.00. *Roquefort, société anonyme des caves et des producteurs réunis,* 1, av. F.-Galtier, ☎ 65.60.23.05. *Centrale hydraulique du Pouget,* ☎ 65.46.58.62.

Handicraft courses : pottery, weaving, wood sculpture, engraving and screen printing, wrought iron, copper enameling, stone sculpture. See **Tarn** and **Aveyron** *C.D.T.* Reservations : *Loisirs-Accueil Tarn.*

Other courses : relaxation, health and well-being (Montbazens, Conques, Entraygues), botanical and ecological walks (Lacalm), yoga (Moyrazès l'Hospitalet-du-Larzac), bioenergetic therapy and personal development (Espalion), flute, guitar, viola and cello (Espalion), music (Cordes, Najac), introduction to computers (Larogue Valzerques). Enq. : *C.D.T. Tarn* and *Aveyron; Assn. des artisans créateurs en Haut-Languedoc,* 42, rue Pharaon, 31000 Toulouse, ☎ 61.52.49.96 ; *Club des vacances actives,* 33, av. V.-Hugo, 12000 Rodez, ☎ 65.68.57.89. Trips on horseback, fishing, golf, making *foie gras,* etc ; reserv. : *Loisirs-Acceui Tarn. Nature and environment : Centre d'initiation à l'environnement du pays des Grands Causses,* La Maladrerie, 12100 Millau, ☎ 65.61.06.57. *ODASPA,* town hall of Espalion 12500, ☎ 65.44.05.46.

Children : *Poney-Club Lillhippus,* l'Hermitage, rte d'Espalion, 12850 Onet-le-Château, ☎ 65.42.06.33. Open all year. Children 4 years and older welcome. Summer courses on farm near lake in Linars. Info : *C.D.T. Aveyron.* 6-12-year-old children welcome on farm during school holidays. Enq. : *Loisirs-Accueil Tarn* and *A.P.A.T.A.R.*

Aquatic sports : nautical centres in Salles-Curan, Arvieu, Saint-Rome-de-Tarn, Rieu, Montagné (Nages), La Borde-Basse (Castres), Aiguelèze, Pont-de-Salars. Enq. : *C.D.T.*

Canoeing : *Comité départemental de canoë-kayak,* M.J.C., rue St-Cyrice, 12000 Rodez, ☎ 65.67.01.13, canoe-kayak centres in **Aveyron :** Millau, Najac, Le Rozier-Peyreleau ; in the **Tarn :** Penne, Trébas. Enq. at *C.D.T.* In Burlats, near Castres, canoe-kayak day trips, at the *Camping-club de France,* 6, av. E.-Villeneuve, 81100 Castres, ☎ 63.35.74.57.

Golf : Pont-de-l'Arn, Mazamet (9 holes), ☎ 63.61.09.00.

Hang-gliding : *Millau Delta,* M. Jullien, 12640 Rivière-sur-Tarn, ☎ 65.60.86.22. Gyro-club U.L.M. : *Aero-club Castres Mazamet,* ☎ 63.35.49.58 ; Delta Club Millavois : ENVOL, la Borie Blangue, 12100 Millau, ☎ 65.59.83.94.

Winter sports : 3 resorts in the Aubrac mountains, situated at between 1 000 and 1 400 m; alpine and cross-country skiing : Brameloup, Laguiole, Aubrac. Enq. : *C.D.T.* and *S.I. du Haut-Rouergue,* in Espalion, ☎ 65.44.05.46.

Spelunking : *Comité dép. de spéléologie,* Michel Ferrières, rue J.-Moulin, 12000 Rodez, ☎ 65.67.23.25.

Country cooking

Charcuterie of all kinds: ham from Najac and Naucelle, sausage from Lacaune, pâté, cracklings and hashed meat (fricandaux); chicken, goose, turkey and duck from Lévezou; mushrooms; trout; river-shrimp (they may only be caught once a year, but there is no law against shrimp-farming); lamb and mutton from the plateaus : these are the local specialities.

Aligot, originally from the Aubrac, is a meal in itself, and simple to make : you need only mix mashed potatoes with *Laguiole cheese* (tomme fraîche). *Truffade* is a variation on the theme : thin slices of cheese melted over fried potatoes. *Tripou* is a regional dish of stuffed mutton tripe braised with white wine, tomatoes and seasonings. More Mediterranean, *aïgo boulido* is a soup made with garlic and croutons.

The numerous regional wines are the perfect accompaniment to these copious dishes : Tarn's reds and rosés, dry white from Entraygues (vin de Fel), rosé from Estaing, and *Marcillac* red (rough, usually consumed young).

Local vocabulary

babissou : *mountain mushroom.*

buron : *in the Aubrac, summer shelter for the shepherds, where cheese is made.*

cabecou : *small goat-cheese.*

cantales : *in the Aubrac, chief shepherd in charge of the buron and cheese-making.*

jasse : *sheepfold in the Larzac.*

laguiole : *shepherd's horn-handled knife, invented more than a century ago by Mr. Clamels of the village of that name.*

megisserie : *sheepskin tanning.*

oustal : *house in Rouergue region.*

pages : *landowner in Rouergue.*

rougier : *valley in the soft sandstone at the foot of the causses; the glistening red stone is characteristic of the landscape and houses.*

raisine : *jam made with autumn fruits.*

Facts and figures

Location : *the Rouergue extends from the Lot Valley to the Tarn Gorges, while the Albigeois mainly represents the middle basin of the Tarn.*

Area : *14 551 km².*

Climate : *very hot in summer. Winter : mild and rainy in the Albigeois, more severe in the Rouergue with heavy rain.*

Population : *637 500.*

Administration : *Aveyron, Prefecture : Rodez; Tarn Department, Prefecture : Albi.*

Hunting and shooting : enq. at the *Féd. dép. des chasseurs.* **Aveyron :** 23, bd de la République, 12000 Rodez, ☎ 65.42.53.48. **Tarn :** 8, rue Louis-Amboise, 81000 Albi, ☎ 63.54.12.23.

Fishing : enq. at the *Féd. dép. des A.P.P.* **Aveyron :** 52, rue de l'Embergue, 12000 Rodez, ☎ 65.68.17.23. **Tarn :** 17, bd du Mal-Foch, 81100 Castres, ☎ 63.59.68.40.

Towns and places

ALBI★★★

Toulouse 76, Rodez 78, Paris 707 km
pop 48021 ⊠ 81000   A3

Albi is called *la ville rouge* (the red town) because of its brickwork. Every shade of brick — pink, ochre, red, brown — is represented. The old centre of town, where administration and commerce are concentrated, is like an outdoor museum brought to life by the daily activity. As early as the Middle Ages, Albi expanded along both banks of the Tarn. The town is now an important industrial centre for agri-business, textiles, glass, construction, chemicals, and engineering.

▶ **Place du Vigan** (C2), the main square linking the old town to newly developed areas to the E, with post office, shops, banks, hotels, restaurants and cafés. On either side of the square, the *lices* (boulevards) Pompidou and Moulin mark the line of former ramparts. ▶ To reach the cathedral, go down Rue de l'**Hôtel de Ville** (Renaissance town hall, 16thC; B2) or Rue Timbal (No. 12, **Reynès Mansion,** same period; now the Chamber of Commerce; half-timbered **Enjalbert House★** with carved decoration). ▶ Between the pedestrian Rues Mariès and Ste. Cécile, **church of St. Salvi** (B2) : 12thC Romanesque, remodeled in the 15thC; triangular cloister reached by marked passages through the surrounding buildings. ▶ **Cathedral of Ste. Cécile★★** (A-B2), an outstanding example of southern Gothic, built between 1282 and the late 14thC, single brick nave, turrets, 78 m bell tower; flamboyant Gothic canopy added to the S entrance in 1535; **inside★,** 16thC Italian Renaissance paintings; late 15thC French fresco of the Last Judgment (W wall), stained glass from the 14th-16thC; choir screen★ and enclosure★ (ca. 1500) showing Burgundian influence. ▶ N of the cathedral, the **Palais de la Berbie★** (former bishops' palace ; 13thC-15thC) overlooks the River Tarn from 17thC terraced gardens: reception rooms; **Toulouse-Lautrec Museum★★** displaying many works (including posters) by the painter Henri de Toulouse-Lautrec (1864-1901), son of the Count of Toulouse-Lautrec, who was especially renowned for his scenes of Parisian life; contemporary art; archaeology *(Easter-Oct., 10-12 & 2-6; Jul.-Aug., 9-12 & 2-6 ; winter season, 2-6).* ▶ S of the cathedral, medieval Albi of narrow streets and old houses; House of Vieil Alby at the corner of Rue Puech-Bérenguier and Rue de la Croix-Blanche. Nearby, **birthplace of Toulouse-Lautrec** in the 18thC Bosc Mansion (No. 14 Rue Toulouse-Lautrec ; B2-3) : furniture, memorabilia, early works, terraced gardens ; in summer, temporary exhibitions on various themes in the painter's work with pictures coming from museums abroad and complementing the museum's own collection *(Jul.-Aug., 10-12 & 2-7).*

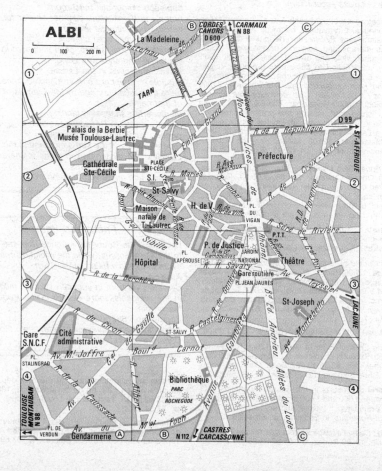

No. 12 next door was home to the navigator Jean-François Galaup de Lapérouse (1741-88), born in Albi: **wax museum** (history of Albi; *daily ex Mon. in Jul.-Aug.; pm only Sep.-Jun.*). At present (between 1985-87), the bicentennial of his last voyage.

Nearby

▶ **Castelnau-de-Lévis** *(9 km NW)* : 12th-15thC castle with 50 m tower overlooking a picturesque village★. ▶ View of Albi and the surrounding country from the chapel of **Notre-Dame-de-la-Drèche** *(5 km N)*. ▶ **Lescure** *(5 km NE)* : 14thC church and Romanesque chapel of St. Michel *(500 m S)*. ▶ **Saint-Juéry** *(6 km NE)* : metallurgic factory on the waterfalls of the Tarn. Farther on *(8 km)*, near Marsal, small icon museum of **La Maurinié.** □

Southern Gothic

Gothic architecture came relatively late to the South, where Romanesque art had flourished. The growing influence of the northern territories over the independent-minded southern states is illustrated by the fact that a northern architect, Jean Deschamps, was placed in charge of cathedral building (Rodez and Narbonne; 1270 onwards), where he introduced the pure Gothic style that had first been developed in Île-de-France in the mid-12thC. The new style soon assumed a southern character, seen in the cathedral at Albi. The main features are : a wide nave roofed by a single vault, a polygonal choir, fortress-like walls supported by buttresses, and narrow windows to keep out the fierce heat and bright sun. In this dissenting region, the walls symbolized the power of the Church, and the single nave its unity.

Practical Information _____

ALBI
🛈 pl. Ste-Cécile (B2), ☎ 63.54.22.30.
✈ *Sequestre*, 3 km SW, ☎ 63.54.45.28. *Air France office*, 24, rue Porte-Neuve, ☎ 63.38.30.30.
SNCF (A4), ☎ 63.54.17.16/63.54.50.50/63.54.74.10.
🚌 pl. J.-Jaurès (B-C3), ☎ 63.54.58.61.
Car rental : *Avis*, train station (A4) ; 270, av. François-Verdier, ☎ 63.54.76.54.

Hotels :
● ★★★★ **Grand Saint-Antoine** (Mapotel), 17, rue Saint-Antoine (C3), ☎ 63.54.04.04, Tx 520850, AE DC Euro Visa, 56 rm P ♨ ♨ 550. Rest. ♦♦ ♪ Fine cuisine in the 'hotel' style, at moderate prices : *truite aux herbes, daube de bœuf albigeoise*, 100-220.
★★★★ **La Réserve** (R.C.), Fonvialane, on the road from Cordes, ☎ 63.60.79.79, Tx 520850, AE DC Euro Visa, 20 rm P ♨ ♨ ♨ ☒ ⌨ closed Oct-Mar, 630. Rest. ♦♦♦ ♨ ♪ Spec : *terrine de foie gras au naturel, papillote de sandre à l'aneth*, 130-230.
● ★★★ **Le Vigan** (Inter-Hôtel), 16, pl. du Vigan (B-C2), ☎ 63.54.01.23, Tx 530328, AE DC Euro Visa, 37 rm P ♨ ♨ ♨ 220. Rest. ♦ ♨ ♨ closed 15-31 Dec. Spec : *tripes à l'albigeoise*, 60-90.
★★★ **Modern'Pujol** (L.F.), 22, av. Col.-Teyssier (C3), ☎ 63.54.02.92, Tx 520411, AE DC Euro Visa, 21 rm P ♨ 230. Rest. ♦ ♪ ♨ closed Fri eve and Sat, Feb school hols, 21 Jun-15 Jul. M. André offers interesting specialties : *foie gras chaud aux fruits et la soupière aux pâtes fraîches et morilles*, 110-190.
★★ **Cantepau**, 9, rue Cantepau (off map B1), ☎ 63.60.75.80, Euro Visa, 33 rm P ♨ ♨ closed 25 Dec-15 Jan, 130.
★★ **Orléans**, pl. Stalingrad (A4), ☎ 63.54.16.56, Tx 521605, Euro Visa, 62 rm P ♨ ♨ ♪ ♨ closed 21 Dec-8 Jan, 180. Rest. ♦ ♪ closed Sun. Access from the

train station ; good, hearty cooking : *jarret de porc haricots, ris de veau financière*, 55-120 ; child : 30.
★★ **Relais Gascon** (L.F.), 3, rue Balzac (C3), ☎ 63.54.26.51, Euro Visa, 15 rm ♨ ♨ half pens, closed Mon eve and Sun eve, 290. Rest. ♦ *Auberge Landaise* ♨ ♪ 60-125 ; child : 35.
● ★ **Le Vieil-Alby** (L.F.), 25, rue Toulouse-Lautrec (B2), ☎ 63.54.14.69, AE DC Euro Visa, 8 rm P ♨ ♨ ♨ half pens, closed Mon eve and Sun eve, 25 Dec-12 Jan, 1-7 May, 1-15 Sep, 260. Rest. ♦ Savoury local specialties served on the terrace : *tripous à l'ail, confits*, 45-100.
★ **Le Parking**, 31, pl. F.-Pelloutier (off map C3), ☎ 63.54.09.07, 15 rm P ♨ 90.

Restaurant :
♦ **Auberge Saint-Loup**, 26, rue du Castelviel (A2), ☎ 63.54.02.75, closed Mon, Oct. Spec : *radis au foie salé, gras double à l'albigeoise*, 60-100.

▲ ★★*Les Avalots*, ☎ 63.55.14.91 ; 8 km E, ★★*Caussels* (100 pl), ☎ 63.60.37.06.

Recommended
Auction house : *Maître Joanny*, 14 bis, bd Castenet, ☎ 63.38.03.05 ; antique dealers nearby on the cathedral square.
Bicycle rental : *Rey-Sport*, 41, bd Soult, ☎ 63.54.08.33.
Nightclubs : at La Barrière, rte de Carmaux, *Le Jumbo*, ☎ 63.60.90.16.
Riding gîte : at Valdériès, 8 km on RN 603, *La Coste*, ☎ 63.55.11.88. Children over 13 only. Riding lessons.
Youth hostel : 13, rue de la République (C2), ☎ 63.54.53.65.
♥ bric-à-brac : 4, rue des Halles, every Sat 2-5pm ; crêperie : *Le 1900*, 1, rue Timbal (B2), ☎ 63.54.86.02 ; dried flower bouquets : *Léo Vrenken*, 7, rue de la Piale, ☎ 63.54.47.96 ; pastry, chocolates : *Michel Belin*, 4, rue Laurent-Camboulive (B3), ☎ 63.54.18.46 ; tea room : *Fournier*, 17, pl. Ste-Cécile (B2), ☎ 63.54.13.86.

Nearby

ALBAN, ☒ 81250, 29 km.

Hotel :
★★ *Au Bon Accueil*, 49, av. de Millau, ☎ 63.55.81.03, AE DC Visa, 13 rm P ♨ closed 4 Feb-3 Mar, 130. Rest. ♦ ♪ closed Mon. Old-fashioned stews, deer, beef, boar, 70-105.

LABASTIDE-DÉNAT, ☒ 81120 Réalmont, 9 km SE.

Hotel :
★★ *Domaine Labastide*, rte de Castres, ☎ 63.56.61.11, AE Euro Visa, 12 rm P ♨ ♨ ☒ ⌨ closed Mon, 4-12 Jan, 250. Rest. ♦ *Le Cécilia* ♪ Regional dishes and seasonal cuisine are M. Gely's trademarks. Gourmets take note! 95-200 ; child : 65.

AMBIALET*

Albi 25, Millau 96, Paris 732 km
pop 400 ☒ 81430 Villefranche-d'Albigeois   B3

Ambialet is a medieval stronghold on a rocky peninsula★★ created by a twist in the River Tarn.

▶ From S to N along the crest : **castle** ruins ; a small Romanesque **church**, cemetery, above the bridge ; square **tower** of ruined church ; at the point, former monastery of **Notre-Dame-de-l'Auder** which includes a very beautiful primitive Romanesque church (missionary museum).

Nearby

▶ **Valence-d'Albigeois** *(11 km N)* : 13thC *bastide* town. ▶ **Villefranche-d'Albigeois** *(10 km SW)* : *bastide* founded in 1239. ▶ **Rassisse★** *(13 km S)* : reservoir in the Dadou Valley. ▶ **Château de Paulin** *(12 km SE)* : 10thC ruins above the **Oulas Gorges★.** ▶ Return to the Tarn Valley via **Saint-André** (15thC castle, restored) and continue to **Trébas** *(15 km E of Ambialet; pleasant surroundings)*. □

Practical Information _____

AMBIALET

Hotel :
★★ *Pont* (L.F.), ☎ 63.55.32.07, AE DC, 13 rm ℙ ⛧ ⊞ ⚲ closed 30 Nov-28 Feb, 135. Rest. ♦ ⛧ ♪ Assorted duck specialties : *cuisses de canard aux parfums des bois, filet de sandre au pouilly*, 60-100 ; child : 30.

⚖ ★★*Au Pont de Courris* (30 pl), ☎ 63.55.32.25 ; ★*La Fédusse* (50 pl), ☎ 63.55.32.10.

Recommended
♥ at La Bastide d'Albignac 11 km N on D 74, *foie gras,* duck *rillettes* and *confits :* ☎ 63.56.42.43.

Nearby

MARSAL, ⊠ 81340 Villefranche-d'Albigeois, 8 km W.

Hotel :
★ *La Bonne Auberge "Chez Cantié"*, ☎ 63.55.15.05, 10 rm ℙ ⚲ ⚲ closed 2-31 Jan, 140. Rest. ♦ 50.

AUBRAC Moutains***

C1

The Aubrac is a region of undulating meadows, magnificent prairies and rounded mountaintops that seem to reach the horizon. Its silence and solitude give it an ethereal quality. It's a land of lakes, streams and volcanic rock, handsome Aubrac cattle, dactyl, lucern, gentian-bitters and absinthe. Though the equipment and huge timbered barns still stand, cheese-making is losing its importance here.

▶ Isolated towns come to life on fair-days. ▶ Laguiole : among upland pastures ; manufacture of pocket-knives and cheese ; Haut Rouergue museum of local crafts ; ski-runs. The bull, symbol of this region, is the main feature at the local fairs. Superb view over the Aubrac and Cantal hills from the church (1659). ▶ Saint-Urcize : regional cattle-fair in mid-Oct ; Romanesque church in Auvergne style with wall-belfry ; 15thC polychrome stone Christ ; old houses. ▶ Nasbinals★ (→ Ardèche, Cévennes) : quiet haven for vacationers in pastureland ; Romanesque church. ▶ Among woods, Aubrac★★ : former priory of the Knights-Hospitallers, who protected pilgrims on the road to Conques or Rocamadour ; square tower (1353) ; Gothic façade on the aimshouse ; remarkable Romanesque church (13thC-15thC) ; now its become a mountain stopover that features such local specialities a *aligot* and *tripou*. ▶ Saint-Chély-d'Aubrac : more southern than Auvergnat ; 15thC church ; hump-backed bridge, pilgrim cross. ▶ Bonnefon : fortified storage tower (15thC). □

Practical Information _____

AUBRAC, ⊠ 12470 Saint-Chély-d'Aubrac, 8 km NE of Saint-Chély.

Hotel :
● ★★ *Moderne* (L.F.), ☎ 65.44.28.42, 26 rm ℙ ⛧ ⊞ ⚲ closed Wed lunch ex Jul-Aug, 9 Mar-23 May, 4 Oct-13 Feb, 190. Rest. ♦ ⛧ 50-100 ; child : 45.

Recommended
Farmhouse-inn : Les Hermaux.

LAGUIOLE, ⊠ 12210, 24 km NE of **Espalion.**
⛷ 1000m.
ℹ ☎ 65.48.44.68.

Hotels :
★★ *Grand Hôtel Auguy* (L.F.), av. de la Pépinière, ☎ 65.44.31.11, Visa, 33 rm ℙ ⚲ closed Sun eve, Mon ex school hols and h.s., 13-23 Apr, 1 Nov-15 Dec, 160. Rest. ♦ 65-120 ; child : 40.

★★ *Lou Mazuc (Michel Bras)*, pl. Prat, ☎ 65.44.32.24, AE Visa, 13 rm, closed Sun eve and Mon, 15 Oct-1 Apr, 220. Rest. ● ♦♦♦ As any gourmet who's made the trip will tell you, the climb to Laguiole is well worth the effort.

Michel Bras will reward your senses with the astonishing 'all vegetable' menu, with his market-fresh herbs, or his grilled sausages with *aligot*, not to mention the *gargouillou* of young vegetables, the *croustillant de lard au saumon et oignons confits, pigeon rôti à l'amertume de cacao jeunes raves, mousse glacée à la gentiane et au citron, coulis aux graines de cassis*, 90-250.
★★ *Régis* (L.F.), ☎ 65.44.30.05, Visa, 15 rm ℙ closed Fri, 1-15 Jun, 1-25 Oct, 160. Rest. ♦ 60-120.

⚖ ★★*La Roseraie* (50 pl), ☎ 65.44.31.91.

Recommended
♥ cooperative cheese dairy : *Jeune Montagne*, for a taste of the real Laguiole cheese, and frozen *aligot ;* hand-crafted cutlery : *Pierre Calmels,* ☎ 65.44.30.03.

SAINT-CHÉLY-D'AUBRAC, ⊠ 12470, 21 km NE of **Espalion.**
⛷ 1250m.

Hotel :
★ *Voyageurs*, ☎ 65.44.27.05, Visa, 14 rm ⚲ closed 2 Dec-31 Mar, 100. Rest. ♦ Nice little restaurant, 45-120.

CAMARÈS

Millau 53, Albi 78, Paris 683 km
pop 1258 ⊠ 12360
C3

Hotel :
● ★★ *La Demeure du Dourdou*, ☎ 65.99.54.08, DC, 11 rm ℙ ⛧ ⚲ closed Oct-Mar, 180. Rest. ♦ ⛧ 60-120.

⚖ ★★*Le Champ Clos* (50 pl), ☎ 65.99.51.93.

CARMAUX

Albi 16, Rodez 62, Paris 685 km
pop 12230 ⊠ 81400
A3

Though coal mining in this area has declined somewhat since the 18thC century, coal is the power source for the EDF thermal station here.

Nearby

▶ Man-made **Roucarié Lake** *(5 km N).* ▶ **Monestiès-sur-Cérou** *(8 km NW),* old town with numerous walks ; St. Pierre church (1550) ; sculpture of Burial of Christ (15thC) and Pietà by an unknown artist, among works in the chapel of St. Jacques hospital ; 3 km S from here, Combefa château ruins (12thC). ▶ Wide view from the priory ruins of **Puy-Saint-Georges** *(approx. 13 km SE of Carmaux).* ▶ 14 km NE, **Pampelonne,** on the edge of the plateau overlooking the Viaur ravine, is an ancient blockhouse, built in 1280 ; 1 km E of the town are the ruins of **Thuriès château** (12thC), situated on a rocky peak above the **Viaur Dam** : reservoir ; view★. ▶ Farther up and overlooking the **Viaur Gorges** *(by foot from Tanus)* is the hamlet of **Las Planques.** Its Romanesque church contains murals from 1696 in the choir. ▶ After **Tanus** *(16 km NE of Carmaux)* can be seen the **Viaur viaduct★** (120 m high, 460 m long, main steel arch 220 m-span) built 1897-1902 by engineer Paul Bodin. □

Practical Information _____

CARMAUX
ℹ pl. Gambetta, ☎ 62.76.76.67 (h.s.).
SNCF ☎ 63.76.50.23.

Hotel :
★ *Terminus* (L.F.), 56, av J.-Jaurès, ☎ 63.76.50.28, 13 rm ℙ closed Sun eve and Mon, Aug, 110. Rest. ♦ 50-120.

⚖ ★★*La Croix du Marquis* (35 pl), ☎ 63.76.52.71.

Nearby

MONESTIÈS-SUR-CÉROU, ⊠ 81400 Carmaux, 8 km NW.

Hotel :
● ★ *A l'Orée du Bois* (L.F.), ☎ 63.76.11.72, Visa, 8 rm ⚲

half pens (h.s.), closed 15 Dec-15 Jan, 130. Rest. ♦ Enjoy savoury cuisine prepared by your hostess in the dining room or in the garden : *soupe de campagne, daube de sanglier*, 60-100.

TANUS, ⊠ 81190 Mirandol-Bourgnounac, 13 km N.

Hotel :
★★ *Voyageurs* (L.F.), pl. de l'Église, ☎ 63.76.30.06, AE Euro Visa, 14 rm ℗ ∭ ℘ closed Fri ex summer, Feb school hols, 1-15 Nov, 150. Rest. ♦♦ ♪ *Cuisine tarnaise : civet de porcelet, ris d'agneau provençale*, 60-120.

CASTRES*

Albi 42, Toulouse 71, Paris 733 km
pop 46880 ⊠ 81100   B4

Once a Roman camp (*castrum*, hence the name) ; the natural advantage of the River Agout and an active cloth industry since the 14thC make Castres a busy town. The textile, pharmaceutical, wood, metallurgic and robotic industries are the driving force behind its economy.

▶ **Place Jean-Jaurès :** the heart of the town has a southern look with plane trees and café-terraces ; open on one side to the Agout, lined with timber-faced and balconied houses. From the other side of the square, pedestrian **Rue Victor-Hugo** leads to **Church of Notre-Dame de la Platé** (18thC ; decoration). ▶ **Cathedral of St. Benoît** (1678-1718) : Southern Gothic ; 18thC paintings ; Romanesque tower from the original abbey. ▶ Opposite, in the former **bishop's palace** (architect, Mansart ; 1666), town hall and **Goya Museum★** *(Jul.-Aug., daily, 9-12 & 2-6 from 10 ou Sun. & hols. ; Sep.-Jun., daily except Mon., 9-12 & 2-5 ; from 10 on Sun. & hols.)* works by the Spanish painter Francisco de Goya (1746-1828) ; other Spanish paintings of 15th-17thC ; famous Caprices etchings★ Hispano-Moorish ceramics ; next door, **Jaurès Museum** *(same hours)* : exhibit on the socialist politician and writer Jean Jaurès, born in Castres in 1859 (assassinated in Paris in 1914). Outside, between the Agout and the town hall : **garden★** by André Le Nôtre. ▶ 16th-17thC buildings ; No. 12 Rue Frédéric-Thomas : Toulousain Renaissance brick and stone 16thC **Nayrac Mansion.**

Nearby

▶ **Lafontasse** *(8 km E)* : 18thC church ; 2 km S in the Lézert Valley : **chaos de la Roquette**, a profusion of rocks over a stream ; farther down, the rock piles form **St. Dominique cave.** ▶ The small industrial city of **Labruguière** *(9 km S)* has a church with an octagonal bell tower begun in 1314 ; 13thC castle ruins at the hospice. ▶ To the S, foothills of the **Montagne Noire** (black mountain ; views★), covered by the forests of Montaud, Fontbruno and Hautaniboul, in the **Parc Naturel du Haut Languedoc** (Upper Languedoc Nature Reserve). ▶ **Escoussens** *(7 km SW of Labruguière)* former Roman town : Renaissance château. ▶ **Dourgne** *(16 km SW of Castres)*, a base for exploring the Montagne Noire : 16thC church ; fountain ; close by are the **Benedictine Abbeys of Eu Calcat** (St. Benoît and St. Scholastique ; 19thC). ▶ **Sorèze** *(24 km SW of Castres)* grew around an abbey founded by the Frankish King Pepin the Short (714-68) there still exist corbelled houses (overhanging storeys) along its streets ; 15thC fortified remains of abbey church ; 16th-18thC abbey with a religious school ; park ; archaeological museum in the Maison du Parc Régional (HQ of the regional nature reserve ; *Jul.-Aug. daily, 9-12 & 3-7*) ; houses with overhanging upper stories. ▶ **Durfort** *(3 km S of Sorèze)* : coppersmiths. Farther up the Sor Valley, **Malamort waterfall.**   □

Practical Information _____

CASTRES
ℹ pl. de la République, ☎ 63.59.92.44.
✈ *Labruguière*, 8 km SE, ☎ 63.35.49.58.
SNCF ☎ 63.59.01.66/63.59.22.00.

🚗 near the jardin du Mail, ☎ 63.35.37.31.
Car rental : *Avis*, Z.-I. de Mélou, ☎ 63.59.11.12 ; train station.

Hotels :
● ★★★ *Grand Hôtel*, 11, rue de la Libération, ☎ 63.59.00.30, AE DC Euro Visa, 40 rm ℗ ₰ closed 1-7 May, 15 Dec-15 Jan, 220. Rest. ● ♦♦ ₰ ₰ closed Fri eve and Sat, 1-7 May, 15 Jun-15 Sep, 15 Dec-15 Jan. Comfortable bourgeois cooking : *blanquette de lotte aux poireaux, aiguillette de canard au poivre vert*, 60-150.
★★ *Occitan* (L.F.), 201, av. du Gal-de-Gaulle, ☎ 63.35.34.20, 30 rm ℗ ℘ closed 20 Dec-2 Jan, 210.

Restaurants :
♦♦♦ *La Caravelle*, 150, av. de Roquecourbe, ☎ 63.59.27.72, AE DC Euro Visa ℗ ₰ ∭ closed Fri eve and Sat, 15 Sep-15 Jun. Spec : *magrets de canard*, fresh grilled salmon, 60-150.
♦♦ *Au Chapon Fin*, 8, quai Tourcaudière, ☎ 63.59.06.17, AE DC Euro Visa ♪ closed Mon and Sun eve , Feb school hols, 1-21 Jul. Spec : *fricassée de ris de veau et rognons de veau aux cèpes, tourte de pigeon aux poires et aux épinards*, 55-150.
♦ *La Ripaille*, Verdalle, Visa ℗ ₰ closed Wed and Thu noon, 1-15 Mar, 15-30 Oct, 55-100.

Recommended
Bicycle rental : *Ets Esclasan*, rue Amiral-Galibert, ☎ 63.59.85.13 ; *Ets Tabarly*, 38, pl. Soult, ☎ 65.35.38.09.

Nearby

MONTREDON-LABESSONNIE, ⊠ 81360, 22 km E.

Hotel :
★ *Parc* (L.F.), rte de Lacaune, ☎ 63.75.14.08, 15 rm ℗ ∭ closed Mon ex summer, hols, Sep, 15 Jan-28 Feb, 100. Rest. ♦ 50-90 ; child : 35.

Le causse COMTAL*

                                                    B2

Round trip N of Rodez *(approx. 53 km ; half-day)*

A *causse* is a plateau marked by underground rivers, springs, caves, waterfalls and ravines. Wheat and sheep-farming in this agricultural area enriched first the Counts of Rodez, and later the citizens. Numerous Romanesque churches, chapels, manors, fortified storehouses and farmsteads were built over the centuries.

▶ **Rodez** (→). ▶ **Aboul :** commandery of the Hospitallers ; Renaissance manor ; Romanesque church. ▶ **Bozouls★ :** site at the edge of the Dourdou canyon ; medieval village on the left bank, modern town on the right ; old sandstone church★ ; view★. ▶ **Rodelle★★**, on a spur over the Dourdou (site★) : castle, Romanesque-Gothic church (16thC Pietà★). ▶ **Muret-le-Château★** : 15thC residence of the bishops of Rodez. ▶ **Villecomtal** *(N of Muret)*, 13thC red sandstone walled town. ▶ **Cruou Valley★** leads to Marcillac. D27, runs EW across the plateau past many châteaux and manor-houses. ▶ **Tindoul de la Vayssière★**, largest sink-hole in the region. ▶ Return to Rodez.   □

Practical Information _____

BOZOULS, ⊠ 12340, 22 km NE of **Rodez.**

Hotels :
● ★★ *Le Belvédère*, rte de Saint-Julien-de-Rochelle, ☎ 65.44.92.66, Euro Visa, 10 rm ₰ ₰ closed Sun eve and Sat lunch, 15 Jan-20 Feb, 125. Rest. ♦♦ 55-120.
★ *La Route d'Argent* (site★) : castle, ☎ 65.44.92.27, AE DC Euro Visa, 20 rm ℗ ∭ closed Sun eve, 1-15 Jan, 105. Rest. ♦ 40-80.

Looking for a locality? Consult the index at the back of the book.

CONQUES***

Rodez 37, Aurillac 57, Paris 603 km
pop 404 ⊠ 12320 Saint-Cyprien-sur-Dourdon   B1

Conques clusters around an abbey church, on a hillside above the Ouche Gorges.

▶ **Ste. Foy** : one of the great pilgrim churches, in the architectural tradition of St. Martin in Tours, St. Sernin in Toulouse and St. Martial in Limoges ; the **tympanum★★★** is a major achievement of Romanesque art, a personal interpretation of the Last Judgement by an anonymous artist of genius : the well-preserved polychrome carvings suggest the original appearance of great medieval sanctuaries. Inside, statuary depicting the Annunciation, probably by the same sculptor ; 15thC painting on the sacristy walls. ▶ Lapidary **Museum** in the former monks' refectory. **Treasury★★** has remained intact over centuries : goldsmiths' work from the 11th to the 16thC ; **Majesté de Ste Foy★★★** (reliquary depicting the saint enthroned, 10thC ; wood covered with gold, enamel and precious stones). A second treasury, opened in the summer of 84, comprises antique furniture, pictures and other ancient relics. ▶ **Village★★**.   ▢

Practical Information _____

Hotel :
● ★★★ *Sainte-Foy*, ☎ 65.69.84.03, Visa, 20 rm Ⓟ ⌂ closed lunch, 15 Oct-1 Apr, 150. Rest. ♦♦ ⌇ ⌘ 100-150.

⚠ ★★*Beau Rivage* (60 pl), ☎ 65.69.82.23.

CORDES***

Albi 25, Montauban 71, Paris 683 km
pop 1044 ⊠ 81170   A3

This town over the River Cérou is protected by four walls ; founded in 1222 as Cordoue on an isolated hill over the Cérou valley. Its magnificent Gothic houses evoke the Middle Ages as powerfully as Mont-Saint-Michel, Carcassonne or the Popes' palace in Avignon.

▶ The main street★ **(Rue Droite)**, from the Ormeaux gate to the Rous gate, lined with **14thC houses★, Maison du Grand Ecuyer** (restaurant), **Maison du Grand Veneur** (carved hunting scene on 2nd storey) and **Maison du Grand Fauconnier** (town hall and museum ; *Sun. and nat. hols. pm, Palm Sun.-last Sun. in Oct.).* ▶ Timbered **market** on stone pillars (1350) ; well (85 m deep). ▶ **Church of St. Michel** : mauve sandstone ; 13thC eastern end ; façade and bell tower 14th-15thC. ▶ At the Rous gate (painted doors), the **Charles Portal Museum** : history of Cordes, *libré ferrat* (chained Bible) on which city officials took their oath *(daily Apr.-Oct. ; Sun. and nat. hols., 2-5 ; Jul.-Aug. daily 2-6).* ▶ **Views★** from La Bride terrace, near the covered market, and from the sentry walk on the S rampart.

Nearby

▶ **Les Cabannes** *(1 km W)* : Gothic church. ▶ **Cayla** *(7 km SW)* : 15th-17thC **château** *(daily ex Fri. am).* ▶ **Vaour** *(17 km W)* : ruined Knights-Templar Commandery ; dolmen *(3 km)*; view from relay-station *(5 km).* ▶ **Grésigne national forest★** (33 km², : oak and hornbeam) ; marked paths ; panoramas.

Valley of the Vère, from Cordes to Bruniquel *(approx. 40 km ; half-day)*

▶ **Cordes.** ▶ **Cahuzac-sur-Vère**, in the valley★, country holidays, vineyards. ▶ **Vieux** : Gothic church (murals). Le Verdier : dovecote ; dolmen just off the road. ▶ Surrounded by the ruins of its 14thC ramparts, **Castelnau-de-Montmiral** *(4 km SW overlooking the valley)* : 14th-15thC houses ; church with 15thC silver-gilt jeweled cross. ▶ **Puycelsi★**, fortified village on the right bank of the Vère (view) ; Gothic houses, 15th-16thC church. ▶ **Larroque** : red cliffs ; caves. ▶ **Bruniquel.**   ▢

Practical Information _____

ⓘ maison du Grand Fauconnier, ☎ 63.56.00.52 (h.s.); mairie, ☎ 63.56.00.40.

Hotels :
● ★★★ *Le Grand Ecuyer*, rue Voltaire, ☎ 63.56.01.03, AE Visa, 15 rm ⌇ ▧ ⌂ closed Mon, 15 Oct-1 Apr, 350. Rest. ● ♦♦♦ ⌇ Ⲩ. Thuries is not just a world-class pastry chef, he's a great all-round cook : *gratin de lapereau, minute de barbue gratinée.* Fabulous desserts, and for those with an uncontrollable sweet tooth, an all-dessert menu, 140-250.
★★ *Cité*, Grand'Rue, ☎ 63.56.03.53, Euro Visa, 11 rm ⌇ ▧ ⌂ closed Dec-Feb, 170. Rest. ♦ ⌇ ⋙ closed 15 Nov-15 Mar, 50-75.
★★ *Hostellerie du Vieux Cordes* (Inter-Hôtel, L.F.), rue de la République, ☎ 63.56.00.12, AE DC Euro Visa, 20 rm Ⓟ ⌇ ▧ ⌂ ⋙ closed Feb, 250. Rest. ♦ ⌇ ⌘ A 13thC house on the heights. Foie gras and over 20 kinds of meat, 85-120 ; child : 50.
★★ *Parc* (L.F.), rte de Montauban, les Cabannes, ☎ 63.56.02.59, AE Visa, 15 rm Ⓟ ▧ ⌂ half pens (h.s.), closed Sun eve and Mon (l.s.), 3 Jan-3 Mar, 400. Rest. ● ♦♦ Energetic Claude Izard, president of the Provincial Restaurateurs Association, is an enthusiastic booster of regional cuisine : *canard Lapeyrade, lapin aux choux, Matelote d'anguilles,* enjoyable Gaillac Awines, 85-250.

⚠ ★★★*Le Moulin de Julien* (130 pl), ☎ 63.56.01.42.

DECAZEVILLE

Rodez 37, Aurillac 68, Paris 612 km
pop 9200 ⊠ 12300   B1

Once the capital of the Rouergue mining industry.

▶ **Lassalle open-cast mine★** : gigantic amphitheatre now open to tourists. ▶ Nearby, **Aubin : Rouergue Departmental Museum★ of Mining** *(daily, Jun-Sep, 10-12 & 3-6 ; low season, Sat and Sun, 3-6) ;* Romanesque and Flamboyant **church★** (15thC statues★ ; Romanesque Christ). ▶ Church of Notre-Dame de Decazeville : Stations of the Cross★ by the 19thC painter Gustave Moreau.

Nearby

▶ **Bournazel** *(12 km S of Aubin)* : château★ ; northern wing, 1545 ; magnificent sculptured Renaissance façade ; *(exterior visits only).* ▶ **Belcastel★** *(15 km S, by the Aveyron Gorge)* : castle, keep ; galleried houses ; Gothic bridge ; mill ; tomb and 15thC sculptures in the church. ▶ **Clairvaux★** *(16 km NE of Belcastel)* : red sandstone hills and houses ; Romanesque church, rebuilt in the 18thC ; 17thC furnishings.   ▢

Practical Information _____

ⓘ ☎ 65.43.06.27 ; pavillon du Tourisme, pl. Wilson, ☎ 65.43.18.36 (h.s.).
🚆 ☎ 65.43.11.81.

Hotels :
★★ *France*, pl. Cabrol, ☎ 65.43.00.07, Euro Visa, 24 rm Ⓟ ⌇ ⌇ ⌂ pens, 200. Rest. ♦ ⌇ ⌂ closed Mon, 60-90.
★ *Moderne*, 16, av. A.-Bos, ☎ 65.43.04.33, Euro Visa, 19 rm Ⓟ closed Jul, 90. Rest. ♦ 45-120.

DOURBIE Gorges**

                          C2-3

From Nant to Millau *(32 km ; approx. 3 hrs)*

Less well known than the Tarn and Ardèche gorges, but just as spectacular.

▶ The River Dourbie runs from the Aigoual mountains into the Tarn through a narrow canyon between Nant and Millau. ▶ **Cuns** : church roofed with fish-scale stone shingles. ▶ **Cantobre★** : site★ ; village built into a mushroom-shaped rock ; Romanesque church. ▶ **Saint-Véran★**, on a narrow cliff road in a fold of the plateau : ruins of Montcalm fortress. ▶ **La-Roque-Sainte-Marguerite**, at the mouth of the Riou Sec ravine from which you can reach the rocks of Montpellier-le-Vieux; 17thC château (dovecote; Romanesque church) overlooks a hump-backed bridge and an old mill. ▶ Continue to Millau between eroded cliffs giving way to gardens and poplars towards the end of the journey.   □

GAILLAC*

Albi 22, Cahors 89, Paris 684 km
pop 10650 ⊠ 81600   A3
On a loop of the Tarn near the Abbey of St. Michel (founded 7thC), Gaillac has been renowned for wine (red, white, sparkling) since the Middle Ages.

▶ **Place d'Hautpoul** and **Place de la Libération** (Friday market) form the centre of town. **Pierre de Brens Mansion** (ca. 1500; brick, flanked by medieval tower) : museum of folklore, wine and vineyards *(visit at 4 pm in summer ex Sun. and Mon.; ask at the TO).* ▶ **Church of St. Pierre :** southern Gothic, on the pedestrian street of **Rue Portal.** At nearby **Place Thiers** (lined with old houses) : **Griffoul fountain** (16th or 17thC). ▶ By the Tarn, **abbey church of St. Michel :** 12th-13thC, restored 17thC, 13thC statue of Virgin and Child.   □

Practical Information _____

🛈 pl. de la Libération, ☎ 63.57.14.65.
SNCF ☎ 63.57.00.23.

Hotels :
★★ *Occitan*, 41, av. Georges-Clemenceau, ☎ 63.57.11.52, AE DC Visa, 13 rm Ⓟ ⑯ 165.
● ★ *Auberge des Barthes*, Les Barthes, Técou, RN 664, ☎ 63.33.02.43, Euro Visa, 8 rm Ⓟ ∦ ⑯ ⚘ ♪ 🖃 half pens (h.s.), closed Mon, 340. Rest. ♦ ∦ ♪ 60-120; child : 30.

Restaurant :
♦♦ *Le Vigneron*, 122, av. Saint-Exupéry, 1.5 km, ☎ 63.57.07.20 Ⓟ ♪ closed Mon and Sun eve ex summer, 1-7 Jan, 55-190.
⚶ ★★*Le Lido* (30 pl), ☎ 63.57.18.30.

Recommended
Guide to wines : *wine festival*, 2nd Sun in Aug.

GRAULHET

Albi 37, Toulouse 58, Paris 703 km
pop 13650 ⊠ 81300   A3
Industrial town on the River Dadou with a long tradition of tanning and leatherwork; the leading European producer of fine leathers.

Nearby

▶ **Lézignac** *(3 km NW)* : remains of 16th-17thC **château.**
▶ **Briatexte** *(7 km W),* walled town founded in 1290 by Simon Brisetête, Sénéchal de Carcassonne and Béziers; arcaded square. ▶ **Lautrec** *(15 km SE)* : gates and remains of fortifications on a hill; church (15th-17th and 18thC) with altarpiece from former collegiate church of Burlats (→ Sidobre and Lacaune mountains); 24 carved stalls; archaeology and local history museum *(pm daily Jul.-Sep.);* limestone cellars.   □

LACAUNE

Castres 47, Montpellier 126, Paris 712 km
pop 3420 ⊠ 81230   B3
▶ Spread out on the left bank of the Gijou River, this large town features some old and interesting tall-storeyed houses. ▶ **Church** (17thC, southern Gothic), across from Griffoul square, the site of the unusual **Pissaïres fountain** (1399). ▶ The rest of the town, on the right bank, is clustered on the foothill under **Calmels château** (18thC; view).

Nearby

▶ **Roc de Montalet** *(7 km SW),* highest point in the Tarn (1 260 m; statue of the Virgin); view★ of Larzac plateau, the Montagne Noire (Black Mountain), Saint-Loup peak and, on clear days, the Mediterranean.   □

Practical Information _____

🛈 pl. du Gal-de-Gaulle, ☎ 63.37.04.98.   ♥

Hotels :
★★ *Fusiés* (Inter-Hôtel, L.F.), 2, rue de la République, ☎ 63.37.02.03, AE DC Euro Visa, 50 rm Ⓟ ⑯ ♪ half pens (h.s.), closed 20 Dec-20 Jan, 370. Rest. ♦♦ ♪ ⚶ Fusiés is given excellent support by chef P.Carpentier : *feuilleté de truites à l'oseille, magret aux pommes,* 65-160; child : 45.
★ *Le Glacier* (L.F.), 4, pl. de la Vierge, ☎ 63.37.03.28, AE Visa, 22 rm Ⓟ ∦ ⑯ ⚘ closed Fri eve and Sat lunch (l.s.), 21 Jan-21 Feb, 125. Rest. ♦ ∦ ⚶ Fantastic value, this local cuisine : *salade tiède au ris de veau et cèpes, crépinette de mérou au jus de truffes,* 50-130.

⚶ ★*Gourp* (33 pl), ☎ 63.37.01.94.

Recommended
♥ pork products : *P. Calas,* rue de la mairie, ☎ 63.37.00.20; *Sablayrolles,* 5, rue Pasteur, ☎ 63.37.02.45.

Causse du LARZAC***
                                                          C3
Round trip from Millau to Le Caylar *(40 km; half-day necessary for good approach)*

The Larzac plateau, where blue Roquefort cheese is made from ewe's milk, is rich in archaeological and architectural remains. The windswept region is dotted with triple-vaulted sheepfolds, traces of Templar and Hospitaller commanderies, fortified farmsteads and villages.

▶ **Millau.** ▶ Long scenic drive along the edge of the plateau. ▶ **Grande Jasse :** sheep-farm 15 km from Millau on N9; information about Larzac : introduction to the region at the **ecomusée du Larzac.** ▶ **Sainte-Eulalie-de-Cernon,** walled town, long the capital of Larzac; 15thC ramparts; church and château remodeled in the 17thC. ▶ **La Couvertoirade★★** : 15thC fortifications built by the Hospitallers, a defensive outlook for 17th-18thC houses and mansions recalling the prosperous wool trade with nearby Lodève (→). ▶ **Le Caylar,** medieval village structure. ▶ View★ over the stony landscape of the Larzac plateau. ▶ Now, the deserted and most Mediterranean part of the plateau, the stepped summer pastures for sheep. ▶ **Escalette Pass★★** and road 200 m above the Lergue Valley down to the Hérault plain (→).   □

LAVAUR

Toulouse 37, Albi 48, Paris 713 km
pop 8264 ⊠ 81500   A3
One-time stronghold built above the left bank of the Agout River.

▶ **St. Alain Cathedral** (13th-14thC), in southern Gothic style; Flamboyant Gothic doorway (15thC) topped by a tower similar to the tower of Albi cathedral; Romanesque tower with a 17thC Jack-o'-the-clock (mechanism and bell, 1523 restored 17thC); inside church polyptych of Christ's Passion (late 16thC). ▶ In former Doctrinaire collegiate chapel (1640), **Vauris Museum** (archaeology and local history; *ask at town hall for schedule).* ▶ In Grand Rue : **Church of St. François** (14th-15thC). ▶ No. 7 Rue du Père-Colin : **Maison du Vieux Lavaur** (museum of regional ethnography).

Nearby

▶ **Ambres** *(5 km N)*, above the junction of the Dadou and Agout rivers; church; panorama. ▶ **Giroussens** *(10 km NW)*, former pottery centre on the right bank of the Agout; pleasant surroundings, château, 16thC church. ☐

Practical Information ―――――――――――

LAVAUR
ℹ mairie, ☎ 63.58.06.71; 22, Grand'Rue, ☎ 63.58.02.00. **SNCF** ☎ 63.58.01.19.

Hotels :
★★ **Terminus** (L.F.), 7, av. de la Gare, ☎ 63.58.31.14, AE DC Visa, 9 rm ℙ ⚑ half pens, closed Sat ex reservations, 248. Rest. ◆ ♪ 50-120.
★ **Central** (L.F.), 7, rue Alsace-Lorraine, ☎ 63.58.04.16, 14 rm ℙ ⚑ ᰒ 100. Rest. ◆ 40-80; child : 25.
★ **Pommiers**, Ambres, 5 km N, ☎ 63.58.05.56, Visa, 7 rm ℙ 120. Rest. ◆ 50-80.

Nearby

GIROUSSENS, ⊠ 81500 Lavaur, 10 km NW on the D 87-D 38.

Hotel :
L'Echauguette, ☎ 63.41.63.65, AE DC Euro Visa, 4 rm ℙ ⚑ ⚑ ᰒ ᰒ closed Mon eve, 1-15 Feb, 1-15 Sep, 150. Rest. ● ◆◆ ⚑ ♪ ᰒ Hearty, inexpensive eating, 55-150.

SAINT-LIEUX-LÈS-LAVAUR, ⊠ 81500 Lavaur, 10 km NW on the D 87.

Hotel :
● ★★ **Château de Saint-Lieux**, ☎ 63.41.60.87, 12 rm ℙ ⚑ ᰒ ᰒ 170. Rest. ◆ ⚑ ᰒ 55-110; child : 35.

LÉVEZOU lakes

B2

From Rodez to Millau via Montjaux *(78 km; winding road in the second half of the trip; full day)*

The high plateau of Lévezou separates north and south Rouergue. In the N, the landscape is similar to Auvergne: moist, wooded and mountainous, whereas the dry limestone country in the S is more Mediterranean. In the S, the roofs are covered with curved pink tiles; stone shingles are used in the N. The Lévezou is a heathland with grazing for sheep and tracts under intensive cultivation. The immense lakes provide excellent fishing and sailing.

▶ **Rodez** (→). **Pont-de-Salars**, in the Viaur valley, once a stopover between Rodez and Millau, today a lakeside resort. ▶ **Salles-Curan**, former stronghold above **Lake Pareloup** (28 km circumference), around the 15thC castle of the bishops of Rodez, now a hotel; Gothic houses, 15thC church (carved stalls). ▶ Rather than seeing the third lake farther S, explore the picturesque villages of the area, situated on the edge of the plateau. ▶ **Bouloc**, on the ridge-line. ▶ **Saint-Beauzély★**, stopover on the road to Rodez until the 18thC; old houses, 16thC château. ▶ **ComBeroumal★** : 1,5 km W from the village, former priory of the order of Grandmont; the austerity of the monastic rule is reflected by the architecture. ▶ Head back to another medieval village, **Castelnau-Pégayrols★** : overlooking the **Muze Gorge**, around the castle of the counts of Lévezou and two Romanesque churches; the dour grey sandstone underlines the fortress outlook of the village; church of St. Victor, in the centre of the village, once belonged to a priory of the same name; the other (11th-12thC), in the cemetery, was the parish church. ▶ **Montjaux★★** (site) : the streets down to the church are lined with old houses of a pretty pink, with climbing plants, architectural details and Gothic or Renaissance windows; small 16th-17thC château; pink sandstone church roofed with blue slate tiles (façade and dome remodeled; inside, the original capitals). ▶ Opposite, view over **Marzials** : terraced medieval fortress. ▶ From Montjaux, to **Mil-**

lau *(26 km →)* via the Tarn Valley (→) or Saint-Affrique *(23.5 km →)*; or go back towards Salles-Curan *(12.5 km)* via **Les Canabières :** Romanesque church and cemetery cross decorated with a Pietà. ☐

Practical Information ―――――――――

BOULOC, ⊠ 12410 Salles-Curan, 9 km E of **Salles-Curan**.

Hotel :
Les Griffouls, ☎ 65.46.35.18, 10 rm ⚑ ᰒ ᰒ closed in winter, 100. Rest. ◆ ♪ Family-style regional cuisine, 65-90.

PONT-DE-SALARS, ⊠ 12290, 33 km SE of **Rodez**.
ℹ mairie, ☎ 65.46.84.27.

Hotel :
★★ **Voyageurs** (L.F.), 1, av. de Rodez, ☎ 65.46.82.08, Euro Visa, 32 rm ℙ half pens (h.s.), closed Sun eve and Mon (l.s.), 380. Rest. ◆◆ ♪ ᰒ Lavish fixed menus, 65-120.

△ ★★★*Le Lac et la Source* (200 pl), ☎ 65.46.84.86.

SALLES-CURAN, ⊠ 12410, 40 km SE of **Rodez**.
ℹ mairie, ☎ 65.46.31.73.

Hotel :
● ★★ **Hostellerie du Levézou** (C.H., L.F.), ☎ 65.46.34.16, AE DC Euro Visa, 25 rm ℙ ⚑ ᰒ closed Sun eve and Mon (l.s.), 15 Oct-1 Apr, 165. Rest. ● ◆◆ ♪ ᰒ In this handsome feudal residence, former home of the bishops of Rodez, the Bouviala family all get into the culinary act ː *tarte aux cèpes sauce au vin de noix, croustade de foie gras chaude sauce aux truffes, tarte de Saint-Jacques au beurre de champagne, magrets*, 70-180.

△ ★★★★*Beau Rivage* (80 pl), ☎ 65.46.36.33; ★★★*Base Nautique Pareloup* (65 pl), ☎ 65.46.36.74; ★★*Les Vernhes* (30 pl), ☎ 65.46.33.62.

Recommended
Farmhouse-inn : *La Baraque*, ☎ 65.46.35.92, Reserve. Spec : *charcuteries*.

LOT Gorges★★

B1

Round trip from Conques to Espalion *(55 km; half-day; see map 1)*.

▶ **Conques**. Drive down the Dourdou Valley. ▶ **Grand-Vabre** : 15th-16thC church; Pietà. ▶ **Saint-Projet** : views over the Lot and Auze gorges. ▶ **Saint-Sulpice**, hamlet opposite **Vieillevie**. ▶ **Entraygues★**, at the junction of the Lot and the Truyère in a vine-growing valley (rosé wine); two medieval bridges over the river; 13th-17thC château on the peninsula; once a busy port for waterway transport between the plateau and Bordeaux. Entraygues : the houses have a medieval appearance (Rue Basse); on the edge of town, Pontet chapel (16th-17thC; statues). ▶ The **Golinhac Dam** has turned the gorge into a lake bordered by chestnut trees. ▶ **Estaing**, in a bend of the Lot (Gothic bridge★); the d'Estaing family was powerful from the 15th to the 18thC; 15thC church (outside, Gothic crosses; inside, 15thC Christ, 17thC altarpieces); 15th-16thC château, now a convent (visits); 16th-18thC houses; town hall in 16thC mansion; balconied houses; bridges over the River Caussane. **Ouradou** *(1 km N)* : Gothic statues★ in the **chapel.** ▶ The valley broadens at **Espalion★★** : view from the Pont-Vieux★ (bridge, late 15thC) to the Renaissance château and the tanners' houses. ▶ **Rouergue Regional Museum★** in the former prison (evolution of thought; *exhibitions in summer*). Joseph Vaylet Museum in converted church : folk art, prehistory, ceramics *(15 Jun.-15 Sep., daily, 10-12 & 2-7; out of season, by request, tel. 65.44.69.18.)*. ▶ Outside the town, church of **Perse★★** *(1 km S)*, pink and white, with blue slate roof, inspired by Conques; doorway with rustic treatment of the Apocalypse; left, re-used Adoration of the Magi; figured capitals; false ogival vaulting; retouched 12thC paintings *(concerts in summer)*. ▶ **Bessuéjouls★** *(3 km W on the left bank)* : church with Romanesque chapel under the bell tower (primitive decoration). ☐

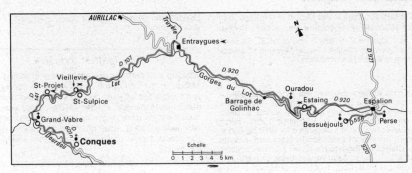

1. Lot gorges

Practical Information ————————

ENTRAYGUES, ✉ 12140, 47 km N of **Rodez**.
ⓘ 30, Tour-de-Ville, ☎ 65.44.56.10.

Hotels :
★★ *La Truyère* (L.F.), 60, av. du Pont-de-Truyère,
☎ 65.44.51.10, Tx 530366, Euro Visa, 26 rm ℙ ⌇ ▒
half pens (h.s.), closed Mon, 17 Nov-1 Mar, 370. Rest. ♦♦
⌇ ♪ ⅋ ⅋ 55-160 ; child : 40.
★★ *Les Deux Vallées* (L.F.), av. du Pont-de-Truyère,
☎ 65.44.52.15, 18 rm ℙ ⅋ pens (h.s.), 200. Rest. ♦ ⌇
⅋ 40-75.

⚊ ★★*Roquepailhol* (70 pl), ☎ 65.44.57.79 ; ★★*Val de
Saures* (200 pl), ☎ 65.44.56.92.

ESPALION, ✉ 12500, 30 km NE of **Rodez**.
ⓘ mairie, ☎ 65.44.05.46.   ♥
SNCF ☎ 65.44.05.38.

Hotel :
★★ *Moderne* (L.F., Inter-Hôtel), 27, bd de Guizard,
☎ 65.44.05.11, Euro Visa, 27 rm ℙ ⅋ ▒ ● ♦
closed Mon and Sun eve (l.s.), 5-31 Jan, 15 Nov-15 Dec.
Varied generous fare. Spec : *persillé de ris d'agneau
et d'écrevisses, terrine de chocolat et de thé d'Aulnac*,
65-125 ; child : 50.

⚊ ★★*Roc de l'Arche* (130 pl), ☎ 65.44.02.49.

Recommended
♥ pork products : *Combacon*, rue Droite, ☎ 65.44.06.26.

ESTAING, ✉ 12190, 40 km SE of **Conques**.
ⓘ rue F.-d'Estaing, ☎ 65.44.70.03 (h.s.).

Hotels :
● ★ *Raynaldy*, rue F.-d'Estaing, ☎ 65.44.70.03, 16 rm ℙ
▒ ◡ closed Oct-Mar, 80. Rest. ♦ ⅋ 40-55 ; child : 30.
★ *Aux Armes d'Estaing* (L.F.), quai du Lot,
☎ 65.44.70.02, Visa, 47 rm ℙ ⅋ ◡ pens (h.s.), closed
15 Dec-15 Mar, 140. Rest. ♦ ⅋ ⅋ 40-80.

⚊ ★★*La Chantellerie* (100 pl), ☎ 65.44.72.77.

LOT Valley**

B1

From Espalion to La Canourgue *(57 km ; poor road ; half-
day)*

At this point, the valley of the Lot divides the dry, cold,
volcanic Aubrac (→) massif from the high plateaus of
the Lozère.

▶ **Espalion**, (→). ▶ On the left, **Flaujac**, fortified hamlet.
▶ **Saint-Côme-d'Olt★**, encircled by ramparts, centred on
a Flamboyant Gothic church (bell tower, carved doorway) ;
town hall in 15thC château. ▶ On a volcanic outcrop to the
S, **Roquelaure★** : feudal château remodeled in the 17thC ;
chapel (16thC Pietà). ▶ **Castelnau Dam** makes a reser-

voir of the Lot Gorges. ▶ **Saint-Geniez-d'Olt :** an orchard
valley, until the 19thC, a centre of the cloth trade ; on the
left bank, former convent (14thC ; 16thC triptych) among
17th-18thC mansions. On the right bank, medieval town.
▶ The villages lining the river are composed of beautiful
houses built of red sandstone with slate roofs and chestnut trees along the Lot separate the walls of Sauveterre
and the Aubrac foothills. ▶ **La Canourgue** (→ Ardèche,
Cévennes).   □

Practical Information ————————

SAINT-GENIEZ-D'OLT, ✉ 12130, 24 km NW of **Séverac-
le-Château**.
ⓘ salle des Cloîtres, ☎ 65.70.43.32 (h.s.).   ♥

Hotel :
★★ *France* (L.F.), ☎ 65.70.42.20, AE DC Euro Visa, 42 rm
ℙ ▒ ◡ ♪ ▱ ⌇ 145. Rest. ♦ ♪ ⅋ closed Sun (l.s.) , Dec,
Jan. Good value, 45-80.

⚊ ★★★*Municipal* (150 pl), ☎ 65.70.40.43 ; at Saint-Côme-
d'Olt, *Belle Rive* (70 pl), ☎ 65.44.05.85.

MARSSAC-SUR-TARN

Albi 10, Gaillac 11, Paris 673 km
pop 1706 ✉ 81150   A3

SNCF ☎ 63.55.44.81.

Hotels :
★ *Fleurs* (L.F.), rte de Toulouse, ☎ 63.55.40.29, 17 rm ℙ
closed Fri eve, 24 Dec-5 Jan, 90. Rest. ♦ 40-100.
★ *Poste* (L.F.), ☎ 63.55.40.26, 19 rm ℙ ▒ 100. Rest. ♦
closed Fri eve, 50.

Restaurant :
● ♦♦♦♦ *Francis Cardaillac*, RN 88, ☎ 63.55.41.90, AE
DC Euro Visa ⅋ ▒ ♪ ▱ closed Mon and Sun eve,
3-24 Jan. In his lovely and much-beloved region, Francis
Cardaillac is a passionate chef. On the banks of the Tarn
he gives his all to satisfy gourmet customers, and spread
the gospel of 'peace and good eating'. It makes the
menu interesting reading : 'duck story', for example.
Wide choice of fixed-price meals. Wines of the month by
the glass or bottle, 85-250.

⚊ ★★*Cévennes-Languedoc* (50 pl), ☎ 63.55.40.31.

MAZAMET

Carcassonne 47, Albi 60, Paris 751 km
pop 13340 ✉ 81200   B4

In spite of religious wars and anti-Protestant hostilities in the 12thC, Mazamet, on the banks of the
Arnette, built an important textile industry and became

one of the busiest cities in the Midi. It is the European centre for processing sheepskin; also a dairy centre.

▶ Place de l'Hôtel de Ville; 18thC church of St. Sauveur.
▶ Near the Casernes carpark : **Fuzier Museum** : Cathars, local history *(daily ex Sun. and Mon.).*

Nearby

▶ On the road to Carcassonne : **Plo de la Bise,** lookout over the town and the hamlet of Hautpoul. ▶ **Montagnès** *(7 km farther)* : reservoir surrounded by woods. ▶ **Hautpoul** *(4 km S),* on a rocky spur : ruined 15thC church of St. Sauveur; two castles destroyed in 1212 by Simon de Montfort, remains of fortifications. Upstream, **Arnette Gorge.** ▶ **Château d'Aiguefonde** *(8 km W),* 16thC, rebuilt in the 18thC. ▶ Near **Saint-Amans-Soult** *(10 km E)* : park, château of Soult-Berg, birthplace of Maréchal Soult (1769-1851), who is buried in the village church (octagonal bell tower with 16thC spire). ▶ **Thoré Valley★** leads to Labastide-Rouairoux (Languedoc-Roussillon →). ▶ **Anglès** *(27 km NE),* between Lakes St. Peyres and Ravièges; 15thC château de Monségou. □

Practical Information _____

MAZAMET
ⓘ rue des Casernes, ☎ 63.61.27.07.
SNCF ☎ 63.61.19.00.

Hotels :
● ★★★ *Château de Montlédier* (R.C.), Pont-de-l'Arn, ☎ 63.61.20.54, Tx 520411, AE DC Visa, 10 rm Ⓟ ⊰ ▨ ◁ 400. Rest. ● ◆◆ ♪ closed Mon and Sun eve , Jan. Light, regional dishes in a 13thC château : *filets de truite, coulis d'écrevisses, jambonnette de volaille forestière,* 85-220.
★★★ *Le Grand Balcon*, sq. G.-Tournier, ☎ 63.61.01.15, AE DC Euro Visa, 24 rm Ⓟ 300. Rest. ◆ ♪ ⊗ closed Sun eve. Interesting dishes by J.-L. Condamines : *foie gras frais, magret de canard aux airelles, cuisses de cailles à l'ail rose,* 90-180.
● ★★ *La Métairie Neuve*, Pont-de-l'Arn, ☎ 63.61.23.31, Euro Visa, 7 rm Ⓟ ⊰ ▨ ◁ ♪ closed 1-15 Aug, 20 Dec-20 Jan, 230. Rest. ◆ ♪ ⓰ closed Sat, 40-180; child : 30.
★ *Le Boulevard* (L.F.), 24, bd Soult, ☎ 63.61.16.08, Euro Visa, 21 rm Ⓟ 228. Rest. ◆ ♪ ⓰ closed Mon ex hols. Spec : *cassoulet aux trois viandes, sandre au beurre blanc,* 50-100.

⚠ ★★★*La Lauze* (60 pl), ☎ 63.61.24.69.

Nearby

ANGLÈS, ✉ 81260 Brassac, 27 km NE.

Hotel :
★ *Auberge de la Souque,* à 4 km S.-E., ☎ 63.70.98.53, 12 rm Ⓟ ▨ closed 11 Nov-15 Mar, 90. Rest. ◆ 80-110.

Rodez 71, Nîmes 166, Paris 631 km
pop 22250 ✉ 12100   C2

Pink-tiled roofs and the Mediterranean trio of sheep, olives and vineyards signal the approach to the deep South. Millau, unlike other towns in the Rouergue, has a strong Protestant tradition. In earlier times, because of its sheep and Tarn River resources, the town was a glove-making centre.

▶ The medieval town is marked by the belfry (view); the centre of the old quarter is Place du Maréchal-Foch (pedestrian zone) with arcaded galleries and fountain in Empire style; corn-market (school); 18thC town hall with archaeological museum (Millau was an important pottery town in Roman times; *daily except Sun., 10-12 & 2-5; Jul.-Aug., 10-12 & 3-7,* visitors to sites of excavation; out of season, daily except Mon. and Tue.; Jul.-Aug., daily except Tue.); 17thC Counter-Reformation church; the Tauriac Mansion contains a glove museum. Centre of

Leather and Skin-tanning *(28 Jun.-7 Sep., 10-12 & 3-7 daily ex Sun.).* □

The leather industry

Tanning and leatherwork are traditional industries in Millau; at the turn of the century, high-fashion gloves were exported all over the world from the town and surrounding villages. By the 1950s, output was more than 4 million pairs of gloves per year, but production has declined as a result of changing fashion, despite the ready supply of fine leather in this sheep-farming region.

Practical Information _____

ⓘ av. Alfred-Merle, ☎ 65.60.02.42.
SNCF ☎ 65.60.02.65/65.60.11.65.
▨ in front of the train station.

Hotels :
● ★★★ *International Hôtel*, 1, pl. de la Tine, ☎ 65.60.20.66, Tx 520629, AE DC Euro Visa, 110 rm Ⓟ ♪ 360. Rest. ◆◆ ⊰ ♪ ⓰ closed Mon and Sun eve (l.s.), 1 Jan-15 Feb. Spec : *suprême de St-Pierre en vert de laitue aux émulsions de poivrons doux, col-vert en salmis aux baies de genièvre,* 95-220.
★★★ *La Musardière* (R.C.), 34, av. de la Musardière, ☎ 65.60.20.63, AE DC Visa, 12 rm Ⓟ ▨ half pens (h.s.), closed 4 Nov-1 Apr. Former private mansion in a shady park, 410. Rest. ● ◆◆◆ ⊰ closed Mon. Updated regional fare : *marmite de baudroie "Musardière", salmis de colvert à l'ancienne avec ses pâtes fraîches,* 80-200.
● ★★ *Château de Creissels*, pl. du Prieur, rte de St-Affrique, ☎ 65.60.16.59, 30 rm Ⓟ ⊰ ▨ ◁ pens, half pens (h.s.), 340. Rest. ● ◆◆ ⊰ ♪ ⓰ closed Wed and Sat noon (l.s.) , Feb. Excellent regional dishes at attractive prices : *confidou de boeuf à la Millavoise, foie de canard chaud aux raisins frais,* 85-155; child : 40.

Restaurants :
◆◆ *Buffet de la Gare*, pl. de la Gare, ☎ 65.60.09.04, AE Euro Visa ♪ closed Tue, Feb and 10 days in Oct. One of France's five best station buffets, with opulent cuisine and an array of fixed-price meals, 60-200.
◆◆ *Capion*, 3, rue J.-F.-Alméras, ☎ 65.60.00.91, AE DC Euro Visa ⓰ ⊗ closed Thu, 1-28 Mar. Spec : *salade de queues d'écrevisses, cassolette de gambas et cuisses de grenouilles.* Good value, 65-130.
◆◆ *La Braconne*, 7, pl. Mal-Foch, ☎ 65.60.30.93, AE DC Visa ▨ ♪ closed Mon and Sun eve, 15-31 Dec. Vaulted 12thC dining room. Spec : *poulet aux écrevisses, fauxfilet aux morilles flambé au cognac,* 80-140.

⚠ ★★★★*Millau Plage* (250 pl), ☎ 65.60.10.97; ★★★★*Millau-Cureplat* (250 pl), ☎ 65.60.15.75; ★★*Saint-Lambert* (135 pl), ☎ 65.60.00.48; at Aguessac, 7 km N, d'*Aguessac*, (70 pl), ☎ 65.59.80.15.

Recommended
♥ leather goods-gloves : *André Sales,* 13, av. J.-Jaurès et 8, pl. du Mandarous, ☎ 65.61.04.55; pastry : *St-Jacques,* 4, pl. du Mandarous, ☎ 65.60.04.03.

C2

Legend has it that this jumble of rocks overlooking the Dourbie is a forgotten city, buried among pines, oaks and arbutus. A marked path leads you to the most interesting sections. From Douminal, view over the Causses down towards **Peyreleau★** on the Tarn and Jonte rivers (→ Cévennes), at the junction of three plateaus. You can see in succession the Jonte Gorges, the Capluc rock at the mouth of the Tarn Gorges (→) and Sauveterre peak (→). □

NAJAC**

Albi 54, Cahors 85, Paris 644 km
pop 820 ⊠ 12270   A2

This stronghold of the Counts of Toulouse was destroyed by Simon de Montfort during the Albigensian Crusade. The feudal castle (illuminated in summer) is silhouetted at the end of the single street, on a spur in a narrow loop of the Aveyron River.

▶ The original town was crowded between the castle and the church; the present village was the suburb. **Place des Arcades★** : at the base of the Najac promontory, the long street winds up to the castle; **Gothic houses**; 1344 fountain; **castle★★** *(Apr.-Sep., 10-12 & 2-5 ex Jun. 2:30-6 and Jul.-Aug., 2:30-7)*, rebuilt by Alphonse de Poitiers in 1253 after a Cathar "heretic" rebellion; Gothic church on the cliff edge built with fines exacted by the Inquisitors (15thC statues; view★).   ☐

Practical Information

ℹ mairie, ☎ 65.65.80.94.
SNCF ☎ 65.65.71.83.

Hotels :
● ★★ **Belle Rive** (L.F.), ☎ 65.65.74.20, 40 rm Ⓟ ⋘ ◬ ⊠ closed 15 Oct-1 Apr, 150. Rest. ♦ ⋞ ♿ ✸ 55-150; child : 35.
★★ **L'Oustal del Barry - Miquel** (L.F.), pl. du Bourg, ☎ 65.65.70.80, Visa, 21 rm Ⓟ ⋘ ◬ ♿ ♪ half pens (h.s.), closed Mon in Apr and Oct, 2 Nov-20 Mar, 320. Rest. ● ♦ ⋞ ♪ ♿ For the same prices as in years past, hearty modern fare : fresh fish, *feuilleté de foie gras de canard aux asperges vertes du pays*, 55-150.

△ ★★★★*Le Paysseyrou* (100 pl), ☎ 65.65.72.06.

NANT*

Millau 34, Albi 127, Paris 665 km
pop 970 ⊠ 12230 La Cavalerie   C3

This village at the entrance to the Dourbie Valley (→) developed around a Benedictine abbey. The monks drained the marshy Durzon Valley to make fertile vineyards and meadows, "the garden of Aveyron".

▶ Surrounded by the steep sides of the Larzac and Bégon plateaus, see the town's arcaded 17thC market on the **Place du Marché★★**; pleasant stroll along the Dourbie River; 14thC **bridge**; Romanesque abbey **church★** (mid-12thC) : each pillar is flanked by eight columns (capitals★★); old houses in neighbouring streets.

Nearby

▶ **Durzon Valley★** *(6 km SW; explore on foot)* : cultivated valley in the Larzac plateau (→) ; trout-stream. **Saint-Martin-du-Vican** (site) : Romanesque chapel. **Foux du Dourzon,** resurgence of the River. ▶ **Saint-Jean-du-Bruel** *(8 km E)* : abundant streams and hump-backed bridge over the Dourbie river; between the Larzac plateau and Mount Aigoual★★ (→), the chestnut woods and dark stone of the Cévennes (→) appear. S, **château d'Algues** (view★), ruins and rocky dolomites.   ☐

Practical Information

Nearby

SAINT-JEAN-DU-BRUEL, ⊠ 12230 La Cavalerie, 6 km E.

Hotel :
★★ **Midi** (L.F.), ☎ 65.62.26.04, 19 rm Ⓟ ⋞ ◬ ♿ closed 11 Nov-11 Apr, 105. Rest. ● ♦♦ ⋞ ♿ In a quiet site on the banks of the Dourbie, enjoy the terrace in fine weather and the Papillon family's delicious, hearty cooking : *filet de saumon de fontaine, confit de canard*, 45-130.

Recommended
♥ pork products : *Papillon*, ☎ 65.62.26.26, duck, thrush and boar pâtés.

PEYRUSSE-LE-ROC*

Figeac 22, Villefranche-de-Rouergue 30, Paris 605 km
pop 375 ⊠ 12220 Montbazens   A2

A majestically-situated former stronghold overlooking the Audierne Gorges.

▶ This was one of the earliest towns in Rouergue, by virtue of its strategic position and its silver mines. At one time Peyrusse boasted a population of 3 000, but cheap silver from Latin America and the consolidation of the French state forced Peyrusse into a decline balanced by the rise of Villefranche, which was better placed for communications. From the 17thC onwards the population of Peyrusse continually dwindled.

▶ Drive down the Diège Valley towards **Capdenac** *(12 km NW); once a citadel* **(Capdenac-le-Haut),** it is now an industrial town on the plain **(Capdenac-Gare).**   ☐

Practical Information

Nearby

CAPDENAC-GARE, ⊠ 12700, 12 km NW.
ℹ bd Paul-Ramadier, ☎ 65.64.74.87.
SNCF ☎ 65.64.70.05.

Hotel :
★ **Paris** (L.F.), 12, rue Gambetta, ☎ 65.64.74.72, Visa, 15 rm, closed Sat eve and Sun (l.s.), 30 Oct-5 Nov, 20 Dec-10 Jan, 100. Rest. ♦ 40-120.

△ ★*Municipal* (53 pl), ☎ 65.80.88.97.

PUYLAURENS

Castres 22, Albi 53, Paris 730 km
pop 2780 ⊠ 81700   A4

The seat of a Protestant college that flourished from 1565 until the 1685 Revocation of the Edict of Nantes. The Wednesday agricultural market dates back to the 12thC. From the hilltop site, view over the Cévennes and the Pyrénées.

▶ **Church** : Romanesque choir, 1675 nave, bell tower rebuilt in 1900; wooden covered market.

Nearby

▶ **Château de Magrin** *(10 km NW),* 12th-16thC ; Pastel Museum explaining development and trade ; Albi art since the 16thC *(Easter, Pentecost, Sun. in Jul.; daily in Aug.; tel. 63.75.63.82).* ▶ **Château de Montgey** *(13 km SW),* on a spur over the Revel plains ; view of Pyrénées ; medieval fortress captured by Simon de Montfort in 1211 ; Romanesque tower, 16th-18thC buildings *(Sun. pm).*   ☐

Practical Information

Hotels :
★ **Grand Hôtel Pagès** (L.F.), sq. Ch.-de-Gaulle, ☎ 63.75.00.09, AE DC Euro Visa, 21 rm, closed Sat (l.s.), 120. Rest. ♦ ♪ Bernard Pagès himself prepares a delicious shepherd's terrine with walnuts and bountiful *magrets de canard aux émincés de cèpes*, 50-100.
● **Château de Garrevaques,** Garrevaques, ☎ 63.75.04.54, Tx 530955, Visa, 10 rm Ⓟ ⋘ ◬ ⊠ ♪ closed 1 Jan-15 Mar, 600. Rest. ♦ 100-250.

Restaurant :
♦♦ **La Gousse d'Ail,** rte de Revel, ☎ 63.75.01.93, AE DC Euro Visa ⋘ ♪ closed Mon and Tue noon, 2 Jan-10 Feb. J.-C. Belaut deserves support for his efforts : *foie gras de canard, ragoût de coquilles Saint-Jacques au safran, tournedos au jus de truffes*, 60-140.

For the translation of a name of a meat, a fish or a vegetable, for the composition of a dish or a sauce, see the Menu Guide in the Practical Holiday Guide; it lists the most common culinary terms.

RABASTENS

Lavaur 22, Toulouse 37, Paris 707 km
pop 3835 ⊠ 81800   A3

Rabastens, known as *Rapistagnum* in ancient times, built from brick on the steep banks of the Tarn, is worth a stop on the route from Albi to Toulouse.

▶ Near the bridge (view), old part of city supported by powerful arch-ways, southern Gothic church of **Notre-Dame du Bourg**★ (13th-14thC) : fortified bell tower; Romanesque doorway with figured capitals showing New Testament scenes (inside, 15thC murals over-restored in the 19thC). ▶ 16th-18thC houses and mansions.

Nearby

▶ **Saint-Sulpice-la-Pointe** *(8 km SW)*, near the junction of the Agout and Tarn rivers : church (rebuilt ca. 1880) with fortified brick façade (14thC Toulouse style). ▶ **Château de Saint-Géry**★ *(4.5 km NE;* 14th-18thC), on the right bank of the Tarn ; furniture from Louis XIII to the Restoration (1814 ; *Sun. and nat. hols. pm, Easter-1 Nov.; daily pm Jul.-Aug.; or by appt. tel. 63.33.70.43).* ▶ **Lisle-sur-Tarn** *(9 km NE)*, a 12thC *bastide* (walled town) amid vineyards (Gaillac wines) : arcaded square ; old houses★ ; Gothic church (13thC Romanesque doorway ; Toulouse-style bell tower). **Raymond Lafage Museum** : drawings of this 17thC artist, local archaeology, history *(Sun. am, or by request for groups)*. View★ of the town from the bridge over the Tarn. ▶ **Salvagnac** *(12 km N)* : 15thC château ; restored mill.   □

Practical Information

RABASTENS
ⓘ 6, pl. St-Michel or mairie, ☎ 63.33.70.18.
SNCF ☎ 63.33.72.14.

Hotel :
★★ **Pré Vert** (L.F.), 54, prom. des Lices, ☎ 63.33.70.51, Visa, 13 rm Ⓟ ⑯ closed Sun eve (l.s.), 250. Rest. ◆◆ ⌡ closed Sun eve, 50-130.

⚐ ★★★**Les Auzerals** (45 pl), ☎ 63.33.70.36.

Nearby

LISLE-SUR-TARN, ⊠ 81310, 9 km NE.
SNCF ☎ 63.33.36.48.

Hotel :
★ **Princinor**, N 88, ☎ 63.33.35.44, Euro Visa, 11 rm Ⓟ ⑯ ⚄ 100. Rest. ◆◆ 50-150.

Recommended
Bicycle rental : *Tonuitti*, at the lake, ☎ 63.33.38.96.
Farmhouse-inn : *Le Noyer Blanc*, domaine du Noyer Blanc, ☎ 63.57.54.58, spec : pork products.

SAINT-SULPICE-LA-POINTE, ⊠ 81370, 8 km SW.

Hotel :
★ **Auberge de la Pointe** (L.F.), rte de Toulouse, ☎ 63.41.80.14, AE DC Visa, 8 rm Ⓟ ⑯ closed Wed, 4-25 Feb, 14-28 Oct, 65. Rest. ◆ ⌡ ⊗ Spec : *foie gras de canard maison, feuilleté de cuisses de grenouilles au gaillac, caille en bécasse aux croquettes d'aïl*, 55-110.

⚐ ★★**Le Borio Blanco** (35 pl), ☎ 63.41.81.19.

RÉALMONT

Albi 20, Toulouse 75, Paris 726 km
pop 2550 ⊠ 81120   A3

A *bastide* founded in 1270 on the Blima River, a refuge for "Albigeois heretics", now a pleasant resort.

▶ Church (15th-17thC ; Baroque altarpiece) on the shady town square. ▶ 13 km SE, ruined **château de Montredon** (12thC view). 17 km SE, 14thC Gothic church of **Notre-Dame-de-Ruffis**. To the E, the **Dadou Valley**.

Nearby

▶ **Saint-Gildas-des-Bois** *(17 km S)* : Romanesque church (12th-13thC), central bell tower from ancient abbey. ▶ 15 km W, near Béganne, **Estier** château (14th-15thC) enlarged 17thC, contains 24 chimneys *(1 Jul.-15 Sep., 2-7 except Tue.)*; 4 km farther W, **Léhélec** château (16th-18thC), sombre red shale and granite façade *(2-7 Sun., 15 May-15 Jun.; daily except Tue., Jul.-Aug.)*; small local museum.   □

Practical Information

RÉALMONT

Hotel :
● ★★ **Noël**, 1, rue de l'Hôtel-de-Ville, ☎ 63.55.52.80, AE DC Euro Visa, 14 rm Ⓟ ⊗ closed Sun eve and Mon (Oct-Jun), 190. Rest. ◆◆ ⚄ ⊗ Spec : *boudin noir au vinaigre, tournedos aux morilles, ris de veau à l'orange et au citron*, 120-200.

⚐ ★★**La Bâtisse** (65 pl), ☎ 63.55.52.80.

Nearby

MONT-ROC-TEILLET, ⊠ 81120 Réalmont, 25 km NE.

Hotel :
★ **Le Cantegrel** (L.F.), ☎ 63.55.70.37, AE Visa, 9 rm Ⓟ ⚄ ⑯ closed Nov-Feb, 105. Rest. ◆ ⚄ ⌡ ⚄ Spec : *écrevisses flambées aux lardons, ballotine de canard, foie gras et magret de canard grillé*, 75-110.

RODEZ*

Albi 78, Brive-la-Gaillarde 157, Paris 609 km
pop 26350 ⊠ 12000   B2

A grey and pink town in a bend of the Aveyron river that is justifiably proud of its mascot bell tower (87 m), its wide panoramas, the Aubrac plateau and its 2000 years of rich history.

▶ In medieval times, Rodez was divided into an episcopal city and a city ruled by the Counts of Rodez. Traces of the division are still apparent in the pedestrian precinct. Relatively prosperous until the 16thC, Rodez became a somewhat forgotten city, a stopover for workers going to more important industrial centres. **Cathedral**★★ (B-C3) : red sandstone structure built over 3 centuries; a masterpiece of religious architecture that was also an integral part of the town's defenses; the fortress-like appearance was relieved by the later addition of a central Flamboyant Gothic upper section★ topped with a Classical pediment, and a Flamboyant bell tower★★ (inside, 16thC chapel enclosure; 15thC choir screen; 17thC carved walnut organ-casing; several Gothic altarpieces★, including a Descent from the Cross). ▶ The **Episcopal Palace** (rebuilt in the 19thC) has a 17thC staircase copied from Fontainebleau (→ Île-de-France). The **Chanoines' quarter** (C2-3, around the Place de la Cité), contains several mansions : Rues Embergue, Bonald, Touat, Bosc and Penavayre. In the rival **Bourg quarter** (C3-4), former domaine of the Counts of Rodez and the merchants, see the Maison de l'Annonciation (16thC, Place du Bourg); the French Classical **Prefecture building**★; the Maison d'Armagnac (Place d'Olmet; façade embellished with sculpted medallions). ▶ Church of St. Amans (C4), rebuilt in 1758; partly Romanesque interior. ▶ **Fenaille museum** (C3) in Renaissance mansion : sculptures, 17 statue-menhirs★ and other archaeological finds from 2000 BC uncovered in southern Rouergue *(15 Jun.-15 Sep. 10-12 & 2:30-5:30, closed Sun., Mon. and nat. hols.; out of season, groups only by request tel. 65.68.02.27).* Former **Jesuit college**★ : chapel with interesting decoration *(ask at S.I.)*. **Studfarm**★ *(past Place du Foirail, via A2)* in a former charterhouse, 17th-18thC *(visits by request tel. 65.68.68.04, preferably during the winter season).*

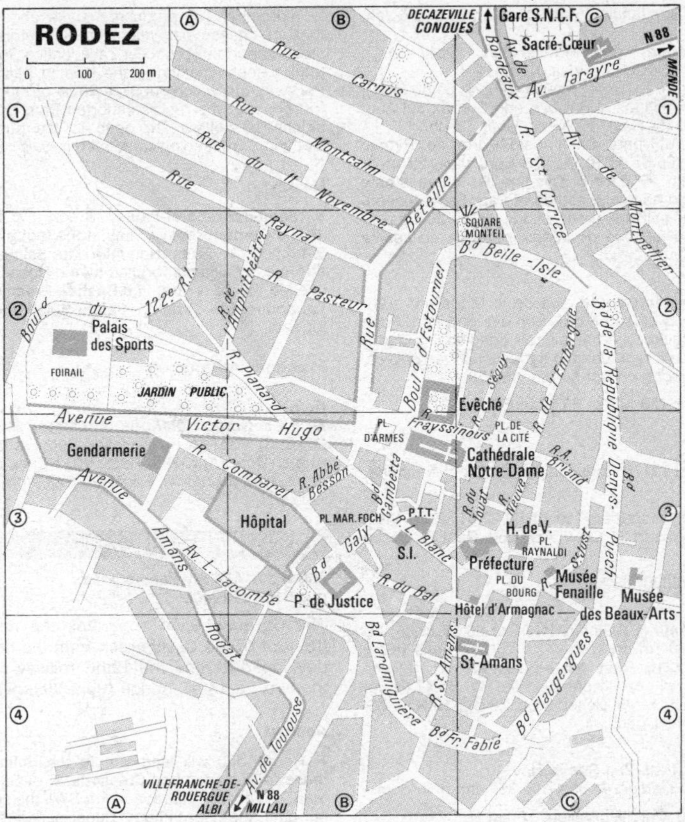
RODEZ
0
100
200 m
DECAZEVILLE
CONQUES
Gare S.N.C.F.
Sacré-Cœur
N 88
MENDE
Av. de Bordeaux
Av. Tarayre
Rue Carnus
Rue Montcalm
Rue du 11 Novembre
Rue Béteille
R. St Cyrice
Av. de Montpellier
SQUARE MONTEIL
Bd Beille-Isle
Rue Raynal
R. de l'Amphithéâtre
R. Pasteur
Rue 122e R.I.
Boul.d du 122e R.I.
Palais des Sports
FOIRAIL
JARDIN PUBLIC
R. Planard
Boul.d d'Estournel
R. Séguy
R. de l'Embergue
Bd de la République
Evêché
R. Frayssinous
PL. DE LA CITÉ
PL. D'ARMES
Avenue Victor Hugo
Gendarmerie
R. Combarel
R. Abbé Besson
Bd Gambetta
Cathédrale Notre-Dame
R. A. Briand
Bd Denys-Puech
Avenue Amans
Hôpital
PL. MAR. FOCH
P.T.T.
R. L. Blanc
R. du Touat
R. Neuve
H. de V.
PL. RAYNALDI
R. St-Just
Bd Galy
S.I.
Préfecture
Av. L. Lacombe
P. de Justice
R. du Bal
PL. DU BOURG
Musée Fenaille
Musée des Beaux-Arts
Hôtel d'Armagnac
Rodat
Bd Laromiguière
R. St Amans
St-Amans
Bd Flaugergues
Av. de Toulouse
Bd Fr. Fabié
VILLEFRANCHE-DE-ROUERGUE
ALBI
N 88
MILLAU
A
B
C
1
2
3
4

Nearby

▶ On the plateau S of Rodez, two pretty villages : ▶ **Sainte-Radegonde★ :** around a Renaissance house and a church★ fortified to shelter the whole village (13thC, fortified 14th-15thC, 13thC frescos). ▶ **Inières★ :** brownish-pink houses around a 15thC church-keep★ (polychrome stone Annunciation★, 16thC). ▶ **Palanges Forest** *(15km E)* : oaks and pines. ▶ Handsome houses on the edge of the plateau N of the forest. **Montrozier★ :** 15th-16thC château. **Anglars :** 16thC polychrome stone entombment of Christ. ▶ Two fortified farmsteads : **Les Bourines★★,** which belonged to the Hospitallers of Aubrac (→); and **Galinières★,** property of Bonneval abbey (richest in the region until the Revolution).

From Rodez to Conques★★ *(37 km, half-day)*

Handsome architecture in the Comtal plateau, beautiful villages, a museum, valleys, a gorge, and finally, Conques.

▶ **Rodez.** ▶ Château de Fontanges, 16thC, now a hotel. ▶ The **Comtal Plateau** (→) is dotted with châteaux : **Floyrac** (17thC) and **Onet** (15th-16thC). ▶ Road through the Faby Gorge (resurgence). ▶ **Salles-la-Source★★** one of the prettiest villages in Aveyron by a waterfall on the edge of the plateau; actually three villages one above the other, each with its church and castle. A few steps from a cave is a Rouergue Departmental Museum★ in a former spinning factory *(daily, Jul.-Aug.; low season group visits by request tel. 65.68.12.86).* ▶ **Sainte-Austremoine★,** another village on the edge of the plateau; Romanesque church★ (15thC Calvary). ▶ **Cougousse,** village around a Renaissance manor. ▶ **Marcillac-Vallon★,** centre of the Marcillac wine area; terraced hillsides★, pretty church. ▶ Chapel of **Saint-Jean-le-Froid★** *(4 km N)* : 16thC Pietà; panorama★ over the plateau, the Aubrac and the Cantal mountains. ▶ The **Cruou Valley★** leads to Bozouls (→) : well-to-do Rodez merchants had their vineyards and summer houses in this area. On the slope, **château de Combret** (17thC). ▶ **Belcaire fortress** overlooks the junction of the Ady and the Dourdou. ▶ Pleasant road to **Mouret★** *(6 km)* along the upper Dourdou Valley. At Mouret★ : feudal fortress composed of four castles within a single defensive wall. This detour leads to Conques along the ridge; poor road (GR62), but spectacular views. ▶ Once the property of Conques, the 16th-18thC mill at Sagnes stands at the entrance to the Dourdou gorges. ▶ Site in **Bancarel★ :** from the right of the village entrance, the best view over Conques (→). □

Practical Information

RODEZ
ℹ pl. Foch (B3), ☎ 65.68.02.27.
✈ *Rodez-Marcillac*, 10 km NW, ☎ 65.68.52.53.
SNCF (C1), ☎ 65.42.50.50/65.42.08.03.
Car rental : *Avis*, train station (C1); 7, av. V.-Hugo (A-B3), ☎ 65.68.00.66.

Hotels :
★★★ ***Biney***, 7, bd Gambetta (B3), ☎ 65.68.01.24, DC Euro Visa, 28 rm P ♨ ♿ closed 15 Dec-7 Jan, 145.
★★★ ***Le Parc*** (France-Accueil), 1, pl. d'Armes (B3), ☎ 65.68.11.22, Tx 530366, AE DC Euro Visa, 20 rm

closed Sat eve , Sun lunch (15 Oct-15 Mar), 23 Dec-5 Jan, 210.
★★★ ***Tour Maje*** (Inter-Hôtel), bd Gally (B3), ☎ 65.68.34.68, AE DC Euro Visa, 48 rm, 210.
★★ ***Midi Dauty*** (L.F.), 1, rue Beteille (B2), ☎ 65.68.02.07, Euro Visa, 34 rm Ⓟ closed Sat eve and Sun ex Jul-Aug, 15 Dec-15 Feb, 175. Rest. ♦ closed Mon, 50-120.
Le Régent (I.L.A.), parc Saint-Joseph, rte de Rignac (off map C1), ☎ 65.67.03.30, AE DC Euro Visa, 20 rm Ⓟ ♨ ♿ 300. Rest. ● ♦♦♦ ♿ This fine old house is new to the Ferries who have just settled at Parc Saint-Joseph. Good cooking is still the order of the day : *queues de langoustines à la julienne de cèpes, daurade au beurre d'orange*, 90-250.

Restaurant :
● ♦♦♦ ***Le Saint-Amans***, 12, rue de la Madeleine (C4), ☎ 65.68.03.18 ♪ ♿ closed Mon , Sun eve and Feb. Posh ambience with background music, air conditioning and a modern decor : *paupiette de ris d'agneau aux deux olives, panaché de poissons en pot-au-feu*, 95-150.

⛺ ★★★★*Layoule* (70 pl), ☎ 65.67.09.52.

Nearby

CASTELPERS, ✉ 12170 Requista, 13 km SE of **Naucelle**.

Hotel :
★★ ***Château de Castelpers***, ☎ 65.69.22.61, Euro Visa, 8 rm Ⓟ ♨ ♿ closed 31 Oct-1 Apr, 260. Rest. ♦ closed Sun, 115-140.

NAUCELLE, ✉ 12800, 33 km.

Hotels :
★★ ***Viaduc du Viaur*** (L.F., Inter-Hôtel), ☎ 65.69.23.86, AE DC Euro Visa, 10 rm Ⓟ ♨ ♿ ♪ half pens (h.s.), closed (Oct-Apr), 210. Rest. ♦♦ ♪ 75-130.
★★ ***Voyageurs***, pl. de l'Hôtel-de-Ville, ☎ 65.47.01.34, Euro Visa, 15 rm Ⓟ closed Mon, 28 Oct-13 Nov, 75. Rest. ♦ 40-85 ; child : 30.

Recommended
Events : *tripe festival*, 2nd Sun in Nov.
Nightclubs : *Le Valadier*, ☎ 65.47.05.36, with grill-room.

NUCES, ✉ 12330 Marcillac-Vallon, 10 km N.

Hotel :
★ ***La Diligence***, route de Rodez, ☎ 65.72.60.20, AE Euro Visa, 7 rm Ⓟ ♨ closed Sun eve and Mon ex Jul.-Aug., 1 Jan-15 Feb, 120. Rest. ♦ ♿ closed Sun eve. Spec : *poêlée de St Jacques et pleurotes au beurre de tomate, filet d'agneau en croûte à l'infusion de thym*, 120 ; child : 35.

ONET-LE-CHÂTEAU, ✉ 12850, 4 km N on the D 601.

Hotels :
● ★★★ ***Hostellerie de Fontanges***, rte de Conques, ☎ 65.42.20.28, Tx 521142, AE DC Euro Visa, 46 rm Ⓟ ♨ night-club, 230. Rest. ● ♦♦ A modern hostelry in an authentic 16thC setting. Spec : *foie gras, confits, magrets*, 65-180 ; child : 35.
★ ***La Rocade*** (L.F.), La Roquette, 3 km, ☎ 65.67.17.12, AE Euro Visa, 17 rm Ⓟ ♨ ♿ closed Fri eve and Sun eve, 27 Jun-13 Jul, 19 Dec-10 Jan, 90. Rest. ♦ ♪ 50-80.

SALLES-LA-SOURCE, ✉ 12330 Marcillac-Vallon, 14 km N.

Restaurant :
♦ ***Auberge de la Cascade***, ☎ 65.71.82.97, closed 1-15 Jan. An interesting little eatery, 50-80.

ROQUEFORT-SUR-SOULZON*

Millau 24, Lodève 65, Paris 655 km
pop 880 ✉ 12250 C3

Roquefort cheese is made with milk from ewes that graze the plateau ; it is matured in the natural caves of the *causse*, where the temperature and humidity remain at the ideal level year-round.

▶ Altogether, 13 producers make about 16,000 metric tons of cheese per year ; the Roquefort *Société* is the most important producer, accounting for 75 % of the total. Cheese-making is the leading pastoral industry of the Aveyron, which supplies 90 % of the milk for Roquefort cheese ; the rest is imported from Corsica. ▶ Several cheese **cellars** are open to the public (take warm clothing). Archaeological Museum *(daily, 9-11 & 12-6)*.

Nearby

▶ **Saint-Jean-Saint-Paul★** *(8 km S)*, fortified village. ▶ The **Cernon Valley★** runs at the foot of the Larzac plateau (→). ▶ From Roquefort to Sainte-Eulalie 25 km through old villages fortified by the Hospitallers (who succeeded the Templars) : **La Bastide-Pradines** and **Mélac★, Lapanouse-de-Cernon, Sainte-Eulalie-de-Cernon★** (→ Larzac). □

Practical Information

Hotel :
● ★★★ ***Grand Hôtel***, rue de Lamas, ☎ 65.59.90.20, AE DC Euro Visa, 16 rm Ⓟ closed Sun eve and Mon ex Jul-Aug, 1 Oct-1 Apr, 295. Rest. ♦♦ ♪ Spec : *biscuit de sole et saumon au basilic, tourte au roquefort*, 80-200.

SAINT-AFFRIQUE

Millau 31, Albi 82, Paris 662 km
pop 9188 ✉ 12400 C3

The Sorgues River separates the medieval city at the foot of the Caylus rock from the new district that developed around the 19thC railway station. Linking the two : a 14thC bridge (Pont-Vieux★).

Nearby

▶ Route D50 will lead you to the **dolmens,** especially those of **Tiergues** and **Crassous,** N of Saint-Affrique plateau. ▶ **Vabres-l'Abbaye** *(4 km SW)*, the seat of a bishopric until the Revolution ; Renaissance houses, French Classical mansions ; the former cathedral was rebuilt in the 18thC (organ★). ▶ **Saint-Izaire** *(16 km W)* : where bishops and canons maintained summer residences on the Dourdou. ▶ The **Sorgues Valley★** leads to the heart of the Larzac plateau *(50 km upstream from Saint-Affrique to La Couvertoirade, on D7)* and invites exploration by bicycle, off the tourist routes. ▶ **Saint-Affrique.** ▶ **Lapeyre :** Gothic bridge at village entrance ; medieval streets ; re-used Romanesque tympanum on the doorway of a house *(le château)* ; another Romanesque tympanum★ on the cemetery church (tomb of the poet Byron's daughter). ▶ On the opposite bank : **château de Montalègre** (16thC). ▶ **Versols,** fortified village around a 15thC keep. ▶ **Saint-Félix-de-Sorgues :** commandery of the Hospitallers ; a Gothic bridge leads to the hamlet of **Saint-Caprazy★** (former priory). ▶ A pleasant road to **Nonenque Abbey,** where noble Rouergue families once consigned their unmarriageable daughters *(no visits)*. ▶ **Château de Latour,** 15thC : fortifications. ▶ **Marnhagues :** Romanesque church. ▶ **Cornus,** in a fold of the Larzac plateau (→) : church. ▶ To N, view over Larzac and Cévennes regions from the rocks at **La Tour d'Aiguillon.** ▶ To S, **source of the River Sorgues★,** near a 15thC keep; the **Mas Raynal sinkhole** opens at the foot of the **Guilhaumard plateau★ :** spectacular. □

Practical Information

SAINT-AFFRIQUE
ℹ bd de Verdun, ☎ 65.99.09.05 (h.s.).
SNCF ☎ 65.99.01.66.

Hotel :
★★ ***Moderne*** (L.F.), 54, av. Alphonse-Pezet, ☎ 65.49.20.44, Euro Visa, 39 rm Ⓟ closed 15 Dec-15 Jan, 150. Rest. ♦ ♪ ♿ 60-145 ; child : 45.

⚠ ★★*Municipal* (50 pl), ☎ 65.99.05.54.

Recommended
Rural-gîte : at St-Victor-et-Melvieu (15 km N), *Le Relais des Raspes*, ☎ 65.62.51.88.

Nearby

BROQUIES, ⊠ 12480, 25 km.

Hotel :
★ *Le Relays du Chasteau* (L.F.), Brousse-le-Château, ☎ 65.99.40.15, Euro Visa, 14 rm Ⓟ ⟨ ⟩ pens (h.s.), closed Fri eve and Sat lunch, 15 Dec-15 Jan, 340. Rest. ♦ 50-100.

SAINT-ROME-DE-CERNON, ⊠ 12490, 10 km NE.

Hotel :
★ *Commerce*, ☎ 65.62.33.92, 13 rm ⟨ ⟩ closed 21 Dec-5 Jan, 100. Rest. ♦ ⟨ 35-80.

SAUVETERRE-DE-ROUERGUE★★

Rodez 40, Albi 54, Paris 664 km
pop 793 ⊠ 12800 Naucelle   B2

A beautiful *bastide* (walled town →), hardly altered since its foundation 7 centuries ago, with all the classic elements of the *bastides* of SW France (chequerboard layout, arcaded square, fortifications, churchkeep). 16thC carved cross ; museum. Up to the 19thC, this was a busy town but it soon found itself too far from railroads and major cities.

Nearby

▶ This area of lower Ségala (→) is wild, difficult to reach and framgented by countless ravines and gorges.
▶ A centre for the Resistance during WWII : **Villelongue** museum-chapel in the **Lézert gorge** (memorabilia of the writer André Malraux, 1901-76). ▶ The painter Toulouse-Lautrec (→ Albi) spent his childhood at the **château du Bosc,** near the Viaur gorges *(13 km SE)* : museum *(10-12 & 2-6).*

Practical Information _____

Hotel :
★★ *Auberge du Sénéchal* (L.F.), ☎ 65.47.05.78, AE DC Euro Visa, 10 rm Ⓟ ⟨ ⟩ closed 31 Oct-1 May, 160. Rest. ♦ ⟨ 50-150.

⚠ *Le Valadier* (30 pl), ☎ 65.47.05.36

SÉGALA Region

                                            B2
Ségala is an isolated region between the Aveyron and the Viaur, a high plateau on the fringe of the Massif Central mountains. Once a poverty-stricken area whose inhabitants lived on little but rye-bread and chestnuts, Ségala is now prosperous farmland, thanks to the railway, the Viaur viaduct and the advent of fertilizers.   ☐

Practical Information _____

BARAQUEVILLE, ⊠ 12160, 19 km SW of **Rodez**.
☎ ☎ 65.69.01.52.

Hotel :
● ★★★ *Ségala Plein Ciel*, ☎ 65.69.03.45, Euro Visa, 47 rm Ⓟ ⟨ ⟩ closed Fri eve and Sun eve, Mon, 220. Rest. ♦ ⟨ ⟩ 80-150.

Recommended
Chambres d'hôtes : *Le Moulinou*, ☎ 65.70.13.55, horseback riding, trout fishing. Farm produce for sale. Disco-restaurant.
Events : *tripe festival*, 3rd Sun in Nov.

RIEUPEYROUX, ⊠ 12240, 21 km W of **Rodez**.

Hotel :
● ★★ *Commerce* (L.F.), rue de l'Hom, ☎ 65.65.53.06, Euro Visa, 28 rm Ⓟ ⟨ ⟩ closed Sun eve and Mon lunch ex Jul-Aug, 20 Dec-20 Jan, 115. Rest. ● ♦ ⟨ Local cuisine at low prices. Spec : *foie gras, confits* and homemade pastries, 50-100 ; child : 40.

SÉVÉRAC-LE-CHÂTEAU

Millau 32, Saint-Flour 109, Paris 600 km
pop 2838 ⊠ 12150   C2

Sévérac : view★ from the rocky outcrop in a valley between the Lévezou and the *causses*.

▶ The old town, on top of a butte (hill) crowned by a ruined **castle**, has a resolutely medieval air. The fortress was rebuilt in the 17thC. The steep narrow streets are lined with 15th-16thC shops.   ☐

Practical Information _____

ⓘ rue des Douves, ☎ 65.46.67.31 (h.s.) ; mairie, ☎ 65.46.62.63.
SNCF ☎ 65.71.61.19.

Hotel :
★ *Causses*, av. A.-Briand, ☎ 65.71.60.15, Euro Visa, 13 rm Ⓟ ⟨ ⟩ closed Sun eve, 15-31 Oct, 90. Rest. ♦ ⟨ closed Mon noon, 50-70 ; child : 30.

⚠ ★★*Les Calquières* (125 pl), ☎ 65.46.64.82.

SIDOBRE and LACAUNE Mounts★★

                                            B4
From Castres to Mazamet *(approx. 170 km ; full day).*
North of the Montagne Noire (Black Mountain) and the Espinouse mountains on the western edge of the Cévennes, the Sidobre Plateau is separated from the Lacaune mountains by the Agout Valley. The granite plateau is strewn with rocks in fantastic shapes and positions. The Lacaune region includes the plateau, a cold, monotonous tableland between 700 m and 1 000 m altitude, and higher up, the wooded slopes of the mountain, contrasting with the surrounding Mediterranean landscapes.

▶ **Castres** (→). ▶ **Burlats :** ruined Benedictine priory ; near the Agout river, Romanesque house. ▶ **Roquecourbe :** 14thC bridge over the Agout ; covered arcades around the square. ▶ Farther up the river, in a loop called Sacaradelle, pinnacle of the **Sainte Juliane hill :** traces of a Celtic sanctuary ; a ruined Cathar cemetery y destroyed during the 12th-13thC. ▶ From **Lacrouzette**, a stone-working town, explore rock formations★ including the balancing rock of **Peyro Clavado★**, as well as **Lake Merle** *(4 km SE).* Along D58 : good views of the valley and the **Agout gorge★.** ▶ **Château de Ferrières :** rebuilt 15th-16thC ; Upper Languedoc Protestant Musuem (historic documents ; *daily 15 Jun-15 Sep ; Sun and Nat. hols pm out of season ; group visits to the furnished apartments by request,* ☎ 63.74.03.53). Maison du Luthier (lute-maker) : organised by the upper Languedoc Nature Reseve ; a lutemaker's workshop, hand printing shop, ethnographic museum *(visits by request, ask at the château) ;* concerts in season. ▶ Beyond Vabre, up the winding Gijou Valley★ on the north flank of the Lacaune plateau : **château de Lacaze** (rebuilt 18thC) ; medieval ruins of **Viane** castle, **Gourp-Fumant,** a natural site near Gijounet. ▶ **Lacaune :** 17thC southern Gothic church, 14thC fountain, 18thC château de Calmels. ▶ Through **Montroucous Forest** to the **Bassine Pass** (alt. 885 m). ▶ **Brassac :** on either bank of the Agout ; two bridges (one 14thC Gothic), ruined ramparts, 17thC château with two towers by the river's edge. ▶ **Vialavert** *(2 km W) :* Sept-Faux trembling rock. 2 km S from **Saint-Salvy :** Balme Rocks. ▶ Through the Rialet

and the Vintrou to the Arn (or Banquet) **gorges,** leading
down to Mazamet (→).   ☐

Practical Information _____

BRASSAC, ⊠ 81260, 24 km E of **Castres.**

Hotel :
★ *Café de Paris* (L.F.), 8, pl. de l'Hôtel-de-Ville,
☎ 63.74.00.31, 11 rm Ⓟ half pens (h.s.), closed Sat-Sun
(l.s.), 30 Oct-10 Nov, 280. Rest. ♦ 45-65.

Recommended
Riding gîte : *ferme La Roussarié,* rte d'Angles,
☎ 65.74.97.32. Full board for children 13 and older ; horseback riding, excursions.
LACROUZETTE, ⊠ 81210 Roquecourbe, 16 km NE
of **Castres.**

Hotel :
★★ *Le Relais du Sidobre* (L.F.), 8, rte de Vabre,
☎ 63.50.60.06, Visa, 22 rm ⫖ ⚱ 150. Rest. ♦ 55-120.

SYLVANÈS**

Camarès 9, Saint-Affrique 23, Paris 685 km
pop 117 ⊠ 12360 Camarès   C3

The Abbey of Sylvanès, one of the finest examples of
Cistercian architecture in the south of France, is set
in a valley between the Lévezou and Lacaune mountains, on the borders of the Rouergue and Albigeois regions.

▶ The abbey was founded in 1138 by a lord in repentance
for a lifetime of brigandage. The **church,** with its single
wide nave, was the model for many others in the south. It
is now an important cultural centre (concerts, exhibitions,
seminars). The abbey buildings are not open to visitors. ▶ **Bains-de-Sylvanès,** a thermal spa built in the
17th-18thC by the monks.   ☐

TARN Valley*

                                                     B3

From Millau to Saint-Sernin *(140 km ; difficult roads ;
full day)*

The Tarn Valley offers more than just its famous Gorges ; between the Camarès and Albigeois regions, the
river runs through schist walls, accompanied part of
the way by the viaducts and tunnels of a ghost railway
that was abandoned before it ever came into service.

▶ **Peyre :** houses huddled against the cliff. ▶ Valleys
and gorges, alternating vines and walnut trees. ▶ Fortifications at **Comprégnac.** ▶ The valley broadens at **Saint-
Rome-de-Tarn :** remains of fortifications and Renaissance
houses ; ruined castle of Auriac. ▶ The **Pouget-Truel**
power station is fed by the Lévezou dams ; other dams on
the Tarn. ▶ **Brousse-le-Château★ :** site overlooking the
junction of the Tarn and the Alrance (Gothic bridge) ; village and fortified castle restored by a youth group ; Romanesque-Gothic church, once a halt for pilgrims to Compostela. ▶ **Coupiac :** 15thC château in a bend of the river ;
good view of the Tarn and the old village of Lincou ; re-
used tympanum on the church. ▶ **Plaisance,** on an outcrop above the Rance River, opposite rival **Curvalle ;**
church★ from former Benedictine abbey, modified in the
15thC (carved decoration). ▶ **Saint-Sernin-sur-Rance★,**
former stronghold on a hillside between two valleys : half-
timbered houses, 15th-16thC mansions ; carved ornamentation in the Gothic church.   ☐

Practical Information _____

BROUSSE-LE-CHÂTEAU, ⊠ 12480 Broquiès, 9 km W
of **Broquiès.**

Hotel :
● ★ *Relays du Château* (L.F.), ☎ 65.99.40.15, Euro Visa,

14 rm Ⓟ ⫖ ⚱ closed Fri eve and Sat lunch, 15 Dec-15 Jan,
110. Rest. ♦ ⚹ Nice little restaurant, 55-75.

COUPIAC, ⊠ 12550, 18 km W of **Saint-Sernin-sur-Rance.**

Hotel :
★ *Renaissance,* ☎ 65.99.78.44, Visa, 10 rm ⫖ ⚱ closed
Sat (l.s.), 100. Rest. ♦ 50-130.

PLAISANCE, ⊠ 12710, 10 km NW of **Saint-Sernin-sur-
Rance.**

Hotel :
Les Magnolias (L.F.), ☎ 65.99.77.34, AE Euro Visa, 5 rm
Ⓟ ⚱ ⫖ closed Mon, Feb, 1-15 Nov, 100. Rest. ● ♦
closed Mon. Modernized regional fare. Superb setting
(16th-17thC), 70-130.

SAINT-SERNIN-SUR-RANCE, ⊠ 12380, 21 km E of **Alban.**

Hotel :
● ★★ *Carayon* (L.F.), pl. du Fort, ☎ 65.99.60.26, AE DC
Euro Visa, 23 rm Ⓟ ⫖ ⚱ ♪ closed Sun eve and Mon
(Nov-Mar), 160. Rest. ● ♦♦ ⚹ ⚱ A splendid view of
the Rance Valley, the better to enjoy the rustic peace
and comfort and the old-fashioned *boudin aux pommes et
oignons confits, le pigeonneau rouergat, la salade gourmande au foie gras d'oie,* 50-180.

VILLEFRANCHE-DE-ROUERGUE**

Cahors 61, Albi 72, Paris 620 km
pop 13869 ⊠ 12200   A2

Medieval silver mines assured the prosperity of this
13thC *bastide,* fortified in the 14thC. Ancient houses
have largely been preserved and are now being restored. The town is a centre of activity for the western
half of the department.

▶ The regular street-plan is still evident ; **Place Notre-
Dame★★** is surrounded by arcaded houses, many richly
ornamented ; best seen on market-day *(Thu.)* or Fair-day
on the fourth Thursday of the month, when the square
is cleared of cars. ▶ The gate-tower of the **collegiate
church of Notre-Dame★★** is integrated into the covered
arcades ; 58 m high, it rivals the tower in Rodez (→). The
church was built over 3 centuries, starting in 1260, from
apse to façade (inside, 15thC stalls). ▶ **Chapel of the
Black Penitents★★ :** 17thC Baroque decor ; choir stalls
from Loc-Dieu, by André Sulpice, a 15thC sculptor
(Jul.-Aug., 9:30-12 & 2:30-6:30). ▶ **Cabrol Museum :** in a
Louis XV mansion, material relating to local personalities ;
antiquities *(same hours as the chapel).* ▶ The 15thC **Char-
terhouse★★,** a great monument of the Rouergue, founded
in 1451 by a rich local merchant and his wife, and completed in very short time *(under restoration ; guided tours
Jul.-Aug. 9:30-12 & 2:30-6 ; unaccompanied visits rest of
year) ;* the large cloister was surrounded by the monks'
cells ; the small cloister★★ is a Flamboyant Gothic structure ; the chapel (stalls by André Sulpice) shelters the
monumental tomb★ of the founders ; 16thC stained glass
in the chapterhouse ; in the refectory : Flamboyant Gothic
pulpit from which the Bible was read aloud during meals.

Nearby

Loc-Dieu Cistercian abbey, on the borders of Rouergue and Quercy, converted into a château in the 19thC ;
cloister★ similar to that at Villefranche *(Jul.-Aug. 10-12 &
3-6:30, closed Tue.).*

Round trip N of Villefranche *(approx. 70 km, half-day)*

▶ The **Villeneuve plateau** begins outside Villefranche :
oak woods, crumbling stone walls, sturdy dovecotes and
turreted houses. ▶ The road around **Villeneuve★** gives a
good view of the layout as well as the remains of the fortifications. The 11thC geometrical plan was based on an
arcaded triangular central area : 14th-16thC houses, grain
measures under the arcades ; 11thC **church** modeled on
that of the Holy Sepulchre in Jerusalem, according to the
donor's wishes when he left on a pilgrimage to the Holy

Land; modified in the 14thC (14thC frescos, stalls, 15thC Christ). ▶ **Foissac** : caverns; traces of men and animals that lived there in the Bronze Age *(Jun.-Sep., 10-11:30 & 2-6, except Jul.-Aug., closes at 6:30; out of season by request tel. 65.64.77.04, for groups.).* ▶ Opposite Saint-Pierre-Toirac, the banks of the Lot (→). ▶ **Salvagnac** : feudal castle; the Romanesque church was its chapel. ▶ Near **Lacapelle-Balaguier** the landscape becomes typical of the plateau (dolmens; 15thC bell tower keep of **Sainte-Croix**). ▶ **Toulonjac,** a suburb of Villefranche built around the 15thC castle and Gothic church : bell tower similar to that at Villefranche (inside, 16thC statues). ☐

Practical Information _____

VILLEFRANCHE-DE-ROUERGUE
ⓘ prom. Guiraudet, ☎ 65.45.13.18.
SNCF ☎ 65.45.03.16.

Hotels :
● ★★ *Lagarrigue*, pl. Bernard-Lhez, ☎ 65.45.01.12, Euro Visa, 20 rm Ⓟ ⌔ ⚐ closed Sun (l.s.), Dec-Easter, 210. Rest. ♦♦ ⌔ ♪ ⚐ 60-130.
★★ *L'Univers* (L.F.), 2, pl. de la République, ☎ 65.45.15.63, Euro Visa, 32 rm ⌔ ḁ 150. Rest. ♦ ⌔ ♪ closed Fri eve and Sat, 1-15 Mar, 15-30 Oct, 45-80.

⋀ ★★★*Le Teulel* (100 pl), ☎ 65.45.16.24.

Nearby

FOISSAC, ⊠ 12200 Villefranche-de-Rouergue, 22 km N.

Hotel :
★★ *Relais de Frejeroques* (L.F.), Fréjeroques, on CD 922, ☎ 65.64.62.80, Euro Visa, 16 rm Ⓟ ⌔ ░ ⚐ ⚐ closed Sat and Sun am (l.s.), 100. Rest. ♦ ⌔ ḁ 40-110.

VILLENEUVE, ⊠ 12260, 10 km N.

Hotel :
★ *La Poste*, ☎ 65.45.62.13, 14 rm Ⓟ ⚐ pens, closed 15 Dec-15 Jan, 130. Rest. ♦ 45-80.

Savoy

▶ Savoy or Savoie, a region of alpine lakes, glaciers and snowy peaks, shares with its Swiss and Italian neighbors the hordes of skiers and mountain climbers, the brilliant wildflowers and hardy animals, chamois, marmots and eagles which thrive at high altitudes. Chamonix is one of the most famous ski resorts in the world — the opening of the Mont-Blanc tunnel in 1965 has helped make it the uncontested capital of skiing and alpine sports in France. But the region has many other ski resorts which are almost as well-known : Les Arcs, La Plagne, Courchevel, Tignes/Val d'Isère. Savoy's history too was linked to its Alpine neighbors, and the region knew many centuries of independence before it came under the sway of the French crown.

The Savoy of the 1980s has adjusted well to the modern era, with its investment in nuclear energy and advanced technology, its healthy and outdoors image, its pure alpine waters which are even more famous than its delicious wines, its winter sports, its sheer falls and outcrops of rock which attract the most seasoned climbers and its deep valleys over which soar modern disciples of Icarus with their multicoloured wings.

Savoy also offers the more tranquil, everyday joys of its villages and hamlets : meadows and running water, the deep blue of the gentian, the silent ballet of the jackdaw. There are flourishing markets and deep forests, creamy Reblochon cheese from Grand-Bornand, wooden crosses on country tracks, the little wooden figurines of the Devils of Bessan repeated in church frescos, the sybilline mottos of ornamental sundials, and the special architecture of the houses, with their wooden galleries and balconies for drying wood and clothes in the winter season. In places you will see the characteristic *greniers* — isolated store houses where fodder for the livestock, the family's Sunday clothes and sometimes their important papers used to be kept to guard against fire. □

Don't miss

★★★ Lake Annecy A2, Lake Bourget A2, Chamonix-Mont-Blanc B2, Grandes Alpes Route B2-3, Lac Léman (Lake Geneva) A-B1.

★★ Annecy A2, The Beaufortain region B2, The Chablais region B1, Évian-les-Bains B1, The Faucigny region B1, Megève B2, Saint-Gervais B2, Vanoise Massif B3.

★ Aix-les-Bains A2, the Bauges region A2, Bessans A-B3, Chambéry A2, La Clusaz A2, Combloux B2, Courchevel B3, La Maurienne A-B3, Menthon-Saint-Bernard A2, Morzine B1, Pralognan-la-Vanoise B3, the Salève region A1, The Tarentaise region B2, Thonon-les-Bains A1, Val d'Isère B3, Valloire A3.

Weekend tips

A few steps from the station at Chamonix, the téléphérique (cable-car) of the Aiguilles du Midi opens the way to the high mountains. Lunch in Chamonix. In the afternoon the train from Montenvers winds past peaks and crests up to the famous Mer de Glace (Ice Sea). Spend the night at Lavanché. The next day discover Les Grands Montets and the Col (Pass) des Montets with its nature reserve.

Savoyard "grenier"

Wooden walls

Wooden tiles

Stone walls

● Brief regional history

Up to the 8thC BC

The discovery of tools, mostly in the Tarentaise and Maurienne areas, shows that **shepherd tribes** from the north of Italy inhabited Savoie from the Bronze Age onward. ● During the Iron Age, the Gauls appeared. From the mouth of the Isère to the banks of the Valance, their communities were more or less united and known as the **Allobroges.** Conquered by Rome (122-118BC), the country of the Allobroges seems to have been from this time on a natural communications link between the valleys of northwestern Italy and the valleys around the Rhône, in spite of the difficulties of terrain. The **highway from Vienne to Milan** runs through the region; Aix (Aquae) and the valley of the Rhône, already much used by shipping, were both flourishing at this time.

9th-12thC

Subject to Lothair (843), later to Burgundy (888), Savoie fell under the nominal authority of the Holy Roman Empire in 1032. At this time, the first representative of the **House of Savoy** appears in the person of **Humbert aux Blanches Mains,** a native of the Vienne region. This dynasty was to Savoie what the Capets were to France. From county to duchy to royalty, this family created a sovereign state of rich and complex character, based on political and economic exploitation of its position at the crossroads of Europe. By dint of shrewd marriages and political alliances, the Blanches Mains eventually ruled both northern and southern slopes of Savoie, "the gatekeepers of the Alps". ● The 11th-12thC also saw the rapid spread of important monastic orders (Cistercians, Carthusians).

13th-14thC

From the reign of Amédée IV to Amédée VIII Savoie grew steadily in power. The Counts of Savoie owned Turin and Geneva, and the passes of Mont-Cenis and Petit St. Bernard, where there were hospices or inns for the benefit of travellers, made Savoie the crossroads for the **constant traffic** into Italy from Champagne, the Germanic countries and the South of France. Small but well governed, Savoie took its place in the affairs of the great European states.

15th-16thC

The Emperor Sigismund made **Amadeus VIII** the Duke of Savoie in 1416, and statesmanship and wisdom made this Prince without doubt the greatest of his dynasty. Under his reign and during the reigns that followed, Chambéry, Annecy and their abbeys became centres of artistic activity and rivals in elegance. ● The Dukes of Savoie, owners also of Nice and Piedmont (1429) began to play off **France against the Hapsburg Empire,** a game that sometimes brought rewards and sometimes losses. It was in fact because of this power that the Duchy was invaded by François I of France (1536), and the Bernese laid waste the Chablais, an area that, converted to Protestantism, passed directly under the control of Calvin. After his subsequent victory over France at Saint-Quentin (1557), Duke Emmanuel-Philibert was able to restore the state of Savoie; however, since Chambéry was too close to France for comfort, the Duke transferred his capital to Turin. Henceforth **Piedmont was**

of greater importance than Savoie, in spite of the impression of riches created by mines, fairs and flourishing commercial life. ● The region was periodically decimated by plagues.

17th-18thC
By the 17thC, Savoie was thoroughly imbued with **French culture.** Honoré d'Urfé (social commentator, 1567-1625) stayed at Chambéry; St. François de Sales (→ Annecy), an exemplary Savoyard, enriched French literature with his "Introduction to the Devout Life" (1608). ● In the confrontation between France and Austria, Savoie played its hand with varying results. Louis XIV invaded on two occasions; but by the Treaty of Utrecht (1713) **Duke Victor-Amédée II** found himself in the winning camp; he received the crown of Sicily, which he soon exchanged for that of Sardinia. At the head of his **Sardinian States,** this Prince began to instigate reforms that were well ahead of their time. ● At that time, 90 out of

100 Savoyards lived from the land; life became less precarious with the introduction of the potato (1750), maize (1780), and communal lands for sheep grazing. The introduction of **watch-making** in Faussigny made full use of the ingenuity and manual dexterity that northern Savoyards had always possessed, and that is exemplified today in the screw-cutting industry of the Haute-Savoie. ● The **first ascent of Mont Blanc** was made in **1786;** in 1792, Savoie was occupied by the forces of the French Revolution, and rechristened the Department of Mont-Blanc.

19th-20thC
By the **Treaty of Paris** (1815), King Victor Emmanuel I of Italy recovered his Sardinian domains together with Savoie. The laws in force before 1792 were re-established and the province settled into what has been called the **Buon Governo,** a conservative era with rigorous morals and severe police controls. ● In 1848, however, the King granted a constitution (Le

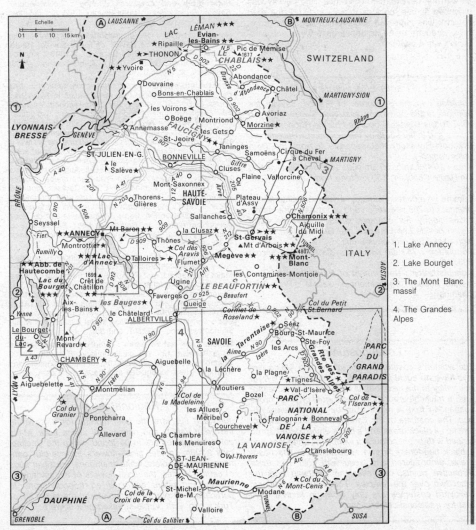

1. Lake Annecy

2. Lake Bourget

3. The Mont Blanc massif

4. The Grandes Alpes

Statuto) that allowed for the creation in Turin of two chambers of Parliament. Savoie was to be represented in terms of its physical importance and not its historical stature. This led to widespread discontent, with grievances ranging from the omnipresence of the Piedmontais in the administration tc the use of Savoyard taxes to benefit foreigners, and the refusal to create a French-language University at Chambéry. At this period the liberal party was reborn. People looked more and more to the France of Napoleon III. ● In 1858, the Italian statesman **Cavour** (1810-61) and **Napoleon III** agreed that in exchange for French aid to drive the Austrians out of Italy, France would receive Savoie and Nice. At the **plebiscite** of 23 and 24 April 1868, the Savoyards voted massively for union with France. ● Thus impoverished Savoie was joined to rich France. After a period of setback stemming from lack of investment and strong commercial competition, the province, divided into the **two departments** of Savoie and Haute-Savoie, became integrated with the development of France : the railway was extended across the Alps to Fréjus (1872), the road network was improved and tourism began to grow ; heavy industry made its appearance with hydroelectricity ("white coal").

Facts and Figures

Location : *In the SE corner of France, Savoie has frontiers in the north and east with Switzerland and Italy. To the west it is bounded by the Rhône and the Guiers and in the south by the mountains (Belledonne, Grandes Rousses) that separate it from the Dauphiné region.*
Area : *10 428 km², 50 km wide between Geneva and the Haute Chablais ; 150 km long from Léman to Galibier.*
Climate : *A mountain climate, varying with altitude and orientation. The vegetation and crops show the differences clearly. For example, vines grow in the warm region beside Lac Léman (Lake Geneva), but on the high peaks the climate is arctic.*
Population : *753 000 (Haute-Savoie 447 795 ; Savoie 305 118).*
Administration : *Department of Haute-Savoie : Prefecture Annecy ; Department of Savoie : Prefecture Chambéry.*

Local costume

The women's costumes worn in the high Alpine valleys have no equal in cut and colour. They vary from one valley to the next, but all have the same accessories ; a multicoloured shawl and a gold or silver cross suspended from a metal heart by a black velvet ribbon. The costume of the Tarentaise region is characteristic : a black dress and a black embroidered apron striped with bright colours, a wimple of white lace and a black headdress known as a frontière. *The headdress, embroidered and laced with gold, has three distinctive points, one over the forehead and the other two over the temples. Today these traditional Savoyard costumes are only worn on festival days and for traditional celebrations.*

Practical information

Information : **Savoie** : *comité régional de tourisme (C.R.T.)* Savoie-Mont-Blanc, 9, bd Wilson, 73100 Aix-les-Bains, ☎ 79.88.23.41. **Haute-Savoie-Mont-Blanc** : *association touristique départementale*, 56, rue Sommeiller, B.P. 348, 74012 Annecy, ☎ 50.51.32.31. **Savoie** : *association départementale de tourisme de Savoie (A.D.T.)*, 24, bd de la Colonne, 73000 Chambéry, ☎ 79.85.12.45. *Dir. dép. de la jeunesse et des sports*, Montée Valérieux, 73000 Chambéry. In **Paris** : *Maison de Savoie* : 16, bd Haussmann, 75009, ☎ 45.23.05.50.

Reservations : **Savoie** : *Loisirs-Accueil Savoie (L.A.)*, 24, bd de la Colonne, 73000 Chambéry, ☎ 79.85.01.09.

S.O.S. : **Savoie** : *SAMU* (Emergency Medical Service), ☎ 79.69.25.25. **Haute-Savoie** : ☎ 50.51.21.21. *Emergency Poisoning Centre* : Grenoble, ☎ 76.42.42.42.

Weather forecast : **Savoie**, ☎ 79.61.58.55. **Haute-Savoie**, ☎ 50.53.03.40.

Rural gîtes and chambres d'hôtes : *Loisirs-Accueil Savoie. Rural gîtes* : **Haute-Savoie** : 52, av. des Iles, 74037 Annecy, ☎ 50.57.82.40.

Holiday villages : list at *fédérations départementales du tourisme social de Savoie et Haute-Savoie*. **Haute-Savoie** : 5, rue Éloi-Serand, 74000 Annecy, ☎ 50.45.60.06 ; **Savoie** : *L.A.*, 24, bd Colonne, 73000 Chambéry, ☎ 79.85.01.09.

Festival and events : **Jan** : *fantastic film festival* in Avoriaz. **May** : *International Festival of Music* in Évian ; *Antiques Salon* in Chambéry. **Jun** : *International Animated Film Festival* in Annecy (odd years only ; every two years) ; *Savoyard costume festival* in Bourg-Saint-Maurice. **Jul** : *fete of the Bellevilles Valley guide ; International Festival of Folklore Dance* in La Clusaz ; *Maurienne festival* in Saint-Jean-de-Maurienne ; *edelweiss festival : international folklore gala* in Bourg-Saint-Maurice ; *advertising festival* in Arcs ; *Chamonix music weeks.* **Aug** : *lake festival* in Annecy ; *procession at the Prés-Plans chapel ; guides' fete* in Les Arcs, Chamonix and Saint-Gervais ; *mountain costume fete* in Peisey-Nancroix ; *auto and moto-cross show* in Val d'Isère ; *baroque music festival* in the church at Haute-Ville-Gondon. **Sep** : *Aix-les-Bains-Lac du Bourget music festival,* in Bourget-du-Lac ; *Savoie fete* in Chambéry ; *local fair* in Annecy. **Oct** : *antiques salon* in Aix-les-Bains.

Sporting events : **Jan** : cross-country skiing in Abundance valley. **Mid-Apr** : *international car rally* at Annemasse. **Mid-May** : *international golf week* at Évian. **Early Jun** : *international rowing-regatta* at Évian. **Late Jun** : *French marathon Championships* at Annecy. **Late Jul** : *national horse-riding competition* at Talloires ; *French rafting Grand Prix.* **Aug** : *artistic skating international Grand Prix* in Saint Gervais. **Dec** : *first snowfall competition* in Val d'Isère. For winter ski contests, enq. at *C.D.T.* and *S.I.*

National and nature parks : *direction du parc national de la Vanoise*, 135, rue du Dr-Julliand, B.P. 705, 73003 Chambéry Cedex, ☎ 79.62.30.54, for lists of shelters and overnight gîtes, topoguides and maps of the park.

Regional flora

June and July are the best months for discovering the great variety and richness of alpine flora. Many colourful species are to be found above the treeline, over 2 200m : golden globe-flowers, intense blue gentians, delicate violets, white anemones, the silver suns of carline thistles, the violet flowers of the soldanelle, pansies and asters, and vivid red rhododendrons. In particular look out for the wonderful martegon lily or Turk's cap, with purple-streaked pink flowers.

Wildlife

Take your binoculars to the high pastures on the upper edge of the forest, and of course to the National Park of the Vanoise (Parc National de la Vanoise), where there is a good chance of seeing various Alpine fauna : ibex, marmot, and the rarer chamois and blue hare.

Alpine ibex : there were fewer than 50 of these mountain goats in Savoie when the Parc de la Vanoise was created in 1963. Heavily built with superb bowed horns.

Chamois : smaller than the ibex, very shy, a real nomad, off at the gallop at the approach of man. May be seen on the upper edges of the Alpine pastures, or perched on rocky outcrops.

Marmot : a ball of reddish fur trotting from one burrow to another, mostly in the high pastures. This pretty rodent lives in families or communities and goes into hibernation at the onset of winter.

Chough and eagle : the chough, connoisseur of picnic leftovers, is a little yellow-beaked crow often seen gliding around the area's peaks. Several pairs of eagles have reappeared in the park.

Blue hare : white in winter and blue-grey in summer, he is the king of camouflage, and doubly difficult to observe in the mountain pastures that are his habitat.

Rambling and hiking : *I.G.N.* maps 1/50 000 and 1/25 000. Didier-Richard in Grenoble publishes maps of the various massifs. GR5 (Haute-Savoie), GR5-55 (Savoie), GR9 and GR96 topoguide, along with GTA n° 15. Nature itineraries : *glacier tours in the Vanoise* by A. Moulin, published by Vanoise national park. For shorter hikes, see *S.I.* brochures. Lists of shelters and gîtes d'étapes are available at the *association départementale de tourisme de la Savoie.* The "Great Crossing of the Alps" *(G.T.A.)* consists of nine routes, from Lake Léman to Menton. Grenoble : *maison du tourisme,* ☎ 76.54.34.36.

Regional specialities : a brochure including a gastronomic map of Savoie is put out by the *Chambre d'agriculture de la Savoie,* 1, rue du Château, 73000 Chambéry, ☎ 79.33.43.36. A brochure describing Savoyard wines is available at the *syndicat des vins de Savoie,* 3, rue du Château, 73000 Chambéry.

Scenic railways : *Alpazur,* Genève-Digne-Nice, daily, end May to end Sep. Enq. : S.N.C.F. *Breda Scenic Railway :* from Poncharra-La Rochette, 2 return trips daily, approx once weekly from Jun to Sep. Enq. : M. Vargel, ☎ 76.48.55.61.

Cycling holidays : *I.G.N.* maps and cycling routes available for purchase in the *O.T.,* **Savoie** and **Haute-Savoie,** enq. at *C.D.,* ☎ 50.60.17.34.

Riding holidays : all enquiries concerning riding centres and activities should be addressed to the *comité départemental Savoie pour le tourisme équestre, l'équitation de loisirs et sportive (C.D.S.T.E.),* Maison des sports, 6, montée Valérieux, 73000 Chambéry, ☎ 79.69.69.69 ; *C.D. sports équestres,* ☎ 50.60.14.41.

Handicraft courses : weaving, stained glass, pottery, silk painting, wickerwork, watercolor, copper enamelling, woodwork, etc. Enq. : *assn. dép. de tourisme de Savoie and Haute-Savoie.*

Other courses : *numerous sports and cultural courses :* dance, music, theatre, photography, *mountain discovery courses, video;* other more novel courses such as microcomputer work, bridge and *nouvelle cuisine.* Enq. : *assn. dép. de tourisme de Savoie* ☎ 79.85.12.45 and Haute-Savoie, ☎ 50.51.32.31.

The produce of Savoie

Savoie produces many cheeses of renown, among them Reblochon and Beaufort. The lakes are still unpolluted and full of fish : pollan, char, salmon-trout and freshwater lotte. The liver of the lotte is a local delicacy. There are also pike, perch and gravanche (fished only in Dec.). The pure mountain air is excellent for curing meat (ham and dry-cured saucisson). Look out for a very special spiced sausage called pormonier. Many varieties of mushroom : mousserons, cêpes, morilles. The gratin de pommes de terre savoyard differs from its Dauphinois cousin in that it is made without milk (potatoes, cheese and stock). The local pastries are very light; try the gâteau de Savoie.

Reblochon

Reblochon was once a fromage de dévotion (tithe or votive cheese), which the peasants of Savoie used to give each year to the Carthusian monks who came to bless their fields. It is a soft, uncooked cheese made from cows' milk and lightly pressed. It is a speciality of the Aravis region (Grand-Bornand). Matured in cold damp cellars for about 4 weeks, the cheese is then washed and presented on round sheets of wood. It contains 50% fat, has a mild, creamy taste and a smooth texture, and should be a pinky yellow with a smooth crust that dimples to the touch. The best season is the end of June to the end of November. The name comes from reblochage, which means "second milking".

Beaufort cheese

This relative of Gruyère is made in the Beaufortin and Tarentaise regions from whole cow's milk. There are two varieties : summer Beaufort from the Alpine pastures and winter Beaufort produced in the valley farms. It is a moulded, firm, cooked cheese, very pale yellow, smooth-textured with holes. It is round, with a concave crust — this distinguishes it from the gruyères— and each cheese weighs from 40 to 60 kilos. It matures for six months in a damp cellar at low temperature. The cheese co-operative in the village of Beaufort is open to visitors.

The wines of Savoie

As Henri Bordeaux, novelist and member of the Académie Française, once said : "These are great wines, subtle and sometimes treacherous." To begin with the whites : Apremont, Abymes, Chignin, Montmélian, dry and fruity. Marignan, Marin, Ripaille, dry and open. The Roussette, fine and heavily perfumed. Roussette de Seyssel and Crépy, light, dry and diuretic. Ayze, pétillant or sparkling, recommended as an apéritif. Finally, the reds : Gamay, full-bodied, fairly fruity; Mondeuse, purple-red with a bouquet of strawberry, raspberry and violet. Good years ·: 1955, 57, 61, 67, 69, 71, 76, 78, 79, 81.

Golf : Aix-les-Bains (18 holes); Annecy-Talloires (18 holes); Bourg-Saint-Maurice-les-Arcs (18 holes); Chamonix (18 holes); Évian (18 holes); Megève (18 holes); Méribel (9 holes); Tignes (9 holes); Flaine-Carroz (18 holes).

Aquatic sports : numerous lake activities, enq. at *C.D.T.* and *S.I.*

Canoeing : list of schools and clubs, and enq. at the *assn. dép. de tourisme de Savoie* and *Haute-Savoie.*

Mountaineering : list of shelters and enq. at the *assn. dép. de tourisme de la Savoie* and *Haute-Savoie.*

Winter sports : *cross-country skiing* : the *assn. dép.* for cross-country skiing at Annecy, ☎ 50.51.32.31 and *C.D.T. Savoie* and *maison de Savoie* in Paris.
Hunting and shooting : *féd. dép. des chasseurs*, 15, rue Nivolet, 73000 Chambéry, ☎ 79.62.04.61. *féd. dép. des chasseurs de Haute-Savoie*, 9 bis, av. Berthollet, 74000 Annecy, ☎ 50.57.14.27.
Fishing : *la féd. dép. des assn. de pêche et de pisciculture de la Savoie*, plage de la Glière, 73240 Saint-Genix-sur-Guiers, ☎ 76.31.61.53, publishes the list of affiliated associations, along with a map of stretches of water : perch, pike, trout, fresh-water char, carp. For Haute-Savoie, enq. at 1, rue de l'Industrie, ☎ 50.45.26.90.

● *Towns and places*

AIX-LES-BAINS*

Chambéry 16, Annecy 34, Paris 567 km
pop 23500 ⊠ 73100   A2

More than 2 000 years ago, the Romans (masters of the art of the hot bath) built baths at Aix. Since the 16thC this resort has been a rendez-vous of the famous, who forgot their rheumatism as they took part in the parade of fashionable life against a backdrop of sumptuously flowered parks and the mirrorlike waters of the Lac du Bourget, made famous by the Romantic poet Lamartine.
Life in Aix centres around the park and its greenery, the Thermes, the Palace of Savoy and the new casino.

The arrow (→) is a reference to another entry.

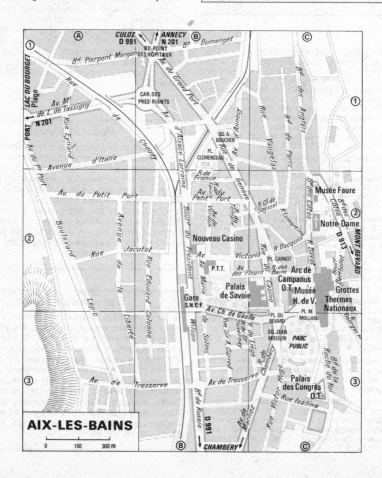

▶ The **Hôtel de Ville★** (town hall; C2) occupies the ancient château (1513; Renaissance staircase★). The nearby **Temple of Diana** (2nd or 3rdC) houses prehistoric and Gallo-Roman antiquities. ▶ In the middle of the Place des Thermes is the Arch of Campanus (3rd or 4thC). The **Thermes Nationaux** (1860, modernized in 1972) include the remains of the Roman baths and the hot springs. ▶ The **Museum of Dr. Faure★** (C2) has a rich collection from the 19th and 20thC (Corot, Degas, Cézanne, Pissarro, Vuillard, Sisley, watercolours by Rodin). Lamartine is not forgotten : furniture from the apartment occupied by the poet at the Perrier *pension,* souvenirs and documents. Porcelain, regional and foreign ceramics *(9-12 & 2-6; Sun. 10-12 & 4-6; closed Sat. pm and Sun. in winter).* ▶ Between the *petit port* (beach★) and the *grand port,* the **Boulevard du Lac★★** (by A1) is the general meeting place for an evening stroll. And in the background are the abbey of Hautecombe and the Dent du Chat ("Cat's Tooth") peak.

Nearby

▶ **Abbey of Hautecombe★★** (→ Lake Bourget) : boat excursion leaving from the Grand-Port. ▶ **Tresserve** *(2 km S)* on the mountain crest overlooking the lake : monument to Lamartine who in 1817 composed his famous poem "Le Lac" here.

Circuit of Mont Revard★★ *(45 km, D913 and 912)*

▶ **Mont-Revard :** a 20 km^2 fir-covered plateau SE of Aix, overlooking Le Bourget. Numerous walks in search of the *martagon* or Turk's cap lily, or more simply looking for mushrooms, blackcurrants and wild strawberries or the *rose du Revard* (a variety of thistle). ▶ **La Féclaz** is the winter sports resort of the inhabitants of Chambéry. This smoothly undulating plateau, bordered by forests, is a beautiful suntrap. The cable car from Oriandaz goes up to 1560m, with a beautiful view over Mont Blanc, Lake Bourget, the Dents du Nivolet and the Revard mountain. ▶ From **Des Déserts,** a road and a path take you to the **Croix du Nivolet** (alt. 1 547m ; view). □

Practical Information

AIX-LES-BAINS
☎ 79.35.38.50, (t.a.).
ℹ pl. M.-Mollard (C2), ☎ 79.35.05.92.
✈ *Chambéry-Aix-les-Bains*, 6 km SW, ☎ 79.61.46.00.
SNCF (B2), ☎ 79.35.03.87.
🚌 pl. Clemenceau (B1), ☎ 79.35.09.33.
⛴ *Cie de navigation du lac du Bourget*, ☎ 79.35.05.19, from from the Grand-Port, regular daily service.
Car rental : *Avis*, Station Avia, 4, bd de Russie (B3), ☎ 79.33.58.54 ; train station.

Hotels :
★★★ ***Le Manoir*** (R.S.), 37, rue Georges-1er (C3), ☎ 79.61.44.00, Tx 980793, DC Euro Visa, 72 rm P ♿ closed 20 Dec-20 Jan, 250. Rest. ♦♦ ♪ ♿ 100-150.
★★ ***Clairefontaine*** (L.F.), Pugny-Chatenod, 3 km D 913, ☎ 79.61.47.09, Euro Visa, 29 rm P ♪ ♿ closed 1 Jan-10 Feb, 170. Rest. ♦ ♪ ♿ closed 15 Oct-10 Feb, 65-130.
★★ ***Davat*** (L.F.), 21, chem. des Bateliers, le Grand-Port (off map A1), ☎ 79.35.09.63, Visa, 20 rm P ♪ closed Mon eve and Tue, 2 Nov-20 Mar, 210. Rest. ♦ ♪ ♿ Classic fare, e.g : *pâté en croûte de canard, filet de perche meunière, filet de bœuf périgueux*, 80-130.
★★ ***La Pastorale***, 221, av. du Grand-Port (B1), ☎ 79.35.25.36, AE DC, 30 rm P closed 1 Feb-31 Mar, 200. Rest. ♦♦ ♪ closed Mon and Sun eve, 75-120.
★★ ***Le Dauphinois*** (L.F.), 14, av. de Tresserve (B3), ☎ 79.61.22.56, AE DC Euro Visa, 84 rm P closed 15 Dec-15 Feb, 195. Rest. ♦ ♪ ♿ closed Sun eve (l.s.), 80-100.

Restaurant :
♦♦ ***Brasserie de la Poste***, 32, av. Victoria (B2), ☎ 79.35.00.65, AE Visa ♪ closed Mon, 2 Nov-10 Dec, 60-110.

⛺ ★★★*Sierroz* (300 pl), ☎ 79.61.21.43.

Recommended
Casino : *Palais de Savoie*, (B2), ☎ 79.35.16.16.

Nearby

RUFFIEUX, ⊠ 73310 Chindrieux, 21 km N on the D991.

Hotel :
★★★ ***Château de Collonges***, (I.L.A., C.H., R.S.), ☎ 79.54.27.38, AE DC Euro Visa, 10 rm P closed Mon and Tue lunch, 5 Jan-14 Feb, 335. Rest. ♦♦ 170-300 ; child : 100.

ALBERTVILLE

Annecy 45, Chambéry 49, Paris 610 km
pop 17530 ⊠ 73200 A2

To replace the fortified city of Conflans (worth a visit for its own sake) King Charles Albert (1798-1849) had a new town planned and built in 1845 to which he gave his name. At the entrance of the Val d'Arly, Albertville is essentially a major highway intersection.

▶ **Conflans★**, on a hill overlooking the junction of the Isère and the Arly, is a typical small military town from the Savoie of earlier times. Numerous craftsmen have given new life to old shops in the ancient Grand' Rue. 17thC pulpit★ in the church. In a charming square, the Maison Rouge★ (16thC Gothic) houses a Savoyard museum. From the Terrace of La Roche there is a view over the valley of the Isère. ▶ **Route du Fort du Mont★** *(11 km E)* panorama★★ over the whole valley of Savoie, the Tarentaise region, Mont-Blanc, etc. □

Practical Information

ALBERTVILLE
ℹ pl. de la Gare, ☎ 79.32.04.22.
SNCF ☎ 79.32.49.83.
🚌 *Cars du Val-d'Arly*, ☎ 79.31.61.14.

Hotels :
★★★ ***Million*** (R.C.), 8, pl. de la Liberté, ☎ 79.32.25.15, AE DC Visa, 29 rm P closed 27 Apr-12 May, 27 Sep-12 Oct, 260. Rest. ● ♦♦♦ closed Mon and Sun eve. Philippe Million serves savoury, traditional cuisine with an original, creative touch. His inviting establishment is a pleasant stop when touring Savoie's resorts : *filet de fera à la mousseline de citron, noix de ris de veau à l'aigre-doux, oreillons d'abricot à la pistache.* All the best local wines are on hand, 130-300 ; child : 80.
★★ ***Le Costaroche***, 1, chem. de la Pierre-du-Roy, ☎ 79.32.02.02, 20 rm P closed Sun eve and Mon lunch (l.s.), 150. Rest. ♦ ♪ ♿ 65-130.

Restaurants :
♦♦ ***Le Ligismond***, pl. de Conflans, ☎ 79.32.53.50 ♪ closed Mon and Sun eve (l.s.). Spec : *émincé d'antilope aux mangues*, 85-200.
♦ ***Uginet***, 8, pl Charles-Albert, ☎ 79.32.00.50, AE DC Visa P closed Tue, 25 Jun-5 Jul, 11 Nov-5 Dec. Alain Rayé sold Uginet when he moved to Paris. Eric Guillot, his former assistant, has taken over : *fricassée de langoustines aux tomates confites, tian de homard et coquilles Saint-Jacques.* Splendid cellar, 110-240.

⛺ ★*Adoubles* (134 pl), ☎ 79.32.06.62.

Recommended
Guided tours : *Maison des Guides*, ☎ 79.32.29.93 ; *C.N.M.H.S.*, enquire at the S.I.
♥ cheese : *Aminthas*, 71, rue de la République ; chocolates : *Parat*, 39, rue de la République.

Nearby

GRÈSY-SUR-ISÈRE, ⊠ 73460 Frontenex, 15 km SW.

Hotel :
★★ ***La Tour de Pacoret*** (R.S.), 1.5 km on D 201, ☎ 79.37.91.59, AE DC Euro Visa, 10 rm P

⚒ half pens (h.s.), closed Tue lunch, 1 Oct-1 Mar, 210. Rest. ♦ ⟨ ♪ ⚒ 150.

La LÉCHÈRE, ⊠ 73260 Aigueblanche, 21 km S.
♨ (1 Apr-31 Oct), ☎ 79.24.11.33.
▯ av. de l'Isère, ☎ 79.22.51.60.

Hotel :
★★★ **Radiana,** Aigueblanche, ☎ 79.22.61.61, Euro Visa, 80 rm ℙ ⚙ ⚐ closed 23 Oct-19 Apr, 290. Rest. ♦♦ ⚒ 90-120.

Restaurant :
♦ *La Sabandia,* ☎ 79.22.51.72 ♪ closed Nov-Mar. On the ski resort circuit; the food here is simple but good. Spec : *ris de rognon de veau façon Céline, millefeuille de sole,* 60-160.

QUEIGE, ⊠ 73720, 12 km.

Hotel :
★ *Auberge des Roches,* on the Beaufort road, ☎ 79.38.02.18, 14 rm ℙ ⚙ ⚙ closed 4-28 May, 12 Nov-15 Dec, 115. Rest. ● ♦ The discreet charm of family-style fare in the no less charming Beaufort valley : *escargots, truite aux amandes, fondue,* 55-90.

SAINT-VITAL, ⊠ 73460 Frontenex, 10 km SW.

Restaurant :
♦ *Au Vieux Pressoir,* ☎ 79.38.54.97, Euro Visa ⚙ ♪ closed Mon and Sun eve, 85-160.

ANNECY**

Genève 57, Lyon 137, Paris 550 km
pop 49965 ⊠ 74000   A2

The lakeside town. The calm, clear waters of Lake Annecy are set against a marvellous backdrop of mountains. The swift currents of the Thiou swirl under the bridges of the old town. This quarter is now a pedestrian precinct at the foot of the château. The quiet streets are bordered by arcades and often decked with flowers. Faithful to the Savoyard tradition of metalwork, Annecy is an important industrial centre (ball-bearings and razors) with a nuclear research centre discreetly hidden in the urban landscape.

▶ The lakeside★★ and old Annecy are the greatest attractions : Champ de Mars (C2); Pont des Amours★; Public Gardens★; Quais du Thiou, a canal into the lake from which the boat trips start. ▶ The old town★★ (market★ *Tue., Fri. and Sun. am*) : church of St. François (B3, 1652); **church of St. Maurice** (15thC) : funerary fresco★ of 1458 and a Descent from the Cross by P. Pourbus the Elder. ▶ In the Thiou river is the **Palais de l'Isle** (B3, 13th-16thC), formerly a prison. ▶ Follow the canal and bear R to the **Cathedral of St. Pierre** (B3) dating from 1535. St. François de Sales, the major figure in Annecy's history, was Bishop here. With St. Jeanne de Chantal (1572-1641), he founded the first monastery of the Visitation. Beside the cathedral, the former Episcopal Palace (1784) occupies the site of the house where Jean-Jacques Rousseau met Madame de Warens (1729) whom he was to remember lovingly. ▶ The **château**★ (B3, 12thC), rebuilt after several fires, now contains the Historical Museum of Annecy and Haute-Savoie : archaeology, ethnography and architecture *(10-12 & 2-6, closed Tue.)*.

Nearby

▶ Lake Annecy (→); the **Gorges du Fier**★ *(11.5 km W)*, with galleries clinging to the cliff wall; remarkably narrow gorges *(entry fee)*. ▶ **Château de Montrottier** (13th and 14thC); varied collections; bas-reliefs★ in bronze cast by the lost-wax method by Hans and Peter Vischer (1520) of Nuremberg *(9-12 & 2-6, Jul.-Aug.; Easter-Oct. closed Tue.)*.   □

Practical Information ――――

▯ 1, rue J.-Jaurès, Bonlieu (B2), ☎ 50.45.00.33.
✈ *Meythet,* 4 km NW, ☎ 50.57.53.42. *Air France office,* rés. du Palais, 17, rue de la Paix, ☎ 50.51.61.51.
▭▭▭ (A2), ☎ 50.51.34.08.
▭▭▭ pl. de la Gare (A2), ☎ 50.45.00.56.
▭▭ *Compagnie des Bateaux du lac d'Annecy,* ☎ 50.51.08.40, tour of the lake with stops in small villages.
Car rental : *Avis,* 14, av. de Genève (A1), ☎ 50.57.47.91; train station (A2).

Hotels :
★★★ *Marquisats,* 6, chem. de Colmyr, ☎ 50.51.52.34, Tx 385230, DC Euro Visa, 25 rm ℙ ⟨ ⚙ ⚐ 260.
★★★ *Splendid,* 4, quai E.-Chappuis (B2), ☎ 50.45.20.00, Tx 385233, Euro Visa, 50 rm ⟨ ♪ 310.
★★ *Au Faisan Doré* (L.F.), 34, av. d'Albigny (C2), ☎ 50.23.02.46, Visa, 41 rm ℙ ♪ 270. Rest. ♦ ♪ closed Mon and Sun eve , Nov-Jan, 80-150.
★ *Château,* 7, chemin du Belvédère (off map B3), ☎ 50.45.04.90, Visa, 9 rm ℙ ⟨ ⚐ ⚒ closed 6 Oct-14 May, 120. Rest. ♦♦ ⟨ ♿ ⚒ closed Mon , Sun eve, Mar, Apr, Nov. The place to go for beautifully cooked ocean fish, 160-220.
★ *Château,* 16, rampe du Château (B3), ☎ 50.45.27.66, 23 rm ℙ ⟨ ⚐ ⚒ closed 15 Oct-15 Dec, 100.

Restaurants :
● ♦♦♦♦ *Auberge de l'Eridan,* 7, av. de Chavoires (off map C2), ☎ 50.66.22.04, AE DC Euro Visa ⟨ ⚙ ♪ ♿ closed Wed and Sun eve, 3 Feb-3 Mar, 16 Aug-3 Sep. Marc Veyrat is cooking in 'peak' form in these Alpine surroundings. The restaurant is plush and comfortable, the view of the lake is superb, and the chef's creations are as attractive as the rest : *omble chevalier* (the famous lake fish) *à la peau, boudin de perche et d'écrevisses, pigeon au lait de cresson.* Mme Veyrat eytends a charming welcome. Flawless service, Savoy wines, 200-450.
● ♦♦ *Le Boutae,* 10, rue Vaugelas, imp. du Pré-Carré (A-B2), ☎ 50.45.62.94, AE DC Euro Visa ♪ closed Tue eve and Sun, 3-24 Aug. Spec : *saumon à l'oseille,* lake fish, 65-170.
● ♦♦ *La Ciboulette,* Cour du Pré-Carré, 10, rue Vaugelas, ☎ 50.45.74.57, AE DC Euro Visa ℙ ⚐ ♪ Light, enjoyable food in the classic style prepared by Georges Paccard : *pithiviers de volaille aux chanterelles, rouget sauté à la crème d'ail et étuvée de cresson,* 135-170.
♦♦ *Le Salino,* 13, rue Jean-Mermoz, ☎ 50.23.07.90, AE DC Euro Visa ⟨ ♿ closed Wed and Sun eve, 28 Jan-5 Feb, 10 Jun-9 Jul. Spec : *gigot de lotte, pigeon de Bresse rôti,* 130-230.

⚑ ★★*Belvédère* (250 pl), ☎ 50.45.48.30; ★★*Petit Port* (100 pl), ☎ 50.23.45.25; ★★*Pré d'Avril* (50 pl), ☎ 50.23.64.46.

Recommended
Guided tours : tour of the old town organized by the friends of Old Annecy : info at the tourist center.
Market : in the old town on Tue (food), Fri and Sun am (food and bric à brac).
♥ *shops in the pedestrian zone* (downtown and in the old town).

Lake ANNECY***

                                    A2

Lake Annecy is one of the loveliest spots in the Savoy Alps, with its mountain backdrop and green shoreline. Hallowed by artists and writers of the last century, the lake is today widely praised for the purity of its water, which has been preserved by herculean efforts to save it from sewage pollution.

Lake statistics : Length 14 km, average width 1.2 km, circumference 35 km, altitude 446 m, max depth 82 m at the Boubioz spring.

Fish : trout, angler fish, perch, char (*omble chevalier,*

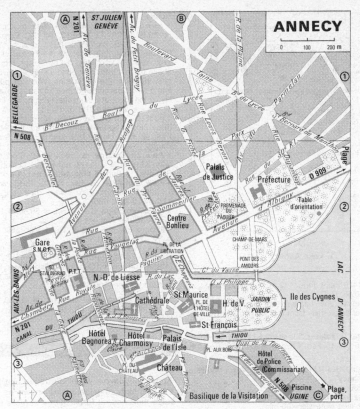

ANNECY

a local delicacy), carp, rudd, roach, pike and other freshwater fish.

Around the lake.

▶ **By boat** : Best way to explore it. Information and departure from the Quais du Thiou in Annecy.
▶ **By road** *(39 km ; 56 km with detour by the La Forclaz Pass).* ▶ **Sévrier** : pleasant country retreat at the foot of Semnoz mountain. ▶ **Saint-Jorioz** : for summer holidays.
▶ **Duingt★** : by the rocky straits near Talloires separating the *Grand Lac* from the *Petit Lac.* The château on its green island makes a splendid tableau for the visitor with a camera. Above is a 15thC château. ▶ **Doussard** : with a forest road up the **Combe d'Ire★,** enlivened by streams that sparkle through the woods. This little valley is today swallowed up in the game reserve of Bauges, where roe deer, chamois, rock partridge, black grouse, marmot and Corsican wild sheep are protected. ▶ Beyond Doussard, continue along **La Forclaz Pass★★,** with superb views over the lake. ▶ **Talloires** : pleasure for both eyes and palate. The most beautiful sight on the lake and a major gastronomic rendez-vous. ▶ **Menthon-Saint-Bernard★** : More family oriented than the neighbouring resort ; château★ (13th-15thC) girdled with walls and turrets *(2-6 Sat., Sun. and Thu. Jun.-Sep.).* Tomb of the historian Taine (d. 1893) on the N face of the Chère Rock. ▶ **Vevier,** surrounded by orchards is dominated by **Mont Baron,** the SE extremity of the Montagne de Vevier. From the summit, magnificent view over the lake, the Semnoz, the Dent du Chat, the Massif des Bauges, the glaciers of the Maurienne ; Mont-Blanc to the East.

Le Semnoz *(18 km to the Crêt de Châtillon)*

▶ The last link in the chain of the Bauges mountains, at the very gates of Annecy, **Le Semnoz★★** gives yet another view of the lake and of the country around Albens. ▶ Numerous paths to lookout points threading through the beautiful forests of the **Crêt du Maure★.** ▶ Climb up to the **Crêt du Chatillon★★★★** *(15 min) ;* view of the Alps from Mont-Blanc to the Chartreuse Massif. □

Practical Information _____

CHAPPARON, ⊠ 74210, 17 km SW of **Annecy.**

Hotel :
★★ *La Châtaigneraie* (L.F.), Lathuille, ☎ 50.44.30.67, Tx 385417, AE DC Euro Visa, 25 rm P ⚹ ⑉ ♨ ♣ ⌚ closed Sun eve and Mon (l.s.), 1 Nov-1 Feb, 230. Rest. ♦ ⚹ ♪ ⚘ 60-170 ; child : 45.

CHAVOIRES, ⊠ 74290 Veyrier-du-lac, 4 km N of **Annecy.**

Hotel :
★★★ *Pavillon de l'Ermitage,* ☎ 50.60.11.09, AE DC Euro Visa, 13 rm P ⚹ ♨ closed 31 Oct-1 Mar, 290. Rest. ♦♦ ⚹ 135-240.

DOUSSARD, ⊠ 74210 Faverges, 19 km SE of **Annecy.**
ⓘ mairie, ☎ 50.44.30.45.

Hotel :
★★★ *Marceau,* ☎ 50.44.30.11, Tx 309346, AE Visa, 18 rm P ⚹ ♨ ⌚ ⌖ pens (h.s.), closed 1 Nov-1 Feb, 700. Rest. ♦ ⚹ 100-250.

⌂ ★★★*La Serraz* (133 pl), ☎ 50.44.30.68 ; ★★★*Le Lac Bleu* (216 pl), ☎ 50.44.30.18.

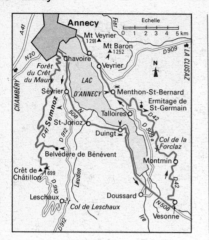

1. Lake Annecy

DUINGT, ✉ 74410 Saint-Jorioz, 12 km SE of **Annecy**.
🛈 mairie, ☎ 50.68.67.07.
🚢 *Compagnie des bateaux du lac d'Annecy*, to Annecy, several times daily from late May to late Oct.

Hotel :
★★ *Auberge du Roselet* (L.F.), ☎ 50.68.67.19, 17 rm P
⧣ ⚏ closed 15 Oct-15 Feb. Private beach, 180. Rest. ♦ 80-130.

MENTHON-SAINT-BERNARD, ✉ 74290 Veyrier-du-lac, 9 km SE of **Annecy**.
🛈 ☎ 50.60.14.30.
🚢 *Compagnie des bateaux du lac d'Annecy*, ☎ 50.51.08.40, lake excursion (90 min).

Hotel :
★★ *Beau Séjour*, ☎ 50.60.12.04, 18 rm P ⚏ ⚏ ⚏ closed Oct-Easter, 200. Rest. ♦ 80-120.

△ ★★*Le Clos Chevalier* (55 pl), ☎ 50.60.20.43 ; ★★*Le Clos Don Juan* (72 pl), ☎ 50.60.18.66.

SAINT-JORIOZ, ✉ 74410, 9 km S of **Annecy**.

Hotel :
★★ *Les Châtaigniers* (L.F.), rte de Lornard, ☎ 50.68.63.29, Tx 385417, Visa, 55 rm P ⧣ ⚏ ⚏ ⚏ ⚏ ⚏ half pens (h.s.), closed 1 Oct-25 Apr. Sauna, 225. Rest. ♦ ♪ 75-105.

△ ★★★*Europa Camping* (150 pl), ☎ 50.68.51.01 ; ★★★*International Lac d'Annecy* (133 pl), ☎ 50.68.67.93 ; ★★*Les Roseaux* (66 pl), ☎ 50.68.66.59.

SÉVRIER, ✉ 74410 Saint-Jorioz, 5 km S of **Annecy**.
🛈 ☎ 50.52.40.56.

Hotels :
★★★ *Auberge de Letraz*, RN 508, ☎ 50.52.40.36, AE DC Euro Visa, 25 rm P ⚏ ⚏ ⚏ ⚏ ⚏ closed Sun eve and Mon lunch, 20 Dec-19 Jan, 600. Rest. ♦ ⧣ ⚏ 175-265.
★★ *Club Riant Port* (L.F.), ☎ 50.52.41.08, AE DC Euro Visa, 36 rm P ⧣ ⚏ ♪ ⚏ ⚏ closed 1 Nov-1 Apr. Riding, sailing, water-skiing, 170. Rest. ♦ ⧣ ♪ 60-120 ; child : 30.

Restaurant :
♦ *Auberge du Bessard*, ☎ 50.52.40.45, Visa ⧣ ⚏ ⚏ closed 1 Nov-20 Mar, 60-110.

△ ★★★*Au Cœur du Lac* (100 pl), ☎ 50.52.46.45 ; ★★★*Le Panoramic* (133 pl), ☎ 50.52.43.09.

TALLOIRES, ✉ 74290 Veyrier-du-lac, 13 km SE of **Annecy**.
🛈 pl. de la Mairie, ☎ 50.60.70.64.

Hotels :
★★★★(L) *Auberge du Père Bise* (R.C.), rte du Port, ☎ 50.60.72.01, Tx 385812, AE DC Euro Visa, 34 rm P ⧣ ⚏ ⚏ half pens (h.s.), closed 15 Dec-1 Feb, 21 Apr-7 May, 750. Rest. ● ♦♦♦♦ ⧣ ♪ closed Tue and Wed noon (1 Oct-7 May), 1 Feb-21 Apr. It is finally time to shake up·this tradition-bound institution. Everything changes, including French cuisine. Why not put some effort into a new selection of dishes ? The prices, given the quality of the food, are unjustifiably high, 300-600.
● ★★★★ *Abbaye* (R.C.), rte du Port, ☎ 50.60.77.53, Tx 385307, AE DC Euro Visa, 33 rm P ⧣ ⚏ ⚏ half pens (h.s.), closed Sun eve and Mon (l.s.), 15 Dec-15 Jan, 600. Rest. ● ♦♦♦ closed Mon and Sun eve. Spec : *fricassée Cailon*, lake fish, 130-250.
★★★★ *Le Cottage*, ☎ 50.60.71.10, Tx 309454, AE DC Visa, 33 rm P ⧣ ⚏ ⚏ ⚏ pens (h.s.), closed Mon eve and Sun eve, 15 Sep-15 Mar, 1400. Rest. ♦♦ ⧣ ⚏ 180-200.
★★★★ *Les Prés du Lac*, (I.L.A., C.H.), ☎ 50.60.76.11, Tx 309288, AE DC Euro Visa, 9 rm P ⧣ ⚏ ⚏ ♪ closed 11 Nov-20 Dec, 600.
★★★ *L'Hermitage*, (L.F., R.S.), ☎ 50.60.71.17, Tx 385196, AE DC Euro Visa, 48 rm P ⧣ ⚏ ⚏ ♪ & ⚏ ⚏ ♪ half pens (h.s.), closed 30 Oct-1 Mar, 360. Rest. ♦♦ ⧣ ♪ & ⚏ 155-195.
● ★★ *La Villa des Fleurs* (L.F.), rte du Port, ☎ 50.61.71.14, Euro Visa, 7 rm P ⧣ ⚏ ⚏ half pens, closed Mon eve and Sun eve, 2-25 Oct. Near the bay of Talloires, 480. Rest. ♦ ⧣ ♪ Meals served on the shaded terrace, 100-120.

△ ★★★*Le Lanfonnet* (166 pl), ☎ 50.60.72.12 ; ★★*Au Cœur des Prés* (90 pl), ☎ 50.23.04.66 ; ★★*L'Horizon* (120 pl), ☎ 50.60.75.36.

The BAUGES Mountains*

A2

Above the Savoie valley between Lake Bourget and Lake Annecy, the mountains known as Les Bauges raise their natural fortifications to more than 1 500 m around a high plateau. Fir, spruce and beech woods alternate with beautiful pastureland ; enormous walnut trees grow in the valleys. Formerly the *Baujus* (the inhabitants of Bauges) spent the winter making studs and wooden dishes that were mockingly known as "Bauges silverware". Bauges includes the *canton* of **Châtelard** and a national nature reserve of more than 50 km². □

The BEAUFORTIN Region**

B2

Albertville to Beaufort *(20 km, full day)*

Between Mont Blanc and the Tarentaise, a land of wide pastures, forests, mountain hikes and long distance cross-country skiing, against the backdrop of Mont-Blanc and La Vanoise mountains. The villages (Beaufort, Arèche, Boudin) are quite unspoilt.

▶ The D925 goes right up the beautiful **valley of the Doron★**. ▶ **Villard-sur-Doron** : with a little road climbing towards the **Signal de Bisanne★★** (panoramic view). ▶ **Beaufort★** has given its name to the region and also to an excellent cheese made in the village co-operative *(visitors welcome)*. With narrow streets and overhanging roofs, Beaufort is a typical example of an old-fashioned Savoyard village. It's a good base for exploration by car : **Hauteluce** *(12 km N)* to see the lake and the Girotte dam★ ; the **Des Saisies Pass** *(20 km NW ; alt. 1 633m)* with skiing facilities ; the **Roselend dam★** *(15 km E)* in an immense and rocky waste ; to Bourg-Saint-Maurice *(40 km from Beaufort)* by D902, which runs down the valley of the Torrent des Glaciers★. □

Practical Information

BEAUFORT-SUR-DORON, ⊠ 73270, 20 km NE of **Albertville.**
ⓘ pl. de la Mairie, ☎ 79.31.23.40.

Hotels :
★ *La Roche*, ☎ 79.31.20.16,, 18 rm Ⓟ ∉ ░░░ ⌕ ♪ ♨ pens, closed 1 Nov-8 Dec, 170. Rest. ♦ ♪ ◈ Food served on the terrace, 46-100; child : 30.
★ *Le Grand Mont* (L.F.), pl. de l'Eglise, ☎ 79.31.20.18, Euro Visa, 15 rm, half pens, closed 25 Sep-5 Nov, 160. Rest. ♦ ♪ 50-60.

△ ★*de Domelin* (100 pl), ☎ 79.31.20.44.

Lake BOURGET***

A2

Since the poet Lamartine sang its praises at the beginning of the 19thC, Lake Bourget has been a continuous source of pleasure to visitors. This mysterious and magical lake lies between the rugged slopes of the Mont du Chat and the Chambotte.

The lake : 18 km long; 1.5 to 3 km wide; max depth 145 m, area 45 km², alt. 231 m; N, the lake is linked to the Rhône by the Canal de Savières.
Fish : trout, char, pike, perch and gudgeon.

Round the lake

▶ **By boat**
Leave from the Grand Port d'Aix-les-Bains; Bourget-du-Lac or Portout-Chanaz (tel. : 79.54.29.26) excursions

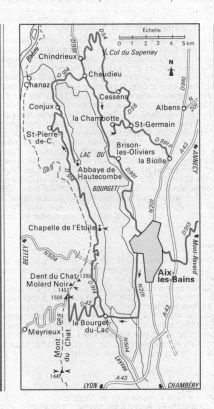

2. Lake Bourget

during the season to the Abbey of Hautecombe, the Savière canal and the Rhône.
▶ **By car** *(52 km; 71 km by the Sapenay Pass and the Chambotte).* ▶ **Le-Bourget-du-Lac,** favourite residence of the Counts of Savoy. This yachting and holiday centre was formerly an important port, linked with Lyons by a steamer service. Visit the church of the old priory (11th-13th-15thC) for its sculptures★★ from a choir-screen (Life and Passion of Christ), 15thC cloister and Italian park *(3-7 pm in summer).* ▶ From Bourget D42 climbs *(14 km)* to the **Mont du Chat★.** GR9 crosses the crest of this peak : a marvellous walk, especially towards the **Molard Noir★★** *(1hr return, alt. 1452 m)* panoramic view★★. ▶ **Chapelle de l'Etoile** *(on right, 5 min on foot);* view★★ over the lake. ▶ **Abbaye de Hautecombe★★** *(4 km right)* isolated in a magnificent site on the W bank of the lake. This abbey contains the tombs of the Princes of the House of Savoie. It was founded in 1125 by St. Bernard and Count Amédée III. The Benedictines of Solesmes have occupied it since 1922. Entirely restored during the 19thC by artists from Piedmont, the church is noted for its profusion of marbles, stucco, paintings and statuary. A beautiful Pieta★ *(cassette-guided visit 9:30-11:30 & 2:30-5:30, Mon.; mass in gregorian chant 9:15 Sun., 9:30 wk; tel. 79.54.26.12).* ▶ After **Conjux,** the road crosses the Canal de Savières at **Portout.** This canal links the lake to the Rhône and runs across the Chautagne marsh, full of rushes and poplars. ▶ At **Chaudieu** there is a choice between the lakeside road (D991) or the magnificent panoramic views from the route over the **Sapenay Pass** *(D991 N to Chindrieux, then right and left on D56).* ▶ At Saint-Germain D991B leads to the peak of the **Chambotte** (restaurant), superb view★★ over the Lac du Bourget. □

Practical Information

Le **BOURGET-DU-LAC,** ⊠ 73370, 9 km SW of **Aix-les-Bains.**
ⓘ ☎ 79.25.01.99 (h.s.); ☎ 75.25.01.43 (l.s.).
⛴ *La Navisavoie,* ☎ 79.25.22.57, toward Aix-les-Bains.

Hotel :
● ★★★★ *Ombremont* (R.C.), RN 504, rte du Tunnel-du-Chat, ☎ 79.25.00.23, Tx 980832, AE DC Euro Visa, 20 rm Ⓟ ∉ ░░░ ⌕ ▭ closed 1 Dec-5 Feb, 550. Rest. ● ♦♦♦ closed Mon noon and Sat noon ex Jul-Aug. On the way to your holiday destination, you'll find quiet, comfort and relaxation beside the lake thanks to the Carlo family's uncessing efforts. In the kitchen, chef J.-J. Barbet puts in overtime, and the results are delicious. Lake fish, *pigeonneau de Bresse.* Fine wines, 160-400.

Restaurants :
● ♦♦♦ *Le Bateau Ivre,* (R.C.), Croix-Verte, ☎ 79.25.02.66, Tx 390162, AE DC Euro Visa ░░░ ♪ ⌕ closed Tue, 12 Nov-10 May. In a converted barn is this charming decor with terrace and stylish service. The summer home of the Jacob family of Courchevel : *escalope de foie gras de canard, tartare de thon frais, escalopine de turbot,* 190-320.
♦♦ *Auberge Lamartine,* rte du Tunnel-du-Chat, Bourdeau, ☎ 79.25.01.03, Euro Visa ∉ ░░░ ⌕ ◈ closed Mon and Sun eve, 30 Nov-20 Jan, 160.

△ ★★★*Ile aux Cygnes* (267 pl), ☎ 79.25.01.76.

The CHABLAIS Region**

B1

Rising in broad steps over Lac Léman (Lake Geneva), this outcrop of the Alps is a complicated landscape of limestone crests and deep valleys. A distinction is usually made between the Bas (lower) Chablais and the Haut (upper) Chablais. The Bas Chablais has slopes planted with vines (the famous Crépy), with chestnut woods along the south bank of Lac Léman (→). Between Évian and the valley of the Dranse d'Abondance lies the Gavot region, forming a broad plateau of woodland and pasture ideal for country walks (GR5). The Haut Chablais around Morzine (→) is segmented by three deep valleys of forest and pastureland. ▶ Thonon (→) and Évian (→) are ideal bases from which to discover this region.

Circuit around the three passes★ *(52 km, half day)*

▶ **Thonon** (→). ▶ Follow D26 to the SE, overlooking the Gorges of the Dranse. The road quickly enters the lovely **valley of Bellevaux**, wooded with beech and fir. ▶ From the hamlet of Jambaz the D236 leads on to the upper valley (Vallon de la Chèvrerie★) : numerous walks, lake, former Charterhouse (Carthusian monastery). ▶ Return via the Col (Pass) de Jambaz and the Terramont and Cou passes.

Gorges de la Dranse ; from Thonon to Morzine *(33 km, 2 hr)*

▶ **Thonon** (→). ▶ D902 takes you past the **Gorges du Pont du Diable** ; a maze of potholes *(entry fee)* and ruins of the Cistercian Abbey of **Notre-Dame d'Aulps** (12th-13thC). ▶ **Morzine** (→).

The Abondance Valley★ ; from Thonon or Évian to the Pas de Morgins *(Swiss frontier ; 42 km, approx 3 hr)*

▶ From Thonon or Évian *(D21)*, rejoin D22 which climbs through the wooded gorges of the **Dranse d'Abondance**. This is one of the valleys of Chablais where the chalets have best preserved their original character. Note the warm red patina of the spruce walls and the beautifully fretted balconies. ▶ **Abondance** (pop. 1 300) : summer and winter resort in a charming location. The old abbey (founded 1128) was an influential religious centre throughout the Middle Ages. The cloister (14thC) has frescos★ illustrating the life of the Virgin *(9-12 & 2-6)*. ▶ **La Chapelle d'Abondance**, small ski village. ▶ **Châtel★** (alt. 1 235 m), the last village in the valley. You can ski at **Super-Châtel** (alt. 1 647 m) surrounded by alpine pasturelands (many good walks). Cable-car from here up the **Pic de Morclan** (alt. 1 970 m ; panoramic view★★). ☐

Practical Information _____

ABONDANCE, ☒ 74360, 28 km SE of **Thonon**.
✆ 950-1800m.
ⓘ ☎ 50.73.02.90.

Hotel :
★ *Touristes*, ☎ 50.73.02.15, 29 rm Ⓟ ≮ ⸫⸫⸫ ⸫⸫ half pens (h.s.), closed 15 Apr-1 Jun, 20 Sep-15 Dec, 350. Rest. ◆ ≮ ⸪ ⸫⸫ 60-120.

La CHAPELLE-D'ABONDANCE, ☒ 74360, 6 km NW on the Châtel.

Hotels :
★★ *Cornettes*, ☎ 50.73.50.24, Euro Visa, 40 rm Ⓟ ⸫⸫ ♿ ⸰⸰ half pens (h.s.), closed 20 Apr-20 May, 30 Oct-15 Dec, 470. Rest. ◆ ⸪ ⸫⸫ 60-120 ; child : 35.
★★ *Le Chabi*, ☎ 50.73.50.14, Euro Visa, 22 rm Ⓟ ≮ ⸫⸫ ⸫⸫ ⸪⸫ closed 15 Apr-30 Jun, 1 Sep-20 Dec, 210. Rest. ◆ ≮ ⸪ 80-90 ; child : 45.
★ *Alpage*, ☎ 50.73.50.25, 25 rm Ⓟ ≮ ⸫⸫ ⸫⸫ closed 15 Apr-15 Jun, 15 Sep-15 Dec, 120. Rest. ◆ ≮ ⸪ ⸫⸫ 55-100 ; child : 40.

CHÂTEL, ☒ 74390, 39 km SW on the Thonon.
✆ 1200-2080m.
ⓘ ☎ 50.73.22.44.

Hotel :
★★★ *Le Macchi*, ☎ 50.73.24.12, 32 rm Ⓟ ≮ closed 20 Apr-15 Jun, 31 Aug-20 Dec, 200.

△ ★★★*L'Oustalet* (100 pl), ☎ 50.73.21.97.

> If you enjoy sports, consult the pages pertaining to the regions ; there you will find addresses for practicing your favorite sport.

Grenoble 55, Lyon 98, Paris 561 km
pop 55000 ☒ 73000   A2

Chambéry was the capital of Savoie when it was a sovereign state, with the rank of County and later Duchy. Proud of its ancient title, this town was the home of Jean-Jacques Rousseau and the seat of Savoie's Senate. Chambéry still has an aristocratic flavour, clearly visible in the elegance of the porticos from the austere château to the famous Fontaine des Éléphants. The Place St. Léger, heart of the pedestrian precinct, is surrounded by houses with the warm colour of Italian buildings.

▶ **La Fontaine des Éléphants** (B2) is a useful reference point. Christened the 'Quatre-Sans-Culs' (the bottomless four) by the Chambériens, the fountain (1838) honours the memory of the Comte de Boigne (1741-1830) who brought back a fortune from the Indies and devoted it to the town. Among his major achievements is the street (B2) that bears his name. Flanked with porticos, this is the main shopping street of Chambéry. ▶ At the **Place St. Léger★** spend some time getting lost in the *trajes* — the labyrinth of alleys and vaulted passages that creates a secret network through the courtyards and apartment buildings adjoining the Place and the Rue de Boigne. The **château★** (B2 ; now the prefecture) is the former dwelling of the Dukes of Savoie. Parts of it date back to 14th and 15thC but the accommodation dates from the 18th and 19thC. The Sainte-Chapelle (15thC) with stained glass from the 16thC is particularly admired *(guided tour of the old town : 15 Jun.-15 Sep., 10:30-12 & 2:15-5 ex Sun. ; departure inner courtyard of the château ; Jul.-Aug., evening visit at 9 pm ex Sun. ; Carillon de la Sainte-Chapelle* (chimes), *concerts Sat. at 11:30 and 6:30).*

Also... ▶ **Savoisien Museum** (B2) in the former Franciscan convent ; excavation finds from lakeside sites round Bourget, history of Chambéry, ethnography, collection★ of Savoie primitives in a gallery of the cloister *(10-12 & 2-6 ; closed Tue.).* ▶ **Cathedral of St. François de Sales** (B2) : the former church of the Franciscan convent, 15thC Gothic ; *trompe-l'oeil* painting of 1848 ; Louis XIII buffets in the sacristy★ ; treasure room with 10thC Byzantine diptych★ *(3-5 Sat., Jun.-Sep.).* ▶ **Fine Arts Museum** (B1) : Italian paintings★ 14th-18thC including 'Portrait of a Young Man' by Uccello, 'Children at Play' attributed to Titian ; Dutch, Flemish and German schools ; French painting of 17th and 18thC *(10-12 & 2-6, closed Tue.).* ▶ **Lémenc church** (15thC) is built over a crypt that is partially Merovingian (Burial of Christ 15thC). ▶ **Les Charmettes** *(2 km on C2)* : the country house of Madame de Warens, where Jean-Jacques Rousseau lived from 1736 to 1742. He describes their idyll in unforgettable terms in book 9 of his "Confessions" *(10-12 & 2-6, Apr.-Sep. ; 10-12 & 2-4:30, Sun. and Wed. Oct.-Mar. ; other days ex Tue. 2-4:30).*

Nearby

▶ **Challes-les-Eaux** *(6 km SE)* : a mineral spa specialising in the treatment of respiratory ailments ; excursion to **Mont-Saint-Michel★** *(9.5 km E and 20 min on foot ; view.)* ▶ **Saint-Pierre-d'Albigny** *(2.6 km E)* : among the Savoy valley vineyards. ▶ 3.5 km NE you can visit the **château de Miolans★★** (10th-14thC), magnificently sited on a rock above the valley. This is an excellent example of mediaeval military architecture *(10-11:30 & 2:30-6, Jun.-Sep., closed Sun. am).* Lake **Aiguebelette★** *(27 km W)* : at the foot of the Montagne de l'Épine ; several summer resorts, ideal for fishing and boating excursions. ☐

Practical Information _____

CHAMBÉRY
ⓘ 24, bd de la Colonne (B1), ☎ 79.33.42.47.
✈ *Chambéry-les-Bains*, 8 km NW, ☎ 79.54.46.05.
🚆 (C1), ☎ 79.85.50.50.

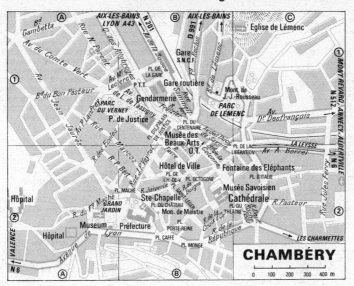

CHAMBÉRY

0 100 200 300 400 m

🔲 pl. de la Gare (C1).
Car rental : *Avis*, Airport, ☎ 79.33.58.54 ; Av. du Docteur-Desfrancois (C1), ☎ 79.33.58.54 ; train station (B1).

Hotels :
★★★★ *Grand Hôtel Ducs de Savoie*, 6, pl. de la Gare (B1), ☎ 79.69.54.54, Tx 320910, AE DC Euro Visa, 55 rm 🅿 ⋙ closed 15-30 Jul, 280.
★★ *Lion d'Or*, 1, av. de la Boisse (B1), ☎ 79.69.04.96, AE DC Euro Visa, 39 rm, 210.

Restaurants :
● ♦♦♦ *Roubatcheff*, 6, rue du Théâtre (B-C2), ☎ 79.33.24.91, AE DC Euro Visa ♪ closed Mon and Sun eve, 17 Jun-17 Jul. The food has a Russian ring to it, like the chef's name : the Caucasus right here in the Alps! Spec : *fondant de saumon frais, panaché de rouget et bar au pinot rouge*, 120-250.
● ♦♦ *Vanoise*, 6, pl. de la Gare (B1), ☎ 79.69.02.78, Tx 320910, AE DC Euro Visa ♪ closed Sun, 13-26 Jul. P. Lenain is a top-notch chef : *filet de rouget, saumon fumé, foie gras chaud de canard*, 110-260.
♦ *La Chaumière*, 14-16, rue Denfert-Rochereau (C2), ☎ 79.33.16.26, Visa ♪ closed Wed eve and Sun (l.s.) , w.e. (h.s.) 1 wk in Mar, 3-26 Aug. A fine variety of good, simple fixed meals, 60-110.
♦ *Le Sporting*, 88, rue Croix-d'Or (B2), ☎ 79.33.17.43, AE Euro Visa ⋙ ♪ For lovers of meat and the wines of Savoie, 50-100 ; child : 30.

Recommended
♥ ice cream, pastries : *Michaud*, 5, bd du Théâtre (near the Elephants).

Nearby

CHALLES-LES-EAUX, ⊠ 73190, 6 km SE.
♨ ☎ 79.85.20.04.
ⓘ av. Chambéry, ☎ 79.85.20.13.

Hotels :
★★★ *Château de Challes*, (Mapotel), ☎ 79.85.21.45, AE DC Euro Visa, 71 rm 🅿 ⋚ ⋙ ⌂ ⌁ closed 30 Oct-1 Feb, 285. Rest. ♦♦ ♪ 90-150 ; child : 50.
★★ *Château de Trivier* (C.H.), ☎ 79.85.07.27, AE DC Euro Visa, 30 rm 🅿 ⋚ ⌂ ♪ ⅋ 400. Rest. ♦♦ ⅋ closed Mon and Sun eve (l.s.). Nice little restaurant, 55-215 ; child : 34.
★ *Mairie* (L.F.), 117, rue Ch.-Pillet, ☎ 79.85.20.24,

Tx 320772, Euro, 18 rm 🅿 ⋙ ⌁ closed Sun eve, 150. Rest. ♦ *La Grinotyère*, closed 15 Oct-20 Apr, 60-120.

⋀ ★★★*Savoy* (88 pl), ☎ 79.70.40.81 ; ★★*Mont Saint-Michel* (100 pl), ☎ 79.85.20.73.

Recommended
Casino : ☎ 79.85.20.07.

NOVALAISE, ⊠ 73470, 7 km N of **Aiguebelette**.

Hotel :
★★ *Novalaise-Plage* (L.F.), ☎ 79.36.02.19, DC Euro Visa, 12 rm 🅿 ⋚ ⋙ closed Mon eve and Tue, 1 Oct-14 Apr. Right on the lake, 185. Rest. ♦ ♪ ⌂ ⅋ 55-185.

⋀ ★★*Le Grand Vernay* (83 pl), ☎ 79.36.02.54 ; ★★*Les Chavannes* (117 pl), ☎ 79.36.02.82.

SAINT-ALBAN-DE-MONTBEL, ⊠ 73610, 7 km NW of **Aiguebelette**.

Hotel :
★★ *Saint-Alban Plage*, ☎ 79.36.02.05, 16 rm 🅿 ⋚ ⋙ ♪ ⅋ closed Oct-Easter. Equipped private beach, 150.

CHAMONIX-MONT BLANC★★★

Genève 80, Annecy 93, Paris 624 km
pop 9000 ⊠ 74400   B2

Chamonix is the uncontested capital of French skiing and mountain climbing. Between Mont-Blanc and the Brévent, it is unrivalled for mountain excursions and rock climbing. The skiing areas, served by numerous ski lifts, are world renowned as are the celebrated mountain guides of Chamonix and Argentière. The opening of the Mont-Blanc tunnel in 1965 greatly aided the expansion of this resort.

▶ Life in Chamonix is dictated by the mountains and the seasons. Activity is greatest along the **Rue du Docteur-Paccard** and in the neighbouring Place de Saussure and Place de Balmat ; these three names honour the memory of the first conquerors of Mont Blanc (1786 and 1787). Their great adventure and the history of the conquest of the alpine peaks are recorded in the **Alpine Museum** in the centre of town (*daily, 2 or 3-7 ; 20 Jun.-15 Sep.*)
▶ Other resorts in the Chamonix Valley : **Les Houches, Les Bossons, Les Praz, Le Lavancher, Argentière and**

3. The Mont Blanc massif

Montroc. ▶ 300 km of paths have been signposted for walking. A map of summer mountain walks may be obtained from the TO in Chamonix. To go up the mountain with a guide contact the Compagnie des Guides in Chamonix or Argentière.

Principal excursions *(see map 3)*

▶ **Aiguilles du Midi** and **Blanche Valley**★★★. This excursion is unique. Take warm clothes and sunglasses. The cable-car goes up to the Aiguilles du Midi (alt. 3 790 m; panoramic view★★★). Continue up to the Helbronner Peak (alt. 3 452 m) by cable-car from the Blanche Valley. Italy is accessible from here, by the road down to Cormayeur. ▶ **Le Brévent**★★ (alt. 2 525 m) : access by ski lift and cable-car. Panoramic view★★★ over the Massif du Mont-Blanc and the Chamonix Valley. ▶ **Les Grands Montets**★★★ : the most beautiful skiing region in Chamonix (and France); alt. 3 297 m. Access from Argentière by ski lift. View★★★ over the glacier of Argentière and the Chamonix valley. ▶ **Les Bossons**★★ : easy access to the most beautiful glacier in the massif, either by ski lift from the top or by foot through the forest *(40 mins)*; ice grotto. ▶ **La Flégère**★★ (alt. 1 894 m) by ski lift and then as far as the Index (alt. 2 385 m) by cable-car. View★★★ over the Massif du Mont-Blanc and particularly over the Aiguille Verte. ▶ **La Prarion**★★ (alt. 1 967 m) : leave from Les Houches by cable-car; allow 35 mins on foot to the top. Panorama★★ over the Massif du Mont-Blanc. ▶ **La Mer de Glace** (Ice Sea)★★. Classic excursion from Chamonix. This famous glacier is reached by **railway to Montenvers.** Site★★ overlooked by the formidable column of the Drus. ▶ **Tour of Mont-Blanc**★★ on foot : allow a minimum of 6 days. Take equipment and a *Topo-guide* ("Topographical Guide of the Sentier de Grande Randonnée"). ▶ **Balme**

Pass★ (alt. 2 204 m) : leave from the cable-car at Montroc, then 20 mins on foot to the frontier pass. Flowers★ and pastures. View★★ over the Chamonix Valley. ▶ **Emosson Dam**★★ : 18 km N of Chamonix (N506; see the church in Vallorcine on the road) to the Swiss frontier, then a small road to the left via Finhaut. From the dam, a view★★ of the Aiguille Verte, Mont-Blanc and the Valais Alps. ▶ **Col des Montets**★ 12 km N of Chamonix (N506) : see the nature reserve of the Aiguilles Rouges★★ (nature museum, flora, ecology trail). ▶ **Bérard**★ *(path to the left approx. 2 km after the Col des Montets)* : a pretty 2hr walk to the Chalet de Pierre-à-Bérard.   □

Practical Information

CHAMONIX-MONT BLANC

☒ 1035-3842m.
ⓘ pl. de l'Eglise, ☎ 50.53.00.24.
✈ Genève, 90 km (bus connections).
SNCF ☎ 50.53.12.98.
Car rental : *Avis*, (St B.P.), 73, rue Ravanel-le-Rouge, ☎ 50.53.13.43; Train station; 200, av. de l'Aiguille-du-Midi, ☎ 50.55.84.34.

Hotels :

● ★★★★ *Auberge du Bois Prin* (R.C.), 69, chem. de l'Hermine, les Moussoux, ☎ 50.53.33.51, AE DC Visa, 11 rm ℗ ⛄ ♪ ♨ ♿ closed 11 May-4 Jun, 12 Oct-17 Dec, 610. Rest. ♦♦ ⛄ ♪ ♿ Quality cuisine, 130-180.

★★★★ *Mont-Blanc*, pl. de l'Eglise, ☎ 50.53.05.64, Tx 385614, AE DC Euro Visa, 50 rm ℗ ⛄ ♨ ♪ ♿ ⌂ ✗ closed 15 Oct-15 Dec, 625. Rest. ● ♦♦♦ *Le Matafan* ⛄ ♪ ♿ closed 11 Oct.-15 Dec. Traditional cuisine. Dishes typical of the Savoy region, 150-300.

★★★ *Albert 1er*, imp. du Montenvers, ☎ 50.53.05.09, Tx 380779, AE DC Visa, 34 rm ℗ ⛄ ♨ ♨ ♿ closed 4-26 May, 12 Oct-4 Dec, 395. Rest. ♦♦♦ ⛄ ♪ ♿ ✗ 120-260.

★★★ *Sapinière-Montana*, 102, rue Mummery, ☎ 50.53.07.63, Tx 305551, AE DC Euro Visa, 30 rm ℗ ⛄ ♨ ♨ ✗ half pens (h.s.), closed 25 Apr-30 May, 26 Sep-12 Dec, 530. Rest. ♦ ⛄ ♪ ✗ 95-150.

● ★★ *Gentianes*, (L.F., R.S.), Le Lavancher, 6 km NE, ☎ 50.54.01.31, Tx 385022, 14 rm ℗ ⛄ ♨ ♪ ♨ ✗ half pens (h.s.), closed 20 Apr-30 May, 25 Sep-20 Dec, 436. Rest. ♦ ⛄ ✗ 85-125.

★★ *Richemond*, 228, rue du Dr-Paccard, ☎ 50.53.08.85, Tx 385417, AE Euro Visa, 52 rm ℗ ⛄ ♨ ♿ closed 11 Apr-15 Jun, 15 Sep-20 Dec, 250. Rest. ♦ ⛄ 65-90.

★★ *L'Aiguille du Midi* (L. F.), 479, chemin Napoléon, Les Bossons, 3.5 km SW, ☎ 50.53.00.65, 50 rm ℗ ⛄ ♨ ♨ ⌂ ✗ pens. (h.s.), closed 5 Jan-14 Feb, 20 Sep-20 Dec, 556. Rest. ♦ ♪ ✗ 70-90.

Restaurants :

♦♦♦ *Neptune,* 78, rue du Lyset, ☎ 50.55.80.80 ♪ closed Sun eve and Mon lunch. Good traditional cuisine, 90-250.

● ♦♦ *Alpina,* 79 pl. du Mt.-Blanc, ☎ 50.53.47.77, Tx 385090 ♪ closed 1 Oct.-15 Dec. Fine panorama. Excellent cuisine 180-250.

● ♦♦ *Lion d'Or*, 255, rue du Dr. Paccard, ☎ 50.53.15.09. AE DC Euro Visa. Closed Mon, 15 Oct.-20 Dec. The friendly halting-place of Josette Dervieux, 70-220.

● ♦♦ *Royin,* 12, pl. Saussure, ☎ 50.53.07.65. Closed for lunch, 110.

● ♦♦ *Velret,* rue Paccard, ☎ 50.53.27.72. Closed for lunch. Excellent meat, 200.

♦♦ *Bartaval,* 26, cours du Bartavel, ☎ 50.53.26.51, AE DC Euro Visa ♪ closed Mon and Sun eve, 9-22 Jun, 16 Nov-14 Dec. Delicious dishes typical of the Quercy region, 100-200.

♦♦ *Plan Joran,* Sehrt, Argentières, ☎ 50.54.00.71. Open in winter. At the foot of the slope, 60.

▲ ★★★ *Les Deux Glaciers* (80 pl), ☎ 50.53.15.84; ★★ *Les Drus* (70 pl), ☎ 50.53.18.05; ★★ *Mont Blanc les Rosières* (120 pl), ☎ 50.53.10.42.

Recommended
Casino : ☎ 50.53.07.65.

Nearby

ARGENTIÈRE, ⊠ 74400 Chamonix-Mont Blanc, 8 km NE.
ℷ 1253-3271m.

Hotels :
★★ *Bellevue*, 274, rue Charlet-Stratton, ☎ 50.54.00.03,
17 rm ∉ ⸬ 🖭 closed , Oct-Nov, 20 May-20 Jun, 255.
★★ *Dahu*, 325, rue Charlet-Straton, ☎ 50.54.01.55, 22 rm
🅿 ∉ closed 15 May-15 Jun, 15 Oct-10 Dec, 180. Rest. ♦
The best raclette in the valley, 50-160.
★★ *Grands Montets*, 340, chemin des Arberons,
☎ 50.54.06.66, Euro Visa, 40 rm 🅿 ∉ ⸬ ⸜ ᕬ 🖭 closed
May, 15 Sep-15 Dec, 260.

Restaurants :
♦♦*Plan Joran*, Sehrt, Argentières, ☎ 50.54.00.71. Open
in winter. At the foot of the slope, 60.

Les HOUCHES, ⊠ 74310, 8 km SW.
ℷ 1113-1900m.
ⓘ ☎ 50.54.40.62.

Hotels :
★★ *Chris-Tal*, ☎ 50.54.50.55, DC Visa, 28 rm 🅿 ∉ ⸬ ♪ ℐ°
closed Wed (2 May-15 Jun), 21 Apr-2 May, 6 Oct-20 Dec,
190. Rest. ♦ ∉ ♪ ᕬ 60-100.
★★ *Piste Bleue*, "Le Fouilly", rte des Chavants,
☎ 50.54.40.66, 25 rm 🅿 ∉ ⸬ ᕬ ➳ closed 15 Apr-15 Jun,
15 Sep-20 Dec, 180. Rest. ♦ ∉ ➳ 58-90 ; child : 32.

Restaurant :
♦ *Fouffion*, rés. du Goûter, ☎ 50.54.46.68, Euro Visa ∉
⸬ ♪ ᕬ closed Mon, 12 Nov-15 Dec. Regional specialties,
40-75 ; child : 30.

▲ ★★★★*Air Hôtel du Bourgeat* (35 pl), ☎ 50.54.42.14 ;
★★★*Le Petit Pont* (100 pl), ☎ 50.54.41.30 ; ★★*Le Clair
de Lune* (50 pl), ☎ 50.54.41.84.

Le LAVANCHEZ, ⊠ 74400 Chamonix-Mont Blanc,
6 km NE.

Hotels :
● ★★*Gentianes*, (L.F., R.S.), ☎ 50.54.01.31, Tx 385022,
14 rm 🅿 ∉ ⸬ ᕬ 🐎 ➳ half pens (h.s.), closed
20 Apr-30 May, 25 Sep-20 Dec, 436. Rest. ♦ ∉ ➳ 85-125.
★★ *Beausoleil*, (L.F.), 60, allée des Peupliers,
☎ 50.54.00.78, 17 rm 🅿 ∉ ⸬ ᕬ 🐎 ℐ° pens (h.s.), closed
20 Sep-20 Dec, 210. Rest. ♦ ∉ ➳ 70-135.
● ★*Beauséjour*, ☎ 50.54.00.76, 13 rm 🅿 ∉ ⸬ ᕬ closed
15 May-20 Jun, 30 Sep-20 Dec, 135. Rest. ♦ ∉ 50-100.

MONTROC, ⊠ 74400 Chamonix-Mont Blanc, 11 km NE.

Hotel :
★★★*Becs Rouges*, ☎ 50.54.01.00, AE DC Visa, 24 rm 🅿
∉ ⸬ ᕬ ∉ closed 15 Apr-15 Jun, 15 Sep-15 Dec, 270.
Rest. ♦ ♦ ♪ ᕬ 75-220.

La CLUSAZ*

Annecy 32, Albertville 40, Paris 568 km
pop 1695 ⊠ *74220*   A2

In the heart of the Aravis, La Clusaz is the largest
summer and winter resort in this part of the Alps. The
village, clustered around its Byzantine-looking bell-
tower, is surrounded by larch woods and Alpine pastures. Highly recommended for walks. In the background is the impressive wall of the Aravis.

Nearby

▶ **Vallon des Confins**★ *(5.5 km E)* : along this valley runs
the little road to Fernuy at the foot of the Aravis escarpment. ▶ **Thônes** and the **valley of Manigod★** *(round trip
of 32 km ; W)*. Thônes is one of the centres of Reblochon
production. This is a delicious farm cheese with a creamy
texture, the speciality of the Aravis region. 3 km NW is the
cemetery of Glières where 105 Resistance fighters from
the Plateau de Glières were buried (Jan-Mar 1944). From
Thônes, follow D12 S then D16 via Manigod and the La
Croix-Fry Pass★. ▶ **Borne Valley★** towards **Bonneville**
(23 km N). Beyond Saint-Jean-de-Sixt, take D12, which

runs through the valley of Etroits★ then after Petit-Bor-
nand, the Gorge of Éveaux★. From **Le Petit-Bornand**
there is a pleasant excursion *(6.5 km)* to Paradis★. ▶ The
Route de la Colombière towards Cluses★ *(3.3 km NE)* : in
Saint-Jean-de-Sixt take D4 through the austere valley of
Chinaillon (old village★) and beyond la Colombière Pass
you will reach the valley of the Reposoir. See also **Le
Grand-Bornand**, source and origin of Reblochon (market★
Wed. am) and the **Chartreuse du Reposoir**, founded in
1151, occupied today by Carmelites ; buildings and clois-
ter 15thC. ▶ Road from the Aravis★★ to Flumet *(19 km
SE)* : without doubt the most beautiful drive in the region.
Plan to arrive at the Aravis Pass (alt. 1 498 m) at the end
of the afternoon for the view★★ over the Massif du Mont-
Blanc in all its glory. The landscape opens out from the
Croix de Fer★★ (alt. 1 649 m ; *2 hr on foot round trip*).
Once the rocky barrier of the Aravis has been crossed,
the road goes down into the gorges of the Arondine★,
cutting through the rocks.   ☐

Practical Information _____

La CLUSAZ
ℷ 1100-2600m.
ⓘ pl. de l'Eglise, ☎ 50.02.60.91.

Hotels :
● ★★★ *Aravis 1500* (L.F.), ☎ 50.02.61.13, 18 rm 🅿 ∉ ⸬
ᕬ 🖭 closed 20 Apr-1 Jul, 1 Sep-20 Dec, 300. Rest. ♦♦♦
♪ ➳ 80-110.
★★★ *Vieux Chalet*, ☎ 50.02.41.53, 7 rm 🅿 ∉ ⸬ ᕬ ♪ ➳
pens (h.s.), closed Tue-Thu (l.s.), 14 Jun-3 Jul, 12-30 Oct,
520. Rest. ♦♦ ∉ ♪ 70-190 ; child : 35.
★★ *Aravis* (L.F.), in the village, ☎ 50.02.60.31, 41 rm 🅿
∉ ⸬ ᕬ ℐ° closed 18 Apr-20 Jun, 6 Sep-20 Dec, 210.
Rest. ♦ ∉ 60-170.
★★ *Christiania* (L.F.), ☎ 50.02.60.60, 30 rm 🅿 ➳ closed
20 Apr-30 Jun, 15 Sep-20 Dec, 200. Rest. ♦♦ ∉ ♪ 70-110.

▲ ★★★*Plan du Fernuy* (33 pl), ☎ 50.02.44.75.

Recommended
Youth hostel : *Le Marcoret*, rte du Col de Croix-Fry, B.P.
47, ☎ 50.02.41.73.

Nearby

Le GRAND-BORNAND, ⊠ 74450, 6 km N.
ℷ 950-1850m.
ⓘ pl. de l'Eglise, ☎ 50.02.20.33.

Hotels :
★★★ *Les Saytels*, ☎ 50.02.20.16, AE Euro Visa, 29 rm 🅿
∉ 🐎 ᕬ closed 1 May-15 Jun, 15 Sep-15 Dec, 300. Rest. ♦
∉ ♪ ᕬ 50-120 ; child : 30.
★★ *Amborzales* (L.F.), Le Chinaillon, ☎ 50.27.02.50,
13 rm 🅿 ∉ ➳ closed 20 Apr-30 Jun, 15 Sep-20 Dec, 170.
★★ *Cortina* (L.F.), Le Chinaillon, ☎ 50.27.00.22, 30 rm 🅿
∉ ᕬ closed 15 Apr-1 Jul, 1 Sep-15 Dec, 210. Rest. ♦ ∉
♪ 80-150.
★★ *Croix Saint-Maurice* (L.F.), ☎ 50.02.20.05, 21 rm 🅿 ∉
closed 20 Apr-20 Jun, 15 Sep-20 Dec, 200. Rest. ♦ closed
Tue, 70-90.

▲ ★★★*L'Escale* (50 pl), ☎ 50.02.20.69.

Recommended
Market : *reblochon cheese market*, Wed am.

THONES, ⊠ 74230, 32 km W.
ⓘ ☎ 50.02.00.26.

Hotel :
★★ *Midi*, pl. de l'Hôtel de Ville, ☎ 50.02.00.44, DC Euro
Visa, 22 rm 🅿 closed 11 Nov-15 Dec, 200. Rest. ♦ ♪
closed Mon and Sun eve (l.s.), 80-180.

▲ ★★*Le Trejeux* (70 pl), ☎ 50.02.06.90 ; ★★*Les Grillons*
(48 pl), ☎ 50.02.06.63.

┌───┐
│ For the translation of a name of a meat, a fish or a │
│ vegetable, for the composition of a dish or a sauce, │
│ see the Menu Guide in the Practical Holiday Guide; │
│ it lists the most common culinary terms. │
└───┘

COURCHEVEL*

Albertville 51, Chambéry 97, Paris 658 km
pop 1651 ⊠ 73120   B3

This is the leading resort in the region of the Trois Vallées ("Three Valleys" : Saint-Bon, Doron-des-Allues and Doron-de-Belleville). The valleys are interlinked by an immense network of ski lifts centred on Courchevel. There are three levels at Courchevel : 1 550 m, 1 650 m., and 1 850 m ; the ski lifts all connect with the lowest level.

Nearby

▶ **La Saulire★★** (alt. 2 693 m) : access by ski lift and cable-car leading from Courchevel 1850. 40 min on foot to the summit. Panoramic view★★. ▶ **Doron de Belleville** : the most remote of the three valleys. There is skiing at **Les Menuires** (alt. 1700 m) and **Val-Thorens** (→ Saint-Martin-de-Belleville); this last resort (2 200 m) is equipped for summer skiing on the Glacier de Péclet. At **Saint-Martin-de-Belleville**, the village in the valley, see the church of St. Martin for its large Baroque altarpiece and the chapel of Notre-Dame de la Vie (Romanesque) for its numerous works of art (Christ★, painting of the German school 1502). ▶ **Doron des Allues**. The central of the three valleys with the second largest winter sports resort (on a par with **Méribel**; alt. 1 600 m) in the area. In the summer Méribel is a good excursion base. From Méribel and its satellite resort of **Méribel-Mottaret** you can go by cable-car to La Saulire★★, and from there down to Courchevel.   ☐

Practical Information _____

COURCHEVEL
🎿 1600-3000m.
ⓘ Courchevel 1650 m, ☎ 79.08.03.29 ; Courchevel 1850 m, ☎ 79.08.00.29.

Hotels :
★★★★(L) **Annapurna**, rte de l'Altiport, ☎ 79.08.04.60, Tx 980324, AE DC Euro Visa, 68 rm 🅿 ≶ ♨ ♪ ⊠ half pens (h.s.), closed 30 Apr-15 Dec, 2540. Rest. ♦♦ ≶ ♪ ᴕ 🍽
Spec : *escalope de loup de mer aux huîtres et au champagne, noisette d'agneau*, 250-380.
★★★★(L) **Le Byblos des Neiges**, Jardin Alpin, ☎ 79.08.12.12, Tx 980580, AE DC Visa, 70 rm 🅿 ≶ ♨ ♪ ⊠ half pens (h.s.), closed 26 Apr-20 Dec. Work on your tan at the foot of the slopes, 1275. Rest. ♦♦♦ ≶ ♪ 🍽 S. Champion is an ace in the kitchen : *minestrone de homard, paupiette de loup*, 230-320.
● ★★★★ **Pralong 2000** (R.C.), rte de l'Altiport, ☎ 79.08.24.82, Tx 980231, AE DC Euro Visa, 72 rm 🅿 ≶ ♨ ♪ ⊠ half pens (h.s.), closed 19 Apr-20 Dec, 1710. Rest. ● ♦♦♦ **Le Paral** ≶ ♪ Albert Parveaux and chef J.-P. Faucher have their winter quarters here : *consommé de crabes aux queues de langoustines, truffe en papillote de choux*, 240-280.
★★★★ **Carlina** (R.C.), ☎ 79.08.00.30, Tx 980248, AE DC Euro Visa, 52 rm 🅿 ≶ ♨ ♪ 🍽 half pens (h.s.), closed 27 Apr-18 Dec, 1800. Rest. ♦♦ ≶ ♪ 🍽 One of the resort's finest restaurants : *foie gras, fricassée de Saint-Pierre aux Saint-Jacques*, 195-300.
★★★ **La Pomme de Pin**, Les Chenus, ☎ 79.08.02.46, Tx 390162, 36 rm 🅿 ≶ ♨ ♪ ♨ half pens (h.s.), closed 22 Apr-20 Dec, 1010. Rest. ● ♦♦♦ **Le Bateau Ivre** ♪ ᴕ closed 10 Apr-20 Dec. One of the resort's finest tables. In the kitchen, the Jacobs give their all to the light, creative cuisine they proudly serve their guests. *Saint-Jacques au foie gras, blanc de volaille aux poireaux*. Savoy wines, 190-430.
★★★ **Le Chabichou**, Les Chenus, ☎ 79.08.00.55, Tx 980416, Visa, 38 rm 🅿 ≶ ♨ ♪ half pens (h.s.), closed 15 Apr-15 Dec, 1100. Rest. ● ♦♦♦ ≶ ♪ ᴕ Summer at the sea, winter in the country : that's the secret ambition of many vacationers. Energetic and talented chef Michel Rochedy has virtually realized that dream, with the help of his wife. With kitchens in Saint-Tropez and Courchevel

(two tables are better than one!) he satisfies a faithful but demanding clientele. We're pleased to welcome him to our chefs' panel, in recognition of his brilliant, airy culinary style : *moules de bouchot en vinaigrette de céleri aux artichauts et champignons des bois, colineau rôti à la crème de laitue, côte de veau au jus simple, casserole de champignons*. Top-drawer desserts. Attractive wines, both modest and great, 180-420.
★★ **Les Peupliers**, ☎ 79.08.11.61, Visa, 31 rm 🅿 ≶ ♨ ♪ ᴕ half pens (h.s.), closed May, 1 Oct-15 Dec, 260. Rest. ♦ ≶ ♪ ᴕ 🍽 65-250.
Restaurant :
● ♦♦ **La Bergerie**, Courchevel 1850, ☎ 79.08.24.70 ≶ ♪ closed 30 Apr.-15 Dec. Lively evenings full of fun, thanks to the humour of the whole crew. Good food, too. Lunch on the terrace, 70-150 ; dinner 150-300.
Recommended
Baby-sitting : ☎ 79.08.07.72.
Events : *classical music*, in the Auditorium, ☎ 79.08.01.61, concerts (28 Dec-15 Apr). Rehearsal space for young people.

Nearby

Les **MENUIRES-VAL-THORENS**, ⊠ 73440, 30 km W.
🎿 1810-2885m.
ⓘ ☎ 79.00.08.08.
Hotels :
★★★ **L'Oisans**, La Croisette, Les Menuires, ☎ 79.00.62.96, Tx 980084, AE DC Euro Visa, 20 rm 🅿 ≶ ♪ 🍽 half pens (h.s.), closed 4 May-9 Dec, 600. Rest. ♦♦ ♪ ᴕ closed for lunch, 75-120.
★★★ **Val Chavière**, Val-Thorens, ☎ 79.00.00.33, 42 rm 🅿 ≶ ♨ ♣ 🍽 half pens (h.s.), closed 5 May-1 Nov, 660. Rest. ♦ ≶ ♪ 🍽 95-200.
★★ **Trois Vallées**, Val Thorens, ☎ 79.00.01.86, Tx 980572, 28 rm ≶ closed 20 May-20 Jun, 31 Aug-20 Oct, 350. Rest. ♦ ≶ ♪ 95.
▲ ♦♦**Caravaneige** (50 pl), ☎ 79.00.60.58.

MÉRIBEL-LES-ALLUES, ⊠ 73550, 30 km W.
🎿 1550-2700m.
ⓘ ☎ 79.08.60.01.
Hotels :
★★★★ **Altiport Hôtel**, ☎ 79.00.52.32, Visa, 42 rm 🅿 ♨ ♨ 🍽 ♪ half pens (h.s.), closed 27 Apr-30 Jun, 31 Aug-15 Dec, 800. Rest. ♦♦ ♪ 🍽 140-230.
★★ **Belvédère**, ☎ 79.08.65.53, 15 rm ♨ ♣ 🍽 pens (h.s.), closed 15 Apr-15 Dec, 290. Rest. ♦ 90-125.
★★ **L'Orée du Bois** (R.S.), rd-pt des Pistes, ☎ 79.00.50.30, Visa, 32 rm, closed 15 Apr-30 Jun, 1 Sep-15 Dec, 205. Rest. ♦ ≶ ♪ 🍽 80-125.
Restaurant :
♦ **L'Estanquet**, rés. la Tougnette, ☎ 79.08.64.25, AE DC Euro Visa, closed 15 Apr-15 Dec. Among other things, many dishes from the Landes region, 80-200.

ÉVIAN-LES-BAINS**

Genève 42, Annecy 84, Paris 588 km
pop 6133 ⊠ 74500   B1

Beautifully situated on the edge of Lac Léman (Lake Geneva), with an air of old-fashioned charm in the grand hotels and casino, Évian is a great spa with a venerable reputation. Modernisation is nonetheless gradually eroding the town's old-world allure ; it has become famous as a bathing, sailing and sports centre as well as for the original Évian water. The busy social and cultural life, the activity in the pedestrians-only streets, the flowered parks and gardens, the beautiful lake front and the white boats all give the season in Évian an air of permanent festivity.

▶ In the **church** (14th-19thC), bas-relief★ of the Virgin (15thC) ; the **Palais des Congrès** (conference building,

ÉVIAN-LES-BAINS

0   100   200   300   400 m

1956) constructed by Novarina and decorated by Quinet; near the port : the English garden★.

Nearby

▶ **Château de Larringes** *(10 km SSW);* the château itself (14thC) is not open to visitors, but the view over Lac Léman and Mont-Blanc is superb. ▶ **Lakes of La Beunaz** and **Bernex** *(11 km SE).* **La Beunaz** (→ **Saint-Paul-en-Chablais**) is a pretty summer resort and **Bernex** is a winter sports centre and a good excursion base (easy ascent of the Dent d'Oche (alt. 2 225 m). ▶ **Thollon** and the **Plateau des Mémises★★** *(11 km* E) : **Thollon** (alt. 992 m) is the starting point of the cable-car for the Plateau des Mémises (alt. 1 600 to 2 000 m). Lookout point over the lake and a nice family resort. □

Practical Information _____

ÉVIAN-LES-BAINS
⚓ ☎ 50.75.02.30.
ℹ️ pl. de la Porte-d'Allinges (B1), ☎ 50.75.04.26.
SNCF ☎ 50.75.25.26.
⛴ *Cie générale de Navigation,* call Office des Baigneurs (C1), ☎ 50.75.27.53, to Lausanne.

Hotels :
★★★★(L) *Royal Club Evian,* south bank of Lac de Genève (C2), ☎ 50.75.14.00, Tx 385759, AE DC Euro Visa, 200 rm Ⓟ ≼ ⋘ ⌕ ♪ ♨ ﴾ ⊡ ⼞ ♩ closed 1 Jan-13 Feb, 15-31 Dec, 500. Rest. ♦♦♦♦ *Café Royal* ≼ ♪ ⼞ 260-315 ♦♦♦ *La Toque Royale* ≼ ♪ ♨ Dinner only. A good place to part with your winnings. Dinners conceived by Roger Lapierre (M.O.F. 54) and prepared by Michel Lentz, F. Félix is the '1er maître d'hôtel', 180-260 ♦♦ *Barbecue Piscine,* 85-120♦♦ *Chalet du Golf* One price gets you shows, health and beauty treatments in an English-style club; golf lessons, tennis, lectures, gala dinners, 100-150 ♦♦ *Rotonde Diététique* Book ahead, 270.
★★★ *La Verniaz* (R.C.), Neuvecelle (C2), ☎ 50.75.04.90, Tx 385715, AE DC Euro Visa, 35 rm Ⓟ ≼ ⋘ ⌕ ⊡ ⼞ half pens (h.s.), closed 1 Jan-6 Feb, 1-31 Dec. 5 chalets, 1050. Rest. ● ≼ ♦♦ ≼ ♪ Enjoyable food. Spec : terrine chaude de truite saumonée du Lac, filet de charolais à la broche, soufflé chaud aux griottes, 160-210.
★★ *Golf et Pavillons,* av. de Larringes, ☎ 50.75.14.47, Visa, 40 rm Ⓟ ≼ ⋘ ⌕ 230. Rest. ♦ *La Bonne Auberge* ≼ ♪ ⼞ closed Oct and Mon, 60-130.

★★ *Terminus,* le Martelay (A2), ☎ 50.75.15.07, 17 rm Ⓟ ≼ ⋘ 180.

⚕ ★★*Grande Rive* (100 pl), ☎ 50.75.50.76.

Recommended
Casino : S.E.A.T., Château de Blonay, ☎ 50.75.03.78.
Events : *international music festival,* in spring.

Nearby

AMPHION-LES-BAINS, ✉ 74500.
ℹ️ Rés. de la Rive, ☎ 50.70.00.63 (h.s.).
⛴ *Cie générale de navigation,* call the S.I. or the Office des Baigneurs, ☎ 50.75.27.53, Excursions, tour of the lake.

Hotels :
★★ *La Plage,* on the edge of Lac Léman, ☎ 50.70.00.06, Tx 385661, Euro Visa, 38 rm Ⓟ ≼ ⋘ ⌕ ⊡ ⼞ half pens (h.s.), closed 25 Sep-25 May, 500. Rest. ♦ ≼ ♪ ⼞ 70-85; child : 45.
★ *L'Amiral,* rue du Lac, ☎ 50.70.00.36, 13 rm Ⓟ ≼ ⌕ ♪ pens (h.s.), closed 1 Oct-1 May, 300. Rest. ♦ ♪ 50-70.

⚕ ★★★*La Plage (caravaneige)* (86 pl), ☎ 50.70.00.46; ★★*Grand Pré* (32 pl), ☎ 50.70.00.45.

La BEUNAZ, ✉ 74500 Evian-les-Bains, 13 km SE.

Hotel :
★★ *Bois Joli* (R.S.), ☎ 50.73.60.11, DC, 24 rm Ⓟ ≼ ⋘ ⌕ ⼞ half pens (h.s.), closed 10-30 Mar, 15 Nov-15 Dec, 420. Rest. ♦ ≼ ⼞ ⊗ closed Wed, 85-115.

THOLLON-LES-MÉMISES, ✉ 74500 Evian-les-Bains, 14 km E.
⛷ 1000-1982m.
ℹ️ ☎ 50.70.90.01.

Hotel :
★★ *Les Gentianes,* ☎ 50.70.92.39, Visa, 22 rm Ⓟ ≼ ⋘ ⌕ ♨ pens (h.s.), closed 25 Apr-1 Jun, 20 Sep-15 Dec, 420. Rest. ♦ ≼ ♪ ⼞ 45-100.

The FAUCIGNY Region★★

B1

Razor-edged crests, gigantic barriers of stone in twisted shapes and the splendid Fer à Cheval (Horseshoe) amphitheatre, give Le Faucigny a special place in the heart of the limestone region of the French Alps. The valley of the Arve from Sallanches to Bonneville, and that of the Giffre, its principal tributary, are the major axes of this area. Regional architecture is seen to best advantage in the high valleys. As in the Chablais region, chalets here are built into the slope; the inhabited part has solid stone walls, while the barn or *fenière* either forms a separate floor or is located under the roof. The *fenière* is usually a wooden structure covered with vertical planks of fir.

The Valley of the Arve, from Bonneville to Sallanches *(31 km by N205, 3 hr)*

▶ **Bonneville** (pop. 10 000) is the former capital of the Faucigny region. Resistance Museum *(Wed. and Sat., 2:30-6)*. 8 km W : **La Roche-sur-Foron** (pop. 6 818) is the major agricultural market of the region; remains of ramparts and of the first château (1016). ▶ Between Bonneville and Cluses try a detour *(5 km farther)* via **Mont Saxonnex★** : a very pleasant holiday resort built on a broad terrace above the valley of the Arve (view★). ▶ **Cluses** (pop. 15 900) is a screw-making and metalworking centre, both Savoyard specialities. ▶ Beyond Cluses, the road runs through a narrow gorge *(cluse)* to which the town owes its name. ▶ At **Balme** *(4 km)* a road runs up to the winter sports resorts of **Les Carroz-d'Arâches** *(9 km)* and **Flaine** *(24 km)*, built (1974) in reinforced concrete sections in an immense valley leading into the **Désert de Platé**. This is a large limestone plateau of 15 km², accessible by cable-car.

The Valley of the Giffre *(24 km from Taninges to the Fer-à-Cheval amphitheatre, 2 hr)*

▶ From Cluses, go on to Taninges and take D907 towards Samoëns. ▶ **Samoëns** and Sixt were formerly renowned for masons and stoneworkers whose craft school was the oldest in France. After working the land during fine weather, stonemasons from the valley of the Giffre would hawk their skills throughout Savoie and beyond. Sculpted lintels, Doric columns, crosses, oratories and fluted stoups for holy water bear witness today to the mastery of the artisans from this valley. In Samoëns, the little capital of Haut-Faucigny, ancient houses cluster around the totem of the market place, a huge lime tree planted in 1438. Flowers are everywhere, and there is a pretty Alpine garden created by Marie-Louise Jay, born in Samoëns, who with her husband, Ernest Cognacq, founded *La Samaritaine*, a well-known chain of French department stores. Don't miss the robust 16thC church. As well as a winter sports resort, **Samoëns** is also a marvellous excursion centre. (**La Rosière**, *6 km N;* view★★ of Mont-Blanc). ▶ At the exit from the village, see the waterfall of Nant d'Ant★, and the Gorges de Tines★. ▶ **Sixt-Fer-à-Cheval** is also a pleasant winter sports resort. All that is left of its abbey is a Gothic church and a 17thC building that is now a hotel (dining room★). ▶ The **Fer-à-Cheval amphitheatre★★**, surmounted by the Pic de Tanneverge, forms a gigantic semicircle of limestone cliffs, where in the month of June some 30 waterfalls can be seen. ▶ Go on foot *(50 min)* to the rocky site of Fond-de-la-Combe★.

　　　　　　　　　　　　　　　　　　　　　　□

Practical Information _____

BONNEVILLE, ⊠ 74130, 41 km NE of **Annecy**.
ℹ pl. de l'Hôtel-de-Ville, ☎ 50.97.38.37.
SNCF ☎ 50.97.00.15.

Restaurant :
● ◆◆◆ *Sapeur et Vivandière*, pl. de l'Hôtel-de-Ville, ☎ 50.97.20.68 ♪ ⚘ closed Sun and Mon (l.s.), 27 Aug-1 Sep, 27 Dec-2 Jan. Friendly atmosphere, tasty food. Spec : *turbot aux cèpes*, 75-200.

Les CARROZ-D'ARACHES, ⊠ 74300 Cluses, 13 km SE of **Cluses**.
⚡ 1150-1850m.
ℹ ☎ 50.90.00.04.

Hotels :
★★★ *Arbaron*, ☎ 50.90.02.67, Tx 385281, AE DC Visa, 30 rm ℙ ⚜ ⚘ ⚘ ♪ ☐ ⤴ pens (h.s.), closed 4 May-20 Jun, 30 Sep-15 Dec, 320. Rest. ◆◆ ⚜ ♪ ⚘ 85-240.
★★ *Croix de Savoie* (L.F.), ☎ 50.90.00.26, Euro Visa, 19 rm ℙ ⚜ ⚘ ⚘ ⚘ pens (h.s.), closed 15 Apr-15 Jun, 15 Sep-15 Dec, 250. Rest. ◆ ⚜ ♪ ⚘ 55-95 ; child : 35.

FLAINE, ⊠ 74300 Cluses, 24 km SE of **Cluses**.
⚡ 1600-2480m.
ℹ ☎ 50.90.80.01.
🚠 ☎ 50.34.40.09.

Hotels :
★★★ *Totem*, ☎ 50.90.80.64, 54 rm ⚜ ⚘ closed 22 Apr-15 Dec, 220. Rest. ◆◆ 220-310.
★★ *Aujon*, ☎ 50.90.80.10, Tx 670512, AE DC Euro Visa, 191 rm ℙ ⚜ ♪ ⚘ closed 3 May-21 Dec, 365. Rest. ◆ ♪ ⚘ 80-110.

Restaurant :
◆ *Le Kris'Eve*, Flaine-Forum, Araches, ☎ 50.90.82.83, DC Euro Visa ⚜ ♪ closed 5 May-1 Jul, 1 Sep-20 Dec, 65-150 ; child : 50.

Recommended
Sports : golf de Flaine-les Carroz, ☎ 50.90.85.44, the highest golf course in Europe. Lessons arranged.

MONT-SAXONNEX, ⊠ 74130 Bonneville, 10 km W of **Cluses**.
ℹ ☎ 50.96.90.56.

Hotel :
★ *Le Jalouvre*, ☎ 50.96.90.67, 15 rm ℙ ⚜ ⚘ ⚘ half pens (h.s.), closed 4 May-1 Jun, 20 Sep-1 Nov, 300. Rest. ◆ ⚘ 65-100.

La ROCHE-SUR-FORON, ⊠ 74800, 8 km W of **Bonneville**.
ℹ pl. Andrevetan, ☎ 50.03.36.68.
SNCF ☎ 50.03.20.62.

Restaurant :
◆◆ *Marie-Jean*, à Vozerier-Amancy, 2 km E, rte de Bonneville, ☎ 50.03.33.30 ♪ closed Mon and Sun eve, 1-22 Aug. An old dwelling. Spec : *soupe de pêches blanches aux langoustines*, 120-200.

SAMOËNS, ⊠ 74340, 21 km NE of **Cluses**.
⚡ 720-2125m.
ℹ ☎ 50.34.40.28.

Hotels :
★★★ *Neige et Roc*, ☎ 50.34.40.72, Euro Visa, 32 rm 17 apt ℙ ⚜ ⚘ ⚘ ♪ ⚘ ⤴ ☐ ⤴ half pens (h.s.), 220. Rest. ◆ ⚜ ♪ ♿ ⚘ 75-125 ; child : 50.
★★ *La Renardière*, ☎ 50.34.45.62, Euro Visa, 23 rm ℙ ⚜ ⚘ ♪ closed 2 May-15 Jun, 10 Sep-20 Dec. Apartment for fam. 2/5 pers, 230.
★ *Edelweiss la Piaz*, ☎ 50.34.41.32, 12 rm ℙ ⚜ ⚘ ⚘ closed 15 Apr-8 Jun, 15 Sep-20 Dec, 160. Rest. ◆ 80-130.

⚠ ★★*Le Giffre* (200 pl), ☎ 50.34.41.92.

Route des GRANDES ALPES★★★
(The Grandes Alpes Road)
　　　　　　　　　　　　　　　　　　B2-3

This road crosses the eastern Alps from north to south and is the most attractive in the Savoie and the Dauphiné regions. From Lac Léman to the La Cayolle Pass (D902), nearly 700 km of hairpin bends, *corniche* roads and deep gorges ; spectacular views.

▶ The best view is the crossing of the passes between Bourg-St. Maurice and La Cayolle Pass. ▶ **Iseran Pass★★** (alt. 2 270 m) : gateway to the Tarentaise and the Haute-Maurienne (view of the glacier peaks of Albaron and Charbonel). **Galibier Pass★★** (alt. 2 640 m) : view of rock wall and sparkling glaciers (Les Écrins, La Meije). ▶ **Lautaret Pass★** (alt. 2 058 m) : between Grenoble and

4. The Grandes Alpes

Briançon. ▶ **Izoard Pass★★** (alt. 2 361 m) and its famous **Casse Déserte**, with tawny needles of rock looking like a lunar landscape. ▶ Finally, **La Cayolle Pass** (alt. 2 326 m) or, even more spectacular, the **Route de la Bonette★★★** (alt. 2 802 m), which leads to one of the most beautiful circular panoramas of the southern Alps. □

Lake LÉMAN***

A-B1

In the heart of the Alps there are two rivieras, one French and one Swiss, linked by great white boats flying the Cross of Savoie of the Cross of Switzerland. Thirteen times longer than Lake Bourget, Léman (580 km², 72 km long, max 13 km wide, 310 m deep) has a microclimate that tends to prolong summer into late autumn.

Cruises

▶ From a simple crossing to a complete tour of the lake (approx. 10 h), visiting all the resorts on both French and Swiss sides. Ask at the embarkation points in Thonon and Évian.

The south bank of the lake (D25 and N5)

▶ In addition to Thonon (→), Évian (→) and their environs, pay a visit to Yvoir★★ between Geneva and Thonon. This ravishing flower-strewn mediaeval city lies at the end of a promontory. Excenevex (shore and scenery★) and Sciez-Bonnatrait. Meillerie★, between Évian and Saint-Gingolph, was much praised by Rousseau, Lamartine and Byron. □

Practical Information ─────────────────

SAINT-GINGOLPH, ⊠ 74500 Evian-les-Bains, 17 km E. ⓘ ☎ 50.76.72.28.

Hotel :
★★ **Ducs de Savoie** (L.F.), ☎ 50.76.73.09, Euro Visa, 14 rm ℗ ⧯ ⬭ ⬭ closed Mon eve and Tue (l.s.), 15 Jan-15 Feb, 140. Rest. ♦ 90-130.

SCIEZ, ⊠ 74140 Douvaine, 10 km SW of **Thonon**.

Hotel :
★★★ **Hôtellerie du Château de Coudrée** (R.C.), ☎ 50.72.62.33, Tx 309047, AE DC Euro Visa, 20 rm ℗ ⧯ ⬭ ⬭ ♪ ⬭ ⬭ half pens, closed 30 Oct-1 May. Private beach, 1120. Rest. ♦ ♪ Spec : galette de truffes et de morilles, petits choux farcis de langoustines, 180-250.

Restaurant :
♦ **Auberge Gourmande**, Massorgy, ☎ 50.94.16.97, AE DC Euro Visa ℗ ⧯ ⬭ ⬭ ♪ ♿ ⬭ closed Wed and Thu noon , school hols, 95-185.

The MAURIENNE Region*

A-B3

From the Iseran Pass to Saint-Jean-de-Maurienne (87 km, full day)

The Maurienne, scored by the valley of the Arc, is one of the great highways of Savoie towards Italy (Col du Mont-Cenis and the Fréjus tunnel). While the high valley has preserved its traditional appearance, the hydro-electric installations in the middle and lower Maurienne have spawned a string of industries including aluminium, special steels and chemical products. Like the Haute-Tarentaise, the 17thC and 18thC Haute-Maurienne was a cradle of Baroque art. Statues, altarpieces, pulpits and stalls, and works by both local artists and Italians embellish even the most modest of the area's mountain churches.

▶ **Iseran Pass** (→ Grandes Alpes Route). ▶ **Bonneval-sur-Arc★** : the houses here are still roofed with stone slabs (lauzes); this winter sports and excursion centre, at the gates of the Parc de la Vanoise★★ (Vanoise Nature Park, →), fosters ancient traditions of woodcarving and cheesemaking. ▶ Don't miss the shepherd villages of the **Vallée d'Avérole** (6 km S). ▶ **Bessans★** is a cradle of popular art and a district rich in traditions (costumes). Frescos of the Diables de Bessans in churches in the region, sculpted in wood. See the sculptures★ of the village church and the paintings★★ in the chapel of St. Antoine. ▶ **Lanslevillard** (15thC paintings in the chapel of St. Sebastian), **Lanslebourg** and **Termignon** together constitute the resort of **Val-Cenis**. Route N6 from Mont-Cenis★ towards Italy (pass, lake, view★★). ▶ **Modane** is an important railway junction, industrial centre and customs inspection post; access to the Fréjus tunnel. ▶ **Saint-Michel-de-Maurienne** : route (D902) from the Télégraph Pass★ towards **Valloire★** (typical village; see the decoration★ of the church; winter sports resort) and the Galibier Pass★★. ▶ **Saint-Jean-de-Maurienne** (pop. 10 420), former capital of Maurienne; **cathedral** (stalls★, ciborium★ and 15thC cloister; pre-Romanesque crypt). ▶ From Saint-Jean : access to winter sports resorts of **La Toussuire** (alt. 1 690 m) and **Corbier** (alt. 1 560 m) and the loop road★★ to the **Glandon Pass★** (63 km D926 and 927) via **Saint-Jean-d'Arves** and the **La Croix de Fer Pass★★** (alt. 2 068 m). □

Practical Information ────────────

BONNEVAL-SUR-ARC, ⊠ 73480 Lanslebourg-Mont-Cenis, 30 km SE of **Val-d'Isère**.
↻ 1800-3250m.
ⓘ ☎ 79.05.95.95.

Hotel :
● ★★ *Bergerie*, ☎ 79.05.94.97, Euro Visa, 22 rm ℗ ⫽ ⚬
♪ half pens (h.s.), closed 1 May-15 Jun, 15 Sep-20 Dec, 390. Rest. ♦ ⫽ ♪ ⁂ 60-80.

Restaurant :
♦♦ *Le Pré Catin*, ☎ 79.05.95.07, Euro Visa ⏏ ♪ ⚬ closed Mon, 4 May-20 Jun, 4 Oct-13 Dec, 70-120 ; child : 45.

LANSLEBOURG-MONT-CENIS, ⊠ 73480, 49 km SW of **Val-d'Isère**.
↻ 1500-2800m.
ⓘ Maison du Val-Cenis, ☎ 79.05.23.66.

Hotels :
★★★ *Alpazur*, (L.F., Inter-Hotel), Val Cenis, ☎ 79.05.93.69, AE DC Euro Visa, 24 rm ℗ ⫽ ⏏ ⚙ closed 4 May-15 Jun, 20 Sep-20 Dec, 235. Rest. ♦ ⫽ 95-160.
★★ *Relais des Deux Cols* (L.F.), ☎ 79.05.92.83, DC Visa, 30 rm ℗ ⫽ ⚙ ▱ half pens (h.s.), closed 20 Apr-25 May, 25 Sep-20 Dec, 280. Rest. ♦ ⫽ 60-90.
★ *Marmottes* (L.F.), ☎ 79.05.93.67, Visa, 16 rm ℗ ♪ closed 30 Apr-10 Jun, 30 Sep-15 Dec, 145. Rest. ♦ ⫽ 55-80.

LANSLEVILLARD, ⊠ 73480 Lanslebourg-Mont-Cenis, 3 km E of **Lanslebourg**.

Hotel :
★★ *Les Prais* (R.S.), ☎ 79.05.93.53, DC Euro, 27 rm ℗ ⫽ ⏏ ⚬ ⚙ ▱ closed 4 May-21 Jun, 13 Sep-20 Dec, 175. Rest. ♦ ♪ 60-130 ; child : 35.

⚠ ★*Municipal* (133 pl), ☎ 79.05.90.52.

MODANE, ⊠ 73500, 23 km SW of **Lanslebourg**.
↻ 1050-2750m.
ⓘ pl. Replaton.
SNCF ☎ 79.05.05.22.
Car rental : *Avis*, train station.

Hotels :
★★ *Le Perce-Neige* (L.F.), 14, av. Jean-Jaurès, ☎ 79.05.00.50, Euro Visa, 18 rm ℗ ⫽ ⚬ ♪ ⚬ ⁂ half pens, closed 1-16 May, 19 Oct-2 Nov, 320. Rest. ♦ ⫽ ♪ ⚬ ⁂ 55-135 ; child : 40.
★★ *Voyageurs* (L.F.), 16, pl. Sommeiller, ☎ 79.05.01.39, AE DC Euro Visa, 19 rm, closed Sun (l.s.), 15 Oct-15 Nov. Rest. ♦ 70-180.

⚠ ★★*Les Combes* (55 pl), ☎ 79.05.00.23.

SAINT-JEAN-DE-MAURIENNE, ⊠ 73300, 60 km S of **Albertville**.
ⓘ pl. de la cathédrale, ☎ 79.64.03.12.
SNCF ☎ 79.64.18.87.
Car rental : *Avis*, train station ; 353, rue des Chaudannes, ☎ 79.64.08.89.

Hotel :
★★ *Saint-Georges*, 334, rue de la République, ☎ 79.64.01.06, AE, 22 rm ℗ ⏏ ♪ 175.

⚠ ★*Municipal* (64 pl), ☎ 79.64.28.02.

SAINT-MICHEL-DE-MAURIENNE, ⊠ 73140, 17 km W of **Modane**.

Hotel :
★ *Galibier*, 32, rue du Temple, ☎ 79.56.50.49, 25 rm ℗ ⫽ ⏏ closed Sun ex Jul-Aug, Oct, 110. Rest. ♦ ⫽ 50-105.

La TOUSSUIRE-FONTCOUVERTE, ⊠ 73300 Saint-Jean-de-Maurienne, 16 km SW of **Saint-Jean**.
↻ 1300-2230m.

Hotel :
★★★ *Les Airelles* (L.F.), Vallée de l'Arvan, ☎ 79.56.75.88, Visa, 31 rm ℗ ⫽ ⚬ ⚙ half pens (h.s.), closed 26 Apr-1 Jul, 6 Sep-21 Dec, 270. Rest. ♦ ⁂ 60-150.

⚠ ★★*Caravaneige du Col* (62 pl), ☎ 79.83.00.80.

VALLOIRE, ⊠ 73450, 21 km S of **Saint-Jean-de-Maurienne**.
↻ 1430-2430m.   ⚘
ⓘ sur la place, ☎ 79.59.03.96.

Hotels :
★★★ *Grand Hôtel de Valloire et Galibier*, (Inter-Hôtel), ☎ 79.59.00.95, Tx 980553, AE DC, 43 rm ℗ ⫽ ⏏ ⚬ ⚬ half pens (h.s.), closed 15 Apr-15 Jun, 15 Sep-15 Dec, 380. Rest. ♦ ⫽ ♪ ⚬ 70-130.
★★★ *Christiania* (L.F.), ☎ 79.59.00.57, DC Euro Visa, 46 rm ℗ ⏏ ⚬ ♪ ⚙ pens (h.s.), closed 15 Apr-15 Jun, 15 Sep-15 Dec, 250. Rest. ♦ ⁂ 55-100 ; child : 35.
★ *Les Gentianes*, ☎ 79.59.03.66, 26 rm ℗ ⫽ ⏏ ⚙ pens (h.s.), closed 25 Apr-30 Jun, 1 Oct-20 Dec, 175. Rest. ♦ 60-80.

MEGÈVE**

Chamonix 36, Annecy 60, Paris 610 km
pop 5375 ⊠ *74120*   B2

Since the 1920s, the queen of French winter sports resorts, Megève is fashionable but retains its Savoyard charm and offers excellent social and sporting activities ; children are particularly welcome here. The sunny slopes of Mont d'Arbois, Rochebrune and the Jaillet provide marvellous skiing and offer a wide choice of walks in summer. See the Place de l'Eglise and the Calvary with figures sculpted in wood.

Nearby

▶ Pleasant views served summer and winter by cable-car : **Mont d'Arbois**★★ (alt. 1 833 m) ; **Croix des Salles**★★ (alt. 1 705 m) ; **Rochebrune-Super-Megève**★ (alt. 1 754 m). From all three sites there are magnificent views★★ over the Massif du Mont-Blanc. ▶ To the SW of Megève, by the N212, the **Arly Valley**, a high valley of prairies and pines studded with ski villages : **Praz-sur-Arly, Flumet** (view★ from the bridge of old wooden houses), **La Giettaz, Notre-Dame-de-Bellecombe, Crest-Voland**. Passing through the beautiful Arly gorges, one arrives at **Ugine**, centre of the valley and renowned for its special steel.   ☐

Practical Information ────────────

MEGÈVE
↻ 1113-2040m.
ⓘ rue de la Poste, ☎ 50.21.27.28/50.21.29.52.
SNCF ☎ 50.21.23.42.

Hotels :
★★★★(L) *Mont Blanc*, pl. de l'Eglise, ☎ 50.21.20.02, Tx 385854, AE DC Euro Visa, 65 rm ℗ ⫽ ⏏ ⚬ ♪ ⚙ ⚬ ▱ half pens (h.s.), closed 15 Apr-15 Jun, 2100. Rest. ♦♦ *Les Enfants Terribles* ♪ ⚬ 150-180.
★★★ *Au Vieux Moulin*, rue A.-Martin, ☎ 50.21.22.29, AE Visa, 35 rm ℗ ⫽ ⏏ ♪ ⚙ ▱ half pens (h.s.), closed 15 Apr-15 May, 20 Sep-15 Dec, 320. Rest. ♦♦ 125-140.
★★ *Perce-Neige*, rte de Rochebrune, ☎ 50.21.22.13, AE DC Euro Visa, 21 rm ℗ ⫽ ⏏ ♪ half pens (h.s.), closed May-Jun, 1 Sep-20 Dec, 480. Rest. ♦ ⫽ ♪ 90-160 ; child : 50.
★★ *Saint-Jean* (L.F.), 97, boucle des Houilles, ☎ 50.21.24.45, 15 rm ℗ ⫽ ⏏ ♪ ⚙ ⁂ closed 15 Apr-1 Jul, 15 Sep-15 Dec, 260. Rest. ♦ ⫽ ♪ ⁂ 70-100.

Restaurants :
♦♦ *Le Capucin Gourmand*, rue du Crêt-du-Midi, ☎ 50.21.01.98, AE DC Euro Visa ⏏ ♪ ⚬ closed Mon (l.s.), 20 Apr-24 Jun, 15 Sep-20 Dec, 145-220.
♦♦ *Le Tire-Bouchon*, rue d'Arly, ☎ 50.21.14.73, Euro Visa ♪ ⚬ closed Mon , Jun, 10 Oct-10 Nov. Spec : *blanc de turbot aux pâtes fraîches*, 70-100.

⚠ ★★*Gai Séjour* (60 pl), ☎ 50.21.22.58.

Recommended
Baby-sitting : info S.I.

Casino : ☎ 50.21.25.11.

Nearby

CREST-VOLAND, ⊠ 73590 Flumet, 16 km S.
⌇ 1134-1500m.
ⓘ ☎ 79.31.62.57.

Hotel :
★★ *Les Aravis*, ☎ 79.31.63.81, 17 rm 🅿 ≼ 🎟 ⌞ closed 15 Apr-30 Jun, 31 Aug-20 Dec, 160. Rest. ♦ ≼ 70-130.

FLUMET-VAL-D'ARLY, ⊠ 73590, 10 km SW.
⌇ 1000-1800m.
ⓘ ☎ 79.31.61.08.

Hotel :
★★★ *Hostellerie le Parc des Cèdres*, prom. des Aravis, ☎ 79.31.72.37, 24 rm 🅿 ≼ 🎟 closed 15 Apr-25 May, 1 Oct-15 Dec, 210. Rest. ♦♦ 90-140.

La GIETTAZ, ⊠ 73590 Flumet, 16 km W.
⌇ 1100-1900m.
ⓘ ☎ 79.32.91.90.

Hotel :
★★ *Relais des Aravis* (L.F.), ☎ 79.32.91.78, 27 rm 🅿 ≼ 🎟 closed 20 Apr-29 Jun, 15 Sep-20 Dec, 130. Rest. ♦ ⅋ 80-120.

Le MONT D'ARBOIS, ⊠ 74190 Le Fayet, 3 km N.

Hotels :
★★★★(L) *Chalet du Mont d'Arbois* (R.C.), rte du Mont-d'Arbois, ☎ 50.21.25.03, Tx 309335, AE DC Euro Visa, 12 rm 🅿 🎟 ⌞ ℘ half pens, closed 6 May-25 Dec, 1300. Rest. ♦♦♦ 230-280.
★★ *Ferme Duvillard*, ☎ 50.21.14.62, Visa, 19 rm 🅿 ≼ 🎟 ⌞ closed 15 Apr-15 Jun, 14 Sep-15 Dec, 300. Rest. ● ♦♦ 140-220.

Restaurant :
♦♦ *Le Chalet dans les Arbres*, ☎ 50.21.19.95 ≼ ⅋ closed Thu, 10 Apr-1 Jul, 15 Sep-15 Dec. A pretty little wooden chalet, 90-150.

PRAZ-SUR-ARLY, ⊠ 74120 Megève, 5 km SW.
⌇ 1000-1800m.
ⓘ rue Nationale, ☎ 50.21.90.57.

Hotel :
★★ *Mont Charvin* (L.F.), ☎ 50.21.90.05, Euro Visa, 31 rm 🅿 ≼ 🎟 ℘ closed 1 May-15 Jun, 1 Nov-20 Dec, 230. Rest. ♦ ⅋ ⅋ 80-130.

⌂ ★★*Chantalouette* (33 pl), ☎ 50.21.90.25.

MORZINE*

Evian 40, Annecy 93, Paris 604 km
pop 2650 ⊠ 74110   B1
The tourist capital of the Chablais region (→), with its chalets distributed around the junction of six valleys, a very popular medium-altitude excursion centre and ski resort. The ski slopes here are linked to those of Avoriaz by cable-car and road.

Nearby

▶ The classic car trip★★ *(29 km)* leads around **Montrond Lake**★ and **Avoriaz**★, the first winter sports resort to ban cars. Highly original architecture ; roofs and façades covered with red cedar shingles. Novarina chapel. ▶ From Morzine to Samoëns, 20 km via the spectacular **Ranfolly Pass**★★ (alt. 1 650 m ; view★★ ; restaurant). ▶ 7 km SE of Morzine is the winter sports resort of **Les Gets**. ▶ 8 km N, ruins of the Cistercian abbey of **Notre-Dame-d'Aulps** (12th-13thC).   □

Practical Information

MORZINE
⌇ 1000-2274m.
ⓘ pl. Cruzaz, ☎ 50.79.03.45.

Hotels :
● ★★★ *Le Dahu*, Le Mas-Métout, ☎ 50.79.11.12, Tx 309514, Visa, 26 rm 🅿 ≼ 🎟 ⌞ ⅋ half pens (h.s.), closed 15 Apr-15 Jun, 15 Sep-15 Dec, 640. Rest. ♦ ≼ 110-150.
★★ *Alpina*, Bois-Venant, ☎ 50.79.05.24, Tx 385620, Visa, 18 rm 🅿 ≼ 🎟 ⌞ closed 26 Apr-27 Jun, 6 Sep-20 Dec, 230. Rest. ♦ ⅋ ⅋ 70-100.
★★ *Chamois d'Or*, ☎ 50.79.13.78, 25 rm 🅿 ≼ 🎟 ⅋ ⅋ half pens (h.s.), closed 10 Apr-20 Dec, 235. Rest. ♦ ≼ ⅋ ⅋ 75-110.
⌂ ★★★*Le Fornay* (60 pl), ☎ 50.79.15.59.

Recommended
Youth hostel : *Beau Site*, ☎ 50.79.14.86.

Nearby

AVORIAZ, ⊠ 74110 Morzine, 14 km NE.
⌇ 1800-2275m.
ⓘ ☎ 50.74.02.11.

Hotel :
★★★ *Dromonts*, at 1 800 m, ☎ 50.74.08.11, AE DC Euro Visa, 37 rm ≼ closed 3 May-15 Dec, 360. Rest. ♦♦ & 200-300.

les GETS, ⊠ 74260, 7 km SW.
⌇ 1172-1850m.
ⓘ rte Nationale, ☎ 50.79.75.55.

Hotels :
★★★ *La Marmotte*, ☎ 50.79.75.39, Euro Visa, 45 rm 🅿 ≼ ⅋ 🖵 pens (h.s.), closed 15 May-28 Jun, 1 Sep-20 Dec, 900. Rest. ♦ ≼ ⅋ & For lodgers only, 100-200.
★★★ *Le Crychar* (C.H.), ☎ 50.79.72.84, Tx 385026, Euro Visa, 12 rm 3 apt 🅿 ≼ 🎟 ⌞ ⅋ closed 30 May-30 Jun, 7 Sep-15 Dec, 280.
★★★ *Les Alpages*, rte de la Turche, ☎ 50.79.82.79, AE Euro Visa, 20 rm 🅿 ≼ ⅋ ⌡ half pens (h.s.), closed 15 Apr-28 Jun, 1 Sep-15 Dec, 860. Rest. ♦ ≼ ⅋ 80-170.
★★ *Alpina*, ☎ 50.79.80.22, 29 rm 🅿 ≼ 🎟 ⌞ ⅋ ⅋ pens (h.s.), closed 15 Apr-1 Jul, 4 Sep-15 Dec, 380. Rest. ♦ ≼ ⅋ ⅋ Guests only, 60.

SAINT-GERVAIS-LES-BAINS**

Chamonix 25, Annecy 87, Paris 605 km
pop 4800 ⊠ 74170   B2
Skiing, with a network of lifts linked to those of Megève and Chamonix, a streetcar named Mont-Blanc, mountaineering and mountain schools, a climate particularly suited to children : Saint-Gervais also has a thermal spa (Fayet), the original source of its renown. The resort is very well situated on a plateau above the valley of the Arve at the exit from the pretty valley of Montjoie. See the **church of Notre-Dame-des-Alpes** (1938 ; architect Novarina, stained glass by Cingria ; fresco by Monier).

Nearby

▶ **Le Bettex** and **Mont d'Arbois**★★ *(8 km SW and cable-car)* : satellite resort of Saint-Gervais, Le Bettex is also a marvellous viewpoint for Mont-Blanc and Les Aravis. Summer or winter, the cable-car goes up to Mont d'Arbois★★ ; from here another cable-car descends to Megève. ▶ **Tramway du Mont-Blanc** (leaves from Fayet or Saint-Gervais). Although somewhat eclipsed by the cable-cars, the TMB offers a fine introduction to the High Alps : Voza Pass (alt. 1 653 m) and the Nid d'Aigle (Eagle's Nest)★ (alt. 2 386 m) : from here it is a 30-minute climb to the glacier of Bionnassay. ▶ **Saint-Nicolas-de-Veroce**★ *(9 km SSE)* occupies an extraordinary site opposite Mont-Blanc. Go up to Le Planey *(1.5 km)* or the plateau of la Croix *(3 km by car)* ; view★★ over the Montjoie Valley and Mont-Blanc. ▶ **Les Contamines-Montjoie** *(9 km S)* : a summer and winter resort in the Montjoie valley★. The road continues *(4 km)* to the **chapel of Notre-Dame de la Gorge,** a place of pilgrimage and a typical example of

Savoyard Baroque. Starting point for the tour of Mont-Blanc on foot (→ Chamonix). ☐

Practical Information

SAINT-GERVAIS-LES-BAINS
⚓ ☎ 50.78.23.47.
⌁ 900-1500m.
ⓘ av. du Mt-Paccard, ☎ 50.78.22.43.
SNCF ☎ 50.66.50.50.

Hotel :
★★★ *Carlina*, 95, rue du Rosay, ☎ 50.93.41.10, AE DC
Euro Visa, 34 rm Ⓟ ⌁ ⚶ ⚘ ⊠ half pens (h.s.), closed
20 Apr-15 Jun, 1 Oct-20 Dec. Near the lift, 625. Rest. ♦♦
⚶ ⚴ ⚘ 100-160.

▲ ★★*Les Dômes de Miage* (90 pl), ☎ 50.93.45.96.

Nearby

Les **CONTAMINES-MONTJOIE,** ⊠ 74190 Le Fayet,
9 km S.
⌁ 1164-2500m.
ⓘ pl. de la Mairie, ☎ 50.47.01.58.

Hotels :
★★★ *La Chemenaz*, les Hameaux du Lac, ☎ 50.47.02.44,
38 rm Ⓟ ⌁ ⚶ ⚴ ⊠ pens (h.s.), closed 15 Apr-15 May,
25 Sep-15 Dec, 700. Rest. ♦ ⚴ closed 15-30 Apr, 70-100.
★★ *Chamois*, ☎ 50.47.03.43, 17 rm Ⓟ ⌁ ⚶ half pens
(h.s.), closed 20 Apr-1 Jul, 1 Sep-18 Dec, 235. Rest. ♦
closed summer, 80-110.

Le **FAYET,** ⊠ 74190, 4 km N.

Hotel :
★★ *La Chaumière*, 222, av. de Genève, ☎ 50.78.15.88,
AE Euro Visa, 22 rm, closed Mon eve, 30 Sep-20 Dec,
220. Rest. ♦ ⚴ ⚵ 55-90 ; child : 35.

SAINT-JULIEN-EN-GENEVOIS

Genève 9, Annecy 35, Paris 538 km
pop 6911 ⊠ 74160   A1

SNCF ☎ 50.49.00.44.

Restaurants :
♦♦♦ *Abbaye de Pomier*, N 201, Présilly, 7 km S,
☎ 50.04.40.64 ⚶ ⚶ ⚴ closed Tue eve and Wed. 12th-C
charterhouse, 190-250.
♦♦ *Diligence et Taverne du Postillon*, rue de Genève,
☎ 50.49.07.55, AE DC Euro Visa, closed Mon and Sun
eve, 1-20 Jul, 30 Dec-10 Jan. Spec : turbot with seaweed
baked in a salt crust, *pigeonneau fermier cocotte*,
110-300.
♦ *Robert Favre*, rue de Genève, ☎ 50.49.07.55, AE
DC Euro Visa ⚵ closed Mon and Sun eve, 1-20 Jul,
30 Dec-10 Jan, 130-250.

Le SALÈVE*

                                                       A1
Le Salève is a huge mass of limestone (alt. 1 380 m)
that towers above Geneva. Although it is on French
territory, it is very much the stamping ground of Swiss
mountaineers (the mountaineering term *varappe*
comes from one of the routes across the Salève).

▶ The **route de Crête**★★ (D41) is easily accessible via
Cruseilles or Annemasse. View★★ over Geneva and the
lake, particularly from the orientation table of the Treize-
Arbres. ▶ **Annemasse** (pop. 28000) is an important crossroads in the heart of Europe. ▶ 1.5 km E of **Cruseilles**
are the leisure resources of the **Dronières Park** (20 acres
of water). ☐

Practical Information

ANNEMASSE, ⊠ 74100, 8 km E of **Genève.**
ⓘ rue de la Gare, ☎ 50.92.53.03.

SNCF ☎ 50.37.00.72.

Hotel :
★★★ *Central'Hôtel*, 2, pl. de l'Hôtel-de-Ville,
☎ 50.38.27.06, AE DC Euro Visa, 28 rm, 240.

BONS-EN-CHABLAIS, ⊠ 74890, 15 km NE of **Annemasse.**

Hotel :
★ *La Couronne*, ☎ 50.36.11.17, AE DC Euro Visa, 12 rm
Ⓟ ⚶ ⚴ ⚘ closed Sun eve and Mon, 24 Dec-28 Jan,
120. Rest. ● ♦♦ ⚘ A sweet little inn, a pretty garden
and fine food. Owner P. Meignan puts quality and reliability over mere show. An address to remember, 90-220.

SALLANCHES

Chamonix 28, Annecy 75, Paris 597 km
pop 8448 ⊠ 74700   B2

One of the best sunset views★★ of Mont-Blanc. This
little town was entirely rebuilt after a great fire
in 1840. The facilities of Mont-Blanc-Plage (shore)
attract numerous summer visitors.

Bassin de Sallanches★

▶ Between two valleys of the Arve, the Bassin de Sal-
lanches seems to have been created to provide views of
Mont-Blanc. ▶ Little roads down the mountain offer
changing views of the massif and the Aravis, including
the chain of the Fiz, spreading over the Plateau d'Assy.
▶ **Cordon** *(4 km SW)* is a charming village★ ; near
Nant-Cruy, see the chapel of Médonnet (panorama★★).
▶ **Combloux**★ *(8 km S)* is a pretty summer and winter holiday resort famous for its view★★ of Mont-Blanc.
▶ **Plateau d'Assy** *(11.5 km E)* : the trip★★ across the plateau in view of Mont-Blanc is a marvel. Facing South with
its back to the Fiz, the Plateau d'Assy stretches across
the shoulders of the mountain chain and is highly reputed
for its climate (numerous sanatoriums and family houses).
The **church of Notre-Dame-de-Toute-Grâce**★★ marks
an important point in the contemporary renewal of sacred
art. Designed by the architect Novarina (1937), consecrated in 1950, this church has been decorated by many
famous artists : on the façade is a mosaic by Fernand
Léger, inside is a tapestry by Lurçat, stained glass by
Rouault and Bazaine, works by Chagall, Bonnard, Matisse,
and a Christ by Germaine Richier. ▶ From the Plateau
d'Assy there is a difficult road★★ around **Plaine-Joux**
and the **Lac Vert** (Green Lake), which reflects Mont-Blanc.
                                                       ☐

Practical Information

SALLANCHES
ⓘ quai de l'Hôtel-de-Ville, ☎ 50.58.04.25.
SNCF ☎ 50.58.00.30.

Hotel :
★★★ *Les Sorbiers* (L.F.), 17, rue de la Paix,
☎ 50.58.01.22, Tx 309422, AE DC Euro Visa, 40 rm Ⓟ ⚶
⚴ ⚵ ⚴ ⚵ 250. Rest. ♦♦ ⚶ ⚴ ⚵ closed Mon noon and Sun
ex school hols, 70-140.

▲ ★★★★*Mont Blanc Village* (130 pl), ☎ 50.58.43.67 ;
★★*Miroir du Mont Blanc* (120 pl), ☎ 50.58.14.28 ;
★★*Relais de la Vallée Blanche* (90 pl), ☎ 50.58.20.05.

Nearby

Le plateau d' ASSY, ⊠ 74480, 12 km E.
ⓘ av. Dr-Arnaud, ☎ 50.58.80.52.

Hotel :
★★ *Le Tourisme*, 6, rue d'Anterne, ☎ 50.58.80.54, 15 rm
Ⓟ ⚶ ⚴ ⚵ 150.

COMBLOUX, ⊠ 74920, 8 km S.
⌁ 1000-1760m.
ⓘ Pavillon savoyard, RN, ☎ 50.58.60.49.

Hotels :

★★★★ *Aux Ducs de Savoie*, Le Bouchet, ☎ 50.58.61.43, AE DC Visa, 50 rm Ⓟ ⊰ 𝔐 ⚲ ᵭ ⊡ closed 26 Apr-12 Jun, 20 Sep-18 Dec, 300. Rest. ◆◆ ⊰ ⌁ ᵭ ⫯ 100-185.

★★★ *Au Cœur des Prés*, ☎ 50.58.70.55, Visa, 34 rm Ⓟ ⊰ 𝔐 ⚲ ⌁⁰ closed 26 Apr-1 Jun, 15 Sep-15 Dec, 220. Rest. ◆ ⊰ ⌁ ᵭ ⫯ 85-115.

★★★ *Les Aiguilles de Warens* (L.F.), ☎ 50.58.70.18, AE Euro Visa, 34 rm Ⓟ closed 10 Apr-20 Jun, 12 Sep-20 Dec, 290. Rest. ◆ ⌁ ⫯ 90-140.

CORDON, ✉ 74700, 5 km S.

Hotels :

★★★ *Le Chamois d'Or*, ☎ 50.58.05.16, AE DC Visa, 32 rm Ⓟ ⊰ 𝔐 ⚲ ⌁ ᵭ ⊡ ⌁⁰ half pens (h.s.), closed 15 Apr-31 May, 15 Sep-20 Dec. On the Mont-Blanc chain, 520. Rest. ◆◆ ⊰ ᵭ 90-130.

★★ *Solneige*, Les Miaz, ☎ 50.58.04.06, 29 rm Ⓟ ⊰ 𝔐 ⚲ half pens (h.s.), closed 30 Sep-18 Dec, 340. Rest. ◆ ⊰ 65-95.

The TARENTAISE*

B2

Trip from Moûtiers to Val-d'Isère *(59 km, half to full day)*

The Tarentaise, formed by the upper valley of the Isère between Conflans (Albertville) and Val d'Isère, owes its name to the ancient *Darentasia,* today's Moûtiers, which was the principal town. The Romans were not the only ones to use this link between Aosta and the Rhone Valley. They were followed by founders of monasteries, upland settlers, pedlars and seasonal migrants who flocked to the valley of the Isère. In modern times it has become a centre for "white coal" (Tignes dam, Isère-Arc diversion) and the electrochemical industry (Moûtiers), in addition to being a winter sports resort (Courchevel, La Plagne, Les Arcs, Tignes).

▶ **Moûtiers** (pop. 4 868) is the gateway to the Trois Vallées (→ Courchevel). Cathedral (11th-15thC; sculptures and wooden panelling) and the Museum of the Académie de Val d'Isère in the former archbishop's palace, now devoted to local history. 6 km SE : **Brides-les-Bains**, a watering place specialising in the treatment of obesity. ▶ **La Léchère** *(6 km NW)*, spa reputed for treatment of circulatory problems. ▶ **Aime** (pop. 2 472). Man has been living on this site since prehistoric times, as attested by the collections in the archaeology museum *(9-12 & 2-6, Jul.-Aug.; closed Tue.).* Built on the remains of a Gallo-Roman site and a 5th-6thC church, the ancient **Basilica of St. Martin**★★ is the best example in Savoie of early Romanesque (11thC) architecture *(9-12 & 2-6, Jul.-Aug.).* Fragments of frescos from 12th-13thC. ▶ 18 km SE : **La Plagne** (1 980 m) a big winter sports resort; access by cable-car to the Grande Rochette★★ (alt. 2 505 m; view) and the slopes of the Bellecôte (2 994 m, view★★). ▶ After Bellentre, a road to the right leads to the pretty **valley of Ponturin**★ and the villages around the summer and winter resort of **Peisey-Nancroix** (alt. 1 300 m). From here explore the Bellecôte and Pourri mountains. ▶ **Bourg-Saint-Maurice** (pop. 5 729) occupies a strategic position on a valley crossroads. 'The Bourg', as they say in Savoie, with the resort of **Les Arcs**, also has its ski-centres farther up the mountain : Arc 1600, Arc 1800 and Arc 2000, which have superb views★★ over the massifs of Beaufortin and Mont-Blanc. North, D902 goes to Le Cormet de Roselend and **the Beaufortin** (→). 31 km NE (route★★ N90) : the **Petit-Saint-Bernard Pass** (alt. 2 188 m), which was historically a very important military and commercial pass to the Aosta Valley. View★ of the Italian slopes of Mont-Blanc (panorama★★★ from the **summit of Lancebranlette**, alt. 2 928 m ; *4 hr round trip).* ▶ D902 now goes back up to the Haute-Tarentaise, under the villages perch on bluffs above the road. ▶ **Barrage de Tignes**★★ (1953 ; vaulted dam), the key construction in

the Haute-Isère electrification project (more than 1 billion kWh). The original village of Tignes, swallowed up by the resulting lake, was rebuilt on the left bank of the Isère. ▶ 5 km SW round a smaller lake is the winter sports centre of **Tignes** (2 100 m), also an excursion centre for trips into the Vanoise (cable-car from the Grande Motte★ alt. 3 450 m ; summer skiing). **Val d'Isère** (→).   ☐

Practical Information

Les ARCS, ✉ 73700 Bourg-Saint-Maurice, 12 km SE of **Bourg**.

↟ 1600-3000m.

ⓘ Maison des Arcs : at 1600 m, at 1800 m, ☎ 79.07.73.73/79.07.26.00; in Paris, 83 and 98 bd du Montparnasse, ☎ (1) 45.44.04.20/(1) 43.22.43.32.

Hotels :

★★★ *Cachette Pierre Blanche*, Arc 1600, ☎ 79.07.73.73, AE DC Euro Visa, 102 rm, closed 3 May-1 Jul, 15 Sep-17 Dec. Reserv. tel. 79.07.70.50. Rest. ◆ Club-hotel, package only, lifts incl, 3500F/wk in season (per pers).

★★★ *Golf*, Arc 1800, ☎ 79.07.25.17, Visa, 288 rm Ⓟ ⊰ 𝔐 ⚲ ⊡ ⌁⁰ closed 3 May-31 Jun, 15 Sep-15 Dec, 870. Rest. ◆◆◆ *Le Green* ⌁ ⫯ 140-400.

★ *Béguin*, Arc 1600, ☎ 79.07.02.92, 34 rm Ⓟ ⊰ ⚲ closed 4 May-30 Jun, 1 Sep-15 Dec, 185. Rest. ◆ 60-100.

BOURG-SAINT-MAURICE, ✉ 73700, 54 km E of **Albertville**.

↟ 800-1600m.

ⓘ pl. de la Gare, ☎ 79.07.04.92.

SNCF ☎ 79.07.00.74.

Car rental : *Avis,* train station.

Hotels :

★★ *Le Concorde* (L.F.), av. Mal-Leclerc, ☎ 79.07.08.90, 32 rm Ⓟ ⊰ ⚲ ⌁ ᵭ half pens (h.s.), closed May, Oct-Nov, 400. Rest. ◆ ⊰ ᵭ 65-160 ; child : 40.

★★ *Petit Saint-Bernard*, 2, av. du Stade, ☎ 79.07.04.32, AE DC Visa, 24 rm Ⓟ ⊰ closed May, 1 Oct-18 Dec, 170. Rest. ◆ 65-80.

Restaurants :

◆ *Edelweiss*, pl. de la Gare, ☎ 79.07.05.55 ⊰ closed June, 1-15 Nov, 40-120.

◆ *La Petite Auberge*, Le Reverset, ☎ 79.07.37.11, Visa ⌁ closed Mon and Sun eve, 50-120.

⚠ ★★★★ *Vallée Haute Renouveau* (37 pl), ☎ 79.07.18.07.

Recommended

Leisure activities : *stages,* courses in canoe-kayak, rafting, mountain climbing, rock collecting, info S.I.

BRIDES-LES-BAINS, ✉ 73600 Moûtiers-Tarentaise, 6 km SE of **Moûtiers**.

♨ (15 Apr-31 Oct), ☎ 79.55.23.44.

ⓘ rue Leray, ☎ 79.55.20.64.

Hotels :

★★★ *Savoy*, ☎ 79.55.20.55, 40 rm Ⓟ ⊰ 𝔐 ⌁ ⊡ closed Oct-Apr, 255. Rest. ◆◆ ⌁ ⫯ 140-170.

★★ *Verseau*, ☎ 79.55.27.44, Euro Visa, 31 rm Ⓟ ⊰ 𝔐 ⚲ ⊡ closed 20 Oct-15 Apr, 550. Rest. ◆ 120-210.

Recommended

Casino : ☎ 79.55.23.07, in the springs park.

MOUTIERS, 26 km NW of **Courchevel**.

Car rental : *Avis,* R.V. Hôtel Moderne, pl. de la Gare, ☎ 79.24.07.93 ; RN 90, Elf service station, ☎ 79.24.01.55.

La PLAGNE, ✉ 73210 Aime, 31 km SW of **Bourg-Saint-Maurice**.

↟ 1970-2700m.

ⓘ ☎ 79.09.02.01.

Hotels :

★★★ *Christina*, ☎ 79.09.28.20, AE DC Euro Visa, 58 rm Ⓟ ⊰ ⚲ closed 10 May-30 Jun, 350. Rest. ◆◆ ⌁ 160-210.

★★★ *Graciosa*, ☎ 79.09.00.18, AE DC Euro Visa, 10 rm 4 apt Ⓟ ⊰ ⚲ ⫪ pens (h.s.), closed 1 May-1 Dec, 580. Rest. ◆◆ ⌁ 125-165.

TIGNES, ⊠ 73320, 30 km SE of **Bourg-Saint-Maurice**.
⚡ 2100-3500m.
ⓘ ☎ 79.06.15.55, closed Wed.

Hotels :
★★★ **Curling**, Val-Claret, ☎ 79.06.34.34, Tx 309605, AE
DC Euro Visa, 35 rm, closed 3 May-3 Jul, 30 Aug-25 Oct,
450.
★★★ **Le Ski d'Or** (R.C.), ☎ 79.06.51.60, 21 rm ≪ ♪ 🎿 ⅙
half pens (h.s.), closed 1 May-15 Dec, 1100. Rest. ♦♦ ≪
♪ 225-250.
★★ **Aiguille Percée**, on the lake, ☎ 79.06.52.22, Visa,
38 rm ℙ ≪ closed May-1 Nov, 380. Rest. ♦ 100-150.

Restaurants :
♦♦ **Caveau**, Val-Claret, ☎ 79.06.52.32, Euro Visa, closed
15 May-1 Nov. Spec : *terrine de saumon, filet de turbot
au riesling*, 100-200.
♦ **La Poutrerie**, Val-Claret, ☎ 79.06.32.64, Visa, closed
15 May-15 Oct. Spec : *fondues et raclettes*, 70-110.

⅄ Le Chantel (400 pl), ☎ 79.06.15.55.

VALMOREL, ⊠ 73260 Aigue-Blanche, 11 km SW of **Moûtiers**.

Restaurant :
♦ **Le Grenier**, hameau du Mottet, ☎ 79.09.82.52 ≪ ♪
closed lunch, 1 May-15 Dec. Spec : *homard rôti au beurre
de corail, pétales de canneton au jus de truffes, symphonie de friandises*. Thursdays, violin and harpsichord,
60-230.

THONON-LES-BAINS*

Genève 33, Annecy 81, Paris 580 km
pop 28200 ⊠ 74200   A1
A flowery town sitting on a terrace overlooking Lac
Léman. This captivating town was the historic capital
of the Chablais region (→). Its waters have long been
sought by those with kidney problems. Geneva and
Lausanne are just a boat trip away and on the Plage
de Ripaille (shore) are excellent sailing facilities.

▶ The **Place du Château**★ offers a fine view of the lake
and the Swiss shore. Nearby : the Anthonioz Garden, the
English Garden★, and the Art and Leisure Centre (architect Novarina, 1966). ▶ From the Place, a funicular provides transportation to **Rives**, the port of Thonon, still retaining a few pretty houses from earlier times. ▶ The
Chablais Museum (history ; popular art ; excavation finds),
is in the 17thC château de Sonnaz *(10-12 & 3-6,
1 Jul.-15 Sep., closed Sun.)*. ▶ The **church of St. Hippolyte** (15th-17thC) made famous by St. François de Sales
during his mission to the Chablais (1594-98) to bring the
country back to Catholicism ; see the decoration★ of the
vault (stucco and paintings) by Italian artists of the 17thC.
Neo-Gothic Basilica of St. François de Sales, Chemin de
Croix★ by Maurice Denis.

Nearby

▶ **Château de Ripaille**★ *(1.5 km, access from Rives and
the Quai de Ripaille)*. It is not certain that the expression
"faire ripaille" (to feast) comes from the many fetes and
galas that were given there, but the former residence of
the House of Savoie (15thC) abounds in charm, in spite
of the numerous remodellings it has suffered. Kitchens★
of the Charterhouse (Carthusian monastery) installed
17th-18thC ; original equipment *(10-12 & 2-6, Apr.-Oct.,
closed Mon.)*. ▶ **Château des Allinges** *(6.6 km S) ;* ruins
of two châteaux (11th-14thC) on the peak ; a chapel from
the end of the 11thC with a Romanesque fresco★ ; view★
over Lake Léman and the Jura mountain region. ▶ Fortified **Château of Avully** (14th and 15thC : *May-Sep.,
10-12 & 2-6)*.   □

Practical Information _____

⚓ ☎ 50.26.17.22, (all year).
ⓘ pl. de l'Hôtel-de-Ville, ☎ 50.71.50.88.
SNCF ☎ 50.66.50.50.

🚢 pl. des Arts.
⚓ *Cie gale de Navigation sur le lac Léman*, Office des
Baigneurs, ☎ 50.71.14.71, from from port de Rives.
Car rental : *Avis*, Croisée d'Anthy, RN 5, ☎ 50.70.34.58 ;
train station.

Hotels :
★★★ **Savoie et Léman**, 40, bd Carnot, ☎ 50.71.13.80,
Tx 385905, AE DC Euro Visa, 35 rm ℙ ≪ closed Sat eve
and Sun (l.s.), school hols, 1-30 Sep. Practical school for
'lycée hôtelier', 300. Rest. ♦♦ ♪ ☀ 100-160.
★★ **Duché de Savoie** (L.F.), 43, av. Gal-Leclerc,
☎ 50.71.40.07, Visa, 15 rm ℙ ≪ 🐾 ☀ pens (h.s.), closed
1 Nov-15 Mar, 360. Rest. ♦ 80-140.
★ **Cygnes**, Port de Sechex, Margencel, ☎ 50.72.63.10,
Euro Visa, 17 rm ℙ ≪ ⚲ closed Mar, Dec-Jan, 150.
Rest. ♦ ≪ ♪ ⅙ 50-100.

⅄ ★★Camp de Morcy (80 pl), ☎ 50.71.32.65 ; ★★Le Lac
Noir (66 pl), ☎ 50.71.12.46 ; ★★Saint-Disdille (733 pl),
☎ 50.71.14.11.

THORENS-GLIÈRES

Annecy 19, Genève 41, Paris 567 km
pop 1376 ⊠ 74570   A1-2
In the heart of the tiny valley of Bornes this modest
summer resort was the home of St. François de Sales
(born 21 Aug. 1567). The **Chapelle de Sales** (1 km E)
marks the site of the château where he was born. His
family moved subsequently to the nearby **Château de
Thorens** (15thC) : souvenirs of the saint, a collection
of pictures and furniture *(9-12 & 2-6:30, Apr.-Nov.)*. □

VAL-D'ISÈRE*

Albertville 85, Chambéry 132, Paris 693 km
pop 1344 ⊠ 73150   B3

This is where the experts ski (including Jean-Claude
Killy and Marielle Goitschel), over varied slopes ranging in altitude from 1 800 m to 3 750 m. The nearby
Vanoise Nature Park and the Iseran Pass make this a
favourite centre for summer excursions.

▶ **Rocher de Bellevarde**★★ (alt. 2 826 m) and the **Tête
du Solaise**★★ (alt. 2 551 m) : both reached by cable-car ;
magnificent views.

Practical Information _____

⚡ 1850-3230m.
ⓘ ☎ 79.06.10.83.

Hotels :
★★★ **Altitude**, ☎ 79.06.12.55, Tx 980077, Visa, 30 rm ℙ
≪ ☀ ▭ closed 5 May-30 Jun, 30 Aug-1 Dec, 400.
Rest. ♦ ≪ ☀ 90-120.
★★★**Blizzard**, ☎ 79.06.02.07, 70 rm, closed May-Nov.
★★★**Christania**, ☎ 79.06.08.25, 46 rm, closed May-Nov.
★★★**Tsanteleina**, ☎ 79.06.12.13, 60 rm, closed
28 Aug.-1st Dec.
★★★**La Savoyarde**, ☎ 79.06.01.55, 46 rm, closed
3 May-1st Dec.
★★ **Bellevue**, ☎ 79.06.00.03, Tx 980296, 25 rm ☀ ♪
half pens (h.s.), closed 5 May-15 Jun, 15 Sep-22 Nov,
230. Rest. ♦ ☀ 70-110.
★★ **Galise**, ☎ 79.06.05.04, 37 rm ℙ pens, closed
23 Apr-5 Dec, 270. Rest. ♦ ☀ 80-130.

Restaurants :
♦♦ **Brussels**, ☎ 79.06.01.58, Euro Visa, closed
1 May-1 Dec. With rooms. Terrace in the centre of town,
at the foot of the trails, 120-210.
♦♦ **Goitschel'Lodge**, ☎ 79.06.02.01, Euro Visa ⚲ ♪
closed 1 Sep-1 Dec. Spec : *huîtres florentines, escalope de
saumon à l'oseille, canard aux oignons confits à l'orange*.
Warm welcome from Marielle, 120-210.
♦ **Bar Jacques**, ☎ 79.06.03.89, AE DC Euro Visa ♪ closed

4 May-28 Jun. A chummy ambience, and Lyonnais bistro dishes washed down with Beaujolais. Open until 4am, 170-230.
♦ *L'Arolay*, Le Fornet, ☎ 79.06.11.68 Ⓟ ≪ ☷ ☌ ♪ closed 3 May-1 Jul, 1 Sep-20 Dec. Spec : *braserade, raclette, fondue*, 80-130.

⚠ ★★*Les Richardes* (75 pl), ☎ 79.06.00.60.

Recommended
Leisure activities : *nature safari*, ☎ 79.06.00.03, Jun-Sep.

VANOISE Massif**

B3

A happy outcome of the difficult marriage between tourism and nature. The **National Park** between Arc and Isère includes the Massif de la Vanoise. The first park of this type created in France (1963), it covers 530 km^2, and is surrounded by an outer park of 1 450 km^2, which attracts tourists from the Maurienne and Tarentaise regions. With its Italian neighbour, the Gran Paradiso, this park pursues the objectives of preserving and protecting alpine flora and fauna and without doubt constitutes one of the most charming initiations to nature study. Ibex, chamois, marmot and blue hare live peacefully here among an extraordinarily rich variety of flowers, especially during June and July. The park is ideal for hikers.

▶ **Pralognan-la-Vanoise**★ (pop. 569) is the best departure point for exploring the park. Surrounded by fir trees and running water at the foot of the Grand Marchet, which looks as if it alone were holding back the sparkling icefields of the Vanoise. It is not uncommon to see summer visitors suddenly scramble from their cars to focus binoculars on the peaks : a troop of chamois has come into view. The **Maison du Parc et du Tourisme** de Pralognan provides all the necessary information for excursions, including details of mountain refuges and overnight lodgings, guided trips and mountain schools with guides from the national park. ▶ **GR55**, which leads from the upper station of Mont Bochor★ cable-car, (alt. 2 023 m) is the best path for visiting the park. ▶ The charming **Doron du Champagny Valley**★ can be reached from Bozel, 14 km NW of Pralognan; this is another excellent way into the park. ▶ Other entrances : Peisey-Nancroix, Tignes (→ Tarentaise), Val d'Isère (→), Bonneval, Bessans, Lanslevillard (→ Maurienne). ☐

Practical Information ────────────

PRALOGNAN-LA-VANOISE, ⊠ 73710, 55 km SE of **Albertville.**
𝔷 1470-2360m.
ⓘ Maison du Parc, ☎ 79.08.71.68.

Hotels :
★★ *Grand Bec* (L.F.), ☎ 79.08.71.10, 39 rm Ⓟ ≪ ☷ ☌ ▱ ⤴ half pens (h.s.), closed 25 Apr-1 Jun, 20 Sep-20 Dec, 480. Rest. ♦ ≪ ♪ ℣ 70-90.
★ *La Vallée Blanche*, ☎ 79.08.70.74, Visa, 11 rm, closed 20 Apr-31 May, 20 Sep-20 Dec, 110. Rest. ♦ ♪ 60-80.

⚠ ★★*Le Chamois* (200 pl), ☎ 79.08.71.54.

Touraine, Blésois, Orléanais

▶ The light of the Val de Loire is different from that of the surrounding Ile-de-France and Normandy regions. Leonardo da Vinci, guest of François I, drew the royal château of Amboise bathed in an ephemeral pink light overlaid with a triumphant patina of gold. In his Notebook he wrote of his concern to "render the light accurately".

Along the embankments built to contain floods — for there have been some very devastating ones — stand little houses in white tufa, which still house bargees and market-gardeners. The region is the "garden of France", and fruit, vegetables and flowers thrive on the rich alluvium deposited by the Loire and its tributaries. The soft, chalky tufa conditions the character of the Loire region and creates an underground world of cave villages, wine cellars, and underground chicory and mushroom beds. The white stone was also hewed out of the earth to build cathedrals, royal châteaux and great buildings of state.

For most people, the Loire Valley is above all the valley of châteaux. Tourists "do" the Loire châteaux, rather as they "do" the Greek islands, visiting three or four a day. Chambord, a fairy castle nestling amidst woods and ponds, shares the stage with Blois and its fabulous staircase, Chaumont with its feudal past, Chenonceaux stretching effortlessly across the river Cher, and Azay-le-Rideau, set like a diamond in the waters of the Indre. All eloquent witnesses to the Renaissance in arts and letters which once flowered along the banks of the Loire.

But Touraine is more than castles — it is also a whole other world of lonely manor-houses in leafy forests, bubbling streams and peaceful villages sleeping in the shadow of their Romanesque and Gothic churches, dense forests where lords and their subjects once hunted fierce packs of wolves, the earthenware factories of Gien and the strange cave villages scattered throughout the region. ☐

 ## Don't miss

★★★ Azay-le-Rideau A2, Chambord B2, Chenonceaux B2, Saint-Benoît-sur-Loire C1, Tours A2.

★★ Amboise A2, Beaugency B1, Blois B2, Chaumont-sur-Loire B2, Cheverny B2, Chinon A2, Langeais A2, Loches A2, Loir Valley A-B1, Vendôme B1, Villandry A2.

★ Cher Valley B2, Gien C2, Le Grand-Pressigny A3, Indre Valley A2, Lavardin A1-2, Montoire-sur-le-Loir B1-2, Montrichard B2, Orléans B1, Richelieu A3, Saché A2, Saint-Aignan B2, the Sologne Region B2, Sully-sur-Loire C1, Ussé A2.

Weekend tips

Near Chambord and Cheverny, the lesser known châteaux around the Sologne : Villesavin, Troussay, Beauregard and Fougères (→ Cheverny). Lunch at Cour-Cheverny or Blois and spend the night at Vendôme (→). The next day see the delightful villages in the Loir Valley (→) : Montoire (lunch), Lavardin and Trôo.

Dovecote, or "fuie", in the Loire Valley

Tufat buil-house

Typical Sologne house

Brief regional history

Up to 1200 BC
In the Neolithic and Paleolithic periods, **Le Grand-Pressigny** (S of Tours) became an important "industrial" centre because of the discovery of flint there : it was used for making saws, hatchets, knives and arrows and for export to Belgium and Switzerland, and was used for trade in the Massif Central and the Alps. ● At the end of the Neolithic Period, a Mediterranean people, the **Ligurians,** overran Brittany and the Loire *(Liger)* to which they gave their name.

1200 BC-4thC AD
The **Celts** came from central Europe, colonizing the Val de Loire (Loire Valley) between 1200 and 800 BC. They founded Orléans and Blois and established a port and a town built on piles at Tours, which controlled trade on the Loire and the Cher. The people of Tours were called **Turones** ("the flooded"). ● In 52BC, **Julius Caesar** arrived with his legions ; thenceforth the Angevins, Bretons and Tourangeaux lived with the *Pax Romana,* Roman gods, paved roads, baths, forums, theatres and aqueducts in their towns. ● Christianity was introduced in the first centuries AD, **St Martin of Tours** (316-97) being its most popular exponent.

Facts and figures
Location : *The Orléanais, the Blois and the Touraine regions belong to what is usually called the Val de Loire (Loire Valley). A distinction is made between the Val d'Orléans, the Val de Loire proper (between Orléans and Tours) and the Val de Touraine. All told, a 300-km strip, three to twelve km wide, with neighbouring regions around the tributaries of the Loire.*
Area : *19 180 km².*
Climate : *Proverbial for its gentle climate ; the Atlantic ocean makes for mild winters and temperate summers. The temperature rarely falls below 10 °C (50 °F). Indian summers are a reality here ; the autumn is an ideal season for visiting the Val de Loire.*
Population : *1 252 476 ; Loiret 490 189 ; Loir-et-Cher 296 200 ; Indre-et-Loire 478 601.*
Administration : *Loiret Department, Prefecture : Orléans ; **Loir-et-Cher** Department, Prefecture : Blois ; **Indre-et-Loire** Department, Prefecture : Tours.*

4th-8thC

During this period of **Barbarian** and later Arab **invasion,** the great abbeys in the Val de Loire struggled to preserve Christian teachings and fragments of Greek and Roman **knowledge.** ● In 448, **Clovis** and the Germanic Merovingians began their **conquest of Gaul** and established themselves in the Val de Loire. On the other bank was the Visigoth kingdom of Alaric. Clovis killed Alaric and the Val de Loire fell under the domain of Germain and his descendants, the Merovingians. Their reign was marked by crime and infighting, until **Clotilde,** the wife of Clovis, and **Radegonde,** Clotaire's wife. Radegonde founded two monasteries, beacons of charity and culture in an otherwise dark age. In 451, the Huns were repelled at Bordeaux, and in 731, the Arabs fought their way to the gates of Tours, before their defeat at Poitiers by Charles Martel.

8thC-1453

The reign of **Charlemagne** was one of stability. Bishop Théodulfe founded the first University at Orléans and established free schooling. The Val de Loire thus became a **centre of learning.** ● But the Vikings were crossing the Channel : Nantes and Tours were soon enveloped in flames. The Normans intensified their attacks. From this troubled period date the castle-keeps, fortified churches and farms of the Loire Valley. The bureaucrats (counts) who governed the towns became more and more powerful in the general confusion. ● When the Count of Anjou, **Henry Plantagenêt,** became King of England (his mother was descended from William the Conqueror), the Val de Loire became the scene of a struggle between the Plantagenêts and the Capetians. Philippe Auguste came off best (Azay-le-Rideau 1189); the peace lasted for a century, only to be followed by the **Hundred Years' War** between France and England (1337-1453).

1453-1589

The appearance of **Joan of Arc** and the establishment on the throne of the House of Valois ended the Hundred Years' War; the Kings of France remained in the Val de Loire. ● Under **Louis XI,** trade was revived; he started the **silk** industry at Tours and, like his father Charles VII, relied on merchants and craftsmen rather than feudal lords as his **administrators.** The beautiful town houses in Blois and Tours were built by these civil servants, as were Chenonceaux, Villandry, Azay-le-Rideau and the Blésois châteaux. ● 1494 to 1559 saw a continual French presence on the Italian peninsula; as a result many Italian artists and artisans came to work in France, and the Italian Renaissance took root along the Loire. ● The **Wars of Religion** between Catholics and Protestants subsequent-

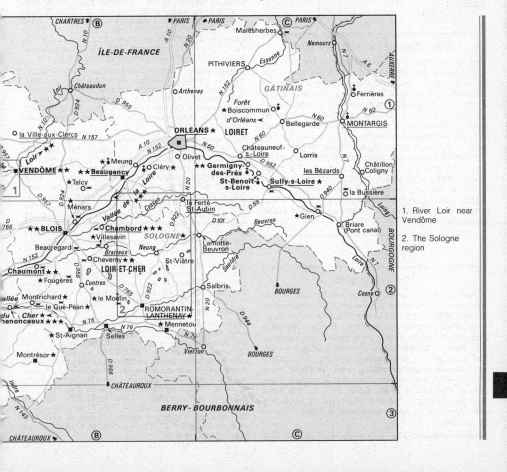

1. River Loir near Vendôme

2. The Sologne region

ly broke out in the Loire Valley and were only partially resolved when the Protestant Henri IV was converted to Catholicism, and moved the seat of government to **Paris.**

17thC to the present
The 18thC mansions of Blois and Tours were built during the commercial and manufacturing **expansion** in the Val de Loire. ● During the Revolution, the Orléanais, suspected of being moderates, were subjected to the excesses of Collot d'Herbois and Barrère. ● During the wars of 1870 and 1940, the government regrouped in the Loire, and the Louvre treasures were hidden in Chambord castle. **Orléans, Blois** and **Tours** were badly damaged during the last war, and were rebuilt in regional architectural style. In the last few years an effort has been made to turn the old *quartiers* into pedestrian zones, and thus rediscover their former ambience. ● **Rungis market,** open at dawn, continues the tradition of Orléanais and Touraine daily life : vegetables, fruits and flowers are sold there. The major industries of the area are **printing,** saw-mills, pharmaceutical products, clothing and shoe manufacture. The **decentralisation** of Paris toward Val de Loire has brought new industries, such as metallurgy, mechanics, computers (at Blois), pneumatics, perfumes, etc. And nuclear power stations are located at Chinon, Avarayon and Saint-Laurent-des-Eaux.

The kings of the Val de Loire

The seat of royalty was transferred to the Touraine region when the English captured Paris during the Hundred Years' War, and the Plantagenêt Kings of England ruled most of France. But Touraine, Berry, Poitou and the Blésois remained faithful to the House of Valois, and in 1422 Charles VII was proclaimed King at Mehun-sur-Yèvre. With the advent of Joan of Arc, the reconquest of the Val de Loire was the first step in the restoration of the French kingdom and Charles VII established himself in the provinces which had supported him. Louis XI and Charles VIII could subsequently have taken up residence in Paris, but preferred the charms of the Touraine. The glow of royalty faded from the Val de Loire with Henri IV and the Protestant question .... Paris was worth a Mass, as he said.

The troglodytes

In the Touraine, around Vendôme and S of the Sarthe, the soft white limestone tufa bordering the river proved ideally suited for carving out semi-subterranean dwellings; even chapels and manors have been partially dug into the rock. These days cellars and terraces are often complemented by a house built against the cliff face. In this wine-growing country, tufa cellars are naturally used for storing wine; many of them are open for wine-tasting (Amboise, Montlouis, Vouvray...). The valleys of the Loire, the Loir, the Indre and the Cher have the best examples of troglodyte dwellings. See especially the village of Trôo (→ Valley of the Loir).

 Practical information

Information : *Comité Régional du Tourisme, (C.R.T.),* Hôtel régional, 9, rue Pierre-Lentin, 45000 Orléans, ☎ 38.54.95.42. **Indre-et-Loire** : *Comité Départemental du Tourisme (C.D.T.),* 16, rue de Buffon, 37032 Tours Cedex, ☎ 47.61.61.23, ext 2160 or 2161. **Loiret** : *C.D.T.,* 3, rue de la Bretonnerie, 45000 Orléans, ☎ 38.54.83.83. **Loiret-Cher** : *C.D.T.,* 11, pl. du Château, 41000 Blois, ☎ 54.78.55.50. *Dir. rég. de la Jeunesse et des Sports,* 1, bd de la Motte-Sanguin, B.P. 14, 45015 Orléans Cedex, ☎ 38.62.70.80. *Dir. rég. des Affaires culturelles,* 6, rue Dupanloup, 45043 Orléans Cedex, ☎ 38.68.11.86.

Reservations : *Loisirs-Accueil* : **Loir-et-Cher,** same address as *C.D.T.;* **Loiret,** same address as *C.D.T.,* ☎ 38.62.04.88.

S.O.S. : **Indre-et-Loire** : *SAMU* (emergency medical service), ☎ 47.28.15.15. **Loir-et-Cher** : *SAMU,* ☎ 54.78.78.78. **Loiret** : *SAMU,* ☎ 38.63.33.33. *Poisoning emergency centre :* Tours, ☎ 47.66.85.11.

Weather forecast : Indre-et-Loire, ☎ 47.54.54.43; **Loiret-Cher,** ☎ 54.74.60.24; **Loiret,** ☎ 38.88.44.83.

Rural gîtes and chambres d'hôtes : Indre-et-Loire : *Chambre d'agriculture,* 38, rue A.-Fresnel, 37170 Chambray-lès-Tours Cedex, ☎ 47.27.56.10. **Loir-et-Cher :** *C.D.T.* **Loiret :** *C.D.T.*

Camping vehicle rental : *Locamat ELS,* centre commercial Petite-Arche, 37000 Tours, ☎ 47.54.20.76. **Loir-et-Cher :** *Bousquet Loisirs,* la Cave, Pouillé, 41110 Saint-Aignan, ☎ 54.71.44.44; *Locamat ELS,* 76, av. de Vendôme, 41000 Blois, ☎ 54.43.48.22. **Loiret :** *Locamat ELS,* zone des Cent-Arpens, 163, rue Thomas-Édison, Saran, 45400 Fleury-les-Aubrais, ☎ 38.73.06.66.

Cultural events : Mar : *musical weekends* in Montbazon, château d'Artigny (until Oct). **Jul :** *Touraine music festival* in La Grange-de-Meslay, Langeais *international music days; festival* in Sully and Loiret. **Aug :** *summer* in Loir-et-Cher, concerts. **Oct-Mar :** *concerts of chimes* at N.-D.-de-la-Trinité in Blois (every other Sat). **Dec :** *international music week* in Orléans.

Fairs and events : Jan : *Vouvray wine fair.* **Feb :** *wine fair* in Bourgueil. **Mar :** *paper fair* in Orléans. **Apr :** *Bourgueil wine fair.* **May :** *andouillette* (chitterling sausages) *fair* in Mennetou-sur-Cher; *rhododendron festival* in Châteauneuf-sur-Loire. **Jun :** *Chinon flower show; folklore* in Saint-Jean-de-la-Ruelle; *dog fair* in Mur-de-Sologne. **Jul :** *garlic fairs* in Bourgueil, Tours; *peasant market* in Loches; *vintage car races* at Blois. **Aug :** *donkey fair* in Savonnières (1st Sun); *world folklore festival* in Montoire-sur-Loir. **Sep :** *wine harvest chapterhouse* in Chinon; *melon festival* in Amboise; *festival du pâté à la citrouille* in Millançay. **End Oct :** *Sologne gastronomy festival* in Romorantin; *apple fair* in Azay-le-Rideau.

Rambling and hiking : Topoguide n° 3; 3/32, 31. I.G.N. map of the Sologne region, 1/100 000, for information concerning access means, activities, unusual excursions and sites, sports groups and accommodation possibilities, enq. : *Tourisme-Accueil Loiret :* see C.D.T. *Tourisme-Accueil Loir-et-Cher.*

Technical tourism : *Faïencerie de Gien,* 78, pl. de la Victoire, 45500 Gien, ☎ 38.67.00.05, by appt. daily ex Sun. and nat. hols. *Orlane,* 7, rue de Chateaubriand, 45100 Orléans-La Source, ☎ 38.63.02.84, by appt. *Porcelaine de Sologne,* 54, av. de Vierzon, 41600 Lamotte-Beuvron, by appt. with dir. techn. *Ets Monmousseau* (regional wines), rte de Vierzon, 41400 Montrichard, ☎ 54.32.07.04, from Easter to All Saints' Day from 9-12 & 2-6, by appt. *Chocolat Poulain,* 41007 Blois, near the train station, 1 hr 30-tour, ☎ 54.78.39.21 (am only, Sat. & Sun. by appt.). *Centrale d'Avoine,* Centrale de Saint-Laurent-des-Eaux, B.P. 23, 37420 Avoine, ☎ 47.93.04.50 (am only by appt. ex Sat).

Scenic railways : *Ligne Chinon-Richelieu-Champigny-Ligré-la-Rivière* with sampling of local produce; mid-May-end Sep : 1 round-trip Sat, 2 round-trip Sun. *Marcilly-sur-Maulne*, 37330 Château-la-Vallière, ☎ 47.24.07.95 and 47.24.04.46. Sun and nat. hols. : May-end Sep. *Blanc Argent*, a small train which traverses the Sologne. Info. *C.D.T.*

Riding holidays : *Tourisme-Accueil du Loiret, Loir-et-Cher, Indre-et-Loire*, see *C.D.T. Association régionale de tourisme équestre du Val de Loire-Centre*, B.P. 7, 36600 Valençay.

Horse drawn wagon or caravan : *Tourisme-Accueil du Loiret, Loir-et-Cher*, ask at *C.D.T. Indre-et-Loire* : Thierry Kuenfer, ☎ 47.26.80.18.

The school of the Loire and the Renaissance

After the Hundred Years' War, the second half of the 15thC proved a period of growth and well-being. A return to more orderly ways allowed security to be gradually sacrificed to comfort; the châteaux became progressively less military and took on the role of country estates. The school of the Loire (Plessis-lès-Tours, Gien, Clos-Lucé, Azay-le-Rideau) is marked by the introduction of Italian designs (Charles VIII brought back a number of artists from his campaigns in Italy), and the conservatism which adhered to traditional concepts. This first French Renaissance period ended with the Pavia Campaign (1525) and was succeeded by a more intellectual phase reflecting the ideas of humanist architects, whose inspiration was drawn first from the Italians and later, more directly, from classical antiquity.

Cycling holidays : *Comité départemental d'Indre-et-Loire*, centre municipal des sports, 37000 Tours. *Association culturelle de la Touraine du Sud*, ☎ 47.94.91.24. *Tourisme-Accueil du Loiret, du Loir-et-Cher* : see *C.D.T.* Train + bike : S.N.C.F. stations and at Tours, ☎ 47.61.46.46.

River and canal cruises : canoe trip down the Loire and Vienne rivers, canoe-kayak excursions on the Loiret : *Dir. dép. de la Jeunesse et des Sports.* Holidays in houseboats or inflatable motorized dinghies : *Tourisme-Accueil du Loiret* : *C.D.T.* Trips in barge-caravans : round-trip Chinon-Monsoreau : *O.T. Chinon*, 12, rue Voltaire, 37500 Chinon, ☎ 47.93.17.85. *Tourisme-Accueil Loir-et-Cher.*

Handicraft courses : weaving (Amboise), ceramics, drawing, painting (Gâtinais), *Tourisme-Accueil Loiret*, see *C.D.T.*, pottery (Indre-et-Loire), see *C.D.T.*

Other courses : archaeology in Vendômois, monument restoration (Lavardin), piloting (aéroclub de Touraine), hang-gliding, ultra-light aircraft, flying acrobatics (aérodrome d'Amboise-Dierre-Chinon), œnology (wine appreciation, château d'Artigny, Blois), cooking (Chinon), genealogy (Blois), marionnettes (Orléans), traditional music (Le Grand-Pressigny), tennis (Blois, ask at *C.D.T. Loir-et-Cher;* Beaugency, ask at *C.D.T. Loiret*), golf (Sully-sur-Loire, ask at *C.D.T. Loiret*) and wind-surfing (Loire lake, ask at *C.D.T. Loir-et-Cher*).

Wine guide : *Comité interprofessionnel des vins de Touraine*, 19 sq. Prosper-Mérimée, 37000 Tours, ☎ 47.05.40.01. Many cellars are open for visits, ask at *C.D.T.*

Golf : Ballan-Miré (18 holes); Sully-sur-Loire (18 holes); Donnery-Orléans (9 holes).

Sailing and wind-surfing : stretches of water : Tours and Saint-Avertin, lac du Rillé, lac de Chemillé-sur-Indrois, lac

The rich table of the Val de Loire

Fruit and vegetables are the speciality of the Touraine and Orléanais regions (Sologne strawberries and Vineuil asparagus). The Loire provides excellent salmon, carp (à la Chambord), shad (with mushrooms) and other river fish. Pork and poultry provide the many forms of andouillette, andouille (chitterling sausages) and rillettes (potted meat), black or white boudin (blood sausage), noisette de porc (with prunes) and poultry (with girolle mushrooms). In the Sologne there are pheasant, boar, lark and game pâtés and wild mushrooms...
Country bread, goat cheese and red wine are the traditional staples of the Tourangeaux (inhabitants of Touraine). Goat cheese comes in a variety of shapes and sizes. In the Orléanais they produce other delicious cheeses : Saint-Benoît, Cendré d'Olivet and Patay.
In the French equivalent of the Gingerbread House, le parquet était de croquet, in other words, the floors were made of a delicious crunchy almond biscuit, only rivalled in popularity by Pithiviers (from the town of the same name), macarons (from Cormery), "Gateaux Royaux" (from Amboise and Loches) and other local specialities.
Confectionery in the Val de Loire still clings to the traditional recipes : pruneaux (prunes) de Tours, crystallized fruit, quince marmalade from Orléans, barley sugar and much more.

The wines of Touraine

Rabelais sang the praises of the red and white wines of Touraine. Vouvray is probably the best known, a dry, demi-sec or sweet white wine. On the opposite side of the Loire, Montlouis is another dry or demi-sec white, which is drinkable earlier than Vouvray and ages well. Other A.C. wines (white and rosé) : Touraine-Amboise, Touraine-Mesland, Touraine-Azay-le-Rideau and Touraine. All go very well with fish and white meat. As for the reds, Chinon, as Rabelais well knew, can be drunk young like Bourgueil. Chinon is full-bodied and ages well, while Bourgueil is a hardier and more sinewy wine which can take fifteen to twenty years in the bottle. Good years : 64, 66, 69, 70, 71, 75, 76, 78, 79, 81, 82 and 83. The Orléanais and the Blésois : red, white and rosé from the Coteaux de Giennois and the Orléanais (Gris-Meunier, Cheverny, Coteaux du Vendômois and Châteaumeillant). Try Jasnières, a well-known dry white from the Coteaux du Loir (communes of Lhomme and Chartre-sur-le-Loir).

de Loire, Montrichard, le Plessis-Dodin : *C.D.T. Indre-et-Loire;* Cerdon : *C.D.T. Loiret;* Châtres-sur-Cher, Salbris : *C.D.T. Loir-et-Cher.*

Hunting and shooting : *Féd. dép. : Indre-et-Loire* : 9, imp. Heurteloup, 37012 Tours Cedex, ☎ 47.05.65.25; **Loir-et-Cher** : 52, av. du Gal-Leclerc, 41000 Blois, ☎ 54.78.51.29; **Loiret** : 31, rue du Bœuf-St-Patern, 45000 Orléans, ☎ 38.53.52.40. With or without dogs, both duck and waterfowl hunting : *Loisirs-Accueil Loir-et-Cher* stag-hunting from Nov-end Mar, ☎ 47.43.49.45.

Fishing : *Féd. dép. : Indre-et-Loir* : 25, rue C.-Gilles, 37000 Tours, ☎ 47.05.33.77. **Loir-et-Cher** : 36, Grande-Rue, Avaray, 41500 Mer, ☎ 54.81.04.28. **Loiret** : 144, rue des Anquignis, 45100 Orléans, ☎ 38.56.62.69.

Towns and places

AMBOISE**

Tours 25, Châteauroux 104, Paris 221 km
pop 11415 ✕ 37400   A2

The kings of France appreciated their residence in this region that is reminiscent of the atmospheric light in Leonardo da Vinci paintings. In 1516 François I invited Leonardo, "the greatest genius of all time", to Amboise. With him he brought the *Mona Lisa...*

► The château★★, terraced high above the river, is flanked by two enormous round towers : the Tour des Minimes beside the Loire once had a spiral ramp for horsemen *(low season, 9-12 & 2-6:30; high season, 9-7; son et lumière, info : 47.57.09.28).* On the left, the **chapel of St. Hubert** (1493) is a Gothic jewel. A stone slab covers a tomb reputed to be that of Leonardo da Vinci. The **Logis du Roi** *(King's Lodge;* late Gothic, end 15thC) was built by Charles VIII, who died there after walking into a very low doorway. Gothic and Renaissance furniture and Aubusson tapestries in the Louis XII-François I wing. The young François spent his youth and the first three years of his reign here, giving magnificent balls, tourneys and masquerades. See the **gardens** and the terraces. ► The Rue Victor-Hugo (old houses) leads to the **Manor of Le Clos-Lucé★** *(9-7 Jun.-15 Sep.; rest of year, 9-12 & 2-7).* This is where Leonardo spent the last three years of his life (d. 1519). He was painter, sculptor, architect, engineer, mathematician, anatomist, writer and musician, and this 15thC manor recalls the period when this great savant drew the plans of the first aeroplane and the first automobile. In the basement are scale models of **machines★** based on his sketches, put together by I.B.M. ► The town itself offers an excellent market *(Sun. am)* and a number of leisurely walks : down the Rue de la Concorde (16thC houses); around the foot of the château; and the pedestrian precinct of **Rue Nationale**, where local specialities such as *rillettes*, goat cheese and pastries tempt the passer-by. ► You arrive eventually at the **church of St. Denis★** (12thC Angevin) with its figured capitals and a 16thC effigy★, possibly of La Belle Babou, mistress of François I.

Nearby

► **Amboise Forest** *(S of town),* covering the plateau between the Loire and the Cher. Marked paths through the park of La Moutonnerie. ► The **Chanteloup Pagoda** *(2.5 km SE, on the edge of the forest)* reflects the taste of the period for Chinese curios *(Jan.-Mar., 9-5, closed Mon.; Apr.-15 Sept., 9-8, closed Mon. am; 16 Sept.-11 Nov., 9-6, closed Mon. am; 12 Nov.-Dec., 9-5, closed Mon.).* ► **Château-Renault** *(22 km N)* : 12th-18thC; 11 km W : church of **Saint-Laurent-en-Gâtines**, in a former 15thC manor.   ☐

Practical Information

AMBOISE
ℹ️ quai du Gal-de-Gaulle, ☎ 47.57.09.28.
SNCF ☎ 47.57.03.89.

Hotels :
★★★ ***Belle-Vue*** (L.F.), 12, quai Charles-Guinot, ☎ 47.57.02.26, Euro Visa, 34 rm ⏀ 🦌 closed 15 Nov-15 Feb, 230.
★★★ ***Château de Pray*** (C.H.), 4 km NE on D 751, ☎ 47.57.23.67, AE DC Euro Visa, 16 rm 🅿 ⏀ ⏲ ⏀ half pens (h.s.), closed 1 Jan-10 Feb, 800. Rest. ◆ ⏀ 145-200.
● ★★ ***Lion d'Or***, 17, quai C.-Guinot, ☎ 47.57.00.23, Visa, 23 rm 🅿 ⏀ ⏲ closed 2 Nov-31 Mar, 190. Rest. ◆ ⏀ ⏲ 105-170.
★★ ***Auberge du Mail***, 32, quai du Gal-de-Gaulle, ☎ 47.57.60.39, AE DC Euro Visa, 15 rm 🅿 ⏀ ⏲ pens

(h.s.), closed 1-15 Mar, 350. Rest. ◆ ⏲ Spec : *foie confit au vouvray,* 90-180.

Restaurant :
◆ ***La Bonne Etape***, La Briquetterie, ☎ 47.57.08.09 ⏲ closed Tue, 75-130.

⏃ ★★*L'Ile d'Or* (520 pl), ☎ 47.57.23.37.

Recommended
Events : *Renaissance show at Château,* eves Jul and Aug.
Guide to wines : *wine festival,* Apr and Aug.
Youth hostel : *Centre Ch.-Péguy,* Entrepont, Ile-d'Or, ☎ 47.57.06.36.
♥ pastry : *Le Fournil,* pl. du château, ☎ 47.57.04.46.

Nearby

CHÂTEAU-RENAULT, ✕ 37110, 22 km N.
ℹ️ parc Vauchevrier, ☎ 47.56.91.35 (h.s.).

Hotels :
★★★ ***Ecu de France*** (L.F.), 37, pl. Jean-jaurès, ☎ 47.29.50.72, AE Visa, 9 rm 🅿 closed Sun eve and Mon lunch ex Jul-Aug, 8-30 Jan, 190. Rest. ◆◆ ⏲ 65-165.
★ ***Le Lion d'Or***, 166, rue de la République, ☎ 47.29.66.50, DC Visa, 10 rm 🅿 ⏲ half pens (h.s.), closed Mon eve and Sun eve, 1-15 Mar, 1-15 Nov, 220. Rest. ● ◆ ⏲ A brief menu based on the freshest market produce : *ragoût de Saint-Jacques sauce corail et petits légumes, salade de ris de veau au kiwi et au vinaigre de framboise,* 65-160.

⏃ ★★*Vauchevrier* (110 pl), ☎ 47.56.54.43.

Recommended
Farmhouse-gîte : at Auzouer, 7 km S, *la Ruellerie,* ☎ 47.56.99.03.

NEUILLE-LE-LIERRE, ✕ 37380 Monnaie, 16 km N.

Restaurant :
◆◆ ***Auberge de la Brenne***, Le Bourg, rue de la Gare, ☎ 47.52.95.05, AE Visa ⏲ ⏀ closed Tue eve and Wed, 22 Jan-26 Feb, 19-25 Oct. Spec : *pain de brochet et géline de Touraine au vouvray,* 55-145.

AZAY-LE-RIDEAU***

Tours 28, Châtellerault 94, Paris 262 km
pop 2915 ✕ 37190   A2

One of the most beautiful châteaux in the Loire Valley, surrounded by trees and reflected in its lake.

► As with many other châteaux in the region, Azay was a replacement for a small fortress, the first appearance (1518) of the Italian Renaissance in Touraine and one of the first examples of the precedence of comfort over security : the corner turrets and machicolations are purely decorative *(9:15-12 & 2-6:30, Apr.-Sep.; 9:15-12 & 2-5, Oct.-15 Nov.; 9:30-12 & 2-4:45, 16 Nov.-Mar., son et lumière info, tel. 47.61.61.23 and at the château tel. 47.43.32.04).* Paintings, furniture and 16thC tapestries make the interior a veritable Renaissance museum. Note the kitchens and the straight flights of stairs★, an innovation for the period. ► The village church has an interesting Carolingian façade★.

Nearby

► **Château de l'Islette★** *(2.5 km NW),* probably built by the craftsmen from Azay, which would explain a certain similarity. ► **Saché★** : 16thC manor, renovated in the 19thC, famous for the writer Honoré de Balzac (1799-1850) who stayed here on many occasions, to write *le Père Goriot* and other famous novels. The writer's room has been preserved as he left it *(9-12 & 2-6, 15 Mar.-Sep.; 9-12 & 2-5, Oct.-14 Mar.; closed Wed., Dec. and Jan.).* Also see stabiles and mobiles installed by Calder on a hill around his house. Before arriving, water-mills at **Pont-de-Ruan** on the Indre. ► **Villaines-les-Rochers** *(6.5 km S),* a village of harness makers and potters; basket weaving has been traditional here since the 9thC. ☐

Practical Information

AZAY-LE-RIDEAU
ℹ️ 26, rue Gambetta, ☎ 47.45.44.40 (h.s.); mairie, ☎ 47.43.32.11 (l.s.).

Hotels :
★★★ *Hostellerie du Château de Montgoger* (C.H.), ☎ 47.65.54.22, AE DC Visa, 12 rm ℗ ≼ 〰 🔔 ᐸ half pens (h.s.), 750. Rest. ◆ ≼ ♪ ᐸ 120-220.
★★ *Le Grand Monarque* (L.F.), pl. de la République, ☎ 47.45.40.08, AE Euro Visa, 30 rm ℗ 〰 ♪ closed 15 Nov-15 Mar, 290. Rest. ◆ ♪ ᐸ 85-180.
Château de Gerfaut, 3 km N, ☎ 47.43.30.16, 3 rm ℗ 〰 🔔 ☜ closed Aug, Dec-May, 260.

⚠ ★★*Municipal du Sabot* (184 pl), ☎ 47.45.42.72.

Recommended
Son et lumière : Pentecost-Sep, tour of château with guides in Renaissance costume, info at S.I.

Nearby
SACHÉ, ✉ 37190 Azay-le-Rideau, 7 km SE.

Restaurant :
◆◆ *Auberge du XIIe s.*, ☎ 47.26.86.58 ℗ 〰 closed Tue and Wed (l.s.), 20 Jan-28 Feb. Menu varies with seasons; game in fall, 180-200.

BEAUGENCY★★

Orléans 25, Tours 87, Paris 151 km
pop 7339 ✉ 45190   B1

Legend has it that the Devil himself offered the 22-arched bridge★ across the Loire to the town of Beaugency in exchange for the soul of the first being to cross it. As it happens, this was a cat; and the people of Beaugency are still nicknamed *chats* (cats). Other colourful medieval characteristics of the town are more realistically dated from the Hundred Years' War between England and France.
▶ The **Tower of St. Firmin** (16thC), the **keep★** (11thC), the **church of Notre-Dame** (12th-17thC, organs★), the former abbey and the château form an unusually beautiful group.
▶ In the 15thC **château** is the **Museum of Orleans Arts and Traditions :** costumes, furniture, vineyards and the Loire *(9-12 & 2-6, 24 Mar.-3 Nov.; 9-12 & 2-4 rest of year ex Tue.).* ▶ The **town hall** is a charming Renaissance building; eight panels of rare 17thC embroidery★. ▶ **Aquarium,** exotic fish *(daily 10-12 & 2-6, closed Wed.).*

Nearby
▶ **Meung-sur-Loire** *(7 km NE)* : 12th-18thC château, former residence of the Bishops of Orléans *(daily 30 Mar.- 11 Nov., 8:30-5:30; weekends only; 1 Jan.-29 Mar. and 12 Nov.-31 Dec., 9-5).* The cruciform **church of St. Liphard** (11th-16thC) is unusual for the region; Gaston Couté and Grand Moulin museums with changing exhibits.
▶ **Cléry-Saint-André** *(12 km NE).* Louis XI was so fond of Cléry that he chose the town's fine 15thC Flamboyant Gothic basilica★ *(8-5, 6:30 in summer)* as his place of burial; visit the vault and the Renaissance chapel of St. Jacques★. ▶ 11 km SW : the **nuclear power stations of Saint-Laurent-Nouan** (A and B); public information office (diagrams, models, viewing platform; *daily 9-6; to visit tel. 94.44.84.09).* ☐

Practical Information

ℹ️ 28, pl. du Martroi, ☎ 38.44.54.42 (h.s.). ♥
SNCF ☎ 38.44.50.28.

Hotels :
★★★★ *La Tonnellerie*, 12, rue des Eaux-Bleues, ☎ 38.44.68.15, Tx 782479, AE DC Euro Visa, 26 rm ℗ 〰

🔔 ᐸ ▣ half pens (h.s.), closed Jan-Apr, 5 Oct-31 Dec, 700. Rest. ◆◆ ♪ ᐸ 🔔 150-190.
★★★ *Abbaye*, 2, quai de l'Abbaye, ☎ 38.44.67.35, 18 rm ℗ 🔔 470. Rest. ◆◆◆ ♪ 160-230.
★★ *Ecu de Bretagne* (L.F.), pl. du Martroi, ☎ 38.44.67.60, AE DC Euro Visa, 26 rm ℗ 〰 ᐸ closed 1 Feb-8 Mar, 150. Rest. ● ◆◆ ♪ ᐸ A friendly stop for food-lovers on the château trail : *oeuf écu (poché au foie gras frais), cul de lapereau au miel*, Loire river fish, game in season, 70-180.
★ *La Maille d'Or* (L.F.), 3, av. de Blois, N 152, ☎ 38.44.53.43, AE Euro Visa, 20 rm ℗ 〰 135. Rest. ◆ ≼ 65-100.

⚠ ★★*Municipal* (130 pl), ☎ 38.44.50.39; at Saint-Laurent Nouan, 9 km S, ★★*Amitié* (60 pl), ☎ 54.87.02.52.

Recommended
Youth hostel : 152, rue de Châteaudun, ☎ 38.44.61.31.

Les BÉZARDS

Montargis 23, Orléans 69, Paris 138 km
pop 468 ✉ 45290 Nogent-sur-Vernisson   C2

Hotels :
● ★★★★(L) *Auberge des Templiers* (R.C.), Boismorand, ☎ 38.31.80.01, Tx 780998, 30 rm ℗ ≼ 〰 🔔 ▣ ℘ closed 15 Jan-15 Feb, 725. Rest. ● ◆◆◆ ≼ ᐸ A fine table in keeping with the setting : Sologne game in season, *fricassée de rognons et pieds de veau en barbouille*, fine wines, 230-400.
★★★★ *Château des Bézards*, ☎ 38.31.80.03, AE DC Euro Visa, 43 rm ℗ ≼ 〰 ♪ ▣ ℘ pens (h.s.), 890. Rest. ◆◆ ≼ ♪ Spec : *fine salade d'artichauts et de faisan à la vinaigrette framboisée, rosace de canard au sabayon de bourgueil, côtelettes de chevreuil*, 100-235.

BLOIS★★

Orléans 59, Angers 152, Paris 181 km
pop 49422 ✉ 41000   B2

Wolves no longer howl at the gates of the town, whose Celtic name (Bleiz) meant "wolf"; but the forests they haunted are still there. Between the Sologne and the Beauce, built of white stone and blue slate, Blois is an important market for corn, wine, strawberries and asparagus. Cocoa used to come up-river from Nantes; today the town is still pervaded by the delicious scent from the Poulain chocolate factories.

▶ The **château★★★** (B2) is a marvelous résumé of French architecture from the Middle Ages to the neo-Classical period *(9-6:30, Easter holidays and Jun.-Aug.; 9-12 & 2-6:30, 15 Mar.-May and Sep.; 9-12 & 2-5, Jan.-14 Mar. and Oct.-Dec.; son et lumière info. at SI, tel. 54.74.06.49).* ▶ Entry to the main square is through the late-Gothic Louis XII wing (1498). **Fine Arts Museum** : 16th-19thC paintings, and **archaeological museum** *(Jan.-Jun., Mon. and Wed. only, 9-12 & 2-5; Jul.-Aug., 2-5:30; Sep.-Dec., 9-12 & 2-5:30, closed Wed.).* ▶ On the right, the **François I wing** (1515 Renaissance) and the dazzling octagonal tower of the **Grand Escalier★★★** (Grand Staircase). In this wing see the Queen's apartments, with Catherine de Medici's Renaissance furniture and tapestries; on the floor above, the apartments of Henri III were the scene of the dramatic assassination of the Duke of Guise (1588). ▶ The **Grand Salle des États★** (State Room; 13thC) between the two wings is a reminder of the former fortress on this site. ▶ Opposite the entrance, the **Gaston d'Orléans wing★** in neo-Classical style was built by François Mansart (1635). ▶ In the **Rue St-Lubin** at the foot of the château there are still some picturesque wooden houses, in spite of the destruction of 1940. ▶ The 12th-13thC **church of St. Nicolas** is a happy marriage of Romanesque and Gothic styles. Nearby, in the Jacobin convent, **Natural History Museum** *(Wed. and Sat., 9-12; daily, 2-6, ex Mon.).* ▶ The **old town★** *(visits Jul.-Aug., 10-3, ex Wed.*

BLOIS

and Sun.) between the château and the cathedral (C2) is now a pedestrian precinct lined with old Renaissance houses★ : Rue de la Fontaine-des-Élus, Rue du Puits-Châtel, Rue des Papegaults, Rue des Juifs, etc. ▶ The **Saint Louis cathedral** was rebuilt in Gothic style after the terrible hurricane of 1678; see the crypt of St. Solenne, 10thC and 11thC. ▶ Behind the cathedral, the **gardens★** of the former Bishops' residence (18thC, Hôtel de Ville) make a magnificent walk above the Loire.

Nearby

▶ **Saint-Denis-sur-Loire** : château (14th-18thC; *exterior visit in summer, 9-12 & 2-6; closed Sun.*). ▶ **Ménars★** *(8 km NE)*: Antoinette Poisson (1721-64), better known as La Marquise de Pompadour, bought the **château★** in 1760 and had it enlarged by Gabriel and Soufflot; Louis XIV and XV furniture; magnificent gardens★ above the Loire. ▶ **Cour-sur-Loire★** *(10 km NE)*: 15thC château (*visit by request, tel. 54.46.81.04*), 15th-16thC church. ▶ **Suèvres** *(13 km NE)*: old houses running down to the Loire; two interesting churches, St. Lubin and St. Christophe (both 12thC, remodeled). ▶ **Mer** *(21 km NE)*: château de Chantecaille (15th-17thC; *visit Apr.-1 Nov., 3-5, closed Thu.*). ▶ **Château de Talcy★** *(28 km NE)*, rebuilt in 1520 : remarkable 18thC interior complete with furnishings★ from the French Regency (1715-23) to the Directoire (1795-99; *9-11:15 & 2-6, Apr.-Sep.; 10-11:15 & 2-4:30, Oct.-Mar.; closed hols.*). Windmill. 10 km NW : Romanesque church of **Saint-Léonard-en-Beauce.**

The châteaux around Blois★★★ *(Round trip 92 km; 2 days)*

▶ Renaissance châteaux in a setting of woods and lakes; **Chambord** (→), **Villesavin** and **Cheverny** (→), **Beaure-**

gard, **Fougères** (→ Cheverny) and **Chaumont** (→). Stopover at **Cour Cheverny** or return to Blois.

The Blois Forest★ *(23 km round trip)*

▶ **Blois**. ▶ D766 to **Molineuf.** 1 km SW, **church of St. Secondin** (11th-16thC) and ruins of **château de Bury** *(500 m).* ▶ **Orchaise**, well known for its wines, picturesque cave. ▶ Return to Blois via **Saint-Lubin-en-Vergonnois.**

Along the Loire★★ *(58 km from Blois to Tours, 2 hr)*

▶ Between the two towns the Loire has a **tourist route★★** on each bank. We recommend the right bank (N152), with magnificent views of **Chaumont** (→) and **Amboise** (→). □

Practical Information _____

BLOIS
ⓘ 3, av. Jean-Laigret (B2), ☎ 54.74.06.49.
✈ *Blois-Le Breuil*, 16 km NW, ☎ 54.20.17.68.
SNCF (A2), ☎ 54.74.24.50/54.78.01.07.
Car rental : *Avis*, train station (A2); 6, rue J.-Moulin, ☎ 54.74.48.15.

Hotels :
★★ *Anne de Bretagne* (L.F.), 31, av. Jean-Laigret (B2), ☎ 54.78.05.38, AE Euro Visa, 29 rm Ⓟ ⌂ closed 15 Feb-15 Mar, 170.
★★ *Grand Cerf* (L.F.), 42, av. Wilson (C3), ☎ 54.78.02.16, 14 rm Ⓟ ❤ closed Fri (l.s.) and Feb, 103. Rest. ♦ 45-160.
★ *Saint-Jacques* (L.F.), pl. de la Gare (A2), ☎ 54.78.04.15, Euro Visa, 28 rm ⌂ 140.

Restaurants :
♦♦ *La Péniche*, prom. du Mail (C2), ☎ 54.74.37.23, AE DC Euro Visa ◊ ❄ A barge on the Loire river. Seasonal, market-fresh fare, 120-250.
♦ *Rendez-Vous des Pêcheurs*, 27, rue du Foix (A-B3),

☎ 54.74.67.48, Visa, closed Sun. A charming little terrace, 110-170.

⚓ ★★★*de la Loire* (80 pl), ☎ 54.74.22.78; at Vineuil, 4 km E., ★★★★*Base du lac de Loire* (250 pl), ☎ 54.78.82.05.

Recommended
Bicycle-rental : *Blot*, 3, rue Henri-Drussy (C2), ☎ 54.78.02.64, closed Sun, Mon and Aug.
Events : *Internat. contemporary theatre festival*, with street animation, in Jun.
Guided tours : *overview of the region and its châteaux*, ☎ 54.20.17.68; *le Vieux Blois*, Jul-Aug ex Wed and Sun.
Son et lumière : at the château.
Youth hostel : *les Grouets*, ☎ 54.78.27.21.
♥ pastry : *Marchan*, 147 bis, av. Maunoury (C1-2), ☎ 54.78.27.78.

Nearby

CHITENAY, ✉ 41120 Les Montils, 12 km S.

Hotel :
★ *La Clé des Champs*, 60, Grande-Rue, ☎ 54.70.42.03, Euro Visa, 10 rm ℗ ⁂ ⚓ closed Mon eve and Tue, 5 Jan-5 Feb, 12-21 Nov, 80. Rest. ♦♦ ♪ ♿ Spec : *terrine aux trois poissons*. In summer, candlelight dinners in the park, 100-140.

COUR-CHEVERNY, ✉ 41700 Contres, 13 km SE.
ℹ 4, av. de la République, ☎ 54.79.95.63.

Hotel :
● ★★ *Saint-Hubert* (L.F.), ☎ 54.79.96.60, Euro Visa, 20 rm ℗ ⁑ closed Tue eve, 5 Dec-15 Jan, 145. Rest. ♦ ♿ 80-200.

Recommended
Events : *fêtes nocturnes*, Jul-Aug.

OUCHAMPS, ✉ 41120 Les Montils, 16 km S.

Hotel :
★★★ *Relais des Landes* (R.S.), (Mapotel), Les Montils, ☎ 54.44.03.33, AE DC Euro Visa, 18 rm ℗ ⁂ ⚓ ♪ ♿ half pens (h.s.), closed 2 Nov-Palm Sun. 10-ha park, bicycle rental, 790. Rest. ♦♦ ⁑ ♿ ⁑ closed Wed and lunch ex Sun. Fresh ingredients, simple cooking, 150-180.

BOURGUEIL

Tours 45, Angers 63, Paris 278 km
pop 4185 ✉ 37140   A2

Wine tasting in a cellar near Chevrette *(2 km N,* wine museum, *10-12:30 & 2-6 or 7:30 in summer).* ▶ In the village, the **church of St. Germain,** 12thC Angevin choir★ and former **abbey** : 18thC Prior's residence, cloister gallery (1472), abbey château (17thC), 13thC storerooms★.

Nearby

▶ 5 km S, **château des Réaux** (15th-18thC), transformed into a château-reception centre. ▶ 5 km E, **Restigné** : remarkable 11thC-12thC church★.   □

Practical Information ─────────────

ℹ mairie, rue Picard, ☎ 47.97.70.50.

Hotel :
★ *Le Thouarsais*, pl. Hublin, ☎ 47.97.72.05, 30 rm ⁂ closed Sun eve (l.s.) , 1 Jan, 21 Feb-9 Mar, 130.

Recommended
Farmhouse-gîte : *Château des Réaux*, (Château-Accueil), Port-Boulet, ☎ 47.95.14.40; at St-Nicolas-de-Bourgueil, *Clos du Vigneau,* 6 km W, ☎ 47.97.75.10.
Guide to wines : *wine fair,* early Feb and early Apr; *Cave de la Dive Bouteille and museum,* daily Feb-Nov.

┌─────────────────────────────────────┐
│ Send us your comments and suggestions; we will │
│ use them in the next edition.   │
└─────────────────────────────────────┘

CHAMBORD★★★

Blois 18, Orléans 45, Paris 175 km
pop 206 ✉ 41250 Bracieux   B2

The château de Chambord is one of the marvels of the French Renaissance, marking the ambitious start of the reign of François I and the first signs of the architectural megalomania which ultimately led to the construction of Versailles. François I's liking for this residence is perhaps explained by his penchant for hunting.

▶ Chambord was a former hunting lodge, rebuilt from 1519. While based on the plan of a feudal château, with a four-towered central keep and enclosing wall, the central keep is actually inspired by Saint Peter's in Rome which was thus, for the first time, adapted to civil architecture. Characteristically, the façades are very simple, almost Classical, while the "keep" is profusely decorated with chimneys, windows, spires and pinnacles, a sort of aerial village appearing above the trees in the park and symbolising "the ideal city" *(daily ex hols. 9-12 & 2-5, 6 or 7 according to season; info at C.D.T.; C.N.M.H.S. (Historical Monuments Board) guided tours and son et lumière,* tel. 54.20.31.32). ▶ The **Grand Escalier**★★★ (Grand Staircase) with its double spiral crowned by the famous lantern, is a marvel of Renaissance ingenuity. There are no less than 440 rooms but the most interesting are the chapel, the guardrooms and the **terraces**★★, together with the apartments of Louis XIV and François I. ▶ The château is surrounded by a magnificent **park**★ of 55 km² where the court could watch the hunt from the terraces. The park is now a national wildlife reserve and only part of it is open to the public; viewing platforms have been set up to watch the deer and wild boar feeding in the early morning or late evening. The GR3 runs through the park.
                                                       □

Practical Information ─────────────

CHAMBORD
ℹ pl. St-Michel, ☎ 54.20.34.86.

Hotel :
★★ *Saint-Michel* (L.F.), ☎ 54.20.31.31, 38 rm ℗ ⁂ ⚓ ⁑ ⁑ closed 12 Nov-22 Dec, 270. Rest. ♦ 90-160.

Recommended
Events : *nightly entertainment,* ☎ 54.78.19.47, May-Sept; *concerts and theatre*, S.I., C.N.M.H.S., ☎ 54.46.31.32, in summer.
Guided tours : *C.N.M.H.S.,* at the porte Royale, ☎ (1) 42.74.22.22.
Night-clubs : at Montliveault, 8 km N, *Le Carioca*, ☎ 54.20.61.06.
Sports : in the former stables of the Marshal of Saxe, ☎ 54.20.31.01, excursions on horseback in the park.

Nearby

SAINT-DYE-SUR-LOIRE, ✉ 41500 Mer, 5 km NW of **Mer.**

Hotel :
● ★★ *Manoir du Bel Air*, ☎ 54.81.60.10, 40 rm ℗ ⁂ ⚓ ♪ ♿ closed 3 Jan-15 Feb, 225. Rest. ♦♦ ⁑ ♿ ⁑ Spec : *rillettes de saumon, cailles aux cèpes,* 78-160.

CHAUMONT-SUR-LOIRE★★

Blois 17, Tours 41, Paris 200 km
pop 842 ✉ 41150 Onzain   B2

High walls and enormous towers surrounding the top of the hill overlooking the Loire.

▶ This ancient feudal fortress (10thC) blends late Gothic (Amboise Tower and W side, 1465-81) and Renaissance styles (the three other towers and the S and E buildings and chapel). Three of the great ladies of French history stayed here, sometimes unwillingly : Catherine de Medicis (1519-89) and her rival, Diane de Poitiers (1499-1566),

wife and mistress respectively of Henri II; and Madame
de Staël (1766-1817), when exiled from Napoleon's court
*(9:30-11:45 & 2:15-5:45, Apr.-Sep.; 9:45-12 & 2-4,
Oct.-Mar.).* ▶ The courtyard has a splendid view N over
the valley. 15th-16thC furniture and works of art in
the apartments. Remarkable **stables★**. □

Practical Information _____

CHAUMONT-SUR-LOIRE
ⓘ ☎ 54.20.78.32; mairie, ☎ 54.20.98.41.

Hotel :
★★★ *Château* (L.F.), rue du Mal-de-Lattre-de-Tassigny,
☎ 54.20.98.04, AE DC Euro Visa, 15 rm ℗ ⁌ ᨏ ⌷ ▭
closed 30 Nov-1 Mar, 290. Rest. ♦ ⁌ ♪ 60-120; child : 40.

Nearby

CANDE-SUR-BEUVRON, ✉ 41120, 6 km E.

Hotel :
★★★ *Hostellerie de la Caillère* (C.H.), 36, rte des Montils, ☎ 54.44.03.08, AE DC Euro Visa, 7 rm ℗ ᨏ ⌷ ♪
closed Wed, 15 Jan-1 Mar, 190. Rest. ♦♦ ♪ Spec : brochet aux morilles et pinot noir, crêpes soufflées sur coulis
de fraise et sorbet mandarine, 100-220; child : 65.

ONZAIN, ✉ 41150, 2 km N.

Hotels :
● ★★★★ *Domaine des Hauts-de-Loire* (R.C.), rte d'Her-
bault, ☎ 54.20.72.57, Tx 751457, AE DC Euro Visa,
28 rm ℗ ᨏ ⌷ ♨ ⁒ closed Sun eve, 1 Dec-1 Mar, 740.
Rest. ♦♦♦ ♪ Spec : saumon cru aux herbes et au citron
vert, émincé de lapereau aux artichauts, 200-280.
★★ *Château de la Haute-Borde*, Rilly-sur-Loire, 4 km W,
☎ 54.20.98.09, Euro Visa, 18 rm ℗ ᨏ ♨ half pens,
closed Sun eve, 15 Nov-15 Mar, 185. Rest. ♦ closed Mon
and Sun eve, 55-80.
★★ *Château des Tertres* (C.H.), rte de Monteaux,
☎ 54.20.83.88, AE Euro Visa, 14 rm ℗ ⁌ ᨏ ⌷ ♨ closed
12 Nov-Palm Sun, 225.
★★ *Domaine de Seillac* (C.H.), ☎ 54.20.72.11,
Tx 751315, AE DC Visa, 11 rm ℗ ᨏ ⌷ ♨ ⁒ half pens,
closed Sun eve and Mon (l.s.), 20 Dec-5 Jan. 24-ha estate,
70 pavilions in the park, pond, 530.

CHENONCEAUX★★★

Tours 35, Châteauroux 89, Paris 224 km
pop 361 ✉ 37150 Bléré   B2

It was Diane de Poitiers, Henri II's mistress, who proposed a five-arched bridge across the Cher as a project for architect Philibert Delorme. However on the
death of Henri II, Catherine de Medici forced her to
exchange Chenonceaux for Chaumont (→) and had
the same architect build the great gallery on the
bridge.

▶ The **château** itself was built in 1515. The great **keep** in
the foreground belongs to a former fortified manor which
was destroyed to build the château *(9-7, 16 Mar.-15 Sep.;
9-6:30, 16-30 Sep.; 9-6, Oct.; 9-5, 1-15 Nov.; 9-12
& 2-4:30, 16 Nov.-15 Feb.; 9-5:30, 16-28 Feb.; 9-6,
1-15 Mar. No guides; boat trips on the Cher, children's
facilities, Jul.-Aug.; restaurant and self-service
15 Feb.-15 Nov.; son et lumière : "At the Time of
the Ladies of Chenonceaux", 10 pm, Jul.-mid-Sep.; tel.
47.29.90.07).* ▶ A magnificent alley of plane trees leads
up to the château. See the Guardroom (**Salle des
Gardes**; 16thC tile work★) with fine Flemish tapestries;
also the **chapel**, and the bedrooms of Diane de Poitiers
and François I. Magnificent Renaissance, 17th and 18thC
paintings (Van Loo, Il Primaticcio, Rubens...) and marvelous furniture. ▶ You can also visit the kitchens and a
wax museum (4 centuries of history, *separate ticket*) and
walk in the **park★**. Refreshments at the orangerie; also,
taste the wine produced on the estate. □

Practical Information _____

ⓘ 1 bis, rue du Château, ☎ 47.23.94.45 (h.s.).
Ⓢ Ⓝ Ⓒ Ⓕ ☎ 47.23.90.64.

Hotels :
★★★ *Bon Laboureur et Château*, 6, rue du Dr-Bretonneau, ☎ 47.23.90.02, AE DC Euro Visa, 30 rm ℗ ᨏ ⌷
half pens (h.s.), closed 15 Dec-1 Mar, 630. Rest. ♦♦ ⁌
ᨏ 140-200.
★ *La Renaudière*, 24, rue du Dr-Bretonneau,
☎ 47.23.90.04, Euro Visa, 12 rm ℗ ᨏ ⌷ ♨ closed
Sun, 20 Nov-1 Mar, 190. Rest. ♦ ♪ ⌷ ♨ closed Mon
noon and Sun eve, 60-150; child : 40.

Recommended
Baby-sitting : ☎ 47.23.90.07, info at the Château. Open
1 Jul-31 Aug.

The CHER Valley*

B2

From Vierzon to Tours *(112 km, half-day)*

On the edge of the Sologne and in Touraine, the Cher
is a slow-running river moving through peaceful countryside dotted with manors, châteaux, attractive towns
and rows of poplars.

▶ **Vierzon.** ▶ **Mennetou-sur-Cher★** : a medieval country town with ramparts and old houses. The church has
a 13thC square choir★. ▶ Charming road along the left
bank through **Saint-Loup** (13thC frescos in the church).
▶ **Villefranche-sur-Cher** : Romanesque capitals★ in the
church. ▶ **Selles-sur-Cher**, clustered around Notre-Dame-
la-Blanche★ (12th-19thC) and the former abbey (17thC),
small museum, *visits by request; tel. 54.97.40.19)*. The
moated château is an ancient feudal fortress transformed
in the time of Henri IV *(9:30-12 & 2-6, Jul.-15 Aug.; Sat.,
Sun. and pm only out of season; closed 12 Nov.-Easter)*.
▶ **Châtillon-sur-Cher** : panel★, school of Leonardo, in
the church. ▶ **Noyers-sur-Cher** where the Canal du
Berry joins the river; 13thC church with Angevin vaulting.
▶ **Saint-Aignan★** (pop. 3680) with old houses, Romanesque and Gothic Collegiate church★ (12th, 13th and 14thC
murals in the crypt) and a château rebuilt in the reign
of François I *(external visit only)*. **Beauval** : ornithological park *(9-nightfall)*. ▶ Past **Thésée** *(1 km)*, museum of
archaeological excavations *(2:30-6:30 ex Tue., Jul.-Aug.)*;
ruins of 2ndC Roman spas at **Tasciaca**, and, on the
opposite bank, the remains of a former potters' village.
▶ 5 km N, through Monthou-sur-Cher the **château
du Gué-Péan★** (16th-17thC), a ravishing building hidden
among oak trees *(9-7, 15 Mar.-15 Oct.; 10-5,
16 Sep.-15 Nov.; 10-5 rest of year)*. ▶ **Montrichard★** (pop.
3786) : the hillsides overlooking this ancient little town
are honeycombed with caves where the white wine of
Touraine goes through the champagne process *(visit and
wine tasting)*. Old houses with wooden facings in the Rue
Nationale. Jeanne de France and the future Louis XII were
married in the **church of St. Croix** (12thC). See also the
church of Nanteuil★ (12th, 13th and 15thC) and the **for-
tress★**. Richard the Lion Heart was imprisoned in the
enormous 12thC keep *(9:30-12 & 2:30-6:30,
11 Jun.-8 Sep.; hols., Sat. and Sun. only rest of year)*; fine
view from the top. ▶ 7.5 km NE, the former **abbey of Pont-
levoy**, founded in 11thC, with 13th-15thC church housing beautiful 17thC altarpieces. 17thC convent buildings
(Apr.-Sep., 10-12 & 2:30-6:30; closed March., low season).
▶ 12 km SW, **château de Montpoupon★** one of the most
graceful early Renaissance buildings in Touraine ; Musée
de la Vénerie (Hunting Museum; *23 Mar.-9 Apr., 2-6;
10 Apr.-11 Jun., 10-12 & 2-7; weekends and hols. only;
15 Jun.-30 Sep., 10-12 & 2-7 daily ex weekends and
hols.)*. The nearby restaurant *(Relais du Moulin Bailly)*
serves regional food. ▶ **Chissay-en-Touraine**, 15th-17thC
château. **"Or" strawberry liqueur distillery** *(visits Easter-
end Sep.)*. □

Practical Information

MENNETOU-SUR-CHER, ⊠ 41320, 50 km NW of **Bourges.**
SNCF ☎ 54.98.00.08.

Hotel :
★★ **Lion d'Or** (L.F.), 2, rue Marcel-Bailly, ☎ 54.98.01.13,
DC Euro Visa, 20 rm P ⋘ ♪ closed Sun eve and Mon,
15 Jan-15 Feb, 170. Rest. ♦ ♪ 55-80 ; child : 35.

MONTHOU-SUR-CHER, ⊠ 41400 Montrichard, 9 km E.

Hotel :
Château du Gué-Péan (C.H.), ☎ 54.71.43.01, 21 rm P ⟨
⋘ ⟨ ⇖ ♪⊙ A private château that takes in guests (55-ha
park), 260. Rest. ♦ ⟨ � 80-130.

MONTRICHARD, ⊠ 41400, 33 km S of **Blois.**
🛈 ☎ 54.32.05.10 (h.s.) ; mairie, ☎ 54.32.00.46.
SNCF ☎ 54.32.03.09.

Hotels :
★★★ **Château de la Ménaudière** (C.H.), ☎ 54.32.02.44,
Tx 751246, AE DC Euro Visa, 25 rm P ⟨ ⋘ ⇖ ♪ closed
1 Dec-1 Mar, 360. Rest. ♦♦ ⟨ ♪ 150-200.
★★★ **Le Bellevue**, (Inter-Hôtel), 16, quai du Cher,
☎ 54.32.06.17, AE DC Euro Visa, 29 rm P ⟨ ⟨ ♪ ở
pens (h.s.), closed Mon eve and Tue, 15 Nov-21 Dec,
710. Rest. ♦♦ ♪ ở 90-170.
★★★ **Tête Noire** (L.F.), 24, rue de Tours, ☎ 54.32.05.55,
Visa, 39 rm P ⋘ half pens (h.s.), closed Fri, 2 Jan-7 Feb,
200. Rest. ♦♦ ở 75-130.
★★ **La Roue à Aubes** (L.F.), 26, rue du Gué-de-l'Arche,
☎ 54.32.42.75, Visa, 12 rm P ⟨ ⋘ ⇖ closed Mon,
15 Nov-15 Mar, 150. Rest. ♦ 75-100.

Restaurant :
♦♦ **Le Grill du Passeur**, 2, Pont de Montrichard,
☎ 54.32.06.80, Euro Visa ⟨ ♪ ở ☞ closed Tue eve,
15 Dec-1 Apr. Historic building. Spec : *rognons de veau
flambés au cognac*, 110-150.

SAINT-AIGNAN, ⊠ 41100, 39 km S of **BLOIS.**
🛈 ☎ 54.75.13.31/54.75.22.85 (h.s.).
SNCF ☎ 54.75.20.14.

Hotel :
★★ **Saint-Aignan** (L.F.), 7, quai J.-J.-Delorme,
☎ 54.75.18.04, 23 rm P ⟨ half pens (h.s.), closed Sun eve
and Mon, 15 Dec-1 Feb, 430. Rest. ♦ ⟨ ở 60-120.

Restaurant :
♦ **Relais de la Poste**, 3, rue de l'Ormeau and 51, rue
Constant-Ragot (angle), ☎ 54.75.23.47 ở Spec : *tripes au
sauvignon, rognons au gamay*, 45-80.

⚏ ★★★*Municipal* (200 pl), ☎ 54.75.15.59.

CHEVERNY★★

B2

Apart from Brissac, Cheverny is the only château on
the Loire still belonging to the family that owned it at
the beginning of the 16thC. It was completed in 1634
and is a transition between Renaissance and Louis
XIV styles.

▶ The principal point of interest is the splendid **interior
decoration★★** dating from the reign of Louis XIII and still
in its original state *(9-6:30 in season ; 9:30-12 & 2:15-5 or
6:30 remainder of year)*. Note the sumptuous furnishings
of the *Chambre du Roi* (King's Bedroom), hung with
magnificent tapestries. The **Cheverny Museum** maintains
the old traditions of the hunt, with more than 2 500 trophies.

Nearby

▶ **Château de Villesavin★** *(8 km NE)*, on the right bank of
the Beuvron, just downstream from **Bracieux** *(10 km NE)* ;
this château, the marble fountain basin and the medallions on the left wing show the influence of the Florentine
craftsmen who built this charming Renaissance structure
in 1537, the same workers who built Chambord. It has

hardly been touched since its construction. 16th-18thC
frescoed chapel. The greenhouse can be rented for
private parties *(May-Sep., 10-7 ; 1 Oct.-20 Dec., 2-5 ;
Mar.-Apr., 10-12 & 2-5)*. ▶ **Château de Troussay★** *(3 km
SW)* : this Renaissance country house is a perfect
example of the small estates in Sologne *(→)* at that time
*(Easter school hols. : 10-12:30 & 2:30-7 ; between Easter
school hols. and summer school hols. : Sun. and nat. hols.
only, same hours ; summer school hols. : daily to 7 ; from
then to 11 Nov : Sunday and nat. hols. only, 10-12:30 &
2-5)*. ▶ **Château de Beauregard★** *(9 km NW)* : this fine
Renaissance building, enlarged 17thC, has a famous **portrait gallery★** of 363 "celebrities" of the period. Note also
the **Delft tiling★** showing an army of the time of Louis XIII
on the march, the oak paneling and the paintings in the
Cabinet des Grelots★ ("cow-bell room" ; *9:30-12 & 2-6:30,
Apr.-Sep. ; 9:30-12 & 2-5 ex Wed. rest of year ;
closed 15 Jan.-15 Feb.)*. ▶ **Fougères-sur-Bièvre castle★**
(11.5 km SW) : a beautiful example of military architecture
at end 15thC *(Apr.-Sep., 9-11 & 2-6 ; Oct.-Mar., 10-11:15
& 2-3:30)*. Beyond **Contres** *(9 km S)*, the village of **Chémery** *(19 km SW)* contains a **château** dating from the
13th, 15th and 16thC *(daily, 10-dusk ; closed Tue.)*. ☐

Practical Information

BRACIEUX, ⊠ 41250, 10 km NE.

Hotel :
★ **Cygne**, 20, rue Roger-Brun, ☎ 54.46.41.07, Euro Visa,
18 rm P ⋘ half pens (h.s.), closed Wed, 1 Jan-1 Mar,
160. Rest. ♦ 80-110.

Restaurant :
● ♦♦ **Relais Bracieux**, 1, av. Chambord, ☎ 54.46.41.22,
Euro Visa P ⟨ ⋘ ⇖ ở ☞ closed Tue eve and Wed.
Reserve. Pretty modern decor with a view of the garden,
moderately priced food : *carpe à la Chambord, rognon et
pied de veau au persil*. Tasty little local wines, 160-270.

⚏ ★★*des Châteaux* (90 pl), ☎ 54.46.41.84.

Recommended
Farmhouse-gîte : at Tour-en-Sologne, 3 km W, *la Bague-
nodière*, ☎ 54.46.45.33.

CONTRES, ⊠ 41700, 9 km S.

Hotel :
★★ **France** (L.F.), 35, rue P.-H.-Mauger, ☎ 38.79.50.14,
42 rm P ♪ ở ☞ ♪⊙ closed Fri (l.s.), 1 Feb-8 Mar, 205.
Rest. ♦ ♪ ☞ closed Thu eve and Fri (l.s.), 65-150.

Restaurant :
♦♦ **La Botte d'Asperges**, 5, rue P.-H.-Mauger,
☎ 54.79.50.49, Euro Visa ♪ ở closed Mon , Jan, 65-170 ;
child : 50.

Recommended
Farmhouse-gîte : at Oisly, 6 km SW, *La Presle*,
☎ 54.79.52.69.

CHINON★★

Tours 49, Poitiers 96, Paris 283 km
pop 8873 ⊠ *37500*   A2

The old town is a lively reminder of the Middle Ages,
where the streets have hardly changed since the day
in March 1429 when Joan of Arc passed through
them on her way from Domrémy to meet the Dauphin
(heir to the throne) and change the destiny of France.

▶ **Rue Haute-St-Maurice** (A1) and its continuation, **Rue
Voltaire** (B2), are lined with picturesque 15th-17thC buildings. Here and in the **Grand-Carroi★★** is the heart of the
old city. ▶ No. 44, the Maison des États Généraux (15thC)
houses the **Vieux-Chinon museum** *(10-12 & 3-7 ex Tue.)*.
▶ The ruined **château★★** was composed of three fortresses separated by deep moats and mounted on a rocky
spur *(Jun.-Aug., 9-6 ; Sep.-May, 9-12 & 2-5 or 6 ; closed
Tue., 1 Oct.-14 Mar. ; son et lumière, mid- Jun.-mid-Sep. ;
Tue. and Fri., live performances ; visit to the underground
passages some Sat. Jul.-Aug. 9 pm)*. ▶ In the E, the

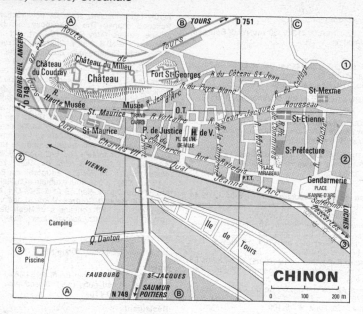

remains of Fort St. Georges. The **Pavillon de L'Horloge** (Joan of Arc Museum) leads to the **château du Milieu** (12th-14thC), scene of the first meeting between Joan of Arc and the Dauphin, when the 18-year-old Joan was able to recognize the future Charles VII, despite his anonymous appearance, in the midst of 300 knights (9 March 1429). A bridge over the moat links this château to the **château du Coudray** (13thC keep★) on the W of the promontory (view★). ▶ The famous **echo★** is ten minutes away on foot *(signposted)*.

Nearby

▶ **"Train 1900"**, steam train from Chinon to Richelieu *(1 hr, 15 km)*, food and wine halt by request at Ligré-Rivière *(regular service Sat. and Sun., 15 May-end Sep.)*. ▶ **Avoine Nuclear power station** *(12 km NW)* : Chinon A (gas-graphite) and Chinon B (enriched uranium; *requests for visits at least 2 weeks in advance : Centrale de Chinon, B.P. 23, 37420 Avoine, tel. 47.93.04.50; visit to Chinon B site, tel. 47.93.20.40)*. ▶ **Château du Rivau** *(11.5 km SE)* : 13th-15thC, period furniture, exhibitions of painting *(Apr.-Oct., 9-12 & 2-6)*. ▶ **Champigny-sur-Veude★** *(15 km SE)* : the **chapel Saint-Louis★★** of the old château is a Renaissance gem with marvelous **stained glass★★** *(1538-61; 9-12 & 2-6, Apr.-15 Oct.; 16 Oct.-3 Nov., closed weekends and hols.)*.

Rabelais territory *(17 km round trip SW, 2 hr)*

▶ **Chinon.** ▶ **La Devinière**, a simple late-15thC building, the former estate of the Rabelais family. François was born there around 1494. All his literary place names are derived from the neighbourhood and in *Gargantua* he made it the scene of the Picrocholine War. Museum of the writer's life and work *(9-12 & 2-6, or 5 out of season; closed Wed., 15 Oct.-15 Mar., and Dec., Jan.)*. ▶ **Seuilly**, Benedictine abbey where one of Rabelais' heroes gave battle to his enemies. ▶ 15thC **château du Coudray-Montpensier**, belonged to Maurice Maeterlinck.

La Vienne upstream from Chinon *(34 km round trip, 1 hr)*

▶ **Chinon.** ▶ **Cravant-les-Coteaux.** 1 km N, in the old town, church with Carolingian elements; small archaeological museum *(2:30-6 ex Tue.)*. ▶ **L'Ile-Bouchard** : on the

left bank, church of St. Maurice (14th-15thC) with carved 16thC pulpit★ and Romanesque ruins of the church of St. Léonard★ (end 11thC; capitals★★). On the right bank, the church of St. Gilles (11th-12thC). ▶ **Tavant**, late-11thC church, crypt decorated with remarkable Romanesque paintings★★ *(Mar.-Nov., 10-12 & 2-6:30, tel. : 47.58.58.06)*.

La Vienne downstream from Chinon *(16 km round trip, 1 hr 30)*

▶ **Candes-Saint-Martin**, in one of the loveliest **sites★★** in the Val de Loire : 13thC church★★, fortified in the15thC, on the site of the house where St. Martin died (397). ▶ **Close by** : Fontevrault-l'Abbaye and Montsoreau★★ (→ Maine-Anjou). ◻

Practical Information ⎯⎯⎯⎯⎯⎯⎯⎯

CHINON
ℹ 12, rue Voltaire (B2), ☎ 47.93.17.85. ⚓
SNCF (off map C2-3), ☎ 47.93.11.04.

Hotels :

● ★★ *Diderot*, 4, rue Buffon (C2), ☎ 47.93.18.87, Euro Visa, 22 rm Ⓟ ▥ ⌕ ⅙ ⚌ closed 15 Dec-15 Jan. Fine old 18th-C house, 215.
★★ *Boule d'Or* (L.F.), 66, quai Jeanne-d'Arc (B2), ☎ 47.93.03.13, AE DC Euro Visa, 20 rm ⋞ ♪ closed Mon (l.s.), 15 Dec-6 Jan, 230. Rest. ♦ ⋞ ♪ Terrace dining. Spec : *omelette créole*, 55-160 ; child : 40.
★★ *France*, 47-49, pl. Gal-de-Gaulle (B2), ☎ 47.93.33.91, Visa, 26 rm Ⓟ ⋞ ♪ ⚌ closed Sun eve (l.s.), 15 Dec-15 Mar, 225.
★★ *Gargantua* (C.H.), 73, rue Haute-Maurienne (A1-2), ☎ 47.93.04.71, AE DC Euro Visa, 11 rm Ⓟ ▥ ⌕ closed Wed (Sep-Nov), 15 Nov-15 Mar, 350. Rest. ● ♦♦ ♪ The 15th-C bailiff who inhabited this old palace was fond of good food ; the tradition continues : *omelette Gargamelle, matelote d'anguille, écrevisses du mont Louis*, 130-250.

Restaurant :

● ♦♦ *Au Plaisir Gourmand*, quai Charles-VII (A2), ☎ 47.93.20.48, Visa, closed Mon and Sun eve, 12 Nov-5 Dec. The young Rigollets have just moved into this splendid house in old Chinon, for our dining pleasure. Appealing fixed-meal : *feuilleté de pointes d'asperges à la ciboulette, jambonnette de canard à l'ancienne.* Marvelous Chinon wine, 145-220.

⚐ ★★*Municipal (A3)* (150 pl), ☎ 47.93.08.35.

Recommended
Guide to wines : *cellar tours*, Dumont, Plouzeau, Château de Ligré, Clos de l'Echo. info. S.I.
Leisure activities : *cruise*, ☎ 49.93.89.46, Chinon-Monsoreau-Saumur.
Youth hostel : rue Descartes (C3), ☎ 47.93.10.48.

Nearby

BEAUMONT-EN-VÉRON, ⊠ 37420 Avoine, 5 km NW.

Hotels :
★★ *Giraudière* (L.F.), ☎ 47.58.40.36, AE DC Euro Visa, 25 rm 🅿 ⟜ ⑅ ⚲ ᕫ 230.
Château de Danzay (C.H.), ☎ 47.58.46.86, 5 rm 🅿 ⑅ ⚲ 🖃 ⥁ closed 30 Oct-1 Apr. Private residence that accepts paying guests, 450.

MARÇAY, ⊠ 37500 Chinon, 7 km S on the D 116.

Hotel :
★★★★ *Château de Marçay* (R.C.), ☎ 47.93.03.47, Tx 751475, AE Visa, 38 rm 🅿 ⟜ ⑅ ⚲ ♪ 🖃 ⥁ closed 10 Jan-10 Mar, 600. Rest. ◆◆ ⟜ ♪ ⌘ Spec : *langoustines sautées aux baies roses, noix de ris de veau au confit d'échalotes*, 135-280.

GIEN*

Orléans 64, Bourges 76, Paris 154 km
pop 16784 ⊠ 45500   C2

One of the first royal châteaux, Gien is the start of the sumptuous route through the Val de Loire. The town was rebuilt after WWII in traditional regional style using cut stone and glazed pink brick.

▶ The **château★** (1484) can be seen above the old town, with its façade of red and black brick in geometrical patterns. It houses the **Musée International de la Chasse ★★** (International Hunting Museum; *9:15-11:45 & 2:15-6:30 or 5:30 out of season*) : paintings★ by François Desportes (1661-1743). ▶ Nearby, the **church of St. Jeanne-d'Arc★** (1954) in brick, with 15thC bell tower. ▶ Place de la Victoire, the **Manufacture de Gien** (ceramics works) houses an interesting **faïence museum** *(9-11:45 & 2-5:45; factory visit on request, no children under 12).*

Nearby

▶ **Château de la Bussière** *(13 km NE)* : 15th-16thC, beside a lake. ▶ **Briare** *(10 km SE)* : canal-bridge★ (1890) over the Loire; automobile museum (1895-1960). ▶ **Ouzouer-sur-Trezee** *(7 km NE)*, château de Pont-Chevron (19thC), Gallo-Roman mosaics *(1 Apr.-15 Sep., 2-6, closed Tue.).*

Practical Information _____

GIEN
ℹ rue Anne-de-Beaujeu, ☎ 38.67.25.28.   ⚑
SNCF ☎ 38.67.01.18.
Car rental : *Avis*, 108, av. Wilson, ☎ 38.67.19.27 ; train station.

Hotels :
★★ *Le Rivage*, 1, quai de Nice, ☎ 38.67.20.53, AE DC Euro Visa, 24 rm 🅿 ⟜ half pens, closed 9 Feb-2 Mar, 260. Rest. ◆ ⟜ ᕫ View on the Loire and the Gaillard family's quality service and cuisine. Pike in season, 75-200.
★ *Beau Site*, 13, quai de Nice, ☎ 38.67.36.05, AE DC Visa, 8 rm 🅿 ⌘ closed Sun eve, 1-15 Jan, 1-8 Sep, 110. Rest. ◆ *Poularde*, 60-140.
⚐ ★★*Municipal* (135 pl), ☎ 38.67.12.50.

Nearby

BRIARE, ⊠ 45250, 10 km SW.
ℹ pl. de la République (C2), ☎ 38.31.24.51 (h.s.).

SNCF ☎ 38.31.24.68.

Hotel :
★★ *Hostellerie Le Canal* (L.F.), 19, rue du Pont-Canal, ☎ 38.31.22.54, AE DC Euro Visa, 12 rm 🅿 ⟜ ⑅ ⚲ half pens (h.s.), closed Mon, 15 Dec-20 Jan, 175. Rest. ◆ ⟜ ♪ ᕫ 50-150 ; child : 40.

Le GRAND-PRESSIGNY*

Poitiers 63, Tours 67, Paris 303 km
pop 1185 ⊠ 37350   A3

This little village on the edge of the Touraine is known principally for its prehistoric finds. Near the ruined château (12thC keep★), the new Renaissance château houses a remarkable **Prehistory Museum★** *(9-12 & 2-6, or 5 out of season ; closed Wed. and Dec.-Jan.).*

Nearby

▶ **La Guerche** *(7 km SW)* : château★ built by Charles VII on the edge of the river *(10-12 & 2-7, Jul.-Aug., ex Sun. am; closed Tue. out of season and Dec.-Mar.).* ▶ **Descartes** *(11.5 km NW)*, further down the captivating **valley of the Claise★** : birthplace of famous French thinker and philosopher René Descartes (1596-1650); small museum *(2-6:30 ex Tue.).*   ☐

Practical Information _____

Hotels :
★ *Savoie Villars* (L.F.), pl. Savoie-Villars, ☎ 47.94.96.86, AE Euro Visa, 8 rm 🅿 ⌘ closed Tue eve and Wed (l.s.), 8 Jan-8 Mar, 150. Rest. ◆ ⌘ 60-100.
Espérance, le Carroir des Robins, ☎ 47.94.90.12, AE Visa, 10 rm 🅿 ⑅ ⚲ ⌘ half pens, closed Mon, 150. Rest. ◆ ᕫ Spec : *galantine de faisan, coussin de loup à la crème de cerfeuil*, 60-150 ; child : 35.

The INDRE Valley*

A2

From Loches to Azay-le-Rideau *(54 km, 4 hr)*

A luminous valley typical of the Touraine where the Indre runs quietly between two walls of tufa, the beautiful white stone used to build so many of the houses in the Val de Loire. Loches (→) and Azay-le-Rideau (→) are high points of medieval and Renaissance architecture respectively.

▶ **Loches.** ▶ **Azay-sur-Indre** (site★ and château, which belonged to La Fayette). ▶ **Reignac** (château, dairy and mill). ▶ **Cormery**, known for its macaroons and the Benedictine abbey founded in the 8thC; St. Paul tower★ (11thC); refectory★ (13thC); kitchens and storerooms etc. *(visit 3 pm Jun.-Sep.; closed Sun. and nat. hols.).* ▶ Further on, the **château de Couzières** (15th-17thC). ▶ **Montbazon** : a formidable rectangular keep★ (12thC; *Jun.-15 Sep., daily 10-10; 15 Oct.-Jan., Mar.-May, Sat., Sun., hols. 10-6; Mon., Tue., Thu., Fri., 10-2).* ▶ **Artannes-sur-Indre** : a picturesque grouping of château, church and mill. ▶ As far as **Saché** (→ Azay-le-Rideau) the itinerary retraces one of Balzac's famous novels, *Le Lys dans la Vallée.*   ☐

Practical Information _____

MONTBAZON, ⊠ 37250 Veigné, 13 km S of **Tours**.
ℹ ☎ 47.26.03.31.   ⚑
SNCF ☎ 47.20.50.50.

Hotels :
★★★★(L) *Château d'Artigny* (R.C.), rte d'Azay-le Rideau, ☎ 47.26.24.24, Tx 750900, Visa, 55 rm 🅿 ⟜ ⑅ ⚲ ᕫ 🖃 ⥁ half pens (h.s.), closed 1 Dec-10 Jan, 1300. Rest. ◆◆◆◆ ⟜ ♪ ᕫ 200-300 ; child : 60.
★★★ *Domaine de la Tortinière* (R.S.), ☎ 47.26.00.19,

Tx 752186, Euro Visa, 21 rm ℗ ⟨ ⬚ ⬚ ⬚ ⬚ ✉ ∕° closed 15 Nov-1 Mar, 500. Rest. ♦♦♦ ⟨ ⬚ ⬚ ⬚ closed Mon and Tue noon Mar-Apr, 15 Oct-15 Nov, 230-250.

⚓ ★★*Municipal* (100 pl), ☎ 47.26.06.43.

VEIGNE, ✉ 37250, 5 km S of **Montbazon** on the N 10 & D37.

Hotel :
★★ *Moulin Fleuri*, (C.H., L.F.), rte de Monts, ☎ 47.26.01.12, AE Visa, 10 rm ℗ ⟨ ⬚ ⬚ ⬚ pens, closed Mon ex hols, 1-20 Feb, 15-30 Oct, 470. Rest. ♦♦ ♪ Tasty regional cooking at affordable prices, 90-180.

LAMOTTE-BEUVRON

Orléans 36, Blois 59, Paris 167 km
pop 4405 ✉ 41600   B-C2

SNCF ☎ 54.88.01.13.

Hotels :
★★ *Bruyères*, Le Rabot, Vouzon, 7 km NW, ☎ 54.88.05.70, DC Euro Visa, 50 rm ℗ ⬚ ⬚ ✉ ∕° ball-trap, hunting, 5-ha pond, fishing, 150. Rest. ♦ ♪ 65-120; child : 40.
★ *Le Monarque*, 2, av. de l'Hôtel-de-Ville, ☎ 54.88.04.47, AE Euro Visa, 13 rm ℗ ⬚ ⬚ ⬚ closed Tue eve and Wed, Feb, 17-24 Aug, 145. Rest. ♦ ⬚ Typical Sologne cuisine, 65-135.
★ *Tatin* (L.F.), 5, av. de Vierzon, ☎ 54.88.00.03, Euro Visa, 15 rm ℗ ⬚ ⬚ ⬚ closed Sun eve and Mon, 12 Jan-24 Feb, 125. Rest. ♦ ♪ For the famous *tarte Tatin*, of course, 60-120.
La Cloche (L.F.), 37, av. de la République, ☎ 54.88.02.20, AE DC Euro Visa, 8 rm ℗ ⬚ ⬚ ⬚ closed Tue, 95. Rest. ♦ ♪ ⬚ Regional fare, 60-130.

Nearby

NOUAN-LE-FUZELIER, ✉ 41600, 8 km S.

Hotel :
● ★ *Le Moulin de Villiers*, ☎ 54.88.72.27, 20 rm ℗ ⟨ ⬚ ⬚ ⬚ ⬚ closed Tue eve , Wed, Nov-Dec, 5 Jan-25 Mar, 30 Aug-14 Sep, 150. Rest. ♦ ⟨ Bucolic atmosphere; simple pleasures around the pond, 65-140.

Restaurant :
♦♦ *Le Dahu*, 14, rue de la Mare, ☎ 54.88.72.88, AE Euro Visa, closed Tue eve and Wed, 10 Feb-20 Mar, 15-20 Jun. Alert J.-L. Germain never stops learning with his confrères : *feuilleté d'asperges au beurre de ciboulette, barbue aux moules et à l'orange, canard sauvage aux pêches*, 80-220; child : 45.

⚓ ★★★*La Grande Sologne* (70 pl), ☎ 54.88.70.22.

SALBRIS, ✉ 41300, 20 km.
SNCF ☎ 54.97.00.05.

Hotels :
★★★ *Parc* (L.F.), 8, av. d'Orléans, ☎ 54.97.18.53, Tx 751164, AE DC Euro Visa, 29 rm ℗ ⬚ ⬚ ⬚ 220. Rest. ♦♦ ♪ closed 12 Jan-15 Feb, 75-200.
★★ *Le Dauphin* (L.F.), 57, bd de la République, ☎ 54.97.04.83, Euro Visa, 10 rm ℗ ⬚ ⬚ ⬚ closed Sun eve and Mon, 12-26 Jan. Rest. ♦ ♪ Spec : *duo de carpe et d'anguille, poularde à la solognote*, 65-190; child : 35.
★ *La Sauldraie*, 81, av. d'Orléans, ☎ 54.97.17.76, Euro Visa, 12 rm ℗ ⬚ ⬚ ⬚ closed Mar (Sep-Easter), 170. Rest. ♦ ♪ ⬚ 80-130.

⚓ ★★★*Sologne* (65 pl), ☎ 54.97.06.38.

SOUVIGNY-EN-SOLOGNE, ✉ 41600, 11 km NW.

Hotel :
★ *Croix Blanche* (L.F.), rue du Gâtinais, ☎ 54.88.40.08, Visa, 9 rm, closed Tue eve and Wed eve, 100. Rest. ♦ 65-150.

Restaurant :
● ♦♦ *La Perdrix Rouge*, 22, rue du Gâtinais, ☎ 54.88.41.05, Euro Visa ⬚ closed Mon eve and Tue, 12-20 Jan, 3-24 Mar, 29 Jun-7 Jul. Fine cuisine. The *noix*

de coquilles Saint-Jacques "Perdrix Rouge" is Dominique and Jean-Noël Beurienne's special pride. A pleasant stopover, 70-200.

LANGEAIS★★

Tours 25, Angers 83, Paris 258 km
pop 4142 ✉ 37130   A2
The château de Langeais was erected in a single operation around 1465; in this severe feudal fortress, Charles VIII of France married Anne, Duchess of Brittany, on 16 December 1491, thus paving the way for the cession of Brittany to France.

▶ A visit to the **apartments★★** will take you straight into the Middle Ages; only the original inhabitants are lacking in this lordly setting; magnificent **tapestries collection★★** *(15 Mar.-Jun., 9-12 & 2-6:30; July-Aug., 9-6:30; Sep., 9-12 & 2-6:30; 1 Oct.-2 Nov., closed at 6; 3 Nov.-14 Mar., closed at 5; 15 Mar.-Sep., closed Mon. am non-hols.; Oct.-14 Mar., closed Mon. non-hols.).*

Nearby

▶ **Cinq-Mars-la-Pile** *(5 km E)* : overlooked by the ruins of a feudal château with huge moats★; interesting historical associations with Richelieu and Louis XIII *(9-12 & 2-7 or dusk Mar.-Sep.; closed Mon. and hols.).*   □

Practical Information _____

LANGEAIS
ℹ ☎ 47.96.58.22 (h.s.); ☎ 47.96.85.75 (l.s.).   ⬚
SNCF ☎ 47.96.82.19.

Hotels :
★★★ *Château de Rochecotte*, Saint-Patrice, ☎ 47.96.90.62, AE DC Euro Visa, 12 rm ℗ ⟨ ⬚ ⬚ ⬚ closed 2-15 Jan, 330. Rest. ♦ ♪ An atmosphere of gentle harmony pervades this dwelling surrounded by a 7-ha park and French gardens, 140-200.
★★ *Hosten*, 2, rue Gambetta, ☎ 47.96.82.12, AE, 12 rm ℗ closed Mon eve and Tue, 15 Jan-5 Feb, 28 Jun-10 Jul, 220. Rest. ♦ *Le Langeais* ♪ 190.

Nearby

CINQ-MARS-LA-PILE, ✉ 37130 Langeais, 5 km E.

Hotel :
Château de Cinq-Mars, (C.A.), ☎ 47.96.40.49, 3 rm ℗ ⟨ ⬚ ⬚ ∕° 300.

LOCHES★★

Tours 42, Châteauroux 70, Paris 258 km
pop 7019 ✉ 37600   A2
The beauty of Loches's trim white houses, set in the idyllic countryside of the Indre, contrasts sharply with the sinister reputation of its fortress, where those unwise enough to displease the kings of France were once imprisoned in damp dungeons.

▶ The **Porte des Cordeliers★** (B2, 15thC) leads to the Grande-Rue; on the right, the Renaissance **Hôtel de Ville★** and the 15thC **Porte Picoys★**. ▶ The Rue du Château (fine Renaissance houses) climbs to the **Cité Médiévale★★** (medieval town) with its impressive 13thC towers and ramparts. Behind the **Porte Royale★** (Royal Gate) is the Regional Museum (Musée du Terroir); paintings by the Vendéen artist Lansyer *(Easter-Sep., 9-11:45 & 2-6; Mar., Oct., 9-11:45 & 2-5; Nov.-Feb., 9-11:45 & 2-4; closed Fri.).* ▶ **Church of St. Ours★★**, 12thC Romanesque, with two octagonal pyramids between the towers, covering the nave. ▶ The **château★★** was inhabited by Charles VII, Louis XI, Charles VIII and Louis XII. The medieval Old Wing (Vieux Logis) is easily distinguished from the Nouveau Logis (New Wing) of the Renaissance. **Triptych★★** (1485, school of Jean Fouquet), **effigy of Agnès Sorel★**, the beautiful favourite of Charles VII

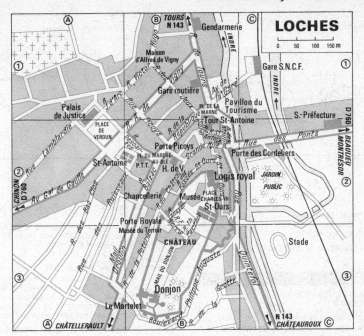

LOCHES

(15 Mar.-Sep., 9-12 & 2-6; 1 Jun.-Aug. 9-6; Oct.-14 Mar., 9-12 & 2-5; closed Wed., Dec., Jan.). ▶ The 11th-15thC **keep★★** is a fine example of the fortifications of the period, with dungeons dug deep into the rock. ▶ **Tour of the ramparts★★** *(opens, closes, 1/2 hr after château).*

Nearby

▶ **Beaulieu-lès-Loches** *(1 km E)* : 11th-15thC abbey church (12thC bell tower★). ▶ **Bridoré** *(15 km SE)* : with a 14th-15thC fortress. ▶ **Loches Forest★** *(7 km E)* : perfect for walks and bicycling; former **Chartreuse du Liget,** founded 1178 *(visits by request).* ▶ **Montrésor** *(17 km E)* : Renaissance **church★** (1519) with contemporary **tombs★** ; fortified Louis XII-style **château★** *(Apr.-Oct., 9-12:30 & 2-6:30).* ▶ **Nouans-les-Fontaines** *(26 km E)* : in 13thC church, **Descent from the Cross★★** by the school of Jean Fouquet (15thC). ☐

Practical Information

ⓘ pl. de la Marne (B1), ☎ 47.59.07.98.
🚃 (C1), ☎ 47.59.00.44.
🚌 3, rue de Tours (B2), ☎ 47.59.06.23.

Hotels :
● *★★ France,* 6, rue Picois (B2), ☎ 47.59.00.32, Visa, 22 rm Ⓟ half pens, closed Sun eve and Mon lunch, 2 Jan-6 Feb, 130. Rest. ♦ ᵹ 50-140.
★★ George Sand, 39, rue Quintefol (C3), ☎ 47.59.39.74, Euro Visa, 17 rm ≤ pens, 460. Rest. ♦♦ ≤ ♪ ᵹ 17th-C coach house on the Indre, 60-160 ; child : 45.

The LOIR Valley**

A-B1

From Vendôme to La Chartre-sur-le-Loir *(40 km, 3 hr; see map 1)*

The Loir (on no account confuse this peaceful little river with the far greater Loire), runs from the Ile-de-France to Anjou through rich meadows and lines of poplars. The surrounding vineyards, gardens, chalky hillsides and white, creeper-covered houses represent the epitome of rural tranquility.

▶ **Vendôme** *(→).* ▶ **Villiers-sur-Loir.** 1.5 km SW : **château de Rochambeau** (16th-18thC). ▶ **Gué-du-Loir** : captivating site★. ▶ **Montoire-sur-le-Loir★** (pop. 4431) : an angler's paradise ; Renaissance houses and town hall ; murals★ (12th-13thC) in the chapel of St. Gilles *(Jan.-Feb., Oct.-Dec., 9:30-7 ; closed Tue., Mar.-Sept., 9:30-7 ; daily).* On the hill, ruins of 12th-14thC château. 2.5 km SE, **Lavardin★** is overlooked by the romantic ruins of the château of the Counts of Vendôme ; 11th-12thC keep★ *(visits by request 9-7 in summer).* In the village, the Romanesque church of St. Genest has 12th-16thC murals★. ▶ **Trôo★** is partially dug into the side of the hill. Passages, narrow streets and **Caforts** (galleries) dug into the rock form an impenetrable maze. Go to see the church of St. Martin★ (12thC), and on the edge of the plateau near a feudal motte (view★) the "Puits-Qui-Parle" (echoing well). There is also a fossil cave. ▶ On the left bank, **Saint-Jacques-des-Guérets** : 12thC church with paintings★ of the same period. ▶ **Manor of La Possonnière★,** Renaissance, where the poet Ronsard was born in 1524. ▶ **L'Isle-Verte,** on the Loir, is Ronsard's burial place. ▶ **Poncé-sur-le-Loir** and **La Chartre-sur-le-Loir** *(→ Maine-Anjou).* ☐

Practical Information

MONTOIRE-SUR-LE-LOIR, ✉ 41800, 19 km NW of **Blois.**
ⓘ ☎ 54.85.39.78 ; mairie, ☎ 54.85.00.29.

Hotel :
● *★★ Cheval Rouge* (L.F.), 1, pl. Foch, ☎ 54.85.07.05, AE Euro Visa, 17 rm Ⓟ ▦ half pens (h.s.), closed Tue eve and Wed, 26 Jan-1 Mar, 360. Rest. ♦ 90-200.

On the maps, a town's name underlined <u>Saulieu</u> means that the locality possesses at least one recommended establishment (blue or red point).

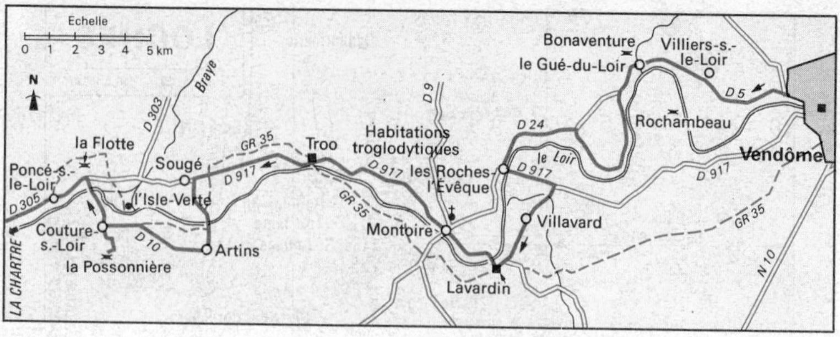

1. River Loir near Vendôme

Restaurant :
● ♦♦ ***Le Cheval Blanc***, rue Auguste-Arnault, Trôo, ☎ 54.85.08.22, Visa 🏞 closed Mon eve and Tue , Feb school hols, 15-31 Oct, 85-190.

⛺ ★★*Reclusages* (40 pl), ☎ 54.85.02.53.

MONTARGIS

Sens 51, Orléans 71, Paris 115 km
pop 17629 ✉ 45200 C1

The numerous parallel branches of the Loing, with their attendant bridges, have gained for Montargis the somewhat grandiose title of "the Venice of the Gâtinais"; despite this exaggeration, the town is undeniably attractive and is a popular fishing and hunting centre.

▶ The local speciality is **pralines** (chocolates or sweets, usually almond flavoured), in all shapes and sizes. Pralines are still sold in the restored building where they were invented. ▶ Next door is the **church of the Madeleine** (12thC nave, 16thC choir★). **Girodet Museum** in the town hall, in large part devoted to this local painter *(9-12 & 1-5:30; closed Mon.).*

Nearby

▶ **Chapelon** *(15 km W) :* Gaillardan Windmill, 15thC *(3-6 Sun., May-Sep.).* ▶ **Pithiviers** *(45 km NW;* pop. 9812) : steam train and Transport Museum *(2:30-6, Sun. and nat. hols., May-10 Oct.);* Kanaka collection in Municipal Museum *(10-12 & 2-6; closed Tue.);* 12th-16thC church. 19 km NE of Pithiviers, 14th-17thC château at **Malesherbes** *(1 Jan.-24 Mar., 2 Nov.-31 Dec., 2-5:30; 25 Mar.-1 Nov., 10-11:30 & 2-6:15);* **leisure centre** at Buthiers. ▶ **Bellegarde** *(23 km W) :* 14th-18thC château, Romanesque church. ▶ 7.5 km NW, 13thC church★ at **Boiscommun.** ▶ **Lorris** *(22 km SW) :* Renaissance town hall★, old covered market and 12th-13thC church. ▶ **Châtillon-Coligny :** outbuildings of the famous Admiral de Coligny's (1519-72) family château (12thC keep★, Renaissance well★). ▶ **Ferrières-en-Gâtinais** *(12 km N) :* 11th-13thC church★. ▶ **Domaine des Barres Arboretum** at **Nogent-sur-Vernisson** *(20 km S) :* 10000 trees of 3500 species *(8-12 & 1:30-5; closed Sat. & Sun. am, 1 Jul., 15 Sep.).* □

Practical Information

MONTARGIS
ℹ pl. du Patis, ☎ 38.98.00.87.
SNCF ☎ 38.85.40.55.
🚌 pl. A.-Briand, ☎ 38.85.08.26.

Hotels :
★★ ***La Gloire***, 74, av. du Gal-de-Gaulle, ☎ 38.85.04.69, 15 rm, closed Tue eve and Wed, 1-25 Feb, 15-25 Aug, 130. Rest. ● ♦♦ J. Jolly's glorious food is nicely priced : *langoustines rôties au riz sauvage*, fabulous desserts, 110-250.
★★ ***Lyon*** (L.F.), 74, rue A.-Coquillet, ☎ 38.85.30.39, Visa, 22 rm 🅿 🏞 closed Sun eve and Mon, 15 Jan-10 Feb, 2-12 Aug, 170. Rest. ♦♦ ♪ 70-90.

Restaurant :
● ♦♦ ***Auberge de l'Ecluse***, 741, rue des Ponts, Amilly, 5 km SE, ☎ 38.85.44.24, Visa ⚘ ♪ ✗ closed Mon and Sun eve , 1 wk late Aug, 21 Dec-10 Jan. His fast friendship with J. Robuchon inspires J.-L. Girault's culinary creations : *vinaigrette de mâche et de foie de canard, sandre gratiné, escalope de bourgeois au poivre rose*, 65-170.

⛺ ★★★*de la Forêt* (100 pl), ☎ 38.98.00.20.

Recommended
Youth hostel : at Cepoy, on the canal, ☎ 38.93.25.45.
♥ *Relais du Miel Villeneuve*, RN 7, 5 km S, ☎ 38.85.32.02; pralines : *Mazet*, 43, rue du Gal-Leclerc.

Nearby

COMBREUX, ✉ 45530, 25 km W.

Hotel :
● ★★ ***Auberge de Combreux*** (C.H.), ☎ 38.59.47.63, Visa, 21 rm 🅿 🏞 🚴 ▭ 🎾 half pens, closed 15 Dec-15 Jan, 480. Rest. ♦ ♪ An ideal spot for a weekend in the Orléans forest, 80-150; child : 35.

COURTENAY, ✉ 45320, 25 km E.

Restaurant :
● ♦♦ ***La Clé des Champs***, Les Quatre Croix, ☎ 38.97.42.68, Euro Visa ⚘ ♪ closed Wed and Thu (l.s.) , Wed and Thu lunch (h.s.), 5-29 Jan, 15-31 Oct. In the heart of the countryside, Marc Delion offers appetizing specialties like *lapin du Gâtinais en gelée, aiguillettes de canette en Pithiviers.* Wide array of desserts and wines, 90-155.

MALESHERBES, ✉ 45330, 60 km NW.
ℹ rue Pilonne, ☎ 38.34.81.94.

Hotel :
★ ***Ecu de France*** (L.F.), 10, pl. du Martroi, ☎ 38.34.87.25, AE Euro Visa, 12 rm 🅿 🏞 120. Rest. ♦ ♿ closed Thu, 55-120.

⛺ ★★★*Municipal* (90 pl), ☎ 38.34.85.63.

PITHIVIERS, ✉ 45300, 45 km NW.
ℹ West Mall, ☎ 38.30.50.02.
SNCF ☎ 38.30.01.31.

Hotel :
★★ ***Chaumière*** (L.F.), 77, av. de la République, ☎ 38.30.03.61, 8 rm, closed Mon, 15 Dec-10 Jan, 160. Rest. ♦ 50-110.

Restaurant :
♦♦♦ ***Au Péché Mignon***, 50, fg de Paris, ☎ 38.30.05.32, closed Mon eve, Tue, Sun eve, 15 Jan-15 Feb. Spec : *savarin d'écrevisses, feuilleté de Saint-Jacques au confit de poireaux*, 100-180.

ORLÉANS*

Chartres 73, Bourges 106, Paris 119 km
pop 105589 ☒ 45000   **B1**

Like all the towns on the Loire, Orléans is best seen from the river. On 7 May 1489, Joan of Arc made her triumphal entry into the town after the English had been driven out. Since then, the Fête de Jeanne d'Arc on the 7th and 8th of May has remained one of the high spots of the town's year. Orléans has always been a thriving commercial town and, to the N, now has an industrialized zone, in addition to its traditional business in corn, potatoes, vegetables, Loire wines and local nursery produce. Across the Loire is a new ecologically oriented town, **Orléans-La Source.** In addition to its widely-known Botanical Gardens, it has managed to surround its offices and factories with woods and greenery.

▶ Orléans, greatly damaged during WWII, has been very carefully rebuilt. **Place du Martroi** (B2) : statue of Joan of Arc. ▶ **Rue Royale**★ nearby has been restored to its 18thC glory. ▶ **Rue d'Escures,** between Martroi and the Place de l'Étape, has fine 17thC mansions. ▶ In 1560 François II died in the Renaissance **Hôtel de Ville**★ (B2, much remodeled, *10-12 & 2-6*). ▶ The **Saint-Croix Cathedral**★ is an unusual example of a great Gothic church rebuilt in the 17th and 18thC, after the Calvinist destruction of 1568. It was rebuilt on the model of the two early 16thC arches left intact in the nave, which explains its unity of style – rare in medieval cathedrals. See the paneling★★ (18thC) in the choir; the remains of primitive sanctuaries in the crypt (4th and 10th-11thC); interesting treasure room. ▶ The **gardens**★ of the former Bishop's residence are charming. ▶ **Fine Arts Museum**★★ (B2), in the Place de la Cathédrale, has an incomparable collection of 17th-18thC portraits★★ (French school), and a series of pastels★★ and busts★ signed Houdon, Pigalle and Germain Pilon. Don't miss *St. Thomas*★ by Velázquez and *L'Ombre*★ by Rodin.

Nearby

▶ **Olivet** *(4 km S)* : fishing, canoeing★, restaurants and cafés along the delightful banks of the Loiret. ▶ **Parc Floral de la Source**★★ *(8 km SE)* : in season, enchanting displays of tulips, iris, roses, dahlias and chrysanthemums; fountains, animals and attractions in the Park, where the Loiret surfaces *(9-6, Apr.-11 Nov.; 2-5 rest of year)*; greenhouse restaurant). ▶ **Tigy** *(29 km SE)* : Museum of Old Rural Crafts *(2:30-6:30 Sun., 15 Apr.-15 Oct.; on request the rest of year).* ▶ **Saint-Denis-de-l'Hôtel** *(16 km E)* : house of Maurice Genevoix *(Easter-15 Sep., Fri., Sun., 10-12 & 3-6).* ▶ **Châteauneuf-sur-Loire** *(25 km E)* : In the château park, arboretum, giant rhododendrons★; Museum of Loire Rivercraft and of Old Châteauneuf *(10-12 & 2-5:30, Jul.-Aug.; closed Oct.-Mar.; request rest of year; tel. : 38.58.41.18).* ▶ **Forest of Orléans**★, NE of town : more than 340 km², mostly pines and oaks; signposted walks, picnic areas and guided tours *(info at SI).* Ecological Museum, Forêt des Loges, at **Nibelle** *(Mar.-Nov. and Sun. year round).* ▶ **Artenay** *(21 km N)* : Moulin de Pierre *(2-6, 3rd Sun. of the month and during local festivals, Mar.-Oct.).* ▶ **Tivernon** *(32 km N)* : traditional farm of Grand Bréau *(visits by request during week, tel. : 38.39.41.46).* ▶ **La Chapelle-Saint-Mesmin** *(6 km W)* : Merovingian crypt in 11thC church.   □

Practical Information _____

ORLÉANS
ℹ️ bd A.-Briand (C2), ☎ 38.53.05.95; C.D.T., 3, rue de la Bretonnerie (B2), ☎ 38.54.83.83.
✈ *Bricy,* 16 km NW, ☎ 38.43.23.60. Air France office, 4, rue de la Cerche, ☎ 38.54.82.10.
🚆 (B1), ☎ 38.53.50.50.
Car rental : *Avis,* 13, rue des Sansonnières, ☎ 38.62.27.04; train station (B1), ☎ 38.62.27.04.

Hotels :
★★★★(L) *Sofitel,* 44-46, quai Barentin (A3), ☎ 38.62.17.39, Tx 780073, AE DC Euro Visa, 110 rm Ⓟ ⚑ ⚓ ⬚ 480. Rest. ◆◆ *La Vénerie* ⚑ ⚓ ⬚ 100-170.
● ★★★ *Cèdres,* (Inter-Hôtel), 17, rue Mal-Foch (A1), ☎ 38.62.22.92, Tx 782314, AE Visa, 36 rm ⬚ 260.
★★★ *Orléans,* 6, rue A.-Crespin (B2), ☎ 38.53.35.34, Euro Visa, 18 rm, 260.
★★ *Marguerite* (L.F.), 14, pl. du Vieux-Marché (A2), ☎ 38.53.74.32, Visa, 25 rm, 130.

Restaurants :
● ◆◆◆ *La Crémaillère (Paul Huyart),* 34, rue N.-D. de Recouvrance (A-B2), ☎ 38.53.49.17, AE DC Euro Visa, closed Mon and Sun eve, Aug. Living quietly in his pleasant establishment, Paul Huyart keeps aloof from culinary fads and trends. His strength lies in this sage approach. He is a great chef, with immense talent for the classical repertory. Spec : *millefeuille de légumes au foie gras, blanc de volailles, cuisses de lapereau rôties avec son jus, soufflé aux fruits,* 190-250.
● ◆◆ *Le Lautrec,* 26, pl. du Châtelet (B2), ☎ 38.54.09.54, Tx 783411, AE Euro Visa Ⓟ closed Sun, 15-28 Feb, 14-30 Jul. The rich cooking of the Tarn region in a turn-of-the-century setting : *œufs de caille au foie gras, saumon à l'ail de lautrec confit, pavé d'onglet à la vapeur de roquefort.* Wonderful array of Armagnacs (1893 to the present), 100-220.
● ◆◆ *Les Antiquaires,* 2-4, rue au Lin (B2-3), ☎ 38.53.52.35 Ⓟ closed Mon and Sun, 1 wk at Easter, Aug, 24 Dec-3 Jan, 100-200.
◆◆ *La Poutrière,* 8, rue de la Brèche (B3), ☎ 38.66.02.30, AE DC Euro Visa Ⓟ ⬚ ⚓ ⬚ closed Mon and Sun eve, 1-7 Mar. Spec : *minute de bar, saumon sauce citronnelle, bœuf mode au raifort,* 120-220.
◆◆ *Le Bigorneau,* 54-56, rue des Turcies (A2), ☎ 38.68.01.10, AE DC Visa ⚑ ⚓ ⚓ ⚓ closed Mon and Sun, hols, Feb, Jul, Aug. Spec : fish and seafood, 120-180.

Recommended
Events : *paper and antiques fair,* weekend early Mar; *feast of Joan of Arc,* early May; *fair-exhibition,* in Apr; *flower show,* parc d'Orléans-La Source; *antiques show,* late Nov.
♥ chocolates : *Chocolaterie Royale,* 53, rue Royale; pastry : *Morin,* 209, rue de Bourgogne (B-C2); at 45400 Fleury-les-Aubrais, old-fashioned vinegar : *Martin-Pouret,* 236, fg Bannier; at Fleury-les-Aubrais, CP 45400, pork products : *Lenormand,* 318, fg Bannier.

Nearby

CHÂTEAUNEUF-SUR-LOIRE, ☒ 45110, 25 km E.
ℹ️ pl. A.-Briand, ☎ 38.58.44.79 (h.s.).
🚆 ☎ 38.58.42.07.

Hotels :
● ★★ *La Capitainerie* (L.F.), 1, Grande-Rue, ☎ 38.58.42.16, Euro Visa, 14 rm Ⓟ ⬚ half pens (h.s.), closed Mon (l.s.), 1 Jan-15 Feb, 190. Rest. ◆◆ ⚓ ⬚ 135-165.
★★ *Loiret,* 4, pl. A.-Briand, ☎ 38.58.42.28, AE DC Euro

ORLÉANS

0 100 200 300 400 m

N 20 ↑ PARIS Ⓑ

Ⓒ Gendarmerie

R. du Ch. au Gaillard

PL. DUNOIS Ⓐ ①

Rue de Patay

Av. de Paris

Emile Zola

P.T.T.

Musée des Sciences Naturelles

Palais des Sports

N 157 LE MANS

Police

Bd Mal Foch

Rue Mal Foch

Av. de Verdun

PLACE GAMBETTA

Gare S.N.C.F.

S.I.

Gare routière

PARC PASTEUR

①

Bd. de Rocheplatte

PLACE ALBERT Iᵉʳ

St-Paterne

Bd. Alex. Martin

Palais de Justice

R. de la Bretonnerie

Patinoire

R. des Champs

Rue d'Illiers

R. de la République

H. de V.

Musée des Beaux-Arts

Bd A. Briand

②

N 152 BLOIS

Hôpital

Rue Jean Jaurès

Pte Madeleine

Rue des Carmes

PL. DU MARTROI · St.de J. d'Arc

St-Pierre

du Martroi

Musée Hôtel Cabu de J. d'Arc

GL DE GAULLE

R. Jeanne d'Arc

PL. DE L'ETAPE

R. Dupanloup

PL. STE-CROIX

Théâtre

Cathédrale

St-Euverte

N 152 PITHIVIERS

②

N.-D. de Recouvrance

R. Croix de Bois

St-Paul

Rue Royale

PL. DU VIEUX MARCHE

PL DU CHÂTELET

Maison de la Coquille

St-Donatien

Préfecture

CLOITRE ST-AIGNAN

Bourgogne

Bd de la Motte Sanguin

St-Aignan

③

PONT MARÉCHAL JOFFRE

Q. Barentin Q. Cypierre

PONT GEORGE-V

Q. du Châtelet

Quai du Fort Alleaume

Ⓐ

LOIRE

③

Av. de Trévise de Prague

Q. du Fort des Tourelles

Quai du

Q. des Augustins

PL. ST-CHARLES

Bd du Gal de Gaulle

D 951 BLOIS

JARDIN BOTANIQUE

FAUBOURG ST-MARCEAU

N 20 ↓ VIERZON Ⓑ

Ⓒ D 951 ↑ SULLY

Visa, 21 rm P closed Sun eve, 1-15 Jan, 148. Rest. ♦ ♪ 69-195.

Restaurant :
● ♦ **Auberge des Fontaines**, 1, rue des Fontaines, ☎ 38.58.44.10 ▨ ⌂ closed Sun eve, Sep. Reserve. Simple, country food : *roulade de saumon beurre blanc, ragoût de l'auberge (lotte, Saint-Jacques, langoustines), rognon de veau aux deux moutardes et noilly*, 160-210.

OLIVET, ⊠ 45160, 5 km S.

Hotel :
★★ **Le Rivage** (R.S.), ☎ 38.66.02.93, Tx 760926, AE DC Euro Visa, 25 rm P ⌂ ▨ ⌂ ♪ᴼ half pens (h.s.), closed 31 Dec-15 Jan, 630. Rest. ♦ ⌂ Spec : *salade de lotte aux pousses d'épinards, vinaigrette de haddock à la mousse d'avocat, pigeonneau au citron*, 100-220 ; child : 80.

Restaurants :
♦♦♦ **Quatre Saisons**, 351, rue de la Reine-Blanche, ☎ 38.66.14.30 P ▨ ⌂ ♪ closed 1 Jan-15 Mar. Spec : seafood pot-au-feu, grilled river perch, 90-180.
♦♦ **Madagascar**, 315, rue de la Reine-Blanche, ☎ 38.66.12.58, AE DC Euro Visa P ⌂ ⌂ closed Tue eve, Wed, Sun eve (l.s.), Wed only (h.s.), 20 Jan-22 Feb, 90-170.

▲ ★★**Municipal** (80 pl), ☎ 38.63.53.94.

SAINT-HILAIRE-SAINT-MESMIN, ⊠ 45580, 10 km SW on the CD 951.

Hotel :
● ♦♦ **Escale du Port-Arthur**, (Inter-Hôtel), 205, rue de l'Eglise, ☎ 38.76.30.36, Tx 782320, AE DC Euro Visa, 21 rm P ⌂ ▨ ⌂ ⛥ 160. Rest. ♦ ⌂ ♪ ⌂ Beside the Loiret, 70-180 ; child : 35.

SAINT-JEAN-DE-BRAYE, ⊠ 45800, 4 km E.

Restaurant :
♦ **La Grange**, 205, fg de Bourgogne, ☎ 38.86.43.36, Euro Visa P ▨ ⌂ ⌂ 75-180.

SAINT-JEAN-DE-LA-RUELLE, ⊠ 45140, 2 km W.

Hotel :
★★★ **Auberge de la Montespan** (C.H.), 31, av. G.-Clemenceau, ☎ 38.88.12.07, Visa, 8 rm P ⌂ ▨ ⌂ ♪ᴼ closed 23 Dec-1 Feb, 350. Rest. ♦♦♦ 130-200.

SURY-AUX-BOIS, ⊠ 45530, 14 km NE of **Châteauneuf-sur-Loire**.

Hotel :
★★ **Domaine de Chicamour** (R.S.), ☎ 38.59.35.42, AE DC Euro, 12 rm P ⌂ ▨ ⌂ ♪ ♪ᴼ closed Dec-Feb, 315. Rest. ♦ ⌂ ♪ 80-170.

VANNES-SUR-COSSON, ⊠ 45510, 17 km S of **Châteauneuf-sur-Loire**.

Restaurant :
♦ **Le Vieux Relais**, rte d'Isdes, ☎ 38.58.04.14, Visa P ⌂ closed Tue eve and Wed, Feb, Sep, 50-130.

RICHELIEU*

Chinon 21, Tours 60, Paris 295 km
pop 2496 ⊠ 37120   A3

Once a little village, then transformed at Cardinal Richelieu's behest into a planned town to provide accommodation for his court near his huge château, now almost entirely destroyed. One of the most beautiful towns in French Classical style (17thC). 28 mansions, all alike, border the Grande-Rue linking two symmetrical squares. Covered market with exceptional 17thC timber structure★.

▶ **Richelieu Museum** in the Hôtel de Ville *(10-12 & 2-6, Jul.-Aug.; 10-12 & 2-4 rest of year; closed Tue., weekends, hols. out of season).* ▶ Château **park★** (1 000 acres, *admission free).* ▶ Tourist railway (→ Chinon). □

Practical Information _____

ⓘ mairie, ☎ 47.58.10.13/47.58.13.62 (h.s.).

Hotel :
★★★ *Château de Milly* (C.H.), Razines, 9 km on the D 749, ☎ 47.95.64.56, AE DC Euro Visa, 15 rm Ⓟ 𝟯 ⌀ ⅃ closed Thu (l.s.), Feb, 400. Rest. ♦ ⅃ 丙 ℅ 150-200; child : 80.

SAINT-BENOÎT-SUR-LOIRE★★★

Orléans 35, Bourges 90, Paris 144 km
pop 1925 ⊠ 45110 Châteauneuf-sur-Loire   C1

The abbey spire here is rich in symbolism. The site has been a place of pilgrimage since the time of the druids; in the Middle Ages the relics of Saint Benedict, the "Father of Western monasticism" were transferred here; under Charlemagne the cultural influence of the Benedictine abbey spread throughout the Christian world.

▶ **The abbey church★★★** (1067-1218) is one of France's most remarkable Romanesque buildings; in front of the façade is an enormous square tower, forming the porch. Don't miss : the **capitals★★** in the porch, the 13thC **sculptures★** by the N doorway and the balanced proportions of the choir (4th-5thC mosaic) and the 11thC **crypt★** containing the relics of St. Benedict *(7 am-10 pm ex during services, guided tour on written request; Gregorian chant; mass Sun. and religious feastdays, 10:45, wkdays 11:45).*

Nearby

▶ **Germigny-des-Prés** *(5.5 km NW)* : little church★★ dating from Charlemagne (806 except 11thC nave) superb 9thC mosaic★★ in E apse *(8-8).*   □

Practical Information _____

Hotel :
★★ *Le Labrador*, 7, pl. de l'Abbaye, ☎ 38.35.74.38, Euro, 22 rm Ⓟ ⅋ 𝟯 ⌀ 丙 ℅ closed 25 Dec-15 Feb, 225.

The SOLOGNE Region*

B2

Round trip *(119 km, half-day)*
The Sologne is a region of woods, heaths and lakes in a loop of the Loire, S of Orléans. It is a paradise for anglers and hunters, but less so for walkers since much of the land is enclosed or private property. The Sologne was once a region of marshes and fevers and was only drained after the Second Empire; the rivers were dredged, one-third of the lakes were filled in, and the woods were replanted. Today almost half the 5 000 km^2 of the Sologne is cultivated land : maize, fruit (especially strawberries), and vegetables (especially asparagus). There are also numerous game farms.
To avoid continually running up against the "No Entry" signs which are numerous in this part of the world, it is worth buying the map of the area, La Carte de la Sologne (I.G.N., 1/100 000), showing all foot- and bridle-paths together with details of leisure facilities and accommodation.
▶ **La Ferté-Saint-Aubin** (pop. 5 498) : low wood-faced brick houses round the château in Louis XIII style; typical of the Sologne. ▶ 6 km E, the **Domaine Solognot du Ciran** *(book beforehand, tel : 38.65.90.93)* : good description of the Sologne countryside; portrayal of past life-

styles. ▶ **Ligny-le-Ribault.** ▶ **La Ferté-Saint-Cyr.** ▶ **Dhuizon.** ▶ **Château de Labord.** ▶ **Courmemin** : 13thC church. ▶ **Mur-de-Sologne,** 3 km NW : château de la Morinière (16thC). ▶ **Gy-de-Sologne** : Straize agricultural museum *(15 Mar.-15 Nov., 10-11:30 & 3-6:30; closed weekends).* ▶ **Château du Moulin★** *(9-11:30 & 2-6:30 Mar.-15 Nov.),* charming 15thC manor with wide moats fed by the Croisne; fine furniture and tapestries (15th-17thC). ▶ **Romorantin-Lanthenay** (pop. 18 187) : a large market town, almost the only important centre in the region. Ancient houses★, gardens and the various arms of the Sauldre make this a charming town. Sologne Museum★ in the town hall : life, folklore, crafts, etc. *(daily 10-11:30 & 2-5:30, ex Tue., Sun. and hols.).* 16thC **Logis,** Rue de la Résistance, 16thC building (the Chancellory, Hôtel Saint-Pol). Remnants of former royal château (15th-16thC). Motor Racing Museum, 29-31 Fbg. d'Orléans *(same hours as the Sologne Museum).* Archaeological Museum, Carroir-Doré *(tel. 54.76.22.06).* 17.5 km E : **château de la Ferté-Imbault,** 16th-17thC. *(Aug.-Sep., Mon., Fri., weekends 2-2:45 & 3:30-4:15).* ▶ **Saint-Viâtre** *(25 km NE of Romorantin)* : four 16thC painted panels★ in the church. □

Practical Information _____

La FERTÉ-SAINT-AUBIN, ⊠ 45240, 21 km S of **Orléans.**
🚄 ☎ 54.91.50.04.

Hotels :
● ★★★ *Hostellerie du Château Les Muids* (C.H.), RN 20, ☎ 38.64.65.14, Tx 650697, AE DC Euro Visa, 13 rm Ⓟ 𝟯 ⅃ 丙 305. Rest. ♦♦ ⅃ 丙 Dream that you are lord of the castle in a 33-ha park, 90-200.
★★ *Perron,* (France-Accueil), 9-11, rue du Gal-Leclerc, ☎ 38.76.53.36, AE DC Euro Visa, 29 rm Ⓟ closed 15-30 Jan, 180. Rest. ♦ 70-160; child : 45.

Restaurants :
● ♦♦ *Ferme de la Lande*, rte de Marcilly, ☎ 38.76.64.37, Visa ⅋ 丙 closed Mon. Youthful cuisine that ought not to be missed, in an old farmhouse, 120-200.
♦♦ *Ecu de France*, 6, rue du Gal-Leclerc, ☎ 38.76.52.20, closed Thu, Feb, 15 Sep-1 Oct, 100-150.
⚑ *Municipal* (40 pl), ☎ 54.91.55.90.

ROMORANTIN-LANTHENAY, ⊠ 41200, 54 km NW of **Poitiers.**
ⓘ pl. de la Paix, ☎ 54.76.43.89.
🚄 ☎ 54.76.06.51.

Hotels :
★★★ *Le Colombier* (L.F.), 10, pl. du Vieux-Marché, ☎ 54.76.12.76, AE DC Euro Visa, 11 rm Ⓟ closed 13 Jan-11 Feb, 15-22 Sep, 160. Rest. ● ♦♦ 丙 closed Mon. A handsome blend of old beams, a blooming terrace and fresh bouquets : *carolines d'asperges à la mousseline de cresson, fricassée de langoustines aux girolles,* 75-200.
★★★ *Lion d'Or* (R.C.), 69, rue G.-Clemenceau, ☎ 54.76.00.28, Tx 750990, AE DC Euro Visa, 10 rm Ⓟ 𝟯 ⅃ 丙 closed 1 Jan-15 Feb, 360. Rest. ● ♦♦♦ ⅃ 丙 In an entirely renovated decor, Didier Clément and his wife bring a youthful new feeling and a burst of talent to this handsome family house. Dishes to share : *escargots, artichauts à la réglisse, langoustines rôtis aux épices douces, agneau de Pauillac en croûte de sel, rouget de roche au caviar et mousse de petits pois.* Loire Valley wines, 240-450.
★★ *Auberge Le Lanthenay* (L.F.), rue N.-D.-de-Lieu, ☎ 54.76.09.19, Euro Visa, 14 rm 𝟯 ⌀ half pens (h.s.), closed Sun eve and Mon, 16 Feb-11 Mar, 27 Sep-6 Oct, 340. Rest. ♦ ⅋ ⅃ 80-200.

⚑ ★★★★*Tournefeuille* (160 pl), ☎ 54.76.16.60.

┌─────────────────────────────────────┐
│ In preparing for your trip, consult the pages pertaining to the regions. You will find there the description of the region you wish to visit, as well as a list of sites that must be seen, a brief history and practical information. │
└─────────────────────────────────────┘

SULLY-SUR-LOIRE*

Orléans 42, Bourges 82, Paris 155 km
pop 5825 ⊠ 45600　　　　　　　　　　　　　C1

Sully is a pleasant little country town facing the Loire, known for its château with water-filled moats and popular as a hunter's rendez-vous.

▶ **The château★★** is linked to the memory of the indefatigable Sully, the great minister of Henri IV. It was he who rebuilt the **"Petit Château"** at the beginning of 17thC, at right angles to the 14thC medieval château, overlooking the Loire *(daily 10-11:45 & 2-4:45; changeable hours — check ahead; closed Dec.-Feb.);* magnificent **beams★★** in the keep. ▶ Place de la Halle, Renaissance house from Henri IV period. ▶ Stained-glass windows in church of **Saint-Ythier** (16thC).　　　　　　　　　　　□

Practical Information _____

ⓘ pl. Gal-de-Gaulle, ☎ 38.35.22.21.
SNCF ☎ 38.36.21.02/38.35.21.02.

Hotel :
● ★★ *Le Pont de Sologne*, 21, rue Porte-de-Sologne, ☎ 38.36.26.34, DC, 25 rm Ⓟ half pens (h.s.), 310. Rest. ♦ 70-150.

TOURS***

Le Mans 82, Orléans 112, Paris 234 km
pop 136483 ⊠ 37000　　　　　　　　　　　　A2

A city of rich merchants, who built the elegant Renaissance and neo-Classic mansions, Tours today is a centre of light industry, research and data processing. The old quarters of the town have been renovated and many are pedestrian precincts. This is a tourist centre for those visiting the châteaux of the Loire, but it is also the scene of important International Fairs in May and September and a world-famous music festival held in the Grange de Meslay *(last Fri. and weekend in Jun., 1st Fri. and weekend in Jul.).*

▶ **Place Jean-Jaurès** (C3), with its café-terraces, flowers and fountains, is the centre of social activity under the watchful eye of the caryatids on the Hôtel de Ville (1905). ▶ Commercial and pedestrian **Rue de Bordeaux.** ▶ **Rue Nationale** (B2) is another street bustling with vendors. ▶ At No. 19 Rue Émile-Zola is the **Hôtel Mame** (18thC), a town mansion with an exhibition of furniture, tapestries and old books *(2:30-6 or 6:30, Apr.-13 Sep.).* ▶ The **cathedral quarter** (C1) is an island of calm ; a gigantic **cedar of Lebanon★** shades the courtyard of the former Archbishop's residence (17th-18thC) which houses the **Musée des Beaux-Arts★★** (Fine Arts Museum; *9-12:45 & 2-6, ex Tue. and nat. hols.).* A remarkable succession of salons decorated with wood paneling and silk wall coverings from Tours evokes French taste from Louis XIV to Louis XVI. French, Flemish and Italian schools are well represented : the museum's masterpieces are *Christ au Jardin des Oliviers★★,* the *Resurrection★★* by Mantegna, a Rubens, and Rembrandt's *Flight into Egypt.* **Public garden★.** ▶ The **cathedral of St. Gatien★★** shows the evolution of Gothic style from 13thC (choir) to 15th-16thC (façade), terminating in the Renaissance lanterns on the two towers ; 13th-15thC stained glass★★. ▶ Close by, the **cloister of La Psalette★** (15th-16thC, frescos) where Balzac located several chapters of his *Curé de Tours.* To the N, the **Tour de Guise** (C1) is one of the remnants of the royal château built in 1160 by Henry II of England. The château, now restored, houses the **Historial de Touraine** (wax museum created by the Grévin Museum of Paris : *summer 9-7; spring, fall 9-11:30 & 2-5; winter 2-5; no tickets sold 1 hr before closing).* ▶ Along the Rue Colbert to the **Place Foire-le-Roi** lined with 15thC gabled houses. At no. 8, **Hôtel Babou de la Bourdaisière★,** Renaissance. ▶ The **church of St. Julien★** (13thC Gothic) originally belonged to an abbey ; its cellars are today the Tou-

raine **Wine Museum** *(9-12 & 2-6; closed Tue.).* Above the Chapter★ *(temporary exhibitions)* is the **Musée du Compagnonnage★** (Craft Guild Museum) where you can see the pieces created by craftsmen to prove their mastery of various trades *(9-12 & 2-6; closed Tue.).* ▶ Nearby in Rue Jules-Favre are the **Palace of Commerce★** (1759), the remains of the Renaissance Hôtel de Semblançay and the **Fontaine de Beaune★** (1511). ▶ Rue du Commerce (B1) : the **Hôtel Gouin★,** Renaissance mansion, housing the **Touraine Archaeological Museum** *(Jan.-14 Mar., 9-12 & 2-5, closed Fri. ; 15 Mar.-Sep., 9-12 & 2-6).* ▶ Now you come to **Vieux Tours★★** (Old Tours), rich in old houses and mansions. Magnificently restored and transformed into a pedestrian precinct, this is an area to see in the daytime for its gabled façades and half timbering ; in the evening the cafés and restaurants come to life. Don't miss the **Place Plumereau★,** centre of the old medieval quarter, the **Rue Briçonnet★** and the **Rue Paul-Louis-Courier★.** In the neighbourhood, **Gemmail Museum** (AB-1), exhibiting stained-glass compositions lit from behind *(10-12 & 2-6, 30 Mar.-15 Oct. ; closed Mon.).* ▶ In the Halles (market) quarter, the Tour de l'Horloge and the Tour Charlemagne (the clock-tower and Charlemagne's tower ; B2) are the only remains of the 12th-13thC **Basilica of St. Martin,** with origins dating from the 5thC. Beside them stands the new basilica (1887-1924).
Also... ▶ The **gardens★** : Jardins de l'Archevêché (C1), the **Préfecture** (C2), the Prébendes, and the **Jardin Botanique★** (animals and exhibitions in the latter). In the new quarter along the banks of the Cher (via C3) is the **Promenade du Lac★** (Olympic swimming pool, sailing).

Nearby

▶ **St. Cosme Priory★** *(3 km W)* : ruins of 11th, 12th and 15thC church where poet Pierre de Ronsard is buried *(9-12 & 2-5 or 6 ; closed Wed. out of season and Dec.-Jan.).* 1.5 km SE, **château de Plessisy-lès-Tours** : exhibition on Louis XI who built it (1463) and died there in 1483 *(10-12 & 2-5, Apr.-Dec. ; closed Tue. and nat. hols.).* ▶ **Luynes** *(12 km W)* : 13th-15thC **château★** *(no visitors).* ▶ **Château de la Roche-Racan** *(26 km NW)* : lovely early-17thC château ; interesting works of art in the **church of St. Paterne-Racan** *(2 km NW).* ▶ **Château-La-Vallière** *(33 km NW)* : to the S, woods and lake, picturesque ruins of **château de Vaujours.** 7 km W, **Marcilly-sur-Maulne** : late-16thC château. ▶ **Grange de Meslay★** *(9 km NE)* : this 1220 tithe barn is the setting for the Touraine Music Festival which attracts internationally famous performers from all over the world. 2 km S, **Parçay-Meslay** : 12thC murals in the church. ▶ **Vouvray** *(9 km E,* right bank of the Loire) and **Montlouis-sur-Loire** *(12 km E,* left bank) both produce white wines of repute (winetasting in the cellars).　　　　　　　　　　□

Practical Information _____

TOURS
ⓘ pl. du Mal-Leclerc (C2), ☎ 47.05.58.08.
✈ *St-Symphorien,* 7 km NE, ☎ 47.54.21.45. *Air France office,* 8-10 pl. de la Victoire (A1-2), ☎ 47.37.54.54.
SNCF (C3), ☎ 47.20.50.50.
🚌 pl. du Mal-Leclerc (C2), ☎ 47.05.30.49.
Car rental : *Avis,* 39 bis, bd Heurteloup (C-D2), ☎ 47.05.59.33/47.20.53.27 ; train station.

Hotels :
● ★★★★ *Jean Bardet,* 57, rue Groison (off map B1), ☎ 47.41.41.11, AE DC Euro Visa, 4 rm 11 apt Ⓟ ≮ ▨ 🍴 ♪ ▭ ⅋ Rest. ● ♦♦♦ ≮ ♪ In a green park that extends over 3ha, with a lake, pool and a tennis court, Sophie and Jean Bardet are utterly at ease in their lovely Napoléon-III residence which counts 15 luxurious rooms. It's the country magically transported to the heart of town. The selection, style and prices that made Châteauroux a gourmet mecca are tangibly the same : *dos de saumon frais vapeur de soja, gésiers de canard et homard rôti, lapin fermier aux artichauts,* 200-400.
★★★★ *Méridien,* 292, av. de Grammont (off map C3), ☎ 47.28.00.80, Tx 750922, AE DC Euro Visa, 125 rm Ⓟ ≮ ▨ 🍴 ▭ ⅋ 530. Rest. ♦♦ *La Crémaillère* ≮ ♪ 130-200.

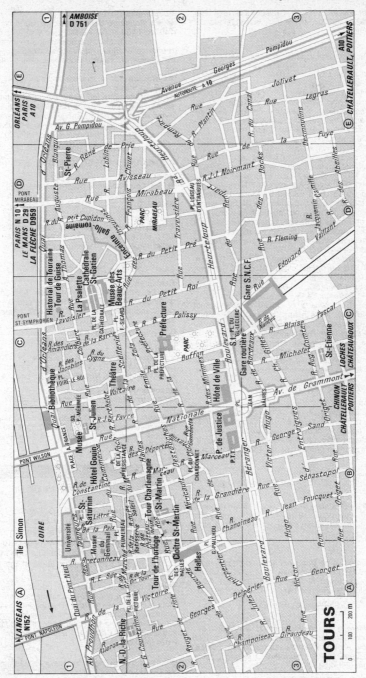

★★★ **Bordeaux** (L.F.), 3, pl. du Mal-Leclerc (C2), ☎ 47.05.40.32, AE DC Euro Visa, 52 rm ⌧ 300. Rest. ♦♦ 100-200.

★★★ **Central**, 21, rue Berthelot (B-C1), ☎ 47.05.46.44, Tx 751173, AE DC Euro Visa, 42 rm ℗ ⌧ ⌧ ᓂ 240.

★★★ **Univers**, 5, bd Heurteloup (C-D2), ☎ 47.05.37.12, Tx 751460, AE DC Euro Visa, 91 rm ⌧ ᓂ 380. Rest. ♦♦ ♪ ᓂ closed Sat, 100-160.

● ★★ *Castel Fleuri*, 10, rue Groison (off map B1), ☎ 47.54.50.99, Tx 752204, 15 rm P ⟡ ఉ 160.

Restaurants :

◆◆◆ *Charles Barrier*, 101, av. de la Tranchée, ☎ 47.54.20.39, Euro Visa P ఉ closed Mon and Sun eve, Feb school hols, 1-31 Jul. In a fresh, trim decor of tidy dimensions, the great Charles Barrier, an ornament of Hachette's panel of chefs, has taken up his pots and pans once more, at an age when many others would retire for a hand-earned rest. Barrier is back at his bread oven (fresh loaves baked daily), in the kitchen he only temporarily abandoned. In this handsome, justly celebrated establishment, you can enjoy the flavourful specialties of Touraine : *matelote d'anguille aux pruneaux et chinon, mousseline de brochet au beurre blanc (échalotes grises), pied de porc pané, farci et grillé, le Challans aux reinettes,* tasty young regional wines. Long may it wave! 180-250.

● ◆◆ *Le Lys*, 63, rue Blaise-Pascal (C3), ☎ 47.27.05.92, AE Visa, closed Sun. Xavier Aubrun and Thierry Jimenez are two gifted young chefs trained by Bernard Loiseau, who worked together at the Barrière de Clichy. Inseparable, they decided to strike out on their own. Pay this talented pair an encouraging visit : *salade de sole aux poivrons rouges, saumon aux huîtres, ris de veau au jus de truffes, gâteau au chocolat aux trois sauces.* Excellent wines from Touraine, 130-220.

● ◆◆ *Les Jardins du Castel*, 10 rue Groison, ☎ 47.41.94.40, AE Euro Visa, closed Mon and Sun eve, Jan. A comfortable house and pleasant garden for the former owners of the "Barger", 140-200.

● ◆◆ *Les Tuffeaux*, 19, rue Lavoisier (C1), ☎ 47.47.19.89, Euro Visa ♪ ఉ closed Mon and Sun, 4-26 Jan, 12-27 Aug. More points for M. Devaux's tasty cuisine : *turbot aux pointes d'asperges, filet de perche au concombre et sauvignon.* Regional wines, 150-230.

◆◆ *Rôtisserie Tourangelle*, 23, rue du Commerce (B1), ☎ 47.05.71.21, AE DC Visa ㎞ ♪ closed Mon and Sun eve, 2-17 Mar, 13 Jul-5 Aug. Spec : *sandre au sabayon de vouvray, aiguillettes de canard au fumet de cabernet,* 145-260.

⚱ ★★*Péron* (62 pl), ☎ 47.61.81.24.

Recommended

♥ antiques : *L'Echiquier*, 74, rue Colbert, ☎ 47.66.69.81 ; *Comparaison*, pl. Plumereau, ☎ 47.61.42.34 ; candy : *Poirault*, 31, rue Nationale ; crafts : *maison de la Touraine*, 4 bis, bd Heurteloup ; Institut français du goût : hôtel Mame, 19, rue E.-Zola ; stuffed prunes : *Sabat*, 76, rue Nationale.

Nearby

JOUE-LES-TOURS, ⊠ 37300, 4 km SW on the D 86.

Hotel :

★★★ *Château de Beaulieu*, (R.S., C.H.), 1 rue de l'Epend, ☎ 47.53.20.26, Euro Visa, 19 rm P ⟡ ㎞ ⟡ half pens (h.s.). An 18th-C manor house, 635. Rest. ◆◆ ♪ 140-220.

LUYNES, ⊠ 37320, 12 km W.

Hotel :

● ★★★★(L) *Domaine de Beauvois* (R.C.), rte de Cléré, D 49, ☎ 47.55.50.11, Tx 750204, Visa, 40 rm P ⟡ ㎞ ⟡ ▱ ✍ half pens (h.s.), closed 15 Jan-15 Mar, 795. Rest. ◆◆ ⟡ ♪ Inspired cuisine featuring the best of Touraine, 120-350.

MONTBAZON, ⊠ 37250 Veigne, 8 km S.

Restaurant :

◆ *La Chancelliere*, 1, pl. des Marronnier, ☎ 47.26.00.67, Euro Visa, closed Mon and Sun eve ex hols, Feb school hols, 15-30 Nov. A great place to eat, definitely a comer, discovered by Jean Didier : *langouste à la nage, caille rotie au vinaigre,* 200-250.

MONTLOUIS-SUR-LOIRE, ⊠ 37270, 10 km E.

🅸 pl. de l'Hôtel-de-Ville, ☎ 47.45.03.06.

SNCF ☎ 47.50.80.77.

Hotel :

★★ *Ville* (L.F.), 2, pl. de la Mairie, ☎ 47.50.84.84, Visa, 29 rm P ㎞ ⟡ closed 15 Dec-15 Jan, 190. Rest. ◆ closed Mon ex Jul-Aug, 80-120.

Restaurants :

● ◆◆ *Relais de Belle Roche*, 14, rue de la Vallée, on D 140, ☎ 47.50.82.43, AE DC Euro Visa ㎞ ♪ ఉ closed Tue eve and Wed, Mar. Unusual dining room arranged in a former cellar. Spec : *ris de veau au Montlouis, estoufade de gésiers de canard.* Good local wines, 80-135 ; child : 45.

◆◆ *Roc en Val*, 4, quai de la Loire, ☎ 47.50.81.96, AE DC Euro Visa ⟡ ㎞ ♪ closed Tue, 21 Jan-28 Feb. On the banks of the Loire, on an 18th-C family estate ; a youthful style reigns thanks to the Régniers, and the light cuisine is the doing of chef F. Gravy : *ragoût d'asperges d'écrevisses et champignons, brochet rôti à la peau, bœuf fondant aux carottes.* Regional wines, 140-200 ; child : 100.

⚱ ★★★*Municipal* (250 pl), ☎ 47.50.81.90.

ROCHECORBON, ⊠ 37210 Vouvray, 3 km NE.

Hotel :

● ★★ *Les Fontaines Saint-Georges* (L.F.), 6, quai de Loire, ☎ 47.52.52.86, AE DC Euro Visa, 15 rm P ⟡ ㎞ ⟡ ♨ ఉ 140.

Restaurant :

◆ *la Lanterne*, 48, quai de la Loire, ☎ 47.52.50.02, Visa ㎞ ♪ closed Mon and Sun eve, 12 Jan-2 Mar. Spec : *petite friture sauce tartare, andouillette à la vouvrillonne,* 55-180.

SAINT-CYR-SUR-LOIRE, ⊠ 37100, 3 km W.

Restaurant :

◆◆ *La Poêle d'Or*, 9, quai des Maisons Blanches, ☎ 47.54.03.62 ⟡ ♪ closed Tue eve and Wed, Aug. Delicious regional fare, tasty desserts, appealing wines, 130-220.

VOUVRAY, ⊠ 37210, 9 km E.

Hotel :

★★ *Grand Vatel* (L.F.), 8, rue Brûlé, ☎ 47.52.70.32, AE DC Visa, 7 rm P ㎞ ఉ ♨ half pens, closed Sun eve and Mon (Oct-Mar), 15 Nov-28 Dec, 380. Rest. ◆ ఉ 110-190.

Recommended

Guide to wines : *la Caillerie*, ☎ 47.52.78.75, cellar tours ; *vallée de Vaux*, ☎ 47.52.93.22, cellar tours ; *vallée Coquette*, ☎ 47.52.75.03, cellar tours ; *viticulteurs du Vouvray*, château de Vaudenuits, ☎ 47.52.60.20, cellar tours. ♥ pork products : *Hardouin*, 9, rue du Commerce, ☎ 47.52.73.37.

USSÉ*

Chinon 14, Châtellerault 65, Paris 295 km
⊠ 37500 Chinon   A2

Charles Perrault (1628-1703 ; author of "Mother Goose" and other stories) is said to have drawn his inspiration for the tale of the Sleeping Beauty from Ussé. This fairytale castle overlooks an enchanting green countryside at the junction of the Indre and the Loire. The tall trees and the lakes in the park add to its charm.

▶ Ussé was built in the 15thC, and is halfway between a medieval castle and a Renaissance château. It stands on the site of a former fortress. The **chapel★** has Flamboyant Gothic architecture and Renaissance decoration *(9-12 & 2-6 or 7 according to season, 15 Mar.-Sep.).* ▶ S of Ussé is the **Forest of Chinon★**, more than 50 km² of oaks and pines (picnic areas). ☐

VENDÔME**

Blois 32, Le Mans 77, Paris 172 km
pop 18218 ⊠ 41100   B1

Vendôme is a charming old town bedecked with bell towers and pointed slate roofs, and situated at the foot of a steep hill crowned by the massive ruins of a feudal château. Round the town run the arms of the

VENDÔME

0   100   200 m

Loire flowing quietly past the washhouses and gardens.

▶ The **Tour St. Martin** (B2), 15th-16thC, marks the centre of Vendôme, a pedestrian precinct. ▶ **La Trinité**★★ (C2). The original abbey was founded in the 11thC by Geoffroi Martel, Count of Anjou, after seeing three fiery lances plunge into a fountain (according to the legend). All architectural styles from 11th to early 16thC are represented; the façade★★ is a masterpiece of Flamboyant Gothic; the magnificent bell tower is a vestige of the feudal abbey. Inside, note the Romanesque capitals★★ of the transept crossing and the 12thC stained-glass★ Virgin and Child in an apsidial chapel. ▶ The buildings of the former Benedictine abbey stand on the S side of the church and house a **museum** of Vendômois religious art, with murals from the valley of the Loir and a section on traditional trades *(daily 9-12 & 2-6 ex Tue.)*. ▶ The **public garden** (C2) has a good view over the town. ▶ **Lycée Ronsard** (B1). Balzac was a student at this former Oratorian school (17th-18thC); Saint-Jacques chapel (1500).

Nearby

▶ **Areines** *(3 km NE)* : interesting murals in the church. ▶ **Mondoubleau** *(28 km NW)* : ruins of 10th-11thC château, Pré-Barré menhir; 7.5 km : **château de St-Agil** (13th-16th-18thC); *visit park)*; 11km NE **Arville** : former Templar Commandery *(visit by request tel. 54.80.91.74)* : fortification walls and 12thC church. ▶ **Sargé-sur-Braye** *(24 km NW)* : 11th-15thC church with 14th-16thC murals. ▶ **Valley of the Loir**★★ *(→)*. □

Practical Information

VENDÔME
ℹ️ hôtel du Bellay le Saillant (B2), ☎ 54.77.05.07. 🚆 **SNCF** (C1), ☎ 54.77.26.42.

Hotels :
● ★★ **Saint-Georges**, 14, rue Poterie (B2),

☎ 54.77.25.42, AE DC Euro Visa, 37 rm Ⓟ 260. Rest. ♦ ♪ closed Sat noon and Sun eve, 1-15 Dec, 70-230.
★★ **Vendôme**, 15, fg Chartrain (C1), ☎ 54.77.02.88, Tx 750383, Euro Visa, 35 rm Ⓟ ♪ pens (h.s.), closed 20 Dec-3 Jan. Rest. ♦♦ *La Cloche Rouge* ♪ & An array of varied, appetizing fixed meals. Spec : *filet de sandre à la crème d'oseille, paupiette de pintadeau Balzac*, 80-210.

Restaurant :
● ♦ *Chez Annette*, 194, bis, fg Chartrain (C1), ☎ 54.77.23.03, AE Euro Visa Ⓟ 🔊 ♪ closed Thu. A choice location for this stopover well known to motorists. In a rustic setting, sample the classic beef dish and the delicate *brochet au beurre blanc*, 55-115.

🅰 ★★★*Municipal* (200 pl), ☎ 54.77.00.27.

Nearby

DROUÉ, ✉ 41270, 14 km NE.

Restaurant :
♦♦ *Le Faisan Doré*, 26, rte de Vendôme, ☎ 54.80.50.51 ⧖ closed eves, ex for groups (reserve), 15-31 Dec. Specialties of Touraine and Quebec by advance order : *coupe faisan doré, ris flambés au marc de Loire*, 45-100; child : 25.

LA VILLE-AUX-CLERCS, ✉ 41160 Morée, 15 km N.

Hotel :
★★ *Manoir de la forêt* (C.H.), Morée, ☎ 54.80.62.83, Visa, 21 rm Ⓟ ⧖ ⬛ 🔊 ♪ 220. Rest. ♦ ♪ This former hunt meeting-place belonging to the duc de La Rochefoucauld boasts a 2-ha park just outside Sologne, 110-250.

VILLANDRY★★

Tours 20, Angers 97, Paris 254 km
pop 742 ✉ 37300 Joué-lès-Tours   A2

Relaid according to the designs of du Cerceau, the Renaissance **gardens**★★★ of Villandry are as famous as the château : a marvelous herb and vegetable garden, box hedges which twine endlessly in astonishing symbolic patterns round the formal French flowerbeds and, on the terrace, the fountains, basins and cascades.

▶ The courtyard has a wide view over the Cher and the Val de Loire. The three 16thC buildings are among the last of the great Renaissance creations in Touraine ; Classical influence is already noticeable in the 1532 reconstruction by Jean le Breton, François I's Secretary of State, who supervised the building of Blois, Chambord and Chenonceaux. The interiors were modified in 18thC with the addition of new windows. All that remains of the original fortress is the keep. Inside, there is a collection of Spanish paintings *(Palm Sun.-12 Nov., 9-6; gardens 9-dusk).*
▶ The village itself, with old houses bordering its quiet streets, makes a pleasant walk (Romanesque church 11th-12thC). ▶ 2.5 km E : **fossilizing caves** at Savonni-ères *(Apr.-15 Sep., 9-6:30; 16 Sep.-Mar., 9-12 & 2-6, closed Thu.).*   □

Practical Information _____

Nearby

SAVONNIÈRES, ⊠ 37510 Joué-lès-Tours, 3 km E.

Hotel :
★★★ *Les Cèdres*, (C.H., R.S.), rte du Château de Villandry, ☎ 47.53.37.58, Tx 750074, Visa, 37 rm Ⓟ ⑭ ᕷ ▤ 320. Rest. ◆◆ ♪ J.-P. Gessier, who took over this establishment, intends to bring it to the highest gastronomic level : *feuillantines d'huîtres chaudes à l'ail doux, noisettes d'agneau aux petits légumes, charlotte de sandre au montlouis.* Sampling menus, splendid fixed menus, fine cellar, 110-280 ; child : 70.

Vendée, Poitou, Charentes

▶ The softness of the Charentes countryside, with its nimbus of light and luminous mist, has always fascinated the traveller. But Poitou is full of paradoxes, and today's travellers, like many before them, tend to hurry through the softly rolling hills and high-growing stands of heather and brushwood, dotted with fertile pastures and marshlands, on their way to the Atlantic coast.

Poitou is an agricultural region and every pore of its being is tuned to the Ocean from which it derives a great part of its wealth, for without the great waterways leading to the sea, Poitou would lose half its solid prosperity. Here, from the most mediocre of local wines, experts distil the most perfect of spirits : cognac. The gentle landscape is dotted with places of interest : estuary ports, old relays, inns and farms, where the traveller can break his journey like the pilgrims of Compostela so many years ago, until he reaches the coast with its clear sky, enormous beaches, villages sparkling in the sun, and wide foreshores where fish farming flourishes and migratory birds add to the richness of the habitat.

The art of the region is imbued with the legendary, as is apparent in the joyous figures found on the great church portals, and in the mysticism which inspired the frescos of Romanesque churches. Manor houses and châteaux bear witness to the wealth of the countryside and the taste and spirit of its inhabitants. This refinement is equally well expressed in the gently-simmered dishes for which the region is famous. Its wine, seafood, snails, sausages and salami, hearty meat dishes and wide variety of cheeses — including 50 varieties of chabichou goat's milk cheese — make Poitou an exciting visit for tourists who appreciate good living and the joys of the table. □

Don't miss

★★★ Poitiers C1, La Rochelle B2, Saint-Savin C1, Saintes B3.

★★ Angoulême C3, Aulnay B2, Chauvigny C1, Ile d'Oléron A2, Ile de Ré A2, Rochefort-sur-Mer B2, Talmont B3, Thouars B1, Ile d'Yeu A1.

★ Airvault C1, Ile d'Aix B2, Angles-sur-l'Anglin C1, Aubeterre-sur-Dronne C3, Brouage B2, Charroux C2, Cognac B3, Coubre forest A3, Esnandes B2, Fontenay-le-Comte B2, Luçon B1-2, Maillezais B2, Marais Poitevin A-B2, Melle B-C2, Mervent forest B1-2, Montmorillon C2, Niort B2, Ile de Noirmoutier A1, Parthenay B1, Pons B3, Pouzauges B1, La Rochefoucauld C3, La Roche-Posay C1, Royan B3, Les Sables-d'Olonne A1, Saint-Gilles-Croix-de-Vie A1, Saint-Jean d'Angely B2, Saint-Palais B3.

Weekend tips

Travel by air or fast train (4 hrs from Paris) to La Rochelle in time for dinner on Friday night. After dark, walk around the town and see the Vieux-Port (old port), the Rue Chaudrier and the flood-lit town hall.
Early Saturday morning, take the boat from La Pallice and spend the day on the Île de Ré (island ; →); lunch at La Flotte, Saint-Martin or Ars); return to La Rochelle at the end of the afternoon (maybe spend the evening in Châtelaillon →).
On Sunday, tour the Marais Poitevin (marshes ; →) : boat-trip before having lunch in Coulon, Arçais or Niort; in the afternoon, visit the abbey of Maillezais, the bird sanctuary at Saint-Denis-du-Payré, Marans ; dinner in Esnandes → (mussels are the speciality here) before returning to La Rochelle.

In the Charente region

Near Confolens

Facts and figures

Location : *Between the Loire river (N), the Gironde river (S), Limousin (E) and the Atlantic (W; 550 km of coast).*
Area : *33 190 km².*
Climate : *One of the sunniest regions in France (over 2 000 hr of sun p.a. : nearly as much as Ajaccio Bay); avg. temp. Jul-Aug : 18-23 °C.*
Population : *2 051 000.*
Administration : *Department of* **Charente;** *Prefecture : Angoulême. Department of* **Charente-Maritime;** *Prefecture : La Rochelle. Department of* **Deux-Sèvres;** *Prefecture : Niort. Department of* **Vendée;** *Prefecture : La Roche-sur-Yon. Department of* **Vienne;** *Prefecture : Poitiers.*

Marshland house, or *bourrine*

In the Poitou region

 # Brief regional history

Up to the Roman conquest

Like his Périgord neighbour, the Lascaux caveman lived in the Clain, Vienne and Anglin Valleys (ca. 15 000BC); but the Angoulême region (Eaux-Claires and Rancogne Valleys) was not inhabited until Neolithic man appeared there around 12 000BC. ● The later **Megalithic** civilisation (6000-4000BC) left many dolmens and covered passages in Upper and Lower Poitou. Their routes are easily traced today, in the coastal Vendée region from Aquitaine to Armorica.

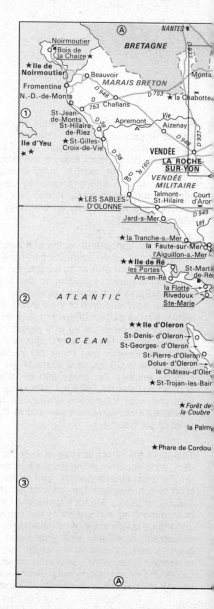

● The most important wave of **Celts** settled in the Clain Valley around 600BC (**La Tène** period); and it was the **Pictons** who first confronted, in 56BC, the Roman legions of **Crassus**. ● The future Poitou and Saintonge regions were lined with roads from **flourishing cities** (like *Mediolanum Santonum*, which would become Saintes), as early as the 1stC AD. This was the flowering of Roman Aquitaine, when the Imperial Legate resided in Poitiers.

From early Christianity to the birth of the County of Poitou

In the 4thC, one of the great bishops, **Hilaire**, spread the Christian faith around Poitiers; and one of his disciples, Martin, founded an abbey in Ligugé in 370. Within the next hundred years, the **Visigoths** occupied the area, setting up their capital in Toulouse. ● **Clovis'** victory at Vouillé in 507 effectively ended the invasion. ● The Duchy of Aquitaine was gradually built up from counties, including Poitou, established in the 7thC. ● Around this time, the **Islamic armies** invaded the region on their way northward. Charles Martel halted their progress near Poitiers in 732. ● But the Carolingian Renaissance was stifled by **Scandinavian invasions**. These gave the local nobility the chance to fortify their domains, building numerous keeps, and also, from the 10thC, religious establishments.

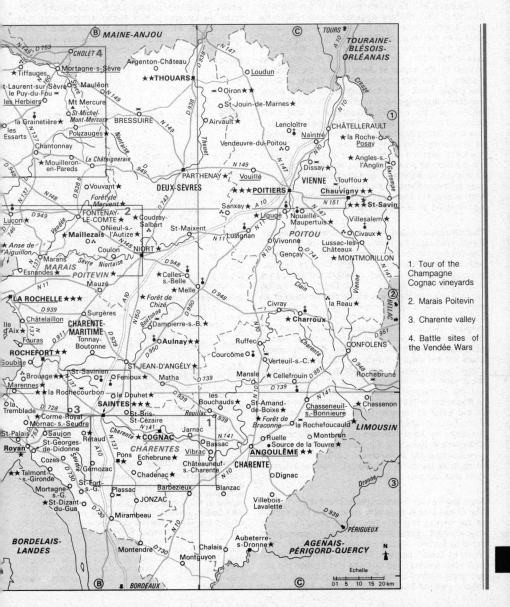

1. Tour of the Champagne Cognac vineyards

2. Marais Poitevin

3. Charente valley

4. Battle sites of the Vendée Wars

The roads to Compostela and the Hundred Years' War

From the 11thC, abbeys and collegiate churches sprang up along the routes of the Compostela **pilgrims**. The political powers conceded more and more terrain to the Church, here represented by the **Cluniacs** (→ Burgundy). The immense areas confided to religious organisations were steadily improved. ● In 1152, this development was halted by the beginning of three centuries of strife : repudiated by Louis VII (King of France), **Eleanor of Aquitaine** married Henry II Plantagenet, who was later to become King of England. ● For the next three centuries the rival houses of Valois and Plantagenet fought for control of Aquitaine and its dependencies. At the death of Eleanor in 1204, **Philippe-Auguste** annexed Poitou for France (although the Angoulême region was not recovered until the reign of Philippe IV, a century later). ● The beginning of the **Hundred Years' War** is officially dated 1337; this long period of bloodshed was marked by the **defeat of Jean II** (John the Good) at Poitiers. It was later confirmed by the **Treaty of Brétigny** (1360), which gave the English all of the Aunis, Saintonge and Angoulême regions; this was followed by the campaigns of **Du Guesclin** who, until 1380, managed to contain France's adversaries around Bordeaux.● Strangely enough, this was a time of **economic prosperity**; northern European merchants, descending upon the region for salt and wine, ensured the growth and prosperity of La Rochelle, the future Protestant stronghold. ● In 1422 **Charles VII** undertook the reconquest of the kingdom, then almost entirely in English hands beginning from Poitiers. But the war dragged on until the victory at **Castillon** in 1453.

The Renaissance and the French Classical period

A new era began for Poitou at the end of the 15thC. The discovery of the New World, as well as commerce with the western islands and later Canada, brought growing prosperity in which the Northern Europeans participated. And thanks to the Dutch, the Poitou region embraced the **ideas of the Reformation** at an early stage. ● Calvin himself taught in Angoulême and the Poitiers region; but the area was torn by religious disputes, which remained unsettled until the Edict of Nantes (1598) gave the Protestants **places of refuge**, among them La Rochelle. ● Nonetheless, **Louis XIII** laid siege to the city in 1627, and in October of the following year it capitulated, only to be razed to the ground by the king's troops. ● The same century saw the invention of **cognac distillation**, the founding of **Rochefort** in 1665 by Colbert, and the **Revocation of the Edict of Nantes** (1685), which forced many Protestants to emigrate. ● During the next century the era of the **Administrators** (Blossac in Poitiers and Châtellerault, Reverseaux in Saintes) was marked by widespread urban development. La Rochelle was not alone in its prosperity; Rochefort, Niort, and Angoulême also expanded rapidly.

From the Vendée Wars to the present day

The Constitutional Assembly created the Department of the Vendée in 1791. Two years later, the region rose in revolt against the forced military **conscription** voted by the Revolutionary Government in Paris. "**The Years of Terror**" began in March **1793** and continued until 1796, leaving dead Charette and Stofflet, the last two great leaders of the Vendée. Napoléon's "pacification" was not truly effective until the beginning of the Empire. ● In the middle of the 19thC, with the introduction of **seaside resorts** and the planting of vegetation to stabilise the dunes, the wealthy middle classes from Bordeaux began to frequent the casino at Royan (1847). ● On the nearby coast, the Portuguese **oyster** made its appearance and La Rochelle came back to life as a fishing centre. **Phylloxeræ** destroyed the vineyards (1876-1882), but a new source of income was soon found : dairy produce. In 1888, the first French **agricultural cooperative** opened at Surgères. ● The cities of Rochefort, Royan and La Rochelle were the last pockets of German resistance at the end of WWII, and sustained heavy damage. ● Reconstruction was accompanied by major **public works** : leasehold housing construction began in 1955 under the initiative of Guy Merlin; bridges were built between the islands and the mainland and across the estuaries; and the "Aquitaine" highway was inaugurated, linking the region to Paris and the motorway network.

 Practical information

Information : *comité régional au tourisme* (*C.R.T.* Vienne, Charente, Charente-Maritime, Deux-Sèvres), 2, rue Sainte-Opportune, 86002 Poitiers Cedex, ☎ 49.88.38.94. **Vendée** : *C.D.T.*, 8, pl. Napoléon, 85000 La Roche-sur-Yon, ☎ 51.05.45.28; **Charente**, *C.D.T.*, 27, pl. Bouillaud, 16021 Angoulême Cedex, ☎ 45.92.27.57. **Charente-Maritime** : *C.D.T.*, 11 *bis*, rue des Augustins, 17008 La Rochelle Cedex, ☎ 46.41.43.33; **Deux-Sèvres**, 74, rue Alsace-Lorraine, 79000 Niort, ☎ 49.24.76.79; **Vienne** : *C.D.T.*, 11, rue V.-Hugo, 86000 Poitiers, ☎ 49.41.58.22. *Dir. rég. de la jeunesse et des sports*, le Capitole, bât. B14, bd Chasseigne, 86020 Poitiers Cedex, ☎ 49.88.04.09. *Dir. rég. des affaires culturelles*, hôtel de Rochefort, 102, Grand-Rue, 86020 Poitiers, ☎ 49.88.12.69. **Paris** : *maison Poitou-Charentes*, 4, av. de l'Opéra, 75001, ☎ (1) 42.96.01.88.

Reservations : *Loisirs-Accueil (L.A.)* : **Charente**, pl. Bouillaud, 16021 Angoulême, ☎ 45.92.24.43; **Charente-Maritime**, 11 *bis*, rue des Augustins, 17000 La Rochelle, ☎ 46.41.43.33; **Vendée**, 124, bd A.-Briand, 85000 La Roche-sur-Yon, ☎ 51.62.33.10; **Vienne**, 11, rue V.-Hugo, 86000 Poitiers, ☎ 49.41.58.22. **Paris** : maison Poitou-Charentes.

S.O.S. : *SAMU* (emergency medical service), Poitiers, ☎ 49.88.33.34; La Roche-sur-Yon, ☎ 51.37.61.34; Angoulême, ☎ 45.92.92.92; Niort, ☎ 49.73.95.15; La Rochelle, ☎ 46.41.23.23.

Weather forecast : **Charente-Maritime**, ☎ 46.41.11.11; **Vendée**, ☎ 51.62.45.99; **Deux-Sèvres**, ☎ 49.24.11.11; **Charente**, ☎ 45.82.21.25; **Vienne**, ☎ 49.58.40.52.

Rural gîtes and chambres d'hôtes : info and bookings at *Loisirs-Accueil (L.A.)*.

Farmhouse-inns, holiday villages, camping : info at *L.A.*

Festivals and concerts : Jan (last week-end) : *international cartoon show* in Angoulême. **Apr** : *police film festival* in Cognac. **May** : *spring music festival* in Poitiers; *jazz festival* in Angoulême; *May cultural festival* in Bressuire. **Whit Sunday** (Pentecost) : *jazz festival* at St-Gilles-Croix-de-Vie. **May-Jun** : *Théâtre du Silence* in La Rochelle. **Jun** : *Saint-Savinien music festival* in Melle; *cinema festival*. **Jul** : *Val de Charente festival* (first two weeks), in Saintes; *early music, jeux santons* (folklore), shows in the arena. **Jul-Aug.** : *downtown festivities* (theatre, concerts) in Poitiers. **Aug** : *rural festivities* in Gençay (Vienne). **Oct** : *musical meetings* in Poitiers; *slide and photo show* in Angoulême.

Son et lumière : Jun-Aug : Le Puy-du-Fou (Vendée, info, ☎ 51.57.65.65), Les Sables-d'Olonne. **Jul-Sep :** Cognac, La Rochefoucauld (last Fri and Sat of Jun to the first week-end of Aug, 10:30 pm), Coulon (summer eve). **Aug :** Angles-sur-l'Anglin. *Evening shows in Brouage, Coulon (boatmen's festival the 15th), La Roche-Courbon, and at the sources of the Trouve (near Angoulême).*

Religious festivals : Christmas : midnight Mass at Ligugé abbey (Vienne) in Gregorian chant; *live nativity scene* in Bressuire.

The pilgrim road to Compostela

Religious buildings sprang up along the roads to Compostela in Northern Spain from the beginning of the 11thC. This was part of the Church's homage to St. Jacques (Santíago in Spanish), Patron Saint of the Christian armies then engaged in reconquering Spain from the Moslems. Pilgrims converged on Compostela from all over Europe. The routes were quite precise, and were adorned not only with churches and convents (more than 300 in Poitou and Saintonge), but also with almshouses, hospitals and resting places of all sorts. The principal routes from the north of France, Normandy, England and Ireland crossed Poitou and Saintonge in the direction of Bordeaux and the Gironde Estuary. For nearly two centuries the Saintes region was travelled each year by half-a-million people going either way. Along the pilgrim roads all services ranging from information to protection were offered. There was even a guidebook, written by a monk from Parthenay. Along the most frequented route, from Châtellerault to Bordeaux (via Poitiers, Saintes, Pons and Blaye), the stopover town of Aulnay only started to lose importance at the beginning of the Renaissance with the decline of the pilgrimage.

Local festivals and folklore : Feb : *wine festival* in Loudun (folklore celebrations, sometimes in Nov), Mimosa festival in Saint-Trojan (Oléron). **Apr :** *flower show and pageant* in La Tranche-sur-Mer. **Easter :** *rose festival* in Brigueil (Charente). **May :** *folklore* (cavalcade) in Parthenay, *festival of the sea* (end May) on the île d'Yeu. **Jun :** Rochefort Carnival (pageant), *traditional festival* in Xanton-Chassenon (Vendée), *Irais procession* (2nd Sun) in Airvault; *cavalcade of St. John's Day,* flowered floats, at Mirebeau; *reconstitution of the battle of 1356 in which Jean le Bon was captured by the Black Prince* at Nouaillé-Maupertuis. **Jun-Sep :** *horticulture show* in La Court-d'Aron (Vendée). **Jul-Aug :** *peasant festivities* organized by the inhabitants of Cherves (Vienne). **Jul :** *sea festivals* in Royan; *flower festival* at Les Sables-d'Olonne. *Records Festival,* Aubigny. Montguyon *international folk festival* (mid-Jul; Charente-Maritime); *peace festival,* including children's folk groups, in Matha. **Aug :** *threshing festival* (1st or 2nd Sun) in Cozes, *historical reenactment* (1st fortnight), in La Flotte-en-Ré, Confolens *international folk festival* (mid-Aug; Charente), *folklore* (end Aug-early Sep) in Gémozac, *agricultural olympics,* La Limouzinière. **Sep :** *festival of the rosebush* (early Sep) in La Mothe-Saint-Héray, *festival of the piglet* in Ranton (Vienne).

Sporting events : May : Montignac-sur-Charente, *canoe rally;* La Rochelle, *international sailing week;* Poitiers, *international fencing competition.* **Jun and Sep :** horse racing at Barbezieux, Châtelaillon, Gémozac, Teruac, Montendre, Le Palmyre. **Jul-Aug;** *international Atlantic fishing week and cruise-race,* in **Aug;** *Côte de lumière marathon,* Saint-Jean-de-Monts; *courses landaises (cow races)* at St-Georges-de-Didonne; *horse and greyhound races* in La Roche-Posay. **Sep :** *grand pavois (ships in full bunting).*

Regional cuisine

La Rochelle is a special shrine for the gourmet, but in fact the entire region has a solid gastronomic reputation. Some of the delights available : oysters (from Marennes or Oléron), mussels (from Aiguillon Bay), shrimp (from the Vendée beaches), prawn (from the Cotinière), éclade (mussels flambée on a bed of pine needles), mouclade (mussels in cream or white wine), eels, fried or in a soup (bouilliture), snails from Niort or the Charente and lobster (large or "baby"). Other entrées include melon served with pineau, ham and sausages, and hare pâté from the Vendée. Fish dishes : stuffed carp, trout, river pike, sardines, salmon, shad from the Gironde; and the chaudrée, a typically Charente version of fish soup (with wine). Among the poultry : Bressuire fatted hen, Barbezieux capon, Challans duck (known as Canard Nantais) and goose prepared with chestnuts. The meats are plentiful as well : ribs of beef à la parthenaise, white veal from Chalais, pig's head soup. Vegetables include : mojettes (beans) from the marshes, salad with walnut oil, and far (stuffed lettuce). There are fifty types of chabichou (goat's milk cheese from the region). Among the cakes and sweets : angélique from Niort, cheesecake (white cheese and eggs, baked), sugar-preserved chestnuts, duchesse de l'Angoumois (chocolate), as well as nougatine and the macaroons of Vivonne and Poitiers.

Fairs : all year round : in Challans, Tue morning (duck fair); Parthenay, Wed morning (butcher's meats). **Feb :** Jaunay-Clan *wine fair* (Vienne). **Mar :** *wine fair* in Thouars. **Apr :** Lezay *goat fair.* **Jun :** *young goose fair* in Javarzay (Deux-Sèvres); *gastronomy fair* in Saint-Maixent; *sheep fair* in Montmorillon (Vienne); *wool fair* (mid-Jun), in Champagné-Saint-Hilaire (Vienne). **Aug :** *La Saint-Louis,* at Mirebeau; *cheese fair* (1st Sat and Sun), in Saint-Maixent; *Saboureau fair,* in Bressuire; Argenton-Château *dog fair* (last Sun); *peasant festival and "festival of the unmarrieds"* in La Génétouze (Charente-Maritime). **Sep :** *grape-harvest festival* in Burie; *Saint Michael's Fair* in Vivonne.

Nature parks, zoos : *nature park* of Marais Poitevin-Val de Sèvre and Vendée : park headquarters, La Ronde presbytery, 17170 Courçon, ☎ 46.01.74.44. *Zoorama and Chizé forest,* 79360 Villiers-en-Bois, ☎ 49.09.60.64 *(daily Apr-Oct 9-7, Sun and hols 9-8; Oct-Mar, 10-12 & 2-nightfall, Sun and hols 10-nightfall).* See also the *Butterfly museum,* ☎ 49.09.61.14. Pheasant preserve at Marigny, featuring 400 bird species on 5-acre aviary, ☎ 49.32.65.35. *(1 May-15 Oct). Aquarium de la Venise Verte,* 8-10, place de l'Église, 79510 Coulon, ☎ 49.35.90.31.

Rambling and hiking : *G.R.4* Méditerranée-Océan (from Limousin to Cognac and Royan); *G.R.36* Channel-Pyrénées (from Thouars and Aulnay to Perigord); *G.R.48* (E of the Charente); *G.R.360* of Romanèsie Saintonge; *G.R.364* Vienne-Vendée (Vivonne-St.-Gilles-Croix-de-Vie). Topoguides for all rambles. Regional representative : M. Pinaud, Biard, 79330 St.-Varent. Excursions : enq. at *délégations dép.* (Angoulême, Saint-Jean-d'Angély, Thouars, La Roche-sur-Yon, Lencloître or Poitiers), and the assn. *pistes nouvelles et traces anciennes,* which recommends the "salt route" in 16thC Vendée, 33, rue de Nantes, 85300 Challans, ☎ 51.68.27.84.

Scenic railways : Oléron, *small train from Saint-Trojan to Gatseau Point (Easter-Sep, 7 km return),* ☎ 46.76.01.26; Mervent, *Pierre-Brune tortillard* (2 km). *Scenic train* from Le Puy-du-Fou (enq. and bookings, ☎ 51.57.64.64). *Scenic train of la Sandre,* 16, pl. de l'Église, 17600 Saujon, ☎ 46.02.40.06. Lambon : *a small circuit around a lake,* ☎ 49.79.80.17.

About cognac

Strangely enough, the wines of the principal cognac-producing areas (Charente and Charente-Maritime, along with their islands) are of mediocre quality; but distilled, they become the best-known French eau-de-vie. The vineyards cover only a small area : less than 250 000 acres, compared to more than 750 000 acres before the vast destruction of vines by phylloxeræ (1876-1882).

The vine-growing areas most highly regarded are those of Grande Champagne (between Cognac, Jarnac and Barbezieux), those surrounding them (Petite Champagne), as far as Pons and Jonzac, and the Borderies (N of the Charente; these vines are cultivated with the greatest care. On the neighbouring clay-soils, the growths of lesser quality are, in descending order : Fins Bois, Bons Bois and Bois Ordinaires (coastal and island vineyards); in the E, the vineyards are confined to the first escarpments of the Limousin, and in the S, to the area of Bordeaux, near Blayais. Of the 250 million bottles produced annually, about 4/5 are destined for export (in value equal to one third of the region's exports).

Cognac is aged in oak barrels, which give it its rich colour. There are three gradings : after 30 months of aging, it merits three stars (★★★); after four and a half years, it is labeled VSOP (or ★★★★); and after ten years, it is called Royal or Napoléon.

Pineau, a popular local aperitif, seems to have been invented quite accidentally. White or red, it is produced from diluted fresh grape must mixed with cognac. Pineau is always drunk chilled.

Cycling holidays : *relais départemental du tourisme rural,* La Rochelle (→ package-deal holidays); *direction départementale de l'agriculture,* pl. de la Vendée, La Roche-sur-Yon; *les comités départementaux de cyclotourismes* (Barbezieux, Bourgneuf, La Jarrie, Thouars, La Roche-sur-Yon). Also itineraries in the Vendée (enq. at *S.L.A.*).

Riding holidays : *association régionale (A.R.T.E.),* M. Josquin, La Vivandière, 79330 Saint-Varent, ☎ 49.67.52.75; or Colonel Cabaret, 16420 Brigueil, Charente; *ligue Poitou-Charente de la fédération équestre française (F.E.F.),* Poursay-Garnaud, 17400 Saint-Jean-d'Angely; *comités départementaux :* aski at the La Rochelle T.O., and *assn. départ. de tourisme équestre Vendée,* M. Courtin, ☎ 51.94.69.75. Also, information at the *C.D.T.'s.*

Horse-drawn holidays : Sainte-Hermine and N.D. de Monts, in the **Vendée** region; in the **Charente-Maritime** region (enq. at the La Rochelle *O.D.T.*) in Aulnay (*Relais de Saintonge*), Matha (*Le Marquisat*), Saint-Savinien, Haimps (near Matha), Aubigny, 79390 Thénezay (*la Chevalerie du Thouet*), ☎ 49.98.26.29.

Boating and sailing holidays : on the Charente, houseboat hire (Charente : *C.D.T.* and *Sté Quiztour,* 19, rue

d'Athènes, Paris, ☎ 45.74.75.70); ocean holidays (houseboat hire in Royan). Inter island and river cruises, *R.D.P.E.* La Rochelle, ☎ 46.42.61.48, and *C.D.T.* Deux-Sèvres, leaving from Arçais, in the Poitevin marshlands (summer only, from 30 mins to 2 hrs); enq. : M. Bardet, ☎ 49.26.31.80.

Technical tourism : *cognac and pineau cellars* in Cognac, Jarnac, Rouillac, and at some wine-growers' properties in the Cognac region; *dairy cooperatives* in Aytré, Celles-sur-Belle, Civray, Matha, Surgères; *oyster beds* at Marennes, La Tremblade, Le Château-d'Oléron, l'île de Ré, Châtelaillon; *slaughterhouses* in Parthenay and Bressuire. Enq. : *O.D.T.* and *C.D.T.*

Handicraft courses : lace-making, embroidery, ceramics, decoration, wood tooling, pottery, sculpture, tapestry, weaving and basket-making. Enq. : *O.D.T.* and *C.D.T.*

Other courses : music and dramatic expression (Saintes), discovering nature (Pugny, 79320 Moncontant), culinary art (Bourcefranc, Oléron), paper-making and molding (*moulin du Verger* in Puymoyen and *moulin de Fleurac* in Nérac). Info and bookings at the *C.D.T.* Archaeological digs (Vivonne, Angoulême, Vieux-Poitiers) and mediaeval excavations (Airvault, Montguyon, Ligugé and with *l'union REMPART :* Coudray-Salbart, Merpins, Saint-Germain-de-Confolens). For more info : *société archéologique et historique de la Charente,* 44, rue de Montmoreau, Angoulême.

Wine guide : *comité national du Pineau de Charentes,* 45, av. Victor-Hugo, 16100 Cognac, ☎ 45.32.09.27.

Young people : holidays on farms in Deux-Sèvres and Charente-Maritime; horseback riding in Vienne and Saint-Varent (ask at *O.D.T.*). *C.I.J.-Poitou,* 64, rue Gambetta, Poitiers, B.P. 176, ☎ 49.88.64.37; *C.D.I.J.-La Rochelle,* 14, rue des Gentilshommes, B.P. 1005, 17007 La Rochelle Cedex, ☎ 46.46.16.99.

Aquatic sports : list of marinas, sailing schools and inland stretches of water at the *O.D.T.*

Canoeing and kayaking : *ligue Poitou-Charente,* 9, av. C.-Coulomb, 16800 Soyaux, ☎ 45.92.06.98; *A.J.* d'Angoulême, courses in the Vienne region, info at *C.D.T.*

Speed-sailing : Notre-Dame and Saint-Jean-de-Monts, Saint-Gilles-Croix-de-Vie.

Golf : Angoulême (9 holes); Poitiers (9 holes); Royan-Saint-Palais (18 holes); Saintes (9 holes); Mazières-en-Gâtine and Loudun-Roiffé (18 holes); La Roche-Posay (18 holes).

Potholing and spelunking : *comité régional,* 20, rue des Cressonnières, 16000 Angoulême, ☎ 45.92.19.95; *comité départemental,* 221, rue de La Tour-d'Auvergne, Angoulême.

Fishing : *fédérations départementales* **Charente :** 31, rue de Bellevue, Angoulême; **Charente-Maritime :** 43, av. Eugène-Normandin, La Rochelle; **Deux-Sèvres :** rue Galucher, Niort, ☎ 49.73.94.06; **Vendée :** 17, rue La Fayette, 85007 La Roche-sur-Yon; **Vienne :** 14, rue Jean-Jaurès, Poitiers. Package-deal holidays in Mansle (Charente), Saint-Savin (Vienne), Tonnay-Boutonne (Charente-Maritime). *Amicale rochelaise de pêche sportive,* 26 bis, rue Thiers, La Rochelle, ☎ 46.41.15.07; *Royan Maritime service,* voûtes du Port, ☎ 46.05.69.49.

Towns and places

L' AIGUILLON-SUR-MER

Luçon 21, La Rochelle 50, Paris 445 km
pop 2152 ☒ 85480   A2

An oyster and mussel producing town on the estuary

of the Lay.

Nearby

▶ **La Faute-sur-Mer,** seaside resort leading to the **Pointe d'Arçay,** where there is a 1 200 acre bird sanctuary and a nature area *(no cars).* ▶ **Anse de l'Aiguillon :** from this cove can be seen all that remains of the former Poitou gulf : slickensides, or striated rock surfaces. ▶ **Saint-Michel-en-l'Herm** *(to the N, rte de Luçon)* is the site of a former abbey partly rebuilt in the 17thC *(10-12 & 3-5 in season)*. ▶ **La Tranche-sur-Mer** *(13 km W)* : immense beach sheltered behind dunes and pines ; the soft climate favours bulb growing *(flower season Easter-Jun.)*; boat trips in summer ; 2 km away, **phare** (lighthouse ; *open to visitors*) on the Pointe du Grouin-du-Cou (panorama). □

Practical Information

L' AIGUILLON-SUR-MER
ⓘ ☎ 51.56.43.87 (h.s.).

Hotel :
● ★★ *Port* (L.F.), 2, rue Bellevue, ☎ 51.56.40.08, Visa, 23 rm, P ⌿ ₩ 🖂 ♪ pens (h.s.), closed 1 Nov-15 Mar, 190. Rest. ♦ ⌿ ♪ Seafood, 55-120.

Å ★★★*Bel Air* (200 pl), ☎ 51.56.44.05.

Nearby

La FAUTE-SUR-MER, ⊠ 85460 L'Aiguillon-sur-Mer, 1 km W.
ⓘ rd-pt Fleuri, ☎ 51.56.45.19 (h.s.).

Hotel :
★★ *Chouans*, rd-pt Fleuri, ☎ 51.56.45.56, Euro Visa, 22 rm, closed Closed Mon, 15 Oct-15 Dec, 200.

Restaurant :
♦ *Délices de la Mer*, rd-pt Fleuri, ☎ 51.56.47.62, Visa P ⌿ ♤ ♪ closed Wed, 20 Nov-20 Dec, 55-150.

Å ★★★*Club Franca* (100 pl), ☎ 51.56.40.62 ; (500 pl).

La TRANCHE-SUR-MER, ⊠ 85360, 12 km NW.
ⓘ pl. de la Liberté, ☎ 51.30.33.96.
🚢 island cruises in summer.

Hotels :
● ★★ *Le Rêve*, ☎ 51.30.34.06, Euro, 42 rm P ⌿ ₩ ♤ ♪ 🖂 pens (h.s.), closed Mon. (l.s.), 1 Oct-31 Mar, 230. Rest. ♦ ♪ ⅋ 65-100.
★★ *Les Cols Verts*, 48, rue de Verdun, ☎ 51.30.35.06, Euro, 33 rm P ₩ ♤ ∂ ⅋ pens (h.s.), closed Mon ex school hols, 478. Rest. ♦ ♪ ∂ ⅋ 60-175.
● ★ *Océan* (L.F.), 49, rue A.-France, ☎ 51.30.30.09, AE DC Euro Visa, 56 rm P ⌿ ₩ ∂ half pens (h.s.), closed 25 Sep-1 Apr, 150. Rest. ♦ ♪ 65-100.

Å ★★★★*Baie d'Aunis* (160 pl), ☎ 51.30.37.36 ; ★★★*Cottage Fleuri* (280 pl), ☎ 51.30.34.57 ; at Longeville, CP 85560 11 km N, ★★★*Les Dunes* (125 pl), ☎ 51.33.32.93 ; at Longeville, CP 85560, 11 km N, *Le Clos des Pins* (120 pl), ☎ 51.90.31.69 ; at Longeville, PC 85560, 11 km N, ★★★★*Fief du Bonair* (100 pl), ☎ 51.33.31.09 ; ★★★★*Jarny* (200 pl), ☎ 51.33.42.21.

Recommended
Events : *floralies internationales*, in Apr and May.

AIRVAULT*

Poitiers 51, Niort 64, Paris 350 km
pop 3847 ⊠ 79600   C1
Remarkable Romanesque church of St. Pierre (narthex★) on the Place du Minage ; half-timbered houses in surrounding streets ; folk art museum in neighbouring 13thC buildings *(daily Jul.-15 Sep., 2:30-6 ; Sun. and nat. hols. out of season, 2-5)*.

Valley of the Thouet *(13 km S and 7 km N ; 2 hr)*

▶ **Airvault** : at the southern exit from the town is the Romanesque Vernay Bridge (11 arches, 12thC). On the opposite bank, the stepped town of **Louin★**, at the village exit toward Saint-Loup-Lamairé, Gallo-Romanesque tomb. ▶ **Saint-Loup-Lamairé**, famous for its goat's milk cheese ; Louis XIII château with Gothic keep and moats *(exterior visit only)*; Gothic and Renaissance houses in

town (staircase★ of the Auditoire). ▶ **Gourgé** : Romanesque church ; bridge used by pilgrims to Compostela ; nearby, château de la Roche-Faton (15th-16thC). ▶ North of Airvault *(6.5 km)*, **Saint-Géneroux★** : 13thC bridge and one of the oldest churches in France (9thC, much restored in the 19thC).

Round trip along the banks of the Dive *(25 km W ; 2 hr)*

▶ **Saint-Jouin-de-Marnes** : large fortified Romanesque church★ ; façade, Angevin vaulting in the nave, stalls. ▶ **Moncontour**, on the opposite bank : massive 12thC keep, rebuilt in the 15thC. ▶ Near Marnes, manor house of **Retournay** (15thC). □

Practical Information

ⓘ mairie, ☎ 49.64.70.13.
SNCF ☎ 49.64.70.63.

Hotel :
● ★★ *Vieux Relais* (L.F.), ☎ 49.64.70.31, 12 rm P ₩ ♤ closed Mon, Feb, Nov-Easter, 170. Rest. ♦♦ ♪ 55-200.

Ile d' AIX*

(Aix Island)

pop 173 ⊠ 17123   B2
From La Fumée Point, a 20 to 30 minute boat-trip (depending on weather and sea conditions, tel. : 46.42.61.48) will take you to this small island (320 acres, 3 km at its longest ; *no cars*) : the only means of transportation are on foot, bicycles or horse-drawn carriages.

▶ Inside the surrounding wall, the village has only three streets, lined with low houses draped with hollyhock ; at the end of the main street, opposite the church (Pre-Romanesque crypt), is a **mother-of-pearl** workshop *(closed nat. hols.)*. ▶ On the Rue Napoléon, two museums : the **Maison de l'Empereur** where Napoleon spent his last nights in France in July 1815 *(10-12 & 2-6, closed Tue.)*; and the **African Museum** (ethnography and zoology ; *same hours, closed Wed.*). □

ANGLES-SUR-L'ANGLIN*

Poitiers 49, Châteauroux 82, Paris 329 km
pop 465 ⊠ 86260 Saint-Pierre-de-Maillé   C1
Beautiful site★, with a nice bridge over the Anglin, near the water wheel of a mill ; impressive mediaeval fortresses (illuminations, *early Aug*). Some of the women here keep up the needlework tradition : Angles has even given its name to a certain kind of stitch : *jours d'Angles*.

Nearby

▶ Romanesque church in **Vicq★** (12thC ; *to N*). ▶ Gorges of the Anglin Valley *(to S)*. ▶ Through the Gartempe Valley, prehistoric caves around **Saint-Pierre-de-Maillé**, and château de la Guittière on the edge of a cliff. □

ANGOULÊME**

Périgueux 85, Bordeaux 116, Paris 446 km
pop 50151 ⊠ 16000   C3
On a bend in the Charente, Angoulême is set on a hilltop, still surrounded by ramparts. A commercial and industrial centre, one of the principal towns of western France.

▶ The **Hôtel de Ville** (town hall) was built in the 19thC (13thC style) on the site of the castle of the Counts of Angoulême, of which two towers remain : the **Tour de Lusignan** (late 13thC) and the **Tour de Valois** (late 15thC). ▶ Walk through **Old Angoulême** (houses from the Renais-

ANGOULÊME

0   100   200   300 m

---

sance to Louis XIV) to reach the cathedral (via Place Lou-vel) or the Esplanade Beaulieu (via Rue Beaulieu) overlook-ing the **Jardin Vert** (gardens; view). The **cathedral★** (12thC) has a storiated façade★★ of great interest. The north transept is topped by a 60 m high Romanesque bell-tower★. ▶ Left of the cathedral façade, the former bishops' residence is now a **Fine Arts Museum** (painting, porcelain, history, African art, ethnology, *10-12 & 2-6, closed Tue.*). ▶ **Musée de la Société archéologique** (Museum of the Archaeological Society), 42, 44 Rue de Montmoreau *(10-12 & 2-5, closed Tue.)*. ▶ Most interest-ing : walk along and around the **ramparts.** ▶ In the old town, restoration projects.

Tour of la Touvre *(30 km E, 3 hr)*

▶ **Ruelle** *(N141; 7 km)* : ▶ D699 : **Magnac-sur-Touvre** : Romanesque church on the river's edge. ▶ **Vauclusi-ennes springs of la Touvre** *(1 km upstream)*, in a vast natu-ral basin. ▶ From the chapel terrace, on the top of a hill, lovely view★ of the springs *(gouffres)* from **Touvres.**

Around Périgord *(70 km SSE, half-day)*

▶ From the château de **la Tranchade** to the Romanesque churches of **Dirac** and **Dignac** *(17 km)*. **Villebois-Lavalette** *(25 km)* is located on a spur in a region inhabited since prehistoric times; castle ruins and Romanesque church (much restored in 19thC). ▶ To the east, 15 km loop by **Gardes-le-Pontaroux** (near prehistoric resort of Quina), **La Rochebeaucourt** (château park, 18thC), and **Blanza-guet-Saint-Cybard** (Romanesque church). ▶ 2.5 km W, Romanesque church at **Ronsenac.** ▶ Return to Angou-lême through **La Mercerie** *(4 km)*, the "Versailles of Cha-rente" begun in 1930 and never finished (part of it has been made into an arboretum, morning visits possible). ▶ Follow the D5 — a route created by the Romans — to the Romanesque church at **Charmant** *(9 km)* : decorat-ed apse.

Eaux-Claires Valley *(32 km round trip; half-day)*

▶ From **Puymoyen** *(4 km;* 13thC church), go down into the **Eaux-Claires Valley** and visit the prehistoric habi-tations; **Le Verger Mill**, where vellum is still produced by traditional methods *(demonstrations, daily visits)*. ▶ **Mouthiers-sur-Boëme** : prehistoric habitations, Roman-esque church, Renaissance château. ▶ **La Couronne** :

vestiges of the former abbey (ruins of the Roman-esque abbey church and cellars from the 13thC; 18thC buildings; *visit on request*). ▶ **Château de L'Oisellerie** (Renaissance). ▶ Romanesque church at **Saint-Michel-d'Entraygues★** *(5 km from Angoulême)*, built in an octa-gonal design (restored in the 19thC). ▶ Nersac : **Fleurac Mill**, traditional paper-making *(instruction)*.

Charente Valley *(85 km round trip north of Angoulême; half-day)*

▶ **Château de Balzac** (home of Guez de Balzac, 17thC). ▶ **Asnières-sur-Nouère** : Romanesque church (more Romanesque churches can be seen at Trois-Palis, Champmillon and Fléac, which can be reached by **Hier-sac**). ▶ **Saint-Cybardeaux** : 1.5 km N, Gallo-Roman theatre at **Les Bouchauds★** (1stC; *admission free, guided visits : S.I.*). **Rouillac** : wine storehouse visits. ▶ **Marcil-lac-Lanville** : beautiful rural architecture. **Montignac-sur-Charente**, château ruins. ▶ **Saint-Amant-de-Boixe** : one of the great Romanesque churches★ of the area (12thC; choir rebuilt 15thC; Gothic murals); right of the façade, remains of cloister (12th-14thC). ▶ Return via N10.   □

Practical Information

ANGOULÊME

ⓘ hôtel de ville (B2), ☎ 45.95.16.84; pl. de la Gare (C1), ☎ 45.92.27.57.
✈ *Air France office*, 19, rue Montmoreau, ☎ 45.95.40.40.
SNCF (C1), ☎ 45.38.50.50.
Car rental : *Avis*, 139, av. Gambetta (C1), ☎ 45.92.49.88; train station, ☎ 45.92.05.80.

Hotels :
● ★★★ *France*, 1, pl. des Halles (B1), ☎ 45.95.47.95, AE DC Euro Visa, 60 rm 🅿 ⫷ ⁂ ⚓ ₺ 230. Rest. ♦♦ ⁊ ⊘ closed Sat and Sun noon, 20 Dec-10 Jan, 100-140.
★★ *L'Epi d'Or*, (Inter-Hôtel) 66, bd René-Chabasse (C2), ☎ 45.95.67.64, AE DC Euro Visa, 30 rm 🅿 ₺ 210.
★ *Le Crab* (L.F.), 27, rue Kléber (C1), ☎ 45.95.51.80, AE DC Euro Visa, 21 rm 🅿 ⚓ 105. Rest. ♦ closed Sat and Sun eve, 40-80.

Restaurant :
♦♦ *La Chamade*, 13, rampe d'Aguesseau (C1), ☎ 45.38.41.33, Visa ⁊ closed Mon noon and Sun, 21-28 Feb, 15 Jul-20 Aug, 135-250.

⚖ ★★★*Ile de Bourgines* (70 pl), ☎ 45.92.83.22.

Recommended
Baby-sitting : *Info 16*, ☎ 45.92.86.73.
Guided tours : *C.N.M.H.S.* (in Jul-Aug daily ex Sun).
Night-clubs : *La nuit des Rois*, rte de Vars.
Youth hostel : île de Bourgines, ☎ 45.92.45.80.
♥ pastry : *Au Palet d'or*, 1, pl. Fr.-Louvel (B1), ☎ 45.95.00.73.

Nearby

ASNIÈRES-SUR-NOUÈRE, ⊠ 16290 Hiersac, 12 km NW.

Hotel :
★★★ ***Moulin du Maine-Brun*** (R.S.), ☎ 45.96.92.62, Tx 791053, AE DC Euro Visa, 20 rm 🅿 ≼ ⋘ ♤ ♪ ⧠ closed Sun eve , Mon, Jan-Mar, 430. Rest. ♦♦ *Le Moulin Gourmand* ♪ ⅙ 160-260 ; child : 45.

CHAMPNIERS, ⊠ 16430, 7 km N of **Asnières-sur-Nouère**.

Hotel :
★★ ***Motel PM 16*** (L.F.), RN 10, ☎ 45.68.03.22, Tx 790345, AE DC Euro Visa, 41 rm 🅿 ⋘ ♪ ♨ ⅙ closed Sat, 23-31 Dec, 200. Rest. ♦ ♪ closed Mon, 4-27 Jan, 50-100.

Restaurant :
● *Auberge de la Chignolle*, RN 10, ☎ 45.69.99.66, AE DC Euro Visa ♪ ⅙ closed Tue and Wed. Winner of the 'best dish of tripe' award, Bernard Laurent is a true specialist; to quench your thirst, try one of his exceptional Bordeaux, Burgundies, or Beaujolais, 90-150.

DIGNAC, ⊠ 16410, 17 km S.

Hotel :
★★ *La Marronnière*, rte de Périgueux, ☎ 45.24.50.42, AE DC Euro Visa, 10 rm 🅿 ⋘ ♤ ⅙ half pens (h.s.), closed Sun eve and Mon, 15 Sep-15 Oct, 185. Rest. ♦ ⅙ 50-95.

NERSAC, ⊠ 16550, 10 km W.

Restaurant :
♦♦ *Auberge du Pont de la Meure*, pont de la Meure, ☎ 45.90.60.48, AE DC Euro Visa 🅿 ≼ ⚲ ⅙ closed Fri eve and Sat , Aug, 80-150.

ROULLET, ⊠ 16440, 10 km SW.

Hotel :
★★★ *La Vieille Etable*, Les Plantes, ☎ 45.66.31.75, AE DC Visa, 23 rm 🅿 ⋘ ⚲ ⧠ ✍ 200. Rest. ♦ ♪ ❀ Spec : duck breast, 60-190.

VOUZAN, ⊠ 16410 Dignac, 17 km SW.

Hotel :
★★ *L'Orée des Bois*, ☎ 45.24.94.38, AE, 11 rm 🅿 ⋘ ⚲ ♪ ⅙ pens, half pens (h.s.), closed Sun eve and Mon (l.s.), 11 Nov-1 Dec, 380. Rest. ♦♦ ⅙ 100-160.

AUBETERRE-SUR-DRONNE*

Chalais 10, Angoulême 46, Paris 492 km
pop 404 ⊠ 16390   C3

Built in the form of an amphitheatre, this village of white buildings and tiled roofs on the road to Compostela resembles the towns of Navarre in Spain, also on the pilgrim route.

▶ At the foot of the castle ruins (14th-15thC) is **Saint John's church** (12thC) cut into the white limestone rock that gives the village its name. ▶ In the upper town, beyond the Renaissance **Chapter-house**, all that remains of the pilgrim **church of St. Jacques** is the imposing storiated façade★.

Nearby

On a hill at the confluence of the Tude and Viveronne rivers, ▶ **Chalais** *(11 km W)*, ▶ W on D2, panoramic view and Roman Gothic church at **Rouffiac**, renowned for its fairs : visit the Talleyrand **Château** (14th-18thC) and the church (**Romanesque doorway**).   □

Practical Information _____

ⅈ pl. Ludovic-Trarieux, ☎ 45.98.50.33.   ♥

Hotel :
★★ ***Périgord***, ☎ 45.98.50.11, 7 rm 🅿 closed Sun eve and Mon (l.s.), 90. Rest. ♦ ❀ 45-140.

⚖ ★★*Dronne* (50 pl), ☎ 51.98.50.33.

AULNAY**

Saint-Jean-d'Angély 18, Poitiers 83, Paris 417 km
pop 1505 ⊠ 17470   B2

Along the main route to Santiago de Compostela, the large Romanesque church (12thC) looms out of the yew trees and stone tombs. Note the three storiated arches of the main doorway★ and the right transept doorway ; sculpted capitals in the nave.

Round trip of the Boutonne *(65 km ; 3 hr)*

▶ **Nuaillé-sur-Boutonne** *(S)* : doorway in the small church (13thC). ▶ **Dampierre : Renaissance château**★ with two superimposed rows of arcades, by a stream *(Nov.-Mar. ; closed Thu.)*. ▶ In the **Chizé Forest** (12 500 acres, remarkable trees : see the "Seven Oaks" group), **zoorama** with more than 600 animals on a 60 acre estate *(closed Tue.)*. The forest, like that of neighbouring Aulnay, is part of the Val de Sèvre Nature Park (→ Marais Poitevin). ▶ **Brioux**, once known for its mule fairs ; return via the forest and **Saint-Mandé-sur-Brédoire** (simple Romanesque church on a knoll).   □

BARBEZIEUX-SAINT-HILAIRE

Angoulême 33, Bordeaux 84, Paris 478 km
pop 5404 ⊠ 16300   B3

Capital of the Grande Champagne area (→ Cognac box), a trading town located on a route used since Neolithic times.

▶ Rochefoucauld **castle** (reconstructed 15thC, restored late 19thC) is today partly occupied by a museum. In the town can be seen two Romanesque churches which have been partly remodelled through the centuries ; old houses.

Nearby

▶ **Condéon** *(8 km S, via D731)* : 12thC church with multifoil doorway (characteristic Romanesque decoration). ▶ **Brossac** *(12 km farther)* : former Gallo-Roman spa overlooking (180 m high) the river Double.   □

Practical Information _____

ⅈ 3, bd Chanzy, ☎ 45.78.02.54 (h.s.) ; mairie, ☎ 45.70.20.22.   ♥

Hotel :
● ★★ *La Boule d'Or*, (Inter-Hôtel), 9, bd Gambetta, ☎ 45.78.22.72, AE Euro Visa, 28 rm 🅿 ⋘ ⚲ pens, 490. Rest. ♦♦ Garden dining in summer, 50-150 ; child : 35.

BLANZAC

Limoges 42, Poitiers 80, Paris 412 km
pop 978 ⊠ 87300 Bellac   C3

Market town of southern Angoulême : remains of 12thC La Rochefoucauld keep and impressive 12th-13thC church.

Nearby

▶ Poet Alfred de Vigny often visited the "Ivory Tower" of the **Maine-Giraud** estate between 1827-63 *(3 km N ; private ; visits daily)*. ▶ Farther on, 12thC Romanesque church★ (apse built on a crypt, bell-tower) at **Plassac-Rouffiac** overlooking the vineyards. ▶ E, via **Pérignac** (church), the former abbey of **Puypéroux** on a beautiful site : fine example of the region's earliest (11thC) Romanesque art. ▶ SE via D10, **Montmoreau-Saint-Cybard** *(13 km)* : 15thC castle on bluff *(visits to chapel only)*; in the town, large 12thC church with multifoil doorway. ▶ S, **Porcheresse** church (late 11thC), with one of the first cupolas in Poitou; at **Cressac**, Templars' chapel with 12thC frescos.   ☐

BRESSUIRE

Cholet 45, Angers 82, Paris 356 km
pop 19502 ⊠ 79300   B1

A former regional capital; its population has declined in modern times. The large agricultural market here was the site of one of the first slaughterhouses in France. Well-known for its fairs *(Aug.)* since the Middle Ages. Remains of 48 towers from a **feudal fortress** with double walls. 12th-16thC **church of Notre-Dame** with Renaissance bell-tower.

Nearby

▶ Long trip through the country of the Vendéen wars (→). ▶ N, via **Voultegon** (Gallo-Roman ruins), **Argenton-Château** *(17 km)* overlooking the confluence of the Ouère and Argenton rivers; church of St. Gilles with interesting sculpted doorway. ▶ On the road to Thouars, ruins of **château d'Ébaupinage** (15thC) burned down during the Vendéen wars, and view from **Grifférus bridge** *(6 km)* of the Argenton pass.   ☐

Practical Information

BRESSUIRE
ℹ pl. de l'Hôtel-de-Ville, ☎ 49.65.10.27.
SNCF ☎ 49.65.00.06.

Hotel :
★ **Boule d'Or** (L.F.), 15, pl. E.-Zola, ☎ 49.65.02.18, Euro Visa, 15 rm ℙ closed Mon lunch, 120. Rest. ♦ ♪ 50-140.

Recommended
Events : *cultural festival* in May, fairs.

Nearby

ARGENTON-CHÂTEAU, ⊠ 79150, 17 km N.
ℹ mairie, ☎ 49.65.70.22; pl. Léopold-Bergeron (h.s.). ♥

Hotel :
★ **Croix Blanche**, pl. Léopold-Bergeron, ☎ 49.65.70.50, 10 rm ℙ closed 1 wk in Mar, 1-20 Oct, 100. Rest. ♦ closed Mon and Sun eve, 45-100.

BROUAGE**

Rochefort 20, Saintes 40, Paris 488 km
pop 476 ⊠ 17320 Marennes   B2

Champlain (1567-1635), who founded Canada, was born in this former fishing port; the town was fortified by Louis XIII.

▶ The **fortified wall**★ is in fine condition; a tour of the sentry walk (1.6 km) will show you the town gates, the produce market, the former arsenal, forges and the underground ports *(son et lumière some summer nights)*.

Tour of the marshes *(35 km N ; 28 km S ; 4 hr)*

▶ To the N, **Moëze** *(6 km)* Renaissance cross *(hosannière :* double vertical cross) church with spire, bell-tower. ▶ **Soubise** *(3 km farther)* and **Port-des-Barques** toward Passe-sur-Bœufs on a road that will take you to **l'île Madame.**

▶ To the S, **Marennes** (pop. 4549) : panorama★ from the bell-tower (15thC; 78 m high) over the marshes now converted to oyster farms; in the village : oyster diorama *(in summer)*; château de La Gataudière (18thC, *10:30-12 & 2:30-6, Jun.-Oct. ; Sun. and hols., Oct.-May, 2-5, on request)* via the yacht harbour to the oyster port of **La Cayenne**

(4 km; organised visit of the parks). ▶ West of Marennes : **Chapus Point** (oyster port); offshore is **Fort Louvois** (17thC), accessible by causeway *(submerged at high tide);* oyster museum *(closed Tue.).*   ☐

Practical Information

Nearby

BOURCEFRANC-LE-CHAPUS, ⊠ 17560, 5 km NW.

Hotel :
● ★★ **Les Claires** (R.S.), rte du Pont-d'Oléron, ☎ 46.85.08.01, Tx 792055, Euro Visa, 19 rm ℙ ⩿ ▩ ⌇ ▱ ⤴ 320. Rest. ♦♦ ♪ よ 130-230; child : 60.

SOUBISE, ⊠ 17780, 9 km S.

Hotel :
★★ **Le Soubise**, 62, rue de la République, ☎ 46.84.92.16, Tx 791171, AE DC Euro Visa, 23 rm ℙ ▩ ⌇ よ closed Sun eve and Mon ex Jul-Aug, 1-30 Oct, 170. Rest. ● ♦♦ ♪ よ A veritable institution in these parts. Spec : *goujonnettes de soles et de langoustines aux pâtes fraîches, émincé de magret et foie tiède aux nouilles et orties, jonchée du marais à la crème fraîche au laurier amande,* 135-250.

CHARROUX*

Poitiers 52, Niort 76, Paris 400 km
pop 1552 ⊠ 86250   C2

Octagonal **lantern-tower**★ on the 11thC church in a Carolingian abbey partially destroyed during the religious wars. **Collection of precious stones** from the abbey's portal, kept in the 14th and 15thC buildings *(closed Oct. and Tue. off season).* Close by : a number of half-timbered Gothic houses.

Nearby

▶ To the W, prehistoric caves of **Chaffaud**. ▶ **Civray** *(11 km)*, on the right bank of the Charente : remarkable storiated façade★★ on the 12thC church; octagonal belltower at the transept crossing. ▶ **Sommières-du-Clain** *(15 km N)* : château de Vareilles (French Classical style). ▶ **La Reau Abbey** *(14 km NE)* : in the middle of the countryside, mediaeval ruins (12thC; burnt during the Hundred Years' War); some constructions were rebuilt in the 15th and 18thC *(10-12 & 2:30-5:15 in summer; closed Tue.).* ▶ On the road to Poitiers : **Usson** Church (Romanesque doorway).   ☐

CHÂTELLERAULT

Poitiers 35, Tours 72, Paris 306 km
pop 36870 ⊠ 86100   C1

Ancient port on the Vienne; splendid bridge; one of Poitou's most important commercial centres.

▶ **Rue Bourbon**, the main street until recent years, is now for pedestrians only : No. 162, former home (16thC) of philosopher Descartes (museum : *closed Tue. and some nat. hols.).* ▶ On the quay : **Chéron de la Martinière Museum** in the castle ruins (local history and craftwork, Nevers faïence; Rue Godeau-Lerpinière, *2-6, closed Tue., Sun. and hols.).* ▶ **Henri IV bridge** (late 16thC) opens onto the Châteauneuf district : upstream, the armaments factory is now partially taken over by an **automobile museum**★ *(closed Tue. out of season).* ▶ On the right bank, rue Sully contains a 16thC hotel of the same name (home of an Acadian and Coiffes museum) and leads to **Saint-Jacques church** (polychrome statue of patron saint of pilgrims, 17thC★), Renaissance houses.

The Châtellerault region (Châtelleraudais)

▶ **Ingrandes** *(N via N10)* : church (partially Carolingian). ▶ **Les Ormes** *(17 km)* : 18thC château. ▶ **Port-de-Piles :** former Romanesque church. ▶ To the NE, **Oyré :** Romanesque church, pillared arcade (ins.de : late 15thC murals). ▶ S, through the Vienne Valley, **Ozon** : former Templar commandery (frescos). ▶ Château de **La Tour d'Oyré**. ▶ Romanesque church at **Bonneuil-Matours**. ▶ SW, through the Clain Valley, **Vieux-Poitiers** *(10 km)* : Gallo-Roman ruins near the supposed site of the Saracen defeat in 732 (Moussais-la-Bataille; *excavations in progress★*). ▶ Via La Tricherie, **Beaumont** : Romanesque church; ruins of 10th-11thC keep.

Hills to the N and W *(60 km; half-day)*
▶ Via **Châtellerault Forest** (3750 acres), Romanesque church at **Colombiers**. ▶ To the NW via **Thuré** : Massardière manor (14th-15thC), and **Scorbé-Clairvaux** château (15th-17thC). ▶ To the N via Saint-Gervais-les-Trois-Clochers : **Marmande Butte**, hill with ruined 14thC keep (40 m high; panorama). Return via **La Motte-d'Usseau** castle (15thC). ☐

Practical Information _____

CHÂTELLERAULT
ⓘ bd Blossac, (cl. Mon l.s. and Sun), ☎ 49.21.05.47.
SNCF ☎ 49.21.00.24/49.21.02.35.
Car rental : Avis, 3, rue de la Paix, ☎ 49.21.07.79.

Hotels :
★★★ *Moderne*, (Mapotel), 74, bd Blossac, ☎ 49.21.30.11, Tx 791801, AE DC Euro Visa, 38 rm Ⓟ 300. Rest. ♦♦ *la Charmille* ♪ ൧ closed Wed , mid-Jan to mid-Feb, Oct, 160-280.
★★ *Le Croissant*, 19, av. Kennedy, ☎ 49.21.01.77, Euro Visa, 20 rm Ⓟ ≶ ⅏ closed Sun eve , Mon lunch, 23 Dec-6 Jan, 120. Rest. ♦ ♪ Spec : *foie gras frais maison, paupiette de moules au roquefort, steak de lotte*, 55-200.
★ *Orée de la Forêt*, 9, av. H.-de-Balzac (exit S), ☎ 49.21.29.78, Euro Visa, 13 rm Ⓟ ⅏ ൧ closed Fri eve and Sat (l.s.), 200. Rest. ♦ ♪ 60-150.

Restaurant :
♦♦ *Buffet de la Gare*, 26, bd Sadi-Carnot, ☎ 49.21.08.93, Visa, closed Sat eve, 45-80.

Recommended
Events : *feast of Saint-Roch*, Sun after 15 Aug; *fair-exhibit*, in Sept.
Leisure activities : 9 km E, *Petites Minaudières park*.
Tables d'hôtes : at Sérigny, CP 86230 St-Gervais, *Château de St-Bonnet*, 25 km E, ☎ 49.86.01.55, closed Oct-May, 350.
Youth hostel : *le Chillou d'Ozon*, exit dir. Chauvigny (20 km NW), ☎ 49.21.29.22.

Nearby
NAINTRÉ, ⊠ 86530, 9 km S.
Restaurant :
♦ *Grillade*, RN 10, ☎ 49.90.03.42, Euro Visa Ⓟ ⅏ ♪ ൧ closed Sun eve. A thatched roof shelters an old-fashioned Charentais kitchen serving fine grills, *daube de bœuf*, eels, 55-120.

CHAUVIGNY★★

Poitiers 23, Montmorillon 26, Paris 336 km
pop 6684 ⊠ 86300   C1
On this steep promontory are the ruins of five enormous fortified castles that once guarded the route to Berry. In the lower section of the city, 11th-12thC church.

▶ The **baronial castle** (or Bishop's), is the first encountered climbing up the hill (large square keep; 12thC); higher up, Harcourt Castle (13th-15thC), followed by Montléon (12th-15thC), Gouzon (with 11thC keep), and finally, the Flins Tower. ▶ The **church of St. Pierre★★** has remarkable storiated capitals★. ▶ Near the entry, a stairway leads to the **museum and panorama** *(folk art and customs, daily Jun.-Sep.; Sun. pm out of season)*.

The Vienne Valley *(43 km; half-day)*
▶ North via **Bonnes** (two Romanesque churches on the left bank) : **Touffou** castle★ *(8 km; Jul.-Aug.; closed Mon. out of season and winter)*, in a park overlooking the Vienne; group of attractive 12th-15thC buildings. ▶ South, along the right bank : small partially Carolingian church at **Saint-Pierre-les-Eglises** *(2 km)* housing the oldest murals in Poitou; cemetery★; Merovingian sarcophagi. ▶ **Gioux** cave, inhabited in prehistoric times. ▶ Cross the river at Valdivienne *(7 km);* 3 km S of Bonneuil, **Morthemer★ :** large castle, Gothic pentagonal keep and adjoining Romanesque church with crypt. ▶ **Civaux** *(5 km farther)* : archaeological dig (Gallo-Roman temple) around the church (Carolingian apse); 200 m away : Merovingian necropolis★ with several thousand tombs. Nuclear power plant under construction. ▶ On the right bank, **Cognons Tower** : ruins of a Romanesque square keep. ▶ **Lussac-les-Châteaux** *(6 km S)* surrounded by **caves** inhabited as early as the Magdalenian era : Marche Cave (engraved flagstones) and Fadets Cave; 18thC pavilion and park of the château where Madame de Montespan was born. ☐

Practical Information _____
CHAUVIGNY
ⓘ pl. du Champ-de-Foire (h.s.); mairie, ☎ 49.46.30.21.

Hotels :
● ★★ *Lion d'Or* (L.F.), 8, rue du Marché, ☎ 49.46.30.28, Visa, 27 rm Ⓟ closed Sat (1 Nov-30 Mar), 15 Dec-15 Jan, 185. Rest. ♦ Spec : *aiguillette à l'ail*, 60-110.
● ★ *Beauséjour*, 20, rue Vassalour, ☎ 49.46.31.30, Euro Visa, 20 rm Ⓟ ⅏ closed Xmas and New Year's Day, 120. Rest. ♦ closed Sun, 45-80.

△ ★★★*La Fontaine* (100 pl), ☎ 49.46.31.94.

Recommended
Guided tours : in the upper town in Jul-Aug, info S.I.

Nearby
LUSSAC-LES-CHÂTEAUX, ⊠ 86320, 21 km S.
ⓘ ☎ 49.48.42.77.
SNCF ☎ 49.48.40.35.

Hotel :
★★ *Montespan*, voie Nouvelle, ☎ 49.48.41.42, 13 rm Ⓟ ൧ ♪ 125.

COGNAC★

Saintes 26, Angoulême 44, Paris 480 km
pop 23000 ⊠ 16100   B3
Cognac was once a small-craft port on the Charente, protected by a fortress where François I was born in 1494. When brandy *(brandevin)* was invented in the middle of the 17thC, the image of the city was changed radically by the wine and spirit warehouses opened along the quays. Here, Dutch and English traders produced the "burntwine" for export. Over the years, the walls of the sidestreets have become covered with a black veneer of mould; this is an effect of alcoholic fumes.

▶ Every visit to Cognac starts with a tour of the cellars *(closed Sat. and Sun. out of season)* and of **Valois Castle** (son et lumière, Cognac cellar, Jul.-Aug., 10-6; Jun., Sep., 10-12 & 2-6 ex. Tue.). ▶ E, a large **wooded park★** in a bend of the Charente river. ▶ Hôtel de Ville : **Cognac and Local Traditions Museum** *(Jun.-Sep., 10-12 & 2-6; out of season, 2-5:30; closed Tue.).* ▶ In the old town, see the **half-timbered houses,** and the largely Romanesque church of St. Léger.

Nearby : *visit the vineyards and storehouses; information : TO*

▶ To the N, **Richemont,** among the smaller estates *(guided visits Sat., Sun., Jul.-Aug.)* : two castles and church (pre-Romanesque crypt). ▶ Romanesque church at

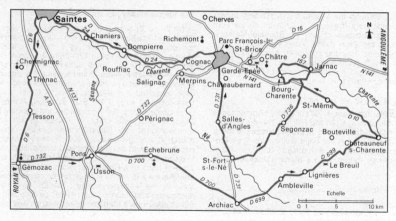

1. Tour of the Champagne Cognac vineyards

Cherves, and Renaissance château in Chesnel. ▶ To the S, passing through Châteaubernard (aerodrome), in "Grande Champagne", is **Salles d'Angles,** inhabited for over 5 000 years, folk arts and traditions museum. ▶ Romanesque churches at **Genté** (interesting façade), **Gensac-la-Pallue** (capitals), **Segonzac** (bell-tower). ▶ To the SW, **Ars Castle★,** church and panorama in Montils. ▶ **Saint-Fort-sur-le-Né** *(1 km)* : prehistoric site (the most beautiful dolmen in the entire Angoulême region).

Tour of the Champagne Cognac vineyards *(round trip, 145 km; one day; see map 1)*

▶ To the W, the Charente Valley *(N141, then D24)* : along the left bank to the mill at Saint-Laurent. ▶ **Merpins** : ruins of Condate Roman spa ; archaeology repository *(Jun., Jul., Aug.).* ▶ **Chaniers** : attractive islands of La Baine ; in the village : Romanesque church (see the chevet). ▶ **Port-Hublé** : former inland port where barges were loaded with wheat. ▶ The trip can be made by boat from Cognac as far as Saintes (→). ▶ Chermignac, Thénac and Tesson (→ Saintes, nearby). ▶ Gémozac (→ Talmont, nearby). ▶ Pons (→). ▶ Echebrune : Romanesque church (portal ★★). ▶ Archiac : feudal remains, panorama over the vineyards. ▶ Via Ambleville and **Lignières-Sonneville** (façade of Romanesque church ; moated castle), **Bouteville** : ruins of castle (17thC), Romanesque church, panorama. ▶ **Châteauneuf-sur-Charente** : leisure activities on the river ; Romanesque church★ (beautiful façade and triple nave). ▶ **Saint-Même-les-Carrières** : prehistoric site, quarries worked since the Roman epoch. ▶ **Bourg-Charente** : bridge over the river (view) ; on the right bank : Renaissance château ; on the left bank : Romanesque and Gothic church. ▶ 2 km away : dolmen. ▶ Former church of **Châtres,** isolated in a valley (cupolas, Saintonge Romanesque façade). ▶ **Château de Garde-Epée** : 15thC dovecote. □

Practical Information ——————————

COGNAC
ℹ️ rue du 14-Juin, ☎ 45.82.10.71, closed Sun.
🚃 ☎ 45.82.25.90/45.82.10.71.
🚢 cruises on the Charente, info and tickets S.I., to Jarnac, Angoulême, Saintes and Rochefort.

Hotels :
● ★★★ *Le Valois,* (Mapotel), 35, rue du 14-juillet, ☎ 45.82.76.00, Tx 790987, AE DC Euro Visa, 27 rm 🅿 ♪ closed 20 Dec-2 Jan, 290.
● ★★★ *Logis de Beaulieu,* (L.F., C.H.), Saint-Laurent-de-Cognac 5 km W, ☎ 45.82.30.50, 21 rm 🅿 ⚡ ♨ 🔥 ♪

closed last 2 wks in Dec, 170. Rest. ♦♦ ♪ Spec : *mousclade charentaise,* 100-160.
★★★ *Pigeons Blancs* (C.H.), 110, rue J.-Brisson, ☎ 45.82.16.36, AE DC Visa, 6 rm 🅿 ♨ 🔥 ♨ pens, closed Sun, Jan, 650. Rest. ♦ ♨ ♪ ♨ Spec : *foie gras frais de canard au pineau, filet de sole à la vapeur de cognac,* 90-230.
★★ *Moderne* (L.F.), 24, rue E.-Mousnier, ☎ 45.82.19.53, DC Euro Visa, 40 rm 🅿 🔥 ♨ ♪ 🔥 closed 15 Dec-6 Jan, 190.

Restaurant :
♦ *Coq d'Or,* 33, pl. François-1er, ☎ 45.82.02.56, AE DC Euro Visa 🅿 ♪ closed Fri eve (l.s.), Sun. Spec. : *huîtres grillées,* 60-110 ; child : 40.

Recommended
Baby-sitting : *Info 16,* ☎ 45.82.62.00.
Events : *fairs,* in May and Nov.
Guide to wines : *Chais Martell,* pl. Ed.-Martell, ☎ 45.82.44.44, guided tour; *Chais Hennessy and barrel museum,* rue de la Richonne, ☎ 45.82.52.22, guided tour; at Gensac-la-Pallue 16130 5 km E, *Chais du Cognac Prince H.-de-Polignac,* Pavillon du Laub, ☎ 45.32.13.85, guided tour (Apr-late Sep).
Guided tours : *industrial plants (St-Gobain...) ; self-guided walk through old Cognac, info S.I.*
Son et lumière : *at château François 1er.*

Nearby

BOURG-CHARENTE, ✉ 16200 Jarnac, 9 km E.

Restaurant :
♦♦ *La Ribaudière,* ☎ 45.81.30.54, AE Euro Visa 🅿 ♨ 🔥 closed Mon and Sun eve, 60-130.

SAINT-FORT-SUR-LE-NÉ, ✉ 16660, 13 km S.

Hotel :
★★★ *Moulin de Cierzac,* ☎ 45.83.01.32, AE DC Visa, 10 rm 🅿 🔥 🔥 closed Mon (l.s.), Feb, 350. Rest. ♦ ♨ ♪ 🔥 Peace and good eating assured in this fine 17th-C house : *crème d'huîtres aux pétoncles, selle d'agneau à la crème d'ail.* Cognac 13 km away, but the best bottles are all here, 105-280.

CONFOLENS

Bellac 36, Angoulême 63, Paris 407 km
pop 3320 ✉ 16500   C2

In an attractive site on the Vienne river at the Gothic Pont-Vieux (bridge), Confolens is known for its international folklore festival in August *(week of the 15th, from Fri. to Mon.)*.

▶ Downstream from the **15thC bridge**, the Vienne and Goire rivers meet; **gorges**, ruins of a keep; half-timbered houses; narrow lanes. Along the right bank of the Vienne, Romanesque **church of St. Barthélemy** (11thC). ▶ **La Fontorse** : curious fountain.

The Confolens area *(Confolentais; E and SE; 65 km; full day)*

▶ **Esse** : church (13thC); megaliths. ▶ **Lesterps** (pronounced : Létère) : Romanesque gate-tower (12thC, 43 m). ▶ **Brigueuil** : fête de la Rosière, famous Easter celebration involving election of most virtuous local maiden; mediaeval granite buildings. ▶ **Etagnac** : **Rochebrune castle★** (11th-16thC) surrounded by moats; mementos of Napoleonic times *(10-12 & 2-6, Palm Sunday-11 Nov.)*. ▶ **Chassenon** *(4 km S)* : Roman ruins of *Cassinomagus* (1st-2ndC; Easter-Nov.). ▶ **Chabanais**, rebuilt in 1946; 16thC bridge. ▶ **Exideuil** : Chétardie château; partially Romanesque church; to the S : Pressac château. ▶ Romanesque church at **Roumazières**. ▶ On the right bank of the Vienne river, church at **Chirac**. ▶ Left bank : **Manot**.

The Vienne downstream of Confolens

▶ **Saint-Germain** *(4 km)* : ruins of a feudal castle. ▶ **Abzac** : La Fayolle castle, Serres castle nearby. ▶ **Availles-Limouzine** : numerous megaliths. ▶ Toward l'Isle Jourdain on the left bank, views of dam-created lakes. ▶ Romanesque church at **Le Vigeant**. ▶ **L'Isle-Jourdain** : vast reservoir, holiday centre. ▢

Practical Information _____

ⓘ pl. des Marronniers, ☎ 45.84.00.77, closed Sun. ♥

Hotels :
★★ *Croix Blanche*, pl. de la Croix Blanche à Chabanais, ☎ 45.89.22.18, AE DC Euro Visa, 17 rm, 100. Rest. ♦ closed Mon, 50-85.
★★ *Emeraude* (L.F.), 20, rue E.-Roux, ☎ 45.84.12.77, AE DC Euro Visa, 18 rm Ⓟ ⋈ closed Feb, 180. Rest. ♦ ≷ ♪ ⋙ closed Mon (l.s.), 70-130.

Å ★★*Municipal* (70 pl), ☎ 45.84.01.97.

COUBRE Forest*

A3

Round trip from Royan on the Arvert Peninsula *(65 km; full day)*

Not until the 18thC was an effort made to halt the progress of the dunes created by the strong winds and wild currents between the Gironde estuary and the straits of the Charente archipelago. The pine groves of the Royan region covering these dunes (64 m high at the Gardour signal) are today traversed by foot- and bridle-paths. The marshes have now been partially drained : the straight seashore to the W, wild and dangerous, is mostly frequented by naturists who come for the sun.

▶ **La Grande Côte** *(9 km from Royan)* : rocky coast beyond the dunes; view from the lighthouse at Cordouan. ▶ **La Palmyre** in the pines : Bonne Anse Bay (beach, aquatic sports); zoological park★ (African animals; *open all year*). ▶ Coubre Lighthouse *(20 km;* 60 m high, panoramic terrace, 300 steps). ▶ **Côte Sauvage** : accessible only by paths, except 30 km along the Espagnole Point (bathing dangerous). ▶ **Ronce-les-Bains** *(35 km)*, seaside resort in the middle of a forest : sheltered beach near the straits of Maumusson; on the straits, beautiful beach of Galon-d'Or *(3 km farther)*. ▶ **La Tremblade** (38 km; pop. 4 687) : large oyster farms; small maritime museum; "inter-island" cruises and visits to the oyster-beds leave from the port at the end of the jetty *(in summer)*. ▶ **Étaules** : oyster

museum (at the *S.I., in summer)*. ▶ **Mornac-sur-Seudre** : artisans' village; partly Romanesque church. ▶ **Breuillet** : church with Saintonge style façade. ▶ Return via **Saint-Sulpice** (another Romanesque church). ▢

Practical Information _____

ARVERT, ⊠ 17530, 5 km S of **La Palmyre**.

Hotel :
★★★ *Villa Fantaisie* (L.F.), rue du Vieux-Moulin, ☎ 46.36.40.09, AE Euro Visa, 23 rm Ⓟ ⋈ ⋈ ♪ ♿ half pens (h.s.), closed Sun eve and Mon, 5 Jan-2 Mar, 580. Rest. ♦ ♪ ♿ Spec : *nage de Saint-Jacques en effilochade, cassolette d'huîtres chaudes au cognac*, 100-220.

CHAILLEVETTE, ⊠ 17890, 15 km of from Royan.

Hotel :
● ★★★ *La Brousse*, ☎ 46.36.60.93, 14 rm Ⓟ ⋙ ⋈ ♪ ⋙ ⊠ half pens (h.s.), closed 8 Sep-30 Jun, 440. Rest. ♦ Half-board only, 80-130.

La PALMYRE, ⊠ 17570 Les Mathes, 17 km NW of **Royan**. ⓘ ☎ 46.22.41.07 ; ☎ 46.02.40.58 (l.s.).

Å ★★★★*La Bonne Anse* (700 pl), ☎ 46.22.40.90; ★★★*Beauséjour* (400 pl), ☎ 46.22.40.05 ; ★★★*la Côte Sauvage* (400 pl), ☎ 46.22.40.18 ; ★★*many sites* (1000 pl).

Recommended
Holiday villages : *les Pins de Cordouan*, ☎ 46.22.41.22; *la Grande Baie*, ☎ 46.42.40.37.

ESNANDES*

La Rochelle 12, Fontenay-le-Comte 40, Paris 450 km
pop 1370 ⊠ 17137 Nieul-sur-Mer   B2

This white village by the cliffs of Aunis and the home of the *mouclade* (mussels with cream), is probably as well known for its miles of mussel pens, as it is for its Romanesque church fortified in the 15thC (doorways★ on the façade).

▶ 6 km N, village of **Charron**, and 1 km farther, the **Pavé** harbour, site of an important mussel-growing industry. ▶ The whole region, similar in many aspects to the Camargue (→), is frequented by migratory birds (→ L'Aiguillon-sur-Mer). ▢

Practical Information _____

Hotel :
★ *Port*, ☎ 46.01.32.11, 13 rm Ⓟ ⋙ ⋈ ⋙ closed Tue (l.s.), Oct, 90. Rest. ♦ ♪ 60-125.

FONTENAY-LE-COMTE*

La Rochelle 49, Cholet 76, Paris 409 km
pop 16650 ⊠ 85200   B2

The town is divided into two different areas on each side of the Vendée river. ▶ On the right bank is an aristocratic district (houses dating from Renaissance to Classical times) : tower of **Notre-Dame** (15th-17thC; inside : Renaissance chapel and Romanesque crypt; in front of the church is the **Vendée Museum** *(in season, 10-12 & 2-6, Sat. and Sun. am only; out of season, 2-6, closed Mon. and Tue.)*; nearby : beautiful buildings along Rue du Pont-aux-Chèvres and **Place Belliard**. ▶ Via Rue de la Fontaine, **Quatre-Tias fountain** (Renaissance). ▶ On the left bank, the town is typified by the busy Rue de la République; parallel, is **Rue des Loges** : older houses (some of them half-timbered) leading to the Gothic and Renaissance **church of St. Jean,** in the district of the same name. ▶ Towards the W exit, along the right bank : **château of Terre-Neuve★** (rich collections, ceilings and fireplaces *(daily 9-12 & 2-5)*.

Nearby

▶ Round trip through the Mervent Forest (→). ▶ Via the Niort road, former **abbey of Nieul-sur-l'Autize** *(10 km)* : Romanesque cloister★★ and chapter room. ▶ 3 km farther, **Oulmes** : church (partially 11thC). ▶ Short tour of the Autize valleys *(N)* : **Saint-Pompain** carvings on the doorway of Romanesque church. ▶ Neo-classic façade on Moulières castle, located in a park (no visits). ▶ **Coulonges-sur-l'Autize** : covered market, Renaissance castle. ▶ **Saint-Hilaire-des-Loges**, site occupied since prehistoric times ; Gallo-Roman and Merovingian ruins ; Romanesque church cupola ; menhirs ; in nearby Niort, reminders of a formerly strong drapery industry. ☐

Practical Information _____

FONTENAY-LE-COMTE
ⓘ quai du Poey-d'Avant, ☎ 51.69.44.99, closed Mon and Sun (l.s.).
🚂 pl. Verdun, ☎ 51.69.46.44.

Hotel :
★★ *Rabelais*, (Inter-hôtel, L.F.), rte de Parthenay, ☎ 51.69.86.20, DC Euro Visa, 37 rm Ⓟ ⫟ 卌 ⟋ ⤳ 🅖 ♿
▭ 230. Rest. ♦ ⫟ ⟋ ♿ 55-120 ; child : 40.

Restaurant :
♦♦ *Les Chouans Gourmets*, 6, rue des Halles, ☎ 51.69.55.92, AE Euro Visa ⫟ 卌 ⟋ closed Mon and Sun eve ex hols, Feb, 1-15 Jul. Fish a specialty, 70-160 ; child : 35.

⚠ ★★★*Chêne Tord* (80 pl), ☎ 51.00.20.63 ; ★★★*La Joletière* (45 pl), ☎ 51.00.26.87.

Recommended
Youth hostel : *F.J.T.*, rue des Gravants.

Nearby

VOUVANT, ✉ 85120, 11 km N.

Hotel :
★★ *Auberge de Maître Pannetier* (L.F.), pl. du Corps-de-Garde, ☎ 51.00.80.12, AE Euro Visa, 7 rm Ⓟ closed Mon (l.s.), 1-15 Oct, 140. Rest. ♦ 55-120.

FOURAS

Rochefort 14, La Rochelle 27, Paris 478 km
pop 3297 ✉ 17450   B2

Seaside resort and fishing port ; Napoléon left from here in July 1815 on his way to the island of Aix.

▶ Beautiful pine and holm oak forest (15 acre Casino Park) overlooking Semaphore beach. ▶ Tour of the 15thC **fort** (regional museum) *(in season : 3-6, daily ; winter : Sun. and nat. hols.).* ▶ **Fumée Point** *(3 km ; departure place for Aix Island).* ☐

Practical Information _____

ⓘ pl. Bujeau and av. du Casino, ☎ 46.88.60.69.
🚂 *R.D.P.E.*, ☎ 46.88.60.50, from Pointe de la Fumée, 3 km to île d'Aix.

Hotel :
★★ *Grand Hôtel des Bains*, 15, rue du Gal-Brüncher, ☎ 46.84.03.44, 36 rm 卌 ⟋ closed 22 Sep-May, 150. Rest. ♦ ⟋ 🎾 70-140.

⚠ ★★*Le Cadoret* (600 pl), ☎ 46.84.02.84.

Les HERBIERS

Cholet 25, La Roche-sur-Yon 40, Paris 374 km
pop 12494 ✉ 85500   B1

In the heart of the hilliest region of Vendée, this is a livestock market town, and a centre of the shoe, pleasure-boat building and furniture industries.

▶ A **Gothic church** with Romanesque bell-tower, and another 15thC **church** in **Petit-Bourg** *(S)*, survived the burning of the town during the Vendée wars in 1794.

Nearby

Beaurepaire *(8 km NW)* : ruined castle, once the headquarters of the Central army. ▶ 4 km farther, **La Gaubretière**, "pantheon of the Vendée military", the starting point for the insurrection. ▶ N, via the road to Cholet : **Mont des Alouettes**★ (alt. 231 m ; orientation table ; panorama). The windmill vanes were used for signalling in 1793 during the Vendée Wars. ▶ **Le Puy-du-Fou** (peak ; *11 km S ;* part of **Epesses**) : Renaissance château partially burnt down during the Vendée Wars *(daily 9-6 ; late evening shows in summer ;* interesting **Ecomuseum**, *Jun.-Sep., 10-12 & 3-6, closed Mon., Oct.-May Sat. and Sun. afternoons only, 10-12 & 2-6, closed Mon. and Tue.).* ▶ Via La Roche-sur-Yon road *(6 km SW)* : **Grainetière Abbey** *(2 km S ;* 12th-15thC) : cloister★ *(daily Jul.-Aug. ; Sun. pm out of season).* ▶ N of crossroads, **La Tricherie** Lake : leisure centre. ▶ Farther on, via **Vendrennes**, château ruins of **Parc-Soubise** burned down during the Vendée wars. ☐

Practical Information _____

ⓘ centre du Lavoir, ☎ 51.91.07.67 (l.s.) ; ☎ 51.67.18.39 (h.s.).

Hotel :
● *Le Centre* (L.F.), 6, rue de l'Eglise, ☎ 51.67.01.75, 8 rm, closed Fri eve, Sat eve, Sun eve (l.s.), 1-15 Jan, 1-22 Aug, 110. Rest. ● ♦ ⟋ A famous site of the Vendée wars, and a gastronomic landmark, too : fresh fish, 45-130.

Recommended
Guided tours : ☎ 51.57.64.64, tour of the region in a steam-engine train, Jun-Oct.

JARNAC

Les Sables-d'Olonne 20, La Rochelle 80, Paris 470 km
pop 4917 ✉ 16200   B3

Great cognac producer *(visit the cellars),* and home town of President François Mitterrand (1916) ; Romano-Gothic crypt in the church.

Nearby

▶ 3 km N, site of **Coussac-les-Métairies** : sepulchral mound. ▶ On the right bank, by way of the Charente valley, **Triac** *(5 km)* : pyramid marking the assassination of Condé by Montesquiou (1569). ▶ **Bassac** *(8 km)* : partially Romanesque abbey★ *(3-6).* ▶ **Vibrac** *(11 km)* : Renaissance church. From Vibrac to Angeac : road with 6 Roman bridges. ☐

Practical Information _____

JARNAC
ⓘ pl. du Château, ☎ 45.81.09.30, closed Sun.   ♥
🚆 ☎ 45.81.07.09.
🚢 cruises on the Charente, info S.I.

Hotels :
● ★★★ *Château de Fleurac* (C.H.), Fleurac, 10 km NE, ☎ 45.81.78.22, 18 rm Ⓟ 卌 ⟋ closed Sun eve and Mon (l.s.), 1 Nov-15 Dec, 300. Rest. ♦♦ ⟋ 🎾 Spec : *crabe gratiné au champagne* 110-160.
★★ *Orangerie*, quai de l'Orangerie, ☎ 45.81.13.72, 10 rm 卌 210.

Restaurant :
♦ *Château*, 15, pl. du Château, ☎ 45.81.07.17, Euro Visa Ⓟ ⟋ closed Mon, Sat noon, Sun eve , Feb school hols, 17 Aug-10 Sep. Spec : *charentaises au cognac et pineau*, seafood, 75-160.

⚠ ★★*Municipal* (200 pl), ☎ 45.81.18.54.

Nearby

VIBRAC, ⊠ 16120 Châteauneuf-sur-Charente, 11 km SE.

Hotel :
● ★★ *Les Ombrages* (L.F.), ☎ 45.97.32.33, Euro Visa, 10 rm P ⬛ 🍴 ⚜ ⌂ ⚲ closed Sun eve and Mon (l.s.), 18-28 Feb, 28 Oct-7 Nov, 15 Dec-3 Jan, 145. Rest. ♦ ⚲ 60-130.

JONZAC

Saintes 49, Angoulême 60, Paris 613 km
pop 4873 ⊠ 17500   B3

Rich in prehistoric sites (e.g. caves in Heurtebise) and buildings from the time of pilgrimages to Compostela, this former Protestant stronghold has become an important market for cognac *(Petite Champagne)*, pineau and Charentes butter.
On the right bank of the Seugne, well-restored castle-keep and doorway of 14th-16thC **château.** ▶ On the left bank, in the "suburb" of **Carmes,** is a former convent housing a cultural center.

Nearby

▶ **Champagnac** *(5 km SE)* : Romanesque church remodelled during the Gothic period ; another Romanesque church at **Fontaines-d'Ozillac** (doorway arches★). ▶ 12 km W on the Pons to Blaye road : **Plassac Château★** (18thC) in a park *(exterior visit only ; pineau tasting).* ▶ 4 km S, remains of the former **abbey of La Tenaille** : Saintonge façade ; 18thC buildings. □

Practical Information

ℹ️ mairie, ☎ 46.48.04.11.
SNCF ☎ 46.48.00.36.

Hotel :
★★ *Le Club*, 8, pl. de l'Eglise, ☎ 46.48.02.27, Euro Visa, 15 rm P 🍴 ⚲ 145.

Restaurants :
● ♦♦ *Moulin de Marcouze*, Mosnac sur Seugne, ☎ 46.70.46.16, Visa P ⚘ Dominique Bouchet, chef at the Tour d'Argent, loves to breathe the bracing air of his native region at this charming Charentais mill. Regional dishes, 150-200.
♦♦ *Du côté des Carmes*, 31, rue des Carmes, ☎ 46.48.21.82, Euro Visa P 🍴 ⚲ closed Mon, Sat noon, Sun eve , Jan, Xmas, 85-110.
♦ *Vieux Logis*, Clam, 6 km, ☎ 46.48.15.11 P ⚘ ⬛ ⚲ ⚲ ⅃ ⛵ closed Mon (l.s.), 15 Nov-10 Dec, 60-180.

LOUDUN

Châtellerault 49, Tours 72, Paris 314 km
pop 8448 ⊠ 86200   C1

Overlooking the town, the "Square Tower" (11th-12thC) provides a panorama.

▶ In the lower town, **St. Croix Church** (11thC choir) converted into a covered market. ▶ Above, Gothic and Renaissance **church of St. Pierre.** ▶ West of the butte, on the **Rue de Martray,** is a **regional museum** (with African collection) and the former Carmelite Gothic and Renaissance church of St. Hilaire ; mediaeval city gate. ▶ To the S, **La Chaussée : Maison de l'Acadie** (Acadia House, books, documents about history of Loudunaise families who emigrated to Acadia in the 17thC ; *by appt., tel. 49.98.15.96).*

Le Loudunois *(approx. 4 hr)*

▶ To the N and NW, numerous megaliths, covered market (Pierre Folle) and dolmens (itinerary of the Dive valley). ▶ In the Dive valley, to the W, underground dove-cote of **Tourtenay,** castle-keep at **Curçay,** and churches at **Glénouze, Saint-Laon, Chasseigne.** ▶ To the NE, **château**

de la Grande-Jaille ; SE, ruins of **Rigny castle** *(10 km)*, church of Dercé, ruins of Renaissance castle **La Roche-du-Maine** in a vast landscape. □

Practical Information

ℹ️ hôtel de ville, ☎ 49.98.15.38.   ♥
SNCF ☎ 49.22.00.32.

Hotel :
★★ *La Roue d'Or* (L.F.), 1, av. d'Anjou, ☎ 49.98.01.23, AE Euro Visa, 16 rm P 🍴 130. Rest. ● ♦ ⅃ Simple cooking : *canard à l'orange, tête de veau,* 55-160.

LUÇON*

La Roche-sur-Yon 32, La Rochelle 51, Paris 433 km
pop 9500 ⊠ 85400   B1-2

Large agricultural market town on a hill at the edge of the drained marshes.

▶ Gothic **cathedral** (13th-14thC) with Classical façade and 85 m spire, lovely Romanesque doorway (south side) and pulpit from which Richelieu preached. ▶ To the S, a Renaissance cloister★ inside the episcopal palace. ▶ Behind the town hall is a landscaped park *(topiary of scenes from La Fontaine's Fables)*, the **Jardin Dumaine★.**

Nearby

▶ **Mareuil-sur-Lay** *(10 km N)* : bell-tower of Romanesque church★ ; ruins and keep of Renaissance castle. ▶ Saint-Cyr-en-Talmondais *(13 km W)* : ornamental fireplaces, tapestries, prehistoric and antique collections in the **La Court-d'Aron Château** *(daily Jun.-Sep., 9-12 & 2-5)*; **flower shows** in park *(May-Oct.)*; **Curzon** *(2 km S)* : Romanesque crypt.★   □

Practical Information

ℹ️ 7, pl. Leclerc, ☎ 51.56.36.52.
SNCF ☎ 51.56.01.49.

Hotel :
● ★★ *Le Bordeaux*, 14, pl. des Acacias, ☎ 51.56.01.35, AE DC Euro Visa, 24 rm P ⅃ ⚲ closed Sun eve, 250. Rest. ● ♦♦ ⅃ 👶 Simple, good and cheap : *huîtres chaudes à la crème de champagne, médaillon de lotte à l'émincé de jeunes poireaux.* Rosé and red Mareuil wines, 70-100 ; child : 35.

LUSIGNAN

Poitiers 24, Niort 47, Paris 360 km
pop 2855 ⊠ 86600   C2

Castle of the Counts (panorama from Blossac promenade), built, according to legend, in one night by the fairy Mélusine. A number of Crusader "Kings" of Jerusalem were born here.

▶ Set back from the fortified site, the Romanesque church★ (bell-tower) with its Gothic gate-tower was badly damaged during the Hundred Years' War between France and England. Bertrand de Got was prior there until he became Pope Clement V ; he was the Pope who transferred the papacy to Avignon (1309), and subsequently suppressed the Order of Templars (1312). ▶ **Jazeneuil** *(6 km NW on the Vonne)* : former priory church (11th-12thC) on a site inhabited since Gallo-Roman times.   □

Practical Information

ℹ️ ☎ 49.43.31.36.   ♥
SNCF ☎ 49.43.31.26.

Hotel :
Les Promenades (L.F.), 19, rte de Poitiers, RN 11, ☎ 49.43.31.35, 10 rm P ⬛ half pens, 195. Rest. ♦ 👶 60-105.

⛺ ★★*Vauchiron* (100 pl), ☎ 49.43.30.08.

MAILLEZAIS*

Fontenay-le-Comte 15, Niort 29, Paris 436 km
pop 939 ⊠ 85420   B2

11thC abbey built on an islet in the middle of a marsh (still at that time the Bay of Poitou). The abbey's mission was to drain and improve the surrounding lands. The ruins of the foundation can still be seen on the oddly-shaped mound. Rabelais spent some time here as a refugee with the Benedictines. At the end of the 16thC, after he was destroyed by the Protestants, a Huguenot fortress was built in his honor by the governor, Agrippa d'Aubigné.

▶ The imposing remains of the **church** (Romanesque choir, Gothic walls in the nave with ogival windows)★ overlook an immense esplanade; S, former **monastic buildings** (13th-14thC), built in a square : the dormitory, monks' refectory, Rabelais' "dungeon" and the kitchen with its octagonal ventilation tower, now a lapidary museum *(daily 9-12 & 2-7, 8 in summer)*. ▶ Boat cruises leave from the port on the Autize, at the foot of the terrace. ▶ In the village centre, a Romanesque **church** heavily restored in the 19thC (12thC façade★ ; 13thC cross in cemetery).   □

MATHA

Angoulême 47, Poitiers 114, Paris 447 km
pop 2303 ⊠ 17160   B2

Crafts centre from which horse-back and horse-drawn caravan excursions are organised; important cereal, wine and dairy market *(visits to distilleries and co-operative dairy)*.

▶ Fortified gate in Gothic town walls. ▶ Large Gothic church with Romanesque façade★ and raised Gothic choir in the **Saint-Hérie** quarter.

Nearby

▶ **Marestay** *(1 km N)* : former Romanesque abbey partly destroyed during the Religious wars. ▶ 12thC Romanesque church at **Blanzac-lès-Matha** *(3 km, toward Saint-Jean)*. ▶ SE, on the road to Angoulême, **Brie-sous-Matha** : choir capitals in the Romanesque church; Renaissance castle of **Neuvicq**, on the side of a hill.   □

MELLE*

Poitiers 46, Saintes 72, Paris 391 km
pop 4575 ⊠ 79500   B-C2

Former stopover for Compostela pilgrims, once renowned for its sanctuaries, inns and mule fairs.

▶ Underground **Loubeau** silver mines *(1 km S of town; Jul.-Aug., 2-6)*. ▶ Three large Romanesque churches : in lower town, **St. Hilaire**★★ with impressive apsidial chapels, equestrian statue above side doorway, interior decoration (cornices, arches over inner doorway). ▶ **St. Savinien** (early 12thC) houses a music festival in May-Jun. ▶ N, church of **St. Pierre** (12th-13thC).

Nearby

▶ **Lezay** *(11 km NE)* : goat, calf and cheese fairs. ▶ **Celles-sur-Belle** *(7 km NW)* : Gothic church with multifoil arches★ over doorway incorporated into narthex★. ▶ **Javarzay** *(15 km SE)* : Renaissance château in park *(Oct.-Apr., by appt.)* and partially Romanesque church. ▶ 2 km farther, **Chef-Boutonne** : well known for goose preserves; feudal mound, ancient buildings.   □

MERVENT Forest*

B1-2
Round trip from Fontenay *(64 km; full day)*

One of the densest and most beautiful forests in Western France, covering 6000 acres NE of Fontenay-le-Comte (→). Mervent is known for its wildness and the quality of its oak and chestnut trees. The forest is now part of the **nature park of Vendé-Val-de-Sèvre**.

▶ **Fontenay-le-Comte** (→). ▶ Follow La Chataigneraie road to Pissotte *(4 km)*, turn right. ▶ **Mervent dam**, on the Vendée river; lake 9 km long, reservoir holding 8.5 million m³. ▶ Via Oulières road, **Gros-Roc zoological park** *(13 km; 10-6, 5 in winter)*. ▶ **Citardière** Château *(15 km, ext. visit only)*. ▶ **Mervent★** *(17 km)* : former fortified town above the Mère river; from the terrace of now-vanished castle, panorama★ *(beach, bathing etc.)*. ▶ Cross the **Pierre-Brune chênaie** (oak-grove). ▶ **Vouvant★** *(31 km)* : **Mélusine Tower** (13thC) and 30 m high keep (panorama); in town, ornamented side doorway★ of church. ▶ **Foussais** *(40 km)* : Romanesque sculptures on façade (Descent from the Cross★). ▶ Saint-Hilaire-des-Loges *(48 km; → nearby Fontenay-le-Comte)*.   □

Practical Information _____

MERVENT, ⊠ 85200 Fontenay-le-Comte, 10 km N of **Fontenay-le-Comte**.
ⓘ le Vieux Château, ☎ 51.00.20.97, closed Mon (l.s.).

Hotel :
★ *Ermitage de Pierre Brune*, ☎ 51.00.25.53, 18 rm Ⓟ ≰ 🍽 ⌣ 𝄢 ⌐ closed 15 Nov-15 Mar, 110. Rest. ♦ ≰ ♪ 45-100; child : 40.

⚐ ★★★*Chêne-Tord* (80 pl), ☎ 51.00.20.63.

MONTENDRE

Bordeaux 62, Saintes 62, Paris 518 km
pop 3383 ⊠ 17130   B3

A park surrounds the well-restored keep (12thC); viewpoints over the pines of Tout-y-Faut *(S)* and Bussac *(SE)* heaths.

Towards the Double river

▶ Via **Montlieux-la-Garde** *(12 km SE)* feudal ruins; **Montguyon** *(19 km)* : known for international folklore festival *(mid-Jul.)*; vestiges of château (12th-15thC), superb keep rising above trees. ▶ 2 km N, Pierre-Folle dolmen.   □

Practical Information _____

MONTENDRE
ⓘ av. de la République, ☎ 46.49.46.45 (h.s.); mairie, ☎ 46.49.20.84.   ♥
🚆 ☎ 46.49.40.04.

Hotel:
★★ *Deux Gares et Pins*, 20, av. de la Gare, ☎ 46.49.43.57, 14 rm Ⓟ 🍽 closed Xmas school hols, Feb, 1 Nov, 150. Rest. ♦ ♪ 65-140.

⚐ ★★★*Forêt* (45 pl), ☎ 46.49.20.17.

Nearby

MONTGUYON, ⊠ 17270, 19 km SE.
ⓘ mairie, ☎ 46.04.10.19.

Hotel:
★ *Poste* (L.F.), 18, av. de la République, ☎ 46.04.19.39, Euro Visa, 18 rm Ⓟ 🍽 ⅙ 🖵 90. Rest. ♦ ⅙ 40-90.

NIORT

0   100   200 m

MONTMORILLON*

Poitiers 48, Limoges 84, Paris 362 km
pop 7541 ⊠ 86500   C2

The chevet of Notre-Dame looms over the old town on the right bank of the Gartempe, across the river from the modern quarter.
▶ The apse of the church (12th-14thC), decorated inside with **frescos**★ (Mystical Marriage of St. Catherine), is built over a crypt decorated with Romanesque frescos.
▶ 500 m S, **archaeological museum** in former Augustinian Maison-Dieu (hospital); storied frieze in Romanesque **St. Laurent church**; strange 12thC building in park, the **Octogone**★, former chapel-mausoleum.

Nearby

▶ In Gartempe Valley (S) : **Plaisance** *(12 km)*, mediaeval church and Merovingian vaults. ▶ Upstream, canoeing and kayaking in the **Gorges d'Enfer.** ▶ To SE, lantern of the dead at Moussac *(via D117)*; **Bourg-Archambault** castle *(13 km;* 13th-15thC), still inhabited. ▶ NE, lantern of the dead at **Journet** *(11 km)*; Romanesque abbey church in **Villesalem** (arches★ of side doorway), classical monastic buildings.   □

Practical Information

ⓘ av. F.-Tribot, ☎ 46.91.11.96, 14-18, closed Sat and Sun.
SNCF ☎ 49.91.00.60.

Hotel :
★★ *France*, 2, bd de Strasbourg, ☎ 49.91.00.51, AE DC Euro Visa, 25 rm ♪ closed Sun eve and Mon, Jan, 150. Rest. ◆◆ ♪ ఉ 95-200.

> Be advised that hotels and restaurants in this Guide have perhaps changed addresses; prices indicated are also subject to modifications.

NIORT*

Rochefort 60, Poitiers 74, Paris 407 km
pop 60230 ⊠ 79000   B2

Formerly a cloth and leather centre, the city has developed into a major centre of the insurance business (more than half the inhabitants are employed in service industries).

▶ Standing above the Vieux-Ponts (Old Bridges), two enormous square towers, attached to the Romanesque **keep**★ house an interesting **museum**★ of arts and local customs and Poitevin ethnology *(daily 9-12 & 2-6, 5 in winter; closed Tue.).* ▶ From the bridges via **Rue du Pont** (old houses) to the **Hôtel du Pilori** (former town hall). Renaissance building housing numismatic and archaeological museum *(daily 9-12 & 2-6, 5 in winter; closed Tue.).*
▶ **Rue St. Jean** (pedestrian); half-timbered houses, leading to **church of Notre-Dame** (tapestries), and the **Hôtel de Ville.** ▶ Natural History and **Fine Arts Museums**★ (paintings★ ; *9-12 & 2-6; 5 in winter; closed Tue.).* ▶ 70 m spires of St. André near the **Jardin des Plantes** (botanical gardens), terraced above the Sèvre (viewpoints).

Nearby

▶ Round trip of the Poitou Marshes *(→).* ▶ N, the Sèvre and Egray valleys : via **Echiré** *(8 km)*, Taillée Château (17thC) and romantic ruins (12th-13thC) of **Coudray-Salbart**★, above the Sèvre *(Mar.-Oct., 9-12 & 2-7, closed Tue.).* ▶ Via the road to **Secondigny, Champdeniers** *(12 km)*; Romanesque church and crypt. ▶ Return via **Egray Valley :** Romanesque church of **Sainte-Ouenne** remarkably well-restored; fortified 15thC manor at Gazeau, château ruins of Mursay where Agrippa d'Aubigné once lived. ▶ SE, **Aiffres** *(6 km)* : lantern of the dead. ▶ 24 km SW, Romanesque church and Renaissance castle in **Mauzé-sur-le-Mignon;** 5 km W, **Olbreuse manor :** organized hikes and excursions.   □

Practical Information

NIORT
ℹ️ pl. de la Poste (B2), ☎ 49.24.18.79, closed Sun.
SNCF ☎ 49.24.50.50/49.24.24.77/49.24.13.20.
🚌 pl. St-Hilaire, ☎ 49.24.50.56.
Car rental : Avis, 89, rue de la Gare (B-C3),
☎ 49.24.36.98 ; train station.

Hotels :
★★★ *Grand Hôtel*, 32, av. de Paris (C2), ☎ 49.24.22.21,
40 rm 🅿 ⚹ ⚘ ❊ 290.
★★★ *La Brèche*, 8, av. Bujault (B2), ☎ 49.24.41.78, 49 rm,
closed 24 Dec-7 Jan, 210.
★★ *Terminus* (L.F.), 82, rue de la Gare (B3),
☎ 49.24.00.38, AE DC Euro Visa, 42 rm 🅶 closed
20 Dec-2 Jan, 200. Rest. ● ◆ *La Poêle d'Or* ⚹ 🅶
closed Sat and Sun eve. J.-L. Tavernier favours tasty regional dishes : magret de canard au blanc du Poitou, sole
pochée au muscadet, 65-200 ; child : 40.

Restaurants :
● ◆◆ *Le Relais Saint-Antoine*, pl. de la Brèche (B2),
☎ 49.24.02.76, AE DC Euro Visa ⚹ 🅶 closed Sat ,
Feb school hols, 5-26 Jul. Modern cuisine prepared by the
capable Thierry Fichet : moisson de la mer en estouffade
aux épinards vapeur, canette truffée aux figues et pruneaux. All this in a contemporary "Design" setting. Dois-
neau, Man Ray, Texier on the walls, 70-200.
◆◆ *La Tuilerie*, rte de La Rochelle, Bessines (2 km),
☎ 49.09.12.45, Euro Visa ⚹ ⚹ 🅶 ☐ closed Sun eve,
80-240 ; child : 35.
● ◆ *Voyageurs*, 32, pl. de l'Hôtel-de-Ville, Beauvoir-sur-
Niort (5 km SW), ☎ 49.09.70.16, Euro Visa ⚹ 🅶 closed
Wed , Sun eve and Feb school hols. J.-C. Batiot's cooking
is rooted in affection for the land : jambon de pays
grillé, 50-230.
◆ *A La Belle Etoile*, 115, quai Maurice-Métayer (A2),
☎ 49.73.31.29, AE DC Euro Visa ⚹ ⚹ closed Mon and
Sun eve. Your choice of menu : regional gastronomy or
market cuisine, 70-160.

🅰 ★★★*Parc des loisirs* (150 pl), ☎ 49.79.05.33 ; ★★*Municipal* (150 pl), ☎ 49.79.05.06.

Recommended
Baby-sitting : *C.D.I.J.,* ☎ 49.24.24.57.
♥ auctions : 52, rue de la Gare, ☎ 49.24.03.03 ; cheese :
La Maison du Fromage, 19, rue St-Jean.

Nearby

La **CRÈCHE**, ✉ 79260, 10 km NE.

Hotel :
● ★★★ *Motel des Rocs* (R.S.), Chavagné,
☎ 49.25.50.38, Tx 790632, AE DC Euro Visa, 51 rm, 300.
Rest. ◆◆ ⚹ 100-250.

île de NOIRMOUTIER*
(Noirmoutier Island)
A1

A large flat island (average altitude 8 m, 15 000 acres),
reached by boat from Pornic, driving through the marshes at low tide via the Gois causeway, or any time
via the toll bridge. There are in fact two islands, connected by the isthmus of Tresson, in the centre of
semi-disused salt marshes. Known for its mild climate
and sunshine ; mimosa bloom in mid-Feb., Mediterranean trees grow in the Chaize woods.

Only N part of the island is touristically interesting.
▶ Beyond the cultivated dunes (pine groves) of **Barbâtre**
(population 1 091, beautiful beaches), is the salt-marsh
region. ▶ **La Guerinière** (population 1 305, to W) : museum
of arts and local traditions (Apr.-Oct.). ▶ **Noirmoutier-en-
l'Ile** (4 327 inhabitants) : fishing port on a 2 km wide
channel : Romanesque keep on the Place d'Armes ; 18thC
mansions ; museum (exceptional collection of English
faïence ; Jun.-Sep., closed Tue.) ; E of esplanade, St. Philibert church, ruins of monastery founded in 7thC and de-

stroyed by the Normans (Romanesque choir, Merovingian
crypt). ▶ 2 km farther are the beaches of Dames and
Souzeaux with a lighthouse tower emerging from the holm
oak of the **Chaize** Woods★. ▶ 5 km NW, **L'Herbaudière** :
sardine port which has become an important leisure centre. □

Practical Information

BARBÂTRE, ✉ 85630, 15 km N of **Fromentine**.
ℹ️ 1, rte du Pont, ☎ 51.39.80.71, closed Sun (l.s.).
🚢 from Pornic to Le Bois-de-la-Chaize (plage des
Dames).

Hotels :
★★★ *Saint-Paul*, Le Bois de la Chaize, ☎ 51.39.05.63,
48 rm ⚹ ⚹ ⚘ ⚹ closed Oct-Apr, 300. Rest. ◆◆ ⚹ ❊
100-160.
● ★★ *Les Prateaux* (R.S.), Le Bois de la Chaize,
☎ 51.39.12.52, Tx 711933, 13 rm 🅿 ⚹ 🅶 ❊ closed
30 Sep-15 Mar, 270. Rest. ◆◆ 🅶 130-150.

🅰 ★★★*Les Onchères* (600 pl), ☎ 51.39.81.31.

La **GUÉRINIÈRE**, ✉ 85680, 5 km S of **Noirmoutier-en-l'Ile**.

Hotel :
★★★ *Punta Lara*, ☎ 51.39.11.58, 60 rm 🅿 ⚹ ⚹ ⚹ ☐ ⚹
closed 15 Oct-30 Mar, 540. Rest. ◆◆ ⚹ 155-220.

NOIRMOUTIER-EN-L'ILE, ✉ 85330.
ℹ️ quai Jean-Bart, ☎ 51.39.12.42 (h.s.).
🚌 ☎ 51.39.04.72.

Hotels :
★★★ *Général d'Elbée*, pl. du Château, ☎ 51.39.10.29,
33 rm ⚹ ☐ closed Oct-Mar. Fine 18th-C residence, 350.
Rest. ◆◆ ⚹ 70-130.
● ★★ *Fleur de Sel* (L.F.), rue des Saulniers,
☎ 51.39.21.59, Tx 701229, Euro Visa, 23 rm 🅿 ⚹ ⚹ ⚹
🅶 ❊ ☐ half pens (h.s.), closed Sun eve and Mon (Feb-
Apr), 15 Nov-31 Jan, 550. Rest. ● ◆ ⚹ ⚹ 🅶 Spec :
moules du Gois gratinées, suprême de bar à la maraîchine,
95-165 ; child : 50.

Restaurant :
● ◆ *Le Grand Four*, 1, rue de la Cure, ☎ 51.39.12.24,
Visa ⚹ closed Tue eve and Wed ex Jul-Aug, 4 Jan-28 Feb.
Seasonal cuisine based on seafood ; warm ambience.
Good homemade desserts, 70-160.

île d' OLÉRON**
(Oléron Island)
A2

Du Pont : Marennes 10, Saintes 49, Paris 496 km

The 3 km toll viaduct from Chapus Point runs to
France's largest Atlantic island (175 km², 30 km NW-
SE). Flat, like Aix and the Île de Ré, with massive
dunes (30 m) on W coast, covered with pine and holm
oak. The mild climate encourages exceptional flower
growth (mimosa festival in Feb.). This "island of perfumes" was always more given to farming than fishing
— Pliny the Elder praised its vineyards. But oyster farming has grown considerably in the last 50 years and
is now a larger industry (at Le Château) than fishing
(from La Cotinière).

Round trip of the island *(full day)*

▶ **Le Château-d'Oléron** (population 3 411), oyster-farming
centre, at the foot of citadel (17thC, seriously damaged
in 1945 ; small oyster museum : guided tours of oyster
parks). ▶ **Dolus-d'Oléron** (population 2 152) : attractive
white houses. ▶ **Boyardville-d'Oléron** (commune of Saint-
Georges) : military port established by Napoleon ; at the
foot of wooded **Saumonards** dunes, beautiful beach
(naturists). ▶ **Saint-Georges-d'Oléron** (population 2 935),
among the vines : doorway★ of Romanesque church (only
historic monument on island). ▶ Via **Saint-Denis-d'Oléron** (population 1 020) (beach and sailing), **Chassiron** Lighthouse (afternoons only, off season ; panorama). ▶ Bird

sanctuary on cliffs of N coast. ▶ **Domino** : **Sables-Vigniers** beach and dunes. ▶ **La Cotinière** fishing port.
▶ **Saint-Pierre-d'Oléron** (population 4 782) : lantern of the dead (13thC) near bell-tower (viewpoint); on the same street, Eleanor of Aquitaine Museum *(15 Jun.-15 Sep., closed Sun., 10-12 & 3-6)*. ▶ Through the beautiful **forests★** of **Remingeasse** and **Vert-Bois** to **Grand-Village** : small Oléron Museum *(in season)*. ▶ **Saint-Trojan-les-Bains** (population 1 470) : one of the country's great coastal spas, on the edge of 5 000 acres of forest★; fishing and pleasure-craft port; small train *(in summer)* to **Gatseau** Point on the straits of Maumusson (beaches).   ☐

Oyster farming
in the Marennes-Oléron basin

The Seudre estuary and the shoals round the Oléron island make this the greatest oyster-producing area in Europe, and perhaps in the world in terms of quality. The 2 500 concessions provide a living for 25 000 people, and an annual yield of 40 000 tons (half of France's production). Guided tours of the farms leave from the ports of Chapus, Bourcefranc and Marennes ; from La Tremblade and Etaules ; and, of course, from Le Château-d'Oléron. The educational museums in Fort-Louvois, Marennes, Etaules and La Tremblade are also worth visiting.

Practical Information _____

BOYARDVILLE, ⊠ 17190 Saint-Georges-d'Oléron, 15 km from **Le pont d'Oléron**.
ℹ ☎ 46.47.04.76.

Hotel :
★★ *Bains*, ☎ 46.47.01.02, AE DC Euro Visa, 10 rm ℗ ≪ half pens (h.s.), closed 15 Sep to Pentecost, 400. Rest. ♦ ≪ ♪ 65-185 ; child : 45.

⚑ ★★★★*Signol* (330 pl), ☎ 46.47.01.22.

Le **CHÂTEAU-D'OLÉRON**, ⊠ 17480, 3 km from **Le pont d'Oléron**.
ℹ pl. de la République, ☎ 46.47.60.51.

Hotel :
★ *France*, ☎ 46.47.60.07, 11 rm ✺ closed Fri and Sat (l.s.), 1-15 Oct, 15 Dec-31 Jan, 160. Rest. ♦ ♪ 70-210.

⚑ ★★★*Montravail* (130 pl), ☎ 46.47.61.82.

Recommended
Leisure activities : tours of oyster beds.

La **COTINIÈRE**, ⊠ 17310 Saint-Pierre-d'Oléron, 16 km from **Le pont d'Oléron**.
ℹ ☎ 46.47.09.08.

Hotel :
★★★ *Le Vivier*, 65, rue du Port, ☎ 46.47.10.31, Visa, 8 rm ≪ ≪ half pens, closed Sun eve and Mon (l.s.), 4 Nov-31 Jan, 625. Rest. ♦♦ ≪ ♪ ✺ Spec : *feuilleté de foie gras et homard, steack de canard aux langoustines et choux verts*, 105-238.

DOLUS-D'OLÉRON, ⊠ 17550, 10 km from **Le Pont d'Oléron**.
ℹ ☎ 46.75.32.84.

Hotel :
★★★★ *Le Grand Large* (L.F.), Baie de la Rémigeasse, ☎ 46.75.37.89, Tx 790395, 31 rm ℗ ≪ ≪ ⚬ ☐ ✺ half pens (h.s.), closed 15 Oct-31 Mar, 1280. Rest. ♦♦ *L'Amiral* ≪ ♪ 160-260.

SAINT-DENIS-D'OLÉRON, ⊠ 17650, 33 km from **Le pont d'Oléron**.
ℹ ☎ 46.47.85.87.

Hotel :
★★ *L'Ormeau*, 1, rue de la Libération, ☎ 46.47.86.72, Visa, 27 rm ℗ ≪ ⚬ ✺ closed Wed (Oct-Easter), 145.

SAINT-GEORGES-D'OLÉRON, ⊠ 17190, 20 km from **Le pont d'Oléron**.

Restaurant :
♦♦ *Les Trois Chapons*, 240, rte de Saint-Pierre, ☎ 46.76.51.51, AE DC Euro Visa ℗ ⚬ ♪ closed Mon eve and Tue, 1 Dec-15 Jan, 100-250.

⚑ ★★★★*Rex, Domino* (450 pl), ☎ 46.76.55.97 ; ★★★*La Désirade* (150 pl), ☎ 46.76.54.43 ; ★★★*Le Suroît* (250 pl), ☎ 46.47.07.25.

SAINT-PIERRE-D'OLÉRON, ⊠ 17310, 14 km from **Le pont d'Oléron**.
ℹ pl. Gambetta, ☎ 46.47.11.39.

Hotel :
★★ *Atlantic*, la Menounière, ☎ 46.47.07.09, Visa, 20 rm ℗ ≪ ⚬ ♪ ⚬ half pens (h.s.), closed Oct-Easter, 360. Rest. ♦ ♪ ⚬ 55-90.

⚑ ★★★*Les Cercelles* (70 pl), ☎ 46.47.19.24.

SAINT-TROJAN-LES-BAINS, ⊠ 17370, 8 km from **Le pont d'Oléron**.
ℹ bd P.-Wiehn and carrefour du Port, ☎ 46.76.00.86, closed Wed and Sun (l.s.).

Hotels :
★★★ *Les Cleunes*, ☎ 46.76.03.08, AE DC Euro Visa, 49 rm ℗ ≪ ≪ ⚬ ✺ ☐ ✎ closed Mon, Mon lunch (Jul-Aug), 5 Nov-20 Mar, 270. Rest. ♦ *La Marée* ≪ ♪ ⚬ 600m from the hotel, 76-150.
★★ *L'Albatros*, 11, bd du Dr-Pineau, ☎ 46.76.00.08, 13 rm ℗ ≪ ≪ ⚬ half pens (h.s.), closed Easter-Feb, 403. Rest. ♦ ✺ 60-120.

PARTHENAY*

Bressuire 32, Niort 42, Paris 374 km
pop 11666 ⊠ 79200   B1

Popular meat market *(fair on Wed. morning)*, this former fortified town was prosperous during the Compostela pilgrimages. The 13thC Saint-Jacques gate★ at the bridge over the Thouet River (view from Pont-Neuf) and the Rue de la Vaux attest to its importance during those times.

▶ Via the steep cobbled **Rue de la Vaux,** lined with old houses★, approach the **upper town,** formerly fortified; enter through the Porte de l'Horloge (13thC) : ruins of **mediaeval churches** and view points from terraces of the former fortress. ▶ Via Niort road *(2 km)* to **Parthenay-le-Vieux** : church★ (12thC) with Poitevin façade.

Nearby

▶ **Secondigny** *(14 kmW)* : church 11thC ; octagonal tower, capitals in the nave. ▶ Via Fontenay-le-Comte road, **Fenioux :** Romanesque church (ornamentation, octagonal bell-tower★, chevet). ▶ S of Parthenay *(E of Niort road)* : churches in **Allonne** and **Saint-Marc-la-Lande** (Flamboyant Gothic and Renaissance façade). ▶ To the SE, view from the highest point in the region, **Terrier de Saint-Martin-du-Fouilloux** (272 m alt.). ▶ Via Bressuire road *(N)* : Tennessus fortified castle (14thC ; *Sat., Sun., hols, 2:30-6:30*).   ☐

Practical Information _____

ℹ palais des Congrès, ☎ 49.64.11.88.   ⚑
SNCF ☎ 49.24.50.50.

Hotels :
★★ *Grand Hôtel*, 85, bd de la Meilleraie, ☎ 49.64.00.16, AE DC Euro Visa, 26 rm ℗ ≪ ⚬ ♪ closed Sun (l.s.), 130. Rest. ♦ ♪ ⚬ 40-95.
★★ *Nord* (L.F.), 86, av. du Gal-de-Gaulle, ☎ 49.94.29.11, AE Euro Visa, 13 rm ℗ ✺ closed Sat, 20 Dec-10 Jan, 130. Rest. ♦ ♪ Spec : *ris de veau flambé Pierrot*, 45-120.

△ ★★*Municipal* (90 pl), ☎ 49.94.39.52; at Verruyes, 16 km S, ★★★*La Fragnée* (65 pl), ☎ 49.63.21.37.

Marais POITEVIN*

(Poitou Marshes)
A-B2

Round trip, passing through 3 departments, from Niort *(205 km; full day; save at least 2 hours for a boat trip from Coulon, La Garette, Arçais, Saint-Hilaire-la-Palud, Magné, Damvix or Maillezais; see map 2)*

N of Niort is the former bay of Poitou, now traversed by the river Sèvre, which floods the area in winter and spring. The abbey has worked since the Middle Ages to reclaim the land; 150 000 acres have been reclaimed, primarily since the 17th-18thC, by the use of techniques developed in the Low Countries by the Dutch. The area, which covers some 600 km² is incorporated in the **Val-de-Sèvre Regional Nature Park**.

Upstream between Niort and Damvix are the "wet" marshes, comprising some 37 000 acres known as "Green Venice" *(La Venise Verte)*, a web of canals under a roof of poplars and beeches; primarily devoted to mixed horticulture, with the farmers moving about by boat. Downstream approx. 100 000 acres of drained marshlands intersected by a network of dyked canals; these are essentially cattle pastures.

▶ **Niort** (→). ▶ **Magné** : gateway to the "wet" marshes; Romanesque and Renaissance church. ▶ **Coulon** *(11 km)*, along the right bank of the Sèvre : a former sailors' village, principle centre for excursions through "Green Venice" *(also from La Garette, 3 km S)*. ▶ **Arçais** *(10 km from Coulon)* : small port at the foot of the château. ▶ **Saint-Hilaire-la-Palud** *(4 km S)* : "capital of the wild marshes"; boat trips and excursions on foot. ▶ Cross the river at **Damvix**, a town stretched out along the right bank. ▶ **Le Mazeau** and Saint-Sigismond, between "wet" marshes and reclaimed land. ▶ **Maillezais** (→). ▶ **Maillé** : small port on the Jeune Autize; façade★ of Romanesque church. ▶ **Vix** was once an island; archaeological remains from Gallo-Roman times. ▶ **L'Ile-d'Elle** : major agricultural centre (dairy co-operative). ▶ **Marans** (pop. 4 307) : along canalised section of the Sèvre, former grain port now devoted to pleasure craft *(at the junction of the maritime canals of Braud and La Rochelle, 23 km)*; leisure park; museum in Hôtel de Ville; nets and basket-weaving; at S exit, ruins of Gothic church. ▶ N, beyond Sableau, the Five Abbots' Channel (dug in the Middle Ages) before reaching *(direction Luçon)* the "Dutch ring" (17thC). ▶ **Chaillé-les-Marais** : at the foot of a 15 m cliff, once

the river bank. ▶ Via Triaize, **Saint-Denis-du-Payré** : bird sanctuary *(daily in season, 9-5)*. ▶ Luçon (→); Nalliers; Fontenay-le-Comte (→); Nieul-sur-l'Autize, Oulmes (→ Fontenay, nearby). ▶ Return via **Benet** : Renaissance doorway of Romanesque church. □

Practical Information _____

COULON, ⊠ 79270 Frontenay-Rohan-Rohan, 10 km W of **Niort**.
🛈 pl. du Colombier, ☎ 49.35.94.74 (h.s.); mairie, ☎ 49.35.90.26.

Hotel :
★★ *Au Marais* (L.F.), 46-48, quai Louis-Tardy, ☎ 49.35.90.43, Visa, 11 rm ⟨ ⟨ 170. Rest. ♦ ⟨ ♪ & closed 21 Dec-14 Jan. Fish is the speciality, 65-190.

Restaurant :
♦ *Auberge de l'Ecluse*, la Sotterie, D 123, ☎ 49.35.90.42, Euro Visa ⟨ ♪ & closed Mon eve and Tue. Spec : garden produce, 85-140; child : 45.

△ ★★*Venise Verte* (100 pl), ☎ 49.25.90.36.

MARANS, ⊠ 17230, 23 km NE of **La Rochelle**.
🛈 jardins de l'Hôtel-de-Ville, ☎ 46.01.12.87.
SNCF ☎ 46.01.10.30.

Hotel :
★ *Pavillon Bleu*, rte de Nantes, ☎ 46.01.11.67, 12 rm 🅿 70. Rest. ♦ closed Fri and Sun eve (l.s.), 50-90.

△ ★★*Municipal* (200 pl), ☎ 46.01.10.51.

POITIERS★★★

Tours 101, Nantes 176, Paris 335 km
pop 82884 ⊠ 86000
C1

The former religious, university and political capital of Poitou is still, architecturally and in terms of monuments, one of the most exciting cities in France.

▶ From **Place du Maréchal-Leclerc** (B2) take the pedestrian Rue Gambetta, at the corner of the theatre : **St. Porchaire church** (16thC; Romanesque gate-tower). ▶ Via Rue P. Guillon, 16thC City Magistracy (Hôtel de l'Echevinage). ▶ **Palais de Justice** (the law courts) is in the former palace of the Counts of Poitou (Maubergeon tower; large Gothic hall whose **gabled wall** from 14thC★ cleverly integrates three monumental fireplaces into the flamboyant window design). ▶ Via Rue des Cordeliers, **Notre-Dame-la-Grande church★★** : small, but nonetheless a major sanctuary for pilgrims during the Middle Ages : perfect proportions and rich ornamentation on the façade★★★; fresco (12thC) on vaulting in the choir. ▶ Via

2. Marais poitevin

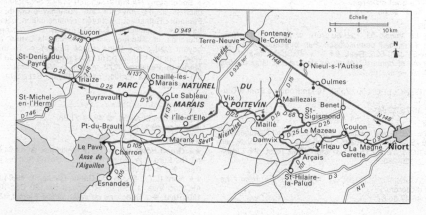

the Rue de la Regratterie (opposite), then the Rue Descartes, visit the 15thC **hôtel Fumé★** in the **Rue de la Chaîne★** (B1) lined with half-timbered houses, access to Berthellot Mansion (Renaissance); further, to right, **St. Jean-de-Montierneuf church** (C1; 11th-14thC, much restored) : high Gothic apse. ► Return to Notre-Dame-la-Grande through the botanical gardens (C1).

► Via Grande-Rue (mansions and houses, 15th-17thC) reach the immense Romanesque **cathedral★** : 13thC doorways★; vast nave lit by stained glass windows★★ (13thC); modern choir stalls. ► **Ste. Radegonde Church★** : gate-tower; apse and crypt (11thC) house the tomb of St. Radegonde (587). ► **St. Jean Baptistry★★**, one of France's oldest Christian monuments (4thC); Merovingian archaeological museum; Romanesque fresco *(in season 10:30-12:30 & 3-6; out of season 2-4).* ► **St. Croix Museum★★** : classical and mediaeval archaeology and fine arts (mainly paintings★ ; *10-12 & 2-5, closed Tue.*).

► From Place Leclerc (B2), S, Renaissance mansion of Jehan Beaussé; further on, former Jesuit school; 17thC chapel *(closed Aug.)*, to reach Rue Carnot. ► Church of **St. Hilaire-le-Grand★★** (11th-12thC), of imposing dimensions (nave and choir); can be viewed at night : illuminated absidial chapels. ► Nearby, former Deanery (Renaissance). ► **Parc de Blossac** (park; 18thC design) on former ramparts : view over the Clain Valley.

Pont-Neuf district *(right bank, via C3)*

► From the **Terrasse des Dunes**, viewpoint★ over the old city. ► Set back in the hillside, tombs of martyrs (underground chapel from 8thC in large **necropolis** of Gallo-Roman origins). ► Via the Rue du Dolmen, **Pierre Levée** (broken foot-plate), memorialized by Rabelais.

Clain Valley

► To N via **Chasseneuil-du-Poitou**, **Vayres** manor (dovecote; *Jul.-Sep. pm, closed Tue.*) and **Dissay Castle★** *(15 km)*, circled by moats (15th-18thC; *pm, closed Wed.*).

Round trip of abbeys *(130 km, full day)*

► To S, sites inhabited since prehistoric era (caves in Saint-Benoît-Ligugé region). ► **Saint-Benoît** *(4 km)*, Romanesque abbey church. ► **Ligugé** : famous Benedictine abbey (Gregorian chant) founded by St. Martin (mid-4thC), of which only a Renaissance building remains; large archaeological dig★. ► **Nouaillé-Maupertuis★★** : Romanesque church and large group of monastic buildings (bell-tower-keep, choirscreen and stalls, crypt). ► Via Nieul-l'Espoir, château de **Chambonneau** (Renaissance). ► **Saint-Maurice-la-Clouère** : church (Romanesque side doorway, 14thC; fresco). ► **Gençay** : ruins of Gothic castle; la Roche-Magné château (Order of Malta museum). ► Romanesque church in **Champagné-Saint-Hilaire.** ► N10 at the Chaunay turning : take the return road. ► Romanesque churches in **Brux** and **Vaux**, then **Couhé.** ► **Vivonne** : ruins of Gothic castle; church (12th-16thC); footpaths. ► **Château-Larcher** : remains of château and church *(son et lumière some summer evenings);* 13thC lantern of the dead cemetery.► N, small roads lead to numerous megaliths. ► Return to Poitiers possible via **Fontaine-le-Comte** *(Niort road)* : Romanesque church★ of former abbey.

Round trip of the Boivre Valley *(W; 56 km; half-day)*

► **Norée Grottos** *(4 km).* ► Site of **Montreuil-Bonnin** Castle, built by Richard the Lion-Hearted; Romanesque church. ► Forest drive. ► Renaissance monuments in **Lavausseau.** □

Practical Information _____

POITIERS

ⓘ 8, rue des Grandes Ecoles (A2), ☎ 49.41.21.24.

✈ *Biard*, 4 km W, ☎ 49.58.27.96. *Air France office*, 11 ter, rue des Grandes-Ecoles, ☎ 49.88.89.63.
SNCF (A3), ☎ 49.58.50.50.
☒☒ ☎ 49.41.14.20.
Car rental : *Avis*, train station (A2); 6, bd de Solférino (A2), ☎ 49.58.28.14 ; 77, av. J.-Coeur, ☎ 49.46.28.48.

Hotels :

★★★★ *France*, (Mapotel), 28, rue Carnot (B3), ☎ 49.41.32.01, Tx 790526, AE DC Euro Visa, 86 rm Ⓟ 🅰 ♪ ♿ Spec : *salade de poitrine de cane, morue à la poitevine, cul de lapin au vin de pêches*, 75-150.

★★★ *Royal Poitou*, 215, rte de Paris (off map B1), ☎ 49.01.72.86, AE DC Euro Visa, 32 rm Ⓟ ♨ 🅰 ♪ ♿ 190. Rest. ♦♦ ♪ Spec : *gratin de langouste au champagne*, 70-155.

● ★★ *Europe*, 39, rue Carnot (B3), ☎ 49.88.12.00, Visa, 50 rm Ⓟ ♨ 🅰 ♿ 200.

★★ *Chapon Fin*, pl. du Mal-Leclerc (B2), ☎ 49.88.02.97, 18 rm Ⓟ closed 21 Dec-5 Jan, 175.

★★ *Terminus*, 3, bd Pont-Achard (A2), ☎ 49.58.20.31, AE Euro Visa, 18 rm, closed Xmas school hols, 130. Rest. ♦ 30-80.

★ *L'Orée du Bois*, 13, rue Naintré, (off map, rte de La Rochelle), ☎ 49.57.11.44, AE Euro Visa, 16 rm 🅰 closed Sun eve and Mon, 1-15 Feb, 150. Rest. ♦ closed Sun eve, 60-100.

Restaurants :

♦♦ *Auberge de la Cigogne*, 20, rue du Planty, Buxerolles (off map B1), ☎ 49.45.61.47, AE Euro Visa ♨ ♪ ♨ closed Mon and Sun, 1-8 Jan, 1-15 Apr, 1-22 Aug, 60-130.

♦♦ *Aux Armes d'Obernai*, 19, rue Arthur-Ranc (B2), ☎ 49.41.16.33, Euro Visa ♪ closed Mon and Sun eve, 18 Feb-10 Mar, 2-15 Sep. Spec : *goujonettes de soles et langoustines, fricassée de rognons, mignons de veau au miel et citron*, 65-160.

♦♦ *Maxime*, 4, rue St-Nicolas (B2-3), ☎ 49.41.09.55, AE DC Euro Visa ♪ closed Sat noon and Sun, 70-220.

♦ *Chez Cul de Paille*, 3, rue Th.-Renaudot (A2-3), ☎ 49.41.07.35 ♪ closed Sun, 1 Aug-1 Sep, 70-100.

Recommended
Baby-sitting : *C.R.I.J.*, ☎ 49.88.64.37.
Youth hostel : 17, rue de la Jeunesse, ☎ 49.58.03.05.

Nearby

CHASSENEUIL-DU-POITOU, ☒ 86360, 8 km N.

Hotel :
★★★ *Relais de Poitiers*, ☎ 49.52.90.41, AE DC Euro Visa, 97 rm, closed Xmas, 290. Rest. ♦♦ ♪ Spec : *foie gras frais, canard maison, blinis de saumon au citron vert*, 70-140.

CROUTELLE, ☒ 86240 Ligugé, 2 km S on the N 10.

Restaurant :
♦♦ *Pierre Benoist*, ☎ 49.57.11.52, AE DC Euro Visa Ⓟ ♨ 🅰 ♿ closed Mon and Sun eve, 28 Jul-12 Aug. Pierre Benoist's enjoyable little gourmet eatery (seats are limited). Spec : *foie gras de canard à la gelée blanche de pineau, pigeonneau à l'ail et à la fleur de thym*. Old vintages in stock, 145-200.

LIGUGÉ, ☒ 86240, 10 km S.

Hotel :
● ★★★ *Bois de la Marche*, (Inter-Hôtel), RN 10, ☎ 49.53.10.10, Tx 790133, AE DC Euro Visa, 45 rm ≼ ♨ 🅰 ♿ ♪° 195. Rest. ♦♦ ≼ ♪ 75-145.

SAINT-BENOÎT, ☒ 86280, 4 km S.

Hotel :
★★ *Le Chalet de Venise*, 6, rue du Square, ☎ 49.88.45.07, 10 rm ≼ ♨ 🅰 ♨ closed Sun eve and Mon, 19-25 Oct, 23 Dec-15 Jan, 160. Rest. ♦ ♪ Spec :

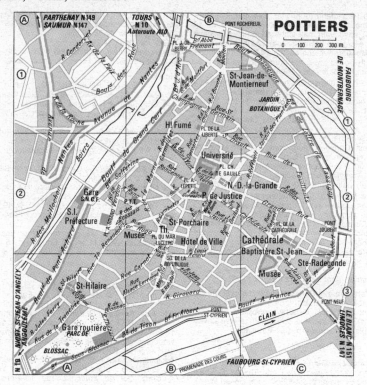

terrine de pâté de lièvre, escargots du chef, chevreau à la poitevine (in season), 55-180.

VIVONNE, ⊠ 86370, 19 km S.
ⓘ mairie, ☎ 49.43.41.05.

Hotel :
La Treille (L.F.), 10, av. de Bordeaux, ☎ 49.43.41.13, AE DC Euro Visa, 4 rm 🅿 ⌀ ⥥ pens (h.s.), closed Wed eve (h.s.), 10-25 Jan, 340. Rest. ♦ closed Wed eve (l.s.). Spec : *paupiettes d'anguilles aux choux verts, mouclade vendéenne,* 60-160.

VOUILLÉ, ⊠ 86190, 17 km NW.

Hotel :
★★★ **Domaine de Périgny,** (I.L.A., R.S., C.H.), ☎ 49.51.80.43, Tx 791400, AE DC Euro Visa, 39 rm 🅿 ⌀ ⥥ ⌀ ⌀ ⌀ ⌀ closed 25 Jan-28 Feb, 440. Rest. ● ♦♦♦ ♪ Luxury, comfort and quality. Spec : *millefeuille de petits gris au coriandre, cervelas de brochet au poivre vert, pigeonneau du pays,* 100-200 ; child : 70.

PONS*

Saintes 22, Bordeaux 96, Paris 494 km
pop 5364 ⊠ 17800　　　　　　　　　　　　　　B3

In what has become one of the best cognac vineyard regions, the old town was built around a castle terrace (view over Seugne Valley). Superb keep★ (late 12thC).

▶ In the lower town, the road goes past the church of St. Vivien (Romanesque façade) through one of the city gates. From here, a vaulted passage★ connects the former Pilgrims' Almshouse to what was once the church of St. Martin. ▶ Renaissance château of Usson★ *(2 km ; ext. visit only, Jul.-15 Sep.).*

Nearby

▶ Short trips to the Romanesque churches of **Colombiers, Montils** and **Bougneau** *(to the N),* **Jazennes** *(to the E)* and **Belluire** *(to the S, on the road to Bordeaux).*

Round trip of Saintonge Romanesque church façades *(47 km ; could take a day)*

▶ Via D142 *(SE) :* **Avy★, Fléac-sur-Seugne, Marignac★, Chadenac** (façade★★), **Jarnac-Champagne★, Lonzac** (Renaissance church), **Coulonges, Pérignac★, Echebrune** (doorways★★) and **Biron★.** ▶ Follow part of the Cognac round trip (→ Nearby Cognac).　　　　　　　□

Practical Information _____

ⓘ hall du Donjon, ☎ 46.96.13.31 (h.s.) ; mairie, ☎ 46.94.30.04 (l.s.).
SNCF ☎ 46.91.30.25.

Hotel :
★★ **Auberge Pontoise,** 23, av. Gambetta, ☎ 46.94.00.99, Euro Visa, 22 rm 🅿 ⌀ ⌀ half pens (h.s.), closed Sun eve and Mon ex Jul-Aug, 22 Dec-26 Jan, 450. Rest. ♦ ⌀ Spec : *feuilleté d'huîtres au beurre rouge, copeaux de lotte à la crème de cèpes,* 85-250.

POUZAUGES*

Bressuire 28, Nantes 81, Paris 384 km
pop 5792 ⊠ 85700　　　　　　　　　　　　　　B1

An excellent centre *(hiking trails)* in the Vendée hills, in a beautiful site★ beneath the woodlands of La Folie (alt. 280 m). In the village : Romanesque and Gothic church and ruins of a 13thC keep.

▶ **Pouzauges-le-Vieux** *(1 km S)* : small isolated Romanesque church★ decorated with 13thC murals.★ ▶ **Puy Crapaud** *(3 km)* : panoramic terrace (alt. 290 m; orientation table).

Round trip of Mount Mercure *(N, approx 25 km, 2 hr)*

▶ Via Pommeraie-sur-Sèvre, **La Flocellière** : feudal castle ruins, superb castle keep intact since the 13thC. ▶ **Saint-Michel-Mont-Mercure** *(7 km)* : at the top of Mont Mercure (alt. 285 m), modern church crowned with huge statue of the archangel; visits to the bell-tower; view to the ocean. ▶ Romanesque church fortified in the 15thC in **Le Boupère**. □

Practical Information _____

ⓘ pl. du Calvaire, ☎ 51.91.82.46 (h.s.); ☎ 51.57.01.37. ◆ *SNCF* ☎ 51.57.02.67.

Hotels :
★★★ *Chouannerie*, 27, rue A.-Delaveau, ☎ 51.57.01.69, Visa, 8 rm P ⪍ ⸿ ⌕ 200.
● ★★ *Auberge de la Bruyère*, (L.F., R.S.), ☎ 51.91.93.46, AE DC Euro Visa, 30 rm P ⪍ ⸿ ⚲ ⅋ ⌕ 225. Rest. ◆ ⪍ ⅃ ⅋ closed Mon and Sun eve (l.s.) ex grill. Spec : *filet de bar au beurre rouge, paletot de canard au pinot noir, cœur de filet de bœuf au poivre vert*, 40-120.

Île de RÉ**
(Ré Island)
A2

28 km long, and 3 to 5 km wide, this is in fact two islands connected by the narrow isthmus of Martray (a few dozen metres). Vineyards and vegetable fields encircle a large lagoon (Le Fiers d'Ars), former salt marshes now partially converted to oyster farming *(visits to oyster parks from villages of Rivedoux, Loix, Ars, Les Portes)*.

▶ The ferry from La Pallice comes to Sablanceaux Point. ▶ After **Rivedoux-Plage** (population 900), to the right in the distance is the 17thC La Prée Fort; ruins of Romanesque and Gothic **abbey of Châteliers.** ▶ **La Flotte** (population 1 879) : fishing and pleasure port. ▶ **Saint-Martin-de-Ré** (population 2 402) *(10 km)* : citadel constructed by Vauban still serves as a prison; the port, once commercial, now used by pleasure craft; remains of old fortifications and city gates; ruins of church (15thC); Renaissance Clerjotte mansion converted into naval and folklore museum *(10-1 & 3-6; Wed. and Sun. pm only out of season)*. ▶ **La Couarde** *(15 km)* : beach and flowered streets; then Isthmus of Martray (Loix road). ▶ **Ars-en-Ré** (population 1 083) *(23 km)* by the broad expanse of the Fier d'Ars (lagoon); Romanesque church façade★ beneath bell-tower painted black to serve as a sea-mark; large yacht harbour. ▶ **Phare des Baleines** ("Whale" Lighthouse, 57 m, 250 steps) near Conche (naturist beach). ▶ **Les Portes** *(visits to oyster beds)* on the edge of Trousse-Chemise Woods. □

Practical Information _____

ARS-EN-RÉ, ⊠ 17590.
ⓘ ☎ 46.29.46.09.

Hotel :
★★ *Le Martray*, 3 km on D 735, ☎ 46.29.40.04, AE DC Visa, 14 rm P ⪍ ⸿ pens (h.s.), closed 1 Nov-31 Mar, 520. Rest. ◆ 80-150.

⚠ ★★★*Soleil* (140 pl), ☎ 46.29.41.74; *Essi* (140 pl) ☎ 46.29.44.73.

Le BOIS-PLAGE, ⊠ 17850.
ⓘ rue des Barjottes, ☎ 46.09.23.26.

⚠ ★★★★*Antioche* (120 pl), ☎ 46.09.23.86; ★★★*Interlude* (180 pl), ☎ 46.09.18.22.

La FLOTTE, ⊠ 17630.
ⓘ quai Sénac, ☎ 46.09.60.38.

Hotels :
★★★ *Le Richelieu*, ☎ 46.09.60.70, Tx 791492, 30 rm P ⪍ ⸿ ⚲ ⅍ ⌕ ⅃° closed 7 Nov-25 Mar, 450. Rest. ● ◆◆ ⪍ ⅃ ⅙ This is the island's best restaurant, which serves a stunning array of seafood delights. Spec : *turbot farci à la mousseline de homard en feuilletage, cassolette de coquilles Saint-Jacques et de langoustines à l'aneth*, 170-300.
★★ *La Belle Rive*, 10, cours F.-Faure, ☎ 46.09.60.02, AE DC Euro Visa, 22 rm P ⪍ ⚲ ⅙ 190. Rest. ◆ ⅃ ⅙ closed 15 Nov-20 Mar, 55-140.

Les PORTES-EN-RÉ, ⊠ 17880, 22 km from **Saint-Martin**.

Restaurants :
● ◆◆ *Le Chasse-Marée*, 1, rue Jules-David, ☎ 46.29.52.03, AE DC Euro Visa ⅃ ⅙ closed Jan-Mar, 4 Nov-31 Mar. Spec : *bavaroise d'artichaut au coulis de tomate, gigot de lotte en papillote*, 120-200.
◆◆ *Le Traversier*, 13, rue de la Grenouillère, ☎ 46.29.57.51, AE DC Euro Visa P ⸿ ⅃ closed Nov-Mar, 80-120.

RIVEDOUX-PLAGE, ⊠ 17940.
ⓘ pl. de la République, ☎ 46.09.80.62 (h.s.); chem. des Coulisses, ☎ 46.09.80.15.

Hotel :
★★★ *Auberge de la Marée* (C.H.), ☎ 46.09.80.02, Visa, 28 rm ⪍ ⸿ ⚲ ⅃ ⌕ half pens (h.s.), closed 1 Oct-15 May, 540. Rest. ◆ ⪍ ⅙ Spec : *escalope de saumon frais à la crème d'oseille, huîtres chaudes au beurre de champagne et fondue de légumes*, 105-220; child : 40.

SAINT-CLÉMENT-DES-BALEINES, ⊠ 17590 Ars-en-Ré.
ⓘ mairie, ☎ 46.29.24.19.

Hotel :
★ *Chat Botté*, 2, rue de la Mairie, ☎ 46.29.42.09, Euro Visa, 22 rm P ⪍ ⚲ ⅃° closed Wed (l.s.), 10 Jan-5 Feb, 15-24 Oct, 120. Rest. ◆ ⅃ Spec : *bar en croûte, feuilleté de turbot*, 60-170.

SAINT-MARTIN-DE-RÉ, ⊠ 17410.
ⓘ hôtel de Clerjotte, ☎ 46.09.20.06 (h.s.).

Hotel :
★★ *Colonnes*, quai Job-Foran, ☎ 46.09.21.58, AE DC Euro Visa, 30 rm ⪍ closed 3rd wk of Oct, 15 Dec-2 Feb, 210. Rest. ◆ ⪍ ⅃ closed Wed, 90-120.

⚠ ★★*Sainte-Thérèse* (200 pl), ☎ 46.09.21.96.

Recommended
Guide to wines : *La Vinatière*, 32, rue de Sully, outstanding wines.

SAINTE-MARIE-DE-RÉ, ⊠ 17740.
ⓘ rue de la République, ☎ 46.30.22.92.

Hotel :
● ★★★ *Atalante*, (Mapotel), ☎ 46.30.22.44, AE DC Euro Visa, 65 rm P ⪍ ⸿ ⚲ ⅃ ⅍ ⅙ ⅃° 380. Rest. ◆ ⪍ Spec : *sole maritaise*, 85-220.

Restaurant :
◆ *Auberge de la Chauvetière*, 1, rue de la Beuretière, ☎ 46.30.21.56, AE DC Euro Visa ⅃ closed Wed, 21 Feb-11 Mar. Late of the Richelieu, the chef also trained at Troisgros. He serves delicious seafood specialities affordably priced : *mouclade, filets de sole royal*, 80-180.

La ROCHE-POSAY*

Châtellerault 23, Poitiers 49, Paris 314 km
pop 1404 ⊠ *86270*
C1

On a high hill, remains of a fortress (12thC keep; *visits*) and bell-tower of Romanesque church (11thC) on site★ inhabited since the Palaeolithic era.

▶ On plateau at the foot of the hill, **thermal spa** : can be reached from the old city via a gateway in the ramparts (12th-14thC).

Nearby

▶ **Coussay-les-Bois** *(6 km NW)* : Romanesque church and close by Vervolière Castle (15thC). ▶ **Château de la Guerche★** *(15 km N)*, built by Charles VII on the banks of the Creuse *(closed Tue. and Sun. am in winter)*.□

Practical Information _____

⚓ (30 Apr-1 Oct), ☎ 49.86.21.03.
ℹ️ cours Pasteur, ☎ 49.86.20.37, closed Sun.

Hotels :
● ★★★★ **Relais du Château**, at the casino, ☎ 49.86.20.10, AE Visa, 13 rm ℙ ✦ ⬛ ⬛ ⬛ 300. Rest. ♦♦ 70-100.
★★★ **Saint-Roch**, Cours Pasteur, ☎ 49.86.21.03, Visa, 45 rm ℙ ⬛ closed 20 Dec-20 Jan, 250. Rest. ♦♦ ❄ 90-130.

La ROCHE-SUR-YON

Nantes 65, La Rochelle 83, Paris 414 km
pop 48156 ⊠ 85000   A1

Created by Napoleon, in a checkerboard pattern, the town is centred on the Place d'Armes (called the "Place Napoléon" due to the equestrian statue of Napoléon). The city now harbours the Prefecture of the Vendée.

▶ W of **Place Napoléon**, Empire façade of the church of St. Louis. ▶ Via Place du Marché (Market Square), crafts museum, place de la Vieille Horloge *(daily 9-12 & 2-5)*. ▶ Opposite the square via Rue Clemenceau *(S.I.)*, the municipal **Historical Museum** (temporary exhibitions, modern painting; *Jun.-Aug. 10-12 & 2-6; closed Sun. and Mon., out of season)*. ▶ S of the Prefecture park is one of the largest **stud farms★** in France *(15 Jul.-15 Feb.; by appt., visits preferably during winter season, closed am)*. ▶ N of the city : Moulin-Papon Lake *(sailing, canoeing, bathing forbidden)*.

Nearby

▶ **Round trips of military Vendée** (→). ▶ 3 km W on the route des Sables, former 13thC **Fontenelles abbey** *(2 km N of the route)*.   □

Practical Information _____

La ROCHE-SUR-YON
ℹ️ galerie Bonaparte, pl. Napoléon, ☎ 51.36.00.85.
✈ *Couzinet*, 6 km NE, ☎ 51.62.31.65.
SNCF ☎ 52.62.50.50.
🚌 pl. Napoléon, ☎ 51.62.18.23.
Car rental : *Avis*, 9, pl. Napoléon, ☎ 51.62.44.45; train station.

Hotels :
● ★★ **Logis de la Couperie** (L.F.), D 80, ☎ 51.37.21.19, Euro Visa, 7 rm ℙ ✦ ⬛ ⬛ ❄ 195.
★★ **Gallet** (L.F.), 75, bd Mal-Leclerc, ☎ 51.37.02.31, AE DC Euro Visa, 12 rm ℙ ♪ ❄ half pens (h.s.), closed Sun (Oct-Mar), 19 Dec-3 Jan, 500. Rest. ♦♦ ♪ ♿ Spec : *navarin de filets de sole au beurre de curry, rognonnade de lapereau à la graine de moutarde*, 100-220; child : 45.

Restaurant :
♦♦ **Le Rivoli**, 31, bd A.-Briand, ☎ 51.37.43.41, AE DC Euro Visa ✦ ♪ ♿ closed Sat eve and Sun, 1-23 Aug. Spec : seafood and grilled fish, 75-140.

Nearby

AIZENAY, ⊠ 85190, 16 km NW.
ℹ️ ☎ 51.94.62.72.   ♥
SNCF ☎ 51.94.60.39.

Hotel :
★ **Gare**, 35, rue du Mal-Leclerc, ☎ 51.94.60.17, 18 rm ℙ ❄ half pens (h.s.), closed Sat, 23 Dec-2 Jan, 195. Rest. ♦ 30-100.

ROCHEFORT-SUR-MER★★

La Rochelle 32, Saintes 40, Paris 465 km
pop 27716 ⊠ 17300   B2

Built between 1666 and 1670, Rochefort was originally a military establishment equipped with a strong arsenal. A veritable town within the town, conceived by Fernand Blondel, the place was run for more than a century using prisoners sentenced to forced labour. The ramparts later gave way to large avenues and promenades, including the Jardin de la Marine. Masterpiece of this ensemble and unique testimony to 17thC industrial architecture : the 17thC Corderie Royale★ (royal rope-makers), perfectly restored, houses today the International Centre of the Sea; permanent and temporary exhibitions, visits to the monument, conferences and symposia *(museum open in summer daily 10-7; out of season 2-6)*.

▶ From the Cours Roy-Bry to the W *(S.I.* building), via Ave. Général de Gaulle going down towards Porte de Soleil : **Fine Arts Museum** *(1:30-6, closed Sun., Mon. and nat. hols.* ; archaeology, painting, Far Eastern art, ethnography, zoology). ▶ The avenue crosses **Rue Pierre-Loti**, named after the writer (1850-1923) whose birthplace (No. 141, on right) is now a **museum★** *(1 Oct.-31 Mar., at 2, 3 and 5; 1 Apr.-30 Sep., at 10, 11, 2, 3 and 4)*. ▶ Near the Charente River : **Navy Museum★** *(daily ex Tue., 10-1 & 2-6)* : models of ships built in Rochefort.

Nearby

▶ **Tonnay-Charente** *(5 km E)* : 1885 suspended bridge reserved for pedestrians and cyclists. ▶ To the W, Charente estuary. ▶ **Martrou** bridges : lifting bridge (1966) carrying the road : upstream, former transporter bridge (1890). ▶ Via La Renaissance, **Échillais** *(4.5 km)* : Romanesque façade★ on the church. ▶ **Saint-Jean-d'Angle** *(14 km)* : Gothic church and castle; 5 km E, **Pont-l'Abbé-d'Arnoult★** : craftwork centre (museum); fortified gate; façade of Romanesque church★. ▶ Via Saint-Symphorien : "Donjon" at **Broue** (11th-12thC keep; *3 km W)* on hillock among marshes; viewpoint. ▶ After the Cadeuil crossroads, to the E, **Le Gua** : Romanesque church. ▶ **L'Éguille** : oyster port on the Seudre.   □

Practical Information _____

⚓ ☎ 46.99.08.64, closed Jan.
ℹ️ av. Sadi-Carnot, ☎ 46.99.08.60.
SNCF ☎ 46.99.01.95.
🚌 pl. de Verdun, ☎ 46.99.23.65; ☎ 46.99.01.36.

Hotel :
★★ **France**, 55, rue Dr-Peltier, ☎ 46.99.34.00, 32 rm, closed Jan-Feb, 180.

Restaurant :
♦♦♦ **Marais**, 10, rue Lesson, ☎ 46.99.47.13, AE DC Euro Visa ♪ closed Sun, 1-8 Jun, 22-31 Nov, 85-180.

Recommended
Baby-sitting : Office Municipal de la Jeunesse, ☎ 46.87.16.42.

La ROCHEFOUCAULD★

Angoulême 22, Limoges 81, Paris 444 km
pop 3328 ⊠ 16110   C3

Large castle (11th-16thC) on the right bank of the Tardoire : Romanesque keep (35 km) on the S façade (partially collapsed 1960).

▶ Access to courtyard *(guided visits)* : 2 wings with three floors of **covered galleries★**; S aisle : superb staircase. ▶ In town : cloister (15thC) of former **Carmelite convent**. ▶ Old half-timbered houses, late 13thC church.

Nearby

▶ Trip through Rancogne woods, valleys of the Tardoire and Bandiat : **Rancogne Grottos** *(5 km)* and Renaissance château (dovecote). ▶ **Prehistoric Fontechevade Cave.** ▶ **Montbron** site : château (12th-15thC), chapel of the Leper hospital, some old houses. ▶ **Marthon** : feudal fortress. ▶ **Pranzac** : lantern of the dead. ▶ **Queroy Grottos** *(visits).* ▶ To W, **Braconne Forest**★ (10 000 acres) and its *fosses* (pits). ▶ To N, Romanesque churches of **Coulgens, Sainte-Colombe, Saint-Amant-de-Bonnieure.** ▶ N, **Cellefrouin**★ *(18 km)* : Romanesque church, lantern of the dead in the cemetery★. ▶ 11 km NE, **Chasseneuil-sur-Bonnieure,** memorial to the martyrs of the Resistance. □

Practical Information ————————————

La ROCHEFOUCAULD
ⓘ 41, rue des Halles, ☎ 45.63.07.45 (h.s.). ✔

Hotels :
★★ *La Vieille Auberge*, 13, fg la Souche, ☎ 45.62.02.72, AE DC Euro Visa, 28 rm 🅿 ⌕ 180. Rest. ♦ ♪ closed Mon noon, 3-23 Jan, 70-200.
★ *France* (L.F.), 13, Grande-Rue, ☎ 45.63.02.29, Euro Visa, 17 rm 🅿 ⌕ closed Fri eve and Sat, Feb, 80. Rest. ♦ 45-100.

Nearby

CHASSENEUIL-SUR-BONNIEURE, ⊠ 16260, 11 km NE.
ⓘ mairie, ☎ 45.39.55.36.
SNCF ☎ 45.39.50.09.

Hotel :
★ *La Gare*, ☎ 45.39.50.36, Euro Visa, 12 rm, closed Sun eve and Mon, Jan, 140. Rest. ♦ 40-200.

MONTBRON, ⊠ 16220, 14 km SE.
ⓘ pl. de l'Hôtel-de-Ville, ☎ 45.23.60.09 (h.s.). ✔

Hotel :
★★★ *Château Sainte-Catherine* (C.H.), rte de Marthon, D 16, 4 km, ☎ 45.23.60.03, Visa, 18 rm 🅿 ☵ ⌕ ♪ ⊡ 200. Rest. ♦ ⌕ ♪ ♿ Spec : *noisette d'agneau au flan de ratatouille, huîtres pochées au beurre de cerfeuil,* 80-180 ; child : 50.
⚲ ★★*La Piscine* (50 pl), ☎ 45.70.60.09.

NIEUIL, ⊠ 16270, 8 km NE.

Hotel :
● ★★★★ *Château de Nieuil* (R.C.), rte de Fontafie, 2 km, ☎ 45.71.36.38, AE Euro Visa, 15 rm 🅿 ☵ ☵ ⌕ ♣ ♿ ⊡ ⌰ closed 12 Nov-14 Apr. 40-ha park. Pond fishing, bicycling, 475. Rest. ● ♦♦ ⌕ ♪ ♿ closed Wed noon ex for hotel guests. The grand old lady of châteaux-hôtels. Luce Bodinaud oversees the kitchen : *effeuillé de morue à l'oseille, sauté d'agneau à la fondue de tomates,* homemade desserts. Magnificent Cognac collection, 175-250.

La ROCHELLE★★★

Saintes 70, Nantes 146, Paris 471 km
pop 78231 ⊠ 17000   B2

A commercial town since 11thC, La Rochelle became a fishing port in the 19thC, then a heavy industry centre ; today it is also a pleasure port. Because it was razed by Cardinal Richelieu in the 17thC, little remains of the city from before that period.

▶ The Chaîne and St. Nicolas towers guard the entrance to the **Vieux-Port**★★ (old harbour ; B3 ; fishing ; in summer departure point for boat tours in summer). ▶ In NW corner, 14thC **Grosse Horloge**★ (Great Clock) **Gate**★ gives access to the town built in the French Classical period (see below). ▶ Opposite is the **Bassin à flot,** the centre of the fishing harbour *(wholesale fish market, early am until 10).* ▶ Standing back from Quai Duperré, **St. Sauveur Church** : 15thC square bell-tower. ▶ **Tour de la Chaîne** (Chain Tower, late 14thC) : the chain was drawn across the harbour mouth to close the port at night *(1 Apr.-30 Sep., 9-12 & 2-6 ex Tue.).* ▶ Via Rue Sur-les-Murs, 15thC **Tour de la Lanterne**★ (Lantern Tower, 1 Apr.-30 Sep. ; 9:30-12 & 2-6:30, closed Tue.) : the lantern on the octagonal spire once served as a lighthouse *(mid-Apr.-Sep. ; panorama).* ▶ **Mail** Promenade : 800 m walk along beach. ▶ N at right angles : **Charruyer Park**★ : more than 1 km long at the foot of the ramparts built by Vauban. ▶ **Tower of St. Nicolas**★ : once a fortress (early 14thC : 35 m keep ; visits to different levels, *10-12:30 & 2:30-6:30),* view★ from the terrace. ▶ Towards Minimes Port, *la ville en bois* (the city of wood) ; wonderful **aquarium**★ *(10-12 & 2-3 daily).* ▶ Via Grosse-Horloge Gate (B3) and Place Fromentin, take **Rue du Palais,** lined with beautiful doorways★ (and see the parallel streets, notably **Rue de l'Escale**★). ▶ Going uphill to the left : **Hôtel de la Bourse** (Exchange ; 18thC ; courtyard★), and above, the Palais de Justice (law courts, late 18thC) ; the street continues into **Rue Chaudrier,** also lined with doorways, to Place de Verdun (B2) : **cathedral** (arch. Gabriel ; 18thC). ▶ To the right, Rue des Augustins : Renaissance house reputedly the former residence of **Diane de Poitiers** (Henri II's mistress). ▶ Still further up on the right : No. 10 Rue Fleurian, *S.I.* and **Musée du Nouveau Monde** (New World Museum ; *10:30-6 Mon.-Sat., 3-6 Sun. ; closed Tue.).* ▶ S from Place de Verdun, **Orbigny Museum**★ (2 Rue St. Côme ; *10-12 & 2-6, closed Sun. am and Tue.) :* history and ceramics. ▶ N of Place de Verdun, via Rue Albert-Ier, Jardin des Plantes (botanical garden) and **Lafaille Museum**★★ *(closed Sun. am and Mon.) ;* oceanography. ▶ E of Place de Verdun, Rue Gargoulleau : **Fine Arts Museum**★ *(2-6, closed Tue.) :* mainly paintings (currently being restored). ▶ From Place du Marché, turn right on **Rue des Merciers**★ (16th-17thC houses), to the **Hôtel de Ville** (town hall ; Gothic and Renaissance) : courtyard **façade**★★★ ; historic collections. ▶ Return to the Vieux-Port via the pedestrian precinct.   □

Nearby

▶ **La Pallice** *(5 km W) :* departure point for the Île de Ré (→). ▶ SE via the new quarter of Périgny to the industrial centre of **Aytré** : from there via Surgères road to **La Jarne** (Romanesque church), and **Burzay Château** (18thC). ▶ Towards Rochefort, the seaside resorts of **Angoulins** and **Châtelaillon**★ : magnificent 4 km beach : viewpoints★ from esplanade and site of Vieux-Châtelaillon ; visit oyster parks by tractor-drawn trailer.   □

Practical Information ————————————

La ROCHELLE
ⓘ 10, rue Fleuriau (B2), ☎ 46.41.14.68, closed Sun ; Accueil de France, at l'O.D.T., 11bis, rue des Augustins, ☎ 46.41.43.33.
✈ *Laleu,* 4 km, ☎ 46.42.18.27. Air France office, 23, rue Fleuriau, ☎ 46.41.65.33.
SNCF ☎ 46.41.09.91/46.41.34.22/46.41.15.98.
🚢 cours des Dames (B3), ☎ 46.41.35.33.
🚤 *R.D.P.E.,* ☎ 46.36.61.48, from La Pallice to Île de Ré, excursions and cruises (on Charente river also).
Car rental : Avis, 166, bd Joffre (C4), ☎ 46.41.13.55 ; train station.

Hotels :
● ★★★ **Les Brises,** chem. de la Digue-Richelieu (B3), ☎ 46.43.89.37, Tx 790754, 46 rm 🅿 ⌕ ⌕ ♪ 390.
★★★ **Champlain,** 20, rue Rambaud (B2), ☎ 46.41.23.99, 37 rm 🅿 ⌕ ⌕ closed 15 Dec-28 Feb, 310.
★★★ **France et Angleterre,** (Mapotel), 22, rue Gargoulleau (B2), ☎ 46.41.34.66, Tx 790717, AE DC Euro Visa, 76 rm 🅿 ⌕ ♪ 250. Rest. ♦♦ *Le Richelieu* ♪ closed Mon noon and Sun, 20 Dec-20 Jan, 110-230.
★★★ **Yachtman,** 23, quai Valin (B3), ☎ 46.41.20.68, Tx 790762, AE DC Euro Visa, 40 rm ⌕ ♪ ⊡ 375. Rest. ● ♦♦ "Le grand Jacques" (Le Divellec) takes the wheel again, supervising the restaurant-grill where Frederic Layec, one of his protégés, mans the kitchen. On the sea-front, 150.
● ★★ **François 1er** (R.S.), 13-15, rue Bazoges (B2), ☎ 46.41.28.46, Visa, 34 rm 🅿 180.

LA ROCHELLE

★★ *Le Rochelois*, 66, bd W.-Churchill (off map A3), ☎ 46.43.34.34, Tx 791410, Visa, 38 rm ℙ ⊱ ☶ ☕ ♿ Free entry to fitness club, 210.

★★ *Le Savary*, 2, rue Alsace-Lorraine (A3), ☎ 46.34.83.44, AE Euro Visa, 28 rm ℙ ⊱ ☶ ☕ closed 3-30 Nov, 175.

★★ *Saint-Jean d'Acre*, (Inter-Hôtel), 4, pl. de la Chaine (B3), ☎ 46.41.73.33, AE DC Euro Visa, 49 rm ⊱ ♪ ♿ 250. Rest. ♦ *Au Vieux Port* ⊱ ♿ closed Fri, 70-200.

★★ *Terminus*, pl. du Cdt-de-la-Motte-Rouge (B3-4), ☎ 46.41.31.94, Euro Visa, 27 rm ℙ 185.

★★ *Trianon et Plage*, 6, rue de la Monnaie (A3), ☎ 46.41.21.35, AE DC Euro Visa, 25 rm ℙ ☶ closed 20 Dec-1 Feb, 200. Rest. ♦♦ closed Fri (l.s.), 75-100.

★ *Bordeaux*, 43, rue St-Nicolas (B3), ☎ 46.41.31.22, AE Euro Visa, closed 25 Feb-3 Mar, 4-12 Nov, 145. Rest. ● ♦ *Le Pré Vert* ♪ ♿ closed Sun eve (Nov-Mar), 25 Feb-1 Mar. Spec : *fricassée d'anguilles au cassis, panaché de turbot et de St-Pierre*, 55-110 ; child : 30.

Restaurants :

● ♦♦♦ *Richard Coutanceau*, pl. de la Concurrence (off map A3), ☎ 46.41.48.19, AE DC Visa ⊱ ♿ closed Mon eve and Sun. Spacious, pleasant decor and outstanding food. Some imitations of the masters (Robuchon, Lenôtre) should be taken off the menu. Spec : *aumonière de langoustines au corail de homard, suprême de turbot aux artichauts, coeur de filet de Charolais au fleurie*, 160-300.

♦♦♦ *La Marmite*, 14, rue St-Jean (A3), ☎ 46.41.17.03, AE DC Euro Visa, closed Wed, 15-31 Jan. Spec : *choucroute du pêcheur au beurre blanc, ris de veau braisé aux jeunes épinards*, 140-250.

● ♦♦ *Serge*, 46, cours des Dames (B3), ☎ 46.41.18.80, AE DC Euro Visa ⊱ closed Tue, 15 Jan-8 Feb. Typical La Rochelle atmosphere. They'll tell you how one really ought to eat fresh fish, 100-160.

♦♦ *Les Flots*, 1, rue de la Chaîne (B2), ☎ 46.41.32.51, Euro Visa ⊱ closed Mon, 26 Jan-4 Mar. Spec : grilled lobster, *bouillabaisse*, 95-170.

● ♦ *Bar André*, 5, rue St-Jean (A3), ☎ 46.41.28.24, AE DC Euro Visa ⊱ The busiest seafood place in town : take a ticket for a table, and wait to be called over the microphone. Huge oyster bar, 100-200.

Recommended

Baby-sitting : *C.D.I.J.*, ☎ 46.41.16.36.

Boat rental : *Locaboat*, ☎ 46.42.44.24, and sailboats.

Events : *decorated boat pageant*, in Sep ; *pageant and international sailing week*, in May.

Guided tours : *C.N.M.H.S.*, official tour guides. In Jul-Aug on request, at 10am and 2 : 30pm ; carriage tour of town, info. S.I. Guilloteau, ☎ 46.41.41.98, boat tour of harbour.

Marina : *Les Minimes*, 3000 pl.

Nearby

AYTRÉ, ⊠ 17440, 5 km SE.

Restaurant :

♦♦ *La Maison des Mouettes*, rte de la Plage, ☎ 46.44.29.12, AE DC Euro Visa 〈 ⋙ ♪ ♿ closed Mon ex hols, 2 Feb-9 Mar, 95-200.

🅰 ★★★*Richelieu* (100 pl), ☎ 46.44.19.24.

CHÂTELAILLON-PLAGE, ⊠ 17340, 12 km S.

ⓘ parc municipal, ☎ 46.56.26.97, closed Sat and Sun (l.s.); mairie, ☎ 46.56.22.24.

Hotels :

★ *Océan*, 121, bd de la République, ☎ 46.56.25.91, Euro Visa, 25 rm 🅿 ⅋ pens (h.s.), closed Sun eve and Mon (l.s.), 15 Dec-15 Jan, 500. Rest. ♦♦ ⅋ 55-160.

🅰 ★★★*Clos des Rivages* (50 pl), ☎ 46.56.26.09 ; and about 10 fields (1000 pl).

DOMPIERRE, ⊠ 17139, 8 km SE.

Restaurant :

♦♦ *Vieux Noyer*, (C.H.), 64, rue du Gal-de-Gaulle, ☎ 46.35.31.32, AE DC Euro Visa 🅿 ⋙ ◿ ♿ 5 rm, closed Mon eve and Tue (l.s.), 15 Jan-15 Feb, 25 Sep-5 Oct, 70-250.

ROYAN*

Saintes 38, Bordeaux 129, Paris 505 km
pop 18125 ⊠ *17200* **B3**

Established in the 19thC around an old port, and known for its small bays with beaches and its numerous parks, Royan was rebuilt after the damage suffered in 1945, and is now the largest seaside resort between La Baule and Biarritz.

▶ More than 4 km of ocean frontage between **Pontaillac★** and **Vallières** Point (St. Georges) : panorama★. ▶ In centre, sardine fishing port and yacht marina, then **Grande-Conche★** beach facing the sea front at the foot of the circular buildings of **Front-de-Mer**. ▶ Farther back, the modern city is laid out on either side of the Blvd A. Briand, which leads to **covered market**. ▶ To the E, **park★**, residential area and garden. ▶ To the W, modern buildings : Casino, Palais des Congrès (Conference Centre) and **church of Notre-Dame★**, entirely in reinforced concrete with 65 m spire. ▶ Beyond is the **Foncillon** residential quarter. ▶ Via Ave. de Pontaillac to the Hôtel de Ville

(town hall ; **museum**) *(in season ; Mon., 1:30-5 ; Wed. and Fri., 10-11:30 & 1:30-5 ; out of season ; Mon., Wed. and Fri., 1:30-5).*

Nearby

▶ To NW, **Vaux-sur-Mer** : Romanesque church and Nauzean Bay. ▶ **Saint-Palais★** : resort ; Maine-Gaudin amusement park. ▶ From here, town of La Coubre. ▶ To SE, **Saint-Georges-de-Didonne** : more than 2 km of beach★. ▶ Forests of Suzac★ and Meschers (→ Nearby Talmont). ▶ Via the Rte. de Saintes, **Médis** *(6 km)* : airport, Romanesque church. ▶ **Saujon** *(11 km)* : thermal spa (neuropsychiatry centre). ▶ 6 km N, former abbey of **Sablonceaux★** (13thC) : domes, bell-tower, Romanesque cellar). ▶ **Sea excursions** : to Saint-Georges, Meschers and Talmont (→) ; Renaissance and 17thC **Courdouan Lighthouse★** *(5 hr round trip, visits to the lower two floors of the tower).* ☐

Practical Information ────────

ROYAN
ⓘ Palais des Congrès (B2), ☎ 46.38.65.11 ; pl. de la Poste (C1), ☎ 46.05.04.71.
✈ *Médis*, 5 km E, ☎ 46.05.08.22.
SNCF (C1), ☎ 46.05.20.10/46.05.62.32.
🚌 (C1), ☎ 46.05.03.81.
⛴ *Trans-Gironde*, ☎ 46.05.23.03, ferry for le Verdon (Gironde).

Hotels :

★★★ *Family Golf Hôtel*, 28, bd Garnier (C2), ☎ 46.05.14.66, Visa, 24 rm 3 apt 🅿 〈 closed 1 Nov-1 Apr, 275.

★★★ *France*, (Inter-Hôtel), 2, rue Gambetta (B2), ☎ 46.05.02.29, Tx 791565, AE DC Euro Visa, 32 rm 🅿 〈 ⋙ ⅋ ♿ 250. Rest. ♦ 〈 ♪ ♿ closed Mon (l.s.), 15 Dec-1 Feb, 65-160.

★★★ *L'Hermitage*, 56, Front-de-Mer (B2), ☎ 46.38.57.33, AE DC Euro Visa, 25 rm 🅿 〈 ⅋ pens, half pens (h.s.), closed 30 Oct-1 Feb, 310. Rest. ♦ 〈 ♪ closed 15 Oct-15 Feb, 65-135 ; child : 35.

★★★ *Le Domino*, 9, rue Pointe-de-Grave, Vaux-sur-Mer (A1), ☎ 46.39.02.22, Euro Visa, 40 rm 🅿 〈 ⋙ ◿ ⅋ half pens (h.s.), closed 12 Oct-17 Apr, 520. Rest. ♦♦ 〈 ♪ ♿ ⅋ 90-120.

★★★ *Le Foncillon*, 5, façade de Foncillon (B2), ☎ 46.38.48.00, Tx 790441, AE DC Euro Visa, 45 rm 🅿 ♪ ⅋ ♿ half pens (h.s.), closed 1 Oct-15 Apr, 590. Rest. ♦ 〈 ♪ ♿ ⅋ closed 1 Oct-15 Jun, 100-150 ; child : 70.

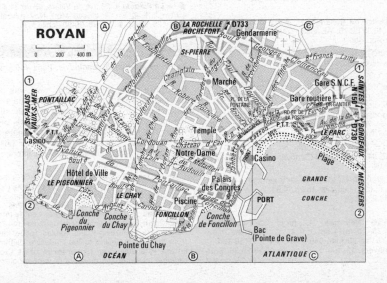

★★★ **Miramar**, plage de Pontaillac, ☎ 46.39.03.64, Tx 790821, AE DC Euro Visa, 27 rm P ⌇ closed 15 Oct-22 Mar, 250.
★★ **Beau Rivage**, 9, façade de Foncillon (B2), ☎ 46.38.73.11, Euro Visa, 22 rm ⌇ & 220.
★★ **Beauséjour**, 32, av. de la Grande-Conche (C1), ☎ 46.05.09.40, 14 rm 𝟙 ⌇ 𝒫 pens (h.s.), closed Oct-Mar, 275. Rest. ♦ ♪ 𝒫 closed Oct-May, 75-100.
★★ **Résidence de Saintonge**, allée des Algues (A2), ☎ 46.39.00.00, Euro Visa, 40 rm P ⌇ 𝟙 ⌇ ♪ & pens (h.s.), closed Oct-Mar, 540. Rest. ♦ *Pavillon Bleu* ♪ 𝒫 55-120.
★★ **Vialard**, 23 bis, bd A.-Briand (B1), ☎ 46.05.84.22, AE Euro Visa, 25 rm ⌇ 𝟙 ♪ & 175. Rest. ♦ ⌇ ♪ & closed Mon noon and Sun (l.s.), Oct, 55-100.

Restaurants :
♦♦♦ **Le Squale**, 102, av. des Semis (off map C2), ☎ 46.05.51.34, DC Euro Visa ♪ closed Tue , Nov-15 Dec. Spec : *foie gras maison, escalope de saumon à la crème persil*, 150.
♦♦ **Chalet**, 6, bd Grandière (off map C1), ☎ 46.05.04.90 ♪ closed Wed ex Jul-Aug, 15 Jan-15 Mar, 90-210.
♦♦ **Le Gigouris**, 37, av. Ch.-Regazzoni (B1), ☎ 46.38.66.31, DC Euro Visa 𝟙 ♪ & closed Mon and Sun eve. Spec : *huîtres farcies, sole grillée au beurre de ciboulette*, 45-130.
🅰 ★★★*Clos Fleuri* (100 pl), ☎ 46.05.62.17; at Médis, 6 km NE, ★★★★*Clairefontaine*, av. Louise (300 pl), ☎ 46.39.08.11.

Recommended
Guide to wines : *Château de Didonne*, 7 km E, ☎ 46.22.12.66, cellar tours.
Riding center : ☎ 46.23.11.44.

Nearby
BREUILLET, ⊠ 17920, 10 km N.
Restaurant :
♦♦ **La Grange**, ☎ 46.22.72.64, Visa ⌇ 𝟙 ♪ ▭ closed 6 Sep-26 Jun. Spec : *ragoût d'huîtres aux salicornes, nage de sole aux fines de claire*, 100-250.

Le GUA, ⊠ 17660, 15 km NE.
Hotel :
● ★★★ **Moulin de Châlons** (C.H.), RD 733, ☎ 46.22.82.72, AE DC Euro Visa, 14 rm P 𝟙 closed Mar. An 18th-C mill, 285. Rest. ♦ ⌇ ♪ & closed 25 Sep-8 May. Spec : *soupe d'huître aux algues, piccata de saumon*, 80-220.

La plage de NAUZAN, ⊠ 17640 Vaux-sur-Mer, 3 km N.
Hotel :
★★★ **Résidence de Rohan**, (C.H., R.S.), parc des Fées, 2.5 km, ☎ 46.39.00.75, AE Visa, 22 rm P ⌇ 𝟙 𝓺 ♪ 𝒫 closed Nov-Apr, 450.

SAINT-GEORGES-DE-DIDONNE, ⊠ 17110, 3 km S.
ℹ️ bd Michelet, ☎ 46.05.09.73 (h.s.).
Hotels :
★ **Colinette**, 16, av. de la Grande-Plage, ☎ 46.05.15.75, 28 rm ⌇ 𝓺 pens (h.s.), closed 15 Nov-15 Feb, 420. Rest. ♦ ♪ & closed Mon and Sun eve (l.s.), 50-100.
★ **Les Bégonias**, 11, pl. Michelet, ☎ 46.05.08.13, AE, 21 rm P ⌇ 𝓺 half pens (h.s.), closed Oct-Easter, 320. Rest. ♦ ⌇ ♪ 𝒫 70-110.
🅰 ★★★★*Le Bois Soleil*, forêt de Suzac (350 pl), ☎ 46.05.05.94 ; ★★★*Idéal-Camping n 1* (400 pl), ☎ 46.05.29.04.

SAINT-PALAIS-SUR-MER, ⊠ 17420, 6 km NW.
ℹ️ ☎ 46.23.11.09 ; mairie, ☎ 46.23.10.64.
🚉 ☎ 46.22.12.66.
Hotels :
● ★★★ **Villa Nausicaa**, 1, prom. de la Plage, ☎ 46.23.14.78, 10 rm 4 apt P ⌇ 𝟙 𝓺 half pens (h.s.), closed Tue, 5 Jan-20 Mar, 640. Rest. ♦♦ ♪ 𝒫 130-185.
● ★★ **Primavera**, 12, rue du Brick, ☎ 46.23.20.35, Euro Visa, 36 rm P ⌇ 𝟙 𝓺 𝒫 ▭ ♪ half pens (h.s.), closed

1 Nov-25 Dec, 300. Rest. ♦♦ closed Tue eve and Wed (Oct-Mar), 80-160.
★★ **Plage**, 1, pl. de l'Océan, ☎ 46.23.10.32, Euro Visa, 20 rm ⌇ 𝟙 half pens (h.s.), closed Wed, Jan, 450. Rest. ♦ 65-120.
🅰 ★★★*Domaine de Bernezac* (100 pl), ☎ 46.39.00.71 ; ★★★*Le Logis* (900 pl), ☎ 46.23.20.23 ; ★★★*Le Puit de l'Auture* (400 pl), ☎ 46.23.20.31 ; ★★★*Les Deux Plages* (200 pl), ☎ 46.23.11.42 ; *Marcel Taburiaux* (120 pl), ☎ 46.38.00.71.

SAUJON, ⊠ 17600, 12 km NE.
⚓ ☎ 46.02.97.55.
ℹ️ pl. du Gal-de-Gaulle (h.s.), ☎ 46.02.83.77, closed Sun.
🚉 ☎ 46.02.80.39, station on the Paris-Royan line.

Hotel :
★★ **Richelieu**, ☎ 46.02.82.43, AE DC Visa, 15 rm P 𝓺 closed Mon, 15 Oct-15 Nov, 160. Rest. ♦ ♪ 60-110.

RUFFEC

Angoulême 43, Poitiers 66, Paris 401 km
pop 4766 ⊠ 16700   C2
An important agricultural market for Poitou and the Angoulême region. Church with Romanesque façade★ and several Renaissance houses.

Nearby
▶ **Courcôme** *(8 km SW)* : 11th-12thC church★. ▶ To S, **Verteuil★** : terraced Renaissance château above the river bank ; Romanesque church (Burial of Christ, 16thC). ▶ **Lichères** : small Romanesque church★. ▶ **Mansle** : church (12th-16thC). ▫

Practical Information _____
RUFFEC
ℹ️ mairie, ☎ 45.31.05.42.   ✦

Nearby
SAINT-GROUX, ⊠ 16230 Mansle, 3 km NW.
Hotel :
● ★★ **Trois Saules** (L.F.), ☎ 45.20.30.40, Visa, 10 rm P 𝟙 𝓺 closed 22 Feb-3 Mar, 3-11 Nov, 160. Rest. ♦ closed Sun eve, 70-160.

VERTEUIL-SUR-CHARENTE, ⊠ 16510, 6 km S.
Hotel :
● ★ **La Paloma** (L.F.), rte de Villars, ☎ 45.31.41.32, Visa, 10 rm P ⌇ 𝟙 𝓺 𝒫 closed Mon, Nov school hols and Feb, 125. Rest. ♦ ⌇ ♪ 𝒫 50-90 ; child : 35.

Les SABLES-D'OLONNE*

La Roche-sur-Yon 36, Nantes 91, Paris 450 km
pop 16657 ⊠ 85100   A1
Built on a dune, this attractive town was created in the middle of the 19thC as the Vendée's first sea-side resort. It is situated between the strand and the mediaeval fishing port of La Chaume, on the narrows. The recent (1978) decision to create the artificial Chasses Harbour has now made Les Sables-d'Olonne one of the most frequented yachting venues on the Atlantic coast.

▶ **Notre-Dame-de-Bon-Port** church (17thC) is the only historic monument of Les Sables. ▶ **La Chaume** (ferryman at the corner of Quai Guiné) : partially Romanesque church, Gothic tower ; near the fort (18thC), pilgrims' church of **St. Nicolas** (12thC), now a cultural centre (after recent restoration) ; nearby, small maritime museum (Taverne de l'Olonais). ▶ Returning to Les Sables, follow the **Remblai** from the Grand Casino to the Rudelière district *(2 km)* : left, via Rue Guynemer, former abbey of **St. Croix,** now a **regional museum** and museum of contemporary art, one

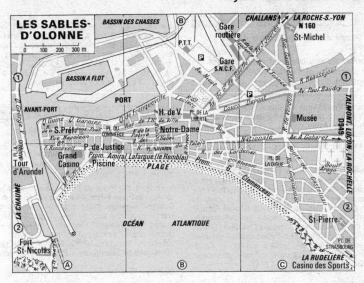

of the very first in France *(closed Mon., Oct. and am Nov.-Jun.)*; close by, Marine Zoo (Rue Chanzy). ▶ Via La Rudelière (Casino des Sports), Le Tanchet **zoological park.** ▶ **Coastal road★** *(corniche)* passes near **Puits d'Enfer** *(3 km),* and the former Orbestier abbey (12thC; *5 km)* before arriving at **Cayola** Cove.

Nearby

▶ N, through the **National Forest★** *(1 km after La Chaume;* 9 km long, 3 300 acres of pine and oak growing on the dunes) : **Ile d'Olonne,** bird sanctuary. ▶ **Olonne-sur-Mer** *(5 km)* : church with Romanesque choir. ▶ **Château de Pierre-Levée★** *(5 km via La Roche road;* 18thC) : park visit only (menhir). ▶ **Talmont-Saint-Hilaire** *(13 km E)* : ruins of castle (11th-16thC; *daily 9-12 & 2-6);* before reaching town, **automobile museum★** (100 old vehicles in running order). ▶ **Avrillé** *(10 km)* in region rich in megaliths : **Le Bernard dolmens** (SE), among which is that of Frébouchère★, one of the largest in France. ▶ From Talmont via L'Aiguillon road : **Jard-sur-Mer** *(7 km)* : 2 km W, **Lieu-Dieu Abbey,** founded in the 12thC by Richard the Lion-Hearted (cellars ; 17thC lodgings); **Saint-Vincent-sur-Jard** *(2 km E)* : on the sea *(1 km),* G. Clemenceau's "shanty", now a museum *(visits, May-Oct.)* of the former French statesman (1841-1929).   ☐

Practical Information _____

Les SABLES-D'OLONNE
ⓘ rue du Mal-Leclerc (B1), ☎ 51.32.03.28, closed Sun (l.s.).
SNCF (B1), ☎ 51.32.00.20.
🚌 *Transvendéens* (B1), ☎ 51.32.08.27 ; *Citroën,* ☎ 51.32.02.28.
⛴ connections with île d'Yeu (in summer).
Car rental : *Avis,* Rue de la Bauduère (Gare Routière) (B1), ☎ 51.95.08.86 ; train station (B1).

Hotels :
★★★ *Atlantic,* 5, prom. Godet (off map C2), ☎ 51.95.37.71, Tx 710474, AE DC Euro Visa, 30 rm ⊰ ♪ & ⊠ half pens (h.s.), 805. Rest. ♦ *Le Sloop* ⊰ & closed Sun (Oct-May), 15 Dec-30 Jan, 105-235.
★★ *Beau Rivage,* 40, prom. Clemenceau (B-C2), ☎ 51.32.03.01, AE DC Euro Visa, 21 rm ⊰ closed Sun eve and Mon, 5-15 Oct, 14 Dec-14 Jan, 200. Rest. ● ♦ ⊰ ♪ A thriving spot, especially in the high season : fine fish, 105-250.

★ *Le Merle Blanc,* 59, av. A.-Briand (off map C2), ☎ 51.32.00.35, 32 rm ⊰ ⌕ closed 30 Oct-15 Mar, 115.
★ *Les Hirondelles,* 44, rue des Corderies (B-C2), ☎ 51.95.10.50, 54 rm ℗ ⊞ closed Apr. Rest. ♦ closed Mon , Jun-20 Sep, 80-130.

Restaurants :
♦♦ *Au Capitaine,* 5, quai Guiné (A1), ☎ 51.95.18.10, AE DC Euro Visa ⊰ ♪ closed Sun eve and Mon (ex Jul-Aug), 5-13 Apr, 28 Sep-30 Oct, 20-28 Dec. Spec : seafood assortment, *huîtres gratinées "Antoinette", soles,* 125-175.
♦♦ *Le Relais de Cayola,* Baie de Cayola, 7 km S on the coastal road, ☎ 51.95.11.16, AE DC Visa ⊰ ♪ closed Mon eve and Tue, 1 Jan-15 Feb, 100-180 ; child : 50.

⚠ ★★★★*Les Roses* (215 pl), ☎ 51.95.10.42 ; at Olonne, ★★★*L'Orée* (270 pl), ☎ 51.33.10.59 ; ★★★*La Loubine* (130 pl), ☎ 51.33.12.92.

Recommended
Baby-sitting : info at the S.I.

Nearby

JARD-SUR-MER, ⊠ 85520, 20 km SE.
ⓘ pl. de la Liberté, ☎ 51.33.40.47.

Hotel :
★★ *Parc de la Grange,* (L.F., France-Accueil), ☎ 51.33.44.88, AE DC Euro Visa, 55 rm ℗ ⊰ ⌕ ⚬ ⊗ ⊰ ⋗⚬ closed Oct-Mar, 230. Rest. ● ♦♦ ⊰ ♪ An English chef working deep in the forest of Vendée : *crabe farci antillais, magret de canard, feuilleté de Saint-Jacques,* 55-130 ; child : 45.

⚠ ★★★★*Les Ecureuils* (190 pl), ☎ 51.33.42.74 ; ★★★*La Coquille* (35 pl), ☎ 51.33.42.67 ; 9 terrains.

TALMONT-SAINT-HILAIRE, ⊠ 85440, 13 km SE.
ⓘ hôtel de ville, ☎ 51.90.65.10.

Hotels :
★★ *Parcs,* at la Guittière port ☎ 51.90.61.24, 21 rm ℗ ⌕ closed 20 Jan-20 Feb. private beach, 180. Rest. ♦ ♪ closed Mon and Sun eve, 50-150.
Boule d'Or, 3, rue du Château, ☎ 51.90.60.23, Euro Visa, 8 rm ℗ ⊰ ⊞ half pens (h.s.), closed Sun eve and Mon, 20 Dec-20 Jan, 280. Rest. ♦ 55-105.

⚠ many sites (around 800 pitches).

SAINT-GILLES-CROIX-DE-VIE*

Les Sables-d'Olonne 30, Nantes 78, Paris 448 km
pop 6339 ⊠ 85800   A1

Two small former fishing ports on either side of the
Havre de Vie (estuary★ of the river Vie) gave birth to
what is today Saint-Gilles : a pleasant seaside resort
as well as a fishing and pleasure craft port.

▶ N, the **Corniche Vendéenne★** (coastal road) runs as far
as **Sion** beach *(4 km)*, part of **Saint-Hilaire-de-Riez** (see
paintings in church of same name).

Round trip of Vie and Jaunay Rivers *(approx 40 km; half-
day)*

▶ **Commequiers** *(12 km)* : ruins of moated 13thC castle; 2 km SW, Pierre-Folle dolmen. ▶ **Apremont★** : ruins
of Renaissance château *(visits in season)* overlooking the
valley road ; water tower in the upper village *(access to
panoramic terrace).* ▶ Through Coex, **La Chaize-Giraud**
(13 km farther) : Romanesque façade★ on the church.
▶ Return past the park of **Beaumarchais Château** (17thC;
no visits). ▶ Via Les Sables road : **Brétignolles-sur-Mer**
(rocks, beaches : La Parée★). Before arriving in Saint-
Martin-de-Brem, 500 m to the left, partially destroyed
church of **St. Nicolas-de-Brem** (11th-12thC).   □

Practical Information _____

SAINT-GILLES-CROIX-DE-VIE
ℹ️ bd de l'Egalité, ☎ 51.55.05.07/51.55.03.66, closed Mon
and Sun (l.s.); mairie, ☎ 51.55.01.57.
SNCF ☎ 51.62.50.50.
🚲 connections with île d'Yeu (Jul-Aug).
Car rental : *Avis,* Esso Station. 39, av. Mal Leclerc,
☎ 51.55.19.25.

Hotels :
★★ *Embruns,* 16, bd de la Mer, ☎ 51.55.11.40, 23 rm ⌁
🍽 closed Fri eve and Sat (l.s.), 21-27 Apr, 4 Nov-8 Dec,
180. Rest. ♦ ⌁ 🍽 Spec : *brochette de coquilles Saint-
Jacques,* 60-130.
★★ *Marina,* 60, av. de la Plage, ☎ 51.55.30.97, Visa,
40 rm Ⓟ ⌁ ♪ ⅃ 🍽 pens (h.s.), closed Mon,
22 Dec-1 Feb, 500. Rest. ♦ ⌁ ♪ ⅃ 🍽 55-70; child : 40.
★ *Ker Louis,* 46, av. Jean-Cristau, ☎ 51.55.01.91, Visa,
16 rm Ⓟ ⌁ half pens (h.s.), closed Dec-Feb, 390. Rest. ♦
♪ 60-85.

Restaurant :
♦♦ *Jean Bart,* Grande-Plage, ☎ 51.55.06.19, closed Mon
and Sun eve , Jan, 110-180.

▲ ★★★★*Le Pas Opton,* at Fenouiller (140 pl),
☎ 51.55.11.98; ★★★*Europa* (170 pl), ☎ 51.55.32.68; at
Givrand,   ★★★★*Domaine   de   Beaulieu* (210   pl),
☎ 51.55.59.46.

Nearby

BRETIGNOLLES-SUR-MER, ⊠ 85470, 10 km SE.
ℹ️ mairie, ☎ 51.90.15.06 (l.s.); ☎ 51.90.12.78 (h.s.).

Hotel :
★★ *Garenne* (L.F.), 26, rue des Dunes, ☎ 51.90.55.33,
Euro Visa, 15 rm Ⓟ 🌐 ⌁ half pens (h.s.), closed
30 Sep-1 Apr, 300. Rest. ♦ 50-100.

▲ ★★★★*Les Dunes* (100 pl), ☎ 51.90.55.32; ★★★*La
Moline* (69 pl), ☎ 51.90.04.42; ★★★*Les Vagues* (185 pl),
☎ 51.90.19.48.

SAINT-HILAIRE-DE-RIEZ, ⊠ 85270, 5 km N.
ℹ️ du pays de Riez, mairie, ☎ 51.54.40.58; pl. Gaston-
Pateau, à Sion, ☎ 51.54.31.97.

Hotels :
★★ *Corniche,* 117, av. de la Corniche, ☎ 51.55.31.37,
36 rm, closed Oct-Easter, 190. Rest. ♦ 70-120.
★★ *L'Atlantique,* 173, av. de la Corniche, ☎ 51.55.09.25,
20 rm, closed Sep-May, 180.

▲ ★★★★*Les Biches* (300 pl), ☎ 51.54.38.82;
★★★★*Municipal* (174 pl), ☎ 51.54.34.23; ★★★*La Parée
des Joncs* (150 pl), ☎ 51.54.32.92; ★★★*La Parée Pre-
neau* (100 pl), ☎ 51.54.33.84; ★★★*Les Chouans* (200 pl),
☎ 51.54.34.90; ★★★*Les Ecureuils* (230 pl),
☎ 51.54.33.71; ★★★*Les Grandes Roselières* (90 pl),
☎ 51.55.11.74; ★★★*Riez à la Vie* (250 pl), ☎ 51.54.30.49;
about 30 sites (about 3000 pitches).

SAINT-JEAN-D'ANGÉLY*

Saintes 27, Angoulême 65, Paris 444 km
pop 9530 ⊠ 17400   B2

Formerly capital of lower Saintonge, later a wine port
for the Boutonne River, this small town shows many
traces of its tumultuous past.

▶ Through the **Porte de l'Horloge** (Clock Gate, 14thC; bell-
tower), to **Pilori Fountain★** (Renaissance). ▶ S, **Audouin-
Dubreuil Museum** (head of Citroën between the two world
wars). ▶ At the foot of the unfinished Baroque church
(called **"the Towers"** : monumental façade★), is a Benedictine abbey destroyed by the Huguenots and partially
rebuilt in the 17th-18thC. ▶ Place de l'Hôtel-de-Ville,
18thC **abbey colonnade** surrounding the town hall.

Nearby

▶ **Varaize** *(8 kmE)* : side doorway★ on Romanesque
church. ▶ In the Boutonne Valley *(W),* **Les Nouillers** :
domed Romanesque church. ▶ **Tonnay-Boutonne** : site
on river bank; Porte St.-Pierre (fortified gate; 14thC).
▶ Return via **Landes** *(11 km NW of Saint-Jean)* : 14thC
wall paintings★ in the Romanesque church. ▶ Château
de **Beaufief** *(2 km),* a Louis XV folly *(2-7, 1 Apr.-1 Nov.).* □

Practical Information _____

ℹ️ hôtel-de-ville, ☎ 46.32.04.72.
SNCF ☎ 46.32.01.01.

Hotels :
★★ *La Paix,* 5, av. du Gal-de-Gaulle, ☎ 46.32.00.93, Euro
Visa, 17 rm Ⓟ 🌐 ⌁ 🖵 190. Rest. ♦ ♪ 60-110.
★ *Chalet,* 66, av. A.-Briand (gare), ☎ 46.32.01.08, Euro
Visa, 19 rm, closed Sun (l.s.), 21 Dec-6 Jan, 130. Rest. ♦
♪ 45-100.

SAINT-JEAN-DE-MONTS

Noirmoutier 32, Nantes 79, Paris 448 km
pop 5611 ⊠ 85160   A1

This resort was created by the promoter Merlin, who
built a façade of apartment houses that today stretch
for several miles along the seashore. A seaside boulevard runs along the dune to Demoiselles Beach.

▶ Nearby, museums at Saint-Hilaire-de-Riez, Grenouillè-
res and Orouet, 6 km S.

Round trip of Breton marshes *(70 km; half or full day)*

▶ **Notre-Dame-de-Monts** : at the end of the dunes road to
the beach, view of Yeu Island (Île d'Yeu). ▶ **La Barre-de-
Monts** : art and local traditions museum, "Davianol" Discovery Centre (recreation of a typical 19thC farm) and a
former water tower with a room which enjoys a panoramic view★. ▶ **Fromentine** : departure point for Île d'Yeu.
▶ **Beauvoir-sur-Mer** : formerly on the shore *(today, a km
away)* : partially Romanesque church; road towards Noirmoutier (covered at high tide ; *see hours posted).* ▶ **Boulin** : island in the marshes. ▶ Through Bois-de-Céné : former abbey of **Ile-Chauvet** *(SW).* ▶ **Challans** (pop. 13 060) :
famous duck market, in the heart of a breeding area. Leisure area. ▶ **Sallertaine** : restored Romanesque church.
▶ **Rairé** : one of two working **windmills** (18thC) in the Vendée, the other being at Châteauneuf *(visits).* ▶ Return via
Le Perrier or Soullans.   □

Practical Information ────────────

SAINT-JEAN-DE-MONTS
ⓘ Palais des Congrès, ☎ 51.58.00.48, closed Sun (l.s.).
🚌 bd du Mal-Leclerc.

Hotels :
★★ *La Cloche d'Or*, 26, av. des Tilleuls and 13, allée
des Ecureuils, ☎ 51.58.00.58, Visa, 24 rm ⌇ ⌇ 🦱
⌇ half pens (h.s.), closed Sun eve and Mon (l.s.),
27 Sep-1 Apr, 350. Rest. ♦ ⌇ ⌇ 55-130.
★★ *Plage*, 1-3, esplanade de la Mer, ☎ 51.58.00.35,
52 rm ℙ ⌇ closed 9 Sep-15 May, 250. Rest. ♦ 120-170.
★★ *Tante Paulette* (L.F.), 32, rue Neuve, ☎ 51.58.01.12,
AE DC Euro Visa, 41 rm ℙ ⌇ pens (h.s.), closed
7 Nov-1 Mar, 430. Rest. ♦ 60-100; child : 40.

⚠ ★★★★*Aux Cœurs Vendéens* (120 pl), ☎ 51.58.84.91 ;
★★★★*l'Abri des Pins* (220 pl), ☎ 51.58.83.86 ; ★★★★*la
Yole* (165 pl), ☎ 51.58.67.17 ; ★★★★*le Bois Masson*
(500 pl), ☎ 51.58.62.62 ; ★★★★*les Amiaux* (380 pl),
☎ 51.58.22.22 ; ★★★★*Les Pins* (140 pl), ☎ 51.58.17.42 ;
★★★*le Clarys-Plage* (140 pl), ☎ 51.58.10.24.

Nearby

BEAUVOIR-SUR-MER, ✉ 85230, 14 km N.
ⓘ ☎ 51.68.71.13 (h.s.) ; mairie, ☎ 51.68.70.32.

Hotel :
★ *Touristes* (L.F.), 1, rue du Gois, ☎ 51.68.70.19, AE DC
Euro Visa, 19 rm ℙ ⌇ half pens (h.s.), closed Mon (l.s.),
5-24 Jan, 230. Rest. ♦ ♪ ⌇ closed Jan. Seafood a speciality, 50-175.

Recommended
Guided tours : Tours of the swamp in carts or skiffs.
Activities in the Grange du Marais Mauvais (info at Tou-
rist Office).

CHALLANS, ✉ 85300, 16 km NE.
ⓘ rue de-Lattre-de-Tassigny, ☎ 51.93.19.75· (h.s.),
closed Sun.
Car rental : *Avis*, 14, pl. de Gaulle, ☎ 51.93.13.25.

Hotels :
★★ *Antiquité*, 14, rue Gallieni, ☎ 51.68.02.84, AE DC Euro
Visa, 12 rm ℙ ⌇ ⌇ closed Fri eve , Sat and Sun (l.s.),
Sep, 190.
★★ *Rocotel*, 9, bd de la Gare, ☎ 51.93.07.48, AE DC
Visa, 21 rm ℙ 230. Rest. ♦ *Le Dauphin* ♪ ⌇ Spec : sea-
food assortment with leeks, *Saint-Jacques aux pom-
mes*, 90-180.

FROMENTINE, ✉ 85550 La Barre-de-Monts, 14 km N.
ⓘ gare maritime, ☎ 51.68.52.32 (h.s.) ; mairie,
☎ 51.68.51.83.
🚢 ☎ 51.68.53.65, to l'île-d'Yeu, 1h10 crossing.

Hotel :
★ *Bretagne*, ☎ 51.68.50.08, 23 rm, closed 1 Oct-1 Apr,
110. Rest. ♦ 50-100.

⚠ ★★★*Le Grand Corseau* (450 pl), ☎ 51.68.52.87 ; ★★*3
terrains (over 1000 sites)*.

NOTRE-DAME-DE-MONTS, ✉ 85690, 7 km NW.
ⓘ mairie, ☎ 51.58.84.97.

Hotel :
★★ *Plage* (L.F.), 2, av. de la Mer, ☎ 51.58.83.09, AE DC
Euro Visa, 39 rm ℙ ⌇ closed Sun eve and Mon, 200.
Rest. ♦ ♪ Spec : *bar poché au beurre rouge*, 70-150.

Restaurant :
♦♦ *Pier'Plot*, rte de Saint-Jean-de-Monts, ☎ 51.58.86.48,
AE Euro Visa ⌇ ♪ closed Wed, 90-160.

⚠ ★★★*Le Bois Soret* (180 pl), ☎ 51.58.84.01 ; ★★★*Le
Grand Jardin* (180 pl), ☎ 51.58.87.76 ; ★★about 10 sites
(700 pl).

SALLERTAINE, ✉ 85300 Challans, 12 km NE.

Hotel :
★ *Relais des Quatre-Moulins*, D 948, ☎ 51.68.11.85, AE
DC Euro Visa, 12 rm ℙ ⌇ ⌇ closed Sun (l.s.), 1-15 Oct,
24 Dec-7 Jan, 120. Rest. ♦ 55-120.

SAINT-MAIXENT-L'ÉCOLE

Niort 24, Poitiers 50, Paris 383 km
pop 9358 ✉ 79400   B2

Primarily a market town, most renowned for its military (infantry) school founded 100 years ago by Colonel Denfert-Rochereau, born in St. Maixent.

▶ Via Châlon Gate, walk across the town : numerous
Renaissance and 17thC mansions and houses. ▶ **St.
Maixent Church★** : former cathedral remodelled in Renaissance style (17thC) after being sacked by the Protestants (11thC doorway, 15thC transept and bell-tower, pre-
Romanesque crypt). ▶ 7thC crypt under the neighbouring
church of St. Léger.

Round trip of Vonne and l'Hermitain *(60 km, 4-5 hr)*

▶ Via Parthenay road *(N)* : right, **Exireuil** Butte (viewpoint).
▶ Pond and ruins of Châteliers Abbey. ▶ **Ménigoute :**
small Flamboyant chapel. ▶ **Sanxay** : along a hillside in
a small valley (40 acres), Roman ruins★ (amphitheatre,
temple, baths). ▶ S, beyond the highway (Seuil de Poitou)
and the N11 : **Pamproux**, attractive village. ▶ Megaliths
along Exoudun road. ▶ **La Mothe-Saint-Héray** : 15thC
church ; orangery★ and two Louis XIII pavilions, last remnants of a château. ▶ Return via Sainte-Eanne *(4 km N)*
or the **Hermitain Forest★** (viewpoint).   ☐

Practical Information ────────────

ⓘ porte Châlon, ☎ 49.05.54.05.
🚄 ☎ 49.24.50.50.

Hotel :
★★ *Cheval Blanc* (L.F.), 8, av. Gambetta, ☎ 49.05.50.06,
AE Euro Visa, 38 rm ℙ ⌇ ⌇ half pens, 280. Rest. ♦ ♪
65-150 ; child : 40.

SAINT-SAVIN★★★

Poitiers 42, Châteauroux 87, Paris 330 km
pop 1058 ✉ 86310   C1

On the Gartempe River, (13thC bridge★) this fishing
centre is known for its **church** (abbey founded in the
Carolingian era ; magnificent 15thC spire, 94 m).

▶ The broad vault of the **nave★★** and the crypt are decorated with **murals★★★** (11th-13thC) restored 1968-74,
showing scenes from the Old Testament.

Gartempe Valley *(15 km to S ; 2 hr)*

▶ **Antigny** : 12thC church and lantern of the dead (with
altar). ▶ Boismorand Gothic and Renaissance château.
▶ Along the side of the valley, La Roche Windmill.
▶ **Jouhet★** : 15th-17thC murals in the funeral chapel.
▶ **Pruniers** : Renaissance château overlooking the river.
▶ Montmorillon (→).   ☐

SAINTES★★★

Royan 38, Bordeaux 116, Paris 470 km
pop 27486 ✉ 17100   B3

Antique *Mediolanum Santonum*, later capital of Saintonge, this town has become both a large regional
market and a craftwork and industrial centre. In terms
of monuments and museums it is one of the richest
towns in France.

▶ Esplanade A. Malraux (SI ; B2) : archaeological
museum★★ (partly outdoor). ▶ Near the water, **Germani-
cus' Arch★** (erected in 19AD in honour of the Roman
Emperor Tiberius, and restored in the 19thC by Mérimée,
Inspector of Historical Monuments, author of "Carmen").
▶ Via the Rue de l'Arc-de-Triomphe, **St. Pallais church**
(12th-13thC) and, nearby, **Abbaye aux Dames** (C2) :
St. Marie church★★ (11th-12thC, restored in 1938 ;
doorways★★, façade, "pinecone" belltower★) ; further

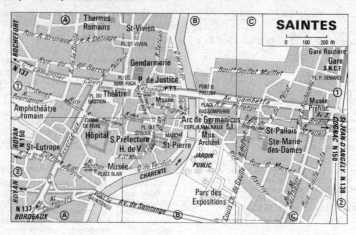

back, the abbey buildings (17thC) where the music festival takes place.▶ Prehistory museum in Ave. Gambetta. Higher up, near the station, is a **stud farm** *(visits)*. ▶ Via Bernard Palissy Bridge the **Cours National** runs up towards the theatre and the boulevard on the former ramparts.▶ Past St. Vivien Church (N), remains of the **Roman baths.** ▶ S, on Rue Victor-Hugo : **Fine Arts Museum★** *(10-12 & 2-5 or 6, closed Tue., paintings, ceramics from Saintonge).* ▶ **Archaeological dig** (information from Archaeological Museum, *in season 10-12 & 2-6; out of season afternoons only; closed Tue.).* ▶ **Church of St. Pierre★** (12th-16thC), former cathedral rebuilt after Protestant destruction : 15thC façade doorway★. ▶ **Dupuy-Mestreau Museum★★** (B2) : history, regional arts and traditions *(Apr.-Oct., at 3 and 5, closed Mon.).* ▶ **St. Eutrope Church★** (11thC; A2; choir, radiating chapels★★ in the apse), enlarged in the 15thC (bell-tower★) and again in the Renaissance, built over a **crypt★★★** housing the 3rdC tomb of the first bishop of Saintes.▶ Imposing ruins of **Roman amphitheatre** *(NW;* site★★) where some of the Festival performances take place on summer nights.

Round trip to the W *(40 km; half-day)*

▶ Along the Charente River : **Port-Hublé,** then Chaniers *(8 km;* round trip of Cognac vineyards.)▶ **La Chapelle-des-Pots,** historical crafts centre where the green ceramic glazes of Saintonges *(Verts de Saintonges)* were created. ▶ **Saint-Bris-Saint-Cézaire** : Maison de la Mérine (local arts and traditions), and zoological garden. ▶ Former **abbey of Fontdouce** (12th-17thC) : archaeological dig; concerts and shows in summer.

Round trip of Charente Valley *(N; 65 km; half-day min.)*

▶ **Le Douhet** *(11 km)* : doorway★ of Romanesque church; **château★** (17thC; *daily in season; closed am and Mon.)* : underground vaulted hall (11thC), Renaissance dovecote, tiled tower (17thC), park, ruins of the Roman aqueduct that brought water to Saintes.▶ **Écoyeux** : Romanesque church with fortified façade (15thC).▶ Saint-Hilaire-de-Villefranche. ▶ **Granjean** : Briacq★ (Saintonge arts and traditions). ▶ **Fenioux** : doorway★ arches of Romanesque church; lantern of the dead (12thC; stairway to the top). ▶ Saint-Savinien (→) : cross the Charente.▶ Via **Saint-Porchaire** (Romanesque and Gothic church), to 15th-17thC **Rochecourbon Château★★,** 2 km away in a splendid park (prehistoric caves, French gardens★); monument ("Château of the Sleeping Beauty") saved from ruin by writer Pierre Loti; halls decorated with paintings, timbered roof★; prehistoric museum in the keep (15thC; *9:30-6:30, closed Wed. out of season).* ▶ Return toward the Charente : **Crazannes** Château (15th-18thC; Gothic

keep, *ext. visit only)* and **Panloy** château (18thC; *in season).* ▶ **Port-d'Envaux :** former wine port, stopover for river cruisers. ▶ **Taillebourg,** where St. Louis vanquished the English in 1242. Overlooking the Charente, ruins of 15thC castle; on right bank, **Chaussée de Saint-James** *(1.2 km road)* supposedly dating from the Gallo-Roman period.

Roman and Romanesque Saintonge *(S; 70 km; full day)*

▶ D737, **Les Arènes** *(7 km)* : right of road, ruins of a Gallo-Roman sanctuary. ▶ **Chermignac** *(7 km W)* : "Hosanna" cross.▶ **Rétaud** : richly decorated pentagonal chevet★ on Romanesque church. ▶ **Rioux** : château; church★, akin to the one in Rétaud. ▶ Small but very charming Romanesque churches in **Saint-André-de-Lidon, Thaims★, Grézac, Corme-Écluse★.** ▶ Saujon (→ Royan, nearby). ▶ **Saint-Romain-de-Bénet** (Romanesque church), then former abbey of Sablonceaux (→ Royan)▶ Balanzac castle (late 16thC). ▶ Church at **Corme-Royal** : Romanesque façade★.   ☐

Practical Information _____

ⓘ espl. A.-Malraux, ☎ 46.74.23.82.
SNCF ☎ 46.92.50.50/46.92.04.19.
🚌 cours Reverseaux, ☎ 94.95.24.82.
⛴ Excursions on the Charente river : info S.I.
Car rental : *Avis,* 7, allée de Castagnary (A2), ☎ 46.93.72.10; train station.

Hotels :
★★★ *Mancini,* rue A.-Lemoyne, ☎ 46.93.06.61, Tx 791012, AE DC Euro Visa, 45 rm ◬ ♪ 240. Rest. ♦♦♦ ♪ Spec : *escalope de bar aux huîtres,* 70-200.
★★★ *Relais du Bois Saint-Georges* (R.S.), rue de Royan, cours Genêt, ☎ 46.93.50.99, Tx 790488, 21 rm Ⓟ ⚞ ☷ ◬ ♪ ᕼ ☐ ⚞ 290. Rest. ♦♦ ⚞ ♪ ᕼ Spec : *turbot à la crème de langoustine,* 105-195.
★★ *Avenue,* 116, av. Gambetta (B-C1), ☎ 46.74.05.91, AE Euro Visa, 15 rm Ⓟ ☷ ◬ ✥ 180. Rest. ♦ *Brasserie Louis* ♪ ᕼ closed Mon (l.s.), 70-130; child : 40.

Restaurant :
♦♦ *La Vieille Forge,* 6 km on the Rochefort road, ☎ 46.92.98.80 ☷ closed Tue, 5-25 Jun, 120-180.

Recommended
Baby-sitting : *C.I.J.,* ☎ 46.93.71.12.
Guided tours : *C.N.M.H.S.,* led by official guides, daily 15 Jun-15 Sep (info S.I.).

On the maps, a town's name underlined <u>Saulieu</u> means that the locality possesses at least one recommended establishment (blue or red point).

TALMONT**

Royan 16, Saintes 35, Paris 517 km
pop 79 ⊠ 17120 Cozes   **B3**

Tiny village with only one small street (full of flowers) : terrace with viewpoint★ over the Gironde; Romanesque church★★★.

▶ Minuscule church situated on the cliff edge, showing the skills of mediaeval builders : carved doorway★; rustic nave; apse★★ ornamented like the prow of a ship. The cliff was reinforced to hold up this edifice.

Nearby

▶ Via Pons road : Romanesque churches in **Arces** and **Cozes**; **Gémozac★** : 13thC choir; château in a park, with wine-tasting in the cellars. ▶ **Meschers** *(6 km N)* : grottos (called *trous*) opened in cliffs *(visits)* and *conches* at Nonnes★ *(beach)*. ▶ Upstream from the estuary *(S, 33 km; half-day)* : **Barzan** *(2 km to left of hill)*, **Fâ Mill**, remains of a Gallo-Roman circular temple. ▶ Drive through vineyards. ▶ **Mortagne-sur-Gironde** : at the foot of a hill, port on the Rive, now used for pleasure boating; 800 m upstream, dug into the cliff, St. Martial hermitage (3rdC?). ▶ **Saint-Fort** : Saintonge façade★ on the 12th-16thC church. ▶ **Saint-Dizant-du-Gua** : "blue fountains" in the park of the Château de Beaulon. ▶ **Saint-Thomas-de-Conac** : village with a number of craftsmen's workshops.   ☐

Practical Information _____

TALMONT
ℹ️ mairie, ☎ 46.90.80.97.

Hotel :
★ *L'Estuaire*, at le Gaillaud port, ☎ 46.90.73.85, Visa, 7 rm ℗ ⇐ 〰️ ⟍ ⌁ closed Tue eve and Wed, 15 Oct-1 Mar, 115. Rest. ♦ ⇐ ♪ closed 5 Jan-5 Feb, 23 Sep-2 Oct, 60-120.

Nearby

GEMOZAC, ⊠ 17260, 22 km E.
ℹ️ mairie, ☎ 46.94.20.35.

⚐ ★★★*Municipal* (40 pl).

Recommended
Guide to wines : *tour of storehouses*, (château).

MESCHERS-SUR-GIRONDE, ⊠ 17132, 5 km N.
ℹ️ pl. de Verdun, ☎ 46.02.70.39 (h.s.).

Restaurant :
♦♦ *Grottes de Matata*, bd de la Falaise, ☎ 46.02.70.02 ⇐ 〰️ ♪ ⌁ closed 15 Sep-31 May, 125-200.

⚐ ★★★*Côte de Beauté* (330 pl), ☎ 46.05.26.93; 6 terrains.

Les MONARDS, ⊠ 17120 Cozés, 5 km SE.

Restaurants :
♦♦♦ *Les Flots*, ☎ 46.90.70.45 ⇐ 〰️ ♪ ⌁ closed 15 Sep-15 Jun. Reserve, 130-210.
♦♦ *Auberge des Monards*, Barzan, ☎ 46.90.78.00 〰️ ♪ closed Thu, 65-140.

THOUARS**

Bressuire 29, Châtellerault 69, Paris 327 km
pop 11913 ⊠ 79100   **B1**

Set on a plateau surrounded by the Thouet river, the town can be entered from the St. Jean district (Loudun to Bressuire road) and the southern access road (below : 15thC bridge).

▶ On the isthmus, French Classical **château** with Cours d'Honneur★ (Grand Courtyard); from the **terrace** (Flamboyant Gothic funeral chapel), viewpoint★. ▶ Follow the **Rue du Château**, lined with ancient houses, to **St. Médard church** (Romanesque : arched doorway★), facing the *S.I.* in a 16thC house. ▶ The old town was built on the plateau

behind the church : 12th-13thC **Prince-de-Galles** (Prince of Wales) **Tower; Renaissance President-Tyndo** mansion, **Prévost's Gate★** (13th-14thC). ▶ Return to the modern part of town and follow Rue de La Trémoille : 100 m to the right, Hôtel de Ville (town hall) in 17thC building of former **St. Laon Abbey;** in its 12th-15thC church is a chapel with Head of Christ Crucified★. ▶ Farther down, small **museum** *(daily; in summer, 10-12 & 2-6; in winter, 2-4)* : prehistory, archaeology, regional crafts, mementos of the Vendéen Wars (18thC).

Nearby

▶ On a bend of the Thouet *(S)*, the *Cirque* (natural amphitheatre) of **Missé** *(4 km)*. ▶ **Pommiers** waterfalls *(3 km W)*. ▶ **Tourtenay** *(12 km NE)* : only troglodyte dovecote in France; small agrarian tools museum *(no visits)*. ▶ **Oiron** *(12 km E)*; **Château★★** (16th-17thC) in French landscaped park *(closed Mon. and Tue.)*; the left wing is considered a masterpiece of Renaissance architecture (open gallery★); inside : guardroom (coffered ceiling, 16thC frescos), grand stairway, banquet hall, king's bedroom (Louis XIII ceiling★), Cabinet des Muses★ (paintings). Gothic, Flamboyant and Renaissance **church★** : 16thC tombs★, altarpieces.   ☐

Practical Information _____

ℹ️ pl. Saint-Médard, ☎ 49.66.17.65.   ⚑
SNCF ☎ 49.66.00.13.

Hotels :
★★ *Château* (L.F.), rte de Parthenay, ☎ 49.66.18.52, Euro Visa, 20 rm ℗ ⇐ 〰️ ⟍ ⌁ closed Sun eve, 140. Rest. ♦ ⇐ 50-180.
★★ *Le Relais*, Louzy, 3 km N., ☎ 49.66.29.45, 15 rm ℗ ⌁ 125.

Restaurant :
● ♦♦♦ *Le Clos Saint-Médard*, 14, pl. St-Médard, ☎ 49.66.66.00, Euro Visa ℗ ⇐ ⟍ ♪ 4 rm, closed Mon and Sun eve. Pierre Aracil (late of les Muses, Hôtel Scribe, Paris) has returned to his native town and is now appearing in a charming old *clos*. Fine regional foods tuffs are painstakingly prepared : *terrine d'écrevisses, sandre aux artichauts, poularde fermière*, 85-200.

The VENDÉE WARS

A-B1

Two tours through the area, involving the principal sites of the 18thC religious and political struggle that raged throughout the Vendée. Places important in the life of the French statesman Clemenceau (1841-1929) are also included.

Round trip from Bressuire *(265 km; 2 days)*

▶ N of Bressuire, La Roche-Jacquelein and La Durbie manors (15th-16thC), followed by **Les Aubiers** and, some distance from the road, the ruins (since 1793 fire) of manor-farm of **La Durbelière**. ▶ **Mauléon** (pop. 8 498; known as Châtillon-sur-Sèvre during the Revolution) : Romanesque doorway★ of La Trinité church : ruins of feudal castle. ▶ **Saint-Laurent-sur-Sèvre** : site★; one of the basilicas houses the tomb of Grignon de Montfort (1716). ▶ **Mortagne-sur-Sèvre** (pop. 5 359): terraced gardens on the old city wall; ruins of 14th-15thC castle long occupied by the Royalists in the Vendée Wars; large granite church (partially 12thC). ▶ **Torfou Crossroads** : monument to the victory of the royalist Vendéens (Whites) over the Revolutionary army (Blues), in September 1793. ▶ **Cholet** *(15 km E → Maine-Anjou)* : scene of the bloodiest encounters during the Vendée Wars. ▶ **Tiffauges** : imposing ruins of the castle★ (13th-15thC), a battle site but also connected with Gilles de Retz, the Bluebeard of legend; site★ *(May-15 Sep., 9-12 & 2-6 daily; out of season Sun. and nat. hols. only)*. ▶ **Montaigu** : horse-back excursion centre in the Maine Valley; Museum of the Northern Vendée. ▶ **La Chabotterie** : Renaissance style 17thC château. ▶ **La**

Roche-sur-Yon (→). ► **La Chaize-le-Vicomte** : Romanesque church in the Boireau valley. ► **Chantonnay** (pop. 7479), where d'Elbée massacred 6000 Revolutionary troops (Blues) in Sep. 1793. ► N, via Les Roches-Baritaud (15thC castle), site of **Mouchamps** *(14 km)* and **Colombier** farm *(4 km farther)*; Clemenceau's tomb. ► S of Chantonnay, via the Grand-Lay gorges and the **Angle-Guignard** reservoir *(6 km long)*, L'Aubraie château (16thC), where Clemenceau spent part of his childhood; then, **Saint-Hermine** *(19 km)* : château (17thC); monument to Clemenceau. ► The route continues as follows : **Mouilleron-en-Pareds** : birthplace of Clemenceau and Maréchal de Lattre de Tassigny; two museums. ► **Cheffois** : 7 km N, **Réaumur** (manor of the physicist of the same name; fortified church). ► **La Châtaigneraie.** ► **Saint-Pierre-du-Chemin** *(6 km farther)*, one of the highest points in the region (alt. 230 m; panorama★). ► **La Forêt-sur-Sèvre** : château burned during the Vendée Wars (rebuilt in the 19thC).

Round trip from La-Roche-sur-Yon *(140 km)*

Besides the trip described above, Charette's steps can be traced in the following manner. ► Via the Nantes route, **Belleville-sur-Vie**, headquarters of Charette's army (Romanesque church door). ► **St-Sulpice-le-Verdon**, La Chabotterie manor; cross erected at the place of the Vendée leader's capture. ► **Le Lucs-sur-Boulogne**, a village burned down in 1793. A chapel built in Charette's honour in Legé. ► **Challans.** ► **La Garnache** : Charette lived in Fonteclose manor before leading the Vendée troops. ► **Nantes** : Charette was executed here, place Viarnes, in 1796.

Round trip from Mortagne-sur-Sèvre *(185 km; full day)*

► Mont des Alouettes (now restored mills used for signals in the Vendée wars), then **Les Herbiers** (→). ► La Grainetière, Le Parc-Soubise (→ Les Herbiers, nearby). ► **Les Essarts** (pop. 3672) : 11thC crypt decorated with frescos from the church; ruins of castle (11th-16thC) in park★. ► La Roche-sur-Yon (→). ► Chantonnay (→ above) ► **Saint-Prouant** *(11 km)* : **La Pellissonnière Château** *(2 km N; 16th-17thC)*. ► **Château de Saint-Mesmin** (14th-16thC), site of intense fighting between Vendéens and Revolutionary forces (1796). ► Former abbey of **Beauchêne**, 13th-15thC chapel. ► **Cerizay** (pop. 4881), industrial centre (gloves, shoes, automobiles), seriously damaged during WWII.   ☐

Practical Information ―――――――――――――――

CERIZAY, ⊠ 79140, 14 km W of **Bressuire.**

Hotel :
★★ *Cheval Blanc* (L.F.), 33, av. du 25-Août, ☎ 49.80.05.77, Euro Visa, 25 rm Ⓟ 🍴 closed Sat eve (l.s.), 18 Dec-5 Jan, 200. Rest. ♦ ♪ 65-85.

CHANTONNAY, ⊠ 85110, 33 km E of **La Roche-sur-Yon.**
ⓘ pl. de la Liberté, closed Sun (h.s.); mairie, ☎ 51.94.46.51.   ♥
SNCF ☎ 51.94.30.14.

Hotel :
★★ *Le Moulin Neuf* (L.F.), ☎ 51.94.30.27, 60 rm Ⓟ 🍴 🐾 ♪ ᪥ ᣰ ☐ 🅿 closed 23 Dec-2 Jan, 150. Rest. ♦ 🍴 ♪ Fresh- and salt-water fish, 45-80; child : 36.

MAULÉON, ⊠ 79700, 22 km NW of **Bressuire.**
ⓘ mairie, ☎ 49.81.45.22.

Hotel :
★★ *L'Europe*, 15, rue de l'Hôpital, ☎ 49.81.40.33, Euro Visa, 11 rm Ⓟ 🍴 half pens, closed Sun eve and Mon (15 Sep-15 Jun), 21 Dec-2 Feb, 245. Rest. ♦ ♪ 50-105.

MORTAGNE-SUR-SÈVRE, ⊠ 85290, 10 km SW of **Cholet.**
ⓘ rue Nationale, ☎ 51.67.71.32.

Hotel :
● ★★ *France*, 4, pl. Dr-Pichat, ☎ 51.67.63.37, Tx 711403, AE DC Euro Visa, 26 rm Ⓟ 🍴 ᣰ 🐾 ᣰ ☐

closed 30 Aug-14 Sep. The charm of a 17thC residence, 260. Rest. ● ♦♦♦ *La Taverne* 🍴 ♪ ᣰ closed Sat and Sun eve (Nov-Mar). We are pleased to tell you about Ph. Gaborit's delicious, creative cooking, inspired by the region : *canette du marais, foie gras frais aux échalotes, turbot pointes d'ortie*, 60-300; child : 45.

Recommended
Leisure activities : tour of the region in a steam train, ☎ 51.57.64.64, Jun-Oct.

SAINT-LAURENT-SUR-SÈVRE, ⊠ 85290 Mortagne-sur-Sèvre, 11 km S of **Cholet.**

Hotels :
● ★★★ *Beaumotel* (C.H.), at 1 km, ☎ 51.67.88.12, AE DC Euro Visa, 20 rm Ⓟ 🍴 ᪥ ᣰ 🐾 ᣰ ☐ half pens, closed 1 wk in Feb. A romantic setting in the heart of Vendée war country, 600. Rest. ♦♦ *La Chaumière* 🍴 ♪ ᣰ An expert pâtissier from Lenôtre's. Spec : *poissons au beurre nantais, trilogie de veau aux morilles*, 95-150; child : 40.
★★ *Hermitage* (L.F.), 2, rue de la Jouvence, ☎ 51.67.83.03, Euro Visa, 17 rm Ⓟ Rest. ♦ 🍴 ♪ Spec : grills over vine-cuttings, 65-100.

SAINTE-HERMINE, ⊠ 85210, 16 km NE of **Luçon.**

Hotel :
★ *Relais de la Marquise*, ☎ 51.30.00.11, Euro Visa, 12 rm Ⓟ closed Fri eve , Sat and Sun eve (l.s.), 15-31 Oct, 26 Dec-20 Jan, 120. Rest. ♦ 🐾 Spec : *saumon grillé au beurre d'anchois*, 60-150.

VENDEUVRE-DU-POITOU

Châtellerault 22, Saumur 71, Paris 370 km
pop 2154 ⊠ 86380   C1

Romanesque and Gothic church (side doorway). ► **Tours Mirandes★** *(1 km N)* : largest archaeological site (1st-2ndC) in western France. ► **Roches Château** *(1 km SE; 15th-16thC)*.

Nearby

► **Avanton** *(8 km S)* : Renaissance château; 14thC church. ► Ruins of castle *(2 km SE)* built by Admiral Bonnivet, favourite of François I. ► **Marigny-Brizay** *(6 km E)* : in a well-known vine-growing area; **Colombiers**, tiny Romanesque church. ► **Lencloître** *(10 km N)* : Romanesque church★ (façade fortified in 15thC).   ☐

Île d' YEU★★
(Yeu Island)

pop 4896 ⊠ 85350   A1

This island of granite and shale, 30km off the Vendée coast, rises 35m above the water at its highest point. Though it enjoys a very mild climate (frost is unknown on the island), its nearly 6000 acres remain barren of flowers due to the strong Atlantic winds. Nonetheless, the islanders do grow some early vegetables. The main activity remains fishing or related occupations; most of the population lives around Port-Joinville, one of the great trawling harbours in France, and disembarcation point from the continent.

The trip around the island *(15 km; can be made on foot (6 hr) or bicycle (3 hr); or by boat; departures for the mainland are determined by high and low tides)*

► **Port-Joinville** : small museum, one room of which is dedicated to Maréchal Pétain, who died on the island in 1951 : his tomb can be seen in the cemetery on the road to Fort Pierre-Levée, where he was in captivity *(no visits)*. ► Grand Phare (lighthouse; *3.5 km; panorama★)*. ► N, many megaliths (mostly dolmens) on the road to the creeks. ► On the **Côte Sauvage** (western coast), ruins of **Vieux-Château** (old castle; site★★), now restored; view from the keep. ▶ From there, footpath along the fjord to **Port de la Meule** (lobstermen), rocks and grottos, and to the cove of Vieilles : view towards the Corbeaux Lighthouse. ▶ Return via **Saint-Sauveur** (Romanesque church) and **Ker Chalon** beach (aquarium nearby). ☐

Practical Information _____

Ile d' YEU

⅄ ★★*Marais de la Guerche* (200 pl), ☎ 51.58.34.20.

Nearby

PORT-JOINVILLE, ✉ 85350 Ile d'Yeu.
ⓘ gare maritime, ☎ 51.58.32.58.
🚢 ☎ 51.68.53.65, 1 to 4 connections daily from Fromentine (1h10 crossing).

Hotel :
★★ *Flux Hôtel*, 27, rue Pierre-Henry, ☎ 51.58.36.25, 15 rm Ⓟ ⸓ ⁓ 180.

Index

A

Abbeville 693
Aber Wrac'h 281
Abers (Côte des) 281
Able 506
Abondance 800
Abondance Valley 800
Aboul 775
Abreschviller 545
Abrest 245
Abriès 417
Abzac 851
Accarias Pass 419
Accolay 346
Acey 441
Acquigny 646
Afrique (Mont) 347
Agay 727
Agde 486
Agde (Cap d') 486
Agen 101
Agincourt 684
Agnac (Château d') 499
Agnetz 460
Agon-Coutainville 639
Agonac 121
Agos-Vidalos 210
Agriates Desert 387
Aguilar (Château d') 510
Ahun 523
Aiffres 855
Aigle (Barrage de l') 518
Aigle (L') 657
Aiglun 732
Aignan 607
Aignay-le-Duc 344
Aigoual (Mont) 158
Aiguebelette (Lake of) 800
Aiguebelle 740
Aiguefonde (Château d') 780
Aigueperse 185
Aigues-Mortes 159
Aigues-Mortes 717
Aiguille du Midi 802
Aiguilles 417
Aiguillon 101
Aiguillon-sur-Mer (L') 844
Aiguillon (Anse de l') 844
Aiguillon (L') 612
Aiguines 765
Aigurande 233
Ailefroide 422
Ailly-sur-Somme 692
Aime 811
Ain Gorges 559
Ainay-le-Vieil 243
Aïnhoa 211
Airaines 693
Aire-sur-l'Adour 262
Aire-sur-la-Lys 673
Airvault 845
Aix-d'Angillon 234
Aix-en-Othe 380
Aix-en-Provence 701
Aix-les-Bains 794
Aix (Ile d') 845
Aizenay 862
Ajaccio 387
Ajaccio (Bay of) 389
Ajol (Val d') 543
Alagnon Valley 192
Alaise 437
Alan 616
Alassac 519
Alba 177
Alban 773
Alban (Mont) 748
Albarine Gorges 563
Albaron (L') 717
Albé 137
Albert 675
Albertville 795
Albi 772
Albigny-sur-Saône 569
Albinhac 202
Albussac 516
Aldudes 224
Alençon 629

Aléria 389
Alès 159
Alet-les-Bains 507
Algajola 394
Algues (Château d') 781
Alincourt 479
Alise-Sainte-Reine 335
Alix 555
Allauch 736
Allègre 196
Allemond 416
Alleuze 201
Allevard 412
Alleyrat 517
Allier Gorges 185
Allier Valley 241
Allimas Pass 420
Allinges (Château des) 812
Allonne 857
Allos 725
Allouville-Bellefosse 662
Alluyes 458
Ally 705
Allymes (Château des) 553
Alonne 454
Alouettes (Mont des) 852
Aloxe-Corton 340
Alpe-D'Huez (L') 416
Alpes-Mancelles (The) 582
Altenstadt 152
Altiani 401
Altier 168
Altkirch 148
Altorf 149
Alzou Gorges 122
Alzous 177
Ambazac 522
Ambérieu-en-Bugey 553
Ambert 185
Ambialet 773
Ambierle 555
Ambleteuse 681
Ambleville 479
Amboise 820
Ambonnay 370
Ambres 778
Ambronay 553
Amélie-les-Bains 487
Ameugny 359
Amiens 674
Ammerschwihr 132
Amou 262
Amphion-les-Bains 805
Ample Gorges 487
Amplepuis 574
Ampus 726
Ancenis 282
Ancizan 210
Ancy-le-Franc 335
Andaines Forest 632
Andelot-lès-Saint-Amour 443
Andelys (Les) 630
Andernos-les-Bains 255
Andlau 132
Andlau 149
Andon 731
Andouze (Signal d') 523
Andrésy 462
Andrézieux-Bouthéon 563
Anduze 160
Anet 453
Angers 582
Angevine (Corniche) 586
Anglards-de-Salers 198
Anglars 783
Angle-Guignard 872
Anglès 780
Angles-sur-L'Anglin 845
Angles (Les) 497
Angles (Les) 712
Anglet 215
Ango (Manoir d') 645
Angotière 663
Angoulême 845
Angoulins 863
Angrie (Moulin d') 597
Anjony 199
Annecy 796
Annecy (Lake) 796
Annemasse 810

Annéot 338
Annesse-et-Beaulieu 121
Annonay 161
Annonciade (L') 742
Annot 703
Anost Forest 344
Anse 555
Ansouis 735
Anterroches 195
Antibes 703
Antibes (Cap d') 704
Antigny 869
Antiques (Les) 754
Antonne-et-Trigonant 121
Antraigues 163
Anzème 521
Anzy-le-Duc 341
Apchon 198
Apothecairerie Cave 285
Appoigny 337
Apremont 868
Apremont-sur-Allier 244
Apt 705
Aragnouet 210
Arago (Canne de l') 510
Aragon 490
Aramits 219
Aravis (The) 803
Arbois 430
Arbonne 454
Arbresle (L') 554
Arc-et-Senans 430
Arcachon Basin 254
Arçais 858
Arçay (Pointe d') 844
Arcenant 354
Arces 354
Arces 871
Archiac 850
Archiane (Cirque d') 411
Arcis-sur-Aube 368
Arcizans-Avant 210
Arconnay 630
Arcouest Point 310
Arcs-sur-Argens (Les) 727
Arcs (Les) 811
Arcy-sur-Cure 346
Ardèche Gorges 162
Ardes-sur-Couze 192
Ardres 683
Aregno 390
Areines 837
Aren 219
Arènes (Les) 870
Aresches 444
Arette-la-Pierre-St-Martin 210
Argein 610
Argelès Valley 210
Argelès-Gazost 210
Argelès-Plage 510
Argelès-sur-Mer 510
Argent-Double Gorges 497
Argent-sur-Sauldre 234
Argentan 630
Argentat 516
Argentelles 630
Argentière 803
Argenton-Château 848
Argenton-sur-Creuse 233
Argilliers 176
Argonne Region (The) 532
Argoules 678
Arguenon 294
Argy 233
Arinthod 443
Arinthod 443
Arlanc 186
Arlay 434
Arlempdes 186
Arles 705
Arles-sur-Tech 487
Arlet 185
Arly Valley 808
Armellière (Château de l') 717
Armentières 372
Armentières 454
Armentières 690
Armentières-en-Brie 468
Armorique Corniche 302
Armorique Nature Park 282

Arnaga 211
Arnage 593
Arnay-le-Duc 335
Arnette Gorge 780
Arpaillargues 176
Arpajon 453
Arpajon-sur-Cère 186
Arques 113
Arques 692
Arques Keep 507
Arques-la-Bataille 645
Arradon (Pointe d') 326
Arraggio 399
Arras 161
Arras-en-Lavedan 222
Arreau 211
Arrée (Monts d') 282
Arrens-Marsous 222
Arromanches-les-Bains 644
Ars Castle 850
Ars-en-Ré 861
Ars-sur-Formans 575
Arsonval 368
Artannes-sur-Indre 827
Artenay 831
Arthies 467
Arthous 272
Artiguelouve 222
Artonne 185
Artouste (Lake) 217
Artzenheim 140
Arudy 222
Arvert 851
Arvieux 417
Arville 837
Arz (L'Île d') 327
Arz (L'Île d') 306
Ascain 211
Asclier Pass 174
Asco 390
Asco Valley 390
Ascou-Pailhères 606
Asnelles-sur-Mer 643
Asnières-sur-Nouère 846
Asnières-sur-Oise 455
Asnières-sur-Vègre 595
Asnières (Abbey of) 594
Aspe Valley 219
Aspet 615
Aspremont 748
Asquins 346
Assas (Château d') 499
Assier 102
Asson 222
Assy (Château d') 648
Assy (Plateau d') 810
Asté 222
Astrée region 554
Aubagne 736
Aubazat 185
Aubazine 519
Aubenas 163
Aubenton 379
Aubépin (Château de l') 572
Auberive 373
Aubeterre-sur-Dronne 847
Aubiac 101
Aubiers (Les) 871
Aubignac 609
Aubigney 441
Aubigny-sur-Nère 234
Aubin 776
Aubin-Saint-Vaast 684
Aubiry (Château d') 493
Aublette 294
Aubrac 774
Aubrac Moutains 774
Aubry-en-Exmes 630
Aubusson 516
Auch 604
Auchy-lès-Hesdin 684
Aucun 222
Aude Gorges 497
Aude Valley 497
Audierne 282
Audignon 262
Audincourt 439
Audinghen 681
Audresse in 609

Audrieu 644
Auffray 662
Auge Region (The) 631
Aullène 400
Aulnay 847
Aulteribe (Château d') 201
Aulus-les-Bains 609
Aumale 634
Aumont-Aubrac 164
Auneau 457
Aups 708
Auray 283
Aure Valley (The Upper) 210
Auribeau-sur-Siagne 720
Aurignac 616
Aurillac 186
Auris 416
Auron 760
Authie Valley 678
Aution (L') 761
Autoire 123
Automne Valley 461
Autrans 408
Autreppes 381
Autrey-lès-Gray 437
Autry-Issards 244
Autun 335
Auvers-sur-Oise 453
Auvillar 102
Auvillers-les-Forges 377
Auxerre 336
Auxerrois Region (The) 337
Auxey-Duresses 340
Auxi-le-Château 678
Auxonne 356
Auzances 520
Auzat 609
Auzers 198
Auzon 188
Availles-Limouzine 851
Avallon 338
Avaloirs (Mont des) 582
Avanton 872
Avenas 555
Avenières (Les) 419
Avensan 270
Aventignan 217
Avernes 467
Avérole (Vallée d') 807
Avesnes-le-Comte 684
Avesnes-sur-Helpe 679
Avesnois Area (The) 678
Aveyron Gorges 123
Avezan (Château d') 612
Avignon 708
Avignonet-Lauragais 611
Avioth 541
Avize 370
Avolsheim 149
Avord 236
Avoriaz 809
Avranches 650
Avrillé 584
Avrillé 867
Avully (Château of) 812
Avy 860
Ax-1400 606
Ax-les-Thermes 606
Ay 370
Aydat Lake 191
Ayet 609
Aytré 863
Azay-le-Ferron 237
Azay-le-Rideau 820
Azay-sur-Indre 827
Azé caves 345
Azergues Valley 555
Azille 497

■ **B**

Babaou (Col de) 740
Baccarat 533
Badefols-d'Ans 114
Badefols-sur-Dordogne 109
Bagatelle (Château de) 693
Bagneaux-sur-Loing 471
Bagnères-de-Bigorre 211
Bagnères-de-Luchon 606
Bagnoles-de-l'Orne 632
Bagnols 555
Bagnols-les-Bains 168
Bagnols-sur-Cèze 164
Baillanouse Pass 490
Bailleul 685
Bailleul (Château de) 648
Bain-de-Bretagne 299
Bains-d'Avène 497

Bains-de-Sylvanès 786
Bains-du-Boulou 493
Bains-les-Bains 533
Baix 172
Balagne Region (The) 390
Balaguier (Fort de) 760
Balaine 241
Balaruc-le-Vieux 508
Balaruc-les-Bains 508
Balazuc 163
Baleines (Phare des) 861
Baleone 389
Balleroy (Château de) 644
Ballersdorf 148
Ballon d'Alsace 132
Ballon de Guebwiller 135
Ballon Keep 593
Balme 806
Balme Pass 802
Balme-de-Rencurel (La) 422
Balmes de Montbrun 166
Balsièges 169
Balzac (Château de) 846
Banca 224
Bancarel 783
Bandol 713
Baneuil 114
Banne d'Ordanche 187
Bannegon 234
Banon 731
Banyuls-sur-Mer 510
Bar-le-Duc 533
Bar-sur-Aube 368
Bar-sur-Loup (Le) 731
Bar-sur-Loup (Le) 731
Bar-sur-Seine 370
Bara-Bahau Cave 111
Barade Forest 102
Baraque-de-Bral Pass 497
Baraqueville 785
Barbaste 118
Barbâtre 856
Barbazan 615
Barbe (Ile) 567
Barben (La) 757
Barbentane 759
Barbery-Saint-Sulpice 380
Barbizon 453
Barbotan-les-Thermes 614
Barcaggio 395
Barcus 219
Bardou 104
Barèges 222
Barentin 662
Barenton 656
Barfleur 638
Barge (La) 201
Bargème 726
Bargemon 726
Barjac 164
Barjols 714
Barles (Clues de) 725
Barneville-Carteret 667
Baronnies Massif 416
Barr 132
Barran 607
Barraques-en-Vercors (Les) 422
Barre-de-Monts (La) 868
Barre-des-Cévennes 165
Barroux (Le) 765
Barsac 273
Barthe-de-Neste (La) 222
Bartrès 217
Barzan 871
Bas-en-Basset 193
Bas-Rupts (Les) 537
Bascons 262
Basque (Pays) 211
Basques (Corniche des) 212
Bassac 852
Basse-Guerche (Manoir de la) 584
Bassée plain (La) 472
Bassillac 121
Bassoues 607
Bastelica 391
Bastelicaccia 389
Bastia 392
Bastide-d'Engras (La) 176
Bastide-de-Besplas (La) 614
Bastide-de-Mazères (La) 614
Bastide-de-Sérou (La) 609
Bastide-Pradines (La) 784
Bastide-Puylaurent (La) 177
Bastide-sur-l'Hers (La) 612
Bastide (La) 177

Bastides of Armagnac (The) 607
Bastides of Périgord (The) 102
Bastié-d'Urfé (La) 554
Bataille Pass 422
Batz Island 319
Batz-sur-Mer 288
Batz-sur-Mer 289
Baucher Cliff 765
Baud 287
Baugé and Baugeois region 586
Bauges Mountains (The) 798
Baule (La) 284
Baume rocks 431
Baume-Cellier Cavern 495
Baume-les-Dames 430
Baume-les-Messieurs 431
Baumes Amphitheatre (Les) 174
Baux-de-Provence (Les) 714
Bavay 431
Bavella Forest 393
Bavella Pass 393
Bavent 636
Bayard (Château) 412
Bayel 368
Bayeux 632
Bayonne 213
Bazadais Region (The) 256
Bazas 256
Bazeilles 378
Baziège 612
Bazincourt 546
Bazoche 454
Bazoche-Gouet (La) 466
Bazoches 346
Bazouges-sur-le-Loir 595
Bazus-Aure 210
Béal Pass 571
Beaubec Abbey 634
Beaucaire 165
Beauce Plain (The) 454
Beaucens 210
Beauchêne 872
Beaucourt 431
Beaudéan 222
Beaudémont 479
Beaufief (Château de) 868
Beaufort 798
Beaufort-en-Vallée 586
Beaufort-sur-Doron 799
Beaufortin 811
Beaufortin Region (The) 798
Beaufremont 543
Beaugency 821
Beaujeu 555
Beaujolais Region (The) 555
Beaulieu 532
Beaulieu-en-Rouergue 104
Beaulieu-lès-Loches 829
Beaulieu-sur-Dordogne 517
Beaulieu-sur-Layon 584
Beaulieu-sur-Mer 752
Beaulon 235
Beaumanois Château 868
Beaumarchès 607
Beaume Gorges 163
Beaumes 177
Beaumesnil 634
Beaumont 104
Beaumont 104
Beaumont 675
Beaumont 849
Beaumont-de-Lomagne 105
Beaumont-en-Auge 631
Beaumont-en-Véron 827
Beaumont-le-Roger 656
Beaumont-Pied-de-Boeuf 587
Beaumont-sur-Oise 455
Beaumont-sur-Sarthe 586
Beaumont-sur-Vingeanne 361
Beaune 339
Beaune Region (The côte de) 340
Beaune-les-Mines 523
Beaupréau 588
Beaurain 381
Beaurains 677
Beauranville 684
Beauregard 576
Beauregard (Château de) 825
Beaurepaire 423
Beaurepaire 852
Beaureteur (Château de) 557
Beausoleil 751
Beausset (Le) 713
Beauvais 454
Beauval 824
Beauvezer 725
Beauville 101

Beauvoir 234
Beauvoir-sur-Mer 868
Beauvois-en-Cambresis 683
Beauzac 193
Bec d'Allier 352
Bec-Hellouin (Le) 657
Bécherel 294
Bédarieux 494
Bédeilhac 609
Bédoin 765
Beg Meil 298
Begadan 270
Bègles 261
Bégude-de-Mazenc (La) 415
Béhérobie 225
Béhuard 586
Belcaire 507
Belcaire Fortress 783
Belcastel 776
Belcastel Château 109
Bélesta 612
Belfort 431
Belfort Territory 431
Belgodère 390
Belinaye 299
Bellac 517
Belle-Île-en-Mer 284
Belle-Isle-en-Terre 305
Belleau (Bois) 371
Bellefontaine 656
Bellegarde 830
Bellegarde-sur-Valserine 556
Bellême 657
Bellerive 246
Bellevarde (Rocher de) 812
Bellevaux (Châteaux of) 441
Belleville 544
Belleville-sur-Loire 345
Belleville-sur-Saône 555
Belleville-sur-Vie 872
Bellevue (Le pont de) 310
Belley 556
Bellignies 678
Bellocq 220
Bellot 457
Bellou Manor 631
Belloy-en-France 455
Belluire 860
Belpuig (Château de) 490
Belvès 104
Belvoir (Château du) 432
Bénerville 639
Benet 858
Bénévent-l'Abbaye 524
Benfeld 143
Bénisson-Dieu (La) 559
Bénodet 285
Bénodet 285
Benonces 557
Bénouville 636
Bénouville 643
Béost 217
Bérarde (La) 416
Berbiguières 109
Bercé Forest 587
Berceau-de-Saint-Vincent-de-Paul 263
Berchères-sur-Vesgres 453
Berck-sur-Mer 678
Berentzwiller 148
Bérenx 220
Bergerac 105
Bergheim 144
Bergheim 149
Bergues 680
Bernardières 116
Bernay 633
Berneval 645
Bernex 805
Bernières-sur-Mer 643
Berre-des-Alpes 748
Berre (Etang de) 715
Berry-au-Bac 374
Berry (Upper) 234
Bertangles 675
Berthenonville 479
Berthenoux 238
Berven 325
Berzé-la-Ville 349
Berzé-le-Châtel 349
Bès-Bédène 202
Besançon 432
Besbre (Valley of the) 234
Besne (Château de) 344
Bessans 807
Besse (Le) 571
Bessay-sur-Allier 241
Besse 126
Besse-en-Chandesse 194
Besse-et-Saint-Anastaise 194
Bessin Region (The) 634

Besson 241
Bessuéjouls 778
Bétharram Caverns 223
Béthisy-Saint-Pierre 461
Bethmale Valley 609
Béthune 680
Betschdorf 141
Bettex (Le) 809
Beuil 725
Beunaz (La) 805
Beuveille 538
Beuvron-en-Auge 631
Beuvry 680
Beuzeville 653
Bévera Valley 742
Beychevelle 270
Beynac-et-Cazenac 109
Bézancourt 634
Bézards (Les) 821
Bèze 361
Béziers 487
Biarritz 215
Bidache 216
Bidarray 211
Bidart 215
Bielle 222
Bienac 524
Bienassis 326
Bierne 680
Bieuzy 286
Bièvre Valley 455
Bièvres 455
Bigouden Region (The) 285
Billanges (Les) 522
Billaude Waterfalls 434
Billom 187
Billy 245
Binic 325
Biot 704
Biozat 185
Biran 607
Biriatou 212
Biron 104
Biron 860
Biscarrosse 271
Biscarrosse-Plage 271
Bissy-sur-Fley 351
Bitche 151
Bitet (Gorges de) 217
Bize-Minervois 497
Blaceret 556
Blagnac 620
Blanc-Nez (Cap) 681
Blancafort 234
Blanche Valley 802
Blanc (Le) 240
Blancs (Côtes des) 370
Blandy (Château de) 468
Blangy-sur-Bresle 667
Blanot 359
Blanot Caves 359
Blanquefort 269
Blanville 477
Blanzac 847
Blanzac-lès-Matha 854
Blanzaguet-Saint-Cybard 846
Blanzy 345
Blanzy 351
Blasimon 264
Blassac 185
Blausasc 749
Blavet River (The) 286
Blavozy 197
Blayais Region (The) 256
Blaye 256
Blécourt 373
Blénod-lès-Toul 547
Blérancourt 378
Blérancourt (Château de) 471
Blériot Plage 681
Blesle 187
Bleu (Lake) 222
Bleurville 534
Bliesbruck 545
Bligny-sur-Ouche 347
Blois 821
Blond 517
Blond (Monts de) 517
Blonville-sur-Mer 639
Blosseville 664
Bocca di Santa Lucia 395
Bochaine 408
Bocognano 393
Bodilis 302
Boen 554
Boersch 149
Boeschepe 685
Bohal 202
Bois Héroult 659
Bois-Chesnu 534
Bois-Chevalier 324

Bois-d'Oingt (Le) 555
Bois-de-Feugères 454
Bois-lès-Pargny 374
Bois-Mauboucher (Château du) 594
Bois-Plage (Le) 861
Bois-Sainte-Marie 342
Boiscommun 830
Boisle (Le) 678
Boisset (Le) 705
Boissonnade (La) 165
Boivre Valley 859
Bollène 750
Bolline (La) 766
Bon Repos 286
Bon-Encontre 101
Bona 353
Bonaguil 105
Bonette (Route de la) 807
Bonheur 159
Bonhomme (Le) 135
Bonifacio 393
Bonifato 394
Bonlieu 435
Bonnat 521
Bonnefont 616
Bonnefoy 193
Bonnes 849
Bonnet 533
Bonnetable 593
Bonneuil-Matours 849
Bonneval 458
Bonneval-sur-Arc 807
Bonnevaux-le-Prieuré 442
Bonneville 803
Bonneville 806
Bonneville (Château de) 631
Bonnières 467
Bonnieux 735
Bono 283
Bonport Abbey 659
Bons-en-Chablais 810
Bontin 348
Boos 659
Boquen Abbey 301
Bordeaux 256
Boréon (Le) 766
Borgo 394
Bormes-les-Mimosas 734
Borne Valley 803
Borne (La) 234
Boron (Mont) 748
Bort-les-Orgues 518
Bosc Cave 123
Bosc-Bordel 659
Boschaud 105
Boscodon (Forest of) 419
Bosserville (Chartreuse de) 541
Bossons (Les) 801
Bostens 262
Boucard 244
Bouchauds (Les) 846
Boucherolles 243
Boucieu-le-Roi 161
Bouconville-sur-Madt 539
Boudou 116
Bouges 240
Bougival 478
Bougneau 860
Bouillac 105
Bouilland 354
Bouillé-Thévalle (Château de) 597
Bouille (La) 666
Bouilly 380
Bouisse (Clue de) 732
Boulbon 759
Boule-d'Amont 490
Bouletternère 490
Bouliac 261
Bouliac 265
Boulieu 161
Boulin 848
Bouloc 778
Boulogne 163
Boulogne-sur-Gesse 615
Boulogne-sur-Mer 681
Boulou (Le) 493
Boumois (Château de) 597
Boupère (La) 861
Bourbansais (La) 294
Bourbilly 357
Bourbon-Archambault (l') 235
Bourbon-Lancy 341
Bourbonnais Mountains 235
Bourbonne-les-Bains 368
Bourboule (La) 187
Bourbourg 687
Bourcefranc-le-Chapus 848
Bourdeilles 106

Bourdon Reservoir 355
Bourg 256
Bourg d'Hem 521
Bourg-Achard 658
Bourg-Archambault 855
Bourg-Argental 572
Bourg-Charente 850
Bourg-d'Oisans (Le) 416
Bourg-d'Oueil 607
Bourg-de-Péage 418
Bourg-Dun (Le) 664
Bourg-en-Bresse 557
Bourg-les-Valence 420
Bourg-Madame 493
Bourg-Saint-Andéol 173
Bourg-Saint-Léonard 630
Bourg-Saint-Maurice 811
Bourganeuf 518
Bourges 235
Bourget-du-Lac (Le) 799
Bourget (Lake) 799
Bourgneuf-en-Retz 314
Bourgoin-Jallieu 419
Bourgonnière (Château de la) 595
Bourgueil 823
Bouriane region 113
Bourines (Les) 783
Bourisp 210
Bourlémont (Château de) 543
Bournazel 776
Bourneville 665
Bourron-Marlotte 470
Boury-en-Vexin 479
Boussac 518
Boussagues 494
Boussens 616
Bout du Monde (Cirque du) 353
Bouteille (La) 379
Bouteville 850
Boutigny-sur-Essonne 464
Boutissaint 355
Bouxières-aux-Chênes 542
Bouxwiller 148
Bouxwiller 151
Bouyon 732
Bouzey Lake 536
Bouzigues 508
Bouzols 196
Bouzy 370
Boves 355
Boyardville-d'Oléron 856
Bozouls 775
Bracieux 825
Braconne Forest 863
Brageac 198
Brahic 177
Braine 379
Bram 492
Bramabiau 159
Bramafan 379
Brancion 359
Branféré 319
Brantôme 105
Brasparts 282
Brassac 116
Brassac 786
Braus Pass 742
Braux-Sainte-Cohière 378
Bray 454
Bray Region (The) 634
Bray-sur-Somme 675
Bréca 288
Brécy 644
Bredons 195
Bréhat (Ile de) 287
Bréhec-en-Plouha 310
Breil 586
Breil-sur-Roya 753
Brêlès 283
Brêmes-lès-Ardres 683
Brenne (La) 237
Brennilis 282
Brès 177
Bresque (Cascade de la) 708
Bresse Region (The) 558
Bresse (La) 537
Bressolles 241
Bresson 414
Bressuire 848
Brest 288
Bretenoux 110
Bretesche 288
Breteuil-sur-Iton 657
Breteuil (Château de) 459
Brétignolles-sur-Mer 868
Bretteville 664
Breuil-Benoist 453
Breuil-en-Auge (Le) 631
Breuil-Yvain 239
Breuil (Le) 346

Breuillet 851
Breuillet 866
Brévennes Valley 576
Brévent (Le) 802
Bréviaires (Les) 473
Bréville-sur-Mer 650
Briançon 409
Briançonnais Region (The) 409
Briançonnet 732
Briare 827
Briatexte 777
Bricquebec 638
Brides-les-Bains 811
Bridjers 524
Bridoré 829
Brie-Comte-Robert 469
Brie-sous-Matha 854
Brie (Château de) 520
Brienne-la-Vieille 368
Brienne-le-Château 368
Brienon-sur-Armançon 356
Brière Nature Park 288
Brignogan-Plage 281
Brignogan-Plage 281
Brignoles 716
Brigue (La) 753
Brigueuil 851
Brimeux 684
Brinay 356
Brinon-sur-Beuvron 355
Brinon-sur-Sauldre 237
Brionnais Region (The) 341
Brionne 656
Brion (Pont de) 419
Brioude 187
Brioux 847
Briscous 214
Brissac 495
Brissac-Quincé 584
Brissac (Château de) 584
Brive-la-Gaillarde 519
Broc (Le) 732
Broglie 634
Brolles 465
Brommat 202
Bron 569
Broquies 785
Brossac 847
Brotonne Forest 665
Brotonne Nature Park 666
Brou 466
Brou 466
Brou 557
Brouage 848
Broualan 296
Broue 862
Brouilla 504
Brousse-le-Château 786
Bruay-en-Artois 681
Bruche Valley 132
Bruère-Alléchamp 243
Bruges 222
Bruley 547
Brumath 133
Bruneaux (Château des) 562
Brunehamel 379
Bruniquel 123
Bruniquel 776
Brux 859
Bruyères 373
Bruzac 106
Bubry 313
Buc 455
Bucey-lès-Gy 437
Budos 273
Buffon Forges 350
Bugue (Le) 111
Buhl 136
Buis-les-Baronnies 416
Buisson Pass 161
Bulat-Pestivien 300
Bulgnéville 534
Bully 554
Buoux (Fort de) 735
Bure (La) 544
Burelles 379
Burlats 785
Bury 460
Bury 477
Burzay 863
Bussang 534
Busséol 202
Bussière-Badil 118
Bussière-sur-Ouche (La) 347
Bussière (Château de la) 827
Bussière (La) 356
Bussières 561
Bussiéval 119
Bussy-le-Grand 335
Bussy-Rabutin 335
Buthiers 441

Buthiers 830
Buxières-les-Mines 244
Buxy 343
Buzancy 381
Buzet-sur-Baïse 118

■ **C**

Cabannes-de-Fleury 501
Cabannes (Les) 776
Cabassols (Les) 702
Cabasson 734
Cabestany 503
Cabourg 639
Cabrerets 115
Cabrières d'Aigues 735
Cabrillac 159
Cabris 731
Cabris 731
Cadéac 210
Cadenet 758
Cadière-d'Azur (La) 713
Cadillac 265
Cadouin 104
Cadourne 270
Cadoux farm 345
Cadouzan 319
Caen 634
Cagnes-sur-Mer 716
Cagnotte 272
Caguo-Ven (Col de) 740
Cahors 106
Cahuzac-sur-Vère 776
Cairn de Barnenez 306
Cajarc 115
Calacuccia 398
Calais 682
Calenzana 390
Calès 122
Callas 726
Callelongue 736
Caluire 569
Calvi 394
Calviac 119
Calvignac 115
Calvinet 195
Camarès 774
Camaret-sur-Mer 289
Camargue (La) 717
Cambes 261
Cambo-les-Bains 211
Cambrai 683
Cambremer 631
Cambronne-lès-Clermont 460
Camembert 631
Campagne 111
Campan 222
Campana 396
Campigny 658
Campodonico 396
Campomoro 400
Canabières (Les) 778
Canadel (Col de) 740
Canalettes Caverns 489
Canapville 631
Canari 395
Cancale 289
Canche Valley 684
Cancon 126
Cande-sur-Beuvron 824
Candes-Saint-Martin 826
Canet-en-Roussillon 503
Canet-Plage 505
Canigou Massif (The) 489
Canigou Peak 506
Canisy 663
Canisy (Mont) 639
Cannes 717
Cannet (Le) 720
Canon (Château de) 636
Canourgue (La) 173
Cantobre 776
Canville 664
Cany-Barville 664
Cany-Barville 664
Cany (Château de) 664
Cap Corse (Le) 395
Cap d'Ail 752
Cap Ferrat (Le) 722
Cap-de-Long-Lakes 210
Cap-Ferret 255
Capbreton 269
Capcir 497
Capdenac-Gare 781
Cape Pertusato 393
Capelle (La) 176
Capendu 490
Capluc Rock 175

Capo Rosso 399
Capoulet 609
Capvern-les-Bains 222
Caradeuc 294
Carança Gorges 497
Carantec 306
Carbini 398
Carcans-Plage 267
Carcassonne 490
Carcès 708
Carcheto 396
Cardaillac 112
Careil 288
Carennac 109
Carentan 644
Cargèse 395
Carla-Bayle 614
Carlit Peak 497
Carluc 735
Carlux 119
Carmaux 774
Carmes 853
Carnac 290
Carnelle Forest 455
Carnoët Forest 316
Carnon-Plage 499
Carolles-Bourg 650
Carolles-Plage 650
Caromb 765
Caronte 715
Carpentras 722
Carqueiranne 732
Carrelet (Plan du) 416
Carros 732
Carrouges 632
Carroux (Mont) 494
Carroz-d'Arâches (Les) 806
Carry-le-Rouet 736
Cars 523
Carsac 108
Carsac 119
Carsac-de-Gurson 116
Cars (Les) 520
Cas 104
Casamozza 394
Casamozza 395
Casinca Region (The) 395
Cassafières Port 486
Cassaigne 607
Cassano 390
Cassel 685
Casseneuil 126
Cassis 723
Cast 291
Casta 387
Castagniccia Heights (The) 396
Castanet 168
Castel-Merle 111
Castelbouc 174
Casteljaloux 116
Castellane 724
Castellar 742
Castellare-di-Casinca 396
Castellet (Le) 713
Castelmore 607
Castelnau 240
Castelnau-Barbarens 605
Castelnau-Bretenoux 110
Castelnau-de-Lévis 773
Castelnau-de-Médoc 270
Castelnau-de-Montmiral 776
Castelnau-Magnoac 217
Castelnau-Montratier 118
Castelnau-Pégayrols 778
Castelnau-Rivière-Basse 227
Castelnaud 109
Castelnaudary 492
Castelnou 504
Castelpers 784
Castelsagrat 116
Castelsarrasin 116
Castelvieil 264
Castennec 286
Castéra-Verduzan 607
Castets 264
Castillon 743
Castillon-du-Gard 167
Castillon-en-Couserans 609
Castillon-la-Bataille 268
Castillonnès 104
Castirla (Le pont de) 397
Castres 775
Castries 499
Cateau (Le) 679
Catteri 391
Catus 113
Caudebec-en-Caux 666
Caudeval (Château de) 613
Caudiès-de-Fenouillèdes 507
Caudry 679

Caulnes 294
Caume (Mont de la) 754
Caum (Mont) 757
Caunes-Minervois 497
Cauro 396
Caussade 108
Cauterets 216
Caux Region (The) 636
Cavaillon 724
Cavalaire-sur-Mer 740
Cavalière 740
Cavaliers (La Falaise des) 765
Cayenne (La) 848
Cayla 776
Caylar (Le) 496
Caylar (Le) 777
Caylus 123
Cayolle Pass (La) 807
Cazals 113
Cazaubon 614
Cazaux-Savès 611
Caze (La) 174
Cazilhac 495
Cazilhac (Château de) 497
Ceffonds 372
Ceillac 418
Celle-Saint-Cyr (La) 349
Celle (Abbey of La) 716
Cellefrouin 863
Celle (La) 243
Celles Valley 546
Celles-sur-Belle 854
Celles-sur-Plaine 546
Cénac 108
Cénevières 115
Centuri-Port 395
Céou Valley 108
Cerbère 510
Cercles 115
Cerdagne Valley (The) 492
Cère Gorges 108
Cergne (Le) 575
Cérisey 216
Cerisiers 354
Cerisy-Belle-Étoile 649
Cerisy-la-Forêt 644
Cerisy-la-Salle 639
Cerizay 872
Cernans 444
Cernay 135
Cernay 135
Cernon Valley 784
Cerny 374
Céron 342
Cérons 273
Cerveyrieu Waterfall 563
Cervières 571
Cervioni 396
Cessenon 507
Cessieu 419
Cévennes Corniche 165
Ceyssat (Col de) 191
Ceyzeriat 559
Cèze Gorges 164
Cézembre Island 295
Châalis 476
Chabanais 851
Chabeuil 420
Chablais Region (The) 799
Chablis 337
Chabotterie (La) 871
Chabrières (Clue de) 725
Chadenac 860
Chaffaud 848
Chagny 340
Chaillé-les-Marais 858
Chaillevette 851
Chaillexon (Lake) 440
Chaillol 409
Chailly-en-Bière 453
Chailly-en-Bière 454
Chailly-sur-Armançon 355
Chaise-Dieu (La) 188
Chaise-Saint-Éloi (La) 233
Chaises (Les) 473
Chaixmill 472
Chaize-Giraud (La) 868
Chaize-le-Vicomte (La) 872
Chaize (Château de La) 555
Chalabre 506

Chalain Lake 437
Chalain-d'Uzore 554
Chalais 847
Chalam Crest 556
Chalamont 560
Chalard (Le) 524
Chalençon 193
Chalet Reynard 765
Chalet-de-la-Maline 765
Challain-la-Potherie 597
Challans 868
Challes-les-Eaux 800
Chalmazel 571
Chalo-Saint-Mars 464
Chalon-sur-Saône 342
Chalonnaise Region (The) 343
Chalonnes-sur-Loire 586
Châlons-sur-Marne 368
Chalosse Region (The) 261
Chalou-Moulineux 464
Châlus 519
Chamalières 189
Chamalières-sur-Loire 193
Chamarande (Château de) 464
Chambaras 177
Chambertin 353
Chambéry 800
Chambles 563
Chambly (Lake) 437
Chambois 630
Chamboëlle-Musigny 353
Chambon-sur-Lac 195
Chambon-sur-Lignon (Le) 203
Chambon-sur-Voueize 520
Chambon (Lake) 195
Chambonneau 859
Chambord 823
Chambost 555
Chambotte 799
Chamboulive 526
Chambray 668
Chamelet 555
Chamonix-Mont Blanc 801
Champ 168
Champ-de-Bataille (Château du) 656
Champ-le-Duc 537
Champagnac 853
Champagnac-de-Belair 105
Champagne 161
Champagne-au-Mont-D'Or 569
Champagné-Saint-Hilaire 859
Champagne-sur-Oise 455
Champagne (La route du) 369
Champagnole 434
Champallement 355
Champdeniers 855
Champdieu 555
Champeaux 328
Champeaux 469
Champeaux 650
Champeix 200
Champigné 585
Champigny-sur-Veude 826
Champillon-Bellevue 372
Champlémy 360
Champlieu 461
Champlitte 434
Champniers 847
Champrepus 650
Champs Pass 725
Champsaur Region (The) 409
Champs (Château de) 468
Champtoceaux 307
Champtoceaux 595
Chamrousse 414
Chanac 173
Chancelade 121
Chandolas-Maisonneuve 177
Changé (Bois de) 593
Change (Le) 121
Chaniers 850
Chanonat 191
Chantemerle 409
Chanteuges 185
Chantilly 456
Chantilly Forest 456
Chantonnay 872
Chaource 370
Chapaize 359
Chapeau 234
Chapelle-aux-Filzméens (La) 292
Chapelle-aux-Pots (La) 454
Chapelle-Caro (La) 301
Chapelle-d'Abondance (La) 800
Chapelle-d'Angillon (La) 234
Chapelle-des-Marais (La) 288
Chapelle-des-Pots (La) 870

Chapelle-en-Valgaudemar (La) 421
Chapelle-en-Valjouffrey (La) 420
Chapelle-en-Vercors (La) 423
Chapelle-Faucher (La) 106
Chapelle-Rainsouin (La) 588
Chapelle-Saint-André (La) 360
Chapelle-Saint-Géraud (La) 517
Chapelle-Saint-Mesmin (La) 831
Chapelle-sous-Brancion (La) 359
Chapelle-sur-Crécy (La) 466
Chapelle-sur-Dun (La) 664
Chapelon 830
Chapparon 797
Chaptuzat 185
Charavines 419
Charbonnières-les-Bains 554
Charbrières Forest 521
Charité-sur-Loire (La) 343
Charlannes Plateau 187
Charleville-Mézières 371
Charlieu 559
Charmant 846
Charmant Som 410
Charmauvillers 436
Charmeil 246
Charmes 534
Charmes-sur-Rhône 166
Charmette Pass (La) 410
Charmettes (Les) 800
Charnay 555
Charny 356
Charolles 342
Charost 240
Charquemont 436
Charron 851
Charroux 848
Chars 472
Chartre-sur-le-Loir (La) 587
Chartres 456
Chartreuse du Reposoir 803
Chartreuse Massif (The) 410
Chassagne-Montrachet 340
Chasseigne 853
Chasselas 349
Chasselay 554
Chasseneuil-du-Poitou 859
Chasseneuil-sur-Bonnieure 863
Chassenon 524
Chassenon 851
Chassey-le-Camp 343
Chassezac Valley 163
Chassiers 163
Chassiron 856
Chassy (Château de) 351
Chastang 516
Chastellux 346
Chastellux 351
Chastenay manor 346
Chastillon Valley 760
Chastreix-Sancy 194
Châtaigneraie (La) 872
Château-Arnoux 759
Château-Chalon 434
Château-Chinon 344
Château-d'Oléron (Le) 856
Château-Gombert 736
Château-Gontier 588
Château-Guillaume 233
Château-la-Vallière 834
Château-Lambert 436
Château-Landon 458
Château-Larcher 859
Château-Queyras 417
Château-Renault 820
Château-Rocher 239
Château-Roussillon 503
Château-Thierry 371
Châteaubourg 172
Châteaubourg 318
Châteaubriant 291
Châteaubrun 239
Châteaudouble Gorges 726
Châteaudun 458
Châteaufort 459
Châteaugiron 318
Châteaulin 291
Châteaumeillant 239
Châteauneuf 342
Châteauneuf 355
Châteauneuf Caves 200
Châteauneuf-de-Contes 748
Châteauneuf-de-Randon 168
Châteauneuf-du-Faou 305
Châteauneuf-du-Pape 750
Châteauneuf-du-Rhône 415

Châteauneuf-en-Thymerais 458
Châteauneuf-les-Bains 188
Châteauneuf-sur-Charente 850
Châteauneuf-sur-Cher 237
Châteauneuf-sur-Loire 831
Châteauneuf-sur-Sarthe 585
Châteauponsac 517
Châteaurenard 709
Châteauroux 237
Chateauvallon 760
Châtel 800
Châtel-Censoir 361
Châtel-de-Neuvre 241
Châtel-de-Neuvre 241
Châtel-Montagne 235
Châtel-sur-Moselle 534
Châtelaillon 863
Châtelaillon-Plage 865
Châtelaudren 300
Châtelet 239
Châtelguyon 188
Châtelier 239
Châtellerault 239
Châtellerault Forest 849
Châtelux-le-Marcheix 522
Châtenois 149
Châtillon-Coligny 830
Châtillon-d'Azergues 555
Châtillon-en-Bazois 344
Châtillon-en-Diois 411
Châtillon-sur-Chalaronne 560
Châtillon-sur-Cher 824
Châtillon-sur-Indre 237
Châtillon-sur-Marne 370
Châtillon-sur-Seine 344
Chatillon (Crêt du) 797
Châtre (La) 238
Châtres 850
Chaudefour Valley 194
Chaudes-Aigues 189
Chaudieu 799
Chaufailles 342
Chauffry 462
Chaulme (La) 186
Chaumeix 521
Chaumont 345
Chaumont 371
Chaumont-sur-Loire 823
Chauriat 187
Chausey Islands 650
Chaussée Neuve (La) 288
Chauve (Mont) 748
Chauvigny 849
Chauvirey-le-Châtel 440
Chaux Forest 430
Chavade Pass (La) 162
Chavanay 571
Chavanges 372
Chavigny 543
Chavoires 797
Chavroches 234
Chazay 555
Chazelet 233
Chazeron 188
Chef-Boutonne 854
Cheffes 585
Cheffois 872
Chéhéry 378
Chémery 825
Chemillé 588
Chemilly 241
Chénas 555
Chenavari 166
Chenecey-Buillon 438
Chênehutte-les-Tuffeaux 584
Chénérailles 523
Chenonceaux 824
Chenôve 353
Cher Valley (The) 824
Cherbourg 637
Cherisy 463
Chermignac 870
Chéroy 358
Chéroy 470
Cherrueix 296
Cherval 115
Cherves 850
Cherville 369
Chesnay (Le) 479
Chevagnes 239
Chevannes 337
Chevenon 353
Cheverny 825
Chèvre Roche 534
Chèvre (Cap de la) 293
Chèvreloup 478
Chevreuse 459
Chevreuse Valley 459
Chevroux 558

Chevry 470
Cheylade 198
Cheylard (Le) 166
Cheylé (Belvédère du) 201
Cheyrac 196
Chezal-Benoît 240
Chezery-Forens 556
Chiavari 389
Chiers Valley 538
Chiffrevast 638
Chinon 825
Chioula Pass 606
Chirac 169
Chirac 851
Chis 227
Chissay-en-Touraine 824
Chissey-lès-Mâcon 359
Chitenay 823
Chitry 338
Chitry (Château de) 361
Chizé Forest 847
Chœurs-Bommiers 240
Cholet 588
Chonas-l'Ambalan 424
Chooz 375
Choranche (Grottes de) 422
Chorey-lès-Beaune 340
Chouvigny 239
Cians Gorges 725
Ciboure 212
Ciboure 224
Cierp-Gaud 615
Cindré 234
Cindre (Mont) 570
Cinq-Mars-la-Pile 828
Cinto (Monte) 390
Ciotat (La) 724
Cirey-sur-Blaise 382
Citardière 854
Cîteaux Abbey 354
Civaux 849
Civrac 270
Civray 848
Clairac 119
Clairvaux 368
Clairvaux 776
Clairvaux-les-Lacs 434
Clamecy 361
Clamouse Cavern 495
Clamoux Gorges 498
Clans 760
Claps 411
Clarée (Valley of the) 409
Claud 119
Claye-Souilly 468
Clayette (La) 342
Clécy 666
Cléden-Cap-Sizun 316
Cléden-Poher 305
Cléder 325
Cleebourg 152
Clères 662
Clergoux 525
Clermont 460
Clermont Abbey 590
Clermont-en-Argonne 532
Clermont-en-Auge 631
Clermont-Ferrand 189
Clermont-l'Hérault 496
Cléron (Château de) 438
Cléry-Saint-André 821
Clisson 291
Cloche Valley 471
Cloyes-sur-le-Loir 458
Cluny 344
Clusaz (La) 803
Cluse-et-Mijoux (La) 442
Cluses 806
Coarraze 221
Coatcouraval 320
Cocalière 159
Coëtquen Forest 294
Cœuvres 381
Cognac 849
Cogolin 740
Cogolin (Marines de) 755
Coiffy-le-Haut 368
Coignières 479
Coincy 372
Coiron Plateau 166
Colayrac 101
Colembert 682
Coligny 558
Colle-sur-Loup (La) 749
Collet-de-Dèze (Le) 166
Collet (Le) 537
Colleville-Montgomery 643
Colleville-Saint-Laurent 643
Collias 176
Collioure 510
Collobrières 740

Collonges-au-Mont-D'Or 569
Collonges-la-Rouge 520
Collonges-lès-Bévy 353
Colmar 133
Colmars-les-Alpes 725
Colmiane (La) 766
Cologne 611
Colombey-les-Deux-Églises 371
Colombiers 849
Colombiers 860
Colombiers 872
Colomby 667
Colroy-la-Roche 132
Combarelles Cave 111
Combe d'Ire 797
Combe-Laval 422
Combeaufontaine 444
Combéroumal 778
Combloux 810
Combourg 291
Combret (Château de) 783
Combreux 830
Combronde 189
Cominac 609
Commagny 356
Commana 302
Commarin 355
Commeaux 630
Commelles Ponds 476
Commequiers 868
Commercy 534
Compains 192
Comper 311
Compiègne 460
Compiègne Forest 461
Comprégnac 786
Compreignac 521
Comps-sur-Artuby 726
Comtal Plateau 783
Comtal (Le causse) 775
Conat 506
Concarneau 292
Concarneau 292
Conches-en-Ouche 657
Conchy 684
Condamine (La) 743
Condat 191
Condat-sur-Vézère 112
Condé-en-Brie 371
Condé-sur-Aisne 379
Condé-sur-Noireau 650
Condéon 847
Condom 608
Condorcet 416
Condrieu 571
Conduché 115
Confins (Vallon des) 803
Conflans 795
Conflans-Sainte-Honorine 462
Confolens 848
Confort 296
Confrançon 558
Conjux 799
Conleau (La presqu'île de) 327
Conliège 438
Connaux 165
Connerré 593
Conques 776
Conques 778
Conques-sur-l'Orbiel 490
Conquet (Le) 293
Conros 186
Cons-la-Grandville 538
Consolation 435
Contamines-Montjoie (Les) 809
Conterne 632
Contes 748
Conteville 658
Contres 825
Contrexéville 534
Coral Hermitage 490
Coray 372
Corbeaux (Lake of) 537
Corbelin (Manor) 360
Corbère (Château de) 504
Corbie 675
Corbier 807
Corbières (Pont des) 409
Corbigny 361

Corbora (Couvent of) 390
Corcelles (Château de) 555
Cordeland de Chamoux 360
Cordès 196
Cordes 776
Cordon 810
Corenc-Montfleury 414
Cormatin 359
Corme-Ecluse 870
Corme-Royal 870
Cormeilles 631
Cormeilles-en-Vexin 472
Cormery 827
Corneilla-de-Conflent 489
Corneville-sur-Risle 658
Corniches (Route des) 606
Cornillon 164
Cornillon-Confoux 715
Cornillon (Château de) 562
Cornus 784
Corps-la-Salette 745
Corrençon-en-Vercors 423
Correrie (La) 410
Corrèze Plateau 520
Corrèze (Valley of the) 519
Corsen Point 281
Corseul 294
Corsican Regional Park 396
Corte 397
Cos d'Estournel 270
Cosne-sur-Loire 345
Cossarieu 256
Cossé-le-Vivien 590
Costabonne Peak 490
Côte d'Opale Corniche 681
Côte de Granit Rose 311
Côte Sauvage 314
Côte-Saint-André (La) 419
Coteau (Le) 573
Cotentin Peninsula (The) 638
Coti-Chiavari 389
Cotignac 708
Cotinière (La) 857
Couarde "peninsula" (La) 286
Couarde (La) 861
Coubre Forest 851
Couches 345
Coucy-le-Château 373
Coudray-Montceaux (Le) 464
Coudray-Montpensier (Château du) 826
Coudray-Salbart 855
Couëlan 294
Cougnac Caves 113
Cougnaguet 122
Cougousse 783
Couiza 507
Coulgens 863
Couloir Samson 765
Coulombs 457
Coulommiers 462
Coulon 858
Coulonges 860
Coulonges-sur-l'Autize 852
Coupesarte 631
Coupiac 786
Coupvray 466
Cour-Cheverny 823
Cour-sur-Loire 822
Courances (Château de) 469
Courbanges 194
Courbons 725
Courcelles 472
Courcelles-Chaussy 541
Courchevel 804
Courcôme 866
Courlans 438
Courmemin 833
Couronne (La) 846
Courpière 201
Cours-la-Ville 574
Coursegoules 732
Courseulles-sur-Mer 644
Courson 453
Court d'Aron (Château de la) 853
Courtalain 458
Courtanvaux (Château de) 595
Courtefontaine 433
Courtenay 830
Courtes 558
Courtils 656
Courtivron 358
Courville 476
Couserans to Plantaurel (From) 609
Couserans Valleys (The Upper) 608
Cousin Valley 338
Cousin-le-Pont 338
Coussac-Bonneval 524

Coussac-les-Métairies 852
Coussay-les-Bois 862
Coussey 543
Coustouges 487
Coutainville 639
Coutances 639
Coutras 268
Couture-Boussey (La) 646
Couvertoirade (La) 777
Couvonges 546
Coux 172
Couzan (Château de) 554
Couzes 192
Couzon-au-Mont-D'Or 570
Cozes 871
Cramant 370
Crancot 438
Cransac 113
Craon 597
Craponne-sur-Arzon 188
Crau plains 707
Cravant 346
Cravant-les-Coteaux 826
Créac'h Ingar 325
Crecey-sur-Tille 358
Crèche (La) 856
Crécy-en-Ponthieu 692
Crécy-la-Chapelle 466
Creil 477
Crémieu 419
Créon 264
Crépy-en-Valois 462
Cressia 443
Crest 191
Crest 411
Crest-Voland 808
Crêtes (Corniche des) 723
Crêtes (Route des) 135
Creully 644
Creuse Gorges 239
Creuse Valley 516
Creusot (Le) 345
Creux Billard 437
Creuzier-le-Vieux 246
Crevant 238
Crèvecoeur-en-Auge 631
Creysse 109
Cricqueville-en-Auge 631
Crillon-le-Brave 765
Croisic (Le) 293
Croisset 666
Croix 691
Croix de Fer 803
Croix de Fer Pass (La) 807
Croix de Revollat 412
Croix-Faron (Fort de la) 760
Croix-Rampeau 569
Croix-Rochette (La) 443
Croix-Valmer (La) 740
Cropières 202
Crossac 288
Crotoy (Le) 685
Crouesty (Le) 318
Croutelle 859
Crouzille (La) 521
Crozant 239
Crozet 354
Crozon Peninsula 293
Crozon-Morgat 293
Cruas 172
Cruou Valley 775
Cruou Valley (The) 783
Cruseilles 810
Crussol 172
Cruzille 359
Cruzy 507
Cublize 574
Cucugnan 510
Cucuron 735
Cucuruzzu 398
Cuisiat 558
Culan 239
Cunault 584
Cuns 776
Curçay 853
Cure Gorges 346
Cure Valley 346
Curtil-Vergy 354
Curvalle 786
Curzac 520
Curzon 853
Cusset 245
Cussey-sur-l'Ognon 441
Cussigny 353
Cussy-en-Morvan 344
Cuxac-Cabardès 498

■ D

Dabo 545
Dabo (Rocher de) 545

Dagny 379
Daluis Gorges 725
Damazan 116
Dambach-la-Ville 149
Dame Jehanne (La) 470
Damery 370
Dampier 459
Dampierre 847
Damprichard 436
Damville 657
Damvillers 548
Damvix 858
Dangeau 458
Dangu 479
Danjoutin 432
Daoulas Gorges 286
Dardilly 554
Darney 534
Darney (Forest of) 534
Daumazan 614
Davayat 189
Dax 262
Deauville 639
Decazeville 776
Decize 346
Delivrande (La) 643
Delle 431
Demoiselles Grotto 495
Denone 185
Denonville Fortress 454
Déols 237
Der-Chantecoq (Lake) 372
Des Saisies Pass 798
Desaignes 161
Descartes 827
Dessoubre Valley 435
Détroits (Les) 174
Deux Amants (La Côte des) 659
Deux-Alpes (Les) 417
Devèze Cavern 494
Devinière (La) 826
Dévoluy Massif (The) 411
Diable (Pont du) 610
Diable (Roche du) 537
Diant (Manor of) 470
Dicy 355
Die 411
Diefmatten 139
Dièlette 638
Dienne 195
Dieppe 645
Dieulefit 411
Dieulouard 544
Dignac 846
Digne-les-Bains 725
Digoin 354
Digoine (Château de) 354
Dijon 346
Dimechaux 679
Dinan 293
Dinard 295
Dingé 292
Dirac 846
Dives-sur-Mer 639
Divonne-les-Bains 559
Dixmont 354
Dol-de-Bretagne 296
Dole 435
Dol (Mont) 296
Dolus-d'Oléron 856
Dombes Plateau (The) 560
Dombrot-le-Sec 534
Domérat 241
Domeyrat 188
Domfront 632
Domino 857
Domjulien 548
Dommartin Abbey 678
Domme 108
Dompierre 865
Dompierre-sur-Besbre 235
Domrémy-la-Pucelle 534
Donges 351
Donnemarie-Dontilly 472
Donon 132
Donon (Col du) 132
Donzenac 519
Donzère 415
Donzère Defile 172
Donzy 345
Donzy-le-Pertuis 359
Donzy-le-Pré 345
Dorat (Le) 519
Dordogne Périgourdine 108
Dordogne Quercynoise 109
Dore-l'Eglise 186
Dormans 370
Dormans 370
Doron de Belleville 804
Doron des Allues 804

Dortan 570
Douai 685
Douains 647
Douarnenez 296
Double Forest 110
Doubs Gorges 440
Doubs (Saut du) 440
Douch 494
Doucier 437
Doue 467
Doué-la-Fontaine 585
Douelle 108
Douhet (Le) 870
Doullens 678
Doullens 684
Dourbie Gorges 776
Dourdan 462
Dourgne 775
Dournazac 520
Doussard 797
Douvrin 687
Doux Gorges 161
Douzes (Les) 175
Drachenbronn 152
Draguignan 726
Drée (Château de) 342
Dreuil-lès-Amiens 676
Dreux 463
Dreux 463
Drevant 243
Droiteval 534
Drôme (Valley of the) 411
Dronières Park 810
Droué 837
Drusenheim 136
Druyes-les-Belles-Fontaines 361
Ducey 651
Duclair 666
Duesme 344
Dugny-sur-Meuse 548
Duingt 797
Dun-le-Palestel 524
Dun-les-Places 351
Dun-sur-Auron 243
Dun-sur-Meuse 534
Dunkerque 686
Dur Ecu Manor 638
Duras 110
Duravel 107
Durban 609
Durbelière (La) 871
Durfort 775
Durolle Valley 201
Durtal 595
Durtol 191
Dury-lès-Amiens 676
Durzon Valley 781

■ E

Eaux-Bonnes 222
Eaux-Chaudes 217
Eaux-Claires Valley 846
Eauze 607
Eawy Forest 634
Ebaupinage (Château d') 848
Ebermunster 143
Ebreuil 239
Ecalgrain Bay 638
Echallon 570
Echebrune 850
Echebrune 860
Echelles de la Mort 436
Echenevex 562
Echets (Les) 560
Echillais 862
Echiré 855
Echourgnac 110
Eckmühl 285
Ecluse Defile 556
Ecluse (L') 494
Ecouché 630
Ecouen 463
Ecouis 830
Ecouves Forest 629
Ecrainville 649
Ecrivains Combattants Forest 494
Ecrouves 547
Ecuisses 345
Egliseneuve-d'Entraigues 192
Egray Valley 855
Egreville 470
Eguille (L') 862
Eguilles 703
Eguisheim 149
Eguzon 239

Ehujarre Ravine 219
Elbeuf 662
Élincourt-Sainte-Marguerite 461
Elne 504
Embiez (Îles des) 757
Embrun 419
Émeraude (Côte d') 297
Emosson Dam 802
Encausse-les-Thermes 615
Énéa (Vale of the) 119
Enfer (Gorges d') 855
Engarran (Château de l') 499
Enghien 463
Englancourt 381
Englesqueville (Château d') 644
Ennezat 199
Ensérune 487
Ensisheim 138
Entrains-sur-Nohain 360
Entraygues 778
Entre-Deux-Mers Region 264
Entrecasteaux 708
Entremont (Oppidum d') 702
Entreportes Pass 442
Entrevaux 725
Enveigt 493
Épau (Abbey of l') 593
Éperlecques Forest 692
Épernay 372
Épernon 474
Epesses 852
Epfig 149
Épinal 534
Épine (L') 369
Épiniac 296
Époisses (Château d') 357
Épône (Château de) 467
Eppe-Sauvage 679
Erbajolo 401
Ercé 609
Erdeven 284
Erdre Valley 307
Ergué-Gabéric 315
Ermenonville 476
Ermenonville (Forest of) 475
Ermenouville 664
Ernée 591
Erquy 297
Erstein 140
Ervy-le-Châtel 370
Escaladieu 222
Escale de l'Ours 506
Escale (Lake of) 759
Escalès (L') 765
Escalette Pass 777
Escarène (L') 748
Eschau 144
Escolives-Sainte-Camille 338
Escos 272
Escot 219
Escoubière Manor 594
Escoussens 775
Escrinet Pass 172
Esmoulières 436
Esmoulières Plateau 436
Esnandes 851
Espagnac-Sainte-Eulalie 115
Espalion 778
Espaly Saint-Marcel 196
Espelette 211
Espérou (L') 159
Espiadet 222
Espinay 328
Espinouse Range (The) 494
Espira-de-l'Agly 503
Espirat 187
Esplantas 201
Esquelbecq 680
Essalois 563
Essarts (Les) 872
Esse 851
Essômes 371
Estables (Les) 193
Estagel 503
Estaing 778
Estavar 493
Esterel Massif (The) 727
Estier 782
Estillac 101
Étables-sur-Mer 325
Etagnac 851
Étain 548
Étalante 344
Étampes 463
Étaples 684
Étaules 851
Étel 298
Étel Estuary 297
Etelan (Château d') 665

Étival 434
Étival-Clairefontaine 546
Étoile-sur-Rhône 420
Étoile (L') 438
Étretat 648
Étroits Défile 411
Étueffont 431
Étuz 441
Eu 667
Eugénie-Lès-Bains 264
Eure Valley 457
Eus 490
Évaux-les-Bains 520
Evenos 757
Éventail 437
Évian-les-Bains 804
Évisa 397
Évreux 646
Évron 588
Évry 464
Excideuil 125
Exideuil 851
Exireuil 869
Eybènes 119
Eybens 414
Eygalières 754
Eyjeaux 521
Eymet 111
Eymoutiers 526
Eyne 493
Eyrieux Corniche and Gorges 166
Eyvigues 119
Eyzies-de-Tayac-Sireuil (Les) 111
Èze 752
Ézy-sur-Eure 453

#F

Fabrezan 501
Faches-Thumesnil 690
Fages 109
Falaise 648
Falgoux Valley 198
Falkenstein 151
Fanges Forest 506
Fanget Pass (Le) 725
Fanjeaux 492
Fanlac 102
Faouët (Le) 298
Faou (Le) 282
Farcheville 463
Faron (Mont) 760
Faucigny Region (The) 805
Faucille (Col de la) 562
Faucogney-et-la-Mer 436
Fauconnière 556
Faugères 177
Faute-sur-Mer (La) 844
Favède (La) 160
Faverges-de-la-Tour 419
Faverolles 201
Favières 685
Favone 389
Favone 401
Faye Pass 745
Fayence 758
Fayet (Le) 810
Faylé-Billot 373
Fayrac 109
Féas 220
Fécamp 648
Féclaz (La) 795
Fédrun (Île de) 288
Feldbach 148
Feliceto 391
Félines-Minervois 497
Felleries 678
Felletin 516
Fénétrange 539
Féniers 192
Fenioux 857
Fenioux 870
Fenouillet 507
Fer à Cheval 430
Fère-Champenoise 372
Fère-en-Tardenois 372
Fère (La) 374
Fermanville 638
Fermont (Fort de) 538
Ferney-Voltaire 562
Ferrals (Château de) 492
Ferrette 148
Ferreux 375
Ferrière-sur-Risle (La) 657
Ferrières 235
Ferrières 464

Ferrières-en-Gâtinais 830
Ferrières (Château de) 785
Ferté Loupière (La) 348
Ferté-Alais (La) 464
Ferté-Bernard (La) 589
Ferté-Imbault (Château de la) 833
Ferté-Macé (La) 632
Ferté-Milon (La) 381
Ferté-Saint-Aubin (La) 833
Ferté-sous-Jouarre (La) 467
Ferté (La) 343
Ferté-Vidame (La) 476
Fervaques (Château de) 631
Feugerolles 562
Feuges 380
Feurs 561
Feytiat 521
Ficajola cove 399
Fier (Gorges du) 796
Figeac 112
Figuerolles Inlet 724
Filain 444
Filhot 273
Filières (Château de) 651
Filitosa 397
Firminy 562
Fiumorbo Region (The) 398
Fixey 353
Fixin 353
Flabémont (Forest of) 534
Flagy 470
Flaine 806
Flamanville 638
Flamarens 612
Flaugergues (Château de) 499
Flaujac 779
Flavigny-sur-Moselle 543
Flavigny-sur-Ozerain 335
Fléac-sur-Seugne 860
Flèche (La) 589
Fléchères (Château de) 575
Fleckenstein 151
Flégère (La) 802
Flers 649
Flers 684
Fleurance 612
Fleurie-en-Beaujolais 556
Fleurigny 358
Fleurines 476
Fleurines 476
Fleurville 349
Fleury-la-Forêt (Château de) 659
Fleury-sur-Orne 636
Fléville (Château de) 541
Flocellière (La) 861
Floirac 265
Florac 166
Florensac 486
Flotte (La) 861
Floyrac 783
Flumet 808
Foce (Belvédère de) 401
Foissac 787
Foissiat 558
Foix 610
Folelli 396
Folgoët (Le) 298
Fonsérânes 487
Font de Gaume Cave 111
Font-Romeu 493
Fontaine-de-la-Pescalerie 115
Fontaine-de-Vaucluse 731
Fontaine-Française 361
Fontaine-Guérard (Abbey of) 659
Fontaine-le-Comte 859
Fontaine-le-Port 474
Fontainebleau 464
Fontainebleau 464
Fontainebleau Forest 465
Fontaines Salées 360
Fontaines-d'Ozillac 853
Fontaines-sur-Saône 569
Fontanaccia 401
Fontanges 198
Fontcaude (Abbey of) 507
Fontdouce (Abbey of) 870
Fontenay (Abbey) 348
Fontenay-le-Comte 851
Fontenay-Saint-Père 467
Fontenay-Trésigny 462
Fontenelles abbey 862
Fontenoy-le-Château 533
Fontenoy 444
Fontestorbes 612
Fontevraud-l'Abbaye 589
Fontfrède Peak 493
Fontfroide Abbey 501
Fontgombault 240

Fontirou 126
Fontjoncouse 502
Fontvieille 714
Forbach 536
Força-Réal (Hermitage of) 504
Forcalquier 731
Forclaz Pass (La) 797
Forêt-Fouesnant (La) 298
Forêt-sur-Sèvre (La) 872
Forges-des-Salles 286
Forges-les-Eaux 634
Forge (Saut de la) 437
Formigny 643
Formiguères 497
Fort la Latte 299
Fort-de-Douaumont 548
Fort-Mahon 678
Fort-Mahon-Plage 678
Fort-Médoc 270
Fos-sur-Mer 715
Fossat (Le) 614
Fossés Blancs 288
Fossette (La) 715
Fou Gorges 490
Foucamont 634
Foucherans 441
Fouesnant 298
Fouesnant 298
Fougères 298
Fougères 299
Fougères-sur-Bièvre 825
Fougerolles 439
Foulletorte (Château de) 588
Fouras 852
Fourcès 607
Fourcharet 476
Fourchaud 241
Fourges 479
Fourmies 679
Fourtou Pass 490
Foussais 854
Foux de Clamouse 495
Foux du Dourzon 781
Framicourt 455
Francescas 118
Francheville 657
Frasne-le-Château 437
Frauenberg 545
Frazé (Château de) 466
Fréhel (Cap) 299
Fréjus 731
Fréjus 731
Freney-d'Oisans (Le) 417
Fresnay-sur-Sarthe 586
Fresnaye (Château de la) 648
Fresnoy-la-Rivière 461
Frespech 126
Fresse 436
Fresse (Forest of) 437
Fresselines 239
Frévent 684
Fromental 524
Fromentine 868
Frontenay 434
Frontignan 508
Fuilla 489
Fuissé 349
Fumay 375
Fuste (La) 736
Futaie des Clos (La) 587
Futeau 532

#G

Gabas 217
Gacé 630
Gadancourt 467
Gaillac 777
Gaillagos 223
Gaillard (Château) 630
Gaillon 668
Gaillon-sur-Montcient 467
Galamus Gorges 507
Galère and Miramar (La) 727
Galeria 395
Galibier Pass 806
Galimas 101
Galinières 783
Gallardon 456
Gambais 469
Gan 221
Gânagobie Priory 731
Ganges 495
Gannat 239
Gap 412
Garabit 202
Garabit Viaduct 201

Garbet (Valley of the) 609
Gard-Maria 312
Garde-Adhémar (La) 415
Garde-en-Oisans (La) 417
Garde-Epée (Château de) 850
Garde-Freinet (La) 740
Garde-Guérin Point (La) 297
Garde-Guérin (La) 167
Gardes-le-Pontaroux 846
Gard (Le pont du) 166
Gardon Gorges 170
Gargan (Mont) 520
Gargas 705
Gargas Caves 615
Gargilesse 239
Garnache (La) 872
Garonne Valley (The) 264
Garons 171
Garris 211
Gas (Gorges des) 411
Gassicourt 467
Gastes 271
Gastines 472
Gatteville-le-Phare 638
Gattières 732
Gaube (Lake) 216
Gaubretière (La) 852
Gaude (La) 716
Gaudiès (Château de) 614
Gau (Pont de) 717
Gaussan (Château de) 501
Gavarnie 218
Gavarnie Valley 218
Gavaudun 104
Gavray 639
Geaune 262
Gèdre 219
Gelos 222
Gémenos 756
Gémozac 871
Gençay 859
Générargues 160
Genevraye (La) 470
Génicourt 548
Génissiat Dam 556
Gennes 584
Génolhac 168
Gensac-la-Pallue 850
Genté 850
Gentioux 526
Gérardmer 536
Géraudot 375
Gerberoy 454
Gerbier de Jonc (Mont) 167
Gergovie 190
Germigny-des-Prés 833
Germolles (Château de) 343
Gets (Les) 809
Gevrey 353
Gevrey-Chambertin 354
Gex 562
Ghisonaccia 398
Ghisoni 398
Gibanel (Château de) 516
Gien 827
Giens 732
Giens Peninsula 732
Gier 570
Giettaz (La) 809
Gif-sur-Yvette 459
Gignac 496
Gigny 443
Gigondas 762
Gillevoisin 464
Gilly 353
Gilocourt 461
Gimel-les-Cascades 525
Gimont 610
Gioux 849
Girolata 399
Giromagny 431
Giroussens 778
Giry 355
Gisors 650
Giverny 479
Givet 375
Givors 562
Givry 343
Givry-en-Argonne 378
Glacière Caverns 430
Glacières 765
Glaine-Montaigut 187
Glandelles 470
Glandieu Waterfall 557
Glandon Pass 807
Glane (Valley of the) 524
Glanum 754
Glénan Islands 292
Gléné 234
Glenic 521
Glénouze 853

Glény 516
Glère 436
Glozel 235
Goa 489
Goldbach 135
Golfe-Juan 745
Gombervaux 547
Gommersdorf 148
Gommerville 651
Gondrecourt-le-Château 533
Gondrin 608
Gorbio 742
Gordes 731
Gordes 731
Gordolasque Valley 766
Gorze 540
Gotein 219
Gouarec 320
Goudargues 164
Goudet 186
Gouézec 305
Gougeonnais (La) 296
Goujounac 113
Goulaine 307
Gouloux (Saut de) 351
Goulven 281
Goumois 436
Goumois Corniche (The) 436
Gour Bleu 437
Gourdon 113
Gourdon 351
Gourdon 731
Gourette 222
Gourgas 496
Gourgé 845
Gourin 305
Gournay-en-Bray 634
Goury 638
Goussaincourt 534
Gouvieux 456
Grainetière Abbey 852
Graisivaudan Valley (The) 412
Gramat 113
Gramat (Causse de) 114
Grambois 735
Gramont (Château de) 612
Grancey-le-Château 358
Grand 543
Grand Ballon (Le) 135
Grande (L'île) 311
Grand Genèvrier 186
Grand Puch 264
Grand Roc Cave 111
Grand Saussaye (Château de) 464
Grand Ventron 537
Grand-Bornand (Le) 803
Grand-Bourg (Le) 524
Grand-Brassac 122
Grand-Combe-Châteleu 440
Grand-Fort-Philippe 686
Grand-Fougeray 299
Grand-Morin Valley 466
Grand-Pressigny (Le) 827
Grand-Quévilly (Le) 663
Grand-Saut waterfall 437
Grand-Vabre 778
Grand-Village 857
Grandcamp-Maisy 644
Grandchamp 631
Grandchamp (Château de) 356
Grande Jasse 777
Grande Trappe (Forest of) 657
Grande-Jaille (Château de la) 853
Grande-Motte (La) 499
Grandes Alpes (Route des) 806
Grandes Dalles (Les) 648
Grandes Landes Region (The) 265
Grandfontaine 132
Grandpré 381
Grands Canalettes Caverns 489
Grands Goulets 422
Grands Montets (Les) 802
Grandval Dam 201
Grane 411
Grange 244
Grangent 563
Granges-les-Beaumont 418
Granges-les-Valence 167
Granjean 870
Granville 650
Grasse 731
Grasse 731
Gratteloup (Col de) 740
Grau de Maury 510
Grau-du-Roi (Le) 499
Graufthal 151

Graulhet 777
Grave (La) 417
Gravelines 686
Gravenne de Montpezat 162
Grave (Pointe de) 267
Gravrinis (L'île de) 306
Gray 437
Grenade 617
Grenade-sur-Adour 262
Grenoble 413
Grentzingen 148
Gréolières 732
Gréolières-les-Neiges 732
Gréoux-les-Bains 736
Grésigne Forest (La) 123
Gresse-en-Vercors 420
Grèsy-sur-Isère 795
Gréville-Hague 638
Grez-sur-Loing 470
Grézac 870
Grignan 414
Grignon 335
Grigny 464
Grigny 562
Grimaud 740
Gris-Nez (Cap) 681
Grisolles 118
Grizy 467
Groix (Île de) 299
Groléjac 119
Gronard 379
Groslée (Château de) 557
Grottes Marines 293
Grozeau 765
Gruissan 501
Guagno 397
Gua (Le) 862
Gua (Le) 866
Gué-du-Loir 829
Gué-Péan (Château du) 824
Gueberschwihr 149
Guebwiller 135
Guécélard 593
Guéhenno 301
Guémar 137
Guentrange (Fort de) 546
Guéra Gorges 487
Guérande 299
Guerche-de-Bretagne (La) 300
Guerche (Château de la) 862
Guerche (La) 827
Guéret 521
Guérigny 352
Guerinière (La) 856
Guerlédan (Lake) 286
Guermantes 468
Guéthary 212
Gueugnon 355
Guiche 216
Guidel 305
Guiers Mort Gorges 410
Guiers Vif Gorges 410
Guildo (Le) 297
Guilhaumard 784
Guillaumes 725
Guillestre 417
Guilvinec (Le) 285
Guimiliau 302
Guingamp 300
Guipry 299
Guirbaden 132
Guiry-en-Vexin 467
Guise 378
Guise 378
Gujan-Mestras 254
Gunsbach 139
Guyancourt 479
Gy 437
Gy-de-Sologne 833
Gy-l'Évêque 338

Graves (La)

■ **H**

Hac 294
Hackenberg 546
Hagenthal 148
Hagetmau 262
Hagondange 541
Hague (Cap de La) 638
Hague (La) 638
Haguenau 136
Haironville 546
Halatte 476
Hallière 546
Ham 687
Hambye (Abbey of) 639
Hamel 675
Hamonière (Château de la) 584

Ham (Roche de) 663
Hanau Lake 151
Hangest-sur-Somme 692
Hannonville 539
Harambels 225
Harcourt 657
Hardelot 682
Harfleur 651
Haroué 546
Hartmannswiller 149
Hasparren 213
Hatten 141
Hattonchâtel 538
Hattstatt 149
Haut Salat Valley 608
Haut-Asco 390
Haut-Barr 143
Haut-de-Cagnes (Le) 716
Haut-Folin peak 335
Haut-Koenigsbourg 136
Haut-Languedoc Nature Park 494
Haut-Ribeaupierre 141
Haute-Isle 479
Haute-Provence Clues (The) 732
Haute-Rivoire 576
Hautecombe (Abbey of) 795
Hautefage-la-Tour 126
Hautefort 114
Hauteluce 798
Hauterive 174
Hauteville-Lompnès 563
Hautpoul 780
Hautvillers 370
Haux 264
Havre-Antifer 651
Havre (Le) 651
Haybes 375
Haye Forest 541
Haye (Château de) 299
Haye-de-Routot (La) 665
Haye-du-Puits (La) 639
Hazebrouck 687
Hèches 211
Heckenransbach 545
Hédé 292
Hédé 294
Hélette 213
Hendaye 211
Hennebont 300
Hénon 305
Hérault Gorges 495
Hérault Valley (The) 495
Herbaudière (L') 856
Herbiers (Les) 852
Héric Gorges 494
Héricy 474
Hérisson 245
Hérisson Falls 437
Hermanville-sur-Mer 643
Hermitage Forest 869
Herm (L') 113
Herpinière (Moulin de la) 594
Hesdin 684
Heudicourt 538
Hierges 375
Hiersac 846
Hirson 381
Hirtzbarch 148
Hoc (Pointe du) 644
Hoffen 141
Hohatzenheim 137
Hohwald (Le) 137
Honfleur 652
Hôpital-Saint-Blaise (L') 219
Hôpital-sous-Rochefort 571
Hôpital-sur-Rhins (L') 573
Hopitâux-Neufs (Les) 442
Hôpitaux (Cluse des) 563
Horme (L') 573
Hornu (Cap) 693
Hospitalet 122
Hospitalet-Près-l'Andorre (L') 606
Hossegor 269
Houches (Les) 803
Houdan 466
Houdelaincourt 547
Houlgate 809
Hourtin 267
Hourtin-Carcans (Lake) 267
Hourtous rock 174
Houssaye (La) 305
Huchet (Courant d') 268
Huelgoat 282
Hume (La) 254
Hunaudaie (La) 294
Hunawihr 149
Hunspach 141
Huriel 241

Hyères 732
Hyères (Îles d') 733

I

Ibos 226
Iffendic 306
Iffs (Les) 294
Ige 350
Iguerande 341
Ilay 437
Ilbaritz 215
Ile-Bouchard (L') 826
Ile-d'Elle (L') 858
Ile-Rousse (L') 390
Ile-Tudy (L') 285
Île-Verte 724
Illhaeusern 137
Illiers-Combray 466
Illzach-Modenheim 139
Ilonse 760
Immerhof 546
Imphy 353
Incudine 401
Indevillers 436
Indre Valley (The) 827
Infernet 495
Ingrandes 848
Ingrandes-sur-Loire 596
Inières 783
Inor 534
Inzecca Defile 398
Irancy 338
Is-sur-Tille 358
Isarlès Lake 167
Iseran Pass 806
Isigny-sur-Mer 644
Isle Briand 594
Isle-Adam (L') 466
Isle-Aumont 380
Isle-d'Abeau (L') 419
Isle-de-Noé 607
Isle-en-Dodon (L') 613
Isle-Jourdain (L') 611
Isle-Jourdain (L') 851
Isle-Savary 237
Isle-sur-la-Sorgue (L') 731
Isle-sur-Serein (L') 358
Isle-Verte (L') 829
Islet of Er Lanic 306
Islette (Château de l') 820
Isola 760
Isola 2000 760
Ispagnac 174
Ispe 271
Issambres-San-Peïre (Les) 731
Issigeac 104
Issigeac 104
Issoire 192
Issoncourt 548
Issoudun 240
Issy-l'Évêque 351
Istres 715
Itterswiller 132
Itxassou 211
Ivry-la-Bataille 646
Izernore 559
Izoard Pass 807
Izoard (L') 409

J

Jade Coast 314
Jaillac 121
Jailly 355
Jaligny-sur-Besbre 234
Jard-sur-Mer 867
Jarnac 852
Jarnac-Champagne 860
Jarne (La) 863
Jars 244
Jas-de-Bouffan 703
Jassans-Riottier 575
Jau (Château de) 504
Jaujac 163
Jaulny 540
Javarzay 854
Javerlhac 118
Jazeneuil 853
Jazennes 860
Jean d'Heurs (Château de) 546
Jeantes 379
Jégun 607
Jemaye Lake (Le) 110
Jeret Valley 216

Jeurre 464
Joigny 348
Joinville 373
Jonas 192
Jonzac 853
Josselin 300
Josselin 301
Jou-sous-Monjou 202
Jouarre 466
Joucas 731
Joucou Defiles 506
Joué-les-Tours 836
Jougne 442
Jougne 442
Jouhet 869
Journet 855
Jours-les-Baigneux 344
Joux Forest 437
Joux (Château de) 442
Jouy 457
Jouy-aux-Arches 540
Jouy-en-Josas 455
Jouy-sous-Thelle 454
Joyeuse 177
Juan-les-Pins 733
Juaye-Mardaye 644
Jublains 594
Juch (Le) 296
Jugon-les-Lacs 294
Juine Valley 464
Jujurieux 572
Juliénas 555
Jumièges 665
Jumilhac-le-Grand 114
Jungholtz 136
Juno Beach 643
Jupilles 587
Jurançon 221
Jussy-Champagne 236
Juzennecourt 382

K

Kakouetta Gorges 219
Kaysersberg 149
Ker Chalon 873
Ker Hoad 302
Keranroux 306
Kérazan 285
Kerbérou 282
Kerbour 288
Kerbreuden 305
Kerfons 302
Kergoff 312
Kergonan 290
Kergrist 302
Kergrist-Moëlou 320
Kerhinet 288
Kerjean 325
Kerjouanno 318
Kerlaz 296
Kerlévenan 318
Kerlever 285
Kerlouan 281
Kernascleden 301
Kérouzéré 325
Kersaint 281
Kervégégan 285
Kervalet 288
Kientzheim 149
Kingersheim 138
Kintzheim 144
Kintzheim 149
Knoeringue 148
Kochersberg Region (The) 137
Kruth-Wildenstein Lake 148
Kuhlendorf 141

L

Laàs 225
Labaroche 141
Labarthe 264
Labarthe-sur-Lèze 620
Labastide-Clairence 216
Labastide-Dénat 773
Labastide-Murat 113
Labastide-Rouairoux 494
Labatut 272
Labeaume 163
Labenne 266
Labéraudie 108
Lablachère 177
Labouiche (River of) 610
Labrède 273
Labruguière 775

Lacanau 267
Lacanau-Océan 267
Lacapelle-Balaguier 787
Lacapelle-Livron 123
Lacapelle-Marival 113
Lacaune 777
Lacaune 785
Lacave 109
Lacaze (Château de) 785
Lachalade (Abbey of) 532
Lacoste 109
Lacoste 735
Lacourtensourt 620
Lacq 216
Lacrouzette 786
Lacs (Vallée des) 537
Ladignac-le-Long 524
Ladoye (Cirque de) 434
Laffrey 745
Lafite-Rothschild (Château) 270
Lafontasse 775
Lagarde (Château de) 608
Lagarde (Château de) 613
Lagat Jar 289
Lagorce 163
Lagrasse 501
Laguiole 774
Laguzon Cavern 497
Lake Abbaye 444
Lake Vaivre 444
Lalande-de-Fronsac 268
Lalbenque 114
Lalinde 114
Lalouvesc 161
Lamagdelaine 108
Lamalou-les-Bains 494
Lamarque 297
Lamartine Territory 349
Lamastre 161
Lamath 539
Lamballe 301
Lambersart 690
Lambesc 734
Lamorlay 456
Lamotte-Beuvron 828
Lamoura 440
Lampaul 310
Lampaul-Guimiliau 302
Lampaul-Plouarzel 293
Lampaul-Ploudalmézeau 281
Lampy Reservoir 498
Lamure-sur-Azergues 555
Lancey 412
Lancharre 359
Lancieux 297
Lançon 715
Landal 296
Landemer 638
Landerneau 301
Landersheim 143
Landes 868
Landes de Gascogne regional park 266
Landes Girondines Coast (The) 266
Landevennec 282
Landivisiau 302
Landsberg 132
Landskron 148
Langeac 185
Langeais 828
Langogne 168
Langoiran 265
Langon 265
Langon 269
Langonnet Abbey 298
Languette Gorges 434
Langres 373
Langrune 643
Languidou 286
Laniscat 286
Lanleff 310
Lanloup 310
Lanmeur 306
Lanne 219
Lannédern 282
Lannemezan 217
Lannilis 281
Lannion 301
Lanouée Forest 301
Lanquais 114
Lanrivain 320
Lans-en-Vercors 423
Lanslebourg 807
Lanslevillard 807
Lantenay (Château de) 347
Lantilly 335
Lantilly 361
Lantosque 766
Lanuéjols 169

Laon 373
Lapalisse 240
Lapanouse-de-Cernon 784
Lapeyre 784
Lapoutroie 140
Larboust Valley 606
Larceveau 213
Larchant 470
Lardin Saint-Lazare (Le) 112
Largentière 163
Largny-sur-Automne 461
Larmont (Fort du) 442
Larmor Baden 306
Larmor Plage 304
Larmor-Baden 306
Larmor-Plage 305
Larnas 173
Laroche-Migennes 348
Larochemillay 356
Larogues-d'Olmes 612
Larone Pass 393
Laroque-Timbaut 126
Laroque-Toirac 115
Laroquebrou 186
Larrau 219
Larressingle 607
Larringes (Château de) 805
Larrivière 262
Larroque 776
Laruns and the Ossau Valley 217
Larzac (Causse du) 777
Las Planques 774
Lasalle 160
Lascaux 114
Lascours 164
Lassay 594
Lasson 643
Lastours 520
Lastours (Châteaux de) 498
Latour (Château de) 784
Latronquière 113
Lattès 499
Lauch Valley 136
Laudun 164
Lauragais Region (The) 611
Laure-Minervois 497
Laurède 261
Lauris 758
Laussac 202
Lautaret Pass 806
Lautenbach 136
Lautenbach 136
Lauterbourg 141
Lautrec 777
Lauzerte 114
Lavagnac 506
Laval 590
Lavanchez (Le) 803
Lavandou (Le) 734
Lavandou (Le) 734
Lavardens 607
Lavardin 829
Lavasina 395
Lavaudieu 188
Lavaufranche 518
Lavaur 777
Lavausseau 859
Laveissenet 195
Lavelanet 612
Laviolle 163
Lavoûte-Chilhac 185
Lavoûte-Polignac 196
Lavoûte-sur-Loire 196
Layon Valley 584
Layrac 607
Léchère (La) 796
Léchère (La) 811
Lechiagat 285
Lectoure 612
Lège 255
Legué (Le) 320
Léhélec 782
Léhon 294
Lelex 556
Lélex 562
Léman (Lake) 807
Lembach 151
Lembeye 227
Lempdes 187
Lencloître 872
Lens 687
Lente Forest 422
Lentigny 554
Lentilles 372
Léon 268
Léon Churchyards (The) 302
Léotoing 187
Lérins (Îles de) 720
Lescar 221
Lesconil 285

Lescun 220
Lescure 773
Lesneven 298
Lesparre-Médoc 270
Lesponne Valley 222
Lesques (Les) 724
Lessay 639
Lestards 523
Lestelle-Bétharram 223
Lesterps 851
Lestournelles 126
Létra 555
Leucate 496
Levant (Ile du) 733
Levens 750
Levernois 340
Levesville-la-Chenard 454
Lévezou lakes 778
Levie 398
Levignac 266
Levroux 240
Lézardrieux 310
Lézat-sur-Lèze 614
Lezay 854
Lézignac 777
Lézignan-Corbières 501
Lezoux 201
Lhuis 557
Lhuître 368
Liaucous 175
Libournais Region (The) 268
Libourne 268
Lichecourt (Château de) 534
Lichères 866
Lichtenberg 151
Licq-Athérey 219
Liercourt 693
Liessies 678
Lieu-Restauré 461
Lieuche 725
Lieurey 654
Liézey 537
Liffol-le-Grand 543
Liffré 317
Liginiac 518
Lignières 237
Lignières-Sonneville 850
Ligny-en-Barrois 533
Ligny-en-Cambresis 684
Ligny-le-Châtel 337
Ligugé 859
Lille 687
Lillebonne 665
Limaton 356
Limay 467
Limeuil 111
Limoëlou Manor 297
Limoges 521
Limogne 114
Limogne (Causse de) 114
Limonest 569
Limousis Cavern 498
Limoux 607
Lion-d'Angers (Le) 594
Lion-sur-Mer 643
Lioran (Le) 192
Liré 282
Liré 595
Lisieux 653
Lisle-en-Rigault 546
Lisle-sur-Tarn 782
Lison (Sources du) 437
Lisores 631
Listrac 270
Lit-et-Mixe 268
Livarot 631
Liverdun 541
Lizines 472
Llagonne (La) 497
Llo 493
Loc-Dieu 786
Loches 828
Locmaria-Berrien 282
Locmariaquer 303
Locminé 327
Locquignol 680
Locquirec 302
Locquirec 302
Locronan 303
Loctudy 285
Lodève 496
Lods 438
Loguivy 302
Loguivy-de-la-Mer 310
Loing 470
Loir Valley (The) 829
Lombez 613
Lombrives (Caves of) 609
Long 693
Longemer (Lake of) 537
Longny-au-Perche 657

Longpont 381
Longpont-sur-Orge 453
Longpré-les-Corps-Saints 693
Longue-Croix 687
Longues-sur-Mer 643
Longuesse 467
Longuyon 538
Longwy 538
Lonlay-l'Abbaye 632
Lons-le-Saunier 438
Lonzac 860
Loos-les-Lilles 691
Lopérec 291
Loqueffret 282
Lordat 606
Loreto-di-Casinca 395
Lorgues 726
Lorie (Château de la) 597
Lorient 303
Lormes 351
Loroux-Bottereau 307
Lorp-Sentaraille 616
Lorraine Nature Park 538
Lorrez-le-Bocage 470
Lorris 830
Losse 111
Lot and Célé Valleys 114
Lot Gorges 778
Lot Valley 779
Louargat 300
Loubaresse 201
Loube (Montagne de la) 716
Loubressac 123
Louch Waterfalls 760
Loudéac 305
Louderville 210
Loudun 853
Loudunois (Le) 853
Loué 591
Loue spring 438
Loue Valley (The) 438
Louez-les-Duisans 677
Louhans 349
Louin 845
Loup Gorges 731
Loup Valley 732
Loupe (La) 477
Loupiac 265
Loupian 508
Louppy-sur-Loison 541
Lourdes 217
Louresse-Rochemenier 584
Lourmarin 735
Louveciennes 468
Louverie 306
Louvie-Juzon 222
Louviers 646
Louvigné-de-Baix 300
Louvigné-du-Désert 299
Louvois (Fort) 848
Louye 453
Loyettes 571
Lozanne 555
Lozère (Mont) 168
Lubéron Heights (The) 734
Luc-en-Diois 411
Luc-sur-Mer 644
Lucéram 761
Lucerne (Abbey of) 650
Luché-Pringé 595
Lucheux 678
Luc (Le) 735
Luçon 853
Lucq-de-Béarn 219
Lucs-sur-Boulogne (Le) 872
Lude (Le) 591
Luère Pass 576
Lumbres 692
Lunain 470
Lunas 497
Lunel 499
Luneray 664
Lunéville 539
Lupersat 520
Luppé-Violles 614
Lurbe-Saint-Christau 219
Lure Mountain 735
Lurs 731
Lus-la-Croix-Haute 408
Lusignan 853
Lussac-les-Châteaux 849
Lussan 176
Luthézieu 563
Luttenbach 139
Lutzelbourg 545
Lux 358
Luxeuil-les-Bains 438
Luxey 265
Luynes 834
Luz-Ardiden 218

Luz-Saint-Sauveur 218
Luzarches 474
Luzech 106
Lyon 563
Lyons-la-Forêt 659
Lys 468
Lys-les-Lannoy 691
Lys-Saint-Georges 238

■ M

Macau 261
Machecoul 324
Machine (La) 352
Macinaggio 395
Maclu Lake 437
Mâcon 349
Madame (Ile) 848
Madeleine grotto (La) 162
Madeleine (La) 111
Madeleine (La) 288
Madiran 227
Maffliers 466
Magagnosc 731
Magescq 268
Magnac-Bourg 520
Magnac-Laval 517
Magnac-sur-Touvre 846
Magné 858
Magnette 241
Magny-Cours 353
Magny-en-Vexin 479
Magny-les-Hameaux 459
Magrin (Château de) 781
Maguelonne Abbey 499
Maîche 436
Mailhac 497
Mailhat 192
Maillane 754
Maillé 858
Maillebois 477
Maillezais 854
Mailly-Champagne 370
Mailly-le-Château 361
Mailly-Maillet 675
Maine-Giraud 847
Maintenon 457
Maisod 445
Maison-Feyne 524
Maisons-Laffitte 474
Maix Lake 546
Malans 441
Malataverne 415
Malaucène 765
Malay 360
Malban (L'île) 311
Malbos 162
Malbuisson 442
Malène (La) 174
Malesherbes 480
Malicorne-sur-Sarthe 595
Malle 273
Mallemort 734
Malleval 572
Malmont (Le) 726
Malo-les-Bains 686
Malromé 265
Malsaucy Lake 431
Malval 521
Malvaux Gorges 434
Malzieu-Ville (Le) 169
Malzy 381
Mamers 591
Manciet 608
Mandailles Valley 186
Mandelieu 720
Mandeure 439
Manerbe 654
Manigod (Valley of) 803
Manosque 736
Manot 851
Mans (Le) 591
Mansle 866
Mantes-la-Jolie 467
Mantes-la-Jolie 467
Manzat 188
Marais Vernier 665
Marais (Château de) 453
Marans 858
Marast 441
Marboué 459
Marçay 821
Marcenais 268
Marcevol 490
Marciac 607
Marcigny 341
Marcilhac-sur-Célé 115
Marcillac-Lanville 846

Marcillac-Vallon 783
Marcilly 361
Marcilly-sur-Maulne 834
Marckolsheim 143
Marcoule 164
Marcoussis (Château de) 453
Marcq-en-Barœul 689
Marennes 848
Marensin Region (The) 268
Marestay 854
Mareuil 115
Mareuil-sur-Ay 370
Mareuil-sur-Lay 853
Margaux 270
Margeride Region (The) 169
Mariana 398
Maridac 607
Marienthal 136
Marignac 860
Marignane 715
Marigny 663
Marigny-Brizay 872
Marigny-le-Cahouët 335
Marina-Baie des Anges 716
Marines 472
Maringues 199
Markstein 135
Marlenheim 149
Marlhes 571
Marlieux 561
Marly-Gomont 381
Marly-le-Roi 467
Marly (Forest of) 468
Marmande 178
Marmande Butte 849
Marmare Pass 606
Marmoutier 137
Marnay 441
Marne Valley 468
Marne-la-Vallée 466
Marnhagues 784
Maroilles 679
Maronne gorges 516
Marquay 125
Marquayssac 109
Marquenterre 692
Marquette 691
Marquèze 266
Marrault 338
Marrous Pass 609
Mars-sur-Allier 352
Marsac-en-Livradois 186
Marsac-sur-Tarn 779
Marsal 539
Marsal 774
Marsan 605
Marsannay 353
Marsannay-la-Côte 354
Marsat 199
Marseillan 508
Marseille 736
Marseilleveyre Massif 736
Marsillargues (Château de) 499
Marsolan 607
Martailly-lès-Brancion 359
Martainville (Château de) 659
Martel 109
Marthon 863
Martignac 107
Martigné-Briand 584
Martigues 715
Martinanches 187
Martinet (Le) 444
Martinvast 637
Martres-Tolosane 616
Martrou 862
Martyre (La) 302
Marvejols 169
Marville 541
Marzials 778
Marzy 352
Mas d'Azil (Caves of) 609
Mas-Cabardès 498
Mas-d'Agenais (Le) 116
Mas-Saint-Chély 174
Mas-Soubeyran (The) 160
Masevaux 148
Masmolène 176
Massat 609
Massay 247
Massebeau 195
Masseube 605
Massiac 187
Massignieu Lake 557
Matelles (Les) 508
Matha 854
Matignon 297
Maubeuge 678
Maubourguet 227
Maubranches 236
Maubuisson 267

Maudéjour 479
Maudétour (Château de) 467
Mauges 588
Mauguio (Lake of) 499
Mauldre Valley 467
Maule 467
Mauléon 871
Mauléon-Barousse 615
Mauléon-Licharre 219
Maupas 234
Maure (Crêt du) 797
Maures Massif 740
Mauriac 193
Mauriac 264
Maurienne Region (The) 807
Maurinié (La) 773
Mauvezin 222
Mauvezin 611
Mauzé-sur-le-Mignon 855
Mauzun 187
Mavaleix 125
Mayenne 593
Mayenne (Valley of) 594
Mayet-de-Montagne (Le) 235
Maye (Tête de la) 416
Mayreste 765
Mazamet 779
Mazan forest 162
Mazeau (Le) 858
Mazères 227
Mazères 607
Maziaux 193
Mazières 233
Meauce 352
Meaux 468
Médavy 630
Médis 865
Médoc Region (The) 269
Médous Caverns 211
Megève 808
Mégrit 294
Mehun-sur-Yèvre 241
Meillant 243
Meillonas 558
Meinsberg 546
Méjanes 717
Méjean (Causse) 169
Mélac 784
Mélas 172
Mêle-sur-Sarthe (Le) 630
Melle 854
Mello 477
Melon 281
Melrand 286
Mels 202
Melun 468
Melun 468
Mémillon 458
Mémises (Château de) 805
Ménars 822
Menat 188
Mende 169
Ménerbes 735
Menessaire 357
Menetou-Salon 234
Menez Bré 305
Menez-Hom 282
Menez-Meur 282
Ménigoute 869
Mennetou-sur-Cher 824
Menou 360
Menoux 239
Mens 419
Menthon-Saint-Bernard 797
Menton 741
Menuires-Val-Thorens (Les) 804
Mer 822
Mer de Glace (La) 802
Mercantour National Park 766
Mercerie (La) 846
Mercœur 517
Mercœur (Château de) 185
Mercoire 168
Mercuès 106
Mercurey 343
Méréville 463
Méribel 804
Méribel-les-Allues 804
Méribel-Mottaret 804
Merkwiller-Pechelbronn 141
Merlande 121
Merle (Tours de) 516
Merlevenez 298
Merlieux 373
Merpins 850
Mers-les-Bains 667
Merval (Château de) 659
Merveilles 123
Mervent 854
Mervent Forest 854

Merville-Franceville-Plage 645
Mery-sur-Marne 467
Meschers 871
Meschers-sur-Gironde 871
Mescla Gorges 760
Mescla (Balcons de la) 765
Meslay 456
Mesnières-en-Bray 634
Mesnil Forest 296
Mesnil-Aubry (Le) 463
Mesnil-Guillaume (Château de) 631
Mesnil-Manger (Le) 631
Mesnil-Saint-Denis (Le) 459
Mesnil-Saint-Père 375
Mesnil-sur-Oger (Le) 370
Mesnil-Voisin (Château de) 464
Mesnil (Le) 467
Mesnuls (Les) 469
Messilbac 202
Métabief 442
Metz 539
Metz-le-Comte 361
Metzig 149
Meulan 467
Meule (Port de la) 873
Meung-sur-Loire 821
Meursault 340
Meuse Valley 375
Méximieux 571
Meymac 525
Meyrargues 758
Meyronne 109
Meyrueis 175
Meyssac 520
Meysse 172
Meyzieu 569
Mez-le-Maréchal 458
Mèze 508
Mézenc 193
Mezenc Massif 193
Mézières-en-Brenne 237
Mézin 118
Mézos 266
Mialet 160
Midi du Bigorre Peak 222
Mièges 441
Miélan 607
Mifaget 222
Mijoux 562
Milandes (Les) 109
Milelli (Les) 387
Millas 560
Millau 777
Millau 780
Milles (Les) 703
Millevaches Plateau 523
Milly-la-Forêt 469
Milly-Lamartine 349
Mimizan 271
Mindin 314
Minerve and the Minervois 497
Minihy-Tréguier 326
Miolans (Château de) 800
Mionnay 560
Mions 569
Mirabeaux Defile 758
Mirabel 108
Miradoux 612
Miramas-le-Vieux 715
Mirande 613
Miraval-Cabardès 498
Mirebeau 361
Mirecourt 546
Mirepoix 613
Mirmande 616
Miromesnil (Château de) 645
Misère (Vallée de) 582
Miserey 646
Missillac 288
Missillac 289
Mittelbergheim 132
Mittelwihr 149
Modane 807
Moëlan-sur-Mer 313
Moëze 848
Mogère (Château de la) 499
Mognéville 546
Moineaudière 537
Moine (Belvédère) 438
Moines (L'île aux) 306
Moines (L'île aux) 311
Moingt 570
Moirax 101
Moissac 116
Moissac 165
Moissat-Bas 187
Molay-Littry (Le) 645
Molesmes 344
Molières 104
Moliets 268

Moligt-les-Bains 506
Molines-en-Queyras 418
Molineuf 822
Mollkirch 132
Molsheim 149
Mommenheim 133
Monaco (Principality of) 741
Monards (Les) 871
Monastier 169
Monastier-sur-Gazelle (Le) 193
Monastir-del-Camp 504
Monbazillac 116
Monbouan 300
Monceaux 516
Monceaux (Château de) 632
Moncley 441
Moncontour 845
Moncontour-de-Bretagne 305
Moncrabeau 118
Mondony Gorges 487
Mondoubleau 837
Monédières Massif (The) 523
Monein 217
Monestier-de-Clermont 419
Monestiès-sur-Cérou 774
Monêtier-les-Bains (Le) 409
Monferrand (Château de) 508
Monflanquin 104
Mongaston 219
Mongie (La) 222
Monistrol-d'Allier 185
Monistrol-sur-Loire 193
Monjardin Pass 159
Monléon-Magnoac 217
Monoblet 174
Monpazier 104
Monpazier 104
Mons 731
Mons-en-Laonnois 373
Mont Beuvray 335
Mont d'Arbois (Le) 808
Mont Sainte-Victoire 702
Mont-d'Or Lyonnais (The) 569
Mont-Dauphin 417
Mont-Dore 194
Mont-de-Marsan 271
Mont-devant-Sassey 534
Mont-Louis 497
Mont-Revard 795
Mont-Roc-Teillet 782
Mont-Saint-Éloi 676
Mont-Saint-Jean 357
Mont-Saint-Martin 538
Mont-Saint-Michel 655
Mont-Saint-Michel 800
Mont-Saint-Vincent 351
Mont-sous-Vaudrey 430
Montady Pool 487
Montagnac 506
Montagnac-sur-Lède 104
Montagne Noire 498
Montagne Noire 775
Montagnès 780
Montagnes Noires (Les) 305
Montaigu 443
Montaigu 871
Montaigu-la-Brisette 638
Montaigu-le-Blin 240
Montaiguët-en-Forez 240
Montaigut-le-Blanc 200
Montaigut-sur-Save 611
Montal 123
Montalègre (Château de) 784
Montalet (Roc de) 777
Montalivet-les-Bains 267
Montaner (Château de) 226
Montargis 830
Montat (Le) 108
Montauban 117
Montauban (Château de) 306
Montaut 261
Montaut 614
Montbazon 827
Montbéliard 439
Montbenoît 440
Montbeton 487
Montbolo 487
Montboucher-sur-Jabron 416
Montboudif 192
Montbozon 441
Montbras 534
Montbrison 570
Montbron 863
Montbrun 116
Montbrun 520
Montcabrier 107
Montcaret 116
Montceau-les-Mines 351
Montceau (Château de) 349
Montceaux-l'Étoile 341

Montceaux-lès-Meaux 468
Montcel Abbey 476
Montchenot 377
Montcient Valley 467
Montcléra 113
Montcornet 377
Montcourt 470
Montcravel 684
Montculot (Château de) 347
Montcuq 114
Montdidier 691
Monte-Carlo 743
Monte-Carlo Beach 743
Montebourg 644
Montecler (Château de) 588
Montégut-en-Couserans 609
Montélimar 415
Montemaggiore 390
Montendre 854
Montépilloy 475
Montereau-Fault-Yonne 469
Monterfil 306
Montesquiou 607
Montets (Col des) 802
Monteux 723
Montfaucon-en-Velay 203
Montfavet 709
Montferrand 189
Montferrand-du-Périgord 104
Montferrer 490
Montfleur 443
Montfleury 202
Montfort 108
Montfort 306
Montfort-L'Amaury 469
Montgaillard 610
Montgenèvre 409
Montgeoffroy (Château de) 584
Montgeroult 472
Montgey (Château de) 781
Montgobert 381
Montguyon 854
Monthelon 335
Monthermé 375
Monthou-sur-Cher 825
Monthureux-sur-Saône 534
Montier-en-Der 372
Montignac 112
Montignac-sur-Charente 846
Montigny 470
Montigny 663
Montigny-sur-Aube 344
Montils 850
Montils 860
Montirail (Château de) 589
Montivilliers 651
Montjaux 778
Montjavoult 479
Montjean (Château de) 590
Montjeu 335
Montjoie-le-Château 436
Montjoie-Volvestre 616
Monthéry 453
Montlieux-la-Garde 854
Montligeon (Chapelle) 657
Montlosier 191
Montlouis-sur-Loire 834
Montluçon 241
Montluel 560
Montmajour Abbey 707
Montmartin-sur-Mer 656
Montmaur 612
Montmédy 541
Montmelas (Château de) 555
Montmerle-sur-Saône 575
Montmeyran 420
Montmirail 375
Montmirail (Dentelles de) 762
Montmoreau-Saint-Cybard 848
Montmorency 470
Montmorillon 855
Montmorin Castle 187
Montmort 372
Montmuran 294
Montoire-sur-le-Loir 829
Montoire-sur-le-Loir 829
Montoulieu 616
Montpellier 498
Montpellier-le-Vieux 780
Montpensier 185
Montpeyroux 116
Montpeyroux 192
Montpezat-de-Quercy 118
Montpinchon 639
Montpoupon (Château de) 824
Montrabe 620
Montréal 163
Montréal 358
Montréal 492
Montréal 607
Montredon-Labessonnie 775

Montréjeau 615
Montrésor 829
Montreuil-Bellay 594
Montreuil-Bonnin 859
Montreuil-sur-Mer 684
Montrevel-en-Bresse 558
Montrichard 824
Montricoux 123
Montroc 803
Montrond Lake 809
Montrond-les-Bains 561
Montrottier (Château de) 796
Montrozier 783
Montsabert (Château de) 584
Montsalvy 195
Montsauche 351
Montsaurès 616
Montsec (Butte de) 538
Montségur 612
Montselgues 177
Mont (Signal du) 341
Montsoreau 594
Montverdun 554
Morbier 444
Morbihan (Gulf of) 306
Morcenx 271
Morclan (Pic de) 800
Moret-sur-Loing 470
Morey 440
Morey-Saint-Denis 353
Morez 440
Morienval 461
Morigny 464
Morigny 464
Morimond 368
Morizécourt 534
Morlaàs 227
Morlaix 306
Morlanne 217
Mormaire (La) 469
Mormal Forest 679
Mornac-sur-Seudre 851
Mornant 570
Mornas 750
Mornay 361
Morogues 234
Morosaglia 396
Morsang-sur-Seine 475
Morsbronn-les-Bains 136
Mortagne-au-Perche 657
Mortagne-sur-Gironde 871
Mortagne-sur-Sèvre 871
Mortain 656
Morteau 440
Mortefontaine 476
Mortemart 517
Mortemer (Abbey of) 659
Morthemer 849
Mortiercrolles (Château de) 597
Mortrée 631
Morvan Lakes 351
Morvan Nature Park 351
Morzine 809
Moselle Valley 534
Mosson (Château de la) 499
Mostuéjouls 175
Mothe-Saint-Héray (La) 869
Motte Lake (La) 437
Motte-d'Usseau (La) 849
Motte-Feuilly (La) 238
Motte-Glain (La) 291
Motte-Josserand (Château de La) 345
Motte-Tilly (Château de) 375
Motte (Château de la) 666
Motte (Château de la) 678
Mottier (Le) 419
Mouans-Sartoux 704
Mouchamps 872
Mouchet (Mont) 201
Moudeyres 193
Moudeyres 193
Mougins 720
Mouguerre 215
Mouillac 658
Mouilleron-en-Pareds 872
Mouliherne 586
Moulin des Bouillons 731
Moulin Neuf 192
Moulin-Cadoux 338
Moulin (Château du) 833
Moulinet Lake 169
Moulineux 464
Moulins 241
Moulins-Engilbert 356
Moulis 270
Moulis 609
Moumour 219
Mourenx 217
Mouret 783

Mourèze 496
Moussages 198
Mousson (Butte de) 544
Moussy 472
Moustier 111
Moustier-en-Fagne 679
Moustiers-Sainte-Marie 743
Moutchic 267
Mouthe 442
Mouthier-Haute-Pierre 438
Mouthiers-sur-Boëme 846
Moutier-d'Ahun 523
Moûtiers 811
Moutiers-en-Beauce 454
Moutiers-Hubert 631
Mouton-Rothschild 270
Moutot (Château de) 358
Mouzens 109
Mouzon 378
Moyenmoutier 546
Mozac 199
Mugron 261
Muhlbach 139
Muids 630
Mulhouse 138
Munster 139
Munster 539
Munster Valley 139
Mur-de-Barrez 202
Mur-de-Bretagne 286
Mur-de-Sologne 833
Murat 195
Murbach 139
Muret 613
Muret-le-Château 775
Murol 195
Mussy-sur-Seine 370
Mutzig 132
Muze Gorge 778
Muzillac 327

■ N

Nacqueville 638
Naguilles dam 606
Naintré 849
Najac 780
Nampont-Saint-Martin 678
Nançay 243
Nancy 541
Nangis 472
Nans-les-Pins 756
Nans-les-Pins 756
Nans-sous-Sainte-Anne 437
Nant 776
Nant 780
Nantes 307
Nantes 872
Nanteuil 824
Nanteuil-sur-Marne 467
Nantua 570
Naours 675
Napoléon (Route) 745
Napoule (La) 720
Narbonne 501
Narbonne-Plage 501
Narlay Lake 437
Natzwiller 133
Naucelle 784
Nauzan (La plage de) 866
Navacelles 495
Navarrenx 225
Naves 177
Naves 525
Nay 221
Nebbio 400
Nébias 506
Nemours 470
Nérac 118
Nerbis 261
Neric-d'Ussel 525
Néris-les-Bains 243
Nersac 847
Nesles 372
Nesque Gorges 745
Neublans 441
Neubourg Plateau (The) 656
Neuf-Brisach 139
Neufchâteau 543
Neufchâtel-en-Bray 634
Neuille-le-Lierre 820
Neuilly-sous-Clermont 460
Neuntelstein 137
Neuvic-d'Ussel 518
Neuvicq 854
Neuville-au-Pont (La) 378
Neuville (Château de) 469
Neuville (La) 675

Neuvy-Saint-Sépulchre 238
Neuvy-Sautour 370
Neuwiller-lès-Saverne 151
Nevers 352
Neyrac-les-Bains 163
Nez de Jobourg 638
Nez de Voidries 638
Niaux 609
Nice 745
Nideck 151
Niderviller 545
Niederbronn-les-Bains 140
Niederhaslach 132
Niedermorschwihr 149
Niedersteinbach 151
Nieuil 863
Nieul 523
Nîmes 170
Nîmes-le-Vieux 175
Nino (Lake) 398
Niolo Region (The) 398
Niort 855
Niou Huella 310
Nissan-lez-Ensérune 487
Nizon 313
Noailles 520
Noé de Bel-Air (La) 291
Noeux-les-Mines 681
Nogaro 614
Nogent-en-Bassigny 371
Nogent-le-Roi 457
Nogent-le-Rotrou 471
Nogent-sur-Oise 476
Nogent-sur-Seine 375
Nogent-sur-Vernisson 830
Nohant 238
Noir (Causse) 172
Noirétable 571
Noirlac 243
Noirmont 533
Noirmoutier-en-l'Ile 856
Noirmoutier (Ile de) 856
Noisiel 468
Nolay 353
Nonenque Abbey 784
Nonette 192
Nontron 118
Nontronnais Region (The) 119
Nonza 395
Norée Grottos 859
Noron-la-Poterie 644
Norrey-en-Bessin 636
Norville 666
Notre-Dame d'Aiguebelle 415
Notre-Dame d'Aubune 762
Notre-Dame d'Aulps 800
Notre-Dame d'Avesnières 590
Notre-Dame de Kérinec 296
Notre-Dame de la Gorge (Chapel of) 809
Notre-Dame de Liesse 373
Notre-Dame de Lorette 313
Notre-Dame de Lumières 735
Notre-Dame de Peygros 720
Notre-Dame de Quilinen 315
Notre-Dame de Tronoën 285
Notre-Dame de Vie 720
Notre-Dame des Fontaines 753
Notre-Dame-d'Aulps 809
Notre-Dame-de-Bellecombe 808
Notre-Dame-de-Bliquetuit 665
Notre-Dame-de-Bon-Cœur 761
Notre-Dame-de-Capimont 494
Notre-Dame-de-Garaison 217
Notre-Dame-de-Grace 496
Notre-Dame-de-Grâce Abbey 638
Notre-Dame-de-l'Aillant 344
Notre-Dame-de-l'Épine 369
Notre-Dame-de-la-Drèche 773
Notre-Dame-de-la-Garde 724
Notre-Dame-de-Laghet 748
Notre-Dame-de-Laval 507
Notre-Dame-de-Londres 508
Notre-Dame-de-Lorette 676
Notre-Dame-de-Marceille 507
Notre-Dame-de-Monts 868
Notre-Dame-de-Pépiole 757
Notre-Dame-de-Pritz 590
Notre-Dame-de-Prouille 492
Notre-Dame-de-Randol 191
Notre-Dame-de-Salagon 731
Notre-Dame-de-Vassivière 194
Notre-Dame-des-Anges 740
Notre-Dame-des-Auzils 501
Notre-Dame-des-Oublieis 501
Notre-Dame-du-Crann 305
Notre-Dame-du-Mai 757
Nouaillé-Maupertuis 859

Nouan-le-Fuzelier 828
Nouans-les-Fontaines 829
Nouillers (Les) 868
Nouveau-Windstein 140
Nouvion-le-Vineux 373
Novalaise 801
Noves 712
Noyal-Pontivy 313
Noyen-sur-Seine 473
Noyer pass 411
Noyers-sur-Cher 824
Noyers-sur-Serein 358
Noyon 471
Nozeroy 441
Nuaillé 588
Nuaillé-sur-Boutonne 847
Nuces 784
Nucourt 472
Nuelles 554
Nuits Vineyards (The côte de) 353
Nuits-Saint-Georges 353
Nuits-sur-Amançon 335
Nyons 416

■ O

Oberhaslach 133
Obermorschwiller 148
Obernai 140
Obersteinbach 151
Objat 519
O (Château d') 630
Octon 496
Odeillo 493
Odenas 555
Odos 227
Oedenbourg 136
Oeyreluy 263
Offemont 432
Offwiller 151
Oger 370
Ognon Valley 441
Ohain 679
Oingt 555
Oiron 871
Oisans Massif (The) 416
Oizon 234
Olargues 494
Olbreuse manor 855
Oléron (Île d') 856
Olette 490
Olhain 677
Olivet 831
Ollières-sur-Eyrieux 172
Ollioules 757
Olmes (Monts d') 612
Olmeto 400
Olonne-sur-Mer 867
Olonne (Ile d') 867
Olonzac 497
Oloron-Sainte-Marie 219
Oltingue 148
Omaha Beach 643
Omerville 479
Omonville-la-Rogue 638
One Valley 606
Onet-le-Château 784
Onzain 824
Oô (Lake of) 606
Oô (Val d') 606
Opio 731
Opme 191
Oppède-le-Vieux 735
Oradour-Saint-Genest 517
Oradour-sur-Glane 524
Orange 750
Orb Gorges 497
Orb Valley 497
Orbais 371
Orbec 653
Orbey 140
Orchaise 822
Orcher (Château d') 651
Orcières-Merlette 409
Orcines 199
Orcival 195
Orédon 210
Orgelet 443
Orgeval 474
Oricourt 441
Orient Lake and Forest 375
Orléaguet 119
Orléans 831
Orlhaguet 202
Ormes (Les) 848
Ornaisons 503
Ornans 441

Ornolac-Ussat-les-Bains 609
Orrouy 461
Orsay 471
Orschwihr 149
Ortenbourg 149
Orthez 220
Orto 397
Orvanne 470
Orvault 310
Osny 472
Ospédale Forest 398
Ossau Valley 217
Osséja 493
Osselle Caves 433
Osterbat 225
Othe Forest 354
Ottmarsheim 138
Ottrott 142
Ouanne 355
Ouarville 454
Ouchamps 823
Ouche Region (The) 657
Ouche Valley 347
Oueil Valley 606
Ouessant (Île d') 310
Ouillat Pass 494
Ouilly (Pont d') 666
Ouistreham-Riva-Bella 645
Oulas Gorges 773
Oulchy-le-Château 372
Oulmes 852
Ouradou 778
Ourscamps (Abbey of) 471
Oursinieres (Les) 761
Oust 610
Outines 372
Outre-Forêt Region (The) 141
Ouveillan 501
Ouye 462
Ouzouer-sur-Trezee 827
Oxocelhaya 211
Oye-et-Pallet 442
Oyonnax 570
Oyré 848
Ozon 849

■ P

Pacaudière (La) 554
Pacy-sur-Eure 646
Padern (Château de) 510
Padirac (Gouffre de) 119
Pail (Corniche du) 582
Pailharès 161
Pailhes castle 614
Paillard (Moulin de) 587
Paillon Gorges 748
Pailly 373
Pailly-sur-Serein 358
Pailly (Le) 562
Paimpol 310
Paimpont 311
Paimpont (Forest of) 311
Païolive Woods 176
Palaggiu 401
Palais du Roi 169
Palaja 490
Palalda 487
Palanges Forest 783
Palavas-les-Flots 499
Paley 470
Pallet 291
Pallice (La) 863
Palloux (Les) 524
Palluau-sur-Indre 237
Palmyre (La) 851
Palombaggia beach 399
Palud-sur-Verdon (La) 765
Paluel 664
Pamiers 614
Pampelonne 774
Pamproux 869
Pancheraccia 401
Panissières 561
Panloy 870
Pannesière-Chaumard Reservoir 351
Paraclet (Le) 375
Paray-le-Monial 354
Parc-de-Saint-Pons (Le) 756
Parçay-Meslay 834
Parcé-sur-Sarthe 595
Parentignat 192
Parentis-en-Born 271
Parfondeval 379
Paris 53
   Acclimatation (Jardin d') 57
   Albert Kahn (Gardens) 56

Aquarium 59
Arc de Triomphe
Armée (Musée de l') 63
Arsenal (Library of the) 66
Art moderne de la Ville de Paris (Musée d') 56
Art Naïf (Museum) 67
Arts de la Mode (Musée des) 57
Arts décoratifs (Musée des) 57
Arts et traditions populaires (Musée des) 57
Aumont (Hôtel d') 66
Bagatelle (Park) 57
Balzac (Museum) 68
Bastille (Opéra de la) 57
Bastille (Place de la) 57
Beauvais (Hôtel de) 66
Belleville 57
Billettes (Cloître des) 66
Biron (Hôtel) 61
Biron (Hôtel) 70
Bois-Préau (Château de) 65
Boulogne (Bois de) 57
Bourdelle (Museum) 67
Bourse 62
Bricart de la Serrure (Museum) 66
Buttes-Chaumont 57
Carnavalet (Hôtel) 66
Carnavalet (Museum) 58
Carrousel (Gardens) 72
Catacombs (The) 58
Centre Georges-Pompidou (Beaubourg) 58
Cernuschi (Museum) 66
Chaillot (Palais de) 58
Champs-de-Mars 59
Champs-Élysées 59
Chasse et de la Nature (Musée de la) 66
Châtelet 59
Cité (Île de la) 59
Cluny (Museum) 60
Cognacq-Jay (Museum) 60
Colonne de Juillet 57
Comédie Française 69
Conciergerie 60
Concorde (Place de la) 60
Contrescarpe (Place de la) 64
Dauphine (Place) 59
Découverte (Palais de la) 62
Défense (La) 60
Déportation (Mémorial de la) 60
Dorée (Maison) 62
Eiffel (Tower) 61
Élysée (Palace) 61
France (Collège de) 64
French History (Museum of) 66
French Monuments (Museum of) 59
Fürstenberg (Place) 71
Géode (The) 73
Grand Palais 61
Grands Boulevards (The) 62
Grévin (Museum) 62
Guénégaud (Hôtel) 66
Guimet (Museum) 62
Halles (Espace des) 62
Halles (Les) 62
Holographie (Museum) 62
Homme (Musée de l') 59
Horloge (Quai de l') 60
Hôtel de Ville 62
Île-de-France (Museum) 72
Innocents (Fountain of) 62
Institut 63
Institut de France (Palais de l') 63
Institut des études musulmanes 63
Invalides (Les) 63
Jardin des Plantes 63
Jeu de Paume (Museum) 72
Justice (Palais de) 60
Lambert (Hôtel) 72
Lamoignon (Hôtel de) 66
Lassay (Hôtel de) 61
Latin Quarter 64
Lauzun (Hôtel) 72
Le Corbusier (foundation) 68
Le Peletier de Saint-Fargeau (Hôtel) 58
Louvre (The) 64
Lutèce (Arènes de) 68

Luxembourg (Gardens and Palace) 65
Madeleine (La) 65
Maine-Montparnasse (Tour) 67
Malmaison (Château de) 65
Marais (Le) 65
Marly (Chevaux de) 60
Marmottan (Museum) 68
Matignon (Hôtel) 61
Ménilmontant 57
Meudon 66
Militaire (École) 59
Monceau (Parc) 66
Monnaie (Hôtel de la) 63
Montmartre 67
Montparnasse 67
Mosque (The) 67
Mouffetard (Rue) 64
Muette (La) 68
National Museum of Modern Art 58
Natural History (Museum of) 63
Naval (Museum) 59
Nissim de Camondo (Museum) 66
Notre-Dame 68
Notre-Dame-de-Lorette 68
Odéon (Theatre) 64
Opéra 68
Opéra-Comique 62
Orangerie (Museum) 72
Orsay (Museum) 69
Palais omnisport de Paris-Bercy 69
Palais-Bourbon 61
Palais-Royal 69
Panthéon (Place du) 64
Panthéon (The) 69
Passages des Grands Boulevards 69
Passy 68
Père-Lachaise (Cemetery) 70
Petit Palais 61
Picasso (Museum) 70
Pigalle 67
Planetarium 62
Pont Neuf 59
Princes (Parc des) 57
Publicité (Musée de la) 70
Ranelagh (Gardens) 68
Renan-Scheffer (Museum) 68
Rodin (Museum) 70
Sacré-Cœur (Basilica of) 67
Saint-Cloud 70
Saint-Denis (Art and History Museum of) 71
Saint-Denis (Basilica of) 70
Saint-Étienne-du-Mont 64
Saint-Eustache 71
Saint-Eustache (Cathedral of) 62
Saint-Germain-des-Prés 71
Saint-Germain (Faubourg) 61
Saint-Honoré (Faubourg) 61
Saint-Julien-Le-Pauvre 71
Saint-Louis (Church of) 72
Saint-Louis (Île) 71
Saint-Merri 72
Saint-Pierre-de-Montmartre 67
Saint-Séverin 72
Saint-Sulpice 64
Sainte-Chapelle 60
Sainte-Geneviève (Library) 64
Salé (Hôtel) 66
Salm (Hôtel de) 61
Sceaux 72
Sens (Hôtel de) 66
Sèvres 72
Sorbonne 64
Soubise (Hôtel) 66
St. Antoine (Faubourg) 57
St. Gervais-St. Protais 65
St. Jacques (Tower) 59
St. Marie (Temple of) 66
St. Martin (Rue) 59
St. Paul-St. Louis 66
Sully (Hôtel de) 66
Techniques (National Museum) 72
Tertre (Place du) 67
Théâtre de la Ville 59
Théâtre Musical de Paris 59
Trinité (The) 59
Trocadéro (Place du) 59
Tuileries (Gardens) 72

Val-de-Grâce (Military hospital) 65
Vendôme (Place) 72
Vert-Galant (Square du) 59
Victoires (Place des) 73
Vieux-Montmartre (Museum) 67
Villette (La) 73
Vincennes (Château of) 73
Vincennes (Forest of) 73
Vosges (Place des) 66
Zadkine (Museum) 67
Parleboscq 608
Parnac 106
Parnes 479
Parnot (Château de) 368
Parthenay 857
Pas de la Case 606
Pas du Miroir 111
Pas-de-l'Escalette 496
Passenans 442
Patrimonio 400
Pau 220
Pauillac 270
Paulin (Château de) 773
Paulnay 237
Paunat 125
Pause Pass 608
Pavé 851
Pavin (Lake) 194
Payzac 177
Peaugres 161
Peaule 319
Pech-Merle Caves 115
Peille 748
Peillon 748
Peïra-Cava 761
Peisey-Nancroix 811
Pellevoisin 233
Pellissonnière Château (La) 872
Pellouailles-les-Vignes 586
Pélussin 571
Pelvoux 422
Pen Hir Point 289
Pencran 302
Pénestin 319
Penly 645
Penmarc'h 285
Pennautier (Château de) 490
Penne 123
Penne d'Agenais 126
Penon 269
Penquelenec 286
Penta-di-Casinca 396
Péone 725
Pépieux 497
Perche Pass 493
Perche Region (The) 657
Percher (Château du) 594
Pérignac 847
Pérignac 860
Pérignat-lès-Sarliève 191
Périgord Blanc Region (The) 119
Périgord Noir Region (The) 119
Périgueux 119
Perjuret Pass 159
Pernand-Vergelesses 340
Pernes-les-Fontaines 722
Péronne 675
Pérouges 571
Perpignan 503
Perray-en-Yvelines (Le) 474
Perrecy-les-Forges 351
Perrier 192
Perriers-sur-Andelle 659
Perros-Guirec 311
Perse 778
Perseigne Forest 629
Perte de l'Ain 434
Perthus (Le) 494
Pertuis 758
Pertuiset (Le) 563
Pescheray (Domaine de) 593
Pesmes 441
Pessac 261
Pessan 605
Petit Drumont 534
Petit-Bornand (Le) 803
Petit-Couronne 665
Petit-Fort-Philippe 686
Petit-Saint-Bernard Pass 811
Petite Meurthe Valley 537
Petite-Pierre (La) 151
Petites Dalles (Les) 648
Peumerit 286
Peyrat-le-Château 526
Peyre 177
Peyre 786
Peyredeyre Gorge 196

Peyrehorade 272
Peyreleau 175
Peyreleau 780
Peyrelevade 523
Peyrepertuse (Château de) 510
Peyriac-de-Mer 501
Peyriac-Minervois 497
Peyrolles-en-Provence 758
Peyrusse 185
Peyrusse-le-Roc 781
Pézenas 505
Pfaffenhofen 136
Pfulgriesheim 145
Phalsbourg 545
Piana 399
Piaon Gorges 742
Piau-Engaly 211
Pibrac 617
Piccovagia peninsula 399
Picquigny 692
Pied-de-Borue 178
Piedicorte-di-Gaggio 401
Piedicroce 396
Piemançon 717
Pierre-Buffière 521
Pierre-Châtel Defile 557
Pierre-d'Albigny 800
Pierre-de-Bresse 356
Pierre-fondue (La) 288
Pierre-Gourde 166
Pierre-la-Treiche 547
Pierre-Levée (Château de) 867
Pierre-Lys Defile 507
Pierre-Percée 546
Pierre-Perthuis 346
Pierre-Pouquelée 638
Pierre-qui-Vire (La) 351
Pierre-Saint-Martin (Pass) 210
Pierreclos (Château de) 349
Pierrefitte-en-Auge 631
Pierrefitte-Nestalas 210
Pierrefonds 461
Pigna 390
Pilat (Mont) 571
Pilon Pass 745
Pin-Sec 267
Pinarello 399
Pin (Château du) 438
Pino 395
Pioggiola 391
Pique (Valley of la) 606
Piriac-sur-Mer 289
Pirou 639
Piscine (Château de la) 499
Pithiviers 830
Pizancon 418
Pizy 358
Pla d'Adet 210
Plagne (La) 811
Plailly 476
Plaimpied 236
Plaine-Joux 810
Plainfaing 538
Plaisance 608
Plaisance 786
Plaisance 855
Plaisir-Fontaine 441
Plaix 237
Plan-de-la-Tour (Le) 757
Planches Caverns 430
Plancoët 294
Planès 497
Plasnes 634
Plassac 853
Plassac-Rouffiac 847
Plazac 111
Plazac 122
Plège (Château de) 351
Pléhédel 311
Pléherel (Plage) 297
Plélauff 320
Plérin 320
Plésidy 300
Pleslin 294
Plessis-Bourré (Château du) 584
Plessis-Brion (Château du) 460
Plessis-Josso 326
Plessis-Macé (Château du) 584
Plessisy-lès-Tours (Château de) 834
Plestin-les-Grèves 302
Pleubian 326
Pleugueneuc 295
Pleumeur-Bodou 302
Pléven 294
Pleyben 312
Pleyber-Christ 302
Plo de la Bise 780
Plobannalec 286
Ploërmel 301

Plogoff 316
Plomb du Cantal 192
Plombières-lès-Dijon 348
Plombières-les-Bains 543
Plomeur 285
Plomion 379
Plomodiern 291
Plonéour-Lanvern 285
Plonévez-Porzay 312
Plouaret 302
Plouarzel 281
Ploubalay 297
Ploudalmézeau 281
Ploudiry 302
Plouescat 325
Plouézec 310
Plougasnou 306
Plougastel-Daoulas 312
Plougescrant 326
Plougonven 302
Plouguerneau 281
Plouharnel 290
Plouhinec 298
Plouider 281
Ploulec'H 302
Ploumanac'h 311
Ploumoguer 281
Plounéour-Ménez 302
Plounérin 307
Plozévet 283
Pluvigner 287
Poët-Laval (Le) 411
Poët-Laval (Le) 415
Poilhes-la-Romaine 488
Point Sublime 174
Point Sublime 765
Poissons 373
Poissy 471
Poitevin (Marais) 858
Poitiers 858
Poix-de-Picardie 691
Poleymieux 569
Polignac 196
Poligny 442
Pollionnay 576
Polminhac 202
Pommard 340
Pommiers 554
Pommiers 871
Pompadour 523
Pompierre 543
Poncé-sur-Loir 587
Poncey-sur-l'Ignon 356
Poncin 572
Pons 202
Pons 860
Pont de Menat 239
Pont des Abarines 160
Pont Sainte-Marie 380
Pont-à-Mousson 543
Pont-Audemer 658
Pont-Aven 313
Pont-Aven 313
Pont-Calleck 301
Pont-Croix 283
Pont-d'Ain 572
Pont-d'Arc 162
Pont-d'Hérault 174
Pont-d'Ouche 347
Pont-de-Briques 682
Pont-de-Chervil 166
Pont-de-l'Arche 659
Pont-de-L'Isère 420
Pont-de-Montvert 168
Pont-de-Pany 347
Pont-de-Salars 778
Pont-de-Vaux 558
Pont-de-Veyle 558
Pont-du-Gard 167
Pont-en-Royans 422
Pont-Évêque 424
Pont-l'Abbé 285
Pont-l'Abbé-d'Arnoult 862
Pont-l'Évêque 631
Pont-Ravagers 165
Pont-Rémy 693
Pont-Saint-Esprit 173
Pont-Saint-Pierre 663
Pont-sur-Yonne 358
Pontailler-sur-Saône 361
Pontaix 411
Pontarion 518
Pontarlier 442
Pontaubault 651
Pontaubert 338
Pontaumur 196
Pontcharra-sur-Turdine 574
Pontchartrain 469
Ponte Leccia 396
Pontécoulant (Château de) 650
Pontécoulant (Château de) 666

Pontet (Le) 712
Pontgibaud 196
Pontgouin 476
Pontigné 586
Pontigny 337
Pontivy 313
Pontoise 41
Pontonx 261
Pontorson 656
Ponts-de-Cé (Les) 584
Popolasca 397
Porcheresse 848
Porge (Le) 267
Pornic 313
Pornichet 284
Porquerolles 733
Porspoder 281
Port Blanc 326
Port Pass 609
Port Tudy 299
Port-Ball 667
Port-Barcarès 503
Port-Blanc 326
Port-Camargues 499
Port-Cros 733
Port-d'Envaux 870
Port-de-Bouc 715
Port-de-By 270
Port-de-Carhaix 305
Port-de-Lanne 272
Port-de-Piles 848
Port-des-Barques 848
Port-du-Salut (La Trappe du) 594
Port-en-Bessin 645
Port-Grimaud 755
Port-Hublé 667
Port-Hublé 502
Port-Joinville 872
Port-la-Nouvelle 502
Port-Lauragais 612
Port-Lesney 438
Port-Leucate 503
Port-Louis 304
Port-Louis 305
Port-Manec'h 313
Port-Manech 313
Port-Navalo 318
Port-Pin (Calanques de) 723
Port-Royal 459
Port-Sainte-Marie 101
Port-sur-Saône 444
Port-Vendres 510
Porta 396
Portel 609
Portel-des-Corbières 501
Portes 168
Portes-en-Ré (Les) 861
Porticcio 389
Porticciolo 395
Portieux 534
Porto 399
Porto-Pollo 399
Porto-Vecchio (Bay of) 399
Porto (Bay of) 398
Portonville 470
Portout 799
Portsal 281
Posanges 361
Possonnière (La) 586
Possonnière (Manor of la) 829
Pouancé 597
Poudenas 118
Poudrey chasm 441
Pougnadoires 174
Pougues 352
Pouilly 349
Pouilly-en-Auxois 355
Pouilly-sur-Loire 344
Poulains Point 285
Pouldavid 296
Pouldreuzic 283
Pouldu (Le) 316
Pouliguen (Le) 284
Pouypardin 608
Pouzac 222
Pouzauges 860
Pouzauges-le-Vieux 861
Poyanne 261
Pra-Loup 713
Prade Ponds 268
Pradelles-Cabardès 498
Prades 174
Prades 185
Prades 506
Prafrance 160
Pralognan-la-Vanoise 813
Pranles 172
Pranzac 863
Prarion (Le) 802

Prats-de-Mollo 490
Praz-sur-Arly 808
Praz (Les) 801
Pré de Madame Carle (Le) 422
Préau Pass 572
Préchac 256
Prémery 355
Prémesques 691
Prémontré (Abbey of) 373
Prény 544
Présilly 443
Presles 373
Presles 466
Preste (La) 489
Preuilly 472
Prévenchères 167
Primel-Trégastel 306
Pringy 355
Prisces 379
Privas 172
Propriano 399
Proumeyssac 111
Provence (Croix de) 702
Provins 472
Provins 472
Prudhomat 110
Prunelli Gorges 391
Prunet-et-Belpuig 490
Prunget 233
Pruniers 869
Puellemontier 372
Puget-Théniers 725
Puisaye Region (The) 355
Pujols 126
Puligny-Montrachet 340
Punta Castle 387
Puntous de Laguian 607
Putanges-Pont-Ecrepin 666
Puy Crapaud 861
Puy de Dôme 199
Puy de Glavenas 203
Puy de Montoncel 235
Puy de Sancy 194
Puy-du-Fou (Le) 852
Puy-l'Évêque 106
Puy-Mary (Le) 198
Puy-Notre-Dame (Le) 584
Puy-Saint-Georges 774
Puy-Saint-Vincent 422
Puycelsi 776
Puyconnieux 520
Puygiron 415
Puyguilhem 105
Puylaroque 108
Puylaurens 781
Puylaurens (Château de) 507
Puylaurent 167
Puy (Le) 196
Puyloubier 702
Puymirol 102
Puymorens Pass 606
Puymoyen 846
Puyoo 220
Puypéroux 847
Puys 645
Pyla-sur-Mer 254
Pyrénées 2000 492
Pyrénées (Passes of the) 222

Q

Quarante 507
Quarré-les-Tombes 351
Quatre Vallées (Les) 659
Quatre Vios 172
Quédillac 295
Queige 796
Quelven 286
Quemigny-sur-Seine 344
Quénécan 286
Quenza 400
Quéribus (Château de) 510
Quérigut 497
Querqueville 638
Quesnoy (Le) 678
Questembert 319
Quetteville 632
Quettreville-sur-Sienne 656
Queue-en-Yvelines (La) 470
Queyras Valley (The) 417
Queyrières 203
Queyssac-les-Vignes 517
Quézac 174
Quiberon 314
Quiévrechain 694
Quillan 506
Quillebeuf 665
Quilly-le-Vicomte 631

Quimper 314
Quimperlé 315
Quincié 556
Quinéville 667
Quinsac 265
Quintenas 161
Quintin 320
Quistinic 287

■ R

Rabastens 782
Rabastens 782
Rabastens-de-Bigorre 227
Rabodanges 666
Raguenes-Plage 313
Raguin (Château de) 597
Rairé 868
Raismes 694
Ramatuelle 755
Rambouillet 473
Rambouillet Forest 473
Ramondens Forest 498
Ramonville-St-Agne 620
Rampillon 472
Rampoux 113
Rance 294
Rancon 517
Randan 199
Ranfolly Pass 809
Ranrouët 288
Rantigny 456
Ranville 645
Raon-L'Étape 533
Raray 476
Rassisse 773
Ratilly 355
Rauzan 264
Ravel 187
Raviège Reservoir 494
Ravières 335
Rayol (Le) 740
Raz Point 316
Razès 521
Razès Region (The) 507
Réalmont 782
Réalville 108
Reau Abbey (La) 848
Réaumur 872
Rebais 467
Rebenty (Valley of) 506
Recques-sur-Hem 683
Reculée des Planches 430
Réding 545
Redon 316
Regalon Gorges 724
Regardoir belvédère 445
Regnéville-sur-Mer 639
Reichstett 147
Reignac 111
Reignac 827
Ré (Ile de) 861
Reillanne 735
Reims 375
Reims (Montagne de) 370
Relanges 534
Relecq (Le) 302
Remarde Valley 453
Remingeasse 857
Remiremont 544
Remoulins 166
Renaison 554
Rennes 316
Rennes-les-Bains 507
Réno-Valdieu (Forest of) 657
Renoso (Monte) 391
Renwez 377
Réole (La) 265
Repaire 115
Replonges 559
République (Col de la) 571
Restigné 823
Restonica Gorges 397
Rétaud 870
Rethondes 461
Retournac 193
Retournay 845
Retournemer (Lake of) 537
Reulle-Vergy 354
Revel 612
Revermont Region (The) 443
Reviers 644
Réville 638
Revin 375
Reygade 517
Rey (Le) 174
Reyssouse 558
Rhinau 140

Rhône Corniche (The) 172
Rhône Pass 161
Rhône Valley (The) 172
Rhue Valley 192
Rhuis 476
Rhune 211
Rhuys Peninsula 318
Riau 241
Ribaouto (Gorges of) 616
Ribeauvillé 141
Ribérac 122
Riberot Valley 608
Ribou (Lake of) 588
Riceys (Les) 370
Richelieu 832
Richemont 105
Richemont 849
Richerenches 761
Riec-sur-Bélon 313
Riec-sur-Belon 313
Riedisheim 139
Rieupeyroux 785
Rieux-Minervois 497
Rieux-Volvestre 616
Riez 736
Rigaud 725
Rignac 113
Rigny castle 853
Rillieux-la-Pape 569
Rilly 370
Rimaison 286
Rimont 609
Rimplas 766
Rinaiu 401
Riolan (Clue du) 732
Riom 198
Riom-Es-Montagnes 198
Rions 265
Rioux 870
Ripaille (Château de) 812
Riquewihr 142
Riscle 614
Risoul (Le) 418
Rivau (Château du) 826
Rive-de-Gier 573
Rivedoux-Plage 861
Riverie 570
Rivesaltes 503
Riviera Corniches (The) 751
Rivière-Bourdet (Château de
la) 666
Rivière-Thibouville (La) 657
Rixheim 138
Roaillan 256
Roaillan 273
Roanne 572
Robert le Diable (Castle of) 665
Robien (Château de) 320
Rocamadour 122
Rochambeau (Château de) 829
Roche aux Fées 300
Roche du Feu (La) 305
Roche du Prêtre 435
Roche-Bernard (La) 318
Roche-de-Maine (La) 853
Roche-en-Brénil (La) 357
Roche-Guyon (La) 479
Roche-Jagu 326
Roche-l'Abeille (La) 524
Roche-Maurice (La) 302
Roche-Posay (La) 861
Roche-Racan (Château de la)
834
Roche-sur-Foron (La) 806
Roche-sur-Yon (La) 862
Rochebeaucourt (La) 846
Rocheblave 174
Rochebloine 161
Rochebronne 166
Rochebrune 202
Rochebrune castle 851
Rochebrune-Super-Megève
808
Rochebrune (Château de) 524
Rochechouart 524
Rochecolombe 163
Rochecorbon 836
Rochecourbon 870
Rochefort 239
Rochefort-en-Terre 319
Rochefort-en-Yvelines 453
Rochefort-sur-Loire 586
Rochefort-sur-Mer 862
Rochefoucauld (La) 862
Roche (La) 177
Rochelambert 196
Rochelle (La) 863
Rochemaure 166
Rochemaure 172
Rochepot (La) 353
Rocher (Château du) 588

Rochers-Sévigné 328
Roches-de-Condrieu (Les) 424
Rochetaillée 573
Rochetaillée-sur-Saône 569
Rochetaillée-sur-Saône 567
Rochette (La) 517
Rocroi 377
Rodelle 775
Rodemack 546
Rodez 782
Roffiac 200
Rogliano 395
Rognes 758
Rogny-les-Sept-Écluses 355
Rolle 354
Rolleboise 467
Romanche Valley 416
Romanèche-Thorins 349
Romanèche-Thorins 555
Romans-sur-Isère 418
Romieu (La) 607
Romorantin-Lanthenay 833
Ronce-les-Bains 851
Ronchamp 443
Ronne 574
Ronsenac 846
Roque-Baignard 631
Roque-Gageac (La) 109
Roque-Gageac (La) 109
Roque-St-Christophe (La) 111
Roque-Ste-Marguerite (La) 777
Roque-sur-Cèze (La) 164
Roquebillière 766
Roquebrun 507
Roquebrune 751
Roquebrune-Cap-Martin 752
Roquebrune-sur-Argens 731
Roquecourbe 785
Roquedols 159
Roquefavour 703
Roquefixade (Château de) 612
Roquefort-sur-Soulzon 784
Roquelaure 779
Roquemaure 753
Roqueston 732
Roquetaillade château 256
Rosay 467
Roscanvel Peninsula 289
Roscoff 319
Roselend dam 798
Rosheim 149
Rosière (La) 806
Rosières 177
Rosières 361
Rosiers-sur-Loire (Les) 597
Rosnay-l'Hôpital 368
Rosny 467
Rosporden 320
Rostrenen 320
Rothéneuf 297
Rotondo (Monte) 397
Rott 152
Roubaix 691
Roubion 760
Rouelles 651
Rouen 659
Rouffach 149
Rouffiac 847
Rouffiac des Corbières 510
Rouffignac (Grotte de) 122
Rouffihac 119
Rougemont-le-Château 431
Rougnat 520
Rougon 765
Rouillac 846
Roullet 847
Roullours 668
Roumazières 851
Roure 760
Rousses Lake 443
Rousses (Les) 443
Rousset Pass 422
Roussillon 106
Roussillon 705
Roussines 233
Rousson 159
Roussy-le-Bourg 546
Rouvray 477
Rouvray (Château de) 469
Rouvres-en-Plaine 347
Rouvres-en-Xaintois 548
Roux (Le) 176
Rouzie (L'Île) 311
Roya Valley 753
Royan 865
Royat 199
Royaumont 474
Roye 691
Rozérieulles 539
Rozier (Le) 175
Ruaudin 593

Rubanel Abyss 495
Rudelle 113
Rudlin Waterfall 537
Rue 572
Rue 691
Ruelle 846
Ruffec 866
Ruffieu 563
Ruffieux 795
Ruillans Pass 416
Rully 343
Rumengol 282
Rumilly-lès-Vaudes 380
Ruoms 163
Ruoms Pass 163
Rupt-aux-Nonnains 546
Rustrel Colorado 705
Ry 659

■ S

Sablé-sur-Sarthe 594
Sables-d'Olonne (Les) 866
Sables-d'Or-les-Pins 297
Sables-Vigniers 857
Sablettes (Les) 760
Sabres 265
Saché 820
Sacy-le-Grand 460
Sagone 395
Sahorre 489
Saignes 193
Saignon 705
Sail-les-Bains 554
Sailhant Waterfall 200
Saillac 520
Saillagouse 493
Saillé 288
Sains-en-Amiénois 675
St Cyprien beach 399
St Cyr-sous-Dourdan 453
St Martin-Valmeroux 198
St Sulpice-de-Favières 463
St Tugen 283
St-Acceul 463
St-Affrique 784
St-Agnan 351
St-Agnant-de-Versillat 524
St-Agrève 166
St-Aignan 286
St-Aignan 824
St-Aignan-en-Vercors 423
St-Alban-de-Montbel 801
St-Alban-les-Eaux 554
St-Agil (Château de) 837
St-Algis 381
St-Alyre-ès-Montagne 192
St-Amand 543
St-Amand-de-Coly 122
St-Amand-en-Puisaye 355
St-Amand-les-Eaux 693
St-Amand-Montrond 243
St-Amand-sur-Fion 381
St-Amand-Tallende 191
St-Amans-Soult 780
St-Amant-de-Boixe 846
St-Amant-de-Bonnieure 863
St-Amarin 148
St-Ambroix 160
St-Amour 443
St-André 773
St-André-d'Allas 119
St-André-d'Apchon 554
St-André-d'Hébertot 653
St-André-de-Bâgé 349
St-André-de-Bâgé 558
St-André-de-Corcy 561
St-André-de-Cubzac 256
St-André-de-Lidon 870
St-André-des-Arques 113
St-André-du-Bois 265
St-André-les-Vergers 380
St-Ange (Château) 470
St-Angel 525
St-Anthème 186
St-Antoine 422
St-Antonin-Noble-Val 122
St-Arnoult 453
St-Astier 110
St-Auban (Clue de) 732
St-Auban-sur-l'Ouvèze 416
St-Aubin 684
St-Aubin-du-Cormier 299
St-Aubin-sur-Loire 341
St-Aubin-sur-Mer 645
St-Augustin 244
St-Aulaye 122
St-Avé 326

St-Avit 104
St-Avit-Sénieur 104
St-Avold 545
St-Barthélemy 287
St-Barthélemy (Château de) 609
St-Baslemont 534
St-Baume Gorges 173
St-Béat 615
St-Beauzély 778
St-Bel 554
St-Benoît 859
St-Benoît-du-Sault 233
St-Benoît-sur-Loire 833
St-Bernard 575
St-Bertrand-de-Comminges 615
St-Blaise 715
St-Blancard 605
St-Bonnet 189
St-Bonnet-en-Champsaur 409
St-Bonnet-la-Rivière 519
St-Bonnet-le-Froid 203
St-Bonnet-Tronçais 245
St-Brévin-les-Pins 314
St-Briac 297
St-Brice-en-Coglès 299
St-Brieuc 320
St-Bris-le-Vineux 338
St-Bris-St-Cézaire 870
St-Brisson 351
St-Cado 298
St-Calais 595
St-Caprazy 784
St-Cassien Lake 720
St-Cast-le-Guildo 297
St-Céneri-le-Gérei 582
St-Céneri-le-Gérei 629
St-Céré 123
St-Cernin 199
St-Cézaire Caverns 731
St-Cézaire-sur-Siagne 731
St-Chamant 199
St-Chamant 516
St-Chamond 573
St-Chartier 238
St-Chély-d'Apcher 164
St-Chély-d'Aubrac 774
St-Chinian 507
St-Christoly-de-Blaye 256
St-Christophe 445
St-Christophe-de-Valains 299
St-Christophe-en-Brionnais 341
St-Christophe-le-Jajolet 630
St-Christophe-les-Gorges 200
St-Cirgues 185
St-Cirgues-la-Loutre 516
St-Cirq-Lapopie 115
St-Clair 740
St-Clar 612
St-Claude 443
St-Claude 443
St-Clément-des-Baleines 861
St-Come 172
St-Côme-d'Olt 779
St-Crépin 119
St-Crépin-aux-Bois 460
St-Cricq château 605
St-Croix 824
St-Croix-en-Jarez 571
St-Cybardeaux 846
St-Cydroine 348
St-Cyprien 109
St-Cyprien 505
St-Cyprien-Plage 503
St-Cyr 570
St-Cyr-L'École 479
St-Cyr-la-Rivière 657
St-Cyr-sur-Loire 836
St-Cyr-sur-Menthon 558
St-Cyr-sur-Morin 467
St-Dalmas 766
St-Dalmas-de-Tende 753
St-Denis-d'Anjou 595
St-Denis-d'Oléron 856
St-Denis-de-l'Hôtel 831
St-Denis-du-Jouhet 238
St-Denis-du-Payré 858
St-Denis-sur-Loire 822
St-Denis-sur-Sarthon 630
St-Désiré 239
St-Didier 569
St-Didier-en-Velay 193
St-Dié 544
St-Dier-d'Auvergne 187
St-Disdier 411
St-Dizant-du-Gua 871
St-Dizier 377
St-Donat Park 756
St-Dye-sur-Loire 823

St-Élophe 543
St-Émilion 272
St-Esprit-des-Bois 294
St-Estèphe 118
St-Estèphe 270
St-Étienne 573
St-Étienne-d'Essensac 495
St-Étienne-de-Baigorry 224
St-Étienne-de-Tinée 760
St-Étienne-en-Dévoluy 411
St-Eugène 497
St-Eulalie 200
St-Évroult-Notre-Dame-du-Bois 657
St-Fargeau 355
St-Fargeau 355
St-Félicien 161
St-Félix-de-Monceau 508
St-Félix-de-Pallières 174
St-Félix-de-Sorgues 784
St-Félix-Lauragais 612
St-Ferme 264
St-Fiacre 298
St-Firmin 745
St-Florent 400
St-Florent-le-Vieil 595
St-Florentin 356
St-Floret 192
St-Flour 199
St-Flour-du-Pompidou 165
St-Fort 871
St-Fort-sur-le-Né 850
St-Fortunade 525
St-Fortunat 569
St-Gabriel 714
St-Galmier 561
St-Gatien 641
St-Gaudens 615
St-Géneroux 845
St-Genès-de-Lombaud 264
St-Genès-du-Retz 185
St-Gengoux-le-National 360
St-Geniès 119
St-Geniez-d'Olt 779
St-Génis-des-Fontaines 504
St-Genou 237
St-Georges Defile 497
St-Georges-d'Oléron 856
St-Georges-de-Didonne 865
St-Georges-la-Pouge 518
St-Georges-Motel 453
St-Gérand-le-Puy 240
St-Germain 851
St-Germain Forest 474
St-Germain-Beaupré 524
St-Germain-de-Livet (Château de) 631
St-Germain-des-Vaux 638
St-Germain-en-Brionnais 342
St-Germain-en-Laye 474
St-Germain-la-Poterie 454
St-Germain-Laprade 196
St-Germain-Laval 554
St-Germain-Lembron 192
St-Germain-les-Belles 520
St-Germain-Lespinasse 573
St-Germer-de-Fly 454
St-Gertrude 665
St-Gervais 256
St-Gervais 479
St-Gervais-les-Bains 809
St-Gervase-d'Auvergne 188
St-Gervazy 187
St-Gery (Château de) 782
St-Gildas-de-Rhuys 318
St-Gildas-des-Bois 782
St-Gilles-Croix-de-Vie 868
St-Gilles-du-Gard 173
St-Gilles-Vieux-Marché 286
St-Girons 268
St-Girons 616
St-Gobain Forest 373
St-Goussaud 521
St-Grat 761
St-Groux 866
St-Guénolé 285
St-Guilhem-le-Désert 495
St-Haon-le-Châtel 554
St-Hermine 872
St-Hernin 305
St-Hilaire-Bonneval 521
St-Hilaire-de-Riez 868
St-Hilaire-de-Villefranche 870
St-Hilaire-des-Landes 299
St-Hilaire-des-Loges 852
St-Hilaire-du-Harcouet 656
St-Hilaire-du-Touvet 412
St-Hilaire-la-Palud 853
St-Hilaire-St-Florent 597
St-Hilaire-St-Mesmin 832

St-Hippolyte 149
St-Hippolyte 436
St-Hippolyte-du-Fort 174
St-Honorat 720
St-Honoré-les-Bains 356
St-Hymetière 443
St-Illide 200
St-Ilpize 185
St-Izaire 784
St-Jacques-des-Guérets 829
St-James (Chaussée de) 870
St-Jaume Gorge 507
St-Jean 298
St-Jean 620
St-Jean d'Abbetot 651
St-Jean-aux-Bois 461
St-Jean-Cap-Ferrat 722
St-Jean-Chazorne 178
St-Jean-d'Angély 868
St-Jean-d'Angle 862
St-Jean-d'Arves 807
St-Jean-de-Beauregard (Château de) 453
St-Jean-de-Boisseau 310
St-Jean-de-Braye 832
St-Jean-de-Côle 106
St-Jean-de-Gonville 562
St-Jean-de-la-Ruelle 832
St-Jean-de-Losne 356
St-Jean-de-Luz 224
St-Jean-de-Maurienne 807
St-Jean-de-Monts 868
St-Jean-de-Pourcharesse 177
St-Jean-de-Verges 610
St-Jean-du-Bleymard 168
St-Jean-du-Bruel 781
St-Jean-du-Doigt 306
St-Jean-du-Gard 160
St-Jean-en-Royans 422
St-Jean-le-Froid 783
St-Jean-le-Vieux 211
St-Jean-le-Vieux 225
St-Jean-Pied-de-Port 225
St-Jean-St-Paul 784
St-Jean-Trolimon 285
St-Jean (Mont) 548
St-Jean-Saverne 143
St-Jeannet 716
St-Jeanvrin 239
St-Jorioz 797
St-Josse 678
St-Jouin-de-Marnes 845
St-Juéry 773
St-Julien 270
St-Julien 343
St-Julien 520
St-Julien-Chapteuil 193
St-Julien-de-Concelles 310
St-Julien-de-Crempse 105
St-Julien-de-Jonzy 341
St-Julien-du-Sault 360
St-Julien-du-Tournel 168
St-Julien-en-Born 266
St-Julien-en-Genevois 810
St-Julien-Molin-Molette 572
St-Junien 524
St-Just-en-Chevalet 563
St-Just-St-Rambert 563
St-Juvin 381
St-Lambert-des-Bois 459
St-Lambert-du-Lattay 586
St-Laon 853
St-Lary-Soulan 210
St-Lattier 418
St-Laurent 270
St-Laurent 644
St-Laurent-de-Cerdans 487
St-Laurent-de-la-Plaine 586
St-Laurent-des-Arbres 164
St-Laurent-du-Pont 410
St-Laurent-en-Gâtines 820
St-Laurent-en-Grandvaux 444
St-Laurent-la-Roche 443
St-Laurent-les-Églises 523
St-Laurent-les-Bains 177
St-Laurent-Nouan 821
St-Laurent-Rochefort 571
St-Laurent-sur-Sèvre 871
St-Léger-en-Yvelines 473
St-Léger-la-Montagne 521
St-Léger-sous-Beuvray 335
St-Léger-Vauban 351
St-Léon-sur-Vézère 111
St-Léonard-de-Noblat 526
St-Léonard-des-Bois 582
St-Léonard-en-Beauce 822
St-Leu-d'Esserent 456
St-Lieux-lès-Lavaur 778
St-Lizier 521
St-Lô 663
St-Louis 826

St-Louis-Artzviller 545
St-Louis-lès-Bitche 151
St-Loup 574
St-Loup 824
St-Loup-de-Naud 472
St-Lôup-Hors 633
St-Loup-Lamairé 845
St-Lunaire 297
St-Lupicin 443
St-Lyphard 288
St-Macaire 265
St-Maixant 516
St-Maixent-l'École 869
St-Malo 321
St-Malo-de-Guersac 288
St-Mammès 470
St-Mandé-sur-Brédoire 847
St-Mandrier 760
St-Marc-Jaumegarde (Château de) 702
St-Marc-la-Lande 857
St-Marcel 233
St-Marcel-d'Ardèche 162
St-Marcel-de-Félines 561
St-Marcel-les-Annonay 161
St-Marcel-lès-Valence 414
St-Marcellin 418
St-Martin-aux-Bois 460
St-Martin-aux-Chartrains 632
St-Martin-Cantalès 200
St-Martin-d'Ardèche 162
St-Martin-d'Auxigny 234
St-Martin-d'Entraunes 725
St-Martin-de-Belleville 804
St-Martin-de-Boscherville 666
St-Martin-de-Castillon 705
St-Martin-de-Fenollar 494
St-Martin-de-Gurson 117
St-Martin-de-Laives 343
St-Martin-de-Limeuil 111
St-Martin-de-Londres 507
St-Martin-de-Ré 861
St-Martin-du-Canigou 489
St-Martin-du-Var 750
St-Martin-du-Vican 781
St-Martin-en-Haut 576
St-Martin-ès-Vignes 380
St-Martin-la-Méanne 525
St-Martin-le-Hébert 638
St-Martin-le-Vinoux 414
St-Martin-Ste-Catherine 522
St-Martin-Terressus 522
St-Martin-Vésubie 766
St-Martory 616
St-Mathieu Point 292
St-Maur (Abbey of) 584
St-Maurice 534
St-Maurice-de-Gourdans 571
St-Maurice-la-Clouère 859
St-Maurice-lès-Châteauneuf 342
St-Maurice-sur-Moselle 534
St-Maurin 101
St-Maximin-La-Ste-Baume 753
St-Mayeux 286
St-Médard 517
St-Médard-Catus 108
St-Méen-le-Grand 306
St-Méloir-des-Ondes 290
St-Même-les-Carrières 858
St-Menoux 235
St-Mesmin (Château de) 872
St-Michel (Abbey of) 381
St-Michel (Plateau) 748
St-Michel-de-Cuxa 489
St-Michel-d'Entraygues 846
St-Michel-de-Frigolet (Abbey of) 759
St-Michel-de-Grandmont 495
St-Michel-de-Maurienne 807
St-Michel-de-Montaigne 116
St-Michel-de-Montjoie 656
St-Michel-de-Veisse 516
St-Michel-en-Grève 302
St-Michel-l'Observatoire 731
St-Michel-Mont-Mercure 861
St-Mihiel 544
St-Mitre-les-Remparts 715
St-Montant 173
St-Moré 346
St-Moreil 518
St-Myon 185
St-Nabord 544
St-Nazaire 323
St-Nazaire 518
St-Nazaire-en-Royans 423
St-Nectaire 200
St-Nic 282
St-Nicodème 286
St-Nicolas 298

St-Nicolas-de-Brem 868
St-Nicolas-de-Campagnac 170
St-Nicolas-de-Port 541
St-Nicolas-de-Veroce 809
St-Nicolas-des-Eaux 286
St-Nicolas-du-Pélem 320
St-Nicolas-lès-Arras 678
St-Nizier-du-Moucherotte 422
St-Omer 692
St-Ouen (Château de) 588
St-Ouen-lès-Parey 534
St-Palais 211
St-Palais 213
St-Palais 234
St-Palais-sur-Mer 866
St-Pancrace 750
St-Papoul 492
St-Parize-le-Châtel 353
St-Paterne-Racan 832
St-Paul-de-Fenouillet 507
St-Paul-de-Jarrat 610
St-Paul-de-Mausole (Monastery of) 754
St-Paul-de-Varax 560
St-Paul-de-Vence 764
St-Paul-le-Jeune 164
St-Paul-lès-Dax 263
St-Paul-les-Monestier 420
St-Paul-Trois-Châteaux 415
St-Paulet 612
St-Paulien 196
St-Pé-de-Bigorre 223
St-Pée-sur-Nivelle 212
St-Péray 167
St-Père-sous-Vézelay 360
St-Pern 294
St-Philbert-de-Grand-Lieu 324
St-Piat 457
St-Pierre-d'Entremont 410
St-Pierre-d'Oléron 857
St-Pierre-de-Bailleul 668
St-Pierre-de-Boeuf 572
St-Pierre-de-Chartreuse 410
St-Pierre-de-Côle 106
St-Pierre-de-Lorouër 587
St-Pierre-de-Maillé 845
St-Pierre-de-Rhèdes 494
St-Pierre-de-Vals 498
St-Pierre-des-Nids 630
St-Pierre-du-Chemin 872
St-Pierre-du-Vauvray 647
St-Pierre-Église 638
St-Pierre-en-Port 648
St-Pierre-Eynac 193
St-Pierre (Gorges) 725
St-Pierre-la-Palud 554
St-Pierre-le-Moutier 352
St-Pierre-les-Eglises 849
St-Pierre-sur-Dives 636
St-Pierre-sur-Mer 501
St-Pierre-Toirac 115
St-Point 349
St-Point Lake 442
St-Pol-de-Léon 324
St-Pol-sur-Ternoise 692
St-Polycarpe 507
St-Pompain 852
St-Pons Park 756
St-Pons-de-Thomières 494
St-Porchaire 870
St-Pourçain-sur-Sioule 243
St-Prest 458
St-Priest 569
St-Priest-en-Jarez 574
St-Privat 516
St-Privat-des-Prés 122
St-Projet 518
St-Projet 778
St-Prouant 872
St-Puy 607
St-Quay-Portrieux 325
St-Quentin 378
St-Quentin-en-Yvelines 459
St-Quintin-sur-Sioule 239
St-Quirin 545
St-Rambert 567
St-Raphaël 753
St-Rémy 343
St-Rémy-de-Provence 754
St-Rémy-de-Provence 754
St-Rémy-la-Varenne 584
St-Rémy-lès-Chevreuse 459
St-Rémy-sur-Durolle 201
St-Renan 281
St-Restitut 415
St-Révérien 355
St-Riquier 692
St-Rivoal 282
St-Robert 118
St-Robert 519
St-Romain 340

St-Romain 443
St-Romain-de-Bénet 870
St-Romain-de-Lerps 172
St-Romain-de-Tousque 165
St-Roman-l'Aiguille 165
St-Roman-le-Puy 570
St-Romans-de-Bellet 750
St-Rome-de-Cernon 785
St-Rome-de-Tarn 786
St-Rouin (Hermitage of) 532
St-Saëns 634
St-Samson-de-la-Roque 665
St-Satur 244
St-Saturnin 191
St-Saturnin-d'Apt 705
St-Saulge 355
St-Sauveur 186
St-Sauveur 225
St-Sauveur 873
St-Sauveur Gorge 218
St-Sauveur-en-Puisaye 355
St-Sauveur-en-Rue 571
St-Sauveur-le-Vicomte 667
St-Sauveur-sur-Tinée 760
St-Sauveur (Château de) 649
St-Savin 210
St-Savin 869
St-Savinien 870
St-Sébastien 291
St-Sébastien 298
St-Seine-l'Abbaye 356
St-Seine-sur-Vingeanne 361
St-Sernin-du-Bois 345
St-Sernin-sur-Rance 786
St-Servais 302
St-Seurin-de-Cadourne 270
St-Sever 261
St-Sever Forest 668
St-Sever-Calvados 668
St-Séver-de-Rustan 226
St-Siffret 176
St-Sorlin-en-Bugey 553
St-Sozy 109
St-Sulpice 778
St-Sulpice 851
St-Sulpice-la-Pointe 782
St-Sulpice-Laurière 521
St-Sulpice-le-Verdon 872
St-Sylvain-d'Anjou 586
St-Symphorien 735
St-Symphorien-de-Lay 572
St-Symphorien-le-Château 458
St-Symphorien-sous-Chomerac 166
St-Thégonnec 302
St-Thibault 244
St-Thibéry 506
St-Thomas-de-Conac 871
St-Thomé 177
St-Tomoso da Pastoreccia 396
St-Trivier-de-Courtes 558
St-Trojan-les-Bains 857
St-Tropez 754
St-Ulrich 141
St-Ulrich 545
St-Urcize Nasbinals Bonnefon 774
St-Vaast-de-Longmont 476
St-Vaast-la-Hougue 638
St-Valbert 439
St-Valérien 358
St-Valéry-en-Caux 664
St-Valéry-sur-Somme 693
St-Vallier 420
St-Vallier-de-Thiey 731
St-Vaury 521
St-Vennec 291
St-Véran 418
St-Véran 776
St-Vérand 555
St-Viâtre 833
St-Victor-la-Coste 164
St-Victor-sur-Loire 563
St-Victor-sur-Ouche 347
St-Victor-sur-Rhins 574
St-Victurnien 524
St-Vidal 196
St-Vigor-d'Ymonville 666
St-Vigor-le-Grand 633
St-Vincent-de-Tyrosse 269
St-Vincent-sur-Jard 867
St-Vital 796
St-Vivant Abbey 354
St-Vrain 464
St-Wandrille 665
St-Yan 341
St-Ybars 614
St-Yorre 245
St-Yrieix-la-Perche 524
St-Yvi 320
Ste Colombe 563

Ste Marguerite Peninsula 281
Ste-Adresse 652
Ste-Agnès 74
Ste-Anne-d'Auray 283
Ste-Anne-la-Palud 303
Ste-Apolline 470
Ste-Austremoine 783
Ste-Avoye 283
Ste-Barbe 298
Ste-Baume Massif 756
Ste-Christie-d'Auch 606
Ste-Colombe 863
Ste-Colome 222
Ste-Cristina 396
Ste-Croix 787
Ste-Croix-d'Offémont 460
Ste-Croix-du-Mont 265
Ste-Croix-Vallée-Française 165
Ste-Croix (Lake of) 745
Ste-Croix (Lake of) 765
Ste-Engrâce 219
Ste-Énimie 174
Ste-Eulalie-de-Cernon 777
Ste-Eulalie-de-Cernon 784
Ste-Feyre 521
Ste-Foy-la-Grande 116
Ste-Foy-lès-Lyon 569
Ste-Gauburge 657
Ste-Gemme 463
Ste-Honorine-la-Chardonne 649
Ste-Jalle 416
Ste-Lucie-de-Tallano 398
Ste-Magnance 339
Ste-Marguerite 720
Ste-Marguerite-Lafigère 178
Ste-Marguerite-sur-Mer 645
Ste-Marie 202
Ste-Marie-Aux-Mines 142
Ste-Marie-Cappel 685
Ste-Marie-de-Ré 861
Ste-Marie-des-Chazes 185
Ste-Marie-du-Lac 372
Ste-Marie-du-Menez-Hom 282
Ste-Marie-du-Mont 644
Ste-Marine 285
Ste-Maxime 756
Ste-Menehould 378
Ste-Mère-Église 644
Ste-Mesme (Château de) 462
Ste-Nathalène 119
Ste-Noyale 313
Ste-Odile (Mont) 142
Ste-Ouenne 855
Ste-Paule 555
Ste-Radegonde 783
Ste-Restituta (Church of) 390
Ste-Roseline (Chapel of) 726
Ste-Savine 380
Ste-Sévère-sur-Indre 238
Ste-Solange 236
Ste-Suzanne 588
Saintes 869
Stes-Maries-de-la-Mer (Les) 717
Stines 461
Saire (Val de) 638
Saison Valley 219
Saissac 498
Saissac 498
Salasc 496
Salau 608
Salaunes 261
Salbris 828
Saleccia Beach 387
Saléchon 615
Salernes 708
Salers 200
Salève (Le) 810
Salies-de-Béarn 220
Salies-du-Salat 616
Salignac-Eyvigues 119
Salin-de-Giraud 717
Salins-d'Hyères (Les) 732
Salins-les-Bains 444
Sallanches 810
Salle-les-Alpes (La) 409
Salletaine 868
Salles 555
Salles d'Angles 850
Salles-Curan 778
Salles-en-Beaujolais 556
Salles-la-Source 783
Salles-sur-l'Hers 492
Salles (Croix des) 808
Salon-de-Provence 757
Salses (Fort de) 503
Salsigne 498
Salvagnac 782
Salvagnac 787

Salvetat-sur-Agout (La) 494
Salviac 113
Samadet 262
Samatan 613
Samoëns 806
Samoreau 474
San Michele 400
San Nicolao 396
San Stefano Pass 400
Sanary-Bandol 713
Sanary-sur-Mer 757
Sancerre 244
Sancoins 244
Sancy-les-Meaux 468
Sand 140
Sandaucourt 543
Sangatte 681
Sanguinaires Islands 389
Sanguinaires (Route des) 389
Sanilhac 163
Sant'Antonino 390
Santa Giulia Bay 399
Santa Manza Bay 393
Santa-Maria-de-Valle-di-Rostino 396
Santenay 340
Santeuil 472
Santo-Pietro-di-Tenda 400
Sanxay 869
Saône Valley (The) 356
Saône (The vale of) 444
Saorge 753
Sappey-en-Chartreuse 410
Saramon 613
Sare 211
Sargé-sur-Braye 837
Sarlat 123
Sarpoil 192
Sarrance 219
Sarrancolin 222
Sarrasine cavern 437
Sarrebourg 545
Sarreguemines 545
Sars-Poteries 678
Sartène 400
Sarzay 238
Sarzeau 318
Sassenage 414
Sassy (Château du) 630
Satillieu 161
Saugues 201
Saujon 866
Saulcet 243
Saulges 595
Saulieu 357
Saulire (La) 804
Saulx Valley 546
Saumane 165
Saumonards 856
Saumur 596
Saurier 192
Sausset-les-Pins 736
Saut-de-la-Mounine (Le) 115
Saut-des-Cuves 537
Sautadet waterfall 164
Sauternais Region (The) 273
Sauternes 273
Sautet Dam 419
Sauvage (Château de) 474
Sauvage (Côte) 851
Sauvagnac 521
Sauvan 731
Sauve 174
Sauve (La) 264
Sauveplantade 163
Sauvetat (La) 607
Sauveterre 753
Sauveterre-de-Béarn 225
Sauveterre-de-Comminges 615
Sauveterre-de-Guyenne 264
Sauveterre-de-Rouergue 785
Sauveterre-la-Lémance 105
Sauveterre (Causse de) 173
Saux 118
Sauze (Le) 713
Save Gorges 615
Savennières 586
Saverdun 614
Saverne 143
Savigny 554
Savigny-en-Septaine 236
Savigny-lès-Beaune 340
Savines-le-Lac 419
Savonnières 838
Saxonnex (Mont) 806
Scaër 320
Scala di Santa Regina 398
Scey-en-Varais 438
Schiltigheim 148
Schirmeck 132

Schleital 141
Schoenenbourg 141
Sciez 807
Scorbé-Clairvaux 849
Scy-Chazelles 539
Sebourg 694
Seclin 689
Secondigny 855
Sedan 378
Seebach 141
Sées 629
Ségala 123
Ségala Region 785
Segonzac 850
Ségos 614
Segré 597
Ségre Gorges 493
Séguret 762
Seignelay 337
Seigneurie Lake 431
Seignosse 269
Seillans 758
Seine Valley 474
Seine Valley (The lower) 665
Seine-Port 475
Sein (Île de) 325
Seissan 605
Sélestat 144
Selles-sur-Cher 824
Seltz 141
Semnoz (Le) 797
Semouille Valley 453
Semur-en-Auxois 357
Semur-en-Brionnais 341
Sénanque Abbey 758
Senez 724
Senlis 475
Senlisse 459
Sennecy-le-Grand 343
Senon 548
Senonches 476
Senones 546
Sens 358
Sens-Beaujeu 244
Sentein 608
Sept Chevaux Lake 438
Sept Îles 311
Sept Laux 412
Sept-Saulx 377
Septeuil 467
Septmonts 379
Sepvigny 534
Sérandon 518
Sercy 360
Sère-Argelès 210
Sérécourt 534
Séreilhac 223
Serein Valley 358
Serein (Mont) 765
Sérézin-du-Rhône 569
Sergeac 111
Sérichamp Signal 537
Sérignan-du-Comtat 750
Sermano 397
Sermizelles 346
Serra di Pigno 400
Serrabone 490
Serrant (Château de) 584
Serre Mt. 191
Serre-Chevalier 409
Serre-Ponçon Lake 419
Serres 408
Serres-sur-Arget 609
Serreyrède Pass 159
Serriera 399
Serrières 161
Serrigny 340
Servières-le-Château 516
Sessenheim 136
Sète 508
Settons (Lake) 351
Seuilly 826
Seurre 356
Sévérac-le-Château 785
Séveraissette 409
Sévignacq-Thèze 227
Sévrier 797
Sewen 148
Seyne-les-Alpes 725
Seyne-sur-Mer (La) 760
Seyssuel 424
Sidobre and Lacaune Mounts 785
Sierck-les-Bains 546
Sigale 732
Sigean 501
Sigean Safari Park 501
Signal de St-Claude 188
Sigolsheim 149
Sigy 472
Sigy-en-Bray 659

Sillé-le-Guillaume 587
Sillegny 540
Sillery 377
Silvacane Abbey 758
Simiane-la-Rotonde 705
Simorre 613
Sion-Vaudemont Hill 546
Sioule Gorges 188
Sioule Gorges 239
Siouville-Hague 638
Sirod 434
Sisco 395
Sisteron 758
Six-Fours-les Plages 757
Sixt-Fer-à-Cheval 806
Sizun 302
Sizun 302
Soccia 397
Sochaux 439
Socoa 212
Sogno Bay 399
Soissons 379
Solaise (Tête du) 812
Solenzara 401
Solerieux 415
Solesmes 595
Solférino 266
Solignac 521
Solliès-Toucas 761
Sologne Region (The) 833
Solre-le-Château 678
Solutré 350
Solutré Rock 349
Somme Valley 692
Sommières 174
Sommières-du-Clain 848
Somport (Col du) 219
Sophia-Antipolis 704
Sorans 441
Sorde-l'Abbaye 272
Sorel (Château de) 453
Sorèze 775
Sorgues Valley 784
Sorinières (Les) 310
Sors 125
Sospel 742
Soubise 848
Soucy 381
Soufflenheim 136
Souillac 125
Soulac-sur-Mer 267
Soulie (Le) 495
Souloise defile 411
Soulor (Col du) 222
Soultz 149
Soultz-sous-Forêts 141
Soultzbach-les-Bains 139
Soultzmatt 149
Soumont-St-Quentin 648
Soumoulou 222
Souppes-sur-Loing 470
Source Bleue 430
Sous-Balme Defile 556
Soustons 269
Souterraine (La) 524
Souvigny 244
Souvigny-en-Sologne 828
Souzon Valley 347
Speloncato 390
Spelunca Gorges 397
Spéracèdes 731
Spesbourg 132
Stainville 546
Stangala 315
Stantari 401
Steige (Col de) 137
Steinbrunn-le-Bas 139
Stello (Monte) 395
Stenay 534
Stival 286
Straiture (Defile de) 537
Strasbourg 144
Strette 398
Struthof 132
Sublime (Corniche) 765
Suc de Bauzon 167
Suèvres 822
Suisse Normande (La) 666
Sully 335
Sully-sur-Loire 834
Sundgau Region (The) 148
Super-Besse 194
Super-Châtel 800
Super-Lioran 193
Super-Sauze 714
Superbagnères 606
Superbloquère 492
Superdévoluy 411
Surbourg 141
Sury-Aux-Bois 832
Sury-le-Comtal 570

Suscinio 318
Suze-la-Rousse 415
Syam 434
Sylvanès 786

■ T

Taillebourg 870
Tain-l'Hermitage 421
Taizé 359
Talcy 358
Talcy (Château de) 822
Tallard 412
Talloires 797
Talmay 361
Talmont 871
Talmont-Saint-Hilaire 867
Tamaris 760
Tamarissière (La) 486
Tamnies 112
Tancarville 665
Tanlay 359
Tanneron Massif 720
Tannois 533
Tanus 774
Taoulet 222
Tarare 574
Tarascon 759
Tarascon-sur-Ariège 609
Tarbes 225
Tarco 401
Tardes (Viaduc de) 520
Tardets-Sorholus 219
Tarentaise (The) 809
Targassonne 493
Tarn and Jonte Gorges 174
Tarn Valley 786
Tarquimpol 539
Tasciaca 824
Tasque 607
Tassin-la-Demi-Lune 569
Taulanne (Clue de) 724
Taulé 307
Tautavel 510
Tavant 826
Tavel 167
Taverny 470
Tavignano Gorges 397
Tavignano Valley 401
Teghime Pass 400
Teich (Le) 255
Tempêtes Pass 765
Tenaille (Abbey of La) 853
Tence 203
Tende 753
Tendu 233
Tergnier 374
Termes 510
Termes d'Armagnac (Château de) 607
Termignon 807
Ternand 555
Ternant 341
Ternant 354
Ternes (Les) 200
Terney Dam 161
Terrans 356
Terraube (Château de) 613
Tertre-Rouge 589
Tessy-sur-Vire 663
Teste (La) 254
Têteghem 687
Teyjat Grotto 118
Teysset (Le) 126
Thaims 870
Thann 148
Thannenkirch 149
Thaon 644
Tharon-Plage 314
Thau Lagoon 508
Thaumiers 243
The D-Day Landing Beaches 643
Theil (Le) 201
Theizé 555
Thémericourt 467
Thémines 113
Théoule-sur-Mer 727
Thérain Valley 477
Théret (Château du) 521
Thérondels 202
Thésée 824
Thévet-Saint-Julien 238
Thiepval 675
Thiérache Region (The) 379
Thiers 201
Thièzac 202
Thil 357

Thillot (Le) 534
Thines 177
Thionville 546
Thivars 458
Thiviers 125
Thizy 358
Thizy 574
Thoirette 559
Thoiry 469
Thoissey 575
Thoisy-la-Berchère 357
Thoisy-le-Désert 355
Thollon-les-Memises 805
Tholonet (Le) 702
Tholy (Le) 537
Thomery 474
Thonac 111
Thônes 803
Thonon-les-Bains 812
Thoré Valley 780
Thorenc 732
Thorens-Glières 812
Thorey-Lyautey 546
Thor (Le) 731
Thoronet Abbey (Le) 759
Thouarcé 584
Thouars 871
Thou (Mont) 569
Thoureil (Le) 584
Thuès-entre-Vals 497
Thuès-les-Bains 497
Thueyts 162
Thueyts 163
Thuillières 534
Thuir 504
Thuré 849
Thuret 199
Thury-Harcourt 666
Tiffauges 871
Tignes 811
Til-Châtel 358
Tillac 607
Tillard 454
Tille Valley 358
Tillières 477
Tilly-sur-Seulles 636
Tindoul de la Vayssière 775
Tinée Valley 760
Tiuccia 395
Tivernon 831
Tizzano 401
Tocqueville 638
Tollare 395
Tomino 395
Tonnay-Boutonne 868
Tonnay-Charente 862
Tonneins 125
Tonnerre 358
Tonquédec 302
Toranchin Valley 574
Torcy 346
Torgan Gorges 510
Torigny-sur-Vire 663
Tornac-Anduze 160
Torre 399
Tortefontaine 678
Tosse 269
Touche-Trébry (La) 305
Toucy 355
Touët-sur-Var 725
Touffou 849
Toul 547
Toul-Goulic 320
Toulon 758
Toulon-sur-Allier 241
Toulon-sur-Arroux 351
Toulonjac 787
Toulouse 617
Toulx-Sainte-Croix 518
Touques 631
Touques 641
Touquet (Le) 684
Tour Blanche (La) 115
Tour d'Aiguillon (La) 784
Tour sans Venin (La) 422
Tour-d'Aigues (La) 758
Tour d'Oyré (La) 849
Tour-du-Pin (La) 419
Tour-en-Bessin 643
Tourcoing 693
Tourette 172
Tourette-sur-Loup 765
Tour (La) 760
Tourlaville 638
Tourmalet (Col du) 222
Tournefeuille 620
Tournemire 199
Tournoël 203
Tournon 161
Tournus 359
Tournus and Cluny (Between) 359

Tourouvre 657
Tourreau (Château de) 722
Tourrette-Levens 748
Tours 834
Tourtenay 853
Tourtenay 871
Tourtoirac 125
Tourtour 708
Tourvéon (Mont) 555
Tourville 639
Toury 234
Toussuire (La) 807
Touvres (La) 846
Trait (Le) 665
Tranchade (La) 846
Tranche-sur-Mer (La) 845
Trayas (Le) 727
Trébas 773
Trébeurden 312
Trécesson 311
Treffort-Cuisiat 558
Tréflaouénan 325
Trégarven 282
Trégastel 311
Trégastel-Bourg 311
Trégoat 286
Tréguennec 286
Tréguier 325
Tréguier 326
Trégunc 292
Tréguron 305
Tréhorenteuc 311
Treignac 523
Treigny 355
Trélazé 584
Trelly 639
Trelon 679
Tremals 313
Trémaouëzan 301
Tremblade (La) 851
Trémilly 368
Tréminou 285
Trémohar-en-Berric 326
Trémolat 125
Trémont-sur-Saulx 546
Tréport (Le) 667
Trépot 441
Treschenu-Creyers 411
Tresserve 795
Trévarez 305
Trévillit 286
Trévou-Tréguignec 326
Trévoux 575
Treyne (La) 109
Tricherie lake 852
Trie-sur-Baïse 226
Trièves Region (The) 419
Trigance 765
Trilport 468
Trimouns 606
Trinité-sur-Mer (La) 290
Trizac 198
Troarn 636
Trois Fontaines 305
Trois Pignons (Massif des) 469
Trois Termes Peak 494
Trois Vallées 612
Trois-Epis (Les) 148
Trois-Fontaines 377
Troissereux (Château de) 454
Tronçais Forest 244
Tronchet Abbey (Le) 296
Trôo 829
Troumouse (Cirque de) 218
Troussay (Château de) 825
Trouville 639
Troyes 379
Truchtersheim 137
Truyère Gorges 201
Tuc de l'Étang 615
Tuchan 510
Tuffé 589
Tulle 525
Tuméjus 547
Turballe (La) 288
Turbie (La) 751
Turckheim 149
Turenne 520
Turini Forest 761
Turpa 288
Turquestein-Blancrupt 545
Tursac 111

■ U

Uchon (Signal d') 345
Ugine 808
Uglas Pass 159

Unac 606
Ungersheim 136
Unieux 562
Upper Ardèche Valley 162
Urbeis 137
Urcel 374
Urfé (Château d') 571
Uriage-les-Bains 414
Urrugne 211
Urt 215
Urtubie 211
Urzumu (Mont) 211
Usclades-et-Rieutord 167
Ussac 519
Ussé 836
Ussel 525
Usson 192
Usson 848
Usson-en-Forez 573
Usson-les-Bains 497
Ustaritz 213
Ustaritz 215
Ustou Valley 608
Utelle 766
Uza 266
Uzemain 533
Uzerche 525
Uzès 175
Uzeste 256

■ V

Vabres-l'Abbaye 784
Vaccarès lake 717
Vache Alliat (La) 609
Vadencourt 381
Vaison-la-Romaine 761
Val Joly (Lake of) 679
Val Richer (Abbey) 631
Val sans Retour 311
Val-André (Le) 326
Val-Cenis 807
Val-d'Isère 812
Val-Suzon 348
Valabres Gorges 760
Valberg cross 725
Valbonnais Valley (The) 420
Valbonne 173
Valbonne 704
Valbonne (Plateau) 704
Valcarlos (Défilé de) 225
Val (Château du) 474
Valdo-Niello Forest 398
Valençay 245
Valence 125
Valence 420
Valence-d'Albigeois 773
Valence-sur-Baïse 607
Valence-sur-Baïse 608
Valenciennes 693
Valensole 736
Valentine 615
Valescure 727
Valescure 754
Valgaudemar Valley (The) 421
Valgorge 164
Valinco 389
Valinco Bay 399
Val (Lake) 437
Vallauris 720
Valle d'Alesani 396
Vallée Française 165
Vallée Noire 238
Valleraugue 158
Vallery 470
Vallet 291
Vallière 476
Vallière 516
Valloire 807
Valloires (Abbey of) 678
Vallon 202
Vallon-Pont-d'Arc 162
Vallouise 422
Vallouise Valley (The) 421
Valmargne 506
Valmont 648
Valmorel 812
Valmy 378
Valognes 667
Valprivas 193
Valras-Plage 487
Valréas 761
Valromey 563
Vals 614
Vals-les-Bains 163
Valsenestre 420
Valserine Valley 556
Van (Pointe du) 316

Vançon Valley 759
Vandenesse (Château de) 356
Vannes 326
Vannes-sur-Cosson 832
Vanoise Massif 813
Vans (Les) 176
Vantoux (Château de) 347
Vaour 776
Var Corniche 716
Varaize 868
Varces 414
Vareilles 342
Varen 123
Varengeville 645
Varenne-l'Arconce 342
Varenne-Valley 634
Varennes-en-Argonnes 532
Varennes-Jarcy 469
Varennes-sur-Allier 244
Varetz 519
Varilhes 614
Varreddes 468
Vars 417
Varzy 360
Vascoeuil 659
Vassivière Lake 526
Vauclair 374
Vaucouleurs 547
Vaudémont 546
Vaudeurs 354
Vaudreuil (Le) 648
Vaufrey 436
Vaugines 735
Vault-de-Lugny 338
Vaumale 765
Vaumas 234
Vausse 350
Vauvenargues (Château de) 702
Vaux 337
Vaux 859
Vaux-de-Cernay 459
Vaux-Douaumont 547
Vaux-le-Pénil 468
Vaux-le-Vicomte 477
Vaux-sur-Mer 865
Vaux (Belvédère de) 675
Vaux (Fort de) 547
Veauce 239
Veigne 828
Velars-sur-Ouche 347
Velay (Château of) 196
Venaco 397
Venanson 766
Venasque 722
Vence 764
Vendée Wars (The) 871
Vendeuil 374
Vendeuvre 636
Vendeuvre-du-Poitou 872
Vendôme 836
Vendrennes 852
Vénéon Valley 416
Venizy 356
Ventabren 702
Ventadour 163
Ventadour (Château de) 525
Ventoux (The) 765
Ventron 537
Ver-sur-Launette 476
Ver-sur-Mer 643
Verberie 461
Verclause 416
Vercors Massif (The) 422
Verdelais 265
Verdelles (Château de) 595
Verdelot 467
Verderonne (Château de) 460
Verdière (La) 714
Verdon-sur-Mer (Le) 267
Verdon (Grand Canyon of) 765
Verdun 547
Verdun-sur-le-Doubs 356
Verdun (Mont) 569
Verfeil 123
Verger Mill (Le) 846
Verghia 389
Vergio (Col de) 397
Verjon 853
Vermeille (La Côte) 510
Vermenton 346
Vernajoul 610
Vernet-les-Bains 489
Verneuil-en-Bourbonnais 243
Verneuil-en-Halatte 476
Verneuil-sur-Avre 657
Vernon 667
Vernouillet 463
Vernoux 558
Verquières 754
Versailles 477

Versilhac 203
Versols 784
Vert-Bois 857
Verteuil 866
Vertheuil 270
Vertus 370
Vervins 380
Verzenay 370
Verzy 370
Vescovato 395
Vesdun 239
Vésigneux (Château de) 351
Vésinet (Le) 474
Vésole (Saut de) 494
Vesoul 444
Vésubie Gorges 766
Vésubie Valley 765
Vétheuil 479
Veules-les-Roses 664
Veulettes-sur-Mer 664
Vevier 797
Vèvre (Tour de) 244
Vexaincourt 546
Vexin Region (The) 479
Vexin (Valleys of the) 467
Veyrignac 119
Veyrines 161
Vez 461
Vézac 109
Vézelay 360
Vézelise 546
Vézénobres 159
Vézère Gorges 519
Vézère Valley 111
Vialas 168
Vialavert 785
Vianne 118
Viarmes 455
Vias 486
Viaur Dam 774
Viaur Gorges 774
Viaur viaduct 774
Vibrac 852
Vibraye 589
Vic 238
Vic-Bilh Region (The) 227
Vic-en-Bigorre 227
Vic-Fezensac 621
Vic-le-Comte 202
Vic-sur-Cère 202
Vic-sur-Seille 539
Vichy 245
Vico 397
Vicq 239
Vicq 845
Vic (Roche de) 516
Victot (Château de) 631
Vieil-Armand 135
Vieil-Baugé (Le) 586
Vieil-Hesdin 584
Vieille-Aure 210
Vieille-Brioude 185
Vieillevie 778
Vienne 423
Vierville-sur-Mer 645
Vierzon 246
Vierzy 381
Vieux 776
Vieux Mareuil 115
Vieux Vera 489
Vieux-Boucau 268
Vieux-Boucau-les-Bains 269
Vieux-Chambord 234
Vieux-Château 872
Vieux-Moulin 461
Vieux-Poitiers 849
Vieux-Port 665
Vieux-Windstein 140
Vigan (Le) 159
Vigan (Le) 174
Vigeant (Le) 851
Vigen 521
Vigeois 526
Vignasse (Mas de la) 163
Vigneaux (Les) 422
Vignes (Les) 174
Vignoles 340
Vignory 373
Vigny (Château de) 467
Vigoulet-d'Auzil 620
Vilhosc 759
Villages Falicon 748
Villaines-les-Rochers 820
Villandraut 837
Villandry 825
Villarceaux 479
Villard-de-Lans 422
Villard-Notre-Dame 416
Villard-Reculas 416
Villard-Reymond 416
Villard-sur-Doron 798

Villars 106
Villars-les-Dombes 560
Villarzel-Cabardès 490
Villé 137
Ville-Aux-Clercs (La) 837
Ville-sur-Saulx 546
Villebois-Lavalette 846
Villecerf 470
Villecomtal 607
Villecomtal 775
Villeconin (Château de) 462
Villecroze 708
Villedieu 200
Villedieu-les-Poêles 650
Villefort 168
Villefranche-d'Albigeois 773
Villefranche-de-Cona 489
Villefranche-de-Conflent 490
Villefranche-de-Lauragais 612
Villefranche-de-Rouergue 786
Villefranche-du-Périgord 126
Villefranche-sur-Cher 824
Villefranche-sur-Mer 751
Villefranche-sur-Saône 575
Villefranque 215
Villegailhenc 490
Villegongis 240
Villelongue Abbey 498
Villemartin 464
Villemaur-sur-Vanne 380
Villemolin (Château de) 361
Villemotier 559
Villemur-sur-Tarn 617
Villeneuve 192
Villeneuve 786
Villeneuve plateau 786
Villeneuve-d'Ascq 689
Villeneuve-de-Berg 177
Villeneuve-de-Haute-Provence 736
Villeneuve-de-Marsan 271
Villeneuve-Jacquelot 287
Villeneuve-l'Archevêque 360
Villeneuve-lès-Avignon 709
Villeneuve-les-Béziers 488
Villeneuve-les-Cerfs 199
Villeneuve-Loubet 716
Villeneuve-sur-Allier 242
Villeneuve-sur-Lot 126
Villeneuve-sur-Yonne 360
Villeneuvette 496
Villeprévost 454
Villequier 665
Villeray 471

Villeréal 104
Villerouge-Termenès 510
Villers-Bocage 636
Villers-Bocage 675
Villers-Bretonneux 675
Villers-Cotterêts 381
Villers-le-Lac 440
Villers-Saint-Sépulcre 477
Villers-sur-Mer 639
Villersexel 441
Villerville 642
Villesalem 855
Villesavin (Château de) 825
Villespassans 507
Villette (Château de) 467
Villeurbanne 569
Villey-le-Sec 547
Villey-sur-Tille 358
Villiers 464
Villiers-Saint-Benoît 355
Villiers-sur-Loir 829
Villy-la-Ferté 541
Vimoutiers 631
Vimy Ridge 676
Vinça 490
Vincelotte 338
Vingeanne (Along the river) 360
Vin (Route du) 149
Violay 575
Viols-le-Fort 508
Vion 161
Viosne Valley 472
Vire 668
Vire (Valley of the) 663
Virieu-le-Grand 563
Virieu (Château de) 419
Vis Valley 495
Visan 764
Vision-de-Sainte-Croix Park 539
Viso (Mount) 418
Vissec 495
Vistaëro (Le) 751
Vitré 327
Vitrolles 715
Vitry-en-Charollais 355
Vitry-le-François 381
Vitry-sur-Orne 546
Vitteaux 361
Vittel 548
Vivarais Cévenol Corniche 177
Vivier-sur-Mer (Le) 296
Viviers 172
Viviers-le-Gras 534

Vivoin 586
Vivonne 859
Vix 344
Vix 858
Vizille 745
Vizzavona 401
Voguë 163
Void 534
Voiron 410
Volhac 196
Vollore-Ville 201
Volnay 340
Volvic 203
Vonnas 559
Voray-sur-l'Ognon 441
Vorges 373
Vosges Region (Northern) 151
Vosne-Romanée 353
Vougeot 353
Vouglans (Lake) 445
Vouillé 859
Voulte-sur-Rhône (La) 166
Voulte-sur-Rhône (La) 166
Voultegon 848
Vouvant 852
Vouvray 834
Vouzan 847
Vouziers 381
Vove (La) 657
Voves 458
Voza Pass 809
Vuillafans 438

Walbourg 136
Wallers-Trélon 679
Wangen 149
Wangenbourg 151
Wantzenau (La) 144
Wasenbourg 140
Wasselonne 137
Wassy 382
Wattwiller 149
Waville 540
Weiterswiller 151
Werentzhouse 148
Western Pyrénées Nat. Park 227
Westhoffen 149
Wethalten 149

Wettolsheim 135
Wimereux 681
Wimy 381
Wingen-sur-Moder 151
Wintersberg 151
Wisques 692
Wissant 681
Wissembourg 151
Woerth 151
Wy 479

■ W

■ X

Xaintrailles 118
Xonrupt-Longemer 538

■ Y

Yaudet (Le) 302
Ydes-Bourg 193
Yeu (Ile d') 872
Yèvres 466
Ygrande 235
Ymonville 454
Yonne Valley (The) 361
Yquem 273
Yssingeaux 203
Yvetot 662
Yvignac 294
Yvoir-Saint-Gingolph 807
Yzeron 576
Yzeure 241

■ Z

Zaglia 397
Zeiterholz 546
Zetting 545
Zicavo 401
Ziegenberg 140
Zonza 393
Zuani 397

Contents

4-5 *How to use the Guide?*
- Get to know the guide
- Symbols and abbreviations

7 *Tourist itineraries*

8 *Gastronomy*
The restaurants of 121 top French chefs (see the list p. 9) are printed in red. These culinary experts have selected their favourite restaurants for you — from unpretentious little inns to celebrated tables. The establishments that represent the finest in French gastronomical tradition are indicated in the guide by a red dot; restaurants that offer both good food and good value are marked with a blue dot.

11 *Faces of France*
An illustrated overview of French history, art and culture, from the prehistoric period to the present.

29 *Practical holiday guide*
Answers to your basic questions about organizing a holiday in France. Nine broad categories: Information — Travel in France — Accommodation — Calendar, events — Holiday themes — Sporting holidays — Menu guide — Weights and measures.

55 *The regions of France*
Where to spend your holiday in France. For each region you will find a thumbnail sketch, a list of sightseeing 'musts' and a wealth of ideas and addresses for leisure activities. All of the region's localities are listed in alphabetical order. Descriptions of cultural treasures are followed by addresses of hotels, restaurants, campsites, rural *gîtes,* activities and events. Look for the addresses marked with a ♥ : they're the 'editor's choices' (gourmet foods, handicrafts, tea rooms...).

906 *Index*
Key to the *Guide,* this is where you will find all the sites, cities and towns described in the text, with their page numbers.

Symbols and abbreviations

● *Maps and sightseeing descriptions*

Sights and places of interest

★ interesting	≼ exceptional view	⚊ château
★★ remarkable	╎ remarkable church	∴ archaeological site
★★★ exceptional	■ architecture worthy of interest	---- hiking *(grande randonnée)* trail

Please note : maps in the guide vary in their scale, which is always indicated by the mention *échelle.* Unless otherwise stated, North is always upwards.

When a town's name is underlined (Saulieu), it possesses a specially recommended hotel or restaurant. (hotels ● and restaurants ◗ and ●)

The → symbol indicates cross-referencing with another entry or section.

● *Practical information*

Towns and places

⊠ postal code	🛳 ferry line	ϟ winter sports resort, with accessible altitudes
ⓘ tourist office	❦ station verte (rural holidays)	
▭ train station	♨ spa (with dates of season)	♥ editor's choice (establishments that particularly caught the fancy of our editorial team)
🚌 bus station	⅄ camping	
✈ airport		

Under the name of each locality is a reference to the regional map (e.g., A2).

Hotels

★	simple
★★	simple but comfortable
★★★	very comfortable
★★★★	first-class hotel
★★★★L	luxury hotel
●	**recommended hotel**
(L.F.)	Logis de France hotel chain
(C.H.)	Château-Hôtel
(R.S.)	Relais du Silence (exceptionally quiet hotel)
(C.A.)	Château-Accueil
(I.L.A.)	International Leading Association

Restaurants

♦	pleasant restaurant
♦♦	comfortable attractive surroundings
♦♦♦	refined decor, high-quality reception and service
♦♦♦♦	exceptional surroundings, decor, reception and service
◉	**recommended restaurant (gourmet food)**
●	**recommended restaurant (good food, good value for money)**

Amenities

rm	room	ᛩ	quiet	▭	swimming pool
Tx	telex	♿	access for the disabled	⚵	tennis
Ⓟ	parking	♪	music	⌣	golf
≼	view	⊗	no pets	h.s.	high season
ᨓ	park or garden	🧒	20% discount for children 5 or over	l.s.	low season

Prices

Prices are noted at the end of each entry.
★★Gare (L.F.) ☎ 99.89.10.46. 62 rm, closed 17 Dec-17 Jan and Sun eve (l.s.), 210. Rest.● ♦♦ A quiet hotel in the country, not far from the seaside. Excellent fixed meals featuring luscious desserts, 85-200; child : 35.

Hotels: the price given is the average price for a double room with bath, breakfast not included. For establishments where board or half-board is obligatory, the price indicated is for board or half-board ('pens or half-pens') per day two persons.

Restaurants: two prices are given: the cheapest fixed-price meal ('menu') and the average prices of a meal 'à la carte' (appetizer, main course and dessert) with wine and coffee, including service.   'Child' indicates the price of the children's menu.

Principal credit cards accepted:

AE	American Express
DC	Diners Club
Euro	Eurocard (Mastercard)
Visa	Visa

Get to know the guide

First, a few figures: 200,000 km covered, thousands of verifications in thousands of hotels and restaurants, 15,000 letters dispatched, 1,000 hours of interviews and some 6,000 telephone calls... For an entire year, a 10-person team traveled throughout France seeking out new addresses, updating and eliminating others, rereading and correcting the results, all with the help of tourist offices, 121 of France's best chefs and the invaluable aid of computerized information systems. This enormous, painstaking effort had but a single goal: to make our readers' holidays in France the best ever. The result is this *Guide to France,* a veritable data bank for planning a holiday in France: 4,000 hotels (360 appearing for the first time in the *Guide*), 5,000 restaurants, 3,500 of them serving meals priced under 100 F and 350 new addresses, 1,300 campsites, 1,000 suggestions for leisure activities, 500 'editor's choice' addresses.

Because we want to make your trip even more rewarding, the *Guide* helps you:
● find answers to your basic questions about holidays in France with our practical holiday guide;
● choose the right restaurant: the *Guide* distinguishes between *haute cuisine* establishments (732 addresses in this new edition) indicated by a red dot, and gourmet restaurants (424 addresses) indicated by a blue dot.

Follow our lead, then, and discover the thousand and one faces of France!

The Editors

THE
HACHETTE
GUIDE
TO
FRANCE

PANTHEON BOOKS

NEW YORK

Special thanks to:

• The French Government Tourist Board, French Government Tourist Offices in New York and London.
• Regional, departmental and local Tourist Authorities.

Originally produced and published in France in 1984 as Guide Hachette France by Hachette Guides Bleus. English edition by Pantheon, New York, and the Automobile Association (Great Britain); Japanese by Kodansha Ltd, Tokyo. Original work conceived under the direction of Adélaïde Barbey and the Guides Bleus, especially Jean-Jacques Fauvel, Patrice Milleron, François Monmarché and Françoise Vibert-Guigue.

Direction: Adélaïde Barbey.

Executive Editor: Marie-Pierre Levallois.

Editor: Isabelle Jendron.

Gastronomy: François Roboth.

Documentation: Florence Guibert.

Contributors: Christian Duponchelle, Françoise Favez, Julie Gaskill, Michèle Hocquet, Harriet Liens, Sheila Mooney-Mall, Alexandra Tufts-Simon, John Tyler Tuttle.

Designer: Pierre Faucheux, A.P.F.

Paste-up: Catherine Riand.

Cartography: René Pineau, Alain Mirande.

Illustrations: Arias Crespo, Dominique Jacomet, Roland Jacoutet, Martine Puchault.

Production: Gérard Piassale, Françoise Jolivot.

Editorial computing: Catherine Julhe, M.C.P.-Orléans, Tadia.

Photocomposition: M.C.P.-Orléans.

Manufactured in France by Maury, S.A. and Reliure Brun (Malesherbes).

First American Edition.

Revised and updated.

Translation first published in the United States by Pantheon Books, a division of Random House, Inc., New York, in 1985.

ISBN 0-394-57046-4

ce in the guide may not always correspond to the official administrative regions.

BELGIUM

PAS-
DE-CALAIS
(62)   NORD
          (59)
'GLISH   PICARDY -
ANNEL   THE NORTH

SOMME (80)

SEINE-
MARITIME   AISNE
(76)   OISE   (02)   ARDENNES   LUX.
          (60)   (08)   WEST GERMANY

'RMANDY   ARDENNE-
/ADOS   (95)   CHAMPAGNE   MEUSE   MOSELLE
     EURE   (78) (93)   (55)   (54) (57)
RNE (27)   (92) PARIS MARNE (51) LORRAINE-
(61)   ÎLE-DE-FRANCE   VOSGES   BAS-RHIN
                 (94)   MEURTHE-ET-   (67)
                                      MOSELLE

     EURE-   ESSONNE   VOSGES   ALSACE
     ET-LOIR (91) (77)   AUBE   (88)
SARTHE (28)   (10)   HAUTE-
(72)   LOIRET   MARNE   HAUT-RHIN
INE-   (45)   YONNE   (52)   HAUTE-   (68)
JOU   TOURAINE-   (89)   SAÔNE
       BLÉSOIS-   (70)   T. de Belfort (90)
NE-   ORLÉANAIS   CÔTE-D'OR   DOUBS
E   LOIR-ET-CHER   (21)   (25)
  INDRE-ET- (41)   CHER   BURGUNDY   FRANCHE-
  LOIRE   (18)   COMTE   SWITZERLAND
  (37)   BERRY-   NIÈVRE
             BOURBONNAIS   (58)
K VIENNE   INDRE   SAÔNE-   JURA
S (86)   (36)   ET-LOIRE   (39)
                   ALLIER   (71)
ARENTES   (03)
     (87)   CREUSE   AIN (01)   HAUTE-
     HAUTE- (23)   SAVOIE
ARENTE VIENNE   LYONNAIS-   (74)
16)   LIMOUSIN PUY-DE-DÔME BRESSE
               (63)   LOIRE RHÔNE   SAVOY
                       (42) (69)   SAVOIE
   DORDOGNE CORRÈZE   ISÈRE (73)
   (24)   (19)   AUVERGNE   (38)   ITALY
             CANTAL HAUTE-
   AGENAIS- LOT (15) LOIRE (07)   DAUPHINÉ
   PÉRIGORD- (46)   (43) ARDÈCHE   HAUTES-
LOT- QUERCY AVEYRON LOZÈRE DRÔME   ALPES
ET-   (12)   (48) (26)   (05) (04)
GARONNE   TARN-ET- ARDÈCHE-   ALPES-DE- (06)
(47)   GARONNE   ROUERGUE CÉVENNES-   HAUTE-   ALPES-
GERS   (82) (31) ALBIGEOIS GARD VAUCLUSE PROVENCE MARITIMES
(32)   HAUTE-   TARN   (30)   (84)   PROVENCE-CÔTE D'AZUR
   MIDI- GARONNE (81) HÉRAULT BOUCHES-
   TOULOUSAIN-   (34)   DU-RHÔNE   VAR (83)
65)   PYRÉNÉES   LANGUEDOC- (13)
UTES-   AUDE ROUSSILLON
ÉNÉES   ARIÈGE   (11)
        (09)
        PYRÉNÉES-
    (66) ORIENTALES

SPAIN

MEDITERRANEAN

SEA

HAUTE-CORSE
(2 B)

CORSICA   (2B)

CORSE-DU-SUD
(2 A)